The Treasury
of the Bible

The Treasury of the Bible

Charles Haddon Spurgeon

Volume VII
Romans 3:27 to Titus

BAKER BOOK HOUSE
Grand Rapids, Michigan 49506

Reprinted 1981 by
Baker Book House Company

ISBN: 0-8010-8210-2   (Eight Volumes)

Printed in the United States of America

GRACE EXALTED—BOASTING EXCLUDED

"Where is boasting then? It is excluded. By what law? of works? Nay: but by the law of faith."—Romans iii. 27.

PRIDE is most obnoxious to God. As a sin, His holiness hates it; as a treason, His sovereignty detests it; as a rebellion, the whole of His attributes stand leagued to put it down. God has touched other sins with His finger, but against this vice He has made bare His arm. There have been, I know, terrible judgments against lust, but there have been ten times as many against that swelling lust of the deceitful heart. Remember, the first transgression had in its essence pride. The ambitious heart of Eve desired to be as God, knowing good and evil, and Adam imagined that he should be lifted up to divine rank if he dared to pluck and eat. The blasting of Paradise, the sterility of the world, the travail of human birth, the sweat of the brow, and the certainty of death, may all be traced to this fruitful mother of mischief, pride. Remember Babel, and how God has scattered us and confounded our tongues. It was man's pride which led him to seek for an undivided monarchy that so he might be great. The tower was to be the rallying-point of all the tribes, and would have been the central throne of all human grandeur, but God scattered us, that pride might not climb to so high a pitch. Pride, thou hast indeed suffered severe strokes from God. Against thee has He furbished His sword, and prepared His weapons of war. The Lord, even the Lord of hosts hath sworn it, and He will surely stain the pride of all human glory, and tread all boasting as straw is trodden for the dunghill. Talk no more so exceeding proudly; let no arrogancy come out of your mouth, for the bows of the mighty have been broken, and the haughtiness of man has been bowed down. Remember Pharaoh and the plagues which God brought on Egypt, and the wonders which He wrought in the field of Zoan. Remember the Red Sea, and Rahab cut, and the dragon broken. Think of Nebuchadnezzar, the mighty architect of Babylon, driven out to eat grass like the oxen till his nails grew like birds' claws, and his hair like eagles' feathers. Remember Herod, eaten of worms, because he gave not God the glory; and Sennacherib, with the Lord's hook in his jaws, turned by the way he came to the place where his sons became his slayers. Time would fail to tell of the innumerable conquerors and emperors and mighty men of earth who have all perished beneath the blast of Thy rebuke, O God, because they lifted up themselves, and said, "I am, and there is none beside Me." He hath turned wise men backward, and made their knowledge foolishness, and no flesh may glory in His presence. Yea, when pride has sought to shelter itself in the hearts of God's chosen people, still the arrows of God have sought it out and have drunk its blood. God loves His servants still, but pride even in them He abhors. David may be a man after God's own heart, but if his pride shall lift him up to number the people, then he shall have a choice between three chastisements, and he shall be fain to choose the pestilence as being the least of the plagues. Or if Hezekiah shall show to the ambassadors of Babylon his riches and his treasures, there shall come to him the rebuke—"What have they seen in thy house?"

and the threatening—"Behold they shall take thy sons to make them eunuchs in the palace of the king of Babylon." Oh, brethren, forget not that God has uttered the most solemn words as well as issued the most awful judgments against pride. "Pride goeth before destruction, and a haughty spirit before a fall." "Him that hath a high look and a proud heart will I not suffer." "Pride and arrogancy do I hate." "The Lord will destroy the house of the proud." "The day of the Lord shall be upon every one that is proud and lofty, and upon every one that is lifted up, and he shall be brought low." "I am against thee, O thou most proud, saith the Lord God of Hosts." There are hundreds of terrible texts like these, but we cannot now recount them all. Now mark, to put an everlasting stigma upon human vanity, and to hurl once for all mire and filth upon all human glorying, God has ordained that the only way in which He will save men shall be a way which utterly excludes the possibility of man's having a single word to say by way of vaunting. He has declared that the only foundation which He will ever lay shall be one by which man's strength shall be broken in pieces, and by which man's pride shall be humbled in the dust. To this subject I ask your attention this morning. It is to enlarge and amplify the sentiment of the text that I seek. "Where is boasting, then? It is excluded. By what law? of works? Nay; but by the law of faith."

We shall notice first of all, *the rejected plan or law ;* then we shall note *the excluded vice ;* having so done, we shall notice in the third place, *that the very fact that boasting is excluded permits of the reception of the worst of sinners ;* and we shall close by observing *that the same system which excludes boasting includes humble and devout gratitude to God for His grace and mercy.*

I. First, then, THE REJECTED PLAN.

There are two ways by which man might have been for ever blessed. The one was by works:—"This do and thou shalt live; be obedient and receive the reward; keep the commandment and the blessing shall be thine, well earned and surely paid." The only other plan was—"Receive grace and blessedness as the free gift of God; stand as a guilty sinner having no merit, and as a rebellious sinner deserving the very reverse of goodness, but stand there and receive all thy good things, simply, wholly, and alone of the free love and sovereign mercy of God." Now, the Lord has not chosen the system of works. The word *law* as used twice in the text is employed, it is believed by many commentators, out of compliment to the Jews, who were so fond of the word, that their antagonism might not be aroused; but it means here, as elsewhere in Scripture, plan, system, method. There were two plans, two systems, two methods, two spirits,—the plan of works and the plan of grace. God has once for all utterly refused the plan of merit and of works, and has chosen to bless men only, and entirely through the plan, or method, or law of faith. Now, brethren, we have put the two before you, and we beg you to mark that there is a distinction between the two, which must never be forgotten. Martin Luther says: —" If thou canst rightly distinguish between works and grace, thank God for thy skill, and consider thyself to be an able divine." This indeed is the bottom of theology, and he who can understand this clearly, it seems to me, can never be very heterodox; orthodoxy must surely follow, and the right teaching of God must be understood when we once for all are able to discriminate with accuracy between that which is of man—works, and that which is of God—faith, and grace received by faith. Now, the plan of salvation by works is impossible for us. Even if God had ordained it to be the way by which men should labour to be saved, yet it is certain that none would have been saved by it, and therefore all must have perished. For if thou wouldst be saved by works, remember O man, that the law requires of thee perfection. One single flaw, one offence, and the law condemns thee without mercy. It requires that thou shouldst keep it in every point, and in every sense, and to its uttermost degree, for its demands are rigorous in the extreme. It knows nothing of freely forgiving because thou canst not pay, but like a severe creditor, it takes thee by thy throat, and says, "Pay me all"; and if thou canst not pay even to the uttermost farthing, it shuts thee up in the prison of condemnation, out of which thou canst not come. But if it were possible for you to keep the law in its perfection outwardly, yet, remember, that you would be required to keep it in your heart as well as in your external life. One single motion of the heart from the right, one reception of even the shadow of a passing temptation, so as to become a partaker of sin, would ruin you. "Thou shalt love the Lord thy God with all thy heart, and with all thy mind, and with all thy soul, and with all thy strength, and thy neighbour as thyself." Fail here, and oh! who among us can be such a hypocrite as to think he has not failed ten thousand times!— fail here, and though your life were virtuous, though your exterior were such as even criticism itself must commend, yet you perish because you have not kept the law and yielded its full demands. Remember, too, that it is clear you can never be saved by the law, because if up to this moment your heart and life have been altogether without offence, yet it is required that it should be so even to your dying day. And do you hope that as temptations come upon you thick as your moments, as your trials invade you numerous as the swarms which once thronged from the gates of Thebes, you will be able to stand against all these? Will there not be found some joint in your harness? Will there not be some moment in which you may be tripped up—some instant when either the eye may wander after lust, or the heart be set on vanity, or the hand stretched out to touch that which is not good? Oh! man, remember, we are not sure that even this life would end that probation, for as long as thou shouldst live and be God's creature, duty would still be due, and the law still thine insatiable creditor. For ever would thy happiness tremble in the scales; even in heaven itself the law would follow thee: even there, as thy righteousness would be thine own, it would never be finished; and even from yonder shining battlements thou mightest fall, and amid those harps, wearing that white robe, if thou wert to be saved by thine own works, there might be a possibility of perishing. The obedience of a creature can never be finished; the duty of a servant of the law is never over. So long as thou wast the creature of God, thy Creator would have demands upon thee. How much better

to be accepted in the Beloved, and to wear His finished righteousness as our glory and security. Now in the face of all this, will any of you prefer to be saved by your works? or, rather, will you prefer to be damned by your works? for that will certainly be the issue, let you hope what you may.

Now I suppose that in this congregation we have but very few—there may be some—who would indulge a hope of being saved by the law in itself; but there is a delusion abroad that perhaps God will modify the law, or that at least He will accept a sincere obedience even if it be imperfect; that He will say, "Well, this man has done what he could, and, therefore, I will take what he has given as though it were perfect." Now, remember against this the Apostle Paul declares peremptorily, "By the works of the law shall no flesh living be justified," so that that is answered at once. But more than this, God's law cannot alter, it can never be content to take less from thee than it demands. What said Christ? "It is easier for heaven and earth to pass, than one tittle of the law to fail," and again He expressly said, "Think not that I am come to destroy the law, or the prophets, I am not come to destroy, but to fulfil." The law's demands were met and fulfilled for believers by Christ; but as far as those demands are concerned to those who are under it, they are as great, as heavy, and as rigorous as ever they were. Unless His law could be altered, and that is impossible, God cannot accept anything but a perfect obedience; and if you are hoping to be saved by your sincere endeavours to do your best, your hopes are rotten things, delusions, falsehoods, and you will perish wrapped up in the shrouds of your pride. "Yes," some say, "but could it not be partly by grace and partly by works?" No. The apostle says that boasting is excluded, and excluded by the law of faith; but if we let in the law of works in any degree, we cannot shut out boasting, for to that degree you give man an opportunity to congratulate himself as having saved himself. Let me say broadly—to hope to be saved by works is a delusion; to hope to be saved by a method in which grace and works are co-acting, is not merely a delusion, but an absurd delusion, since it is contrary to the very nature of things, that grace and merit should ever mingle and co-work. Our apostle has declared times without number, that if it be of grace it is not of works, otherwise grace is no more grace; and if it be of works, then it is not of grace, otherwise work is no more work. It must be either one or the other. These two cannot be married, for God forbids the banns. He will have it all grace or all works, all of Christ or all of man; but for Christ to be a make-weight, for Christ to supplement your narrow robes by patching on a piece of His own, for Christ to tread a part of the wine-press, and for you to tread the rest; oh! this can never be. God will never be yoked with the creature. You might link an angel with a worm and bid them fly together, but God with the creature—the precious blood of Jesus with the foul ditch-water of our human merits—never, never. Our paste gems, our varnished falsehoods, our righteousnesses which are but filthy rags, put with the real, true, precious, everlasting, divine things of Christ! Never! Unless heaven should blend in alliance with hell, and holiness hold dalliance with impurity! It must be one or the other, either man's merit absolutely and alone, or unmixed, unmerited favour from the Lord. Now, I suppose if I were to labour never so arduously to hunt out this evil spirit from the sons of men, I should miss it still, for it hides in so many shapes, and therefore let me say, that in no shape, in no sense, in no single case, and in no degree whatsoever, are we saved by our works or by the law. I say in no sense, because men make such shifts to save alive their own righteousness. I will show you one man who says, "Well, I don't expect to be saved by my honesty; I don't expect to be saved by my generosity, nor by my morality; but then, I have been baptized; I receive the Lord's Supper; I have been confirmed; I go to church, or I have a sitting in a meeting-house; I am, as touching the ceremonies, blameless." Well, friend, in that sense you cannot be saved by works, for all these things have no avail whatever upon the matter of salvation, if you have not faith. If you are saved, God's ordinances will be blessed things to you, but if you are not a believer you have no right to them; and with regard to Baptism and the Supper, every time you touch them you increase your guilt. Whether it be Baptism or the Lord's Supper, you have no right to either, except you be saved already, for they are both ordinances for believers, and for believers only. These ordinances are blessed means of grace to living, quickened, saved souls; but to unsaved souls, to souls dead in trespasses and sins, these outward ordinances can have no avail for good, but may increase their sin, because they touch unworthily the holy things of God. Oh! repose not in these; oh! dream not that a priestly hand and sacred drops, or a God-ordained baptism in the pool, can in any way redeem you from sin, or land you in heaven: for by this way salvation is impossible. But if I drive the lover of self-righteousness out of this haunt, he runs to another. You will find others who suppose that at least *their feelings*, which are only their works in another shape, may help to save them. There are thousands who think, "If I could weep so much, and groan so deeply, and experience so much humiliation, and a certain quantity of repentance, and so much of the terrors of the law, and of the thunders of conscience, then I might come before God." Souls, souls, this is work-mongering in its most damnable shape, for it has deluded far more than that bolder sort of work-trusting, which says, "I will reply upon what I do." If you rely upon what you feel, you shall as certainly perish as if you trust to what you do. Repentance is a blessed grace, and to be convinced of sin by God the Holy Ghost is a holy privilege, but to think that these in any way win salvation, is to run clean counter to all the teachings of the Word, for salvation is of the free grace of God alone. There are some, moreover, who believe that if their feelings cannot do it, still *their knowledge can*. They have a very sound creed; they have struck out this doctrine and that; they believe in justification by faith, and their sound creed is to them a confidence. They think that because they hold the theory of justification by faith, therefore they shall be saved. And oh! how they plume their feathers; how they set up their peacock tail because they happen to be orthodox! With what awful pride do they exult over their fellow professors because they hold *the truth*, and all the rest of the Church they think is deluded with a lie. Now this is nothing but salvation by works, only they are works performed by the head instead of by the hand, and oh! sirs, I will tell you—if you rest in creeds, if you hope to be saved because you can put your hand to the thirty-nine articles of an Episcopalian prayer-book, or to the solemn league and covenant of the Presbyterian, or to the confession of faith of the Calvinist—if you fancy that because you happen to receive truth in the head you shall be saved, you know not the truth, but still do lie, because you cling to Satan's falsehood—that salvation is of man and not of God. I know that self-righteousness was born in our bone and that it will come out in our flesh, and even that man in whom its reigning power is kept down will still feel it sometimes rising up. When he has preached a sermon and has got on pretty well, the devil will come up the pulpit stairs and say "Well done." When he has prayed in public and has had unusual fluency, he will have to be careful lest there should be a whisper behind—"What a good and gifted man you are." Aye, and even in his hallowed moments, when he is on the top of the mountain with his Lord, he will have to watch even there, lest self-congratulation should suggest—"Oh, man, greatly-beloved, there must surely be something in thee, or else God would not have done thus unto thee." Brethren, when you are thinking of your sanctification, if you are tempted to look away from Christ—away with it; and if when you are repenting of sin you cannot still have one eye on Christ, recollect it will be a repentance that will need to be repented of, for there is nothing in ourselves that can be offered to God. There is a stench and putridity in everything that is done of the creature, and we can never come before God save through Christ Jesus, who is made of God unto us, wisdom, and righteousness, and sanctification, and redemption. I have thus tried to denounce the plan which God has rejected.

II. I shall now, in the second head, SHOW THAT BOASTING IS EXCLUDED, for in a blessed sense God has accepted the second plan, namely the way of salvation by faith through grace.

The first man that entered heaven, entered heaven by faith. "By faith Abel offered a more acceptable sacrifice than Cain." Over the tombs of all the goodly who were accepted of God, you may read the epitaph —"These all died in faith." By faith they received the promise; and among all yonder bright and shining throng, there is not one who does not confess, "We have washed our robes and made them white in the blood of the Lamb." The plan, then, which God has chosen, is one of grace alone. I will try and picture that plan before our mind's eye. We will imagine Boasting to be exceedingly desirous to enter into the kingdom of heaven. He marches to the door and knocks. The porter looks out and demands, "Who stands there?" "I am Boasting," saith he, "and I claim to have the highest seat; I claim that I should cry aloud and say, Glory be unto man, for though he has fallen, he has lifted himself up, and wrought out his own redemption." And the angel said, "But hast thou not heard that the salvation of souls is not of man, nor by man, but that God will have mercy on whom He will have mercy, and will have compassion on whom He will have compassion? Get thee gone, Boasting, for the highest seat can never be thine, when God, in direct opposition to human merit, has rejected the Pharisee, and chosen the publican and the harlot, that they may enter into the kingdom of heaven." So Boasting said, "Let me take my place, then, if not in the highest seat, yet somewhere amid the glittering throng; for instance, let me take my place in the seat of *election ;* let it be said and taught, that albeit God did choose His people, yet it was because of their works which He foresaw, and their faith which He foreknew, and that, therefore, foreseeing and foreknowing, He did choose them because of an excellence which His prescient eye discovered in them; let me take my seat here." But the porter said, "Nay, but thou canst not take thy place there, for election is according to the eternal purpose of God, which He purposed in Christ Jesus before the world was. This election is not of works, but of grace, and the reason for God's choice of man is in Himself, and not in man; and as for those virtues which thou sayest God did foreknow, God is the author of all of them if they exist, and that which is an effect cannot be a first cause; God foreordained these men to faith and to good works, and their faith and good works could not have been the cause of their fore-ordination." Then straight from heaven's gate the trumpet sounded— ("For the children being not yet born, neither having done any good or evil, that the purpose of God according to election might stand, not of works, but of Him that calleth;) it was said unto her, The elder shall serve the younger." Then Boasting found that as works had no place in election, so there was no room for him to take his seat there, and he bethought himself where next he could be. So after a while Boasting said to the porter, "If I cannot mount the chair of election, I will be content to sit in the place of conversion, for surely it is man that repents and believes." The porter did not deny the truth of that, and then this evil spirit said, "If one man believes and not another, surely that must be the act of the man's will, and his will being free and unbiassed, it must be very much to that man's credit that he believes and repents and is therefore saved, for others, having like opportunities with himself, and having the same grace no doubt, reject the proferred mercy and perish, while this man accepts it and therefore let me at least take my seat there." But the angel said in anger, "Take thy seat there! Why, that were to take the highest place of all, for this is the hinge and turning-point, and if thou leavest that with man then thou givest him the brightest jewel in the crown. Does the Ethiopian change his skin and the leopard his spots? Is it not God that worketh in us to will and to do of His own good pleasure? Of His own will begat He us with the word of truth, and it is not of the will of man, nor of blood, nor of birth. Oh, Boaster, thy free-will is a lie; it is not man that chooses God, but God that chooses man; for what said Christ, "Ye have not chosen Me but I have chosen you"; and what said He to the ungodly multitude, "Ye will not come unto Me that ye might have life;" in which He gave the death-blow to all ideas of free-will, when He declared that man *will not* come to Him that he might have life; and when He said again in another place, as if that were not enough, "No man can come unto Me except the Father which hath sent Me draw him." So Boasting, though he were fain not to admit it, was shut out, and could not take his place in heaven upon the stool of conversion; and while he stood there but little abashed, for bashfulness he knows not, he heard a song floating over the battlements of heaven from all the multitude who were there, in accents like these, "Not unto us, not unto us, but unto Thy name, O Lord, be all the praise."

"'Twas the same love that spread the feast
    That gently forced us in;
Else we had still refused to taste,
    And perished in our sin."

"But then," said Boasting, "if I may not have so high a place, let me at least sit on the lowly stool of perseverance, and let it at least be said that while God saved the man and is therefore to have the glory, still the man was faithful to grace received; he did not turn back unto perdition, but watched and was very careful, and kept himself in the love of God, and therefore there is considerable credit due to him; for while many drew back and perished, and he might have done the same, he struggled against sin, and thus by his using his grace he kept himself safely; let me sit, then, on the chair of perseverance." But the angel replied, "Nay, nay, what hast thou to do with it? I know it is written, 'Keep yourselves in the love of God,' but the same apostle forbids all fleshly trust in human effort by that blessed doxology,— 'Now unto Him that is able to keep you from falling, and to present you faultless before the presence of His glory with exceeding joy, to the only wise God our Saviour, be glory and majesty, dominion and power, both now and ever, Amen.' That which is a command in one Scripture is a covenant in another, where it is written, 'I will put My fear in their hearts that they shall not depart from Me.'" Oh, brethren, well do you and I know that our standing does not depend upon ourselves. If that Arminian doctrine, that our perseverance rests somewhere in our own hands, were true, then damnation must be the lot of us all. I cannot keep myself a minute, much less year after year.

"If ever it should come to pass,
    That sheep of Christ should fall away;
My fickle, feeble soul, alas!
    Would fall a thousand times a day."

But what saith the Scripture?—"I give unto My sheep eternal life, and they shall never perish, neither shall any man pluck them out of My hand; My Father which gave them Me is greater than all, and no man is able to pluck them out of My Father's hand." And what says the apostle—"I am persuaded, that neither death, nor life, nor angels, nor principalities, nor powers, nor things present, nor things to come, nor height, nor depth, nor any other creature, shall be able to separate us from the love of God, which is in Christ Jesus our Lord." I have not time to quote all the innumerable passages, but it is absolutely certain that if there be one doctrine in Scripture more clearly revealed than another, it is the doctrine of the perseverance of the saints by the power of the Holy Ghost, and the man who doubts that precious truth, has quite as much reason to doubt the Trinity, to doubt the divinity of Christ, or the fact of the atonement; for nothing can be more clear in the plain, common-sense meaning of the words than this, that they who are in Christ have, even to-day, eternal life and shall never perish. Now since this perseverance is not dependent upon our works, but like all the rest of salvation is an efflux from the bottomless love of God, boasting is manifestly excluded. But once again, and lastly, Boasting sometimes asks to be admitted a little into glorification. I fear sometimes that a doctrine which is popular in the Church, about degrees of glory, is not altogether unassociated with that old self-righteousness of ours which is very loath to die. "One star differeth from another star in glory" is a great truth—but this the stars may do without differing in degrees. One star may shine with one radiance, and another with another; indeed, astronomers tell us that there are many varieties of colour among stars of the same magnitude. One man may differ from another, without supposing a difference in rank, honour, or degree. For my part, I do not see anything about degrees in glory in Scripture, and I do not believe in the doctrine; at least if there be degrees, mark this, they cannot be according to works, but must be of grace alone. I cannot consider that because one Christian has been more devoted to Christ than another, therefore there will be an eternal difference, for this is to introduce works; this is to bring in again the old Hagar marriage, and to bring back the child of the bond-woman, whereof God has said, "The son of the bond-woman shall not be heir with My son, even with Isaac." Oh! brethren, I think we can serve God from some other motive than that base one of trying to be greater than our brethren in heaven. If I should get to heaven at all, I do not care who is greater than I am, for if any one shall have more happiness in heaven than I shall, then I shall have more happiness too; for the sympathy between one soul and another will there be so intense and so great, that all the heavens of the righteous will be my heaven, and therefore, what you have I shall have, because we shall all be one in fellowship far more perfectly than on earth. The private member will there be swallowed up in the common body. Surely, brethren, if any of you can have brighter places in heaven, and more happiness and more joy than I, I will be glad to know it. 'The prospect does not excite any envy in my soul now, or if it did *now*, it certainly would not *then*, for I should feel that the more *you* had the more *I* should have. Perfect communion in all good things is not compatible with the private enrichment of one above another. It is all joint-stock in heaven. Even on earth the saints had all things common when they were in a heavenly state, and I am persuaded they will have all things common in glory. I do not believe in gentlemen in heaven, and the poor Christians behind the door; I do believe that our union with each other will be so great, that distinctions will be utterly lost, and that we shall all have such a joint communion, and interest, and fellowship, that there will be no such thing as private possession, private ranks, and private honours—for we shall there, to the fullest extent, be one in Christ. I do believe that Boasting is shut out there, but I think that if there were these degrees in glory, I mean if they are dependent on works done on earth, Boasting would at least get his tail in; if it did not insinuate its whole body, it would at least get some of its unhallowed members over the wall, whereas, the text says it is excluded. Let me enlarge this one word, and then proceed. It does not say, "Boasting, you are to be allowed to come in and sit down on the floor." No, shut the door and do not let him in at all. "But let me in," says he, "and I will be quiet." No, shut him out altogether. "But at least let me put my foot in." No, exclude him; shut him out altogether. "But at least let me sometimes go in and out." No, shut him out altogether; exclude him; bolt the door; put double padlocks on it. Say once for all, "Boasting, get thee gone: thou art hurled down and broken in pieces, and if thou canst refit thyself, and come once more to the gate to ask admittance, thou shalt be driven away with shame." It is *excluded;* it cannot be let in, in any sense, in any term, nor in any degree. As Calvin says, "Not a particle of boasting can be admitted, because not a particle of work is admitted into the covenant of grace;" it is of grace from top to bottom, from Alpha to Omega; it is not of man nor by man, not of him that willeth, nor of him that runneth, but

of God that showeth mercy, and therefore, boasting is excluded by the law of faith.

III. And now, thirdly, and very briefly. Beloved in Christ Jesus, what a precious truth I have now to hold up to the eyes of poor lost sinners, who to-day are aware that they have no merits of their own. Soul, THE VERY GATE WHICH SHUTS OUT BOASTING, SHUTS IN HOPE AND JOY FOR YOU.

Let me state this truth broadly, that the ignorant may catch it. You say to-day, "Sir, I never attend the house of God, and up to this time I have been a thief and a drunkard." Well, you stand to-day on the same level as the most moral sinner, and the most honest unbeliever, in the matter of salvation. They are lost, since they believe not, and so are you. If the most honest be saved, it will not be by their honesty, but by the free grace of God; and if the most roguish would be saved, it must be by the same plan. There is one gate to heaven for the most chaste and the most debauched. When we come to God, the best of us can bring nothing, and the worst of us can bring no less. I know when I state it thus, some will say, "Then what is the good of morality?" I will tell you. Two men are overboard there; one man has a dirty face, and the other a clean one. There is a rope thrown over from the stern of the vessel, and only that rope will save the sinking men, whether their faces be fair or foul. Is not this the truth? Do I therefore underrate cleanliness. Certainly not; but it will not save a drowning man; nor will morality save a dying man. The clean man may sink with all his cleanliness, and the dirty man may be drawn up with all his filth, if the rope do but get its hold of him. Or take this case. Here we have two persons, each with a deadly cancer. One of them is rich and clothed in purple, the other is poor and wrapped about with a few rags; and I say to them—"You are both on a par now, here comes the Physician Himself—Jesus, the king of disease; His touch can heal you both; there is no difference between you whatever." Do I therefore say that the one man's robes are not better than the other's rags? Of course they are better in some respects, but they have nothing to do with the matter of curing disease. So morality is a neat cover for foul venom, but it does not alter the fact that the heart is vile and the man himself under condemnation. Suppose I were an army-surgeon, and there had been a batte. There is one man there—he is a captain and a brave man; he led his rank into the thick of the battle, and he is bleeding out his life from a terrible gash. By his side there lies a man of the rank and file, and a great coward too, wounded in the same way. I come up to both of them, and I say, "You are both in the same condition; you have both the same sort of wound, and I can heal you both." But if either of you should say, "Get you gone; I'll have nothing to do with you," your wound will be your death. If the captain should say, "I do not want you; I am a captain, go and see to that poor dog yonder." Would his courage and rank save his life? No, they are good things, but not saving things. So is it with good works, men can be damned with them as well as without them if they make them their trust. Oh! what a gospel is this to preach in our theatres; to tell those hedge-birds, those who are full of all manner of loathsomeness, that there is the same way of salvation open to them as to a peer of the realm, or a bishop on the bench; that there is no difference between us in the way of mercy, that we are all condemned; that there may be degrees as to our guilt, but that the fact of our condemnation is quite as certain to the best as to the worst! "Oh," you say, "this is a levelling doctrine!" Ah! bless God if you are levelled. "Oh," you say, "but this cuts at everything that is good in man!" Ah! thank God, if it kills everything in which man glories, for that which man thinks to be good is often an abomination in the sight of God. And oh! if all of us together, moral or immoral, chaste or debauched, honest or unholy, can come with the rope about our neck, and with the weeds of penitence upon our loins, and say, "Great God, forgive us; we are all guilty; give us grace; we do not deserve it; bestow upon us Thy favour, we have no right to it, but give it to us because Jesus died." Oh! He will never cast out one that way, for that is the way of salvation. And if we can put our hand this morning—no matter though it was black last night with lust, or red up to the elbow with murder—yet if we can put our hand on Jesu's head, and believe on Him—the blood of Jesus Christ, God's dear Son, cleanseth us from all sin. Where is boasting now? You who have done so much for humanity—you cannot boast, for you have nothing to boast of. You fine gentlemen and noble ladies, what say you to this. O be wise, and join in the prayer, "But Thou, O Lord, have mercy upon us, miserable sinners!" And may the Lord then pronounce over us His sentence, "Ye are clean, go and sin no more; your iniquities are all forgiven you."

IV. I close by just observing, that THE SAME PLAN WHICH SHUTS OUT BOASTING LEADS US TO A GRACIOUS GRATITUDE TO CHRIST.

We are sometimes asked by people, "Do you think that such a thing is necessary to salvation?" or, perhaps, the question is put in another way, "How long do you think a man must be Godly in order to be saved?" I reply, dear friend, you cannot understand us, for we hold that these things do not save in any sense, "Why, then," they say, "are you baptized?" or, "Why do you walk in holiness?" Well, not to save myself, but because I am saved. When I know that every sin of mine is forgiven, that I cannot be lost, that Christ has sworn to bring me to the place where He is; then I say, Lord what is there that I can do for Thee? Tell me. Can I burn for Thee? Blessed were the stake if I might kiss it. If Thou hast done so much for me, what can I do for Thee? Is there an ordinance that involves self-denial? Is there a duty which will compel me to self-sacrifice? So much the better.

> "Now for the love I bear His name,
>   What was my gain I count my loss;
>   My former pride I call my shame,
>   And nail my glory to His cross."

This is the way to do good works; and good works are impossible until we come here. Anything that you do by which to save yourself is a selfish act, and therefore cannot be good. Only that which is done for God's glory is good in a Scriptural sense. A man must be saved before he can do a good work; but when saved, having nothing to get and nothing to lose; standing now in Christ, blessed and accepted—he begins to serve God out of pure gratitude and love. Then, virtue is possible, and he may climb to its highest steeps, and stand safely there without fear of the boasting which would cast him down, though he will feel even then that his standing is not in what he has done, nor in what he is, nor in what he hopes to be, but in what Christ did, and in the "It is finished," which made his eternal salvation secure.

Oh, for grace, that we may live to the praise of the glory of His grace, wherein He hath made us accepted in the beloved, bringing forth the fruits of righteousness, which are by Jesus Christ unto the glory and praise of God. Of Him, and through Him, and to Him are all things; to Him be glory for ever. Amen.

HOW IS SALVATION RECEIVED?

"Therefore it is of faith, that it might be by grace; to the end the promise might be sure to all the seed; not to that only which is of the law, but to that also which is of the faith of Abraham; who is the father of us all."—Romans iv. 16.

WE shall turn during yet another Sabbath morning to one of the great vital truths of the gospel. I feel it to be important more and more to bring forward the fundamental doctrines, since they are in certain quarters placed so much in the background. I met with a remark the other day that even the evangelical pulpit needs to be evangelized: I am afraid it is too true, and therefore we will give such prominence to the gospel, and to its central doctrine of justification by faith, that no such remark shall be applicable to us. We have heard it said if an instrument could be invented which would serve the same purpose towards sermons as the lactometer does towards milk, you would with great difficulty be able to discover any trace of the unadulterated milk of the Word in large numbers of modern discourses. I shall not subscribe to any sweeping censure, but I am afraid there is too much ground for the accusation. In abundance of sermons the polish of the rhetoric is greatly in excess of the weight of the doctrine, and "the wisdom of words" is far more conspicuous than the cross of Christ.

Besides, the gospel is always wanted. There are always some persons who urgently need it, and will perish unless they receive it. It is a matter of hourly necessity. There may be finer and more artistic things to speak about than the simplicities of Christ, but there are certainly no more useful and requisite things. The sign-posts at the cross roads bear very simple words, generally consisting of the names of the towns and villages to which the roads lead; but if these were painted out and their places supplied with stanzas from Byron, or stately lines from Milton, or deep thoughts from Cowper or Young, I am afraid there would be grievous complaints from persons losing their way. They would declare that however excellent the poetry might be they thought it an impertinence to mock them with a verse when they needed plain directions as to the king's highway. So let those who will indulge in poetical thoughts and express them in high-flown language, it shall be ours to set up the hand-posts marking out the way of salvation, and to keep them painted in letters large and plain, so that he who runs may read.

There is another reason for giving the gospel over and over, again and again. It is the reason which makes the mother tell her child twenty times, namely, because nineteen times are not enough. Men are so forgetful about the things of Christ, and their minds are so apt to start aside from the truth, that when they have learned the gospel they are very easily bewitched by falsehood, and are readily deceived by that "other gospel" which is not another: therefore we need to give them "line upon line and precept upon precept." I scarcely remember the old rustic rhyme, but I recollect hearing it sung in my boyish days when the country people were dibbling beans, and according to the old plan were putting three into each hole,— I think it ran thus—

> "One for the worm and one for the crow,
> And let us hope the other will grow."

We must be content to plant many seeds in the hope that one will take root and bear fruit. The worm and crow are always at work, and will be sure to get their full share of our sowing, and therefore let us sow the more.

Come we, then, to our text and to the gospel of faith. Last Sabbath the theme was, For whom is the gospel meant? and the reply was, for sinners. The question to-day is, *How is the gospel received?* The answer is, *by faith.*

Our first head shall be, *the fact,*—"it is of faith": secondly, *the first reason for this,*—"that it might be by grace": and thirdly, *the further reason,*—"to the end that the promise might be sure to all the seed."

I. First, then, here is THE FACT, *it is of faith.* What does the "it" refer to? *It* is of faith. If you will read the context, I think you will consider that it refers to the promise, although some have said that the antecedent word or thought is "the inheritance." This matters very little if at all: it may mean the inheritance, the covenant, or the promise, for these arc one. To give a wide word which will take in all,—the blessedness which comes to a man in Christ, the blessedness promised by the covenant of grace is of faith: in one word, salvation is of faith.

And what is faith? It is believing the promise of God, taking God at His word, and acting upon that belief by trusting in Him. Some of the Puritans used to divide faith, improperly but still instructively, into three parts. The first was self renunciation, which is, perhaps, rather a preparation for faith than faith itself, in which a man confesses that he cannot trust in himself, and so goes out of self and all confidence in his own good works. The second part of faith they said was reliance in which a man believing the promise of God trusts Him, depends upon Him, and leaves his soul in the Saviour's hands; and then the third part of faith they said was appropriation by which a man takes to himself that which God presents in the promise to the believer, appropriates it as his own, feeds upon it, and enjoys it. Certainly there is no true faith without self-renunciation, reliance, and at least a measure of appropriation; where these three are found there is faith in the soul. We shall, however, better understand what faith is as we proceed with our subject, if God the Holy Ghost will be pleased to enlighten us. Dear friends, you can easily see that the blessing was of faith in Abraham's case, and it is precisely the same with all those who by faith are the children of believing Abraham.

First, *it was so in the case of Abraham.* Abraham obtained the promise by faith and not by works nor by the energy of the flesh. He relied alone upon the divine promise. We read in the seventeenth verse ("As it is written, I have made thee a father of many nations), before Him whom he believed, even God, who quickeneth the dead, and calleth those things which be not as though they were." Abraham's faith consisted in *believing the promise* of God, and this he did firmly and practically. He was far away in Chaldea when the Lord called him out and promised to give him a land and a seed, and straightway he went forth, not knowing whither he went. When he came into Canaan he had no settled resting place, but wandered about in tents, still believing most fully that the land wherein he sojourned as a stranger was his own. God promised to give him a seed, and yet he had no children. Year followed year, and in the course of nature he grew old and his wife was long past the age of childbearing, and yet there was no son born to them. When at last Ishmael was born his hope in that direction was dashed to the ground, for he was informed that the covenant was not with Ishmael. Believing Abraham had stepped aside to carnal expediency, and had hoped in that way to realise the lingering promise, but he had fourteen years more to wait, till he was a hundred years old, and till Sarah had reached her ninetieth year. Yet he believed the word of the Lord and fell upon his face and laughed with holy joy and said in his heart, "Shall a child be born unto him that is an hundred years old?" So, too, when Isaac was born and grown up he believed that in Isaac should the covenant be established, nor did he doubt this when the Lord bade him take Isaac and offer him up as a sacrifice. He obeyed without questioning, believing that God was able to raise Isaac from the dead, or in some other way to keep His word of promise. Now consider that we have multiplied promises, and those written down in black and white in the inspired Word, which we may consult at any time we please, while Abraham had only now and then a verbal promise, and yet he clung to it and relied upon it. Though there was nothing else to rely upon, and neither sign nor evidence of any offspring to fulfil the promise that he should be heir of the world and father of many nations, yet he needed no other ground of confidence but that God had said it, and that He would make His word good.

There was in Abraham, also, *an eye to the central point of the promise,* the Messiah, Jesus, our Lord. I do not know that Abraham understood all the spiritual meaning of the covenant made with him, probably he did not; but he did understand that the Christ was to be born of him, in whom all nations should be blessed. When the Lord said that He would make him a blessing, and in him should all nations of the earth be blessed, I do not suppose Abraham saw all the fulness of that marvellous word; but he did see that he was to be the progenitor of the Messiah. Our Lord Himself is my authority for this assertion: "Abraham saw My day, he saw it and was glad." Though there appeared to this man, old and withered, with a wife ninety years of age, no likelihood that he should ever become a father, yet did he fully believe that he would be the father of many nations, and that upon no ground whatever but that the living God had so promised him, and therefore so it must be.

This faith of Abraham we find *considered no difficulties whatever.* "Who against hope believed in hope, that he might become the father of many nations, according to that which was spoken, so shall thy seed be. And being not weak in faith, he considered not his own body now dead, when he was about an hundred years old, neither yet the deadness of Sarah's womb; he staggered not at the promise of God through unbelief." Brethren, these were in themselves terrible difficulties, enough to make a man fear that the promise did but mock him, but Abraham did not consider anything beyond the promise and the God who gave it. The difficulties were for God to consider, and not for him. He knew that God had made the world out of nothing, and that He supported all things by the word of His power, and therefore he felt that nothing was too hard for Him. His own advanced years and the age of his wife were of no consequence, he did not even take them into the reckoning, but saw only a faithful Almighty God, and felt content. O noble faith! Faith such as God deserves! Faith such as none render to Him but those whom He calls by effectual grace! This it was which justified Abraham, and made him the father of believers.

Abraham's faith also *gave glory to God.* I stopped in the middle of the twentieth verse just now, but we must now complete the reading of it. "But was strong in faith, giving glory to God." God had promised, and he treated the Lord's promise with becoming reverence; he did not impiously suspect the Lord of falsehood, or of mocking His servant or of uttering to-day what He might take back to-morrow. He knew that Jehovah is not a man that He should lie, nor the son of man that He should repent. Abraham glorified the truth of God, and at the same time he glorified His power. He was quite certain that the Lord had not spoken beyond His line, but that what He had promised He was able to perform. It belongs to puny man to speak more than he can do; full often his tongue is longer than his arm; but with the Lord it is never so. Hath He said, and shall He not do it? Is anything too hard for the Lord? Abraham adoringly believed in the immutability, truth, and power of the living God, and looked for the fulfilment of His word.

All this strong, unstaggering faith which glorified God *rested upon the Lord alone.* You will see that it was so by reading the twenty-first verse. "Being fully persuaded that, what He had promised, He was able also to perform." There was nothing whatever in his home, his wife, himself, or anywhere else, which could guarantee the fulfilment of the promise. He had only God to look to: only, did I say—what could a man have more? Yet so it was, there were no signs, marks, tokens, or indications to substantiate the confidence of Abraham: he rested solely upon the unlimited power of God. And this, dear brethren, is the kind of faith which God loves and honours, which wants no signs, marks, evidences, helps, or other buttresses to support the plain and sure word of the Lord; but simply knows that Jehovah has said it, and that He will make it good. Though all things should give the promise the lie, we believe in it because we believe in God. True faith ridicules impossibility, and pours contempt upon improbability, knowing that omnipotence and immutability cannot be thwarted or hindered. Has God said it? Then so it is. Dictum! Factum! Spoken! Done! These twain are one with the Most High.

Well, now, *the faith of every man who is saved must be of this character.* Every man who receives salvation receives it by a faith like that of Abraham, for, my brethren, when we are saved *we too take the promise of God and depend upon it.* To one believer one word of God is applied, to another another, but some sweet word, most sure and steadfast, is discovered upon which we fix our hope, and find anchorage for our spirit. Yea, and as we search the word by faith we take each promise as we find it, and we say "this

is true" and "this is true," and so we rest upon all of them. Is it not so with all of you who have peace with God? Did you not gain it by resting upon the promise of God as you found it in the word and as it was opened up to you by the Holy Spirit? Have you any other ground of confidence but God's promise? I know you have not, my brethren, nor do you desire any.

And *we also believe in God over the head of great difficulties.* If it was hard for Abraham to believe that a son should be born unto him, methinks it is harder for a poor burdened sinner, conscious of his great guilt, conscious that God must punish him also for that guilt, to believe nevertheless in the hopeful things which the gospel prophesies unto him. Can I believe that the righteous God is looking upon me, a sinner, with eyes of love? Can I believe that though I have offended Him and broken all His laws He nevertheless waits to be gracious to me? While my heart is heavy and the prospect is black around me and I see nothing but a terrible hell to be my eternal portion, can I at such a time believe that God has planned my redemption and given His Son to die for me, and that now He invites me to come and receive a full, perfect, and immediate pardon at His hands? Can the gospel message be true to such a worthless rebel as I am? It seems as if the law and justice of God set themselves against the truth of such wonderful deeds of mercy as the gospel announces, and it is hard for a stricken heart to believe the report; but the faith which saves the soul believes the gospel promise in the teeth of all its alarms, and notwithstanding all the thunders of the law. Despite the trepidation of the awakened spirit, the Holy Spirit enables it to accept the great Father's word, to rest upon the propitation which He has set forth, and to quiet itself with the firm persuasion that God for Christ's sake doth put away its sin.

At the same time another grand miracle is also believed in, namely, regeneration. This seems to me to be quite as great an act of faith as for Abraham to believe in the birth of a child by two parents who were both advanced in years. The case stands thus: here am I, dead by nature, dead in trespasses and sins. The deadness of Abraham and Sarah according to nature was not greater than the deadness of my soul to every good thing. Is it possible, then, that I should live unto God, that within this stony heart there should yet throb eternal life and divine love, and that I should come to delight in God? Can it be that with such a depraved and deceitful heart as mine I should yet rise to fellowship with the holy God and should call Him my Father and feel the spirit of adoption within my heart? Can I who now dread the Lord yet come to rejoice in Him? "Oh," says the poor troubled sinner, "can I that have fought against the throne of God, I that even tried to doubt His existence, ever come to be at perfect peace with Him, so that He shall call me His friend and reveal His secret to me and listen to my voice in prayer? Is it possible?" The faith which saves the soul believes in the possibility of regeneration and sanctification, nay, more, it believes in Jesus and obtains for us power to become children of God and strength to conquer sin. This is believing God indeed.

Look this way yet again, for here is another difficulty. We know that we must persevere to the end, for only he that endureth to the end shall be saved. Does it not seem incredible that such feeble, fickle, foolish creatures as we are should continue in faith and the fear of God all our lives? Yet this we must do; and the faith which saves enables us to believe that we shall persevere, for it is persuaded that the Redeemer is able to keep that which we have committed unto Him, that He will perfect that which concerneth us, that He will suffer none to pluck us out of His hand, and that having begun the good work in us He will carry it on. This is faith worthy of the father of the faithful.

Once again, let us behold another difficulty for faith. We believe according to God's promise that we shall one day be "without spot or wrinkle, or any such thing." I do believe that this head shall wear a crown of glory, and that this hand shall wave a palm branch. I am fully assured that He will one day sweetly say to me—

"Close thine eyes that thou may'st see
What I have in store for thee.
Lay thine arms of warfare down,
Fall that thou may'st win a crown."

We, all, who are believers in Jesus, shall one day be without fault before the throne of God; but how is this to be? Surely our confidence is that He who has promised it is able to perform it. This is the faith which finds its way to glory—the faith which expects to enter into the Redeemer's joy, because of the Redeemer's love and life. Brethren, in this matter we see the difficulties, but we do not consider them; we count them as less than nothing since omnipotence has come into the field. "Thanks be unto God which giveth us the victory through our Lord Jesus Christ." We know that our Redeemer liveth, and that because He lives we shall also live, and be with Him where He is.

At the end of the chapter we are told that *this saving faith rests in the power of God as manifested in Jesus,*—" If we believe in Him who was delivered for our offences, and was raised again for our justification." Beloved, we believe that Jesus died, as certainly died as ever man died, and yet on the morning of the third day He rose again from the dead by divine power. It is not to us a thing incredible that God should raise the dead; we therefore believe that because God has raised the dead He hath raised us also from our death in sin, and that He will raise our bodies from the tomb after they shall have slept awhile in the earth. We believe also that our Lord Jesus died for our offences, and put them away. Our faith builds upon the substitution of the Lord Jesus on our behalf, and it rests there with firm confidence. We believe also that He arose again because His substitution was accepted, and because our offences were for ever put away,—rose again to prove that we are justified in Him. This is where we stand then. I expect to be saved, not at all because of what I am, nor of what I can do, nor because of anything I ever shall be able to be or to do; but only because God has promised to save those who believe in Jesus Christ through what the Lord Jesus has suffered in their stead. Because Jesus has risen to prove that His suffering was accepted on the behalf of believers, there do we rest and trust, and that is the way in which every believer is saved,—that way and nohow else. Even as Abraham believed so do we. Here is the fact, it is of faith.

II. Now we come to the second point; and here we are to consider THE FIRST REASON why God has chosen to make salvation by faith, "*that it might be of grace.*"

Now, dear friends, the Lord might have willed to make the condition of salvation a mitigated form of works. If He had done so it would not have been of grace, for it is a principle which I need not explain now, but a fixed principle, that if the blessing be of grace it is no more of works, otherwise grace is no more grace; and if it be of works it is no more of grace, otherwise work is no more work. As water and oil will not mix, and as fire and water will not lie down side by side in quiet, so neither will the principle of merit and the principle of free favour. You cannot make a legal work to be a condition of a gracious blessing without at once introducing an alien element and really bringing the soul under the covenant of works, and so spoiling the whole plan of mercy. Grace and faith are congruous, and will draw together in the same chariot, but grace and merit are contrary the one to the other and pull opposite ways, and therefore God has not chosen to yoke them together. He will not build with incongruous materials, or daub with untempered mortar. He will not make an image partly of gold and partly of clay, nor weave a linsey-woolsey garment: His work is all of a piece and all of grace.

Again, *in Abraham's case*, inasmuch as he received by faith the blessing which God promised him, *it is very evident that it was of grace.* You never heard any one ascribe Abraham's salvation to his merits, and yet Abraham was an eminently holy man. There are specks in his life—and in whose life will there not be found infirmities?—but yet he was one of the grandest characters of history. Still, no man thinks of Abraham as a self-justifying person, or as at all related to the Pharisee who said, "God, I thank thee that I am not as other men." I never heard anybody hint that the great patriarch had whereof to glory before God. His name is not "the father of the innocent," but "the father of the faithful." When we read Abraham's life we see that God called him by an act of sovereign grace, that God made a covenant with him as an act of grace, and that the promised child was born, not of the power of the flesh, but entirely according to promise. Grace reigns through righteousness unto eternal life in the life of the patriarch, and it is illustrated in a thousand ways whenever we see his faith receiving the promises. The holiness of Abraham, since it arose out of his faith, never leads us to ascribe his blessedness to anything but the grace of God.

Now, inasmuch as we are saved by faith, *every believer is made to see for himself that, in his own instance, it is by grace.* Believing is such a self-renunciating act that no man who looks for eternal life thereby ever talked about his own merits, except to count them but dross and dung. No, brethren, the child of the promise cannot live in the same house with the son of the bondwoman; when Isaac grows up Ishmael must depart: the principle of believing unto everlasting life will not endure a hint about human deservings. Those who believe in justification by faith are the only persons who can believe in salvation by grace. The believer may grow in grace till he becomes fully assured of his own salvation; yes, and he may become holiness unto the Lord in a very remarkable manner, being wholly consecrated to God in body, soul, and spirit, but you will never hear the believing man speak of his experience, or attainments, or achievements as a reason for glorying in himself, or as an argument for becoming more confident as to his safety. He dares not trust his words, or states of feeling, for he feels that by faith he stands.

He cannot get away from simple faith, for the moment he attempts to do so he feels the ground going from under him, and he begins to sink into horrible confusion of spirit; therefore he returns unto his rest, and resolves to abide in faith in his risen Saviour, for there he abides in the grace of God.

Through the prominence given to faith, the truth of salvation by grace is so conspicuously revealed that *even the outside world are compelled to see it,* though the only result may be to make them cavil threat. They charge us with preaching too much concerning grace, because they hear us magnifying and extolling the plan of salvation by faith, and they readily perceive that a gift promised to faith must be a boon of grace, and not a reward for service done. Only begin to preach salvation by works or ceremonies, and nobody will accuse you of saying too much of grace, but keep to faith and you are sure to keep to the preaching of grace.

Moreover, *faith never did clash with grace yet.* When the sinner comes and trusts to Christ, and Christ saith to him, "I forgive thee freely by My grace," faith says, "O Lord, that is what I want, and what I believe in; I ask Thee to deal with me even so." "But if I give thee everlasting life it will not be because thou deservest it, but for Mine own name's sake." Faith replies, "O Lord, that also is precisely as I desire; it is the sum and substance of my prayer." When faith grows strong and takes to pleading in prayer (and oh how mighty she is with God in supplication, moving His omnipotence to her mind). yet all her pleadings are based on grace, and none of them upon the merit of the creature. Never yet did faith borrow weapons from Mount Sinai, never once did she ask as though the favour were a debt, but she always holds to the promise of the gracious God, and expects all things from the faithfulness of her God.

Aye, and when faith grows strongest and attains to her highest stature, and is fullest of delight, so that she danceth for very joy, yet she never in all her exultation boasts or exalts herself. Where is boasting, then? It is excluded. By the law of works? nay, but by the law of faith. Faith and carnal boasting never yet walked together. If a man should boast of the strength of his faith, it would be clear evidence that he had none at all, or at least that he had for the time fallen into vainglorious presumption. Boasting? No, faith loves to lie low, and behave herself as a little child, and when she lifts herself up it is to exalt her Lord, and her Lord alone.

Faith, too, is well calculated to show forth the grace of God, because, *faith is the child of grace.* "Ah," says faith, "I have grasped the covenant, I have laid hold on the promises, I have seen Christ, I have gazed into heaven, I have enjoyed foretastes of eternal joys. But," says she, " I am of the operation of God; I should never have existed if the Spirit of God had not created me." The believer knows that his faith is not a weed indigenous to the soil of his heart, but a rare plant, an exotic which has been planted there by divine wisdom, and he knows too that if the Lord does not nourish it his faith will die like a withered flower. He knows that his faith is a perpetual miracle; for it is begotten, sustained, and preserved by a power not less mighty than that which raised our Lord Jesus Christ from the dead. If I met with an angel in a hovel I should know that he was not born there, but that he came from above; and so it it with faith, its heavenly descent is manifest to all. Faith, then, tracing her very existence to grace, never

can be anything but the friend, the vindicator, the advocate, and the glorifier of the grace of God: therefore it is of faith that it might be by grace.

III. Now, thirdly, there is A FURTHER REASON for faith and grace being the Lord's chosen method of salvation,—"*To the end that the promise might be sure to all the seed.*" Look at this, dear friends, very carefully. Salvation was made to be of faith, and not of works, that the promise might be sure to all the seed, for first, *it could not have been sure to us Gentiles by the law,* because in a certain sense we were not under the law of Moses at all. Turn to the text and you find that it runs thus: "Sure to all the seed, not to that only which is of the law, but to that also which is of the faith of Abraham, who is the father of us all." That is to say, the Jew, receiving the seal of circumcision and coming under the ceremonial law, eating its passover, and presenting its sacrifices, might possibly have been reached by a legal method, but we who are Gentiles would have been altogether shut out. As to the covenant according to the flesh, we are aliers and have never come under its bonds, or participated in its privileges, therefore grace chooses to bless us by faith in order that the Gentile may partake of the blessing of the covenant as well as the Jew.

But there is a still wider reason: it is of faith, because *the other method has failed already in every case.* We have all broken the law already, and so have put ourselves beyond the power of ever receiving blessing as a reward of merit. Failure at the outset has ruined our future prospects and henceforth by the deeds of the law shall no flesh be justified. What remaineth, then, if we are to be saved at all, but that if should be of faith? This door alone is open, let us bless God that no man can shut it.

Again, it is of faith that it *might be sure.* Now, under the system of works nothing is sure. Suppose, my dear brethren, you were under a covenant of salvation by works, and you had fulfilled those works up till now, yet you would not be sure. Are you seventy years of age, and have you kept your standing till now? Well, you have done a great deal more than father Adam did, for though he was a perfect man without any natural corruption, I do not suppose that he kept his first estate for a day. But after all you have done for these long years you may lose everything before you have finished your next meal. If your standing depends upon your own works you are not safe, and can never be safe until you are out of this present life, for you might sin, and that one offence against the conditions would destroy the covenant. "When the righteous turneth from his righteousness, and committeth iniquity, he shall even die thereby." But see the excellence of salvation by grace, for when you reach the ground of faith in the promises you are upon *terra firma*, and your soul is no longer in jeopardy. Here is a sure foundation, for the divine promise cannot fail. If my salvation depends upon the Lord, and is received by me on the ground that the Lord hath decreed it, promised it in covenant, and ensured it to me by the blood of Jesus Christ, then it is so mine that neither life nor death nor Satan nor the world shall ever rob me of it. If I live to the age of Methuselah my faith will have the same promises to rest upon, and clinging there she will defy the lapse of years to change her immutable security. The promise would not be sure to one of the seed by any other means than that of grace through faith, but now it is sure to all.

Moreover, if the promise had been made to works there are some of the seed to whom most evidently it never could come. One of the seed of Abraham hung dying upon a cross, and within an hour or two his bones were broken that he might the more quickly die and be buried. Now, if salvation to that poor dying thief must come by works, how can he be saved? His hands and feet are fastened up and he is in the very article of death, what can he do? The promise would not have been sure *to him*, my brethren, if there had been any active condition; but he believed, cast a saving eye upon the Lord Jesus and said, "Lord remember me," and the promise was most sure to him, for the answer was—"To-day shalt thou be with Me in Paradise." Many a chosen one of God is brought into such a condition that nothing is possible to him except faith, but grace has made the act of believing divinely possible. Well was it for those bitten by serpents that all that was asked of them was a look, for this was possible even when the hot venom made the blood to boil and scalded all the frame with fever. Faith is possible to the blind, the lame, the deaf, the dumb; faith is possible to the almost idiot, the desponding and the guilty; faith can be possessed by babes and by the extremely aged, by the illiterate as well as by the instructed; it is well chosen as the cup to convey the living water, for it is not too heavy for the weak, nor too huge for the little, nor too small for the full-grown.

Now, brothers and sisters, I have done when I have said just this. I will ask you who have believed in Christ one question,—you who are resting in the promise of God, you who are depending upon the finished work of Him who was delivered for your offences—how do you feel? Are you rejoicing in your unquestionable safety? As I have turned this matter over, and thought upon it, my soul has dwelt in perfect peace. I cannot conceive anything that God Himself could give to the believer which would make him more safe than the work of Christ has made him. God cannot lie, are you not sure of this? He must keep His promise, are you not certain of this? What more do you want? As a little child believes its father's word without any question, even so would we rest on the bare, naked promise of Jehovah, and in so doing we became conscious of a peace that passeth all understanding, which keeps your hearts and minds by Christ Jesus. I dare not say otherwise, nor be silent, for I am conscious of being able to say, "Therefore being justified by faith, I have peace with God." In that peace of the soul much love springs up, and inward unity to God and conformity to Christ. Faith believes her God and trusts Him for time and eternity, for little things and great things, for body and for soul, and this leads on to still higher results. O blessed God, what a union of desire, and heart, and aim exists between Thee and the soul that trusts Thee! How are we brought into harmony with Thy mind and purposes! How is our heart made to delight in Thee! How completely is our soul "bound up in the bundle of life with the soul of the Lord our God"! We grow up into Him in all things who is our Head, our life, our all.

I charge you, dear children of God, "as ye have received Christ Jesus the Lord so walk ye in Him." Live in His peace, and abound in it more and more; do not be afraid of being too peaceful, "rejoice in the Lord always, and again I say rejoice." When you have to condemn yourself for shortcomings, yet do not question the promise of the Lord. When sin overcomes you, confess the fault, but do not doubt the pardon which Jesus still gives you. When sharp temptations and severe trials arise from divers quarters do not suffer them to carry you by storm; let not the stronghold and castle of your spirit be captured— "let not your heart be troubled." Stagger not at the promise through unbelief, but hold to it whether you walk in the sunshine or in Egyptian darkness. That which the Lord has promised He is able also to perform, do not doubt it. Lean hard on the faithful promise, and when you feel sad at heart lean harder and harder still, for "faithful is He that hath promised, who also will do it."

Last of all, you sinners here this morning, who have heard all about this salvation by trusting; I charge you do not rest till you have trusted the Lord Jesus Christ, and rested in the great promises of God. Here is one: "I will be merciful to their unrighteousness, and their sins and their iniquities will I remember no more for ever." Here is another which is very cheering: "Whosoever calleth upon the name of the Lord shall be saved." Call upon Him in prayer, and then say, "Lord I have called, and Thou hast said I shall be saved." Here is another gracious word: "He that believeth and is baptized shall be saved." Attend thou to these two commands and then say, "Lord, I have Thy word for it that I shall be saved, and I hold Thee to it." Believe God, sinner. Oh, that He would give thee grace this morning by His Holy Spirit to say, "How can I do otherwise than believe Him? I dare not doubt Him." O poor tried soul, believe in Jesus so as to trust thy guilty soul with Him. The more guilty thou feelest thyself to be, the more is it in thy power to glorify God, by believing that He can forgive and renew such a guilty one as thou art. If thou liest buried like a fossil in the lowest stratum of sin, yet He can quarry for thee and fetch thee up out of the horrible pit, and make thy dry, petrified heart to live. Believest thou this? "If thou canst believe, all things are possible to him that believeth." Trust the promise that He makes to every believer that He will save him, and hold thou to it, for it is not a vain thing, it is thy life. "But what if I obtain no joy or peace?" Believe the promise still, and joy and peace will come. "But what if I see no signs?" Ask for no signs, be willing to trust God's word without any other guarantee but His truthful character, and thou wilt thus give Him glory. "Blessed are they that have not seen, and yet have believed." Believe that Jehovah cannot lie, and as He has promised to forgive all who believe in Jesus, hang on to that word and thou shalt be saved. Sinners, I have set before you the way of salvation, as simply as I can, will you have it or not? May the Spirit of God sweetly lead you to say, "Have it, aye, that I will." Then go in peace and rejoice henceforth and for ever. God bless you. Amen.

PEACE: A FACT AND A FEELING

"Therefore being justified by faith, we have peace with God through our Lord Jesus Christ."—Romans v. 1.

WONDERFUL is the power of faith. In the Epistle to the Hebrews our apostle tells us of the marvellous exploits which it has wrought in subduing kingdoms and obtaining promises, in quenching the violence of fire and stopping the mouths of lions, in braving perils and doing deeds of prowess. Still, to us personally one of the most wonderful of its effects is that it brings us justification and consequent peace. "Being justified by faith, we have peace with God." If we know the justifying power of faith, and the way in which, like a hand, it puts upon us the matchless garment of the Saviour's righteousness, we shall value that faith as our first parents did the gracious hand of God which made for them coats of skins and therewith covered their nakedness. The little faith we have will make us crave for more; and every need we feel will make us long to prove its virtue in our own souls to meet our own personal case, by the operation of the Holy Ghost.

Now, fault brings to the soul, according to the text, two blessings. It is not the creator of these things, but the conveyance, the channel, the conduit pipe through which these favours come to us. First, *it brings us a state of peace*—"being justified by faith"; and, secondly, *it brings us a sense of peace*— "we have peace with God through our Lord Jesus Christ."

I. Our first thoughts shall cluster about that most important of all matters—A STATE OF PEACE WITH GOD.

Naturally we have no peace. God is angry with us because we are sinful, and we are at variance with God because He is holy. God cannot agree with us—"Can two walk together except they be agreed?" And we cannot agree with God, for "the carnal mind is enmity against God: for it is not subject to the law of God, neither indeed can be." There is a breach between the rebellious creature and the righteous Creator. Sad that it should be so, but such is the case by nature with every man that is born of woman. We are set against the Lord. We kick against His providence, we rebel against His commands, we resist His Holy Spirit, we reject His love as manifested in the death of Christ, and we should live and die in this hostility if it were not for His almighty grace. Before ever we can enjoy peace within our hearts there must be a state of peace established between us and God. We must submit ourselves to the Lord, and He must forgive the past, and make with us a covenant of peace, or else there is no peace for us; for "there is no peace, saith my God, unto the wicked."

Let me briefly explain to you the way in which we come to possess peace with God. We are criminals condemned, though we do not consider ourselves to be in such a critical condition. We persist that we are righteous, we decline to acknowledge the jurisdiction of the law, and we refuse to own the justice of its sentence. Therefore or ever we can have peace with God we must be brought **into court, hear** the indictment preferred **against** us,

and be put on our trial. When thus arraigned we must put in our pleading. Dost thou say "Not guilty?" Then, man, thou challengest thine accuser to bring forth the evidence which will soon spoil thy conceit, and crush thee with its weight. But before there can be peace between us and God *we must with all our hearts plead "guilty."* We must confess the truth, for God will never agree with liars, nor with those who indulge self-deception. He is a God of truth, and dissemblers can have no communion with Him. Being guilty, we must take the place of the guilty: it is our proper position, and it is due to the judge of all the earth that we take it; to refuse to do so is contempt of court. There is mercy for a sinner, but there is no mercy for the man who will not own himself a sinner. "If we confess our sins He is faithful and just to forgive us our sins"; but if any man say that he has no sin he is a liar, and the truth is not in him, and there cannot be peace between him and God while he is in that humour.

It seems a stern demand, and very galling for our pride, to have to stand in the dock, and in answer to the question, "Guilty or not guilty?" to reply, "Guilty, Lord, guilty. Whatever the consequences may be, guilty." But to some of us it no longer seems to be hard, because we could not now plead otherwise. We are so conscious of our guilt that we cannot escape from a sense of it. "If I wash myself with snow water, and make my hands never so clean, yet shalt Thou plunge me in the ditch, and mine own clothes shall abhor me." We cannot look upon a single day without being convinced of sin; and in reviewing our past lives from our childhood, we are over and over constrained to blush at the memory of our waywardness and our wilfulness, our perverseness and our provocation. The faults and the follies that have tracked our course haunt us, till our very looks would tell the truth though our tongues were silent. To plead guilty has now become a positive though a painful relief to us; it is the ending of a vain show which we found it hard to keep up; it is coming to the bottom of the matter, and knowing the worst of our case. Dear hearer, before thou canst have peace with heaven thou must take up thy true position, and plead guilty. I pray the Holy Spirit to lead thee to do so. It is His work to convince us of sin, and if He shall exercise His divine office upon any of us we shall no longer profess like the Pharisee that we are not as other men, but like the publican we shall heartily pray, "God be merciful to me a sinner."

Supposing that with confusion of face, contrition of heart, and aroused conscience we own and acknowledge our inexcusable guilt, *the next thing requisite to our peace is that we should admit the justice of the divine sentence*, and reverence instead of reviling the Judge of all the earth, against whom we have so grossly revolted. There are men who will say, "Yes, I am guilty and sinful, but still the penalty is out of proportion to my criminality; I cannot believe that God will deal so severely with the offences of His creatures." Now, however rational such reflections may sound they certainly are not acceptable with God. Of this thing, my friend, I warrant thee: if the Holy Spirit has ever shown thee sin in its natural hideousness and deformity, thou wilt think nothing too bad for it. Thou wilt cry from the depths of thy soul, "Let it be condemned, let it be punished." I would not, if I could, lift a finger to prevent God from punishing sin. Whatsoever a man soweth, that must he reap: the result of sin must follow its commission. The foundations of society would be undermined and there would be no living in the world if there were no laws, or if laws might be violated with impunity. There would indeed be no proof that there was a great Judge of all the earth if He did not do right; and if He does right, He must punish sin, for it ought to be punished. Were I the judge of quick and dead the first thing that I would do would be to condemn myself, for I deserve condemnation and punishment. Neither would it yield my heart the least comfort to be told that God could wink at sin. I want not such a God, neither could I endure to think that the law of righteousness was thus relaxed. My conscience would not be relieved of a sense of obligations I could not deny, nor of impurities I could not cleanse, nor of wrongs I could not rectify, by a suspicion that the Majesty of heaven had threatened a damnation which did not exist. I pray the Spirit of God to bring you, my hearer, not only to be convinced of sin, but of righteousness and of judgment to come. God is righteous in fixing a day in which He will judge the world by the man Christ Jesus, according to our gospel.

This appears to be a painful process, to be bound to confess your guilt, and then to bare your neck to the sword of vengeance, and to say, "Thou wilt be justified when thou judgest, and wilt be clear when thou condemnest; for against Thee, Thee only have I sinned, and done this evil in Thy sight"; yet, there cannot be any peace with God till we come to it: because there can be no peace with the God of truth where there is any prevarication. Lasting peace must be founded upon everlasting truth. The fact is, we are guilty, and we deserve the punishment which God apportions to guilt, and we must agree with that truth, grim as it looks, or else we cannot be friends with God.

The next essential to our receiving justification is this: the prisoner is guilty, sentence is pronounced, and he admits the righteousness of it; he is asked if he has anything to say why the sentence should not be executed, and he stands speechless: and now comes in the abounding mercy of *God, who in order to our peace, finds a substitute to bear our penalty, and reveals to us this gracious fact.* He puts His Son into the sinner's place. Voluntarily doth the divine Saviour take upon Himself our nature, and come under the law, and by a sovereign act Jehovah lays upon Him the iniquity of us all. That sin having been laid on Christ, He has borne it and carried it away. In His own body he bore it on the tree. The transgressions of His people were made to meet upon His devoted person: those five wounds tell what He suffered, that marred countenance bears the tokens of His inward grief, and that cry, "My God, My God, why hast Thou forsaken Me?" indicates to us, as far as we are able to understand it, what He endured when He stood in the sinner's stead, the sin-bearer and the sacrifice.

When the Lord enables the soul to perceive that Christ stood in its stead, then the work of appropriating the justification is going on. Christ died "the just for the unjust, that He might bring us to God"; for He "made Him to be sin for us, who knew no sin; that we might be made the righteousness of God in Him." He was "made a curse for us: as it is written, Cursed is every one that hangeth on a tree." Christ hath once suffered for sin, and this is the foundation of our peace.

The point wherein faith comes into contact with pardon is when faith believes that the Son of God did come and stand in the sinner's stead, and when faith accepts that substitution as a glorious boon of grace, and rests in it, and says, "Now I see how God is just, and smites Christ in my stead. Seeing He condemned me before I had personally sinned, because of Adam's sin, I see how He can absolve me, though I have no righteousness, because of Christ's righteousness. In another did I fall, and in another do I rise. By one Adam I was destroyed: by another Adam am I restored. I see it. I leap for joy as I see it, and I accept it as from the Lord."

This is not quite all, for now here stands the guilty one, who has owned the sentence, and he has seen the sentence executed upon another. What then? *He takes his place as no longer liable to that sentence.* The penalty cannot be exacted twice. It were neither in accord with human or divine righteousness that two individuals should be punished for the same offence unless both were guilty. When God devised the plan of substitution the full penalty demanded of the guiltless surety was clearly intended to bring exemption to the guilty sinners. That Jesus should suffer vicariously and yet those for whom He paid the quittance in drops of blood should obtain no acquittal could not be. When God laid sin upon Christ it must have been in the intent of His heart that He would never lay it on those for whom Christ died. So then there standeth the man who was once guilty, but he is no more condemned, because another has taken upon Him the condemnation to which he was exposed. Still more, inasmuch as the Lord Jesus Christ came voluntarily under the law, obeyed the law, fulfilled the law, and made it honourable, according to the infinite purpose and will of God the righteousness of Christ is imputed to the believer. While Christ stands in the sinner's place, the believing sinner stands in Christ's place. As the Lord looked upon Christ as though He had been a sinner, though He was no sinner, and dealt with Him as such, so now the Lord looks upon the believing sinner as though he were righteous, though indeed he has no righteousness of his own; and He loves him and delights in his perfect comeliness, regarding him as covered with the mantle of his Redeemer's righteousness, and as having neither spot nor wrinkle nor any such thing.

This is a wonderful doctrine, but it is the doctrine of the word of God. It is the doctrine whereon faith can feed and rest; and when faith receives it she says to the soul, "Soul, thou art free from sin, for Christ has borne thy sin in His own body on the tree. Soul, thou art righteous before God, for the righteousness of Christ is thine by imputation." Without any works of thine own thou art yet justified according to the righteousness of faith, even as faithful Abraham, of whom it is written, "He believed God, and it was counted unto him for righteousness." This is a wonderful exchange, the putting of Christ where the sinner was, and of the sinner where Christ was. And, now, what does the court say? The court says, "Not guilty; absolved; acquitted." And what is the condition of the man towards God? Why, he can say—

> "'Now freed from sin, I walk at large;
> My Saviour's blood's my full discharge.
> At His dear feet my soul I lay,
> A sinner saved I'll homage pay.'

Now do I love the Lord, and I know that the Lord loveth me."

By this process we have come to the truth before God, and we have dealt with each other on the line of truth. There has been no fabrication or falsehood. Justice has been vindicated, mercy has been magnified, and we are justly forgiven. Strange fusion of vehement grace and vindictive wrath! Behold how judgment and mercy have linked hands together in the person of the dying, bleeding, rising Son of God. This is the way by which we obtain justification.

The soul may well have a settled peace when it has realized and received such a justification as this, seeing it is a peace consistent with justice. The Lord has not winked at sin; He has not treated sin as if it were a trifle; the Lord has punished transgression and iniquity. The rod has been made to fall, and the blessed shoulders of our Lord have been made to smart under the infliction. If justice had never been satisfied the human conscience would not have been content. The proclamation of unconditional mercy would never have satisfied a human mind. If we had to preach to you that God forgave you irrespectively of an atonement, no awakened conscience would welcome the tidings; we should still have to confront the question, "Where is justice, then?" We should be unable to see how the law could be vindicated, or the moral government of God maintained. We are quite at rest, when we see that there is as much justice as there is mercy in the forgiveness of a believing soul, and that God is as glorious in holiness when He passes by sin as He would have been if He had cast the whole race into the abyss of unfathomable woe.

Nor need there be any morbid apprehension as to whether all the evidence that could be produced against us at our trial has been brought forward. Nobody can come in and say "Though you have been exonerated upon a partial trial, upon a more searching investigation your guilt could have been proved." We can reply, "But it was proved." There was the best of evidence to prove it, for we confessed it. There was no other evidence wanted, and nothing further could have been brought, since we pleaded guilty to every charge. If you bring any further accusation, we can only say that we pleaded guilty without reserve. It was all in the indictment; we did not attempt for a moment to cloak or conceal any guilt we had incurred. We confessed it all before the Lord, and owned to it; and since the Lord Jesus Christ took it all there is no cause for reopening the proceedings. There cannot be a second trial through a writ of error: the case is thoroughly disposed of; the prisoner has pleaded guilty to the capital charge, and has borne the utmost penalty of the law by his Substitute, which penalty God Himself has accepted. His acquittal is such as he can rest upon with implicit reliance.

Moreover we know that, being justified, we are now at peace with God, because there cannot be any more demands made against us. All that was against us Christ took away. "The blood of Jesus Christ His Son cleanseth us from all sin." The death of our great Redeemer has abounding merit in it, seeing that He was the Son of God. All the transgressions and iniquities that could ever be raked up against us were all laid to His charge, and His atonement by one offering has put an end to them all. We are not afraid, therefore, that anything fresh will be raised against us.

Again, our acquittal is certified beyond all question, and the certificate is always producible. Somebody might say to a prisoner "How do you know that you were acquitted?" He cannot produce any writing. On the record of the court it stands; and yet, mayhap, he has no means of access to the court record. But, beloved, you and I have a writ of acquittal which is always visible. Faith can see it to-night. "What is that?" say you. It is the risen Christ, for Jesus Christ "died for our sins, and rose again for our justification." You all know how that was. He was cast into the prison of the grave until it had been certified that our liabilities were fully discharged, and

> "If Jesus ne'er had paid the debt
> He ne'er had been at freedom set."

He was our hostage, and His body was held in durance till it was certified that there was no further claim against any one of His people. That done, He rose again from the dead for our justification. He is at the Father's right hand, and He could not be there if any of our iniquity remained on Him. He took our sin, but He has our sin no longer, for on the cross He discharged and annihilated it all so that it ceased to be, and He has gone into the glory as the representative and the substitute of His people, cleared from their imputed liabilities—clean delivered from anything that could be brought against Him on their account. So long as we see the Lord Jesus sitting in the throne of glory, we may boldly ask, "Who is he that condemneth? Christ that died, yea rather, hath risen again, who is even at the right hand of God, who also maketh intercession for us." We know our justification to be for ever complete, and beyond challenge, for Jesus keeps the place of acceptance for us.

And lastly, on this point, it was a justification from the very highest court. You know how it is in law: a matter may be decided in your favour, but there is an appeal to a higher court; and such are the glorious uncertainties of law that a sentence which has been confirmed in several courts may after all be reversed when it comes before the highest authorities. But you and I pleaded guilty *before God*. There is no higher authority than that of God Himself. When Jesus stood in our stead *we* did not put Him there; nor did He put Himself there; it was the act and deed of the Eternal Father. Is it not written—"The Lord hath laid on Him the iniquity of us all." It is not only true as a matter of personal faith that

> "I lay my sins on Jesus,"

but as a matter of fact of a far earlier date the Lord laid them on Him. There is no higher authority than the Lord's, and therefore do we cry, "it is God that justifieth, who is he that condemneth?" We have been taken into the highest court of all, and there we have been cleared through Jesus's blood; have we not cause to be fully at peace with God, "being justified by faith?" Precious doctrine! Oh to rest in it with a childlike confidence henceforth and for evermore!

II. I now come to the second part of the subject, which is this. Faith brings us into the state of peace which I have explained, and afterwards FAITH GIVES US THE SENSE OF PEACE. "Therefore being justified by faith, we have peace with God."

Will you please to notice that the sense of peace follows upon the state of peace. We do not get peace before we are justified, neither is peace a means of justification. No, brethren, we are justified first. "While we were yet without strength, in due time Christ died for the ungodly." God justifies the ungodly. We have no peace till that is done. At least there may seem to be peace, a horrible peace—the peace of death and of daring presumption—when a man says, "Peace, peace," when there is no peace, and talks about rest when he has a conscience seared as with a hot iron—and a mind drugged with presumption, so that he sleeps that awful sleep which is the presage of waking up in hell. From such peace may God deliver us! But real peace—the peace of God—and peace with God must spring out of our being justified in the way which I have been trying to describe. The man who is justified, according to the text, at this moment has a sense of peace with God, but this is only true of those who by faith are justified.

Here I want you to observe—for every word is instructive—that we have peace with God "through Jesus Christ our Lord." Many children of God lose their peace in a measure, and part of the reason of it is because they begin to deal with God absolutely. None of us will ever experience true peace with God except through Jesus Christ. I like that strong expression of Luther, bald and bare as it is, when, in commenting on the Epistle to the Galatians, he says, "I will have nothing to do with an absolute God." If you have anything to do with God absolutely, you will be destroyed. There cannot be any point of contact between absolute deity and fallen humanity except through Jesus Christ, the appointed Mediator. That is God's door; all else is a wall of fire. You can by Christ approach the Lord, but this is the sole bridge across the gulf.

Whenever you, dear soul, begin to deal with God according to your own experience, according to your own frames and feelings, or even according to the exercises of your own faith, unless that faith keeps its eye on Christ, you will lose your peace. Stand out of Christ, and what a wretched creature you are! Have you attempted to approach the Eternal King without His chosen ambassador? How presumptuous is your attempt! The throne of divine sovereignty is terrible apart from the redeeming blood. Peace with God must come to us by the way of the cross. Through our Lord Jesus Christ we gain it, and through Him we keep it.

There be some among you who, I trust, are really believers in Christ, who are constantly prone to fret and say, "I have no lasting peace. I am a believer in Jesus, and I have a measure of peace at times, but I do not enjoy fulness of peace." Well, now we must look at this a little, and the more closely we inspect it the more convinced we shall be that peace is the right of every believer. What is there now between him and God? Sin is forgiven. What is more, righteousness is imputed. He is the object of eternal love; he is more than that; he is the object of divine complacency. God sees him in His Son, and loves him. Why should he not be at peace? "Let not your heart be troubled; ye believe in God," said Jesus, "believe also in Me." Christian, there is no ground of quarrel between you and your heavenly Father. God for Christ's sake has forgiven you. To you the Lord virtually says, "Come now and let us reason together, though your sins be as scarlet, I have made them as wool. Though they be red like crimson, I have already made them as snow." When He says, "They shall be," He is speaking to the sinner; but to you they *are* so. You are justified. Why have you not peace, then? You have a claim to it, and you ought to enjoy it. What is the reason why you do not possess it? I will tell you. It is your unbelief. You are justified by faith, remember; and it is by faith that you obtain peace with God; and when you are doubting and fearing instead of simply believing—when you are questioning and grumbling, then it is that you lose your peace; but in proportion as your faith stands so will your peace with God abide.

I feel certain that the text tells us that every justified man has peace with God; and if so how is it that I hear poor souls crying, "I do believe, but I do not enjoy peace." I think I can tell you how it is. You make a mistake as to what this peace is. You say, "I am so dreadfully tempted. Sometimes I am drawn this way, and sometimes the other, and the devil never lets me alone." Listen. Did you ever read in the Bible that you were to have peace with the devil? Look at the text—"Therefore being justified by faith, we have peace *with God*." That is a very different thing from having peace with Satan. If the devil were to let you alone and never to tempt you I should begin to think that you belonged to him; for he is kind to his own in his own way, for a while. He has a way of whispering soft things into their ears, and with dulcet notes and siren songs he lures them to eternal destruction. But he worries with a malicious joy those whom he cannot destroy; for in their case he has great wrath, knowing that his time is short. He expects to see you soon in heaven out of gunshot of him; and so he makes the best of his opportunities to try if he can distress and injure you while you are here. You will soon be so far above him that you will not be able to hear the hell-dog bark, and so he snaps at you now to see if he can hurt you, as once he did your Master when he wounded his heel. You never had a promise of being at peace with the prince of darkness, but there is another promise which is far better: it is this—"The Lord shall bruise Satan under your feet shortly." A bruise it shall be when we have him under our feet; we will triumph like our Master in the breaking of his head. Till then depend upon it the enmity between the seed of the serpent and the seed of the woman will continue, and there will be no truce to the war.

Do I hear another tried one saying, "Alas, it is not the devil; it is myself that I fear. I feel the flesh revolting and rebelling. Lusts that I thought were slain have a terrible resurrection. When I would do good, evil is present with me. Sin assails me with an awful power by reason of the weakness of my spirit and the strength of my flesh, and I cry, 'O wretched man that I am!'" Hearken again. Did the Lord ever promise that you should have peace with the flesh? Oh no, the moment you were converted there began a battle between the flesh and the spirit, and the battle will last till that flesh of yours shall lie low in the dust from whence it came, and your spirit, delivered from its bondage, shall ascend to God. You must not suppose that as long as you are in this body the flesh will help you. Ah no, you will cry with Paul, "O wretched man that I am, who shall deliver me from the body of this death?" You are harassed and hampered by the rising corruption of your nature, and it will still rise. Your brethren will still say of you, "What will ye see in the Shulamite? As it were the company of two armies." The flesh is striving against the spirit, and the spirit against the flesh; and though the lion shall one day lie down with the lamb, the flesh will never agree with the spirit. As the Lord hath war with Amalek for ever and ever, so there is war between the spirit and the flesh so long as the two are in the same man. There is no promise of peace with the flesh, then; but we have peace with God.

"Ah," says another, "I have little peace, for I am surrounded by those that vex me. When I serve the Lord they malign and misrepresent me with scoff and slander. They take up an evil report against me. Woe is me that I sojourn in Mesech, that I dwell in the tents of Kedar. My soul is among lions, even amongst them that are set on fire of hell. They give me no rest." Yes, but I smile as I think of it. Did you ever dream of having peace with the wicked, peace with such as turn aside to their crooked ways, peace with the workers of iniquity? Vain thought! Peace in this world where your Lord was crucified—peace with those that hate you for His sake? Why did He not say to you at the first, "If the world hate you, ye know that it hated Me before it hated you. If ye were of the world, the world would love his own: but because ye are not of the world, but I have chosen you out of the world, therefore the world hateth you." What! do you expect to wear a crown of gold where He wore a crown of thorns? The confessors and martyrs of ancient times never reckoned upon peace with the world. Nor did the apostle Paul, for he said, "The world is crucified to me, and I unto the world." You have no promise of the world's love, but you have a promise of this sort, "These things have I spoken unto you, that in Me ye might have peace. In the world ye shall have tribulation: but be of good cheer; I have overcome the world." "And this is the victory which overcometh the world, even our faith." I pray you, then, do not misconstrue the text. It does not say that you shall either have peace with the devil, or peace with the flesh, or peace with the world; but it does say that you have peace with God, which is infinitely better.

"Still," says one, "I find every day that I sin, and I hate myself for sinning. I cannot get to my bed at night but I feel grieved in my soul that I am not more like Christ, and that I cannot grow in grace as I desire. I do not seem to make the advance in the divine life that I hoped I should, and I am full of sin. Whatever I do is stained with defilement. Wherever I go I seem to fall one way or another into something that wounds my conscience and hurts me." Yes; and the Lord never said that you should have peace with sin. I am delighted to find that sin stings you, and that you hate it. The more hatred of sin the better. A sin-hating soul is a God-loving soul. If sin never distresses you, then God has never favoured you. Unless you hate sin you do not love holiness; and if you hate sin you cannot have any peace with it. You will never be satisfied till you are perfect, and when will you be perfect?

Why, when you wake up in your Lord's likeness. That will be the hour of your perfection, but till then sin will vex you. Then shall you have no Canaanite to harass you, and there shall be war with Amalek no more, when the last enemy is slain, when sin is extirpated, and you shall be near and like your God. You have no promise of peace with sin, nor need you wish for one, but you have peace with God.

To come back again to what is promised, and indeed to what is not only promised but really bestowed and communicated to us—"Being justified by faith, *we have peace with God.*"

Most assuredly we do enjoy peace with God in this respect—that *we know He loves us.* He would not have given His Son to die for us if He had not. He would not have devised this matchless plan of justification if He had not loved us. Moreover, we feel a fervent love to Him in return. We do not love Him as we wish to do, nor as we hope to do, but we do love Him for all that. We can say, "Lord, Thou knowest all things; Thou knowest that I love Thee."

"Yes, I love Thee and adore,
Oh for grace to love Thee more."

Of the excellence and virtue of this peace we make daily, hourly proof; for now *we are not afraid to go to our covenant God* for all necessary things, and to seek His face for help in time of trouble. Why, to some of us this resorting to God has become so habitual, that we speak with Him every hour of the day. Nothing happens but we fly to Him for counsel or for succour. We no longer ask leave to do so, for He has given to us the private key and the perpetual permit of access. We have not always such settled peace with our fellow creatures, for at times we so much lack confidence in them that we could not divulge to them our troubles; but we have peace with God; such an amity that we can always have recourse to Him, assured of His sympathy and His readiness to come to our relief in every time of need. Our habitude of prayer proves that we have peace with God; we should not think of praying to Him if we believed that He was our adversary, or if we doubted His goodwill. If we felt any enmity in our hearts to Him we should not go to Him as we do, with a childlike hope, in time of distress.

This peace with God makes us *delight in Him.* I am sure that every soul here that has been justified by faith delights in God. You do not always feel Him equally near, but when He is near it is the joy of your spirit. What are the best and happiest moments you ever know? Are they not those in which you have communion with God? What days can you reflect upon with the greatest satisfaction and ardently wish to have repeated? Are they not those in which His majesty and mercy have been so revealed to your spirit that with mingled awe and sweetness you have realized intensely His power and His presence? Oh, what a good God He is! Bad as we are, how good He is! Now, take care that you indulge this delight very often. If you delight in anything else you will be an idolater, but He has said, "Delight thyself in the Lord, and He will give thee the desire of thy heart." You cannot be too delighted with your God. Is He not perfection itself? Are we not, in all respects, rejoiced to have such a God? We would not have one attribute changed; nor one appointment of His sovereign will in the least degree moved from its order. Let Him be as He is, and do as He pleases, and our souls shall delight in Him. "Yea, though He slay me, yet will I trust in Him." Now, when you can delight in God, though you cannot delight in yourself, it shows that you have peace with Him, and are justified.

Then, brethren, this peace also shows itself in our *acquiescing in all that He does in His rough providences.* You know that a hypocrite is like a strange dog that will follow a man as long as he casts him a bone or a bit of meat; but a true believer is like a man's own dog that will follow him when he gives him nothing, and even when he deals him a cuff or a blow. A true believer says, "Shall I receive good from the hand of the Lord, and shall I not also receive evil? If He chasten me, I would sooner be chastened by my Father than I would be caressed by Satan." It were better to smart till one were black and blue under the rod of God, than to be set upon a high throne by the world or the devil. When he offers thee the kingdoms of this world be sure that thou say to the foul fiend, "Get thee behind me"; but when the Lord hands thee the bitter cup be sure to say, "Thy will be done," and take it cheerfully at His hands. If we feel an agreement with our Lord's will it shows that we are at peace with Him.

One more evidence of being at peace with God is when you can *with confidence look forward to the time of your departure* out of this world and say, "I can die, if Thou, O Lord, be with me." When you can fall in with the words of the hymn we were singing just now—

"Bold shall I stand in that great day,
For who aught to my charge shall lay?
While through Thy blood absolved I am,
From sin's tremendous curse and shame."

We are not afraid of the day of judgment because we have peace with God, and hence we are not afraid to die.

There is concord and harmony between the righteous God and His redeemed people, and hence fear is banished. He has given to us His Spirit to dwell in our hearts, and now we desire that each rising wish may be prompted by His will. Our mind is agreed with the mind of God. He wishes us to be holy, and we wish to be holy. He would kill sin in us, and we long to have it killed. He wishes us to obey, and we desire to obey. He would have us seek His glory, and we desire that He should be glorified in us, in our whole spirit, soul, and body. The lines of our life run parallel with the life of God, though upon a lower level: we can never be as He is in the glory of His nature, but still we desire to be holy as He is holy. The life within us is divine, for we have been begotten again by Himself, and henceforth we are in Christ, and Christ in us, and so we are at peace with God.

Go your way, my brethren, and swim in this peace. Bathe your weary souls in seas of heavenly rest until you come to the place where not a wave of trouble shall ever roll across your peaceful breasts; and the very God of peace sanctify you wholly, and preserve you blameless unto the coming of our Lord Jesus Christ. Faithful is He that calleth you, who also will do it. Amen.

FOR WHOM DID CHRIST DIE?

"Christ died for the ungodly."—Romans v. 6.

IN this verse the human race is described as a sick man, whose disease is so far advanced that he is altogether without strength: no power remains in his system to throw off his mortal malady, nor does he desire to do so; he could not save himself from his disease if he would, and would not if he could. I have no doubt that the apostle had in his eye the description of the helpless infant given by the prophet Ezekiel; it was an infant—an infant newly born—an infant deserted by its mother before the necessary offices of tenderness had been performed; left unwashed, unclothed, unfed, a prey to certain death under the most painful circumstances, forlorn, abandoned, hopeless. Our race is like the nation of Israel, its whole head is sick, and its whole heart faint. Such, unconverted men, are you! Only there is this darker shade in your picture, that your condition is not only your calamity, but your fault. In other diseases men are grieved at their sickness, but this is the worst feature in your case, that you love the evil which is destroying you. In addition to the pity which your case demands, no little blame must be measured out to you: you are without will for that which is good, your "cannot" means "will not," your inability is not physical but moral, not that of the blind who cannot see for want of eyes, but of the willingly ignorant who refuse to look.

While man is in this condition Jesus interposes for his salvation. "When we were yet without strength, in due time Christ died for the ungodly"; "while we were yet sinners, Christ died for us," according to "His great love wherewith He loved us, even when we were dead in trespasses and sins." The pith of my sermon will be an endeavour to declare that the reason of Christ's dying for us did not lie in our excellence; but where sin abounded grace did much more abound, for the persons for whom Jesus died were viewed by Him as the reverse of good, and He came into the world to save those who are guilty before God, or, in the words of our text, "Christ died for the ungodly."

Now to our business. We shall dwell first upon *the fact*—"Christ died for the ungodly;" then we shall consider the *fair inferences* therefrom; and, thirdly, proceed to think and speak of *the proclamation* of this simple but wondrous truth.

I. First, here is THE FACT—"*Christ died for the ungodly.*" Never did the human ear listen to a more astounding and yet cheering truth. Angels desire to look into it, and if men were wise they would ponder it night and day. Jesus, the Son of God, Himself God over all, the infinitely glorious One, Creator of heaven and earth, out of love to men stooped to become a man and die. Christ, the thrice holy God, the pure-hearted man, in whom there was no sin and could be none, espoused the cause of the wicked. Jesus, whose doctrine makes deadly war on sin, whose Spirit is the destroyer of evil, whose whole self abhors iniquity, whose second advent will prove His indignation against transgression, yet undertook the cause of the impious, and even unto death pursued their salvation. The Christ of God, though He had no part or lot in the fall and the sin which has arisen out of it, has died to redeem us from its penalty, and, like the psalmist, He can cry, "Then I restored that which I took not away." Let all holy beings judge whether this is not the miracle of miracles!

Christ, the name given to our Lord, is an expressive word; it means "Anointed One," and indicates that He was sent upon a divine errand, commissioned by supreme authority. The Lord Jehovah said of old, "*I have laid* help upon One that is mighty, *I have exalted* One chosen out of the people;" and again, "*I have given Him* as a covenant to the people, a leader and commander to the people." Jesus was both set apart to this work, and qualified for it by the anointing of the Holy Ghost. He is no unauthorised saviour, no amateur deliverer, but an ambassador, clothed with unbounded power from the great King, a Redeemer with full credentials from the Father. It is this ordained and appointed Saviour who has "died for the ungodly," Remember this, ye ungodly! Consider well who it was that came to lay down His life for such as you are.

The text says Christ *died*. He did a great deal besides dying, but the crowning act of His career of love for the ungodly, and that which rendered all the rest available to them, was His death for them. He actually gave up the ghost, not in fiction, but in fact. He laid down His life for us, breathing out His soul, even as other men do when they expire. That it might be indisputably clear that He was really dead, His heart was pierced with the soldier's spear, and forthwith came there out blood and water. The Roman governor would not have allowed the body to be removed from the cross had he not been duly certified that Jesus was indeed dead. His relatives and friends who wrapped Him in linen and laid Him in Joseph's tomb, were sorrowfully sure that all that lay before them was a corpse. The Christ really died, and in saying that, we mean that He suffered all the pangs incident to death; only He endured much more and worse, for His was a death of peculiar pain and shame, and was not only attended by the forsaking of man, but by the departure of His God. That cry, "My God. My God! why hast Thou forsaken Me?" was the innermost blackness of the thick darkness of death.

Our Lord's death was penal, inflicted upon Him by divine justice. and rightly so, for on Him lay our iniquities, and therefore on Him must lay the suffering. "It pleased the Father to bruise Him; He hath put Him to grief." He died under circumstances which made His death most terrible. Condemned to a felon's gibbet, He was crucified amid a mob of jesters, with few sympathizing eyes to gaze upon Him; He bore the gaze of malice and the glance of scorn; He was hooted and jeered by a ribald throng, who were cruelly inventive in their taunts and blasphemies. There He hung, bleeding from many wounds, exposed to the sun, burning with fever, and devoured with thirst, under every circumstance of contumely, pain, and utter wretchedness; His death was of all deaths the most deadly death, and emphatically "Christ died."

But the pith of the text comes here, that "Christ died *for the ungodly*"; not for the righteous, not for the reverent and devout, but for the *ungodly*. Look at the original word. and you will find that it has the meaning of "impious, irreligious, and wicked."

Our translation is by no means too strong, but scarcely expressive enough. To be ungodly, or godless, is to be in a dreadful state, but as use has softened the expression, perhaps you will see the sense more clearly if I read it, "Christ died for the *impious*," for those who have no reverence for God. Christ died for the godless, who, having cast off God, cast off with Him all love for that which is right. I do not know a word that could more fitly describe the most irreligious of mankind than the original word in this place, and I believe it is used on purpose by the Spirit of God to convey to us the truth, which we are always slow to receive, that Christ did not die because men were good, or would be good, but died for them as ungodly —or, in other words, "He came to seek and to save that which was lost."

Observe, then, that when the Son of God determined to die for men, He viewed them as ungodly, and far from God by wicked works. In casting His eye over our race He did not say, "Here and there I see spirits of nobler mould, pure, truthful, truth-seeking, brave, disinterested, and just; and therefore, because of these choice ones, I will die for this fallen race." No; but looking on them all, He whose judgment is infallible returned this verdict, "They are all gone out of the way; they are together become unprofitable; there is none that doeth good, no, not one." Putting them down at that estimate, and nothing better, Christ died for them. He did not please Himself with some rosy dream of a superior race yet to come, when the age of iron should give place to the age of gold,—some halcyon period of human development, in which civilisation would banish crime, and wisdom would conduct man back to God. Full well He knew that, left to itself, the world would grow worse and worse, and that by its very wisdom it would darken its own eyes. It was not because a golden age would come by natural progress, but just because such a thing was impossible, unless He died to procure it, that Jesus died for a race which, apart from Him, could only develop into deeper damnation. Jesus viewed us as we really were, not as our pride fancies us to be; He saw us to be without God, enemies to our own Creator, dead in trespasses and sins, corrupt, and set on mischief, and even in our occasional cry for good, searching for it with blinded judgment and prejudiced heart, so that we put bitter for sweet and sweet for bitter. He saw that in us was no good thing, but every possible evil, so that we were lost,—utterly, helplessly, hopelessly lost apart from Him: yet viewing us as in that graceless and godless plight and condition, He died for us."

I would have you remember that the view under which Jesus beheld us was not only the true one, but, for us, the kindly one; because had it been written that Christ died for the better sort, then each troubled spirit would have inferred "He died not for me." Had the merit of His death been the perquisite of honesty, where would have been the dying thief? If of chastity, where the woman that loved much? If of courageous fidelity, how would it have fared with the apostles, for they all forsook Him and fled? There are times when the bravest man trembles lest he should be found a coward, the most disinterested frets about the selfishness of his heart, and the most pure is staggered by his own impurity; where, then, would have been hope for one of us, if the gospel had been only another form of law, and the benefits of the cross had been reserved as the rewards of virtue? The gospel does not come to us as a premium for virtue, but it presents us with forgiveness for sin. It is not a reward for health, but a medicine for sickness. Therefore, to meet all cases, it puts us down at our worst, and, like the good Samaritan with the wounded traveller, it comes to us where we are. "Christ died for the impious" is a great net which takes in even the leviathan sinner; and of all the creeping sinners innumerable which swarm the sea of sin, there is not one kind which this great net does not encompass.

Let us note well that in this condition lay the need of our race that Christ should die. I do not see how it could have been written, "Christ died for the *good*." To what end for the good? Why need they His death? If men are perfect, does God need to be reconciled to them? Was He ever opposed to holy beings? Impossible! On the other hand, were the good ever the enemies of God? If such there be are they not of necessity His friends? If man be by nature just with God, to what end should the Saviour die? "*The just for the unjust*" I can understand; but the "just dying for the just" were a double injustice—an injustice that the just should be punished at all, and another injustice that the just should be punished for them. Oh no! If Christ died, it must be because there was a penalty to be paid for sin committed, hence He must have died for those who had committed the sin. If Christ died, it must have been because "a fountain filled with blood" was necessary for the cleansing away of heinous stains; hence, it must have been for those who are defiled. Suppose there should be found anywhere in this world an unfallen man—perfectly innocent of all actual sin, and free from any tendency to it, there would be a superfluity of cruelty in the crucifixion of the innocent Christ for such an individual. What need has he that Christ should die for him, when he has in his own innocence the right to live? If there be found beneath the copes of heaven an individual who, notwithstanding some former slips and flaws, can yet, by future diligence, completely justify himself before God, then it is clear that there is no need for Christ to die for him. I would not insult him by telling him that Christ died for him, for he would reply to me, "Why should He? Cannot I make myself just without Him?" In the very nature of things it must be so, that if Christ Jesus dies He must die for the ungodly. Such agonies as His would not have been endured had there not been a cause, and what cause could there have been but sin?

Some have said that Jesus died as our example; but that is not altogether true. Christ's death is not absolutely an example for men, it was a march into a region of which He said, "Ye cannot follow Me now." His life was our example, but not His death in all respects, for we are by no means bound to surrender ourselves voluntarily to our enemies as He did, but when persecuted in one city we are bidden to flee to another. To be willing to die for the truth is a most Christly thing, and in that Jesus is our example; but into the winepress which He trod it is not ours to enter, the voluntary element which was peculiar to His death renders it inimitable. He said, "I lay down My life of Myself; no man taketh it from Me, but I lay it down of Myself." One word of His would have delivered Him from His foes; He had but to say "Begone!" and the Roman guards must have fled like chaff before the wind. He died because He

willed to do so; of His own accord He yielded up His spirit to the Father. It must have been as an atonement for the guilty; it could not have been as an example, for no man is bound voluntarily to die. Both the dictates of nature, and the command of the law, require us to preserve our lives. "Thou shalt not kill" means "Thou shalt not voluntarily give up thine own life any more than take the life of another." Jesus stood in a special position, and therefore He died; but His example would have been complete enough without His death, had it not been for the peculiar office which He had undertaken. We may fairly conclude that Christ died for men who needed such a death; and, as the good did not need it for an example—and in fact it is not an example to them—He must have died for the ungodly.

The sum of our text is this—all the benefits resulting from the Redeemer's passion, and from all the works that followed upon it, are for those who by nature are ungodly. His gospel is that sinners believing in Him are saved. His sacrifice has put away sin from all who trust Him, and, therefore, it was offered for those who had sin upon them before. "He rose again for our justification," but certainly not for the justification of those who can be justified by their own works. He ascended on high, and we are told that He "received gifts for men, yea, for the rebellious also." He lives to intercede, and Isaiah tells us that "He made intercession for the transgressors." The aim of His death, resurrection, ascension, and eternal life, is towards the sinful sons of men. His death has brought pardon, but it cannot be pardon for those who have no sin—pardon is only for the guilty. He is exalted on high "to give repentance," but surely not to give repentance to those who have never sinned, and have nothing to repent of. Repentance and remission both imply previous guilt in those who receive them: unless, then, these gifts of the exalted Saviour are mere shams and superfluities, they must be meant for the really guilty. From His side there flowed out water as well as blood—the water is intended to cleanse polluted nature, then certainly not the nature of the sinless, but the nature of the impure; and so both blood and water flowed for sinners who need the double purification. To-day the Holy Spirit regenerates men as the result of the Redeemer's death; and who can be regenerated but those who need a new heart and a right spirit? To regenerate the already pure and innocent were ridiculous; regeneration is a work which creates life where there was formerly death, gives a heart of flesh to those whose hearts were originally stone, and implants the love of holiness where sin once had sole dominion. Conversion is also another gift, which comes through His death, but does He turn those whose faces are already in the right direction? It cannot be. He converts the sinner from the error of his ways, He turns the disobedient into the right way, He leads back the stray sheep to the fold. Adoption is another gift which comes to us by the cross. Does the Lord adopt those who are already His sons by nature? If children already, what room is there for adoption? No; but the grand act of divine love is that which takes those who are "children of wrath even as others," and by sovereign grace puts them among the children, and makes them "heirs of God, joint heirs with Jesus Christ."

To-day I see the Good Shepherd in all the energy of His mighty love, going forth into the dreadful wilderness. For whom is He gone forth? For the ninety and nine who feed at home? No, but into the desert His love sends Him, over hill and dale, to seek the one lost sheep which has gone astray. Behold, I see Him arousing His church, like a good housewife, to cleanse her house. With the besom of the law she sweeps, and with the candle of the Word she searches, and what for? For those bright new coined pieces fresh from the mint, which glitter safely in her purse? Assuredly not, but for that lost piece which has rolled away into the dust, and lies hidden in the dark corner. And lo! grandest of all visions! I see the Eternal Father, Himself, in the infinity of His love, going forth in haste to meet a returning child. And whom does He go to meet? The elder brother returning from the field, bringing his sheaves with him? An Esau, who has brought Him savoury meat such as His soul loveth? A Joseph whose godly life has made him lord over all Egypt? Nay, the Father leaves His home to meet a returning prodigal, who has companied with harlots, and grovelled among swine, who comes back to Him in disgraceful rags, and disgusting filthiness! It is on a sinner's neck that the Father weeps; it is on a guilty cheek that He sets His kisses; it is for an unworthy one that the fatted calf is killed, and the best robe is worn, and the house is made merry with music and with dancing. Yes, tell it, and let it ring round earth and heaven, Christ died for the ungodly. Mercy seeks the guilty, grace has to do with the impious, the irreligious and the wicked. The physician has not come to heal the healthy, but to heal the sick. The great philanthropist has not come to bless the rich and the great, but the captive and the prisoner. He puts down the mighty from their seats, for He is a stern leveller, but He has come to lift the beggar from the dunghill, and to set him among princes, even the princes of His people. Sing ye, then, with the holy Virgin, and let your song be loud and sweet,—"He hath filled the hungry with good things, but the rich He hath sent empty away." "This is a faithful saying, and worthy of all acceptation, that Jesus Christ came into the world to save sinners." "He is able to save to the uttermost them that come unto God by Him, seeing He ever liveth to make intercession for them." O ye guilty ones, believe in Him and live.

II. Let us now consider THE PLAIN INFERENCES FROM THIS FACT. Let me have your hearts as well as your ears, especially those of you who are not yet saved, for I desire you to be blessed by the truths uttered; and oh, may the Spirit of God cause it to be so. It is clear that those of you who are ungodly— and if you are unconverted you are that—*are in great danger.* Jesus would not interpose His life and bear the bloody sweat and crown of thorns, and nails, and spear, and scorn unmitigated, and death itself, if there were not solemn need and imminent peril. There is danger, solemn danger, for you. You are under the wrath of God already, and you will soon die, and then, as surely as you live, you will be lost, and lost for ever; as certain as the righteous will enter into everlasting life, you will be driven into everlasting punishment. The cross is the danger signal to you, it warns you that if God spared not His only Son, He will not spare you. It is the lighthouse set on the rocks of sin to warn you that swift and sure destruction awaits you if you continue to rebel against the Lord. Hell is an awful place, or Jesus had not needed to suffer such infinite agonies to save us from it.

It is also fairly to be inferred that *out of this danger only Christ can deliver the ungodly, and He only through His death.* If a less price than that of the life of the Son of God could have redeemed men, He would have been spared. When a country is at war, and you see a mother give up her only boy to fight her country's battles—her only well-beloved, blameless son—you know that the battle must be raging very fiercely, and that the country is in stern danger: for, if she could find a substitute for him, though she gave all her wealth, she would lavish it freely to spare her darling. If she were certain that in his heart a bullet would find its target, she must have strong love for her country, and her country must be in dire necessity ere she would bid him go. If, then, "God spared not His Son, but freely delivered Him up for us all," there must have been a dread necessity for it. It must have stood thus: die He, or the sinner must, or justice must; and since justice could not, and the Father desired that the sinner should not, then Christ *must;* and so He did. Oh, miracle of love! I tell you, sinners, you cannot help yourselves, nor can all the priests of Rome or Oxford help you, let them perform their antics as they may; Jesus alone can save, and that only by His death. There on the bloody tree hangs all man's hope; if you enter heaven it must be by force of the incarnate God's bleeding out His life for you. You are in such peril that only the pierced hand can lift you out of it. Look to Him, at once, I pray you, ere the proud waters go over your soul.

Then let it be noticed—and this is the point I want constantly to keep before your view—*that Jesus died out of pure pity.* He must have died out of the most gratuitous benevolence to the undeserving, because the character of those for whom He died could not have attracted Him, but must have been repulsive to His holy soul. The impious, the godless—can Christ love these for their character? No, He loved them notwithstanding their offences, loved them as creatures fallen and miserable, loved them according to the multitude of His lovingkindnesses and tender mercies, from pity, and not from admiration. Viewing them as ungodly, yet He loved them. This is extraordinary love! I do not wonder that some persons are loved by others, for they wear a potent charm in their countenances, their ways are winsome, and their characters charm you into affection; "but God commendeth His love towards us in that while we were yet sinners Christ died for us." He looked at us, and there was not a solitary beauty spot upon us: we were covered with "wounds, and bruises, and putrefying sores," distortions, defilements, and pollutions; and yet, for all that, Jesus loved us. He loved us because He would love us; because His heart was full of pity, and He could not let us perish. Pity moved Him to seek the most needy objects that His love might display its utmost ability in lifting men from the lowest degradation, and putting them in the highest position of holiness and honour.

Observe another inference. If Christ died for the ungodly, *this fact leaves the ungodly no excuse if they do not come to Him,* and believe in Him unto salvation. Had it been otherwise they might have pleaded, "We are not fit to come." But you are ungodly, and Christ died for the ungodly, why not for you? I hear the reply, "But I have been so very vile." Yes, you have been impious, but your sin is not worse than this word ungodly will compass. Christ died for those who were wicked, thoroughly wicked. The Greek word is so expressive that it must take in your case, however wrongly you have acted. "But I cannot believe that Christ died for such as I am," says one. Then, sir, mark! I hold you to your words, and charge you with contradicting the Eternal God to His teeth, and making Him a liar. Your statement gives God the lie. The Lord declares that "Christ died for the ungodly," and you say He did not, what is that but to make God a liar? How can you expect mercy if you persist in such proud unbelief? Believe the divine revelation. Close in at once with the gospel. Forsake your sins and believe in the Lord Jesus, and you shall surely live. The fact that Christ died for the ungodly renders self-righteousness a folly. Why need a man pretend that he is good if "Christ died for the ungodly?" We have an orphanage, and the qualification for our orphanage is that the child for whom admission is sought shall be utterly destitute. I will suppose a widow trying to show to me and my fellow trustees that her boy is a fitting object for the charity; will she tell us that her child has a rich uncle? Will she enlarge upon her own capacities for earning a living? Why, this would be to argue against herself, and she is much too wise for that, I warrant you, for she knows that any such statements would damage rather than serve her cause. So, sinner, do not pretend to be righteous, do not dream that you are better than others, for that is to argue against yourself. Prove that you are not by nature ungodly, and you prove yourself to be one for whom Jesus did not die. Jesus comes to make the ungodly godly, and the sinful holy, but the raw material upon which He works is described in the text not by its goodness but by its badness; it is for the ungodly that Jesus died. "Oh, but if I felt!" Felt what? Felt something which would make you better? Then you would not so clearly come under the description here given. If you are destitute of good feelings, and thoughts, and hopes, and emotions, you are ungodly, and "Christ died for the ungodly." Believe in Him and you shall be saved from that ungodliness.

"Well," cries out some Pharisaic moralist, "this is dangerous doctrine," How so? Would it be dangerous doctrine to say that physicians exercise their skill to cure sick people and not healthy ones? Would that encourage sickness? Would that discourage health? You know better; you know that to inform the sick of a physician who can heal them is one of the best means for promoting their cure. If ungodly and impious men would take heart and run to the Saviour, and by Him become cured of impiety and ungodliness, would not that be a good thing? Jesus has come to make the ungodly godly, the impious pious, the wicked obedient, and the dishonest upright. He has not come to save men in their sins, but from their sins; and this is the best of news for those who are diseased with sin. Self-righteousness is a folly, and despair is a crime, since Christ died for the ungodly. None are excluded hence but those who do themselves exclude; this great gate is set so wide open that the very worst of men may enter, and you, dear hearer, may enter now.

I think it is also very evident from our text that when they are saved, *the converted find no ground of boasting;* for when their hearts are renewed and made to love God they cannot say, "See how good I am," because they were not so by nature; they were ungodly, and, as such, Christ died for them. Whatever goodness there may be in them after conversion they ascribe it to the grace of God, since by nature

they were alienated from God, and far removed from righteousness. If the truth of natural depravity be but known and felt, free grace must be believed in, and then all glorying is at an end.

This will also keep the saved ones from thinking lightly of sin. If God had forgiven sinners without an atonement they might have thought little of transgression, but now that pardon comes to them through the bitter griefs of their Redeemer they cannot but see it to be an exceeding great evil. When we look to Jesus dying on the cross we end our dalliance with sin and utterly abhor the cause of so great suffering to so dear a Saviour. Every wound of Jesus is an argument against sin. We never know the full evil of our iniquities till we see what it cost the Redeemer to put them away.

Salvation by the death of Christ is the strongest conceivable promoter of all the things which are pure, honest, lovely, and of good report. It makes sin so loathsome that the saved one cannot take up even its name without dread. "I will take away the name of Baali out of thy mouth." He looks upon it as we should regard a knife rusted with gore, wherewith some villain had killed our mother, our wife, or child. Could we play with it? Could we bear it about our persons or endure it in our sight? No, accursed thing! stained with the heart's blood of my beloved, I would fain fling thee into the bottomless abyss! Sin is that dagger which stabbed the Saviour's heart, and henceforth it must be the abomination of every man who has been redeemed by the atoning sacrifice.

To close this point. Christ's death for the ungodly is *the grandest argument to make the ungodly love Him when they are saved.* To love Christ is the mainspring of obedience in men—how shall men be led to love Him? If you would grow love, you must sow love. Go, then; and let men know the love of Christ to sinners, and they will, by grace, be moved to love Him in return. No doubt all of us require to know the threatenings of the wrath of God; but that which soonest touches my heart is Christ's free love to an unworthy one like myself. When my sins seem blackest to me, and yet I know that through Christ's death I am forgiven, this blest assurance melts me down.

> "If Thou hadst bid Thy thunders roll,
>   And lightnings flash, to blast my soul,
>   I still had stubborn been;
>   But mercy has my heart subdued,
>   A bleeding Saviour I have view'd,
>   And now I hate my sin."

I have heard of a soldier who had been put in prison for drunkenness and insubordination several times, and he had been also flogged, but nothing improved him. At last he was taken in the commission of another offence, and brought before the commanding officer, who said to him, "My man, I have tried everything in the martial code with you, except shooting you; you have been imprisoned and whipped, but nothing has changed you. I am determined to try something else with you. You have caused us a great deal of trouble and anxiety, and you seem resolved to do so still; I shall, therefore, change my plans with you, and I shall neither fine you, flog you, nor imprison you; I will see what kindness will do, and therefore I fully and freely forgive you." The man burst into tears, for he reckoned on a round number of lashes, and had steeled himself to bear them, but when he found he was to be forgiven, and set free, he said, "Sir, you shall not have to find fault with me again."

Mercy won his heart. Now, sinner, in that fashion God is dealing with you. Great sinners! Ungodly sinners! God says, "My thoughts are not your thoughts, neither are My ways your ways. I have threatened you, and you hardened your hearts against Me. Therefore, come now, and let us reason together: though your sins be as scarlet, they shall be as white as snow; though they be red like crimson, they shall be as wool." "Well," says one, "I am afraid if you talk to sinners so they will go and sin more and more." Yes, there are brutes everywhere, who can be so unnatural as to sin because grace abounds, but I bless God there is such a thing as the influence of love, and I am rejoiced that many feel the force of it, and yield to the conquering arms of amazing grace. The Spirit of God wins the day by such arguments as these; love is the great battering-ram which opens gates of brass. When the Lord says, "I have blotted out thy transgressions like a cloud, and like a thick cloud thine iniquities," then the man is moved to repentance.

I can tell you hundreds and thousands of cases in which this infinite love has done all the good that morality itself could ask to have done; it has changed the heart and turned the entire current of the man's nature from sin to righteousness. The sinner has believed, repented, turned from his evil ways, and become zealous for holiness. Looking to Jesus he has felt his sin forgiven, and he has started up a new man, to lead a new life. God grant it may be so this morning, and He shall have all the glory of it.

III. So now we must close—and this is the last point—THE PROCLAMATION OF THIS FACT, that "Christ died for the ungodly." I would not mind if I were condemned to live fifty years more, and never to be allowed to speak but these five words, if I might be allowed to utter them in the ear of every man, and woman, and child who lives. "CHRIST DIED FOR THE UNGODLY" is the best message that even angels could bring to men. In the proclamation of this the whole church ought to take its share. Those of us who can address thousands should be diligent to cry aloud—"Christ died for the ungodly"; but those of you who can only speak to one, or write a letter to one, must keep on at this—"Christ died for the ungodly." Shout it out, or whisper it out; print it in capitals, or write it in a lady's hand—"Christ died for the ungodly." Speak it solemnly; it is not a thing for jest. Speak it joyfully; it is not a theme for sorrow, but for joy. Speak it firmly; it is an indisputable fact. Facts of science, as they call them, are always questioned: this is unquestionable. Speak it earnestly; for if there be any truth which ought to arouse all a man's soul it is this: "Christ died for the ungodly." Speak it where the ungodly live, and that is at your own house. Speak it also down in the dark corners of the city, in the haunts of debauchery, in the home of the thief, in the den of the depraved. Tell it in the gaol; and sit down at the dying bed and read in a tender whisper—"Christ died for the ungodly." When you pass the harlot in the street, do not give a toss with that proud head of yours, but remember that "Christ died for the ungodly"; and when you recollect those that injured you, say no bitter word, but hold your tongue, and remember "Christ died for the ungodly." Make this henceforth the message of your life—"Christ died for the ungodly."

And, oh, dear friends, you that are not saved, take care that you receive this message. Believe it.

Go to God with this on your tongue—"Lord save me, for Christ died for the ungodly, and I am of them." Fling yourself right on to this as a man commits himself to his lifebelt amid the surging billows. "But I do not feel," says one. Trust not your feelings if you do; but with no feelings and no hopes of your own, cling desparately to this, "Christ died for the ungodly." The transforming, elevating, spiritualising, moralising, sanctifying power of this great fact you shall soon know and be no more ungodly; but first, as ungodly, rest you on this, "Christ died for the ungodly." Accept this truth, my dear hearer, and you are saved. I do not mean merely that you will be pardoned, I do not mean that you will enter heaven, I mean much more; I mean that you will have a new heart; you will be saved from the love of sin, saved from drunkenness, saved from uncleanness, saved from blasphemy, saved from dishonesty. "Christ died for the ungodly"—if that be really known and trusted in, it will open in your soul new springs of living water which will cleanse the Augean stable of your nature, and make a temple of God of that which was before a den of thieves. Trust in the mercy of God through the death of Jesus Christ, and a new era in your life's history will at once commence.

Having put this as plainly as I know how, and having guarded my speech to prevent there being anything like a flowery sentence in it, having tried to put this as clearly as daylight itself,—that "Christ died for the ungodly," if your ears refuse the precious boons that come through the dying Christ, your blood be on your own heads, for there is no other way of salvation for any one among you. Whether you reject or accept this, I am clear. But oh! do not reject it, for it is your life. If the Son of God dies for sinners, and sinners reject His blood, they have committed the most heinous offence possible. I will not venture to affirm, but I do suggest that the devils in hell are not capable of so great a stretch of criminality as is involved in the rejection of the sacrifice of Jesus Christ. Here lies the highest love. The incarnate God bleeds to death to save men, and men hate God so much that they will not even have Him as He dies to save them. They will not be reconciled to their Creator, though He stoops from His loftiness to the depths of woe in the person of His Son on their behalf. This is depravity indeed, and desperateness of rebellion. God grant you may not be guilty of it. There can be no fiercer flame of wrath than that which will break forth from love that has been trampled upon, when men have put from them eternal life, and done despite to the Lamb of God. "Oh," says one, "would God I could believe!" "Sir, what difficulty is there in it? Is it hard to believe the truth? Darest thou belie thy God? Art thou steeling thy heart to such desperateness that thou wilt call thy God a liar?" "No; I believe Christ died for the ungodly," says one, "but I want to know how to get the merit of that death applied to my own soul." Thou mayest, then, for here it is—"He that believeth in Him," that is, he that trusts in Him, "is not condemned." Here is the gospel and the whole of it—"He that believeth and is baptized shall be saved: he that believeth not shall be damned."

I am but a poor weak man like yourselves, but my gospel is not weak; and it would be no stronger if one of "the mailed cherubim, or sworded seraphim" could take the platform and stand here instead of me. He could tell to you no better news. God, in condescension to your weakness, has chosen one of your fellow mortals to bear to you this message of infinite affection. Do not reject it! By your souls' value, by their immortality, by the hope of heaven and by the dread of hell, lay hold upon eternal life; and by the fear that this may be your last day on earth, yea, and this evening your last hour, I do beseech you now, "steal away to Jesus." There is life in a look at the crucified one; there is life at this moment for you. Look to Him now and live. Amen.

LOST THROUGH ONE; SAVED THROUGH ONE

"And not as it was by one that sinned, so is the gift: for the judgment was by one to condemnation, but the free gift is of many offences unto justification."—Romans v. 16.

MY one and only desire, at this time, is to help those who are sincerely seeking salvation, that they may find it, and find it speedily. Ignorance often hinders sinners from coming to Christ. I know that it did so in my own case. I have often thought that, if I had understood the plan of salvation more clearly, I should have accepted Christ sooner than I did; and I feel very little doubt that there are many other anxious enquirers who are a long time looking for what is close to them all the while. They are like Hagar in the wilderness, dying of thirst while a well of water is near their feet. They are asking the way to Zion because they are ignorant of the road.

Even the reading of the Scriptures will sometimes not suffice for the enlightenment of such troubled souls, for they are in the condition of the Ethiopian eunuch, who, in reply to Philip's question, "Understandest thou what thou readest?" said, "How can I, except some man should guide me?" It needs, sometimes, only just a few words to cast light upon the passage which is not understood, and then the eye sees it, the understanding perceives it, the heart accepts it, and the captive soul is set at liberty. Pray, you who love the Lord, and are rejoicing in free justification through Christ Jesus,—pray that the Lord may direct the sin-smitten where to look. Here is Christ lifted up, as the brazen serpent was set upon a pole in the wilderness; but they look to the right or to the left, above or below, anywhere except to the point where we direct them. Divine Spirit, give them sight, and direct that sight to the Saviour, even while we are speaking about Him!

I am not going to enter into any theological subtleties concerning the imputation of the sin of Adam, or even into any questions about the imputation of the righteousness of Christ. I shall try to speak very simply upon the two points to which the apostle here refers, and to show you that, as we are lost through one, so we are saved through one.

It pleased God, of old, to commence the human race with a single pair of individuals. One man, Adam, was the representative of the entire race of mankind, for God determined to deal with men in the mass through one chosen representative. In that one man, they stood in perfection for a while. How long or how short Adam's obedience was, we cannot tell. There are some who think that he stood scarcely for a day. The psalmist says, "Man being in honour abideth not." But, at all events, after a time he was tempted, and he fell. He broke the one commandment which was given him as a test,—by no means a hard one,—by no means savouring of severity or austerity; but he broke it wilfully, and, straightway, our representative was found to be faulty. He was expelled from Paradise, and upon all his seed, seeing that they were all represented in him, there came judgment unto condemnation. The result was that,

as men grew up, and advanced in years, they died; and from Adam to Moses, and from Moses to this present day, it has been the rule that men should die; so that the sin of Adam has prevailed over the race, and left to it a life of toil and sorrow, by-and-by to end in death. This might cause us the deepest gloom if it were all that we had to tell; but, thank God, there is another and a brighter side to the story.

There are some who cavil at the justice of this representative arrangement, but there are many others who believe in it, and rejoice over it. I always contend that it is a happy circumstance for us that we did fall and were condemned in the bulk in our representative; because, had we, each one of us, been individually put upon the like probation, we should, to a certainty, all of us have fallen. We are none of us better than our first parent was; and if the experiment had been repeated in the case of each one of us, it would have ended in the same sorrowful way. But then it must have ended finally and fatally;—at least, so we believe; for when the angels fell, sinning individually, there was no hope of restoration for them. Whether infinite wisdom might not have devised a plan, consistent with justice, by which the angels who had apostatized might have been restored, is more than we can tell. We know that the Lord did not devise any such plan. They individually sinned, and, sinning, fell past all hope of recovery; and now they are "reserved in everlasting chains under darkness unto the judgment of the great day." No gospel was ever preached to them,—no atonement was ever made for them; but they were left to abide in their sinful condition, willingly to persevere in perpetual rebellion against the Most High.

But we, happily, had fallen through a representative: and, therefore, we could be restored by another Representative; so, in the infinite wisdom and mercy of God, there came into the world the second Adam,—man, really man, though much more than man, for He was also God, and He offered an atonement for the offence committed against the law,—such an atonement that whosoever believeth in Him hath his sins for ever put away. Thus, we rise in the same manner as we fell, only in a very different Person. We fell in the first Adam; we rise in the second Adam; we fell, in the first Adam, through no fault of our own; we rise, in the second Adam, through no merit of our own; it is of the free grace of God that we are received back into his favour.

There is much that might be said upon this matter; but I only intend, as I have already said, to touch the points mentioned here. So, first, *let us contemplate the contrast which the apostle here sets before us ;* and when we have done so, *let us adore the manner of the divine mercy.*

I. First, LET US CONTEMPLATE THE CONTRAST DEPICTED IN THE TEXT.

Paul tells us that, "by one man's disobedience many were made sinners." But it is not so with the free gift; one transgression ruined us, but the free gift takes away many transgressions. *It was one offence of one man which brought ruin upon our race.* Adam offended once, and by that one offence he brought us all into disfavour with God, and the race became a judged and condemned race, toiling and ultimately dying. Now, if one offence had such power that the whole race was ruined by it, will you not, with all your hearts, adore the wondrous atoning work of Christ, by which many offences are removed by the free gift of pardon which He has come into the world to bring? When, through Jesus Christ, we obtain the remission of our sins, all the mischief of Adam's fall is undone. As to any guilt which has fallen upon the race, all the members of that race are set free from guilt as soon as they believe in Jesus Christ.

Adam brought a great mortgage upon our estate, which it would not have been possible for any of us to discharge; but, to every believer, that first and heaviest mortgage is entirely removed, and the estate is free. In addition to this, however, we have, each one of us, sinned. The estate was encumbered at first, but we have encumbered it much more; like an heir, who comes into an encumbered estate, yet straightway beginneth to burden it with debts more and more, multiplying them until the mortgage is a crushing load too grievous to be borne. But whosoever believeth in Jesus Christ may have this for his consolation,—that "the free gift is of many offences unto justification." Do not try to count your sins, your arithmetic will fail you if you attempt such a task as that; but if it will benefit you to go over the transgressions of your life from your youth up even until now, do so with repentent heart; but when you have added them up as best you can, and tried to conceive the total sum of your iniquities, then write at the bottom, "But the free gift is of many offences unto justification;"—"of *many* offences,"—however many there may be;—though they should outnumber the sands on the seashore, or the drops that make up the ocean, yet the free gift of divine pardon sweeps them all away.

Think a little of the many forms that sin has taken in this world,—from that crimson sin which startles even the ungodly man himself, such as murder, adultery, fornication, theft, drunkenness, blasphemy, and the like, to the lighter shades of sin, as we are apt to think them, though it may be that, in God's sight, there is as much evil in these faults as in those more glaring crimes. I will not attempt to catalogue our transgressions. I should have to use a roll like that of the prophet which was written within and without, and it would have to be so long that I know not where space could be found to put it away. Our sins and iniquities are innumerable. They have gone over our heads like the waves of the sea. Personally and individually, there is not one person, who looks at his own character and heart aright, who will not see that his life has teemed and swarmed with sin; yet the free gift of divine love puts all those sins away the moment we believe in Jesus. The Romish Church divides sin into two sorts, sins mortal and sins venial; but, to me, it is of no consequence how the sins of a believer are described, seeing that Christ has taken them as a whole, and cast them into the depths of the sea. You may, if you will, classify sins under various heads,—sins of thought, sins of word, sins of deed;—sins against the first table, which concerns God; or sins against the second table, which concerns man;—sins of ignorance, and sins of wilfulness; the sins of youth, the sins of middle life, and the sins of old age; but though you pile them together, mountain upon mountain, as in the old fable,—Pelion upon Ossa;—yet, still, Christ taketh them all away from all who believe on Him. "The free gift is of many offences unto justification."

This thought grows to startling dimensions when you remember that all the sins of each man must be multiplied by the number of men who, being believers in Christ, find in Him justification from their many offences. Oh, what a seething mass of sin would lie upon this poor world, in the sight of the living God, if there were none but His own people upon it, had not Christ swept it away by His infinite atonement! One cannot think, without horror, of his own sins alone; but when we think of the sin of all the saints who have ever lived upon the earth, and the sin of all the blood-bought sinners who are yet to be born, and who shall many of them, perhaps, live to old age,—what a heap and mass of sin it is! "But the free gift is of many offences unto justification," and covers the whole vast mass.

As I want practically to use each separate thought, let me say,—Soul, if thou art willing to be saved in Christ,—if thou art willing to be saved in this way in the second Adam as thou art assuredly lost in the first Adam,—let not the number of thy sins confound thee, so as to prevent thee from having hope of eternal salvation in Christ Jesus. Let thy sins so confound thee as to drive thee to despair if thou hast any hope in thyself or in thine own merits, in thine own feelings, or doings, or weepings, or in anything that is thine; but if salvation is to be had through the blood of Another, through the merits of Another, and thou art willing to have it so, then, though thy sins be as scarlet, they shall be as white as snow; though they be red like crimson, they shall be as wool; and though they be more in number than the hairs of thy head, they shall, in one single instant, be taken from thee never to return. Yes, in a moment shall they disappear, and shall never be mentioned against thee any more for ever. Is not this good news? You do not want me to embellish it with fine words; you only need to believe it, and to say to yourself, "Yes, there is a possibility of the blotting out of all my transgressions." Say that, thou who hast gone in for sin like a very leviathan who needs the great deep to swim in. If thou hast oceans of iniquity, it mattereth not, in the sight of God, though thou hadst oceans more, for "the free gift" of pardon and eternal life "is of many offences unto justification." One sin has slain us, but Christ's mercy bringeth us the death of all our multitudes of sins.

The second point in our text is that *the one transgression of Adam led to judgment:* "for the judgment was by one." That first sin of our first parent did not go long unjudged. Sometimes, among the sons of men, there is a long period between the commission of a crime and the assizes at which the prisoner is tried; but, in Adam's day, God had short sessions. Ere the sun had gone down, the Lord God walked in the garden in the cool of the day, and He called to Adam, and said unto him, "Where art thou?" Then Adam stood before his Maker in a different relationship from that which he had ever occupied before,—as an offender to be judged; and though there was no great white throne for him to see, yet there was a pure throne of justice there, and his transgression received the condemnation with which God had threatened him; and he went forth from the garden of Eden to toil, and, by-and-by, to return to the dust whence he was taken,—respited, but still condemned,—condemned to drag his chain about, and at last to die. One transgression, then, brought judgment upon Adam, and will bring judgment upon all who are not protected and preserved by the second Adam, the Lord from heaven. When the time arrives for the sitting of the Judge of all upon the great white throne, men and angels will be present to watch the distribution of His impartial justice. Then will come the sentence of condemnation against all sin; but the mercy for all who are trusting in Christ is that "the free gift is of many offences unto justification." That free gift has anticipated the judgment, for it says to the believer, "Thou art already condemned in the person of thy Substitute. The verdict in thy case has been given; thy judgment is past already."

Let me repeat what I have often said, for I find that it is still needed. I frequently read in books. or hear ministers say, that we are in a state of probation; but nothing can be more false. We are not in any sense in a state of probation; we are condemned already. The time for probation was over in Adam's day; and, now, we are criminals under sentence of condemnation, or else we have been absolved. God's free gift of pardon implies that we admit our condemnation, that the sentence has already rung in our ears, and that then God has said to each one of us who has trusted to the blood and merit of His Son, "I absolve thee; thy transgressions are all put away for His sake."

Have you, dear friend, ever gone through that experience? Did you ever stand before the judgment-seat of your own spirit? Did you ever judge yourself, that you might not be condemned with the world? Did you ever feel that you were condemned, and then did you, with trembling faith, accept that free pardon which puts you past the judgment? For, when a man has committed an offence against the law of the land, and the Queen gives him a free pardon for it, he is not afraid that the police will break into his house, and take him off to further trial. No. it is tantamount to this,—that he has had his trial, and passed it, for he has received a free pardon from the highest authority in the country; and, beloved, no child of God needs to stand in fear of the judgment. He has been judged; he has been condemned; what is more, he has been punished; for, in the person of his glorious Representative, the guilt of his transgression has been laid upon his Substitute, and expiation has been made for it so that it is for ever put away, according to that wondrous word of the prophet, "In those days, and in that time, saith the Lord, the iniquity of Israel shall be sought for, and there shall be none; and the sins of Judah, and they shall not be found: for I will pardon them whom I reserve." How can he be amenable to justice who has already acknowledged his transgression, and has received pardon? Does not the divine forgiveness clear him? Aye, that it does; such is the pardon, stamped and sealed with the atoning blood of Jesus Christ, which the Judge of all the earth has given to us who have believed on His Son.

The one offence, then, brought man to judgment; but the glorious free gift of grace takes away from us even the fear of that tremendous day when Christ shall come in His glory; for, in that day, who shall lay anything to our charge? That man need not fear to go to the last great assize who feels that he can walk into the court and say, "Who is he that can even bring a charge against me?" and who feels, in addition, that if the devils in hell were base enough to fabricate a charge yet, "it is God that justifieth: who is he that condemneth?" Since Christ hath died, and risen again, and now sitteth at the right hand of God, and maketh intercession for us, what judgment have we to fear? Glory be to God for that free gift!

Note, also,—I have already partly anticipated this point,—that *the one transgression not only led to judgment, but it led to condemnation.* Adam must have felt that when he picked up the first dead bird, and when he saw the deer lie bleeding beneath the paw of the lion. He must have realized it still more painfully when he gazed upon the pale face of Abel, smitten to death by his own brother; aye. and when Adam had to pause in his work because he felt weary, or that he might wipe the sweat from his brow, he felt more and more that he was under condemnation. When he could no longer walk through Eden's garden, and converse with God,—when he saw the fiery sword uplifted at the gate of what had once been his own *pleasaunce* and place of delight, and when he knew that he could never again enter there, he understood what it was to be under condemnation.

That condemnation, dear friends, is a thing to tremble at; but our text tells us that "the free gift is of many offences unto justification." What a glorious word that word "justification" is! It means the opposite of "condemnation." When God comes, in infinite mercy, and gives a free pardon to a guilty soul, through Christ, He makes that man to be the same as if he were perfectly just. Instead of standing there condemned, he is absolved;—nay, more than that,—he is justified, made just, and to be treated now as though he never had sinned at all, but had always been a just and righteous man. Oh, wondrous change of condemnation into justification! Just as thou hast trembled when God has condemned thee, so do thou with as much force rejoice when God justifies thee; for, if He says thou art just, then just thou art,—so just that, as I have already said, none shall ever dare to lay anything to thy charge.

This, too, is a matter of present possession. As soon as we believe in Jesus, we are justified,—made righteous,—"made the righteousness of God in Him." It is a very wonderful thing; it is, perhaps, the grandest doctrine that could possibly be proclaimed; but it is true. Hark, thee, friend; dost thou understand that, just as, in Adam, thou wast condemned, and so came under the sentence of death, so, if thou believest in Jesus Christ, thou shalt be cleansed altogether from thy many offences, and God will look upon thee as perfectly just in Christ Jesus. Thou shalt, by faith, have peace with God, and there shall be a reason for that peace, for everything which made God angry with thee shall have been put away, and thou shalt sing,—

> "I will praise Thee every day!
> Now Thine anger's turned away;
> Comfortable thoughts arise
> From the bleeding sacrifice;"—

and that may be done now, at this very moment. It need not take thee a day, a month, a year; but, in an instant God can speak the pardoning word, strike His pen through the long list of thy sins, and write thee in His book as "Righteous," and righteous thou shalt be there and then. Oh, wondrous grace! Shall we ever be able to say sufficient to express our gratitude for it?

Now I want you to notice that *this one offence involved death*, as well as judgment and condemnation; for we find, in the next and succeeding verses, that "death reigned." The apostle puts it very strongly. "By one man's offence death reigned by one;" He sat upon His throne swaying His grim sceptre over the entire race of mankind, and He even claimed, as His victims, babes "that had not sinned after the similitude of Adam's transgression," and their little bodies were laid in the grave. Oh, the awful power which sin had thus to turn the world into one vast cemetery, and to slay the whole human race! But, beloved, when Jesus Christ comes to your soul and mine, He takes away the punishment,—not merely of that one offence of Adam, but of "many offences." Sin brought death into the world, with all its woe, but Christ comes, and takes death away, removing all punishment for sin; so that whosoever believeth in Him will, for His sake, never be punished, and cannot be for this best of reasons,—that it is not consistent with divine justice that there should be two punishments for the same offence; and as God accepted Christ as the Substitute for all of us who believe in Him, He cannot afterwards punish us for the sin that was laid upon Him. There can never be such injustice as that which would be perpetrated by the Judge of all the earth if he took Christ to stand vicariously to suffer in the believer's stead, and then caused the believer to suffer, too.

"But," someone asks, "will not the believer be afflicted and chastened?" Yes, but that is quite another thing from being punished for his guilt. Not penally, as with the severity of a judge; but lovingly may He be chastened by His Father who takes Him into His family. There is a great difference between punishing for an offence and chastening for it. Punishment looks at the guilt of it; but chastening comes from a Father who has already forgiven it, and who chastens with a view to the profit of the child, that he may not offend again. There is and always must be a grave distinction between the rectorial character of God as a judge, and the paternal character of God towards His own people; and you and I, who have received Christ, are dealt with as children, no more to be punished in the penal sense, but as dear children who must be scourged that we may no more offend him.

Do you understand this, poor seeking sinner,—that you need not dread the punishment of your sin if you will but trust in Jesus? You need then have no dread of hell; for, if you believe in Jesus, and so prove that you are one of those who are in Jesus, and that He stood as the Substitute for you, and made atonement for you, there is for you no sword of vengeance, for you there are no flames of hell, for you there is no wrath of God. You are free from condemnation; and, as a natural result, you must be free from punishment.

I will only just mention two or three things on which I meant to have spoken at greater length, and then leave this point. The first is this, that *the one offence brought condemnation immediately.* As soon as ever Adam committed the offence, he underwent the sentence of spiritual death which God had threatened as the result of disobedience. In like manner, the free gift, the instant it is bestowed, brings justification immediately.

"The moment a sinner believes,
And trusts in his crucified God,"—

he is as much justified as he ever will be even in heaven. He is clean in God's sight; he is cleared of all guilt by that one act of God's free grace as soon as he believes in Jesus.

Next, *the offence of one was manifested* very speedily. Adam felt ashamed of his nakedness. Very soon, he realized what toil meant, and he saw the signs of death's dominion, for the graves began to multiply. Now, in the same fashion, the free gift soon manifests itself. It does not give us a something merely to dream about, but it gives us a justification which our spiritual senses are able to perceive, for "we have peace with God through our Lord Jesus Christ." When God puts away our sins, He gives us a manifest joy,—not a thing that is hidden or wrapped up, but a joy that can be seen by all whose eyes are open.

Further, *the one offence operated universally.* All who were represented by Adam have had to feel the consequence of his transgression; and, in like manner, the free gift operates universally upon all who receive it. There was never a sinner yet, who trusted in Christ, who did not receive strength, life, absolution, and justification; neither shall anyone ever trust in Christ, and yet be left to perish.

And *the one offence acted completely and fatally.* It slew the whole race; see how they have died! Ask every hill or valley whether still it doth not hold the relics of the slain. And, in similar but more blessed fashion, the free gift operates effectually and finally. In the first case, God overrides its effects; but, in the second case, He never will do so. He whom God justifies is justified for ever, and so shall he stand, as long as he lives, and throughout eternity, a just man in the sight of God. This just man shall live by his faith; he shall hold on his way, and wax stronger and stronger. What a glorious piece of news is this that I have to tell to every soul that feels its need of such a great salvation! Would God that you would all believe it, and trust the Saviour whom I thus proclaim unto you!

II. My time has fled, so I can only tell you very briefly what I meant to have said at greater length upon my second head, which is, LET US ADORE THE MANNER OF DIVINE MERCY.

Let us, first, *thank God that He treats us representatively.* I was pleased with a passage, which I met with in the writings of Dr. Chalmers, where he rejoices that he fell in Adam, that so it became possible for God to raise him up again in the same way that he fell, that is representatively. Because, my dear brethren, if you and I were standing now in perfect innocence, we should always have to feel that there was a possibility that we might fall; nay, more than that, by this time we should all have fallen, whatever our age or position may be. Even these dear girls and boys would have fallen into some sin or other. It would always be an insecure standing if we had to stand by ourselves upon our own merits. But, now, although we have fallen in Adam, and have been broken to shivers, we who have believed in Jesus have been lifted up again in Him who never can or will fall. Do you see Him up yonder in glory? Never did the so-called everlasting hills stand upon their solid basis as firmly as He stands at the right hand of God. What power can ever remove Him? And He stands there for me, —for you, my brother or sister,—for every soul that believeth on Him; and until He falls, you will never fall. You will never perish until He perishes, for you form a part of His mystical body, as the apostle Paul puts it, "we are members of His body, of His flesh, and of His bones." There are some people who think that Christ may lose certain of His members. In fact, according to their representations of the theory of falling from grace, you would think that He was like a lobster, or some other creature that sheds its limbs, and grows new ones. But our Lord Jesus represents Himself as a man, and a man will not willingly lose so much as his little finger. If he did, he would be imperfect; and Christ will not lose the humblest, meanest member of His mystical body, for, as the apostle says, that body is His fullness, "the fullness of Him that filleth all in all." Oh, what a standing it is to be made to stand in Christ! He raised me from the gates of gaping hell, and made my standing more secure than ever it was even before Adam fell, and I fell in Him, blessed be His holy name!

The next thing for which we ought to adore the method of God's mercy is, that *it is all a free gift*: "The free gift is of many offences." "The free gift." I like Paul's way of putting those two words together," —"free" and "gift." A gift, of course, is free, so this expression is tautological; but it is blessedly tautological. Someone asked me once, "Why do you say 'free grace'? Of course, if it is grace, it is free." "Oh, well!" I replied, "I do so to make assurance doubly sure." We will always call it, not only grace, but free grace, to make it clear that God gives His grace freely to sinners,—the undeserving and ungodly. He gives it without any condition. If, in one place, He says that He requires repentance, in another place He promises it; if He demands faith at the moment, He bestows it at another. So grace is always God's free gift, and that suits a man who has not a penny in his pocket. I have walked—as I daresay some of you have—by the goldsmiths' and jewellers' shops in the Palais Royal at Paris, and seen the vast amount of wealth that is exhibited there; and many of you have gone along the great streets of our city, and seen perfect mines of wealth displayed, and you have said to yourself, "Ah! I cannot purchase any of these things, because there is a little ticket hanging down below with certain pounds marked on it, and I cannot afford to buy them. It is all I can do to get bread and cheese for those who are at home, so I must leave these luxuries to others." But if I should ever pass by a goldsmith's shop, and see a ticket bearing the words, "Free Gift!" I should be willing to take a few things at that price. I am glad that you smile at that expression, because those are my Master's terms. He has treasures worth more than the most glorious jeweller's shop ever contained, and they are all free gifts to all who trust Him. I dare not laugh at you, but I shall have to blame and condemn you, if eternal life be God's free gift, and yet you will not say, "I will take it, and have it for ever." You would like to take jewellery for nothing, but you will not accept everlasting life and pardon for nothing by simply trusting in the Lord Jesus Christ.

Lastly, we ought specially to adore the love and mercy of God in that *His plan is to save us by Christ Jesus*. To my mind, it makes every blessing all the sweeter because it comes through Him; the very glory of our salvation is that we are saved in Him, "saved in the Lord with an everlasting salvation." I have sometimes thought, when I have seen a ship beautifully fitted up,—a fast-sailing clipper,—that I would like to go to sea in her, not simply for the sake of the place to which I should be going, but because I should like to be in such a ship, with such company, and under such-and-such a captain. Well, here is Jesus, the great Captain of the glorious ship of salvation; and who does not feet that, while it would be well to go to heaven anyhow, it is best of all to go with Him and in Him? Oh, to be linked with Him,— with God's darling Son,—with the delight of the angels —with the Father of all the ages.—the Wonderful, —the Counsellor,—the Mighty God,—the Altogetherlovely,—the Best-beloved of our soul! It makes the sweetness of salvation all the sweeter because it comes to us by Christ Jesus.

The Lord bless you, beloved, and give you to know all this in your own souls, for His dear Son's sake! Amen.

GRACE ABOUNDING OVER ABOUNDING SIN

"Moreover, the law entered, that the offence might abound. But where sin abounded, grace did much more abound." Romans v. 20."

THE first sentence will serve as a preface; the second sentence will be the actual text.

"Moreover the law entered, that the offence might abound." Man was a sinner before the law of Ten Commandments had been given. He was a sinner through the offence of his first father, Adam; and he was, also, practically a sinner by his own personal offence; for he rebelled against the light of nature, and the inner light of conscience. Men, from Adam downward, transgressed against that memory of better days which had been handed down from father to son, and had never been quite forgotten. Man everywhere, whether he knew anything about the law of Moses or not, was alienated from his God. The Word of God contains this truthful estimate of our race: "They are all gone out of the way, they are together become unprofitable; there is none that doeth good, no, not one."

The law was given, however, according to the text, "that the offence might abound." Such was the effect of the law. It did not hinder sin, nor provide a remedy for it; but its actual effect was that the offence abounded. How so?

It was so, first, because it revealed the offence. Men did not in every instance clearly discern what was sin; but when the law came, it pointed out to man that this evil, which he thought little of, was an abomination in the sight of God. Man's nature and character was like a dark dungeon which knew no ray of light. Yonder prisoner does not perceive the horrible filthiness and corruption of the place wherein he is immured, so long as he is in darkness. When a lamp is brought, or a window is opened and the light of day comes in, he finds out to his dismay the hideous condition of his den. He spies loathsome creatures upon the walls, and marks how others burrow out of sight because the light annoys them. He may, perhaps, have guessed that all was not as it should be, but he had not imagined the abundance of the evils. The light has entered, and the offence abounds. Law does not make us sinful, but it displays our sinfulness. In the presence of the perfect standard we see our shortcomings. The law of God is the looking-glass in which a man sees the spots upon his face. It does not wash you—you cannot wash in a looking-glass; but it prompts you to seek the cleansing water. The design of the law is the revealing of our many offences, that, thereby, we may be driven out of self-righteousness to the Lord Jesus, in whom we have redemption through His blood, the forgiveness of sin.

The law causes the offence to abound by making an offender to stand without excuse. Before he knew the law perfectly, his sin was not so wilful. While he did but faintly know the commands, he could, as it were, but faintly break them; but as soon as he distinctly knows what is right, and what is wrong, then every cloak is taken away from him. Sin becomes exceeding sinful when it is committed against light and knowledge. Is it not so with some of you? Are you not forced to admit that you commit many sins in one, now that you have been made to know the law, and yet wilfully offend against it, by omission or commission? He who knows his Master's will and does it not, will be beaten with many stripes, because he is guilty of abounding offences. The law enters to strip us of every cloak of justification, and so to drive us to seek the robe of Christ's righteousness.

Next, I think the law makes the offence to abound by causing sin to be, more evidently, a presumptuous rebellion against the great Law-giver. To sin in the front of Sinai, with its wonderful display of divine majesty, is to sin indeed. To rebel against a law promulgated with sound of trumpet, and thunders, and pomp of God, is to sin with a high hand and a defiant heart. When thou hast heard the Ten Commands, when thou knowest the law of the kingdom, when thy Maker's will is plainly set before thee, then to transgress is to transgress with an insolence of pride which will admit of no excuse.

Once more: the entrance of the law makes the offence to abound in this sense, that the rebellious will of man rises up in opposition to it. Because God commands, man refuses; and because He forbids, man desires. There are some men who might not have sinned in a particular direction if the commandment had not forbidden it. The light of the law, instead of being a warning to them to avoid evil, seems to point out to them the way in which they can most offend. Oh, how deep is the depravity of human nature! The law itself provokes it to rebel. Men long to enter, because trespassers are warned to keep away. Their minds are so at enmity against God, that they delight in that which is forbidden, not so much because they find any particular pleasure in the thing itself, but because it shows their independence and their freedom from the restraints of God. This vicious self-will is in all of us by nature; for the carnal mind is enmity against God; and therefore the law, though in itself holy and just and good, provokes us to do evil. We are like lime, and the law is as cold water, which is in itself of a cooling nature; yet, no sooner does the water of the law get at the lime of our nature, than a heat of sin is generated: thus, "the law entered, that the offence might abound."

Why, then, did God send the law? Is it not an evil thing that the offence should abound? In itself it may seem so to be; but God dealeth with us as physicians sometimes deal with their patients. A disease, which will be fatal if it spends itself within the patient, must be brought to the surface: the physician therefore prescribes a medicine which displays the evil. The evil was all within, but it did not abound as to its visible effects; it is needful that it should do so, that it may be cured. The law is the medicine which throws out the depravity of man, makes him see it in his actions, and even provokes him to display it. The evil is in man, like rabbits in yonder brushwood: the law sets alight to the cover, and the hidden creatures are seen. The law stirs the mud at the bottom of the pool, and proves how foul the waters are. The law compels the man to see that sin dwelleth in him, and that it is a powerful tyrant over his nature. All this is with a view to his cure. God be thanked when the law so works as to take off the sinner from all confidence in himself! To make the leper confess that he is incurable is going a great way towards compelling him to go to that Divine Saviour, who alone is able to heal him. This is the object and end of the law towards men whom God will save.

Consider for a moment. You may take it as an axiom, a thing self-evident, that there can be no grace where there is no guilt: there can be no mercy where there is no sin. There can be justice, there can be benevolence; but there cannot be mercy unless there is criminality. If you are not a sinner God cannot have mercy upon you. If you have never sinned God cannot display pardoning grace towards you, for there is nothing to pardon. It were a misuse of words to talk of forgiving a man who has done no wrong, or to speak of bestowing undeserved favour upon a person who deserves reward. It would be an insult to innocence to offer it mercy. You must, therefore, have sin or you cannot have grace—that is clear.

Next, consider that there will be no seeking after grace where there is no sense of sin. We may preach till we are hoarse, but you good people, who have never broken the law, and are not guilty of anything wrong, will never care for our message of mercy. You are such kind people that, out of compliment to religion, you say, "Yes, we are sinners. We are all sinners." But you know in your heart of hearts you do not mean it. You will never ask for grace; for you have no sense of shame or guilt. None of you will seek mercy, till first you have pleaded guilty to the indictment which the law of God presents against you. Oh, that you felt your sins! Oh, that you knew your need of forgiveness! for then you would see yourselves to be in such a condition that only the free, rich, sovereign grace of God can save you.

Furthermore, I am sure that there will be no reception and acceptance of grace by any man, till there is a full confession of sin and a burdensome sense of its weight. Why should you receive grace when you do not want it? What is the use of it to you? Why should you bow your knee to God, and receive, as the free gift of His charity, that which you feel you deserve? Have you not already earned eternal life? Are you not as good as other people? Have you not some considerable claim upon God? Do I startle you with these plain questions? Have I not heard you say much the same? The other day when we preached the electing love of God, you grumbled and muttered that God was unjust to choose one rather than another. What did this mean? Did it not mean that you felt you had some claim upon God? O sir, if this is your spirit, I must deal plainly with you! If you have any claim upon your Maker, plead it, and be you sure that He will not deny you your just rights. But I would advise you to change your method of dealing with your Judge! you will never prevail in this fashion. In truth you have no claim upon Him; but must appeal to His pure mercy. You are not in a position for Him to display free grace to you till your mouth is shut, and you sit down in dust and ashes, silently owning that you deserve nothing at His hands but infinite displeasure. Confess that whatever He gives you that is good and gracious must be given freely to one who deserves nothing. Hell gapes at your feet: cease from pride, and humbly sue out a pardon.

You see, then, the use of the law: it is to bring you where grace can be fitly shown you. It shuts you up that you may cry to Jesus to set you free. It is a storm which wrecks your hopes of self-salvation, but washes you upon the Rock of Ages. The condemning sentence of the law is meant to prepare you for the absolution of the gospel. If you condemn yourself and plead guilty before God, the royal pardon can then be extended towards you. The self-condemned shall be forgiven through the precious blood of Jesus, and the sovereign grace of God. Oh, my hearer, you must sit down there in the dust, or else God will not look at you! You must yield yourself to Him, owning His justice, honouring His law: this is the first condition of His mercy, and to this His grace brings all who feel its power. The Lord will have you bow before Him in self-abhorrence, and confess His right to punish you. Remember, "He will have mercy on whom He will have mercy, and He will have compassion on whom He will have compassion," and He will have you know this, and agree to it. His grace must reign triumphantly, and you must kiss its silver sceptre.

Thus has the first sentence served us for a preface: God bless it to us!

I. The doctrine of the text itself is this, that "where sin abounded, grace did much more abound"; and I shall try to bring out that truth, first, by saying that THIS IS SEEN IN THE WHOLE WORK OF GRACE, from beginning to end.

I would direct your attention to the context. The safest way to preach upon a text, is to follow out the idea which the inspired writer was endeavouring to convey. Paul has, in this place, been speaking of the abounding result for evil of one sin in the case of Adam, the federal head of the race. That one sin of Adam's abounded terribly. Look at the multitudinous generations of our race which have gone down to death. Who slew all these? Sin is the wolf which has devoured the flocks of men. Sin has poisoned the streams of manhood at their fountain-head, and everywhere they run with poisoned waters. Concerning this, Paul says, "Where sin abounded, grace did much more abound."

First, then, *sin abounded in its effect upon the whole human race :* one sin overthrew all humanity; one fatal fault, the breach of a plain and easy law, made sinners of us all. "By one man's disobedience many were made sinners." Simple as was the command which Adam broke, it involved obedience or disobedience to the sovereignty of God. All the trees of the garden were generously given to happy Adam in Paradise: "Of every tree of the garden thou mayest freely eat." There was but one tree reserved for God by the prohibition, "Thou shalt not eat of it: for in the day that thou eatest thereof thou shalt

surely die." Adam had no need to touch that fruit, there were all the other trees for him. Nothing was denied him which was really for his good; he was only forbidden that which would ruin him. We all look back to that Paradisaical state and wish we could have been put in some such a position as he: yet he dared to trespass on God's reserves, and thus to set himself up above his Maker. He judged it wise to do what God forbade: he ran the risk of death in the foolish hope of rising into a still higher state.

See the consequences of that sin on all sides, the world is full of them. Yet, saith Paul, "Where sin abounded, grace did much more abound," and he gives us this as a proof of it: "And not as it was by one that sinned, so is the gift: for the judgment was by one to condemnation, but the free gift is of many offences unto justification" (Rom. v. 16). The Lord Jesus came into the world, not alone to put away Adam's sin, but all the sins which have followed upon it. The second Adam has repaired the desperate ruin of the first, and much more. By His death upon the cross, our Divine Substitute has put away those myriads of sins, which have been committed by men since the first offence in Eden. Think of this! Take the whole aggregate of believers, and let each one disburden his conscience of its load of sin. What a mountain! Pile it up! Pile it up! It rises huge as high Olympus! Age after age believers come and lay their enormous loads in this place. "The Lord hath made to meet on Him the iniquities of us all." What Alps! What Himalayas of sin! If there were only mine and yours, my brother, what mountains of division would our sins make! But the great Christ, the free gift of God to us, when He bare our sins in His own body on the tree, took all those countless sins away. "Behold the Lamb of God, which taketh away the sin of the world"! Here is infinite grace to pardon immeasurable sin! Truly the "one man's offence" abounded horribly; but the "one man's obedience," the obedience of the Son of God, hath superabounded. As the arch of heaven far exceedeth in its span the whole round globe of the earth, so doth grace much more abound over human sin.

Follow me further, when I notice, secondly, that *sin abounded in its ruinous effects.* It utterly destroyed humanity. In the third chapter of the Romans you see how, in every part of his nature, man is depraved by sin. Think of the havoc which the tyrant, sin, has made of our natural estate and heritage. Eden is withered—its very site is forgotten. Our restfulness among the trees of the field, freely yielding their fruit, is gone, and God hath said, "In the sweat of thy face shalt thou eat bread." The field we till has lost its spontaneous yield of corn: "Thorns also and thistles shall it bring forth to thee." Our life has lost its glory and immortality; for "Dust thou art, and unto dust shalt thou return." Every woman in her pangs of travail, every man in his weariness of labour, and all of us together in the griefs of death, see what sin has done for us as to our mortal bodies. Alas, it has gone deeper: it has ruined our souls. Sin has unmanned man. The crown and glory of his manhood it has thrown to the ground. All our faculties are out of gear; all our tendencies are perverted. Beloved, let us rejoice that the Lord Jesus Christ has come to redeem us from the curse of sin, and He will undo the evil of evil. Even this poor world He will deliver from the bondage of corruption; and He will create new heavens and a new earth, wherein dwelleth righteousness. The groans and painful travail of the whole creation shall result in a full deliverance, through the grace of our Lord Jesus Christ, and somewhat more. As for ourselves, we are lifted up to a position far higher than that which we should have occupied had the race continued in its innocence. The Lord Jesus Christ found us in a horrible pit and in the miry clay, and He not only lifted us up out of it, but He set our feet upon a rock, and established our goings. Raised from hell, we are lifted not to the bowers of Eden, but to the throne of God. Redeemed human nature has greater capacities than unfallen human nature. To Adam the Lord did not say, "Thou art a son of God, joint heir with the Only-Begotten"; but He has said that to each believer redeemed by the precious blood of Jesus. Beloved, such a thing as fellowship with Christ in His sufferings could not have been known to Adam in Paradise. He could not have known what it is to be dead, and to have his life hid with Christ in God. Blessed be His name, our Lord Jesus Christ can say, "I restored that which I took not away"! He restored more than ever was taken away from us; for He hath made us to be partakers of the divine nature, and in His own person He hath placed us at God's right hand in the heavenly places. Inasmuch as the dominion of the Lord Jesus is more glorious than that of unfallen Adam, manhood is now more great and glorious than before the Fall. Grace has so much more abounded, that in Jesus we have gained more than in Adam we lost. Our Paradise Regained is far more glorious than our Paradise Lost.

Again, *sin abounded to the dishonour of God.* I was trying the other day to put myself into the position of Satan at the gates of Eden, that I might understand his diabolical policy. He had become the arch-enemy of God, and when he saw this newly-made world, and perceived two perfectly pure and happy creatures placed in it, he looked on with envy, and plotted mischief. He heard the Creator say, "In the day that thou eatest thereof thou shalt surely die," and he hoped here to find an opportunity for an assault upon God. If he could induce those new-made creatures to eat of the forbidden fruit, he would place their Maker upon the horns of a dilemma: either He must destroy the creatures which He had made, or else He must be untrue. The Lord had said, "Ye shall surely die," and He must thus undo His own work, and destroy a creature which He had made in His own image, after His own likeness. Satan, probably, perceived that man was an extra-ordinary being, with a wonderful mystery of glory hanging about his destiny; and, if he could make him sin, he would cause God to destroy him, and so far defeat the eternal purpose. On the other hand, if the Lord did not execute the sentence, then He would not be truthful, and throughout all His great universe it would be reported that the Lord's word had been broken. Either He had changed His mind, or He had spoken in jest, or He had been proven to have threatened too severe a penalty. In either case, the evil spirit hoped to triumph. It was a deep, far-reaching scheme to dim the splendour of the King of kings.

Beloved, did it not seem as if sin had abounded beyond measure, when first the woman and then the man had been deceived, and had done despite to God? Behold how grace, through our Lord Jesus Christ, did much more abound! God is more honoured in the redemption of man than if there had never been a Fall. The Lord has displayed the majesty of His justice, and the glory of His grace, in the great sacrifice of His dear Son, in such a manner that angels, and principalities, and powers will wonder throughout all ages. More of God is to be seen in the great work of redeeming love than could have been reflected in the creation of myriads of worlds, had each one of them been replete with marvels of divine skill, and goodness, and power. In Jesus crucified, Jehovah is glorified as never before. Where sin abounded to the apparent dishonour of God, grace doth much more abound to the infinite glory of His ever-blessed name.

Again, *sin abounded by degrading human character.* What a wretched being man is, as a sinner against God! Unchecked by law, and allowed to do as he pleases, what will not man become? See how Paul describes men in these progressive times—in these enlightened centuries: "This know also, that in the last days perilous times shall come. For men shall be lovers of their own selves, covetous, boasters, proud, blasphemers. disobedient to parents, unthank-ful, unholy, without natural affection, trucebreakers, false accusers, incontinent, fierce, despisers of those that are good, traitors, heady, highminded, lovers of pleasures more than lovers of God; having a form of godliness, but denying the power thereof." Human nature was not at all slandered by Whitefield when he said that, "left to himself, man is half beast and half devil." I do not mean merely men in savage countries, I am thinking of men in London. Only the other day a certain newspaper gave us plenty of proof of the sin of this city: I will say no more—could brutes or demons be worse? Read human history, Assyrian, Roman, Greek, Saracenic, Spanish, English; and if you are a lover of holiness, you will be sick of man. Has any other creature, except the fallen angels, ever become so cruel, so mean, so false? Behold what villains, what tyrants what monsters sin has made!

But now look on the other side, and see what the grace of God has done. Under the moulding hand of the Holy Spirit a gracious man becomes the noblest work of God. Man, born again and rescued from the Fall, is now capable of virtues, to which he never could have reached before he sinned. An unfallen being could not hate sin with the intensity of abhor-rence which is found in the renewed heart. We now know by personal experience the horror of sin, and there is now within us an instinctive shuddering at it. An unfallen being could not exhibit patience, for it could not suffer, and patience has its perfect work to do. When I have read the stories of the martyrs in the first ages of the Christian church, and during the Marian persecution in England, I have adored the Lord, who could enable poor feeble men and women thus to prove their love to their God and Saviour. What great things they suffered out of love to God; and how grandly did they thus honour Him! O God, what a noble being Thy grace has made man to be! I have felt great reverence for sanctified humanity, when I have seen how men could sing God's praises in the fires. What noble deeds men have been capable of, when the love of God has been shed abroad in their hearts! I do not think angels, or archangels, have ever been able to exhibit so admirable an all-round character as the grace of God hath wrought in once fallen men whom He has, by His grace, inspired with the divine life. In human character, "where sin abounded, grace did much more abound." I believe God looks out of heaven to-day, and sees in many of His poor, hidden people such beauties of virtue, such charms of holiness, that He Himself is delighted with them. "The Lord taketh pleasure in them that fear Him." These are such true jewels that the Lord has a high estimate of them, and sets them apart for Himself: "They shall be Mine, saith the Lord of hosts, in that day when I make up My jewels."

Again, dear friends, *sin abounded to the causing of great sorrow.* It brought with it a long train of woes. The children of sin are many, and each one causeth lamentation. We cannot attempt to fathom the dark abysses of sorrow which have opened in this world since the advent of sin. Is it not a place of tears—yea, a field of blood? Yet by a wonderful alchemy, through the existence of sin, grace has produced a new joy, yea, more than one new joy. The calm, deep joy of repentance must have been unknown to perfect innocence. This right orient pearl is not found in the rivers of Eden. Yea, and that joy which is in heaven in the presence of the angels of God over sinners that repent is a new thing, whose birth is since the Fall. God Himself knows a joy which He could not have known had there been no sin. Behold, with tearful wonder, the great Father as He receives His returning prodigal, and cries to all about Him, "Let us eat, and be merry: for this My son was dead, and is alive again; he was lost, and is found." O brethren, how could almighty love have been victorious in grace had there been no sin to battle with? Heaven is the more heaven for us, since there we shall sing of robes washed white in the blood of the Lamb. God hath greater joy in man, and man hath greater joy in God, because grace abounded over sin. We are getting into deep waters now! How true our text is!

Once more, *sin abounded to hinder the reign of Christ.* I believe that Satan's design in leading men into sin at the first, was to prevent the supremacy of the Lord Jesus Christ as man and God in one person. I do not lay it down as a doctrine, specifically taught in Scripture, but still it seems to me a probable truth, that Satan foresaw that the gap which was made in heaven by the fall of the angels was to be filled up by human beings, whom God would place near His throne. Satan thought that he saw before him the beings who would take the places of the fallen spirits, and he envied them. He knew that they were made in the image of the Only-Begotten, the Christ of God, and he hated him because he saw united in his person God whom he abhorred, and man whom he envied. Satan shot at the second Adam through the breast of the first Adam. He meant to overthrow the Coming One; but, fool that he was, the Lord Jesus Christ, by the grace of God, is now exalted higher than ever we could conceive Him to have been, had there been no sin to bear, no redemption to work out. Jesus, wounded and slain, has about Him higher splendour than before. O King of kings and Lord of lords, Man of Sorrows, we sing hallelujahs unto Thee! All our hearts beat true to Thee! We love Thee beyond all else! Thou art He whom we will praise for ever and ever! Jesus sits on no precarious throne in the empire of love. We would each one maintain His right with the last pulse of our hearts. King of kings and Lord of lords! Hallelujah! Where sin abounded, grace hath much more abounded to the glory of the Only-Begotten Son of God.

II. I find time always flies fastest when our subject is most precious. I have a second head, which deserves a lengthened consideration; but we must be content with mere hints. This great fact, that where sin abounded, grace did much more abound, crops up everywhere. THIS IS TO BE SEEN IN SPECIAL CASES.

The first special case is *the introduction of the law.* When the law of Ten Commands was given, through man's sin, it ministered to the aboundings of the offence; but it also ministered to the aboundings of grace. It is true there were ten commands; but there was more than tenfold grace. With the law there came forward a High Priest. The world had never seen a High Priest before, arrayed in jewelled breastplate, and garments of glory and beauty. There was the law; but at the same time there was the holy place of the Tabernacle of the Most High with its altar, its laver, its candlestick, and its table of shewbread. There was, also, the secret shrine where the majesty of God dwelt. God had, by those symbols and types, come to dwell among men. It is true, sin abounded through the law; but, then, sacrifices for sin also abounded. Heretofore, there had been no morning and evening lambs; there had been no day of atonement; no sprinkling of blood; no benediction from the Lord's High Priest. For every sin that the law revealed, a sacrifice was provided. Sins of ignorance, sins of their holy things, sins of all sorts were met by special sacrifices; so that the sins uncovered to the conscience were also covered by the sacrifice.

The story of Israel is another case in point. How often the nation rebelled; but how often did mercy rejoice over judgment! Truly the history of the chosen people shows how sin abounded, and grace did much more abound.

Run your eye down history and pause at *the crucifixion of our Lord Jesus.* This is the highest peak of the mountains of sin. They crucified the Lord of glory. Here sin abounded. But do I need to tell you that grace did here much more abound? You can look at the death of Christ till Pilate vanishes, and Caiaphas fades away, and all the clamour of the priests and Jews is hushed, and you see nothing and hear nothing but free grace and dying love.

There followed upon the crucifixion of our Lord, *the casting away of the Jewish people for a while.* Sin abounded when the Lord thus came to His own and His own received Him not. Yes; but the casting away of them was the saving of the nations. "We turn to the Gentiles," said the apostle; and that was a blessed turning for you and for me. Was it not? They that were bidden to the feast were not worthy, and the master of the house, being angry, invited other guests. Mark, "being angry"! What did he do when he was angry? Why, he did the most gracious thing of all; he said, "Go ye out into the highways and hedges, and as many as ye shall find bid to the supper." Sin abounded, for Israel would not enter the feast of love; but grace did much more abound, for the heathen entered the kingdom.

The heathen world at that time was sunk in the blackest darkness, and sin abounded. You have only to study ancient history and you will fetch a heavy sigh to think that men could be so vile. A poor and unlettered people were chosen of God to receive the gospel of Jesus, and they went about telling of an atoning Saviour, in their own simple way, until the Roman empire was entirely changed. Light and peace and truth came into the world, and drove away slavery and tyranny and bestial lust. Where sin abounded, grace did much more abound. **What** wonderful characters were produced in the terrible reign of Diocletian! What consecration to God was seen in the confessors! What fearlessness in common Christians! What invincible loyalty to Christ in the martyrs! Out of barbarians the Lord made saints, and the degraded rose to holiness sublime.

If I were to ask you, now, to give the best illustrations of grace abounding in individuals, I think your impulse would be to choose *men in whom sin once abounded*. What characters do we preach of most, when we would magnify the grace of God? We talk of David, and Manasseh, and swearing Peter, and the dying thief, and Saul of Tarsus, and the woman that was a sinner. If we want to show where grace abounded, we naturally turn our eyes to the place where sin abounded. Is it not so? Therefore, I need not give you any more cases—it is proven that where sin abounded, grace did much more abound.

III. Lastly; and this is what I want to hold you to, dear friends, at this time: THIS HOLDS TRUE TO EACH ONE OF US.

Let me take the case of the *open sinner*. What have you been? Have you grossly sinned? Have you defiled your body with unhallowed passions? Have you been dishonest to your fellow-men? Does some scarlet sin stain your conscience. even as you sit in the pew? Have you grown hardened in sin by long perseverance in it? Are you conscious that you have frequently, wilfully, and resolutely sinned? Are you getting old, and have you been soaking these seventy years in the crimson dye of sin till you are saturated through and through with its colour? Have you even been an implacable opponent of the gospel? Have you persecuted the saints of God? Have you tried by argument to batter down the gospel, or by ridicule to put it to reproach? Then hear this text: "Where sin abounded, grace did much more abound"; and as it was in the beginning, it is now and ever shall be, till this world shall end. The grace of God, if thou believest in the Lord Jesus Christ, will triumph over the greatness of thy wickedness. "All manner of sin and blasphemy shall be forgiven unto men." Throw down your weapons of rebellion; surrender at discretion; kiss the pierced hand of Jesus which is now held out to you, and this very moment you shall be forgiven, and you shall go your way a pardoned man, to begin a new life, and to bear witness that "where sin abounded, grace did much more abound."

Perhaps this does not touch you, my friend. Listen to my next word which is addressed to *the instructed sinner*. You are a person whose religious education has made you aware of the guilt of sin; you have read your Bible, and you have heard truthful preaching; and although you have never been a gross open sinner, yet you know that your life teems with sins of omission and commission. You know that you have sinned against light and knowledge. You have done despite to a tender conscience very often; and therefore you rightly judge that you are even a greater sinner than the more openly profane. Be it so; I take you at that. Do not run back from it. Let it be so; for "where sin abounded, grace did much more abound." Oh, that you may be as much instructed in the remedy, as you are instructed in the disease! Oh, that you may have as clear a view of the righteousness of Christ, as you have of your own unrighteousness! Christ's work is a divine work, broad enough to cover all your iniquity, and to conquer all your sin. Believe this! Give glory to God by believing

it; and according to your faith, so be it unto you.

I address another, who does not answer either of these two descriptions exactly; but he has lately begun to seek mercy, and the more he prays the more he is *tempted*. Horrible suggestions rush into his mind; damnable thoughts beset and bewilder him. Ah, my friend, I know what this means: the nearer you are to mercy, the nearer you seem to get to hell-gate! When you most solemnly mean to do good you feel another law in your members bringing you into captivity. You grow worse where you hoped you would have grown better. Very well, then; grip my text firmly as for your life: "Where sin abounded, grace did much more abound." If a whole legion of devils should be let loose upon you, Christ will glorify Himself by mastering them all. If now you cannot repent, nor pray, nor do anything, remember that text, "When we were yet without strength, in due time Christ died for the ungodly." Look over the heads of all these doubts, and devils, and inabilities, and see Jesus lifted on the cross, like the brazen serpent upon the pole; and look thou to Him, and the fiery serpents shall flee away from thee, and thou shalt live. Believe this text to be true, for true it is; "Where sin abounded, grace did much more abound."

"Ah!" saith another, "my case is still worse, sir; I am of a *despondent* turn of mind; I always look upon the black side of everything, and now if I read a promise I am sure it is not for me. If I see a threatening in God's Word, I am sure it is for me. I have no hope. I do not seem as if I should ever have any. I am in a dungeon into which no light can enter: it is dark, dark, dark, and worse darkness is coming. While you are trying to comfort me, I put the comfort away." I know you. You are like the poor creature in the Psalm, of whom we read—"His soul abhorreth all manner of meat." Even the gospel itself he cannot relish. Yes; I know you: you are writing bitter things against yourself: this morning you have been newly dipping your pen in gall; but your writing is that of a poor bewildered creature; it is not to be taken notice of. I see you writing, in text hand, great black words of condemnation; but there is nothing in them all. Verily, verily I say unto thee, thine handwriting shall be blotted out, and the curse, causeless, shall not come. Thus saith the Lord, " Your covenant with death shall be disannulled, and your agreement with hell shall not stand, for the Lord Jesus Christ has redeemed you, and where sin abounded, grace shall much more abound." Broken in pieces, all asunder, ground between the millstones, reduced to nothing, yet believe this revelation of God, that where sin abounded, grace did much more abound." Notice that "*much more*"—"much more abound." If thou canst grip it, and know it to be of a certainty the great principle upon which God acts, that grace shall outstrip sin, then there is hope of thee; nay, more than hope, there is salvation for thee on the spot. If thou believest in Jesus, whom God has set forth to be a propitiation for sin, thou art forgiven.

Oh, my hearers, do not despise this grace! Come, and partake of it. Does any one say, as Paul foresaw that some would say, "Let us sin, that grace may abound"? Ah, then, such an infamous inference is the mark of the reprobate, and your damnation is just. He that turns God's mercy into a reason for sin, has within him something worse than a heart of stone: surely his conscience is seared with a hot iron.

Beloved, I hope better things of you, for I trust that on the contrary, the sound of the silver bells of infinite love, free pardon, abounding grace, will make you hasten to the hospital of mercy, that you may receive healing for your sinfulness, strength for your feebleness, and joy for your sorrow. Lord, grant that in this house, in every case wherein sin has abounded, grace may yet more abound, for Jesus' sake! Amen.

THE DOCTRINES OF GRACE DO NOT LEAD TO SIN

"For sin shall not have dominion over you: for ye are not under the law, but under grace. What then? shall we sin, because we are not under the law, but under grace? God forbid."—Romans vi. 14, 15.

LAST Sabbath morning I tried to show that the substance and essence of the true gospel is the doctrine of God's grace—that, in fact, if you take away the grace of God from the gospel you have extracted from it its very life-blood, and there is nothing left worth preaching, worth believing, or worth contending for. Grace is the soul of the gospel: without it the gospel is dead. Grace is the music of the gospel: without it the gospel is silent as to all comfort. I endeavoured also to set forth the doctrine of grace in brief terms, teaching that God deals with sinful men upon the footing of pure mercy: finding them guilty and condemned, He gives free pardons, altogether irrespective of past character, or of any good works which may be foreseen. Moved only by pity He devises a plan for their rescue from sin and its consequences—a plan in which grace is the leading feature. Out of free favour He has provided, in the death of His dear Son, an atonement by means of which His mercy can be justly bestowed. He accepts all those who place their trust in this atonement, selecting faith as the way of salvation, that it may be all of grace. In this He acts from a motive found within Himself, and not because of any reason found in the sinner's conduct, past, present, or future. I tried to show that this grace of God flows towards the sinner from of old, and begins its operations upon him when there is nothing good in him: it works in him that which is good and acceptable, and continues so to work in him till the deed of grace is complete, and the believer is received up into the glory for which he is made meet. Grace commences to save, and it perseveres till all is done. From first to last, from the "A" to the "Z" of the heavenly alphabet, everything in salvation is of grace, and grace alone; all is of free favour, nothing of merit. "By grace are ye saved through faith; and that not of yourselves: it is the gift of God." "So then it is not of him, that willeth, nor of him that runneth, but of God that sheweth mercy."

No sooner is this doctrine set forth in a clear light than men begin to cavil at it. It is the target for all carnal logic to shoot at. Unrenewed minds never did like it, and they never will; it is so humbling to human pride, making so light of the nobility of human nature. That men are to be saved by divine charity, that they must as condemned criminals receive pardon by the exercise of the royal prerogative, or else perish in their sins, is a teaching which they cannot endure. God alone is exalted in the sovereignty of His mercy; and the sinner can do no better than meekly touch the silver sceptre, and accept undeserved favour just because God wills to give it—this is not pleasant to the great minds of our philosophers, and the broad phylacteries of our moralists, and therefore they turn aside, and fight against the empire of grace. Straightway the unrenewed man seeks out artillery with which to fight against the gospel of the grace of God, and one of the biggest guns he has ever brought to the front is the declaration that the doctrine of the grace of God must lead to licentiousness. If great sinners are freely saved, then men will more readily become great sinners; and if when God's grace regenerates a man it abides with him, then men will infer that they may live as they like, and yet be saved. This is the constantly-repeated objection which I have heard till it wearies me with its vain and false noise. I am almost ashamed to have to refute so rotten an argument. They dare to assert that men will take license to be guilty because God is gracious, and they do not hesitate to say that if men are not to be saved by their works they will come to the conclusion that their conduct is a matter of indifference, and that they may as well sin that grace may abound.

This morning I want to talk a little about this notion; for in part it is a great mistake, and in part it is a great lie. In part it is a mistake because it arises from misconception, and in part it is a lie because men know better, or might know better if they pleased.

I begin by admitting that the charge does appear somewhat probable. It does seem very likely that if we are to go up and down the country, and say, "The very chief of sinners may be forgiven through believing in Jesus Christ, for God is displaying mercy to the very vilest of the vile," then sin will seem to be a cheap thing. If we are everywhere to cry, "Come, ye sinners, come and welcome, and receive free and immediate pardon through the sovereign grace of God," it does seem probable that some may basely reply, "Let us sin without stint, for we can easily obtain forgiveness." But that which looks to be probable is not, therefore, certain: on the contrary, the improbable and the unexpected full often come to pass. In questions of moral influence nothing is more deceptive than theory. The ways of the human mind are not to be laid down with a pencil and compasses; man is a singular being. Even that which is logical is not always inevitable, for men's minds are not governed by the rules of the schools. I believe that the inference which would lead men to sin because grace reigns is not logical, but the very reverse; and I venture to assert that, as a matter of fact, ungodly men do not, as a rule, plead the grace of God as an excuse for their sin. As a rule they are too indifferent to care about reasons at all; and if they do offer an excuse it is usually more flimsy and superficial. There may be a few men of perverse minds who have used this argument, but there is no accounting for the freaks of the fallen understanding. I shrewdly suspect that in any cases in which such reasoning has been put forward it was a mere pretence, and by no means a plea which satisfied the sinner's own conscience. If men do thus excuse themselves, it is generally in some veiled manner, for the most of them would be utterly ashamed to state the argument in plain terms. I question whether the devil himself would be found reasoning thus—"God is merciful, therefore let us be more sinful." It is so diabolical an inference, that I do not like to charge my fellow-men with it, though our moralist opposers do not hesitate thus to degrade them. Surely, no intelligent being can really persuade itself that the goodness of God is a reason for offending Him more than ever. Moral insanity produces strange reasonings, but it is my solemn conviction that very rarely do men practically consider the grace of God to be a motive for sin. That which seems so probable at the first blush, is not so when we come to consider it.

I have admitted that a few human beings have turned the grace of God into lasciviousness; but I trust no one will ever argue against any doctrine on account of the perverse use made of it by the baser sort. Cannot every truth be perverted? Is there a single doctrine of Scripture which graceless hands have not twisted into mischief? Is there not an almost infinite ingenuity in wicked men for making evil out of good? If we are to condemn a truth because of the misbehaviour of individuals who profess to believe it, we should be found condemning our Lord Himself for what Judas did, and our holy faith would die at the hands of apostates and hypocrites. Let us act like rational men. We do not find fault with ropes because poor insane creatures have hanged themselves therewith; nor do we ask that the wares of Sheffield may be destroyed because edged tools are the murderer's instruments.

It may appear probable that the doctrine of free grace will be made into a license for sin, but a better acquaintance with the curious working of the human mind corrects the notion. Fallen as human nature is, it is still human, and therefore does not take kindly to certain forms of evil—such, for instance, as inhuman ingratitude. It is hardly human to multiply injuries upon those who return us continued benefits. The case reminds me of the story of half-a-dozen boys who had severe fathers, accustomed to flog them within an inch of their lives. Another boy was with them who was tenderly beloved by his parents, and known to be so. These young gentlemen met together to hold a council of war about robbing an orchard. They were all of them anxious to get about it except the favoured youth, who did not enjoy the proposal. One of them cried out, "You need not be afraid: if our fathers catch us at this work, we shall be half-killed, but your father won't lay a hand upon you." The little boy answered, "And do you think because my father is kind to me, that therefore I will do wrong and grieve him? I will do nothing of the sort to my dear father. He is so good to me that I cannot vex him." It would appear that the argument of the many boys was not overpoweringly convincing to their companion: the opposite conclusion was quite as logical, and evidently carried weight with it. If God is good to the undeserving, some men will go into sin, but there are others of a nobler order whom the goodness of God leadeth to repentance. They scorn the beast-like argument—that the more loving God is, the more rebellious we may be; and they feel that against a God of goodness it is an evil thing to rebel.

By-the-way I cannot help observing that I have known persons object to the evil influence of the doctrines of grace who were by no means qualified by their own mortality to be judges of the subject. Morals must be in a poor way when immoral persons become their guardians. The doctrine of justification by faith is frequently objected to as injurious to morals. A newspaper some time ago quoted a verse from one of our popular hymns—

"Weary, working, plodding one,
   Why toil you so?
Cease your doing; all was done
   Long, long ago.

Till to Jesus' work you cling
   By a simple faith,
'Doing' is a deadly thing,
   'Doing' ends in death."

This it styled mischievous teaching. When I read the article I felt a deep interest in this corrector of Luther and Paul, and I wondered how much he had drunk in order to elevate his mind to such a pitch of theological knowledge. I have found men pleading against the doctrines of grace on the ground that they did not promote morality, to whom I could have justly replied, "What has morality to do with you, or you with it?" These sticklers for good works are not often the doers of them. Let legalists look to their own hands and tongues, and leave the gospel of grace and its advocates to answer for themselves.

Looking back in history, I see upon its pages a refutation of the oft-repeated calumny. Who dares to suggest that the men who believed in the grace of God have been sinners above other sinners? With all their faults, those who throw stones at them will be few if they first prove themselves to be their superiors in character. When have they been the patrons of vice, or the defenders of injustice? Pitch upon the point in English history when this doctrine was very strong in the land; who were the men that held these doctrines most firmly? Men like Owen, Charnock, Manton, Howe, and I hesitate not to add Oliver Cromwell. What kind of men were these? Did they pander to the licentiousness of a court? Did they invent a Book of Sports for Sabbath diversion? Did they haunt ale-houses and places of revelry? Every historian will tell you, the greatest fault of these men in the eyes of their enemies was that they were too precise for the generation in which they lived, so that they called them Puritans, and condemned them as holding a gloomy theology. Sirs, if there was iniquity in the land in that day, it was to be found with the theological party which preached up salvation by works. The gentlemen with their womanish locks and essenced hair, whose speech savoured of profanity, were the advocates of salvation by works, and all bedabbled with lust they pleaded for human merit; but the men who believed in grace alone were of another style. They were not in the chambers of rioting and wantonness; where were they? They might be found on their knees crying to God for help in temptation; and in persecuting times they might be found in prison, cheerfully suffering the loss of all things for the truth's sake. The Puritans were the godliest men on the face of the earth. Are men so inconsistent as to nickname them for their purity, and yet say that their doctrines lead to sin?

Nor is this a solitary instance—this instance of Puritanism; all history confirms the rule: and when it is said that these doctrines will create sin, I appeal to facts, and leave the oracle to answer as it may. If we are ever to see a pure and godly England we must have a gospelized England; if we are to put down drunkenness and the social evil it must be by the proclamation of the grace of God. Men must be forgiven by grace, renewed by grace, transformed by grace, sanctified by grace, preserved by grace; and when that comes to pass the golden age will dawn; but while they are merely taught their duty, and left to do it of themselves in their own strength, it is labour in vain. You may flog a dead horse a long while before it will stir: you need to put life into it, or else all your flogging will fail. To teach men to walk who have no feet is poor work, and such an instruction in morals before grace gives a heart to love holiness. The gospel alone supplies men wth motive and strength and therefore it is to the gospel that we must look as the real reformer of men.

I shall fight this morning with the objection before us as I shall find strength. The doctrine of grace the whole plan of salvation by grace, is most promotive of holiness. Wherever it comes it helps us to say, "God forbid," to the question, "Shall we sin, because we are not under the law, but under grace?" This I would set out in the clear sunlight.

I wish to call your attention to some six or seven points.

I. First, you will see that the gospel of the grace of God promotes real holiness in men by remembering that THE SALVATION WHICH IT BRINGS IS SALVATION FROM THE POWER OF SIN. When we preach salvation to the vilest of men, some suppose we mean by that a mere deliverance from hell and an entrance into heaven. It includes all that, and results in that, but that is not what we mean. What we mean by salvation is this—deliverence from the love of sin, rescue from the habit of sin, setting free from the desire to sin. Now listen. If it be so, that that boon of deliverance from sin is the gift of divine grace, in what way will that gift or the free distribution of it, produce sin? I fail to see any such danger. On the contrary, I say to the man who proclaims a gracious promise of victory over sin, "Make all speed: go up and down throughout the world, and tell the vilest of mankind that God is willing by his grace to set them free from the love of sin and to make new creatures of them." Suppose the salvation we preach be this:—you that have lived ungodly and wicked lives may enjoy your sins, and yet escape the penalty—that would be mischievous indeed; but if it be this,—you that live the most ungodly and wicked lives may yet by believing in the Lord Jesus be enabled to change those lives, so that you shall live unto God instead of serving sin and Satan,—what harm can come to the most prudish morals? Why, I say spread such a gospel, and let it circulate through every part of our vast empire, and let all men hear it, whether they rule in the House of Lords or suffer in the house of bondage. Tell them everywhere that God freely and of infinite grace is willing to renew men, and make them new creatures in Christ Jesus. Can any evil consequences come of the freest proclamation of this news? The worse men are, the more gladly would we see them embracing this truth, for these are they who most need it. I say to every one of you, whoever you may be, whatever your past condition, God can renew you according to the power

of His grace; so that you who are to Him like dead, dry bones, can be made to live by His Spirit. That renewal will be seen in holy thoughts, and pure words, and righteous acts to the glory of God. In great love He is prepared to work all these things in all who believe. Why should any men be angry at such a statement? What possible harm can come of it? I defy the most cunning adversary to object upon the ground of morals, to God's giving men new hearts and right spirits even as He pleases.

II. Secondly, let it not be forgotten as a matter of fact that THE PRINCIPLE OF LOVE HAS BEEN FOUND TO POSSESS VERY GREAT POWER OVER MEN. In the infancy of history nations dream that crime can be put down by severity, and they rely upon fierce punishments; but experience corrects the error. Our forefathers dreaded forgery, which is a troublesome fraud, and interferes with the confidence which should exist between man and man. To put it down they made forgery a capital offence. Alas for the murders committed by that law! Yet the constant use of the gallows was never sufficient to stamp out the crime. Many offences have been created and multiplied by the penalty which was meant to suppress them. Some offences have almost ceased when the penalty against them has been lightened.

It is a notable fact as to men, that if they are forbidden to do a thing they straightway pine to do it, though they had never thought of doing it before. Law commands obedience, but does not promote it; it often creates disobedience, and an over-weighted penalty has been known to provoke an offence. Law fails, but love wins.

Love in any case makes sin infamous. If one should rob another it would be sufficiently bad; but suppose a man robbed his friend, who had helped him often when he was in need, everyone would say that his crime was most disgraceful. Love brands sin on the forehead with a red-hot iron. If a man should kill an enemy, the offence would be grievous; but if he slew his father, to whom he owes his life, or his mother, on whose breasts he was nursed in infancy, then all would cry out against the monster. In the light of love sin is seen to be exceeding sinful.

Nor is this all. *Love has a great constraining power towards the highest form of virtue.* Deeds to which a man could not be compelled on the ground of law, men have cheerfully done because of love. Would our brave seamen man the life-boat to obey an Act of Parliament? No, they would indignantly revolt against being forced to risk their lives; but they will do it freely to save their fellow-men. Remember that text of the apostle, "Scarcely for a righteous (or merely just) man will one die: yet peradventure," says he, "for a good (benevolent) man some would even dare to die." Goodness wins the heart, and one is ready to die for the kind and generous. Look how men have thrown away their lives for great leaders. That was an immortal saying of the wounded French soldier. When searching for the bullet the surgeon cut deeply, and the patient cried out, "A little lower and you will touch the Emperor," meaning that the Emperor's name was written on his heart. In several notable instances men have thrown themselves into the jaws of death to save a leader whom they loved. Duty holds the fort, but love casts its body in the way of the deadly bullet. Who would think of sacrificing his life on the ground of law? Love alone counts not life so dear as the service of the beloved. Love to Jesus creates a heroism of which law knows nothing.

All the history of the church of Christ, when it has been true to its Lord, is a proof of this.

Kindness also, working by the law of love, has often changed the most unworthy, and therein proved that it is not a factor of evil. We have often heard the story of the soldier who had been degraded to the ranks, and flogged and imprisoned, and yet for all that he would get drunk and misbehave himself. The commanding officer said one day, "I have tried almost everything with this man, and can do nothing with him. I will try one thing more." When he was brought in, the officer addressed him, and said, "You seem incorrigible: we have tried everything with you; there seems to be no hope of a change in your wicked conduct. I am determined to try if another plan will have any effect. Though you deserve flogging and long imprisonment I shall freely forgive you." The man was greatly moved by the unexpected and undeserved pardon, and became a good soldier. The story wears truth on its brow: we all see that it would probably end so.

That anecdote is such good argument that I will give you another. A drunkard woke up one morning from his drunken sleep, with his clothes on him just as he had rolled down the night before. He saw his only child, his daughter Millie, getting his breakfast. Coming to his senses he said to her, "Millie, why do you stay with me?" She answered, "Because you are my father, and because I love you." He looked at himself, and saw what a sottish, ragged, good-for-nothing creature he was, and he answered her, "Millie, do you really love me?" The child cried, "Yes, father, I do, and I will never leave you, because when mother died she said, 'Millie, stick to your father, and always pray for him, and one of these days he will give up drink, and be a good father to you'; so I will never leave you." Is it wonderful when I add that, as the story has it, Millie's father cast away his drink, and became a Christian man? It would have been more remarkable if he had not. Millie was trying free grace, was she not? According to our moralists she should have said, "Father, you are a horrible wretch! I have stuck to you long enough: I must now leave you, or else I shall be encouraging other fathers to get drunk." Under such proper dealing I fear Millie's father would have continued a drunkard till he drank himself into perdition. But the power of love made a better man of him. Do not these instances prove that undeserved love has a great influence for good?

Hear another story: In the old persecuting times there lived in Cheapside one who feared God and attended the secret meetings of the saints; and near him there dwelt a poor cobbler, whose wants were often relieved by the merchant; but the poor man was a cross-grained being, and, most ungratefully, from hope of reward, laid an information against his kind friend on the score of religion. This accusation would have brought the merchant to death by burning if he had not found a means of escape. Returning to his house, the injured man did not change his generous behaviour to the malignant cobbler, but, on the contrary, was more liberal than ever. The cobbler was, however, in an ill mood, and avoided the good man with all his might, running away at his approach. One day he was obliged to meet him face to face, and the Christian man asked him gently, "Why do you shun me? I am not your enemy. I know all that you did to injure me, but I never had an angry thought against you. I have helped you, and I am willing to do so as long as I live, only let us be friends."

Do you marvel that they clasped hands? Would you wonder if ere long the poor man was found at the Lollards' meeting? All such anecdotes rest upon the assured fact that grace has a strange subduing power and leads men to goodness, drawing them with cords of love, and bands of a man. The Lord knows that bad as men are the key of their hearts hangs on the nail of love. He knows that His almighty goodness, though often baffled, will triumph in the end. I believe my point is proved. To myself it is so. However, we must pass on.

III. There is no fear that the doctrine of the grace of God will lead men to sin, because ITS OPERATIONS ARE CONNECTED WITH A SPECIAL REVELATION OF THE EVIL OF SIN. Iniquity is made to be exceeding bitter before it is forgiven or when it is forgiven. When God begins to deal with a man with a view to blotting out his sins and making him His child, He usually causes him to see his evil ways in all their heinousness; He makes him look on sin with fixed eyes, till he cries with David, "My sin is ever before me." In my own case, when under conviction of sin, no cheering object met my mental eye, my soul saw only darkness and a horrible tempest. It seemed as though a horrible spot were painted on my eyeballs. Guilt, like a grim chamberlain, drew the curtains of my bed, so that I rested not, but in my slumbers anticipated the wrath to come. I felt that I had offended God, and that this was the most awful thing a human being could do. I was out of order with my Creator, out of order with the universe; I had damned myself for ever, and I wondered that I did not immediately feel the gnawing of the undying worm. Even to this hour a sight of sin causes the most dreadful emotions in my heart. Any man or woman here who has passed through that experience, or anything like it, will henceforth feel a deep horror of sin. A burnt child dreads the fire. "No," says the sinner to his tempter, "you once deceived me, and I so smarted in consequence, that I will not again be deluded. I have been delivered, like a brand from the burning, and I cannot go back to the fire." By the operations of grace we are made weary of sin; we loathe both it and its imaginary pleasures. We would utterly exterminate it from the soil of our nature. It is a thing accursed, even as Amalek was to Israel. If you, my friend, do not detest every sinful thing, I fear you are still in the gall of bitterness; for one of the sure fruits of the Spirit is a love of holiness, and a loathing of every false way. A deep inward experience forbids the child of God to sin; he has known within himself its judgment and its condemnation, and henceforth it is a thing abhorrent to him. An enmity both fierce and endless exists between the chosen seed and the serpent brood of evil: hence the fear that grace will be abused is abundantly safeguarded.

IV. Remember also that not only is the forgiven man thus set against sin by the process of conviction, but EVERY MAN WHO TASTES OF THE SAVING GRACE OF GOD IS MADE A NEW CREATURE IN CHRIST JESUS. Now if the doctrine of grace in the hands of an ordinary man might be dangerous, yet it would cease to be so in the hands of one who is quickened by the Spirit, and created anew in the image of God. The Holy Spirit comes upon the chosen one, and transforms him: his ignorance is removed, his affections are changed, his understanding is enlightened, his will is subdued, his desires are refined, his life is changed—in fact, he is as one new-born, to whom all things have become new. This change is compared in Scripture to the resurrection from the dead, to a creation, and to a new birth. This takes place in every man who becomes a partaker of the free grace of God. "Ye must be born again," said Christ to Nicodemus; and gracious men are born again. One said the other day, "If I believed that I was eternally saved, I should live in sin." Perhaps *you* would; but if you were renewed in heart you would not. "But," says one, "if I believed God loved me from before the foundation of the world, and that therefore I should be saved, I would take a full swing of sin." Perhaps *you* and the devil would; but God's regenerate children are not of so base a nature. To them the abounding grace of the Father is a bond to righteousness which they never think of breaking: they feel the sweet constraints of sacred gratitude, and desire to perfect holiness in the fear of the Lord. All beings live according to their nature, and the regenerated man works out the holy instincts of his renewed mind; crying after holiness, warring against sin, labouring to be pure in all things, the regenerate man puts forth all his strength towards that which is pure and perfect. A new heart makes all the difference. Given a new nature, and then all the propensities run in a different way, and the blessings of almighty love no longer involve peril, but suggest the loftiest aspirations.

V. One of the chief securities for the holiness of the pardoned is found in the way of CLEANSING THROUGH ATONEMENT. The blood of Jesus sanctifies as well as pardons. The sinner learns that his free pardon cost the life of his best Friend; that in order to his salvation the Son of God Himself agonized even to a bloody sweat, and died forsaken of His God. This causes a sacred mourning for sin, as he looks upon the Lord whom he pierced. Love to Jesus burns within the pardoned sinner's breast, for the Lord is his Redeemer; and therefore he feels a burning indignation against the murderous evil of sin. To him all manner of evil is detestable, since it is stained with the Saviour's heart's blood. As the penitent sinner hears the cry of, "Eloi, sabachthani!" he is horrified to think that One so pure and good should be forsaken of heaven because of the sin which He bore in His people's stead. From the death of Jesus the mind draws the conclusion that sin is exceedingly sinful in the sight of the Lord; for if eternal justice would not spare even the Well-beloved Jesus when imputed sin was upon Him, how much less will it spare guilty men? It must be a thing unutterably full of poison which could make even the immaculate Jesus suffer so terribly. Nothing can be imagined which can have greater power over gracious minds than the vision of a crucified Saviour denouncing sin by all His wounds, and by every falling drop of blood. What! live in the sin which slew Jesus? Find pleasure in that which wrought His death? Trifle with that which laid His glory in the dust? Impossible! Thus you see that the gifts of free grace, when handed down by a pierced hand, are never likely to suggest self-indulgence in sin, but the very reverse.

VI. Sixthly, a man who becomes a partaker of divine grace, and receives the new nature, is ever afterwards a PARTAKER OF DAILY HELPS FROM GOD'S HOLY SPIRIT. God the Holy Ghost deigns to dwell in the bosom of every man whom God has saved by His grace. Is not that a wonderful means of sanctifying? By what process can men be better kept from sin than by having the Holy Spirit Himself to dwell as Vicegerent within their hearts? The Ever-

blessed Spirit leads believers to be much in prayer, and what a power for holiness is found in the child of grace speaking to the heavenly Father! The tempted man flies to his chamber, unbosoms his grief to God, looks to the flowing wounds of his Redeemer, and comes down strong to resist temptation. The divine word also, with its precepts and promises, is a never-failing source of sanctification. Were it not that we every day bathe in the sacred fountain of eternal strength we might soon be weak and irresolute; but fellowship with God renews us in our vigorous warfare with sin. How is it possible that the doctrines of grace should suggest sin to men who constantly draw near to God? The renewed man is also by God's Spirit frequently quickened in conscience; so that things which heretofore did not strike him as sinful are seen in a clearer light, and are consequently condemned. I know that certain matters are sinful to me to-day which did not appear so ten years ago: my judgment has, I trust, been more and more cleared of the blindness of sin. The natural conscience is callous and hard; but the gracious conscience grows more and more tender till at last it becomes as sensitive as a raw wound. He who has most grace is most conscious of his need of more grace. The gracious are often afraid to put one foot before another for fear of doing wrong. Have you not felt this holy fear, this sacred caution? It is by this means that the Holy Spirit prevents your ever turning your Christian liberty into licentiousness, or daring to make the grace of God an argument for folly.

Then, in addition to this, the good Spirit leads us into high and hallowed intercourse with God, and I defy a man to live upon the mount with God, and then come down to transgress like men of the world. If thou hast walked the palace floor of glory, and seen the King in His beauty, till the light of His countenance has been thy heaven, thou canst not be content with the gloom and murkiness of the tents of wickedness. To lie, to deceive, to feign, as the men of the world do, will no longer beseem thee. Thou art of another race, and thy conversation is above them: "Thy speech betrayeth thee." If thou dost indeed dwell with God, the perfume of the ivory palaces will be about thee, and men will know that thou hast been in other haunts than theirs. If the child of God goes wrong in any degree, he loses to some extent the sweetness of his communion, and only as he walks carefully with God does he enjoy full fellowship; so that this rising or falling in communion becomes a sort of parental discipline in the house of the Lord. We have no court with a judge, but we have home with its fatherhood, its smile and its rod. We lack not for order in the family of love, for our Father dealeth with us as with sons. Thus, in a thousand ways, all danger of our presuming upon the grace of God is effectually removed.

VII. THE ENTIRE ELEVATION OF THE MAN WHO IS MADE A PARTAKER OF THE GRACE OF GOD is also a special preservative against sin. I venture to say, though it may be controverted, that the man who believes the glorious doctrines of grace is usually a much higher style of man than the person who has no opinion upon the matter. What do most men think about? Bread-and-butter, house-rent and clothes. But the men who consider the doctrines of the gospel muse upon the everlasting covenant, predestination, immutable love, effectual calling, God in Christ Jesus, the work of the Spirit, justification, sanctification, adoption, and such like noble themes. Why, it is a refreshment merely to look over the catalogue of these grand truths! Others are as children playing with little sand-heaps on the seashore; but the believer in free grace walks among hills and mountains. The themes of thought around him tower upward, Alps on Alps; the man's mental stature rises with his surroundings, and he becomes a thoughtful being, communing with sublimities. No small matter this, for a thing so apt to grovel as the average human intellect. So far as deliverance from mean vices and degrading lusts must in this way be promoted, I say, it is no small thing. Thoughtlessness is the prolific mother of inquity. It is a hopeful sign when minds begin to roam among lofty truths. The man who has been taught of God to think will not so readily sin as the being whose mind is buried beneath his flesh. The man has now obtained a different view of himself from that which led him to trifle away his time with the idea that there was nothing better for him than to be merry while he could. He says, "I am one of God's chosen, ordained to be His son, His heir, joint-heir with Jesus Christ. I am set apart to be a king and priest unto God, and as such I cannot be godless, nor live for the common objects of life." He rises in the object of his pursuit: he cannot henceforth live unto himself, for he is not his own, he is bought with a price. Now he dwells in the presence of God, and life to him is real, earnest, and sublime. He cares not to scrape together gold with the muck-rake of the covetous, for he is immortal, and must needs seek eternal gains. He feels that he is born for divine purposes, and enquires "Lord, what wouldst Thou have me to do?" He feels that God has loved him that His love may flow forth to others. God's choice of any one man has a bearing upon all the rest: He elects a Joseph that a whole family, a whole nation, nay, the whole world, may be preserved alive when famine had broken the staff of bread. We are each one as a lamp kindled that we may shine in the dark, and light up other lamps.

New hopes come crowding on the man who is saved by grace. His immortal spirit enjoys glimpses of the endless. As God has loved him in time, he believes that the like love will bless him in eternity. He knows that his Redeemer lives, and that in the latter days he shall behold Him; and therefore he has no fears for the future. Even while here below he begins to sing the songs of the angels, for his spirit spies from afar the dawn of the glory which is yet to be revealed. Thus with joyous heart and light footstep he goes forward to the unknown future as merrily as to a wedding-feast.

Is there a sinner here, a guilty sinner, one who has no merit, no claim to mercy whatever; is there one willing to be saved by God's free grace through believing in Jesus Christ? Then let me tell thee, sinner, there is not a word in God's book against thee, not a line or syllable, but everything is in thy favour. "This is a faithful saying, and worthy of all acceptation, that Christ Jesus came into the world to save sinners," even the chief. Jesus came into the world to save thee. Only do thou trust Him, and rest in Him. I will tell thee what ought to fetch thee to Christ at once, it is the thought of His amazing love. A profligate son had been a great grief to his father; he had robbed him and disgraced him, and at last he ended by bringing his grey hairs with sorrow to the grave. He was a horrible wretch of a son: no one could have been more graceless. However, he attended his father's funeral, and he stayed to hear the will read: perhaps it was the chief reason why he was there. He had fully made up his mind that his father would cut him off with a shilling, and he meant to make it very unpleasant for the rest of the family. To his great astonishment, as the will was read it ran something like this: "As for my son Richard, though he has fearfully wasted my substance, and though he has often grieved my heart, I would have him know that I consider him still to be my own dear child, and therefore, in token of my undying love, I leave him the same share as the rest of his brothers." He left the room; he could not stand it, the surprising love of his father had mastered him. He came down to the executor the next morning, and said, "You surely did not read correctly?" "Yes I did: there it stands." "Then," he said, "I feel ready to curse myself that I ever grieved my dear old father. Oh, that I could fetch him back again!" Love was born in that base heart by an unexpected display of love. May not your case be similar? Our Lord Jesus Christ is dead, but He has left it in His will that the chief of sinners are objects of His choicest mercy. Dying He prayed, "Father, forgive them." Risen He pleads for transgressors. Sinners are ever on His mind: their salvation is His great object. His blood is for them, His heart for them, His righteousness for them, His heaven for them. Come, O ye guilty ones, and receive your legacy. Put out the hand of faith and grasp your portion. Trust Jesus with your souls, and He will save you. God bless you. Amen.

OUR CHANGE OF MASTERS

"Being then made free from sin, ye became the servants of righteousness."—Romans vi. 18.

MAN was made to rule. In the divine original he was intended for a king, who should have dominion over the beasts of the field, and the fowl of the air, and the fish of the sea. He was designed to be the lord-lieutenant of this part of creation, and the form of his body and the dignity of his countenance betoken it. He walks erect among the animals, while they move upon all-fours; he subjugates and tames them to perform his will, and the fear and dread of him is upon all creatures, for they know their sovereign. Yet is it equally true that man was made to serve. At his beginning he was placed in the garden to keep it, and to dress it, and so to serve his Maker. His natural feebleness, his dependence upon rain, and sun, and dew, his instinctive awe of an unseen and omnipotent spirit, indicate that he is not the chief of the universe, but a subordinate being, whose lot it is to serve. We find within man various powers and propensities seeking to get dominion over him, so that his mind also is capable of servitude. The appetites which are essential for the sustenance of his bodily frame, even such as eating and drinking, endeavour to master him and if they can they will do so, and reduce him below the level of the swine. Man is in part spirit, but he is also in part animal, and the animal strives to get dominion over the spiritual; and in many, many men it does so, till they are utterly degraded. Nothing can be worse than a soul enslaved by such a body as that of man. The brute nature of man is the worst sort of brute. There is no beast in wolf, or lion, or serpent that is so brutish as the beast in man. Did I not tell you last Sabbath day that whereas, according to the Levitical law, he that touched a dead animal was unclean till the evening, he who touched a dead man was unclean seven days, for man is a seven times more polluting creature than any of the beasts of the field when his animal nature rules him.

If evil aims at ruling man the good Spirit also strives with him. When God of His infinite mercy visits man by His Spirit, that Spirit does not come as a neutral power to dwell quietly within man, and to share his heart with the Prince of Darkness, but He enters with full intent to reign. Hence there is a conflict which cannot be ended by an armistice, but must be carried on to the end, and that end will be found either in the driving out of the evil or in the thrusting out of the good; for one or the other, either the Prince of Darkness or the King of Light, will have dominion over man. Man must have a master: he cannot serve two masters, but he must serve *one.* Of all sorts of men this has been true, and it has perhaps been most clearly seen in those who were evidently made to lead their fellow men: it is specially seen in such a man for instance, as Alexander, a true king of men, so heroic and great-hearted that one does not wonder that armies were fired with enthusiasm by his presence, and drove everything before them. Alexander conquered the world, and yet on occasions he became the captive of drunkenness and the bondsman of his passionate temper. At such times the king of men, the vanquisher of armies, was little better than a raving maniac. Look for further illustration at the busts of the emperors of Rome, the masters of the world; study their faces, and mark what grovelling creatures they must have been. Rome had many slaves, but he who wore her purple was the most in bonds. No slave that ground at the mill, or died in the amphitheatre, was more in bondage than such men as Tiberius and Nero, who were the bond-slaves of their passions. High rank does not save a man from being under a mastery: neither does learning nor philosophy deliver men from this bondage, for the teachers of liberty have not themselves been free, but it has happened as the apostle saith, "While they promise them liberty they themselves are the servants of corruption." Solomon himself, with all his wisdom, played the fool exceedingly, and though he was the most sagacious ruler of his age he became for awhile completely subject to his fleshly desires.

Man is born to be a servant, and a servant he must be. *Who shall be his master?* That is the question. Our text proves the point with which I have started, for it speaks of "being made free from sin," and in the same breath it adds, "Ye became the servants of righteousness." There is no interregnum: there does not appear to be a moment left for an independent state, but out of one servitude we pass into another. Do not think I made a mistake in the use of the word servitude; I might have translated the Greek word by that of slave, and have been correct. "Being made free from sin, ye were enslaved to righteousness." The apostle makes an excuse for using the figure, and says, "I speak after the manner of men, because of

the infirmity of your flesh." He did not know how else to describe it, for when we come from under the absolute power of sin we come at once into a like subjection to righteousness; as we were governed and swayed by the love of sin, so we become in a similar manner subject to the forces of grace and truth. As sin took possession of us and controlled our acts, so grace claims us as its own, takes possession of us, and rules us with an absolute sway. Man passes from one master to another, but he is always in subjection. Free will I have often heard of, but I have never seen it. I have met with will, and plenty of it, but it has either been led captive by sin or held in blessed bonds of grace. The passions drive it hither and thither like a rolling thing before a whirlwind; or the understanding sways it, and then, according as the understanding is darkened or enlightened, the will acts for good or evil. In any case the bit is in its mouth, and it is guided by a power beyond itself.

However, I leave that question, and call attention this morning first of all to *our change of masters*— "Being made free from sin, we become the servants of righteousness": secondly, to *the reasons for that change*; and thirdly, to *the consequence of that change.*

I. We begin with OUR CHANGE OF MASTERS. We must have a master, but some of us by divine grace have made a change of masters infinitely to our advantage. In describing this inward revolution we will begin with a word or two upon our old master. The apostle says in the verse preceding our text, "*Ye were the servants of sin.*" How true that is! Those of us who now believe, and are free from sin, were all without exception the servants of sin. We were not all alike enslaved, but we were all under bondage. Sin has its liveried servants. Did you ever see a man dressed in the full livery of sin? A fine suit, I warrant you! Sin clothes its slave with rags, with shame, and often with disease. When fully dressed in Satan's uniform the sinner is abominable, even to his fellow sinners. If you want to see sin's liveried servants dressed out in their best or their worst, go to the prison, and you will find them there; or go to the dens of infamy in this great city, or to the liquor-bars, or to the places of vicious amusement, and you will find them there. Many of them wear the badge of the devil's drudgery upon their backs in poverty and rags, upon their faces in the blotches born of drunkenness, and in their very bones in the consequences of their vice. Satan has regimentals for his soldiers, and they are worthy of the service.

But great folks have many servants who are out of livery, and so has sin. We were not all open transgressors before our new birth, though we were all the servants of sin. There are many slaves of evil whom you would not know to be such if you only saw the surface of their characters. They do not swear, or steal, or commit adultery, or even break the Sabbath outwardly; on the contrary, they are most moral in their conduct. They are the servants of sin, but they are secretly so, for fear of rebuke; they are non-professing sinners and yet sincerely in love with sin. They stood up and sung the hymn just now, they bowed their heads in prayer, and they are now listening to the sermon, and no one will know the difference between them and the servants of Christ by their exterior; but at heart they reject the Son of God, and refuse to believe in Him, for they love the pleasures of sin and the wages of unrighteousness. A kind of selfish caution restrains them from overt acts of transgression, but their heart loves not God, and their desires are not towards His ways. Oh, my dear hearer, if thou art setting up thine own righteousness in thy soul as an anti-Christ against God's Christ, if thou art kicking against the sway of the Divine Spirit, if thou art secretly living in sin, if thou art following out some sweet sin in secret, even though thou darest to appear in the livery of Christ, yet still thou art the slave of sin. Hypocrites are worse slaves than any others, because they are laid under the restraints of religious men without enjoying their consolations, and they practise the sins of the ungodly without their pleasures. Every hypocrite is a fool and a coward; he has not the will to serve the Lord and yet he has not the courage to serve the devil out and out. These go-betweens are of all sorts of people the most to be pitied and the most to be blamed.

As long as we are unbelievers we are the servants of sin, but we are not all outdoor servants of sin. Sin has its domestic servants who keep quiet, as well as its soldiers who beat the drum. Many keep their sin to themselves: nobody hears of them in the street, they raise no public scandal, and yet at heart they are the faithful followers of wickedness and rebellion. Their idols are set up in secret chambers, but they are heartily loved. Their desires and aspirations are all selfish, but they try to conceal this fact even from themselves; they will not serve God, they will not bow before His Son, and yet they would shrink from avowing their rebellion. They are amiable, admirable, and excellent in their outward deportment; but they are the indoor servants of Satan for all that, and their heart is full of enmity against God. Some of us confess that it was so with us. When none found fault with us we were, nevertheless, rotten in heart. We used to pray, but it was a mockery of God; we went up to God's house, but we regarded not His word, and yet in all this we prided ourselves that we were righteous.

There are, however, many believers, who were once outdoor servants of Satan, sinning openly and in defiance of all law. I thank God that there are some here who are now the servants of Christ, upon whom I can look with great delight, although they were once the open, overt, zealous, diligent servants of the devil. Now they are washed, renewed, and sanctified. Glory be to God for it. Oh that the Lord would bring some more great sinners inside this house and turn them into great saints, for bold offenders make zealous lovers of Jesus when He puts away their sins. They love much because they have had much forgiven, and inasmuch as they desperately sinned so do they devoutly love; and their surrender to Christ is as entire and unreserved as their former surrender to the service of evil. In this let God be praised. Still, let us all humbly bow before the truth we are now speaking of, and own with great humiliation of spirit that we were the servants of sin.

In passing on we notice next the expression of the apostle, "*Being made free from sin.*" Through divine grace we have been led to trust the Lord Jesus Christ for eternal salvation, and having done so we are at this moment free from sin. Come you who trust the Saviour's name, and rejoice in the words before us, for they describe you. You *are* made free from sin—not you *shall be,* but you *are.* In what sense is this true?

First, in the sense of condemnation. The believer is no more condemned for sin. Your sin was laid on Christ of old, and He as your scapegoat took it all away. "There is therefore now no condemnation to

them which are in Christ Jesus." You are acquitted and justified through the Lord your righteousness. Clap your hands for joy! It is a mercy worth ten thousand worlds. You are made free from the damning power of sin, now and for ever.

Next, you are made free from the guilt of sin. As you cannot be condemned so does the truth go further, you cannot even be accused; your transgression is forgiven you, your sin is covered. "As far as the east is from the west, so far hath He removed our transgressions from us." "Who shall lay anything to the charge of God's elect? It is God that justifieth. Who is he that condemneth? It is Christ that died, yea, rather, that is risen again, who is even at the right hand of God, who also maketh intercession for us." You are delivered from sin's guilt at this moment—"made free from sin."

You are in consequence free from the punishment of sin. You shall never be cast into hell, for Jesus has suffered in your stead, and the justice of God is satisfied. As a believer in Christ, for you there is no bottomless pit, for you no undying worm, for you no fire unquenchable; but, guilty as you are by nature, Christ hath made you so completely clean that for you is reserved the "Come, ye blessed of My Father, inherit the kingdom prepared for you before the foundation of the world."

Nor is this all. You are made free from sin as to its reigning power, and this is a point in which you greatly delight. Sin once said to you, "Go," and you went: it says "Go" now, but you do not go. Sometimes sin stands in your way when grace says "Go," and then you would gladly run but sin opposes and hinders; and yet you will not yield to its demands, for grace holds dominion. You push, you struggle, you resolve that sin shall not be lord of your life, for you are not under the law but under grace. Sin hides itself in holes and corners of your nature, skulks in the dark about the streets of Mansoul, plots and plans if it can to get the mastery over you: but it never shall: it is cast out of the throne, and the Holy Ghost sits there ruling your nature, and there He will sit until you shall be perfected in holiness, and shall be caught up to dwell with Christ for ever and ever.

"Made free from sin." I wish I could now leave off preaching, and get into a quiet pew, and sit down with you and meditate upon that thought; chewing the cud as you farmers say, and getting the juice out of this rich pasturage. "Made free from sin!" Why, as I pronounce those blessed words I feel like an escaped negro in the old slave days when he leaped upon British soil in Canada. After all his running through the woods, and crossing of hills and rivers, he was free! How he leaped for joy! How he cried with delight! Even so did we exult in our liberty when at the first our Lord Jesus set us free. You who were never slaves, and never felt the taskmaster's lash, you do not know the value of liberty; and so in spiritual things, if you have never felt the slavery of sin, and have never escaped therefrom into the good land of grace where Christ hath made you free indeed, you do not know the joy of the redeemed. I am free! I am free! I am free!—I that was once a slave to every evil desire! I am made free by omnipotent love! I have escaped from the taskmaster's fetters, and I am the Lord's free man! Let all the angels praise my redeeming Lord. Let all the spirits before the throne praise the Lord, who hath led His people out of bondage, for He is good, for His mercy endureth for ever.

Now, how came we to be free? We have become free in three ways. First, by *purchase*, for our Saviour has paid the full redemption money for us, and there is not a halfpenny due upon us. Blessed be His name, there is no mortgage on His inheritance: the price is all paid and we are Christ's unencumbered property for ever. Here we stand at this moment free, because we are ransomed, and we know that our Redeemer liveth. Our body, soul, and spirit are all bought with a price, and in our complete manhood we are Christ's.

Next, we are free by *power* as well as by purchase. Just as the Israelites were the Lord's own people, but He had to bring them out of Egypt with a high hand and an outstretched arm, so has the Lord by power broken the neck of sin and brought us up from the dominion of the old Pharaoh of evil and set us free. The Spirit's power, the same power which raised Christ from the dead, aye, the same power which made the heavens and the earth, hath delivered us, and we are the ransomed of the Lord.

And then we are free by *privilege*. "Unto as many as believed Him, to them gave He the privilege to become the sons of God." God has declared us free. His own royal, majestic, and divine decree has bidden the prisoners go forth. The Lord Himself looseth the prisoners, and declares that they shall no more be held in captivity. Price and power and privilege meet together in our liberty.

How came we to be free? I will tell you another story. We are free in a strange way. According to the chapter in which we find our text we are free because *we have died*. If a slave dies his master's possession in him is ended. The tyrant can rule no longer, death has relaxed his hold. "He that is dead is free from sin." Sin comes to me and asks me why I do not obey its desires. I have a reply ready. "Ah, Master Sin, I am dead! I died some thirty years ago, and I do not belong to you any more. What have you to do with me?" Whenever the Lord brings a man to die in Christ the blessed, heavenly death unto sin, how hath sin any more dominion over him? He is clear from his old master, because he is dead. Our old master lives to us, but we do not live to him. He may make what suit he pleases, we will not acknowledge his right. Some of us have made a public claim of our freedom by death, for *we have been buried*, and the apostle saith, "Know ye not, that so many of us as were baptized into Jesus Christ were baptized into His death? Therefore we are buried with Him by baptism into death: that like as Christ was raised up from the dead by the glory of the Father, even so we also should walk in newness of life." We do not trust in the burial of baptism, for we know that there would have been no truth in it if we had not been dead first; but still it is a blessed sign to us that inasmuch as we died we have also been buried. Whenever the devil comes to us we can each one say to him, "I am no servant of yours, I died and was buried, did you not see me laid in the liquid tomb?" Oh, it is a blessed thing when the Lord enables us to feel a clear assurance that our baptism was not a mere form, but the instructive token of a work within the soul wrought by the divine Spirit, which set us free from the thraldom of sin.

A third thing has happened to us: *we have risen again*. According to Paul's teaching we have risen in the resurrection of Christ: a new life has been given to us: we are new creatures in Christ Jesus. We are not the same people that we once were; old things

have passed away, behold all things have become new. If some of you were to meet your old selves you would not know yourselves, would you? My old self does not know me, and cannot make me out. I am dead to him as to his reigning power, and buried too, so that I can never be his subject, nor can he ever be the king of my heart, yet he struggles to dwell within me, and seems to have as many lives as a cat. Every now and then my old self sneeringly cries to my true self, "What a fool you are." My true self answers, "No, I was a fool when you had sway, but now I have come to my right mind." Sometimes that old self whispers, "There is no reality in faith," and the new self replies, "There is no reality in the things which are seen. This world is a shadow, but heaven is eternal." "Ah," says the old self, "you are a hypocrite." "No," says the new self, "I was false when I was under your power, but now I am honest and true." Yes, brethren, we are risen with Christ: with Him we died and were buried, and with Him we are risen, and hence we are free. What slave would remain under the dominion of a master if he could say, "I died, sir: you cannot own me now, for your ownership only extended over one life. I was buried; did you own me when I was buried? I have risen again, and my new life is not yours; I am not the same man that I was, and you have no rights over me." We have undergone this wondrous death and resurrection, and so we can say this morning with heartfelt joy, "We are made free from sin."

We are also free from sin in our hearts: we do not love it now, but loathe the thought of it. We are free from sin as to our new nature: it cannot sin because it is born of God. We are free from sin as to God's purpose about us, for He will present us ere long blameless and faultless before His presence with exceeding great joy. We do not belong to sin; we refuse to serve sin; we are made free from it by the grace of God.

Now, the third part of this change of masters is this—"*ye became the servants of righteousness.*" So we have done, and we are now in the possession of righteousness and under its rule. A righteous God has made us die to sin: a righteous God has redeemed us: a new and righteous life has been infused into us, and now righteousness rules and reigns in us. We do not belong to ourselves, but we yield ourselves up entirely to the Redeemer's sway through His Spirit, and the more completely He rules us the better. The text says we are enslaved to righteousness, and so we wish to be. We wish we were so enslaved that we could not even will a wrong thing nor wish an evil thing. We desire to give ourselves up wholly and absolutely to the divine sway, so that the right, and the true, and the good may hold us in perpetual bonds. We abandon ourselves to the supremacy of God, and we find our liberty in being entirely subjected to the will of the Most High. This is a change of masters with which I know that some of you are well acquainted. I am afraid, however, that others of you know nothing about it. May the Lord grant that you may be made to know it before you go to sleep to-night. May you be delivered from the black tyrant and brought into the service of the Prince of Peace, and that straightway.

II. Secondly, let us survey the REASONS FOR OUR CHANGE. How do we justify this change of masters? A man who makes frequent shifts is not good for much. But we changed our old master because he never had any right to us, and we were illegally detained by him. Why should sin have dominion over us? Sin did not make us, sin does not feed us, sin has no right to us whatever; we never owed it a moment's homage; we are not debtors to the flesh to live after the flesh. Our old master cannot summon us for desertion, for he stole our services. Besides, our old master was as bad as bad could be. You never saw his portrait; but he that would paint a picture of sin would have to put upon the canvas all the monstrosities that ever existed, and all the horrors that were ever imagined, and these would have to be exaggerated and condensed into one, before they could fairly depict the deformity of sin. Sin is worse than the devil, for sin made the devil a devil; he would have been an angel if it had not been for sin. Oh, who would serve the destroying tyrant who of old cast down even the stars of light and turned angels into fiends? Who ran away from our old master because we had never any profit at his hands. The apostle says, "What fruit had he then?" Ask the drunkard, "What did you get by the drink?" Who hath woe? Who hath redness of the eyes? Ask the spendthrift what he gained by his debauchery. He would hardly like to tell you, and I certainly should not like to repeat his tale. Ask any man that lives in sin what he has gained by it, and you will find it is all loss; sin is evil and only evil, and that continually. We have found that out, and therefore we have quitted the old master, and taken up with the new. Besides that, our old master, sin, brought us shame. There was no honour in serving him. His work is called by Paul, "those things whereof ye are now ashamed." We are in the sight of God, aye, and in our own sight, ready to blush scarlet at the very thought of the evil in which we once took delight. Sin is a grovelling, mean, despicable thing, and we are ashamed of having been connected with it. Moreover, its wages are death, and this is dreadful to think upon. Sin at one time was pleasant to us, but when we found out that sin led its servants down to hell, and plunged them into fire unquenchable, we renounced its rule, and found another lord.

But why did we take up with our new Master? We could not help it, for it was He that set us free; it was He that bought us, it was He that fought for us, it was He that brought us into liberty. Ah, if you could see Him you would not ask us why we became His servants. In the first place, we owe ourselves wholly to Him; and in the next place, if we did not, He is so altogether lovely, so matchless, and so charming, that if we had a free choice of masters we would choose Him a thousand times over, for He is the crown and glory of mankind, among the sons there is none to be compared to Him.

If you want us to justify our service of Him, we tell you that His service is perfect freedom and supreme delight. We have had to suffer a little sometimes when His enemy and ours has barked at us, and the ungodly have called us ill names, but we count it honour to suffer for Jesus' sake; or He is so sweet, and so good, that if we had a thousand lives, and could give each one away by a martyr's death, we count Him worthy of those lives, so sweet is He to our heart's love. Why have we taken our new Master? Why, because He gives us even now a present payment in His service. If there were no hereafter we would be satisfied with the present delight He gives us, but in addition to that He has promised us, as a future reward, life eternal at His right hand. We

think, therefore, that we have more than sufficient reason for becoming the servants of Jesus Christ, who is made of God unto us righteousness. Dear hearers, how I wish that you would all enter my Lord's service by faith in His name.

III. In the third place, and very practically, I want to talk to those who are servants of God upon THE CONSEQUENCES OF THIS CHANGE. Ye have become the servants of righteousness, and the first consequence is that you belong wholly to your Lord? Have you recognized this? I know numbers of Christian people —I hope they are Christian people, for in some points they seem as if they were—but if I were asked to look at their lives, and give an opinion as to whom they belong, I should be compelled to say, "They seem mostly to belong to themselves." To whom does their property belong? "To themselves." To whom does their time belong? "To themselves." To whom does their talent belong? "To themselves." As far as I can see they lay all out upon themselves, and live for themselves. And what do they give to God? If they are rather generous they give Him the candle-ends and the parings of the cheese, and little odds and ends, threepenny-bits, and things they do not want, and can give without missing them. There are hundreds of professors who never gave God anything that cost them a self-denial; no, not so much as going without a dish on the table, or a picture on the wall, or a ring on the finger. There are numbers of professing Christians who spend a deal more on the soles of their boots than on Christ, and many women who spend more on the feathers and the flowers which deck their bonnets than on their Saviour. Yes, and I have heard of men who said they were perfect, and yet they were worth half a million of money, and were hoarding up more! Sinners dying and being damned and missionaries without support, and yet these absolutely perfect men are piling up gold and letting the cause of Christ stop for means. It is not my theory of perfection, nay, it does not seem to me to come up to the idea of a common Christian who says he is not his own. If you are really saved, brethren, not a hair of your heads belongs to yourselves: Christ's blood has either bought you or it has not, and if it has, then you are altogether Christ's, every bit of you, and you are neither to eat nor drink, nor sleep, but for Christ. "Whatsoever ye do, do all to the glory of God." Have you ever got a hold of that? Just as a negro used to belong to the man that bought him, every inch of him, so you are the slave of Christ; you bear in your body the brand of the Lord Jesus, and your glory and your freedom lie therein. That is the first consequence of being set free from sin,— ye became the servants of righteousness.

What next? Why, because you are Christ's His very name is dear to you. You are not so His slave that you would escape from His service if you could; no, but you would plunge deeper and deeper into it. You want to be more and more the Lord's. His very name is sweet to you. If you meet with the poorest person who belongs to Christ you love him, and though perhaps some who are like Christ in other respects may have awkward tempers, you put up with their infirmities for His sake. Where there is anything of Christ there your love goes forth. I remember when I left the village where I first preached I felt that if I had met a dog that came from Waterbeach I should have petted him; and such is the love we have for Christ that the lowest and weakest thing that belongs to Him we love for His sake; the very sound of His name is music to us, and those who do not love Him we cannot endure. Haydn, the great musician, one day walked down a London street and turning into a music-seller's shop, he asked the salesman if he had any select and beautiful music? "Well sir," said he. "I have some sublime music by Mr. Haydn." "Oh," said Haydn. "I'll have nothing to do with that." "Why, sir, you come to buy music and will have nothing to do with Mr. Haydn's composition! What fault can you find with it?" "I can find a great deal of fault with it, but I will not argue with you: I do not want any of his music." "Then," said the shop-keeper, "I have other music, but it is not for such as you," and he turned his back on him. A thorough enthusiast grows impatient of those who do not appreciate what he so much admires. If we love Jesus we shall sometimes feel an impatient desire to get away from those who know Him not. You do not love Christ? What kind of man can you be to be so blind, so dead? You can be no friend of mine if you are not a friend of Christ's. I would do anything for your good, but you cannot yield me delight or be my bosom friend unless you love my Lord, for He has engrossed my heart and taken entire possession of my spirit. If you have thus become a servant of righteousness you will weary of that which does not help you in His service, but the name of your Master will be as choicest music to you.

And now, dear friends, let me mention another result. All your members are henceforth reserved for Christ. What does the apostle say? "When ye were the servants of sin ye were free from righteousness." When Satan was your master you did not care about Christ, did you? You had no respect for Him, and if anybody brought the words of Jesus before you you said, "Take them away—I do not want to hear them." You went wholly in for evil. Now, just in the same way yield yourself up wholly to Christ, and say, "Now, Satan, when I was yours I did not yield obedience to Jesus, and now that I am Christ's I can yield no obedience to you." If Satan brings sin before you, say, "I cannot see it: my eyes are Christ's": and if he would charm you with the sweet sound of temptation say, "I cannot hear it: my ears are Christ's." "Oh," saith he, "seize on this delight." You answer, "I cannot reach it; my hands are Christ's." "But taste this sweet draught," saith he. You say, "I cannot take it, my lips are Christ's, my mouth is Christ's, all my members are Christ's." "Well, but you can form a judgment, cannot you, about this error?" "No, I do not want to know anything about it; my understanding is Christ's." "Oh, but hear this new thing." "No, I do not want to hear it; I have found Christ, who is new enough for me; I do not want your novel discoveries; I am dead to them. I do not want to be worried with arguments which dishonour my Lord: take them away. When I was a servant of sin I would not meddle with the truth, and now that I am a servant of Christ I will not trifle in the opposite direction; I have done with all but Jesus."

Think, my brethren, when we were servants of sin in what way we served it; for just as we used to serve sin, so ought we to work for Jesus. I do not speak to all here present, but I speak to many who were sinners of an open kind: how did you serve sin? I will answer for them. They did not require to be egged on to it; they did not want any messenger of the devil to plead with them and urge them to unholy pleasures and unclean delights. Far from it;

some even of their own companions thought them too imprudent. Now, dear friends, you ought not to want your ministers or Christian friends to stir you up to good works; you ought to be just as eager after holiness as you were after sin. Evil was very sweet to you once. You used to watch for the day when you could indulge in a sweet sin; did you not? When the time was coming round when you could take a deep draught of iniquity you took the almanack and looked for it as a child for his holidays. You did not mind travelling from town to town to make a round of dissipation. Brother, serve Christ in the same way. May His Holy Spirit help you to do so. Watch for opportunities of doing good; do not need whipping to duty. Instead of requiring to be urged forward in evil we needed holding back: did we not? Our parents had to put the rein upon us! Sometimes mother would say, "John, do not so," and father would cry, "My boy, do not this." We wanted a deal of restraint. I wish I had a band of Christians round me who needed holding back in the service of Christ: I have not met with that sort yet. I am prepared with any kind of curb when I meet with a high-mettled Christian, who goes at too great a rate in his Lord's service. For the most part my Master's horses are fonder of getting into the stables than out into the hunting field. I have not met with one who has done too much for the Lord. I shall never be guilty of too much work myself; I wish I could go like the wind in serving Jesus.

Brethren, be just as hot to honour Christ as you once were to dishonour him. As you have given the devil first-rate service, let Christ have the same. You recollect in the days of your sin, some of you who went in for it thoroughly, that you never stood at any expense—did you? Oh no, if you wanted pleasure in sin, away went the five pounds, and the hundreds. How often do I meet with men, particularly those given to drink, who get pounds in their pockets and never know how they go; but they will never leave off till all is spent, be it little or much. Poor fools, poor fools. Yet I wish we could serve Jesus Christ thus unstintedly. No expense should be reckoned so long as we can honour Him and bless His name. Bring forth the alabaster box; break it, never mind the chips and pieces; pour out the oil, and let Jesus have it all. It was thus I served Satan and thus would I serve Christ.

Aye, and the poor slaves of sin not only do not stop at expense, but they are not frightened by any kind of loss. See how many lose their characters for the sake of one short hour of sin. How many are wringing their hands now because none will trust them, and they are cut off from decent society because of one short-lived sin. They ruin their peace and think nothing of it. A quiet conscience is the brightest of jewels, but they fling it away to enjoy their sin. They will lose their health, too, for the sake of indulging their passions. The devil says, "Drink, drink; drink yourselves blind"; and they do it as eagerly as if it were for their good. They are martyrs for Satan. Never did a Zulu fling himself upon death for his king so recklessly as these servants of Satan yield themselves for his service. They will do anything; they will destroy their health, and, what is worst of all, destroy their souls for ever for the sake of sin's brief delights. They know that there is a hell, they know that the wrath of God abideth for ever on guilty men, but they risk all and lose all for sin. In that same way should we serve our Lord. Be willing to lose character for Him; be willing to lose health for Him; be willing to lose life for Him; be willing to lose all, if by any means you may glorify Him whose servant you have become.

Oh, who will be my Master's servant? Here He comes! Do you not see Him? He wears upon His head no diadem but the crown of thorns; adown His cheeks you see the spittle flowing, His feet are still rubied with their wounds, and His hands are still bejewelled with the marks of the nails. This is your Master, and these are the insignia of His love for you. What service will you render Him? That of a mere professor, who names His name but loves Him not? That of a cold religionist, who renders unwilling service out of fear? I pray you, brethren, do not so dis-

honour Him. I lift the standard this morning to enlist beneath the banner of Christ those who will henceforth be Christ's men from head to foot; and happy shall the church be, and happy the entire Israel of God if a chosen number shall enlist and remain true to their colours. We need no more of your nominal Christians, your lukewarm Christians, whom my Master spues out of His mouth: we need men on fire with love, all over consecrated, intensely devoted, who, by the slavery from which they have escaped, and by the liberty into which they have entered, are under bond to spend and be spent for the name of Jesus, till they have filled the earth with his glory, and made all heaven ring with His praise. The Lord bless you, beloved, for Jesus' sake. Amen.

DEATH AND LIFE: THE WAGE AND THE GIFT

"For the wages of sin is death; but the gift of God is eternal life through Jesus Christ our Lord."—Romans vi. 23.

IN the fifth chapter of this Epistle, Paul had shown at considerable length our justification from sin through the righteousness of Jesus Christ our Saviour. Our apostle goes on to speak of our sanctification in Christ; that as by the righteousness of Christ we have been delivered from the guilt and penalty of sin, so by the power and life of Christ in us we are delivered from the dominion of sin, so as not to live any longer therein. His object is to show that true servants of God cannot live in sin; that by reason of our newness of life in Christ, it is not possible that we should continue to yield our members instruments unto iniquity. We have passed out of the realm of death, we have come into the domain of life; and, therefore, we must act according to that life; and that life being in its essence pure, holy and heavenly, we must proceed from righteousness unto holiness.

Whilst he is driving at this argument, our apostle incidentally lets fall the text which may be regarded as a Christian proverb, a golden sentence, a divine statement of truth worthy to be written across the sky. As Jesus said of the woman who anointed Him to His burial, "Wheresoever this gospel shall be preached, in the whole world, there shall also this, that this woman hath done, be told for a memorial of her"; so I may say, "Wheresoever the gospel is preached, there shall this golden sentence, which the apostle has let fall, be repeated as a proof of his clearness in the faith." Here you have both the essence of the gospel, and a statement of that misery from which the gospel delivers all who believe. "The wages of sin is death; but the gift of God is eternal life through Jesus Christ our Lord."

First, it will be my painful duty to dwell for a while upon *death as the wages of sin* ; and then, more joyfully, we shall close our morning's meditation by considering *eternal life as the gift of God.*

I. First, DEATH IS THE WAGES OF SIN. The apostle has in his mind's eye the figure of a soldier receiving his pay. Sin, the captain, pays his hired soldiers a dreadful wage. The original word signifies "rations," or some translate it "stipend." It means the payment which soldiers receive, put in the plural as wages, because pay can be given in different forms: soldiers might be paid in meat, or in meal, or in money, or in part by their clothing, or by lands promised when the time of service came to an end.

Now that which sin, the grim captain, pays to those who are under him, is comprehended in this terrible term "death." It is a word as full as it is short. A legion of terrors are found around this "king of terrors." Death is the rations which sin pays to those who enlist beneath its banner.

Now "sin is any want of conformity to, or transgression of the law of God." Sin is that evil power which is in the world in rebellion against the good and gracious power of righteousness which sits upon the throne of God. This evil power of unholiness, untruth, sin, contrariety to the mind of God, holds the great mass of our fellow-men beneath its sway at this hour. The rations with which it rewards the most desperate valour of its champions is death.

To set forth this terrible fact, I shall make a few observations. First, *death is the natural result of all sin.* When man acts according to God's order he lives; but when he breaks his Maker's laws he wrecks himself, and does that which causes death. The Lord warned Adam thus: "In the day that thou eatest thereof thou shalt surely die." Dying does not mean ceasing to exist, for Adam did not cease to exist, nor do those who die. The term "death" conveys to me no such idea as that of ceasing to exist, or how could I understand that word in 1 John iii. 14: "He that loveth not his brother abideth in death"? How could a man abide in annihilation? A grain of wheat falls into the ground and dies; but it does not cease to be; nay, rather, it bringeth forth much fruit. That Adam did die in the day when he ate of that fruit is certain, or else the Lord spake not the truth. His nature was wrecked and ruined by separation from God, and by a fall from that condition which constitutes the true life of man. When any man commits sin, he dies to holiness and purity. No transgression is venial, but every sin is mortal, and gendereth death.

The further a man goes in lust and iniquity, the more dead he becomes to purity and holiness: he loses the power to appreciate the beauties of virtue, or to be disgusted with the abominations of vice. Our nature at the very outset has lost that delicacy of perception which comes of healthy life; and as men proceed in unchastity, or injustice, or unbelief, or sin of any kind, they enter deeper and deeper into that awful moral death which is the sure wage of sin.

You can sin yourself into an utter deadness of conscience, and that is the first wage of your service of sin.

All desire after God, and all delight in Him, die out where sin reigns. Death is the separation of the soul from God. Alas, this death hath passed upon all men. Can two walk together except they be agreed? Man may continue to believe in the existence of God, but for all practical purposes God to him is really non-existent. The fool hath said in his heart, "No God"—he does not desire God; indeed, he wishes there were no God. As for seeking after God, and delighting himself in the Almighty, the sinner knows nothing thereof; his sin has killed him towards all desire for God, or love to Him, or delight in Him. He is to God dead while he liveth. "To be carnally minded is death."

As there is through sin a death to God, so is there a death to all spiritual things. "The natural man receiveth not the things of the Spirit of God: for they are foolishness unto him: neither can he know them, because they are spiritually discerned." The man doth not perceive and discern spiritual things, for he is dead to them. Talk to him of the sorrows of the spiritual life, he has never felt them, and he despises them as mean cant. Speak to him of the joys of the spiritual life, and you will soon discover that you are casting your pearls before swine: he has never sought such joys, he does not believe in them, and he thinks you a fanatic for talking such nonsense. He is as dead to spiritual realities as a mole is blind to astronomy, or a stone is dead to music. To him it is as though there were neither angel, nor spirit, nor God, nor mercy-seat, nor Christ, nor holiness, nor heaven, nor hell. Giving himself up to the dominion of sin, the sinner receives more and more the result of his sin; even as the apostle says, "Sin, when it is finished, bringeth forth death." "He that soweth to his flesh shall of the flesh reap corruption."

Inasmuch as in holy and spiritual things dwells the highest happiness of our manhood, this man becomes an unhappy being: at first by deprivation of the joy which spiritual life brings with it, and afterwards by suffering the inevitable misery of spiritual death. God has justly appointed that if a man will not be conformed to God he shall not taste of happiness; and if a man will follow after that which is evil, that evil shall of necessity bring with it sorrow and unrest (Romans ii. 9). Since sin as naturally brings spiritual death upon men as fire brings burning, death is spoken of as the wages of sin.

I would observe next, that *the killing power of some sins is manifest to all observers;* for it operates upon the body and the mind as well as upon the spirit. This spiritual death of which I speak may not strike some of you with fear: you may think it a small matter, though to me I do confess that hell, however painted, is never so terrible a thing as the death which fills it. Some sins are murderous to a degree which is clear to all. For instance, if a man takes to drunkenness, or if he indulges in lasciviousness, it is manifest even to the unspiritual that the wages of sin is death. See how by many diseases and deliriums the drunkard destroys himself: he has only to drink hard enough, and his grave will be digged. The horrors which attend upon the filthy lusts of the flesh I will not dare to mention; but many a body rotting above ground shall be my silent witness. All know, or ought to know, the mischief which is occasioned to men and women by the violation of that law which commands us to be pure. I spoke the other day to an aged brother who feels the result of natural decay, but is in all other respects sound and healthy, and I congratulated him upon retaining so much vigour at such an age. "Yes," he replied, "I owe it to the grace of God that I never abused myself in my younger days, and hence I have a store of strength in my old age." How many, on the contrary, feel the sins of their youth in their bone, and in their flesh. We have all known that sins of the flesh kill the flesh; and therefore we may infer that sins of the mind kill the mind. Death in any part of our manhood breeds death to the whole. Death drags man down from the power, beauty, and joy of life to the wretched existence, the feebleness, the abominableness of death. The man is no more a man, but the wreck of a man; and his body is not the house of his soul, but a ruin, in which his poor spirit seeks in vain for comfort. A withered heart, a blinded mind, a blasted being; such is the death which comes of sin. The wage of sin is openly death when it assumes certain forms, and it is always really so, take what form it may.

Now *this tendency is in every case the same,* "the wages of sin is death" everywhere to everyone. It is so not only where you can see it operating upon the body, but where you cannot see it. I may perhaps startle you when I say that the wages of sin is death even in the man who has eternal life. Sin has the same deadly character to one as to the other, only an antidote is found. You, my Christian brother, cannot fall into sin without its being poison to you as well as to anybody else; in fact, to you it is more evidently poison than to those hardened to it. If you sin it destroys your joy, your power in prayer, your confidence towards God. If you have spent evenings in frivolity with worldlings, you have felt the deadening influence of their society. What about your prayers at night? You cannot draw nigh unto God. The operation of sin upon your spirit is most injurious to your communion with God. You are like a man who has taken a noxious drug, whose fumes are stupefying the brain, and sending the heart into slumber. If you, being a child of God, fall into any of the sins which so easily beset you, I am sure you will never find that those sins quicken your grace or increase your faith; but on the contrary, they will work you evil, only evil, and that continually. Sin is deadly to any man and every man, whoever he may be; and were it not for the mighty curative operation which the indwelling Spirit of God is always carrying on upon the believer's nature, not one of us would survive the deadly effects of even those sins of infirmity, and ignorance into which we fall. I wonder not that Paul cried aloud, "O wretched man that I am! who shall deliver me from the body of this death?" If a man takes poison, if it does not absolutely kill him, it injures him, and thus proves its killing tendency. In certain places the air is pestilential, and though a very healthy man may pass through them and seem none the worse, yet this does not disprove the general deadly tendency of the malarious district, nor does it even prove that the healthy person is not secretly but really injured by having been there. Evils caused by sin may be too deep to be at once visible, just as the most serious of diseases have their periods of incubation, during which the person affected has no idea of the ill which is hatching within him. Sin is in itself an unmitigated evil, a root which beareth wormwood. Sin is death.

Wonder not therefore that the apostle saith, "the wages of sin is death." As the sparks fly upward, and as the rain falleth to the ground, so sin leads to death. As the river takes its leap in the thundering cataract, so must the stream of sin create the fall of death.

Moreover, when we read of anything being a wage, what does it mean? It means that it is a reward for labour. *Death is sin's due reward, and it must be paid.* A master employs a man, and it is due to that man that he should receive his wages. If his master did not pay him his wages, it would be an act of gross injustice. Now, if sin did not bring upon man death and misery, it would be an injustice. It is necessary for the very standing of the universe that sin should be punished. It must be so. They that sow must reap. The sin which hires you must pay you. Wrong cannot produce right. Iniquity, transgression and sin must, in the nature of things, become darkness, sorrow, misery, death. Every transgression and disobedience must receive its just recompense of reward. There is no use in attempting to alter it so long as God and justice reign: those who do sin's work must receive sin's wage, and "the wages of sin is death."

Now, observe, that this death, *this wage of sin, is in part received by men now as soldiers receive their rations, day by day.* It is a terrible thing that they do so receive it. The Scripture saith, "If evil ye after the flesh, ye shall die"—such a life is a continued dying. Again, it is written, "She that liveth in pleasure is dead while she liveth." The wrath of God abideth on him that believeth not on the Son of God; it is there already. I would that men here who are not converted would recollect where they now are—they are "dead in trespasses and sins." O men, you are not merely sick, but you are "dead in your sins"! You are already dead to the highest spiritual enjoyments, and can never know them except by passing from death unto life. You cannot rejoice in God, you cannot know spiritual truth, you cannot taste of spiritual bliss, for your sin deadens you to these things every day that you live in it. To all that which is worthy of a man, to all that which is the true life of manhood, you are dead through sin.

But then a Roman solider did not enlist merely for his rations; his chief pay often lay in the share of the booty which he received at the end of the war. He expected to share in his captain's triumph, and to be a partaker in the spoil. *Death is the ultimate wage of sin.* The death which is here intended is the eternal loss and wreckage of the soul, the destruction of all about it that is worth having, the drifting of the guilty being for ever upon the full tide of those evil tendencies which caused his sin, and were further increased by sin. When all comes to all, this is where sin will drive you: it will perpetuate itself, and so for ever kill the soul to God, and goodness, and joy and hope. You will enter upon a world in which the highest enjoyments which even God Himself can provide for men will be revealed, but they will be hidden from your eyes because you will be utterly incapable of knowing, appreciating, and enjoying them. Being under the ever-growing power of sin, it will become more and more a hopeless thing that you should escape from the death which thus settles down upon you. All the agencies which could have recovered you from the clutch of death have failed to bless you in the life which has come to an end and now in eternity neither the death of Christ, nor the Holy Ghost, nor the ministry of the word, will ever again operate upon you. Till your last moments you chose sin, and through eternity you will still choose it; for this death is the reward of your sin. Our Lord Himself said, "These shall go away into everlasting punishment." Then you shall come to know to the full what that awful word "death" really means as God intends it. Meanwhile, if you would escape this dreadful doom, read your Bible and see how the result of sin is expounded. As our Saviour taught, that future death includes within itself the fire which never shall be quenched, the worm that never dieth, the outer darkness, the weeping and wailing and gnashing of teeth, and the departure into everlasting fire which begins with a curse from the lip of love. Alienation from God is death, and can never be otherwise. The Holy Ghost, speaking of the ungodly, saith, "In flaming fire taking vengeance on them that know not God, and that obey not the gospel of our Lord Jesus Christ: who shall be punished with everlasting destruction from the presence of the Lord, and from the glory of His power." This will be the ultimatum of sin. As surely as rivers run into the sea, so surely must sin run into death; there is no help for it. This hard and impenitent heart heaps up for itself wrath against the day of wrath and revelation of the righteous judgment of God. Sin inevitably pays to all who are its servants the death by which bondage to its power is sealed for ever. O my God, grant us grace to see what a wretched service this is which pays such terrible rations now, and gives such a terrible dividing of the spoil in the end.

I shall not longer dwell upon it, the subject is so distressing to me; save that I must add a few solemn words. *The misery of the misery of sin is that it is earned.* Every pang that shall fall upon the ungodly either in this life or in the life to come will have this for its sting,—that it was duly earned. The sinner may well say, "I worked for this; I laid myself out to earn this; I now feel the misery of what I wilfully did." Death is the result of being out of gear with God. But the sinner puts himself into that condition. If men in the world to come could say, "This misery of ours has come upon us by an arbitrary arrangement on the part of God, quite apart from its just results," then they would derive from that fact some kind of comfort to their conscience, some easement of their biting remorse. But when they will be obliged to own that all their woe was their own choice in choosing sin, and is still their own choice in abiding in sin, this will scourge them indeed. Their sin is their hell. The worm which gnaws at the heart of the lost soul is its own wilful hate of God, and love of evil. O lover of sin, you are under the power of this death—this worse than death! You are dead to God, and dead to holiness, and dead to love, and dead to true happiness; and you have brought this death upon yourself, every part and particle of it. You have chosen that which has made you a wreck and a ruin, and that in the teeth of many warnings and admonitions. It must be so, that "the wages of sin is death," and the terror of that death is that it comes as a wage. Why will you die? Why will you earn death? Why will you choose your own delusions? Have you wickedly determined to prove what outer darkness means? Have you turned your back on God just to see how a man must fare who wars with his Maker? Have not enough dashed themselves to pieces on the rock of sin? Why will you do the same? If you will do so, this shall be the misery of your misery: that you brought it on yourselves, and that you rejected the one remedy provided of the Lord in the person of His Son Jesus Christ.

Note, next—and I speak with the truest compassion—that *it will be the folly of follies to go on working for such a wage.* Hitherto they that have worked for sin have found no profit in it. What fruit have you had, any of you, in the things whereof you have cause to be ashamed? Has sin ever brought you any real benefit? Come, now, and let us reason together:—up till now has doing wrong ever worked for your health, or your happiness? Are you the better for hate, or greed, or lust, or drink? Has sin ever developed your inner self into anything worth calling life? You know it has not. It has rather destroyed you than improved you, and you know it. Why, then, will you go further in sin? Have you not learned enough already of the deadly nature of evil? Why will you press further into this barren region, which will become more and more a howling wilderness to you as you advance into it? Why will you go where it will be more and more difficult to return? Oh, may God's infinite mercy prevent our being such madmen as to labour in the very fire to earn nothing else but death! God forbid that we should plunge from sin to sin by an inventiveness of rebellion, only to discover more and more what it is to be dead for ever to God, and heaven, and hope, and everything that is to be desired.

Let me add, *it ought to be the grief of griefs to each of us that we have sinned.* Oh, misery, to have wrought so long in a service which brings such terrible wages! Though I have known the Lord now these six-and-thirty years, I still regret most deeply every sin that I have ever committed against the perfect law of the Lord. I take it that repentance is not the temporary act of a certain period of time, but it is the spirit of the whole life after conversion. When we know we are forgiven, we repent all the more that ever we loved that sin which is so abominable unto God, and so evil in every way. Evil seems most evil when we have the clearest sense of divine goodness. Its constant wage is death, and only death; and our lamentation is that we harboured this assassin, yea, even became its slave. Let us humble ourselves before God, because we have played the fool exceedingly by sinning against Him; we have wounded, injured, and destroyed ourselves, and all for nothing—our only wage being a still deeper destruction.

Oh you that have never repented, but are still abiding in this spiritual death, how I long that the voice of Jesus may echo in that sepulchre of sin in which you now lie asleep: may it arouse you, and make you dread the death that never dies! Oh that you may turn over, as it were, in your grave, and begin to moan, "O God, deliver me!" If there be such a thought as that in your soul, I shall hope that the Spirit of God has begun to bring life into your spirit. But what an awful thing it is to have spent all these days—and some of you are getting grey—in only doing that which is your undoing, in giving life to that which is your death! The sole wage that some of you have yet earned is death. Is not this a poor reward for all the risk, labour, and perseverance with which you have served sin? God help you to see your folly, and repent of it.

One thought more ere I leave this point, and that is, *it must certainly be a miracle of miracles if any sinner here does not remain for ever beneath the power of sin.* Sin has this mischief about it, that it strikes a man with spiritual paralysis; and how can such a palsied one ward off a further blow? It makes the man dead; and to what purpose do we appeal to him that is dead? I have tried to describe what a dreadful thing it is to be dead to God, and purity, and happiness; but the dead man does not know or care for these things. Our preaching may well be called foolishness, since it is addressed to ears that cannot, or, rather, will not, hear. What a miracle of miracles it is when the Divine life comes streaming down into the heart that sin has chilled into death! What a blessedness it is when God interposes and finds a way by which the wage most justly due shall not be paid! It is a necessity, that every transgression should have its recompense; but in the person of the Lord Jesus such an expiation is made, that sin pays its wage of death to Him who did not earn it, while those who did earn it go free. O sinner, none can save you but the God who made you! You, as dead in sin, are in such a state that you will rot into corruption, and go on for ever rotting into a yet fouler and filthier corruption throughout the ages; and none can prevent it but Almighty God Himself. Only one power is capable of affording you the help you need; and that power worketh through the Lord Jesus, who is at this moment mighty to save. Oh! that the miracle of miracles might be wrought upon you: for if not, there it stands, "The wages of sin is death." Alas! I fear that sin will pervert even the ministry of the word, and make it a savour of death unto death. This is the first teaching of the text, and I pray the Holy Ghost to impress it on every conscience!

II. And now I am glad to pass into liberty and joy while I speak on the second subject: ETERNAL LIFE IS THE GIFT OF GOD.

Note well the change: death is a *wage,* but life is a *gift.* Sin brings its natural consequences with it; but eternal life is not the purchase of human merit, but the free gift of the love of God. The abounding goodness of the Most High alone grants life to those who are dead by sin. It is with clear intent to teach us the doctrine of the grace of God that the apostle altered the word here from wages to gift. Naturally he would have said, "The wages of sin is death, but the wages of righteousness is eternal life." But he wished to show us that life comes upon quite a different principle from that upon which death comes. In salvation all is of free gift: in damnation everything is of justice and desert. When a man is lost, he has earned it; when a man is saved, it is given him.

Let us notice, first, that *eternal life is imparted by grace through faith.* When it first enters the soul it comes as God's free gift. The dead cannot earn life; the very supposition is absurd. Eternal life enjoyed on earth comes to us as a gift. "What!" saith one, "do you mean to say that eternal life comes into the soul here?" I say yes, here, or else never. Eternal life must be our possession now; for if we die without it, it will never be our possession in the world to come, which is not the state of probation, but of fixed and settled reward. When the flame of eternal life first drops into a man's heart, it is not as the result of any good works of his which preceded it, for there were none; nor as the result of any feelings of his, for good feelings were not there till the life came. Both good works and good feelings are the fruit of the heavenly life which enters the heart, and makes us conscious of its entrance by working in us repentance and faith in our Lord Jesus Christ. "Eternal life is the gift of God in Jesus Christ." By faith we come consciously into Christ. We trust Him, we rest upon Him, we become one with Him, and thus eternal life manifests itself. Has He not said, "I give unto My sheep eternal life"; and again, "He that believeth in Him hath everlasting life"? O beloved, you that have been quickened by the Spirit of God, I am sure you trace that first quickening to the grace of God. Whatever your doctrinal views may be, you are all agreed in the experimental acknowledgment that by the grace of God you are what you are. How could you, being dead, give yourself life? How could you, being the slave of sin, set yourself free? But the Lord in mercy visited you as surely as the Lord Jesus Christ visited the tomb of Lazarus; and He spoke with His almighty voice, and bade you come to life, and you arose and came to life at His bidding. You remember well the change that came upon you. If any man here could have been literally dead, and then could have been made to live, what a wonderful experience his would have been! We should go a long way to hear the story of a man who had been dead, and then was made alive again. But I tell you, his experience, if he could tell it, would not be any more wonderful than our experience as quickened from death in sin; for we have suffered the pains that come through the entrance of life into the soul, and we know the joys which afterwards come of it. We have seen the light that life brings to the spiritual eye; we have felt the emotions that life brings to the quickened heart; we have known the joys which life, and only life, can bring to the entire man. We can tell you something about these things; but if you want to know them to the full, you must feel them for yourselves. "Ye must be born again." We bear our witness that eternal life within our spirit is not of our earning, but the gift of God.

Beloved, since we received eternal life, we have gone on to grow, and we have made great advances in the divine life; our little trembling faith has now grown to be full assurance; that zeal of ours which burned so low that we hardly dared to attempt anything for Jesus has now flamed up into full consecration, so that we live to His praise. Whence has this growth come? Is it not still a free gift? Have you received an increase of life by the law, or has it come to you as the free gift of God? I know what you will say; and if any of you have so grown in grace that you have become ripe Christians; if any of you have been taught of God so that you can teach others; if any of you have been led by the Holy Spirit so that your sanctification is known unto all men, and you have become saintly men and women; I am sure that your holiness and maturity are still gifts received, and not wages earned. I will put the question to you again: Did this abundant life come to you by the works of the law, or by grace through faith which is in Christ Jesus? Your instantaneous answer is, "It is all of grace, in the latter as well as in the earlier stages." Yes, in every degree the gift of God is eternal life in Christ Jesus.

Yes; and when we get to heaven, and the eternal life shall there be developed as a bud opens into a full-blown rose; when our life shall embrace life, and God's life shall encompass ours; when we

shall be abundantly alive to everything that is holy, divine, heavenly, blessed, and eternally glorious; oh, then we shall confess that our life was all of the grace of God, the free gift of God in Jesus Christ our Lord! I am sure that our heavenly education will only make us know more and more fully that while death is the well-earned wages of sin, eternal life is from beginning to end the gift of infinite grace.

Beloved, observe gratefully what a wonderful gift this is,—"*the gift of God*,"—the gift which Jesus bestows upon every believer; for "to as many as received Him, to them gave He power to become the sons of God, even to as many as believed on His name; which were born, not of blood, nor of the will of the flesh, nor of the will of man, but of God." How express is our Lord's statement: "He that believeth on the Son hath everlasting life: and he that believeth not the Son shall not see life; but the wrath of God abideth on him"! What a life this is! It must be of a wonderful sort, because it is called "life" *par excellence*, emphatically "life," true life, real life, essential life. This does not mean mere existence, as some vainly talk. There never was a greater blunder than to confound life with existence, or death with non-existence; these are two totally different and distinct ideas. The life of man means the existence of man as he ought to exist—in union with God, and consequently in holiness, purity, health, and happiness. Man, as God intended him to be, is man enjoying life; man, as sin makes him, is man abiding in death. All that man can receive of joy and honour the Lord gives to man to constitute life eternal in the world to come. What a life is this! The life that is imparted to us in regeneration is God's own life, brought into us by "the living and incorruptible seed which liveth and abideth for ever." We are akin to God by the new birth, and by loving union with His Son Jesus Christ. What must life mean in God's sense of it?

Moreover, we have life *eternal*, too, never ending. Whatever else may end, this never can. It can neither be killed by temptation, nor destroyed by trial, nor quenched by death, nor worn out by the ages. The gift of the eternal God is eternal life. Those who talk about a man having everlasting life, and losing it, do not know the force of language. If a man has eternal life, it is eternal, and cannot therefore end or be lost. If it be everlasting, it is "everlasting"; to lose it would prove that it was not everlasting. No, if you have eternal life, you can never perish; if God has bestowed it upon you, it will not be recalled, "for the gifts and calling of God are without repentance." This eternal life is evidently a free gift; for how could any man obtain it in any other way? It is too precious to be bought, too divine to be made by man. If it had to be earned, how could you have earned it? You, I mean, who have already earned death. The wage due to you already was death, and by that wage you were effectually shut out from all possibility of ever earning life. Indeed, the earning of life seems to me to be from the beginning out of the question. It has come to us as a free gift; it could not come in any other way.

Futhermore, remember that it is life *in Jesus*; the "through" of our version is "in" in the original. We are in everlasting union with the blessed Person of the Son of God, and therefore we live. To be in Christ is a mystery of bliss. The apostle felt that this was an occasion for again rehearsing our blessed

Master's names and titles of honour—"in Jesus Christ our Lord." I noted to you on a former occasion how, at certain seasons, the various honours and titles of great men are proclaimed by heralds with becoming state; and so here, to the praise of the Lord Jesus, Paul writes his full degree—"Eternal life in Jesus Christ our Lord." He writes at large the august name before which every knee shall bow, and he links our life therewith. Here we read the cheering and precious name of Jesus. By that name He is nearest to man; when He was born into our nature He was named Jesus, "for He shall save His people from their sins." The life which comes in connection with Him is salvation from sin. In this Saviour is life. The next name is "Christ," or anointed, by which name He is nearest to God, being sent forth and anointed of God to treat with us on God's behalf. He is the Lord's Christ, and our Jesus. Next He is called "Our Lord." Herein lieth the glory of our anointed Saviour: we through grace becoming servants participate in the life and glory of our Lord. He reigneth as our Lord, and by His reigning power He shows Himself to be the Lord and giver of life. "All live unto Him." Our Lord hath life in Himself, and breathes it into us. What a life this is, a life saved from sin, a life anointed of the Holy Ghost, a life in union with Him who is Lord of all. This is the life which is peculiarly the gift of God.

Thus I have set forth this doctrine, and I desire to apply it by adding a little more of practical importance. First, *let us come at this time, one and all, and receive this divine life as a gift in Christ Jesus.* If any of you have been working for it by going about to establish your own righteousness, I beseech you to end the foolish labour by submitting yourselves to the righteousness of God. If you have been trying to feel so much, or to pray so much, or to mourn so much, forbear from thus offering a price, and come and receive life as a free gift from your God. Pull down the idol of your pride, and humbly sue for pardoning grace on the plea of mercy. Believe and live. You are not called upon to earn life, but to receive it; receive it as freely as your lungs take in the air you breathe. If you are dead in sin at this moment, yet the gospel of life has come nigh unto you. With that gospel there comes the life-giving wind of the eternal Spirit. He can call you out of your ruin, and wreckage, and death, and make you live. This is His word, "Awake, thou that sleepest, and rise from the dead, and Christ shall give thee life." Will you have it as a gift? If there be any true life in you your answer will be quick and hearty. You will be lost if you do not receive this gift. Your earnings will be paid into your bosom, and dread will be the death which will settle down upon you. The acceptance of a free gift would not be difficult if we were not proud. Accept it—God help you to accept it at once! Even that acceptance will be God's gift; for the will to live is life; and all true life, from beginning to end, is entirely of the Lord.

Beloved, have we accepted that free gift of eternal life? *Let us abide in it.* Let us never be tempted to try the law of merit; let us never attempt to live by our earnings. No doubt eternal life is a reward in one sense, but it is always a reward of grace, not a reward of debt. The Lord shall give us a crown of life at last as a reward; but even then we shall confess that He first gave us the work by which the crown was won. The Lord first gives us good works, and then rewards us for them. The labour of love is in itself a gift of love. Grace reigns all along; not only in removing sin, but in working virtue.

Finally, are we now abiding in eternal life, trusting in the Son of God, and clinging to His skirts? then *let us live to His glory.* Do we know that because He lives, we shall live also? If so, let us show by our gratitude how greatly we prize this gift. We dwell in a world where death is everywhere manifesting itself in various forms of corruption; therefore let us see from what the Lord has delivered us. Let no man boast in his heart that he is not subject to the vile influences which hold the world in its corruption. Let no pride because of our new life ever cross our spirit. Chase every such thought as that away with detestation. If our life be of grace, there is no room for boasting, but much space for soul-humbling. When you walk the streets, and hear the groans of the dead in the form of oaths and blasphemies, thank the Lord that you have been taught a more living language. Think of drunkenness and lust as the worms that are bred of the putridity of the death which comes of sin. You are disgusted and horrified, my brethren; but these things would have been in you also but for the grace of God. We are like living men shut up in a charnel-house; wherever we turn we see the dreary works of death; but all this should make us grateful to the sacred power which has brought us out of death into spiritual life.

As for others, let us anxiously ask the question—"Can these dry bones live?" Then let us be obedient to the heavenly vision when the divine word saith to us, "Son of man, prophesy upon these bones." We must cherish the faith which will enable us to do this. Moreover, a sight of the universal death of unrenewed nature should drive us to prayer, so that we cry, "Come from the four winds O breath, and breathe upon these slain, that they may live." This prayer being offered, we should live in hopeful expectancy that the Lord will open the graves of His people, and cause them to come forth and live by His Spirit. Oh for grace to prophesy believingly upon these bones, and say, "O ye dry bones, hear the word of the Lord. Thus saith the Lord God unto these bones, Behold I will cause breath to enter into you, and ye shall live." Beloved, we shall yet see them stand up an exceeding great army, quickened of the Lord our God. He delights to burst the bonds of death. Resurrection is one of His chief glories. He heralds resurrection work with trumpets, and angels, and a glorious high throne, because He delighteth in it. The living Jehovah rejoices to give life, and especially to give it to the dead. Corruption flies before Him, grave clothes are rent, and sepulchres are broken open. "I am the resurrection, and the life," saith Jesus; and so He is even at this hour. O God, save this congregation to the praise of the glory of Thy grace, wherein Thou hast made us to live, and to be accepted in Thy well-beloved Son. Amen and Amen.

THE MONSTER DRAGGED TO LIGHT

"Sin, that it might appear sin, working death in me by that which is good; that sin by the commandment might become exceeding sinful."—Romans vii. 13.

"Philosophers have measured mountains,
Fathom'd the depths of seas, of states, and kings,
Walked with a staff to heav'n and traced fountains:
But there are two vast, spacious things,
The which to measure it doth more behove:
Yet few there are that sound them; Sin and Love."

SO sang George Herbert, that sweet and saintly poet, and of one of those "two vast spacious things" we are about to speak this morning—namely, sin. May the Holy Spirit direct us in thought and speech while into the very centre of our subject we plunge at once, keeping to the words of our text.

I. Our first point to consider this morning shall be that TO MANY MEN SIN DOES NOT APPEAR SIN; aye, and in all men in their natural blindness there is an ignorance of what sin is. It needs the power of the divine omnipotence, the voice of that same Majesty, which said, "Let there be light," and there was light to illuminate the human mind, or else it will remain in darkness as to much of its own actual sin, and the deep and deadly evil which belongs to it. Man, with wretched perverseness of misconception, abides content in a wrong idea of it; his deeds are evil, and he will not come to the light lest he should know more concerning that evil than he wishes to know. Moreover, such is the power of self-esteem that though sin abounds in the sinner he will not readily be brought to feel or confess its existence. There are men in this world steeped up to the throat in iniquity, who never dream that they have committed anything worse than little faults. There are those whose souls are saturated with it till they are like the wool that has been lying in the scarlet dye; and yet they conceive themselves to be white as snow. This is due in part to that dulness of conscience which is the result of the fall. Though I have heard ten thousand times that conscience is the vicegerent of God in the soul of man, I have never been able to subscribe to that dogma. It is no such thing. In many persons conscience is perverted, in others only a fragment of it remains, and in all it is fallible, and subject to aberrations. Conscience is in all men a thing of degrees dependent upon education, example, and previous character; it is an eye of the soul, but it is frequently purblind and weak, and always needs light from above, or else it does but mock the soul. Conscience is a faculty of the mind, which, like every other, has suffered serious damage through our natural depravity, and it is by no means perfect. It is only the understanding acting upon moral subjects; and upon such matters it often puts bitter for sweet and sweet for bitter, darkness for light and light for darkness. Hence it is that men's sins do not appear to them sin. In all probability there is not one, even among renewed men, who fully knows the evil of sin, nor will there be until in heaven we shall be perfect; and then, when we shall see the perfection of divine holiness, we shall understand how black a thing was sin. Men who have lived underground all their lives do not know how dark the mine is, nor can they know it until they stand in the blaze of a summer's noon.

In a great measure, our inability to see sin as sin arises from the exceeding deceitfulness both of sin and of the human heart. Sin assumes the brightest forms even as Satan attires himself as an angel of light. Such a thing as iniquity walking abroad in its own nakedness is seldom seen; like Jezebel it tires its head and paints its face. And, indeed, the heart loves to have it so and is eager to be deceived. We will, if we can, extenuate our faults. We are all very quick-sighted to perceive something, which, if it does not quite excuse our fault, at all events prevents its being placed in the first-class of atrocities. Sometimes we will not understand the commandment; we are willing not to know its force and stringency; it is too keen and sharp, and we try to blunt its edge, and if we can find a milder meaning for it we are glad to do so. "The heart is deceitful above all things, and desperately wicked"—hence it invents a thousand falsehoods. As the deceivableness of sin is very great, so that it adorns itself with the colours of righteousness, and makes men believe that they are pleasing God when they are offending Him, so is man himself an eager self deceiver, and, like the fool in Solomon's Proverbs, he readily follows the flatterer.

In most men their not seeing sin to be sin arises from their ignorance of the spirituality of the law. Men read the ten commandments and they suppose them to mean nothing more than the superficial sense. If they read, for instance, "Thou shalt do no murder," straightway they say, "I have never broken that law." But they forget that he that hateth his brother is a murderer, and that unrighteous anger is a distinct violation of the command. If I wilfully do anything which tends to destroy or shorten life, either my own or my neighbour's, I am breaking the command. A man finds it written, "Thou shalt not commit adultery." "Well, well," says he, "I am clear there." Straightway he plumeth himself upon the supposition that he is chastity itself. But if he be given to understand that the command touches the heart, and that a licentious look is adultery, and that even a desire to do that which is evil condemns the soul, then straightway he sees things in a very different light, and sees that to be sin which had never troubled him before. Commonly—aye, universally—until the Spirit of God comes into the soul, there is a total ignorance as to what the law means, and men say, with a light heart, "Lord, have mercy upon us, and incline our hearts to keep this law;" whereas, if they did but know it, they would say, "Lord, have mercy upon us, and cleanse us of our innumerable infractions of a law which we cannot keep, and which must for ever condemn us as long as we abide under its power."

Thus you see a few of the reasons why sin does not appear in its true light to the unconverted, but cheats impenitent and self-righteous minds. This is one of the most deplorable results of sin. It injures us most by taking from us the capacity to know how much we are injured. It undermines the man's constitution, and yet leads him to boast of unfailing health; it beggars him, and tells him he is rich; it strips him, and makes him glory in his fancied robes. In this it resembles slavery, which, by degrees, eats into the soul and makes a man contented in his chains. Bondage at length degrades a man, so that at last he forgets the misery of slavery and the dignity of freedom, and is unable to strike the blow when a happy hour offers him the chance of liberation. Sin, like the deadly frost of the northern regions, benumbs its victim ere it slays him. Man is so diseased that he fancies his disease to be health, and judges healthy men to be under wild delusions. He loves the enemy which destroys him, he warms at his bosom the viper whose fangs cause his death. The most unhappy thing that can happen to a man is for him to be sinful and to judge his sinfulness to be righteousness. The Papist advances to his altar and bows before a piece of bread; but he does not feel that he is committing idolatry—nay, he believes that he is acting in a praiseworthy manner. The persecutor hounded his fellow creature to prison and to death, but he thought he verily did God service. You and I can see the idolatry of the Papist, and the murder committed by the persecutor, but the guilty persons do not see it themselves. The passionate man imagines himself to be rightly indignant, the greedy man is proud of his own prudence, the unbeliever rejoices in his independence of mind; these are the aspects under which iniquity presents itself to the spiritually blind. There is the mischief of sin, that it throws out of gear the balances by which the soul discerns between good and evil. What horrible beings those must have been who could run down a vessel crowded with living souls, and then, while hearing them shriek and cry for help, could go steaming away from them, leaving them all to perish in the overwhelming waters! To what a state of inhumanity must they have sunk to be able to do such a thing. The wreck of the vessel is hardly more dreadful than the wreck of all moral sense and common humanity in those who left the hundreds to die, when they might have saved them. To be able to stab a man would be horrible; but, to be so bad that after stabbing him you felt no sense of wrong doing would be far worse; yet with every act of sin, there goes a measure of heart-hardening, so that he who is capable of great crimes is usually incapable of knowing them to be such. With the ungodly this pestilential influence is very powerful, leading them to cry "peace, peace," where there is no peace, and to rebel against the most Holy God without fear or compunction. And, alas, since even in the saints there remains the old nature, even they are not altogether free from the darkening power of sin, for I do not hesitate to say, that we all unwittingly allow ourselves in practices, which clearer light would show to be sins. Even the best of men have done this in the past. For instance, John Newton, in his trading for slaves in his early days, never seemed to have felt that there was any wrong in it; and Whitefield in accepting slaves for his orphanage in Georgia, never raised or dreamed of raising the question as to whether slavery was in itself sinful. Perhaps advancing light will shew that many of the habits and customs of our present civilisation are essentially bad, and our grandsons will wonder how we could have acted as we did. It may need centuries before the national conscience, or even the common Christian conscience, will be enlightened up to the true standard of right; and the individual man may need many a chastisement and rebuke from

the Lord ere he has fully discerned between good and evil. O thou demon, sin, thou art proved to be sin with a vengeance, by thus deluding us. Thou dost not only poison us, but make us imagine our poison to be medicine—thou dost defile us, and make us think ourselves the more beautiful—slay us, and make us dream that we are enjoying life!

My brethren, before we can be restored to the holy image of Christ, which is the ultimatum of every Christian; we must be taught to know sin to be sin: and we must have a restoration of the tenderness of conscience which would have been ours had we never fallen. A measure of this discernment and tenderness of judgment is given to us at conversion; for conversion, apart from it, would be impossible. How can a man repent of that which he does not know to be sin? How shall he humble himself before God concerning that which he does not recognize to be evil in God's sight? He must have enlightenment. Sin must be made to appear sin to him. Moreover, man will not renounce his self-righteousness till he sees his sinfulness. As long as he believes himself to be righteous, he will hug that righteousness, and stand before God with the Pharisee's cry, "God, I thank Thee that I am not as other men are!" As long as it is possible for us to swim on the bladders of our own righteousness we will never take to the life-boat of Christ's righteousness. We can only be driven to free grace by sheer stress of weather; and as long as our leaky barque of self-will only keeps us above the flood, we will hold to it. It is a miracle of grace to make a man see himself, so as to loathe himself, and confess the impossibility of being saved by his own works. Yet, till this is done, faith in Jesus is impossible; for no man will look to the righteousness of another while he is satisfied with his own righteousness; and every one believes he has a righteousness of his own till he sees sin in its native hideousness. Unless sin is revealed to you as a boundless evil, whoever you may be, where God and Christ are you can never come. You must be made to see that your heart reeks with evil—that your past life has been defiled with iniquity; and you must also be taught that this evil of yours is no trifle, but a monstrous and horrible thing. You must be made to loathe yourselves as in the presence of God, or else you never will fly to the atoning blood for cleansing. Unless sin is seen to be sin, grace will never be seen to be grace, nor Jesus to be a Saviour, and without this salvation is impossible.

Here then we leave this important point—bearing witness again that to the natural man sin does not appear sin; and, therefore, a work of grace must be wrought in him to open his blind eyes, or he cannot be saved. These are no soft speeches, and fair words, but hard truths: may the Holy Spirit lead many hearts to feel how sorrowfully true they are.

II. This leads us to our second consideration—WHERE SIN IS MOST CLEARLY SEEN, IT APPEARS TO BE SIN: its most terrible aspect is its own natural self. Sin at its worst appears to be sin. Do I seem to repeat myself? Does this utterance sound like a mere platitude? Then I cannot help it, for the text puts it so; and I know you will not despise the text. But indeed there is a depth of meaning in the expression, "Sin, that it might appear sin"—as if the apostle could find no other word so terribly descriptive of sin as its own name. He does not say, "Sin, that it might appear like Satan." No, for sin is worse than the devil, since it made the devil what he

s. Satan as an existence is God's creature, and this sin never was; its origin and nature are altogether apart from God. Sin is even worse than hell, for it is the sting of that dreadful punishment. Anselm used to say that if hell were on one side, and sin on the other, he would rather leap into hell than willingly sin against God. Paul does not say, "Sin, that it might appear madness." Truly it is moral insanity, but it is worse than that by far. It is so bad that there is no name for it but itself. One of our poets who wished to show how evil sin looks in the presence of redeeming love, could only say,

> "When the wounds of Christ exploring,
> Sin doth *like itself* appear."

If you need an illustration of what is meant, we might find one in Judas. If you wanted to describe him, you might say he was a traitor, a thief, and a betrayer of innocent blood, but you would finish up by saying, "he was a Judas"—that gives you all in one: none could match him in villainy. If you wished a man to feel a horror of murder, you would not wish murder to appear to him as manslaughter, or as destruction of life, or as mere cruelty, but you would want it to appear as *murder;* you could use no stronger expression. So here, when the Lord turns the strong light of His eternal Spirit upon sin and reveals it in all its hideousness and defilement, it appears to be not only moral discord, disorder, deformity, or corruption, but neither more nor less than sin. "Sin," says Thomas Brooks, "is the only thing that God abhors, it brought Christ to the cross, it damns souls, it shuts heaven, and it laid the foundations of hell."

There are persons who see sin as a misfortune, but this is far short of the true view, and indeed, very wide of it. How commonly do we hear one sort of sinner called "an unfortunate." This indicates a very lax morality. Truly it is a calamity to be a sinner, but it is much more than a calamity; and he who only sees sin as his misfortune has not seen it so as to be saved from it. Others have come to see sin as folly, and so far they see aright, for it is essentially folly, and every sinner is a fool. A fool is God's own name for a sinner—commonly used throughout the book of Psalms. But for all that, sin is more than folly. It is not mere want of wit or mistaken judgment, it is the knowing and wilful choice of evil, and it has in it a certain maliciousness against God which is far worse than mere stupidity. To see sin as folly is a good thing, but it is not a gracious thing, nor a saving thing. Some, too, have seen certain sins to be crimes, and yet have not viewed them as sins. Our use of the word "crime" is significant. When an action hurts our fellow-men, we call it a crime, when it only offends God, we style it a sin. If I were to call you criminals, you would be disgusted with me; but if I call you sinners, you will not be at all angry; because to offend man is a thing you would not like to do, but to offend God is to many persons a small matter, scarcely worth a moment's thought. Human nature has become so perverted that if men know that they have broken human laws they are ashamed, but the breach of a command, which only affects the Lord Himself, causes them very small concern. If we were to steal, or lie, or knock another down, we should be ashamed of ourselves, and so we ought to be; but, for all that, such shame would be no work of grace. Sin must appear to be *sin* against God— that is the point; we must say with David, "Against

Thee, Thee only, have I sinned, and done this evil in Thy sight." With the prodigal we must cry, "Father, I have sinned against heaven and before Thee, and am no more worthy to be called Thy son." That is the true view of it. The Lord bring us to confess our transgressions after that sort.

And here lend me your ears a minute or two. Think how odious a thing sin is. Beloved, our offences are committed against a law which is based upon right. It is holy, and just, and good; it is the best law which could be conceived. To break a bad law may be more than excusable, but there can be no excuse for transgression when the commandment commends itself to every man's conscience. There is not one command in God's word which is either harsh, arbitrary, or unnecessary. If we ourselves were perfect in holiness and infinitely wise, and had to write a law, we should have written just the law which God has given us. The law is just to our fellow men, and beneficial to ourselves. When it forbids anything, it does but set up danger signals where real danger to ourselves exists. The law is a kind of spiritual police to keep us out of harm's way; those who offend against it injure themselves. Sin is a false, mean, unrighteous thing, it does evil all round, and brings good to nobody. It has not one redeeming feature; it is evil, only evil and that continually. It is a wicked, wanton, purposeless, useless rejection of that which is good and right, in favour of that which is disgraceful and injurious.

We ought also to remember that the divine law is binding upon men because of the right and authority of the lawgiver. God has made us, ought we not to serve Him? Our existence is prolonged by His kindness; we could not live a moment without Him: should we not obey Him? God is superlatively good, He has never done us any harm, He has always designed our benefit, and has treated us with unbounded kindness. Why should we wilfully insult Him by breaking laws which He had a right to make, and which He has made for our good? Is it not shameful to do that which He hates, when there can be nothing to gain thereby, and no reason for doing it? How I wish every heart here could hear that plaintive lamentation of the Lord—it is wonderful condescension that He should describe Himself as uttering it—"The ox knoweth his owner and the ass his master's crib, but Israel doth not know; My people doth not consider." That other word of pleading is equally pathetic where the Lord expostulates and cries "O, do not this abominable thing that I hate!"

After all His tenderness, in which He has acted towards us, as a father to his child, we have turned against Him and harboured His enemy; we have found our pleasure in grieving Him, and have called His commands burdens, and His service a weariness. Shall we not repent of this? Can we continue to act thus basely? This day, my God, I hate sin not because it damns me, but because it has done Thee wrong. To have grieved my God is the worst of grief to me. The heart renewed by grace feels a deep sympathy with God in the ungrateful treatment which He has received from us. It cries out, "How could I have offended Him? Why did I treat so gracious a God in so disgraceful a manner? He has done me good and no evil, wherefore have I slighted Him?" Had the Eternal been a tyrant and had His laws been despotic, I could imagine some dignity in a revolt against Him; but seeing He is a Father full of gentleness and tenderness, whose loving kindnesses are beyond all count, sin against Him is exceeding sinful. Sin is worse than bestial, for the beasts only return evil for evil, it is devilish—for it returns evil for good. Sin is lifting our heel against our benefactor—it is base ingratitude, treason, causeless hate, spite against holiness, and a preference for that which is low and grovelling—but whither am I going? Sin is sin, and in that word we have said all.

It would appear that Paul made the discovery of sin as sin through the light of one of the commands. He gives us a little bit of his own biography, which is most interesting to notice. He says, "I had not known lust except the law had said thou shalt not covet." It strikes me that when Paul was struck down from his horse on his way to Damascus, the first thought that came to him was, "this Jesus whom I have been persecuting, is after all the Messiah and Lord of all. Oh, horror of horrors, I have ignorantly warred against Him. He is Jesus, the Saviour who saves from sins; but what are my sins? Wherein have I offended against the law?" In his lonely blindness his mind involuntarily ran over the ten commandments; and as he considered each one of them with his poor half-enlightened judgment, he cried to himself, "I have not broken that! I have not broken that!" till at last he came to that command, "Thou shalt not covet," and in a moment, as though a lightning flash had cut in twain the solid darkness of his spirit, he saw his sin, and confessed that he had been guilty of inordinate desires. He had not known lust if the law had not said, "thou shalt not covet." That discovery unveiled all the rest of his sins, the proud Pharisee became a humble penitent, and he who thought himself blameless cried out, "I am the chief of sinners." I pray God by some means to let the same light stream into every soul here, where as yet it has not penetrated. O my hearers, I beseech the Lord to let you see sin as sin, and so lead you to Jesus as the only Saviour.

III. I shall need your best attention to the third point, which is this: THE SINFULNESS OF SIN IS MOST CLEARLY SEEN IN ITS PERVERTING THE BEST OF THINGS TO DEADLY PURPOSES. So the text runs: "Sin, that it might appear sin, working death in me by that which is good." It is evident that we are atrociously depraved since we make the worst conceivable use of the best things. Here is God's law, which was ordained to life, for "He that doeth these things shall live in them," is wilfully disobeyed, and so sin turns the law into an instrument of death. It does worse still. The sin that is in us, when it hears the commandment, straightway resolves to break it. It is a strangely wicked propensity of our nature, that there are many things which we should not care for otherwise, which we lust after at once, as soon as they are forbidden. Have you ever noticed, even in regard to human law, that when a thing is prohibited, persons long after it? I do not remember, in all the years I have lived in London, any cravings of the populace to hold meetings in Hyde Park till an attempt was made to keep them out, and then, straightway, all the railings were pulled down, and the ground was carried by storm. The park has been a field of battle every since. Had liberty of speech in the park never been interfered with as it was, most unwisely, nobody would have cared to hold forth at the Reformer's tree or any other tree. They would have said, "What's the use of dragging up there all through the mud for miles, when we can meet more comfortably in a hall under cover," but because they must not do it, they resolve to do it. That is the way with our common nature, it kicks at restraint—if we must not do a thing, then we will do it! Even before she fell, our mother Eve felt drawn to the forbidden tree, and the impulse in her fallen sons and daughters is far more forcible; as by one common impulse we wander from the road appointed, and break hedges to leap into fields enclosed against us. Law to our depraved nature is but the signal for revolt. Sin is a monster indeed, when it turns a preventive law into an incentive to rebellion. It discovers evil by the law, and then turns to it and cries, "evil be thou my good."

This is far from being the only case in which good is turned to evil through our sin. I might mention many others. Very briefly then, how many there are who turn the abounding mercy of God, as proclaimed in the gospel, into a reason for further sin! The preacher delights to tell you in God's name, that the Lord is a God ready to forgive and willing to have mercy upon sinners, and that whosoever believes in Jesus shall receive immediate pardon. What do these men say, "O, if it be so easy to be forgiven, let us go on to sin. If faith be so simple a matter, let us put it off until some future time." O, base and cruel argument! To infer greater sin from infinite love! What if I call it devilish reasoning—for so it is—to make of the very goodness of a gracious God, a reason for continuing to offend! Is it so that the more God loves the more you will hate? The better He is the worse you will be? Shame! Shame! Then, again, there are individuals who have indulged in very great sin, and have very fortunately escaped from the natural consequences of that sin, and what do they gather from this forbearance on God's part? God has been very longsuffering and pitiful to them; and, therefore, they defy Him again, and return presumptuously to their former habits. They dream that they have immunity to transgress, and even boast that God will never punish them, let them act as they may. Sin appears sin, indeed, when the longsuffering which should lead to repentance is regarded as a license for further offending. What a marvel that the Eternal does not crush His foes at once, when they count His gentleness to be weakness, and make His mercy a ground for further disobedience! Look again at thousands of prosperous sinners whose riches are their means of sinning. They have all that heart can wish, and instead of being doubly grateful to God they are proud and thoughtless, and deny themselves none of the pleasures of sin. The blessings entrusted to them become their curses, because they minister to their arrogance and worldliness. They war against God with weapons from His own armoury; they are indulged by providence, and then they indulge their sins the more. Fulness of bread too often breeds contempt of God. Men are lifted up, and then look down upon religion and speak loftily against the people of God, and even against the Lord Himself. With His meal in their mouths they blaspheme their benefactor, and with the wealth which is the loan of His charity they purchase the vile pleasures of iniquity. This is horrible, but so it is, that the more God gives to man the more man hates his God, and he to whom God multiplies His mercies returns it by multiplying his transgressions. I remember in our Baptist martyrology the story of one of the Baptists of Holland escaping from his persecutors. A river was frozen over, and the good man crossed it safely, but his enemy was of greater bulk, and the ice gave way under him. The Baptist, like a child of God as he was, turned round and rescued his persecutor just as he was sinking beneath the ice to certain death. And what did the wretch do? As soon as ever he was safely on the shore, he seized the man who had saved his life, and dragged him off to the prison, from which he was only taken to be put to death! We wonder at such inhumanity; we are indignant at such base returns—but the returns which the ungodly make to God are baser far. I wonder myself as I talk to you, I wonder that I speak so calmly on so terribly humbling a theme; and remembering our past lives, and our long ingratitude to God, I marvel that we do not turn this place into one vast Bochim or place of weeping, and mingle our tears in a flood, with expressions of deep shame and self abhorrence for our dealings towards God.

The same evil is manifested when the Lord reveals His justice and utters threats. When a threatening sermon is delivered, you will hear men say as they go out from hearing such a discourse, although the preacher has spoken most affectionately, "We will have no more of this hell-fire preaching, we are wearied and worried with these threatenings of judgment."

> "Thy judgments, too, unmoved they hear,
> Amazing thought! which devil's fear
> Goodness and wrath in vain combine,
> Their heart betrays no feeling sign."

Try the same man with God's tenderness, and speak of God's love, and he will be hardened by it, for the gospel hardens some men and becomes a savour of death unto death unto many. O sin, thou art sin indeed to make the gospel of salvation a reason for deeper damnation!

When great judgments are abroad in the land not a few of the ungodly become more insolent against God, and even rail at Him as a tyrant. The fire which ought to melt them only makes them harder. The terrors of God they defy, and like Pharaoh they demand, "Who is the Lord?"

We have known persons in adversity—very poor and very sick, who ought to have been led to God by their sorrow, but instead thereof, they have become careless of all religion, and cast off all fear of God. They have acted like Ahaz of whom it is written, "In the time of his distress did he trespass yet more against the Lord: this is that king Ahaz." The rod has not separated them from sin, but whipped them into a worse state. Their medicine has become their poison. The more the tree has been pruned, the less fruit it has yielded. Ploughing has only made the field more barren. That which has often proved so great a blessing to believers, has been utterly lost upon them. Why should they be smitten any more, they will revolt more and more?

One very singular instance of the heart's perversity is the fact that familiarity with death and the grave often hardens the heart, and none become more callous than grave-diggers and those who carry dead men to their graves. Men sin openly when graves are open before them. It is possible to work among the dead, and yet to be as wild as the man possessed of a devil in our Lord's day, who dwelt among the tombs. The Egyptians were accustomed to hold their riotous festivals in the presence of a corpse, not to sober their mirth, as some have said, but to make them the more wanton, gluttonous, and drunken because they should so soon die. Coffins and shrouds should be good sermons, but they seldom are so to those who see them every day. In times when cholera has raged, and in seasons when the pest, in the olden times, carried off its thousands, many men have not been at all softened but have grown callous in the presence of God's grim messenger, and even jested at Him. Hervey finds holy "meditations among the tombs," but unholy men are as far off from God in a churchyard as in a theatre.

Another strange thing I have often noticed—as a proof of sin's power to gather poison from the most healthful flowers, I have observed that some transgress all the more because they have been placed under the happy restraints of godliness. Though trained to piety and virtue, they rush into the arms of vice as though it were their mother. As gnats fly at a candle as soon as ever they catch sight of it, so do these infatuated ones dash into evil. Young people who are placed in the providence of God where no temptations ever assail them, in the midst of holy and quiet homes, where the very name of evil scarcely comes, will often fret and worry themselves to get out into what they call "life," and thrust their souls into the perils of bad company. The sons and daughters of Adam long to eat of the tree of the knowledge of good and evil. Their very preservation from temptation grows irksome to them, they loathe the fold and long for the wolf. They think themselves hardly done by that they have not been born in the midst of licentiousness and tutored in crime. Strange infatuation, and yet many a parent's heart has been broken by this freak of depravity, this reckless lust for evil. The younger son had the best of fathers, and yet he could never be quiet till he had gained his independence, and had brought himself to beggary in a far country, by spending his living with harlots.

Observe another case. Men who live in times when zealous and holy Christians abound, are often the worse for it. What effect has the zeal of Christians upon such? It excites them to malice. All the while the church is asleep the world says, "Ah, we do not believe your religion, for you do not act as if you believed it yourselves," but the moment the church bestirs herself, the world cries, "They are a set of fanatics; who can put up with their ravings? We could have believed their religion had it been brought to us with respectful sobriety, but accompanied by enthusiasm it is detestable." Nothing will please sinners but their sins, and if their sins could be made into virtues they would fly to their virtues at once, so as to remain in opposition. Contrary to God man will go, his very nature is enmity against his Creator. The quaint poet with whose verse we commenced our sermon, has truly said—

> "If God had laid all common, certainly
> Man would have been th' encloser: but since now
> God hath impal'd us, on the contrary
> Man breaks the fence, and every ground will plough.
> O what were man, might he himself misplace!
> Sure to be cross he would shift feet and face."

Sin is thus seen to be exceeding sinful. That plant must possess great vitality which increases by being uprooted and cut down. That which lives by being killed is strangely full of force. That must be a very hard substance which is hardened by lying in the blast furnace, in the central heat of the fire, where iron melts and runs like wax. That must be a very terrible power which gathers strength from that which should restrain it, and rushes on the more violently in proportion as it is reined in. Sin kills men by that which was ordained to life. It makes heaven's gifts the stepping stones to hell, uses the lamps of the temple to show the way to perdition, and makes the ark of the Lord as in Uzzah's case, the messenger of death. Sin is that strange fire which burns the more fiercely for being damped, finding fuel in the water which was intended to quench it. The Lord brings good out of evil, but sin brings evil out of good. It is a deadly evil—judge ye how deadly! O that men knew its nature and abhored it with all their hearts! May the Eternal Spirit teach men to know aright this worst of ills, that they may flee from it to Him who alone can deliver.

Now, what is all this about, and what is the drift of this discourse? Well, the drift of it is this. There is in us by nature a propensity to sin which we cannot conquer, and yet conquered it must be, or we can never enter heaven. Your resolutions to overcome sin are as feeble as though you should try to bind Leviathan with a thread, and lead him with a string. As well as hope to bind the tempest and rein in the storm, as to govern yourself by your own resolutions as to sin. Nor is sin to be overcome by philosophy, it laughs at such a spider's web. Nor can it be prevented: nor will the soul be cleansed from it by any outward observances. Genuflections, penances, fastings, washing, are all in vain. What then must be done? We must be new created. We are too far gone for mending; we must be made afresh; and for cleansing there is no water beneath the skies, nor any above them, that can remove our stain. But there is a fountain filled with the blood of God's own Son. He that is washed there shall be made white. And there is an all-creating Holy Spirit, who can fashion us anew in Christ Jesus into holiness. I would to God you all despaired of being saved, except by a miracle of grace. I would God you utterly despaired of being saved except by the supernatural power of the Holy Spirit. I would you were driven to look away from self, each one of you, to Him who on the bloody tree bore the wrath of God, for there is life in a look at Him, and whosoever looks at Him shall be saved—saved from the power of sin, as well as its guilt. That which the brazen serpent took away was the burning poison in the veins of the men who had been bitten by the serpents. They were diseased with a deadly disease, and they looked, and it was healed. It was not filth that was taken from them, it was disease that was healed by their simple look. And so a look at Christ does not merely take away sin, but it heals the disease of sin; and, mark you, it is the only possible healing for the leprosy of iniquity. Faith in Jesus brings the Holy Spirit with His sacred weapons of invincible warfare into the field of the human heart, and He overthrows the impregnable strongholds of sin, makes lust a captive, and slays the enmity of the heart. Sin being made to appear sin, grace is made to appear grace: God's Holy Spirit gets the victory, and we are saved. God grant that this may be the experience of us all. Amen and Amen.

WHY AM I THUS?

"I delight in the law of God after the inward man: but I see another law in my members, warring against the law of my mind, and bringing me into captivity to the law of sin which is in my members."—Romans vii. 22, 23.

LAST Thursday evening, as many of you will remember, I addressed you upon the final perseverance of the saints. I have been greatly surprised and gratified during the week to learn how many persons found comfort and cheer from the simple explanation of that doctrine, which I then gave you. In fact, on the two past Thursday evenings we have been handling a *precept* and a *promise* both relating to the same matter, though each putting it in a different light. The one admonished us to *perseverance* by holding fast; the other assured us of *preservation*, because we are fast held. The welcome you gave to these familiar expositions has led me to think it would be acceptable, specially, to such of you as have been lately brought into the sacred household, and who may not even know the rudiments of religious experience, were I to-night to follow up those two elementary discourses with some little account of the great inward conflict to which the believer's life is exposed.

The passage before us tells a portion of the experience of the Apostle Paul. We all of us concede that he was a most eminent saint. Indeed, we place him in the front rank. For this reason his experience is the more valuable to us. If the greatest saints have their inward struggles, how much more should we expect to have them who have not attained the same degree of grace the apostle did. If he who was not a whit behind the very chief of the apostles yet had to say, "When I would do good evil is present with me," then you and I, who can only take the position of babes in grace, or of ordinary disciples of Jesus Christ, must not be surprised if we have to bear assaults that surprise us and enter into struggles that distress us, and often are fain by stress of emotion to cry out, "O wretched man that I am, who shall deliver me from the body of this death?"

I shall ask you, therefore, for your personal consolation to notice, first of all, that the ruling power in the Christian's mind is a strong affection, and, therefore, an intense pleasure in that which is pure and holy,—"I delight in the law of God after the inward man;" secondly, that there are passions and propensities within the breast of a man which come into direct conflict with this holy principle,—"I see another law in my members warring against the law of my mind;" and, thirdly, that the discipline involved in this constant hostility, despite all the fretfulness and irritation it causes, is not without true and satisfactory evidence of our spiritual welfare. "I thank God through Jesus Christ our Lord."

I. It may be said of every true Christian that the ruling power in him delights in the law of God. The new nature which God has created in every believer cannot sin because it is born of God. This is the work of the Holy Spirit, and as such without guile, unblemished, incorruptible. We are made partakers of the divine nature. The divine nature, so far as it is communicable, is given to us when we are begotten again unto a lively hope by the resurrection of Jesus Christ from the dead. We are born not of the flesh, not of blood, nor of the will of man, but of God. We receive from God a new nature at the time of our regeneration. This new nature, though it is the younger, compels the older nature within us to submit to it. It has a struggle, but it gets the victory; that significant augury, "The elder shall serve the younger," is abundantly fulfilled in the little kingdom within our souls. It has a long struggling trial before the full subjugation; there are many harassing rebellions to encounter, but at length that which is born of the Spirit shall overcome that which is born of the flesh, and the divine nature within us shall vanquish the sensual nature. The Christian man because of this new nature implanted in him delights in the law of God. He has no desire to change that law in any way whatever. When we read the ten commandments, our conscience approves the ordinances of God while it reproves our own culpable shortcomings; yea, we feel that only God could have drawn up so complete, so perfect a code. We would not wish to have one single iota, word, or syllable of that law altered, though it condemns us. Though we know, apart from the precious blood of Christ, it would have cast us into hell, and most justly so, yet with holy instinct, pure taste, and righteous judgment we consent unto the law that it is good. It expresses God's mind of the difference between right and wrong, good and evil, truth and falsehood, harmony and discord, and our mind agrees with God's mind. We perceive it not as truth established by investigation, but as truth all radiant, shining in its own majesty. We would willingly take our place on Mount Ebal or Mount Gerizim to give our tremulous Amen to the curses pronounced on disobedience, or to hail with solemn joy the blessings avouched to those who observe and do His commandments. Nor, beloved, would the Christian man wish to have the spirituality of the law in any degree compromised. He is not only pleased with the law as he reads it, though, as I have said, it condemns him, but he is pleased with the very spirit of the law. What if the law condemns in him an unchaste look as well as an unchaste action? He condemns that unchaste look in himself. What if the law reaches to the heart and says, "Thou shouldst not even desire thy neighbour's goods, much less shouldst thou steal them?" He feels in his soul that it is sin, and that it is a bitter thing in him even to covet where he does not defraud. He never thinks that God is too exacting. He never for a moment says, "I knew that Thou wast an austere man, gathering where Thou hadst not strewed," but he consents to the law though it be high and broad, exceedingly broad. Though the thunderings, the lightnings, and the voices which usher in that law do terrify him, yet the wisdom, the equity, and the benevolence which ordained it resolves this awe into admiration. Being born from above, in fellowship with Christ, at peace with God, his very constitution is in unison with the law of the Lord. Is the law spiritual, so is he. The pact is unbroken, the concord perfect. I trust full many of you, my hearers, can endorse this; for, doubtless, as many of us as have been born again can bear witness that we delight in the law of God after the inward man.

Again, no Christian desires to have any dispensa-tion to exempt him from complying with any one of the Lord's commands. His old nature may desire it, but the inner man saith, "No; I do not wish to get or to give any concession to the flesh, to have an allowance or make an excuse for sin in any point whatever. The flesh craves for liberty, and asks to have provision made for it. But, does any believer here want liberty to sin? My brother, if it were possible to conceive without blasphemy that the Lord should say to you, "My child, if there be one sin that you love, you may continue in it," would you desire any sin? Would you not rather say, "Oh, that I may be purged from every sin, for sin to me is misery, it is but another term for sorrow. Moral evil is its own curse; a plague, a pest, at the thought of which I shudder." It is thought a blessing in the Church of Rome, that a dispensation be given to men from certain religious duties. We ask no such favour; we value not their boon. Liberty to sin would mean putting double fetters upon us. A license even for a moment to relax our obedience to Christ would be but a license to leave the paths of light and the way of peace to wander awhile in darkness and danger; to exchange the glow of health for sore distemper and smarting pain. Brethren, I am sure you never did, and never will, if you be believers, ask the Lord for permission to transgress His statutes. You may have taken leave to do what you did not know was sinful at the time. There may have been a desire in your heart after something that was wrong. I grant you that. But the new-born nature, the moment it discovers its culpability, recoils at it and turns from it; it could do no otherwise. It cannot sin, for it is born of God. The new nature that is in you shudders at sin; it is not its element; it cannot endure it, whereas before you could riot in it and take pleasure in it, and drink iniquity like water. You ask no dispensation that you may escape from the law. You delight in it after the inward man.

The new-born nature of the Christian also laboriously desires to keep the holy law according to the mind of God. If it were proposed to any one of us that we should have whatever we would ask for,—if in a vision of the night the Lord should appear to us, and to say to us as He did to Solomon, "Ask what I shall give you," I do not think any of us would hesitate. I cannot imagine myself asking for riches or honour, or even for wisdom, unless it were wisdom of a far higher order than is commonly esteemed among the sons of men. But the gift which I feel I should crave beyond every other boon is holiness, pure and immaculate holiness. Possessing now an interest in Christ, knowing that my sins are forgiven me for His name's sake, the one thing I desire beyond everything else is to be perfectly free from sin, and to lead an unblemished life without sin of omission or sin of commission. Now, every Christian that has that desire within his soul will never be satisfied until that desire is fulfilled; and this shows that we delight in the law of God after the inward man. Nor is it long ere that desire will be fulfilled. Why, we shall be like Him when we shall see Him as He is; and until we do see Him as He is and are like Him, we shall always have restlessness of spirit, and always be crying out for more grace, and labouring against the evil that is in us, if by any means we may subdue it. O yes, beloved, in the fact that this is what we hope for, this is what we pray for, this is what we fight for, this is what we would be willing to die for, that we might be entirely conformed to the mind and will of God, there is evidence that we see that the law of God is good and delight in it after the inward man.

This, however, is proved in a more practical way to onlookers when the Christian shews that the life of God is enabling him to overcome many of the desires of the flesh and of the mind. Oftentimes in striving to be holy he has to put himself to much stern self-denial; but he does it cheerfully. For instance, should it happen in business that by using a very common trick in trade he might gain more profit, he will not do it if he is a Christian; he feels he cannot do this evil and sin against his God. Or should the young convert find that a little divergence from the right path would please the worldly people with whom he is obliged to associate, he may, perhaps, turn aside in his weakness, but the new life within him will never be easy if he does. The inner life, when it is in its vigour, will make him say, "Though I should lose the goodwill of these people, let me serve my Lord and Master. I must forfeit my situation if it come to that sooner than I can do wrong. I must be put even in peril of my daily bread sooner than I will be found wilfully breaking a commandment of Christ. I cannot do it." Now, I know many of God's people who have often suffered very severely, and have passed through a great many trials and troubles because they would not flinch from following their Lord. This is one of the proofs that they delight in the law of God after the inner man. When a man is willing to bear reproach, to be scorned at, to be ridiculed, and taunted as mad for righteousness sake, when he is willing that men should sneer at him as a hypocrite and yclept him a Pharisee, when he braves the cold shoulder from those whose company he would otherwise have enjoyed, and all because he must and will follow the mind and direction of God's Spirit, I say then it is that the man gives proof that he delights in the law of God. I thank God there are in this Church those who have given that proof, and I pray that you and I, all of us who have received the divine nature, may give constant evidence by using the good art at all hazards, and taking up the cross at all risks, that our soul, even if it cannot be perfect in action, at any rate, would be perfect in aim, and determined by God's help to cherish a love and desire in all things to do Jehovah's will. Is there any one here who is obliged to say, "Well, I do not consent to the law of God: I do not delight in it. When I hear it said, 'Thou shalt not covet,' 'Thou shalt not commit adultery,' 'Remember the Sabbath day to keep it holy;' I wish it were not evil to do those things that are forbidden. Pity 'tis our pleasure and our profit, our duty and our delight, should be so much at variance. I would rather there were less law and more license. Those commandments, especially, that touch our thoughts, and trench on the freedom of our will, are harsh and unpalatable. I am not content to be bound by them. I would rather live as I like." Well, my dear friend, I will say nothing more severe to you than this, you have no part or lot in this matter at all. If you had, if your heart had been renewed, you would talk after a very different matter. Whenever you hear persons commending a low standard of religion, a low standard of morality, whenever you find them vindicating lax views of right and wrong, you may rest assured that the spirit that is in them is not the spirit of the holy God, but it is the spirit of their sinful nature; yea, the spirit of Satan may have come in to make the human spirit even worse than it

was before. But, does your heart delight in God's law? Is there a charm in that which is right to your soul? Is there a beauty in that which is virtuous to your Spirit's eye? Do you especially admire the character of Jesus because "in His life the law appears drawn out in living characters?" If so, then I trust, dear friends, you give evidence that you have been made partakers of the divine nature, that you are regenerate, and though there is evil in you still, yet there is the life of God in you which will resist the evil and subdue it, till you are brought safely to his right hand.

II. Now, secondly, we come to the conflict. Where there is this delight in the law of God, yet there is another law in the members. So Paul says, and he seems to me to speak of it in three different stages. He could see it first, and then he had to encounter it, and at length to some extent he was enthralled by it; for he says, "bringing me into captivity."

There is in each one of us a law of sin. It may always be seen even when it is not in active operation, if our eyes are lightened. Whenever I hear a man say he has no propensity to sin, I infer at once that he does not live at home. I should think he must live a long way from home, or else he has never been anywhere except in the front parlour of his house where he keeps his profession. He cannot have gone through all the chambers and searched them thoroughly, or he would somewhere have discovered that there is an evil heart of unbelief in departing from the living God. This is true of the believer; he has to cry out against another nature, and say, "Help thou mine unbelief." It is always in the man. Sometimes it is dormant. I do not know whether the devil ever goes to sleep, but our sinful nature seems for a time to do so; not, indeed, that it is any the less sinful when asleep than when it is awake. It is just as bad as it can be. Gunpowder is not always exploding, but it is always explosive. Bring but the spark to it and anon it bursts out, as though it had been ready and waiting to exert its powers of explosion. The viper may be coiled up doing no damage; but it hath a deadly virus beneath its fangs. It is still a viper even when it is not putting forth its poisonous tooth. There is within our nature that which would send the best saint to hell if sovereign grace did not prevent. There is a little hell within the heart of every child of God, and only the great God of heaven can overmaster that mischievous indwelling sin. This sin will crop up when it is least expected, generally it breaks forth suddenly, taking us by surprise. I have known it to my sorrow. I am not going to stand here and make many confessions with regard to myself. Howbeit I did know a man once who, in attending a prayer-meeting felt his heart much lifted up in the ways of God, drew very near to his heavenly Father, held sweet communication with Christ, and enjoyed much of the fellowship of the Spirit. Little did he think that the moment the prayer-meeting was over somebody in the congregation would insult and bitterly affront him. Because he was taken unawares his anger was roused, and he spake unadvisedly with his tongue. He had better have held his peace. Now, I believe, that man if he had been met at any other time, for he was of a tolerably quiet temper, would have taken the insult without resenting it or making any reply whatever; but he had been unwarned, therefore he was unguarded. The very love shed abroad in his heart caused the animosity he encountered to shock his feelings the more. He had been so near heaven that he expected everybody present had thoughts in harmony with his own; he had not reckoned upon being assailed then. When there is most money in the house, then is the likeliest time for thieves to break in; and when there is most grace in the soul the devil will try, if he can, to assault it. Pirates were not accustomed to attack vessels when they went out to fetch gold from the Indies: they always waylaid them when they were coming home, with a view of getting rich spoil worth the capture. If you have enjoyed a sermon, if you have got near to God in prayer, if the Scriptures have been very precious to you, you may expect just then that the dragon that sleeps within will wake up and disturb the peaceful calm of your soul:

> "We should expect some danger nigh,
> When we receive too much delight."

Let us be the more watchful then in seasons of tranquillity. This evil nature, you see, will sometimes be excised, as if by jealousy, when we are being refreshed with good. It will certainly be developed when we are exposed to evil. The man who congratulates himself because he feels no sinful proclivities, no unholy thoughts, no impure imaginations, no conceited ideas, no turbulent passions had need be reminded of that saying of old Rutherford— "When the temptation sleepeth the madman is wise, the harlot is chaste; but when the vessel is pierced out cometh that which is within, be it wine or water." O my soul, thou hast only been at rest awhile, because there was not any exciting cause for a time. Put into the company of godly people and the mind occupied with good things continually, the bad instincts may sleep; but cast into other society, it only needs a slight provocation, and oh, how soon the evil that always was within manifests itself abundantly. There are weeds in almost every soul. If you throw up the soil from ten or twenty feet deep there will be found the seeds from which they grow. Now, those seeds cannot germinate until they are put in a convenient place; then let the sun shine and the dews fall, and the weeds begin to show themselves. There may be many weeds in our nature, deep down, out of sight, but should they be thrown up by some change of circumstances, we shall find in ourselves evils we never dreamt of. Oh, let no man boast; let no man say, "I should never fall into that particular sin." How knowest thou, my brother? thou mayst never have been in that position in which such a sin would have allured you? Beware! perhaps where thou thinkest thou art iron, thou art clay; and when thou thinkest that the gates are closed with bars of brass it may be but rotten wood. With respect to none of us, even the holiest, is there reason to trust his best faculties, his best desires, his best resolutions; we are utter weakness through and through, and to transgressions prone, notwithstanding all that God's grace has done for us. The sin which is in us as a taint in our constitution, might easily break out as a loathsome distemper, spreading over the entire man from head to foot, and spoiling all the character. I pray God it never may.

It is remarkable how sin will show itself in the Christian, even in the holiest of his duties. Suppose it is prayer. When you feel that you ought to pray, and would draw near to God, do you not find sometimes an unwillingness as if the knees were stiff and the heart was hard. In prayer, when your soul is led away with thoughts of things divine, straight across your soul like some carrion crow flying across a landscape, there comes a bad thought and you cannot get rid of it, or perhaps you get through your devotion with much delight in God; but you have not got out of your little room before an alien pleasure steals over your mind, a self-satisfaction that you have prayed so well that you are growing in grace; that you are rising to the fullness of the stature of a man in Christ. Is it so, that you come from the chamber of reverent worship musing on your own importance; meditating your fitness to occupy a place above the common rank and file of the soldiers of Christ—or that you might very well take a lieutenant's rank in the church of God. Perhaps, again you did not feel any liberty in prayer, and then with a peevish fretful temper you will inwardly murmur, if you do not actually say, you might as well give up praying such prayers as those, there can be no use in them. So do what you may, or leave undone what you may, yet still the evil that is within will rise; it will intrude upon you at some time or other to let you know of its existence. You may bolt the door, and you may fancy that no thief can get in, and begin to take off your clothes and go to rest, while yet the thief is under the bed. So many a man has thought "I have barred the door against those temptations," and, lo, they have been hidden in his soul like the images which Rachel took that were concealed under the camel's furniture. Somewhere or other they were secreted where he had not discovered them. Take it for granted, dear friends, and do not doubt it. The Apostle Paul saw it, so you may if you choose to look. He said, "I see another law in my members."

And this law in his members, he goes on to tell us, was "warring against the law of his mind." It strove to get the mastery, and the new nature, on the other hand resisted and would not let it get the mastery. The old lusts fight and then the new life fights too, for there must be two sides to a war. Such is the warfare going on within the renewed soul. We have known this warfare take different shapes. At times it has been on this wise. A wrong desire has come into a Christian, and he has loathed it, utterly loathed it, but that desire has followed him again and again. He has cried to God against it; he has wept over it; he has not consented to it; he fears lest he may have found it sweet or palatable to him for the moment, but when he has had time for reflection he shudders at the very thought of giving way to that temptation; and yet by the restiveness of his own flesh and by the reprisals of Satan that hateful desire will come up and up and up again. He will hear it baying behind him like a bloodhound following his prey, and sometimes it will take a leap and grip him by the throat and cast him down. It will be as much as that poor man can do to keep down that ferocious temptation that has arisen in his spirit. I can bear witness that such warfare is a very terrible ordeal, for it sometimes lasts for days and weeks, and months together. I have known thoughtful Christians who have been harassed with doubts which have been suggested about the inspiration of Scripture, about the deity of our Lord, about the sureness of the covenant of grace, or some other fundamental doctrine of our most holy faith; or even it may be the temptation has been to blasphemies, which the believer has abhorred from his very soul. Yet the more bitterly he has detested it the more relentlessly it has pursued him. Would he drive it away, it returned with redoubled force. "Is it true?" "Is it so?" Mayhap, that a hideous sentiment is wrapped up in a neat epigram, and then it will haunt the memory, and he will strive in vain to dislodge it He would gladly hurl the thought and the words that clothe the thought into the bottomless pit. Out, cursed spectre, he will cry. Back, like the ghost of one's own crimes, it comes. Whence these evils? May they sometimes be traced to Satan? Ay, but most commonly temptation derives its strength, as well as its opportunity, from the moods or habits to which our own constitution is prone. In the discharge of public duties, when straining every nerve to serve the Lord, we may meet with men whose temper acts on our temper to stir up the bile and make us think evil of those to whom we are bent on doing good. In the peaceful shades of retirement which wise men seek out as a relief from the distractions of society, what strange fancies and monstrous vagaries will often come into the heart and confuse the brain. Or, sad to tell, in the walks of study where thoughtful men set out reverently to enquire into the counsels of God, how frequently have they been lured from the open paths to trespass on dangerous ground, to lose themselves in labyrinths, to leave the footsteps of the flock; and so to become giddy and high minded. Anywhere, everywhere, we are challenged to fight, and we must give battle to the sin that besets us.

But, the war carried on by this evil nature is not always by the continual besieging of the soul, at times it tries to take us by assault. This is a favourite mode of warfare with our own corrupt heart. When we are off our guard up it will come and attack us, and as I have said before, we are apt to be off our guard when we have been brought up into the high mountain apart, when we have been near the Lord. In that exalted sphere of communion we have not thought of the devil, his existence has not come across our mind; but when we go down again into the plain, we soon find that he is still living, still distressing our brethren, still lying in wait to ensnare us. For this cause, our experience should quicken our sympathy. Full many a Christian has been surprised into a sin for which he was to be greatly blamed, but for which he ought not to have been condemned by his fellow Christians with so much severity. They ought to condemn the sin, but to remember themselves lest they also should be tempted. Many a man has been good because he had not a chance of being bad, and, I believe, many a professing Christian has stood because the road did not happen to be very smooth, and there was not much to be gained by falling down. We do not judge each other as God does. He knows the infirmities of His dear children. While He does not make excuses for their sin—He is too pure and holy for that—yet, having blotted out their sins through the atonement of Christ Jesus, He does not cast them off and turn them out of fellowship, as sometimes His people do their poor brethren, who may, after all, be as true children as they are themselves, and have as much real love to their Father. This evil nature when it is warring, laughs at our own resolutions, and mocks our own attempts to put it down. It must be warred against by grace. No arm but the Almighty arm can overcome our natural corruption. Like a leviathan it laugheth at the spear: it counteth it but as rotten wood. You cannot come at a besetting sin as you would. At times you fancy, "I'll wound it to its deadly hurt;" and in the very act of wounding one sin you are calling another into play. Many a man has tried to overcome his propensity to faintheartedness,

and he has run into presumption. Some have tried to be less profuse in their expenditure, and they have become penurious. Some have said, "I will be no more proud, and then they have become mean-spirited. I have known some that were so stern for the truth, they became bigoted, who have afterwards become latitudinarian and hold the truth with so loose a hand that their constancy could hardly be relied on. Look straight on and "do the duty that next lies before you." It is no easy thing, believe me, to defend yourself from the surprises of sin. It is a thing impossible, unless God who created the new nature shall come to its rescue, shall feed it with the bread of heaven, shall give it water out of the Rock of Ages, and lead it on its way to the goodly land where the Canaanite shall never be, and where our soul shall feast on milk and honey.

I must not linger on this point, but pass on to notice the next. It is a sadder one The apostle said this warring brought him into captivity to the law of sin. What does he mean by this? I do not think he means he wandered into open flagrant immoralities. No observer may have noticed any fault in the apostle's character. He could see it in himself, and he saw flaws in his life where we are not able to detect them, and probably that was a habit with the apostle. When I hear a good man lamenting his faults I know what the world will say: they will take him at his word and think that he is as they are, whereas with every godly man, if you knew him and marked his life and conversation you would be compelled, if you judged him candidly, to say that he was like Job, perfect and upright, one that feared God and eschewed evil. Yet that very man would be the first to see spots in himself, because he has more light than others, because he has a higher idea of what holiness is than others, and chiefly because he lives nearer to God than others, and he knows that God is so infinitely holy that the heavens were not pure in his sight, and he charged his angels with folly; therefore, every one who sees himself in the glass of the law sees in himself a filthiness that he never saw before. As Job said, "I have heard of Thee by the hearing of the ear; but now mine eye seeth Thee. Wherefore I abhor myself, and repent in dust and ashes." But I think the apostle was not referring here to acts of gross misdemeanour having brought him into captivity so far as he himself was concerned; though many who are God's children, get into sorry captivity because the law of sin and death in their members gets the mastery over them sometimes. Oh, watch against this: weep against this: I was about to say wrestle unto blood against this. Brethren, they that have committed great sins who have been God's children, though they have been saved, have been saved so as by fire; and if they could tell you how many times they were chastened, how sore the chastening was, how their very bones were broken, how the Lord made them see that He hated sin in His own family even more than anywhere else,—could you hear them confess how they lost the light of His countenance, lost enjoyments, lost the sweet savour of the promises, oh, it would make you say, "My God, be pleased not only to save me at the last but all the journey through. Hold up my footsteps in Thy way that they slip not: make me to run in the way of Thy commandments." It is a captivity like that of the Israelites in Babylon itself when a child of God is suffered to fall into some great sin. But, long before it comes to that pass, and I hope in your case it may never go so far, I think this law of sin brings us unto captivity in other respects. While you are fighting and contending against inbred sin doubts will invade your heart. "Am I a child of God? If it be so, why am I thus? I cannot pray as I would. Surely if I were a child of God I should not be hampered in devotion or go out to a place of worship and feel I have no enjoyment, while others feast and sing for joy of heart." Oh, what a captivity the soul is brought into when it allows inbred sin to cast any doubts upon its safety in Christ. We are saved because we are believers in Christ. Christ, having been all our confidence, is always in us the hope of glory. To as many as received Him to them gave He power to become the sons of God, even to as many as believed on His name. If I have believed on His name, whatever my inward experience may be, or may not be in my own estimation, if I have believed on the name of Jesus I have the privilege to be a child of God. But sometimes doubts will come over us, and so we are brought into captivity. I have known those who were almost driven to despair. The child of God, has written bitter things against himself and signed his own death-warrant. Thank God, if we sign our own death-warrant it does not stand for anything. Nobody can sign that but the King, and He will never sign it for any soul that believes in Him, however feeble his love may be. We may be brought into captivity by a sense of sin, a temptation to sin, or a yielding to sin. If we ever come to that it will make us weak in serving, cold in prayer; restless when alone, and joyless in the society of the saints; nay, we shall feel almost lifeless. Oh, may God save us from it! Oh, may we wrestle hard; may we wrestle every day that we may keep sin down; may divine grace, even that grace which is treasured up in Christ Jesus, secure to us the victory.

III. It is some comfort when we feel a war within the soul, to remember that it is an interesting phase of Christian experience. Such as are dead in sin have never made proof of any of these things. Time was when we were self-righteous, lost, and ruined, and without the law, and sin was dead in us, so we thought. We were dead, in trespasses and sins, though we boasted of our own righteousness. These inward conflicts, show that we are alive. There is some life in the soul that hates sin, even though it cannot do as it would. I have known what it is to bless God for the times when my soul has felt inward war, and I would have been glad to feel the war renewed. Rest assured that the strong man of the soul while he keeps the house will keep it in peace. It is when a stronger than he comes to eject him, that there is a fight within your soul; I would suggest it therefore to you as a cause for consolation and thankfulness. Do not be depressed about it. Say—"after all, there is some life here." Where there is pain there is life. The best of God's saints have suffered in this very manner. Your way to heaven is not a bad one. Some, I know, are not so troubled to any great extent, but the majority of God's saints have to endure fightings without and fears within. You read of Martin Luther. That great bold man became a master of theology, by being taught in the school of temptation. Even his last hours were full of stern conflict. He was a man of war from his youth up. How constantly did he have to contend against himself. We get the same testimony from this chapter of the life of Paul. Be not, therefore, downcast as though some strange thing had happened unto you. Look up yonder to those saints above in their white robes singing their

unending song! Ask them whence their victory came? They will tell you that it did not come to them because they were sinless or perfect in themselves, but through the blood of Jesus.

> "Once they were wrestling here below,
> And wet their couch with tears,
> They wrestled hard as we do now,
> With sins, and doubts, and fears."

The richest consolation comes from the last verse of the chapter. Paul having asked how he should be delivered, answers the question, "I thank God through Jesus Christ our Lord." "They shall call His name Jesus, for He shall save His people from their sins," not only from the guilt of their sins, but from the power of their sins. What a mercy it is that the Lord Jesus has struck a deadly blow at our sin. He has broken the head of it. It is a monster, and has immense vitality; but it is a broken-backed, broken-legged, broken-headed monster. There it is: it lies hissing and spitting, and writhing, capable of doing us much mischief, but He that has wounded it will smite it again and again, until at last it shall utterly die. Thank God it has not vitality enough to get across the river Jordan. No sinful desire shall ever swim on that stream. They are not molested there with tendencies and propensities to sin, and when they shall be restored to their bodies, and their bodies shall rise again, they shall have bodies not of flesh. Bodies of flesh shall not inherit the kingdom of heaven, neither shall their bodies see corruption, but with bodies fit for celestial minds, they shall be eternally free from their former sin. Let us rejoice that Jesus Christ can do it all. He can save us from all sin. He who has bought us with His blood, He will not cheaply lose that which He has dearly bought. He will deliver us from all sin, and He will bring us into His eternal kingdom and glory without fail. So we fall back upon this sweet consolation. Though the fight may be long and arduous, the result is not doubtful. Remember the text of last Thursday night. That shall settle the point. "I give unto My sheep eternal life, and they shall never perish, neither shall any pluck them out of My hand." "My Father who gave them Me is greater than all, and none shall pluck them out of My Father's hand." You will have to get to heaven fighting for every inch of the way; but you will get there. Some on boards and some on broken pieces of the ship, they all came safe to land in Paul's shipwreck, and so shall it be with the saints. When the sheep shall pass again under the hand of Him that telleth them one by one, there shall not be one of them missing. They were all so weak that the wolf could have rent them in pieces; they were all so foolish that if left to themselves they would have wandered on the mountains and in the woods, and have been destroyed; but the eternal shepherd makes this a point of honour—"Of all them that Thou hast given Me, I have lost none. Here am I, and the children that thou hast given Me." It ought to make you quite well now to know that you are sure of victory. Oh, by the lilies of the love of Christ, and by the strong right arm that once smote Rahab, and cut the dragons in twain, let every Christian be of good courage. The Omnipotent is with us; the Invincible is for us. Forward to the charge, onward to the conflict, though the fight wax warmer and sterner still, onward ever, onward without fear or a moment's hesitation. "He that hath loved us bears us through, and makes us more than conquerors too." "The breaker is come up before them; they have broken up, and have passed through the gate, and are gone out by it, and their king shall pass before them, and the LORD on the head of them." They have put to the rout their foes. Thus shall it be spoken of all those that follow under the leadership of Christ; this is the heritage of the saints and their righteousness is of Me saith the Lord. God grant us to be victors in this holy war, for Christ's sake. Amen.

HOW GOD CONDEMNED SIN

"For what the law could not do, in that it was weak through the flesh, God sending His own Son in the likeness of sinful flesh and for sin, condemned sin in the flesh."—Romans viii. 3.

EVER since man has fallen away from God, two things have been highly desirable. The one, that he should be forgiven all his offences; the other, equally if not more important, that he should be led to hate the sin into which he has fallen, and love the purity and holiness from which he has become alienated. These two disabilities must be removed; or, looking at the matter from a loftier point of view, these two purposes of divine mercy must be accomplished together. It were impossible to make a man happy unless both be equally and simultaneously realised. If his sins were forgiven, and yet he loved sin, his prospects were dark; over his future the direst portents would loom. If he ceased to love sin, and yet were lying under the guilt of it, his present condition would rather be deeply miserable than happy —his conscience pure and sensitive being tortured with pangs of remorse. By what process can the two requirements be met, or the double purpose be achieved? To use our common words, how can man be both justified and sanctified, obtain clearance from his guilt in the sight of God, and then be made holy and meet to appear in His presence?

Human reason suggests that a law should be given to man which he should keep. This has been tried, and the law which was given was the best law that could be framed. The law of God written on the conscience, of which the law given by Moses recorded in the book of Exodus is but a copy, is a perfect law. There is not a command in it that could be omitted; there is not one single arbitrary precept. The right must be true, the true must be right, and God's law is never otherwise than right and true. "Of law," said the judicious Hooker, "there can be no less acknowledged, than that her seat is the bosom of God, her voice the harmony of the world; all things do her homage, the very least as feeling her care, and the greatest as not exempt from her power." If, therefore, that law which is promulgated from heaven should fail to make men what they should be, the fault will not be in the law, but in the man. As the text says, it was "weak through the flesh." Because of our flesh and our tendency to sin, our weakness and our defilement of nature, it could not do what, indeed, God never intended it should do, but what some have thought law might do, to repair the breach and to renovate the depraved. The principle of law, which is, "Do this and you shall be rewarded"; or, "Do that and you shall be punished," never can by any means achieve either of these two purposes. The law cannot forgive past sin. It evidently has nothing to do with that question. The law says, "The soul that sinneth it shall die." It can execute the sentence, but it can do no more. It ceases to be law if it lays aside the sword, and does not exact its own penalty. Yet it has been thought that surely law might make men love holiness, albeit experience and observation prove that it never has that effect. Very often men have needed nothing more than the knowledge of sin to enamour them of it, and they have loved sin all the better for knowing it to be sin. The apostle Paul tells us that he had not known lust if the law had not said, "Thou shalt not covet." There was a citizen of Gaunt who had never been outside the city walls. For some reason or other the magistrate passed an order that he should not go outside. Strange to tell, up to the moment that the command had passed, the man had been perfectly easy, and never thought of passing the line, but as soon as ever he was forbidden to do it, he pined, and sickened, and even died moaning over the restriction. If a man sees a thing to be law, he wants to break that law. Our nature is so evil that, forbid us to do a thing, and at once we want to do the thing that is forbidden, and in many minds the principle of law instead of leading to purity has even offered opportunities for greater impurity. Beside, although you may point out the way of uprightness to a man, and tell him what is right and what is wrong with all the wisdom and force of counsel and caution, unless you can give him a heart to choose the right, and a heart to love the true, you have not done much for him. This is just the province of law. It can write out its precepts on the brazen tablets, and it can brandish its fiery sword, and say, "Do this or else be punished," but man, carnal man, only wraps himself the more closely in his self-conceit, and perseveres the more doggedly in his obstinate rebellion. He defies God, defers to his own reprobate mind, goes on in sin, and waxes worse and worse, knowing the judgment threatened, yet committing the transgressions prohibited, and taking pleasure in those that do such things, as his boon companions. Because of the malignity, as well as the infirmity of our flesh, the mere principle of law will never do anything to purify or ennoble our moral nature. It has been tried by eminent teachers and social reformers. Dr. Chalmers tells us that in his early ministry, he used to preach morality, and nothing but morality, till, he said, he had hardly a sober or an honest man left in the parish. The preaching of morality seemed to lead to immorality. Something more is wanted than merely to din into men's ears what they ought to be, and what they ought to do. Something is wanted more effectually to renovate the heart and move the springs of action. The water is nought, and if you make it flow it is bitter. You want an ingredient to be cast into it that will heal its poison springs, and make them sweet and clear.

Now, in the text, we are told how God interposed to do by His grace what His law could not do. I will read it to you again: "For what the law could not do, in that it was weak through the flesh, God sending His own Son in the likeness of sinful flesh, and for sin, condemned sin in the flesh." There are here, then, two things; first, *what God did*; He sent His own Son in the likeness of sinful flesh for sin; and then, *what was the immediate result of this*, He condemned sin in the flesh. After expounding these matters, I will try, in the third place, to show you *how this bears upon the two desirable things I speak of*, namely, the forgiving the offender, and the making the offender from thenceforth yearn after holiness and purity.

I. First, and very briefly, let me tell you WHAT, ACCORDING TO THE TEXT, GOD DID—He sent His Son.

We believe in one God, but though we understand not the mystery of the Divine Existence, we accept the propositions declared in Scripture, clearly apprehending the obvious sense of the terms employed, and heartily assenting to the truth of the facts revealed. Thus we believe that the Father is God, and the Son is God, and the Holy Ghost is God, and we worship these three as the one God, the triune God of Israel. The second person of that blessed unity in Trinity was sent by the Father to this earth. He is God the Father's Son, "the only-begotten of the Father." What that means we do not attempt to define: of the matter of fact we feel no doubt, of the manner thereof we can offer no explanation. We suppose that the relationship implied in the words "Father" and "Son" is the nearest description that the Divine Mind can present to our feeble intelligence of that ineffable fellowship, but we do not assume therefore that it explains to us anything, or was intended to explain anything as the basis of an argument, or of a theory concerning the profound doctrine itself. It is a great mystery. Indeed, were there no mystery in God, He were no God to us; for how then should we fear Him with the reverence due unto His name? The fact of there being mysteries should never stagger us, poor worms of a day, when we have to think or speak of the infinitely glorious Jehovah. So, however, it came to pass, that in the fulness of time God sent His son. He is called in the text, "His own Son," to distinguish Him from us who are only His sons by Creation, or His sons by regeneration and adoption. He sent His own Son, and He sent Him in the flesh. Jesus Christ, the Son of God, was born into this world; He took upon Himself our manhood. The Word was made flesh, and dwelt among us, and the apostles declare that they beheld His glory, the glory as of the only-begotten of the Father, full of grace and truth. The text uses very important words. It says that God sent His Son "in the likeness of sinful flesh," not in the likeness of flesh, for that would not be true, but in the same likeness as our *sinful flesh*. He was to all intents and purposes like ourselves, tempted in all points like as we are, though without sin, with all our sinless infirmities, with all our tendencies to suffer, with everything human in Him except that which comes to be human through human nature having fallen. He was perfectly man; He was like ourselves; and God sent Him in the likeness of sinful flesh. Though it is eighteen hundred years ago and more, the Christmas bells seem to ring on. The joy of His coming is still in our hearts. He lived here His two or three and thirty years, but He was sent, the text tells us, for a reason which caused Him to die. He was sent for sin. This may mean that He was sent to do battle with sin, or that He was sent because sin was in the world; or, best of all, He was sent to be a sin-offering. He was sent that He might be the substitute for sinners. God's great plan was this, that inasmuch as His justice could not overlook sin, and sin must be punished, Jesus Christ should come and take the sin of His people upon Himself, and upon the accursed tree, the cross of ignominious note,

should suffer what was due on our behalf, and that then through His sufferings the infinite love of God should stream forth without any contravention of His infinite justice. This is what God did. He sent His Son to Bethlehem; He sent His Son to Calvary: He sent His son down to the grave, and He has now recalled Him unto the excellent glory where He sitteth at the right hand of God.

II. Ask you now, secondly, WHAT WAS THE IMMEDIATE RESULT OF THIS?

Why, brethren, the immediate result was that God condemned sin. Let me show you how He did it. The very fact that God—I must use language which is for us, not for Him—was under necessity, if He would save men and yet not violate His justice, to send His Son, *condemned sin*, for it said, "This sin is such an evil, such a plague, such a curse, that it cannot be stamped out of the world unless God Himself comes down among the sons of men." His usual presence among men in the power that sustains nature, it seemed, was not enough to put out sin. So venomous the serpent, that there must be born a seed of the woman that should bruise that serpent's head. This world of ours was such an Augean stable, that omnipotence itself must come down and turn the sluices of divine perfection right through the hideous heap, or else washed it never could be; therefore down from the highest glory came the Saviour, that He might achieve a task which the law could not do in that it was weak through the flesh, but which He in the likeness of sinful flesh undertook to accomplish.

Moreover, *the life of our Lord Jesus Christ* on earth *condemned sin*. You can often condemn an evil best by putting side by side with it the palpable contrast, the purity to which it is so thoroughly alien, so totally opposite. So blameless was the conduct of this most blessed Man of Nazareth throughout His entire career, that even those who accept not His deity, do homage to His integrity. We have had in our own day, and in our midst, we grieve to say, some who have blasphemed our faith with bitterest words, but even they have paused as if they stood abashed when they came to survey the character of Him whose divinity and mission they refused to acknowledge. They have seen about His life a something that they saw nowhere else, and if they have not adored they have admired. There was a condemnation of sin in His very look. The Pharisees felt it. They could not meet or encounter Him without discovering and exposing what hypocrites they were. All sorts of men felt it. They could not fail to see through the purity of His life what crooked, ugly, deformed lives their own were in comparison with His, and thus the very existence of Christ, and the example of Christ, condemned sin. But what shall we who are His disciples say to that assemblage of graces found only in Him, each sparkling with peerless lustre, and all blending with such exquisite gracefulness that we are at once moved with awe and touched with love as we contemplate Him? Such majesty, yet such meekness in His mien; such solemnity, yet such tenderness in His speech; so impartial in judgment, yet so forgiving in temper; so full of zeal, yet so equally full of patience; so keen to detect malice, yet so slow to resent it; such a wise Mentor in the inner circle of His followers, yet such a gentle sympathising friend. Say, my brethren— why I think some of us never commit a trespass or betray an infirmity, but we say, and say it to ourselves, Would Christ have done this? And the remembrance of His holy, harmless life, condemns sin in our conscience.

God condemned sin still further, *by allowing it to condemn itself.* The scoff has always been on this wise, "Oh, sin, sin! well, it is a mere trifle," and the most of men disdain to allow that their particular transgressions are at all heinous. "No, we never killed anybody; we never committed adultery; we are not thieves; ours are only sins of a common sort; there can be no harm in us." But see now, God seemed to say, "I will let sin do what it can; I will let sin ripen in this world; I will let it grow to its perfection; and men shall see henceforth what sin is from that sample." "What am I aiming at, do you ask?" Why, there came into this world a Man perfectly innocent, harmless, gentle, meek, loving, tender. All His words were love; all His actions were kindness. He raised the dead; He healed the sick; He spake nothing but peace and goodwill towards men. And what did sin do? Sin said, "Away with such a fellow from the earth; it is not fit that He should live." Sin murdered the perfect Man, as it would lay violent hands on all who interfere with its evil maxims and base habits, and utterly destroy all goodness if it could. It convicted itself. Ferocious as a wild beast, it is always to be feared and hated, for it never can be tamed or trusted. That Man came into this world on an errand, and that errand was one of disinterested mercy and pure affection. He need not have come; He had nothing to gain by it; He never did gain anything while here. They would have made Him a king, but He would not be a king. His was all disinterested kindness, benevolence, to his bitterest foes. When they nailed His hands to the wood, they could get nothing vindictive from His lips, but He said, "Father, forgive them, for they know not what they do." He came to save His enemies. Now, surely sin will not touch such a blessed Being as this! Surely sin will say, "I hate His holiness, but I reverence His philanthropy"! Not so, sin shouted: "Crucify Him! crucify Him!" Sin made a jest of His prayers, and mocked at His tears. As we hold and believe, *this Man was no other than God, God's Son.* You know how the wilfulness and atrocity of this sin against Christ is represented to us in the parable of a certain man that had let out his vineyard unto husbandmen. He sent unto them his servant that at the time of the crops they should pay a portion of the produce, but they treated him despitefully, and when he sent another they beat him, and stoned another. At last he said, "I will send my son; they will surely reverence my son." But they said, "This is the heir; let us kill Him! and the inheritance shall be ours." And so with this very God, they seemed to say, "Let us kill Him;" and though they could not give a death blow to His deity, they showed that they would if they could, and redhanded sin stands out before the world this day as a deicide. It would wreak its vengeance on Him that inhabiteth eternity if it could, and hurl destruction at the lawgiver, to secure a triumph for its own lawlessness. The fool hath said in his heart, "There is no God," and the great aim of human nature is to get rid of God in fact as well as in faith; this it attempts to do, either by discoursing of Him in an abstraction, or by setting up blocks of wood and stone in simple credulity, as a correct representation of His fashion or His attributes. To the one true and glorious God men will not pay any allegiance. If sin had power equivalent to its purpose, had its means to accomplish its menace, it would cast down the throne of the Most

High, and assail Jehovah Himself in the heaven of His dwelling. Oh, thou abominable thing, sin! Thou standest convicted. God shall smite thee, thou accursed thing. Thou hast condemned thyself by thine own act and deed, even where thy craftiness has been foiled and thy desperate prowess has issued in defeat.

Thus, brethren, I have shown you that Christ's coming condemned sin, Christ's life condemned it, and by putting Christ to death, sin condemned itself. But here comes the peculiar doctrine of our faith. God condemned sin *by bruising Christ,* by suffering Him to be put to death, by deserting him in the hour of nature's extremity, by permitting His soul to undergo an agony beyond all conception. Sirs, our sin, your sin, my sin, the sin of as many as do believe or ever shall believe in Jesus, was laid on Him, "who His own self bare our sins in His own body on the tree." He was the Father's Best-beloved. He had never offended, and the Father loved Him. Will He not spare Him? Will He not spare Him? Infinite love loved us, and infinite love loved Christ, but infinite love said, "I cannot pass by sin without punishment; what justice demands must be done;" and it was love that made the Father pour forth the vials of His wrath upon the head of the Only-begotten Son, till in the garden He sweat, as it were, great drops of blood falling down to the ground. Oh, there was an inner sweat, of which those outward drops were but the faint types! His soul was exceeding sorrowful even unto death, and then on the cross He died. I have often painted you that scene, but for the present I forbear. His inward sufferings, his soul-sufferings, were the soul of His sufferings.

"'Twas thus the Lord of life appeared,
And sigh'd, and groan'd, and pray'd, and fear'd;
Bore all incarnate God could bear,
With strength enough, and none to spare."

There and then He made expiation for man's guilt. What a condemnation that was of sin! Methinks it were as though the righteous Judge of all the earth had said, "I cannot suffer sin, I cannot pass by sin, even if it lie on the innocent one; I must smite even My own Son if sin be imputed to Him; I cannot and will not clear the guilty; the Judge of all the earth am I. If My Son should be spared, or My law should be put on one side, the thousands of worlds I govern might well be in high revolt against Me." Poised was the cause in the impartial scales of justice, and on His Son He visited our transgressions, into His hands the cup of wrath was given; against Him the sword of vengeance was unsheathed; of Him the uttermost penalty was exacted; that we for whom He surety stood might be clear by His dying, justified by His rising from the dead, and henceforth accepted in the Beloved.

Now, I know it will be said, "But why did not God exercise the sovereign prerogative of mercy, and at once forgive sin? Why did He not by His own absolute fiat condone the offence and pardon the offenders?" I reply, how then could God have condemned sin? If sin be only such a simple misdemeanour as an arbitrary act of God can forgive, then its evil were not infinite in turpitude, the prolific parent of crimes and curses numberless. But if there must be an atonement for it, an atonement as wonderful as that which I have essayed to preach to you, then sin descried in the light of that altar-fire where it was propitiated, appears worse than felonious.

worse than any word I can use, more hideous than any ghastly form I can depict. Its summary condemnation alone could vindicate the unimpeachable holiness of the Judge. Some one else may say, "But if the righteous law be really so spiritual, and carnal man so weak, why not alter the law and adapt it to the exigency?" I reply again, because such a procedure would not condemn the sin. On the contrary, it would condemn the law. It would be an admission that the law originally was too severe. It would be making an apology for sinners, and henceforth encourage them to sin with both hands greedily. To relax the prescript, and forego the punishment, were to trifle with sin and make the law to be a thing contemptible. The criminal will ask o have it altered still, and lowered to suit his basest passions. But would not a part-punishment have sufficed, and then let the rest be excused? I answer, No; that, too, would have condemned the law for having asked a greater punishment than was absolutely necessary. Whatever was laid down as being the necessary punishment of sin must be enforced, *or else God* changes, the statute is set aside, and the law breaks down altogether. The only way to condemn sin to the full is this—let the sin be punished, and if there be one found who, without a breach of justice, may be permitted to suffer in the stead of another, let him so suffer; but let care be taken that it is no sham, but a reality; that sin, from the dignity of the sufferer, from the amount of the suffering, from the completeness of the atonement, is effectually and thoroughly condemned.

Thus far have I led you. God has sent His Son into the world, and has thus condemned sin by His Son's life and death.

III. Now, thirdly, I come to the main business of this evening, which is TO SHOW YOU HOW THIS DOES WHAT THE LAW COULD NOT DO.

There were two desirable things, you will remember, that I started with. The first was, that the offender should be pardoned. You can clearly see how that is done. If Jesus did suffer in my stead, henceforth it becomes not only mercy that absolves me, but justice that seals my acquittal.

> "Since Christ hath my discharge procured,
> And freely, in my room, endured
> The whole of wrath divine;
> Payment God cannot twice demand,
> First at my bleeding Surety's hand,
> And then again at mine."

If Jesus paid the debt, it is paid, and I am clear. There is, therefore, now no condemnation to them that are in Christ Jesus. Your only question, dear hearers, is—have you a part in the sufferings of Christ? Was He a substitute for you? According to this grand old Book, on which we fix our trust as an infallible guide in this matter, Jesus died for every soul that trusts Him. So is it written—"He that believeth, and is baptized, shall be saved." Have you these personal evidences? Do you unfeignedly trust Him? Then you are forgiven. You are this night absolved; you may rejoice in God through our Lord Jesus Christ, by whom you have now received the atonement. Your sins, past, present, and to come, are all blotted out.

> "Here's pardon for transgressions past,
> It matters not how black their caste;
> And, O my soul, with wonder view,
> For sins to come, here's pardon too."

The red mark is drawn across the bill, it is discharged. The load of obligation is gone, from its thraldom thou art released. The sin of the believer has ceased to be. Christ has been punished in his stead. Is not that simple enough for all of you to understand, and scriptural enough for all of you to receive?

But how comes the second necessity to be supplied? How does this tend henceforth to make such a man pure in heart, and produce in his very soul an aversion and a total abhorrence of sin? This is not difficult to apprehend, if you will give it a little quiet consideration. When the Holy Spirit comes with power into a man's heart, and renews his nature (oh, matchless miracle!)—a miracle that has been wrought many times in this house; forthwith the unhallowed and the impure are made chaste, the dishonest are made honest, and the ungodly are made to love God— "for if any man be in Christ he is a new creature." Such motives as the following now begin to influence his mind. The man says, "Did God, instead of forgiving my sin without a penalty, make the anointed Substitute smart for it? Then I reverence the lawgiver, the mighty lawgiver who would not, even though He is love itself, suffer His law to be broken. I reverence that dreadful Judge of all the earth. who, though I be His child, yet since I had offended, would not spare me for my sin, but executed the penalty that was due to me upon Himself. Himself! for Christ His Son was one with Him, and dear to His Father's soul. Why, more than that, it makes me feel an intense love to Him. What, was He so just and yet was He so determined to save me, that He would not spare His only Son. but freely gave Him up to die? O blessed God, I tremble at Thy justice, which yet I come to admire; but oh! Thy love— what shall I say of it? It wins my love.' I must love Thee, my God; the just and yet the gracious One. I must love Thee."

Then there comes into the heart *an enmity against the sin which caused the suffering of Christ.* "What," says the heart, "did sin make my Redeemer, who gave Himself for me, suffer? Then, away with it; it must be a'foul, vile thing, to put such a blessed One as He to death; I will not tolerate it." It makes the soul cry, "Revenge" against itself; a blessed vengeance it decrees against all sin. "Bring out the gallows, and let sin be hanged thereon. The dearest idol I have known, bring out the hammer and the axe, and let it be broken in pieces. The choicest transgression I have ever nurtured in my bosom, I see what a viper it is, and I shake it into the fire; away with it. If it grieves my Christ, and makes Him bleed, my own beloved Saviour, away with it, away with it!"

And let me tell you, there is another matter that comes in and supplies the basis for holiness, such a basis as cannot be found anywhere else. The man says, "Now I am pardoned through the love of Jesus Christ and the shedding of His precious blood; I have God for my Father, and He is my friend; there is no one to part me from Him; my sin was laid on another, it has been expiated, and it is gone: I am saved, I am forgiven." The man is happy; the man is cheerful; the man is joyful, and what springs up? "Now," says he, "there is that glorious Christ of God who has wrought this for me, and I see Him with the eye of faith; I see Him in heaven, and I am His man—body soul, and spirit; I am not my own; He has bought me with His blood; I lay myself at His feet; what He bids me do I will do; what He asks of me I will give; what He forbids me, it shall be my joy never to touch."

Here breaks forth in the soul an enthusiastic love to the person of Jesus Christ, which, as it burns and glows like a refining fire, becomes a great motive-power to the spirit to pursue holiness in the power of God. When do the soldiers fight best, sirs? When you have read their rules to them as to how they must keep place, and how they must load their guns, and fire in due order? No; law does not inflame the soldier with martial ardour, though it is good in its place. But just when the battle lingers—take an instance from our own history—just when the battle was about to turn with the Ironsides, and the Cavaliers were coming on with one of Rupert's hot charges, ready to break the line, and the brave old Ironsides were half inclined to turn, up came the general old Noll, riding on his horse, and they passed the word along, "'Tis he, boys; here he comes!" and every man grew into a giant at once; they stood like iron columns, like walls of granite, and the Cavaliers as they came on broke like waves against rocks, and dashed away, and were heard of no more. It was the presence of the man that fired each soldier. And so it is now with us. We believe in Jesus Christ. We know that He is with His church. He was dead, but He rose again. He has gone to heaven, but His spirit is with us— King of Kings, and Lord of lords is He. If He seems to sleep in the midst of our ship, yet He sleeps with His hand on the helm, and He will steer the vessel rightly; and now the love that we bear His name steers our souls to holiness, to self-denial, to seek after God, to make full proof of the faith and the fellowship of the gospel, to seek to become like God, and to be absorbed into God that He may be all in all. This is what was wanted—a stimulus potent enough, under God's grace, to break through the barriers of sin. What the law could not do in that it was weak through the flesh, God has accomplished by sending His own dear Son in the likeness of sinful flesh for sin, and having condemned sin in the flesh, He has now removed its guilt, and destroyed its power.

To the best of my ability, I have thus set before you a doctrine in which my own heart finds perfect rest. I would that you all had the like rest, the same sweet heart's ease in your breasts. Two words of counsel I must address to you before I close. One is, *I do beseech you to receive this doctrine*. It is of God; it is true. They who first bore witness to it were humble fishermen. Unsophisticated as they were, they had no motive for inventing it; indeed, it is a theory which they had not the brains to invent if they had tried. They nearly all of them died for it. They never gained honour or emolument by professing or publishing it, but they endured contumely and persecution even to the loss of their lives, for testifying to what they saw and heard. Ah! since then the church has had long lines of martyrs. Who could help bearing the same witness, fortified with the same assurances, whatever it might cost them, however they might be ridiculed as ignorant, old-fashioned, and not up to the progress of the age? I pray you accept this—specially would I address myself to those of you whom I have preached to so long, who yet are unsaved. I do not know what forms of speech to use with some of you, or in what shape to fashion my appeal. If I thought that coming round to your pews and kneeling down before you, and entreating you to receive Christ would have any effect upon you,

I would fain do it. I have prayed very anxiously that if perhaps my voice should not be the one, that God would bless to your conversion, my brother's voice next Sabbath-day, or that of some one else on the following Sabbath on which I shall be absent, may have the effect of leading you to Christ. O that you may but be saved! I will make no terms with God if you will but accept Christ. I am somewhat of the mind of a dear little girl, who is now dying, if she has not already departed. She sent a little note in pencil to her minister, and it was delivered at the prayer-meeting. "A little believer in Christ, nine years of age, asks the prayers of the people for her father, for he is an unbeliever." She was visited by her minister, and she said to him, "O sir, I have asked father to come and hear you preach; I thought he might get saved, but he mocks at it, and will not come; but, sir, he must hear you preach one day, and that is when I shall be buried, for I shall soon be with Jesus. O sir! when he stands at the grave do be sure to tell him about the love of Christ, and say that I asked you to do so, for perhaps when I am dead that might help to break his heart." Oh, yes! if anything would break your hearts, that were a mercy if it happened. If the preacher himself were dead, if his interment in the grave could bring you to the Saviour, it were a cheap price to pay. Only may God save you; may the Holy Ghost renew you; may the Saviour wash you in His precious blood; and I shall be well content.

The other word is this. You that profess to be Christians, to believe what I have told you, *take care that you do not give the lie to it*. Not everyone that says, "I am a Christian" is so. Nay, nay. It is a heathenish nation this, that has had the impudence to call itself Christian. "Strait is the gate, and narrow is the way, which leadeth unto life, and few there be that find it," is as true to-day as when Christ uttered it. To be a Christian in name is nothing worth; to be a Christian in the power of these truths, having received Christ Jesus the Lord, and being rooted and built up in Him, and stablished in the faith as ye have been taught, that is to be a Christian in all good conscience. If your lives should be unholy, if you tradespeople should be dishonest, if you rich people should be proud and selfish, if you poor people should be envious, if any of you should be drunken, if you should be loose in speech, if you should be unclean in deed or in conversation, men may say: "The preacher has only laid down a theory, let him show us facts." Well; but I can show facts. I bless God that I have it in my own soul to say that I believe the most of you do so live as to prove these things; even though there should be others of you of whom I tell you even weeping that you are the enemies of the cross of Christ. Enemies! of all enemies the worst of enemies, too, because whilst professing to be actuated by them you live in opposition to the teachings of Jesus. O blessed Saviour! wounded worse by Thy treacherous friends than by Thine open foes. O holy faith! more damaged by Thy professors than by Thy antagonists. The Lord grant us to walk and live in holiness, and in His fear, till the Master shall come, as come He will a second time without a sin-offering unto salvation.

Finally, brethren and sisters, farewell. Let me dismiss you with a blessing.

HEIRS OF GOD

"And if children, then heirs; heirs of God, and joint-heirs with Christ."—Romans viii. 17.

THIS chapter—the 8th of Romans—is, like the garden of Eden, full of all manner of delights. Here you have all the necessary doctrines to feed upon, and luxurious truths with which to satisfy your soul. One might well have been willing to be shut up as a prisoner in paradise, and one might well be content to be shut up to this one chapter, and never to be allowed to preach from any other part of God's Word. If this were the case, one might find a sermon in every line; nay, more than that, whole volumes might be found in a single sentence by anyone who was truly taught of God. I might say of this chapter, "All its paths drop fatness." It is among the other chapters of the Bible like Benjamin's mess which was five times as much as that of any of his brothers. We must not exalt one part of God's Word above another; yet, as "one star differeth from another star in glory," this one seems to be a star of the first magnitude, full of the brightness of the grace and truth of God. It is an altogether inexhaustible mine of spiritual wealth, and I invite the saints of God to dig in it, and to dig in it again and again. They will find, not only that it hath dust of gold, but also huge nuggets, which they shall not be able to carry away by reason of the weight of the treasure.

I notice, in this chapter, and also in many other parts of Paul's writings, that it is his habit to make a kind of ladder—a sort of Jacob's ladder, let me call it,—which he begins to climb. But every step he takes leads to another, and that one to another, and that again to yet another. You see it here. "As many as are led by the Spirit of God,"—there is the leading of the Spirit,—"they are the sons of God." And when he gets to sonship, then he says, "And if children, then heirs." So he gets to heirship, and he climbs still higher when he says, "heirs of God, and joint-heirs with Christ." I think he means us to judge, by this mode of writing, that this ought to be the style of our Christian experience. Every measure of grace which we receive should lead us to seek after something higher still. We are never to say, "This is the pinnacle of grace; I cannot get beyond this." Self-satisfaction is the end of progress; so we are constantly to cry, "Higher, and yet higher still; onward and upward,"—and still to ask to be filled yet more completely with all the fulness of God.

My text is far too large for me to attempt to preach from it in an exhaustive style; so I will just make four observations upon it; and even those observations will only give you a bird's-eye view of the great truths here revealed. May God grant that, in each of those four things, there may be food for your souls!

I. The first thing that I see in the text is THE GROUND OF HEIRSHIP: "If children, then heirs." The children of God are heirs of God, and they come to be heirs through being His children, and in no other way.

Mark that *we are not heirs of God as the result of creation*. I cannot say what we might have been

by reaction had the Fall not ruined us; but that fatal disobedience of our first parent robbed us of any inheritance that might have come to us in that way; and now, by nature, we are "children of wrath, even as others," but certainly not heirs of the promise or heirs of the grace of God. No, beloved friend, nature will never entitle you to be a joint-heir with Christ. Whatever you may think of your human nature,—and you may suppose that it is not so depraved as the nature of others,—you may even get the notion that yours is a very superior sort of human nature;—well, let it be what it may, it will not entitle you to this inheritance. For as it was not the children of the flesh who were necessarily the heirs of the old covenant, even as Ishmael, born after the flesh, was not the heir, but Isaac, born after the spirit; and not Esau, but Jacob; so is it now. It is not what you are by nature,—not that which is born of the flesh, but what you are by grace,—that which is born of the Spirit,—that is the ground upon which heirship may be claimed before God. So, my dear hearer, if you are in a state of nature,—if you have never passed out of that state into a state of grace,—this text has nothing to do with you.

And, further, as our heirship with God depends upon our being the children of God, *it does not depend upon our natural descent.* I have already shown you that it does not depend upon our nature, but there is another phase of that truth which needs to be mentioned. There were some, of old, who said, "We have Abraham to our father"; but being born as sons of Abraham after the flesh availed not to give them any part in the inheritance which was according to the Spirit. And, to-day, there are some who say, "We are the children of godly parents. We were born in a Christian land, so, of course, we are Christians." Not so, you are no more Christians, on that ground, than if you were the children of the Hottentot in his kraal. You need as much to be born again as does "the heathen Chinee"; you need to be regenerated by the Holy Spirit as much as if you had been taught from your childhood to bow your knee to a block of wood or stone. O ye, who are the inhabitants of this so-called Christian country, you stand before the living God in no sort of preference to the heathen, except that you have the privilege of hearing the gospel; but if you reject it, it shall be more tolerable for the people of Sodom and Gomorrah, and the inhabitants of heathen lands, in the day of judgment than for you. Did not our Lord Jesus Christ say that "many shall come from the east and west, and shall sit down with Abraham, and Isaac, and Jacob, in the kingdom of heaven; but the children of the kingdom"—the favoured ones of His day, or of our day,—"shall be cast out into outer darkness: there shall be weeping and gnashing of teeth"?

Further, as the inheritance is not by creation, nor by natural descent, *neither can it come by meritorious service*. The apostle says, "If *children*, then heirs"; —not, "if *servants*." You may toil, and keep on toiling all your life, but that will not make you an heir of God. The servant in your house, however diligent, is not your heir; for a servant to claim to be the heir, would not be tolerated for a moment in a court of law. The servant may be able truthfully to say, "I have been in my master's house these many years, neither transgressed I at any time his commandments; and all that is right for a servant to do, I have done for him from my youth up;" but if he were to go on to ask, "What lack I yet?" the reply would be, "You lack the one thing that is absolutely essential to heirship, namely, sonship." Oh, how this truth cuts at the root of all the efforts of those who hope to win heaven by merit, or to obtain the favour of God by their own exertions! To them all, God says what Jesus said to Nicodemus, "Ye must be born again." Birth alone can make you children, and you must be children if you are to be heirs. O sirs, if you remain what you are by nature, you may strive to do what you please; but, when you have dressed out the child of nature in its finest garments, it is still only the child of nature, finely dressed, but not the child of God. Ye must be, by a supernatural birth, allied to the living God, for, if not, all the works that you may perform will not entitle you to the possession of the inheritance of the Most High.

And as good works cannot do this, *neither can any ceremonial observances*. You know that there is a ceremony of which children are taught to say, "In my baptism, wherein I was made a member of Christ, a child of God, and an inheritor of the kingdom of heaven." It does not matter what people may say in order to make an excuse for believing that this statement is true, for it is as gross a falsehood as was ever put into human language. We know it is not true. Look where we may, we can see numbers of persons who were sprinkled in their infancy, or were even baptized after they had reached years of discretion, but their conduct shows that they are not members of Christ, children of God, or inheritors of the kingdom of heaven. And as that ceremony cannot make them Christians, neither can any other, whether it be devised by man, or ordained by God himself, for God never intended that any ceremony should take the place of the new birth, the regeneration, which must be wrought by the Spirit of God himself.

"Not all the outward forms on earth,
  Nor rites that God has given,
Nor will of man, nor blood, nor birth,
  Can raise a soul to heaven.

"The sovereign will of God alone
  Creates us heirs of grace;
Born in the image of His Son,
  A new peculiar race."

And, without the Holy Spirit to carry out that sovereign will of God by making us to be born into the image of His Son, we are not His heirs, for thus it stands in our text, "*If children*, then heirs;" which implies that, if we are not children, we are not heirs.

So this is the all-important enquiry for us to make. Do we, beloved friends, possess this qualification which is absolutely essential to our heirship? Have we been born again? We cannot have been born into God's family when we were born the first time, for Christ himself said, "That which is born of the flesh is flesh," and nothing more;—"and that which is born of the Spirit is spirit," so we must be born of the Spirit, we must be born again, born from above, if we are to be children of God. Did you ever undergo that great change? Do you know what regeneration means? I do not mean, have you read of it in the Confession of Faith, but have you experienced it in your own soul? Are you new creatures in Christ Jesus? For, as the Lord liveth, before whom I stand, if any of us have not been created anew in Christ Jesus, if we have not been born again by the regenerating power of the Holy Spirit, we cannot possibly be the children of God, and heirs according to the promise.

If we have been thus regenerated, we shall certainly know it. There may be times when we shall doubt it; but we shall know it, partly by the indwelling of the Spirit, as Paul wrote to the Galatians, "Because ye are sons, God hath sent forth the Spirit of His Son into your hearts, crying, Abba, Father;" and in the verse before our text, we read, "The Spirit himself beareth witness with our spirit, that we are the children of God." Do you know anything, dear friend, about this witness-bearing by the Holy Spirit? I have often asked myself that question, so I feel free to ask you the same. This is not a thing that you may know, or may not know, and yet possibly may be safe; but you must have this witness of the Holy Spirit, or else the witness of your own spirit will be a very doubtful thing indeed. The Holy Spirit never confirms a false witness, but a true witness He will confirm; and if the witness of your spirit be true, you will have, more or less definitely, the witness of the Spirit within you, bearing confirmatory testimony that it is even so.

Those who are truly the children of God have yet another mark by which they can be recognized, namely, that there is a likeness to their Heavenly Father begotten in them. If a man says to you, "I am the son of So-and-so,"—some old friend of yours,—you look into his face to see whether you can trace any likeness to his father. So, when a man says to us, "I am a child of God," we have the right to expect that there shall be at least some trace of the character of God visible in his walk and conversation. Come, dear friend, with all your imperfections, are you seeking to be an imitator of God, as one of His dear children? Do you try to do that which He wishes you to do? Do you make His Son to be your Exemplar? Do you strive after holiness? Are you aiming at obedience to those divine commands, "Be ye holy; for I am holy": "be ye therefore perfect, even as your Father which is in heaven is perfect?" Do you feel that, because you are a child of God, it becomes you to walk even as His firstborn Son walked while He was here below? Remember that, without holiness no man shall see the Lord; because, without holiness, no man has the evidence that he is indeed a child of God.

And, once more, the main evidence of our being children of God, by the new birth, lies in our believing in the Lord Jesus Christ. "As many as received Him, to them gave He power to become the sons of God, even to them that believe on His name; which were born, not of blood, nor of the will of the flesh, nor of the will of man, but of God." There are many evidences of the life of God in the soul, but there is no other that is so abiding as the possession of faith in Jesus Christ. Perhaps, dear friend, you are afraid to say that you have the likeness of God upon you, although others can see it; but I hope you are not afraid to say, "I do believe that Jesus is the Christ," and the apostle John says, "Whosoever believeth that Jesus is the Christ is born of God." If you accept him as appointed and anointed of God to be your Saviour, and commit your soul into His hands, then be you sure that you are a child of God, for true, simple, sincere faith in the Lord Jesus exists only in the heart of the regenerate. No unregenerate man ever did, or ever could, believe in Jesus Christ; but where the Lord has given the divine life, He gives faith at the same time,—faith which is the surest proof of the existence of that divine life in the soul.

God grant to each one of you the grace to test yourself by these four questions:—"Have I been born again? Have I the Spirit of adoption? Have I at least some likeness to my Heavenly Father? Do I believe in Jesus Christ?" If so, then you are a child of God, and that childhood is the ground of heirship, so we can leave that point, and go on to the next.

II. The text teaches, in the second place, THE UNIVERSALITY OF HEIRSHIP TO ALL THE CHILDREN OF GOD: "If children, then heirs;"—not some of them heirs, but, "if children, then heirs," all of them without an exception. Proven that they are children, it is also proven that they are heirs. It is not so among men, for, often, it is only the firstborn sons who are the heirs; but, with God, the rule is, "If children,"—whenever born,—"then heirs."

Why is it that all the children of God are His heirs? First, *because the principle of priority as to time cannot possibly enter into this question.* There is a Firstborn, who had priority by nature, and honour, and right; but He is "the firstborn among many brethren;" and in Him all the rest of the children of God are also firstborn, for Paul writes of "the general assembly and church of the firstborn, which are written in heaven." The question of the time of birth is, sometimes, a matter of very great concern on earth. In the case of twins, a few minutes may make all the difference between "his lordship" and his brother who is no lord at all,— between the brother who shall be heir of many broad acres, and the one who shall go forth upon the broad ocean to earn his bread. But, with God's children, there is no difference in point of time. Adam, if he was the first man converted, certainly has no priority over Paul, although Paul says that he was as "one born out of due time." Noah, an early member of God's great family, has no preference over Abraham; indeed, Abraham seems to be mentioned with greater honour than any of those who had gone before him; certainly, they had no priority over him. Time has to do with time, but time has not to do with eternity; so, whether you, my brother, were born to God fifty years ago, and I five-and-twenty years ago, and our young friend over there five-and-twenty days ago, it makes no difference. "If children, then heirs," because the date of birth cannot come into our reckoning when we have to do with eternal things.

Again, we know that *the love of God is the same toward all His children.* They are all His children,—all chosen, all redeemed, all regenerated, all called, all justified, and they shall be all glorified. Where a father loves all his children alike, his disposition leads him to treat them all alike, both as to what he gives them now, and also as to what he will leave them as an inheritance; but, sometimes, circumstances—such as the law of the land and the title-deeds of estates—prevent the father from treating all alike. But, in the case of the children of God, laws cannot hamper or hinder Him. He is the great Law-Maker, and He can control circumstances so as to do everything according to the dictates of His own heart; and His heart of love says, "I have loved all My children alike, and they shall all have the blessing;" and so they shall, beloved. Though you, my dear friend, think yourself obscure, and one of the least in God's Israel, your name is just as prominently written upon the heart of Christ as the names of His apostles are, and you are as dear to the Lord as the very noblest among His saints. Indeed, He carries the lambs in His bosom, so the little ones have the best chariot of all. He may leave the sheep to walk, but He carries the lambs; and He always takes special care of the weak and feeble. "If children, then heirs," because all God's children are qually partakers of their Father's love.

Again, we know, from Scripture, that *all the children of God are favoured with the same promise.* If you turn to the 6th chapter of the Epistle to the Hebrews, and the 18th verse, you will find there what Paul says to all the Lord's children. What a precious passage that is where he tells us that, "be two immutable things, in which it was impossibly for God to lie, we might have a strong consolation, who have fled for refuge to lay hold upon the hope set before us." In the previous verse, he mentions the heirs of promise, and by that expression he means all the children of God, for they are all heirs according to the promise, and all heirs of the promise. Well, then, as God has given them a promise, He will fulfil it; and that promise is that they shall be heirs of this world, and also heirs of the world to come; and He will fulfil it to them all, and keep His oath by which He has confirmed it to them, so they shall surely be His heirs.

Notice, again, that all God's children are His heirs *because they are all equally related to Him through whom the heirship comes,* for every child of God is neither more nor less than brother to the Lord Jesus Christ, yea, a member of His body, of His flesh, and of His bones. In this brotherhood with Christ, there can be no degrees; a man is not partly a brother, and partly not a brother. If he is a brother of Christ, he *is* His brother. A man is not partly in Christ, and partly out of Christ. If one with Christ, he *is* one with Christ; and all the members of Christ's mystical body are quickened with the same life, and shall have the same heaven to dwell in for ever. Seeing, then, that we are all one in Christ Jesus, the heirship which comes to us by way of the Firstborn must come equally to all the children.

And there is one more very comforting reflection, and that is, that *the inheritance is large enough for all the children.* Rich men sometimes have to let their estates go to the eldest son, according to the stupid regulations of this age, "to keep up the family dignity." There are some great lords, who find that they can accumulate wealth enough to set up two or three sets of families, and they do so; but, in other families, there generally are some of the children who must remain lean in order that the firstborn son may grow fat. Now, it is not so with the inheritance of God, because there is enough for all; and there is this peculiarity about it, that every child of God has all the inheritance, yet there is not any the less for all the rest of the family. It can never be said, in relation to human affairs, that each heir has all the inheritance, yet no one else has any less than all. You, my brother, if you are a child of God, are an heir of God, and so am I; and I have not any the less of God because you have Him, and you have not any the less of God because I have Him. Nay, if it were possible for it to be so, I should have the more in the joy that you also have the same blessing, and you would have the more in the joy of seeing others partaking in the same privilege as you have. The whole of God belongs to Christ, and the whole of God belongs to the least member of Christ, all are "heirs of God." So, you see that there was no reason for the exclusion of the younger branches of God's family in order to make up a greater estate for the older ones. All the children of God are the heirs of God, because the inheritance is an infinite one, and there is an infinite inheritance for each one of them.

O beloved, let us dwell for a moment or two on this theme! The text says, "If children, then heirs." It does not say, "If children, then apostles." None of us could attain to that high office. It does not say, "If children, then preachers." Here and there, one of us could claim that title. It does not say, "If children, then deeply-experienced saints." Some of us may never be that. It does not say, "If children, then mighty men of valour." Perhaps some of us are too timid ever to grow to that. It does not say, "If children, then rich men," because some of us are poor. It does not say, "If children, then favoured with health," for some of us have little enough of that boon. It does not say, "If children, then filled with full assurance," for some of us are vexed with many doubts and fears. But it does say, "If children, then heirs." So let us rejoice that we are "heirs; heirs of God, and joint-heirs with Christ." Let us rejoice in that fact now, and let us begin to live worthily of our rank as heirs of God. Let us strive after holiness, and seek to live as becometh the heirs of eternal life, considering what manner of persons we ought to be in all holy conversation and godliness.

Thus I have spoken of the universality of the heirship to all the children of God.

III. Now, thirdly, I want to speak concerning THE INHERITANCE ITSELF: "If children, then heirs; heirs of God."

That little phrase, which I have just uttered, is one which none of us can fully comprehend, and none of us may even attempt to do so. This is the glory of our inheritance, that we are "heirs of God." Will you give me your most earnest attention while I remind you of some of the descriptions of our inheritance which are given in Scripture?

Here is one, which you will find in the 21st chapter of the Revelation, and the 7th verse: "He that overcometh shall inherit all things." That is the extent of your inheritance, "all things"; and it is not a singular expression, for you have it again in 1 Cor. iii. 21, 22: "All things are yours; whether Paul, or Apollos, or Cephas, or the world, or life, or death, or things present, or things to come; all are yours." The richest man who ever lived could not say that all things were his; but the poorest Christian who ever lived can say that. If you turn to the 1st chapter of the Epistle to the Hebrews, the 14th verse, you will find that we are there called "heirs of salvation." Looking on a little further in the same Epistle, in the 6th chapter, and the 17th verse, you will find that we

are called "the heirs of promise." In his Epistle to Titus, the 3rd chapter, and the 7th verse, Paul calls us "heirs according to the hope of eternal life;" while James says, in the 2nd chapter of his Epistle, at the 5th verse, that we are "heirs of the kingdom which God hath promised to them that love Him;" and Peter says, in his first Epistle, the 3rd chapter, and 7th verse, that we are "heirs together of the grace of life." If any preacher wants to deliver a series of sermons upon the heirship of the saints, let him take these texts, and preach upon them. I have not time to do that to-night, and even if I should say all that I could upon all these texts put together, I should not then have said so much as my text says, for that does not speak of "the heirs of promise," or the "heirs of salvation," or the "heirs of the kingdom," but it says, "heirs of God."

"Heirs of God,"—what does that mean? Well, it means, first of all, that *we are heirs to all that God has.* Suppose I am my father's heir, and that he has an old thatched cottage worth a shilling a week,—well, that is what I am heir to; but if I happened to be the heir of the Duke of Westminster, he might take me over a county, and say to me, "That is what you are heir to." Ah, just so! Whatever the father has, that is what the child is heir to. Now think what God has. Stretch your wings, most vivid imagination! Fly abroad, most capacious thought, and when the remotest bounds of space have been crossed, you have only just commenced your endless journey. We will not attempt such a flight as that. We will stop at home, and meditate upon the great truth that all God has is ours because we are His,—heirs of God.

Yet even that, great as it is, is only part of the meaning of our text, for the apostle next means that *God Himself belongs to us.* David said, "The Lord is the portion of mine inheritance," and this is what every child of God can say; so that the portion of each child of God is not only what God has, but what God Himself is. O child of God, thou hast God's power to protect thee, God's eye to guide thee, God's justice to defend thee, God's immutability to be constant to thee, God's infinity to enrich thee! Thou hast God's heart of love, God's hand of power, God's head of glory —time would fail me to tell all that thou hast, for thou hast all that God is to be thine for ever and ever.

All the world's that at present have been created are but as mere trifles compared with what God could make if He so pleased. A thousand, thousand, thousand, thousand worlds, when they were all made, would be but as a handful of dust scattered from His almighty hand, and He could, if He willed, do the like again a thousand, thousand, thousand, thousand times over. "Behold, the nations are as a drop of a bucket, and are counted as the small dust of the balance: behold, He taketh up the isles as a very little thing. And Lebanon is not sufficient to burn, nor the beasts thereof sufficient for a burnt offering." Think of the whole mountain range as one great altar, and all the cedars set ablaze, and then all the beasts that feed there offered up as a burnt sacrifice; yet the prophet says that is not sufficient for God. Then, how great He must be! Oh, make Him great in your hearts, and reverence and adore Him; but when you do so, do not forget to say, "My God! my God! my God!" How often you have that expression in the Psalms! It never could have been there, as the utterance of any mere man, if it had not been first in the eternal purpose of God as the utterance which was to be on the lip of Christ in that dread hour when He cried, "My God, my God, why hast Thou forsaken me?" So, now, each believer can say, "*my* God;" for Jesus Christ Himself puts it, "My Father and your Father; my God, and your God." In some aspects God is as much my God as He is Christ's God, and as much my Father as He is Christ's Father. O beloved, I have got out of my depth now! I wish I were able to go even deeper into this wondrous truth, but there I must leave off what I have to say concerning the inheritance itself: "heirs of God."

IV. My last point is, perhaps, as blessed as any in the whole text. It is, THE PARTNERSHIP OF THE CLAIMANTS TO THE INHERITANCE: "joint-heirs with Christ."

This is, first of all, *the test of our heirship*. Listen. You are not an heir of God alone; you cannot be. You can only be an heir of God through being "in Co."—in company—joint-heir with Christ. Now, are you and Christ in company? That is a simple question. Are you and Christ in company, or do you stand alone? If you stand alone, you are a poor miserable bankrupt, gazetted in the court of heaven; so do not try to stand alone. You will perish if you do. But are Christ and you thus joined together? Have you learned to trust in Christ, to live in Christ, to pray in Christ, to trade with heaven through Christ, and to have everything in Christ? That is the test of heirship. God's child is born God's heir, but it is because He is in Christ, and is born in union with Christ, that He becomes God's heir. If we are out of Christ, we are out of the family of God, and out of the heirship of God. "Without Christ," you are "without God in the world;" but in Christ, joined in company with Christ. you are an heir of God.

This, beloved, seems to me to be *the sweetest part of all the inheritance*. Once let me know that I am one with Christ, and so have become a fellow-heir with Him, and it is like heaven below to my soul. Indeed, I shall like heaven itself all the better, and I shall like all that God is going to give me by-and-by all the better, because I am going to share it with Christ. A good deal depends upon the company we may meet in going to any place to which we may be invited. A person might ask you to his house, and you might not know whether you cared to go there. But suppose the host were to tell you that a very dear friend of yours was going to be there, you would say, then, "Oh, yes, I will go for the sake of having his company!" Now, wherever Jesus Christ is,—I do not care whether it is in the house of a Pharisee, or on some lonely hillside, —it is good to be where He is, and to go shares with Him; it makes everything more sweet to be able to enjoy it with Him. So, beloved, while you are heirs of God, you are not the only heirs; for you are joint-heirs with Christ, and you will share the inheritance with Him. When the Lord Jesus Christ prayed the best prayer that He could pray for His people, do you remember what He asked for? It was this: "Father, I will that they also, whom Thou hast given Me, be with Me where I am;" that they may behold My glory, which Thou hast given Me;"—as if He knew that His people would prize something that belonged to Him better than anything else in all the world, or even in heaven itself. If Christ sups with us, it is a blessed supper though it is only a dish of herbs; but if Christ is absent, it is a poor dinner though there may be joints enough to make the table groan. To my mind, then, this is the sweetness of our inheritance, that it is a joint-heirship with Christ.

This also shows *the greatness of the inheritance;* because, if we are to be joint-heirs with Christ, it cannot be a little thing that we are to share with Him. Can you imagine what the Father would give to His Son as the reward of the travail of His soul? Give yourself time to think what the everlasting God would give to His equal Son, who took upon Himself the form of a servant, and was made in the likeness of men, and who humbled Himself, and became obedient unto death, even the death of the cross. Can you think of a reward that would be large enough for Him? Let the Father's love and the Father's justice judge. Oh, it must be a large inheritance, for such a well-beloved Son, and such an obedient Son as He was! I, a poor worm of the dust, cannot think of anything that I consider good enough for Him. Lord, I would have Him crowned with many crowns, and set up on a glorious, high throne. But what must be the reward which His Father devises for Him? What must be the greatness of the infinite recompense which the infinite God will bestow upon His Only-Begotten? Follow that line of thought as far as you can, and then recollect that you are to be joint-heir with Christ. What he has, you are to share. I will read those wonderful words again; "If children, then heirs; heirs of God, and joint-heirs with Christ; if so be that we suffer with Him, that we may be also glorified together." The same glory that is to be His, He will have us to enjoy with Him.

Again, this joint-heirship *ensures the inheritance to us.* I am quite sure that I should not like to go into partnership with just anybody whom I might meet in the street; indeed, if I had a share in any limited liability company, I would do with it as the man did with the bad bank-note,—lay it down, and run away from it as fast as ever I could. What multitudes of people have been ruined by taking shares in companies which seemed to be the nicest, neatest, most money-getting schemes under heaven! But one need not mind going shares if one has nothing at all, and the other partner is the wealthiest person in the whole world. So, what a blessing it is to go shares with Christ, because we know that He cannot fail. I was thinking, just now, that, if I ever should lose heaven, seeing that I am joint-heir with Christ, it would be "the firm" that would lose it, because we must stand or fall together if we are joint-heirs. Somebody once said to a holy man, "Your soul will be lost." "Then," said he, "Christ will be the loser." He was like the negro, who was quite unconcerned when the ship was being wrecked. He said that he should not lose anything, for he belonged to his massa, and his massa would lose it. Well, what the negro said in his simplicity, we may say in real earnest. If our souls are lost, it will be Christ who will be the loser, for He bought us with His blood, and He will lose what He purchased at so great a cost. And His Father gave us to Him, so He will lose His Father's gift. And He has loved us, and is married to us, so He will lose His spouse, the beloved of His soul. But He will *not* lose us,—He cannot lose us; and if Christ cannot lose His inheritance, then none of His people can lose theirs, for we are joint-heirs with Him. If two partners go into a court of law, and the case is decided against the one, it is against the other also, for the two are one in that matter. So, if the decision could, by any possibility, be given against anyone who is in Christ Jesus, it would be given equally against the Lord Jesus Christ Himself; but that cannot be. How secure, then, is the inheritance of the saints! We are joint-heirs with Christ.

And, my brethren, to conclude, *how this endears*

His love to us,—that He should thus put Himself on the same footing with us as to His heirship, first taking us into union with Himself, making us joint-heirs with Himself, and then Himself going back to heaven to plead for us, and to make it part of His glory up there to prepare the place which we are to share with Him. Does not this bind us fast to Him? If He lets us be sharers in His inheritance in glory, will we not gladly be sharers here in His sufferings and in His shame? Is there anybody who desires to spit upon Christ as they did of old? Then, let him do me the honour to spit upon me for Christ's sake. Is there anyone who has an evil word for Christ? Then, let that word fall upon my ears. Do you not feel, beloved, that it is an honour for you to endure any reproach for Christ's sake? Surely, if we are to be with Him there for ever, it is but right that we should be with Him here; if we are to share the splendour of His throne, we may be joyful to share the dishonour of His cross so far as we may.

I have thus set before you the heirship of the saints, and the way to attain it. I pray God the Holy Spirit to apply the message to His own people, and to make them feel glad in the Lord. As for the others, I have shown that they can only be heirs through being children, and if you are not the children of God by faith in Christ Jesus, I pray the Lord to reveal to you whose children you must be, and what inheritance you must expect to have at the last. Yet I pray you to remember that the way of salvation lies in simply looking to Jesus Christ. May you look to Him to-night,—not to-morrow; ere you leave this place, present this prayer, "O Lord, give me the nature of Thy children, and the spirit of Thy children, and faith in Jesus, as all Thy children have it, for His dear name's sake! Amen."

GLORIOUS PREDESTINATION

"For whom He did foreknow, He also did predestinate to be conformed to the image of His Son, that He might be the first-born among many brethren."—Romans viii. 29.

YOU will have noticed that in this chapter, Paul has been expounding a very deep inward, spiritual experience. He has written concerning the spirit of bondage, and the spirit of adoption; the infirmities of the flesh, and the helpings of the spirit; the waiting for the redemption of the body, and the groanings which cannot be uttered. It was most natural, therefore, that a deep spiritual experience should bring him to a clear perception of the doctrines of grace, for such an experience is a school in which alone those great truths are effectually learned. A lack of depth in the inner life accounts for most of the doctrinal error in the church. Sound conviction of sin, deep humiliation on account of it, and a sense of utter weakness and unworthiness naturally conduct the mind to the belief of the doctrines of grace, while shallowness in these matters leaves a man content with a superficial creed. Those teachings which are commonly called Calvinistic doctrines are usually most beloved and best received by those who have had much conflict of soul, and so have learned the strength of corruption and the necessity of grace.

Note, also, that Paul in this chapter has been treating of the sufferings of this present time; and though by faith he speaks of them as very inconsiderable compared with the glory to be revealed, yet we know that they were not inconsiderable in his case. He was a man of many trials; he went from one tribulation to another for Christ's sake; he swam through many seas of affliction to serve the church. I do not wonder, therefore, that in his epistles he often discourses upon the doctrines of foreknowledge, and predestination, and eternal love, because these are a rich cordial for a fainting spirit. To be cheered under many things, which otherwise would depress him, the believer may betake himself to the matchless mysteries of the grace of God, which are wines on the lees well refined. Sustained by distinguishing grace, a man learns to glory in tribulations also; and strengthened by electing love, he defies the hatred of the world and the trials of life. Suffering is the college of orthodoxy. Many a Jonah, who now rejects the doctrines of the grace of God, only needs to be put into the whale's belly and he will cry out with the soundest free-grace man, "Salvation is of the Lord." Prosperous professors, who do no business amid David's billows and waterspouts, may set small store by the blessed anchorage of eternal purpose and everlasting love; but those who are "tossed with tempest, and not comforted, are of another mind." Let these few sentences suffice for a preface. I utter them not in the spirit of controversy, but the reverse.

Our text begins by the expression, "Whom He did foreknow, He also did predestinate," and many senses have been given to this word "foreknow," though in this case one commends itself beyond every other. Some have thought that it simply means that God predestinated men whose future history he foreknew. The text before us cannot be so understood, because the Lord foreknows the history of every man, and angel, and devil. So far as mere prescience goes, every man is foreknown, and yet no one will assert that all men are predestinated to be conformed to the image of the Lord Jesus. But, it is further asserted that the Lord foreknew who would exercise repentance, who would believe in Jesus, and who would persevere in a consistent life to the end. This is readily granted, but a reader must wear very powerful magnifying spectacles before he will be able to discover that sense in the text. Upon looking carefully at my Bible again I do not perceive such a statement. Where are those words which you have added, "Whom he did foreknow to repent, to believe, and to persevere in grace"? I do not find them either in the English version or in the Greek original. If I could so read them the passage would certainly be very easy, and would very greatly alter my doctrinal views; but, as I do not find those words there, begging your pardon, I do not believe in them. However wise and advisable a human interpolation may be, it has no authority with us; we bow to holy Scripture, but not to glosses which theologians may choose to put upon it. No hint is given in the text of foreseen virtue any more than of foreseen sin, and, therefore, we are driven to find another meaning for the word. We find that the word "know" is frequently used in Scripture, not only for knowledge, but also for favour, love, and complacency. Our Lord Jesus Christ will say, in the judgment, concerning certain persons, "I never knew you," yet in a sense He knew them, for He knows every man; He knows the wicked as well as the righteous; but there the meaning is, "I never knew you in such a respect as to feel any complacency in you or any favour towards you." See also John x. 14, 15, and 2 Tim. ii. 19. In Rom. xi. 2, we read, "God hath not cast away His people which He foreknew," where the sense evidently has the idea of fore-love; and it is so to be understood here. Those whom the Lord looked upon with favour as He foresaw them, He has predestinated to be conformed to the image of His Son. They are, as Paul puts it in his letter to the Ephesians, "predestinated according to the purpose of Him who worketh all things after the counsel of His own will."

I am anxious not to tarry over controverted matters, but to reach the subject of my sermon this morning. Here we have in the text *conformity to Christ* spoken of as *the aim of predestination ;* we have, secondly, *predestination as the impelling force by which this conformity is to be achieved ;* and we have, thirdly, *the firstborn Himself set before us as the ultimate end of the predestination and of the conformity.*—"that HE might be the firstborn among many brethren."

I. Mark then, with care, that OUR CONFORMITY TO CHRIST IS THE SACRED OBJECT OF PREDESTINATION. Into predestination itself I will not now pry. The deeper things shall be left with God. I think it was Bishop Hall who once said, "I thank God I am not of His counsels, but I am of His court." If I cannot understand I will not question, for I am not His counsellor, but I will adore and obey, for I am His servant. Now, to-day, seeing we are here taught the object of His predestination, it will be our business to labour after it, to bless God that He has set such an object before Him, and pray that we may be partakers in it. Here stands the case. Man was originally made in the image of God, but by sin he has defaced that image, and now we who are born into this world are fashioned, not in the heavenly image of God, but in the earthy image of the fallen Adam. "We have borne," says the Apostle, in the first Epistle to the Corinthians, "the image of the earthy." The Lord in boundless grace has resolved that a company whom no man can number, called here "many brethren," shall be restored to His image, in the particular form in which His Eternal Son displays it. To this end Jesus Christ came into the world and bore our image, that we, though His grace, might bear His image. He became a partaker of our infirmities and sicknesses that we might be partakers of the divine nature in all its excellence and purity. Now, therefore, the one thing to which the Lord is working us through His Spirit, both by providence and by grace, is the likeness of the Lord from heaven. He is evermore transforming the chosen, removing the defilement of sin, and moulding them after the perfect model of His Son, Jesus Christ, the second Adam, who is the firstborn amongst the "many brethren."

Now, observe, that this conformity to Christ lies in several things. First, we are to be conformed to Him as to our *nature*. What was the nature of Christ, then, as divine? We must not pry into it, but we know that He was verily of the nature of God. "Begotten, not made," says the Athanasian Creed, and it says truly too, "being of one substance with the Father." Now, we also, though we at our conversion are new creatures, are also said to be "*begotten* again unto a lively hope." To be begotten is something more than to be made: this is a more personal work of God; and that which is begotten is in closer affinity to Himself than that which is only created. As Christ was, as the only begotten of the Father, far above mere creatures; so also to be begotten of God, in our case, means far more than even the first and perfect creation could imply. As to His humanity our blessed Lord, when He came into this world, underwent a birth which was a remarkable type of our second birth. He was born into this world in a very humble place, amidst the oxen, and in the manger; but yet He lacked not the songs of angels and the adoration of the heavenly hosts. Even so we also were born of the Spirit without human observation; men of this world saw no glory whatsoever in our regeneration, for it was not performed by mystic rites, or with sacerdotal pomp. The Spirit of God found us in our low estate, and quickened us without outward display. Yet at that self-same moment, where human eyes saw nothing seraphic, eyes beheld marvels of grace, and angels in heaven rejoiced over one sinner that repented, singing once again, "Glory to God in the highest." When our Lord was born a few choice spirits welcomed His birth; an Anna and a Simeon were ready to take the new-born child into their arms and bless God for Him: and even so there were some that hailed our new birth with much thanksgiving; friends and well-wishers who had watched for our salvation were glad when they beheld in us the true heavenly life, and gladly did they take us up into the arms of Christian nurture. Perhaps, also, there was one who had travailed in birth till Christ was formed in us the hope of glory, and how happy was that spirit to see us born unto God; how did our spiritual parent ponder each gracious word which we uttered, and thank God for the good signs of grace which could be found in our conversation. Then, too, a worse than Herod sought to kill us. Satan was eager that the new-born child of grace should be put to death, and, therefore, sent forth fierce temptations to slay us; but the Lord found a shelter for our infant spiritual life, and preserved the young child alive. In us the living and incorruptible seed abode and grew. As many of you as have been born again have been conformed to the image of Christ in the matter of His birth, and you are now partakers of His nature. It is not possible for us to be divine, yet it is written that we are made "partakers of the divine nature." We cannot be precisely as God is, yet as we have borne the image of the earthy, we shall also bear the image of the heavenly, whatever that image may be. The new birth as surely stamps us with the image of Christ as our first birth impressed us with a resemblance to the fathers of our flesh. Our first birth gave us humanity; our second birth allies us with Deity. As we were conceived in sin at the first, and shapen in iniquity, even so in regeneration our new man is renewed in knowledge after the image of Him that created us. He that sanctifieth and they that are sanctified are all of one; for which cause He is not ashamed to call them brethren.

Furthermore, this conformity to Christ lies in *relationship* as well as in nature. Our Lord is the Son of the Highest,—the Son of God; and truly, beloved, now are we the sons of God, and it doth not yet appear what we shall be, but we know that when

He shall appear we shall be like Him, for we shall see Him as He is. Jehovah has declared that He will be a father unto us, and that we shall be His sons and His daughters. As surely as Jesus is a son, so surely are we, for the same Spirit bears witness to both, as it is written "And because ye are sons, God hath sent forth the Spirit of His Son into your hearts, crying, Abba, Father." When Jesus came into the world as God's Son, He was not left without attesting proofs. His first public appearance, when He came to the waters of baptism, was signalled by a voice out of the excellent glory, which said, "This is my beloved Son," and the descending Spirit, like a dove, rested upon Him. So is it also with us. The voice of God in the word has testified to us our heavenly Father's love; and the Holy Spirit has borne witness with our spirits that we are the children of God. When first we dared to come forward and say "we are on the Lord's side," some of us had sacred tokens of sonship which have never been forgotten by us, and oftentimes since then we have received renewed seals of our adoption from the great Father of our spirits. "He that believeth on the Son hath the witness in himself," so that he can with his brethren say plainly, "we know that we have passed from death unto life." God has given us full assurance, and infallible testimony, and in all this we rejoice. We have believed in Jesus, and it is written, "as many as received Him, to them gave He power to become the sons of God, even to them which believed on His name."

Our Lord was declared to be the Son of God by the actions which He performed, both towards God and towards man. As a Son He served His Father, you could see the nature of God in Him, in His deep sympathy with God and in His exact imitation of God. Whatever God would have done under the circumstances, that Jesus did. You perceive at once by His deeds that His nature was Godlike. His works bore witness of Him. It was evermore most clear that He acted towards God as a son towards a father. Now, in proportion as God's determination has been carried out in us, we also act to God as children towards a loving father, and whereas the children of darkness speak of their own, and like their father, who is a liar, speak the lie; and like their father, who is a murderer, act out wrath and bitterness, even so the children of God speak the truth, for God is true, and they are full of love, for God is love; and their life is light, for their God is light. They feel that they must act, under the circumstances in which they are placed, as they would suppose Jesus would have acted, who is the Son of the ever blessed Father. Moreover, Christ wrought miracles of mercy towards men, which proved Him to be the Son of God. It is true we can work no miracles, yet can we do works which mark God's children. We cannot break the bread and multiply it, we can, however, generously distribute what we have, and thus in feeding the hungry we shall prove ourselves children of our Father who is in heaven; we cannot heal the diseased with our touch, still we can care for the sick, and so in love towards the suffering we can prove ourselves to be children of the tender and ever-pitiful God. But our Lord has told us that greater works than His own shall we do, because He is gone to His Father; and these greater works we do. We can work spiritual miracles. To-day, can we not stand at the grave of the dead sinner, and say, "Lazarus, come forth"? And has not God

often made the dead to rise at our word, by the power of His Spirit! To-day, also, we can preach the gospel of Jesus Christ, casting it about us as it were as our garment, and He that toucheth the hem thereof shall he not also be made whole to-day, even as when Jesus was among men? This day, if we do not break fish and barley loaves, we bring you better food; this day, if we cannot give to men opened eyes and unstopped ears, yet in the teaching of the gospel of Jesus, by the power of the Spirit, the mental eye is cleansed, and the soul's ear also is purged; so that in every child of God, in proportion as he labours in the power of the Spirit for Christ, the works which he does bear witness of him that he is a son of God. His zeal in doing them proves that He has the spirit of a child of God, and the result of those works proves that God works in Him as He will never do in any but His own children. Thus, in relationship, as well as in nature, we are conformed to the image of Christ.

Thirdly, we are to be conformed to the image of Christ in our *experience*. This is the part of the subject from which our craven spirit often shrinks, but if we were wise it would not be so. What was the experience of Christ in this world? for that ours will be. We may sum it up as referring to God, to men, to the devil, and to all evil.

His experience with regard to God, what was that? "Though He were a Son yet learned He obedience by the things which He suffered." Though without sin, He was not without suffering. The firstborn of the divine family was more sorely chastened than any other of the household; He was smitten of God and afflicted till, as the climax of all, He cried *Eloi, Eloi, lama sabachthani.* Oh, the bitterness of that cry— "My God, My God, why hast thou forsaken Me?" It was the Father bruising the firstborn Son; and, if you and I, brethren, are to be conformed to the image of the firstborn, though we may expect from God much fatherly love, we may also reckon that it will show itself in parental discipline. If ye be without chastisement, whereof all are partakers, then are ye bastards, and not sons; but, if ye be true sons, like to the firstborn, the rod will make you smart, and sometimes you will have to say, "My God, my God, why hast thou forsaken me?" "For whom the Lord loveth He chasteneth, and scourgeth every son whom He receiveth. If ye endure chastening, God dealeth with you as with sons; for what son is he whom the father chasteneth not?" If we are predestinated to be conformed to the image of His son, the Lord has predestinated us to much tribulation, and through it shall we inherit the kingdom.

Next survey our dear covenant Head in His experience in relation to men. "He came unto His own, and His own received Him not." "He was despised and rejected of men." He said, "Reproach hath broken Mine heart, and I am full of heaviness." Now, brethren, in the very proportion in which we are conformed to the image of Christ we shall have to "go forth unto Him without the camp, bearing His reproach;" for the disciple, if he be a true disciple, is not above his Master, or the servant about his Lord. If they have called the Master of the house Beelzebub, much more will they call them of His household by some yet more opprobrious title, if they can invent it. The saints of God must not expect crowns where Christ found a cross; they must not reckon to ride in triumph through those streets which saw the Saviour hurried to a malefactor's death. We must suffer with Him if we would be glorified with Him. Fellowship in His sufferings is needful to communion with His glory.

Then, consider our Lord's experience with regard to the prince of the power of the air. Satan was no friend to Christ, but finding Him in the desert he came to Him with this accursed "if"—"If thou be the Son of God." With that attack upon His Sonship the fiend commenced the battle. "If thou be the Son of God." You know how thrice he assailed Him with those temptations which are most likely to be attractive to poor humanity, but Jesus overcame them all. The arch enemy, the old dragon, was always nibbling at the heel of our great Michael, who has for ever crushed his head. We are predestinated to be conformed to Christ in that respect; the serpent's subtlety and cruelty will assail us also. A tempted Head involves tempted members. Satan desires to have us and to sift us as wheat. He attacked the Shepherd, and he will never cease to worry the sheep. Inasmuch as we are of the seed of the woman, there must be enmity between us and the seed of the serpent.

And, as to all evil, our Lord's entire life was one perpetual battle. He was fighting evil in the high places and evil in the low, evil among the priests and evil among the people, evil in a religious dress, in Pharisaism, and evil in the dress of philosophy amongst the Sadducees; He fought it everywhere: He was the foe of everything that was wrong, false, selfish, unholy or impure. And you and I must be conformed to Christ in this respect. We are to be holy, harmless, undefiled and separate from sinners. Ye are of God, little children, and the whole world lieth in the wicked one. We are chosen out of the world to be a peculiar people, adversaries to all evil, never sheathing our sword till we enter into our rest. We are to be like Him then in nature, in relation, in experience.

Fourthly. We are to be conformed to Christ Jesus as to *character*. Time and ability alike fail us to speak of this. I only pray that God's Spirit may make our lives to speak of it. He was consecrated to God; so are we to be. The zeal of God's house ate Him up; so should it consume us also. He went about His Father's business; so should we ever be occupied. Towards man He was all love; it becomes us to be the same. He was gentle and kind and tender; as He was, so are we to be in this world. He did not break the bruised reed, nor quench the smoking flax; neither should we. Yet was He stern in the denunciation of all evil; so should we be. Purity, holiness, unselfishness, all the virtues, should glow in us as they shone in Him. Ah, and blessed be God they will too, by the work of the Spirit. Our text speaks not only of what we ought to be, but of what we shall be, for we are predestinated to be conformed to the image of God's Son. My brethren, what a glorious model! Behold it, wonder at it, and bless God for it. You are not to be conformed to the mightiest of the apostles, you will one day be purer than were Paul or John while here below; you are not to be conformed to the sublimest of the prophets, you shall be like the prophets' Master; you are not to be content with your own conception of that which is beautiful and lovely, but God's perfect conception incarnated in His own Son is that to which you shall certainly be brought by the predestination of God.

Just a sentence upon another point. We are to be conformed to the image of His Son, fifthly, as to our *inheritance*, for He is heir of all things, and what less are we heirs of, since all things are ours? He is heir of this world. "Thou madest Him to have dominion over all the works of Thy hands: thou hast put all things under His feet, all sheep and oxen, yea, and the fowl of the air and the fish of the sea, and whatsoever passeth through the paths of the sea." We see not yet all things put under man, but we see Jesus, who was made a little lower than the angels for the suffering of death crowned with glory and honour; and in the person of Christ Jesus this day we, the men who are made in His image, have dominion over all things, being all made kings and priests unto God, and in Christ Jesus ordained to reign with Him for ever and ever. "If children then heirs," says the apostle; therefore, whatever Christ has we have, and though we may be very poor and unknown, yet whatever belongs to Christ belongs to us. "The good of all the land of Egypt is yours," said Joseph to his brethren, and Jesus saith this to all His people, "All are yours, for ye are Christ's, and Christ is God's."

I must close this point—time goes much too swiftly this morning when descanting upon this delightful theme—by observing that we are to be conformed to Christ in His *glory*. We will think of our bodies, for that is a point surrounded with consolation, since He shall change our vile body and make it like unto His glorious body. We are like Adam now in weakness and pain, and we shall soon be like him in death, returning to the ground whence we were taken; but we shall rise again to a better life, and then shall we wear in glory and incorruption the image of the second Adam, the Lord from heaven. Conceive the beauties of the risen Redeemer. Let your faith and your imagination work together to pourtray the unutterable glories of Immanuel, God with us, as He sits at the right hand of the Father. Such and so bright shall our glories be in the day of the redemption of the body. We shall behold His glory, we shall be with Him where He is, and we shall be ourselves glorious in His glory. Is He exalted? you also shall be lifted up. Is He a King? you shall not be uncrowned. Is He a victor? you also shall bear a palm. Is He full of joy and rejoicing? so also shall your soul be filled to the brim with delights. Where He is every saint shall be ere long.

Thus much upon the sacred end of predestination.

II. Now, observe that PREDESTINATION IS THE IMPELLING FORCE TOWARDS THIS CONFORMITY. This truth divides itself thus: it is the *will* of God that conforms us to Christ's image rather than our own will. It is our will now, but it was God's will when it was not our will, and it only became according to our will when we were converted, because God's grace had made us willing in the day of its power. We cannot be made like Christ unwillingly; a consenting will is essential to the likeness of Christ; unwilling obedience would be disobedience. Naturally we never will towards good without God, but God works in us to will and to do. God treats us as men responsible and intelligent, and not as stone or metal; He made us free agents, and He treats us as such. We are willing now to be conformed to the image of Jesus, yea, we are more than willing, we are anxious and desirous for it; but still the main and first motive power lay not in our will but in His will, and to-day the immutable force which is best to be depended upon does not lie in our fickle, feeble will, but in the unchanging and omnipotent will of God. The force that is conforming us to Christ is the will of God in predestination.

And so, too, it is rather God's *work* than our work. We are to work with God in the matter of our becoming like to Christ. We are not to be passive like wood or marble; we are to be prayerful, watchful, fervent, diligent, obedient, earnest, and believing, but still the work is God's. Sanctification is the Lord's work in us. "Thou hast wrought all our works in us." From the first, and now, and to the last, "He that hath wrought us for the self-same thing is God, who also hath given to us the earnest of the Spirit." There is no holiness in us of our own creating; no good thing in us of our own fashioning. "Every good gift and every perfect gift is from above." "Not unto us, not unto us, but unto Thy name be praise." Still, true as it is that we are free agents, yet the Lord is the potter and we are the clay upon the wheel, and it is His work, and not ours, that makes us like to Christ. If there be a touch of our finger anywhere upon the vessel, it mars and does not beautify. It is only where God's hand has been that the vessel begins to assume the form of the model.

Therefore, beloved, all the *glory* must be unto God and not to us. It is a great honour to any man to be like Christ; God does not intend that His children should have no honour, for He puts honour upon His own people; but, still, the true glory lies with Him, since He has made us and not we ourselves. Cannot we say this morning with thankful hearts, "By the grace of God I am what I am"? and do we not feel that we shall lay all our honours, whatever they may be, at His dear feet, who hath according to His abundant mercy predestinated us to be conformed to the image of His Son?

III. Now I must come to the third point, upon which with brevity. It sweetly appears that the ULTIMATE END OF ALL THIS IS CHRIST. "Predestinated to be conformed to the image of His Son, that HE,"—"that HE"—God is always driving at something for Him, His well-beloved Son. He aims at His own glory in the glory of His dear Son; if He blesses us the text of last Sabbath is still true, "not for your sakes do I this"; it is for the sake of a higher, a better one than we are, it is "that *He* might be the first-born." Now, if I understand the passage before us, it means this. First, God predestinates us to be like Jesus that His dear Son might be the first of a new order of beings, elevated above all other creatures, and nearer to God than any other existences. He was Lord of angels, seraphim and cherubim obeyed His behests; but the Son desired to be at the head of a race of being mores nearly allied to Him than any existing spirits. There was no kinship between the Lord Jesus and angels, for to which of the angels had the Father said at any time, "Thou art my Son"? They are by nature servants, and He is the Son, this is a wide distinction. The Eternal Son desired association with beings who should be sons as He was, towards whom He could stand in a close relationship as being like to them in nature and sonship, and the Father therefore ordained that a seed whom He has chosen should be conformed to the image of the Son, that His Son might head up and be chief among an order of beings more nearly akin to God than any other. The serpent said to Eve, "God doth know that ye shall be as gods, know-ing good and evil." That lie had in it a residuum of truth, for by sovereign grace we have become such. There were no obedient creatures in the world of that sort, knowing good and evil, in the days of Eden's glory. The angels in heaven had known good, and only good, and preserved by grace had not fallen; the evil spirit had fallen, and he knew evil, but he had forgotten good, and was incapable of ever choosing it again; he is now for ever banished from hope of restoration. But here are we who know both good and evil; we understand the one, and the other too, and now there is begotten in us a nature which loves holiness and cannot sin, because it is born of God; we are left free agents, yea, we are freer than ever we were, and yet in this life, and in the life to come, our path is like that of the just which shineth more and more unto the perfect day. Angels know not evil; they have never had to battle with evil known and felt within; they have not tried the paths of sinful pleasure, and through grace been turned from them, so as with full purpose of heart to cleave to holiness for ever. Jesus now heads a race assailed but victorious; sorely tempted but enabled to overcome. Joyfully and cheerfully for ever shall it be our delight to do the Father's will. For ever with Christ at our head we shall be the nearest to the eternal throne; the most attached of servants, because also sons; the most firmly adhesive to good, because we once knew the bitterness of evil. Even as Christ had to drink the cup of suffering for sin, we also have sipped of it. We have known horror caused by guilt, and, therefore, for the future shall be throughout eternity a nobler race, freer to serve, and serving God after a nobler fashion than any other creatures in the universe. I take it that it is the meaning of the text, that the Lord would have Christ to be the first of a nobler order of beings.

But, secondly, the object of grace is that there may be some in heaven with whom Christ can hold brotherly converse. Note the expression, "Many brethren"—not that he might be the firstborn among many, but among "many brethren," who should be like Himself. Our blessed Lord delights in fellowship; such is the greatness of His heart that He would not be alone in His glory, but would have associates in His happiness. Now, I speak with bated breath. God can do all things, but I see not any way by which He could give to His only begotten Son beings that should be akin to Himself, except through the processes which we discover in the economy of grace. Here are beings that know evil, and know also good, beings placed under infinite obligations by bonds of love and gratitude to choose for ever the good, beings with a nature so renewed that they always must be holy beings; and these beings can commune with the incarnate God upon suffering as angels cannot, upon the penalty of guilt as angels cannot, upon heart-throes, conflicts, reproaches, and brokenness of spirit as angels cannot: and to them the Lord Jesus can reveal the glory of holiness, the bliss of conquering sin, and the sweetness of benevolence as only they can comprehend them. Renewed men are made fit companions for the Son of God. He shall feast all the more joyously because they shall eat bread with Him in His kingdom. He shall be joyful when He declares the Lord's name unto His brethren. He shall joy in their joy, and be glad in their gladness.

No doubt, however, the text means that these will for ever love and honour the Lord Jesus Christ

Himself. The children look up to the firstborn. In the East the firstborn is the lord and king of the household. We love Jesus now, and esteem Him our head and chief. How will we, when we once get to heaven, love and adore Him as our dear elder brother with whom we shall be on terms of the closest familiarity and most reverent obedience. How joyfully will we serve Him, how rapturously adore Him. Shall we not want to have our voices made more loud till they become as thunders, or like many waters, or surely we shall not be able to praise Him as we would? If there be work to do for Him in future ages, we will be the first to volunteer for service; if there be battles to be fought in times to come with other rebellious races, if there be wanted servants to fly over the vast realms of the infinite to carry Jehovah's messages, who shall fly so swiftly as we shall, when once we feel that in His courts we shall dwell not as mere servants, but as members of the royal family, partakers of the divine nature, nearest to God Himself. What bliss to know that He who is "very God of very God," and sits on the eternal throne, is also of the same nature with ourselves, our kinsman, who is not ashamed even amidst the royalties of glory to call us brethren, O brethren, what honours are ours! What a heritage lies before us! Who among us would change with Gabriel? We shall have no need to envy angels, for what are they but ministering spirits, servants in our Father's halls; but we are sons, and sons of no inferior order, no sons of a secondary rank like Abraham's children born of Keturah, or like the son of the bondwoman, but we are the Isaacs of God, born according to the promise, heirs of all that He hath, a seed beloved of the Lord for ever. Oh, what joy ought to fill our spirits this morning, at the prospect which this text reveals, and which pre-destination secures!

Perhaps our fullest thought upon the text is this. God was so well pleased with His Son, and saw such beauties in Him, that He determined to multiply His image. "My beloved," said He, "Thou shalt be the model by which I will fashion my noblest creature, I will for Thy sake make men able to converse with Thee, and bound to Thee by bands of love, who shall be next akin to Myself, and in all things like to Thee." Behold from heaven's mint golden pieces of inestimable value are sent forth, and each one bears the image and superscription of the Son of God. The face of Jesus is more lovely to God than all the worlds, His eyes are brighter than the stars, His voice is sweeter than bliss; therefore doth the Father will to have His Son's beauty reflected in ten thousand mirrors in saints made like to Him, and His praises chanted by myriads of voices of those who love Him, because His blood has saved them. The Father knew how happy His Son would be to associate His chosen with Himself, for of old His delights were with the sons of men. As a shepherd loves his sheep, as a king loves his subjects, so Jesus loves to have His people around Him; but deeper yet is the mystery, as it is not good for a man to be alone, and as for this cause doth a man leave his father and mother and is joined unto his wife, and they twain are one flesh, even so is it with Christ and His church. He was made like to her for her salvation, and now she is made like to Him for His honour. In what way could the Father put greater honour on His Son than by forming a race like to Himself, who shall be the many brethren among whom He is the well-beloved firstborn?

Now, brethren, this word I say and send you home. Keep your model before you. You see what you are to come to, therefore, set Christ before your eyes always. You see what you are predestinated to be: aim at it, aim at it every day. God worketh, and He worketh in you not to sleep, but to will and to do according to His own good pleasure. Brethren, grieve at your failures; when you see anything in yourselves that is not Christlike mourn over it, for it must be put away, it is so much dross that must be consumed; you cannot keep it, for God's pre-destination will not let you retain anything about you which is not according to the image of Christ. Cry mightily to the Holy Spirit to continue His sanctifying work upon you; beseech Him not to be grieved and vexed, and, therefore, in any measure to stay His hand. Cry, "Lord, melt me, pour me out like wax, and set Thy seal upon me until the image of Christ be clearly there." Above all, commune much with Christ. Communion is the fountain of conformity. Live with Christ and you will soon grow like Christ. They said of Achilles, the greatest of the Grecian heroes, that when he was a child they fed him upon lion's marrow, and so made him brave; feed upon Christ and be Christlike. They record on the other hand of blood-thirsty Nero, that he became so because he was suckled by a woman of a ferocious, barbaric nature. If we drink in our nutriment from the world, we shall be worldly; but, if we live upon Christ and dwell in Him, our conformity with Him shall be readily accomplished, and we shall be recognised as brethren of that blessed family of which Jesus Christ is the firstborn. How I wish every one here had a share in the text: I mourn that some have not, for he that believeth not on the Son hath not life, and therefore cannot have conformity to a living Christ. God grant to you all to be believers in Christ, now and for ever. Amen and Amen.

JESUS, THE SUBSTITUTE FOR HIS PEOPLE

"Who is he that condemneth? It is Christ that died, yea rather, that is risen again, who is even at the right hand of God, who also maketh intercession for us."—Romans viii. 34.

THE most dreadful alarm that can disturb a reasonable man is the fear of being condemned by the Judge of all. To be condemned of God now, how dreadful! To be condemned of Him at the last great day, how terrible! Well might Belshazzar's loins be loosed when the hand-writing on the wall condemned him as weighed in the balances and found wanting; and well may the conscience of the convicted one be comparable to a little hell when at its lesser judgment-seat the law pronounces sentence upon him on account of his past life. I know of no greater distress than that caused by the suspicion of condemnation in the believer's mind. We are not afraid of tribulation, but we dread condemnation.

We are not ashamed when wrongly condemned of men, but the bare idea of being condemned of God makes us like Moses "exceeding fear and quake." The bare possibility of being found guilty at the great judgment-seat of God is so alarming to us that we cannot rest until we see it removed. When Paul offered a loving and grateful prayer for Onesiphorus he could ask no more for him than, "the Lord grant that he may find mercy in that day." Yet, though condemnation is the most fatal of all ills, the apostle Paul in the holy ardour of his faith dares ask, "Who is he that condemneth?" He challenges earth and hell and heaven. In the justifiable venturesomeness of his confidence in the blood and righteousness of Jesus Christ he looks up to the excellent glory and to the throne of the thrice holy God, and even in His presence before whom the heavens are not pure, and who charged His angels with folly, he dares to say, "Who is he that condemneth?"

By what method was Paul, who had a tender and awakened conscience, so completely delivered from all fear of condemnation? It certainly was not by any depreciation of the enormity of sin. Amongst all the writers who have ever spoken of the evil of sin none have inveighed against it more heartily, or mourned it more sincerely from their very soul, than the apostle. He declares it to be exceeding sinful. You never find him suggesting apologies or extenuations; he neither mitigates sin nor its consequences. He is very plain when he speaks of the wages of sin and of what will follow as the consequences of iniquity. He sought not that false peace which comes from regarding transgression as a trifle, in fact he was a great destroyer of such refuges of lies. Rest assured, dear hearer, that you will never attain to a well-grounded freedom from the fear of condemnation by trying to make your sins appear little. That is not the way: it is far better to feel the weight of sin till it oppresses your soul than to be rid of the burden by presumption and hardness of heart. Your sins are damnable, and must condemn you unless they are purged away by the great sin-offering.

Neither did the apostle quiet his fears by confidence in anything that he had himself felt or done. Read the passage through and you will find no allusion to himself. If he is sure that none can condemn him, it is not because he has prayed, nor because he has repented, nor because he has been the apostle of the Gentiles, nor because he has suffered many stripes and endured much for Christ's sake. He gives no hint of having derived peace from any of these things, but in the humble spirit of a true believer in Jesus he builds his hope of safety upon the work of his Saviour; his reasons for rejoicing in noncondemnation all lie in the death, and resurrection, the power and the plea of his blessed Substitute. He looks right out of himself, for there he could see a thousand reasons for condemnation, to Jesus through whom condemnation is rendered impossible, and then in exulting confidence he lifts up the challenge, "Who shall lay anything to the charge of God's elect?" and dares to demand of men and angels and devils, yea of the great Judge Himself, "Who is he that condemneth?"

Now since it is not an uncommon thing for Christians in a weakly state of mind, exercised with doubts and harassed with cares, to feel the cold shadow of condemnation chilling their spirits, I would speak to such, hoping that the good Spirit may comfort their hearts.

Dear child of God, you must not live under fear of condemnation, for "there is therefore now no condemnation to them which are in Christ Jesus," and God would not have you fear that which can never come to you. If you be not a Christian, delay not till you have escaped from condemnation by laying hold on Christ Jesus; but if you have indeed believed in the Lord Jesus you are not under condemnation, and you never can be either in this life or in that which is to come. Let me help you by refreshing your memory with those precious truths concerning Christ, which show that believers are clear before the Lord. May the Holy Spirit apply them to your souls and give you rest.

I. And first you, as a believer, cannot be condemned because CHRIST HATH DIED. *The believer has Christ for his substitute,* and upon that substitute his sin has been laid. The Lord Jesus was made sin for His people. "The Lord hath made to meet upon Him the iniquity of us all." "He bare the sin of many." Now our Lord Jesus Christ by His death has suffered the penalty of our sin, and made recompense to divine justice. Observe, then, the comfort which this brings to us. If the Lord Jesus has been condemned for us, how can we be condemned? While justice survives in heaven, and mercy reigns on earth, it is not possible that a soul condemned in Christ should also be condemned in itself. If the punishment has been meted out to its substitute, it is neither consistent with mercy nor justice that the penalty should a second time be executed. The death of Christ is an all-sufficient ground of confidence for every man that believeth in Jesus; he may know of a surety that his sin is put away; and his iniquity is covered. Fix your eye on the fact that you have a substitute who has borne divine wrath on your account and you will know no fear of condemnation.

"Jehovah lifted up His rod—
O CHRIST, it fell on Thee!
Thou wast sore stricken of Thy God;
There's not one stroke for me."

Observe, dear brethren, *who it was that died,* for this will help you. Christ Jesus *the Son of God* died, the just for the unjust. He who was your Saviour was no mere man. Those who deny the Godhead of Christ are consistent in rejecting the atonement. It is not possible to hold a proper substitutionary propitiation for sin unless you hold that Christ was God. If one man might suffer for another, yet one man's sufferings could not avail for ten thousand times ten thousand men. What efficacy could there be in the death of one innocent person to put away the transgressions of a multitude? Nay, but because He who carried our sins up to the tree was God over all, blessed for ever; because He who suffered His feet to be fastened to the wood was none other than that same Word who was in the beginning with God, and who also was God; because He who bowed His head to death was none other than the Christ, who is immortality and life:—His dying had efficacy in it to take away the sins of all for whom He died. As I think of my Redeemer and remember that He is God Himself, I feel that if He took my nature and died, then indeed my sin is gone. I can rest on that. I am sure that if He who is infinite and omnipotent offered a satisfaction for my sins I need not enquire as to the sufficiency of the atonement, for who dares to suggest a limit to its power? What Jesus did and suffered must be equal to any emergency. Were my sins even greater than they are His blood could make them whiter than snow. If God incarnate died in my stead my iniquities are cleansed.

Again, remember who it was that died, and take another view of Him. It was *Christ* which being interpreted means "*the anointed.*" He who came to save us did not come unsent or uncommissioned. He came by His Father's will, saying, "Lo, I come, in the volume of the book it is written of Me, I delight to do Thy will, O God." He came by the Father's power, "for Him hath God set forth to be a propitiation for our sins." He came with the Father's anointing, saying, "The Spirit of the Lord is upon Me." He was *the* Messiah, sent of God. The Christian need have no fear of condemnation when he see Christ die for him, because God Himself appointed Christ to die, and if God arranged the plan of substitution, and appointed the substitute, he cannot repudiate the vicarious work. Even if we could not speak as we have done of the glorious person of our Lord, yet if the divine sovereignty and wisdom elected such an one as Christ to bear our sin we may be well satisfied to take God's choice, and rest content with that which contents the Lord.

Again, believer, sin cannot condemn you because Christ *died*. His sufferings I doubt not were vicarious long before He came to the cross, but still the substance of the penalty due to sin was death, and it was when Jesus died that He finished transgression, made an end of sin, and brought in everlasting righteousness. The law could go no further than its own capital sentence, which is death: this was the dire punishment pronounced in the garden,—"In the day that thou eatest thereof thou shall surely die." Christ died physically, with all the concomitants of ignominy and pain, and His inner death, which was the bitterest part of the sentence, was attended by the loss of His Father's countenance and a horror unutterable. He descended into the grave, and for three days and three nights he slept within the tomb really dead. Herein is our joy, our Lord has suffered the extreme penalty and given blood for blood, and life for life. He has paid all that was due, for He has paid His life; He has given himself for us, and borne our sins in His own body on the tree, so that His death is the death of our sins. "It is Christ that died."

I speak not upon these things with any flourishes of words, I give you but the bare doctrine. May the Spirit of God apply these truths to your souls, and you will see that no condemnation can come on those who are in Christ.

It is quite certain, beloved, that the death of Christ must have been effectual for the removal of those sins which were laid upon Him. It is not conceivable that Christ died in vain—I mean not conceivable without blasphemy, and I hope we could not descend to that. He was appointed of God to bear the sin of many, and though He was God himself, yet He came into the world and took upon Himself the form of a servant and bore those sins, not merely in sorrow but in death itself, and it is not possible that He should be defeated or disappointed of His purpose. Not in one jot or tittle will the intent of Christ's death be frustrated. Jesus shall see of the travail of His soul and be satisfied. That which He meant to do by dying shall be done, and He shall not pour His blood upon the ground in waste in any measure or sense. Then, if Jesus died for you there stands this sure argument, that as He did not die in vain you shall not perish. He has suffered and you shall not suffer. He has been condemned and you shall not be condemned. He has died for you, and now He gives you the promise—"Because I live you shall live also."

II. The apostle goes on to a second argument, which he strengthens with the word "rather." "It is Christ that died, yea *rather*. THAT IS RISEN AGAIN." I do not think we give sufficient weight to this "rather." The death of Christ is the rocky basis of all comfort, but we must not overlook the fact that the resurrection of Christ is considered by the apostle to yield richer comfort than His death—"yea rather, that is risen again." How can we derive more comfort from Christ's resurrection than from His death, if from His death we gained a sufficient ground of consolation? I answer, because our *Lord's resurrection denoted His total clearance from all the sin which was laid upon Him*. A woman is overwhelmed with debt: how shall she be discharged from her liabilities? A friend, out of his great love to her, marries her. No sooner is the marriage ceremony performed than she is by that very act clear of debt, because her debts are her husband's, and in taking her he takes all her obligations. She may gather comfort from that thought, but she is much more at ease when her beloved goes to her creditors, pays all, and brings her the receipts. First she is comforted by the marriage, which legally relieves her from the liability, but much more is she at rest when her husband himself is rid of all the liability which he assumed. Our Lord Jesus took our debts; in death He paid them, and in resurrection He blotted out the record. By His resurrection He took away the last vestige of charge against us, for the resurrection of Christ was the Father's declaration that He was satisfied with the Son's atonement. As our hymnster puts it—

> "The Lord is risen indeed,
> Then justice asks no more;
> Mercy and truth are now agreed,
> Which stood opposed before."

In His prison-house of the grave the hostage and surety of our souls would have been confined to this very hour, unless the satisfaction which He offered had been satisfactory to God, but being fully accepted He was set free from bonds, and all His people are thereby justified. "Who is He that condemneth? Christ is risen again."

Mark further that *the resurrection of Christ indicated our acceptance with God*. When God raised Him from the dead He thereby gave testimony that He had accepted Christ's work, but the acceptance of our representative is the acceptance of ourselves. When the French ambassador was sent away from the Court of Prussia it meant that war was declared, and when the ambassador was again received peace was re-established. When Jesus was so accepted of God that He rose again from the dead everyone of us who believe in Him was accepted of God too, for what was done to Jesus was in effect done to all the members of His mystical body. With Him are we crucified, with Him are we buried, with Him we rise again, and in His acceptance we are accepted.

Did not His resurrection also indicate that *He had gone right through with the entire penalty*, and that His death was sufficient? Suppose for a moment that one thousand eight hundred and more years had passed away, and that still He slumbered in the tomb. In such a case we might have been enabled to believe that God had accepted Christ's substitutionary sacrifice, and would ultimately raise Him from the the dead, but we should have had our fears. But now we have before our eyes a sign and token, as consoling as the rainbow in the day of rain, for Jesus is risen, and it is clear that the law can exact no more from Him. He lives now by a new life, and the law has no claim against Him. *He* against whom the claim was brought has died, His present life is not that against which the law can bring a suit. So with us: the law had claims on us once, but we are new creatures in Christ Jesus, we have participated in the resurrection life of Christ, and the law cannot demand penalties from our new life. The incorruptible seed within us has not sinned, for it is born of God. The law cannot condemn us, for we have died to it in Christ, and are beyond its jurisdiction.

I leave with you this blessed consolation. Your surety has discharged the debt for you, and being justified in the Spirit has gone forth from the tomb. Lay not a burden upon yourselves by your unbelief. Do not afflict your conscience with dead works, but turn to Christ's cross and look for a revived consciousness of pardon through the blood washing.

III. I must pass on now to the third point upon which the apostle insists. "WHO IS EVEN AT THE RIGHT HAND OF GOD." Bear in mind still that what Jesus is His people are, for they are one with Him. His condition and position are typical of their own. "Who is even at the right hand of God." That means *love*, for the right hand is for the beloved. That means *acceptance*. Who shall sit at the right hand of God but one who is dear to God? That means *honour*. To which of the angels has He given to sit at His right hand? *Power* also is implied! No cherub or seraph can be said to be at the right hand of God. Christ, then, who once suffered in the flesh is, in love, and acceptance, and honour, and power at the right hand of God. See you the force then, of the interrogation, "Who is he that condemneth?" It may be made apparent in a twofold manner. "Who can condemn me while I have such a friend at court? While my representative sits near to God how can I be condemned?" But next, I am where He is, for it is written, "He hath raised us up together, and made us sit together in heavenly places in Christ Jesus." Can you suppose it possible to condemn one who is already at the right hand of God? The right hand of God is a place so near, so eminent, that one cannot suppose an adversary bringing a charge against us there. Yet there the believer is in his representative, and who dare accuse him? It was laid at Haman's door as his worst crime that he sought to compass the death of queen Esther herself, so dear to the king's heart; and shall any foe condemn or destroy those who are dearer to God than ever Esther was to Ahasuerus, for they sit at His right hand, vitally and indissolubly united to Jesus. Suppose you were actually at the right hand of God, would you then have any fear of being condemned? Do you think the bright spirits before the throne have any dread of being condemned, though they were once sinners like yourself? "No," say you, "I should have perfect confidence if I were there." But you are there in your representative. If you think you are not I will ask you this question, "Who shall separate us from the love of Christ?" Is Christ divided? If you are a believer you are one with Him, and the members must be where the head is. Till they condemn the head they cannot condemn the

members? Is not that clear? If you are at the right hand of God in Christ Jesus who is he that condemneth? Let them condemn those white-robed hosts who for ever circle the throne of God, and cast their crowns at His feet; let them attempt that, I say, before they lay anything to the charge of the meanest believer in Christ Jesus.

IV. The last word which the apostle gives us is this, "WHO ALSO MAKETH INTERCESSION FOR US." This is another reason why fear of condemnation should never cross our minds if we have indeed trusted our souls with Christ, for if Jesus intercedes for us He must make a point of interceding that we may never be condemned. He would not direct His intercession to minor points and leave the major unheeded. "Father, I will that they also whom Thou hast given Me be with Me where I am" includes their being forgiven all their sins, for they could not come there if their sins were not forgiven. Rest assured that a pleading Saviour makes secure the acquittal of His people.

Reflect that our Lord's intercession must be prevalent. It is not supposable that Christ asks in vain. He is no humble petitioner at a distance who, with moan and sigh, asks for what He deserves not, but with the breast-plate on, sparkling with the jewels which bear his people's names, and bringing His own blood as an infinitely satisfactory atonement to the mercy-seat of God, He pleads with unquestioned authority. If Abel's blood, crying from the ground, was heard in heaven and brought down vengeance, much more shall the blood of Christ, which speaketh within the veil, secure the pardon and salvation of His people. The plea of Jesus is indisputable, and cannot be put aside. He pleads this,—"I have suffered in that man's stead." Can the infinite justice of God deny that plea? "By Thy will, O God, I gave Myself a substitute for these My people. Wilt Thou not put away the sin of these for whom I stood?" Is not this good pleading? There is God's covenant for it, there is God's promise for it, and God's honour involved in it, so that when Jesus pleads, it is not only the dignity of His person that has weight, and the love which God bears to His only begotten, which is equally weighty, but His claim is overwhelming, and His intercession omnipotent.

How safe is the Christian since Jesus ever liveth to make intercession for him! Have I committed myself into His dear hands? Then may I never so dishonour Him as to mistrust Him. Do I really trust Him as dying, as risen, as sitting at the Father's right hand, and as pleading for me? Can I permit myself to indulge a solitary suspicion? Then, my Father, forgive this great offence, and help Thy servant by a greater confidence of faith to rejoice in Christ Jesus and say, "There is therefore now no condemnation." Go away, ye that love Christ, and are resting on Him, with the savour of this sweet doctrine on your hearts; but, oh, you that have not trusted Christ there is present condemnation for you. Ye are condemned already, because ye have not believed on the Son of God; and there is future condemnation for you, for the day cometh, the dreadful day, when the ungodly shall be as stubble in the fire of Jehovah's wrath. The hour hasteneth when the Lord will lay justice to the line, and righteousness to the plummet; and sweep away the refuges of lies. Come, poor soul, come and trust the crucified, and you shall live, and with us you shall rejoice that none can condemn you.

MORE THAN CONQUERORS

"Nay, in all these things we are more than conquerors through Him that loved us."—Romans viii. 37.

THE distinguishing mark of a Christian is his confidence in the love of Christ, and the yielding of his affections to Christ in return. First, faith sets her seal upon the man by enabling the soul to say with the apostle, "Christ loved me and gave Himself for me." Then love gives the countersign, and stamps upon the heart gratitude and love to Jesus in return. "We love Him because He first loved us." "God is love," and the children of God are ruled in their inmost powers by love; the love of Christ constraineth them. They believe in Jesus' love, and then they reflect it; they rejoice that divine love is set upon them; they feel it shed abroad in their hearts by the Holy Ghost which is given unto them, and then by force of gratitude they love the Saviour with a pure heart, fervently.

In those grand old ages, which are the heroic period of the Christian religion, this double mark was very clearly to be seen in all believers in Jesus. They were men who knew the love of Christ, and rested upon it as a man leaneth upon a staff whose trustiness he has tried. They did not speak of Christ's love as though it were a myth to be respected, a tradition to be reverenced; they viewed it as a blessed reality, and they cast their whole confidence upon it, being persuaded that it would bear them up as upon eagles' wings, and carry them all their days; resting assured that it would be to them a foundation of rock, against which the waves might beat, and the winds blow, but their soul's habitation would stand securely if founded upon it. The love which they felt towards the Lord Jesus was not a quiet emotion which they hid within themselves in the secret chamber of their souls, and which they only spake of in their private assemblies when they met on the first day of the week, and sung hymns in honour of Christ Jesus the Crucified, but it was a passion with them of such a vehement and all-consuming energy, that it permeated all their lives, became visible in all their actions, spoke in their common talk, and looked out of their eyes, even in their commonest glances. Love to Jesus was a flame which fed upon the very marrow of their bones, the core and heart of their being; and, therefore, from its own force burned its way into the outer man, and shone there. Zeal for the glory of King Jesus was the seal and mark of all genuine Christians. Because of their dependence upon Christ's love they *dared* much; and because of their love to Christ they *did* much. Because of their reliance upon the love of Jesus they were not afraid of their enemies; and because of their love to Jesus they scorned to shun the foe even when he appeared in the most dreadful forms. The Christians of the early ages sacrificed themselves continually upon the altar of Christ with joy and alacrity. Wherever they were they bore testimony against the evil customs which surrounded them. They counted it foul scorn for a Christian to be as others were; they would not conform themselves to the world: they could not, for they were transformed by the renewing of their minds; their love to Christ compelled them to bear their witness against everything which dishonoured

Christ by being contrary to truth, and righteousness, and love. They were innovators, reformers, image-breakers, everywhere; they could not be quiet and let others do as they pleased, whilst they followed out their own views, but their protest was continual, incessant, annoying to the foe, but acceptable to God. In every place the Christian was a speckled bird, because love to Jesus would not allow him to disguise his convictions; he was everywhere a stranger and an alien, because the very language of his everyday life differed from that of his neighbours. Where others blasphemed, he adored; where others used oaths habitually, his "yes" was yea, and his "nay," nay; where others girt on the sword, he resisted not evil; where others were each man seeking his own and not his brother's welfare, the Christian was known as being one whose treasure was in heaven, and who had set his affections upon things above. This love to Jesus made the Christian a perpetual protestor against evil for the sake of Jesus. It led him yet further—he became a constant witness to the truth which he had found so precious in his own soul. Christian men were like Naphtali, of whom it was said: "Naphtali is a hind let loose: he giveth goodly words." Tongue-tied Christians, silent witnesses, were scarcely known in apostolic days. The matron talked of Christ to her servants; the child, having learned of Jesus, spake of Him in the schools; whilst the Christian workman at the shop testified, and the Christian minister (and these were many in those days, for all men ministered according to their ability) stood in the corners of the streets, or met in their own hired houses with tens or twenties, as the case might be, always declaring the doctrine of the resurrection, and of the incarnation of Christ, and of His death and resurrection, and of the cleansing power of His blood.

The love of Jesus, I have said at the commencement, was a real passion with those men, and their confidence in Jesus was real and practical; hence their testimony for Jesus was bold, clear, and decided. There was a trumpet ring in ancient Christian testimony which startled the old world which was lying in a deep sleep, dreaming filthy dreams; that world loved not to be so aroused, and turning over in its sleep, muttered curses deep and many, and vowed revenge against the disturber who dared break its horrible repose. Meanwhile believers in Jesus, men not satisfied with witnessing by their lives and testifying by their tongues in the places where their lot was cast, but were continually commissioning fresh bands of missionaries to carry the word into other districts. It was not enough for Paul to preach the gospel at Jerusalem or Damascus, he must needs journey into Pisidia and Pamphylia, he must journey to the utmost verge of Asia Minor, and then, so full of Christ is he, that he dreams of eternal life, and when he falls asleep, he hears in a vision a man of Macedonia across the blue Ægean, entreating him, "Come over and help us." And with the morning light Paul rises, fully resolved to take ship and preach the gospel among the Gentiles. Having preached

Christ throughout all Greece, he passed over to Italy, and though chained, he entered as God's ambassador within the walls of the imperial city of Rome; and it is believed that after that, his sacredly restless spirit was not satisfied with preaching throughout Italy, but he must needs cross into Spain, and it is said even into Britain itself. The ambition of the Christian for Christ was boundless; beyond pillars of Hercules, to the utmost islands of the sea, believers in Jesus carried the news of a Saviour born for the sons of men. Those were days of ardour. I fear these are days of lukewarmness. Those were times when the flame was like coals of juniper, which have a most vehement heat, and neither shipwreck, nor peril by robbers, nor peril by rivers, nor peril by false brethren, nor the sword itself, could stay the enthusiasm of the saints, for they believed, and therefore spake; they loved, and therefore served, even to the death.

Thus I introduce to you our text. Behold the men and their conflict for Christ! It was natural, it was inevitable, that they should provoke enmity. You and I do not love Christ much, nor believe much in His love—I mean the most of us. We are a sickly, unworthy, degenerate generation. We let the world alone, the world lets us alone. We conform a great deal to worldly customs, and the world is not annoyed by us. We do not dog the world's heels, perpetually declaring the truth as we ought to do, and therefore the world is not impatient with us—it thinks us a very good sort of people,—a little whimsied, crazed about the head perhaps, but still very bearable and well behaved—and so we do not meet with half the enemies which they did of old, because we are not half such true Christians, nay, not one-tenth such saints as they. But if we were more holy, in proportion as we were so, we should meet with the same battle, though it may be in another shape. Though I spoke thus censoriously of all, there are some few here, I trust, who have been enabled by divine grace to know the power of the love of Jesus, and who are living under its influences, and contending for the sovereignty of the thorn-crowned King—these are they who will endure the same fight in other forms as the conflict of apostolic days, and these are they who may use without falsehood the language of my text: "In all these things we are more than conquerors through Him that loved us."

I will ask you, this morning, as we are assisted by the Holy Spirit, first, to consider *the victories already won* ; secondly, *the laurels of the fight* ; thirdly, *the men who won them* ; and fourthly, *the power by which their conquest was achieved.*

1. First, this morning, we shall view THE VICTORIES ALREADY WON by those who have been possessed by the love of Jesus.

Look attentively at the champion. It needs no stretch of imagination to conceive this place to be a Roman amphitheatre. There in the midst of the arena stands the hero. The great doors of the lion's dens are lifted up by machinery, and as soon as the lairs are open, rushing forth with fury come bears and lions, and wild beasts of all kinds, that have been starved into ferocity, with which the champion is to contend. Such was the Christian in Paul's day, such is he now. The world is the theatre of conflict: angels and devils look on; a great cloud of witnesses view the fight— and monsters are let loose against him, with whom he must contend triumphantly.

The apostle gives us a little summary of the evils with which we must fight, and he places first, "*tribula-*

tion." The word "tribulation," in the Latin, signifies threshing, and God's people are often cast upon the threshing-floor to be beaten with the heavy flail of trouble; but they are more than conquerors, since they lose nothing but their straw and chaff, and the pure wheat is thus separated from that which was of no benefit to it. The original Greek word, however, suggests pressure from without. It is used in the case of persons who are bearing heavy burdens, and are heavily pressed upon. Now, believers have had to contend with outward circumstances more or less in all ages. At the present day, there are very few who do not at some time or other in their lives meet with outward pressure, either from sickness or from loss of goods, or from bereavements, or from some other of the thousand and one causes from which affliction springs. The Christian has not a smooth pathway. "In the world, ye *shall have* tribulation," is a sure promise, which never fails of fulfilment. But under all burdens, true believers have been sustained, no afflictions have ever been able to destroy their confidence in God. It is said of the palm-tree, that the more weights they hang upon it the more straight and the more lofty doth it tower towards heaven; and it is so with the Christian. Like Job, he is never so glorious as when he has passed through the loss of all things, and at last rises from his dung-hill more mighty than a king. Brethren, you must expect to meet with this adversary so long as you are here; and if you now suffer the pressure of affliction, remember you must overcome it, and not yield to it. Cry unto the strong for strength, that your tribulation may work out for you patience, and patience experience, and experience hope that maketh not ashamed.

The next in the list is "*distress.*" I find that the Greek word rather refers to mental grief than to anything external. The Christian suffers from external circumstances; but this is probably a less affliction than internal woe. "Straitness of place" is something like the Greek word. We sometimes get into a position in which we feel as if we could not move, and are not able to turn to the right hand or to the left: the way is shut up; we see no deliverance, and our own consciousness of feebleness and perplexity is unbearably terrible. Do you never get into this state in which your mind is distracted, you know not what to do; you cannot calm and steady yourself; you would if you could consider calmly the conflict, and then enter into it like a man with all his wits about him; but the devil and the world, outward trial and inward despondency combined, toss you to and fro like the waves of the sea, till you are, to use John Bunyan's Saxon expression, "much tumbled up and down in your mind." Well, now, if you are a genuine Christian, you will come out of this all right enough. You will be more than a conqueror over mental distress. You will take this burden as well as every other to your Lord, and cast it upon Him; and the Holy Ghost, whose office it is to be the Comforter, will say to the troubled waves of your heart, "Be still." Jesus shall say, as He walks the tempest of your soul, "It is I, be not afraid;" and though the outward tribulation and the inward distress meet together like two contending seas, they shall both be calmed by the power of the Lord Jesus.

The third evil the apostle mentions is "*persecution,*" which has always fallen upon the genuine lovers of Christ; their good name has been slandered. I should blush to repeat the villanies which have been uttered against the saints of the olden times. Suffice it to say, there is no crime in the category of vice which has not been falsely laid to the door of the followers of the pure and holy Jesus. Yet slander did not crush the church; the fair name of Christianity outlived the reputation of the men who had the effrontery to accuse her. Imprisonment followed slander, but in prisons God's saints have sung like birds in cages, better than when they were in the fields of open liberty. Prisons have glowed into palaces, and been sanctified into the dwelling places of God Himself, more sacred far than all the consecrated domes of gorgeous architecture. Persecution has sometimes taken to banishing the saints, but in their banishment they have been at home, and when scattered far and wide, they have gone everywhere preaching the word, and their scattering has been the gathering together of others of the elect. When persecution has even resorted to the most cruel torments, God has had many a sweet song from the rack. The joyful notes of holy Lawrence, broiling upon the gridiron, must have been more sweet to God than the songs of cherubims and seraphims, for he loved God more than the brightest of them, and proved it in his bitterest anguish; and holy Mr. Hawkes, when his lower extremities were burnt, and they expected to see him fall over the chain into the fire, lifted his flaming hands, each finger spurting fire, and clapped them three times, with the shout of "None but Christ, none but Christ!" God was honoured more by that burning man than even by the ten thousand times ten thousand who ceaselessly hymn His praises in glory. Persecution, in all its forms, has fallen upon the Christian church, and up to this moment it has never achieved a triumph, but it has been an essential benefit to the church, for it cleared her of hypocrisy; when cast into the fire the pure gold lost nothing but its dross and tin, which it might well be glad to lose.

Then the apostle adds "famine." We are not exposed to this evil so much nowadays; but, in Paul's time, those who were banished, frequently were carried to places where they could not exercise their handicraft to earn their bread. They were taken away from their situations, from their friends, from their acquaintance; they suffered the loss of all their goods, and consequently they did not know where to find even the necessary sustenance for heir bodies; and no doubt there are some now who are great losers by their conscientious convictions—who are called to suffer, in a measure, even famine itself. Then, the devil whispers, "You ought to look after your house and children; you must not follow your religion so as to lose your bread." Ah! my friend, we shall then see whether you have the faith that can conquer famine; that can look gaunt hunger in the face; look through the ribs of the skeleton, and yet say, "Ah! famine itself I will bear sooner than sell my conscience, and stain my love to Christ."

Then comes nakedness, another terrible form of poverty. The Christian banished from house to house, and prevented from working at his trade, was not able to procure necessary funds, and therefore his garments gradually fell to rags, and the rags one by one disappeared. At other times the persecutors stripped men and women naked, to make then yield to shame; but nakedness, even in the case of the most tender and sensitive spirits, though such have been exposed to this evil in the olden days, has been unable to daunt the unconquerable spirit of the saints.

There are stories in the old martyrologies of men and women who have had to suffer this indignity; and it is reported by those who looked on, that they never seemed to be so gloriously arrayed; for when they stood naked before the whole bestial throng, that they might gaze upon them with their cruel eyes, their very bodies seemed to glow with glory, as with calm countenance they surveyed their enemies, and gave themselves up to die.

The apost e mentions next to nakedness, peril— that is, constant exposure to sudden death. This was the life of the early Christian. "We die daily," said the apostle. They were never sure of a moment's mercy, for a new edict might come forth from the Roman emperor to sweep the Christians away. They went literally with their lives in their hands wherever they went. Some of their perils were voluntarily encountered for the spread of the gospel; perils by rivers and by robbers were the lot of the Christian missionary going through inhospitable climes to declare the gospel. ther perils were the result of persecution; but we are told here that believers in Jesus so steadily reposed upon Christ's love, that they did not feel peril to be peril; and the love of Christ so lifted them up above the ordinary thoughts of flesh and blood, so that even when perils became perils indeed, they entered upon them with joy, out of love to their Lord and Master.

And to close the list, as if there were a sort of perfection in these evils, the seventh thing is the sword, that is to say, the apostle Paul singles out one cruel form of death as a picture of the whole. Ye know, and I need not tell you, how the noble army of my Master's martyrs have given their necks to the sword, as cheerfully as the bride upon the marriage day gives her hand to the bridegroom. Ye know how they have gone to the stake and kissed the faggots; how they have sung on the way to death, though death was attended with the most cruel torments; and have rejoiced with exceeding great joy, even to leaping and dancing at the thought of being counted worthy to suffer for Christ's sake. The apostle tells us that the saints have suffered all these things put together. He does not say in some of these things we are conquerors, but in all; many believer literally passed through outward want, inward trial, persecution, want of bread want of raiment, the constant hazard of life, and at last laid down life itself; and yet in every case through the whole list of these gloomy fights, believers were more than conquerors. Beloved, this day you are not, the most of you, called to peril, or nakedness, or sword: if ye were, my Lord would give you grace to bear the test; but I think the troubles of a Christian man, at the present moment, though not outwardly so terrible, are yet more hard to bear than even those of the fiery age. We have to bear the sneer of the world—that is litt e; its blandishments, its soft words, its oily speeches, its fawning, its hypocrisy, are far worse. O sirs, your danger is lest you grow rich and become proud, lest you give yourselves up to the fashions of this present evil world, and lose your faith. If you cannot be torn in pieces by the roaring lion, you may be hugged to death by the bear, and the devil little cares which it is so long as he gets your love to Christ out of you, and destroys your confidence in Him. I fear me that the Christian church is far more likely to lose her integrity in these soft and silken days than she was in those rough times. Are there not many professing Christians whose methods of trade are just as vicious as the methods of trade of the most shifty and tricky of the unconverted? Have we not some professed Christians who are worldly altogether? whose non-attendance at our meetings for prayer, whose want of liberality to Christ's cause, whose entire conduct indeed proves that if there be any grace in them at all, it is not the grace which conquers the world, but the pretended grace which lets the world put its foot upon its neck. We must be awake now; for we traverse the enchanted ground, and are more likely to be ruined than ever, unless our faith in Jesus be a reality, and our love to Jesus a vehement flame. We are likely to become bastards and not sons, tares and not wheat, hypocrites with fair vineyards, but not the true living children of the living God. Christians, do not think that these are times in which you can dispense with watchfulness or with holy ardour; you need these things more now than ever, and may God the eternal Spirit display his omnipotence in you, that you may be able to say, in all these softer things as well as in the rougher, "We are more than conquerors through Him that loved us."

II. I shall with great brevity turn to the second head of the discourse. Let us inspect THE LAURELS OF THE FIGHT.

Hitherto believers have been conquerors, but the text says they have been "*more than conquerors.*" How is that? The word in the original is one of the apostle Paul's strong expressions; it might be rendered, "more exceeding conquerors." The Vulgate, I think, has a word in it which means, "over-over-comers," over and above conquering. For a Christian to be a conqueror is a great thing: how can he be more than a conqueror? I think in many respects, first, a Christian is better than some conquerors because *the power by which he overcomes is nobler far.* Here is a champion just come from the Greek games; he has well nigh killed his adversary in a severe boxing match, and he comes in to receive the crown. Step up to him, look at that arm, and observe the thews and sinews. Why! the man's muscles are like steel, and you say to him, " I do not wonder that you beat and bruised your foe; if I had set up a machine made of steel, and worked by a little watery vapour, it could have done the same, though nothing but mere matter would have been at work. You are a stronger man and more vigorous in constitution than your foe: that is clear; but where is the particular glory about that? One machine is stronger than another. No doubt, credit is to be given to you for your endurance, after a sort; but you are just one big brute beating another big brute. Dogs, and bulls, and game-cocks, and all kinds of animals, would have endured as much, and perhaps more. Now, see the Christian champion coming from the fight, having won the victory! Look at him! He has overcome human wisdom; but when I look at him, I perceive no learning nor cunning: he is a simple, unlettered person, who just knows that Jesus Christ came into the world to save sinners; yet he has won the victory over profound philosophers: then he is more than a conqueror. He has been tempted and tried in all sorts of ways, and he was not at all a crafty person; he was very weak, yet somehow he has conquered. Now this is being more than a conqueror, when weakness overcomes strength, when brute force is baffled by gentleness and love. This is victory indeed, when the little things overcome the great things; when the base things of this world overthrow the mighty; and the things that are not bring to nought the things that are: yet this is just the triumph of grace. The Christian is, viewed according to the eye of sense, weak as water; yet faith knows him to be irresistible. According to the eye of sense, he is a thing to be trampled upon, for he will not resist; and yet, in the sight of God, he becomes in this very way, by his gentleness and patience, more than a conqueror.

The Christian is more than a conqueror again, because the conqueror fights for victory—*fights with some selfish motive.* Even if the motive be patriotism, although from another point of view, patriotism is one of the highest of worldly virtues, yet it is only a magnificent selfishness by which one contends for one's own country, instead of being subject to the far more generous cosmopolite thought of caring for all men. But the Christian fights neither for any set of men nor for himself: in contending for truth he contends for all men, but especially for God; and in suffering for the right he suffers with no prospect of earthly gain. He becomes more than a conqueror, both by the strength with which he fights and the motives by which he is sustained, which are better than the motives and the strength which sustain other conquerors.

He is more than a conqueror, because *he loses nothing even by the fight itself.* When a battle is won, at any rate the winning side loses something. In most wars, the gain seldom makes any recompense for the effusion of blood; but the Christian's faith, when tried, grows stronger; his patience, when tempted, becomes more patient. His graces are like the fabled Anteus, who, when thrown to the ground, sprang up stronger than before, by touching his mother earth; for the Christian, by touching his God and falling down in helplessness into the arms of the Most High, grows stronger by all that he is made to suffer. He is more than a conqueror, because he loses nothing even by the fight, and gains wondrously by the victory.

He is more than a conqueror over persecution, because *most conquerors have to struggle and agonise to win the conquest.* But, my brethren, many Christians, ay and all Christians, when their faith in Christ is strong, and their love to Christ is fervent, have found it even easy to overcome suffering for the Lord. Look at Blandina, enveloped in a net, tossed upon the horns of bulls, and then made to sit in a red hot iron chair to die, and yet unconquered to the close. What did the tormentors say to the emperor —"Oh! emperor," said the tormentors, "we are ashamed, for these Christians mock us while they suffer thy cruelties." Indeed, the tormentors often seemed to be themselves tormented; they were worried to think they could not conquer timid women and children. They devoured their own hearts with rage; like the viper, which gnaws at the file, they broke their teeth against the iron strength of Christian faith; they could not endure it, because these people suffered without repining, endured without retracting, and glorified Christ in the fires without complaining. I love to think of Christ's army of martyrs, ay, and of all His church, marching over the battlefield, singing as they fight, never ceasing the song, never suffering a note to fall, and at the same time advancing from victory to victory; chanting the sacred hallelujah while they tramp over their foes. I saw one day upon the lake of Orta, in northern Italy, on some holyday of the church of Rome, a number of boats coming from all quarters of the lake towards the church upon the central islet of the lake, and it was singularly beautiful to hear the splash of the oars and the sound of song as the boats came up in long processions, with all the villagers in them, bearing their banners, to the appointed place of meeting. As the oars splashed they kept time to the rowers, and the rowers never missed a stroke because they sang, neither was the song marred because of the splash of the oars, but on they came, singing and rowing: and so has it been with the church of God. That oar of obedience, and that other oar of suffering—the church has learned to ply both of these, and to sing as she rows: "Thanks be unto God, who always maketh us to triumph in every place! Though we be made to suffer, and be made to fight, yet we are more than conquerors, because we are conquerors even while fighting; we sing even in the heat of the battle, waving high the banner, and dividing the spoil even in the centre of the fray. When the fight is hottest, we are then there most happy; and when the strife is sternest, then most blessed; and when the battle grows most arduous, then, "calm 'mid the bewildering cry, confident of victory." Thus the saints have been in those respects more than conquerors.

More than conquerors I hope, this day, because *they have conquered their enemies* by doing them good, converting their persecutors by their patience. To use the old Protestant motto, the church has been the anvil, and the world has been the hammer; and though the anvil has done nothing but bear the stroke, she has broken all the hammers, as she will do to the world's end. All true believers who really trust in Jesus' love, and are really fired with it, will be far more glorious than the Roman conqueror when He drove his milk white steeds through the imperial city's streets; then the young men and maidens, matrons and old men gathered to the windows and chimney-tops, and scattered flowers upon the conquering legions as they came along; but what is this compared with the triumph which is going on even now as the great host of God's elect come streaming through the streets of the New Jerusalem? What flowers are they which angels strew in the path of the blessed? What songs are those which rise from yonder halls of Zion, conjubilant with song as the saints pass along to their everlasting habitations?

III. The time has almost failed me, and therefore, in the third place, but two or three words. Who are THE PERSONS THAT HAVE CONQUERED?

Attentively regard these few words which I utter. The men who conquered in the fight up till now have been known only by this—the two things I mentioned at the first—men who believed in Christ's love to them, and who were possessed with love to Christ; for there has been no other distinction than this. They have been rich: Cæsar's household yielded martyrs. They have been poor: the inscriptions on the tombs of the catacombs are few of them spelt correctly; they must have been very poor and illiterate persons who constituted the majority of the first Christian churches, yet all classes have conquered. At the stake, bishops have burned and princes have died, but more numerous still have been the weavers, and the tailors, and the seamstresses. The poorest of the poor have been as brave as the wealthy; the learned have died gloriously, but the unlearned have almost stolen the palm. Little children have suffered for Christ; their little souls, washed in the blood of Jesus, have also been encrimsoned with their own; meanwhile, the aged have not been behindhand. It must have been a sad but glorious sight to see old Latimer, when past seventy, putting off all his garments but his shirt, and then standing up and saying, as he turned round to Mr. Ridley, "Courage, brother! we shall this day light such a candle in England as, by the grace of God, shall never be put out." Oh! if you wish to serve my Master, old men, you have not passed the prime of your days for that. Young men, if you would be heroes, now is the opportunity. You who are poor, you may glow with as great a glory as the rich; and you who have substance, may count it your joy if you are called in the high places of the field to do battle for your Lord. There is room for all who love the Lord in this fight, and there are crowns for each. O that God would only give us the spirit and the strength to enlist in His army, and to fight till we win the crown! I leave that point, beloved friends, hoping that you will enlarge upon it in your thoughts.

IV. And now to close. The apostle distinctly tells us, THE POWER, MYSTERIOUS AND IRRESISTIBLE, WHICH SUSTAINED THESE MORE THAN CONQUERORS, it was "*Through Him that loved us.*"

They conquered through Christ's being their captain. Much depends upon the leader. Christ showed them how to conquer, by personally enduring suffering, and conquering as their example. They triumphed through Christ as their teacher, for His doctrines strengthened their minds, made them masculine, made them angelic, made them divine, for He made them partakers of the divine nature. But, above all, they conquered because Christ was actually with them. His body was in heaven, for He has risen, but His Spirit was with them. We learn from all the history of the saints, that Christ has a way of infusing supernatural strength into the weakest of the weak. The Holy Spirit, when He comes into contact with our poor, wavering, feeble spirits, girds us up to something which is absolutely impossible to man alone. You look at man as he is, and what can he do? Brethren, he can do nothing. "Without Me ye can do nothing." But look at man with God in him, and I will reverse the question—What can he not do? I do not see a man burning in yonder fires, I see Christ suffering in that man. I do not see a martyr in prison, so much as the divine power, laughing at the thought of imprisonment, and scorning iron bands. I do not so much see a simple-minded virgin, uneducated, contending with sophists and cavillers, as I see the Spirit of the living God speaking through her simple tongue, teaching her in the same hour what she shall speak, and proving the truth that the foolishness of God is greater than the wisdom of man, and the feebleness of God is stronger than the power of man. Oh! it is glorious to think that God should thus take the meanest, poorest, feeblest things, and should put Himself into them, and then say, "Come on, all ye that are wise and great, and I will baffle you through those that are foolish and feeble! Now, come, ye devils of hell; come, ye men of earth, who breathe out threatenings, and foam with cruelty; come all of you, and this poor defenceless one shall laugh you all to scorn, and triumph even to the last!" It is the power of Christ. And did you notice the name by which the apostle called our Lord in the text? It is so significant, that I think it is the key to the text, "Through Him that loved us." Yes, love yielded them victory. They knew He loved them, had loved them, always would love them. They knew that if they suffered for His sake, it was His love which let them suffer for their ultimate gain, and for His permanent honour. They felt that He loved them; they could not doubt it, they never mistrusted that fact, and this it was that made them so strong. O beloved, are ye weak to-day? Go to Him that loved you. Does your love grow cold to-day? Do not go to Moses to get it improved; do not search your own heart with a view of finding anything good there, but go at once to Him that loved you. Think, this morning, of our Lord's leaving heaven, and of His incarnation upon earth. Think especially of the bloody sweat of Gethsemane, the wounds of Calvary, the dying thirst, the "My God! My God! why hast Thou forsaken Me?" Think of all that. Get Christ's love to you burnt into your inmost consciousness; and in the strength of this, fear no difficulties, dread no tribulations, but march to your life-battle as the heroes of old went to theirs, and you shall return with your crowns of victory as they returned with theirs, and you shall find that verse which we just now sang, to be most divinely true.

"And they who, with their Leader, have conquered in the fight,
    For ever and for ever, are clad in robes of white."

PAUL'S PERSUASION

"For I am persuaded that neither death, nor life, nor angels, nor principalities, nor powers, nor things present, nor things to come, nor height, nor depth, nor any other creature, shall be able to separate us from the love of God which is in Christ Jesus our Lord."—Romans viii. 38, 39.

A CHRISTIAN brother was asked, on day, "To what persuasion do you belong?" He parried the question at first, for he did not think that it was very important for him to answer it. So the enquirer asked him again, "But what is your persuasion?" "Well," said he, "if you must know my persuasion, this is it: 'I am persuaded that neither death, nor life, nor angels, nor principalities, nor powers, nor things present, nor things to come, nor height, nor depth, nor any other creature, shall be able to separate us from the love of God which is in Christ Jesus our Lord.'" I also am of that persuasion. Somebody says, "That is Calvinistic doctrine." If you like to call it so, you may; but I would rather that you made the mistake of the good old Christian woman who did not know much about these things, and who said that she herself was "a high Calvarist." She liked "high Calvary" preaching, and so do I; and it is "high Calvary" doctrine that I find in this passage. He who hung on high Calvary was such a lover of the souls of men that from that glorious fact I am brought to this blessed persuasion, "I am persuaded that neither death, nor life, nor angels, nor principalities, nor powers, nor things present, nor things to come, nor height, nor depth, nor any other creature, shall be able to separate us from the love of God which is in Christ Jesus our Lord."

Paul was fully persuaded of this great truth. Did he not learn it by revelation? I doubt not that God at first supernaturally revealed it to him; but yet, in order that he might be still more sure of it, God was pleased to reveal it to him again and again, till his trembling heart was more and more completely persuaded of it. It may have seemed to him, as it does to some of us, to be almost too good to be true, and therefore the Holy Spirit so shed abroad this truth in the apostle's mind that he yielded to it, and said, "I am persuaded." He may have thought, with a great many in the present day, that it was necessary to caution believers against falling from grace, and to be a little dubious about their final perseverance in the ways of God; but, if he ever had such fears, he gave them up, and said, "I am,—yes, I am persuaded that nothing can separate us from the love of God which is in Christ Jesus our Lord."

Besides that, I suppose that the apostle was persuaded through reasoning with himself from other grand truths. He said to himself, "If, when we were enemies, we were reconciled to God by the death of His Son, much more, being reconciled, we shall be saved by His life." He argued that, if the death of Christ reconciled God's enemies to Himself, the life of Christ will certainly preserve safely those who are the friends of God; that was good argument, was it not?

I have no doubt that Paul also argued with himself from the nature of the work of grace, which is the implantation of a living and incorruptible seed which liveth and abideth for ever. Christ spoke of it as the putting of a well into us, and He said, "The water that I shall give him shall be in him a well of water springing up into everlasting life." And as Paul thought of the nature of this new life, he felt persuaded that it would not die; he was convinced that he would never be separated from the love of God.

Moreover, I doubt not that Paul remembered the doctrine of the union of believers with Christ, and he said to himself, "Shall Christ lose the members of His body? Shall a foot or an arm be lopped off from Him? Shall an eye of Christ be put out in darkness?" And he could not think that it could be so; as he turned the matter over mentally, he said, "If they be indeed one with Christ, I am persuaded that nothing can separate them from the love of God which is in Christ Jesus our Lord."

Now, dear brethren, if I could extend the time for this service to four-and-twenty hours, I might give you all the arguments, or the most of the arguments, which support the blessed truth of the non-separation of believers from the love of Christ. As for my own convictions, I never can doubt it, I am fully persuaded concerning it. This truth seems to me to have struck its roots into all the other truths of Scripture, and to have twisted itself among the granite rocks which are the very foundation of our hope. I, too, am persuaded by a thousand arguments, and persuaded beyond all question, that nothing shall be able to separate us from the love of God which is in Christ Jesus our Lord.

Yet more, I fancy that Paul had been persuaded of this truth by his own experience. He had endured persecution, imprisonment, famine, shipwreck; he had suffered from scorn and scandal, pain of body, and depression of spirit. "A night and a day," said he, "I have been in the deep," and I will warrant you that many a night and many a day he had been in spiritual deeps; yet he had survived them all, and he could testify to the faithfulness of his God, and say at the end, as the issue of his sufferings, "I am persuaded that nothing in creation is able to separate us from the love of God which is in Christ Jesus our Lord."

Thus he was persuaded of this truth by revelation, by argument, and by experience; and I should like you to notice that he was not only persuaded that none of the powers he mentions will separate us from the love of Christ, but that they cannot do it. He puts it thus, they are not able to separate us. Yet these are the strongest forces imaginable—death, life, angels, principalities, powers, the dreary present and the darker future. Paul summons all our foes, and sets them in battle array against us, and when he has added up the total of all their legions, he says that he is persuaded that they shall not be able—shall not be able, mark you,—to separate us from the love of God which is in Christ Jesus our Lord.

I. In this discourse I am only going to handle the topic of Paul's persuasion. Paul says, "I am persuaded," and it is implied that, first, HE IS PERSUADED OF THE LOVE OF GOD. He could not be persuaded that nothing could separate us from a thing which did not exist, so he is persuaded, first of all, of the love of God which is in Christ Jesus our Lord.

Come, my brothers and sisters, *are you persuaded of the love of God?* Are you intelligently persuaded not only that God is love, but that God loves *you?* Are you fully persuaded of the love of God,—the love of the Father who chose us, because He would choose us, for nothing but His love; the love of Jesus, the Son of God, who bowed Himself from His glory that He might redeem us from our shame; the love of the Holy Ghost who has quickened us, and who comes to dwell in us that we may by-and-by dwell with Him? Are you persuaded of this love of God to you? Happy man, happy woman, who can truly say, "I am persuaded that God loves me. I have thought it over, I have fully considered it, I have thoroughly weighed it, and I have come to this persuasion, that the love of God is shed abroad in my heart."

Then, next, it is *the love of God in Christ Jesus our Lord.* That is, His great love in giving His dear Son to die for us. I am not going to expatiate upon this wondrous theme. The thoughts are too great to need to be spun out, or you can do that in your private meditations. Is it not a wonderful thing that God loved *me,* and loved *you* (let us individualize it,) that God so loved *us* that he gave His only-begotten Son, that whosoever believeth in Him should not perish, but have everlasting life? He gave His Son for you; and for me. It is as though one bartered a diamond to buy a common pebble from the brook, or gave away an empire to purchase some foul thing not worthy of being picked off a dunghill. Yet we are persuaded that He did it, and that the love of God is most clearly to be seen in the fact that He gave His Son Jesus Christ to die instead of us.

And, once more, we are persuaded of *the love of God to all who are in Christ.* We believe in Christ, and so we come to be in Christ by our believing; and now we are persuaded that, to as many as receive Christ, to them gives He power to become the sons of God, even to them that believe on His name, and therefore all who believe in Jesus are beloved of the Lord, not because of anything good in them, but for Jesus Christ's sake. He loves Christ so much that He loves us notwithstanding our unloveliness, because Jesus Christ has covered us with His robe of righteousness, and He has said, "My Father, consider them as lost in Me, hidden in Me, made one with Me." And the Father says, "Yes, My beloved Son, I will love them; Jesus, I will love them for Thy sake."

So we are persuaded of these three things: first, that God loves us; next, that God has shown His love to us by the gift of His Son Jesus Christ; and then, that His divine love comes streaming down to us because we are in Christ, and are loved for His sake. I want you, dear friends, to get this persuasion into you. If you are not so persuaded, here is honey, but you do not taste it; here is light, but you do not see it; here is heaven, but you do not enter the pearly gate. Beloved, if you would be saved, you must be persuaded of this truth; and when you are persuaded of it, you will know the joy of it.

II. That leads me to pass on to the second thing of which Paul was persuaded. It does not appear on the surface of the text; but if you look a minute, you will see that PAUL WAS PERSUADED THAT HE AND ALL THE SAINTS ARE JOINED TO GOD BY LOVE. Otherwise, he could not have said, "I am persuaded that things present and things to come shall not be able to separate us." We must be joined together, or else the apostle would not talk of separation. There is a picture for you to contemplate,—God and ourselves joined together by the bonds of love in Christ Jesus. God loves Christ, and we love Christ, so we have a meeting-place; we love the same blessed Person, and that brings us to love one another.

There are two things that join God and a believer together; the first is, God's love to the believer, and the second is, the believer's love to God. It is as when two dear friends lovingly embrace with their arms around each other's neck, there is a double link binding them together. Or, to come nearer the truth, it is as when a mother puts her arms around the neck of her little child, and her child puts its tiny arms about the mother's neck; that is how we and God are joined together.

Are you persuaded that it is o with you, dear friends? Can you each one say, as you sit in your pew to-night, "*God loves me, and that love joins Him to me;*" and "*I love God, and that love joins me to Him*"? I believe that the apostle was persuaded that these two blessed links existed between him and the great God, and he was persuaded that neither of those two links would ever be broken. God could not withdraw from Paul His embrace of love, and Paul felt that, by divine grace, he could not withdraw his embrace of love from his God; but he must have been first of all persuaded that both those embraces were there. Are *you,* my dear hearer, persuaded that it is so with you? Are your arms about the neck of the great Father? Are the great Father's loving arms about your neck? Be persuaded of that truth, and you are indeed happy men and happy women; what more could you wish to say than to be able truthfully to say that?

III. Now, to come to what is evidently in the text, and to dwell upon it for a little while, Paul being thus persuaded that there was a love of God, and that there was a union through love between the soul and its God, now says that HE IS PERSUADED THAT NOTHING CAN EVER BREAK THOSE BONDS.

He begins by mentioning some of the things that are supposed to separate, and the first is, *death.* It sends a shiver through some when we begin to speak of death, and the bravest man who ever lived may well tremble at the thought that he must soon meet the king of terrors; but, brothers and sisters, if Christ loves us, and we love Christ, we may well be persuaded that death will not break the union which exists between us. I have lately seen one or two of our friends almost in the very article of death; I think that they cannot long survive, but I have come out from their bed-chamber greatly cheered by their holy peacefulness and joy. I can see that death does not break the believer's peace; it seems rather to strengthen it. I can see that there is no better place than the brink of Jordan, after all. I have seen the brethren, and the sisters, too, sit with their feet in the narrow stream, and they have been singing all the while. Death has not abated a single note of their song; nay, more, I have known some of them who are like the fabled swan which is said never to sing till it dies. Some of them who were rather heavy and sad of spirit in their days of health have grown joyous and glad as they have neared the eternal kingdom. There is nothing about death that the believer should construe it into a fear that it will separate him from the love of Christ. Christ loved you when He died; He will love you when you die. It was after death— remember that,—it was after death that His heart poured out the tribute of blood and water by which we have the double cure; see, then, how He loves us in death and after death. There is nothing about death that should make Christ cease to love us; our bodies will be under His protection and guardian care, and our souls shall be with Christ, which is "far better" than being anywhere else. Do not, therefore, fear death. In the days when this Epistle was written, the saints had to die very cruel deaths by fire, by the cross, by wild beasts in the amphitheatre; they were sawn asunder, they wandered about in sheep skins and goat skins, being destitute, afflicted, tormented; yet they never feared death. It is very wonderful how the Church of Christ seems always to brighten up at the idea of death by martyrdom. The grandest, most heroic, days in Christendom were the days of the Pagan persecutions, when, to be a Christian, meant to be doomed to die. In English history, the days of Mary, when the saints at Smith-field bore witness for Christ at the stake, were grand days; and in Madagascar,—did you ever read a more thrilling story than the record of the bravery of those Christian men and women who suffered the tyrant's cruelty? And at the present moment, in Central Africa, where Bishop Hannington has been put to death, we hear that there is an edict for the killing of Christians, yet hundreds of black men come forward to confess that they are followers of Christ. It is a wonderful thing. We do not ask for these persecu-tions, but they might do us great good if they came. Certainly, this wondrous ship of Christ's Church, when she ploughs her way through waves of blood, makes swifter headway to the heavenly haven than she does in times of calm. So, beloved friends, there is nothing in death to separate us from the love of God in Christ Jesus.

The apostle says next, *"nor life."* I must confess that I am more afraid of life than of death. "Oh!" says one, "but dying is such hard work." Do you think so? Why, dying is the end of work; it is living that is hard work. I am not so much afraid of dying as I am of sinning; that is ten times worse than death. And what if some of us should live very many years? "There's the respect that makes calamity of so long life," that there is so much longer time for temptation and trial. If one might have his choice, one might be content to have a short warfare, and to enter upon the crown at once. But we may be permitted to live on to extreme old age; do you dread it? There is nothing about old age to separate you from the love of Christ; He hath made, and He will bear; even to hoar hairs will He carry you; therefore, be not afraid. The ills of life are many, the trials of life are many, the temptations of life are more; O life, life, life here below, thou art, after all, little better than a lingering death! The true life is hereafter. "Yet," says Paul, "I am persuaded that life cannot separate us from the love of God in Christ Jesus." He means that, if we were tempted by the love of life to deny Christ, we should be strengthened so that we should not deny Him even to save our lives, for His people have been brave enough in this respect in all times. Paul himself counted not his life dear unto him that he might win Christ, and be found in Him; wherefore he says that he is persuaded that neither death, nor life, shall be able to separate us from the love of God which is in Christ Jesus our Lord.

Then he mentions *angels, principalities, and powers.* Well, the good angels cannot separate us from the love of God; we are sure that they would not wish to do so, and whatever spiritual creatures may frequent this earth, they cannot separate us from the love of Christ. Does the apostle mean devils,— fallen angels, that would overthrow us, some of them as "principalities" by their dignity, others of them as "powers" by their subtle, crafty force,—does he refer to devils? I think he does, and this, then, is our comfort, that, if we have to meet the arch-fiend himself foot to foot in terrible duel,—and we may, for men of God have had so to meet him, and he that does battle with this adversary will gain nothing by it but sweat of blood and aching heart, even if he shall win the victory, so that we may well pray, "Lead us not into temptation, but deliver us from the evil one,"— still we have this comfort, that even though he may rejoice over us for a moment, and may cast us down, he cannot separate us from the love of Christ; he may open many of our veins, and make us bleed even to utter weakness, but the life-vein he can never touch. There is a secret something about the Christian of which Satan wishes to spoil him, but which is entirely out of his reach, so the saint sings, "I am persuaded that neither angels, nor princi-palities, nor powers can separate me from the love of Christ. You may come on, battalions of the adversary, with all your terrible might, sweeping hypocrites and deceivers before you, like chaff before the wind, but as many as are linked to Christ by His eternal love shall stand firm against you, like the solid rocks against the billows of the sea." Wherefore, be confident, dear brethren, that these spiritual beings, these unseen forces, these strange and mysterious powers which you cannot fully understand, can none of them separate you from the love of God which is in Christ Jesus, your Lord.

Having summarily disposed of all of them, Paul adds, *"nor things present."* I like this thought. He is persuaded that things present cannot separate us from Christ. I wonder what the things present are with you, my dear hearers. One of you says, "Well, it is an empty pocket with me." Others will say, " It is a family of children who have no bread." Some may say, "It is the prospect of bankruptcy." Another will say, "Ah, it is an insidious disease that will soon carry me to my grave!" A mother will say, "It is rebellious children who are breaking my heart." Well whatever it may be,—and the woes of the present are very small,—there is nothing that can separate us from the love of Christ.

I was feeling very heavy, I scarcely knew why, when I caught at this text; and it seemed to come in so pleasantly for me when my spirits were down. "Things present." Even a depressed and desponding state of mind, whatever the cause of it is, whether weariness of brain or heaviness of heart, cannot separate us from the love of God in Christ Jesus. Then, what can it do? Why, sometimes, it can drive us to Christ; let us pray that it may. But anyhow, things present cannot separate us from the love of God in Christ Jesus.

Then the apostle says, "*nor things to come.*" Well, I wonder what is "to come." O friends, I sometimes feel a strange trembling when I stand upon this platform to speak to you, because the words that I utter are often so remarkably fulfilled of God as really to amaze me. Two Sunday nights ago, when I stood here to preach about the long-sueffring of God being salvation, I spoke, in the middle of the sermon, as if personally addressing someone who was present, who had lately been ill with fever, and who had come to the Tabernacle, still weakly, and scarcely recovered. There was a young man here, who exactly answered to the description I gave, and who wrote home to his mother something like this (I have the letter):—" I went to Spurgeon's Tabernacle on Sunday night, and I heard such a sermon. I never felt anything like it before. He looked at me, and picked me out as if I was the only man there, and described me exactly." Then he gave the words I used, and continued, " It was a true description of myself. If the sermon is printed, pray get me a copy that I may read it when I come home, for I felt the power of it, and I prayed there and then that God would bring me to my mother's God, and save me." That was on the Sunday, mark you; on the Wednesday, he was at Gravesend, there was a collision, and he and five others were drowned. The mother received that letter about an hour before she heard the news that her son was dead, and the parents write to tell me what a balm it was to their spirits that God's providence should bring their boy in here just before he was to meet his God.

So, you see, I cannot help wondering what the "things to come" will be for you who are here. With some,—who can tell?—as the Lord liveth, there may be but a step between you and death; and if you have no Christ ι nd have never tasted of His love, you are running awful risks even in going one step further. You have walked on, and on, and on, and there has hitherto always been something beneath your footfall; but the next step may precipitate you into the abyss. Wherefore, seek the Lord now ere it be too late. As for the child of God, he knows no more about his immediate future than you do; but he knows this, that there is nothing in the future that can separate him from the love of God which is in Christ Jesus our Lord. Therefore, let the future bring with it what it may, all will be well with him.

Now the apostle adds two more expressions, "*nor height, nor depth.*" There are some brethren who dwell in the heights; I am rather pleased to meet with dear friends who never have any doubts or fears, but are always full of joy and ecstasy, and who go on to tell us that they have left all these things behind, and have risen to the heights of bliss. But what I do not like is when they look down from those awful heights upon us poor Christians, and say that they cannot believe in us because we are anxious, because we practise self-examination, because we have to struggle against sin. They do not struggle; they have risen beyond all struggling, they rub their hands, and sing of everlasting victory. Well, my dear brother,—you up there on the topmost bough,—you will not frighten me with all your heights, though I cannot get up there, and I could not stay there if I could get up so high. This one thing I know, I am sure that there is nothing in those heights that can separate me from the love of Christ; I will stick to that, whatever revelations there may be to the enthusiastic, whatever raptures and ecstasies and extreme delights any may have, they cannot separate me from Christ. I am glad that you have them, brother, may you always keep them; and if I cannot have them, I shall sit down in my struggles and temptations and still say that there is nothing in the heights,—in high doctrine or in high living,—that can separate me from the love of Christ.

I am a little more acquainted with the depths, and I meet with many Christian people who are very familiar with those depths. I could indicate some dear friends here who I hope are not in the depths now, but I have seen them there. You were very low down, brother; we had to stoop to call to you; the waters of God's waves and billows seemed to have gone over you; you have been down to the depths, and I have been there with you. But there is nothing in the depths that can separate us from the love of Christ. Jonah went down to the depths of the sea, but he came up with this testimony, that there was nothing there to separate us from the love of God. No; though you should be weary of your life, though you should never have a ray of light by the month together, there is nothing there to separate you from the love of Christ. You may go down, down, down, till you seem to have got beyond the reach of help from mortal man; but there are cords and bands which bind you to Christ that even these depths can never break, come what may.

The apostle ends the list by saying, "*nor any other creature.*" It may be read, "Nor anything in creation, nor anything that ever is to be created," nothing shall ever separate us from the love of Christ. Oh, what a sweet persuasion is this! Let us go forward into the future, however dark it is, with this confidence, that, one thing at least we know,—the love of Christ will hold us fast, and by His grace we will hold fast to Him. We are married to Him, and we shall never be divorced. We are joined to Him by a living, loving, lasting union that never shall be broken.

IV. I have done when I have called your attention to one more thing. Did you notice how the text begins? It begins with the word "for." " *For* I am persuaded." What does that mean? That shows that this is used as an argument drawn from something mentioned before. What is that? "Nay, in all these things we are more than conquerors through Him that loved us, *for* I am persuaded, that neither death, nor life," and so on. It seems, then, dear friends, that PAUL'S PERSUASION HELPED TO BRING HIM TO VICTORY.

He was persuaded that Christ would not leave him, and that he would not be allowed to leave Christ, and *this stirred him up to deeds of daring.* Oh, where there is real cause for fighting, there cannot be victory without striving! Paul was so persuaded that Christ would never leave him that he became a fighter, and he went in with all his might against the world, the flesh, and the devil. Some say that this doctrine would send us to sleep; it never does, it wakes us up. The doctrine that I am quite sure to gain the victory makes me fight. If I did not know that I should win it, I might think that I would let discretion be the better part of my valour; but, being assured that Christ will be with me all through, I feel incited to war against all that is evil that I may overcome it in His strength.

Yes, and the apostle seems to hint that this persuasion that Christ would not leave him *made him aspire to a very great victory.* Men do not reach what they do not aspire to, and Paul says, "We are more than conquerors." Therefore, he aspired to be a complete and perfect conqueror. And this persuasion *helped him to gain his aspiration.* By God's grace, the man who trusts in Christ's eternal love, and believes in the immutability of the divine purpose, and

therefore is persuaded that he can never be separated from the love of God which is in Christ Jesus, he is the man to win a glorious victory by his faith in his great God. Wherefore, let us be encouraged to go on, and fight against everything that is evil, especially in ourselves, and tread down all the powers of darkness, since nothing can stand against us while Christ is for us; and for us He must be for ever and ever.

I wish that all here present had a share i my blessed text. It is an intense regret to me that i cannot present it to some of you. You do not know the love of Christ. Oh, that you would come and learn it! May the sweet Spirit lead you to Jesus, cause you to look to Him upon the cross, and trust in Him; then you will have something worth having, for you will have a love that changeth never, a love that shall never be separated from you nor you from it. God bless you, for Christ's sake. Amen.

JACOB AND ESAU

" Jacob have I loved, but Esau have I hated."—Romans ix. 13.

DO not imagine for an instant that I pretend to be able thoroughly to elucidate the great mysteries of predestination. There are some men who claim to know all about the matter. They twist it round their fingers as easily as if it were an everyday thing; but depend upon it, he who thinks he knows all about this mystery, knows but very little. It is but the shallowness of his mind that permits him to see the bottom of his knowledge; he who dives deep, finds that there is in the lowest depth to which he can attain a deeper depth still. The fact is, that the great questions about man's responsibility free-will, and predestination, have been fought over, and over, and over again, and have been answered in ten thousand different ways; and the result has been, that we know just as much about the matter as when we first began. The combatants have thrown dust into each other's eyes, and have hindered each other from seeing; and then they have concluded, that because they put other people's eyes out, they could therefore see.

Now, it is one thing to refute another man's doctrine but a very different matter to establish my own views. It is very easy to knock over one man's hypothesis concerning these truths, not quite so easy to make my own stand on a firm footing. I shall try to-night, if I can, to go safely, if I do not go very fast; for I shall endeavour to keep simply to the letter of God's Word. I think that if we kept more simply to the teachings of the Bible, we should be wiser than we are; for by turning from the heavenly light of revelation, and trusting to the deceitful will-o'-the-wisps of our own imagination, we thrust ourselves into quags and bogs where there is no sure footing, and we begin to sink; and instead of making progress, we find ourselves sticking fast. The truth is, neither you nor I have any right to want to know more about predestination than what God tell us. That is enough for us. If it were worth while for us to know more, God would have revealed more. What God has told us, we are to believe, but to the knowledge thus gained, we are too apt to add our own vague notions, and then we are sure to go wrong. It would be better, if in all controversies, men had simply stood hard and fast

by "Thus saith the Lord," instead of having it said, "Thus and thus I think," I shall now endeavour, by the help of the Holy Spirit, to throw the light of God's Word upon this great doctrine of divine sovereignty, and give you what I think to be a Scriptural statement of the fact, that some men are chosen, other men are left,—the great fact that is declared in this text,—"Jacob have I loved, but Esau have I hated."

It is a terrible text, and I will be honest with it if I can. One man says the word "hate" does not mean hate; it means "love less."—"Jacob have I loved, but Esau have I loved less." It may be so; but I don't believe it is. At any rate, it says "hate" here; and until you give me another version of the Bible, I shall keep to this one. I believe that the term is correctly and properly translated; that the word "hate" is not stronger than the original; but even if it be a little stronger. it is nearer the mark than the other translation which is offered to us in those meaningless words, "love less." I like to take it and let it stand just as it is. The fact is, God loved Jacob, and He did not love Esau; He did choose Jacob, but He did not choose Esau; He did bless Jacob, but He never blessed Esau; His mercy followed Jacob all the way of his life, even to the last, but His mercy never followed Esau; He permitted him still to go on in his sins, and to prove that dreadful truth, "Esau have I hated." Others, in order to get rid of this ugly text, say, it does not mean Esau and Jacob; it means the nation; it means Jacob's children and Esau's children; it means the children of Israel and Edom. I should like to know where the difference lies. Is the difficulty removed by extending it? Some of the Wesleyan brethren say, that there is a national election; God has chosen one nation and not another. They turn round and tell us it is unjust in God to choose one man and not another. Now, we ask them by everything reasonable, is it not equally unjust of God to choose one nation and leave another? The argument which they imagine overthrows us overthrows them also. There never was a more foolish subterfuge than that of trying to bring out national election. What is the election of a nation but the election of so many *units*, of so many people? and it is tantamount to the same thing as the particular election of individuals. In thinking, men cannot see clearly that if—which we do not for a moment believe—that if there be any injustice in God choosing one man and not another, how much more must there be injustice in His choosing one nation and not another. No! the difficulty cannot be got rid of thus, but is greatly increased by this foolish wrestling of God's Word. Besides, here is the proof that that is not correct; read the verse preceding it. It does not say anything at all about nations; it says, "For the children being not yet born, neither having done any good or evil, that the purpose of God according to election might stand, not of works, but of Him that calleth; It was said unto her, The elder shall serve the younger,"—referring to the children, not to the nations. Of course the threatening was afterwards fulfilled in the position of the two nations; Edom was made to serve Israel. But this text means just what it says; it does not mean nations, but it means the persons mentioned. "Jacob,"—that is the man whose name was Jacob—"Jacob have I loved, but Esau have I hated." Take care, my dear friends, how any of you meddle with God's Word. I have heard of folks altering passages they did not like. It will not do, you know, you cannot alter them; they are really just the same. Our only power with the Word of God is simply to let it stand as it is, and to endeavour by God's grace to accommodate ourselves to that. We must never try to make the Bible bow to us, in fact we cannot, for the truths of divine revelation are as sure and fast as the throne of God. If a man wants to enjoy a delightful prospect, and a mighty mountain lies in his path, does he commence cutting away at its base, in the vain hope that ultimately it will become a level plain before him? No, on the contrary, he diligently uses it for the accomplishment of his purpose by ascending it, well knowing this to be the only means of obtaining the end in view. So must we, do; we cannot bring down the truth of God to our poor finite understandings; the mountain will never fall before us, but we can seek strength to rise higher and higher in our perception of divine things, and in this way only may we hope to obtain the blessing.

Now, I shall have two things to notice to-night. I have explained this text to mean just what it says, and I do not want it to be altered—"Jacob have I loved, but Esau have I hated." To take off the edge of this terrible doctrine that makes some people bite there lips so, I must just notice that *this is a fact* and, after that, I shall try to answer the question,— *Why was it that God loved Jacob and hated Esau?*

I. First, then THIS IS A FACT. Men say they do not like the doctrine of election. Verily, I do not want them to; but is it not a fact that God has elected some? Ask an Armenian brother about election, and at once his eye turns fiercely upon you, and he begins to get angry, he can't bear it; it is a horrible thing, like a war-cry to him, and he begins to sharpen the knife of controversy at once. But say to him, "Ah, brother! was it not divine grace that made you to differ? Was it not the Lord who called you out of your natural state, and made you what you are?" "Oh, yes," he says, "I quite agree with you there." Now, put this question to him: "What do you think is the reason why one man has been converted, and not another?" "Oh," he says, "the Spirit of God has been at work in this man." Well, then, my brother, the fact is, that God *does* treat one man better than another; and is there anything wonderful in this fact? It is a fact we recognize every day. There is a man up in the gallery there, that work as hard as he likes, he cannot earn more than fifteen shillings a week; and here is another man that gets a thousand a year; what is the reason of this? One is born in the palaces of kings, while another draws his first breath in a roofless hovel. What is the reason of this? God's providence. He puts one man in one position, and another man in another. Here is a man whose head cannot hold two thoughts together, do what you will with him; here is another who can sit down and write a book, and dive into the deepest of questions; what is the reason of it? God has done it. Do you not see the fact, that God does not treat every man alike? He has made some eagles, and some worms; some He has made lions, and some creeping lizards; He has made some men kings, and some are born beggars. Some are born with gigantic minds, and some verge on the idiot. Why is this? Do you murmur at God for it? No, you say it is a fact, and there is no good in murmuring. What is the use of kicking against facts? It is only kicking against the pricks with naked feet, and you hurt yourself and not them. Well, then, election is a positive fact; it is as clear as daylight, that God does, in matters of religion, give to one man more than to another. He gives to me opportunities of hearing the word, which He does not give to the Hottentot. He gives to me, parents who, from infancy, trained me in the fear of the Lord. He does not give that to many of you. He places me afterwards in situations where I am restrained from sin. Other men are cast into places where their sinful passions are developed. He gives to one man a temper and disposition which keeps him back from some lust, and to another man He gives such impetuosity of spirit, and depravity turns that impetuosity so much aside, that the man runs headlong into sin. Again, He brings one man under the sound of a powerful ministry, while another sits and listens to a preacher whose drowsiness is only exceeded by that of his hearers. And even when they are hearing the gospel, the fact is God works in one heart when He does not in another. Though I believe to a degree the Spirit works in the hearts of all who hear the Word, so that they are all without excuse, yet I am sure He works in some so powerfully, that they can no longer resist Him, but are constrained by His grace to cast themselves at His feet, and confess Him Lord of all ; while others resist the grace that comes into their hearts ; and it does not act with the same irresistible force that it does in the other case, and they perish in their sins, deservedly and justly condemned. Are not these things facts ? Does any man deny them ? *can* any man deny them ? What is the use of kicking against facts ? I always like to know when there is a discussion, what is the fact. You have heard the story of King Charles the Second and the philosophers—King Charles asked one of them, " What is the reason why, if you had a pail of water, and weighed it, and then put a fish into it, that the weight would be the same ? " They gave a great many elaborate reasons for this. At last one of them said, " Is it the fact ? " And then they found out that the water did weigh more, just as much more as the fish put into it. So all their learned arguments fell to the ground. So, when we are talking about election, the best thing is to say, "Put aside the doctrine for a moment, let us see what is the fact?" We walk abroad; we open our eyes; we see, there is the fact. What, then, is the use of our discussing any longer? We had better believe it, since it is an undeniable truth. You may alter an opinion, but you cannot alter a fact. You may change a mere doctrine, but you cannot possibly change a thing which actually exists. There it is—God does certainly deal with some men better than He does with others. I will not offer an apology for God; He can explain His own dealings; He needs no defence from me,

"God is His own interpreter,
And He will make it plain";

but there stands the fact. Before you begin to argue upon the doctrine, just recollect that whatever you may think about it, you cannot alter it; and however much you may object to it, it is actually true that God did love Jacob, and did not love Esau.

For now look at Jacob's life and read his history; you are compelled to say that, from the first hour that he left his father's house, even to the last, God loved him. Why, he has not gone far from his father's house before he is weary, and he lies down with a stone for his pillow, and the hedges for his curtain, and the sky for his canopy; and he goes to sleep, and God comes and talks to him in his sleep; he sees a ladder, whereof the top reaches to heaven, and a company of angels ascending and descending upon it; and he goes on his journey to Laban. Laban tries to cheat him, and as often as Laban tries to wrong him, God suffers it not, but multiplies the different cattle that Laban gives him. Afterwards, you remember, when he fled unawares from Laban, and was pursued, that God appears to Laban in a dream, and charges him not to speak to Jacob either good or bad. And more memorable still, when his sons Levi and Simeon have committed murder in Shechem, and Jacob is afraid that he will be overtaken and destroyed by the inhabitants who were rising against him, God puts a fear upon the people, and says to them, "Touch not Mine anointed, and do My prophet no harm." And when a famine comes over the land, God has sent Joseph into Egypt, to provide corn in Goshen for his brethren, that they should live and not die. And so the happy end of Jacob—"I shall see my son Joseph before I die." Behold the tears streaming down his aged cheeks, as he clasps his own Joseph to his bosom! See how magnificently he goes into the presence of Pharaoh, and blesses him. It is said, "Jacob blessed Pharaoh." He had God's love so much in him, that he was free to bless the mightiest monarch of his times. At last he gave up the ghost and it was said at once, "This was a man that God loved." There is the fact that God did love Jacob.

On the other hand, there is the fact that God did not love Esau. He permitted Esau to become the father of princes, but He has not blessed His generation. Where is the house of Esau now? Edom has perished. She built her chambers in the rock, and cut out her cities in the flinty rock; but God has abandoned the inhabitants thereof, and Edom is not to be found. They became the bond-slaves of Israel; and the kings of Edom had to furnish a yearly tribute of wool to Solomon and his successors; and now the name of Esau is erased from the book of history. Now, then, I must say, again, this ought to take off at least some of the bitterness of controversy, when we recollect that it is the fact, let men say what

they will, that God did love Jacob, and He did not love Esau.

II. But now the second point of my subject is, WHY IS THIS? Why did God love Jacob? why did He hate Esau? Now, I am not going to undertake too much at once. You say to me, "Why did God love Jacob? and why did He hate Esau?" We will take one question at a time, for the reason why some people get into a muddle in theology is because they try to give an answer to two questions. Now, I shall not do that; I will tell you one thing at a time. I will tell you why God loved Jacob; and, then, I will tell you why He hated Esau. But I cannot give you the same reason for two contradictory things. That is wherein a great many have failed. They have sat down and seen these facts, that God loved Jacob and hated Esau, that God has an elect people, and that there are others who are not elect. If, then, they try to give the same reason for election and non-election, they make sad work of it. If they will pause and take one thing at a time, and look to God's Word, they will not go wrong.

The first question is, *why did God love Jacob?* I am not at all puzzled to answer this, because when I turn to the Word of God, I read this text;—"Not for your sakes, do I this saith the Lord God, be it known unto you: be ashamed and confounded for your own ways O house of Israel." I am not at a loss to tell you that it could not be for any good thing in Jacob, that God loved him, because I am told that "the children being not yet born, neither having done any good or evil, that the purpose of God, according to election might stand, not of works but of Him that calleth." I *can* tell you the reason why God loved Jacob; *It is sovereign grace.* There was nothing in Jacob that could make God love him; there was everything about him, that might have made God hate him, as much as He did Esau, and a great deal more. But it was because God was infinitely gracious, that He loved Jacob, and because He was sovereign in His dispensation of this grace, that He chose Jacob as the object of that love. Now, I am not going to deal with Esau, until I have answered the question on the side of Jacob. I want just to notice this, that Jacob was loved of God, simply on the footing of free grace. For, come now, let us look at Jacob's character; I have already said in the exposition, what I think of him. I do think the very smallest things of Jacob's character. As a natural man, he was always a bargain-maker.

I was struck the other day with that vision that Jacob had at Bethel: it seemed to me a most extraordinary development of Jacob's bargain-making spirit. You know he lay down, and God was pleased to open the doors of heaven to him, so that he saw God sitting at the top of the ladder, and the angels ascending and descending upon it. What do you suppose he said as soon as he awoke? Well, he said, "Surely the Lord is in this place; and I knew it not. And he was afraid, and said, How dreadful is this place! this is none other but the house of God, and this is the gate of heaven." Why, if Jacob had had faith, he would not have been afraid of God: on the contrary, he would have rejoiced that God had thus permitted him to hold fellowship with Him. Now, hear Jacob's bargain. God had simply said to him, "I am the Lord God of Abraham thy father, and the God of Isaac: the land whereon thou liest, to thee will I give it, and to thy seed." He did not say anything about what Jacob was to do; God only said, "I will do it,'—"Behold I am with thee, and will keep thee in all places whither thou goest, and will bring thee again into this land; for I will not leave thee, until I have done that which I have spoken to thee of." Now, can you believe, that after God had spoken face to face with Jacob, that He would have had the impudence to try and make a bargain with God? But he did. He begins and says "*If*—" There now, the man has had a vision, and an absolute promise from God, and yet he begins with an "*If.*" That is bargain-making with a vengeance! "*If* God will be with me, and will keep me in the way that I go, and will give me bread to eat, and raiment to put on, so that I come again to my Father's house in peace, *then*"—not without—mark, he is going to hold God to His bargain— "*then* shall the Lord be my God; and this stone which I have set up for a pillar, shall be God's house; and of all that Thou shalt give me I will surely give the tenth unto Thee." I marvel at this! If I did not know something about my own nature, I should be utterly unable to understand it. What! a man that has talked with God, then begin to make a bargain with Him! that has seen the only way of access between heaven and earth, the ladder Christ Jesus, and has had a covenant made between himself and God, a covenant that is all on God's part—all a promise— and yet wants after that to hold God to the bargain: as if he were afraid God would break His promise! Oh! this was vile indeed!

Then notice his whole life. While he lived with Laban, what miserable work it was. He had got into the hands of a man of the world; and whenever a covetous Christian gets into such company, a terrible scene ensues! There are the two together, greedy and grasping. If an angel could look down upon them, how would he weep to see the man of God fallen from his high place, and become as bad as the other. Then, the device that Jacob used, when he endeavoured to get his wages was most extraordinary. Why did he not leave it to God, instead of adopting such systems as that? The whole way through we are ashamed of Jacob; we cannot help it. And then, there is that grand period in his life, the turning point, when we are told, that "Jacob wrestled with God, and prevailed." We will look at that—I have carefully studied the subject, and I do not think so much of him as I did. I thought Jacob wrestled with God, but I find it is the contrary; he did not wrestle with God; God wrestled with him. I had always set Jacob up, in my mind, as the very model of a man wrestling in prayer; I do not think so now. He divided his family, and put a person in front to appease Esau. He did not go in front himself, with the holy trust that a patriarch should have felt; guarded with all the omnipotence of heaven, he might boldly have gone to meet his brother, but no! he did not feel certain that the latter would bow at his feet, although the promise said, "The elder shall serve the younger." He did not rest on that promise; it was not big enough for him. Then he went at night to the brook Jabbok. I do not know what for, unless he went to pray; but I am afraid it was not so. The text says, "And Jacob was left alone: and there wrestled a man with him until the breaking of the day." There is a great deal of difference between a man wrestling with me, and my wrestling with him. When I strive with anyone, I want to gain something from him, and when a man wrestles with me, he wants to get something out of me. Therefore, I take it, when the man wrestled with Jacob, he wanted to get his cunning and deceit out of him, and prove what a poor sinful creature he was, but he could not do it. Jacob's craft was so strong, that he could not be overcome; at last, the angel touched his thigh, and showed him his own hollowness. And Jacob turned round and said, "Thou hast taken away my strength, now I will wrestle with *thee;*" and when his thigh was out of joint, when he fully felt his own weakness, then, and not till then, is he brought to say, "I will not let *thee* go, except thou bless me." He had had full confidence in his own strength, but God at last humbled him, and when all his boasted power was gone, then it was that Jacob became a prevailing prince. But, even after that, his life is not clear. Then you find him an unbelieving creature; and we have all been as bad. Though we are blaming Jacob, brethren, we blame ourselves. We are hard with him, but we shall be harder with ourselves. Do you not remember the memorable speech of the patriarch, when he said, "Joseph is not, and Simeon is not, and ye will take Benjamin away: all these things are against me?" Ah, Jacob, why cannot you believe the promise? All other promises have been fulfilled. But no! he could not think of the promise: he was always wanting to live by sight.

Now, I say if the character of Jacob, be as I have described it, and I am sure it is—we have got it in God's word—there was, there could have been nothing in Jacob, that made God love him; and the only reason why God loved him, must have been because of His own grace, because "He will have mercy on whom He will have mercy." And rest assured, the only reason why any of us can hope to be saved is this, the sovereign grace of God. There is no reason why I should be saved, or why you should be saved, but God's own merciful heart, and God's own omnipotent will. Now that is the doctrine; it is taught not only in this passage, but in multitudes of other passages of God's Word. Dear friends, receive it, hold fast by it, and never let it go.

Now, the next question is a different one: *Why did God hate Esau?* I am not going to mix this question up with the other, they are entirely distinct, and I intend to keep them so, one answer will not do for two questions, they must be taken separately, and then can be answered satisfactorily. Why does God hate any man? I defy anyone to give any answer but this, because that man deserves it; no reply but that can ever be true. There are some who answer, divine sovereignty; but I challenge them to look that doctrine in the face. Do you believe that God created man and arbitrarily, sovereignly—it is the same thing —created that man, with no other intention, than that of damning him? Made him, and yet, for no other reason than that of destroying him for ever? Well, if you can believe it, I pity you, that is all I can say: you deserve pity, that you should think so meanly of God, whose mercy endureth for ever. You are quite right when you say the reason why God loves a man, is because God does do so; there is no reason in the man. But do not give the same answer as to why God hates a man. If God deals with any man severely, it is because that man deserves all he gets. In hell there will not be a solitary soul that will say to God, O Lord, thou hast treated me worse than I deserve! But every lost spirit will be made to feel that he has got his deserts, that his destruction lies at his own door and not at the door of God; that God had nothing to do with his condemnation, except as the Judge condemns the criminal, but that he himself brought damnation upon his own head, as the result of his own evil works. Justice is that which damns a man; it is mercy, it is free grace, that saves; sovereignty holds the scale of love; it is justice holds the other scale. Who can put that into the hand of sovereignty? That were to libel God and to dishonour Him.

Now, let us look at Esau's character, says one, "did he deserve that God should cast him away"? I answer, he did. What we know of Esau's character, clearly proves it. Esau lost his birthright. Do not sit down and weep about that, and blame God. Esau sold it himself; he sold it for a mess of pottage. Oh, Esau, it is in vain for thee to say, "I lost my birthright by decree." No, no. Jacob got it by decree, but you lost it because you sold it yourself—didn't you? Was it not your own bargain? Did you not take the mess of red pottage of your own voluntary will, in lieu of the birthright? Your destruction lies at your own door, because you sold your own soul at your own bargain, and you did it yourself. Did God influence Esau to do that? God forbid, God is not the author of sin. Esau voluntarily gave up his own birthright. And the doctrine is, that every man who loses heaven gives it up himself. Every man who loses everlasting life rejects it himself. God denies it not to him—he will not come that he may have life. Why is it that a man remains ungodly and does not fear God? It is because he says "I like this drink, I like this pleasure, I like this sabbath-breaking, better than I do the things of God." No man is saved by his own free-will, but every man is damned by it if that is damned. He does it of his own will; no one constrains him. You know, sinner, that when you go away from here, and put down the cries of conscience, that you do it yourself. You know that, when after a sermon you say, "I do not care about believing in Christ," you say it yourself—You are quite conscious of it, and if not conscious of it, it is notwithstanding a dreadful fact, that the reason why you are what you are, is because you *will* to be what you are. It is your own will that keeps you where you are, the blame lies at your own door, your being still in a state of sin is voluntary. You are a captive, but you are a voluntary captive. You will never be willing to get free until God makes you willing. But you are willing to be a bond slave. There is no disguising the fact, that man loves sin, loves evil, and does not love God. You know, though heaven is preached to you through the blood of Christ, and though hell is threatened to you as the result of your sins, that still you cleave to your iniquities; you will not leave them, and will not fly to Christ. And when you are cast away, at last it will be said of you, "you have lost your birthright." But you sold it yourself. You know that the ball-room suits you better than the house of God; you know that the pot-house suits you better than the prayer-meeting; you know you trust yourself rather than trust Christ; you know you prefer the joys of the present time to the joys of the future. It is your own choice—keep it. Your damnation is your own election, not God's; you richly deserve it.

But, says one, "Esau repented." Yes, he did, but what sort of a repentance was it? Did you ever notice his repentance? Every man who repents and believes will be saved. But what sort of a repentance was his? As soon as he found that his brother had got the birthright, he sought it again with repentance, he sought it with tears, but he did not get it back. You know

he sold his birthright for a mess of pottage; and he thought he would buy it back by giving his father a a mess of pottage. "There," he says, "I will go and hunt venison for my father. I have got over him with my savoury meat, and he will readily give me my birthright again." That is what sinners say: "I have lost heaven by my evil works: I will easily get it again by reforming. Did I not lose it by sin? I will get it back by giving up my sins." "I have been a drunkard," says one, "I will give up drinking, and I will now be a teetotaller." Another says, "I have been an awful swearer; I am very sorry for it, indeed; I will not swear any more." So all he gives to his father is a mess of pottage, the same as that for which he sold it. No, sinner, you may sell heaven for a few carnal pleasures, but you cannot buy heaven by merely giving them up. You can get heaven only on another ground, viz., the ground of free grace. You lose your soul justly, but you cannot get it back by good works, or by the renunciation of your sins.

You think that Esau was a sincere penitent. Just let me tell you another thing. This blessed penitent, when he failed to get the blessing, what did he say? "The days of mourning for my father are at hand: then will I slay my brother Jacob." There is a penitent for you. That is not the repentance that comes from God the Holy Spirit. But there are some men like that. They say they are very sorry they should have been such sinners as that, very sorry that they should have been brought into such a sad condition as that; and then go and do the same that they did before. Their penitence does not bring them out of their sin, but it leaves them in it, and, perhaps, plunges them still deeper into guilt. Now, look at the character of Esau. The only redeeming trait in it was that he did begin with repentance, but that repentance was even an aggravation of his sin, because it was without the effects of evangelical repentance. And I say, if Esau sold his birthright he did deserve to lose it, and, therefore, am I not right in saying, that if God hated Esau, it was because he deserved to be hated. Do you observe how Scripture always guards this conclusion? Turn to the ninth chapter of Romans, where we have selected our text, see how careful the Holy Spirit is here, in the 22nd verse. "What if God, willing to shew His wrath, and to make His power known, endured with much longsuffering the vessels of wrath fitted to destruction: And that He might make known the riches of His glory on the vessels of mercy, which He had afore prepared unto glory." But it does not say anything about *fitting* men for destruction; they fitted themselves. *They* did that: God had nothing to do with it. But when men are saved, God fits them for that. All the glory to God in salvation; all the blame to men in damnation.

If any of you want to know what I preach every day, and any stranger should say, "Give me a summary of his doctrine," say this, "He preaches salvation all of grace, and damnation all of sin. He gives God all the glory for every soul that is saved, but he won't have it that God is to blame for any man that is damned." That teaching I cannot understand. My soul revolts at the idea of a doctrine that lays the blood of man's soul at God's door. I cannot conceive how any human mind, at least any Christian mind, can hold any such blasphemy as that. I delight to preach this blessed truth—salvation of God, from first to last—the Alpha and the Omega; but when I come to preach damnation, I say, damnation of man, not of God; and if you perish, at your own hands must your blood be required. There is another passage. At the last great day, when all the world shall come before Jesus to be judged, have you noticed, when the righteous go on the right side, Jesus says, "Come, ye blessed of My Father,"—("of My Father," mark,)—"inherit the kingdom prepared"—(mark the next word)—"*for you*, from the foundation of the world." What does He say to those on the left? "Depart, ye cursed." He does not say, "ye cursed of My Father," but, "ye cursed." And what else does He say? "into everlasting fire, prepared"—(*not for you*, but)—"for the devil and his angels." Do you see how it is guarded. Here is the salvation side of the question. It is all of God. "Come, ye blessed of My Father." It is a kingdom prepared for them. There you have election, free grace in all its length and breadth. But, on the other hand, you have nothing said about the Father—nothing about that at all. "Depart, ye cursed." Even the flames are said not to be prepared for sinners, but for the devil and his angels. There is no language that I can possibly conceive that could more forcibly express this idea, supposing it to be the mind of the Holy Spirit, that the glory should be to God, and that the blame should be laid at man's door.

Now, have I not answered these two questions honestly? I have endeavoured to give a scriptural reason for the dealings of God with man. He saves man by grace, and if men perish they perish justly by their own fault. "How," says some one, "do you reconcile these two doctrines?" My dear brethren, I never reconcile two friends, never. These two doctrines are friends with one another; for they are both in God's word, and I shall not attempt to reconcile them. If you show me that they are enemies then I will reconcile them. "But," says one, "there is a great deal of difficulty about them." Will you tell me what truth there is that has not difficulty about it? "But," he says, "I do not see it." Well, I do not ask you to see *it*; I ask you to believe it. There are many things in God's word that are difficult, and that I cannot see, but they are there, and I believe them. I cannot see how God can be omnipotent and man be free; but it is so, and I believe it. "Well," says one, "I cannot understand it." My answer is, I am bound to make it as plain as I can, but if you have not any understanding, I cannot give you any; there I must leave it. But then, again, it is not a matter of understanding; it is a matter of faith. These two things are true; I do not see that they at all differ. However, if they did, I should say, if they appear to contradict one another, they do not really do so, because God never contradicts Himself. And I should think in this I exhibited the power of

my faith in God, that I could believe Him, even when His word seemed to be contradictory. That is faith. Did not Abraham believe in God even when God's promise seemed to contradict His providence? Abraham was old, and Sarah was old, but God said Sarah should have a child. How can that be? said Abraham, for Sarah is old; and yet Abraham believed the promise, and Sarah had a son. There was a reconciliation between providence and promise; and if God can bring providence and promise together, He can bring doctrine and promise together. If I cannot do it, God can, even in the world to come.

Now, let me just practically preach this for one minute. Oh, sinners, if ye perish, on your own head must be your doom. Conscience tells you this, and the word of God confirms it. You shall not be able to lay your condemnation at any man's door but your own. If you perish you perish by suicide. You are your own destroyers, because you reject Christ, because you despise the birthright and sell it for that miserable mess of pottage—the pleasures of the world. It is a doctrine that thrills through me. Like a two-edged sword, I would make it pierce to the dividing asunder of the joints and marrow. If you are damned it shall be your own fault. If you are found in hell, your blood shall be on your own head. You shall bring the faggots to your own burning; you shall dig the iron for your own chains; and on your own head will be your doom. But if you are saved, it cannot be by your merits, it must be by grace—free, sovereign grace. The gospel is preached to you; it is this: "Believe on the Lord Jesus Christ and thou shalt be saved."

May grace now be given to you to bring you to yield to this glorious command. May you now believe in Him who came into the world to save sinners, of whom I am chief. Free grace, who shall tell thy glories? who shall narrate thy achievements, or write thy victories? Thou hast carried the cunning Jacob into glory, and made him white as the angels of heaven, and thou shalt carry many a black sinner there also, and make him glorious as the glorified. May God prove this doctrine to be true in your own experience! If there still remains any difficulty upon your minds about any of these points, search the word of God, and seek the illumination of His Spirit to teach you. But recollect after all, these are not the most important points in Scripture. That which concerns you most, is to know whether *you* have an interest in the blood of Christ? whether you really believe in the Lord Jesus. I have only touched upon these, because they cause a great many people a world of trouble, and I thought I might be the means of helping some of you to tread upon the neck of the dragon. May God grant that it may be so for Christ's sake.

S. S.: OR, THE SINNER SAVED

"What shall we say then? That the Gentiles, which followed not after righteousness, have attained to righteousness, even the righteousness which is of faith. But Israel, which followed after the law of righteousness, hath not attained to the law of righteousness. Wherefore? Because they sought it not by faith, but as it were by the works of the law. For they stumbled at that stumblingstone; as it is written, Behold, I lay in Sion a stumblingstone and rock of offence: and whosoever believeth on Him shall not be ashamed."—Romans ix. 30–33.

FOR several Sabbath mornings I have sought the comfort and edification of God's people, although I trust I have not, even in such discourses, overlooked the unconverted. How can we forget them while they are in such peril? At the same time, the main drift of the service has been for the people of God, and it will not be wise to continue long in that line. We must not forget the lost sheep: it were better that we left the ninety and nine than that we neglected the rambler. We must, therefore, this morning seek to go after that which is gone astray until we find it. Oh, that God the Holy Spirit would make every word to be full of His power! He can fill each sentence with a celestial dynamite, an irresistible energy, which will blast the rocks of self-righteousness, and make a way for the gospel of the grace of God through the impenetrable barriers of sin. For that end I am anxious that, while I speak on God's behalf, the prayers of the faithful may bring down God's power, and make the feeble voice of man to be the vehicle for the omnipotence of God.

It is very necessary often to go over the elements—the foundation truths of the gospel. Schools may rise to the classics, but they can never dispense with the spelling-book. All over the country there must be the repetition of the alphabet, and words of one syllable, or there will be no scholarship. I feel that it is necessary to give line upon line, precept upon precept, as to the first principles of the gospel of our Lord Jesus Christ. Multitudes of persons are in bondage, and will continue to be so until they hear a very clear and simple description of the way of salvation. This is the key of their liberty. You that know these first things must be willing often to hear them; indeed, I find that you are the people that never grow tired of viewing that stone which God has laid in Sion for a foundation; for it never becomes a rock of offence to you. To you the repetitions of Jesus are more acceptable than the novelties of human invention. The system and method of salvation, therefore, will come before you again this morning. Oh, that to some it may seem to be heard for the first time, though they may with the outward ear have heard "the old, old story" a thousand times! Oh, that they may now understand it, grasp it, and find the blessing of it, and so rejoice in God their Saviour!

Paul had two facts before him: the first was, that wherever he went preaching Jesus Christ certain Gentiles believed the doctrine, and straightway became justified persons, receiving at once forgiveness of sins, and a change of heart. He had been in Ephesus and Thessalonica, in Corinth and in Rome, and at his preaching of the word of life the heathen who were outside of the pale of true religious profession had believed in the Lord Jesus, and so had attained to righteousness, and proved that they had done so by their righteous, pure, devout lives. On the other hand, there was the sad fact that whereas he had usually commenced his ministry in the synagogues, and so had opened his commission by addressing the seed of Abraham, to whom belonged the covenants of promise, yet they had almost everywhere rejected the Messiah, and refused the grace of the gospel. At the same time, it was evident that they had missed the righteousness which they conceived they had obtained; for, as a nation, they were in bondage to superstitious prejudice, and were fallen low, both as to morality and spirituality, insomuch that they were correctly described by the prophet when he said, "Except the Lord of Sabaoth had left us a seed, we had been as Sodoma, and been made like unto Gomorrha." There were these two facts before the apostle's mind: the Gentiles, who had been far off, had attained to righteousness; and the Israelites, on the border of it, yet perished there, and did not attain to the law of righteousness. To this he calls our attention, and I shall ask you to look, first of all, at a *wonder of grace*: "The Gentiles, which followed not after righteousness, have attained to righteousness." Secondly, I shall ask you to note a *marvel of folly*: "Israel, which followed after the law of righteousness, hath not attained to the law of righteousness"; and when I have done that, I shall have to throw my whole strength into a *discourse of affectionate concern* about those of you who, as yet, have not attained unto the righteousness which is of faith. Oh that you may see yourselves, and then see the Lord Jesus by the light of the Holy Spirit! Like the prodigal, may it be said of each one of you, "he came to himself," and then "he arose, and came to his Father."

I. First, I crave your earnest attention to A WONDER OF GRACE. *Certain men had attained to righteousness.* They had, so to speak, "put their hand upon righteousness." They had grasped the righteousness of faith, which is the righteousness of God. They could say, "Therefore being justified by faith, we have peace with God through our Lord Jesus Christ." These without boasting could declare that Jesus Christ was made of God unto them wisdom and righteousness. In them the righteousness of the law was fulfilled. They were at peace, for the fruit of righteousness is peace; they were grateful, earnest, devoted, zealous, and they yielded their members instruments of righteousness unto God. The Lord had covered them with the righteousness of Christ, and had infused into them the righteousness of His indwelling Spirit. Saintly men and saintly women were produced among those who once had used "curious arts" and enchantments: in those in whom sin abounded grace reigned through righteousness unto eternal life by Jesus Christ. There were people in the world whom God, the Judge of all, accepted as righteous. Now that alone is a great wonder; for we are all sinners both by nature and by practice, and it is as great a marvel as the making of a world, that anyone of our race should attain to righteousness. Sit down, Christian man, and rejoice in the righteousness which you have received by faith, and you will be filled with amazement. The more you consider the righteousness which you have received in Christ Jesus by your faith in Him, the more you will cry out, "Oh, the depths!" It is indeed a miracle of love that we, who by nature were under the curse, have now obtained the blessing of righteousness, as it is written, "For He hath made Him to be sin for us, who knew no sin; that we might be made the righteousness of God in Him."

The wonder grows when we consider that *these persons who had attained to righteousness had come to it under great disadvantages ;* for they were Gentiles. The Gentiles were considered by the Jews to be offcasts and outcasts, aliens from the commonwealth of grace. They were given up to idolatry or to atheism, and lusts the most degrading were rife among them. They had gone very far from original righteousness. A true picture of the Gentile world in the days of Paul would have terribly dark colours in it: it would be injurious to morals to describe in public the details of the lives of the best of the heathen. If you speak of the manners of the common people, you must be prepared to hear of vices which crimson the cheek of modesty. There are virtues for which the heathen had no name; and they practised vices for which, thank God, you have no name. The Gentiles were filled with all unrighteousness; and withal they were ignorant of the requirements of the law and of the holiness of God. The light which shone upon the seed of Israel had not yet dawned on them. There may have been here and there a chosen few, like Cornelius the centurion, and others, who followed the light which is found in nature and in the human conscience, and so welcomed all that they learned from Israel; but, taken in the bulk, John fitly described the Gentiles when he said, "The whole world lieth in wickedness." The strange thing is that such originally were those men who attained unto righteousness. The gospel came into their streets, and at first they heard it with opposition, saying, "What will this babbler say?" Their attention was attracted, and they were willing to hear the preacher again concerning this matter. Conscience was aroused, and soon they began to enquire, "What must we do to be saved?" Having no righteousness of their own, and being convinced that they needed one, they fled at once to the righteousness which God has prepared in His dear Son for all who believe in Him; and multitudes believed and turned to God. Thus those who knew not the Lord became His obedient worshippers, and those who were far off were made nigh by faith.

Are there not persons here whose condition is somewhat similar to that of the Gentiles? You are not religious: you are not members of godly families, neither are you frequenters of our sanctuaries; but why should not you also attain to righteousness by faith? Wonders of grace are things which God delights in; why should He not work such wonders in you? At any rate, while I preach I am exercising faith concerning you, that you shall at once be brought to salvation and eternal life.

The marvel of grace in the case of these Gentiles was all the greater because, as the apostle says, " *They followed not after righteousness.*" They had originally felt no desire after righteousness before God. Some of them were thoughtful, just, and generous towards men; but righteousness and holiness towards God was not a matter after which they laboured. The Gentile mind ran more upon "What shall we eat? What

shall we drink?" than upon "What is righteousness before God?" Gold or glory, power or pleasure, were the objects for which they ran; but they ran no race for the prize of holiness. They were ignorant of such matters as salvation, reconciliation with God, the inward life, sanctification, and all the other mysteries and blessings of the covenant, and therefore they followed not after them. They were content, most of them, to live like the cattle that ploughed their fields, or like the dogs that prowled through their streets; they followed the devices and desires of their own hearts. Yet when the gospel burst in upon the midnight of their souls they received its light with joy, and accepted the good news from heaven with much readiness of mind. They had not sought the Shepherd, but He had sought them, and, laying them on His shoulders, He brought them to His fold. It was a wonderful thing that, though they did not follow after righteousness, yet they found it. They are like that Indian who, passing up the mountain side pursuing game, grasped a shrub to prevent his slipping, and as its roots gave way they uncovered masses of pure silver, and thus the richest silver mine was discovered by a happy accident by one who looked not for it. These Gentiles discovered in Christ the righteousness which they needed, but which they had never dreamed of finding. This reminds us of our Lord's own parable: the man was ploughing with oxen, and on a sudden the ploughshare struck upon an unusual obstacle. He stopped the plough and turned up the soil, and lo! he found a crock of gold! This "treasure hid in a field" at once won his heart, and for joy thereof he sold all that he had, and bought the field. Grace finds men who else would never have found grace. Oh, the glorious grace of God, which brings the righteousness of Christ full often to those who never sought it, to those who had no religiousness, nor even tendencies that way! Saul, the son of Kish, went to seek his father's asses, and found the kingdom; and even thus have careless and worldly persons been made to know the Lord when it seemed highly improbable that they would ever do so. This is a great wonder, for which all heaven rings with hallelujahs to God.

Observe that *these unlikely persons did really believe, and so attain to righteousness.* When the gospel came to them they heard it with deep attention. There was a something about it which powerfully attracted them. You know who hath said, "I, if I be lifted up, will draw all men unto Me." This divine charm drew them to consider the doctrine, and when they came to understand it, they perceived that it suited their need as a shoe fits a foot. It revealed their secret needs and wounds, but it also provided for them; and so, having considered the thing, they accepted with joy the blessings brought to them in the gospel. They at once believed in the Lord Jesus: the thing was done suddenly, but it was well done. Their first hearing of the gospel saved them. We read of one of them, that he had shut up the preacher in the prison, and had gone to bed; but in the middle of the night an earthquake shook the prison; and that night he not only became a believer, but he was baptized, and all his household. These Gentiles did not want hammering at so long as some of you do; they did not require the preacher to rack his brains to find fresh illustrations and arguments, and then labour in vain year after year. At the first summons they surrendered. They no sooner saw the light than they rejoiced in it. They rose at a bound from depths of sin to heights of righteousness. Those who had been ringleaders in the service of the devil became zealots in the service of Jesus Christ. The change was as complete as it was startling—"they attained unto righteousness": they were accepted before God as righteous men.

The apostle asks us, "What we shall say, then?" We say this: *herein is seen the sovereign appointment of the Lord.* He will have mercy on whom He will have mercy. He will fulfil His promise to His Son, "Behold, Thou shalt call a nation that Thou knowest not, and nations that knew not Thee shall run unto Thee because of the Lord Thy God, and for the Holy One of Israel: for He hath glorified Thee." Here I see the Almighty Lord of all speaking to the darkness, and saying, "Let there be light," and there is light. Here I see the word of the Lord coming forth out of His mouth, and accomplishing the thing whereto He sent it. The voice of the Lord which breaketh the cedars of Lebanon also breaks the hard hearts of men: "the voice of the Lord which maketh the hinds to calve," creates new life in the minds of the ungodly. The gospel is full of power, and it works according to the eternal purpose of God. The calling of the Gentiles in Paul's day is only one illustration of the frequent action of sovereign grace.

This also is according to divine prophecy. What said the Lord by His servant Hosea? "I will call them My people, which were not My people; and her beloved, which was not beloved. And it shall come to pass, that in the place where it was said unto them, Ye are not My people; there shall they be called the children of the living God." Thus spake the prophet, and so it must be. The Lord has many more such chosen ones to call forth from their death in sin. I expect as I stand here that God's infinite power is about to save certain of you. I do not know to whom this grace will be vouchsafed, but I know that the Word of the Lord will not return unto Him void. He may bless the least likely of you. He may call the man who now says, "I do not believe a word of it." Friend, you do not know what you will believe before this day is over. I trust that God's power is going forth to bring you within the bounds of salvation. It may be that some persecuting Saul of Tarsus will at this hour cry, "Lord what wilt Thou have me to do?" And, on the other hand, it may be that some young man who lacks only one thing will this day find it. So doth God work in the majesty of His power, that persons who have not sought after righteousness nevertheless are led to faith in Christ, and by that faith they are immediately made righteous before God. This is what we have reason to expect, for many promises declare that it shall be so. Did not Esaias boldly say, "I was found of them that sought me not; I was made manifest unto them that asked not after me"?

This is, in fact, the gospel of the grace of God. That God smiles upon worthy people and rewards their goodness is not the gospel. The gospel is, that God hath mercy upon the guilty and undeserving. The gospel gives us this "faithful saying, and worthy of all acceptation, that Christ Jesus came into the world to save sinners." It is not the gospel that you will be saved who do your best, and will, therefore, have some claim upon mercy. , No, no! By such statements you sail upon quite another tack. But the gospel declares to you that though you have done your worst, the Lord will yet have mercy upon you if you believe in the atonement of His dear Son. If you were turned upside down and shaken for a week, not even a dust of goodness would fall from some of you; and yet even you shall be made the children of God if you believe in Christ Jesus. Repent and be converted; believe in Jesus and live. That the most guilty may yet attain to righteousness, this is the glorious gospel of the blessed God, which it is my delight to preach. Behold, I set before you an open door of grace, and beseech you to enter in just as you are. We come not to mend the garments of those of you who are clothed already, but to present the naked with the robe of Christ's righteousness. We come not hither to search for your beauties, but to unveil your deformities, your wounds, and bruises, and putrefying sores; and then to point you to the Lord Jesus, who can heal you, and cause the beauty of the Lord to rest upon you. We preach not merit, but mercy; not human goodness, but divine grace; not works of law, but wonders of love. This is the gospel of which the salvation of the Gentiles was a blessed result.

II. We see, in the second place, A MARVEL OF FOLLY: "Israel, which followed after the law of righteousness, hath not attained to the law of righteousness." *Multitudes have never yet found true righteousness.* I fear that many of my present congregation are in the number; they are not righteous, though, perhaps, they trust in themselves that they are so. Their consciences are not at ease; they are conscious of serious shortcomings; they have not yet found a safe anchorage. I commend to their study the case of Israel.

In Paul's day *these people were, first of all, very advantageously placed.* They were of the chosen race of Israel. They had been born, as it were, within the visible church, and circumcised, and brought up to know the law of Moses; and yet they had never attained to righteousness. Like Gideon's fleece, they were dry while the floor around was wet. There are those present who were nursed in the lap of piety; from their babyhood they heard the name of Jesus; they have scarcely been a single Sabbath-day absent from the courts of the Lord's house. They went from the Sunday-school to the Bible-class, and it was hoped that they would go thence to the church; but it has not proved so. Now that they have reached riper years they are still hovering around the gates of mercy; but they have not entered upon the way of life. My hearer, I am frightened for you, and such as you. I tremble for you who are so good, so religious, so zealous, and yet are not regenerate. You are the child of nature finely dressed, but not the living child of grace. You look somewhat like a Christian; but as you are not converted, and have never become as a little child, you have not entered the kingdom of heaven. It is a misery of miseries that you should stand on such a vantage ground, as many of you do, and yet be lost. Shall it be so? Turn ye, turn ye, why will ye die?

It was not merely that they had many advantages, but *these Israelites were earnest and zealous in following after the law of righteousness.* Alas! many who have never forgotten a single outward rite or ceremony of the church, and are evermore zealous for taking the sacrament, and regular attendance at their place of worship, are nevertheless quite dead as to spiritual things. Some even kneel down every morning and night and repeat a prayer; they pay everybody their own, they are always kind to their neighbours, and they do not refuse their help to the subscription list; and yet they are quite out of the running. Some of you know that it is so; you dare not die as you are; in fact, you can hardly go on living as you now feel. Nobody could put a finger upon an open fault in you, and yet you are like a rosy apple which is rotten at the core. You know it is so; at least, you have a shrewd suspicion that all is not right between you and God. You have no peace, no joy, and when you hear others rejoicing in the Lord, you either think they are presumptuous, or else you envy them, as well you may. Thousands of people in England are perishing in the light, even as the heathen perish in the dark. Many are wrapping themselves up in their own righteousness, and are as sure to be lost as if the nakedness of their sin could be seen of all men. I pray you, take heed to yourselves, you that follow after the law of righteousness. It is concerning such as you that the apostle Paul had great heaviness and continual sorrow of heart. Remember, you may be in the visible church, and yet may be strangers to the grace of God. You may be earnestly seeking righteousness in the wrong way, and this is a terrible thing.

Notice that these people made a mistake at the very beginning; it may not seem a great one, but it was so in reality. *Israel did not follow after righteousness, but after "the law of righteousness."* They missed the spirit, which is righteousness, and followed after the mere letter of the law. To be really righteous was not their aim, but to do righteousness was their utmost notion. They looked at "Thou shalt not kill," "Thou shalt not commit adultery," "Remember the Sabbath-day to keep it holy," and so forth; but to love God with all their heart was not thought of, and yet this is the essence of righteousness. They looked at the letter of the law, and were careful to pay tithe upon mint and anise, and to attend to all sorts of small points and niceties; but to cleanse the heart and purify the motive did not occur to them. They thought of what a man *does*, but they forgot the importance of what a man *is*. Love to God, and likeness to God, were forgotten in a servile attempt to observe the letter of the law. So we see everywhere, people nowadays consider what kind of dress a clergyman ought to wear on a certain day, and which position he should occupy at the communion, and what should be the decoration of the place of worship, and what should be the proper music for the hymn, and so forth; but to what purpose is all this? To be right in heart with God, to trust in His dear Son, and to be renewed in His image, is better than all ritual. Among ourselves there are certain people who are nothing if they are not orthodox: they make a man an offender for a word, and are never so happy as when they are up to their necks in controversy. In each case the external and the letter are preferred to the inward and the spiritual. O my dear hearers, escape from this error; be not so eager for the shell as to lose the kernel, so zealous for the form of godliness as to deny the power thereof!

What was the reason why these zealous Israelites did not attain to righteousness? *They went upon a wrong principle.* The principle of these Israelites was that of works. They said within themselves "We must keep the law, and in that way we shall be saved." In this way no man ever was saved, nor ever will be. Hearken diligently to what I now say. The principle of salvation by our own works *exalts man*, and you may be sure that it must be an error for that reason. On that principle you are your own Saviour. Everything hinges upon what *you* do and what *you* feel, and Jesus Christ is nowhere. If you were to get to heaven by this road, you would sing to your own praise and glory. This system puffs you up, and makes you feel what an important person you are to deserve so well of God. It smells of that pride which the Lord abhors.

While it thus lifts man up, *it altogether ignores the great fact that you have sinned already*. Are you going to be saved by your works? What about the past? If I am going to pay my way for the future, this will not discharge my old debts. What have you to say for your former sins and follies? Do you imagine that you can make up for wasted years by using the rest of life as you ought to do? If you do your best in future you will do no more than you are bound to do: this will not remove your old sins. Why, man, if you could start afresh as a new-born babe, and keep God's law perfectly throughout all time, yet the faults of the past would remain like blots indelible. Sin is sin, and God will punish it, and all your future obedience can be no atonement for it.

Note again, that this principle of salvation by works, while it makes much of man, *makes nothing of God*. It shuts out both His justice and His mercy. Do you really know what you are? You think you are somebody, and can merit something of God; but this is a delusion. I will tell you where you are. You are already convicted of rebellion; you are "condemned already." Nothing that you can do can reverse that condemnation which is already passed upon you; and your only hope lies in the royal prerogative of God, who can grant a free pardon if He pleases to do so. You can never deserve pardon, it must be an act of pure grace. Nothing but the longsuffering of God at this moment keeps you out of hell. Yes, I mean you who think so much of yourselves. I mean you who set yourselves down among the naturally good. I would fain strip you of your finery, and throw away the false jewellery with which you have decorated yourselves; for a self-righteous man's religion is nothing but a painted pageantry to go to hell in. Oh, how I loathe to see the plumes and feathers of self-confidence, which are an awful mockery, the lying ensigns of a false hope, flaunted by a soul that is on its way to sure damnation! O presuming souls, may God in His mercy make you see where you are! Let your cry be, "God be merciful to me a sinner." Until you have taken the sinner's place, you are in a false position, and God will treat you as one of those liars who shall not tarry in His sight.

Moreover, dear friends, the system of salvation by works *is impossible to you*. You cannot perfectly keep the law of God, for you are sold under sin. I recollect when I resolved never to sin again. I sinned before I had done my breakfast. It was all up for that day; so I thought I would begin the next day, and I did, but my failure was repeated. Who can get clean water from a polluted spring? You will never keep the commandment without spot; it is so pure, and you are so impure; it is so spiritual, and you are so earthly. "There is not a just man upon earth that doeth good and sinneth not."

But suppose you could outwardly keep the law of God out of a sense of obligation to do so, yet the work is not done unless you yourself are made right with God. Your heart must love God, as well as your hands serve Him. If you only obey Him from fear of hell and hope of heaven, what are you? Nothing but a mere hireling. This is not the filial nature of a child, whose service is all for love. As for myself, I serve God this day with my whole heart; but it is not from fear of hell. My sins are forgiven me, and there is no hell for me. Neither do I serve the Lord because I hope for heaven thereby, but because I love Him who loved me, and gave Himself for me. There is evidence of righteousness in this, but no claim of any. Mere obedience to the Lord, if there were no heart in it, would be a poor affair. We have many servants who regard their work as drudgery, and though they do their duties, they do them with no regard for our interests: but the old-fashioned servants were of another kind. If you have any such, you will prize one of such above a thousand others. They love their master, and they identify themselves with his interests. Old John did not want orders, he was a law to himself, he served from love. When his master one day spoke about their parting, he wanted to know where his master was going, for he had no idea of going himself: he was part and parcel of the household, and was worth his weight in diamonds. You may well say, "I would give my eyes to get such a servant as that." I dare say you would. Our Lord Jesus gave Himself that He might make such servants out of us. Mere work-mongering will never do this; it leaves the man still a self-seeker, a slave working under fear of the lash, with no delight either in his master or in his work. O my hearers, "ye must be born again," or ye cannot attain to righteousness; and there is no being born again on the principle of the works of the law; that must be a gift of grace, and it can only be given into that hand of faith which receives Christ Jesus the Lord.

Once more, *the full development of the unrighteousness of these zealous Israelites came when they stumbled at Christ.* "They stumbled at the stumblingstone." Jesus Christ came among them, and became to them a rock of offence. They seemed to stand upright until then; but when He came among them, down they went into actual rebellion against the Lord and His Anointed. Yes, your moralists are the great enemies of the Cross. They do not want an atonement: they can hardly endure the doctrine. "Washed in the blood!" they cannot bear the sound of the word; they need no washing. They have kept the law; and what do they lack? Jesus came to proclaim salvation by grace; but these men spurn the idea of grace. When Jesus told them of a certain creditor who frankly forgave those debtors who had nothing to pay, such parables were worthless to them; for they were not in debt to God, but quite the reverse. The reception of returning prodigals might make a pretty picture, but it had no relation to themselves. They were not sinners like the publican, and they did not need to be taught, like the Samaritan woman, to look to Jesus for the living water. "He that believeth on Me hath everlasting life" was not doctrine that they cared to hear. They could see, and needed not to have their eyes opened: they were free-born, and were never in bondage to any man; in fact, they were the whole who had no need of a physician. They regarded the mission of Christ as an insult to their virtues, and therefore they crucified Him. Self-righteousness is the enemy of the cross: it does despite to the blood of Jesus; it sets itself up in rivalry with the divine sacrifice, and hence it rejects the gospel, and rails at imputed righteousness. "They followed after the law of righteousness," but Christ, who was righteousness itself, they would have nothing to do with; for their proud self-conceit thought itself above all need of Him.

III. In the last place, I am to come to close-handed fighting. I must deliver A DISCOURSE OF AFFECTION.

As I love you, I would have you saved at once. It is the first of May. Londoners in the olden time used to go into the country on the first of May to wash their faces in the dew. Oh, that God would make His heavenly dew to wash your hearts this May morning! Oh, that you may enjoy the perfume of the Plant of renown at this hour! Some Gentiles have attained to righteousness by faith, why should not you? Believe in Jesus, and His righteousness is yours: to you God imputeth righteousness without works (Rom. iv. 6). Why do you not trust my Lord, my bleeding Lord, my risen Lord, my interceding Lord? There is no conceivable reason for doubting Him. Come and rely upon Him, and righteousness is yours. Did I hear you say, "But—"? Away with your buts: others have been just where you now are, and they have believed in Jesus, and have attained to righteousness; and why should not you? Try it. Believe, I pray you, and God's righteousness is yours. Why should you not believe? Do I hear you say, "I cannot feel"? Did I say anything about feeling? Salvation by feelings is only another form of salvation by works, and it is not to be thought of. Salvation is by Jesus Christ, and it is received by faith alone. It is bestowed as a free gift, and it must be received as a free gift, or not at all. Trust Jesus to save you, and you are saved: believe Him, and be happy. Take to yourself what is freely presented to you in the gospel. If thou canst believe, thou art saved. I cannot help quoting my brother Hill's expression the other day: "He that believeth on Me hath everlasting life" (John vi. 47). You know how he put it: "H.A.T.H. spells *got it.*" So it does, it is a curious but a perfectly correct way of spelling it. If you take Christ to yourself, He will never be taken from you. Breathe the air, and the air is yours; receive Christ, and Christ is yours, and you have attained to righteousness.

Next, see why it is that you have failed hitherto to find rest. You have been earnest and sincere for a great many years, and you have kept on hearing and reading, and, after a fashion, you have even kept on praying; but all the while you have been on the wrong road. Suppose yonder young man should start with his bicycle to go to Brighton, and he should travel due north; he will never get there. The faster he travels the further he will go from the place. If you follow after righteousness by the works of the law, the more you do the further off you will be from the righteousness of God. It must be so. Hear a parable. Yonder is a river, deep and broad. You imagine that the proper way to cross it is to wade or swim through it. You will not hear of any other way. The king has built a bridge; it is open free and without toll: the passage is as safe as it is plain. You refuse to be beholden to His Majesty. You mean to get across by your own exertions. Already you are wet and cold, but you mean to persevere. You are nearly up to your neck in the stream, and the current is too strong for you. Come back, O foolish man, come back, and cross the river by the bridge. The way of faith is so safe, so simple, so blessed; do try it! Have you not had enough of self-saving? After years of struggling you are no forwarder, and have no more comfort: quit the struggle, and rest in the Lord Jesus. Give up your self-confiding folly, and confide in the Son of God, the bleeding Substitute for guilty men. May the blessed Spirit sweetly help you now to receive Jesus!

Do you not see, my friend, that in all your selfish trustings you are really fighting against your God. Jesus says, "Trust Me, I will save you"; and you reply, "I prefer my own doings." Is not that a great insult to Jesus? Have you not attacked the great Father upon a tender point? May He not appoint His own way of saving you? He has chosen the way of grace through faith. What arrogance to refuse that way! God gives without money and without price, why do you provoke Him with your fancied merits? You are flying in the face of the great God, and therefore your very religion is a sin. Let me justify so strong a charge. Your very good works are evil works, because you are doing them to set aside the gift of God by Jesus Christ. The Lord appoints Jesus to be your righteousness, and you laboriously endeavour to manufacture a righteousness of your own. You reject the sacrifice of Calvary in which you are bidden to trust, and virtually say that for you it is a needless thing, for you can reach heaven by your own doings and feelings. O sirs, if you could be saved by your own works, and your proud hopes could be fulfilled, then the death of our Lord would be proved to be a gross mistake. What need of the great sacrifice if you can save yourself? The cross is a superfluity if human merit can suffice. There was no need for the Father to put His Son to grief if, after all, men can work out a righteousness of their own. If works can save you, why did Jesus die? Do you see what you are driving at? Do you mean to trample under foot the blood of Jesus? I beseech you, abhor all notion of self-justification. Dash down the idol which would rival your Lord.

> "Cast your deadly 'doing' down,
>   Down, at Jesus' feet;
> Stand in Him, in Him alone,
>   Gloriously complete!"

"Well," saith one, "you seem to know the ins and outs of a soul aiming at self-salvation." I do, for I long laboured to climb up to heaven upon the tread-mill of my own works. At length I grew weary, and gave myself up to Jesus, that He might bear me there in His own arms. Will you not do the same?

Now, my hearer, it will be an awful thing for you to understand this way of grace, and yet to neglect it. How long am I to preach to some of you? How long am I to wear my heart out in crying, "Come to Jesus; believe in Jesus?" If anybody had said twenty years ago that yonder seat-holder would still remain an unconverted man he would have replied "Impossible: I am near to the kingdom; I am almost persuaded, and before long I shall decide." Yes, you are persuaded on Sundays, but you forget it all on Mondays, and all because faith is not exercised. You believe in faith, but you do not believe in Jesus. You know that Jesus could save you if you trusted Him, but you do not trust Him. Oh that this moment you would end this delay! To trust in Jesus is described in Scripture as looking. As the man bitten by the serpent looked to the serpent of brass hung high upon the pole, and as he looked healing and life came to him, so if you look to Jesus now you will be saved. I see God's only begotten Son, who has deigned to become man for our sakes, and to die in our room and place, and from the cross I entreat Him to speak to you. Speak, O my Master! He does speak, and these are His words—"Look unto Me, and be ye saved, all the ends of the earth: for I am God, and there is none else." Look, I pray you! Look and live!

CHRIST THE END OF THE LAW

"For Christ is the end of the law for righteousness to every one that believeth."—Romans x. 4.

YOU remember we spoke last Sabbath morning of "the days of the Son of man." Oh that every Sabbath now might be a day of that kind in the most spiritual sense. I hope that we shall endeavour to make each Lord's Day as it comes round a day of the Lord, by thinking much of Jesus, by rejoicing much in Him, by labouring for Him, and by our growingly importunate prayer, that to Him may the gathering of the people be. We may not have very many Sabbaths together, death may soon part us; but while we are able to meet as a Christian assembly, let us never forget that Christ's presence is our main necessity, and let us pray for it and entreat the Lord to vouchsafe that presence always in displays of light, life and love! I become increasingly earnest that every preaching time should be a soul-saving time. I can deeply sympathize with Paul when he said, "My heart's desire and prayer to God for Israel is that they might be saved." We have had so much preaching, but, comparatively speaking, so little believing in Jesus; and if there be no believing in Him, neither the law nor the gospel has answered its end, and our labour has been utterly in vain. Some of you have heard, and heard, and heard again, but you have not believed in Jesus. If the gospel had not come to your hearing you could not have been guilty of refusing it. "Have they not heard?" says the apostle. "Yes, verily:" but still "they have

not all obeyed the gospel." Up to this very moment there has been no hearing with the inner ear, and no work of faith in the heart, in the case of many whom we love. Dear friends, is it always to be so? How long is it to be so? Shall there not soon come an end of this reception of the outward means and rejection of the inward grace? Will not your soul soon close in with Christ for present salvation? Break! Break, O heavenly day, upon the benighted ones, for our hearts are breaking over them.

The reason why many do not come to Christ is not because they are not earnest, after a fashion, and thoughtful and desirous to be saved, but because they cannot brook God's way of salvation. "They have a zeal for God, but not according to knowledge." We do get them by our exhortation so far on the way that they become desirous to obtain eternal life, but "they have not submitted themselves to the righteousness of God." Mark, "submitted themselves," for it needs submission. Proud man wants to save himself, he believes he can do it, and he will not give over the task till he finds out his own help-lessness by unhappy failures. Salvation by grace, to be sued for in forma pauperis, to be asked for as an undeserved boon from free, unmerited grace, this it is which the carnal mind will not come to as long as it can help it: I beseech the Lord so to work that some of you may not be able to help it. And oh, I have been praying that, while this morning I am trying to set forth Christ as the end of the law, God may bless it to some hearts, that they may see what Christ did, and may perceive it to be a great deal better than anything they can do; may see what Christ finished, and may become weary of what they themselves have laboured at so long, and have not even well commenced at this day. Perhaps it may please the Lord to enchant them with the perfection of the salvation that is in Christ Jesus. As Bunyan would say, "It may, perhaps, set their mouths a watering after it," and when a sacred appetite begins it will not be long before the feast is enjoyed. It may be that when they see the raiment of wrought gold, which Jesus so freely bestows on naked souls, they will throw away their own filthy rags which now they hug so closely.

I am going to speak about two things, this morning, as the Spirit of God shall help me: and the first is, *Christ in connection with the law*—he is "the end of the law for righteousness"; and secondly, *ourselves in connection with Christ*—"to everyone that believeth Christ is the end of the law for righteousness."

I. First, then, CHRIST IN CONNECTION WITH THE LAW. The law is that which, as sinners, we have above all things cause to dread; for the sting of death is sin, and the strength of sin is the law. Towards us the law darts forth devouring flames, for it condemns us, and in solemn terms appoints us a place among the accursed, as it is written, "Cursed is every one that continueth not in all things that are written in the book of the law to do them." Yet, strange infatuation! like the fascination which attracts the gnat to the candle which burns its wings, men by nature fly to the law for salvation, and cannot be driven from it. The law can do nothing else but reveal sin and pronounce condemnation upon the sinner, and yet we cannot get men away from it, even though we show them how sweetly Jesus stands between them and it. They are so enamoured of legal hope that they cling to it when there is nothing to cling to; they prefer Sinai to Calvary, though Sinai has nothing for them but thunders and trumpet warnings of coming judgment. O that for awhile you would listen anxiously while I set forth Jesus my Lord, that you may see the law in Him.

Now, what has our Lord to do with the law? He has everything to do with it, for He is its end for the noblest object, namely, for righteousness. He is the "end of the law." What does this mean? I think it signifies three things: first, that Christ is *the purpose and object* of the law; secondly, that He is *the fulfilment* of it; and thirdly, that He is *the termination* of it.

First, then, *our Lord Jesus Christ is the purpose and object of the law.* It was given to lead us to Him. The law is our schoolmaster to bring us to Christ, or rather our attendant to conduct us to the school of Jesus. The law is the great net in which the fish are enclosed that they may be drawn out of the element of sin. The law is the stormy wind which drives souls into the harbour of refuge. The law is the sheriff's officer to shut men up in prison for their sin, concluding them all under condemnation in order that they may look to the free grace of God alone for deliverance. This is the object of the law: it empties that grace may fill, and wounds that mercy may heal. It has never been God's intention towards us, as fallen men, that the law should be regarded as a way to salvation to us, for a way of salvation it can never be. Had man never fallen, had his nature remained as God made it, the law would have been most helpful

to him to show him the way in which he should walk: and by keeping it he would have lived, for "he that doeth these things shall live in them." But ever since man has fallen the Lord has not proposed to him a way of salvation by works, for He knows it to be impossible to a sinful creature. The law is already broken; and whatever man can do he cannot repair the damage he has already done; therefore he is out of court as to the hope of merit. The law demands perfection, but man has already fallen short of it; and therefore let him do his best he cannot accomplish what is absolutely essential. The law is meant to lead the sinner to faith in Christ, by showing the impossibility of any other way. It is the black dog to fetch the sheep to the shepherd, the burning heat which drives the traveller to the shadow of the great rock in a weary land.

Look how the law is adapted to this; for, first of all, *it shows man his sin.* Read the ten commandments and tremble as you read them. Who can lay his own character down side by side with the two tablets of divine precept without at once being convinced that he has fallen far short of the standard? When the law comes home to the soul it is like light in a dark room revealing the dust and the dirt which else had been unperceived. It is the test which detects the presence of the poison of sin in the soul. "I was alive without the law once," said the apostle, "but when the commandment came sin revived and I died." Our comeliness utterly fades away when the law blows upon it. Look at the commandments, I say, and remember how sweeping they are, how spiritual, how far-reaching. They do not merely touch the outward act, but dive into the inner motive and deal with the heart, the mind, the soul. There is a deeper meaning in the commands than appears upon their surface. Gaze into their depths and see how terrible is the holiness which they require. As you understand what the law demands you will perceive how far you are from fulfilling it, and how sin abounds where you thought there was little or none of it. You thought yourself rich and increased in goods and in no need of anything, but when the broken law visits you your spiritual bankruptcy and utter penury stare you in the face. A true balance discovers short weight, and such is the first effect of the law upon the conscience of man.

The law also shows *the result and mischief of sin.* Look at the types of the old Mosaic dispensation, and see how they were intended to lead men to Christ by making them see their unclean condition and their need of such cleansing as only He can give. Every type pointed to our Lord Jesus Christ. If men were put apart because of disease or uncleanness, they were made to see how sin separated them from God, and from His people; and when they were brought back and purified with mystic rites in which were scarlet wool and hyssop and the like, they were made to see how they can only be restored by Jesus Christ, the great High Priest. When the bird was killed that the leper might be clean, the need of purification by the sacrifice of a life was set forth. Every morning and evening a lamb died to tell of daily need of pardon, if God is to dwell with us. We sometimes have fault found with us for speaking too much about *blood ;* yet under the old testament the blood seemed to be everything, and was not only spoken of but actually presented to the eye. What does the apostle tell us in the Hebrews? "Whereupon neither the first testament was dedicated without blood. For when Moses had spoken every precept to all the people according to the law, he took the blood of calves and of goats, with water, and scarlet wool, and hyssop, and sprinkled both the book, and all the people, saying, this is the blood of the testament which God hath enjoyed unto you. Moreover he sprinkled with blood both the tabernacle, and all the vessels of the ministry. And almost all things are by the law purged with blood; and without shedding of blood is no remission." The blood was on the veil, and on the altar, on the hangings, and on the floor of the tabernacle: no one could avoid seeing it. I resolve to make my ministry of the same character, and more and more sprinkle it with the blood of atonement. Now the abundance of the blood of old was meant to show clearly that sin has so polluted us that without an atonement God is not to be approached: we must come by the way of sacrifice or not at all. We are so unacceptable in ourselves that unless the Lord sees us with the blood of Jesus upon us He must away with us. The old law, with its emblems and figures, set forth many truths as to men's selves and the coming Saviour, intending by every one of them to preach Christ. If any stopped short of Him, they missed the intent and design of the law. Moses leads up to Joshua, and the law ends at Jesus.

Turning our thoughts back again to the moral rather than the ceremonial law, it was intended to teach men *their utter helplessness.* It shows them how short they fall of what they ought to be, and it also shows them, when they look at it carefully, how utterly impossible it is for them to come up to the standard. Such holiness as the law demands no man can reach of himself. "Thy commandment is exceeding broad." If a man says that he can keep the law, it is because he does not know what the law is. If he fancies that he can ever climb to heaven up the quivering sides of Sinai, surely he can never have seen that burning mount at all. Keep the law! Ah, my brethren, while we are yet talking about it we are breaking it; while we are pretending that we can fulfil its letter, we are violating its spirit, for pride as much breaks the law as lust or murder. "Who can bring a clean thing out of an unclean? Not one." "How can he be clean that is born of a woman?" No, soul, thou canst not help thyself in this thing, for since only by perfection thou canst live by the law, and since that perfection is impossible, thou canst not find help in the covenant of works. In grace there is hope, but as a matter of debt there is none, for we do not merit anything but wrath. The law tells us this, and the sooner we know it to be so the better, for the sooner we shall fly to Christ.

The law also shows us *our great need*—our need of cleansing, cleansing with the water and with the blood. It discovers to us our filthiness, and this naturally leads us to feel that we must be washed from it if we are ever to draw near to God. So the law drives us to accept of Christ as the one only person who can cleanse us, and make us fit to stand within the veil in the presence of the Most High. The law is the surgeon's knife which cuts out the proud flesh that the wound may heal. The law by itself only sweeps and raises the dust, but the gospel sprinkles clean water upon the dust, and all is well in the chamber of the soul. The law kills, the gospel makes alive; the law strips, and then Jesus Christ comes in and robes the soul in beauty and glory. All the commandments, and all the types direct us to

Christ, if we will but heed their evident intent. They wean us from self, they put us off from the false basis of self-righteousness, and bring us to know that only in Christ can our help be found. So, first of all, Christ is the end of the law, in that He is its great purpose.

And now, secondly, He is *the law's fulfilment.* It is impossible for any of us to be saved without righteousness. The God of heaven and earth by immutable necessity demands righteousness of all His creatures. Now, Christ has come to give to us the righteousness which the law demands, but which it never bestows. In the chapter before us we read of "the righteousness which is of faith," which is also called "God's righteousness"; and we read of those who "shall not be ashamed" because they are righteous by believing, "for with the heart man believeth unto righteousness." What the law could not do Jesus has done. He provides the righteousness which the law asks for but cannot produce. What an amazing righteousness it must be which is as broad and deep and long and high as the law itself. The commandment is exceeding broad, but the righteousness of Christ is as broad as the commandment, and goes to the end of it. Christ did not come to make the law milder, or to render it possible for our cracked and battered obedience to be accepted as a sort of compromise. The law is not compelled to lower its terms, as though it had originally asked too much; it is holy and just and good, and ought not to be altered in one jot or tittle, nor can it be. Our Lord gives the law all it requires, not a part, for that would be an admission that it might justly have been content with less at first. The law claims complete obedience without one spot or speck, failure, or flaw, and Christ has brought in such a righteousness as that, and gives it to His people. The law demands that the righteousness should be without omission of duty and without commission of sin, and the righteousness which Christ has brought in is just such an one that for its sake the great God accepts His people and counts them to be without spot or wrinkle or any such thing. The law will not be content without spiritual obedience, mere outward compliances will not satisfy. But our Lord's obedience was as deep as it was broad, for His zeal to do the will of Him that sent Him consumed Him. He says Himself, "I delight to do Thy will, O My God, yea Thy law is within My heart." Such righteousness He puts upon all believers. "By the obedience of one shall many be made righteous"; righteous to the full, perfect in Christ. We rejoice to wear the costly robe of fair white linen which Jesus has prepared, and we feel that we may stand arrayed in it before the majesty of heaven without a trembling thought. This is something to dwell upon, dear friends. Only as righteous ones can we be saved, but Jesus Christ makes us righteous, and therefore we are saved. He is righteous who believeth on Him, even as Abraham believed God and it was counted unto him for righteousness. "There is, therefore, now no condemnation to them that are in Christ Jesus," because they are made righteous in Christ. Yea, the Holy Spirit by the mouth of Paul challengeth all men, angels, and devils, to lay anything to the charge of God's elect, since Christ hath died. O law, when thou demandest of me a perfect righteousness, I, being a believer, present it to thee; for through Christ Jesus faith is accounted unto me for righteousness. The righteousness of Christ is mine, for I am one with Him by faith, and this is the name wherewith He shall be called—"The Lord our righteousness."

Jesus has thus fulfilled the original demands of the law, but you know, brethren, that since we have broken the law there are other demands. For the remission of past sins something more is asked now than present and future obedience. Upon us, on account of our sins, the curse has been pronounced, and a penalty has been incurred. It is written that He "will by no means clear the guilty," but every transgression and iniquity shall have its just punishment and reward. Here, then, let us admire that the Lord Jesus Christ is the end of the law as to penalty. That curse and penalty are awful things to think upon, but Christ has ended all their evil, and thus discharged us from all the consequences of sin. As far as every believer is concerned the law demands no penalty and utters no curse. The believer can point to the Great Surety on the tree of Calvary, and say, "See there, oh law, there is the vindication of divine justice which I offer to thee. Jesus pouring out His heart's blood from His wounds and dying on my behalf is my answer to Thy claims, and I know that I shall be delivered from wrath through Him." The claims of the law both as broken and unbroken Christ has met: both the positive and the penal demands are satisfied in Him. This was a labour worthy of a God, and lo, the incarnate God has achieved it. He has finished the transgression, made an end of sins, made reconciliation for iniquity, and brought in everlasting righteousness. All glory be to His name.

Moreover, not only has the penalty been paid, but Christ has put great and special honour upon the law in so doing. I venture to say that if the whole human race had kept the law of God and not one of them had violated it, the law would not stand in so splendid a position of honour as it does to-day when the man Christ Jesus, who is also the Son of God, has paid obeisance to it. God Himself, incarnate, has in His life, and yet more in His death, revealed the supremacy of law; He has shown that not even love nor sovereignty can set aside justice. Who shall say a word against the law to which the Lawgiver Himself submits? Who shall now say that it is too severe when He who made it submits Himself to its penalties. Because He was found in fashion as a man, and was our representative, the Lord demanded from His own Son perfect obedience to the law, and the Son voluntarily bowed Himself to it without a single word, taking no exception to His task. "Yea, Thy law is My delight," saith He, and He proved it to be so by paying homage to it even to the full. Oh wondrous law under which even Emmanuel serves! Oh matchless law whose yoke even the Son of God does not disdain to bear, but being resolved to save His chosen was made under the law, lived under it and died under it, "obedient to death, even the death of the cross."

The law's stability also has been secured by Christ. That alone can remain which is proved to be just, and Jesus has proved the law to be so, magnifying it and making it honourable. He says, "Think not that I am come to destroy the law, or the prophets: I am not come to destroy, but to fulfil. For verily I say unto you, till heaven and earth pass, one jot or one tittle shall in no wise pass from the law, till all be fulfilled." I shall have to show you how He has made an end of the law in another sense, but as to the settlement of the eternal principles of right and wrong, Christ's life and death have achieved this for ever. "Yea, we establish the law," said Paul, "we do not make void the law through faith." The law is proved to be holy and just by the very gospel of faith, for the gospel which faith believes in does not alter or lower the law, but teaches us how it was to the uttermost fulfilled. Now shall the law stand fast for ever and ever, since even to save elect man God will not alter it. He had a people, chosen, beloved, and ordained to life, yet He would not save them at the expense of one principle of right. They were sinful, and how could they be justified unless the law was suspended or changed? Was, then, the law changed? It seemed as if it must be so, if man was to be saved, but Jesus Christ came and showed us how the law could stand firm as a rock and yet the redeemed could be justly saved by infinite mercy. In Christ we see both mercy and justice shining full orbed, and yet neither of them in any degree eclipsing the other. The law has all it ever asked, as it ought to have, and yet the Father of all mercies sees all His chosen saved as He determined they should be through the death of His Son. Thus I have tried to show you how Christ is the fulfilment of the law to its utmost end. May the Holy Ghost bless the teaching.

And now, thirdly, He is the end of the law in the sense that He is *the termination of it*. He has terminated it in two senses. First of all, His people are not under it as a covenant of life. "We are not under the law, but under grace." The old covenant as it stood with father Adam was "This do and thou shalt live"; its command he did not keep, and consequently he did not live, nor do we live in him, since in Adam all died. The old covenant was broken, and we became condemned thereby, but now, having suffered death in Christ, we are no more under it, but are dead to it. Brethren, at this present moment, although we rejoice to do good works, we are not seeking life through them, we are not hoping to obtain divine favour by our own goodness, nor even to keep ourselves in the love of God by any merit of our own. Chosen, not for our works, but according to the eternal will and good pleasure of God; called, not of works, but by the Spirit of God, we desire to continue in this grace and return no more to the bondage of the old covenant. Since we have put our trust in an atonement provided and applied by grace through Christ Jesus, we are no longer slaves but children, not working to be saved, but saved already, and working because we are saved. Neither that which we do, nor even that which the Spirit of God worketh in us is to us the ground and basis of the love of God toward us, since He loved us from the first, because He would love us, unworthy though we were; and He loves us still in Christ, and looks upon us not as we are in ourselves, but as we are in Him; washed in His blood and covered in His righteousness. Ye are not under the law, Christ has taken you from the servile bondage of a condemning covenant and made you to receive the adoption of children, so that now ye cry, Abba, Father.

Again, Christ is the terminator of the law, for we are no longer under its curse. The law cannot curse a believer, it does not know how to do it; it blesses him, yea, and he shall be blessed; for as the law demands righteousness and looks at the believer in Christ, and sees that Jesus has given him all the righteousness it demands, the law is bound to pronounce him blessed. "Blessed is he whose transgression is forgiven, whose sin is covered. Blessed is the man unto whom the Lord imputeth not iniquity, and in whose spirit there is no guile." Oh, the joy of being redeemed from the curse of the law by Christ, who was "made a curse for us," as it is written, "Cursed is every one that hangeth on a tree." Do ye, my brethren, understand the sweet mystery of salvation? Have you ever seen Jesus standing in your place that you may stand in His place? Christ accused and Christ condemned, and Christ led out to die, and Christ smitten of the Father, even to the death, and then you cleared, justified, delivered from the curse, because the curse has spent itself on your Redeemer. You are admitted to enjoy the blessing because the righteousness which was His is now transferred to you that you may be blessed of the Lord world without end. Do let us triumph and rejoice in this evermore. Why should we not? And yet some of God's people get under the law as to their feelings, and begin to fear that because they are conscious of sin they are not saved, whereas it is written, "He justifieth the ungodly." For myself, I love to live near a sinner's Saviour. If my standing before the Lord depended upon what I am in myself and what good works and righteousness I could bring, surely I should have to condemn myself a thousand times a day. But to get away from that and to say, "I have believed in Jesus Christ and therefore righteousness is mine," this is peace, rest, joy, and the beginning of heaven! When one attains to this experience, his love to Jesus Christ begins to flame up, and he feels that if the Redeemer has delivered him from the curse of the law he will not continue in sin, but he will endeavour to live in newness of life. We are not our own, we are bought with a price, and we would therefore glorify God in our bodies and in our spirits, which are the Lord's. Thus much upon Christ in connection with the law.

II. Now, secondly, OURSELVES IN CONNECTION WITH CHRIST—for "Christ is the end of the law *to every one that believeth.*" Now see the point "to every one that believeth," there the stress lies. Come, man, woman, dost thou believe? No weightier question can be asked under heaven. "Dost thou believe on the Son of God?" And what is it to believe? It is not merely to accept a set of doctrines and to say that such and such a creed is yours, and there and then to put it on the shelf and forget it. To believe is, to trust, to confide, to depend upon, to rely upon, to rest in. Dost thou believe that Jesus Christ rose from the dead? Dost thou believe that He stood in the sinner's stead and suffered the just for the unjust? Dost thou believe that He is able to save to the uttermost them that come unto God by Him? And dost thou therefore lay the whole weight and stress of thy soul's salvation upon Him, yea, upon Him alone? Ah then, Christ is the end of the law for righteousness to thee, and thou art righteous. In the righteousness of God thou art clothed if thou believest. It is of no use to bring forward anything else if you are not believing, for nothing will avail. If faith be absent the essential thing is wanting: sacraments, prayers, Bible reading, hearings of the gospel, you may heap them together, high as the stars, into a mountain, huge as high Olympus, but they are all mere chaff if faith be not there. It is thy believing or not believing which must settle the matter. Dost thou look away from thyself to Jesus for righteousness? If thou dost He is the end of the law to thee.

Now observe that there is no question raised about the previous character, for it is written, "Christ is the end of the law for righteousness to *every one that believeth.*" But, Lord, this man before he believed was a persecutor and injurious, he raged and raved against the saints and haled them to prison and sought their blood. Yes, beloved friend, and that is the very man who wrote these words by the Holy Ghost, "Christ is the end of the law for righteousness to every one that believeth." So if I address one here this morning whose life has been defiled with every sin, and stained with every transgression we can conceive of, yet I say unto such, remember "all manner of sin and of blasphemy shall be forgiven unto men." If thou believest in the Lord Jesus Christ thine iniquities are blotted out, for the blood of Jesus Christ, God's dear Son, cleanseth us from all sin. This is the glory of the gospel that it is a sinner's gospel; good news of blessing not for those without sin, but for those who confess and forsake it. Jesus came into the world, not to reward the sinless, but to seek and to save that which was lost; and He, being lost and being far from God, who cometh nigh to God by Christ, and believeth in Him, will find that He is able to bestow righteousness upon the guilty. He is the end of the law for righteousness to everyone that believeth, and therefore to the poor harlot that believeth, to the drunkard of many years standing that believeth, to the thief, the liar, and the scoffer who believeth, to those who have aforetime rioted in sin, but now turn from it to trust in Him. But I do not know that I need mention such cases as these; to me the most wonderful fact is that Christ is the end of the law for righteousness *to me,* for I believe in Him. I know whom I have believed, and I am persuaded that He is able to keep that which I have committed to Him until that day.

Another thought arises from the text, and that is, that there is nothing said by way of qualification as to the strength of the faith. He is the end of the law for righteousness to everyone that believeth, whether he is Little Faith or Greatheart. Jesus protects the rear rank as well as the vanguard. There is no difference between one believer and another as to justification. So long as there is a connection between you and Christ the righteousness of God is yours. The link may be very like a film, a spider's line of trembling faith, but, if it runs all the way from the heart to Christ, divine grace can and will flow along the most slender thread. It is marvellous how fine the wire may be that will carry the electric flash. We may want a cable to carry a message across the sea, but that is for the protection of the wire, the wire which actually carries the message is a slender thing. If thy faith be of the mustard-seed kind, if it be only such as tremblingly touches the Saviour's garment's hem, if thou canst only say "Lord, I believe, help thou mine unbelief," if it be but the faith of sinking Peter, or weeping Mary, yet if it be faith in Christ, He will be the end of the law for righteousness to thee as well as to the chief of the apostles.

If this be so then, beloved friends, all of us who believe are righteous. Believing in the Lord Jesus Christ we have obtained the righteousness which those who follow the works of the law know nothing of. We are not completely sanctified, would God we were; we are not quit of sin in our members, though we hate it; but still for all that, in the sight of God, we are truly righteous, and being qualified by faith we have peace with God. Come, look up, ye believers that are burdened with a sense of sin. While you chasten yourselves and mourn your sin, do not doubt your Saviour, nor question His righteousness. You are black, but do not stop there, go on to say as the spouse did, "I am black, but comely."

"Though in ourselves deform'd we are,
And black as Kedar's tents appear,
Yet, when we put Thy beauties on,
Fair as the courts of Solomon."

Now, mark that the connection of our text assures us that being righteous we are saved; for what does it say here, "If thou shalt confess with thy mouth the Lord Jesus, and shalt believe in thine heart that God hath raised Him from the dead, thou shalt be *saved.*" He who is justified is saved, or what were the benefit of justification? Over thee, O believer, God hath pronounced the verdict "*saved,*" and none shall reverse it. You are saved from sin and death and hell; you are saved even now, with a present salvation; "He hath saved us and called us with a holy calling." Feel the transports of it at this hour. "Beloved, now are we the sons of God."

And now I have done when I have said just this. If any one here thinks he can save himself, and that his own righteousness will suffice before God, I would affectionately beg him not to insult his Saviour. If your righteousness sufficeth, why did Christ come here to work one out? Will you for a moment compare your righteousness with the righteousness of Jesus Christ? What likeness is there between you and Him? As much as between an emmet and an archangel. Nay, not so much as that: as much as between night and day, hell and heaven. Oh, if I had a righteousness of my own that no one could find fault with, I would voluntarily fling it away to have the righteousness of Christ, but as I have none of my own I do rejoice the more to have my Lord's. When Mr. Whitefield first preached at Kingswood, near Bristol, to the colliers, he could see when their hearts began to be touched by the gutters of white made by the tears as they ran down their black cheeks. He saw they were receiving the gospel, and he writes in his diary "as these poor colliers had no righteousness of their own they therefore gloried in Him who came to save publicans and sinners." Well, Mr. Whitefield, that is true of the colliers, but it is equally true of many of us here, who may not have had black faces, but we had black hearts. We can truly say that we also rejoice to cast away our own righteousness and count it dross and dung that we may win Christ, and be found in Him. In Him is our sole hope and only trust.

Last of all, for any of you to reject the righteousness of Christ must be to perish everlastingly, because it cannot be that God will accept you or your pretended righteousness when you have refused the real and divine righteousness which He sets before you in His Son. If you could go up to the gates of heaven, and the angel were to say to you, "What title have you to entrance here?" and you were to reply, "I have a righteousness of my own," then for you to be admitted would be to decide that your righteousness was on a par with that of Immanuel Himself. Can that ever be? Do you think that God will ever allow such a lie to be sanctioned? Will He let a poor wretched sinner's counterfeit righteousness pass current side by side with the fine gold of Christ's perfection. Why was the fountain filled with blood if you need no washing? Is Christ a superfluity? Oh, it cannot be. You must have Christ's righteousness or be unrighteous, and being unrighteous you will be unsaved, and being unsaved you must remain lost for ever and ever.

What! has it all come to this, then, that I am to believe in the Lord Jesus Christ for righteousness, and to be made just through faith? Yes, that is it: that is the whole of it. What! trust Christ alone and then live as I like! You cannot live in sin after you have trusted Jesus, for the act of faith brings with it a change of nature and a renewal of your soul. The Spirit of God who leads you to believe will also change your heart. You spoke of "living as you like," you will like to live very differently from what you do now. The things you loved before your conversion you will hate when you believe, and the things you hated you will love. Now, you are trying to be good, and you make great failures, because your heart is alienated from God; but when once you have received salvation through the blood of Christ, your heart will love God, and then you will keep His commandments, and they will be no longer grievous to you. A change of heart is what you want, and you will never get it except through the covenant of grace. There is not a word about conversion in the old covenant, we must look to the new covenant for that, and here it is—"Then will I sprinkle clean water upon you, and ye shall be clean: from all your filthiness, and from all your idols, will I cleanse you. A new heart also will I give you, and a new spirit will I put within you: and I will take away the stony heart out of your flesh, and I will give you an heart of flesh. And I will put My spirit within you, and cause you to walk in My statutes, and ye shall keep My judgments, and do them." This is one of the greatest covenant promises, and the Holy Ghost performs it in the chosen. Oh that the Lord would sweetly persuade you to believe in the Lord Jesus Christ, and that promise and all the other covenant engagements shall be fulfilled to your soul. The Lord bless you! Spirit of God, send Thy blessing on these poor words of mine for Jesus' sake. Amen.

HOW CAN I OBTAIN FAITH?

"So then faith cometh by hearing, and hearing by the word of God."—Romans x. 17.

IT is difficult to make men understand that the salvation of the gospel is not by works but entirely by grace, that it is not presented to men as the reward of their own endeavours, but is given to them freely upon their accepting it by an act of simple faith or trust in Jesus Christ. However plainly we may preach this truth, there will always be some who will misunderstand us, and as many who will raise objections against it, as if it were their part to give an opinion, and not to do as they are bidden by the Lord. But when men are brought under the teaching of the word, to see that the pardon of their sins, and the acceptance of their souls does not lie with any merit of their own, or any doings of their own, another difficulty generally presents itself: they say, "What is this faith of which you speak?" and when we assure them that it is a simple trust or confidence in the finished work of Christ, then straightway they say, "How can we get this faith? How can we obtain this confidence?" To us, who have faith, this question is very easy to answer, for when we heard the gladsome news of a finished salvation for lost sinners, complete forgiveness for the guilty, and acceptance for the ungodly, simply upon believing in Jesus, we came to Jesus, and we trusted in Him, and we continue still to trust, and we have joy and peace through believing. We see far more reasons for belief than for doubt. Yet, nevertheless, there are hundreds and thousands who are awakened, and seriously enquiring, to whom this is a great difficulty—"How can I get the faith which gives me possession of Christ Jesus, and brings me salvation?" Our text is the ready answer, practically a complete answer; not doctrinally or theologically complete, but practically perfect. "Faith cometh by hearing, and hearing by the word of God." "But faith is the work of the Holy Spirit in the soul, is it not?" Certainly. "And it is given by the Spirit to God's own chosen?" Assuredly; yet, nevertheless, it was not necessary for the apostle to mention those facts here. Some persons are always for having a whole system of theology in every sermon, but it is not needful that they should be gratified. Paul is clear enough about the work of the Spirit in other places, and it is not needful that he should introduce that subject into every line he writes. It was practically unnecessary for him to mention that subject in the present instance, and, therefore, he did not do so. It would sometimes puzzle rather than instruct an enquirer if we were to go into the full details of a matter. For instance, if I am thirsty, how shall I quench my thirst? By a draught of water. But in what way can I obtain water? It quite suffices for practical purposes for you to tell me to go to the tap or the fountain. There is no need to explain to me before I drink that the water is supplied by a company, and forced to the spot by sundry machines, having been first extracted from the great fountains beneath by artesian wells, or drawn from the river at Thames Ditton. Nor would it be needful in answer to my question to trace the river to the clouds, and to treat upon the formation of vapour by the skill and wisdom of God. Practically, to the thirsty man all you want to say is, "There's the water, drink." I will add another illustration. A man is hungry, and he asks you, "How can I get bread?" "Go to the baker's," you say. The answer is complete enough for him; it meets the case at once. If he wants a larger declaration of how bread is obtained, we can give it to him at another time, when he is no longer hungry; we will tell him how the corn is sown in the furrowed earth, and how by mysterious processes of nature it germinates, grows, and ripens; we will trace it from the reaper to the thresher, and from the thresher to the mill, and we will also show that daily bread is as much a gift from heaven as the manna which dropped down upon the hungry people in the wilderness. But, it is not needful for the feeding of the hungry that we should on every occasion go into all those details, although we hold very sound views upon them. And when you are dealing with an anxious person, it will suffice to say to him, "Faith cometh by hearing;" further information can be supplied under happier circumstances. I mean to keep to our text this morning, and if any shall charge me with an omission of the work of the Spirit, or a failure to trace all saving faith to the electing grace of God, I shall bear the charge without murmuring,

only saying that my soul rejoices as much as that of any man living in the work of the Spirit of God; and, that the electing love of God and His determinate purposes are precious truths to me. If the text was sufficient for Paul; it will, I trust, be sufficient for you.

May the Spirit of God assist us while we meditate upon *the way by which faith cometh*. This shall be followed by a brief indication of *certain obstructions which often lie in that way ;* and then we will conclude by dwelling upon *the importance that faith should come to us by that appointed road.*

I. First, then, THE WAY BY WHICH FAITH COMES TO MEN. "Faith cometh by hearing."

It may help to set the truth out more clearly, if we say, *negatively*, that it does not come by any other process than by hearing—not by any mysterious and strange method, but in the most simple and natural mode conceivable, namely, by the hearing of the word.

Some imagine that faith comes by *hereditary descent*, and they act upon the supposition. Hence, in certain churches, birthright membership is thought to be a proper practice, and the child of a Christian is thought to be a Christian. In some other churches, though the theory would not be stated in so many words, yet it is practically accepted, and children of pious parents are regarded as scarcely needing conversion. The text is forgotten which saith that the heirs of salvation are born, "not of blood, nor of the will of the flesh, but of God." The typical covenant secured outward privileges to the children born after the flesh, but under the covenant of grace the blessing is secured to the spiritual and not to the natural seed. "He who was of the bondwoman was born after the flesh; but he of the freewoman was by promise" (Gal. iv. 23). That which is born of the flesh is flesh, and nothing more: the new-born nature is not transmissible from father to son like a natural temperament or a cast of countenance. I know the answer will be that "the promise is to us and to our children," but it will be well for the objector to reply to himself by completing the quotation,—"even to as many as the Lord your God shall call." The fact is, that nothing spiritual is inherited by carnal generation. Our children, even if we are far advanced in grace, will still be "shapen in iniquity." No matter how high the sainthood of the professing Christian, his child (when capable of understanding) must for himself become a personal believer in Jesus.

It appears to be thought possible to infuse grace by *sacraments*. There are persons yet alive who teach that a babe may be regenerated by certain aqueous processes, and be thereby placed in "a state of salvation." But is not faith a perpetual concomitant of regeneration? and what is that regeneration worth which leaves a person an unbeliever, and, consequently, "condemned already, because he hath not believed on the Son of God?" Rest assured, that as faith does not come by descent, neither can it be produced by any rite which recognizes that descent: it comes in one way, and in one way only in every case, and that is, by the hearing of the word. To every person, whoever he may be, though nursed in the bosom of the church, and introduced to that church by the most solemn ritual, we are bound to say, You must hear as well as others, and you must believe as the result of that hearing as well as others, or else you will remain short of saving grace. Faith is not a mystery juggled into us by the postures, genuflexions, and mumblings of priests. We have heard a great deal about sacramental efficacy, but I think a man must have extraordinary hardihood who would say that either baptism, or the so-called Eucharist, are the sure creators of faith; yet see I not what saving service these forms can render to unbelieving men if they leave them in an unbelieving condition, and, consequently, in a state of condemnation. Seeing that without faith it is impossible to please God, the grace supposed to be conveyed by the mere participation in sacraments is of small value, if it cannot give the cardinal requisite for acceptance before God. Faith cannot be washed into us by immersion, nor sprinkled upon us in christening; it is not to be poured into us from a chalice, nor generated in us by a consecrated piece of bread. There is no magic about it; it comes by hearing the word of God, and by that way only.

These are superstitions, you tell me, and scarcely need to be mentioned here; very well, then, we will have done with them, and treat of superstitions which linger in our own congregations. There are some who fancy that faith cometh by *feeling*. If they could feel emotions either of horror or of exquisite delight, they would then, they think, be the possessors of faith; but till they have felt what they have heard described in certain biographies of undoubtedly good men, they cannot believe, or even if they have a measure of faith, they cannot hope that it is true faith. Faith doth not come by feeling, but through faith arises much of holy feeling, and the more a man lives in the walk of faith, as a rule, the more will he feel and enjoy the light of God's countenance. Faith hath something firmer to stand upon than those ever-changing frames and feelings which, like the weather of our own sunless land, is fickle and frail, and changeth speedily from brightness into gloom. You may get feeling from faith, and the best of it, but you will be long before you will find any faith that is worth the having, if you try to evoke it from frames and feelings.

> "My hope is built on nothing less
> Than Jesus' blood and righteousness;
> I dare not trust the sweetest frame;
> But wholly lean on Jesus' name;
> On Christ the solid rock I stand,
> All other ground is sinking sand."

Some, also, have supposed that true faith will come to men by *dreams and visions*. It is surprising how a belief in these things lingers still in what is called this age of light; the notion is still current that if you dream of seeing Jesus, or fancy you have seen Him while awake, or if a passage of Scripture strikes you, or if you hear or imagine that you hear a voice speaking to you, you are then a believer. Now, faith in Christ is like faith in anyone else, it comes to us by the same kind of mental processes, and is based upon simple principles and plain matters of fact, and needs no vision of the night. Though you should see all the angels in heaven, it would not prove that you would go to heaven, any more than my having seen the Pope's bodyguard would be a proof that I shall be made a Cardinal. Things which are seen of the eye save not, for the things which are seen are temporal, and cannot work eternal salvation. Moreover, men saw Christ, and yet pierced Him and blasphemed Him. Visions have been seen by heathens like Nebuchadnezzar, and angels have appeared to bad men like Balaam who, though he sighed out, "Let me die the death of the righteous," yet perished, fighting against the God of Israel. True faith has a more solid basis for its fabric than the fleeting fancies of the mind.

I beg you to notice, too, that it does not say in the text that faith comes through the *eloquence*, earnestness, or any other good quality of the preacher. Faith cometh by hearing, and hearing by the word, not of man, but of God. The word of God is the substance of faith-creating preaching; it is by the hearing of God's word, and not by any other hearing that saving faith comes to the soul. I may hear a man descant upon the gospel with all the eloquence that can be commanded by the most fluent tongue, yet if my faith comes to me because the man spoke pathetically, or poetically, or argumentatively, or rhetorically, it is a poor miserable faith; being born of the power of the flesh, it will die, and so prove itself unlike the faith which springs from the incorruptible word of God, for that liveth and abideth for ever. On the other hand, I may hope for faith if I am listening to the true gospel, the very word of God, though the man who speaks it may be of stammering lips, and his voice may be disagreeable to my ear, and there may be much about his manner that does not commend itself to me. If he preaches truth it is by hearing not him, the man, but by hearing the word of God, that I shall come to faith. I do desire ever, as a preacher, to feel that it is not my word but God's word that saves souls; we are to explain it and expound it, but we are not to add to it, take from or conceive that we can improve it. We must not go into the pulpit and say, "I have been working out a subject from my own mind, and I am going to give you the result of my thoughts." We had better keep our own thoughts for some other place, and give the people the revealed truth of God. The theory nowadays is that all preachers worth hearing by this refined generation must be profound thinkers, and inventors of improved theologies. Brethren, let man's thoughts perish for ever; the thoughts of God and not the thoughts of man will save souls. The truth of God should be spoken simply, with as little as possible of the embellishments of metaphysics, and philosophy, and high culture, and all that stuff. I say the word of God delivered as we find it is that which, when heard, brings faith to the souls of men. I counsel you, my occasional hearers, you who perhaps have come freshly to this city, or who reside where you have a choice of ministry, seek not that which tickles your ear, but that which your conscience approves as consistent with the word of God; and, though we or an angel from heaven should preach to you that which is not God's word, do not listen to us, for it will be mischievous to you. Hear you what God the Lord speaketh, and hear nothing else. What though He shall sound forth His word through a ram's-horn, if it be God's Spirit that giveth forth a certain sound, it shall be more profitable to your soul than though the silver trumpet should be set to the mouth of falsehood, and the sweetest music should regale your ear. The matter of a discourse is far more important than the manner. Saving faith never comes from hearing falsehood, but from the word of God alone.

I ought, perhaps, to add that the expression "by hearing," though of course literally it must be confined to the hearing of words vocally uttered, is meant to include in its spirit the reading of the word; for reading is a sort of hearing with the eyes, and faith has often come and will often come to men while they are reading the word of God for themselves. We must not kill the spirit of the text by excessive regard to the mere letter of it, and we should do so if we excluded reading, which is a quiet hearing of the still small voice of the printed page. Faith comes by the word of God reaching our minds, and our knowing and understanding it. The entrance of God's word giveth light. "Incline your ear and come unto Me, hear and your soul shall live." Thus, we have spoken of it negatively.

Now, *positively* : "Faith cometh by hearing." Sometimes faith has come into men's minds by *hearing the simple statement* of the gospel. They have longed to be saved, and they have been told that Jesus the Son of God condescended to come into this world and to take upon Himself the form of man, and as man to be partaker of our infirmities, and to offer Himself as a sacrifice in the room, place, and stead of sinners; they have, moreover, been told that whosoever trusts in this substitutionary sacrifice shall be saved, and straightway they have believed. All they have wanted has been merely to be informed of the way of salvation. God's Spirit has so prepared them that they have believed almost as soon as they have heard the saving truth. In many cases the only difficulty in the way of salvation has been a want of understanding the word. I know in my own case I would have given all I had, if I might but have been informed what I must do to be saved. Though I frequented places where the gospel was preached, I did not catch the meaning of believing, it puzzled me much. I do not remember to have heard the simple declaration that to trust in Jesus Christ would save my soul; or, possibly, I did hear it with my outward ears, but I must have been strangely infatuated, for I did not understand the sense; and I have often thought if I could have heard the way of faith simply stated, my soul would have leaped into liberty long before. I will not so say; but I am persuaded that faith often comes by hearing the simple declaration that God accepts sinners, not for what they are in themselves but for what Christ is, and that when sinners believe in Jesus they are saved there and then, and are acceptable with God through Jesus Christ His dear Son. The mere statement of this has brought, by the operation of the Spirit of God, faith into the soul. "How is this?" saith one. Well, it is because the gospel commends itself to some hearts as true upon the very first blush of it, it strikes them as being undoubtedly the gospel of God. It is the same in other matters; you sometimes hear a story about which you say, "Well, I do not now, it may be correct, but I shall have to look a little into that before I am certain;" but you often hear statements which you accept at once, because they commend themselves to your understanding, and you feel that they must be true. There are minds which God has so prepared that the moment they hear the gospel they respond to it. I think I hear the seeker after truth exclaim when he heard the gospel, "True? Why, how could it be otherwise? It is so divinely grand, so harmonious, so good, so gracious, so unexpected—nobody could have thought of it but God Himself—it must be the truth." Having long sought goodly pearls of truth, the illuminated eye catches the gleam of the gospel and discerns it to be a priceless gem. Those are blessed indeed who are thus at once brought unto faith by the statement of the gospel.

To some others, the convincing point has been *the suitability of the gospel to their case*, for while they have heard it preached as a gospel for sinners, they have felt that they were certainly among that class. When the preacher has gone on to describe the misery of the fall, the utter ruin of human nature, its deceitfulness, feebleness, fickleness, and folly, the hearer has said, "Is the gospel sent to those who are thus lost, guilty, and impotent? Why, I am precisely in that condition?" And, then, when its great command is stated, namely, simple trust in Jesus, the soul perceives the suitability of the way of grace. We do not go to heaven to bring Christ down, or dive into the deeps to bring Him up from the dead; we can neither keep the law nor find an atonement for our transgressions; but this simple trust, oh how suitable it is to undone sinners. Nothing to do—I can do nothing; nothing to bring—I have nothing to bring; it suits my case. Glory be to God for devising a plan so adapted to our wants. From the suitability of the gospel to the sinner, many have been by God's Spirit led to saving faith in Jesus, and so faith has come by hearing.

In many, I do not doubt, faith has come through hearing of *the condescending pity and the melting love of Jesus*. Oh, that we dwelt more on this; that He loved His enemies, that He died for the ungodly, that His heart yearns over the lost sheep, that He is willing to receive prodigal sons, for He is full of grace and truth.

> "His heart is made of tenderness,
> His bowels melt with love."

When such texts as the following have been preached on:—"This man receiveth sinners." "Come unto Me all ye that labour." "Ho, every one that thirsteth," etc. "All manner of sin and transgression shall be forgiven unto men." "Whosoever will, let him come and take the water of life freely." "Him that cometh unto Me I will in no wise cast out," that melting strain has touched the heart, and led the most hardened to believe in a Saviour so kind to the undeserving. Men have found it impossible not to believe in a friend so self-sacrificing, a Redeemer so altogether lovely. The sweet love of Jesus has an omnipotence in it to win souls. They yield "by mighty love subdued," unable to resist its charms, and as if they could hold out no longer, they throw themselves by an act of faith into the Saviour's arms. I can well understand their singing, "I do believe, I must believe in such a Friend as this." Faith comes by hearing of the free forgiveness procured by the agony, the stripes, the wounds, the death of Jesus, the lover of our souls.

At other times, faith has come not so much through hearing the statement of the gospel as from hearing of *its authority*. I may believe a statement because it looks like truth. I may, on the other hand, accept it not at all because I have myself perceived the apparent truth of it, but because of the person who tells it to me. And this is a very right and acceptable kind of faith. What has God said about my salvation? Before I hear it I am prepared to believe it on the testimony of God. He says it, and that is enough for me. I believe this Bible to be His book; I hear what it says, and whatsoever the Lord God hath said I must and will receive, whether it appears plain or not. There are persons who when they have heard the gospel preached have not at first believed it, but if it has pleased the Spirit of God to lead the minister to show that the gospel is of divine appointment, that the way proclaimed is ordained by God himself, and that God has set the sanction of His promise upon it —"He that believeth and is baptized shall be saved" —and has also set upon it the second sanction of His threatening—"He that believeth not shall be damned"—then they have yielded and given over all further question. God bids them trust in Jesus, and they do so through His grace. Without canvassing the statement itself they receive what God teaches, and since He hath set forth Christ to be a propitiation for sin they receive Him as such: since He has said, "Look unto Me and be saved," they look because God bids them look, and they are saved. To believe in Jesus is a command from God's own mouth, and is, therefore, to be obeyed, and the more so, because "he that believeth not God hath made Him a liar, because he believeth not the record that God gave of His Son; and this is the record, that God hath given to us eternal life, and this life is in His Son."

In some cases, too, the coming of faith has been helped by hearing and perceiving *the veracity of the subordinate testifiers of the gospel*,—I mean the writers of the sacred book, the prophets, and chiefly the apostles. These men are worthy of credit—they were honest, unsophisticated men, and they certainly gained nothing by testifying that Christ was the Messiah, and that He died and rose again from the dead. One of them, the Apostle Paul, lost his position, which was one of great eminence, and spent his whole life in toil, and suffering, and reproach, and ended with a bloody death because of what he preached, and thus he proved that he was a sincere, honest, upright man. If Paul or any other of the apostles were in the witness-box, nobody could demur to their evidence; whatever they said we should believe, because the men were truthful witnesses. Now, sometimes, persons have been led into faith in Christ, by feeling that those whom He sent to be testifiers to his person, death, and resurrection were evidently true to the core, and, therefore, their word was worthy of all acceptation.

I believe, dear friends, that faith has come by hearing in another way. Perhaps the preacher has not so much stated the gospel, and brought forward its authority, as *explained it*, and so faith has come. If we spent our time in nothing else but just explaining the text, "He that believeth and is baptized shall be saved," we might achieve a blessed life-work, and perhaps might see greater results than when our ministry takes a wider range. When the preacher takes up one by one the soul difficulties which prevent man from seeing what faith is, and keep him away from looking to Christ, and when he tries to show, as he should, that all the hope of the sinner lies out of himself, none of it in himself, that all his help for salvation is laid upon one that is mighty, even Jesus Christ the Son of God, and that he must look away from his own feelings, and prayings, and doings, and even away from his own believings as any ground of confidence, and must rest simply and alone upon the one sacrifice of Jesus; it has often happened that faith has come through the hearing of such an explanatory word.

In some cases, too, faith has come when the word has possessed a peculiar *soul-revealing pointedness* in it to the hearer's particular case. Remember the Samaritan woman. Our Lord Jesus Christ explained to her the gospel, but she does not appear to have been enlightened by His explanations: it was that home stroke of His—"Go, call thy husband and come hither," which won her to faith. Such revealings of the thoughts and intents of the heart will occur in any God-sent preaching of the gospel, just because the word pierces to the dividing of soul and spirit, and lays bare the secrets of the soul. Then it is that hearers cry, "Come, see a man that told me all things that ever I did; is not this the Christ?" Thus, by the guidance of the Spirit, the word finds out the man, and faith cometh by hearing.

Faith, also, comes in to many by hearing, when we detail *the experience* of those who have tasted and handled the good word of life; when the preacher or teacher tells how he trusted in Jesus, and found pardon, peace, and life eternal; when he is able to point to others who have felt the same, some of whom, perhaps, were even greater offenders than the person addressed, then conviction and faith are wrought in the mind. We bid you see what Jesus has done for us, in the hope that you will trust and try Him for yourselves. Jesus prayed for those who shall believe on Him through our word, and we hope you will be among the number.

To set the whole matter clearly, we will suppose that you are labouring under a very serious disease, and a physician professes to heal you. You are quite willing to believe in him, but you cannot blindly follow any man, for there are thousands of quacks and impostors. You naturally want to know something about him. Now, in what way would you go to work to get faith in him? How would faith be likely to come to you? It would come by hearing. You hear him speak, and you perceive that he understands your case, for he describes exactly all your symptoms, even those which none know but yourself and a skilful physician. You feel already some confidence in him. He next describes to you as much of the method of cure as you can comprehend, and it seems to you to be very reasonable, and withal suitable to the requirements of your case. His proposal commends itself to your best judgment, and you are already a stage nearer submission to his mode of operation. Then you enquire as to the man's character; you find that he is no mere pretender, but an authorised, skilful, long-established practitioner, well known for truthfulness, uprightness, and every good quality. Moreover, suppose in addition to this he charges you nothing whatever, but does everything gratis, having evidently no motive of gain, but being altogether disinterested, moved only by real pity for you, and a kind desire to remove your pain and save your life. Can you any longer refuse to believe and submit? But if, in addition to all this, he shows you his case-book, and bids you read case after case similar to your own in which he has affected perfect cure, and if some of these are your own acquaintances, if they are persons whom you know and esteem, why, sir, you will not insult him by saying, "I wish I could believe you;" but you will be unable to help trusting him, unless you are unwilling to be cured. Faith, in such a case, does not depend upon the will at all; you are convinced by hearing, and you become a believer. In the same way faith comes by hearing. You are unreasonable if you sit still and say, "I cannot make myself believe;" of course you cannot, but you hear, do you not, of how Christ heals sinners; you hear that He is backed by divine authority; you see that He really does save those who trust Him, and what more of evidence do you want? O soul! it seems to me a harder thing not to believe in Jesus than to believe in Him, if you are indeed willing to be made whole. When one has heard these things, and understands them, surely the mind, if it be not wilfully blinded, must receive the Saviour. May God forgive your long perverseness, and by His Spirit open your eyes to see the simplicity of that faith which comes by hearing the word of God.

II. My time, however, flies much too rapidly this morning, and I must be brief on the second very important head, namely, OBSTRUCTIONS WHICH OFTEN BLOCK UP THIS WAY.

One is a *want of intention*, by which I mean that many persons come to hear, but they have no wish to be led into faith. Like the butterflies which flit from flower to flower, they extract no honey because they come not for such a purpose; while the bees dive into the cups and bells of the flowers, and come up loaded with their luscious food. Oh, if men came to hear, praying to be endowed with faith in Jesus, faith would surely come to them by hearing. Many persons in hearing a sermon, are like children looking at a cornfield—it is full of yellow garlic, or perhaps of scarlet poppies, and they cry "What a lovely field; ' but the farmer thinks not so, he is looking for the wheat. Many a hearer watches for pretty speeches and flowery metaphors, and cries, "How well he puts it! What a well-turned sentence! How sweetly he quotes poetry!" and so on. Bah! Is that what you come to God's house for? O fools and slow of heart, is this your end in hearing the life-giving gospel of the bleeding Lamb? I assure you it is not this that we are aiming at in preaching to you. If you came to look after the good corn, you would care little for the gaudy poppies of a flaunting eloquence so much regarded by the men of these days. Come with the intent to find faith in Jesus; cry to God to make His word effectual to your salvation, and then hearing will be quite another business with you. Alas! I fear you will perish, let us preach as we may, while we are regarded by you as mere orators to be criticised, and not as witnesses whose testimony is to be weighed.

Some do not hear aright for *want of attention*. Sleepy hearers are not likely to be led to faith. Eutychus may fall from the third loft and be taken up for dead, but he is not likely to become a believer by sleeping, even though Paul should be the preacher. We want attention in order to the real reception of the word. Oh how pleasant it is to preach to earnest hearers who lean forward to catch every syllable, anxious to know how they can be saved. Wandering hearts lose the benefit of the truth, and vain minds trifle away the privilege of a gospel ministry. Take heed how ye hear, otherwise ye may remain hearers only, and so perish in unbelief.

With many a *want of candour* is another reason why faith does not come by hearing. If a man hears with a prejudiced heart, making up his mind beforehand what he will believe, he is not likely to be convinced, he puts himself as far as he can out of the reach of benefit. When the heart rebels against the word: when it says, "If this be true I am living a bad life, and I shall have to give up my pleasures, therefore I will not accept it." Well then, faith does not come and cannot come by such hearing. Faith comes by hearing when a man does, as it were, give himself up to the word of God, like a person who is badly wounded and surrenders himself to the surgeon's hand. Oh, if I had a gangrened limb and it must be taken off, I think I would pray for patience enough to say, "O sir, if you can but spare my life, cut to the very bone." When it is the soul that is concerned I would say to the preacher, "Sir, do not flatter me, do not tell me that which will please but delude me; I do not want your flattery, I do not want your fine

words. Sir, tell me what I am, and where I am in the sight of God, and how I can be saved; for it will little satisfy me to wake up in hell and remember that I used to hear a fine orator. I want to be saved in deed and of a truth." "Ah," says one, "but some preachers are not only bold, but rough in their expression." Yes, but suppose you were nearly drowned, and a strong swimmer plunged into the stream and plucked you out just as you were sinking for the last time, if he dislocated your arm would you grumble? No, you would say, "The bone can be set at another time, but my life could not have been restored." And so with the preacher, though he be rough, if it be the truth which he speaks, only pray that it may save your soul, and be content to put up with the man's infirmity, if by any means you may attain to salvation by Jesus Christ.

With some, however, hearing does not bring faith, because they hear *without any after meditation*. There is a great trial going on, as you know, in the Tichborne case. Every juryman, I doubt not, wants to judge righteously. I am sure the sleepy one is not likely to do so, and I am pretty clear that the juryman who is most likely to get at the truth will be the man who, when he gets away from the court, having heard attentively all the time, takes home the notes of the evidence, weighs it, and makes comparisons, and endeavours to sift out the truth. So I would say to you when you hear us preach, sift the sermon afterwards, turn our sermons over, pick holes in them if you like, and find out our mistakes; but oh, do search into the truth, and be not content till you find it. If you want to find Christ, the wisdom of God, you should seek for Him as for silver. You are likely to believe the truth when your mind turns it over and over. Here is a bag, and I am willing to make a man rich, and, therefore, I drop into it pound after pound, but I find that the bag is just as empty as before: the reason is plain,— there are holes in the bag, and the money drops through. Too many hearers are as a bag full of holes, and golden sermons will not bless them because they wilfully forget all. They will never come to faith because they do but look at their face in the glass of the word, and go their way and forget what manner of men they are. Oh for hearers who only need to know the gospel, and the evidence of it, and then consent thereto, saying, "It is the truth of God, I cannot quarrel with it; I joyfully receive it." Such are saved souls.

III. But, now, I am sorry to be so brief, but I must conclude by speaking of THE IMPORTANCE THAT FAITH SHOULD COME TO US BY HEARING. I will let my words drop rapidly without any ornament, and remind you, dear friend, that if you have been a hearer and faith has not come to you, you are, this moment, in the gall of bitterness and in the bonds of iniquity. You believe not in Christ, and you make God a liar, because ye have not believed in His only-begotten Son. The wrath of God abideth on you. You are dead while you live. Without God, without Christ, and stranger to the covenant of promise. My soul pities you—will you not pity yourselves? Hearers only; faithless, graceless, Christless! Christ died, but you have no part in His death. His blood cleanses from sin, but your sin remains upon you. Christ has risen, and he pleads before the throne,— you have no part in that intercession. He is preparing a place for His people, but that place is not for you. Oh, unhappy soul! oh, wretched soul! out of favour with God, at enmity with eternal love, destitute of eternal life! Truly, if Jesus were here He would weep over you, as He did over Jerusalem, and say, "How often would I have gathered you as a hen gathereth her chickens under her wings, and ye would not."

Ah, remember, though your present state is terrible it is not all. You will soon die, and you will die without faith. Remember that word of Christ, it is one of the most terrible I know of, "if ye believe not that I am He, ye shall die in your sins." To die in a ditch, to die in a prison, to die on the gallows, none of us would desire it; but to die in your sins! O God, it is hell, it is eternal damnation. May the great Lord save you! But to perish for ever will be your lot as surely as you live, except you believe in Jesus and that speedily, for soon you will be out of the reach of all hearing. No more sermons, no more invitations of grace. Oh, what would you give to have the gospel once more when you are cast away from it! No more the preacher's voice, saying, "Turn ye, turn ye, why will ye die!" No more the pitiful accents of one who loves your souls, and fain would snatch you as firebrands from the flame; around you all will be dark, and hard, and the only message for you will be this,—"He that is filthy, let him be filthy still."

"There are no acts of pardon passed,
 In that cold grave to which we haste;
 But darkness, death, and long despair,
 Reign in eternal silence there."

Ah! then it will be no assuagement of your miseries that you once heard the gospel; it will rather increase your torment. Conscience will cry aloud—"I heard the gospel of grace, and I heard the arguments which proved it true, but I rejected a gospel which God Himself proclaimed, a gospel which was genuine on the face of it, a gospel full of such love as ought to have melted a rock, a gospel that was brought to me without money and without price, a gospel that was pressed upon me from my infancy to my hoar hairs— I rejected it, I wilfully rejected it, not because it was not true, but because I would believe a lie, and would not believe the living God." Eternal Father, Thou who art mighty to save, let not one among us go down into the pit with a lie in his right hand, refusing to accept the gospel of Thy blessed Son! The Lord save you all, for Christ's sake. Amen.

WAKE UP! WAKE UP!

"That, knowing the time, that now it is high time to awake out of sleep: for now is our salvation nearer than when we believed."—Romans xiii. 11.

THIS exhortation, as you will readily perceive, is not addressed to the ungodly. These words are not spoken to those who are dead in sin, but to those who are alive unto God, though somewhat given to slumber. There are many expostulations and admonitions which do appeal to the wilful and wicked, to the indifferent and unbelieving, to those who err and are out of the way, but this is not one of them. Here we have a special charge to disciples of Jesus who know the time, and also know that their salvation draweth nigh. They are represented as being asleep and needing to awake from their present sluggishness; but they are not described as those who had ceased to be Christians, or whose salvation was in jeopardy. Though it is admitted that it is high time for them to awake out of sleep, their salvation is never questioned, but on the contrary they are reminded that now it is nearer than when they believed. The tone and tenor of this call to circumspection suggest to us that when we address the Lord's people and find occasion to rebuke and reprove them we should never insinuate that they are likely to be banished from the household of faith, or to be cast away from the presence of God, or to be treated as reprobates. Even if we feel convinced that they are asleep, and that they must be aroused, we ought not to denounce them with railing accusations, or threaten them with the wailings of the lost and the doom of unquenchable fire. You would not be pleased if anyone should touch your child with a horsewhip; nor will the Lord allow us to strike His chosen with the rod of the wicked. Legal thunders are not intended for justified saints.

"The terrors of law and of God
 With us can have nothing to do,
 Our Saviour's obedience and blood
 Hide all our transgressions from view."

Even if the saints' hearts are dull, their eyes heavy, and they are evidently fast asleep, we are not warranted in raising a false alarm. It is not for us to tell the heirs of salvation to awake because they are in danger of the wrath to come, for they are in no such danger; that is past and gone. Rather let us remind them that their salvation is nearer than when they believed, and so stir them up to watchfulness and activity by appropriate motives. The whip is for the slave, not for the child. The dread of punishment is for the condemned, not for the justified. The fear of wrath is not for those who are "accepted in the beloved," but for those who reject the Saviour and put from them the eternal mercy of God. While, then, I endeavour to speak frankly and faithfully to the Lord's people, I shall try to avoid anything like a legal tone. I would fain talk to God's children as their Father in heaven would have them talked to, somewhat sharply, perhaps, but still without a trace of the threatening which belongs to the ungodly, but not to those who are saved in the Lord.

From the connection it appears to me that Paul had in his mind's-eye a kind of sleepy state into which God's people may fall with regard to others; and upon that state of slumber we shall speak to-night.

I. Looking at the text in its true bearings, this is the lesson—SOME PROFESSING CHRISTIANS SEEM TO BE ALTOGETHER IN A DEAD SLEEP WITH REGARD TO OTHERS.

It is all very well to take a passage of Scripture, isolate it from the context, and use it as the motto of a sermon; but it is evidently not the natural and fair way of treating the word of God. You may do so for the most part with tolerable safety, for God's truth, even when it is broken up into little pieces, still retains its purity and perfection like certain crystals, which, however much they may be subdivided, always bear the same crystalline form. So true in every particle and detail is the revelation of God, that though you should take it up and dash it to pieces, yet every little fragment will bear the original impress. But this is no excuse for treating the Scriptures in an unjustifiable manner instead of expounding them according to the rules of common sense. Texts ought always to be handled with a reverential deference to the mind of the divine Spirit who indited them. When we attempt to rivet your attention to a verse or the fraction of a verse of the Bible we desire you also to be scrupulously attentive to the affinities in which it stands. If any of my published sermons should in any instance appear to violate this rule, you will bear me witness that it has been my constant habit throughout all my ministry among you to read and open up, as best I could, the whole chapter from which I have selected a few words as the motto of my discourse. I have honestly endeavoured to give you the special mind of the Spirit either in the exposition or in the sermon.

Now, you will see that the connection here is this. Paul has been bidding us to pay attention to relative duties. As citizens, he bids us render honour to magistrates, and to those who are in authority, and to pay all lawful dues and customs, and the like, telling us that we are to owe no man anything except to "love one another"; and then he shows us that the law of love is the abstract and the essence of that great table of the law which concerns a man's relation to his neighbours. He goes on to exhort us to keep that law of love, to manifest love more and more; and, when he has done so, he interjects this sentence, "And that, knowing the time, that now it is high time to awake out of sleep." Now, I gather that he means that many Christians are in a sleepy state with reference to the law of love, with reference to their obligations to others. Beloved friends, true godliness makes a man look to himself. It commences by convincing him of his own sin, and by leading him personally to lay hold on Christ by faith that in His blood he may find salvation. It then makes the man feel his personal obligations and his individual responsibilities. It sets him free from many of the yokes with which his fellow men would load him, and bids him obey his own conscience before his God, to be a law unto himself and to stand and walk as before the Most High, judging righteous judgment as to the Lord's will, and not basely bending to evil at the advice and persuasion of other men. I would to God we could get some Christians, some professed Christians, to be a little more independent; but so many of them are like the rotten houses of which we have not a few in this neighbourhood; they could not stand alone, they must keep together, for they prop one another up. If you were to pull down one of the houses in some of our streets, they must all fall; and so there are sets of Christian professors that lean one upon another, upon the custom of their set and sect, and church and community. They have never dared to study Scripture for themselves and follow it, nor have they ever tried to form their own personal conscientious convictions. One of the first works of the Holy Spirit is to make the man look at home, and to consider the condition of his own soul.

When the Spirit of God has made a man thus to stand on his own footing before God, and to feel his personality, there springs up a danger that such a man may say, "I shall henceforth keep myself to myself. My chief business will be indoor work, to see after the rightness of my own spirit and to keep myself prospering before the Lord. Other people must see to themselves, and I must see to myself." The principle of individuality might be thus pushed to an extreme, till what at first was necessary grit in the spiritual constitution, making the man truly a man, may be so unduly increased that he becomes at last an unkind, ungenerous, cruel, selfish thing, deprived of the best part of his humanity. Thus, then, we are brought back to this, that albeit every man must give an account of himself before God, and must personally be born again, and personally be reconciled to God by Jesus Christ, yet, "no man liveth to himself," nor was he ever meant to do so. No man can compass the ends of life by drawing a little line around himself upon the ground. No man can fulfil his calling as a Christian by seeking the welfare of his wife and family only, for these are only a sort of greater self. There are outgoing lines of life that bind us not only with some men, but, in fact, with all humanity; so that, if we did but know it, the thought of one brain, the utterance of one lip, the movement of one pair of hands does in its measure influence the whole human race to some degree and will do so till time shall be no more. We are placed, therefore, in a most solemn position; and it is with regard to this that it is high time that we should awake out of sleep.

Into what a deep slumber some professing Christians have fallen! How utterly insensible they are to the sins and sorrows of those around them. They believe God has a people, and they are very glad He has, as far as they are capable of being glad of anything that does not concern themselves. But, "the world lieth in the wicked one," and multitudes are perishing. They are sorry it is so, that is to say, they go the length of saying they are sorry. It does not cause them any sleepless nights, it does not disturb their digestion, it in no way interferes with their comfort, for they do not seem to think that it has anything to do with them. I know some that are in such a sleep who drug themselves with almost as much regularity as they feed themselves. They take that great and precious truth of the divine sovereignty, and turn it to a most detestable use: for they say, "What is to be will be, and the Lord's purpose will be fulfilled. There will be some saved and others lost." All this is said as coolly as if they were talking of a wasp's nest. As for those that are lost! They dare not injure their logic by indulging a little mournful emotion. Were their minister to weep over the lost, as Jesus wept over Jerusalem, they would say he was unsound—a duty-faith man, certainly, and, probably, an Arminian. And they would straightway quit him, and think that he could not have really received the mind of the Spirit of God. Yet, in the judgment of all who think aright, one of the finest traits in a Christian's character is the deep sorrow which he feels over souls that are being lost and the great longing of his own soul that men would turn unto God and find peace through Jesus Christ. O sirs, I fear there are many professors in a deep sleep as to whether others are going to heaven or to hell! The drunkenness that is around them they look upon as a matter of course. The blasphemy which greets their ears does not chill their blood: they say it is very usual and very shocking. The Sabbath breaking they take to be a kind of necessary evil. The rejection of Christ by men they look upon as no sin at all, and they even quarrel and cavil with those who think that sinners are blameworthy in rejecting the Son of God, the Saviour of sinners.

I trust that many of these are God's people, and, if they be, it is high time that they should awake out of such a sleep as that, so unlike Christ, so alien to the spirit of love, so contrary to the mind which God would have His Spirit work in all His people. Alas! that they should have sunk into so dead a sleep.

Others there are, dear friends, who are prone to be overtaken with an oft-recurring sleep. I know a brother who often takes forty winks in the day-time: you may nudge him, and he will wake and listen to you, but he goes to sleep again in a few minutes if you let him alone. He will attend to you with much pleasure if you pull his coat again; but he soon returns to his dozing. Who can blame the sleeper when it is a question of infirmity or sheer exhaustion? I never like to blame people too hastily when they go to sleep in a place of worship, for I remember thinking rather hardly of a brother, who went to sleep one Sunday morning under my sermon; but when I found that he had been sitting up two nights with a sick wife and had been doing a full day's work besides, then I was sorry enough to have thought a hard thought of a worthy man. I rather wondered, when I understood the case, whether I should have been able to come to worship at all. Well, without blaming any of you, then, for the weakness of the flesh, I take this sleepy habit to be a fit illustration of the state in which some Christians are to be found. They go to sleep and then they wake up for a little; they have fits and starts of wakefulness, and then off to sleep again they drop. Does this describe you, dear friend? At that missionary meeting you woke up when you heard the cry of the perishing heathen. You wanted to get out into the street at once and tell poor sinners about Christ; and you did empty your pockets into the plate before you left the building. Have you cared much about China or India since then, though you know that there are millions of people,—millions dying for lack of knowledge? They have not troubled you much, have they, since that missionary meeting? Perhaps to-night I shall pull your coat tail a little and you will be awake again, and youw ill be very much concerned, and you will pray earnestly for your neighbours and your ungodly friends. But, I fear, you will soon go to sleep again. You have gone back to your slumbers so many times before that now it is "sleeping made easy." Could not your ministers lodge a grievous complaint against you for this? You do get on fire with love for souls when the discourse is specially arousing, but then after the sermon is over, and the week of special services has ended, you go to sleep again. Many Sunday-school teachers there are of that kind. They do sometimes talk to their children about their souls with tears in their eyes; and then, again, their ardour evaporates, and they get through their duties in little better form than merely reading the Scriptures, and explaining them in a dry, dull fashion. My slumbering brethren, you could be awake. You might be awake! For sometimes you are so. There are times when your whole soul seems on fire. If anybody had spoken of you then, they would have said, "What a fine man that is! What love he has for Christ! What concern for the souls of men! He ought to be sent forth as a missionary at once." Wait till you see him asleep! He can sleep very soundly! In fact, he is as great at sleeping as at waking. He can descend into depths of stupidity and indifference as naturally as he just now rose into heights of fervour and enthusiasm. Yes, there are many such, and I would say to any brothers and sisters who are conscious of a propensity in that direction—is it not high time that you, that I, that any, that all of us should awake out of sleep?

There are those, again, who fall into a kind of somnambulistic state. They are doing a good deal for their Lord and Master, but yet they are asleep. If we judged them by their outward actions we should think they were wide awake, and they do what they do very well. But have you never seen a person who has a habit of walking in his sleep? It is a strange sight. Persons have been known to walk along giddy heights safely enough when they have been fast asleep, where they would not have thought of venturing if they had been wide awake. And we have known, sometimes, professors going on very safely, carefully, exactly, in positions where others have fallen, and we have admired their prudence and discretion, and attributed it to the grace of God, whereas in part it has been attributable to the fact that they were spiritually asleep all the time. It is very possible to walk long and far and yet remain asleep; it is very possible to appear very devout when, indeed, you are very sleepy. It is very possible to sing hymns when you are not awake to the sense; yes, and it is very probable that you will betray your absence of mind by sitting down at the last verse, although there is going to be a chorus afterwards. You know it is coming, but your part of the worship is performed so mechanically that you dropped down in your pews as a mere matter of habit, and then were all in a flurry to be up again. I have detected many of you doing it. I have felt convinced that you were virtually asleep at the time, not really drinking in the spirit of the hymn, or else it would not have happened. It is very easy to hear sermons and to be asleep all the while, at least with one ear open and one eye, but the major part of the faculties of the soul still steeped in slumber. And you can keep on teaching in the Sunday-school, pay your religious contributions punctually, maintain the habit of family prayer, and even your private devotions may not be wholly neglected, and yet you may be a somnambulist. All these duties may be done with a sort of sleep-walking life and action, and not at all with the life of a thoroughly wakeful man. Oh, I would like to hear a man speak about heaven who was altogether awake to it. I would like to hear a man preach about hell who was aroused to the true pitch. It would make your very hair stand on end, as you should hear how he told of the terrors of the wrath to come. It would make every drop of blood dance in your veins to hear a man speak of Christ who is all on fire with love divine, and all awake with divine delight in him. But that slumber is apt to come over the most lively minister. Who will not confess it? Oh, if you have ever read a chapter of the Bible when your soul has been all awake, how the promises have glowed and burned. How bright have they been like "the terrible crystal." But too often we have nodded over the Bible, nodded over the promises, nodded over the precepts, till there seemed neither life nor power in them. The life was there, but we were asleep.

Well, dear friends, I must add, and then I shall have said enough about sleep, that a very large number of us are half asleep. Whether there is one man alive that is spiritually awake all over, I do not know. Such a man as Rutherford, who loved his Lord so that he scarcely ever thought of anything but Jesus—that was a man all awake. Such a man as Mr. Whitefield again, preaching his very heart out morning, noon, and night with a seraphic eloquence—that was a man wide awake. There have been many such; I trust there is a remnant of such now. But the most of us are painfully conscious that we are waking, and need greatly to be more awake still. O God, make us to feel the solemn weight of those eternal things in which we believe. Thou hast saved us, make us awake to feel from what Thou hast saved us, and by whom Thou hast saved us, and to what thou hast saved us, and what the privileges are which belong to us now that we are saved. Oh, when I think how trivial are the things of time, and how all-important are the unseen realities of eternity, I cannot but again conclude that most of us are nothing more than about half awake as to the things of God, and if it be so it is high time that we wake out of sleep.

II. Now, in the second place, I want to occupy a few minutes by saying, that whereas many believers are asleep IT IS HIGH TIME THAT THEY SHOULD AWAKE. And why high time that they should be awake?

Why, first, because what right have we who are believers to be asleep at all? The Lord has saved us—saved us from death—saved us from the sleep which is the first cousin to death—saved us from indifference—saved us from unbelief—saved us from hardheartedness—saved us from carelessness. Well, now, if the Lord has done this for us, what business have we to be in a sleepy state? When the five wise virgins went out to meet the bridegroom, and took their lamps with them, what right had they to be asleep? I can very well understand those sleeping who had no oil in the vessels with their lamps, because when their lamps went out they would be in the dark, and darkness suggests sleep, but those who had their lamps well trimmed, should they go asleep in the light? Those that had the oil, should they go to sleep while the oil was illuminating them? They needed to be awake to put the oil into the lamp. Besides, they had come out to meet the bridegroom. Could they meet him asleep? When he should come, would it be fit that he should find those who attended his wedding all asleep in a row, insulting his dignity and treating his glory with scorn? Child of God, thou art expecting Christ soon to come, and He may come to-night, or He may, if He pleases, delay His coming, but why, oh why, dost thou think of sleeping? What is there congruous to thy character—what is there suitable to thy expectations—in thy sleep? If then thou hast caught thyself having a sinful nap, bestir thyself, and ask the Holy Spirit to arouse thee, for since thou hast no right to sleep at all it is high time that thou shouldest awake out of sleep.

It is high time because a great many opportunities have already slipped away. I address myself to some of you who have been converted, say these ten years. And what have you done for Christ? You are saved—we are not going to question that; and your glorious salvation is nearer than when you believed. But what have you done during these many years? You have been eating the fat and drinking the sweet, but have you fed the hungry? Have you brought in the wandering? You have enjoyed the means of grace, you tell me. And is this all you were created for—to enjoy, ay, even to enjoy good things? Have you not asked yourself the question "What shall I render to the Lord for all His benefits toward me?" Dear friend, if you have been saved a week, and you have done nothing for Christ during that week, you have already wasted more than enough time in having lived through seven fruitless days. Let the time past suffice you to have suffered opportunities to pass before your door unwelcomed.

But some professors are growing old; grey hairs are upon them. How long hast thou been a Christian? Hast thou loved the Lord these thirty years, and done so little? Or what, if though thou be an old man, and yet only a babe in grace? That is worse still, is it not? As to all the past, is thine account grievously unprofitable?—a wilderness where there might have been a garden, a desert where there might have been a fruitful field? Can you endure the painful retrospect? Oh, when I look back, one of the joys of my life is to have been converted to God while yet a child, and to have begun to preach the name of Jesus when still a youth, and yet though that be a subject for joy, I find abundant reason for accusing myself of wasting opportunities of service. If it be so with me, though for years I have lived unto the Lord, I am sure it must be so with many of my Master's servants; so let me say to them, by all those wasted opportunities, it must be high time for you to awake out of sleep. Time is hastening on, my brethren; each flying moment holds another by the heel. Life rushes on as a rapid stream; it bears us along swiftly and silently. If you are going to do something it must be done very soon, young man. You are not a child now. Your sun has not quite reached its zenith, but it is rising high. It may go down ere it is noon. If something is to be accomplished before you die, get at it, man, get at it, or your life will be a failure. And you of middle life. Well, you are in the very strength and prime of your days. If God is to be glorified by you, and souls brought to Christ by you, I urge you, in the name of all that is reasonable, get at it, and lay to, for if you do not work now, when will you? When the days of weakness come, and those that look out of the windows are darkened, you will say, "I am too old." Oh, now, let the prime of your days be the Lord's! Or, has the evening of life descended upon you? Are the shadows lengthening, and does strength fail? Brother, sister, thou art saved. Thou wouldest not like to go to heaven, wouldest thou, without glorifying Christ somewhat here below? Then do it now. All hand, all heart, all mind, all thought must be given to the present pressing duty. Thou hast such a little while before thee—so scanty an evening is left thee—surely it should be all spent with the utmost diligence in the Master's service. "Knowing the time, that now it is high time to awake out of sleep."

Do you not see that it is high time to awake out of sleep, because there were so many people that had a claim upon us, who are beyond our power now, even if we do wake? Have you ever felt the sadness of neglecting to visit a person who was ill until you heard that he was dead? You said to yourself, "Why did I not go and speak at least one word of warning before that soul was gone into eternity?" Death is sweeping away multitudes of our neighbours and friends, and it is high time that we were diligent in seeking those that remain, if we are to do them any good, for when that knell is tolling, and that grave is closing, our regrets will be useless to the departed, but, at the same time, bitter to ourselves. Many are passing away from us and from the sphere of our influence in the common course of providence. Your children, for instance. They were little. Some of you have little children still. Well, they will not be little long. Already, mother, that boy is beginning to show a good deal of independence of spirit; he will not even now listen to you as he did, and you feel a little grieved at it. It will be more so soon. If you do not bend the twig when it is a twig, you will not do much with it when it gets to be a tree. We let our children slip from under our fingers while they are plastic We forget to mould them, and then they get into manhood, and become less amenable to our counsels and our cautions, and we grieve that we did not do something more to train them up in the way they should go. Now is your time, mother, God helping you. Now is your time, father. Parents, avail yourselves of your opportunities; and remember that good is done by constant watching and by small degrees. And your servants, too. Cannot you recollect some servants that lived with you, and you always meant to talk to them about their souls, and to pray with them? But they left you, and they were gone before you had commenced to bless them. They are very worldly now. Perhaps if you were to trace them out you would find they were Christless, and you would hear them say that they once lived with a religious mistress, with a pious master, and they hoped they would never do so again, for it was the most miserable time they ever had, "and whatever religion master might have had, he kept it all pretty well to himself, for they never heard much of it." "Oh," you say, "I hope they do not say so." I hope so too, but I have known such things said. And it is very possible that men and women may be so asleep about the souls of those round about them that opportunities which were in their way may be sliding away never to return. I believe that if we were awake we might often avail ourselves of opportunities to speak to men who otherwise hold themselves aloof from any religious conversation. There is a time with almost every man when conscience is awake. Perhaps he is saddened by affliction, is cowed by adversity: then he will respect as friendly what he might otherwise resent as insulting. The most hardened do at some season or other become amenable to reproof, or exhortation, or direction. If you are ready, take a shot at him, and you will have him. But, if not at that moment, you may never have another occasion of getting the truth where the man will feel it. We ought to be ready in a minute. Those who would shoot the running deer have to be very, very clever in taking sight and seizing the moment while it is running by, and those that would take running souls—and the most of our fellow-countrymen are just such—must be sharp sighted and quick witted. They only run by us, and we must have them in a minute or else they will have gone beyond our reach. We cannot do this unless we are awakened out of our sleep. God grant we may be so awakened.

Meanwhile, dear friends, there is this reason why we should be awake; we have plenty of enemies that are awake if we are not. You may sleep, but you cannot induce the devil to close his eyes. Protestantism may slumber, but I will warrant you Jesuitism never does. You may see evangelicals asleep, but you will not find ritualists slumbering. The prince of the power of the air keeps his servants well up to their work. Is it not a strange thing that the servants of the devil serve him so enthusiastically, while the servants of the Lord often serve Him at a poor, cold, dead-alive rate. Oh, may the Lord quicken us! If we could with a glance see the activities of the servants of Satan we should be astonished at our own sluggishness. It is while men sleep that the enemy comes and sows tares among the wheat, and it is because men sleep that the tares are sown in the Lord's field. If we were more awake, the adversary would not have the opportunity of scattering his evil grain.

It is high time that we awake out of sleep, for it is daylight. The sun has risen. Will you sleep now? We are getting far into the gospel dispensation. Can you sleep still? It is time that we were awake, for our Lord was awake. What wakefulness He exhibited! How did His eyes stream with tears over perishing Jerusalem! He was all heart. The zeal of God's house consumed Him. Ought it not to consume us? We ought to be awake, for our own day may be over within an hour or two. The preacher may be delivering his last sermon. You may go home to-night to offer the last prayer at the family altar which you will ever utter on earth. You shall open shop to-morrow morning for the last time. Should not these possibilities bestir you? How near, how very near, is the ultimatum of every man here present. Have you fixed upon a grand purpose, brother? Fulfil it. You have scarcely time to get through it, therefore waste not an hour. Have you been planning? Leave off planning and get to executing your work. You have been speaking about being generous. Be generous. You have been talking about being spiritually minded. Leave off talk, and get at it, man. You have intended to be consecrated to God. Come, do not squabble about consecration and about perfectionism, but be ye consecrated and be ye perfect. Go in for the highest possible form of devotion and service. We have lived long enough at this poor half-and-half rate. If there be any higher platform, the Lord lift us up to it. If there be a way of living, spirit, soul, and body, wholly, unreservedly devoted every moment to the Lord, oh for His Spirit to conduct us into such a state. This is our ambition. After this we aspire. We dare not say, as some do, that we have gained it, for if we did we believe that we should give evidence that we knew not what it was, or else we should not talk so loftily. But brethren, while the Master's personal coming may be so near, and while His coming to us by death may be nearer still, it is high time that we awoke out of sleep.

III. I close with a third remark. IT IS WORTH WHILE WAKING, FOR THERE IS SOMETHING WORTH WAKING FOR.

He says, that it is high time that we wake out of sleep, for now is our salvation nearer than when we believed. As I already remarked, he does not say, "for if you do not wake you will be lost." Neither does He say, "You Christian people, if you remain in this dull state, will perish without hope." No, that is the threatening of the law, and suits the tongue of Moses, but Jesus does not talk so. No, no, He sets His servant speaking to us in a gospel tone, "Now is your salvation nearer than when you believed."

Undoubtedly, dear brother, it is nearer in order of time. How long is it since you believed? Ten years? You are ten years nearer heaven, then. Your salvation, that is, your ultimate, complete salvation, the display and manifestation of your complete deliverance from evil, from sin, from death, from hell, is nearer by so many years than when you believed. Some of us are five-and-twenty years nearer than we were. Ought we not to be more awake? The farther we are off from heaven, the less we may feel its influence; but we are getting so much nearer that we ought to be increasingly sensitive to its mysterious spell. Oh, to feel more of its power! We shall soon be in heaven, brothers. We shall soon be there, sisters. Do not let us go to sleep now with the golden gate right before us, and Jesus waiting to admit us. Nearer glory! Is it not good argument for being more alive unto God?

Some of you are sixty years nearer to heaven than you were. You have been in Christ now more than half a century. Well, well, brother, are you not glad of it? Would you like to live those sixty years over again? Would you like to go back and tread that weary road a second time, clambering again the hill Difficulty, and sliding down again into the Valley of Humiliation. Would you wish to march a second time through the Valley of the Shadow of Death, and into Giant Despair's castle? "No," say you; and you need not fear the return journey, for you shall not go back again. Rejoice that you are so much nearer heaven in the matter of time. Therefore, keep wide awake, and looking out for it. When little children have been taken from their inland homes to the sea they have been very eager to see the ocean, and yet they have been ready to go to sleep as they approached the end of the journey. They have never seen the sea before, but mother says, "Wake up, children, you are coming near the sea." Soul, soul, soul, we have never seen heaven, but we are getting nearer. Let us keep awake. Jerusalem, my happy home, shall I enter thy sacred precincts sleeping? Shall I come to the last hill, from which I am to take a view of thy glittering vanes and golden streets, and shall I be half asleep within view of them? Come, no, no, no; my heart, wake up! Heart, wake up! thou art getting nearer home. "A day's march nearer home" thou hast come even this day, be ashamed to slumber.

And, if we are getting nearer in point of time, I hope we are getting nearer in point of *preparation*. Christ is preparing heaven for us, and His Spirit is preparing us for heaven. Well, then, if we are getting more ready for heaven, we ought to be more awake, for sleepiness is not the state of heavenly spirits. Heaven is the home of activity, not the dormitory of unconsciousness. When our bodies shall have been raised from the dead, they shall enjoy life and energy, and be for ever free from fatigue and sluggishness. Let us, as we are getting ready for celestial company, be fuller of life and fuller of energy.

More ready for heaven, then reap, reap, reap with stronger arm. Do another man's work, if thou canst, as well as thine own. Thou hast nearly accomplished thy life's labour, therefore throw all thy strength into that little which remaineth. So near heaven; then

pluck another brand out of the burning. If thou art more fit for heaven thou hast more love, more grace, more pity; then reach out both hands to bring another poor soul to Christ. If the golden gate shall soon be open to thee, and thou shalt be shut in for ever in the blest place of rest, be sure to show others the way to that gate, that thou enter not alone. Your salvation is nearer than when you believed, therefore do something more to prove that you are ready for it.

And, lastly, as your salvation is nearer than when you believed, let us hope your realization of it is more clear. Have you tried to realize the glory to be revealed? Within a short time you will be with Jesus—

> "Far from this world of grief and sin,
> With God eternally shut in."

Your head will wear a crown, your hand shall grasp the palm of victory; you, even you, shall walk the golden streets, and see that face which is brighter than the sun. It may be that to-night you will be made free of the New Jerusalem: to-night you may leave that narrow room and that hard bed, the abode of poverty and care, and you may be away up where they keep eternal sabbath, and the congregations never break up. You will be there, brother, even you. There is a crown in glory which no head can wear but yours. You will be there. Well, now, it really seems to me that, if I can realize that in so short a time my eternal salvation shall be consummated, and I, even I, shall be among the blood-washed throng, to see my Saviour's face, I cannot any longer neglect a single opportunity of serving my Master—cannot any longer let poor souls go down to hell without endeavouring to save them—cannot any longer neglect prayer—neglect opportunities of usefulness, or live otherwise than as a man should live who has his foot upon the doorstep of heaven and his finger on the latch. What manner of persons ought ye to be to whom heaven is guaranteed by promise, and to whom it has been sealed by blood to be your special heritage,—the portion of a people whom every moment brings nearer to eternal felicity? What manner of persons ought ye to be? May the Spirit of God make you to be just that now, and He shall have praise for ever. Amen.

I have said nothing to the unconverted because I have been admonishing *you* to say something to them. If you will catch the spirit of my text, you will each one feel for them and begin to speak. But if I were to wrench the text from its connection, and apply it to the unconverted, what a sledge hammer it would be! Shall I read the text as I should have to read it if it spoke to the unregenerate? It runs to the Christian, "Now is your salvation nearer than when ye believed." Oh, ye unconverted men, must I read the text as it would have to run if it were written to you? "It is high time that you should awake out of sleep, for now is your damnation nearer than when you first heard the gospel and rejected it." Take heed, take heed. God grant you grace to take heed and to believe in Christ. Amen and Amen.

CHRIST PUT ON

"But put ye on the Lord Jesus Christ, and make not provision for the flesh, to fulfil the lusts thereof."—Romans xiii. 14.

CHRIST must be in us before He can be on us. Grace puts Christ within, and enables us to put on Christ without. Christ must be in the heart by faith, before He can be in the life by holiness. If you want light from a lantern, the first business is to light the candle inside of it; and then, as a consequence, the light shines through, to be seen of men. When Christ is formed in you, the hope of glory, do not conceal your love to Him; but put Him on in your conduct as the glory of your hope. As you have Christ within as your Saviour, the secret of your inner life, so put on Christ to be the beauty of your daily life. Let the external be brightened by the internal; and this shall be to you that "armour of light" which all the soldiers of the Lord Jesus are privileged to wear. As Christ is your food, nourishing the inner man, so put Him on as your dress, covering the outer man.

"Put ye on the Lord Jesus Christ." It is a very wonderful expression. It is most condescending on our Lord's part to allow of such an exhortation. Paul speaks the mind of the Holy Spirit, and the word is full of meaning. Oh, for grace to learn its teaching! It is full of very solemn warning to us, for we need a covering thus divinely perfect. Oh, for grace to practise the command to put it on! The apostle does not so much say, "Take up the Lord Jesus Christ, and bear Him with you;" but, "Put on the Lord Jesus Christ," and thus wear Him as the garment of your life. A man takes up his staff for a journey, or his sword for a battle; but he lays these down again after a while; you are to put on the Lord Jesus as you put on your garment; and thus He is to cover you, and to become part and parcel of your outward appearance, surrounding your very self, as a visible part of your manifest personality.

"Put ye on the Lord Jesus Christ." This we do when we believe in Him: then we put on the Lord Jesus Christ as our robe of righteousness. It is a very beautiful picture of what faith does. Faith finds our manhood naked to its shame; faith sees that Christ Jesus is the robe of righteousness provided for our need, and faith, at the command of the gospel, appropriates Him, and gets the benefit of Him for it. By faith the soul covers her weakness with His strength, her sin with His atonement, her folly with His wisdom, her failure with His triumphs, her death with His life, her wanderings with His constancy. By faith, I say, the soul hides itself within Jesus; till Jesus only is seen, and the man is seen in Him. We take not only His righteousness as being imputed to us, but we take Himself to be really ours; and so His righteousness becomes ours as a matter of fact. "By the obedience of one shall many be made righteous." His righteousness is set to our account, and becomes ours because He is ours. I, though long unrighteous in myself, believe in the testimony of God concerning His Son Jesus Christ, and I am accounted righteous, even as it is written, "Abraham believed God, and it was counted to him for righteousness." The riches of God in Christ Jesus become mine as I take the Lord Jesus Christ to be everything to me.

But, you see, the text does not distinctly refer to this great matter, for the apostle is not referring to the imputed righteousness of Christ. The text stands in connection with precepts concerning matters of every-day practical life, and to these it must refer. It is not justification, but sanctification that we have here. Moreover, we cannot be said to put on the imputed righteousness of Christ after we have believed, for that is upon us as soon as we believe, and needs no more putting on. The command before us is given to those who have the imputed righteousness of Christ, who are justified, who are accepted in Christ Jesus. "Put ye on the Lord Jesus Christ" is a word to you that are saved by Christ, and justified by His righteousness. You are to put on Christ, and keep on putting Him on in the sanctifying of your lives unto your God. You are every day continually more and more to wear as the dress of your lives the character of your Lord.

I will handle this subject by answering questions. First, Where are we to go for our daily dress? "Put ye on the Lord Jesus Christ." Secondly, What is this daily dress? "Put ye on the Lord Jesus Christ." Thirdly, How are we to act towards evil when we are thus clad? "And make not provision for the flesh, to fulfil the lusts thereof." And then I will finish with the consideration of the question, Why should we hasten to put on this matchless dress? For "The night is far spent, the day is at hand; let us put on the armour of light."

I. May the Holy Spirit help us while we, in the first place, answer the inquiry, WHERE ARE WE TO GO FOR DAILY DRESS? Beloved, there is but one answer to all questions as to our necessities. We go to the Lord Jesus Christ for everything. To us "Christ is all." "He is made of God unto us wisdom, and righteousness, and sanctification, and redemption." When you have come to Christ for pardon and justification, you are not to go elsewhere for the next thing. Having begun with Jesus, you are to go on with Him, even to the end; "for ye are complete in Him," perfectly stored in Christ, fully equipped in Him. "It pleased the Father that in Him should all fulness dwell." Every necessity that can ever press upon you between this Marah in the wilderness and yonder sea of glass before the throne, will be found to be met in Christ Jesus. You ask, What am I to do for a vesture which will befit the courts of the Lord? for armour that will protect me from the assaults of the foe? for a robe that will enable me to act as a priest and king unto God? The one answer to the much-including question is, "Put ye on the Lord Jesus Christ." You have no further need. You need not look elsewhere for a thread or a shoe latchet.

So, dear friends, I gather from this, that if we seek an example, we may not look elsewhere than to our Lord Jesus Christ. It is not written, "Put ye on this man or that"; but "Put ye on the Lord Jesus Christ." The model for a saint is his Saviour. We are very apt to select some eminently gracious or useful man to be a pattern to us. A measure of good may result from such a course, but a degree of evil may also come of it. There will always be some fault about the most excellent of our fellow-mortals; and as our tendency is to caricature virtues till we make them faults, so is it our greater folly to mistake faults for excellences, and copy them with careful exactness, and generally with abundant exaggeration. By this plan, with the best intentions, we may reach very sad results. Follow Jesus in the way, and thou wilt not err: let thy feet go down exactly in His foot-prints, and thou canst not slide. As His grace enables us, let us make it true, that "as He was, so are we in this world." You need not look beyond your Lord for example under any circumstances. Of Him you may enquire as of an unfailing oracle. You need never enquire what is the general custom of those about you: the broad road of the many is no way for you. You may not ask, "What are the rulers of the people doing?" You follow not the fashion of the great, but the example of the greatest of all. "Put ye on the Lord Jesus Christ" will apply to each one of us. If I am a tradesman, I am not to ask myself—On what principles do other traders conduct their busness? Not so. What the world may do is no rule for me. If I am a student I should not enquire—How do others feel towards religion? Let others do as they will, it is for us to serve the Lord. In every relationship, in the domestic circle, in the literary world, in the sphere of friendship, or in business connections, I am to "put on the Lord Jesus Christ." If I am perplexed, I am bound to ask—What would Jesus do? and His example is to guide me. If I cannot conceive of His acting in a certain way, neither must I allow myself to do so; but if I perceive, from His precept, His spirit, or His action, that He would follow such and such a course, to that line I must keep. I am not to put on the philosopher, the politician, the priest, or the popularity hunter; but I am to put on the Lord Jesus Christ, by taking His life to be the model upon which I fashion my own life.

From our text I should also gather that we are to go to the Lord Jesus Christ for *stimulus*. We want not only an example, but a motive, an impulse and constraining power to keep us true to that example. We need to put on zeal as a cloak, and to be covered with a holy influence which will urge us onward. Let us go to the Lord Jesus for motives. Some fly to Moses, and would drive themselves to duty by the thunders of Sinai. Their design in service is to earn eternal life, or prevent the loss of the favour of God. Thus they come under law, and forsake the true way of the believer, which is faith. Not from dread of punishment or hope of hire do believers serve the living God; but we put on Christ, and the love of Christ constraineth us. Here is the spring of true holiness: "Sin shall not have dominion over you, for ye are not under the law, but under grace." A stronger force than law has gripped you: you serve God, not as servants, whose sole thought is the wage, but as children, whose eye is on the Father and His love. Your motive is gratitude to Him by whose precious blood you are redeemed. He has put on *your* cause, and therefore you would take up *His* cause. I pray you, go not to the steep sides of Sinai to find motives for holiness; but hasten to Calvary, and there find those sweet herbs of love, which shall be the medicine of your soul. "Put ye on the Lord Jesus Christ." Covered with a consciousness of His love, fired with love to Him in return, you will be strong to be, to do, or to suffer, as the Lord God may appoint.

Need I say, never find a reason for doing right in a desire to win the approbation of your fellow-men? Do not say, "I must do this or that in order to please my company." That is poor life which is sustained by the breath of other men's nostrils. Followers of Jesus will not wear the livery of custom, or stand in awe of human censure. Love of commendation, and fear of disapprobation, are low and beggarly motives: they sway the feeble many, but they ought not to rule the man in Christ. You must be moved by a far higher consideration: you serve the Lord Christ, and must not, therefore, become the lackey of men. His glory is to be your one aim; and for the joy of this you must treat all else as a light thing. Here we find our spur—"The love of Christ constraineth us."

Beloved, the text means more than this. "Put ye on the Lord Jesus Christ"; that is, find in Jesus your *strength*. Although you are saved, and are quickened by the Holy Spirit, so as to be a living child of the living· God, yet you have no strength for heavenly duty, except as you receive it from above. Go to Jesus for power. I charge you, never say, "I shall do the right because I have resolved to do it. I am a man of strong mind; I am determined to resist this evil, and I know I shall not yield. I have made up my mind, and there is no fear of my turning aside." Brother, if you rely upon yourself in that way, you will soon prove to be a broken reed. Failure follows at the heel of self-confidence. "Put ye on the Lord Jesus Christ."

I charge you, do not rely upon what you have acquired in the past. Say not in your heart, "I am a man of experience, and therefore I can resist temptation, which would crush the younger and greener folk. I have now spent so many years in persistent well-doing that I may reckon myself out of danger. Is it likely that I should ever be led astray?" O sir, it is more than likely! It is a fact already. The moment that a man declares he cannot fall, he has already fallen from sobriety and humility. Your head is turned, my brother, or you would not talk of your inward perfection; and when the head turns, the feet are not very safe. Inward conceit is the mother of open sin. Make Christ your strength, and not yourself; nor your acquirements or experiences. "Put ye on the Lord Jesus Christ" day by day, and make not the rags of yesterday be the raiment of the future. Get grace fresh and fresh. Say with David, "All my fresh springs are in Thee." Get all your power for holiness and usefulness from Jesus, and from Him alone. "Surely in the Lord have I righteousness and strength." Rely not on resolves, pledges, methods, prayers; but lean on Jesus only as the strength of your life.

"Put ye on the Lord Jesus Christ." This is a wonderful word to me, because it indicates that in the Lord Jesus we have *perfection*. I shall in a moment or two show you some of the virtues and graces which are resplendent in the character of our Lord Jesus Christ. These may be likened to different parts of our armour or dress—the helmet, the shoes, the breast-plate. But the text does not say, "Put on this quality or virtue of the Lord Christ"; but "Put ye on the Lord Jesus Christ." He Himself, as a whole, is to be our array. Not this excellence or that; but Himself. He must be to us a sacred over-all. I know not by what other means to bring out my meaning: He is to cover us from head to foot. We do not so much copy His humility, His gentleness, His love, His zeal, His prayerfulness, as Himself. Endeavour to come into such communion with Jesus Himself that His character is reproduced in you. Oh, to be wrapped about with Himself; feeling, desiring, acting, as He felt, desired, and acted. What a raiment for our spiritual nature is our Lord Jesus Christ! What an honourable robe for a man to wear! Why, in that case, our life would be hid in Christ, and He would be seen over us in a life quickened by His Spirit, swayed by His motives, sweetened with His sympathy, pursuing His designs, and following in His steps. When we read, "Put ye on the Lord Jesus Christ," it means, Receive the whole character of Christ, and let your whole character be conformed to His will. Cover your whole being with the whole of the Lord Jesus Christ. What a wonderful precept! Oh, for grace to carry it out! May the Lord turn the command into an actual fact. Throughout the rest of our lives may we be more and more like Jesus, that the purpose of God may be fulfilled wherein we are "predestinated to be conformed to the image of His Son."

Once more, observe the *speciality* which is seen in this dress. It is specially adapted to each individual believer. Paul does not say merely to one person, "Put *thou* on the Lord Jesus Christ," but to all of us, "Put *ye* on the Lord Jesus Christ." Can all the saints put on Christ, whether babes, young men, or fathers? You could not all of you wear my coat, I am quite certain; and I am equally certain that I could not wear the garments of many of the young people now present; but here is a matchless garment, which will be found suitable for every believer, without expansion or contraction. Whoever puts on the Lord Jesus Christ has put on a robe which will be His glory and beauty. In every case the example of Jesus is admirably suited for copying. Suppose a child of God should be a king; what better advice could I give to him, when about to rule a nation, than this, "Put on the Lord Jesus Christ"? Be such a king as Jesus would have been. Nay, copy His royal character. Suppose, on the other hand, that the person before us is a poor woman from the workhouse; shall I say the same to her? Yes, and with equal propriety; for Jesus was very poor, and is a most suitable example for those who have no home of their own. O worker, put on Christ, and be full of zeal! O sufferer, put on the Lord Jesus Christ, and abound in patience! Yonder friend is going to the Sunday-school this afternoon. Well, in order to win those dear children to the Saviour, "put on the Lord Jesus Christ," who said, "Suffer the little children to come unto me, and forbid them not." In His sacred raiment you will make a good teacher. Are you a preacher, and about to address thousands of grown-up persons? How better can I advise you then that you put on Christ and preach the gospel in His own loving, pleading, earnest style. The preacher's model should be his Lord. This is our preaching gown, our praying surplice, our pastoral robe—the character and spirit of the Lord Jesus; and it admirably suits each form of service.

No man's example will precisely fit his fellow-man; but there is this strange virtue about the character of Christ, that you may all imitate it, and yet be none of you mere imitators. He is perfectly natural who is perfectly like Christ. There need be no affectation, no painful restraint, no straining. In a life thus fashioned there will be nothing grotesque or disproportionate, unmanly or romantic. So wonderfully is Jesus the Second Adam of the new-born race, that each member of that family may bear a likeness

to Him, and yet exhibit a clear individuality. A man advanced in years and wisdom may put Him on, and so may the least instructed, and the freshest comer among us. Please remember this; we may not choose examples, but each one is bound to copy the Lord Jesus Christ. You, dear friend, have a special personality; you are such a person that there is not another exactly like you, and you are placed in circumstances so peculiar that no one else is tried exactly as you are;—to you, then, is this exhortation sent: "Put on the Lord Jesus Christ." It is absolutely certain, that for you, with your personal singularity, and peculiar circumstances, there can be nothing better than that you array yourself in this more than royal robe. You, too, who live in ordinary circumstances, and are only tried by common temptations, you are to "put on the Lord Jesus Christ"; for He will be suitable for you also. "Oh," cries one, "but the Lord Jesus never was exactly where I am!" You say this from want of knowing better, or from want of thought. He has been tempted in all points like as you are. There are certain relationships which the Lord could not literally occupy; but then, He took their spiritual counterpart. For instance, Jesus could not be a husband after the flesh. Does anyone demand how He could be an example for husbands? Hearken! "Husbands, love your wives, even as Christ also loved the church, and gave Himself for it." He is your model in a relationship which, naturally, He never sustained. but which, in very deed, He has more than fulfilled. Wherever you may be, you find that the Lord Jesus has occupied the counterpart of your position, or else the position is sinful, and ought to be quitted. In any place, at any hour, under any circumstances, in any matter, you may put on the Lord Jesus Christ, and never fear that your array will be unsuitable. Here you have a summer and winter garment—good in prosperity, as well as in adversity. Here you have a garment for the private chamber or the public forum, for sickness or for health, for honour or for reproach, for life or for death. "Put ye on the Lord Jesus Christ," and in this raiment of wrought gold you may enter into the King's palace, and stand among the spirits of just men made perfect.

II. Secondly, trusting to the Holy Spirit, let us enquire WHAT IS THIS DAILY DRESS? The Lord Jesus Christ is to be put on. May the Spirit of God help us to do so!

We see how the sacred dress is *here described* in three words. The sacred titles of the Son of God are spread out at length: "Put ye on the Lord—Jesus—Christ." Put Him on as *Lord*. Call Him your Master and Lord, and you will do well. Be you His servant in everything. Submit every faculty, every capacity, every talent, every possession to His government. Submit all that you have and are to Him, and delight to own His superior right and His royal claim to you. Be Christ's man; His servant. under bonds to His service for ever, finding therein life and liberty. Let the dominion of your Lord cover the kingdom of your nature. Then put on *Jesus*. Jesus means a Saviour: in every part be covered by Him in that blessed capacity. You, a sinner, hide yourself in Jesus, your Saviour, who shall save you from your sins. He is your sanctifier driving out sin, and your preserver keeping sin from returning. Jesus is your armour against sin. You overcome through His blood. In Him you are defended against every weapon of the enemy; He is your shield, keeping you from all evil.

He covers you all over like a complete suit of armour, so that when arrows of temptation fly like a fiery shower, they may be quenched upon heavenly mail, and you may stand unharmed amid a shower of deaths. Put on Jesus, and then put on *Christ*. You know that Christ signifies "anointed." Now, our Lord is anointed as Prophet, Priest, and King, and as such we put Him on. What a splendid thing it is to put on Christ as the anointed *Prophet*, and to accept His teaching as our creed! I believe it. Why? Because He said it. This is argument enough for me. Mine not to argue, or doubt, or criticize; the Christ has said it, and I, putting Him on, find in His authority the end of all strife. What Christ declares, I believe; discussion ends where Christ begins. Put Him on also as your *Priest*. Notwithstanding your sin, your unworthiness, your defilement, go to the altar of the Lord by Him who, as Priest, has taken away your sin, clothed you with His merit, and made you acceptable to God. In our great High Priest we enter within the veil. We are in Him; by faith we realize this, and so put Him on as our Priest, and lose ourselves in His accepted sacrifice. Our Lord Jesus is also anointed to be *King*. Oh, put Him on in all His imperial majesty, by yielding your every wish and thought to His sway! Set Him on the throne of your heart. As you have submitted your thought and understanding to His prophetic instruction, submit your action and your practical life to His kingly government. As you put on His priesthood and find atonement in Him, so put on His royalty and find holiness in Him.

I now wish to show *the description given in Colossians iii.* from the twelfth verse. I will take you to the wardrobe for a minute, and ask you to look over the articles of our outfit. See here, "Put on therefore"; you see everything is to be put on; nothing is to be left on the pegs for the moth to eat, nor in the window to be idly stared at: you *put on* the whole armour of God. In true religion everything is designed for practical use. We keep no garments in the drawer; we have to put on all that is provided. "Put on therefore, as the elect of God, holy and beloved, bowels of mercies, kindness." Here are two choice things: mercy and kindness—silken robes indeed! Have you put them on? I am to be as merciful, as tender-hearted, as kind, as sympathetic, as loving to my fellow-men as Christ himself was. Have I reached this point? Have I ever aimed at it? Who among us has put on these royal gloves?

See what follows—these choice things come in pairs—"humbleness of mind, meekness." These choice garments are not so much esteemed as they should be. The cloth of one called "Proud-of-heart" is very fashionable, and the trimmings of Mr. Masterful are much in request. It is a melancholy thing to see what great men some Christians are. Truly, the footman is bigger than his master. How some who would be thought saints can bluster and bully! Is this to put on the Lord Jesus Christ? Point me to a word of our Lord's in which He scolded, and tyrannized, and overrode any man. He was meek and lowly, even He, the Lord of all: what ought we to be, who are not worthy to loose the latchets of His shoes? Permit me to say to any dear brother who has not a very tender nature, who is naturally hard and rasping, "Put on the Lord Jesus Christ," my brother, and make not provision for that unfeeling nature of yours. Endeavour to be lowly in mind, that you may be gentle in spirit.

See, next, we are to put on longsuffering and forbearance. Some men have no patience with others: how can they expect God to have patience with them? If everything is not done to their mind they are in a fine fury. Dear me! whom have we here? Is this a servant of Mars, or of the Fire-god? Surely, this fighting man does not profess to be a worshipper of Christ! Do not tell me that the man lost his temper. It would be a mercy if he had lost it, so as never to find it again. He is selfish, petulant, exacting, and easily provoked. Has this man the spirit of Christ? If he be a Christian, he is a naked Christian, and I would urge him to "put on the Lord Jesus Christ," that he may be fitly clothed. Our Lord was full of forbearance. "Consider Him that endured such contradiction of sinners against Himself, lest ye be wearied, and faint in your minds." Put on the Lord Jesus Christ, and bear and forbear. Put up with a great deal that really ought not to be inflicted upon you, and be ready to bear still more rather than give or take offence.

"Forgiving one another, if any man have a quarrel against any; even as Christ forgave you, so also do ye." Is not this heavenly teaching? Put it in practice. Put ye on your Lord. Have you fallen to loggerheads with one another, and did I hear one of you growling, "I'll, I'll I'll——"? Stop, brother! What will you do? If you are true to the Lord Jesus Christ you will not avenge yourself, but give place unto wrath. Put the Lord Jesus on your tongue, and you will not talk so bitterly; put Him on your heart, and you will not feel so fiercely; put Him on your whole character, and you will readily forgive, not only this once, but unto seventy times seven. If you have been unjustly treated by one who should have been your friend, lay aside wrath, and begin again; and perhaps your brother will begin again also, and both of you by love will overcome evil. "Put ye on the Lord Jesus Christ."

"And above all these things put on charity, which is the bond of perfectness." Love is the girdle which binds up the other garments, and keeps all the other graces well braced, and in their right places. Put on love—what a golden girdle! Are we all putting on love? We have been baptized into Christ, and we profess to have put on Christ; but do we daily try to put on love? Our baptism was not true if we are not buried to all old enmities. We may have a great many faults, but God grant that we may be full of love to Jesus, to His people, and to all mankind!

How much I wish that we could all put on, and keep on, the next article of this wardrobe! "And let the peace of God rule in your hearts, to the which also ye are called in one body; and be ye thankful." Oh, for a peaceful mind! Oh, to rest in the Lord! I recommend that last little word, "Be ye thankful," to farmers and others whose interests are depressed. I might equally recommend it to certain tradespeople, whose trade is quite as good as they could expect. "Things *are* a little better," said one to me; and at that time he was heaping up riches. When things are extremely well, people say they are "middling," or a "little better"; but when there is a slight falling off, they cry out about "nothing doing, stagnation, universal ruin." Thankfulness is a rare virtue; but let the lover of the Lord Jesus abound in it. The possession of your mind in peace, keeping yourself quiet, calm, self-possessed, content—this is a blessed state; and in such a state Jesus was; therefore, "put ye on the Lord Jesus Christ." He was never in a fret or fume. He was never hurried or worried; He never repined or coveted. Had He nothing to worry Him? More than you have, brother. Had He not many things to distress Him? More than all of us put together. Yet He was not ruffled, but showed a prince-like calm, a divine serenity. This our Lord would have us wear. His peace He leaves with us, and His joy He would have fulfilled in us. He wishes us to go through life with the peace of God keeping our hearts and minds from the assaults of the enemy. He would have us quiet and strong—strong because quiet, quiet because strong.

I have read of a great man, that he took two hours and a half to dress himself every morning. In this he showed rather littleness than greatness; but if any of you put on the Lord Jesus Christ you may take what time you will in making such a toilet. It will take you all your lives, my brothers and sisters, fully to put on the Lord Jesus Christ, and to keep Him on. For let me again say, that you are not only to put on all these garments which I have shown to you in the wardrobe of the Colossians, but, more than this, you are to put on all else that makes up Christ Himself. What a dress is this! "Put on Christ," says the text.

Put on the Lord Jesus Christ for daily wear. Not for high days and holy days only, but for all time, and every time. Put on the Lord Jesus Christ on the Lord's day, but do not lay Him aside during the week. Ladies have ornaments which they put on occasionally for display on grand occasions: as a rule, these jewels are hidden away in a jewel-case. Christians, you must wear your jewels always. Put on the Lord Jesus Christ, and have no casket in which to conceal any part of Him. Put on Christ to keep Him on. I saw a missionary from the cold north the other day, and he was wearing a coat of moose-skin, which he had worn among the Red Indians. "It is a capital coat," he said, "there's nothing like leather. I have worn it for eleven years." In the arctic region through which he had travelled, he had worn this garment both by night and by day; for the climate was much too cold to allow the taking off of anything. Brethren, the world is far too cold to allow of our taking off Christ even for an hour. So many arrows are flying about that we dare not remove a single piece of our armour even for an instant. Thank God, we have in our Lord a dress which we may always wear. We can live in it, and die in it; we can work in it, and rest in it, and, like the raiment of Israel in the wilderness, it will never wax old. Put it on more and more.

If you have put on something of Christ, put on more of Christ. I dare not say much in commendation of apparel, here in England, for the tendency is to exceed in that direction; yet I noticed, the other day, the remark of a missionary in the South Sea Islands, that as the heathen people became converted they began to clothe themselves, and as they acquired tenderness of conscience, and delicacy of feeling, they gave more attention to dress—wearing more clothes, and of a better sort. However that may be as to dress for the body, it is certainly so as to the arraying of the soul. As we make spiritual progress, we have more graces and more virtues than in the beginning. Once we were content to wear faith only, but now we put on hope and love. Once if we wore humbleness, we failed to wear thankfulness; but our text exhorts us to wear a full dress, a court suit; for we are to "put on the Lord Jesus Christ." You cannot wear too much of Him. Be covered from head to foot with Him.

Put on the Lord in every time of trial. Do not take Him off when it comes to the test. Quaint Henry Smith says that some people wear the Lord Jesus as a man wears his hat, which he takes off to everybody he meets. I am afraid I know persons of that kind, who wear Christ in private, but they off with Him in company, especially in the company of the worldly, the sarcastic, and the unbelieving. Put on Christ, intending never to put Him off again. When tempted, tried, ridiculed, hear in your ear this voice, "Put ye on the Lord Jesus Christ." Put Him on the more as others tempt you to put Him off.

III. My time fails me, and I must hurriedly notice, in the third place, HOW WE ARE TO ACT IN THIS DRESS TOWARDS EVIL. The text says, "Put ye on the Lord Jesus Christ, and make not provision for the flesh, to fulfil the lusts thereof." By the flesh is here meant the evil part of us, which is so greatly aided by the appetites and desires of the body. When a man puts on Christ, has he still the flesh about him? Alas! it is even so. I hear some brethren say that they have no remaining corruptions. I claim liberty to believe as much as I like of a man's statements as to his own personal character. When he bears witness concerning himself, his witness may or may not be true. When a man tells me that he is perfect, I hear what he has to say, but I quietly think within myself that if he had been so, he would not have felt the necessity of spreading the information. "Good wine needs no bush"; and when our town once holds a perfect man within its bounds there will be no need to advertise him. Goods that are puffed probably need puffery. Brethren, I fear we have all very much of the flesh about us, and therefore we need be on our guard against it. What does the apostle say? "Make no provision for the flesh." By this, he means several things.

First, give *no tolerance* to it. Do not say, "Christ has sanctified me so far; but you see I have a bad temper naturally, and you cannot expect it to be removed." Dear brother, do not make provision for thus sheltering and sparing one of your soul's enemies. Another cries, "You know I always was a good deal desponding; and therefore I can never have much joy in the Lord." Don't make room for your unbelief. If you find a kennel for this dog, it will always lie in it. "But," says another, "I was always rather fond of gaiety, and so I must mix up with the world." Well, if you cook a dinner for the devil, he will take a seat at your table. This is to make provision for the flesh, to fulfil the lusts of it. Do not so; but slay the Canaanites, break their idols, throw down their altars, and fell their groves.

Moreover, give sin *no time*. Allow no furlough to your obedience. Do not say to yourself, "At all other times I am exact, but once in a year, at a family meeting, I take a little liberty." Is it liberty to you to sin? I am afraid there is something rotten in your heart. "Ah!" cries one, "I only allow myself an hour or two occasionally with questionable company. I know it does me harm; but we must all have a little relaxation, and the talk is very amusing, though rather loose." Is evil a relaxation to you? It ought to be worse than slavery. What a trial is foolish talking to a child of God! How can you find pleasure in it? Give no license to the flesh; you cannot tell how far it will go. Keep it always under subjection, and make no space for its indulgence.

Provide *no food* for it. Carve it no rations. Starve it out; at any rate, if it wants fodder, let it look elsewhere. When you are allotting your provision to the body, the soul, the spirit, allot nothing to the depraved passions. If the flesh says, "What is for me?" say, "Nothing." Some people like a little bit of reading for the flesh. As some people like a little bit of what they call "rather high" meat, so do these folk enjoy a portion of tainted doctrine, or questionable morality. Thus they make provision for the flesh, and the flesh takes care to feed thereon, and to give its lusts a meal. I have known professors, whom I would not dare to judge, dabble just a little in matters which they would forbid to others, but they think them allowable to themselves, if done in secret. "You must not be too exact," they say. But the apostle says, "Make not provision for the flesh." Do not give it a morsel; do not even allow it the crumbs that fall from your table. The flesh is greedy, and never hath enough; and if you give it some provision, it will steal much more.

"Put ye on the Lord Jesus Christ," and then you will leave *no place* for the lusts of the flesh. That which Christ does not cover is naked unto sin. If Christ be my livery, and I wear Him, and so am known to be His avowed servant, then I place myself entirely in His hands always and for ever, and the flesh has no claim whatsoever upon upon me. If, before I put on Christ, I might make some reserve, and duty did not call, yet now that the Lord Jesus Christ is upon me, I have done with reserves, and am openly and confessedly my Lord's. "Know ye not," saith the apostle, "that as many of you as were baptized into Christ have put on Christ?" Being buried with Him, we are dead to the world, and live only unto Him. The Lord bring us up to this mark by His mighty Spirit; and He shall have the glory of it.

IV. If this be the case, and we have indeed "put on the Lord Jesus Christ," we will thank God evermore; but if it be not so, let us not delay to be arrayed in this dress. WHY SHOULD WE HASTEN TO PUT ON CHRIST? A moment is all that remains. It is dark. Here is armour made of solid light; let us put on this attire at once; then the night will be light about us, and others beholding us will glorify God, and ask for the same raiment. With so dense a night round about us, a man needs to be dressed in luminous robes; he needs to wear the light of God, he needs thus to be practically protected from the darkness around him.

"Put on the Lord Jesus Christ," moreover; for the night will soon be over: the morning will soon dawn. The rags of sin, the sordid robes of worldliness, are not fit attire for the heavenly morning. Let us dress for the sun-rising. Let us go forth to meet the dawn with garments of light about us.

"Put on the Lord Jesus Christ," for He is coming, the beloved of our souls! Over the hills we hear the trumpet sounding; the heralds are crying aloud, "The bridegroom cometh! The bridegroom cometh!" Though He has seemed to tarry, He has been always coming post haste. To-day we hear His chariot-wheels in the distance. Nearer and nearer is His advent. Let us not sleep as do others. Blessed are they who will be ready for the wedding when the Bridegroom cometh. What is that wedding dress that shall make us ready? Nothing can make us more fit to meet Christ, and to be with Him in His glory, than for us to put on Christ to-day. If I wear Christ as my dress I do great honour to Christ as my Bridegroom. If I take Him for my glory and my beauty while I am here, I may be sure that He will be all that and more to me in eternity. If I take pleasure in Jesus here, Jesus will take pleasure in me when He shall meet me in the air, and take me up to dwell with Himself for ever. Put on the wedding-dress, ye beloved of the Lord! Put on the wedding dress, ye brides of the Lamb, and put it on at once, for behold He cometh! Haste, haste, ye slumbering virgins! Arise and trim your lamps! Put on your robes, and be ready to behold His glory, and to take part in it. O ye virgin souls, go forth to meet Him; with joy and gladness go forth, wearing Himself, as your gorgeous apparel, fit for the daughters of a King. The Lord bless you, for Christ's sake! Amen.

THE JUDGMENT SEAT OF GOD

"But why dost thou judge they brother? or why dost thou set at nought thy brother? for we shall all stand before the judgment seat of Christ. For it is written, As I live, saith the Lord, every knee shall bow to me, and every tongue shall confess to God. So then every one of us shall give account of himself to God."—Romans xiv. 10-12.

NO doubt there is an error in our version, for where in the tenth verse we read, "The judgment seat of Christ," it should be "The judgment seat *of God*." I suppose the word "Christ" slipped into certain manuscripts because Paul had been speaking of Christ, and it was thought to be natural that he should continue to use the same name. Paul did not say "Christ," but "God," but by that word he meant the same person. Paul knew that Christ is God, and when he was speaking of Christ it was no deviation from the subject for him to speak concerning Him under the title of "God." It was necessary here for him to use the word "God," because he was about to quote from the Old Testament Scripture a passage which speaks concerning the sovereignty of God, which is to be acknowledged and confessed by all mankind. The passage runs, "We shall all stand before the judgment seat of God, for it is written, As I live, saith the Lord, every knee shall bow to Me, and every tongue shall confess to God. So then every one of us shall give account of himself to God." I beg you to notice how strongly this passage goes to prove the divinity of our Lord Jesus Christ; because of the whole run of the passage is concerning Christ. "To this end Christ both died, and rose, and revived, that He might be Lord both of the dead and living." And then the apostle immediately, without any break in the sense whatever, speaks of God, because he was speaking of the same person, and he quotes a passage which relates to God himself, and uses it as relating to Christ. It does, indeed, relate to our Lord Jesus Christ, for He is "very God of very God," and God shall judge the secrets of men by Jesus Christ. In another place Paul most distinctly declares that it is Christ who is to judge the world. Look into the fifth chapter of the second epistle to the Corinthians, at the ninth verse, "We labour, that, whether present or absent, we may be accepted of Him; for we must all appear before the judgment seat of Christ; that every one may receive the things done in his body, according to that he hath done, whether it be good or bad." Therefore, though the reading should be God, the sense is "Christ."

It would have been a most important point with Paul to draw a distinction between Christ and God if there had been any doubt as to His divinity. It would have been a most necessary thing to prevent us from idolizing a mere man. But here, so far from taking any pains to make such distinction between Christ Jesus and God, as would have been needful if He were not God, he interchanges the two words. He speaks of them in the same breath, for they are one. "The Lord shall judge His people," and it is "the Lord Jesus Christ, who shall judge the quick and the dead at His appearing and His kingdom" (2 Tim. iv. 1). "Behold, He cometh with clouds; and every eye shall see Him, and they also which pierced Him" (Rev. i. 7). This judgment by Christ is by our apostle proved from an Old Testament prophecy which certainly refers to Jehovah Himself. Read Isaiah xlv. 23, and learn from it that our Lord Jesus is Jehovah, and let us joyfully adore Him as our Saviour and God, to whom be glory for ever and ever.

The doctrine of eternal judgment, upon which I shall speak this morning, is introduced to us for a certain reason. Paul saw among Christians a much too common habit of judging one another. I suppose if Paul were to come among us now he would not see any remarkable difference upon that point. Just then the bulk of the converts were Jews, and as such, they brought into the Christian Church their former religious habits; those men who had devoutly kept the ceremonial law felt as if they would violate their consciences if they did not continue to keep its more prominent precepts; and though they gave up certain of its observances which were evidently abolished by the gospel, they kept up others, such as special days for religious fasts and feasts. Many true but weak believers were very scrupulous about what they should eat, thinking to keep up the legal distinction between meats clean and unclean. At the same time the church had in her midst men who said, and said correctly, "The coming of Christ has done away with the old dispensation; these holy days are all types and shadows whose substance is in Christ. Has not the Lord shown to Peter, who is the minister of the circumcision, that henceforth nothing is common or unclean?" The men of strong faith blamed their weaker brethren for being superstitious, and by their superstition bringing a yoke of bondage upon themselves. "No," replied the weaker sort, "we were not superstitious; we are conscientious, while you go much too far in your liberty, and cause us to stumble." Thus while the strong looked down upon the weak, almost doubting whether they could have come into the liberty of Christ at all, the weak condemned the strong, almost charging them with turning their liberty into licence. They were both wrong, for they were judging one another. Paul, who was himself most strongly opposed to the Judaizing party, and in every respect came out clear and straight upon the bold lines of Christian liberty, was, nevertheless, so actuated by the spirit of his Master that he was ready to be all things to all men, and seeing grave peril of dissension where all should be love, he rushed into the breach,

and he said, "Do not judge one another: what have ye to do with judging? There is a judgment yet to come." He mentioned the future judgment on purpose that by its powerful influence upon their minds they might be taken away from the frivolous amusement, for it does not come to much more—the frivolous amusement, the mischievous meddlesomeness of judging one another, when already the Judge is at the door.

Let us linger a moment over this practical point, and see how Paul rebukes the spirit of judging one another. First, he says in effect that it is *unnatural.* "Why dost thou judge thy brother? Why dost thou set at nought thy brother? He whom thou judgest or despisest is thy brother. Thou hast called the weak one superstitious, but he is thy brother: thou hast called the strong man licentious because he enjoys his liberty; but he is thy brother." If we must needs judge, certainly it should not be those who are linked to us by the ties of spiritual relationship. Are not all believers one family in Christ? Wherever the root of the matter is to be found there exists an overwhelming argument for undying unity. Why, then, wilt thou take thy brother by the throat and drag him before thy judgment seat, and make him answer to thee, brother to brother, and then condemn him? Shall a brother condemn a brother? When the outside world censures Christians we understand it, for they hated our Master, and they will hate us; but inside the charmed circle of Christian communion there should be esteem for one another, a defending of each other: we should be anxious rather to apologise for infirmity than to discover imperfection. Far be it from us to find flaws where they do not exist. Would to God it were so, that perfect love cast out all suspicion of one another, and that we had confidence in each other, because Christ our Lord will hold up our brethren, even as He has upheld ourselves.

This judging among Christians, then, is, first of all, unnatural; and, next, it is *an anticipation of the judgment day.* There is to come a day when men shall be judged—judged after a better fashion than you and I can judge. How dare we, then, travesty God's great assize by ourselves mounting the throne and pretending to rehearse the solemn transactions of that tremendous hour? Judgment will come soon enough: may the Lord have mercy upon us in that day. My brother, why needest thou hurry it on by thyself ascending the throne? Cannot God do His own work? "Vengeance is mine: I will repay," saith the Lord. We need not spend our time in perpetually trying to discern between the tares and the wheat. The tares to which the Saviour referred in that parable were so like the wheat that men could not tell which was which, and His command was, "Let both grow together until the harvest." At harvest time He will give the reapers directions for separating between the real wheat and that which was a mockery of it. As for us, the saints shall judge the world, but for the present the order is "judge nothing before the time." We can separate between the outwardly vile and the outwardly pure, by marks which God has given us, such as these, "By their fruits ye shall know them," and "If any man love not the Lord Jesus let him be anathema." As guardians of the church's honour we are bound to use these rules; but between brother and brother, differing on minor points, between Christian and Christian, each one obeying his conscience, we are not to exercise mutual condemnation. Come hither, brethren! Here is work enough for you all in dragging the great net to shore. What are you at there? Sitting down and trying to put the good into vessels, and cast the bad away? That work may be left till later on; but now let us drag the net to shore. Haul away, brethren, with all your might! By-and-by shall come the time for reckoning up the results of our fishery, and separating between the seeming and the true.

Moreover, we not only anticipate the judgment, but we *impudently intrude ourselves into the office and prerogative of Christ* when we condemn the saints. "We must all appear before the judgment seat of Christ": that is the true throne of judgment. How many times I have had to appear before the judgment seat of my fellow-men! Sometimes one's motives are impugned; another time one's actions, or mode of speech, or way of managing church affairs. Well, it is a small matter for us to appear before men's judgment seat: we may very well refuse to put in an appearance at all, for man is not our master, and we are not bound to answer to his summons. Why is it that so many brethren seem to think that they are masters, and have a right to judge the Lord's servants? I know some Christians who not only form judgments, and very severe judgments, upon all that are round about them as to the facts that come under their notice; but they, also, without any facts whatever, conceive notions concerning persons whom they have never seen, and are full of obstinate prejudices against them. Many twist words into meanings which they were never intended to mean by the person who used them; and others, even without so much as the excuse of misunderstanding words, sit down and imagine evil against their brethren. They dream that they are slighted, and then hard judgments follow. Once imagine that you are badly treated, and then you will think that everything is done out of spite to you, and the next thing is to think spitefully of others. There are persons about who are liberally gifted in the line of gossip who by their talk would make you think that you were living in Sodom and Gomorrah, if not in Tophet. You are made to fear that everyone you have trusted is a vile deceiver, that every man who is zealous is mercenary, that every minister is preaching in public what he secretly disbelieves, that every generous subscriber only gives out of pride; that, in fact, you are living in a place where the race of Judas Iscariot is to be seen, reproduced ten thousand times over. One goes to bed and cannot sleep after talking to these tale-bearers. The consolation is that there is no truth in their wonderful discoveries. These slanderous statements are a base burlesque of judgment, and nothing more. Why are they thought so much of? After you and I have done our best to hold our mimic court and have summoned this man and that man before us, what is it at its best but child's play, and at its worst a violent usurpation of the rights of Christ Jesus, who alone reigns as lawgiver in the midst of His church to-day, and who will sit as judge on the clouds of heaven by-and-by to judge the world in righteousness?

The apostle argues strongly against this evil spirit of censoriousness in the Christian Church; and to give a knock-down blow to it he says, "It is all *needless;* you need not judge one another, for both your brother and yourself will stand before the judgment seat of God. There is no need of your

condemnation, for if any man be worthless the Judge will condemn him: you may not interfere with the business of the great Supreme; He will manage the affairs of men far better than you can."

Yet more, your judgment is *unprofitable*: you would spend your time much more profitably if you would recollect that you also who can be so exact and severe in pointing out this fault here, and the other fault there, will be yourselves examined by an unerring eye. Your own account books have to be sent in, and to be examined item by item; therefore look well to your own matters. If you were watching your own heart, out of which are the issues of life; if you were watching your own tongue and bridling it, and so mastering your whole body; if you were watching your own opportunities for usefulness; if you were observing your Master's eye as a handmaiden looks to her mistress, you would be doing something that would pay you far better than censuring others, something much more to the glory of God, much more to the gain of the church, much more to the comfort of your own soul. So the apostle winds up by saying, according to the most forcible rendering of the original, "We must each one of us give an account of himself to God."

Brothers, sisters, I bring these truths before you because they are meant for brothers in Christ, and not so much for the outside world. It is to those who have faith, and are in the family of love, that the word of warning is given that we do not judge, and to us the argument is addressed that we shall each one give an account for himself to God. I do not know that you specially need a warning against unkind judgments, but I know that you may need it, even as other churches have done. I am very thankful that we have not been much disturbed with this great evil; but, still, it does come up among all Christian people more or less. I read the other day in an interesting pamphlet upon the Apocalypse, a note which furnishes me with an illustration: the writer endeavours to describe why the tribe of Dan is not mentioned in the Book of Revelation as having its chosen twelve thousand. All the other tribes are there, but Dan is missed, and Manasseh is put in his place. The author says it is because Dan signifies "judgment," or "one that judges." He says: "These 'judges of evil thoughts' have been sad troublers in Israel in all ages; not fearing to judge their brother and set at nought their brother, they have judged everything and everybody but themselves. All who have not pronounced their Shibboleth, nor seen eye to eye with them, have been adjudged as heretics, not to be tolerated, but tabooed to the extent of their ability. In vain for them has it been written, 'Judge nothing before the time, until the Lord come, who will bring to light the hidden things of darkness, and make manifest the counsels of the heart.' Like their great ancestor of this tribe, they deal in foxes and firebrands, and too often set on fire their neighbours' standing corn, an act we have never been able to commend even in Samson. This predilection for foxes and firebrands has unhappily developed in the seed of Dan to this day. And so in the place of Dan, *The Judge*, we get Manasseh, *One who forgets*, one who, though cast off by his brethren, forgets and forgives their injuries, and we account it a *good exchange;* and in the New Jerusalem home, where failure will be no more, Dan, 'a serpent in the way,' or 'a lion's whelp,' would be as much out of *work* as out of *place*." If any of the

Danites hear or read this let them pray for grace to change their habits and natures.

I. Now I come to the doctrine itself, the solemn doctrine of judgment to come. May God make it impressive to our hearts. Our thoughts are now directed to the future judgment, and we notice concerning it, first, that THE JUDGMENT WILL BE UNIVERSAL: "For we shall all stand before the judgment seat of God. For it is written, As I live, saith the Lord, every knee shall bow to me, and every tongue shall confess to God." There will come a judgment, then, for all classes of persons; for the strong brother who with his knowledge of Christian liberty went as far as he should, perhaps further than he ought to have gone. He judged himself to be right in the matter, but he must stand before the judgment seat of Christ about it. There will also be a judgment for the weak brother. He who was so scrupulous and precise ought not to be censuring the other man who felt free in his conscience, for he will himself stand before the judgment seat of God. No elevation in piety will exclude us from that last solemn test, and no weakness will serve as an excuse. The man of one and the man of ten talents must alike be reckoned with. Weak Christians are exempted from many trials by the gentleness of God, but not from the ultimate trial, for we shall each one of us give an account of himself unto God: the strong and the weak. The men who bore office in the church will have to answer for it, even as saith the apostle Paul, in Hebrews xiii. 17, "They watch for your souls, as they that must give an account." And again, "It is required in stewards, that a man be found faithful: He that judgeth me is the Lord." I could on bended knees ask your pity for myself, having to minister to so large a congregation, and with so much larger a congregation outside to whom I weekly minister through the press. Ah me, who is sufficient for these things? Who shall be found faithful in such a position? I think all ministers might with tears in their eyes cry to you, "Brethren, pray for us." It will be the height of my ambition to be clear of the blood of all men. If, like George Fox, I can say in dying, "I am clear, I am clear," that were almost all the heaven I could wish for. Oh to discharge one's ministry aright, and to be able to render an account like that of Paul, who said, "I have fought a good fight, I have kept the faith." This is my soul's longing.

Yes, but not only will ministers, and deacons, and elders, and persons who had high standing in the church have to appear before the judgment seat of Christ, but so will the most obscure members of the church, and those secret ones who never dared to take up membership at all. You will not be able to hide away for ever. The man with the one talent must be summoned before his Lord as certainly as the man with ten, and of each one a reckoning shall be taken. In our Lord's parable it is ever the King's own servants that are called before him. "the lord of those servants cometh and reckoneth with them." Our Master will say to each one of His servants, "Give an account of thy stewardship." "God shall judge the righteous and the wicked," "for we shall all stand before the judgment seat of God." I have not time or space to enter into the differences of that judgment as it regards the righteous and the wicked, but I confine myself to the one fact that all mankind will be judged, according to the word of the Lord in the second chapter of the

Epistle to the Romans, at the fifth verse: "The day of wrath and revelation of the righteous judgment of God; who will render to every man according to his deeds: to them who by patient continuance in well doing seek for glory and honour and immortality, eternal life: but unto them that are contentious, and do not obey the truth, but obey unrighteousness, indignation and wrath, tribulation and anguish, upon every soul of man that doeth evil, of the Jew first, and also of the Gentile; but glory, honour, and peace, to every man that worketh good, to the Jew first, and also to the Gentile: for there is no respect of persons with God."

What a motley throng will gather at that assize, of all nations and peoples and tongues! Persons of all ages, too. You boys and girls, and you who have lived through a long life. Kings and princes will be there to give in their weighty account, and senators and judges to answer to their Judge; and then the multitude of the poor and needy, and those that live neglecting God, and forgetful of their souls,—they must all be there. It is a universal judgment. John says, "I saw the dead, small and great, stand before God." Both sheep and goats shall gather before the great dividing shepherd: the wise and foolish virgins shall both hear the midnight cry; the house on the rock and the house on the sand shall alike be tested by the last tremendous storm; tares and wheat alike shall ripen; bad fish and good shall be sorted out from the net, while the multitudes outside, the nations that knew not God, shall all without exception hear with trembling the summons to the dread tribunal.

Saints and sinners too, only on what a different footing, are all to be judged out of the books, and out of the Book of Life. Thus saith the word of the Lord,—"We must all appear before the judgment seat of Christ; that every one may receive the things done in his body, according to that he hath done, whether it be good or bad." To the saints the judgment of the things done shall be according to righteousness, for these things shall be taken in evidence that they were indeed reconciled to God. The Judge will say, "Come, ye blessed of my Father, inherit the kingdom prepared for you from the foundation of the world." And then shall come the evidence: "For I was an hungred, and ye gave me meat; thirsty, and ye gave me drink," and so on. These fruits shall be the evidence that they were in Christ, the evidence of their being justified by faith; while on the other hand the sour and bitter fruit of the ungodly shall be an evidence that they were not planted of the Lord: "I was an hungred, and ye gave me no meat; I was thirsty, and ye gave me no drink; sick and in prison, and ye did not minister unto me." We need have no fear of the judgment to come when we know that we are in Christ, for who fears to enter a just court when he knows that by the highest authority he has already been cleared? How complete the Christian's safety! For there will be no accuser. So bright will be the righteousness of a saint through faith that no accuser will appear. Hark, the herald gives forth the challenge! "Who shall lay anything to the charge of God's elect?" All through the court it rings; and God is there— the faithful and all-seeing God. Does He lay anything to their charge? Far from it. "It is God that justifieth." Outside the court the voice demands, "Who shall lay anything to the charge of God's elect?" They hear it in heaven, and angels who have watched the race of every believer, and seen how he has been running towards the goal, are silent as to any accusation. The challenge is heard in hell, where devils hate the godly, but they dare not forge a lie against them. Happy he who can also say, "There is laid up for me a crown of righteousness which the righteous Judge shall give me at that day." Mark, He will give it as Judge, and on that day: how say some among you that there is no judgment for the saints? Who, then, need fear to enter the court when every accusation is silenced and a reward is expected?

But still you say that the believer has sinned. Yes, but that sin has been forgiven, and he has a righteousness with which to answer the law. I will show you ere I have done how the Christian has been judged, condemned, and tried, and in reference to him the essence of the judgment is past already, so that there can be no condemnation. Hence that second challenge, "Who is he that condemneth?" The Judge is the only one who can condemn, and we are sure that He will not, for "it is Christ that died, yea rather, that has risen again, who also maketh intercession for us." Tremble not, therefore, at the doctrine that we shall all appear before the judgment seat of Christ, but pray that, as John puts it, "we may have boldness in the day of judgment, because as Jude saith, the Lord Jesus "is able to present you faultless before the presence of His glory with great joy."

Not a single person shall escape the judgment. There shall be no omission from the calendar; every being of the race of Adam shall answer for himself. "The kings of the earth, and the great men, and the chief captains and the mighty men, and every bond-man, and every free man" must see the face of Him that sitteth upon the throne. We shall have to put in an appearance as men do in court when they are subpœnaed to attend. The word of Jesus is, "Behold I come quickly, and My reward is with Me, to give every man according as his work shall be." Ah, how unwillingly will rebels come before that throne! Pharaoh! you must see a greater than Moses. Herod! you must see the young child upon His throne. Judas! you hanged yourself to escape the judgment of your conscience, but by no means can you escape the judgment of your God. Though four thousand years have elapsed since men died, and their bodies may have melted quite away, yet when the trumpet ringeth out clear and shrill their bodies shall live again, and they must all come forth, each one to answer for himself at that grand assize before the Judge of all the earth, who must do right with each of them. Let us, then, bow before the solemn truth that God hath appointed a day in which He will judge the world in righteousness by that Man whom He hath ordained.

The second truth, which we must make as prominent as ever we can, is that IT WILL BE A PERSONAL JUDGMENT for each one. This is the pith of what the apostle is saying: "So then every one of us shall give account of himself to God." The judgment will not proceed in a rough, indiscriminate manner, as upon a race or tribe, but each man will have to stand apart, and the account reckoned will not be of a family or a band, but of each individually for himself. Note this carefully, O men: We shall have to give an account each man for his own actions, for his own thought, for his own words, for his own intention; nay, not only of that, but *of himself*. We shall each man have to give account of the state of his own heart, of the condition of his mind before God, whether he repented, whether he believed, whether he loved God, whether he was zealous, whether he was truthful, whether he was faithful. If it only dealt with actions, words, and thoughts, the account would be solemn enough, but we must each one give an account *of himself*, of what he *was* as well as what he *did*, of what was in his heart as well as of that which came out of it in his deeds. Oh, what a trial will this be!

We shall then have to give an account of our judgments of others. We shall not have to answer for what they did, but for our daring to judge and condemn them. Did you ever think of this, you that judge others, that you are laying down the standard by which you will have to be judged yourselves? I generally find that those who are most severe towards others need and often expect great leniency towards themselves, but it will not be so at the last, for thus it is written, "With what judgment ye judge ye shall be judged." How easy it will be to judge the fault-finding at the judgment day. The Judge will only have to say, "They have already condemned themselves: they have condemned their own faults as they saw them in others; they have used the sharpest judgments against less faults than their own; out of their own mouth let them take the sentence and depart." You will have to render no account for other people, but you will have to render an account of yourself and how you judged other people. The last account will be wholly personal, therefore see ye to it.

That account will, according to my text, have connected with it full *submission*. "As I live, saith the Lord, every knee shall bow to me." You may to-day say, "I do not care about God": you will have to care about Him. As truly as God lives you will have to bow. You may say, "What matters it to me what Scripture says?" It will matter to you, as certainly as God lives, which is putting it on the most solemn certainty that can be. God has taken an oath about it, and declares that you shall own His sway. You had better bend at once, for you must either break or bow. God means to have His sovereignty acknowledged by all mankind. Hath He not made us? Do we not owe everything to Him? He will not have His crown rights denied for ever. He is Lord of all, and He swears by Himself that every knee shall bow and own it. You will have to come to it, my friend. Next, you will have to *confess;* so the text saith. By this I understand that you will have to acknowledge that God is your Lord and Master, and had a right to your services; that you ought to have kept His law; that in sinning you have done unrighteously and acted as you ought not to have acted. That confession you will not be able to withhold. Oh how the wicked will bite their tongues when they have to acknowledge their folly and wrong-doing; but it will have to come out of every man's mouth. When God pronounces sentence, and the ungodly are sent down to hell, they will give their own assent to His righteousness in condemning and punishing them. The verdict of the castaways in hell is that they deserve it; and this is, indeed, the hell of hell, that they cannot deny the justice of those pains which come upon them as the result of their disobedience. God will see to it that we shall justify Him either in life or in death, by confessing that He is righteous.

I appeal to you, my dear hearers, whether you

are ready with your account which you will have to render to God: have you kept one at all? Sometimes when men appear before a court they plead that they have no books, and it is always a bad sign. You know what the judge thinks of him. Can you dare to examine yourself, and answer questions? Can you give an account of your stewardship? Have you kept it correctly, or have you credited yourself with large things where you ought to have debited yourself? Your fraud will be discovered, for the great Accountant will read it through, and will detect an error in a single moment. Is your account kept correctly, and are you ready to render it in at this moment? Christian brother, you and I might hold back a little before we could say "Aye" to that. and yet I trust we could say it, for we know ourselves to be accepted with God. As for those who have scarcely thought of their God, their Maker, what will they do? what can they do, when each one of them must give an account before God, and they have no account except that which will condemn them for having wasted their Master's goods, for having defrauded the eternal God of that which was justly His due, and having spent upon their lusts that which ought to have been dedicated to their God? This judgment, then, will be personal. You cannot put your godly mother into the scale with yourself; you cannot associate your dear old father with yourself in judgment. O children, you cannot be judged by your ancestry, but by your acts; for it is written: "the Son of man shall come in the glory of His Father with His angels; and then He shall reward every man according to his works." Oh, see ye to it: God help you to do so.

III. Thirdly, THIS JUDGMENT WILL BE DIVINE. "We shall stand before the judgment seat of God." The judgment will be universal, personal, divine; and because it is the judgment seat of God, it will be a judgment according to truth. God will make no mistakes: He will not impute any wrong to us undeservedly, and He will not give us credit for right because we bore the appearance of it. He will search to the very core and essence of the matter. Are you ready to be tried as by fire? Trial by fire is but a scant figure of trial by the searching eye of the Most High God. He will test us by the supreme standard of perfect justice. We judge by one another, and if we are as liberal, or as prayerful, or as gracious as others we consider that it is all right. But the balances of the sanctuary are far more exact. It will not be you in one scale and I in another; and if I am as gracious as you, we shall both be accepted. Ah, no; there is another standard than that, the standard of truth and grace in the heart, and real love to God, and conformity to the image of Christ. Judge ye whether ye can stand that test. That judgment will be most searching. "The Lord pondereth the hearts." He will not judge after the sight of the eyes, but search out our secrets. Then shall the foundations be tested, then shall all that the man rested on and stayed himself upon be tried, whether it be the Rock of Ages or whether it be the mere sand of presumption. There will be no such trial day before or after as that day of the assize of God. "For God shall bring every work into judgment, with every secret thing, whether it be good, or whether it be evil."

That judgment will be impartial. You and I are always partial in weighing ourselves. We generally give the most lenient verdict except when we happen to be despondent in spirit, and then we are morbidly sensitive. But God will judge us without partiality. Rich friend, that diamond ring will answer no purpose in that day: my ladies, those fine garments will make no impression in that court. My learned friend, that handle to your name will be of no avail; and you, fine sir, with your knighthood, earldom, or dukedom, will be none the better off; for coronets, and even imperial crowns all go for nothing before the throne of God, who is no respecter of persons.

This judgment will be final. The sentence of the Supreme Court will settle all. Doth He say, "Depart ye cursed"? They can do no other. Doth He say, "Come ye blessed"? Oh, how blessed to enter into the eternal home. May none of you ever hear Him say, "Depart"; for He will never reverse the sentence: you will have to depart, and keep on departing, going further, further, and further away from Him who is hope and life and joy. There is no hope held out that He shall ever say, "Come back again, ye cursed"; but no, "Depart into everlasting fire in hell." God save us from such an ultimatum as that.

At the last judgment certain sins will prove to be of heavy weight. I will do no more than mention a few of them. There is one that is never treated leniently by any judge; it is contempt of court. God will speedily condemn those who have despised His authority. Are there any such here who have despised the Lord their God, and set at nought His counsel? They seldom or never think of God or His law, or even regard His day; but they say, "Who is the Lord that we should obey His voice?" Beware, ye despisers, and wonder and perish, for the Lord our God is jealous of His great name, and He hears the voices of them that scoff at Him.

Rejection of mercy is also a high crime and misdemeanour. The Judge who shall sit upon the throne has already presented mercy to all of you, and the unconverted among you have refused it. Surely they deserve the deepest hell who slight eternal love. If the Judge can say, "The prisoner at the bar has had the glad tidings of forgiveness presented to him, but has refused to listen to the gracious message, or having listened, and being almost persuaded, he nevertheless puts it off to a more convenient time, and here he stands a trampler on the blood of Christ." This will be the fiercest heat of the eternal burnings. Ye refused mercy; ye put from you eternal life, and counted yourselves unworthy of salvation. This sin will be a millstone about the soul for ever.

Then there is the crime of wilful, deliberate sinning, with intent so to do. Have any of you been guilty of this fact, and have you not fled to Christ? Did you choose sin, knowing it to be sin? Are you still choosing sin, and living in it against the voice of conscience? Ah, believe me, sin repeated, sin continued in will bring swift and sure destruction. These sins go beforehand to judgment, and there lodge solemn plaints against the guilty.

I cannot close amid these clouds. Break forth, O sun! Turn to the passage from which Paul quoted; for there you shall hear a sweet gospel word which may fitly end my discourse. Paul's mind was at Isaiah xlv. 23. He did not quote the words literally, but he gave the sense. Here is the passage: "I have sworn by Myself, the word is gone out of My mouth in righteousness, and shall not return, that unto me every knee shall bow, every tongue shall swear."

Now, what words do you think come before these? You shall look for yourselves. I will wait while you open your Bibles Do you see the blessed lines? God declares that every man shall bow before Him, and confess His authority; but what word of exhortation stands before that oath of His? I wish I could make it flash out at this moment in letters of light right round the building,—"Look unto Me, and be ye saved, all the ends of the earth: for I am God, and there is none else." That mercy-message stands side by side with the judgment prophecy. Come, then, dear hearts, you that are guilty, come and bow before your God ere He ascends the throne of judgment. Come and do willingly what you will have to do by-and-by unwillingly. Come now, and confess that He is judge and ought to be honoured; confess that He is king and ought to be obeyed; confess that you are His subject and are bound to serve Him; confess that you have done wrong, grievous wrong, in having broken His law; come and make out your own indictment; come and be your own accuser;

come and condemn yourself; come and bow your head when God's law condemns you; come and own that you deserve divine wrath, and submit yourself to the Lord's justice. Then give another look to your God and Saviour and say, "My Lord, I know Thou art my Judge; but Thou art also my Redeemer: I accept the place of condemnation, but I see that Thou didst stand there in my behalf, the just for the unjust, my substitute, bearing my sin and punishment. Blessed Lord, I accept Thee as my substitute; I yield myself up to Thee; I stand now tried, condemned, punished, dead, raised again in Thee, and therefore pardoned, acquitted, justified, beloved, accepted for Jesus' sake." Oh, is not this a blessed ending to a solemn sermon?

> "Bold shall I stand in that great day,
> For who aught to my charge shall lay?
> While through Thy blood absolved I am
> From sin's tremendous curse and shame."

God bless you. Amen.

A ROUND OF DELIGHTS

"Now the God of hope fill you with all joy and peace in believing, that ye may abound in hope, through the power of the Holy Ghost."—Romans xv. 13.

THIS is one of the richest passages in the Word of God. It is so full of instruction that I cannot hope to bring out even so much as a tithe of its teaching. The apostle desired for the Roman Christians that they might be in the most delightful state of mind, that they should be filled with joy and peace, and that this should lead on to yet further expectations, and create an abundance of hope in their souls. See, dear friends, the value of prayer, for if Paul longs to see his friends attain the highest possible condition, he prays for them. What will not prayer do? Whatsoever thou desirest for thyself, or for another, let thy desire be prepared like sweet spices and compounded into a supplication, and present it unto God, and the benediction will come.

I gather, also, from Paul's making this state of happiness a subject of request unto God, that it is possible for it to be attained. We may be filled with joy and peace in believing, and may abound in hope. There is no reason why we should hang our heads and live in perpetual doubt. We may not only be somewhat comforted, but we may be full of joy; we may not only have occasional quiet, but we may dwell in peace, and delight ourselves in the abundance of it. These great privileges are attainable, or the apostle would not have made them the subjects of prayer. Ay, and they are possible for us, as the meaning of the Epistle to the Romans was not exhausted upon the Romans, so this text belongeth to us also; and the words before us still rise to heaven as the prayer of the apostle for us, upon whom the ends of the earth are come, that we also may be filled with joy and peace, and abound in hope through the Holy Ghost. The sweetest delights are still grown in Zion's gardens, and are to be enjoyed by us; and shall they be within our reach and not be grasped? Shall a life of joy and peace be attainable, and shall we miss it through unbelief? God forbid. Let us, as believers, resolve that whatsoever of privilege is to be enjoyed we will enjoy it; whatsoever of lofty experience is to be realized, we will, by God's gracious

help, ascend to it: for we wish to know to the full the things which are freely given to us of God.

Not, however, in our own strength will we thus resolve, for this condition of faith, and joy, and peace must be wrought in us by God alone. This is clear enough in the text, for it is the God of hope who alone can fill us with joy and peace; and yet again, our hope which is to abound will only abound through the power of the Holy Ghost. The fact that the happy condition described is sought by prayer is a plain evidence that the blessing comes from a divine source, and the prayer itself is so worded that the doctrine is prominently presented to the mind. So, brethren, while we resolve to obtain everything of privilege that is obtainable, let us set about our effort in divine power, not depending upon our resolutions, but looking for the power of the Holy Ghost and the energy of the God of hope.

I shall want you to follow me whilst I notice concerning the blessed state of fulness of joy and peace, first, *whence it comes;* secondly, *what it is,* taking its delights in detail; and then, thirdly, *what it leads to.* We are to be filled with joy and peace, that "we may abound in hope through the power of the Holy Ghost."

I. If there be, then, such a condition as being divinely filled with all joy and peace in believing, WHENCE DOES IT COME? The answer is, it comes from "the God of hope." But in order that we may see how it comes let us look a little at the chapter in which we find our text, for the connection is instructive.

To know joy and peace through believing we must begin by knowing what is to be believed, and this we must learn from holy Scripture, for there *He is revealed as the God of hope.* Unless God had revealed Himself, we could not have guessed at hope, but the Scriptures of truth are windows of hope to us. Will you kindly read the fourth verse of the chapter and note how strikingly parallel it is to our text—"For whatsoever things were written aforetime were written for our learning, that we through patience and comfort of the Scriptures might have hope." See, then, the God of hope is revealed in Scripture with the design of inspiring us with hope. If we would be filled with faith, joy, and peace, it must be by believing the truths set forth in the Scriptures. Before we have any inward ground of hope, God Himself, as revealed in the Bible, must be our hope. We must not ask for joy first and then found our faith upon it, but our joy must grow out of our faith, and that must rest upon God alone. Our apostle sets us an example of how to use the Scriptures, for in this chapter he searches out the truth from Moses, and David, and Isaiah, and then places one text with another and gets a clear view of the testimony of God. What is very much to our point, he sees in those Scriptures that to us Gentiles God has of old been set forth in the Scriptures as the God of hope. Aforetime it seemed as if salvation were of the Jews and of the Jews alone, and we were shut out; but now, on turning to the Old Testament itself, we discover that God had spoken good things concerning us before we knew Him. There was always hope for the Gentiles, and though Israel perceived it not, yet patriarchs and kings and prophets full often spake words which could not otherwise be interpreted. "In thee and in thy seed shall all the nations of the earth be blessed" is a promise which overleaped the bounds of Canaan. As, then, by searching the apostle found in the word of God hope for the Gentiles, so will the most heavy laden and burdened spirit discover sources of consolation if the Bible be diligently read and faithfully believed. Every promise is meant to inspire the believer with hope; therefore use it to that end. Use the written word as the source of comfort, and do not look for dreams, excitements, impressions, or feelings. Faith deals with the Scriptures and with the God of hope as therein revealed, and out of these it draws its fulness of joy and peace. Beloved, if you desire to get faith in Christ, or to increase it, be diligent in knowing and understanding the gospel of your salvation as set forth in the word of God. "Faith cometh by hearing," or by reading the word of God. How shall you believe that which you do not know? Do not at once make an effort to believe before you are instructed, but first know what God hath revealed, see how He hath displayed to you the hope of everlasting life, and then believe with all your heart the testimony of God. Every promise and word of God must be to you a foundation most sure and steadfast whereon to build your hope. Let your anchor grasp and hold to each revealed truth, whatever your feelings may be. We begin then by saying that fulness of joy and peace comes to us from the God of hope as He reveals Himself in holy writ. As it is written, "Hear, and your soul shall live," so do we find that we must hear if our soul is to rejoice.

Now, it so happens that the Scriptures were not only written that the Gentiles might have hope, but that they might have joy. I ask you to notice the passages quoted by the apostle, for at least the last three of them call us to joy. Thus in verse 10, Moses saith, "Rejoice, ye Gentiles, with His people." If there be any joy for the elect nation, it is for us also who believe. If there be any joy for Israel redeemed out of Egypt, led through the Red Sea, fed with manna, and brought to the borders of Canaan, that joy is for us also; if any joy over the burnt offering, if any joy at the paschal supper, if any delight at the jubilee, all that joy may be shared by us, for thus saith the Lord, "Rejoice, ye Gentiles, with His people." Joy in their joy. Again, David saith (verse 11), "Praise the Lord, all ye Gentiles; and laud Him, all ye people." Now, where there is praise there is joy, for joy is a component element of it. They that praise the Lord aright rejoice before Him. Go, ye Gentiles, when David bids you thus unite with Israel in praising God, he bids you take full possession of the joy which moves the favoured nation to magnify the Lord. Again, Isaiah says, "There shall be a root of Jesse, and He that shall rise to reign over the Gentiles; in Him shall the Gentiles trust," or, as it should be translated, "hope." Now, hope is ever the source of joy. So, then, in the Scriptures we see God is the God of hope, and on further search we see that the hope of the Gentiles permits them to rejoice with His people; in fine, we see that God Himself is the hope of all those who know Him, and the consequent source of joy and peace.

Again, then, I am brought to this, that, to begin with, the joy and peace which we all desire to obtain must be sought through a knowledge of the God of hope, as He is revealed to us by the Scriptures. We must begin with that sure word of testimony whereunto we do well if we take heed as unto a light that shineth in a dark place. There must be belief in God as revealed in the word, even though as yet we see no change within ourselves, nor any conceivable internal ground in our nature for hope or joy. Blessed is he who hath not seen and yet hath believed. He who can hang upon God without the comfort of inward experience is on the high road to being filled with joy and peace.

But the apostle in the text leads us through the Scriptures to God Himself, who is personally to fill us with joy and peace; by which I understand that He is to become *the great object of our joy.* As Israel in the Red Sea triumphed in the Lord, even so do we joy in God by our Lord Jesus Christ. Like David, we say, "Then will I go unto the altar of God, unto God my exceeding joy"; and with Isaiah we sing, "I will greatly rejoice in the Lord; my soul shall be joyful in my God." When first the Lord looked upon us through the windows of His word we began to hope; by-and-by His good Spirit caused our hoping to grow into believing, and since then, as our knowledge of the Lord has increased, our believing has risen to fulness of joy. Our God is a blessed God, so that to believe in Him is to find rest unto the soul, and to commune with Him is to dwell in bliss. Beloved, when you think of God, the just one, apart from Christ, you might well tremble, but when you see Him in Jesus, His very justice becomes precious to you as "the terrible crystal," and you learn to build it into the foundation of your joy. The holiness of God which aforetime awed you becomes supremely attractive when you see it revealed in the person of Jesus Christ your Lord. How charming is "the glory of God in the face of Christ." As for the love of God, as you see it set forth in this book and in His Son, it inspires you with every sacred passion. As for His eternal immutability, it becomes the groundwork of your peace, for if He changes not, then all His promises will stand sure to you and to all His people from generation to generation. His power, which was once so terrible in the thunder and in the storm, now becomes delightful to you as you see it, yoked to the promise, that the promise may be fulfilled, and behold it concentrated in the man Christ Jesus that His purposes may be achieved. In fine, there is no attribute of God, there is no purpose of God, there is no deed of God, there is no aspect under which God is seen, but what becomes the object of the Christian's joy when he has seen Him and believed in Him as revealed in the Scriptures. To the believer God is his sun, his shield, his portion, his delight, his all. His soul delights herself in the Lord. At first he hoped in God, that peradventure he would smile upon him: he turned to the Scriptures, and he found there many a cheering declaration, and these he knew to be true, and therefore he believed God that He would do as He had said: and now not only has his hope become faith, but his faith has budded and blossomed and brought forth the almonds of joy and peace. You see, then, how the Lord is the author of all our holy gladness.

Our God is, however, called the God of hope, not only because He is the object of our hope, and the ground of our joy and peace, but because *He it is that worketh hope and joy in us*. No joy is worth the having unless the Lord is the beginning and the end of it, and no joy is worth receiving except it springs from hope in Him. He must breathe peace upon us, or else the storm-tossed waters of our spirit will never rest, nor is it desirable that they should, for peace without God is stupefaction, joy without God is madness, and hope without God is presumption. In true believers their hope, faith, joy, and peace are all alike of divine workmanship. Our spiritual raiment is never homespun; we are divinely arrayed from head to foot.

This blessed name of "God of hope" belongs to the New Testament, and is a truly gospel title. Livy tells us that the Romans had a god of hope, but he says that the temple was struck by lightning, and in an after book he adds that it was burned to the ground. Exceedingly typical this of whatever of hope can come to nations which worship gods of their own making. All idol hopes must perish beneath the wrath of the Most High. The God of human nature unenlightened, or only sufficiently enlightened to discover its sin, is the God of terror; in fact, to many, the Lord is the God of despair: but when you turn to the revelation of God in Scripture, you find Him to be a God whose gracious character inspires hope, and henceforth you turn away from everything else to fix your hope on God alone. "My soul, wait thou only upon God, for my expectation is from Him." God, in Christ Jesus, has ceased to be the dread of men, and has become their hope. Our Father and our Friend, we look for all to Thee. And blessed be God, the hope which He excites is a hope worthy of Him. It is a God-like hope—a hope which helps us to purify ourselves. At first we hope in God for cleansing from every sin, and then for acceptance here and hereafter. We hope for pardon through the atonement which is in Christ Jesus, and when we have it, we hope for sanctification by the Spirit. Our hope never ceases to rise higher and higher, and to receive fulfilment after fulfilment, and we know that it shall continue to do so till we rise to dwell at His right hand for ever and ever. He who graspeth this hope hath a soul-satisfying portion, for which a man might well be content to suffer a thousand martyrdoms if he might but abide in it. It is a hope which only God would have contrived for man—a hope founded in Himself; a hope presented to the sons of men in Christ Jesus because His sacrifice has been presented and accepted; a hope which God alone can inspire in men, for even if they hear the gospel they do not find hope till He comes in power to their souls; a hope which always

adores God, and lies low at His feet, never dreaming of being independent of Him; a hope which layeth her crown at His feet, and taken Him to be her Lord for ever and ever. This is the hope which is the mother of our joy and peace, and only as it is wrought in us by the Lord can we be truly happy and restful.

II. Secondly, let us enquire, WHAT IS THIS BLESSED STATE OF MIND of which we have spoken a little? Let us look into the words. He says, "That the God of hope may fill you with all joy and peace in believing." It is a state of mind *most pleasant*, for to be filled with joy is a rare delight reminding one of heaven.

It is, however, a state as *safe* as it is pleasant, for the man has a joy which God gives him may be quite easy in the enjoyment of it. The best of the world's joy is but a season; while you are enjoying it you are in fear because it will soon be over, and what then? Earth's best candles will soon burn out. The day of this world's mirth will end in a night of misery. This thought mars and sours all fleeting joys; but the joy which God gives has no afterthought about it. It is wholesome and safe and *abiding*. We may drink our full without being sickened, yea, revel in it without surfeit.

At the same time it is most *profitable* joy, for the more a man has of this joy the better man he will be. It will not soften him and render him effeminate, for it has a singular strengthening power about it. There is, doubtless, a tonic influence in sorrow, but holy joy is also exceedingly invigorating, for it is written, "The joy of the Lord is your strength." The more happy we can be in our God the more thoroughly will the will of Christ be fulfilled in us, for He desired that our joy might be full. The more you rejoice in God the more you will recommend true religion. The more full of delight you are, especially in trying times, the more you will glorify God. Few things are at the same time both pleasant and profitable, but holy joy and peace possess that double excellence. Fulness of spiritual joy is both the index and the means of spiritual strength. I commend this state, therefore, to you. I trust that we shall not be so unbelieving as to be afraid of heaven's own consolations, nor so unreasonable as to decline to be filled with joy and peace when they may be had by believing.

Now, notice, that it is *a state which has varieties in it*. It is joy and peace; and it may be either. Sometimes the believer is full of joy. Joy is active and expressive; it sparkles and flashes like a diamond; it sings and dances like David before the ark. To be filled with holy joy is a delicious excitement of the sweetest kind; may you often experience it, until strangers are compelled to infer that the Lord hath done great things for you. Nevertheless, the flesh is weak, and might hardly endure continuous delight, and so there comes a relief, in the lovely form of peace, in which the heart is really joyous, but after a calm and quiet manner. I have seen the ringers make the pinnacles of a church tower reel to and fro while they have made the joy bells sound out to the full, and then they have played quietly, and let the fabric settle down again. Even thus does joy strain the man, but peace comes in to give him rest. In this peace there is not much to exhilarate, not much which could fittingly be spoken out in song; but silence, full of infinite meaning, becomes the floodgate of the soul. You seek not the exulting assembly, but the calm shade and the quiet chamber. You are as happy as you were in your joy, but not so stirred and moved. Peace is joy resting, and joy is peace dancing. Joy cries hosanna before the Well-beloved, but peace leans her head on His bosom. In the midst of bereavements and sickness we may scarcely be able to rejoice, but we may be at peace. When faith cannot break through a troop with her sacred joy she stands still and sees the salvation of God in hallowed peace. We work with joy and rest with peace. What a blessing it is that when we come to die if we cannot depart with the banners of triumphant joy all flying in the breeze, we can yet fall asleep safely in the arms of peace. How pleasant a life do they lead who are not the subjects of any very great excitement, but maintain calm and quiet communion with God. Their heart is fixed, trusting in the Lord. They neither soar nor sink, but keep the even tenor of their way. It is a state of mind, then, which admits of variations; and I really do not know which to choose out of its two forms. I should not like to be without joy, and yet methinks there is something so solid about peace that I might almost give it the preference. I think I love the quiet sister the better of the two. That famous text in Isaiah—"They shall mount up with wings as eagles; they shall run, and not be weary; and they shall walk and not faint" looks somewhat like an anti-climax; it would appear to place the greatest first, and then the less, and then the least; but it is not so. The mounting up with wings as eagles must always be more or less temporary: we are not eagles, and cannot always be on the wing. The Lord renews our strength like the eagles, and this shows we are not always up to the eagle mark. Well, though it is a grand thing to be able to fly, it is a better thing to be able to run; this is more like a man, involves less danger, and is more practically useful. It is good to run, but even that is not the best journey pace: it is best of all to walk, for this is a steady persevering pace to move at. "Enoch walked with God." This is God's pace, who even when He makes clouds His chariot is described as walking upon the wings of the wind. We read of the walk of faith, and the walk of holiness, for, walking is practical, and is meant for every day. You young people, I like to see you run, and I am glad to take a turn at it myself, but, after all, steady, sober, unwearied walking is the best. To walk without fainting is a high experimental attainment, and is none the less valuable because at first sight there seems nothing striking about it. Walking is the emblem of peace, and running and mounting up with wings as eagles are the emblems of joy.

But, beloved, *this blessed state is also a compound*, for we are bidden at one and the same time to receive both wine and milk—wine exhilarating with joy, and milk satisfying with peace. "Ye shall go out with joy, and be led forth with peace." You shall lie down in the green pastures of delight, and be led by the still waters of quietness. Our heart may be as an ocean, gloriously casting upward its spray of joy, and lifting up its waves on high in delight, as one clappeth his hands for joy; and yet, at the same time, as down deep in the coral caverns all is still and undisturbed, so may the heart be quiet as a sleeping babe. We see no difficulty in understanding both lines of the hymn:—

"My heart is resting, O my God,
I will give thanks and sing."

We rest and praise, as trees hold to the earth by their roots, and perfume the air with their bloom;

as morning comes without sound of trumpet, and yet awakens the music of birds by its arising. Ours is no froth of joy; there is solid peace beneath our effervescence of delight. Happy are we to have learned how to combine two such choice things.

"Joy is a fruit that will not grow
In nature's barren soil;
All we can boast, till Christ we know,
Is vanity and toil.

"But where the Lord has planted grace,
And made His glories known,
These fruits of heavenly joy and peace
Are found, and there alone."

Now, I want you to lay stress on the next observation I am about to make, because I began with it, and wish to leave it upon your minds as the chief thought. *The joy and peace here spoken of are through believing.* You come to know the God of hope through the Scriptures, which reveal Him; by this you are led to believe in Him, and it is through that believing that you become filled with joy and peace. It is not by working, nor by feeling, that we become full of joy; our peace does not arise from the marks, and evidences, and experiences which testify to us that we are the sons of God, but simply from believing. Our central joy and peace must always come to us, not as an inference from the internal work of the Spirit in our souls, but from the finished work of the Lord Jesus, and the promises of God contained in the Scriptures. We must continue to look out of self to the written word wherein the Lord is set forth before us, and we must rest in God in Christ Jesus as the main basis of our hope; not depending upon any other arguments than those supplied by the Bible itself. I will show by-and-by how we shall afterwards reach to a hope which flows out of the work of the Spirit within us; but at the first, and, I think, permanently and continuously, the main ground of the surest joy and truest peace must come to us through simply believing in Jesus Christ. Beloved, I know that I have been converted, for I am sure that there is a change of heart in me; nevertheless, my hope of eternal life does not hang upon the inward fact. I rest in the external fact that God hath revealed Himself in Jesus as blotting out the sin of all His believing people, and, as a believer, I have the word of God as my guarantee of forgiveness. This is my rest. Because I am a believer in Christ Jesus, therefore have I hope, therefore have I joy and peace, since God hath declared that "he that believeth in Him hath everlasting life." This joy can only safely come through believing, and I pray you, brothers and sisters, never be drifted away from child-like faith in what God hath said. It is very easy to obtain a temporary joy and peace through your present easy experience, but how will you do when all things within take a troublous turn? Those who live by feeling change with the weather. If you ever put aside your faith in the finished work to drink from the cup of your own inward sensations, you will find yourself bitterly disappointed. Your honey will turn to gall, your sunshine into blackness; for all things which come of man are fickle and deceptive. The God of hope will fill you with joy and peace, but it will only be through believing. You will still have to stand as a poor sinner at the foot of the cross, trusting to the complete atonement. You will never have joy and peace unless you do. If you once begin to say, "I am a saint; there is something good in me," and so on, you will find joy evaporate and peace depart. Hold on to your believing.

Come back to the text again, and you will find that *this joy and peace, according to Paul, are of a superlative character*, for, after his manner, Paul makes language for himself. He often manufactures a superlative by the use of the word "*all*," as here, "Fill you with all joy." He means with the best and highest degree of joy, with as much joy as you can hold, with the very choicest and most full of joys in earth or in heaven. God give you the joy of joys, the light of delight, the heaven of heaven.

Then notice *the comprehensiveness* of his prayer. "All joy"; that is joy in God the Father's love, joy in God the Son's redeeming blood, joy in God the Holy Ghost's indwelling; joy in the covenant of grace, joy in the seal and witness of it, joy in the promises, joy in the decrees, joy in the doctrines, joy in the precepts, joy in everything which cometh from God, "all joy." Paul also requests for them all peace, peace with God, peace of conscience, peace with one another, peace even with the outside world, as far as peace may be. May you all have it.

And now observe the degree of joy and peace which he wishes for them—"that ye may be *filled*," and that by the God of hope Himself. God alone knows our capacity and where the vacuum lies which most needs filling. A man might try to fill us and fail, but God, who made us, knows every corner and cranny of our nature, and can pour in joy and peace till every portion of our being is flooded, saturated, and overflowed with delight. I like to remember David's word, "The rain also filleth the pools," for even thus doth the Lord pour His grace upon the thirsty soil of our hearts till it stands in pools. As the sun fills the world with light, and enters into all places, even so the God of hope by His presence lights up every part of our nature with the golden light of joyous peace, till there is not a corner left for sadness or foreboding. This is Paul's prayer, and he expects its answer to come to us *through believing*, and in no other way; he does not ask for us mysterious revelations, dreams, visions, or presumptuous persuasions; he seeks for us no excitement of fanaticism nor the intoxication of great crowds and pleasing oratory, neither does he seek that we may imagine ourselves to be perfect, and all that kind of lumber, but that we may be happy through simply believing in the God of hope as He is set forth in the Bible. I take this book of God into my hands and say, "Whatsoever things are written here were written for my learning, that through patience and comfort of the Scriptures I might have hope"; I do have hope, for I believe this book, and now I feel joy and peace welling up within my soul. Brethren, receive ye this benediction! O Lord, fulfil it in the heart of every believer before Thee.

III. Now thirdly, WHAT DOES THIS LEAD TO? "Lead to?" says one, "Lead to, why surely it is enough in itself. What more is wanted?" When a man brings you into a chamber vaulted with diamonds and amethysts, and pearls and rubies; with walls composed of slabs of gold, and the floor made of solid pavements of silver, we should be astonished if he said, "This is a passage to something richer still." Yet the apostle directs us to this fulness of joy and peace through believing that we may by its means reach to something else,—"that you may abound in hope through the power of the Holy Ghost." How often do great things in the Bible, like the perpetual cycles of nature, begin where they end and end where

they begin. If we begin with the God of hope, we are wound up into holy joy and peace, that we may come back to hope again and to abounding in it by the power of the Holy Ghost.

First, I notice that the hope here mentioned arises, not out of pure believing, but out of the joy created in us by our having believed. Hope led to faith, faith to joy, and now joy back again to hope. This is the story as far as I am concerned:—I began with believing. I felt nothing good within me, but I believed in what God revealed concerning Himself. I saw nothing, but I believed, on the ground that God said so. I soon had joy and peace in my soul as the result of my faith, and now, because of this joy and peace, I hope and expect further blessings. Though still resting my soul upon the finished work of Jesus, yet hopes do arise from the work of the Holy Ghost within me. The God who has given me by believing to rejoice that the past is all atoned for, and who has given me peace because my sins are forgiven me for His name's sake, will not dash that joy by revoking my pardon. He who has given me joy, because He has quickened me, and has, up to this day, preserved me, will not, I am persuaded, forsake me, and suffer me to perish. Surely He will never leave me, after having done so much for me. My present joy gives me a hope, most sure and steadfast, that He will never turn His back upon me. If He did not intend to bless me in the future, He would not have done so much for me in the past, and He could not and would not be doing so much for me now.

This hope, you perceive, drinks its life at the fountain of personal experience. The first hope we ever know comes together with our simply believing the Word of God, but now there arises in us an abounding of hope, which is the outgrowth of the inward life. Fear is banished now, for we have looked to the God of hope, and found acceptance in the Beloved. Now, therefore, in the chamber where fear formerly dwelt hope takes up its habitation; azure-winged, bright-eyed hope makes its nest there, and sings to us all the day long.

The text speaks of an abounding hope, and if you consider for awhile you will see that very much hope must arise to a Christian out of his spiritual joy. If you have once been in the bosom of Jesus, and known His joy, your hope will overflow. For instance, you will argue—He has pardoned my sin, and made me to rejoice as a forgiven man: will He condemn me after all? What meaneth the pardon if, after all, the transgressions are to be laid upon me, and I am to suffer for my sin? The believer hath great joy because God's love is shed abroad in his soul, and he argues that if the Lord loves him so intensely now, He will not undergo a change, and remove His love. He who in love redeemed me by the blood of His Son will love me eternally, for He changes not. Is not this sound argument? Grace enjoyed is a pledge of glory. Redeeming love is the guarantee of preserving love. Acceptance with God to-day creates a blessed hope of acceptance for ever. Faith and joy within the soul sing to one another somewhat after this fashion:—

"His smiles have freed my heart from pain,
  My drooping spirits cheer'd;
And will He not appear again
  Where He has once appeared?

"Has He not form'd my soul anew,
  And caused my light to shine;
And will He now His work undo,
  Or break His word divine?"

Perfectly assured of the Lord's goodness, the man confronts the future without fear, and in due time approaches death without dismay. Since the Lord has begun to make us like His Son we conclude that He will perfect His work, and raise us from our graves in the full image of our Redeemer. He has given us already to know something of the joy of Christ, who prayed that His joy might be fulfilled in us that our joy might be full, and therefore we are sure that we shall bask in the joy of heaven. We will, therefore, lie down in peace, and rest when our last day on earth shall come, for we shall rise with Jesus: of this we have no doubt. We shall enter into the joy of the Lord, for we have entered into it already. Thus out of peace and joy there grow the noblest of human hopes. Little enjoyment, like a weak telescope, gives us but a faint prospect, but great enjoyment is an optic glass of marvellous power, and brings great things near to us. Joy and peace are specimens of heaven's felicities, and set the soul both hoping and hungering. Having tasted of the grapes of Eshcol, we believe in the land which floweth with milk and honey, and long to rest under the boughs which bear such luscious clusters. We have seen the celestial city far away, but the light of it is so surpassing that we have longed to walk its golden streets, ay, and have felt sure of doing so ere long. He who has seen a little of the light of the morning expects the more eagerly the noonday. He who has waded into the river of joy up to the ankles, becomes eager to enter it still further, till he finds it a river to swim in, wherein the soul is borne along by a sacred current of unutterable delight. Up, ye saints, to your Pisgah of joy, for there you shall have a full view of Canaan which stretches before you, and is soon to be yours. Whatever your joy and peace may be now you ought to see at once that they are meant to be only a platform from which you are to look for something brighter and better still: ye are filled with joy and peace that ye may abound in hope.

Our apostle rightly adds, "*by the power of the Holy Ghost*," for I take it that this is partly mentioned by way of caution, because there are hopes arising out of inward experience which may turn out to be fallacious, and therefore we must discriminate between the hope of nature and the hope of grace. I have heard young people say, "I know I am saved, because I am so happy." Be not too sure of that. Many people think themselves very happy, and yet they are not saved. The world has a happiness which is a fatal sign, and a peace which is the token of spiritual death. Discernment, therefore, is needed lest we mistake the calm before a storm for the rest which the Lord giveth to those who come unto Him. Hope may arise out of our joy, but we must mind that we do not fix our confidence in it, or we shall have a sandy foundation.

The solid grace of hope which abides and remains in the soul is born of faith through the Word; it is only *the abounding* of hope which comes out of our joy and peace. Let me begin again with you lest there should be any mistake. You hear of the God of hope, and are led to believe in God as He is revealed in Scripture. So far all is plain sailing. If you believe in the Christ of God, you obtain joy and peace, but these are results, not causes: you must not begin with your own joy and peace, and say, "My hope of salvation is built upon the happiness I have felt of late." This will never do. Begin first of all with the Scriptures, not with your feelings or fancies, nor with your impressions and excitements: these will be ruinous as a foundation. Begin with God revealed in Christ Jesus as the God of hope, and let your joy and your peace come from your believing in Him: then afterwards it will be fair enough to draw arguments for the aboundings of hope, but it must be by the Holy Ghost. That hope which is worth having, which springs from inward experience, must still be wrought in us by the Holy Spirit, and I will show you how it is natural that it should be so. We ask ourselves, "How shall I hold on to the end?" The answer will be suggested by another question, "How have I held on till now?" I feel now a joy and peace because my faith has been sustained until this day, how have I been preserved hitherto? By the Holy Spirit. Then He is able to keep me to the end. I feel joy and peace already, because in some measure sin is conquered in me. How will my soul be yet further sanctified and sin cast out of me? Why, by the same Holy Spirit, who has already renewed me. I have had an earnest of what He can do, and therefore I have an abounding of hope of what He will do. My joyful experience of His indwelling, comforting, illuminating, and sanctifying power leads me into a full and confident assurance that He will carry on the work of grace, and present me complete at the last great day.

Beloved, go forward, keeping close to the groundwork of faith, and you will feel joy and peace in your hearts. At such times give full play to your hope. Expect what you will. "Eye hath not seen, nor ear heard, neither have entered into the heart of man, the things which God hath prepared for them that love Him." Expect great things, expect things beyond all expectation. Your largest hopes shall all be exceeded. Hope, and hope, and yet hope again, and each time hope more and more, but the Lord will give you more than you have hoped for. When you enter His palace gates at the last, you will say, "My imagination never conceived it, my desires never compassed it, my hope never expected it; the glory surpasses all. The tenth hath not been told me of the things which God had provided for me." "Rejoice in the Lord alway: and again I say, rejoice." Amen.

OUR URGENT NEED OF THE HOLY SPIRIT

"Through the power of the Holy Ghost."—Rom. xv. 13.
"By the power of the Spirit of God."—Rom. xv. 19.

I DESIRE to draw your attention at this time to the great necessity which exists for the continual manifestation of the power of the Holy Spirit in the church of God if by her means the multitudes are to be gathered to the Lord Jesus. I did not know how I could much better do so than by first showing that the Spirit of God is necessary to the church of God for its own internal growth in grace. Hence my text in the thirteenth verse, "Now the God of hope fill you with all joy and peace in believing, that ye may abound in hope, through the power of the Holy Ghost,"—where it is evident that the apostle attributes the power to be filled with joy and peace in believing, and the power to abound in hope, to the Holy Ghost. But, then, I wanted also to show you that the power of the church outside, that with which she is to be aggressive and work upon the world for the gathering out of God's elect from among men, is also this same energy of the Holy Spirit. Hence I have taken the nineteenth verse, for the apostle there says that God had through him made "the Gentiles obedient by word and deed, through mighty signs and wonders, by the power of the Spirit of God." So you see, dear friends, that first of all to keep the church happy and holy within herself there must be a manifestation of the power of the Holy Spirit, and secondly, that the church may invade the territories of the enemy and may conquer the world for Christ she must be clothed with the self-same sacred energy. We may then go further and say that the power of the church for external work will be proportionate to the power which dwells within herself. Gauge the energy of the Holy Spirit in the hearts of believers and you may fairly calculate their influence upon unbelievers. Only let the church be illuminated by the Holy Spirit and she will reflect the light and become to onlookers "fair as the moon, clear as the sun, and terrible as an army with banners."

Let us by two or three illustrations show that the work outward must always depend upon the force inward. On a cold winter's day when the snow has fallen and lies deep upon the ground you go through a village. There is a row of cottages, and you will notice that from one of the roofs the snow has nearly disappeared, while another cottage still bears a coating of snow. You do not stay to make enquiries as to the reason of the difference, for you know very well what is the cause. There is a fire burning inside the one cottage and the warmth glows through its roof, and so the snow speedily melts: in the other there is no tenant; it is a house to let, no fire burns on its hearth and no warm smoke ascends the chimney, and therefore there lies the snow. Just as the warmth is within so the melting will be without. I look at a number of churches, and where I see worldliness and formalism lying thick upon them, I am absolutely certain that there is not the warmth of Christian life within; but where the hearts of believers are warm with divine love through the Spirit of God, we are sure to see evils vanish, and beneficial consequences following therefrom. We need not look within; in such a case the exterior is index sufficient.

Take an illustration from political life. Here is a trouble arising between different nations; there are angry spirits stirring, and it seems very likely that the Gordian knot of difficulty will never be untied by diplomacy, but will need to be cut with the sword. Everybody knows that one of the hopes of peace lies in the bankrupt condition of the nation which is likely to go to war; for if it be short of supplies, if it cannot pay its debts, if it cannot furnish the material for war, then it will not be likely to court a conflict. A country must be strong in internal resources before it can wisely venture upon foreign wars. Thus is it in the great battle of truth: a poor starveling church cannot combat the devil and his armies. Unless the church is herself rich in the things of God and strong with divine energy, she will generally cease to be aggressive, and will content herself with going on with the regular routine of Christian work, crying, "Peace! peace!" where peace should not be. She will not dare to defy the world, or to send forth her legions

to conquer its provinces for Christ, when her own condition is pitiably weak. The strength or weakness of a nation's exchequer affects its army in its every march, and in like manner its measure of grace influences the church of God in all its action.

Suffer yet another illustration. If you lived in Egypt, you would notice, once in the year, the Nile rising; and you would watch its increase with anxiety, because the extent of the overflow of the Nile is very much the measure of the fertility of Egypt. Now the rising of the Nile must depend upon those far-off lakes in the centre of Africa—whether they shall be well filled with the melting of the snows or no. If there be a scanty supply in the higher reservoirs, there cannot be much overflow in the Nile in its after-course through Egypt. Let us translate the figure, and say that, if the upper lakes of fellowship with God in the Christian Church are not well filled—if the soul's spiritual strength be not sustained by private prayer and communion with God—the Nile of practical Christian service will never rise to the flood.

The one thing I want to say is this: you cannot get out of the Church what is not in it. The reservoir itself must be filled before it can pour forth a stream. We must ourselves drink of the living water till we are full, and then out of the midst of us shall flow rivers of living water; but not till then. Out of an empty basket you cannot distribute loaves and fishes, however hungry the crowd may be. Out of an empty heart you cannot speak full things, nor from a lean soul bring forth fat things full of marrow, which shall feed the people of God. Out of the fulness of the heart the mouth speaketh, when it speaks to edification at all. So that the first thing is to look well to home affairs, and pray that God would bless us and case His face to shine upon us that His way may be known upon earth, and His saving health among all people.

> "To bless Thy chosen race,
>   In mercy, Lord, incline,
> And cause the brightness of Thy face
>   On all Thy saints to shine.
>
> "That so Thy wondrous way
>   May through the world be known;
> Whilst distant lands their tribute pay,
>   And Thy salvation own."

This morning, in trying to speak of the great necessity of the Church, namely, her being moved vigorously by the power of the Holy Spirit, I earnestly pray that we may enter upon this subject with the deepest conceivable reverence. Let us adore while we are meditating; let us feel the condescension of this blessed Person of the Godhead in deigning to dwell in His people and to work in the human heart. Let us remember that this divine person is very sensitive. He is a jealous God. We read of His being grieved and vexed, and therefore let us ask His forgiveness of the many provocations which He must have received from our hands. With lowliest awe let us bow before Him, remembering that, if there be a sin which is unpardonable, it has a reference to Himself—the sin against the Holy Ghost, which shall never be forgiven, neither in this world nor in that which is to come. In reference to the Holy Ghost we stand on very tender ground indeed; and if ever we should veil our faces and rejoice with trembling, it is while we speak of the Spirit, and of those mysterious works with which He blesses us. In that lowly spirit, and under the divine overshadowing follow me while I set before you seven works of the Holy Spirit which are most necessary to the Church for its own good, and equally needful to her in her office of missionary from Christ to the outside world.

I. To begin, then, the power of the Holy Ghost is manifested in the QUICKENING of souls to spiritual life. All the spiritual life which exists in this world is the creation of the Holy spirit, by whom the Lord Jesus quickeneth whomsoever He will. You and I had not life enough to know our death till He visited us, we had not light enough to perceive that we were in darkness, nor sense enough to feel our misery: we were so utterly abandoned to our own folly that, though we were naked, and poor, and miserable, we dreamed that we were rich, and increased in goods. We were under sentence of death as condemned criminals, and yet we talked about merit and reward; yea, we were dead, and yet we boasted that we were alive—counting our very death to be our life. The Spirit of God in infinite mercy came to us with His mysterious power, and made us live. The first token of life was a consciousness of our being in the realm of death, and an agony to escape from it; we began to perceive our insensibility, and, if I may be pardoned such an expression, we saw our blindness. Every growth of spiritual life, from the first tender shoot until now, has also been the work of the Holy Spirit. As the green blade was His production, so is the ripening corn. The increase of life, as much as life at the beginning, must still come by the operation of the Spirit of God, who raised up Christ from the dead. You will never have more life, brother, except as the Holy Ghost bestows it upon you; yea, you will not even know that you want more, nor groan after more, except as He worketh in you to desire and to agonize, according to His own good pleasure. See, then, our absolute dependence upon the Holy Spirit; for if He were gone we should relapse into spiritual death, and the Church would become a charnel-house.

The Holy Spirit is absolutely needful to make everything that we do to be alive. We are sowers, brethren, but if we take dead seed in our seed-basket there will never be a harvest. The preacher must preach living truth in a living manner if he expects to obtain a hundred-fold harvest. How much there is of church work which is nothing better than the movement of a galvanized corpse. How much of religion is done as if it were performed by an automaton, or ground off by machinery. Nowadays men care little about heart and soul, they only look at outward performances. Why, I hear they have now invented a machine which talks, though surely there was talk enough without this Parisian addition to the band of prattlers. We can preach as machines, we can pray as machines, and we can teach Sunday-school as machines. Men can give mechanically, and come to the communion-table mechanically: yes, and we ourselves shall do so unless the Spirit of God be with us. Most hearers know what it is to hear a live sermon which quivers all over with fulness of energy; you also know what it is to sing a hymn in a lively manner, and you know what it is to unite in a live prayer-meeting; but, ah, if the Spirit of God be absent, all that the church does will be lifeless, the rustle of leaves above a tomb, the gliding of spectres, the congregation of the dead turning over in their graves.

As the Spirit of God is a quickener to make us alive and our work alive, so must He specially be with us to make those alive with whom we have to deal for Jesus. Imagine a dead preacher preaching a dead sermon to dead sinners: what can possibly come of it? Here is a beautiful essay which has been admirably elaborated, and it is coldly read to the cold hearted sinner. It smells of the midnight oil, but it has no heavenly unction, no divine power resting upon it, nor, perhaps, is that power even looked for. What good can come of such a production? As well may you try to calm the tempest with poetry or stay the hurricane with rhetoric as to bless a soul by mere learning and eloquence. It is only as the Spirit of God shall come upon God's servant and shall make the word which He preaches to drop as a living seed into the heart that any result can follow His ministry; and it is only as the Spirit of God shall then follow that seed and keep it alive in the soul of the listener that we can expect those who profess to be converted to take root and grow to maturity of grace, and become our sheaves at the last.

We are utterly dependent here, and for my part I rejoice in this absolute dependence. If I could have a stock of power to save souls which would be all my own apart from the Spirit of God, I cannot suppose a greater temptation to pride and to living at a distance from God. It is well to be weak in self, and better still to be nothing: to be simply the pen in the hand of the Spirit of God, unable to write a single letter upon the tablets of the human heart except as the hand of the Holy Spirit shall use us for that purpose. That is really our position, and we ought practically to take it up; and doing so we shall continually cry to the Spirit of God to quicken us in all things, and quicken all that we do, and quicken the word as it drops into the sinner's ear. I am quite certain that a church which is devoid of life cannot be the means of life-giving to the dead sinners around it. No. Everything acts after its kind, and we must have a living church for living work. O that God would quicken every member of this church! "What," say you, "do you think some of us are not alive unto God?" Brethren, there are some of you concerning whom I am certain, as far as one can judge of another, that you have life, for we can see it in all that you do; but there are some others of you concerning whose spiritual life one has to exercise a good deal of faith and a great deal more charity, for we do not perceive in you much activity in God's cause, nor care for the souls of others, nor zeal for the divine glory. If we do not see any fruits, what can we do but earnestly pray that you may not turn out to be barren trees?

That is the first point, and we think it is as clear as possible that we must have the quickening power of the Spirit for ourselves if we are to be the means in the hand of God of awakening dead souls.

II. Next it is one of the peculiar offices of the Holy Spirit to ENLIGHTEN His people. He has done so by giving us His word, which He has inspired; but the Book, inspired though it be, is never spiritually understood by any man apart from the personal teaching of its great Author. You may read it as much as you will, and never discover the inner and vital sense unless your soul shall be led into it by the Holy Ghost Himself. "What," saith one, "I have learned the shorter catechism and I have got the creed by heart, and yet do I know nothing?" I answer, you have done well to learn the letter of truth, but you still need the Spirit of God to make it the light and power of God to your soul. The letter you may know, and know it better than some who know also the spirit, and I do not for a moment depreciate a knowledge of the letter, unless you suppose that there is something saving in mere head knowledge; but the Spirit of God must come, and make the letter alive to you, transfer it to your heart, set it on fire and make it burn within you, or else its divine force and majesty will be hid from your eyes. No man knows the things of God save he to whom the Spirit of God has revealed them. No carnal mind can understand spiritual things. We may use language as plain as a pikestaff, but the man who has no spiritual understanding is a blind man, and the clearest light will not enable him to see. Ye must be taught of the Lord, or you will die in ignorance. Now, my brethren, suppose that in a church there should be many who have never been thus instructed, can you not see that evil must and will come of it? Error is sure to arise where truth is not experimentally known. If professors be not taught of the Spirit their ignorance will breed conceit, pride, unbelief, and a thousand other evils. Oh, hadst thou known more of truth, my brother, thou hadst not boasted so! Oh, hadst thou seen that truth which as yet has not been revealed to thee because of thy prejudice, thou hadst not so fiercely condemned those who are better than thyself! With much zeal to do good, men have done a world of mischief through want of instruction in divine things. Sorrow too comes of ignorance. O, my brother, hadst thou known the doctrines of grace thou hadst not been so long a time in bondage! Half of the heresy in the church of God is not wilful error, but error which springs of not knowing the truth, not searching the Scriptures with a teachable heart, not submitting the mind to the light of the Holy Ghost. We should, as a rule, treat heresy rather as ignorance to be enlightened than as crime to be condemned; save, alas, that sometimes it becomes wilful perversity, when the mind is greedy after novelty, or puffed up with self-confidence; then other treatment may become painfully necessary. Beloved, if the Spirit of God will but enlighten the church thoroughly there will be an end of divisions. Schisms are generally occasioned by ignorance, and the proud spirit which will not brook correction. On the other hand, real, lasting, practical unity will exist in proportion to the unity of men's minds in the truth of God. Hence the necessity for the Spirit of God to conduct us into the whole truth. My dear brother, if you think you know a doctrine, ask the Lord to make you sure that you know it, for much that we think we know turns out to be unknown when times of trial put us to the test. Nothing do we really know unless it be burnt into out souls as with a hot iron by an experience which only the Spirit of God can give.

I think you will now see that, the Spirit of God being thus necessary for our instruction, we pre-eminently find in this gracious operation our strength for the instruction of others; for how shall those teach who have never been taught? How shall men declare a message which they have never learned? "Son of man, eat this roll"; for until thou hast eaten it thyself thy lips can never tell it out to others. "The husbandman that laboureth must first be a partaker of the fruits." It is the law of Christ's vineyard that none shall work therein till first of all they know the flavour of the fruits which grow in the sacred enclosure. Thou must know Christ, and grace, and love, and truth thyself before thou canst even be an instructor of babes for Christ.

When we come to deal with others, earnestly longing to instruct them for Jesus, we perceive even more clearly our need of the Spirit of God. Ah, my brother, you think you will put the gospel so clearly that they *must* see it; but their blind eyes overcome you. Ah! you think you will put it so zealously that they *must* feel it; but their clay-cold hearts defeat you. Old Adam is too strong for young Melancthon, depend upon that. You may think you are going to win souls by your pleadings, but you might as well stand on the top of a mountain and whistle to the wind, unless the Holy Spirit be with you. After all your talking, your hearers will, perhaps, have caught *your* idea, but the mind of the Spirit, the real soul of the gospel, you cannot impart to them; this remains, like creation itself, a work which only God can accomplish. Daily, then, let us pray for the power of the Spirit as the Illuminator. Come, O blessed light of God! thou alone canst break our personal darkness, and only when thou hast enlightened us can we lead others in Thy light. An ignorant Christian is disqualified for great usefulness; but he who is taught of God will teach transgressors God's ways, and sinners shall be converted unto Christ. Both to burn within and shine without you must have the illuminating Spirit.

III. One work of the Spirit of God is to create in believers the spirit of ADOPTION. "Because ye are sons, God hath sent forth the Spirit of His Son into your hearts, whereby ye cry, Abba, Father!" "For ye have not received the spirit of bondage again to fear, but ye have received the spirit of adoption, whereby we cry, Abba, Father!" We are regenerated by the Holy Spirit, and so receive the nature of children; and that nature, which is given by Him, He continually prompts, and excites, and develops, and matures; so that we receive day by day more and more of the child-like spirit. Now, beloved, this may not seem to you to be of great importance at first sight; but it is so; for the church is never happy except as all her members walk as dear children towards God. Sometimes the spirit of slaves creeps over us: we begin to talk of the service of God as though it were heavy and burdensome, and are discontented if we do not receive present wages and visible success, just as servants do when they are not suited; but the spirit of adoption works for love, without any hope of reward, and it is satisfied with the sweet fact of being in the Father's house, and doing the Father's will. This spirit gives peace, rest, joy, boldness, and holy familiarity with God. A man who never received the spirit of a child towards God does not know the bliss of the Christian life; he misses its flower, its savour, its excellence, and I should not wonder if the service of Christ should be a weariness to him because he has never yet got to the sweet things, and does not enjoy the green pastures, wherein the Good Shepherd makes His sheep to feed and to lie down. But when the Spirit of God makes us feel that we are sons, and we live in the house of God to go no more out for every, then the service of God is sweet and easy, and we accept the delay of apparent success as a part of the trial we are called to bear.

Now, mark you, this will have a great effect upon the outside world. A body of professors performing religion as a task, groaning along the ways of godliness with faces full of misery, like slaves who dread the lash, can have but small effect upon the sinners around them. They say, "These people serve, no doubt, a hard master, and they are denying themselves this and that; why should we be like them?" But bring me a church made up of children of God, a company of men and women whose faces shine with their heavenly Father's smile, who are accustomed to take their cares and cast them on their Father as children should, who know they are accepted and beloved, and are perfectly content with the great Father's will; put them down in the midst of a company of ungodly ones, and I will warrant you they will begin to envy them their peace and joy. Thus happy saints become most efficient operators upon the minds of the unsaved. O blessed Spirit of God! let us all now feel that we are the children of the great Father, and let our childlike love be warm this morning; so shall we be fit to go forth and proclaim the Lord's love to the prodigals who are in the far-off land among the swine.

These three points are self-evident, I think. Now to pass to a fourth.

IV. The Holy Spirit is especially called the Spirit of HOLINESS. He never suggested sin nor approved of it, nor has He ever done otherwise than grieve over it: but holiness is the Spirit's delight. The church of God wears upon her brow the words, "Holiness to the Lord." Only in proportion as she is holy may she claim to be the church of God at all. An unholy church! Surely this cannot be her of whom we read, "Christ also loved the church, and gave Himself for it; that He might sanctify and cleanse it with the washing of water by the word, that He might present it to Himself a glorious church, not having spot, or wrinkle, or any such thing." Holiness is not mere morality, not the outward keeping of divine precepts out of a hard sense of duty, while those commandments in themselves are not delighted to us. Holiness is the entirety of our manhood fully consecrated to the Lord and moulded to His will. This is the thing which the church of God must have, but it can never have it apart from the Sanctifier, for there is not a grain of holiness beneath the sky but what is of the operation of the Holy Ghost. And, brethren, if a church be destitute of holiness what effect can it have upon the world? Scoffers utterly contemn and despise professors whose inconsistent lives contradict their verbal testimonies. An unholy church may pant and struggle after dominion, and make what noise she can in pretence of work for Christ, but the kingdom comes not to the unholy, neither have they themselves entered it. The testimony of unholy men is no more acceptable to Christ than was the homage which the evil spirit gave to Him in the days of His flesh, to which He answered, "Hold thy peace." "Unto the wicked God saith, What has thou to do to declare my statutes?" The dew is witholden, and the rain cometh not in its season to the tillage of those who profess to be the servants of God and yet sow iniquity. After all, the acts of the church preach more to the world than the words of the church. Put an anointed man to preach the gospel in the midst of a really godly people and his testimony will be marvellously supported by the church with which he labours; but place the most faithful minister over an ungodly church, and he has such a weight upon him that he must first clear himself of it, or he cannot succeed. He may preach his heart out, he may pray till his knees are weary, but conversions will be sorely hindered, if indeed they occur at all. There is no likelihood of victory to Israel while Achan's curse is on the camp. An unholy church makes Christ to say that He cannot do many mighty works there because of its iniquity.

Brethren, do you not see in this point our need of the Spirit of God? And when you get to grappling terms with sinners, and have to talk to them about the necessity of holiness, and a renewed heart, and a godly life coming out of that renewed heart, do you expect ungodly men to be charmed with what you say? What cares the unregenerate mind for righteousness? Was a carnal man ever eager after holiness? Such a thing was never seen. As well expect the devil to be in love with God as an unredeemed heart to be in love with holiness. But yet the sinner must 'ove that which is pure and right, or he cannot enter heaven. *You* cannot make him do so. Who can do it but that Holy Ghost who has made you to love what once you also despised? Go not out, therefore, to battle with sin until you have taken weapons out of the armoury of the Eternal Spirit. Mountains of sin will not turn to plains at your bidding unless the Holy Ghost is pleased to make the word effectual. So then we see that as the Spirit of holiness we need the Holy Spirit.

V. Fifthly, the church needs much PRAYER, and the Holy Spirit is the Spirit of grace and of supplications. The strength of a church may pretty accurately be gauged by her prayerfulness. We cannot expect God to put forth His power unless we entreat Him so to do. But all acceptable supplication is wrought in the soul by the Holy Ghost. The first desire which God accepts must have been excited in the heart by the secret operations of the Holy One of Israel, and every subsequent pleading of every sort which containeth in it a grain of living faith, and therefore comes up as a memorial before the Lord, must have been effectually wrought in the soul by Him who maketh intercession in the saints according to the will of God. Our great High Priest will put into his censer no incense but that which the Spirit has compounded. Prayer is the creation of the Holy Ghost. We cannot do without prayer, and we cannot pray without the Holy Spirit; and hence our dependence on Him.

Furthermore, when we come to deal with sinners, we know that they must pray. "Behold he prayeth" is one of the earliest signs of the new birth. But can *we* make the sinner pray? Can any persuasion of ours lead him to his knees to breathe the penitential sigh and look to Christ for mercy? If you have attempted the conversion of a soul in your own strength you know you have failed; and so you would have failed if you had attempted the creation of one single acceptable prayer in the heart of even a little child. Oh then, dear brethren, let us cry to our heavenly Father to give the Holy Spirit to us; let us ask Him to be in us more and more mightily as the spirit of prayer, making intercession in us with groanings that cannot be uttered, that the church may not miss the divine blessing for lack of asking for it. I do verily believe this to be her present weakness, and one great cause why the kingdom of Christ does not more mightily spread; prayer is too much restrained, and hence the blessing is kept back; and it will always be restrained unless the Holy Ghost shall stimulate the desires of His people. O blessed Spirit, we pray Thee make us pray, for Jesus' sake.

VI. Sixthly, the Spirit of God is in a very remarkable manner the giver of FELLOWSHIP. So often as we pronounce the apostolic benediction we pray that we may receive the communion of the Holy Ghost. The Holy Ghost enables us to have communion with spiritual things. He alone can take the key and open up the secret mystery, that we may know the things which be of God. He gives us fellowship with God

Himself; through Jesus Christ by the Spirit we have access to the Father. Our fellowship is with the Father, and with His Son Jesus Christ, but it is the Spirit of God who brings us into communion with the Most High. So, too, my dear brethren, our fellowship with one another, so far as it is Christian fellowship, is always produced by the Spirit of God. If we have continued together in peace and love these many years, I cannot attribute it to our constitutional good tempers, nor to wise management, nor to any natural causes, but to the love into which the Spirit has baptized us, so that rebellious nature has been still. If a dozen Christian people live together for twelve months in true spiritual union and unbroken affection, trace it to the love of the Spirit; and if a dozen hundred, or four times that number shall be able to persevere in united service, and find themselves loving each other better after many years than they did at the first, let it be regarded as a blessing from the Comforter, for which he is to be devoutly adored. Fellowship can only come to us by the Spirit, but a church without fellowship would be a disorderly mob, a kingdom divided against itself, and consequently it could not prosper. You need fellowship for mutual strength, guidance, help, and encouragement, and without it your church is a mere human society.

If you are to tell upon the world you must be united as one living body. A divided church has long been the scorn of Antichrist. No sneer which comes from the Vatican has a greater sting in it than that which taunts Protestants with their divisions; and as it is with the great outward church so it is with any one particular church of Christ. Divisions are our disgrace, our weakness, our hindrance, and as the gentle Spirit alone can prevent or heal these divisions by giving us real loving fellowship with God and with one another, how dependent we are upon Him for it. Let us daily cry to Him to work in us brotherly love, and all the sweet graces which make us one with Christ, that we all may be one even as the Father is one with the Son, that the world may know that God hath indeed sent Jesus, and that we are His people.

VII. Seventhly, we need the Holy Spirit in that renowned office which is described by our Lord as THE PARACLETE, or Comforter. The word bears another rendering, which our translators have given to it in that passage where we read, "If any man sin we have an Advocate (or Paraclete) with the Father." The Holy Spirit is both Comforter and Advocate.

The Holy Spirit at this present moment is our friend and *Comforter*, sustaining the sinking spirits of believers, applying the precious promises, revealing the love of Jesus Christ to the heart. Many a heart would break if the Spirit of God had not comforted it. Many of God's dear children would have utterly died by the way if He had not bestowed upon them His divine consolations to cheer their pilgrimage. That is His work, and a very necessary work, for if believers become unhappy they become weak for many points of service. I am certain that the joy of the Lord is our strength, for I have proved it so, and proved also the opposite truth. There are on earth certain Christians who inculcate gloom as a Christian's proper state. I will not judge them, but this I will say, that in evangelistic work they do nothing, and I do not wonder. Till snow in harvest ripens wheat, till darkness makes flowers blossom, till the salt sea yields clusters bursting with new wine, you will never find

an unhappy religion promotive of the growth of the kingdom of Christ. You must have joy in the Lord, brethren, if you are to be strong *in* the Lord, and strong *for* the Lord. Now, as the Comforter alone can bear you up amid the floods of tribulation which you are sure to meet with, you see your great need of His consoling presence.

We have said that the Spirit of God is the *Advocate* of the church—not with God, for there Christ is our sole Advocate,—but with man. What is the grandest plea that the church has against the world? I answer, the indwelling of the Holy Ghost, the standing miracle of the church. External evidences are very excellent. You young men who are worried by sceptics will do well to study those valuable works which learned and devout men have with much labour produced for us, but, mark you. all the evidences of the truth of Christianity which can be gathered from analogy, from history, and from external facts, are nothing whatever compared with the operations of the Spirit of God. These are the arguments which convince. A man says to me, "I do not believe in sin, in righteousness, or in judgment." Well, brethren, the Holy Ghost can soon convince him. If he asks me for signs and evidences of the truth of the gospel, I reply, "Seest thou this woman; she was a great sinner in the very worst sense, and led others into sin, but now you cannot find more sweetness and light anywhere than in her. Hearest thou this profane swearer, persecutor, and blasphemer? He is speaking with purity, truth, and humbleness of mind. Observe yon man, who was aforetime a miser, and see how he consecrates his substance. Notice that envious, malicious spirit, and see how it becomes gentle, forgiving, and amiable through conversion. How do you account for these great changes? They are happening here every day; how come they to pass? Is that a lie which produces truth, honesty, and love? Does not every tree bear fruit after its kind? What then must that grace be which produces such blessed transformations? The wonderful phenomena of ravens turned to doves, and lions into lambs, the marvellous transformations of moral character which the minister of Christ rejoices to see wrought by the Gospel, these are our witnesses, and they are unanswerable." Peter and John have gone up to the temple, and they have healed a lame man, they are soon seized and brought before the Sanhedrim. This is the charge against them—"You have been preaching in the name of Jesus, and this Jesus is an impostor." What do Peter and John say? They need say nothing, for there stands the man that was healed; he has brought his crutch with him, and he waves it in triumph, and he runs and leaps. He was their volume of evidences, their apology, and proof. "When they saw the man that was healed standing with Peter and John, they could say nothing against them."

If we have the Spirit of God amongst us, and conversions are constantly being wrought, the Holy Spirit is thus fulfilling his advocacy, and refuting all accusers. If the Spirit works in your own mind, it will always be to you the best evidence of the gospel. I meet sometimes one piece of infidelity, and then another; for there are new doubts and fresh infidelities spawned every hour, and unstable men expect us to read all the books they choose to produce. But the effect produced on our mind is less and less. This is our answer. It is of no use your trying to stagger us, for we are already familiar with everything you suggest; our own native unbelief has outstripped you. We have had doubts of a kind which even you would not dare to utter if you knew them; for there is enough infidelity and devilry in our own nature to make us no strangers to Satan's devices. We have fought most of your suggested battles over and over again in the secret chamber of meditation, and have conquered. For *we have been in personal contact with God.* You sneer, but there is no argument in sneering. We are as honest as you are, and our witness is as good as yours in any court of law; and we solemnly declare that we have felt the power of the Holy Spirit over our soul as much as ever old ocean has felt the force of the north wind: we have been stirred to agony under a sense of sin, and we have been lifted to ecstasy of delight by faith in the righteousness of Christ. We find that in the little world within our soul the Lord Jesus manifests Himself so that we know Him. There is a potency about the doctrines we have learned which could not belong to lies, for the truths which we believe we have tested in actual experience. Tell us there is no meat? Why, we have just been feasting. Tell us there is no water in the fountain? We have been quenching our thirst. Tell us there is no such thing as light? We do not know how we can prove its existence to you, for you are probably blind, but *we* can see. That is enough argument for us, and our witness is true. Tell us there is no spiritual life? We feel it in our inmost souls. These are the answers with which the Spirit of God furnishes us, and they are part of His advocacy.

See, again, how entirely dependent we are on the Spirit of God for meeting all the various forms of unbelief which arise around us; you may have your societies for collecting evidence, and you may enlist all your bishops and doctors of divinity and professors of apologetics, and they may write rolls of evidence long enough to girdle the globe, but the only person who can savingly convince the world is the Advocate whom the Father has sent in the name of Jesus. When He reveals a man's sin, and the sure result of it, the unbeliever takes to his knees. When He takes away the scales and sets forth the crucified Redeemer, and the merit of the precious blood, all carnal reasonings are nailed to the cross. One blow of real conviction of sin will stagger the most obstinate unbeliever, and afterwards, if his unbelief return, the Holy Ghost's consolations will soon comfort it out of him. Therefore, as at the first so say I at the last, all this dependeth upon the Holy Ghost, and upon Him let us wait in the name of Jesus, beseeching Him to manifest His power among us. Amen.

THE WORD OF THE CROSS

" For the preaching of the cross is to them that perish foolishness; but unto us which are saved it is the power of God."—1 Corinthians i. 18.

NOTE well that in the seventeenth verse Paul had renounced the "wisdom of words." He says that he was sent to preach the gospel, " not with wisdom of words, lest the cross of Christ should be made of none effect." It is very clear, therefore, that there is an excellence, elegance, and eloquence of language which would deprive the gospel of its due effect. I have never yet heard that the cross of Christ was made of none effect by great plainness of speech, nor even by ruggedness of language; but it is the "wisdom of words" which is said to have this destroying power. Oh, dreadful wisdom of words! God grant that we may be delivered from making attempts at it, for we ought earnestly to shun anything and everything which can be so mischievous in its influence as to make the cross of Christ of none effect.

The "wisdom of words" works evil at times by veiling the truth which ought to be set forth in the clearest possible manner. The doctrine of atonement by blood, which is the essence of the preaching of the cross, is objectionable to many minds, and hence certain preachers take care not to state it too plainly. Prudently, as they call it,—craftily, as the apostle Paul would call it, they tone down the objectionable features of the great sacrifice, hoping by pretty phrases somewhat to remove the " offence of the cross." Proud minds object to substitution, which is the very edge of the doctrine; hence theories are adopted which leave out the idea of laying sin upon the Saviour, and making Him to be a curse for us. Self-sacrifice is set forth as possessing a high, heroic influence by which we are stimulated to self-salvation, but the Lord's suffering as the just for the unjust is not mentioned. The cross in such a case is not at all the cross by which self-condemned sinners can be comforted, and the hardened can be subdued, but quite another matter. Those who thus veil an unwelcome truth imagine that they make disciples, whereas they are only paying homage to unbelief, and comforting men in their rejection of the divine propitiation for sin. Whatever the preacher may mean in his heart, he will be guilty of the blood of souls if he does not clearly proclaim a real sacrifice for sin.

Too often the " wisdom of words " explains the gospel away. It is possible to refine a doctrine till the very soul of it is gone; you may draw such nice distinctions that the true meaning is filtered away. Certain divines tell us that they must adapt truth to the advance of the age, which means that they must murder it and fling its dead body to the dogs. It is asserted that the advanced philosophy of the nineteenth century requires a progressive theology to keep abreast of it; which simply means that a popular lie shall take the place of an offensive truth. Under pretence of winning the cultured intellects of the age, " the wisdom of words " has gradually landed us in a denial of those first principles for which the martyrs died. Apologies for the gospel, in which the essence of it is conceded to the unbeliever, are worse than infidelity. I hate that defence of the gospel which razes it to the ground to preserve it from destruction.

The " wisdom of words," however, is more frequently used with the intent of adorning the gospel, and making it to appear somewhat more beautiful than it would be in its natural form. They would paint the rose and enamel the lily, add whiteness to snow and brightness to the sun. With their wretched candles they would help us to see the stars. O superfluity of naughtiness! The cross of Christ is sublimely simple; to adorn it is to dishonour it. There is no statement under heaven more musical than this : " God was in Christ reconciling the world unto Himself, not imputing their trespasses unto them " : all the bells that you could ring to make it more harmonious would only add a jingle jangle to its heavenly melody, which is in itself so sweet that it charms the harpers before the throne of God. The doctrine that God descended upon the earth in human nature, and in that nature bore our sins, and carried our sorrows, and made expiation for our transgressions by the death of the cross, is in itself matchless poetry, the perfection of all that is ennobling in thought and creed. Yet the attempt is made to decorate the gospel, as though it needed somewhat to commend it to the understanding and the heart. The result is that men's minds are attracted from the gospel either to the preacher or to some utterly indifferent point. Hearers carry home charming morsels of poetry, but they forget the precious blood ; they recollect the elaborate metaphors so daintily wrought out, but they forget the five wounds, and fail to look unto the Lord Jesus and be saved. The truth is buried under flowers. Brethren, let us cut out of our sermons everything that takes men's minds away from the cross. One look at Jesus is better than the most attractive gazing at our gems of speech. One of the old masters found that certain vases which he had depicted upon the sacramental table attracted more notice than the face of the Lord, whom he had painted sitting at the head of the feast, and therefore he struck them out at once : let us, my brethren, do the same whenever anything of ours withdraws the mind from Jesus. Christ must ever be in the foreground, and our sermons must point to Him, or they will do more harm than good. We must preach Christ crucified, and set Him forth like the sun in the heavens, as the sole light of men.

Some seem to imagine that the gospel does not contain within itself sufficient force for its own spreading, and therefore they dream that if it is to have power among men it must either be through the logical way in which it is put—in which case all glory be to logic, or through the handsome manner in which it is stated—in which case all glory be to rhetoric. The notion is current that we should seek the aid of prestige, or talent, or novelty, or excitement ; for the gospel itself, the doctrine of the cross, is in itself impotent in its hands and lame upon its feet, and must be sustained by outside power, and carried as by a nurse whithersoever it would go. Reason, elocution, art, music, or some other force must introduce and support it, or it will make no advance—so some injuriously dream. That is not Paul's notion ; he speaks of the cross of Christ as being itself the power of God, and he says that it is to be preached "not with wisdom of words," lest the power should be attributed to the aforesaid wisdom of words, and the cross of Christ should be proven to have in itself no independent power, or, in other words, to be of none effect. Paul would not thus degrade the cross for a moment, and, therefore, though qualified to dispute with schoolmen and philosophers, he disdained to dazzle with arguments and sophistries ; and, though he himself could speak with masterly energy—let his epistles bear witness to that—yet he used great plainness of speech, that the force of his teaching might lie in the doctrine itself, and not in his language, style or delivery. He was jealous of the honour of the cross,

and would not spread it by any force but its own, even as he says in the fourth and fifth verses of the second chapter of this epistle—" My speech and my preaching was not with enticing words of man's wisdom, but in demonstration of the Spirit and of power : that your faith should not stand in the wisdom of men, but in the power of God."

Having cleared our way of the wisdom of words, we now come to the word of wisdom. Paul preached the cross, and our first head shall be *the word of the cross.* Many give the cross a bad word, and so our second head shall be *the word of its despisers concerning it,* they called it foolishness : and then, thirdly, we will think upon *the word applied to the cross by those who believe it ;* it is to them "the power of God." O that the Holy Spirit may use it as the power of God to all of us this day.

I. First, then, we speak upon " THE WORD OF THE CROSS." I borrow the term from the Revised Version, which runs thus :—" The word of the cross is to them that are perishing foolishness, but unto us who are being saved it is the power of God." This is, to my mind, an accurate translation. The original is not " the preaching of the cross," but " the word of the cross." This rendering gives us a heading for our first division and at the same time brings before us exactly what the gospel is, it is " the word of the cross."

From which I gather, first, that *the cross has one uniform teaching,* or word. We are always to preach the word of the cross, and the cross hath not many words, but one. There are not two gospels any more than there are two Gods : there are not two atonements any more than there are two Saviours. There is one gospel as there is one God, and there is one atonement as there is one Saviour. Other gospels are not tolerated among earnest Christians. What said the apostle, " If we or an angel from heaven preach any other gospel unto you than that which we have preached unto you, *let him be candidly heard and quietly fraternized with.*" Nothing of the sort. I will quote the Scripture. Paul saith, " Let him be accursed." He has no more tolerance than that for him, for Paul loved the souls of men, and for to tolerate spiritual poison is to aid and abet the murder of souls. There is no gospel under heaven, but the one gospel of Jesus Christ. But what about other voices and other words ? They are not voices from heaven, nor words from God, for he hath not in one place spoken one thing, and in another place another ; neither is it according to the spirit of the gospel that there should be one form of gospel for the first six centuries, and then another mood of it for the nineteenth century. Is it not written, " Jesus Christ, the same yesterday, to-day, and for ever " ? If the atonement were in progress, if the great sacrifice were not complete, then I could understand that there should be progress in the preaching of it ; but inasmuch as " It is finished " was pronounced by Christ upon the tree, and then He bowed His head and gave up the ghost, there can be no further development in the fact or in the doctrine. Inasmuch as the word of the Lord which describes that atonement is so complete that he that addeth thereunto shall have the plagues that are written in this book added unto him, I gather that there is no such thing as a progressive word of the cross, but that the gospel is the same gospel to-day as it was when Paul in the beginning proclaimed it. The word of the cross, since it is the express word of God, endureth for ever. Generations of men come and go like yearly growths of the grass of the field, but the word of the Lord abideth evermore the same in all places, the same to all nationalities, the same to all temperaments and constitutions of the mind. "Other foundation can no man lay than that which is laid."

From that word I gather, next, that the doctrine of the atonement is *one word in contradistinction from many other words which are constantly being uttered.* We preach Christ crucified, and His voice from the cross is "Look unto Me and be ye saved"; but another voice cries aloud, "This do and thou shalt live." We know it, it is the voice of the old covenant which the Lord Jesus hath removed, taking away the first covenant that He may establish the second. The doctrine of salvation by works, salvation by feelings, salvation by outward religiousness, is not the word of the cross, which speaketh in quite another fashion. The call to salvation by works is a strange voice within the fold of the church, and the sheep of Christ do not follow it, for they know not the voice of strangers. The word of the gospel speaketh on this wise—"The word is nigh thee, even in thy mouth, and in thy heart: that is, the word of faith, which we preach; that if you shalt confess with thy mouth the Lord Jesus, and shalt believe in thine heart that God hath raised Him from the dead, thou shalt be saved." "Believe and live" is the word of the cross.

Much less do we regard the word of ceremonialism and priestcraft which still lingers among us. We had thought it was a dull echo of the dead past, but, alas, it is a powerful voice, and is constantly lifting up itself. Priestcraft is crying, "Confess to me and thou shalt have forgiveness. Perform this ceremony, and undergo the other rite, and thou shalt receive a sacred benediction through men ordained of heaven." This voice we know not, for it is the voice of falsehood. He that believeth in Christ Jesus hath everlasting life: we are complete in Him, and we know nothing of any priest save that one High Priest, who, by His one sacrifice, hath perfected for ever them that are set apart. Voices here and there are heard like mutterings from among the tombs; these are the maunderings of superstition, saying, "Lo, here," and "Lo, there," and one man hath this revealed to him, and another that; but to none of these have we any regard; for God hath spoken, and our preaching henceforth is nothing but "the word of the cross," which is none other than the word of the crucified Son of God who loved us and gave Himself for us.

Brethren, let us hear this word of the cross, for in effect my text says, "*Let the cross speak for itself.*" That is to be our preaching. We bid reasoning and speculation hold their tongues that the cross itself may speak. We let the cross speak its own word.

First, it cries aloud, *God must be just.* The dreadful voice of justice in its certainty and severity rings through the world in the sighs and cries and death-groans of the Son of the Highest. Jesus has taken man's sin upon Himself, and He must die for it, for be sin where it may, God must smite it. The Judge of all the earth must do right, and it is right that sin should involve suffering. Supreme justice must visit iniquity with death: and therefore Jesus on the cross, though in Himself perfectly innocent and unspeakably lovely, must die the death, deserted by His Father because the iniquity of us all has been made to meet upon Him. The cross cries unto the sons of men,

"Oh, do not this abominable thing which God hates, for He will by no means spare the guilty." God must make bare His arm, and bathe His sword in heaven to smite sin wherever it is found, for He smites it even when it is imputed to His own Son! The cross thunders more terribly than Sinai itself against human sin. How it breaks men's hearts to hear its voice! How it divides men from their sins, even as the voice of the Lord breaketh the cedars of Lebanon and rends the rock in pieces! If God smites the perfect One who bears our sin, how will He smite the guilty one who rejects His love?

Let the cross speak again, and what does it say with even louder voice? *God loves men, and delights in mercy.* Though He loveth righteousness and hateth wickedness, yet He loves the sons of men, so much so that He gives His only Begotten to die that sinners may live. What more could God have done to prove His love to mankind? "God commendeth His love to us, in that, while we were yet sinners, Christ died for us." The love within that glorious deed needs no telling, it tells itself. God had but one Son, one with Himself by mystic union, and He sent Him here below to take our nature, that, being found in fashion as a man, He might die on our behalf, made sin for us that we might be made the righteousness of God in Him. "God so loved the world, that He gave His only begotten Son, that whosoever believeth in Him might not perish, but have everlasting life." The word of the cross is, "God is love"; He willeth not the death of the sinner, but that he turn unto Him and live.

What next does the cross say? Mark, we are not speaking of the crucifix. The crucifix represents Christ on the cross, but He is not on the cross any longer, He has finished His sacrificial work and has ascended to His glory. If He were still on the cross He could not save us. We now preach the cross as that on which He died who now liveth and reigneth full of ability to save. Let the bare cross speak, and it declares that *the one sacrifice is accepted and the atonement is complete.* Sin is put away, the work of reconciliation is accomplished, and Jesus hath gone up on high unto His Father's throne to plead for the guilty. Christ being raised from the dead dieth no more, death hath no more dominion over Him: He is risen for our justification, and we are accepted in Him.

> "No more the bloody spear,
> The cross and nails no more,
> For hell itself shakes at His name,
> And all the heavens adore."

Let the cross speak and it tells of ransom paid and atonement accepted. The law is magnified, justice is satisfied, mercy is no longer bound by the unsatisfied demands of judgment. "God was in Christ, reconciling the world unto Himself, not imputing their trespasses unto them; and hath committed unto us the word of reconciliation," which also is the word of the cross.

When we let the cross speak still further we hear it say—*Come and welcome!* Guilty sons of men, come and welcome to the feast of mercy, for God hath both vindicated His law and displayed His love, and now for the chief of sinners there is free and full forgiveness to be had—to be had for nothing, for the cross gives priceless blessings without price: "Whosoever will, let him take the water of life freely." Free pardon, free justification, perfect cleansing, complete salvation, these are gifts of grace bestowed upon the unworthy so soon as they believe in Christ Jesus and trust themselves with Him. This is the word of the cross ; what more can we desire to hear ? We may be forgiven in a way which shall not violate the claims of justice. God is just, and yet the justifier of Him that believeth. He is merciful and just to forgive us our sins. Oh that I knew how to be quite still, and to let the cross itself speak out with its matchless tones of mercy and majesty, love and blood, death and life, punishment and pardon, suffering and glory. It speaks in thunder and in tenderness. If we will but listen to what it hath to say it is a word by which the inmost heart of God is revealed.

Now speak I yet further the word of the cross, for in the name of Him that did hang upon the cross *I call for faith in His atonement.* The death of Christ was no ordinary matter : the dignity of His nature made it the event of the ages. He who died on the cross was very God of very God, as well as man, and His sacrifice is not to be neglected or rejected with impunity. Such a divine marvel demands our careful thought and joyful confidence. To do despite to the blood of the Son of God is to sin with a vengeance. God demands faith in His Son, and especially in His Son dying for our sakes. We ought to believe every word that God has spoken, but above all the word of the cross. Shall we doubt the good faith and love of God when He gives His Son a hostage for His word, and offers up the Only-begotten as the token of His grace ! Oh, men, whatever ye trifle with, disregard not the Son of God ! Whatever presumption ye commit, yet trample not upon the cross of Jesus. This is the highest thought of God, the centre of all His counsels, the topmost summit of the mighty alp of divine lovingkindness. Do not think little of it or turn away from it. I beseech you, nay command you, in the name of Him that liveth and was dead, look to the dying Saviour and live : if ye do not so ye shall answer for it in that day when He shall come upon the clouds of heaven to avenge Him of His adversaries. Thus have I set before you the word of the cross ; may the Holy Ghost bless the message.

II. We have the unpleasant task, in the second place, of listening to THE WORD OF ITS DESPISERS. They call the doctrine of the atonement "*foolishness.*" Numbers of men call the doctrine of salvation by the blood of Christ " foolishness." It is most assuredly the wisdom of God, and the power of God, but they stick at the first assertion and will not acknowledge the wisdom of the wondrous plan, it is therefore no wonder that they never feel its power. No, it is foolishness to them ; a thing beneath their contempt. And why foolishness ? " Because," say they, " see how the common people take it up. Everybody can understand it. You believe that Jesus is a substitute for you, and you sing with the poorest of the poor—

> ' I do believe, I will believe
>   That Jesus died for me ;
> And on the cross He shed His blood
>   From sin to set me free.' "

" There," say they, " that's a pretty ditty for educated men. Why, the very children sing it, and are able to believe it, and talk of it. Pshaw, it is sheer foolishness ! We don't want anything so vulgar and commonplace. Don't you know that we take in a high-class review, and read the best thought of the times ? You don't suppose we are going to believe just as common ploughboys and servant girls may do ? " Ah me ! How mighty wise some people think themselves ! Is every truth which can be understood by simple minds to be thrown aside as foolishness ? Is nothing worth knowing except the fancy thinking of the select portion of humanity ? Are the well-known facts of nature foolishness because they are open to all ? Is it quite certain that all the wisdom in the world dwells with the superfine gentlemen who sneer at everything and take in a review ? These superficial readers of superior literature, are they the umpires of truth ? I wish that their culture had taught them modesty. Those who glorify themselves and sneer at others are usually not wise, but otherwise ; and those who call other people fools may be looking in the glass, and not out of the window. He who is truly wise has some respect for others, and the profoundest respect for the word of God.

But why is it that you count the gospel of the cross to be foolishness ? It is this : because this religion of ours, this doctrine of the cross, is not the offspring of reason, but the gift of revelation. All the thinkers of the ages continued to think, but they never invented a plan of salvation in which divine justice and mercy should be equally conspicuous. The cross was not in all their thoughts. How could it be ? As a thought it originated with the infinite mind, and could have originated nowhere else. The doctrine of the cross is not a speculation, but a revelation : and for this reason the learned ones cannot endure it. It is God telling men something which they could not else have known, and this suits not the profound thinkers, who cannot bear to be told anything, but must needs excogitate everything, evolving it from their inner consciousness, or from the depths of their vast minds. Now, inasmuch as nothing can come out of a man that is not in him, and as the supreme love of God never was in such an unlovely thing as an unregenerate man, it happens that the doctrine of atonement never originated with man but was taught to him by God at the gates of Eden. The plan which blends vengeance and love, was never invented by human imagination. Since man has such an aversion to the great atonement, he could not have been the author of the idea, and he was not the author of it ; God alone reveals it in language that babes may understand and therefore carnal pride calls it " foolishness."

Besides, the carnal man thinks it foolishness because it makes him out to be a fool, and you may take my word for it that anything which proves either you or me to be a fool will at once strike us as being very foolish. Our conscience is dull, and therefore we retaliate upon those who tell us unpleasant truth. " Why, am I nobody after all ? I, bound in the best black cloth, and wearing a white cravat ? So religious and so respectable, so thoughtful, so studious, so profound, am I to be nobody ? Do you dare to say to me, ' Except ye be converted and become as little children, ye shall in no wise enter the kingdom ' ! My dear sir, you cannot know what you are talking about. Why, I am a professor, a philosopher, a doctor of divinity, and therefore you cannot really mean that I am to receive truth as a little child ! Such talk is foolishness." Of course they say so. We always reckoned that they would say so. I have rejoiced when I have read the sceptical papers, and have seen how they sneer at the old-fashioned gospel. The Bible said that carnal men could not receive spiritual things ; how truthful is its statement ? It is written, " There shall come in the last days scoffers." Here, they are hastening to prove by their conduct the things which they deny. One is grieved that any should scoff, and yet in a measure we are rejoiced to find such confirmation of truth from the lips of her enemies. As long as the world lasts ungodly men will despise a revelation which they are unable to understand ; it is beyond their sphere, and therefore its preachers seem to be babblers and its doctrines to be foolishness.

But, in very deed, it may well seem foolishness to them, for it treats on subjects for which they have no care. If I were able to explain to a general audience how to make unlimited profit upon the Stock Exchange, or in some other market, all the world would listen with profound attention ; and if I put my point clearly I should be pronounced a really clever preacher, a man well worth hearing ; but when the sermon is only about the word of God, and eternity, and the soul, and the blood of Jesus— most people turn on their heel ; they are not sure that they have souls, and they refuse to argue upon the supposition of a future existence, which is an old wife's fable to them. As for eternity their philosophy has no room for it, and they do not concern themselves about it. One said in argument the other day, " I believe I shall die like a dog." I could give him no better reply on the spur of the moment than to say, " If I had known that you were a dog I would have brought you a bone." As I had the notion that he would live for ever I came to talk to him upon subjects suitable to an immortal being, but as I found out that he was going to die like a dog, what could I do for him but provide such cheer as the creature could enjoy ? These men call the gospel foolishness because they look after the main chance, and care more for the body than for the soul. One of their wise men said, " Why do you preach so much about the world to come, why not preach about the world which now is ? Teach these people how to ventilate their sewers, that is a much more needful matter than their believing on Jesus." Well, sanitary matters are important, and if any of you feel that you have nothing to live for but ventilating sewers I wish you would live at a great rate, and get it done as quickly as you can. Meanwhile, as we are convinced of the need of other things besides drainage, and as many of us expect soon to take our happy flight to a place where there are no sewers to ventilate, we shall look into those things which concern our future life, seeing they also fit us for the life which now is.

They call the word of the cross foolishness, because they regard all the truths with which it deals as insignificant trifles. " Soul ! " say they, " what matters whether we have a soul or not ? Sin—what is it but the blunder of a poor creature who knows no better ? " Of all things, the eternal God is the greatest trifle to unbelieving men. It is merely a name to swear by, that is all. They admit that there may be a great master force in nature, or an energy co-extensive with the existence of matter, hence they allow Theism or Pantheism, but they will not endure a personal God whom they are bound to obey. Theism and pantheism are only masks for atheism. These men will have no personal God who loves them, and whom they love. God is a nonentity to them, and therefore when we speak of God as real,

and sin as real, and heaven as real—and God knoweth they are the only real things—then straightway they mutter " Foolishness." As for us, we deplore their folly, and pray God to teach them better. Having entered by a new birth into the realm of spiritual things we know the reality and power of the word of the cross.

Now, brethren, I say of these gentlemen who pronounce the gospel foolishness that you need not take much notice of them, because they are not capable witnesses, they are not qualified to form a judgment upon the subject. I do not depreciate their abilities in other respects, but it is certain that a blind man is no judge of colours, a deaf man is no judge of sound, and a man who has never been quickened into spiritual life can have no judgment as to spiritual things. How can he ? I, for instance, have felt the power of the gospel, and I assert that I have done so. Another man declares that I am not speaking the truth. Why not ? Because he has not himself felt that power. Is that sound reasoning ? Have you not heard of the Irishman who, when five men swore that they saw him commit a theft, made answer that he could produce fifty people who did not see him do it. Would there have been any force in that negative evidence ? And what if all the world except two men should say, " We do not feel the power of the cross," would that be any evidence against the fact asserted by the two ? I trow not. Two honest men who witness to a fact are to be believed, even though twenty thousand persons are unable to bear such witness. The unspiritual are incapable witnesses ; they put themselves out of court, for at the outset they assert that they are not cognizant of those things concerning which we bear testimony. Their assertion is that they never were the subjects of spiritual influences, and we quite believe what they say ; but we do not believe them when they go further, and assert that therefore what we have seen, and tasted, and handled is all a delusion. Concerning that matter they are not capable witnesses.

And I beg you to notice that those who call the gospel of the cross folly are themselves, if rightly looked at, proofs of their own folly and of the sad results of unbelief. The Christians in Paul's days felt that the gospel had emancipated them from the bondage of idolatry and vice, and when they heard others that were captives under these delusions telling them that the emancipating force was foolish- ness, they looked at them, and smiled at the absurdity of the statement. They noticed that such men were themselves perishing. What a calamity it is for a man to be perishing ! A house is unoccupied, its floor is untrodden, its hearth knows no genial glow. It suffers from neglect, it is perishing. Men who are not living to God are missing the end of their being, and like deserted houses are falling into ruin : they are perishing. While unoccupied by good, such minds are surrounded by powers of evil. Yonder is a tree, I have seen many such : around its trunk the ivy has twisted itself, grasping it like a huge python, and crushing it in its folds. The tree is perishing, its very life is being sucked out by the parasite that grasps it. Multitudes of men have about them lusts and sins, and errors that are eating out their life— they are perishing. Their souls and characters are as timber devoured by dry rot, it remains in the fabric of the house, but it is perishing. Ungodly men are devoured by their own pride, eaten up by self-confidence. Unbelieving men are comparable to a ship that is drifting to destruction : it has snapped its cable, it is nearing the rocks, it will be broken to pieces, it is perishing ! Those that believe not in Jesus are drifting towards a sure immortality of misery, they are daily perishing ; and yet while they perish, they condemn the means of rescue. Fancy drowning mariners mocking at the life-boat ! Imagine a diseased man ridiculing the only remedy. That which we have tried and proved they call "foolishness" : we have only to answer them, "Ye are yourselves, as ye remain captives to your sins, the victims of foolishness. Ye are yourselves, as ye waste your lives, as ye drift to destruction, proofs that the foolishness is not in the cross, but in you that reject it." The preaching of the cross is to them that perish foolishness, but to nobody else. O that their hearts were changed by the power of the word, then would they see all wisdom in the word of the cross.

III. We come, in the third place, to notice THE WORD OF THOSE WHO BELIEVE. What do they say of the cross ? They call it *power*, the power of God. The more we study the gospel the more we are surprised at the singular display of wisdom which it contains ; but we will not say much upon that point, for we are not qualified to be judges of wisdom. But we do say this, the word of the cross is power ; it has been the power of God to us, it has worked upon us as nothing else has ever done. Its work upon many of us has been so remarkable that even onlookers must have been surprised at it.

The phenomenon of conversion is a fact. Men and women are totally changed, and the whole manner of their life is altered. It is of no use to deny the fact, for instances of it come before us every day ; unbelievers become devout, the immoral become pure, the dishonest become upright, the blasphemous become gracious, the unchaste become holy. Evil ways are on a sudden deserted, and penitents struggle towards virtue. We see persons in all ranks of society undergoing a radical transformation,—self-satisfied people are humbled by the discovery of their unworthiness, and others who were steeped in immorality renounce their vicious pleasures and seek happiness in the service of God. How do you account for this ? We who are the subjects of such a change account for it in this way,—it is wrought by the doctrine of the cross, and the power which accomplishes the change is the power of God. No force less than divine could have effected so great a change. The word of the cross has delivered us from the love of sin : no sin is now our master, we have broken every fetter of evil habit. We fall into sin, but we mourn over it, and hate the sin, and hate ourselves for committing it. We have been clean delivered from the bondage of corruption, and made free to serve the Lord. We have also been delivered from the dread which once bowed us down, a horrible dread which held us in bondage, and made us tremble before our Father and our friend. We thought hardly of God and fled from Him ; from this we are now delivered, for now we love Him and delight in Him, and the nearer we can approach Him the happier we are.

We have been delivered, also, from the power of Satan. That evil prince has great power over men, and once we were led captive at his will. Even now he attacks us, but we overcome him through the blood of the Lamb. We are also daily delivered from self and from the world, and from all things that would enthral us. We are being saved ; yes, we are saved.

Every day a saving force is operating upon us to set us free from the thraldom of corruption. This we feel and know. We are bound for the kingdom, and nothing can keep us back : we are bound for purity, for ultimate perfection : we feel eternal life within us, urging us upward and onward, beyond ourselves and our surroundings. We sit here like eagles, chained to the rock by the feebleness of our bodies, but the aspiration within us tells us that we are born to soar among pure and glorified spirits. We feel that heaven is born within us,—born by the word of the cross through the Spirit. We could tell the histories of some here present, or, better still, they could tell them themselves, histories of changes sudden but complete, marvellous but enduring, changes from darkness to light, from death to life. How gladly could we detain you with details of our being upheld when our temptations have been almost overwhelming, and kept pressing forward in Christ's service when we had been altogether without strength had not the word of the cross poured new energy into us. We have been ready to die in despair until we have looked to the cross, and then the clouds have yielded to clear shining. A sight of the bleeding Saviour, and a touch of His hand have made us men again, and we have lifted up our heads as from among the dead. Under the power of the cross we still advance from strength to strength : there is power in the word of the cross to make a man grow into something nobler than he ever dreamed of. We shall not know what we shall be till we shall see our Lord and Saviour as He is.

Why, brethren, the power with which God created the world was no greater than the power with which He made us new men in Christ Jesus. The power with which He sustains the world is not greater than the power by which He sustains His people under trial and temptation ; and even the raising of the dead at the end of the world will be no greater display of divine power than the raising of dead souls out of their spiritual graves. These wonders of power are being performed in our own experience every day of the week, entirely through the cross. I appeal to you who are truly converted, were you converted through the wisdom of man ? I appeal to you that are kept from sinning, are you led towards holiness by the power of elocution, of rhetoric, or of logic ? I appeal to you who are despairing, are you ever revived by musical words and rhythmical sentences ? Or do you owe all to Jesus crucified ? What is your life, my brethren, but the cross ? Whence comes the bread of your soul but from the cross ? What is your joy but the cross ? What is your delight, what is your heaven, but the Blessed One, once crucified for you, who ever liveth to make intercession for you ? Cling to the cross, then. Put both arms around it ! Hold to the Crucified, and never let Him go. Come afresh to the cross at this moment, and rest there now and for ever ! Then, with the power of God resting upon you, go forth and preach the cross ! Tell out the story of the bleeding Lamb. Repeat the wondrous tale, and nothing else. Never mind how you do it, only proclaim that Jesus died for sinners. The cross held up by a babe's hand is just as powerful as if a giant held it up. The power lies in the word itself, or rather in the Holy Spirit who works by it and with it.

Brethren, believe in the power of the cross for the conversion of those around you. Do not say of any man that he cannot be saved. The blood of

Jesus is omnipotent. Do not say of any district that it is too sunken, or of any class of men that they are too far gone : the word of the cross reclaims the lost. Believe it to be the power of God, and you shall find it so. Believe in Christ crucified, and preach boldly in His name, and you shall see great things and gladsome things. Do not doubt the ultimate triumph of Christianity. Do not let a mistrust flit across your soul. The cross must conquer ; it must blossom with a crown, a crown commensurate with the person of the Crucified, and the bitterness of His agony. His reward shall parallel His sorrows. Trust in God, and lift your banner high, and now with psalms and songs advance to battle, for the Lord of hosts is with us, the Son of the Highest leads our van. Onward, with blast of silver trumpet and shout of those that seize the spoil. Let no man's heart fail him ! Christ hath died ! Atonement is complete ! God is satisfied ! Peace is proclaimed ! Heaven glitters with proofs of mercy already bestowed upon ten thousand times ten thousand ! Hell is trembling, heaven adoring, earth waiting. Advance, ye saints, to certain victory ! You shall overcome through the blood of the Lamb.

THE FOURFOLD TREASURE

" But of Him are ye in Christ Jesus, who of God is made unto us wisdom, and righteousness, and sanctification, and redemption : that, according as it is written, he that glorieth, let him glory in the Lord."—1 Corinthians i. 30-31.

WE meet somewhere in the Old Testament with the expression " salt without prescribing how much." Beyond all question the name, person, and work of Jesus are the salt and savour of every true gospel ministry, and we cannot have too much of them. Alas ! that in so many ministries there is such a lack of this first dainty of the feast, this essence of all soul-satisfying doctrine. We may preach Christ without prescribing how much, only the more we extol him the better. It would be impossible to sin by excess in preaching Christ crucified. It was an ancient precept, " With all thine offerings thou shalt offer salt " ; let it stand as an ordinance of the sanctuary now : " With all thy sermonisings and discoursings thou shalt ever mingle the name of Jesus Christ ; thou shalt ever seek to magnify the alpha and omega of the plan of redemption." The apostle in the first chapter of this epistle was anxious to speak to the Corinthians about their divisions and other serious faults ; but he could not confine himself to that unpleasant theme ; as naturally as possible his heart bounded over the mountains of division to his Lord and Master. Divisions did but remind him of the great uniting one who has made all his people one, and human follies did but drive him nearer to the infallible Christ who is the wisdom of God. Though Paul had to write many sharp things to those ancient Plymouth Brethren at Corinth, yet how sweetly did he prevent all bitterness by dipping his pen in the honeyed ink of love to the Lord Jesus, and admiration of His person and work ! Let us, dear friends, if we have to preach, preach Christ crucified ; and if we are private persons, let us in our household life, and in all our conversation, make His name to be as ointment poured forth. Let your life be Christ living in you. May you be like Asher, of whom it is said, he dipped his foot in oil ; may you be so anointed with the Spirit of your Lord that wherever you put down your foot, you may leave an impression of grace. The balmy south wind bears token of having passed over sunny lands ; may the ordinary bent and current of your life bear evidence in it that you have communed with Jesus.

To-night we have before us a text which is extraordinarily comprehensive, and contains infinitely more of meaning than mind shall grasp, or tongue shall utter at this hour. Considering it carefully, let us observe, first, that the apostle here attributes the fact that we are in Christ Jesus to the Lord alone. He shows that there is a connection between our very being as Christians, and the love and grace of God in Christ. " Of Him " (that is of God) " are ye in Christ Jesus." So we will first speak about our *spiritual existence*. Then Paul goes on to write of *our spiritual wealth*, which he sums up under four heads : wisdom, righteousness, sanctification, and redemption ; but which indeed, I might say, he sums up under one head, for he declares that Christ is made of God unto us all these four things : and then he closes the chapter by telling us where *our glorying* ought to go—it should return to the source of our spiritual existence and heavenly wealth. " He that glorieth, let him glory in the Lord."

I. To begin, then, where God began with us— OUR SPIRITUAL EXISTENCE.

" Of him are ye in Christ Jesus." Different translators have read this passage in divers ways. " Of Him," they think properly should be " Through Him " : that is, " Through God we are in Christ Jesus." Are you this day united to Christ—a stone in that building, of which He is both foundation and topstone—a limb of that mystical body, of which He is the head ? Then you did not get there of yourself. No stone in that wall leaped into its place ; no member of that body was its own creator. You come to be in union with Christ through God the Father. You were ordained unto this grace by His own purpose, the purpose of the Infinite Jehovah, who chose you, or ever the earth was. " Ye have not chosen Me, but I have chosen you." The first cause of your union with Christ lies in the purpose of God who gave you grace in Christ Jesus from before the foundation of the world. And as to the purpose, so to the power of God is your union with Christ to be attributed. He brought you into Christ ; you were a stranger, He brought you near ; you were an enemy, He reconciled you. You had never come to Christ to seek for mercy if first of all the Spirit of God had not appeared to you to show you your need, and to lead you to cry for the mercy that you needed. Through God's operation as well as through God's decree you are this day in Christ Jesus. It will do your souls good, my brethren, to think of this very common-place truth. Many days have passed since your conversion, it may be, but do not forget what a high day the day of your new birth was ; and do not cease to give glory to that mighty power which brought you out of darkness into marvellous light. You did not convert yourself ; if you did, you still have need to be converted again. Your regeneration was not of the will of man, nor of blood, nor of birth ; if it were so, let me tell you the sooner you are rid of it the better. The only true regeneration is of the will of God and by the operation of the Holy Ghost. " By the grace of God I am what I am." He " hath begotten us again unto a lively hope." " He that hath wrought us to the selfsame thing is God." " Of Him are ye in Christ Jesus." Through the operation and will and purpose of God are you this day a member of Christ's body and one with Jesus. Give all the glory, then, to the Lord alone.

But suppose we read it as we have it in the text, and then we shall not have an illusion to the source of our spiritual life, but to the dignity of it. " Of God are ye in Christ Jesus." Being in Christ you are of God. Not of the earth earthy now, not of Satan, not of the bondage of the law, not of the powers of evil, but of God are you ; God's husbandry, God's people, God's children, God's beloved ones. " Ye are of God," little children, " and the whole world lieth in wickedness." On you hath God's light shone, to you hath God's life come, in you God's love is made manifest, and in you shall God's glory be fully revealed. What a dignity is this to be " of God ! " Some have thought it a great thing to have it said, " These are they which are of the prince's household," and others have been yet more boastful when they have been pointed at as parts of an imperial court ; but you are of the divine family, descended from Him who only hath immortality. " They shall be Mine, saith the Lord, in the day when I make up My jewels." " For the Lord's portion is His people, Jacob is the lot of His inheritance." Of God, are you, every one of you who are in Christ Jesus : ye are Christ's, and Christ is God's. The Creator, the Upholder, the Sublime, the Invisible, the Infinite, the Eternal claims you. You have a part and lot with Him, and you are herein uplifted to the highest degree of exaltation because you are in Christ.

Here, then, you have the dignity of the Christian life—it is of God, as its source is through God.

But note the essence of the Christian life. " Of God are ye in Christ Jesus." You have no life before the Lord, except as you are in Christ Jesus. Apart from Him, you are as the branch that is severed from the vine—dead, withered, useless, obnoxious, rotten. Men gather these branches, and cast them into the fire, and they are burned. A ghastly sight it must be on the battle-field, to see on all sides arms, legs, and various portions of limbs torn away from the bodies to which they belonged, and scattered in hideous disorder ! Once of the utmost service, these severed limbs are useless now. Every one knows that they are dead, for they cannot live divided from the vital regions : even thus if you and I could be separated from Christ, our vital head, death—spiritual death—must be the inevitable result. Our life hinges upon union to our Lord. " Because I live, ye shall live also." Out of Christ we abide in death, but in Christ we live, and we are of God. Our spiritual being, and the fact that our spiritual being is an exalted one, both hang upon this—that we are in Christ. Beloved Christian friends, I can congratulate you upon your being able to know that you are in Christ, and that so you are of God; but I must not speak so broadly to all this congregation. I must rather put a grave enquiry, and ask each of my hearers : Are you all in Christ Jesus ? Could the apostle write to you, and say, " Of God are you in Christ Jesus." Have you ever been the subject of a work of God, putting you into Christ Jesus ? Are you now of God in Christ Jesus, so as to be depending for everything upon Him, dwelling in Him, and He in you ; feeling His life within you, and that your life is hid with Him in God ? Beloved hearer, there is no joy in this world like union with Christ. The more we can feel it, the happier we are, whatever our circumstances may be. But if you are without Christ, you are without hope. Joy comes not where Jesus comes not. No Saviour, then no peace in life or death. Oh remember, beloved hearer, that you will soon die. Where, where will you look for consolation in your last moments ? Your soul will soon have to fly through tracks unknown, and face the burning throne of judgment. What will you do then, without the hand of love to guide you and the righteousness of Christ to cover you ? He who wraps Himself about with Christ's matchless robe can say—

" Bold shall I stand in that great day,
For who aught to my charge shall lay ?
While through Thy blood absolved I am
From sin's tremendous curse and shame."

But he that hath no Saviour, it were better for him that he had never been born. That day is cursed and hath no blessing, on which he first saw the light. Jesus Christ is willing to receive you if you desire to come to Him. Noah's ark was shut, but not until the flood came, it was open till then ; Christ is the ark of the covenant, and the door is not shut yet. Let not this, however, cause you to delay, for the flood will rise, and the rains will fall and then to those who shall knock at the door, it will be said, " Too late ! too late ! Ye cannot enter now."

Of Him, beloved believers in Christ, are ye in Christ Jesus. All you are, even to your bare existence as Christians, you have to trace to "the God and Father of our Lord Jesus Christ, which according to His abundant mercy hath begotten us again unto a lively hope by the resurrection of Jesus Christ from the dead, to an inheritance incorruptible and undefiled and that fadeth not away."

II. Now let us turn to the second part of our subject, and contemplate OUR SPIRITUAL WEALTH. Christ Jesus is of God made unto us wisdom, righteousness, sanctification, and redemption. Here are four things—only it is to be noticed that in the original Greek the second and third have a peculiar connecting link, which the others have not. The wisdom stands alone, and the redemption, but the righteousness and sanctification have a special link, as though we should be taught that they always go together, that they should always be considered as united,—a warning to modern theology, which so often divideth what God hath joined together.

Let us take the first blessing first, asking to be partakers of it at this very moment. Jesus Christ is made unto us wisdom. You noticed when we read the chapter that the apostle had been speaking of some other wisdom which he treated somewhat roughly. It had set itself up in opposition to the cross of Christ, and the apostle handled it with no gentle handling. There have always been those in the world who have conceived that wisdom would come to them as the result of the exercise of their own thoughts assisted by culture ; that is to say, they hoped to know divine truth by their own thoughts and the additional light arising from the thoughts of other men. They fancied that wisdom would rise out of the human mind, and would not need to be taught us from above. There were those in Paul's days who were always ruminating, considering, contemplating with themselves, and then disputing, dialoguing, and conversing with others. These were the philosophers of the time. They looked for wisdom through man, and expected to find it in the shallow brain of a poor son of Adam. They so believed that they themselves were wise ; that though they affected modesty and did not call themselves "the Sophoi, or wise," but "the Philosophoi," or lovers of wisdom, yet for all that, in their innermost hearts they esteemed themselves to be an inner circle of instructed persons, and they looked upon the rest of mankind as the unilluminated and the ignorant. They had found a treasure which they kept to themselves, and virtually said to their fellow-men, "You are almost without exception hopelessly ignorant," Now, the apostle, instead of pointing to his own brain, or pointing to the statue of Socrates or Solon, says Jesus Christ is made of God unto us wisdom. We look no more for wisdom from the thoughts that spring of human mind, but to Christ Himself ; we do not expect wisdom to come to us through the culture that is of man, but we expect to be made wise through sitting at our Master's feet and accepting Him as wisdom from God Himself. Now, as it was in the apostle's day, so is it very much at this present. There are those who will have it that the gospel—the simple gospel—such as might have been preached by John Bunyan, or Whitfield, or Wesley, and others, was very well for the many, and for the dark times in which they lived——the great mass of mankind would be helped and improved by it ; but there is wanted, according to the wiseacres of this intensely luminous century, a more progressive theology, far in advance of the Evangelism now so generally ridiculed. Men of mind, gentlemen of profound thought, are to teach us doctrines that were unknown to our fathers ; we are to go on improving in our knowledge of divine truth till we leave Peter and Paul, and those other old dogmatists far behind. Nobody knows how wise we are to become. Brethren, our thoughts loathe this ; we hate this cant about progress and deep thought : we only wish we could know as much of Christ as the olden preachers did. We are afraid that instead of getting into greater light through the thinkings of men, the speculations and contemplations of the scribes, ancient and modern, and the discoveries of the intellectual and eclectic, have made darkness worse, and have quenched some of the light that was in the world. Again has it been fulfilled : "I will destroy the wisdom of the wise, and will bring to nothing the understanding of the prudent. Where is the wise ? where is the scribe ? where is the disputer of this world ? hath not God made foolish the wisdom of this world ? " It seemeth to me to be greater wisdom to believe what Christ hath said than to believe what my deepest thoughts have discovered ; and though I have thought long upon a subject, and turned it over and over, and think I know more of it than another man, yet, in one single word of Christ there is more wisdom than in all my thoughts and ruminatings. I am never to look to myself for wisdom, and to fancy that I am the creator of truth or the revealer of it ; but ever to go to Him, my Lord, my teacher, my all, and to believe that the highest culture, the best results of the highest education are to be found by sitting at His feet and the best results of the deepest meditation, too,

are to be gained in lying down in the green pastures, beside the still waters, where He, as the Good Shepherd, leads me. Brethren, when we read that Christ is made of God unto us wisdom, let us recollect what wisdom is. Wisdom is, I suppose, the right use of knowledge. To know is not to be wise. Many men know a great deal, and are all the more fools for what they know. There is not fool so great a fool as a knowing fool. But to know how to use knowledge is to have wisdom. Now, that man is wise in three respects who has Christ for his wisdom. Christ's *teaching* will make him wise of thought, and wise of heart. All you want to know of God, of sin, of life, of death, of eternity, of predestination, of man's responsibility, Christ has either personally, or by His Spirit in the word of God, taught you. Anything that you find out for yourself, anything over and above revelation, is folly, but whatever He has taught is wisdom ; and He has so taught it that if you learn it, in the spirit in which He would have you learn it, it will not be dry, dead doctrine to you, but spirit and life ; and His teaching will endow you with wisdom as well as knowledge. Scholars at the cross-foot let us always be. Never let us go to any other school than Schola crucis, for the learners of the cross are the favourites of wisdom. Let Corpus Christi be the college in which we study. To know Jesus, and the power of His resurrection, this is wisdom.

But, in addition to profiting by our Lord's instruction, the Christian learns wisdom through his Master's *example*. " Wherewithal shall a young man cleanse his way ? " How shall I be made wise in action ? Policy says, " Adopt this expedient and the other " ; and the mass of mankind at this age are guided by the policy of the hour ; but policy is seeming wisdom and real folly. Remember it is always wisest to act in any condition as Jesus would have acted, supposing Him to have been in that condition. Never did He temporise. Principle guided Him, not fashion nor personal advantage. You shall never be a fool if you follow Christ, except in the estimation of fools ; and who wishes to be wise in a fool's esteem ? But, sometimes it may be said : " To do as Christ would have done would involve me in present difficulty or loss." It is true : but there is no man that loseth aught in this life for Christ's sake who shall remain a loser, for he shall receive tenfold in this life, and in the world to come life everlasting. The wisest action is not always the most pecuniarily profitable. It is wise sometimes for men to be poor, ay, even to lose their lives. Truest wisdom—not sham wisdom, not temporary wisdom—you shall manifest by following the example of Christ, though it lead you to prison or to death. His teachings and His example, together, will give you the wisdom which cometh from above.

Above all, if you have the Redeemer's *presence*, He will be made of God unto you wisdom in a very remarkable sense. Never forget or doubt that Jesus is still with His people. They who know how to enter into the secret place of the tabernacles of the Most High, find Him still at the mercy-seat. He feedeth among the lilies, and they who know the lilies know where to find Him ; and those who live with Him, and catch His spirit, have their garments perfumed as His are with myrrh, and aloes, and cassia. These may be thought to be mad by some, and others may call them fanatical enthusiasts ; but these are the wisest of mankind. O happy men that live at the gates of heaven while yet on earth, that sit at the feet of the blessed in the heavenly places in Christ Jesus while they are toiling along through the pilgrimage of this life ! This is to be wise, to have Christ's teaching, Christ's example, and above all, Christ's presence ; so may the poorest find the Lord Jesus made of God unto them wisdom.

Pause just a minute. Let none of us ever be so foolish as to suppose that when we have received Jesus and His gospel, we have occasion to blush when we are in the company of the very wisest of the present day. Carry a bold face when you confront the brazen faced philosophy which insults your Lord. The man who does not believe the Bible does not know so much as thou dost. Blush not, though with mimic wisdom the unbeliever tries to laugh or argue thee down. He who knows not Christ, though he propounds wonderful theories as to the creation of mankind and the formation of the world, and though he has a glib tongue, is only an educated fool, a learned idiot, who thinks his own rushlight brighter than God's own sun. "Ah ! but he has been to college, and he has a degree, and he is esteemed by men ; for he has written books that nobody can comprehend." "The fool hath said in his heart, There is no God " ; and I do not care even if he be a Solon, if he has said that there is no God, he is a fool. Do not blush, then, if you find yourself in his company; do not make yourself the blushing one because the fool is there. Self-conceit were to be avoided and loathed ; but this is not self-conceit, but a holy courage in a case which demands of you to be courageous. To know Christ is the best of all philosophy, the highest of all sciences. Angels desire to look into this ; but I do not know that they care a fig for half the sciences so valued among men. If you know Christ you never need be afraid of being ashamed and confounded whatever company you may be in. If you stood in a senate of emperors, or amidst a parliament of philosophers, and only told them of the God that came in human flesh, and loved, and lived, and died to redeem mankind, you would have told them a greater mystery and a profounder secret than reason could discover. Be not ashamed, then, amid the intellectual pride of this boastful age.

At the same time let me remind you of another evil ; do not seek to complete your wisdom at any other source : be satisfied that in keeping close to Christ you have the highest and truest wisdom. As I would not have you cowed before the pretender, neither would I have you envy him, or seek to supplement the wisdom that is in Christ Jesus by the wisdom that is of man. Are you so foolish, having begun with Jesus, will you end with a German neologian, or a French wit, or a Puseyite dreamer ? Have you taken Christ's word to be your guide, and will you go and tack on to that some decree of Convocation, some rubric of a church, some minute of Conference, or other invention of human brain and fallen fancy ? God forbid ! Array yourself solely in this armour of gold, and go forth and gleam in the sun, and angels themselves shall marvel at you as they see your brightness. "Jesus Christ is made of God unto you wisdom."

It is high time for us to proceed to review the next blessing. He is made of God unto us *righteousness*. This was a great want of ours, for naturally we were unrighteous, and to this hour in ourselves we are the same. Righteous we must be to be acceptable with God, but righteous we certainly are

not personally, and by merit. All our righteousnesses are as filthy rags, and we are unable to stand before the Great King ; but there is one who says : " Take away his filthy garments from him," and that same Deliverer, even the Lord Jesus Christ, is made of God unto us righteousness. You know how we usually speak of this as a double work. His blood cleanseth us from all guilt ; by it pardon is bestowed upon the believer. He that looks to Christ is absolved from all sin—completely so. Then, in addition to that cleansing, which we call pardon, there is the clothing, the arraying in the righteousness of Christ— in a word, there is justification by faith. The doctrine of imputed righteousness seems to me to be firmly established in the word of God. Yet I have sometimes fancied I have heard a little too much stress put upon the word "imputed," and scarcely enough upon the word "righteousness" ; for though I know that righteousness is imputed to us, yet I believe it is not all the truth that we are righteous by imputation. It is true, most true, but there is something true beyond it. Not only is Christ's righteousness imputed to me, but it is mine actually, for Christ is mine. He who believes in Jesus, has Jesus Christ to be his own Christ, and the righteousness of Christ belongs to that believer, and is his. We are not merely imputedly righteous, but the righteousness of our Substitute is legally, actually, truly our righteousness. I am not now speaking of nature—that would have to do with sanctification—but I am speaking of repute before God. He reckons us to be righteous in Christ, and he does not reckon wrongly; the imputation is not a legal fiction or a charitable error. We are righteous. Depend upon it, God's imputation is not like human imputation, which makes a thing to be what it is not : we are in Christ made actually righteous, because we are one with Him. Do you think that there is an unrighteous member of Christ's body ? God forbid ! Do you think Christ mystical to be a building with an unholy stone in it ? Is Christ a vine with branches, which bear deadly fruit ? As He is, so are we also in this respect. His salt has seasoned the whole lump. In the mystical body, every member is made righteous before God, because joined to the living head. Here is an actual righteousness given to us through the righteousness of Jesus Christ our Lord. He is made of God unto us righteousness. Consider this, O believer—you are to-night righteous before God. You are a sinner in yourself worthy to be condemned, but God does not condemn you, nor ever will He do so, for before the eye of His justice you are arrayed in perfect righteousness. Your sin is not upon you : it was laid upon the Scapegoat's head of old. All your iniquities were made to meet upon the head of the Crucified Saviour : He bore your transgressions in His own body on the tree. Where are your sins now ? You may ask the question without fear, for they have ceased to be. "As far as the east is from the west, so far hath He removed our transgressions from us." "He hath cast our iniquities into the depths of the sea." Glory be to His name, there is no sin in existence against a believer. Is it not written : "He hath finished transgression, made an end of sin [what stronger expression can there be ?], and brought in everlasting righteousness " ? And that is true of you to-night, Christian, as true of you to-night as it will be when you are in heaven. You are not so sanctified to-night as you will be in the glory land, but you are as righteous as you can be even there. In God's sight you are as much "accepted in the Beloved," as you will be when you stand on the sea of glass mingled with fire. You are beloved of God, and dear to Him and justified, so that even to-night you can say : " Who shall lay anything to the charge of God's elect ? It is God that justifieth. Who is he that condemneth ? " You cannot lift up a louder boast than that, even when you shall see your Saviour, and shall be like Him because you see Him as He is. By faith this righteousness is yours at this present moment, and will always be yours without a change : yours when your spirit is cast down, as much as when your joys abound. You are accepted not because of anything in yourself, but because you stand in the Lord your righteousness.

I remarked some time ago that the next blessing in our text is pinned on to this one. I need not say much about that fact, but just note it. Righteousness and sanctification must always go together, and though they are two different things, or else there would not have been two different words, yet they blend into each other most remarkably, hence the Greek joins the two words by a close link. Our *sanctification* is all in Christ ; that is to say, it is because we are in Christ that we have the basis of sanctification, which consists in being set apart. A thing was sanctified of old, under the law, when it was set apart for God's service. We were sanctified in Christ Jesus when we were set apart by the divine Spirit to be the Lord's own peculiar people for ever. Election is the basis of sanctification. Moreover, the power by which we are sanctified comes to us entirely by virtue of our union with Christ. The Holy Spirit who sanctifies us through the truth, works in us by virtue of our union with Jesus. That which becomes holy in us is the new life. The old nature never changes into a holy thing ; the carnal mind is not reconciled to God, neither, indeed, can be. The old man is not sent to the hospital to be healed, but to the cross to be crucified. It is not transformed and improved, but doomed to die and to be buried. The ordinance of baptism, which is placed at the outset of Christian life, is meant to show, by our immersion in the liquid tomb, that it is by death and burial that we pass into life by the power of resurrection. If any man be in Christ, he is not an old creature mended up : he is a new creature. " Old things are passed away ; behold all things are become new." Now, it is because this new life is the great, the true matter of sanctification, and because it comes to us by virtue of our oneness with Christ, that Jesus Christ is made to us the power and the life by which we are sanctified. Beloved, let your hearts add another meaning : let Jesus always be the motive for your sanctification. Is it not a strange thing that some professors should look to Christ alone for pardon and justification, and run away to Moses when they desire sanctification ? For instance, you will hear persons preach this doctrine : " The Christian is to be holy, because if he be not holy he will fall from grace and perish." Do you not hear the crack of the old legal whip in all that ? What is that but the yoke of that covenant which none of our fathers were able to bear ? It is the bondage of Egypt, not the freedom of the children of God. Christ talks not so, nor His gospel. Think not to make thyself holy by motives of that kind. They are not right motives for a child of God. How then should we urge the child of God to holiness ? Should it not be in this way : " Thou art God's

child : walk worthy of Him who is thy Father " ? His love to thee will never cease. He cannot cast thee away : He is faithful and never changes, therefore love Him in return. This is a motive fit for the child of the free woman, and it moves His heart. The child of the bond woman is driven by the whip, but the child of the free woman is drawn by cords of love. " The love of Christ constraineth us " ; not fear of hell, but love of Christ ; not fear that God will cast us away, for that He cannot do, but the joy that we are saved in the Lord with an everlasting salvation constrains us to cling to Him with all our heart and soul, for ever and ever. Rest assured, if motives fetched from the gospel will not kill sin, motives fetched from the law never will. If you cannot be purged at Calvary, you certainly cannot be cleansed at Sinai. If " the water and the blood, from the riven side which flowed," are not sufficient to purify thee, no blood of bulls or of goats—I mean, no argument from the Jewish law, or hope of salvation by your own efforts—will ever furnish motives sufficiently strong to cast out sin. Let your reasons for being holy be found in Christ, for He is made of God unto you sanctification ! I have ever found, and I bear my witness to it, that the more entirely for the future as well as for the present, I lean upon my Lord, the more conscious I am of my own emptiness and unworthiness ; and the more completely I rest my whole salvation upon the grace of God in Christ Jesus, the more carefully do I walk in my daily life. I have always found that self-righteous thoughts very soon lead to sinful actions ; but that, on the other hand, the very faith which leads to assurance, and makes the heart rest in the faithfulness of God in Christ, purifies the soul. " He that hath this hope in him purifieth himself, even as he is pure." Jesus, the Saviour, saves us from our sins, and is made of God to us " sanctification."

Now, the last item of our boundless wealth catalogued in the text is " *redemption*." Somebody says : " That ought to have come first ; because redemption, surely, is the first blessing that we enjoy." Ay, but it is the last as well. It is the *alpha* blessing, I grant you that—but it is the *omega* blessing too. You are not yet redeemed altogether. By price you are—for He that redeemed you on the tree did not leave unpaid a penny of your ransom ; but you are not yet altogether redeemed by power in a measure, you are set free by divine power, for you have been brought up out of the Egypt of your sin, you have been delivered from the galling bondage of your corruption, and led through the Red Sea, to be fed upon the heavenly manna ; but you are not altogether redeemed by power as yet. There are links of the old chains yet to be snapped from off you, and there is a bondage still about you from which you are ere long to be delivered. You are " waiting for the adoption, to wit, the redemption of the body." You will fall asleep, rejoicing that you were redeemed ; but you will not, even when you die, have received the full redemption. When will that come—the full redemption ? Only at the second advent of the Lord Jesus ; for when the Lord shall descend from heaven with a shout, then the bodies of His saints, which have long been lying in the prison-house of the sepulchre, shall be redeemed by a glorious redemption from the power of death. " I know that my Redeemer liveth." The bodies of the saints shall come again from the land of the enemy. Then their body, soul, and spirit—their entire manhood, which Christ hath bought, shall be altogether free from the reign of the enemy. Then will redemption be completed. Remember the saints in heaven without us cannot be made perfect, that is to say, they wait till we arrive among them; and when all the rest of the chosen ones shall be gathered in, and the fulness of time has come, then shall the bodies of the dead arise; and then, in body and soul made perfect, the year of the redeemed shall have fully come. "Lift up your heads; for your redemption draweth nigh." Here, then, is my joy, that Christ is my redemption. My soul is free from slavery, but my poor trembling and much suffering body feels the chains of death. Weakened by pain, my body shall in all probability bow before the stroke of death's sword. Unless the Lord soon come, it must be the portion of this frame to feed the worm and mingle with the dust; but, O my body, thou art redeemed, and thou shalt rise in power and incorruption; thou shalt yet adore the Lord without weariness, and without pain shalt thou serve Him day and night in His temple. Even thou, O my weary body; even thou shalt be made glorious like unto the Lord Himself. Thou shalt rise and live in the brightness of His presence.

All, then, that you can possibly want, O Christian, is in Christ. You cannot conceive a need which Jesus does not supply. "Wisdom, righteousness, sanctification, redemption," you have all in Him. Some gather a flower here; some gather another there; some will go farther, and pluck another there; and some will go yet beyond to grasp a fourth; but when we win Christ we have a posy; we have all sweet flowers in one.

> "All human beauties, all divine,
> In my Beloved meet and shine;
> Thou brightest, sweetest, fairest One,
> That eyes have seen or angels known."

But we cannot stay on this tempting subject, though even amid my present pain I would fain talk on by the hour together; and therefore I must finish with the last point; and on that only a word.

You see then, brethren, our very existence as Christians, and all that we possess as Christians, we get from God by Jesus Christ; *let all our glory then be unto Him.* What insanity it is to boast in any but in our Lord Jesus! How foolish are they that are proud of the beauty of their flesh—worms' meat at the best! How foolish are they who are proud of their wisdom! The wisdom of which a man is proud, is but folly in a thin disguise. How foolish

are they that are vain of their wealth! He must be a poor man who can think much of gold. He must be a beggar indeed who counts a piece of dirt a treasure. They that know Christ, always value these things at their right estimate, and that is low indeed. If any glory—and I suppose it is natural to us to glory, there is a boasting bump on all our heads—let us glory in the Lord; and here is a wide field and ample sea-room. Now, put out every stitch of canvas, run up the topgallants, seek as stiff a breeze as you will, there is no fear of running on a lee shore here, or striking a rock, or drifting on a quicksand! O men, O angels, O cherubim, O seraphim, boast in Jesus Christ! Wisdom, righteousness, sanctification, and redemption is He, therefore ye may boast and boast, and boast again! You will never exaggerate. You cannot exceed His worth, or reach the tithe of it. You can never go beyond the truth, you do not even reach beyond the skirts of His garments. So glorious is God that all the angels' harps cannot sound forth half His glory. So blessed is Christ that the orchestra of the countless multitudes of the redeemed, though it continue for ever and for ever its pealing music, can never reach to the majesty of His name or the glory of His work. "Give unto the Lord, O ye mighty, give unto the Lord glory and strength. Give unto the Lord the glory due unto His name." Let time and space become great mouths for song; let the infinite roll up its waves; let all creatures lift up their voices in praise of Him that liveth and was dead; but chiefly, O my soul, since to Him thou owest in a double sense thine existence, give thy praise to Him from whom all blessing comes. Give thou the homage of thine intellect to Him who is thy wisdom. Let thy conscience and love of rectitude adore Him who has made thee righteous. Give the tribute of thy soul to Him who sanctifies thee; let thy sanctified nature consecrate itself continually; and to Him that hath redeemed thee give thou never-ceasing praise. I wish it were possible for me to rise to the height of my text, but my wings flag; I cannot ascend as the eagle, and face the full blaze of the sun; I can but mount a little as the lark, and sing my song, and then return to my nest. God grant you to know the Lord Jesus in His fulness in your personal experience.

O you to whom Christ is no wisdom, how foolish are you! O you to whom He is no righteousness, you are condemned sinners! O you to whom He is no sanctification, the fire of God's wrath will consume you! O you to whom He is no redemption, you are slaves in hopeless bondage! God deliver you! May you be led to put your trust in Jesus even now.

THE MAN OF ONE SUBJECT

"For I determined not to know anything among you, save Jesus Christ, and Him crucified."—1 Corinthians ii. 2.

PAUL was a very determined man, and whatever he undertook he carried out with all his heart. Once let him say "I determined," and you might be sure of a vigorous course of action. "This one thing I do" was always his motto. The unity of his soul and its mighty resoluteness were the main features of his character. He had once been a great opposer of Christ and His cross and shown

his opposition by furious persecutions; it was not so very much to be wondered at that when he became a disciple of this same Jesus, whom he had persecuted, he should become a very ardent one, and bring all his faculties to bear upon the preaching of Christ crucified. His conversion was so marked, so complete, so thorough, that you expect to see him as energetic for the truth as once he had been violent against it.

A man so whole-hearted as Paul, so thoroughly capable of concentrating all his forces as the apostle was, and so entirely won over to the faith of Jesus, was likely to enter into his cause with all his heart and soul and might, and determined to know nothing else but his crucified Lord. Yet do not think that the apostle was a man easily absorbed in one thought. He was, above the most of men, a reasoner, calm, judicious, candid, and prudent. He looked at things in their bearings and relations, and was not a stickler for minor matters. Perhaps even more than might perfectly be justified he made himself all things to all men that he might by all means win some, and therefore any determination which he came to was only arrived at after taking counsel with wisdom. He was not a zealot of that class which may be likened to a bull which shuts its eyes and runs straight forward, seeing nothing which may lie to the right or to the left ; he looked all round him calmly, and quietly, and though he did in the end push forward in a direct line at his one object, yet it was with his eyes wide open, perfectly knowing what he was doing, and believing that he was doing the best and wisest thing for the cause which he desired to promote. If, for instance, to have opened his ministry at Corinth by proclaiming the unity of the Godhead, or by philosophically working out the possibilities of God's becoming incarnate,—if these had been the wisest plans for spreading the Redeemer's kingdom Paul would have adopted them ; but he looked at them all, and having examined them with all care, he could not see that anything was to be got by indirect preaching, or by keeping back a part of the truth, and therefore he determined to go straight forward, and promote the gospel by proclaiming the gospel. Whether men would hear or whether they would forbear, he resolved to come to the point at once, and preach the cross in its naked simplicity. Instead of knowing a great many things which might have led up to the main subject, he would not know anything in Corinth, save Jesus Christ, and Him crucified. Paul might have said " I had better beat about the bush, and educate the people up to a certain mark before I come to my main point ; to lay bare my ultimate intent at the first might be to spread the net in the sight of the birds and frighten them away. I will be cautious and reticent and will take them with guile, enticing them on in pursuit of truth." But not so : looking at the matter all round as a prudent man should, he comes to this resolve, that he will know nothing among them save Jesus Christ and Him crucified. I would to God that the " culture " we hear of in these days, and all this boasted " modern thought " would come to the same conclusion. This most renowned and scholarly divine after reading, marking, learning, and inwardly digesting everything as few men could do, yet came to this as to the issue of it all,—" I determined not to know anything among you, save Jesus Christ, and Him crucified." May God grant that the critical skill of our contemporaries, and their laborious excogitations may land them on the same shore, by the blessing of the Holy Spirit.

I. Our first consideration this morning will be, WHAT WAS THIS SUBJECT TO WHICH PAUL DETERMINED TO SHUT HIMSELF UP WHILE PREACHING TO THE CHURCH AT CORINTH ? That subject was one, though it may also be divided into two ; it was *the person* and *the work* of our Lord Jesus Christ : laying special stress upon that part of his work which is always the most objected to, namely, His substitutionary sacrifice, His redeeming death. Paul preached Christ in all His positions, but he especially dwelt upon Him as the Crucified One.

The apostle first preached his great Master's *person*—Jesus Christ. There was no equivocation about Paul when he spoke of Jesus of Nazareth. He held Him up as a real man, no phantom, but One who was crucified, dead and buried, and rose again from the dead in actual bodily existence. There was no hesitation about his Godhead either. Paul preached Jesus as the Son of the Highest, as the wisdom and the power of God, as One " in whom dwelleth all the fulness of the Godhead bodily." You never doubted when you heard Paul but what he believed in the divinity and the humanity of the Lord Jesus Christ, and worshipped and adored Him as very God of very God. He preached His person with all clearness of language and warmth of love. The Christ of God was all in all to Paul.

The apostle spoke equally clearly upon the Redeemer's *work*, especially laying stress upon His death. " Horrible ! " said the Jew. " How can you boast in a Man who died a felon's death, and was cursed because He was hanged on a tree ! " " Ah," said the Greek, " tell us no more about your God that died ! Babble no longer about resurrection. We never shall believe such unmitigated foolishness." But Paul did not, therefore, put these things into the background and say, " Gentlemen, I will begin with telling you of the life of Christ, and of the excellency of His example, and by this means I shall hope to tempt you onward to the conclusion that there was something divine in Him, and then afterwards to the further conclusion that He made an atonement for sin." But no, he began with His blessed person, and distinctly described Him as he had been taught it by the Holy Spirit, and as to His crucifixion he put it in the front and made it the main point. He did not say, " Well, we will leave the matter of His death for a time," or " We will consider it under the aspect of a martyrdom by which He completed His testimony," but he gloried in the crucified Redeemer, the dead and buried Christ, the sin-bearing Christ, the Christ made a curse for us, as it is written, " Cursed is every one that hangeth on a tree," This was the subject to which he confined himself at Corinth : beyond this he would not stir an inch. Nay, he does not merely determine to keep his preaching to that point, but he resolves not even to *know* any other subject ; he would keep his mind fast closed among them to any thought but Jesus Christ and Him crucified.

Very impolitic this must have seemed. Call in a council of worldly wise men, and they will condemn such a rash course ; for in the first place such preaching would drive away all the Jews. Holding as the Jews did the Old Testament Scriptures, and receiving therefore a great deal of teaching about the Messiah, and holding very firmly to the unity of the Godhead, the Jews had gone a long way towards the light, and if Paul had kept back the objectionable points a little while, might he not have drawn them a little further, and so by degrees have landed them at the cross ? Wise man would have remarked upon the hopefulness of the Israelites, if handled with discretion, and their advice would have been, " We do not say, renounce your sentiments, Paul, but disguise them for a little while. Do not say what is untrue, but at the same time be a little reticent about what is true, or else you will drive away these hopeful Jews." The apostle yielded to no such policy, he would not win either Jew or Gentile by keeping back the truth, for he knew that such converts are worthless. If the man who is near the kingdom will be driven right away from the gospel by hearing the unvarnished truth, that is no guide as to Paul's duty ; he knows that the gospel must be a "savour of death unto death" to some, as well as of "life unto life" unto others, and therefore whichever may occur he must deliver his own soul : consequences are not for him, but for the Lord. It is ours to speak the truth boldly, and in every case we shall be a sweet savour unto God ; but to temporise in the hope of making converts is to do evil that good may come, and this is never to be thought of for an instant.

Another would say "But, Paul, if you do this you will arouse opposition. Do you not know that Christ crucified is a byword and a reproach to all thinking men ? Why, at Corinth there are a number of philosophers, and I tell you it will create unbounded ridicule if you so much as open your mouth about the Crucified One and His resurrection. Do not you remember on Mars' Hill how they mocked you when you spoke upon that theme ? Do not provoke their contempt. Argue with their Gnosticism, and show them that you too are a philosopher. Be all things to all men ; be learned among the learned, and rhetorical among the orators. By these means you will make many friends, and by degrees your conciliatory conduct will bring them to accept the gospel." The apostle shakes his head, puts down his foot, and with firm voice utters his decision. "I have *determined*," says he, "I have already made up my mind, your counsels and your advice are lost upon me ; I have *determined* to know nothing among the Corinthians, however learned the Gentile portion of them may be, or however fond of rhetoric, save Jesus Christ, and Him crucified." He stands to that.

It is further worthy of note that the apostle had resolved that his subject should so engross the attention of his hearers that he would not even speak it with excellency of speech or garnish it with man's wisdom. You have heard perhaps of the famous painter who drew the likeness of James I. He represented him sitting in a bower with all the flowers of the season blooming around him, and nobody ever took the smallest notice of the king's visage, for all eyes were charmed by the excellency of the flowers. Paul resolved that he would have no flowers at all, that the portrait which he sketched should be Christ crucified, the bare fact and doctrine of the cross without so much as a single flower from the poets or the philosophers. Some of us need not be very loud in our resolution to avoid fine speech, for we may have but slender gifts in that direction ; but the apostle was a man of fine natural powers and of vast attainments, a man whom the Corinthian critics could not have despised, and yet he threw away all ornaments to let the unadorned beauty of the cross win its own way.

As he would not add flowers, so he would not darken the cross with smoke : for there is a way of preaching the gospel amid a smother of mystification and doubt, so that men cannot perceive it. A numerous band of men are always boiling and stirring up a huge philosophic caldron, which steams with dense vapour, beclouding the cross of Christ most horribly. Alas for that wisdom which conceals the wisdom of God, it is the most guilty form of folly. Some people preach Christ as I have seen representations of a man-of-war in battle. The painter painted nothing but the smoke, and you have said, "Where is the ship ?" Well, if you looked long you might discern a fragment of the top of one of the masts, and, perhaps, a portion of the boom ; the ship was there, no doubt, but the smoke concealed it. So there may be Christ in some men's preaching, but there is such a cloud of thinking, such a dense pall of profundity, such a horrid smoke of philosophy, that you cannot see the Lord. Paul painted beneath a clear sky, he would have no learned obscurity, he determined not to know how to speak after the manner of the orators, not to know how to think deeply according to the mode of the philosophers, but only to know Jesus Christ, and Him crucified, and just to set Him forth in His own natural beauties unadorned. He dispensed with those accessories which are so apt to attract the eye of the mind from the central point—Christ crucified. "A rash experiment," says one. Ah, brethren, it is the experiment of faith, and faith is justified of all her children. If we rely upon the power of mere suasion, we rely upon that which is born of the flesh ; if we depend upon the power of logical argument, we again rely upon that which is born of men's reason ; if we trust to poetic expressions and attractive turns of speech, we look to carnal means ; but if we rest upon the naked omnipotence of a crucified Saviour, upon the innate power of the wondrous deed of love which was consummated upon Calvary, and believe that the Spirit of God will make this the instrument for the conversion of men, the experiment cannot possibly end in failure.

But oh, my brethren, what a task this must have been for Paul ! He was not like some of us, who are neither familiar with philosophy, nor capable of oratory. He was so great a master of both, that he must have found it needful to keep himself constantly in check. I think I can see him every now and then when a deeply intellectual thought has come across his mind and a beautiful mode of utterance has suggested itself, reining himself up and saying to his mind, "I will leave these deep thoughts for the Romans, I will give them all this in the eighth chapter ; but as for these Corinthians they shall have nothing but Christ crucified, for they are so carnal, so grossly slavish before talent that they will run away with the idea that my excellent way of putting the truth was the power of it. They shall have Christ only, and only Christ. They are children, and I must speak to them as such ; they are mere babes in Christ, and have need of milk, and milk alone must I give them. They claim to be clever and learned, they are conceited, high-minded, full of divisions and controversies ; I will give them nothing but 'the old, old story of Jesus and His love,' and I will tell them that story simply as to a little child." Boundless love to their souls thus made him concentrate his testimony upon the one central point of Jesus crucified.

Thus I have shown you what his subject was.

II. Now, secondly, ALTHOUGH PAUL THUS CONCENTRATED HIS ENERGIES UPON ONE POINT OF TESTIMONY, IT WAS QUITE SUFFICIENT FOR HIS PURPOSE. If the apostle had aimed at pleasing an intelligent audience, Christ and Him crucified would not have done at all. If again he had designed to set himself up as a profound teacher he would naturally have looked out for something new, something a little more dazzling than the person and work of the Redeemer. And if Paul had desired, as I am afraid some of my brethren do, to collect together a class of highly independent minds, which is I believe the euphemism for free-thinkers—to draw together a select church of the men of culture and intellect, which generally means a club of men who despise the gospel, he certainly would not have kept to preaching Jesus Christ and Him crucified. This order of men would deny him all hope of success with such a theme. They would assure him that such preaching would only attract the poorer sort and the less educated, the servant maids and the old women ; but Paul would not have been disconcerted by such observations, for he loved the souls of the poorest and feeblest : and, besides, he knew that what had exercised power over his own educated mind was likely to have power over other intelligent people, and so he kept to the doctrine of the cross, believing that he had therein an instrument which would effectually accomplish his one design with all classes of men. Brethren, what did Paul wish to do ? Paul desired first of all to arouse sinners to a sense of sin, and what has ever accomplished this so perfectly as the doctrine that sin was laid upon Christ and caused His death ? The sinner, enlightened by the Holy Spirit, sees at once that sin is not a trifle, that it is not to be forgiven without an atonement, but must be followed by penalty, borne by some one or other. When the guilty one has seen the Son of God bleeding to death in pangs unutterable in consequence of sin, he has learned that his sin is an enormous and crushing burden. If even the Son of God cries out beneath it, if His death agony rends the heavens and shakes the earth, what an awful evil sin must be. What must it involve upon my soul if in my own person I shall be doomed to bear its consequences ? Thus the sinner rightly argues, and thus he is aroused to a sense of guilt.

But Paul wanted also to awaken in the minds of the guilty that humble hope which is the great instrument of leading men to Jesus. He desired to make them hope that forgiveness might be given consistently with justice. Oh, brethren, Christ crucified is the one ray of light that can penetrate the thick darkness of despair, and make a penitent heart hope for pardon from the righteous Judge. Need a sinner ever doubt when he has once seen Jesus crucified ? When he understands that there is pardon for every transgression through the bleeding wounds of Jesus, is not the best form of hope at once kindled in his bosom, and is he not led to say " I will arise and go unto my Father, and will say unto Him, Father, I have sinned " ?

Paul longed yet further to lead men to actual faith in Jesus Christ. Now, faith in Jesus Christ can only come by preaching Jesus Christ. Faith cometh by hearing, but the hearing must be upon the subject concerning which the faith is to deal. Would you make believers in Christ, preach Christ. The things of Christ, applied by the Spirit, lead men to put their reliance upon Christ. Nor was that all. Paul wanted men to forsake their sins, and what should lead them to hate evil so much as seeing the sufferings of Jesus on account of it. You and I know the power of a bleeding Saviour to make us take revenge upon sin. What indignation, what searching of heart, what stern resolve, what bitterness of regret, what deep repentance have we felt when we

have seen that our sins became the nails, the hammer, the spear, yea, the executioners of the Well-beloved ?

And Paul longed to train up in Corinth a church of consecrated men, full of love, full of self-denial, a holy people, zealous for good works ; and let me ask you, what more is there necessary to preach to any man to promote his sanctification and his consecration than Jesus Christ, who hath redeemed us and so made us for ever His servants ? What argument is stronger than the fact that we are not our own, for we are bought with a price ? I say that Paul had in Christ crucified a subject equal to his object ; a subject that would meet the case of every man however degraded or however cultured, and a subject which would be useful to men in the first hours of the new birth and equally useful when they were made meet to be partakers of the inheritance of the saints in light. He had a subject for to-day and to-morrow, and a subject for next year, for Jesus Christ is the same yesterday, to-day, and for ever. He had in the crucified Jesus a subject for the prince's palace and a subject for the peasant's hut, a subject for the market place and a subject for the academy, for the heathen temple and for the synagogue. Wherever he might go, Christ would be both to Jew and Gentile, to bond and free, the wisdom of God and the power of God, and that not to one form of beneficial influence alone, but unto full salvation to every one that believeth.

III. But I must pass on to a third remark, that THE APOSTLE'S CONFINING HIMSELF TO THIS SUBJECT COULD NOT POSSIBLY DO HARM. You know, brethren, that when men dwell exclusively upon one thing they get pretty strong there, but they generally become very weak in other points. Hence a man of one thought only is generally described as riding a hobby : well this was Paul's hobby, but it was a sort of hobby which a man may ride without any injury to himself or his neighbour : he will be none the less a complete man if he surrenders himself wholly and only to this one theme.

But let me remark that Christ crucified is the only subject of which this can be said. Let me show you that it is so. You know a class of ministers who preach doctrine—and doctrine only. Their mode of preaching resembles the counting of your fingers—" one, two, three, four, five," and for a variety, " five, four, three, two, one,"—always a certain set of great truths and no others. What is the effect of this ministry ? Well, generally to breed a generation of men who think they know everything, but really do not know much : very decided, and so far good ; but very narrow, very exclusive, very bigoted, and so far bad. You cannot preach doctrine alone without contracting your own mind and that of your hearers.

There are others who preach experience only. They are very good people ; I am not condemning either them or their doctrinal friends, but they also fall into mischief. Some of them take the lower scale of experience, and they tell us that nobody can be a child of God, except he feels the horrible character of his inbred sin, and groans daily, being burdened. We used to hear a good deal of that some years ago, there is less of it now. Am I wrong in saying that this teaching trains up a race of men who show their humility by sitting in judgment upon all who cannot groan down to as deep a note as they can ?

Another class has lately arisen who preach

experience, but theirs is always upon the high key. They soar aloft, as I think, a little in the balloon line. They own only the bright side of experience, they have nothing to do with its darkness and death. For them there are no nights, they sing through perpetual summer days. They have conquered sin, and they have ignored themselves. *So they say,* but we should not have thought so if they had not told us so ; on the contrary, we might have fancied that they had a very vivid idea of themselves and their own attainments. I hope I am mistaken, but it has appeared to some of us poor fallible beings, that in some beloved brethren self had grown marvellously big of late ; certainly their conventions and preachings largely consist of very wonderful declarations of their own admirable condition. I should be pleased to learn of their progress in grace, *if it be real ;* but I had sooner have made the discovery myself, or have heard it from somebody else besides themselves, for there is an inspired proverb which says ; " Let another praise thee, and not thine own lips," and, for my part, if any other man thought it right to praise me, I would rather that he held his tongue, for man-magnifying is a poor business. Let the Lord alone be magnified. I think it is clear that grave faults arise, one of exclusively preaching an inner life, instead of preaching Christ, who is the life itself.

Another class of ministers have preached the precepts and little else. We want these men as we want the others, they are all useful, and act as antidotes to each other, but their ministries are not complete. If you hear preaching about duty and command, it is very proper, but if it be the one sole theme the teaching becomes very legal in the long run ; and after a while the true gospel which has the power to make us keep the precept gets flung into the background, and the precept is not kept after all. Do, do, do, generally ends in nothing being done.

If a brother were to undertake to preach the ordinances only, like those who are always extolling what they are pleased to call the holy sacraments— well, you know where that teaching goes—it has a tendency towards the south-east, and its chosen line runs across the city of Rome.

Moreover, beloved brother, even if you preach Jesus Christ you must not keep to any other phase of Him but that which Paul took, namely, " Him crucified," for under no other aspect may you exclusively regard Him. For instance, the preaching of the second advent, which, in its place and proportion, is admirable, has been by some taken out of its place, and made the end-all and be-all of their ministry. That, you see, is not what Paul had selected, and it is not a safe selection. In many cases sheer fanaticism has been the result of exclusively dwelling upon prophecy, and probably more men have gone mad on that subject than on any other religious question. Whether any man ever could become fanatical about Christ crucified I cannot say, I have never heard of such an instance. Whether a man ever went insane with love to the crucified Redeemer I do not know, but I have never met such a case. If I should ever go mad, I should like it to be in that direction, and I should like to bite a great many more ; for what a blessed subject it would be for one to be carried away with, to become unreasonably absorbed in Christ crucified, to have gone out of your senses with faith in Jesus. The fact is, it never can

injure the mind, it is a doctrine which may be heard for ever, and will be always fresh, new, and suitable to the whole of our manhood.

I say that the keeping to this doctrine cannot do hurt, and the reason is this : it contains all that is vital within itself. Keep within the limit of Christ, and Him crucified, and you have brought before men all the essentials for this life and for the life to come ; you have given them the root out of which may grow both branch and flower, and fruit of holy thought and word and deed. Let a man know Christ crucified, and he knows Him whom to know is life eternal. This is a subject which does not arouse one part of the man, and send the other part to sleep ; it does not kindle his imagination and leave his judgment uninstructed, nor feed his intellect and starve his heart. There is not a faculty of our nature but what Christ crucified affects for good. The perfect manhood of Christ crucified affects mind, heart, memory, imagination, thought, everything. As in milk there are all the ingredients necessary for sustaining life, so in Christ crucified there is everything that is wanted to nurture the soul. Even as the hand of David's chief minstrel touched every chord of his ten-stringed harp, so Jesus brings sweet music out of our entire manhood.

There is also this to be said about preaching Christ exclusively, that it will never produce animosities. It will not impregnate men's minds with questions and contentions, as those nice points do which some are so fond of dealing with. When certain questions are settled by my judgment and by your judgment, and by a third and a fourth man's judgment, a contest is sure to ensue ; but he who stands at Christ's cross, and keeps there, stands where he may embrace the whole brotherhood of true Christians, for we are perfectly joined together in one mind and judgment there. There is no vaunting of man's judgment at the cross. " I am of Paul, I am of Apollos, I am of Christ," comes from not keeping to Jesus crucified ; but if we keep to the cross as guilty sinners needing cleansing through the precious blood, and finding all our salvation there, we shall not have time to set ourselves up as religious leaders, and to cause divisions in the church of Christ. Was there ever yet a sect created in Christendom by the preaching of Christ crucified ? No, my brethren, sects are created by the preaching of something over and above this, but this is the soul and marrow of Christianity, and consequently the perfect bond of love which holds Christians together.

IV. I shall not say more, but pass on to my last reflection, which is this : Because, then, Paul made this his one sole subject amongst the Corinthians, and he did not hurt by so doing, which cannot be said of any other subject, I COMMEND TO YOU THAT WE SHOULD ALL OF US MAKE THIS THE MAIN SUBJECT OF OUR THOUGHTS, PREACHING AND EFFORTS.

Unconverted men and women, to you I speak first. To you I have nothing else to preach but Jesus Christ and Him crucified. Paul knew there were great sinners at Corinth, for it was common all over the then world to call a licentious man a Corinthian. They were a people who pushed laxity and lasciviousness of manners to the greatest possible excess, yet among them Paul knew nothing but Christ and Him crucified, because all that the greatest sinner can possibly want is to be found there. You have nothing in yourself, sinner, and you need not wish for anything to carry to Jesus. You tell me you know nothing about the profound doctrines of the gospel : you need not know them when coming to Christ. The one thing you need to know is this, Jesus Christ, the Son of God, came into the world to save sinners, and whosoever believeth in Him shall not perish, but have everlasting life. I shall be glad for you to be further instructed in the faith, and to know the heights and depths of that love which passeth knowledge, but just now the one thing you require to know is Jesus Christ crucified, and if you never get beyond that, if your mind should be of so feeble a cast that anything deeper than this you should never be able to grasp, I for one shall feel no distress whatever, for you will have found that which will deliver you from the power of sin and from the punishment of it, and that which will take you up to heaven to dwell where that same Jesus who was crucified sits enthroned at the right hand of God. Oh, dear broken heart, if thou wouldest find healing, it is in those wounds. If thou wouldest find rest thou must have it from those pierced hands. If thou wouldest hear absolution, it must be spoken from those same lips which said so sweetly, " It is finished." God forbid that we should know anything among sinners except Christ and Him crucified. Look to Him, and Him only, and you shall find rest unto your souls.

As for you, my brethren and sisters, who know Christ, I have this to say to you : keep this to the front, and nothing else but this, for it is against this that the enemy rages. That part of the line of battle which is most fiercely assailed by the enemy is sure to be that which he knows to be most important to carry. Men hate those they fear. The antagonism of the enemies of the gospel is mainly against the cross. From the very first it was so. They cried " Let Him come down from the cross and we will believe in Him." They will write us pretty lives of Christ and tell us what an excellent Man He was, and do our Lord such homage as their Judas' lips can afford Him ; they will also take His sermon on the mount and say what a wonderful insight He had into the human heart, and what a splendid code of morals He taught, and so on. " We will be Christians," say they, " but the dogma of atonement we utterly reject." Our answer is, we do not care one farthing what they have to say about our Master if they deny His substitutionary sacrifice, whether they give Him wine or vinegar is a small question so long as they reject the claims of the Crucified. The praises of unbelievers are sickening ; who wants to hear polluted lips lauding Him? Such sugared words are very like those which came out of the mouth of the devil when he said " Thou Son of the Highest," and Jesus rebuked him and said " Hold thy peace, and come out of him," Even thus would we say to unbelievers who extol Christ's life : " Hold your peace ! We know your enmity, disguise it as you may. Jesus is the Saviour of men or He is nothing ; if you will not have Christ crucified you cannot have Him at all." My brethren in Jesus, let us glory in the blood of Jesus, let it be conspicuous as though it were sprinkled upon the lintel and the two side posts of our doors, and let the world know that redemption by blood is written upon the innermost tablets of our hearts.

Brethren, this is the test point of every teacher. When a fish goes bad they say it first stinks at the head, and certainly when a preacher becomes heretical it is always about Christ. If he is not clear about Jesus crucified, and you hear one sermon from him—that is your misfortune : but if you go and hear him again, and hear another like the first, it will be your fault : go a third time, and it will be your crime. If any man be doubtful about Christ crucified, recollect Hart's couplet, for it is a truth—

" You cannot be right in the rest,
    Unless you think rightly of Him."

I do not want to examine men upon all the doctrines of the Westminster Assembly's Confession. I begin here, " What think ye of Christ ? " If you cannot answer that question, go and publish your own views where you like, but you and I are wide as the poles asunder, neither do I wish to have fellowship with you. We must have plain speaking here.

It is " Christ crucified " which God blesses to conversion. God blessed William Huntingdon to the conversion of souls : I am sure of that, though I am no Huntingdonian. He blessed John Wesley to the conversion of souls : I am quite as clear about that, though I am not a Wesleyan. The point upon which the Lord blessed them both was that wherein they bore testimony to Christ ; and you shall find that in proportion as Jesus Christ's atonement is in a sermon it is the life-blood of that sermon, and is that which God sanctifies to the conversion of the sons of men. Therefore, keep it always prominent.

And I ask you now, my brethren, one thing more ; is not Christ and Him crucified the thing to live on and the thing to die on ? Worldlings can live upon their flimsies, they can delight themselves under their Jonah's gourds while they last ; but when a man is depressed in spirit, and tortured in body, where does he look ? If he be a Christian, where does he fly ? Where, indeed, but to Jesus crucified ? How often have I been glad to creep into the temple and stand in the poor publican's shoes, and say " God be merciful to me a sinner," looking only to that mercy-seat which Jesus sprinkled with His precious blood. This will do to *die* with. I do not believe we shall die seeking consolation from our peculiar church organisations ; nor shall we die grasping with a dying clutch either ordinance or doctrine by itself. Our soul must live and die on Jesus crucified. Notice all the saints when they die whether they do not get back to Calvary's great sacrifice. They believed a great many things ; some of them had many crotchets and whims and oddities, but the main point comes uppermost in death. " Jesus died for me. Jesus died for me "— they all come to that. Well, where they get at last do you not think it would be well to go at first ; and if that be the bottom of it all, and it certainly is, would it not be as well for us to keep to that ? While some are glorying in this, and some in that, some have this form of worship and some that, let us say, " God forbid that I should glory, save in the cross of our Lord Jesus Christ, by whom the world is crucified to Me and I unto the world."

Brethren, I commend to you more and more the bringing of the cross of Christ into prominence, because it is this which will weld us more and more closely to one another, and will keep us in blessed unity. We cannot all understand those peculiar truths which depend very much upon nice points, and shades of meaning in the Greek, which only critics can bring out. If you are going in for these pretty things, brother, you must leave behind many of us poor fools, for we cannot go in for these things, and you only puzzle us. I know you have got that dainty point very beautifully in your own mind, and you think a great deal of it, and I do not wonder, for it has cost you a good deal of thinking, and it shows your powerful discernment. At the same time, do you not think you ought to condescend to some of us who never will as long as ever we live take up with these knotty points? Some of our brains are of an ordinary sort. We have to earn our bread and we mingle with ordinary people; we know that twice two will make four; but we are not acquainted with all the recondite principles which lie concealed in the lofty philosophy to which you have climbed. I do not know much about it, I do not climb to such elevations myself, and I shall never get up there along with you: might it not be better for the unity of the faith that you would kindly leave some of these things alone, agree better with your friends at home, show more love to your fellow Christians, and attend a little more to common-place duties? I do not know but what it might do you good, and bring a little of your humility to the front, if you kept down there with Jesus Christ and Him crucified. Personally I might know a host of things—I specially might, for everybody tries to teach me something. I get advice by the waggon-load: one pulls this ear and one pulls that. Well, I might know a great deal, but I find I should have to leave some of you behind if I went off to those things, and I love you too well for that. I am determined to know nothing among you but Jesus Christ and Him crucified. If any man will keep to that, I will say, "Give me your hand, my brother, Jesus washed it with His blood as He did mine. Come, brother, let us look up together at the same cross. What dost thou make of it?" There is a tear in your eye, and there is one in mine, but yet there is a flush of joy upon both our faces, because of the dear love that nailed Jesus there. "What shall we do in the sight of this cross?" My brother says, "I will go and win souls," and I say, "So will I." He says, "I have one way of speaking," and I reply, "I have another, for our gifts differ, but we will never clash, for we are serving one Lord and one Master, and we will not be divided, either in this world or in that which is to come." Let Apollos say what he likes, or Paul or Peter, we will learn from them all, and be very glad to do so, but still from the cross we will not move, but stand fast there, for Jesus is the first and the last, the Alpha and the Omega. Amen.

THE ONE FOUNDATION

"For other foundation can no man lay than that is laid, which is Jesus Christ."—1 Corinthians iii. 11.

UPBUILDING is very important, but the first question must always concern the foundation. However quickly, however cleverly a man may build, if the foundation be unsound he is a foolish builder; and however slowly, however laboriously a man may proceed, his building will not put him to shame if he has set his walls erect upon a firm basis. This is emphatically true in spiritual things, for there the foundation is of the utmost importance. The hearer of the word, who is not a doer also, comes to a fatal end, because, as the Saviour says, he has built upon the sand, and therefore his fabric in the day of storm and flood is swept away, while he who hears the word and does it is secure because he digs deep and lays his foundation upon a rock, and therefore his building survives the rains of trial from above, the floods of persecution from without, and the mysterious winds of Satanic temptation which howl from ever quarter. The best masonry must crack and fall if the groundwork is unstable: the higher the pinnacle the speedier its fall if the base is insecure.

As to what the foundation is in the religion of Jesus Christ there is no question. This verse declares it to be decided beyond controversy. A man may build the superstructure in some measure according to his own taste and judgment, but it must be based upon the one foundation; there may be room for varieties of style in the upper building, but there can be no variety in the groundwork. That is fixed for ever by the unchanging God, who says, "Behold, I lay in Zion a foundation stone." It must be acknowledged that all Christian minds and lives do not take exactly the same form and fashion: there are among the best of Christian builders certain grades of excellences,—one man builds with gold, another with silver, and a third with precious stones; but as to the foundation, all are on a level, Christ is all and in all. Whether the gracious life be rich as a golden palace, or pure as a temple of silver, or substantial as a tower of marble, whether it be public or obscure, wide or narrow, it must in every case be built upon the same basement of eternal rock: "for other foundation can no man lay than that is laid." You may say "we will agree to differ" about matters which concern the superstructure, but we must agree to agree as to the foundation; for if we are not at one with the plain statement of the text we are in the wrong.

The apostle is dogmatic to the very last degree: "Other foundation can no man lay." "But," saith one, "various teachers did lay other foundations." The apostle will not admit that they were foundations: they were not worthy of the name, the imposture was too shallow to succeed. No builder if he looked upon a heap of sand poured into an excavation would admit that it was a foundation. If he saw a mass of decayed vegetation and garden rubbish heaped together no architect would for one moment allow it to be spoken of as a "foundation." Paul declareth that there is but one foundation, and that there is none beside it, or beyond it; and that the one only, unalterable, immovable, everlasting foundation is Jesus Christ. It is not to be imagined that there are other foundations somewhat differing and only a little inferior to the Lord Jesus: there is no other, and no other can be laid. It is not a question of comparison, but of monopoly. All other groundworks and principles, whatever may be said in their praise, are mere falsehoods if they are set forth as foundations, for the Lord Jesus has exclusive possession of that title, and in Him alone all that is fundamental is summed up; "Neither is there salvation in any other : for there is none other name under heaven given among men, whereby we must be saved."

And truly, when you think that God from all eternity has made His only-begotten Son to be the foundation and corner stone, it will be seen that this rock goes deep into the very nature of things, ay, deep as infinity itself ; and, therefore, there cannot be two of the kind, for of whom else is it written that verily He was fore-ordained before the foundation of the world ? Of whom else is it said, " I was set up from everlasting, from the beginning, or ever the earth was " ? When you think that this foundation is nothing less than divine, for Christ is very God of very God, it is as impossible that there should be two foundations as that there should be two Gods. You must imagine two redemptions before you can conceive of two groundworks for our confidence. Who will dream of two atonements, two Saviours, two Christs ? Yet must such a thing be ere there can be two foundations. None but Jesus, the divine Saviour, could sustain the weight of a single soul with all its sins, much less of all the souls which are built up into the temple of God. Jesus alone can sustain our eternal interests, deliver us from eternal wrath, or lift us into eternal bliss. "There is one God, and one Mediator between God and men, the Man Christ Jesus." His own words in prophecy are very positive—" I, even I, am the Lord, and beside Me there is no Saviour"; and equally express is His personal declaration—" I am the way, the truth, and the life : no man cometh unto the Father, but by Me."

I will sketch out my discourse with these four lines, which I may not always be able to keep from intersecting each other, but they shall each be marked deeply and broadly, so that none can help seeing them. First, *no church but what is built on Christ ;* secondly, *no gospel but what is built on Christ ;* thirdly, *no hope of salvation but what is built on Christ ;* and fourthly, *no Christian but what is built on Christ.*

I. First, there is NO CHURCH BUT WHAT IS BUILT ON CHRIST. I mean, of course, no true, no real church. There are many churches in the world, so called, but this may be laid down as a first principle that there is but one church, and that this one church is built upon Christ alone. Whatever community, congregation, hierarchy, sect, or corporation may call itself a church, or even *the* church, if it is not built upon Christ it is not a church at all. No matter how great in numbers, nor how ancient, nor how wealthy, nor how learned, nor how pretentious, bigoted, dominant, or exclusive, it may be, it is not Christ's church if it is not built upon Christ.

To begin with, *a foundation is the first portion* of a building ; and so is the Lord Jesus first and foremost with His church, for His people were chosen in Him. God has always had in His purpose and decree a chosen people, but He has had no such people apart from Christ. The apostle saith : " Blessed be the God and Father of our Lord Jesus Christ, who hath blessed us with all spiritual blessings in heavenly places in Christ : according as He hath chosen us in Him before the foundation of the world." We were chosen in Christ Jesus ; He is " the first born among many brethren," and the Lord has " predestinated us to be conformed to the image of His Son." The first setting apart of the church and making it to

be the peculiar inheritance of God was in connection with Christ.

> " ' Christ, be my first elect,' he said,
>   Then chose our souls in Christ our head."

We were never otherwise chosen, nor otherwise beloved, nor otherwise appointed to eternal life than as regarded in Christ Jesus, and one with Him. No single soul can be said to be elect otherwise than as it is considered in connection with Christ ; much less then is there a church of God apart from the eternal purpose concerning Christ Jesus, the covenant head, and federal representative of His people. The foundation must be laid first, and so was our Lord Jesus Christ first appointed. " Therefore thus saith the Lord God, Behold, I lay in Zion for a foundation a stone, a tried stone, a precious corner stone, a sure foundation." Jesus is called by the Father " Mine elect in whom My soul delighteth," and there are none elect except such as are in Him in the eternal purpose of grace.

But next, *a foundation is the support of all*, and there is no church but that which derives all its support from Christ Jesus. If there be any company of people calling themselves a church who depend for salvation and eternal life upon anything beside, or beyond the merit of Christ's atoning blood, they are not a church. That all things are of God, and that He hath reconciled us unto Himself by Christ Jesus, is a truth never to be doubted. The atoning Saviour is the corner-stone of the church. He is the one rock of our salvation, the one pillar of our strength. As living stones we are built up into a spiritual house, but we one and all rest and depend upon Him, and upon no other. To us the word of the Lord has come with power,—" Therefore let all the house of Israel know assuredly, that God hath made that same Jesus, whom ye have crucified, both Lord and Christ." The great atoning sacrifice of Christ must be the sole reliance of the whole church as well as of each individual, and this must be set forth with great clearness and distinctness as its first and greatest doctrine—salvation by Christ Jesus : " In whom we have redemption through His blood, the forgiveness of sins, according to the riches of His grace." The atonement taken away, no church remains. Call the community a religious club if you like, but it is no church when once the atonement made by the Lord Jesus, through His death in the room and stead of His people, is denied or ignored.

Nor do we judge a community to be worthy of the name of a church which places its dependence for its present power and future progress anywhere but in the almighty Saviour. Jesus saith, " Because I live ye shall live also," and the church must draw its daily life from the immortality of her glorious Head. He that loved us and died for us and rose again is pledged to keep His own, and on that pledge let them repose their faith. Because all power is given unto Him in heaven and in earth, therefore go we forth to teach the nations. He has said, " Lo, I am with you alway, even unto the end of the world," therefore have we strength to go forth for the conquest of the world. But if we depend upon an arm of flesh, upon the secular power, upon carnal wisdom, upon education, or eloquence, or prestige, or upon our own zeal and ardour, and not upon Christ, we are leaving the rock for the sand. We cannot thus build up Christ's church, nor ought we to attempt it. The strength of a living church is the living Christ. We must be very careful on this point, that when we are zealous in building we build only upon Christ and by Christ, for edifices otherwise erected will fall in heaps. We must as a church not only rely upon the Christ that died, but upon the Christ who is gone into the glory and sits at the right hand of God, ruling and reigning on our behalf, who also shall shortly come to gather together the scattered, and to reign amongst His own. The true church, like a vine, derives the life-sap of its branches from Jesus the stem, and from no other source. She can say of her glorious Redeemer, " My soul, wait thou only upon the Lord, for my expectation is from Him." Other communities may lean on princes, but she comes up from the wilderness leaning on her Beloved ; other congregations may look to human greatness for support, but her eyes are towards the hills whence cometh her help ; her help cometh from the Lord which made heaven and earth.

Furthermore, *a foundation has the shaping of the building*, and the true church shapes and forms itself upon the Lord Jesus as its ground-plan and outline. The shape of the building must, to a very large extent, be determined by its foundation. If you have ever traced the foundations of an ancient abbey or castle, as they have appeared on a level with the soil, you have proceeded to infer the form of the building from the run of the ground line. Here was a sharp angle, there was a circular tower ; there was a buttress, and there was a recess. The building must have followed the ground line, and so must every true church be built upon Christ, in the sense of following His word and ordinances to the best of its knowledge and understanding. The law of Christ is the law of the church. All the decrees of popes and councils, all the resolutions of assemblies, synods, presbyteries, and associations, and all the ordinances of men as individuals, however great they be, when they are all put together, if they at all differ from the law of Christ, are mere wind and waste paper, nay, worse, they are treasonable insults to the majesty of King Jesus. Those who build apart from the authority of Christ build off of the foundation, and their fabric will fall. There is no law and no authority in a true church but that of Christ Himself ; we who are His ministers are His servants and the servants of the church, and not lords or law-makers. To His law a faithful church brings all things as to the sure test. As churches we are not legislators, but subjects ; it is not for us to frame constitutions, invent offices, and decree rites and ceremonies, but we are to take everything out of the mouth of Christ, and to do what He bids us, as He bids us, and when He bids us. Parliaments and kings have no authority whatever in the church, but Christ alone rules therein. If any portion of a church be not based upon Christ it is a mere deforming addition to the plan of the great Architect, and mars the temple which God has built, and not man. What a blessed thing it is to feel that you belong to a church which has a rock under it, because it is constituted by Christ's authority. We feel safe in following an ordinance which is of His commanding, but we should tremble if we had only custom and human authority for it. How secure we feel in believing a doctrine which is of our Lord's teaching, for we can say, " this is not mere opinion, this is not the judgment of a wise man, this is not the decree of councils, but this is the Master's own declaration." Not one of His words shall ever fall to the ground.

There is in His authority no change, for ever is His word settled in heaven, and He is in Himself the same yesterday, to-day, and for ever. Steadfast is that church which carefully follows His guiding line, but that which departeth from His fixed rule and authority hath left the foundation, and therein ceased to be a church.

A foundation is indispensable to a building, and so Christ is indispensable to a true church. In a house you could do without certain of the windows, you might close a door, and you might remove parts of the roof, and still it might be a house, but you cannot have a house at all if you take away the foundation ; and so you cannot have a church of Christ if Jesus Christ be not there as the foundation and corner stone. When sermons are preached without so much as the mention of Christ's name, it takes more than charity, it requires you to tell a lie to say " That was a Christian sermon " ; and if any people find their joy in a teaching which casts the Lord Jesus into the background, they are not His church, or else such teaching would be an abomination to them. Yet have I heard it said that from some ministries you may go away like Mary Magdalene from the sepulchre, exclaiming, " They have taken away my Lord, and I know not where they have laid Him." One told me the other day that he had heard a discourse from a Christian pulpit which would have been applauded by Jews and Mahometans, for there was not a trace of Christ in it. Another declared that in another place he heard priests, and clergy, and sacraments so much puffed up that as for faith in the Lord Jesus it seemed to be a very small matter. Brethren, this is not so in the church of Christ. There the Lord Jesus is Alpha and Omega—first and last, beginning and end. True Christians make much of Christ ; indeed, they make all of Him : and as for priests and preachers they say, " Who then is Paul, and who is Apollos, but ministers by whom ye believed, even as the Lord gave to every man " ? O brethren, let us see to this. If anything be put into Christ's place we make it an antichrist, and we are not Christians, but anti-Christians. The true church saith, " Give us what learning and eloquence you will, but we cannot be content except Christ be glorified ; preach us what you may, we will never be satisfied unless He who is the express image of the Father shall be set forth in our midst." Then, I say, she speaketh like the true bride of Christ, but if she can be content to see her Lord dishonoured, she is no chaste spouse of Christ.

Let us put this, our first point, in a few sentences. It is not the union of men with men that makes a church if Jesus Christ be not the centre and the bond of the union. The best of men may come into bonds of amity, and they may form a league, or a federation, for good and useful purposes, but they are not a church unless Jesus Christ be the basis upon which they rest. He must be the ground and foundation of the hope of each and of all.

Neither can a church be created by a mere union to a minister. It is most good and pleasant to see brethren dwelling together in unity ; it is most advantageous that between the pastor and his flock there should be perfect love, but the relationship must not be exaggerated beyond due bounds. Brethren, there must be no glorying in men, nor blind following of them. A body formed of individuals whose religion lies in drinking in the theories and opinions of a religious teacher falls short of being a church of God. The church is not built on Paul, nor upon Apollos, nor upon Cephas, but upon the sole authority of Jesus Christ. We are not to be believers in Luther, Calvin, Wesley, or Whitefield, but in Christ. Of such believers a true church must be composed. Neither is a church made by the following of any particular form or rite. We have one Lord, one faith, one baptism ; and we are bound to be loyal to Christ in His ordinances as in all else, but it is not the practice of an ordinance which constitutes a church. It is well to be united and bound together in loyalty to the faith once delivered to the saints, but, unless there is vital, personal union with the person of Christ on the part of the members of the church, their association may constitute a league for the defence of orthodoxy, or a confederation for the maintenance of a form of religious thought, but it is not a church. No, most blessed Lord, Thou must be there, or nothing is there ! Pastors, elders, deacons, teachers, evangelists, these are courses of precious stones in the heavenly temple, but without Thee they are no church, for the foundation is wanting. All Thy saints come to Thee and rest on Thee, O Christ ; and in Thee all the building, fitly framed together, groweth unto an holy temple in the Lord. Thou, O Christ, art the seed-corn out of which the church grows, the stem from which it branches, the head in which it lives, the shepherd by whom it is fed, the captain by whom it is marshalled, the husband to whom it is married : Thou art, indeed, the all in all of the church which Thou hast redeemed with Thine own blood.

> " God hath a sure foundation given,
> Fixed as the firm decrees of heaven
> The changeless everlasting rock,
> That braves the storm, and bides the shock.
> *There build :* the gates of hell in vain
> Against that rock their war maintain.
> Christ is the rock, the corner stone,
> God rears His beauteous house thereon."

Thus far, then, we have declared that there is no church except that which is built on Jesus Christ. This truth we assert in the face of all men, let them make what they will of it.

II. Secondly, we assert that there is NO GOSPEL BUT WHAT IS BUILT ON JESUS CHRIST. There are many pretended gospels in the world. Paul said once " another gospel," and then he corrected himself, and said, " which is not another," for strictly speaking there is only one gospel and there cannot be two. The good news, God's good news to men, is one. There never were two gospels, for there never were two Saviours or two redemptions, and there never will be ; but a Saviour and a redemption are necessary to a gospel, and therefore there can be only one. The foundation of the gospel is one, namely Jesus Christ, and there is no other possible foundation. For, first, *there is but one Mediator, by whom God speaks words of grace.* " There is one God, and one Mediator between God and men, the Man Christ Jesus." If then, beloved, any man shall come to you and say, " God hath spoken to me, and bidden me to say to you somewhat other and above what Jesus hath said," receive him not. If any man say unto you, " I have a revelation from heaven, and God bids me speak," if he speak not according to the words of Christ Jesus he is a false prophet, and cometh not from God at all. Yea, moreover, if bishop, or council, or church speak otherwise than Christ has spoken, the truth is not in any of them. All that ever spake from God, both before Christ and after Christ, have spoken after their manner and measure in the same fashion as Christ Jesus the Lord, for the voice of God is not two, but one, and the word of God is not two or three, but one ; and now at this day ye may rest quite certain that, if God hath anything to say unto us, He hath in these last days spoken to us by His Son, and His own hand has closed and sealed the revelation of God. Woe unto us if we hear Him not, and woe unto us if we listen to other voices. Indeed, if we be the sheep of Christ we shall not regard new voices, for our Lord hath said it, " A stranger will they not follow, for they know not the voice of strangers." The true gospel comes through Christ as the Mediator, and through Him alone, and that which comes otherwise is not the gospel.

The true gospel has Christ's divine person as its glory, and there can be no gospel without this. Christ is God, and in Him dwelleth all the fulness of the Godhead bodily. In the person of Christ the divinity has come down to us to heal our diseases and remove our griefs. Now, if you hear of a gospel which begins by saying that Christ is not the Only-begotten of the Father, or that He is not the Son of God, close your ears to it, for it is not the gospel of God. Unless Jesus be extolled as certainly God over all, blessed for ever, the preaching is not the gospel.

Jesus Christ is the essence of the gospel : He Himself is the good news, as well as the medium of it. The good news is that God hath sent His only-begotten Son into the world that we might live through Him. Eternal redemption has been obtained for us by the life, death, and resurrection of the Lord Jesus, and this is the gospel. There is pardon through His blood, justification through His righteousness, and sanctification through His Spirit. Complete salvation is freely provided for believers in Him, and the grace of God through Him is abundantly displayed to the very chief of sinners. God hath made Him to be unto us wisdom, and righteousness, and sanctification, and redemption ; in fact, all the blessings that are needed to lift man up into the favour of God, and keep him there for ever, are stored up in the person of Jesus, in whom God's love hath displayed itself to the fullest degree. Jesus is the sum and substance, crown and glory of the gospel. If, then, you hear a gospel in which the freewill of man is spoken of as the main agent, in which the works of man, or the forms and ceremonies practised by priests, are set up as being fundamental things, reject such teaching, for it is not the good news from heaven. The one good news is this,—" God was in Christ, reconciling the world unto Himself, not imputing their trespasses unto them." Let others preach what they please ; as for us, " we preach Christ crucified." Jesus Himself preached the very gospel of the gospel when He cried, " Come *unto Me,* all ye that labour and are heavy laden, and I will give you rest."

Now then, brethren, for I speak to many of you who teach the gospel, I beseech you to recollect my simple text of to-day, and henceforth teach nothing apart from Christ. The teaching of doctrines is not the teaching of the gospel if those doctrines be held in a dry, didactic style apart from Christ. Suppose I preach the doctrine of election—that is one thing ; but unless I preach that we are chosen in Christ I have left out the foundation, and my teaching crumbles to the ground : as a bowing wall shall it be, and as a tottering fence. Suppose I preach final perseverance, it is well; but I have not preached the gospel unless I show that it is because Jesus lives we shall live also, and that the preservation of the saints depends on their union with Him. Suppose I am teaching justification, it is not the true justification unless it is the righteousness of God in Christ Jesus which I hold forth. Herein I commend to you the example of the earlier preachers of the church. From such of their writings as remain we gather that they dwelt much upon the actual events of the Redeemer's life. They are not always so clear as one could wish upon the great doctrines as Paul gives them to us, but there is one point in which they excel. You may not hear enough from them about justification by faith, but you hear a great deal concerning the precious blood of Christ : they do not always speak so clearly upon regeneration as we could desire, but they speak much of the resurrection of Christ, and of the newness of life which His saints enjoy in virtue thereof. Pardon to them is a washing in the blood of Christ : conversion is being called by Christ : resurrection is a risen Christ. Everything is brought out as a matter of fact arising from the actual life and death of the Saviour, and I am free to confess that I greatly admire this way of preaching the gospel. How does Paul put it ? What was the gospel to Him ? Hear him : "Moreover, brethren, I declare unto you the gospel which I preached unto you, which also ye have received, and wherein ye stand ; by which also ye are saved, if ye keep in memory what I preached unto you, unless ye have believed in vain. For I delivered unto you first of all that which I also received, how that Christ died for our sins according to the scriptures ; and that He was buried, and that He rose again the third day according to the scriptures ; and that He was seen of Cephas, then of the twelve." Thus, you see, Paul's body of divinity was the life and death of that only embodied divinity, the Lord Jesus. My brethren, always set forth the gospel in close connection with your Lord, fetching it, as it were, out of Him. The juice of the grape is pleasant, but if you would know what it is in all its purity keep the grapes near you, and press them in the vineyard where they grow. So the gospel is the wine of Christ, but it is sweetest when it flows fresh from the cluster. Preach Jesus Christ Himself when you preach His doctrine, or else you may make the doctrine to be like the stone at the door of His sepulchre, whereas it ought to be like a throne of ivory on which, like another Solomon, your Lord sits resplendent.

Some preach experience, and they do well ; but they should be exceedingly careful to keep Jesus very prominent. We have a school of brethren who preach little else than experience, and I do not condemn them ; but what is the experience of a poor fellow-sinner to me ? How does it help me to hear that he groans as I do, or sings as I do ? It may be of some small service to me, but there are more excellent things. I want to know how Jesus felt, and what Christ can do for my brother and for me. Experience is admirable when Jesus Christ is set forth in it ; but if you take up an experimental vein of things, whether of human corruption, or of human perfection, and Jesus Christ is put in the background, you are marring the gospel. Jesus is the one foundation, and there is no gospel apart from Him.

So, too, with practice. By all means let us have practical preaching, and plenty of it, and let it come down sternly and faithfully on the vices of the times ; but merely to preach against this and that vice, and extol this and that virtue, is a mission fit enough for Socrates or Plato, but does not well beseem a minister of Jesus Christ. Set Jesus forth, my practical brother. His example shames vice and encourages virtue. Set Him up as the mirror of perfection, and in Him men will see what they ought to be, and learn how to come at it. Jesus Christ, then, is the only gospel. We leave that point, being abundantly sure that you are persuaded of it.

III. Thirdly. THERE IS NO HOPE OF SALVATION BUT THAT WHICH IS BUILT UPON CHRIST. This is another point upon which I need not speak much. I will only spend a few minutes in talking upon certain other hopes. No doubt some think it must be well with them because they were brought up from their childhood most respectably, their parents were excellent Christian people, and they believe that they themselves, having never done anything very wrong, are no doubt safe. Ah, my dear hearers, if this is your only hope, you are lost, for you are dead in sin. That which is born of the flesh—the best of flesh that ever was—is flesh, and flesh and blood cannot inherit the kingdom of God. You must be born again, you must have a far better hope than any which can spring out of your birth and your relations. "Ay, but," saith another, "I had all the ceremonies of the church performed upon me." Yes, and it makes no difference to me what church it was. If you are building even upon rites which God has given, they will not suffice you ; they cannot bear the weight of your soul. Baptism, the Lord's Supper, or fifty thousand sacraments, if men were to make so many, would not help you one solitary inch. The only foundation for your soul's hope must be Christ, and none of these outward things. "Ah," saith another, "but I have diligently performed a great many good works." I would to God you had ten times as many good works ; but if you have committed one single sin no works can save you. All the good works of the best men that ever lived would make but a rotten foundation for them if they were to place reliance thereon. Abound in good works, but do not trust them. Human merit is a foundation of sand. "But I have had special spiritual feelings," says one ; "I have been broken down, I have been lifted up." Yes, you may have been crushed down to hell's door, and lifted up to heaven's gate, but there is nothing in feelings and excitements which can be a ground of hope. "Why," says one, "it has troubled me that I have not had these feelings." Do not let it trouble you, but go to Jesus Christ and rest in Him, feelings or no feelings. High frames and low frames are delusions all, if they be trusted in. We can no more be saved by our feelings than by our works. "Oh, but," saith another, "I have confidence that I am saved, for I have had a wonderful dream, and, moreover, I heard a voice, and saw a vision." Rubbish all ! Dreams, visions, voices ! Throw them all away. There is not the slightest reliance to be placed upon them. "What, not if I saw Christ ?" No, certainly not, for vast multitudes saw Him in the days of His flesh, and died and perished after all. "But surely a dream will save me." It will give you a dreamy hope, and when you awake in the next world your dream will be gone. The one thing to rest upon is the more sure word of testimony :—Christ Jesus came into the world to save sinners, and whosoever believeth in Him is not condemned. I believe in Him, and, therefore, I am not condemned. Why do I believe my sin to be forgiven ? Because Jesus died to put away the sins of believers, and there is no condemnation to those who are in Him. Why do I believe myself to be justified ? Because he that believeth is justified ; the word of God says so. How do I know that I am saved ? Because Jesus Christ has declared that whosoever believeth in Him is not condemned. To believe in Him is to trust in Him, to make Him my foundation. I do trust in Him, He is my foundation, and I am saved, or else His word is not true. I know that His word is true, and therefore I am at rest. It is written, " He that believeth in Him hath everlasting life." I believe in Him, therefore I have everlasting life. I have His promise that I shall never perish, neither shall any pluck me out of His hand ; therefore I shall never perish, neither shall any separate me from His love.

You see, then, there is no hope of salvation but what is fixed upon Christ alone ; and I do invite and entreat you, if any of you have any hope which goes beyond Christ or beside Christ, get rid of it, throw it on a dunghill, and loathe it as an insult to God. Do as the man did with the bad bank note. When he found it was a forgery he buried it, and ran away as fast as he could, for fear anybody should think the note had ever been in his possession. So, if you are trusting in anything that is not of Christ, bury your faith, and run away from it, for it is a false confidence, and will work ill to your soul. Let your faith cry, " None but Christ " ; all-saving faith delights in that cry. For eternal salvation, " other foundation can no man lay than that is laid."

IV. Our last point is this,—there is NO CHRISTIAN BUT THE MAN BUILT ON JESUS CHRIST. Here is a Christian, and of one thing in him I am sure : I cannot tell whether he holds Arminian views or Calvinistic views, but if he is a Christian he has no foundation but Christ. Here is a person who reverences the Pope, here is another who glories in the name of Protestant, here is a third who is a Baptist : which is the Christian out of these ? I answer, he is the Christian that is built on Christ, whoever he may be ; but if he can do without Christ he is not worthy the name of Christian. What do we mean ? Why this. I mean first, every man to be a Christian must *rest his whole soul upon Christ* as to eternal salvation. There must be no stuttering or stammering over that ; there must be no mixing up the merits of Jesus with priests or ceremonies : no, it must be a clear, straight line—Christ for me, Christ everything for me, my sole and only hope. Any deviation here is fatal. On the cross is written, *Spes unica*, and it remains the one only hope of a burdened soul.

Next, if you are to be a Christian, *Christ must be your model :* by the aid of His Holy Spirit, you must try to do what He would have done in your position and under your circumstances. You are not to say, " I cannot follow Christ in this " : you are never to renounce His leadership. If you do you must give up being a Christian, because you are bound to take up His cross and follow Him. He claims to be your King when He becomes your Saviour. A true Christian is a man who builds upon Christ as his model as walls are built on a foundation. A true Christian is one whose growing up is in Christ, for, strange to say, the temple of God grows. Nor need we wonder, for it is a living temple. I have seen magnificent pieces of architecture, masterpieces, and it has struck me when I looked at them that they must have grown. An ordinary, clumsy bit of work displays the mason and the carpenter, but perfect architecture looks as if it grew ; and Christ's church does grow, for Christ's people grow. But all our up-growing must come out of Christ. When a man says, " Years ago I used to worship with these Christian people, and I felt very happy with them, but I have now more education and have got beyond them," he is guided by his pride and not by grace. No true Christian talks so. The higher he grows the more he grows into Christ ; the wiser he is the more he shows the wisdom of Christ. If he has begun aright he may advance as far as he can, but he never can advance beyond Christ ; he will get to be less and Christ will be more and more to him, for he is not a Christian who does not still stick to this,— that the foundation goes as far as he means to go, and he builds never beyond that, but builds upward upon that, and upon that alone.

And he, again, is the true Christian who *lives for Christ*, to whom Christ's glory is the great object of his being. He is a Christian who reckons that time wasted which is not used for Jesus, that substance wasted which is not used in obedience to Jesus : who considers that he does not live except as Christ lives in him.

Brothers and sisters, I pray that you may all be Christians of this sort, only do let it be with you evermore Jesus Christ. I do not like to preach a sermon without feeling the presence of my Master. I have done so, but never to my own comfort. I cannot bear to come away from the Monday evening prayer-meeting without feeling that the Lord has been there, and He generally is. The true heart does not like to engage in any kind of enterprise without first consulting Him, and doing it in His sight. We are a very busy church, and I want you, as a busy church doing a great deal, always to keep the Master near you. The most holy work gets to be mere routine, to be done mechanically, unless we enjoy His dear love, and sweet presence, and blessed smile in the doing of His will. Sit at Jesus' feet with Mary as well as work for Him like Martha. May He be the foundation of everything, not only of the church, but of our hope, of our character, of every little thing we do. When you are laying the first stone of a new enterprise, lay it upon Christ with fair colours. Set it in the vermilion of His precious blood ; perfume it with the oil of gratitude, and lay it upon Him alone ; so shall you build for eternity, and glorify His precious name.

PRIDE CATECHIZED AND CONDEMNED

" For who maketh thee to differ from another ? and what hast thou that thou didst not receive ? now if thou didst receive it, why dost thou glory, as if thou hadst not received it ? "—1 Corinthians iv. 7.

PRIDE grows apace like other ill weeds. It will live on any soil. In the natural heart it flourishes, springing up without sowing, and growing without watering ; and even in the renewed heart it all too readily takes root when Satan casts abroad a handful of its seed. Of all creatures in the world the Christian is the last man who ought to be proud ; and yet, alas, we have had mournful evidence both in past history and in our own observation, and worst of all in our own personal experience, that Christian men may become lifted up, to their own shame. Paul set himself very earnestly to deal with this disease when he saw it raging among the Corinthians. He felt it needful to do so, for it was leading to other mischiefs of the most disgraceful kind. Pride and self-conceit had led the members of the church in Corinth to choose for themselves distinct leaders, and to arrange themselves under separate banners : the followers of this man thinking themselves better than the followers of that. Thus the body of Christ was divided, and and all sorts of ill feeling, jealousy, emulation, and envy sprang up in the church of God where all ought to have been mutual helpfulness and loving unity. Paul therefore earnestly, and with great wisdom, assailed the spirit of pride.

Paul was well aware of one fact, namely, that pride is shallow and superficial. It cannot endure honest questioning, and so Paul tried it by the Socratic method, and put it through a catechism. He puts three questions to it in this verse, and these three all called upon his friends to go a little lower in their contemplation of themselves than their pride had before allowed them to go. Pride said, " I have such and such gifts " ; but Paul replied, " What hast thou that thou didst not receive ? " Thus he digged deeper and undermined pride. The receipt of those gifts from God it had forgotten altogether ; therefore, by bringing that fact to mind the apostle took pride right under the root, and that is always the best way to destroy a weed. To cut off the green top, and leave the crown of the root so that it may spring up in the next shower, or the next sunshine, is of no avail ; but to go deep down and tear up the root is effectual : this Paul did with pride by reminding the vainglorious Corinthians that the gifts which they possessed were no ground of glory, because they had received them as alms from the charity of God.

Another truth is also illustrated by Paul's procedure, namely, that pride is always inconsistent with the true doctrine of the gospel. You may use this test concerning any preaching or teaching that you meet with : if it legitimately and logically leads a man to boast of himself, it is not true. Our chemists use litmus to discover the presence of acid in any liquid submitted to them, for the paper then takes a reddish tint ; and you may use this as your test, that when a doctrine makes you red with pride it contains the acid of falsehood. That which puffs up is not of God, but that which lays the man low, and exalts Jesus Christ, has at least two of the tokens of truth. That which glorifies man cannot have been revealed by God, for He has said that no flesh shall glory in His presence. Such teaching may appear very lustrous with affected holiness, and very fascinating with pretended spirituality, and there may be much in your fondest desires which inclines your heart towards it, as there always is in the novelties of the present day, but try it whether it be of God by the test which is here suggested. If with a sleek hand it brushes your feathers the right way, and makes you feel " What a fine fellow I am," you ought at once to flee from it. The very fact that it flatters you should be to you like a foghorn to warn you of danger. Say to every doctrine which fosters pride, " Get thee behind me, Satan, for thou savourest not the things that be of God and of truth, or thou wouldst not speak so well of me."

My object this morning shall be to attempt to do with our own pride what Paul sought to do with that of the Corinthians, namely, to go a little deeper then we generally go when measuring our own abilities ; and then I shall try to use the silver spade of the doctrines of grace, so that this hemlock of pride may be taken up by the roots. Looking at the text I notice, first, *a question to be answered with ease*— " Who maketh thee to differ from another ? and what hast thou that thou didst not receive ? " secondly, *a question to be answered with shame*— " Now if thou didst receive it, why dost thou glory, as if thou hadst not received it ? " and then, thirdly, I shall occupy your attention a few minutes with *other questions which these questions suggest.* May the Holy Spirit graciously bless the word.

I. In a two-fold form the apostle gives us A QUESTION TO BE ANSWERED WITH EASE. There may be some who would be puzzled with these questions, but I do not suppose there are any such people present ; at any rate, there are no such members of our church. When we are asked, " Who maketh thee to differ from another ? " our answer is immediately, " God by His grace has made us to differ " : and if we are asked, " What hast thou that thou didst not receive ? " we reply, " We have nothing but our sin ; for every good gift and every perfect gift is from above, and cometh down from the Father of lights."

We are the more glad to hear Paul say this, because he was what is nowadays styled a " self-made " man. It very frequently happens that a man who makes himself has very great respect for his maker. Is it not natural that he should worship his creator ? Paul was a man who, as far as the Christian church is concerned, at any rate, had forced his way up without aid from others. He began in that church with no respect, but under very much suspicion. The brethren had heard that he persecuted the saints, so that at first they would scarce receive him ; his name was a terror rather than a pleasure ; but Paul, with that high spirit, that consecrated ardour, that indefatigable industry, that wondrous courage of his, backed, of course, by the grace of God, came to the front until he could honestly claim, without egotism, that he was "not a whit behind the very chief of the apostles, though," said he, "I be nothing." Paul was a man who had not been borne upon the crest of the wave into an eminent position, he did not wake up one morning and find himself famous, but he had put forth all his powers in the struggle of life, and laboured with persistent energy year after year. When he persecuted the saints of God he did it ignorantly, in unbelief, and thought he did God service; and all his life-long for him to know a thing to be right was to strive after it. He had been kept from self-seeking and deceit, he had been an intensely active, strong-minded, high-souled man, and he had done a grand life-work by which the church is still affected; and yet Paul himself had nothing whereof to glory. His testimony to his own indebtedness to God's grace is so plain, and given so many times over, that we cannot mistake it. He says distinctly, "By the grace of God I am what I am." He counted his own righteousness as worthless, and only desired that he might be found in Christ, arrayed in the righteousness which is of God by faith. Do we address to-day any self-made man, as the world calls men who have risen from the ranks? Have you taken credit to yourself, dear friend, for your success in life? Do you plume yourself upon your having risen by your own exertions? Then cease from such boasting, and in the spirit of the apostle ask yourself the question, "Who maketh thee to differ, and what hast thou that thou didst not receive?"

Our question is easy to answer, whether it be applied to natural gifts or to spiritual ones. There is a tendency to boast in *natural gifts*, but if questioned concerning them we must give the self-evident answer that any natural gifts we possess are not to be set to our credit, but were bestowed on us by God. Some gifts come to us as the result of *birth*, and of course in that matter we had no hand. It may be we were born of Christian parents, and that pedigree is one for which we shall always be thankful: we had sooner number our parents with the saints of God than with the peers of the realm: but truly, brethren, we should be foolish to boast of godly ancestors, for we had not the choosing of them. Children of pious parents, you cannot look with disdain even upon those who are basely born, for you did not cause yourselves to be born any more than they did.

From their birth some derive physical strength. It always seems to me to be a very insane thing for a man to glory in his animal force, for there can be no merit in it; yet there are some who do so. In the strength of those brawny limbs of theirs, and those powerful muscles, some vaunt themselves abundantly. Though the Lord taketh not pleasure in the legs of a man, yet some count it a very wonderful thing that they can outleap or outrun their fellows. O athlete, though thou be strong as Samson, or swift as Asahel, what hast thou that thou hast not received? Hadst thou been born with a tendency to consumption, or with some other hereditary weakness, couldst thou have prevented it? And now that thou art strong, art thou to be praised for that any more than a horse or a steam engine?

The same is true of beauty of person, which too frequently is the cause of vanity. Beauty is often a snare on this account. What if thy features be delicately chiselled, what if thine eyes are bright as the morning, and thy countenance fair as the lily, what if there be a charm in thine every glance; what hast thou in all these for which to praise thyself? Jezebel also was fair to look upon, and is she to be praised? Is not thy beauty the gift of God? Bless thy Creator for it, but do not despise those who are less comely, for in so doing thou wilt despise their Maker. How often do we hear a laugh raised behind their backs against persons who are somewhat grotesque, or it may be deformed; but God made them, and who is he that shall dare to taunt the Maker with what He has done? What hast thou, O thou fairest among women; what hast thou, O thou comeliest among the sons of men, but what thou hast received? Cease, then, those mincing airs and tossings of the head.

The same is true with regard to the rank which comes of birth. Some men are born—according to heraldic arrangements—noble. In what way is a new-born babe noble? Can true nobility arise out of anything but personal character? They are, however, born with the repute of nobility, and are at once regarded with respect. Are they not our future rulers? Through no deed or desert, or talent or heroism of their own, some are as it were by accident, or rather by the sovereign ordinance of providence, placed above others, wherefore then should they glory in what is so purely a matter of gift? O thou who art great and honourable amongst men, what hast thou but what thou hast received? Walk in lowly gentleness, and live with true nobility of character, and so make thy rank a blessing.

Brethren and sisters, how much all of us owe in the matter of birth for which we sometimes take to ourselves credit. We have never fallen, perhaps, into the grosser immoralities, but should we not readily have done so if we had been huddled together in chambers where decency struggles for existence, or been compelled to take our walks abroad where blasphemy and vice contend with law and order, and are not to be subdued? If the worst of examples had been before us instead of the best, what might we not have become? We have sinned enough as it is, but very much of the fact that we have not sinned more must be laid rather to the account of our having commenced life under favourable circumstances than to any meritorious conduct of our own. In this respect, what have we that we did not receive? You have been honest, thank God for it: but you might have been a thief if your father had been so. You have been chaste and modest, be glad of it: you might not have been so had you been encompassed with other surroundings. You are at this time respected and reputable, and you carry on business in an upright manner; had you been as poor as some, you might have been tempted to as dirty transactions as they are chargeable with. In these common matters of morality we cannot tell how much we owe to birth, and how little to ourselves. Certainly self-applause ceases as we hear the question, "What hast thou that thou didst not receive?"

In the matter of *talent* there are very great differences. One man will very soon make his way in the world where others fail. Put him where we will, he will make his fortune; and his friends laughingly say that if he were transported to the desert of Sahara he would sell the sand at a profit. But who gave him that talent? What has he that he has not received? Another can study an art or a science and become proficient in it in a short time ; as a boy he is a leader at school, and as a man he is eminent in his sphere ; still, are not his wisdom and insight gifts from heaven ? Another man has the gift of eloquence, and can speak well, while his fellow has the pen of a ready writer. In either of these gifts a man may take so much content as by-and-by to become vainglorious, but the truth taught in our text ought always to prevent that folly. " What hast thou that thou didst not receive ? " That which God gave to thee He might have with-held, and the man whom thou despisest might have had thy gifts : he would have been foolish to despise thee if thou hadst been without them, and thou art foolish now to despise him.

What differences there are, too, as to what men are helped to make of themselves by *education*. Nowadays there is a better opportunity of education for all ranks and conditions of men, for which I am earnestly thankful, and hope that true religion will be connected with the advantage ; but all boys trained in the same school do not leave it equally educated. One is quick, and another dull ; one manages to place himself foremost, and another is doomed to be in the rear. Whether the difference be in the original conformation of the man, or be the result of different teaching, the result must alike be subject for thankfulness to God, for whether it be natural talent or excellent education, both are received.

Equally so is it with *wealth*. I may address some one to whom God has given large substance ; but, my dear friend, in the course of the accumulation of that substance you have had plenty of evidence that " it is God that giveth thee power to get wealth." There was a time when you had little enough, and it was a singular providence which put you in the way of rising. There have been times, too, when a little turn of the scale would have sent you into bankruptcy, but the markets went the other way, and you were made. You have seen others who were ahead of you in the race of prosperity left far behind, and though God has prospered you I know there have been anxious moments when you have had to lift up your eyes to the Most High, and beseech Him by His tenderness and mercy to help and deliver you. Well, inasmuch as this wealth is a blessing if you know how to use it rightly, ascribe the posses-sion of it to God, who has made you His steward. Do you tell me that you have had a keener eye and exercised more industry than others, as well as a better judgment ? True, but who gave you the judg-ment, and who gave you the health with which to be industrious ? Many another man has been as industrious, and yet has failed ; many another has been as willing to work, but he has been disabled by sickness ; many another man has had as keen an eye, but alas, his judgment has been baffled by misfortune ; another man began life with as clear a brain as you, but now he is confined in the asylum and you still are in possession of all your faculties. O sirs, never sacrifice to your own net and drag, and say, " We brought up these treasures from the deep " ; but bless God who gave you all that you have of earthly things, for what have you that you have not received ? I would that you felt more than you do that you are only stewards, that your possessions are lent to you to be used for God's glory and the good of others, and neither to be squandered nor hoarded for yourselves.

But now, brothers and sisters, this is very em-phatically true as to *our spiritual gifts*, and I invite you to consider this truth—" What hast thou that thou didst not receive ? There has long been a great doctrinal discussion between the Calvinists and the Arminians upon many important points. I am my-self persuaded that the Calvinist alone is right upon some points, and the Arminian alone is right upon others. There is a great deal of truth in the positive side of both systems, and a great deal of error in the negative side of both. If I was asked, " Why is a man damned ? " I should answer as an Arminian answers, " He destroys himself." I should not dare to lay man's ruin at the door of divine sovereignty. On the other hand, if I were asked, " Why is a man saved ? " I could only give the Calvinistic answer, " He is saved through th esovereign grace of God, and not at all of himself." I should not dream of ascrib-ing the man's salvation in any measure to himself. I have not found, as a matter of fact, that any Christ-ian people care seriously to quarrel with a ministry which contains these two truths in fair proportions. I find them kicking at the inferences which are supposed to follow from one or the other of them, and sometimes needlessly crying to have them " reconciled " ; but the two truths together, as a rule, commend themselves to the conscience, and I feel sure that if I could bring them both forward this morning with equal clearness I should win the assent of most Christian men. At this time, however, I have to confine myself to the statement that all the grace we have is the gift of God to us, and I trust none will, therefore, suppose that I deny the other side of the question. I believe assuredly that we have nothing good in us but what we have received. For instance, we were dead in trespasses and sin, and we were quickened into spiritual life : my brethren, did that life spring out of the ribs of death ? Did the worm of our corruption beget the living seed of regeneration ? It were absurd to think so. God be praised for His great love wherewith He loved us, even when we were dead in sin, which led Him to quicken us by His grace. We have been forgiven our great sins—wholly forgiven ; through the precious blood of Christ we have been made clean. Did we deserve it ? Does any man who professes to be a Christian say for a single moment that he deserved the ransom paid by Christ, and deserved the pardon of his sin ? It would be monstrous blasphemy even to imagine such a thing. Oh no ; " By grace are ye saved, through faith, and that not of yourselves, it is the gift of God : not of works, lest any man should boast." God forgave us freely ; there could not possibly have been any quality in sin which could have called forth forgiving love. He had mercy upon us because He would have mercy upon us ; not because we could claim anything at His hand.

Everything, dear friend, that makes you to *differ from the common sinner* is the gift of God's grace to you. You know it is. You have faith in Christ : yes, but did not the Holy Spirit work it in you ? Do you not cheerfully subscribe to the doctrine that faith is of the operation of God ? You have repentance of sin, but was the repentance natural to you ? Did you not receive it from Him who is exalted on high to give repentance ? Is not your repentance His gift ? " Truly," one will say, " but then the same gospel was preached to others as to us." Precisely so. Perhaps the very sermon which was the means of your conversion left others as they were. What made the difference then? Do you reply, "We willed to believe in Jesus." That is true; an unwilling faith would be no faith: but then who influenced your will? Was your will influenced by some betterness of nature in you so that you can claim credit for it? I for one reject with abhorrence any such an idea. Do you reply, "Our will was influenced by our understanding, and we chose what we knew to be best." But then, who enlightened your understanding? Who gave you the light which illuminated your mind, so that you chose the way of life? "Oh," say you, "but our hearts were set towards salvation, and the hearts of others were not." That also is true, but then who set your heart that way, who was the prime mover? Were you or God? There is the question, and if, my dear brother, you dare affirm that in the matter of your own salvation you were the prime mover I am at a loss to understand you, and I hope there are few of your creed. Jesus is not Alpha to you. You do not love Him because He first loved you. You were evidently not converted, or turned at all, but you turned yourself. You are not a new creature, but are your own new-creator. Do you look to see the same thing in others? Why, then, do you act as you do? Why do you pray the Lord to turn others if you believe that He did not turn you? Do you pray the Lord to convert your children? Why do you do it? If it is left entirely to them to be the prime movers, why pray to God about them? "Ah," says one, "God must treat all alike." I ask again, why do you pray for your children? You ask God to do a wrong thing in blessing your children in preference to other people, if it be true that He is bound to treat all alike. When you go practically to work these sentiments do not hold water. The man who knows that the Holy Spirit was first in His operations upon the mind, and who calls Christ Jesus the Alpha and the Omega of his salvation, is the man who can fairly go to the Lord, and pray for the conversion of this man or that; and he too is sure to give God all the glory of his salvation, and magnify and bless the grace of the Most High.

Perhaps, my dear brother, there is a difference *between you and other saints*. I am sure there is reason for some saints to eclipse others, for some professors are very poor things indeed. Well, brother, you have a great deal more faith than others; where did you get it? If you received it from anywhere but from God, you had better get rid of it. Dear brother, you have more joy than some, and possibly you feel ashamed of your fellow Christians who are so doubting and sad: beware that you do not become vain of your joy, and remember, that if your joy is true joy you received it of the Lord. Are you more useful than others? You cannot help looking at certain professors who are idle and wishing that you could stir them up. I know I do; I would put a sharp pin into their downy cushions if I could: but for all that, who gives us activity, who gives us usefulness, who gives us zeal, who gives us courage, who gives us everything? If you, dear friend, get into such a condition that you begin to whisper to yourself, "I have improved my gifts and graces at a very noble rate, and am getting on exceedingly well in spiritual things," you will soon have to come down from your high places. If you register yourself A 1 at Lloyd's I will not sail with you, brother, for I fear your proud barque will tempt the tempest; I would rather sail with some poor Christian man whose

weather-beaten vessel would go to the bottom if Jesus were not on board, for I am persuaded he is safe. "Blessed is the man that feareth always." Blessed is the man who lies low at the foot of the cross, and who, concerning everything that he has, whether temporal or spiritual, ascribes all to the Giver of all Good.

Now we must pass on briefly to think of the second point.

II. HERE IS A QUESTION TO BE ANSWERED WITH SHAME. "If thou didst receive it, why dost thou glory, as if thou hadst not received it?" If any of us have fallen into vainglory, and we all have more or less done so, let us answer this question with confusion of face. Brother, sister, have you glorified in anything you have received? Then bethink you how wrongly you have acted, for you have robbed God of His honour. To glory in man is altogether inconsistent with glorying in God. Depend upon it every particle of praise we take to ourselves is so much stolen out of the revenues of the King of kings. Will a man rob God? Will a redeemed man rob God? Will a poor sinner snatched from between the jaws of death and hell by undeserved mercy, rob God? Lord have mercy upon us.

When we boast we also leave our truthful position, and every Christian ought to be ashamed to stand anywhere but in the truth. When I confess myself to be weak, helpless, and ascribe all I have to grace, then I stand in the truth; but if I take even the remotest praise to myself, I stand in a lie. The Lord have mercy upon us if we have dared to act falsehood in His presence.

Let us remember, too, that whensoever we prize ourselves highly we are sure to esteem our Lord less. Do you see any spiritual beauty in yourself? Then it is because you do not know what true beauty is? Do you say, "I am rich and increased in goods"? Then you know nothing, or very little, of what true wealth is. You have mistaken gilt for gold, and rags for raiment. I counsel thee buy of Jesus gold tried in the fire, and fine linen wherewith thou mayest be clothed. Depend upon it our judgment is very much like a pair of scales: if Christ goes up self goes down; and if self rises Jesus falls in our esteem. No man ever sets a high price upon self and Christ at the same time.

"The more Thy glories strike mine eyes
The humbler I shall be,"

is a rule without exception.

Besides, if you and I have gloried in what we possess we have undervalued our fellow Christians, and that is a great sin. They are very dear to Jesus, and He accounts even their deaths precious. "Take heed that ye despise not one of these little ones that believe in Me"; but if we over-estimate ourselves the natural consequence is that we under-estimate others. Have I ever thought, "I am a rich man; and these poor people, though good Christians, are nobodies compared to me; I am of far more consequence to the church"? Have I conceived, because I have a measure of talent, that those holy men and women who cannot speak for Christ are of no great account? Or have I, because I happened to be an old, experienced Christian, snuffed out the young ones, and said, "They are only a pack of boys and girls"? Is this the way to speak of those who were bought with the blood of Christ, and are members of Christ's body? It will not do for us to despise the meanest saint. I believe there are many who are now pushed into the background and shoved into any hole and corner whom Christ looks upon with special delight, and will place first when He comes. Verily I say unto you, " There are first that shall be last, and there are last that shall be first."

Besides, all this honouring of ourselves generally puts us off from the right course as to our gifts, and makes us forget that these things are only lent us, to be used for our Master. It is required of stewards that they be found faithful, not that they vaunt themselves and deck themselves in their Master's goods. We have too much to do to afford to boast. Look at yonder young soldier who has just received his armour and his helmet. He has just entered the service. Look with what pleasure he sees his comely face reflected in his breastplate; how much he admires his plume; he thinks how grand he shall look in such gear. My dear fellow, all this while you have forgotten that to wear these things in the thick of the battle, where they will bear the dint of the sword, is what awaits you, and you do not consider that, not your gallant appearance, but your valour is what we want to see. When a man exalts himself because of what he possesses, he does not act as a soldier of the cross should do.

Here we will insert an illustration or two. There is a tendency in some to exalt themselves because God has placed them in *office*. They are ministers, deacons, elders, superintendents, or something. What mighty airs they give themselves ! " Honour to whom honour is due "—they seem to have learned the text by heart, and to have seen a personal reference in it. Have you never seen the footmen of princes when they are playing the great man ? What wonders of nature and art they often are. I was admiring one of them the other day, with all the reverence due. The vision of his pomp quite staggered me, for he was so gorgeous to look upon. I feel sure that his royal master was nothing like so striking, and certainly could not have been more pompous or aristocratic. While I was looking on with due wonder and reverence, somebody cruelly remarked, " What a flunkey ! "—a most irreverent observation, and yet very natural. My brothers, whenever you and I, because we have our best clothes on, and are ministers, or deacons, or elders, act as if we were very great men, somebody or another is sure to call us flunkeys too ; not perhaps exactly in so many words, but in language to the same effect. Do not let us expose ourselves to such contempt, and if ever we have done so, let us be rebuked at once by the thought of what we have seen in others.

Some persist in boasting about their experience. This also is vanity. Suppose a man here, who is a great pedestrian, has been over the Alps, and traversed Europe ; here is his walking-stick, and it boasts, " I am the most travelled walking-stick in creation, I have smitten the craggy brows of the Alps and bathed myself in the Nile." " Well," says one, " but wherever you have gone you have been carried by a power beyond yourself." So let the man who boasts in experience remember that in the paths of peace he has gone nowhere except as the Lord's hand has borne him onward ; he has been nothing but a staff in God's hands, and while he should be grateful he should never be proud.

I was in a beautiful garden the other day, upon the rocks, where the choicest of flowers and tropical plants are growing : while all around the rocks are bare, with scarce a trace of vegetable life. Now, suppose that garden were proud, and boasted of its fruitfulness. The answer would be, " Every basketful of earth had to be carried up to you, and you would not bear fruit now if it was not for the stream of water that is turned on, and tracked through many little mazes, and brought to the root of each plant you bear ; you would be a rock again in a few months if you were left to yourself ; therefore let the former of the garden rejoice in his work, but the garden itself may not glory." That is what the most fruitful believer would be if God let him alone—a barren rock, a wilderness.

Suppose I address some Christian who is happy, and joyous, and cheerful, and has such dainty bits sent home to him out of the promises, such precious words from Scripture applied to his heart. Dear friend, are you apt to think that there is something specially good about you because you get all these remarkable enjoyments ? Then let me disabuse your mind. It is your weakness which gets you these favours. When you are living in a hotel you will remark that certain persons have their dinners sent upstairs. What for ? Oh, that is because they are ill. If you are well you must go down to the *table d'hôte* with the rest ; but if you are ill they will send it upstairs, and pay you extra attention. These very comforts that God gives you ought to make you enquire whether there is not something amiss with you, and instead of thinking you are strong and well you should search and see if there is not some weakness which the Lord in His mercy intends to remove by the double comforts which He gives to you. Nothing in the world ought to be a cause of self-exaltation ; nothing that our God gives us ought to make us think highly of ourselves. Lower down, brother, lower down, and so you will rise. The way to heaven is downhill, not uphill. As Christ went down to the grave that He might come up again and fill all things, so must you go to the cross, and down to the grave of self and be buried with Christ, and learn the meaning of your baptism, and make it true that you are buried with Him to all the world, and to yourself also, for so only can you rise into the fulness of the new life.

III. Other questions which these questions suggest shall now, in the third place, occupy our attention. What are they ?

The first is this. *Have I ever given to God His due place in the matter of my salvation ?*—a question that I may very well put, for I recollect when I was converted to God, and truly converted too, but I did not know that it was the work of the Spirit in my heart ; I did not understand that it was the result of special grace. I had heard the gospel generally preached, but I had not learned the peculiar doctrines of grace ; and I recollect very well sitting down and thinking to myself, " I am renewed in my mind, I am forgiven, I am saved : how came that about ? " and I traced it to this, that I had heard the gospel, but as I knew that many never had an opportunity of hearing it, I saw special grace in my having had the opportunity to hear it. But then I said, " There are others who have heard it, but it was not blessed to them : how came it to be blessed to me ? " and I cogitated for awhile whether it could be something good in me that made the gospel useful to me, for if so I deserved to have the credit of it. Somehow the grace which God had given me made me fling that theory to the winds, and I came to this conclusion, " It must be God that made the difference," and having got that one thought into my mind, the doctrines of grace followed as a matter of course. Only by experimentally knowing that there has been a special work of grace in your own soul, will you be likely to place the Lord where He should be in your creed, for some provide a very inferior place for the Lord in the matter of their salvation. With them man is very great, and God is made little of ; but true theology makes God the very sun of the system, the centre, the head, the first, and chief. Have *you* done so ? If not, correct your views, and get a clearer view of the gospel of grace. May the Holy Spirit help you therein. To know the doctrines of grace will be much to your comfort, will tend to your stability, and will also lead you to seek the glory of God.

The next question is this, Have I this morning the spirit of humble gratitude ? How do I feel ? Do I take God's mercy as a matter of course, and view my own gifts without thankfulness ? Then I act like the brutes that perish, but let me pray this morning that humble, lowly gratitude may daily rule my spirit. Such gratitude will make you cheerful, it will make you earnest, it will in fact be an atmosphere in which all Christian graces will grow by the blessing of God's Spirit.

Next, seeing I have been a receiver, what have I done towards giving out again ? It cannot have been intended that I should receive and never give out, for if that be the case there is a sad lot for me. You know they used to make, and do still make, in the North of England, earthenware saving boxes for the children. You can put what you like in, but you cannot get it out any more until you break the box ; and there are persons of that sort among us. Some have died lately, and their estates have been reported in the Probate Court. There was plenty put in to them, but you could never get anything out, and consequently they had to be broken up. I only hope when they were broken up the gold and silver went the right way. What a pity to be like money boxes, to be of no good until you are broken up. One would like to get and give at the same time. We ought not to be as a stagnant pond, a Dead Sea, which receives from rivers all the year round, but gives forth no stream in return, and so becomes a stagnant, putrid lake. Let us be like the great lakes of America, which receive the mighty rivers and pour them out again, and consequently keep fresh and clear.

The next question is—Since what I have had I have received by God's grace, might I not receive more ? Come, brothers and sisters, with regard to gracious things I want you to be covetous. Covet earnestly the best gifts. If you have had faith, why should you not have more ? If God gave you hope, joy, experience, why not more ? You are not straitened in Him ; you can be only straitened in yourself. Try to remove those hindrances, and ask the Lord to give you more grace.

One other question—If all that Christians have they have received, sinner, why should not you receive as well as they ? If it were true that Christians got these good things out of themselves, then you, poor sinner, might despair, for you know you have no good thing in you ; but if the best of saints, the best Christian in heaven, has not anything but what he received, why should not you receive ? To receive, you know, is never a difficult thing. I warrant you that out of all the people in London there is not a man but what could receive. Try it on the present occasion. Let it be a thousand pounds, and see how many among us would be unable to receive. If there be a person about who would not receive, I tell you who it is—it is the man who thinks himself so rich that he does not care to have any more. Even so the proud, self-righteous Pharisee cannot receive; but you poor, good-for-nothing, empty sinners can receive ; and here is the mercy—" to as many as *received* Him, to them gave He power to become the sons of God, even to as many as believed on His name." Open that empty hand, open that empty heart : God grant they may be opened now by His own divine Spirit, and may you receive, and then I know you will join with us in saying, " Of His fulness have all we received, and grace for grace."

PURGING OUT THE LEAVEN

" Know ye not that a little leaven leaveneth the whole lump ? Purge out, therefore, the old leaven, that ye may be a new lump, as ye are unleavened. For even Christ our passover is sacrificed for us : therefore let us keep the feast, not with old leaven, neither with the leaven of malice and wickedness ; but with the unleavened bread of sincerity and truth."—1 Corinthians v. 6-8.

" WHAT God hath joined together, let no man put asunder." Evermore in Scripture the doctrines of grace are married to the precepts of holiness. Where faith leads the way, the virtues follow in a goodly train. The roots of holiness and happiness are the same, and in some respects they are but two words for the same thing. There have been persons who have thought it impossible that holiness should come out of the preaching of salvation by faith. If you tell men that "there is life in a look at the Crucified One," will they not conclude that cleanness of life is unnecessary ? If you preach salvation by grace through faith, and not at all by the works of the law, will they not draw the inference that they need not be obedient to Christ, but may live as they list ? To this the best answer is found in the godly, honest, and sober lives of the men who are most zealous for the gospel of the grace of God. On the other hand, there have been others of Antinomian spirit, who have dared to say that because they are saved, and Christ has finished His work for them, so that nothing is left undone by way of merit, therefore, henceforth they may act as they please, seeing that they are not under the law, but under grace. Our reply is, that the faith which saves is not an unproductive faith, but is always a faith which produces good works and abounds in holiness. Salvation *in* sin is not possible, it always must be salvation *from* sin. As well speak of liberty while yet the irons are upon a man's wrists, or boast of healing while the disease waxes worse and worse, or glory in victory when the army is on the point of surrendering, as to dream of salvation in Christ while the sinner continues to give full swing to his evil passions. Grace and holiness are as inseparable as light and heat in the sun. True faith in Jesus in every case leads to an abhorrence of every false way, and to a perseverance in the paths of holiness even unto the end.

The apostle Paul while he was showing the Corinthians how wrong they were to tolerate an incestuous person in their midst, compared the spirit of uncleanness to an evil leaven ; then the leaven suggested to him the passover, and turning aside for a moment he applied the type of the paschal feast, so as to make his argument yet more cogent. He would urge purity upon them by every conceivable reason, and his keen eye saw an argument in the celebration of the passover. In using this type he furnishes me with another proof of the fact, that hard by any Scripture wherein you find the safety of the believer guaranteed, you are sure to see needful holiness set side by side with it. Here you have at the passover a favoured people safe beneath the sprinkled blood, safe in that dire hour when the destroying angel's sword was unsheathed, but you find that people busily engaged in purging out the defiling leaven from their houses : they were not saved by purging out the leaven, but being preserved by the sprinkled blood, they were obedient to the divine precept, and diligently put away the corrupt and forbidden thing. The purity of the house from leaven went side by side with its safety by the blood.

We shall, this morning, first, consider *the happy condition of believers* ; next, *the holy duty commended to them*, running side by side with their privilege ; and thirdly, we shall show how *their happiness and holiness, their holiness and happiness*, act and re-act upon each other.

I. We have set forth to us THE HAPPY CONDITION OF ALL TRUE BELIEVERS IN CHRIST. " Christ our passover is sacrificed for us, therefore let us keep the feast."

The habitual, normal state of a Christian is that of one keeping a feast in perfect security. We are to be, as a rule, like the Israelites who stood at the table of the passover festival, with loins girt, and staves in their hands, expectant of a joyful deliverance. Observe how the apostle puts it ; take his words one by one. " Christ our passover is sacrificed for us." " Our passover," that by which God's wrath makes a transition, and passes over from us who deserve its full vengeance. It passed upon the Lamb of God, and therefore it passes over us. Christ is sacrificed or slain, His life is taken, for He gave Himself for us ; His life and blood, yea, His truest self He yielded up for us. The word *for us* implies substitution. Christ is sacrificed for or instead of us. We should never think of saying that Paul was sacrificed for us, though it is true Paul did lay down his life for the church of God, to promote the interests of the faithful, and in a certain sense, since his exertions handed down the gospel, he died even for us ; but we use the term so generally and so correctly in the sense of substitution, that we should not think of applying it to any but our Lord, who alone in the fullest sense was sacrificed *for* us. He is the Lamb of our passover, sacrificed in our behalf, that we might not be sacrificed, roasted in the fire of suffering that we might go free. It is by the process of substitution that, according to abundant Scriptures, believing sinners are passed over in judg-

ment, and so escape eternal condemnation. " For Christ also hath once suffered for sins, the just for the unjust, that He might bring us to God." " For He hath made Him to be sin for us, who knew no sin ; that we might be made the righteousness of God in Him." Christ hath redeemed us from the curse of the law, being made a curse for us : for it is written, Cursed is every one that hangeth on a tree." " For as by one man's disobedience many were made sinners, so by the obedience of one shall many be made righteous." No one can doubt this doctrine who believes the word of the Lord by the prophet Isaiah in his fifty-third chapter, " But He was wounded for our transgressions, He was bruised for our iniquities : the chastisement of our peace was upon Him ; and with His stripes we are healed. All we like sheep have gone astray ; we have turned every one to his own way ; and the Lord hath laid on Him the iniquity of us all." " He shall see of the travail of His soul, and shall be satisfied : by His knowledge shall my righteous servant justify many ; for He shall bear their iniquities." " He was numbered with the transgressors, and He bare the sin of many, and made intercession for the transgressors."

Our great joy is that the sacrifice through which we are passed over is already slain. No new victim is expected or required. The sacrifice by which we are delivered is complete. Accursed be all those who say that there is offered to God continually a sacrifice in the mass by which the sacrifice of Jesus Christ is rendered complete. He hath said, " It is finished," and they are liars before God who say otherwise. " This Man, after He had offered one sacrifice for sins for ever, sat down on the right hand of God." Do you think me severe in my speech, I say no other than Paul said, " If any man preach any other gospel, let him be accursed." All that was wanted to atone for our sin, all that was required to vindicate the law of God, is already offered, there is nothing left to be presented by so-called priests on earth, or to be made up by the penances and payments of their dupes. Our passover is sacrificed ; let others offer what they will, ours is the Lamb once slain, and there remaineth no more sacrifice for sin.

This completeness of sacrifice indeed is the main part of the festival which the Christian should perpetually keep. If there were anything yet to be done—if the substitutionary sacrifice were imperfect, how could we celebrate the feast ? Anxiety would destroy all enjoyment. " It is finished," is the joyous peal which rings us into the celestial banquet of present peace ; the fact that we are complete in Him, perfect in Christ Jesus, is our soul's deepest delight.

Our sacrifice is slain : " therefore," says the apostle—and it is a natural inference from it—" let us keep the feast." By which I understand this : Jesus Christ, the Paschal Lamb, not only was offered as a sacrifice towards God, but He has become a festival towards ourselves ; in Him we have communion with God, and joy and peace through believing. We are to keep the feast by feeding upon Christ. The paschal lamb was not slain to be looked at, to be laid by in store, or merely made the subject of conversation ; but it was slain to be fed upon. So, Christian, it is your daily business to feed upon Christ Jesus, whose flesh is meat indeed, and whose blood is drink indeed. Jesus is the food on which your faith must be nourished ; and what rich nourishment He is ! God over all, blessed for ever, hath redeemed us ; the Word made flesh, who dwelt among us, has been sacrificed for us. My soul, what more could be required ? What more canst thou desire, or can the Almighty One demand ? A sacrifice divine, a perfect Man in union with the eternal God, dies for thee. What more is needed to make thy faith firm and unmoved ? Come and feed thyself on this bread which came down from heaven. The infinite love of the great Sacrifice, the amazing wisdom of it, the transcendent merit of it, the abounding fulness of the blessings which it secures ; let your souls consider these things, and feed upon them until they are satisfied with favour and full of the goodness of the Lord. Here is a festival the viands of which never can be exhausted, and from which the guests need never depart. Remember that at the paschal supper the whole of the lamb was intended to be eaten ; and even thus, O believer, the whole of Christ thou art to feed upon. No part of Christ is denied thee, neither His humiliation nor His glory, His kingship nor His priesthood, His Godhead nor His manhood ; all this has He given to thee and for thee, and thou art now to nourish thy soul by meditating upon Him.

Forget not, moreover, that a feast is not only for nourishment, it is for something more, for joy, for exhilaration. Let us in this sense also keep a lifelong feast. The Christian is not only to take the doctrines which concern Christ, to build up his soul with them as the body is built up with food, but he may draw from them the wine of joy and the new wine of delight. It is meet that we rejoice in Christ Jesus. He is the bliss of the saints. Is it not a joy unspeakable and full of glory, that my sin will never be laid to my charge if I am a believer ; that my sin has been laid at Jesus' door, and He has put it all away, so that if it be searched for it shall not be found ? Is it not an intense delight to believe that Jesus has so effectually put away sin that no destroying angel can touch one of His saints ? There being no condemnation, there can be no punishment for us either in this world or in that which is to come. We are as safe as Israel when the door was sprinkled with the blood. And more, being justified, we rise to a higher position, we are adopted into the family of God, and if children, then heirs. What a vista of glory opens before our eyes at the mention of that word, heirs of God ! All things are ours, because Christ our passover has been slain for us. My brethren, do not let your religion merely keep you calm and quiet, look for bursts of joy. "Praise Him upon the cymbals, praise Him upon the high-sounding cymbals." Surely there should be an excitement of delight created by truths so grand, by blessings so inestimable as those of which we are partakers ! Let us not treat our religion as merely an ordinary meal for our souls, but as a holy banquet of wine wherein our souls may be exceeding glad.

When the Jews came together at the passover, we find that they were accustomed to sing. They did not close the paschal supper without chanting some portions of the great "Hallel," which consisted of those Psalms at the end of the book, dedicated to the praise of God. Let us keep the feast in the same way, nourishing our souls with Christ's sacrifice, making our hearts glad by reflecting upon the blessing which this has brought us, and never forgetting to magnify Jehovah, the Father, the giver

of Christ, the founder of the covenant, our God in Christ Jesus. Let your praises never cease. You remember what I started with, that when the apostle says, "let us keep the feast," having drawn his exhortation as an inference from the fact that the passover is killed, he does not mean, "let us sometimes keep the feast," but let us always keep it. Our passover is perpetual. It has no times and seasons, it is lifelong. Salute ye your God each morning with your hymn of praise, ye redeemed ones ; let not the sun go down without another hymn of thanksgiving. Praise Him, praise Him, praise Him. Ceaseless as your mercies let His praises be. O for the life of heaven on earth, to be always praising God ! Our sacrifice is slain, therefore let us keep this feast of daily adoration and hourly thankfulness to Him who passed us by in mercy when He might have smitten us in wrath.

At the passover the devout Jew was accustomed to teach his family the meaning of the feast. The children said, "What mean ye by this ordinance ? " And then the father explained to them how they came out of Egypt, saying, "With a high hand and an outstretched arm Jehovah brought us forth, and on the night when He smote the first-born of Egypt, He smote not us, for the lamb was slaughtered, and when the Lord saw the blood upon the door He passed over us." Let it be a part of our continual festival—and I do not know a more delightful duty—to tell to others what our Redeeming Lord has done. Too many of you need to be stirred up to this pleasant duty. When you once break through those wicked, cowardly habits—for I cannot help thinking them so in many of you—which lock your mouths and prevent your giving Jesus praise, you will find it sweet to tell to your children and kinsfolk the story of the atoning sacrifice. While blessing them you will obtain a double blessing in your own souls, and if it should please the Holy Spirit to bless your teaching to the salvation of your fellow men, you will be happy indeed.

Do not suppose that I am exhorting you to keep the feast when you come to the Lord's-supper. I do not refer to that emblematic feast at all. I refer to our daily life-long fellowship with Jesus. "Christ our sacrifice is slain for us, therefore let us keep the feast " ; the inference is of continuous force. When is Jesus slain ? Is He not slain at this hour ; was not His sacrifice completed upon Calvary's bloody tree ? Therefore let us keep the feast always, for the Lamb is always slain. Our keeping of the feast is not a matter for times and seasons, for festivals and holidays, it is always our position. O you who go with your heads bowed down like bulrushes, and yet are the Lord's true people, I would fain put my hand on your shoulders and say, " Christ our passover is sacrificed for us, therefore let us keep the feast." Wherefore should we lie in the dungeon when liberty is ours ? "Alas," saith a downcast one, " I have so many corruptions." I know you have, my dear brother. We will talk about that directly, but " Christ our passover is sacrificed for us, therefore let us keep the feast." " But I have so many troubles and I am so very poor." So were many of the Israelites, but when they had slain the passover they kept the feast ; so notwithstanding all these things which make you sorrow, you must feast, for " our passover is sacrificed." " Ah ! my cares," saith one. What business hath a believer with cares ? Is it not written, " Cast thy burden upon the Lord, He will sustain thee,

He will never suffer the righteous to be moved"? You cannot keep a feast while care, like a harpy, hovers above the table; but let us, like Abram, drive away the birds of prey, and keep the feast. "Ah! but I am thinking about the past, my old sins still haunt me." What, after Christ your passover is slain? Surely the past is blotted out and forgiven. "Still," says one, "my mind is heavy, my harp is on the willows." Will not a sight of Calvary relieve you? Jesus Christ was made a curse for you that you might not be regarded any longer as accursed. Will not this make you lift up the note of thanksgiving? Certainly it ought. It should be always feast time with God's servants, since Christ their passover is slain. "But I have nothing to rejoice in," says one, "except my religion." What more do you want? What was there brought on the table at that paschal supper by way of good cheer, except the paschal lamb? I grant you there was something else upon the table, but what was it? Bitter herbs. Surely those were not an addition to the joy? It was not sharp sauce such as we ordinarily use, but bitter, pungent herbs. These did not please the palate, yet they kept the feast upon the lamb, which was all they needed. So you may bring the bitter herbs of your deep repentance that your sin made it necessary that the Lamb of God should die; but all the feast is *in Him*, and all the world can contribute nothing to that feast but bitter herbs. If you had all the world, and derived comfort from it for a time, in the end it would become bitter as wormwood. Bitter herbs all things beneath the sky must be, only Jesus is the true feast. My soul, rejoice in the Lord always, for thou hast always reason to triumph, since Jesus Christ is slain.

II. Close side by side with the picture of the lifelong feast, we find A HOLY DUTY COMMENDED to us. "Purge out, therefore, the old leaven." "Let us keep the feast; not with old leaven, nor with the leaven of malice and wickedness, but with the unleaven of sincerity and truth."

Leaven is used in Scripture, we believe in every case—there is only one case in which the question could possibly be raised—as the emblem of sin. This arises partly from its sourness. We being ourselves leavened with evil, find leaven somewhat palatable at first, but God, who hates all evil, puts away the type in all its stages. Sin, which for awhile may seem pleasant, will soon be nauseous even to the sinner; but the very least degree of sin is obnoxious to God. We cannot tell how much God hates sin. With the entire intensity of His infinite nature He loathes it; He cannot look upon iniquity, it is detestable to Him, the fire of His wrath will burn for ever against it, because sin is infinitely loathsome to His pure and holy nature. He calls it leaven, then, because of its sourness. Leaven is, moreover, the offspring of a sort of corruption, and tends towards further corruption. Sin is a corruption, it dissolves the very fabric of society, it dissolves the constitution of man, wherever it gets into our nature it puts it out of order, disjoints it, destroys its excellence, and poisons its purity. Leaven is also very spreading. No matter how great the measure of flour, the leaven will work its way. There is no saying, "Hitherto shalt thou go, but no further," a little leaven leaveneth the whole lump. Even thus it is with sin. When that leaven had place among angels, it brought a multitude of them down to hell. One woman sinned, and the whole human race was leavened by her fault. One sin drops into the nature, and it becomes entirely deprived, corrupt through and through, by the leavening influence.

Now, according to the apostle, if the leaven of evil is permitted in a church, it will work its way through the whole of it. In the Christian church a little false doctrine is sure to pave the way for greater departures from truth, so that no one can predict the end and result of the first false teaching. You cannot say, "I will be so far unorthodox"; you might as well break the dykes of Holland, and bid the sea be moderate in its encroachments. The doctrines of the gospel have such a close relation to one another, that if you snap a link, you have broken the whole chain, and we may say of the system of truth what is written concerning the law, "He that offendeth in one point is guilty of all." The renunciation of one truth almost necessarily leads to the giving up of another, and before a man is half aware of it himself he has let go the gospel. I greatly fear that the denial of the eternity of future punishment is but one wave of an incoming sea of infidelity. Deny the awful character of the desert of sin, and the substitutionary work of Christ will soon follow. Indeed we have living proofs of this at this day, and we shall see many more before long. The new teaching eats as doth a canker. It speaks fair, but in its heart there is a deadly enmity to the gospel itself, and the sooner it is seen to be so the better for the church of God.

The leaven of evil living, too, is equally obnoxious in the church; tolerated in one it will soon be excused in another, and a lower tone of thought with regard to sin will rule the church. The toleration of sin in the church soon leads to the excusing of it, and that to the free indulgence of it, and to the bringing in of other sins yet more foul. Sin is like the bale of goods which came from the east to this city in the olden time, which brought the pest in it. Probably it was but a small bale, yet it contained in it the deaths of hundreds of the inhabitants of London. In those days one piece of rag carried the infection into a whole town. So, if you permit one sin or false doctrine in a church knowingly and wittingly, none can tell the extent to which that evil may ultimately go. The church, therefore, is to be purged of practical and doctrinal evil as diligently as possible. That sour and corrupting thing which God abhors must be purged out, and it is to be the business of the Christian minister, and of all his fellow helpers, to keep the church free from it.

We will, however, view the text as relating to ourselves, and let me remark that the apostle had in his mind's eye the custom of the Jews at the passover. In consequence of the command that they should purge out the leaven at the passover, the head of the household among the Jews in the olden times, especially when they grew more strict in their ritual, would go through the whole of the house on a certain day to search for every particle of leavened bread. It was generally done in the evening with a candle, and the servants and others would accompany the good man of the house to search for every crumb. Clothes were shaken, cupboards were emptied, drawers were opened, and if a mouse ran across the room and might be supposed to carry a crumb of bread into its hole, they trembled lest a curse should rest on the home. So strict did they become that our Saviour might have rebuked them as straining at a gnat while swallowing a camel. We, however, have no need to fear excessive strictness in getting rid of sin. With as scrupulous a care as the Israelite purged out the leaven from his house we are to purge out all sin from ourselves, our conduct, and our conversation. Here is a task set before you, then, my brethren. Note well, we do not urge you to purge out sin in order that you may save yourselves, for Christ our passover is slain, and our salvation is secured. But that being done, in order that we may keep the feast and unbrokenly possess the joy of salvation, we are to purge out the leaven of sin. We may suppose that the Jewish householder would very soon put away all the large loaves of leavened bread that remained in the house ; just as you and I, when we were sorrowing for sin, gave up at once all those gross outward sins in which we indulged before. Some of these have never tempted us again. Drunkenness, profanity, uncleanness— I have known men give up these sins at once, in a moment, and they appear to be delivered from their power henceforth and for ever. Then perhaps there were some stray crusts which the children had left. These were put away also. So there may be certain minor sins in the judgment of the world which the Christian man, when converted, may not put away the first week ; but when they are seen he says, " I must have done with these ; Christ my passover has been offered, I cannot do this wickedness. I am a child of God, more is expected of me than of others." But the most trouble would be caused by the little crumbs of leaven : these might be hidden away in the cupboard, and perhaps it was a long time after the search began before the householder found these out ; but when he did, he said, " Put them away, they must not remain." And, beloved, many a Christian man has not found out the sinfulness of some actions for years after his conversion. I am very conscious that certain matters which I thought very lightly of years ago would greatly trouble my conscience now. As I have obtained light upon certain sins I have through grace put them away, and I expect as long as I live to find something which, viewed in a brighter light, and from a higher standing, will be discovered to be sinful, and I desire grace to have done with it. We must not hesitate for a moment ; we must not retain even a crumb of the evil leaven ; we must earnestly desire to sweep it all out.

The whole house was searched. I have seen a picture in which the servant is represented as cleansing the cooking vessels in the kitchen, the housewife is searching garments and cups in the dining room, and the master and his sons are opening cupboards, and chests, and diligently investigating. A Christian man may feel that he has got rid of all the leaven from his shop, he is upright, and honest himself, and his system of business is just ; yet it may be there is leaven in his private house, for the children are uncorrected, the Sabbath is disregarded, or the servants' souls are neglected. Perhaps, however, the home is right, and then there may be leaven in the bed-chamber. Your conversation with yourself and your God may be in a sad condition. Prayer may be restrained. Suppose you have purged out the leaven of hypocrisy and are sincere, are you also free from the leaven of anger ? May you not still be slow to forgive ? Are you clear of the leaven of pride, or of covetousness ? Every part of our nature needs searching, the reins, the heart, the judgment, all must be cleansed. Purge out the old leaven wherever it has penetrated : it must come away or else, though

we are safe beneath the blood, we shall not know and enjoy our safety. The feast cannot be kept while the old leaven is wilfully left within us.

I told you that the head of the household usually performed the search ; let your best powers of judgment be exercised upon yourself, my dear brother. Too many exercise their understandings in criticizing others, but they do not judge themselves in the same way. Let your main and chief thought be, now that you are saved, to get rid of sin, let the master powers of your soul be called into this purging work, and ask the Master Himself to aid you. Doth He not sit as a refiner to purify the sons of Levi ? Search me, O God ; try me, and know my ways. Thine eyes can see what mine cannot. May the great Purifier put forth from us every crumb of the old leaven of our natural corruption.

I said that a candle was used to throw a light into every corner of the house, that no leaven might escape notice. Take you the candle of God's Word, the candle of His Holy Spirit. Do you say, " There is nothing wrong in me if I judge myself by my fellow men " ? My brother, it is a small thing to be able to say no more than this. To be approved of men is but a poor standard for a Christian. Does thine own heart reproach thee ? Does the word of God reproach thee ? To be measuring myself by my fellow men, and saying, " Compared with them I am generous to the poor, and diligent in God's service." This is to be proud because you are taller than pigmies or fairer than blackamoors. Compare yourself with Paul, with John, with Brainerd or Rutherford, and even that is ill advice, for what were the best disciples compared with their Master ? There must be no lower standards for us than the perfection of Christ. No attainment must ever satisfy us until we are conformed to His image who is the firstborn among many brethren. You will tell me I am holding up a high standard. I am ; but then you have a great helper, and I will show you in a moment how you may be of good cheer concerning this business.

To purge out the old leaven many sweepings of the house will be wanted ; one certainly will not suffice. You must search, and search, and search on, until you get to heaven. The motto of your life must be, " Watch, watch, watch." For, mark you, you are sure to leave some leaven, and if you leave a little it will work and spread. Sin has evermore a swelling tendency, and until the Holy Spirit has cut up the last root of sin, evil will grow up again in the heart, at the scent of water it will bud and put forth once again its shoots. Here is work for all time, enough to keep us busy till we land in eternity.

It is hinted in the text that there are forms of evil which we must peculiarly watch against, and one is malice. Is a Christian man likely to be malicious ? I trust in the strong sense of that term we have done with malice, but, alas ! I have known believers who have had a very keen sense of right, and therein have been commendable, who have too much indulged the spirit deprecated here ; that is to say, they have been very severe, censorious, and angry—angry with people for not being perfect. Though not perfect themselves, and though they know that if they are better than others, the grace of God has made them so, yet they are bitter and untender towards the imperfections of Christian people, and they cherish feelings of prejudice, suspicion, and ill-will. They do not seek the improvement of the faulty, but their exposure and condemnation.

They hunt down sincere but faulty people, and denounce them, but never by any chance offer an excuse for them. In some believers there is too much of the leaven of unkind talking; they speak to one another about the faults of their brethren, and, in the process of retailing, characters are injured and reputations marred. Now harsh judgments and evil speakings are to be put away from us as sour leaven. If a man has injured me, I must forgive him; and if I find him to be faulty, I must love him till he gets better, and if I cannot make him better by ordinary love, I must love him more, even as Christ loved His church and gave Himself for it, "that he might present it to Himself a glorious church, not having spot or wrinkle, or any such thing." He did not love her because she was without spot or wrinkle, but to get the spots and wrinkles out of her; He loved her into holiness.

Take good heed also that every form of hypocrisy be purged out, for the apostle tells us to eat the passover with the unleavened bread of sincerity and truth. Do let us leave off talking beyond our experience, let us never pray beyond what we mean. Ask God, my brother, to clean us from all unreality, that nothing may be in us but true metal. There is a strong temptation among Christian ministers, and Christian men of all sorts, to seem to be a little more than they are. God save us from it. The slightest taint of hypocrisy should be abhorred by the Christian man. All illwill and all mere seeming should be detestable to the Christian, for where these are there can be little or no communion with Jesus. The fellowship of heaven is not enjoyed where the leaven of hell is endured.

III. Our last point shall be touched briefly. THE HAPPINESS OF THE BELIEVER ACTS UPON HIS HOLINESS, AND HIS HOLINESS UPON HIS HAPPINESS.

First of all, *the happiness acts upon the holiness.* We have drawn a picture of the paschal feast. Set it before you again. If I know that I feed upon Christ day by day, who has been sacrificed for me, the happiness I feel leads me to say, "Yet it was dearly purchased; my sins slew my Saviour, and therefore will I slay my sins." Every taste you get of redeeming love makes you feel that sin is a cruel and detestable thing, and therefore you will destroy it. Sitting as you do within the house, and knowing that you are all safe because the blood is on the lintel outside—what next? Why, you will say, "The firstborn sons of Egypt are slain, and am I preserved; what then? Why I must be God's firstborn, and must belong to Him." "Ye are not your own, but ye are bought with a price," is the voice of the angel as he passes by the house which he must not enter to destroy. Has Christ loved me and died for me? Then I am His, and if I am His I cannot live in sin. If I am redeemed, how can I continue a slave? If I belong to Jesus I cannot serve the devil, I must be rid of sin. Then, further, if I feel that all is safe my mind is calm, and I am able to care about the state of my heart. The Israelite was safe within his house, he needed not to keep watch and ward outside, the sprinkled blood was his security, and therefore he had time and space to see to the interior of his abode. Now, said the believer, "I have nothing to do with saving myself, for my salvation is finished, and therefore I will see to my growth in grace." He who has outdoor work done for him may well see to his indoor work, and earnestly turn his thoughts to the purging out of the old leaven. The freedom you have from fear through the blood of Jesus gives you the peace of mind needful for a thorough search after your sins. Moreover, the Christian man is encouraged to put away his leaven of sin because he has the foresight of a profitable exchange. The Israelite gave up leavened bread, but he soon had angels' food in the place of it. So the Christian says, "I give up these sins; they were sweet to me once, now they are sour, stinking, corrupt leaven; I shall receive nobler enjoyments, fellowship with heaven shall be my portion. I may gladly part with leaven, for I am called to eat the bread of angels, nay, the bread of God.

The Christian, too, who knows that his sin is forgiven, feels that the God who could put away his load of sin, will surely help to conquer his corruptions. When I see Calvary I believe everything to be possible. If Jesus can blot out sin, His Spirit can subdue it. The holy peace created in the soul by feeding upon Christ, nerves the spirit for conflict with inbred sin. We will overcome it, we will drive out the Canaanites which defile our souls, we will be pure, we will be perfect, for greater is He that is with us than all they that be against us. So you see our happiness in many ways promotes our holiness.

I am quite sure you will not need me to enlarge upon the fact that *holiness produces happiness.* How quiet doth the soul become when the man feels, "I have done that which was right, I have given up that which was evil." I grant you that the deep peace of the believer arises from the sprinkled blood, but it is enjoyed by purging out the leaven. You question yourself and say, "Can I believe in Christ if I am living in sin?" and you get back the comfortable sense that Jesus is yours when you can honestly feel that you have, by the Holy Spirit, renounced your old sins. Purging out the leaven clears your evidences, and so enables you to keep the feast. You were safe enough through the blood, but now you find happiness in a sense of security, a happiness which would have been taken from you had you fallen into sin. My brethren, how can we expect to enjoy communion with Jesus Christ while we indulge in sin? I am sure you will find that at the bottom our want of fellowship with Christ arises from our want of careful walking before the Lord. I read sometimes holy Rutherford's letters, and say, "I wish I lived like this." Now, if I do not do so it is either Christ's fault or mine. Can I say it is Christ's fault? I dare not. He is as willing to reveal Himself to me as to any other of His servants. It is my fault then. My dear brother, if you do not walk in the light as Christ is in the light, it is not because He is not willing that you should walk in His light, it is because you keep at a distance from Him, and so walk in darkness. Do you believe that the sad faces among God's servants are caused by their poverty? Some of the very poorest of saints have been the most joyful. Do you think they are caused by their sicknesses? Why, we have known persons confined to the bed of sickness twenty years together, who have found a very heaven below in their chamber of languishing. What is it that makes God's people look so sad? It is the old leaven. "Let us keep the feast," says the apostle, but it is useless to hope to do so while we keep the leaven. Perhaps there is one thing which we know to be our duty, but we have not attended to it: that one neglect will break up our festival. "He that knoweth his master's will, and doeth it not shall be beaten with many stripes." Are these stripes to be given in the next world? I do not believe it, it is in this world that erring believers will be beaten, and very often depression of spirit, losses and bereavements, happen to a Christian because he has knowingly violated his conscience by neglecting a duty or permitting a sin. Jesus will not commune with neglecters of His will. Jesus will have no leaven where He is. If you tolerate that which is nauseous to Him expect not a comfortable word from Him. If you walk contrary to Him He will walk contrary to you. Can two walk together unless they be agreed? I would with much affection press these considerations upon you, for I have pressed them upon my own heart. I fear we shall not enjoy the blessing we have had as a church unless there is more jealousy for holiness among us. I am afraid some of us are barren of spiritual usefulness because we do not watch against sin. O keep your conscience tender! Beware of getting it seared. It is like the pond in the winter; a very thin scale of ice is formed at first, but afterwards the whole surface becomes hard enough to bear half a town. Beware of the thin scale over your conscience. Keep your heart tender before God, ready to be moved by the faintest breath of His Spirit. Ask to be like sensitive plants, that you may shrivel up at the touch of sin, and only open out in the presence of your Lord and Master. God grant it to you. God grant it, for Jesus' sake.

This last sentence, and I have done. There are some here who are not saved. Do notice how salvation comes—not through purging out the leaven; no, that operation is to be seen to afterwards, but salvation comes because the Paschal Lamb is slain, the soul feeds on Jesus, His blood is sprinkled, and the soul is saved; afterwards comes the purging out of sin. Dear soul, if thou wouldst be saved, do not begin at the wrong end, begin with the Saviour's blood, begin with Calvary's cross; go there as a poor sinner, and look to Him, and then after that we will say, "Let us keep the feast," and we will diligently see to it in His strength that the leaven be put away. God bless you for Christ's sake.

"BOUGHT WITH A PRICE"

"Ye are not your own: for ye are bought with a price: therefore glorify God in your body, and in your spirit, which are God's."—1 Corinthians vi. 19-20.

OUR beloved brother, Thomas Cook, who has for so long a time served this church as an honoured deacon, has fallen asleep in Christ. We have laid his earthly remains in the tomb: his spirit rejoices before the throne of God. This day we thank God for his useful life, and ask for grace to imitate it. Before he closed his eyes in death he left a text of Scripture for the pastors: "Christ is all, and in all"; and he left another for his fellow church members, for all of you this day who are members of the body of Christ; and this is the legacy, which now, as a spiritual executor, I present to you: "Ye are not your own: for ye are bought with a price: therefore glorify God in your body, and in your spirit, which are God's." I have no doubt the intention of our departed brother was to promote God's glory by speaking to us even after he was dead concerning our sanctification, that so we might be stirred up to a greater consecration to the Lord our Saviour.

You will notice that in this chapter the apostle Paul has been dealing with sins of the flesh, with fornication and adultery. Now, it is at all times exceedingly difficult for the preacher either to speak or to write upon this subject; it demands the strictest care to keep the language guarded, so that while we are denouncing a detestable evil we do not ourselves promote it by a single expression that should be otherwise than chaste and pure. Observe how well the apostle Paul succeeds, for though he does not mask the sin, but tears the veil from it, and lets us know well what it is that he is aiming at, yet there is no sentence which we could wish to alter. Herein he is a model for all ministers, both in fidelity and prudence.

Be sure also to note that the apostle, when he is exposing sin, does not trifle with it, but like a mighty hunter before the Lord, pursues it with all his might; his hatred to it is intense; he drags it forth to the light; he bids us mark its hideous deformity; he hunts it through all its purlieus, hotfoot, as we say. He never leaves it breathing time; argument after argument he hurls like javelins upon it; he will by no means spare the filthy thing. He who above all others speaks most positively of salvation by grace, and is most clear upon the fact that salvation is not by the works of the law, is at the same time most intensely earnest for the holiness of Christians, and most zealously denounces those who would say, "Let us do evil, that good may come." In this particular instance he sets the sin of fornication in the light of the Holy Spirit; he holds up, as it were, the seven-branched candlesticks before it, and lets us see what a filthy thing it is. He tells us that the body is the temple of the Holy Ghost, and therefore ought not to be profaned; he declares that bodily unchastity is a sacrilegious desecration of our manhood, a violation of the sacred shrine wherein the Spirit takes up its dwelling-place; and then, as if this were not enough, he seizes the sin and drags it to the foot of the cross, and there nails it hand and foot, that it may die as a criminal; for these are his words: "Ye are not your own: for ye are bought with a price": the price being the blood of Jesus. He finds no sharper weapon, no keener instrument of destruction than this. The redemption wrought on Calvary by the death of Jesus must be the death of this sin, and of all other sins, wherever the Spirit of God uses it as His sword of execution. Brethren and sisters, it is no slight thing to be holy. A man must not say, " I have faith," and then fall into the sins of an unbeliever; for, after all, our outer life is the test of our inner life; and if the outer life be not purified, rest assured the heart is not changed. That faith which does not bring forth the fruit of holiness is the faith of devils. The devils believe and tremble. Let us never be content with a faith which can live in hell, but rise to that which will save us—the faith of God's elect, which purifies the soul, casting down the power of evil, and setting up the throne of Jesus Christ, the throne of holiness within the spirit.

Noticing this as being the run of the chapter, we now come to the text itself, and in order to discuss it we must take it to pieces, and I think we shall see in it at once three things very clearly. The first is *a blessed fact*, " Ye are," or as it should be rendered, " Ye were bought with a price " ; then comes *a plain consequence* from that fact, a consequence of a double character, negative and positive : " Ye are not your own " ; " your body and your spirit are God's " ; and out of that there springs inevitably *a natural conclusion :* " Therefore, glorify God in your body, and in your spirit."

I. Let us begin, then, first of all, with this BLESSED FACT—" *Ye are bought with a price.*" Paul might, if his object were to prove that we are not our own, have said : " Ye did not make yourselves." Creation may well furnish motives for obedience to the great Lawgiver. He might also have said, " Ye do not preserve yourselves : it is God who keeps you in life ; you would die if He withdrew His power." The preservation of divine providence might furnish abundant arguments for holiness. Surely He who feeds, nourishes, and upholds our life should have our service. But He prefers, for reasons known to Himself, which it would not be hard to guess, to plead the tenderer theme, redemption. He sounds that note, which if it do not thunder with that crash of power which marked the six days' labour of Omnipotence, yet has a soft, piercing, subduing tone in it, which, like the still small voice to which Elias listened, has in it the presence of God.

The most potent plea for sanctity is not " Ye were made," or, " Ye are nourished," but " Ye are bought." This the apostle selects as a convincing proof of our duty, and as a means to make that duty our delight. And truly, beloved, it is so. If we have indeed experienced the power of redemption we fully admit that it is so. Look ye back to the day when ye were bought, when ye were bondslaves to your sins, when ye were under the just sentence of divine justice, when it was inevitable that God should punish your transgressions ; remember how the Son of God became your substitute, how He bared His back to the lash that should have fallen upon you, and laid His soul beneath the sword which should have quenched its fury in your blood. You were redeemed then, redeemed from the punishment that was due to you, redeemed from the wrath of God, redeemed unto Christ to be His for ever.

You will notice the text says, " Ye were bought *with a price.*" It is a common classical expression to signify that the purchase was expensive. Of course, the very expression, " Ye were bought," implies a price, but the words " *with a price* " are added, as if to show that it was not for nothing that ye were purchased. There was a something inestimably precious paid for you ; and ye need scarcely that I remind you that " ye were not redeemed with corruptible things, as silver and gold " ; " but with the precious blood of Christ, as of a lamb without blemish and without spot." Ah ! those words slip over our tongue very glibly, but we may well chide ourselves that we can speak of redemption with dry eyes. That the blood of Christ was shed to buy our souls from death and hell is a wonder of compassion which fills angels with amazement, and it ought to overwhelm us with adoring love whenever we think of it, glance our eye over the recording pages, or even utter the word " redemption." What meant this purchasing us *with blood ?* It signified pain. Have

any of you lately been racked with pain ? Have you suffered acutely ? Ah ! then at such times you know to some degree what the price was which the Saviour paid. His bodily pains were great, hands and feet nailed to the wood, and the iron breaking through the tenderest nerves. His soul-pains were greater still, His heart was melted like wax, He was very heavy, His heart was broken with reproach, He was deserted of God, and left beneath the black thunder-clouds of divine wrath, His soul was exceeding sorrowful, even unto death. It was pain that bought you. We speak of the drops of blood, but we must not confine our thoughts to the crimson life-floods which distilled from the Saviour's veins ; we must think of the pangs which He endured, which were the equivalent for what we ought to have suffered, what we must have suffered had we endured the punishment of our guilt for ever in the flames of hell. But pain alone could not have redeemed us ; it was by death that the Saviour paid the ransom. Death is a word of horror to the ungodly. The righteous hath hope in His death ; but as Christ's death was the substitute for the death of the ungodly, He was made a curse for us, and the presence of God was denied Him. His death was attended with unusual darkness ; He cried, " My God, My God, why hast Thou forsaken Me ? " O think ye earnestly on this. The Ever-living died to redeem us ; the Only Begotten bowed His head in agony, and was laid in the grave that we might be saved. Ye are bought then " with a price "—a price incalculable, stupendous, infinite, and this is the plea which the apostle uses to urge upon us that we should " be holiness to the Lord."

I desire upon this theme, which is a very simple and every-day one, but which is nevertheless of the weightiest consideration, to remind you, dearly beloved, who profess to be followers of Christ, that this matter of your being " bought with a price " is *an indisputable fact* to every Christian. To every person here present it either is a fact or not. I scarcely need to ask whether any of you are prepared to abjure your redemption ; and yet, professor of the faith of Christ, I shall put it to you now : Are you willing to have the negative put upon this ? will you deny that you were " bought with a price ? " Will you now confess that you were not redeemed on Calvary ? You dare not, I am sure. You would sooner die than abjure your belief of it. Well, then, as certain as is your redemption, so certain is it that you " are not your own," but belong to God, and should glorify Him. It is inevitable that if you be " bought with a price," you have ceased to be your own property, and belong to Him who bought you. Holiness, therefore, is necessary to all the redeemed. If you cast off your responsibility to be holy, you at the same time cast away the benefit of redemption. Will you do this ? As I am sure you could not renounce your salvation, and cast away your only hope, so I charge you by the living God be not so inconsistent as to say : " I am redeemed, and yet I will live as I list." As redeemed men, let the inevitable consequences follow from the fact, and be ye evidently the servants of the Lord Jesus.

Remember, too, that *this fact is the most important one in all your history.* That you were redeemed " with a price " is the greatest event in your biography. Even your birth, what was it unless a second birth had been yours ? Might you not say : " Let the day perish wherein I was born, and the night in which it was said, there is a man child conceived " ? Would it not have been to you the direst calamity to be born into the world if you had not been rescued from the wrath of which you were the heir ? You left your father's house, and it was an important step in life ; perhaps you crossed the great and wide sea ; it may be you aspired to high office in the state and you obtained it ; it is possible you have been sore sick, or it may be you have sunk from affluence to poverty. Such events leave their impress upon the memory ; men cannot forget these great changes in their lives ; but they all shrivel into less than nothing compared with this fact that you were " bought with a price." Your connection with Calvary is the most important thing about you. Oh, I do beseech you then, if it be so, prove it ; and remember the just and righteous proof is by your not being your own, but consecrated unto God. If it be the most important thing in the world to you, that you were " bought with a price," let it exercise the most prominent influence over your entire career. Be a man, be an Englishman, but be most of all Christ's man. A citizen, a friend, a philanthropist, a patriot : all these you may be, but be most of all a saint redeemed by blood.

Recollect, again, that your being " bought with a price " *will be the most important fact in all your future existence.* What say they in heaven when they sing ? They would naturally select the noblest topic and that which most engrosses their minds, and yet in the whole range of their memory they find no theme so absorbing as this : " Thou wast slain, and hast redeemed us to God by Thy blood." Redeeming love is the theme of heaven. When you reach the upper realms your most important memory will not be that you were wealthy or poor in this life, nor the fact that you sickened and died, but that you were " bought with a price." We do not know all that may occur in this world before the close of its history, but certainly it will be burnt up with fire, and you in yonder clouds with Christ may witness the awful conflagration. You will never forget it. There will be new heavens and new earth, and you with Christ may see the new-born heavens and earth, laughing in the bright sunlight of God's good pleasure ; you will never forget that joyous day. And you will be caught up to dwell with Jesus for ever and ever ; and there will come a time when He shall deliver up the kingdom to God, even the Father and God shall be all in all. You will never forget the time of which the poet sings—

> " Then the end, beneath His rod
> Man's last enemy shall fall.
> Hallelujah, Christ in God,
> God in Christ is all in all."

All these divinely glorious events will impress themselves upon you, but not one of them will make an impression so lasting, so clear, so deep as this, that you were " bought with a price." High over all the mountain tops, Calvary, that was but a little mount in human estimation, shall rise ; stars shall the events of history be ; but this event shall be the sun in whose presence all others hide their diminished heads. " Thou wast slain," the full chorus of heaven shall roll it forth in thundering accents of grateful zeal. " Thou wast slain, and hast redeemed us to God by Thy blood " ; the saints shall remember this first and foremost ; and amidst the cycles of eternity this shall have the chief place in every glorified memory. What then, beloved ? Shall it

not have the chief place with you now ? It has been *the fact* of your life hitherto, it will be the fact of your entire eternal existence : let it saturate your soul, let it penetrate your spirit, let it subdue your faculties, let it take the reins of all your powers and guide you whither it will ; let the Redeemer, He whose hands were pierced for you, sway the sceptre of your spirit and rule over you this day, and world without end.

If I had the power to do it, how would I seek to refresh in your souls a sense of this fact that you are " bought with a price." There, in the midnight hour, amidst the olives of Gethsemane, kneels Immanuel the Son of God ; He groans, He pleads in prayer, He wrestles ; see the beady drop stand on His brow, drops of sweat, but not of such sweat as pours from men when they earn the bread of life, but the sweat of Him who is procuring life itself for us. It is blood, it is crimson blood ; great gouts of it are falling to the ground. O soul, thy Saviour speaks to thee from out Gethsemane at this hour, and He says : " Here and thus I bought thee with a price." Come, stand and view Him in the agony of the olive garden, and understand at what a cost He procured thy deliverance. Track Him in all His path of shame and sorrow till you see Him on the Pavement ; mark how they bind His hands and fasten Him to the whipping-post ; see, they bring the scourges and the cruel Roman whips ; they tear His flesh ; the ploughers make deep furrows on His blessed body, and the blood gushes forth in streams, while rivulets from His temples, where the crown of thorns has pierced them, join to swell the purple stream. From beneath the scourges He speaks to you with accents soft and low, and He says, " My child, it is here and thus I bought thee with a price." But see Him on the cross itself when the consummation of all has come ; His hands and feet are fountains of blood ; His soul is full of anguish even to heartbreak ; and there, ere the soldier pierces with a spear His side, bowing down He whispers to thee and to me, " It was here, and thus, I bought thee with a price." Oh, by Gethsemane, by Gabbatha, by Golgotha, by every sacred name connected with the passion of our Lord, by sponge and vinegar, and nail and spear, and everything that helped the pang and increased the anguish of His death, I conjure you, my beloved brethren, to remember that ye were " bought with a price," and " are not your own." I push you to this ; you either were or were not so bought ; if you were, it is the grand fact of your life ; if you were, it is the greatest fact that ever will occur to you : let it operate upon you, let it dominate your entire nature, let it govern your body, your soul, your spirit, and from this day let it be said of you not only that you are a man, a man of good morals and respectable conduct, but this, above all things, that you are a man filled with love to Him who bought you, a man who lives for Christ, and knows no other passion. Would God that redemption would become the paramount influence, the lord of our soul, and dictator of our being ; then were we indeed true to our obligations : short of this we are not what love and justice both demand.

II. Now, let us pass on to the second point. Here is A PLAIN CONSEQUENCE arising from the blessed fact. Ye were " bought with a price," Then first it is clear as a *negative*, that " Ye are not your own " ; and secondly, it is clear as a *positive*, that " your body and spirit are God's."

Take first *the negative :* if bought, you are not your own. No argument is needed for this, and indeed it is so great a boon in itself that none of us could find it in our hearts to demur to it. It is a great privilege not to be one's own. A vessel is drifting on the Atlantic hither and thither, and its end no man knoweth. It is derelict, deserted by all its crew; it is the property of no man; it is the prey of every storm, and the sport of every wind: rocks, quicksands, and shoals wait to destroy it: the ocean yearns to engulf it. It drifts onward to no man's land, and no man will mourn its shipwreck. But mark well yonder barque in the Thames which its owner surveys with pleasure. In its attempt to reach the sea, it may run ashore, or come into collision with other vessels; or in a thousand ways suffer damage; but there is no fear, it will pass through the floating forest of "the Pool"; it will thread the winding channel, and reach the Nore because its owner will secure it pilotage, skilful and apt. How thankful you and I should be that we are not derelict to-day! we are not our own, not left on the wild waste of chance to be tossed to and fro by fortuitous circumstances; but there is a hand upon our helm; we have on board a Pilot who owns us, and will surely steer us into the Fair Havens of eternal rest. The sheep is on the mountain side, and the winter is coming on; it may be buried in the snow; perhaps the wolf may seize it, or by-and-by, when the summer crops have been eaten, there may be little fodder for it, and it may starve; but the sheep's comfort, if it could think at all, would be this: it is not its own, it belongeth to the shepherd, who will not willingly lose his property; it bears the mark of its owner, and is the object of his care. O happy sheep of God's pasture, what a bliss it is to you that you are not your own! Does any man here think it would be a pleasure to be his own? Let me assure him that there is no ruler so tyrannical as self. He that is his own master, has a fool and a tyrant to be his lord. No man ever yet governed himself after the will of the flesh but what he by degrees found the yoke heavy and the burden crushing. Self is a fierce dictator, a terrible oppressor; imperious lusts are cruel slave-drivers. But Christ, who says we are not our own, would have us view that truth in the light in which a loving wife would view it. She, too, is not her own. She gave herself away on a right memorable day, of which she bears the golden token on her finger. She did not weep when she surrendered herself and became her husband's; nor did they muffle the bells, or bid the organ play the "Dead March" in Saul: it was a happy day for her; she remembers it at this moment with glowing joy. She is not her own, but she has not regretted the giving herself away: she would make the same surrender again to the self-same beloved owner, if it were to be done. That she is her husband's does not bespeak her slavery, but her happiness; she has found rest in her husband's house, and to-day, when the Christian confesses that he is not his own, he does not wish that he were. He is married to the Saviour; he has given himself up, body, soul, and spirit, to the blessed Bridegroom of his heart; it was the marriage day of his true life when he became a Christian, and he looks back to it with joy and transport. Oh, it is a blissful thing not to be our own, so I shall not want arguments to prove that to which every gracious spirit gives a blissful consent.

Now, if it be true that we are not our own, and I hope it is true to many here present, then, the inference from it is, "I have no right to *injure*

myself in any way." My body is not my own, I have no right then, as a Christian man, to do anything with it that would defile it. The apostle is mainly arguing against sins of the flesh, and he says, "the body is not for fornication, but for the Lord; and the Lord for the body." We have no right to commit uncleanness, because our bodies are the members of Christ and not our own. He would say the same of drunkenness, gluttony, idle sleep, and even of such excessive anxiety after wealth as injures health with carking care. We have no right to profane or injure the flesh and blood which are consecrated to God; every limb of our frame belongs to God; it is His property; He has bought it "with a price." Any honest man will be more concerned about an injury done to another's property placed under his care, than if it were his own. When the son of the prophet was hewing wood with Elisha, you remember how he said, when the axe head flew off into the water, "Alas! master, for it was borrowed." It would be bad enough to lose my own axe, but it is not my own, therefore I doubly deplore the accident. I know this would not operate upon thievish minds. There are some who, if it was another man's, and they had borrowed it, would have no further care about it: "Let the lender get it back, if he can." But we speak to honest men, and with them it is always a strong argument: Your body is another's, do it no injury. As for our spirit too, that is God's, and how careful we should be of it. I am asked sometimes to read an heretical book: well, if I believed my reading it would help its refutation, and might be an assistance to others in keeping them out of error, I might do it as a hard matter of duty, but I shall not do it unless I see some good will come from it. I am not going to drag my spirit through a ditch for the sake of having it washed afterwards, for it is not my own. It may be that good medicine would restore me if I poisoned myself with putrid meat, but I am not going to try it: I dare not experiment on a mind which no longer belongs to me. There is a mother and a child, and the child has a book to play with, and a blacklead pencil. It is making drawings and marks upon the book, and the mother takes no notice. It lays down one book and snatches another from the table, and at once the mother rises from her seat, and hurriedly takes the book away, saying: "No, my dear, you must not mark that, for it is not ours." So with my mind, intellect, and spirit; if it belonged to me I might or might not play tomfool with it, and go to hear Socinians, Ritualists, Universalists, and such like preach, but as it is not my own, I will preserve it from such fooleries, and the pure word shall not be mingled with the errors of men. Here is the drift of the apostle's argument—I have no right to injure that which does not belong to me, and as I am not my own, I have no right to injure myself.

But, further, I have no right to let myself *lie waste*. The man who had a talent, and went and dug in the earth and hid it, had not he a right to do so? Yes, of course, if it was his own talent, and his own napkin. If any of you have money and do not put it out to interest, if it is all your own, nobody complains. But this talent belonged to the man's master, it was only intrusted to him as a steward, and he ought not to have let it rust in the ground. So I have no right to let my faculties run to waste since they do not belong to me. If I am a Christian I have no right to be idle. I saw the other day men using picks in the road in laying down new gas-pipes; they had been resting, and just as I passed the clock struck one, and the foreman gave a signal. I think he said, "*Blow up*"; and straightway each man took his pick or his shovel, and they were all at it in earnest. Close to them stood a fellow with a pipe in his mouth, who did not join in the work, but stood in a free-and-easy posture. It did not make any difference to him whether it was one o'clock or six. Why not? Because he was his own: the other men were the master's for the time being. He as an independent gentleman might do as he liked, but those who were not their own fell to labour. If any of you idle professors can really prove that you belong to yourselves, I have nothing more to say to you, but if you profess to have a share in the redeeming sacrifice of Christ, I am ashamed of you if you do not go to work the very moment the signal is given. You have no right to waste what Jesus Christ has bought "with a price."

Further than that, if we are not our own, but "are bought with a price," we have no right to exercise any *capricious government* of ourselves. A man who is his own may say, "I shall go whither I will, and do what I will"; but if I am not my own but belong to God who has bought me, then I must submit to His government; His will must be my will, and His directions must be my law. I desire to enter a certain garden, and I ask the gardener at the gate if I may come in. "You should be very welcome, sir, indeed," says he, "if it were mine, but my master has told me not to admit strangers here, and therefore I must refuse you." Sometimes the devil would come into the garden of our souls. We tell him that our flesh might consent, but the garden is not ours, and we cannot give him space. Worldly ambition, covetousness, and so forth, might claim to walk through our soul, but we say, "No, it is not our own; we cannot, therefore, do what our old will would do, but we desire to be obedient to the will of our Father who is in heaven." Thy will be done, my God, in me, for so should it be done where all is thine own by purchase.

Yet, again, if we are not our own, then we have no right *to serve ourselves*. The man who is living entirely for himself, whose object is his own ease, comfort, honour, or wealth, what knows he concerning redemption by Christ? If our aims rise no higher than our personal advantages, we are false to the fact that we "are bought with a price," we are treacherous to Him in whose redemption we pretend to share.

But time would fail me if I dwelt upon this, or, indeed, at any length upon *the positive side* of this blessed fact: I will therefore only say a word or two concerning it. Our body and our spirit are God's; and, Christian, this is certainly a very high honour to you. Your body will rise again from the dead at the first resurrection, because it is not an ordinary body, it belongs to God: your spirit is distinguished from the souls of other men; it is God's spirit, and He has set His mark upon it, and honoured you in so doing. You are God's, because a price has been paid for you. According to some, the allusion price here is to the dowry that was paid by a husband for his wife in ancient days. According to the Rabbis there were three ways by which a woman became the wife of a man, and one of these was by the payment of a dowry. This was always held good in Jewish law; the woman was not her own from the moment when the husband had paid to her father or natural guardian the stipulated price for her. Now,

at this day, you and I rejoice that Jesus Christ has espoused us unto Himself in righteousness or ever the earth was; we rejoice in that language which He uses by the prophet Hosea, "I will betroth thee unto Me for ever"; but here is our comfort, the dowry money has been paid, Christ has redeemed us unto Himself, and Christ's we are, Christ's for ever and ever.

Remember that our Lord has paid all the price for us; there is no mortgage or lien upon us; we have therefore no right to give a portion of ourselves to Satan. And He has bought us entirely from head to foot, every power, every passion, and every faculty, all our time, all our goods, all that we call our own, all that makes up ourselves in the largest sense of that term; we are altogether God's. Ah! it is very easy for people to say this, but how very difficult it is to feel it true and to act as such! I have no doubt there are many persons here who profess to be willing to give God all they have, who would not actually give Him five shillings. We can sing—

"Here, Lord, I give myself away";

and yet if it comes to yielding only a part of ourselves, if it requires self-denial, or self-sacrifice, straightway there is a drawing back. Now, was the cross a fiction? Was the death of Christ a fable? Were you only fancifully "bought with a price," and not in deed and in truth? If redemption be a fable, then return a fabled consecration; if your purchase be a fiction, then lead the fictitious lives that some of you do lead with regard to consecration to Christ. If it be only an idea, a pretty something that we read of in books, then let our belonging unto God be a mere idea and a piece of sentiment; but a real redemption demands real holiness. A true price, most certainly paid, demands from us a practical surrendering of ourselves to the service of God. From this day forth even for ever, "ye are not your own," ye are the Lord's.

III. And now I must close, and oh, may God give power to His word while I beg to speak upon the last point, namely, THE NATURAL CONCLUSION "Therefore glorify God in your body, and in your spirit." I am not clear that the last few words are in the original. A large number of the old manuscripts and versions, and some of the more important of them, finish the verse at the word "body"— "Therefore glorify God in your body." It was the body the apostle was speaking about, and not the spirit, and there is no necessity for the last words: still we will not further raise the question, but take them as being the inspired word of God: but still, I must make the remark, that according to the connection the force of the apostle's language falls upon the body; and perhaps it is so, because we are so apt to forget the truth, that the body is redeemed and is the Lord's, and should be made to glorify God.

The Christian man's body should glorify God by its chastity. Pure as the lily should we be from every taint of uncleanness. The body should glorify God by temperance also; in all things, in eating, drinking, sleeping, in everything that has to do with the flesh. "Whether ye eat or drink, or whatsoever ye do, do all to the glory of God," or as the apostle puts it elsewhere, "whatsoever ye do in word or deed, do all in the name of the Lord Jesus, giving thanks to God and the Father by Him." The Christian man can make every meal a sacrament, and his ordinary avocations the exercise of his spiritual priesthood. The body ought to glorify God by industry. A lazy servant is a bad Christian. A working man who is always looking for Saturday night, a man who never spends a drop of sweat except when the master is looking on, does not glorify God in his body. The Christian is the man who is not afraid of hard work when it is due, who works not as an eye-servant or man pleaser, but in singleness of heart seeks to glorify God. Our bodies used to work hard enough for the devil; now they belong to God we will make them work for Him. Your legs used to carry you to the theatre; be not too lazy to come out on a Thursday night to the house of God. Your eyes have been often open upon iniquity, keep them open during the sermon: do not drop asleep! Your ears have been sharp enough to catch the word of a lascivious song, let them be quick to observe the word of God. Those hands have often squandered your earnings in sinfulness, let them give freely to the cause of Christ. Your body was a willing horse when it was in the service of the devil, let it not be a sluggish hack now that it draws the chariot of Christ. Make the tongue speak His praises, make the mouth sing of His glory, make the whole man bow in willing subservience to the will of Him who bought it.

As for your spirit, let that glorify God. Let your private meditations magnify God; let your songs be to Him when no one hears you but Himself, and let your public zeal, let the purity of your conversation, let the earnestness of your life, let the universal holiness of your character, glorify God with your body and with your spirit.

Beloved Christian friends, I want to say these few things and have done. Because you are God's, you will be looked at more than others, therefore, glorify Him. You know it is not always the thing itself, but the ownership that causes curiosity. If you were to go to a cattle-show, and it were said "such and such a bullock belongs to Her Majesty," it may be it is no better than another, but it would be of interest to thousands as belonging to royalty. See here, then, such and such a man belongs to God; what manner of person ought he to be? If there be any one in this world who will not be criticized, depend upon it, Christian, it is not the Christian; sharp eyes will be upon him, and worldly men will find faults in him which they would not see if he were not a professor. For my part I am very glad of the lynx eyes of the worldlings. Let them watch if they will. I have heard of one who was a great caviller at Christian people, and after having annoyed a church a long time, he was about to leave, and therefore, as a parting jest with the minister, he said, "I have no doubt you will be very glad to know that I am going a hundred miles away?" "No," said the pastor, "I shall be sorry to lose you." "How? I never did you any good." "I don't know that, for I am sure that never one of my flock put half a foot through the hedge but what you began to yelp at him, and so you have been a famous sheep-dog for me." I am glad the world observes us. It has a right to do so. If a man says, "I am God's," he sets himself up for public observation. Ye are lights in the world, and what are lights intended for but to be looked at? A city set on a hill cannot be hid.

Moreover, the world has a right to expect more from a Christian than from anybody else. He says he is "bought with a price," he says he is God's, he therefore claims more than others, and he ought to render more. Stand in fancy in one of the fights of the old civil war. The Royalists are fighting desperately and are winning apace, but I hear a cry from the other side that Cromwell's Ironsides are coming. Now we shall see some fighting. Oliver and his men are lions. But, lo! I see that the fellows who come up hang fire, and are afraid to rush into the thick of the fight; surely these are not Cromwell's Ironsides, and yonder captain is not old Noll? I do not believe it: it cannot be. Why, if they were what they profess to be, they would have broken the ranks of those perfumed cavaliers long ago, and have made them fly before them like chaff before the wind. So when I hear men say, "Here is a body of Christians." What! those Christians? Those cowardly people, who hardly dare speak a word for Jesus! Those covetous people who give a few cheese-parings to his cause! Those inconsistent people whom you would not know to be Christian professors if they did not label themselves! What! such beings followers of a crucified Saviour? The world sneers at such pretensions; and well it may. With such a Leader let us follow bravely; and bought with such a price, and being owned by such a Master, let us glorify Him who condescends to call such poor creatures as we are His portion, whom He hath set apart for Himself.

And let us remember that by men who profess to be "bought with a price," the name of Christ is compromised if their behaviour is unseemly. If we are not holy and gracious, ungodly men are sure to say, "That is one of your believers in God; that is one of your Christians." Do not let it be so. Every soldier in a regiment ought to feel that the renown of the whole army depends upon him, and he must fight as if the winning of the battle rested upon himself. This will cause every man to be a hero. Oh, that every Christian felt as if the honour of God and the Church rested upon him, for in a measure it certainly does!

May we so seek God, that when we come to die we may feel that we have lived for something; that although our hope has rested alone in what Jesus did, yet we have not made that an excuse for doing nothing ourselves. Though we shall have no good works in which to glory, yet may we bring forth fruit that shall be for the glory of our Lord. I feel I so desire to glorify God, body, soul, and spirit while I breathe, that I would even do so on earth after I am dead. I would still urge my brethren on in our Lord's cause. Old Zizka, the Hussite leader, when about to die, said to his soldiers: "Our enemies have always been afraid of my name in the time of battle, and when I am dead take my skin, and make a drum-head of it, and beat it whenever you go to battle. When the foemen hear the sound they will tremble, and you will remember that Zizka calls on his brethren to fight valiantly." Let us so live that when we die, we live on, like Abel, who being dead yet speaketh. The only way to do this is to live in the power of the Immortal God, under the influence of His Holy Spirit: then out of our graves we shall speak to future generations. When Doctor Payson died, he desired that his body should be placed in a coffin, and that his hearers should be invited to come and see it. Across his breast was placed a paper bearing these words, "Remember the words which I spake unto you, being yet present with you." May our lives be such that even if we are not public speakers, yet others may remember our example, and so may hear what our lives spake while we were yet on earth. Your bodies and your spirits are God's : oh, live to God, and glorify Him in the power of His Spirit as long as you have any breath below, that so when the breath is gone, your very bones, like those of Joseph, shall be a testimony. Even in the ashes of the saints their wonted fires live on. In their hallowed memories they rise like a phœnix from their ashes.

The Lord make us more and more practically His own, and may His name be glorious, for ever and ever. Amen, and amen.

"BY ALL MEANS SAVE SOME"

" That I might by all means save some."—1 Corinthians ix. 22.

THE apostle speaks very broadly, and talks about saving men. Some of our extremely orthodox brethren would say at once, " *You* save men ? How can man do that ? The expression is inaccurate in the extreme. Is not salvation of the Lord from first to last ? How can you, Paul, dare to speak of saving some ? " Yet Peter had spoken very like this when he said, " Save yourselves from this untoward generation " ; indeed, the expression is a little more bold, if anything, and if Peter were alive now he would be called to account. When Paul wrote to Timothy he said to him, " Take heed unto thyself, and unto the doctrine ; continue in them : for in doing this thou shalt both save thyself and them that hear thee," which is another instance of language used in a popular sense by a man who had not the fear of critics before his eyes. The apostle did not intend to insinuate that he could save anybody by his own power, and no one thought that he did. He used expressions without guarding them, because he was writing to people who mixed candour with their knowledge of doctrine, and would not wilfully misunderstand him. He did not write for those who must have all the creed in every sermon, and require all statements of the truth to be cut into one shape. The doctrine that salvation is of God alone, and is the work of the Holy Spirit, was dear to him as life itself, and having often proclaimed it he was not afraid of being misunderstood. Our testimony also has for many years been clear upon this point, and therefore we shall venture to be as accurately inaccurate as was the apostle, and to speak of saving souls and winning souls after the manner of ordinary speech.

The expression used gives great prominence to instrumentality, and this is the use and wont of Scripture. There is not much danger just now of exaggerating the power of instrumentality, and looking to the men instead of their Master. The danger seems to lie in the opposite direction, in the habit of depreciating both an organised church and a recognized ministry. Frequently have we heard it said of certain revivals that no particular person was engaged in them, neither evangelist nor minister had a hand in the work, and this is thought to be a recommendation, but indeed it is none. I fear that many hopeful beginnings have come to a sudden collapse because faithful and holy ministers have been despised, and a slur has been cast upon ordinary instrumentalities. Men talk thus under the notion that they are honouring God ; they are off the track altogether, for God still owns and blesses His chosen ministers, and is honoured thereby, and as He still works by them He would not have us speak disparagingly of them.

The topic of this morning is this : it has pleased God to save souls by His people, and therefore He places in them a sacred longing by all means to save some. He might if He had pleased have called all His chosen to Himself by a voice out of the excellent glory, just as He called Saul the persecutor ; or He might have commissioned angels to fly throughout the length and breadth of the world, and carry the message of mercy ; but in His inscrutable wisdom He has been pleased to bring men to Himself by men. The atonement is complete, and the Spirit's power is fully given ; all that is needed is that men be led to believe for the salvation of their souls and this part of salvation is accomplished by the Holy Ghost through the ministries of men. Those who have themselves been quickened are sent to prophesy upon the dry bones. In order that this divine arrangement may be carried out, the Lord has implanted in the hearts of all genuine believers a passion for the salvation of souls : in some this is more lively than in others, but it ought to be a leading feature in the character of every Christian. I shall speak upon this sacred instinct, and deal with it thus : first, *why is it implanted in us ?* secondly, *how does it exercise itself ?* thirdly, *why is it not more largely manifested ?* and fourthly, *how can it be quickened and made more practically efficient ?*

I. WHY IS THIS PASSION FOR SAVING OTHERS IMPLANTED IN THE BREASTS OF THE SAVED ? For three reasons, I think, among many others ; namely, for God's glory, for the good of the church, and for the profiting of the individual.

It is implanted there, first, *for God's glory*. It is greatly to the glory of God that He should use humble' instruments for the accomplishment of His grand purposes. When Quintin Matsys had executed a certain wonderful well-cover in iron, it was the more notable as a work of art because he had been deprived of the proper tools while he was executing it, for I think he had little more than his hammer with which to perform that wonderful feat in metal. Now, when we look at God's work of grace in the world, it glorifies Him the more when we reflect that He has achieved it by instruments which in themselves would rather hinder than promote His work. No man among us can help God ; it is true He uses us, but He could do better without us than with us : by the direct word of power He could do in a moment that which, through the weakness of the instrument, now takes months and years, yet He knows best how to glorify His own name. He puts a longing to save others into our souls, that He may get glory by using us, even us who have little fitness for such work except this passion which He has implanted in our breasts. He graciously uses even our weak points, and makes our very infirmities to illustrate the glory of His grace, blessing our poorest sermons, prospering our feeblest efforts, and giving us to see results even from our stray words. The Lord glorifies Himself by making our feebleness to be the vehicle of His power, and to this end He makes us pant for a work far out of our reach, and sets our hearts a-longing to " save some."

It brings glory to God also that He should take sinful men such as we are, and make us partakers of His nature, and He does this by giving us fellowship in His bowels of compassion, communion in His overflowing love. He kindles in our breasts the same fire of love which glows in His own bosom. In our own little way we look down upon the prodigal sons, and see them a great way off, and have compassion on them, and would fain fall on their necks and kiss them. The Lord loves men, however, after a holy fashion, He desires their sanctification, and their salvation by that means ; and when we desire the good of our fellow-men by means of their conversion, we are walking side by side with God. Every real philanthropist is a copy of the Lord Jesus ; for though it is too low a term to apply to His infinite excellence, yet truly the Son of God is the grandest of all philanthropists. Now, that God should, by the power of His matchless grace, produce in such cold hearts as ours a burning passion for the salvation of others is a singular proof of His omnipotent power in the world of mind. To change sinful men so that they pant after the increase of holiness, to render stubborn wills eager for the spread of obedience, and to make wandering hearts earnest for the establishment of the abiding kingdom of the Redeemer, this is a mighty feat of the grace of God. That a perfect angel should cleave the air to perform His message is a simple matter enough, but that a Saul of Tarsus, who foamed at the mouth with enmity to Christ, should live and die for the winning of souls to Jesus, is a memorable illustration of the grace of God.

In this way the Lord gets great glory over the Arch-enemy, the Prince of the power of the air, for He can say to Satan, " I have defeated thee, not by the sword of Michael, but by the tongues of men ; I have conquered thee, O thou enemy, not with thunderbolts, but with the earnest words and prayers and tears of these My humble servants. O Mine adversary, I have pitted against thee feeble men and women, into whom I have put the love of souls, and these have torn away from thee province after province of thy dominions, these have snapped the fetters of the bondaged ones, these have burst open the prison doors of those who were thy captives." How illustriously is this truth seen when the Lord seizes the ringleaders of Satan's army and transforms them into captains of His own host ! Then is the enemy smitten in the house of his former friends. Satan desired to sift Peter as wheat, but Peter sifted him in return on the day of Pentecost ; Satan made Peter deny his Master, but when restored Peter loved his Lord all the more, and all the more earnestly did he proclaim his Master's name and gospel. The fury of the foe recoils on himself, love conquers, and where sin abounded grace doth much more abound. As for Saul, who persecuted the saints, did not he become the apostle of Christ to the Gentiles, labouring more than any other for the good cause ? Beloved, the ultimate triumph of the cross will be the more admirable because of the manner of its achievement.

Good will conquer evil, not by the assistance of governments and the arms of potentates, not by the prestige of bishops and popes, and all their pompous array, but by hearts that burn, and souls that glow, and eyes that weep, and knees that bend in wrestling prayer. These are the artillery of God, by using such weapons as these He not only foils His foes, but triumphs over them in it, confounding the mighty by the weak, the wise by the simple, and the things which are by the things which are not.

Next, the passion for saving souls is implanted for *the church's good*, and that in a thousand ways, of which I can only mention a few. First, there can be no doubt that the passion for winning souls expends the church's energy in a healthy manner. I have observed that churches which do not care for the outlying population speedily suffer from disunion and strife. There is a certain quantity of steam generated in the community, and if we do not let it off in the right way, it will work in the wrong way, or blow up altogether, and do infinite mischief. Men's minds are sure to work, and their tongues to move, and if they are not employed for good purposes they will assuredly do mischief. You cannot unite a church so completely as by calling out all its forces for accomplishing the Redeemer's grand object. Talents unused are sure to rust, and this kind of rust is a deadly poison to peace, and acrid irritant which eats into the heart of the church. We will therefore by all means save some, lest by some other means we become disunited in heart.

This passion for saving souls not only employs but also draws forth the strength of the church, it awakens her latent energies, and arouses her noblest faculties. With so divine a prize before her she girds up her loins for the race, and with her eye upon her Lord presses forward to the goal. Many a commonplace man has been rendered great by being thoroughly absorbed by a noble pursuit, and what can be nobler than turning men from the road which leads to hell ? Perhaps some of those ignoble souls who have lived and died like dumb, driven cattle, might have reached the majesty of great lives if a supreme intent had fired them with heroic zeal, and developed their concealed endowments. Happy is the man whose task is honourable, if he do but honourably fulfil it. Lo, God has given to His church the work of conquering the world, the plucking of brands from the burning, the feeding of His sheep and lambs, and this it is which trains the church to deeds of daring and to nobility of soul.

Dear brethren, this common passion for souls knits us together. How often do I feel a fresh bond of union with my beloved brethren and fellow-workers, when I find that I was the means of the conviction of a sinner, whom one of them comforted, and led him to the Saviour, and thus we have a joint possession in the convert. Sometimes I have been blest of God to the salvation of my hearer, but that hearer was first brought here by yonder friend, and so we become sharers in the joy. Communion in service and success welds the saints together, and is one of the best securities for mutual love.

And, moreover, when new converts are brought into the church, the fact that they are brought in by instrumentality tends to make their fusion with the church an easy matter. It is in this case much the same as with our families. If God had been pleased to create each of us as individual men and women, and drop us down somewhere on the earth, and leave us to find our way to somebody's house, and unite with his family, I daresay we should have had to wander long before we should have been welcomed : but now we come as little ones to those who rejoice to see us, and sing, " Welcome, welcome, little stranger ! " We become at once parts of the family, because we have parents and brothers and sisters, and these make no debate about our introduction and consider it no trouble to receive us, though I fear we have never duly rewarded them for their pains. So is it in the church : if God had converted all men one by one, by His Spirit, without instrumentality, they would have been separate grains of sand, hard to unite into a building, and there would have been much difficulty in forming them into one body ; but now we are born into the church, and the pastor and others look upon those converted under their in- strumentality as their own children, whom they love in the Lord, and the church having shared in the common service by which they are converted feels, " These belong to us, these are our reward " ; and so they are taken cordially into the Christian family. This is no small benefit, for it is at once the joy and the strength of the church to be made one by vital forces, by holy sympathies and fellowships. We have spiritual fathers among us, whom we love in the Lord, and spiritual children whose welfare is our deepest concern, and brethren and sisters to whom we have been helpful, or who have been helpful to us, whom we cannot but commune with in heart. As a common desire to defend their country welds all the regiments of an army into one, so the common desire to save souls makes all true believers akin to each other.

But this passion is most of all for *the good of the individual possessing it*. I will not try this morning to sum up in the short time allotted to me the immense benefits which come to a man through his labouring for the conversion of others, but I will venture this assertion, that no man or woman in the church of God is in a healthy state if he or she be not labouring to save some. Those who are laid aside by suffering are taking their part in the economy of the household of Christ, but with that exception, he that doth not work neither shall he eat, he that doth not water others is not watered himself, and he who cares not for the souls of others may well stand in jeopardy about his own.

To long for the conversion of others makes us Godlike. Do we desire man's welfare ? God does so. Would we fain snatch them from the burning ? God is daily performing this deed of grace. Can we say that we have no pleasure in the death of Him that dieth ? Jehovah has declared the like with an oath. Do we weep over sinners ? Did not Jehovah's Son weep over them ? Do we lay out ourselves for their conversion ? Did He not die that they might live ? Ye are made Godlike when this passion glows within your spirit.

This is a vent for your love to God as well as your love to men. Loving the Creator, we pity His fallen creatures, and feel a benevolent love towards the work of His hands. If we love God, we feel as He does, that judgment is His strange work, and we cannot bear that those whom He has created should be cast away for ever. Loving God makes us sorrow that all men do not love Him too. It frets us that the world lieth in the wicked one, at enmity to its own Creator, at war with Him who alone can bless it. O beloved, you do not love the Lord at all unless you love the souls of others.

Trying to bring others to Christ does us good by renewing in us our old feelings, and reviving our first love. When I see an inquirer penitent for sin, I recollect the time when I felt as he is feeling ; and when I hear the seeker for the first time say, " I do believe in Jesus," I recollect the birthday of my own soul, when the bells of my heart rang out their merriest peals, because Jesus Christ was come to dwell within me. Soul-winning keeps the heart lively, and preserves our warm youth to us ; it is a mighty refresher to decaying love.

If you feel the chill of scepticism stealing over you, and begin to doubt the gospel's power, go to work among the poor and ignorant, or comfort souls in distress, and when you see the brightness of their countenances as they obtain joy and peace in believ- ing, your scepticism will fly like chaff before the wind You must believe in the cause when you see the result ; you cannot help believing when the evidence is before your eyes. Work for Jesus keeps us strong in faith, and intense in love to Him,

Does not this holy instinct draw forth all the faculties of a man ? One strong passion will fre- quently bring the whole man into play, like a skilful minstrel whose hand brings music from every chord. If we love others, we shall, like Paul, become wise to attract them, wise to persuade them, wise to convince them, wise to encourage them ; we shall learn the use of means which had lain rusted by, and discover in ourselves talents which else had been hidden in the ground if the strong desire to save men had not cleared away the soil.

And I will add here that love to souls will in the end bring to every one who follows it up the highest joy beneath the stars. What is that ? It is the joy of knowing that you have been made the spiritual parent of others. I have tasted of this stream full often, and it is heaven below. The joy of being saved one's self has a measure of selfishness about it, but to know that your fellow-men are saved by your efforts brings a joy pure, disinterested, and heavenly, of which we may drink the deepest draughts without injury to our spirits. Yield yourselves, brethren, to the divine appetite for doing good, be possessed with it, and eaten up by it, and the best results must follow. Be this henceforward your aim, " That I may by all means save some."

II. How DOES THIS PASSION EXERCISE ITSELF ? Differently in different persons, and at different periods. At first it shows itself by *tender anxiety*. The moment a man is saved he begins to be anxious about his wife, his child, or his dearest relative, and that anxiety leads him at once to pray for them. As soon as the newly opened eye has enjoyed the sweet light of the Sun of Righteousness it looks lovingly round on those who were its companions in darkness, and then gazes up into heaven with a tearful prayer that they also may receive their sight. Hungry ones while they are eating the first mouthful at the banquet of free grace groan within themselves and say, " Oh, that my poor, starving children could be here to feed on the Saviour's love with me." Com- passion is natural to the new-born nature ; as common humanity makes us pity the suffering, so renewed humanity makes us pity the sinful. This, I say, happens at the very dawn of the new life. Further on in the heavenly pilgrimage this passion manifests itself in the *intense joy* exhibited when news reaches us of the conversion of others. I have often seen at church meetings, and missionary meetings, a hearty and holy joy spread throughout an audience when some new convert, or returned missionary, or successful minister, has given details of the wonders of saving grace. Many a poor girl who could do but little for the Saviour has, nevertheless, shown what she would have done if she could, by the tears of joy which have streamed down her cheeks when she has heard that sinners have been led to Jesus. This is one of the ways in which those who can personally do little can share in the joy of the most useful, yea, can have fellowship with Jesus Himself.

The hallowed instinct of soul-winning also shows itself in *private efforts, sacrifices, prayers, and agonies* for the spread of the gospel. Well do I remember when I first knew the Lord how restless I felt till I could do something for others. I did not know that I could speak to an assembly, and I was very timid as to conversing upon religious subjects, and therefore I wrote little notes to different persons setting forth the way of salvation, and I dropped these written letters with printed tracts into the post, or slipped them under the doors of houses, or dropped them into areas, praying that those who read them might be aroused as to their sins, and moved to flee from the wrath to come. My heart would have burst if it could not have found some vent. I wish that all professors kept up their first zeal, and were diligent in doing little things as well as greater things for Jesus, for often the lesser agencies turn out to be as effectual as those which operate upon a larger area. I hope that all of you young people who have been lately added to the church are trying some mode of doing good, suitable for your capacity and position, that by all means you may save some. A word may often bless those whom a sermon fails to reach, and a personal letter may do far more than a printed book.

As we grow older, and are more qualified, we shall take our share in the more *public agencies* of the church. We shall speak for Jesus before the few who meet at the cottage prayer-meeting, we shall pray with as well as for our families, or we shall enlist in the Sabbath-school, or take a tract district. Ultimately the Lord may call us to plead His cause before hundreds or thousands, and so beginning with littles our latter end shall greatly increase.

There is one point in which zeal for the salvation of others will show itself in all who possess it, namely, in *adapting ourselves to the condition and capacity of others for their good.* Notice this in Paul. He became all things to all men, if by any means he might save some. He became a Jew to the Jews. When he met with them he did not rail at their ceremonies, but endeavoured to bring out their spiritual meaning. He did not preach against Judaism, but showed them Jesus as the fulfiller of its types. When he met with a heathen he did not revile the gods, but taught him the true God and salvation by His Son. He did not carry about with him one sermon for all places, but adapted his speech to his audience. What a very wonderful address that was which Paul delivered to the council of philosophers upon Mars' Hill. It is most courteous throughout, and it is a pity that our translation somewhat destroys that quality, for it is eminently conspicuous in the original. The apostle began by saying, " Ye men of Athens, I perceive that ye are on all points very God-fearing." He did not say, " Too superstitious," as our version has it, that would have needlessly provoked them at the outset. He went on to say, " For as I passed through the city and observed your sacred things, I found an altar

bearing the inscription, ' To an unknown God.' What, therefore, ye worship without knowing it, that I announce unto you." He did not say, " Whom ye ignorantly worship." He was far too prudent to use such an expression. They were a collection of thoughtful men, of cultured minds, and he aimed at winning them by courteously declaring to them the gospel. It was most adroit on his part to refer to that inscription upon the altar, and equally so to quote from one of their own poets. If he had been addressing Jews, he would neither have quoted from a Greek poet nor referred to a heathen altar : his intense love for his hearers taught him to merge his own peculiarities in order to secure their attention. In the same manner we also sink ourselves, and instead of demanding that others submit to us, we cheerfully submit to them in all unessential matters, that we may gain their favourable consideration of the claims of Jesus. Mark you, there was never a man more stern for principle than Paul ; in things where it was necessary to take his stand he was firm as a rock, but in merely personal and external matters he was the servant of all. Adaptation was his *forte*. Beloved, if you have to talk to children, be children, and do not expect them to be men. Think their thoughts, feel their feelings, and put truth into their words. You will never get at their hearts till your heart is in sympathy with their childhood. If you have to comfort the aged, enter also into their infirmities, and do not speak to them as if they were still in the full vigour of life. Study persons of all ages, and be as they are, that they may be led to be believers, as you are. Are you called to labour among the educated ? Then choose out excellent words, and present them apples of gold in baskets of silver. Do you work among the illiterate ? Let your words be as goads ; speak their mother tongue, use great plainness of speech, so that you may be understood, for what avails to speak to them in an unknown tongue ? Are you cast among people with strange prejudices ? Do not unnecessarily jar with them, but take them as you find them. Are you seeking the conversion of a person of slender understanding ? Do not inflict upon him the deeper mysteries, but show him the plain man's pathway to heaven in words which he who runs may read. Are you talking with a friend who is of a sorrowful spirit ? Tell him of your own depressions, enter into his griefs, and so raise him as you were raised. Like the good Samaritan, go where the wounded man lies, and do not expect him to come to you. A real passion for winning souls reveals the many sides of our manhood, and uses each one as a reflector of the divine light of truth. There is a door to each man's heart, and we have to find it, and enter it with the right key, which is to be found somewhere or other in the Word of God. All men are not to be reached in the same way, or by the same arguments, and as we are by all means to save some, we must be wise to win souls, wise with wisdom from above. We desire to see them conquered for Christ, but no warrior uses always the same strategy ; there is for one open assault, for another a siege, for a third an ambush, for a fourth a long campaign. On the sea there are great rams which run down the enemy, torpedoes under water, gunboats, and steam frigates, one ship is broken up by a single blow, another needs a broadside, a third must have a shot between wind and water, a fourth must be driven on shore, even thus must we adapt ourselves, and use the sacred force entrusted to us with grave consideration and solemn judgment, looking ever to the Lord for guidance and for power. All the real power is in the Lord's hands, and we must put ourselves fully at the disposal of the divine Worker, that He may work in us both to will and to do of His good pleasure ; so shall we by all means save some.

III. Why is not this passion more largely developed among Christians ? The preacher needs not answer that question, each of his hearers may do that for himself. Why is it that we do not yearn more over the perishing souls of men ? Is it not that we have but very little grace ? We are dwarfish Christians, with little faith, little love, little care for the glory of God, and therefore with little concern for perishing sinners. We are spiritually naked, and poor, and miserable, when we might be rich and increased in goods if we had but more faith. That is the secret of the matter, and is the fountain of all the mischief, but if we must come to particulars, do you not think that men are careless about the souls of others because they have fallen into *one-sided views of gospel doctrines*, and have turned the doctrines of grace into a couch for idleness to rest upon ? "God will save His own," say they. Yes, but His own do not talk in that fashion ; they are not like Cain, who said, "Am I my brother's keeper ? " Unquestionably the Lord will see that His own elect are called in due season, but He will do this by the preaching or teaching of the word. Predestination is not a legitimate reason for inaction ; men do not consider it so in other matters, why then in religion ? Except the Lord prospers us in business all our efforts are vain, and yet we do not say, " I shall have as many pounds in my pocket as God intends I shall have, and therefore I need not work or trade." No, men save their fatalism to play the fool with in spiritual things : in all other things they are not such idiots as to suffer predestination to paralyse their minds, but here, since idleness wants an excuse for itself, they dare to abuse this sacred truth to stultify their consciences.

In some professors downright *worldliness* prevents their seeking the conversion of others. They are too fond of gain to care for saving souls, too busy about their farms to sow the seed of the kingdom, too much occupied with their shops to hold up the cross before the sinner's eye, too full of care to care for the salvation of the lost. Covetousness eats up the very soul of many. They have far more business than they can manage, without injury to their spiritual health, and yet they are eager after more. Prayer-meetings are neglected, the class in the school is given up, efforts for the poor and ignorant are never made, and all because they are so taken up with the world and its cares. This age is peculiarly tempted in that direction, and it needs strong piety to be able to love the souls of men practically.

With some I fear that the cause of indifference is *want of faith*. They do not believe that God will bless their efforts, and therefore they make none. They have a vivid recollection of far-gone times when they tried to be useful and failed, and instead of past failure being made a reason for double exertion in the present, to make up for lost time, they have given up labour for the Lord as a bad case, and do not attempt anything more. It is to be feared that with many church-members the reason of the absence of this passion is that they love ease, and are worm eaten with *indolence*. They say, " Soul, take thine ease, eat, drink, and be merry ; why trouble

about others ? " " Send the multitude away," said the disciples. They did not want to be worried with them. True, the people were very hungry and weary, and it was a painful thing to see them fainting ; but it was easier to forget their needs than to relieve them. London is perishing, millions are dying in their sins, the world still lieth in the wicked one, and sloth calls forgetfulness to her aid to ignore the whole matter. Such people do not want to be made uncomfortable, neither do they wish to spend and be spent for the glory of Christ.

The secret of all is that the great majority of Christians are *out of sympathy with God*, and out of communion with Christ. Is not this an evil ? O eyes that never wept over dying men, do ye expect to see the King in His beauty ? O hearts that never throbbed with anxiety for those that are going down to the pit, do ye hope to leap for joy at the Master's coming ? O lips that never speak for Jesus, how will ye answer to the searching questions of the last great day ? I do beseech you, Christian people, if you have grown indifferent to the conversion of those around you, search out the secret reason, find what is the worm at the root of your piety, and in the name of Christ seek to be delivered therefrom.

IV. How can this passion be more fully aroused ? It can be aroused only, first, by our *obtaining a higher life*. The better man shall do the better deed ; the stronger in grace the stronger to save some. I do not believe in a man's trying to pump himself up beyond his level. The man must be up, and then all that comes out of the man will have risen. If love to God glows in your soul, it must show itself in your concern for others. Make the tree good and the fruit will be good. It will not do for you to begin a more earnest career by stimulating yourself to a hectic zeal which will come and go like the flush on the consumptive's cheek ; the life within must be permanently strengthened, and then the pulsings of the heart, and the motion of the whole man will be more vigorous. More grace is our greatest need.

This being granted, it will greatly help us to care for the conversion of sinners if we are *fully cognisant of their misery and degradation*. How differently one feels after seeing with your own eyes the poverty, filth, and vice of this city. I wish some of you respectable people, who have never seen any part of London except the broad thoroughfares, would take a stroll down the courts which open into the narrow side streets. I would like you to go down courts such as Queen Victoria never saw, and alleys far from green. Ladies, you may leave some of that finery at home ; and gentlemen, you may put away your pocket-handkerchiefs and your purses, unless you would like to empty them out among the wretched beings you will meet. There are sights to be seen close to your own homes which might well make our hearts bleed and harrow up our spirits. When you have seen them you will begin to feel aright towards the sinful. We sit at home comfortably at our fires in the winter time and think the weather is not so very cold, but if we go out and see the poor shivering in their rags, or find them cowering over their empty grates, we begin to think that cold is a greater evil than we dreamed : we come here to this place of worship, and while we are listening to the Word we forget the destitution of those who hear it not. Why, at this very moment around the doors of the gin-palaces and public-houses of

London there are thousands standing waiting till the blessed hour of one, when they can obtain the cheering draught which their souls thirst after. The assemblies now tarrying for the god Bacchus can be counted by thousands. What have these men been doing with the Sabbath hours up till now ? Reading the Sunday newspaper, lying in bed, or loafing about their little gardens in their shirt sleeves. That is the occupation of hundreds of thousands this day all around us and at our doors ; have we done our best to bring them to the house of prayer ? Hundreds of thousands hard by have never heard the gospel in their lives, and never think of entering places where it is preached. Of course, if they had lived in Calcutta we should have thought about them ; living in London close to us shall we neglect them ? One of the best things that could be done for us all would be to go round for a week with a city missionary to houses in the worst parts of the city, that we might see for ourselves what is to be seen ; then would sin and poverty become palpable and stand out in grim reality. Your fellow-countrymen, men born of women, who are of the same flesh and blood as yourselves, are living in daily neglect of your dear Saviour, living in jeopardy of their immortal souls ; if you did but realise this it would quicken you by all means to save some.

Brethren, the strongest argument I have ever seen for the doctrine of the eternity of future punishment is an argument which is often used against it. They say, " If the eternity of future punishment be true, we wonder that believers in it can rest in their beds, or eat their meals, for the truth is so horrible that it ought to stir them to incessant efforts to deliver others from going into this boundless misery." It is true, and spoken as by a prophet, and that is one reason why I believe the doctrine, because it has a tendency, if anything has, to move us to compassion and rouse us to action. If the advocate of other views is prepared to teach me a doctrine which will make me think more lightly of sin, and make me feel more easy about the damnation of my fellow-men, I do not want his doctrine, for I am too careless now, and have a dread of being more so. If with the most terrible argument for incessant sorrow for the ruin of the souls of my hearers, I cannot be as tender as I would, what should I be if I could lay the flattering unction to my soul that after all it was of smaller consequence than I had thought whether they were damned or saved ? Ah, dear friends, can you bear to think of it, that all around you there are men and women who will, in a few years, suffer the terrible wrath of God, and be banished for ever from His presence ? If you could but realise hell and its horrors, you must be stirred by all means to save some.

Many other things might move us, but certainly this last ought to do it. A sense of *our own solemn obligations* to the grace of God should arouse all our energies. If we are what we profess to be, we are saved men, redeemed by the heart's blood of the Son of God : do we not owe something to Christ for this ? Shall we be easy till we have found many jewels for His crown ? Can we be content while so many myriads are ignorant of Him, or opposed to Him ? If ye love Him, what will ye do for Him ? Show Him a proof of your love, and the best proof you can give is your own personal holiness and persevering effort to gather in His redeemed. Brother, sister, do something for Jesus. Do not talk about it : do it. Words are leaves ; actions are fruits. Do something for Jesus ; do something for Jesus to-day ! Ere the sun goes down think of some one action which may tend to the conversion of some one person, and do it with your might ; let the object of the effort be your child, your servant, your brother, your friend—but do make the effort to-day. Having done it to-day, do it to-morrow, and every day ; and doing it in one way, do it in another way ; and doing it in one state of heart, do it in another. Let your joy enchant, let your sorrow arouse, let your hope attract ; let your changeful moods help you to attack sinners from different quarters, as your varying circumstances bring you into contact with differing persons. Be always awake. Turn yourself about like a gun on a swivel to reach persons who are found in any direction, so that some may fall wounded by the gospel's power. By all means save some : God grant it may be so. And, oh, that some might be saved this morning by simply believing in Christ Jesus, for that is the way of salvation. Jesus puts away sin wherever there is a simple trust in Him ; may seekers exercise that trust now, and live for ever. Amen.

THE HEAVENLY RACE

" So run, that ye may obtain."—1 Corinthians ix. 24.

WE are continually insisting upon it from day to day, that salvation is not of works, but of grace. We lay this down as one of the very first doctrines of the gospel. " Not of works, lest any man should boast." " By grace are ye saved, through faith, and that not of yourselves ; it is the gift of God." But we find, that it is equally necessary to preach the absolute necessity of a religious life for the attainment of heaven at last. Although we are sure that men are not saved for the sake of their works, yet are we equally sure that no man will be saved without them ; and that he who leads an unholy life, who neglects the great salvation, can never inherit that crown of life which fadeth not away. In one sense, true religion is wholly the work of God ; yet there are high and important senses in which we must ourselves " strive to enter in at the strait gate." We must run a race ; we must wrestle even to agony ; we must fight a battle, before we can inherit the crown of life. We have in our text the course of religion set down as a race ; and inasmuch as there be many who enter upon a profession of religion, with very false motives, the apostle warns us that although all run in a race, yet all do not obtain the prize : they run all, but only one is rewarded : and he gives us, therefore, the practical exhortation to run that we may obtain ; for unless we are the winners we had better not have been runners at all, for he that is not a winner is a loser ; he who makes a profession of religion, and does not at last obtain the crown of life, is a loser by his profession ; for his profession was hypocrisy or else formality, and he had better not have made a profession, than fall therein.

And now, in entering upon the text, I shall have to notice *what it is we are to run for* : " So run that ye may *obtain* " ; secondly, *the mode of running, to which we must attend*—" *So* run that ye may obtain " ; and then I shall give a few *practical exhortations*, to stir those onward in the heavenly race who are flagging and negligent, in order that they may at last " obtain."

I. In the first place, then, WHAT IS IT WE OUGHT TO SEEK TO OBTAIN ?

Some people think they must be religious, *in order to be respectable*. There are a vast number of people in the world who go to church and to chapel, because everybody else does so. It is disreputable to waste your Sundays, not to be found going up to the house of God ; therefore they take a pew and attend the services, and they think they have done their duty : they have obtained all that they sought for, when they can hear their neighbours saying, " Such-and-such a man is a very respectable person ; he is always very regular at his church ; he is a very reputable person, and exceedingly praiseworthy." Verily, if this be what you seek after in your religion, you shall get it ; for the Pharisees who sought the praise of men " had their reward." But when you have gotten it, what a poor reward it is ! Is it worth the drudgery ? I do not believe that the drudgery to which people submit in order to be called respectable is at all compensated by what they gain. I am sure, for my own part, I would not care a solitary rap what I was called, or what I was thought ; nor would I perform anything that was irksome to myself for the sake of pleasing any man that ever walked beneath the stars, however great or mighty he may be. It is the sign of a fawning, cringing spirit, when people are always seeking to do that which renders them respectable. The esteem of men is not worth the looking after, and sad it is, that this should be the only prize which some men put before them, in the poor religion which they undertake.

There are other people who go a little farther : they are not content with being considered respectable, but they want something more ; *they desire to be considered pre-eminently saints*. These persons come to our places of worship, and after a little time they venture to come forward and ask whether they may unite with our churches. We examine them, and so hidden is their hypocrisy that we cannot discover its rottenness : we receive them into our churches ; they sit at the Lord's Supper ; they come to our church-meetings : mayhap, they are even voted into the deacon's office ; sometimes they attain to the pulpit, though God has never called them, and preach what they have never felt in their hearts. Men may do all this merely to enjoy the praise of men ; and they will even undergo some persecution for the sake of it ; because to be thought a saint, to be reckoned by religious people to be everything that is right and proper, to have a name among the living in Zion, is to some persons a thing exceedingly coveted. They would not like to be set down among the " chief of sinners," but if they may have their names written among the chief of saints they will consider themselves exceedingly exalted. I am afraid we have a considerable admixture of persons of this sort in our churches who only come for the mere

sake of keeping up their religious pretensions and obtaining a religious status in the midst of the church of God. " Verily, I say unto you, *they have* their reward," and they shall never have any but what they obtain here. They get their reward for a little time ; for a short time they are looked up to ; but perhaps even in this life they make a trip, and down they go ; the church discovers them, and they are sent out like the ass stripped of the lion's skin to browse once more among their native nettles, no longer to be glorious in the midst of the church of the living God. Or mayhap, they may wear the cloak until the last day of their lives, and then death comes, and strips them of all their tinsel and gewgaw ; and they who acted upon the stage of religion as kings and princes, are sent behind the stage to be unrobed and to find themselves beggars to their shame, and naked to their eternal disgrace. It is not this which you and I would seek after in religion. Dearly beloved, if we do run the race, we would run for a higher and more glorious prize than any of these things.

Another set of people take up with religious life *for what they can get by it*. I have known tradespeople attend church for the mere sake of getting the custom of these who went there. I have heard of such things as people knowing which side their bread was buttered, and going to that particular denomination where they thought they could get the most by it. Loaves and fishes drew some of Christ's followers, and they are very attracting baits, even to this day. Men find there is something to be gotten by religion. Among the poor it is, perhaps, some little charity to be obtained, and among those that are in business, it is the custom which they think to get. " Verily I say unto you, they have their reward " ; for the church is ever foolish and unsuspicious. We do not like to suspect our fellow creatures of following us from sordid motives. The church does not like to think that a man would be base enough to pretend to religion for the mere sake of what he can get ; and, therefore, we let these people easily slip through, and they have their reward. But ah ! at what a price they buy it ! They have deceived the Lord's servants for gold, and they have entered into His church as base hypocrites for the sake of a piece of bread ; and they shall be thrust out at last with the anger of God behind them, like Adam driven out of Eden, with the flaming Cherubim with a sword turning every way to keep the tree of life ; and they shall for ever look back upon this as the most fearful crime they have committed—that they pretended to be God's people when they were not, and entered into the midst of the fold when they were but wolves in sheeps' clothing.

There is yet another class, and when I have referred to them I will mention no more. These are the people who take up with religion for the sake of *quieting their conscience* ; and it is astonishing how little of religion will sometimes do that. Some people tell us that if in the time of storm men would pour bottles of oil upon the waves, there would be a great calm at once. I have never tried it, and it is most probable I never shall, for my organ of credulity is not large enough to accept so extensive a statement. But there are some people who think that they can calm the storm of a troubled conscience by pouring a little of the oil of a profession about religion upon it ; and it is amazing how wonderful an effect this really has. I have known a man who was drunk many times in a week, and who got his money dishonestly, and yet he always had an easy conscience by going to his church or chapel regularly on the Sunday. We have heard of a man who could "devour widows' houses"—a lawyer who could swallow up everything that came in his way, and yet he would never go to bed without saying his prayers; and that stilled his conscience. We have heard of other persons, especially among the Romanists, who would not object to thieving, but who would regard eating anything but fish on a Friday as a most fearful sin, supposing that by making a fast on the Friday, all the iniquities of all the days in the week would be put away. They want the outward forms of religion to keep the conscience quiet; for Conscience is one of the worst lodgers to have in your house when he gets quarrelsome: there is no abiding with him; he is an ill bed-fellow; ill at lying down, and equally troublesome at rising up. A guilty conscience is one of the curses of the world: it puts out the sun, and takes away the brightness from the moonbeam. A guilty conscience casts a noxious exhalation through the air, removes the beauty from the landscape, the glory from the flowing river, the majesty from the rolling floods. There is nothing beautiful to the man that has a guilty conscience. He needs no accusing; everything accuses him. Hence people take up with religion just to quiet them. They take the sacrament sometimes; they go to a place of worship; they sing a hymn now and then; they give a guinea to a charity; they intend to leave a portion in their will to build alms-houses; and in this way conscience is lulled asleep, and they rock him to and fro with religious observances, till there be sleeps while they sing over him the lullaby of hypocrisy, and he wakes not until he shall wake with that rich man who was here clothed in purple, but in the next world did lift up his eyes in hell, being in torments, without a drop of water to cool his burning tongue.

What, then, is it, for which we ought to run in this race? Why heaven, eternal life, justification by faith, the pardon of sin, acceptance in the Beloved, and glory everlasting. If you run for anything else than salvation, should you win, what you have won is not worth the running for. Oh! I beseech every one of you, make sure work for eternity; never be contented with anything less than a living faith in a living Saviour; rest not until you are certain that the Holy Spirit is at work in your souls. Do not think that the outside of religion can be of use to you: it is just the inward part of religion that God loveth. Seek to have a repentance that needeth not to be repented of—a faith which looks alone to Christ, and which will stand by you when you come into the swellings of Jordan. Seek to have a love which is not like a transient flame, burning for a moment and then extinguished; but a flame which shall increase and increase, and still increase, till your heart shall be swallowed up therein, and Jesus Christ's one name shall be the sole object of your affection. We must, in running the heavenly race, set nothing less before us than that which Christ did set before Him. He set the joy of salvation before Himself, and then He did run, despising the cross and enduring the shame. So let us do; and may God give us good success, that by His good Spirit we may attain unto eternal life, through the resurrection of Jesus Christ our Lord!

II. Thus have I noticed what it is we are to run for. And now the Apostle says, "So run that ye may obtain." I shall notice some people who never will obtain, and tell you the reason why, and in so doing, I shall be illustrating THE RULES OF THE RACE.

There are some people who certainly never will obtain the prize, because they are not even *entered*. Their names are not down for the race, and therefore it is quite clear that they will not run, or if they do run, they will run without having any warrant whatever for expecting to receive the prize. There are some such here this afternoon: who will tell you themselves, "We make no profession, sir—none whatever." It is quite as well, perhaps, that you do not; because if you did, you would be hypocrites, and it is better to make no profession at all than to be hypocrites. Still, recollect, your names are not down for the race, and therefore you cannot win. If a man tells you in business that he makes no profession of being honest, you know he is a confirmed rogue. If a man makes no profession of being religious, you know what he is—he is irreligious—he has no fear of God before his eyes, he has no love to Christ, he has no hope of heaven. He confesses it himself. Strange that men should be so ready to confess this. You don't find persons in the street willing to acknowledge that they are confirmed drunkards. Generally a man will repudiate it with scorn. You never find a man saying to you, "I don't profess to be a chaste living man." You don't hear another say, "I don't profess to be anything but a covetous wretch." No; people are not so fast about telling their faults; and yet you hear people confess the greatest fault to which man can be addicted: they say, "I make no profession"—which means just this—that they do not give God His due. God has made them, and yet they won't serve Him; Christ hath come into the world to save sinners, and yet they will not regard Him; the gospel is preached; and yet they will not hear it; they have the Bible in their houses, and yet they will not attend to its admonitions; they make no profession of doing so. It will be short work with them at the last great day. There will be no need for the books to be opened, no need for a long deliberation in the verdict. They do not profess to be pardoned; their guilt is written upon their own foreheads, their brazen shamelessness shall be seen by the whole world, as a sentence of destruction written upon their very brows. You cannot expect to win heaven unless your names are entered for the race. If there be no attempts whatever made, even at so much as a profession of religion, then of course you may just sit down and say, "Heaven is not for me; I have no part nor lot in the inheritance of Israel; I cannot say that my Redeemer liveth; and I may rest quite assured that Tophet is prepared of old *for me*. I must feel its pains and know its miseries; for there are but two places to dwell in hereafter, and if I am not found on the right hand of the Judge, there is but one alternative—namely, to be cast away for ever into the blackness of darkness."

Then there is another class whose names are down, but they *never started right*. A bad start is a sad thing. If in the ancient races of Greece or Rome a man who was about to run for the race had loitered, or if he had started before the time, it would not matter how fast he ran if he did not start in order. The flag must drop before the horse starts; otherwise, even if it reach the winning post first, it shall have no reward. There is something to be noted, then, in the starting of the race. I have known men run the race of religion with all their might, and yet they have lost it because they did not start right. You say, "Well, how is that ?" Why, there are some people who on a sudden leap into religion. They get it quickly, and they keep it for a time, and at last they lose it because they did not get their religion the right way. They have heard that before a man can be saved, it is necessary that, by the teaching of the Holy Spirit, he should feel the weight of sin, that he should make a confession of it, that he should renounce all hope in his own works, and should look to Jesus Christ alone. They look upon all these things as unpleasant preliminaries and therefore, before they have attended to repentance, before the Holy Spirit has wrought a good work in them, before they have been brought to give up everything and trust to Christ, they make a profession of religion. This is just setting up in business without a stock in trade, and there must be a failure. If a man has no capital to begin with, he may make a fine show for a little time, but it shall be as the crackling of thorns under a pot, a great deal of noise and much light for a little time, but it shall die out in darkness. How many there are who never think it necessary that there should be heart work within ! Let us remember, however, that there never was a true new birth without much spiritual suffering ; that there never was a man who had a changed heart without his first having a miserable heart. We must pass through that black tunnel of conviction before we can come out upon the high embankment of holy joy ; we must first go through the Slough of Despond before we can run along the walls of Salvation. There must be ploughing before there is sowing ; there must be many a frost, and many a sharp shower, before there is any reaping. But we often act like little children who pluck flowers from the shrubs and plant them in their gardens without roots ; then they say how fair and how pretty their little garden is ; but wait a little while, and all their flowers are withered, because they have no roots. This is all the effect of not having a right start, not having the " root of the matter." What is the good of outward religion, the flower and the leaf of it, unless we have the " root of the matter " in us—unless we have been digged into by that sharp iron spade of conviction, and have been ploughed with the plough of the Spirit, and then have been sown with the sacred seed of the gospel, in the hope of bringing forth an abundant harvest ? There must be a good start ; look well to that, for there is no hope of winning unless the start be right.

Again, there are some runners in the heavenly race who cannot win because they *carry too much weight.* A light weight, of course, has the advantage. There are some people who have an immensely heavy weight to carry. " How hardly shall a rich man enter into the kingdom of heaven ! " What is the reason ? Because he carries so much weight ; he has so much of the cares and pleasures of this world ; he has such a burden that he is not likely to win, unless God should please to give him a mighty mass of strength to enable him to bear it. We find many men willing to be saved, as they say ; they receive the word with great joy, but by-and-by thorns spring up and choke the word. They have so much business to do ; they say they must live ; they forget they must die. They have such a deal to attend to, they cannot think of living near to Christ. They find they have little time for devotions ; morning prayer must be cut short,

because their business begins early ; they can have no prayer at night, because business keeps them so late. How can they be expected to think of the things of God ? They have so much to do to answer this question—"What shall I eat ? what shall I drink ? and wherewithal shall I be clothed ? " It is true they read in the Bible that their Father who is in heaven will take care of them in these things if they will trust Him. But they say, " Not so." Those are enthusiasts according to their notions who rely upon providence. They say, the best providence in all the world is hard work ; and they say rightly ; but they forget that into the bargain of their hard work " it is in vain to rise up early and sit up late, and eat the bread of carefulness ; for except the Lord build the house, they labour in vain that build it." You see two men running a race. One of them, as he starts, lays aside every weight ; he takes off his garment and away he runs. There goes the other poor fellow ; he has a whole load of gold and silver upon his back. Then around his loins he has many distrustful doubts about what shall become of him in the future, what will be his prospects when he grows old, and a hundred other things. He does not know how to roll his burden upon the Lord. See how he flags, poor fellow, and how the other distances him, leaves him far behind, has gained the corner, and is coming to the winning post. It is well for us if we can cast everything away except that one thing needful, and say, " This is my business, to serve God on earth, knowing that I shall enjoy Him in heaven." For when we leave our business to God, we leave it in better hands than if we took care of it ourselves. They who carve for themselves generally cut their fingers ; but they who leave God to carve for them shall never have an empty plate. He who will walk after the cloud shall go aright, but he who will run before it shall soon find that he has gone a fool's errand. " Blessed is the man who trusteth in the Lord, and whose hope the Lord is." " The young lions do lack and suffer hunger, but they that wait upon the Lord shall not want any good thing." Our Saviour said, " Consider the lilies of the field, how they grow ; they toil not, neither do they spin, and yet I say unto you that even Solomon in all his glory was not arrayed like one of these." " Behold the fowls of the air, for they sow not, neither do they reap, nor gather into barns, yet your heavenly Father feedeth them ; are ye not much better than they ? " " Trust in the Lord and do good, and verily thou shalt be fed." " His place of defence shall be the munitions of rocks ; bread shall be given him ; his waters shall be sure." " Seek ye first the kingdom of God and His righteousness, and all these things shall be added unto you." Carry the weight of this world's cares about you, and it will be as much as you can do to carry them and to stand upright under them, but as to running a race with such burdens, it is just impossible.

There is also another thing that will prevent man's running the race. We have known people who stopped on their way to *kick their fellows.* Such things sometimes occur in a race. The horse, instead of speeding onwards to the mark, is of an angry disposition, and sets about kicking those that are running beside him—there is not much probability of his coming in first. " Now they that run in a race run all, but one receiveth the prize." There is one, however, who never gets it, and that is the man who always attends to his fellow-creatures instead of himself. It is a mysterious thing that I never yet saw a man with a hoe on his shoulder going to hoe his neighbour's garden; it is a rarity to see a farmer sending his team of horses to plough his neighbour's land; but it is a most singular thing that every day in the week I meet with persons who are attending to other people's character. If they go to the house of God, and hear a trite thing said, they say at once "How suitable that was for Mrs. Smith and Mrs. Brown?" The thought never enters their head, how suitable it was to themselves. They lend their ears to everybody else, but they do not hear for themselves. When they get out of chapel, perhaps as they walk home, their first thought is, "Well, how can I find fault with my neighbours?" They think that putting other people down is going up themselves (there never was a greater mistake); that by picking holes in their neighbour's coat they mend their own. They have so few virtues of their own that they do not like anybody else to have any, therefore they do the best they can to despoil everything good in their neighbour; and if there be a little fault, they will look at it through a magnifying glass; but they will turn the glass the other way when they look at their own sins. Their own faults become exceedingly small while those of others become magnificently great. Now this is a fault not only among professing religious men, but among those who are not religious. We are all so prone to find fault with other people instead of attending to our own home affairs. We attend to the vineyards of others, but our own vineyard we have not kept. Ask a worldly man why he is not religious, and he tells you "Because so-and-so makes a profession of religion and is not consistent." Pray is that any business of yours? To your own Master you must stand or fall, and so must he; God is their judge, and not you. Suppose there are a great many inconsistent Christians—and we are compelled to acknowledge that there are—so much the more reason why you should be a good one. Suppose there are a great many who deceive others; so much the more reason why you should set the world an example of what a genuine Christian is. "Ah! but," you say, "I am afraid there are very few." Then why don't you make one? But after all, is that your business? Must not every man bear his own burden? You will not be judged for other men's sins, you will not be saved by their faith, you will not be condemned for their unbelief. Every man must stand in his own proper flesh and blood at the bar of God, to account for the works done in his own body, whether they have been good or whether they have been evil. It will be of little avail for you to say at the day of judgment, "O Lord, I was looking at my neighbours; O Lord, I was finding fault with the people in the village; I was correcting their follies." But thus saith the Lord: "Did I ever commission thee to be a judge or a divider over them? Why, if thou hadst so much time to spare, and so much critical judgment, didst thou not exercise it upon thyself? Why didst thou not examine thyself, so that thou mightest have been found ready and acceptable in the day of God?" These persons are not very likely to win the race, because they turn to kicking others.

Again, there is another class of persons who will not win the race—namely, those who, although they seem to start very fair, very soon *loiter*. They dart ahead at the first starting, and distance all the others. There they fly away as if they had wings to their heels; but a little further on in the race, it is with difficulty that with whip and spur they are to be kept going at all, and they almost come to a standstill. Alas! this race of persons are to be discovered in all our churches. We get young people who come forward and make a profession of religion, and we talk with them, and we think it is all well with them; and for a little while they do run well; there is nothing wanting in them; we could hold them up as patterns for the imitation of others. Wait a couple of years; they drop off just by little and little. First, perhaps, there is the attendance on a week-day service neglected; then it is altogether discontinued; then one service on Sabbath; then perhaps family prayer, then private prayer—one thing after another is given up, until at last the whole edifice which stood upright and looked so fair, having been built upon the sand, gives way before the shock of time, and down it falls, and great is the ruin thereof. Recollect, it is not starting that wins the race; it is running all the way. He that would be saved, must hold on to the end: "He that endureth to the end, the same shall be saved." Stop and loiter in the race before you have come to the end thereof, and you have made one of the greatest mistakes that could possibly occur. On, on, on! while you live; still onward, onward, onward! for until you come to the grave, you have not come to your resting place; until you arrive at the tomb, you have not come to the spot where you may cry "Halt!" Ever onward if ye would win. If you are content to lose; if you would lose your own soul, you may say, "Stop," if you please; but if you would be saved evermore, be on, on, till you have gained the prize.

But there is another class of persons, who are worse than these. They start well too, and they run very fast at first, but at last they leap over the posts and rails; they *go quite out of the course* altogether, and you do not know where they are gone. Every now and then, we get such people as this. They go out from us, because they were not of us, for had they been of us, doubtless they would have continued with us. I might point out in my congregation on the Sabbath-day, a man whom I saw start myself. I saw him running so well, I almost envied him the joy he seemed always able to preserve, the faith which ever seemed to be so buoyant and full of jubilee. Alas! just when we thought he was speeding onwards to the prize, some temptation crossed his path, and he turned aside. Away he is scrambling far over the heath, out of the path of right, and men say, "Aha! aha! so would we have it; so would we have it." And they laugh and make merriment over him, because, having once named the name of Jesus Christ, he hath afterwards gone back again, and his last end is worse than the first. Those whom God starts never do this, for they are preserved in Christ Jesus. Those who have been "entered" in the great roll of the Covenant before all eternity shall persevere, by the aid of the good Spirit. He that began the good work in them, shall carry it on even unto the end. But, alas! there are many who run on their own account and in their own strength; and they are like the snail, which, as it creeps, leaves its life as a trail upon its own path. They melt away; their nature decayeth; they perish, and where are they? Not in the church, but lost to all hope. They are like the dog that returned to his vomit, and the sow that was washed to her wallowing in the mire. " The last end of that man shall be worse than the first."

I do not think I shall now mention any other class of persons. I have brought before you the rules of the race, if you would win; if you would " so run that you may obtain," you must first of all take care to start well; you must keep to the course; you must keep straight on; you must not stop on the road, or turn aside from it, but, urged on by Divine grace, you must ever fly onwards, " like an arrow from the bow, shot by an archer strong." And never rest until the march is ended, and you are made pillars in the house of your God, to go out no more for ever.

III. But now I am about to give you some few reasons to URGE YOU ONWARD IN THE HEAVENLY RACE—those of you who are already running.

One of my reasons shall be this—" *We are compassed about by so great a cloud of witnesses.*" When zealous racers on yonder heath are flying across the plain, seeking to obtain the reward, the whole heath is covered with multitudes of persons, who are eagerly gazing upon them, and no doubt the noise of those who cheer them onward, and the thousand eyes of those who look upon them, have a tendency to make them stretch every nerve, and press with vigour on. It was so in the games to which the apostle alludes. There the people sat on raised platforms, while the racers ran before them, and they cried to them, and the friends of the racers urged them forward, and the kindly voice would ever be heard bidding them go on. Now, Christian brethren, how many witnesses are looking down upon you. Down! do I say? It is even so. From the battlements of heaven the angels look down upon you, and they seem to cry to-day to you with sweet, silvery voice, " Ye shall reap if ye faint not; ye shall be rewarded if ye continue steadfast in the work and faith of Christ." And the saints look down upon you—Abraham, Isaac, and Jacob; martyrs and confessors, and your own pious relatives who have ascended to heaven, look down upon you; and if I might so speak, methinks sometimes you might hear the clapping of their hands when you have resisted temptation and overcome the enemy; and you might see their suspense when you are lagging in the course, and you might hear their friendly word of caution as they bid you gird up the loins of your mind, and lay aside every weight, and still speed forward; never resting to take your breath, never staying for a moment's ease till you have attained the flowery beds of heaven, where you may rest for ever. And recollect, these are not the only eyes that are looking upon you. The whole world looks upon a Christian: he is the observed of all observers. In a Christian every fault is seen. A worldly man may commit a thousand faults, and nobody notices him; but let a Christian do so, and he will very soon have his faults published to the wide world. Everywhere men are looking at Christians, and it is quite right that they should do so. I remember a young man, a member of a Christian church, who went to a public-house ball of the lowest character; and he was no sooner mounting up the stairs, than one of them said, " Ah! here comes the Methodist; we will give it to him." As soon as they had him in the room, they first of all led him up and down to let everybody see the Methodist who had come among them, and then they kicked him down stairs. I sent them my respectful compliments for doing so, for it served him right; and I took care that he was kicked down stairs in another sense afterwards, and kicked out of the church. The world would not have him and the church would not have him. The world, then, looks upon you; it never misses an opportunity of throwing your religion in your teeth. If you don't give sixteen ounces to the pound of morality, if you don't come up to the mark in everything, you will hear of it again. Don't think the world is ever asleep. We say, " as sound asleep as a church," and that is a very good proverb; but we cannot say, " as sound asleep as the world," for it never sleeps; it always has its eyes open; it is always watching us in all we do. The eyes of the world are upon you. " We are compassed about with a great cloud of witnesses "; " let us run with patience the race that is set before us." And there are darker and yet more malignant eyes that scowl upon us. There are spirits that people this air, who are under the prince of the power of the air, who watch every day for our halting.

" Millions of spiritual creatures walk this earth,
Both when we wake and when we sleep."

And alas! those spiritual creatures are not all good. There be those that are not yet chained and reserved in darkness, but who are permitted by God to wander through this world like roaring lions, seeking whom they may devour, ever ready to tempt us. And there is one at the head of them called Satan, *the enemy*, and you know his employment. He has access to the throne of God, and he makes most horrid use of it, for he accuses us day and night before the throne. The accuser of the brethren is not yet cast down—that is to be in the great day of the triumph of the Son of man; but as Jesus stands our Advocate before the throne, so does old Satan first watch us and tempt us, and then stands as our accuser before the bar of God. O my dear brothers and sisters, if you have entered into this race, and have commenced it, let these many eyes urge you forward.

" A cloud of witnesses around
Hold thee in full survey;
Forget the steps already trod,
And onward urge thy way."

And now a more urgent consideration still. Recollect, your race is win or lose—death or life, hell or heaven, eternal misery or everlasting joy. What a stake that is for which you run! If I may so put it, you are running for your life; and if that does not make a man run nothing will. Put a man there on yonder hill, and put another after him with a drawn sword seeking his life. If there is any *run* in him you will soon see him run; there will be no need for us to shout out to him, " Run, man, run! " for he is quite certain that his life is at hazard, and he speeds with all his might—speeds till the veins stand like whipcords on his brow, and a hot sweat runs from every pore of his body—and still flees onward. Now, he looks behind, and sees the avenger of blood speeding after him; he does not stop; he spurns the ground, and on he flees till he reaches the city of refuge, where he is safe. Ah! if we had eyes to see, and if we knew who it is that is pursuing us every day of our lives, how we should run! for lo! O man, hell is behind thee, sin pursues thee, evil seeks to overtake thee; the City of Refuge has its gates wide open; I beseech thee, rest not till thou canst say with confidence, " I have entered into this rest, and now I am secure; I know that my Redeemer liveth." And rest not even then, for this is not the place for rest; rest not until thy six days' work is done; and thy heavenly Sabbath is begun. Let this life be thy six days of ever-toiling faith. Obey thy Master's commandment; "labour therefore to enter into this rest," seeing that there are many who shall not enter in, because through their want of faith they shall not be able. If that urge not a man to speed forward, what can?

But let me picture yet one more thing; and may that help you onward! Christian, run onward, for remember *who it is that stands at the winning post.* You are to run onward, always looking unto Jesus: then Jesus must be at the end. We are always to be looking forward, and never backward; therefore Jesus must be there. Are you loitering? See Him with His open wounds. Are you about to leave the course? See Him with His bleeding hands; will not that constrain you to devote yourself to Him? Will not that impel you to speed your course, and never loiter until you have obtained the crown? Your dying Master cries to you to-day, and He says, " By My agony and bloody sweat; by My cross and passion, onward! By my life, which I gave for you; by the death which I endured for your sake, onward!" And see! He holds out His hand, laden with a crown sparkling with many a star, and He says, " By this crown, onward!" I beseech you, onward, my beloved; press forward, for " I know that there is laid up for me a crown of life which fadeth not away, and not for me only, but for all them that love His appearing."

I have thus addressed myself to all sorts of characters. Will you this afternoon take that home to yourself which is the most applicable to your case. Those of you who make no profession of religion, are living without God and without Christ, strangers to the commonwealth of Israel,—let me affectionately remind you that the day is coming when you will want religion. It is very well now to be sailing over the smooth waters of life, but the rough billows of Jordan will make you want a Saviour. It is hard work to die without a hope; to take that last leap in the dark is a frightful thing indeed. I have seen the old man die when he has declared he would not die. He has stood upon the brink of death, and he has said, " All dark, dark, dark! O God, I cannot die." And his agony has been fearful when the strong hand of the destroyer has seemed to push him over the precipice. He " lingered shivering on the brink, and feared to launch away." And frightful was the moment when the foot slipped and the solid earth was left, and the soul was sinking into the depths of eternal wrath. You will want a Saviour then, when your pulse is faint and few; you will need an angel then to stand at your bedside; and when the spirit is departing, you will need a sacred convoy to pilot you through the dark clouds of death and guide you through the iron gate, and lead you to the blessed mansion in the land of the hereafter. Oh, " seek ye the Lord while He may be found, call ye upon Him while He is near: Let the wicked forsake his way, and the unrighteous man his thoughts: and let him return unto the Lord and He will have mercy upon him; and to our God, for He will abundantly pardon. For my thoughts are not your thoughts, neither are your ways My ways, saith the Lord. For as the heavens are higher than the earth, so are My ways higher than your ways, and My thoughts than your thoughts." O Lord, turn us and we shall be turned. Draw us and we will run after Thee; and Thine shall be the glory; for the crown of our race shall be cast at Thy feet, and Thou shalt have the glory for ever and ever.

COMFORT FOR THE TEMPTED

" There hath no temptation taken you but such as is common to man: but God is faithful, who will not suffer you to be tempted above that ye are able; but will with the temptation also make a way to escape, that ye may be able to bear it."—1 Corinthians x. 13.

THE children of God are all subject to temptation; some of them are tempted more than others, but I am persuaded that there is not one, except those who are too young to be conscious of evil, who will enter heaven without having endured some temptation. If anyone could have escaped, surely it would have been "the Firstborn among many brethren"; but you will remember how He was led of the Spirit, straight from the waters of His baptism, into the wilderness to be tempted of the devil; and the apostle Paul informs us that He " was in all points tempted like as we are, yet without sin." Truly, the Lord Jesus might say to us who are His followers, " If I, your Master and Lord, have been tempted, you must not expect to escape temptation; for the disciple is not above his Master, nor the servant above his Lord."

The fact that we are tempted ought to humble us, for it is sad evidence that there is sin still remain-ing in us. I am old enough to remember the times when we used to strike with a flint upon the steel in order to get a light in the morning, and I recollect that I always left off trying to produce a spark when I found that there was no tinder in the box. I believe that the devil is no fool, and that, if there be a man who has no tinder in the box,—that is, no corruption in his nature,—depend upon it, Satan will not long continue to tempt him. He does not waste his time in such a useless exercise. The man who believes that he is perfect can never pray the Lord's prayer; he must offer one of his own making, for he will never be willing to say, " Lead us not into temptation"; but, beloved, because the devil thinks it worth his while to tempt us, we may conclude that there is something in us that is temptable, —that sin still dwells there, notwithstanding that the grace of God has renewed our hearts.

The fact that we are tempted ought also to

remind us of our weakness. I referred just now to the model prayer of our Lord Jesus Christ, which contains the sentence, " Lead us not into temptation." The reason for presenting that petition must be because we are so weak and frail. We ask that we may not be burdened, for our back is not strong ; and we plead that we may not have sin put before us in any of its enticing forms, for, oftentimes, the flesh borrows strength from the world, and even from the devil, and these allied powers will be too much for us unless the omnipotence of God shall be exerted on our behalf to hold us up lest we fall.

Some children of God, whom I know of, are very greatly troubled because they are tempted. They think they could bear trial if it were trial dissociated from sin, though I do not see how we can, as a general rule, separate trial from temptation, for every trial that comes to us has in it some kind of temptation or other, either to unbelief, or to murmuring, or to the use of wrong means to escape from the trial. We are tempted by our mercies, and we are tempted by our miseries ; that is, tempted in the sense of being tried by them ; but, to the child of God, the most grievous thing is that, sometimes, he is tempted to do or say things which he utterly hates. He has set before him, in a pleasant aspect, sins which are perfectly abhorrent to him ; he cannot bear the very name of them. Yet Satan comes, and holds before the child of God the unclean meats which he will never touch ; and I have known the devil to tempt the people of God by injecting into their mind blasphemous thoughts, hurling them into their ear as with a hurricane. Ay, even when you are in prayer, it may happen to you that thoughts the very opposite of devotional will come flocking into your brain. A little noise in the street will draw you off from communion with God ; and, almost before you are aware of it, your thoughts, like wild horses, will have gone galloping over hill and dale, and you hardly know how you shall ever catch them again. Now, such temptations as these are dreadfully painful to a child of God. He cannot bear the poisoned breath of sin ; and when he finds that sin stands knocking at his door, shouting under his window, pestering him day and night, as it has occurred with some,—I hope not with many,—then he is sorely beset, and he is grievously troubled.

It may help such if I remind him that there is no sin in being tempted. The sin is that of the tempter, not of the tempted. If you resist the temptation, there is something praiseworthy about your action. There is nothing praiseworthy about the temptation ; that is evil, and only evil ; but you did not tempt yourself, and he that tempted you must bear the blame of the temptation. You are evidently not blameworthy for thoughts that grieve you ; they may prove that there is sin still remaining in you, but there is no sin in your being tempted. The sin is in your yielding to the temptation, and blessed shall you be if you can stand out against it. If you can overcome it, if your spirit does not yield to it, you shall even be blessed through it. " Blessed is the man that endureth temptation." There is a blessedness even in the temptation, and though for the present it seemeth not to be joyous, but grievous, nevertheless, afterward, it yieldeth blessed fruit to those who are exercised thereby.

Moreover, there are worse things in this world than being tempted with painful temptations. It is much worse to be tempted with a pleasant temptation,—to be gently sucked down into the destroyer's mouth,—to be carried along the smooth current, afterwards to be hurled over the cataract. This is dreadful ; but to fight against temptation,—this is good. I say again that there are many worse things than to be tried with a temptation that arouses all the indignation of your spirit. An old divine used to say that he was more afraid of a sleeping devil than he was of a roaring one, and there is much truth in that observation ; for, when you are left quite alone, and no temptation assails you, you are apt to get carnally secure, and boastfully to say, " I shall never be moved." I think no man is in such imminent danger as the man who thinks that there is no danger likely to befall him, so that anything that keeps us on the watch-tower, even though it be in itself evil, is, so far, overruled for good. The most dangerous part of the road to heaven is not the Valley of the Shadow of Death ; we do not find that Christian went to sleep there when the hobgoblins were all about him, and when he found it hard to feel the path, and keep to it ; but when he and Hopeful came to the Enchanted Ground, " whose air naturally tended to make one drowsy," then were the pilgrims in great peril until Christian reminded his fellow-traveller that they were warned by the shepherds not to sleep when they came to that treacherous part of the way. I think, then, that to be tempted with painful temptations, those that goad the spirit almost to madness,—bad as that trial is,—grievous as it is to be borne,—may be, spiritually, not the worst thing that can possibly happen to us. Of all evils that beset you, always choose that which is less than another ; and as this is less than something else might be, do not be utterly driven to despair if it falls to your lot to be tempted as many before you have been.

This will suffice by way of preface to a little talk about temptation, with a view of comforting any who are sorely tempted of Satan. I know that I am speaking to many such, and I would repeat to them the words of my text : " There hath no temptation taken you but such as is common to man : but God is faithful, who will not suffer you to be tempted above that ye are able ; but will with the temptation also make a way to escape, that ye may be able to bear it." Remember, dear tried friend, that you must not sit down in despair, and say, " I am greatly tempted now, and I am afraid that I shall be tempted worse and worse, until my feet shall slide, and I shall fall and utterly perish." Do not say as David did when he had been hunted like a partridge upon the mountains, " I shall now perish one day by the hand of Saul " ; but believe that the Lord, who permits you to be tempted, will deliver you in His own good time.

I. Here is your first comfort. THERE HAS BEEN A LIMIT IN ALL YOUR FORMER TRIALS : " There hath no temptation taken you but such as is common to man."

Temptations has sometimes laid hold of you, like a garroter takes a man by the throat, on a sudden. It has seized you—perhaps that is as correct a word as I can use—temptation has seized you, unawares, pinioned you, and seemed to grip you fast ; and yet, up till now, the temptations you have had to endure, have only been such as are common to man.

First, *they are such as have been endured by your fellow-Christians.* I know that you are tempted to think that you are a lone traveller on a road that nobody has ever traversed before you; but if you carefully examine the track, you can discover the footprints of some of the best of God's servants who have passed along that wearisome way. It is a very dark lane, you say,—one that might truly be called, "Cut-throat Lane." Ah! but you will find that apostles have been along that way, confessors have been that way, martyrs have been that way, and the best of God's saints have been tempted just as you now are. "Oh, but!" says one, "I am tempted, as you said a little while ago, with blasphemous and horrible thoughts." So was Master John Bunyan; read his *Grace Abounding to the Chief of Sinners*, and see what he had to pass through. Many others have had a similar experience, and among them are some of us who are alive to tell you that we know all about this special form of temptation, yet the Lord delivered us out of it. "Oh, but!" says another tried soul, "I have been even tempted to self-destruction." That also has not been an unusual temptation even to God's dearest saints; and, though He has preserved them, and kept them alive, yet they have often felt like Job when he said, "My soul chooseth strangling, and death rather than my life." "Ah!" cries another, "I am tempted to the very worst sins, the foulest sins, I should not dare even to mention to you the abominations Satan tempts me to commit." You need not tell me; and I trust that you will be kept from them by the almighty power of God's Holy Spirit; but I can assure you that even the saints in heaven, if they could speak to you at this moment, would tell you that some of them were hard beset—even some of the bravest of them who walked nearest to God were beset by temptations which they would not have told to their fellow-men, so troubled were they by them. Perhaps yet another friend says, "I have been actually tempted to self-righteousness, which is as great a temptation as can befall a man whose whole confidence is in Christ." Well, so was Master John Knox, that grand preacher of justification by faith. When he lay dying, he was tempted to glory in his own bravery for Christ, but he fought against that evil thought, and overcame it, and so may you.

You think that, when a man is very patient, he is not tempted to impatience. Brother, the Spirit of God says, by the pen of the apostle James, "Ye have heard of the patience of Job." I suggest to you this question,—Have you not heard of the impatience of Job? You have heard, no doubt, of the strong faith of Peter; have you never heard of Peter's unbelief? God's people usually fail in the very point for which they are most famous; and the man who has the greatest renown for any work of the Spirit of God in him, so far as the Bible biographies are concerned, has usually been the man who has made a failure just at the place where he thought he was strongest. "I have been reading the life of a good man," say you, "and I am not like him." Shall I tell you why? Because the whole of his life was not written; but when the Holy Ghost writes a man's life, he gives it all. When biographers write the lives of good men, of course they do not put down their inward struggles and fears, unless the subject happens to be a man like Martin Luther, whose life seemed to be all an inward struggle, and who, while he was brave without, was often a trembler within. When they write my life, they will tell

you that I had strong faith; but they will not tell you all about the other side of it. And then you will, perhaps, get thinking, "Oh, I cannot reach even to such a height as Mr. Spurgeon attained!" That all comes of your not knowing the inside of us, for if you knew the inside and the outside of the man who walks nearest to God,—if he is a sincere, true-hearted man, he will tell you that the temptations you have to endure are just such temptations as he has had, and as he expects to have again and again, and that, as the apostle says, "there hath no temptation taken you but such as is common to man."

Then, again, *no temptation has assailed you but such as is fit for men to be tried with while they are in this state of trial.* This is not the time for the final victory, brother; this is the hour of battle, and the weapons that are used against us are only such as have been employed against the armies of the faithful in all ages. You and I never were tempted as were the angels who kept their first estate and overcame the temptation. I cannot tell you how the prince of darkness was tempted, or how he went about tempting his fellow-servants from their loyalty to the great King; but of this I am sure, you were never tried with temptation suitable to an angel. Your temptation has only been such as is suitable to a man, and *such as other men like yourself have overcome.* Others have fought valiantly against similar temptations to yours, and you must do the same, yea, and you shall do the same by the power of God's Spirit resting upon you. It is said, in the affairs of common life, that what man has done man can do, and that is true with regard to the spiritual life. Temptations that have been grappled with by other men, can be grappled with by you if you seek the same source of strength, and seek it in the same name as they did. The strength to overcome temptation comes from God alone, and the conquering name is the name of Jesus Christ; therefore, go forward in that strength and in that name against all your temptations. Up and at them, for they have been routed long before, and you shall rout them again. Tremble not to go from fight to fight and from victory to victory, even as did the others who have gone before you, and who have now entered into their rest.

"Once they were mourning here below,
  And wet their couch with tears;
They wrestled hard, as we do now,
  With sins, and doubts, and fears."

If you ask them whence their victory came, they ascribe it to the resources which are as open to you as they were to them,—even to the mighty working of God the Holy Spirit and the blood and righteousness of the Lord Jesus Christ. There has no temptation happened to you but such as human beings can grapple with and overcome by the help of God.

Again, there has no temptation hitherto happened to you but such as is common to man in this sense,—that *Christ has endured it.* That great Head of manhood, that representative Man, has suffered from the very temptation which is now pestering you. "In all their affliction"—that is, the affliction of His people in the wilderness, which is just the same as yours if you are in the wilderness,—"in all their affliction He was afflicted, and the angel of His presence saved them." He was compassed with infirmity, "a Man of sorrows and acquainted with grief." To repeat the text I have already quoted, and which is so suitable here, He " was in all points tempted like as we are." " In all things it behoved Him to be made like unto His brethren, that He might be a merciful and faithful high priest in things pertaining to God, to make reconciliation for the sins of the people. For in that He Himself hath suffered being tempted, He is able to succour them that are tempted." He knows all about the case of each one of us, and He knows how to deal with it, and how to bear us up and bear us through.

So you see, dear friends, there hath no temptation happened to you but such as is common to man in the sense of having been endured by men like yourselves, having been overcome by men such as you are, and having been endured and vanquished by your blessed Representative, our Lord and Saviour Jesus Christ.

Come, then, beloved, let all mystery with regard to your temptations be banished. Mystery puts an edge upon the sword of trial ; perhaps the hand that wrote upon the wall would not have frightened Belshazzar if he could have seen the body to which that hand belonged. There is no mystery about your trouble, after all. Though you did write it down as being bigger than any that ever happened to a human being before, that is not the truth ; you are not an emperor in the realm of misery. You cannot truly say, " I am the man that hath seen affliction above all others," for your Lord endured far more than you have ever done, and many of His saints, who passed from the stake to the crown, must have suffered much more than you have been called to undergo thus far.

II. Now let us turn to the second comfort revealed in our text ; that is, THE FAITHFULNESS OF GOD : " There hath no temptation taken you but such as is common to man : *but God is faithful.*"

Oh, what a blessed word is this, " God is faithful " ! Therefore, *He is true to His promise.* Even Balaam said, " God is not a man, that He should lie ; neither the son of man, that He should repent : hath He said, and shall He not do it ? or hath He spoken, and shall He not make it good ? " One of God's promises is, " I will never leave thee, nor forsake thee " ; " God is faithful," so He will fulfil that promise. Here is one of the promises of Christ, and Christ is God : " My sheep hear My voice, and I know them, and they follow Me : and I give unto them eternal life ; and they shall never perish, neither shall any man pluck them out of My hand." " God is faithful," so that promise shall be fulfilled. You have often heard this promise, " As thy days, so shall thy strength be." Do you believe it, or will you make God a liar ? If you do believe, then banish from your mind all dark forebodings with this blessed little sentence, " God is faithful."

Notice, next, that not only is God faithful, but *He is master of the situation, so that He can keep His promise.* Note what the text says : " Who will not suffer you to be tempted above that ye are able to bear." Then you could not have been tempted if God had not suffered it to happen to you. God is far mightier than Satan. The devil could not touch Job except by divine permission, neither can he try and tempt you except as God allows him ; he must have a permit from the King of kings before he can tempt a single saint. Why, Satan is not allowed to keep the key of his own house, for the keys of death and of hell hang at the girdle of Christ ; and without God's permission, the dog of hell cannot even open

his mouth to bark at a child of God, much less can he come and worry any of the sheep whom the Lord has called by His grace into His fold. So, then, beloved, you have great cause for comfort from the fact that the temptation that tries you is still under the control of the faithful Creator, " who will not suffer you to be tempted above that ye are able."

That is a second reason for comfort ; roll it under your tongue as a sweet morsel.

III. The third comfort lies in THE RESTRAINT WHICH GOD PUTS UPON TEMPTATION. He " will not suffer you to be tempted above that ye are able." The tide of trial shall rise to high-water mark, and then God shall say, " Hitherto shalt thou come, but no further : and here shall thy proud waves be stayed."

He " will not suffer you to be tempted above that ye are able." That may apply, sometimes, to *the period when the temptation comes.* I have carefully watched how God times the trials of His people. If such-and-such a trial had come to one of His children when he was young, I believe he could not have borne it ; or if he had lost some dear friend while he was himself sick, the double trouble would have crushed him. But God sends our trials at the right time ; and if He puts an extra burden on in one way, He takes something off in another. " He stayeth His rough wind in the day of the East wind." It is a very simple thing to say, but it is true ; if the wind blows from the North, it does not at the same time blow from the South ; and if one set of troubles comes to a Christian man, another set of troubles generally departs from him. John Bradford, the famous martyr, was often subject to rheumatism and depression of spirit, in which I can greatly sympathize with him ; but when he was laid by the heels in a foul damp dungeon, and knew that he would never come out except to die, he wrote, " It is a singular thing that, ever since I have been in this prison, and have had other trials to bear, I have had no touch of my rheumatism or my depression of spirit." Was not that a very blessed thing ? And you will usually find that it is so ; you shall not be tempted above what you are able to bear, because God will permit the trial to come at a time when you are best able to stand up under it.

There is also great kindness on God's part *in the continuance of a trial.* If some of our trials lasted much longer, they would be too heavy for us to bear. Concerning the destruction of Jerusalem, our Lord said, " Except those days should be shortened, there should no flesh be saved : but for the elect's sake those days shall be shortened." And I have no doubt that, oftentimes, God makes quick work of His children's trials because, if they were continued longer, they would have not a good but an evil effect upon us. If a child must be whipped, let not the punishment last as if he were a criminal who must be sentenced for a long period ; let him have his chastisement, and have done with it. So is it often in the discipline of God's house ; yet there are other trials which are protracted year after year because trial is an ingredient in their efficacy, and they might not be blessed to us if they were shortened. In every case, there is an infinite wisdom which makes our troubles to be just as long as they are, and no longer.

So there is *in the number of the trials.* Blessed be God,—

" If He ordains the number ten,
They ne'er can be eleven."

If He intends His servants to pass through the fire, and not through the water, Satan himself cannot make them go through the water. God counts the drops of bitter tonic that He administers to His ailing saints, and not a drop more shall they possibly have than He measures out to them. So, dear tried children of God, you shall not be tempted above what ye are able so far as the number of your temptations and trials is concerned.

It is the same, also, *in the stress with which the temptation comes.* Have you never seen a great tree in the full blast of a tremendous tempest ? It sways to and fro, and seems scarcely able to recover itself from the powerful blows of the storm ; yet the roots hold it. But now comes another tornado ; and it seems as if the tree must be torn up out of the earth ; but the strain ceases just in time for the old oak to rock back into its place again ; yet, if there were a pound or two more force in that tremendous blast, the trees would be laid prone upon the grass ; but God, in His people's case at any rate, just stops at the right point. You may be tried till you have not an ounce of strength left. Sometimes, the Lord tests His people till it seems as if one more breath from Him would assuredly cause them to sink. Then it is that He puts under them the everlasting arms, and no further trial is laid upon them. This is a blessed thing, for all of you have troubles of one sort or another, and you who are the people of God may take this text, and rely implicitly upon it : " God is faithful, who will not suffer you to be tempted above that ye are able."

As for you who are not His people, I am very sorry for you. I am holding up these precious things, but they are not for you. God's Word declares, " Many sorrows shall be to the wicked." If you have no God to flee to, what will you do when the storms beat upon your barque ? To whom or whither can you flee ? As for the Christian, he can sing,—

> " Jesu, lover of my soul,
> Let me to Thy bosom fly,
> While the nearer waters roll,
> While the tempest still is high !
> Hide me, O my Saviour, hide,
> Till the storm of life be past ;
> Safe into the haven guide ;
> Oh receive my soul at last ! "

But, poor dear souls who love not Christ, where can you find comfort in your seasons of sorrow and trial ? You who have lost wife and children,—you who are pinched with poverty,—you who are racked with sickness, and yet have no Saviour, what can you do ? Poor houseless people in a snow-storm,—what can they do without even a bush to shelter them ? That is just your state, and I grieve for you, and plead with you not to remain in such a pitiful condition even a moment longer.

> " Come, guilty souls, and flee away
> Like doves to Jesu's wounds ;
> This is the welcome gospel-day,
> Wherein free grace abounds."

Oh, that your sense of need might drive you to accept Christ as your Saviour this very hour ! As for His believing people, there is this solid comfort for them, they shall never be tempted above what they are able.

IV. The next comfort we gather from our text relates to THE PROVISION WHICH THE LORD MAKES FOR THE TEMPTED : " God is faithful, who . . . will with the temptation also make a way to escape."

The Greek has it, " who will with the temptation also make *the* way to escape " ; for *there is a proper way to escape from a temptation.* There are twenty improper ways ; and woe to the man who makes use of any one of them ; but there is only one proper way out of a trial, and that is the straight way, the way that God has made for His people to travel. God has made *through* all trials the way by which His servants may rightly come out of them. When the brave young Jews were tried by Nebuchadnezzar, there was one way by which they might have kept out of the burning fiery furnace. They had only to bow their knees before the great image when the flute, harp, sackbut, and psaltery sounded ; that way of escape would never have answered, for it was not the right one. The way for them was to be thrown down into the furnace, and there to have the Son of God walking with them in the midst of the fire that could not hurt them. In like manner, whenever you are exposed to any trial, mind that you do not try to escape from it in any wrong way.

Notice specially that *the right way is always of God's making* ; therefore, any of you who are now exposed to temptation or trial have not to make your own way of escape out of it. God, and God alone, has to make it for you, so do not attempt to make it for yourselves. I knew a man who was in trouble because he was short of money ; and the way he made for himself was to use somebody else's money, with which he had been entrusted. That was not God's way of escape for him, so he only plunged himself into a worse trial than he was in before. I have known a man of business in great trouble, and things were going wrong with him, so he speculated, and gambled, and ruined both his business and his personal character. That was not God's way for him to escape from his troubles. Sometimes, the best thing a man in trouble can do, is to do nothing at all, but to leave all in the hands of God. " Stand still, and see the salvation of the Lord." When the Israelites came out of Egypt, God led them in a way at which men might well have cavilled ; there was nothing before them but the sea, and behind them came Pharaoh in all his rage, crying, " I will pursue, I will overtake, I will divide the spoil ; my lust shall be satisfied upon them ; I will draw my sword, my hand shall destroy them." Now, then, what was God's way of escape for them ? Right through the Red Sea, and on the other side they sang, when the Egyptians were drowned, " Sing ye to the Lord, for He hath triumphed gloriously ; the horse and his rider hath He thrown into the sea." It would have been a great pity if they had tried to escape by any way of their own, or had attempted to turn round, and fight Pharaoh ; that would not have done at all, but the Lord made for His people the very best way of escape that could possible have been devised.

Notice, also, that *the Lord makes the way of escape* " *with the temptation.*" He suffered the trial to come, and at the same time He made the way of escape from it. God has planned it all, my brother, how you, His champion, shall go forth, and fight valiantly in His strength ; and how He will be your shield and your exceeding great reward. He will lead you into the dangerous defile ; but then He can see the way out of it as well as the way into it, and He will take you safely through. Did not the psalmist sing, " To

Him which led His people through the wilderness : for His mercy endureth for ever " ? He not only led them into the wilderness, but He led them through it, blessed be His holy name ! And if He has brought you into the wilderness of trouble and affliction, He made the way out of it at the same time that He made the trouble. " Trust in the Lord, and do good ; so shalt thou dwell in the land, and verily thou shalt be fed. Delight thyself also in the Lord ; and He shall give thee the desires of thine heart. Commit thy way unto the Lord ; trust also in Him ; and He shall bring it to pass. And He shall bring forth thy righteousness as the light, and thy judgment as the noonday. Rest in the Lord, and wait patiently for Him : fret not thyself because of him who prospereth in his way, because of the man who bringeth wicked devices to pass." " Seek ye first the kingdom of God and His righteousness," and all else that you need shall be added unto you. Keep clear of the sin of the temptation, and you need not fear the sorrow of the temptation. If the trials do not drive you to your own devices, but drive you to your knees, they will, after all, be blessings to you.

That is the fourth comfort, that God has made the way of escape for His people out of their trials. " Well, then," says some one, " I shall escape from this trial." Wait a moment, my friend, and listen to the closing words of the text, with which I will conclude my discourse.

V. This is the last point of comfort, THE SUPPORT WHICH GOD SUPPLIES IN THE TRIAL : " that ye may be able to bear it."

God's way of escape from trial is not for His people to avoid it, so as not to pass through it, but such an escape as leads them through the trouble, and out at the other end ; not an escape *from* the Red Sea, but an escape *through* the Red Sea from a still greater trial. If you, beloved, are exposed to trial or temptation, you are to be made able to bear it. Now, pray, before you leave this building, that this last word, upon which I have not time to enlarge, may be fulfilled in your experience : " that ye may be able to bear it."

Suppose you are to be poor. Well, if God has so appointed it, you will be poor ; therefore, pray that you may be able to bear it. With honest industry and stern integrity struggle to attain to a better position ; but, if all your efforts fail, then say to the Lord, " Nevertheless, not as I will, but as Thou wilt." Perhaps your dear child is dying, or your wife is sickening ; you dread the thought of losing them, and you would willingly give your life, if you could, for them. Well, do all you can for their recovery, for life is precious, and any money spent to save it will be well spent ; but, if health is not to be granted to them, pray that you may be able to bear even that heavy trial. It is wonderful how God does help His people to bear troubles which they thought would

crush them. I have seen poor feeble women, that I thought would die under their bereavement, become brave and strong ; and men, who were faint-hearted in the prospect of trouble, have nevertheless blessed the Lord for it when the blow has actually fallen ; and you may do the same.

Suppose you are to be sick. Well, that is a sore trial, and I know that, personally, I would do anything I could to escape from the affliction that often besets me ; but if it must not be, then I must change my note, and pray that I may be able to bear it. I had a letter from a man of God, this morning, which sustained me very much. He says, " My dear brother, I was sorry to hear that you were again in pain, and depressed in spirit, and so forth ; but, as I remembered how God had blessed you in so many ways, I thought to myself, ' Perhaps Mr. Spurgeon would not have kept to preaching the doctrines of grace, and would not have been so able to comfort God's poor people, if he did not get these smart touches sometimes.' So," he said, " I congratulate you upon these trials " ; and I accepted the congratulation. Will not you do the same, my afflicted brother or sister ? Pray, " Lord, if it be possible, let this cup pass from me " ; but, if it must not, then here comes that other form of comfort, " that ye may be able to bear it."

And remember, dear friends, while I tell you to make this passage into a prayer, it is really a promise ; and there is no prayer like a promise that is turned, as it were, roundabout, and cut prayerwise. God Himself has said, by His inspired apostle, that He " will not suffer you to be tempted above that ye are able ; but will with the temptation also make a way to escape, that ye may be able to bear it." Up with the banners, then ! Forward, whatever obstructs the way ! Let us sing, with good old John Ryland,—

" Through floods and flames, if Jesus lead,
    I'll follow where He goes ;
' Hinder me not,' shall be my cry,
    Though earth and hell oppose."

The immortal life within us can never be destroyed ; the divine nature, which God the Holy Ghost has implanted, shall never be trodden under foot. " Rejoice not against me, O mine enemy ; when I fall, I shall arise ; when I sit in darkness, the Lord shall be a light unto me."

But, oh, sorry, sorry, sorry, sorry am I, from the bottom of my soul, for you who know not the Lord, for this comfort is not for you ! Seek Him, I pray you ; seek Him as your Saviour. Look to Him, and trust in Him ; and then all the blessings of the everlasting covenant shall be yours, for the Father has given Him to be a Leader and Commander unto the people, and they that look to Him, and follow Him, shall live for ever and ever. God bless you, for Christ's sake ! Amen.

NOW, AND THEN

" For now we see through a glass, darkly ; but then face to face."—1 Corinthians xiii. 12.

IN this chapter the apostle Paul has spoken in the highest terms of charity or love. He accounts it to be a grace far more excellent than any of the spiritual gifts of which he had just before been speaking. It is easy to see that there were good reasons for the preference he gave to it. Those gifts, you will observe, were distributed among godly men, to every man his several portion, so that what one had another might have lacked; but this grace belongs to all who have passed from death unto life. The proof that they are disciples of Christ is found in their love to Him and to the brethren. Those gifts, again, were meant to fit them for service, that each member of the body should be profitable to the other members of the body; but this grace is of personal account; it is a light in the heart and a star on the breast of every one who possesses it. Those gifts, moreover, were of temporary use: their value was limited to the sphere in which they were exercised; but this grace thrives at all times and in all places, and it is no less essential to our eternal future state than it is to our present welfare. By all means covet the best gifts, my dear brother, as an artist would wish to be deft with all his limbs and quick with all his senses; but above all, cherish love, as that same artist would cultivate the pure taste which lives and breathes within him—the secret spring of all his motions, the faculty that prompts his skill. Learn to esteem this sacred instinct of love beyond all the choicest endowments. However poor you may be in talents, let the love of Christ dwell in you richly. Such an exhortation as this is the more needful, because love has a powerful rival. Paul may have noticed that in the academies of Greece, as indeed in all our modern schools, knowledge was wont to take all the prizes. Who can tell how much of Dr. Arnold's success, as a schoolmaster, was due to the honour in which he held a good boy in preference to a clever boy? Most certainly Paul could discern in the church many jealousies to which the superior abilities of those who could speak foreign tongues, and those who could prophesy or preach well, gave rise. So, then, while he extols the grace of love, he seems rather to disparage knowledge; at least, he uses an illustration which tends to show that the kind of knowledge we pride ourselves in, is not the most reliable thing in the world. Paul remembered that he was once a child. A very good thing for any of us to bear in mind. If we forget it, our sympathies are soon dried up, our temper is apt to get churlish, our opinions may be rather overbearing, and our selfishness very repulsive. The foremost man of his day in the Christian church, and exerting the widest influence among the converts to Christ, Paul thought of the little while ago when he was a young child, and he thought of it very opportunely too. Though he might have hinted at the attainments he had made or the high office he held, and laid claim to some degree of respect, he rather looks back at his humble beginnings. If there is wisdom in his reflection, there is to my mind a vein of pleasantry in his manner of expressing it. "When I was a child I spake as a child, I understood as a child, I thought as a child: but when I became a man, I put away childish things." Thus he compares two stages of his natural life, and it serves him for a parable. In spiritual knowledge he felt himself to be then in his infancy. His maturity, his thorough manhood, lay before him in prospect. He could easily imagine a future in which he should look back on his present self as a mere tyro, groping his way amidst the shadows of his own fancy. "For now," he says, "we see through a glass, darkly; but then face to face: now I know in part; but then shall I know even as also I am known." Here he employs one or two fresh figures. " Through a glass ! " What kind of a glass he alluded to, we may not be able exactly

to determine. Well; we will leave that question for the critics to disagree about. It is enough for us that the meaning is obvious. There is all the difference between viewing an object through an obscure medium, and closely inspecting it with the naked eye. We must have the power of vision in either case, but in the latter case we can use it to more advantage. "Now we see through a glass, darkly." Darkly—in a riddle ! So weak are our perceptions of mind, that plain truths often puzzle us. The words that teach us are pictures which need explanation. The thoughts that stir us are visions which float in our brains and want rectifying. Oh, for clearer vision ! Oh, for more perfect knowledge ! Mark you, brethren, it is a matter of congratulation that we do see ; though we have much cause for diffidence, because we do but " see through a glass, darkly." Thank God we do know ; but let it check our conceit, we know only in part. Beloved, the objects we look at are distant, and we are near-sighted. The revelation of God is ample and profound, but our understanding is weak and shallow.

There are some things which we count very precious now, which will soon be of no value to us whatever. There are some things that we know, or think we know, and we pride ourselves a good deal upon our knowledge ; but when we shall become men we shall set no more value upon that knowledge than a child does upon his toys when he grows up to be a man. Our spiritual manhood in heaven will discard many things which we now count precious, as a full grown man discards the treasures of his childhood. And there are many things that we have been accustomed to see that, after this transient life has passed, we shall see no more. Though we delighted in them, and they pleased our eyes while sojourning on earth, they will pass away as a dream when one awaketh ; we shall never see them again, and never want to see them ; for our eyes in clearer light, anointed with eye-salve, shall see brighter visions, and we shall never regret what we have lost, in the presence of fairer scenes we shall have found. Other things there are that we know now and shall never forget ; we shall know them for ever, only in a higher degree, because no longer with a partial knowledge ; and there are some things that we see now that we shall see in eternity, only we shall see them there in a clearer light.

So we shall speak some things that we do see now, which we are to see more fully and more distinctly hereafter ; then enquire how it is we shall see them more clearly ; and finish up by considering what this fact teaches us.

I. Among the things that we see now, as many of us as have had our eyes enlightened by the Holy Spirit, is OURSELVES.

To see ourselves is one of the first steps in true religion. The mass of men have never seen themselves. They have seen the flattering image of themselves, and they fancy that to be their own fac-simile, but it is not. You and I have been taught of God's Holy Spirit to see our ruin in the fall ; we have bemoaned ourselves on account of that fall ; we have been made conscious of our own natural depravity ; we have been ground to the very dust by the discovery ; we have been shown our actual sinfulness and how we have transgressed against the Most High. We have repented for this, and have fled for refuge to the hope set before us in the gospel. Day by day we see a little more of ourselves—

nothing very pleasing, I grant you—but something very profitable, for it is a great thing for us to know our emptiness. It is a step towards receiving His fulness. It is something to discover our weakness; it is a step essential towards our participation of divine strength. I suppose the longer we live the more we shall see ourselves; and we shall probably come to this conclusion: "Vanity of vanities; all is vanity": and cry out with Job, "I am vile." The more we shall discover of ourselves, the more we shall be sick of ourselves. But in heaven, I doubt not, we shall find out that we never saw even ourselves in the clearest light, but only as "through a glass, darkly," only as an unriddled thing, as a deep enigma; for we shall understand more about ourselves in heaven than we do now. There we shall see, as we have not yet seen, how desperate a mischief was the Fall, into what a horrible pit we fell, and how fast we were stuck in the miry clay. There shall we see the blackness of sin as we have never seen it here, and understand its hell desert as we could not till we shall look down from yonder starry height whither infinite mercy shall bring us. When we shall be singing, "Worthy is the Lamb that was slain," we shall look at the robes that we have washed in His blood, and see how white they are. We shall better understand then than now how much we needed washing—how crimson were the stains and how precious was that blood that effaced those scarlet spots. There, too, shall we know ourselves on the bright side better than we do now. We know to-day that we are saved, and there is therefore now no condemnation to them that are in Christ Jesus; but that robe of righteousness which covers us now, as it shall cover us then, will be better seen by us, and we shall discern how lustrous it is, with its needlework and wrought gold—how much better than the pearls and gems that have decked the robes of monarchs are the blood and righteousness of Jehovah Jesus, who has given Himself for us. Here we know that we are adopted. We feel the spirit of sonship; "we cry, Abba, Father"; but there we shall know better what it is to be the sons of God, for here it doth not yet appear what we shall be; but when we shall be there, and when Christ shall appear, we shall be like Him, for we shall see Him as He is, and then we shall understand to the full what sonship means. So, too, I know to-day that I am a joint-heir with Christ, but I have a very poor idea of what it is I am heir to; but there shall I see the estates that belong to me; not only see them, but actually enjoy them. A part shall every Christian have in the inheritance undefiled and that fadeth not away, that is reserved in heaven for him, because he is in Christ Jesus; one with Christ—by eternal union one. But I am afraid that is very much more a riddle to us than a matter of understanding. We see it as an engima now, but there our oneness with Christ will be as conspicuous to us and as plain as the letters of the alphabet. There shall we know what it is to be a member of His body, of His flesh, and of His bones; there shall I understand the mystical marriage bond that knits the believer's soul to Christ; there shall I see how, as the branch springs from the stem, my soul stands in union, vital union, with her blessed Lord Jesus Christ. Thus, one thing that we see now which we shall see in a much clearer light hereafter, is "ourselves."

Here, too, we see the CHURCH, but WE SHALL SEE THE CHURCH MUCH MORE CLEARLY BY-AND-BY.

We know there is a church of God. We know that the Lord has a people whom He hath chosen from before the foundation of the world: we believe that these are scattered up and down throughout our land, and many other lands. There are many of them we do not know, many that we should not particularly like, I daresay, if we did know them, on account of their outward characteristics; persons of very strange views, and very odd habits perhaps; and yet, for all that, the people of the living God. Now, we know this church, we know its glory, moved with one life, quickened with one Spirit, redeemed with one blood, we believe in this church, and we feel attachment to it for the sake of Jesus Christ, who has married the church as the Bride. But, oh! when we shall get to heaven, how much more we shall know of the church, and how we shall see her face to face, and not "through a glass, darkly." There we shall know something more of the numbers of the chosen than we do now, it may be to our intense surprise. There we shall find some amongst the company of God's elect, whom we in our bitterness of spirit had condemned, and there we shall miss some who, in our charity, we have conceived to be perfectly secure. We shall know better then who are the Lord's and who are not than we ever can know here. Here all our processes of discernment fail us. Judas comes in with the apostles, and Demas takes his part amongst the saints, but there we shall know the righteous, for we shall see them; there will be one flock and one Shepherd, and He that on the throne doth reign for evermore shall be glorified. We shall understand then, what the history of the church has been in all the past, and why it has been so strange a history of conflict and conquest. Probably, we shall know more of the history of the church in the future. From that higher elevation and brighter atmosphere we shall understand better what are the Lord's designs concerning His people in the latter day; and what glory shall redound to His own name from His redeemed ones, when He shall have gathered together all that are called and chosen and faithful from among the sons of men. This is one of the joys we are looking for, that we shall come to the general assembly and church of the firstborn whose names are written in heaven; and have fellowship with those who have fellowship with God through Jesus Christ our Lord.

Thirdly. Is it not possible, nay, is it not certain, that in the next state WE SHALL SEE AND KNOW MORE OF THE PROVIDENCE OF GOD THAN WE DO NOW?

Here we see the providence of God, but it is in a glass, darkly. The apostle says "through" a glass. There was glass in the apostles' days, not a substance such as our windows are now made of, but thick, dull coloured glass, not much more transparent than that which is used in the manufacture of common bottles, so that looking through a piece of that glass you would not see much. That is like what we now see of divine providence. We believe all things work together for good to them that love God; we have seen how they work together for good in some cases, and experimentally proved it to be so. But still it is rather a matter of faith than a matter of sight with us. We cannot tell how "every dark and bending line meets in the centre of His love." We do not yet perceive how He will make those dark dispensations of trials and afflictions that come upon His people really to subserve His glory and their lasting happiness; but up there we shall see Providence, as it were, face to face; and I suppose it will be amongst our greatest surprises, the discovery of how the Lord dealt with us. "Why," we shall some of us say, "we prayed against those very circumstances which were the best that could have been appointed for us." "Ah!" another will say, "I have fretted and troubled myself over what was, after all, the richest mercy the Lord ever sent." Sometimes I have known persons refuse a letter at the door, and it has happened, in some cases, that there has been something very valuable in it, and the postman has said, afterwards, "You did not know the contents, or else you would not have refused it." And often God has sent us, in the black envelope of trial, such a precious mass of mercy, that if we had known what was in it, we should have taken it in, and been glad to pay for it—glad to give it house room, to entertain it; but because it looked black we were prone to shut our door against it. Now, up there we shall know not only more of ourselves, but perceive the reasons of many of God's dealings with us on a larger scale; and we shall there perhaps discover that wars that devastated nations, and pestilences that fill graves, and earthquakes that make cities tremble, are, after all, necessary cogs in the great wheel of the divine machinery; and He who sits upon the throne at this moment, and rules supremely every creature that is either in heaven, or earth, or hell, will there make it manifest to us that His government was right. It is good to think in these times when everything seems loosening, that "the government shall be upon His shoulder: and His name shall be called Wonderful, Counsellor, The mighty God, The everlasting Father, The Prince of Peace." It must come out right in the long run; it must be well; every part and portion must work together with a unity of design to promote God's glory and the saint's good. We shall see it there, and we shall lift up our song with new zest and joy, as fresh displays of the wisdom and goodness of God, whose ways are past finding out, are unfolded to our admiring view.

Fourthly. It is surely no straining of the text to say, that, though here we know something of THE DOCTRINES OF THE GOSPEL, AND THE MYSTERIES OF THE FAITH, by-and-by, in a few months or years at the longest, *we shall know a great deal more than we do now.* There are some grand doctrines, brethren and sisters, we dearly love, but though we love them, our understanding is too feeble to grasp them fully. We account them to be mysteries; we reverently acknowledge them, yet we dare not attempt to explain them. They are matters of faith to us. It may be that in heaven there shall be counsels of eternal wisdom into which no saints or angels can peer. It is the glory of God to conceal a matter. Surely, no creature will ever be able, even when exalted to heaven, to comprehend all the thoughts of the Creator. We shall never be omniscient—we cannot be. God alone knoweth everything, and understandeth everything. But how much more of authentic truth shall we discern when the mists and shadows have dissolved; and how much more shall we understand when raised to that higher sphere and endowed with brighter faculties, none of us can tell. Probably, things that puzzle us here will be as plain as possible there. We shall perhaps smile at our own ignorance. I have fancied sometimes that the elucidations of learned doctors of divinity,

if they could be submitted to the very least in the kingdom of heaven, would only cause them to smile at the learned ignorance of the sons of earth. Oh! how little we do know, but how much we shall know! I am sure we shall know, for it is written, "Then shall I know even as also I have known." We now see things in a mist—"men as trees, walking"—a doctrine here, and a doctrine there. And we are often at a loss to conjecture how one part harmonizes with another part of the same system, or to make out how all these doctrines are consistent. This knot cannot be untied, that gnarl cannot be unravelled, but—

> "Then shall I see, and hear, and know
> All I desired or wish'd below;
> And every power find sweet employ
> In that eternal world of joy."

But, my dear brethren and sisters, having kept you thus far in the outer courts, I would fain lead you into the temple; or, to change the figure, if in the beginning I have set forth good wine, certainly I am not going to bring out that which is worse; rather would I have you say, as the ruler of the feast did to the bridegroom, "thou has kept the good wine until now." HERE WE SEE JESUS CHRIST, BUT WE DO NOT SEE HIM AS WE SHALL SEE HIM SOON. We have seen Him by faith in such a way, that we have beheld our burdens laid on Him, and our iniquities carried by Him into the wilderness, where, if they be sought for, they shall not be found. We have seen enough of Jesus to know that "He is altogether lovely"; we can say of Him, He "is all my salvation, and all my desire." Sometimes, when He throws up the lattice, and shows Himself through those windows of agate and gates of carbuncle, in the ordinances of His house, at the Lord's Supper especially, the King's beauty has entranced us even to our heart's ravishment; yet all we have ever seen is somewhat like the report which the Queen of Sheba had of Solomon's wisdom. When we once get to the court of the Great King we shall declare that the half has not been told us. We shall say, "mine eyes shall behold, and not another." Brethren, is not this the very cream of heaven? There have been many suggestions of what we shall do in heaven, and what we shall enjoy, but they all seem to me to be wide of the mark compared with this one, that we shall be with Jesus, be like Him, and shall behold His glory. Oh, to see the feet that were nailed, and to touch the hand that was pierced, and to look upon the head that wore the thorns, and to bow before Him who is ineffable love, unspeakable condescension, infinite tenderness! Oh, to bow before Him, and to kiss that blessed face! Jesu, what better do we want than to see Thee by Thine own light—to see Thee and speak with Thee, as when a man speaketh with his friend? It is pleasant to talk about this, but what will it be there when the pearl gates open? The streets of gold will have small attraction to us, and the harps of angels will but slightly enchant us, compared with the King in the midst of the throne. He it is who shall rivet our gaze, absorb our thoughts, enchain our affection, and move all our sacred passions to their highest pitch of celestial ardour. We shall see Jesus.

Once again (and here we come into the deep things), beyond a doubt WE SHALL ALSO SEE GOD. It is written that the pure in heart shall see God. God is seen now in His works and in His word.

Little indeed could these eyes bear of the beatific vision, yet we have reason to expect that. as far as creatures can bear the sight of the infinite Creator. we shall be permitted to see God. We read that Aaron and certain chosen ones saw the throne of God, and the brightness as it were of a sapphire stone—light, pure as jasper. In heaven it is the presence of God that is the light thereof. God's more immediately dwelling in the midst of the new Jerusalem is its peerless glory and peculiar bliss. We shall then understand more of God than we do now; we shall come nearer to Him, be more familiar with Him, be more filled with Him. The love of God shall be shed abroad in our hearts; we shall know our Father as we yet know Him not; we shall know the Son to a fuller degree than He has yet revealed Himself to us, and we shall know the Holy Spirit in His personal love and tenderness towards us, beyond all those influences and operations which have soothed us in our sorrows and guided us in our perplexities here below. I leave your thoughts and your desires to follow the teaching of the Spirit. As for me, I cower before the thought while I revel in it. I, who have strained my eyes while gazing at nature, where the things that are made show the handiwork of God; I, whose conscience has been awe-struck as I listened to the voice of God proclaiming His holy law; I, whose heart has been melted while there broke on my ears the tender accents of His blessed gospel in those snatches of sacred melody that relieve the burden of prophecy; I, who have recognised in the babe of Bethlehem the hope of Israel; in the man of Nazareth, the Messiah that should come; in the victim of Calvary, the one Mediator; in the risen Jesus, the well-beloved Son— to me, verily, God incarnate has been so palpably revealed that I have almost seen God, for I have, as it were, seen Him in whom all the fulness of the Godhead bodily doth dwell. Still I " see through a glass, darkly." Illumine these dark senses, waken this drowsy conscience, purify my heart, give me fellowship with Christ, and then bear me up, translate me to the third heavens; so I may, so I can, so I shall see God. But what that means, or what it is, ah me! I cannot tell.

II. We proposed to enquire, in the second place, HOW THIS VERY REMARKABLE CHANGE SHALL BE EFFECTED? WHY IS IT THAT WE SHALL SEE MORE CLEARLY THEN THAN NOW? We cannot altogether answer the question, but one or two suggestions may help us. No doubt many of these things will be more clearly revealed in the next state. Here the light is like the dawn: it is dim twilight. In heaven it will be the blaze of noon. God has declared something of Himself by the mouth of His holy prophets and apostles. He has been pleased, through the lips of His Son, whom He hath appointed heir of all things, to speak to us more plainly, to show us more openly the thoughts of His heart and the counsel of His will. These are the first steps to knowledge. But there the light will be as the light of seven days, and there the manifestation of all the treasures of wisdom shall be brighter and clearer than it is now; for God, the only-wise God, shall unveil to us the mysteries, and exhibit to us the glories of His everlasting kingdom. The revelation we now have suits us as men clad in our poor mortal bodies : the revelation then will suit us as immortal spirits. When we have been raised from the dead, it will be suitable to our immortal spiritual bodies. Here, too, we are at a distance from many of the things we long to know something of, but there we shall be nearer to them. We shall then be on a vantage ground, with the entire horizon spread out before us. Our Lord Jesus is, as to His personal presence, far away from us. We see Him through the telescope of faith, but then we shall see Him face to face. His literal and bodily presence is in heaven, since He was taken up, and we need to be taken up likewise to be with Him where He is that we may literally behold Him. Get to the fountain-head, and you understand more; stand in the centre, and things seem regular and orderly. If you could stand in the sun and see the orbits in which the planets revolve round that central luminary, it would become clear enough; but for many an age astronomers were unable to discover anything of order, and spoke of the planets as progressive, retrograde, and standing still. Let us get to God, the centre, and we shall see how Providence in order revolves round His sapphire throne. We, ourselves, too, when we get to heaven, shall be better qualified to see than we are now. It would be an inconvenience for us to know here as much as we shall know in heaven. No doubt we have sometimes thought that if we had better ears it would be a great blessing. We have wished we could hear ten miles off; but probably we should be no better off; we might hear too much, and the sounds might drown each other. Probably our sight is not as good as we wish it were, but a large increase of ocular power might not be of any use to us. Our natural organs are fitted for our present sphere of being; and our mental faculties are, in the case of most of us, properly adapted to our moral requirements. If we knew more of our own sinfulness, we might be driven to despair; if we knew more of God's glory, we might die of terror; if we had more understanding, unless we had equivalent capacity to employ it, we might be filled with conceit and tormented with ambition. But up there we shall have our minds and our systems strengthened to receive more, without the damage that would come to us here from overleaping the boundaries of order, supremely appointed and divinely regulated. We cannot here drink the wine of the kingdom, it is too strong for us; but up there we shall drink it new in our heavenly Father's kingdom, without fear of the intoxications of pride, or the staggerings of passions. We shall know even as we are known. Besides, dear friends, the atmosphere of heaven is so much clearer than this, that I do not wonder we can see better there. Here there is the smoke of daily care; the constant dust of toil; the mist of trouble perpetually rising. We cannot be expected to see much in such a smoky atmosphere as this; but when we shall pass beyond, we shall find no clouds ever gather round the sun to hide His everlasting brightness. There all is clear. The daylight is serene as the noonday. We shall be in a clearer atmosphere and brighter light.

III. The practical lessons we may learn from this subject demand your attention before I close. Methinks there is an appeal to our *gratitude*. Let us be very thankful for all we do see. Those who do not see now—ah, not even " though a glass, darkly " —shall never see face to face. The eyes that never see Christ by faith shall never see Him with joy in heaven. If thou hast never seen thyself a leper, defiled with sin and abashed with penitence, thou shalt never see thyself redeemed from sin, renewed by grace, a white-robed spirit. If thou hast no sense of God's presence here, constraining thee to worship and love Him, thou shalt have no sight of His glory hereafter, introducing thee to the fulness of joy and pleasure for evermore. Oh! be glad for the sight you have, dear brother, dear sister. It is God that gave it to thee. Thou art one born blind; and "Since the world began was it not heard that any man opened the eyes of one that was born blind." This miracle has been wrought on thee; thou canst see, and thou canst say: " One thing I know, that whereas I was blind, now I see."

Our text teaches us that this feeble vision is very *hopeful*. *You shall see better by-and-by.* Oh, you know not how soon—it may be a day or two hence—that we shall be in glory! God may so have ordained it, that betwixt us and heaven there may be but a step.

Another lesson is that of *forbearance* one with another. Let the matters we have spoken of soften the asperity of our debates; let us feel when we are disputing about points of difficulty, that we need not get cross about them, because after all there are limits to our present capacity as well as to our actual knowledge. Our disputes are often childish. We might as well leave some questions in abeyance for a little while. Two persons in the dark have differed about a colour, and they are wrangling about it. If we brought candles in and held them to the colour, the candles would not show what it was; but if we look at it to-morrow morning, when the sun shines, we shall be able to tell. How many difficulties in the word of God are like this! Not yet can they be justly discriminated; till the day dawn, the apocalyptic symbols will not be all transparent to our own understanding. Besides, we have no time to waste while there is so much work to do. Much time is already spent. Sailing is dangerous; the winds are high; the sea is rough. Trim the ship; keep the sails in good order; manage her and keep her off quicksands. As to certain other matters, we must wait till we get into the fair haven, and are able to talk with some of the bright spirits now before the throne. When some of the things they know shall be opened unto us, we shall confess the mistakes we made, and rejoice in the light we shall receive.

Should not this happy prospect excite our *aspiration* and make us very desirous to be there? It is natural for us to want to know, but we shall not know as we are known till we are present with the Lord. We are at school now—children at school. We shall go to the college soon—the great University of Heaven—and take our degree there. Yet some of us, instead of being anxious to go, are shuddering at the thought of death—the gate of endless joy we dread to enter! There are many persons who die suddenly; some die in their sleep, and many have passed out of time into eternity when it has scarcely been known by those who have been sitting at their bedsides. Depend upon it, there is no pain in dying; the pain is in living. When they leave off living here, they have done with pain. Do not blame death for what it does not deserve; it is life that lingers on in pain: death is the end of it. The man that is afraid of dying ought to be afraid of living. Be content to die whenever the Master's will shall bid thee. Commit thy spirit to His keeping. Who that hath seen but the glimpses of His beaming countenance doth not long to see His face, that is as the sun shining in His strength? O Lord! Thy will be done. Let us speedily behold Thee, if so it may be—only this one word, if so it may be. Do we now see, and do we expect to see better? Let us bless the name of the Lord, who hath chosen us of His mercy and of His infinite lovingkindness. On the other hand, let it cause us great anxiety if we have not believed in Jesus, for he that hath not believed in Him, dying as he is, will never see the face of God with joy. Oh! unbeliever, be concerned about your soul, and seek thou after Him, repair thou to Him. Oh! that God would open thy eyes now in this very house of prayer. Blessed for thee to know in part. Thrice blessed, I say; for as surely as thou knowest in part now, thou shalt fully know hereafter. Be it your happy lot to know Him, whom to know is life eternal. God grant it, for Jesus' sake. Amen.

"ALAS FOR US, IF THOU WERT ALL, AND NOUGHT BEYOND, O EARTH"

" If in this life only we have hope in Christ, we are of all men most miserable."—1 Corinthians xv. 19.

YOU will understand that the apostle is arguing with professedly Christian people, who were dubious about the resurrection of the dead. He is not saying that all men are now miserable if there be no hope of the world to come, for such an assertion would be untrue. There are very many who never think of another life, who are quite happy in their way, enjoy themselves, and are very comfortable after a fashion. But he speaks of Christian people—" If *we*, who have hope in Christ, are led to doubt the doctrine of a future state and of a resurrection, then *we* are of all men most miserable." The argument has nothing to do with some of you who are not Christians; it has nothing to do with you who have never been brought out of a state of nature into a state of grace; it only respects those who are real, living followers of the Saviour, and who are known by this, that they have *hope in Christ*—hope in His blood for pardon, in His righteousness for justification, in His power for support, in His resurrection for eternal glory. " If we who have hope in Christ, have that hope for this life only, then we are of all men most miserable." You understand the argument; he is appealing to their consciousness; they, as Christians, had real enjoyments, " but," says he, " you could not have these enjoyments if it were not for the hope of another life: for once take that away, if you could still remain Christians and have the same feelings which you now have, and act as you now do, you would become of all men most miserable." therefore to justify your own happiness and make it all reasonable, you must admit a resurrection ; there is no other method of accounting for the joyous peace which the Christian possesses. Our riches are beyond the sea ; our city with firm foundations lies on the other side of the river : gleams of glory from the spirit-world cheer our hearts, and urge us onward ; but if it were not for these, our present joys would pine and die.

We will try and handle our text this morning in this way. First, *we are not of all men most miserable ;* but secondly, *without the hope of another life we should be*—that we are prepared to confess—because thirdly, *our chief joy lies in the hope of a life to come ;* and thus, fourthly, *the future influences the present ;* and so, in the last place, *we may to-day judge what our future is to be.*

I. First then, WE ARE NOT OF ALL MEN MOST MISERABLE. Who ventures to say we are ? He who will have the hardihood to say so knoweth nothing of us. He who shall affirm that Christianity makes men miserable, is himself an utter stranger to it, and has never partaken of its joyful influences. It were a very strange thing indeed, if it did make us wretched, for see *to what a position it exalts us !* It makes us sons of God. Suppose you that God will give all the happiness to His enemies, and reserve all the mourning for His sons ? Shall His foes have mirth and joy and shall His own home-born children inherit sorrow and wretchedness ? Are the kisses for the wicked and the frowns for us ? Are we condemned to hang our harps upon the willows, and sing nothing but doleful dirges, while the children of Satan are to laugh for joy of heart ? We are heirs of God, and joint-heirs with Christ Jesus. Shall the sinner, who has no part nor lot in Christ, call himself happy, and shall we go mourning as if we were penniless beggars ? No, we will rejoice in the Lord always, and glory in our inheritance, for we "have not received the spirit of bondage again to fear ; but ye have received the Spirit of adoption, whereby we cry, Abba, Father." The rod of chastisement must rest upon us in our measure, but it worketh for us the comfortable fruits of righteousness ; and therefore by the aid of the divine Comforter, we will rejoice in the Lord at all times. We are, my brethren, married unto Christ ; and shall our great Bridegroom permit His spouse to linger in constant grief ? Our hearts are knit unto Him : we are members of His body, of His flesh, and of His bones, and though for awhile we may suffer as our Head once suffered, yet we are even now blessed with heavenly blessings in Him. Shall our Head reign in heaven, and shall we have a hell upon earth ? God forbid : the joyful triumph of our exalted Head is in a measure shared by us, even in this vale of tears. We have the earnest of our inheritance in the comforts of the Spirit, which are neither few nor small. Think of a Christian ! He is a king, and shall the king be the most melancholy of men ? He is a priest unto God, and shall He offer no sweet incense of hallowed joy and grateful thanksgiving ? We are fit companions for angels : He hath made us meet to be partakers of the inheritance of the saints in light ; and shall we have no days of heaven upon earth ? Is Canaan ours from Dan to Beersheba, and shall we eat no fruit from Eshcol's vine on this side of Jordan ? Shall we have no taste of the figs, and of the pomegranates, and of the flowing milk and honey ? Is there no manna in the wilderness ? Are there no streams in the desert ? Are there no streaks of light to herald our eternal sunrising ? Heritors of joy for ever, have we no foretastes of our portion ? I say again, it were the oddest thing in the world if Christians were more miserable than other men, or not more happy. Think again of *what God has done for them !* The Christian knows that his sins are forgiven ; there is not against the believer a single sin recorded in God's book. " I have blotted out, as a thick cloud, thy transgressions, and, as a cloud, thy sins." More than that, the believer is accounted by God as if he had perfectly kept the law, for the righteousness of Christ is imputed to him, and he stands clothed in that fair white linen which is the righteousness of the saints. And shall the man whom God accepts be wretched ? Shall the pardoned offender be less happy than the man upon whom the wrath of God abideth ? Can you conceive such a thing ? Moreover, my brethren, we are made temples of the Holy Ghost, and is the Holy Ghost's temple to be a dark dolorous place, a place of shrieks and moans, and cries, like the Druidic groves of old ? Such is not like our God. Our God is a God of love, and it is His very nature to make His creatures happy ; and we, who are His twice-made creatures, who are the partakers of the divine nature, having escaped the corruption which is in the world through lust, is it to be supposed that we are bound by a stern decree to go mourning all our days ? Oh ! if ye knew the Christian's privilege, if ye understood that the secret of the Lord is laid open to him, that the wounds of Christ are his shelter, that the flesh and blood of Christ are his food, that Christ Himself is his sweet companion and his abiding friend, oh ! if ye knew this, ye would never again foolishly dream that Christians are an unhappy race. " Happy art thou, O Israel : who is like unto thee, O people saved by the Lord ? " Who can be compared with the man who is " satisfied with favour and full with the blessing of the Lord." Well might the evil prophet of Bethor exclaim, " Let me die the death of the righteous, and let my last end be like his."

We will go a step farther. We will not only say that from the nature of his position and privileges, a Christian should be happy, but we declare that he is so, and that among all men there are none who enjoy such a *constant peace* of mind as believers in Christ. Our joy may not be like that of the sinner, noisy and boisterous. You know what Solomon says—" The laughter of fools is as the crackling of thorns under a pot "—a great deal of blaze and much noise, and then a handful of ashes, and it is all over. " Who hath woe, who hath redness of the eyes ? They that tarry long at the wine—men of strength to mingle strong drink." The Christian, in truth, does not know much of the excitement of the bowl, the viol and the dance, nor does he desire to know ; he is content that he possesses a calm deep-seated repose of soul. " He is not afraid of evil tidings, his heart is fixed, trusting in the Lord." He is not disturbed with any sudden fear ; he knows that " all things work together for good to them that love God, to them who are the called according to His purpose." He is in the habit, in whatever society he may be, of still lifting up his heart to God ; and therefore he can say with the Psalmist, " My heart is fixed, O God, my heart is fixed : I will sing and give praise."

" He waits in secret on his God ;
    His God in secret sees ;
Let earth be all in arms abroad,
    He dwells in heavenly peace.

His pleasures rise from things unseen,
　Beyond this world and time,
Where neither eyes nor ears have been,
　Nor thoughts of sinners climb.

He wants no pomp nor royal throne
　To raise his figure here :
Content and pleased to live unknown,
　Till Christ his life appear.

" There is a river the streams whereof make glad the city of God." Believers drink of that river and thirst not for carnal delights. They are made " to lie down in green pastures," and are led " beside the still waters." Now this solid, lasting joy and peace of mind sets the Christian so on high above all others, that I boldly testify that there are no people in the world to compare with him for happiness. But do not suppose that our joy never rises above this settled calm ; for let me tell you, and I speak experimentally, we have our seasons of *rapturous delight* and overflowing bliss. There are times with us when no music could equal the melody of our heart's sweet hymn of joy. It would empty earth's coffers of every farthing of her joy to buy a single ounce of our delight. Do not fancy Paul was the only man who could say, " Whether in the body or out of the body, I cannot tell ; God knoweth," for these ecstasies are usual with believers ; and on their sunshiny days, when their unbelief is shaken off and their faith is strong, they have all but walked the golden streets ; and they can say, " If we have not entered within the pearly gate, we have been only just this side of it ; and if we have not yet come to the general assembly and Church of the firstborn, whose names are written in heaven, if we have not joined the great congregation of the perfect in actual body, yet still—

　　" E'en now by faith we join our hands
　　　With those that went before,
　　And greet the blood-besprinkled bands
　　　On the eternal shore."

I would not change one five minutes of the excessive joy my soul has sometimes felt for a thousand years of the best mirth that the children of this world could give me. O friends, there is a happiness which can make the eye sparkle and the heart beat high, and the whole man as full of bounding speed of life as the chariots of Amminadib. There are raptures and high ecstasies, which on festival days such as the Lord allotteth to His people, the saints are permitted to enjoy. I must not fail to remind you that the Christian is the happiest of men for this reason, that *his joy does not depend upon circumstances.* We have seen the happiest men in the most sorrowful conditions. Mr. Renwick, who was the last of the Scotch martyrs, said a little before his death, " Enemies think themselves satisfied that we are put to wander in mosses and upon mountains, but even amidst the storm of these last two nights I cannot express what sweet times I have had when I have had no coverings but the dark curtains of night : yea, in the silent watch my mind was led out to admire the deep and inexpressible ocean of joy wherein the whole family of heaven do swim. Each star led me to wonder what He must be who is the star of Jacob, and from whom all stars borrow their shining." Here is a martyr of God driven from house and home and from all comforts, and yet having such sweet seasons beneath the curtains of the black night as kings do not often know beneath their curtains of silk. A

minister of Christ going to visit a very, very poor man, gives this description. He says, " I found him alone, his wife having gone out to ask help of some neighbour. I was startled by the sight of the pale emaciated man, the living image of death, fastened upright in his chair by a rude mechanism of cords and belts hanging from the ceiling, totally unable to move hand or foot, having been for more than four years entirely deprived of the use of his limbs, and suffering extreme pain from swellings in all his joints. I approached him full of pity, and I said, " Are you left alone, my friend, in this deplorable situation ? " He answered with a gentle voice—his lips were the only parts of his body which he appeared to have power to move—" No, sir, I am not alone, because the Father is with me." I began to talk with him, and I soon observed what was the source of his consolation, for just in front of him lay the Bible upon a pillow, his wife having left it open at some choice Psalm of David so that he might read while she was gone, as he had no power to turn over the leaves. I asked him what he had to live upon, and found that it was a miserable pittance, scarcely enough to keep body and soul together, " But," said he, " I never want anything, for the Lord has said, ' Your bread shall be given you, and your water shall be sure,' and I trust in Him, and I shall never want while God is faithful to His promise." " I asked him," says this minister, " whether he did not often repine on account of suffering so acutely for so many years. " Sir," said he, " I did repine at first, but not for the last three years, blessed be God for it, for I know whom I have believed, and though I feel my own weakness and unworthiness more and more, yet I am persuaded that He will never leave me nor forsake me ; and so graciously does He comfort me that, when my lips are closed with lock-jaw and I cannot speak a word for hours together, He enables me to sing His praises most sweetly in my heart." Now here was a man to whom the sun of all earthly comfort was set, and yet the sun of heaven shone full in his face, and he was more peaceful and happy in deep poverty and racking pain than all you or I have been in the health and strength of youth. John Howard spent his time in visiting the gaols and going from one haunt of fever to another, he was asked how he could find any ground of happiness when he was living in miserable Russian villages, or dwelling in discomfort in an hospital or a gaol. Mr. Howard's answer was very beautiful. " I hope," said he, " I have sources of enjoyment which depend not upon the particular spot I inhabit. A rightly cultivated mind, under the power of divine grace and the exercise of a benevolent disposition affords a ground of satisfaction that is not to be affected by *heres* and *theres.*" Every Christian will bear you his witness that he has found his sad times to be his glad times, his losses to be his gains, his sicknesses means to promote his soul's health. Our summer does not depend upon the sun, nor our flood-tide upon the moon. We can rejoice even in death. We look forward to that happy hour when we shall close our eyes in the peaceful slumbers of death, believing that our last day will be our best day. Even the crossing of the river Jordan is but an easy task, for we shall hear Him say, " Fear not ; I am with thee : be not dismayed, I am thy God ; when thou passest through the rivers I will be with thee, and the floods shall not overflow thee." We dare to say it, then, very boldly, we are *not* of all men most miserable : we would not change with unconverted men for all their riches, and their pomp, and their honour thrown into the scale.

II. This brings us to the second point—WITHOUT THE HOPE OF ANOTHER LIFE, WE WILL ADMIT, THAT WE SHOULD BE OF ALL MEN MOST MISERABLE.

" Go you that boast in all your stores,
    And tell how bright they shine,
Your heaps of glittering dust are yours,
    And my Redeemer's mine."

Especially was this true of the apostles. They were rejected by their countrymen ; they lost all the comforts of home ; their lives were spent in toil, and were daily exposed to violent death. They all of them suffered the martyr's doom, except John, who seems to have been preserved not *from* martyrdom, but *in* it. They were certainly the twelve most miserable of men apart from that hope of the world to come, which made them of all men the most happy. But this is true, dear friends, not merely of persecuted, and despised, and poverty-stricken Christians, but of all believers. We are prepared to grant it, that take away from us the hope of the world to come we should be more miserable than men without religion. The reason is very clear, if you think that the Christian has *renounced those common and ordinary sources of joy from which other men drink*. We must have some pleasure : it is impossible for men to live in this world without it, and I can say most truthfully I never urge any of you to do that which would make you unhappy. We must have some pleasure. Well then, there is a vessel filled with muddy filthy water which the camels' feet have stirred : shall I drink it ? I see yonder a rippling stream of clear flowing water, pure as crystal and cooling as the snow of Lebanon, and I say, " No, I will not drink this foul, muddy stuff ; leave that for beasts ; I will drink of yon clear stream." But if I be mistaken, if there be no stream yonder, if it be but the deceitful *mirage*, if I have been deluded, then I am worse off than those who were content with the muddy water, for they have at least some cooling draughts ; but I have none at all. This is precisely the Christian's case. He passes by the pleasures of sin, and the amusements of carnal men, because he says, " I do not care for them, I find no pleasure in them : my happiness flows from the river which springs from the throne of God and flows to me through Jesus Christ—I will drink of that," but if there were no hereafter, if that were proved to be a deception, then were we more wretched than the profligate and licentious.

Again, the Christian man has *learned the vanity of all earthly joys*. We know when we look upon pomp that it is an empty thing. We walk through the world, not with the scorn of Diogenes, the cynical philosopher, but with something of his wisdom, and we look upon the common things in which men rejoice, and say with Solomon, " Vanity of vanities, all is vanity." And why do we say this ? Why, because we have chosen eternal things in which there is no vanity, and which are satisfying to the soul. But, my brethren, it is the most unhappy piece of knowledge which a man can acquire, to know that this world is vain, if there be not another world abundantly to compensate for all our ills. There is a poor lunatic in Bedlam, plaiting straw into a crown which he puts upon his head, and calls himself a king, and mounts his mimic throne and thinks that he is

monarch over all nations, and is perfectly happy in his dream. Do you think that I would undeceive him ? Nay, verily, if I could, I would not. If the delusion makes the man happy, by all means let him indulge in it ; but, dear friends, you and I *have been* undeceived ; our dream of perfect bliss beneath the skies is gone for ever ; what then if there be no world to come ? Why then it is a most sorrowful thing for us that we have been awakened out of our sleep unless this better thing which we have chosen, this good part which shall not be taken from us, should prove to be real and true, as we do believe it is.

Moreover, the Christian man is a man who has had *high, noble, and great expectations*, and this is a very sad thing for us if our expectations be not fulfilled, for it makes us of all men most miserable. I have known poor men waiting and expecting a legacy. They had a right to expect it, and they have waited, and waited, and borne with poverty, and the relative has died and left them nothing ; their poverty has ever afterwards seemed to be a heavier drag than before. It is an unhappy thing for a man to have large ideas and large desires, if he cannot gratify them. I believe that poverty is infinitely better endured by persons who were always poor, than by those who have been rich and have had to come down to penury, for they miss what the others never had, and what the originally poor would look upon as luxuries they consider to be necessary to their existence. The Christian has learned to think of eternity of God, of Christ, of communion with Jesus, and if indeed it be all false, he certainly has dreamed the most magnificent of all mortal visions. Truly, if any man could prove it to be a vision, the best thing he could do would be to sit down and weep for ever to think it was not true, for the dream is so splendid, the picture of the world to come so gorgeous, that I can only say, if it be not true, it ought to be—if it be not true, then there is nothing here worth living for, my brethren, and we are disappointed wretches indeed—of all men most miserable.

The Christian, too, *has learned to look upon everything here on earth as fleeting*. I must confess every day this feeling grows with me. I scarce look upon my friends as living. I walk as in a land of shadows, and find nothing enduring around me. The broad arrow of the great skeleton king is, to my eye, visibly stamped everywhere. I go so often to the grave, and with those I least expected to take there, that it seems to be rather a world of dying than of living men. Well, this is a very unhappy thing—a very wretched state of mind for a man to be in, if there be no world to come. If there be no resurrection of the dead, then is the Christian indeed committed to a state of mind the most deplorable and pitiable. But, O my brethren, if there be a world to come, as faith assures us there is, how joyous it is to be weaned from the world, and to be ready to depart from it ! To be with Christ is far better than to tarry in this vale of tears.

" The cords that bound my heart to earth
    Are broken by His hand ;
Before His cross I find myself
    A stranger in the land.

My heart is with Him on His throne,
    And ill can brook delay ;
Each moment listening for the voice,
    ' Make haste, and come away.' "

May I not pant to be in my own sweet country with my own fair Lord, to see Him face to face ? Yet, if it be not so and there be no resurrection of the dead, " we are of all men most miserable."

III. OUR CHIEF JOY IN THE HOPE OF THE WORLD TO COME. Think of the world to come, my brethren, and let your joys begin to kindle into flames of delight, for heaven offers you all that you can desire. You are, many of you, weary of toil ; so weary, perhaps, that you can scarcely enjoy the morning service because of the late hours at which you have had to work at night. Ah ! there is a land of *rest*—of perfect rest, where the sweat of labour no more bedews the worker's brow, and fatigue is for ever banished. To those who are weary and spent, the word " rest " is full of heaven. Oh ! happy truth, there remaineth a rest for the people of God. " They rest from their labours, and their works do follow them." Others of you are always in the field of battle ; you are so tempted within, and so molested by foes without, that you have little or no peace. I know where your hope lies. It lies in the *victory*, when the banner shall be waved aloft, and the sword shall be sheathed, and you shall hear your Captain say, " Well done, good and faithful servant ; thou hast fought a good fight ; thou hast finished thy course : henceforth wear thou the crown of life which fadeth not away." Some of you are tossed about with many troubles ; you go from care to care, from loss to loss : it seems to you as if all God's waves and billows had gone over you ; but you shall soon arrive at the land of *happiness*, where you shall bathe your weary soul in seas of heavenly rest. You shall have no poverty soon ; no mud-hovel, no rags, nor hunger. " In My Father's house are many mansions," and there shall you dwell, satisfied with favour, and full of every blessing. You have had bereavement after bereavement ; the wife has been carried to the tomb, the children have followed, father and mother are gone, and you have few left to love you here ; but you are going to the land where graves are unknown things, where they never see a shroud, and the sound of the mattock and the spade are never heard ; you are going to your Father's house in the land of the *immortal*, in the country of the hereafter, in the home of the blessed, in the habitation of God Most High, in the Jerusalem which is above, the mother of us all. Is not this your best joy, that you are not to be here for ever, that you are not to dwell eternally in this wilderness, but shall soon inherit Canaan ? With all God's people their worst grief is sin. I would not care for any sorrow, if I could live without sinning. Oh ! if I were rid of the appetites of the flesh and the lusts thereof, and the desires which continually go astray, I would be satisfied to lie in a dungeon and rot there, so as to be delivered from the corruption of sin. Well but, brethren, we shall soon attain unto *perfection*. The body of this death will die with this body. There is no temptation in heaven, for the dog of hell can never cross the stream of death ; there are no corruptions there, for they have washed their robes and made them white in the blood of the Lamb ; there shall by no means enter into that kingdom anything which defileth. Methinks as I hear the joyous song of the glorified this morning, as I catch floating down from heaven the sound of that music which is like many waters and like the great thunder, and as I hear the harmony of those notes which are sweet as harpers harping with their harps, my soul desireth to stretch her wings, and fly straight to yonder worlds of joy. I know it is so with you, my

brethren, in the tribulation of Christ—as you wipe the sweat from your brow, is not this the comfort : there is rest for the people of God ? As you stand out against temptation and suffer for Christ's sake, is not this your comfort : " If we suffer with Him, we shall also reign with Him." When you are slandered and despised by men, is not this your hope : " He will remember me when He cometh into His kingdom. I shall sit upon His throne, even as He has overcome, and sitteth down upon His Father's throne ? " Oh ! yes, this is the music to which Christians dance ; this is the wine which maketh glad their hearts ; this is the banquet at which they feast. There is another and a better land, and we, though we sleep with the clods of the valley, shall in our flesh see God, when our Redeemer shall stand in the latter days upon the earth. I think you catch my drift—we are *not* of all men most miserable ; apart from the future hope we should be, for our hope in Christ for the future is the mainstay of our joy.

IV. Now, dear friends, this brings me to a practical observation in the fourth place, which is, that THUS THE FUTURE OPERATES UPON THE PRESENT.

I had some time ago a conversation with a very eminent man whose fame is familiar to you all, but whose name I do not feel justified in mentioning, who was once a professed believer but is now full of scepticism. He said to me in the course of our argument, " Why, how foolish you are, and all the company of preachers. You tell people to think about the next world, when the best thing they could do would be to behave themselves as well as they can in this ! " I granted the truth of the observation ; it would be very unwise to make people neglect the present, for it is of exceeding great importance, but I went on to show him that the very best method to make people attend to the present was by impressing them with high and noble motives with regard to the future. The potent force of the world to come supplies us through the Holy Spirit with force for the proper accomplishment of the duties of this life. Here is a man who has a machine for the manufacture of hardware. He wants steam power to work this machine. An engineer puts up a steam engine in a shed at some considerable distance. " Well," saith the other, " I asked you to bring steam power here, to operate upon my machine." " That is precisely," says he, " what I have done. I put the steam engine there, you have but to connect it by a band and your machine works as fast as you like ; it is not necessary that I should put the boiler, and the fire, and the engine close to the work, just under your nose : only connect the two, and the one will operate upon the other." So God has been pleased to make our hopes of the future a great engine wherewith the Christian man may work the ordinary machine of every-day life, for the band of faith connects the two, and makes all the wheels of ordinary life revolve with rapidity and regularity. To speak against preaching the future as though it would make people neglect the present is absurd. It is as though somebody should say, " There, take away the moon, and blot out the sun. What is the use of them—they are not in this world ? " Precisely so, but take away the moon and you have removed the tides, and the sea becomes a stagnant, putrid pool. Then take away the sun—it is not in the world —take it away, and light, and heat, and life ; everything is gone. What the sun and moon are to this natural world, the hope of the future is to the Christian in this world. It is his light—he looks upon all things in that light, and sees them truly. It is his heat; it gives him zeal and energy. It is his very life; his Christianity, his virtue would expire if it were not for the hope of the world to come. Do you believe, my brethren, that apostles and martyrs would ever have sacrificed their lives for truth's sake if they had not looked for a hereafter? In the heat of excitement, the soldier may die for honour, but to die in tortures and mockeries in cold blood needs a hope beyond the grave. Would yon poor man go toiling on year after year, refusing to sacrifice his conscience for gain; would yon poor needle-girl refuse to become the slave of lust if she did not see something brighter than earth can picture to her as the reward of sin? O my brethren, the most practical thing in all the world is the hope of the world to come; and you see the text teaches this, for it is just this which keeps us from being miserable; and to keep a man from being miserable, let me say, is to do a great thing for him, for a miserable Christian—what is the use of him? Keep him in a cupboard, where nobody can see him; nurse him in the hospital, for he is of no use in the field of labour. Build a monastery, and put all miserable Christians in it, and there let them meditate on mercy till they learn to smile; for really there is no other use for them in the world. But the man who has a hope of the next world goes about his work strong, for the joy of the Lord is our strength. He goes against temptation mighty, for the hope of the next world repels the fiery darts of the adversary. He can labour without present reward, for he looks for a reward in the world to come. He can suffer rebuke, and can afford to die a slandered man, because he knows that God will avenge His own elect who cry day and night unto Him. Through the Spirit of God the hope of another world is the most potent force for the product of virtue; it is a fountain of joy; it is the very channel of usefulness. It is to the Christian what food is to the vital force in the animal frame. Let it be said of any of us, that we are dreaming about the future and forgetting the present, but let the future sanctify the present to highest uses. I fear our prophetical brethren err here. They are reading continually about the last vials, the seventy weeks of Daniel, and a number of other mysteries; I wish they would set to work instead of speculating so much, or speculate even more if they will, but turn their prophecies to present practical account. Prophetical speculations too often lead men away from present urgent duty, and especially from contending earnestly for the faith once delivered to the saints; but a hope of the world to come is, I think, the best practical power which a Christian can have.

V. And now, to conclude, this will let us see very clearly WHAT OUR FUTURE IS TO BE.

There are some persons here to whom my text has nothing whatever to say. Suppose there were no hereafter, would they be more miserable? Why, no; they would be more happy. If anybody could prove to them that death is an eternal sleep, it would be the greatest consolation that they could possibly receive. If it could be shown, to a demonstration, that as soon as people die they rot in the grave and there is an end of them—why some of you could go to bed at night comfortable, your conscience would never disturb you, you would be molested by none of those terrible fears which now haunt you.

Do you see, then, this proves that you are not a Christian; this proves as plainly as twice two make four, that you are no believer in Christ; for if you were, the taking away of a hereafter would make you miserable. Since it would not tend to make you happy to believe in a future state, this proves that you are no believer in Christ. Well, then, what have I to say to you? Why just this—that in the world to come, *you will be of all men most miserable.* "What will become of you?" said an infidel once to a Christian man, "supposing there should be no heaven?" "Well," said he, "I like to have two strings to my bow. If there be no hereafter I am as well off as you are; if there be I am infinitely better off. But where are you? Where are you?" Why then we must read this text in the future—"If in this life there be indeed a hope of a life to come, then you shall be in the next life of all men most miserable." Do you see where you will be? Your soul goes before the great Judge, and receives its condemnation and begins its hell. The trumpet rings; heaven and earth are astonished; the grave heaves; yonder slab of marble is lifted up, and up you rise in that very flesh and blood in which you sinned, and there you stand in the midst of a terrified multitude, all gathered to their doom. The Judge has come. The great assize has commenced. There on the great white throne sits the Saviour who once said, "Come unto Me, ye weary, and I will give you rest"; but now He sits there as a Judge and opens with stern hand the terrible volume. Page after page He reads, and as He reads He gives the signal, "Depart, ye cursed, into everlasting fire," and the angels bind up the tares in bundles to burn them. There stand you, and you know your doom; you already begin to feel it. You cry to the lofty Alps to fall upon you and conceal you. "O ye mountains, can ye not find in your rocky bowels some friendly cavern where I may be hidden from the face of Him who sits upon the throne?" In terrible silence the mountains refuse your petition and the rocks reject your cry. You would plunge into the sea, but it is licked up with tongues of fire; you would fain make your bed even in hell if you could escape from those dreadful eyes, but you cannot! for now your turn is come, that page is turned over which records your history; the Saviour reads with a voice of thunder and with eyes of lightning. He reads, and as He waves His hand you are cast away from hope. You shall then know what it is to be *of all men most miserable.* Ye had your pleasure; ye had your giddy hour; ye had your mirthful moments; you despised Christ, and you would not turn at His rebuke; you would not have Him to reign over you; you lived His adversary; you died unreconciled, and now where are you? Now, what will ye do, ye who forget God, in that day when He shall tear you in pieces, and there shall be none to deliver you? In the name of my Lord and Master I do conjure you, fly away to Christ for refuge. "He that believeth in Him shall be saved." To believe is to trust; and whosoever this morning is enabled by faith to cast himself upon Christ, need not fear to live, nor fear to die. You shall not be miserable here; you shall be thrice blessed hereafter if you trust my Lord.

> "Come, guilty souls, and flee away
> To Christ, and heal your wounds;
> This is the welcome gospel-day
> Wherein free grace abounds."

O that ye would be wise and consider your latter end ! O that ye would reflect that this life is but a span, and the life to come lasts on for ever ! Do not, I pray you, fling away eternity ; play not the fool with such solemn things as these, but in serious earnestness lay hold upon eternal life. Look to the bleeding Saviour ; see there His five wounds, and His face bedewed with bloody sweat ! Trust Him, trust Him, and you are saved. The moment that you trust Him your sins are gone. His righteousness is yours ; you are saved on the spot, and you shall be saved when He cometh in His kingdom to raise the dead from their graves. O that the Lord might lead us all thus to rest on Jesus, now and ever. Amen.

CHRIST THE DESTROYER OF DEATH

" The last enemy that shall be destroyed is death."—i Corinthians xv. 26.

DURING four previous Sabbaths we have been following our Lord and Master through His great achievements : we have seen Him as the end of the law, as the conqueror of Satan, as the overcomer of the world, as the creator of all things new, and now we behold Him as the destroyer of death. In this and in all His other glorious deeds let us worship Him with all our hearts.

May the Spirit of God lead us into the full meaning of this, which is one of the Redeemer's grandest characters.

How wonderfully is our Lord Jesus *one with man !* For when the Psalmist David had considered " the heavens the work of God's fingers," he said, " Lord, what is man that Thou art mindful of him, or the son of man that Thou visitest him ? " He was speaking of Christ. You would have thought he was thinking of man in his humblest estate, and that he was wondering that God should be pleased to honour so frail a being as the poor fallen son of Adam. You would never have dreamed that the glorious gospel lay hid within those words of grateful adoration. Yet in the course of that meditation David went on to say, " Thou madest him to have dominion over all the works of Thy hands, Thou hast put all things under his feet." Now, had it not been for the interpretation of the Holy Spirit, we should still have considered that he was speaking of men in general, and of man's natural dominion over the brute creation but behold while that is true, there is another and a far more important truth concealed within it, for David, as a prophet, was all the while chiefly speaking of the man of men, the model man, the second Adam, the head of the new race of men. It was of Jesus, the Son of man, as honoured of the Father, that the psalmist sang, " He hath put all things under his feet." Strange, was it not, that when He spake of man He must of necessity speak also of our Lord ? And yet, when we consider the thing, it is but natural and according to truth, and only remarkable to us because in our minds we too often consider Jesus and man as far removed, and too little regard Him as truly one with man.

Now, see how the apostle infers from the psalm the necessity of the resurrection, for if all things must be put under the feet of the man Christ Jesus, then every form of evil must be conquered by Him, and death among the rest. " He must reign till He hath put all enemies under His feet." It must be so, and therefore death itself must ultimately be overcome. Thus out of that simple sentence in the psalm, which we should have read far otherwise without the light of the Holy Spirit, the apostle gathereth the doctrine of the resurrection. The Holy Spirit taught His servant Paul how by a subtle chemistry he could distil from simple words a precious fragrant essence, which the common reader never suspected to be there. Texts have their secret drawers, their box within a box, their hidden souls which lie asleep till He who placed them on their secret couches awakens them that they may speak to the hearts of His chosen. Could you ever have guessed resurrection from the eighth Psalm ? No, nor could you have believed, had it not been told you, that there is fire in the flint, oil in the rock, and bread in the earth we tread upon. Man's books have usually far less in them than we expect. but the book of the Lord is full of surprises, it is a mass of light, a mountain of priceless revelations. We little know what yet lies hidden within the Scriptures. We know the form of sound words as the Lord has taught it to us, and by it we will abide, but there are inner store-houses into which we have not peered ; chambers of revelation lit up with bright lamps, perhaps too bright for our eyes at this present. If Paul, when the Spirit of God rested upon him, could see so much in the songs of David, the day may come when we also shall see still more in the epistles of Paul, and wonder at ourselves that we did not understand better the things which the Holy Ghost has so freely spoken to us by the apostles. May we at this time be enabled to look deep and far, and behold the sublime glories of our risen Lord.

To the text itself then : *death is an enemy : death is an enemy to be destroyed : death is an enemy to be destroyed last :*—" the last enemy that shall be destroyed is death."

I. DEATH AN ENEMY. *It was so born,* even as Haman the Agagite was the enemy of Israel by his descent. Death is the child of our direst foe, for " sin when it is finished bringeth forth death." " Sin entered into the world and death by sin." Now, that which is distinctly the fruit of transgression cannot be other than an enemy of man. Death was introduced into the world on that gloomy day which saw our fall, and he that had the power of it is our arch enemy and betrayer, the devil : from both of which facts we must regard it as the manifest enemy of man. Death is an alien in this world, it did not enter into the original design of the unfallen creation, but its intrusion mars and spoils the whole. It is no part of the Great Shepherd's flock, but it is a wolf which cometh to kill and to destroy. Geology tells us that there was death among the various forms of life from the first ages of the globe's history, even when as yet the world was not fitted up as the dwelling of man. This I can believe and still regard death as the result of sin. If it can be proved that there is such an organic unity between man and the lower animals that they would not have died if Adam had not sinned, then I see in those deaths before Adam the antecedent consequences of a sin which was then uncommitted. If by the merits of Jesus there was salvation before He had offered His atoning sacrifice I do not find it hard to conceive that the foreseen demerits of sin may have cast the shadow of death over the long ages which came before man's transgression. Of that we know little, nor is it important that we should, but certain is it that as far as this present creation is concerned death is not God's invited guest, but an intruder whose presence mars the feast. Man in his folly welcomed Satan and sin when they forced their way into the high festival of Paradise, but he never welcomed death : even his blind eyes could see in that skeleton form a cruel foe. As the lion to the herds of the plain, as the scythe to the flowers of the field, as the wind to the sere leaves of the forest, such is death to the sons of men. They fear it by an inward instinct because their conscience tells them that it is the child of their sin.

Death is well called an enemy, for *it does an enemy's work* towards us. For what purpose doth an enemy come but to root up, and to pull down, and to destroy ? Death tears in pieces that comely handiwork of God, the fabric of the human body, so marvellously wrought by the fingers of divine skill. Casting this rich embroidery into the grave among the armies of the worm, to its fierce soldiery death divideth " to every one a prey of divers colours, of divers colours of needlework " ; and they ruthlessly rend in pieces the spoil. This building of our manhood is a house fair to look upon, but death the destroyer darkens its windows, shakes its pillars, closes its doors and causes the sound of the grinding to cease. Then the daughters of music are brought low, and the strong men bow themselves. This Vandal spares no work of life, however full of wisdom, or beauty, for it looseth the silver cord and breaketh the golden bowl. Lo, at the fountain the costly pitcher is utterly broken, and at the cistern the well-wrought wheel is dashed in pieces. Death is a fierce invader of the realms of life, and where it comes it fells every good tree, stops all wells of water, and mars every good piece of land with stones. See you a man when death has wrought his will upon him, what a ruin he is ! How is his beauty turned to ashes, and his comeliness to corruption. Surely an enemy hath done this.

Look, my brethren, at the course of death throughout all ages and in all lands. What field is there without its grave ? What city without its cemetery ? Whither can we go to find no sepulchres ? As the sandy shore is covered with the upcastings of the worm, so art thou, O earth, covered with those grassgrown hillocks beneath which sleep the departed generations of men. And thou, O sea, even thou, art not without thy dead ! As if the earth were all too full of corpses and they jostled each other in their crowded sepulchres, even into thy caverns, O mighty main, the bodies of the dead are cast. Thy waves must become defiled with the carcases of men, and on thy floor must lie the bones of the slain ! Our enemy, death, has marched as it were with sword and fire ravaging the human race. Neither Goth, nor Hun, nor Tartar could have slain so universally all that breathed, for death has suffered none to escape. Everywhere it has withered household joys and created sorrow and sighing ; in all lands where the sun is seen it hath blinded men's eyes with

weeping. The tear of the bereaved, the wail of the widow, and the moan of the orphan—these have been death's war music, and he has found therein a song of victory.

The greatest conquerors have only been death's slaughtermen, journeymen butchers working in his shambles. War is nothing better than death holding carnival, and devouring his prey a little more in haste than is his common wont.

Death has done the work of an enemy to those of us who have as yet escaped his arrows. Those who have lately stood around a new-made grave and buried half their hearts can tell you what an enemy death is. It takes the friend from our side, and the child from our bosom, neither does it care for our crying. He has fallen who was the pillar of the household ; she has been snatched away who was the brightness of the hearth. The little one is torn out of its mother's bosom though its loss almost breaks her heartstrings ; and the blooming youth is taken from his father's side though the parent's fondest hopes are thereby crushed. Death has no pity for the young and no mercy for the old ; he pays no regard to the good or to the beautiful. His scythe cuts down sweet flowers and noxious weeds with equal readiness. He cometh into our garden, trampleth down our lilies and scattereth our roses on the ground ; yea, and even the most modest flowers planted in the corner, and hiding their beauty beneath the leaves that they may blush unseen, death spieth out even these, and cares nothing for their fragrance, but withers them with his burning breath. He is thine enemy indeed, thou fatherless child, left for the pitiless storm of a cruel world to beat upon, with none to shelter thee. He is thine enemy, O widow, for the light of thy life is gone, and the desire of thine eyes has been removed with a stroke. He is thine enemy, husband, for thy house is desolate and thy little children cry for their mother of whom death has robbed thee.

He is the enemy of us all, for what head of a family among us has not had to say to him, " Me thou hast bereaved again and again ! " Especially is death an enemy to the living when he invades God's house and causes the prophet and the priest to be numbered with the dead. The church mourns when her most useful ministers are smitten down, when the watchful eye is closed in darkness, and the instructive tongue is mute. Yet how often does death thus war against us ! The earnest, the active, the indefatigable are taken away. Those mightiest in prayer, those most affectionate in heart, those most exemplary in life, those are cut down in the midst of their labours, leaving behind them a church which needs them more than tongue can tell. If the Lord does but threaten to permit death to seize a beloved pastor, the souls of his people are full of grief, and they view death as their worst foe, while they plead with the Lord and entreat Him to bid their minister live.

Even *those who die* may well count death to be their enemy : I mean not now that they have risen to their seats, and, as disembodied spirits, behold the King in His beauty, but aforetime while death was approaching them. He seemed to their trembling flesh to be a foe, for it is not in nature, except in moments of extreme pain or aberration of mind, or of excessive expectation of glory, for us to be in love with death. It was wise of our Creator so to constitute us that the soul loves the body and the body loves the soul, and they desire to dwell together as long as they may, else had there been no care for self-preservation, and suicide would have destroyed the race.

> " For who would bear the whips and scorns of time,
> The oppressor's wrong, the proud man's contumely,
> When he himself might his quietus make
> With a bare bodkin ? "

It is a first law of our nature that skin for skin, yea, all that a man hath will he give for his life, and thus we are nerved to struggle for existence, and to avoid that which would destroy us. This useful instinct renders death an enemy, but it also aids in keeping us from that crime of all crimes the most sure of damnation if a man commit it wilfully and in his sound mind ; I mean the crime of self-murder.

When death cometh even to the good man he cometh as an enemy, for he is attended by such terrible heralds and grim outriders as do greatly scare us.

> " Fever with brow of fire ;
> Consumption wan ; palsy, half-warmed with life,
> And half a clay-cold lump ; joint-torturing gout,
> And ev er-gnawing rheum convulsion wild ;
> Swoln dropsy ; panting asthma ; apoplex
> Full gorged."

None of these add to the aspect of death a particle of beauty. He comes with pains and griefs ; he comes with sighs and tears. Clouds and darkness are round about him, an atmosphere laden with dust oppresses those whom he approaches, and a cold wind chills them even to the marrow. He rides on the pale horse, and where his steed sets its foot the land becomes a desert. By the footfall of that terrible steed the worm is awakened to gnaw the slain. When we forget other grand truths and only remember these dreadful things, death is the king of terrors to us. Hearts are sickened and reins are loosened, because of him.

But, indeed, he is an enemy, for what comes he to do to our body ? I know he doeth that which ultimately leadeth to its betterness, but still it is that which in itself, and for the present, is not joyous, but grievous. He comes to take the light from the eyes, the hearing from the ears, the speech from the tongue, the activity from the hand, and the thought from the brain. He comes to transform a living man into a mass of putrefaction, to degrade the beloved form of brother and friend to such a condition of corruption that affection itself cries out, " Bury my dead out of my sight." Death, thou child of sin, Christ hath transformed thee marvellously, but in thyself thou art an enemy before whom flesh and blood tremble, for they know that thou art the murderer of all of woman born, whose thirst for human prey the blood of nations cannot slake.

If you think for a few moments of this enemy, you will observe some of his points of character. He is the *common* foe of all God's people, and the enemy of all men : for however some have been persuaded that they should not die, yet is there no discharge in this war ; and if in this conscription a man escapes the ballot many and many a year till his grey beard seems to defy the winter's hardest frost, yet must the man of iron yield at last. It is appointed unto all men once to die. The strongest man has no elixir of eternal life wherewith to renew his youth amid the decays of age : nor has the wealthiest prince a price wherewith to bribe destruction. To the grave must thou descend, O crowned monarch, for sceptres and shovels are akin. To the sepulchre must thou go down, O mighty man of valour, for sword and spade

are of like metal. The prince is brother to the worm, and must dwell in the same house. Of our whole race it is true, " Dust thou art, and unto dust shalt thou return."

Death is also a *subtle* foe, lurking everywhere, even in the most harmless things. Who can tell where death hath not prepared his ambuscades ? He meets us both at home and abroad ; at the table he assails men in their food, and at the fountain he poisons their drink. He waylayeth us in the streets, and he seizeth us in our beds ; he rideth on the storm at sea, and he walks with us when we are on our way upon the solid land. Whither can we fly to escape from thee, O death, for from the summit of the Alps men have fallen to their graves, and in the deep places of the earth where the miner goeth down to find the precious ore, there hast thou sacrificed many a hecatomb of precious lives. Death is a subtle foe, and with noiseless footfalls follows close at our heels when least we think of him.

He is an enemy whom *none of us will be able to avoid*, take what by-paths we may, nor can we escape from him when our hour is come. Into this fowler's nets, like the birds, we shall all fly ; in his great *seine* must all the fishes of the great sea of life be taken when their day is come. As surely as sets the sun, or as the midnight stars at length descend beneath the horizon, or as the waves sink back into the sea, or as the bubble bursts, so must we all early or late come to our end, and disappear from earth to be known no more among the living.

Sudden too, full often, are the assaults of this enemy.

> " Leaves have their time to fall,
> And flowers to wither at the north wind's breath,
> And stars to set—but all,
> Thou hast all seasons for thine own, O Death ! "

Such things have happened as for men to die without an instant's notice ; with a psalm upon their lips they have passed away ; or engaged in the daily business they have been summoned to give in their account. We have heard of one who, when the morning paper brought him news that a friend in business had died, was drawing on his boots to go to his counting-house, and observed with a laugh that as far as he was concerned, he was so busy he had no time to die. Yet, ere the words were finished, he fell forward and was a corpse. Sudden deaths are not so uncommon as to be marvels if we dwell in the centre of a large circle of mankind. Thus is death a foe not to be despised or trifled with. Let us remember all his characteristics, and we shall not be inclined to think lightly of the grim enemy whom our glorious Redeemer has destroyed.

II. Secondly, let us remember that death is AN ENEMY TO BE DESTROYED. Remember that our Lord Jesus Christ has already wrought a great victory upon death so that He has delivered us from lifelong bondage through its fear. He has not yet *destroyed death*, but he has gone very near to it, for we are told that He has " abolished death and hath brought life and immortality to light through the gospel." This surely must come very near to having destroyed death altogether.

In the first place, our Lord has subdued death in the very worst sense by having delivered His people from spiritual death. " And you hath He quickened who were dead in trespasses and sins." Once you had no divine life whatever, but the death of original depravity remained upon you, and so you were dead to all divine and spiritual things ; but now, beloved, the Spirit of God, even He that raised up Jesus Christ from the dead, has raised you up into newness of life, and you have become new creatures in Christ Jesus. In this sense death has been subdued.

Our Lord in His lifetime also conquered death by restoring certain individuals to life. There were three memorable cases in which at His bidding the last enemy resigned his prey. Our Lord went into the ruler's house, and saw the little girl who had lately fallen asleep in death, around whom they wept and lamented : He heard their scornful laughter, when He said, " She is not dead but sleepeth," and He put them all out and said to her, " Maid, arise ! " Then was the spoiler spoiled, and the dungeon door set open. He stopped the funeral procession at the gates of Nain, whence they were carrying forth a young man, " the only son of his mother, and she was a widow," and he said " Young man, I say unto thee arise." When that young man sat up and our Lord delivered him to his mother, then again was the prey taken from the mighty. Chief of all when Lazarus had laid in the grave so long that his sister said " Lord, by this time he stinketh," when, in obedience to the word, " Lazarus come forth ! " forth came the raised one with his grave-clothes still about him, but yet really quickened, then was death seen to be subservient to the Son of man. " Loose him and let him go," said the conquering Christ, and death's bonds were removed, for the lawful captive was delivered. When at the Redeemer's resurrection many of the saints arose and came out of their graves into the holy city then was the crucified Lord proclaimed to be victorious over death and the grave.

Still, brethren, these were but preliminary skirmishes and mere foreshadowings of the grand victory by which death was overthrown. The real triumph was achieved upon the cross,—

> " He hell in hell laid low ;
> Made sin, He sin o'erthrew :
> Bow'd to the grave, destroy'd it so,
> And death, by dying, slew."

When Christ died He suffered the penalty of death on the behalf of all His people, and therefore no believer now dies by way of punishment for sin, since we cannot dream that a righteous God would twice exact the penalty for one offence. Death since Jesus died is not a penal infliction upon the children of God : as such He has abolished it, and it can never be enforced. Why die the saints then ? Why, because their bodies must be changed ere they can enter heaven. " Flesh and blood " as they are " cannot inherit the kingdom of God." A divine change must take place upon the body before it will be fit for incorruption and glory ; and death and the grave are, as it were, the refining pot and the furnace by means of which the body is made ready for its future bliss. Death, it is true thou art not yet destroyed, but our living Redeemer has so changed thee that thou art no longer death, but something other than thy name ! Saints die not now, but they are dissolved and depart. Death is the loosing of the cable that the bark may freely sail to the fair havens. Death is the fiery chariot in which we ascend to God : it is the gentle voice of the Great King, who cometh into His banqueting hall, and saith " Friend, come up higher." Behold, on eagle's wings we mount, we fly, far from this land of mist and cloud, into the

eternal serenity and brilliance of God's own house above. Yes, our Lord has abolished death. The sting of death is sin, and our great Substitute has taken that sting away by His great sacrifice. Stingless, death abides among the people of God, but it so little harms them that to them " it is not death to die."

Further, Christ vanquished death and thoroughly overcame him when He rose. What a temptation one has to paint a picture of the resurrection, but I will not be led aside to attempt more than a few touches. When our great Champion awoke from His brief sleep of death and found Himself in the withdrawing-room of the grave, He quietly proceeded to put off the garments of the tomb. How leisurely He proceeded ! He folded up the napkin and placed it by itself, that those who lose their friends might wipe their eyes therewith ; and then He took off the winding sheet and laid the graveclothes by themselves that they might be there when His saints come thither, so that the chamber might be well furnished, and the bed ready sheeted and prepared for their rest. The sepulchre is no longer an empty vault, a dreary charnel, but a chamber of rest, a dormitory furnished and prepared, hung with the arras which Christ Himself has bequeathed. It is now no more a damp, dark, dreary prison ; Jesus has changed all that.

> " 'Tis now a cell where angels use
> To come and go with heavenly news."

The angel from heaven rolled away the stone from our Lord's sepulchre and let in the fresh air and light again upon our Lord, and He stepped out more than a conqueror. Death had fled. The grave had capitulated.

> " Lives again our glorious King !
> ' Where, O death, is now thy sting ? '
> Once He died our souls to save ;
> ' Where's thy victory, boasting grave ? ' "

Well, brethren, as surely as Christ rose so did He guarantee as an absolute certainty the resurrection of all His saints into a glorious life for their bodies, the life of their souls never having paused even for a moment. In this He conquered death ; and since that memorable victory, every day Christ is overcoming death, for He gives His Spirit to His saints, and having that Spirit within them they meet the last enemy without alarm : often they confront him with songs, perhaps more frequently they face him with calm countenance, and fall asleep with peace. I will not fear thee, death, why should I ? Thou lookest like a dragon, but thy sting is gone. Thy teeth are broken, oh old lion, wherefore should I fear thee ? I know thou art no more able to destroy me, but thou art sent as a messenger to conduct me to the golden gate wherein I shall enter and see my Saviour's unveiled face for ever. Expiring saints have often said that their last beds have been the best they have ever slept upon. Many of them have enquired,

> " Tell me, my soul, can this be death ? "

To die has been so different a thing from what they expected it to be, so lightsome, and so joyous ; they have been so unloaded of all care, have felt so relieved instead of burdened, that they have wondered whether this could be the monster they had been so afraid of all their days. They find it a pin's prick, whereas they feared it would prove a swordthrust : it is the shutting of the eye on earth and the opening of it in heaven, whereas they thought it would have been a stretching upon the rack, or a dreary passage through a dismal region of gloom and dread. Beloved, our exalted Lord has overcome death in all these ways.

But now, observe, that this is not the text :—the text speaks of something yet to be done. The last enemy that *shall be* destroyed is death, so that death in the sense meant by the text is not destroyed yet. He is to be destroyed, and how will that be ?

Well, I take it death will be destroyed in the sense first that, at the coming of Christ, *those who are alive and remain shall not see death.* They shall be changed ; there must be a change even to the living before they can inherit eternal life, but they shall not actually die. Do not envy them, for they will have no preference beyond those that sleep ; rather do I think theirs to be the inferior lot of the two in some respects. But they will not know death : the multitude of the Lord's own who will be alive at His coming will pass into the glory without needing to die. Thus death, as far as they are concerned, will be destroyed.

But the sleeping ones, the myriads who have left their flesh and bones to moulder back to earth, death shall be destroyed even as to them, for when the trumpet sounds they shall rise from the tomb. *The resurrection is the destruction of death.* We never taught, nor believed, nor thought that every particle of every body that was put into the grave would come to its fellow, and that the absolutely identical material would rise ; but we do say that the identical body will be raised, and that as surely as there cometh out of the ground the seed that was put into it, though in very different guise, for it cometh not forth as a seed but as a flower, so surely shall the same body rise again. The same material is not necessary, but there shall come out of the grave, aye, come out of the earth, if it never saw a grave, or come out of the sea if devoured by monsters, that selfsame body for true identity which was inhabited by the soul while here below. Was it not so with our Lord ? Even so shall it be with His own people, and then shall be brought to pass the saying that is written, " Death is swallowed up in victory. O death, where is thy sting ! O grave where is thy victory ! "

There will be this feature in our Lord's victory, that death will be fully destroyed because *those who rise will not be one whit the worse for having died.* I believe concerning those new bodies that there will be no trace upon them of the feebleness of old age, none of the marks of long and wearying sickness, none of the scars of martyrdom. Death shall not have left his mark upon them at all, except it be some glory mark which shall be to their honour, like the scars in the flesh of the Wellbeloved, which are His chief beauty even now in the eyes of those for whom His hands and feet were pierced. In this sense death shall be destroyed because he shall have done no damage to the saints at all, the very trace of decay shall have been swept away from the redeemed.

And then, finally, there shall, after this trumpet of the Lord, be no *more death,* neither sorrow, nor crying, for the former things have passed away. " Christ being raised from the dead dieth no more, death hath no more dominion over Him " ; and so also the quickened ones, His own redeemed, they too shall die no more. Oh dreadful, dreadful supposition, that they should ever have to undergo temptation or pain, or death a second time. It cannot be. " Because

I live," says Christ, " they shall live also." Yet the doctrine of the natural immortality of the soul having been given up by some, certain of them have felt obliged to give up with the eternity of future punishment the eternity of future bliss, and assuredly as far as some great proof texts are concerned, they stand or fall together. " These shall go away into everlasting punishment, and the righteous into life eternal " ; if the one state be short so must the other be : whatever the adjective means in the one case it means in the other. To us the word means endless duration in both cases, and we look forward to a bliss which shall never know end or duration. Then in the tearless, sorrowless, graveless country death shall be utterly destroyed.

III. And now last of all, and the word " last " sounds fitly in this case, DEATH IS TO BE DESTROYED LAST. Because he came in last he must go out last. Death was not the first of our foes : first came the devil, then sin, then death. Death is not the worst of enemies ; death is an enemy, but he is much to be preferred to our other adversaries. It were better to die a thousand times than to sin. To be tried by death is nothing compared with being tempted by the devil. The mere physical pains connected with dissolution are comparative trifles compared with the hideous grief which is caused by sin and the burden which a sense of guilt causes to the soul. No, death is but a secondary mischief compared with the defilement of sin. Let the great enemies go down first ; smite the shepherd and the sheep will be scattered ; let sin, and Satan, the lord of all these evils, be smitten first, and death may well be left to the last.

Notice, that death is the last enemy to each individual Christian and the last to be destroyed. Well now, if the word of God says it is the last I want to remind you of a little piece of practical wisdom,— leave him to be the last. Brother, do not dispute the appointed order, but let the last be last. I have known a brother wanting to vanquish death long before he died. But, brother, you do not want dying grace till dying moments. What would be the good of dying grace while you are yet alive ? A boat will only be needful when you reach a river. Ask for living grace, and glorify Christ thereby, and then you shall have dying grace when dying time comes. Your enemy is going to be destroyed, but not to-day. There is a great host of enemies to be fought to-day, and you may be content to let this one alone for a while. This enemy will be destroyed, but of the times and the seasons we are in ignorance ; our wisdom is to be good soldiers of Jesus Christ as the duty of every day requires. Take your trials as they come, brother ! As the enemies march up slay them, rank upon rank, but if you fail in the name of God to smite the front ranks, and say " No, I am only afraid of the rear rank," then you are playing the fool. Leave the final shock of arms till the last adversary advances, and meanwhile hold you your place in the conflict. God will in due time help you to overcome your last enemy, but meanwhile see to it that you overcome the world, the flesh, and the devil. If you live well you will die well. That same covenant in which the Lord Jesus gave you life contains also the grant of death, for " All things are yours, whether things present or things to come, or life or death, all are yours, and ye are Christ's, and Christ is God's."

Why is death left to the last ? Well, I think it is because Christ can make much use of him. The last enemy that shall be destroyed is death, because death is of great service before he is destroyed. Oh, what lessons some of us have learned from death ! " Our dying friends come o'er us like a cloud to damp our brainless ardours," to make us feel that these poor fleeting toys are not worth living for ; that as others pass away so must we also be gone, and thus they help to make us set loose by this world, and urge us to take wing and mount towards the world to come. There are, perhaps, no sermons like the deaths which have happened in our households ; the departure of our beloved friends have been to us solemn discourses of divine wisdom, which our heart could not help hearing. So Christ has spared death to make him a preacher to His saints.

And you know, brethren, that if there had been no death the saints of God would not have had the opportunity to exhibit the highest ardour of their love. Where has love to Christ triumphed most ? Why, in the death of the martyrs at the stake and on the rack. O Christ, Thou never hadst such garlands woven for Thee by human hands as they have brought Thee who have come up to heaven from the forests of persecution, having waded through streams of blood. By death for Christ the saints have glorified Him most.

So is it in their measure with saints who die from ordinary deaths ; they would have had no such test for faith and work for patience as they now have if there had been no death. Part of the reason of the continuance of this dispensation is that the Christ of God may be glorified, but if believers never died, the supreme consummation of faith's victory must have been unknown. Brethren, if I may die as I have seen some of our church members die, I court the grand occasion. I would not wish to escape death by some by-road if I may sing as they sang. If I may have such hosannas and hallelujahs beaming in my very eyes as I have seen as well as heard from them, it were a blessed thing to die. Yes, as a supreme test of love and faith, death is well respited awhile to let the saints glorify their Master.

Besides, brethren, without death we should not be so conformed to Christ as we shall be if we fall asleep in Him. If there could be any jealousies in heaven among the saints, I think that any saint who does not die, but is changed when Christ comes, could almost meet me and you, who probably will die, and say " My brother, there is one thing I have missed, I never lay in the grave, I never had the chill hand of death laid on me, and so in that I was not conformed to my Lord. But *you* know what it is to have fellowship with Him, even in His death." Did I not well say that they that were alive and remain should have no preference over them that are asleep ? I think the preference if anything shall belong to us who sleep in Jesus, and wake up in His likeness.

Death, dear friends, is not yet destroyed, because he brings the saints home. He does but come to them and whisper His message, and in a moment they are supremely blessed.

" Have done with sin and care and woe,
And with the Saviour rest."

And so death is not destroyed yet, for he answers useful purposes.

But, beloved, he is going to be destroyed. He is the last enemy of the church collectively. The church as a body has had a mass of foes to contend with, but after the resurrection we shall say, " This is the last enemy. Not another foe is left." Eternity shall roll on in ceaseless bliss. There may be changes, bringing new delights ; perhaps in the eternity to come there may be eras and ages of yet more amazing bliss, and still more superlative ecstasy ; but there shall be

" No rude alarm of raging foes,
No cares to break the last repose."

The last enemy that shall be destroyed is death, and if the last be slain there can be no future foe. The battle is fought and the victory is won for ever. And who hath won it ? who but the Lamb that sitteth on the throne, to whom let us all ascribe honour, and glory, and majesty, and power, and dominion, and might, for ever and ever. The Lord help us in our solemn adoration. Amen.

DYING DAILY

" I die daily."—1 Corinthians xv. 31.

IN a certain sense we all do this. The very moment we begin to live we commence to die. We are like hour-glasses ; there are fewer sands left to run from the very moment they begin to trickle down. The whole of our life is like an ebbing tide : our first months and years may look like advancing waves, but the whole is retreating, and by-and-by the living flood will be replaced by the mire of death.

" Our pulse, like muffled drums, are beating
Funeral marches to the tomb " ;

Or, as Watts words it—

" Every beating pulse we tell,
Leaves but the number less."

This is no land of the living, but the land of the dying, and this so-called life is but one protracted act of death. This is not our rest, our soul is ever on the wing ; like the swallows, we must depart for another land. Life is a long descent to the valley of the shadow of death, it shelves gradually to the precipice, and no man can prevent his feet from sliding down it every hour. We fly like arrows to that common target of mankind—the grave. So that we may all say in the words of the text, " I die daily."

Of some also this may be affirmed in a very painful and unhappy sense. They die daily because they feel a thousand deaths in fearing one. They are those of whom the apostle writes, " who through fear of death were all their lifetime subject to bondage." This nightmare oppresses them and breaks their rest ; this ghost stalks before them at all hours, and makes life grim with forebodings ; this gall-drop makes all their pleasant things bitter. They are afraid to die, and yet are so fascinated by death that they cannot take their eyes off it. They cannot shake off the chill horror of the grave, their clothes seem to them to smell of the vault, and their bread tastes of the charnel. They are slaves to a fear whose chains are heavy. These timorous doves ought to remember that Jesus Christ came into this world on purpose that He might deliver such as they are. It was never His intention that any of His people should be subject to the fear of death, nor ought they to be, nor indeed would they be if they walked by faith, for what can there be in death for a Christian to fear? " The sting of death is sin," but that is pardoned ; " the strength of sin is the law," but Christ has fulfilled it. What is dying but departing to be with Christ, which is far better ? And why should a man fear that which is far better for him, which will rid him of all his ills, admit him into unlimited blessedness, take him away from all fear and all care, and conduct him to the fulness of the glory which is laid up in Christ Jesus ? I trust you and I may never have to moan out, in that mournful and gloomy sense, " I die daily," but with holy joy may we look forward to the hour of our departure, which is so near at hand.

Paul used this expression in an heroic sense, to which I fear you and I are not very likely to attain. He said, " I die daily," because every day he deliberately put his life in jeopardy for the cause of Jesus Christ. One day he went into the Jewish synagogue, knowing that in all probability they would drag him out, scourge him with rods, or, perhaps, in fanatic zeal, stone him with stones. Another day he was found in the street preaching to a multitude of idolaters, and denouncing their gods, irritating them by exposing their vices, and by advancing truths which were novelties, and so contrary to their prejudices that they could not endure them. Behold him often crossing the sea in a frail barque, or passing over rugged mountains, among robbers ; in perils from the mountain-torrents, and from cold and nakedness. In all places he lived the life of one whose neck was always on the block, who stood ready at any minute to offer up himself a sacrifice for Christ. In these more silken days, we cannot run such serious risks, and it is to our shame that there are some who are not willing to run even the little risks which the times may demand. We know professors who cannot imperil their business by an avowal of their faith, and others who cannot venture the breaking of some fond connection for the sake of the cross of Christ. Alas ! there are many who are ashamed of Jesus, because a father or a mother or a brother might perhaps ridicule them or sneer at them. They are ashamed to bear the loss of anything, when our apostle rejoiced to suffer the loss of all things, and did count them but dung that he might win Christ. May the heroic age of Christianity return to us, and even if it should be necessary that the furnace should be heated once again, yet if God's gold may but glow with that clear, bright lustre which it exhibited in the former days, we may well be satisfied with the fury of the blazing coals. The persecuted were happy men despite their sorrows, and honoured men notwithstanding their shame ; they were earth's princes, heaven's peers ; for they could say that for Christ's sake they every day were delivered unto death, but did rejoice and were exceeding glad that they were privileged to suffer for the cross of Christ.

Our text we shall now take in a practical spiritual sense. Neither fixing our minds upon its universal sense, nor yet upon its mournful nor even upon its heroic meaning, but taking it in a spiritual way, common to all the saints, " I die daily." Our subject this morning is the art and mystery of dying every day.

First, we shall notice some *previous necessaries* for this art ; secondly, we shall speak upon *wherein this art consists* ; and thirdly, upon *the great benefits* which will accrue to those who shall learn to die daily.

I. First, there are CERTAIN THINGS PREVIOUSLY NECESSARY before a man can be a scholar to this great art of dying every day.

The first necessary is, that *he must be willing to die* ; for if he shall shrink at death, and covet life, and dread even the thought of departure, it will be a miserable necessity to him that he will have to die one day, but he will not be at all likely to be an apt pupil in the art of dying to-day, and to-morrow, and the next day, and every day that he lives. With a natural disinclination, with an awful fear, and a terrible shrinking from the very fact of dissolution, he will not be at all forward to bring his mind to find delight and satisfaction in contemplation of the grave. In order that a man should be willing to die daily he must be a saved man, he must have his sins forgiven, and he must know it by infallible assurance, or else death will be to him of all things the most terrible. He must be clad in the righteousness of Jesus Christ as with armour of proof, and he must know that he has it on, or else death will be a dart that will afflict him terribly, and from it he will shrink with all his soul. He must be a man perfectly at peace with his Creator, not ashamed to look into his Maker's face in Christ Jesus, nor afraid to stand before Jehovah's solemn bar. He must, in fact, have looked by faith to the blood-stained tree, and he must have seen Jesus making a full atonement there for sin ; he must have accepted that atonement as being made for him ; he must be resting on it with an unstaggering faith, believing that all his sin is put away through that one dread sacrifice. He must know that the righteousness of Christ is wrapped about him, and that he is accepted in the Beloved, or else to talk to him of dying daily would be somewhat analogous to inviting the thief to be hanged daily, or asking a culprit to be transported daily. It will be enough, he thinks, to endure on e that dread sharp stroke which will separate him from his joys ; he certainly will not foredate and anticipate the period, but be glad to forget it while he can, crying, " Let us drown care, and live while we live."

Yet more is necessary than this to make a good student of the art of daily dying. A man must not only submissively await his dissolution, but *he must be even desirous of departure, and cheered with the hope of the better land.* A hard thing, say you, yet not impossible. Impossible perhaps to nature, for it shrinks from the hard thought of dissolution, but possible enough to grace, for grace overlooks the temporary separation, anticipating the bright resurrection and the everlasting glory. To an ungodly man, to die can never be a thing to be desired, for what remaineth to him after death ? His possessions go from him. Like birds that have rested for a little while upon the field, but take to their wings when the traveller claps his hands, so all the worldling's riches must take to themselves wings and fly away, and what remaineth to the sinner in the next world ? A fearful looking for of judgment, and of fiery indignation. Ungodly men and women, you know what you have to expect when you shall be called to the unknown land, to face the Judge upon his throne. You will be condemned, banished, accursed, executed, destroyed for ever. It is not possible that death should be a welcome thing to drunkards and unclean persons, or even to merely moral men. But the believer, what of him ? To him death is gain. What he loses of comfort here is made up to him a thousandfold by the joys of the hereafter. He knows that for him there is the crown of triumph and the palm of victory ; for him the harp of ecstatic joy ; for him the robe of immaculate purity ; for him a place at the right hand of God, even the Father, in eternal security, and ineffable delight. Hence the Christian not only regards death as a necessity through which he hopes to be supported as a patient through a painful operation, but he looks for his departure as an heir looks forward to the day of his majority, as the bride anticipates her wedding-day.' It is the time when his manhood shall burst its shell, when his imprisoned soul shall snap its fetters, when that which was long like a shrivelled corn shall bud and blossom, and bear sweet fruit in the garden of God. When he is in his right mind and his faith is in active exercise, he longs to depart and to be with Christ, which is far better. Endowed with such a longing, he becomes an apt pupil in the art of dying daily.

Once more, if a man would learn to die daily, it is necessary that *he should have a good understanding, and a clear knowledge as to what death really is*, and what are the matters that follow upon it. Nothing is more becoming our study than the departure of our souls from this mortal stage to the immortal glory. What is it to die ? Is it to cease to be ? If it were so, then indeed we should be idiotic to speak of dying daily. To die ! is it to part with every comfort, and lose every joy ? If it were so, and we had to be driven forth from the body as naked spirits, houseless, restless, drifted about with ever-lasting winds, we might indeed be excused if we shut our eyes to the dreary prospect. To die is nothing, but for the soul to be separated from the body, the body remaining to rest in the grave and moulder back to mother earth, the soul ascending to God who gave it, to be at once with Jesus, immediately in paradise, without the body, a disembodied spirit, naked for a time, but yet most sweetly blessed. To die is, in its after consequences, to wait a little in a state of bliss, and then at the trump of the archangel to return to put on the body yet again— the selfsame body which was buried, the same in identity but marvellously changed—as changed as the flower from the seed, or the crocus with its golden cup from the fashionless bulb which was put into the soil. I say our souls shall come back to their bodies to a new marriage. The spirit and the body shall be knit together once again, so that our manhood shall be again entire, body, soul, and spirit, all being in glory even as we are here on earth, but far more gloriously developed. Believers in Christ know that the first resurrection delivers them from all fear of the second death. We shall reign with Christ upon the earth : a thousand years of glory shall be given unto the saints ; on this selfsame globe in which they suffered with their Master they shall triumph with Him. Then in the last time, when Jesus shall have delivered up the kingdom unto God, even the Father, then the people of God shall reign for ever and ever in unsurpassed and unimaginable delight.

This it is, then, to die. There is nothing dreadful at all about it ; it is altogether the very simplest of operations, although it involves afterwards the most wonderful of results. I suppose that to die is but a pin's prick, or less than that. The pains which we call dying pains are really pains caused by life's struggling to hold its own. Death gives us no pain whatever ; it is the anodyne that lulls us into a blessed slumber ; it is the obstinate grasp of life within us which causes all the agony of separation ; but as soon as life relaxes its stern grip grief is ended. As for death, his hand is gentle and tender, and to those who know him his voice is musical and his countenance delightsome.

Now, Christian, if you can get an intelligent view of what dying is, and a clear view of what will follow dying, you will then be able to learn to die daily, and by the grace of God you may yet be able to achieve it, and every day ere you have mingled with the din of this world's turmoil, you may bathe in Jordan's river, and be refreshed thereby.

II. Secondly, WHEREIN DOES DYING DAILY CONSIST ? Many things go to make up this high achievement.

The first is *to consider with much care every day the certainty of death* to all those who shall not remain at the coming of Christ, and to let the certainty of our own death or change go with us as an undivided companion. We ought always to feel that we are mortal ; it should be to us a garment that we never shake off ; the fact that we are here but as sojourners and wayfarers, should be painted on our eyeballs. We are never right-hearted when we imagine that we are abiding inhabitants of this land. We are but strangers and sojourners in it ; we are only right when we act as such. The Lord knowing that we should try to shake off the remembrance of death has so helped us as almost to force us to it. We have before us the frequent departures of others : the path to the cemetery is well trodden. It is well for us that we live not always in the house of feasting : the grave's brink is a healthier resort than the table of luxury. Bethink you how often you have seen strong men who appeared to be as likely to live as yourselves taken away in their strength ! How often have we marked others sickening gradually before our eyes like slowly fading lilies ! God rings the funeral knell in our ears, and bids us remember that the bell may next toll for us. Our dying friends cast their shadows over us, and cool our worldly heats and madnesses. In the presence of the corpse we gather up our skirts, and gird up the loins of our mind, because as surely as the soul is gone from yonder lifeless body we too must follow. We have no lease of life, we have no earthly immortality guaranteed to us. Let us then remember the myriads who have marched before us ; let us keep their track before our eye, feeling that we are wending our way to the selfsame goal.

The whole of nature around us also helps us to recollect that we are mortal. Look at the year. It is born amid the songs of birds and the beauty of upspringing flowers, it comes to its ripeness amid luscious fruits and shouts of harvest home ; but anon the old age of autumn comes, and a lamentation is heard, " The harvest is passed and the summer is ended." Amidst the fall of decaying leaves, and the howling of the cold winds of winter the year finds its end. So too with every day. Well does Herbert sing—

" Sweet day, so calm, so bright,
The bridal of the earth and sky,
The dew must weep thy fall to-night,
For thou must die."

Every flower we see lavishing its fragrance on the breeze, trembles because it hears the footsteps of death. It blooms that it may wither ; " Its root is ever in its grave, and it must die." Where see you immortal things beneath the moon ? Lift up your eyes, look where ye may, see you not everywhere change, and mutability, and departure, written upon nature's brow ! and all this God hangeth up, as it were, as a notice upon the wall, like the mystic characters which amazed Belshazzar, that we may not dare to forget that it is appointed unto all men once to die. Nay, as if this were not all, not only is nature full of helps to make us familiar with the grave, but our own bodies also tell us of our appointed change. What is that grey hair but the beginning, the first sign, the foretoken of the coming winter which shall freeze the life current within the vein and chill the heart itself ? What is that loosened tooth but a part of the fabric crumbling to let us know that the whole tenement must soon come down ? What are those aches and pains, and what that decay of the eyesight, and that dulness of hearing, what those tottering knees, and wherefore that staff, but that we may receive clear warnings that the whole tabernacle is shaking in the rude winds of time, and must soon totter to its fall ? The Lord will not suffer us to win a freehold here, but He puts affliction into our family, and disease into our flesh, in order that we may seek after a better country, even a heavenly. Let me exhort you then, beloved brethren in Christ, seeing you have all these mementoes, to keep the lamp of the sepulchre always burning in your chambers, and to be well acquainted with the shroud and the winding-sheet. Every time you take off your clothes at night, think how you must be unrobed for your last narrow bed ; and when you put on your garments in the morning, familiarize yourself with the time of the resurrection, when you shall put on your glittering garments, in which you are to rejoice for ever. Do not, I pray you, put aside these reflections because at first sight they may seem sombre. Familiarize yourself a little with the grey tints of death, and they will brighten before your eyes ; and ere long you will see a transcendent beauty in such meditations to which you would not be a stranger if you could. Thus the first part of dying daily is to think constantly of death.

The next part of dying daily is to *put your soul, by faith, through the whole process of death.* It is a wise thing to sit down quietly and to picture your departure. You need not stretch your fancy much. You have seen the like with others ; you can picture it for yourselves. There you lie, upon that bed grown hard with weeks of weariness, and loving watchers whisper in the silent chamber ; they are anxious that you should not catch the sound, but your quick ear hears it, and you wistfully enquire " What is it the physician says ? " You gather, though they tell you not, that you must soon depart. As a believer in Jesus you are glad to hear it. You have had enough of this world. You are like a child tired out with its day's play, and you are glad to fall asleep upon your father's breast. The solemn article comes nearer and nearer, the pulse is fainter, you have enough consciousness left to perceive that the eye is being glazed, and outward objects are lost ; perhaps you have also enough strength to sing your last song, for heaven has met you while you are yet here, and your soul is flooded with a joy you never knew before. You have evidently arrived at the border land, for there are flowers beneath your feet, the like of which never bloomed in the wilderness, and you hear songs such as you never before heard in the desert. Then you yourself begin to sing. Perhaps it is some such song as this—

" And when ye hear my eye-strings break,
How sweet the minutes roll ;
A mortal paleness on my cheek,
But glory in my soul " ;

or perhaps you burst out with a song concerning the new Jerusalem, " your happy home," name ever dear to you, and rejoice that you are about to end your labours in the joy and peace which remaineth for the people of God. The solemn instant has come, but will you be able precisely to distinguish it ? May there not be so sweet a gradation from the earnest of the Spirit to the bliss itself that at no exact moment shall there be a wrench from time to eternity ? All may be so divinely ordered that pilgrims may advance by degrees from the tabernacle of earth to the temple of heaven. There will be a matchless change, but it will not necessarily be a shock to the spirit ; the folding gates of paradise may be opened by degrees, that our eyes may be gradually prepared to endure the excessive glory. But while we linger, the spirit has mounted. Now, oh, joy of joys ! you are in *His* bosom who loved you with an everlasting love. The hand that embraces you wears the nailprint still, and as you bow to kiss those sacred feet, and cast the crown which has been placed upon your head before that Man, that God, you see that the feet are the feet of Him who was nailed to the tree for you. What joy ! what blessedness to see that your Father smiles upon you ! The Spirit of God fills you and you know Him, and you grieve Him no more. The Son of God gives you to partake in all His glory, for you are with Him where He is. Now be sure that you rehearse such thoughts as these as though they were sacred drama in which you are soon to take your part. Traverse the azure way. Plume your wings for the last solemn flight. Let faith like a courier march before to track the way. Every semblance of affectation upon dying beds is shocking. I have never been able to admire the oft-quoted death-bed of Addison. " Come," said he, " and see how a Christian can die." It seems to me too like a brag to be a fitting utterance for a soul humbly resting at the cross-foot, and looking out over the black waters which fringe the eternal shore. The true idea of a Christian's dying speech is a humble and gracious witness to those who look around, that though a sinner, he has found peace with God through the precious blood of Jesus, and would have others trust in the same Saviour. Prepare to deliver such a testimony. Often picture yourself as bidding adieu to every earthborn thing. Anticipate the final stroke, the upward mounting, the soaring through tracts unknown, the sight of the judgment throne, the eternal beatific vision. So will you die daily.

But we have not come into the soul of the matter yet. The way to die daily, practically, is *to hold this world with a very loose hand.* Birdlime so much abounds. When a man wins a little gain in this world it sticks to him, holds him, prevents his aspiring to heavenly things, and holds him bound to earth. Our dear friends, and our beloved children, are all strong chains, binding our eagle-souls to the rock of earth. "Ah!" said one, as he was shown a rich man's ample house and luxuriant gardens, "these are the things that make it hard to die"; and I suppose they are. When they are misused and wrongly applied, they birdlime us; they hold us to the soil when we would fain mount. But, brethren, ye must not be the servants of the present. Look on your lands as a dying man would look on them. Look on your children and the comforts of your fireside, and your little savings, as so much hoar-frost to vanish in the sun. Look on your hourly cares and daily joys as on things which perish in the using; mere visions of the night; things that flit at the rising of the sun. You will never enjoy earth rightly unless you know it to be a poor mutable thing. Earthliness eats as doth a canker, and if you become so great a fool as to think that mortal things are eternal, or that you yourself will long endure, you will reserve for yourself many sorrows. See you not how the glittering dew-drops exhale as the day grows old—such and so fleeting are human joys. Mark how the meteor marks the brow of night, and anon is seen no more—such and so hasty is mortal bliss. Hold not earth's treasures with too firm a grasp. Give them all up to your Father, and use them as temporary comforts borrowed for awhile, to be returned anon. Our bereavements would not be half so sharp if we always viewed our friends as being lent to us. A man does not cry when he has to return a tool which he has borrowed. No; but as an honest man, he knew he borrowed it; he never called it his own, and he hands it back, thankful that he has had it so long. When you weep, who have lost your friends, you do well; but if you carry that weeping to repining, you ought to recollect the mercy of God in letting you retain these dear ones at all, and in sparing them to you so long; and you should mourn that a rebellious spirit should so reign in you as to make you lament, because your God takes back His own. Gracious souls, rejoice to say, "The Lord gave, and the Lord hath taken away; blessed be the name of the Lord." To die daily, then, is to hold this world with a loose hand and to look upon earthly possessions as fickle joys.

To die daily, again, is *to test our hope and our experience very solemnly every day.* Alas! for that evil habit of taking our religion for granted, of looking back to some period a few years ago, and believing that we were then converted, and reckoning that it must be all right now because of something that happened then! Brethren, it is most mischievous to live in the past and to be afraid at any moment to try our faith by present tests. We may live on experience if we will use experience in its proper place, but any man who is afraid to search present evidences and to try the foundation of his faith before God to-day, is treating his soul most wretchedly. How would you like to die to-day, dear friend? would you like to die with a hope too weak and tender to endure to be questioned? Can you enter into eternity with a hope that you dare not put into the crucible? Oh, no! you feel you want sure work when it comes to the last; you need a safe and stable foundation to build your soul upon in

the trying moment. Well, then, beloved, see that your hope is stable now. Each day examine yourself whether you be in the faith; whether you have really repented of sin; whether you have actually and truly laid hold of Jesus Christ; search; see whether the root of the matter is in you, and the fruits of the Spirit proceeding from you, whether God dwells in you, whether you walk after the flesh or walk after the Spirit. I would not foment doubts and fears, but I would above all things press professors to avoid presumption. The man who is in a sound business does not object to overhaul his stock and examine his books; but the man to whom bankruptcy is imminent generally seeks to shut his eyes to his actual position. O sirs, if you are right with God, you will desire to be quite sure, you will not flinch at heart-searching preaching, you will be anxious to be put into the sieve and to be tried even as by fire; your prayer will be, "Cleanse me, O God, from secret faults! search me and try me, and know my ways!" You will not be among those who hunt after prophets with smooth tongues, who prophesy in gentle strains. You will not desire to have your cradle rocked that you may be lulled into presumption, but you will labour to make sure work for eternity, lest you suffer irreparable loss. Beloved, do this every day, look into the glass of the Word, and see what manner of men you are, and purge yourselves from all filthiness of the flesh and of the spirit. Put yourself under the lash of the severest texts of Scripture, and by all means labour that you be not deceived, for God will not be mocked, but will deal with you according to fact.

To die daily, it will be necessary that you *come every day, just as you did at conversion, to the cross of Christ, as a poor guilty sinner, and rest in Him.* I do not know anything that is more delightful, more necessary, or more profitable, than a renewal of the look of faith. I have always found, when I have been in fear as to my safety, or have had hard thoughts of death pressing heavily upon me, that my only resort has been a humble resort to the atonement. Carey ordered that they should write on his tombstone—

"A guilty, weak, and helpless worm,
On Christ's kind arms I fall;
He is my strength and righteousness,
My Jesus, and my all."

Here is an epitaph for each one of us. Just come with nothing of your own, no good feelings and no good works, fall before the cross of Jesus, and rest there. Take Jesus to be everything that God's law and your conscience can require. Methinks, dear friends, this is the way to die daily; and if you can always live as an empty sinner filled with the fulness of Christ, as a lost sinner saved wholly by a precious Saviour, you are then fit to live and fit to die.

But I have not quite concluded. To die daily the Christian should *take care to be always in such a place and state that he should not be ashamed to die therein.* Hence, the possessor of faith in Jesus Christ has no licence to be found in the places of ungodly and unclean amusement. How would he like to die there? The old story has it that the devil once carried off a very hopeful young man, hurrying him on a sudden to hell. A monk of great saintliness called after the devil, "You have taken one of mine; you have no business with him!"

"Well," said Satan, " I found him in the theatre ; he was on my premises, and I took him." I should not wonder if many a professor is carried off in that style. If professors of religion go astray into the purlieus of iniquity, no wonder if they are shot at by that old hunter after souls. Where your treasure is there your heart is. Tell me where you go to find your amusement, and I will tell you what you are, for where a man finds his highest joy, there his heart most truly abides. It may serve you as a guide when you have to question yourself, " Ought I to do this, or to go to this or that place ? " then ask yourself, " Should I be prepared to die in such company and in such an occupation ? " If you could not, leave it alone ; if you would, you may fairly go.

The Christian, also, should never be in a state of temper in which he would be ashamed to die. Who would like to die bearing malice against any man ? Who would wish to die with hard thoughts of a neighbour ? Who would like to die in a passion ? You have no business to get into a passion at any time, but to die daily. Thus the aim and strife of a Christian should be to keep himself in that delightfully equable frame of mind, in which he should be prepared at any moment to stand before his God with his present emotions and feelings upon him. You say that is hard work : so it is, but you have a glorious helper—the Holy Ghost shall enable you, and by His power you may accomplish miracles of holiness.

To die daily, *a Christian man should have all his affairs in such a condition that he is ready to die.* I admire that habit in Whitfield, who was a man so very orderly that he would not go to bed at night until everything was in order, for he said,“ I should not like to die with a pair of gloves out of place ” ; and yet I know some believers who have not made their wills, and if they were to die to-day, and they may, their property would go far otherwise than it ought to do, and a wife whom they love so well might be put to serious suffering. A Christian man has no right to leave his affairs in a tangle. If he careth not for the affairs of his own household, he is worse than a heathen man and a publican. Many traders keep their business transactions in such a confusion that if they were taken away, their very character might be impugned ; but such should not be. We must set our house in order, for we must die, and not live. We should watch, because the Master comes as a thief, and a good servant would fain have all things in good order at his lord's appearing.

So should it be with all our acts towards God. Some of you have not yet fulfilled the Master's command with regard to baptism. Now, if you died unbaptized you would be saved, but still I am sure you would not wish to be taken away till you had fulfilled your Master's bidding. Make haste, then, and delay not to keep His commandments.

Some of you have dear children who are unconverted, and you have not spoken to them about their souls ; now, if you were called this afternoon to sleep upon the bed of death, I am sure you would wish that you had delivered your soul fully to these dear ones. This afternoon, then, call them into your room and plead with them. A thousand other things may press upon your conscience, but you have been putting them off ; attend to them, I pray you, at once, as a dying man should do.

Who would wish to die with a duty left undone ? I would like to depart when the day's work is quite finished, my last sheaf reaped. I would desire to go home to my house when I have tended my corner of the vineyard, and pruned the vines, and cleaned my pruning knife, and put it in its place. It must be so delightful to feel, " It is all done ; I may just go home, for I have fulfilled, as a hireling, my day." It is said that that venerable divine, Watts Wilkinson, asked of God that he might never know consciously what it was to die, and he died, as many of you will recollect, in his sleep ; so that his admission into heaven must have been almost without any recognition of death. In his case death was swallowed up in victory. Perhaps such an end may be given to us. I would choose so to die, that I should have nothing to disturb my mind of matters left undone, but be found waiting and ready. If we are thus prepared, we have acquired the art of dying daily.

III. What would be THE PRACTICAL BENEFIT OF such daily dying ? *It will help us to live well,* and this is no small matter. We should not be covetous and grasping if we knew that the heap would soon melt or we should be taken from it. We should not be so impetuous, and attach so much importance to trifles, if we felt that there were grander things close at our heels. We should not be so obstinate, and take so long to be persuaded to Christian duty, if we felt that the time was short, and it behoved us to get much done in a little time. If we saw our candle flickering in its socket, we should be far more diligent. We should not be so grovelling and so earthly, if we saw that the world is founded on the floods, and therefore is utterly unstable. Next to living close to Christ, I do not know of any better prescription for overcoming worldly-mindedness than this dying every day. He whose mind anticipates a departure to be with Jesus, is armed with weapons for warring a good warfare.

But mark, brethren, the best practical effect is that *it would help us to die.* No man would find it difficult to die who died every day. He would have practised it so often, that he would only have to die but once more ; like the singer who has been through his rehearsals, and is perfect in his part, and has but to put forth the notes once for all, and have done. Happy are they who every morning go down to Jordan's brink, and wade into the stream in fellowship with Christ, dying in the Lord's death, being crucified on His cross, and raised in His resurrection. They, when they shall climb their Pisgah, shall behold nothing but what has been long familiar to them, as they have studied the map of death.

I do not know how wide the benefits of dying daily may be, but they seem to me to be commensurate with the whole period of human existence. You young people, you would not be likely to plunge into youthful gaieties to your own damage, if you felt that you might die while yet you are young. That wild oat sowing would never cause you a harvest of regrets if you felt that you might perish in the midst of sin. Graves are often short trenches for little prattlers. Beware, ye boys and girls. You men of middle age, how it would check you in that eager pursuit after gold, that hasting to be rich which never leaves a man innocent, if you felt that it is little matter after all to gain wealth since so soon you must be parted from it. And you who totter on a staff, I cannot conceive of anything which would keep you in a holier frame of mind, or in a happier and calmer state than to be always dying the death of Jesus that you might live His life.

Put the Christian man in any position, and this art of dying daily will be useful to him. Is he rich ? He will not be purse proud, because he knows that he must soon be removed from all his treasures. Is he poor ? He will not murmur, for he recollects the streets of gold which are so speedily to be his portion. This is useful to a Christian in all pursuits. If he is seeking after knowledge, as he may, he will mingle with it the knowledge of Christ crucified, for he knows that all else will not serve him. If he be toiling for a livelihood, as he may and as he should, he will seek first the kingdom of God and His righteousness, because these things last when all else shall perish like faded leaves.

Make a believer a king or a pauper, and the art of dying daily will help him in either position ; and whether he shall rule as a potentate, or smart as a slave, daily dying will be an equal benefit to his soul. Put him under every temptation, and this will help him, for he will not be tempted by the offers of so brief a happiness—his soul has a grip upon eternal realities, and vain shows it utterly despises. " See here, tempter," saith he, " I have a kingdom which cannot pass away ; vain is your offer of the kingdoms of this world. See here, foul fiend, I have the beauty and the joy which never can fade : wherefore tempt ye me with these vanities, these painted nothings ? " Above temptation's billows the believer lifts his head with calm joy, because he breathes the atmosphere of heaven. Daily dying is as useful to the saint in his joys as in his griefs, in his exaltations as in his depressions. It is a blessed thing for him in the vale and on the mountain, in strength and in sickness, on the battlefield of activity or in the hospital of suffering. He shall be tutored for immortality, trained for bliss, fitted for heaven, by learning to die daily.

God teach us this art, and He shall have the glory of it. Amen.

SENTENCE OF DEATH, THE DEATH OF SELF-TRUST

" But we had the sentence of death in ourselves, that we should not trust in ourselves, but in God which raiseth the dead."—2 Corinthians i. 9.

WE are justified, dear friends, in speaking about our own experience when the mention of it will be for the benefit of others. Especially is this the case with leaders in the church such as Paul ; for their experience is rich and deep, and the rehearsal of it comes with great weight, and is peculiarly valuable. We are all the better when we are distressed for discovering that such an one as Paul was also subject to heaviness : we feel safe in following the line of conduct which was marked out by the great apostle, and we are hopeful that if he came out of his troubles which were so great, we may also be delivered out of ours which are comparatively so little. These footprints on the sand of time help us to take heart. By tracing the footsteps of the flock, we are helped to return to the fold and to the Shepherd. It would have been a great calamity if such men as David and Paul had, through a fear of seeming egotistical, withheld from us a sight of their inner selves. God has been pleased to fill a large part of the Bible with biographies and histories of human actions, in order that we who are men ourselves may learn from them. Where a biography concerns mainly the inner rather than the outer life, as in the Psalms and in Paul's epistles, we are all the more strengthened, instructed, directed, and comforted, for it is in the inner life that we are most perplexed, and most in danger of going astray. God grant us grace to make good use of the treasure of experience which is stored up for us in His Word ! How rich, how varied, how admirably selected ! If one man can learn by the life of another, surely we ought to learn from such memorable lives as those immortalized in the Scriptures. Especially may we see ourselves as in a mirror while we steadily look into the heart of Paul.

As to our own experience of trial and of delivering mercy, it is sent for our good, and we should endeavour to profit to the utmost by it : but it was never intended that it should end with our private and personal benefit. In the kingdom of God no man liveth unto himself. We are bound to comfort others by the comfort wherewith the Lord hath comforted us. We are under solemn obligation to seek out mourners, and such as are in tried circumstances, that we may communicate to them the cheering testimony which we are able personally to bear to the love and faithfulness of God. Our Lord has handed out to us spiritual riches of joy that we may communicate thereof to others who are in need of consolation through great tribulation. You may think that you are not called upon to preach, and possibly you may neither have the ability nor the opportunity for such public witness-bearing ; but your experience is a treasure, of which you are the trustee, and you are bound by the law of gratitude to make use of all you know, all you have felt, all you have learned by personal experience for the comforting and the upbuilding of your brethren. To be reticent is sometimes to be treacherous : you may be found unfaithful to your charge unless you endeavour to improve for the general good the dealings of the Lord with your soul. I would exhort every Christian to reflect the light which falls upon him. Brother, echo thy Master's voice faithfully and clearly. What the Lord has whispered to thee in thine ear in closets, that do thou proclaim according to thine ability upon the housetops. It thou hast found honey, eat of it ; yet eat not the feast alone, but call in others who can appreciate its sweetness that they may rejoice with thee. If thou hast discovered a well, drink and quench thy thirst ; but hasten forthwith to call the whole caravan, that every traveller may drink also. If thou hast been sick, and thou hast been healed, tell the glad news to all sick folk around thee, and let them know where they too may find a cure. Peradventure thy telling of the news may have more weight with men than all our preachings : they know thee, and have seen the change which grace has wrought in thee, and thou wilt by thine own experience give them proof and evidence which they cannot gainsay. May the Holy Ghost help thee in this thing.

Let this stand for the preface to our sermon, and let us learn, once for all, that, as Paul used his experience for the comfort and edification of the churches, so is every believer called upon to use his experience for the benefit of his fellow Christians.

The particular experience of which Paul speaks was a certain trial, or probably series of trials, which he endured in Asia. You know how he was stoned at Lystra, and how he was followed by his malicious countrymen from town to town wherever he went, that they might excite the mob against him. You recollect the uproar at Ephesus, and the constant danger to which Paul was exposed from perils of all kinds ; but it must not be forgotten that he appears to have been suffering at the same time grievous sickness of body, and that the whole together caused very deep depression of mind. His tribulations abounded : without were fightings and within were fears. I call to your notice the strong expressions which he uses in the eighth verse : " We were pressed," he says. The word is such as you would use if you were speaking of a cart loaded with sheaves, till it could not bear up under the weight : it is over-loaded, and threatens to break down and fall by the way. Or the word might be used if you spoke of a man who was weighted with too great a burden, under which he was ready to fall : or perhaps, better still, if you were speaking of a ship which had taken too much cargo, and sank nearly to the water's edge, looking as if it must sink altogether through excessive pressure. Paul says that this was his condition of mind when he was in Asia,—" We were pressed." To strengthen the language he adds, " out of measure." He was pressed out of measure ; he could convey no idea of the degree of pressure put upon him—it seemed to be beyond the measure of his strength. All trials, we are taught in the Scripture, are sent to us in measure, and so were Paul's, but for the time being he himself could see no limit to them, and he seemed to be quite crushed. Paul could not tell how much he was tried ; he could not calculate the pressure ; it was more severe than he could estimate. So great, so heavy was the burden upon his mind, that he gave up calculating its weight. Then he adds another word, " above strength," because a man may be pressed out of measure, and yet he may have such remarkable strength that he may bear up under all. The posts, and bars, and gates of Gaza must have pressed Samson, and they must have pressed him out of measure, but still not beyond his strength, because gigantic force was given to those mighty limbs of his, so that he carried readily what would have crushed another man. Paul says that the pressure put upon him was beyond his strength, he was quite unable to cope with it, and his spirits so failed him that he adds, " insomuch that we despaired even of life." He gave himself up for a dead man, for no way of escape was visible to him. Into whatsoever town he entered he was followed by the Jews ; the fickle mob soon turned against him ; even the converts were not always faithful. He had been stoned and beaten with rods, and men had sworn to take his life. Perils of robbers beset him in lonely

places, while tumult and assault befell him in the cities. Meanwhile, the thorn in his flesh worried him, afflictions and cares of all kinds weighed upon him, and altogether his mind was bowed down under the pressure which had come upon him. What a deep bass there is in this note, " We were pressed out of measure, above strength, insomuch that we despaired even of life " ! May we be spared so grievous a condition, or if that cannot be, may we be profited by it.

We shall in the sermon of this morning, as the Holy Spirit, the Comforter, may help us, endeavour to show the reason for such affliction, and the good effect of it. First, I shall direct your attention to *the disease* mentioned in the text as one to be prevented by the sentence of death—" that we should not trust in ourselves." Secondly, we shall dwell for a little upon *the treatment*, " we had the sentence of death in ourselves " ; and, thirdly, we will observe *the cure*, " we should not trust in ourselves, but in God which raiseth the dead."

I. The first point is THE DISEASE—the tendency to trust in ourselves.

And we remark upon it, first, that this is *a disease to which all men are liable, for even Paul was in danger of it.* I do not say that Paul did trust in himself, but that he might have done so, and would have done so, if it had not been for the Lord's prudent dealings with him both in the matter of this great trial in Asia and in the incident of the thorn in the flesh. Where a sharp preventive is used it is clear that a strong liability exists. My brethren, I should have thought that Paul was the last man to be in danger of trusting in himself : so singularly converted, so remarkably clear in his views of the gospel ; indeed, so thorough in his faith, so intense in his zeal, so eminent in his humility was Paul that all could see that his reliance was upon grace alone. No writer that ever lived has set in so clear a light the fact that all things are of God, and that we must walk by faith and depend alone upon God if we would find salvation and eternal life : and yet you see, my brethren, it was possible that the great teacher of grace should have trusted in himself. He was a man in whose life we see no sort of self-confidence. I cannot recall anything that he did or said which looks like vanity or pride. He exhibits deep humility of spirit, and great faith in God, but he evidently has no confidence in himself—such confidence he is always disclaiming. He looks upon his own works and his own righteousness as dross and dung, that he may win Christ ; and when he does speak of himself it is generally with special self-denials—" I, yet not I, but the grace of God which was with me." " By the grace of God," saith he, " I am what I am." It is plain then that no clearness of knowledge, no purity of intent, and no depth of experience can altogether kill in our corrupt nature the propensity to self-reliance. We are so foolish that we readily yield to the witchery which would cause us to trust in ourselves. This widespread folly has no respect for knowledge, age, or experience, but even feeds upon them. I have heard men say several times and I have been ashamed as I have heard the boast—" I am sure there is no likelihood that I should ever trust in myself ; I know better." Brother, you are trusting in yourself when you say so : the subtle poison is in your veins even now. You do not know what folly you can commit. You are such a fool that even while you say, " I know my folly," you are probably even then betraying your self-conceit. What do we know? We know not what spirit we are of. We are capable of almost everything that the devil is capable of. Aye, and if the grace of God should leave us, though we had been exalted to stand like Paul and say, " I am not a whit behind the very chief of the apostles," yet should we fall, like Lucifer, and perish with pride. The silliest of the vices may overcome the wisest of saints. Trust in self is one of the most foolish of sins, though the commonness of it hides its contemptible character. When we say, " I am surprised that I should have acted so unwisely," we betray our secret pride, and confess that we thought ourselves wonderfully wise. If, my brother, you knew yourself you would not be surprised at anything that you might do. If you had a proper estimate of yourself it would rather cause you surprise that you were ever right than that you were sadly wrong, for such is the natural weakness, folly, and vanity of our deceitful hearts, that when we err even in the most foolish way, it may be said of us that we are only acting out our own selves, and we should do the same again, if not worse, were we left by the Spirit of God.

Notice, secondly, that *trusting in self is evil in all men, since it was evil in an apostle.* Paul speaks of it as a fault, which God in mercy prevented, " that we should not trust in ourselves." Why, beloved, if you or I were to trust in ourselves, we should be fit objects for ridicule and derision, for what is there in us that we can trust to ? But as for Paul, in labours more abundant, in stripes above measure, laying himself out for the church of God with heroic zeal, and wearing himself out with self-denials, at first sight it seems that there was somewhat in him whereof he might glory. He walked with God, and was like his Master and Lord. He was a humble but admirable imitation of the Lord Jesus, and the mind that was in Christ was also in him : he was a noble man ; take him for all in all we know not where to find his like. His was one of the most beautiful, well-balanced, forceful, and influential of human characters, and yet it would have been a most injurious thing to him to have trusted in himself in any degree. He was singularly judicious, far-seeing, and prudent, and yet he might not rely on himself. If this be so : if his revelations from God, if his deep experience, if his intense consecration, if his remarkable wisdom, if his splendid education, if his logical mind, and fervent spirits,—if all these combined could not warrant him in trusting to himself, what folly would be ours if we became self-sufficient ? If a lion's strength be insufficient, what can the dogs do ? If the oak trembles, how can the brambles boast ? If such poor things as we are dare to be self-confident, we deserve to smart for it. May God keep us from this evil in all its disguises, whether it beguiles us in the form of boastfulness of our own righteousness, or flatters us into reliance upon our own judgment ; for in any shape it is a sin against God, and a mischief to ourselves. May the God of all grace destroy it, root and branch.

We see, dear friends, in the next place, that *it must be highly injurious to trust in ourselves, since God Himself interposed to prevent His dear servant from falling into it.* The Lord warded off the evil by sending Paul a great trouble when he was in Asia : thus doth our all-wise and almighty God arrange providence to prevent His servants from falling into self-trust. Depend upon it, He is doing the same for us, since we have even greater need, He is arranging all our ways and steps that we may not wander into self-conceit. Peradventure, our heavenly Father is at this present time afflicting some of you, denying you your heart's desire, or taking from you the delight of your eyes, placing you in circumstances where you are puzzled and bewildered, and do not know what to do at all ; and all for this reason, that you may become sick of yourself and fond of Christ ; that you may know your own folly, and may trust yourself with purpose of heart to the divine wisdom : for, rest assured, nothing can happen to you that is much worse than to trust yourselves. A man may escape from poverty, but if he falls into self-confidence he has of two evils fallen into the worse : a man may escape from a great blunder, and yet if he grows proud because he was so prudent, it may happen that his conceit of his own wisdom may be a worse evil than the mistake which he might have made. Anything is better than vainglory and self-esteem. Self-trust before God is a monster evil which the Lord will not endure ; indeed, He so abhors it that he has pronounced a curse upon it : " Cursed is the man that trusteth in man and maketh flesh his arm." That dread word of warning emphatically applies to those who trust in themselves.

Let me, then, think most solemnly of the fact that if I am relying upon myself for acceptance with God, or for power to serve Him, I am cursed. I am so, and I must be so, because trusting in myself means idolatry, and idolatry is a cursed thing. The self-truster puts himself into God's place, for God alone is to be relied upon. " Trust in *Him* at all times ; ye people, pour out your heart before *Him*." Trusting in yourself, you lift yourself into the throne where God alone may sit, and so you become a traitor. To trust yourself is the result of a gross falsehood, and it also imputes falsehood to the God of truth ; for you do, as it were, deny that God can be believed, and you assert that you can be trusted ; whereas, the Lord declares that no man is the proper object of trust. " He that trusteth in His own heart," saith He, " is a fool " ; but you will not have it so, and therefore you give God the lie.

To trust in one's self is a piece of impertinent pride insulting to the majesty of heaven. It is a preference of ourselves to God, so that we take our own opinion in preference to His revelation. We follow our own whim in preference to His providential direction ; we, as it were, become gods to ourselves, and act as if we knew better than God. It is, therefore, a very high crime and misdemeanour against the majesty of heaven that we should trust in ourselves ; and in whomsoever this exists, it makes a man intolerable to God.

Yet, brethren, this fourth remark must be made, that *this evil is very hard to cure* ; for it seems that to prevent it in Paul it was necessary for the Great Physician to go the length of making him feel the sentence of death in himself ; nothing short of this could cure the tendency. On another occasion it is written, " Lest I should be exalted above measure, there was given to me a thorn in the flesh, the messenger of Satan to buffet me." In the case mentioned in our text the buffeting of Satan does not seem to have sufficed ; but God in His providence and love saw it necessary to cause the sentence of death to ring out its knell in the apostle's heart. A sentence of death ! Can you conceive the feeling of a man who has just seen the judge put on the black cap and pronounce sentence of death ? The condemned cell, the iron bars, the prison fare, the grim warders, these are nothing, but sentence of death—sentence of death ! This is terrible. Paul must feel that woe. A sharp knife was needful to cut out the cancer of self-trust even from such an one as Paul. This bitter potion, bitter as gall, he must drink even to the dregs. The sentence must not only be in his ear, but be in his very self. "We had the sentence of death *in ourselves."* Nothing short of this could prevent his being polluted with self-trust ; for if less suffering would have sufficed, the Lord would have spared him so dread a sorrow. As stones fall towards the earth, so do we gravitate towards self. If we are zealous, self-trust says, "What a zealous man you are, you can certainly carry everything before you." If we grow diffident, then this same pride whispers, "What a humble, modest person you are ; you are not conceited or rash, you can well be trusted." If God grants us a little success in working for Him we blow the trumpets that all men may be aware of it. Our Lord can scarecely send us on the commonest errand without danger of our becoming like Jack-in-office, too proud to be borne with. The Lord cannot allow us a little sweet communion with Christ but what we say, "Oh, what joy I have had. What delights at His table ! What a precious season of private prayer ! I am somebody." Yes, we are prone to sacrifice before this basest of idols—I say the basest of idols, for surely there is no idolatry so utterly degrading as the worship of one's self. Alas, we cannot get rid of the flavour of the Egyptian leeks and onions ; self clings to us as a foul odour not to be got out of our unclean flesh. Does the Lord teach us much of His word ? Then we grow proud of knowledge. Does the Lord help us to comfort His people ? Then we set up at once for something wonderful in the church. Does Christ reveal Himself to us as He does not to the world ? Ah, then our heads are ready to smite the stars, we are so great. God save us from this subtle malady, this spiritual leprosy. I think I may add even if nothing else but the sentence of death in ourselves can stop us from trusting in ourselves, then let even this remedy be used.

II. But now I invite you for a few minutes to look at THE TREATMENT ordained for the apostle's cure : "We had the sentence of death in ourselves," which means, first, that *he seemed to hear the verdict of death passed upon him by the conditions which surrounded him.* So continually hounded by his malicious countrymen, he felt certain that one day or other they would compass his destruction : so frequently subject to popular violence, he felt that his life was not worth a moment's purchase : and, withal, so sick in body and so depressed in spirit he felt that he might at any moment expire. The original conveys the idea, not only of a verdict from without, but of an answer of assent from within. *There was an echo in his consciousness ;* an inward dread ; a sort of presentiment that he was soon to die. The world threatened him with death, and he felt that one of these days the threat would be carried out, and that very speedily. And yet it was not so : he survived all the designs of the foe. My brethren, we often feel a thousand deaths in fearing one. We die before we die, and find ourselves alive to die again. Death seems certain, and yet the bird escapes even out of the fowler's hand. Just when he was about to wring its neck it flew aloft. Hark, how it sings, far above his reach. "Unto God the Lord belong the issues from death." A witty saying puts it, "Let us never say

die till we are dead " ; but then we shall most truly say we live for ever and ever. Let us postpone despair till the evil comes.

Into a low state of spirit was Paul brought : death appeared imminent, and his eye of faith gazed into the eternities, and this prevented his trusting in himself. The man who feels that he is about to die is no longer able to trust in himself. After this manner the remedy works our health. What earthly thing can help us when we are about to die ? Paul needed not to say, "My riches will not help me," for he had no wealth. He had no need to say, "My lands and broad acres cannot comfort me now," for he had no foot of land to call his own : his whole estate lay in a few needles, with which he made and mended tents. His trade implements and a manuscript book or two were all his store. He says, in effect, "Nothing on earth can help me now. My tongue, with which I preached, cannot plead with death, whose deaf ear no oratory can charm. My epistles and my power of writing cannot stand me in any stead, for no pen can arrest the death-warrant : it is written, and I must die. Friends cannot help me. Titus, Timothy, none of these can come to my aid. Neither Barnabas nor Silas can pass through the death-stream with me : I must ford the torrent alone." He felt as every man must who is a true Christian, and is about to die, that he must commit his spirit unto Christ, and watch for His appearing. He determined, whether he did die or live, that he would spend and be spent for the Lord Jesus. Brethren, we do not yet know what dying is : the way to the other land is an untrodden path as yet. We read about heaven, and so on, but we know very little of the way thither. To the mind of one about to die the unknown frequently causes a creeping sensation of fear, and the heart is full of horror. Paul felt the chill of death coming over him, and by this means his trust in himself was killed, and he was driven to rely upon his God. If nothing else will cure us of self-confidence we may be content to have the rope about our neck, or to lay our neck upon the block, or to feel the death-rattle in our throats : we may be satisfied to sink as in the deep waters, if this would cure us of trusting in ourselves. Such was the case with Paul, when his gracious Master put forth His hand to turn him aside from all glorying in the flesh.

What was more, I think Paul means here that *the sentence of death which he heard outside wrought within his soul a sense of entire helplessness.* He was striving to fight for the kingdom and gospel of Christ, but he saw that he must be baffled if he had nothing to rely upon but himself ; he was hampered and hemmed in on every side by the opposing Jews, who would not permit him to go about his work in peace. He despaired even of his life. He was not able to get at his work, for these persons were always about him, howling at him, uttering falsehoods against him, and hindering him. He became so worried and wearied that he was pressed and oppressed, immeasurably loaded and brought into such a state of mind that all inward comfort failed him, and he was obliged to look above for succour. His faculties were cramped as with a mortal rigour, his reason argued against him, and his imagination rather created terrors than expectations. He knew the experience so poetically described by Kirke White in his hymn upon the star of Bethlehem :—

" Deep horror, then, my vitals froze,
Death-struck, I ceased the tide to stem."

And he also knew the joy of the other two lines of the verse :—

> " When suddenly a star arose,
> It was the star of Bethlehem."

Paul's mind was so struck with death within himself that he could not stem the torrent, and would have drifted to despair had he not given himself up into the hands of grace divine, and proved the loving power of God.

My brethren, you may never have experienced this, and I do not wish that you may do so to the same extent as the apostle, for the Lord may not bring you into a condition of exaltation, where you are so exposed to the peril of self-confidence, and therefore it may not be necessary to make you feel to the same extent this sentence of death ; but I am aware that some of God's people here know what it is to see death written upon everything within them and around them, and these dare not trust in themselves. Ah, there are times with some of us when we appear to lose all power to think aright, when we set ourselves to a subject, and our brain will not exercise itself upon it : when we wish to do right, and cannot tell which of two courses is the proper one. At times we cannot make out our way ; we kneel to pray, and find that we cannot pray as we were wont to do, the whole energy and force of our spirit seems to be shrivelled up as though the simoom had blown over the meadow of our soul, and left every blade of grass and floweret dead beneath its burning breath. Such things do happen unto men, and when they happen this is God's severe but effectual treatment, whereby He prevents their trusting in themselves. You have said sometimes of a very useful person—" God honours that man, and I am afraid he will be proud." You might well tremble for him were it not that behind the door God whips the man, and makes him loathe himself in dust and ashes. If the great Father favours any one of you with usefulness to any great extent or degree, depend upon it He will favour you also with humiliations and spiritual conflicts, unless, indeed, you have so much grace that you do not need these correctives, and this is not the case with many. Brethren, take the bitter with the sweet ; all things work *together* for good, not one alone, neither the exaltation nor the depression alone, but " all things work *together* for good to them that love God." The compound brings the benefit to us : as one drug in a compound medicine counteracts another, and the whole result is health, so is it with the total sum of divers providences, it brings benefit to us and glory to God.

I think I need not say any more about this remedy, except to notice that the Lord uses the same treatment in dealing with men who as yet are not saved. Why is it that one of the first works of grace on a man is to take away all his comfort and hope ? I will soon tell you. Suppose that a poor man had fallen into such a state of mind that he could not bear the sun, but lived in perpetual candle light. He dreamed that no light could equal his poor tapers, and he despised the sun :—candles for him, he hated daylight. By the way, I am not wild in this supposition, for there are people who cannot worship God without candles, even in the daylight, and yet are not said to be insane. But to return to the imaginary case, our poor, weak-minded friend is prejudiced against the sun, and we aim to bring him into brightness. How shall we proceed ? I think we had better blow out his candles, and leave him in the dark, and then, perhaps, he will be willing to try the light of heaven. Then I would take him out of doors, and let him see the sun ; and, after he had once beheld its superior light, he would never be able to praise his poor candles again. The first thing is to blow his candles out, and the first thing to bring a man to Christ, the divine light, is to put out his own feeble tapers of self-trust. I have heard of one who fell into the water and sank, and a strong swimmer standing on the shore did not at the same instant plunge in, though fully resolved to rescue him. The man went down the second time, and then he who would rescue him was in the water swimming near him, but not too near, waiting very cautiously till his time came. He who was drowning was a strong, energetic man, and the other was too prudent to expose himself to the risk of being dragged under by his struggles. He let the man go down for the third time, and then he knew that his strength was quite exhausted, and swimming to him he grasped him and drew him to shore. If he had seized him at first, while the drowning man had strength, they would have gone down together. The first part of human salvation is the sentence of death upon all human power and merit. When all hope in self is quite gone, Christ comes in, and with His infinite grace rescues the soul from destruction. As long as you think you can swim, you will kick, and struggle, and drown ; but when you see the futility of all your own efforts, and perceive that you are without strength, you will leave yourselves with Jesus, and be saved. The eternal power will come in when your power goes out. The sentence of death in yourselves will prevent your trusting in yourselves : death recorded and death confessed to be a just penalty will expel all vain hope, and grace will be welcomed, and the heart will believe with a true faith wrought in it by the Spirit of God.

III. Thirdly, let us think of THE CURE. It was sharp medicine, but it worked well with Paul, for we find first that Paul's self-trust was prevented : any rising token of it was effectually removed. He says, " We had the sentence of death in ourselves, that we should not trust in ourselves." Under this influence he preached as though he ne'er might preach again, a dying man to dying men. I have heard of brethren who do not expect to die. I do not wish to disturb their hope if it gives them comfort, but I know there is something very salutary in my own sense of the nearness of death. Christ may come, it is true, and this faith has the same effect as the expectation of going home to Him, but one way or the other, the sense of the insecurity of this mortal life is good for us. To bring death very near to the mind is a solemn, searching, sanctifying exercise. Our forefathers of centuries ago were wont to have a death's head on the table where they read their Bibles. I do not recommend so sickening a device ; we can have a *memento mori* in better form than that ; still, it is greatly wise to talk with our last hours, to be familiar with the grave, to walk among those little hillocks where our predecessors sleep, and to remember that all the world is like a sandy sea-beach, where after the tide has gone innumerable little worm-casts cover all the plain. Such a worm-cast I too shall leave behind me. This world is full of death's handiwork, a very charnel-house ; nay, better, name it a God's acre, a sleeping-place, where myriads lie waiting for the awakening trumpet. We, too, may expect to sleep with them, and therefore we must not confide in ourselves. Art thou a dying man, and canst thou trust thyself ? More frail than the moth, driven up and down like a sere leaf in the tempest, canst thou trust thyself ? I hope a sense of death will work a cure of that tendency in us.

When the sentence of death assumes the form of an experience of despair as to everything that is of our own selves, then it has thoroughly wrought the cure. I have gone up and down in my own soul where once sweet things did sing and fair hopes bloomed, and I have searched in every chamber to hear a note or find a flower, and I have found nought but silence and death. I have gone abroad into the fields of my imagination, where once I saw much that made ny heart right glad, and I have seen a valley of dry bones, where death reigned alone. Everything which I formerly rejoiced in was touched by the paralysing hand ; all was dead within me, sentence was passed, and apparently executed upon my whole being. If a man does not trust God then, when will he ? and if this does not take him off from self-confidence, what is to do it ? This treatment never fails when the Holy Spirit uses it.

Remember, this was only half the result in Paul's case, for he does not only say that by this sentence of death he was delivered from trusting in himself, but he was led to trust " in God which raiseth the dead." Now, my brethren, we have come out of the gloom of the sepulchre into the glory of the resurrection. " God which raiseth the dead " is our hope. The doctrine of the resurrection is essential to the Christian system, and Paul takes it for granted. When he was delivered from trusting in himself because of the sentence of death, the first thing he did was to trust in the God and Father of his risen Lord.

For first he argued thus,—If I die, what matters it ? God can raise me from the dead. If they stone me, if they smite me with the sword, if they fling me headlong into the sea, I shall rise again. I know that my Redeemer liveth, and that I shall see Him when He appeareth.

He inferred, also, that if God could raise him from the dead He could preserve him from a violent death. He that could restore him if he were dead and rotten in the tomb could certainly keep him from dying till all his life-work was accomplished. This inference is unquestionably true.

> " Plagues and deaths around me fly,
> Till He bids I cannot die ;
> Not a single shaft can hit
> Till the God of love thinks fit."

Immortal is every believer till his work is done. Paul felt this and was comforted.

He argued yet further that if God can raise the dead and call together the separate atoms of a body long since dissolved, and rebuild the house out of such ruin, then surely He could take His fainting powers, over which the sentence of death has passed, and He could use them for His own purposes. Thus would I also reason with myself when I am deeply depressed. He can make me feel His life within me again ; and He can make great use of me under all my weaknesses and difficulties. It needs omnipotence to wake the dead ; that same omnipotence can make me triumph and enable me to do its will, whatever may stand in my way. Is not this a blessed form of argument—that God who raiseth the dead can do for me, can do in me, can do by me great things, for which His name shall have glory for ever and ever ?

Brethren, we need to get away more and more from ourselves, and we shall never do it till we write this down in our books, that self is dead—we must make a corpse of it. We sometimes hear that in setting forth the balance sheet of a banking establishment a mistake was committed by putting down a doubtful asset at too high a value : we must keep clear of such a blunder in making up our spiritual balances. There is no fear of undue depreciation if you say of anything which belongs to self, " it is good for nothing : set it down as worthless." If then you have written yourself down at twenty shillings in the pound, my dear brother, I warn you that you will never realize it. But you say, " I never thought to get more than half-a-crown in the pound out of self "—you will never get that in good money. " Well, I will put it down at a farthing in the pound." You will never realize even that : it will cost you more to get it than it is worth : it is a deception altogether.. He that trusts in himself not only gets not a farthing in the pound out of what he trusted in, but he is a loser by his foolish confidence. I should not like to realize myself ; it would be an awful loss, and leave a great gap in my exchequer ; for what am I but a mass of wounds, a bag of necessities, a mountain of weakness, a world of infirmities, and nothing else worth mentioning ? Do not put yourself down in your spiritual assets at all except as a debt, a liability, and an encumbrance. Say, " Self is dead," and you will be happy if you find that he is dead, for the most of your trouble will come from his being too much alive. That old corrupt nature—ah, the vagabond, if he were indeed dead, and would never struggle again, what a mercy ! But there is life in the old dog yet, life of a troublesome sort, full of mischief. Wisdom reckons self as a dead and worthless thing, to be mortified, but never to be trusted. Folly talks otherwise, and bids you think well of yourself, but do not listen to its dotings. He says, " You are getting an old man now ; those grey hairs have brought experience and wisdom : you are not like those young chits of children that have just come into the church." No ; but there is no fool like an old fool ; mind you do not become another example of that old saying. Do not say to yourself, " Ah ! now you are a man of wide experience, you are : you are not like those narrow-minded people who never went beyond their cottage or the hedges of their little farm. You have had a splendidly wide experience." Ah ! but no blunder is so great as the blunder of a great man : no man is capable of doing so much mischief as the man who has capacity for doing great good. " Oh, but," says another, " I am so careful, so guarded, that there can be no fear of me." Yet no one is so likely to sleep as the watchman who flatters himself that he does not even doze. So it used to be in the old days ; and you watchful people are sure to go wrong if you are proud of being watchful. If, on the other hand, you feel that you are not as watchful as you ought to be, and pray to be made more so, you will be kept right. Trust in ourselves is a kind of manna which will breed worms and stink, and it will make our house unbearable, and ourselves sick. Sweep it out ! Oh, for a state of weakness that is strong in the divine strength. Oh, to be nothing, to be nothing, that God may be all in all ! Amen and amen. So let it be.

THE GLORY OF GOD IN THE FACE OF JESUS CHRIST

" For God, who commanded the light to shine out of darkness, hath shined in our hearts, to give the light of the knowledge of the glory of God in the face of Jesus Christ."—2 Corinthians iv. 6.

THE apostle is explaining the reason for his preaching Christ with so much earnestness : he had received divine light, and he felt bound to spread it. One great motive power of a true ministry is trusteeship. The Lord has put us in trust with the gospel ; He has filled us with a treasure with which we are to enrich the world. The text explains in full what it is with which the Lord has entrusted us : He has bestowed upon us " the light of the knowledge of the glory of God in the face of Jesus Christ," and it is ours to reflect the light, to impart the knowledge, to manifest the glory, to point to the Saviour's face, and to proclaim the name of Jesus Christ our Lord. Having such a work before us, we faint not, but press onward with our whole heart.

I. With no other preface than this we shall ask your attention this morning, first, to THE SUBJECT OF THAT KNOWLEDGE in which Paul delighted so much. What was this knowledge which to his mind was the chief of all, and the most worthy to be spread ? It was the knowledge of God. Truly a most needful and proper knowledge for all God's creatures. For a man not to know his Maker and Ruler is deplorable ignorance indeed. The proper study of mankind is God. Paul not only knew that there is a God, for he had known that before his conversion : none can more surely believe in the God head than did Paul as a Jew. Nor does he merely intend that he had learned somewhat of the character of God, for that also he had known from the Old Testament Scriptures before he was met with on the way to Damascus ; but now he had come to know God in a closer, clearer, and surer way, for he had seen Him incarnate in the person of the Lord Jesus Christ.

The apostle had also received the knowledge of " the glory of God." Never had the God of Abraham appeared so glorious as now. God in Christ Jesus had won the adoring wonder of the apostle's instructed mind. He had known Jehovah's glory as the One and only God, he had seen that glory in creation declared by the heavens and displayed upon the earth, he had beheld that glory in the law which blazed from Sinai and shed its insufferable light upon the face of Moses ; but now, beyond all else, he had come to perceive *the glory of God in the face, or person, of Jesus Christ*, and this had won his soul. This special knowledge had been communicated to him at his conversion when Jesus spake to him out of heaven. In this knowledge he had made great advances by experience and by new revelations ; but he had not yet learned it to the full, for he was still seeking to know it perfectly by the teaching of the divine Spirit, and we find him saying, " That I may know Him, and the power of His resurrection, and the fellowship of His sufferings, being made conformable unto His death."

Paul knew not merely God, but God in Christ Jesus ; not merely " the glory of God," but " the glory of God in the face of Jesus Christ." The knowledge dealt with God, but it was Christward knowledge. He pined not for a Christless Theism, but for God in Christ. This, beloved, is the one thing which you and I should aim to know. There are parts of the divine glory which will never be seen by us in this life, speculate as we may. Mysticism would fain pry into the unknowable ; you and I may leave dreamers and their dreams, and follow the clear light which shines from the face of Jesus. What of God it is needful and beneficial for us to know He has revealed in Christ, and whatsoever is not there, we may rest assured it is unfit and unnecessary for us to know. Truly the revelation is by no means scant, for there is vastly more revealed in the person of Christ than we shall be likely to learn in this mortal life, and even eternity will not be too long for the discovery of all the glory of God which shines forth in the person of the word made flesh. Those who would supplement Christianity had better first add to the brilliance of the sun or the fulness of the sea. As for us, we are more than satisfied with the revelation of God in the person of our Lord Jesus, and we are persuaded of the truth of His words " he that hath seen Me hath seen the Father."

Hope not, my brethren, that the preacher can grapple with such a subject. I am overcome by it. In my meditations I have felt lost in its lengths and breadths. My joy is great in my theme, and yet I am conscious of a pressure upon brain and heart, for I am as a little child wandering among the mountains, or as a lone spirit which has lost its way among the stars. I stumble among sublimities, I sink amid glories. I can only point with my finger to that which I see, but cannot describe. May the Holy Spirit Himself take of the things of Christ and show them unto you.

We will for a minute or two consider this glory of God in the face of Jesus Christ *historically*. In every incident of the life of Jesus of Nazareth, the Lord's anointed, there is much of God to be seen. What volumes upon volumes might be written to show God as revealed in every act of Christ from His birth to His death ! I see Him as a babe at Bethlehem lying in a manger, and there I perceive a choice glory in the mind of God, for He evidently despises the pomp and glory of the world, which little minds esteem so highly. He might have been born in marble halls, and wrapped in imperial purple, but He scorns these things, and in the manger among the oxen we see a glory which is independent of the trifles of luxury and parade. The glory of God in the person of Jesus asks no aid from the splendour of courts and palaces. Yet even as a babe He reigns and rules. Mark how the shepherds hasten to salute the new-born King, while the magi from the far-off East bring gold, frankincense, and myrrh, and bow at His feet. When the Lord condescends to show Himself in little things He is still right royal, and commands the homage of mankind. He is as majestic in the minute as in the magnificent, as royal in the babe at Bethlehem as in after days in the man who rode through Jerusalem with hosannas. See the holy child Jesus in the temple when He is but twelve years old, sitting in the midst of the doctors, astonishing them with His questions! What wisdom there was in that child! Do you not see therein an exhibition of the truth that " the foolishness of God is wiser than men " ? Even when God reserves His wisdom, and gives forth utterances fitted for a child, He baffles the wisdom of age and thought. Watch that youth in the carpenter's shop. See Him planing and sawing, cutting and squaring, working according to His parent's command, till He is thirty years of age. What learn we here when we see the incarnate God tarrying at the workman's bench ? See we not how God can wait ? Is not this a masterly display of the leisure of the Eternal ? The Infinite is never driven out of His restful pace of conscious strength. Had it been you and I, we should have hastened to begin our life-work long before ; we could not have refrained from preaching and teaching for so long a period ; but God can wait, and in Christ we see how prudence tempered zeal, and made Him share in that eternal leisure which arises out of confidence that His end is sure. The Godhead was concealed at Bethlehem and Nazareth from the eyes of carnal men ; but it is revealed to those who have spiritual sight wherewith to behold the Lord. Even in those early days of our Lord, while yet He was preparing for His great mission, we behold the glory of God in His youthful face, and we adore.

As for His public ministry, how clearly the Godhead is there ! Behold Him, brethren, while He feeds five thousand with a few loaves and fishes, and you cannot fail to perceive therein the glory of God in the commissariat of the universe ; for the Lord God openeth His hand and supplieth the lack of every living thing. See Him cast out devils, and learn the divine power over evil. Hear Him raise the dead, and reverence the divine prerogative to kill and to make alive. See Him cure the sick, and think you hear Jehovah say, " I wound, I heal." Hear how He speaks, and infallibly reveals the truth, and you will perceive the God of knowledge to whom the wise-hearted owe their instruction. Set over against each other these two sentences,—" Behold, God exalteth by His power ; who teacheth like Him ? " and " Never man spake like this man." It is ever the Lord's way to make His truth known to those of humble and truthful hearts, and so did Jesus teach the sincere and lowly among men. Observe how Jesus dwelt among men, wearing the common smock-frock of the peasant, entering their cottages, and sharing their poverty. Mark how He even washed His disciples' feet. Herein we see the condescension of God, who must stoop to view the skies, and bow to see what angels do, and yet does not disdain to visit the sons of men. In wondrous grace He thinks of us, and has pity upon our low estate. See, too, the Christ of God, my brethren, bearing every day with the taunts of the ungodly, enduring " such contradiction of sinners against Himself," and you have a fair picture of the infinite patience and the marvellous longsuffering of God, and this is no small part of His glory.

Note well how Jesus loved His own which were in the world, yea, loved them to the end, and with what tenderness and gentleness He bore with them, as a nurse with her child, for here you see the tenderness and gentleness of God, and the love of the great Father towards His erring children. You read of Jesus receiving sinners and eating with them, and what is this but the Lord God, merciful and gracious, passing by transgression, iniquity, and sin ? You see Jesus living as a physician among those diseased by sin, with the one aim of healing their sicknesses ; and here you see the pardoning mercy of our God, His delight in salvation, and the joy which He has in mercy. Beloved, I cannot go through the whole life of Jesus Christ, it were impossible, for time would fail us ; but if you will yourselves select any single incident in which Jesus appears, whether in the chamber of sickness or at the grave, whether in weakness or in power, you shall in each case behold the glory of God. Throughout His ministry, which was mainly a period of humiliation, there gleams forth in the character, acts, and person of Jesus the glory of the everlasting Father. His acts compel us not only to admire but to adore ; He is not merely a man whom God favours, He is God Himself.

What shall I say of His death ? Oh never did the love of God reveal itself so clearly as when He laid down His life for His sheep, nor did the justice of God ever flame forth so conspicuously as when He would suffer in Himself the curse for sin rather than sin should go unpunished, and the law should be dishonoured. Every attribute of God was focussed at the cross, and he that hath eyes to look through his tears, and see the wounds of Jesus, shall behold more of God there than a whole eternity of providence or an infinity of creation shall ever be able to reveal to Him. Well might the trembling centurion, as he watched the cross, exclaim, " Truly this was the Son of God."

Shall I need to remind you, too, of the glory of God in the person of Christ Jesus in His resurrection, when He spoiled principalities and powers, led death captive, and rifled the tomb. That is indeed a godlike speech, " I am He that liveth and was dead, and behold I am alive for evermore, and have the keys of hell and of death." His power, His immortality, His eternal majesty, all shone forth as He left the shades of death.

I will not linger over His ascension when He returned to His own again. Then His Godhead was conspicuous, for He again put on the glory which He had with the Father or ever the world was. Then amid the acclamations of angels and redeemed spirits the glory of the conquering Lord was seen. By His descent He had destroyed the powers of darkness, and then He ascended that He might fill all things as only God can do.

I would only hint at His session at the right hand of God, for there you know how—

> " Adoring saints around Him stand,
> And thrones and powers before Him fall ;
> The God shines gracious through the Man,
> And sheds sweet glories on them all."

In heaven they never conceive of Jesus apart from the divine glory which perpetually surrounds Him. No one in heaven doubts His deity, for all fall prostrate before Him, or anon, all seize their harps and wake their strings to the praise of God and the Lamb.

The glory of God will most abundantly be seen

in the second advent of our Lord. Whatever of splendour we may expect at the advent, whatever of glory shall surround that reign of a thousand years, or the end when He shall deliver up the kingdom to God, even the Father, in every transaction which prophecy leads us to expect, God in Christ Jesus will be conspicuous, and angelic eyes shall look on with adoring admiration as they see the eternal Father glorious in the person of His Son. These are great themes ; we do but indicate them, and leave them to your quiet thought. It is enough to point to a table if men have appetites for them.

But now I will ask you to think of the glory of God in the face of Jesus Christ, in the same line of thought, only putting it in another fashion. Treat it *by way of observation.* When you look upon the material universe you can see, if your eyes are opened, somewhat of the glory of God   The reverent mind perceives enough to constrain the heart to worship, and yet after awhile it pines for more. I have often heard the earth spoken of as the mirror of God's image, but when I was travelling among the Alps, and saw many of the grandest phenomena of creation, such as glacier, avalanche, and tempest, I was so impressed with the narrowness of visible things in comparison with God that I wrote such lines as these :

> The mirror of the creature lacketh space
> To bear the image of the Infinite.
> 'Tis true the Lord hath fairly writ His name,
> And set His seal upon creation's brow,
> But as the skilful potter much excels
> The vessel which he fashions on the wheel,
> E'en so, but in proportion greater far,
> Jehovah's self transcends His noblest works.
> Earth's ponderous wheels would break, her axles snap,
> If freighted with the load of Deity.
> Space is too narrow for th' Eternal's rest,
> And time too short a footstool for His throne.

If your mind has ever entered into communion with God, you will become conscious of the dwarfing of all visible things in His presence. Even when your thought sweeps round the stars, and circumnavigates space, you feel that heaven, even the heaven of heavens, cannot contain Him. Everything conceivable falls short of the inconceivable glory of God. When you come, however, to gaze upon the face of Christ Jesus, how different is the feeling ! Now you have a mirror equal to the reflection of the eternal face, for " In Him dwelleth all the fulness of the Godhead bodily." His name is " Wonderful, Counsellor, the mighty God." He is the image of God ; " the brightness of His glory, and the express image of His person." If your conception of Christ be truthful it will coincide with the true idea of God, and you will exclaim, " This is the true God and eternal life." Like Thomas, you will salute the wounded Saviour with the cry, " My Lord and my God." Truly, " God was manifest in the flesh "— not a part of Him, but God in perfection. In the visible creation we see God's works, but in Christ Jesus we have God Himself, Emmanuel, " God with us." The glory of God in the face of Jesus Christ is most sweetly conspicuous, because you are conscious that not only are God's attributes there, but God Himself is there.

In the person of Jesus we see the glory of God *in the veiling of His splendour.* The Lord is not eager to display Himself : " Verily Thou art a God that hidest Thyself, said the prophet of old." The world seems to be created rather to hide God than to manifest Him : at least, it is certain that even in the grandest displays of His power we may say with Job, " There was the hiding of His power." Though His light is brightness itself, yet it is only the robe which conceals Him. " Who coverest Thyself with light as with a garment." If thus God's glory is seen in the field of creation as a light veiled and shaded to suit the human eye, we certainly see the like in the face of Jesus Christ where everything is mild and gentle—full of grace as well as truth. How softly breaks the divine glory through the human life of Jesus : a babe in grace may gaze upon this brightness without fear. When Moses' face shone the people could not look thereon : but when Jesus came from His transfiguration the people ran to Him and saluted Him. Everything is attractive in God in Christ Jesus. In Him we see God to the full, but the Deity so mildly beams through the medium of human flesh that mortal man may draw near, and look, and live. This glory in the face of Jesus Christ is assuredly the glory of God, even though veiled ; for thus in every other instance doth God in measure shine forth. In providence and in nature such a thing as an unveiled God is not to be seen, and the revelation of God in Christ is after the same divine manner.

In our Lord Jesus we see the glory of God *in the wondrous blending of the attributes.* Behold His mercy, for He dies for sinners ; but see His justice, for He sits as judge of quick and dead. Observe His immutability, for He is the same yesterday, to-day, and for ever ; and see His power, for His voice shakes not only earth but also heaven. See how infinite is His love, for He espouses His chosen ; but how terrible His wrath, for He consumes His adversaries. All the attributes of Deity are in Him : power that can lull the tempest, and tenderness that can embrace little children. The character of Christ is a wonderful combination of all perfections making up one perfection ; and so we see the glory of God in the face of Jesus Christ, for this is God's glory, that in Him nothing is excessive and nothing is deficient. He is all that is good and great : in Him is light, and no darkness at all. Say, is it not so seen in Jesus our Lord ?

When I think of God I am led to see His glory *in the outgoing of His great heart ;* for He is altogether unselfish and unsparingly communicative. We may conceive a period when the Eternal dwelt alone and had not begun to create. He must have been inconceivably blessed ; but He was not content to be enwrapped within Himself, and to enjoy perfect bliss alone. He began to create, and probably formed innumerable beings long before this world came into existence ; and He did this that He might multiply beings capable of happiness. He delighted to indulge His heart by deed of beneficence, manifesting the inherent goodness of His nature. In whatever God is doing He is consulting the happiness of His creatures ; being in Himself independent of all, He loves to bless others. He is living—we speak with awe in His presence—He is living, even He, not unto Himself, but living in the lives of others, rejoicing in the joy of His creatures. This is His glory, and is it not to be seen most evidently in Christ Jesus, who " saved others, Himself He could not save " ? Do you not see the great unselfish glory of God in Christ Jesus ? When did He ever live unto Himself ? What single act of His had a selfish purpose? What word ever sought His own honour? In what deed did He consult His own aggrandisement? Neither in life nor in death did Christ live within Himself: He lived for His people, and died for them. See the glory of God in this!

There are two things I have noticed in the glory of God whenever my soul has been saturated with it, and these I have seen in Jesus. I have stood upon a lofty hill and looked abroad upon the landscape, and seen hill, and dale, and wood, and field, and I have felt as if God had gone forth and spread His presence over all. I have felt *the outflow of Deity*. There was not a pleasant tree, nor a silvery stream, nor a corn-field ripening for the harvest, nor mount shaggy with pines, nor heath purple with heather, but seemed aglow with God. Even as the sun pours himself over all things, so does God; and in the hum of an insect as well as in the crash of a thunderbolt we hear a voice saying, "God is here." God has gone forth out of Himself into the creation, and filled all things. Is not this the feeling of the heart in the presence of Christ? When we come near Him He is the all-pervading spirit. In any of the scenes in which Jesus appears He is omnipresent. Who but He is at Bethlehem, or at Nazareth, or at Jerusalem? Who but He is in the world? Is not He to us the every-body, the one only person of His age? I cannot think of Cæsar or Rome, or all the myriads that dwell on the face of the earth as being anything more than small figures in the background of the picture when Jesus is before me. He is to my mind most clearly the fulness, filling all in all; all the acces-sories of any scene in which He appears are submerged in the flood of glory which flows from His all-subduing presence. Verily the outgoing glory of God was in Christ.

But you must have had another thought when you have felt the glory of God in nature: you must have felt *the indrawing of all things towards God*. You have felt created things rising unto God as steps to His throne. As you have gazed with rapture on the landscape every tree and hill has seemed to drift towards God, to tend towards Him, to return, in fact, to Him from whom it came. Is it not just so in the life of Christ? He seems to be drawing all things to Himself, gathering together all things in one in His own personality. Some of these things will not move, but yet His attraction has fallen on them, while other fly with alacrity to Him, according to His word. "I, if I be lifted up, will draw all men unto Me." Thus those observations of the glory of God, which have been suggested to us by nature, are also abundantly verified in Christ, and we are sure that the glory is the same.

I cannot express my own thought to you so clearly and vividly as I would, but this I know, if you ever get a vision of the glory of God in nature, and if you then turn your thoughts towards the Lord's Christ, you will see that the same God is in Him as in the visible universe, and that the same glory shines in Him, only more clearly. There is one God, and that one God is gloriously manifested in Christ Jesus. "No man hath seen God at any time; the only begotten Son, which is in the bosom of the Father, He hath declared Him."

Let us now treat this thought of the glory of God in the person of Christ *by way of experience*. Have you ever heard Christ's doctrine in your soul? If so, you have felt it to be divine, for your heart has perceived its moral and spiritual glory, and you have concluded that God is in it of a truth. Has your heart heard the voice of Christ speaking peace and pardon through the blood? If so, you have known Him to be Lord of all. Did you ever see the fulness of His atonement? Then you have felt that God Himself was there reconciling the world unto Himself. You have understood the union of the two titles, "God, our Saviour." Beloved, you have often felt your Lord's presence, and you have been admitted into intimate communion with Him. Then I know that a profound awe has crept over you which has made you fall at His feet, and in the lowliest reverence of your spirit you have owned Him to be Lord and God. But when He has bent over you in love and said, "Fear not"; when He has opened His heart to you and shown you how dear you are to Him, then the rapture you have felt has been so divine that you have, beyond all question, known Him to be God. There are times when the elevating influence of the presence of Christ has put His Godhead beyond the possibility of question, when we have felt that all the truth we ever heard before had no effect upon us compared with the truth that is in Him; that all the spirits in the world were ineffectual to stir us till His Spirit came into contact with our spirit. In this manner His omnipotent, all-subduing, elevating love has proved Him to be none other than "very God of very God."

Thus have we spoken of the supremely precious object of Christian knowledge.

II. Secondly, let us spend a few words in noticing THE NATURE OF THIS KNOWLEDGE. How, and in what respects, do we know the glory of God in the face of Jesus Christ?

Briefly, first. We know it *by faith*. Upon the testimony of the infallible word we believe and are sure that God is in Christ Jesus. The Lord hath spoken and said, "This is My beloved Son, hear ye Him." We accept as a settled fact the Godhead of the Lord Jesus, and our soul never permits a question upon it. "We know that the Son of God is come, and hath given us an understanding, that we may know Him that is true, and we are in Him that is true, even in His Son Jesus Christ. This is the true God, and eternal life."

Knowing our Lord's divinity by faith, we next have used our perceptive faculty, and *by consideration and meditation we perceive* that His life furnishes abundant evidence that He was God, for God's glory shines in that life. The more carefully we pay attention to the details given us by the four evan-gelists, the more is our understanding persuaded that no mere man stands before us. If, my brethren, your spiritual nature was set this task, to try and describe how God would act if He were here, what God would be if He became incarnate and dwelt among men—I am sure you would not have been able to imagine the life of Christ; but if someone had brought to you the description given by the evangelists you would have said, "My task is done: this is indeed a noble conception of God manifest in the flesh." I do not say that the wise men of this world would suppose God to have thus behaved, for their suppositions are sure to be the reverse of the simple, unaffected, open-hearted conduct of Jesus: but this I say, that the pure in heart will at once see that the acts of Christ are like the doings of God. He hath done exactly what a pure intelligence might suppose God would have done. The more we **have** studied the more we have seen the glory of God in Christ.

And now we have come rather further than this, for we feel an *inward consciousness* that the Deity is in Christ Jesus. It is not merely that we have believed it, and that we somewhat perceive it by observation, but we have come into contact with Christ, and have known therefore that He is God. We love Him, and we also love God, and we perceive that these two are one ; and the more we love truth and holiness, and love, which are great traits in the character of God, the more we see of these in Christ Jesus. It is by the heart that we know God and Christ, and as our affections are purified we become sensible of God's presence in Christ. Ofttimes when our soul is in rapt fellowship with Jesus we laugh to scorn the very thought that our Beloved can be less than divine.

Moreover, there is one other thing that hath happened to us while we have been looking at our Lord. Blessed be His name, we begin to grow like Him. Our beholding Him has purified the eye which has gazed on His purity : His brightness has helped our eyesight, so that we see much already, and shall yet see more. The light of the sun blinds us, but the light of Jesus Christ strengthens the eye. We expect that as we grow in grace we shall behold more and more of God's glory ; but we shall see it best in the Well-beloved, even in Christ Jesus our Lord. What a sight of God we shall enjoy in heaven ! We are tending that way, and, as we get nearer and nearer, our sight and vision of the glory of God in Christ is every day increased. We know it, then ; we know it : we belive it, we are conscious of it, we are affected by it, we are transformed by it ; and thus at this day we have " the light of the knowledge of the glory of God in the face of Jesus Christ."

III. Thirdly, let us gratefully review THE MEANS OF THIS KNOWLEDGE. How have we come at it ? That brings us to read the text again :— " For God, who commanded the light to shine out of darkness, hath shined in our hearts, to give the light of the knowledge of the glory of God in the face of Jesus Christ." Why did not everybody see the glory of God in Jesus Christ when He was here ? It was conspicuous enough. Answer : it mattereth not how brightly the sun shineth among blind men. Now, the human heart is blind, it refuses to see God in creation except after a dim fashion, but it utterly refuses to discern God in Christ, and therefore He is the despised and rejected of men. Moreover, there is a god of this world, the prince of darkness, and since he hates the light he deepens and confirms the natural darkness of the human mind, lest the light should reach the heart. He blinds men's minds with error and falsehood and foul imaginations, blocking up the windows of the soul either with unclean desires, or with dense ignorance, or with pride. The reason why we did not at one time perceive the glory of God in Christ was because we were blind by nature, and were darkened by the evil one. As only the pure in heart can see God, we, being impure in heart, could not see God in Christ. What, then, hath happened to us ? To eternal grace be endless praise, God Himself hath shined into our hearts : that same God who said " Light be," and light was, hath shined into our hearts. You know creation's story, how all things lay in black darkness. God might have gone on to make a world in darkness if He had pleased, but if He had done so it would

have been to us as though it had never been, for we could not have perceived it ; therefore He early said, " Let there be light." Now, God's glory in the face of Jesus Christ might have been all there, and we should never have discerned it, and as far as we are concerned it would have been as though it had never been, if the Lord had not entered into us amid the thick darkness and said, " Let there be light." Then burst in the everlasting morning, the light shined in the darkness, and the darkness fled before it. Do you recollect the incoming of that illumination ? If you do, then I know the first sight you saw by the new light was the glory of God in Jesus Christ : in fact, that light had come on purpose that you might see it ; and at this present moment that is the main delight of your soul, the choice subject of your thoughts. In the light of God you have seen the light of the glory of God, as it is written, " In Thy light we shall see light."

One thing I want to say to comfort all who believe. Beloved, do you see the glory of God in Christ Jesus ? Then let that sight be an evidence to you of your salvation. When our Lord asked His disciples, " Whom do men say that I the Son of man am ? " Simon Peter answered, " Thou art the Christ, the Son of the living God." Now, note the reply of the Lord Jesus to that confession : " Blessed art thou, Simon Bar-jona ; for flesh and blood hath not revealed it unto you, but My Father which is in heaven." If thou canst delight in God in Christ Jesus, then remember, " no man can say that Jesus is the Christ but by the Holy Ghost," and thou hast said it, and this morning thou art saying it, and therefore the Holy Ghost has come upon thee. " Whosoever believeth that Jesus is the Christ is born of God." Thou believest this, and therefore thou art born of the Father. " Whosoever denieth the Son, the same hath not the Father : but he that acknowledgeth the Son hath the Father also." Thou lovest God, and thou art His : the Spirit of God hath opened thine eyes and thou art saved.

While I have been preaching this morning a number of my hearers have been saying, " We care nothing about Jesus Christ. His name is a most respectable one in our religion ; we call ourselves Christians, but as to seeing the glory of God in Him when He was a babe, and when He was despised and rejected of men, we know nothing of it. No doubt He is exalted now in heaven, and we worship Him, though we hardly know why. But we see no special glory in Him." Others of you have been saying, " Yes, God was in Christ Jesus reconciling the world unto Himself, and He has reconciled me to Himself. I never loved God till I saw Him in Christ. I could never have any familiarity with God till I saw His familiarity with me in the person of His Son. I never understood how I could be God's son till I understood how God's Son became a man. I never saw how I could be a partaker of the divine nature till I saw how His Son become a partaker of the human nature, and took me up unto Himself that He might take me up unto His Father." Oh, beloved, do you delight in Jesus Christ ? Is He all your salvation and all your desire ? Do you adore Him, do you consecrate yourself to His honour, do you wish to live for Him, and to die for Him ? Then be sure that you belong to Him, for it is the mark of the children of God that they love God in Christ Jesus.

IV. So I finish by mentioning, in the fourth

place, THE RESPONSIBILITIES OF THIS KNOWLEDGE. There have been considerable debates among the interpreters as to the precise bearing of this text, and some of them think it means that Paul is giving a reason why he preached the gospel. This makes the verse run thus :—" For God, who commanded the light to shine out of darkness, hath shined in our hearts, that we might give out again the light of the knowledge of the glory of God in the face of Jesus Christ." God gave light to the apostles that they might show forth the light of the knowledge of God in the face of Jesus Christ to the nations. I do not know whether this is the exact run of the text, but I know it is true anyhow. Never is a gleam of light given to any man to hide away, and to spiritual men the great object of their lives, after they have received light, is to reflect that light in all its purity. You must not hoard up the light within yourself ; it will not be light to you if you do. Only think of a person when his room is full of sunlight saying to his servant, " Quick, now ! Close the shutters, and let us keep this precious light to ourselves." Your room will be in the dark, my friend. So, when a child of God gets the light from Christ's face He must not say " I shall keep this to myself," for that very desire would shut it out. No, let the light shine through you ; let it shine everywhere. you have the light that you may reflect it. An object which absorbs light is dark, and we call it black ; but hang up a reflector in its place when the sun is shining, and it will not appear black, it will be so bright that you will hardly bear to look at it. An object is itself bright in proportion as it sends back the light which it receives. So you shall find, as a Christian, that, if you absorb light into yourself, you will be black, but if you scatter it abroad you yourself shall be brilliant : you shall be changed into the very image of the light which you have received, you shall become a second sun. I noticed last Sabbath evening, when I came into this pulpit, that, at the angle of the building before me, on the left hand the sun seemed to be setting, and I saw the brightness of his round face, and yet I knew it to be the wrong quarter of the heavens for the sun to be setting there. Perhaps you will observe that there is a peculiar window on the other side of the street, and it was reflecting the sun so well that I thought it was the sun himself, and I could hardly bear the light. It was not the sun, it was only a window, and yet the radiance was dazzling ; and so a man of God, when he receives the light of Christ, can become so perfect a reflector that to common eyes, at any rate, he is brightness itself. He has become transformed from glory to glory as by the image of the Lord.

Brothers and sisters, if you have learned the truth, manifest it, and make it plain to others. Proclaim *the gospel*, not your own thoughts ; for it is Christ that you are to make manifest. Teach, not your own judgments, and conclusions, and opinions, but the glory of God in the face of Jesus Christ. Let Jesus manifest Himself in His own light ; do not cast a light on Him, or attempt to show the sun with a candle. Do not aim at converting men to your views, but let the light shine for itself and work its own way. Do not colour it by being like a painted window to it, but let the clear white light shine through you that others may behold your Lord.

Scatter your light in all unselfishness. Wish to shine, not that others may say " How bright he is," but that they getting the light may rejoice in the source from which it came to you and to them. Be willing to make every sacrifice to spread this light which you have received. Consecrate your entire being to the making known among the sons of men the glory of Christ. Oh, I would we had swift messengers to run the world over to tell the story that God has come down among us. I wish we had fluent tongues to tell in every language the story that, coming down among us, God was arrayed in flesh like to our own ; and that He took our sins and carried our sorrows. Oh, that we had trumpet tongues, to make the message peal through heaven and earth that God has come among men, and cries, " Come unto Me all ye that labour and are heavy laden, and I will give you rest." Oh, for a thunder voice, to speak it, or a lightning pen to write it athwart the heavens, that God hath reconciled the world unto Himself by the death of His Son, not imputing their trespasses unto them ; and that whosoever believeth in Christ Jesus hath everlasting life. I cannot command thunder or lightning, but here are your tongues, go and tell it this afternoon : here is my tongue, and I have tried to tell it, and may it be silent in the dust of death ere it ceases to declare that one blessed message, that God in Christ Jesus receives the sons of men in boundless love. Tell it, brother, with broken accents, if thou canst not speak it more powerfully. Whisper it, sister, gently whisper, if to none other yet to thy little children, and make the name of " Emmanuel, God with us," to be sweet in thine infant's ears. Thou art growing in strength and talent, young man, come, consecrate thyself to this. And thou, grey-beard, ere thou dost lie down on thy last bed to breathe out thy spirit, tell the love of Jesus to thy sons that they may tell it to their sons, and hand it down to coming generations, that mankind may never forget that the " word was made flesh and dwelt among us, and we beheld His glory, the glory as of the only begotten of the Father, full of grace and truth." God bless you. Amen.

" OUR LIGHT AFFLICTION "

" Our light affliction."—2 Corinthians iv. 17.

PERHAPS someone here thoughtlessly says, " Well, whoever calls affliction ' light ' must have been a person who knew very little about what affliction really is. If he had suffered as I have done, he would not have written about ' our light affliction.' He must have been in robust health, and known nothing of sickness and pain." " Just so," says another, " and if he had been as poor as I am, and had to work as hard as I do to maintain a sickly wife, and a large family, he would not have written about ' our light affliction.' I expect the gentlemen who used that expression lived very much at his ease, and had all that his heart could wish." "Aye," says another, " and if he had stood by an open grave, and had to lament the loss of loved ones, as I have done, and if he had known what it was to be desolate and forsaken, as I have known it, he would not have written about ' our light affliction.' "

Now, if you do talk like that, you are all of you mistaken, for the man who wrote these words was probably afflicted more than any of us have ever been. The list of his afflictions that he gives us is perfectly appalling : " in stripes above measure, in prisons more frequent, in deaths oft. Thrice was I beaten with rods, once was I stoned, thrice I suffered shipwreck, a night and a day I have been in the deep ; in journeyings often, in perils of waters, in peril of robbers, in perils by mine own countrymen, in perils by the heathen, in perils in the city, in perils in the wilderness, in perils in the sea, in perils among false brethren ; in weariness and painfulness, in watchings often, in hunger and thirst, in fastings often, in cold and nakedness." Is there anyone here who could truthfully make out such a catalogue of personal afflictions as the apostle Paul endured ?

Well then," says one, " he must have been so hardened that he took no notice of it, like the Red Indian who will endure terrible torture without a groan, or like the Stoic philosopher who concealed his inward feelings beneath an unmoved countenance." No ; you also are mistaken. If you read Paul's letters to his private friends and to the churches, you will see that they bear abundant evidences that he was a man of great tenderness of spirit and of intense emotion, one who could suffer and who did suffer most acutely. His education and training had fitted him for a life amongst the most learned and refined of his countrymen, yet he had to support himself by labouring as a tent-maker, and to journey hither and thither in peril and privation ; and though he endured all this in absolute submission to the will of God, yet there was nothing stoical about his resignation.

" Well then," says another, " he must have been one of those careless, light-hearted people who never trouble about anything that happens, and whose motto is, ' Let us eat and drink, for to-morrow we die.' " Oh, no ! the apostle Paul was not at all that kind of man ; he was the most thoughtful, logical, careful, considerate man of whom I have ever read. He knew what it was to be joyful, yet there was never any sign of levity about him. He had a grandly buoyant spirit which lifted him above waves of sorrow in which most men would have sunk, yet he was never frivolous. He wrote of " our light affliction " even when he was heavily afflicted, and while he acutely felt that affliction. The sailor forgets the storm when he is again safely on shore, and we are all apt to think less of our sickness when we have been restored from it ; but Paul was in the midst of affliction when he called it " light." He felt the weight of it, and was fully conscious of the pressure of it upon his spirit ; but the elastic spring of faith within his soul was so vigorously in action that he was enabled at that very time to call it " our light affliction."

We must not forget that Paul had afflictions which were peculiarly his own. There are afflictions which Christians have because they are Christians, and which those who are not Christians do not have ; and Paul, as an apostle of Jesus Christ, had sufferings which were peculiarly his because he was an apostle.

Because he was specially called to be the apostle of the Gentiles, because he was chosen to carry the gospel to many nations, because he was called to stand even before the cruel Emperor Nero,—for that very reason, he who was peculiarly gifted and specially chosen above all others to do most arduous and onerous work was also called to endure unusual trial. He had spelt out the word " AFFLICTION " as perhaps no other mere man had done, he had seen it written in capital letters across his whole life ; so he could speak, not as a novice, but as one who had graduated in the school of affliction, and yet he wrote concerning " our light affliction." Before I have finished my discourse, I hope that most if not all here will agree with the apostle, and say, " We also call our affliction light."

I. I am going to speak, first, specially TO CHRISTIAN WORKERS ; and to them I would say,— Dear brethren and sisters in Christ, *our affliction is light compared with the objects we have in view.*

Much of the affliction that the apostle had to endure came upon him because he was seeking the conversion of the heathen and the ingathering of the elect into the kingdom of Christ. If this is the object you also have in view, my dear friend, and you are made to suffer through your sedulous and faithful pursuit of it, I think you may truly call anything you have to endure a light affliction. If you have ever seen a mother sit up night after night with her sick child, you must have sometimes wondered that her eyes did not close in slumber. You were amazed that she did not permit someone else to share her task, but she seemed to think nothing of the cost to herself if she might only be the means of saving her little one's life. 'Twas love that made her labour light, and he who truly loves the souls of sinners will willingly bear any affliction for their sakes if he may but bring them to the Saviour. Yes, and he will also patiently endure affliction from them as he remembers how, in his own wilfulness and waywardness, he caused his Saviour to suffer on his behalf. If a man could know that, all through his life, he would have to wear a threadbare garment and exist upon very scanty fare ; if he were sure that, throughout his life, he would meet with but little kindness from Christians, and with nothing but persecution from worldlings ; and if, at the close of his career, he could only expect to be devoured by dogs or his body to be cast to the carrion crows, yet might he think all this to be but a light affliction if he might but win one soul from the unquenchable flame. Such trials as these are, happily, not necessary ; but if they were, we might count them as nothing in comparison with the bliss of bringing up from the depths of sin the precious pearls that are for ever to adorn the crown of the Redeemer.

Still speaking to Christian workers, I have next to say that *our affliction is light compared with our great motive.*

What should be the great motive of all who seek to spread the gospel, and to win sinners for Christ ? Surely there is no motive comparable to that of seeking to bring glory to God by gathering into the kingdom of Christ those for whom He shed His precious blood. Ever keep in memory, beloved, what Jesus has done for us. He left His radiant throne in glory, and condescended to take upon Himself our nature, and also our sin,—

" Bearing, that we might never bear,
    His Father's righteous ire."

Saved by His almighty grace, cleansed by His ever-precious blood, living because we have been made partakers of His life, how can we help loving Him who has made us what we are ? When that sacred passion burns vehemently within our hearts, we feel that any affliction that we have to endure in order to glorify Christ is too light to be even worth mentioning. O ye devoted lovers of the Saviour, have ye not known hours when ye have envied the martyrs, and wished that ye too might be allowed to wear the ruby crown ? When you have read about how thay had to lie for years in cold, damp dungeons, and then at last were dragged forth to die at the block, the stake, or the scaffold, have you not felt that your lives were poor and mean compared with theirs, and that you would gladly sacrifice all the comforts you now enjoy if you might be permitted to die for Christ as they did ? I hope that many of you could truthfully say to your dear Lord and Saviour,—

> " Would not my ardent spirit vie
>   With angels round the throne,
> To execute Thy sacred will,
>   And make Thy glory known ?
>
> " Would not my heart pour forth its blood
>   In honour of Thy name,
> And challenge the cold hand of death
>   To damp the immortal flame ? "

It was such a spirit as this that must have possessed the apostle Paul when he wrote concerning " our light affliction." Let us also, as workers for Christ, reckon as light affliction anything we have to endure by which we may glorify Him who bore such a terrible weight of suffering and sorrow for us.

II. Now, secondly, I am going to speak TO THOSE WHO COMPLAIN OF THE WEIGHT OF THEIR AFFLICTION.

Dear brethren and sisters, let me remind you that *your affliction is light compared with that of many others.* Think of the horrors of a battlefield, and of the agonies of the poor wounded men who have to lie there so long untended. Living in peace in our happy island home, it is difficult for us to realize the misery and wretchedness that are being endured in Paris even while I am preaching to you. Some of you complain of shortness of bread, but you have not to suffer the pangs of hunger as so many of the inhabitants of the French capital are at this moment suffering. There are some who are miserable as soon as any little ache or pain seizes them, yet their affliction is very light compared with that of many who never know what it is to be well and strong. Even if we are called to suffer pain, let us thank God that we have not been deprived of our reason. If we could go through the wards of Bethlehem Hospital, not far away from us, and see the many forms of madness represented, I think each one of us would be moved to say, " My God, I thank Thee that, however poor or sick I am, Thou hast preserved me from such mental affliction as many have to bear." How thankful we all ought to be that we are not in prison ! Does it seem improbable that such good people as we are could ever be numbered amongst the law-breakers of the land ? You know how Hazael said to Elisha, " Is thy servant a dog, that he should do this great thing ? " yet he did all that the prophet foretold ; and but for the restraining grace of God, you and I, dear friends, might have been suffering the agony and remorse that many are to-night enduring in the prisons of this and other lands. I need not go on multiplying instances of those who are suffering in various ways in mind or body or estate ; but I think I have said sufficient to convince you that our affliction, whatever form it may assume, is light compared with that of many others.

Next, *our affliction is light compared with our deserts.* We can truly say, with the psalmist, " He hath not dealt with us after our sins ; nor rewarded us according to our iniquities." If the Lord had not dealt with us in mercy and in grace, we might have been at this moment beyond the reach of hope, like that rich man who in vain begged " Father Abraham " to send Lazarus to dip his finger in water to cool his parched tongue. Yes, ungodly ones, you might have been in hell to-night, in that outer darkness where there is weeping and wailing and gnashing of teeth. Let the goodness of God in preserving you alive until now lead you to repent of your sin, and to trust in the Saviour. Thank God, you are still out of the pit ; the iron gate has not yet been opened to admit you, and then been closed upon you for ever. Yet remember that you are, as it were, standing upon a narrow neck of land between two unbounded seas, and that the waves are every moment washing away the sand from beneath your feet, and rest no longer upon such an unsafe footing, lest it should give way altogether, and you should sink down into the fathomless abyss. As for any affliction that you ever can have to endure on earth, it is not merely light, it is absolutely unworthy of mention in comparison with the eternal woe that is the portion of the lost. Be thankful that, up to the present moment, this has not been your portion ; and lest it should be, flee at once for refuge to lay hold upon the hope set before you in the gospel.

Then next, *our affliction is very light compared with that of our Lord.* Do you, dear friend, murmur at the bitterness of the draught in the cup which is put into your hand ? But what heart can conceive of the bitterness of that cup of which Jesus drank ? Yet He said, " The cup which My Father hath given Me, shall I not drink it ? " Is the disciple to be above is Master, and the servant above his Lord ? Did Christ have to swim through stormy seas, and—

> " Must you be carried to the skies
>   On flowery beds of ease ? "

I think there is no consolation for an afflicted child of God so rich as that which arises from the contemplation of the sufferings of Jesus. The remembrance of the agony and bloody sweat of Gethsemane has often dried up the sweat of terror upon the anguished brow of the believer. The stripes of Jesus have often brought healing to His wounded followers. The thirst, the desertion, and the death on Golgotha— all the incidents of our Saviour's suffering, and the terrible climax of it all,—have been most helpful in assuaging the sorrows of stricken saints. Brethren and sisters in Christ, your sufferings are not worth a moment's thought when compared with the immeasurable agonies of Jesus your Redeemer. My soul would prostrate herself at His dear pierced feet, and say, " I have never seen any other affliction like Thine affliction. I have beheld and seen, but I have never seen any sorrow like unto Thy sorrow. Thou art indeed the incomparable Monarch of misery, the unapproachable King of the whole realm of grief. Of old, Thou wert the 'Man of sorrows, and acquainted with grief,' and no man has ever been able to rob Thee of Thy peculiar title." I think that such reflections as these will help us to realize that, however heavy our affliction appears to us to be, it is very light compared with that of our dear Lord and Master.

> " Sons of God, in tribulation,
>   Let your eyes the Saviour view,
> He's the rock of our salvation,
>   He was tried and tempted too :
>   All to succour
>   Every tempted, burden'd son."

And further, beloved, *our affliction is very light compared with the blessing which we enjoy.* Many of us have had our sins forgiven for Christ's sake, and the blessing of full and free forgiveness must far outweigh any affliction that we ever have to endure. When we were lying in the gloomy dungeon of conviction, and had not a single ray of hope to lighten the darkness, we thought that, even though we had to be kept in prison all our days, and to be fed only upon bread and water, we could be quite joyous if we could but be assured that God's righteous anger was turned away from us, and that our sins and iniquities He would remember against us no more for ever. Well, that is just what many of us have experienced ; our transgressions have been forgiven, and our sin has been covered by the great atoning sacrifice of Jesus Christ our Lord and Saviour. Then let us rejoice and be glad all our days. But this is not all the blessing that we have received, for we have been clothed in the righteousness of Christ, and adopted into the family of God. Now we are heirs of God, and joint-heirs with Jesus Christ. We share even now in all the privileges of the children of God, and there are still greater favours and honours reserved for us in the future, as the apostle John saith. " Beloved, now are we the sons of God, and it doth not yet appear what we shall be ; but we know that, when He shall appear, we shall be like Him ; for we shall see Him as He is." We already have a foretaste of the bliss that is laid up in store for us, for—

> " The men of grace have found
>   Glory begun below ;
> Celestial fruits on earthly ground
>   From faith and hope do grow."

So it is quite true that, in comparison with our blessings and privileges, our affliction is indeed light. And, dear friends, we specially realize that *our affliction is light as we prove the power of the Lord's sustaining grace.* Some of you have never personally proved its power, but many of you do know by practical experience what I mean. There are times when, through acute physical pain or great mental anguish, the soul is at first utterly prostrate ; but at last it falls back, in sheer helplessness, upon the bosom of Jesus, gives up struggling, and resigns itself absolutely to His will ; and then—I speak what I do know, and testify what I have felt,—there comes into the soul a great calm, a quiet joy so deep and so pure as never is experienced at any other time. I have sometimes looked back upon nights of pain,—pain so excruciating that it has forced the tears from my eyes,—and I have almost asked to have such suffering repeated if I might but have a repetition of the seraphic bliss that I have often enjoyed under such circumstances. I made a mistake when I said

" seraphic " bliss, for seraphs have not the capacity for suffering that we have, and therefore they can never experience that deep, intense, indescribable bliss that is our portion when, by grace, we are enabled to glorify God even in the furnace of affliction.

> " Let me but hear my Saviour say,
>   Strength shall be equal to Thy day ! '
> Then I rejoice in deep distress,
>   Leaning on all-sufficient grace.
>
> " I can do all things, or can bear
>   All sufferings, if my Lord be there :
> Sweet pleasures mingle with the pains,
>   While His left hand my head sustains."

We may well say that no affliction weighs more than a gnat resting upon an elephant when the Lord's upholding grace is sweetly manifested to our soul in times of perplexity, anxiety, and pain. It is just then that Jesus often so graciously reveals Himself to us that we even come to love the cross that brings Him specially near to us. I can understand that strange speech of Rutherford, as some have regarded it, when he said that he sometimes feared lest he should make his cross into an idol by loving affliction too much because of the blessed results that flowed from it. The bark of the tree of affliction may be bitter as gall ; but if you get to the pith of it, you will find that it is as sweet as honey.

Once more, affliction—*sanctified affliction becomes very light when we see to what it leads.* Sin is our great curse, and anything that can help to deliver us from the dominion of sin is a blessing to us. It seems that, in the constitution of our nature, and in the divine discipline under which we are being trained, our growth in grace is greatly assisted by affliction and trial. There are certain propensities to evil that can only be removed in the furnace, as the dross is burnt away from the pure metal ; and surely, brethren, you who know the exceeding sinfulness of sin would not think any affliction too severe that should humble your pride, or subdue your passions, or slay your sloth, or overcome any other sin that so easily besets you. You will not merely acquiesce in the Lord's dealings with you, but you will devoutly thank Him for using the sharp knife of affliction to separate you from your sin. A wise patient will gratefully thank the surgeon who cuts his flesh, and makes it bleed, and who will not allow it to heal up too quickly ; and when God, by His gracious Spirit's operation, uses the stern surgery of trial to eradicate the propensity to sin, we do well to kiss the hand that holds the knife, and to say with cheerfulness as well as with resignation, " The will of the Lord be done."

> " It needs our hearts be wean'd from earth,
>   It needs that we be driven,
> By loss of every earthly stay,
>   To seek our joys in heaven."

Now, lastly, *our affliction is light compared with the glory which is so soon to be revealed to us and in us.* Some of us are much nearer to our heavenly home than we have ever imagined. Possibly, we are reckoning upon another twenty or even forty years of service, yet the shadows of our life's day are already lengthening although we are unaware that it is so. Perhaps we are anticipating long periods of fightings without and fears within, but those anticipations will never be realized, for the day of our final victory is close at hand, and then doubts and fears shall never again be able to assail our spirits. In this house to-night there may be some who are sitting on the very banks of the Jordan, and just across the river lies the land that floweth with milk and honey, the land which is reserved as the inheritance of the true children of God. Their eyes are so dimmed with tears that they cannot see—

> "Canaan's fair and happy land,
> Where their possessions lie."

They even imagine that they are captives by the waters of Babylon, and they hang their harps upon the willows, for they fear there are many years of banishment still before them. Yet the King's messenger is already on the way with the summons to bid them to appear before Him very soon. Even if the call does not come to some of us at once, if the Master has need of us in this world a little longer, how soon our mortal life must end! What is our life? "It is even a vapour, that appeareth for a little time, and then vanished away." "As for man, his days are as grass; as a flower of the field, so he flourisheth. For the wind passeth over it, and it is gone; and the place thereof shall know it no more." But does the brevity of life cause us any anxiety? Oh, no! "For we know that if our earthly house of this tabernacle were dissolved, we have a building of God, a house not made with hands, eternal in the heavens"; and when once we reach that blest abode of all the saints, and look back upon our earthly experiences, we shall feel that any affliction we had to endure was light indeed compared with the unutter-able bliss that shall then be our eternal portion. We are pilgrims to Zion's city bound, and we necessarily have certain privations and difficulties; but when our journey is at an end,—

> "One hour with our God
> Will make up for it all."

If we have not this good hope through grace, we may well say that our affliction is *not* light. I cannot imagine how any of you, my hearers, can go on living without a Saviour;—you poor people, you hard-working people, you sickly, consumptive people, how can you live without a Saviour? I wonder how those who are rich, and who have an abundance of earthly comforts, can live on year after year without any hope (except a false one) of comfort and blessing in the life that is to come. But as for you who have so few earthly comforts, you whose life is one long struggle for bare existence, you who scarcely know what it is to have a day without pain, how can *you* live without a Saviour? Remember that "godliness, is profitable unto all things, having promise of the life that now is, and of that which is to come." So, "seek ye the Lord while He may be found, call ye upon Him while He is near: let the wicked forsake his way, and the unrighteous man his thoughts: and let him return unto the Lord, and He will have mercy upon him; and to our God, for He will abundantly pardon." May the Lord give you the grace to come unto Him this very moment, and to Him shall be all glory for ever, for Jesus Christ's sake. Amen.

THE TENT DISSOLVED AND THE MANSION ENTERED

" For we know that if our earthly house of this tabernacle were dissolved, we have a building of God, an house not made with hands, eternal in the heavens."—2 Corinthians v. 1.

PAUL ranks among the bravest of the brave. We note also with admiration how the hero of so many dangers and conflicts, who could glow and burn with fervour, was yet among the calmest and quietest of spirits. He had learned to live beyond those present circumstances which worry and disturb; he had stolen a march upon the shadows of time, and entered into possession of the realities of eternity. He looked not on the things which are seen, but he set his whole regard on the things which are not seen; and by this means he entered into a deep and joyful peace which made him strong, resolute, steadfast, immovable. I would to God that we had all acquired Paul's art of being "always confident,"—his habit of having the inward man renewed day by day. The most of us are far too like the insect of the summer hour, which sports away its life of moments among the flowers, and lo! all is over. Are we not too apt to live in the immediate present which is revealed by the senses? The ox projects no thought upward or beyond: to stand in the cool brook or lie down in the fat pasturage is its all in all; even thus is it with the mass of men, their souls are tethered to their bodies, imprisoned within the circumstances of the day. If we could be completely delivered from the thraldom of things seen and felt, and could feel the full influence of the invisible and the eternal, how much of heaven we might enjoy before the celestial shores are reached!

Paul's life was rough and stormy, yet who might not desire it? Had there been no life to come, he would have been of all men the most miserable, for he was one of the poorest, most persecuted, most despised, most slandered, most wearied, and most suffering of mortals: and yet if I had to put my finger upon happy lives I should not hesitate to select among the foremost the life of the Apostle Paul, for whom to live was Christ. It is also to be specially noted as to his happiness that he had a reason for it. My text begins with the word, "For." Paul is always argumentative, the leaning of his mind is in that direction; hence, if he is cast down he has a reason for it, and if he is calm he can show just cause for his peace. Some religionists are deliriously happy, but they cannot tell you why. They can sing and shout, and dance, but they can give no reason for their excitement. They see an enthusiastic crowd, and they catch the infection: their religion is purely emotional; I am not going to condemn it, yet show I unto you a more excellent way. The joy which is not created by substantial causes is mere froth and foam, and soon vanishes away. Unless you can tell why you are happy you will not long be happy. If you have no principle at the back of your passion your passion will burn down to a black ash, and you will look in vain for a living spark. Some professors have not enough emotion, their hearts are too small, though I cannot say that their heads are too large ; but there are others whose hearts are their main force, who are soon on fire, blazing away like shavings and brush-wood when first the flame lights upon them ; but their brains are an uncertain quantity, never sufficient to manage the furnace of their emotions. It was not so with Paul : he was a well-balanced man. If able to defy the present and rejoice in prospect of the future, he had a solid reason for so doing. I like a man who is fervent and enthusiastic, and yet in his fervour is as reasonable as if he were some cool logician. Let the heart be like a fiery, high-mettled steed, but take care that it is curbed and managed by discretion. An instructed Christian man is rational even in his ecstasies : ready to give a reason for the hope that is in him, when that hope seems to rise above all reason. He is glad, gladdest of the glad, but he knows the why and the wherefore of his gladness ; and so he can bear the cruel tests to which the world exposes spiritual joy. The true believer's peace can answer the cavils of men or devils ; it can justify itself in its opposition to all appearances. This is a house built upon a foundation, a tree which has a firmly settled root, a star fixed in its sphere ; and thus it is infinitely superior to the house upon the sand, the tree plucked up, the fleeting vapour of mere emotion. May God, the Holy Spirit, instruct us so that we may know the truth out of which solid happiness is sure to grow!

I see in the text before us, first of all, *a catastrophe which Paul saw to be very possible*—" If our earthly house of this tabernacle were dissolved " ; secondly, *the provision which he surely knew to be made* should that catastrophe occur—" We have a building of God, a house not made with hands, eternal in the heavens " ; and thirdly, I shall dwell for a minute or two upon *the value of this knowledge to Paul and to the rest of us in our present trying condition.*

I. First, then, consider THE CATASTROPHE WHICH PAUL SAW TO BE VERY POSSIBLE : " If our earthly house of this tabernacle were dissolved."

He did not fear that he himself would be dissolved : he had not the slightest fear about that. The catastrophe which he looked forward to is known among us by the name of " death " ; but he calls it the dissolving of the earthly house of his tabernacle ; the taking down of his tent-house body. He does not say, " If I were to be destroyed," or " If I were to be annihilated " ; he knows no supposition of that character ; he feels assured that he himself is perfectly safe. There is latent within the text an element of deep quiet as to his real self. " *We* know that if *our* earthly house of this tabernacle were dissolved, *we* have a building of God." The " we " is all unharmed and unmoved ; if our house were dissolved *we* should not be undone ; if we were to lose this earthly tent we have " a building of God, eternal in the heavens." The real man, the essential self, is out of harm's way ; and all that he talks about is the falling to pieces of a certain tabernacle or tent in which for the present he is lodging. Many people are in a great fright about the future, yet here is Paul viewing the worst thing that could happen to him with such complacency that he likens it to nothing worse than the pulling down of a tent in which he was making shift to reside for a little season. He was afraid of nothing beyond that, and if that happened he had expectations which reconciled him to the event, and even helped him to anticipate it with joy.

Paul was not absolutely sure that his body would be dissolved. He hoped that he might be alive and remain at the coming of the Lord, and then he would be changed and be for ever with the Lord, without passing through death. Still, he was willing to leave this in the Lord's hands, and when he saw it to be possible that he should be numbered among the blessed dead who die in the Lord he did not shrink from the prospect, but bravely found a metaphor which set forth the little fear which he entertained concerning it.

The apostle perceived that the body in which he lived *was frail in itself.* Paul was accustomed to make tents. I do not suppose he ever manufactured any very large or sumptuous ones—probably he did not own capital enough for that, but he was a tent worker and mender. The use of tents was common enough among the Roman people in Paul's day. The gentry delighted in bright pavilions which they could set up at pleasure, and the commoner folk found pleasure in spending a part of their time under canvas. Whilst he was sitting writing this letter it is most likely that Paul had a tent or two to repair lying near his hand, and this suggested to him the language of the verse before us. When a tent is newly placed it is but a frail structure, very far removed from the substantiality of a house ; in that respect it is exactly like this feeble corporeal frame of ours, which is crushed before the moth. Paul felt that his body would not need any great force to overthrow it ; it was like the tent which the Midianite saw in his dream, which only needed to be struck by a barley cake, and lo ! it lay along. A house of solid masonry may need a crowbar and a pick to start its stones from their places, but feebler tools will soon overturn a tent and make a ruin of it. The body is liable to dissolution from causes so minute as to be imperceptible—a breath of foul air, an atom of poisonous matter, a trifle, a mere nothing, may end this mortal life. I hope that you and I duly remember the frailty of our bodies. We are not so foolish as to think that because we are in robust health to-day we must necessarily live to old age. We have had among ourselves lately abundant evidence that those who appear to be the healthiest are often the first to be taken away, while feeble persons linger on among us, whose lives are a continued wonder and a perpetual struggle. When we think of the brittle ware whereof our bodies are made it is not strange that they should soon be broken. Is it not a wonderful thing that we continue to live ? much more wonderful than that we should die ? Dr. Watts has wisely said—

" Our life contains a thousand springs,
And dies if one be gone ;
Strange ! that a harp of thousand strings
Should keep in tune so long "

Some small affair interferes with a minute valve or organ of secretion, mischief is engendered by it, the whole current of life is hindered, and by-and-by death ensues. It is a very delicate process by which dust remains animated ; a thousand things can stay that process, and then our body is dissolved. Paul, therefore, because he saw his body to be frail as a bubble, looked forward to the time when the earthly house of his soul would be dissolved.

When he was writing this epistle *he had many signs about him that his body would be dissolved.* His many labours were telling upon him ; he was worn down with fatigue, he was spent in his Master's service. He was so full of the heavenly fire that he could never rest : after he had evangelized one city he was forced to hasten to another ; if he was driven out of one village he hurried to the next, for he was eager to deliver the message of salvation. He wore himself out with labour, and he felt, therefore, that the day would come when his body would give way under the intense excitement of his life-agony. In addition to this he endured cold and hunger, and nakedness, and sickness, and infirmities brought upon him by his missionary self-sacrifice. He had a hard time of it as to physical endurance, and I should think there was scarcely a limb of the man that did not suffer in consequence of the imprisonments, scourings, stonings, and other hardships which he had suffered. He felt that one of these days in all probability the house of his tent would come down through the violence of his persecutors. Once he most touchingly spoke of himself as " such an one as Paul the Aged " ; and aged men cannot get away from the consciousness that their body is failing. Certain crumbling portions warn the old man that the house is dilapidated ; the thatch which has grown thin or blanched tells its tale. There are signs about the aged which warn them that their earthly house was not built to stand for ever ; it is a tabernacle or tent set up for a temporary purpose, and it shows signs of waxing old, and being ready to pass away. Hence, then, Paul was led to feel that both from the natural frailty of the body, and also from the injuries which it had already sustained, there was before him the evident probability that the earthly house of his tabernacle would be dissolved.

Besides, Paul's frail body had been *subject to exceeding great perils*. I saw the other day an encampment of gipsies out upon the common ; many of this wandering race were sitting under a coarse covering sustained by sticks, I should exaggerate if I called them poles ; and I could not help feeling that such an abode was all very well on a warm day, but not at all desirable when the east-wind was blowing, or a shower of sleet was driving along, or a deluge of rain descending. The apostle's body was a tent which was subjected to great stress of weather. God had not screened him ; though one of the most precious men that ever lived, yet he was exposed to more danger than almost any other of the Lord's servants. Here is his own account of the matter ;— " Thrice was I beaten with rods, once was I stoned, thrice I suffered shipwreck, a night and a day I have been in the deep ; in journeyings often, in perils of waters, in perils of robbers, in perils by mine own countrymen, in perils by the heathen, in perils in the city, in perils in the wilderness, in perils in the sea, in perils among false brethren ; in weariness and painfulness, in watchings often, in hunger and thirst, in fastings often, in cold and nakedness." Well might he reckon that ere long his poor shepherd's shanty would give way under such rude blasts.

Besides, Paul knew that so *many others whom he had known and loved had already died*, and he gathered from this that he would himself die. There used to sit in this house a brother who has often assured me that he should not die, and that if any Christian man did die it was because he grieved the Lord. I am sorry to say that I have missed that brother for many months ; I hope he has not yet disproved his own theory ; but I am sure that he will do so sooner or later unless our Lord should hasten his advent. Whenever I meet with an enthusiast who boasts that he shall never die, I find it best to let him wait and see. One fine old Irish clergyman has frequently sought to instruct me in the art of being immortal, and he has been grieved and angry because I never set much store by the long life which he offered me. Though an old man, he assured me that he should never die ; he expected in a short time to throw out all the infirmities of his years in the form of a rash, and then he should be as vigorous as ever. Alas ! the good rector is buried, and his crazy brain is at rest. It is appointed unto men once to die. I should have thought that since so many of the excellent of the earth have fallen asleep, nobody would ever have been so mad as to raise a question about its being the common lot. Our crowded cemeteries supply ten thousand arguments why each one of us may expect to die in due time. This earthly house of our tabernacle will be dissolved ; all things unite to warrant the belief.

Now, brethren, this was all that Paul did expect on the sad side ; and truly it is not much. Is it ? Certain Swiss peasants not very long ago were feeding their flocks on one of the lofty upland valleys. On one side of the pasturage stood a number of *chȃlets*, or wooden huts, in which they were accustomed to live during the summer, poor shelters which were left as soon as the winter set in. One day they heard a strange rumbling up in the lofty Alps, and they understood what it meant ; it meant that a mass of rock or snow or ice had fallen, and would soon come crushing down in the form of an avalanche. In a brief space their fears were realized, for they saw a tremendous mass come rushing from above, bearing destruction in its course. What did it destroy ? Only the old, crazy *chȃlets :* that was all. Every man of the shepherds was safe, and untouched : the event was rather to them a matter which caused a Te Deum to be sung in the village church below than a subject for mourning and sorrow. They said, " The avalanche is terrible, but it has not slain the aged mother, nor crushed the babe in its cradle : it has injured none of us, but only buried a few hovels which we can soon rebuild." Their case is a picture of ours. The avalanche of death will fall ; but O ye saints, when it comes this is all it will do for you—your earthly house will be dissolved ! Will you fret over so small a loss ? No evil will come nigh to you ; the poor hut of the body will be buried beneath the earth, but as for yourself, what will you have to do but to sing an everlasting Te Deum unto Him who delivered you from death and danger, and raised you to His own right hand ?

It would not long affect a man if his tent should be overthrown ; he would shake himself clear of it and come forth ; it would not otherwise disturb him. So death shall not affect us for the worse, but for the better ; the dissolution of this hampering frame shall give us liberty. To-day we are like birds in the egg ; so long as the shell is whole we are not free : death breaks the shell. Does the fledgling lament the dissolution of the shell ? I never heard of a bird in its nest pining over its broken shell ; no, its thought runs otherwise : to wings, and flight, and sunny skies. So let it be with us. This body will be dissolved : let it be so ; it is meet it should be. We have been glad of it while we have needed it, and we thank God for the wondrous skill displayed in it ; but when we no longer require it we shall escape from it as from imprisonment, and never wish to return to its narrow bounds. Death, as it pulls away our sackcloth canopy, will reveal to our wondering eyes the palace of the King wherein we shall dwell for ever, and, therefore, what cause have we to be alarmed at it ? I have set out the whole catastrophe before you, and surely no believer trembles in view of it.

II. So now we pass on to the second head, THE PROVISION OF WHICH THE APOSTLE PAUL MOST SURELY KNEW. He knew that if his tent-dwelling was overthrown he would not be without a home ; he knew that he would not have to open his eyes in a naked condition, and cry, " Woe's me, whither am I to fly ? I have no dwelling place." No, he knew that if this tent-house were gone he had " a building of God." Paul was not afraid of going to purgatory : though of late some even among Protestants have in a modified form revived that grim fiction, and have told us that even believers will have much to bear before they will be fit for eternal happiness. The apostle held no such opinion ; but, on the contrary, he wrote—" We know that if our earthly house of this tabernacle were dissolved, we have a building of God." He did not expect to be roasted alive for the next thousand years, and then to leap from purgatory to Paradise ; but he did expect to go, as soon as ever his earthly house was dissolved, into his eternal house which is in the heavens. He had not even the thought of lying in a state of unconsciousness till the resurrection. He says, " We know that if the earthly house of this tabernacle were dissolved, we have [we have already] a building of God." He says not " we shall have it," but " we have it " ; " we know that we have it." The picture seems to me to be as though one of you should dwell in his garden in a tent for a while. Somebody inquires what would happen if a gale of wind should blow your tent away in the night. " Oh," say you, " I have a house over yonder ; I should go within doors and live there." What a comfort to know that, whatever occurs to our temporary gear, we have a fixed and settled abode to which we can at once repair. This makes us feel independent of all dangers, and helps us joyfully to welcome the inevitable, come when it may.

What did the apostle mean, however ? for this text is said to be a very difficult one. He meant, first—the moment his soul left its body it would at once enter into that house of which Jesus said, " In my Father's house are many mansions : if it were not so, I would have told you." Do you want to know about that house ? Read the Book of the Revelation, and learn of its gates of pearl, its streets of gold, its walls of rarest gems, of the river which windeth through it, and of the trees which bear their fruit every month. If after that you desire to know more concerning this house, I can but give you the advice which was given by John Bunyan in a similar case. One asked of honest John a question which he could not answer, for the matter was not opened in God's word ; and therefore honest John bade his friend live a godly life, and go to heaven, *and see for himself.* Believe no dreams, but bide thy time, believing in the Lord Jesus, and thou shalt shortly know all about the house not made with hands, eternal in the heavens.

Paul, however, did mean that in the fulness of time he would again be clothed upon with a body. He regarded the waiting time as so short that he

almost overlooked it, as men forget a moment's pause in a grand march. Ultimately, I say he expected to be housed in a body : the tent-house which was blown down and dissolved would be developed into a building, so rich and rare as to be fitly called " a building of God, a house not made with hands." This also is our prospect. At this present in this mortal body we groan being burdened, for our spirit is liberated from bondage, but our body is not yet emancipated, although it has been bought with a price. We are " waiting for the adoption, to wit, the redemption of our body," and so " the body is dead because of sin ; but the Spirit is life because of righteousness." Our soul has been regenerated, but the body waits for the process which in its case is analogous to regeneration, namely, the resurrection from the dead. Disembodied saints may have to wait a few thousand years, more or less, dwelling in the Father's house above ; but there shall come eventually the sounding of the trumpet and the raising of the dead, and then the perfected spirit shall dwell in a body adapted to its glory. The certainty of the resurrection raises us above the dread which would otherwise surround the dissolution of our body. A child sees a man throwing precious metal into a melting pot, and he is sad because fair silver is being destroyed ; but he that knows the business of the refiner understands that no loss will come of the process ; only the dross of that silver will be taken away, and the pure molten mass poured out into a comely mould will yet adorn a royal table. Well, my brethren, are we assured that to lose this vile body is clear gain since it will be fashioned according to the glorious body of the Lord Jesus ?

Let us pass on to *consider how Paul could say he knew this.* This wonderfully enlightened nineteenth century has produced an order of wise men who glory in their ignorance. They call themselves " Agnostics," or know-nothings. When I was a boy it would have seemed odd to me to have met with a man who glorified in being an ignoramus, and yet that is the Latin for that Greek word " Agnostic." Is it not singular to hear a man boastfully say, " I am an ignoramus " ? How different is our apostle ! He says " we know." Whence came this confidence ? How did He know ?

First, Paul knew that he had a Father in heaven, for he felt the spirit of sonship ; he knew also that his Father had a house, and he was certain that if ever he lost the tent in which he lived he should be sure to be welcomed into his own Father's house above. How do our children know that if ever they are in need of a house they can come home to us ? Did they learn that from their tutors at school ? No, their childhood's instinct teaches them that our house is their home, just as chickens run under the mother-hen without needing to be trained. Because they are our children they feel that as long as we have a house they have a house too ; Paul, therefore, unhesitatingly said, " We know " ; and, brethren, we know the same through like confidence in our Father's love. In the house of the many mansions we feel quite sure of a hearty welcome in due time. Shut out from our Father's home we cannot be ! Houseless wanderers while our royal Father dwells in His palace we cannot be ! We are not merely hopeful on this matter, but certain ; and therefore we say, " We know."

Paul knew, again, that he had an elder brother,

and that this brother had gone before to see to the lodging of the younger brethren. Paul remembered that Jesus had said, " I go to prepare a place for you, and if I go and prepare a place for you, I will come again, and receive you unto Myself, that where I am ye may be also." So Paul had no question whatever ; if the Lord had gone to prepare a place there would be a place for him ; for he never knew his divine Lord set about anything and fail therein. Can we not all trust our Forerunner ? Have we any doubts of Him who has entered within the veil as our representative ? No ; as we are sure that Jesus has passed into the heavens on our behalf, so are we sure that when this tent-house body is dissolved, there remains a rest and home for our souls.

Doubtless, Paul also thought of the Holy Ghost, that blessed One who deigns to live with us in this frail house of clay, which is in many ways an uncomfortable and unsuitable abode for Him by reason of the sin which has defiled it. He condescends to dwell in these mortal bodies, and, therefore, when we leave our earthly house He will leave it too ; and we are persuaded that a place will be found where we may still abide in fellowship. As our bodies have been honoured to entertain the Holy Ghost we may be sure that in our hour of need He will find an abode for us. He has been our guest, and in His turn He will be our host ; this we know, for we know the love of the Spirit. He who has made our body His temple will find a rest for our souls. Thus, from the Father, the Son, and the Holy Ghost, we gather assurance that we shall not wander to and fro unhoused, even though this mortal frame should be dissolved.

Besides, let me tell you something. Paul knew that when he died there was a Paradise prepared, for he had been there already. You remember how he locked up that story till he could keep it no longer, and, then, fifteen years after its occurrence, he let out the blessed secret. Let me read his words, " I knew a man in Christ above fourteen years ago (whether in the body, I cannot tell ; or whether out of the body, I cannot tell ; God knoweth), such an one caught up to the third heaven. And I knew such a man (whether in the body, or out of the body, I cannot tell : God knoweth), how that he was caught up into Paradise, and heard unspeakable words, which is not lawful for a man to utter." He says he was taken up to the third heaven ; it was, therefore, idle to tell Paul that there was no home for him hereafter, for he had seen the place. " Well," say you, " I have not seen it." No ; but you fully believe the witness of Paul, do you not ? For my own part I am sure that Paul would not say that which is false, and inasmuch as he went into the third heaven or Paradise, and saw it, I believe that there is such a place. Remember that this is the place to which the Lord Jesus admitted the dying thief, " To-day shalt thou be with Me in Paradise." This is the place where Jesus is, and where we shall be with Him for ever, when the earthly house of this tabernacle shall be dissolved.

Yet, again, dear brothers and sisters, you and I know that when this earthly tabernacle is dissolved there will be a new body for us, because our Lord Jesus Christ has risen from the dead. In my mind the ultimate answer to my deepest unbelief is the fact of the rising of Jesus from the dead. No matter of history is anything like so well attested as the fact that our Lord was crucified, dead and buried, and that He did upon the third day rise again from the dead. This I unhesitatingly accept as a fact, and this

becomes my anchorage. Inasmuch as Jesus is the representative of all who are in Him, it is as certain that the believer will rise as that Jesus has risen. The apostle says, " We know," and remembering these grand truths I am sure that His words are not a bit too strong. Nay, if I knew any word in the English language which would express more assurance than the word to know, I would use it this morning for myself. Much more, then, might the apostle use it for himself.

This we are also sure of, namely, that if our Lord Jesus be alive and in a place of rest He will never leave His chosen and redeemed ones without house or home. Where He has found a throne His people shall find a dwelling. Delightful is our old-fashioned ditty :—

" And when I shall die, Receive me, I'll cry,
For Jesus has loved me, I cannot tell why ;
But this I do find, we two are so joined,
He won't be in glory and leave me behind."

There is such an attachment between Christ and the believer ; yea, more, such a vital, essential, indissoluble, tender marriage union that separation is impossible. As no man among us would ever be content to see his wife in prison if he could set her free, or to leave her outside in the cold when he could bring her to his fireside in comfort, so Christ, to whom our soul is espoused in eternal wedlock, will never rest until He has brought every one of His own beloved to be with Him where He is, that they may behold His glory, the glory which the Father hath given Him. No believer in Jesus has any doubts about that. I am sure you can all say, as Paul did, " We know that if our earthly house of this tabernacle were dissolved, we have a building of God, an house not made with hands."

" Ah," says one, " but how is a man to know that *he* has an interest in all this ? Suppose I do know that the children of God are thus favoured, how am I to know that I am one of them ? " I invite you to self-examination on this point. Dost thou believe in the Lord Jesus Christ with all thine heart ? Then it is written, " He that believeth in Me though he were dead yet shall he live. He that liveth and believeth in Me shall never die." Having believed in Christ the apostle knew that he was safe ; for the promises are to believers, and if any man be a believer every promise of the covenant belongs to him. We obtain further assurance of this by our possessing the new life. Dear friend, have you entered into a new world ? Do you feel within you a new heart and a right spirit ? Have old things passed away, and have all things become new ? Are you a new creature in Christ Jesus ? Then it is all right with you : that new life cannot die, your new-born nature must inherit everlasting bliss. " Fear not, little flock ; it is your Father's good pleasure to give you the kingdom." In addition to this, do you commune with God ? Do you speak with Christ ? None perish who commune with the Father and the Son. Jesus cannot say at the last " I never knew you ; depart from Me " ; for He does know you, and you know Him. " Oh," say you, " He knows enough of me, for I am always begging." Just so, go on with that trade ; be always a spiritual mendicant. The Lord of love will never cast away a pleading suppliant : he who frequents the throne of grace shall infallibly reach the throne of glory. Beside, does not " the Spirit itself also bear witness with our spirit that we are the children of God " ? And if children and heirs, are we afraid of being left naked in the world to come ? I hope that many of us have now reached the full assurance of faith, so that we believe and are sure. Can you not say each one for himself,—" I know whom I have believed, and I am persuaded that He is able to keep that which I have committed to Him until that day " ? These are the ways in which believers know that they are believers, and then by the word of God they know that all things are theirs, so that if their earthly house should fail they would be received into everlasting habitations.

III. Lastly, as to THE VALUE OF THIS KNOWLEDGE TO US. To be sure that when this body dies all is well, is not that worth knowing ? Secularists twit us with taking men's minds away from the practical present that they may dream over a fancied future. We answer that the best help to live for the present is to live in prospect of the eternal future. Paul's confident belief that if his body should be dissolved he would be no loser, kept him from fainting. He knew what the worst would be, and he was prepared for it. Great storms were out, but the apostle knew the limit of his possible loss, and so was ready. All we can lose is the frail tent of this poor body. By no possibility can we lose more. When a man knows the limit of his risk it greatly tends to calm his mind. The undiscoverable and the unmeasured are the worst ingredients of dread and terror : when you can gauge your fears, you have removed them. Our apostle felt that he had been sent into the world with the great design of glorifying God, winning souls, and building up saints, and he was fully resolved to keep to the ministry which he had received. He argues with himself that his most dangerous course would be to faint in his life-service, for perseverance in his calling could bring with it no greater risk than death, and that he summed up as losing a tent and gaining a mansion. The Roman emperor might strike off his head, or a mob might stone him to death, or he might be crucified like his Master : but he made light of such a fate ! It was to him only the coming down of the old tent ; it did not affect his undying spirit ; he smiled and sang, " For our light affliction, which is but for a moment, worketh for us a far more exceeding and eternal weight of glory."

The prospect of his heavenly house made his present trials seem very light ; for he felt like a man who sojourns for a night at a poor inn, but puts up with it gladly because he hopes to be home on the morrow. If we were trying tent life for a season we should probably cry out, " A fearful draught comes in at that corner ! How damp it is under foot ! How cramped up one feels ! " Yet we should smile over it all, and say, " It will not be for long. We shall soon be in our house at home." Ah, brethren, an hour with our God will make up for all the trials of the way. Wherefore, be of good courage, and press on.

This changed for Paul the very idea of death ; death was transformed from a demon into an angel : it was but the removal of a tottering tent that he might enter into a permanent palace. Some of God's own children are much troubled through fear of death, because they do not know what it is. If they were better taught they would soon discover in their present source of sorrow a subject for song. I would like here to say that I have known some of my Master's doubting and fearing servants die splendidly. Do you remember how Mr. Feeble-mind, when he crossed the

river, went over dry-shod. Poor soul, he thought he should surely be drowned, and yet he scarcely wet the soles of his feet. I have known men of God go like Jacob all day long weary and faint, feeling banished from their Father's house ; and yet when they have laid their head down for their final sleep they have had visions of angels and of God. The end of their journey has made amends for the rough places of the way. It shall be so with you, brother believer. There is usually a dark place in every Christian's experience : I have seen some travel in sunlight almost the whole of the way, and then depart in gloom, and I have thought none the worse of them for it ; and I have seen others struggle forward through a fog for the first part of their pilgrimage, and then come out into cloudless day. At one period or another beneath these lowering skies the shadow falls across our way, but surely " light is sown for the righteous, and gladness for the upright in heart."

As I have thought of some of my dear brothers and sisters that I have seen die very sweetly, and I have remembered that they were, in life, lowly and self-distrustful, I have compared them to persons who, when they drink their tea, forget to stir the sugar at the bottom of the cup. How doubly sweet the drink becomes as they near the bottom : they have more sweetness than they can well bear. Would it not be wise to stir the tea at once and enjoy the sweetness from the brim to the bottom ? This is the benefit of faith as to the future, for it flavours the present with delight. But what if saints should miss immediate comfort for awhile, how richly will they be compensated ! What will it be to open your eyes in heaven ! What a joy to fall asleep on the bed of languishing and to wake up amid the celestial Hallelujahs ! " What am I ? Where am I ? Ah, my God ! my Christ ! my heaven ! my all ! I am at home." Sorrow and sighing shall flee away. Does not this view of things give a transfiguration to death ? O you poor unbelievers, how I pity you, since you have no such glorious hopes. O that you would believe in the Lord Jesus and enter into life eternal.

Faith had such an effect upon Paul that it made him always calm, and brave. Why should he be afraid of a man that could not do him harm ? Even if his persecutor killed him he would do him a service. What had he to fear ? This made Paul wise and prudent. He could use his judgment, for he was not fluttered. He was not like some of you that are only a little ill, and straightway you are filled with fright, and so you make yourselves worse than you otherwise would be, so that the doctor has to contend with an affrighted mind as well as a diseased body. He who is calm, restful, happy is already on the road to a cure. He is quiet because he is in his Father's hands, and whether he lives or dies all is well ; and this conviction helps the physician to remove his bodily malady. I say again, there is no way to live like learning to die, and he who can afford to be careless whether he lives or dies is the man who will so live as to die triumphantly. Oh, that all of you felt the quiet which comes of trusting in the Lord Jesus. How sad to know that you may die at any moment, and to be unprepared for the change ! I do not wonder that you are unhappy : you have good reason for being so. Oh that you were wise, and would make the future sure by faith in the risen Lord.

In Martin Luther's time, and before his era, men who had lived evil lives were often in great fear when they came to die, and in their terror they would send to a monastery and procure a monk's dress in which to be buried. What a foolish fancy! Yet so it was that they hoped to fare better in the day of judgment for being wrapped in brown serge, and covered with a cowl! Be ours a better garment. Here is a wish of holy Rutherford—" His believed love shall be my winding-sheet, and all my grave-clothes; I shall roll up my soul, and sew it up in the web of His sweet and free love." Is not that your idea? It is surely mine! If we are laid to sleep in such a cerecloth, there will be no fear of our waking. It will happen

to us as to the man who was laid in Elisha's grave, and at once arose as soon as he touched the prophet's bones. No man can lie dead if wrapped up in the love of Christ, for His love is life. He that has touched the love of Christ has touched the heart of the life of God, and he must live. So let us give ourselves up to that divine love, and trusting in our Lord, let us go onward to eternal bliss till the day break and the shadows flee away: let us triumph and rejoice that there is prepared for us a " building of God, a house not made with hands, eternal in the heavens."

THE BELIEVER IN THE BODY AND OUT OF THE BODY

" Now He that hath wrought us for the selfsame thing is God, who also hath given unto us the earnest of the Spirit. Therefore we are always confident, knowing that, whilst we are at home in the body, we are absent from the Lord: (for we walk by faith, not by sight): we are confident, I say, and willing rather to be absent from the body, and to be present with the Lord. Wherefore we labour, that, whether present or absent, we may be accepted of Him. For we must all appear before the judgment seat of Christ; that every one may receive the things done in his body, according to that he hath done, whether it be good or bad."—2 Corinthians v. 5-10.

IT is quite clear that the apostle did not consider his body to be himself. He speaks of it as being the frail tent or tabernacle in which he dwelt, and again as the garment with which for a while he was clothed. That tent or tabernacle he expected to see dissolved, and that garment he expected to put off. He distinguished between the outward man which would perish, and the inward man, which was his true self, which he speaks of as " renewed day by day." The apostle reckoned upon living here in the body, according to the divine will, till he had finished the work which was given him to do, and then he expected to put off his mortal flesh, and to be a spirit unclothed and disembodied. Such is the condition at the present time of all the saints who have departed; they are well described as " the spirits of just men made perfect." With the exception of Enoch and Elias, who carried their bodies with them into the celestial world, all departed believers are now spirits unclothed of their bodies, and wearing only such array as befits spiritual existences. Is it difficult to conceive of them in that condition? I do not think it should be. Spirits *without* bodies are not such marvellous things as spirits *in* bodies. You every day as you walk the streets meet spirits in bodies, spirits that quicken flesh and bone and muscle, and move a mass of material from place to place. If we had never seen such a thing as a body kept in life and filled with power by an immaterial, invisible, and spiritual substance, it would be a very hard thing to realize it. No man among us knows how it is that this inner spirit of ours is connected with the body. Where is the point of union? What is the link between soul and sinew? Where does spirit begin and where does matter end? We know that if we will to move our arm it is moved, but how does the mind that wills manage to grasp the materialism which obeys its bidding? How is spirit capable of acting upon matter at all? How is it that a spirit can dwell within an abode of flesh, look out of these eyes, listen through these ears, speak by these lips, and perform its will by these hands? Eyes and ears and hands are but earth; they are made of such matter as we meet with in other parts of the solid

world, mere dust of the earth, materialism wisely moulded, but yet corruptible materialism; and yet the soul somehow manages to indwell and inhabit its house of clay—a far more wonderful thing it seems to me than for a spirit to exist without a body. We shall find it easy to conceive of a spirit disentangled of materialism in proportion as we have learned to meditate upon spiritual things, and to feel the powers of the world to come. Multitudes around us know nothing of anything which does not appeal to their senses, but the man who has been renewed by the Spirit of God is himself made spiritually minded, and hence the idea of disembodied spirits is not strange to him. Let us, according to Scripture, look forward to a condition in which our perfected spirits shall abide with Christ, " waiting for the adoption, to wit, the redemption of our body " (Romans viii. 23).

Yet Paul did not expect that the disembodied state would last for ever, for he was assured of the resurrection of the body. He did not despise the body so as to hope never to see it again, but he reckoned that after it had been put off it would undergo a change, and thus would be so renovated that at the coming of the Lord he would put it on afresh, and so his spirit would again be clothed. He expected that mortality would be swallowed up of life, and we also confidently indulge the same hope. The fabric which was put into the ground when the believer was buried was sown in corruption, we expect to see it raised in incorruption. That which we laid in the tomb the other day was a poor dishonoured corpse on which decay was working its fierce will, but we shall see it raised in glory, radiant with the light which made Moses' face to shine. That which we committed to mother earth we lowered into the grave in weakness, but it shall as surely rise in power. That which was buried was a soulish body, only fit for the natural soul, but not adapted for the movements and aspirations of the regenerated spirit; but we know that when it shall rise it will be a spiritual body adapted to our highest nature, fitted to be the palace of that gracious life which makes us sons of God. The apostle's great expectation was the perfection of his entire manhood, spirit, soul and body in

Christ Jesus. He was confident in the expectation that though he would be unhoused for awhile by the dissolving of his earthly tabernacle, he would soon enter into a building of God, a house not made with hands, eternal in the heavens, and stand before the presence of God both as to his body and his soul made perfect in Christ Jesus. This was his confident expectation.

From the text it is clear that this belief had a powerful influence over the apostle. It had especially two effects upon him : one was to make him " always confident," and the other was to create in him a high ambition : " wherefore," says he, " we labour, that, whether present or absent, we may be accepted of Him." He felt that whatever he might be, and in whatever condition he might exist, the only thing he had to care for was that he might be pleasing to Him who had redeemed him with His precious blood ; and so whether in the body or out of the body it mattered little to him so long as he could but be accepted of the Lord in Jesus Christ.

Of the apostle's *confidence* and *ambition* we are going to speak this morning as the Spirit of God may graciously help us.

I. And first, dear friends, THE BELIEVER HAS GROUND FOR CONSTANT CONFIDENCE. The apostle tells us, " Therefore we are always confident " ; and then again, lest we should lose the sense by the interjected sentence in the seventh verse, he says again, " We are confident, I say." The condition, then, of the Christian, when he is living in faith of resurrection and eternal life, is a condition of continual confidence, a confidence which regards both the life which now is, and the state in which we expect to live before we reach the fulness of the promised glory : a confidence which concerns the present state,—for while we are at home in the body we are always confident : a confidence which equally concerns, and rather more, so the state which is to come, for " we are confident, I say, and willing rather to be absent from the body, and to be present with the Lord."

First, let me speak with you upon *the confidence which the believer has in reference to his present condition while he is at home in the body.* Our translators have been somewhat unfortunate in their choice of terms in this instance, for they have lost part of the interest of the passage. We should have seen more beauty in these words if they had given us their literal meaning a little more closely. Let me read them to you as they may be read : " We are always confident, knowing that, while we are at home in the body, we are from home as to the Lord. We are confident, I say, and willing rather to be from home as to the body, and to be at home with the Lord. Wherefore we labour, that, whether from home, or at home, we may be accepted of Him." You see the point lies in *at home* and *from home.* These words are as near an approach to the original as could readily be found, though they do not exhaust the sense of the Greek terms. Here, then, in the present state we are said to be at home in the body ; but we are at home in a very modified sense, for it is a home which is not a home, but only a frail lodging, a temporary tenement to accommodate us till we reach our true and real home in the New Jerusalem. It is such a home as a soldier has in the camp at a bivouac, or as a passenger has when he is crossing from continent to continent. Abraham, Isaac, and Jacob had each a home, but it was in a strange country, and they were daily looking for a city which

hath foundations whose builder and maker is God. While we are in this present state we are at a disadvantage, for we are dwelling in a house which is not as yet in our home-country, and by it we are kept from our real home in the Fatherland above. In a sense, however, this body is a home, for here dwells the living, thinking, active mind, somewhere in the brain, whence it spreads itself and rules all the members of the body. We know that within the walls of this earthly fabric our spirit is ordained to live for awhile, a lamp burning within a pitcher, a precious jewel set in a ring of clay. It is a house for which we have no little affection, and we are loath to quit it.

> " For who to dumb forgetfulness a prey,
> This pleasing, anxious being e'er resigned,
> Left the warm precincts of this house of clay,
> Nor cast one longing, lingering look behind ? "

We complain of the infirmities of our bodies, but we are in no hurry to leave them ; they threaten to fall upon us in their decay, but we linger in them still, till death serves a writ of ejectment, and at the same time pulls down the tenement. We have some of us lived in our body for forty years, some of you for sixty or seventy years, and it is natural that we should have made a home of it, such as it is, and it is small marvel that we are in no haste to emigrate, and even the temptation of that brighter home, and the " many mansions," is not always enough to make us wish to be gone.

But yet this body is not a fitting home for us, and we often discover by experience how inconvenient it is. It is a poor old tent, easily overturned, constantly getting rent, and the older it gets the more trouble it takes to patch it up and to keep it in habitable repair. In the course of years it has become soiled and creased, and worn like the tents of Kedar ; with the wear and tear of many years it becomes more and more evident that it is not a worthy dwelling-place for the child of a King, nor a fit abode for an immortal spirit, born from on high. We have suffered many inconveniences from this crumbling tabernacle in many ways, but especially in spiritual things : we have been willing to watch, but the body has been inclined to sleep, the spirit has been willing, but the flesh has been very weak. We have been cumbered with weariness, pain, care, and bodily appetite when we have desired to be altogether engrossed with heavenly things. Sometimes, when we would sing, a throbbing headache makes us sigh ; when we would rejoice with joy unspeakable a palpitating heart depresses us ; and when we would go about our Master's business a lame foot or a decaying constitution hinders us, so that we dwell in a house which is beneath the quality of so noble a creature as a spirit. We have to put up with flesh and blood, but we are outgrowing them—we feel we are ; there is a something within us which warns us that, like certain of the sea creatures which have to break their shells up as they grow, so we are growingly in need of another and better abode. We are like the young chick within the egg-shell—it has been a home for us until now, but it is becoming too strait for us, we begin to chip it, and we sometimes wish it would break altogether, that we might enjoy fuller liberty. " We that are in this body do groan, being burdened," and groan we shall till the day of our full redemption and the deliverance of the body from the bondage of corruption.

> " Welcome, sweet hour of full discharge,
> That sets my longing soul at large,
> Unbinds my chains, breaks up my cell,
> And gives me with my God to dwell."

According to the expression of the Greek, ours is a home in a foreign country, we are not dwelling among our own people at this present, but we are exiles in a far off land. We are not alone, for a numerous band of our brothers and sisters are with us, even as the Jews found company of their own race in Babylon, in whose songs and sighs they could unite ; but this is exile to us, we have no inheritance here. "A possession of a burying place " is all that we need ask for, and all that we shall soon have, for this world is not our rest. The Lord has not been pleased to give us our portion in this life, our inheritance lies on the other side of Jordan. We are at home in the body, but, as I have already said, it is but a lodging place in the midst of a strange country in which we are pilgrims and sojourners, as all our fathers were. We are wayfaring men hastening away and passing through a foreign land amongst people who speak not our tongue, know not our customs, understand nothing of the place to which we are going, and therefore cannot comprehend us, but even think us mad when we talk about another country, of which they have no idea, and for which they have no longing. We are at home only in a narrow sense, as a man may be said to be at home when, being in banishment, he takes up his abode for awhile in a foreign town ; it can never be more than this.

It is a home, too, which keeps us from our true home. We are not yet where we can see our Lord, and hear His voice : we are not yet in the " rest which remaineth for the people of God." To-day we are at school, like children whose great holiday joy is to go home. We are labourers, and this is the work field ; when we have done our day's work we shall go home, but this is the workshop, not the home. It is a very sweet thing after a week of hard work to reach home at last, to take off one's dusty clothes and throw them aside, and feel that toil is over for the present, and rest has come. In this world we cannot find a total rest so as to be completely at ease and at home; and we shall only reach that happy condition when we are out of this foreign world. No sense of perfect home rest ever comes over the soul while we are here, except as faith anticipates the joys prepared above. There remaineth a rest for the people of God, but in this body and in this world it is not to be had.

Home is the place where one feels secure ; our house is our castle. Outside in the world men watch your words, and if they can they misrepresent or misinterpret them. You have to fight a battle of life outside, but it is a very blessed thing if the battle is over when you cross your own threshold ; when you are no longer misunderstood, but are appreciated and loved around your own fireside. Beneath our own dear rooftree there is nobody to catch us up, nobody to cavil at us, but wife and children and friends love us and delight in us. Well, brethren, we find no such home spiritually in this world, for this is the place of conflict and watchfulness. Here we dwell among enemies, and we have sorrowfully

to cry, " My soul is among lions, among those that are set on fire of hell." We sing

> " Woe's me that I in Mesech am
> A sojourner so long ;
> That I in tabernacles dwell
> To Kedar that belong.
>
> My soul with him that hateth peace
> Hath long a dweller been ;
> I am for peace ; but when I speak
> For battle they are keen.
>
> My soul distracted mourns and pines
> To reach that peaceful shore,
> Where all the weary are at rest,
> And troubles vex no more."

In heaven there will be no foes to watch against, nor men of our own household to be our worst enemies. Home, sweet home, is to be found above, and from that home our present home in the body is keeping us.

Home, too, is the place of the closest and sweetest familiarities. There all unbend. The judge takes off his gown, and the soldier his sword, and both sport with their children. He who wears his buckram out of doors, finds himself stripped of it when he comes amongst his own kith and kin. There is the kiss of affection, there are the blandishments of love. Here, alas, our spirits cannot take their fill of heavenly familiarities, for distance comes between. We long for the vision of love, but it comes not as yet : but up there, what indulgence shall be accorded to us ! What discoveries of the love of God in Christ Jesus ! Then shall the cry of the spouse in the song be fulfilled for ever and ever—" Let him kiss me with the kisses of his mouth : for thy love is better than wine." Then shall the inmost heart of Christ be known to us, and we shall dwell in Him for ever and ever in closest communion. This home of ours in the body keeps us away from such intercourse with God as the glorified ones above enjoy without ceasing : said I not truly that our present state has its drawbacks, such as make a man sigh and cry to be gone ?

But, dear friends, the main point in which the present state is at a disadvantage compared with the future one is this, that here we have to live entirely by faith. We walk here by faith, not by sight. You believe in God, but you have not beheld His glory as the blessed dead have done. You believe in our Lord Jesus Christ, but it is in one " whom having not seen you love." You believe in the Holy Spirit, and you have been conscious of His presence by faith, but there is a something better yet ; a clearer sight is yet to be had, which we cannot enjoy while we tarry here. At present we take everything on the testimony of God's word and the witness of His Spirit : but we have not yet seen the celestial city, nor heard the voice of harpers harping with their harps, nor eaten at the banquets of the glorified. We enjoy a foretaste of all these, and anticipate them by faith, but actual enjoyments are not for this world. What a man seeth why doth he yet hope for ? As this is the realm of hope we cannot expect to see, but we are going to the place where we shall not so much believe as behold, where we shall not so much credit as enjoy. We are nearing the country where we shall

> " See, and hear, and know,
> All we desired or wished below."

And faith shall be exchanged for the clearest sight. Here we gaze through the telescope at heavenly things, but we cannot get into contact with them as we wish to do ; but when we have shaken thee off, O flesh, then shall we come actually into sight and fruition, and shall behold the Saviour, as He is, face to face.

These are the inconveniences, then, of this present state, but Paul despite all these disadvantages was confident. "We are always confident," says he. He was contented, he was happy, he was courageous, he was steadfast still : and why ? Why, brethren, because he had a hope of the immortality to be revealed. He knew that as soon as ever he shook off this body his soul would be with Christ. He knew that in some future day, when Christ should come, his body and his soul, re-married, should be for ever beatified with the Lord, and therefore he counted all the disadvantages of this life to be as nothing— "these light afflictions which are but for a moment." He laughed to scorn anything he had to suffer here below, because of the "exceeding weight of glory" which his faith realised as soon to be revealed.

Observe, also, that his confidence came from God's work in his soul. "He that hath wrought us to the selfsame thing is God." He was sure he should one day be perfect and immortal, because God had begun to work in him to that very end. When the statuary takes the block of stone and begins to carve it into a statue we get the promise of that which is to be. I no sooner see the master workman take the first stroke than I feel sure of a work of art, because I see that he has begun to work towards that end. From that work the mason may turn aside, or he may die, and therefore I cannot be sure that from the chosen stone there will leap out by-and-by the statue. But God never undertakes what He does not finish, He never fails for want of power, or because of a change of mind ; and so if to-day I be the quarried block of marble, if He has begun to make the first chippings in me of genuine repentance and simple faith towards God, I have the sure prophecy that He intends to work upon me till He has worked me up into the perfect image of Christ, to be immortal and immaculate like my Lord. Paul by faith knew that by a divine decree before all worlds he was predestinated to be made a perfect and immortal being. He saw that God had created him for that very purpose, and new created him to that end : he felt the working of God within him—he could feel the Spirit of God operating in him, giving him newness of life, causing him to hate sin and to receive more and more fully the likeness of Christ his Master. "He has worked me up to the selfsame thing," said the apostle, and therefore he felt confident that to this end he should be brought.

Again, there was another ground of confidence— "who also hath given unto us the earnest of the Spirit." You know what an "earnest" is. It is not a mere pledge, for a pledge is returned when that which it certifies is given ; but an earnest is a part of the promise itself. A man is to receive a wage at the end of the week ; in the middle of the week he obtains a part of the money, and this is more than a pledge of the rest : it is an earnest of the whole, a most sure and positive pledge of that which remains unpaid. The man who has received the Spirit of God in his soul has obtained the immortal seed which will expand into perfection, he is forgiven and accepted, and the Spirit helps his infirmities in prayer, fills him with faith, perfumes him with love, adorns him with holiness, and makes him commune with God—all this is the earnest of his perfected condition, and the beginning of the joys to come, the infallible assurance of all those joys which the Lord hath prepared for them that love Him. No man ever had the Spirit of God dwelling in him, moulding him to the divine will, but what he ultimately obtained the heavenly state, for the Spirit of God leaves not His work undone, neither does He bestow gifts to take them away again. "Therefore," says Paul, "we are always confident." We have a hope which entereth into that which is within the veil, we know what image the Lord is working in us, and we have received the Holy Spirit as the earnest of eternal blessedness : therefore, come what may, we are filled with a sacred courage and a sublime peace which make us await the future with calmest confidence.

Now we shall pass on to the next point, which is, that *Paul was equally confident about the next state into which he expected soon to pass*, namely, the condition of a disembodied spirit. Nature when it acts apart from grace shrinks from the thought of dying, but death can have no terrors for the man whom it lands in a condition which he prefers. By turning to the text, we see that Paul preferred the state into which death would cast him. "We are confident, I say, and willing rather to be absent from the body, and to be present with the Lord," that is, we have a preference for being away from this home in the body, that we may be at home with the Lord. He looked at the state into which he would soon come by the dissolution of his body as a more desirable one than even his life of confidence here below. Yet let us observe that it was not because Paul thought it would be better to be without a body than with one that he thus spoke. He has told us already "not for that we would be unclothed": he did not desire to be a disembodied spirit for its own sake. There are certain mystics who look upon the body as a wretched incumbrance ; the thought of resurrection has no pleasure to them, and therefore they spiritualize the doctrine, and make it to be no resurrection at all. The apostle was not of their mind, he called the body the temple of God, and desired its perfection, not its destruction. The Lord has constituted man to be a wonderful combination of many forms of existence, a link between the angel and the animal, a mixture of the divine and the material, a comprehensive being taking up into himself the heaven which is above him and the earth on which he treads. Our great Creator does not mean us to be maimed creatures for ever, He intends us to dwell with Him eternally in the perfection of our humanity. When our Lord Jesus died He did not redeem one half of man, but the whole man, and He means not to leave any part of the purchased possession in the enemy's hands. We ought not to think that to be half a man would be more desirable than to be a whole man, for our Lord Jesus thinks not so. We should be waiting for the second advent of our Lord, who will call His saints from their tombs, and redeem them altogether from the power of the grave. We should even now rejoice that this corruptible must put on incorruption, and this mortal must put on immortality.

It will be evident to you all, dear friends, that if Paul preferred the disembodied state to this, as the text tells us he did, then the spirits of those saints who have left their bodies in the grave are not annihilated—they live on. Paul could not have counted it better to be annihilated than to lead a life of holy confidence. The saints are not dead ; our Lord gave a conclusive answer to that error when He said, " Now that the dead are raised, even Moses shewed at the bush, when he calleth the Lord the God of Abraham, and the God of Isaac, and the God of Jacob. For He is not a God of the dead, but of the living : for all live unto Him." Those who have departed this life are still alive : we are sure of that, or else Paul would not have preferred that state. Neither are they unconscious, as some say, for who would prefer torpor to active confidence ? Whatever trials there may be in the Christian life here below, the man of faith does really enjoy life, and could not prefer unconsciousness. Neither are the saints in purgatorial fires, as the Babylonish harlot says, for nobody would desire to be tormented, and we may be sure that the apostle Paul would not have been willing rather to be in purgatory than to live here and serve his Lord. Brethren, the saints live, they live in consciousness and in happiness. Moses came and talked with Christ on the mount of Transfiguration, though he had no body, just as readily as Elias did, though that mighty prophet carried his body with him when he ascended in a chariot of fire. The body is not necessary to consciousness, or to happiness. The best of all is, the spirits of the departed are with Christ. " To be with Christ, which is far better," saith the apostle. " For ever with the Lord," their portion is allotted them. It is the Lord's own prayer : " I will that they also whom Thou hast given Me be with Me where I am, that they may behold My glory," and the prayer is fulfilled in them. " Blessed are the dead which die in the Lord from henceforth : yea, saith the Spirit, that they may rest from their labours ; and their works do follow them."

This made the apostle something more than confident and courageous in the prospect of death ; he was willing to depart into the disembodied state because he knew he would be at home with the Lord in it. I wish you to dwell a minute on that thought of being at home with the Lord. We rejoice that we have Christ with us here spiritually, for His presence brings us spiritual blessings of a very high order, and joys prophetic of the joys of heaven ; but still we have not His bodily presence. We have now a sight of our Lord through a telescope as it were ; but we do not see Him near at hand. We speak to Him as through a trumpet across the sea, we do not talk to him face to face. Ah, what will it be to be at home with Christ ! When we reach His own palace gate, and sit at His own board, we shall know Him far better than we do now, and He will look more lovely in our eyes than ever because we shall see Him more clearly. The sound of His voice will be much sweeter than anything we have heard in the gospel here below, for we shall actually hear Him speak. Will we not take our fill of Him when we once behold Him ? Methinks I shall never want to take my eyes off Him, but find a heaven, an eternity, an infinity of bliss in drinking Him in with all my eyes and all my heart. To be at home with Him will be to understand infinitely more of Him than we have ever dreamed of as yet. Ah, you do not know His glory, you could not bear to behold it as yet ; you would fall at His feet as dead, in a swoon of delight, if you could but gaze upon it while you are yet in this frail body. When disembodied you shall not have the flesh to throw a mist over your eyes, but you shall behold the King in His beauty, and be able to bear the joy.

In that condition to which we are speeding we shall also be beyond all doubt as to the truth of our holy faith. There will be no more mistrust of our Lord or of His promises, and no more shall we doubt the power of His blood or our share in His atoning sacrifice. Sometimes the dark atheistic thought will come, " Is it not all a dream ? " You shall never have such a thought there, for you will be at home with Jesus. Now there arises the troublesome question, Are you a real believer ? Has Jesus really washed you in His blood ? You will be beyond all such enquiries when you are absent from the body and present with the Lord. Now you have to walk by faith, and you must not try to get beyond faith, for that is the mode of spiritual life for this present state ; but after death you will no more walk by faith, you will have sight, and fruition, and these will banish all the doubts which will try your faith while in the body. How pleasant and desirable does the prospect of actual fruition cause heaven to become even though we know that for awhile we shall be away from the body.

In the future state we shall comunicate with Christ more sensibly than we do now. Here we do speak with Him, but it is by faith through the Spirit of God ; in the glory land we shall actually speak to Him in His immediate presence, and hear His voice while He personally speaks to us. Ah ! what we shall have to tell Him ! What will He have to tell us ! Truly, I dare not venture into these great deeps of expectation lest I drown myself in the delights of hope. Oh, the joy which awaits us ! It is almost too much for me to think of.

When we are at home with Him, without the body, and also, I suppose, even more when we are at home *in* the resurrection body, we shall have greater capacity for taking in the glory of our Lord than we have now. Sometimes He fills us with His love which passeth knowledge, and then we think we know very much of Him, but oh, my brethren, our knowledge is but that of little babes as yet. We are such small and shallow vessels that a few drops of Christ's love soon fill us up, and we begin running over : but He will enlarge us till we hold great measures of Him, and then He will fill us with all the fulness of God. You have sometimes tried to imagine what heaven must be. Well, you shall have many such heavens ; nay, ten thousand times as much delight in God as you have dreamed of. If even here He does for us exceeding abundantly above what we ask or think, what will He do for us there ? As for His person, and His sweetness, and His excellence, and His glory, you have only touched the hem of His garment. You have only, like Jonathan, dipped the end of your rod in that flood of honey, and it has enlightened your eyes : but oh, when you shall be at home with Him you shall feast to your heart's content. Here we sip, but there we shall drink full bowls ; here we eat our daily morsel, but there the heavenly feast will never break up.

Now, putting these two things together, the present state and the next, we have great reason, like the apostle, to go on from day to day with holy courage and confidence. If the way be rough, it leads to an unspeakably joyful end, so let us trip over it cheerfully ; and if the way should grow rougher still, let us show still greater confidence, for one hour with our God will make up for it all, and infinitely more.

II. The last point I can only spend a few minutes upon: it is this—THE BELIEVER HAS REASONS FOR AN ABSORBING AMBITION. According to the text, we are to live alone for Jesus,—" Wherefore we labour, that, whether present or absent, we may be accepted of Him." From henceforth, my brethren, the one great thing we have to care about is to please our Lord. You are saved, and heaven is your portion: now from this time concentrate all your thoughts, your faculties, and your energies upon this one design, —to be acceptable with Jesus Christ. Live for Him as He has died for you; live for Him alone. Believer, it ought to be your ambition to please Christ in every act you do. Do not say " How will this please myself or please my neighbour?" but " How will this please my Lord?" And, remember, it is not by the action alone that He will be pleased, but the motive must be right or you will fail. Oh cry to Him to keep your motives clean, pure, elevated, heavenly; for grovelling aims will be a sour leaven, and will render the whole loaf unfit to offer. Nor is it merely the motive, it is the spirit in which the whole thing is done. Labour, brethren, with a divine ambition to please Jesus Christ in your thoughts, in your wishes, in your desires, in everything that is about you. I know you will have to lament many shortcomings and errors; there will be much about you that will be displeasing to Him, take care that it is also displeasing to you, and never be pleased with that which does not please Him. Never accept anything in yourself which He would not accept. With all your ardent spirit watch every movement of your soul that no power or passion so moves as to vex His Holy Spirit. Seek to please Him every moment while you are upon the earth. You know what sort of things Jesus did, and what He would like you to do; follow His every step, obey His every word. He has bidden you walk in holiness as He did, O sin not against Him. He bids you clothe the naked, feed the hungry, teach the ignorant, visit the sick, look after the fatherless and widows,— all these things He speaks of as peculiarly pleasing to Himself, and as mentionable to the honour of His saints, in the day of His appearing; let these things be in you and abound. Be fruitful in those graces which were most conspicuous in Him. Do not let a day pass without doing something with the one object of pleasing Christ in it. We do a great deal because it is customary, or because church opinion expects it, but to do holy acts directly for Christ, simply and alone for love of Him,—this should be our constant habit. Have we not some alabaster box to break to anoint *His* head, some tears with which to wash *His* feet? Need I urge that something, however humble, should frequently be done, even at the cost of self-denial, for His dear sake? Yea, let everything be done as unto Him.

For then, mark this last, we shall please Him in the next state, for " we must all appear before the judgment seat of Christ." The child of God is glad of this. The text might be translated " we shall be all manifested before the judgment seat of Christ." To-day men do not understand us, but they will know us in that day. I will warrant you this one thing, if you will live the most devoted and disinterested life possible, you will find people sneering at you and imputing your actions to selfish motives, and putting a cruel construction on all you do or say. Well, it does not matter, for we shall all be manifested at the judgment-seat of Christ, before God, and men, and angels. Let us live to please Him, for our integrity of motive will be known at the last, and put beyond all dispute. The world said of one man that he preached from selfish motives, while all the time he had no thought but for God's glory: the Lord will make it clear how false was the judgment of men. They said of another man that he was very earnest, but that he wanted to win popularity; yet all the while he cared not one straw for human praise. Such a man need not trouble himself, the smoke will clear away in that great day, and he will be seen in his uprightness. If you have lived only to please Christ you need not be afraid of His coming, for in that day He shall clear away all slander and misrepresentation, and you shall stand out vindicated and justified before an assembled universe. In that day, when God shall publicly justify His saints, He will make all men, and angels, and devils know that they are truly just. The solemn verdict of God will be one to which the whole universe of intelligent spirits will give in their assent. They will say " aye " to the sentence passed by the Lord Jesus; they themselves would bring in a verdict in favour of believers in that last testing day if it were left to them. As for the ungodly, the condemning sentence shall be not only just, but such as the whole universe shall assent to. The punishment which God will lay upon sinners for the evil deeds done in the body, will not then be cavilled at as too severe. It will be such a sentence as every intelligent spirit shall be compelled to own to be right. But, my brethren, let us so live that while our lives shall challenge no judgment on the score of merit—for that thought we utterly abhor—yet there shall be in our lives evidences of our having received grace from God, evidences of our being acceptable with Christ; for if we do not so live, we may talk what we like about faith, and boast what we please about experience, but without holiness no man shall see the Lord. If our life has never had in it that which pleases Christ, then the evidence will be taken against us that we were not pleasing unto Him, that we had no spiritual life, that we had no grace in the heart, and that we were not saved. Then there will remain nothing for us but to be condemned with the ungodly. Come, then, brothers and sisters, do not let us care whether we live or die, let us not suffer ourselves to be alarmed about the passage out of this world into the next state, but let us be " stedfast, unmoveable, always abounding in the work of the Lord."

I have been twice to the grave this week, with two of our aged friends, a sister and a brother, who have passed into the glory, and the lesson which they have left behind for our edification is—let us not be careful whether we be at home in the body or whether we be at home with Christ: but, living or dying, let us be careful to please Jesus. I wish I knew how to enforce this lesson, and send it home to every believer's heart, but I must rather pray the Holy Spirit so to do. May He write it on my soul and on yours, and may we all be found practising it from this time forth even for ever. Amen.

UNDER CONSTRAINT

" For the love of Christ constraineth us; because we thus judge, that if One died for all, then were all dead."— 2 Corinthians v. 14.

THE apostle and his brethren were unselfish in all that they did. He could say of himself and of his brethren that when they varied their modes of action they had ever the same object in view; they lived only to promote the cause of Christ, and to bless the souls of men. He says, " Whether we be beside ourselves, it is to God : or whether we be sober, it is for your cause." Some may have said that Paul was too excitable, and expressed himself too strongly. " Well," said he, " if it be so, it is to God." Others may have noticed the reasoning faculty to be exceedingly strong in Paul, and may perhaps have thought him to be too cooly argumentative. " But," said Paul, " if we be sober, it is for your cause."

Viewed from some points the apostle and his co-labourers must have appeared to be raving fanatics, engaged upon a Quixotic enterprise, and almost if not quite out of their minds. One who had heard the apostle tell the story of his conversion exclaimed, " Paul, thou art beside thyself; much learning doth make thee mad "; and no doubt many who saw the singular change in his conduct, and knew what he had given up and what he had endured for his new faith, had come to the same conclusion. Paul would not be offended by this judgment, for he would remember that his Lord and Master had been charged with madness, and that even our Lord's relatives had said, " He is beside Himself." To Festus He had replied, " I am not mad, most noble Festus ; but speak forth the words of truth and soberness "; and to Corinthian objectors He gave a still fuller reply. Blessed are they who are charged with being out of their mind through zeal for the cause of Jesus, they have a more than sufficient answer when they can say, " If we be beside ourselves, it is to God." It is no unusual thing for madmen to think others mad, and no strange thing for a mad world to accuse the only morally sane among men of being fools and lunatics : but wisdom is justified of her children. If others assailed the apostle with another charge, and insinuated that there was a method in his madness, that his being all things to all men showed an excess of prudence, and was no doubt a means to an end, which end it is possible they hinted at was a desire for power, he could reply most conclusively, " If we be sober, it is for your cause." Paul had acted so unselfishly that he could appeal to the Corinthian church and ask them to bear him witness that he sought not theirs but them, and that if he had judged their disorders with great sobriety it was for their cause. Whatever it did, he felt, or suffered, or spake, he had but one design in it, and that was the glory of God in the perfecting of believers and the salvation of sinners.

Every Christian minister ought to be able to use the apostle's words without the slightest reserve ; yea, and every Christian man should also be able to say the same : " If I be excited, it is in defence of the truth ; if I be sober, it is for the maintenance of holiness : if I seem extravagant, it is because the name of Jesus stirs my inmost soul ; and if I am moderate in spirit and thoughtful in mood, it is that I may in the wisest manner subserve the interests of my Redeemer's kingdom." God grant that weeping or singing, anxious or hopeful, victorious or defeated, increasing or decreasing, elevated or depressed, we may still follow our one design, and devote ourselves to the holy cause. May we live to see churches made up of people who are all set on one thing, and may those churches have ministers who are fit to lead such a people, because they also are mastered by the same sacred purpose. May the fire which fell of old on Carmel fall on our altar, whereon lieth the sacrifice, wetted a second and a third time from the salt sea of the world, until it shall consume the burnt sacrifice, and the wood, and the stones, and the dust, and lick up the water that is in the trench. Then will all the people see it, and fall upon their faces, and cry, " The Lord, He is the God ; the Lord, He is the God."

The apostle now goes on to tell us why it was that the whole conduct of himself and his co-labourers tended to one end and object. He says, " The love of Christ constraineth us, because we thus judge, that if One died for all, then the all died." I give you here as exact a translation as I can.

Two things I shall note in the text : first, under constraint ; secondly, under constraint which His understanding justified.

I. Our main point will come under the head " UNDER CONSTRAINT." Here is the apostle, a man who was born free, a man who beyond all others enjoyed the greatest spiritual liberty, glorying that he is under constraint. He was under constraint because a great force held him under its power. " The love of Christ constraineth us." I suppose " constraineth us " is about the best rendering of the passage that could be given ; but it might be translated " restraineth." The love of Christ restrains true believers from self-seeking, and forbids them to pursue any object but the highest. Whether they were beside themselves or sober, the early saints yielded to divine restraint, even as a good ship answers to her helm or as a horse obeys the rein. They were not without a restraining force to prevent the slightest subjection to impure motives. The love of Christ controlled them, and held them under its power. But the word " restrained " only expresses a part of the sense, for it means that he was " coerced or pressed," and so impelled forward as one carried along by pressure. All around him the love of Christ pressed upon him as the water in a river presses upon a swimmer, and bears him onward with its stream. Bengel, who is a great authority, reads it, " Keep us employed " : for we are led to diligence, urged to zeal, maintained in perseverance, and carried forward and onward by the love of Jesus Christ. The apostles laboured much, but all their labour sprang from the impulse of the love of Jesus Christ. Just as Jacob toiled for Rachel solely out of love to her, so do true saints serve the Lord Jesus under the omnipotent constraint of love. One eminent expositor reads the word, " containeth us," as though it signified that the Lord's servants were kept together and held as a band under a banner or standard ; and he very appropriately refers to the words of the church in the Song, " His banner over me was love." As soldiers are held together by rallying to the standard, so are the saints kept to the work and service of their Lord by the love of Christ, which constrains them to endure all things for the Elect's sake, and for the glory of God, and like an ensign is uplifted high as the centre and loadstone of all their energies. In our Lord's love we have the best motive for loyalty, the best reason for energy, and the best argument for perseverance.

The word may also signify " compressed," and then it would mean that all their energies were pressed into one channel, and made to move by the love of Christ. Can I put restraint and constraint, and all the rest, into one by grouping them in a figure ? I think I can. When a flood is spread over an expanse of meadow land, and stands in shallow pools, men restrain it by damming it up, and they constrain it to keep to one channel by banking it in. Thus compressed it becomes a stream, and moves with force in one direction. See how it quickens its pace, see what strength it gathers ; it turns yonder wheel of the mill, makes a sheep wash, leaps as a waterfall, runs laughing through a village as a brook wherein the cattle stand in the summer's sun. Growing all the while it develops into a river, bearing boats and little ships ; and this done, it still increases, and stays not till it flows with mighty flood into the great sea. The love of Christ had pressed Paul's energies into one force, turned them into one channel, and then driven them forward with a wonderful force, till he and his fellows had become a mighty power for good, ever active and energetic. " The love of Christ," saith he, " constraineth us."

All great lives have been under the constraint of some mastering principle. A man who is everything by turns and nothing long is a nobody : a man who wastes life on whims and fancies, leisures and pleasures, never achieves anything : he flits over the surface of life and leaves no more trace upon his age than a bird upon the sky ; but a man, even for mischief, becomes great when he becomes concentrated. What made the young prince of Macedon Alexander the Great but the absorption of his whole mind in the desire for conquest. The man was never happy when he was at ease and in peace. His best days were spent on the battle-field or on the march. Let him rush to the forefront of the battle and make the commonest soldier grow into a hero by observing the desperate valour of his king, and then you see the greatness of the man. He could never have been the conqueror of the world if the insatiable greed of conquest had not constrained him. Hence come your Cæsars and your Napoleons—they are whole men in their ambition, subject to the lust of dominion. When you carry this thought into a better and holier sphere the same fact is clear. Howard could never have been the great philanthropist if he had not been strangely under the witchery of love to prisoners. He was more happy in an hospital or in a prison than he would have been at Court or on the sofa of the drawing room. The man could not help visiting the gaols, he was a captive to his sympathy for men in bondage, and so he spent his life in seeking their good. Look at such a man as Whitfield or his compeer Wesley. Those men had but one thought, and that was to win souls

for Christ ; their whole being ran into the one river-bed of zeal for God, and made them full and strong as the rushing Rhone. It was their rest to labour for Christ : it was their honour to be pelted while preaching and to be calumniated for the name of Jesus ; a bishopric and a seat in the House of Lords would have been the death of them ; even a throne would have been a rack if they must have ceased hunting for souls. The men were under the dominion of a passion which they could not understand, and did not wish to weaken. They could sing—

> " The love of Christ doth me constrain
> To seek the wandering souls of men ;
> With cries, entreaties, tears, to save,
> To snatch them from the fiery wave."

Their whole life, being, thought, faculty, spirit, soul, and body became one and indivisible in purpose, and their sanctified manhood was driven forward irresistibly, so that they might be likened to thunder-bolts flung from the eternal hand, which must go forward till their end is reached. They could no more cease to preach than the sun could cease shining or reverse his course in the heavens.

Now, this kind of constraint implies no compulsion, and involves no bondage. It is the highest order of freedom ; for when a man does exactly what he likes to do, if he wants to express the enthusiastic joy and delight with which he follows his pursuit, he generally uses language similar to that of my text. " Why," saith he, " I am engrossed by my favourite study ; it quite enthrals me ; I cannot resist its charms, it holds me beneath its spell." Is the man any the less free ? If a man gives himself up to a science, or to some other object of pursuit, though he is perfectly free to leave it whenever he likes, he will commonly declare that he cannot leave it ; it has such a hold upon him that he must addict himself to it. You must not think, therefore, that when we speak of being under constraint from the love of Christ we mean by it that we have ceased to exercise our wills, or to be voluntary agents in our service. Far from it, we own that we are never so free as when we are under bonds to Christ. No, our God does not constrain us by physical force ; His cords are those of love, and His bands are those of a man. The constraint is that which we are glad to feel ; we give a full assent to its pressure, and therein lies its power. We rejoice to admit that " The love of Christ constraineth us," we only wish the constraint would increase every day.

We have seen that Paul had a great force holding him : we advance a step further and note that *the constraining force was the love of Christ.* He does not speak of *his* love to Christ : that was a great power too, though secondary to the first ; but he is content to mention the greater, for it includes the less : " The love of Christ constraineth us," that is, Christ's love to us is the master force. And O, brethren, this is a power to which it is joy to submit : this is a force worthy to command the greatest minds. " The love of Christ." Who shall measure this omni-potent force ? That love, according to our text, is strongest when seen in His dying for men. Mark the context " because we thus judge, that if one died for all." The peculiar display of the love of Christ which had supreme sway over Paul was the love revealed in His substitutionary death. Think of it a moment. Christ the ever blessed, to whom no pain, nor suffering, nor shame could come, loved men. O singularity of love! He loves guilty men, yea, loves His enemies! Loving poor fallen men, He took their nature and became a man. Marvellous condescension! The Son of God is also Son of Mary, and being found in fashion as a man He humbles Himself, and is made of no reputation. See Him taken before human judges and unjustly condemned; seized by Roman lictors and lashed with the scourge! Gazing a little longer, you see Him nailed to a gibbet, hung up for a felon, left amid jeer and jibe and cruel glance and malicious speech to bleed away His life, till He is actually dead, and laid in the grave. At the back of all this there is the mystery that He not only dying, but dying in the stead of others, bearing almighty wrath, enduring that dread sentence of death which is attached to human sin. Herein is love indeed, that the infinitely pure should suffer for the sinful, the Just for the unjust, to bring us to God. Love did never climb to so sublime a height as when it brought Jesus to the bloody tree to bear the dread sentence of inexorable law. Think of this love, beloved, till you feel its constraining influence. It was love eternal, for long before the earth was fashioned the eternal Word had set His eye upon His people, and their names were graven on His heart. It was love unselfish, for He had nothing to gain from His redeemed; there were harps enough in heaven and songs enough in the celestial city without their music. It was love most free and spontaneous, for no man sought it, or so much as dreamed thereof. It was love most persevering, for when man was born into the world, and sinned, and rejected Christ, and He came to His own and His own received Him not, He loved them still, loved them even to the end. It was love,—what shall I say of it? If I were to multiply words I might rather sink your thoughts than raise them: it was love infinite, immeasurable, inconceivable! It passeth the love of women, though the love of mothers is strong as death, and jealousy is cruel as the grave. It passes the love of martyrs, though that love has triumphed over the fury of the flame. All other lights of love pale their ineffectual brightness before this blazing sun of love, whose warmth a man may feel but upon whose utmost light no eye can gaze. He loved us like a God. It was nothing less than God's own love which burned within that breast, which was bared to the spear that it might redeem us from going down into the pit. It is this force, then, which has taken possession of the Christian's mind, and as Paul says, "constraineth us."

Now we may advance another step and say that *the love of Christ operates upon us by begetting in us love to Him.* Brethren beloved, I know you love our Lord Jesus Christ, for all His people love Him. "We love Him because He first loved us." But what shall I say? There are scarcely any themes upon which I feel less able to speak than these two— the love of Christ to us and our love to Him, because somehow love wanteth a tongue elsewhere than this which dwells in the mouth. This tongue is in the head, and it can therefore tell out our thoughts; but we need a tongue in the heart to tell out our emotions, which have now to borrow utterances from the brain's defective orator. There is a long space between the cool brain and the blazing heart, and matters cool on the road to the tongue, so that the burning heart grows weary of chill words. But oh, we love Jesus; brothers and sisters, we truly love Him. His name is sweet as the honeycomb,

and His word is precious as the gold of Ophir. His person is very dear to us: from His head to His foot He is altogether lovely. When we get near Him and see Him at the last, methinks we shall swoon away with excess of joy at the sight of Him, and I for one ask no heaven beyond a sight of Him, and a sense of His love. I do not doubt that we shall enjoy all the harmonies, and all the honours, and all the fellowships of heaven, but if they were all blotted out, I do not know that they would make any considerable difference to us, if we may but see our Lord upon His throne, and have His own prayer fulfilled, "Father, I will that they also whom Thou hast given Me be with Me where I am, that they may behold My glory." He is happiness to us, yea, He is all in all. Do you not feel that the sweetest sermons you ever hear are those which are fullest of Him? When I can sometimes hear a sermon it sickens me to listen to fine attempts to philosophise away the gospel, or to pretty essays which are best described as a jingle of elegant words: but I can hear with rapture the most illiterate and blundering brother if his heart burns within him, and he heartily speaks of my Lord, the Well-beloved of my soul. We are glad to be in the place of assembly when Jesus is within; for whether on Tabor with two or three, or in the congregation of the faithful, when Jesus is present it is good to be there. This joyful feeling when you hear about Jesus shows that you love His person; and your endeavours to spread the gospel show that you love His cause. The love of Christ to you has moved you to desire the coming of His kingdom, and you feel that you could give your life to extend the borders of His dominions, for He is a glorious King, and all the world should know it. Oh that we could see all the nations bowing before His sceptre of peace. We love Him so much that till the whole earth smiles in the light of His throne we can never rest.

As to His truth, a very great part of our love to Christ will show itself by attachment to the pure gospel. I have not much patience with a certain class of Christians nowadays who will hear anybody preach so long as they can say, "He is very clever, a fine preacher, a man of genius, a born orator." Is cleverness to make false doctrine palatable? Why, sirs, to me the ability of a man who preaches error is my sorrow rather than my admiration. I cannot endure false doctrine, however neatly it may be put before me. Would you have me eat poisoned meat because the dish is of the choicest ware? It makes me indignant when I hear another gospel put before the people with enticing words, by men who would fain make merchandise of souls; and I marvel at those who have soft words for such deceivers. "That is your bigotry," says one. Call it so if you like, but it is the bigotry of the loving John who wrote—" If there come any unto you, and bring not this doctrine, receive him not into your house, neither bid him God speed: for he that biddeth him God speed is partaker of his evil deeds." I would to God we had all more of such decision, for the lack of it is depriving our religious life of its backbone, and substituting for honest manliness a mass of the tremulous jelly of mutual flattery. He who does not hate the false does not love the true; and he to whom it is all the same whether it be God's word or man's, is himself unrenewed at heart. Oh, if some of you were like your fathers you would not have tolerated in this age the wagon loads of trash under which the gospel has been of late buried by ministers of your own choosing. You would have hurled out of your pulpits the men who are enemies to the fundamental doctrines of your churches, and yet are crafty enough to become your pastors and undermine the faith of a fickle and superficial generation. These men steal the pulpits of once orthodox churches, because otherwise they would have none at all. Their powerless theology cannot of itself arouse sufficient enthusiasm to enable them to build a mousetrap at the expense of their admirers, and therefore they profane the houses which your sires have built for the preaching of the gospel, and turn aside the organisations of once orthodox communities to help their infidelity : I call it by that name in plain English, for " modern thought " is not one whit better, and of the two evils I give infidelity the palm, for it is less deceptive. I beg the Lord to give back to the churches such a love to His truth that they may discern the spirits, and cast out those which are not of God. I feel sometimes like John, of whom it is said that, though the most loving of all spirits, yet he was the most decided of all men for the truth ; and when he went to the bath and found that the heretic, Cerinthus, was there, he hurried out of the building, and would not tarry in the same place with him. There are some with whom we should have no fellowship, nay, not so much as to eat bread ; for though this conduct looks stern and hard, it is after the mind of Christ, for the apostle spake by inspiration when he said, " If we or an angel from heaven preach to you any other gospel than that ye have received, let him be accursed." According to modern effeminacy he ought to have said, " Let him be kindly spoken with in private, but pray make no stir. No doubt the good brother has his own original modes of thought, and we must not question his liberty. Doubtless, he believes the same as we do, only there is some little difference as to terms." This is treason to Christ, treachery to truth, and cruelty to souls. If we love our Lord we shall keep His words, and stand fast in the faith, coming out from among the false teachers ; nor is this inconsistent with charity, for the truest love to those who err is not to fraternize with them in their error, but to be faithful to Jesus in all things.

The love of Jesus Christ creates in men a deep attachment to the gospel, especially to the doctrines which cluster around the person of our Lord ; and I think more especially to that doctrine which is the corner stone of all, namely, that Christ died in the stead of men. He who toucheth the doctrine of substitution toucheth the apple of our eye : he who denies it robs our soul of her only hope, for thence we gather all our consolation for the present and our expectation for days to come. A great force, then, held the apostle : that force was the love of Christ, and it wrought in him love to Christ in return. Now, this force acts proportionately in believers. It acts in every Christian more or less, but it differs in degree. We are all of us alive, but the vigour of life differs greatly in the consumptive and the athletic, and so the love of Jesus acts upon all regenerate men, but not to the same extent. When a man is perfectly swayed by the love of Christ he will be a perfect Christian : when a man is growingly under its influence he is a growing Christian ; when a man is sincerely affected by the love of Christ he is a sincere Christian ; but he in whom the love of Christ has no power whatever is not a Christian at all.

" I thought," says one, " that believing was the main point." True, but faith worketh by love, and if your faith does not work by love it is not the faith which will save the soul. Love never fails to bloom where faith has taken root.

Beloved, you will feel the power of the love of Christ in your soul in proportion to the following points. In proportion as you know it. Study, then, the love of Christ : search deep and learn its secrets. Angels desire to look into it. Observe its eternity— without beginning, its immutability—without change, its infinity—without measure, its eternity—without end. Think much of the love of Christ, till you comprehend with all saints what are its breadths and lengths, and as you know it you will begin to feel its power. Its power will also be in proportion to your sense of it. Do you feel the love of God shed abroad in your heart by the Holy Ghost ? Knowing is well, but enjoyment as the result of believing is better. Does it not sometimes force the tears from your eyes to think that Jesus loved you and gave Himself for you ? On the other hand does it not at times make you feel as if, like David, you could dance before the ark of the Lord, to think that the love of God should ever have been set on you, that Christ should die for you ? Ah, think and think again : for you the bloody sweat, for you the crown of thorns, for you the nails, the spear, the wounds, the broken heart,—all, all for love of you who were His enemy ! In proportion as your heart is tender and is sensitive to this love it will become a constraining influence to your whole life. The force of this influence will also depend very much upon the grace which dwells within you. You may measure your grace by the power which the love of Christ has over you. Those who dwell near their Lord are so conscious of His power over them that the very glances of His eyes fill them with holy ardour. If you have much grace you will be greatly moved by the love which gave you that grace, and wondrously sensitive to it, but he who hath little grace, as is the case with not a few, can read the story of the cross without emotion, and can contemplate Jesus' death without feeling. God deliver us from a marble heart, cold and hard. Character also has much to do with the measure in which we feel the constraint of Jesus' love : the more Christlike the more Christ-constrained. You must get, dear brother and sister, by prayer, through the Holy Spirit, to be like Jesus Christ, and when you do, His love will take fuller possession of you than it does at this moment, and you will be more manifestly under its constraining power.

Our last point upon this head is that wherever its energy is felt it will operate after its kind. Forces work according to their nature : the force of love creates love, and the love of Christ begets a kindred love. He who feels Christ's love acts as Christ acted. If thou dost really feel the love of Christ in making a sacrifice of Himself thou wilt make a sacrifice of thyself. " Hereby perceive we the love of God, because He laid down His life for us : and we ought to lay down our lives for the brethren." We shall for our Lord's sake count all things but dross for the excellency of His knowledge. O soul, thou wilt have no choice left after thou hast once known and chosen thy Lord. That road leads to wealth, but if it does not glorify Christ thou wilt at once say, " Farewell wealth." That road leads to honour ; thou wilt be famous if thou wilt take that path ; but if it will bring no glory to Christ, if thou feelest the power of His love in thy soul, thou wilt say, "Farewell honour: I will embrace shame for Christ, for my one thought is to sacrifice myself for Him who sacrificed Himself for me."

If the love of Christ constrain you it will make you love others, for His was love to others, love to those who could do Him no service, who deserved nothing at His hands. If the love of Christ constrain you, you will specially love those who have no apparent claim upon you, and cannot justly expect anything from you, but on the contrary deserve your censure. You will say, " I love them because the love of Christ constraineth me." Dirty little creatures in the gutter, filthy women polluting the streets, base men who come out of jail merely to repeat their crimes,—these are the fallen humanities whom we learn to love when the love of Christ constraineth us. I do not know how else we could care for some poor creatures, if it were not that Jesus teaches us to despise none and despair of none. Those ungrateful creatures, those malicious creatures, those abominably blasphemous and profane creatures whom you sometimes meet with and shrink from, you are to love them because Christ loved the very chief of sinners. His love to you must be reflected in your love to the lowest and vilest. He is your sun, be you as the moon to the world's night.

The love of Jesus Christ was a practical love. He did not love in thought only and in word, but in deed and in truth, and if the love of Christ constraineth us we shall throw our souls into the work and service of love ; we shall be really at work for men, giving alms of our substance, enduring our measure of suffering, and making it clear that our Christianity is not mere talk, but downright work ; we shall be like the bullock of the burnt offering, laid upon the altar wholly to be consumed ; we shall consider nothing but how we can most completely be eaten up with the zeal of God's house, how without the reserve of one single faculty we may be entirely consumed in the service of our Lord and Master. May the Lord bring us to this.

II. THE CONSTRAINT OF WHICH WE HAVE SPOKEN WAS JUSTIFIED BY THE APOSTLE'S UNDERSTANDING. "The love of Christ constraineth us ; *because we thus judge*." Love is blind. A man may say that in the affairs of love he exercises a calm discretion, but I take leave to doubt it. In love to Christ, however, you may be carried right away and be as blind as you like, and yet you shall act according to the soundest judgment. The apostle saith warmly, "The love of Christ constraineth us," and yet he adds with all coolness, "because we thus judge." When understanding is the basis of affection, then a man's heart is fixed and his conduct becomes in a high degree exemplary. So it is here. There is a firm basis of judgment,—the man has weighed and judged the matter as much as if the heart were out of the question ; but the logical conclusion is one of all-absorbing emotion and mastering affection as much as if the understanding had been left out of the question. His judgment was as the brazen altar, cold and hard, but on it He laid the coals of burning affection, vehement enough in their flame to consume everything. So it ought to be with us. Religion should be with a man a matter of intellect as well as of affection, and his understanding should always be able to justify the strongest possible passion of his soul, as the apostle says it did in the case of himself and brethren. They had reasons

for all that they did. For, first, *he recognized substitution :* "We thus judge, that if One died for all." O brethren, this is the very sinew of Christian effort—Christ died in the sinner's stead. Christ is the surety, the sacrifice, the substitute, for men. If you take the doctrine of vicarious sacrifice out of the Christian religion I protest that nothing is left worth calling a revelation. It is the heart, the head, the bowels, the soul, the essence of our holy faith,—that the Lord hath laid on Him the iniquity of us all, and with His stripes we are healed. The apostle firmly believed this to be a matter of fact, and then out of his belief there grew an intense love to Jesus, as well there might. Did Jesus stand in my stead ? Oh, how I love Him. Did He die for me ? Then His love hath mastered me, and henceforth it holds me as its willing captive. O sacred Substitute, I am Thine, and all that I have.

In the next place *he recognized union to Christ*, for, said he, " If One died for all, then the all died," for so it runs, that is to say the all for whom Christ died died in His death. His dying in their stead was their dying ; He dies for them, they die in Him ; He rises, they rise in Him ; He lives, they live in Him. Now if it be really so, that you and I who have believed in Christ are one with Christ, and members of His body, that truth may be stated coolly, but like the flint it conceals a fire within it ; for if we died in Jesus, we are henceforth dead to the world, to self, to everything but our Lord. O Holy Spirit, work in us this death even to the full. The apostle recognizes the natural consequence of union with the dying Lord, and resolves to carry it out. Brethren, when Adam sinned we sinned, and we have felt the result of that fact ; we were constituted sinners by the act of our first representative, and every day we see it to be so : every little child that is carried to the grave bears witness that death passeth upon all men, for that all have sinned in Adam, even though they have not personally sinned after the similitude of his transgression. Now, just as our sin in Adam effectively operates upon us for evil, so must our death with Christ effectively operate upon our lives for good. It ought to do so. How can I live for myself ? I died more than eighteen centuries ago. I died and was buried, how can I live to the world ? Eighteen hundred years ago and more the world hung me up as a malefactor ; ay, and in my heart of hearts I have also crucified the world, and henceforth regard it as a dead malefactor. How shall I fall in love with a crucified world, or follow after its delights ? We thus died with Christ. "Now," saith the apostle, "the love of Christ constraineth us ; because we thus judge, that if one died for all, then the all died." All who were in Christ, for whom He died, died when He died, and what follows from it, but that henceforth they should not live unto themselves, but unto Him that died for them, and rose again ? We are one with Christ, and what He did for us we did in Him, and therefore we are dead because He died ; hence we ought no longer to live in the old selfish way, but should live to the Lord alone. There is the basis upon which the intellect rests, and then the affections yield themselves to the sacred forces of Jesus' dying love.

I close with the following reflections, putting them very briefly.

The first reflection is,—how different is the inference of the apostle from that of many professors. They say, " If Christ died once for all, and so finished the work of my salvation, then I am saved, and may sit down in comfort and enjoy myself, for there is no need for effort or thought." Ah, what a mercy to feel that you are saved, and then to go to sleep in the corner of your pew. A converted man, and therefore curled up upon the bed of sloth! A pretty sight surely, but a very common one. Such people have but little or no feeling for others who remain unconverted. "The Lord will save His own," say they, and they little care whether He does so or not. They appear to be dreadfully afraid of doing God's work, though there is not the slightest need for such a fear, since they will not even do their own work. These are presumptuous persons, strangers to the grace of God, who know not that a main part of salvation lies in our being saved from selfishness and hardness of heart. It is the devil's inference, that because Christ did so much for me I am now to do nothing for Him; I must even beg the devil's pardon, for I scarcely think that even he is base enough to draw such an inference from the grace of God. Assuredly he has never been in a position to attempt so detestable a crime. It is to the last degree unutterably contemptible that a man who is indebted to the Lord Jesus Christ for so much should then make the only consequence of his indebtedness to be a selfish indolence. Never will a true child of God say, "Soul, take thine ease: thou art all right: what matters anything else?" Oh no, "The love of Christ constraineth us."

How much more ennobling, again, is such conduct as that of the apostle than that of many professed Christians? I am not about to judge any one, but I would beg you to judge yourselves. There are some, and I would try to hope that they may be Christians—the Lord knoweth them that are His—who do give to the cause of God, who do serve God after a fashion; but still the main thought of their life is not Christ nor His service, but the gaining of wealth. That is their chief object, and towards it all their faculties are bent. There are other church members—God forbid we should judge them—whose great thought is success in their profession. I am not condemning their having such a thought, but the chief ambition of the apostle and of those like him was not this, but something higher. The chief aim of all of us should be nothing of self, but serving Christ. We are to be dead to everything but our Lord's glory, living with this mark before us, this prize to be strained after, that Christ shall be glorified in our mortal bodies. In our business, in our studies, in everything, our motto must be, Christ, Christ, Christ. Now, is it not a far more noble thing for a man to have lived wholly unto Christ than for mammom, or honour, or for himself in any shape? I speak as unto wise men, judge ye what I say.

Do you not think also that such a pursuit as this is much more peace-giving to the spirit? People will judge our conduct, and they are sure to judge as severely as they can: if they see us zealous and self-denying they will say of us, "Why, the man is beside himself." This will not matter much to us if we can reply, "It is for God"; or if they say, "Oh, you old sobersides; how grave you are," we shall not be offended, if we can reply, "Ah, but it is for the good of others I am sober." You will be very little distressed by sharp criticisms if you know that you motive is wholly unselfish. If you live for Christ, and for Christ alone, all the carpings of men or devils will never cast you down.

Do you not think that a life spent for Jesus only is far more worth looking back upon at the last than any other? If you call yourselves Christians how will you judge a life spent in money-making? It cannot be very much longer before you must gather up your feet in the bed and resign your soul to God. Now, suppose yourself sitting in your chamber all alone, making out the final balance-sheet of your stewardship, how will it look if you have to confess, "I have been a Christian professor; my conduct has been outwardly decent and respectable, but my chief purpose was not my Master's glory. I have lived with the view of scraping together so many thousands, and I have done it." Would you like to fall asleep and die with that as the consummation of your life? Or shall it be, "I have lived to hold up my head in society and pay my way and leave a little for my family"? Will that satisfy you as your last reflection? Brethren, we are not saved by our works, but I am speaking now upon the consolation which a man can derive from looking back upon his life. Suppose he shall have felt the power of my text, and shall be able to say, "I have been enabled by the grace of God, to which I give all the glory, to consecrate my entire being to the entire glorification of my Lord and Master; and whatever my mistakes, and they are many, and my wanderings and failures, and they are countless, yet the love of Christ has constrained me, for I judged myself to have died in Him, and henceforth I have lived to Him. I have fought a good fight. I have kept the faith." Why, methinks it were worth while so to die. To be constrained by the love of Christ creates a life heroic, exalted, illustrious: no, I must come down from such lofty words—it is such a life as every Christian ought to live; it is such a life as every Christian must live if he is really constrained by the love of Christ, for the text does not say the love of Christ ought to constrain us, it declares that it does constrain us. Men and brethren, if it does not constrain *you*, judge yourselves, that ye be not judged and found wanting at the last. God grant we may feel the love of God shed abroad in our hearts by the Holy Ghost. Amen.

IS CONVERSION NECESSARY?

" Therefore if any man be in Christ, he is a new creature: old things are passed away; behold, all things are become new."—2 Corinthians v. 17.

A FEW days ago I was preaching in Lancashire upon the putting away of sin by our Lord Jesus, and the consequent peace of conscience enjoyed by the believer. In the course of the sermon I related my own conversion, with the view of showing that the simple act of looking to Jesus brought peace to the soul. Now, the diocese of Manchester is presided over by a bishop who has a deservedly high place in public esteem for his zeal, industry, and force of character; and, feeling that he did not agree with me, he has very properly taken an opportunity to warn the working men whom he addressed against drawing improper inferences from my story, and he has done this in a manner so courteous that I only wish all discussions were conducted in the same spirit. The best return I can make for his courtesy is to enlarge upon the subject, and carefully guard his utterances from injurious inferences, even as he has protected mine. The idea of controversy is not upon my mind at all, nor have I any other feeling towards Bishop Fraser than that which is honestly expressed in a hearty prayer that God may bless him ; but I am thinking of the many who will read his remarks who, I trust, may afterwards read mine : and as the point is one of the utmost conceivable importance, and deeply concerns the souls of our hearers, it is well that neither should be misunderstood, and that by all means a truth so vital should be brought into prominence.

The bishop does not doubt for a moment that my own conversion was correctly described by me, and that like cases have occurred at other times : but he fears lest others should suppose that they must be converted in exactly the same manner. In that fear I fully participate, and it has ever been a special point with me to show that God's Spirit calls men to Jesus in divers ways. Some are drawn so gently that they scarce know when the drawing began, and others are so suddenly affected that their conversion stands out with noonday clearness. Perhaps no two conversions are precisely alike in detail ; the means, the modes, the manifestations, all vary greatly. As our minds are not cast in the same mould, it may so happen that the truth which affects one is powerless upon another ; the style of address which influences your friend may be offensive to yourself, and that which leads him to decide may only cause you to delay. " The wind bloweth where it listeth." The Holy Ghost is called " the free Spirit," and in the diversity of His operations that freeness is clearly seen. Again and again have I warned you against imitating others in the matter of conversion, lest you be found counterfeits, and it is well when another voice unites with me in the warning.

Yet in all true conversions there are points of essential agreement : there must be in all a penitent confession of sin, and a looking to Jesus for the forgiveness of it, and there must also be a real change of heart such as shall affect the entire after life, and where these essential points are not to be found there is no genuine conversion.

The bishop goes on to remark upon Bunyan's " Pilgrim's Progress," and its description of the burdened pilgrim and his finding rest at the cross. The bishop mistakes honest John, for he says that " the pilgrim having failed to get his wife to take the same gloomy view of fleeing from the wrath to come, and to accompany him in his flight, set out alone. There they had a man who deserted his home and home duties, leaving them to take care of themselves ; but if a man stayed at home and his heart was right, he would have been saved in the day of doom." Surely allegory is not to be read in this fashion. John Bunyan never meant to teach that any man should forsake his home and neglect his family ; no one ever charged him with doing so himself ; in his imprisonment he worked hard at tagging laces to support his family, and his affection for his poor blind child is well known.

John Bunyan was no monk, but as true a father, citizen, and friend as ever lived. The passage is part of an allegory, and represents an awakened man as resolving to seek the Saviour, whether others would do so or not ; a man alive to his own condition and responsibility, and therefore determined to pursue the right road, even if the nearest and dearest refused to bear him company. It is not implied that he left the company of his family in temporal things, for with these the allegory has nothing to do. I feel sure the bishop knows too well the value of decision of mind, and of that strong resolve to be right which dares to be singular, to say a word wittingly against one of the bravest of the virtues.

The bishop continues, " The pilgrim went on his journey, and at the sight of the cross, the great bundle, which was the burden of his past sins, fell off his back. Falling down before the cross, he thought of Him who hung upon it, and of the great doctrine of atonement, and the burden dropped from his back, and he rose what is called ' a converted man.' " The bishop is inclined to think that this story of Bunyan's conversion has given a colour to a great part of what is called Protestant theology in these days. He has noticed that a great number of our theological ideas come rather from Milton and " the Pilgrim's Progress " than from the Bible, for he does not find a single case in the Bible at all analogous to or resembling the case of John Bunyan. He then denies that the case of the penitent thief is at all to the point, or even the conversion of the apostle Paul, and he bids his hearers remember that it is " better not to dream those dreams of conversion that might happen to one and not to another." Now, so far as Milton is concerned, the bishop is right, but I demur to his statement with regard to Bunyan's " Pilgrim," and differ from him altogether in his judgment of Paul's conversion. He fears that some may imagine a particular manner of conversion to be necessary, but my fear is much greater than from Bishop Fraser's words far more will infer that no conversion is necessary at all. My fear is not so much that they should say, " I must be converted like John Bunyan," but that they will whisper, " It is all an idle tale ; the Bishop means that we have only to do our duty and be sober and honest, and all will be well, whether we are converted or not." Our text says that " if any man be in Christ, he is a new creature : old things are passed away ; behold, all things are become new " ; and my point is just this, that any man who is united to Christ has experienced a great change. I do not lay down hard and fast lines about how the conversion is to be wrought, but the word is imperative which says, " Ye must be born again," and the exhortation speaks to all mankind, " Repent, and be converted, that your sins may be blotted out." Even to this hour our Lord saith, " Verily I say unto you, except ye be converted and become as little children, ye shall not enter into the kingdom of heaven."

My line of discourse will be as follows : according to our text and many other Scriptures, *a great change is needed in any man who would be saved ;* secondly, *this great change is frequently very marked ;* and thirdly, *this change is recognisable by distinct signs.*

I. IN ORDER TO SALVATION A RADICAL CHANGE IS NECESSARY. This change is a thorough and sweeping one, and operates upon the nature, heart, and life of the convert. Human nature is the same to all time, and it will be idle to try to turn the edge of scriptural quotations by saying that they refer to the Jews or to the heathen, for at that rate we shall have no Bible left us at all. The Bible is meant for mankind, and our text refers to *any* man, of any country, and any age. " If any man be in Christ, he is a new creature : old things are passed away ; behold, all things are become new."

We prove this point by reminding you, first, *that everywhere in Scripture men are divided into two classes*, with a very sharp line of distinction between them. Read in the gospels, and you shall find continual mention of sheep lost and sheep found, guests refusing the invitation and guests feasting at the table, the wise virgins and the foolish, the sheep and the goats. In the epistles we read of those who are " dead in trespasses and sin," and of others to whom it is said, " And you hath He quickened " ; so that some are alive to God, and others are in their natural state of spiritual death. We find men spoken of as being either in darkness or in light, and the phrase is used of " being brought out of darkness into marvellous light." Some are spoken of as having been formerly aliens and strangers, and having been made fellow-citizens and brethren. We read of " children of God," in opposition to " children of wrath." We read of believers who are not condemned, and of those who are condemned already because they have not believed. We read of those who have " gone astray," and of those who have " returned to the shepherd and bishop of their souls." We read of those who are " in the flesh and cannot please God," and of those who are chosen and called and justified, whom the whole universe is challenged to condemn. The apostle speaks of " us who are saved," as if there were some saved while upon others " the wrath of God abideth." " Enemies " are continually placed in contrast with those who are " reconciled to God by the death of His Son." There are those that are " far off from God by wicked works," and those who are " made nigh by the blood of Christ." I could continue till I wearied you. The distinction between the two classes runs through the whole of the Scriptures, and never do we find a hint that there are some who are naturally good, and do not need to be removed from the one class into the other, or that there are persons between the two who can afford to remain as they are. No, there must be a divine work, making us new creatures, and causing all things to become new with us, or we shall die in our sins.

The Word of God, besides so continually describing two classes, very frequently and in forcible expressions speaks of an inward change by which men are brought from one state into the other. I hope I shall not weary you if I refer to a considerable number of Scriptures, but it is best to go to the fountain-head at once. This change is often described as a *birth*. See the third chapter of the gospel of John, which is wonderfully clear and to the point, " Except a man be born again he cannot see the kingdom of God." This birth is not a birth by baptism, for it is spoken of as accompanied by an intelligent faith which receives the Lord Jesus. Turn to John i. 12, 13, " But as many as received Him, to them gave He power to become the sons of God, even to them that believed on His name : which were born not of blood, nor of the will of the flesh, nor of the will of man, but of God." So that believers are " born again," and

receive Christ through faith : a regeneration imparted in infancy and lying dormant in unbelievers is a fiction unknown to Holy Scripture. In the third of John our Lord associates faith and regeneration in the closest manner, declaring not only that we must be born again, but also that whosoever believeth in Him shall not perish, but have everlasting life. We must undergo a change quite as great as if we could return to our native nothingness and could then come forth fresh from the hand of the Great Creator. John tell us, in his first epistle, v. 4, that " Whatsoever is born of God overcometh the world," and he adds, to show that the new birth and faith go together, " This is the victory that overcometh the world, even our faith." To the same effect is 1 John v. 1, " Whosoever believeth that Jesus is the Christ is born of God." Where there is true faith, there is the new birth, and that term implies a change beyond measure complete, and radical.

In other places this change is described as a *quickening.* " And you hath He quickened who were dead in trespasses and sins." (Eph. ii. 1.) We are said to be raised from the dead together with Christ, and this is spoken of as being a very wonderful display of omnipotence. We read (Eph. i. 19) of " the exceeding greatness of His power to us-ward who believe, according to the working of His mighty power, which He wrought in Christ when He raised Him from the dead, and set Him at His own right hand in the heavenly places." Regeneration is a very prodigy of divine strength, and by no means a mere figment fabled to accompany a religious ceremony.

We find this change frequently described as a *creation*, as, for instance, in our text, " If any man be in Christ, he is a new creature " ; and this also is no mere formality, or an attendant upon a rite, for we read in Galatians vi. 15, " For in Christ Jesus neither circumcision availeth anything, nor uncircumcision, but a new creature." No outward rites, though ordained of God Himself, effect any change upon the heart of man, there must be a creating over again of the entire nature by the divine hand ; we must be " created in Christ Jesus unto good works " (Eph. ii. 10), and we must have in us " the new man, which after God is created in righteousness and true holiness " (Eph. iv. 24). What a wonderful change that must be which is first described as a birth, then as a resurrection from the dead, and then as an absolute creation.

Paul, in Colossians i. 13, further speaks of God the Father, and says, " Who hath delivered us from the power of darkness, and hath translated us into the kingdom of His dear Son." John calls it a " passing from death unto life " (1 John iii. 14), no doubt having in his mind that glorious declaration of his Lord and Master : " Verily, verily, I say unto you, He that heareth My word, and believeth on Him that sent Me, hath everlasting life, and shall not come into condemnation ; but is passed from death unto life " (John v. 24).

Once more, as if to go to the extremity of forcible expression, Peter speaks of our conversion and regeneration as our being "begotten again." Hear the passage (1 Peter i. 3), " Blessed be the God and Father of our Lord Jesus Christ, which according to His abundant mercy hath begotten us again unto a lively hope by the resurrection of Jesus Christ from the dead." To the same purport speaks the apostle James in his first chapter, at the eighteenth verse : " Of His own will begat He us with the word of truth, that we should be a kind of firstfruits of His creatures."

My dear friends, can you conceive of any language more plainly descriptive of a most solemn change ? If it be possible with the human tongue to describe a change which is total, thorough, complete, and divine, these words do describe it ; and if such a change be not intended by the language here used by the Holy Spirit, then I am unable to find any meaning in the Bible, and its words are rather meant to bewilder than to instruct, which God forbid we should think. My appeal is to you who try to be contented without regeneration and conversion. I beseech you, do not be satisfied, for you never can be in Christ unless old things are passed away with you, and all things become new.

Further, *the Scriptures speak of this great inner work as producing a very wonderful change in the subject of it.* Regeneration and conversion, the one the secret cause, and the other the first overt effect, produce a great change in the character. Read Romans vi. 17, " But God be thanked, that ye were the servants of sin, but ye have obeyed from the heart that form of doctrine which was delivered you." Again at verse 22, " Now being made free from sin, and become servants to God, ye have your fruit unto holiness, and the end everlasting life." Mark well the description the apostle gives in Colossians iii. 9, when, having described the old nature and its sins, he says, " Lie not one to another, seeing that ye have put off the old man with his deeds ; and have put on the new man." The Book swarms with proof texts. The change of character in the converted man is so great, that " they that are Christ's have crucified the flesh with the affections and lusts " (Gal. v. 24).

And as there is a change in character, so there is a change in feeling. The man had been an enemy to God before, but when this change takes place he begins to love God. Read Colossians i. 21, "And you, that were some time alienated and enemies in in your mind by wicked works, yet now hath He reconciled in the body of His flesh through death, to present you holy and unblamable and unreprovable in His sight."

This change from enmity to friendship with God arises very much from a change of man's judicial state before God. Before a man is converted he is condemned, but when he receives spiritual life we read " there is therefore now no condemnation to them which are in Christ Jesus, who walk not after the flesh, but after the Spirit." This altogether changes his condition as to inward happiness. " Therefore, being justified by faith, we have peace with God, through Jesus Christ our Lord " ; which peace we never had before. " And not only so, but we also joy in God through our Lord Jesus Christ, by whom we have now received the atonement."

O brethren, conversion makes a difference in us most mighty indeed, or else what did Christ mean when He said, " Come unto Me, all ye that labour and are heavy laden, and I will give you rest " ? Does He after all give us no rest ? Is the man who comes to Jesus just as restless and as devoid of peace as before ? God forbid ! Does not Jesus say that when we drink of the water which He gives to us we shall never thirst again ? What ! And are we to be told that there is never a time when

we leave off thirsting, never a time when that living water becomes in us a well of water, springing up unto everlasting life ? Our own experience refutes the suggestion. Does not Paul say in Heb. iv. 3, " We which have believed do enter into rest " ? Our condition before God, our moral tone, our nature, our state of mind, are made by conversion totally different from what they were before. " Old things are passed away ; behold, all things are become new." Why, beloved, instead of supposing that we can do without conversion, the Scriptures represent this as being the grand blessing of the covenant of grace. What said the Lord by His servant Jeremiah ? " This shall be the covenant that I will make with the house of Israel ; after these days, saith the Lord, I will put My law in their inward parts, and write it in their hearts, and I will be their God, and they shall be My people " (Jer. xxxi. 33). This passage Paul quotes in the Hebrews x. 16, not as obsolete, but as fulfilled in believers. And what has the Lord said by Ezekiel ? (Ezek. xxxvi. 26, 27). Listen to the gracious passage, and see what a grand blessing conversion is ;— " A new heart also will I give you, and a new spirit will I put within you : and I will take away the stony heart out of your flesh, and I will give you a heart of flesh ; and I will put My spirit within you and cause you to walk in My statutes ; and ye shall keep My judgments and do them." Is not this *the* blessing of the gospel by which we realise all the rest ? Is not this the great work of the Holy Ghost by which we know the Father and the Son ? And is not this needful to make us in accord with future glory ? " He that sat upon the throne said, Behold, I make all things new " (Rev. xxi. 5). There is to be a new heaven and a new earth, for the first heaven and the first earth shall pass away ; and can we believe that the old carnal nature is to enter into the new creation ? Is that which is born of the flesh to enter into the spiritual kingdom ? Never can it be. No ; a change as wonderful as that which will pass over this world when Christ shall re-create it, must pass over each one of us, if it be not so already. In a word, if we be in Christ Jesus we are new creatures ; old things are passed away ; behold, all things are become new.

Do you know anything about this ? I trust that a great number of you have experienced it, and are showing it in your lives ; but I fear me some are ignorant of it. Let those who are unconverted never rest till they have believed in Christ and have a new heart created and a right spirit bestowed. Lay it well to heart, that a change must come over you which you cannot work in yourselves, but which must be wrought by divine power. There is this for your comfort, that Jesus Christ has promised this blessing to all who receive Him, for He gives them power to become the sons of God.

II. Secondly, I now remark that THIS CHANGE IS FREQUENTLY VERY MARKED AS TO ITS TIME AND CIRCUMSTANCES. Many souls truly born of God could not lay their finger upon any date, and say, " At such a time I passed from death unto life." There was such a time, however, though they may not be able to fix upon it. The act of conversion is often as to many of its circumstances so surrounded by preceding works of restraining grace that it appears to be a very gradual thing, and the rising of the sun of righteousness in the soul is comparable to the dawning of day, with a grey light at first, and a gradual increase to a noonday splendour. Yet, as there is a time when the sun rises, so is there a time of new birth. If a dead man were restored to life, he might not be able to say exactly when life began, but there is such a moment. There must be a time when a man ceases to be an unbeliever and becomes a believer in Jesus. I do not assert that it is necessary for us to know the day, but such a time there is. In many cases, however, the very day and hour and place are fully known, and we might expect this, first, *from many other works of God.* How very particular God is about the time of creation ! " The evening and the morning were the first day." " God said, ' Let there be light,' and months afterwards there came a little grey dawning, and a solitary star." Oh no, you say, you are quoting from imagination ! I am. The Scripture has it, " God said, Let there be light : and there was light." Immediate work is God's method of creating ; all through the six days' work He spake and it was done, He commanded and it stood fast. There is generally a likeness between one act of God and another, and if in the old creation the fiat did it all, it does seem likely upon the very face of things that in the new creation the fiat of the eternal Word should be equally quick and powerful in its working. Look at the acts of God in the person of Christ when He was here among men. The water turns at once to wine, the fig-tree immediately withers away, the loaves and fishes are at once multiplied in the hands of the disciples. Miracles of healing were as a rule instantaneous. In one instance the Lord puts clay on the blind man's eyes, and sends him to wash ; but lengthen the operation as much as you like, it is still very briefly summed up in " I washed and do see." Yonder paralytic man is lying on his bed, Jesus says to him, " Take up thy bed and walk," and he does so at once. The leprosy was cured with a touch, devils fled at a word, ears were unstopped instantly, and withered limbs restored. He spake to the waves and the winds and they were calm at once ; and as to the resurrections which Christ worked, which are His acted parables of regeneration, they were all instantaneous. Jesus took the little girl by the hand, and said, " *Talitha cumi,*" she opened her eyes and sat up. He bade the bier stand still on which was the young man : He said—" Young man, I say unto thee arise " ; and he arose straightway. Even the carcase of Lazarus, which had begun to corrupt, yielded at once to His word. He did but say, " Lazarus, come forth," and there was Lazarus. As the Master worked on men's bodies, so does He constantly work upon men's souls, and it is according to analogy to expect that His works will be instantaneous. Such they constantly are, for are they not daily before us ?

We might also look for many instances of vividness if we consider the work itself. If it be worthy to be called a resurrection, there must manifestly be a time in which the dead man ceases to be dead and becomes alive. Take the opposite process of dying : we commonly say that such a man was long in dying ; that is a popular description, but strictly speaking, the actual death must be instantaneous. There is a time in which there is breath in the body, and another time in which there is none. So must it be in the reception of life ; that life may seem to come by slow degrees into the soul, but it cannot really be so ; there must be an instant up to which there was no life, and beyond which life began. Is

not that self-evident ? Is it wonderful that that instant should fix itself on the memory, and in many cases be the most prominent fact in a man's whole history ?

It is called a creation. Now creation is necessarily a work which happens in an instant, for a thing either is or is not. There is no intervening space between non-existence and existence ; there is the sharpest conceivable line between that which is not and that which is. So in the new creation, there must be a time when grace is not received, and a time when renewing it is, and we may naturally expect that in so grand a work there would be, in many cases, a marked boundary line at which the work begins.

But, brethren, we need not talk of what we might expect ; let us look at the facts. What are the facts about the conversions mentioned in Scripture ? We hear much of educational processes which supersede conversion, but they are among the many inventions unknown to apostolic history. The bishop tells us that he does not find a single case in the Bible at all resembling the case of John Bunyan. It is very curious how very differently we read. I at once turn to Paul, but the bishop says he is not a case in point, for he did not feel the burden of sin fall off his back. I cannot guess how the bishop knows what Paul endured during his three days' blindness, but my own notion, gathered from Paul's after sayings and doings, is very different. The man was one moment an opponent of Christ, and the next moment was crying, " Who art thou, Lord ? " For three days he was blind and fasted ; was he not then feeling the power of the law, and casting away his own righteousness ? And when Ananias came to tell him more fully the gospel, and to bid him arise and be baptized, and wash away his sins, was there no removal of sin ? Did he remain as before ? There were two things spoken of, he was to be baptized, and also to receive another and spiritual washing : was the first real and not the second ? The apostle always speaks of the whole thing as if he had cast away his own righteousness, and counted it but dung, to lay hold on Christ, and he continually glories in having peace with God, though he did not claim perfection in the flesh. He had not attained perfection, but he had attained salvation. He calls himself the chief of sinners, but this was as a retrospect ; surely Bishop Fraser does not really mean to insinuate that the great apostle still remained the chief of sinners ? If so, I must say the morality of his teaching is not such as one would expect from him.

Some have said that Paul's case is a special and solitary one. But this is an error, for he says himself, that Jesus Christ in him showed forth all long-suffering *for a pattern to them which should hereafter believe on Him to life everlasting* (1 Tim. i. 15, 16.) That which is a pattern is not a special case. Though the Lord does not always work to pattern in details, yet the case of Paul suddenly converted is the pattern rather than the exception.

Let us look at other instances. A Samaritan woman comes to the well to draw water, Christ speaks to her, she is converted, and goes away to tell the men of the city. Is not that a case of sudden conversion ? Zacchæus, is in the tree, he is a rich publican, and a sinner. Jesus cries, " Zacchæus, make haste, and come down " ; he comes down, receives Jesus into his house, and proves his salvation by his works. Is not that a sudden conversion? Matthew sits at the receipt of custom, another publican and sinner: Jesus says, "Follow me"; he rises and follows Jesus. Is not that a sudden conversion? Three thousand persons gathered at Pentecost, Peter preaches to them, and tells them that Jesus whom they had murdered was really the Christ of God; they are pricked in the heart, they believe, and are baptized on the same day. Have we not here three thousand sudden conversions? Sudden enough to prove my point. Further on, the jailer has gone to his bed, having fastened Paul and Silas in the stocks; his prisoners pray and sing praises unto God, there is an earthquake, the jailer in alarm cries, "What must I do to be saved?" He believes in Jesus there and then, and is baptized with his believing household. Are not these "at all analogous to John Bunyan's pilgrim" and his losing his load? It really seems to me as if it would be much more difficult to find gradual conversion in Scripture than a sudden one, for here they come, one after another, men and women brought to Jesus Christ who knew Him not before, in whom the Scripture is fulfilled, "I am found of them that sought Me not."

Furthermore, we need not go back to Scripture for this. The matter of the conversion of souls is one about which I feel it a weariness to argue, because these wonders of grace happen daily before our eyes, and it is like trying to prove that the sun rises in the morning. By the space of twenty years there has certainly never occurred to me a single week, and I might with truthfulness say scarcely a solitary day, in which I have not heard of persons being converted by the simple preaching of the gospel either here or elsewhere, when I have borne witness for Christ; and these conversions have been in far the greater majority of instances very clear and well-defined. Sometimes the children of godly parents who have been long hearing the word are converted, and in them the inward change is as marked as if they had never heard the gospel before. Infidels become believers, Romanists forsake their priests, harlots become chaste, drunkards leave their cups, and, what is equally remarkable, Pharisees leave their self-righteous pride, and come as sinners to Jesus. Why, if this were the proper time and place, I might say to you now assembled, "Brothers and sisters, you who have experienced a great change, and know that you have experienced it, and can tell how it came about, stand up!" and you would rise in numbers like a host and declare, "Thus and thus, God met with us under the preaching of His truth, and thus did He turn us from darkness to marvellous light." I would to God that every man that heareth me this day had received such a distinct conversion that it would be so plain to him that he was a new creature that he could no more doubt it than he can doubt his existence.

III. Thirdly, THIS CHANGE IS RECOGNISABLE BY CERTAIN SIGNS. It has been supposed by some that the moment a man is converted he thinks himself perfect. It is not so among us, for we rather question the conversion of any man who thinks himself perfect. It is thought by others that a converted man must be henceforth free from all doubts. I wish it were so. Unhappily, although there is faith in us, unbelief is there also. Some dream that the converted man has nothing more to seek for, but we teach not so; a man who is alive unto God has greater needs than

ever. Conversion is the beginning of a life-long conflict; it is the first blow in a warfare which will never end till we are in glory.

In every case of conversion there are these signs following. There is always *a sense of sin*. No man, rest assured, ever found peace with God without first repenting of sin, and knowing it to be an evil thing. The horrors which some have felt are not essential, but a full confession of sin before God, and an acknowledgment of our guilt, is absolutely required. "The whole," says Christ, "have no need of a physician, but they that are sick; I came not to call the righteous but sinners to repentance." Christ does not heal those who are not sick, He never clothes those who are not naked, nor enriches those who are not poor. True conversion always has in it a humbling sense of the need of divine grace.

It is also always attended with simple, true, and real faith in Jesus Christ; in fact, that is the king's own mark, and without it nothing is of any worth. "Like as Moses lifted up the serpent in the wilderness, even so must the Son of man be lifted up, that whosoever believeth in Him should not perish, but have everlasting life"; and that passage is put side by side with "ye must be born again," in the same address, by the same Saviour, to the same inquirer. Therefore we gather that faith is the mark of the new birth, and where it is, there the Spirit has changed the heart of man; but where it is not, men are still "dead in trespasses and sin."

Conversion may be known, next, by this fact, that it changes the whole man. It changes the principle upon which he lives; he lived for self, now he lives for God; he did right because he was afraid of punishment if he did wrong, but now he shuns evil because he hates it. He did right because he hoped to merit heaven, but now no such selfish motive sways him, he knows that he is saved, and he does right out of gratitude to God. His objects in life are changed: he lived for gain, or worldly honour; now he lives for the glory of God. His comforts are changed: the pleasures of the world and sin are nothing to him, he finds comfort in the love of God shed abroad in his heart by the Holy Ghost. His desires are changed: that which he once panted and pined for he is now content to do without; and that which he once despised he now longs after as the hart panteth after the water brooks. His fears are different; he fears man no more, but fears his God. His hopes are also altered. His expectations fly beyond the stars.

"He looks for a city which hands have not piled;
He pants for a country by sin undefiled."

The man has begun a new life. A convert once said, "Either the world is altered or else I am." Everything seems new. The very faces of our children look different to us, for we regard them under a new aspect, viewing them as heirs of immortality. We view our friends from a different standpoint. Our very business seems altered. Even taking down the shutters of a morning is done by the husband in a different spirit, and the children are put to bed by the mother in another mood. We learn to sanctify the hammer and the plough by serving the Lord with them. We feel that the things which are seen are shadows, and the things which we hear are but voices out of dreamland, but the unseen is substantial, and that which mortal ear hears not is truth. Faith has become to us "the substance of things hoped for, the evidence of things not seen."

I may go on to talk about this, but none will understand me except those who have experienced it, and let those who have not experienced it say it is not true. How do they know? How can a man bear witness to what he has *not* seen? What is the value of testimony from a man who begins by saying "I know nothing about it"? If a credible witness declares that he knows such a thing to have happened it would be easy to find fifty persons who can say that they did not see it, but their evidence goes for nothing. Here are men of position, quite as keen in business, and able to judge between fact and fiction as other men, and they tell you solemnly that they have themselves experienced a wonderful, thorough, and total change of nature. Surely if their honest testimony would be taken in any court of law, it ought to be taken in this case. Brethren, I pray that we may know what this change is, and if we do know it, I again pray that we may so live that others may see the result of it upon our characters, and inquire what it means.

The phenomena of conversion are the standing miracles of the church. " Greater things than these shall ye do," said Christ, " because I go to My Father " ; and these are some of the greater things which the power of the Holy Ghost still performs. This day the dead are raised, blind eyes are opened, and the lame are made to walk. The spiritual miracle is greater than the physical one. These spiritual miracles show that Jesus lives and puts life and power into the gospel. Tell me of a ministry which never reclaims the drunkard, never calls back the thief to honesty, never pulls down the self-righteous and makes him confess his sin ; that, in a word, never transforms its hearers ; and I am sure that such a ministry is not worth the time which men spend in listening to it. Woe unto the man who at the last shall confess to a ministry fruitless in conversions. If the gospel does not convert men, do not believe in it ; but if it does, it is its own evidence, and must be believed. It may be to some of you a stumbling-block, and to others foolishness, but unto those who believe it is the power of God unto salvation, saving them from sin.

Beloved hearers, may we all meet in heaven ; but to meet in heaven we must all be renewed, for inside yonder gates of pearl none can enter but those who are new creatures in Christ Jesus our Lord. God bless you, for Christ's sake. Amen.

THE CONDESCENSION OF CHRIST

" For ye know the grace of our Lord Jesus Christ, that, though He was rich, yet for your sakes He became poor, that ye through His poverty might be rich."—2 Corinthians viii. 9.

THE apostle, in this chapter, was endeavouring to stir up the Corinthians to liberality. He desired them to contribute something for those who were the poor of the flock, that he might be able to minister to their necessities. He tells them, that the churches of Macedonia, though very much poorer than the church at Corinth, had done even beyond their means for the relief of the Lord's family, and he exhorts the Corinthians to do the same. But suddenly recollecting that examples taken from inferiors seldom have a powerful effect he lays aside his argument drawn from the church of Macedonia, and he holds before them a reason for liberality which the hardest heart can scarcely resist, if once that reason be applied by the Spirit. " My brethren," said he, " there is One above, by whom you hope you have been saved, One whom you call Master and Lord, now if you will but imitate Him, you cannot be ungenerous or illiberal. For, my brethren, I tell you a thing which is an old thing with you and an undisputed truth—' For ye know the grace of our Lord Jesus Christ, that, though He was rich, yet for your sakes He became poor, that ye through His poverty might be rich.' Let this constrain you to benevolence." O Christian, whenever thou art inclined to an avaricious withholding from the church of God, think of thy Saviour giving up all that He had to serve thee, and canst thou then, when thou beholdest self-denial so noble,—canst thou then be selfish, and regard thyself, when the claims of the poor of the flock are pressed upon thee? Remember Jesus ; think thou seest Him look thee in the face and say to thee, " I gave Myself for thee, and dost thou withhold thyself from Me? For if thou dost so, thou knowest not My love in all its heights and depths and lengths and breadths."

An now, dear friends, the argument of the apostle shall be our subject to-day. It divides itself in an extremely simple manner. We have first, *the pristine condition of our Saviour*—" He was rich." We have next, *His condescension*—" He became poor." And then we have *the effect and result of His poverty*— " That we might be made rich." We shall then close by giving you a doctrine, a question, and an exhortation. May God bless all these, and help us to tell them aright.

I. First, then, our text tells us THAT JESUS CHRIST WAS RICH. Think not that our Saviour began to live when He was born of the Virgin Mary ; imagine not that He dates His existence from the manger at Bethlehem ; remember He is the Eternal, He is before all things, and by Him all things consist. There was never a time in which there was not God. And just so, there was never a period in which there was not Christ Jesus our Lord. He is self-existent, hath no beginning of days, neither end of years ; He is the immortal, invisible, the only wise God, our Saviour. Now, in the past eternity which had elapsed before His mission to this world, we are told that Jesus Christ was rich ; and to those of us who believe His glories and trust in His divinity, it is not hard to see how He was so. Jesus was rich *in possessions*. Lift up thine eye, believer, and for a moment review the riches of my Lord Jesus, before He condescended to become poor for thee. Behold Him, sitting upon His throne and declaring His own all sufficiency. " If I were hungry, I would not tell thee, for the cattle on a thousand hills are Mine. Mine are the hidden treasures of gold ; Mine are the pearls that the diver cannot reach ; Mine every precious thing that earth hath seen." The Lord Jesus might have said, " I can stretch My sceptre from the east even to the west, and all is Mine ; the whole of this world, and yon worlds that glitter in far off space, all are Mine. The illimitable expanse of unmeasured space, filled as it is with worlds that I have made, all this is Mine. Fly upward, and thou canst not reach the summit of the hill of My dominions ; dive downwards, and thou canst not enter into the innermost depths of My sway. From the highest throne in glory to the lowest pit of hell, all, all is Mine without exception. I can put the broad arrow of My kingdom upon everything that I have made."

But He had besides that which makes men richer still. We have heard of kings in olden times who were fabulously rich, and when their riches were summed up, we read in the old romances, " And this man was possessed of the philosopher's stone, whereby he turned all things into gold." Surely all the treasures that He had before were as nothing compared with this precious stone that brought up the rear. Now, whatever might be the wealth of Christ in things created, He had the *power of creation*, and therein, lay His boundless wealth. If He had pleased He could have spoken worlds into existence ; He had but to lift His finger, and a new universe as boundless as the present would have leaped into existence. At the will of His mind, millions of angels would have stood before Him, legions of bright spirits would have flashed into being. He spake, and it was done ; He commanded, and it stood fast. He who said " Light be," and light was, had power to say to all things, " Be," and they should be. Herein, then, lay His riches ; this creating power was one of the brightest jewels of His crown.

We call men rich, too, who have *honour*, and though men have never so much wealth, yet if they be in disgrace and shame, they must not reckon themselves amongst the rich. But our Lord Jesus had honour, honour such as none but a divine being could receive. When He sat upon His throne, before He relinquished the glorious mantle of His sovereignty to become a man, all earth was filled with His glory. He could look both beneath and all around Him, and the inscription, " Glory be unto God," was written over all space ; day and night the smoking incense of praise ascended before Him from golden viols held by spirits who bowed in reverence ; the harps of myriads of cherubim and seraphim continually thrilled with His praise, and the voices of all those mighty hosts were ever eloquent in adoration. It may be, that on set days the princes from the far off realms, the kings, the mighty ones of His boundless realms, came to the court of Christ, and brought each his annual revenue. Oh, who can tell but that in the vast eternity, at certain grand eras, the great bell was rung, and all the mighty hosts that were created gathered together in solemn review before His throne. Who can tell the high holiday that was kept in the court of heaven when these bright spirits bowed before His throne in joy and gladness, and, all united, raised their voices in shouts and hallelujahs such as mortal ear hath never heard. Oh, can ye tell the depths of the rivers of praise that flowed hard by the city of God ? Can ye imagine to yourselves the sweetness of that harmony that perpetually poured into the ear of Jesus, Messias, King, Eternal, equal with God His Father ? No ; at the thought of the glory of His kingdom, and the riches and majesty of His power, our souls are spent within us, our words fail, we cannot utter the tithe of His glories.

Nor was He poor in any other sense. He that hath wealth on earth, and honour, too, is poor if he hath not *love*. I would rather be the pauper, dependant upon charity, and have love, than I would be the prince, despised and hated, whose death is looked for as a boon. Without love, man is poor—give him all the diamonds, and pearls, and gold that mortal hath conceived. But Jesus was not poor in love. When He came to earth, He did not come to get our love because His soul was solitary. Oh no, His Father had a full delight in Him from all eternity. The heart of Jehovah, the first person of the Sacred Trinity, was divinely, immutably linked to Him ; He was beloved of the Father and of the Holy Spirit ; the three persons took a sacred complacency and delight in each other. And besides that, how was He loved by those bright spirits who had not fallen. I cannot tell what countless orders and creatures there are created who still stand fast in obedience to God. It is not possible for us to know whether there are, or not, as many races of created beings as we know there are created men on earth. We cannot tell but that in the boundless regions of space, there are worlds inhabited by beings infinitely superior to us : but certain it is, there were the holy angels, and they loved our Saviour ; they stood day and night with wings outstretched, waiting for His commands, hearkening to the voice of His word ; and when He bade them fly, there was love in their countenance, and joy in their hearts. They loved to serve Him, and it is not all fiction that when there was war in heaven, and when God cast out the devil and His legions, then the elect angels showed their love to Him, being valiant in fight and strong in power. He wanted not our love to make Him happy, He was rich enough in love without us.

Now, though a spirit from the upper world should come to tell you of the riches of Jesus He could not do it. Gabriel, in thy flights thou hast mounted higher than my imagination dares to follow thee, but thou hast never gained the summit of the throne of God.

" Dark with insufferable light thy skirts appear."

Jesus, who is he that could look upon the brow of Thy Majesty, who is he that could comprehend the strength of the arm of Thy might ? Thou art God, Thou art infinite, and we poor finite things, are lost in Thee. The insect of an hour cannot comprehend Thyself. We bow before Thee, we adore Thee ; Thou art God over all, blessed for ever. But as for the comprehension of Thy boundless riches, as for being able to tell Thy treasures, or to reckon up Thy wealth, that were impossible. All we know is, that the wealth of God, that the treasures of the infinite, that the riches of eternity, were all Thine own : Thou wast rich beyond all thought.

II. The Lord Jesus Christ then was rich. We all believe that, though none of us can truly speak it forth. Oh, how surprised angels were, when they were first informed that Jesus Christ, the Prince of Light and Majesty, intended to shroud Himself in clay and become a babe, and live and die ! We know not how it was first mentioned to the angels, but when the rumour first began to get afloat among the sacred hosts, you may imagine what strange wonderment there was. What ! was it true that He whose crown was all bedight with stars, would lay that crown aside ? What ! was it certain that He about whose shoulders was cast the purple of the universe, would become a man, dressed in a peasant's garment ? Could it be true that He who was everlasting and immortal, would one day be nailed to a cross ? Oh ! how their wonderment increased ! They desired to look into it. And when He descended from on high, they followed Him ; for Jesus was " seen of angels," and seen in a special sense ; for they looked upon Him in rapturous amazement, wondering what it all could mean. " He for our sakes became poor." Do you see Him as on that day of heaven's eclipse He did ungird His majesty ? Oh, can ye conceive the yet increasing wonder of the heavenly hosts when the deed was actually done, when they saw the tiara taken off, when they saw Him unbind His girdle of stars, and cast away His sandals of gold ? Can ye conceive it, when He said to them, " I do not disdain the womb of the virgin ; I am going down to earth to become a man ? " Can ye picture them as they declared they would follow Him ! Yes, they followed Him as near as He would permit them. And when they came to earth, they began to sing, " Glory to God in the highest, on earth peace, good will towards men." Nor would they go away till they had made the shepherds wonder, and till heaven had hung out new stars in honour of the new-born King. And now wonder, ye angels, the Infinite has become an infant ; He, upon whose shoulders the universe doth hang, hangs at His mother's breast, He who created all things, and bears up the pillars of creation, hath now become so weak, that He must be carried by a woman ! And oh, wonder ye that knew Him in His riches, whilst ye admire His poverty ! Where sleeps the new-born King ? Had He the best room in Cæsar's palace ? hath a cradle of gold been prepared for Him, and pillows of down, on which to rest His head ? No, where the ox fed, in the dilapidated stable, in the manger, there the Saviour lies, swathed in the swaddling bands of the children of poverty ! Nor there doth He rest long ; on a sudden His mother must carry Him to Egypt : He goeth there, and becometh a stranger in a strange land. When He comes back, see Him that made the worlds handle the hammer and the nails, assisting his father in the trade of a carpenter ! Mark Him who has put the stars on high, and made them glisten in the night ; mark Him without one star of glory upon His brow—a simple Child as other children. Yet leave for a while the scenes of His childhood and His earlier life ; see Him when He becomes a man, and now ye may say, indeed, that for our sakes He did become poor. Never was there a poorer man than Christ ; He was the Prince of poverty. He was the reverse of Crœsus— *he* might be on the top of the hill of riches, *Christ* stood in the lowest vale of poverty. Look at His dress, it is woven from the top throughout, the garment of the poor ! As for His food, He oftentimes did hunger, and always was dependent upon the charity of others for the relief of His wants ! He who scattered the harvest o'er the broad acres of the world, had not sometimes wherewithal to stay the pangs of hunger. He who digged the springs of the ocean, sat upon a well and said to a Samaritan woman, " Give Me to drink ! " He rode in no chariot, He walked His weary way, foot sore, o'er the flints of Galilee. He had not where to lay His head. He looked upon the fox as it hurried to its burrow, and the fowl as it went to its resting place, and He said, " Foxes have holes, and the birds of the air have nests, but I, the Son of man, have not where to lay My head." He who had once been waited on by

angels, becomes the servant of servants, takes a towel, girds Himself and washes His disciples' feet ! He who was once honoured with the hallelujahs of ages, is now spit upon and despised ! He who was loved by His Father, and had abundance of the wealth of affection, could say, " He that eateth bread with Me hath lifted up his heel against Me." Oh for words to picture the humiliation of Christ ! What leagues of distance between Him that sat upon the throne, and Him that died upon the cross ! Oh, who can tell the mighty chasm between yon heights of glory, and the cross of deepest woe ! Trace Him, Christian, He has left thee His manger, to show thee how God came down to man. He hath bequeathed thee His cross, to show thee how man can ascend to God. Follow Him, follow Him, all His journey through ; begin with Him in the wilderness of temptation, see Him fasting there, and hungering, with the wild beasts around Him ; trace Him along His weary way, as the Man of Sorrows, and acquainted with grief. He is the byword of the drunkard, He is the song of the scorner, and He is hooted at by the malicious ; see Him as they point their finger at Him, and call Him " drunken man and wine-bibber ! " Follow Him along His *via dolorosa*, until at last you meet Him among the olives of Gethsemane ; see Him sweating great drops of blood ! Follow Him to the pavement of Gabbatha ; see Him pouring out rivers of gore beneath the cruel whips of Roman soldiers ! With weeping eye follow Him to the cross of Calvary, see Him nailed there ! Mark His poverty so poor, that they have stripped Him naked from head to foot, and exposed Him to the face of the sun ! So poor, that when He asked them for water they gave Him vinegar to drink ! So poor, that His unpillowed head is girt with thorns in death ! Oh, Son of Man, I know not which to admire most, Thine height of glory, or Thy depths of misery ! Oh, Man, slain for us, shall we not exalt Thee ? God, over all, blessed for ever, shall we not give Thee the loudest song ? " He was rich, yet for our sakes He became poor." If I had a tale to tell you this day of some king, who, out of love to some fair maiden, left his kingdom and became a peasant like herself, ye would stand and wonder, and would listen to the charming tale ; but when I tell of God concealing His dignity to become our Saviour, our hearts are scarcely touched. Ah ! my friends, we know the tale so well, we have heard it so often ; and, alas, some of us tell it so badly that we cannot expect that you would be as interested in it as the subject doth demand. But surely, as it is said of some great works of architecture, that though they be seen every morning, there is always something fresh to wonder at ; so we might say of Christ, that though we saw Him every day, we should always see fresh reason to love, and wonder, and adore. " He was rich, yet for your sakes He became poor."

I have thought that there is one peculiarity about the poverty of Christ, that ought not to be forgotten by us. Those who are nursed upon the lap of want feel less the woes of their condition. But I have met with others whose poverty I could pity. They were once rich ; their very dress which now hangs about them in tatters, tells you that they once stood foremost in the ranks of life. You meet them amongst the poorest of the poor ; you pity them more than those who have been born and bred to poverty, because they have known something better. Amongst all those who are poor, I have always found the greatest amount of suffering in those who had seen better days. I can remember, even now, the look of some who have said to me when they have received assistance—and I have given it as delicately as I could, lest it should look like charity—" Ah, sir, I have known better days." And the tear stood in the eye, and the heart was smitten at bitter recollections. The least slight to such a person, or even too unmasked a kindness, becomes like a knife cutting the heart. " I have known better days," sounds like a knell over their joys. And verily our Lord Jesus might have said in all His sorrows, " I have known better days than these." Methinks when He was tempted of the devil in the wilderness, it must have been hard in Him to have restrained Himself from dashing the devil into pieces. If I had been the Son of God, methinks, feeling as I do now, if that devil had tempted me I should have dashed him into the nethermost hell, in the twinkling of an eye! And then conceive the patience our Lord must have had, standing on the pinnacle of the temple, when the devil said, " Fall down and worship me." He would not touch him, the vile deceiver, but let him do what he pleased. Oh! what might of misery and love there must have been in the Saviour's heart when He was spit upon by the men He had created; when the eyes He Himself had filled with vision, looked on Him with scorn, and when the tongues, to which He Himself had given utterance, hissed and blasphemed Him! Oh, my friends, if the Saviour had felt as we do, and I doubt not He did feel in some measure as we do— only by great patience He curbed Himself—methinks He might have swept them all away; and, as they said, He might have come down from the cross, and delivered Himself, and destroyed them utterly. It was mighty patience that could bear to tread this world beneath His feet, and not to crush it, when it so ill-treated its Redeemer. You marvel at the patience which restrained Him; you marvel also at the poverty He must have felt, the poverty of spirit, when they rebuked Him and He reviled them not again; when they scoffed Him, and yet He said, " Father, forgive them, for they know not what they do." He had seen brighter days; that made His misery more bitter, and His poverty more poor.

III. Well, now we come to the third point— WHY DID THE SAVIOUR COME TO DIE AND BE POOR ? Hear this, ye sons of Adam—the Scripture says, " For your sakes He became poor, that ye through His poverty might be made rich." For *your* sakes. Now, when I address you as a great congregation, you will not feel the beauty of this expression, " For *your* sake." Husband and wife, walking in the fear of God, let me take you by the hand and look you in the face, let me repeat those words, " for *your* sakes He became poor." Young man, let a brother of thine own age look on thee and repeat these words, " Though He was rich, yet for your sake He became poor." Grey-headed believer, let me look on you and say the same, " For *your* sake He became poor." Brethren, take the word home, and see if it does not melt you—" Though He was rich, yet for *my* sake He became poor." Beg for the influences of the Spirit upon that truth, and it will make your heart devout and your spirit loving—" I the chief of sinners am, yet for my sake He died." Come let me hear you speak ; let us bring the sinner here, and let him soliloquize—" I cursed Him, I blasphemed, and yet for my sake He was made poor ; I scoffed at His minister, I broke His Sabbath, yet for my sake was He made poor. What! Jesus, couldst Thou die for

one who was not worth Thy having? Couldst Thou shed Thy blood for one who would have shed Thy blood, if it had been in his power? What! couldst Thou die for one so worthless, so vile?" " Yes, yes," says Jesus, " I shed that blood for thee." Now let the saint speak ; " I," He may say, " have professed to love Him, but how cold my love, how little have I served Him! How far have I lived from Him ; I have not had sweet communion with Him as I ought to have had. When have I been spending and spent in His service ? And yet, my Lord, Thou dost say, ' for *thy* sake I was made poor.' " " Yes," saith Jesus, " see Me in My miseries ; see Me in My agonies ; see Me in My death—all these I suffered for *thy* sake." Wilt thou not love Him who loved thee to this great excess, and became poor for thy sake ?

That, however, is not the point to which we wish to bring you, just now ; the point is this, *the reason why Christ died* was, " that we through His poverty might be rich." He became poor from His riches, that our poverty might become rich out of His poverty. Brethren we have now a joyful theme before us—those who are partakers of the Saviour's blood are rich. All those for whom the Saviour died, having believed in His name and given themselves to Him, are this day rich. And yet I have some of you here who cannot call a foot of land your own. You have nothing to call your own to-day, you know not how you will be supported through another week ; you are poor, and yet if you be a child of God, I do know that Christ's end is answered in you ; *you are rich*. No, I did not mock you when I said you were rich ; I did not taunt you—you are. You are really rich ; you are *rich in possessions* ; you have in your possession now things more costly than gems, more valuable than gold and silver. Silver and gold, have I none, thou mayest say ; but if thou canst say afterwards, " Christ is all," thou hast outspoken all that the man can say, who had piles of gold and silver. " But," thou sayest, " I have nothing." Man, thou hast all things. Knowest thou not what Paul said ? He declares that " things present and things to come, and this world, and life and death, all are yours and ye are Christ's, and Christ is God's." The great machinery of providence has no wheel which does not revolve for you. The great economy of grace with all its fulness is yours. Remember that adoption, justification, sanctification, are all yours. Thou hast everything that heart can wish in spiritual things ; and thou hast everything that is necessary for this life ; for you know who hath said, " having food and raiment, let us therewith be content." You are rich ; rich with true riches, and not with the riches of a dream. There are times when men by night do scrape gold and silver together, like shells upon the sea shore ; but when they wake in the morning they find themselves penniless. But, yours are everlasting treasures ; yours are solid riches. When the sun of eternity shall have melted the rich man's gold away, yours shall endure. A rich man has a *cistern* full of riches ; but a poor saint has got a *fountain* of mercy ; and he is the richest who has a fountain. Now if my neighbour be a rich man, he may have as much wealth as ever he pleases, it is only a cistern full, it will soon be exhausted ; but a Christian has a fountain that ever flows, and let him draw, draw on for ever, the fountain will still keep on flowing. However large may be the stagnant pool, if it be stagnant, it is but of little worth ; but the flowering stream, though it seem to be but small, needs but time, and it will have produced an immense volume of precious water. Thou art never to have a great pool of riches, they are always to keep on flowing to thee ; " Thy bread shall be given thee, and thy water shall be sure." As old William Huntingdon says, " The Christian has a hand-basket portion. Many a man, when his daughter marries, does not give her much ; but he says to her, ' I shall send you a sack of flour one day, and so-and-so the next day, and now and then a sum of gold ; and as long as I live I will always send you something.' " Says he, " She will get a great deal more than her sister who has had a thousand pounds down. That is how my God deals with me ; He gives to the rich man all at once, but to me day by day." Ah, Egypt, thou wert rich when thy granaries were full, but those granaries might be emptied : Israel were far richer when they could not see their granaries, but only saw the manna drop from heaven, day by day. Now, Christian, that is thy portion—the portion of the fountain always flowing, and not of the cistern-full and soon to be emptied.

But remember, O saint, that thy wealth does not all lie in thy possession just now ; remember thou art rich in *promises*. Let a man be never so poor as to the metal that he hath, let him have in his possession promissory notes from rich and true men ; and he says, " I have no gold in my purse, but here is a note for such-and-such a sum—I know the signature, I can trust the firm—I am rich, though I have no metal in hand." And so the Christian can say, " If I have no riches in possession, I have the promise of them ; my God hath said, ' No good thing will I withhold from them that walk uprightly,'—that is a promise that makes me rich. He has told me, ' My bread shall be given me, and my water shall be sure.' I cannot doubt His signature, I know His word to be authentic ; and as for His faithfulness, I would not so dishonour Him as to think He would break His promise. No, the promise is as good as the thing itself. If it be God's promise, it is just as sure That I shall have it, as if I had it."

But then the Christian is very rich in *reversion*. When a certain old man dies that I know of, I believe that I shall be so immensely rich that I shall dwell in a place that is paved with gold, the walls of which are builded with precious stones. But, my friends, you have all got an old man to die, and when he is dead, if you are followers of Jesus, you will come in for your inheritance. You know who that man is, he is very often spoken of in Scripture ; may the old man in you die daily, and may the new man be strengthened in you. When that old man of corruption, your old nature, shall totter into his grave, then you will come in for your property. Christians are like heirs, they have not much in their minority, and they are minors now : but when they come of age they shall have the whole of their estate. If I meet a minor, he says, " That is my property." " You cannot sell it sir ; you cannot lay hold of it." " No." says he, " I know I cannot ; but it is mine when I am one-and-twenty, I shall then have complete control ; but at the same time it is as really mine now as it ever will be. I have a legal right to it, and though my guardians take care of it for me it is mine, not theirs." And now, Christian, in heaven there is a crown of gold which is thine to-day ; it will be no more thine when thou hast it on thy head than it is now. I remember to have heard it reported that I once spoke in metaphor, and bade Christians look at all the crowns hanging in rows in heaven—very likely I did say it—

but if not, I will say it now. Up, Christian, see the crowns all ready, and mark thine own ; stand thou and wonder at it ; see with what pearls it is bedight, and how heavy it is with gold ! And that is for thy head, thy poor aching head ; thy poor tortured brain shall yet have that crown for its arraying ! And see that garment, it is stiff with gems, and white like snow ; and that is for thee ! When thy week-day garment shall be done with, this shall be the raiment of thy everlasting Sabbath. When thou hast worn out this poor body, there remaineth for thee, " A house not made with hands eternal in the heavens." Up to the summit, Christian, and survey thine inheritance ; and when thou hast surveyed it all, when thou hast seen thy present possessions, thy promised possessions, thine entailed possessions, then remember that all these were bought by the poverty of thy Saviour ! Look thou upon all thou hast, and say, " Christ bought them for me." Look thou on every promise, and see the blood stains on it ; yea, look, too, on the harps and crowns of heaven and read the bloody purchase ! Remember, thou couldst never have been anything but a damned sinner unless Christ had bought thee ! Remember, if He had remained in heaven, thou wouldst for ever have remained in hell ; unless He had shrouded and eclipsed His own honour thou wouldst never have had a ray of light to shine upon thee. Therefore bless His dear name, extol Him, trace every stream to the fountain ; and bless Him who is the source and the fountain of everything thou hast. Brethren, " Ye know the grace of our Lord Jesus Christ, that, though He was rich, yet for your sakes He became poor, that ye through His poverty might be rich."

IV. I have not done ; I have three things now to say, and I shall say them as briefly as possible.

The first *is a doctrine ;* the doctrine is this : If Christ in His poverty made us rich, what will He do now that He is glorified. If the Man of Sorrows saved my soul, will the man now exalted suffer it to perish ? If the dying Saviour availed for our salvation, should now the living, interceding Saviour, abundantly secure it ?

> " He lived, He lives and sits above,
> For ever interceding there ;
> What shall divide us from His love,
> Or what shall sink us in despair ? "

If when the nail was in Thine hand, O Jesus, Thou didst rout all hell, canst Thou be defeated now that Thou hast grasped the sceptre ? If, when the thorn crown was put about Thy brow Thou didst prostrate the dragon, canst Thou be overcome and conquered now that the acclamations of angels are ascending to Thee ? No, my brethren, we can trust the glorified Jesus, we can repose ourselves on His bosom ; if He was so strong in poverty, what must He be in riches ?

The next thing was a *question,* that question was a simple one. My hearer hast thou been made rich by Christ's poverty ? Thou sayest, " I am good enough without Christ ; I want no Saviour." Ah, thou art like her of old who said, " I am rich and increased in goods, and have need of nothing, whereas, said the Lord, ' Thou art naked and poor and miserable.' " O ye that live by good works, and think that ye shall go to heaven because you are as good as others ; all the merits you can ever earn yourselves are good for nothing. All that human nature ever made turns to a blot and a curse. If those are your riches, you are no saints. But can you say this morning, my hearers, " I am by nature without anything, and God has by the power of His Spirit taught me my nothingness."

My brother, my sister, hast thou taken Christ to be thine all in all ? Canst thou say this day, with an unfaltering tongue, " My Lord, my God, I have nothing ; but Thou art my all ? " Come, I beseech thee, do not shirk the question. Thou art careless, heedless ; answer it, then, in the negative. But when thou hast answered it, I beseech thee, beware of what thou hast said. Thou art sinful, thou feelest it. Come, I beseech thee, and lay hold on Jesus. Remember, Christ came to make those rich that have nothing of their own. My Saviour is a physician ; if you can heal yourself, He will have nothing to do with you. Remember, my Saviour came to clothe the naked. He will clothe you if you have not a rag of your own ; but unless you let Him do it from head to foot, He will have nothing to do with you. Christ says He will never have a partner ; He will do all or none. Come then, hast thou given up all to Christ ? Hast thou no reliance and trust save in the cross of Jesus ? Then thou hast answered the question well. Be happy, be joyous ; if death should surprise thee the next hour, thou art secure. Go on thy way, and rejoice in the hope of the glory of God.

And now I close with the third thing, which was *an exhortation.* Sinner, dost thou this morning feel thy poverty ? Then look to Christ's poverty. O ye that are to-day troubled on account of sin—and there are many such here—God has not let you alone ; He has been ploughing your heart with the sharp ploughshare of conviction ; you are this day saying, " What must I do to be saved ? " You would give all you have to have an interest in Jesus Christ. Your soul is this day sore broken and tormented. O sinner, if thou wouldst find salvation thou must find it in the veins of Jesus. Now, wipe that tear from thine eye a moment, and look here. Dost thou see Him high where the cross rears its terrible form ? There He is. Dost see Him ? Mark His head. See the thorn-crown, and the beaded drops still standing on His temples. Mark His eyes ; they are just closing in death. Canst see the lines of agony, so desperate in woe ? Dost see His hands ? See the streamlets of blood flowing down them. Hark, He is about to speak. " My God, My God,

Why hast Thou forsaken Me ! " Didst hear that, sinner ? Pause a moment longer, take another survey of His person ; how emaciated His body, and how sick His spirit ! Look at Him ; But Hark, He is about to speak again—" It is finished." What means He by that ? He means, that He has finished thy salvation. Look thou to Him, and find salvation there. Remember, to be saved, all that God wants of a penitent, is to look to Jesus. My life for this—if you will risk your all on Christ you shall be saved. I will be Christ's bondsman to-day, to be bound for ever if He breaks His promise. He has said, " Look unto Me, and be ye saved, all the ends of the earth." It is not your hands that will save you ; it must be your eyes. Look from those works whereby you hope to be saved. No longer strive to weave a garment that will not hide your sin, throw away that shuttle ; it is only filled with cobwebs. What garment can you weave with that ? Look thou to Him, and thou art saved. Never sinner looked and was lost. Dost mark that eye there ? One glance will save thee, one glimpse will set thee free. Dost thou say, " I am a guilty sinner " ? Thy guilt is the reason why I bid thee look. Dost thou say " I cannot look " ? Oh, may God help thee to look now. Remember, Christ will not reject thee ; thou mayest reject Him. Remember now, there is the cup of mercy put to thy lip by the hand of Jesus. I know if thou feelest thy need, Satan may tempt thee not to drink, but he will not prevail ; thou wilt put thy lip, feebly and faintly, perhaps, to it. But oh, do but sip it ; and the first draught shall give thee bliss ; and the deeper thou shalt drink, the more of heaven shalt thou know. Sinner, believe on Jesus Christ ; hear the whole gospel preached to thee. It is written in God's Word, " He that believeth and is baptized shall be saved." Hear me translate it—He that believeth and is *immersed* shall be saved. Believe thou, trust thyself on the Saviour, make a profession of thy faith in baptism, and then thou mayest rejoice in Jesus, that He hath saved thee. But remember not to make a profession till thou hast believed ; remember, baptism is nothing until thou hast faith. Remember, it is a farce and a falsehood until thou hast just believed ; and afterwards it is nothing but the profession of thy faith. Oh, believe that ; cast thyself upon Christ, and thou art saved for ever ! The Lord add His blessing, for the Saviour's sake Amen.

THE GIFT UNSPEAKABLE

" Thanks be unto God for His unspeakable gift."—2 Corinthians ix. 15.

PAUL had spoken of the liberality of the Corinthian believers, and he had endeavoured to stir them up to a prudent preparation for displaying it. " Now, therefore," said he, " perform the doing of it, that as there was a readiness to will, so there may be a performance also out of that which you have." He closes his exhortation by this remarkable sentence : " Thanks be unto God for His unspeakable gift " ; intending no doubt thereby to give expression to his own hearty thankfulness, and also to deliver a master stoke of argument for Christian liberality. Nothing can so excite God's people to give to Him as the remembrance of what

God has given to them. " Freely ye have received, freely give," is our Lord's own argument. Gospel graces are best stimulated by gospel motives. It is wrong to appeal to believers by reasons drawn from the law of works, for they are not under it ; children are to be ruled as children, not as oxen. Appeal should be made to renewed hearts by arguments distilled from the law of love under which they live : seeing God has loved them with an infinite love, this love has become the most mighty of forces within them :—" The love of Christ constraineth us." Nothing can move a man to complete consecration to God like the fact that He so loved us that He gave His only begotten Son, that whosoever believeth in Him should not perish, but have everlasting life.

The gospel is founded upon giving, and its spirit is giving. Buying and selling are unknown in spiritual things, unless we buy without money and without price. Payment is for the law ; under the gospel everything is a gift. God gives us Jesus, gives us eternal life, gives us grace and glory, gives us everything, in fact ; and then moved by love to Him we give ourselves back to Him and to His people. As it is the glory of the sun that He gives light and heat to our world, so is it God's glory that He gives mercy and peace to the sons of men ; and moreover, as the sun is the author of reflected heat, and is all the more valued because his beams can be reflected, so is God glorified by that part of His goodness which we are able to impart to others. God is glorified in the thanksgiving which is excited by the gifts of His people to the poor, as well as by their personal thanksgivings for His own gift. He gives to us, and we thank Him ; we give to others, and they thank God for the kindness which He has inspired in us. Thus a round of thanksgiving to God is created by the spirit of giving, which first of all displayed itself in the unspeakable gift of God. We are as cups filled at the spring, and from us the thirsty drink and praise the fountain.

Paul had been boasting of the liberality of the Corinthians, and he somewhat feared that by their delay he might be made ashamed ; he seemed almost alarmed lest he had said too much about their gifts. He could speak upon that subject and say all that should be said, but he felt that he could not describe the liberality of God. The gifts of the Corinthians were such as he could speak of, but when he thought of what God had given he could only cry, " Thanks be unto God for His unspeakable gift." You can readily put down in black and white, and count up, the largest contributions of the most self-sacrificing believers, but you cannot estimate the gift of God. You cannot estimate the value of God's own dear Son : you could certainly give no expression to any estimate you had formed if it were in the least degree worthy of the subject. The love which is seen in Jesus is inconceivable, infinite, unspeakable.

During this meditation I desire to aid you as the Holy Spirit shall aid me, for in my case the power to speak of this unspeakable gift must itself be a gift. I trust it shall be given me in the selfsame hour what I shall speak. We will first consider that *Christ Jesus is the gift unspeakable ;* but we are not going to be silent because of this, for our second head is, *Christ Jesus is a gift to be very much spoken of.* The gift unspeakable is to be for ever spoken of by way of gratitude—" Thanks be unto God for His unspeakable gift."

I. First, then, the eternal Son of God given of God unto men, CHRIST JESUS, IS THE GIFT UN-SPEAKABLE, and He is so in many ways.

To begin with : *no man can doctrinally lay down the whole meaning of the gift of Christ to men.* The church has produced thoughtful scholars whom it has called " divines," and described as " eminent theologians " : from these teachers we have no doubt received much help in the exposition of the Word ; and yet if we put them all together they have never been able to unfold to us the entire meaning of the gift of the Son of God to men. The devout and studious have themselves cried, " O the depths," but they have not pretended to fathom this abyss of mystery. Certain teachers have fallen far short of the mark, and have done great mischief by their low estimate of the unspeakable gift. What they have said may have been true, but their sin has been one of omission—omission where none should have been possible. They have said far too little about Christ, and have seemed to be afraid of extolling Him too highly. In the estimation of such persons the gift of the Saviour has been simply a display of God's good will to the race, and nothing more : Jesus was a divine philanthropist and nought beside, according to their gospel. This is to use other balances than those of the sanctuary, and to give short weight to the great Householder. It is true that God commended His love to man by the death of His Son, and none can say too much upon this point ; but there is far more in the gift of Christ than mere good will. We are glad that these men admit the divine benevolence, but we wish they could see more than that : for that view of our Lord which sees in Him only a display of benevolence to men does but dimly discern His character and value. Certainly He is " unspeakable " by those who only think of Him after this fashion.

Others have spoken of Christ as a wonderful declaration of God's opposition to moral evil. The death of Christ has been received by them as a vague expression of divine displeasure against sin, of course not dissociating it from His benevolence towards men. Herein is truth also, for how shall we ever see the purity of God more fully vindicated than in the exhibition of sin's result in the mortal agony and death throes of our divine Lord ? Yet, if this be all that any man has to say, he has failed to comprehend the gift of God, for the great Father has done far more for men by the gift of His Son than merely to intimate the kindness of His nature and the results of moral evil. We admit that in the death of His Son the Lord has declared His love to man, and His hatred of sin, but He has done infinitely more : the cross is not only a school but a hospital : the crucifixion not only reveals man's evil, but provides a remedy for it ; Christ is not merely a lesson, but a gift—a gift unspeakable.

Some of our brethren dwell very much, perhaps none too much, upon the general aspect of Christ's death towards all mankind. It is a grand fact that the human race is spared because Jesus died ; and that it is not only reprieved, but uplifted from degradation and put in a position to hear messages of mercy, which if believed will bring salvation. The Lord Jesus is described in Scripture as " the Saviour of all men, specially of them that believe " ; His mission is glad tidings both to Israel and to all people ; all Adam's seed are affected by His death. They do well who freely proclaim the common salvation ; they cannot dwell too much upon its freeness, though I would have them not overlook its fulness and sovereignty. We like well to hear of the effect of the incarnation and the atonement upon the entire human family as placing it under a mediator, but we would also hear of the special application of redemption and its actual results. No one can say too much of the great redemption, the matchless propitiation ; yea, though one should speak with the tongues of men, and of angels, concerning Jesus Christ in His relation to the human family, he need not fear that he would magnify the Lord too loftily. The sinner's Friend, the mighty Saviour, the gracious

Pardoner cannot be too much spoken of, for under that aspect He is unspeakable.

We delight in addition to this to speak of Christ's special relationship to His own people, and we lay a great emphasis upon the fact of His substitution in their behalf. We rejoice to speak of His bearing the sin of many, His being numbered with the transgressors, His being made sin for us though He knew no sin, that we might be made the righteousness of God in Him. Our heart expands, our eyes o'erflow, whenever we dilate upon His suretyship and consequent substitution. His wondrous condescending love in taking our place, His standing in the sinner's stead that we might stand in His place and be accepted in the Beloved—this carries our heart away, and we never weary of the theme. O divine doctrine! Full of consolation! Teeming with highest hopes! Fain would we preach for ever the sublime truth of the substitution of our Lord for us! Yet if this were our one theme we should still fail to express the unspeakable. We are apt to think that when we have laid down this doctrine clearly and distinctly, and have admitted all that others have well said, that we have believed and taught all that can be known concerning the gift of Jesus Christ to men : but, beloved, I am persuaded that it is not so. Beside the purpose of declaring benevolence and censuring sin, of uplifting the race and of effectually saving the chosen, there is more yet to be subserved by the incarnation and atonement. The purposes of God are manifold, and a wheel is ever within a wheel with Him. I will not at this time even try to speak doctrinally beyond what I have already attempted, for we must stop somewhere, and I will pause here, at the truth of His vicarious suffering : the gift is unspeakable when we have spoken our very best, and so let this suffice. I bid you peer over the brink upon which I would set you. Look down into this abyss of love. Be you sure of this, that this depth is unfathomable. It is idle to attempt a definition of infinity, and therefore vain to hope to declare how wide, how high, how deep, how broad, is the wondrous gift of God to the sons of men. Theology can speak on many themes, and she hath much to say on this, but her voice fails to speak the whole. From the pulpit when occupied by a gracious man the confession freely comes, that the heralds of the cross are not able to tell out all that is hidden in Christ Jesus.

The gift is unspeakable for another reason : no man can ever set forth the manner of this gift. The way and method of the giving are unknown, perhaps unknowable, and hence unspeakable. Just think awhile. Do you understand, and could you possibly explain, the manner of the Father's giving the Only-Begotten to us ? For Jesus Christ is not only the Father's Son, but He is God Himself, one with God : the gift of the Son is virtually God's giving Himself to men. There can be no separation between God the Son and God the Father, for, saith Christ, " I and My Father are one." " Believe Me," saith He, " that I am in the Father, and the Father in Me." Do you understand this ? Is it not unspeakable ? Do not, therefore, be drawing hard and fast lines, and speaking of Christ as suffering, and of the Father as scarcely participating in the sacrifice, for this may grow into grievous error. It has been laid down by divines that God is impassable, and not capable of any form of suffering. It may be so, but I fail to see scriptural authority for the statement. That God can do what He pleases I do believe, and there-

fore He can suffer too if so He wills. To me a God who has no feelings is further off from me a great deal than my Father who is in heaven, who can be grieved by my sin, and can feel for my sorrow. It may be true that Scripture only speaks after the manner of men, but then it is as a man that I understand it ; and it does seem to me to reveal not only a living God, but a feeling God. Is God glorified by being petrified ? Read Paul's words to the Ephesian elders when he speaks of " the church of God, which He hath purchased with His own blood " (Acts xx. 28). The blood of God—is not that a mistake ? Certainly not, since inspiration thus speaks. Sometimes expressions which are mistakes in logic may be more accurate descriptions than the best arranged sentences. The expression which looks to be a contradiction may better express the truth than that which is verbally accurate. Scripture is infallible, and yet it uses none of the red tape of systematic theology. We swim in mysteries when we speak of the Father and the Son. How, then, God could give the Son to die, He being one with Himself—shall any man explain it ? Or, if he could explain the mystery, can he tell us what it cost the Father to give His Son ? Can a mother tell us how it pains her heart to part with her child ? Can any father tell us the anguish of losing his only begotten ? What must it be to give up your well-beloved son to be despised and spit upon, maltreated and murdered! No ; you do not know what it is, and therefore you cannot tell what it is! You that have been bereaved of your dearest, you know the pang which tears the heart, but you cannot express your loss to others : your grief is inexpressible. Who shall tell what the Father felt when He did, as it were, cast the glory of the Well-beloved to the dogs, by sending Him among the wicked husbandmen, who said, " This is the heir, let us kill Him " ? Who shall tell what the Eternal felt when the brightness of His glory, the express image of His person, was bound like a felon, and accused like a criminal, mocked as an impostor, and scourged as a transgressor, rejected as vile, and slain as worthy of death ? To see His Well-beloved hung up like a thief, and made to bear infinite agony—what thought the Father of this ? True, " it pleased Jehovah to bruise Him : He hath put Him to grief," but not without great self-denial on the part of the great Father. All the agony of Abraham when he unsheathed the knife to slay his son was but a faint type of what it cost the Father when He gave the Only-Begotten that He might die for us.

A further sense of the unspeakableness of this gift will come over you if you attempt to measure our Lord's sufferings when He was made sin for us. None can declare the greatness of His sacrifice. Think of the glory of Christ throughout all ages at the right hand of God, and remember that all this was laid aside. What a descent from heaven's majesty to Bethlehem's manger ; from the throne of Jehovah to the breast of Mary! Think of the perfect nature of Christ's humanity, and its consequent rest in God, and yet He stooped out of His spirit's peace to endure the contradiction of sinners against Himself. Think of His infinite perfections and boundless deservings, and of the shameful contempt that was poured upon Him. The cruel asp of ingratitude stung Him, and the serpent of malice bit Him : yet all the while was He Lord of all. Every step of His way of love is full of wonders. His becoming one with us according to the flesh is a great marvel. Think, if you can, of what it must mean that "the Word was made flesh and dwelt among us." Incarnation is but the first step, but of that first descent of love who shall declare the mystery? But this was merely the beginning : He became a man that He might go further, and become man's substitute. Try, if you can, to conceive of incarnate God as having sin imputed to Him, transgression laid upon Him. Why, the very idea must have been horror to His perfect spirit. Conceive of justice with its iron rod bruising and pounding the innocent Son of God with griefs vicarious, borne for us !

> "Much we talk of Jesu's love.
> But how little's understood !
> Of His sufferings, so intense,
> Angels have no perfect sense."

"Thine unknown sufferings," says the Greek Liturgy, and unknown they must for ever be. O Jesus, what a price it was that Thou didst pay ! What griefs they were to which Thou didst bow Thyself till Thou wast covered with a bloody sweat ! O Lord Jesus, the brightest spirit before Thy throne who has dwelt with Thee ever since Thine ascension cannot tell us what Thou didst endure. Thy groans are a gift unspeakable. How it was that He died who is the resurrection and the life ? and how it was He bore sin, even He who is none other than eternal perfection ? None of us can speak here, for He is the gift unspeakable.

I ask you to follow me in another line of thought, while I still talk upon the unspeakable. *None can describe the boons which have come to us through the gift of Christ.* Think of what we have been delivered from : think awhile of what you were by nature, and what you would have continued to have been had not grace interposed, and what you would have become if Jesus had not been given to save the lost. Ah, my brothers and sisters, we are fallen already, but the full results of the fall are not seen on earth. The ripe result of sin is gathered in the dark region where castaways dwell for ever, finally banished from hope ; where ring of Sabbath bell is never heard, for they rest not day nor night ; where voice of mercy can never enter, for this doleful knell tolls through that dreary land with awful tone, " He that is unjust, let him be unjust still : and he which is filthy, let him be filthy still." And you and I might have been there now, and shall be there yet, if Jesus Christ be not ours. Yea, and the brightest saints in heaven, upon whom the eternal light has risen never to set, would have been now in the outer darkness, weeping and wailing and gnashing their teeth, if it had not been for this unspeakable gift. The distance between the depth unfathomable of deserved woe and the height unutterable of infinite grace and glory an angel's wing cannot measure ; hence it will always be impossible to tell the height and depth of this unspeakable gift.

But now think for awhile what are the boons which we enjoy at this hour. There is, first of all, the forgiveness of sins according to the riches of His grace. We are washed, washed in the blood, clothed in the righteousness of the Son of God, adopted into the family of the Eternal, and " if children, then heirs ; heirs of God, and joint heirs with Jesus Christ." There comes to us by way of adoption all the provision, nurture, education, and paternal love which the heavenly Father gives to all the children of His family. Brethren, I have not time to mention one by one all the covenant blessings. All things are in the covenant, whether things present, or things to come, or life, or death, all things are yours, and ye are Christ's and Christ is God's ; and all these things come to us through Christ. God spared not His own Son, and in giving Him to us He hath also freely given us all things. Now, who is he that can speak of such a theme as this, for if he do but dwell upon the blessings which flow to us from Jesus Christ he must be lost in wonder ? Other gifts may amaze us, but this utterly overwhelms us. If the streams be fathomless, who shall find a plummet wherewith to measure the fountain ? I preached last Sabbath night to a great congregation that had come for many miles, and being faint and thirsty, they emptied many buckets of water which were set for them : their thirst consumed a great quantity, yet an observer might soon have known how much they drank ; but who shall tell what the earth drinks in during a single thunder-shower ? Who shall measure the floods which roll down the great rivers ? Who shall compute the volume of the sea ? Yet all these are finite, and may be reckoned up in order : our Lord Jesus Christ is infinite. Of man's gifts to man we may readily make estimate, but when you come to the gift of Christ arithmetic is baffled, and even imagination is outstripped. Other themes we may hope to compass by study and careful speech, but before this we are dumb with astonishment. Boundless grace, unutterable mercy, divine love—these are heavenly things, and tongues of clay can never fully declare them.

Furthermore, the gift of God must always be unspeakable because *when it is best realized the effect it produces upon the emotions is so great that speech fails.* I would not give much for the man who can at all times fluently talk about the love of God in Christ Jesus. When he feels most his obligations his heart will check his lips ! Utterance belongs not to the deepest emotion. Only believe thou in thy heart that God has given Christ to thee, and all that comes with Him, and thou wilt rise from thy bended knees weeping for joy. A sense of sin forgiven through the atoning sacrifice will master thee ! When Jesus bares His heart before thee, canst thou speak then ? I will defy thee to play the orator when love holds thee beneath its spell. Thou wilt have a longing to tell the story, but an incapacity to fulfil thy desire. Some feelings are too big for expression. The griefs that prattle are but small : great griefs are silent. Mercies which make us talk are common, and no longer wondered at ; but those which come with an unveiled divinity about them are like Moses, too bright to look upon. A sense of covenant love binds a man to his place and makes him sit down like David before the Lord, and bow his head and cry, " Whence is this to me ? " Is this according to the manner of man, O Lord God ? " Yes, the gift must be unspeakable, because the more it is appreciated the more are we silenced : the deeper our sense of its value the less is our power to impart it to others. Power to speak of the love of Christ is not always to be taken as an evidence of true religion, nor is its absence a matter for alarm. I remember one dear lover of Christ who wished to join a certain church, but her testimony of experience was very slender ; indeed, she said too little to satisfy the brethren who came to speak with her, and they told her so ;

when, bursting through all bonds she cried out, " I cannot speak for Him, but I could die for Him." Many are in a like plight, and in a measure all true souls lie under the like difficulty. We could more easily die for Christ than hope to tell out fully our sense of His dear love. He is a gift unspeakable. Heaven cannot match Him ; how can earth describe Him ?

When this gift is best expressed, even when the Spirit of God helps men to speak upon it, they yet feel it to be unspeakable. When men sing like poets, or write like apostles, they own that the wing of their thought cannot soar to the full height of this grand mystery : they have not even expressed what they have felt, and they have not felt what they inwardly know they ought to have felt in connection with so divine a theme.

He who before his fellow men has given the most vivid description of the love of God in Christ Jesus is the very man who best knows that it is inexpressible. You shall not be able to soar amongst the mysteries and bask in the eternal light of Jehovah's face, and then come back from thence and say, " I can declare it all to you." No, Paul said that " he heard things which it were not lawful for a man to utter." Joys revealed in the innermost place of holy fellowship are not to be commonly published : we should mar them in the attempt at their utterance. You can often feel what you cannot possibly describe to those who most eagerly listen to you. Often my preaching of the love of Christ is to my own mind, when I have done, as sad a failure as if I had gilded gold or enamelled the lily. I was one day in the ruins of Nero's palace, and he who guided us there had a series of rods fitted in telescopic manner into one another. On the top of these was a candle, and he held it high up to let us read the inscriptions on the arch of the vault overhead. We can do that with mortal things, and so make men see them, but when we have done our best to describe the love of Christ we have felt as though we had held aloft those silly rods with a farthing candle upon them to show the sun at noon. God is very gracious to let His dear Son be seen at all through such poor narrow windows as we are. Poor, poor work is our best preaching concerning the adorable Lord Jesus. But this is one thing we can say with respect to Him from our very hearts, that He has filled us to the full and satisfied us. They said of Alexander that he had an ambition so vast that if his body had been as large as his soul he would have stood with one foot on the sea and the other on the shore, and would have grasped the east with his right hand and the west with his left. If our souls were thus boundless in desire Christ's love could fill them. Nothing else contents a man ; but with Jesus we are satisfied. Though a man were, like Solomon, to get to himself all the wisdom and the riches of the world, " Vanity of vanities " would be his verdict ; but he who wins Christ, and has Christ's love shed abroad in his heart, has no vacant corner in his heart, no vacuum within his soul : Christ has filled him to running over. We can say, " filled with all the fulness of God," but as to containing the fulness of God, he that hath most of it knows how impossible a thing it is. You may frame the fairest picture that ever man painted, but you cannot frame the Alps ; though his daring pencil should cover many a yard, you may hang up the master's canvas upon your walls, but when you stand upon the mountain's brow, and look o'er hill and vale, and sea and shore, you dream not of frames and picture-

galleries, but leave the panorama in its own setting, for it cannot be encompassed by human invention. You may take the population of a city, a kingdom, or if needs be of the world, and make a census thereof, and set down the millions ; but who shall take a census of the birds of heaven, the insects which swarm the air, the fish which teem the sea, the stars which stud the sky, and the sands which bound the main ? All these things are countable by some sort of reckoning, but the love of Christ is infinite. " Thanks be unto God for His unspeakable gift."

Thus have we dealt with the unspeakable, and we now feel even more truly than when we began that language fails us.

II. Let me have all your hearts for a few minutes while I now dwell on the other truth, that CHRIST IS A GIFT OF GOD TO BE VERY MUCH SPOKEN OF. To be spoken of, first, *by thanks to God.* " Thanks be unto God for His unspeakable gift." Brethren, we do not thank God as we ought for anything : we are not half as thankful as we ought to be. Luther was wont to tell a story of two cardinals who were riding to the council of Constance. One of them stopped because he saw a shepherd sitting down in the meadow weeping. Dismounting, he tried to comfort him, and asked him why he wept. The poor man was slow to answer, but being pressed he said, " Looking upon this toad I wept because I have never thanked God as I ought for making me a man possessed of reason, and of excellent form, and not a loathsome toad." The cardinal fainted as he saw the piety of the peasant, and as he went away he exclaimed, " O St. Augustine ! how truly didst thou say the unlearned rise and take heaven by force, and we with all our learning rise not above flesh and blood." Might not some of us faint under a like sense of ingratitude ? Did you ever bless God for your creation, your reason, your continued life ? I have known what it is to thank God with all my heart for being able to move my limbs and turn in bed. Perhaps you have always enjoyed good health : do you thank Him for that ? To be out of the hospital, to be out of the lunatic asylum, to be out of prison, to be out of hell,—do we ever glorify God for these things ? As for the unspeakable gift of Christ, who among us has ever worthily blessed the Lord on this account ? Brethren, if we have Jesus to be our salvation, when ought we to thank God for Him ? Why, every morning when we wake. How long should we continue to praise God on this account ? Till we go to sleep again. From the rising of the sun to the going down of the same His name is to be extolled. Let us praise God till sleep steeps our senses in a sweet forgetfulness. It is even pleasant to go on singing unto the Lord in visions of our bed, as if the chords of grateful emotion vibrated after the hand of thought had ceased to play on them. It is good when even this wayward fancy of our dreams wanders towards the Well-beloved, never rambling outside of holy ground. Let even the fairies of our night-dream sing hymns to Jesus, and the cowslip bells of dream-land harbour imaginings of the fair plant of renown. Oh, to get into such a state that we shall be still praising Him ; praising, and praising, and praising, and never ceasing. When we become low in spirit, it will be a sad reflection if we have to own that in fairer weather we forgot our Beloved. Let us give double praise while we can. While we are in good spirits and happy in the Lord let us pour forth our hymns. Tamerlane said to the mighty Bajazet, when he had overcome him in battle and taken him for a prisoner, " Didst thou ever give God thanks for making thee so great an emperor ? " Bajazet confessed that he had never thought of that. " Then," said Tamerlane, " it is no wonder that so ungrateful a man should be made a spectacle of misery." Conscience will taunt us when we are sorrowful by saying, " You did not praise God when you were in health ; and now you are ill and hoarse, and cannot lift up your voice ; you did not praise Him for His unspeakable gift when you knew you had it ; and now you are full of doubts about it, and Satan has you upon the hip, you well deserve all the sorrow that your mind shall feel." Therefore, brothers and sisters, let us praise the Lord ; let us vow unto ourselves to-day that, His grace helping us, we will praise Him, praise Him, praise Him, and praise Him again, and again, and again, and again, as long as we have any being, for His unspeakable gift. We shall never get to the end of this work ; the unspeakable gift is for ever telling, and telling, yet never shall it all be told. Help us, all that know His salvation ! Help us, angels ! Help us, all ye coming ages ! Help us, all ye stars of light ! but still the thing shall be unspeakable even to the end.

Next, *let us show our gratitude to God in deeds of praise.* " Thanks be unto God for His unspeakable gift." If we cannot speak it, let us try if we cannot *do* something that will show forth the praise of God. Actions speak more loudly than words. If our words have failed, let us try actions. And the first thing to do is to give yourself away to your Lord. Come, beloved, if God has given you Jesus Christ, give Him yourself. Ye are not your own, ye are bought with a price, wherefore present your bodies as living sacrifices. Don't talk about it, but really do it : live for Him who died for you. Then, in consequence of having already given yourself, give of your substance to God, and give freely. Give not the lame and the blind, but look ye out the best of the flock. Let this be a great joy to you ; not the payment of a tax, but the tribute of delighted love. Give to God cheerfully, for He loveth a cheerful giver. Buy Him the sweet cane with money, and fill Him with the fat of your sacrifices. Nothing can be too good or great for our ever blessed Lord. Our Loving Master will accept at our hands the alabaster box when we break it joyfully for His dear sake. Let deeds of holy consecration mark the whole of our lives, for with such sacrifices God is well pleased, when they are not brought as a price to purchase merit, but as a love-token and tribute to His grace. Think of this exhortation, and carry it out abundantly : it shall turn to your temporal and eternal enrichment.

I am sure, however, that deeds of patience are among the thanks which best speak out our gratitude to God. Did it ever strike you that patience is a noble sort of psalmody ? Perhaps you will see this truth if I tell you an anecdote. In the old church stories we read of one called Didymus, a famous preacher, who brought many souls to Christ ; but he was blind, and Didymus grieved greatly over the loss of his sight. Those who heard him perceived that his blindness gave a mournful tinge to his discourses. A certain godly man named Alexander went to him and spoke to him in private after this fashion : " Didymus," said he, " does not thy blindness cause thee great sorrow ? " " Brother Alexander," said he, " it is my constant grief that I have lost the light. I can scarcely endure my existence, because I am always in the dark." Then Alexander said to him,

" Thou art doing a work which an angel might envy thee, and thou hast the honour of an apostle in speaking for Jesus Christ, and wilt thou fret because thou hast lost that which rats and mice and brute beasts have in common with men ? " This was not a very tender thing to say, but it strengthened Didymus patiently to endure his trial and to bless God for His unspeakable gift. What is there, after all, that we have not, if we have Christ ? If you have lost everything but Christ, yet if you have Christ left you what have you lost ? Why fret for pins when God gives pearls ? Why grieve over the loss of a few pence when God has heaped upon us talents of gold ? Submit in gracious joy to the divine will, and let your patience say, " I will thank God, I will thank God still for His unspeakable gift."

Now, dear friends, there is one way in which I want you to thank God and show your gratitude for Christ, and that is *by always holding a thankful creed.* Believe nothing which would rob God of thanks, or Christ of glory. I set great store by a sound creed in these evil days when the gospel is but little valued by many. Hold a creed of which the top and bottom is this, " Grace, grace, grace ; salvation all of grace." Whenever you hear a preacher, no matter who he may be, making out that salvation is not completely of the grace of God, just say in your hearts, " Thanks be unto God for His unspeakable gift." Do not go an inch away from that standpoint. Salvation is altogether a gift : it is not of works, it is not of merit ; it is of grace, and grace alone. Turn away from the man who stutters when he says " grace " ; he will never feed your soul.

Hold a theology which magnifies Christ, a divinity which teaches that Christ is God's unspeakable gift. When a man gets cutting down sin, paring down depravity, and making little of future punishment, let him no longer preach to you. Some modern divines whittle away the gospel to the small end of nothing. They make our divine Lord to be a sort of blessed nobody ; they bring down salvation to mere salvability, make certainties into probabilities, and treat verities as mere opinions. When you see a preacher making the gospel small by degrees and miserably less, till there is not enough of it left to make soup for a sick grasshopper, get you gone. Such diminution and adulteration will not do for me : my heart cries, " Thanks be to God for His unspeakable gift." These gentlemen, you know, are highly cultivated and can tell us all about it ; they have a theology which is suited to their educated reason : to them grace can be weighed in scales and atonement in balances ; unless indeed both be as the drop of a bucket, not worthy of being mentioned at all. Every grand truth with them is dwarfed and dwindled down into utter insignificance. The thought of the nineteenth century makes men the heirs of apes, while it declares their souls to be mortal, and their sins to be trifles. Our Bibles are made to be mere human records, and our hopes are treated as childish dreams. These pigmy thinkers shorten all things to their pigmy scale. As for me, I believe in the colossal : a need deep as hell and grace as high as heaven. I believe in a pit that is bottomless, and in mercy above the heavens. I believe in an infinite God and an infinite atonement, infinite love and infinite mercy, an everlasting covenant ordered in all things and sure, of which the substance and the seal is an infinite Christ. Christ is all ; Christ is unspeakable, the unspeakable gift of God. Hold to that, or you will not thank God as you should.

Nor rest in a thoroughly sound creed, but *try to bring others to accept God's unspeakable gift.* You know how the birds stir up each other to sing. One bird in a cage will excite its fellow, who looks at him and seems to say, " You shall not outstrip me : I will sing with you." Then another joins the strain, saying, " I will sing with you," till all the little minstrels quiver with an ecstasy of song, and form a choir of emulating songsters. Hark how the early morning of the spring is rendered musical by the full orchestra of birds ! One songster begins the tune, and the rest hasten to swell the music ! Let us be like these blessed birds. Let us try to lead our families to praise the Lord. Bless the Lord till you set the fashion, and others bless Him with you. Seek out those who do not know the Lord Jesus Christ, and tell them " the old, old story of Jesus and His love." Thus, if you cannot sing more yourself, nor praise God more yourself, you will have increased His praise by bringing in others to sing with you. See you to this, and let this be henceforth the motto of your lives. Write it over your doors ; emblazon it on the walls of your chambers ; let it hang over your bed-head by night, " THANKS BE UNTO GOD FOR HIS UNSPEAKABLE GIFT." O Holy Spirit, write this line of gratitude upon the tablets of our hearts. Amen.

FORTS DEMOLISHED AND PRISONERS TAKEN

" Casting down imaginations, and every high thing that exalteth itself against the knowledge of God, and bringing into captivity every thought to the obedience of Christ."—2 Corinthians x. 5.

THIS chapter presents the remarkable spectacle of a minister of the gospel of peace going forth to war. At first sight we wonder how the meek and gentle Paul should speak about warring and talk of pulling down strongholds, and " having a readiness to revenge all disobedience." The surprise is all the greater because he is going to war in the church : a shepherd entering the fold with a sword. One would not so much marvel that he carried his weapons against the outside world, but on this occasion it is within the church at Corinth that he is about to commence a campaign. Yet observe how earnestly he deprecates the conflict, how he beseeches them by the meekness and gentleness of Christ to spare him a task which was so unpleasant to his feelings as to deal sternly with those whom he would far rather have commended. But the wonder ceases when we find that the shepherd fights only with grievous wolves, and even in that conflict declares, " though we walk in the flesh, we do not war after the flesh." Note, moreover, that his weapons are of a peculiar kind,—" The weapons of our warfare are not carnal." He is not about to assault his antagonists in the church with bitter words of railing such as they used against himself ; he is not about to meet the philosophers with such philosophies and sophisms as those with which they assailed the gospel ; neither is he coming forth with any kind of temporal weapon to inflict aught of injury upon the leaders in error ; his weapons are of a very different sort. They are not carnal, but spiritual. Trials under a Public Worship Act he knew nothing of, an appeal to Cæsar upon church matters never crossed his mind. For the church of God ever to avail itself of force or compulsion in order to propagate its doctrines would be clean contrary to the spirit of Christianity : for the Christian bishop to become a soldier, or employ the secular arm, would seem to be the very climax of contradiction. A warrior ambassador is a dream of folly. I remember a story which illustrates that absurdity. When a certain bishop-prince in the olden times went forth himself personally to battle, and was taken prisoner, the Pope sent word to the king who had captured him that he was to set him at liberty at once, for he was a son of the church. The king, with considerable wit, sent back to the Pope the coat of armour which the bishop had worn on the field with this message, " This have we found : know now whether it be thy son's coat or no." And so we might send back, I think, to the nominal church the black and bloodstained gown of the Inquisition, the garb of the headsman and the hangman, the smoke-browned raiment of those who lighted the Smithfield fires, and even the parchments on which are written the Test and Corporation Acts, and the Act of Uniformity, and say, " Know now whether these be thy sons' coats or no." Is the raiment of a man of war the vestment of a servant of the Lord ? Are robes of legal authority the adornments of heralds of peace ? Jesus Christ did not thus array His apostles when He sent them forth to the war, and not with such weapons did Paul arm himself when he entered the conflict.

" The weapons of our warfare are not carnal " ; yet the spiritual weapons which can be wielded by the Christian minister, and indeed by every Christian man, are not to be despised, for while not fleshly, they are mighty through God. God is in them ; God is with those who use them. The sword of the Spirit, which is the word of God, the arrows of truth which pierce the consciences of men, the weapon of all prayer, the influence of the Holy Ghost—that divine power—such weapons as these are by God's power made mighty to the overthrow of spiritual principalities and powers. Truth and holiness are the appointed engines for the pulling down of the castles of evil. Blessed is he who in every conflict for God takes heed to use none other weapons than those which the Lord hath hung up in the tower of David, builded for an armoury, wherein do hang a thousand bucklers, all shields of mighty men. Those only can fight the Lord's battles successfully who come to Him to be armed for the fight, and reject all fleshly force. The spiritual shall be victorious, but others must fail.

The passage, if I were to confine it to its immediate connection, would represent Paul as dealing with those lofty ones who had usurped authority in the church at Corinth, who denied his apostleship, and set themselves up as superior to him, while they themselves preached error, and led the people astray. Paul declared that when he came among them armed with the power with which God had clothed him, he should overthrow every proud opposition, and convince them all of the truth to their conversion or to their confusion. But I shall speak rather of a warfare carried on in individuals, a warfare in our own souls, for what is true of the triumphs of the gospel in the mass is true because it gains the like conquest over individuals. While I am speaking of the war of the gospel against sin within the heart of man, may you who have never felt its power be praying that it may conquer even you, and may those who have experienced its sacred omnipotence be pleading to be yet more completely subjugated to its sway.

> " Great King of Grace, our hearts subdue,
>   May we be led in triumph too,
>   As willing captives to our Lord,
>   To sing the victories of His word."

observation. The first is *fortresses demolished*— " casting down imaginations, and every high thing that exalteth itself against the knowledge of God " ; then, secondly, *prisoners seized*—" bringing into captivity every thought " ; and thirdly, *prisoners led away captive*—for such is the force of the Greek " bringing into captivity every thought to the obedience of Christ,"—as if the captured ones were taken away and put under new service to the anointed Prince.

I. First, let us look at FORTRESSES DEMOLISHED. When the gospel endeavours to penetrate the human heart it meets with earthworks of prejudice, which men have cast up to screen their minds from the force of the truth. Many things are opposed to the knowledge of God. The object sought for is that men may be brought to know God, to know who He is and what He is, to know their relation to Him as fallen men, to know His plan of restoration, to know Him in Christ Jesus, and so to know as to love Him, to obey Him, and to become like Him. This is the great object for which the gospel is sent into the world, that the knowledge of the glory of God may cover the earth as the waters cover the sea. But men desire not the knowledge of God's ways, and shut up their hearts against the entrance of divine light by many reasonings and imaginings.

Some are garrisoned against the knowledge of God by the feeling that *they do not want to know God*. The masses of our fellow-countrymen are not so much opposed to the gospel as indifferent to it. They pass by our places of worship and they see their neighbours entering, and they sometimes say, " Who preaches there ? " ; but " What is preached there ? " is a question seldom asked. Religious enquiry seems to be very dull at the present time. Time was when the announcement of evangelical doctrine excited universal attention, though at the same time almost universal opposition : that opposition was better than a state of stagnation like the present. Men nowadays pass by the cross as if a dying Saviour were nothing to them. Graceless zealots, as they call them, may fight about their creeds ; as for them, they have something more practical to think of. " What shall we eat ? what shall we drink ? and wherewithal shall we be clothed ? " are far more important questions to them, than " What must we do to be saved ? " This entrenchment has to be carried, and the gospel does carry it by the power of the Holy Ghost, for it flashes conviction on the soul, creates alarm, arouses apprehension, and so storms the stronghold of indifference and utterly demolishes it. When the Holy Ghost convinces a man of sin, of righteousness

and of judgment to come, he is indifferent no longer. We call him an " enquirer," and the name is correct, for he does enquire about the weightiest matters, which concern eternity, and God, and heaven, and hell, and his own immortal destiny. He wants to know at first more than he is at that time capable of learning : he questions about high mysteries which are for men in Christ rather than for babes ; but most of all he wants to know " How can I be at peace with God ? " If the Holy Spirit does but apply to a man's heart such a truth as this,—that he is condemned already because he hath not believed in Christ, then indifference is as a bowing wall, and as a tottering fence. Even if a man had no other sin whatsoever, it is quite sufficient to condemn him for ever, that he neglects his God and turns away from his Saviour ; for unbelief is an act of high treason against the divine majesty, plucking at the crown jewel of Jehovah's truthfulness. Hence " the wicked shall be turned into hell *with all the nations that forget God*." Lay this Krupp gun in proper position, and let it be fired by the Eternal Spirit against the indifference of the human heart and it soon casts down the wall of carelessness. Then the sinner discovers that if he does not know his God it were better for him that he had never been born. He finds out that if he does not know his Saviour he is doomed to endless woe, and this makes him cry out in anguish of heart : " Men and brethren, what shall we do ? "

Amongst the other " imaginations " with which man fortifies himself is the idea of many that *they know already*. Trained from their childhood in false doctrine, they hold fast to it, and defy the gospel to reach them. They are Christians by birth, they say, forgetting the inspired declaration,—" that which is born of the flesh is flesh ; and that which is born of the Spirit is spirit." Others make up their minds as to what the knowledge of God ought to be, and of course they quarrel with God's view of things. They fashion a god and a gospel after their own fond notions, and then they dream that they had reached the sum of wisdom. They refuse to go to school to Christ, and when He says, " Except ye be converted and become as little children, ye shall in no wise enter into the kingdom of God," they turn from Him with disdain. They know quite enough, and are resolved to learn no more. A large proportion of our fellow men are in this condition, and are perfectly content and satisfied to remain as they are. Graduates in the university of self-importance, full of ignorance and equally full of pride, they scarcely deign to give Christ a hearing, and hardly go as far as the Athenians who said, " What will this babbler say ? " Nothing shuts the heart more completely against the knowledge of God than the conceit that we know already and need no teaching from above. It is written of the true church, " All thy children shall be taught of the Lord," but many are not such children, for they are wise in their own eyes and refuse instruction. But, O sirs, how the Holy Spirit casts down this imagination when He makes men feel that they are blind by nature, and lets them know that the natural man understandeth not the things which be of God, for they are spiritual and must be spiritually discerned. A little heavenly light suffices to reveal to men their darkness, for if they will but think they must admit that if God deigns to teach us in the Scriptures it must be because apart from them we are ignorant. There is no need of revelation, and the Bible is worthless ; there is no need of an incarnate deity, and Calvary is a superfluity, if men already know God apart from the Lord Jesus, and the word by which He is pleased to reveal Himself. Let but the Holy Spirit bring this home to a man's heart and he begins to cry out against his own pride, he bemoans his own blindness, and he is quite willing to become a fool that he may be wise, a child that he may sit at Jesus' feet.

Another entrenchment, behind which many are hiding securely, is the idea that *if they do not know God they can find Him out without His help.* This is a very general notion nowadays. Scientific thought is supposed to be the way for finding out God Himself, and the old Scripture is out of date which says, "Incline your ear, and come unto Me : hear, and your soul shall live." Plain truth is in this wonderful century of small account ; men crave to be mystified by their own cogitations. Many glory in being too intellectual to receive anything as absolute certainty : they are not at all inclined to submit to the authority of a positive revelation. God's word is not accepted by them as final, but they judge it. and believe what they like of it. This is madness. I speak to those who believe in the Scriptures, and I say if, indeed, there be a revelation, it becomes us to be silent before it, and accept it without dispute. The Lord knows what He is better than we can ever know, and if He has been pleased to speak in His Word plainly and solemnly, it is ours to believe what He says, because He says it. It may be all very well to prove that such and such a revelation of God is consistent with reason, consistent with analogy, consistent with a thousand things ; but the spirit which needs such argument is a spirit of rebellion against God. If there be a revelation, every part of it is of authority, and must be believed. Human thought is not the arbiter of truth, but the infallible Word is the end of all strife. It is not ours to say what the truth must be, or what we think it should be, or what we would like it to be, but reverently to sit down with open ear and willing heart to receive what God has spoken. If an astronomer were to forbear to examine the stars, and teach an astronomy invented in his own brain, he would be an idiot : and those who treat theology in like fashion are not much better. "Surely," saith one, "we ought to modify our beliefs by public opinion, and the current of thought." I say "*no*" a thousand times. The incorruptible word of God liveth and abideth for ever, and is incapable of modification. To modify is to adulterate and nullify it, and render it of none effect, so that it becomes another gospel, and, indeed, no gospel. The thought of tampering with revealed truth is vicious, and ought not to be tolerated by any Christian for a second. The gospel of Jesus Christ is not a thing which is to be moulded according to the fashion of the period : it is "Jesus Christ the same yesterday, to-day, and for ever." Whether the Greek philosophy rules or is exploded, whether some more modern theory blazes up or smoulders down, is small concern of ours, for we are set to preach the one unvarying gospel of Jesus Christ, with the Holy Ghost sent down from heaven. No man was ever led to a saving faith by our meeting him half way, and consenting to his unbelief. No real faith was ever wrought in man by his own thoughts and imaginations ; he must receive the gospel as a revelation from God, or he cannot receive it at all. Faith is a supernatural work wherever it is found,

and if we think that we can beget faith in ourselves or others by the use of the fleshly weapons of philosophy we shall certainly be foiled. The Scriptures pressed home by the Holy Ghost are God's power unto salvation, and not men's cogitations and imaginations. There is the revealed gospel,—reject it at your peril ; there is Jehovah's revelation of Himself to men,—receive it or be lost ; this is the ground to go upon if we would speak as the oracles of God. God grant that proud thinkers may come upon this ground and become believers.

Here we are boldly met by some who say, "We do not want this doctrine which you call the knowledge of God : *we know of something better already.* We tell you that your gospel, about which you make such a fuss, is outworn and done with." Treat it so, sirs, and perish, if you will, but as for us, we will mourn day and night over your unbelief. You will surely destroy your souls in rejecting the divine testimony, but in so doing you will prove that word to be true, which saith that the gospel is a savour of death unto death as well as of life unto life. You know better, you say ; but how can this be ? Do you know God better than God knows Himself ? Do you know more about His way of reconciling men to Himself than His own messenger, the Lord Jesus Christ, knows ? Do you profess to know better than the Eternal Spirit who inspired the Scriptures ? It is to those Scriptures that we crave your reverent attention, and not to any assertions of ours ; we pray you do not reject them. I heard one say the other day that he never felt any desire to pray, and never had prayed in all his life ; and, though I looked at him with sorrow, I could only say to him, "Dead men never cry : you are dead in sin, and so have not the breath divine. You have not been born again, you have not a new nature or a right spirit : if you had you could not help praying and believing." To me his statements were confirmations of Bible teaching concerning the real state of all unregenerate men. The gospel, as we have said before, wherever it creates faith begets it by its own power, and by the power of the Eternal Spirit convincing men of the truth, and enlightening those whom the Lord our God hath chosen. Now, where the gospel comes, it undermines and overturns everything which opposes the truth of God, and makes a man feel that of himself he knows nothing, until the Lord reveals it to him. Find a sinner made conscious of sin and you have found a man who does not know better than his God : find a man with an awakened conscience, and you have found a man who does not know better than his God : find one who believes in Christ, and sits at Jesus' feet, and the more he learns the more surely have you found in him a man who does not know better than his God, but who still cries out to be taught more, that he may possess to the full the knowledge of the glory of God in the face of Jesus Christ.

There is yet another entrenchment behind which some hide themselves from the knowledge of God, and that is "*I never can know. I do not know, and I never can know. I despair of ever being able to know the Lord.*" In this despair the rebel entrenches himself as in a very Malakoff, and becomes desperate in his resistance to the gospel. Yet even this rampart is cast down by mighty grace. When the Holy Ghost comes with the word of reconciliation the sinner catches at the idea of an atonement by a substitute. He is charmed by the truth—"I am lost in myself, but saved in Christ. I am in myself judged and condemned for sin, but in Christ I see my sin laid on another and put away." He catches at that truth, so simple, so sublime, and as he believes it he begins to know Him whom to know is life eternal. The Spirit of God, as He shines with light divine into the soul, soon sweeps away the Egyptian darkness of despair, and in the light of God the man sees light.

You see what my drift is. It is just this, that there are certain walls of reasonings, reckonings, thinkings,—our version calls them "imaginations," which are to be cast down, and the gospel does this when used by the Holy Ghost. Nor is this all, for with the walls the battlements fall. Man having devised the fortress of reasoning, erects thereon towers of pride, which the apostle calls "high things," of which he says that the power of God casts down "every high thing that exalteth itself against the knowledge of God." These lofty castles are such as the following :—" I have a noble nature within me : my instincts are towards right. I have not done much amiss. I am as good as my neighbours. I can overcome any temptation. I am persuaded that I can fight my own way into eternal felicity,"— and all such vain ideas. Let but the gospel come with power, and all these citadels are laid low. Away they go, like Jericho's old bulwarks, rocking and reeling, till in a cloud of dust they thunder to their fall. In how many cases we have seen this to be so ! Fine men have come into this place, men that knew a great deal better than anything they could find in the Bible, quite confident that nothing would ever alter them. These have sat down like ancient knights, mailed from head to foot, invulnerable to any shafts of ours, but the blessed Spirit has found an arrow in some simple saying that we have gathered from God's blessed word, and, lo, the proud warriors have fallen in the dust. Convinced that they were ignorant and foolish, the formerly proud boasters have begun to cry, " What must we do to be saved ? " and ere long, made champions of the faith, it has been their delight humbly to yield judgment and will and heart to the obedience of Christ. O that the Lord would thus storm the prejudices and self-conceits of all my unconverted hearers and sweep them away by His mighty love.

II. After a breach has been made and the city has been taken, PRISONERS ARE MADE : this is our second point. The text runs thus, " Bringing into captivity every thought." The word translated " thought " has a very broad meaning, but its best explanation is that which is placed first in the lexicon, " everything which comes from the mind." The mind is like a city, and when it is captured the inhabitants which swarm its streets are the thoughts, and these are taken prisoners. Look at the process, which I will rapidly describe. The gospel comes with power to the heart of a man, and he begins to fear the wrath of God and the judgment to come. See how he trembles. Christ has captured his thoughts of self-security. He no more says, " Though I add drunkenness to thirst, it shall surely be well with me." On the contrary he cries, " I am guilty ; I have broken God's law, and I am condemned." The Lord has captured his thoughts of self-righteousness. This is the man who yesterday boasted in himself that he was righteous : the pure and holy law of God has come near his conscience, and he feels himself guilty, and therefore sues for mercy. Now he begins to pray, " God be merciful

to me a sinner," and it is clear that his thoughts of independence, his ideas that he could do without his God, are made prisoners. His thoughts of pleasure in alienation from the Great Father are now slain, for he desires to draw near to the Most High. See ! a little hope begins to dawn, he hopes that there may be salvation for him. His thoughts of rebellious despair are led captive in fetters of iron. Praise ye the Lord ! Watch him still further. The Spirit of God encourages him, and he comes to believe in Jesus : his self-trust is a prisoner. That Jesus died for sinners is a truth which he accepts, and he casts himself upon it ; his proud intellect is a captive, and he gladly bows at the Redeemer's feet. Hear him as he sings, " I am forgiven : God assures me of it. I am justified because I have believed in Jesus. Oh, how I love His precious name." His inmost heart is captured, all the thoughts of his love are now subdued, and the Saviour whom he once despised he now adores. See how with gratitude he brings his alabaster box to break it, and pour the sweet perfume on the Saviour's feet. Jesus has won his heart, and holds it in a willing captivity, and henceforth the man consecrates himself to Christ, to live and to die for Him. Thus the whole mind of the man, yea, the whole man, has thrown down its rebellious weapons and surrendered unconditionally to the conquering arm of the Lord Jesus.

I dwell very briefly upon this point, because I wish to enlarge upon the last.

III. These prisoners are to be LED AWAY INTO CAPTIVITY,—" Bringing every thought into captivity to the obedience of Christ." Monarchs of the olden times, such as the kings of Assyria and Babylon, when they subdued a country, removed the people to a distance away from their old haunts, to find new homes. Now, when the Lord captivates the thoughts of our mind He leads them all away, conducting them to another region altogether. The offspring of the mind he guides into the spiritual realm, wherein they delight in the Lord, and bow themselves before Him. Let us see this procession of captives led away to grace the triumph of the conqueror and to settle down in another region under another King than they ever knew before. From the highest to the lowest all the faculties of the soul are made to pass under the yoke. I shall not attempt a list according to mental science, but mention them as they occur to me. He who being made conscious of his sin believes in Jesus Christ submits all the thoughts of his *judgment* and *understanding* to the obedience of Christ, and this is a great point gained. Before, he put bitter for sweet and sweet for bitter, darkness for light and light for darkness : but now, when he is in difficulty about a moral question he asks his Lord ; now, if pleasure tempts him he judges whether it be sweet by the question whether it would be sweet to his Lord ; now, if a certain doctrine is stated he weighs it not in the balances of his own thoughts, much less in the scales of popular opinion, but he asks, " What did my Master say ? How would the Lord Jesus think of this ? " He suspends his own judgment upon his Master's judgment. He does not say " I am a law unto myself," but he says, " Christ is the way, and in His steps I desire to follow." Thus his reason is led into captivity to the higher reason and understanding of his supreme Lord. If there be a truth which he does not know he tries to learn it, if his Lord sets it before him as a lesson, and if it be hidden from him, he is content not to know. His prayer is, "Lord, teach me, for else I shall never learn. I wish to have my understanding developed to the full, but let it be under Thy sweet light. Let my mind blossom and open all its flowers beneath the sunlight of Thy divine instruction." I know it is not so with some professed Christians, for they too often invent their own doctrines, and think out their opinions apart from their Master. To think is admirable, but not if we mean thereby to supplement the teachings of Christ, or to improve upon them, or to accommodate them to popular theories in science and philosophy. For my part, true science may say what it will, and never lack for an attentive listener while I live : the more loudly it shall speak the better, if it will speak facts and not theories, if it will tell me what God has done and not what man has dreamed. All that true science ever can discover must tally with the word of revelation, for God speaks in nature no lie, but the selfsame truth as He has written in the holy Scriptures. Let our wise men ransack earth to its centre, and climb to heaven and make inquisition through every star, the testimony of universal nature if heard aright shall never contradict the inspired utterances of the Holy Ghost. The evil is that the wise men add their own inferences to the facts as if they were of equal authority. What, then, is to be done ? Shall we alter the deductions of the fallible, or try to shape the declarations of the infallible ? The question is not hard to answer. We are not to revise the statements of the Book, but the inferences of the philosophers. When philosophy contradicts revelation, what say I ? So much the worse for philosophy. The Word of God is no lie ; the lie is on the other side. In spite of the perpetual restlessness which I see in many who are for ever mending that which is perfect in itself, my understanding is happy to delight in the infallible testimonies of Jehovah. Let those fellows alter, we shall not ! Let them come up to us ; verily, believers in God's revelation will never go down to them, for that would be to be disloyal to our Master Christ, whose teachings are too sacred for us knowingly to alter a letter of them. Whatever others may do, it is the delight of those who have felt the overwhelming power of the divine Spirit to find in Christ the wisdom with which their intellect is more than content.

The same power of truth and of the Holy Ghost leads captive *the will*. My Lord Will-be-will, as Bunyan describes Him, is a very stout fellow. In some men He is exceedingly obstinate,—" I will, and I will, and I will,"—and by no means can they be made to yield. In truth the will has a wonderful power over all the faculties, and rules them like a despot. It is boasted that the will of man is free, yet was Luther quite correct when he called it a slave. Never is it so much a slave as when it brags of its own liberty. Let the Spirit of God come into the heart and apply with power the gospel of Jesus Christ, and the human will no longer glories in its freedom, but surrenders, and is subjugated. It remains a will still, but the will of God is supreme over it. Hear it describe itself,—" Lord, this is my will, or what I want to be my will—' Not as I will, but as Thou wilt.' " See how the will wears its golden fetters, and kisses them with happy lips, so glad to find true freedom in being subdued to the obedience of Christ.

It is very beautiful also to see how human *hopes* are spell-bound by grace. These winged things were wont to flutter no higher than the tainted atmosphere of this poor world ; but now they find stronger pinions and soar aloft to things not seen as yet, eternal in the heavens. The man's *fears*, too, all nestled in the ruins of his sinful joys, or were aroused by the voices of his fellow man, but now, ennobled by grace, they ascend into another sphere, they cover their faces with their wings before the throne of God, while the man fears to grieve the Holy Spirit, fears to offend against the Father's love, fears to do anything which would dishonour the Saviour. His joys and sorrows are now found where they never went before ; he rejoices in the Lord, and he sorrows after a godly sort. His *memory* also now retains the precious things of divine truth, which once it rejected for the trifles of time, and his *powers of meditation* and consideration keep within the circle of truth and holiness, finding green pastures there. This done, you shall see the same enthralment cast over the Christian man's *desires and aspirations*. He has flung away his old ambitions, and aspires to nobler things. He is not without his longings, but he longs for heavenly blessings. His wishes and desires fly to Christ as doves to their windows. His affection, which is no longer set upon things upon the earth, but on things above, draws upward his desires. He pines for holiness, for usefulness, for the glory of God. His own glory he discards, and is willing to be of no repute, so long as he may but make the name of Jesus famous among the sons of men. I would to God, dear brothers and sisters, that this sacred vassalage would be more fully felt by every motion of the mind, so that no desire would dare to wander beyond bounds even for a moment.

The same blessed servitude binds the man's *plots and designings*. He plans still, but it is not for his own aggrandisement : his grandest design is to bring jewels to the crown of Christ. He arranges his life now with circumspection and with diligence, but not with cunning and craftiness, for holiness is his policy, and his scheme of life is sanctity. Does not this talk of mine sound rather like sarcasm to some who profess to be Christians ? If it does, stand convicted, for it is not I that am wrong in this, but you ; for every thought is to be brought into captivity to the obedience of Christ, and even when we are thinking about common things, matters that have to do with business, we are to be serving our Lord, for " *every* thought," not *some* thought, is to be bowed unto the obedience of Christ. It is a wicked error to conceive that so much of our life ought to be religious and so much to be secular. A Christian's whole life is to be his religion, and his religion is to saturate his whole life. You are as religiously to eat your meals as you eat at the sacred supper, as religiously to speak the truth in your parlour as you would in the pulpit. Whether you eat or drink, or whatsoever you do, it is all to be done to the glory of God. The great thought you are to have in opening your shops, in trading, in toiling, in furnishing your houses, in nursing your children, and even in taking recreation, is still to be, " How can I glorify God in all this ? " All, all must be brought into captivity to Christ. When a man yields himself to Jesus he should comprehend his house, his money, his body, his time, his wife, his children,—everything in the deed of surrender ; for He who bought us with His precious blood did not buy us with a reserve and leave the devil a mortgage upon us, but we are our Lord's unencumbered freehold for ever. We are His own conquered portion, which He took out of the hand of the Amorite with his sword and with his bow, and therefore over the whole of our being He has an absolute and undivided right of property.

The renewed man's *love and hate* are both held captive by the power of grace. He loves Jesus truly and intensely ; he hates sin with his whole soul. Indignation is a hard thing to tame, but to my mind it is a grand thing to see a man's anger made the servitor of Christ, so that he only grows indignant when he wars with that which is mean, cruel, unjust, un-Christlike. Then he doth well to be angry, for his anger is but virtue on a blaze. It is a fair sight to see Christ's sacred bands worn by our *tastes*, which are so volatile and hard to constrain. Concerning tastes it is never wise to dispute, but Jesus' love creates a delicacy of mind, a discernment of that which is tender and gentle, and pure and heavenly, an abhorrence of that which is evil, so that the Lord's redeemed become very connoisseurs in things moral and divine. *The fancy*, too, that impalpable cloud, painted as by the setting sun, that will-o'-th'-wisp of the spirit, even this is impressed into royal service, and made to wear the livery of Christ, so that men even dream eternal life. When godly men give their imagination rein even Pegasus bears a royal burden, and in his flight from the actual to the imaginative he feels the golden bridle of the King's rule restraining and directing all his airy motions. Yes, the Holy Spirit wins an undisputed sway, " bringing into captivity every thought to the obedience of Christ."

Do you not wish for this complete subjection, you to whom Jesus is God and Lord ? I know you do, and what is more, I am sure you wish for the time when that which is wrought in yourselves shall be accomplished in all mankind. Christ's gospel has not come into the world to be co-equal with other faiths and share a divided kingdom with differing creeds. False gods may stand face to face to each other in one Pantheon, and be at peace, for they are all false together, but where Christ comes, Dagon must go down, not even the stump of him must stand. Truth is of necessity intolerant of falsehood, love wars with hate, and justice battles with wrong. Christ Jesus will be all in all, and sit upon the throne alone. May the day come in which obedience to Christ shall be universal. What a scene would present itself if every thought of every human being were in holy subjection to Christ ! Not a poor woman would muse beneath her lowly roof of thatch without rendering holy adoration, while on the throne neither queen nor prince would purpose anything but what should be for the glory of Jesus. No council chamber would know a policy which would be contrary to the Prince of love, nor would the freest thinker think ought contrary to the thoughts of Jesus. The wild men of the plain would cease to forget the Lord, and the civilized dwellers in cities would no longer cast off His fear. The common people would seek unto Him in multitudes, and the nobles would study how to honour Him. How happy will the time be when all inventive genius shall own the sway of Jesus, and man shall desire no more to fashion weapons of war, but only to design that which shall minister to the well-being of mankind ; when art with pencil and chisel shall refrain from all which excites lascivious thoughts and perpetuates the memory of blood and slaughter, and shall bow at Jesus' feet to honour God by setting nature's beauties before reverent eyes ; when learning poring over its classic tomes shall find in human wisdom trophies for the surer wisdom of Jesus ; and study, searching by the midnight lamp, shall seek out the heights and depths of love divine. It charms me to think of every poet singing divine songs for earth's great King, drinking no more from the Castalian fount, but finding all his springs in God alone. Then, too, shall music compose her most harmonious symphonies, and pour forth her richest notes in worship of the redeeming Lord ; while eloquence, no longer declaiming in the defence of wrong, shall spend her force in the maintenance of peace and righteousness, and in the extolling of the Lord. Dawn even now, auspicious day. Why hangs the night so heavy ? Why bides the darkness around us for so many ages ?

Great Captain of salvation, Thou canst achieve the victory. We have compassed this Jericho these many days, but still the walls fall not. Up, Thou mighty man of war, for Thou art such, and come Thou to the battle and then the battlements of sin will fall. " The Lord is a man of war : Jehovah is His name." Awake, awake, put on strength, O arm of the Lord ; awake as in the ancient days, in the generations of old. Art Thou not it that hath cut Rahab and wounded the dragon ? Because of truth and righteousness, ride forth in Thy majesty. For peace on earth and glory to God in the highest, come forth in the glory of Thy might with the everlasting gospel, " Casting down imaginations, and every high thing that exalteth itself against the knowledge of God, and bringing into captivity every thought to the obedience of Christ."

STRENGTHENING WORDS FROM THE SAVIOUR'S LIPS

" And He said unto me, My grace is sufficient for thee : for My strength is made perfect in weakness. Most gladly therefore will I rather glory in my infirmities, that the power of Christ may rest upon me."—2 Corinthians xii. 9.

PAUL, when buffeted by the messenger of Satan, addressed his power to the Lord Jesus Christ, and not, as he usually did, to the heavenly Father. This is a somewhat remarkable fact, but it is clear from the passage before us. He says, " For this thing I besought *the Lord* thrice," and that the Lord here is the Lord Jesus is pretty clear from the fact that he says in the next verse, " that the power *of Christ* may rest upon me." His prayer was not directed to God absolutely considered, nor does he speak of the power of God, but his prayer was directed to the Lord Jesus Christ, and it was the power of the Lord Jesus Christ which he desired to rest upon him. It is an infallible proof of our Lord's divinity, that He may be addressed in prayer ; and this is one instance, with several others, which show to us that we may legitimately present our petitions, not only to the ever-blessed Father, but also to His Son Jesus Christ. There seems to me to be a peculiar fitness in a prayer to Jesus when the temptation came from a messenger of Satan, because the Lord Jesus has endured the like temptation Himself, and knows how to succour them that are tempted. Moreover, He has come to earth to destroy the works of the devil. In His lifetime He manifested peculiar power over unclean spirits, and was constantly casting them out from those whom they tormented. It was one of His few rejoicing notes, " I saw Satan like lightning fall from heaven." It was by the name of Jesus that devils were expelled after Christ had risen into the glory. " Jesus I know," said the spirits whom the sons of Sceva endeavoured in vain to exorcise. Devils felt the power of Jesus, and therefore it was wise and natural that the apostle Paul should, when buffeted of Satan, turn to Jesus and ask Him to bid the evil spirit depart from him.

It is not a little remarkable also that this prayer was not only addressed to Jesus, but was offered in much the same manner as the prayer of our Lord in the garden. The apostle prayed three times, even as our Lord did when He too was sorely buffeted by the powers of darkness. The thrice-repeated cry was intensely earnest, for he " besought " the Lord thrice. And Paul, singularly enough, met with very much the same answer as his Master, for our Lord was not permitted to put aside the cup (it could not pass away from Him except He drink it), but an angel appeared unto Him strengthening Him, and so in Paul's case the trial was not taken away from him, but he was strengthened by kind, assuring words, and by being led to see that God would be glorified by his enduring the trial. I see, then, the Lord Jesus reflected in His servant Paul as in a mirror ; I hear the three-times repeated prayer, I mark the cup standing unremoved, and I see the strength imparted in the midst of weakness.

Our text fell from the lips of Jesus Christ Himself, and if anything could make its language more sweet than it is in itself it would be this fact, that He Himself delivered the words to His chosen apostle. It is Jesus who says in the words of the text, " My grace is sufficient for thee ; My strength is made perfect in weakness." This truth casts a soft, mellow light upon the words, helps us to interpret them, and enables us to derive all the greater comfort from them. When Jesus speaks, a special charm surrounds each syllable.

The exact tense of the Greek words it is not easy to translate into English. The apostle does not merely tell us that his Lord said these words to him fourteen years ago, but the tense connects the past with the present, as if he felt that the answer was not simply something past, but something which continued with him in its consoling power. The echoes of what his Lord had said were still sounding through his soul. I should not miss the apostle's meaning if I read it, " He has been saying to me, ' My strength is sufficient for thee.' " The words had an abiding effect upon the apostle's mind, not merely for the time reconciling him to the particular trouble which had afflicted him, but cheering him for all the rest of his life, constraining him in all the future trials to glory in his infirmities and render praise to God. It is a sweet thing to have a text of Scripture laid home to the heart

for present uses, but when God the Holy Spirit so applies a promise that it abides in the heart for the term of one's natural life, then are we favoured indeed. Elijah's meat gave him strength for forty days, but what is that meat which endureth unto life eternal ? What bread must that be which feeds me through the whole period of my pilgrimage ? Here, then, we have before us food which Jesus Himself provides, so nutritive that His Spirit can cause us to remember the feast to our dying day. O Lord, feed us now and give us grace to inwardly digest Thy gracious word.

With this preface, which I beg you to remember during the discourse, since it indicates my line of thought, we now come to the text itself—a mass of diamonds, bright and precious. In the text we notice three things—first, *grace all-sufficient* ; secondly, *strength perfected* ; and, thirdly, *power indwelling*.

I. In the text even the most superficial observer notices a promise of GRACE ALL-SUFFICIENT. In the case of our Lord Jesus, the Spirit so rested upon Him as to be sufficient for Him at all times. Never did the Spirit of God fail to uphold the man Christ Jesus under the most arduous labours, the most terrible temptations, and the most bitter sufferings ; and therefore He completed the work which His Father gave Him to do, and in death He was able to exclaim, " It is finished." The Lord here assures His chosen servant that it should be the same with him,—" My grace," saith He, " is sufficient for thee."

To bring out the full meaning of these few words, I will give you four readings of them. The first is a strictly grammatical one, and is the first sense which they bear. Taking the word translated grace to mean favour or love—for that also is included in the word *charis*—how does the passage run ? " My favour is sufficient for thee." Do not ask to be rid of your trouble, do not ask to have ease, comfort, or any other form of happiness,—My favour is enough for thee ; or, as good Dr. Hodge reads it, " *My love is enough for thee.*" If thou hast little else that thou desirest, yet surely it is enough that thou art My favoured one, a chosen subject of My grace. " My love is enough for thee." What a delicious expression. You do not need an explanation. Repeat the words to yourselves, and even now conceive that the Well-beloved looks down on you, and whispers, " My love is enough for thee." If you have been asking Him three times to deliver you from your present affliction, hear Him reply, " Why need you ask Me any more ? My love is enough for you." What say you to that ? Do you not answer, " Aye, Lord, indeed it is. If I am poor, if Thou willest me to be poor, I am content to be severely tried, for Thy love is enough for me : If I am sick, so long as Thou wilt come and visit me and reveal Thy heart to me, I am satisfied, for Thy love is enough for me. If I am persecuted, cast out, and forsaken, cheerfully will I bear it, if a sense of Thy love sustains me ; for Thy love is enough for me. Aye, and if I should be left so alone as to have no one to care for me in the whole world, if my father and my mother should forsake me, and every friend should prove a Judas,—Thy love is enough for me." Do you catch the meaning, and do you see how Paul must have been comforted by it if he understood it in this primary and most natural sense ? " O Paul, it is sufficient for thee that I have made thee to be a chosen vessel to bear My name among the Gentiles ; it is enough for Thee that I have loved thee from before the foundation of the world, that I redeemed thee with My precious blood, that I called thee when thou wast a blasphemer and injurious, that I changed thy heart and made thee love Me, and that I have kept thee to this day, and will keep thee even to the end by Mine inimitable love. My love is enough for thee ; ask not to be set free from this buffeting ; ask not to be delivered from weakness and trial, for these will enable thee the better to enjoy My favour, and that is enough for thee."

We will now read our text another way, keeping to our authorized version, but throwing the stress on the first word—" *My* grace is sufficient for thee." What grace is this ? Note who it is that promises. It is Jesus who speaks ; therefore it is mediatorial grace, the grace given to Jesus Christ as the covenant Head of His people which is here intended. Think of it a minute. It is the head speaking to the member, and declaring that its grace is enough for the whole body. The anointing oil has been poured upon the head that it may go down the beard and descend to the skirts, and, lo, one poor member of the body is mourning and complaining, for it is fearful of being omitted in the plenteous anointing, but the head comforts it by saying, " *My* anointing is enough for thee, since it is enough for all My members." It is the Head ; Christ, in whom all fulness dwells, speaking to one of the members of His mystical body, and saying, " The grace which God has given to Me without measure on behalf of all the members of My body is sufficient for thee as well as for the rest of them." Beloved, seize the thought. The Lord has made over to Christ all that the whole company of His people can possibly want ; nay, more than that, for " it pleased the Father that in Him should all fulness dwell," and of His fulness have all we received, and grace for grace, and from that fulness we hope continually to draw for evermore. This is the grace which is sufficient for us. It greatly tends to help faith when you can see the relation that exists between the Redeemer and yourself ; for Jesus is your covenant Head, and God has been pleased to give Himself and all His infinite riches to the Lord Jesus Christ as your federal representative ; and as your covenant Head the Lord Jesus assures you that the stores laid up in Him on your behalf are sufficient for you. Can you limit the mediatorial power of Christ ? Do you not know that God giveth not the Spirit by measure unto Him ? Be ye, then, assured that Christ's grace is sufficient for you.

I will read the text again, and this time put the stress in the centre. "My grace *is sufficient* for thee." It *is now* sufficient. Thou art buffeted by this evil spirit, but My grace is sufficient for thy present need. Paul, thou hast been beaten of rods, and stoned and shipwrecked, and in perils often, and in all these My grace has been sufficient ; and now I tell thee this present trouble, though it be somewhat different in shape from the rest, is nevertheless such as I am well able to meet. My grace is sufficient for thee in this also. The nearness of an object increases its apparent bulk, and so the affliction under which we are at present labouring seems greater than any we have known before. Past trials appear when we have passed them to have been small things compared with present troubles, and therefore the difficulty is to see the sufficiency of grace for present and pressing afflictions. It is easy to believe in grace for the past and the future, but to rest in it for the immediate necessity is true faith. Believer, it is *now* that grace is sufficient : even at this moment it *is* enough for thee. Do not say this is a new trouble, or if you do say it remember the grace of God is always new. Do not complain that some strange thing has happened unto you, or if you do, remember blessings are provided in the grace of God to meet your strange difficulties. Tremble not because the thorn in the flesh is so mysterious, for grace is mysterious too, and so mystery shall be met by mystery. At this moment, and at all moments which shall ever occur between now and glory, the grace of God will be sufficient for you. This sufficiency is declared without any limiting words, and therefore I understand the passage to mean that the grace of our Lord Jesus is sufficient to uphold thee, sufficient to strengthen thee, sufficient to comfort thee, sufficient to make thy trouble useful to thee, sufficient to enable thee to triumph over it, sufficient to bring thee out of ten thousand like it, sufficient to bring thee home to heaven. Whatever would be good for thee, Christ's grace is sufficient to bestow ; whatever would harm thee, His grace is sufficient to avert ; whatever thou desirest, His grace is sufficient to give thee if it be good for thee ; whatever thou wouldst avoid, His grace can shield thee from it if so His wisdom shall dictate. O child of God, I wish it were possible to put into words this all-sufficiency, but it is not. Let me retract my speech : I am glad that it cannot be put into words, for if so it would be finite, but since we never can express it, glory be to God it is inexhaustible, and our demands upon it can never be too great. Here let me press upon you the pleasing duty of taking home the promise personally at this moment, for no believer here need be under any fear since for him also, at this very instant, the grace of the Lord Jesus is sufficient.

In the last reading which I will give, I shall lay the emphasis upon the first and last words : " *My* grace is sufficient for *thee*." I have often read in Scripture of the holy laughter of Abraham, when he fell upon his face and laughed ; but I do not know that I ever experienced that laughter till a few evenings ago, when this text came home to me with such sacred power as literally to cause me to laugh. I had been looking it through, looking at its original meaning, and trying to fathom it, till at last I got hold of it this way : " *My* grace," says Jesus, " is sufficient for *thee*," and it looked almost as if it were meant to ridicule my unbelief : for surely the grace of such a One as my Lord Jesus is indeed sufficient for so insignificant a being as I am. It seemed to me as if some tiny fish, being very thirsty, was troubled with fear of drinking the river dry, and Father Thames said to him, " Poor little fish, my stream is sufficient for thee." I should think it is, and inconceivably more. My Lord seems to say to me, " Poor little creature that thou art, remember what grace there is in Me, and believe that it is all thine. Surely it is sufficient for thee." I replied, " Ah, my Lord, it is indeed." Put one mouse down in all the granaries of Egypt when they were fullest after seven years of plenty, and imagine that one mouse complaining that it might die of famine. " Cheer up," says Pharaoh ? " poor mouse, my granaries are sufficient for thee." Imagine a man standing on a mountain, and saying, " I breathe so many cubic feet of air in a year ; I am afraid that I shall ultimately inhale all the oxygen which surrounds the globe." Surely the earth on which the man would stand might reply, " My atmosphere is sufficient for thee." I should think it ; let him fill his lungs as full as ever he can, he will never breathe all the oxygen, nor will the fish drink up all the river, nor the mouse eat up all the stores in the granaries of Egypt. Does it not make unbelief seem altogether ridiculous, so that you laugh it out of the house, and say, " Never come this way any more, for with a mediatorial fulness to go to, with such a Redeemer to rest in, how dare I for a moment think that my wants cannot be supplied." Our great Lord feeds all the fish of the sea, and the birds of the air, and the cattle on the hills, and guides the stars, and upholds all things by the power of His hand, how then can we be straitened for supplies, or be destitute of help ? If our needs were a thousand times larger than they are they would not approach the vastness of His power to provide. The Father hath committed all things into His hand. Doubt Him no more. Listen, and let Him speak to thee : " *My* grace is sufficient for thee. What if thou hast little grace, yet *I* have much : it is *My* grace thou hast to look to, not thine own, and *My* grace will surely be sufficient for thee." John Bunyan has the following passage, which exactly expresses what I myself have experienced. He says that he was full of sadness and terror, but suddenly these words broke in upon him with great power, and three times together the words sounded in His ears, " My grace is sufficient for thee ; My grace is sufficient for thee ; My grace is sufficient for thee." And " Oh ! methought," says he, " that every word was a mighty word unto me ; as ' *My*,' and ' *grace*,' and ' *sufficient*,' and ' *for thee* ' ; they were then, and sometimes are still, far bigger than others be." He who knows, like the bee, how to suck honey from flowers, may well linger over each one of these words and drink in unutterable content.

> " Have we forgot the Almighty name
> That form'd the earth and sea ;
> And can an all-creating arm
> Grow weary or decay ?
>
> Treasures of everlasting might
> In our Jehovah dwell ;
> He gives the conquest to the weak,
> And treads their foes to hell.
>
> Mere mortal power shall fade and die,
> And youthful vigour cease ;
> But we that wait upon the Lord
> Shall feel our strength increase."

II. Secondly, in the text we have STRENGTH PERFECTED,—" For My strength is made perfect in weakness." Now, running the parallel still between Jesus and Paul, remember, beloved, that it was so with our Lord Jesus Christ. He was strong as to His Deity, in Him dwells all strength, for He is the mighty God ; but how was His strength as Mediator made perfect ? The Scripture says, "Perfect through suffering": that is to say, the strength of Christ to save His people would never have been perfected if He had not taken upon Himself the weakness of human nature, and if He had not in that feeble nature descended lower and lower in weakness. Had He saved Himself He could not have saved us, but His giving up of all that He had, made Him rich towards us, and His putting on of weakness made Him strong to redeem us. O incarnate God, Thou couldst not redeem till Thou wast swaddled as a babe in Bethlehem ; nay, Thou couldst not redeem till Thou wast made to bear a cross like a felon ; nay,

Thou couldst not perfect redemption till Thou didst hang a ghastly corpse upon a gibbet ; nay, it was even essential that Thou shouldst be laid in the grave ; Thy work was not fulfilled till three days and nights Thou didst abide in the heart of the earth amongst the dead. The Lord Jesus could say—" My strength is made perfect in weakness." This was to be realized in Paul, and is to be fulfilled in all the saints. Of course the strength of God is always perfect ; we do not understand that anything is necessary to make perfect the divine power, but the words fell from the lip of Jesus as our Mediator and representative, and it is His strength which is made perfect in weakness. In us this is true, first because *the power of Jesus can only be perfectly revealed in His people by bearing them up, keeping them, and sustaining them when they are in trouble.* Who knows the perfection of the strength of God till he sees how God can make poor puny creatures strong ? Yonder is a timid, sickly woman, who lives a life of agony ; almost every breath is a spasm, and every pulse a pang ; each member of her body is subject to tortures of which others scarcely dream ; but look at her cheerful patience ! As much as possible she conceals her pain that she may not distress others ; you hear no murmur of complaint, but oftentimes she utters words as cheery as those which fall from persons in robust health ; and when she must tell of her afflictions she always speaks of them in such a tone that you feel she has accepted them at the Lord's hands with complete resignation, and is willing to bear them as many years as the Lord may appoint. I do not wonder when strong men say strong things, but I have often marvelled when I have heard such heroic sentences from the weak and trembling. To hear the sorrowing comfort others, when you would think they needed comfort themselves ; to mark their cheerfulness, when if you and I suffered half as much we should have sunk to the earth—this is worthy of note. God's strength is perfectly revealed in the trials of the weak. When you see a man of God brought into poverty, and yet in that poverty never repining ; when you hear his character assailed by slander, and yet he stands unmoved like a rock amidst the waves ; when you see the gracious man persecuted and driven from home and country for Christ's sake, and yet he takes joyfully the spoiling of his goods and banishment and disgrace—then the strength of God is made perfect in the midst of weakness. While the man of God suffers, and is under necessities and distresses and infirmities, then it is that the power of God is seen. It was when tiny creatures made Pharaoh tremble that his magicians said, " This is the finger of God," and evermore God's greatest glory comes from things weak and despised.

This is equally true to the man himself. *God's strength is made perfect to the saint's own apprehension when he is weak.* Brothers, if you have prospered in business all your lives, and have had an easy path of it, I will tell you something : you do not know much about the strength of God. If you have been healthy all your lives and never suffered, if your families have never been visited by bereavements, and if your spirits have never been cast down, you do not know much about the strength of God. You may have read about it in books, and it is well you should ; you may have seen it in others, and observation is useful ; but a grain of experience is worth a pound of observation, and you can only get knowledge of the power of God by an experimental acquaintance with your own weakness, and you will not be likely to get that except as you are led along the thorny, flinty way which most of God's saints have to travel, which is described by the word "tribulation." Great tribulation brings out the great strength of God. If you never feel inward conflicts and sinking of soul, you do not know much of the upholding power of God ; but if you go down, down, into the depths of soul-anguish till the deep threatens to shut her mouth upon you, and then the Lord rides upon a cherub and does fly, yea, rides upon the wings of the wind and delivers your soul, and catches you away to the third heaven of delight, then you perceive the majesty of divine grace. Oh, there must be the weakness of man, felt, recognized, and mourned over, or else the strength of the Son of God will never be perfected in us. Thus have I given you two meanings of the text : others see the strength of God in our weakness, and we ourselves discover it when our weakness is most manifest.

I think the term "made perfect" also means *achieves its purposes*. Read it thus : "For my strength fully achieves its design in weakness." Brethren, God has not done for us what He means to do except we have felt our own strengthlessness; as long as a portion of strength remains we are but partially sanctified. When our Lord has accomplished in us what He is aiming at, the result will be to empty us out and to make us discover the utter vanity of self. If the Lord ever takes you like a dish and turns you upside down and wipes you right out, and sets you away on a shelf, you will then feel what He means you to feel : that is to say, you will feel as if you were waiting there for the Lord to take you down and use you, and then, be sure, He will come in due time and use you for His honourable purposes, laying meat upon you for His hungry people and making you an ornament at His banquets of love. If you feel yourself to be a full dish, I will tell you what there is in you : you hold nothing but the slops and filthiness of depraved nature. The Lord will never use you till all that is poured out, and you are wiped quite clean and put away with nothing of yourself remaining in you wherein you may glory. All the saints who are ready to go to heaven feel themselves to be less than the least ; but those professors who are by no means ready for glory are highly self-conscious, and feel that there is a great deal in them which is very commendable. Those who enter heaven carry nothing of self with them, neither will any of us enter there so long as we talk proudly of our attainments. Those who claim to possess " the higher life " have been heard to boast of their purity, but those who enjoy the highest life in glory cry, " Not unto us ! Not unto us, be glory." It is a mark of fitness for heaven when self is dead and grace alone reigns. The strength of God is never perfected till our weakness is perfected. When our weakness is consciously and thoroughly felt, then the strength of God has done its work in us.

There is yet another meaning. *The strength of God is most perfected or most glorified by its using our strengthlessness.* Suppose the world had been converted to Christ by twelve emperors ; the establishment of Christianity might have been readily accounted for without glorifying God. Imagine that Christianity had been forced upon men with the stern arguments which Mahomet placed in the hands of his first disciples, the glory would have redounded to human courage and not to the love of God. We wonder not that the gods of the heathen were dashed to the ground when the scimitars were so sharp, and were wielded by such ferocious warriors ; but when we know that twelve humble fishermen, without arms or armour, without patronage or prestige, without science or sophistry, overthrew colossal systems of error and set up the cross of Christ in their place, we adoringly exclaim, " This is the finger of God." And so the other day, when the Lord took a consecrated cobbler and sent him out to Hindostan, whatever work was done by William Carey was evidently seen to be of the Lord. If societies would send out distinguished scholars it is thought by some that in all probability heathen intelligence would recognize their abilities and genius, and respect them and, convinced by reasoning and influenced by talent, they would bow before superior Western culture. Yes, and so they would be converted by a conversion in which the Lord would not be glorified, but proud man would have the praise. In what way would that increase the glory of God ? God uses weakness rather than strength, and so His power is revealed. All that you have that is strong, my brother, will be of small service in this matter, for the Lord will not exalt your strength and make you proud of your attainments : your weakness and infirmities, in all probability, the Lord will see fit to use, for He delights to take the base things and the things that are despised, and use them to achieve His purposes, that the excellency of the power may be all His own.

Let me notice last of all on this point, that all history shows that the *great strength of God has always been displayed and perpetuated in human weakness.* Brothers, what made Christ so strong ? Was it not that He condescended to be so weak ? And how did He win His victory ? By His patience, by His suffering : that is to say, by those things wherein His human weakness appeared. Now, look at Christ mystical, namely, the church. How has the church ever been strong ? Of course you reply, " By the strength of God ! " I know it : but what has brought forth the strength of God so that it has been undeniably manifest, and consequently operative upon mankind ? Has it been the strength of the church ? No, but the weakness of the church, for when men have seen believers suffer and die it is then that they have beheld the strength of God in His people. The sufferings of the saints have been the victories of the truth. The martyrs led the van ; they suffered most, and consequently are the champions of the elect army : the weakness which allowed of their being destitute, afflicted, tormented, has been the battle-axe and the weapons of war with which the Lord has procured conquest for the gospel. When one of the pastors of a church in London was put to death in Smithfield one early morning, while yet the frost was unmelted by the sun, there stood around the stake a number of young people who had been accustomed to listen to his teachings. Strange thing for young believers to be up so very early to see their pastor burned to death ! What do you think they were there for ? No idle curiosity could have brought them to such a spectacle. It is written that they went there *to learn the way.* Do you see ? They saw him burn, and came there with that intention, to learn the way to die for Christ themselves. The church of Rome could do nothing with a people who from the weakness which compelled them to suffer gathered strength to die triumphantly. The weakness of the martyr as he suffered revealed the strength of God in him, which held him fast to his principles while he was gradually consumed by the cruel flames. Had not men been poor worms, capable of being crushed, and capable of agonising sufferings, the upholding grace of God could never have been so conspicuously revealed. Blessed be the name of the Almighty, He displays His might in our weakness even as He shone forth in the midst of the burning bush. He spake, and lo ! the heavens and the earth stood forth. A marvellous creation ! But then there was nothing to oppose the fiat of His power : His all-powerful word was not hampered by using weak instrumentalities. How, then, is God to show yet greater power ? How shall *omnipotence* or all kinds of power be seen ? Why, brethren, He will not use His unfettered word alone, but He will clog and encumber it by using instruments infirm and weak. He will in the kingdom of grace work by men compassed with infirmities, and achieve His purposes by agencies in themselves unfitted for His ends, and then His power will be doubly seen. The celebrated Quentin Matsys had to make a well-cover in iron one morning. He was a master in the art of fashioning the metal, and could shape it as though it were so much wax. His fellow-workmen were jealous, and therefore they took from him the proper tools, and yet with his hammer he produced a matchless work of art. So the Lord with instruments which lend Him no aid, but rather hinder Him, doeth greater works of grace to His own glory and honour. He takes us poor nothings who are weak as water, and uses us to accomplish His designs, and thus is His almightiness gloriously displayed. Omnipotence when it does what it wills by its bare word is one, but when it takes weakness into league with it and performs its powerful deeds by means of weakness, it counts for two, and by the weakness it doubly manifests itself.

III. The most blessed part of the text remains,— POWER INDWELLING. Dr. Adam Clarke here furnishes us on the last part of our text with a most useful observation, " Most gladly therefore will I glory in infirmity, that the power of Christ may rest upon me." Now mark, the Greek word here used, interpreted " rest," is the same word employed by John, when he says, " The word was made flesh, and," as the Greek runs, " tabernacled among us, and we beheld His glory, the glory as of the only begotten of the Father, full of grace and truth." The passage before us means just this, " I glory in infirmities that the power of Christ may tabernacle in me." Just as the Shekinah light dwelt in the tent in the wilderness beneath the rough badger skins, so I glory to be a poor frail tent and tabernacle, that the Shekinah of Jesus Christ may dwell in my soul. Do you catch the thought ? Is it not full of beauty ? See, then, what he means,— First, he puts the power of Christ in opposition to his own power, because if he is not weak, then he has strength of his own ; if then what he does is done by his own strength, there is no room for Christ's strength ; that is clear, but if his own power be gone there is space for the power of Christ. If my life be sustained by my own strength, and my good works are done in my own strength, then there is no room for Christ's strength ; but the apostle found that it was not so, and therefore he said, " I glory in my strength-lessness, that the power of Christ may tabernacle in me."

But what is the power of Christ ? Let the text I quoted tell you—" The glory as of the only begotten of the Father, full of grace and truth." What power, then, was this which Paul expected to tabernacle in him but the power of grace and the power of truth ? It must be so, because God had said, " My *grace* is sufficient for thee." Paul catches at that promise, and he cries " this is truth, and I rely upon it " ; and he therefore expects that the grace of God and the faithfulness of God would tabernacle in him, and shine forth within his soul. This is the power of Christ which he expected to rest upon him. What more could we desire ?

What is the power of Christ ? I answer next, it is Christly power : the kind of power which is conspicuous in the life of Jesus. There was a power in Christ peculiar to Himself, as all can see who read the New Testament : a power unique and altogether His own. You know what the power of Alexander was : it was a power to command men, inspire them with courage for great enterprises, and keep them in good heart when called to endure hardships. You know what the power of Demosthenes was : it was the power of eloquence, the power to stir the patriotic Greeks, to break the fetters of the Macedonian. But what was the power of Jesus ? It was power to suffer, power to be made nothing of, power to descend to the very depths for love of God and love of men. There lay His power, in those five conquering wounds, in that majestic mournful face, more marred than that of any man, in that great agonizing heart which sent forth sweat of blood when men were to be pleaded for before the Lord. Love and patience were Christ's power, and even now these subdue the hearts of men, and make Jesus the sufferer to be Jesus the King. Therefore Paul says, " I glory in my infirmities that this same power may tabernacle in me. I triumph in weakness, in reproaches, in necessities, in persecutions, in distresses, for Christ's sake, that I may suffer, and humble myself, and be obedient, and prove my love to God even as Jesus did. When I am weak then am I strong "—strong to prove my love by enduring the weaknesses and afflictions which I accept for my Master's sake.

What was this power of Christ ? I answer again, it was part of the " all power " which our Lord declared was given unto Him in heaven and in earth ; " Go ye, therefore, and teach all nations." Paul desired to have that power tabernacling in himself, for he knew right well that if he had to " go and teach all nations " he would have to suffer in so doing, and so he takes the suffering cheerfully, that he might have the power. Even as beneath the badger skins of the tabernacle the glory of the Lord shone forth, so the mighty converting power of Christ which dwelt in Paul was gloriously revealed while he endured reproaches and persecutions, sufferings and death for Jesus' sake.

What was Christ's power again ? I answer, to complete my sermon, His power lay in His weakness, His humiliation, His dependence upon God, His faith in God, His self-abnegation, His perfect consecration to the Father ; and Paul says that he was made to suffer, and to be weak, that this same power to become nothing that God might be glorified, might rest in him.

I have done when I say just this. Dear brothers and sisters, go home and never ask the Lord to make you strong in yourselves, never ask Him to make you anybody or anything, but be content to be nothing and nobody. Next ask that His power may have room in you, and that all those who come near you may see what God can do by nothings and nobodies. Live with this desire, to glorify God. Sometimes when God honours us in His service a great " I " stands in the Lord's way. Tremble when you see a poor, weak preacher made useful in converting souls : then all the papers and magazines begin to blaze his name abroad, and silly Christians—for there are plenty of them—begin to talk him up as if he were a demigod, and say such great things about him, and describe him as wise, and eloquent, and great. Thus they do all they can to ruin the good brother. If the man is sensible he will say, " Get thee behind me, Satan, for thou savourest not the things that be of God " ; and, if God gives him great grace, he will retire more and more into the background, and lie lower and lower before his God : but, if you once get a man to feel himself to be great and good, either a fall will happen, or else the power of God will withdraw from him, or in some other way the Lord will make His people feel that His glory He will not give to another. The best of men are flesh and blood, and they have no power except as God lends them power, and He will make them know and feel this. Therefore, neither exalt others nor exalt yourselves, but beseech the Lord to make and keep you weakness itself, that in you His power may be displayed. God grant it may be so, for Christ's sake. Amen.

EVERYDAY RELIGION

" The life which I now live in the flesh I live by the faith of the Son of God."—Galatians ii. 20.

I AM not about to preach from this whole verse, for I have done that before : this single sentence will suffice me. I shall not attempt to enter into the fulness of the spiritual meaning of this very deep and fruitful passage ; I am merely going to bring out one thought from it, and to try to work that out, I trust, to practical ends. It has sometimes been objected to the preaching of the gospel, that we exhort men to live for another sphere, and do not teach them to live well in the present life. Nothing can be more untrue than this : I venture to say that more practical moral teaching is given by ministers of the gospel than by all the philosophers, lecturers, and moralists put together. While we count ourselves to be ordained to speak of something higher than mere morals, we nevertheless, nay, and for that very reason, inculcate the purest code of duty, and lay down the soundest rules of conduct. It would be a great pity, dear brethren, if in the process of being qualified for the next life we became disqualified for this ; but it is not so. It would be a very strange thing if, in order to be fit for the company of angels, we should grow unfit to associate with men ; but it is not so. It would be a singular circumstance if those who speak of heaven had nothing to say concerning the way thither ; but it is not so. The calumny is almost too stale to need a new denial. My brethren, true religion has as much to do with this world as with the world to come ; it is always urging us onward to the higher and better life ; but it does so by processes and precepts which fit us worthily to spend our days while here below. Godliness prepares us for the life which follows the laying down of this mortal flesh ; but as Paul tells us in the text, it moulds the life which we now live in the flesh. Faith is a principle for present use ; see how it has triumphed in ordinary life according to the record of the eleventh chapter of the Epistle to the Hebrews. Godliness with contentment is great gain : it hath the promise of the life that now is, as well as of that which is to come. The sphere of faith is earth and heaven, time and eternity ; the sweep of its circle takes in the whole of our being—spirit, soul, and body ; it comprehends the past and the future, and it certainly does not omit the present. With the things that now are the faith of Christians has to do ; and it is concerning the life that we now live in the flesh that I shall now speak, trying, by the help of God's Spirit, to show the influence which faith has upon it.

There are seven points in which faith in Him who loved us and gave Himself for us will have a distinct influence upon the life which we now live in the flesh.

I. To begin. FAITH INCLINES A MAN TO AN INDUSTRIOUS LIFE. *It suggests activity.* I will venture to say of any lazy man that he has little or no faith in God ; for faith always worketh,—" worketh by love." I lay it down as a thesis which shall be proved by observation that a believing man becomes an active man, or else it is because he cannot act, and, therefore, what would have been activity runs into the channel of patience, and he endures with resignation the will of the Most High. He who does nothing believes nothing—that is to say, in reality and in truth. Faith is but an empty show if it produces no result upon the life. If a professor manifests no energy, no industry, no zeal, no perseverance, no endeavour to serve God, there is cause gravely to question whether he is a believer at all. It is a mark of faith that, whenever it comes into the soul, even in its lowest degree, it suggests activity. Look at the prodigal, and note his early desires. The life of grace begins to gleam into his spirit, and its first effect is the confession of sin. He cries, " Father, I have sinned against heaven and before thee, and am no more worthy to be called thy son." But what is the second effect ? He desires to be doing something. " Make me as one of thy hired servants." Having nothing to do had helped to make him the prodigal he was. He had wasted his substance in riotous idleness, seeking enjoyment without employment. He had plunged into the foulest vices because he was master of money but not master of himself. It was not an ill thing for him when he was sent into the fields to feed swine ; the company which he met with at the swine trough was better than that which he had kept at his banquets. One of the signs of the return of his soul's sanity was his willingness to work, although it might be only as a menial servant in his father's house. In actual history observe how Saul of Tarsus, even before he had found peaceful faith in Christ, cried, " Lord, what wilt Thou have me to do ? " Faith arouses the soul to action. It is the first question of believing anxiety, " Sirs, what must I do to be saved ? " Hence faith is such a useful thing to men in the labour and travail of this mortal life, because it puts them into motion and supplies them with a motive for work. Faith does not permit men to lie upon the bed of the sluggard, listless, frivolous, idle ; but it makes life to appear real and earnest, and so girds the loins for the race.

Everyone should follow an honourable vocation. It was a rule of the old church, and it ought to be one of the present—" If any man will not work neither let him eat." It is good for us all to have something to do, and plenty of it. When man was perfect God placed him in a paradise, but not in a dormitory. He set him in the garden to " dress it and to keep it." It would not have been a happy place for Adam if he had had nothing to do but to smell the roses and gaze at the flowers : work was as essential to the perfect man as it is to us, though it was not of the kind which brings sweat to the face or weariness to the limbs. In the garden of grace faith is set to a happy service, and never wishes to be otherwise than occupied for her Lord.

The text says, " The life which I now live in the flesh I live by the faith of the Son of God." Does faith in the Son of God, who loved him and gave Himself for him, suggest to the redeemed man that he should be industrious and active ? Assuredly it does ; for it sets the divine Saviour before him as an example, and where was there ever one who worked as Jesus did ? In His early youth He said, " Wist ye not that I must be about My Father's business ? " He was no loitering heir of a gentleman, but the toiling son of a carpenter. In after life it was His meat and His drink to do the will of Him that sent Him. He says, " My Father worketh hitherto, and I work." His was stern labour and sore travail : the zeal of God's house did eat Him up, and the intensity of love consumed Him. He worked on until He could say, " I have finished the work which Thou gavest Me to do." Now, it is no small thing for a man to be roused by such an example, and to be made a partaker of such a spirit.

True faith in Him who loved us, and gave Himself for us, also *seeks direction* of the Lord as to the sphere of its action, and waits upon Him to be guided by Him in the choice of a calling. This part of our discourse may be useful to young persons who have not settled upon what they are to do in life. Faith is a great service to us here. Much depends upon the choice of our pursuits. Very grievous mistakes have been made here—as grievous mistakes as if a bird in the air should have undertaken the pursuits of a fish, or a labouring ox should have entered into competition with a race-horse. Some people are trying to do what they were never made for, ambitious beyond their line. This is a grievous evil. There should, therefore, be a seeking unto God for guidance and direction ; and faith leads us to such seeking. This prayer may be used in many senses : " Show me what Thou wouldest have me to do." In the choice of a calling faith helps a Christian to refuse that which is the most lucrative if it be attended with a questionable morality. If the Christian could have huge purses of that gold which is coined out of the drunkenness, the lust, or the ungodliness of men, he would scorn to put them among his stores. Trades which are injurious to men's minds and hearts are not lawful callings before God. Dishonest gain is awful loss. Gold gained by deceit or oppression shall burn into the soul of its owner as the fire of hell. " Make money," said the worldling to his son ; " make it honestly if you can, but, anyhow, make money." Faith abhors this precept of Mammon, and having God's providence for its inheritance, it scorns the devil's bribe. Choose no calling over which you cannot ask God's blessing, or you will be acting contrary to the law of faith. If you cannot conceive of the Lord Jesus wishing you success in a certain line of trade, do not touch it. If it is not possible to think of your Lord as smiling upon you in your daily calling, then your calling is not fit for a Christian to follow.

Callings should be deliberately chosen with a view to our own suitableness for them. Faith watches the design of God, and desires to act according to His intent. It had been ill for David to have lived in retirement, or for the prophet Nathan to have aspired to the throne. The law of the kingdom is—" Every man in his own order " ; or in other words, " Every man according to his several ability." If the Lord has given us one talent let us use it in its own market ; or if two, or five, let us trade with them where they can be most profitably employed, so that we may be found faithful servants in the day of the Master's coming.

We should also by faith desire such a calling as Providence evidently has arranged and intended for us. Some persons have never had a free choice of what vocation they would follow ; for from their birth, position, surroundings, and connections they are set in a certain line of things, like carriages on the tram lines, and they must follow on the appointed track, or stand still. Faith expects to hear the voice behind it saying, " This is the way, walk ye in it." Trusting to our own judgment often means following our own whims ; but faith seeks direction from infallible wisdom, and so it is led in a right way. God knows your capacity better than you do ; entreat Him to choose your inheritance for you. If the flowers were to revolt against the gardener, and each one should select its own soil, most of them would pine and die through their unsuitable position, but he who has studied their nature knows that this flower needs shade and damp ; and another needs sunlight and a light soil ; and so he puts his plants where they are most likely to flourish. God doeth the same with us. He hath made some to be kings, though few of those plants flourish much. He has made many to be poor, and the soil of poverty, though damp and cold, has produced many a glorious harvest for the great Reaper. The Lord has set some in places of peril, places from which they would gladly escape, but they are there preserved by His hand ; He has planted many others in the quiet shade of obscurity, and they blossom to the praise of the great Husbandman.

So, then, you see, faith has much to do with the force and direction of our life in the flesh. It provides impetus by giving a man something to live for ; it shows him the far-reaching influences of the thoughts and deeds of to-day, and how they issue in eternal results ; and faith also takes the helm and steers the vessel along a safe channel towards the haven of holy rest. Happy are they who in the early days of their youth believe in Him who loved them and gave Himself for them, and so begin their life-walk with Jesus. Blessed be God for converting some of us while we were yet boys and girls. O happy young people, who begin life with the early dew of grace upon them ! No prince of eastern empires was ever so richly bejewelled ! You will not in after-days have to lament a score years spent in error, or half a life wasted in sin, or a whole seventy years frittered away in idleness. O that you, who are yet young, who have the world before you, may now be led by the Spirit to follow Christ, who pleased not Himself but did the will of His Father, so shall the life that you live in the flesh be lived by the faith of the Son of God who loved you and gave Himself for you.

II. Secondly, FAITH LEADS A MAN TO LOOK TO GOD FOR HELP IN HIS ORDINARY AVOCATION. Here, again, it has a great influence over him. A believer may seek of God the *qualifications* for his particular calling. "What," say you, "may we pray about such things ?" Yes. The labourer may appeal to God for strength ; the artisan may ask God for skill ; the student may seek God for help to quicken his intelligence. David was a great warrior, and he attributed his valour to God who taught his hands to war and his fingers to fight. We read of Bezaleel, and of the women that were wise-hearted, that God had taught them, so that they made all manner of embroidery and metal work for the house of the Lord. In those days they used to reckon skill and invention to be the gifts of God ; this wretched century has grown too wise to honour any God but its own idolized self. If you pray over your work I am persuaded you will be helped in it. If for your calling you are as yet but slenderly qualified, you may every morning pray God to help you that you may be careful and observant as an apprentice or a beginner ; for has He not promised that as your day your strength shall be ? A mind which is trusting in the Lord is in the best condition for acquiring knowledge, and getting understanding.

As to your *behaviour* also in your work, there is room for faith and prayer. For, O brethren, whether qualified or not for any particular offices of this life, our conduct is the most important matter. It is well to be clever, but it is essential to be pure. I would have you masters of your trades, but I am even more earnest that you should be honest, truthful, and holy. About this we may confidently go to God and ask Him to lead us in a plain path, and to hold up our goings that we slip not. He can and will help us to behave ourselves wisely. "Lead us not into temptation" is one sentence of our daily prayer, and we may further ask that when we are in the temptation we may be delivered from the evil. We need prudence, and faith remembers that if any lack wisdom he may ask of God. Godliness teaches the young men prudence, the babes knowledge and discretion. See how Joseph prospered in Egypt because the Lord was with him. He was placed in very difficult positions, on one occasion in a position of the most terrible danger, but he escaped by saying, "How can I do this great wickedness and sin against God ?" A sense of God's presence preserved him then and at all other times. He was set over all the house of Potiphar because God was with him. And so, dear friends, engaged in service or in business, you may go to your heavenly Father and ask Him to guide you with His counsel, and you may rest assured that He will order all your way, so that your daily calling shall not hinder your heavenly calling, nor your conduct belie your profession.

Faith bids you seek help from God as to the *success* of your daily calling. Know ye not what David says, "Except the Lord build the house, they labour in vain that build it. It is vain for you to rise up early, to sit up late, to eat the bread of sorrows : for so He giveth His beloved sleep." It is a most pleasant thing to be able by faith to consult the holy oracle about everything, whether it arises in trade, or in the family, or in the church. We may say with Abraham's servant, " O Lord, I pray Thee send me good speed this day." You may expect success if you thus seek it : and peradventure some of you would have prospered more if you had more believingly sought the Lord. I say " peradventure," because God does not always prosper even His own people in outward things, since it is sometimes better for their souls that they should be in adversity, and then the highest prosperity is a want of prosperity. Faith quiets the heart in this matter by enabling us to leave results in the hand of God.

Faith acts also in reference to our *surroundings*. We are all very much influenced by those about us. God can raise us up friends who will be eminently helpful to us, and we may pray Him to do so : He can put us into a circle of society in which we shall find much assistance in this life's affairs, and also in our progress towards heaven ; and concerning this we know that " The steps of a good man are ordered of the Lord." Faith will keep you clear of evil company, and constrain you to seek the society of the excellent of this earth, and thus it will colour your whole life. If there be no friends to help him, the believer's dependence is so fixed upon God, that he goes forward in cheerful confidence knowing that the Lord alone is sufficient for him ; yet, if he be encouraged and assisted by friends, he looks upon it as God's doing, as much as when David was strengthened by those who came to him in the cave.

Do you say, We see the connection of this with faith, but how with faith upon the Son of God who loved us and gave Himself for us ? I answer,—Our Saviour as the object of our faith is also the object of our imitation, and you know, brethren, how in all things He rested upon God. Whenever He undertook a great enterprise you find Him spending a night in prayer. If anybody could have dispensed with prayer it was our Lord Jesus ; if any man that ever lived could have found his own way without heavenly guidance it was Christ the Son of God. If then He was much in prayer and exercised faith in the great Father, much more should you and I bring everything before God. We should live in the flesh expecting that the Lord Jesus will be with us even to the end, and that we shall be upheld and comforted by His sympathetic love and tenderness. Faith enables us to follow Jesus as the great Shepherd of the sheep, and to expect to be led in a right way, and daily upheld and sustained until the Redeemer shall come to receive us unto Himself.

III. Thirdly, faith exercises a power over a man's life of a remarkable kind because IT LEADS HIM TO SERVE GOD IN HIS DAILY CALLING. Never is life more ennobled than when we do all things as unto God. This makes drudgery sublime, and links the poorest menial with the brightest angel. Seraphs serve God in heaven, and you and I may serve Him in the pulpit or in the kitchen, and be as accepted as they are. Brethren, Christian men are helped by faith to serve God in their calling *by obedience to God's commands*, by endeavouring to order everything according to the rules of love to God and love to men. In such a case integrity and uprightness preserve the man, and his business becomes true worship. Though there be no straining after eccentric unworldliness and superstitious singularity, yet in doing that which is right and just, the common tradesman is separated unto the service of the Lord. Jesus says, " If any man serve Me let him follow Me," as much as to say that obedience to the divine command is the true mode of showing love to Jesus. If thou wishest to do something great for God, be greatly careful to obey His commands : for " to obey is better than sacrifice, and to hearken than the fat of rams."

Godly men exercise faith in God in their callings by trying to *manifest a Christian spirit* in all that they do. The spirit which actuates us may seem to be a small matter so long as we are outwardly right ; but it is in reality the essence of the whole thing. Take away the flavour from the fruit, or the fragrance from the flower, and what is left ? such is correct living without the savour of grace. The same thing can be done in several ways : you can do a right thing in so wrong a way as to make it wrong. Even in giving to the poor, a churl will trample upon their feelings in the very act of his charity ; while I have known others who have been unable to give who, nevertheless, have expressed their inability in so kindly a form that they have comforted the disappointed applicant. Oh, to act in your trade and your calling as Christ would have acted had He been in your place. Hang that question up in your houses, " What would Jesus do ? " and then think of another, " How would Jesus do it ? " for what He would do, and how He would do it, may always stand as the best guide to us. Thus faith puts a man upon serving God by leading him to exhibit the spirit of Christ in what he ordinarily does, showing all courtesy, gentleness, forbearance, charity, and grace.

Furthermore, in all that we do, we should be *aiming at God's glory.* We should do everything as unto God, and not unto men. There would be no eye-service if we left off being men pleasers and began to please God. Neither would there be impatience under injustice ; for if men do not accept our service when we have done it with all our hearts, we shall comfort ourselves with the reflection that our Master in heaven knows how little we deserve the unrighteous censure. To live as kings and priests unto God is the cream of living. Then will you be the Lord's free men. Serve God in serving men, and serve men by serving God : there is a way of working out those two sentences even to the full, and thus rendering life sublime. May God the Holy Spirit teach us to do this. If we really live to serve God we shall live intensely day by day, allowing no time to waste. Sophia Cook sought Mr. Wesley's counsel as to what she should do in life, and he answered, " Live to-day " : a very short direction, but one that is full of wisdom. " Live to-day," and to-morrow you may do the same. Plans for the whole term of life many of you may not be able to construct, but mind that you work while it is called to-day. " Son, go work to-day in My vineyard " is the great Father's word. How would a man live if he felt that he was specially to live for God *this day ?* Suppose that to-day there was a vow upon you, or some other bond, by which you felt that this whole day was solemnly consecrated to the Lord ; how would you behave yourself ? So ought you to behave this day, and every day ; for you belong wholly to Him who loved you, and gave Himself for you. Let the love of Christ constrain us in this matter : let us put on the yoke of Christ, and feel at once that we are His blood-bought possession, and His servants for ever, because by faith He has become ours and we are His. We ought to live as Christ's men in every little as well as in every great matter ; whether we eat or drink, or whatsoever we do, we should do all to the glory of God, giving thanks unto God and the Father by Christ Jesus. Thus, you see, faith in Him who gave Himself for us leads us to spend our energies in His service, and to do our ordinary work with an eye to His glory, and so our life is coloured and savoured by our faith in the Son of God.

IV.   Fourthly, faith has a very beneficial influence upon the life that we live in the flesh, for IT RECON-CILES A MAN TO THE DISCOMFORTS OF HIS CALLING. It is not every calling that is easy or lucrative, or honoured among men. It is a happy circumstance when a man has espoused a business which is so congenial with his taste that he would not change it for another if he could : but some find their trades irksome to them. This is an evil under the sun. Some employments are despised by the thoughtless, and involve much self-denial, and hence those who follow them need much faith to enable them to live above the trials of their position. Faith teaches the humble worker to see Jesus in all His lowliness, condescending to take upon Himself the form of a servant for our sakes. Faith reads, " Jesus, knowing that he came forth from God and went to God, took a towel, and girded Himself, and washed His disciples' feet." That was one of the most menial of employments, and if our Lord and Master did not disdain it why should we be ashamed of the humblest form of service ? From henceforth let no man trouble you, but rejoice because the poor man's Saviour was a servant even as you are, and He too was " despised and rejected of men."

Your faith ought to help you by arousing your gratitude for deliverance from a far worse drudgery. You did for Satan things of which you are now ashamed. Any work for the devil, and for his black cause, would be dishonourable : to rule an empire for Satan would disgrace us ; to wear the crown put on our heads by sinning would be a horrible curse, but to wash feet for Christ is glorious service. There is no degradation in anything that is done for God. Faith in God sanctifies the man, and his calling, too, and makes it pleasant to him to carry the cross of Christ in his daily labour. There are some who hold their heads high, who, nevertheless, do things that are disgraceful to humanity, but surely you and I ought never to think anything a hardship which falls to our lot by the appointment of divine providence.

Faith is a great teacher of humility ; for it bids us think little of ourselves, and rest alone in God ; and because it fosters humility it renders a man's task pleasant when else it would be irksome. Pride makes a man stiff in the back : there are some works which he cannot do though he would be happy enough in doing them if he had not such foolish ideas of his own importance. Hard work is no disgrace to any man ; it is far more degrading to be leading the life of a fashionable do-nothing. When the Lord makes us feel that we are poor, undeserving creatures, we do not mind taking the lowest room, or doing the meanest work, for we feel that as long as we are out of hell and have a hope of heaven, the meanest service is an honour to us. We are glad enough to be where God would have us be, seeing Christ has loved us and given himself for us.

Faith also removes discomforts by reminding us that they will not last long. Faith says of trial, "Bear it! The time is short. Soon the Saviour cometh, and the poorest of His followers shall then reign with Him." Toil on, O weary one, for the morning light will put an end to thy labour, which lasts only through the hours of darkness. The glory breaks; the night is wearing away, and the dawn appeareth. Therefore patiently wait and quietly hope, for thou shalt see the salvation of God. Thus faith takes the thorns from our pillow, and makes us learn in whatsoever state we are therewith to be content. Call you this nothing? Has not Jesus done much for us when by faith in Him we have learned to endure the ills of life with sweet content?

V. Fifthly, faith has this further influence upon ordinary life—THAT IT CASTS ALL THE BURDEN OF IT UPON THE LORD. Faith is the great remover of yokes, and it does this in part by making us submissive to God's will. When we have learned to submit we cease to repine. Faith teaches us so to believe in God, infallible wisdom and perfect love, that we consent unto the Lord's will and rejoice in it. Faith teaches us to look to the end of every present trial, and to know that it works together for good; thus again reconciling us to the passing grief which it causes. Faith teaches us to depend upon the power of God to help us in the trial, and through the trial, and in this way we are no longer stumbled by afflictions, but rise above them as on eagles' wings. Brethren, if any of you are anxious, careworn, and worried, stop not in such a state of mind; it cannot do you any good; and it reflects no honour upon your great Father. Pray for more faith, that you may have no back-breaking load to carry, but may transfer it to the great Burden-bearer. Pray to your great Lord so to strengthen and ease your heart that your only care may be to please Him, and that you may be released from all other care. By this means will you be greatly helped, for if the burden be lightened, it comes to much the same thing as if the strength were multiplied. Content with the divine will is better than increase of riches, or removal of affliction, for with wealth no peace may come; and out of prosperity no joy in the Lord may arise, but contentment is peace itself.

Whatever burden faith finds in her daily avocation she casts it upon God by prayer. We begin with God in the morning, seeking help to do our work, and to do it well. At His hands we seek guidance and prosperity from hour to hour. We pray Him to prevent our doing any wrong to others, or suffering any wrong from them; and we ask Him to keep our temper and to preserve our spirit while we are with worldly men. We beg that we may not be infected by the evil example of others, and that our example may be such as may be safely followed. These are our great concerns in business; we tremble lest in anything we should dishonour God, and we trust in Him to keep us. A believer goes to God with the matters of each day, and looks for the morning dew to fall upon him; he looks up through the day expecting the Lord to be his constant shield, and at night ere he goes to rest he empties out the gathered troubles of the day, and so falls to a happy sleep. Then doth a man live sweetly when he lives by the day, trusting his Lord with everything, and finding God to be ever near.

To all this the example of the Saviour leads us, and His love within our hearts draws us. "He trusted on the Lord that He would deliver him," and "was heard in that he feared."

VI. Sixthly, faith hath a happy influence upon the present life, for IT MODERATES A MAN'S FEELINGS AS TO THE RESULT OF HIS WORK. Sometimes the result of our work is prosperity, and here the grace of God prevents a surfeit of worldly things. There is a keen test of character in prosperity. Everybody longs for it, but it is not every man that can bear it when it comes. True faith forbids our setting great store by worldly goods and pleasures and enjoyments, for it teaches us that our treasure is in heaven. If we begin to idolize the things that are seen, we shall soon degenerate and turn aside from God. How easily we may spoil a blessing! Two friends gathered each a rose: the one was continually smelling at it, touching its leaves and handling it as if he could not hold it too fast; you do not wonder that it was soon withered. The other took his rose, enjoyed its perfume moderately, carried it in his hand for a while, and then placed it on the table in water, and hours after it was almost as fresh as when it was plucked from the bough. We may dote on our worldly gear until God becomes jealous of it, and sends a blight upon it; and, on the other hand, we may with holy moderateness use these things as not abusing them, and get from them the utmost good which they are capable of conveying to us. Many pursue wealth or fame as some eager boy hunts the painted butterfly: at last, after a long and weary run, he dashes it down with his cap, and with the stroke he spoils its beauty. Many a man hath reached the summit of a life-long ambition and found it to be mere vanity. In gaining all he has lost all; wealth has come, but the power to enjoy it has gone; life has been worn out in the pursuit, and no strength is left with which to enjoy the gain. It shall not be so with the man who lives by faith, for his chief joys are above, and his comfort lies within. To him God is joy so rich that other joy is comparatively flavourless.

But perchance the result of all our work may be adversity. Some men row very hard, and yet their boat makes no headway. When an opportunity presents itself the tide of trade suddenly turns against them. When they have corn in the mill the wind does not blow. Perhaps they lose all but their character, and then it is that faith comes in to cheer them under the disaster. I am deeply grieved when I hear of persons committing suicide because they were in difficulties: it is a dreadful thing thus to rush before one's Creator unbidden. Faith sustains the heart and puts aside all thought of such desperate attempts to fly from present griefs by plunging into far more awful woes. We shall bear up and come through our trials triumphantly if we have faith in God. If our heavenly Father has appointed a bitter cup for us shall we not drink it? If the fields which we have tilled yield no harvests, and the beasts that we have foddered die in the stall, shall we not bow the head and say, "The Lord hath done it"? Must it not be right if the Lord ordains it? let us bless Him still. If not, it will be our unbelief which hinders. How many have been happy in poverty, happier than they were in wealth! How often have the saints rejoiced more during sickness than in their health. Payson declared that during illness he felt happier than he had ever been, far happier than he had ever expected to be. Though bereavement has come into the family, and sickness unto the household, yet faith has learned to sing in all weathers because her God is still the same.

O brothers and sisters, faith is a precious preparative for anything and everything that comes; mind that you have it always ready for action. Do not leave it at home in time of storm as the foolish seaman left his anchor. It is not a grace to be shut up in a closet, or fastened to a communion table, or boxed up in a pew, but it is an everyday grace which is to be our companion in the shop and in the market, in the parlour and in the kitchen, in the workroom and in the field; ay, it may go into the workhouse with the poor, as well as into the mansion with the rich; it may either cheer the dreary hours of the infirmary, or sanctify the sunny weeks of holiday. Faith is for every place in which a good man may lawfully be found. "Should fate command you to the utmost verge of the green earth, to rivers unknown to song," yet shall a childlike faith in God find you a home in every clime, under every sky. Oh, to feel the power of it, as to all that comes of our labour, that the life which we live in the flesh may be lived by faith in the Son of God, who loved us and gave Himself for us.

VII. Seventhly, faith has this sweet influence upon our present life, that IT ENABLES A MAN CHEERFULLY TO LEAVE HIS OCCUPATION WHEN THE TIME COMES. A Christian may have to quit a favourite vocation on account of circumstances over which he has no control; he may have to emigrate to a distant land, or altogether to change his mode of living, and this may involve many a wrench to his feelings. It is not always easy to leave the old house, and all its surroundings, and to take a long journey; nor is it pleasant to change one's settled habits and begin life anew; yet true faith sets loose by worldly things, and is ready to haul up the anchor and make sail at the divine bidding. The believer says, "Command my journey, and I go." I am but a tent dweller, and must expect to be on the move. Like Israel in the desert, we must follow the cloud, and journey or rest as the cloud ordains, for here we have no continuing city, but we seek one to come. Faith has the same gracious influence upon those who enjoy unbroken prosperity; it keeps them from taking root in the soil of earth, and this is a miracle of grace.

Sometimes our vocations have to be given up through weakness or old age. It is a hard pinch to many a busy man when he feels that he has no more strength for business, when he perceives that other and more vigorous minds must be allowed to step into the long occupied position. The workman cannot bear to feel that his hand has lost its cunning: it is a sharp experience. Faith is of essential service here. It helps a man to say, "My Master, I am one of the vessels of Thy house; if Thou wilt use me I will be glad; but if Thou wilt put me on the shelf, I will be glad too. It must be best for me to be as Thou wouldst have me." If faith resigns herself to the supreme wisdom and love and goodness of Christ, and says, "Do with me even as Thou wilt: use me, or set me aside," then retirement will be a release from care and no source of distress. The evening of advanced age may be spent as joyfully as the noontide of manhood if the mind be stayed on God. "They shall bring forth fruit in old age" is a promise full often realized by believers, for all around me are venerable brethren who are more useful and more happy than ever, though the infirmities of years are growing upon them.

And then comes at last the leaving of your vocation by death, which will arrive in due time to us all. Then faith displays its utmost energy of blessing. Brethren, may we meet death as Moses did, who when God bade him climb the mountain, for there he must die, uttered no word of sorrow, but like a child obeyed his father, went upstairs to bed, looked wistfully out at the window upon the promised land, and then fell asleep. How sweet to look upon the goodly land and Lebanon, and then to be kissed to sleep by his Father's own mouth, and to be buried man knoweth not where. His work was done, and his rest was come. Beautiful are the departing words of Samuel when, laying down his office, he can challenge all men to bear witness to his character. Happy man, so spent amid universal blessing. O that each one of us may be ready to render in his account before the judgment-seat of Christ—let the last day come when it may.

Our Master, by whose love we have been endowed with faith, has taught us how to die as well as how to live. He could say, "I have finished the work which Thou gavest me to do," and He would have us say it. Thrice happy man who, in laying down the shepherd's crook or the carpenter's plane, in putting aside the ledger or the class-book, never to open them again, can exclaim, "I have fought a good fight; I have kept the faith; henceforth there is laid up for me a crown of life which fadeth not away." Good old Mede, the Puritan, when he was very old, and leaning on his staff, was asked how he was, and he answered, "Why, going home as fast as I can; as every honest man ought to do when his day's work is done: and I bless God I have a good home to go to." Dear aged saints, so near home, does not faith transform death from an enemy into a friend, as it brings the glory so near to you? You will soon be in the Father's house and leave me behind; and yet I cannot tell: I remember that the other disciple did outrun Peter, and came first to the sepulchre, and so, perhaps, may I. You have the start of us in years, but we may be called home before you, for there are last that shall be first. Let death come when it may we shall not be afraid, for Jesus, who has loved us and given Himself for us, is the resurrection and the life. Living this life in the flesh by faith upon the Son of God, we are waiting for the usher of the black rod to bring a message from the King to summon us to meet Him in the upper house. Why should we be loth to go? What is there here that we should wait? What is there on this poor earth to detain a heaven-born and heaven-bound spirit? Nay, let us go, for He is gone in whom our treasure is, whose beauties have engrossed our love. He is not here, why should we desire to linger? He has risen, let us rise.

Thus, from the beginning to the end of the life that we live in the flesh, faith upon the Son of God answereth all things, and all its paths drop fatness.

CHRISTUS ET EGO

" I am crucified with Christ : nevertheless I live ; yet not I, but Christ liveth in me : and the life which I now live in the flesh I live by the faith of the Son of God, who loved me, and gave Himself for me."—Galatians ii. 20.

IN great ranges of mountains there are lofty peaks which pierce the clouds, but, on the other hand, there are, here and there, lower parts of the range which are crossed by travellers, become national highways, and afford passages for commerce from land to land. My text rises before my contemplation like a lofty range of mountains, a very Andes for elevation. I shall not attempt, this morning, to climb the summits of its sublimity : we have not the time, we fear we have not the skill for such work, but I shall, to the best of my ability, conduct you over one or two practical truths, which may be serviceable to us this morning, and introduce us to sunny fields of contemplation.

I. At once to our work. I call upon you to observe very carefully, in the first place, THE PERSON-ALITY OF THE CHRISTIAN RELIGION *as it is exhibited in the text before us.*

How many personal pronouns of the first person are there in this verse ? Are there not as many as eight ? It swarms with *I* and *me.* The text deals not with the plural at all ; it does not mention some one else, nor a third party far away, but the apostle treats of himself, his own inner life, his own spiritual death, the love of Christ to *him,* and the great sacri-fice which Christ made for *him.* " Who loved *me,* and gave himself for *me."* This is instructive, for it is a distinguishing mark of the Christian religion, that it brings out a man's individuality. It does not make us selfish ; on the contrary, it cures us of that evil, but still it does manifest in us a self-hood by which we become conscious of our personal individuality in an eminent degree. In the nocturnal heavens there had long been observed bright masses of light : the astronomers called them " nebulæ " ; they supposed them to be stores of unfashioned chaotic matter, until the telescope of Herschell resolved them into distinct stars. What the telescope did for stars, the religion of Christ, when received into the heart, does for men. Men think of them-selves as mixed up with the race, or swamped in the community, or absorbed in universal manhood ; they have a very indistinct idea of their separate obligations to God, and their personal relations to His govern-ment, but the gospel, like a telescope, brings a man out of himself, makes him see himself, as a separate existence, and compels him to meditate upon his own sin, his own salvation, and his own personal doom unless saved by grace. In the broad road there are so many travellers, that as one takes a bird's eye view of it, it appears to be filled with a vast mob of men moving on without order ; but in the straight and narrow way which leadeth unto life eternal, every traveller is distinct ; he attracts your notice ; he is a marked man. Having to go against the general current of the times, the believer is an individual upon whom observant eyes are fixed. He is a distinct individual, both to himself and the rest of his kind. You will very readily see how the religion of Jesus Christ brings out a man's in-dividuality *in its very dawn ;* it reveals to him his own personal sin and consequent danger. You know

nothing about conversion if you merely believe in human depravity and human ruin, but have never felt that *you* are depraved, and that *you yourself* are ruined. Over and above all the general woes of the race, there will be one particular woe of your own, if you have been by the Holy Spirit convinced of sin ; you will cry, like that shrill-voiced prophet of Jerusalem, in the days of the siege, " Woe unto myself also " ; you will feel as if the arrows of God were mainly aimed at you, and as if the curses of the law would surely fall upon you if upon none else. Certainly, beloved hearer, you know nothing about salvation unless you have *personally looked with your own eye to Jesus Christ.* There must be a personal reception of the Lord Jesus into the arms of your faith, and into the bosom of your love ; and, if you have not trusted in the Crucified while standing alone in contemplation at the foot of the cross, you have not believed unto life eternal.

Then, in consequence of a separate personal faith, the believer enjoys *a personal peace ;* he feels that if earth were all at arms abroad, he would still find rest in Christ, that rest being peculiarly his own, independently of his fellows. He may talk of that peace to others, but he cannot communicate it ; others cannot give it to him, nor can they take it from him. Wherever the Christian religion is truly in the soul, it soon leads to *a personal consecration* to God. The man comes to the altar of Christ, and he cries, " Here I am ; O most glorious Lord, I feel it to be my reasonable service to give spirit, soul, and body, unto Thee. Let others do as they will ; as for me and my house, we will serve the Lord." The renewed man feels that the work of others does not exonerate him from service, and the general lukewarmness of the Christian church cannot be an excuse for his own indifference. He stands out against error, if need be, as a lone protestor, like Athanasius, crying, " I, Athanasius, against the whole world," or he works for God in the building up of Jerusalem, like Nehemiah, being content to work alone if others will not assist him. He has discovered himself to have been personally lost, and to have been saved personally, and now his prayer is, " Lord, show me what Thou wouldst have *me* to do ; here am *I,* send *me."* I believe that in proportion as our piety is definitely in the first person singular, it will be strong and vigorous. I believe, moreover, that in proportion as we fully realise our personal responsibility to God, we shall be likely to discharge it ; if we have not really understood it, we are very likely to dream of work for God by proxy, to pay the priest or the minister to be useful for us, and act as if we could shift our responsibility from our own shoulders to the back of a society or a church. From its dawn up to its noonday glory, the personality of true godliness is most observable. All the teaching of our holy faith bears in this direction. We preach personal election, personal calling, personal regenera-tion, personal perseverance, personal holiness, and we know nothing of any work of grace which is not personal to the professor of it. There is no doctrine in Scripture which teaches that one man can be saved by the godliness of another. I cannot discover anything like salvation by sponsorship, except in the one case of the sponsorship of the Lord Jesus Christ. I find no human being placed in the stead of another, so as to be able to take another's burden of sin, or perform another's duty. I do find that we are to bear one another's burdens in respect of sympathy, but not in the sense of substitution. Every man must bear his own burden, and give an account for himself before God. Moreover, the ordinances of the Christian religion teach us the same. When a man is typically buried with Christ by the public act of baptism, he cannot be dead for another, or buried for another, nor can he rise again instead of another. There is the personal act of immersion to show forth our personal death to the world, personal burial with Christ, and personal resurrection with Him. So also, in the Supper of the Lord, the distinct act of each man eating and drinking for himself, most manifestly sets forth that we stand as individuals before the Lord our God in our connection with the Lord Jesus Christ. Now, I feel earnest that nothing should ever spoil the effect of this truth upon our minds. It is so simple a truth, that when I make the statement, you perhaps wonder that I should repeat it so often; but simple as it is, it is constantly being forgotten. How many church members shelter themselves behind the vigorous action of the entire community! The church is being increased, the church opens schools, the church builds new houses of prayer, and so the church member flatters himself that he is doing somewhat, whereas that very man may not have, either by his contributions, or his prayers, or his personal teachings, done anything at all. O idle church member, I beseech thee, shake thyself from the dust ; be not so mean as to appropriate other men's labours. Before thine own Master, thou shalt stand or fall upon thine own individual service or neglect, and if thou bringest forth no fruit thyself, all the fruit upon the other boughs shall not avail thee. "Every tree which bringeth not forth good fruit is hewn down, and cast into the fire." Every branch in Me that beareth not fruit He taketh away."

Common enough is it, also, for persons to shelter themselves behind a society. A small annual contribution has often been a cloak for gross indifference to holy effort. Somebody else is paid to be a missionary, and to do your mission-work : is this the Lord's way ? Is this the path of obedience ? Does not our Lord say to me, "As My Father hath sent Me, even so send I you"? Now the Father did not send Christ that He might procure a proxy and be a nominal Redeemer, but Jesus gave Himself for us in personal service and sacrifice : even so does Jesus send us forth to suffer and to serve. It is well to support the minister ; it is well to pay the city missionary that he may have his time to give to needful work ; it is well to assist the Bible-woman that she may go from house to house, but remember, when all the societies have done all that is possible, they cannot exonerate you from your own peculiar calling, and however large your contributions to assist others to serve the Master, they cannot discharge on your behalf one single particle of what was due from you personally to your Lord. Let me pray you, brethren and sisters, if you have ever sheltered behind the work of others, stand forth in your own proper character, and remember that before God you must be estimated by what *you* have felt, what *you* have known, what you have *learned*, and what you have done.

The worst form of the mischief is when persons imagine that family piety and national religion can ever be available in lieu of individual repentance and faith. Absurd as it may seem, yet a very common thing it is for people to say, " Oh, yes ! we are all Christians—of course, we are all Christians—every Englishman is a Christian. We do not belong to the Brahmins or Mahometans: we are all Christians." What grosser lie can a man invent than that ? Is a man a Christian because he lives in England ? Is a rat a horse because it lives in a stable ? That is just as good reasoning. A man must be born again or he is no child of God. A man must have living faith in the Lord Jesus Christ, or else he is no Christian, and he does but mock the name of Christian when he takes it upon himself without having part or lot in the matter.

Others say, "My mother and my father always professed such a religion, therefore I am bound to do the same." Glorious reasoning, fit for idiots most surely ! Have you never heard of that old Pagan monarch who professed conversion, and was about to step into the baptismal font, when, turning round to the bishop, he said, " Where did my father go when he died, before your religion came here, and where did his father go, and all the kings that were before me who worshipped Woden and Thor ? Where did they go when they died ? Tell me at once ! " The Bishop shook his head, and looked very sorrowful, and said he was afraid they were gone to a very dark place. " Ah ! then," said he, " I will not be separated from them." Back he started, and remained an unwashed heathen still. You suppose that this folly expired in the dark ages ! It survives and flourishes in the present. We have known persons impressed under the gospel, who have nevertheless clung to the false hopes of superstition or human merit, and have excused themselves by saying, " You see, I have always been brought up to it." Does a man think that because his mother was poor, or his father a pauper, that he himself must necessarily remain a beggar ? If my parent was blind, am I bound to put out my own eyes to be like him ? Nay, but if I have beheld the light of the truth of Jesus Christ, let me follow it, and not be drawn aside by the idea that hereditary superstition is any the less dangerous or erroneous because a dozen generations have been deluded by it. You must appear before God, my dear friend, on your own feet, and neither mother nor father can stand in your stead, therefore judge for yourself ; seek for yourself eternal life ; lift up your eyes to Christ's cross for yourself, and let it be your own earnest endeavour that you yourself may be able to say, " He loved *me*, and gave Himself for *me*." We are all born alone : we come as sorrowful pilgrims into this world to traverse a path which only our own feet can tread. To a great extent we go through the world alone, for all our companions are but vessels sailing with us side by side, vessels distinct and bearing each one its own flag. Into the depths of our heart no man can dive. There are cabinets in the chamber of the soul which no man can open but the individual himself. We must die alone, friends may surround the bed, but the departing spirit must take its flight by itself. We shall hear no tramp of thousands as we descend into the dark river, we shall be solitary travellers into the unknown land.

We expect to stand before the judgment seat in the midst of a great assembly, but still to be judged as if no other man were there. If all that multitude be condemned, and we are in Christ, we shall be saved, and if they should all be saved, and we are found wanting, we shall be cast away. In the balances we shall each be placed alone. There is a crucible for every ingot of gold, a furnace for every bar of silver. In the resurrection every seed shall receive his own body. There shall be an individuality about the frame that shall be raised in that day of wonders, an individuality most marked and manifest. If I am condemned at the last, no man can be damned for my spirit ; no soul can enter the chambers of fire on my behalf, to endure for me the unutterable anguish. And, blessed hope, if I am saved, it will be *I* who shall see the King in His beauty : mine eyes shall behold Him, and not another in my stead. The joys of heaven shall not be proxy joys, but the personal enjoyments of those who have had personal union with Christ. You all know this, and therefore, I pray you, let the weighty truth abide with you. No man in his senses thinks that another can eat for him, or drink for him, or be clothed for him, or sleep for him, or wake for him. No man is content nowadays with a second person's owning money for him, or possessing an estate for him : men long to have riches themselves ; they wish to be personally happy, to be personally honoured ; they do not care that the good things of this life shall be merely nominally theirs, while other men grasp the reality ; they wish to have a real grasp and grip of all temporal goods. O let us not play the fool with eternal things, but let us desire to have a personal interest in Christ, and then let us aspire to give to Him, who deserves it so well, our personal service, rendering spirit, soul, and body, unto His cause.

II. Secondly, our text very plainly TEACHES US THE INTERWEAVING OF OUR OWN PROPER PERSONALITY WITH THAT OF JESUS CHRIST.

Read the text over again, " I am crucified with Christ : nevertheless I live ; yet not I, but Christ liveth in me : and the life which I now live in the flesh I live by the faith of the Son of God, who loved me, and gave Himself for me." Here is the man, but here is the Son of God quite as conspicuously and the two personalities are singularly interwoven. I think I see two trees before me. They are distinct plants growing side by side, but as I follow them downward, I observe that the roots are so interlaced and intertwisted that no one can trace the separate trees and allot the members of each to its proper whole. Such are Christ and the believer. Methinks I see before me a vine. Yonder is a branch, distinct and perfect as a branch ; it is not to be mistaken for any other, it is a branch, a whole and perfect branch, yet how perfectly is it joined to the stem, and how completely is its individuality merged in the one vine of which it is a member ! Now, so is it with the believer in Christ.

There was one parent man who threw his shadow across our path, and from whose influence we never could escape. From all other men we might have struggled away and claimed to be separate, but this one man was part of ourselves, and we part of him—Adam the first, in his fallen state : we are fallen with him, and are broken in pieces in his ruin. And now, glory be to God, as the shadow of the first man has been uplifted from us, there appears a second man, the Lord from heaven ; and across

our path there falls the light of His glory and His excellence, from which also, blessed be God, we who have believed in Him cannot escape : in the light of that Man, the second Adam, the heavenly federal Head of all His people—in His light we do rejoice. Interwoven with our history and personality is the history and personality of the Man Christ Jesus, and we are for ever one with Him.

Observe the points of contact. First Paul says, *I am " crucified with Christ " ;* what does he intend ? He means a great many more things than I can tell you this morning ; but, briefly, he means this : he believed in the representation of Christ on the cross ; he held that when Jesus Christ hung upon the tree, He did not hang there as a private person, but as the representative of all His chosen people. As the burgess in the House of Commons votes not for himself alone, but in the name of the township which has sent him to Parliament, so the Lord Jesus Christ acted in what He did as a great public representative person, and the dying of Jesus Christ upon the tree was the virtual dying of all His people. Then all His saints rendered unto justice what was due, and made an expiation to divine vengeance for all their sins. *" I am crucified with Christ."* The apostle of the Gentiles delighted to think that as one of Christ's chosen people, he died upon the tree in Christ. He did more than believe this doctrinally, however ; he accepted it confidently, resting his hope upon it. He believed that by virtue of Jesus Christ's death, he had himself paid the law its due, satisfied divine justice, and found reconciliation with God. Beloved, what a blessed thing it is when the soul can, as it were, stretch itself upon the cross of Christ, and feel " I am dead ; the law has killed me, cursed me, slain me, and I am therefore free from its power, because in my Surety I have borne the curse, and in the person of my Substitute the whole that the law could do, by way of condemnation, has been executed upon me, for I am crucified with Christ." Oh, how blessed it is when the cross of Christ is laid upon us, how it quickens us ! Just as the aged prophet went up, and stretched himself upon the dead child, put his mouth upon the child's mouth, and his hands upon the child's hands, and his feet upon the child's feet, and then the child was quickened, so when the cross is laid upon my soul, it puts life, power, warmth, and comfort into me. Union with the suffering, bleeding Saviour, and faith in the merit of the Redeemer, are soul cheering things : O for more enjoyment of them ! Paul meant even more than this. He not only believed in Christ's death and trusted in it, but he actually felt its power in himself in causing the crucifixion of his old corrupt nature. If you conceive of yourself as a man executed, you at once perceive that, being executed by the law, the law has no further claim upon you ; you resolve, moreover, that having once proven the curse of sin by the sentence passed upon you, you will not fall into that same offence again, but henceforth, being miraculously delivered from the death into which the law brought you, you will live in newness of life. You must feel so if you feel rightly. Thus did Paul view himself as a criminal upon whom the sentence of the law had been fulfilled. When he saw the pleasures of sin, he said, " I cannot enjoy these : I am dead to them. I once had a life in which these were very sweet to me, but I have been crucified with Christ ; consequently, as a dead man can have no delight in the joys which once were delights to him, so neither can I." When Paul looked upon the carnal things of the world, he said, " I once allowed these things to reign over me. What shall I eat ? what shall I drink ? and wherewithal shall I be clothed ? These were a trinity of questions of the utmost importance : they are of no importance now, because I am dead to these things ; I cast my care upon God with regard to them ; they are not my life ; I am crucified to them." If any passion, if any motive, if any design should come into our mind, short of the cross of Christ, we should exclaim, " God forbid that I should glory in any of these things ; I am a dead man. Come, world, with all thy witchery ; come, pleasure, with all thy charms ; come, wealth, with all thy temptations ; come, all ye tempters that have seduced so many ; what can you do with a crucified man ? How can you tempt one who is dead to you ? " Now, it is a blessed state of mind when a man can feel that through having received Christ, he is, to this world, as one who is utterly dead. Neither does he yield his strength to its purposes, nor his soul to its customs, nor his judgment to its maxims, nor his heart to its affections, for he is a crucified man through Jesus Christ ; the world is crucified unto him, and he unto the world. This is what the apostle meant.

Notice next another point of contact. He says, "Nevertheless I live," but then he corrects himself, "yet not I, but Christ liveth in me." You have seen the dead side of a believer : he is deaf, and dumb, and blind, and without feeling to the sinful world, yet he adds, "Nevertheless I live." He explains what his life is—his life is produced in him by virtue of Christ's being in him and his being in Christ. Jesus is the source of the Christian's life. The sap in the vine lives even in the smallest of the tendrils. No matter how minute may be the nerve, the anatomist will tell you that the brain-life lives in its most distant extremity. So in every Christian ; though the Christian may be insignificant, and possessed of little grace, yet still, if he be truly a believer, Jesus live in him. The life which keeps his faith, his hope, his love still in existence, comes from Jesus Christ, and from Him alone. We should cease to be living saints if we did not daily receive grace from our covenant Head. As the strength of our life comes from the Son of God, so is He the ruler and moving power within us. How can he be a Christian who is ruled by any but Christ ? If you call Christ "Master and Lord," you must be His servant ; nor can you yield obedience to any rival power, for no man can serve two masters. There must be a master-spirit in the heart ; and unless Jesus Christ be such a master-spirit to us, we are not saved at all. The life of the Christian is a life which springs from Christ, and it is controlled by His will. Beloved, do you know anything about this ? I am afraid it is dry talking to you about it unless you feel it. Has your life been such during the past week ? Has the life which you have lived been Christ's living in you ? Have you been like a book printed in plain letters, in which men might read a new edition of the life of Jesus Christ ? A Christian ought to be a living photograph of the Lord Jesus, a striking likeness of his Lord. When men look at him they should see not only what the Christian is, but what the Christian's Master is, for he should be like his Master. Do you ever see and know that within your soul Christ looks out at your eyes, regarding poor sinners and considering

how you may help them ? that Christ throbs in your heart, feeling for the perishing, trembling for those who will not tremble for themselves ? Do you ever feel Christ opening your hands in liberal charity to help those who cannot help themselves ? Have you ever felt that a something more than yourself was in you, a spirit which sometimes struggles with yourself, and holds it by the throat and threatens to destroy its sinful selfishness—a noble spirit which puts its foot upon the neck of covetousness, a brave spirit that dashes to the ground your pride, an active fervent spirit that burns up your sloth ? Have you never felt this ? Truly we that live unto God feel the life of God within, and desire to be more and more subdued under the dominant spirit of Christ, that our manhood may be a palace for the Well-beloved. That is another point of contact.

Further on, the apostle says—and I hope you will keep your Bibles open to follow the text—" The life which I now live in the flesh I live by the faith of the Son of God." Every moment the life of the Christian is to be a life of faith. We make a mistake when we try to walk by feeling or by sight. I dreamed the other night, while musing upon the life of the believer, that I was passing along a road which a divine call had appointed for me. The ordained pathway which I was called to traverse was amid thick darkness, unmingled with a ray of light. As I stood in the awful gloom, unable to perceive a single inch before me, I heard a voice which said, "Let thy feet go right on. Fear not, but advance in the name of God." So on I went, putting down foot after foot with trembling. After a little while the path through the darkness became easy and smooth, from use and experience ; just then I perceived that the path turned : it was of no use my endeavouring to proceed as I had done before ; the way was tortuous, and the road was rough and stony ; but I remembered what was said, that I was to advance as I could, and so on I went. Then there came another twist, and yet another, and another, and another, and I wondered why, till I understood that if ever the path remained long the same, I should grow accustomed to it, and so should walk by feeling ; and I learned that the whole of the way would constantly be such as to compel me to depend upon the guiding voice, and exercise faith in the unseen One who had called me. On a sudden it appeared to me as though there was nothing beneath my foot when I put it down, yet I thrust it out into the darkness in confident daring, and lo, a firm step was reached, and another, and another, as I walked down a staircase which descended deep, down, down, down. Onward I passed, not seeing an inch before me, but believing that all was well, although I could hear around me the dash of falling men and women who had walked by the light of their own lanterns, and missed their foothold. I heard the cries and shrieks of men as they fell from this dreadful staircase ; but I was commanded to go right on, and I went straight on, resolved to be obedient even if the way should descend into the nethermost hell. By-and-by the dreadful ladder was ended, and I found a solid rock beneath my feet, and I walked straight on upon a paved causeway, with a balustrade on either hand. I understood this to be the experience which I had gained, which now could guide and help me, and I leaned on this balustrade, and walked on right confidently till, in a moment, my causeway ended and my feet sank in the mire, and as for my other comforts, I groped for them, but they were gone, for still I was to know that I must go in dependence upon my unseen Friend, and the road would always be such that no experience could serve me instead of dependence upon God. Forward I plunged through mire and filth and suffocating smoke, and a smell as of death-damp, for it was *the* way, and I had been commanded to walk therein. Again the pathway changed, though all was midnight still: up went the path, and up, and up, and up, with nothing upon which I could lean; I ascended wearily innumerable stairs, not one of which I could see, although the very thought of their height might make the brain to reel. On a sudden my pathway burst into light, as I woke from my reverie, and when I looked down upon it, I saw it all to be safe, but such a road that, if I had seen it, I never could have trodden it. It was only in the darkness that I could have performed my mysterious journey, only in child-like confidence upon the Lord. The Lord will guide us if we are willing to do just as He bids us. Lean upon Him, then. I have painted a poor picture, but still one which, if you can realise, it will be grand to look upon. To walk straight on, believing in Christ every moment, believing your sins to be forgiven even when you see their blackness, believing that you are safe when you seem in the utmost danger, believing that you are glorified with Christ when you feel as if you were cast out from God's presence—this is the life of faith.

Furthermore, Paul notes other points of unity. "*Who loved me.*" Blessed be God, before the mountains uplifted their snow-crowned heads to the clouds, Christ had set His heart upon us. His "delights were with the sons of men." In His "book all our members were written, which in continuance were fashioned, when as yet there was none of them." Believer, get a hold of the precious truth that Christ loved you eternally—the all-glorious Son of God chose you, and espoused you unto Himself, that you might be His bride throughout eternity. Here is a blessed union indeed.

Observe the next, "*and gave Himself for me*"; not only gave all that He had, but gave Himself; not merely laid aside His glory, and His splendour, and His life, but yielded up His very self. O heir of heaven, Jesus is yours at this moment. Having given Himself once for you upon the tree, to put your sin away, at this moment He gives Himself to you to be your life, your crown, your joy, your portion, your all in all. You have found out yourself to be a separate personality and individuality, but that personality is linked with the person of Christ Jesus, so that you are in Christ, and Christ is in you; by a blessed indissoluble union you are knit together for ever and ever.

III. Lastly, the text *describes* THE LIFE WHICH RESULTS FROM THIS BLENDED PERSONALITY.

If you will have patience with me, I will be as brief as I can while I go over the text again word by word. Brethren, when a man finds and knows himself to be linked with Christ, his life is altogether *a new life*. I gather that from the expression, " I am crucified, nevertheless I live." Crucified, then dead; crucified, then the old life is put away—whatever life a crucified man has must be new life. So is it with you. Upon your old life, believer, sentence of death has been pronounced. The carnal mind, which is enmity against God, is doomed to

die. You can say, " I die daily." Would to God the old nature were completely dead. But whatever you have of life was not given you till you came into union with Christ. It is a new thing, as new as though you had been actually dead and rotted in the tomb, and then had started up at the sound of the trumpet to live again. You have received a life from above, a life which the Holy Spirit wrought in you in regeneration. That which is born of the flesh is flesh, but your grace-life did not come from yourself: you have been born again from above.

Your life is *a very strange one*—" I am crucified, nevertheless I live." What a contradiction! The Christian's life is a matchless riddle. No worldling can comprehend it; even the believer himself cannot understand it. He knows it, but as to solving all its enigmas, he feels that to be an impossible task. Dead, yet alive; crucified with Christ, and yet at the same time risen with Christ in newness of life! Do not expect the world to understand you, Christian, it did not understand your Master. When your actions are misrepresented, and your motives are ridiculed, do not be surprised. " If ye were of the world, the world would love his own: but because ye are not of the world, but I have chosen you out of the world, therefore the world hateth you." If you belonged to the village, the dogs would not bark at you. If men could read you, they would not wonder; it is because you are written in a celestial language that men cannot comprehend you, and think you worthless. Your life is new; your life is strange.

This wonderful life, resulting in the blended personality of the believer and the Son of God, is *a true life*. This is expressed in the text, " Nevertheless I live "—yes, live as I never lived before. When the apostle declares himself to be dead to the world, he would not have us imagine that he was dead in the highest and best sense; nay, he lived with a new force and vigour of life. It seemed to me, brethren, when I woke up to know Christ, that I was just like the fly newly burst from the chrysalis, I then began really to live. When a soul is startled by the thunder claps of conviction, and afterwards receives pardon in Christ, it begins to live. The worldling says he wants to see life, and therefore plunges into sin! Fool that he is, he peers into the sepulchre to discover immortality. The man who truly lives is the believer. Shall I become less active because I am a Christian? God forbid! Become less industrious, find less opportunities for the manifestation of my natural and spiritual energies? God forbid! If ever a man should be like a sword too sharp for the scabbard, with an edge which cannot be turned, it should be the Christian: He should be like flames of fire burning his way. Live while you live. Let there be no drivelling and frittering away of time. Live so as to demonstrate that you possess the noblest form of life.

Clear is it, also, that the new life which Christ brings to us is a life of *self-abnegation*, for he adds, " I live, yet not I." Lowliness of mind is part and parcel of godliness. He who can take any credit to himself knows not the spirit of our holy faith. The believer when he prays best says, " Yet not I, but the Spirit of God interceded in me." If he has won any souls to Christ, he says, " Yet not I; it was the gospel; the Lord Jesus wrought in me mightily." " Not unto us, not unto us, but unto Thy name be all the praise." Self-humiliation is the native spirit of the true-born child of God.

Further, the life which Christ works in us is a life of *one idea*. Is the believer's soul ruled by two things? Nay, he knows but one. Christ liveth in me. Two tenants in the chamber of my soul? Nay, one Lord and Master I serve. "Christ liveth in me." An old divine desired that he might eat and drink and sleep eternal life. Do you thus live! Alas! I mourn that I live too much in the old life, and too little does Jesus live in me; but the Christian, if he should ever come to perfection, and God grant we each may come as near to it as possible even now, will find that the old "*I* live," is kept under, and the new Christ-life reigns supreme. Christ must be the one thought, the one idea, the one master-thought in the believer's soul. When he wakes in the morning the healthy believer enquires, "What can I do for Christ?" When he goes about his business he asks, "How shall I serve my Lord in all my actions?" When he makes money he questions himself, "How can I use my talents for Christ?" If he acquires education, the enquiry is, "How can I spend my knowledge for Christ?"

To sum up much in little, the child of God has within him the *Christ-life*; but how shall I describe that? Christ's life on earth was the divine mingled with the human—such in the life of the Christian; there is something divine about it: it is a living, incorruptible seed, which abideth for ever. We are made partakers of the divine nature, having escaped the corruption which is in the world through lust, yet our life is thoroughly human life. The Christian is a man among men; in all that is manly he labours to excel, yet he is not as other men are, but wears a hidden nature which no mere worldling understands. Picture the life of Christ on earth, beloved, and that is what the life of God in us ought to be, and will be in proportion as we are subject to the power of the Holy Spirit.

Notice again, keeping close to the text, that the life which God worketh in us is still *the life of a man*. "The life that I now live in the flesh," says the apostle. Those monks and nuns who run away from the world for fear its temptations should overcome them, and seclude themselves for the sake of greater holiness, are as excellent soldiers as those who retire to the camp for fear of being defeated. Of what service are such soldiers in the battle, or such persons in the warfare of life? Christ did not come to make monks of us: He came to make *men* of us. He meant that we should learn how to *live in the flesh*. We are neither to give up business nor society, nor in any right sense to give up life. "The life I live in the flesh," says the apostle. Look at him busy at his tent-making. What! an apostle making tents? What say you, brethren, to the Archbishop of Canterbury stitching away for his living? It is too low for a state bishop certainly, but not too low for Paul. I do not think the apostle was ever more apostolic than when he picked up sticks. When Paul and his companions were shipwrecked at Melita, the apostle was of more service than all the Pan-Anglican synod with their silk aprons, for he set

to work like other people to gather fuel for the fire; he wanted to warm himself as other men, and therefore he took his share at the toil. Even so you and I must take our turn at the wheel. We must not think of keeping ourselves aloof from our fellow men, as though we should be degraded by mingling with them. The salt of the earth should be well rubbed into the meat, and so the Christian should mingle with his fellow men, seeking their good for edification. We are men, and whatever men may lawfully do, we do; wherever they may go, we may go. Our religion makes us neither more nor less than human, though it brings us into the family of God. Yet the Christian life *is a life of faith*. "The life which I live in the flesh, I live by the faith of the Son of God." Faith is not a piece of confectionery to be put upon drawing room tables, or a garment to be worn on Sundays; it is a working principle, to be used in the barn and in the field, in the shop and on the exchange; it is a grace for the housewife and the servant; it is for the House of Commons and for the poorest workshop. "The life which I live in the flesh, I live by faith." I would have the believing cobbler mend shoes religiously, and the tailor make garments by faith, and I would have every Christian buy and sell by faith. Whatever your trades may be, faith is to be taken into your daily callings, and that is alone the truly living faith which will bear the practical test. You are not to stop at the shop door and take off your coat and say, "Farewell to Christianity till I put up the shutters again." That is hypocrisy; but the genuine life of the Christian is the life which we live *in the flesh by faith of the Son of God*.

To conclude: the life which comes out of the blended personality of the believer and Christ is a life of *perfect love*. "He gave Himself for me." My question is, therefore, What can I do for Him? The new life is a life of *holy security*, for, if Christ loved me, who can destroy me? It is a life of *holy wealth*, for, if Christ gave His infinite self to me, what can I want? It is a life of *holy joy*, for, if Christ be mine, I have a well of holy joy within my soul. It is *the life of heaven*, for, if I have Christ, I have that which is the essence and soul of heaven.

I have talked mysteries, of which some of you have not understood so much as a sentence. God give you understanding that you may know the truth. But if you have not understood it, let this fact convince you: you know not the truth because you have not the Spirit of God; for the spiritual mind alone understands spiritual things. When we talk about the inner life, we seem like those that dote and dream to those who understand us not. But if you have understood me, believer, go home and live out the truth, practise that which is practicable, feed upon that which is full of savour, rejoice in Christ Jesus that you are one with Him, and then, in your own proper person, go out and serve your Master with might and main, and the Lord send you His abundant blessing. Amen and Amen.

A CALL TO THE UNCONVERTED

" For as many as are of the works of the law are under the curse : for it is written, Cursed is every one that continueth not in all things which are written in the book of the law to do them."—Galatians iii. 10.

MY hearer, art thou a believer, or no ? for according to thine answer to that question must be the style in which I shall address thee to-night. I would ask thee as a great favour to thine own soul, this evening to divest thyself of the thought that thou art sitting in a chapel, and hearing a minister who is preaching to a large congregation. Think thou art sitting in thine own house, in thine own chair, and think that I am standing by thee, with thine hand in mine, and am speaking personally to thee, and to thee alone ; for that is how I desire to preach this night to each of my hearers—one by one. I want thee, then, in the sight of God, to answer me this all-important and solemn question before I begin—Art thou in Christ, or art thou not ? Hast thou fled for refuge to Him who is the only hope for sinners ? or art thou yet a stranger to the commonwealth of Israel, ignorant of God, and of His holy Gospel ? Come—be honest with thine own heart, and let thy conscience say yes, or no, for one of these two things thou art to-night—thou art either under the wrath of God, or thou art delivered from it. Thou art to-night either an heir of wrath, or an inheritor of the kingdom of grace. Which of these two ? Make no " ifs " or " ahs " in your answer. Answer straightforward to thine own soul ; and if there be any doubt whatever about it, I beseech thee rest not till that doubt be resolved. Do not take advantage of that doubt to thyself, but rather take a disadvantage from it. Depend upon it, thou art more likely to be wrong than thou art to be right ; and now put thyself in the scale, and if thou dost not kick the beam entirely, but if thou hangest between the two, and thou sayest, " I know not which," better that thou shouldest decide for the worst, though it should grieve thyself, than that thou shouldest decide for the better, and be deceived, and so go on presumptuously until the pit of hell shall wake thee from thy self-deception. Canst thou then, with one hand upon God's holy word, and the other upon thine own heart, lift thine eye to heaven, and say, " One thing I know, that whereas I was blind, now I see ; I know that I have passed from death unto life ; I am not now what I once was ; ' I the chief of sinners am, but Jesus died for me.' And if I be not awfully deceived, I am this night, ' A sinner saved by blood, a monument of grace ? ' " My brother, God speed you ; the blessing of the Most High be with you. My text has no thunders in it for you. Instead of this verse, turn to the 13th, and there read your inheritance—" Christ hath redeemed *us* from the curse of the law, being made a curse for us : for it is written, Cursed is every one that hangeth on a tree." So Christ was cursed in the stead of you, and you are secure, if you are truly converted, and really a regenerated child of God.

But my hearer, I am solemnly convinced that a large proportion of this assembly dare not say so ; and thou to-night (for I am speaking personally to thee), remember thou art one of those who dare not say this, for thou art a stranger to the grace of God. Thou durst not lie before God and thine own conscience, therefore thou dost honestly say, " I know I was never regenerated ; I am now what I always was, and that is the most I can say." Now, with you I have to deal, and I charge you by Him who shall judge the quick and the dead, before whom you and I must soon appear, listen to the words I speak, for they may be the last warning you shall ever hear, and I charge my own soul also, be thou faithful to these dying men, lest haply on thy skirts at last should be found the blood of souls, and thou thyself shouldst be a castaway. O God, make us faithful this night, and give the hearing ear, and the retentive memory, and the conscience touched by the Spirit, for Jesus' sake.

First, to-night, we shall *try the prisoner ;* secondly, we shall *declare his sentence ;* and thirdly, if we find him confessing and penitent, we shall *proclaim his deliverance ;* but not unless we find him so.

I. First, then, we are about to TRY THE PRISONER. The text says—" Cursed is every one that continueth not in all things which are written in the book of the law to do them." Unconverted man, are you guilty, or not guilty ? Have you continued " in all things that are written in the book of the law to do them ? " Methinks you will not dare to plead, " Not guilty." But I will suppose for one moment that you are bold enough to do so. So then, sir, you mean to assert that you have continued " in all things which are written in the book of the law." Surely the very reading of the law would be enough to convince thee that thou art in error. Dost thou know what the law is ? Why, I will give thee what I may call the outside of it, but remember that within it there is a broader spirit than the mere words. Hear thou these words of the law—" *Thou shalt have no other gods before Me.*" What ! hast thou never loved anything better than God ? Hast thou never made a god of thy belly, or of thy business, or of thy family, or of thine own person ? Oh ! surely thou durst not say thou art guiltless here. " *Thou shalt not make unto thee any graven image, or any likeness of anything that is in heaven above, or that is in the earth beneath, or that is in the water under the earth.*" What ! hast thou never in thy life set up anything in the place of God ? If thou hast not, I have, full many a time. And I wot, if conscience would speak truly it would say, " Man thou hast been a mammon worshipper, thou hast been a belly worshipper, thou hast bowed down before gold and silver ; thou hast cast thyself down before honour, thou hast bowed before pleasure, thou hast made a god of thy drunkenness, a god of thy lust, a god of thy uncleanness, a god of thy pleasures ! " Wilt thou dare to say thou hast never taken *the name of the Lord thy God in vain ?* If thou hast never sworn profanely, yet surely in common conversation thou hast sometimes made use of God's name when thou oughtest not to have done so. Say, hast thou always hallowed that most holy name ? Hast thou never called upon God without necessity ? Hast thou never read His book with a trifling spirit ? Hast thou never heard His gospel without paying reverence to it ? Surely thou art guilty here. And as for that fourth commandment, which relates to the keeping of the Sabbath—" *Remember the Sabbath day to keep it holy*," —hast thou never broken it ? Oh, shut thy mouth, and plead guilty, for these four commandments were enough to condemn thee ! " *Honour thy father and thy mother*." What ! wilt thou say thou hast kept that ? Hast thou never been disobedient in thy youth ? Hast thou never kicked against a mother's love, and striven against a father's rebuke ? Turn over a page of your history till you come to your childhood : see if you cannot find it written there ; aye, and your manhood too may confess that you have not always spoken to your parents as you should, or always treated them with that honour they deserved, and which God commanded you to give unto them. " *Thou shalt not kill* " ; you may never have killed any, but have you never been angry ? He that is angry with his brother is a murderer ; thou art guilty here. " *Thou shalt not commit adultery*." Mayhap thou hast committed unclean things and art here this very day stained with lust ; but if thou hast been never so chaste, I am sure thou hast not been quite guiltless, when the Master says, " He that looketh on a woman to lust after her, hath committed adultery already with her in his heart." Has no lascivious thought crossed thy mind ? Has no impurity ever stirred thy imagination ? Surely if thou shouldest dare to say so, thou wouldest be brazen-faced with impudence. And hast thou never stolen ? " *Thou shalt not steal* " : you are here in the crowd to-night with the product of your theft mayhap, you have done the deed, you have committed robbery ; but if you have been never so honest, yet surely there have been times in which you have felt an inclination to defraud your neighbour, and there may have been some petty, or mayhap some gross frauds which you have secretly and silently committed, on which the law of the land could not lay its hand, but which, nevertheless, was a breach of this law. And who dare say he has not borne *false witness against his neighbour?* Have we never repeated a story to our neighbour's disadvantage, which was untrue ? Have we never misconstrued his motives ? Have we never misinterpreted his designs ? And who among us can dare to say that he is guiltless of the last—" *Thou shalt not covet ?* " for we have all desired to have more than God has given us ; and at times our wandering heart has lusted after things which God has not bestowed upon us. Why, to plead not guilty, is to plead your own folly ; for verily, my brethren, the very reading of the law is enough, when blessed by the Spirit, to make us cry, " Guilty, O Lord, guilty."

But one cries, " I shall not plead guilty, for though I am well aware that I have not continued ' in all things which are written in the book of the law,' yet I have done the best I could." That is a lie— before God a falsehood. You have not ! You have not done the best you could. There have been many occasions upon which you might have done better. Will that young man dare to tell me that he is doing the best he can *now ?* that he cannot refrain from laughter in the house of God ? It may be possible that it is hard for him to do so, but it is just possible he could, if he pleased, refrain from insulting his Maker to His face. Surely we have none of us done the best we could. At every period, and at every time, there have been opportunities of escape from temptation. If we had had no freedom to escape from the sin, there might have been some excuse for it ; but there have been turning points in our history when we might have decided for right or for wrong, but when we have chosen the evil and have eschewed the good, and have turned into that path which leadeth unto hell.

" Ah, but," saith another, " I declare, sir, that while I have broken that law, without a doubt, I have been no worse than my fellow-creatures." And a sorry argument is that, for what availeth it thee ? To be damned in a crowd is no more comfortable than to be damned alone. It is true, thou hast been no worse than thy fellow-creatures, but this will be of very poor service to thee. When the wicked are cast into hell, it will be very little comfort to thee that God shall say, " Depart ye cursed," to a thousand with thee. Remember, God's curse, when it shall sweep a nation into hell, shall be as much felt by every individual of the crowd as if there were but that one man to be punished. God is not like our earthly judges. If their courts were glutted with prisoners, they might be inclined to pass over many a case lightly ; but not so with Jehovah. He is so infinite in His mind, that the abundance of criminals will not seem to be any difficulty with Him. He will deal with thee as severely, and as justly as if there were ne'er another sinner in all the world. And pray, what hast thou to do with other men's sins ? Thou art not responsible for them. God made thee to stand or fall by thyself. According to thine own deeds thou shalt be judged. The harlot's sin may be grosser than thine, but thou wilt not be condemned for her iniquities. The murderer's guilt may far exceed thy transgressions, but thou wilt not be damned for the murderer. Religion is a thing between God and thine own soul, O man ; and therefore, I do beseech thee, do not look upon thy neighbour's, but upon thine own heart.

" Aye, but," cries another, " I have very many times striven to keep the law, and I think I have done so for a little." Hear ye the sentence read again—" Cursed is every one that *continueth* not in all things which are written in the book of the law to do them." Oh ! sirs ; it is not some hectic flush upon the cheek of consumptive irresolution that God counts to be the health of obedience. It is not some slight obedience for an hour that God will accept at the day of judgment. He saith, " continueth " ; and unless from my early childhood to the day when my grey hairs descend into the tomb, I shall have continued to be obedient to God, I must be condemned. Unless I have from the first dawn of reason, when I first began to be responsible, obediently served God, until, like a shock of corn, I am gathered into my Master's garner, salvation by works must be impossible to me, and I must (standing on my own footing) be condemned. It is not, I say, some slight obedience that will save the soul. Thou hast not continued " in all things which are written in the book of the law," and therefore thou art condemned.

" But," says another, " there are many things I have not done, but still I have been very virtuous." Poor excuse, that, also. Suppose thou hast been virtuous ; suppose thou hast avoided many vices : turn to my text. It is not my word, but God's— turn to it—" *all things*." It does not say " *some things* "—" Cursed is every one that continueth not in *all things* which are written in the book of the law to do them." Now, hast thou performed all virtues ? Hast thou shunned all vices ? Dost thou stand up and plead, " I never was a drunkard " ?—Yet shalt thou be damned, if thou hast been a fornicator. Dost thou reply, "I never was unclean " ? Yet thou hast broken the Sabbath. Dost thou plead guiltless of that charge ? Dost thou declare that thou hast never broken the Sabbath ? Thou hast taken God's name in vain, hast thou not ? Somewhere or other God's law can smite thee. It is certain (let thy conscience now speak and affirm what I assert)—it is certain that thou hast not continued " in *all things* which are written in the book of the law." Nay, more, I do not believe thou hast even continued in any one commandment of God to the full, for the commandment is exceeding broad. It is not the overt act, merely, that will damn a man ; it is the thought, the imagination, the conception of sin, that is sufficient to ruin a soul. Remember, my dear hearers, I am speaking now God's own word, not a harsh doctrine of my own. If you had never committed one single act of sin, yet the thought of sin, the imagination of it would be enough to sweep your soul to hell for ever. If you had been born in a cell, and had never been able to come out into the world, either to commit acts of lasciviousness, murder, or robbery, yet the thought of evil in that lone cell might be enough to cast your soul for ever from the face of God. Oh ! there is no man here that can hope to escape. We must every one of us bow our heads before God, and cry, " Guilty, Lord, guilty—every one of us guilty—' Cursed is *every one* that continueth not in *all things* which are written in the book of the law to do them.' " When I look into thy face, O law, my spirit shudders. When I hear thy thunders, my heart is melted like wax in the midst of my bowels. How can I endure Thee ? If I am to be tried at last for my life, surely I shall need no judge, for I shall be my own swift accuser, and my conscience shall be a witness to condemn.

I think I need not enlarge further on this point. O thou that art out of Christ, and without God, dost thou not stand condemned before Him ? Off with all thy masks, and away with all excuses ; let every one of us turn our idle pretences to the wind. Unless we have the blood and righteousness of Jesus Christ to cover us, we must every one of us acknowledge that this sentence shuts the gates of heaven against us, and only prepares us for the flames of perdition.

II. Thus have I singled out the character, and he is found guilty ; now I have to DECLARE THE SENTENCE.

God's ministers love not such work as this. I would rather stand in this pulpit and preach twenty sermons on the love of Jesus than one like this. It is very seldom that I meddle with the theme, because I do not know that it is often necessary ; but I feel that if these things were kept altogether in the background, and the law were not preached, the Master would not own the gospel ; for He will have both preached in their measure, and each must have its proper prominence. Now, therefore, hear me whilst I sorrowfully tell you what is the sentence passed upon all of you who this night are out of Christ. Sinner, thou art cursed to-night. *Thou are cursed*, not by some wizard whose fancied spell can only frighten the ignorant. Thou art cursed—not cursed by some earthly monarch who could turn his troops against thee, and swallow up thy house, and thy patrimony quick. Cursed ! Oh ! what a thing a curse is anyhow ! What an awful thing is the curse of a father. We have heard of fathers, driven to madness by the undutiful and ungracious conduct of their children, who have lifted their hands to heaven, and have implored a curse, a withering curse upon their children. We cannot excuse the parent's mad and rash act. God forbid we should exempt him from sin ; but oh, a father's curse must be awful. I cannot think what it must be to be cursed by Him that did beget me. Sure, it would put out the sunlight of my history for ever, if it were deserved. But to be cursed of God—I have no words with which to tell what that must be. " Oh, no," you say, " that is a thing of the future ; we do not care about the curse of God ; it does not fall upon us now." Nay, soul but it does. The wrath of God *abideth* on you even now. You have not yet come to know the fulness of that curse, but you are cursed this very hour. You are not yet in hell ; not yet has God been pleased to shut up the bowels of His compassion, and cast you for ever from His presence ; but notwithstanding all that, you are cursed. Turn to the passage in the book of Deuteronomy, and see how the curse is a present thing upon the sinner. In the 28th chapter of Deuteronomy, at the 15th verse, we read all this as the sentence of the sinner : " Cursed shalt thou be in the city,"—where you carry on your business God will curse you. " Cursed shalt thou be in the fields,"—where you take your recreation ; where you walk abroad, there shall the curse reach you. " Cursed shall be thy basket and thy store. Cursed shall be the fruit of thy body, and the fruit of thy land, the increase of thy kine, and the flocks of thy sheep. Cursed shalt thou be when thou comest in, and cursed shalt thou be when thou goest out." There are some men upon whom this curse is very visible. Whatever they do is cursed. They get riches, but there is God's curse with the riches. I would not have some men's gold for all the stars, though they were gold : and if I might have all the wealth of the world, if I must have the miser's greed with it, I would rather be poor than have it. There are some men who are visibly cursed. Don't you see the drunkard ? He is cursed, let him go where he may. When he goes into his house, his little children run upstairs to bed, for they are afraid to see their own father ; and when they grow a little older, they begin to drink just as he did, and they will stand and imitate him ; and they too will begin to swear, so that he is cursed in the fruit of his body. He thought it was not so bad for him to be drunk and to swear ; but oh, what a pang shoots through the father's conscience, if he has a conscience at all, when he sees his child following his footsteps. Drunkenness brings such a curse upon a man that he cannot enjoy what he eats. He is cursed in his basket, cursed in his store. And truly, though one vice may seem to develop the curse more than others, all sin brings the curse, though we cannot always see it. Oh ! thou that art out of God, and out of Christ, and a stranger to Jesus, thou art cursed where thou sittest, cursed where thou standest ; cursed is the bed thou liest on ; cursed is the bread thou eatest ; cursed is the air thou breathest. All is cursed to thee. Go where thou mayest, thou art a cursed man. Ah ! that is a fearful thought. Oh ! there are some of you that are cursed to-night. Oh, that a man should say that of his brethren ! but we must say it, or be unfaithful to your poor dying souls. Oh! would to God that some poor soul in this place would say, "Then I am cursed to-night; I am cursed of God, and cursed of His holy angels—cursed! cursed! cursed!—for I am under the law." I do think, God the Spirit blessing it, it wants nothing more to slay our carelessness than that one word—"cursed!" "Cursed is every one that continueth not in all things which are written in the book of the law to do them."

But now, my hearer, thou that art in this state, impenitent and unbelieving, I have more work to do before I close. Remember, the curse that men have in this life is as nothing compared with the curse that is to come upon them hereafter. In a few short years, you and I must die. Come, friend, I will talk to you personally again—young man, we shall soon grow old, or, perhaps, we shall die before that time, and we shall lie upon our bed—the last bed upon which we shall ever sleep—we shall wake from our last slumber to hear the doleful tidings that there is no hope; the physician will feel our pulse, and solemnly assure our relatives that it is all over! And we shall lie in that still room, where all is hushed except the ticking of the clock, and the weeping of our wife and children; and we must die. Oh! how solemn will be that hour when we must struggle with that enemy, Death! The death-rattle is in our throat—we can scarce articulate—we try to speak; the death-glaze is on the eye: Death hath put his fingers on those windows of the body, and shut out the light for ever; the hands well-nigh refuse to lift themselves, and there we are, close on the borders of the grave! Ah! that moment, when the Spirit sees its destiny; that moment, of all moments the most solemn, when the soul looks through the bars of its cage, upon the world to come! No, I cannot tell you how the spirit feels, if it be an ungodly spirit, when it sees a fiery throne of judgment, and hears the thunders of Almighty wrath, while there is but a moment between it and hell. I cannot picture to you what must be the fright which men will feel, when they realize what they often heard of! Ah! it is a fine thing for you to laugh at me to-night. When you go away, it will be a very fine thing to crack a joke concerning what the preacher said; to talk to one another, and make merry with all this. But when you are lying on your death-bed, you will not laugh. Now, the curtain is drawn, you cannot see the things of the future, it is a very fine thing to be merry. When God has removed that curtain, and you learn the solemn reality, you will not find it in your hearts to trifle. Ahab, on his throne, laughed at Micaiah. You never read that Ahab laughed at Micaiah when the arrow was sticking between the joints of his harness. In Noah's time, they laughed at the old man; they called him a grey-headed fool, I doubt not, because he told them that God was about to destroy the earth with a flood. But ah! ye scorners, ye did not laugh in that day when the cataracts were falling from heaven, and when God had unloosed the doors of the great deep, and bidden all the hidden waters leap upon the surface; then ye knew that Noah was right. And when ye come to die, mayhap ye will not laugh at me. You will say, when you lie there, "I remember such-and-such a night I strolled into Park Street; I heard a man talk very solemnly; I thought at the time I did not like it, but I knew he was in earnest, I am quite certain that he meant good for me; oh, that I had hearkened to his advice; oh, that I had regarded his words! What would I give to hear him again!" Ah! it was not long ago that a man who had laughed and mocked at me full many a time, went down one Sabbath day to Brighton, to spend his day in the excursion—he came back that night to die! On Monday morning, when he was dying, who do you suppose he wanted? He wanted Mr. Spurgeon! the man he had laughed at always; he wanted him to come and tell him the way to heaven, and point him to the Saviour. And although I was glad enough to go, it was doleful work to talk to a man who had just been Sabbath-breaking, spending his time in the service of Satan, and had come home to die. And die he did, without a Bible in his house, without having one prayer offered for him except that prayer which I alone did offer at his bedside. Ah! it is strange how the sight of a death-bed may be blessed to the stimulating of our zeal. I stood some year or so ago, by the bedside of a poor boy, about sixteen years of age, who had been drinking himself to death, in a drinking bout, about a week before, and when I talked to him about sin and righteousness, and judgment to come, I knew he trembled, and I thought that he had laid hold on Jesus. When I came down from those stairs, after praying for him many a time, and trying to point him to Jesus, and having but a faint hope of his ultimate salvation, I thought to myself, O God! I would that I might preach every hour and every moment of the day, the unsearchable riches of Christ; for what an awful thing it is to die without a Saviour. And then, I thought how many a time I had stood in the pulpit, and had not preached in earnest as I ought to have done; how I have coldly told out the tale of the Saviour, when I ought to have wept very showers of tears, in overwhelming emotion. I have gone to my bed full many a season, and have wept myself to sleep, because I have not preached as I have desired, and it will be even so to-night. But, oh, the wrath to come! the wrath to come! the wrath to come!

My hearers, the matters I now talk of are no dreams, no frauds, no whims, no old wives' stories. These are realities, and you will soon know them. O sinner, thou that hast not continued in all things written in the book of the law; thou that hast no Christ; the day is coming when these things will stand before thee, as dread, solemn, real things. And then; ah! then; ah! then; ah! then, what wilt thou do?—"And after death *the judgment*."—Oh, can ye picture—

> "The pomp of that tremendous day,
> When Christ with clouds shall come."

I think I see that terrible day. The bell of time has tolled the last day. Now comes the funeral of damned souls. Your body has just started up from the grave, and you unwind your cerements, and you look up. What is that I see? Oh! what is that I hear? I hear one dread, tremendous blast, that shakes the pillars of heaven, and makes the firmament reel with affright; the trump, the trump, the trump of the archangel shakes creation's utmost bound. You look and wonder. Suddenly a voice is heard, and shrieks from some, and songs from others—He comes—He comes—He comes; and every eye must see Him. There He is; the throne is set upon a cloud, which is white as alabaster. There

He sits. 'Tis He, the Man that died on Calvary—I see His pierced hands—but ah, how changed! No thorn-crown now. He stood at Pilate's bar, but now the whole earth must stand at His bar. But hark! the trumpet sounds again: the Judge opens the book, there is silence in heaven, a solemn silence: the universe is still. "Gather mine elect together, and my redeemed from the four winds of heaven." Swiftly they are gathered. As with a lightning flash, the angel's wing divides the crowd. Here are the righteous all in-gathered; and sinner, there art thou, on the left hand, left out, left to abide the burning sentence of eternal wrath. Hark! the harps of heaven play sweet melodies; but to you they bring no joy, though the angels are repeating the Saviour's welcome to His saints. "Come ye blessed, inherit the kingdom prepared for you from the foundations of the world." You have had that moment's respite, and now His face is gathering clouds of wrath, the thunder is on His brow; He looks on you that have despised Him, you that scoffed His grace, that scorned His mercy, you that broke His Sabbath, you that mocked His cross, you that would not have Him to reign over you; and with a voice louder than ten thousand thunders, He cries, "Depart, ye cursed." And then—— No, I will not follow you. I will not tell of quenchless flames: I will not talk of miseries for the body, and tortures for the spirit. But hell is terrible; damnation is doleful. Oh, escape! escape! Escape, lest haply, being where you are, you should have to learn what the horrors of eternity must mean, in the gulf of everlasting perdition. "Cursed is the man that hath not continued in *all things* that are written in the book of the law to do them."

III. DELIVERANCE PROCLAIMED.

"You have condemned us all," cries one. Yes, but not I—God has done it. Are you condemned? Do you feel you are to-night? Come, again, let me take thee by the hand, my brother: yes, I can look around upon the whole of this assembly, and I can say, there is not one now in this place whom I do not love as a brother. If I speak severely unto any of you, it is that you may know the right. My heart, and my whole spirit are stirred for you. My harshest words are far more full of love than the smooth words of soft-speaking ministers, who say, "Peace, peace," when there is no peace. Do you think it is any pleasure to me to preach like this? Oh! I had far rather be preaching of Jesus; His sweet, His glorious person, and His all-sufficient righteousness. Now come, we will have a sweet word before we have done. Do you feel you are condemned? Do you say, "O God, I confess thou wouldest be just, if Thou shouldest do all this to me"? Dost thou feel thou canst never be saved by thine own works, but that thou art utterly condemned through sin? Dost thou hate sin? Dost thou sincerely repent? Then, let me tell thee how thou mayest escape.

Men and brethren, Jesus Christ, of the seed of David, was crucified, dead and buried; He is now risen, and He sitteth on the right hand of God, where He also maketh intercession for us. He came into this world to save sinners, by His death. He saw that poor sinners were cursed: He took the curse on His own shoulders, and He delivered us from it. Now, if God has cursed Christ for any man, He will not curse that man again. You ask me then, "Was Christ cursed for me?" Answer me this question,

and I will tell you—Has God the Spirit taught you that you are accursed? Has He made you feel the bitterness of sin? Has He made you cry, "Lord, have mercy upon me, a sinner"? Then, my dear friend, Christ was cursed for you; and you are not cursed. You are not cursed now. Christ was cursed for you. Be of good cheer; if Christ was cursed for you, you cannot be cursed again. "Oh!" says one, "if I could but think He was cursed for me." Do you see Him bleeding on the tree? Do you see His hands and feet all dripping gore. Look unto Him, poor sinner. Look no longer at thyself, nor at thy sin; look unto Him, and be saved. All He asks thee to do is to look, and even that He will help thee to do. Come to Him, trust Him, believe on Him. God the Holy Spirit has taught you that you are a condemned sinner. Now, I beseech you, hear this word and believe it: "This is a faithful saying, and worthy of all acceptation, that Christ Jesus came into the world to save sinners." Oh, can you say, "I believe this Word—it is true—blessed be His dear name; it is true to me, for whatever I may not be, I know I am a sinner; the sermon of this night convinces me of that, if there were nothing else; and, good Lord, Thou knowest when I say I am a sinner, I do not mean what I used to mean by that word. I mean that I am a real sinner. I mean that if Thou shouldest damn me, I deserve it; if thou shouldest cast me from Thy presence for ever, it is only what I have merited richly. O my Lord I am a sinner; I am a hopeless sinner, unless Thou savest me; I am a helpless sinner, unless Thou dost deliver me. I have no hope in my self-righteousness; and Lord, I bless Thy name, there is one thing else, I am a sorrowful sinner, for sin grieves me; I cannot rest, I am troubled. Oh, if I could get rid of sin, I would be holy even as God is holy. Lord I believe." But I hear an objector cry out, "What, sir, believe that Christ died for me simply because I am a sinner!" Yes; even so. "No, sir, but if I had a little righteousness; if I could pray well, I should then think Christ died for me." No, that would not be faith at all, that would be self-confidence. Faith believes in Christ when it sees sin to be black, and trusts in Him to remove it all. Now poor sinner, with all thy sin about thee, take this promise in thy hands, go home to-night, or if thou canst, do it before thou gettest home—go home, I say, up-stairs, alone, down by the bedside, and pour out thine heart, "O Lord, it is all true that that man said; I am condemned, and Lord I deserve it. O Lord, I have tried to be better, and I have done nothing with it all, but have only grown worse. O Lord, I have slighted Thy grace, I have despised Thy gospel: I wonder Thou hast not damned me years ago; Lord, I marvel at myself, that Thou sufferest such a base wretch as I am to live at all. I have despised a mother's teaching, I have forgotten a father's prayer. Lord I have forgotten Thee; I have broken Thy Sabbath, taken Thy name in vain. I have done everything that is wrong; and if Thou dost condemn me, what can I say? Lord, I am dumb before Thy presence. I have nothing to plead. But Lord, I come to tell Thee to-night, Thou hast said in the Word of God, 'Him that cometh unto Me, I will in no wise cast out.' Lord, I come: my only plea is that Thou hast said, 'This is a faithful saying, and worthy of all acceptation, that Christ Jesus came into the world to save sinners.'

Lord, I am a sinner; He came to save *me*; I trust in it—sink or swim—Lord, this is my only hope: I cast away every other, and hate myself to think I ever should have had any other. Lord, I rely on Jesus only. Do but save me, and though I cannot hope by my future to blot out my past sin, O Lord, I will ask of Thee to give me a new heart and a right spirit, that from this time forth even for ever, I may run in the way of Thy commandments: for, Lord, I desire nothing so much as to be Thy child. Thou knowest, O Lord, I would give all, if Thou wouldest but love me; and I am encouraged to think that Thou dost love me; for my heart feels so. I am guilty, but I should never have known that I was guilty if Thou hadst not taught it to me. I am vile, but I never should have known my vileness unless Thou hadst revealed it. Surely, Thou wilt not destroy me, O God, after having taught me this. If Thou dost, Thou art just, but,

'Save a trembling sinner, Lord,
Whose hopes still hovering round Thy Word,
Would light on some sweet promise there;
Some sure support against despair.' "

If you cannot pray such a long prayer as that, I tell you what to go home and say. Say this, " Lord Jesus, I know I am nothing at all; be Thou my precious all in all."

Oh, I trust in God there will be some to-night that will be able to pray like that, and if it be so, ring the bells of heaven; sing ye seraphim; shout, ye redeemed; for the Lord hath done it, and glory be unto His name for ever and ever.

LIFE BY FAITH

" The just shall live by faith."—Galatians iii. 11.

THE apostle quotes from the Old Testament, from the second chapter of Habakkuk, at the fourth verse, and thus confirms one inspired statement by another. Even the just are not justified by their own righteousness, but by faith; it follows then, most conclusively, that no man is justified by the law in the sight of God. If the best of men find no justification coming to them through their personal virtues, but stand accepted only by faith, how much more such imperfect beings, such frequent sinners as ourselves?

Men who are saved by faith become just. The operation of faith upon the human heart is to produce love, and through love, obedience, and obedience to the divine law is but another name for morality, or, what is the diviner form of it, holiness; and yet, wherever this holiness exists, we may make sure that the holiness is not the cause of spiritual life and safety, but faith is still the wellspring of all. You saw, a few weeks ago, the hawthorn covered with a delicious luxuriance of snow-white flowers, loading the air with fragrance; now, no one among the admiring gazers supposed that those sweet May blossoms caused the hawthorn to live. After awhile you noticed the horse chestnut adorned with its enchanting pyramids of flowers, but none among you foolishly supposed that the horse chestnut was sustained by its bloom: you rightly conceived these forms of beauty to be the products of life and not the cause of it. You have here, in nature's emblems, the true doctrine of the inner life. Holiness is the flower of the new nature. It is inexpressibly lovely and infinitely desirable; nay, it must be produced in its season, or we may justly doubt the genuineness of a man's profession; but the fair graces of holiness do not save, or give spiritual life, or maintain it—these are rills from the fount, and not the fountain itself. The most athletic man in the world does not live by being athletic, but is athletic because he lives and has been trained to a perfection of animal vigour. The most enterprising merchant holds his personal property not on account of his character or deservings, but because of his civil rights as a citizen. A man may cultivate his land up to the highest point of production, but his right to his land does not depend upon the mode of culture, but upon his title deeds. So the Christian man should aim after the highest degree of spiritual culture and of heavenly perfection, and yet his salvation, as to its justness and security, depends not on his attainments, but rests upon his faith in a crucified Redeemer, as it is written in the text, " The just shall live by faith." Faith is the fruitful root, the inward channel of sap, the great life-grace in every branch of the vine. In considering the text, this morning, we shall use it perhaps somewhat apart from the connection in which it stands, and yet not apart from the mind of the Spirit, nor apart from the intention of the apostle, if not here yet in other places.

I. In the first place, IN THE PUREST SPIRITUAL SENSE IT IS TRUE THAT THE JUST SHALL LIVE BY FAITH.

It is through faith that a man becomes just, for otherwise, before the law of God he is convicted of being unjust: being justified by faith, he is enrolled among the just ones. It is through faith that he is at first quickened and breathes the air of heaven, for naturally he was dead in trespasses and sins. Faith is the first sure sign of the spiritual life within the human breast. He repents of sin and looks to Jesus, because he believes the testimony of God's Son; he believes that testimony because he has received a new life. He depends upon the atoning blood of Jesus because his heart has received the power to do so by the Holy Ghost's gift of spiritual life. Ever afterwards you shall judge of the vigour of the man's inner life by the state of his faith: if his faith groweth exceedingly, then his life also is increasing in power; if his faith diminishes, then depend upon it the vital spark burns low. Let faith ebb out, and the life-floods are ebbing too; let faith roll in with a mighty sweep, in a flood-tide of full assurance, then the secret life-floods within the man are rising and filling the man with sacred energy. Were it possible for faith to die, the spirit-life must die too; and it is very much because faith is imperishable that the new life is incorruptible. You shall find men only live before God as they believe in God and rest in the merit of His dear Son; and in proportion, also, as they do this you shall find they live in closer fellowship with heaven. Great saints must be great believers: Little-faith never can be a matured saint.

Observe that this truth proves itself in all the characteristics of spiritual life. The *nobility* of the inner life—who has not noticed it ? A man whose life is hid with Christ in God is one of the aristocrats of this world. He who knows nothing of the inner life is but little above a mere animal, and is by no means comparable to the sons of God, to whom is given the royal priesthood, the saintly inheritance. In proportion as the spiritual life is developed, the man grows in dignity, becoming more like the Prince of glory, yet the very root and source of the dignity of the holy life lies in faith. Take an instance. The life of Abraham is remarkable for its placid nobility. The man appears at no time to be disturbed. Surrounded by robber bands, he dwells in his tent as quietly as in a walled city. Abraham walked with God, and does not seem to have quickened or slackened his pace ; he maintained a serene, obedient walk, never hastening through fear, nor loitering through sloth ; he kept sweet company with his God—and what a noble life was his ! The father of the faithful was second to no character in history ; he was a kingly man, yea, a conqueror of kings, and greater than they. How calm is his usual life ! Lot following his carnal prudence is robbed in Sodom, and at last loses all : Abraham following his faith, abides as a pilgrim, and is safe. Lot is carried away captive out of a city, but Abraham remains securely in a tent, because he cast himself on God. When does Abraham fail ? When does that mighty eagle suddenly drop as with wounded wing ? It is when the arrow of unbelief has pierced him : he begins to tremble for Sarah his wife ; she is fair, perhaps the Philistine king will take her from him ; then in an unbelieving moment, he says, " She is my sister." Ah ! Abraham, where is thy nobility now ? The man who so calmly and confidently walked with God while he believed, degrades himself to utter the thing that is not, and so falls to the common level of falsehood. Even so will you, so shall each of us, be strong or weak, noble or fallen, according to our faith. Walking confidently with God, and leaning upon the everlasting arm, you shall be as a celestial prince surrounded by ministering spirits, your life shall be happy and holy, and withal glorious before the Lord ; but the moment you distrust your God, you will be tempted to follow degrading methods of evil policy, and you will pierce yourself through with many sorrows.

As the dignity, so *the energy* of the spiritual life depends upon faith. Spiritual life when in sound health is exceedingly energetic ; it can do all things. Take the apostles as an instance, and see how over sea and land, under persecutions and sufferings, they nevertheless pressed forward in the Holy War, and declared Christ throughout all nations. Whereever the spiritual life fairly pervades man, it is a force which cannot be bound, fettered, or kept under ; it is a holy fury, a sacred fire in the bones. Rules, and customs, and proprieties, it snaps as fire snaps bonds of tow. But its energy depends, under God the Holy Ghost, entirely upon the existence and power of faith. Let a man be troubled with doubts as to the religion which he has espoused, or concerning his own interest in the privileges which that religion bestows, and you will soon find all the energy of his spiritual life is gone—he will have little more than a name to live, practically he will be powerless. Take Abraham again. Abraham finds that certain kings from the east have pounced upon the cities

of the plain. He cares very little for Sodom or Gomorrha, but among the prisoners his nephew Lot has been carried away. Now, he has a great affection for his kinsman, and resolves to do his duty and rescue him. Without stopping to enquire whether his little band was sufficient, he relies entirely upon the Lord his God, and with his servants and neighbours hastens after the spoilers, nothing doubting, but expecting aid from the Most High God. That day did Jehovah, who raised up the righteous man from the east, give his enemies to his sword, and as driven stubble to his bow, and the patriarch returned from the slaughter of the kings laden with spoil. He could not but fight while he believed. It was impossible for him to sit still and yet believe in God ; but if he had not believed, then had he said, " The matter must go by default ; it is a sorrowful misfortune, but my nephew Lot must bear it : perhaps God's providence will interpose for him." Faith believes in providence, but she is full of activity, and her activity, excited by reliance upon providence, leads like wheel within a wheel to the fulfilment of the providential decree. My brethren, it is necessary for us to believe much in God, or we shall do but little for Him. Believe that God is with you, and you will have an insatiable ambition to extend the Saviour's kingdom. Believe in the power of the truth, and in the power of the Holy Ghost who goes with the truth, and you will not be content with the paltry schemes of modern Christendom, but you will glow and burn with a seraph's ardour, longing and desiring even to do more than you can do, and practically carrying out with your utmost ability what your heart desireth for the glory of the Lord.

Further, it is quite certain that all *the joy* of the spiritual life depends upon faith. You all know that the moment your faith ceases to hang simply upon Jesus, or even if it suffers a little check, your joy evaporates. Joy is a welcome angel, but it will not tarry where faith does not entertain it. Spiritual joy is a bird of paradise, which will build its nest only among the boughs of faith. Faith must pipe, or joy will not dance. Unbelieving Jacob finds his days few and evil, but believing Abraham dies an old man, and full of years. If you would anoint your head and wash your face, and put away the ashes and the sackcloth, you must trust more firmly in the faithfulness of the Lord your God. Doubts and fears never could strike so much as a spark with which to light the smallest candle to cheer a Christian ; but simple trust in Jesus makes the sun to rise in his strength with healing beneath his wings, even upon those that sit in the valley of the shadow of death. In proportion as you lean on Christ, in that proportion shall life's burden grow light, heaven's joys grow real, and your whole being more elevated.

I might thus continue to mention each point in the secret life, but I rather choose to proceed in order to observe only, that all our *growth* in the spiritual life depends upon our faith. True life must grow in its season. You can tell the difference between two stakes which are driven into the ground : the one may happen to have life in it, and if so, before long it sprouts, while the dead one is unchanged. So with the Christian. If he be living he will grow. He must make advances. It is not possible for the Christian to sit still and remain in the same state month after month ; but if he is to increase in spiritual riches, he must of necessity exert a constant and increasing faith in the Lord Jesus Christ. Peter cannot walk the waters except he believes ; doubting does not help him, but it sinks him. I fear me that some of my brethren and sisters try to grow in spiritual life by adopting methods which are not of faith. Some think that they will set themselves rules of self-denial or extra devotion—these plans are lawful, but they are not in themselves effective ; for vows may be observed mechanically, and rules obeyed formally, and yet the heart may be drifting away yet further from the Lord ; yea, these vows and rules may be a means of deluding us into the vain belief that all is well, whereas we are nearing to spiritual shipwreck. I have found in my own spiritual life, that the more rules I lay down for myself, the more sins I commit. The habit of regular morning and evening prayer is one which is indispensable to a believer's life, but the prescribing of the length of prayer, and the constrained remembrance of so many persons and subjects, may gender unto bondage, and strangle prayer rather than assist it. To say I will humble myself at such a time, and rejoice at such another season, is nearly as much an affectation as when the preacher wrote in the margin of his sermon, " cry here," " smile here." Why, if the man preached his sermon rightly, he would be sure to cry in the right place, and to smile at a suitable moment ; and when the spiritual life is sound, it produces prayer at the right time, and humiliation of soul and sacred joy spring forth spontaneously, apart from rules and vows. The kind of religion which makes itself to order by the almanack, and turns out its emotions like bricks from a machine, weeping on Good Friday, and rejoicing two days afterwards, measuring its motions by the moon, is too artificial to be worthy of your imitation. The liberty of the spiritual life is a grand thing, and where that liberty is maintained constantly, and the energy is kept up, you will need much faith, for the fading of faith will be the withering of devotion, liberty will degenerate into license, and the energy of your life will drivel into confidence in yourself. Let who will bind himself with rules and regulations in order to advance himself in grace, be it ours, like Abraham, to believe God, and it shall be counted us for righteousness, and like Paul, to run the race which is set before us, looking unto Jesus. Faith enriches the soil of the heart. Faith fills our treasuries with the choicest gold, and loads our tables with the daintiest food for our souls. By faith we shall do valiantly, stopping lions' mouths, and quenching violent flames ; but faith in Jesus, the Saviour, faith in the heavenly Father, faith in the Holy Spirit, this we must have, or we perish like foam upon the waters.

As the other side of all this, let me notice that some Christians appear to try to live by experience. If they feel happy to-day, they say they are saved, but if they feel unhappy to-morrow, they conclude that they are lost. If they feel at one moment a deep and profound calm overspreading their spirits, then are they greatly elevated ; but if the winds blow and the waves beat high, then they suppose that they are none of the Lord's people. Ah, miserable state of suspense ! To live by feeling is a dying life ; you know not where you are, nor what you are, if your feelings are to be the barometer of your spiritual condition. Beloved, a simple faith in Christ will enable you to remain calm even when your feelings are the reverse of happy, to remain confident when your emotions are far from ecstatic. If, indeed, we be saved by Jesus Christ, then the foundation of our salvation does not lie within us, but in that crucified Man who now reigns in glory. When He changes, ah, then what changes must occur to us ! But since He is the same yesterday, to-day, and for ever, why need we be so soon removed from our steadfastness ? Believe in Jesus, dear heart, when thou canst not find a spark of grace within thyself ; cast thyself as a sinner into the Saviour's arms when thou canst not think a good thought, nor uplift a good desire ; when thy soul feels like a barren wilderness that yields not so much as one green blade of hope, or joy, or love, still look up to the great Husbandman, who can turn the desert into a garden. Have confident faith in Jesus at all times, for if thou believest in Him thou art saved, and canst not be condemned. However good or bad thy state, this shall not affect the question ; thou believest, therefore thou shalt be saved. Give up living from hand to mouth in that poor miserable way of frames and feelings, and wait thou only upon the Lord, from whom cometh thy salvation.

Many professors are even worse : they try to live by experiments. I am afraid a great many among Dissenters are of that kind. They must have a revival meeting once a week at least ; if they do not get a grand display quite so often, they begin to fall dreadfully back, and crave an exciting meeting, as drunkards long for spirits. It is a poor spiritual life which hangs on eloquent sermons, and such-like stimulants. These may be good things and comforting things : be thankful for them, but I pray you do not let your spiritual life depend upon them. It is very much as though a man should, according to scriptural language, feed on the wind and snuff up the east wind ; for your faith is not to stand in the wisdom of man, nor in the excellency of human speech, nor in the earnestness of your fellow Christians, but in your simple faith in Him who is, and was, and is to come, who is the Saviour of sinners. A genuine faith in Christ will enable you to live happily even if you be denied the means of grace ; will make you rejoice on board ship, keep Sabbath on a sick bed, and make your dwelling-house a temple even if you find a log-hut in the far West, or a shanty in the bush of Australia. Only have faith, and thou needest not look to these excitements any more than the mountains look to the summer's sun for their stability.

Shall I need further to say, by way of caution, that I am afraid many professors live *anyhow* ? I know not how otherwise to describe it. They have not enough caution to look at their inward experience, they have not enough vigour to care about excitement, but they live a kind of listless, dreamy, comatose life. I mean *some of you*. You believe that you were saved years ago. You united yourselves to a Christian church, and were baptized, and you conclude that all is right. You have written your conversion in your spiritual trade-books as a good asset, you consider it as a very clear thing. I am afraid it is rather doubtful, still you think it sure. Since that time you have kept up the habit of prayer, you have been honest, you have subscribed to church funds, have done your duty outwardly as a Christian, but there has been very little vitality in your godliness ; it has been surface work, skin-deep consistency. You have not been grievously exercised about sin, you have not been bowed under the weight of inward corruption ; neither have you been, on the other hand, exhilarated by a sense of divine love and a delightful recognition of your interest in it. You have gone on dreamily, as I have heard of soldiers marching when they were asleep. O for a thunderbolt to wake you, for this is dangerous living ! Of all modes of living, if you be a Christian, this is one of the most perilous ; and if you be not a Christian, it is one of the most seductive ; for while the outward sinner may be got at by the preaching of the gospel, you are almost beyond the reach of gospel ministry, because you will not allow that warnings are meant for you. You wrap yourselves up and say, " It is well with me," while you are really naked, and poor, and miserable in the sight of God. Oh, if you could but get back to live by faith !

II. Secondly, " the just shall live by faith "— this means that FAITH IS OPERATIVE IN OUR DAILY LIFE.

It is operative in many ways, but three observations will suffice. Faith is *the great sustaining energy* with the just man under all his trials, difficulties, sufferings, or labours. It is a notion with some that true religion is meant to be kept shut up in churches and chapels, as a proper thing for Sundays, which ought to be attended to, since a man is not respectable if he does not take a pew somewhere, even if he does not need sit in it, or, sitting in it, pays no more attention to the word preached than to a ballad singer in the street ; there is a decent show of religion which people, as a rule, must keep up, or they cannot be received into polite society ; but the idea of bringing religion down to the breakfast table, introducing it to the drawing-room, taking it into the kitchen, keeping it on hand in the shop, in the workshop, or the corn exchange, carrying it out to sea in your vessel—this is thought by some to be sheer fanaticism ; and yet if there is anything taught by the revelation of the Lord Jesus Christ, it is just this : that religion is a matter of common, everyday life ; and no man understands the Christian religion at all unless he has fully accepted it as not a thing for Sundays, and for certain places and certain times, but for all places and all times, and all conditions and all forms of life. An active, operative faith is by the Holy Spirit implanted in the Christian and it is sent to him on purpose to sustain him under trial. I shall put this to some of you as a test by which you may try whether you have obtained the faith of God's elect. You have lost a large sum of money : well, are you distracted and bewildered ? Do you almost lose your senses ? Do you murmur against God ? Then I ask you what are you better than the man who has no religion at all ? Are you not an unbeliever ? for if you believed that all things work together for your good, would you be so rebellious ? Yet that is God's own declaration. Now is the time when your faith in God should enable you to say, " The Lord gave, and the Lord hath taken away ; blessed be the name of the Lord." What do you more than others unless you can thus speak with submission and resignation—aye, even with alacrity ? Where is your new nature if you cannot say, " It is the Lord, let Him do as seemeth him good." ? By this shall you test whether you have faith or no. Or it may be you have lost a darling child, and that loss has cut you to the very quick. You are scarcely able to reconcile yourself at present to it, yet I trust you do not so repine as to accuse your God of cruelty, but I shall trust your faith helps you to say, " I

shall go to Him, though He shall not return to me ; I would not have it other than my heavenly Father has determined." Here will be a crucible for your faith. Those two instances may serve as specimens. In all positions of life a real faith is to the believer like the hair of Samson, in which his great strength lieth. It is his Moses' rod dividing seas of difficulty, his Elijah's chariot in which he mounts above the earth. So, too, in difficult labours, for instance, in labours for Christ's cause, a man who feels it his duty to do good in his neighbourhood, yet may say " I do not know what I can do, I am afraid to commence so great a matter, for I feel so unfit, and so feeble." My dear friend, if it is your duty to do it, you not being able to do it cannot excuse you, because you have only to go and tell your heavenly Father of your weakness, and ask for strength, and He will give it liberally. Some of us who can now speak with ease were once very diffident in public. Those preachers who are now most useful, were poor stammerers before their gifts were developed ; and those who are our best teachers and most successful soul-winners, were not always so ; but they had faith, and they pressed forward, and God helped them. Now, if your religion is not worth an old song, you will not persevere in holy work ; but if it is real and true, you will press forward through all difficulties, feeling it to be an essential of your very existence, that you should promote the Redeemers cause. I would quite as soon not be, as live to be a useless thing. Better far to fatten the field with one's corpse, than to lie rotting above ground in idleness. To be a soldier in Immanuel's ranks, and never fight, never carry a burden, nor uphold a banner nor hurl a dart—aye, better that the dogs should eat my worthless carrion, than that such should be the case. Feeling this, then, you will press forward with the little power you have, and new power will come upon you, and so you will prove that your faith is sincere, because it comes to your support in the ordinary work of Christian life. Under all difficulties and labours, then, the just shall live by faith.

Furthermore, faith in ordinary life *has an effect upon the dispensations of divine providence.* It is a riddle which we cannot explain how everything is eternally fixed by divine purpose, and yet the prayer of faith moves the arm of God. Though the enigma cannot be explained, the fact is not to be denied. My brethren and sisters, I may be thought fanatical, but it is my firm belief that in ordinary matters, such as the obtaining of your living, the education of your children, the ruling of your household, you are to depend upon God as much as in the grand matter of the salvation of your soul. The hairs of your head are all numbered : go to God then about your trifles. Not a sparrow falls to the ground without your Father : cast upon the Lord your minor trials. Never think that anything is too little for your heavenly Father's love to think upon. He who rides upon the whirlwind, walks in the garden at evening in the cool breath of the zephyr ; he who shakes the avalanche from its Alp, also makes the sere leaf to twinkle as it falls from the aspen ; he whose eternal power directs the spheres in their everlasting marches, guides each grain of dust which is blown from the summer's threshing-floor. Confide in Him for the little as well as for the great, and you shall not find Him fail you. Is He God of the hills only, and not the God of the valleys ?

" Do we expect miracles then ? " saith one. No, but we expect the same results as are compassed by miracles. I have sometimes thought that for God to interpose by a miracle to accomplish a purpose is a somewhat clumsy method, if I may be allowed such a word, but for Him to accomplish the very same thing without interfering with the wheels of His providence, seems to me the more thoroughly God-like method. If I were hungry to-day, and God had promised to feed me, it would be as much a fulfilment of His promise if my friend here brought my food unexpectedly, as if the ravens brought it ; and the bringing of it by ordinary means would all the better prove that God was there, not interrupting the machinery of providence, but making it to educe the end which He designed. God will not turn stones into bread for you, but perhaps He will give you stones to break, and you will thus earn your bread. God may not rain manna out of heaven, and yet every shower of rain falling upon your garden brings you bread. It will be the better for you to earn your food than to have it brought by ravens, or better that Christian charity should make you its care than that an inexhaustible barrel and cruse should be placed in your cupboard. Anyhow, your bread shall be given you, and your water shall be sure. My witness is, and I speak it for the honour of God, that God is a good provider. I have been cast upon the providence of God ever since I left my father's house, and in all cases He has been my Shepherd, and I have known no lack. My first income as a Christian minister was small enough in all conscience, never exceeding forty pounds, yet I was as rich then as I am now, for I had enough ; and I had no more cares, nay, not half as many then as I have now ; and when I breathed my prayer to God then, as I do now, for all things temporal and spiritual, I found him ready to answer me at every pinch—and pinches I have had full many. Many a pecuniary trial since then have I had in connection with the college work, which depends for funds upon the Lord's moving His people to liberality : my faith has been often tried, but God has always been faithful, and sent supplies in hours of need. If any should tell me that prayer to God was a mere piece of excitement, and that the idea of God's answering human cries is absurd, I should laugh the statement to scorn, for my experience is not that of one or two singular instances, but that of hundreds of cases, in which the Lord's interposition for the necessities of His work has been as manifest as if He had rent the clouds, and thrust forth His own naked arm and bounteous hand to supply the needs of His servant. This, my testimony, is but the echo of the witness of the Lord's people everywhere. When they look back they will tell you that God is good to Israel, and that when they have walked by faith they have never found that God has failed them. The Red Sea of trouble has been divided, the waters have stood upright as a heap, and the depths have been congealed in the heart of the sea ; as for their doubts and their difficulties, like the Egyptians, the depths have covered them, there has not been one of them left ; and standing on the further shore to look back upon the past, the redeemed of the Lord have shouted aloud, " Sing unto the Lord, for He hath triumphed gloriously," for faith has conquered all their difficulties, and brought supplies for all their needs. Do not let me be misunderstood, however. Faith is never to be regarded as a premium for idleness. If

I sit down and fold my arms, and say, " The Lord will provide " ; He will most likely provide me a summons to the County Court, and a place in the parish workhouse. God has never given any promise to idle people that He will provide for them, and therefore they have no kind of right to believe that He will. To trust in God to make up for our laziness, is not faith, but wicked presumption. Neither does the power of faith afford ground for fanaticism. I have no right to say, " I should like to have so-and-so, and I will ask for it, and shall have it." God has never promised to give to us everything which our whimsies may select. If we really want any good thing, we may plead the promise, " No good thing will I uphold from them that walk uprightly," but we must never dream that God will pander to our fooleries. The God of wisdom will not be art and part with our mere whims. Nor is faith to be a substitute for prudence and economy. I have known some who have, to a great degree, abstained from energetic action, because they feared to interfere with the Lord. This fear never perplexes me. My faith never leads me to believe that God will do for me what I can do for myself. I do not believe that the Lord works needlessly. Up to the highest pitch that my own prudence, and strength, and judgment can carry me, I am to go, depending upon divine guidance ; then I stop, for I can go no further ; and I plead with my Father thus—" Now, Lord, the promise reaches further than this, it is Thy business to make up the deficiency." There I pause, and God is as good as His word. But if I stop short when I might advance, how dare I ask the Lord to pander to my sloth ? I believe, in Christian work, we ought for God to exert ourselves to the utmost, both in the giving of our substance and in the collecting help from our fellow Christians ; and come in faith and prayer to the Lord for help. Faith is operative in the land of the unseen, not in the seen. Faith is to come to your help where creature-power fails you. Up to the point at which you can work you must work, and with God's blessing upon it, your work will not hinder your faith, but be an exhibition and display of it.

Thus with a simple faith in God, not fanatical, not idle, but going on in the path of prudence, desiring to glorify God, you shall find that all difficulties will vanish, and your doubts and fears shall fly away. Do understand that even faith itself will be no guarantee against trials and against poverty, for it is good for God's people to be tried, and there are some of them who would not glorify God if they were not poor. Therefore, you are not to suppose that you have no faith because you are in need, neither are you to expect that in answer to prayer God will necessarily keep you in easy circumstances. If it be best for you that you should not be poor, He will keep you from it ; but if it be better that you should be, He will sustain you in it. Resignation should walk hand-in-hand with faith, and they each will minister to the other's beauty.

III. Lastly, THIS IS ALSO TRUE IN THE HISTORY OF THE CHRISTIAN CHURCH AS A WHOLE.

The Christian church lives by faith. She lives by faith in opposition to *speculation*. Every now and then a fit of speculative philosophy seizes the church, and then her vitality withers. In the days of the schoolmen, just before Luther's time, good men were fighting and squabbling from morning to night, gathered like so many carrion crows around the dead body of Aristotle, fighting about nobody knows what. It is said that they held sage discussions upon how many angels could poise themselves upon the point of a needle! While such foolish and unlearned questions as these were being raised, the poor people in the Christian church were starved, and the church lost all its energy, sinners were not converted, fundamental truth was despised. Then came Luther and the notable revival. In more modern days, in the period after Doddridge and Watts, amongst Dissenters, the habit of philosophising upon the Trinity was common. Brethren tried to be very exact and precise, as exact and precise as the Athanasian creed, while others combated their dogmatism, and the result was that a large proportion of the Dissenting churches fell asleep practically, degenerated doctrinally, and Socinianism threatened to eat out the very life of evangelical Dissent. Speculation is not the life of the Christian church, but faith, a reception of the Bible truth in its sublimity and authority; an obedient belief in revelation, not because we understand all its teachings, but because, not understanding, we nevertheless receive the Lord's word upon the *ipse dixit* of the Most High. Whenever the church is simple-minded enough to require no out-works to her faith, to care very little about evidences, internal or external, but just to fight the battle on the ground of divine authority, saying, " This is of God, and at your peril reject it," she has been " fair as the sun, clear as the moon, and terrible as an army with banners " : let her begin to split hairs, try to move away objections, and spend all her time upon her out-works, and then her glory departs.

In the next place, faith is the life of the Church in opposition to *retiring despondency*. In our own churches, it used to be the habit for our friends to be very well content if they built a chapel in the lowest part of a town, down two courts, three alleys, and a turning ; and as to attendants, the members appeared to be particularly anxious to avoid anything like the excitement of a crowd. They were a most retiring people as a rule, but as to coming out into the forefront to set their city on a hill, and make their light shine by evangelizing the masses, that was a forgotten business. At the present hour from other quarters you constantly hear expressions defiled with the most dastardly timidity, denoting the most shameful cowardice. For instance, lately we have heard that " The Church is in danger ! " " The Church is in danger ! " Christians with their Bibles, and all the truths in the Bibles ; with their ministers and all their earnestness, with the Holy Spirit, with God's promises, with the foundations against which the gates of hell shall not prevail, and yet in danger ! Really, such remarks and such fears are quite unworthy of the manhood of those who believe in the divinity of the Christian faith. No church can make progress till she believes enough in her God to be sure that in Him she is strong. While she imagines that she is weak she is weak, fear paralyses her, dread kills her energies ; but when she believes in the divine strength with which she is enceintered as with a golden girdle, then she marches on with certainty of triumph. May we as a church always believe that resting upon the strength of God nothing can hurt us : I defy the House of Lords, the House of Commons, the Pope, the Turk, and all the nations in all the world, and all the devils in hell, to put this church in danger. I do not know anything that they could take away from us, for I know of nothing which

they have given us. If they had endowed and established us, they could take away what they gave, but as they have not given us a thread to a shoe-latchet, they can do whatever they please, and we shall not even call a church meeting to consider it. Yet here are other churches, with lord bishops, and deans, and prebends, and I know not what beside, which are horribly shaken because an arm of flesh is failing them. The pay of their preachers will by-and-by, by a gradual process, be withdrawn, and they tremble for the ark of the Lord ! Shame on your little minds, to be thus afraid ! Surely, you have lost confidence in truth and in God, or you would not fear because of the talents of gold which will be justly withheld from you. Remember that truth allied with earthly power has often been defeated by error, but truth alone has always defeated error, even when that error has had physical might upon its side. Let truth have her fair chance and stand alone. She is most strong when least hampered with human strength, and most sure to be victorious when she hath no might but that which dwells in herself, or comes from her God.

In the next place, the Christian church lives by faith, that is, faith in opposition to a *squeamishness* which I see springing up nowadays as to the slection of instruments. Let me be understood. I hear it is said, " Why allow these men to preach in the street ? Is it not a pity that illiterate persons should preach at all ? Some of them are very ungrammatical, and really what they say at the very best is very so-so. Is it not better that none should go out but the best trained men ? " Then, for missions, it is said, the very best picked men only should be sent forth. As to young men, full of zeal, not having had experience, and not having learned all the classics, and being well up in mathematics, it is of no use thinking to send them. Many a church indeed thinks that all her officers ought to be rich, all her ministers learned, all her agents Masters of Arts at least, if not Doctors of Divinity. This was not so in the olden time. Thus it was not when the church of God grew mightily, for of old the church of God had faith—in what ? Why, faith in weakness, faith in the things that were not. Did not she believe that " Not many noble, not many wise men after the flesh, not many mighty, are called ; but God hath chosen the foolish things of the world to confound the wise ; and God hath chosen the weak things of the world to confound the things which are mighty ; and base things of the world, and things which are despised." It is very memorable that in the catacombs of Rome, among those remarkable inscriptions which are now preserved with so much care as the memorials of the departed saints, it is rare to find an inscription which is all of it spelt correctly, proving that the persons who wrote them, who were no doubt the very pick of the Christian flock, could neither write nor spell correctly ; and yet these were the men that turned the world upside down. When Wesley began his career, our churches were nearly dead with the disease called " proprieties," but Mr. Wesley employed men, some of whom were quite unlettered, to go about to preach, and by those men this nation was revived. To this day, our Primitive Methodist friends are doing a great and noble work, for which God be thanked, because they use almost every man they have, and they use the men till they become fit to be used, trained and tutored by practice. In this church, I thank God, I have always encouraged every brother and sister to do all they can, and I do still urge all so to do. I trust there is not a young man here who can say that I ever held him back in desiring to serve his Master. If I have, I am sure I am very sorry for it. Oh! do all of you all that you can ; for this church at any rate has faith in you all, that though you make a thousand blunders, yet it is better to have the gospel preached blunderingly than not at all ; and while three millions and more in London are perishing for lack of knowledge, it is better that you spoil the Queen's English and make ever such mistakes, than that you should not preach Jesus Christ. God will not be angry with you for all your ignorance, if you be not ignorant of the one thing needful.

So, brethren, it comes to this, that we must not as a Christian church calculate our resources, nor take out our note books and count up how much we have to rely upon. The exchequer of the church is the liberality of God ; the power of the church is the omnipotence of Jehovah ; the persuasions of the church are the irresistible influences of the Holy Ghost ; the destiny of the church is an ultimate conquest over all the sons of men. Advance then, every one of you to the fray, for you advance also to conquest ! Rely upon Him who has said, " Lo, I am with you alway, even unto the end of the world ! " and you shall find that as the just you shall live by faith ; while if you sit down and waste your time, or turn your backs and retire from the battle, you shall be written among the cravens whose memorial is in the dust ; but if you stand fast and are immovable, " always abounding in the work of the Lord," your record shall be on high, and your portion shall be at the right hand of the Father, where Christ sitteth, and where you also shall sit for ever and ever. God bless these words for His name's sake. Amen.

CHRIST MADE A CURSE FOR US

" Christ hath redeemed us from the curse of the law, being made a curse for us: for it is written, Cursed is every one that hangeth on a tree."—Galatians iii. 13.

THE apostle had been showing to the Galatians that salvation is in no degree by works. He proved this all-important truth in the verses which precede the text, by a very conclusive form of double reasoning. He showed, first, that the law could not give the blessing of salvation, for, since all had broken it, all that the law could do was to curse. He quotes the substance of the twenty-seventh chapter of Deuteronomy, " Cursed is every one that continueth not in all things which are written in the book of the law to do them " ; and as no man can claim that he has continued in all things that are in the law, he pointed out the clear inference that all men under the law had incurred the curse. He then reminds the Galatians, in the second place, that if any had ever been blessed in the olden times, the blessing came not by the law, but by their faith, and to prove this, he quotes a passage from Habakkuk ii. 4, in which it is distinctly stated that the just shall live by faith : so that those who were just and righteous did not live before God on the footing of their obedience to the law, but they were justified and made to live on the ground of their being believers. See, then, that if the law inevitably curses us all, and if the only people who are said to have been preserved in gracious life were justified not by works, but by faith, then is it certain beyond a doubt that the salvation and justification of a sinner cannot be by the works of the law, but altogether by the grace of God through faith which is in Christ Jesus. But the apostle, no doubt feeling that now he was declaring that doctrine, he had better declare the foundation and root of it, unveils in the text before us a reason why men are not saved by their personal righteousness, but saved by their faith. He tells us that the reason is this : that men are not saved now by any personal merit, but their salvation lies in another—lies, in fact, in Christ Jesus, the representative Man, who alone can deliver us from the curse which the law brought upon us ; and since works do not connect us with Christ, but faith is the uniting bond, faith becomes the way of salvation. Since faith is the hand that lays hold upon the finished work of Christ, which works could not and would not do, for works lead us to boast, and to forget Christ, faith becomes the true and only way of obtaining justification and everlasting life. In order that such faith may be nurtured in us, may God the Holy Spirit this morning lead us into the depths of the great work of Christ ; may we understand more clearly the nature of His substitution, and of the suffering which it entailed upon Him. Let us see, indeed, the truth of the stanzas whose music has just died away—

" He bore that we might never bear
His Father's righteous ire."

I. Our first contemplation, this morning, will be upon this question, WHAT IS THE CURSE OF THE LAW HERE INTENDED ?

It is the curse of God. God who made the law has appended certain penal consequences to the breaking of it, and the man who violates the law, becomes at once the subject of the wrath of the Lawgiver. It is not the curse of the mere law of itself ; it is a curse from the great Lawgiver whose arm is strong to defend His statutes. Hence, at the very outset of our reflections, let us be assured that the law-curse must be supremely just, and morally unavoidable. It is not possible that our God, who delights to bless us, should inflict an atom of curse upon any one of His creatures unless the highest right shall require it ; and if there be any method by which holiness and purity can be maintained without a curse, rest assured the God of love will not imprecate sorrow upon His creatures. The curse, then, if it fall, must be a necessary one, in its very essence needful for the preservation of order in the universe, and for the manifestation of the holiness of the universal Sovereign. Be assured, too, that when God curses, it is a curse of the most weighty kind. The curse causeless shall not come ; but God's curses are never causeless, and they come home to offenders with overwhelming power. Sin must be punished, and when by long continuance and impenitence in evil, God is provoked to speak the malediction, I wot that he whom He curses, is cursed indeed. There is something so terrible in the very idea of the omnipotent God pronouncing a curse upon a transgressor, that my blood curdles at it, and I cannot express myself very clearly or even coherently. A father's curse, how terrible! but what is that to the malediction of the great Father of Spirits! To be cursed of men is no mean evil, but to be accursed of God is terror and dismay. Sorrow and anguish lie in that curse; death is involved in it and that second death which John foresaw in Patmos, and described as being cast into a lake of fire. Rev. xx. 14. Hear ye the word of the Lord by His servant Nahum, and consider what His curse must be: "God is jealous, and the Lord revengeth; the Lord revengeth, and is furious; the Lord will take vengeance on His adversaries, and He reserveth wrath for His enemies . . . . The mountains quake at Him, and the hills melt, and the earth is burned at His presence, yea, the world, and all that dwell herein. Who can stand before His indignation? and who can abide in the fierceness of His anger? His fury is poured out like fire, and the rocks are thrown down by Him." Remember also the prophecy of Malachi: "For behold, the day cometh, that shall burn as an oven; and all the proud, yea, and all that do wickedly, shall be stubble: and the day that cometh shall burn them up, saith the Lord of hosts, that it shall leave them neither root nor branch." Let such words, and there are many like them, sink into your hearts, that ye may fear and tremble before this just and holy Lord.

If we would look further into the meaning of the curse that arises from the breach of the law, we must remember that a curse is first of all a sign of displeasure. Now, we learn from Scripture that God is angry with the wicked every day; though towards the persons of sinners God exhibits great longsuffering, yet sin exceedingly provokes His holy mind; sin is a thing so utterly loathsome and detestable to the purity of the Most High, that no thought of evil, nor an ill word, nor an unjust action, is tolerated by Him; He observes every sin, and His holy soul is stirred thereby. He is of purer eyes than to behold iniquity; He cannot endure it. He is a God that will certainly execute vengeance upon every evil work. A curse implies something more than mere anger. It is suggested by burning indignation; and truly our God is not only somewhat angry with sinners, but His wrath is great towards sin. Wherever sin exists, there the fulness of the power of the divine indignation is directed; and though the effect of that wrath may be for awhile restrained through abundant longsuffering, yet God is greatly indignant with the iniquities of men. We wink at sin, yes, and even harden our hearts till we laugh at it and take pleasure in it, but oh! let us not think that God is such as we are; let us not suppose that sin can be upheld by Him and yet no indignation be felt. Ah! no, the most holy God has written warnings in His word which plainly inform us how terribly He is provoked by iniquity, as, for instance, when He saith, "Beware, ye that forget God, lest I tear you in pieces, and there be none to deliver." "Therefore saith the Lord, the Lord of hosts, the mighty One of Israel, Ah, I will ease Me of Mine adversaries, and avenge Me of Mine enemies." "For we know Him that hath said, Vengeance belongeth unto Me, I will recompense, saith the Lord. And again, the

Lord shall judge His people. It is a fearful thing to fall into the hands of the living God." Moreover, a curse imprecates evil, and is, as it comes from God, of the nature of a threat. It is as though God should say, "By-and-by I will visit thee for this offence. Thou hast broken My law which is just and holy, and the inevitable penalty shall certainly come upon thee." Now, God has throughout His word given many such curses as these: He has threatened men over and over again. "If He turn not, He will whet His sword; He hath bent His bow, and made it ready." Sometimes the threatening is wrapped up in a plaintive lamentation. "Turn ye, turn ye from your evil ways; for why will ye die, O house of Israel?" But still it is plain and clear that God will not suffer sin to go unpunished, and when the fulness of time shall come, and the measure shall be filled to the brim, and the weight of iniquity shall be fully reached, and the harvest shall be ripe, and the cry of wickedness shall come up mightily into the ears of the Lord God of Sabaoth, then will He come forth in robes of vengeance and overwhelm His adversaries.

But God's curse is something more than a threatening; He comes at length to blows. He uses warning words at first, but sooner or later He bares His sword for execution. The curse of God, as to its actual infliction, may be guessed at by some occasions wherein it has been seen on earth. Look at Cain, a wanderer and a vagabond upon the face of the earth! Read the curse that Jeremiah pronounced by the command of God upon Pashur; "Behold, I will make thee a terror to thyself, and to all thy friends: and they shall fall by the sword of their enemies, and thine eyes shall behold it." Or, if you would behold the curse upon a larger scale, remember the day when the huge floodgates of earth's deepest fountains were unloosed, and the waters leaped up from their habitations like lions eager for their prey. Remember the day of vengeance when the windows of heaven were opened, and the great deep above the firmament was confused with the deep that is beneath the firmament, and all flesh were swept away, save only the few who were hidden in the ark which God's covenant mercy had prepared—when sea-monsters whelped and stabled in the palaces of ancient kings, when millions of sinners sank to rise no more, when universal ruin flew with raven wing over a shoreless sea vomited from the mouth of death. Then was the curse of God poured out upon the earth. Look ye yet again further down in time. Stand with Abraham at his tent door, and see towards the east the sky all red at early morning with a glare that came not from the sun; sheets of flames went up to heaven, which were met by showers of yet more vivid fire, which preternaturally descended from the skies. Sodom and Gomorrah, having given themselves up to strange flesh, received the curse of God, and hell was rained upon them out of heaven until they were utterly consumed. If you would see another form of the curse of God, remember that bright spirit who once stood as servitor in heaven, the son of the morning, one of the chief of the angels of God. Think how he lost his lofty principality when sin entered into him! See how an archangel became an arch-fiend, and Satan, who is called Apollyon, fell upon his lofty throne, banished for ever from peace and happiness, to wander through dry places, seeking rest and finding none, to be reserved in chains of darkness unto the judgment of the last great day.

Such was the curse that it withered an angel into a devil, it burned up the cities of the plain, it swept away the population of a globe. Nor have you yet the full idea. There is a place of woe and horror, a land of darkness as darkness itself, and of the shadow of death, without any order, and where the light is darkness. There those miserable spirits who have refused repentance, and have hardened themselves against the Most High, are for ever banished from their God and from all hope of peace or restoration. If your ear could be applied to the gratings of their cells, if you could walk the gloomy corridors wherein damned spirits are confined, you would then with chilled blood, and hair erect, learn what the curse of the law must be—that dread malediction which comes on the disobedient from the hand of the just and righteous God. The curse of God is to lose God's favour; consequently, to lose the blessings which come upon that favour; to lose peace of mind, to lose hope, ultimately to lose life itself; for " the soul that sinneth, it shall die " ; and that loss of life, and being cast into eternal death, is the most terrible of all, consisting as it does in everlasting separation from God and everything that makes existence truly life. A destruction lasting on for ever, according to the scriptural description of it, is the fruit of the curse of the law. Oh, heavy tidings have I to deliver this day to some of you ! Hard is my task to have to testify to you thus the terrible justice of the law. But you would not understand or prize the exceeding love of Christ if you heard not the curse from which He delivers His people, therefore hear me patiently. O unhappy men, unhappy men, who are under God's curse to-day ! You may dress yourselves in scarlet and fine linen, you may go to your feasts, and drain your full bowls of wine ; you may lift high the sparkling cup, and whirl in the joyous dance, but if God's curse be on you, what madness possesses you ! O sirs, if you could but see it, and understand it, this curse would darken all the windows of your mirth. O that you could hear for once the voice which speaks against you from Ebal, with doleful repetition. " Cursed shalt thou be in the city, and cursed shalt thou be in the field. Cursed shall be thy basket and thy store. Cursed shall be the fruit of thy body, and the fruit of thy land, the increase of thy kine, and the flocks of thy sheep. Cursed shalt thou be when thou comest in, and cursed shalt thou be when thou goest out." How is it you can rest while such sentences pursue you ? Oh ! unhappiest of men, those who pass out of this life still accursed. One might weep tears of blood to think of them. Let our thoughts fly to them for a moment, but O let us not continue in sin, lest our spirits be condemned to hold perpetual companionship in their grief. Let us fly to the dear cross of Christ, where the curse was put away, that we may never come to know in the fulness of its horror what the curse may mean.

II. A second enquiry of great importance to us this morning is this : WHO ARE UNDER THIS CURSE ?

Listen with solemn awe, O sons of men. First, especially and foremost, the Jewish nation lies under the curse, for such I gather from the connection. To them the law of God was very peculiarly given beyond all others. They heard it from Sinai, and it was to them surrounded with a golden setting of ceremonial symbol, and enforced by solemn national covenant. Moreover, there was a word in the commencement of that law which showed that in a certain sense it peculiarly belonged to Israel. " I am the Lord thy God, which brought thee out of the land of Egypt, from the house of bondage." Paul tells us that those who have sinned without law shall be punished without law ; but the Jewish nation, having received the law, if they broke it, would become peculiarly liable to the curse which was threatened for such breach. Yet further, all nations that dwell upon the face of the earth are also subject to this curse, for this reason : that if the law was not given to all from Sinai, it has been written by the finger of God more or less legibly upon the conscience of all mankind. It needs no prophet to tell an Indian, a Laplander, a South Sea Islander, that he must not steal ; his own judgment so instructs him. There is that within every man which ought to convince him that idolatry is folly, that adultery and unchastity are villanies, that theft, and murder, and covetousness, are all evil. Now, inasmuch as all men in some degree have the law within, to that degree they are under the law ; the curse of the law for transgression comes upon them. Moreover, there are some in this house this morning who are peculiarly under the curse. The apostle says, " As many as are of the works of the law are under the curse." Now, there are some of you who choose to be under the law ; you deliberately choose to be judged by it. How so ? Why, you are trying to reach a place in heaven by your own good works ; you are clinging to the idea that something you can do can save you ; you have therefore elected to be under the law, and by so doing you have chosen the curse ; for all that the law of works can do for you, is to leave you still accursed, because you have not fulfilled all its commands. O sirs, repent of so foolish a choice, and declare henceforth that you are willing to be saved by grace, and not at all by the works of the law. There is a little band here who feel the weight of the law, to whom I turn with brightest hope, though they themselves are in despair. They feel in their consciences to-day that they deserve from God the severest punishment ; this sense of His wrath weighs them to the dust. I am glad of this, for it is only when we come consciously and penitently under the curse that we accept the way of escape from it. You do not know what it is to be redeemed from the curse till you have first felt the slavery of it. No man will ever rejoice in the liberty which Christ gives him till he has first felt the iron of bondage entering into his soul. I know there are some here who say, " Let God say what He will against me, or do what He will to me, I deserve it all. If He drive me for ever from His presence, and I hear the Judge pronounce that awful sentence, ' Depart, accursed one,' I can only admit that such has been my heart and such my life, that I could expect no other doom." O thou dear heart, if thou art thus brought down, thou wilt listen gladly to me while I now come to a far brighter theme than all this. Thou art under the curse as thou now art, but I rejoice to have to tell thee that the curse has been removed through Jesus Christ our Lord. O may the Lord lead thee to see the plan of substitution and to rejoice in it.

III. Our third and main point, this morning, is to answer the question, HOW WAS CHRIST MADE A CURSE FOR US ?

The whole pith and marrow of the religion of Christianity lies in the doctrine of " substitution," and I hesitate not to affirm my conviction that a very large proportion of Christians are not Christians at all, for they do not understand the fundamental doctrine of the Christian creed ; and alas ! there are preachers who do not preach, or even believe this cardinal truth. They speak of the blood of Jesus in an indistinct kind of way, and descant upon the death of Christ in a hazy style of poetry, but they do not strike this nail on the head, and lay it down that the way of salvation is by Christ's becoming a substitute for guilty man. This shall make me the more plain and definite. Sin is an accursed thing. God, from the necessity of His holiness, must curse it ; He must punish men for committing it ; but the Lord's Christ, the glorious Son of the everlasting Father, became a man, and suffered in His own proper person the curse which was due to the sons of men, that so, by a vicarious offering, God having been just in punishing sin, could extend His bounteous mercy towards those who believe in the Substitute. Now for this point. But, you enquire, how was Jesus Christ a curse ? We beg you to observe the word "made." "He was *made* a curse." Christ was no curse in Himself. In His person He was spotlessly innocent, and nothing of sin could belong personally to Him. In Him was no sin. "God made Him to be sin for us," the apostle expressly adds, "who knew no sin." There must never be supposed to be any degree of blameworthiness or censure in the person or character of Christ as He stands as an individual. He is in that respect without spot or wrinkle, or any such thing, the immaculate Lamb of God's Passover. Nor was Christ made a curse of necessity. There was no necessity in Himself that He should ever suffer the curse ; no necessity except that which His own loving suretyship created. His own intrinsic holiness kept Him from sin, and that same holiness kept Him from the curse. He was made a sin *for us*, not on His own account, not with any view to Himself, but wholly because He loved us, and chose to put Himself in the place which we ought to have occupied. He was made a curse for us not, again I say, out of any personal desert, or out of any personal necessity, but because He had voluntarily undertaken to be the covenant head of His people, and to be their representative, and as their representative to bear the curse which was due to them. We would be very clear here, because very strong expressions have been used by those who hold the great truth which I am endeavouring to preach, which strong expressions have conveyed the truth they meant to convey, but also a great deal more. Martin Luther's wonderful book on the Galatians, which he prized so much that he called it his Catherine Bora (that was the name of his beloved wife, and he gave this book the name of the dearest one he knew). In that book he says plainly, but be assured he did not mean what he said to be literally understood, that Jesus Christ was the greatest sinner that ever lived ; that all the sins of men were so laid upon Christ that He became all the thieves, and murderers, and adulterers that ever were, in one." Now, he meant this, that God treated Christ as if he had been a great sinner ; as if He had been all the sinners in the world in one ; and such language teaches that truth very plainly : but, Luther-like in his boisterousness, he overshoots his mark, and leaves room for the censure that he has almost spoken blasphemy against the blessed person of our Lord. Now, Christ never was and never could be a sinner ; and in His person and in His character, in Himself considered, He never could be anything but well-beloved of God, and blessed for ever and well-pleasing in Jehovah's sight ; so that when we say to-day that He was a curse, we must lay stress on those words, "He was *made* a curse"—constituted a curse, set as a curse ; and then again we must emphasise those other words, "*for us*"—not on His own account at all ; but entirely out of love to us, that we might be redeemed, He stood in the sinner's place and was reckoned to be a sinner, and treated as a sinner, and made a curse for us.

Let us go farther into this truth. How was Christ made a curse ? In the first place, He was made a curse because all the sins of His people were actually laid on Him. Remember the words of the apostle— it is no doctrine of mine, mark you ; it is an inspired sentence, it is God's doctrine—"He made Him to be sin for us " ; and let me quote another passage from the prophet Isaiah, "The Lord hath laid on Him the iniquity of us all " ; and yet another from the same prophet, "He shall bear their iniquities." The sins of God's people were lifted from off them and imputed to Christ, and their sins were looked upon as if Christ had committed them. He was regarded as if He had been the sinner ; He actually and in very deed stood in the sinner's place. Next to the imputation of sin came the curse of sin. The law, looking for sin to punish, with its quick eye detected sin laid upon Christ, and, as it must curse sin wherever it was found, it cursed the sin as it was laid on Christ. So Christ was made a curse. Wonderful and awful words, but as they are scriptural words, we must receive them. Sin being on Christ, the curse came on Christ, and in consequence, our Lord felt an unutterable horror of soul. Surely it was that horror which made Him sweat great drops of blood when He saw and felt that God was beginning to treat Him as if He had been a sinner. The holy soul of Christ shrunk with deepest agony from the slightest contact with sin. So pure and perfect was our Lord, that never an evil thought had crossed His mind, nor had His soul been stained by the glances of evil, and yet He stood in God's sight a sinner and therefore a solemn horror fell upon His soul ; the heart refused its healthful action, and a bloody sweat bedewed His face. Then He began to be made a curse for us, nor did He cease till He had suffered all the penalty which was due on our account. We have been accustomed in divinity to divide the penalty into two parts, the penalty of loss and the penalty of actual suffering. Christ endured both of these. It was due to sinners that they should lose God's favour and presence, and therefore Jesus cried, "My God, My God, why hast Thou forsaken Me ? " It was due to sinners that they should lose all personal comfort ; Christ was deprived of every consolation, and even the last rag of clothing was torn from Him, and He was left, like Adam, naked and forlorn. It was necessary that the soul should lose everything that could sustain it, and so did Christ lose every comfortable thing ; He looked and there was no man to pity or help ; He was made to cry, "But I am a worm, and no man ; a reproach of men, and despised of the people." As for the second part of the punishment, namely, an actual infliction of suffering, our Lord endured this also to the uttermost, as the evangelists clearly show. You have read full often the story of His bodily sufferings ; take care that you never depreciate them.

There was an amount of physical pain endured by our Saviour which His body never could have borne unless it had been sustained and strengthened by union with His Godhead ; yet the sufferings of His soul were the soul of His sufferings. That soul of His endured a torment equivalent to hell itself. The punishment that was due to the wicked was that of hell, and though Christ suffered not hell, He suffered an equivalent for it ; and now, can your minds conceive what that must have been ? It was an anguish never to be measured, an agony never to be comprehended. It is to God, and God alone that His griefs were fully known. Well does the Greek liturgy put it, " Thine unknown sufferings," for they must for ever remain beyond guess of human imagination. See, brethren, Christ has gone thus far ; He has taken the sin, taken the curse, and suffered all the penalty. The last penalty of sin was death ; and therefore the Redeemer died. Behold, the mighty conqueror yields up His life upon the tree ! His side is pierced ; the blood and water flows forth, and His disciples lay His body in the tomb. As He was first numbered with the transgressors, He was afterwards numbered with the dead. See, beloved, here is Christ bearing the curse instead of His people. Here He is coming under the load of their sin, and God does not spare Him but smites Him, as He must have smitten us, lays His full vengeance on Him, launches all His thunderbolts against Him, bids the curse wreak itself upon Him, and Christ suffers all, sustains all.

IV. And now let us conclude by considering WHAT ARE THE BLESSED CONSEQUENCES OF CHRIST'S HAVING THUS BEEN MADE A CURSE FOR US.

The consequences are that He hath redeemed us from the curse of the law. As many as Christ died for, are for ever free from the curse of the law ; for when the law cometh to curse a man who believeth in Christ, he saith, " What have I to do with thee, O law ? Thou sayest, ' I will curse thee,' but I reply, ' Thou hast cursed Christ instead of me. Canst thou curse twice for one offence ? ' " Behold how the law is silenced ! God's law having received all it can demand, is not so unrighteous as to demand anything more. All that God can demand of a believing sinner, Christ has already paid, and there is no voice in earth or heaven that can henceforth accuse a soul that believes in Jesus. You were in debt, but a friend paid your debt ; no writ can be served on you. It matters nothing that *you* did not pay it, it is paid, and you have the receipt. That is sufficient in any court of equity. So with all the penalty that was due to us, Christ has borne it. It is true I have not borne it ; I have not been to hell and suffered the full wrath of God, but Christ has suffered that wrath for me, and I am as clear as if I had myself paid the debt to God and had myself suffered His wrath. Here is a glorious bottom to rest upon ! Here is a rock upon which to lay the foundation of eternal comfort ! Let a man once get to this. My Lord without the city's gate did bleed for me as my surety, and on the cross discharged my debt. Why, then, great God, Thy thunders I no longer fear. How canst Thou smite me now ? Thou hast exhausted the quiver of Thy wrath ; every arrow has been already shot forth against the person of my Lord, and I am in Him clear and clean, and absolved and delivered, even as if I had never sinned. " He hath redeemed us," saith the text. How often I have heard certain gentry of the modern school of theology sneer at the atonement, because they charge us with the notion of its being a sort of business transaction, or what they choose to call " the mercantile view of it." I hesitate not to say that the mercantile metaphor expresses rightly God's view of redemption, for we find it so in Scripture ; the atonement is a ransom—that is to say, a price paid ; and in the present case the original word is more than usually expressive ; it is a payment for, a price instead of. Jesus did in His sufferings perform what may be forcibly and fitly described as the payment of a ransom, the giving to justice a *quid pro quo* for what was due on our behalf for our sins. Christ in His person suffered what we ought to have suffered in our persons. The sins that were ours were made His ; He stood as a sinner in God's sight; though not a sinner in Himself, He was punished as a sinner, and died as a sinner upon the tree of the curse. Then having exhausted His imputed sinnership by bearing the full penalty, He made an end of sin, and He rose again from the dead to bring in that everlasting righteousness which at this moment covers the persons of all His elect, so that they can exultingly cry, " Who shall lay anything to the charge of God's elect ? It is God that justifieth. Who is he that condemneth ? It is Christ that died, yea, rather, that is risen again, who is even at the right hand of God, who also maketh intercession for us."

Another blessing flows from this satisfactory substitution. It is this, that now the blessing of God, which had been hitherto arrested by the curse, is made most freely to flow. Read the verse that follows the text : " That the blessing of Abraham might come on the Gentiles through Jesus Christ ; that we might receive the promise of the Spirit through faith." The blessing of Abraham was that in his seed all nations of the earth should be blessed. Since our Lord Jesus Christ has taken away the curse due to sin, a great rock has been lifted out from the river-bed of God's mercy, and the living stream comes rippling, rolling, swelling on in crystal tides, sweeping before it all human sin and sorrow, and making glad the thirsty who stoop down to drink thereat. O my brethren, the blessings of God's grace are full and free this morning ; they are as full as your necessities. Great sinners, there is great mercy for you. They are as free as your poverty could desire them to be, free as the air you breathe, or as the cooling stream that flows along the water-brook. You have but to trust Christ, and you shall live. Be you who you may, or what you may, or where you may, though at hell's dark door you lie down to despair and die, yet the message comes to you, " God hath made Christ to be a propitiation for sin. He made Him to be sin for us who knew no sin, that we might be made the righteousness of God in Him." Christ hath delivered us from the curse of the law, being made a curse for us. He that believeth, hath no curse upon him. He may have been an adulterer, a swearer, a drunkard, a murderer, but the moment he believes, God sees none of those sins in him. He sees him as an innocent man, and regards his sins as having been laid on the Redeemer, and punished in Jesus as He died on the tree. I tell thee, if thou believest in Christ this morning, my hearer, though thou be the most damnable of wretches that ever polluted the earth, yet thou shalt not have a sin remaining on thee after believing. God will look at thee as pure ; even Omniscience shall not detect a sin in thee, for thy sin shall be put on the scapegoat, even Christ, and carried away into forgetfulness, so that if thy transgression be searched for, it shall not be found. If thou believest—there is the question—thou art clean ; if thou wilt trust the incarnate God, thou art delivered. He that believeth is justified from all things. " Believe on the Lord Jesus Christ, and thou shalt be saved," for " he that believeth and is baptized, shall be saved ; and he that believeth not shall be damned."

I have preached to you the gospel, God knows with what a weight upon my soul, and yet with what holy joy. This is no subject for gaudy eloquence, and for high-flying attempts at oratory ; this is a matter to be put to you plainly and simply. Sinners—you must either be cursed of God, or else you must accept Christ, as bearing the curse instead of you. I do beseech you, as you love your souls, if you have any sanity left, accept this blessed and divinely-appointed way of salvation. This is the truth which the apostles preached, and suffered and died to maintain ; it is this for which the Reformers struggled; it is this for which the martyrs burned at Smithfield ; it is the grand basis doctrine of the Reformation, and the very truth of God. Down with your crosses and rituals, down with your pretensions to good works, and your crouchings at the feet of priests to ask absolution from them ! Away with your accursed and idolatrous dependence upon yourself ; Christ has finished salvation-work, altogether finished it. Hold not up your rags in competition with His fair white linen : Christ has borne the curse ; bring not your pitiful penances, and your tears all full of filth to mingle with the precious fountain flowing with His blood. Lay down what is your own, and come and take what is Christ's. Put away now everything that you have thought of being or doing, by way of winning acceptance with God ; humble yourselves, and take Jesus Christ to be the Alpha and Omega, the first and last, the beginning and end of your salvation. If you do this, not only shall you be saved, but you are saved : rest, thou weary one, for thy sins are forgiven ; rise, thou lame man, lame through want of faith, for thy transgression is covered ; rise from the dead, thou corrupt one, rise, like Lazarus from the tomb, for Jesus calleth thee ! Believe and live. The words in themselves, by the Holy Spirit, are soul-quickening. Have done with thy tears of repentance and thy vows of good living, until thou hast come to Christ ; then take them up as thou wilt. Thy first lesson should be none but Jesus, none but Jesus, none but Jesus. O come thou to Him ! See, He hangs upon the cross ; His arms are open wide, and He cannot close them, for the nails hold them fast. He tarries for thee ; His feet are fastened to the wood, as though He meant to tarry still. O come thou to Him ! His heart has room for thee. It streams with blood and water ; it was pierced for thee. That mingled stream is—

> " Of sin the double cure,
> To cleanse *thee* from its guilt and power."

An act of faith will bring thee to Jesus. Say, " Lord, I believe, help thou mine unbelief " ; and if thou so doest, He cannot cast thee out, for His word is, " Him that cometh to me I will in no wise cast out." I have delivered to you the weightiest truth that ever ears heard, or that lips spoke, put it not from you. As we shall meet each other at the last tremendous day, when heaven and earth are on a blaze, and the trumpet shall ring and raise the dead, as we shall meet each other then, I challenge you to put this from you. If you do it, it is at your own peril, and your blood be on your own heads ; but the rather accept the gospel I have delivered to you. It is Jehovah's gospel. Heaven itself speaks in the words you hear to-day. Accept Jesus Christ as your substitute. O do it now, this moment, and God shall have glory, but you shall have salvation. Amen.

THE GREAT JAIL, AND HOW TO GET OUT OF IT

" But the Scripture hath concluded all under sin, that the promise by faith of Jesus Christ might be given to them that believe."—Galatians iii. 22.

IN every work which we undertake it is most important that we should act upon right principles ; for if we are misled upon essential points, our efforts will be wasted, since success cannot possibly be the result. A man may study the stars as long as he pleases, but he certainly will not come to right conclusions if he calculates their courses upon the theory that they daily revolve around the earth as a centre. The alchemists were earnest even to enthusiasm, but the object of their pursuit was unattainable, and the theories which guided their investigations were absurd, and, therefore, they exhibited a sorrowful spectacle of perseverance misapplied, and labour thrown away. In mechanics the most ingenious contriver must fail if he forgets the law of gravitation. You must proceed upon right principles, or disappointment awaits you. If a man in London believed that he would reach the city of York by travelling rapidly to the south, he would certainly fail, even though he had a special express attached to his carriage. If another should be sincerely of opinion that by drinking a strong poison he would restore himself to health, his friends and survivors would have to regret his infatuation. The earnestness of his belief will not alter the fact ; the principles which make the deadly drug so murderous will not yield because the man was sincere, but he will certainly die for his obstinacy. Now, the greatest matter of concern for any one of us is the eternal salvation of our soul. We need to be saved, and, according to the Scriptures of truth, there is but one way of salvation ; but that way does not happen to be in favour among the sons of men. The great popular principle, popular all over the world, no matter whether the people happen to be Protestant or Catholic, Parsee of Mahomedan, Brahminist or Buddhist, is *self-salvation*—they would reach eternal life by merit. There are differences about what is to be done, but the great universal principle of unregenerate man is that he is, somehow or other, to save himself. This is his principle ; and the further he goes in it the less likely is he to be saved. My object this morning is to bring before you the much despised principle which God has revealed as the only true one, namely, salvation by the grace of God, through Jesus Christ, by simple faith in Him. We preach, at God's commands, the way of salvation by mercy, not by merit ; by faith, not by works ; by grace, not by the efforts of men. May God help us so to set forth that principle, that many may accept it. I do not care one snap of my finger about preaching so that the style shall please the ear, but I long to reach your hearts. I want you to receive the only sure method of salvation, and I pray the Holy Ghost to baptize my words in His own mighty fire, and make them to burn their way into your hearts, and subdue you to the obedience of faith.

The text divides itself into two parts, but my sermon will not end there, for I shall try to enforce its great truths. Upon two points we will speak at once. The first is *a crowded prison*,—" The Scripture hath shut up all under sin " : and the second is *a glorious jail delivery*,—" that the promise by faith of Jesus Christ might be given to them that believe." After that we will try to show how excellent is that plan which God has marked out—the plan of deliverance from sin by the promise of aith in Christ Jesus.

I. Behold THE CROWDED PRISON.—" *The Scripture hath concluded or shut up all under sin.*" The *jailer* is the Scripture,—a *lawful* authority, for the Scripture is not the word of man, but of the Spirit of God. If any man reject the Scripture, I have little to say to him at this moment, for I am speaking mainly to those who accept the Bible as having been written by an infallible pen. If the Scriptures then, which you admit to be written by God, shut you up in sin, you are shut up by a lawful authority, against which you cannot rebel. God has done it ; God's own voice has declared you to be a prisoner under sin. No authority is more *powerful* than that of Scripture, for it is not only true, but it has force to support it. Where the word of the Lord is, there is power ; the Scripture, when it comes home to the heart, like a hammer breaks in pieces, and like a fire burns its way. We need not be alarmed when judged of men, but the voice of the Lord is full of terrible majesty, and awes the spirit which it condemns.

But how does the Scripture shut up all men under sin ? I reply, first, it has been well observed by Martin Luther that the very promises of Scripture shut up all mankind under sin. To begin with the first—that morning star of promise which shone over this world when first our parents left the gates of blighted Eden—" The seed of the woman shall bruise the serpent's head." Since such a promise was needed, it is clear that the blessing could only come to men through the Redeemer, the seed of the woman, and that in the case of all men the serpent's head must be broken, or they would remain under his dominion. When a blessing is promised, there must have been a need for it ; where a deliverer is predicted, there must have been a necessity for Him. If a blessing could come to men by the way of merit, or in the course of nature, there would be no need of a promise ; a promise implies a want, and the very first promise of deliverance by the woman's seed from the power of the serpent implies that men were under that evil power.

The promise of grace is clear in the covenant with Noah, in which the Lord declared that He would no more destroy the earth with a flood. Had the race of men been holy, God could not have destroyed it with a flood, for He would have violated justice by destroying an innocent race. To a pure race there could be no necessity for a covenant of preservation, for there would be no conceivable reason for the destruction of the innocent. The very making of a covenant that the earth should not again be swept with an overwhelming flood implies that, apart from such a gracious covenant, the earth might justly have been destroyed at any time. The lovely rainbow, while it comfortably reminds us of the divine faithfulness, is also a memorial of that universal depravity of our race which necessitated a covenant of grace to stand as a barrier for our protection, lest the righteous wrath of God should break forth upon us.

The yet more explicit covenant which God made with Abraham plainly shows men to be shut up under sin, because it runs thus, " In Thy seed shall all the nations of the earth be blessed," proving that the nations were not originally in a blessed state, and could only be blessed through the promised seed. If some of them were blessed already, or could be blessed by their works, then the words of the promise would not be true. The covenant blessing comes to the nations only through Jesus Christ, the seed, and, consequently, it is clear that the nations were in need of a blessing.

The fact is that the very existence of the gospel and its provisions of grace, pardon, and so on, the coming of a Saviour, His death upon the tree, and His intercession in heaven, all prove that men were shut up under sin. If they had not been so, what need of thee, O Calvary ? What need of Thy five wounds, O Son of God ? Surely all this vast machinery for redemption is ridiculous if men be not slaves ; this wondrous filling of a fountain with blood is a vain superfluity if men are not foul. So that the very Scripture which is brightest with life to the sons of men carries within it convincing evidence that men, apart from the grace of God, are shut up under sin.

I have no doubt the apostle alluded more immediately to that part of Scripture which deals with *law*. Turn, I pray you, to the twentieth chapter of Exodus, which I hope you carry in your memories. Let me ask you to read those Ten Commands with deep solemnity, and see whether they do not shut you up under sin. What man can read them and then say, " I am clear of all these " ? The Ten Commands surround us on all sides, and encompass all the movements of body, soul, and spirit, comprising under their jurisdiction the whole range of moral action ; they hold us under fire from all points, and nowhere are we out of range. These ten precepts are condensed into two comprehensive precepts. " Thou shalt love the Lord thy God with all thy heart, and with all thy soul, and with all thy mind, and with all thy strength, and thy neighbour as thyself." Can you listen to those two precepts, which are the essence of the ten, without feeling that you have not loved God with all your heart and soul and mind and strength, but very far from it ; and that you have not loved your neighbour as yourself, but have gone far aside. A man who can read the law and not tremble, if he be out of Christ, must be dead in his sin ; he must be ignorant altogether of its meaning, or else he must have hardened his heart against its terrible import. The awakened conscience knows that the law curses every one of us, without exception, for we have broken it.

The law as given on Sinai does that ; and let us remember that the law as repeated by Mosaic command upon Mounts Ebal and Gerizim, at the time of the entrance of Israel into the Holy Land, is not less express than the thunders of the mount which might not be touched. Read the passage in Deuteronomy xxvii. 26. Perhaps of all the verses of the Word of God this is the most sweeping and utterly crushing to self-righteous hopes. " Cursed be he that confirmeth not all the words of the law to do them. And all the people shall say, Amen " ; which the apostle quotes in another form : " Cursed is every one that continueth not in all things which are written in the book of the law to do them." The law roars like a lion upon us in this sentence. If there be in any one of us a solitary violation of the command of God, we are cursed by Him ; if we have at any time throughout life, in any measure or degree, in deed, word, or thought, by omission or commission, diverged from absolute perfection, we are cursed. Such is the statement of God Himself, by the mouth of His servant Moses, in this book of Deuteronomy. There is no exception made whatever ; all sins are included in it, and we are all of us included : " Cursed is *every one* that continueth not in *all things* that are written in the book of the law to do them." Right well does our text say that the Scripture hath shut all of us up under sin.

We are putting no strain upon the Scripture, for such was the understanding of the law by the saints of old. Turn to Psalm cxliii. 2, and remember, while I quote this, that this is by no means a solitary passage, but only selected as one of many. There David says, " Enter not into judgment with Thy servant, for in Thy sight shall no man living be justified." He stood before God, a man whose heart was sincere and true, but he did not dare to bring his works into judgment ; and, speaking by the Spirit of God as a prophet, he declared that in God's sight no man could be clear of guilt.

And yet further, brethren, the law of God shuts us up, not only as it was delivered from Sinai, as it was repeated at Gerizim, as it was understood by the saints, but especially as it was expounded by the Saviour. He did not come to break the bars of this prison, nor to remove this jailer from being its marshal : His deliverance is not by violence, but by fair legal process. He came to strengthen rather than to weaken the law ; for what does He say concerning it ? He does not merely forbid adultery, but He expounds the command by saying, " He that looketh upon a woman to lust after her committeth adultery with her already in his heart." He shows what had been so much forgotten by the Jews, that the commandments are spiritual, and that they reach infinitely further than mere outward actions ; that, for instance, " Thou shalt not kill " does not merely mean " Thou shalt do no murder," but is to be understood in the sense given it by the Lord Jesus : " I say unto you that whosoever is angry with his brother without a cause shall be in danger of the judgment." As Christians understand it, the law forbids our doing anything whereby the natural or spiritual life of another may be placed in jeopardy. Now, since the law is to be so understood, its commandments are exceeding broad. Since it touches our thoughts, our imaginations, and our casual wishes, who among us can stand before it ? Verily the law shuts us up as in a terrible Bastille, and we are each one of us prisoners under sin.

Here will be the time for us to say that not only do the Scriptures of promise and the Scriptures of law shut us up, but so do all the Scriptures of the old ceremonial law of the Jews. " Oh," say you, " how is that ? " I reply, " When the destroying angel went through Egypt on that memorable night, not one man, woman, or child was delivered except through the sprinkling of the blood upon the doorposts and the lintel of the houses where they dwelt. What did that mean ? Why, that they were all under sin ; and had it not been for the blood, the same angel who smote the first-born of Egypt must have smitten every one of them, God's people as they were, for they were all under sin. When they had reached the wilderness, there were divers rites and ceremonies, but it is remarkable that everything under the law was sprinkled with blood, because the people and all that they did were polluted with sin before God, and needed to be cleansed by an atonement. When an Israelite came to worship God at the Tabernacle, he could not come without a sacrifice. Atonement for sin was the way to God—the altar and the slaughtered lamb were the way of approach. There must be blood to cleanse the comer, because every comer was in himself unclean. Note also that the Holy Place in the Tabernacle in the wilderness was closed, and into it no man went but the High Priest, and he but once a year ; this was a most solemn declaration of God that no man was fit to come near to His infinite holiness, that every man, even of the chosen people, was so polluted that there must be hung up a veil between him and God ; and the one man who did come near at all must approach with sprinkled blood and smoking incense, typical of the coming sacrifice of the Lord Jesus. There was nothing about the Mosaic economy to say to man, " You are good, or you can be good, and you can save yourself " ; but everywhere the declaration was, " Ye have rebelled and have not served the Lord ; ye cannot come nigh unto Him until ye are purged by the blood of the great sacrifice ; God cannot accept you as you are ; you are polluted and defiled." The sinfulness of all men is abundantly taught in Scripture ; indeed, it is to be found on every page of it.

I have spoken of the jailer ; now notice his prisoners. " The Scripture hath concluded *all* under sin "—all, all. The heathen ? Yes, for the first chapter of the Epistle to the Romans tells us that, though they have not God's written law, they have sufficient of it upon their consciences to accuse them if they do wrong, and every heathen has violated the law of God by sinning against the light of nature. To us who have heard that law the " all " of the text is very emphatic. But you have been very moral, you say. Yes, but you are shut up under sin, for, outwardly moral as you have been, you dare not say that you have never thought of evil so as to long for it, that you have never indulged wrong imaginations, that you have never spoken a rash word, that you have never sinned in action. Surely you dare not say that you have loved God with all your heart, and all your soul, and all your strength, nor that you have always loved your neighbour as yourself ? My friend, you, who are so fair to look upon when you look in the glass of your own self-adulation, if you could see yourself as God sees you, would discover that you are leprous from head to foot ; your sins are abundant and loathsome, though you perceive them not. And this is true of the most religious of those men who are resting in outward observances. They have prayed every night and morning since they were children ; they have never absented themselves from assemblies for worship ; they have attended to baptism, and communion, and the like. Ah, sirs, but the law takes no account of this ; if you have not kept its ten commandments perfectly, it accepts no ceremonies as a recompense. God requires of His creatures that they obey His law completely, without flaw, and one sin of omission or commission will bring down that dreadful sentence which I have already quoted, Cursed is every one that continueth not in all things that are written in the book of the law to do them." Religious or irreligious, the broken law shuts up all men in the selfsame prison.

Now, notice for a minute the prison itself. It is one from which we cannot escape by any efforts of our own. Brethren, if we say, " We will never sin again," we shall sin ; and our never sinning again would make no atonement for past offences. Suppose we were to resolve from this time forth that we would suffer mortifications of body, and sorrow of heart, to make atonement for sin, it would be useless, for the law speaks nothing of repentance. When a man has broken the law, he must be punished for it ; there is no space left for repentance under the law, and the sure result of our being shut up in the prison of the law, apart from the grace of God, is to be taken from that prison to execution, and to be destroyed for ever by the wrath of God. There is the prison of the text ; there is the jailer, and his prisoners.

II. It is our great happiness to know that we are not shut up in this way with a view to our hopeless destruction, but in order that the grace of God may come to us, and so we have to speak of A GLORIOUS JAIL-DELIVERY. The jail-delivery which I have to speak of is evidently *of those who are shut up in the prison.* " The Scripture hath concluded all under sin, that the promise by faith of Jesus Christ might be given to them that believe." Christ came into this world to save those who have broken the law, those whom the law curses, and those who have no means whatever of escaping from the curse, unless Jesus open the way. He has not come to save the righteous. If there be any among you who will not believe that you are shut up in the prison of the law, I have no gospel to preach to you. Why send a physician to a man who is not sick ? and why offer alms to a man who is not poor ? If you can save yourselves by your works, go and do so, fools that you are, for you might as well hope to drink dry the Atlantic. If you believe in self-salvation, I am hopeless of doing you any good till you are exhausted of your strength. When you are weak and sick, and ready to die, then will you be willing to accept the free salvation of Christ. But remember, Christ came to save the ungodly ; the guilty alone are objects of mercy.

The Lord Jesus Christ has come to bring to all those who believe in Him *a complete deliverance* from the bondage of the law. The man who believes in Jesus is forgiven ; the very moment he believes, all his transgressions are blotted out, and from that moment he is just in the sight of God. " Being justified by faith, we have peace with God through Jesus Christ our Lord." Having believed, he becomes

at once a child of God, a son of the Most High, and since God will never cast away His children, nor reject those whom He has loved, the man is there and then saved, and saved eternally. He was a slave before, and deserved the lash, and felt it ; he is a child now, and is no longer under the law, but under grace. The principle which guides him now is not " This do and thou shalt live," but this— " I am saved, and now I love to serve my God." Now he does not work for wages, and expect to win a reward by merit ; he is a saved man, and he has all that he needs ; for Christ is his, and Christ is all. Now a higher principle burns within his bosom than that of self-salvation, he loves God, and is selfish no longer.

Observe that this jail-delivery *comes to men by promise.* It is salvation according to promise. The promise is given, says the text. Now, if any man be saved on the Bible plan of salvation, it is not the result of anything he has done, he has never deserved it, it is not the result of a bargain between him and God. No, the Lord says freely, " I will blot out your sins ; I will accept you ; I will hear your prayer ; I will save you." He does this, because He chooses to do it, of His own sovereign good will and pleasure. " I will have mercy on whom I will have mercy, and I will have compassion on whom I will have compassion." " So, then, it is not of him that willeth, nor of him that runneth, but of God that sheweth mercy."

The promise is not made to works, but only *to faith.* It is " the promise of faith by Christ Jesus." If God had made His promise to a certain measure of holiness, or a certain amount of feeling, then, brethren, we might have despaired ; but the promise is to faith. If thou believest, thou art saved. Thou poor harlot, if thou believest, thou art saved ; thou thief, thou murderer, thou vilest of wretches, however far thou mayest have gone, if thou believest in Jesus Christ, thy transgressions are forgiven thee, and thou art a child of God. It is thy believing, not thy doing ; thy trusting, thy relying upon Christ, not thy prayers, tears, preachings, hearings, or anything else thou canst do, or be, or feel: Thou art saved by giving up self entirely, and resting wholly on Him whom God hath set forth to be a propitiation, namely, the crucified Redeemer.

Observe that the faith spoken of in the text is faith *in Christ Jesus.* It must not be faith in yourself, nor faith in a priest, nor faith in sacraments, nor faith in a set of doctrines ; the promise is to faith in Christ Jesus : that is to say, you must believe that Christ the Son of God came on earth and became a man, took your sins upon His shoulders, bore them up to the tree, and suffered what was due for your sins in His own person on the cross ; and you must trust yourself with Him, with Him fully, with Him alone, and with all your heart ; and if you do so, the promise is given to faith in Christ Jesus, and it will be fulfilled to you, and you shall be blessed and saved.

This promise of faith in Christ Jesus is given *to all believers,* weak as well as strong, young as well as old. Dear friend, if you have only believed in Jesus during the present service, you are as certainly forgiven as if you had been a believer fifty years ; for, if you only believed in Jesus when the last word escaped my lip, yet still your faith has saved you. Go in peace. Faith is the vital matter. " But there must be works," saith one, " to follow." Brother, there will be works to follow. There **was** never a true faith which did not produce works ; but the works do not save us : faith alone saves. How strong is the apostle Paul upon this point ! Read the Epistle to the Romans carefully, and the Epistle to the Galatians, and you will see that they come down like a Nasmyth hammer upon all notion of salvation by our own doings. No reasoning could be more cogent, no expressions more plain. " Not of works, lest any man should boast," says the apostle ; and he puts it over again : " If by grace, then it is no more of works : otherwise grace is no more grace. But if it be of works, then it is no more grace : otherwise work is no more work." He will have it that we are saved as poor sinners by the sovereign grace of God, through faith in Christ Jesus, and not by works, or forms, or ceremonies, or anything whatsoever of our own doing.

Now, there is the plan of salvation. I put it before you, and I pray through Jesus Christ that many may receive it, for it is not a matter of human opinion, but of divine ordinance. I am not setting up the dogma of a sect ; I am preaching to you the very truth of God. If there be salvation by any other way than by Jesus Christ I am a false prophet among you, and this Bible also is false ; but if there be salvation to believers in Jesus, I am a saved man, and all of you who have believed in Jesus are saved also, effectually and eternally saved.

Having thus spoken upon the text itself, I desire to say a few things upon the subject in general. Objections are continually raised to this plan of salvation. The world's plan of salvation is " Do " ; the Bible plan of salvation is " It is all done, accept it as a free gift." The gospel way of salvation is, Christ has saved His people, and as many as trust in Him are His people, and are saved. Just think for a minute, is not this way of salvation which we have preached to you the only one which would be suited to all sorts and conditions of men ? Dear sir, you yourself may be a man of excellent disposition, and of admirable habits ; I will suppose that the salvation to be preached by us was exactly such as would be suitable to such a person as you believe yourself to be, would not this be a very unfortunate thing for many others ? Are there not living within your observation many persons who are far below you in moral character ? Do you not know of whole swarms of your fellow creatures whose outward life is utterly defiled ? Some of these are conscious of their degradation, and would fain rise out of it : would you have them left to despair ? A way of salvation suited to the righteous it is clear would not suit them : are they to be overlooked ? Would you have salvation put up to an examination like a place in the Civil Service, and only those allowed to pass who are as good as you are ? Are all beneath your level to perish ? I am speaking to you on your own ground, and I feel sure that you love your fellow-men enough to say, " No, let the plan of salvation be such as to save the most reprobate of men." Then, I ask you, what plan could there be but this one, that God freely forgives for Christ's sake even the greatest offenders if they turn to Him and put their trust in His dear Son ? We have here a gospel which reaches to the lowest depths and saves to the uttermost.

But I shall put another argument. Would any other salvation than that which I have preached suit any man ? O excellent sir, would any other, after all, suit you ? I admit, and I admire your excellences ; I would that all men were such as you are, rather than dissolute and depraved ; but, sir, can you really sit down in the quietude of your chamber, and as a thoughtful man weigh your own character in the scales, and say that it is so perfect that you could die with it in perfect peace, and stand before your Maker without fear ? I am sure it is not so. It is very remarkable that some persons who have been exceedingly moral have never seen their sinfulness till they have been on the borders of the grave, and then they have realised eternity, and have abhorred themselves in dust and ashes. I have heard of some who, in the very hour of imminent peril of death by drowning, have in the act of sinking seen the whole panorama of their lives pass before them, and they have seen, as they never saw before, the evil nature of that which they aforetimes thought so excellent : then they have said, " I must be saved by the merits of Jesus ; I cannot be saved by my own." My dear friend, whoever you may be, I am not about to decry you, but I must believe God's word before I believe your estimate of yourself ; and as God's word has declared that you have sinned, and are condemned, I am sure that for you, as well as for the rest of your fellow-men, there is no plan of salvation at all available but that of salvation by the free mercy of God, through Jesus Christ His Son.

Now, observe a few of the beauties of the plan of salvation by faith in Jesus Christ. It prevents men from having low thoughts of sin, because if a man says, " I have not kept this law of God perfectly, but still I have done very well, and any mistakes I have made are little sins ; God is merciful, He will wipe them out,"—he is sure to be a believer in self-salvation. It always is connected with narrow thoughts of sin. A man knows he has sinned, but he thinks little of the wrong ; he cannot believe that sin is such a great evil that men should be cast into hell for it. He kicks against the doctrine of damnation, he will not believe it just, because he does not know and will not admit that sin is a great and tremendous evil. So long as the idea of self-salvation exists, sin is lightly thought of ; but oh, when we see that sin could not be put away till the incarnate God Himself did hang upon the tree and bled to death for men, then we see sin in its true colours, and loathe it as a deadly thing, and with our joy for pardoned guilt we mingle abhorrence of the sin which required such an atoning sacrifice.

The plan of salvation by grace has this beauty about it, that it gives men high thoughts of God. In the other system their idea of God is that He is very much like themselves. See the Catholic's God. He is pleased with candles and delights in incense ; He is a God who likes show and gewgaws, garments of blue and scarlet, and dolls dressed up, and flowers on His altars. I do not know what kind of God to call him. However, that is their notion of Him. They try to save themselves, and they pull down God to their standard ; and every man who is a self-saver, even if he be a Protestant, lowers God in some manner. He fancies that God will accept something short of perfection. Each man has a different standard. That miserly old gentleman— his standard is that he will build a row of almshouses with his mouldy leavings, and that will content the Most High. Another says, " I never open my shop on a Sunday." Perhaps he cheats enough on Monday to make up for it, but Sunday's rest, that will do for his God. Another, who is living a wicked life in private, believes the doctrines of grace, and that will satisfy his God. But the man who is saved by the grace of God says, " My God is infinitely just ; nothing will content Him but a perfect righteousness ; as a moral lawgiver, He will not put away sin till He had laid punishment upon One who stood in the sinner's stead. He is so loving that He gave His Son ; He is so just that He slew His Son on my behalf." All the divine attributes flame with splendour forth before the eyes of the man who is saved by faith, and he is led to reverence and to adore.

The way of salvation by grace, beloved, is the best promoter of holiness in all the world. " There," says yonder gentleman, " I went to hear Spurgeon in the Tabernacle this morning, and he was crying out against salvation by good works. Of course the worst results will come of such teaching." Ah, that has been the cuckoo-cry from the very first, whereas salvation by grace promotes good works far better than the teaching of salvation by works ever did, for those who hope to be saved by their works have generally very scanty works to be saved by, and those who put works aside altogether as a ground of hope, and look to grace alone, are the very people who are most zealous to perform good works, and I will tell you why. Who loved Christ best at the Pharisee's feast ? Simon, the Pharisee, who had kept the law ? Ah ! no : he was to be saved by his doings, and yet Christ said to him, " Thou gavest Me no kiss ; thou gavest Me no water to wash My feet." Simon did not love the Master. He did what he did because he thought he ought to do it and must do it ; but there was a poor woman there who was a sinner, and she had had much forgiven, and she it was that did wash His feet with her tears, and wipe them with the hairs of her head. Simon shows how self-righteous men love the Saviour : they do not even was His feet or kiss His cheeks ; but those who are saved by grace love Jesus, and therefore kiss His feet and bathe them with their tears, and would willingly lay down their lives for Him. Law ! There is no power for holiness in it ! Law drives our spirits to rebellion, but love has magic in it. Has God forgiven me ? Did Christ die for me ? Am I God's child ? Has He forgiven me, not because of anything I did, but just because He would do it, out of love to my poor guilty soul ? O God, I love Thee. What wouldest Thou have me to do ? There speaks the man who will perform good works, I warrant you, sir ; and while he will tread under foot with the deepest detestation any idea that he can merit anything of God, he is the man who will lay himself out, as long as he lives, for the honour of that dear Lord and Master by whose precious blood he has been redeemed. The law does not furnish me with a constraining principle, but the gospel does. The law treats me like a mere hireling, and a hireling never can serve with the zeal which is born of love. There is a better place with double wages, and naturally enough the servant leaves your house, but your child will not. You do not give your child wages, and you do not bind him by indentures or agreements. He loves you, and his sense of your love leads him to a tender obedience, and what he does is doubly sweet to you. Missionaries and martyrs have done and borne for love's sake what law could not have forced from them. Oh yes, the doctrine of salvation by grace, by teaching men to love, transforms them, and makes new creatures of them. I have seen it hundreds of times. There are some here, but I will not speak of them, but of cases parallel to theirs. They have been to a place of worship, and they have read the Bible, and have thought it was all about what was required from their own efforts, but all the while they have felt no obedience of heart, no love to Christ, and no joy in God. But those same persons have heard the gospel, and found that there is nothing to do, that Jesus Christ had done it all, that sin was put away by His death, and righteousness was wrought out ; and they have just taken what God has presented to them, and believed in Jesus and been saved, and from that very moment the difference has been evident. They have cried, " I never felt any love to God before, but now I do. I love Him with all my soul for what He has done for me." You hear them say, " I used to go to the house of God as a matter of duty, and I might almost as well have been away, for it was no enjoyment to me ; but now I go as a matter of privilege, and I take my heart with me, and sing God's praises with all my soul, because He has done so much for me." Those people will tell you that, whereas they resolved to be good, and to give up vice, and to practise virtue, they never did it till they believed in Jesus ; and when they believed in Him, love to Him made service easy, and sin hateful, and they became new creatures in Christ Jesus, by the Spirit's power. There is the pith of it all. If you want to get rid of the guilt of sin, you must believe in Jesus ; but equally, if you would be rid of the chains of sin, the tyranny of your passions, the domination of your lusts, you must believe in Him ; for from His side there flows not merely blood but water—blood to take away your criminality, and water to take away your tendencies to sin—so that henceforth you shall not serve sin, or live any longer therein. It is all there in that pierced heart, it is all there in that crimson fount, opened on Calvary's bloody tree. Look to Jesus, and ye shall be saved. It is all in that nutshell.

" There is life in a look at the crucified One."

I may never have an opportunity of preaching this gospel to some of you again : it may be the first time you have heard it, and perhaps the last. O sirs, I charge you accept it, and may the Spirit of God constrain you so to do. We will meet in heaven if it be so ; but if you put it from you, you are like a man who flings away the only lifebelt that can keep him alive in the angry flood ; you put from you the only medicine under heaven that can heal your soul, for I am holding up before you the only gospel in the world. If any man preach any other gospel, let him be accursed. Intolerant ! Content am I to be as intolerant as my Master, and He bade me say, " He that believeth and is baptized shall be saved ; he that believeth not shall be damned." " But may I not be saved some other way ? " No, sir. " But may I not reject with impunity this which you have preached ? " No, sir ; at your peril is it, and before God I will put it right plainly before you. You must believe in Jesus, and if you reject Him your blood be upon your own head, for other way of salvation there is none. The Lord grant you may receive it, for Jesus' sake. Amen.

THE STERN PEDAGOGUE

"Wherefore the law was our schoolmaster to bring us unto Christ, that we might be justified by faith. But after that faith is come, we are no longer under a schoolmaster."—Galatians iii. 24-25.

NEITHER the Jewish law of ten commands, nor its law of ceremonies was ever intended to save anybody. It was not the intent of the ceremonial law in itself to effect the redemption of the soul: by a set of pictures it set forth the way of salvation, but it was not itself the way. It was a map, not a country, a model of the road, not the road itself. The blood of bulls, and of goats, and the ashes of an heifer, could not really take away sin. These sacrifices and offerings were but types of the great sacrifice which in due time was presented by the true priest. There was no inherent virtue in the victims that were slain, or in the services that were observed by the worshippers! Those sacred rites were intended to portray to the minds of the people the real sacrifice which was in the fulness of time to be offered by our Lord Jesus Christ, but they could do nothing more. The king's portrait is not himself, the engraving of a banquet is not the feast itself, and so the grand old ceremonial law was a shadow of good things to come, but contained not the substance of spiritual blessings.

Neither was the moral law of ten commands proclaimed on Mount Sinai ever given with the view of sinners being saved by it. When that law was announced by God, He knew that every one to whom He gave that law had already broken it, and that consequently they could not keep its precepts, or claim justification by their conformity to its requirements. He never intended it to be a way of salvation. Hundreds of years before He had revealed His covenant of grace and the way of faith to His servant Abraham, and the law was not meant to disannul the ancient promise. To look at the law as a Saviour is to place Sinai in the place of Zion, and so to misuse and abuse the law. It was sent with quite a different purpose, as we shall presently try to show you. It was sent to be our schoolmaster till Christ came—the schoolmaster of a world in its minority, that had need to be under tutelage until it attained full age, which would not happen until Christ should be born of a woman, and the doctrine of salvation by faith in Him should be fully preached and known.

Now I shall try and show, first, *the office of the law*; then, secondly, *the design of that office*—"to bring us to Christ;" and, thirdly, *the termination of that office*: "After that faith is come, we are no longer under a schoolmaster."

I. We begin with THE OFFICE OF THE LAW. It is to be a schoolmaster. Here I must endeavour to explain the figure. A schoolmaster nowadays is not at all like the personage Paul intended. He speaks of a *pedagogue*, an official seldom if ever now seen among men. This was not a person who actually officiated as master in the school, and gave instruction in the school itself; but one—a slave generally—who was set to take the boys to school, and to watch over them, and to be a sort of general supervisor of them, both in school and out of school, and at all times. A pedagogue was very generally employed in the training of the young: indeed, it was a common and customary thing for the sons of the Greek and Roman nobility to have appointed over them some trustworthy servant of the family who took them in charge. The boys were entirely under these servants; and thus had their spirits broken in, and their vivacity restrained. As a rule, these pedagogues were very stern and strict—they used the rod freely, not to say cruelly, and the condition of the boys was sometimes no better than slavery. The boys (as it was supposed to be for their good) were kept in perpetual fear. Their recreations were restricted; even their walks were under the surveillance of the grim pedagogues. They were sternly held in check in all points, and were thus disciplined for the battle of life. As for the young women, they also had some elderly woman of grim appearance who tried to keep them out of mischief, and suppress anything like cheerfulness or girlish glee. It was considered necessary for young people that they should suffer from rigid discipline and bear the yoke in their youth; so they were all put under pedagogues, whoever they might be,—pedagogues armed with penalties but devoid of sympathies.

Now Paul, taking up this thought, which was his idea in the word "schoolmaster," says the law was our pedagogue, our guardian, our custodian, ruler, tutor, governor until Christ came.

Well, then, what is the business of the law as a pedagogue? The business of the law is, first, *to teach us our obligations to God*. Let us ask ourselves if we have ever heard the law teaching us in that way. Brethren, read the law of ten commands, and study each separate precept, and you will find that in those ten short precepts you have all the moral virtues, the full compass of your accountability to God, and of your relationship to your fellow-men. It is a wonderful condensation of morals. The essence of all just decrees and statutes lies there. Perfection is there photographed, and holiness mapped out. No one has ever been able to add to it without creating an excrescence, not a word could be taken from it without causing a serious omission. It is the perfect law of God, and tells us exactly what we ought to be; if we are in any degree deficient, we are to that extent guilty before God. Now, when the law comes to a man's conscience it reveals to him the divine standard of right—holds it up before him—makes him look at it—and apprizes him that the commandments do not merely refer to acts and deeds, but with equal force to the words and thoughts from whence they proceed. I warrant you it is a humbling day when a man gets to understand that for every idle word that he has spoken he will be brought to account; and when he hears again that his desires and imaginations will all come under divine scrutiny. How startled is the purest mind when it understands that whosoever looketh upon a woman to lust after her hath committed adultery with her already in his heart, so that even glances of the eye and thoughts of the heart are offences of the law. The law of God takes cognisance of the entire nature, and reveals the evil which lurks in every faculty. The mere imagination of sin is sinful—the very conception of it, albeit that we should reject it, and never carry it into act, would still be a stain upon our minds, and render us impure before the thrice holy God. This is one of the first works of the law—to show us what spotless purity it demands, and to reveal to us the matchless perfection which alone can meet its requirements. He who has once gazed upon the blinding light of legal holiness will tremble at the memory of it, and abhor himself in dust and ashes as he feels how far short of it he falls.

Having done that, the law acts as a schoolmaster next by *showing us our sinfulness*. We are naturally prone to account ourselves very good. Our own opinion of ourselves is seldom too low ; most generally it is a rather high one ; but just as a stern pedagogue would say to a boy who was getting a little proud, " Come along sir ; I must take you down a little " ; so the law takes us down. It says, " Look at that precept ; you have not kept that ; and consider this other precept, for you appear to have forgotten it." " Look," says the law, " you talk about your holiness ; but have you loved the Lord your God with all your heart, and all your soul, and all your might ? And have you loved your neighbour as yourself ? " And then, when conscience, who is a great friend of this pedagogue, replies, " Indeed I have done nothing of the kind," the conviction of sin comes home to the soul, and sadness reigns. You will tell me, " This is very unpleasant—to be made to feel that you are sinful." Ay, but it is very necessary, there is no getting to Christ in any other way. Christ died for sinners, and if you are not sinners, what interest can you have in His death ? why should you think that He died for you ? You must be convinced of your sinfulness before you can possibly realize the value and need of salvation. It is the business of the law to lay before you the straight line, that you may see your crooks, and put before you the pure gold, that you may discern the humbling fact that what you thought to be pure metal is only so much worthless dross. It is the part of this pedagogue to bring you down, to humble you, and make you feel how sinful you have been.

When the law has carried our education thus far, its next business is to *sweep away all our excuses*, and stop our mouths as to all self-justifying pleas. Did you ever know a boy without an excuse ? I never did. I think I never knew a girl either. We all make excuses readily enough. But those rough, surly pedagogues always answered the boy's idle apologies by giving the offender an extra stroke of the whip for daring to impose upon his guardian ; and that is what the law does with us. We say to it, " We have not done exactly as we ought, but then think of pure human nature ! " Ah ! how often we make that excuse, and the law says, " I have nothing to do with the poverty of human nature. This is what God commands, and if you do not obey you will have to be cast away for ever from His presence." The law makes no diminution of its claims because of fallen human nature ; and what is more, when the law comes with power to a man's conscience he does not himself dare to plead human nature, for of all pleas that is one of the most fallacious. A man will say, " Well, I know I drank to intoxication, but that is merely gratifying an instinct of human nature." Now, just suppose that this drunkard when he gets sober falls into the hands of a thief, will he not give the rogue in charge to a

policeman ? But what if the defence be set up that it was human nature robbed him ? See what he will say about it. Says he, " I will get human nature locked up for twelve months if I can." He does not recognize soft speeches about human nature when any one does wrong to him ; and he knows, in his own soul, that there is no valid defence in such a plea when he does wrong to God. What if human nature be bad ? That only proves that the man ought to be punished the more. A man stands before my Lord Mayor to-morrow morning ; he is brought up for a thief, charged with having picked somebody's pocket, and he says, " My Lord Mayor, I ought to be forgiven, for the fact is, it is my nature to steal. I have stolen so long that whenever I see a pocket I feel a disposition at once to put my hand into it ; such is the infirmity of my nature." What does the Lord Mayor say ? He replies very gravely, " Why, I see that it is not merely in actions that you are guilty, but your very nature is poisoned with dishonesty. I shall give you a double punishment ; your plea is no excuse, but an aggravation." So when the law comes it sweeps all excuses away, and makes us see how hollow, false, and even wicked they are. Men, like boys, will say that circumstances were such that they could not help doing amiss ; but the law, like a stern pedagogue, says, " I have nothing to do with circumstances. Whatever your circumstances are there is your duty, and you have not done it, and, not having done it, you must be punished for your offence." Where does Moses, in the twentieth chapter of Exodus, speak about exonerating or even extenuating circumstances ? God spake all these words, saying, " I am the Lord thy God, which have brought thee out of the land of Egypt, out of the house of bondage. Thou shalt have no other gods before Me. Thou shalt not make unto thee any graven image, or any likeness of anything that is in heaven above, or that is in the earth beneath, or that is in the water under the earth : Thou shalt not bow down thyself to them, nor serve them." That is to say, not under any circumstances. " Thou shalt not steal," not under any circumstances. Circumstances are not taken into account, the law sweeps that excuse away, and makes men speechless before the judgment-seat.

Many transgressors argue, " Well, but I have not done worse than other people " ; to which the law replies, " What hast thou to do with other people ? Each individual must stand or fall on his own account before the law. The law is to *thee*. If another has broken it he shall be punished even as thou shalt, inasmuch as thou hast broken it." Then the man cries, " But I have been better than others." But, says the law, " If thou hast not perfectly walked in all the ways of the Lord thy God to do them, I have nothing to do with comparing thee with others : for this is my sentence, ' Cursed is every man that continueth not in all things that are written in the book of the law to do them.' " Now, my dear hearers, these are not my words, they are the words of God by His servant Moses, and there they stand like a flaming sword, turning every way, and blocking up the legal road to the tree of life. Conscience, when it is really awakened by the law, confesses herself condemned, and ceases to uphold her plea of innocence. How can it be otherwise when the law is so stern ? Then, peradventure, the man will say, " I mean to do better in the future " ; to which the law replies, " What have I to do with that ?

It is already due that thou shouldst be perfect in the future ; and if thou shouldst be perfect, in what way would that wipe out thine old offences ? Thou hast only done what thou oughtest to have done." But the man cries, " I do repent of having done wrong." " Ay," says the law, " but I have nothing to do with repentance." There is no provision in the ten commands for repentance. Cursed is the man that breaks the law ; and that is all that the law has to say to him. Over the top of Sinai there were flames exceeding bright, and a trumpet sounded exceeding loud, but there were no drops of rain of pity there. Storm and tempest, thundering and lightnings appalled the people, so that they trembled in the camp, and such must be the sights and sounds we witness as long as we are under the law.

Having thus swept away excuses, this pedagogue does the next thing which the pedagogues did to the boys. It begins *to chide us and to chasten us.* And it will *chide* too. I know it. I had the law frowning and shaking its fist at me for years before I got from under it. Glad enough was I to escape from it, for well do I remember the weight of its cudgel—that cudgel of crabtree of which John Bunyan speaks. I warrant you it can give you sore bones, so that you cannot lie down upon the bed of your self-confidence to take rest. " Why," says the law, " thou hast done this, and that, and the other, and thou knowest thou hast ; thou hast sinned against light, and against knowledge, and against conscience, and against love, and against mercy " ; and every one of these brings another blow from the great rod, till we are all wounds and bruises, and we seem to ourselves to be covered with putrefying sores. The law will serve us as the pedagogue did the boy—it will accompany and follow us up everywhere. The old pedagogue went with the boy to the play-ground : he did not let him play in peace. He went upstairs to bed with him : he did not let him go to sleep without a last frown ; and he woke him up in the morning much earlier than he liked to be awakened, and made him come out of his bed, whether he liked it or not. He could never go anywhere without this pedagogue with him, poor child. And so it is when the law gets hold of a man—really gets hold of him. Does he go to the theatre to find pleasure in sin ?—the law will go with him there and make him feel more wretched there than when he was at home. He may get among the frivolous, and try to sing some old song to get rid of his feelings, but the more he tries to drown his misery, the more the dark forebodings come before his mind. He cannot rest. The law keeps on saying, " What are you doing now ? Why, you are only going from bad to worse." The law also smites the awakened conscience again and again, and frightens him with what is soon to come. " Suppose you were to die where you now are," says the law ; " suppose you were now to appear before your Maker, unforgiven, where would you be ? " Perhaps in this kind of feeling a man goes to the house of God. The law follows him there. If the preacher preaches a comforting sermon, the law says, " This is not for you. You have nothing to do with that. You are under my government, not under Christ." The sweeter the promise, the more bitter will be the taste of the sermon in the poor sinner's mouth ; for the law says, " You have broken my injunctions ; you have violated my statutes. There is nothing for you but eternal punishment—to be driven for ever from the presence of God." " Hard lines," say you. You do not like this pedagogue. No, nor did I, when I was under him. Glad was I when the day came that I was of age.

Do you see what the drift of it all is ? Why, the drift of it is to make you despair of being saved by your good works, and to make you feel that you can do nothing right apart from Jesus. You are forced by the law to cry out, " Why, I cannot do anything right. I have tried and failed ; I have tried again and have failed. I thought I was going to improve myself into an angel, but I seem to be worse every day. I thought surely the law would have smiled on me and said, ' That is well done,' but when I have done my best I am still condemned, I am allowed no peace." No, dear soul, and if God means to save you, you never will have any peace till you come to Christ. The man whom God does not intend to save is often left without the law, to enjoy his portion in this life as best he may. What is the use of worrying that man ? He may as well have peace in this life, for he will never see the face of the Lord in heaven. But the Lord's elect are made to feel the rod, and by that rod they are so beaten that they are driven out of all heart and confidence in themselves, and made to turn away to Jesus, to find salvation by some better method than by their own works. The law is our schoolmaster to whip us to Christ—our pedagogue to flog us and beat us till we are heartily sick of self, and look for our hope and confidence to some other source.

II. Thus I have shown you the office of the law, and I have entrenched upon the second head, which is, THE DESIGN OF THIS OFFICE.

The law is not intended to conduct any man to despair. " But did not you say it was, just now ? " No, I did not. I said it was sent to drive a man to despair *of himself.* That is the despair which hails the gospel, and the sooner we have it the better ; It would be quite another matter if we were driven to despair absolutely.

Brethren, the law says, " You shall not indulge the hope of being saved by me. I will whip it out of you." And it does this effectually, but it is not meant that the man should say, " Well, if I cannot be saved by my works there is no hope of my being saved at all." Oh, no ! it is that he may then ask, " What *must* I do to be saved ? " and may get this answer, " Believe on the Lord Jesus Christ, and thou shalt be saved."

Its office is not to urge us to make an amalgam of works and faith, as some suppose. There are those who say, " I cannot keep the law, but if I believe in Jesus, then the blood of Jesus will make up for my sins and deficiencies." That is not the way of salvation. Nobody will ever get to heaven that way. If you have any engagements with the law, you must pay it twenty shillings in the pound. It will not take a composition of any sort whatever. you must satisfy its utmost demands, or it will give you no rest, either in time or in eternity. If you say to the law, " I will give you so much in works and so much in grace," the law does not deal in that way, it must be paid by a legal tender of current coin of the king's realm. It demands works, and it will have nothing but works, and those absolutely perfect, and in full tale and measure. The law repudiates amalgamation, and so does the gospel of free grace. If you have anything to do with Jesus, you must get right away from your own good works; I mean from all reliance upon them, and come to rest in Him, and Him alone, for it never will be Christ and company. He will save from top to bottom, from first to last, or else not at all. Not a drop of His blood and then a drop of your tears; not a work from Christ and then a work from you. Oh no! Such hideous patchwork cannot be endured. It is not the object of the law to drive you to a compromise.

But its object is this—to make you accept salvation as the free gift of God—to make you stand and own that you are a sinner, and accept a free, full, perfect forgiveness, according to the infinite grace of the eternal Father. The law is meant to keep you always holding on to salvation by grace. For my part, I cannot bear that preaching which is partly law and partly grace. I have had enough of the law. If you had known five years of its rigor—five years discipline of the pedagogue—you would never want to see even his back any more. When a man knows what law-work is in his soul, he knows the difference between that and the gospel, and he will not have linsey-woolsey: he wants to have the pure white linen all of one material, and that material free grace. It must be not " Yea, nay," but " Yea, yea,"—grace, grace, all grace, nothing but grace, and not grace and works, not Moses and Christ, but Jesus only; the grace must be pure and un-adulterated. It is a grand thing when this school-master makes a man stick to grace, and so flogs and whips him that he never wants to go back to the law any more; for, brethren, nobody is so happy in the liberty of Christ as the man who has thoroughly known the bondage of the law. I think I have repeated to you a story my old friend Dr. Alexander Fletcher told me. He said he was passing by the Old Bailey, or some other of our gaols, and he saw a couple of boys turning somersaults, standing on their heads, making wheels of themselves, and all sorts of things, and he stopped and said, " Why, boys, whatever are you at? You seem to be delighted "; and one of them said, " Ay, and you would be delighted too if you had been locked up in that gaol three months. You would jump when you came out." And the good old doctor said, he thought it was very likely he should. If he had been a prisoner there he should hardly know how to express his delight in getting out. Now, if a man has once been pommeled by the law, if he has felt his sin and misery, and the impossibility of obtaining any relief by the way of human merit, when he comes to see that Christ has kept the law for him, comes to know that he is saved, and saved perfectly by an act of faith in Jesus Christ, that henceforth he lives under new conditions, and is not under the law but under grace, he is the man to know the sweets of liberty, because aforetime the iron had entered into his soul. He is the man to kiss the emancipator's feet, for was he not heavily ironed in the days of his former estate?

This, then, is the design of the law—to make us sick of self and fond of Christ, to condemn us that we may accept free grace, to empty us that God may fill us, to strip us that God may clothe us, in a word, to kill us that Christ may make us alive.

III. Now to our last point—THE TERMINATION OF THE LAW'S OFFICE. When does it terminate? The text says, " But after that faith is come we are no longer under a schoolmaster." We come to believe in Jesus, and then the pedagogue troubles us no more. No, there is a great change in his behaviour. When the young Roman, or we will say a young Hebrew, who had come under the Greek law, was under thirteen and a-half years old, this pedagogue was always beating, and cuffing, and buffeting him for his faults; but when he was a day over the time, then, according to the law, he was free from the tutelage of the pedagogue. Do you think the pedagogue struck him that morning? He knew better. He had whipped him yesterday, but now he must know his master, and render him another sort of service. The lad is come to his full age, and is under other regulations. Under the old Roman law a man was not of full age till he was twenty-five. According to that law the peda-gogue might be insulting and domineering over him when he was three or four-and-twenty; but when his young master had come of age he changed his talk altogether; matters wore another phase. And so when a man becomes a believer he has come of age, and the schoolmaster's rule is over, he is no longer under his former tutors and governors, for his time of liberty appointed by the Father is come. He is not under the pedagogy of the law any longer, for Christ's work has set him entirely free therefrom.

Certainly, a man sees the office of the law as pedagogue ended when he ascertains that Christ has fulfilled it. I read the ten commands and say, " These thundered at me and I trembled at them, but Christ has kept them, kept them for me. He was my Representative in every act of His obedient life and death, and before God it is as if I had kept the law, and I stand accepted in the Beloved. When Jesus Christ is seen of God, God sees His people in Him, and they are justified through His righteous-ness, because they have faith in Him. " He that believeth in Him is not condemned." Oh, is it not a thousand mercies in one that the grand old cannons of the law are no longer turned against us? Christ has either spiked them or else turned them on our enemies, by fulfilling the law, so that they are on our side instead of against us.

The law ceases its office as schoolmaster when it comes to be written on our hearts. Boys have their lessons on slates, but men have their laws in their minds. We trust a man where we should carefully watch a boy. When the child becomes a man his father and mother do not write down little rules for him, as they did when he was a child in petticoats, neither do they set servants over him to keep him in order. He is trusted. His manliness is trusted; his honour is trusted; his best feelings are trusted. So now, brethren, we who have believed in Jesus have the law written here in our hearts, and it corresponds with what is written there in the Scriptures, and now we do not say of a sin, " I am afraid to do that, for I should be lost if I did." We do not want to do it. We loathe it. And of a virtue we do not say, " I must do that, or else I shall not be a child of God." No, we love to do it: we want to do it: the more of holiness the better. We love the law of the Lord and desire to keep its statutes unto the end. We no longer have, " Thou *shall* " and " Thou *shall not*," constantly sounding in our ears as we did when we were children; but we are men in Christ Jesus, and now our sacred passions delight to run in the ways of God's commandments; and if the old nature rebels grace is given to put it down: there is a daily conflict, but the new life that is within us cannot sin, because it is born of God, and it keeps down the old nature, so that we walk in the ways of righteousness after the example of our Lord. A warfare goes on, but we are no longer children; when faith is come, we are no longer under a schoolmaster. This is not Antinomianism, for we are not against the law, but the law that once was on the stony table, and there was broken, is now written on the fleshy tablet of a renewed heart, and the Lord sweetly inclines us to keep His testimonies and observe His statutes.

Moreover, we get free from the law when we take up our heirship in Christ. I am afraid some Christians have never fully done this. Can you say, beloved, " I have believed in Jesus, and therefore I am one with Him. Whatever Christ is before God that I am, for I am a member of His body, of His flesh, and of His bones.

" So near, so very near to God,
    I cannot nearer be,
For in the person of His Son
    I am as near as He.

So dear, so very dear to God,
    I cannot dearer be,
The love wherewith He loves His Son,
    Such is His love to me.' "

Can you say, " He hath made with me an everlasting covenant, ordered in all things and sure ? As long as Jesus lives I cannot die, for it is written, ' Because He lives, I shall live also.'

' My name from the palms of His hands
    Eternity cannot erase,
Impressed on His heart it remains
    In marks of indelible grace.' "

When a man gets there, and knows that his standing does not depend on himself, but that he is what he is in Christ, that Christ has done everything for him, and has saved him, so that he can challenge every accuser in the words of Paul. " Who shall lay anything to the charge of God's elect ? It is God that justifieth, who is he that condemneth ? " —when he gets there, then he can truly say that he is no longer under a schoolmaster. O brethren, read the eighth and ninth of Romans. Get into the spirit of the apostle when he rejoiced and triumphed in the complete salvation of Christ ; get away from all beliefs that you have something still to do in order to save yourself ; get to know that you have only to work out what God works in ; with fear and trembling to fetch out from within, and show in your outward life, what God by the eternal Spirit works in your heart, and you will find that you are no longer under the law.

If there be any unconverted person here, and I am afraid there are a great many, I beseech you do not abide with the law, for the law can do nothing for you but curse you. Give up all hope of being saved by anything that you can do, and agree to be saved by what Christ has done. Plead guilty ; plead guilty, and then God will say, " I absolve you." Plead guilty, and plead the blood of Jesus, and, this done, you are accepted in the Beloved.

" There is life for a look at the Crucified One ;
    There is life at this moment for thee,"

for every soul that will confess its guiltiness, and renounce all hope of self-salvation, and fly away to the wounds of Jesus.

And how shall I urge you, O Christian, never to go back to the law. Do not begin to judge yourself as if you were under the law. What if you are a sinner ? It is true you are. Confess your sin and mourn over it ; but remember there is a fountain open for sin and uncleanness in the house of David. That sin of yours was laid on Christ before you committed it. It was laid on the scapegoat's head of old, and put away ; and at this moment you are still clean in the sight of God through the great washing which you have received in the precious blood. Do not imagine that God will change His mind about you ; He never did and never can change his mind. He has said concerning each soul that believes in His dear Son, " He that believeth in Him is not condemned." Ye are complete in Christ Jesus, in Him you have righteousness and strength, in Him you may even glory. Get away from legal doctrines, and stand upon the gospel rock, and you will be happy and holy all your days.

Let me speak to those of you who are engaged in Christian service. When you try to teach others always keep the law in its proper place. I remember hearing a sermon from this text, " They that sow in tears shall reap in joy," in which the preacher so thoroughly missed the mark as to leave the inference upon the minds of his hearers that, after all, our good works and repentance would save us. Now, that is not the gospel ; neither ought it to be preached as such. We preach up good works with all our might as the result of faith, as the outgrowth of faith, but not as the groundwork of salvation. We tell you that the tree of human nature must be altered first, or the fruit cannot be good. There will be no pears upon that crab-tree till you change the stock. Do not, therefore, go preaching to crab-trees and tell them to bear pears and apples. We testify that Christ is able to change man's nature, and then good fruits will come as a matter of course : but I am afraid that in many Sunday-schools the children are taught a different doctrine, somewhat after this fashion—" Now, dear children, be very good, and obey your parents, and love Jesus, and you will be saved." That is not the gospel, and it is not true. Often do I hear it said, " Love Jesus, dear children." That is not the gospel. It is " Trust Him "—" Believe." Not love, but faith is the saving grace ; and that love of Jesus of a sentimental kind, which does not spring out of faith in Him is a spurious emotion, a counterfeit of love, not at all the love of God, shed abroad in the heart by the Holy Spirit. The root of the matter is, " Believe in the Lord Jesus Christ and thou shalt be saved ; " and that is the gospel for a child of two years of age, and the gospel for a man of a hundred. There is only one gospel for all that are born on the face of the earth—" Believe in Jesus." Not your doing, not your obeying the law ; you have broken that ; you have put yourself out of all possible hope in that direction ; but your acceptance of what Christ has done will save you at once, save you for ever. But why should I multiply words ? I know not how to put the whole matter in a simpler form, or to commend it more plainly to your understanding. It is not the mere exposition of a few verses of Scripture, or the clearing up of some small critical difficulty. Rather would I have you consider it a direction of vital importance to every seeking soul, a council of thrilling interest to every tried and exercised heart. Oh, how anxious I am to make straight paths for your feet, lest that which is lame be turned out of the way ! I wish that all of you, especially our young friends, would learn and often repeat that hymn of Dr. Watts, till it becomes indelibly fixed on their memory—

" The law commands and makes us know
    What duties to our God we owe ;
But 'tis the gospel must reveal
    Where lies our strength to do His will.

" The law discovers guilt and sin,
    And shows how vile our hearts have been ;
Only the gospel can express
    Forgiving love and cleansing grace.

" What curses doth the law denounce
    Against the man that sins but once !
But in the gospel Christ appears,
    Pardoning the guilt of numerous years.

" My soul, no more attempt to draw
    Thy life and comfort from the law ;
Fly to the hope the gospel gives,
    The man that trusts the promise lives."

And remember, last of all, that the law which is so sharp and terrible to men when it only deals with them for their good, will if you and I die without being brought to Christ be much more terrible to us in eternity, when it deals with us in justice for our punishment. Then it will not be enshrined in the body of Moses, but, terrible to tell, it will be incarnate in the person of the Son of God sitting upon the throne. He will be at once the Lawgiver, the Judge, and the Saviour ; and you that have despised Him as the Saviour will have to appear before Him as your Judge. No such Judge as He, His justice will be clear and undiluted now that His mercy has been scorned. Oil is soft, but set it on fire, and see how it burns ! Love is sweet, but curdle it to jealousy, and see how sour it is ! If you turn the Lamb of Zion into the Lion of the tribe of Judah, beware, for he will tear you in pieces, and there shall be none to deliver. Rejected love will change its hand. The pierced hand was outstretched with invitations of mercy, but if these be rejected—O, sirs, I am telling you solemn truth, and hear it, I pray you, ere I send you away—if from that hand that was pierced you will not take the perfect salvation which He is prepared to give to all who confess their guilt, you will have to receive from that selfsame hand the blows of that iron rod which shall break you in pieces as a potter's vessel. Fly now, and kiss the Son, lest He be angry, and ye perish from the way while His wrath is kindled but a little. Blessed are all they that put their trust in Him ! Amen.

ADOPTION—THE SPIRIT AND THE CRY

" And because ye are sons, God hath sent forth the Spirit of His Son into your hearts, crying, Abba, Father,"—Galatians iv. 6.

WE do not find the doctrine of the Trinity in Unity set forth in Scripture in formal terms, such as those which are employed in the Athanasian creed ; but the truth is continually taken for granted, as if it were a fact well known in the church of God. If not laid down very often, in so many words, it is everywhere held in solution, and it is mentioned incidentally, in connection with other truths in a way which renders it quite as distinct as if it were expressed in a set formula. In many passages it is brought before us so prominently that we must be wilfully blind if we do not note it. In the present chapter, for instance, we have distinct mention of each of the three divine Persons. " God," that is the Father, " sent forth the Spirit," that is the Holy Spirit ; and He is here called " the Spirit of His Son." Nor have we the names alone, for each sacred person is mentioned as acting in the work of our salvation : see the fourth verse, " God sent forth His Son " ; then note the fifth verse, which speaks of the Son as redeeming them that were under the law ; and then the text itself reveals the Spirit as coming into the hearts of believers, and crying Abba, Father. Now, inasmuch as you have not only the mention of the separate names, but also certain special operations ascribed to each, it is plain that you have here the distinct personality of each. Neither the Father, the Son, nor the Spirit can be an influence, or a mere form of existence, for each one acts in a divine manner, but with a special sphere and a distinct mode of operation. The error of regarding a certain divine person as a mere influence, or emanation, mainly assails the Holy Ghost ; but its falseness is seen in the words—" crying, Abba, Father ": an influence could not cry ; the act requires a person to perform it. Though we may not understand the wonderful truth of the undivided Unity, and the distinct personality of the Triune Godhead, yet, nevertheless, we see the truth revealed in the Holy Scriptures : and, therefore, we accept it as a matter of faith.

The divinity of each of these sacred persons is also to be gathered from the text and its connection. We do not doubt the divinity of the Father, for He is here distinctly mentioned as " God " : twice is the Father evidently intended when the word " God " is used. That the Son is God is implied, for though made of a woman, as to His human nature, He is described as " sent forth " and, therefore, He was pre-existent before He was sent forth and made of a woman ; this, together with His being called the Son of God, and His being spoken of as able to redeem, are to our minds sufficient proofs of deity. The Spirit is said to do what only God can do, namely, to dwell in the heart of all believers. It were not possible for any being to cry in the hearts of a multitude of men if He were not omnipresent and therefore divine. So that we have the name of each divine Person, the working of each, the personality of each, and in some degree the deity of each, within the compass of a few lines. As for believers in the Lord Jesus Christ, they know how needful is the co-operation of the entire Trinity to our salvation, and they are charmed to see the loving union of all in the work of deliverance. We reverence the Father, without whom we had not been chosen or adopted : the Father who hath begotten us again unto a lively hope by the resurrection of Jesus Christ from the dead. We love and reverence the Son by whose most precious blood we have been redeemed, and with whom we are one in a mystic and everlasting union : and we adore and love the divine Spirit, for it is by Him that we have been regenerated, illuminated, quickened, preserved, and sanctified ; and it is through Him that we receive the seal and witness within our hearts, by which we are assured that we are indeed the sons of God. As God said of old, " Let us make man in our image, after our likeness," even so do the divine Persons take counsel together, and all unite in the new creation of the believer. We must not fail to bless, adore, and love each one of the exalted Persons, but we must diligently bow in lowliest reverence before the one God—Father, Son, and Holy Ghost. " Glory be to the Father, and to the Son, and to the Holy Ghost ; as it was in the beginning, is now, and ever shall be, world without end. Amen."

Having noted this most important fact, let us come to the text itself, hoping to enjoy the doctrine of the Trinity while we are discoursing upon our adoption, in which wonder of grace they each have a share. Under the teaching of the divine Spirit may we be drawn into sweet communion with the Father through His Son Jesus Christ, to His glory and to our benefit.

Three things are very clearly set forth in my text : the first is *the dignity of believers*—" ye are sons " ; the second is *the consequent indwelling of the Holy Ghost*—" because ye are sons, God hath sent forth the Spirit of His Son into your hearts " ; and the third is *the filial cry*—crying, " Abba, Father."

I. First, then, THE DIGNITY OF BELIEVERS. Adoption gives us the rights of children, regeneration gives us the nature of children : we are partakers of both of these, for we are sons.

And let us here observe that *this sonship is a gift of grace received by faith*. We are not the sons of God by nature in the sense here meant. We are in a sense " the offspring God " by nature, but this is very different from the sonship here described, which is the peculiar privilege of those who are born again. The Jews claimed to be of the family of of God, but as their privileges came to them by the way of their fleshly birth, they are likened to Ishmael, who was born after the flesh, but who was cast out as the son of the bondwoman, and compelled to give way to the son of the promise. We have a sonship which does not come to us by nature, for we are " born, not of blood, nor of the will of the flesh, nor of the will of man, but of God." Our sonship comes by promise, by the operation of God as a special gift to a peculiar seed, set apart unto the Lord by His own sovereign grace, as Isaac was. This honour and privilege come to us, according to the connection of our text, by faith. Note well the twenty-sixth verse of the preceding chapter (Gal. iii. 26) : " For ye are all the children of God by faith in Christ Jesus." As unbelievers we know nothing of adoption. While we are under the law as self-righteous we know something of servitude, but we know nothing of sonship. It is only after that faith has come that we cease to be under the schoolmaster, and rise out of our minority to take the privileges of the sons of God.

Faith worketh in us the spirit of adoption, and our consciousness of sonship, in this wise : first, *it brings us justification*. Verses twenty-four of the previous chapter says, " The law was our schoolmaster to bring us unto Christ, that we might be justified by faith." An unjustified man stands in the condition of a criminal, not of a child : his sin is laid to his charge, he is reckoned as unjust and unrighteous, as indeed he really is, and he is therefore a rebel against his king, and not a child enjoying his father's love. But when faith realizes the cleansing power of the blood of atonement, and lays hold upon the righteousness of God in Christ Jesus, then the justified man becomes a son and a child. Justification and adoption always go together. " Whom He called them He also justified," and the calling is a call to the Father's house, and to a recognition of sonship. Believing brings forgiveness and justification through our Lord Jesus ; it also brings adoption, for it is written, " But as many as received Him, to them gave He power to become the sons of God, even to them that believe on His name."

Faith brings us into the realization of our adoption in the next place by *setting us free from the bondage of the law*. " After that faith is come, we are no longer under a schoolmaster." When we groaned under a sense of sin, and were shut up by it as in a prison, we feared that the law would punish us for our iniquity, and our life was made bitter with fear. Moreover, we strove in our own blind self-sufficient manner to keep that law, and this brought us into yet another bondage, which became harder and harder as failure succeeded to failure : we sinned and stumbled more and more to our soul's confusion. But now that faith has come we see the law fulfilled in Christ, and ourselves justified and accepted in Him : this changes the slave into a child, and duty into choice. Now we delight in the law, and by the power of the Spirit we walk in holiness to the glory of God. Thus it is that by believing in Christ Jesus we escape from Moses, the taskmaster, and come to Jesus, the Saviour ; we cease to regard God as an angry Judge and view Him as our loving Father. The system of merit and command, and punishment and fear, has given way to the rule of grace, gratitude, and love, and this new principle of government is one of the grand privileges of the children of God.

Now, *faith is the mark of sonship in all who have it*, whoever they may be, for " ye are all the children of God by faith in Christ Jesus " (Gal. iii. 26). If you are believing in Jesus, whether you are Jew or Gentile, bond or free, you are a son of God. If you have only believed in Christ of late, and have but for the past few weeks been able to rest in His great salvation, yet, beloved, now are you a child of God. It is not an after privilege, granted to assurance or growth in grace ; it is an early blessing, and belongs to him who has the smallest degree of faith, and is no more than a babe in grace. If a man be a believer in Jesus Christ his name is in the register-book of the great family above, " for ye are all the children of God by faith in Christ Jesus." But if you have no faith, no matter what zeal, no matter what works, no matter what knowledge, no matter what pretensions to holiness you may possess, you are nothing, and your religion is vain. Without faith in Christ you are as sounding brass and a tinkling cymbal, for without faith it is impossible to please God. Faith then, wherever it is found, is the infallible token of a child of God, and its absence is fatal to the claim.

This according to the apostle is further illustrated by our baptism, for in baptism, if there be faith in the soul, there is an open putting on of the Lord Jesus Christ. Read the twenty-seventh verse : " For as many of you as have been baptized into Christ have put on Christ." In baptism you professed to be dead to the world and you were therefore buried into the name of Jesus : and the meaning of that burial, if it had any right meaning to you, was that you professed yourself henceforth to be dead to everything but Christ, and henceforth your life was to be in Him, and you were to be as one raised from the dead to newness of life. Of course the outward form avails nothing to the unbeliever, but to the man who is in Christ it is a most instructive ordinance. The spirit and essence of the ordinance lie in the soul's entering into the symbol, in the man's knowing not alone the baptism into water, but the baptism into the Holy Ghost and into fire : and as many of you as know that inward mystic baptism into Christ know also that henceforth you have put on Christ and are covered by Him as a man is by his garment. Henceforth you are one in Christ, you bear His name, you live in Him, you are saved by Him, you are altogether His. Now, if you are one with Christ, since He is a Son, you are sons also. If you have put on Christ, God seeth you not in yourself but in Christ, and that which belongeth unto Christ belongeth also unto you, for if you be Christ's then are you Abraham's seed and heirs according to the promise. As the Roman youth when he came of age put on the *toga*, and was admitted to the rights of citizenship, so the putting on of Christ is the token of our admission into the position of sons of God. Thus are we actually admitted to the enjoyment of our glorious heritage. Every blessing of the covenant of grace belongs to those who are Christ's, and every believer is in that list. Thus, then, according to the teaching of the passage, we receive adoption by faith as the gift of grace.

Again, *adoption comes to us by redemption*. Read the passage which precedes the text : " But when the fulness of the time was come, God sent forth His Son, made of a woman, made under the law, to redeem them that were under the law, that we might receive the adoption of sons." Beloved, prize redemption, and never listen to teaching which would destroy its meaning or lower its importance. Remember that ye were not redeemed with silver and gold, but with the precious blood of Christ, as of a lamb without blemish. You were under the law, and subject to its curse, for you had broken it most grievously, and you were subject to its penalty, for it is written, "the soul that sinneth, it shall die "; and yet again, "cursed is every one that continueth not in all things that are written in the book of the law to do them." You were also under the terror of the law, for you feared its wrath ; and you were under its irritating power, for often when the commandment came, sin within you revived and you died. But now you are redeemed from all ; as the Holy Ghost saith, " Christ hath redeemed us from the curse of the law, being made a curse for us : for it is written, Cursed is every one that hangeth on a tree." Now ye are not under the law, but under grace, and this because Christ came under the law and kept it both by His active and His passive obedience, fulfilling all its commands and bearing all its penalty on your behalf and in your room and stead. Henceforth you are the redeemed of the Lord, and enjoy a liberty which comes by no other way but that of the eternal ransom. Remember this ; and whenever you feel most assured that you are a child of God, praise the redeeming blood ;

whenever your heart beats highest with love to your great Father, bless the "firstborn among many brethren," who for your sakes came under the law, was circumcised, kept the law in His life, and bowed His head to it in His death, honouring, and magnifying the law, and making the justice and righteousness of God to be more conspicuous by His life than it would have been by the holiness of all mankind, and His justice to be more fully vindicated by His death that it would have been if all the world of sinners had been cast into hell. Glory be to our redeeming Lord, by whom we have received the adoption !

Again, we further learn from the passage that *we now enjoy the privilege of sonship*. According to the run of the passage the apostle means not only that we are children, but that we are full-grown sons. " Because ye are sons," means,—because the time appointed of the Father is come, and you are of age, and no longer under tutors and governors. In our minority we are under the schoolmaster, under the regimen of ceremonies, under types, figures, shadows, learning our A B C by being convinced of sin ; but when faith is come we are no longer under the schoolmaster, but come to a more free condition. Till faith comes we are under tutors and governors, like mere boys, but after faith we take our rights as sons of God. The Jewish church of old was under the yoke of the law ; its sacrifices were continual and its ceremonies endless ; new moons and feasts must be kept ; jubilees must be observed and pilgrimages made : in fact, the yoke was too heavy for feeble flesh to bear. The law followed the Israelite into every corner, and dealt with him upon every point : it had to do with his garments, his meat, his drink, his bed, his board, and everything about him : it treated him like a boy at school who has a rule for everything. Now that faith has come we are full-grown sons, and therefore we are free from the rules which govern the school of the child. We are under law to Christ, even as the full-grown son is still under the discipline of his father's house ; but this is a law of love and not of fear, of grace and not of bondage. " Stand fast therefore in the liberty wherewith Christ hath made us free, and be not entangled again with the yoke of bondage." Return not to the beggarly elements of a merely outward religion, but keep close to the worship of God in spirit and in truth, for this is the liberty of the children of God.

Now, by faith *we are no more like to bond-servants*. The apostle says that " the heir, as long as he is a child, differeth nothing from a servant, though he be lord of all ; but is under tutors and governors till the time appointed of the father." But beloved, now are ye the sons of God, and ye have come to your majority : now are ye free to enjoy the honours and blessings of the Father's house. Rejoice that the free spirit dwells within you, and prompts you to holiness ; this is a far superior power to the merely external command and the whip of threatening. Now no more are you in bondage to outward forms, and rites, and ceremonies ; but the Spirit of God teacheth you all things, and leads you into the inner meaning and substance of the truth.

Now, also, saith the apostle, *we are heirs*—" Wherefore thou art no more a servant, but a son ; and if a son, then an heir of God through Christ." No living man has ever realised to the full what this means. Believers are at this moment heirs, but what is the estate ? It is God Himself ! We are heirs of God! Not only of the promises, of the covenant engagements, and of all the blessings which belong to the chosen seed, but heirs of God Himself. "The Lord is my portion, saith my soul." "This God is our God for ever and ever." We are not only heirs to God, to all that He gives to His first-born, but heirs of God Himself. David said, "The Lord is the portion of mine inheritance and of my cup." As He said to Abraham, "Fear not, Abraham, I am thy shield and thine exceeding great reward," so saith He to every man that is born of the Spirit. These are His own words—"I will be to them a God, and they shall be to Me a people." Why, then, O believer, are you poor? All riches are yours. Why then are you sorrowful? The ever-blessed God is yours. Why do you tremble? Omnip-otence waits to help you. Why do you distrust? His immutability will abide with you even to the end, and make His promise steadfast. All things are yours, for Christ is yours, and Christ is God's; and though there be some things which at present you cannot actually grasp in your hand, nor even see with your eye, to wit, the things which are laid up for you in heaven, yet still by faith you can enjoy even these, for "He hath raised us up together, and made us sit together in the heavenlies in Christ," "in whom also we have obtained an inheritance," so that "our citizenship is in heaven." We enjoy even now the pledge and earnest of heaven in the indwelling of the Holy Ghost. Oh what privileges belong to those who are the sons of God!

Once more upon this point of the believer's dignity, *we are already tasting one of the inevitable consequences of being the sons of God.* What are they? One of them is the opposition of the children of the bondwoman. No sooner had the apostle Paul preached the liberty of the saints, than straightway there arose certain teachers who said, "This will never do; you must be circumcised, you must come under the law." Their opposition was to Paul a token that he was of the free woman, for behold the children of the bondwoman singled him out for their virulent opposition. You shall find, dear brother, that if you enjoy fellowship with God, if you live in the spirit of adoption, if you are brought near to the Most High, so as to be a member of the divine family, straightway all those who are under bondage to the law will quarrel with you. Thus saith the apostle, "As then He that was born after the flesh persecuted Him that was born after the Spirit, even so it is now." The child of Hagar was found by Sarah mocking Isaac, the child of promise. Ishmael would have been glad to have shown his enmity to the hated heir by blows and personal assault, but there was a superior power to check him, so that he could get no further than "mocking." So it is just now. There have been periods in which the enemies of the gospel have gone a great deal further than mocking, for they have been able to imprison and burn alive the lovers of the gospel; but now, thank God, we are under His special protection as to life and limb and liberty, and are as safe as Isaac was in Abraham's house. They can mock us, but they cannot go any further, or else some of us would be publicly gibbetted. But trials of cruel mockings are still to be endured, our words are twisted, our sentiments are misrepresented, and all sorts of horrible things are imputed to us, things which we know not, to all which we would reply with Paul, "Am I therefore become your enemy because I tell you the truth?"

This is the old way of the Hagarenes, the child after the flesh is still doing his best to mock him that is born after the Spirit. Do not be astonished, neither be grieved in the least degree when this happens to any of you, but let this also turn to the establish-ment of your confidence and to the confirmation of your faith in Christ Jesus, for He told you of old, "If ye were of the world, the world would love his own: but because ye are not of the world, but I have chosen you out of the world, therefore the world hateth you."

II. Our second head is THE CONSEQUENT IN-DWELLING OF THE HOLY GHOST IN BELIEVERS—"God hath sent forth the Spirit of His Son into your hearts." *Here is a divine act of the Father.* The Holy Ghost proceedeth from the Father and the Son: and God hath sent Him forth into your hearts. If He had only come knocking at your hearts and asked your leave to enter, He had never entered, but when Jehovah sent Him He made His way, without violat-ing your will, but yet with irresistible power. Where Jehovah sent Him there He will abide, and go no more out for ever. Beloved, I have no time to dwell upon the words, but I want you to turn them over in your thoughts, for they contain a great depth. As surely as God sent His Son into the world to dwell among men, so that His saints beheld His glory, the "glory as of the only begotten of the Father, full of grace and truth," so surely hath God sent forth the Spirit to enter into men's hearts, there to take up His residence that in him also the glory of God may be revealed. Bless and adore the Lord who hath sent you such a visitor as this.

Now, note the style and title under which the Holy Spirit comes to us: *He comes as the Spirit of Jesus.* The words are "the Spirit of His Son." by which is not meant the character and disposition of Christ, though that were quite true, for God sends this unto His people, but it means the Holy Ghost. Why, then, is He called the Spirit of His Son, or the Spirit of Jesus? May we not give these reasons? It was by the Holy Ghost that the human nature of Christ was born of the Virgin. By the Spirit our Lord was attested at His baptism, when the Holy Spirit descended upon Him like a dove, and abode upon Him. In Him the Holy Spirit dwelt without measure, anointing Him for His great work, and by the Spirit He was anointed with the oil of gladness above His fellows. The Spirit was also with Him, attesting His ministry by signs and wonders. The Holy Ghost is our Lord's great gift to the church; it was after His ascension that He bestowed the gifts of Pentecost, and the Holy Spirit descended upon the church to abide with the people of God for ever. The Holy Ghost is the Spirit of Christ, because, also, He is Christ's witness here below; for "there are three that bear witness on earth, the Spirit, and the water, and the blood." For these and many other reasons He is called "the Spirit of His Son," and it is He who comes to dwell in believers. I would urge you very solemnly and gratefully to consider the wondrous condescension which is here displayed. God Himself the Holy Ghost, takes up His residence in believers. I never know which is the more wonderful, the incarnation of Christ or the indwelling of the Holy Ghost. Jesus dwelt here for awhile in human flesh untainted by sin, holy, harmless, undefiled, and separate from sinners; but the Holy Ghost dwells continually in the hearts of all believers, though as yet they are imperfect and prone to evil. Year after year, century after century, He still abideth in the saints, and will do so till the elect are all in glory. While we adore the incarnate Son, let us adore also the indwelling Spirit whom the Father hath sent.

Now notice *the place wherein He takes up His residence.*—" God hath sent forth the Spirit of His Son *into your hearts.*" Note, that it does not say into your heads or your brains. The Spirit of God doubtless illuminates the intellect and guides the judgment, but this is not the commencement nor the main part of His work. He comes chiefly to the affections, He dwells with the heart, for with the heart man believeth unto righteousness, and " God hath sent forth the Spirit of His Son into your hearts." Now, the heart is the centre of our being, and therefore doth the Holy Ghost occupy this place of vantage. He comes into the central fortress and universal citadel of our nature, and thus takes possession of the whole. The heart is the vital part ; we speak of it as the chief residence of life, and therefore the Holy Ghost enters it, and as the living God dwells in the living heart, taking possession of the very core and marrow of our being. It is from the heart and through the heart that life is diffused. The blood is sent even to the extremities of the body by the pulsings of the heart, and when the Spirit of God takes possession of the affections, He operates upon every power, and faculty, and member of our entire manhood. Out of the heart are the issues of life, and from the affections sanctified by the Holy Ghost all other faculties and powers receive renewal, illumination, sanctification, strengthening, and ultimate perfection.

This wonderful blessing is ours " because we are sons " ; and *it is fraught with marvellous results.* Sonship sealed by the indwelling Spirit brings us peace and joy ; it leads to nearness to God and fellowship with Him ; it excites trust, love, and vehement desire, and creates in us reverence, obedience, and actual likeness to God. All this, and much more, because the Holy Ghost has come to dwell in us. Oh, matchless mystery ! Had it not been revealed it had never been imagined, and now that it is revealed it would never have been believed if it had not become matter of actual experience to those who are in Christ Jesus. There are many professors who know nothing of this ; they listen to us with bewilderment as if we told them an idle tale, for the carnal mind knoweth not the things that be of God ; they are spiritual, and can only be spiritually discerned. Those who are not sons, or who only come in as sons under the law of nature, like Ishmael, know nothing of this indwelling Spirit, and are up in arms at us for daring to claim so great a blessing : yet it is ours, and none can deprive us of it.

III. Now I come to the third portion of our text—THE FILIAL CRY. This is deeply interesting. I think it will be profitable if your minds enter into it. Where the Holy Ghost enters there is a cry. " God hath sent forth the Spirit of His Son, crying, ' Abba, Father.' " Now, notice, *it is the Spirit of God that cries*—a most remarkable fact. Some are inclined to view the expression as a Hebraism, and read it, He " makes us to cry " ; but, beloved, the text saith not so, and we are not at liberty to alter it upon such a pretence. We are always right in keeping to what God says, and here we plainly read of the Spirit in our hearts that He is crying " Abba, Father." The apostle in Romans viii. 15 says,

" Ye have received the Spirit of adoption, whereby *we* cry, Abba, Father," but here he describes the Spirit himself as crying " Abba, Father." We are certain that when he ascribed the cry of " Abba, Father " to us, he did not wish to exclude the Spirit's cry, because in the twenty-sixth verse of the famous eighth of Romans he says, " Likewise the Spirit also helpeth our infirmities : for we know not what we should pray for as we ought : but the Spirit itself maketh intercession for us with groanings which cannot be uttered." Thus He represents the Spirit Himself as groaning with unutterable groanings within the child of God, so that when he wrote to the Romans he had on his mind the same thought which he expressed to the Galatians,—that it is the Spirit itself which cries and groans in us " Abba, Father." How is this ? Is it not ourselves that cry ? Yes, assuredly ; and yet the Spirit cries also. The expressions are both correct. The Holy Spirit prompts and inspires the cry. He puts the cry into the heart and mouth of the believer. It is His cry because He suggests it, approves of it, and educates us to it. We should never have cried thus if He had not first taught us the way. As a mother teaches her child to speak, so He puts this cry of " Abba, Father " into our mouths ; yea, it is He who forms in our hearts the desire after our Father, God, and keeps it there. He is the Spirit of adoption, and the Author of adoption's special and significant cry.

Not only does He prompt us to cry, but He works in us a sense of need which compels us to cry, and also that spirit of confidence which emboldens us to claim such relationship to the great God. Nor is this all, for He assists us in some mysterious manner so that we are able to pray aright ; He puts His divine energy into us so that we cry " Abba, Father " in an acceptable manner. There are times when *we* cannot cry at all, and then He cries in us. There are seasons when doubts and fears abound, and so suffocate us with their fumes that we cannot even raise a cry, and then the indwelling Spirit represents us, and speaks for us, and makes intercession for us, crying in our name, and making intercession for us according to the will of God. Thus does the cry " Abba, Father " rise up in our hearts even when we feel as if we could not pray, and dare not think ourselves children. Then we may each say, " I live, yet not I, but the Spirit that dwelleth in me." On the other hand, at times our soul gives such a sweet assent to the Spirit's cry that it becometh ours also, but then we more than ever own the work of the Spirit, and still ascribe to Him the blessed cry, " Abba, Father."

I want you now to notice a very sweet fact about this cry ; namely, that *it is literally the cry of the Son.* God hath sent the Spirit of His Son into our hearts, and that Spirit cries in us exactly according to the cry of the Son. If you turn to the gospel of Mark, at the fourteenth chapter, thirty-sixth verse, you will find there what you will not discover in any other evangelist (for Mark is always the man for the striking points, and the memorable word), he records that our Lord prayed in the garden, " Abba, Father, all things are possible unto Thee ; take away this cup from Me : nevertheless not what I will, but what Thou wilt." So that this cry in us copies the cry of our Lord to the letter—" Abba, Father." Now, I dare say you have heard these words " Abba, Father " explained at considerable length at other times, and if so, you know that the first word is

Syrian or Aramaic; or, roughly speaking, Abba is the Hebrew word for "father." The second word is in Greek, and is the Gentile word, " πατηs," or *patēr*, which also signifies father. It is said that these two words are used to remind us that Jews and Gentiles are one before God. They do remind us of this, but this cannot have been the principal reason for their use. Do you think that when our Lord was in His agony in the garden that He said, "Abba, Father," because Jews and Gentiles are one? Why should He have thought of that doctrine, and why need He mention it in prayer to His Father? Some other reason must have suggested it to Him. It seems to me that our Lord said "Abba" because it was His native tongue. When a Frenchman prays, if he has learned English he may ordinarily pray in English, but if ever He falls into an agony he will pray in French, as surely as he prays at all. Our Welsh brethren tell us that there is no language like Welsh—I suppose it is so *to them*: now they will talk English when about their ordinary business, and they can pray in English when everything goes comfortably with them, but I am sure that if a Welshman is in a great fervency of prayer, he flies to his Welsh tongue to find full expression. Our Lord in His agony used His native language, and as born of the seed of Abraham He cries in his own tongue, "Abba." Even thus, my brethren, we are prompted by the spirit of adoption to use our own language, the language of the heart, and so to speak to the Lord freely in our own tongue. Besides, to my mind, the word "Abba" is of all words in all languages the most natural word for father. I must try and pronounce it so that you see the natural childishness of it, "Ab—ba," "Ab—ba." Is it not just what your children say, ab, ab, ba, ba, as soon as they try to talk? It is the sort of word which any child would say, whether Hebrew, or Greek, or French, or English. Therefore, Abba is a word worthy of introduction into all languages. It is truly a child's word, and our Master felt, I have no doubt, in His agony, a love for child's words. Dr. Guthrie, when he was dying, said, "Sing a hymn," but he added, "Sing me one of the bairns' hymns." When a man comes to die he wants to be a child again, and longs for bairns' hymns and bairns' words. Our blessed Master in His agony used the bairns' word, "Abba," and it is equally becoming in the mouth of each one of us. I think this sweet word "Abba" was chosen to show us that we are to be very natural with God, and not stilted and formal. We are to be very affectionate, and come close to Him, and not merely say "Patēr," which is a cold Greek word, but say "Abba," which is a warm, natural, loving word, fit for one who is a little child with God, and makes bold to lie in His bosom, and look up into His face and talk with holy boldness. "Abba" is not a word, somehow, but a babe's lisping. Oh, how near we are to God when we can use such a speech! How dear He is to us and dear we are to Him when we may thus address Him, saying, like the great Son Himself, "Abba, Father."

This leads me to observe that *this cry in our hearts is exceedingly near and familiar*. In the sound of it I have shown you that it is childlike, but the tone and manner of the utterance are equally so. Note that it is *a cry*. If we obtain audience with a king we do not cry, we speak then in measured tones and set phrases; but the Spirit of God breaks down our measured tones, and takes away the formality which

some hold in great admiration, and He leads us to *cry*, which is the very reverse of formality and stiffness. When we cry, we cry "Abba": even our very cries are full of the spirit of adoption. A cry is a sound which we are not anxious that every passer-by should hear; yet what child minds his father hearing him cry? So when our heart is broken and subdued we do not feel as if we could talk fine language at all, but the Spirit in us sends forth cries and groans, and of these we are not ashamed, nor are we afraid to cry before God. I know some of you think that God will not hear your prayers, because you cannot pray grandly like such-and-such a minister. Oh, but the Spirit of His Son cries, and you cannot do better than cry too. Be satisfied to offer to God broken language, words salted with your griefs, wetted with your tears. Go to Him with holy familiarity, and be not afraid to cry in His presence, "Abba, Father."

But then *how earnest it is*: for a cry is an intense thing. The word implies fervency. A cry is not a flippant utterance, nor a mere thing of the lips, it comes up from the soul. Hath not the Lord taught us to cry to Him in prayer with fervent importunity that will not take a denial? Hath He not brought us so near to Him, that sometimes we say, "I will not let Thee go except Thou bless me"? Hath He not taught us so to pray that His disciples might almost say of us as they did of one of old, "Send her away, for she crieth after us." We do cry after Him, our heart and our flesh crieth out for God, for the living God, and this is the cry, "Abba, Father, I must know Thee, I must taste Thy love, I must dwell under Thy wing, I must behold Thy face, I must feel Thy great fatherly heart overflowing and filling my heart with peace." We cry, "Abba, Father."

I shall close when I notice this, that *the most of this crying is kept within the heart*, and does not come out at the lips. Like Moses, we cry when we say not a word. God hath sent forth the Spirit of His Son *into our hearts*, whereby we cry, "Abba, Father." You know what I mean: it is not alone in your little room, by the old arm-chair, that you cry to God, but you call Him "Abba, Father," as you go about the streets or work in the shop. The Spirit of His Son is crying, "Abba, Father," when you are in the crowd or at your table among the family. I see it is alleged as a very grave charge against me that I speak as if I were familiar with God. If it be so, I make bold to say that I speak only as I feel. Blessed be my heavenly Father's name, I know I am His child, and with whom should a child be familiar but with his father? O ye strangers to the living God, be it known unto you that if this be vile, I purpose to be viler still, as He shall help me to walk more closely with Him. We feel a deep reverence for our Father in heaven, which bows us to the very dust, but for all that we can say, "truly our fellowship is with the Father and with His Son, Jesus Christ." No stranger can understand the nearness of the believer's soul to God in Christ Jesus, and because the world cannot understand it, it finds it convenient to sneer, but what of that? Abraham's tenderness to Isaac made Ishmael jealous, and caused him to laugh, but Isaac had no cause to be ashamed of being ridiculed, since the mocker could not rob him of the covenant blessing. Yes, beloved, the Spirit of God makes you cry "Abba, Father," but the cry is mainly within your heart, and there it is so commonly uttered that it becomes the habit of your soul to be crying to your heavenly Father. The text does not say that He had cried, but the expression is " crying " —it is a present participle, indicating that He cries every day " Abba, Father." Go home, my brethren, and live in the spirit of sonship. Wake up in the morning, and let your first thought be " My Father, my Father, be with me this day." Go out into business, and when things perplex you let that be your resort—" My Father, help me in this hour of need." When you go to your home, and there meet with domestic anxieties, let your cry still be, " Help me, my Father." When alone you are not alone, because the Father is with you : and in the midst of the crowd you are not in danger, because the Father Himself loveth you. What a blessed word is that— " The Father Himself loveth you " ! Go, and live as His children. Take heed that ye reverence Him, for if He be a Father where is His fear ? Go and obey Him, for this is right. Be ye imitators of God as dear children. Honour Him wherever you are, by adorning His doctrine in all things. Go and live upon Him, for you shall soon live with Him. Go and rejoice in Him. Go and cast all your cares upon Him. Go henceforth, and whatever men may see in you may they be compelled to own that you are the children of the Highest. " Blessed are the peacemakers, for they shall be called the children of God." May you be such henceforth and evermore. Amen and amen.

THE FIRST FRUIT OF THE SPIRIT

" But the fruit of the Spirit is love."—Galatians v. 22.

THE worst enemy we have is the flesh. Augustine used frequently to pray, " Lord, deliver me from that evil man, myself." All the fire which the devil can bring from hell could do us little harm if we had not so much fuel in our nature. It is the powder in the magazine of the old man which is our perpetual danger. When we are guarding against foes without, we must not forget to be continually on our watch-tower against the foe of foes within. " The flesh lusteth against the Spirit." On the other hand, our best friend, who loves us better than we love ourselves, is the Holy Spirit. We are shockingly forgetful of the Holy Ghost, and therein it is to be feared that we greatly grieve Him ; yet we are immeasurably indebted to Him : in fact, we owe our spiritual existence to His divine power. It would not be proper to compare the love of the Spirit with the grace of our Lord Jesus Christ, so as even by implication to set up a scale of degrees in love ; for the love of the regenerating Spirit is infinite, even as is the love of the redeeming Son. But yet for a moment we will set these two displays of love side by side. Is not the indwelling of the Spirit of God equal in lovingkindness to the incarnation of the Son of God ? Jesus dwelt in a pure manhood of His own ; the Holy Spirit dwells in our manhood, which is fallen, and as yet imperfectly sanctified. Jesus dwelt in His human body, having it perfectly under His own control ; but, alas, the Holy Spirit must contend for the mastery within us, and though He is Lord over our hearts, yet there is an evil power within our members, strongly intrenched, and obstinately bent on mischief. " The flesh lusteth against the Spirit, and the Spirit against the flesh." Our Lord Jesus dwelt in His body only for some thirty years or so ; but the blessed Spirit of all grace dwelleth in us evermore, through all the days of our pilgrimage : from the moment when He enters into us by regeneration. He continueth in us, making us meet to be partakers of the inheritance of the saints in light. You sing

" Oh, 'twas love, 'twas wondrous love,"

in reference to our Lord Jesus and His cross : sing it also in reference to the Holy Spirit and His long-suffering. He looks at us from within, and therefore He sees the chambers of imagery where hidden idols still abide. He sees our actions ; not from without, for therein, perhaps, they might be judged favourably, but He discerns them from within, in their springs and in the pollution of those springs ; in their main currents and in all their side eddies and back waters. O brethren, it is wonderful that this blessed Spirit should not leave us in indignation ; we lodge Him so ill, we honour Him so little. He receives so little of our affectionate worship that He might well say, " I will no longer abide with you." When the Lord had given up His people to the Roman sword, there was heard in the temple at Jerusalem a sound as of rushing wings, and a voice crying, " Let us go hence." Justly might the divine presence have left us also because of our sins. It is matchless love which has caused the Holy Spirit to bear with our ill manners, and bear our vexatious behaviour. He stays though sin intrudes into His temple ! He makes His royal abode where evil assails His palace ! Alas, that a heart where the Spirit deigns to dwell should ever be made a thoroughfare for selfish or unbelieving traffic ! God help us to adore the Holy Ghost at the commencement of our discourse, and to do so even more reverently at its close !

The Holy Ghost when He comes into us is the author of all our desires after true holiness. He strives in us against the flesh. That holy conflict which we wage against our corruption cometh entirely of Him. We should sit down in willing bondage to the flesh, if He did not bid us strike for liberty. The good Spirit also leads us in the way of life. If we be led of the Spirit, says the apostle, we are not under the law. He leadeth us by gentle means, drawing us with cords of love, and bands of a man. " He leadeth me." If we take a single step in the right road, it is because He leadeth us, and if we have persevered these many years in the way of peace, it is all due to His guidance, even to Him who will surely bring us in and make us to enjoy the promised rest.

" And every virtue we possess,
And every victory won,
And every thought of holiness,
Are His alone."

The Holy Ghost not only creates the inward contest against sin, and the agonizing desire for holiness, and leads us onward in the way of life, but He remains within us, taking up His residence and somewhat more : for the text suggests a still more immovable steadfastness of residence in our hearts, since according to the figure, the Spirit strikes root within us. The text speaks of " fruit," and fruit cometh only of a rooted abidance ; it could not be conceived of in connection with a transient sojourning, like that of a wayfaring man. The stakes and tent pins that are driven into the ground for an Arab's tent bear no fruit, for they do not remain in one stay ; and inasmuch as I read of the " fruit of the Spirit," I take comfort from the hint, and conclude that He intends to abide in our souls as a tree abides in the soil when fruit is borne by it. Let us love and bless the Holy Ghost ! Let the golden altar of incense perfume this earth with the sweet savour of perpetual adoration to the Holy Ghost ! Let our hearts heartily sing to Him this solemn doxology :—

> " We give Thee, Sacred Spirit, praise,
> Who, in our hearts of sin and woe,
> Makes living springs of grace arise,
> And into boundless glory flow."

I. Now, coming to our text, I shall notice the matters contained in it, and the first thing which my mind perceives is A WINNOWING FAN. I would like to be able to use it, but it is better far that it should remain where it is, for " the fan is in *His* hand, and *He* will throughly purge His floor." The handle of this winnowing fan is made of the first word of the text, that disjunctive conjunction, that dividing monosyllable, " *But*." " *But* the fruit of the Spirit is love " !

That " but " is placed there because the apostle had been mentioning certain works of the flesh, all of which He winnows away like chaff, and then sets forth in opposition to them " the fruit of the Spirit." If you will read the chapter, you will notice that the apostle has used no less than seventeen words, I might almost say eighteen, to describe the works of the flesh. Human language is always rich in bad words, because the human heart is full of the manifold evils which these words denote. Nine words are here used to express the fruit of the Spirit ; but to express the works of the flesh, see how many are gathered together !

The first set of these works of the flesh which have to be winnowed away are *the counterfeits of love to man*. Counterfeited love is one of the vilest things under heaven. That heavenly word, *love*, has been trailed in the mire of unclean passion and filthy desire. The licentiousness, which comes of the worship of Venus, has dared to take to itself a name which belongs only to the pure worship of Jehovah. Now, the works which counterfeit love are these : " *adultery*, fornication, uncleanness, lasciviousness." To talk of " love " when a man covets his neighbour's wife, or when a woman violates the command, " Thou shalt not commit adultery," is little less than sheer blasphemy against the holiness of love. It is not love, but lust ; love is an angel, and lust a devil. The purities of domestic life are defiled, and its honours are disgraced when once the marriage bond is disregarded. When men or women talk of religion, and are unfaithful to their marriage covenant, they are base hypocrites. Even the heathen condemned this infamy, let not Christians tolerate it. The next fleshly work is " *fornication*," which was scarcely censured among the heathen,

but is most sternly condemned by Christianity. It is a wretched sign of the times that in these corrupt days some have arisen who treat this crime as a slight offence, and even attempt to provide for its safer indulgence by legislative enactments. Has it come to this ? Has the civil ruler become a panderer to the lusts of corrupt minds ? Let it not be once named among you, as it becometh saints. " *Unclean-ness* " is a third work of the flesh, and it includes those many forms of foul offence which defile the body, and deprive it of its true honour ; while to bring up the rear we have " *lasciviousness*," which is the cord which draws on uncleanness, and includes all conversation which excites the passions, all songs which suggest lewdness, all gestures and thoughts which lead up to unlawful gratification. We have sadly much of these two evils in these days, not only openly in our streets, but in more secret ways. I loathe the subject. All works of art which are contrary to modesty are here condemned and the most pleasing poetry if it creates impure imaginations. These unclean things are the works of the flesh in the stage of putridity—the very maggots which swarm within a corrupt soul. Bury these rotten things out of our sight ! I do but uncover them for an instant that a holy disgust may be caused in every Christian soul ; and that we may flee therefrom as from the breath of pestilence. Yet remember, O you that think yourselves pure, and imagine you would never transgress so badly, that even into these loathsome and abominable criminalities high professors have fallen ; aye, and sincere believers trusting in themselves have slipped into this ditch, from whence they have escaped with infinite sorrow, to go with broken bones the rest of their pilgrimage. Alas, how many who seemed to be clean escaped from pollution have so fallen that they have had to be saved so as by fire ! Oh, may we keep our garments unspotted by the flesh ; and this we cannot do unless it be in the power and energy of the Spirit of holiness. He must purge these evils from us, and cause His fruit so to abound in us that the deeds of the flesh shall be excluded for ever.

The winnowing fan is used next against the *counterfeits of love to God ;* I refer to the falsities of superstition—" Idolatry and witchcraft "—" but the fruit of the Spirit is love." Alas, there are some that fall into *idolatry ;* for they trust in an arm of flesh, and exalt the creature into the place of the Creator ; " their God is their belly, and they glory in their shame." The golden calf of wealth, the silver shrines of craft, the goddess of philosophy, the Diana of fashion, the Moloch of power, these are all worshipped instead of the living God. Those who profess to reverence the true God, yet too generally worship Him in ways which He has not ordained. Thus saith the Lord, " Thou shalt not make unto thee any graven image, or any likeness of anything that is in heaven above, or that is in the earth beneath, or that is in the water under the earth : thou shalt not bow down thyself to them, nor serve them." Yet we have Christians (so called) who say they derive help in the exercise of devotion from images and pictures. See how their places of assembly are rendered gaudy with pictures, and images, and things which savour of old Rome. What idolatry is openly carried on in certain buildings belonging to the National Church ! What sensuous worship is now approved ? Men cannot worship God nowadays unless their eyes, and ears, and noses are gratified : when these senses of the flesh are pleased, they are satisfied with themselves ; "but the fruit of the Spirit is love." Love is the most perfect architecture, for " love buildeth up " ; love is the sweetest music, for without it we are become as a sounding brass or a tinkling cymbal ; love is the choicest incense, for it is a sacrifice of sweet smell ; love is the fittest vestment,—" Above all things put on charity, which is the bond of perfect-ness." Oh, that men would remember that the fruit of the Spirit is not the finery of the florist, the sculptor, or the milliner, but the love of the heart. It ill-becomes us to make that gaudy which should be simple and spiritual. The fruit of the Spirit is not idolatry,—the worship of another god, or of the true God after the manner of will-worship. No, that fruit is obedient love to the only living God.

" Witchcraft," too, is a work of the flesh. Under this head we may rightly group all that prying into the unseen, that rending of the veil which God has hung up, that interfering with departed spirits, that necromancy which calls itself spiritualism, and pays court to familiar spirits and demons—this is no fruit of the Spirit, but the fruit of a bitter root. Brother Christians, modern witchcrafts and wizardry are to be abhorred and condemned, and you will be wise to keep clear of them, trembling to be found acting in concert with those who love darkness rather than light, because their deeds are evil. Idolatry and witchcraft are caused by a want of love to God, and they are evidences that the Spirit's life is not in the soul. When you come to love God with all your heart, you will not worship God in ways of your own devising, but you will ask, "Wherewithal shall I draw near unto the most high God ? " and you will take your direction from the Lord's inspired word. The service which He prescribes is the only service which He will accept. The winnowing-fan is at work now : I wonder whether it is operating upon any here present ?

But next, this great winnowing-fan drives away with its " but " all the forms of hate. The apostle mentions " hatred," or an habitual enmity to men, usually combined with a selfish esteem of one's own person. Certain men cherish a dislike to everybody who is not of their clique, while they detest those who oppose them. They are contemptuous, to the weak, ready to take offence, and little careful whether they give it or no. They delight to be in minorities of one, and the more wrongheaded and pugnacious they can be, the more are they in their element. " Variance," too, with its perpetual dislikes, bickerings, and quarrellings, is a work of the flesh. Those who indulge in it are contrary to all men, pushing their angles into everybody's eyes, and looking out for occasions of faultfinding and strife. " Emulations,"—that is, jealousy. Jealousy in all its forms is one of the works of the flesh : is it not cruel as the grave ? there is a jealousy which sickens if another be praised, and pines away if another prospers. It is a venomous thing, and stingeth like an adder : it is a serpent by the way, biting the horse's heels, so that his rider shall fall backward. " Wrath " is another deed of the flesh : I mean the fury of angry passion, and all the madness which comes of it. " But I am a man of very quick temper," says one. Are you a Christian ? If so, you are bound to master this evil force, or it will ruin you. If you were a saint of God to the very highest degree in all but this one point, it would pull you down ;

aye, at any moment an angry spirit might make you say and do that which would cause you life-long sorrow. " Strife " is a somewhat milder, but equally mischievous, form of the same evil ; if it burns not quite so fast and furiously, yet it is a slow fire kindled by the self-same flame of hell as the more ardent passion. The continual love of contention, the morbid sensitiveness, the overweening regard to one's own dignity, which join together to produce strife, are all evil things. What is the proper respect which is due to poor creatures like ourselves ? I ween that if any one of us did get our " proper respect," we should not like it long : we should think that bare justice was rather scant in its appreciation. We desire to be flattered when we cry out for " proper respect." Respect, indeed ! Why if we had our desert, we should be in the lowest hell ! Then our apostle mentions " seditions," which occur in the State, the Church, and the family. As far as our church life is concerned, this evil shows itself in an opposition to all sorts of authority or law. Any kind of official action in the Church is to be railed at because it is official ; rule of any sort is objected to because each man desires to have the pre-eminence, and will not be second. God save us from this evil leaven ! Heresy is that kind of hate which makes every man set up to create his own religion, write his own Bible, and think out his own gospel. We have heard of " Every man his own lawyer," and now we are coming to have " Every man his own God, every man his own Bible, every man his own instruc-tor." After this work of the flesh, come " Envyings "; not so much the desire to enrich one's self at another's expense, as a wolfish craving to impoverish him, and pull him down for the mere sake of it. This is a very acrid form of undiluted hate, and leaves but one stronger form of hate. To desire another's dishonour merely from envy of his superiority is simply devilish, and is a sort of murder of the man's best life. The list is fitly closed by " murders," a suitable corner-stone to crown this diabolical edifice ; for what is hate but murder ? And what is murder but hate bearing its full fruit ? He who does not love has within him all the elements that make a murderer. If you have not a general feeling of benevolence towards all men, and a desire to do them good, the old spirit of Cain is within you, and it only needs to be unrestrained, and it will strike the fatal blow, and lay your brother dead at your feet. God save you, men and brethren, every one of you, from the domination of these dark principles of hate, which are the works of the flesh in its corrup-tion. " But the fruit of the Spirit is love."

Next time you begin to boil over with wrath, think you feel a hand touching you and causing you to hear a gentle voice whispering, " But the fruit of the Spirit is love." Next time you say, " I will never speak to that man again, I cannot endure him," think you feel a fresh wind fanning your fevered brow, and hear the angel of mercy say, " But the fruit of the Spirit is love." Next time you are inclined to find fault with everybody, and set your brethren by the ears, and create a general scuffle, I pray you let the chimes ring out, " But the fruit of the Spirit is love." If you wish to find fault, it is easy to do so ; you may begin with me and go down to the last young member that was admitted into the church, and you will not have to look long before you can spy out something which needs improvement ; but to what end will you pick holes in our coats ? Whenever you are bent on the growling business, pause awhile and hear the Scripture admonish you, " The fruit of the Spirit is love." When you wax indignant because you have been badly treated, and you think of returning evil for evil, remember this text, " The fruit of the Spirit is love." " Ah," you say, " it was shameful ! " Of course it was : and therefore do not imitate it : do not render railing for railing, but contrariwise blessing, for " the fruit of the Spirit is love."

The winnowing-fan is at work : God blow your chaff away, brethren, and mine too !

The next thing which the winnowing-fan blows away is *the excess of self-indulgence*—" drunkenness, revellings, and such like." Alas, that Christian people should ever need to be warned against these animal offences, and yet they do need it. The wine-cup still has its charms for professors. Nor is this all : it is not merely that you may drink to excess, but you may eat to excess, or clothe your body too sumptuously, or there may be some other spending of money upon your own gratification which is not according to sober living. Drunkenness is one of those trespasses of which Paul says " that they which do such things shall not inherit the kingdom of God." The revelling which makes night hideous with its songs so-called—call them howlings and you are nearer the mark—the revelling which spends hour after hour in entertainments which heat the blood, and harden the heart, and chase away all solid thought, is not for us who have renounced the works of darkness : for us there is a better joy, namely, to be filled with the Spirit, and " the fruit of the Spirit is love."

II. The second thing which I see in the text is A JEWEL,—that jewel is *love*. " The fruit of the Spirit is love." What a priceless Kohinoor this is ! It is altogether incalculable in value. What a heavenly grace love is ! It has its centre in the heart, but its circumference sweeps, like omnipresence, around everything. Love is a grace of boundless scope. We love God : it is the only way in which we can embrace Him fully. We can love the whole of God, but we cannot know the whole of God. Yes, we love God, and even love that part of God which we cannot comprehend or even know. We love the Father as He is. We love His dear Son as He is. We love the ever-blessed Spirit as He is. Following upon this, for God's sake we love the creatures He has made. It is true in a measure that

" He prayeth best that loveth best
Both man and bird and beast."

Every tiny fly that God has made is sacred to our souls as God's creature. Our love climbs to heaven, sits among the angels, and anon bows among them in lowliest attitude ; but in due time our love stoops down to earth, visits the haunts of depravity, cheers the garrets of poverty, and sanctifies the dens of blasphemy, for it loves the lost. Love knows no outcast London, it has cast out none. It talks not of the " lapsed masses," for none have lapsed from its regard. Love hopes good for all, and plans good for all : while it can soar to glory it can descend to sorrow.

Love is a grace which has to do with eternity ; for we shall never cease to love Him who first loved us. But love has also to do with this present world for it is at home in feeding the hungry, clothing the naked, nursing the sick, and liberating the slave.

Love delights in visiting the fatherless and the widows, and thus it earns the encomium,—" I was an hungred, and ye gave Me meat : I was thirsty, and ye gave Me drink : I was a stranger, and ye took Me in : naked, and ye clothed Me : I was sick, and ye visited Me : I was in prison, and ye came unto Me." Love is a very practical, home-spun virtue, and yet it is so rich and rare that God alone is its author. None but a heavenly power can produce this fine linen ; the love of the world is sorry stuff.

Love has to do with friends. How fondly it nestles in the parental bosom ! How sweetly it smiles from a mother's eye ! How closely it binds two souls together in marriage bonds ! How pleasantly it walks along the ways of life, leaning on the arm of friendship ! But love is not content with this, she embraces her enemy, she heaps coals of fire upon her adversary's head ; she 'prays for them that despitefully use her and persecute her. Is not this a precious jewel indeed ? What earthly thing can be compared to it ?

You must have noticed that *in the list of the fruit of the Spirit it is the first*—" The fruit of the Spirit is love." It is first because in some respects it is best. First, because it leads the way. First, because it becomes the motive principle and stimulant of every other grace and virtue. You cannot conceive of anything more forceful and more beneficial, and therefore it is the first. But *see what followeth at its heel*. Two shining ones attend it like maids of honour, waiting upon a queen. " The fruit of the spirit is love, joy, peace " ; he that hath love hath joy and peace. What choice companions ! To love much is to possess a deep delight, a secret cellar of the wine of joy which no man else may taste. He that loveth is like to God, who is the God of peace. Truly the meek and loving shall inherit the earth, and delight themselves in the abundance of peace. He is calm and quiet whose soul is full of love ; in his boat the Lord stands at the helm, saying to the winds and waves, " Peace ; be still ! " He that is all love, though he may have to suffer, yet shall count it all joy when he falleth into divers trials. See then what a precious jewel it is that hath so many shining brilliants set at its side.

Love has this for its excellence, that it fulfils the whole law : you cannot say that of any other virtue. Yet, while it fulfils the whole law, it is not legal. Nobody ever loved because it was demanded of him ; a good man loves because it is his nature to do so. Love is free—it bloweth where it listeth, like the Spirit from which it comes. Love, indeed, is the very essence of heart liberty. Well may it be honoured ; for while it is a true grace of the gospel, it nevertheless fulfils the whole law. If you would have law and gospel sweetly combined, you have it in the fruit of the Spirit, which is love.

Love, moreover, is Godlike, for God is love. Love it is which prepares us for heaven, where everything is love. Come, sweet Spirit, and rest upon us till our nature is transformed into the divine nature by our becoming burning flames of love. Oh, that it were so with us this very day !

Mark, beloved, that the love we are speaking of is not a love which cometh out of men on account of their natural constitution. I have known persons who are tenderly affectionate by nature ; and this is good ; but it is not spiritual love : it is the fruit of nature and not of grace. An affectionate disposition is admirable, and yet it may become a danger, by leading to inordinate affection, a timid fear of offending, or an idolatry of the creature. I do not condemn natural amiability; on the contrary, I wish that all men were naturally amiable: but I would not have any person think that this will save him, or that it is a proof that he is renewed. Only the love which is the fruit of the Spirit may be regarded as a mark of grace. Some people, I am sorry to say, are naturally sour; they seem to have been born at the season of crab-apples, and to have been fed on vinegar. They always take a fault-finding view of things. They never see the sun's splendour, and yet they are so clear-sighted as to have discovered his spots. They have a great speciality of power for discerning things which it were better not to see. They do not remember that the earth has proved steady and firm for centuries, but they have a lively recollection of the earthquake, and they quake even now as they talk about it. Such people as these have need to cry for the indwelling of the Spirit of God, for if He will enter into them His power will soon overcome the tendency to sourness, for "the fruit of the Spirit is love." Spiritual love is nowhere found without the Spirit, and the Spirit is nowhere dwelling in the heart unless love is produced. So much for this jewel!

III. I see in the text a third thing, and that is A PICTURE: a rich and rare picture painted by a Master, the great designer of all things beautiful, the divine Spirit of God. What doth He say? He saith, "The fruit of the Spirit is love." We have seen many fine fruit pictures; and here is one. The great artist has sketched fruit which never grows in the gardens of earth till they are planted by the Lord from heaven. Oh, that every one of us might have a vineyard in His bosom, and yield abundance of that love which is "the fruit of the Spirit."

What does this mean? "Fruit," how is love a fruit? The metaphor shows that love is a thing which comes out of life. You cannot fetch fruit out of a dead post. The pillars which support these galleries have never yielded any fruit, and they never will; they are of hard iron, and no life-sap circulates within them. A dead tree bringeth forth no fruit. God implants a spiritual life in men, and then out of that life comes love, as the fruit of the Spirit.

Love appears as a growth. Fruit does not start from the tree perfectly ripe at once: first comes a flower; then a tiny formation which shows that the flower has set; then a berry appears, but it is very sour. You may not gather it. Let it alone a little while, and allow the sun to ripen it. By-and-by if fills out, and there you have the apple in the full proportions of beauty, and with a mellow flavour which delights the taste. Love springs up in the heart, and increases by a sure growth. Love is not produced by casting the mind in the mould of imitation, or by fastening the grace to a man's manner as a thing outside of himself. Little children go to a shop where their little tastes are considered, and they buy sticks upon which cherries have been tied; but everybody knows that they are not the fruit of the sticks, they are merely bound upon them. And so have we known people who have borrowed an affectionate mannerism and a sweet style; but they are not natural to them; they are not true love. What sweet words! What dainty phrases! You go among them and at first you are surprised with

their affection, you are a "dear sister" or a "dear brother," and you hear a "dear minister," and you come to the "dear Tabernacle," and sing dear hymns to those dear old tunes. Their talk is so sweet that it is just a little sticky, and you feel like a fly which is being caught in molasses. This is disgusting; it sickens one. Love is a fruit of the Spirit, it is not something assumed by a man, but something growing out of his heart. Some men sugar their conversation very largely with pretentious words because they are aware that the fruit it is made of is unripe and sour. In such a case their sweetness is not affection but affectation. But true love, real love for God and man, comes out of a man because it is in him, wrought within by the operation of the Holy Ghost, whose fruit it is. The outcome of regenerated manhood is that a man lives no longer unto himself but for the good of others.

Fruit again calls for care. If you have a garden you will soon know this. We had a profusion of flowers upon our pear trees this year, and for a few weeks the weather was warm beyond the usual heat of April, but nights of frost followed and cut off nearly all the fruit. Other kinds of fruit which survived the frost are now in danger from the dry weather which has developed an endless variety of insect blight, so that we wonder whether any of it will survive. If we get over this trial and the fruit grows well we shall yet expect to see many apples fall before autumn, because a worm has eaten into their hearts and effectually destroyed them. So is it with Christian: I have seen a work for the Lord prospering splendidly, like a fruitful vine, when suddenly there has come a frosty night and fond hopes have been nipped: or else new notions, and wild ideas have descended like insect blights and the fruit has been spoiled; or if the work has escaped these causes of damage, some immorality in a leading member, or a quarrelsome spirit, has appeared unawares like a worm in the centre of the apple, and down it has fallen never to flourish again. "The fruit of the Spirit is love." You must take care of your fruit if you wish to have any laid up in store at the end of the year; and so must every Christian be very watchful over the fruit of the Spirit, lest in any way it should be destroyed by the enemy.

Fruit is the reward of the husbandman and the crown and glory of the tree. The Lord crowns the year with His goodness by giving fruit in due season: and truly the holy fruit of love is the reward of Jesus and the honour of His servants.

How sweet is the fruit of the Spirit! I say "fruit" and not fruits, for the text says so. The work of the Spirit is one, whether it be known by the name of love, or joy, or peace, or meekness, or gentleness, or temperance. Moreover, it is constant; the fruit of the Spirit is borne continually in its season. It is reproductive, for the tree multiplies itself by its fruit; and Christianity must be spread by the love and joy and peace of Christians. Let the Spirit of God work in you, dear brethren, and you will be fruitful in every good work, doing the will of the Lord, and you will rear others like you, who shall, when your time is over, occupy your place, and bring forth fruit to the great Husbandman.

IV. Lastly, you see in my text A CROWN. "The fruit of the Spirit is love." Let us make a diadem out of the text, and lovingly set it upon the head of the Holy Spirit, because He has produced in the people of God this precious thing which is called "Love."

How comes heavenly love into such hearts as yours and mine ? It comes, first, because the Holy Ghost has given us a new nature. There is a new life in us that was not there when we first came into the world, and that new life lives and loves. It must love God who has created it, and man who is made in His image. It cries, " My Father," and the essence of that word, " My Father," is love.

The Spirit of God has brought us into new relationships. He has given us the spirit of adoption towards the Father ; He has made us to feel our brotherhood with the saints, and to know our union with Christ. We are not in our relationships what we used to be, for we were " heirs of wrath even as others " ; but now we are " heirs of God, joint heirs with Jesus Christ " ; and consequently we cannot help loving, for love alone could make the new relation to be fully enjoyed.

The blessed Spirit has also brought us under new obligations. We were bound to love God and serve Him as creatures, but we did not do it : now the Holy Spirit has made us to feel that we are debtors to infinite love and mercy through redemption. Every drop of Jesus' blood cries to us to love ; every groan from yonder dark Gethsemane cries love, The Spirit of God works in us, so that every shiver of yonder cross moves us to love. The love of Christ constraineth us : we must love, for the Spirit hath taken of the things of the loving Christ and hath revealed them unto us.

The Spirit of God has so entered into us that He has caused love to be our delight. What a pleasure it is when you can preach a sermon full of love to those to whom you preach it, or when you can visit the poor, full of love to those you relieve ! To stand at the street corner and tell out of Jesus' dying love—why, it is no irksome task to the man who does it lovingly ; it is his joy, and his recreation. Holy service in which the emotion of love is indulged is as pleasant to us as it is to a bird to fly, or to a fish to swim. Duty is no longer bondage, but choice ; holiness in so longer restraint, but perfect liberty ; and self-sacrifice becomes the very crown of our ambition, the loftiest height to which our spirit can aspire. It is the Holy Ghost that does all this.

Now, my dear hearer, have you this love in your heart ? Judge by your relation to God. Do you live without prayer ? Do you very seldom read God's word ? Are you getting indifferent as to whether you go and worship with His people ? Ah, then, be afraid that the love of God is not in you. But if you feel that everything that has to do with God you love—His work, His service, His people, His day, His book—and that you do all that in you lies in spread His kingdom, both by prayer, by word of mouth, by your liberality, and by your example , if you do love you can easily see it, I think, and there are many ways by which you can test yourself.

Well, suppose that to be satisfactorily answered, then I have this further question :—Do you and I—who can say, " Lord, Thou knowest that I love Thee "—do we sufficiently bless the Holy Spirit for giving us this jewel of love ? If you love Christ, then say, " This love is given to me : it is a rare plant, an exotic, it never sprang out of my natural heart. Weeds will grow apace there, but not this fair flower." Bless the Holy Spirit for it. " Oh, but I do not love God as I ought ! " No, brother, I know you do not, but bless Him that you love Him at all. Love God for the very fact that He has led you to love Him ; and that is the way to love Him more. Love God for letting you love Him. Love Him for taking away the stone out of your heart, and giving you a heart of flesh. For the little grace that you see in your soul, thank God. You know when a man has been ill ; the doctor says to him, " You are not well by a long way, but I hope you are on the turn." " Yes," says the man, " I feel very ill ; but still I think I am a little better : the fever is less, and the swelling is going down." He mentions some little symptom, and the doctor is pleased, because he knows that it indicates much : the disease is past the crisis. Bless God for a little grace ! Blame yourself that you have not more grace, but praise Him to think you have any. Time was when I would have given my eyes and ears to be able to say, " I do love God " ; and now that I do love Him, I would give my eyes and ears to love Him more. I would give all I have to get more love into my soul ; but I am grateful to think I have a measure of true love and I feel its power. Do be grateful to the Holy Ghost. Worship and adore Him specially and peculiarly. You say, " Why specially and peculiarly ? " I answer— Because He is so much forgotten. Some people hardly know whether there be any Holy Ghost. Let the Father and the Son be equally adored ; but be careful in reference to the Holy Spirit, for the failure of the church towards the Holy Trinity lies mainly in a forgetfulness of the gracious work of the Holy Spirit. Therefore I press this upon you, and I beg you to laud and magnify the Holy Ghost, and sedulously walk in all affectionate gratitude towards Him all your days. As your love increases, let your worship of the Holy Spirit become daily more and more conspicuous, because love is *His* fruit although it be *your* vital principle. To the God of love I commend you all. Amen.

MESSRS. MOODY AND SANKEY DEFENDED;
OR
A VINDICATION OF THE DOCTRINE OF JUSTIFICATION BY FAITH

" They that are Christ's have crucified the flesh with the affections and lusts."—Galatians v. 24.

FROM several quarters we have heard lately intense earnest objections to *the matter and tenor* of the preaching of the evangelists from America, who have been working among us. Of course, their teaching as well as our own is open to honest judgment, and they, we feel sure, would rather court than shun investigation of the most searching sort. Criticisms upon their style of speaking and singing, and so on, are unimportant, that nobody has any need to answer them, " Wisdom is justified of her children." It is a waste of time to discuss mere matters of taste, for no men, however excellent, can please all, or even become equally adapted to all constitutions and conditions : therefore we may let such remarks pass without further observation. But upon the matter of doctrine very much has been said, and said also with a good deal of temper not always of the best. What has been affirmed by a certain class of public writers comes to this, if you boil it down—that it cannot really do any good to tell men that simply by believing in Jesus Christ they will be saved, and that it may do people very serious injury if we lead them to imagine that they have undergone a process called conversion, and are now safe for life. We are told by these gentlemen, who ought to know, for they speak very positively, that the doctrine of immediate salvation through faith in Christ Jesus is a very dangerous one, that it will certainly lead to the deterioration of the public morality, since men will not be likely to set store by the practical virtues when faith is lifted up to so very lofty a position. If it were so it were a grievous fault. and woe to those who led men into it. That it is not the fact we are sure ; but meanwhile let us survey the field of battle.

Will you please to notice that this is no quarrel between these gentlemen and our friends Messrs. Moody and Sankey alone. It is a quarrel between these objectors and the whole of us who preach the gospel ; for, differing as we do in the style of preaching it, we are all ready to set our seal to the clearest possible statement that men are saved by faith in Jesus Christ, and saved the moment they believe. We all hold and teach that there is such a thing as conversion, and that when men are converted they become other men than they were before, and a new life begins which will culminate in eternal glory. We are not so dastardly as to allow our friends to stand alone in the front of the battle, to be looked upon as peculiar persons, holding strange notions from which the rest of us dissent. So far as salvation through faith in the atoning blood is concerned, they preach nothing but what we have preached all our lives ; they preach nothing but what has the general consent of Protestant Christendom. Let that be known to all, and let the archers shoot at us all alike.

Then, further, if this be the point of objection, we should like those who raise it to know that they do not raise it against us merely, and these friends who are more prominent, but against the Protestant faith which these very same gentlemen most probably profess to glory in. The Protestant faith, in a nutshell, lies in this very same justification by faith which they hoot at. It was the discovery that men are saved by faith in Jesus Christ which first stirred up Luther. That was the ray of light which fell upon his dark heart, and by the power of which he came into the liberty of the gospel. This is the hammer by which popery was broken in the old time, and this is the sword with which it still is to be smitten —the very " Sword of the Lord and of Gideon." Jesus is the all-sufficient Saviour, and " He that believeth in Him is not condemned." Luther used, in fact, to say—and we endorse it—that this matter of justification by faith is the article by which a church must stand or fall. That so-called church which does not hold this doctrine is not a church of Christ, and it is a church of Christ that does hold it, notwithstanding many mistakes into which it may have fallen. The contest lies really between the Popish doctrine of merit and the Protestant doctrine of grace, and no man who calls himself a Protestant can logically dispute the question with us and our friends.

We shall go somewhat further than this. The objection is not against Messrs. Moody and Sankey, but against all evangelical ministers ; not against them only, but against our common protestantism ; and yet more, it is against the inspired word of God ; for if this book teaches anything under heaven, it certainly teaches that men are saved by faith in our Lord Jesus. Read the Epistle to the Galatians, and your judgment may be perverse, but you cannot, by any common wresting of words, expel that doctrine from the Epistle. It was written on purpose to state that truth plainly, and defend it fully. Neither can you get rid of that doctrine from the whole New Testament. You shall find it not merely seasoning all the epistles, but positively saturating them, till, as you take chapter by chapter, you may wring out of them, as out of Gideon's fleece, this one truth, that justification before God is by faith, and not by the works of the law. So that the objection is against the Bible ; and let those who shoot their arrows understand that they fight against the Eternal Spirit of God and the witness which He has borne by His prophets and apostles. Deny inspiration, and you have ground to stand on ; but while you believe the Bible you must believe in justification by faith.

But now let us look this matter in the face. Is it true or not that persons who believe in Jesus Christ do become worse than they were before ? We are not backward to answer the inquiry, and we stand in a point of observation which supplies us with abundant data to go upon. We solemnly affirm that men who believe in Jesus become purer, holier, and better. At the same time I confess that there has been a good deal of injudicious and misleading talk at times by uninstructed advocates of free grace. I fear, moreover, that many people think that they believe in Jesus Christ, but do nothing if the sort. We do not defend rash statements, or deny the existence of weakminded followers ; but we ask to be heard and considered. Some persons say, " You tell these people that they will be saved upon their believing in Christ." Exactly so. " But will you kindly tell me what you mean by being saved, sir ? " I will, with great pleasure. We do not mean that these people will go to heaven when they die, irrespective of character ; but, when we say that if they believe in Jesus they will be saved, we mean that they will be saved from living as they used to live—saved from being what they are now, saved from licentiousness, dishonesty, drunkenness, selfishness, and any other sin they may have lived in. The thing can be readily put to the test, if it can be shown that those who have believed in the Lord Jesus have been saved from living in sin, no rational man ought to entertain any objection to the preaching of such a salvation. Salvation from wrongdoing is the very thing which every moralist should commend and not censure, and that is the salvation which we preach. I am afraid that some imagine that they have only to believe something or other, and they will go to heaven when they die, and that they have only to feel a certain singular emotion, and it is alright with them. Now, if any of you have fallen into that error, may God in His mercy lead you out of it, for it is not *every* faith that saves, but only *the* faith of God's elect. It is not *any* sort of emotion that changes the heart, but the work of the Holy Ghost. It is a small matter to go into an enquiry room and say, " I believe " : such an avowal as that proves nothing at all, it may even be false. It will be proved by this—if you have rightly believed in Jesus Christ you will become from that time forward a different man from what you were. There will be a change in your heart and soul, in your conduct and your conversation ; and, seeing you thus changed, those who have been honest objectors will right speedily leave off their objections, for they will be in the condition of those who saw the man that was healed standing with Peter and John ; and therefore they could say nothing against them. The world demands facts, and these we must supply. It is of no use to cry up our medicine by words, we must point to cures. Your change of life will be the grandest argument for the gospel, if that life shall show the meaning of my text— " They that are Christ's have crucified the flesh with the affections and lusts."

Let us discuss this text in an apologetic manner, hoping to overcome prejudice, if God permit.

Notice, first of all, that THE RECEPTION OF JESUS CHRIST BY FAITH IS, IN ITSELF, AN AVOWAL THAT WE HAVE CRUCIFIED THE FLESH WITH THE AFFECTIONS AND LUSTS. If faith be such an avowal, why say that it is not connected with holy living ?

Let me show that this is the case. Faith is the accepting of Jesus Christ. In what respects ? Well, principally as a substitute. He is the Son of God, and I am a guilty sinner. I deserve to die : the Son of God stands in my stead and suffers for me, and when I believe in Him I accept Him as standing for me. To believe in Jesus was very beautifully set forth in the old ceremony of the law, when the person bringing a sacrifice laid his hands upon the head of the bullock or the lamb, and thereby accepted the victim as standing in his place, so that the victim's sufferings should be instead of his sufferings. Now, our faith accepts Jesus Christ as standing in our stead. The very pith and marrow of faith's confidence lies in this—

> " He bore, that I might never bear,
> His Father's righteous ire."

Christ for me, Christ in my room and stead.

Now, try to catch the following thought.—When you believe, you accept Christ as standing instead of you, and profess that what He did He did for you ; but what did Christ do upon the tree ? He was crucified and died. Follow the thought, and note well that by faith *you regard yourself as dead with Him*—crucified with Him. You have not really grasped what faith means unless you have grasped this. With Him you suffered the wrath of God, for He suffered in your stead : you are now in Him— crucified with Him, dead with Him, buried with Him, risen with Him, and gone into glory with Him— because He represents you, and your faith has accepted the representation. Do you see, then, that you did in the moment when you believed in Christ, register a declaration that you were henceforth dead unto sin. Who shall say that our gospel teaches men to live in sin, when the faith which is essential to salvation involves an avowal of death to it ? The convert begins with agreeing to be regarded as dead with Christ to sin : have we not here the foundation stone of holiness ?

Observe also that, if he follows the command of Christ, the very first step which a Christian takes after he has accepted the position taken up by the Lord Jesus on his behalf is another avowal more public than the first, namely, *his baptism*.

By faith he has accepted Christ as dead, instead of him, and he regards himself as having died in Christ. Now, every dead man ought to be buried, sooner or later ; and so, when we come forward and confess Christ, we are " buried with Him in baptism unto death, that like as Jesus Christ rose from the dead by the glory of the Father, even so we also might rise to newness of life." Though baptism does not avail anything as a ceremony, having no power or efficacy in and of itself, yet as a sign and a symbol it teaches us that true believers are dead and buried with Christ. So, you see, the two ways in which, according to the gospel, we actually and avowedly give ourselves to Christ, are by faith and baptism. He that believeth, and is baptized, shall be saved." Now, the essence of faith is to accept Christ as representing me in His death : and the essence of baptism is to be buried with Christ because I am dead with Him. Thus at the very doorstep of the Christian religion, in its first inward act and its first outward symbol, you get the thought that believers are henceforth to be separated from sin and purified in life. He who truly believes, and knows what it is to be really buried with Christ, has begun—nay, he has, in a certain sense, effected completely— what the text describes as the crucifixion of the flesh with the affections and lusts. For, dear friends, let it never be forgotten that the grand object for which we lay hold on Christ is the death of sin. Who among us has believed in Christ that he might escape the pangs of hell ? Oh, brother, you have but a very poor idea of what Jesus Christ has come into the world to do : He is proclaimed to be a Saviour who " shall save His people *from their sins.*" This is the object of His mission. True, He comes to give pardon, but He never gives pardon without giving repentance with it ; He comes to justify, but He does not justify without also sanctifying. He has come to deliver us, not from thee, O death, alone ! nor from thee, O hell, alone ! but from thee, O sin, the mother of death, the progenitor of hell ! The Redeemer lays His axe at the root of all the mischief, by killing sin, and thus, as far as we are concerned, He puts an end to death and hell. Glory be to God for this ! Now, it does seem to me that if the very commencement of the Christian faith be so manifestly connected with death to sin, they do us grievous injustice who suppose that in preaching faith in Jesus Christ we ignore the moralities or the virtues, or that we think little of sin and vice. We do not so, but we proclaim the only method by which moral evil can be put to death and swept away. The reception of Christ is an avowal of the crucifixion of the flesh with the affections and lusts, what more can the purest moralist propose ? What more could he avow himself ?

II. But secondly, AS A MATTER OF FACT, THE RECEPTION OF CHRIST IS ATTENDED WITH THE CRUCIFIXION OF SIN. I shall now state my own experience when I believed in Jesus ; and while I am doing so I rejoice to remember that there are hundreds, if not thousands in this place who have experienced the same, and millions in this world, and millions more in heaven, who know the truth of what I declare. When I believed that Jesus was the Christ, and rested my soul in Him, I felt in my heart from that moment an intense hatred to sin of every kind I had loved sin before, some sins particularly, but those sins became from that moment the most obnoxious to me, and, though the propensity to them was still there, yet the love of them was clean gone ; and when I at any time transgressed I felt an inward grief and horror at myself for doing the things which aforetime I had allowed and even enjoyed. My relish for sin was gone. The things I once loved I abhorred, and blushed to think of.

Then I began to search out my sins. I see now a parallel between my experience in reference to sin, and the details of the crucifixion of Christ. They sent Judas into the garden to search for our great substitute, and just in that way I began to search for sin, even for that which lay concealed amid the thick darkness of my soul. I was ignorant, and did not know sin to be sin, for it was night in my soul ; but, being stirred up to destroy the evil, my repenting spirit borrowed lanterns, and torches, aud went out as against a thief. I searched the garden of my heart through and through, with an intense ardour to find out every sin ; and I brought God to help me, saying, " Search me, O God, and try me, and know my ways " ; nor did I cease till I had spied out my secret transgressions. This inward search is one of my most constant occupations ; I patrol my nature through and through to try and arrest these felons, these abhorred sins, that they may be crucified with Christ. O ye in whom iniquity lurks under cover of your spiritual ignorance, arouse yourself to a strict scrutiny of your nature, and no longer endure that your hearts should be the lurking-places of evil. I remember when I found my sin. When I found it I seized it, and dragged it off to the judgment-seat. Ah, my brethren, you know when that occurred to you, and how stern was the judgment which conscience gave forth. I sat in judgment on myself. I took my sin to one court, and to another. I looked at it as before men, and trembled to think that the badness of my example might have ruined other men's souls : I looked at my sin as before God, and I abhorred myself in dust and ashes. My sin was as red as crimson in His sight and in mine also. I judged my sin, and I condemned it—condemned it as a felon to a felon's death. I heard a voice within me which, Pilate-like, pleaded for it—" I will chastize him and let him go ; let it be a little put to shame ; let not the wrong deed be done quite so often ; let the lust be curbed and kept under." But, ah, my soul said, " Let it be crucified ! Let it be crucified ! " and nothing could shake my heart from this intent, that I would slay all the murderers of Christ if possible, and let not one of them escape ; for my soul hated them with a deadly hatred, and would fain nail them all to the tree. I remember, too, how I began to see the shame of sin. As my Lord was spit upon, and mocked, and despitefully used, so did my soul begin to pour contempt upon all the pride of sin, to scorn its promises of pleasure, and to accuse it of a thousand crimes. It had deceived me, it had led me into ruin, it had well nigh destroyed me, and I despised it, and poured contempt upon its briberies, and all it offered of sweetness and of pleasure. O sin, how shameful a thing didst thou appear to be ! I saw all that is base, mean, and contemptible concentrated in thee. My heart scourged sin by repentance, smote it with rebukes, and buffeted it with self-denials. Then was it made a reproach and a scorn. But this sufficed not—sin must die. My heart mourned for what sin had done, and I was resolved to avenge my Lord's death upon myself. Thus my soul sang out her resolve—

> " Oh, how I hate those lusts of mine
> That crucified my God ;
> Those sins that pierced and nail'd His flesh
> Fast to the fatal wood !
>
> " Yes, my Redeemer, they shall die ;
> My heart has so decreed :
> Nor will I spare the guilty things
> That made my Saviour bleed."

Then I led forth my sins to the place of crucifixion. They would fain have escaped, but the power of God prevented them, and like a guard of soldiery, conducted them to the gibbet of mortification. The hand of the Lord was present, and His all-revealing Spirit stripped my sin as Christ was stripped ; setting it before mine eyes, even my secret sin in the light of His countenance. Oh, what a spectacle it was as I gazed upon it ! I had looked before upon its dainty apparel, and the colours with which it had bedizened itself, to make it look as fair as Jezebel when she painted her face : but now I saw its nakedness and horror, and I was well nigh ready to despair ; but my spirit bore me up, for I knew that I was forgiven, and I said " Christ Jesus has pardoned me, for I have believed in Him ; and I will put the flesh to death, by crucifying it on His cross." The driving of the nails I do remember, and how the flesh struggled to maintain its liberty. One, two, three, four, the nails went in, and fastened the accursed thing to the wood with Christ, so that it could neither run nor rule ; and now, glory be to God, though my sin is not dead, it is crucified, and must eventually die. It hangs up there : I can see it bleeding out its life. Sometimes it struggles to get down, and it tries to wrench away the nails, for it would fain go after vanity ; but the sacred nails hold it too fast, it is in the grasp of death, and it cannot escape. Alas, it dies a lingering death, attended with much pain and struggling : still it dies, and soon its heart shall be pierced through with the spear of the love of Christ, and it shall utterly expire. Then shall our immortal nature no more be burdened with the body of this death, but, pure and spotless, it shall rise to and behold the face of God for ever.

Now, I am not talking allegorically of things which ought to be realized, but as a matter of fact remain mere ideas. I am describing in figure what happens in reality ; for every man who believes in Jesus immediately bestirs himself to get rid of sin ; and you may know whether he has believed in Jesus Christ or not by seeing whether there is a change in his motives, feelings, life, and conduct. Do you say that you doubt this ? You may doubt what you like, but facts speak for themselves. There will come before me, I dare say, before this week is over, as there have almost every week of my life, men who have been slaves to intoxication made sober at once by believing in Jesus Christ ; women, once lost to virtue, who have become pure and chaste by believing in Jesus ; men who were fond of all manner of evil pleasures, who have turned instantly from them, and have continued to resist all temptation, because they are new creatures in Jesus Christ. The phenomenon of conversion is singular, but the effect of conversion is more singular still ; and it is not a thing done in a corner, it can be seen every day. If it were merely an excitement in which men felt a distress of mind, and then by-and-by thought they were at peace, and became happy because self-satisfied, I should not see any particular good in it ; but if it be true that regeneration changes men's tastes and affections, that it, in fine, changes them radically, making them altogether new creatures ; if it be so, I say, then may God send us thousands of conversions ! And that this is so we are quite sure, for we see it perpetually.

III. Thirdly, we go a step farther, and say that THE RECEPTION OF JESUS CHRIST INTO THE HEART BY SIMPLE FAITH IS CALCULATED TO CRUCIFY THE FLESH.

When a man believes in Jesus the first point that helps him to crucify the flesh is that *he has seen the evil of sin,* inasmuch as he has seen Jesus, his Lord, die because of it. Men think that sin is nothing ; but what will sin do ? What will it *not* do ? The virus of sin, what will it poison ? Aye, what will it *not* poison ? Its influence has been baleful upon the largest conceivable scale. Sin has flooded the world with blood and tears through red-handed war ; sin has covered the world with oppression, and so has crushed the manhood of many, and broken the hearts of myriads ; sin begat slavery, and tyranny, and priestcraft, and rebellion, and slander, and persecution ; sin has been at the bottom of all human sorrows ; but the crowning, culminating point of sin's villainy was when God Himself came down to earth in human form—pure, perfect, intent on an errand of love—came to work miracles of mercy, and re-demption. Then sinful man could never rest till he had crucified his incarnate God. They coined a word when the Parliamentary party executed the king in England, and called the king's destroyers " regicides," and now we must make a word to describe sin : sin is a *deicide.* Every sinner, if he could, would kill God, for he says in his heart, " No God." He means he wishes there were none. He would be rejoiced indeed if he could learn for certain that there was no God. In fact, that is the bugbear of his life, that there is a God, and a just God, who will bring him into judgment. His secret wish is that there were no religion and no God, for he might then live as he pleased.

Now, when a man is made to see that sin in its essence is the murderer of Emmanuel, God with us, his heart being renewed, he hates sin from that very moment. " No," he says, " I cannot continue in such evil. If that be the true meaning of every offence against the law of God—that it would put God Himself out of His own world if it could—I cannot bear it." His spirit recoils with horror, as he feels—

" My sins have pull'd the vengeance down
    Upon His guiltless head :
Break, break, my heart, oh burst mine eyes !
    And let my sorrows bleed.

" Strike, mighty grace, my flinty soul,
    Till melting waters flow,
And deep repentance drown mine eyes
    In undissembled woe."

Then *the believer has also seen in the death of Christ an amazing instance of the great grace of God ;* for if sin be an attempt to murder God—and it is all that—then how wonderful it is that the creatures who committed this sin were not destroyed at once. How remarkable that God should consider it worth His while to devise a plan for their restoration ; and yet He did, with matchless skill, contrive a way which involved the giving up of His only-begotten and well-beloved Son. Though this was an expense unequalled, yet He did not withdraw from it. He " so loved the world, that He gave His only-begotten Son, that whosoever believeth in Him should not perish, but have everlasting life " : and this for a race of men who were the enemies of their good and gracious God. " Henceforth," says the believer in Christ, " I can have nothing to do with sin, since it does despite to so gracious a God. O, thou accursed sin, to drive thy dagger at the heart of Him who was all grace and mercy ! This makes sin to be exceedingly sinful."

Further, *the believer has had a view of the justice of God.* He sees that God hates sin intensely, for when His only begotten Son took sin upon Himself, God would not spare even Him. That sin was not His own, in Him was no sin, but when He voluntarily took it upon Himself, and was made a curse for us, the Judge of all the earth did not spare Him. Down from His armoury of vengeance He took His thunderbolts and hurled them at His Son, for His Son stood in the sinner's stead. There was no mercy for the sinner's substitute. He had to cry as never one cried before or since, " My God, My God, why hast Thou forsaken Me ? " Torrents of woe rushed through His spirit ; the condemnation of sin overwhelmed Him ; all God's waves and billows went o'er Him.

Now, when a man sees this wonderful fact he can no longer think lightly of transgression. He trembles before the thrice holy Jehovah, and cries in his secret heart, "How can I sin if this be God's opinion of it ? If in His justice He smote it so unsparingly, even when it was only laid by imputation upon His Son, how will He smite it when its actual guilt lies on me ? O God deliver me from it."

The believer has also had one more sight which, perhaps, more effectually than any other changes his view of sin. *He has seen the amazing love of Jesus.* Did you ever see it, my hearer ? If you have seen it you will never love sin again. O think, that He who was Master of all heaven's majesty came down to be the victim of all man's misery ! He came to Bethlehem, and dwelt among us, offering thirty years and more of toilsome obedience to His Father's will ; and at the close He reached the crisis of His griefs, the crowning sorrow of His incarnation—His bloody sweat and death agony. That was a solemn passover which He ate with His disciples, with Calvary full in view. Then He rose and went to Gethsemane.

> " Gethsemane, the olive-press,
> (And why so called let Christians guess);
> Fit name, fit place, where vengeance strove,
> And griped and grappled hard with love.
>
> 'Twas there the Lord of life appeared,
> And sighed, and groaned, and pray'd, and feared ;
> Bore all incarnate God could bear,
> With strength enough, and none to spare."

Behold how He loved us ! He was taken to Pilate's hall, and there was scourged—scourged with those awful Roman whips weighted with little bullets of lead, and made of the intertwisted sinews of oxen, into which they also inserted small slivers of bone, so that every blow as it fell tore off the flesh. Our beloved Lord had to suffer this again and again, being scourged often as that verse seems to intimate which says, " He was *wounded* for our transgressions, He was *bruised* for our iniquities : the *chastisement* of our peace was upon Him ; and with His *stripes* we are healed." Yet He loved us, loved us still. Many waters could not quench His love, neither could the floods drown it. When they nailed Him to the tree, He loved us still. When, every bone being dislocated, He cried in sad soliloquy, " I am poured out like water, all My bones are out of joint," He loved us still. When the dogs compassed Him and the bulls of Bashan beset him round, He loved us still. When the dread faintness came upon Him till He was brought into the dust of death, and His heart melted like wax in the midst of His bowels, He loved us still. When God forsook Him, and the sun was blotted out, and midnight darkness covered the midday, and a denser midnight veiled His spirit —a darkness like that of Egypt, which might be felt, He loved us still. Till He had drunk the last dregs of the unutterable bitter cup, He loved us still. And when the light shone on His face, and He could say, " It is finished," that light shone on a face that loved us still. Now, every man to whom it has been given to believe in Jesus, and to know His love, says, " How can I offend *Him* ? How can I grieve *Him* ? There are actions in this life which I might otherwise indulge in, but I dare not now, for fear to vex my Lord." And if you say " Dare not, are you afraid of Him ? " the answer will be, " I am not slavishly afraid, for into hell I can never go." What am I afraid of, then ? I am afraid of that dear face, on which I see the gutterings of tears which He once shed for me. I am afraid of that dear brow which

wore the thorn-crown for me ; I cannot rebel against such kindness, His bleeding love enchains me. How can I do so great a wickedness as to put my dying Lord to shame ? " Do you not feel this, my beloved brother ? If you have ever trusted the Lord Jesus, you crouch at His feet, and kiss the prints of His nails, for very love ; and if He would use you as a footstool, if it would raise Him any higher, you would count it the highest honour of you life. Aye, if He bade you go to prison and to death for Him, and would say it Himself, and put His pierced hand on you, you would go there as cheerfully as angels fly to heaven. If He bade you die for Him, though the flesh is weak, your spirit would be willing ; ay, and the flesh would be made strong enough, too, if Jesus did but look upon you, for He can with a glance cast out selfishness and cowardice, and everything that keeps us back from being whole burnt-offerings to Him. Is it not so ?

> " Speak of morality ! Thou bleeding Lamb
> The best morality is love of Thee ! "

When we once are filled with love to Thee, O Jesus' sin becomes the dragon against which we wage a lifelong warfare ; holiness becomes our noblest aspiration, and we seek after it with all our heart and soul and strength. If candid minds will but honestly consider the religion of Jesus Christ, they will see that Christian men must hate sin if they are sincere in their faith. I might go farther into that, but I will not.

IV. The last thing of all is this. THE HOLY SPIRIT IS WITH THE GOSPEL, AND WHERE HE IS HOLINESS MUST BE PROMOTED.

Let it never be forgotten that—while the reception of Jesus Christ by simple faith is an avowal of death to sin, and does bring with it an experience of hating sin, and is calculated to do so—there is one thing more. If, dear friends, in any work of revival, or ordinary ministry, there was nothing more than you could see or hear, I think that many criticisms and cavils might be, at least, rational, but they are not so now ; for one grand fact makes them for ever unreasonable. Wherever Jesus Christ is preached, there is present One sublime in rank and high in degree. You will not suppose that I am speaking of any earthly potentate. No, I am speaking of the Holy Ghost—the ever blessed Spirit of God. There is never a gospel sermon preached by an earnest heart but what the Holy Ghost is there, taking of the things of Christ and revealing them unto men. When a man turns his eye to Jesus, and simply trusts Him—for we adhere to that as being the vital matter —there is accompanying that act—nay, I must correct myself, there is as the cause of that act—a miraculous, supernatural power which in an instant changes a man, as completely as if it flung him back into nothingness and brought him forth into new life. If this be so, then believing in Christ is something very marvellous. Now, if you will turn to the third chapter of John's gospel, and also to his Epistles, you will see that faith is always linked with regeneration, or the new birth, which new birth is the work of the Spirit of God. That same third of John which tells us, " Ye must be born again," goes on to say, " And as Moses lifted up the serpent in the wilderness, even so must the Son of Man be lifted up ; that whosoever believeth in Him should not perish, but have eternal life." Wherever there is faith in Jesus Christ a miracle of purification has been wrought in the heart. Deny this and you deny the testimony of the Scriptures, which say plainly, that "whosoever believeth that Jesus is the Christ is born of God." "And whosoever is born of God sinneth not; but he that is begotten of God keepeth himself, and that wicked one toucheth him not." Wherefore do you doubt, for we who are personal examples can assure you that it has been so in our case? I mean not that myself and one or two others affirm this, but the witnesses may be met with by hundreds and thousands, and they all agree in asserting that the power of the Holy Ghost has changed the current of their desires, and made them love the things which are holy, and just, and true. Therefore, sirs, whether you believe it or not, you must be so kind as to understand one thing from us very decidedly, namely, that if to preach salvation through faith be vile we purpose to be viler still. Surely you cannot blame us for acting as we do if our stand-point be correct. If the preaching of the cross, though it be to them that perish foolishness, be to them that believe in Christ the wisdom of God and the power of God, we shall not give up preaching Christ for you. If it be so that men are made new creatures—that, while others are talking about morals, our gospel plants and produces them—we shall not give up work for talk, nor the efficient agency of the gospel for the inventions of philosophy.

To the front, my brethren, with the cross, more and more; in your schools and in your pulpits set forth Christ crucified as the sinner's hope more and more plainly. Bid the sinner look to Jesus! Look and live! The gospel is the great promoter of social order, the great reclaimer of the waifs and strays of society, the elevator of the human race; this doctrine of free pardon and gracious renewal, freely given to the most worthless upon their believing in Jesus, is the hope of mankind. There is no balm in Gilead, and never was; but this is the balm of Calvary, for there is the true medicine, and Jesus Christ is the infallible Physician. Do but try it, sinners! Do but try it! Look to Jesus, and the passions which you cannot else overcome shall yield to His cleansing power. Believe in Jesus, and the follies which cling to you, and crush you as the snakes engirdled Laocoon and his sons, you shall be able to untwist. Yea, they shall die at Jesus' glance, and shall fall off from you. Believe in Jesus, and you have the spring of excellency, the bath of purity, the source of virtue, the destruction of evil, the bud of perfection.

God grant us still to prove the power of the Lord Jesus in ourselves, and to proclaim His power to all around us.

> "Happy if, with our latest breath,
> We may but gasp His name;
> Preach Him to all, and cry in death
> 'Behold, behold, the Lamb!'"

THREE CROSSES

"But God forbid that I should glory, save in the cross of our Lord Jesus Christ, by whom the world is crucified unto me, and I unto the world."—Galatians vi. 14.

WHENEVER we rebuke other people we should be prepared to clear ourselves of their offence. The apostle had been rebuking those who wished to glory in the flesh. In denouncing false teachers and upbraiding their weak-minded followers he used sharp language, while he appealed to plain facts and maintained his ground with strong arguments; and this he did without fear of being met by a flank movement, and being charged with doing the same things himself. Very fitly, therefore, does he contrast his own determined purpose with their plausible falseness. They were for making a fair show in the flesh, but he shrunk not from the deepest shame of the Christian profession; nay, so far from shrinking, he even counted it honour to be scorned for Christ's sake, exclaiming, "God forbid that I should glory, save in the cross of our Lord Jesus Christ." The Galatians, and all others to whom his name was familiar, well knew how truly he spoke; for the manner of his life as well as the matter of his teaching had supplied evidence of this assertion, which none of his foemen could gainsay. There had not been in all his ministry any doctrine that he extolled more highly than this of "Christ crucified"; nor any experience that he touched on more tenderly than this "fellowship with Christ in His sufferings"; nor any rule of conduct that he counted more safe than this following in the footsteps of Him who "endured the cross, despising the shame, and is set down at the right hand of the throne of God." His example accorded with his precept. God grant, of His grace, that there may always be with us the like transparent consistency. Some-times when we notice an evil, and protest as boldly and conscientiously as we can against it, we feel that our protest is too obscure to have much influence; it will then be our very best resource resolutely to abstain from the evil ourselves, and so, at least in one person, to overthrow its power. If you cannot convert a man from his error by an argument, you can at least prove the sincerity of your reasoning by your own behaviour; and thus, if no fortress is captured, you will at least "hold the fort," and you may do more: your faithfulness may win more than your zeal. Vow faithfully within your own heart, and say frankly to your neighbour, "You may do what you will; but as for me, God forbid that I should remove the old landmarks, or seek out new paths, however inviting, or turn aside from that which I know to be the good old way." A determined resolution of that sort, fully adhered to, will often carry more weight and exert more influence on the mind of an individual, especially of a waverer, than a host of arguments. Your actions will speak more loudly than your words.

The apostle in the present case warms with emotion at the thought of anybody presuming to set a carnal ordinance in front of the cross, by wishing to glory in circumcision or any other outward institution. The idea of a ceremony claiming to be made more of than faith in Jesus provoked him, till his heart presently grew hot with indignation, and he thundered forth the words, "God forbid!" He never used the sacred name with lightness; but when the fire was hot within him he called God to witness that he did not, and could not, glory in anything but the cross. Indeed, there is to every true-hearted believer something shocking and revolting in the putting of anything before Jesus Christ, be it what it may, whether it be an idol of superstition or a toy of scepticism, whether it be the fruit of tradition or the flower of philosophy. Do you want new Scriptures to supplement the true sayings of God? Do you want a new Saviour who can surpass Him whom the Father hath sealed? Do you want a new sacrifice that can save you from sins which His atoning blood could not expiate? Do you want a modern song to supersede the new song of "Worthy is the Lamb that was slain"? "O foolish Galatians!" said Paul. O silly Protestants! I am inclined to say. We might go on in these times to speak warmly to many of the parties around us—the doting Ritualists, the puffed-up Rationalists, and the self-exalting school of modern thought. I marvel not at Paul's warmth. I only wish that some who think so little of doctrinal discrepancies, as they call them, could but sympathise a little with his holy indignation when he saw the first symptoms of departure from godly simplicity and sincerity. Do you not notice that a little dissembling of a dear brother made him withstand him to his face? When a whole company turned the cold shoulder to the cross of Christ it made him burn with indignation. He could not brook it. The cross was the centre of his hopes; around it his affections twined; there he had found peace to his troubled conscience. God forbid that he should allow it to be trampled on. Besides, it was the theme of his ministry. "Christ crucified" had already proved the power of God to salvation to every soul who had believed the life-giving message as he proclaimed it in every city. Would any of you, he asks, cast a slur on the cross—you who have been converted—you before whose eyes Jesus Christ hath been evidently set forth crucified among you? How his eyes flash; how his lips quiver; how his heart grows hot within him; with what vehemence he protests: "God forbid that I should glory, save in the cross of our Lord Jesus Christ." He spreads his eagle wing, and rises into eloquence at once, while still his keen eye looks fiercely upon every enemy of the cross whom he leaves far beneath. Oftentimes in his epistles you observe this. He burns, he glows, he mounts, he soars, he is carried clean away as soon as his thoughts are in fellowship with his Lord Jesus, that meek and patient Sufferer, who offered Himself a sacrifice for our sins. When his tongue begins to speak of the glorious work which the Christ of God has done for the sons of men it finds a sudden liberty, and he becomes as "a hind let loose; he giveth goodly words." May we have something of that glow within our breasts to-night, and whenever we think of our Lord. God forbid that we should be cold-hearted when we come near to Jesus; God forbid that we should ever view with heartless eye and lethargic soul the sweet wonders of that cross on which our Saviour loved and died.

Let us, then, in that spirit approach our text; and we notice at once three crucifixions. These are the summary of the text. "God forbid that I should glory, save in the cross of our Lord Jesus Christ"; that is, *Christ crucified.* "By whom," or, "by which" (read it whichever way you like), "the world is crucified unto me"; that is, *a crucified world.* "And I unto the world"; that is, *Paul himself, or the believer, crucified with Christ.* I see,

again, Calvary before me with its three crosses—Christ in the centre, and on either side of Him a crucified person: one who dies to feel the second death, and another who dies to be with Him in paradise. At these three crosses let us proceed to look.

I. First, then, the main part of our subject lies in CHRIST CRUCIFIED, in whom Paul gloried. I call your attention to the language; "God forbid that I should glory, save in the cross." Some popular authors and public speakers, when they have to state a truth, count it necessary to clothe it in very delicate language. They, perhaps, do not quite intend to conceal its point and edge; but, at any rate, they do not want the projecting angles and bare surfaces of the truth to be too observable, and therefore they cast a cloak around it; they are careful to scabbard the sword of the Spirit. The apostle Paul might have done so here, if he had chosen, but he disdains the artifice. He presents the truth "in the worst possible form," as his opponents say—"in all its naked hideousness," as the Jew would have it; for he does not say, "God forbid that I should glory, save in the *death* of Christ"; but in the *cross.* You do not realize, I think—we cannot do so in these days—how the use of that word "cross" would grate on ears refined in Galatia and elsewhere. In those days it meant the felon's tree, the hangman's gibbet; and the apostle, therefore, does not hesitate to put it just so: "Save in that gibbet on which my Master died." We have become so accustomed to associate the name of "the cross" with other sentiments that it does not convey to us that sense of disgrace which it would inflict upon those who heard Paul speak. A family sensitively shrinks if one of its members has been hanged; and much the same would be the natural feeling of one who was told that his leader was crucified. Paul puts it thus badly, he lets it jar thus harshly, though it may prove to some a stumbling-block, and to others foolishness; but he will not cloak it, he glories in "*the cross!*"

On the other hand, I earnestly entreat you to observe how he seems to contrast the glory of the person with the shame of the suffering; for it is not simply the death of Christ, nor of Jesus, nor of Jesus Christ, nor of *the* Lord Jesus Christ, but of "*our* Lord Jesus Christ." Every word tends to set forth the excellence of His person, the majesty of His character, and the interest which all the saints have in Him. It *was* a cross, but it was the cross of our Lord: let us worship Him! It was the cross of our Lord Jesus the Saviour: let us love Him! It was the cross of our Jesus Christ the anointed Messiah: let us reverence Him! Let us sit at His feet and learn of Him! Each one may say, "It was the cross of *my* Lord Jesus Christ"; but it sweetens the whole matter, and gives a largeness to it when we say, "It was the cross of *our* Lord Jesus Christ." Oh yes, we delight to think of the contrast between the precious Christ and the painful cross, the Son of God and the shameful gibbet. He was Immanuel, God with us; yet did He die the felon's death upon the accursed tree. Paul brings out the shame with great sharpness, and the glory with great plainness. He does not hesitate in either case, whether he would declare the sufferings of Christ or the glory that should follow.

What did he mean, however, by the cross? Of course he cared nothing for the particular piece of wood to which those blessed hands and feet were nailed, for that was mere materialism, and has perished out of mind. He means the glorious doctrine of justification—free justification—through the atoning sacrifice of Jesus Christ. This is what he means by the cross—the expiation for sin which our Lord Jesus Christ made by His death, and the gift of eternal life freely bestowed on all those who by grace are led to trust in Him. To Paul the cross meant just what the brazen serpent meant to Moses. As the brazen serpent in the wilderness was the hope of the sin-bitten, and all that Moses had to do was to bid them look and live, so to-day the cross of Christ —the atonement of Jesus Christ—is the hope of mankind, and our mission is continually to cry, " Look and live ! Look and live ! " It is this doctrine, this gospel of Christ crucified, at which the present age, with all its vaunted culture and all its vain philosophies, sneers so broadly, it is this doctrine wherein we glory. We are not ashamed to put it very definitely : we glory in substitution, in the vicarious sacrifice of Jesus in our stead. He was " made sin for us who knew no sin, that we might be made the righteousness of God in Him." " All we like sheep have gone astray ; we have turned every one to his own way ; and the Lord hath laid on Him the iniquity of us all." " Christ hath redeemed us from the curse of the law, being made a curse for us : for it is written, Cursed is every one that hangeth on a tree." We believe in the imputation of sin to the innocent person of our covenant Head and Representative, in the bearing of the penalty by that substituted One, and the clearing by faith of those for whom He bore the punishment of sin.

Now we glory in this. We glory in it, not as men sometimes boast in a creed, which they have received by tradition from their forefathers, for we have learned this truth, each one for himself by the inward teaching of the Holy Ghost, and therefore it is very dear to us. We glory in it with no empty boast, but to the inward satisfaction of our own hearts ; we prove that satisfaction by the devout consecration of our lives to make it known. We have trusted our souls to its truth. If it be a fable our hopes are for ever shipwrecked, our all is embarked in that venture. We are quite prepared to run that risk, content to perish if this salvation should fail us. We live upon this faith. It is our meat and our drink. Take this away there is nothing left us in the Bible worth the having. It has become to us the head and front of our confidence, our hope, our rest, our joy. Instead of being ashamed to preach it, we wish that we could stand somewhere where all the inhabitants of the earth should hear us, and we would thunder it out day and night. So far from being ashamed of acknowledging it, we count it to be our highest honour and our greatest delight to tell it abroad, as we have opportunity, among the sons of men.

But why do we rejoice in it ? Why do we glory in it ? The answer is so large that I cannot do more than glance at its manifold claims on our gratitude. We glory in it for a thousand reasons. We fail to see anything in the doctrine of atonement that we should not glory in. We have heard a great many dogs bark against it, but dogs will bay the moon in her brightness, and therefore we mind not their howlings. Their noise has sometimes disturbed, though never yet has it frightened us. We have not yet heard a cavil against our Lord or an argument against His atoning blood which has affected our faith the turn of a hair. The Scriptures affirm it, the Holy Ghost bears witness to it, and its effect upon our inner life assures us of it. The analogy between Jewish fasts and festivals and our Christian faith endorses it ; there is a chasm that no man yet has been able to bridge without it ; it lightens our conscience, gladdens our hearts, inspires our devotion, and elevates our aspirations ; we are wedded to it, and daily glory in it.

In the cross of Christ we glory, because we regard it as a matchless exhibition of the attributes of God. We see there the love of God desiring a way by which He might save mankind, aided by His wisdom, so that a plan is perfected by which the deed can be done without violation of truth and justice. In the cross we see a strange conjunction of what once appeared to be two opposite qualities—justice and and mercy. We see how God is supremely just ; as just as if He had no mercy, and yet infinitely merciful in the gift of His Son. Mercy and justice in fact become counsel upon the same side, and irresistibly plead for the acquittal of the believing sinner. We can never tell which of the attributes of God shines most glorious in the sacrifice of Christ ; they each one find a glorious high throne in the person and work of the Lamb of God that taketh away the sin of the world. Since it has become, as it were, the disk which reflects the character and perfections of God it is meet that we should glory in the cross of Christ ; and none shall stay us of our boasting.

We glory in it, next, as the manifestation of the love of Jesus. He was loving inasmuch as He came to earth at all ; loving in feeding the hungry, in healing the sick, in raising the dead. He was loving in His whole life ; He was embodied charity, the Prince of philanthropists, the King of kindly souls. But oh, His death !—His cruel and shameful death— bearing, as we believe He did, the wrath due to sin, subjecting Himself to the curse, though in Him was no sin—this shows the love of Christ at its highest altitude, and therefore do we glory in it, and will never be ashamed to do so.

We glory in the cross, moreover, because it is the putting away of sin. There was no other way of making an end of sin, and making reconciliation for iniquity. To forgive the transgressions without exacting the penalty would have been contrary to all threatenings of God. It would not have appeased the claims of justice, nor satisfied the conscience of the sinner. No peace of mind can be enjoyed without pardon, and conscience declares that no pardon can be obtained without an atonement. We should have distracted ourselves with the fear that it was only a reprieve, and not a remission, even if the most comforting promises had been given unsealed with the atoning blood. The instincts of nature have convinced men of this truth, for all the world over religion has been associated with sacrifice. Almost every kind of worship that has ever sprung up among the sons of men has had sacrifice for its most prominent feature ; crime must be avenged, evil and sin cry from the ground, and a victim is sought to avert the vengeance. The heart craves for something that can calm the conscience : that craving is a relic of the ancient truth learned by man in primeval ages. Now, Christ did make His soul an offering for sin, when His own self He bare our sins in His own body on the tree. With His expiring breath He said, " It is finished !" Oh, wondrous grace ! Pardon is now freely published among the sons of men, pardon of which we see the justice and validity. As far as the east is from the west, so far hath God removed our transgressions from us by the death of Christ. This and this alone will put away sin, therefore in this cross of Christ we glory ; yea, and in it alone will we glory evermore.

It has put away our sins, blessed be God, so that this load and burden no more weigh us down ! We do not speak at random now. It has breathed hope and peace and joy into our spirits. I am sure that no one knows how to glory in the cross unless he has had an experimental acquaintance with its peace-breathing power. I speak what I do know, and testify what I have felt. The burden of my sin laid so heavy upon me that I would sooner have died than have lived. Many a day, and many a night, I felt the flames of hell in the anguish of my heart, because I knew my guilt, but saw no way of righteous forgiveness. Yet in a moment the load went from me, and I felt overflowing love to the Saviour. I fell at His feet awe-stricken that ever He should have taken away my sin and made an end of it. That matchless deed of love won my heart to Jesus. He changed my nature and renewed my soul in that same hour. But, oh, the joy I had ! Those who have sunk to the very depths of despair, and risen in a moment to the heights of peace and joy unspeakable, can tell you that they must glory in the cross and its power to save. Why, sirs, we must believe according to our own conscience. We cannot belie that inward witness. We only wish that others had been as deeply convinced of sin, and as truly led to the cross to feel their burden roll from off their shoulder as we have been, and then they, too, would glory in the cross of Christ. Since then we have gone with this remedy in our hands to souls that have been near despair, and we have never found the medicine to fail. Many and many a time have I spoken to people so depressed in spirit that they seemed not far from the madhouse, so heavy was their sense of sin ; yet have I never known the matchless music of Jesus' name, in any case, fail to charm the soul out of its despondency. "They looked unto Him, and were lightened : and their faces were not ashamed." Men who, because they thought there was no hope for them, would have desperately continued in sin, have read that word "hope" written in crimson lines upon the Saviour's dying body, and they have sprung up into confidence, have entered into peace, and henceforth have begun to lead a new life. We glory in the cross because of the peace it brings to every troubled conscience which receives it by faith : our own case has proved to our own souls its efficacy, and what we have seen in others has confirmed our confidence.

Yet we should not glory so much in the cross, were we not convinced that it is the greatest moral power in all the world. We glory in the cross because it gets at men's hearts when nothing else can reach them. The story of the dying Saviour's love has often impressed those whom all the moral lectures in the world could never have moved. Judged and condemned by the unanswerable reasonings of their own consciences, they have not had control enough over their passions to shake off the captivity in which they were held by the temptations that assailed them at every turn, till they have drawn near to the cross of Jesus, and from pardon have gathered hope, and from hope have gained strength to master sin.

When they have seen their sin laid on Jesus, they have loved Him, and hated the sin that made Him to suffer so grievously as their substitute. Then the Holy Ghost has come upon them, and they have resolved, with divine strength, to drive out the sin for which the Saviour died ; they have begun a new life, aye, and they have continued in it, sustained by that same sacred power which first constrained them, and now they look forward to be perfected by it through the power of God. Where are the triumphs of infidelity in rescuing men from sin ? Where are the trophies of philosophy in conquering human pride ? Will you bring us harlots that have been made chaste ; thieves that have been reclaimed ; angry men, of bear-like temper, who have become harmless as lambs, through scientific lectures ? Let our amateur philanthropists, who suggest so much and do so little, produce some instances of the moral transformations that have been wrought by their sophistries. Nay ; they curl their lips, and leave the lower orders to the City Missionary and the Bible Woman. It is the cross that humbles the haughty, lifts up the fallen, refines the polluted, and gives a fresh start to those who are forlorn and desperate. Nothing else can do it. The world sinks lower and lower into the bog of its own selfishness and sin. Only this wondrous lever of the atonement, symbolized by the cross of Christ, can lift our abject race to the place of virtue and honour which it ought to occupy.

We glory in the cross for so many reasons that I cannot hope to enumerate them all. While it ennobles our life, it invigorates us with hope in our death. Death is now deprived of its terrors to us, for Christ has died. We, like Him, can say, "Father, into Thy hands we commend our spirit." His burial has perfumed the grace ; His resurrection has paved the road to immortality. He rose and left a lamp behind which shows an outlet from the gloom of the sepulchre. The paradise He immediately predicted for Himself and for the penitent who hung by His side has shown us how quick the transition is from mortal pains to immortal joys. "Absent from the body, present with the Lord," is the cheering prospect. Glory be to Christ for ever and for ever that we have this doctrine of "Christ crucified" to preach.

II. The second cross exhibits THE WORLD CRUCIFIED. The apostle says that the world was crucified to Him. What does he mean by this ? He regarded the world as nailed up like a felon, and hanged upon a cross to die. Well, I suppose he means that its character was condemned. He looked out upon the world which thought so much of itself, and said, "I do not think much of thee, poor world ! Thou art like a doomed malefactor." He knew that the world had crucified its Saviour—crucified its God. It had gone to such a length of sin that it had hounded perfect innocence through the streets. Infinite benevolence it had scoffed at and maligned. Eternal truth it had rejected, and preferred a lie ; and the Son of God, who was love incarnate, it had put to the death of the cross. "Now," says Paul, " I know thy character, O world ! I know thee ! and I hold thee in no more esteem than the wretch abhorred for his crimes, who is condemned to hang upon the gibbet and so end his detested life." This led Paul, since he condemned its character, utterly to despise its judgment. The world said, "This Paul is a fool. His gospel is foolishness and he himself is a mere babbler." "Yes," thought Paul, " a deal you know of it!" In this we unite with him. What is your judgment worth? You did not know the Son of God, poor blind world! We are sure that He was perfect, and yet you hunted Him to death. Your judgment is a poor thing, O world! You are crucified to us. Now, there are a great many people who could hardly endure to live if they should happen to be misjudged by the world or what is called "society." Oh yes, we must be respectable. We must have every man's good word, or we are ready to faint. Paul was of another mind. What cared he for aught the world might say? How could he wish to please a world so abominable that it had put his Lord to death! He would sooner have its bad opinion than its good. It were better to be frowned at than to be smiled upon by a world that crucified Christ. Certainly, its condemnation is more worth having than its approbation if it can put Christ to death: so Paul utterly despised its judgment, and it was crucified to him. Now, we are told to think a great deal about "public opinion," "popular belief," "the growing feeling of the age," "the sentiment of the period," and "the spirit of the age." I should like Paul to read some of our religious newspapers; and yet I could not wish the good man so distasteful a task, for I dare say he would sooner pine in the Mammertine prison than do so; but, still, I should like to see how he would look after he had read some of those expressions about the necessity of keeping ourselves abreast with the sentiment of the period. "What," he would say, "the sentiment of the world! It is crucified to me! What can it matter what its opinion is? We are of God, little children, and the whole world lieth in the wicked one; would ye heed what the world that is lying in the wicked one thinks of you or of the truth of your Lord? Are you going to smooth your tongue, and soften your speech, to please the world that lieth in the wicked one!" Paul would be indignant with such a proposition. He said, "the world is crucified to me." Hence he looked upon all the world's pleasures as so much rottenness, a carcase nailed to a cross. Can you fancy Paul being taken to the Colosseum at Rome? I try to imagine him made to sit on one of those benches to watch a combat of gladiators. There is the emperor: there are all the great peers of Rome and the senators; and there are those cruel eyes all gazing down upon men who shed each others' blood. Can you picture how Paul would have felt if he had been forced to occupy a seat at that spectacle? It would have been martyrdom to him. He would have closed his eyes and ears against the sight of what Rome thought to be the choicest pleasure of the day. They thronged the imperial city; they poured in mighty streams into the theatre each day to see poor beasts tortured, or men murdering one another; that was the world of Paul's day; and he rightly judged it to be a crucified felon. If he was compelled to see the popular pleasures of to-day upon which I will say but little, would he not be well-nigh as sick of them as he would have been of the amusements of the amphitheatre at Rome?

To Paul, too, all the honours of the age must have been crucified in like manner. Suppose that Paul settled his mind to think of the wretches who were reigning as emperors in his day! I use the word advisedly, for I would not speak evil of dignities: but really I speak too well of them when I call them wretches. They seem to have been inhuman monsters —"tyrants whose capricious folly violated every law of nature and decency," to whom every kind of lust was a daily habit, and who even sought out new inventions of sensuality, calling them new pleasures. As Paul thought of the iniquities of Napoli, and all the great towns to which the Romans went in their holidays—Pompeii and the like—oh, how he loathed them! And I doubt not that if the apostle were to come here now, if he knew how often rank and title are wont to sink all true dignity in shameful dissipation, and what flagrant profligacy is to be found in high quarters, he might as justly consider all the pomps and dignities and honours of the world that now is to be as little worth as a putrid carcase hanging on a tree and rotting in the sun. He says, "The world is crucified to me: it is hanging on the gallows to me, I think so little of its pleasures and of its pomps."

Alike contemptuously did Paul judge of all the treasures of the world. Paul never spent as much time as it would take to wink his eye in thinking of how much money he was worth. Having food and raiment he was therewith content. Sometimes he had scarcely that. He casually thanks the Philippians for ministering to his necessities, but he never sought to store anything, nor did he live with even half a thought of aggrandizing himself with gold and silver. "No," he said, "this will all perish with the using," and so he treated the world as a thing crucified to him. Now, Christian man, can you say as much as this—that the world in its mercantile aspect, as well as in its motley vices and its manifold frivolities, is a crucified thing to you? Now, look what the world says. "Make money, young man, make money! Honestly if you can, but by all means make money. Look about you, for if you are not sharp you will not succeed. Keep your own counsel, and rather play the double than be the dupe. Your character will rise with the credit you get on 'Change." Now, suppose that you get the money, what is the result? The net result, as I often find it, is a paragraph in one of the newspapers to say that So-and-so Esquire's will was proved in the Probate Court under so many thousands. Then follows a grand squabble among all his relatives which shall eat him up. That is the consummation of a life of toil and care and scheming. He has lived for lucre, and he has to leave it behind. There is the end of that folly. I have sometimes thought of the contrast between the poor man's funeral and the rich man's funeral. When the poor man dies there are his sons and daughters weeping with real distress, for the death of the father brings sadness and sympathy into that house. The poor man is to be buried, but it can only be managed by the united self-denials of all his sons and daughters. There is Mary out at service; she, perhaps, contributes more than the others towards the funeral, for she has no family of her own. The elder son and the younger brothers all pinch themselves to pay a little; and the tears that are shed that evening when they come home from the grave are very genuine: they *do* suffer, and they prove their sorrow by rivalling one another in the respect they pay to their parent. Now you shall see the rich man die. Of course everybody laments the sad loss: it is the proper thing. Empty carriages swell the procession to the grave by way of empty compliment. The mourners return, and there is the reading of that blessed document the will; when that is read the time for tears is over in almost every case. Few are pleased; the one whom fortune favours is the envy of all the rest. Sad thoughts and sullen looks float on the surface, not in respect of the man's departure, but concerning the *means* he has left and the mode in which he has disposed of them. Oh, it is a poor thing to live for, the making of money and the hoarding of it. But still the genius of rightly getting money can be consecrated to the glory of God. You can use the wealth of this world in the service of the Master. To gain is not wrong. It is only wrong when grasping becomes the main object of life, and grudging grows into covetousness which is idolatry. To every Christian that and every other form of worldliness ought to be crucified, so that we can say, " For me to live is not myself, but it is Christ ; I live that I may honour and glorify Him."

When the apostle said that the world was crucified to him, he meant just this. " I am not enslaved by any of its pursuits. I care nothing for its maxims. I am not governed by its spirit. I do not court its smiles. I do not fear its threatenings. It is not my master, nor am I its slave. The whole world cannot force Paul to lie, or to sin, but Paul will tell the world the truth, come what may." You recollect the words of Palissy, the potter, when the king of France said to him that if he did not change his religion, and cease to be a Huguenot, he was afraid that he should have to deliver him up to his enemies. " Sire," said the potter, " I am sorry to hear you say, ' I am afraid,' for all the men in the world could not make Palissy talk like that. I am afraid of nobody, and I *must* do nothing but what is right." Oh, yes ; the man that fears God and loves the cross has a moral backbone which enables him to stand, and he snaps his fingers at the world. " Dead felon ! " says he, " dead felon ! Crucifier of Christ ! Cosmos thou callest thyself. By comely names thou wouldst fain be greeted. Paul is nothing in thine esteem ; but Paul is a match for thee, for he thinks as much of thee as thou dost of him, and no more." Hear him as he cries, " The world is crucified unto me, and I unto the world." To live to serve men is one thing, to live to bless them is another ; and this we will do, God helping us, making sacrifices for their good. But to fear men, to ask their leave to think, to ask their instructions as to what we shall speak, and how we shall say it—that is a baseness we cannot brook. By the grace of God, we have not so degraded ourselves, and never shall. " The world is crucified to me," says the apostle, " by the cross of Christ."

III.   Then he finishes up with the third crucifixion, which is, *I* AM CRUCIFIED TO THE WORLD. We shall soon see the evidence of this crucifixion if we notice how they poured contempt upon Him. Once Saul was a great rabbi, a man profoundly versed in Hebrew lore, a Pharisee of the Pharisees, and much admired. He was also a classic scholar and a philosophic thinker, a man of great mental powers, and fit to take the lead in learned circles. But when Paul began to preach Christ crucified—" Bah," they said, " he is an utter fool ! Heed him not ! " Or else they said, " Down with him ! He is an apostate ! " They cursed him. His name brought wrath into the face of all Jews that mentioned it, and all intelligent Greeks likewise. " Paul ? He is nobody ! " He was everybody when he thought their way : he is nobody now that he thinks in God's way.

And then they put him to open shame by suspecting all his motives, and by misrepresenting all his actions. It did not matter what Paul did they were quite certain that he was self-seeking ; that he was endeavouring to make a fine thing of it for himself. When he acted so that they were forced to own that he was right, they put it in such a light that they made it out to be wrong. There were some who denied his apostleship, and said that he was never sent of God ; and others questioned his ability to preach the gospel. So they crucified poor Paul one way and another to the full.

They went further still. They despised, they shunned him. His old friends forsook him. Some got out of the way, others pointed at him the finger of scorn in the streets. His persecutors showed their rancour against him, now stoning him with lynch-law, and anon with a semblance of legality dragging him before the magistrates. Paul was crucified to them. As for his teaching, they decried him as a babbler—a setter-forth of strange gods. I dare say they often sneered at the cross of Christ which he preached as a nine days' wonder, an almost exploded doctrine, and said, " If you do but shut the mouths of such men as Paul, it will soon be forgotten." I have heard them say in modern times to lesser men, " Your old-fashioned Puritanism is nearly dead, ere long it will be utterly extinct ! " But we preach Christ crucified ; the same old doctrine as the apostles preached, and for this by the contempt of the worldly wise we are crucified.

Now, dear Christian friends, if you keep to the cross of Christ you must expect to have this for your portion. The world will be crucified to you, and you will be crucified to the world. You will get the cold shoulder. Old friends will become open foes. They will begin to hate you more than they loved you before. At home your foes will be the men of your own household. You will hardly be able to do anything right. When you joined in their revels you were a fine fellow ; when you could drink, and sing a lascivious song, you were a jolly good fellow ; but now they rate you as a fool ; they scout you as a hypocrite ; and slanderously blacken your character. Let their dislike be a badge of your discipleship, and say, " Now also the world is crucified to me, and I unto the world. Whatever the world says against me for Christ's sake is the maundering of a doomed malefactor, and what do I care for that ? And, on the other hand, if I be rejected and despised, I am only taking what I always expected—my crucifixion—in my poor, humble way, after the manner of Christ Himself, who was despised and rejected of men."

The moral and the lesson of it all is this. Whatever comes of it, still glory in Christ. Go in for this, dear friends, that whether ye be in honour or in dishonour, in good report or in evil report, whether God multiply your substance and make you rich, or diminish it and make you poor, you will still glory in the cross of Christ. If you have health, and strength, and vigour to work for Him, or if you have to lie upon a bed of languishing and bear in patience all your heavenly Father's will, resolve that you will still glory in the cross. Let this be the point of your glorifying throughout your lives. Go down the steeps of Jordan, and go through Jordan itself, still glorying in the cross, for in the heaven of glory you will find that the blood-bought hosts celebrate the cross as the trophy of their redemption.

Are you trusting in the cross ? Are you resting in Jesus ? If not, may the Lord teach you this blessed privilege. There is no joy like it. There is no strength like it. There is no life like it. There is no peace like it. At the cross we find our heaven. While upon the cross we gaze all heavenly, holy things abound within our hearts. If you have never been there, the Lord lead you there at this very hour ; so shall you be pardoned, accepted, and blest for aye. The Lord grant that you all may be partakers of this grace for Christ's sake. Amen.

BLESSING FOR BLESSING

"Blessed be the God and Father of our Lord Jesus Christ, who hath blessed us with all spiritual blessings in heavenly places in Christ: according as He hath chosen us in Him before the foundation of the world, that we should be holy and without blame before Him in love."—Ephesians i. 3, 4.

GOD blesses us; let us bless Him. I pray that every heart here may take its own part in this service of praise.

"O thou, my soul, bless God the Lord,
And all that in me is,
Be stirred up His holy name
To magnify and bless!"

Sit in your seats, and keep on blessing God from the first word of the sermon to the last; and then go on blessing God till the last hour of life, and enter into heaven, into the eternal glory, still blessing God. It should be our life to bless Him who gave us our life. It should be our delight to bless Him who gives us all our delights. So says the text, and so let us do: "Blessed be the God and Father of our Lord Jesus Christ."

I. Our first occupation, at this time, will be that of BLESSING GOD.

But how can we bless God? Without doubt the less is blessed of the Greater. Can the Greater be blessed by the less? Yes, but it must be in a modified sense. God blesses us with all spiritual blessings; but we cannot give Him any blessings. He needs nothing at our hand; and if He did, we could not give it. "If I were hungry," saith the Lord, "I would not tell thee: for the world is Mine, and the fullness thereof." God has an all-sufficiency within Himself, and can never be thought of as dependent upon His creatures, or as receiving anything from His creatures which He needs to receive. He is infinitely blessed already; we cannot add to His blessedness. When He blesses us, He gives us a blessedness that we never had before; but when we bless Him, we cannot by one iota increase His absolutely infinite perfectness. David said to the Lord, "My goodness extendeth not to Thee." This was as if he had said, Let me be as holy, as devout, and as earnest as I may, I can do nothing for Thee; Thou art too high, too holy, too great for me to be really able to bless Thee in the sense in which Thou dost bless me.

How, then, do we bless God? Well, I should say, first, that this language is the expression of gratitude. We say with David, "Bless the Lord, O my soul," and we say with Paul, "Blessed be the God and Father of our Lord Jesus Christ." We can bless God by praising Him, extolling Him, desiring all honour for Him, ascribing all good to Him, magnifying and lauding His holy name. Well, we will do that. Sit still, if you will, and let your heart be silent unto God; for no language can ever express the gratitude that, I trust, we feel to Him who has blessed us with all spiritual blessings in Christ Jesus. Praise Him also in your speech. Break the silence; speak to His glory. Invite others to cry with you, "Hallelujah!" or "Hallels unto Jah!" "Praise unto

Jehovah!" Ascribe ye greatness unto our God. Oh, that all flesh would magnify the Lord with us!

This language is also the utterance of assent to all the blessedness that is ascribed to the Lord. After hearing how great He is, how glorious He is, how happy He is, we bless Him by saying, "Amen; so let it be! So would we have it. He is none too great for us, none too glorious for us, none too blessed for us. Let Him be great, glorious, and blessed, beyond all conception." I think that we bless God when we say concerning the whole of His character, "Amen. This God is our God for ever and ever." Let Him be just what the Bible says He is; we accept Him as such. Sternly just, He will not spare the guilty. Amen, blessed be His name! Infinitely gracious, ready to forgive. Amen, so let it be! Everywhere present, always omniscient. Amen, so again do we wish Him to be! Everlastingly the same, unchanging in His truth, His promise, His nature. We again say that we are glad of it, and we bless Him. He is just such a God as we love. He is indeed God to us, because He is really God, and we can see that He is so, and every attribute ascribed to Him is a fresh proof to us that Jehovah is the Lord. Thus, we bless Him by adoration.

We also bless God in the spreading of His kingdom. We can win hearts to Him through His mighty grace blessing our service. We can fight against evil; we can set up a standard for the truth. We can be willing to suffer in repute, and every way else, for His name's sake. We can by His grace do all this, and thus we are blessing God. Surely, dear friends, if it is well-pleasing in God's sight that sinners should repent, if it makes heaven the gladder, and makes joy in the presence of the angels that men should repent, we are in the best and most practical way blessing God when we labour to bring men to repentance through faith in Christ Jesus.

There is also another way of blessing God which, I trust, we shall all endeavour to practise; and that is by the doing good to His children. When they are sick, visit them. When they are downcast, comfort them. When they are poor, relieve them. When they are hard pressed by outward adversaries, stand at their side, and help them. You cannot bless the Head, but you can bless the feet; and when you have refreshed the feet, you have refreshed the Head. He will say, "Inasmuch as ye have done it unto one of the least of these My brethren, ye have done it unto Me." If they be naked, and you clothe them; if they be sick, and you visit them; if they be hungry, and you feed them; you do in this respect bless God. David not only said, "Thou art my Lord: my goodness extendeth not to Thee"; but he added, "but to the saints that are in the earth, and to the excellent in whom is all my delight." You can be good to them, and in that respect you may be blessing God. He has done so much for us, that we would fain do something for Him; and when we have reached the limit of our possibilities, we long to do more. We wish that we had more money to give, more talent to use, more time that we could devote to His cause, we wish that we had more heart and more brain; sometimes we wish that we had more tongue, and we sing,—

> "Oh, for a thousand tongues to sing
> My great Redeemer's praise!"

This word "blessed" is an attempt to break the narrow circle of our capacity. It is an earnest endeavour of a burning heart to lay at God's feet crowns of glory which it cannot find: "Blessed be the God and Father of our Lord Jesus Christ."

II. But now, secondly, we shall spend a little time in VIEWING GOD in the light in which Paul sets Him before us: "Blessed be the God and Father of our Lord Jesus Christ."

We bless the God of nature. What beauties He has strewn around us! We bless the God of providence. How bountifully doth He send us harvests and fruitful seasons! We bless the God of grace who hath redeemed us, and adopted us as His children. But here is a peculiar aspect of God, which should call forth our highest praises; for He is called "the God and Father of our Lord Jesus Christ."

When we see God *in connection with Christ*, when we see God through Christ, when we see God in Christ, then our hearts are all aflame, and we burst out with, "Blessed be the God and Father of our Lord Jesus Christ." God apart from Christ—that is a great and glorious theme; but the human mind fails to grasp it. The infinite Jehovah, who can conceive Him? "Our God is a consuming fire." Who can draw near to Him? But in the Mediator, in the Person of the God, the Man, in whom we find blended human sympathy and divine glory, we can draw nigh to God. There it is that we get our hands upon the golden harp-strings, and resolve that every string shall be struck to the praise of God in Christ Jesus.

But note carefully that God is described here as *the God of our Lord Jesus Christ*. When Jesus knelt in prayer, He prayed to our God. When Jesus leaned in faith upon the promises, He trusted in God that He would deliver Him. When our Saviour sang on that passover night, the song was unto God. When he prayed in Gethsemane, with bloody sweat, the prayer was unto our God. Jesus said to Mary at the sepulchre, "Go to My brethren, and say unto them, I ascend unto My Father, and your Father; and to My God, and your God." How we ought to bless God when we think that He is the God whom our Redeemer blesses! This is the God who said of Christ, "This is My beloved Son, in whom I am well pleased." Delightful thought! When I approach Jehovah, I approach the God of our Lord Jesus Christ. Surely, when I see His blood-stained footprints there on the ground before me, though I put my shoe from off my foot, for the place is holy ground, yet I follow with confidence where my Friend, my Saviour, my Husband, my Head has been before me; and I rejoice as I worship the God of our Lord Jesus Christ.

He is also called *the Father of our Lord Jesus Christ*. This is a great mystery. Think not that we shall ever understand the high relationship between the first and second Persons of the blessed Trinity, the Father and the Son. We speak of eternal filiation, which is a term that does not convey to us any great meaning; it simply covers up our ignorance. How God is the Father of our Lord Jesus Christ as God, we do not know; and perhaps to wish to gaze into this tremendous mystery were as great a folly as to look at the sun, and blind ourselves with its brilliance. It is so; that ought to be enough for us. God the Father is the Father of Jesus Christ as to His divine nature: "Thou art My Son; this day have I begotten Thee." He is also His Father as to the human side of His nature. He was begotten of the Holy Ghost. That body of His, that human life, came of God; not of Joseph, not of man. Born of a woman, God sent forth His Son; but He was His Son then. It was God's Son that was born at Bethlehem. Gabriel said to the Virgin Mary, "That holy thing which shall be born of thee shall be called the Son of God." Now take the two natures in their wondrous blending in the person of the Lord Jesus Christ, and you see how the great God is the God and Father of our Lord Jesus Christ. Yet, sweet thought, He is my Father, too; my Father is Christ's Father. Jesus Christ's Father is our Father, and He teaches us to call Him, "Our Father, which art in heaven." Often in prayer He said, "Father"; and he bids us say the same, putting the plural pronoun before it, "Our Father." Now will you not bless the Lord, who is the God and Father of our Lord Jesus Christ? Do you not feel a glowing in your hearts, as you think of the near and dear relationship into which you are brought through Jesus Christ? The God of Jesus Christ, the Father of Jesus Christ, is my God, my Father, too. Blessed, blessed, blessed, for ever blessed be that dear name!

III. Our third occupation, at this time, is that of RECOUNTING HIS GREAT MERCIES. I will read the rest of the third verse: "Blessed be the God and Father of our Lord Jesus Christ, who hath blessed us with all spiritual blessings in heavenly places in Christ."

This recapitulation of mercies is written with *full assurance;* and you will not bless God unless you have a touch of that same experience. Paul does not say, "Who has, we hope and trust, blessed us," but he writes, "Who hath blessed us." Ah, beloved, if you have a full assurance that God has blessed you in Christ, and that now His smile rests upon you, and all the benisons of the covenant are stored there for you, I think that you cannot help saying, "Blessed, blessed be the name of the Most High!" That doubt, that trembling, this it is that empties out the marrow from the bone of our blessedness. If you have suspicions about the truth of this precious Book, if you have questions about the truth of the doctrines of grace, if you have doubts about your own interest in those things, I do not wonder that you do not praise God, for a blessing which is only mine by peradventure, well, peradventure I shall be grateful for it; but peradventure I shall not. But if I know whom I have believed, if I have a firm grip of spiritual mercies, if all heavenly things are mine in Christ my Lord, I can sing, "Wake up, my glory; awake psaltery and harp; I myself will awake right early." "Blessed be the God and Father of our Lord Jesus Christ, who hath blessed us with all spiritual blessings."

With this full assurance should come *intense delight:* "Who hath blessed us." God has blessed us. Come brethren, He has not done some trifle for us, which we can afford to ignore. He has not merely given us some absolutely necessary boons, which we must have, for we could not live without them; but He has in grace dealt still more abundantly with us. He has gone beyond workhouse fare, and made us feast with saints and princes. He has given us more than home-spun garments; He has put upon us robes of beauty and of glory, even His own spotless righteousness. He has blessed us; we are blessed; we feel that we are. Each believer can say:

"I feel like singing all the time,
My tears are wiped away;
For Jesus is a Friend of mine,
I'll praise Him every day.
I'll praise Him! praise Him! praise Him all the time!"

We are not sitting here, and groaning, and crying, and fretting, and worrying, and questioning our own salvation. He has blessed us; and therefore we will bless Him. If you think little of what God has done for you, you will do very little for Him; but if you have a great notion of His great mercy to you, you will be greatly grateful to your gracious God.

Let me also remark, next, that as assurance and delight lead to blessing God, so does a *right understanding* of His mercies. To help your understanding, notice what Paul says; "Blessed be the God and Father of our Lord Jesus Christ, who hath blessed us with all spiritual blessings." An enlightened man is grateful to God for temporal blessings; but he is much more grateful to God for spiritual blessings, for temporal blessings do not last long; they are soon gone. Temporal blessings are not definite marks of divine favour, since God gives them to the unworthy, and to the wicked, as well as to the righteous. The corn, and wine, and oil, are for Dives; and Lazarus gets even less than his share. Our thanks are due to God for all temporal blessings; they are more than we deserve. But our thanks ought to go to God in thunders of hallelujahs for spiritual blessings. A new heart is better than a new coat. To feed on Christ is better than to have the best earthly food. To be an heir of God is better than being the heir of the greatest nobleman. To have God for our portion is blessed, infinitely more blessed than to own broad acres of land. God hath blessed us with spiritual blessings. These are the rarest, the richest, the most enduring of all blessings; they are priceless in value. Wherefore, let me beg you to join in blessing the God and Father of our Lord Jesus Christ, who hath blessed you with spiritual blessings.

But did you notice that little word "all"? I must bring that out clearly. I must turn the microscope on it. "Who hath blessed us with all spiritual blessings." Surely, Paul means that we have not a spiritual blessing which God did not give. We have never earned one; we could never create one. All spiritual blessings come from the Father; He has really given us all spiritual blessings. "I have not received them," says one. That is your own fault. He hath blessed us with all spiritual blessings in Christ. A new heart, a tender conscience, a submissive will, faith, hope, love, patience, we have all these in Christ. Regeneration, justification, adoption, sanctification, perfection are all in Christ. If we do not take them out, it is the fault of our palsied hand, that has not strength enough to grasp them; but He has given us all spiritual blessings in Christ. Whenever you read your Bible, and see a great promise, do not hesitate to claim it. He hath given us all spiritual blessings in Christ. "I am afraid," says one, "that I should be presuming if I took some of the promises." He hath given us all spiritual blessings in Christ. You are in your Father's house; you cannot steal; for your Father says, "Help yourself to what you like." He has made over His whole estate of spiritual wealth to every believing child of His; wherefore take freely, and you will, by so doing, glorify God. He hath blessed us with all spiritual blessings in Christ.

This He has done in the "heavenly places." What does that mean, "Who hath blessed us with all spiritual blessings in heavenly places"? Does it not mean that He is working upon us all spiritual blessings out of the heaven where He dwells? Or does it mean much more, that He is sending us all these spiritual blessings to bring us to the heaven where He dwells, and where He would have us dwell?

I want to stir up your heart by reminding you that all the spiritual blessings we receive are the richer and the rarer because they are given to us "in Christ." Here are the blessings; and Christ is the golden casket that holds them all. When the City of London makes a man a freeman of the city, the document giving him his liberty is usually presented to him enclosed in a golden casket. Christ is that golden casket, in which we find the charter of our eternal liberty. He hath blessed us with all spiritual blessings in Christ. If they came to us any other way, we might lose them; or we might not be sure that they were genuine; but when they come to us in Christ, they come to stay, and we know that they are real. If Christ is mine, all blessings in heavenly places are mine.

I seem, to myself, to be talking very drily of things that ought to be swimming in a sea of joy and delight. Beloved, do not let my faint words rob my Lord of any of His glory. He has done such great things for you; bless His name. We cannot stand up, and ask for instruments of music with which to sound His praise; but we can sit still, and each one say, "Blessed be His name! It is all true; He has blessed me; I know that He has. He has blessed me, with a liberal hand, with all spiritual blessings. He has blessed me just where I wanted blessing, where I was poorest in spiritual things. I could make my way in business, but I could not make my way in grace; so He has blessed me with all spiritual blessings; and He has made the garments all the dearer because of the wardrobe in which He has hung them. He has given me these royal things in Christ; and as I look to my dear Lord, and see what there is for me stored up in Him, I prize each thing the more because it is in Him. Come, Holy Spirit, set our hearts on fire with blessing and praise to God for all the great things that He has done for us!"

IV. I shall close with this fourth remark: Let us bless God, BEHOLDING THE MANNER OF HIS GIFTS. That is described in the fourth verse: "According as He hath chosen us in Him before the foundation of the world, that we should be holy and without blame before Him in love."

Now, brethren, we are to praise God because all spiritual blessings have come to us in the same way as our election came, "according as He hath chosen us in Him." How did that come? Well, it came of *His free, sovereign grace.* He loved us because He would love us. He chose us because He chose us.

"Ye have not chosen me; but I have chosen you." If there be any virtue, if there be any praise in us now, He put it there. To the bottomless abyss of His own infinite goodness we must trace the election of His grace. Well, now, every blessing comes to us in the same way. God hath not blessed thee, my brother, with usefulness because thou didst deserve it; but because of His grace. He did not redeem thee, or regenerate thee, or sanctify thee, or uphold thee, because of anything in thee. Again and again, by the prophet Ezekiel, did the Lord remind His ancient people that the blessings He bestowed upon them were all gifts of His grace. "Therefore say unto the house of Israel, Thus saith the Lord God, I do not this for your sakes, O house of Israel, but for Mine holy name's sake." And again, "Not for your sakes do I this, saith the Lord God, be it known unto you: be ashamed and confounded for your own ways, O house of Israel." Every blessing comes to us with the hall-mark of sovereign grace upon it. As the Lord distributes the gifts of His grace, He says, "May I not do as I will with My own?" He does so, and we bless, and praise, and adore the sovereign grace of God, which, having chosen us, continues to bless us according as He hath chosen us in Christ.

Next, we have to bless God that all His gifts come to us *in Christ*. Notice Paul's words, "according as He hath chosen us in Him." God called us in Christ. He justified us in Christ. He sanctified us in Christ. He will perfect us in Christ. He will glorify us in Christ. We have everything in Christ, and we have nothing apart from Christ. Let us praise and bless the name of the Lord that this sacred channel of His grace is as glorious as the grace itself. There is as much grace in the gift of Christ to save us as there is in the salvation which Christ has wrought out for us. "Blessed be the God and Father of our Lord Jesus Christ."

Again, all our blessings come from *the divine purpose*. Listen: "Who hath blessed us with all spiritual blessings in heavenly places in Christ: according as He hath chosen us in Him." No spiritual blessing comes to any man by chance. No man gets a boon from God through his "good luck"; it all comes according to the eternal purpose of God, which He purposed or ever the earth was.

> "Long e'er the sun's refulgent ray
> Primeval shades of darkness drove,
> They on His sacred bosom lay,
> Loved with an everlasting love."

"Before the foundation of the world," says the text, there was a purpose in the heart of God, and in that purpose we were chosen, and by that same purpose God continues to bless us. Look, beloved, God never gives His people either a gift or a grace without His purpose. Has God given you a brain clear, quick, capacious? Think for Him. Has God given you a tongue fluent, eloquent? Speak for Him. He does not give you these gifts without a purpose. Has God given you influence among your fellow-men? Use it for Him. Your election came according to His purpose; and so have all your gifts, and much more, all your graces. Have you strong, bright-eyed faith? Have you burning zeal? Have you vehement love? Have you any of the gifts of the covenant? Use them for a purpose. God has given them for a purpose; find out what that purpose is, and glorify God thereby.

Lastly, the text tells us that God blesses us with all spiritual blessings in heavenly places in Christ: according as He hath chosen us in Him before the foundation of the world, "that we should be holy and without blame before Him in love." God's choice of us was not because we were holy, but *to make us holy;* and God's purpose will not be fulfilled unless we are made holy. Some people, when they talk about salvation, mean escaping from hell, and getting into heaven by the skin of their teeth. We never mean any such thing. We mean deliverance from evil, deliverance from sin. I often wonder why some people grumble because God has chosen to deliver others from sin when they themselves do not want to be delivered from sin. Like a dog in the manger, they cannot eat the hay themselves, and they growl at those who can. If you wish to be safe from sin, ask God for that great blessing, and He will give it to you; but if you do not want it, do not complain if God says, "I shall give it to such and such a person, and you that do not even ask for it shall be left without it." If you do not care to be holy, you shall not be holy. If you did care for it, and wish for it, you might have it, for God denies it to none who seek it at His hands. But if you neither wish for it, nor value it, why do you lift your puny fist against the God of heaven because He hath chosen others, that they should be holy and without blame before Him in love?

The object of our election is our holiness, and the object of every spiritual blessing is our holiness. God is aiming at making us holy. Are you not glad of that? May I not say, "Blessed be the God and Father of our Lord Jesus Christ, because His aim in every gift is to make us holy"? Brothers and sisters, would we not sacrifice everything that we have, and count it no sacrifice, if we might be perfectly holy? I said to a young girl, who came to join the church, "Mary, are you perfect?" She looked at me, and said, "No, sir." I said, "Would you like to be?" "Oh, that I would! I long for it; I cry for it." Surely, the God who makes us long to be perfect, has already wrought a great work in us; and if we can say that, to be perfect, would be heaven to us, then we are already on the road to heaven, and God is working out in us His eternal purpose, which is, "that we should be holy."

There is one thing more: "That we should be holy and *without blame before Him in love*." Does that mean that we are to be loving, full of love, and without blame in that matter? Well, I am afraid that there are not very many Christians who are without blame on the score of love. I know a man, a noble man intellectually, and, in some respects, spiritually. I believe that he would die at the stake for the grand old Calvinistic faith; but he is as hard as iron; you cannot feel any kind of love to him, for he does not seem to feel any kind of love to anybody else. That man is not without blame before God in love. I have known others; wonderful Christians they appear to be, they could pray for a week; but if you are poor, and ask them for a little help, your asking will be all in vain. I do not think that they are without blame before God in love. O brothers, God has chosen us to be loving, He has ordained us to be loving; and all the innumerable blessings which He has given to us, He sends to win us to a loving spirit, that we may be without blame in that matter. Our dear friend, Mr. William Olney, whom we remember here still, and never can forget, was, I think, without blame in that matter of love. I sometimes thought that he used to shed his love on some who might have been the better for a hard word; for they were deceivers; but he could not bring his mind to think that anybody could be a deceiver; and if anybody was in want of help, no matter though their own misconduct had brought them into poverty, his hand was in his pocket, and out again, very quickly with help for them. He never failed in love; and I pray that you and I, with prudence and wisdom mixed with it, may be without blame before God in the matter of love. Love your fellow-Christians. Love poor sinners to Christ. Love those that despitefully use you. Love those round about you who are strangers to the love of God. It may be that they will see in your love some little image of the love of God, as in a drop of water you may some-times see the sun and the heavens reflected. God make us to be reflections of the love of God! His purpose is that we may be holy and without blame before Him in love.

Now, I have set before you a rare treasury. Does this treasury belong to you? My dear hearers, is Christ yours? Are you trusting Him? If not, there is nothing yours. Without Christ, you can do nothing, and you are nothing, and you have nothing. Come to Jesus as you are, and put your trust in Him, and then all things are yours. If Christ be yours, beloved, then I charge you bless the Lord, aye, bless the Lord again and again, for you will never bless Him as much as He deserves to be blessed. Let us finish this service as we closed our worship this morning, by singing the doxology,—

"Praise God from whom all blessings flow."

ACCEPTED OF THE GREAT FATHER

"He hath made us accepted in the beloved."—Ephesians i. 6.

A FEW Sabbath mornings ago I spoke to you upon those memorable words of the great Father, "This is My beloved Son, in whom I am well pleased." We now go a step farther, and see how the love of God to His beloved Son overflows, and runs like a river of life to all those who are in Christ Jesus. To Him He saith, "This is My beloved Son," and then He turns to all who are in union with Him and says, "These also are My beloved for His sake." As believers we are assured by the text that we are "Accepted *in the Beloved*," to the praise of the glory of God's grace. Why is that peculiar title here used? It might have been said, we are accepted in Christ, or accepted in the Mediator; there must be some motive for giving Him this special name in this place. The motive is declared to be that we may praise the glory of divine grace. God did not want for a beloved when He made us His beloved: His heart was not pining for an object; His affections were not lone and desolate. His only-begotten Son was His delight, and there was room enough in Him for all the Father's love; it was *we* that needed to be loved, and so the Beloved is mentioned that we may remember the unselfishness of divine grace. He makes us His beloved, but He had a Beloved before.

We are also reminded that we are "accepted in the Beloved" to let us know that God has not shifted His love—His first Beloved is His Beloved still. We have not supplanted His dear Son, nor even diverted a beam of love from Him. The Lord has called us a beloved who were not so, and made us a people who were not a people; but He has not withdrawn a grain of love from Jesus, whom He still calls "Mine elect, in whom My soul delighteth." All the infinite love of God still flows to Jesus, and then to us in Him. It pleased the Father that to Him a fulness of love should be given, that out of it we might each one receive. God's love to us is His love to His Son flowing in a hundred channels. For His sake He makes the wedding-feast, and we are the happy guests who sit at the table. Not for our sakes is this done, but for Jesus' sake, that so it might be all of grace. His perpetual acceptance with God is our acceptance, that nothing legal, nothing whereof we might boast, might be mingled with the work of sovereign grace.

We are "accepted in the Beloved." Do you not love that sweet title? Is it not the highest quality of the acceptance, that it comes through such an One? He is beloved in the highest conceivable degree by the Father, and in this you imitate the great God, for to you also the Lord Jesus is altogether lovely. He is your Beloved as well as God's Beloved, and this is one proof that you are accepted; for all who truly love the Son are approved by the Father. Thus saith the Scripture: "Because He hath set His love upon Me, therefore will I deliver Him: I will set Him on high because He hath known my name." Is Christ your Beloved? Then, as He is the Father's Beloved, you and the Father have evidently come to a sweet agreement; you have come to look at things from the same standpoint as the glorious Jehovah; the Lord and you evidently have a mutual interest in one common person—the incarnate God. Your recognition of Christ as your Beloved is thus a sure proof that you are accepted in the Beloved. See you not this? It is because He is the Father's Beloved that the Father loves you in Him, and because He is your Beloved therefore you have an evidence within yourself that you have come to an agreement with the Father, and so to an acceptance by Him. I delight in being *accepted* all the more because therein I am still further linked with Him who joins God and man in one grand affection.

God's love of His dear Son covers all believers, as a canopy covers all who come beneath it. As a hen covereth her chickens with her wings, so God's love to Christ covers all the children of promise. As the sun shining forth from the gates of the morning gilds all the earth with golden splendour, so this great love of God to the Well-beloved, streaming forth to Him, enlightens all who are in Him. God is so boundlessly pleased with Jesus that in Him He is altogether well pleased with us. Oh, the joy of this blending of our interests with those of the Well-beloved! I scarcely know whither I am borne even by a single word of my precious text.

Let this stand for our preface, and now let us come close to our subject, upon which I do not desire so much to descant myself as to lead you individually to meditate, and personally to feed. I would much rather put the text into your mouths as a sweet fruit from the garden of the Lord, most mellow and ripe, than be judged myself to handle it well. I seek not to exhibit my own skill in words, but I long that you may be refreshed with the marrow and fatness of the choice word. I desire that you may this morning experimentally enjoy the precious drop of honey from the rock Christ Jesus which is contained in the four words—"Accepted in the Beloved." Oh that the Holy Spirit may make you enter into the treasures which they contain!

I. I will begin by treating the text by way of CONTRAST. Brethren and sisters, the grace of God hath made us to be this day "accepted in the Beloved"; but it was not always so. As many of us as have, through grace, believed in Christ are now, to a certainty, at this very moment "accepted in the Beloved"; but in times past it was very different. It is not a matter of question, nor of imagination, nor of sentiment; but a matter of fact, declared by the Holy Ghost Himself, that the Lord hath "made us accepted in the Beloved"; but it was far otherwise a little while ago. What a contrast is our present condition of acceptance to our position under the law through Adam's fall. By actual sin we made ourselves to be the very reverse of accepted, for we were utterly refused. It might have been said of us, "Reprobate silver shall men call them, because God hath rejected them." Our way was contrary to God's way, our thoughts were not His thoughts, our hearts were not according to His heart. Oh, if He had dealt with us then after our sins what must have become of us? At that time we were condemned, "condemned already," because we had not believed on the Son of God. We had no acceptableness before God; He could take no complacency is us; His pure and holy eyes could not look upon us, we were so full of everything that provoked Him to jealousy; but now we are—(oh, let me pronounce it like music!) —"accepted in the Beloved." The criminal is now a child, the enemy is now a friend, the condemned one is now justified. Mark, it is not said that we are "acceptable," though that were a very great thing, but we are actually accepted; it has become not a thing possible that God might accept us, but He has accepted us in Christ. Lay this to your soul, and may it fill you with delight. The Lord has chosen you; He has received you to Himself, and set His love upon you, and His delight is in you now. What a contrast from what you were a season ago in your own consciousness, in your own judgment. Refresh your memories a little. If you passed through the same state of mind as I did, you loathed your very selves in the sight of God; you felt that God must abhor you, for you abhorred yourselves; you saw sin to be exceeding sinful, and that sinful thing was permeating your entire being, saturating your thoughts, putrefying your aims, making you to be corrupt and offensive in the sight of the Most High. I know I felt that if the Lord swept me away with the besom of destruction, and cast me into the lowest hell, I well deserved it. But now that condemnation is no more to be dreaded; we receive not the spirit of bondage, but the spirit of adoption. Lift up your eyes out of the thick darkness, and behold the light. You, who in your own judgment were cast away for ever; you, who thought that the Lord would never be favourable to you, nor blot out your sins, are this day accepted, "accepted in the Beloved." No contrast could be more sharp and clear, and no reflections could be more joyful than this contrast suggests to the heart.

Think, again, of the contrast between what you are now and what you would have been had not grace stepped in. Left out of Christ as we then were, we might at this time have been going from sin to sin, revelling and rioting in it, as so many do: we might at this moment have been sinning with a high hand, finding even in the Sabbath-day a special opportunity for double transgression. In our daring rebellion we might have been crying, "The better the day the better the deed," and so might have shown how completely we had thrown off the yoke of allegiance to the great King. Aye, by this time we might have been dead, as the result of our own sins. The measure of our iniquity might have been full, and we might have been in hell. Be startled, my soul, at this thought, that nothing but infinite long-suffering has kept thee out of the pit that is bottomless, "where their worm dieth not, and their fire is not quenched." But, brothers, we are not in hell, and, what is more, we never shall be, for those iron gates can never close upon a soul that is "accepted in the Beloved," and that is our condition now. We have fled for refuge to the hope set before us, and now no more need we be in terror of the great white throne and the righteous Judge, and the stern sentence, "Depart, ye cursed." Clinging to the cross, and beholding ourselves covered with the righteousness of Christ, we know that we are saved, and, what is far more, we are *accepted*. This blessed fact is true of those who might have been among the damned. Our laments might have been going up to-day amidst the wailings of the wretched who are eternally cast away from hope; and now, instead thereof, we lift the joyful song of praise unto our God, and bless and magnify His name in whom we are accepted this day. Oh, my soul, sing thou thine own song to thy Beloved—

> "Just as thou art—how wondrous fair,
> Lord Jesus, all Thy members are!
> A life divine to them is given—
> A long inheritance in heaven.
>
> "Just as I was I came to Thee,
> An heir of wrath and misery;
> Just as Thou art before the throne,
> I stand in righteousness Thine own.
>
> "Just as Thou art—nor doubt, nor fear,
> Can with Thy spotlessness appear;
> Oh timeless love! as Thee, I'm seen,
> The 'righteousness of God in Him.'"

One more point I cannot quite pass over, and that is, the contrast between what we now are and all we ever could have been in the most favourable circumstances apart from the Beloved. If it had been possible for us out of Christ to have had desires after righteousness, yet those desires would all have run in a wrong direction; we should have had a zeal of God, but not according to knowledge, and so, going about to establish our own righteousness, we should not have submitted ourselves to the righteousness of God. We should have been weaving a righteousness of our own with heavy labour, which would have proved no better when completed than a cobweb that could never conceal our nakedness. At this moment the prayers we offered would never have been received at the throne; the praises we presented would have been all ill savour unto God; all that we could have aimed to accomplish in the matter of good works, had we striven to our utmost, would have been done in wilfulness and pride, and so must necessarily have fallen short of acceptance. We should have heard the voice of the Eternal saying, "Bring no more vain oblations; incense is an abomination unto Me"; for out of Christ our righteousness is as unacceptable as our unrighteousness, and all our attempts to merit acceptance increase our unworthiness. Oh, strive as ye will, ye self-righteous; labour as ye may after a righteousness of your own, what can come of it but confusion? Whence is it that the people labour as in the very fire? This shall they have at the Lord's hands—they shall lie down in sorrow. The bed is shorter than that a man may stretch himself on it, and the covering is narrower than that a man may wrap himself in it. Woe is unto the man who is out of Christ, wherever he may be. In any case the wrath of God abideth on him. But we are not out of Christ, we are not striving in vain, we are not spending our strength for naught, for here is the blessed contrast, we are "accepted in the Beloved."

A touch of the black pencil brings out the bright lights, and therefore I have laid on these shades. Such were some of you, but now ye are washed, now ye are sanctified, now ye are justified, now ye are "accepted in the Beloved." All glory be unto the grace by which we have received this heavenly benefit.

II. Secondly, we will say a little by way of EX- PLANATION, that the text may sink yet deeper into your hearts, and afford you richer enjoyment. Recollect, brethren, that once we were pitied of God as poor, lost, self-destroyed creatures: that was in a degree hopeful. We were chosen of God while in that pitiable condition, and although forlorn, wretched, and ruined, yet were we marked by His electing love —this was still more encouraging. Then came a time of dealing with us, and we were pardoned, our transgressions were put away, we were renewed in the spirit of our minds by the Holy Ghost, and the righteousness of Christ was imputed to us, and at length burst forth the light of this word, "He hath made us accepted in the Beloved." Much went before this, but, oh, what a morning without clouds rose upon us when we knew our acceptance and were assured thereof. Acceptance was the watchword, and had troops of angels met us we should have rejoiced that we were as blest as they.

Understand that this acceptance comes to us entirely as a work of God—"He hath made us accepted in the Beloved." We never made ourselves acceptable, nor could we have done so, but He that made us first in creation, hath now new made us by His grace, and so hath made us accepted in the Beloved.

That this was an act of pure grace there can be no doubt, for the verse runs thus, "Wherein He hath made us accepted in the Beloved"—that is, in His grace. There was no reason in ourselves why we should have been put into Christ, and so accepted; the reason lay in the heart of the Eternal Father Himself. He will have mercy on whom He will have mercy, and by this will we were saved. To the great First Cause we must ever trace the motive for our acceptance. Grace reigns supreme. It is a gracious acceptance of those who but for grace had been rejected. Do notice this, and dwell upon the truth, glorifying God therein. Again, our acceptance is "in the Beloved." It is only as we are in Christ that we are accepted. Let no man steal out of Christ, and then say, "God has accepted me." Nothing of the

kind. If the Lord views you apart from Christ, whoever you may be, you are a thing to be consumed, and not to be accepted. "In the Beloved," that is, as it were, within the gates of the city of refuge. You must abide within that wall of fire of which the cross is the centre, or else you are not accepted. You must remain within the arms of the Well-beloved, living in the very heart of Christ, and then you shall know yourself to be "accepted in the Beloved." For Christ's sake, and because you are a part of Him, you shall be approved of the Father. He has taken you into covenant union, so that you can say with the favoured apostle, "Truly our fellowship is with the Father and with His Son Jesus Christ." Therefore the Father accepts you, because He cannot dissociate you from His Son, nor His Son from you, nor think of Christ without you, nor of you without Christ; hence it is you are "accepted in the Beloved." That explains the words.

The following remarks may make the sense somewhat more transparent. No man, my brethren, can be accepted of God while he is guilty of sin, so that our acceptance in the Beloved involves the fact that our sin at this moment is for ever put away. Covered is our unrighteousness, and therefore from condemnation we are free, and we are accepted. Realize this truth. It does not require any oratory to set it forth; it needs only that your faith should fully apprehend it. Realize that you are forgiven to-day. With your eye upon the wounds of Christ, say unto your soul by the Spirit, "I am without spot or wrinkle in the sight of God; for Christ hath washed me whiter than the driven snow." He has said of His people, "Ye are clean every whit." Rejoice in this. You could not be accepted if He had not made you clean, for the filthy are not accepted of the Lord.

Neither could God accept a man devoid of righteousness. A mere colourless person, whose sin was forgiven, but who had no righteousness, could not be acceptable with Him. I cannot suppose the existence of such a being; but if there were such, he would be like one who was neither cold nor hot, and must be spued out of God's mouth. He that is accepted with God must be positively righteous. Very well, then, if He has made believers "accepted in the Beloved," they that believe in Christ are righteous in the sight of God. Mark you, they are not righteous with a sham righteousness, an imaginary, fictitious righteousness; no, the righteousness which is of faith is the most real righteousness under heaven. The righteousness of works may be questioned, but the righteousness of faith cannot be, for it is the righteousness of God Himself. Now drink that in. Do not let me hold it up, and show you what a draught it is; but drink it up for yourselves. You are righteous in Christ, or else you could not be accepted. Sin is gone, and righteousness is positively yours.

Now to come back again. If we be indeed "accepted in the Beloved," does it not show how close, how real our union with the Beloved must be? Do we even share in Christ's acceptance with God? Then we are one with Him in everything. Here is a father who has no particular interest in such and such a woman, but his son takes to himself that woman to be his wife, and now the loving father says, "That woman is my daughter," and so she is received into his love for his son's sake. He says to her, "You are my dear son's wife; therefore you are my daughter, and dear to me, and welcome to my house at any time." Thus it is with the great God,

He says to us, whom Christ had espoused unto Himself, that we may be His bride in blessed conjugal union for ever and ever. "Come to My heart, My children, for He is My Son, and I love you for His sake; I accept you in Him." Is not that a wonderful union, closer than the marriage bond, which causes us to share in Christ's righteousness, so that the holy God can say to us who are sinful by nature, "You are acceptable to Me because of your connection with My Son"? If a woman of base character were married to the best of men it would not make her acceptable. A father would scarcely know what to do with such a daughter-in-law: we should try and carry out our relationship as far as we could with all kindness, but we could hardly say that such a person brought into our family by marriage would be acceptable to us; but, oh, the Lord sees His people so wrapped up in Christ that He must accept them in Him. If I accept a man, I cannot quarrel with his little finger; if I accept a man, I accept his whole body; and so, since the Father accepts Christ, He accepts every member of His mystical Body. If I am one with Christ, though I be but as it were only the sole of His foot, and exposed oftentimes to the mire of the streets, yet, because the glorious Head is accepted, the meanest member joined in living union to that Head is accepted too. Is not this glorious? Can you get a firm hold of it? Unless you intelligently grasp its full significance you will not heartily enjoy this unspeakable privilege. But if your faith receives and welcomes it, you will not need any further explanation. You are "accepted in the Beloved," and it is clear that there is a blessed union between you and Christ. The acceptance which the Father gives to Christ He gives to you. Now, see if you can measure it. How acceptable is Christ to God? Must it not be an infinite acceptance? for it is an infinite Being infinitely accepting an infinitely holy and well-pleasing One, and then accepting us who are in Him with the self-same acceptance. Oh, how acceptable is every believer to the eternal Father in Christ Jesus!

III. Can we get a step farther? Will the Holy Spirit help us while I say a few words by way of ENLARGEMENT? If we are "accepted in the Beloved," then, first, our persons are accepted: we ourselves are well-pleasing to Him. God looks upon us now with pleasure. Once He said of men that it repented Him that He had made them, but now when He looks at His people He never repents that He made us; He is glad He made us, He takes delight in us. Look at your own children; sometimes they grieve you, but still you are pleased with them; it is a pleasure to have them near you; and if they are long out of your sight you grow anxious about them. They are coming home for their holidays soon; they are glad to return home, and I am sure their mothers are glad at the thought of seeing them again. Our Father is as truly pleased with us: our very persons are accepted of God. He delights in us individually; He thinks of us with joy, and when we are near to Him it gives pleasure to His great heart.

Being ourselves accepted, the right of access to Him is given us. When a person is accepted with God he may come to God when he chooses; he is one of those sheep who may go in and out and find pasture; he is one of those courtiers who may come even to the royal throne and meet with no rebuff. No chamber of our great Father's house is closed against us; no blessing of the covenant is withheld from us; no sweet smile of the Father's face is refused us. He that accepted us gives us access into all blessings. "See, I have accepted thee concerning this thing also." You remember the story of King Ahasuerus and his poor trembling spouse Esther, how she ventured in at peril of her life, for if her royal lord and master did not stretch out the golden sceptre then the guards that stood about the throne would cut her down, the queen royal though she was, for daring to come unbidden into the despot's presence; but to-day, when you and I come to God, we have no fear of that kind, because we are accepted first; He hath already stretched out to us the golden sceptre, and He bids us come boldly. All is well between us and Him. We have access with boldness into this grace wherein we stand.

And, being accepted ourselves, our prayers are also accepted. Children of God, can you sincerely believe this? Do you not sometimes pray as if you were beggars in the street, pleading with unwilling persons to give you a gratuity of coppers? I believe many children of God do so; but when we know we are "accepted in the Beloved" we speak to God with a sweet confidence, expecting Him to answer us. To us it is no surprise that our heavenly Father should hear our prayers. He does it so often and so generously that we expect Him to do so always. It is a way of His to hear the prayers of the Well-beloved. When unaccepted men pray they pray unaccepted prayers, but when accepted men plead with God He says, "In an acceptable time have I heard thee, and in a day of salvation have I succoured thee." When God delights in men He gives them the desires of their hearts. Oh, the splendour of that man's position who is "accepted in the Beloved!" To him the Lord seems to say, "Ask what thou wilt, and it shall be given to thee, not even to the half of My kingdom, but My kingdom itself shall be Thine: Thou shalt sit with Me upon My throne." Oh, the blessedness of being "accepted in the Beloved," because the acceptance makes our prayers to be as sweet incense before the Lord!

It follows, then, as a pleasant sequence, that our gifts are accepted, for those who are accepted with God find a great delight in giving of their substance to the glory of His name. I know that when money is wanted for the church of God, and one of the brethren goes round to collect the offerings, the subjects of the kingdom are wont to say, "Here comes the tax-gatherer again." Yes, that is what the subjects say. Oh, but when the children are about, they cry, "Here is another opportunity of presenting an offering to our Father, a welcome occasion of proving that our love to Him is pure, without greed or grudging." They clap their hands to think that they may come before the Lord with their sacrifices. Their only question is, "Will He accept it? Oh, what would I not give if I did but know that He would accept it!" Many a poor woman will take her two mites, and not more stealthily than joyfully cast them into the treasury, as she says, "Will He really accept them when dropped into the offering-box; will He even know about them?" And some of God's children get schemes into their heads of doing great things for God, but they say, "May I not after all be working for myself? May it not be that pride and vain-glory so leaven my labours that 'the odour of a sweet smell,' like to that 'sacrifice acceptable' which the Philippians presented, will be all a-wanting." Nay, my friends my helpers in every good work, you need not ask that question if He has accepted you, for the accepted man brings an accepted offering. It is wonderful how God sees good things in His people where we cannot see them. He saw in Abijah some good thing towards the Lord God of Israel when perhaps no one else saw it. Mistress Sarah once made a rather naughty speech; yet there was one good word in it. I doubt very much if any one of us would have been quick enough to discern it. Yet the Holy Spirit picked out that one word, and put it into the New Testament to her praise. She spoke unbelievingly as to her bearing a child at her advanced age, though the promise was pronounced that she should bring forth a son. She said "Shall it be, I being old, my lord being old also?" This was a bad speech, but we are somewhat startled to read in the New Testament, "As Sarah also obeyed her husband, calling him lord." If God can find a speck of good in us He will. Then let us try what we can do for Him. Here is a great lump of quartz, but if the Lord can see a grain of gold He will save the quartz for the sake of it. He says, "Destroy it not, for a blessing is in it." I do not mean that the Lord deals thus with all men. It is only for accepted men that He has this kind way of accepting their gifts. Had you seen me, when a young man, and an usher, walking through the street with rolls of drawings from a boys' school, you would have guessed that I considered them of no value and fit only to be consigned to the fire; but I always took a great interest in the drawings of my own boy, and I still think them rather remarkable. You smile, I dare say, but I do so think, and my judgment is as good as yours. I value them because they are his, and I think I see budding genius in every touch, but you do not see it because you are so blind. I see it since love has opened my eyes, God can see in His people's gifts to Him and their works for Him a beauty which no eyes but His can perceive. Oh, if He so treats our poor service what ought we not to do for Him? What zeal, what alacrity should stimulate us! If we are ourselves accepted our sacrifices shall be acceptable. The Almighty will permit us to be called His servants, and we shall find His blessing resting on all that we do. If the tree be good the fruit is good. As is the man so is his strength; and as is his prestige, so is his power. "Accepted in the Beloved" has for its accompaniment "God hath accepted thy works."

IV. We have thus pursued our train of thought in a contrast, an explanation, and an enlargement; let us now indulge in a few REFLECTIONS.

"Accepted in the Beloved." May not each believer talk thus with himself—I have my sorrows and griefs, I have my aches and pains, and weaknesses, but I must not repine, for God accepts me. Ah me! How one can laugh at griefs when this sweet word comes in, "accepted in the Beloved." I may be blind, but I am "accepted in the Beloved": I may be lame, I may be poor, I may be despised, I may be persecuted, I may have much to put up with in many ways, but really these troubles of the flesh count for little or nothing to me since I am "accepted in the Beloved."

I have to mourn over a multitude of infirmities and imperfections, and there is never a day but what when night comes on I have repenting work to do, and feel compelled to fly to the precious blood again for a renewed sense of pardon. Yes, but I am "accepted in the Beloved." Ah me, I have been struggling with this evil and that, and I hope I have got the victory, though I have had many a wound in the battle; yes, but I am "accepted in the Beloved." I have just now been blaming myself for my shortcomings, and mourning, over my many slips and failures: yes, but I am "accepted in the Beloved." I am speaking for you, or at least I am trying to interpret your meditations: I want you to let this blessed fact go down sweetly with you, that whatever may be the trials of life, whatever the burdens that oppress you, whatever the difficulties of the way, whatever the infirmities of the body, whatever the frailties of the mind, yet still, as being "in the Beloved" you are accepted. Oh, will you not be accepted when you stand where golden harps ring out perpetual hallelujahs, where every robe is spotless, and every heart is sinless? Yes, but you will not be a jot more accepted then than you are now, in all this noise, and strife, and turmoil of everyday life, for you are "accepted in the Beloved" now. Is not this present grace in the highest perfection? What more can you have till you behold the unveiled face of infinite love. Drink down that truth, I pray you.

Let a further reflection be added also to the sweetness of your enjoyment. Think of who it is that doth accept you. It is no common person who admits us to His favour: it is the God whose name is Jehovah, the jealous God. "Holy, holy, holy," cry the seraphim unceasingly, and nothing that is defiled can ever enter His palace-gates, nor can His heart endure the thought of iniquity, and yet it is He that hath accepted you. Did your brethren cast you out? Did your friend condemn you? Did your own heart accuse you? Did the devil roar upon you? What matters it, for He hath accepted you. "Who shall lay anything to the charge of God's elect? It is God that justifieth. Who is he that condemneth?" He hath made us "accepted in the Beloved," and if that be so, we need not fear what men can do unto us.

Now, just think again, He has made you "accepted in the Beloved." He, that is, God, has accepted you in Christ. Would you have liked any other way of acceptance one half as well? For my part, I had infinitely rather receive everything through Christ than reach it from myself. Mercy seems so much the sweeter and the better from the fact that it all comes from that dear, pierced hand. If I were this day accepted in myself, I should fear that I might lose my acceptance, for I am a poor, changeable being, but if I am "accepted in the Beloved," then the Beloved will never change, and I always must and shall be accepted, come what may. Is not this a word to die with? We will meet death and face his open jaws with this word, "Accepted in the Beloved." Will not this be a word to rise with amidst the blaze of the great judgment-day? You wake up from your tomb, lift up your eyes, and ere you gaze upon the terrors of that tremendous hour, you say, "I am accepted in the Beloved," what can then fill you with alarm? For ever and ever, as the cycles of eternity revolve, will not this be the core and centre of heaven's supremest bliss, that still we are "accepted in the Beloved"? I hear strange theories nowadays of what may happen to the saints: they tell us the sinners will die out, or be restored, or something else; for they are not content with the Scripture teaching of eternity, but must needs invent strange notions about the punishment of the ungodly. Then they begin to picture new destiny for saints too, and the heaven of our fathers has sad doubts cast on it. I care not for their dreams, for I am "accepted in the Beloved." It matters nothing what all the eternities can reveal: he that is accepted in Christ, and eternally one with Him, has nothing before him at which he need tremble.

My time is gone: I heard the warning bell just now, and so I must forbear to amplify on the many reflections that spontaneously flew out of our text; all fitted to stifle anxious care, to sweeten mortal life, and to set our souls a-longing for the home which is above where so hearty a welcome awaits us.

V. And now I wish to finish with this one PRACTICAL USE. If it be so that we are "accepted in the Beloved," then let us go forth and tell poor sinners how they can be accepted too. Are you, to-day though unconverted, anxious to be found right at last? Listen, friend. If you, want to be accepted, you must accept. "And what," do you ask, "must I accept?" You must accept Christ as the free gift of God; you must accept Christ as God's way of accepting you, for if you get into Christ you are accepted. The guiltiest of the guilty *may be* accepted in Christ; no matter how great and grievous their transgressions may have been, the atoning sacrifice can take all their guilt away, and the perfect righteousness can justify the most heinous sinner before God. You may be accepted. Listen. If you come to Christ now and trust Him you *will be* accepted. Never did one come to Christ to be rejected. You shall not be the first. Try it; and though you came into this house condemned you shall go out accepted, if you come now and hide in those dear wounds of His as doves do hide them in the clefts of the rocks.

Listen again. It is not only that *you may be* accepted; it is rather that *you will be* accepted, *you cannot but be* accepted in Christ: there is no sort of fear nor possibility that you shall come to Christ and be cast out. Christ must change, truth must change, God must change towards His Well-beloved, He must cease to love Him ere he could refrain from loving a soul that is in Him. Guilty as you are, come to Christ this morning. Come, despise not the exhortation, for you must be accepted; it cannot but be that you should be accepted if you come. And you shall be accepted *at once*. If at this moment you are as vile as vile can be, if while I speak you know that you are black as hell's dark night, yet the moment that you come to Christ you are "accepted in the Beloved." Trust Him; trust Him. Have you done so? Your sin is gone; righteousness is imputed; you are saved.

And, then, to close, if you get into Christ you shall be accepted as long as you are in Christ, and as the grace of God will never let you go out of Christ you shall be accepted for ever, "accepted in the Beloved," world without end. If that be the verdict of this day it shall be the verdict of every day till days shall be no more; the hope for you dying, the song for your rising again, the verdict which shall be given out when the great assize shall sit, and you shall be tried for your life for the last time. They that sit in judgment shall say, "Let that man go; he is accepted in the Beloved." If thou believest in Jesus it shall be so; it is so; it shall be so for ever and ever. God bless you all by His good Spirit, for Christ's sake. Amen.

REDEMPTION THROUGH BLOOD, THE GRACIOUS FORGIVENESS OF SINS

"In whom we have redemption through His blood, the forgiveness of sins, according to the riches of His grace."—Ephesians i. 7

READ the chapter, and carefully note how the apostle goes to the back of everything, and commences with those *primeval blessings* which were ours before time began. He dwells on the divine love of old, and the predestination which came out of it; and all that blessed purpose of making us holy and without blame before Him in love, which was comprehended in the covenant of grace. It does us good to get back to these antiquities—to these eternal things. You shake off something of the dust of time, as you no longer walk adown its restless ages; but traverse the glorious eternity, where centuries seem no more than fallen leaves by the way. Thousands of years are less than a drop of a bucket compared with the lifetime of the Almighty. How sublime a thing to climb, in contemplation, to the everlasting God and the eternal council-chamber, and to see the heart of love beating towards the chosen people before all time, and the infinite mind of God devising and purposing their good! This is an exceeding great refreshment, and the wonder is that so few believers dare to ascend this sublime hill of the Lord, there to commune with Him that was, and is, and is to come.

After the apostle had briefly touched upon that subject, he then began to speak of *present blessings* —matters of actual experience; and he commenced by saying, "In whom we have redemption." The grace of the eternal past is a matter of faith; but here is something which is within our grasp and enjoyment. The other we believe; but this we actually and literally receive. "We have redemption through His blood, the forgiveness of sins."

And here let me say what a charming thing it is to deal with experimental divinity; not with theories, but with matters of fact, great facts which are dear to you, because they have been wrought in you, and you have not been merely a delighted spectator of them, but you have been the subject and object of them. "In whom we have redemption." Whether others have it or not, *we* have "redemption through His blood, the forgiveness of sins." We do not hope for it, but we *have* it. We do not merely think so, but we know that we have it. We are redeemed; we are free from bondage; we are forgiven, and are no longer under condemnation.

At this time, as God shall help me, I shall dwell upon the forgiveness of sins. We have not time to plunge into the deeps of the eternal purpose, nor even to dive into the full doctrine of redemption; but, as the swallow with his wing touches the brook, and then is up and away, so must it be with my thoughts at this time—a mere touch of the river of the water of life will be a blessing to myself; and as I cast a little spray over you, I hope it will refresh you also. May the Holy Spirit help our meditation!

I. The first observation, taken distinctly from the text, is this—THAT THE FORGIVENESS OF SINS IS A GRAND BLESSING. The apostle has mentioned it, if you notice, amongst the great things of God—His electing love, His adoption of us by Jesus Christ, His acceptance of us in the Beloved. Side by side with these colossal mercies He puts this one, that we have "the forgiveness of sins according to the riches of His grace." This is a blessing of no mean stature, for it marches with the giants of election and adoption. Let it stand prominently out before us at this time.

What is this "forgiveness of sins?" Too often, in popular talk, it is supposed that the chief and main thought of the forgiven sinner is that he has escaped from hell. Salvation means much more than this; and what it further means is too much kept in the background, but yet I will begin with rescue from punishment; for if sin be pardoned, *the penalty is extinguished.* It would not be possible for God to forgive, and yet to punish. That would be a forgiveness quite unworthy of God. It would, indeed, be no forgiveness at all. We are certain that the everlasting punishment of sin declared in Scripture, will never happen to the man who is forgiven. When transgression is removed the soul stands clear at the bar of God, and there can be no further penalty. "I absolve thee," says the great Judge; and that carries with it weight, so that a man that is forgiven is cleared of the punishment which he must otherwise have borne. "Blessed is he whose transgression is forgiven, whose sin is covered." "There is therefore now no condemnation to them which are in Christ Jesus."

Yet *divine favour restored* is a still brighter result of forgiveness to many. Speaking from my own experience, while I was under conviction of sin I had less apprehension of the punishment of sin than I had of sin itself. I do not know that I very frequently trembled at the thought of hell: I did so whenever it came before my mind; but when I was in the hand of the Holy Ghost, as a Spirit of bondage convincing me of sin, my great trouble was that God was angry with me—properly and rightly so. I mourned that I had offended my Maker, that I had grieved the living God, that I had sinned against His righteous will, and that I could not rejoice in His favour, nor sun myself in His smile. I felt that it was right on the part of the holy God to be displeased with me. I believe that the great joy of forgiveness, to the believer, is that God has taken away His anger from him. That sweet hymn, which we often sing, is a paraphrase of a passage in Isaiah—

"I will praise Thee every day,
Now Thine anger's turned away;
Comfortable thoughts arise
From the bleeding sacrifice."

"Though Thou wast angry with me, Thine anger is turned away, and Thou comfortedst me." Forgiveness means this among men. A person has grieved and wronged me. I feel hurt in my mind about it. When I forgive him, I no longer feel grieved or angry with him: I think of him as aforetime, and we are on good terms. If my forgiveness is genuine—and in God's case it is emphatically so—then there is no resentment left. The offence is as though it had never been committed. I say to the person who did me wrong, "I take a sponge, and I wipe it all off the slate: give me your hand, let us stand as we stood before." The pardon of sin by God is after such a fashion. He blots out the sin as the Oriental erases with his pencil the record made upon his waxen tablet, so that no trace of it remains. He smiles where else He must have frowned; He gives complacent love where else there must have been indignation and wrath. Do you not think that this is the sweetest way of looking at the forgiveness of sins? If you are at this time under legal work, feeling the tortures of a guilty conscience, you will appreciate such a pardon very highly. In the case of the poor penitent prodigal, it was the kiss of his father's lip, it was his restoration to his father's heart, it was the cheering words of his father's love, that constituted to him the sweetest fragrance of the rose of forgiveness. Yes, the Lord Jesus Christ has come, that we poor, guilty ones may be restored to the favour of God, and walk consciously in the light of His countenance, because sin is removed.

This pardon of sin, being of this full and sweet character, involving both the reversal of the penalty of sin, and the ending of the distance that intervened between us and God, brings with it *the removal of much distress and sorrow from the heart!* I do not think that there can be any grief outside of hell that is more terrible to bear than the wounds of conscience. We read that "David's heart smote him"; and, believe me, the heart can smite as with an iron mace, and smite where the bruise is felt intensely. Give me into the power of a roaring lion, but never let me come under the power of an awakened, guilty conscience. Aye, shut me up in a dark dungeon, among all manner of loathsome creatures—snakes and reptiles of all kinds—but, oh, give me not over to my own thoughts when I am consciously guilty before God! This, surely, is the worm that dieth not, and the fire that is not quenched. I do not speak now what I have merely heard of; though, if you will read Mr. Bunyan's "Grace Abounding," you will find a striking account of it there; but I speak of what I have felt in my own soul. No pains of body can rival, for a moment, the agonized feeling of the heart, when the hot irons of conviction burn their way through the soul. When God sets up the conscience, and makes it a target for His arrows, they drink up the life blood of our spirit, till we cry out, and wonder how such anguish can come to a creature so insignificant. Our soul seems too small a cup to contain such an ocean of misery—too narrow a field for so cruel a battle. It is not the Lord that is the author of the misery; but He is giving us up for a while, that we may be filled with our own ways, and learn the bitterness of our own sin. When the Lord comes to us with a forgiving word, these sorrows are gone, like the mists of the morning when the sun arises. We grieve still to think that we have sinned; but that gnawing remorse, that vulture eating up the liver, is smitten with death, and the man breathes hopefully again. Though the penitence remains, the torment is removed from me, when God has forgiven me.

Let me say here, that full forgiveness of sin, consciously enjoyed, will not only lift an enormous weight from off the soul, but *it will breathe into the heart a great joy.* When you know that sin is forgiven, you cannot be sad as before. The thought of perfect pardon, if it does but fill the spirit, will thrust out gloom, and remove apathy. It will make the lame man leap as a hart: he may still be lame, but he will leap as if he were not. And the tongue of the dumb, even though untrained to speech, shall be made to sing concerning free grace and dying love.

When the thoughts are concentrated upon the enjoyment of complete forgiveness, full reception into the divine favour, and the blotting out of sin, then is the heart lifted into the suburbs of heaven. My dear hearers, do you know what I am talking about? Some of you do, blessed be the name of the Lord; but I am afraid that some of you do not; and you never can know the sweetness of mercy until you first have tasted the bitterness of sin. You will never know how grace can heal until you have felt how sin can wound. There is no clothing you till you are stripped; there is no making you alive till you are killed; there is no filling you till you are empty. The Lord filleth the hungry with good things, but the rich He sends empty away. God Himself will never comfort you till you are driven to self-despair; and if you have already come to that, it is a great privilege to me to be allowed to tell you that the fact of forgiveness of sin is not only a doctrine of the creed, but it is a promise of God's word. "I believe in the forgiveness of sins:" this is no mere formula, but a realized fact with me. Removal of the penalty, removal of God's offence against us, the clearing away of all the turbid waters within the heart, and the creation of joy and peace through perfect reconciliation to God—this is a summary account of the forgiveness of sins. It is a blessing vast and rich.

II. And now, secondly, THE FORGIVENESS OF SINS IS BOUND UP WITH REDEMPTION BY BLOOD. Take the text, "In whom we have *redemption through His blood*, the forgiveness of sins." Redemption and forgiveness are so put together, as to look as if they were the same thing. Assuredly they are so interlaced and intertwisted that there is no having the one without the other. Do you ask—"How is it that there should always need to be redemption by blood, in order to the forgiveness of sins?" I call your attention to the expression, "Redemption through His blood." Observe, it is not redemption through His power, it is *through His blood*. It is not redemption through His love, it is through His blood. This is insisted upon emphatically, since in order to the forgiveness of sins it is redemption through His blood, as you have it over and over again in Scripture. "Without shedding of blood is no remission." But they say—they say—that substitution is not just. One said, the other day, that to lay sin upon Christ, and to treat Him as guilty, and let Him die for the unjust, was not just. Yet the objector went on to say that God forgave men freely without any atonement at all. Of this wise critic I would ask—Is that just? Is it just to pass by breaches of the law without a penalty? Why any law at all? and why should men care whether they keep it or break it? It was stated by this critic that God, out of His boundless love, treated the guilty man as if he were innocent. I would ask—if that be right, where is the wrong of God's treating us as innocent because of the righteousness of Christ? I venture to affirm that pardon is needless, if not impossible, upon the theory that the man, though guilty, is treated as if he were not guilty. If all are treated alike, whether guilty or not guilty, why should any one desire pardon? It were easy to answer cavillers, but they really are not worth the answering. It is to me always sufficient if I find a truth taught in Scripture: I ask no more. If I do not understand it, I am not particularly anxious to understand it: if it be in the Scriptures, I believe it. I like those grand, rocky truths of the Bible which I cannot break with the hammer of

my understanding, for on these I lay the foundations of my soul's confidence. Redemption by blood is here linked with forgiveness of sins, and in many other Scriptures we find it plainly stated. *It is so.* Let that stand for a sufficient answer to all objectors.

And *it is so*, if we come to think of it, *because this reflects great honour upon God*. They say, "Let God simply forgive the sin, and have done with it." But where, then, were His justice? "Shall not the Judge of all the earth do right?" He threatened sin with punishment. If He does not execute His threatening, what then? Can we be sure that He will fulfil His promise? If He breaks His word one way, might He not break it another? If the Lord should not execute the penalty which He has threatened to sin, would it not look as if He made a mistake in threatening a penalty at all? Would it not seem as if He had been too severe at the first, and then had to catch Himself up, and revise His own judgments afterwards? And shall that be? Might it not be supposed that, after all, God made much ado about nothing, and that He was really jesting with men when He threatened them with fearful punishment on account of sin? Shall God say, "Yea," and "Nay"? Shall He speak and unspeak? This is according to the folly of man. Sometimes it may even be wisdom in a fallible man to reverse his word, and retract his declaration; but with God this cannot be. It is needful for the vindication of His own justice, His wisdom, and His holiness, that He shall not forego one of His threatenings, any more than one of His promises; and since it is just that sin should be punished, and that, though the sinner should in wondrous mercy be permitted to go free, it is wise and just that Another should step in—God's own Self should step in—and bear for the sinner what is due to the justice of the Most High. The substitution of our Lord in our room and stead is the central doctrine of the gospel, and it greatly glorifies the name of God.

Besides that, beloved, *that sin should not be pardoned without an atonement is for the welfare of the universe.* This world is but a speck compared with the universe of God. We cannot even imagine the multitudes of beings over which the great Lawgiver has rule; and if it could be whispered anywhere in that universe that, on this planet, God tampered with law, set aside justice, or did anything, in fact, to save His own chosen, so that He threw His own threatening behind His back, and disregarded His own solemn ordinance; why, this report would strike at the foundations of the eternal throne! Is God unjust in any case? Then how can He judge the universe? What creatures, then, would fear God, when they knew that He could play fast and loose with justice? It were a calamity even greater than hell itself that sin should go unpunished. The very reins of moral order would be snatched from the hand of the great Charioteer, and I know not what of mischief would happen. Evil would then have mounted to the high throne of God, and would have become supreme throughout His domains. It is for the welfare of the universe, throughout the ages, that in the forgiveness of sins there should be redemption by blood. Let lovers of anarchy cavil at it; but let good men accept the sacrifice of the Son of God with joy as the great establishment of law and justice.

Moreover, *this also is arranged for our comfort and assurance of heart.* I protest before you all that, if I had been anywhere assured, when I was under conviction of sin, that God could forgive me outright without any atonement, it would have yielded no sort of satisfaction to me; for my conscience was sitting in judgment upon myself, and I felt that if I were on the throne of God, I must condemn myself to hell. Even if I could have derived a temporary comfort from the notion of forgiveness apart from atonement, the question would afterwards have come up—how is this just? If God does not punish me, He ought to do so; how can He do otherwise? He must be just, or He is not God. It must be that such sin as mine should bring punishment upon itself. Never, until I understood the great truth of the substitutionary death of Christ, could my conscience get a moment's peace. If an atonement was not necessary for God, it certainly was necessary for me; and it seems to me necessary to every conscience that is fairly instructed as to the absolute certainty that sin involves deserved sorrow, and that every transgression and every iniquity must have its just recompense of reward. It was necessary for the perpetual peace of every enlightened conscience that the glorious atonement should have been provided.

Besides that, the Lord meant to save us in a safe way *for the promotion of our future reverence for the law.* Now, if sin had been blotted out so readily, and nothing more said of it, what effect would that have had on us in the future? I think that everyone who has felt the burden of sin, and has stood at the foot of the cross, and heard the cries of the great Sacrifice, and read God's wrath against sin written in crimson lines upon the blessed and perfect person of the innocent Saviour—every such person feels that sin is an awful thing. You cannot trifle with transgression after a vision of Gethsemane. You cannot laugh at it, and talk about the littleness of its demerit, if you have once stood on Golgotha, and heard the cry, "Eli, Eli, lama sabachthani?" The death of the Son of God upon the cross is the grandest of all moral lessons, because it is a lesson that affects the very soul of the man, and changes his whole idea of sin. The cross straightens him from the desperate twist which sin gave him at the first. The cure of the first Adam's fall is the second Adam's death—the second Adam's grace, which comes to us through His great sacrifice. We love sin till we see that it killed our best Friend, and then we loathe it evermore. I say, again, that if the great Father did forgive you, and said, "There is nothing in it; go your way, it is all over"; you would have lacked that grandest source of sanctified life which now you find in the wounds of Him who has made sin detestable to you, and has made perfect obedience, even unto death, the subject of your soul's admiration. Now you long to be unto the great Father, in your measure, what your great Redeemer was to Him when He magnified the law, and made it honourable. This is no mean benefit.

O beloved friends, I do bless the Lord, at this time, for the forgiveness of sins through redemption by blood. There is something worth preaching in this truth. You can live on it; you can die on it. I am constantly—almost every week—at the deathbeds of our members here; we are so large a church that one or two every week are going home. When we begin to talk about the precious blood of Jesus— the blood of the everlasting covenant, you should see the brightness of dying eyes! I mark the quiet of the departing spirit; and as my dear friends grip my hand, their testimony is unvaryingly, "Jesus is the Rock of our confidence, and all is well."

O Lord Jesus, hold Thou Thy cross before my closing eyes! O blessed Redeemer, what will a man do in death who has not Thy death to be the death of his sin? How can a man live who has never seen Thee lay down Thy life in his stead, "the Just for the unjust to bring us to God"? Whatever others may say, let us repeat our text, with solemn assurance, "In whom we have redemption through His blood, the forgiveness of sins."

III. But now, thirdly—and the text is very clear upon this, as upon the other two points—THE FORGIVENESS OF SINS IS STILL A MATTER OF GRACE, AND OF RICH GRACE. "We have redemption through His blood, the forgiveness of sins, *according to the riches of His grace.*"

I admit that the forgiveness of sins, on God's part, is a matter of justice, now that the redemption by blood has been completed. The man believes; the man confesses his sin; and it is written, "If we confess our sins, He is faithful and just to forgive us our sins." The sacrifice is so great that it justly puts away the sin, and it is righteously forgiven. But observe this: the act of God in forgiving is not one atom the less gracious, because, in His infinite wisdom, He has so contrived that it is unquestionably just. If any make this assertion, they will be called upon to prove it; and they can prove it.

Pardon is the more gracious to us that it does not come to us in an unrighteous way. We see God's great prudence and wisdom in planning the method by which He may "be just, and the Justifier of him that believeth." Those thoughts and plans on God's part are all tokens of great love to us. Beloved, it is only by grace that we are justified; yet that this grace is exercised in a way of justice causes the grace to be not less, but even manifestly more gracious.

The death of Christ, the redemption by blood, instead of veiling the grace of God, only manifests it. Put the thing before your own minds. Suppose that somebody has offended you, and you say, "Think no more of it; it is all forgiven." Very well: that is kind of you, and commendable. It shows the graciousness of your character. But suppose, on the other hand, you were in office as a judge, and felt compelled to say, "I am willing to forgive you, but your offence has resulted in such and such great mischiefs, and all these things have to be cleared away. I will tell you what I will do; I will clear them away myself. I will bear the result of your sin in order that my pardon may be seen to be most sure and full. I will pay the debt in which you have involved yourself. I will go to the prison to which you ought to go, as the consequence of what you have done. I will suffer the effect of your wrongdoing instead of condemning you to suffer it." Well, now, the forgiveness that cost you so much would manifest your graciousness much more than that which costs you nothing beyond a kind will, and a tender heart. Oh, if it be so, that God, the Divine Ruler, the Judge of all the earth, says to guilty man, "I will pardon you, but it is imperative that My law be carried out; and this cannot be done except by the death of My dear Son, who is one with Me, who is very God of very God, who Himself wills to stand in your stead, and vindicate My justice, by suffering the penalty due to you" —then I say that the grace of God is a thousandfold more clearly shown than by the free forgiveness which "modern thought" pleads for! Pardon which has cost God more than it cost Him to make all worlds—which has cost Him more than to manage all the empires of His providence—which has cost Him His only-begotten Son, and has cost that only-begotten Son a life of sorrow and a death of unutterable and immeasurable anguish—I say that this pardon is pre-eminently gracious. Love is more displayed in this, infinitely more, than by a mere word and a wave of the hand, which would dismiss the sinner, without any attempt at an atoning sacrifice.

Besides, beloved, be this always remembered, that it is in the application of redemption, and the personal pardon of any sinner, through the blood of Jesus, that the grace of God is best seen by that sinner. To each one pardon through the Lord Jesus comes, not only according to grace, but "according to the riches of His grace." I can understand that God should forgive *you*, all of you. I could hear it with full belief, and it would not astonish me. But that He should pardon *me*—that I should have the forgiveness of sins, and redemption by blood—that does astonish me. And I believe that any person, under a sense of sin, sees more of the grace of God in his own salvation than in the salvation of anybody else. He may be quite conscious that he has never been a thief, or a drunkard, or a murderer; and yet, when he comes to look at it, he may see reasons why the pardon of sin in his case should be more remarkable than even in the case of a drunkard, or a thief, or a murderer. There may be elements in his own case which may make him seem to have sinned even more grievously than open transgressors, because he transgressed against greater light, with less temptation thereto, and with a direr presumption of rebellion against the Most High. That Jesus died, is unutterable grace; but that He loved me, and gave Himself for me, this is overwhelming grace, and makes the heir of heaven say with emphasis, Blessed be God that, in Jesus, I have redemption through His blood, the forgiveness of sins, according to the riches of His grace!

Do you not feel at this time, you that have been pardoned, that nothing but the riches of God's grace could ever have pardoned you? No scanty grace could have provided an atonement equal to your iniquities. Poverty of grace would have left you ruined by your debt of sin. Riches of grace would have left you ruined by your debt of sin. Riches of grace were wanted, and riches of grace were forthcoming in redemption by blood, and in the full, perfect, irreversible forgiveness which God gave you in the day when you believed on Jesus Christ your Saviour. Oh, that the Holy Spirit would help you to sing of the grace of God to-day and every day!

IV. Thus far have I brought you, then, in three remarks. Kindly follow me in the fourth one, upon which I will not be long.

Fourthly, THIS FORGIVENESS OF SINS IS ENJOYED BY US NOW. "In whom we have!"—*we have*—"redemption through His blood, the forgiveness of sins, according to the riches of His grace." I remember the astonishment with which I sat in a ministers' meeting, and heard one, who professed to be a preacher of the gospel, assert that he did not think that any one of us could be sure that he was forgiven. I ventured at once to say that I was sure; and I was pleased, but by no means surprised, to find that others dared to say the same. I hope I have hundreds before me who enjoy the same assurance.

Brethren, if there be no consciousness of the forgiveness of sins possible, *how can there be any rest for the conscience?* Yet Jesus says, "Come unto Me, all ye that labour and are heavy laden, and I will give you rest." What rest is possible to the condemned? Can you go to bed to-night with your sins unforgiven? Some of you may have the foolhardiness to do that, but I would not dare to do it. See where you are. Within a moment you may be dead. Within that moment you will be in hell, past all hope. In a single instant you may be eternally lost: can you endure the thought? Our breath has but to stop, or the heart to cease beating, and instantly life is over. How can you be at peace, while sin is unforgiven? Unless sin had made men mad, they would never rest till they were cleared from their sins. There cannot be any true rest without a consciousness of forgiveness. Yet that rest is promised; therefore the present enjoyment of an assurance of forgiveness must be possible.

And, next, *where could there ever be that great love in the hearts of m n and women which we read of in Scripture?* She that washed the Saviour's feet with her tears, and wiped them with the hairs of her head—would she have done so if she had not known that she was forgiven? She loved much, because she had had much forgiven her. And the stimulus, the zeal, the fervour that spurs on a man in his service and suffering for the Lord Jesus, must arise out of the consciousness that the Lord has done great things for him, and the conclusion that therefore he must do great things for his Lord. Surely, you have robbed Christianity of its highest moral force, if you have denied the possibility of knowing that you are pardoned.

Moreover, *where is there any testimony of the power of grace?* We that come and preach to you may be liars unto you, if we ourselves have never tasted and handled pardoning grace. We do, at any rate, but retail to you a second-hand gospel, which we have never tested and proved for ourselves. If I did not know, in my very soul, that the blood of Jesus Christ His Son cleanseth us from all sin, how could I dare to face you with the gospel message? I have not impudence enough to tell you of what might be, or might not be, about which I am uncertain myself. God grant me grace to break stones, or sweep chimneys, sooner than come and tell you a cunningly-devised fable, or a tale about which I have no assured certainty, derived from personal knowledge! Could I say to you, "I dare say there is bread, but I myself am hungry, I have never eaten a mouthful of the provision which I offer you"? Think of my saying to one perishing of thirst, "There is living water flowing from the rock; but personally I am thirsty." You might say to me at once, "Then go home to your house, and next time you appear, be sure of the truth of what you tell us. If *you* do not believe it, how should we believe it?" Beloved, there are thousands, there are tens of thousands, on earth still who know that the Son of God has power on earth to forgive sins; and there are myriads in heaven who passed to their felicity confident that they had been forgiven, and they sang on earth the same song that they sing in heaven, "Worthy is the Lamb that was slain." They have washed their robes and made them white in the blood of the Lamb. They know it, they have no doubt about it. Many of us know it here, and rejoice therein at this moment.

Dear friend, what would you give to have this assurance? Thou mayest have it—"Believe on the Lord Jesus Christ, and thou shalt be saved." "He that believeth and is baptized shall be saved." Whoso believeth in Him is justified from all sin. "He that believeth in Him hath everlasting life." Oh, that God's grace may lead you to cast away all other confidences, and to lay your guilty spirit down at Jesus' feet! Then shall you go your way rejoicing that you also, with us, can say, "In whom we have redemption through His blood, the forgiveness of sins."

V. Fifthly—and this is only a brief head; but it is a point that must not be left out—THE FORGIVENESS OF SINS BINDS US TO OUR LORD JESUS CHRIST. Let us read the text again. "*In whom* we have redemption through *His* blood." We have nothing apart from Jesus. Every blessing of the covenant binds us to Christ. Covenant gifts are so many golden chains to fasten the soul of the believer to His Lord. Our wealth of mercy is all in Christ. There is nothing good outside of Christ. When are we pardoned, brethren? When have we forgiveness? Why, when we are in Him, "*in whom* we have redemption through His blood, the forgiveness of sins." O son of Adam, living without Jesus, hear and take warning! So long as thou art out of Christ, thou must bear thine own burden till it crush thee to the dust; but as soon as thou hast touched the hem of His garment, there is a link of connection; and if thou canst rise from that to holding Him by the feet, the union is closer; and if thou canst from that become like Simeon, who took Him up in his arms, then mayest thou cry, "Mine eyes have seen Thy salvation." When thou hast Christ to the full, thou hast grace to the full. It is as you are in Christ—in connection and communion with Christ—that you receive the pardon of sin, for all the pardon is in Him. Do you see that?

"*In whom* we have redemption through His blood, the forgiveness of sins." The forgiveness is not so much in His office, and in His work, as in Himself. When thou gettest Christ, thou hast redemption; for He is redemption. When thou gettest Christ, thou hast forgiveness of sins; for He is the propitiation for our sins. He has put the sin away by the sacrifice of Himself. Get Christ, and thou hast the proof, the evidence, the sum, the substance of perfect pardon. If thou acceptest the Beloved, thou art "accepted in the Beloved." When thou art in Him, then thou art forgiven; but thy forgiveness is alone in Him. In Him thou hast redemption: out of Him thou art in bondage.

Beloved, every day, as we go afresh to God for a sense of pardon, let us know that we can never get it except as we come still viewing Jesus. I notice that some believers, when they get rather dull and cold, begin the work of self-examination. This may appear very proper, but it is dreary work. I do not believe,

dear friends, if you are very poor, that you will ever get rich by looking through all your empty cupboards. If it is very cold, and you have no coals in the cellar, you will not become warm by going into the cellar, and seeing that there is nothing below but an empty coal-hole. No, no; if our graces are to be revived, we must begin with a renewed consciousness of pardon through the precious blood; and the only way to get that sense of pardon is to go to the cross again, even as we went at the first. I sometimes wonder that you do not get tired of my preaching, because I do nothing but hammer away on this one nail. I have driven it in up to the head, and I have gone round to the other side to clinch it; but still I keep at it. With me it is, year after year, "None but Jesus! None but Jesus!" Oh, you great saints, if you have outgrown the need of a sinner's trust in the Lord Jesus, you have outgrown your sins, but you have also outgrown your grace, and your saintship has ruined you! He that has the mind of Christ within him must still come to his Lord, just as he came at the first.

I frankly confess that still I cry to my Lord Jesus—

"Nothing in my hand I bring,"
Simply to Thy cross I cling."

Still, to this day, I have no redemption in myself, but only in Jesus. I am not an inch forwarder as to the ground of my trust. Is it not so with you? Do we not still say of Jesus—"In whom we have redemption through His blood"? To this day we find no reason for forgiveness in ourselves. The precious blood is still our one plea. Lost and condemned are we apart from the one offering of our Great High Priest. But cleansed and justified are we in Him.

"Oh! how sweet to view the flowing
Of His sin-atoning blood,
With divine assurance knowing,
He has made my peace with God!"

You know the story of the poor bricklayer, who fell from a scaffold, and when they took him up, he was so much injured that they fetched a minister to him, who, stooping over him, said, "My dear man, you have a very short time to live. I entreat you to make your peace with God." To the surprise of the minister, the man opened his eyes, and said, "Make my peace with God, sir? It was made for me nearly nineteen hundred years ago, upon the cross of Calvary, by Him that loved me, and gave Himself for me." Oh, the joy which this creates in the heart! Yes, it is in Jesus that the peace is made—effectually made, made for you, made for all believers. In Jesus is perfect redemption. In Jesus pardon is provided, proclaimed, presented, and sealed upon the conscience. Go and live on Jesus; live with Jesus; live in Jesus; never go away from Jesus; and may He be dearer to you every day of your lives! Blessed be His adorable name! Amen, and Amen.

THE MIGHTY POWER WHICH CREATES AND SUSTAINS FAITH

"The exceeding greatness of His power to us-ward who believe, according to the working of His mighty power, which He wrought in Christ, when He raised Him from the dead, and set Him at His own right hand in the heavenly places, far above all principality, and power, and might, and dominion, and every name that is named, not only in this world, but also in that which is to come: and hath put all things under His feet, and gave Him to be the Head over all things to the church, which is His body, the fulness of Him that filleth all in all."—Ephesians i. 19-23.

TO believe on the Lord Jesus Christ with all our heart is one of the simplest things imaginable. To trust Christ, to depend upon His power and faithfulness, is such a childlike act that one sees no extraordinary difficulty in it. Yet, to bring the human mind to exercise simple faith in Jesus is a work of the most astounding power. To bring down the pride of man, to subjugate his will and to captivate his passions, so that he shall cheerfully accept that which God presents to him in the person of Christ Jesus, is a labour worthy of a God. How strangely vile are they who cannot be brought to know their own mercies, except by an omnipotent power. The blessed Spirit of God is always the secret Author of faith; it is not of ourselves, it is the gift of God. Our text twice over uses the strongest words which could be employed to set forth the Almighty power exhibited in bringing a soul to believe in Jesus, and in bringing that believing soul onward till it ascends to heaven. You will carefully notice we have first of all this expression, "The exceeding greatness of His power;" and then we have on the other side of the word "Believe," lest it should escape anyhow from the sacred barrier, these words, "According to the working of His mighty power." Now, the first expression is a very amazing one. It might be read thus: "The super-excellent, sublime, overcoming, or triumphing greatness of His power;" and the other is even more singular: it is a Hebrew mode of speech forced to do duty in the Greek tongue: "The effectual working of the might of His strength:" or "The energy of the force of His power,"—some such strong expression as that. As if the apostle was not content to say, "You believe through the power of God," nor "through the greatness of that power," but "through the *exceeding* greatness of His power," and not satisfied with declaring that the salvation of man is the fruit of God's might, he must needs put it, His mighty power: nay, as if that were not enough, he writes, the energy, the efficacious activity of the power of that might. No amount of straining at the passage can ever get rid of the grand doctrine which it contains, namely, that the bringing of a soul to simple faith in Jesus, and the maintenance of that soul in the life of faith, displays an exercise of omnipotence such as God alone could put forth.

Nor need we, dear friends, be at all surprised at this, when we recollect what the work of salvation really is. Be it never forgotten by us that the salvation of a soul is *a creation*. Now, no man has ever been able to create a fly, nor even a single molecule of matter. Man knows how to fashion created substance into divers forms; but to create the minutest atom, is utterly beyond his might. Jehovah alone creates. "All things were created by Him and for Him." No human or angelic power can intrude upon this glorious province of divine power. Creation is God's own domain. Now, in every Christian there is an absolute creation—"Created anew in Christ Jesus." "The new man, after God, is created in righteousness." Regeneration is not the reforming of principles which were there before, but the implantation of a something which had no existence; it is the putting into a man of a new thing called the Spirit, the new man—the creation not of a soul, but of a principle higher still—as much higher than the soul, as the soul is higher than the body. Since the life and principle created are the most glorious of all God's works, being in fact a part of the divine nature itself, I may say most boldly, that in the bringing of any man to believe in Christ, there is as true and proper a manifestation of creating power, as when God made the heavens and the earth.

Further than this, there is more than creation— there is *destruction* No man can destroy anything. Since the world began, not a single particle of matter has ever been annihilated. You may cast matter into the depths of the sea, but there it is; it still exists. Cast it into the fire, and the fire consumes it; but either in the ash or in the smoke, every atom survives. Fire does not destroy a single particle. There is as much matter in the world now as when God first spoke it out of nothing. It is as great an exercise of divinity to destroy as it is to create.

> "Know that the Lord is God alone—
> He can create *and He destroy*."

In the regeneration of every soul there is a destruction as well as a creation. The old man has to be destroyed —the stony heart has to be taken away out of our flesh; and though this is not done in all of us—nay, nor in any of us completely—yet the day shall come when sin shall be utterly destroyed, both root and branch, and all evil principles shall be torn up by the roots, and, like our sins, they shall cease to be, so that if they were searched for they could not be found. When the morning stars sang together because a world was made, creation was their one theme. God made the world out of nothing. That was an easy task, compared with making a new heart and a right spirit, for "nothing" at least could not oppose God: "nothing" could not stand out against Him; but here, in salvation, God had to deal with an opposing something which he has to fight with and to destroy; and when that has been reduced and overcome, then comes in the creating power by which we are made new creatures in Christ Jesus; so that it is a double miracle, something more than creation: it is creation and destruction combined.

The work of salvation is most truly a *transformation*. "Be ye transformed by the renewing of your mind." You who have been made anew in Christ Jesus, know in your own hearts how great that transformation is. The wolf, with all its bloodthirsty tendencies, feeds quietly with all the amiable gentleness of the lamb; the lion eats straw like the ox; the desert becomes a garden, and the dry land springs of water; nay, what is more wonderful still, stones of the brook become children unto Abraham. The Lord takes the man who is like the leopard, covered with spots, and cleanses him till he is whiter than snow. He takes the Ethiopian, black as night, and doth but touch him with the matchless blood of Jesus, and he becomes altogether fair and lovely. None of the fanciful transformations of which Ovid sang of old, could ever rival the matchless work of God when he displays His power upon the human mind. Oh, what a difference between a sinner and a saint, between "dead in trespasses and sins," and quickened by divine grace! If God should speak to Niagara, and bid its floods in their tremendous leap suddenly stand still, that were a trifling demonstration of power compared with the staying of a desperate human will. If He should suddenly speak to the broad Atlantic, and bid it be wrapped in flames, we should not even then see such a manifestation of His greatness as when He commands the human heart, and makes it submissive to His love.

Remember, too, as if this were not enough, that the conversion of a soul is constantly compared to *quickening*—the quickening of the dead. How great the miracle when the dry bones in Ezekiel's vision suddenly became a great army! greater still is the transcendant work of might when dead souls are quickened, and made to serve the living God. Indeed it is not only the first act of conversion which displays divine power, but the whole of the Christian's career, until he comes to perfection, is a clear display of the same. The spiritual life may be likened unto *the burning* bush which Moses saw in Horeb; it burnt, but it was not consumed. Such is the Christian—like a bush, he is most fitting fuel for the flame; yet the flame does not hurt him. It kindles about him, but he is not destroyed. Or the Christian life may be likened to *walking upon water*. As Peter trod the waves and did not sink so long as his faith looked to Jesus, so the believer every day, in every footstep that he takes, is a living miracle. Faith, too, in its life may be compared to *flying*—"They shall mount up with wings as eagles." "I bear you as upon eagles' wings." The believer every day takes venturesome flights into the atmosphere of heaven, rises above the world, leaves its cares and its wants beneath his feet, and that too with no other wings but those of faith and love. Herein is a continued and splendid miracle of the divine power.

But to come to our text— laying it down, then, as being most certain that the work of the conversion and sanctification of a believer is an amazing display of divine might, we have in the text given to us a most singular analogy. The apostle declares to us by the Holy Ghost that the very same power which raised Jesus Christ from the dead and exalted Him to the highest heaven is seen in the conversion and preservation of every individual believer.

Now, we shall first *notice the analogy;* secondly, we shall *consider the reason of it;* and thirdly, we shall observe the *inferences which come from it.*

I. First of all, we shall consider THE ANALOGY WHICH THE APOSTLE HERE POINTS OUT.

Conceive that you hold a great pair of golden compasses. You are to put one foot of the compass here upon the grave of Christ; you are to open those compasses till you reach Christ ascending up into heaven. Widen them again, and again, and again, till you put down the other foot of the compass where Christ is Head over all things to the Church, which is His fulness. Now, can you imagine such a stretch as that? You have to conceive of the power by which the dead body of Christ is brought to all that preeminence of honour, and then to remember that just such power is seen in you if you are a believer.

In examining the wonderful picture before us, we begin with Christ in the grave, by noticing that it was in Christ's case *a real death.* Those loving hands have taken Him down from the cross; those weeping eyes have let fall hallowed drops upon His face. Tenderly have the women wrapped Him about with spices and fine linen, and now He is about to be put into the tomb. He is assuredly dead. The pericardium of the heart has been pierced; blood and water have both freely flowed. Lift up the pierced hand and it falls at once to His side. The lids of yon eyes, so red with weeping, do but cover eyes glazed with death. The foot has no power of motion. Take up the corpse, ye loving bearers, carry it and put it into the tomb—this is no trance, but a most certain death. So is it with us; by nature we are really dead. We were dead in trespasses and sins. Try to stir the natural man to spiritual action, and you cannot do it. Lift up his hand to good works, he has no power to perform them. Try to make the feet run in the ways of righteousness; they will not move an inch. The fact is that *the heart* is dead. The living pulse of spiritual life which was in our parent Adam has long ago ceased. Neither can the eye perceive any beauty in Immanuel, nor can the nostril discover the fragrance of the Lord's sweet spices, nor can the ear hear the voice of the Beloved. The man is absolutely and entirely dead as to anything like spiritual life. There he lays in the grave of his corruption, and must lay there and rot too, unless divine grace shall interpose.

In Christ's case, He was not only dead, but as the text tells us, He was *among the dead.* "He hath raised up Jesus Christ *from the dead.*" Do notice that. He lay for some time sleeping among those who dwelt in the tomb—among the dead. Three days and nights He is a denizen of the lonely shades; He was numbered among the victims of death's dart. "He made His grave with the wicked, and with the rich in His death." Such were some of us—we were among the dead—and "were by nature the children of wrath," even as others. In the case of some of us, our outward life was just that of other ungodly men. Were they drunkards? so were we. Were they immoral? so were we. Did they love the delights of the flesh? so did we. Did they follow the desires of the mind? so did we. Were they hard-hearted, and impenitent, and unbelieving? so were we. Whatever may be said of any ungodly man, may be said of at least some of those whom God has quickened by His divine power. We, like Jesus, were reckoned among the dead. If you had seen His corpse, you would have discovered no difference between it and the body of another, save only that He saw no corruption. Dear brethren, in this our case is lower than that of our Lord, for we did see corruption; the old man is "'corrupt' according to the deceitful lusts." Yea, more, we were "children that are corrupters," and in nothing did we differ from others, save that the Lord had predestinated that no bands of death should hold us for ever, for He was determined to save and to bring us to His right hand.

Come with me again to the new tomb in the garden

Will that sleeper ever rise? Will that hallowed tomb ever be burst? No, never while time and eternity shall last, unless God shall interfere. Here comes a *heavenly messenger*. His face is like lightning, and his raiment white as snow; and for fear of him the keepers do quake and become as dead men. So, when the time comes, in God's great power, He sends His messenger: it is no angelic spirit whose face is like lightning, but it is some humble minister of Christ, who, nevertheless, is clothed with power. He hath in his mouth a sharp two-edged sword, and when he speaks of Christ, for fear of Him sins tremble, and the prejudices and enmities of men's hearts become as dead men. The divine power is seen all the more in the fact that the messenger in the second case is an earthen vessel, a poor creature of flesh and blood. There is a divine mandate for our resurrection, as much as for that of Jesus Christ.

There came with that messenger *a mysterious life*. You cannot see it, but inside that tomb a spirit has fallen upon those once bleeding limbs, and entered that lifeless corpse; the eye shall soon see the light, for the hands are already unwinding the napkin from the brow; the cerements are unbound, one by one; the feet are free, and the whole frame is clear of every incumbrance. No one saw the life come back. If any one had watched that corpse, they could not have seen the vital spark of heavenly flame return to its proper altar. No, it was a mysterious thing. Ah! there was a time with us when the messenger of God came, but *he* could not quicken us; he could only make the keepers shake and tremble; but a myterious life from God the Holy Ghost fell into our souls, and we were as we never were before. We trembled with a new fear, rejoiced with a new joy, believed with a fresh confidence, and hoped with a divine hope. We lived! And, oh! can we ever forget the moment when first we began to live unto God? Divine Spirit, Thou didst it. Let all the glory be unto Thy name.

Then came an *earthquake*, by which the stone was rolled away, showing that the power put forth was enough to shake the earth, and to make all the elements obedient. Surely when God shakes but common dust and clay, and rock, and stone, we wonder, and men stand in awe; but when He rends the harder marble of our hearts, and moves the grosser dust and heavier earth of our spirits, there is reason to praise and bless His name.

The stone being removed, *forth came the Saviour*. He was free; *raised up no more to die ;* He stood erect, beheld by His followers, who, alas! did not know Him. And even so we, when the divine life has come, and the divine energy has burst our tomb, come forth to a new life—no more to die; then men of the world know us not, because they knew *Him* not; they misunderstand our motives, they misrepresent our actions, they contort our words, because now we have a life of which they are not the subjects, and have come into a resurrection-state to which they are utter strangers.

You see the parallel holds. We, too, in the same manner as Christ was raised from the dead, have been made to live in newness of life, even as the Master Himself said, "As the Father raiseth up the dead, and quickeneth them; even so the Son quickeneth whom He will."

Please to note here, dearly beloved friends, that in the resurrection of Christ, as in our salvation, there was put forth nothing short of a *divine power*. It was not angelic or archangelic, much less was it human. What shall we say of those who think that conversion is wrought by the free will of man—who ascribe man's salvation to his own betterness of disposition, or to his willingness to accept that which God presents to him? Beloved, when we shall see the dead in the graves rise therefrom by their own power, then expect to see ungodly sinners turn to Christ. It is not the ministry, it is not the word preached, nor the word heard in itself; all the power proceeds from the Holy Ghost.

Observe again, that this power was *irresistible*. All the soldiers and the high priests could not keep the body of Christ in the tomb. Death himself could not hold Christ in his bonds. When the life-pangs first began to move in Jesus, He could no longer be holden of death. Then was death swallowed up in victory. The Father brought forth His begotten Son, and said, "Let all the angels of God worship Him." He was the first begotten from the dead. Irresistible is the power put forth, too, in the Christian. No sin, no corruption, no temptation, no devils in hell, nor sinners upon earth can ever stay the hand of God's grace when it intends to convert a man. If God says, "Thou shalt," man shall not say, "I will not," or, if he does, as the trees of the wood before the hurricane are torn up by the roots, so shall the human will give place to the irresistible power of grace.

Observe, too, that the power which raised Christ from the dead was *glorious*. It reflected great honour upon God and brought great dismay upon the hosts of evil. So there is great glory to God in the conversion of every sinner.

Lastly, it was *everlasting power*. "Christ being raised from the dead dieth no more; death hath no more dominion over Him." So we, being raised from the dead, go not back to our dead works nor to our old corruptions, but we live unto God. Because He lives we live also, for we are dead and our life is hid with Christ in God. The parallel will hold in every point, however minute. "Like as Christ was raised up from the dead by the glory of the Father, even so we also should walk in newness of life."

You see I have not stretched the compasses halfway yet. We have only proceeded so far as to see Christ raised from the dead; but the power exhibited in the Christian goes farther than this—it goes onward to the ASCENSION. If you will carefully read the story of the ascension, you will notice first that Christ's ascension was *contrary to nature*. How should the body of a man without any means be borne upward into the air? "While He blessed them He was taken out of their sight." So the Christian's rising above the world, His breathing another atmosphere, is clean contrary to nature. How would you wonder if you saw a man suddenly rise up into the sky? Wonder more when you see a Christian rise above temptation, worldliness, and sin; when you discover him forsaking those things which once were his delight, and mounting towards heaven.

You will observe again, that the disciples *could not long see the rising Saviour*. "A cloud received Him out of their sight." So in our case, too, if we rise as we should rise, if the Spirit of God worketh in us all the good pleasure of His will, men will soon lose sight of us. They will not understand us; they will be certain to run hither and thither, wondering at this and marvelling at that; they will call us mad, fanatical, wild and enthusiastic, and I know not what. And we, on our part, must not wonder at it, for now we look down and wonder at them as much as they wonder at us. They think it strange that we should be looking for unseen things, and hoping for that which we see not. We, on the other hand, look down upon them, and wonder how it is that they can heap together things of clay, and find a living joy in dying things, and fix eternal hopes on shadows that are soon—so soon—to melt away for ever.

Jesus Christ continued to ascend by that same divine power, until He had reached the seat of heaven above; He was gone, really gone from earth altogether. Such is the Christian's life. He continues to ascend, the Lord makes him dead to the world, and the carnal multitude know him no more. Where his treasure is, his heart is also. He is risen with Christ, and His affection is set on things above, not on things on the earth.

See, beloved, we have stretched our compass somewhat wide now, when we say that there is as much divine power seen in raising the Christian above the world, as in raising Christ from the grave into heaven. But that is not all. When the Master had come to heaven, we are told in the text, that He was made *to sit down at the right hand of God*. Sitting at the right hand implies *honour, pleasure,* and *power*. Conceive the change! "He was despised and rejected of men; a man of sorrows, and acquainted with grief." They spat in His face and bowed the knee, saying, "Hail, King of the Jews." He hath sat down at the right hand of the Majesty on high. He was full of misery: "My soul is exceeding sorrowful, even unto death," said He. The ploughers made deep furrows upon His back, and His visage was more marred than that of any man. But now His joy is full; He is at the right hand of God, where there are pleasures for evermore. He was a worm and no man—the despised of the people. "All they that see me laugh Me to scorn." They shake the head; they thrust out the lip, saying, "He trusted in God that He would deliver Him; let Him deliver Him, seeing He delighteth in Him." But see Him now! He hath sat down for ever at the right hand of God, even the Father. Note the change from depths of reproach to heights of glory; from fearful deeps of sorrow to glorious summits of bliss; from weakness, shame, and suffering, to strength, and majesty, and dominion, and glory. Such is the change in the Christian—just such a change. You, too, what were you? Were you worthy to have been cast upon a dunghill? Nay, scarcely fit for that; you were like salt which had lost its savour, neither fit for the land nor yet for the dunghill, and God and man might have cast you out; you were utterly worthless and fit for nought. As for suffering, ah, how were your bones broken by convictions of sin! The sorrows of death compassed you, and the pains of hell gat hold upon you, for the arrows of God stuck fast in your loins, and the sword of God pierced to the dividing asunder of your soul and spirit. As for power, what power had you? You could not lift a finger; you could not pray; you could not believe; and yet, where are you now? Why, if you know where you are, you are this day as a believer sitting down at the right hand of God—God's beloved one, ministered unto of angels—God's son, endowed with power and made to sit and reign together with the Lord Jesus Christ. All that sitting at the right hand of God can mean in respect to the man Christ Jesus, it means in respect to every believer. For the apostle Paul writes concerning man in Christ Jesus, "What is man, that thou art mindful of him? or the son of man, that thou visitest him? Thou madest him a little lower than the angels; thou crownedst him with glory and honour,

and didst set him over the works of thy hands: thou hast put all things in subjection under his feet. For in that he put all in subjection under him, he left nothing that is not put under him. But now we see not yet all things put under him. But we see Jesus, who was made a little lower than the angels for the suffering of death, crowned with glory and honour." At the right hand of God is the believer's place at this very day. May an act of faith give you a sweet enjoyment of it.

But note next, that Christ was not only put at God's right hand, but He had a complete triumph given—*far above all principalities and powers*, that neither good angels have eminence compared with Him, nor evil angels any power in contrast with Him. It is not only said that He was above them, but *far* above them. And so is the believer. As for evil angels, the Lord shall tread Satan under your feet shortly; as for holy angels, "Are they not all ministering spirits, sent forth to minister for them that shall be heirs of salvation?" so that we, in the person of our Lord, are far above all principalities and powers.

You will not fail to observe that He has also universal dominion. Follow the passage—"*And hath put all things under His feet.*" And so hath the Lord put all things under His people's feet. Their sins and corruptions, their sorrows and afflictions, this world and the world to come, are all made subject unto us, when He makes us kings and priests, that we may reign for ever. Nay, as if this were not enough, Christ is then honoured with a gracious Headship. He is made to be Head over all things to His Church, and He is made the fulness of that Church, for "He filleth all in all." But, as if the believer must be made like his Lord even here, observe that if Christ filleth all in all, the Church is His fulness. In Christ, the Church is the head of the universe under God. For Thou hast made Him a little lower than the angels, and hast crowned Him with glory and honour. Thou madest Him to have dominion over the works of Thy hands; Thou hast put all things under His feet: all sheep and oxen, yea, and the beasts of the field; the fowl of the air, and the fish of the sea, and whatsoever passeth through the paths of the sea.

I do not know whether I have brought forth the parallel completely. If you view our Lord as descending in His agony never so deep, and then behold Him in His glory never so high; if by combining judgment and imagination, hope and fear, you can get some glimmering of a thought of how low the Saviour went, and how loftily He climbed, then you may transfer that to your own state, for the same power is at work to-day, has been at work, and will be at work in you, to lift you up from equal depths to equal heights, that in all things you may be like unto Christ; and having been like Him numbered with the transgressors, you may like Him obtain the lot and the heritage to reign for ever and ever at the right hand of the Majesty in the heavens.

I cannot speak on such a topic as this—it o'ermasters me: it is by far too grand for my limited gifts of utterance, but I trust not too great for human delectation. We can delight in it, and suck honey, marrow, and fatness from it.

II. Now we must note, in the second place, THE REASON OF THIS.

Why does God put forth as much power towards every Christian as He did in His beloved Son? Well, my brethren, I believe the reason is not only that the same power was required, and that by this means He getteth great glory, but the reason is this—*union*. It lays in the word—union. There must be the same divine power in the member that there is in the Head, or else where is the union? If we are one with Christ, members of His body, of His flesh, and of His bones, there must be a likeness. Note, first, that *there cannot be a body at all*—I mean not a true living body—unless the members are of the same nature as the head. If you could conceive a human head joined to bestial limbs, you would at once understand that you were not looking upon a natural body. If here were a dog's foot, and there a lion's mane, and yet a man's eyes and a human brow, you could never conceive of it as a body of God's creation; you would look upon it as a strange monstrosity, a thing to be put out of sight, or to be shown for fools to gaze at as a nine-day's wonder; but certainly not as a thing to display divine wisdom and power. Nebuchadnezzar's dream, you remember, had an image, of which the "head was of fine gold, his breast and his arms of silver, his belly and his thighs of brass, his legs of iron, his feet part of iron and part of clay." Do you think that the person of Christ is to be so odd a medley? Our Head, we know, is like much fine gold. Thanks be unto God, we are well persuaded that a body of God's making will be of the same material all the way through. He will not have, I say, a perfectly glorious Head allied to members in which the divine energy has never been seen. The same power which sparkles about the Head must shine in the members, or else it cannot be a body constituted according to the analogy of nature, or according to the usual methods of the Divine Worker.

This is not the most forcible mode of putting it. Let us notice that if all the members were not like the Head and did not display the same power *it would not be glorious to God*. Some of the old tapestries were made at different times and in different pieces, and occasionally the remark is heard, "That part of the battle-scene must have been wrought by a different needle from the other. You can see here an abundance, and there a deficiency of skill; that corner of the picture has been executed by a far inferior hand. Now, suppose in this great tapestry which God is working—the great needlework of His love and power—the mythical person of Christ—that we should say, "The Head has been wrought, we can see, by a divine hand; that glorious brow, those fire-darting eyes, those honey-dropping lips are of God, but that hand is by another and an inferior artist, and that foot is far from perfect in workmanship." Why, it would not be glorious to our Great Artist; but when the whole picture is by Himself we see that He did not begin what He could not finish, and that He had not inserted a single thread of inferior value.

Note again, that *it would not be glorious to our Head*. I saw the other day, a cathedral window in the process of being filled with the richest stained glass. Methinks the great person of Christ may be compared to that great cathedral window. The artists had put in the head of the chief figure in the most beautiful glass that ever human skill could make, or human gold could purchase; I have not seen it since, but imagine for an instant that the workers afterwards found that their money failed them, and they were obliged to fill in the panes with common glass. There is the window, there is nothing but a head in noble colours, and the rest is, perhaps, white glass, or some poor ordinary blue and yellow. It is never finished. What an unhappy thing, for who will care to see the head? It has lost its fulness. There is the head, but it is strangely circumstanced. If you complete it with anything inferior, you mar and spoil it; it is the head of an imperfect piece of workmanship. But, dear friends, when all the rest of the picture shall have been wrought out with just the same costly material as the first part, then the head itself shall be placed in a worthy position, and shall derive glory as well as confer glory upon the body. Ye can read this parable without an interpreter.

I must add, that if anything, the power manifested in the member should be greater than that manifested in the head—*If anything, it should be greater*. A marble palace is to be built. Well, now, if they build (and oh, how many people do this kind of thing in their houses) the front with costly stone, and then erect the back with common stock bricks; if the pinnacles be made to soar with rich Carrara to the skies, and then down in the walls common stone is seen, everybody says, "This was done to save money." But if the whole structure throughout, from top to bottom, is of the same kind, then it reflects much honour upon the great builder, and declares the wealth which he was able to expend upon the structure. But suppose that some of the blocks of marble used in the foundation have lain in a very dark quarry, and have been subject to damaging influences, so that they have lost their gloss and polish, then surely they will want more polishing, more workmanship, to make them look like that bright corner-stone, that noble pinnacle which is brought out with shoutings. Christ Jesus was in His nature *fit*, without any preparing, to be a part of the great temple of God. We in our nature were unfit; and so, if anything, the power should be greater; but we are constrained to rejoice that we find in Scripture that it is just the same power which lifted the man Christ Jesus to the throne of God, which now shall lift each one of us to live and reign with him.

Moreover, to conclude this point, the loving promise of our Lord will never be fulfilled (and He will never be contented unless it be), unless His people do have the same power spent upon them as He has. What is His prayer? "I will that they also, whom Thou hast given Me, be with Me where I am; that they may behold My glory;" and then He adds, "The glory which Thou gavest Me I have given them." You know how the union stands—"I in them, and Thou in Me." We must be like our Head. Is He crowned—we must be crowned too. He is a good husband; He will enjoy nothing without His spouse. When she was poor, He became poor for her sake; when she was despised, He was spit upon too; and now that He is in heaven, He must have her there. If He sits on a throne, she must have a throne too; if He has fulness of joy, and honour, and glory for ever—then so must she. He will not be in heaven, and leave her behind; and He will not enjoy a single privilege of heaven, without her being a sharer with Him. For all this reason, then you see it is clear why there should be the same power in the believer as there was in Christ.

III. Well, WHAT ARE THE INFERENCES FROM ALL THIS. Two or three—they will only be hinted at, so do not grow weary.

The first inference is this—*what a marvellous thing a Christian is*. A marvellous personage am I if I am a believer in Christ. I am by doubting and fearing led to look down upon myself as despicable, but when I reflect that the Eternal has put His graving-tool upon me—nay, that He has exerted the whole of His omnipotence in me, and will continue to exert it till He brings me to Himself—Lord, what is man! How strangely honoured! How near hast thou brought Him to thyself, so that now there is no creature between God and man! God first, man as a creature far distant, but yet second, as an adopted and regenerated being, brought as near to God as a son is brought to a father; and who shall tell how near this may be? Lord, what a mighty thing can Thy grace make out of that poor crawling worm called man! How hast Thou exalted him, and make him to be higher even than principalities and powers! Let us love and bless God who has done thus much for us.

Then, secondly, *why should I doubt God's power for others?* If God has put forth so much power to save me, cannot He save anyone? The might which brought Christ from the dead and took Him to heaven is such a tremendous power that it surely can bring the drunkard, the harlot, the blasphemer to Christ. Let me pray, then, for the chief of sinners; let me encourage the vilest of the vile to believe in Jesus, for there is ability in Christ to save just such.

Again, *why should I ever have any doubts about my ultimate security?* Is this irresistible power engaged to save me? Then I must be saved. Does the devil vow that he will destroy me? Do my corruptions threaten to overwhelm me? Who can stay Omnipotence? Who shall come into the struggle with the Most High, or match himself with the Eternal? Aha! aha! ye enemies of my soul; I laugh ye to scorn. If God be with us, who can be against us?

And lastly, *how doleful the state of those who are not converted.* See where you lie; so dead, so helpless, so ruined, so undone, needing nothing less than this eternal power to save you from the wrath to come! Ah, indeed I know this to be the case with many present here. Our preaching does you very little good. You come here in the morning, and I know what you do in the afternoon. You would not be absent from listening to the morning's sermon, nor would you be absent from the evening's pleasure; and when the Bible and the hymn book have been put up, the newspaper will take the place. There are some who sit under our earnest appeals (and thank God they are earnest and often prevalent), and yet they are as unmoved as slabs of marble when oil runs down them. In a state of death and ruin are you. I see no human power can help you; in vain the minister, in vain the preaching; your damnation is sure, you will go down to hell and perish, and that without mercy. Yet fain would I hope that God would have pity upon you yet. Still Christ is lifted up, and "whosoever believeth in Him shall not perish, but have everlasting life." If you can now believe in Christ, the mighty power of God is working in you. Trust Him now, and you give the best evidence that Jesus's irresistible might has been displayed upon you, as it was upon the person of the King of kings. The Lord bless you with His mercy, for Christ's sake. Amen.

LIFE FROM THE DEAD

"And you hath He quickened, who were dead in trespasses and sins."—Ephesians ii. 1.

OUR translators, as you observe, have put in the words "hath He quickened," because Paul had thrown the sense a little farther on, and it was possible for the reader not to catch it. They have but anticipated the statement of the fourth and fifth verses: "God, who is rich in mercy, for His great love wherewith He loved us, even when we were dead in sins, hath quickened us together with Christ."

Here is the point. God has quickened us, who were dead in trespasses and sins, spiritually dead. We were full of vigour towards everything which was contrary to the law of the holiness of God, we walked according to the course of this world; but as for anything spiritual, we were not only somewhat incapable, and somewhat weakened; but we were actually and absolut ly dead. We had no sense with which to comprehend spiritual things. We had neither the eye that could see, nor the ear that could hear, nor the power that could feel.

We were dead, all of us; and yet we were not all like one another. Death may be universal over a certain number of bodies, and yet those bodies may look very different. The dead that lie on the battlefield, torn of dogs or kites, rotting, corrupting in the sun, what a horrible sight! Your lately-departed one, lying in the coffin, how beautiful! The corpse looks like life still; yet is your beloved one in the coffin as dead as the mangled bodies on the battle-field. Corruption has not yet done its work, and tender care has guarded the body as yet from what will surely come to it; yet is there death, sure, complete death, in the one case as well as in the other.

So we have many who are lovely, amiable, morally admirable, like him whom the Saviour looked upon and loved; yet they are dead for all that. We have others who are drunken, profane, unchaste; they are dead, not more dead than the others; but their death has left its terrible traces more plainly visible. Sin brings forth death, and death brings forth corruption. Whether we were corrupt or not, is not a question that I need raise here; let every one judge concerning himself. But dead we were, most certainly. Even though trained by godly parents, though well instructed in the gospel scheme, though saturated with the piety that surrounded us, we were dead, as dead as the harlot of the street, as dead as the thief in the jail.

Now, the text tells us that, though we were dead, yet Christ has come, and by His Spirit He has raised us out of the grave. This text brings us Easter tidings; it sings of resurrection; it sounds in our ear the trumpet of a new life, and introduces us into a world of joy and gladness. We were dead; but we are quickened by the Spirit of God. I cannot help stopping a minute to know whether it is so with you, my dear hearers, and praying that what I may have to say may act as a kind of sieve, separating between the really living and those who only think that they are alive, so that, if you have not been quickened, if you are only "a child of nature, finely dressed," but not spiritually alive, you may be made aware of it. If you have been quickened, even though your life be feeble, you may cry to the living God with the "Abba, Father," which never comes from any lip but that which has been touched and quickened by the Holy Spirit.

I. First, let us talk a little about OUR QUICKENING. You who have been quickened will understand what I say. To those who have not, I daresay it will seem as an idle tale.

Well, dear friends, if we have been quickened, we have been *quickened from above.* "You hath HE quickened." God Himself has had dealings with us. He has raised us from the dead. He made us at the first; He has new-made us. He gave us life when we were born; but He has given us now a higher life, which could not be found anywhere else. He must always give it. No man ever made himself to live. No preacher, however earnest, can make one hearer to live. No parent, however prayerful, no teacher, however tearful, can make a child to live unto God. "You hath HE quickened," is true of all who are quickened. It is a divine spark, a light from the great central Sun of light, the great Father of lights. Is it so with us? Have we had a divine touch, a superhuman energy, a something which all the learning and all the wisdom and all the godliness of man could never work in us? Have we been quickened from above? If so, I daresay that we remember something of it. We cannot describe it; no man can describe his first birth; it remains a mystery. Neither can he describe his new birth; that is a still greater mystery, for it is a secret inward work of the Holy Ghost, of which we feel the effect, but we cannot tell how it is wrought.

I think that, usually, when the divine life comes, the first consciousness that we get of quickening is *a sense of pain.* I have heard that when a man is nearly drowned, while he lies under the power of death, he feels little or nothing, perhaps has even pleasurable dreams; but when, in the process of restoring him, they have rubbed him till the blood begins to flow, and the life begins to revive a little he is conscious of pricking and great pain. One of the tokens that life is coming back to him is, that he wakes up out of a pleasant sleep, and feels pain. Whether it be so or not with every person restored from drowning, I do not know; but I think that it is so with every person restored from drowning in the river of sin. When the life begins to come to him, he feels as he never felt before; sin that was pleasant becomes a horror to him. That which was easy to him becomes a bed of thorns. Thank God, dear hearer, if you have living pangs. It is an awful thing to have your conscience hardened, as in the very fires of hell, till it becomes like steel. To have consciousness is a great mercy, even if it be only painful consciousness and if every movement of the life within seems to harrow up your soul. This divine life usually begins with pain.

Then, *everything surprises you.* If a person had never lived before, and had come into life a full-grown man, everything would be as strange to him as it is to a little child; and everything is strange to a new-born man in the spiritual realm into which he is born. He is startled a hundred times. Sin appears as sin; he cannot understand it. He had looked at sin before, but had never seen it to be sin. And Christ appears now so glorious to him; he had heard of Christ before, and had some apprehension of Him; but now he is surprised to find that the One who he said had no form or comeliness is, after all, altogether lovely. To the new-born soul everything is a surprise. He makes no end of blunders; he makes many miscalculations because everything is new to him. He that sitteth upon the throne saith, "Behold, I make all things

new;" and the renewed man says, "My Lord, it is even so." One said to me, when joining the church, "Either I am a new creature, or else the world is altogether altered from what it was. There is a change somewhere;" and that change is from death to life, from darkness into God's marvellous light.

Now, as life comes thus with strange surprises, and mingled with pain, so, dear friends, it comes often *with many questions.* The child has a thousand things to ask; it has to learn everything. We little think of the experiments that children have to go through before they arrive even at the use of their eyes. They do not know that things are at a distance; they have to learn that fact by looking many times. So long as the object falls upon the retina, the child is not aware of whether it is a distant or a near object till some time after. What you think that you and I knew from our birth, we did not so know; we had to learn it. And when a man is born into the kingdom of God, he has to learn everything; and consequently, if he is wise, he questions older and wiser believers about this and about that. I pray you that are instructed, and have become fathers, never to laugh at babes in grace, if they ask you the most absurd questions. Encourage them to do so; let them tell you their difficulties. You, by God's grace are a man; this little one is but a new-born babe; hear what he has to say. You mothers, do this with your little children. You are interested, you are pleased, you are amused, with what they say. Thus ought instructed saints to deal with those who have been newly quickened. They come to us, and ask, "What is this? What is that? What is the other?" It is a time of asking, a time of enquiring. It is well, also, if it is a time of sitting at Jesus' feet, for there is no other place so safe to a new-born believer as the feet of Jesus. If he gets to the feet of anybody else, he is apt to get ill-instructed at a time when everything warps his judgment, when he is exceedingly impressionable, and not likely to forget the mistakes that he has made, if he has borrowed them from others. So you see what the divine life does when it comes into the soul. It comes to us with pain; it gives us many surprises; and it suggests a large number of questions.

We begin then to *make a great many attempts* at things which we never attempted before. The new-born child of God is just like the new-born child of man in some things; and after a time that child begins to walk. No, it does not; it begins to crawl; it does not walk at first. It creeps along, pleased to make any kind of progress; and when it gets upon its little feet, it moves from one chair to another, trembling at every step it takes, and presently down it goes. But it gets up again, and so it learns to walk. Do you remember when the new life came into you? I do. I remember the first week of that new life, and how, on the second Sabbath, I went to the place where I had heard the gospel to my soul's salvation, thinking that I would attend there. But, during that week, I had made many experiments, and tumbled down a great many times, and the preacher took for his text, "O wretched man that I am! who shall deliver me from the body of this death?" I thought, "Yes; I know all about that; that is my case." When the preacher said that Paul was not a Christian when he wrote those words, though I was only seven days old in divine things, I knew better than that, so I never went there any more. I knew that no man but a Christian ever could or would cry out against sin with that bitter wail; and that, if the grace of God was not with him, he would rest satisfied and contented; but that, if he felt that sin was a horrible thing, and he was a wretched man because of it, and must be delivered from it, then he surely must be a child of God, especially if he could add, "Thanks be to God, which giveth us the victory through our Lord Jesus Christ."

Beloved, we make many mistakes, and we shall continue to do so. At the same time, we learn by our experiments. You remember when you began to pray; would you like to have your first prayer printed? I believe that God liked it better than many of the collects. You might not like it so well; it would not look well in print. You remember when you first began to confess Christ to a friend. Oh, you did stutter and stammer over it! There were more tears than words; it was not a "dry" discourse; you wetted it well with tears of grief and anxiety. That was the new life putting forth powers with which it was not itself acquainted; and I believe that there are some of God's children who have powers that they will never find unless they try to use them. I should like some of you young men who do not pray at the prayer-meeting to make a start. And some of you older men, perhaps, have never preached yet; but you might if you tried; I wish you would. "I should break down," says one. I wish you would. A break-down sermon, that breaks the preacher down, might break the people down, too. There might be many advantages about that kind of discourse.

This, then, was the way in which the new life, spiritual life, came into us. We did not know what it was when it came; we had never felt like that before; we could not think that we really had passed from death to life; and yet, in looking back, we are persuaded that the throes within, the anguish of heart, the longing, and the pleading, and the wrestling, and the crying, would never have been in a dead heart, but were the sure marks that God had quickened us, and we had passed into newness of life.

II. Now, secondly, let us think of OUR PRESENT LIFE. "You hath He quickened." Well, then we have a new life. What is the effect of this life upon us? I speak to you who are quickened by grace.

Well, first, we have become now *sentient towards God*. The unconverted man lives in God's world, sees God's works, hears God's Word, goes up to God's house on God's day, and yet he does not know that there is any God. Perhaps he believes that there is, because he was brought up to believe it; but he is not cognizant of God; God has not entered into him; he has not come into contact with God. Beloved brethren and sisters in Christ, I think that you and I can say, that to us the surest fact in all the world is that there is a God. No God? I live in Him. Tell the fish in the sea that there is no water. No God? I live by Him. Tell a man who is breathing that there is no air. No God? I dare not come downstairs without speaking to Him. No God? I would not think of closing my eyes in sleep unless I had some sense of His love shed abroad in my heart by the Holy Ghost. "Oh!" says one, "I have lived fifty years, and I have never felt anything of God." Say that you have been dead fifty years; that is nearer the mark. But if you had been quickened of the Holy Spirit fifty minutes, this would have been the first fact in the front rank of all facts, God is, and He is my Father, and I am His child. Now you become sentient to His frown, His smile, His threat,

or His promise. You feel Him; His presence is photographed upon your spirit; your very heart trembles with awe of Him, and you say with Jacob, "Surely God is in this place." That is one result of spiritual life.

Now you have become also *sympathetic with similar life in others*. You have a wide range, for the life of God, His life in His new-born child, is the same life that is in every Christian. It is the same life in the new-born believer as in yonder bright spirits that stand before the throne of God. The life of Christ, the life of God, is infused into us in that moment when we are quickened from our death in sin. What a wonderful thing it is to have become sympathetic with God! What He desires, we desire. His glory is the first object of our being. He loves His Son, and we love His Son. We desire to see His kingdom come as He does, and we pray for His will to be done on earth, even as it is done in heaven. We wish that death did not remain, the old nature hampering us; but, in proportion as the new life is really in us, we now run parallel with God. The holiness which He delights in we aspire after. Not with equal footsteps, but with tottering gait, we follow in that selfsame path that God has marked out for Himself. "My soul followeth hard after Thee; Thy right hand upholdeth me."

The new life that made us sympathetic with God, and holy angels, and holy men, and with everything that is from above, has also made us *capable of great pleasure*. Life is usually capable of pleasure, but the new life is capable of the highest conceivable pleasure. I am certain that no ungodly man has any conception of the joy which often fills the believer's spirit. If worldlings could only know the bliss of living near to God, and of basking in the light of His countenance, they would throw their wealth into the sea, and ten thousand times as much, if they might but get a glimpse of this joy that can never be bought, but which God gives to all who trust His dear Son. We are not always alike. Alas! we are very changeable; but when God is with us, when the days are spiritually bright and long, and we have come into the midsummer of our heavenly bliss, we would not change places with the angels, knowing that by-and-by we shall be nearer to the throne than they are; and, while they are God's honoured servants, yet they are not beloved sons as we are. Oh, the thrill of joy that has sometimes gone through our spirits! We could almost have died with delight at times when we have realized the glorious things that God has prepared for them that love Him. This joy we never knew till we received the new life.

But I must add that we are also *capable of acute pain* to which we were strangers once. God has made our conscience quick as the apple of the eye; He has made our soul as sensitive as a raw wound, so that the very shadow of sin falling on the believer's heart will cause him great pain; and, if he does go into actual sin, then, like David, he talks about his bones being broken, and it is not too strong a figure of the sorrow that comes upon the believing heart when sin has been committed, and God has been grieved. The heart itself, then, is broken, and bleeds at ten thousand wounds. Yet this is one of the results of our possessing the new life; and I will say this, the sharpest pang of spiritual life is better than the highest joy of carnal life. When the believer is at his worst, he is better than the unbeliever at his best; his reasons for happiness are always transcendently above all the reasons for joy that worldlings can ever know.

Now, dear friends, if we have received spiritual life, you see what a range of being we have, how we can rise up to the seventh heaven or sink down into the abyss. This new life makes us *capable of walking with God;* that is a grand thing. We speak of Enoch walking with God, and we look at the holiness of his life; but did anybody ever think of the majesty of his life? How does God walk? It needs a Milton to conceive of the walk of God; but he that hath the divine life walks with God; and sometimes he seems to step from Alp to Alp, over sea and ocean, accomplishing what, unaided, he would never even attempt. He that has the divine life is lifted up into the infinities; he gets to hear that which cannot be heard, and to see that which cannot be seen, for "Eye hath not seen, nor ear heard, neither have entered into the heart of man, the things which God hath prepared for them that love Him. But God hath revealed them unto us by His Spirit," when He has given us the new life.

One effect of this divine life is to *put life into everything that we do.* They tell me that "creeds are dead." Yes, yes! It is a pleasant thing to hear an honest confession; they are dead to dead men. To me, that which I believe is not dead; it is a part of myself. I hold nothing as a truth that I can put away on the shelf, and leave there, My creed is a part of my being. I believe it to be true; and, believing it to be true, I feel its living force upon my nature every day. When a man tells you that his creed is a dead thing, do not deny it for a minute; there is no doubt of the fact. He knows about himself better than you do. Oh, dear friends, let *us* never have a dead creed! That which you believe, you must believe up to the hilt; believe it livingly, believe it really, for that is not believed at all which is only believed in the letter, but is not felt in the power of it.

If you have been quickened by the Spirit of God, your prayers are living prayers. Oh, the many dead prayers that are heard at the bedside; so many good words rushed through at a canter! He that is alive unto God asks for what he wants, and he believes that he shall have it, and he gets it. That is living prayer. Beware of dead prayers; they are a mockery to the Most High. I do not think that a living man can always pray by clockwork, at such a time and such a time. It would be something like the minister's sermon which he "got up" beforehand, and upon which he wrote in the margin "weep here," "here you must show great emotion." Of course that was all rubbish; it cannot be done to order. You cannot resolve to "groan at one o'clock, and weep at three o'clock." Life will not be bound like that. I love to have an appointed season for prayer, and woe unto the man who does not have his time for prayer! But, at the same time, our living prayer bursts out hours before the appointed time, or sometimes it will not come at the time. You have to wait till another season, and then your soul is like a hind let loose. Why, sometimes we can pray, and prevail, and come off conquerors; and at another time, we can only bow at the throne, and groan out, "Lord, help me; I cannot pray; the springs seem to be all sealed." That is the result of life. Living things change. There are some personages in St Paul's Cathedral; I have not seen them lately, but I have seen them. When I lived in the country, I came up to look at the notabilities in St. Paul's Cathedral. I have

heard that they have never had a headache during the last hundred years, and no rheumatic pains, nor have they ever been troubled with the gout. The reason is that they are cut in marble, and they are dead; but a living man feels the fogs and the winds; he knows whether it is an east wind or a west wind that is blowing. Before he gets up in the morning, he begins to feel sometimes lively and sometimes dull; he does not understand himself. Sometimes he feels merry, and can sing hymns; at another time, he can do nothing else but sigh and cry, though he scarcely knows wherefore. Yes, life is a strange thing; and if you have the life of God in your soul, you will undergo many changes, and not always be what you want to be.

If we are alive unto God, every part of our worship should be living. What a deal of dead worship there is! If we go on with our services in regular routine, a large number of our friends find it difficult to keep awake. I fear that some people go to a place of worship because they get a better sleep there than they do anywhere else. That is not worship which consists of doing as Hodge did, when he said, "I like Sunday, for then I can go to church, and put my legs up, and think of nothing at all." That is all the worship a great many render to God, just getting to a place of worship, and there sitting still, and thinking of nothing at all. But if you are a living child of God, you cannot do that. If, sometimes, through infirmity of the flesh, you fall into that state of slumber, you loathe yourselves for it, but you rouse yourself up, and say, " I must worship my God; I must sing, I must praise God. I must draw near to Him in prayer."

III. I must come to my third point; for our time flies. Notice what OUR PRESENT POSITION IS, if God has quickened us.

Our present position is this, first, that *we are raised from the dead.* "He hath quickened us together with Christ, and hath raised us up together." We cannot live where we used to live. We cannot wear what we used to wear. There is nobody here who would like to go and live in a grave. If you had been raised from the dead, after you had been buried in Norwood Cemetery, I will warrant you that you would not go there to-night to sleep. So the man, who has once been raised by the quickening power of the Holy Spirit, quits the dead; his old company does not suit him. If you had been raised from the dead, and had come out of your tomb, you would not go about London streets with your shroud on. You are a living man. How is it that I find some who say that they are the people of God; but yet are rather fond of wearing their grave-clothes? I mean that they like the amusements of the world; they like to put on their shroud sometimes just for a treat. Oh, do not so! If God has made you to live, come away from the dead; come away from their habits, and manners, and customs. Life sees no charms in death. The living child of God likes to get as far as ever he can away from the death that once held him bound. "Come out from among them, and be ye separate, saith the Lord, and touch not the unclean thing; and I will receive you, and will be a Father unto you, and ye shall be my sons and daughters, saith the Lord Almighty." That is the first part of our position, that we have come to live a separated life now, and have quitted the path we trod before.

Next to that, we are *one with Christ.* He hath "quickened us together with Christ, and hath raised us up together." I told you just now that the life which the Holy Spirit gives us when we are born again, is the life of God. We are made partakers of the divine nature, of course, in a modified sense, but still in a true sense. The life everlasting, the life that can never die, is put into us then, even as Christ said, "The water that I shall give him shall be in him a well of water springing up into everlasting life." The believer's life is the life of Christ in the believer. "Because I live, ye shall live also." What a mystic union there is between the believer and his Lord! Realize that; believe in it; rejoice in it; triumph in it. Christ and you are one now, and you are made to live together with Him. God grant you to know the joy of that condition!

Once more, we are told, "He hath raised us up together, and made us sit together in heavenly places in Christ Jesus." That is very wonderful. We have not only left the dead, and become joined to Christ, but we are made to *sit in heaven with Christ*. A man is where his head is, is he not? and every believer is where his Head is; and if we are members of Christ's body, we are in heaven. It is a very blessed experience to be able to walk on earth, and look up to heaven but it is a higher experience to live in heaven, and look down on the earth; and this is what the believer may do. He may sit in the heavenlies; Christ is there as his Representative. The believer may take possession of what his Representative is holding on his behalf. Oh, to live in heaven, to dwell there, to let the heart be caught up from this poor life into the life that is above! This is where we should be, where we may be if we are quickened by the divine life.

One thing more, and I have done. We are in this position, that God is now working in us, through this divine life, to make *us the most wonderful reflectors of His grace* that He has yet formed. He has raised us up together, and made us sit together in heavenly places in Christ Jesus, "that in the ages to come He might shew the exceeding riches of His grace in His kindness toward us through Christ Jesus." The ages to come will have for their wonder the quickened children of God. When God made the world, it was a wonder, and the angels came from afar to see His handiwork. But when Christ makes the new creation, they will say no more that God made the heaven and the earth, but they will say in higher strains, "He made these new-born men and women. He made for them, and in them, new heavens and a new earth."

Ah! beloved, "It doth not yet appear what we shall be." God has given us a life that is more precious than the Koh-i-noor, a life that will outlast the sun and moon. When all the things that are shall be like old ocean's foam, which dissolves into the wave that bears it, and is gone for ever; we shall still live, and we shall live in Christ and with Christ, glorified for ever. When the moon has become black as sackcloth of hair, the life that is within us shall be as bright as when God first gave it to us. Thou hast the dew of thy youth, O child of God; and thou shalt have yet more of it, and be like thy Lord, when He shall take thee away from every trace of death, and the corrupt atmosphere of this poor world, and thou shalt dwell with the living God in the land of the living for ever and for ever!

The practical outcome of all this is, that some of you do not know anything at all about it. If you do not, let that fact impress you. If there be a divine life to which you are a stranger, how long will you be a stranger to it? If there be a spiritual death, and you are dead, be startled; for within a little while God will say, "Bury My dead out of My sight." And what will happen to you when the word of God is, "Depart, depart, depart, depart," and unto the grave-yard of souls, to the fire that never shall be quenched, you and the rest of the dead are taken away? "God is not the God of the dead, but of the living," and, unless we are made alive unto Him, He cannot be our God either here or hereafter. The Lord impress this solemn truth on all your hearts by His own Spirit; for Jesus Christ's sake! Amen.

WHAT CHRISTIANS WERE AND ARE

"And were by nature the children of wrath, even as others."—Ephesians ii. 3.

"The Spirit itself beareth witness with our spirit, that we are the children of God: and if children, then heirs; heirs of God, and joint-heirs with Christ."—Romans viii. 16,–17.

THESE two texts will furnish me with two familiar but most important themes,—*what Christians were*, and *what they are*. There are great and vital differences between what they once were and what they now are, and these are implied or indicated by the two expressions "the children of wrath" and "the children of God." There is so much instruction in each of our texts that we will proceed at once to consider them without any further introduction.

I. So, first, let us consider WHAT CHRISTIANS WERE.

The apostle tells us that we "were by nature the children of wrath, even as others." "*By nature*," mark you, not merely by practice, but "by nature *the children of wrath*." The expression is a Hebraism. When a person was doomed to die, he would be called by the Jews "the child of death." One who was very poor would be called by them "the child of poverty." So, because we were, by nature, under the wrath of God, we are called "the children of wrath."

When the apostle says that we "were by nature the children of wrath," he means that *we were born so*. David expressed what is true of us all when he said, "Behold, I was shapen in iniquity; and in sin did my mother conceive me." Our first parent, Adam, sinned and fell as the representative of the whole human race. "By one man sin entered into the world, and death by sin; and so death passed upon all men." If any object to this principle of representation, that does not affect its truth, and I would also remind them that, by this very principle of representation, a way was left open for our restoration. The angels did not sin representatively, they sinned personally and individually; and therefore there is no hope of their restoration, but they are "reserved in everlasting chains under darkness unto the judgment of the great day." But men sinned representatively, and this is a happy circumstance for us, "for as by one man's disobedience many were made sinners, so by the obedience of One shall many be made righteous." As we fell through one representative, it was consistent with the principles upon which God was governing mankind that He should allow us to rise by another Representative. At first, we fell not by our own fault; so now, by grace, we rise not by our own merit. Death by sin came to us through Adam ere we were born, so did life come to us through Christ Jesus. Thus our first text sets before us this terrible fact,—as true as it is terrible, and as terrible as it is true,—that we were by nature under the wrath of God from the very first. The whole race of mankind was regarded by God as descended from an attainted traitor; we were all born "children of wrath."

This expression also implies that *there was within us a nature which God could not look upon except with wrath.* The way in which some cry up the excellence of human nature is all idle talk. "The heart is deceitful above all things, and desperately wicked: who can know it?" Our Lord Jesus Christ has told us that "out of the heart proceed evil thoughts, murders, adulteries, fornications, thefts, false witness, blasphemies." Everything that is evil lurks within the heart of everyone that is born of a woman. Education may restrain it, imitation of a good example may have some power in holding the monster down; but the very best of us, apart from the grace of God, placed under certain circumstances which would cause the evil within us to be developed rather than restrained, would soon prove to a demonstration that our nature was evil, and only evil, and that continually. You may take a bag of gunpowder, and play with it if you care to do so, for it is quite harmless as long as you keep the fire from it; but put just one spark of fire to it, and then you will discover the force for evil that was latent in that innocent-looking powder. You may tame a tiger if you begin training it early enough, and you may treat it as if it was only a big cat; but let it once learn the taste of blood, and you will soon see the true tiger nature flashing from its eyes, and seeking to destroy all that come within reach of its cruel claws. In a similar fashion to that, sin was originally latent within every one of us; and whatever better qualities God may, by His grace, have planted there, it is still true that we "were by nature the children of wrath, even as others."

I need not say any more about the original sin of Adam, or about the sinfulness of our nature, for those of us who have been saved know that *our practice was according to our nature.* Who can deny that the fountain was defiled when he is compelled to confess that polluted streams flowed from it? Can you look back with complacency upon the days of your unregeneracy? I feel sure that you cannot think of the sins that you committed then without weeping over them; and especially sorrowing over that sin which so many forget,—the sin of not believing on the Son of God, the sin of so long rejecting the Saviour, the sin of not yielding to the gentle calls of His grace, the sin of bolting and barring the door of your heart while He stood without, and cried, "Open to Me, My sister, My love, My dove, My undefiled: for My head is filled with dew, and My locks with the drops of the night." But we would not rise, and let Him in. What a horrible sin it

was not to see the loveliness of Christ, and not to admire the infinitude of His love! Had we not been sinful by nature and by practice too, our opposition or our indifference would have been melted by the coming of Jesus, and we should at once have opened our hearts to receive Him.

Not only were we "children of wrath" by descent, by nature, and by practice; but, had not God, in his long-suffering patience, spared us until we were converted, *we should have had to endure the wrath of God for ever* in that dark realm where not a single ray of hope or one cooling drop of consolation will mitigate the miseries of any child of wrath who hears the dread sentence, "Depart from Me; I never knew you." We cannot bear even to think of the doom of those who have died impenitent. I confess that my flesh creeps when I read those terrible words of the Lord Jesus concerning the worm that never dies, and the fire that never shall be quenched; and yet, instead of sitting in these seats at this moment, rejoicing in the good hope through grace, we might have been there; aye, and without any very great change in the order of God's providence before our conversion, we might have been there. We were sick with the fever, and if only the disease had taken an unfavourable turn, we should have been there. We were shipwrecked; and if only the waves had washed us out to sea instead of washing us up upon a rock, we should have been there. Possibly, some of us have been in battle, and as "every bullet has its billet," if one had found its billet in our brain or heart, we should have been there. Some of us have been in many accidents; if one of them had been fatal before we knew the Lord, we should have been there. All of us are in jeopardy every day and every hour; we are constantly being reminded of the frailty of human life; yet God spared us by His grace, and did not cut us off, as so many others were, while we were unrepentant and unregenerated. Had he done so, we should indeed have been "the children of wrath" in the most terrible of all senses, for we should even now have been enduring the wrath of God on account of our sin. Children of God, as you realize the truth of what I have been saying to you, I trust that you will feel intensely grateful to the Lord who has so graciously interposed on your behalf, and delivered you from going down into the pit.

Notice also that Paul says that we "were by nature *the children of wrath, even as others.*" God's grace has made a great difference between His children and others, but there was no such difference originally; they were "the children of wrath, even as others," that is, in the same sense as others were children of wrath. I know that God's children have been from eternity the objects of His distinguishing love, for there never was a period when He did not love those whom He had chosen as His own; but regarding us as sinners, unforgiven sinners, dead in trespasses and sins, we "were by nature the children of wrath, even as others."

We were also "the children of wrath, even as others" who remain unconverted. You have, perhaps, a daughter for whose conversion you have long prayed; you have brought her to hear the gospel since she was a child; but, up to the present moment, it has not touched her heart. Do not forget that you also were a child of wrath, even as she is. You have a friend who ridicules the gospel, even though he comes with you to listen to it. Yet you were an heir of wrath, even as he is; and if it had not been for the super-natural work of the Holy Spirit, you also would have been only a hearer and not a doer of the Word; you would have been like so many others in this congregation, and you might have said, with Cowper,—

> "I hear, but seem to hear in vain.
> Insensible as steel."

But you are not "insensible as steel" now; you do feel the power of the Word. It makes you tremble, but it also makes you rejoice, for you know that it is the Word of your Father in heaven who has loved you with an everlasting love, and who therefore with loving-kindness has drawn you to Himself. While you remember all this with devout gratitude to Him who has made you to differ from others, and also to differ from what you yourself used to be, never forget that you were once a child of wrath, even as others still are.

Yes, beloved brethren and sisters in Christ, you "were by nature the children of wrath, even as others" who still revel in sin. As you pass along the street, you see such sights and hear such language that you are shocked and horrified that men and women can so grievously sin against the God who made them, and who still permits them to live; yet do not look down upon them with an affectation of superior holiness and say, "What shameful sinners those people are in comparison with us!" but rather say, "We, too, were by nature the children of wrath, even as others still are."

Yes, and to emphasize what I have previously said, we "were by nature the children of wrath, even as others" who pass away impenitent, and in due time must stand before the judgment bar of God. They will stand shivering before that great white throne whose spotless lustre will reveal to them, as in a wondrous mirror, the blackness of their lives and the guiltiness of their impenitence; and when the King sits down upon His throne, even though it will be the Lamb Himself, who died for sinners, who will sit as their Judge, they will cry to the mountains and rocks, "Fall on us, and hide us from the face of Him that sitteth on the throne, and from the wrath of the Lamb: for the great day of His wrath is come, and who shall be able to stand?" There is nothing so terrible to look upon as injured love. Fiercer than a lion leaping upon its prey is love when once it is incensed. Oil flows smoothly, but it burns furiously; and when the love of Jesus has been finally rejected, then the sight of Him whose head was once crowned with thorns will be more terrifying than anything else to the eyes of those who have rejected Him. They will wish they had never been born; and, indeed, it would have been better for them if they had never had an existence. Had it not been for the grace of God, their portion would also have been our portion; for, by nature, we were the children of wrath even as they were, and amidst that shivering, trembling crowd we must have taken our station. But, believing in Jesus, our place shall be at His right hand "when He shall come to be glorified in His saints, and to be admired in all them that believe." We shall be amongst those to whom the King will then say, "Come, ye blessed of my Father, inherit the kingdom prepared for you from the foundation of the world." Yet, by nature, we were "the children of wrath, even as others."

II. Now I must turn from that sad, solemn knell—"children of wrath, even as others," to the joyous peal that rings out from our second text, which tells us what CHRISTIANS ARE, what we now are if we have believed in Jesus: "The Spirit itself beareth witness with our spirit, that we are the children of God."

It is such a wonderful thing that those who were the children of wrath should now be the children of God that *there are two witnesses to it;* first, our own spirit says that we are the children of God; and then the Holy Spirit comes, and says, "Ay, and I also divinely bear witness that you are the children of God."

Now, beloved, do you realize that God has wrought this great miracle of mercy in you? *Does your spirit bear witness that you are now a child of God?* When you go out of this building, and look up at the stars, will you say to yourself, "My Father made them all?" Will you feel that you must talk to your Father? And when you go to your bed to-night, should you lie sleepless, will you begin to think of your heavenly Father as naturally as a little child, when it lies in the dark, thinks of its mother, and calls to her? If you are a true believer, this is the case with you. The Spirit of adoption is given to you, by which you are enabled to cry, "Abba, Father." Do you not also know what it is sometimes, when you are sitting down quietly by yourself, to think, "The God who made the heavens and the earth, and who upholds all things by the word of His power, is my Father?" Then very likely a flood of tears will come as you stand silently before the Lord just as the lilies do, for at times there is no form of worship that seems possible to our joyous spirit except standing still, and letting the love of the heart silently breathe itself out before the Lord like the fragrance of flowers ascending in a gentle breeze. In such a frame of mind as that, your spirit may well bear witness that you are a child of God.

Then comes the Holy Spirit, the infallible Witness, and through the Word, and through His own mysterious influence upon our heart, *he bears witness that we are the children of God.* Two witnesses were required, under the law, to establish a charge that was made against any man; and, under the gospel, we have two witnesses to establish our claim to be the children of God,—first, the witness of our own spirit, and then the second and far greater Witness, the Holy Spirit himself; and by the mouth of these two witnesses shall our claim be fully established. If our own spirit were our only witness, we might hesitate to receive its testimony, for it is fallible and partial; but when the infallible and impartial Spirit of God confirms the unfaltering witness of our own heart and conscience, then may we have confidence toward God, and believe without hesitation that we are indeed the children of the Most High God. One of the points on which the Holy Spirit beareth witness with our spirit that we are the children of God is this: "We know that we have passed from death unto life, because we love the brethren." When we really love those who are God's children, it is strong presumptive evidence that we are ourselves members of His family; and when we truly love God the Father, God the Son, and God the Holy Spirit, when we have a compassionate love to the souls of men, and an intense love of holiness, and hatred of sin, and desire for God's glory, all these are the further witness of the Spirit with our spirit that we are the children of God.

Then, as there are two witnesses that we are the children of God, so are there *two ways in which we become the children of God*.

First, we are the children of God *by adoption*. When God asked Himself the question, "How shall I put the children of wrath among My children?" He Himself answered by saying, "I will do it by adopting them into My family." We were far off from God by wicked works, "aliens from the commonwealth of Israel, and strangers from the covenants of promise, having no hope, and without God in the world"; yet, by the grace of God, we have been adopted into the divine family.

Now you know that a child may be adopted into a nobleman's family, and yet he will not really be one of the nobleman's kindred; so there is a second way in which we become the children of God, that is *by regeneration*. We are born into the family of God as well as adopted into it, and thus we become "partakers of the divine nature." So Peter writes, "Blessed be the God and Father of our Lord Jesus Christ, which according to His abundant mercy hath begotten us again unto a lively hope by the resurrection of Jesus Christ from the dead, to an inheritance incorruptible, and undefiled, and that fadeth not away, reserved in heaven for you, who are kept by the power of God through faith unto salvation ready to be revealed in the last time." Adoption gives us the privileges of the children of God, regeneration gives us the nature of the children of God. Adoption admits us into the divine family, regeneration makes us akin to the Divine Father; it creates us anew in Christ Jesus, and puts into us a spark from the eternal Spirit himself, so that we ourselves become spiritual beings. Before regeneration, we are only body and soul; but when we are born again, born from above, we become body, soul, and spirit; being born of the Spirit, we understand spiritual things, and have spiritual perceptions which we never possessed before.

Becoming the children of God, we are entitled to all the privileges of childhood. It is the privilege of a child to enjoy its father's love, its father's care its father's teaching, its father's protection, its father's provision, and last, but by no means least, its father's chastening. Whatever a child receives as its right from its father, we also receive from our Father who is in heaven. "If ye then, being evil, know how to give good gifts unto your children; how much more shall your heavenly Father give" to you who are His children every blessing that you can possibly need while you are here on earth, and heaven itself to crown it all?

Then the apostle further says, *"and if children, then heirs;* heirs of God, and joint-heirs with Christ." Now, in this country, it is not always true that, if children, then heirs, because we have laws (of which some may approve, though I fail to see the justice of them,) which made one son to be the heir just because he happens to be the firstborn. It is not so in God's family; it is "if children, then heirs"; that is to say, all the children in the divine family are God's heirs. The last one who ever will be born into the family of God will be as much an heir as the first who ever said, "My Father, who art in heaven." And the least of the children of God—Little-faith, Ready-to-halt, and Miss Much-afraid, are just as much the heirs of God as Faithful, Valiant-for-Truth, and Mr. Great-heart himself. "If children," that is all; "if children, then heirs." Are they true-born children of God? Have they the faith which is the characteristic mark of all who are in God's family? Are they truly converted? Have they been born again, born into the family of God? If so, then it follows of necessity that, "if children, then heirs." Does not this truth encourage poor Miss Despondency over there, and you, Mr. Fearing, and friend Little-faith over yonder? "If children, then heirs." Not "if big children," nor "if firstborn children," nor "if strong children," but simply "if children, then heirs." If you have received the Spirit of adoption, whereby you cry, "Abba, Father," you are an heir of God, and a joint-heir with Jesus Christ.

There is another remarkable thing in the family of God; if we, who were by nature the children of wrath, become by grace the children of God, we thereby become, all of us, the heirs of all that God has. Now, this can never happen in an earthly family. If the father were rich, and all his children were his heirs, one son would have one farm, and another son would have another farm, and each of the girls would have so many thousands of pounds for her dowry; but each one of them could not have all that there was, it would have to be divided between them; one would have what the others had not, and could not have anything that they had. But, in God's family, all the children are heirs of all that is His. My dear brother or sister in Christ, if you have a choice privilege that is yours because you are a Christian, I rejoice that you have it, but I have it too; and if I have a precious promise that belongs to me because I am one of the Lord's children, you may be thankful for it, for it belongs equally to you. No child of God can keep Christ all to himself, for He is the portion of all His people. Some dear brethren, whom I know, would like to plant a very prickly hedge around their little gardens, so as to keep all their Christian privileges to themselves; but God's birds of paradise can fly over those hedges, and share in all the good things they are intended to enclose.

"If children, then heirs; *heirs of God.*" You, my dear brother or sister, have Christ, and I have Christ. You have the Spirit, and I have the Spirit. You have the Father, and I have the Father. You have pardon, you have peace, you have the righteousness of Christ, you have union with Christ, you have security in life, you have safety in death, you have the assurance of a blessed resurrection and of eternal glory; but so have all those who have believed in Jesus. There is the same inheritance for all the children of God; not a part for one, and another part for another. The covenant is not, "Manasseh shall have this portion of the promised land, and Issachar that portion, and Zebulun that other portion"; but to every believer the Lord says, "Lift up now thine eyes to the North, and to the South, to the East, and to the West, for all this goodly heritage have I given to thee by a covenant of salt for ever."

There is another thing about this inheritance that makes it still more precious to us, and that is, that every one of the heirs shall certainly inherit it, and that is more than you can say about any earthly inheritance. If you know that somebody has made a will in your favour, do not reckon that the estate or money is really yours until you are actually in possession of it, for "there's many a slip 'twixt the cup and the lip." The will may be cancelled, and the new one may leave you out; or there may be a flaw in it, so that the estate will get into Chancery, and remain there for the term of your natural life. Even if there is no doubt that you are the heir, there may be many who will dispute your right to the inheritance; but if you are really a child of God, not even the devil himself shall be able to rob you of your heavenly inheritance. Satan may deny that you are an heir of God, but your heavenly Father will say, " Yes, he is indeed My child, and heir to all I have. I remember his first tear of penitence, and I have preserved that in My bottle. I remember his first true prayer, his first look of faith, his first note of praise, they are all registered in My records that none can erase. I have his name here in the book of life of the Lamb slain from the foundation of the world, and it can never be blotted out. Yes, he is My child, and My heir; all that I have belongs to him." There is a day coming when all Christ's sheep shall pass again under the hand of Him that telleth them; and in that day, not one of the whole redeemed flock shall be missing. As the long roll of God's ransomed family is called, it shall be asked, " Is Little-faith here?" and he will answer to his name not at all in the trembling way in which he used to speak when he was upon earth. When it is asked, " Is Miss Much-afraid here?" she will reply, in jubilant tones, " Glory be to God, I am here!" No matter how weak and feeble you may be, if you are a child of God, you shall certainly be there, and the inheritance shall assuredly be yours.

I have not yet done with this expression, "heirs of God." Paul does not say that the children of God are heirs of heaven. Our inheritance is much bigger than that, for heaven has its bounds, but God has none. Heaven and earth shall pass away, but God never will; we are heirs, therefore, of unending bliss, for we are "heirs of God." There is no one here, there is no one on earth, there is no man or angel in heaven who can tell the full meaning of this expression: "heirs of God." The words are simple enough for even a child to utter, but only God fully understands what they mean, and we shall go on learning throughout eternity all that is included in those three short syllables. To have God himself as our inheritance, to be able to say, "The Lord is my portion," is a thousand heavens in one. And all the children of God are the heirs of God; no one of them will ever have to say, "My portion will have

to be stinted because my elder brother has taken such a large share"; but every one shall have God to enjoy here on earth, and then to enjoy for ever in glory.

Finally the apostle says, " *and joint-heirs with Christ.*" It always adds to our enjoyment of any pleasure if we have someone whom we greatly love to share it with us; then how much more shall we enjoy our heavenly inheritance because we are to occupy it with Christ Jesus, our Lord and Saviour, to whose incarnation, and life, and death, and resurrection, and intercession we are indebted for it all! Oh, who would not be a child of God, to have such bliss for ever, and to enjoy it in such blessed company? Yet is there anyone here who despises this inheritance? Is there anyone here like Esau, "who for one morsel of meat sold his birthright," and who, "afterward, when he would have inherited the blessing, was rejected: for he found no place of repentance, though he sought it carefully with tears?" Is there someone here who was once a professor of religion, who has gone back to the world, in the hope of getting a better living or a little praise, among men? Poor soul, poor soul, h w I pity you! But, O child of God, have you been kept faithful even to this hour? Then let Naboth rather than Esau be your model. Ahab offered Naboth a better vineyard than his own, or the worth of it in money if he would sell it, but he would neither exchange nor sell his inheritance even though his refusal to do so cost him his life; and it would be better for us to die a thousand deaths than ever even to think of parting with our heavenly patrimony. Happily, if we are really the children of God, He who has, by His grace, made us His children, will keep us His children; and He will both keep us for the inheritance, and keep the inheritance for us. There is, however, such a danger of being only children of God in name, and not in truth, that we shall all do well to give heed to the apostle's warning, "Let us therefore fear, lest, a promise being left us of entering into His rest, any of you should seem to come short of it." Having put our hand to the plough, let us not even think of looking back; but may we be proved to be the living children of the living God by walking in His ways until we come into His blessed presence to go no more out for ever, for His dear Son's sake! **Amen.**

" HIS GREAT LOVE "

" His great love wherewith He loved us, even when we were dead in sins."—Ephesians ii. 4, 5.

YOU notice, in this chapter, the remarkable change of subject which commences at the 4th verse. Paul had been giving a very sad description of what even the saints are by nature, and of their conduct before conversion; and then, as if he was quite weary of writing upon that painful topic, he says, "But *God*"—and goes on to tell what God has done. What a relief it is to turn from ourselves, and from our fellow-men, to God! And I do not know when God, in His rich mercy, ever seems so lovely in our eyes as when we have just gazed upon our own abundant sins. The diamond shines all the more brilliantly when it has a suitable foil to set off its brightness; and man seems to act as a foil for the goodness and the mercy of God. Perhaps you remember that the psalmist, when he had said in his haste, "All men are liars,"

turned abruptly from that theme, and said, "What shall I render unto the Lord for all His benefits toward me?" It is as if He had said, "I will not have anything more to do with man. I find him to be only like a broken cistern that can hold no water; but as for my God, He has never failed me, and He never will, so ' I will take the cup of salvation, and call upon the name of the Lord.'"

I want, at this time, just to intertwist these two subjects,—ourselves in our fall, and God in His grace, —ourselves in our sin, and God in His love: "His great love wherewith He loved us, even when we were dead in sins." I shall not need so much to preach as just to refresh your memories,—to revive your recollections of the great things which the Lord, in His grace, hath done for you. I want you, who know the Lord, to remember what you were, and what God has done for you. Those two themes will bring out the greatness of His love, so they shall be our two subjects for meditation; first, *what we were;* and, secondly, *what God did for us.*

I. First, then, WHAT WE WERE. The text says that "we were dead in sins."

O believer, whatever life, of a spiritual kind, thou hast in thee to-day, was given to thee by God; it was not thine by nature. Before God looked upon thee in love and pity, and said unto thee, "Live!" thou wast dead. That is to say, as far as spiritual things are concerned, *thou wast insensible,*—insensible alike to the terrors of divine wrath and to the melodies of divine love. Thou couldst even lie at the foot of Sinai, and not shake with affright, although Moses did exceedingly fear and quake, and thou couldst lie at the foot of the cross, and yet not be melted by the death-cries of Immanuel, although the earth did quake, and the rocks were rent, and the graves were opened at that doleful sound. Do you not remember, beloved, when you passed through such a time as that? I do,—when utter callousness and hardness of heart reigned supreme within us, when the world— painted harlot, as she is,—could attract us, but we were insensible to the inexpressible beauties of Him who is altogether lovely, Jesus Christ our Lord and Saviour.

And as we were insensible to spiritual things, being dead, so *we were, at that time, without power to do anything.* We were preached to, called, and bidden to come; but, as far as all goodness was concerned, we were like a corpse, unable to hear the sweetest music, or the crack of doom resounding overhead. Do you not remember, dear friends, when it was so with you? You thought then that you could do something good in your own strength, but it was a dreadful failure when you attempted it. Your resolutions, when you got as far as resolving, all fell to the ground, for you were, in the emphatic words of Paul, "without strength." Yes, you were insensible and powerless.

And, what is worse still, we were then *without will or desire to come to God.* We had no disposition to move towards the Lord, no aspirations after holiness, no longings after communion with our Creator. We loved the world, and were content to fill our treasury with its paltry pelf; this seemed to be the only portion for which we cared. If we could have become rich, and increased with goods, we should have said, "Soul, take thine ease; there is nothing more for thee to desire."

That was our state by nature; we were dead. And did the Lord love us then, when there was nothing whatever in us to commend us to Him,—nothing by which we could possibly rise into a condition that would be estimable in His sight? Did He love us then? Yes, He did; and there must have been surprising grace in that "great love wherewith He loved us, even when we were dead in sins."

While we were dead as to spiritual things, *there was, alas! a life in us of another kind.* If you read the chapter from which our text is taken, you will find that these dead people are described as walking. They were walking corpses,—a strange commingling of metaphors, and yet most certainly true with regard to all ungodly men. They are dead to goodness; but, as for the evil within them, how full of life it is! The devil within them and the flesh within them were active enough. And, as the corpse gives forth corruption, and fills the tomb with putridity, so did

our sin continually give forth evil emanations which must have been most nauseous to God; yet, notwithstanding all this, "He loved us, even when we were dead in sins."

Let me just mention some of the unlovely and unlovable things which God saw in us while we were in that dead state. One of the first was this; *we were ungrateful.* It is very difficult to continue to love ungrateful persons. If you seek to do them good, and yet you receive no thanks from them;—if you persevere in doing them good, and yet still, for all that, they are unkind to you;—it is not in flesh and blood to continue still to love them. Yet, my brethren and sisters in Christ, what ingratitude to God was in our hearts once! What favours the Lord bestowed upon us;—not merely daily bread and temporal blessings, but there were real spiritual gifts of His grace presented to us; yet we turned our backs upon them all, and worse still, we turned our backs upon Him who gave them to us. How sad it is that many people live, year after year, without ever recognizing the God who gives them so many mercies and blessings! Perhaps, now and then, there is a "thank God!" just uttered in idleness or as a compliment; but there is no heart in it. The ingratitude of some of us was greater even than that of others, for we were born of godly parents, we were nurtured in the home of piety, we heard scarcely a sound in our infancy that was not mingled with the name of Jesus; and yet, as we grew up, these very things we regarded as restraints and sometimes we wished that we could do as other people's children did, and half regretted that we had godly friends who watched so carefully over our conduct. The Lord might have said to us, "I have done so much for you, yet you exhibit no gratitude, It will therefore leave you, and give these favours to others;" but, in His great mercy, He did not act like that although we were so ungrateful.

What is even worse, *we were complaining and murmuring.* Do you not remember, in your unconverted state, my friend, how scarcely anything seemed to please you? This thing happened quite contrary to your wishes, and that was not at all to your mind; and the other was not according to your notion of what should be. The prophet Jeremiah asked, "Wherefore doth a living man complain?" But we seemed to ask, "Why should we leave off complaining?" We murmured against the Lord notwithstanding the great mercies that He gave to us; we rebelled against Him, and waxed worse and worse. It is a difficult thing for us to love a murmurer. When you try to do a man good, and he only grumbles at what you do for him, you are very apt to say, "Very well, I will take my favours where they will be better appreciated." But God did not act like that towards us; "His great love wherewith He loved us" was not to be turned away from us even by our murmurings and complainings.

And all that while, dear friends, *we were trifling with spiritual things.* Like those people mentioned in the parable who, when they were invited to the marriage feast, "made light of it," so did we. We were warned to escape from hell, but it seemed to us like an idle tale. We were bidden to seek after heaven, but we loved the things of this world too well to barter them for joys unseen and eternal. We were told that "Christ Jesus came into the world to save sinners," and it seemed to be a story that we had heard so often that we called it "a platitude." We were adjured to lay hold on Christ, and to find eternal life in Him; but we said, "Perhaps we will to-morrow;" proving that we did not care about it, but would make God wait at our beck and call when it should be convenient for us. You know that, if a man is in an ill state of health, and you, as a doctor, go to help him; but he merely laughs at his illness, and says that he does not care about it, you are very apt to say, "Then, why should I care? You are sick, and I am anxious to heal you; but you say that you do not care to be healed. Very well, then, I will go to some other patient who will entreat me to use my best skill on his behalf, and who will be grateful to me when I have used it." But the Lord did not act like that with us. Notwithstanding our trifling. He was in earnest; He meant to heal our soul-sickness, and He did heal it. Determined to save us, He would not heed the rebuff of our carelessness and callousness, but still persevered in manifesting toward us that "great love wherewith He loved us, even when we were dead in sins."

To make the deformity of our character still worse, —we were all the while proud,—as proud as Lucifer. We had not any righteousness of our own, yet we thought we had. We were far off from God by wicked works, yet we stood before Him, like the Pharisee in the temple, and thanked Him that we were not as other men! We were quite content, though we had nothing to be content with. We were "wretched, and miserable, and poor, and blind, and naked," yet we said that we were "rich, and increased with goods, and had need of nothing." As for shedding penitential tears, we left that work to those who had sinned more deeply than we had, for we imagined that we had kept all the commandments from our youth up. Thus we despised the Saviour because we exalted ourselves. We thought little of Christ because we thought much of ourselves. And so, in our pride, we dared to strut before the eternal throne as if we were some great ones, though we were but worms of the dust. I think that it is one of the most difficult things in the world to love a proud man. You can love a man, even though he has a thousand faults, if he is not proud and boastful; but when he is very proud, human nature seems to start back from him; yet God, in His "great love wherewith He loved us, even when we were dead in sins," loved us although we were proud, and loved us out of that sinful state.

If worse could be, there was something even worse than pride in us, for we were deceptive as well as proud. "No," says one, "surely you cannot truthfully lay that to our charge." Well, I have to confess that it was so with myself. I remember that, when I was ill, I said that, if God would only spare my life, I would live so differently in future; but my promise was not kept, though God did spare my life. Often, after a stirring sermon, I have sought a place where I could weep in secret, and I have said, "Now will I be decided for the Lord;" but it was not so. Oh, how many times have we broken the promises and vows we made unto the Lord! Child of God, before your conversion, how many vows and covenants you made; yet your goodness was like the morning cloud or the early dew, which soon passes away. Who can love one who is not to be trusted? Yet God, in "His great love wherewith He loved us, even when we were dead in sins," loved us while we so many times deceived Him.

These things, which I have mentioned, have appertained to all the children of God; but there are some of them whose sins have been even greater than these. I ask every converted man here just to look through his own biography. Some of you were, perhaps, converted while you were young, and so were kept from the grosser sins into which others fall; but there were some who were suffered to go into drunkenness, or into uncleanness and all manner of iniquity. God has forgiven you, my brother, and has washed all that evil away in the precious blood of Jesus; but you feel that you can never forgive yourself. I know that I am bringing some very unhappy memories before you, of which you say, "Would God that night had never been, or that day had never passed over my head!" The Lord grant that, as you look back upon those sins of yours, you may feel deeply humbled, and, at the same time, may be devoutly grateful to God for "His great love" wherewith He hath loved you!

There have been some, who seem as if they had gone to the utmost extremity of sin,—as if they dared and defied the Most High; and yet, notwithstanding their atrocious sins, free grace has won the day. There has seemed, in some cases, to be a stern struggle between sin and grace, as if sin said, "I will provoke God till grace shall leave Him;" but grace has said, "Provoked as the Lord is, yet still will He stand to His purpose of mercy; He will not turn away from the decree of His love." Dear brothers and sisters in Christ, I ask you to think this subject over in your own private meditations. There are some things that it would not be right to mention in any ear but the ear of God; for it certainly was a horrible pit out of which He took us, and miry clay indeed out of which He drew us; so we may well praise "His great love wherewith He loved us even when we were dead in sins."

II. The second subject for our meditation is, WHAT GOD DID FOR US "even when we were dead in sins."

Well, first of all, he remained faithful to His choice of us. He had chosen His people or ever the earth was, and He did not choose them in the dark. He knew right well what their nature would be, and also the practice which would grow out of their nature; so that nothing that has happened has ever surprised the Lord concerning any one of His people. He was well aware beforehand of all their corruption and filthiness; so, when He saw them acting as I have described, He did not turn from His purpose to save them. Blessed be His name for this. It is one of the wonders of His grace, and proves the greatness of His love.

Then, next, as He did not repent of His choice, so neither did He repent of His redemption of His people. You will find it recorded in Scripture that "it repented the Lord that He had made man on the earth, and it grieved Him at His heart;" but you never read that He repented of redemption. Nowhere in Scripture is there such a passage as this, "It grieved the Lord at His heart that He had given His Son to die for such unworthy ones." No, my friends, He had bought us with a price beyond all calculation, even the heart's blood of His only-begotten Son; so that, although we went from sin to sin, and for a time resisted all the calls of the gospel, He did not turn from His purpose of love and mercy, nor make His atonement for us null and void.

Then, further, in His great love for us, God would not let us die till He had brought us to Christ. Possibly, we passed through many perils, and had many escapes. John Bunyan, you will remember, was to have stood as sentinel, one night, but another soldier took his place, and was shot.   John Bunyan did not know, at the time, why the exchange was made, but God had ordained that he should not die till he had been brought to Christ.   So fool-hardy was he that, on one occasion, he plucked the sting out of a viper with his bare hand, yet he was unhurt, for God would not let him die while he was such a desperado.   And what wonderful escapes from shipwreck, from murder, from fever, from accidents in a thousand forms, some men have had, simply because God will not let them perish, for He means that they shall yet be brought as sheep into His fold.   I told you, some time ago, that I once talked with a gentleman who was in the famous charge at Balaclava; and I felt moved to say to him, "Surely God had some designs of love toward you, or He would not have spared you when so many were being taken away."   Well, in whatever way our lives have been spared, we ascribe it to the great love wherewith God loved us even when we were dead in sins.

We see that great love also manifested *in the way in which God restrained us from many sins.*   There have been times in our history when, if it had not been for a mysterious check that was put upon us, we should have sinned much worse even than we did.   Something of that kind happened in the case of the well-known Colonel Gardiner.   He had made an appointment for the commission of a very gross sin, but the Lord had chosen him unto eternal life, so that night, which he intended to spend in sin, became the time of his conversion to God; and you know what a devout and earnest Christian he became.   The Lord knows the right time to say to anyone, "Thus far shalt thou go, but no farther."   He makes men's minds and hearts, like the sea, to know His will, and to move or be still at His divine command.   Cannot some of you, my brethren, recollect the way in which God thus restrained you from going to an excess of riot?

And, then, His great love was seen *by the way in which He kept on calling us by His grace.*   Some of us can scarcely tell when we were first bidden to come to the Saviour.   A mother's tears and a father's prayers are, however, among the fondly-cherished memories of that early call.   Do not some of you remember that loving Sabbath-school teacher, and the earnestness with which she pleaded with you; and that godly minister, and how he seemed to throw his whole soul into the work of entreating you to yield yourself to the Saviour?   Others of you cannot forget how, with good books, letters, entreaties, and persuasions from Christian friends, you have been followed, as if the Lord had hunted you out of your sins by all the agencies that could possibly be used, yet you dodged, and twisted, and doubled, this way and that way, trying to escape from your gracious Pursuer.   You were like a bird that the fowler cannot take for a long while, or like a wandering sheep that the shepherd cannot find for many a day.   But the good Shepherd never gave up the search; He meant to find you, and He did.   He had determined to save you, and from that determination He would not be turned aside, do whatever you might.   And, at last, there came the blessed day when He subdued you unto Himself.   The weapons of your rebellion fell from your hands, for Christ had conquered you; and how did He do it?   By "His great love"—His omnipotent grace.   You were dead in sins when His Spirit came to work thus upon you; but the Spirit came, in the name of the risen Saviour, with such almighty force or irresistible love that you were carried captive—a willing captive—

at the chariot wheels of your Divine Conqueror.   Shall we ever forget that blessed time?   We sing "Happy day! Happy day!" and well we may, for that conquest is the chief and foremost token of "His great love wherewith He loved us, even when we were dead in sins."

I will not say more about this precious truth, but I will use the few minutes still at my disposal in making a practical application of my subject.

If, dear friends, the Lord loved us with such great love even when we were dead in sins, *do you think that He will ever leave us to perish?*   Have you indulged the notion that, under your present trial, whatever it may be, you will be deserted by your God?   My dear widowed sister, do you fear that the Lord will forsake you now that your husband is dead?   My friend over there,—you who have had heavy losses in business,—do you not believe that the Lord will help you through?   Did He love you when you were dead in sins, and is He going to desert you now?   Do you think you will ever have to ask, with the psalmist, "Is His mercy clean gone for ever? doth His promise fail for evermore?   Hath God forgotten to be gracious? hath He in anger shut up His tender mercies?   If you do talk like that, then ask yourself why the Lord ever began His work of love upon you if He did not mean to finish it, or if He meant, after all, to cast you off?   Do you think, if that was His intention, He would ever have begun with you?   He knew all that would happen to you, and all that you would do, so that nothing comes unexpectedly to Him.   Known unto the Lord, from the beginning, were all your trials and all your sins, so that, as He still loved you, in the foresight of all that was to happen to you, do you think that He will now, or ever, cast you away from Him?   You know that He will not.

Again, if He so loved you even when you were dead in sins, *will he deny you anything that is for His own glory, and for your own and others' good?*   You have been praying, but you have feared that the mercy you asked would never come.   Think for a moment,—He that spared not His own Son, but delivered Him up for you centuries before you were born, will He not freely give to you all that you ought to ask of Him now that you are alive unto Him?   George Herbert speaks of the dew that falls upon the grass, although the grass cannot call for the dew; but you do call upon God to give you His grace, so shall not His grace come as copiously to you as the dew falls where God sends it?   Doth He water the earth when its dumb mouth opens?   Doth He provide food for the "dumb driven cattle"?   Then, will He not attend to your cries and prayers when you call upon Him in the name of His well-beloved Son?   If He loved you when you were a mass of corruption, will He not answer your supplications now that He has made you to be an heir of heaven, and formed you in the likeness of His Son?   O, beloved, be of good comfort, and let no thought of despondency, or of unbelief, ever cross your mind!

Further, if the Lord loved you thus even when you were dead in sins, *ought you not now to love Him very much?*   Oh, the love of God!   The apostle does not say that God pitied us, though that is true.   He does not say that the Lord had compassion upon us, though that also is true; but Paul speaks of "His great love."   I can perfectly understand God's pitying me; I can perfectly understand God's having compassion on me; but I cannot comprehend God's loving me; nor can you.   Think what it means,—He *loves* you.

Sweet above all other things is love;—a mother's love, a father's love, a husband's love, a wife's love;—but all these are only faint images of the love of God. You know how greatly you are cheered by the earthly love of one who is dear to you; but Paul says that *God* loves you. He that made the heavens and the earth, before whom you are as an emmet, has set His heart's affection upon you. He loves you so much that He has made great sacrifices for you, He is daily blessing you, and He will not be in heaven without you. So dear, so strong is His love to you, and it was so even when you were dead in sins. Oh, then, will you not love Him much in return for His "great love" to you? Is anything too hard for you to bear for His dear sake, or anything too difficult for you to do for Him who loved you so? Dear Lord, we give ourselves to Thee; 'tis all that we can do.

Another reflection for you, my Christian friend, is this. If God so loved you even when you were dead in sins, *ought not you to love those who treat you badly*? There are many people, in this world, who seem as if they could not do anything but ugly things. They have not a generous spot in their nature; they are cross-grained, ever quarrelling, and he who would fain live peaceably with them sometimes finds it very hard work. I know some gentle spirits that are deeply wounded by the hard and cruel things that are said or done to them by their relatives or companions. Well, dear friends, if any of us are treated thus, let us love these cruel people, let us cover their unkindness over with our love; for, if God loved us even when we were dead in sins,—when He could not see anything in us to love, we also ought to love others for His sake. Even when we see a thousand faults in them, we must say, "As God, for Christ's sake, has forgiven us, so do we forgive you." It is a grand thing to be able to bury in eternal forgetfulness every unkind word or act that has ever caused us pain. If any of you have any thought of anger in your heart against anyone,—if you have any feeling of resentment,—if you have any recollection of injuries,—if there is aught that vexes and grieves you, come and bury it all in the grave of Jesus; for if He loved you when you were dead in sins, it cannot be half so wonderful for you to love your poor fellow-sinner whatever ill-treatment you may have received at his hands.

My last word is to the unconverted, and it is a very sweet and precious word. Do you see, unconverted man, that you need never say, "I dare not come to God through Jesus Christ, because there is nothing good in me"? You need never say that, for Paul speaks of "His great love wherewith He loved us, even when we were dead in sins." Now, if all His people were loved by Him when they were dead in sins, how can you think that God requires anything good in man as the cause or reason for His love? Of all the saints in heaven it may be said that God loved them because He would do it; for, by nature, there was nothing more in them for God to love than there was in the very devils in hell. And as to His saints on earth, if God loves them,—and He does,—it is simply because He will do it, for there was no goodness whatever in them by nature; God loves them in the infinite sovereignty of His great loving nature. Well, then, poor soul, why should not God love *you*? And since He bids you come to Him, however empty you may

be of everything that is good, come to Him, and welcome. Let the text knock on the head, once for all, all ideas of doing anything to win the love of God; and if you feel yourself to be the very worst, and lowest, and meanest of the human race, I rejoice that you feel that, for the Lord loves to look upon those who are self-emptied, and who have nothing good of their own to plead before Him. These are the people who will value His love, and upon such people as these it is that He bestows His love. "The whole have no need of a physician, but they that are sick." The hospital is for the man who is diseased, not for the one who is in health; and the Lord Jesus Christ has opened a Hospital for Incurables,—for those who cannot be cured by all the medicines of human morality and outward religion. Christ bids them come to Him that He may make them whole.

I wish I had the power to speak of the love of God to the sinner in such a way that he would come to the Lord Jesus Christ, but I will try to put the truth very plainly and simply, and then I will close my discourse. My hearer, whatever thou mayest have been up to this moment,—if thou hast been a despiser of God, an infidel, a blasphemer,—if thou hast added sin to sin, if thou hast made thyself black as hell with enormous transgressions,—yet all this is no reason why God should not have chosen thee, and loved thee; and all this is no reason why He should not now forgive thee, and accept thee. Nay, He puts it thus in His Word: "Come now, and let us reason together, saith the Lord: though your sins be as scarlet, they shall be as white as snow; though they be red like crimson, they shall be as wool." Come, then, ye blackest of sinners, —ye who feel yourselves unfit to be found in a house of prayer,—ye who, like the publican in the temple, scarcely dare to lift up your eyes to heaven,—ye self-condemned ones, who fear that there is no hope for you,—let me assure you that in you there is space for God's mercy to be displayed, elbow-room for His grace to work. Come to Jesus just as you are; accept the atonement made by His own blood, and be saved here and now, for He waiteth to be gracious, and He hath said, "Him that cometh to Me, I will in no wise cast out." I recollect the time, many years ago, when I would have given both my eyes to hear such truth as I have preached to-night. It would not have mattered to me who had told it to me. If it had been a man of stammering tongue and faulty grammar, if he had but said to me, "Salvation is of God's grace, not of your merit; it is of God's goodness, not of your holiness; you have nothing to do but to rest on what Christ has done, for God loves even those who are dead in sins,"—if I had known that, I think I should have found peace with God long before I did. Does anyone say, "But I want to feel, and I want to do, and I want to find out this, and that, and the other"? You want nothing of the kind, sinner. Christ has done it all. To take any merit of your own to Christ, would be worse than carrying coals to Newcastle. Come just as you are, empty-handed sinner, bankrupt sinner, starving sinner, thou who art at the very gates of hell, for—

"There is life for a look at the Crucified One;
     There is life at this moment for thee;
  Then look, sinner,—look unto Him, and be saved,—
     Unto Him who was nailed to the tree."

FAITH: WHAT IS IT? HOW CAN IT BE OBTAINED?

"By grace are ye saved through faith."—Ephesians ii. 8.

I MEAN to dwell mainly upon that expression, "Through faith." I call attention, however, first of all, to the fountain head of our salvation, which is the grace of God. "By grace are ye saved." Because God is gracious, therefore sinful men are forgiven, converted, purified, and saved. It is not because of anything in them, or that ever can be in them, that they are saved; but because of the boundless love, goodness, pity, compassion, mercy, and grace of God. Tarry a moment, then, at the well-head. Behold the pure river of water of life as it proceeds out of the throne of God and of the Lamb. What an abyss is the grace of God! Who can fathom it? Like all the rest of the divine attributes, it is infinite. God is full of love, for "God is love"; God is full of goodness, and the very name "God" is but short for "good." Unbounded goodness and love enter into the very essence of the Godhead. It is because "His mercy endureth for ever" that men are not destroyed; because "His compassions fail not" that sinners are brought to Himself and forgiven. Right well remember this, or else you may fall into error by fixing your minds so much upon the faith which is the channel of salvation as to forget the grace which is the fountain and source even of faith itself. Faith is the work of God's grace in us. No man can say that Jesus is the Christ but by the Holy Ghost. "No man cometh unto Me," said Christ, "except the Father which hath sent Me draw him." So that faith, which is coming to Christ, is the result of divine drawing. Grace is the first and last moving cause of salvation, and faith, important as it is, is only an important part of the machinery which grace employs. We are saved "through faith," but it is "by grace." Sound forth those words as with the archangel's trumpet: "By grace are ye saved."

Faith occupied the position of a channel or conduit-pipe. Grace is the fountain and the stream: faith is the aqueduct along which the flood of mercy flows down to refresh the thirsty sons of men. It is a great pity when the aqueduct is broken. It is a sad sight to see around Rome the many noble aqueducts which no longer convey water into the city, because the arches are broken and the marvellous structures are in ruins. The aqueduct must be kept entire to convey the current; and, even so, faith must be true and sound, leading right up to God and coming right down to ourselves, that it may become a serviceable channel of mercy to our souls. Still, I again remind you that faith is the channel or aqueduct, and not the fountain head, and we must not look so much to it as to exalt it above the divine source of all blessing which lies in the grace of God. Never make a Christ out of your faith, nor think of it as if it were the independent source of your salvation. Our life is found in "looking unto Jesus," not in looking to our own faith. By faith all things become possible to us; yet the power is not in the faith, but in the God upon whom faith relies. Grace is the

locomotive, and faith is the chain by which the carriage of the soul is attached to the great motive power. The righteousness of faith is not the moral excellence of faith, but the righteousness of Jesus Christ which faith grasps and appropriates. The peace within the soul is not derived from the contemplation of our own faith, but it comes to us from Him who is our peace, the hem of whose garment faith touches, and virtue comes out of Him into the soul.

However, it is a very important thing that we look well to the channel, and therefore at this time we will consider it, as God, the Holy Ghost, shall enable us. Faith, *what is it?* Faith, *why is it selected as the channel of blessing?* Faith, *how can it be obtained and increased?*

I. FAITH, WHAT IS IT? What is this faith concerning which it is said, "By grace are ye saved *through faith?*" There are many descriptions of faith, but almost all the definitions I have met with have made me understand it less than I did before I saw them. The negro said when he read the chapter that he would confound it, and it is very likely that he did so, though he meant to expound it. So, brethren, we may explain faith till nobody understands it. I hope I shall not be guilty of that fault. Faith is the simplest of all things, and perhaps because of its simplicity it is the more difficult to explain.

What is faith? *It is made up of three things—knowledge, belief, and trust. Knowledge* comes first. Romanist divines hold that a man can believe what he does not know. Perhaps a Romanist can; but I cannot. "How shall they believe in Him of whom they have not heard?" I want to be informed of a fact before I can possibly believe it. I believe this, I believe that; but I cannot say that I believe a great many things of which I have never heard. "Faith cometh by hearing"; we must first hear, in order that we may know what is to be believed. "They that know Thy name will put their trust in Thee." A measure of knowledge is essential to faith: hence the importance of getting knowledge. "Incline your ear, and come unto Me; hear, and your soul shall live,"—such was the word of the ancient prophet, and it is the word of the gospel still. Search the Scriptures and learn what the Holy Spirit teacheth concerning Christ and His salvation. Seek to know God,—"that God is, and is the rewarder of them that diligently seek Him." May He give you "the spirit of knowledge and of the fear of the Lord." Know the gospel: know what the good news is, how it talks of free forgiveness, and of change of heart, of adoption into the family of God, and of countless other blessings. Know God, know His gospel, and know especially Christ Jesus the Son of God, the Saviour of men, united to us by His human nature, and united to God, seeing He is divine, and thus able to act as Mediator between God and man, able to lay His hand upon both, and to be the connecting link between the sinner and the Judge of all the earth. Endeavour to know more and more of Christ. After Paul had been converted more than twenty years, he tells the Philippians that he desired to know Christ; and depend upon it, the more we know of Jesus, the more we shall wish to know of Him that so our faith in Him may increase. Endeavour especially to know the doctrine of the sacrifice of Christ, for that is the centre of the target at which faith aims; that is the point upon which saving faith mainly fixes itself, that "God was in Christ, reconciling the world unto Himself, not imputing their trespasses unto them." Know that He was made a curse for us, as it is written, "Cursed is everyone that hangeth on a tree." Drink deep into the doctrine of the substitutionary work of Christ, for therein lies the sweetest possible comfort to the guilty sons of men, since the Lord "made Him to be sin for that we might be made the righteousness of God in Him." Faith, then, begins with knowledge; hence the value of being taught in divine truth, for to know Christ is life eternal.

Then the mind goes on to *believe* that these things are true. The soul believes that God is. and that He hears the cries of sincere hearts; that the gospel is from God; that justification by faith is the grand truth that God hath revealed in these last days by His Spirit more clearly than before. Then the heart believes that Jesus is verily and in truth our God and Saviour, the Redeemer of men, the Prophet, Priest, and King unto His people. Dear hearers, I pray that you may at once come to this. Get firmly to believe that "the blood of Jesus Christ, God's dear Son, cleanseth us from all sin"; that His sacrifice is complete and fully accepted of God on man's behalf, so that He that believeth on Jesus is not condemned. So far you have made an advance towards faith, and one more ingredient is needed to complete it, which is *trust*. Commit yourself to the merciful God; rest your hope on the gracious gospel; trust your soul on the dying and living Saviour; wash away your sins in the atoning blood; accept His perfect righteousness, and all is well. Trust is the life-blood of faith: there is no saving faith without it. The Puritans were accustomed to explain faith by the word "recumbency." You know what it means. You see me leaning upon this rail, leaning with all my weight upon it; even thus lean upon Christ. It would be a better illustration still if I were to stretch myself at full length and rest my whole person upon a rock, lying flat upon it. Fall flat upon Christ. Cast yourself upon Him, rest in Him, commit yourself to Him. That done, you have exercised saving faith. Faith is not a blind thing; for faith begins with knowledge. It is not a speculative thing; for faith believes facts of which it is sure. It is not an unpractical, dreamy thing; for faith trusts, and stakes its destiny upon the truth of revelation. Faith *ventures* its all upon the truth of God; it is not a pleasant word to use, but the poet employed it, and it suggests my meaning:

"Venture on Him, venture wholly;
Let no other trust intrude."

That is one way of describing what faith is: I wonder whether I have "confounded" it already.

Let me try again. *Faith is believing that Christ is what He is said to be, that He will do what He has promised to do, and expecting this of Him.* The Scriptures speak of Jesus Christ as being God, God in human flesh; as being perfect in His character; as being made a sin-offering on our behalf; as bearing sins in His own body on the tree. The Scripture speaks of Him as having finished transgression, made an end of sin, and brought in everlasting righteousness. The Scriptures further tell us that He "rose again," that He "ever liveth to make intercession for us," that He has gone up into the glory, and has taken possession of heaven on the behalf of His people, and that He will shortly come again "to judge the world in righteousness and His people with equity." We are most firmly to believe that it is even so; for this is the testimony of God the Father when He said, "This is my beloved Son; hear ye Him." This also is testified by God the Holy Spirit; for the Spirit has borne witness to Christ, both by the word and by divers miracles, and by His working in the hearts of men. We are to believe this testimony to be true.

Faith also believes that Christ will do what He has promised; that if He has promised to cast out none that come to Him, it is certain that He will not cast us out if we come to Him. Faith believes that if Jesus said, "The water that I shall give him shall be in him a well of water springing up into everlasting life," it must be true; and if we get this living water from Christ it will abide in us, and will well up within us in streams of holy life. Whatever Christ has promised to do He will do, and we must believe this so as to look for pardon, justification, preservation, and eternal glory from His hands, according as He has promised.

Then comes the next necessary step. Jesus is what He is said to be, Jesus will do what He says He will do; therefore we must each one *trust Him*, saying, "He will be to me what He says He is, and He will do to me what He has promised to do; I leave myself in the hands of Him who is appointed to save, that He may save me. I rest upon His promise that He will do even as He has said." This is a saving faith, and he that hath it hath everlasting life. Whatever his dangers and difficulties, whatever his darkness and depression, whatever his infirmities and sins, he that believeth thus on Christ Jesus is not condemned, and shall never come into condemnation. May that explanation be of some service. I trust it may be used by the Spirit of God.

But now I thought, as it was a very hot and heavy morning, that I had better give you a number of illustrations, lest anybody should be inclined to go to sleep. If anybody should be drowsy, will his next neighbour just nudge him a little by accident; for it may be as well while we are here to be awake, especially with such a subject on hand as this. The illustrations will be such as have been commonly used, and perhaps I may be able to give one or two of my own. Faith exists in various degrees, according to the amount of knowledge, or other cause. Sometimes faith is little more than a simple *clinging* to Christ: a sense of dependence, and a willingnes, so to depend. When you are down at the seasides as we might all of us wish to be, you will see the limpet sticking to the rock; you walk with a soft tread up to the rock with your walking stick and strike the limpet with a rapid blow, and off he comes. Try the next limpet in that way. You have given him warning; he heard the blow with which you struck his neighbour, and he clings with all his might. You will never get him off; not you! Strike, and strike again, but you may as soon break the rock. Our little friend, the limpet, does not know much, but he clings. He cannot tell us much about what he is clinging to, he is not acquainted with the geological formation of the rock, but he clings. He has found something to cling to, that is his little bit of knowledge, and he uses it by clinging to the rock of his salvation; it is the limpet's life to cling. Thousands of God's people have no more faith than this; they know enough to cling to Jesus with all their heart and soul, and this suffices. Jesus Christ is to them a Saviour strong and mighty, and like a rock immovable and immutable; they cleave to Him for dear life, and this clinging saves them.

God gives to His people the propensity to cling. Look at the sweet pea which grows in your garden. Perhaps it has fallen down upon the gravel wall. Lift it up against the laurel or the trellis, or put a stick near it, and it catches hold directly, because there are little hooks ready prepared with which it grasps anything which comes in its way: it was meant to grow upwards, and so it is provided with tendrils. Every child of God has his tendrils about him— thoughts, and desires, and hopes with which he hooks on to Christ and the promise. Though this is a very simple sort of faith, it is a very complete and effectual form of it, and, in fact, it is the heart of all faith, and that to which we are often driven when we are in deep trouble, or when our mind is somewhat bemuddled by our being sickly or depressed in spirit. We can cling when we can do nothing else, and that is the very soul of faith. O poor heart, if thou dost not yet know as much about the gospel as we could wish thee to know, cling to what thou dost know. If as yet thou art only like a lamb that wades a little into the river of life, and not like leviathan who stirs the mighty deep to the bottom, yet drink; for it is drinking, and not diving, that will save thee. Cling, then! Cling to Jesus; for that is faith.

Another form of faith is this, in which a man depends upon another from a knowledge of the superiority of that other, and *follows* him. I do not think the limpet knows much about the rock, but in this next phase of faith there is more knowledge. A blind man trusts himself with his guide because he knows that his friend can see, and trusting, he walks where his guide conducts him. If the poor man is born blind he does not know what sight is; but he knows that there is such a thing as sight, and that it is possessed by his friend, and therefore he freely puts his hand into the hand of the seeing one, and follows his leadership. This is as good an image of faith as well can be; we know that Jesus has about Him merit, and power, and blessing which we do not possess, and therefore we gladly trust ourselves to Him, and He never betrays our confidence.

Every boy that goes to school has to exert faith while *learning*. His schoolmaster teaches him geography, and instructs him as to the form of the earth, and the existence of certain great cities and empires. The boy does not himself know that these things are true, except that he believes his teacher, and the books put into his hands. That is what you will have to do with Christ if you are to be saved—you must just know because He tells you, and believe because He assures you it is even so and trust yourself with Him because He promises you that salvation will be the result. Almost all that you and I know has come to us by faith. A scientific discovery has been made, and we are sure of it. On what ground do we believe it? On the authority of certain well-known men of learning, whose repute is established.

We have never made or seen their experiments, but we believe their witness. Just so you are to do with regard to Christ: because He teaches you certain truths you are to be His disciple, and believe His words, and trust yourself with Him. He is infinitely superior to you, and presents Himself to your confidence as your Master and Lord. If you will receive Him and His words you shall be saved.

Another and a higher form of faith is that faith which *grows out of love*. Why does a boy trust his father? You and I know a little more about his father than he does, and we do not rely upon him quite so implicitly; but the reason why the child trusts his father is because he loves him. Blessed and happy are they who have a sweet faith in Jesus, intertwined with deep affection for Him. They are charmed with His character and delighted with His mission, they are carried away by the lovingkindness that He has manifested, and now they cannot help trusting Him because they so much admire, revere, and love Him. It is hard to make you doubt a person whom you love. If you are at last driven to it, then comes the awful passion of jealousy, which is strong as death and cruel as the grave: but till such a crushing of the heart shall come, love is all trustfulness and confidence.

The way of loving trust in the Saviour may thus be illustrated. A lady is the wife of the most eminent physician of the day. She is seized with a dangerous illness, and is smitten down by its power; yet she is wonderfully calm and quiet, for her husband has made this disease his special study, and has healed thousands similarly afflicted. She is not in the least troubled, for she feels perfectly safe in the hands of one so dear to her, in whom skill and love are blended in their highest forms. Her faith is reasonable and natural, her husband from every point of view deserves it of her. This is the kind of faith which the happiest of believers exercise towards Christ. There is no physician like Him, none can save as He can; we love Him, and He loves us, and therefore we put ourselves into His hands, accept whatever He prescribes, and do whatever He bids. We feel that nothing can be wrongly ordered while He is the director of our affairs, for He loves us too well to let us perish, or suffer a single needless pang.

Faith also *realizes* the presence of the living God and Saviour, and thus it breeds in the soul a beautiful calm and quiet like that which was seen in a little child in the time of tempest. Her mother was alarmed, but the sweet girl was pleased; she clapped her hands with delight. Standing at the window when the flashes came most vividly, she cried in childish accents, "Look, mamma! How beautiful! How beautiful!" Her mother said, "My dear, come away, the lightning is terrible;" but she begged to be allowed to look out and see the lovely light which God was making all over the sky, for she was sure God would not do His little child any harm. "But hearken to the terrible thunder," said her mother. "Did you not say, mamma, that God was speaking in the thunder?" "Yes," said her trembling parent. "O," said the darling, "how nice it is to hear Him. He talks very loud, but I think, it is because He wants the deaf people to hear Him. Is it not so, mamma?" Thus she went talking on; as merry as a bird was she, for God was real to her, and she trusted Him. To her the lightning was God's beautiful light, and the thunder was God's wonderful voice, and she was happy. I dare say her mother knew a good deal about the laws of nature and the energy of electricity; and little was the comfort which her knowledge brought her. The child's knowledge was less showy, but it was far more certain and precious. We are so conceited nowadays that we are too proud to be comforted by self-evident truth, and prefer to make ourselves wretched with questionable theories. Hood sang a deep spiritual truth when he merrily said,

> "I remember, I remember,
> The fir trees dark and high;
> I used to think their slender tops
> Were close against the sky;
> It was a childish ignorance,
> But now 'tis little joy
> To know I'm farther off from heav'n
> Than when I was a boy."

For my own part I would rather be a child again than grow perversely wise. Faith, is to be a child towards Christ, believing in Him as a real and present person, at this very moment near us, and ready to bless us. This may seem to be a childish fancy; but it is such childishness as we must all come to if we would be happy in the Lord "Except ye be converted, and become as little chilren, ye shall not enter into the kingdom of heaven." Faith takes Christ at His word, as a child believes His father, and trusts Him in all simplicity with past, present, and future. God give us such faith!

A firm form of *faith arises out of assured knowledge ;* this comes of growth in grace, and is the faith which believes Christ because it knows Him, trusts Him because it has proved Him to be infallibly faithful. This faith asks not for signs and tokens, but bravely believes. Look at the faith of the master mariner—I have often wondered at it. He looses his cable, he steams away from the shore. For days, weeks, or even months he never sees sail or shore, yet on he goes day and night without fear, till one morning he finds himself just opposite to the desired haven towards which he has been steering. How has he found his way over the trackless deep? He has trusted in his compass, his nautical almanack, his glass, and the heavenly bodies, and obeying their guidance, without sighting shore, he has steered so accurately that he has not to change a point to get into port. It is a wonderful thing that sailing without sight. Spiritually it is a blessed thing to leave the shores of sight, and say, "Good-bye to inward feelings, cheering providences, signs, tokens, and so forth: I believe in God, and I steer for heaven straight away." "Blessed are they that have not seen and yet have believed:" to them shall be administered an abundant entrance at the last, and a safe voyage on the way.

This is the faith which makes it easy *to commit our soul and all its eternal interests into the Saviour's keeping.* One man goes to the bank and puts his money into it with a measure of confidence; but another has looked into the bank's accounts, and has been behind the scenes and made sure of its having a large reserve of well invested capital; he puts in his money with the utmost assurance. He knows and is established in his faith, and so he cheerfully commits his all to the bank. Even so, we who know Christ are glad to place our whole being in His hands, knowing that He is able to keep us even unto the end.

God give us more and more of an assured confidence in Jesus until it comes to be an unwavering faith, so that we never doubt, but unquestioningly believe. Look at the ploughman; he labours with his plough in the wintry months, when there is not a bough on the tree nor a bird that sings to cheer him, and after he has ploughed he takes the precious corn from the granary, of which perhaps he hath little enough, and he buries it in the furrows, assured that it will come up again. Because he has seen a harvest fifty times already he looks for another, and in faith he scatters the precious grain. To all appearance, the most absurd thing that ever was done by mortal man is to throw away good corn, burying it in the ground. If you had never seen or heard of its results, it would seem the way of waste and not the work of husbandry; yet the farmer has no doubt, he longs to be allowed to cast away his seed, in faith he even covets fair weather that he may bury his corn; and if you tell him that he is doing an absurd thing, he smiles at your ignorance, and tells you that thus harvests come. This is a fair picture of the faith which grows of experience: it helps us to act in a manner contrary to appearances, it leads us to commit our all to the keeping of Christ, burying our hopes and our very lives with Him in joyful confidence that if we be dead with Him we shall also live with Him. Jesus Christ who rose from the dead will raise us up through His death unto newness of life, and give us a harvest of joy and peace.

Give up everything into the hand of Christ, and you shall have it back with an abundant increase. May we get strong faith, so that as we have no doubt of the rising and setting of the sun, so we may never doubt the Saviour's working for us in every hour of need. We have already trusted in our Lord, and have never been confounded, therefore let us go on to rely upon Him more and more implicitly; for never shall our faith in Him surpass the bounds of His deservings. Have faith in God, and then hear Jesus say, "Ye believe in God, believe also in Me."

II. Thus far have I done my best to answer what faith is; we shall now enquire, WHY FAITH IS SELECTED AS THE CHANNEL OF SALVATION? "By grace are ye saved *through faith.*" It becomes us to be modest in answering such a question, for God's ways are not always to be understood; but, as far as we can tell, faith has been selected as the channel of grace because *there is a natural adaptation* in faith to be used as the receiver. Suppose that I am about to give a poor man an alms: I put it into his hand—why? Well, it would hardly be fitting to put it into his ear, or to lay it upon his foot; the hand seems made on purpose to receive. So faith in the mental body is created on purpose to be a receiver: it is the hand of the man, and there is a fitness in bestowing grace by its means. Do let me put this very plainly. Faith which receives Christ is as simple an act as when your child receives an apple from you, because you hold it out and promise to give it the apple if it comes for it. The belief and the receiving relate only to an apple, but they make up precisely the same act as the faith which deals with eternal salvation, and what the child's hand is to the apple that your faith is to the perfect salvation of Christ. The child's hand does not make the apple, nor alter the apple, it only takes it; and faith is chosen by God to be the receiver of salvation, because it does not pretend to make salvation, nor to help in it, but it receives it.

Faith, again, is doubtless selected because *it gives all the glory to God.* It is of faith that it might be by grace, and it is of grace that there may be no boasting; for God cannot endure pride. Paul saith, "Not of works, lest any man should boast." The hand which receives charity does not say, "I am to be thanked for accepting the gift"; that would be absurd. When the hand conveys bread to the mouth it does not say to the body, "Thank me, for I feed you." It is a very simple thing that the hand does, though a very necessary thing; but it never arrogates glory to itself for what it does. So God has selected faith to receive the unspeakable gift of His grace because it cannot take to itself any credit, but must adore the gracious God who is the giver of all good.

Next, God selects faith as the channel of salvation because *it is a sure method, linking man with God.* When man confides in God there is a point of union between them, and that union guarantees blessing. Faith saves us because it makes us cling to God, and so brings us into connection with Him. I have used the following illustration before, but I must repeat it, because I cannot think of a better. I am told that years ago above the Falls of Naigara a boat was upset, and two men were being carried down the current, when persons on the shore managed to float a rope out to them, which rope was seized by them both. One of them held fast to it and was safely drawn to the bank; but the other, seeing a great log come floating by, unwisely let go the rope and clung to the log, for it was the bigger thing of the two, and apparently better to cling to. Alas, the log with the man on it, went right over the vast abyss, because there was no union between the log and the shore. The size of the log was no benefit to him who grasped it: it needed a connection with the shore to produce safety. So when a man trusts to his works, or to sacraments, or to anything of that sort, he will not be saved, because there is no junction between him and Christ; but faith, though it may seem to be like a slender cord, is in the hand of the great God on the shore side; infinite power pulls in the connecting line, and thus draws the man from destruction. Oh, the blessedness of faith, because it unites us to God!

Faith is chosen, again, because *it touches the springs of action.* I wonder whether I shall be wrong if I say that we never do anything except through faith of some sort. If I walk across this platform it is because I believe my legs will carry me. A man eats because he believes in the necessity of food. Columbus discovered America because he believed that there was another continent beyond the ocean: many another grand deed has also been born of faith, for faith works wonders. Commoner things are done on the same principle; faith in its natural form is an all-prevailing force. God gives salvation to our faith, because He has thus touched the secret spring of all our emotions and actions. He has, so to speak, taken possession of the battery, and now He can send the sacred current to every part of our nature. When we believe in Christ, and the heart has come into the possession of God, then are we saved from sin, and are moved towards repentance, holiness, zeal, prayer, consecration, and every other gracious thing.

Faith, again, *has the power of working by love;* it touches the secret spring of the affections, and draws the heart towards God. Faith is an act of the understanding; but it also proceeds from the heart. "With the heart man believeth unto righteousness;" and hence God gives salvation to faith because it resides next door to the affections, and is near akin to love, and love, you know, is that which purifies the soul. Love to God is obedience, love is holiness;

to love God and to love man is to be conformed to the image of Christ, and this is salvation.

Moreover, *faith creates peace and joy;* he that hath it rests, and is tranquil, is glad, and joyous; and this is a preparation for heaven. God gives all the heavenly gifts to faith, because faith worketh in us the very life and spirit which are to be eternally manifested in the upper and better world. I have hastened over these points that I might not weary you on a day when, however willing the spirit may be, the flesh is weak.

III. We close with the third point: How CAN WE OBTAIN AND INCREASE OUR FAITH? A very earnest question this to many. They say they want to believe but cannot. A great deal of nonsense is talked upon this subject. Let us be practical in our dealing with it. "What am I to do in order to believe?" The shortest way is to believe, and if the Holy Spirit has made you honest and candid, you will believe as soon as the truth is set before you. Anyhow, the gospel command is clear: "Believe in the Lord Jesus Christ, and thou shalt be saved."

But still, *if you have a difficulty, take it before God in prayer.* Tell the great Father exactly what it is that puzzles you, and beg Him by His Holy Spiri' to solve the question. If I cannot believe a statement in a book I am glad to enquire of the author what he meant, and if he is a true man his explanation will satisfy me: much more will the divine explanation satisfy the heart of the true seeker. The Lord is willing to make Himself known; go to Him, and see if it be not so.

Furthermore, if faith seem difficult, it is possible that God the Holy Spirit will enable you to believe if you *hear very frequently and earnestly that which you are commanded to believe.* We believe many things because we have heard them so often. Do you not find it so in common life, that if you hear a thing fifty times a day, at last you come to believe it? Some men have come to believe that which is false by this process: I should not wonder but what God often blesses this method in working faith concerning that which is true, for it is written, "Faith cometh by hearing." If I earnestly and attentively hear the gospel, it may be that one of these days I shall find myself believing that which I hear, through the blessed operation of the Spirit upon my mind.

If that, however, should seem poor advice, I would add next, *consider the testimony of others.* The Samaritans believed because of what the woman told them concerning Jesus. Many of our beliefs arise out of the testimony of others. I believe that there is such a country as Japan: I never saw it, and yet I believe that there is such a place because others have been there. I believe I shall die: I have never died, but a great many have done so whom I once knew, and I have a conviction that I shall die also; the testimony of many convinces me of this fact. Listen, then, to those who tell you how they were saved, how they were pardoned, how they have been changed in character: if you will but listen you will find that somebody just like yourself has been saved. If you have been a thief, you will find that a thief rejoiced to wash away his sin in the fountain of Christ's blood. You that have been unchaste in life, you will find that men who have fallen that way have been cleansed and changed. If you are in despair, you have only to get among God's people, and enquire a little, and some who have been equally in despair with yourself will tell you how He saved them. As you listen to one after another of those who have tried the word of God, and proved it, the divine Spirit will lead you to believe. Have you not heard of the African who was told by the missionary that water sometimes became so hard that a man could walk on it? He declared that he believed a great many things the missionary had told him; but he never would believe that. When he came to England it came to pass that one frosty day he saw the river frozen, but he would not venture on it. He knew that it was a river, and he was certain that he would be drowned if he ventured upon it. He could not be induced to walk the ice till his friend went upon it; then he was persuaded, and trusted himself where others had ventured. So, mayhap, while you see others believe, and notice their joy and peace, you will yourself be gently led to believe. It is one of God's ways of helping us to faith.

A better plan still is this,—*note the authority upon which you are commanded to believe*, and this will greatly help you. The authority is not mine, or you might well reject it. It is not even the Pope's, or you might even reject that. But you are commanded to believe upon the authority of God Himself. *He* bids you believe in Jesus Christ, and you must not refuse to obey your Maker. The foreman of a certain works in the north had often heard the gospel, but he was troubled with the fear that he might not come to Christ. His good master one day sent a card round to the works—"Come to my house immediately after work." The foreman appeared at his master's door, and the master came out, and said somewhat roughly, "What do you want, John, troubling me at this time? Work is done, what right have you here?" "Sir," said he, "I had a card from you saying that I was to come after work." "Do you mean to say that merely because you had a card from me you are to come up to my house and call me out after business hours?" "Well, sir," replied the foreman, "I do not understand you, but it seems to me that, as you sent for me, I had a right to come." "Come in, John," said his master, "I have another message that I want to read to you," and he sat down and read these words—"Come unto Me, all ye that labour and are heavy laden, and I will give you rest." "Do you think after such a message from Christ that you can be wrong in going to Him?" The poor man saw it all at once, and believed, because he saw that he had good warrant and authority for believing. So have you, poor soul; you have good authority for coming to Christ, for the Lord Himself bids you trust Him.

If that does not settle you, *think over what it is that you have to believe*,—that the Lord Jesus Christ suffered in the room and place and stead of men, and is able to save all who trust Him. Why, this is the most blessed fact that ever men were told to believe: the most suitable, the most comforting, the most divine truth that ever was set before men. I advise you to think much upon it, and search out the grace and love which it contains. Study the four Evangelists, study Paul's epistles, and then see if the message is not such a credible one that you are forced to believe it.

If that does not do, then *think upon the person of Jesus Christ*—think of who He is and what He did, and where He is now, and what He is now; think often and deeply. When He, even such an one as He, bids you trust Him, surely then your heart will be persuaded. For how can you doubt *Him?*

If none of these things avail, then there is something wrong about you altogether, and my last word is, *submit yourself to God!* May the Spirit of God take away your enmity and make you yield. You are a rebel, a proud rebel, and that is why you do not believe your God. Give up your rebellion; throw down your weapons; yield at discretion; surrender to your King. I believe that never did a soul throw up its hands in self-despair, and cry, "Lord, I yield," but what faith became easy to it before long. It is because you still have a quarrel with God, and intend to have your own will and your own way, that therefore you cannot believe. "How can ye believe," said Christ, "that have honour one of another?" Proud self creates unbelief. Submit, O man. Yield to your God, and then shall you sweetly believe in your Saviour. God bless you, for Christ's sake, and bring you at this very moment to believe in the Lord Jesus. Amen.

A SOLEMN DEPRIVAL

"Without Christ."—Ephesians ii. 12.

WE shall have two things to consider this evening—*the misery of our past estate, and the great deliverance which God has wrought for us.* As for:—

I. THE MISERY OF OUR PAST ESTATE, be it known unto you that, in common with the rest of mankind, believers were once without Christ. No tongue can tell the depth of wretchedness that lies in those two words. There is no poverty like it, no want like it, and for those who die so, there is no ruin like that it will bring. Without Christ! If this be the description of some of you, we need not talk to you about the fires of hell; let this be enough to startle you, that you are in such a desperate state as to be without Christ. Oh! what terrible evils lie clustering so thick within these two words!

The man who is without Christ *is without any of those spiritual blessings which only Christ can bestow.* Christ is the life of the believer, but the man who is without Christ is dead in trespasses and sins. There he lies; let us stand and weep over his corpse. It is decent and clean, and well laid out, but life is absent, and, life being absent, there is no knowledge, no feeling, no power. What can we do? Shall we take the word of God and preach to this dead sinner? We are bidden to do so, and, therefore, we will attempt it; but so long as he is without Christ no result will follow, any more than when Elisha's servant laid the staff upon the child—there was no noise, nor sound, nor hearing. As long as that sinner is without Christ, we may give him ordinances, if we dare; we may pray for him, we may keep him under the sound of the ministry, but everything will be in vain. Till thou, O quickening Spirit, come to that sinner, he will still be dead in trespasses and sins. Till Jesus is revealed to him there can be no life.

So, too, Christ is the light of the world. *Light is the gift of Christ.* "In Him was light, and the light was the life of men." Men sit in darkness until Jesus appears. The gloom is thick and dense; not sun, nor moon, nor star appeareth, and there can be no light to illumine the understanding, the affections, the conscience. Man has no power to get light. He may strike the damp match of reason, but it will not yield him a clear flame. The candle of superstition, with its tiny glare, will but expose the darkness in which he is wrapped. Rise, morning star! Come, Jesus, come! Thou art the sun of rghteousness, and healing is beneath Thy wings. Without Christ there is no light of true spiritual knowledge, no light of true spiritual enjoyment, no light in which the brightness of truth can be seen, or the warmth of fellowship proved. The soul, like the men of Napthali, sits in darkness, and seeth no light.

Without Christ *there is no peace.* See that poor soul hunted by the dogs of hell. It flies swift as the wind, but faster far do the hunters pursue. It seeks a covert yonder in the pleasures of the world, but the baying of the hell-hounds affright it in the festive haunts. It seeks to toil up the mountain of good works, but its legs are all too weak to bear it beyond the oppressor's rule. It doubles; it changes its tack; it goes from right to left but the hell-dogs are too swift of foot, and too strong of wind to lose their prey, and till Jesus Christ shall open His bosom for that poor hunted thing to hide itself within, it shall have no peace.

Without Christ *there is no rest.* The wicked are like the troubled sea, which cannot rest, and only Jesus can say to that sea, "Peace, be still."

Without Christ *there is no safety.* The vessel must fly before the gale, for it has no anchor on board: it may dash upon the rocks, for it has no chart and no pilot. Come what may, it is given up to the mercy of wind and waves. Safety it cannot know without Christ. But let Christ come on board that soul, and it may laugh at all the storms of earth, and e'en the whirlwinds which the Prince of the Power of the air may raise need not confound it, but without Christ there is no safety for it.

Without Christ again, *there is no hope.* Sitting wrecked upon this desert rock, the lone soul looks far away, but marks nothing that can give it joy. If, perchance, it fancies that a sail is in the distance, it is soon undeceived. The poor soul is thirsty, and around it flows only a sea of brine, soon to change to an ocean of fire. It looks upward, and there is an angry God—downward, and there are yawning gulfs —on the right hand, and there are accusing sounds— on the left hand, and there are tempting fiends. It is all lost! lost! lost! without Christ, utterly lost, and until Christ comes not a single beam of hope can make glad that anxious eye.

Without Christ, beloved, remember that *all the religious acts of men are vanity.* What are they but mere air-bags, having nothing in them whatever that God can accept? There is the semblance of worship, the altar, the victim, the wood laid in order, and the votaries bow the knee, or prostrate their bodies, but Christ alone can send the fire of heaven's acceptance. Without Christ the offering, like that of Cain's, shall lie upon the stones, but it shall never rise in fragrant smoke, accepted by the God of heaven. Without Christ your church-goings are a form of slavery, your chapel-meetings a bondage. Without Christ your prayers are but empty wind, your repentances are wasted tears, your almsgivings and your good deeds are but a coating of thin veneer to hide your base iniquities. Your professions are white-washed sepulchres, fair to look upon, but inwardly full of rottenness. Without Christ your religion is dead, corrupt, a stench, a nuisance before God—a thing of abhorrence, for where there is no Christ there is no life in any devotion, nothing in it for God to see that can possibly please Him. And this, mark you, is a true description, not of some, but of all who are without Christ. You moral people without Christ, you are lost as much as the immoral. You rich and respectable people, without Christ, you will be as surely damned as the prostitute that walks the streets at midnight. Without Christ, though you should heap up your charitable donations, endow your almshouses and hospitals, yea, though you should give your bodies to be burned, no merit would be imputed to you. All these things would profit you nothing. Without Christ, e'en if you might be raised on the wings of flaming zeal, or pursue your eager course with the enthusiasm of a martyr, you shall yet prove to be but the slave of your own passion, and the victim of your own folly. Unsanctified and unblest, you must, then, be shut out of heaven, and banished from the presence of God. Without Christ, you are destitute of every benefit which He, and He alone, can bestow.

Without Christ, implies, of course, that you are without the benefit of *all those gracious offices of Christ, which are so necessary to the sons of men,* you have no true *prophet.* You may pin your faith to the sleeve of man, and be deceived. You may be orthodox in your creed, but unless you have Christ in your heart, you have no hope of glory. Without Christ truth itself will prove a terror to you. Like Balaam, your eyes may be open while your life is alienated. Without Christ that very *cross* which does save some will become to you as a *gallows* upon which your soul shall die. Without Christ you have no *priest* to atone or to intercede on your behalf. There is no fountain in which you can wash away your guilt; no passover blood which you can sprinkle on your lintel to turn aside the destroying angel; no smoking altar of incense for you; no smiling God sitting between the cherubim. Without Christ you are an alien from everything which the priesthood can procure for your welfare. Without Christ you have no shepherd to tend, no King to help you; you cannot call in the day of trouble upon one who is strong to deliver. The angels of God, who are the standing army of King Jesus, are your enemies and not your friends. Without Christ, Providence is working your will, and not your good. Without Christ you have no *advocate* to plead your cause in heaven; you have no representative to stand up yonder and represent you, and prepare a place for you. Without Christ you are as sheep without a shepherd; without Christ you are a body without a head; without Christ you are miserable orphans without a father, and your widowed soul is without a husband. Without Christ you are without a *Saviour*; how will you do? what will become of you when you find out the value of salvation at the last pinch, the dreary point of despair? and without a *friend* in heaven, you must needs be if you are without Christ. To sum up all, you are without anything that can make life blessed, or death happy. Without Christ, though you be rich as Crœsus, and famous as Alexander, and wise as Socrates, yet are you naked, and poor, and miserable, for you lack Him by whom are all things, and for whom are all things, and who is Himself all in all.

Surely this might be enough to arouse the conscience of the most heedless? But ah! without any of the blessings which Christ brings, and to miss all the good offices which Christ fills—this is only to linger on the side issues! The imminent peril is to be *without Christ Himself.* Do you see, there, the Saviour in human form—God made flesh, dwelling among us? He loves His people, and came to earth to wipe out—an iniquity which had stained them most vilely, and to work out a righteousness which should cover them most gloriously, but without Christ that living Saviour is nothing to you. Do you see Him led away as a sheep to the slaughter, fastened to the cruel wood—bleeding, dying? Without Christ you are without the virtue of that great sacrifice; you are without the merit of that atoning blood. Do you see Him lying in the tomb of Joseph of Arimathea, asleep in death? That sleep is a burial of all the sins of His people, but without Christ your sins are not atoned for; your transgressions are yet unburied; they walk the earth; they shall go before you to judgment; they shall clamour for your condemnation; they shall drag you down without hope. Without Christ, remember, you have no share in His resurrection. Bursting the bonds of death, you, too, shall rise, but not to newness of life, nor yet to glory, for shame and everlasting contempt shall be your portion if you be without Christ. See Him as He mounts on high; He rides in His triumphal car through the streets of heaven; He scatters gifts for men, but without Christ there are none of those gifts for you. There are no blessings for those who are without Christ. He sits on that exalted throne, and pleads and reigns for ever, but without Christ you have no part in His intercession, and you shall have no share in His glory. He is coming. Hark! the trumpet rings. My ear prophetic seems to catch the strain! He comes, surrounded by majestic pomp, and all His saints shall reign with Him, but without Christ you an have no part nor lot in all that splendour. He goes back to His Father, and surrenders His kingdom, and His people are for ever safe with Him. Without Christ there shall be none to wipe away the tears from your eyes; no one to lead you to the fountain of living waters; no hand to give you a palm-branch; no smile to make your immortality blessed. Oh! my dear hearers, I cannot tell you what unutterable abysses of wretchedness and misery are comprised here within the fulness of the meaning of these dreadful words—without Christ.

At this present hour, if you are without Christ, you lack the very essence of good, by reason of which your choicest privileges are an empty boast, instead of a substantial boon. Without Christ *all the ordinances and means of grace are nothing worth.* Even this precious Book, that might be weighed with diamonds, and he that was wise would choose the Book, and leave the precious stones—even this sacred volume is of no benefit to you. You may have Bibles in your houses, as I trust you all have, but what is the Bible but a dead letter without Christ? Ah! I would you could all say what a poor woman once said. "I have Christ here," as she put her hand on the Bible, "and I have Christ here," as she put her hand on her heart, "and I have Christ there," as she raised up her eyes towards heaven; but if you have not Christ in the heart, you will not find Christ in the Book, for He is discovered there in His sweetness, and His blessedness, and His excellence, only by those who know Him

and love Him in their hearts. Do not get the idea that a certain quantity of Bible-reading, and particular times spent in repeating prayers, and regular attendance at a place of worship, and the systematic contribution of a guinea or so to the support of public worship and private charities will ensure the salvation of your souls. No, you must be born again. And that you cannot be; for it is not possible that you could have been born again if you are still living without Christ. To have Christ is the indispensable condition of entering heaven. If you have Him, though compassed about with a thousand infirmities, you shall yet see the brightness of the eternal glory; but if you have not Christ, alas! for all your toil, and the wearisome slavery of your religion, you can but weave a righteousness of your own, which shall disappoint your hope, and incur the displeasure of God.

And without Christ, dear friends, there comes the solemn reflection *that ere long ye shall perish.* Of that I do not like to talk, but I would like you to think of it. Without Christ you may live, young man—though, mark you, you shall miss the richest joys of life. Without Christ you may live, hale, strong man, in middle age—though mark, without Him you shall miss the greatest support amidst your troubles. Without Christ you may live, old man, and lean upon your staff, content with the earth into which you are so soon to drop, though, mark you, you shall lose the sweetest consolation which your weakness could have found. But remember, man, thou art soon to die. It matters not how strong thou art; death is stronger than thou, and he will pull thee down, even as the stag-hound drags down his victim, and then "how wilt thou do in the swellings of Jordan," without Christ? How wilt thou do when the eyes begin to close, without Christ? How wilt thou do, sinner, when the death-rattle is in thy throat, without Christ? When they prop thee up with pillows, when they stand weeping round thine expiring form, when the pulse grows faint and few, when thou hast to lift the veil, and stand disembodied before the dreadful eyes of an angry God, how wilt thou do without Christ? And when the judgment-trump shall wake thee from thy slumber in the tomb, and body and soul shall stand together at that last and dread assize, in the midst of that tremendous crowd, sinner, how wilt thou do without Christ? When the reapers come forth to gather in the harvest of God, and the sickles are red with blood, and the vintage is cast into the wine-press of His wrath, and it is trodden until the blood runs forth up to the horse's girdles—how wilt thou do then, I conjure thee, without Christ? Oh! sinner, I pray thee let these words sound in thine ears till they ring into thy heart. I would like you to think of them to-morrow, and the next day, and the next. Without Christ! I would like to make thee think of dying, of being judged, of being condemned, without Christ! May God in His mercy enable thee to see thy state, and fly to Him who is able to save, even unto the uttermost, all them that come unto God by Him. Christ is to be had for the asking. Christ is to be had for the receiving. Stretch out thy withered hand and take Him; trust Him, and He will be thine evermore; and thou shalt be with Him where He is, in an eternity of joy. Having thus reviewed the misery of our past estate, let us endeavour, with the little time we have left, to:—

II. Excite the thankfulness of God's people for what the Lord has done for them.

We are not without Christ now, but let me ask you,

who are believers, where you would have been now without Christ? As for some of you, you might, indeed you would have been, to-night in the ale-house or gin-palace. You would have been with the boisterous crew that make merriment on the Lord's Day; you know you would, for "such were some of you." You might have been ever worse; you might have been in the harlot's house; you might have been violating the laws of man as well as the laws of God, "for even such" were some of you, but ye are washed, but ye are sanctified. Where might you not have been without Christ? You might have been in hell; you might have been shut out for ever from all mercy, condemned to eternal banishment from the presence of God. I think the Indian's picture is a very fair one of where we should have been without Christ. When asked what Christ had done for him, he picked up a worm, put it on the ground, and made a ring of straw and wood round it, which he set alight. As the wood began to glow the poor worm began to twist and wriggle in agony, whereupon he stooped down, took it gently up with his finger, and said, "That is what Jesus did for me; I was surrounded, without power to help myself, by a ring of dreadful fire that must have been my ruin, but His pierced hand lifted me out of the burning." Think of that Christians, and, as your hearts melt, come to His table, and praise Him that you are not now without Christ.

Then think what His blood has done for you. Take only one thing out of a thousand. It has put away your many, many sins, You were without Christ, and your sins stood like yonder mountain, whose black and rugged cliff threaten the very skies. There fell a drop of Jesus's blood upon it, and it all vanished in a moment. The sins of all your days had gone in that instant by the application of the precious blood! Oh! bless Jehovah's name that you can now say:—

"Now freed from sin I walk at large,
My Saviour's blood my full discharge,
Content at His dear feet I lay,
A sinner saved, and homage pay."

Bethink you, too, now that you have Christ, of *the way in which He came* and made you partaker of Himself. Oh! how long he stood in the cold, knocking at the door of your heart. You would not have Him; you despised Him; you resisted Him; you kicked against Him; you did, as it were, spit in His face, and put Him to open shame to be rid of Him. Yet He would have you, and so, overcoming all your objections, and overlooking all your unworthiness, at length He rescued you and avouched you to be His own.

Consider, beloved, *what might have been your case had He left you to your own free agency.* You might have had His blood on your head in aggravation of your guilt. Instead of that, you have got His blood applied to your heart, in token of your pardon. You know right well what a difference *that* makes. Oh! that was a dreadful cry in the streets of Jerusalem, "His blood be on us and our children," and Jerusalem's streets flowing with gore witnessed how terrible a thing it is to have Christ's blood visited on His enemies. But, beloved, you have that precious blood for the cleansing of your conscience. It has sealed your acceptance, and you can, therefore, rejoice in the ransom he Has paid, and the remission you have received with joy unspeakable and full of glory.

And I would not have you forget the vast *expense which it cost to procure this priceless boon.* Christ could not have been yours had He lived in heaven. He must come down. o earth, and even then He could not be fully yours till He had bled and died. Oh! the dreadful portals through which Christ had to pass before He could find His way to you! He finds you now right easily, but before He could come to you He must Himself pass through the grave! Think of *that*, and be astonished!

And *why are you not left to be without Christ?* I suppose there are some persons whose minds naturally incline towards the doctrines of free will. I can only say that mine inclines as naturally towards the doctrines of sovereign grace. I cannot understand the reason why I am saved, except upon the ground that God would have it so. I cannot, if I look ever so earnestly, discover any kind of reason in myself why *I* should be a partaker of divine grace. If I am not to-night without Christ, it is only because Christ Jesus would have His will with me, and that will was that I should be with Him where He is, and should share His glory. I can put the crown nowhere but upon the head of Him whose mighty grace has saved me from going down into the pit.

Beloved, let us mention one thing more out of the thousand things which we must leave unsaid. *Remember what you have got to-night now that you have got Christ.* No, no, no, do not be telling me what you have *not* got. You have not got a certain income, you say; you have not got a competence; you have not got wealth; you have not got friends; you have not got a comfortable house. No, but you have got your Saviour; you have got Christ, and what does that mean? "He that spared not His own Son, but freely delivered Him up for us all, how shall He not with Him, also, freely give us all things?" The man who has got Christ has got everything. There are all things in one in Christ Jesus, and if you once get Him you are rich to all the intents of bliss. What, have Jesus Christ, and be discontented? Have Christ and murmur? Beloved, let me chide you gently, and pray you to lay aside that evil habit. If you have Christ, then you have God the Father to be your protector, and God the Spirit to be your comforter. You have present things working together for your good, and future things to unravel your happier portion; you have angels to be your servitors both on earth and in heaven. You have all the wheels of Providence revolving for your benefit; you have the stones of the field in league with you; you have your daily trials sanctified to your benefit; and you have your earthly joys hinged from their doors and hallowed with a blessing; your gains and your losses are alike profitable to you; your additions and your diminutions shall alike swell the tide of your soul's satisfaction; you have more than any other creatures can boast as their portion; you have more than all the world beside could yield to regale your pure taste, and ravish your happy spirits. And now, will you not be glad? I would have you come to this feasting-table this evening, saying within yourselves, "Since I am not without Christ, but Jesus Christ is mine, I do rejoice, yea, and I will rejoice."

And oh! dear Christian friends, if you have lost your evidences, go to Christ to find them all. Do not go striking your matches to light your candles, but go direct to the sun and get your light from his full orb. You who are doubting, desponding, and cast down, do not get foraging up the mouldy bread of yesterday, but go and get the manna which falls fresh to-day at the foot of the cross. Now you who have been wandering and backsliding, do not stay away from Jesus because of your unworthiness, but let your very sins impel you to come the faster to your Saviour's feet. Come, ye sinners; come, ye saints; come, ye who dare not say that ye are His people; come, you whose faith is but as a grain of mustard seed; come, you who have not any faith at all; come now to Jesus, who says, "Whosoever will, let him come and take of the water of life freely."

May God grant that some who feel that they are without Christ because they have no enjoyment, nor any sense of communion with Him, may now take hold of His name, His covenant, His promises with a lively faith, nay more, may they find Him to the rapture of their souls, and He shall have all the praise. Amen.

OUR GLORIOUS TRANSFORMING

"But now in Christ Jesus, ye who sometimes were far off are made nigh by the blood of Christ."—Ephesians ii. 13.

I DO not want you to feel at this time as if you were listening to a sermon, or to any sort of set discourse, but rather I should like, if it were possible, that you should feel as if you were alone with the Saviour, and were engaged in calm and quiet meditation; and I will try to be the prompter, standing at the elbow of your contemplation, suggesting one thought and then another; and I pray, dear brethren and sisters in Christ, as many of you as are truly in Him, that you may be able so to meditate as to be profited, and to say at the close, "My meditation on Him was sweet. I will be glad in His name." There are three very simple things in the text. The first is *what we were*. Some time ago "we were far off." But secondly, *what w are*—we are "made nigh." And then there is the how, *the means of this great change*. It is "in Christ Jesus," and it is added, "by the blood of Christ." First, then, let us with humility consider, as believers:—

I. WHAT WE WERE.

There was a day when we passed from death unto life. All of us who are children of God have undergone a great and mysterious change; we have been new created, we have been born again. If any of you have not experienced this great change, I can only pray that you may, but you will not be likely to take much interest in the theme of meditation this evening. As many of you as have experienced this great change are now asked to recollect what you were. You were far off, first, in the respect that *you were aliens* from the commonwealth of Israel. The Jew was brought nigh. The Jewish people were favoured of God with light, while the rest of the world remained in darkness. To them He gave the oracles; with them He made a covenant; but as for the rest of the nations, they were left unclean and far off. They could not come near to God. This was our condition. We were Gentiles. We had no participation in the covenant that God had made with Abraham; we had no share in the sacrifices of Aaron or his successors. We could not come in by the way of circumcision. We were not born after the flesh, and we had no right to that fleshly covenant, however great its privileges. We are brought nigh now. All that the Jew ever had we have. We have all his privileges, and more. He had but the shadow: we have the substance. He had but the type: we have the reality. But aforetime we had neither shadow nor substance; we were afar off, and had no participation in them.

And, beloved, when we think of our distance from God, there are three or four ways in which we may illustrate it. We were far off from God, for *a vast cloudland of ignorance hung between our souls and Him.* We were lost as in a tangled wood in which there was no pathway. We were like some bird drifted out to sea that should be bereft of the instinct which guides it on its course, driven to and fro by every wind, and tossed like a wave by every tempest. We knew not God, neither did we care to know. We were in the dark with regard to Him and His character; and when we did make guesses concerning God, they were very wide of the truth, and did not help to bring us at all near. He has taught us better now; He has taught us to call Him Father, and to know that He is love. Since we have known God, or, rather, have been known of God, we have come nigh, but once our ignorance kept us very far off. Worse than that, there was between us and God a vast range of the *mountains of sin*. We can measure the Alps, the Andes have been scaled, but the mountains of sin no man has ever measured yet. They are very high. They pierce the clouds. Can you think of the mountains of your sin, beloved? Reckon them all up since your birth—sins of childhood, and youth, and manhood, and riper years; your sins against the gospel, and against the law; sins with the body, and sins with the mind; sins of every shape and form—ah! what a mountain range they make! And you were on one side of the mountain, and God was on the other. A holy God could not wink at sin, and you, an unholy being, could not have fellowship with the thrice Holy One. What a distance!—an impassable mountain sundered you from your God. It has all gone now. The mountains have sunk into the sea, our transgressions have all gone, but, oh! what hills they were once, and what mountains they were but a little while ago! In addition to these mountains, there was, on the other side nearest to God, *a great gulf of divine wrath*. God was angry, justly angry, with us. He could not have been God if sin had not made Him angry. He that plays with sin is very far from knowing anything of the character of the Most High. There was a deep gulf. Ah! even the lost in hell know not how deep it is. They have been sinking in it, but this abyss hath no bottom. God's love is infinite. Who knoweth the power of Thine anger, O Most High? It is all filled now, as far as we are concerned. Christ has bridged the chasm. He has taken us to the other side of it; He has brought us nigh; but what a gulf it was! Look down and shudder. Have you ever stood on a glacier and looked down a crevasse and taken a great stone and thrown it down, and waited till at last you heard the sound as it reached the bottom? Have you not shuddered at the thought of falling down that steep? But there you stood but a little while ago, an heir of wrath, even as others. So the Apostle puts it, "even as others." Oh! how far off you were!

Nor was this all, for there was another division

between you and God. When, dear friends, we were brought to feel our state, and to have some longings after the Most High, had the mountains of sin been moved and the chasm of wrath been filled, yet there remained another distance of our own making. There was *a sea of fear* rolling between us and God. We dare not come to Him. He told us He would forgive, but we could not think it true. He said that the blood would cleanse us—the precious blood of the atoning sacrifice—but we thought our stains too crimson to be removed. We dared not believe in the infinite compassion of our Father. We ran from Him; we could not trust Him. Do you not remember those times when to believe seemed an impossibility, and salvation by faith appeared to be as difficult a thing as salvation by the works of the law? That sea has gone away now. We have been ferried o'er its streams. We have no fear of God now in the form of trembling, slavish fear; we are brought nigh and say, "Abba Father," with an untrembling tongue. You see then something of the distance there was between us and God, but I will illustrate it in another way. Think of God a moment. Your thoughts cannot reach Him: He is infinitely pure; the heavens are not clean in His sight; and He charges His angels with folly. That is one side of the picture. Now look at yourself, a worm that has rebelled against its Creator, loathsome with sin, through and through defiled. When I see a beggar and a prince stand together I see a distance, but ah! it is but an inch, a span, compared with the infinite leagues of distance in character and nature between God and the fallen man. Who but Christ could have lifted up from so low an estate to so high a condition—from fellowship with devils unto communion with Jehovah himself? The distance was inconceivable. We were lost in wonder at the greatness of the love that made it all to vanish. We were afar off.

Now I have stated that very simply. Think it over a minute. And what do you feel as the result of your thought? Why, humility rises. Suppose you are a very experienced Christian, and a very intelligent reader of the Bible; suppose that for many years you have been able to maintain a consistent character. Ah! my dear brother, my dear sister, you have nothing whereof to glory when you recollect what you were, and what you would have been still if it had not been for sovereign grace. You, perhaps, have forgotten a little that you were just what the Bible says. You have been so contemplating your present privileges that you have for a while failed to remember that it is only by the grace of God that you are what you are. Let these considerations bring you back to your true condition. And now with lowly reverence at the cross-foot bow down your soul and say, "My Lord, between me and the greatest reprobate there is no difference but what Thy grace has made: between me and lost souls in hell there is no difference, except what Thine infinite compassion has deigned to make. I humbly bless Thee, and adore Thee, and love Thee, because Thou hast brought me nigh."

And now we shall continue our contemplation, but take the second point. We have a bitter pill in this first one, but the next consideration kills it, takes the bitterness away and sweetens it. It is:

II. WHAT WE ARE—WHAT WE ARE.

"We are made nigh through the blood of Christ." You will please to observe that the Apostle does not say, "We hope we are"; he speaks positively, as every believer should. Nor does he say, "We shall be." There are privileges reserved for the future, but here he is speaking of a present blessing, which may be now the object of distinct definite knowledge, which ought to be, indeed, a matter of present experimental enjoyment. We are brought nigh. What means he by this? Does not he mean, first, what I have already said, that as we were far off, being Gentiles, and not of the favoured commonwealth of Israel, we are now brought nigh, that is to say, *we have all the privileges of the once favoured race.* Are they the seed of Abraham? So are we, for He was the Father of the faithful, and we, having believed have become His spiritual children. Had they an altar? We have an altar whereof they have no right to eat which serve the tabernacle. Had they any high priest? We have an high priest—we have one who has entered into the heavenly. Had they a sacrifice and paschal supper? We have Christ Jesus, who, by His one offering, hath for ever put away our sin, and who is to-day the spiritual meat on which we feed. All that they had we have, only we have it in a fuller and clearer sense. "The law was given by Moses, but grace and truth came by Jesus Christ," and they have come to us. But we are brought a great deal nearer than the Jew—than most of the Jews were, for you know, brethren, the most devout Jew could not offer sacrifice to God; I mean, as a rule. Prophets were exceptions. They could not offer sacrifices themselves; they could bring the victim, but there were some special persons who must act as priests. The priest came nigh to God on the behalf of the people. Listen, O ye children of God, who were once afar off! It is the song of heaven. Let it be your song on earth—"Thou wast slain and hast redeemed us unto God by Thy blood, and hath made us priests and kings." *We are all priests* if we love the Saviour. Every believer is a priest. It is for him to bring his sacrifice of prayer and thanksgiving, and come in, even into the holy place in the presence of the Most High. And I might say more, for no priests went into the most holy place of all, save one, the high priest, and he once in the year, not without blood and not without smoke and perfume of incense, ventured into the most holy place. But we, brethren, see the veil taken right away, and we come up to the mercy-seat without the trembling which the high priest felt of old, for we see the blood of Jesus on the mercy-seat and the veil rent, and we come boldly to the throne of heavenly grace to obtain grace in time of need. Oh! how near we are; nearer than the ordinary Jew; nearer than the priest; as near as the high priest himself, for in the person of Christ we are where He is, that is, at throne of God. Let me say, dear brethren, that we are near to God to-day, for *all that divides us from God is gone.* The moment a sinner believes, all that mountain of sin ceases to be. Can you see those hills—those towering Andes? Who shall climb them? But lo! I see one come who has the scar of one that has died upon a cross. I see Him hold up His pierced hand, and one drop of blood falls on the hills, and they smoke; they dissolve like the fat of rams; they turn to vapour, and they are gone. There is not so much as a vestige of them left. Oh! glory be to God, there is no sin in God's book against the believer; there is no record remaining; He hath taken it away and nailed it to His cross, and triumphed in the deed. As the Egyptians were all drowned in the sea, and Israel said, "The depths have covered them; there was not one of them left," so may every believer say, "All sin is gone, and we are pure, accepted in the Beloved, justified through the blood and righteousness of Jesus Christ." Oh! how glorious this nearness is when all distance is gone!

And now, brethren, we are near to God, for *we are His friends*. He is our mighty friend, and we love Him in return. Better than that, *we are His children*. A friend might be forgotten, but a child—a father's bowel's yearn towards Him. We are His children. He has chosen us that we may approach unto Him, that we may dwell in His courts and abide, and go no more out for ever. "The servant abideth not in the house for ever, but the son abideth ever." And this is our privilege. And yet even more than that. Can anybody here imagine how near Jesus Christ is to God? So near are we, for that is truth which the little verse sings:—

> "So near—so very near to God,
> More near I cannot be;
> For in the person of His Son,
> I am as near as He."

If we are, indeed, in Christ, we are one with Him; we are members of His body, of His flesh, and of His bones; and He has said, "Where I am, there shall also my servant be," and He has declared that we shall receive the glory—the glory which He had with the Father before the world was. What nearness is this!

Now I have stated that truth, I want you now to feed on it for a minute, and draw the natural conclusions, and feel the fit emotion. Beloved, if you are brought so near to God, what manner of lives ought you to lead? Common subjects ought never to speak a traitorous word, but a member of the Privy Council, one who is admitted to the Court, should certainly be loyal through and through. Oh! how we ought to love God, who has made us nigh!—a people near unto Him. How ought heavenly things and holy things to engross our attention! How joyously we ought to live too, for with such high favours as these it would be ungrateful to be unhappy! We are near to God, brethren. Then God sees us in all things—our heavenly Father knows what we have need of; He is always watching over us for good. We are near to Him—let us pray as if we were near God. There are some prayers that are dreadful from the distance there is evidently in the mind of the offerer. Too generally liturgies are addresses to a God too far off to be reached, but the humble familiarity which boldly comes trembling with fear, but rejoicing with faith, into the presence of God—this becomes those who are made nigh. When a man is near a neighbour whom he trusts he tells him his griefs, he asks his help. Deal thus with God; live on Him, live for Him, live in Him. Be never distant from a God who has made you nigh unto Himself. Our life ought to be a heavenly one, seeing that we are brought nigh to God —the God of heaven. Brethren, how assured every one of us may be of our safety if we are, indeed, believers in Christ, for if we are made nigh by love and friendship to our God, He cannot leave us. If, when we were enemies, He brought us nigh, will He not keep us now He has made us friends? He loved us so as to bring us up from the depths of sin, when we had no thoughts, nor desires towards good, and now He has taught us to love Him and to long for Him, will He forsake us? Impossible! What confidence this doctrine gives?

And once more, dear brethren and sisters, if the Lord has brought us nigh, what hope we ought to have for those who are farthest off from God to-day! Never be you amongst that Pharisaical crew who imagine that fallen women or degraded men cannot be uplifted again. Ye were sometimes far off, but He has made you nigh. The distance was so great in your case that surely He who met that can also meet the distance in another case. Have hope for any who can be got under the sound of the gospel, and labour on until the more hopeless, the most hopeless, are brought there. Oh! let us gird up our loins for Christian work! believing that if God has saved us, there remain no impossibles. The chief of sinners was saved years ago. Paul said so. He had no mock modesty. I believe he said the truth. The chief of sinners has gone through the gate into heaven, and there is room for the second worst to get through— there is room for thee, friend, as there is room for me. The God that brought me nigh has taught me to know that no man is beyond the reach of His grace. But I must leave that with you, hoping that it will flavour all your thoughts to-night. Once more. The last thing we are to consider is:—

III. How THE GREAT CHANGE WAS WROUGHT.

We were put into Christ, and then through the blood we were made nigh. The doctrine of the Atonement is no novelty in this house. We have preached it often, nay, we preach it constantly, and let this mouth be dumb when it prefers any other theme to that old, old story of the passion, the substitution, and consequent redemption by blood. Beloved, it is the blood of Jesus that has done everything for us. Our debts Christ has paid; therefore, those debts have ceased to be. The punishment of our sin Christ has borne, and, therefore, no punishment is due to us; substitution has met a case that is never to be met by any other means. The just has suffered for the unjust to bring us to God. We deserved the sword, but it has fallen upon Him who deserved it not, who voluntarily placed Himself in our room instead, that He might give compensation to justice and full liberty to mercy. It is by the blood that we are brought nigh then. Christ has suffered in our stead, and we are, therefore, forgiven. But think about that blood a minute. It means suffering; it means a life surrendered with agony. Suffering—we talk about it; ah! but when you feel it, then you think more of the Saviour. When the bones ache, when the body is racked, when sleep goes from the eyelids, when the mind is depressed, when the heads turns; ah! then we say, "My Saviour, I see a little of the price that redeemed me from going down into the pit." The mental and physical suffering of Christ are both worthy of our consideration, but depend upon it His soul's sufferings were the soul of His sufferings; and when we are under deep depression, brought near even unto death with sorrow, then again we guess how the Saviour bought us. The early Church was noted in its preaching for preaching facts. I am afraid now that we are too noted for forgetting facts and preaching doctrine. Let us have doctrine by all means, but, after all, the fact is the great thing. When Paul gave a summary of the gospel which he had preached, he said, "This is the gospel that I have preached—that Jesus Christ was crucified, died, was buried, rose again." There in Gethsemane, where bloody sweat bedews the soil; there on the pavement, where the lash tears again and again into those blessed shoulders till the purple streams gush down, and the ploughers make their furrows, and the blood fills them; there when they hurl Him on

His back to the ground, and fasten His hands to the wood with rough iron; there when they lift Him up and dislocate His bones, when they fix the cross into the earth; there when they sit and watch Him, and insult His prayers, and mock His thirst, while He hangs naked to His shame in the midst of a ribald crew; there where God Himself forsakes Him, where Jehovah turns His face away from Him, where the sufferer shrieks in agony, "My God, my God, why hast Thou forsaken Me?"—there it is that we were brought nigh, even we that were far off. Adore your Saviour, my brethren—bow before Him. He is not here, for He is risen; but your hearts can rise, and you can bow at His feet. Oh! kiss those wounds of His; ask that by faith you may put your finger into the print of His nails, and your hand into His side. "Be not faithless, but believing," and let all your sacred powers of mind assist your imagination and faith to realise now the price with which the Saviour brought you from bondage intolerable. God grant you grace to feel something of this.

I have laid the truth before you. Now sit down and quietly turn it over in your mind. And what will strike you? Why, surely first *the heinousness of sin.* Was there nothing that could wash out sin but blood, and was there no blood that could wash it out but the blood of the Son of God? O sin! O sin! what a black, what a damning thing thou art! Only the blood of an incarnate God can wash out the smallest stain of sin. My heart, I charge thee to hate it; my eyes, look not on it; my ears, listen not to its siren charm; my feet, run not in its paths; my hands, refuse to handle it; my soul, loathe, loathe that which murdered Christ, and thrust a spear through the tenderest heart that ever beat.

Next to that, do you not feel emotions of *intense gratitude* that, if such a price was needed, such a price was found? God had but one son, dearer to Him than Isaac was to Abraham, and though there was none to command Him to do it, as there was in Abraham's case, yet voluntarily the gracious Father led His son up to the cross, and it pleased the Father to bruise Him; He put Him to grief; He gave Him up for us. Which shall I most admire—the love of the Father, or the love of the Son? Blessed be God, we are not asked to make distinctions, for they are one. "I and my Father are one," and in that sacred act of the sacrifice for the sins of men the Father and the Son are both to be worshipped with equal love. You see, then, the heinousness of sin in some degree, for its needing for its pardon the love of Jesus, and the love of God that gave the Saviour's blood.

But, dear friends, ere I sit down, let me remark that we learn from our text and from the whole contemplation, what it is that would bring us nearer experimentally than we are to-night. How did I get nigh first? Through the blood. Do I want to get near to God to-night? Have I been wandering? Is my heart cold? Have I got into a backsliding state? Do I want to come close now to my blessed Father, and again to look up to Him, and say, "Abba," and rejoice in that filial spirit? There is no way for me to come nearer except the blood. Let me think of it then, and let me see its infinite value; it is sufficient, let me hear its everlasting, ever-prevalent plea, and oh! then I shall feel my soul drawn; for that which draws us nearer to God, and will draw us right up to heaven, is none other than the crimson cord of the Saviour's endless, boundless, dying, but ever-living love.

And this teaches me, and teaches you, too, and here I have done, *what it is we ought to preach and teach* if we would bring the far-off ones in—if we would bring near to God those that now wander from Him. Philosophy, bah! You will philosophize men into hell, but never into heaven. Ceremonies—you can amuse children, and you can degrade men into idiots with them, but you can do nothing else. The gospel, and the essence of that gospel, which is the blood of Jesus Christ—it is this which is an omnipotent leverage to uplift the filth, debauchery, and poverty of this city into life, into light, and into holiness. There is no battering-ram that will ever shake the gates of hell except that which every time it strikes sounds this word, "Jesus, Jesus, the Crucified." "God forbid that we should glory, save in the cross of our Lord Jesus Christ." If it will save us, it will save others; only let us spread the good news, let us tell the good tidings. Every one of us ought to preach the gospel somehow. You that speak in common conversation forget not to speak of Him. Scatter such tracts as are most full of Christ—they are the best; others will be of little use. Write letters concerning Him. Remember His name is like ointment, full of sweetness, but to get the perfume you must pour it forth. Oh! that we could make fragrant all this neighbourhood with the savour of that dear name! Oh! that wherever we dwell every one of us might so think of Christ in our hearts that we could not help speaking of Him with our lips! Living, may we rejoice in Him; dying, may we triumph in Him. May our last whisper on earth be what our first song shall be in heaven, "Worthy is the Lamb that was slain and hath redeemed us unto God by His blood." Oh! I pray God to make this season of communion very sweet to you, and I think it will be if you have the key of our meditation to-night, and can unlock the door—if you know how far off you were, and see how near you are by the precious blood.

Oh! there are some far-off ones here to-night, however, to whom I must say just this word. Far-off one, God can make you nigh; you can be made nigh to-night. Whoever you may be, He is able still to save, but the blood must make you nigh—the blood of Jesus. Trust him. To believe is to live, and to believe means only and simply to trust, to depend upon. That is faith. Have confidence in Christ's sacrifice, and you are saved. God grant you may be enabled to do it, for Jesus' sake. Amen.

JESUS CHRIST HIMSELF

" Jesus Christ Himself."—Ephesians ii. 20.

"JESUS CHRIST Himself " is to occupy all our thoughts this morning. What an ocean opens up before me ! Here is sea-room for the largest barque ! In which direction shall I turn your thoughts ? I am embarrassed with riches. I know not where to begin : and when I once begin, where shall I end ? Assuredly we need not go abroad for joys this morning, for we have a feast at home. The words are few, but the meaning vast—" Jesus Christ Himself."

Beloved, the religion of our Lord Jesus Christ contains in it nothing so wonderful as Himself. It is a mass of *marvels*, but He is THE miracle of it ; the wonder of wonders is " The Wonderful " Himself. If *proof* be asked of the truth which He proclaimed, we point men to Jesus Christ Himself. His character is unique. We defy unbelievers to imagine another like Him. He is God and yet man, and we challenge them to compose a narrative in which the two apparently incongruous characters shall be so harmoniously blended,—in which the human and divine shall be so marvellously apparent, without the one overshading the other. They question the authenticity of the four Gospels ; will they try and write a fifth ? Will they even attempt to add a few incidents to the life which shall be worthy of the sacred biography, and congruous with those facts which are already described ? If it be all a forgery, will they be so good as to show us how it is done ? Will they find a novelist who will write another biography of a man of any century they choose, of any nationality, or of any degree of experience, or any rank or station, and let us see if they can describe in that imaginary life a devotion, a self-sacrifice, a truthfulness, a completeness of character at all comparable to that of Jesus Christ Himself ? Can they invent another perfect character even if the divine element be left out ? They must of necessity fail, for there is none like unto Jesus Himself.

The character of Jesus has commanded respect even from those who have abhorred His teaching. It has been a stumbling-stone to all objectors who have preserved a shade of candour. Jesus' doctrine they could refute, they say ; His precepts they could improve, so they boast ; His system is narrow and outworn, so they assert : but Himself—what can they do with Him ? They must admire Him even if they will not adore Him ; and having done so they have admired a personage who must be divine, or else He wilfully left His disciples to believe a lie. How will they surmount this difficulty ? They cannot do so by railing at Him, for they have no material for accusation. Jesus Christ Himself silences their cavillings. This is a file at which these asps do bite, but break their teeth. Beyond all argument or miracle, Jesus Christ Himself is the proof of His own gospel.

And as He is the proof of it, so, beloved, He is the *marrow* and essence of it. When the apostle Paul meant that the gospel was preached he said, " Christ is preached," for the gospel is Christ Himself. If you want to know what Jesus taught, know Himself. He is the incarnation of that truth which by Him and in Him is revealed to the sons of men. Did He not Himself say, " I am the way, the truth, and the life " ? You have not to take down innumerable tomes, nor to pore over mysterious sentences of double meaning in order to know what our great teacher has revealed, you have but to turn and gaze upon His countenance, behold His actions, and note His spirit, and you know His teaching. He lived what He taught. If we wish to know Him, we may hear His gentle voice saying, " Come and see." Study His wounds, and you understand His innermost philosophy. " To know Him and the power of His resurrection " is the highest degree of spiritual learning. He is the end of the law and the soul of the gospel, and when we have preached His word to the full, we may close by saying, " Now, of the things which we have spoken this is the sum,—we have an high priest who is set on the right hand of the throne of the majesty in the heavens."

Nor is He alone the proof of His gospel and the substance of it, but He is the *power* and force by which it spreads. When a heart is truly broken for sin, it is by Him that it is bound up. If a man is converted, it is by Christ, the power of God. If we enter into peace and salvation it is by the gracious manifestation of Jesus Himself. If men have enthusiastically loved Christianity, it is because first of all they loved Christ : for Him apostles laboured, and for Him confessors were brave ; for Him saints have suffered the loss of all things, and for Him martyrs have died. The power which creates heroic consecration is " Jesus Christ Himself." The memories stirred by His name have more influence over men's hearts than all things else in earth or heaven. The enthusiasm which is the very life of our holy cause comes from Himself. They who know not Jesus know not the life of truth, but those who dwell in Him are filled with power, and overflow so that out of the midst of them streams forth living water. Nor is it only so, beloved ; for the power which propagates the gospel is Jesus Himself. In heaven He pleads, and therefore does His kingdom come. " The pleasure of the Lord shall prosper in His hand." It is from heaven that He rules all things so as to promote the advance of the truth. All power is given unto Him in heaven and in earth, and therefore are we to proclaim His life-giving word with full assurance of success. He causes the wheel of providence to revolve in such a manner as to help His cause ; He abridges the power of tyrants, overrules the scourge of war, establishes liberty in nations, opens the mysteries of continents long unknown, breaks down systems of error, and guides the current of human thought. He works by a thousand means, preparing the way of the Lord. It is from heaven that He shall shortly come, and when He cometh, when Christ Himself shall put forth all His might, then shall the wilderness rejoice and the solitary place be glad. The reserve force of the gospel is Christ Jesus Himself. The latent power which shall at last break every bond, and win universal dominion, is the energy, the life, the omnipotence of Jesus Himself. He sleeps in the vessel now, but when He arises and chides the storm there will be a deep calm. He now for awhile concealeth Himself in the ivory palaces of glory, but when He is manifested in *that day* His chariot wheels shall bring victory to His church militant.

If these things be so, I have a theme before me which I cannot compass. I forbear the impossible task, and I shall but briefly note some few apparent matters which lie upon the surface of the subject.

Brethren, "Jesus Christ Himself" should always be the prominent thought of our minds as Christians. Our theology should be framed upon the fact that He is the Centre and Head of all. We must remember that "in Him are hid all the treasures of wisdom and knowledge." Some of our brethren are mainly taken up with the doctrines of the gospel, and are somewhat bitter in their narrow orthodoxy. We are to love every word of our Lord Jesus and His apostles, and are to contend earnestly for the faith once delivered unto the saints, but yet it is well always to hold truth in connection with Jesus and not as in itself alone the sum of all things. Truth isolated from the person of Jesus grows hard and cold. We know some in whom the slightest variation from their system arouses their indignation, even though they admit that the brother is full of the Spirit of Christ. It is with them doctrine, doctrine, doctrine; with us, I trust, it is Christ Himself. True doctrine is to us priceless as a throne for our living Lord, but our chief delight is not in the vacant throne, but in the King's presence thereon. Give me not His garments, though I prize every thread, but the blessed wearer whose sacred energy made even the hem thereof to heal with a touch.

There are others of our brethren who delight above measure in what they call experimental preaching, which sets forth the inner life of the believer, both the rage of depravity and the triumph of grace: this is well in due proportion, according to the analogy of faith: but still Jesus Himself should be more conspicuous than our frames and feelings, doubts and fears, struggles and victories. We may get to study the action of our own hearts so much that we fall into despondency and despair. "Looking unto Jesus" is better than looking unto our own progress: self-examination has its necessary uses, but to have done with self and live by faith in Jesus Christ Himself is the best course for a Christian.

Then, there are others who rightly admire the precepts of the gospel, and are never so happy as when they are hearing them enforced, as, indeed, they ought to be; but after all, the commands of our Lord are not our Lord Himself, and they derive their value to us and their power over our obedience from the fact that they are *His* words, and that He said, "If ye love Me, keep My commandments." We know the truth of His declaration, "If a man love Me, he will keep My sayings," but there must be the personal love to begin with. Brethren, all the benefits of these three schools will be ours if we live upon Jesus Himself. They gather each a flower, but our divine "plant of renown" has all the beauty, and all the fragrance, of all that they can gather; and without the thorns which are so apt to grow on their peculiar roses. Jesus Christ Himself is to us precept, for He is the way: He is to us doctrine, for He is the truth: He is to us experience, for He is the life. Let us make Him the pole star of our religious life in all things. Let Him be first, last, and midst; yea, let us say, "He is all my salvation and all my desire." And yet

do not, I beseech you, disdain the doctrine, lest in marring the doctrine you should be guilty of insult to Jesus Himself. To trifle with truth is to despise Jesus as our Prophet. Do not for a moment underrate experience, lest in neglecting the inner self you also despise your Lord Himself as your cleansing Priest; and never for a moment forget His commandments lest if ye break them ye transgress against Jesus Himself as your King. All things which touch upon His kingdom are to be treated reverently by us for the sake of Himself: His Book, His day, His Church, His ordinances, must all be precious to us, because they have to do with Him; but in the front of all must ever stand "Jesus Christ Himself," the personal, living, loving Jesus; Christ in us the hope of glory, Christ for us our full redemption, Christ with us our guide and our solace, and Christ above us pleading and preparing our place in heaven. Jesus Christ Himself is our captain, our armour, our strength, and our victory. We inscribe His name upon our banner, for it is hell's terror, heaven's delight, and earth's hope. We bear this upon our hearts in the heat of the conflict, for this is our breastplate and coat of mail.

I shall not endeavour to say anything this morning which will strike you as beautiful in language, for to endeavour to decorate the altogether Lovely One would be blasphemy. To hang flowers upon the cross is ridiculous, and to endeavour to adorn Him whose head is as the most fine gold, and whose person is as bright ivory overlaid with sapphires, would be profane. I shall but tell you simple things in simple language: yet are these the most precious and soul-satisfying of the truths of revelation.

I. With Jesus Christ Himself we begin by saying, first, that Jesus Himself is THE ESSENCE OF HIS OWN WORK, and therefore *how readily we ought to trust Him.* Jesus Himself is the soul of His salvation. How does the apostle describe it? "He loved me, and gave *Himself* for me." He gave His crown, His throne, and His joys in heaven for us, but that was not all—He gave Himself. He gave His life on earth, and renounced all the comforts of existence, and bore all its woes; He gave His body, He gave His agony, He gave His heart's blood: but the summary of it is, He gave Himself for me. "Christ loved the church and gave Himself for it." "Who His own self bare our sins in His own body on the tree." No proxy service here! No sacrifice which runs as far as His own person and there stops! There was no limit to the grief of Jesus like that set upon the suffering of Job,—"Only on himself lay not thine hand," or "Only spare his life." No, every reserve was taken down, for He gave Himself. "He saved others; Himself He could not save," because He Himself was the very essence of His own sacrifice on our behalf. It is because He is what He is that He was able to redeem us: the dignity of His person imparted efficacy to His atonement. He is divine, God over all, blessed for ever, and therefore infinite virtue is found in Him; He is human, and perfect in that humanity, and therefore capable of obedience and suffering in man's place and stead. He is able to save us because He is Immanuel—"God with us." If it were conceivable that an angel could have suffered the same agonies, and have performed the same labours, as our Lord, yet it is not conceivable that the same result would have followed. The pre-eminence of His person imparted weight to His work. Always think then when you view the atonement, that it is Jesus Himself who is the soul of it.

Indeed the efficacy of His sacrifice lies there ; hence the apostle in the Hebrews speaks of Him as having " by Himself purged our sins." This purging was wrought by His sacrifice, but the sacrifice was Himself. Paul says, " He offered up Himself." He stood as a priest at the altar offering a bloody sacrifice, but the offering was neither bullock, nor ram, nor turtle dove ; it was Himself. " Once in the end of the world hath He appeared to put away sin by the sacrifice of Himself." The sole reason why we are well-pleasing with God is because of Him, for He is our sweet savour-offering ; and the only cause for the putting away of our sin is found in Him because He is our sin-offering. The cleansing by the blood, and the washing by the water, are the result, not of the blood and the water in and of themselves and separate from Him, but because they were the essentials of Himself. You see this, I am persuaded, without my enlarging upon it.

Now, because of this, *the Lord Jesus Christ Himself* is the object of our faith. Is He not always so described in Scripture ? " Look unto *Me*, and be ye saved, all ye ends of the earth,"—not " look to My cross," nor " look to My life," nor " to My death," much less " to My sacraments or to My servants," but " look unto *Me*." From His own lips the words sound forth, " Come *unto Me* all ye that labour and are heavy laden, and I will give you rest." In fact, it is the Christian's life motto, " Looking unto Jesus, the author and finisher of our faith." May I not go further and say, *how very simple and how very easy and natural ought faith to be henceforth?* I might be puzzled with various theories of the atonement, but I can believe in Jesus Himself : I might be staggered by the divers mysteries which concern theology, and overpower even master-minds, but I can confide in Jesus Himself. He is one whom it is difficult to distrust : His goodness, gentleness, and truth command our confidence. We can and do trust in Jesus Himself. If He be proposed to Me as my Saviour, and if faith in Him be that which saves me, then at His dear feet I cast myself unreservedly, and feel myself secure while He looks down on me. He who bled that sinners might be saved cannot be doubted any more : " Lord, I believe ; help Thou mine unbelief." Now you who have been looking to your faith, I want you to look to Jesus Himself rather than at your poor feeble faith. Now you who have been studying the results of faith in yourselves and are dissatisfied, I beseech you turn your eyes away from yourselves and look to Jesus Himself. Now you who cannot understand this and cannot understand that, give up wanting to understand for the while, and come and look at Jesus Christ Himself, " that the God of our Lord Jesus Christ, the Father of glory, may give unto you the spirit of wisdom and revelation in the knowledge of Him." The Lord grant us grace to view Jesus Christ Himself in the matter of our salvation as all in all, so that we may have personal dealings with Him, and no more think of Him as a mere idea, or as an historical personage, but as a personal Saviour standing in the midst of us, and bidding us enter into peace through Him.

II. " Jesus Christ Himself is, as we have said, THE SUBSTANCE OF THE GOSPEL, *and therefore how closely should we study Him.* While He was here He taught His disciples, and *the object of His teaching was that they might know Himself*, and through Him might know the Father. They did not learn very fast, but

you see what He meant them to learn by the observation He made to Philip, " Have I been so long time with you, and yet hast Thou not known *Me*, Philip " ? He meant them to know Himself ; and when He had risen from the dead the same object was still before Him. As He walked with the two disciples to Emmaus they had wide choice of subjects for conversation, but He chose the old theme, and " beginning at Moses and all the prophets, He expounded unto them in all the Scriptures the things concerning Himself." No topic was one half so important or profitable. No mere man may come to teach himself, but this divine One can have nothing better to reveal, for He Himself, the incarnate God, is the chief of all truth. Hence our Lord was concerned to be known to His people, and therefore again and again we read that " Jesus showed Himself unto His disciples." Whatever else they may be ignorant of, it is essential to disciples that they know their Lord. His nature, His character, His mind, His spirit, His object, His power, we must know—in a word, we must know Jesus Himself.

This also, beloved, is the work of the Holy Spirit. " He shall glorify Me : for he shall receive of Mine, and shall shew it unto you." The Holy Ghost reveals Christ to us and in us. Whatsoever things Christ hath spoken while He was here, the Holy Ghost opens to the mind and to the understanding, and thus by speaking of Christ within us He carries on the work work which our Lord began when here below. The Comforter is the instructor and Jesus is the lesson. I dare say you long to know a thousand things, but the main point of knowledge to be desired is Jesus Himself. This was His teaching, and this is the Holy Spirit's teaching, and *this is the end and object of the Bible.* Moses, Esaias, and all the prophets spake of Him, and the things which are recorded in this book were written that ye might believe that Jesus is the Christ, and that believing ye might have life through His name. Precious is this book, but its main preciousness lies in its revealing Jesus Himself, it is the field which contains the pearl of great price, the casket which encloses heaven's brightest jewel. We have missed our way in the Bible if its silken clue has not led us to the central chamber where we see Jesus Himself. We have never been truly taught of the Holy Ghost, and we have missed the teaching of the life of Christ, unless we have come to abide in Jesus Himself. To know Him is our beginning of wisdom and our crown of wisdom. To know Him is our first lesson on the stool of penitence and our last attainment as we enter heaven. Our ambition is that we may know the love of Christ which passeth knowledge. Here is our life study, and we have good associates in it, for these things the angels desire to look into. May the Lord grant that the eyes of your understanding may be enlightened, that we may know what is the hope of His calling, and what the riches of the glory of His inheritance in the saints.

Beloved, because Jesus is the sum of the gospel *He must be our constant theme.* " God forbid that I should glory save in the cross of our Lord Jesus Christ." " I determined not to know anything among you save Jesus Christ and Him crucified." So spake men of old, and so say we. When we have done preaching Christ we had better have done preaching ; when you have done teaching in your classes Jesus Christ Himself, give up Sunday school work, for nothing else is worthy of your pains. Put out the sun, and light is gone, life is gone, all is gone. When

Jesus is pushed into the background or left out of a minister's teaching, the darkness is darkness that might be felt, and the people escape from it into gospel light as soon as they can. A sermon without Jesus in it is savourless, and worthless to God's tried saints, and they soon seek other food. The more of Christ in our testimony the more of light and life and power to save. Some preachers are guilty of the most wearisome tautology, but this is not laid to their charge when their theme is Jesus. I have heard hearers declare that their minister appeared to have bought a barrel organ on which he could grind five or six tunes and no more, and these he ground out for ever and ever, amen. They have been weary, very weary, of such vain repetitions; but to this day I never heard of anybody against whom the complaint was urged that He preached Christ too much, too often, too earnestly, or too joyfully. I never recollect seeing a single Christian man coming out of a congregation with a sorrowful face saying, " He extolled the Redeemer too highly : He grossly exaggerated the praises of our Saviour." I do not remember ever meeting with a case in which the sick upon the bed of languishing have complained that thoughts of Jesus were burdensome to them. I never recollect that a single book has been denounced by earnest Christian men because it spoke too highly of the Lord, and made Him too prominent. No, my brethren, He who is the study of the saints must be the daily theme of ministers if they would feed the flock of God. No theme so moves the heart, so arouses the conscience, so satisfies the desires, and so calms the fears. God forbid we should ever fail to preach Jesus Himself. There is no fear of exhausting the subject, nor of our driving away our hearers, for His words are still true, " I, if I be lifted up, will draw all men unto Me."

III. Jesus Christ Himself is THE OBJECT OF OUR LOVE, and *how dear He should be*. We can all of us who are really saved declare that " We love Him because He first loved us." We have an intense affection for His blessed person as well gratitude for His salvation. The personality of Christ is a fact always to be kept prominently in our thoughts. The love a truth is all very well, but the love of a person has far more power in it. We have heard of men dying for an idea, but it is infinitely more easy to awaken enthusiasm for a person. When an idea becomes embodied in a man it has a force which in its abstract form it never wielded. Jesus Christ is loved by us as the embodiment of everything that is lovely, and true, and pure, and of good report. He Himself is incarnate perfection, inspired by love. We love His offices, we love the types which describe Him, we love the ordinances by which He is set forth, but we love Himself best of all. He Himself is our beloved ; our heart rests only in Him.

Because we love Him we love His people, and through Him we enter into union with them. Our text is taken from a verse which says, " Jesus Christ Himself being the chief corner stone." He is the binder at the corner, joining Jew and Gentile in one temple. In Jesus those ancient differences cease, for He " hath made both one, and hath broken down the middle wall of partition between us ; to make in Himself of twain one new man, so making peace." We are at one with ever man who is at one with Christ. Only let our Lord say, " I love that man," and we love him at once ; let us only hope that our friend can say, " I love Jesus," and we hasten to respond, " And I love you for Jesus' sake." So warm is the fire of our love to Jesus that all His friends may sit at it, and welcome. Our circle of affection comprehends all who in any shape or way have truly to do with Jesus Himself.

Because we love Himself we delight to render service to Him. Whatever service we do for His church, and for His truth, we do for His sake, even if we can only render it to the least of His brethren we do it unto Him. The woman with the alabaster box of precious ointment is a type which we greatly prize, for she would only break the precious box *for Him*, and every drop of its delicious contents must be poured only upon His head. The bystanders complained of waste, but there can be no waste in anything that is done for Jesus. If the whole world, and the heavens, and the heaven of heavens were all one great alabaster box, and if all the sweets which can be conceived were hived within it, we would wish to see the whole broken, that every drop of the sweetness might be poured out for Jesus Christ Himself.

" Jesus is worthy to receive
Honour and power divine ;
And blessings more than we can give,
Be Lord, for ever Thine."

Oh, our Beloved, if we can do anything for Thee, we are charmed at possessing such a privilege. If we are allowed to wash Thy disciples' feet, or to care for the poorest of Thy poor, or the least lamb of Thy flock, we accept the office as a high honour, for we love Thee with all our hearts. Our love to Jesus should be as much a matter of fact as our affection for our husband, wife, or child, and it should be far more influential upon our lives. Love to our Lord is, I trust, moving all of you to personal service. You might have paid a subscription and allowed others to work, but you cannot do it when you see that Jesus gave Himself for you. Jesus Himself demands that I myself should be consecrated to His praise. Personal service is due to a personal Christ, who personally loved and personally died for us. When nothing moves us to zeal, when the jaded spirit cannot follow up its industries, let but Jesus Himself appear, and straightway our passions are all in a blaze, and the fiery spirit compels the flesh to warm to its work again. We even glory in infirmity when Jesus is near, and venture upon works which else had seemed impossible. We can do anything and everything for " Jesus Christ Himself."

IV. Fourthly, our Lord Jesus Christ Himself is THE SOURCE OF ALL OUR JOY. *How ought we to rejoice when we have such a springing well of blessedness.* In times of sorrow our solace is Jesus Himself. It is no small ground of comfort to a mourner that Jesus Himself is a man. How cheering to read, " Forasmuch as the children are partakers of flesh and blood, He also Himself took part of the same." The humanity of Christ has a charm about it which the quietly sorrowful alone discover. I have known what it is to gaze upon the incarnation with calm repose of heart when my brain has seemed to be on fire with anguish. If Jesus be indeed my brother man, there is hope at all times. This is better balm than that of Gilead, " Himself took our infirmities, and bare our sicknesses " ; " For in that He Himself hath suffered, being temped, He is able also to succour them that are tempted." Pain, hunger, thirst, desertion, scorn, and agony Jesus Himself has borne. Tempted in all points like as we are, though without sin, He has become the chief Comforter of the sorrowful. Many and many a sufferer in the lone watches of the night has thought of Him and felt his strength renewed. Our patience revives when we see the Man of Sorrows silent before His accusers. Who can refuse to drink of His cup and to be baptized with His baptism ?

"His way was much rougher and darker than mine :
Did Christ, my Lord, suffer, and shall I repine ? "

The darkness of Gethsemane has been light to many an agonized soul, and the passion even unto death has made the dying sing for joy of heart. Jesus Himself is the solace of our soul in sorrow, and when we emerge from the storm of distress into the deep calm of peace, as we often do, blessed be His name, He is our peace. Peace He left us by legacy, and peace He creates in person. We never know deep peace of heart until we know the Lord Jesus Himself. You remember that sweet word when the disciples were met together, the doors being shut for fear of the Jews, " Jesus Himself stood in the midst of them, and said, Peace be unto you." Jesus Himself you see brought the message ; for nothing but His presence could make it effectual. When we see Him our spirit smells a sweet savour of rest. Where can an aching head find such another pillow as His bosom ?

On high days and holidays our spirits soar beyond rest : we ascend into the heaven of joy and exultation ; but then it is our Lord's joy which is in us making our joy full. " Then were the disciples glad when they saw the Lord," and then are we glad also. By faith we see Jesus Himself enthroned, and this has filled us with delight, for His glorification is our satisfaction. " Him also hath God highly exalted, and given Him a name which is above every name." I care not what becomes of me so long as He is glorified. The soldier dies happy when the shout of victory salutes his ear, and his failing sight beholds his prince triumphant. What a joy to think that Jesus is risen—risen to die no more : the joy of resurrection is superlative. What bliss to know that He has ascended, leading capitivity captive, that He sitteth now enthroned in happy state, and that He will come in all the glory of the Father to break His enemies in pieces as with a rod of iron. Here lies the grandest joy of His expectant church. She has in reserve a mighty thunder of hosannahs for that auspicious day.

If there is any joy to be had, O Christian, that is both safe and sweet, a joy of which none can know too much, it is to be found in Him whom as yet you see not, but in whom believing you rejoice with joy unspeakable and full of glory.

We must tear ourselves away from that thought to turn to another, but assuredly it is rich in happy memories and in blessed expectations.

V. Fifthly, JESUS CHRIST HIMSELF IS THE MODEL OF OUR LIFE, and therefore *how blessed it is to be like Him.* As to our rule for life, we are like the disciples on the mount of transfiguration when Moses and Elias had vanished, for we see " no man save Jesus only." Every virtue found in other men we find in Him in greater perfection ; we admire the grace of God in them, but Jesus Himself is our pattern. It was once said of Henry VIII, by a severe critic, that if the characteristics of all the tyrants that had ever lived had been forgotten, they might all have been seen to the life in that one king : we may more truly say of Jesus, if all graces, and virtues, and sweetnesses which have ever been seen in good men could all be forgotten, you might find them all in Him : for in Him dwells all that is good and great. We, therefore, desire to copy His character and put our feet into His footprints. Be it ours to follow the Lamb whithersoever He goeth. What saith our Lord Himself ? " Follow Me," and again, " Take My yoke upon you and learn of Me, for I am meek and lowly in heart, and ye shall find rest unto your souls." Not Christ's apostle, but Christ Himself, is our guide ; we may not take a secondary model, but must imitate Jesus Himself. By the indwelling of the Holy Spirit and His gracious operations we are developing into the the image of Christ till Christ be formed in us ; an we thus develop because the heavenly life in us is His own life. " I in them," said He, and again, " I am the life." For " we are dead, and our life is hid with Christ in God." " He that hath the Son hath life, and he that hath not the Son of God hath not life." It is not passing through baptism, nor bearing the name of Christ, it is having Jesus Himself in our hearts that makes us Christians, and in proportion as He is formed in us and the new life grows we become more and more like Him. And this is our prospect for eternity, that we are to be with Him and like Him, for " when He shall appear, we shall be like Him, for we shall see Him as He is." Think of Him, you that mourn your imperfectness to-day—think of Jesus Christ Himself, and then be assured that you are to be like Him. What a picture ! Come, artist, bring your best skill here. What can you do ? All pencils fail to depict *Him.* It needs a poet's eye as well as an artist's hand to picture the Lovely One. But what can the poet do ? Ah, you also fail ; you cannot sing Him any more than your friend can paint Him. Fruitful conception and soaring imagination may come to your aid, but they cannot prevent your failure. He is too beautiful to be described—He must be seen. Yet here comes the marvel—" We shall be like Him "—like Jesus Christ Himself. O saint, when thou art risen from the dead how lovely thou wilt be ! Wilt thou know thyself ? To-day thou art wrinkled with old age, scarred with the marks of disease and pain, and perhaps deformed by accident, or blanced with consumption, but none of these shall blemish thee then. Thou wilt be without spot of wrinkle, faultless before the throne.

" O glorious hour ! O blest abode !
I shall be near and like my God."

And not in bodily form alone shall we be like unto Him whose eyes are as the eyes of doves, and whose cheeks are as beds of spices ; but in spirit and in soul shall we be perfectly conformed to the Well-beloved. We shall be holy even as He is holy, and happy as He is happy. We shall enter into the joy of our Lord—the joy of Jesus Himself. I say not that we can be divine—that cannot be ; but still, brothers to Him that is the Son of God, we shall be very near the throne. O what rapture to know that my next of kin liveth, and when He shall stand in the latter day upon the earth I shall not only see God in this my flesh, but I shall be like Him, for I shall see Him as He is. Christ Himself then becomes to us unspeakably precious, as the model of our present life and the image of the perfection towards which the Holy Ghost is working us.

VI. Lastly, HE IS THE LORD OF OUR SOUL. *How sweet it will be to be with Him.* We find to-day that His beloved company makes everything move pleasantly whether we run in the way of His commands, or traverse the valley of the shadow of death.

Saints have lain in dungeons, and yet they have walked at liberty when He has been there ; they have been stretched on the rack, and even called it a bed of roses when He has stood by. One lay on a gridiron, with the hot fires beneath him ; but amidst the flames he challenged his tormentors to do their worst, and laughed them to scorn, for his Lord was there. Martyrs have been seen to clap their hands when every finger burned like a lighted candle, and they have been heard to cry, " Christ is all," " Christ is all." When the Fourth, like unto the Son of God, walks in the furnace, all the fire can do is but to snap their bonds and set the sufferers free. Oh, brethren, I am sure your only happiness that has been worth the having has been found in knowing that He loved you and was near you. If you have ever rejoiced in the abundance of your corn and wine and oil, it has been a sorry joy ; it has soon palled upon your taste, it never touched the great deeps of your spirit ; and anon it has gone and left you sore wearied in heart. If you have rejoiced in your children, and your kinsfolk, and your bodily health, how readily has God sent a blight upon them all. But when you have rejoiced in Jesus you have heard a voice bidding you proceed to further delights. That voice has cried, " Drink, O friends, yea, drink abundantly, O beloved " ; for to be inebriated with such joy as this is to come to the best condition of mind, and to fix the soul where it should be. We are never right till we come out of ourselves and into Jesus ; but when the ecstatic state comes, and we stand right out of self, and stand in Him, so that whether in the body or out of the body we can scarcely tell, God knoweth ; then are we getting back to where God meant man to have been when He walked with Him in Eden, getting near to where God means we shall be when we shall see Him face to face. Brethren, what must the unveiled vision be ! If the sight of Him here be so sweet, what must it be to see Him hereafter ! It may be we shall not live till He cometh, for the Master may tarry ; but if He doth not come, and we therefore are called to pass through the gate of death, we need not fear I should not wonder if when we pass under the veil and come out in the disembodied state, one of our astonishments will be to find Jesus Himself there waiting to receive us. The soul hoped that a convoy of ministering angels would be near the bed and would escort it across the stream and up the mountains to the Celestial City ; but no : instead thereof the spirit will be saluted by the Lord Himself. Will it be amazed and cry : " It is He, e'en He, my best Beloved, Jesus Himself ; He has come to meet me. Heaven might have been too great a surprise ; even my disembodied spirit might have swooned away, but it is he, the man Christ Jesus whom I trusted down below, and who was the dear companion of my dying hours. I have changed my place and state, but I have not changed my Friend nor changed my joy, for here He is ! " What a glance of love will that be which He will give to us and which we shall return to Him. Shall we ever take our eyes away from Him ? Shall we ever wish to do so ? Will not the poet's words be true.

" Millions of years my wondering eyes,
Shall o'er Thy beauties rove ;
And endless ages I'll adore
The glories of Thy love."

Within a week it may be our meeting with Jesus Himself may take place ; perhaps within an hour. A poor girl lying in the hospital was told by the doctor or the nurse that she could only live another hour ; she waited patiently, and when there remained only one quarter of an hour more, she exclaimed : " One more quarter of an hour, and then— " she could not say what, neither can I ; only Jesus Himself hath said, " Father, I will that they also, whom Thou hast given me, be with me where I am ; that they may behold my glory." And as He has prayed, so shall it be, and so let it be. Amen and Amen.

THE TABERNACLE OF THE MOST HIGH

"In whom ye also are builded together for an habitation of God through the Spirit."—Ephesians ii. 22.

UNDER the old Mosaic dispensation God had a visible dwelling-place among men. The bright shekinah was seen between the wings of the cherubim which overshadowed the mercy-seat ; and in the tabernacle while Israel journeyed in the wilderness, and in the temple afterwards, when they were stablished in their own land, there was a visible manifestation of the presence of Jehovah in the place which was dedicated to His service. Now, everything under the Mosaic dispensation was but a type, a picture, a symbol of something higher and nobler. That form of worship was, as it were, a series of shadow-pictures, of which the gospel is the substance. It is a sad fact, however, that there is so much Judaism in all our hearts, that we frequently go back to the old beggarly elements of the law, instead of going forward and seeing in them a type of something spiritual and heavenly, to which we ought to aspire. It is disgraceful to the present century to hear some men talk as they do. They had better at once espouse the Jewish creed. I mean it is disgraceful to hear some men speak as they do with regard to religious edifices. I remember to have heard a sermon once upon this text—" If any man defile the temple of God, him will God destroy." And the first part of the sermon was occupied with a childish anathema against all who should dare to perform any unhallowed act in the churchyard, or who should lean the pole of a tent during the fair of the coming week against any part of that edifice, which, it seemed to me, was the god of the man who occupied the pulpit. Is there such a thing as a holy place anywhere? Is there any spot wherein God now particularly dwells? I trow not. Hear ye the words of Jesus, "Believe me, the hour cometh, when ye shall neither in this mountain, nor yet at Jerusalem, worship the Father. But the hour cometh, and now is, when the true worshippers shall worship the Father in spirit and in truth: for the Father seeketh such to worship Him." Remember, again, the saying of the apostle at Athens, "God that made the world and all things therein, seeing that He is Lord of heaven and earth, dwelleth not in temples made with hands."

When men talk of holy places they seem to be ignorant of the use of language. Can holiness dwell in bricks and mortar? Can there be such a thing as a sanctified steeple? Can it possibly happen that there can be such a thing in the world as a moral window or a godly post? I am lost in amazement, utterly lost, when I think how addled men's brains must be when they impute moral virtues to bricks and mortar, and stones, and stained glass. Pray how deep down this consecration go, and how high? Is every crow that flies over the edifice at that time in solemn air? Certainly it is as rational to believe that, as to conceive that every worm that is eating the body of an Episcopalian is a consecrated worm, and therefore there must necessarily be a brick wall, or a wide grave-path to protect the bodies of the sanctified from any unhallowed worms that might creep across from the Dissenters' side of the cemetery. I say again, such child's play, such Popery, such Judaism, is a disgrace to the cemetery. And yet, notwithstanding, we all find ourselves at diver times and seasons indulging in it. That at which you have just now smiled is but pushing the matter a little further, an error into which we may very readily descend; it is but an extravaganza of an error into which we all of us are likely to fall. We have a reverence for our plain chapels; we feel a kind of comfort when we are sitting down in the place which somehow or other we have got to think must be holy.

Now let us if we can, and perhaps it takes a great sturdiness and independence of mind to do it—let us drive away once and for ever, all idea of holiness being connected with anything but with a conscious active agent; let us get rid once and for ever of all superstitions with regard to place. Depend upon it, one place is as much consecrated as another, and wherever we meet with true hearts reverently to worship God, that place becomes for the time being God's house. Though it be regarded with the most religious awe, that place which has no devout heart within it, is no house of God; it may be a house of superstition, but a house of God it cannot be. "But, still," says one, "God hath a habitation; doth not your text say so?" Yes, and of that house of God, I am about to speak this morning. There is such a thing as a house of God; but that is not an inanimate structure, but a living and a spiritual temple. "In whom," that is Christ, "ye also are builded together for a habitation of God through the Spirit." The house of God is built with the living stones of converted men and women, and the church of God, which Christ hath purchased with His blood—this is the divine edifice, and the structure wherein God dwelleth even to this day. I would, however, make one remark with regard to places in which we worship. I do think, albeit that there can be no sanctity of superstition connected with them, there is at the same time, a kind of sacredness of association. In any place where God has blessed my soul, I feel that it is none other than the house of God, and the very gate of heaven. It is not because the stones are hallowed, but because there I have met with God, and the recollections that I have of the place consecrate it to me. That place where Jacob laid him down to sleep, what was it but his sleeping chamber for the time being, but his sleeping chamber was none othe than the house of God. Ye have rooms in your houses, I hope, and closets there more sacred in truth than any gorgeous cathedral that ever lifted its spire to heaven. Where we meet with God there is a sacredness, not in the place but in the associations connected with it. Where we hold fellowship with God and where God makes bare His arm, though it be in a barn or a hedgerow, or on a moor, or on a mountain side, there is God's house to us, and the place is consecrated at once, but yet not so consecrated as that we may regard it with superstitious awe, but only consecrated by our own recollections of blessed hours which we have spent there in hallowed fellowship with God. Leaving that out of the question, I come to introduce you to the house which God has builded for His habitation.

We shall regard the church this morning thus— first, as a *building ;* secondly, as *a habitation ;* and thirdly, as what she is soon to become, namely—*a glorious temple.*

I. First, then, we shall regard the church as A BUILDING. And here let us pause to ask the question first of all what is a church—what is the church of God? One sect claims the title for itself of *the church*, while other denominations hotly contend for it. It belongs to none of us. The church of God consisteth not of any one peculiar denomination of men; the church of God consisteth of those whose names are written in the book of God's eternal choice; the men who were purchased by Christ upon the tree, the men who are called of God by His Holy Spirit and who being quickened by that same Spirit partake of the life of Christ, and become members of His body, of His flesh, and of His bones. There are to be found in every denomination among all sorts of Christians; some stray ones where we little dreamed of them; here and there a member of the church of God hidden in the midst of the darkness of accursed Rome; now and then, as if by chance, a member of the church of Christ, connected with no sect whatever, far away from all connection with his brethren, having scarcely heard of their existence yet still knowing Christ, because the life of Christ is in him. Now this church of Christ, the people of God, throughout the world, by whatever name they may be known, are in my text compared to a building in which God dwells.

I must now indulge in a little allegory with regard to this building. The church is not a heap of stones shot together; she is a building. Of old her Architect devised her. Methinks I see Him, as I look back into old eternity making the first outline of His church. "Here" said He in His eternal wisdom, "shall be the corner stone, and there shall be the pinnacle." I see Him ordaining her length, and her breadth, appointing her gates and her doors with matchless skill, devising every part of her, and leaving no single portion of the structure unmapped. I see Him, that mighty Architect, also choosing to Himself every stone of the building, ordaining its size and its shape; settling upon His mighty plan the position each stone shall occupy, whether it shall glitter in front, or be hidden in the back, or buried in the very centre of the wall. I see Him marking not merely the bare outline, but all the fillings up; all being ordained, decreed, and settled, in the eternal covenant, which was the divine plan of the mighty Architect upon which the church is to be built. Looking on, I see the Architect choosing a corner stone. He looks to heaven, and there are the angels, those glittering stones, He looks at each one of them from Gabriel down; but, saith He, "None of you will suffice, I must have a corner stone that will support all the weight of the building, for on that stone every other one must lean. O Gabriel, thou wilt not suffice! Raphael thou must lay by; I cannot build with thee." Yet was it necessary that a stone should be found, and one too that should be taken out of the same quarry as the rest. Where was he to be discovered? Was there a man who would suffice to be the corner stone of this mighty building? Ah no! neither apostles, prophets, nor teachers would. Put them altogether, and they would be as a foundation of quicksand, and the house would totter to its fall. Mark how the divine mind solved the difficulty—"God shall become man, very man, and so He shall be of the same substance as the other stones of the temple, yet shall He be God, and therefore strong enough to bear all the weight of this mighty structure, the top whereof shall reach to heaven." I see that foundation laid. Is there singing at the laying of it? No. There is weeping there. The angels gathered round at the laying of this first stone; and look ye men and wonder, the angels weep; the harps of heaven are clothed in sackcloth, and no song is heard. They sang together and shouted for joy when the word was made, why shout they not now? Look ye here and see the reason. That stone is imbedded in blood, that corner stone must lie nowhere else but in His own gore. The vermillion cement drawn from His own sacred veins must imbed it. And there He lies, the first stone of the divine edifice. Oh, begin your songs afresh, ye angels, it is over now. The foundation stone is laid; the terrible ceremony is complete, and now, whence shall we gather the stones to build this temple? The first is laid, where are the rest? Shall we go and dig into the sides of Lebanon? Shall we find these precious stones in the marble quarries of kings? No. Whither are ye flying ye labourers of God? Whither are ye going? Where are the quarries? And they reply—"We go to dig in the quarries of Sodom and Gomorrah, in the depths of sinful Jerusalem and in the midst of erring Samaria." I see them clear away the rubbish. I mark them as they dig deep into the earth, and at last they come to these stones. But how rough, how hard, how unhewn. Yes, but these are the stones ordained of old in the decree, and these must be the stones, and none other. There must be a change effected. These must be brought in and shaped and cut and polished, and put into their places. I see the workmen at their labour. The great saw of the law cuts through the stone, and then comes the polishing chisel of the gospel. I see the stones lying in their places, and the church is rising. The ministers, like wise master-builders, are there running along the wall, putting each spiritual stone in its place: each stone is leaning on that massive corner stone, and every stone depending on the blood, and finding its security and its strength in Jesus Christ, the corner stone, elect, and precious. Do you see the building rise as each one of God's chosen is brought in, called by grace and quickened? Do you mark the living stones as in sacred love and holy brotherhood they are knit together? Have you ever entered the building, and see how these stones lean one upon another bearing each other's burden, and so fulfilling the law of Christ? Do you mark how the church loveth Christ, and how the members love each other. How first the church is joined to the corner stone, and then each stone bound to the next, and the next to the next, till the whole building becometh one? Lo! the structure rises, and it is complete, and at last it is built. And now open wide your eyes, and see what a glorious building this is—the church of God. Men talk of the splendour of their architecture—this is architecture indeed; neither after Grecian nor Gothic models, but after the model of the sanctuary which Moses saw in the holy mountain. Do you see it? Was there ever a structure so comely as this—instinct with life in every part? Upon one stone shall be seven eyes, and each stone full of eyes and full of hearts. Was ever a thought so massive as this—a building built of souls—a structure made of hearts? There is no house like a heart for one to repose in. There a man may find peace in his fellow-man; but here is the house where God delighteth to dwell—built of living hearts, all beating with holy love—built of redeemed souls, chosen of the Father, bought with the blood of Christ. The top of it is in heaven. Part of them are above the clouds. Many of the living stones are now in the pinnacle of paradise. We are here below, the building rises, the sacred masonry is heaving, and, as the corner stone rises, so all of us must rise until at last the entire structure from its foundation to its pinnacle shall be heaved up to heaven, and there shall it stand for ever—the new Jerusalem—the temple of the majesty of God.

With regard to this building I have just a remark or two to make before I come to the next point. Whenever architects devise a building they make mistakes in forming the plan. The most careful will omit something; the most clever find in some things he has been mistaken. But mark the church of God; it is built according to rule, and compass, and square, and it shall be found at last that there has not been one mistake. You, perhaps, my dear brother, are a little stone in the temple, and you are apt to think you ought to have been a great one. There is no mistake about that. You have but one talent; that is enough for you. If you had two you would spoil the building. You are placed perhaps in a position of obscurity, and you are saying, "Oh that I were prominent in the church!" If you were prominent you might be in a wrong place; and but one stone out of its place in architecture so delicate as that of God, would mar the whole. You are where you ought to be; keep there. Depend on it there is no mistake. When at last we shall go round about her, mark her walls, and tell her bulwarks, we shall each of us be compelled to say, "How glorious is this Zion!" When our eyes shall have been enlightened, and our hearts instructed, each part of the building will command our admiration. The topstone is not the foundation, nor does the foundation stand at the top. Every stone is of the right shape; the whole material is as it should be, and the structure is adapted for the great end, the glory of God, the temple of the Most High. Infinite wisdom then may be remarked in this building of God.

Another thing may be noticed, namely, her impregnable strength. This habitation of God, this house which is not made with hands, but is of God's building, has often been attacked, but it has never been taken. What multitudes of enemies have battered against her old ramparts! but they have battered in vain. "The kings of the earth stood up, and the rulers took counsel together," but what happened? They came against her, every one of them with mighty men, each man with his sword drawn, but what became of them? The Almighty scattered kings in Hermon like snow in Salmon. As the snow is driven from the mountain side before the stormy blast, even so didst Thou drive them away, O God, and they melted before the breath of Thy nostrils.

"Then should our souls in Zion dwell,
Nor fear the rage of Rome or hell."

The church is not in danger, and she never can be.

Let her enemies come on, she can resist. Her passive majesty, her silent rocky strength, bids them defiance now. Let them come on and break themselves in pieces, let them dash themselves against her, and learn the ready road to their own destruction. She is safe, and she must be safe even unto the end. Thus much then we can say of the structure: it is built by infinite wisdom, and it is impregnably secure.

And we may add, it is glorious for beauty. There was never structure like this. One might feast his eyes upon it from dawn to eve, and then begin again. Jesus Himself takes delight in it. So pleased is God in the architecture of His church, that He has rejoiced with His church as He never did with the world. When God made the world He heaved the mountains, and digged the seas, and covered its valleys with grass; He made all the fowls of the air, and all the beasts of the field; yea, and He made man in His own image, and when the angels saw it they sang together and they shouted for joy. God did not sing; there was no sufficient theme of song for Him that was "Holy, holy, holy." He might say it was very good; there was a goodness of fitness about it, but not moral goodness of holiness. But when God built His church He did sing; and that is the most extraordinary passage, I sometimes think, in the whole Word of God, where He is represented as singing:—"Thy Redeemer in the midst of thee is mighty, He will save, He will rest in His love, He will rejoice over thee with singing." Think, my brethren, of God Himself looking at His church; and so fair and beautiful is the structure, that He sings over His work, and as each stone is put in its place, Divinity itself sings. Was ever song like that? Oh, come, let us sing, let us exalt the name of God together; praise Him who praiseth His church—who hath made her to be His peculiar dwelling-place.

Thus, then, have we in the first place regarded the church as a building.

II. But the true glory of the church of God consists in the fact that she is not only a building, but that she is A HABITATION. There may be great beauty in an uninhabited structure, but there is always a melancholy thought connected with it. In riding through our country, we often come upon a dismantled tower, or castle; it is beautiful, but it is not a thing of joy; there is a sorrowful reflection connected with it. Who loves to see desolate palaces? Who desireth that the land should cast out her sons, and that her houses should fail of tenants? But there is joy in a house lit up and furnished, where there is the sound of men. Beloved, the church of God hath this for her peculiar glory, that she is a tenanted house, that she is a habitation of God through the Spirit. How many churches there are that are houses, yet not habitations! I might picture to you a professed church of God; it is built according to square and compass, but its model has been formed in some ancient creed, and not in the Word of God. It is precise in its discipline according to its own standard, and accurate in its observances according to its own model. You enter that church, the ceremony is imposing; the whole service perhaps attracts you for a while; but you go out of that place conscious that you have not met with the life of God there—that it is a house, but a house without a tenant. It may be professedly a church, but it is not a church possessing the indwelling of the Holy One: it is an empty house that must soon be dilapidated and fall. I do fear that this is true of many of our churches, Established and Dissenting, as well as Romanist. There are too many churches that are nothing but a mass of dull, dead formality; there is no life of God there. You might go to worship with such a people, day after day, and your heart would never beat more quickly, your blood would never leap in its veins, your soul would never be refreshed, for it is an empty house. Fair may be the architecture of the structure, but empty is its storehouse; there is no table spread, there is no rejoicing, no killing of the fatted calf, no dancing, no singing for joy. Beloved, let us take heed, lest our churches become the same, lest we be combinations of men without spiritual life, and consequently houses uninhabited, because God is not there. But a true church, that is visited by the Spirit of God, where conversion, instruction, devotion, and the like, are carried on by the Spirit's own living influences—such a church has God for its inhabitant.

And now we will just turn over this sweet thought. A church built of living souls is God's own house. What is meant by this? I reply, a house is a place where a man solaces and comforts himself. Abroad we do battle with the world: there we strain every nerve and sinew that we may stem a sea of troubles, and may not be carried away by the stream. Abroad, among men, we meet those of strange language to us, who often cut us to the heart and wound us to the quick. We feel that there we must be upon our guard. We could often say, "My soul is among lions. I lie even among those that are set on fire of hell." Going abroad in the world we find but little rest, but the day's work done, we go home, and there we solace ourselves. Our weary bodies are refreshed. We throw away the armour that we have been wearing, and we fight no more. We see no longer the strange face, but loving eyes beam upon us. We hear no language now which is discordant in our ears. Love speaks, and we reply. Our home is the place of our solace, our comfort, and our rest. Now, God calls the church His habitation—His *home*. See Him abroad; He is hurling the thunderbolt and lifting up His voice upon the waters. Hearken to Him; His voice breaks the cedars of Lebanon and makes the hinds to calve. See Him when He makes war, riding the chariot of His might, He drives the rebellious angels over the battlements of heaven down to the depth of hell. Behold Him as He lifteth Himself in the majesty of His strength! Who is this that is glorious? It is God. most high and terrible. But see He lays aside His glittering sword; His spear He bears no longer. He cometh back to His home. His children are about Him. He taketh His solace and His rest. Yes, think not I venture too far—He shall rest in His love! and He doth do it. He resteth in His church. He is no longer a consuming fire, a terror, and a flame. Now, is He love and kindness and sweetness, ready to hear the prattle of His children's prayer, and the disjointed notes of His children's song. Oh how beautiful is the picture of the church as God's house, the place in which He takes His solace! "For the Lord hath chosen Zion; He hath desired it for His habitation. This is My rest for ever: here will I dwell; for I have desired it."

Furthermore, a man's home is the place where he shows his inner self. You meet a man at the market, he deals sharply with you; he knows with whom he has to deal, and he acts with you as a man of the world. You see him again at home, talking with his children, and you say, "What a different man! I could not have believed it was the same being."

Mark, again, the professor in his chair; he is instructing students in science. Mark his sternness as he speaks upon recondite themes. Would you believe that that same man will in the evening have his little one upon his knee, and will tell it childish tales, and repeat the ballads of the nursery? And yet it is even so. See the king as he rides through the street in his pomp; thousands gather round him; acclamation rends the sky. With what majestic port he bears himself! He is all a king, every inch a monarch, as he towers in the midst of the multitude. Have you seen the king at home? He is then just like other men; his little ones are about him; he is on the floor with them in their games. Is this the king? Yes, it is even he. But why did he not do this in his palace?—in the streets? Oh, no, that was not his home. It is in his home that a man unbends himself. Even so with regard to our glorious God: it is in His church that He manifests Himself as He does not unto the world. The mere worldling turns his telescope to the sky, and he sees the pomp of God in the stars, and he says, "O God, how infinite art Thou?" Devoutly he looks across the sea, and beholds it lashed with tempest, and he says, "Behold the might and majesty of the Deity!" The anatomist dissects an insect, and discovers in every part of it divine wisdom, and he says, "How wise is God!" Aye; but it is only the believer who as he kneels in his chamber can say, "My Father made all these," and then can say, "Our Father, which art in heaven, hallowed be Thy name." There are sweet revelations which God makes in His church, which He never makes anywhere else. It is there He takes the children to His bosom it is there He opens His heart, and lets His people know the fountains of His great soul, and the might of His infinite affection. And is it not a sweet thing to think of God at home with His family, happy in the house of His church?

But yet, furthermore, another thought strikes me now. A man's home is the centre of all he doth. Yonder is a large farm. Well, there are outhouses, and hay ricks, and barns, and the like; but just in the middle of these there is the house, the centre of all husbandry. No matter how much wheat there may be, it is to the house the produce goes. It is for the maintenance of the household that the husband carries on his husbandry. You may hear the cattle lowing yonder, you may mark the sheep upon the hills, but the fleece cometh home, and the full udders must yield the milk for the children of the house, for the house is the centre of all. Every river of industry cometh down towards the sweet soft inland lake of home. Now God's church is God's centre? He is abroad in the world, He is busy here and there and everywhere, but to what does all His business tend? To His church. Why doth God clothe the hills with plenty? *For the feeding of His people?* Why is providence revolving? Why those wars and tempests, and then again this stillness and calm? *It is for His church.* Not an angel divides the ether who hath not a mission for the church. It may be indirectly, but nevertheless truly so. There is not an archangel that fulfils the behests of the Most High but really carries the church upon his broad wings, and bears up her children lest they dash their feet against a stone. The storehouses of God are for His church. The depths beneath of hidden treasures, of God's unutterable riches—all these are for His people. There is nothing which He hath from His blazing crown to the darkness that is beneath His throne, that is not for His redeemed. All things must

minister and work together for good for the chosen church of God which is His *house*—His daily habitation. I think if you will turn that over and over again, when you are away, you will see there is much in the beautiful fact, that as the house is the centre, so is the church the centre of everything with God.

One other thought and I will have done. We have heard much talk of late about the French invasion. I shall begin to be alarmed about it when I see it, but certainly not till then. However, there is one thing we may say pretty safely. We are many of us peace men and would not like to wield the sword; the first sight of blood would sicken us; we are peaceful beings, we are not for fighting and war. But let the most peaceful man imagine that the invader has landed on our shore, that our house is in danger, and our homes about to be sacked by the foe, our conscientiousness I fear would give way; notwithstanding all we might say about the wrongness of war, I query whether there be a man among us who would not take such weapon as he could find next to hand to repel the enemy. With this for our war cry, "Our hearths and our homes," we would rush upon the invader, be he who he may or what he may. There is no might so tremendous that it could paralyse our arm; until we were frozen in death we would fight for our home; there would be no command so stern that it could quiet us; we should break through every band and bond, and the weakest of us would be a giant, and our women would become heroines in the day of difficulty. Every hand would find its weapon to hurl at the invader. We love our homes, and we must and will defend them. Aye, and now lift up your thou hts—the church is God's home, will He not defend it? will He suffer His own house to be sacked and stormed? shall the hearth of divinity be stained with the blood of His children? Shall it be that the church is overthrown, and her battlements stormed, her peaceful habitations given up to fire and sword? No, never, not while God hath a heart of love, and while He calleth His people His own house and His habitation. Come, let us rejoice in this our security; let earth be all in arms abroad, we dwell in perfect peace, for our Father is in the house and He is God Almighty. Let them come on against us, we need not fear, His arm shall fell them, the breath of His nostrils shall blast them, a word shall destroy them, they shall melt away like the fat of rams, as fat of lambs shall they be consumed, into smoke shall they consume away. All these thoughts seem to me naturally to arise from the fact that the church is God's habitation.

III. I was about to show you in the third place, that the church is, by-and-bye, to be GOD'S GLORIOUS TEMPLE. It doth not yet appear what *she* shall be. I have, however, already mentioned this precious fact. The church is rising to-day, and she shall continue to rise until the mountain of the Lord's house shall be established upon the top of the mountains, and then when all nations call her blessed, and Him blessed too—when they shall all say "Come and let us go up to the house of our God that we may worship Him," then shall the church's glory begin. When this earth shall pass away, when all the monuments of empires shall be dissolved and run down in the common lava of the last burning, then shall the church be caught up in the clouds and afterwards be exalted to heaven itself, to become a temple such as eye hath not seen.

And now, brethren and sisters, in conclusion I make these remarks. If the church of God is God's house, what should you and I do? Why we should earnestly seek as being a part of that temple always to retain the great inhabitant. Let us not grieve His Spirit lest He leave His church for awhile; above all let us not be hypocrites lest He never come into our hearts at all. And if the church be God's temple and God's house, let us not defile it. If you defile yourselves you defile the church, for your sin if you be a church member is the church's sin. The defilement of one stone in a building virtually mars its perfection. Take care that thou be holy even as He is holy. Let not thine heart become a house for Belial. Think not that God and the devil can dwell in the same habitation. Give thyself wholly to God. Seek for more of His Spirit, that as a living stone thou mayest be wholly consecrated; and never be content unless thou feelest in thyself the perpetual presence of the divine inhabitant who dwelleth in His church. May God now bless every living stone of the temple. And as for you that as yet are not hewn out of the quarries of sin, I pray that divine grace may meet with you, that you may be renewed and converted, and at last be partakers of the inheritance of the saints of light.

THE UNSEARCHABLE RICHES OF CHRIST

"Unto me, who am less than the least of all saints, is this grace given, that I should preach among the Gentiles the unsearchable riches of Christ."—Ephesians iii. 8.

THE apostle Paul felt it to be a great privilege to be allowed to preach the gospel. He did not look upon his calling as a drudgery, or a servitude, but he entered upon it with intense delight. All God's truly-sent servants have experienced much delight in the declaration of the gospel of Jesus; and it is natural that they should, for their message is one of mercy and love. If a herald were sent to a besieged city with the tidings that no terms of capitulation would be offered, but that every rebel without exception should be put to death, methinks he would go with lingering footsteps, halting by the way to let out his heavy heart in sobs and groans; but if instead thereof, he were commissioned to go to the gates with the white flag to proclaim a free pardon, a general act of amnesty and oblivion, surely he would run as though he had wings to his heels, with a joyful alacrity, to tell to his fellow-citizens the good pleasure of their merciful king. Heralds of salvation, ye carry the most joyful of all messages to the sons of men! When the angels were commissioned for once to become preachers of the gospel, and it was but for once, they made the welkin ring at midnight with their choral songs, "Glory to God in the highest, and on earth peace, good will toward men." They did not moan out a dolorous dirge as of those proclaiming death, but the glad tidings of great joy were set to music, and announced with holy mirth and celestial song. "Peace on earth; glory to God in the highest" is the joy-note of the gospel—and in such a key should it ever be proclaimed. We find the most eminent of God's servants frequently magnifying their office as preachers of the gospel. Whitefield was wont to call his pulpit his throne; and when he stood upon some rising knoll to preach to the thousands gathered in the open air, he was more happy than if he had assumed the imperial purple, for he ruled the hearts of men more gloriously than doth a king. When Dr. Carey was labouring in India, and his son Felix had accepted the office of ambassador to the king of Burmah, Carey said, "Felix has drivelled into an ambassador"—as though he looked upon the highest earthly office as an utter degradation if for it the minister of the gospel forsook his lofty vocation. Paul blesses God that this great grace was given to him, that he might preach among the Gentiles the unsearchable riches of Christ; he looked upon it not as toil but as a grace. Aspire to this office, young men whose souls are full of love to Jesus. Fired with sacred enthusiasm, covet earnestly the best gifts, and out of love to Jesus try whether you cannot in your measure tell to your fellow-men the story of the cross. Men of zeal and ability, if you love Jesus, make the ministry your aim; train your minds to it; exercise your souls towards it; and may God the Holy Spirit call you to it, that you also may preach the word of reconciliation to the dying thousands. The labourers still are few, may the Lord of the harvest thrust you into His work.

But while Paul was thus thankful for his office, his success in it greatly humbled him. The fuller a vessel becomes the deeper it sinks in the water. A plenitude of grace is a cure for pride. Those who are empty, and those especially who have little or nothing to do, may indulge a fond conceit of their abilities, because they are untried; but those who are called to the stern work of ministering among the sons of men, will often mourn their weakness, and in the sense of that weakness and unworthiness, they will go before God and confess that they are less than the least of all saints. I prescribe to any of you who seek humility, try hard work; if you would know your nothingness, attempt some great thing for Jesus. If you would feel how utterly powerless you are apart from the living God, attempt especially the great work of proclaiming the unsearchable riches of Christ. You will come back from the proclamation thankful that you were permitted to attempt it, but crying, "Who hath believed our report? and to whom is the aim of the Lord revealed?" and you will know, as you never knew before, what a weak unworthy thing you are.

Although our apostle thus knew and confessed his weakness, there is one thing which never troubled him: he was never perplexed as to the subject of his ministry. I do not find the apostle in all his writings proposing to himself the question, "What shall I preach?" No, my brethren, he had been taught in the college of Christ, and had thoroughly learned his one subject, so that preferring it beyond all else, he said, with solemn decision, "I determined not to know any thing among you, save Jesus Christ, and Him crucified." From his first sermon to his last, when he laid down his neck upon the block to seal his testimony with his blood, Paul preached Christ, and nothing but Christ. He lifted up the cross, and extolled the Son of God who bled thereon. His one and only calling here below was to cry, "Behold the Lamb!

Behold the Lamb of God which taketh away the sin of the world."

I pause to ask, on my own account, the prayers of God's people yet again, that the Holy Spirit may be my helper this morning. O deny not my earnest request! I call the attention of you all to this great master subject, which engrossed all the powers and passions of such a one as Paul, and I shall beg you to notice first *a glorious person mentioned*—the Lord Jesus Christ; secondly, *unsearchable riches sp ken of;* and thirdly, which shall make our practical conclusion —*a royal intention implied*, the intention which Jesus had in His heart when He bade His servants preach His unsearchable riches.

I. First then, may the Spirit of God strengthen us in our weakness while we try to speak upon THIS GLORIOUS PERSON, the Lord Jesus Christ.

The Lord Jesus Christ was the first promise of God to the sons of men after the Fall. When our first parents had been banished from the garden, all was dark before them. There was not a star to gild the cheerless midnight of their guilty and despairing souls until their God appeared to them, and said in mercy, "The seed of the woman shall bruise the serpent's head." That was the first star which God set in the sky of man's hope. Years rolled after years, and the faithful looked up to it with comfort; that one promise stayed the soul of many a faithful one, so that he died in hope, not having received the promise, but having seen it afar off, and having rejoiced in its beams. Whole centuries rolled away, but the seed of the woman did not come. Messiah, the great bruiser of the serpent's head, did not appear. Why tarried He? The world was foul with sin and full of woe, where was the Shiloh who should bring it peace? Graves were digged by millions, hell was filled with lost spirits, but where was the promised One, mighty to save? He was waiting till the fulness of time should come; He had not forgotten, for He had God's will in His inmost bowels; His desire to save souls was consuming His heart; He was but waiting until the word should be given. And when it was given, lo! He came delighting to do the Father's will. Seek ye Him? Behold, in Bethlehem's manger Emmanuel is born, God is with us. Before your eyes He lies who was both the Son of Mary, and the Son of the Blessed, an infant, and yet infinite, of a span long, and yet filling all eternity, wrapped in swaddling bands, and yet too great for space to hold Him. Thirty and more years He lived on earth: the latter part of His life was spent in a ministry full of suffering to Himself, but fraught with good to others. "We beheld His glory, the glory as of the only begotten of the Father, full of grace and truth." Never man spake like that Man. He was a Man on fire with love; a Man without human imperfections, but with all human sympathies; a Man without the sins of manhood, but with something more than the sorrows of common manhood piled upon Him. There was never such a Man as He, so great, so glorious in His life, and yet He is the pattern and type of manhood. He reached His greatest when He stooped the lowest. He was seized by His enemies one night when wrestling in prayer, betrayed by the man who had eaten bread with Him; He was dragged before tribunal after tribunal, through that long and sorrowful night, and wrongfully accused of blasphemy and sedition. They scourged Him; though none of His works deserved a blow, yet the ploughers made deep furrows on His back. They mocked Him; though He merited

the homage of all intelligent beings, yet they spat in His face, and smote Him with their mailed fists, and said, "prophesy, Who is he that smote Thee?" He was made lower than a slave even the abjects opened their mouths with laughter at Him, and the slaves scoffed at Him. To end the scene, they took Him through the streets of the Jerusalem over which He had wept; they hounded Him along the Via Dolorosa, out through the gate, to the mount of doom. Methinks I see Him, as with eyes all red with weeping, He turns to the matrons of Salem, and cries, "Daughters of Jerusalem, weep not for Me, but for yourselves, and for your children." Can you see Him bearing that heavy cross, ready to faint beneath the burden? Can you endure to see Him, when, having reached the little mound outside the city, they hurl Him on His back, and drive the cruel iron through His hands and feet? Can you bear to see the spectacle of blood and anguish as they lift Him up between heaven and earth, made a sacrifice for the sin of His people? My words shall be few, for the vision is too sad for language to depict. He bleeds, He thirsts, He groans, He cries—at last He dies—a death whose unknown griefs are not to be imagined, and were they known would be beyond expression by human tongue.

Now, it was the history of the crucifixion which Paul delighted to preach—Christ crucified was his theme—this old, old story, which ye have heard from your childhood, the story of the Son of God, who loved us and gave Himself for us. Ye all know that our Lord, after He had been taken down from the cross and laid in the tomb, lingered there but a few short hours, and then on the third day rose again from the dead, the same, yet not the same—a Man, but no more despised and rejected. He communed with His servants in a familiar and yet glorious manner for forty days, and cheered and comforted their hearts, and then, from the top of Olivet, in the sight of the company, He ascended to His Father's throne. Follow Him with your hearts, if ye cannot with your eyes. Behold Him as the angels meet Him, and

"Bring His chariot from on high,
To bear Him to His throne;
Clap their triumphant hands, and cry,
'The glorious work is done.'"

There He sits—faith sees Him this very day—at the right hand of God, even the Father, pleading with authority for His people; ruling heaven, and earth, and hell, for the keys thereof swing at His girdle; waiting till, on the flying cloud, He shall descend to judge the quick and dead, and distribute the vengeance or the reward. It was this glorious person of whom Paul delighted to speak. He preached the doctrines of the gospel, but he did not preach them apart from the person of Christ. Do not many preachers make a great mistake by preaching doctrine instead of preaching the Saviour? Certainly the doctrines are to be preached, but they ought to be looked upon as the robes and vestments of the man Christ Jesus, and not as complete in themselves. I love justification by faith—I hope I shall never have a doubt about that grand truth; but the cleansing efficacy of the precious blood appears to me to be the best way of putting it. I delight in sanctification by the Spirit; but to be conformed to the image of Jesus, is a still sweeter and more forcible way of viewing it. The doctrines of the gospel are a golden throne upon which Jesus sits, as king—not a hard, cold stone rolled at the door of the sepulchre in which Christ is hidden. Brethren, I believe this to be the mark of God's true minister, that he preaches Christ, as his one choice and delightful theme. In the old romance, they tell us that at the gate of a certain noble hall there hung a horn, and none could blow that horn but the true heir to the castle and its wide domains. Many tried it. They could make sweet music on other instruments; they could wake the echoes by other bugles; but that horn was mute let them blow as they might. At last, the true heir came, and when he set his lips to the horn, shrill was the sound and indisputable his claim. He who can preach Christ is the true minister. Let him preach anything else in the world, he has not proved his calling, but if he shall preach Jesus and the resurrection, he is in the apostolical succession. If Christ crucified be the great delight of his soul, the very marrow of his teaching, the fatness of his ministry, he has proved his calling as an ambassador of Christ. Brethren, the Christian minister should be like these golden spring flowers which we are so glad to see. Have you observed them when the sun is shining? How they open their golden cups, and each one whispers to the great sun, "Fill me with Thy beams!" but when the sun is hidden behind a cloud, where are they? They close their cups and droop their heads. So should the Christian feel the sweet influences of Jesus; so especially should the Christian minister be subject to his Lord. Jesus must be his sun, and he must be the flower which yields itself to the Sun of Righteousness. Happy would it be for us if our hearts and our lips could become like Anacreon's harp, which was wedded to one subject, and would learn no other. He wished to sing of the sons of Atreus, and the mighty deeds of Hercules, but his harp resounded love alone; and when he would have sung of Cadmus, his harp refused—it would sing of love alone. Oh! to speak of Christ alone—to be tied and bound to this one theme for ever; to speak alone of Jesus, and of the amazing love of the glorious Son of God, who "though He was rich, yet for our sakes became poor." This is the subject which is both "seed for the sower, and bread for the eater." This is the live coal for the lip of the preacher, and the master-key to the heart of the hearer. This is the tune for the minstrels of earth, and the song for the harpers of heaven. Lord, teach it to us more and more, and we will tell it out to others.

Before I leave this subject, I feel bound to make two or three remarks. You will perceive that the apostle Paul preached the unsearchable riches of Christ, not the dignity of manhood, or the grandeur of human nature; he preached not man, but man's Redeemer. Let us do the same. Moreover, he did not preach up the clergy and the church, but Christ alone. Some of the gentlemen who claim to be in the apostolical succession, could hardly have the effrontery to claim to be the successors of Paul. I believe that our modern priests are in the apostolical succession, I have never doubted that they are the lineal successors of Judas Iscariot, who betrayed his Master; but no other apostle would endure them for so much as an hour. Look ye, if Paul had been their leader, would he not have preached the unsearchable riches of priestcraft, as they do? Do not they preach up their own priestly power? Did Paul do this? Is not their one great theme the unsearchable riches of baptism; the unsearchable riches of the Eucharist, the blessed bread and the blessed wine; the unsearch-

able riches of their confession and absolution; the unsearchable riches of their albs, and their dalmatics, and their chasubles, and I know not what else of the rags of the whore of Babylon? A fine day is this in which we are to go back to the superstitions of the Dark Ages—so dark that our forefathers could not bear them—and for the unsearchable cunning of priests are to give up the unsearchable riches of Christ! We are told that the Reformation was a mistake; but we tell these false priests to their faces that they lie, and know not the truth. Beloved, Paul cared nothing for priestcraft; and this Book has not a word in it in favour of priestcraft. With Paul and with this Book all believers in Jesus are priests, and God's only clergy. Paul never posted bills upon the walls of Jerusalem, with black crosses on them, warning men that they would not be able to meet Christ at the Day of Judgment, if they did not keep Good Friday; but I will tell you what Paul did, he wrote to the Galatians, "Ye observe days, months, and times, and years. I am afraid of you, lest I have bestowed upon you labour in vain." This whole abomination of ritualism was the utter abhorrence of the apostle: in its first form of Judaism it stirred up his whole soul with indignation; it brought the blood into his cheek; he never was mightier in denouncing anything than when dealing heavy blows at ceremonialism; he said, "Neither circumcision availeth anything, nor uncircumcision, but faith that worketh by love." Paul preached up no priest, whether he lived at Rome or Canterbury; he exalted no class of men arrogantly pretending to have power to save. He would have been out of all patience with a set of simpletons decked out as guys, and dressed up as if they were meant to amuse children in a nursery. He never taught the worship of these calves, but Jesus alone was his subject, and the unsearchable riches of His grace. Mark you, on the other hand, Paul did not preach up the unsearchable riches of philosophy, as some do. "Yes," say some, "we must please this thinking age, this thoughtful people; we must educate a people who will reject all testimony because they will not be credulous; who will believe nothing but what they can understand, because, forsooth, their understanding is so amazingly clear, so perfect, so all but divine!" Not so, the apostle: he would have said to these philosophical gentlemen, "Stand away; I have nothing at all that can make me kindred with you, I preach the unsearchable riches of Christ, not the uncertainties of philosophical speculation; I give the people something to believe, something tangible to lay hold of, not superstitious, it is true, but divinely accredited; not concocted by the wisdom of man, but revealed by the wisdom of God." My dear friends, we must come back to the gospel of Paul, and may God bring all His ministering servants more and more clearly back to it, that we may have nothing to preach but that which clusters around the cross; which glows and glistens like a sacred halo of light around the head of the Crucified One; that we may lift up nothing but Jesus, and say, "God forbid that we should glory, save in the cross of our Lord Jesus Christ."

II. Secondly, Paul preached THE UNSEARCHABLE RICHES OF CHRIST.

Paul had no stinted Saviour to present to a few, no narrow-hearted Christ to be the head of a clique, no weak Redeemer who could pardon only those little offenders who scarcely needed it, but he preached a great Saviour to the great masses, a great Saviour to great sinners; he preached the Conqueror with dyed garments, travelling in the greatness of His strength, whose name is "Mighty to Save." Let us enquire in what requests we may ascribe to our Lord Jesus the possession of unsearchable riches? Our answer is, first, He has *unsearchable riches of love to sinners as they are.* Jesus so loved the souls of men that we can only use the "*so*," but we cannot find the word to match with it. In the French Revolution, there was a young man condemned to the guillotine, and shut up in one of the prisons. He was greatly loved by many, but there was one who loved him more than all put together. How know we this? It was his own father; and the love he bore his son was proved in this way: when the lists were called, the father, whose name was exactly the same as his son's, answered to the name, and the father rode in the gloomy tumbril out to the place of execution, and his head rolled beneath the axe instead of his son's, a victim to mighty love. See here an image of the love of Christ to sinners; for thus Jesus died for the ungodly, viewed as such. If they had not been ungodly, neither they nor He had needed to have died; if they had not sinned, there would have been no need for a suffering Saviour, but Jesus proved His boundless love in "that, while we were yet sinners, Christ died for us." Your name was in the condemned list, my fellow-sinner, but, if you believe in Jesus, you shall find that your name is there no longer, for Christ's name is put in your stead, and you shall learn that He suffered for you, the just for the unjust, that He might bring you to God. Is not this the greatest wonder of divine love, that it should be set upon us *as sinners.* I can understand God's loving reformed sinners and repenting sinners; but here is the glory of it, "God commendeth His love toward us, in that, while we were yet sinners [*yet sinners!*] Christ died for us." O my hearers, from my inmost heart I pray that this boundless wealth of love on the part of Jesus to those who were rebels and enemies, may win your hearts to love the heavenly Lover in return.

In the next place, Jesus has *riches of pardon for those who repent of their sins.* My Lord Jesus, by His death, has become immensely rich in pardoning power —so rich indeed that no guiltiness can possibly transcend the efficacy of His precious blood. There is one sin which He never will forgive—there is but one— and I am convinced that you have not committed that sin against the Holy Ghost if you have any feeling of repentance or desire towards God; for the sin which is unto death brings death with it to the conscience, so that when once committed the man ceases to feel. If thou desirest pardon, sinner, there is no reason why thou shouldst not have it, and have it now. The blood of Christ can wash out blasphemy, adultery, fornication, lying, slander, perjury, theft, murder. Though thou hast raked in the very kennels of hell till thou hast blackened thyself to the colour of a devil, yet, if thou wilt come to Christ and ask mercy, He will absolve thee from all sin. Do but wash in the bath which He has filled with blood, and "though your sins be as scarlet, they shall be as white as snow; though they be red like crimson, they shall be as wool." Do not misunderstand me, I mean just this, that the gospel of Jesus Christ is not meant exclusively for you respectable people, who always appear to be so religious, but for you who are irreligious, for you who are not even moral, or sober, or honest. I tell you the gospel of Christ is meant for the scum of the population; it is meant for the lowest of the low, for the worst of the worst. There is no den in London where the Saviour cannot work; there is no loathsome haunt of sin too foul for Him to cleanse. The heathen fabled of their Hercules that he cleansed the Augean stables by turning a river through them, and so washing away the filth of ages; if your heart be such a stable, Christ is greater than the mightiest Hercules —He can cause the river of His cleansing blood to flow right through your heart, and your iniquities, though they are a heap of abominations, shall be put away for ever. Riches of love to sinners as such, and riches of pardon to sinners who repent, are stored up in the Lord Jesus.

Again, *Christ has riches of comfort for all that mourn.* Have I the happiness of having before me some who mourn before the Lord? Blessed are you, for you shall be filled. What is the cause of your weeping? Is it your sin? Christ has a handkerchief that can wipe away such tears. He can blot out your sins like a cloud, and like a thick cloud your iniquities. Do but come to Him, and your deepest sorrow shall disappear beneath the influence of His sympathetic love. Are you sorrowful because you have lost a friend? He will be a friend to you. Have you been deceived and betrayed? My Master can meet that craving of your nature after friendship and sympathy. Confide in Him, and He will never forsake you. Oh! I cannot tell you how rich He is in consolation, but the Holy Ghost can tell you. If you do but get Jesus, you shall find, as Bernard used to say, that He is "honey to the mouth, music to the ear, and heaven to the heart." Win Christ, and you shall want nothing, beyond Him: lay hold of Him, and you shall say with the apostle, "I have learned in whatsoever state I am, therewith to be content," for He hath said, "I will never leave thee, nor forsake thee."

My Master's unsearchable rich s are also of another kind. Do you thirst for knowledge? *Jesus has riches of wisdom.* The desire to know has sent men roving over all the world, but he who finds Jesus may stay at home and be wise. If you sit at His feet, you shall know what Plato could not teach you, and what Socrates never learned. When the old schoolmen could not answer and defend a proposition, they were wont to say, "I will go to Aristotle: he shall help me out." If you do but learn of Christ, He shall help you out of all difficulties; and that which is most useful for your soul to know, the knowledge which will last you in eternity, Christ shall teach to you. Think not that the gospel of Christ, because it is simple, is therefore mere child's play. Oh, no! it has that in it which an angel's intellect unillumined of the Holy Spirit might fail to master; the highest ranks of seraphim still lost in wonder gaze upon it. Come to my Master, and you shall be made wise unto salvation.

Let me not weary you with so great a message. Perhaps I tell it badly, but the matter of it is worthy of your ears, and worthy of your hearts. *My Master has ri hes of happiness to bestow upon you.* After all, He is the rich man who wears heart's-ease in His button hole. The man who can say, " I have enough," is richer than the peer of the realm who is discontented. Believe me, my Lord can make you to lie down in green pastures, and lead you beside still waters. There is no music like the music of His pipe, when He is the Shepherd and you are the sheep, and you lie down at His feet. There is no love like His, neither earth or heaven can match it. If you did but know it, you would prize it beyond all mortal joys, and say with our poet—

> "Such as find Thee find such sweetness
> Deep, mysterious, and unknown;
> Far above all worldly pleasures,
> If they were to meet in one;
> My Beloved,
> O'er the mountains haste away."

I speak experimentally. I have had more joy in half-an-hour's communion with Christ than I have found in months of other comforts. I have had much to make me happy—divers successes and smiles of providence which have cheered and comforted my heart; but they are all froth on the cup, mere bubbles—the foam of life, and not its true depths of bliss. To know Christ and to be found in Him—oh! this is life, this is joy, this is marrow and fatness, wine on the lees well refined! My Master does not treat His servants churlishly; He gives to them as a king giveth to a king; He gives them two heavens—a heaven below in serving Him here, and a heaven above in delighting in Him for ever.

And now I shall close this poor talk of mine about these priceless riches, by saying that *the unsearchable riches of Christ will be best known in eternity*. The riches of Christ are not so much to be enjoyed here as *there*. He will give you by the road and on the way to heaven all your needs; your place of defence shall be the munitions of rocks, your bread shall be given you, and your water shall be sure; but it is there, *there*, THERE, where you shall hear the song of them that triumph, the shout of them that feast. My dear hearer, if you get Christ, you have obtained riches which you can take with you in the hour of death. The rich man clutched his bags of money, and as he laid them on his heart, he murmured, "They will not do, they will not do; take them away!" If you receive Jesus into your heart, He will be death's best antidote. When your disembodied spirit quits this poor clay carcass, as it must, what will your silver and gold do for you then? What will your farms and your broad acres do for you then? You must leave them all behind. Even if men buy you a coffin of gold, or bury you in a sarcophagus of marble, yet of what avail will that be? But oh! if you have Christ, you can fly up to heaven to your treasure, and there you shall be rich to all the intents of bliss, world without end.

Now, dear friends, if I could have spoken as Paul would have spoken, I would have done so, but the subject would have been the same. Paul preached the gospel better than I do, but even he could not preach a better gospel. Let me close this point by a few words. My Master has such riches that you cannot count them; you cannot guess them, much less can you convey their fulness in words. They are *unsearchable!* You may look, and search, and weigh, but Christ is a greater Christ than you think Him to be when your thoughts are at the greatest. My Master is more able to pardon than you to sin, more able to forgive than you to transgress. My Master is more ready to supply than you are to ask, and ten thousand times more prepared to save than you are to be saved. Never tolerate low thoughts of my Lord Jesus. Your highest estimates will dishonour Him; when you put the crown on His head, you will only crown Him with silver when He deserves gold; when you sing the best of your songs, you will only give Him poor, discordant music, compared with

what He deserves, but oh! do believe in Him, that He is a great Christ, a mighty Saviour. Great sinner, come and do Him honour by trusting in Him as a great Saviour. Come with your great sins and your great cares, and your great wants! Come, and welcome. Come to Him now, and the Lord will accept you, and accept you without upbraiding you.

III. Lastly, there must have been A ROYAL INTENTION in the heart of Christ in sending out Paul to preach of His unsearchable riches, because every man must have a motive for what he do s, and beyond all question, Jesus Christ has a motive.

Did you ever hear of a man who employed a number of persons to go about to proclaim his riches, and call hundreds of people together, and thousands as on this occasion, simply to tell them that So-and-so was very rich? Why, the crowds would say, "What is that to us?" But if at the conclusion the messenger could say, "But all these riches he presents to you, and whoever among you shall desire to be made rich, can be enriched now by him"—Ah! then you would say, "Now we see the sense of it. Now we perceive the gracious drift of it all." Now, my Lord Jesus Christ is very strong, but all that strength is pledged to help a poor weak sinner to enter into heaven. My Lord Christ is a great king, and He reigns with irresistible power; but all that sovereign power He swears to give to believers to help them to reign over their sins. My Lord Jesus is as full of merit as the sea is full of salt, but every atom of that merit He vows to give to sinners who will confess that they have no merits of their own, and will trust in Him. Aye, and once more, my Lord Christ is so glorious that the very angels are not bright in His presence, for He is the Sun, and they are but as twinkling stars; but all this glory He will give to you, poor sinner, and make you to be glorious in His glory, if you will but trust Him. There is a motive, then, on our Lord's part for bidding us preach a full Christ.

I think I hear a whisper somewhere; there is a poor heart standing crowded in the aisle, and it is saying to itself, "Ah! I am full of sin; I am weak; I am lost; I have no merit." My dear hearer, thou dost not need any merit, nor any strength, nor any goodness in thyself, for Jesus presents thee with an abundance of all these in Himself. I will not care whether I have money in my own purse or not, if I have a kind friend who says, "All that I have is thine"; if I may go and draw upon Him whenever I please for whatever I wish, I will not desire to be independent of Him, but I will live upon His fulness. Poor sinner, you must do the same. You do not need merits of strength apart from Christ: take my Master and He will be enough for you, while you shall joyfully sing, "Christ is my all."

Two or three words, then. The first is this: *How rich those must be who have Christ for a friend!* Will you not seek to be friends with Him? If it be true that all Christ has He gives to His people—and this is asserted over and over again in this Book—then, oh! how unspeakably blest must those be who can say, "My Beloved is mine, and I am His!" They who get Christ to be their own property, are like the man who, having long eaten of fruit from a certain tree, was no longer satisfied with having the fruit, but he must needs take up the tree and plant it in his own garden. Happy those who have Christ planted as the tree of life in the soil of their hearts! You not only have His grace, and His love, and His merit, but you have HIMSELF. He is all your own. Oh, that sweet word, Jesus is mine ! Jesus is mine ! All that there is in His humanity, in His deity, in His living and in His dying, in His reigning and in His second advent, all is mine, for Christ is mine.

How transcendently foolish, on the other hand, must those be who will not have Christ when He is to be had for the asking ! who prefer the baubles and the bubbles of this world, and let the solid gold of eternity go by ! O fools, to play with shadows and miss the substance ! to dig and toil, and cover your faces with sweat, and lose your nightly rest, to get this world's fleeting good, while you neglect Him who is the eternal good ! O fools and slow of heart to court this harlot world, with her painted face, when the beauties of my Master are infinitely more rich and rare ! Oh ! if you did but know Him, if you could but see His unspeakable riches, you would fling your toys to the wind, and follow after Him with all your heart and soul.

" But may I have Him ? " says one. May you, indeed ! Who is to say you nay ? Did not you hear the sweet notes of the hymn just now. " Come and welcome, come and welcome ? " When heaven's big bell rings, it always sounds forth that silver note for sinners—" Come and welcome ! Come and welcome ! " Leave your sins, leave your follies, leave your self-righteousness. Jesus Christ stands at the open door of grace, more willing to receive you than you are to be received by Him. " Come and welcome, come and welcome." At the top of the Hospice of St. Bernard, in the storm, when the snow is falling fast, the monks ring the great bell, and when the way cannot be seen, the traveller can almost hear the way to the house of refuge across the snowy waste. So would I ring that bell this morning. Poor lost traveller, with thy sins and thy fears blowing cold into thy face, " Come and welcome, come and welcome," to a Saviour once dead and buried for thee, but now risen and pleading at the right hand of God. If thou canst not see thy way, yet hear it. " Hear, and your soul shall live ; and He will make an everlasting covenant with you, even the sure mercies of David.

You need nothing but Christ, dear heart ; you need pump up no tears of repentance to help Christ, for He will give you repentance if you seek it of Him. You must come to Him to get repentance ; you must not seek the gospel blessing anywhere but at the cross. You will need no baptisms and Lord's Suppers to rely upon ; it will be your duty as a believer to profess your faith in Him, and to remember Him at His table, but these things will not help your salvation, you will be saved by Jesus and by Him alone. You need experience no terrors, you need undergo no preparation, Christ is ready to receive you *now*. Like the surgeon whose door is open for every accident that may occur ; like the great hospitals on our side the river, where, let the case be what it may, the door swings open the moment an entrance is demanded—such is my Master. Unsearchable riches are in Him, though unsearchable poverty may be in you.

> " Let not conscience make you linger,
> Nor of fitness fondly dream,
> All the *fitness* He requireth,
> Is to feel your need of Him :
> This He gives you ;
> 'Tis His Spirit's rising beam."

All this week long I have been fretting and worrying because I cannot preach to you as I wish, and when each of my sermons here has been over, I have wished that I could preach it over again in a more earnest and fervent manner. But what can I do ? O my hearers, I can preach Christ to you, but I cannot preach you to Christ. I can tell you that if you trust Him you shall be saved ; I can declare to you that as the Son of God now risen He is able to save to the uttermost them that come to Him, but I cannot make you come. Yet, thank God, since last Sunday I have heard of some who have come ; I have heard good news of some who, by the Holy Ghost's power, have believed in Jesus. Are there no more eyes that will look at my Master's wounds ? Are there no more hearts that will fall in love with my Master's beauties ? Must I come a wooing for Him, and get so small a return ? Must it be ones and twos out of the twenty thousands of you ? God forbid it ! God send a greater rate of fruit than this, a hundredfold harvest to a hundredfold congregation. Pray, believers, pray for a blessing. Pray that God may strike this lip dumb before next Sunday if He will do more good by some other preacher than by me. Ask nothing for me, but ask large things for my Lord, for the Crucified One. Do pray that these great gatherings may not be without a permanent result which shall tell upon the impiety of this city ; aye, and tell upon the piety of it too, slaying the first, and stimulating the second. God send forth the Spirit of His grace, and unto Him shall be the praise, world without end. Amen.

A GRATEFUL SUMMARY OF TWENTY VOLUMES

"Unto me, who am less than the least of all saints, is this grace given, that I should preach among the Gentiles the unsearchable riches of Christ."—Ephesians iii. 8.

THIS is a very remarkable day to me, for, if I am spared to preach this present sermon, I shall have completed twenty years of printed discourses issued week by week. This will be the last sermon of my twentieth volume, making 1,209 in all. This is by no means a common occurrence; indeed, I have not heard of another case in which for so long a time published discourses have been welcomed by the Christian church, and scattered broadcast over the land. Having obtained help of God, I continue unto this day testifying the gospel of Christ Jesus.

For this I magnify the name of the Lord, and ask my dear friends associated with me to assist me in the expression of my thankfulness to Almighty God for such special lovingkindness. I could not find even in the rich volume of inspiration any language more expressive of the deep emotions of my soul than the verse which is now before us, "Unto me, who am less than the least of all saints, is this grace given, that I should preach among the Gentiles the unsearchable riches of Christ." How long or how short the time allotted to my future ministry may be I do not wish to know, whether I shall complete another twenty years or become silent in a few months, but for these twenty years of blessed assistance in the ministration of the gospel of Jesus Christ I must and will adore the name of the Lord, even if never again He should permit me to open my lips in His service. It is enough of mercy for one man to have enjoyed, even if there were no more to follow. Bless the Lord, O my soul.

While we shall consider the verse as Paul's own expression, we shall retain our own hold upon it, and use it very much as a summary of our own emotions. Note from the text that *Paul thought very little of himself.*—"Unto me, who am less than the least of all saints," saith he, "is this grace given." I am sure Paul was never guilty of mock modesty, and never pretended to be humbler than he really was. At suitable times he could vindicate himself, and claim his position among his fellow men. If any denied his apostleship, he proved it by abundant arguments. Yea, he even became on one occasion what he calls a "fool in glorying"; he recounted his abundant labours, and his frequent sufferings; he pointed to his success, and protested that he was not a whit behind the very chief of the apostles, though he was nothing. Although all this was true, and Paul expressed only the bare truth, when he thus defended himself, yet in his heart of hearts he chose to take the lowest seat in the lowest room, and because there were no adjectives in correct language which could express his opinion of himself, he did violence to language, and said that he was "less than the least of all saints." His straining of words is not to be censured, for language was made for man, and not man for language, and when within the bounds of grammar a mighty heart cannot express itself, it does well to snap the bonds and let its strength have space to exercise itself. I do not quarrel with Paul's language, but I do dispute his right to push me out of my place. Less than the least is a position which I had hoped to occupy, but he has taken it from me, and I would fain give him a touch on the shoulder and say, "Friend, go up higher"; for as there are no lower seats, and we could not think of sitting above the great apostle, he must allow us to allot him a higher place.

Was Paul really less than the least of all saints? Was not this too low an estimate of himself? Brethren, I suppose he meant that he felt this to be the case when he looked at himself from certain aspects. He was one of the late converts, many of his comrades were in Christ before him, and he yielded precedence to the older ones. He had been aforetime a persecutor and injurious, and, though God had forgiven him, he had never forgiven himself; and when he recollected his share in the sufferings and martyrdom of the saints, he felt that, though now numbered among them, he could only dare to sit in the lowliest place. Besides, any devout man, however eminent he may be in most respects, will find that there are certain other points in which he falls short; and the apostle, instead of looking at the points in which he excelled, singled out with modest eye those qualities in which he felt he failed, and in those respects he put himself down as "less than the least of all saints." This strikes us as being a very different mode of speech from that which is adopted by certain brethren. One friend asserts that he has ceased from known sin for some months; and then another brother, to go a little further, asserts that the very being of sin in him has been destroyed, root and branch; of which I believe in both cases not one single word. If those brethren had said that they were sixteen feet high, that their eyes were solid diamonds, and that their hair was Prussian blue, I should feel towards them very much as I do now. They simply do not know themselves, and the best article of furniture they could have in their houses would be a looking-glass which would let them see their own selves; if they had once had such a sight, I warrant you they would sing another tune, pitched to a far lower key. Many who now shine in the highest places of self-estimation, will one day be glad enough to sit at the feet of the poorest of the saints, unless I am greatly mistaken; for every one that exalteth himself shall be abased. For my part I had sooner hear Paul say that he was less than the least of all the saints, than I would hear the holiest brother out of heaven say that he had been living without sin. I could believe the one, but I could not believe the other. Paul was as holy as the holiest now upon earth, but among the humble he was the humblest. The Lord make us each so.

Our next remark is, that *Paul thought very much of his brethren.* These two things usually go together—a low opinion of one's self and a high estimate of others. He calls himself less than the least—not of all the apostles, though even that would have been a lowly judgment, but less than the least of all *saints*; and yet there were some very imperfect saints among his acquaintance. His pastoral observation had discovered many weak, trembling, half-instructed, and even backsliding brethren. Remember how he differed from Barnabas about John Mark, and how he rebuked Peter to his face, because he was to be blamed. He was not insensible of the defects of the saints, for in some of his epistles he gives us a very sad picture of the condition of some of the members of the churches; aye. and of some who were true saints: he tells them that he could only write unto them as unto carnal, as unto babes in Christ, and that when they ought to have been teachers they needed themselves to be taught the very elements of the faith; and yet he says he was less than the least of them. He must have thought very highly of the least instructed and most imperfect of the divine family. After all, dear brethren, though we hear much fault found with professing Christians and church-members, and hear it said that they are no better than men of the world, we dare not be among their detractors. If we cannot find saints in the church of God, certainly we shall find them nowhere else. They are faulty, no doubt, but still they are the Lord's elect, and the people on whom His heart is set. They are the excellent of the earth, and if we may but be numbered with them we shall be thankful even if our name should stand lowest and last on the list. We count the regenerate and the sanctified to be the true aristocracy, the real nobility of the world. "O God, thou art my God, my goodness extendeth not to Thee, but to the saints that are in the earth, and to the excellent in whom is all my delight." The church, notwithstanding her spots, is fairest among women, and though her garments are sometimes stained (would God they were not), yet for all that she is all glorious within, her clothing is of wrought gold. She is beautiful in the eyes of her Lord, He loved her well enough to redeem her with His precious blood, and to make her His bride; it would be shameful on our part to despise her. She ought to be lovely in our eyes, yea, and she is, for we love the people of God beyond all others. My inmost soul can say of the church of God—

"My soul shall pray for Zion still
While life or breath remains;
There my best friends, my kindred dwell
There God my Saviour reigns."

The next reflection suggested by the text is that *Paul thought very highly of his work.* He says, "Unto me, who am less than the least of all saints, is this grace given, that I should preach." He looked upon his ministry as a great gift from God, an honour bestowed, a favour granted. Yet, my brethren, Paul's office was not such a very attractive thing after all, looking upon it after the manner of men. Paul was not a Lord Bishop or a right reverend, his salary was less than nothing; he received no homage from men; his greatest gains were his losses, his honours came from his dishonours, and his glory from his sufferings. Stripes and imprisonments awaited him in every city; stoning and shipwreck, perils of robbers and perils of traitors, care and grief, were his portion. He was made an outcast for Christ's sake; his Jewish brethren even foamed at the mouth at the very thought of the renegade Pharisee who preached to the Gentiles. He had suffered the loss of all things for Christ's sake, and he says he "counted them but dung that he might win Christ and be found in Him." If the advowson and next presentation of Paul's office had been put up at Garraway's, our modern imitators of Simon Magus would have been very slow in the bidding, they would rather have paid a heavy sum to be excused. Paul himself said of it, " If in this life only we have hope, we are of all men most miserable." Yet so contented was he to preach the gospel that, notwithstanding all the hardships and reproaches which went with it, he considered it to be a special favour granted him of the Lord that he was permitted to proclaim the unsearchable riches of Christ among the Gentiles.

The apostle even lifts up his hands in grateful astonishment that so great an honour should be bestowed upon him. He says "Unto *me*—unto me, who am less than the least of all saints, is this grace given, that *I*—the persecutor, the man who breathed out threatenings and slaughter—that *I* should preach among the Gentiles." He marvels at it; he cannot make it out; the passage reads as if he paused in his writing, and burst into a song of adoring gratitude because the Lord had honoured him so exceedingly as to put him in trust with the gospel. How deeply do I sympathise with him in his wonder at electing love! My heart cries, "Why me, Lord, why me?"

Note well that the apostle had a very clear view of what he had to do. "That I should preach," says he, "among the Gentiles." Paul does not claim to be sent to regenerate the Gentiles by sprinkling them, to hear their confessions of secret sin, to pry into their private lives with filthy questions, and to absolve them on the fulfilment of appointed penances; he has not a word to say about playing the priest; he does not glory in the grace which enabled him to display a comely ritual, or restore a pompous ceremonialism; he boasts not of carrying a crucifix or a banner in a procession up and down the aisles to delight the Gentiles; nor, in a word, does he set himself up as a sort of demi-god, able to kill and to make alive, to distribute pardons and to regenerate babes. Paul was quite satisfied to preach the gospel, that was as far as his commission went, and whenever God the Holy Spirit sends forth a minister to bless the Church that is the purport of his mission and nothing else,— he is to preach among the Gentiles the unsearchable riches of Christ. Neither our Lord nor His apostles command us to set up altars, but the grand command is "preach the gospel to every creature." O ye priests of the Church of England, take off your tag-rags, and stand out like men and preach the gospel, if indeed ye be ministers of God, and not sappers and miners for the Pope of Rome. God sends men to preach the gospel, but He never sends them to intrude into the office of Christ, and set themselves up as priests offering sacrifice for the quick and dead, when in Him the priesthood is fulfilled. Paul knew what his vocation was, and he kept to it. Find me one instance of his acting the priest. Wherever he went he was preaching and teaching, preaching and teaching, preaching and teaching, that was the one object of his life; whether in Damascus or Corinth, Jerusalem or Rome, he must preach. When he was amid the Areopagites on Mars' Hill why did he not show them the beauty of divine service as performed in the most approved fashion? Why at Lystra did he not offer a sacrifice to God, and wave a censer?—all the materials were ready. No; but he *preached* everywhere. When detained at Rome he did not train a choir, or instruct a company of clergy in ecclesiastical calisthenics, or Church millinery, but he taught Jesus to all around. We read nothing of his genuflexions and intonations, but a great deal of his preaching the word in season and out of season. This too is our work. The Church must see to it that this ordinance be used above every other for the conversion of men. It pleases God by the foolishness of preaching to save them that believe. Stand to your guns, my brethren; preach the word; make full proof of your ministry, and cease not to teach all men the truth concerning Jesus.

Remark how Paul calls his ministry a "grace." Every true preacher of the gospel will have to thank God that he has been permitted to preach. I do not know how my soul would have been kept alive if it had not been for the searching of Scripture, the prayer, the faith, and the joy which preaching has involved. Though it may be true that professional familiarity with sacred things is apt to breed a want of personal enjoyment in them, I do not find it so. To me it is a great blessing to have to prepare for preaching; often the best means of grace to my own soul are the groaning, the pleading, the meditation, and the communion needed for the selection of the right subject upon which to feed your souls. Preachers ought to grow in grace, for their very calling places them at a great advantage, since they are bound to search the Scriptures, and to be much in prayer. It is a choice mercy to be permitted to preach the gospel. I wish some of you would be ambitious of it, for earnest preachers are wanted. There are several brethren here who ought to preach, and I believe they would preach with great power if they were once driven to the attempt. A modesty which may be cowardice silences many; a diffidence, which may also be culpable love of ease, keeps them back from speaking in the name of the Lord. Brethren, let it be so no longer.

Thus, you see, Paul thought little of himself, much of his brethren, and highly of his work.

Again, *Paul thought very lovingly of his congregation.* He counted it a great grace that he was permitted to preach *among the Gentiles.* Peter had a much more respectable sphere, for he was the apostle of the circumcision, and preached to the ancient aristocratic race of the Hebrews; but Paul was sent to preach to the Gentile dogs, who were despised by the Jews as uncircumcised and unclean. Our Lord Jesus Christ Himself gave the Gentiles a sad character, or when speaking of worldly things, He said, "After all these things do the Gentiles seek," as if they were utterly gross and carnal, and entirely besotted with grovelling pursuits. Paul, however, rejoiced to preach to these worldly-minded Gentiles, he was glad to bring the outcasts to Jesus. They were such an ignorant crew,—these Gentiles, ignorant of the true God and eternal life; though they were some of them wise in their own conceits, yet were they sunk in spiritual ignorance. There were the Greeks, proud of their learned folly, the Romans, boasting of brute force and despising a merely spiritual kingdom, the Scythians, barbarous and uncouth, and the bondsmen, sunk in vice and degradation; but he who was sent to labour among them preferred them to any other audience. Paul thanked God for his congregation, ignorant as they were. Worse than ignorant, they were worshippers of idols; they had gods many and lords many, and they bowed themselves before the personifications of their own wickedness; yet Paul was glad to preach to idolaters. The first chapter of his epistle to the Romans contains a fearful indictment against the Gentiles, for their horrible vices. They were sunk in a horrible slough of corruption, and yet Paul considered it a great privilege to preach among these ignorant, heathenish, debased, vicious Gentiles the unsearchable riches of Christ; and a privilege it was. It is a royal honour to preach to the lowest of the low. Dear brethren and sisters, wherever you and I are called to labour we ought to be thankful that God has given us that particular place to labour in. I like to see Christian workers fall in love with their spheres: for instance, the brethren who work in Golden Lane and Seven Dials do well to look upon their districts as the most important in London; and every city missionary, if he is to succeed, must feel that his particular part of the city is that which is best for him. I like to hear Mr. Moffat speak as if there were no people in the world of more consequence than Bechuanas and Hottentots. I never knew a man succeed among a people unless he preferred them to all others as the objects of his care. When ministers despise their congregations, their congregations are very likely to despise them, and then usefulness is out of the question. When a man thinks himself above his work the probability is that he is in the clouds altogether, or stands in the way of some practical worker of a more commonplace kind, who would do the work which he is despising. Oh you who teach little children, love them or you cannot teach them. If you preach in the street feel a sympathy with the people who gather around you, or you had better give over. Paul became a Gentile for the Gentiles' sake. Pharisee as he had been, we see nothing of his phylacteries or the broad borders of his garment. He always loved his kinsmen according to the flesh, and would have gladly died to save them, but Jew as he was, and at one time bound by the strongest possible Jewish prejudices, he had broken them all down, and had made the Gentiles his clients, his flock, his children. It was his daily joy that he was ordained to preach among the Gentiles the unsearchable riches of Christ.

Upon our next remark we will more fully enlarge, it is this,—*Paul thought most of all of his subject.* That he had to preach the unsearchable riches of Christ was his highest bliss. The glories of Jesus, whom once

he had persecuted, were his one and only theme. All he had to say was contained within the circumference of that word Christ, and all that he aimed at was to glorify his Lord. Neither ceremonies, nor orthodoxies, nor philosophies, nor sects, nor parties did Paul labour for, but he exalted Christ Jesus the Lord. Nor did he feel that his engrossment by one solitary subject restricted him in his thought or speech, for he looked upon his theme as full of riches, riches altogether unsearchable. He had a deep insight into the truth which he had to proclaim, and saw within it veins of precious thought which he could never exhaust, lodes of more than golden treasure which no research could ever fully explore. O to be in this fashion enamoured of the gospel, absorbed in it, and wholly carried away by its charms.

Let us meditate a few minutes upon the unsearchable riches of Christ, which it has been our joy to preach, even as it was Paul's.

Notice, first, that the apostle dwelt much upon *the essential riches of Christ's person.* Beloved, there are unsearchable riches in Christ, for He is by nature "God over all, blessed for ever." Others may make Him a mere man, but we behold the unsearchable riches of the Deity in Jesus Christ, "In whom dwelleth all the fulness of the Godhead bodily." He is the Creator, without whom was not anything made that was made. He is the preserver of all things, and by Him all things consist. What riches there must be in Him who both makes and sustains the universe by the word of His power. In Jesus Christ all the attributes of God are manifest: the wisdom, the power, the immutability, the truth, the faithfulness, the justice, and love of God are all to be found in the character of Jesus Christ our Lord. Even while He was here on earth, and clothed Himself in mortal flesh, the Godhead shone through the veil. The winds knew Him and were silent, the waves knew Him and kissed His feet; the angels ministered to Him and the devils fled before Him; diseases were healed, for His touch was omnipotent; the dead lived, for His voice was almighty. He was God even while to mortal eye He was only the carpenter's son. To-day He has put off His servant's garments, and laid aside the towel wherewith He wiped His disciples' feet, and all power is given unto Him in heaven and in earth; let us then proclaim His unsearchable riches. Now is He crowned with universal sovereignty, and the government is upon His shoulder, and His name is called "Wonderful, Counsellor, the mighty God, the Everlasting Father, the Prince of Peace." Riches beyond compare belong to Him who for our sakes became poor; riches unsearchable, for He is God, and "Who by searching can find out God? Who can find out the Almighty unto perfection?" Jesus is "very God of very God," and as such we adore Him, and glory in the wealth of His nature.

Jesus our Lord is also man, man of the substance of His mother, bone of our bone. And here we may descant upon the wealth of human love which is treasured up in Him and manifested to His brethren; His wealth of sympathy with His people, for He has been tempted in all points like as they are; His wealth of discernment, for He knows the secrets of our nature, having worn that nature Himself. Because of the riches of His love, He is not ashamed to call His redeemed ones brethren. It is a wonderful subject, the wealth of pure manhood which dwelt in Jesus, for He both thought, and spake, and acted as man, with a richness of perfect manhood which never dwelt in any other son of man. He was the true Adam—the sum of humanity's best glory, made to have dominion over all the works of Jehovah's hands. Thus in the two natures which make up His mysterious person, Son of man and Son of God, there was a measureless wealth, and this Paul preached.

My brethren, I boldly appeal to you whether during these twenty years I have not tried to set forth the unsearchable riches of my Lord and Master in His blessed person. I have preached Him to you as no mere abstraction, but as a real Christ. I have not talked of Him as if He were a myth, I have spoken of Him always as an actual personage, who lived and died, and is risen and gone into heaven. I have also preached Him as still amongst you in spirit, Head of the Church, and Lord over all. Neither have I preached to you a Christ stinted in power or glory. I have endeavoured, according to my ability, to set Him forth as King of kings and Lord of lords. Your hearts have rejoiced to hear concerning Him, and mine has rejoiced to speak of one so altogether lovely, so good, so kind, so ready to forgive, so faithful, and mighty. In a word, I have preached the unsearchable riches of His person.

Next, we have to preach the riches of our Lord Jesus *as the Christ*; that is to say, in His relationship towards us. Now, think a minute or two. In the old eternity, or ever the earth was, the unsearchable riches of Christ were displayed when He entered into covenant with the Father on our behalf. What matchless love it was which prompted the second person of the Divine Unity to become the surety of the covenant of grace for His elect. Unsearchable were the riches of love which suggested the covenant, and the riches of the wisdom which planned it. It was worthy of a God.

Remember, that as time rolled on His people as they were one by one created were saved simply on the ground of His word and pledge; and if the bare bond of Christ, before He had shed a drop of His blood, was able to save myriads of His elect, what riches there must be in His atonement itself. If His promise to redeem was enough for thousands of years to save multitudes from death and hell, what must be the riches of the finished righteousness and the accomplished substitution?

Think of the riches of Christ's grace from the day of man's fall until the day of his redemption. He saw man in his waywardness, and knew what he would be under the best conditions, yet He did not turn aside from His pledge of love because of the baseness of fallen humanity. He knew that men would prove ungrateful, yet did He resolve to redeem His people. He had throughout those ages an opportunity of estimating what the pangs of death would be, He knew the cost at which He must seek and save the lost; but through those thousands of years such were the riches of His infinite love that He never started back from the compact which He had made, but determined to push on till by His death He had delivered man from sin, and the earth from the curse. Wealth of mercy! What can transcend this?

Down the Lord descends to Bethlehem's manger, and there He lies a babe wrapped in swaddling clothes. Who shall tell the riches of the condescending love which made the Infinite incarnate? Amongst the sons of men He tarries, going about doing good: calculate if you can the riches of that generous heart which detained Him for years amongst a sinful and gainsaying generation. The life of Jesus on earth is a mint of grace. But oh, the unsearchable love which led Him to give His hands to the nails and His heart to the spear! What love unspeakable is centred in the cross! What riches of grace that He should deign to die a malefactor's death for His enemies! Can any of us conceive the unsearchable riches of merit which must lie in the holy life and painful death of our beloved Lord. If the Son of God Himself deigns to die, the just for the unjust, surely no limit can be set to the virtue of that death, neither indeed can we calculate how precious it must be in the Father's sight. O thou bleeding Saviour, when Thou hadst become poorest of all in Thine own glory, surely Thou didst also become richest of all for the redemption of the sons of men! None shall ever know, nor even eternity itself fully declare, the infinite value of Thy tears, and bloody sweat, and agony and death!

But see, He rises again, for the tomb could not contain Him; He rises for our justification. In the risen Saviour what wealth may be seen, for while He justifies all His people by His rising, He also secures to them eternal life, and guarantees to their bodies a glorious resurrection. Think of our Lord as the first fruits of them that sleep, and you will see in His resurrection a truth which is the corner stone of the entire gospel, and the sure pledge of eternal bliss.

But lo, He spurns the acclivity of Olivet and mounts into the opened heavens, a cloud receiving Him from mortal sight. As He ascends, He scatters gifts among the sons of men. The Holy Ghost is given, He rests in tongues of fire upon the heads of chosen men; He gave "some apostles, some pastors and teachers," for the building up of His church. Those gifts He still continues to bestow, for He "received gifts for men, yea, for the rebellious also, that the Lord God might dwell among them." The riches of the ascended Saviour it is not possible for the mind to calculate.

Look ye again! Behold Him in heaven! There He sits at the right hand of the Father to represent His people, is there not a wealth of comfort in that representation? He sits on the throne to rule for His people; there is another mine of consolation. His presence is the guarantee of our being there—is not this full of richness? He intercedes for all His saints before the eternal throne; there is another treasure house of marvellous instruction and delight. Jesus for ever sits at the right hand of God, because His work is done, He waits until His enemies become His footstool, is He not to us a treasure of unsearchable riches?

But He is soon to come, and who shall tell the riches which then shall be revealed, when sin shall fly before Him, and this burdened earth shall be eased of the load which has made her groan continually; when instead of thorn and thistle, shall come up the cedar and the rose, when the desert shall rejoice and blossom, and men down-trodden and weary, shall lift up their eyes to behold a new paradise, and enjoy a glory such as eye hath not seen nor ear heard, a splendour of millennial bliss, of which may every one of us be partakers? All this shall be because He cometh. There are unsearchable riches in Christ, whether living, dying, rising, dwelling in heaven, or descending a second time to earth. See what a subject Paul had to preach; and we have preached it too. These twenty years our one theme has been Christ Jesus in His relationship to His people, in His everlasting love, in His once-offered, completely-atoning sacrifice, in His pleading before the Father's throne, and in the kingdom which is yet to subdue all things to itself. What a mercy it is to have been privileged to preach all this!

Thirdly and briefly, Paul had preached the unsearchable riches of Jesus Christ *in and to his people*. He had told them that Christ had paid their debts, and they were free. How wondrously had he put it —"There is therefore now no condemnation to them that are in Christ Jesus." We cannot stop to repeat the texts, but Paul had been clear enough upon the point, that the riches of Christ in pardoning sin were unsearchable. He had told the saints that Christ had provided all that could be needed by them between where they were and the gates of heaven, for, said he, "ye are complete in Him." "All things are yours, whether things present or things to come." Paul had delighted to dive into the depth of overflowing grace. What a grand swimmer he was in the sea of joy.

He had also told the saints that they might have whatever they asked for in answer to believing prayer. How often had He put it before them that He who spared not His own Son, but delivered Him up for them, would also with Him freely give them all things. What riches of Christ are found at the mercy seat! He who knows how to draw nigh to God by Jesus Christ will find great store of wealth therein.

He had assured them that the Lord Himself was theirs, yea, said he, "all things are yours, and ye are Christ's, and Christ is God's. He had told them that heaven was theirs, for they had obtained an inheritance in Christ, and were on their way to the glory, every hour bringing them nearer. Truly, if you want to know the deep things of God, you must listen to Paul, for he tells us of the eternity of Christ's love, a love without beginning and without end. He tells us of the immutability of that love, for Jesus Christ is "the same yesterday, and to-day, and for ever." He tells us of the infinity of that love, and delights to declare that it passeth knowledge. In fact, he tells us that God Himself is ours, to be our portion for ever. Oh, children of God, if you are straitened, you are not straitened in the preaching of the apostle, you are straitened in yourselves. I venture also to say that in my own preaching I have not knowingly restrained any of the blessings of the covenant of grace, nor spoken lightly of the boons which Jesus gives to His beloved. No, I have delighted to expatiate upon what the Lord has given to His saints, and have bidden believers enjoy the fat things full of marrow which He has provided for them. Happy people to have such a Saviour.

But lastly, the point Paul most rejoiced to preach upon was this—*the unsearchable riches of our Lord towards sinners*, for he says that he preached *among the Gentiles*, the sinners, the unsearchable riches of Christ. This is the most delightful theme of all, to tell poor sinners that there is an unspeakably rich Saviour. I lament to say that there are brethren who do not preach this among the Gentiles. They have a great deal to say to God's own people, but they have nothing to say to the Gentiles, to the sinners, to the insensible, unquickened sinners, nothing to say to them. I have known them close a sermon by saying "The election hath obtained it, the rest are blinded," and sit down with not a word for those dead in sin. Brethren, we have not so learned Christ; we delight to preach among the *Gentiles* the unsearchable riches of Christ, and to make all men see what is the fellowship of the mystery. What have we to say to Gentile sinners? Why, we have to tell them that our Lord Jesus is so rich in grace that He keeps open house all day and all night long, and "Come and welcome" is written over His palace gates. "Whosoever will, let him come and take of the water of life freely." We have to tell you that, though millions of sinners have already come, the banqueting table is as loaded as it ever was; He has as much grace and mercy to distribute as He had eighteen hundred years ago; He is as able to cleanse from sin, as able to justify and to sanctify as He was when first He began His work of mercy. There is no limit to His grace to those that come to Him; whosoever cometh to Him shall receive eternal salvation. My Master is so rich that He wants nothing from any of you. You need not bring a rag with you, He will cover you from head to foot; you need not bring a mouldy crust, He will give you of the bread of heaven. You need not stop to cleanse away a single spot, He will wash you white as snow. Help from you! Does the sun want help from darkness? Christ wants no help from sinners. Let them come empty-handed, naked, sick, helpless, and believe that He is able to do for them all that they require. I am bold to tell you that my Master's riches of grace are so unsearchable, that He delights to forgive and forget enormous sin; the bigger the sin the more glory to His grace. If you are over head and ears in debt, He is rich enough to discharge your liabilities. If you are at the very gates of hell, He is able to pluck you from the jaws of destruction. So mighty is His mercy, that no case did ever exceed His power to save or ever will.

I will challenge you to a contest with regard to my dear Lord and Master, that if you will sit down and think the best and largest thoughts you can of Him, you will not think Him to be so good and loving as He really is: if you will try and wish for the largest blessings you can conceive you shall not be able to wish for such blessings as He is prepared to bestow; and if you will open your mouth wide, and make request for the greatest favour that ever human being asked of God or man, you shall not ask for a tenth of what He is prepared to give. Come and try Him! Let it be a wrestling match between your wants and Christ's abundance—and see which will win the day. I tell you that as Aaron's rod swallowed up the rods of the magicians, so my Master's all-sufficiency will swallow up all the demands of your dreadful necessities. Only come and try Him now! All that you want between the gates of hell and the gates of heaven you shall find in Christ, and you shall have it all for nothing, all for the asking for. Open your hand and take it, it is all He asks of you, that you believingly receive what He freely bestows; trust in Him, in Him as dead and risen, and ascended, and reigning; rely upon Him, and by so doing you shall find that there are unsearchable riches of grace in Him.

Now, I have done when I have said just this. I have no doubt Paul would not have been so pleased to preach Christ as he was unless something had come of it. Now, at the close of twenty years of printed sermons, my great delight in having preached the unsearchable riches of Christ lies in this, that something has come of it. How many souls have been converted it is not in my power to tell. I do not think I ever pass a single day, nor have done so for some years, without having intimations of some persons at the very ends of the earth, or at home, having been led to the Saviour by the reading of the sermons. I am not prepared to say how many persons have gone through this church to other churches or to heaven; the number can hardly be far short of those which remain, and of these it may suffice to say that four thousand seven hundred souls are with us, still kept by the power of grace, and knit together in church fellowship. Is not this matter of great thankfulness to God? During these twenty years the dew has never ceased to fall, the church has been planted like a tree by rivers of water, she has brought forth her fruit in her season, and whatsoever she has attempted has prospered. I joy, therefore, and will joy in this.

Yet once more I think Paul must have felt an especial gladness that through his preaching the unsearchable riches of Christ others had been raised up to preach it too. So has it been with us. How many tongues this day are preaching Christ, out of our church members and students, I cannot assert definitely, but that they are to be counted by hundreds is certain; would to God they were ten times as many. I wish all the rest of this congregation who love Christ would go and talk about Him too. Some among you are very diligent, and I bless God for you. I wish more of you were trying to bring these unsearchable riches of Christ within the knowledge of the ignorant and sinful. It is the last Sabbath of the year. Could we not begin next year with a great deal more industry than we have shown last year? I am afraid there are many members who have no work to do for Jesus, and these are the sort of people to backslide. You that have neither to do nor to suffer are the baggage of the army, the impedimenta which prevent the host from marching on to victory. Bestir yourselves, feed upon Jesus, and then take of the good cheer to those who do not know the riches of Christ, and as God gives you grace, go you and fulfil this ministry, and you will then say, as I do, and as the apostle said of old, "Unto me, who am less than the least of all saints, is this grace given, that I should preach among the Gentiles the unsearchable riches of Christ." The Lord bless you. Amen.

ANOTHER AND A NOBLER EXHIBITION

"To the intent that now unto the principalities and powers in heavenly places might be known by the Church the manifold wisdom of God."—Ephesians iii. 10.

ALL the world has been talking during the last three days of the splendid pageant which adorned the opening of the International Exhibition. Crowds have congregated in the palace of universal art; representatives of all the nations of the earth have journeyed for many a league to view its wonders; eminent personages of all empires have appeared in the gorgeous spectacle, and such a scene has glittered before the eyes of all men, as has never before in all respects been equalled, and may not for many a year find a successor to rival it. Wherefore all these gatherings? Why muster ye, all ye nations? Wherefore come ye hither, ye gazing sons of men? Surely your answer must be, that ye have come together that ye may see *the manifold wisdom of* MAN. As they walk along the aisles of the great Exhibition, what see they but the skill of man, first in this department, and then in the other—at one moment in the magnificent, at the next in the minute —at one instant in a work of elegance in ornament, in the next in a work of skill and usefulness: "manifold wisdom," the works and productions of many minds, the different hues and colours of thought, embodied in the various machines, and statues, and so forth, which human skill has been able to produce. We grant you that God has been most rightly recognized there, both in the solemn prayer of the Archbishop, and in the hymn of the Laureate; but still the great object, after all, was to behold the manifold wisdom of man; and had they taken away man's skill and man's art, what would there have been left? Brethren, may the greatest results follow from this gathering! We must not expect that it, or anything else short of the gospel, will ever bring about the universal reign of peace; we must never look to art and science to accomplish that triumph which is reserved for the second advent of the Lord Jesus Christ; yet may it spread the feelings of benevolence —may it bind together the scattered children of Adam—may it fuse into a happy and blessed union the kindreds of men that were scattered abroad at Babel, and may it prepare the way, and open the gates, that the gospel may proceed to the uttermost ends of the earth!

It is, however, very far from my mind to direct your attention to the marvels which crown the area of the huge temple of 1862. I invite you, rather, to follow me to a nobler exhibition than this, where crowds are gathering—not of mortals, but of immortal spirits. The temple is not of art and science, but of grace and goodness, built with living stones, cemented with the fair colours of atoning blood, "built upon the foundation of the apostles and prophets, Jesus Christ Himself being the chief corner stone,"—that temple, the Church of the living God, "the pillar and ground of the truth." Into this great palace crowd ten thousand times ten thousand of the host of God, "cherubim and seraphim," or by whatsoever other names those bright intelligences may be known among themselves —"principalities and powers," the different degrees in the hierarchy of immortal spirits, if such there be —they are all represented as intently gazing upon the wondrous fabric which God has reared. Along the aisles of that Church, along the ages of its dispensations, stand the various trophies of divine grace and love—the jewel cases of virtues and graces which adorn the believer, the mementoes of triumphs gotten over sin and hardness of heart, and of victories achieved over temptation and trial; and as the spirits walk along these corridors full of divine workmanship, they stand, they gaze, they admire, and wonder, and speed back their way to heaven, and sing mor loudly than before, hallelujah to the God whose manifold wisdom they have beheld in the Church of God below.

Beloved friends, our text is a strange one. If you will reflect that the angels, the elder-born of creatures when compared with us, have been with God for many an age; and yet I do not know that it is ever said that by anything else they ever learned "the manifold wisdom of God." They were with Him when He made the earth and the heavens; perhaps during those long periods when the earth was a-forming—"In the beginning," when "God created the heavens and the earth," the angels were wont to visit this world, and to behold alive and in their glory those strange shapes of mystery which now we dig up in fossil from the earth. Certainly in that day when "the earth was without form and void, and darkness was upon the face thereof," the angels knew the hidden treasure; and when He said, "Let there be light, and there was light," when that first ray of light seemed like a living finger to touch the earth and waken it to beauty, then seraphic fingers swept their heavenly harps, and "the morning stars sang together, and the sons of God shouted for joy." Yet I do not learn, though they were with the Great Worker during the seven days of creation, though they saw "the cattle after their kind, and the fowls of the air after their kind," and the fish of the sea, and all the plants and herbs, yet I see not that in all this there was made known unto them "the manifold wisdom of God." Nay, more, when man, the Master's last work, walked through Eden,—when, with his fair consort by his side, he stood up to praise his Maker, though he was "fearfully and wonderfully made," though in his mind and body there was a display of wisdom unrivalled before,—yet I do not learn that even in man, as a creature, there was made known "the manifold wisdom of God." Yes, and more than this, when other worlds were made, when the stars were kindled like glowing flames by light of Deity, if there be other peoples, and other kindreds, and other tribes in those myriads of far-off lands, I do not find in the creation of all those hosts of worlds which bestud the wide fields of ether, that there was then made known to celestial spirits "the manifold wisdom of God." Nay, more, in all the dispensations of divine Providence apart from the Church, in all the mystic revolutions of those wondrous wheels that are full of eyes, apart from the Church, there has not been made known to these beings to the fullest extent the wisdom of God. Ah! and, brethren, remember yet once more, that they with undimmed eye look upon the glory of Him that sits upon the throne, so far as it can be seen by created vision; they behold the beatific vision; they are glistening in the splendours of Deity, and veil their faces when at His footstool they cry, "Holy, holy, holy, Lord God of Sabaoth"; and yet, though standing, as it were, in the sun, though they are foremost of all the creatures, nearest to the eternal throne, I do not read that by all this they have in the highest sense learned "the manifold wisdom of God."

What an idea, then, does this give us of the importance of the Church! Brethren, never let us despise any more the meanest member of it, since there is more to be beheld in the Church than in creation in its utmost breadth; more of the wisdom of God in the saving of souls than in the building the arches of the sky; nay, more of God to be seen than even heaven with all its splendours can otherwise reveal. Oh! let us open our eyes that we lose not those divine mysteries which angels desire to look into!

I have now already explained the meaning of the text; we have therefore, but to direct your attention to those points of interest upon which angelic intelligence would be sure to linger; and we shall pray that, while we mention these in brief and running catalogue, our hearts may be led to meditate much upon the manifold, the varied wisdom of God displayed in the Church which Christ has bought with His blood.

I. And first, dear brethren, we think that the grand object of attention in the Church to the principalities and powers, is THE SCHEME AND PLAN OF SAVING THE CHURCH. It is this that they so much admire and wonder at. It has been exceedingly well said by others, that if a Parliament had been held of all the spirits in heaven and in earth, and if it had been committed to this general assembly to ordain and fix upon a plan whereby God might be just and yet the justifier of the ungodly, they must all have failed to achieve the task. Those lofty minds, doubtless, consider with delight the fact that in God's way of saving His Church, all His attributes shine out with undiminished lustre. God is just; they know it in heaven, for they saw Lucifer fall like lightning when God cast him out of His dwelling-place on account of sin. God is just; and as much so upon Calvary, where His Son hangs and bleeds "the just for the unjust, to bring us to God," as He was when He cast down the Son of the Morning. The angels see in salvation this great wonder of justice and peace embracing each other—God as sternly just as if there were not a particle of mercy in His being, smiting His Son for the sin of His people with all the force of His might—God, yet as merciful as if He were not just, embracing His people as though they had never sinned, and loving them with a love which could not have been greater had they never transgressed. They understand how God so hated sin that He laid vengeance on His only begotten, and yet "God so loved the world that He gave His only begotten Son, that whosoever believeth in Him might not perish, but have everlasting life." As in the crowns of Oriental princes the most precious jewels shone in clusters, so as in one wonderful *corona* all the infinite attributes of God shine out at once in all their combined glory around thy cross, O Jesu, earth's wonder and heaven's prodigy! This difficulty, so delightfully met, so completely disposed of by the atonement of Christ, causes the angels to behold "the manifold wisdom of God."

But, further, when the angels see that by this great plan all the ruin that sin brought upon mankind is removed, they again wonder at the wisdom of God; and when they especially notice the way in which it was removed, the strange and mysterious methods which God used for rolling away the stone from the door of the human sepulchre, they yet more bow down with awe. Did we lose Eden in Adam? Lo, the Lord Jesus Christ has given us a better than Paradise! Did we lose the dignity of manhood? Lo, to-day we regain it in Christ; "for thou hast put all things under His feet." Did we lose spotless purity? Again we have obtained it in Christ; for we are justified through His righteousness and washed in His blood. Did we lose communion with God? We have obtained it this day; for "we have access by faith into this grace wherein we stand." Did we lose heaven itself? Ah! heaven is ours again; for in Him we have obtained an inheritance, and are "made meet to be partakers of the inheritance of the saints in light." And all this mischief is made to destroy itself, God overruling it to be its own destruction; the dragon stung with his own sting; Goliath killed with his own sword; Death is slain by the death of the Man who was crucified; sin is put away by the great sin-offering, who "bare our sins in His own body on the tree"; the grave is plagued by its own victim since Christ lay a captive within it. Satan casteth out Satan in this case. We rise by man as by man we fell: "As in Adam all died, so in Christ shall all be made alive." The worm in whom Satan triumphed, is the worm in whom God is glorified. It was man whom Satan sought to make the instrument of divine dishonour, and it is man in whom God triumphs over all the crafts and cruelties of hell. This the angels wonder at, for they see in this scheme of salvation, meeting as it does every mischief, and meeting it on its own ground, "the manifold wisdom of God."

Observe, also, that through the great scheme of salvation by the atonement, God is more glorified than He would have been if there had been no Fall, and consequently no room for a redemption. The angels admire "the manifold wisdom of God" in the whole story of the human race, seeing that in the whole of it, from the beginning to the end, God is more glorified than He would have been had it all been written in letters of gold, without one sin or one suffering on the part of the human race. O Lord! when Thou didst permit for a moment Thy people to go astray like lost sheep, there might have been silence in heaven, since Thine enemy had triumphed, since the precious ones whom Thou hast loved were given up into the hand of the enemy; when the jewels of Christ were lost for a little season amidst the miry clay and ruins of the Fall, there might have been a furling of Jehovah's banner; for perhaps it seemed to angels as though God had been defeated in His highest praise; but when Christ comes back "from Edom, with dyed garments from Bozrah," wearing upon His royal head the crown in which every jewel is securely set that once was in the hand of the enemy—when the shepherd comes back from the mountains, bearing on his shoulders the lost sheep which had gone astray, there is more joy in heaven over the lost ones that are found again than there could have been over all of them had they never gone astray. The deep bass of the Fall shall swell the song of the restoration; the hollow moans, as they seemed to be, when heard alone, shall but make a part of the grand swell of the eternal song, as it shall peal up to the throne of the Lord God of hosts. Brethren, if you would think for awhile upon the whole work of God, taking in it the Fall as being foreseen and foreknown, until the day when all the chosen seed shall meet around the throne, I think you will be struck with its glory as a whole. It was within the compass of the power of God to make creatures that would love Him, to make beings that would be attached to Him by the very closest ties; but—I speak with reverence—I do not see how omnipotence itself, apart from the fall and the redemption by the sacrifice of Christ, when He gave Himself to die for us, could have made such creatures as the redeemed will be in heaven. Brethren, if we had never fallen and never been redeemed, we could never have sung of redeeming grace and dying love. We could not, and the angels could not; we could not have known the heights and depths, and lengths and breadths of the love of Christ which passeth knowledge. Feasted with heavenly food, we might have admired His bounty, but not as we now do when we eat the flesh of Christ; made to drink the wine pressed from heaven's own clusters, we might have blessed the giver of the feast, but not as we now can do, when we drink the blood of Jesus as our sweet wine: pure and holy, we could have praised Him, and we should have done so, but not as we now can, when we have "washed our robes and made them white in the blood of the Lamb." There is a nearer relationship now than there could have been in any

other way, if God had not taken humanity into alliance with Himself, if the Word had not been made flesh and dwelt among us. I say there may have been other plans, but certainly no mortal mind can conceive any other. This seems to be the most wonderful, the most Godlike, the most divine, that a creature shall be made perfectly free; that that creature shall offend, shall discover the justice of God through the punishment being laid upon a substitute, but shall learn the love of God through that substitute being God Himself. This creature was ordained to be attached to the Eternal One by ties of filial relationship, by bonds of affection so strong that the pains of the rack and the flames of the fire shall not be able to separate it from the love of God; and in heaven this creature shall feel that it owes nothing to itself, nothing to its own natural efforts, but all to Him who loved it and who bought it with His blood; and therefore this grateful being shall praise God after a sort superior by many high degrees to the attainment of any other. Oh! dear friends, I think if we study the subject for a few hours alone, we shall see that in nothing that God has done is there such a discovery of His wisdom as in the plan of redeeming love. Go round about her, O angels of the Lord; mark ye well her bulwarks, and tell the towers thereof; consider her palaces; behold the impregnable strength of covenant engagements; see the largeness and broadness of electing love; behold the veracity and truthfulness of divine promises; see the fulness of grace and efficacy in the pardoning blood; see the faithfulness and the immovability of the divine affection, when once it is set on men; and when ye have admired the whole, go back, ye spirits, and more sweetly than before unite with us in our song—"Worthy is the Lamb that was slain to receive honour, and blessing, and majesty, and power, and dominion for ever and ever."

II. Secondly, without a doubt the wisdom of God is made known to angels and principalities in THE VARIOUS DISPENSATIONS THROUGH WHICH THE CHURCH HAS PASSED. At first the Church was indeed a little flock, a few chosen out of the mass—Abram, the Syrian, ready to perish, and a few godly ones in his household. Then the stream widened a little, and there became twelve tribes; and soon the dispensation became more clear; Moses was raised up, and Aaron, whom God had chosen. Then the angels desired to look into the typical rites and ceremonies of that ancient dispensation. They were pictured standing on the mercy seat, with wings outstretched, with their faces bent downwards as if they would fain behold the secret which the golden lid concealed. Doubtless, as they saw the sacrifice, whether it was the burnt-offering, the peace-offering, or the sin-offering—as they saw the gorgeous ceremonies of the tabernacle, or the yet more splendid rites of the temple, they admired the wisdom of God, as it was set forth in the dim symbol and shadow; how much more must they have admired it, when the Sun of Righteousness arose with healing beneath His wings, when they saw the sacrifice superseded by the one great offering, the high priest set aside by the Man, who having once offered one sacrifice for ever, sat down at the right hand of the Majesty on high; how they have marvelled since that time as truth after truth has been expounded in the experience of believers, as doctrine after doctrine has been revealed to the Church of Christ by the illuminations of the Holy Spirit! Oh! brethren, the angels, when they compare the past with the present, and again, the present with the past, the choosing of the Jewish olive, and the leaving out of the rest of the trees, and anon, the grafting-in of the Gentiles from the wild olive, and the casting out of the natural branches, how much they must have admired the singular variety of God's dispensations, when they know, as certainly they do, that His grace remains the same!

In climbing or in descending a lofty mountain, one is struck with the sudden change of views. You looked on the right just now, and you saw a populous city in the plain; but you turn a corner, and looking through a break in the forest you see a broad lake; and in a moment or two your road winds again, and you will see a narrow valley and another range of mountains beyond. Every time you turn, there is a new scene presented to you. So it would seem to the angelic spirits. When first they began to ascend the hill on which the Church stands, "Mount Zion, which is above, the mother of us all," they saw the wisdom of God manifested as Abraham saw it; a turn in the road, and they saw it as Moses beheld it; another, and they had a view as David was wont to gaze upon it; and anon, when they ascended to clearer light, and the mists that hung about the mountain-side had all been scattered, and had fallen in one gracious shower of grace, they saw it as the apostles beheld it when they stood upon Mount Olivet; and since then, through every trial of the Church, as the eighteen centuries have rolled on since the Master went up to heaven, they have been constantly catching fresh views and seeing fresh manifestations of the varied and constantly-changing wisdom of the unchanging God, as it is manifested in His dealings to the Church. So that both in the dispensations, as well as in the plan, there is made known to principalities and powers "the manifold wisdom of God."

III. Thirdly, to be brief upon each point, we may conclude, without any doubt, that they mainly see the wisdom o God in His Church, IN THE CHURCH'S COVENANT HEAD AND REPRESENTATIVE. Oh! when first they heard that the Lord of life and glory was to be made flesh and to dwell among us, how they must have admired the plan of heaven's going down to earth that earth might come up to heaven! The babe in the manger commanded all their songs. When they saw that babe become a man, and heard Him preach, how they must have marvelled at the wisdom of sending God Himself to be God's own prophet! When they saw that man living a life of perfect holiness, how they must have clapped their wings at the thought that man could see perfection now in God's own self, shrouded in human form! But when it came to atonement, and they learned that God's people must be crucified in Christ, how struck must they have been, as the thought burst upon them for the first time, that the whole host of the elect were to sweat great drops of blood through one man, —that they were to be flagellated, to be scourged, bruised, and spat upon, in one man,—that the host of the chosen were to carry the cross of their condemnation upon one man's shoulders,—that that one man was for them all, to take all their load of guilt, and, nailed to the tree, bleed away His life for the whole Body. Oh! I say, when they saw that lowly man, with all the sins of the whole chosen company resting upon His shoulders, and knew this solitary man to be God—able to carry the whole—they must have marvelled, indeed, at the wisdom of God. And

when that triumphant man cried, "It is finished!" having drained the cup of damnation to its utmost dregs, till there remained not one black drop for another of the elect to drink,—when that one man descended into the grave, and the whole company of the faithful were buried with Him, oh, how they marvelled! When again they beheld the second Adam bursting His cerements, rending the chains of death as though, like another Samson, he had broken the green withes of the Philistines as though they were but tow, how astonished they were when they thought that the elect were risen in that glorified person! And when that man was received up into heaven and the cloud hid Him from mortal view, how they rejoiced to see Him rise! but much more to think that we also were risen in Him, and in Him had descended up.on high,—in Him the whole Church, I say, leading their captivity captive! When that representative personage, with acclamation beyond all measure, rose to the throne of the Father, and took His seat at the right hand of the dreadful Majesty on high, how wonderful must have been the admiration of the spirits when they thought that He had raised *us* up together, and made *us* sit together in heavenly places in Christ Jesus! Perhaps there is no doctrine that is more astounding to Christians than this. I know if we want a theme that will enlarge our mind, the subject of the union of the chosen with Christ is certainly the most expansive.

> "O sacred union, firm and strong,
>   How great the grace, how sweet the song,
>   That worms of earth should ever be
>   One with incarnate Deity!
>
> One when He died, one when He rose,
>   One when He triumphed o'er His foes;
>   One when in heaven He took His seat,
>   And angels sang all hell's defeat.
>
> This sacred tie forbids all fears,
>   For all He has and is is ours;
>   With Him our Head we stand or fall,
>   Our life, our surety, and our all."

"The manifold wisdom of God," in thus constituting Christ the covenant Head and representative of the elect in all its various shapes and shades, must have been discovered to angelic beings.

IV. Though that were a theme that might require a full discourse, we leave it at once to turn to another. In the fourth place, the manifold wisdom of God is made known to principalities and powers IN THE CONVERSION OF EVERY CHILD OF GOD.

There are some very singular implements in this present Great Exhibition; marvellous feats of human skill; but there is one thing they have not there that is to be found in the Church of the living God, and that is a heart-melter, an instrument for turning stone to flesh. There are inventions for melting granite, and for liquifying flints, but I know of no invention but one, and that is not to be found in any earthly show, for melting the adamant of the human heart. Now when the Lord takes the profane man, or the infidel, or the proud self-righteous Pharisee, or some tall, hectoring, careless sinner, and casts his heart into a fountain filled with Jesus' blood, and it begins to melt with penitence, the angels see the matchless wisdom of God. But I am sure, also, that there is not in the Exhibition another instrument called a heart-healer, an invention for binding up broken hearts and making them one again, and healing all their wounds; but the Lord is pleased by the same instrument by which He breaks hearts to heal them. That blood which melts the flint restores us the heart of flesh. Having first melted the heart, He next shows His matchless skill by taking away despair, despondency, and terror, and giving to the poor conscience perfect peace and rest, nay, exulting joy and boundless liberty. As the angels see the proud man bow his knee, as they hear him in his silent chamber pour out his heart in sighs and groans, they say. 'It is well, great God; it is well"; and as they see him come down from that chamber light of foot and joyous of heart because his sin is all forgiven, with his groans all turned into songs, the angels say, "It is well, great God; it is well; Thou woundest, but Thou dost heal; Thou killest, and Thou makest alive." Conversion is the greatest prodigy that we know of. If there be no such things as miracles to-day, believe me I have neither eyes nor ears. But you say, "What miracles?" I answer, not miracles in smitten rocks that yield rivers of water or seas that are divided by prophetic rod, but miracles in hearts and consciences, obedient to holy, heavenly power. I have seen in my short life more miracles and stranger than Moses ever wrought, and wonders great as Christ Jesus Himself ever performed on flesh and blood; for they are His miracles to-day that are wrought through the gospel. If it were well just now, I might point to some in these galleries and on this ground-floor, and ask them to tell what miracles God did for them, and how they here are in one happy circle to-day met for the praise of God; men who once were everything that was vile; but they are washed, but they are sanctified. The tear starts in their eye now when they think of the drunkard's cup and of the swearer's oath with which they were once so well acquainted; ah! too, and of the dens and kens of filth and of lasciviousness which they once knew; and they are here, loving and praising their Lord. Oh! there are some in this house to-day who, if they could speak, would say they are the greatest sinners out of hell, and the mightiest wonders out of heaven. If our gospel be hid, it is only hid to those who wilfully shut their eyes to it. When one sees harlots reclaimed, thieves, drunkards, swearers made to be saints of the living God, do not tell us that the gospel has lost its power. O Sirs! do not dream that we shall believe you while we can see this power, while we can feel it in our own souls, while every day we hear of conversions, while scarce a week rolls on without some score of brands being plucked from the eternal burnings. And I say, if the Church of God on earth admires these conversions, what must angels do who are more acquainted with the guilt of sin, and know more of the loveliness of holiness, and understand better the secret heart of man than we do? How must they gladly and exultingly admire in each distinct conversion as it presents phases different from any other, the "manifold wisdom of God!" That ingenious toy called the kaleidoscope at every turn presents some new form of beauty, so the different converts who are brought to Christ by the preaching of the word are every one unlike the other; there is something to distinguish each case; hence by them to the very letter our text is proved, the manifold wisdom, the much varied wisdom of God is displayed. I have sometimes understood the word "manifold" as comparing grace to a precious treasure that is wrapped up in many folds, first this, then the next, then the next must be unfolded, and

as you unwrap fold after fold, you find something precious each time; but it will be long ere you and I shall have unwrapped the last fold and shall have found the wisdom of God in its pure glittering lustre, lying stored within as the angels behold it in the Church of the living God.

V. But time has failed me, and therefore I must leave points upon which I wanted to dwell. The principalities and powers to this day find great opportunities for studying the wisdom of God in THE TRIALS AND EXPERIENCE OF BELIEVERS, in the wisdom which subjects them to trial, in the grace which sustains them in it, in the power which brings them out of it, in the wisdom which overrules the trial for their good, in the grace which makes the trial fit the back or strengthens the back for the burden. They see wisdom in the prosperity of Christians when their feet stand like hinds' feet upon their high places; they see the same in the despondencies of believers when even in the lowest depths they still say, "Though He slay me, yet will I trust in Him." As every day brings to us our daily bread, so every day brings to heaven its daily theme of wonder, and the angels receive fresh stores of knowledge from the ever-new experience of the people of God. They lean from the battlements of heaven to-day to gaze on you, ye tried believers; they look into your furnace as did the King of Babylon, and they see the fourth man with you like unto the Son of God. They track you, O ye children of Israel in the wilderness; they see the places of your encampment and the land to which you are hastening; and as they mark the fiery cloudy pillar that conducts you and the angel of God's host that leads the van and brings up the rear, they discover in every step of the way the wonderful wisdom of God.

VI. And lastly, beyond all controversy, WHEN THE LAST OF GOD'S PEOPLE SHALL BE BROUGHT IN, and the bright angels shall begin to wander through the heavenly plains and converse with all the redeemed spirits, they will then see "the manifold wisdom of God." Let the angel speak awhile for himself. "Here," saith he, "I see men of all nations, and kindreds, and tongues, from Britain to Japan, from the frozen north to the burning zone beneath the equator; here I see souls of all ages, babes hither snatched from the womb and breast, and spirits that once knew palsied age to whom the grasshopper was a burden. Here I see men from all periods, from Adam and Abel down to the men who were alive and remained at the coming of the Son of God from heaven. Here I see them from the days of Abraham, and the times of David, and the period of the Apostles, and the seasons of Luther and of Wickliffe, even to the last times of the Church. Here I see them of all classes. There is one who was a king, and at his side, as his fellow, is another that tugged the oar as a galley-slave. There I see a merchant prince who counted not his riches dear unto him, and by his side a poor man who was rich in faith and heir of the kingdom. There I see the poet who could sing on earth of *Paradise Lost and Regained*, and by his side one who could not put two words together, but who knew the Paradise Lost and the Paradise Regained within the Eden of his own nature, the garden of his own heart. Here I see Magdalene and Saul of Tarsus, repenting sinners of all shades and saints of all varieties, those who showed their patience on a lingering sick bed, those who triumphed with holy boldness amid the red flames, those who wandered about in sheepskins and goatskins, destitute, afflicted, tormented, of whom the world was not worthy; the monk who shook the world, and he who cast salt into the stream of doctrine and made it wholesome and pure; the man who preached to his millions, and brought tens of thousands of souls to Christ, and the humble cottager who knew but the Bible true, and herself the partaker of the life of Christ—here they all are, and as the spirits wander and look first at this and then at that—first one trophy of grace, and then at another monument of mercy, they will all exclaim, 'How manifold are Thy works, O God! In wisdom hast Thou made them all. Heaven is full of Thy goodness which Thou hast wrought for the sons of men.'"

And now, dear friends, the sermon is done, when I ask you just these questions; the first sha'l be a question for the children of God, and the other for those who know Him not.

First, to the children of God. Do you think you and I have sufficiently considered that we are always looked upon by angels, and that they desire to learn by us the wisdom of God? The reason why our sisters appear in the House of God with their heads covered is "because of the angels." The apostle says that a woman is to have a covering upon her head, because of the angels, since the angels are present in the assembly and they mark every act of indecorum, and therefore everything is to be conducted with decency and order in the presence of the angelic spirits. Think of that, then, when this afternoon we shall be talking together. Let us not talk in such a way that a visitor from heaven might be grieved with us; and when we are in our general assemblies met together, let us not discuss ignoble themes, but let the matters which we discuss be truly edifying, seasoned with salt. Especially in our families, might we not say more about Christ than we do? Do we not often spend days, perhaps weeks without making any mention of such things as we could wish angels to hear? Ye are watched, brethren, ye are watched by those that love you. The angels love us and bear us up in their hands lest we dash our feet against the stones. They encamp about our habitations; let us entertain these royal guests. Since they cannot eat our bread and sit at our table to partake of our good cheer, let us talk of subjects which will delight them, in a manner with which they shall be gratified, and let their presence be to us a motive why we should so conduct ourselves that to angels and principalities may be made known by us the wisdom of God.

And, lastly, what think some of you, would angels say of *your* walk and conversation? Well, I suppose you don't care much about them, and yet you should. For who but angels will be the reapers at the last, and who but they shall be the convoy to our spirits across the last dark stream? Who but they shall carry our spirit like that of Lazarus into the Father's bosom? Surely we should not despise them. What has your conduct been? Ah, sirs, it need not that the preacher speak. Let Conscience have her perfect work. There are some here over whom angels, could their eyes have known a tear, would have wept day and night. Ye have been almost persuaded to be Christians. Ye have known the struggles of conscience, and ye have said, "I would to God I were altogether such as the saints are!" but ye are unconverted still. Stay, spirit, guardian spirit, thou who hast watched over this son of a sainted mother, wing not back thy disappointed flight to heaven! He relents, he relents. Now the Spirit of God is moving in him. "*It shall be*," saith he, "*it shall be*," "I repent and believe in Jesus," but oh, spirit, thou wilt be disappointed yet, for he is about to say, "In a little time, go thy way for a little season, when I have a more convenient season I will send for thee." Angel, thou wilt be disappointed yet, but if the soul shall say "Now, even now, in this house of prayer, I cast myself upon the finished atonement of Christ; I trust in Him to save me"; wing thy flight aloft, thou glorious angel, tell the cherubs around the throne that the prodigal has returned, and an heir of heaven has been born; let heaven keep holiday and let us go into our homes rejoicing, for he that was dead is alive again, and he that was lost is found.

May the Spirit of God do this, for Jesus' sake! Amen.

SAINTS IN HEAVEN AND EARTH ONE FAMILY

"The whole family in heaven and earth."—Ephesians iii. 15.

BEREAVEMENTS are among the sorest griefs of this mortal life. We are permitted by God to love those whom He gives to us, and our heart eagerly casts its tendrils around them, and therefore when suddenly the beloved objects are withdrawn by death, our tenderest feelings are wounded. It is not sinful for us to lament the departure of friends, for Jesus wept; it would be unnatural and inhuman if we did not mourn for the departed, we should be less feeling than the beasts of the field. The Stoic is not a Christian, and his spirit is far removed from that of the tender-hearted Jesus.

The better the friend the greater our regret at his loss, although there also lie within that fact more abundant sources of consolation. The mourning for Josiah was very sore, because he was so good a prince. Because Stephen was so full of the Holy Ghost, and so bold for the faith, devout men carried him to his burial, and made great lamentation over him. Dorcas was wept and bewailed because of her practical care for the poor. Had they not been true saints, the mourning had not been so great; and yet, had they been wicked, there would have been graver cause for woe. Brethren, we cannot but sorrow this day, for the Lord has taken away a sister, a true servant of the church, a consecrated woman, whom He honoured above many, and to whom He gave many crowns of rejoicing; and we cannot but sorrow all the more, because so loving a mother in Israel has fallen asleep, so useful a life has come to a close, and so earnest a voice is hushed in silence. I have this day lost from my side one of the most faithful, fervent, and efficient of my helpers, and the church has lost one of her most useful members.

Beloved, we need comfort, let us seek it where it may be found. I pray that we may view this source of grief, not with our natural, but with our spiritual eyes. The things external are for the natural eye, and from that eye they force full many a tear, for in his natural life man is the heir of sorrow; but there is an inward and spiritual life, which God has given to believers, and this life has an inner eye, and to this inner eye there are other scenes presented than the senses can perceive. Let that spiritual vision indulge itself now. Close your eyes as much as your tears will permit you to the things which are seen, for they are temporal, and shadowy, and look to the eternal, secret, underlying truths, for these are realities. Take a steady look into the invisible, and the text, I think, sets before us something to gaze upon which may minister comfort to us. The saints in heaven, though apparently sundered from us, are in reality one with us; though death seems to have made breaches in the church of God, it is in fact perfect and entire; though the inhabitants of heaven and believers on earth might seem to be two orders of beings, yet in truth they are "one family."

> "Let all the saints terrestrial sing,
> With those to glory gone;
> For all the servants of our King,
> In earth and heaven, are one."

So sings the poet. The text tells us that there is a "whole family"; it speaks not of a broken family, nor of two families, but of "the whole family in heaven and earth." It is one undivided household still, notwithstanding all the graves which crowd the cemetery. To this thought I shall call your attention, hoping that thereby you may enter into that "one communion," in which saints above are bound up with saints below. I invite you to consider the ties which bind us to those who have gone before, and the indissoluble kinship in Christ which holds us as much as ever in one sacred unity.

I. First, let us think of THE POINTS OF THIS GREAT FAMILY UNION. In what respects are the people of our God in heaven and earth one family? We answer, in very many; for their family relation.hip is so ancient, so certain, and so paramount, that it may be seen in a vast variety of ways.

Let us note, first, concerning those in heaven and earth whom he Lord loves that their names are all *written in one family register*. That mystical roll which eye hath not seen containeth all the names of His chosen. They are born by degrees, but they are chosen at once; by one decree set apart from the rest of mankind, by one declaration "They shall be Mine," separated for ever as hallowed things unto the Most High. "Blessed be the God and Father of our Lord Jesus Christ, who hath blessed us with all spiritual blessings in heavenly places in Christ: according as He hath chosen us in Him before the foundation of the world, that we should be holy and without blame before Him in love: having pre-destinated us unto the adoption of children by Jesus Christ to Himself, according to the good pleasure of His will, to the praise of the glory of His grace, wherein He hath made us accepted in the beloved." We like to keep our own family registers; we are pleased to look back to the place where our parents recorded our names with those of our brothers and sisters. Let us gaze by faith upon that great book of life where all the names of the redeemed stand indelibly written by the hand of everlasting love, and as we read those beloved names let us remember that they make but one record. The faithful of modern times are on the same page with the saints of the Old Testament, and the names of the feeblest among us are written by the same hand which inscribed the apostles and the martyrs. We confidently believe hat Mrs. Bartlett's name is found in the same roll which contains yours, my sister, though you may be the most obscure of the Lord's daughters. "Even as ye are called in one hope of your calling," so were ye all comprehended in one election of grace.

The saints above and below are also *one family in the covenant*, "ordered in all things and sure," made with them in the person of their one great federal Head, the Lord Jesus Christ. Sadly one are all the members of the human race in our first father Adam, for in Adam we all fell. We realise that we are one family by the common sweat of the face, the common tendency to sin, the common liability to death: but there is a second Adam, and all whom He represented are most surely one family beneath His blessed Headship. What the Lord Jesus has accomplished was achieved for all His people; His righteousness is theirs, His life is theirs, His resurrection is the pledge of their resurrection, His eternal life is the source and guarantee of their immortal glory.

> "With Him, their Head, they stand or fall—
> Their life, their surety, and their all."

Let us think how close we are together then, for we are in very truth nearer to the saints in heaven than we are to the ungodly with whom we dwell. We are in one covenant Headship with just men made perfect, but not with the unregenerate. We are fellow citizens with the glorified, but we are strangers and foreigners among worldlings. Christ Jesus represented us even as He represented the glorified ones in the old eternity, when the covenant was signed and in that hour when the covenant stipulations were fulfilled upon the bloody tree, and He represents us with the glorified ones still as He takes possession of the inheritance in the names of all His elect, and dwells in the glory which He is preparing for His one church.

It is sweet to remember that all the saints in heaven and earth have *the covenant promises se ured to them by the selfsame seal*. Ye know the seal of the covenant; your eyes delight to dwell upon it, it is the sacrifice of the bleeding Lamb. And what, my brethren, is the ground of the security of the saints above, but the covenant of divine grace, sealed and ratified by the blood of the Son of God? We are rejoiced to see that, in the Epistle to the Hebrews, in connection with the spirits of just men made perfect, the Holy Spirit mentions Jesus the mediator of the new covenant, and the blood of sprinkling, which speaketh better things than that of Abel. The promise and the oath of God, those two immutable things, in which it is impossible for God to lie, are given to all the heirs of promise whether they be militant or triumphant, and to them all hath the Lord said, "I will be to them a God, and they shall be to Me a people." Glory be to His name, the blood which is the ground of our hope of heaven guarantees to the perfected that they shall abide in their bliss. They are there as the "redeemed from among men," which we also are this day. That same blood which has made white their robes has also cleansed us from all sin.

The family in heaven and earth, again, will be plainly seen to be one if you remember that they are *all born of the same Father*, each one in process of time. Every soul in heaven has received the new birth, for that which is born of the flesh cannot inherit a spiritual kingdom, and therefore even babes snatched away from the womb and breast ere yet they had fallen into actual sin, have entered heaven by regeneration. All there, whether they lived to old age or died in childhood, have been begotten again into a lively hope by the resurrection of Jesus Christ from the dead, and are born as to their heavenly state, not of blood, nor of the will of the flesh, nor of the will of man, but of God.

The nature of all regenerate persons is the same, for in all it is the living and incorruptible seed which liveth and abideth for ever. The same nature is in the saints above as in the saints below. They are called the sons of God and so are we; they delight in holiness and so also do we; they are of the church of the firstborn and so are we; their life is the life of God and so is ours; immortality pulses through our spirits as well as through theirs. Not yet, I grant, is the body made immortal, but as to our real life we know who hath said "Whosoever liveth and believeth in Me shall never die." Is it not written, "Ye are made partakers of the divine nature, having escaped the corruption which is in the world through lust"? I trow there is no higher nature than the divine, and this is said to have been bestowed upon the saints below. The new life in heaven is more developed and mature; it has also shaken off its dust, and has put on its beautiful garments, yet it is the same. In the sinner born to God but yesterday there is a spark of the same fire which burns in the breasts of the glorified above. Christ is in the perfected and the same Christ is in us, for we are "all of one" and He calls us all brethren. Of the same Father begotten, into the same nature born, with the same life quickening us, are we not one family? Oh, it needs but little alteration in the true saint below to make him a saint above. So slight the change that in an instant it is accomplished. "Absent from the body and present with the Lord." The work has proceeded so far that it only remains for the Master to give the last touch to it, and we shall be meet for glory and shall enter into the heavenly rest with capacities of joy as suitable for heaven as the capacities of those who have been there these thousand years.

We are one yet further brethren, because all saints, whether in heaven or earth, are *partakers in the same divine love*. "The Lord knoweth them that are His," not merely those in heaven but those below. The poor struggling child of God in poverty is as well known by God as yon bright songster who walks the golden streets. "The eyes of the Lord are upon the righteous, and His ears are open to their cry." I tell you timid, trembling woman, humbly resting on your Saviour, that you are as truly beloved of God as Abraham, Isaac, and Jacob, who sit down at His table in glory. The love of God toward His children is not affected by their position, so that He loves those in heaven better and those on earth less. God forbid. You, being evil, are not so partial as to bestow all your love upon a son who has prospered in the world, and give none of it to another who is bearing the burden of poverty. Our great Father loves the world of His elect with love surpassing thought, and has given Himself to each one of them to be the portion of each individual for ever. What more can He do for those in heaven? What less has He done for us on earth? Jesus has engraved the names of all the redeemed upon His hands and heart, and loves them all unto perfection. If then they all dwell in the bosom of God as the dearly beloved of His soul are they not indeed one family?

As they all receive the same love so are they all *heirs of the same promises* and the same blessed inheritance. I am bold to say that as a believer in Christ, heaven is as much mine as it is Paul's or Peter's; they are there to enjoy it, and I am waiting to obtain it, but I hold the same title deeds as they do, and as an heir of God, and joint heir with Jesus Christ, my heritage is as broad and as sure as theirs. Their only right to heaven lay in the grace of God which brought them to believe in Jesus; and if we also have been brought by grace to believe in Jesus our title to eternal glory is the same as theirs. Oh, child of God, do not think that the Lord has set apart some very choice and special blessings for a few of His people—all things are yours. The land is before you, even the land which floweth with milk and honey, and the whole of it is yours, though you may be less than the least of all saints. The promise is sure to all the seed, and all the seed have an interest in it. Remember that blessed passage. "If children, then heirs, heirs of God, joint heirs with Jesus Christ,"—not if full-grown children, not if well-developed children, not if strong, muscular children, but "if children," and that is all; regeneration proves you to be heirs, and alike heirs, for there can be no difference in the heirship if they are all heirs of God and joint heirs with Jesus Christ. Will you think of this, you who are little in Israel? You who rank with the Benjamites, will you sit down and think of this? You are one of the same family as those bright spirits who shine as the stars for ever and ever, and their inheritance is also yours, though as yet you have not come of age, and like a minor must wait till you have been trained under tutors and governors and educated for heaven. You are a prince, though as yet an infant; one of the Redeemer's kings and priests, as yet uncrowned; waiting, waiting, but still secure of the inheritance; tarrying till the day break and the shadows flee away, but sure that in the morning the crown of life so long reserved will be brought forth, and you also shall sit with Jesus on His throne.

So might I continue showing the points in which the saints above and the saints below are akin, but this last must suffice.

They are all members of one body, and are necessary to the completion of one another. In the Epistle to the Hebrews we are told concerning the saints above that "they without us cannot be made perfect." We are the lower limbs as it were of the body, but the body must have its inferior as well as its superior members. It cannot be a perfect body should the least part of it be destroyed. Hence it is declared that in the dispensation of the fulness of times, He will gather together in one all things in Christ, both which are in heaven and which are on earth. The saints above with all their bliss must wait for their resurrection until we also shall have come out of great tribulation; like ourselves they are waiting for the adoption, to wit, the redemption of the body. Until all who were predestinated to be conformed to the image of the firstborn shall have been so conformed, the Church cannot be complete. We are linked to the glorified by bonds of indispensable necessity. We think that we cannot do without them, and that is true; but they also cannot do without us. "As the body is one and hath many members, and all the members of that one body, being many are one body, so also is Christ." How closely this brings us together. Those for whom we sorrow cannot be far away, since we are all "the body of Christ and members in particular." If it be dark, my hand knows that the head cannot be far off, nor can the foot be far removed: eye, ear, foot, hand, head, are all comprised within the limits of one body; and so if I cannot see my beloved friend, if I shall not again hear her pathetic voice on earth, nor see her pleading tears, yet am I sure she is not far away, and that the bond between us is by no means snapped, for we are members of our Lord's body, of which it is written, "not a bone of Him shall be broken."

Thus have I according to my ability set forth some of the points of this family union; may the Holy Spirit give us to know them for ourselves.

II. Let us now speak upon THE INSEPARABLENESS OF THIS UNION. "The *whole* family in heaven and earth," not the two families nor the divided family, but the whole family in heaven and earth. It appears at first sight as if we were very effectually divided by the hand of *death*. Can it be that we are one family when some of us labour on, and others sleep beneath the greensward? There was a great truth in the sentence which Wordsworth put into the mouth of the little child when she said, "O master, we are seven."

> "'But they are dead: those two are dead!
> Their spirits are in heaven!'
> 'Twas throwing words away; for still
> The little maid would have her will,
> And said 'Nay, we are seven.'"

Should we not thus speak of the divine family, for death assuredly has no separating power in the household of God. Like the apostle, we are persuaded that death cannot separate us from the love of God. The breach caused by the grave is only apparent; it is not real, the family is still united: for if you think of it, when there is a loss in a family the father is bereaved, but you cannot conceive of our heavenly Father's being bereaved. Our Father which art in heaven, Thou hast lost none of Thy children. We wept and went to the grave, but Thou didst not, for Thy child is not dead; rather had Thy child come closer unto Thy bosom to receive a sweeter caress, and to know more fully the infinity of Thy love! When a child is lost from a family the elder brother is a mourner, for he has lost one of his brethren, but our Elder Brother is not bereaved; Jesus has lost none of His; nay, has He not rather brought home to Himself His own redeemed? Has He not rejoiced exceedingly to see His good work perfected in one whom He loved? There is no break towards the Father, and no break towards the Elder Brother, and therefore it must be our mistake to fancy that there is any break at all. It cannot be that death divides our Israel; were not the tribes of Reuben and Gad and Manasseh one with the rest of Israel, though the Jordan rolled between? It is a *whole* family, that redeemed household in heaven and in earth.

How little death prevents actual intercourse it is impossible for us to tell. Some attractive, but worthless books have been written pretending to unfold to us the connection between departed spirits and ourselves, but I trust you will not be led into such idle speculations. God has not revealed these things to us, and it is not for us to go dreaming about them, for we may dream ourselves into grievous errors if we once indulge our fancies. We know nothing about the commerce of the glorified with earth, but we do know that all departed saints are supremely blest, and that they are with Christ; and if they be with Christ, and we are with Christ, we cannot be far from each other. We meet all the saints of every age whenever we meet with God in Christ Jesus. In fellowship with Jesus ye are come unto the city of the living God, the heavenly Jerusalem, and to an innumerable company of angels, to the general assembly and church of the firstborn, whose names are written in heaven, and to the spirits of just men made perfect. It is impossible to restrict our communion with the people of God by the bounds of sect, race, country, or time, for we are vitally one with them all. Come, brethren, let us join our hands with those who have gone before, and let us with equal love join hands with those below, who before long will be numbered with the self-same company. Death has removed part of the family to an upper room, but we are one family still: there may be two brigades, but we are one army; we may feed in two pastures, but we are only one flock; we may dwell awhile in separate habitations, but one homestead will ere long receive us all.

As a matter which grows out of death, it may be well to say that *space* makes no inroads into the wholeness of the Lord's family. So far as spirits are limited to place, there must be a vast distance between the saint in heaven and the saint on earth; but we ought to remember that space, which seems vast to us, is not vast relatively, either as to God or to spiritual beings. Space is but the house of God; nay, God comprehends all space, and space, therefore, is but the bosom of the Eternal. Space also is scarcely to be reckoned when dealing with spiritual beings. We can love and commune with those who are across the Atlantic with as much ease as we can have fellowship with those in the next house. Our friends in Australia, though on the other side of the world, are by no means too distant for our spiritual embrace. Thought flies more swiftly than electricity; spirits defy space and annihilate distance; and we, in spirit, still meet with the departed in our songs of praise, rejoicing with them in our Lord Jesus Christ. Space does not divide: there are many mansions, but they are all in our Father's house.

And, dear brethren, it is such a great mercy that *sin*, that greatest of all separators, does not now divide us; for we are made nigh by the blood of Christ. When we think of those bright spirits before the throne, they seem to be of a superior race to us, and we are half tempted to bow at their feet; but this feeling is rebuked in us, as it was in John, by the voice which said, "See thou do it not: for I am thy fellow-servant, and of the prophets: worship God." They are one with us, after all; for they have washed their robes, and made them white in the blood of the Lamb, and that is exactly what we have done. Beloved in Christ, we are already justified and accepted in the Beloved as much as the glorified. The veil is rent for us as well as for them, the dividing mountains of sin are overturned for us as well as for them. Sinners as we are, we have access to God by the blood of Jesus, and with joy we draw near the throne. They have attained to perfectness, and we are following after: they see the Lord face to face, but we also who are pure in heart have grace given us to see God. The atoning blood has removed the middle wall, and we are one in Christ Jesus.

Neither do *errors* and failures of understanding divide the family of God; if, indeed, they did, who among us could be of the same family as those who know even as they are known? The little child makes a thousand mistakes, and his elder brethren smile sometimes, but they do not deny that he is their brother because he is so ignorant and childish. Even so, dear brothers and sisters, we know very little now; like the apostle we may ea h one say, "I spake as a child, I understood as a child, I thought as a child." For now we see through a glass darkly, and only know in part, but this does not disprove our kinship with those who see "face to face." We are of the same school, though on a lower form, and it is written "All thy children shall be taught of the Lord." What they know they learned at those same feet at which we also sit.

Neither can *sorrow* separate us. Ah, they know no tears, their griefs are ended and their toils, but we must abide awhile in the stern realities of life's battle, to wrestle, and to suffer; but it is evident that we are not divided from them, for we are all spoken of in one sentence, as "These are they that are coming out of great tribulation," for so the translation may run. Those who are already arrived and those who are on the way are described as one company. The sick child is of the same family as his brother in perfect health; soldiers who are enduring the brunt of the battle are of the same army as those who have gained their laurels. To deny that your warring soldier is a part of the host would be a great mistake; to say that he is not of the army because he is in the midst of the conflict would be cruel and false. The saints militant are of the same host as the triumphant; those who are suffering are of the same company as the beatified. None of these things part us, we are still one family in Christ Jesus. Who shall separate us?

III. A topic of deep interest now comes before us —THE PRESENT DISPLAY OF THIS UNION. We have been speaking of our being one family, but perhaps it appears to you to be only a pleasing theory, and therefore we will notice certain points in which our unity practically appears.

I like to think, first, that the *service* of those who have departed blends with ours. I do not mean that they can descend to earth to preach and teach and labour, but I do mean this, that they being dead, yet speak; their service projects itself beyond this life. A good man is not dead as to his influential life and real service for God as soon as the breath leaves his body; his work has a momentum in it which makes it roll on; his influence abides. "Even in their ashes live their wonted fires." A very large part of the power which the Holy Spirit gives to the church is found in the form of influence derived from the testimonies and examples of departed saints. To-day the Church of God feels the influence of Paul and Peter; at this very moment the work of the apostles is telling upon the nations. Is it not certain that the energetic souls of Luther and Calvin have left vital forces behind them which throb and pulsate still? Perhaps the Reformers are doing as much to-day as they did when they were alive. So each man, according to his talent and grace, leaves behind him not merely his arrow and his bow, his sword and his shield, for other hands to use; but the arrows which he shot before he died are still flying through the air, and the javelin which he hurled before his hand was paralysed in death is yet piercing through the bucklers of the foe. The influence of my dear sister, Mrs. Bartlett, will operate upon some of you as long as you live; and

you will transmit it to your successors. You Christians will be the more intense because of her glowing example; and you sinners will find it the harder to live in sin, when you remember her tearful warnings. Some of you, I do not doubt, will be her posthumous children, born unto her after she has entered into her rest. Do not let the living think that they are the sole champions in this holy war, for, to all intents and purposes, the spirits of the just made perfect stand side by side with them; and the battle is being carried on, in no small measure, by cannon which they cast, and weapons which they forged. Though the builders be absent in body, yet the gold, silver, and precious stones which they builded their Lord will establish for ever.

Then again, we are one family in heaven and earth, and that very visibly, because the influence of *the prayers* of those in heaven still abides with us. Do not mistake me, I am no believer in the intercession of the saints above. I believe that they pray, but I believe it to be a damnable error to urge anyone to seek their intercession. What I mean is very different. I mean that prayers offered while they were here, and unanswered in their lifetime, still remain in the church's treasury of prayer. Many a mothers dies with her children unsaved, but the prayers she continually offered for them will prevail after her death. Many a minister, and many a private member pleads with God for blessing on the Church, and perhaps does not see it; but prayer must be answered, and fifty years afterwards it is possible that the church will reap the result of those supplications. Is not Scotland to-day the better and the holier for the prayers of John Knox? Is not England the brighter for the prayers of Latimer and Ridley? The august company of the glorified have ceased to kneel with us in person, but in effect they do so. They have gone to other work, but the incense which they kindled when they were below still perfumes the chambers of the Church of God.

Further, the unity of the Church will be seen in this, that their *testimony* from above blends with ours. The Church is ordained to be a witness. My brethren, we try to witness as God helps us to the truth as it is in Jesus, even as those who are above once witnessed with us here in life and in death. What a sweet witness dying Christians often bear when they cannot speak, in the gleam of the eye, in the perfect rest of soul, which others may well envy, enjoyed just in the moment when pain was most severe, and the flesh was failing. But now that these spirits have entered within the veil do they cease their testimony? No. Hear them. They bear witness to the Lamb, saying "for Thou wast slain, and hast redeemed us to God by Thy blood." They make known to angels and principalities and powers in heavenly places the manifold wisdom of God, according to the eternal purpose which He purposed in Christ Jesus our Lord. We are engaged with them in revealing the abundant mercy and all-sufficiency of the Lord. Ye are comrades with us, ye shining ones; ye are fellow-witnesses for Jesus, and therefore ye are one with us.

The main employment of saints above is *praise*. Beloved, what is ours but praise too? Is it not well put by our poet,

"They sing the amb in hymns above,
And we in songs below?"

Their music is sweeter than ours, freer from discord,

and from all that is cold or wandering, but still the theme is the same, and the song springs from the same motive, and was wrought in the heart by the same grace. I think I shall never praise my Lord in heaven more sincerely than I often praise Him now, when my mouth cannot speak for the overfloodings of my soul's delight and joy in my God. who hath taken me up out of the horrible pit and out of the miry clay, and set my feet upon a rock, and established my goings, and put a new song in my mouth. The deep obligations of every day overwhelm me with indebtedness; I cannot but praise my God, when I think of dire necessities perpetually supplied, multiplied sin continually pardoned, wretched infirmity graciously helped. Yes, we are one family, because when holy worship goeth up into the ear of the Eternal our praise blendeth with the praise of those who are glorified above, and we are one.

Brethren, I believe we are one in some other points as well. Do you not rejoice over sinners? Is it not one of our holidays on earth when the prodigal returns? "Verily I say unto you there is joy in the presence of the angels of God over one sinner that repenteth." Do you ever cry out against sin and groan because of the power of error in the land? Know ye not that the souls under the altar also cry with the selfsame indignation, "O Lord, how long! Wilt Thou not judge and avenge Thine own elect?" Do you not expect each day the coming of your Lord, and look for it with rapture? They also do the same. They say there is no hope in heaven, but who told them so? The saints, like ourselves, are looking for the blessed hope, the glorious appearing of our Lord and Saviour Jesus Christ. Your joy, your desire, your hope, are not these the same as theirs before the throne?

Towering over all is the fact that *The Well-beloved is the common joy of saints in heaven and on earth.* What makes *their* heaven? Who is the object of all their worship? Who is the subject of all their songs? In whom do they delight themselves all the day long? Who leads them to living fountains of waters, and wipes all tears from their eyes? Beloved, He is as much all in all to us as He is to them. Jesus, *we* know Thee and *they* know Thee; Jesus, we love Thee and they love Thee; Jesus, we embrace Thee and they embrace Thee; Jesus, we are oft-times lost in Thee, and they are lost in Thee. Thou Sun of our soul, Thou life of our life, Thou light of our delight, Thou art that to us which Thou art to them, and herein we are all one.

IV. Last of all, there is to come, before long, A FUTURE MANIFESTATION OF THIS FAMILY UNION, much brighter than anything we have as yet seen. We are one family, and we shall meet again. If they cannot come to us we shall go to them by-and-by. It does not often happen that we carry to the grave one who is known to all of this congregation, but seldom does a week pass but what one or other of our number, and frequently two or three, are taken home. I have to look upon you and upon myself as so many shadows, and when I meet you, how often does the question occur to me, "Who will go next?" Naturally, I think of some of you who have grown grey in your Master's service, and have passed your threescore years and ten. You must go soon, my brethren and my sisters; and I know you are not grieved at the prospect. Yet the young as well as the old are taken home, and men in middle life, with the marrow moist in their bones, are removed, even as those who lean upon their staff for very age. Who knoweth but what *I* may leave you soon? My brother, who knoweth but that *you* may be called away? Well, in that blessed day when we leave the earth, we shall perceive that as we were free of the Church below, we are citizens of the Church above. Whenever some of us enter an assembly of believers, they recognize and welcome us; the like reception awaits us above! We shall be quite at home in heaven, when we get there. Some of you have more friends in heaven than on earth. How few are left of your former friends, compared with the many who have gone above. In the day when you enter into heaven, you will perceive that the Church is one family, for they will welcome you heartily, and recognize in you a brother, and a friend, and so, together with them, you shall adore your Lord.

Remember there is coming another day in which the family union of the Church will be seen, and that is when the trumpet shall sound and the dead shall be raised. It may be that we shall all be of the company of those who sleep, and if so, when the trumpet sounds, the dead in Christ shall rise first, and we shall have our share in the first resurrection. Or, if our Lord should come before we die, we shall be "alive and remain;" but we shall undergo a change at the same moment as the dead are raised, so that this corruptible shall put on incorruption. What a family we shall be when we all rise together, and all the changed ones stand with us, all of one race, all regenerate, all clothed in the white robe of Jesus' righteousness! What a family! What a meeting it will be!

> "How loud shall our glad voices sing,
>   When Christ His risen saints shall bring
>   From beds of dust, and silent clay,
>   To realms of everlasting day."

Beloved, I cannot dwell upon what glory will follow on earth, but if our Lord shall live and reign on earth a thousand years, and if there shall be set up a great empire, which shall outshine all other monarchies as much as the sun outshines the stars, we shall all share in it, for He will make us all kings and priests unto God, and we shall reign with Him upon the earth. Then, when cometh the end, and He shall deliver up the kingdom to God, even the Father, and God shall be all in all, we shall for ever be with the Lord. My soul anticipates that grandest of all family meetings, when all the chosen shall assemble around the throne of God. It is but a little while and it shall come; it is but the twinkling of an eye, and it shall all be matter of fact. We talk of time as though it were a far reaching thing; I appeal to you grey heads who know what seventy years mean; are they not gone as a watch in the night? Well, let the waiting be prolonged for ten thousand years, if the Lord pleases; the ten thousand years will end, and then for ever and for ever we shall be as one family where Jesus is. This hope should cheer us. Death, where is thy sting? Grave, where is thy victory? Cheered by the prospect of an everlasting reunion, we defy thee to sadden us! Encouraged by the glory which God has decreed, we laugh at thy vain attempts to make breaches in the ranks of the one and indivisible family of the living God!

The practical point is—*Do we belong to that family?* I will leave that naked question to work in every heart. Do I belong to that family? Am I born of God? Am I a believer in Jesus? If not, I am an heir of wrath, and not in the family of God.

If we do belong to the family *let us show our relationship* by loving all the members of it. I should not like a brother to be gone to heaven and to reflect that I was unkind to him; I should not like to think that I might have smoothed his pathway, and I did not; or I might have cheered him, and refused. Dear brethren, we shall live together in heaven for ever, let us love each other now with a pure heart fervently. Help your poor brethren, cheer your desponding sisters; let no man look only on his own things, but every man also on the things of others. Brother, be brotherly; sister, be a true sister. Let us not love in word only, but in deed and in truth, for we shall soon be at home together in our Father's house on high.

PAUL'S DOXOLOGY

"Now unto Him that is able to do exceeding abundantly above all that we ask or think, according to the power that worketh in us, unto Him be glory in the Church by Christ Jesus throughout all ages, world without end. Amen."—Ephesians iii. 20, 21.

THIS chapter has a whole service of worship within itself. It certainly contains a sermon, for Paul gives a very earnest address upon the unveiling of the hidden mystery, so that the Gentiles are made partakers of the promise in Christ by the gospel: it contains a prayer, for one of the verses begins, "For this cause I bow my knees"; and in the verses before us it closes with a hymn, a hymn of incomparable praise. Thus, in the compass of a short chapter, we have all those devout exercises with which our assemblies for worship are familiar, namely, instruction, supplication, and praise. It was meet that the apostle should close the chapter as he does, for the doxology here given grows out of the chapter: it is its natural outcome and crowns the whole, even as the flower of the lily is upborne by the stem, completes it, and adorns it. The chapter would have been altogether incomplete without the ascription of praise —not perhaps in its sense, but certainly in its spiritual development. Mount Zion doubtless possessed in itself both glory and beauty, but the temple on its summit constituted its most sacred charm; even so to a noble chapter this doxology is a divine climax, adding glory and sanctity to all the rest.

If you look the chapter through, you will see that the apostle has represented the gospel in its various aspects to different persons, and generally has set it forth with the word *nto*. In the fifth verse he speaks of it as manifested *unto the sons of men*. It was not revealed to them in the olden time so clearly as now, but now unto the holy apostles and prophets by the Spirit the gospel is revealed, and we live in its clear light, for which we have reason for great thankfulness. It were a good subject to dwell upon—the relation of the gospel unto the sons of men. The apostle, a little lower down, in the eighth verse, speaks of the relation of the gospel *unto himself*, "Unto me, who am less than the least of all saints, is this grace given." What the gospel may do unto other men it is of great importance for us to know, but the knowledge will little avail us unless we can testify of what it has done unto each one of us personally. All the gold mines of California are of less worth to a man than the money in his own possession. Can you, beloved hearers, speak each one for himself and say of the gospel—"unto me is this grace given." Further on, the apostle speaks of the angels, and in the tenth verse he says, "To the intent that now *unto the principalities and powers* in heavenly places might be made known by the Church the manifold wisdom of God." The gospel has a relation to angels; they have always had something to do with it, for of old they desired to look into it, and it is written of our Lord that He was "seen of angels"; we know also that they rejoice over penitent sinners, and that they join in those ascriptions of glory which the redeemed in heaven present to the Lamb of God. Yet further, the apostle, without exactly using the word "unto," dwells upon the relation of the gospel *to the people whom he addressed*, when he declares that he had prayed to the Lord that He would grant them according to the riches of His glory, to be strengthened with might by His Spirit in the inner man. Thus having mentioned how the gospel bears upon mankind at large, upon inspired men, upon himself, upon angels, and then upon the saints to whom he was writing, he turns with a full heart to look at its bearings upon God Himself. And now it is no longer "unto principalities and powers," no longer even "unto me," or "unto the holy apostles and prophets," but his theme is "*unto HIM*." I pray God the Holy Spirit to fulfil my desire at this time that every one of us who have tasted that the Lord is gracious, may look wholly *unto the Lord*, and spend the little time appointed for our discourse in reverent adoration of Him from whom all grace comes, and to whom all the glory ought therefore to return, "for of Him, and through Him, and to Him, are all things." If unto Him there should be glory in the Church throughout all ages, then, to Him should there be glory in this Church at this present moment. O Lord, help us to render it unto Thee.

In our text we have adoration; not prayer, the apostle had done with that: adoration—not even so much the act of praise as the full sense that praise is due, and far more of it than we can render. I hardly know how to describe adoration. Praise is a river flowing on joyously in its own channel, banked up on either side that it may run towards its one object, but adoration is the same river overflowing all banks, flooding the soul and covering the entire nature with its great waters; and these not so much moving and stirring as standing still in profound repose, mirroring the glory which shines down upon it, like a summer's sun upon a sea of glass; not seeking the divine presence, but conscious of it to an unutterable degree, and therefore full of awe and peace, like the sea of Galilee when its waves felt the touch of the sacred feet. Adoration is the fulness, the height and depth, the length and breadth of praise. Adoration seems to me to be as the starry heavens, which are always telling the glory of God, and yet "there is no speech nor language, where their voice is not heard." It is the eloquent silence of a soul that is too full for language. To prostrate yourself in the dust in humility, and yet to soar aloft in sublime thought; to sink into nothing, and yet to be so enlarged as to be filled with all the fulness of God; to have no thought and yet to be all thought; to lose yourself in God; this is adoration. This should be the frequent state of the renewed mind. We ought to set apart far longer time for this sacred engagement, or what shall we call it? act or state? It were for our highest enrichment if we made it our daily prayer that the blessed Spirit would frequently bear us right out of ourselves and lift us above all these trifles which surround us, till we were only conscious of God and His exceeding glory. Oh that He would plunge us into the Godhead's deepest sea till we were lost in His immensity, and could only exclaim in wonder, "Oh! the depths! Oh! the depths!" In that spirit I desire to approach the text, and I ask you to turn your eyes away from all else to Him, even to the Lord God Almighty and the Lamb. I do not ask you to remember what the gospel does for you except as you remember it to render praise for it; I do not ask you to contemplate the gospel in its reference to men and angels, but only to consider the Lord Himself, and to render Him glory for ability to bless, and enrich, and sanctify, above all our asking or thinking. Looking to the Lord alone, let us draw nigh unto Him in spirit and in truth.

I. Our first consideration shall be, UPON WHAT PART OF HIS GLORIOUS CHARACTER SHALL OUR MINDS REST? The text guides us to *the divine ability.* "Now unto Him that is able to do exceeding abundantly;" and it selects the divine ability to bless—"to do according to the power that worketh in us." This, then, is the subject.

What does the apostle say to it? He declares that the divine ability to bless is *above what we ask.* We have asked great things in our time. We do remember when it seemed the greatest thing conceivable for us to say, "Father, forgive me." We asked a large thing when we requested the pardon of all our sins, and an equally great thing when we prayed to be cleansed in spirit. When we felt our hearts hard and our natures depraved, it seemed almost too great a boon to expect the heart of stone to be turned to flesh. We did, however, cry for gracious renewal, and the prayer was heard. Full many a time since then in deep distress we have besought the Lord for great deliverances; in abject need we have sought great supplies, and in terrible dilemmas we have asked for great guidance, and we have received all these again and again. The blessings sought and obtained have assuredly been neither few nor small.

Some of us would almost seem to have tried the limit of prayer in the matters for which we have cried unto the Lord; we have in times of holy boldness and sacred access asked large things, such as one could only ask of the Great King: and yet our asking has been too short a line to reach the bottom of divine ability, He is able to do above what we ask. Our prayer at its best and boldest has many a boundary. It is limited often by our sense of need; we scarce know what we want; we need to be taught what we should pray for, or we never ask aright. We mistake our condition, we know not how deep and numerous our necessities are. Our soul's hunger is not keen enough, sin has taken the edge from our spiritual appetites, and therefore we stint and cramp our prayers: but, blessed be God, He is not limited by our sense of need; His guests do but ask for bread and water, but behold His oxen and fatlings are killed, and a feast is made of fat things, "of fat things full of marrow, of wines on the lees well refined."

Yes, and our need itself is limited. We do not want everything. Empty as we are there are some things that can fill us even to the full: but God is able to go beyond our absolute needs, and He has often

already done so. He has given to His redeemed more than, as creatures, they absolutely required to make them happy and blessed. We might have been restored to the full stature of unfallen manhood, and in consequence have been as Adam was before his sin; but, wonder of wonders, the Lord has done more, for He has made us His children, and His heirs, heirs of God, joint heirs with Jesus Christ. This is not the supply of necessity, it is the bestowal of honour, dignity, and exceeding great glory. And now, although our needs are in themselves very terrible, and far greater than can be supplied by anything short of all-sufficiency, yet God is able to do exceeding abundantly above all that we actually need, and He will do it. He will not treat us as men treat a pensioner, to whom they allot barely enough to live upon, and count themselves generous for doing so, but He will treat us as kings and princes, and do exceeding abundantly above all that we need. Thus does He leave our prayers far behind, outstripping both our sense of need and the need itself.

Our prayer is also limited by our desire. Of course a man does not pray any further than his desires go, and our desires are not always as much awake as they should be. We are sometimes very cold and slow in desiring good things; the nether springs make us forget the upper fountains. Alas, like the foolish king of Israel, we shoot but two or three arrows when we ought to have emptied out our quiver. We bring but small cups to the well, and take home but little water. Our mouths are not opened wide enough, for our hearts are not warm enough to melt the ice which closes our lips; but blessed be God, He is not limited by our desires; He is able to bless us beyond what our souls have yet learned to wish for.

And, alas, when we do desire great things our faith is often weak, and there we are restrained; we cannot believe God to be so good as to give us such unspeakable blessings, and so we fail. How much we lose thereby I scarcely dare pause to consider. Our unbelief is a great impoverishment to us. Yea, even when faith has become developed, and sometimes it does, yet I warrant you its stature never reaches the height of the promise. No man ever believed God as much as He might be believed, nor trusted His promise so implicitly as He might do, nor put so large a construction upon the divine word as it would bear. O brethren, we have to thank God that He is not bounded by our narrow faith, but even goes beyond what we believe concerning Him.

How often, too, we are limited in prayer by our want of comprehension; we do not understand what God means. Query, if there be a single promise in the whole covenant of grace which any child of God perfectly understands. There is a meaning in the covenant promises, a breadth, a length, a height, a depth, not compassed yet. God condescends to use human language, and to us the words mean silver but He uses them in a golden sense. He never means less than He says, but He always means far more than we think He says. For this let us magnify the Lord. His power to bless us is not bounded by our power to understand the blessing. Grace is not measured to us according to our capacity to receive, but according to His efficacy to bestow. He can enlarge us, my brethren. O that He would do so now! Prayer is an exercise in which our minds ought to be expanded, and our hearts enlarged; has not the Lord said, "Open thy mouth wide and I will fill it"? Yet our widest mouth is not the measure of what He can give us; our boldest prayer is not the boundary of what He is able to bestow. Pray at your utmost, like Elias upon Carmel; pray as you will till the keys of heaven seem to swing at your girdle, and yet you can never outrun that omnipotence to bless which dwells in the Lord God Almighty.

The apostle then goes on to say that *the ability of God to bless is above what we think.* Now, we can think of some things we dare not pray for. Thought is free, and scarcely can space contain it, its wings bear it far beyond all visible things, it can even soar into the impossible; yet thought cannot attain to the power of God to bless, for that is immeasurable. Have you not at times been filled with great thoughts of what God might do with you? Have you not imagined how He might use you for His glory? He can do more than you have dreamed! Turn your pleasant dreams into fervent prayers, and it may yet please the Lord to make you useful to an amazing degree, so that you shall be astonished at what you will accomplish. If of a humble shepherd lad He made a David, He may do the like with you. Have you not at other times conceived great ideas of what the Lord will make out of you when you shall be washed, and cleansed, and delivered from sin, and carried away to serve Him in heaven? Ah, but you have no idea what you will be; you do not know, when you have guessed your greatest, how perfect and pure and blessed you will be in your Father's house on high, when He has completed in you all the good pleasure of His will. You have sung sometimes

"What must it be to dwell above!"

And your thoughts and imaginations have gone to very great lengths in picturing the repose, the security, the wealth, the enjoyment, the perfect satisfaction of heaven. Ah, yes, but the Lord is able to do more than has ever entered into your heart. There, fling the bridle on the neck of your imagination, and let it like a winged horse, not only scour the plains of earth, but fly through the clouds, and mount above the stars; but its furthermost flight on the most rapid wing shall not bring you near the confines of the possibilities of God. Your thoughts even at their best, are not His thoughts: as high as the heavens are above the earth, so high are His thoughts above yours. think however, you may. How amazing a subject is now before us! What language of mine can adequately set forth the divine ability to bless, when both the eagle eye of prayer, and the eagle wing of thought fail to discover a boundary.

Now, I want to call your attention in this passage to every word of it. for every word is emphatic. "He is able to do exceeding abundantly above *all* that we ask or think;" not above some things that we ask, but "all"; not above some of our dimmer conceptions. our lower thoughts, but above "all" that we think. Now just put together all that you have ever asked for. Heap it up, and then pile upon the top thereof all that you have ever thought of concerning the riches of divine grace. What a mountain! Here we have hill on hill, Pelion on Ossa, as though Alp on Alp were heaped on end, to build a staircase or a Jacob's ladder to the very stars. Go on! go on! It is no Babel tower you build, and yet its top will not reach unto heaven. High as this pyramid of prayers and contemplations may be piled, God's ability to bless is higher still, —"above *all* that we ask or even think." Some render it, "Now unto him that is able to do above all things exceeding abundantly," and so on. Well,

take it so. God is able to bless us above all things; above all the blessings that others could give us— that is little; above all the blessedness which resides in creatures—that is great, but not comparable to what He can do: above all the blessings which can be imagined to be conveyed to us by all the creatures that are useful and beneficial to us—He is able to do above all good things for us. O Lord, help us to understand all this; give us faith to get a grip of this, and then to magnify and adore Thee. Alas, our adoration can never be proportionate to Thy goodness!

Now dwell on another word, "He is able to do exceeding abundantly above all that *we* ask or think." The *we* refers to the apostles as well as to ourselves. Paul was a mighty man in prayer. What a wonderful prayer this chapter contains,—how he finishes up, "That ye might be filled with all the fulness of God." I will defy any man to bring out the meaning of those words to the full. Yet when he had prayed that prayer Paul felt that God could go far beyond his comprehension of it. I do not know how, but he says so—above all that *we* ask, and of course this includes himself. Paul in that *we* may be viewed as including the apostles: *we*, the Twelve who have come nearest to Jesus, and have been personally taught how to pray by Him, we who have seen Him face to face, and upon whom His Spirit specially rests,—"He is able to do exceeding abundantly above that *we* ask"! The apostles were inspired; the Spirit of God was in them to an unusual degree, their thoughts were larger than ours, but, saith Paul, He is able to do above what *we* think, even *we* His apostles. the best, the most holy, the most spiritual, of Christian men! Oh, then, brethren, I am sure He is able to do exceeding abundantly above what we ask or think, for it is a terrible come down from the apostles' asking and thinking to ours. He must be able to do exceeding abundantly above the askings or thinkings of such poor, puny saints as we are.

Now, notice the apostle's use of the word "*abundantly.*" He says, not only that God is able to do above what we ask or think, but "abundantly." We might say of a man, "He has given much, but he has still something left." That expression would fall sadly short if applied to the Most High: He has not only something left, but an abundance left. We have already understood but a part of His ways. We have been able to comprehend the mere remnant of His glorious grace; but the reserve of goodness, the things which God hath prepared for them that love Him far exceed our thoughts. Our apostle, not content with the use of the word "abundantly," adds another word, and says, "*exceeding abundantly.*" He has constructed here in the Greek an expression which is altogether his own. No language was powerful enough for the apostle.—I mean for the Holy Ghost speaking through the apostle,—for very often Paul has to coin words and phrases to shadow forth his meaning, and here is one, "He is able to do exceeding abundantly," so abundantly that it exceeds measure and description. Yonder ship is on the sea, and the sea can bear it up, though it weighs several thousands of tons. Does that surprise you, my brethren? No. for you know that the ocean could float not merely one such ship, but a navy, yea, and more navies than you could count if you continued to number them throughout the livelong day. The far-reaching main is able to bear upon its bosom ships innumerable, it supports them "exceeding abundantly." God is as the great ocean. What you have seen Him do is but as it were the floating of one single bark, but what He can do, ah, that is "exceeding abundantly" above what you ask or think. There flows our beautiful river among the meadows, and the child dips its cup to drink, and is fully refreshed, yet all that the child can take is as nothing compared with what still remains, and if along the banks of Father Thames crowds of thirsty ones should congregate and drink their fill, both men and cattle, yet all they could abstract from the waters would bear a very inconsiderable proportion to the volume which would still flow to the sea. Lo, I see thousands of the redeemed crowding down to the all-sufficiency of God; I see them lie down to drink like men that must take draughts both long and deep, or die; but after they have all drunk, and all the creatures that live have all been supplied, I see no diminution in the blessedness which pours forth from the throne of God and of the Lamb, which can only be described in these words, "He is able to do exceeding abundantly above all that we ask or think."

Now to help you to adore the Lord—for that is my one object this morning—think how blessed you are in having such an all-sufficient God. It is always pleasant to take out of a great heap, and to know that what you receive does not deprive others of their share. Who cares to sit at a table where every morsel must be counted, for if you have more somebody must have less? It is a scant feast where the provision is exactly measured. Here, at the table of our God, there is need of no such economy. "Eat, O friends, drink, yea drink abundantly, O beloved," for the feast is of a king, and His provisions are infinite.

Thus we see that there need be no limit to our prayer. You need never rise from your knees, and say, "Perhaps I was presumptuous; perhaps I have asked more than God will give?" Down on your knees, brother, and ask God to forgive you for dishonouring Him by harbouring such a thought. He is able to give exceeding abundantly above what you ask.

Thus, we see also that He is still able to bless us, upon whom the ends of the earth are come; for if He was able to do exceeding abundantly in the apostle's time, He is quite as able still, and we may come to Him without fear. Now, I see, also, that if my case be very special, still I need not tremble or stand in dread of want. What if I require superabundant grace? I may have it. If I want exceeding abundant help, I can have it. Ah, if I need more grace than I dare ask for, I can have it. Yes, and if I require more than I think, I may have it, for still my Lord is able to give it me, and what He is able to do, He is willing to do.

What comfort this should afford even to poor sinners who are far away from God. He is able to give you great forgiveness for the greatest possible sin; sins that you have not yet thought of He can pardon. Do but come to God in Christ Jesus, and you shall find Him able to save to the uttermost. If this little hint be taken up by some despairing heart, it may give it immediate peace. It cannot be true that God cannot forgive, for in Christ Jesus, "He is able to do exceeding abundantly above what we ask or even think."

II. Our second business is to answer the enquiry, IN WHAT WAY DO WE PERCEIVE THIS ABILITY? We cannot well praise what we cannot in any measure discern. The apostle says, "*according to the power*

that worketh in us." We know that God can give us more than we ask or think, for *He has given us more than we have asked or thought.* Our regeneration came to us before prayer, for prayer was the first sign of the new birth already given. To pray for life is not a faculty of the dead; but regeneration puts into us the living desire and the spiritual longing. The first principle of life imparted makes us long after more life. We were dead in sins and far from God, and He surprised us with His preventing mercy, and in us was fulfilled the words, "I was found of them that sought me not." In this case He did for us above what we asked or thought.

Redemption again,—whoever sought for that? Had it not been provided from of old, who would have dared to ask the Lord to give His Son as a substitute to bleed and die for man? Sirs, in providing for us a substitute from before the foundation of the world, the Lord has already gone beyond man's thoughts or requests. Thanks be unto Him for His unspeakable gift. He gave us Christ, and then gave us His blessed Spirit, another surprising boon which man could not have supposed it possible for Him to have obtained. Having done that which we never sought for, nor thought of, He is still able to amaze us with unlooked for grace.

Moreover, *where prayer has been offered, our heavenly Father has gone far beyond what we have asked or thought.* I said unto the Lord in the anguish of my soul that if He would forgive my sins I would be content to be the meanest servant in His house, and would gladly lie in prison all my life, and live on bread and water; but His mercy did not come to me in that scanty way, for He put me among His children and gave me an inheritance. "Make me as one of Thy hired servants" is a prayer the Father does not hear; He puts His hand on His child's mouth when he begins to talk so, and says, "Bring forth the best robe and put it on him, put a ring on his hands, and shoes on his feet." We have asked for a stone and He has given us bread; we have asked for bare bread and He has given us angels' food. For brass He has given silver, and for silver gold. We looked for a drop and the rain has filled the pools; we sought a morsel and He has filled us with good things; and therefore we are warranted in expecting that in future He will still outdo our prayers.

Look at the plan of salvation, in the next place, and you will see how *it suggests the ability of God to do more for us.* Who is He that chose us? Who is He that hath begotten us again unto a lively hope? It is God the Father; and when you mention Him as having put His hand to the work of grace, you have opened a wide door of hope, for what is there He cannot do? He who has filled yon heavens with stars, scattering them broadcast as the sower soweth corn, and could have made a thousand universes, alike full of worlds, with as much ease as man speaks a word, —has He begun to bless us, and can there be any limit to His power to deal graciously with us? Impossible!

Look next at His dear Son. He that created the heavens and the earth is made a man and lies in a manger; He whom angels obey is despised and rejected of men; He who only hath immortality hangs on a tree and bleeds and dies. There must be in those groans, and those drops of sweat, and those wounds, and that death of His, a power to save altogether inconceivable. Immanuel made a sacrifice! What ability to bless must dwell in Him! He must be able to do exceeding abundantly above what we ask or think

And who is this, the divine Spirit, who comes to dwell in us? Yes, literally to dwell in these mortal bodies, and make these tabernacles of clay His temples! He has already mortified our lusts, already changed our hearts, already made us partakers of the divine nature: my brethren, is there any limit to the possibilities of the Spirit's work in us? May we not fairly conclude that when God Himself comes to inhabit our bodies He will deliver us from every sin, and make us spotless as God is spotless, till in us shall be fulfilled the command, "Be ye holy, for I am holy."

Look at the plan: it is drawn to a wondrous scale. The Trinity in Unity is manifest in the divine working within us, and there must be something inconceivably great possible to us through the working of such mighty power. Come then, dear friend, and for a moment think of the power which actually dwells in you. If you are a Christian you must be conscious of a power in you far too great for your mental or physical constitution to bear if it were not restrained. Do you never experience groanings which cannot be uttered, deep and terrible, like the moving of an earthquake, as though everything were loosed within you with extreme heaviness, anguish, and travailing in birth? These pangs and throes betray the latent God within you, cramped for room within the narrow bounds of your new created and growing spiritual nature. Have you never felt the workings and strivings of strong desires, fierce hungers, and insatiable thirsts? Have you not felt mysterious energies working like pent-up springs within your spirit, demanding space and vent, or threatening to burst your heart? Are you never conscious of the infinite, struggling within you? Have you never felt like a little bird shut up within its egg, chipping at the shell to gain liberty? Are you not conscious that you are not what you shall be? Do you not feel omnipotence rush through you sometimes with unutterable joy, till you have to cry, "Hold, my Lord, this joy becomes not man—it is the joy of Christ fulfilled in me; and if I feel it longer I must die, for in this body it is insupportable." There are ecstacies, but we must not tell of them here; there are high mysterious delights of which it is scarce lawful to speak, upliftings wherein man so communes with his Maker as to rise above himself, and to be far more than man; even as the bush in Horeb, though but a bush, was rendered capable of burning with fire without being consumed, and so was more than a bush, for it blazed with Deity. Are not your hearts familiar with these sacred mysteries of the heaven-born life? If they are, then you have the means of guessing at the apostle's meaning when he said, "He is able to do exceeding abundantly above all that we ask or even think, according to the power that worketh in us." God grant us to know this more fully.

Our third consideration is—

III. What, then, shall be rendered to God. "Unto Him be glory in the Church by Christ Jesus throughout all ages, world without end." "Unto Him be glory." O, my soul, adore Him! Feel His splendour, let His exceeding goodness shine full upon thy soul and warm thee with its rays, and let the warmth be adoring love! O, my soul, tell out His goodness, and reflect the light which falls upon thee from Himself; and so glorify Him by manifesting to the sons of men what He manifests to thee! Yea, my soul, let all that is within thee bathe in His boundless goodness, and then glorify Him by perpetual service. Bow thy strength to obedience; be yoked to that mighty chariot in which Jesus rides forth conquering and to conquer, saving the sons of Adam. God deserves glory in the most emphatic sense, and in the most practical meaning of that term. O, my brethren and sisters, let us try to render it to Him.

But the apostle felt that he must not say, "Unto Him be glory in my soul." He wished that, but his one soul afforded far too little space, and so he cried "unto Him, be glory in the church." He calls upon all the people of God to praise the divine name. If all the world beside were dumb, the Church must always proclaim the glory of God. If moon and stars and sun and sea no more reflect the majesty of the Creator, yet let the redeemed of the Lord praise him, even those whom He hath redeemed out of the hand of the enemy. As Israel sung at the Red Sea, with dances and timbrel, so let the Church of God exult, for He has brought us through the sea and drowned our adversaries: "the depths have covered them, there is not one of them left." Thou, O Jesus, hast redeemed our souls with blood, hast set the prisoners free, and made us to be a royal priesthood, and therefore Thy Church must praise Thee without ceasing.

But as if he felt that the Church herself was unequal to the task, though she is ordained to be the sphere of the divine glory, note how he puts it. "In the Church by Christ Jesus." Thou, Lord Jesus, Thou art He alone among men eloquent enough to express the glory of God. Grace is poured into Thy lips, and Thou canst declare our praises for us. Brethren, do you not remember how our blessed Lord vowed to praise the divine name amongst His brethren. Read the twenty-second Psalm, and you will see how He becomes the chief musician, the leader of the choirs of the blessed. By Christ it is that our praises ascend to heaven, He is the spokesman for us, the interpreter, one of a thousand before the throne of the infinite majesty. O Christ—we are Thy Body, and every member of the Body praises God, but Thou art the Head, and Thou must speak for us with those dear lips that are like lilies dropping sweet smelling myrrh; Thou must offer our praises to the great High Priest, and they shall be accepted at Thy hands.

Yet the apostle was not satisfied, for he adds, "Unto Him be glory in the church by Christ Jesus through all ages;" and the Greek runs exactly thus, "unto all the generations of the age of ages." Perhaps the apostle half expected the world to last for ages yet, although he did not know when Christ might come, and therefore stood watching for Him. At any rate, He desired that generation after generation might show forth the glory of God, and when there were no more succeeding races of men, He desired that that age of ages, the golden age, God's age, the age of peace and joy and blessedness, whatever phases it might pass through, might never cease to resound with the glory of God. O, blessed words of the apostle! We cannot reach their meaning, and if we did, still that meaning would be short of what God deserves.

"I'll praise Him while He lends me breath;
And when my voice is lost in death!
Praise shall employ my nobler powers:
My days of praise shall be ne'er past,
While thought and life and being last,
Or immortality endures."

Our children shall follow after us, and they shall praise the Lord, and their children and they shall praise Him, and their children and they shall praise Him;

and when the time comes that earth grows old, and Christ Himself shall descend from heaven to renew all things, His saints shall magnify Him when He comes. When He smites His foes, and breaks them in pieces like potters' vessels, the saints shall adore Him still. And when cometh the end and He shall have delivered up the power to God, even the Father, still the everlasting song shall go up to God and the Lamb; and through the ages of ages when God shall be all in all, it shall be the bliss of every redeemed one for ever and for ever to say, "Unto Him be glory, unto Him be glory for ever and ever."

IV. I have done when you have done, and the last point concerns what you have to do. WHAT SHALL WE SAY TO ALL THIS?

The text tells in one word. It concludes with your part of it —"Amen." Some of you have newly been born to God, you are babes in His family. I pray you to glorify Him this morning, who can do for you exceeding abundantly above what you ask or think. Say "Amen" while we unite in ascribing glory to Him. And you, my brethren, who like myself are in the vigour of manhood, in the very prime of life, working for God, let us heartily say "Amen," as well we may; for all the grace we have had and still have comes from Him. And you, my venerable brothers and sisters who are getting near to heaven, there is more mellowness in your voices than in ours; for there is a ripeness, and maturity in your experience, therefore say you first and foremost, "Unto Him be glory in the Church." Say it now, all classes of believers: you who are rejoicing in the Lord this morning, and you who are sorrowful and bowed down, say "Amen." Though you have not the present joy, yet say "Amen" in the expectation of it. Be not laggard any one of you to say "Unto Him be glory in the Church throughout all ages. Amen." Say it, O Church, below, without exception; say it all ye militant ones. Ye saints that lie upon your sick beds, and ye that are near to die, yet say "Amen." Ye that suffer and ye that labour ye who sow and ye who reap, say "Amen." And when the whole church below has said "Amen," O Church above take up the grand "Amen." Ye triumphant ones who have washed your robes in the blood of the Lamb, I need not challenge you to say, "Amen," for I know ye do it louder and more sweetly than saints below.

Ye sinners who have not yet tasted of His grace, I think I might almost urge you to say "Amen," for if you have not yet obtained mercy He is able to give it you. You have come here this morning thirsty like Hagar, and God sees you. You are searching for a little water to fill your bottle. See, yonder is a well, a well which flows freely. Drink of it, drink and live, and say "Amen," as you bless the Lord who looks on you in love. Perhaps you came here like Saul seeking your father's asses, or some such trifles. Behold, He gives you a kingdom—He gives you more than you ask or think—freely He gives it according to the riches of His grace. Accept it, and then say, "Amen." Oh, with one heart and one soul let all of you that have been redeemed from death and hell, or even hope to be so, join in this ascription,

"Now to the Lord, whose power can do
More than our thoughts or wishes know,
Be everlasting honour done,
By all the Church, through Christ His Son."

Amen and Amen.

THE ASCENSION OF CHRIST

"Unto every one of us is given grace according to the measure of the gift of Christ. Wherefore He saith, when He ascended up on high, He led captivity captive, and gave gifts unto men. (Now that He ascended, what is it but that He also descended first into the lower parts of the earth? He that descended is the same also that ascended up far above all heavens, that He might fill all things.) And He gave some, apostles; and some, prophets; and some, evangelists; and some, pastors and teachers; for the perfecting of the saints, for the work of the ministry, for the edifying of the body of Christ."—Ephesians iv. 7-12.

OUR blessed Lord and Master has gone from us. From the mount of Olives, the place where in dread conflict His garments were rolled in blood, He has mounted in triumph to His throne. After having shown Himself for forty days amongst His beloved disciples, giving them abundant evidence that He had really risen from the dead, and enriching them by His divine counsels, He was taken up. Slowly rising before them all, He gave them His blessing as He disappeared. Like good old Jacob, whose departing act was to bestow a benediction on his twelve sons and their descendants, so ere the cloud received our Lord out of our sight, He poured a blessing upon the apostles, who were looking upward and who were the representatives of His Church. He is gone! His voice of wisdom is silent for us, His seat at the table is empty, the congregation on the mountain hears Him no more. It would be very easy to have found reasons why He should not have gone. Had it been a matter of choice to us, we should have entreated Him to tarry with us till the dispensation closed. Unless, peradventure, grace had enabled us to say: "Not as we will, but as Thou wilt," we should have constrained Him, saying, "Abide with us." What a comfort to disciples to have their own beloved Teacher visibly with them! What a consolation to a persecuted band to see their leader at their head; difficulties would disappear, problems would be solved, perplexities removed, trials made easy, temptations averted! Let Jesus Himself, their own dear Shepherd be near, and the sheep will lie down in security. Had He been here we could have gone to Him in every affliction, like those of whom it is said, "they went and told Jesus."

It seemed expedient for Him to stay, to accomplish the conversion of the world. Would not His presence have had an influence to win by eloquence of gracious word and argument of loving miracle? If He put forth His power the battle would soon be over, and His rule over all hearts would be for ever established. "Thine arrows are sharp in the heart of the king's enemies; whereby the people fall under Thee." Go not from the conflict, thou mighty bowman, but still cast thine all-subduing darts abroad. In the days of our Lord's flesh, before He had risen from the dead, He did but speak, and those who came to take Him fell to the ground; might we but have Him near us no persecuting hand could seize us; at His bidding, the fiercest enemy would retire. His voice called the dead out of their graves; could we but have Him still in the Church His voice would awaken the spiritually dead. His personal presence would be better to us than ten thousand apostles, at least, so we dream; and we imagine that with Him visibly among us the progress of the Church would be like the march of a triumphant army.

Thus might flesh and blood have argued, but all such reasoning is hushed by our Lord's declaration, "It is expedient for you that I go away: for if I go not away, the Comforter will not come unto you." He might have told us that His majestic presence was expected by the saints in heaven to complete their felicity; He might have said that for Himself it was fitting that after so long an exile and the performance of such stupendous labours, He should rise to His reward; He might also have added that it was due to His Father that He should return into the bosom of His love; but, as if He knew that their trembling at His departure was mainly occasioned by fear for their own personal interests, He puts the consoling word into this form: "It is expedient *for you* that I go away." He has gone then, and whether our weak understandings are able to perceive it or not, it is better for us that Jesus should be at the right hand of God than here corporeally in our assemblies below. Fain would a hundred Bethanies entertain Him, a thousand synagogues would rejoice to see Him open the Scriptures; women there are among us who would kiss His feet, and men who would glory to unloose the latchets of His shoes; but He has gotten Him away to the mountains of myrrh and the hills of frankincense. He no more sits at our tables, or walks with us on our highways; He is leading another flock to living fountains of waters, and let not His sheep below imagine that He has injured them by His removal; unerring wisdom has declared that it is expedient for us that He is gone.

This morning, instead of standing here gazing up into heaven, like the men of Galilee, deploring that we have lost our Lord, let us sit down in quiet contemplation, and see if we cannot gather profitable reflections from this great thing which has come to pass. Let our meditations ascend the yet glowing trackway of our Lord's ascension,—

> "Beyond, beyond this lower sky,
> Up where eternal ages roll."

We shall, by the Holy Spirit's aid, first consider, with a view to practical good, *the fact of His ascension;* secondly, *the triumph of that ascension;* thirdly, *the gifts of that ascension;* and then we shall conclude by noticing *the bearings of that ascension upon the unconverted*.

I. First, then, let our earnest thoughts gaze upward, viewing THE FACT OF THE ASCENSION. We lay aside all controversy or attempt at mere doctrinal definition, and desire to meditate upon the ascension with a view to comfort, edification, and soul profit. *It should afford us supreme joy* to remember that He who descended into the lower parts of the earth has now "ascended up far above all heavens." The descent was a subject of joy to angels and men, but it involved Him in much humiliation and sorrow, especially, when, after having received a body which, according to the Psalmist, was "curiously wrought in the lowest parts of the earth," He further descended into the bowels of the earth, and slept as a prisoner in the tomb. His descent on earth, though to us

the source of abounding joy, was full of pain, shame, and humiliation to Him. In proportion, then, ought to be our joy that the shame is swallowed up in glory, the pain is lost in bliss, the death in immortality. Did shepherds sing at His descent, let all men sing at His rising. Well deserves the warrior, to receive glory, for He has dearly won it. Our love of justice and of Him compels us to rejoice in His rejoicing. Whatever makes the Lord Jesus glad makes His people glad. Our sympathy with Him is most intense; we esteem His reproach above all wealth, and we set equal store by His honour. As we have died with Him, were buried with Him in baptism, have also risen with Him through the faith of the operation of God who raised Him from the dead, so also have we been made to sit together in the heavenly places, and have obtained an inheritance. If angels poured forth their sweetest minstrelsy when the Christ of God returned to His royal seat, much more should we. Those celestial beings had but slight share in the triumphs of that day compared with us; for it was a man who led captivity captive, it was one born of a woman who returned victoriously from Bozrah. We may well say with the Psalmist, in the sixty-eighth Psalm, to which our text refers, "Let the righteous be glad; let them rejoice before God: yea, let them exceedingly rejoice. Sing unto God, sing praises to His name: extol Him that rideth upon the heavens by His name JAH, and rejoice before Him." It was none other than Christ, bone of our bone and flesh of our flesh; it was the second Adam who mounted to his glory. Rejoice, O believers, as those who shout because of victory, divide ye the spoil with the strong.

> "Bruisèd is the serpent's head,
> Hell is vanquish'd, death is dead,
> And to Christ gone up on high,
> Captive is captivity.
>
> All His work and warfare done,
> He into His heaven is gone,
> And beside His Father's throne,
> Now is pleading for His own.
>
> Sing, O heavens! O earth, rejoice!
> Angel harp and human voice,
> Round Him, in His glory, raise
> Your ascended Saviour's praise."

Reflect yet again that from the hour when our Lord left it, *this world has lost all charms to us*. If He were in it, there were no spot in the universe which would hold us with stronger ties; but since He has gone up He draws us upward from it. The flower is gone from the garden, the first ripe fruit is gathered. Earth's crown has lost its brightest jewel, the star is gone from the night, the dew is exhaled from the morning, the sun is eclipsed at noon. We have heard of some who, when they lost a friend or favourite child never smiled again, for nothing could supply the dreary vacuum. To us it could not be that any affliction should bring us such grief, for we have learned to be resigned to our Father's will; but the fact that "Jesus, our all, to heaven is gone," had caused something of the same feeling in our souls, this world can never be our rest now, its power to content us is gone. Joseph is no more in Egypt, and it is time for Israel to be gone. No, earth, my treasure, is not here with thee, neither shall my heart be detained by thee. Thou art, O Christ, the rich treasure of Thy people, and since Thou art gone Thy people's hearts have climbed to heaven with Thee.

Flowing out of this is the great truth that *"our conversation is in heaven,"* from whence also we look for the Saviour, the Lord Jesus Christ." Brethren, inasmuch as Christ is gone our life is hid with Him in God. To the glory-land our Head is gone, and the life of the members is there. Since the Head is occupied with things celestial, let not the members of the body be grovelling as slaves to terrestrial things. "If ye then be risen with Christ, seek those things which are above, where Christ sitteth on the right hand of God. Set your affection on things above, not on things on the earth." Our Bridegroom has gone into the ivory palaces, He dwelleth in the midst of His brethren; do we not hear Him calling us to commune with Him? Hear ye not His voice, "Rise up my love, my fair one, and come away"? Though awhile our bodies linger here, let our spirits even now walk the golden streets, and behold the King in His beauty. Begin, O faithful souls, to-day the occupation of the blessed, praising God even while ye linger yet below, and honouring Him if not by the same modes of service as the perfect ones above, yet with the same obedient delight. "Our conversation is in heaven." May you and I know what that means to the full. May we take up our celestial burgess-rights, exercise our privileges and avocations as heavenly citizens, and live as those that are alive from the dead, who are raised up together and made partakers of His resurrection life. Since the head of the family is in the glory, let us by faith perceive how near we are to it, and by anticipation live upon its joys and in its power. Thus the ascension of our Lord will remind us of heaven, and teach us the holiness which is our preparation for it.

Our Lord Jesus Christ has gone from us. We return again to the thought. We cannot speak into His ear and hear His voice reply in those dear accents with which He spoke to Thomas and to Philip. He no longer sits at feasts of love with favoured friends, such as Mary and Martha and Lazarus. He has departed out of this world unto the Father, and what then? Why He has taught us by this the more distinctly, that *we must henceforth walk by faith and not by sight.* The presence of Jesus Christ on earth would have been, to a great extent, a perpetual embargo upon the life of faith. We should all have desired to see the Redeemer; but since, as man, He could not have been omnipresent, but could only have been in one spot at one time, we should have made it the business of our lives to provide the means for a journey to the place where He might be seen; or if He Himself condescended to journey through all lands we should have fought our way into the throng to feast our eyes upon Him, and we should have envied each other when the turn came for any to speak familiarly with Him. Thank God we have no cause for clamour or strife or struggle about the mere sight of Jesus after the flesh; for though once He was seen corporeally by His disciples, yet now after the flesh know we even Him no more. Jesus is no more seen of human eyes; and it is well, for faith's sight is saving, instructing, transforming, and mere natural sight is not so. Had He been here we should have regarded much more the things which are visible, but now our hearts are taken up with the things which are not seen, but which are eternal. This day we have no priest for eyes to gaze upon, no material altar, no temple made with hands, no solemn rites to satisfy the senses; we have done with the outward and are rejoicing in the inward.

Neither in this mountain nor in that do we worship the Father, but we worship God, who is a Spirit, in spirit and in truth. We now endure as seeing Him who is is visible; whom, having not seen, we love; in whom, though now we see Him not yet believing, we rejoice with joy unspeakable and full of glory. In the same fashion as we walk towards our Lord, so walk we towards all that He reveals; we walk by faith, not by sight. Israel, in the wilderness, instructed by types and shadows, was ever prone to idolatry; the more there is of the visible in religion, the more is there of difficulty in the attainment of spirituality. Even baptism and the Lord's Supper, were they not ordained by the Lord Himself, might be well given up, since the flesh makes a snare of them. and superstition engrafts on them baptismal regeneration and sacramental efficacy. Our Lord's presence might thus have become a difficulty to faith, though a pleasure to sense. His going away leaves a clear field for faith; it throws us necessarily upon a spiritual life, since He who is the head, the soul, the centre of our faith, hope, and love is no more within the range of our bodily organs. It is poor believing which needs to put its finger into the nail-prints; but blessed is he that hath not seen and yet hath believed. In an unseen Saviour we fix our trust, from an unseen Saviour we derive our joy. Our faith is now the substance of things hoped for, the evidence of things not seen.

Let us learn this lesson well, and let it never be said to us, "Are ye so foolish? Having begun in the Spirit, are ye now made perfect by the flesh?" Let us never attempt to live by feeling and evidence. Let us banish from our soul all dreams of finding perfection in the flesh, and equally let us discard all cravings for signs and wonders. Let us not be like the children of Israel, who only believed while they saw the works of the Lord. If our Beloved has hidden Himself from our sight, let Him even hide everything else, if so it pleases Him. If He only reveals Himself to our faith, the eye which is good enough to see Him with is good enough to see everything else with, and we will be content to see His covenant blessings, and all else with that one eye of faith, and no other, till the time shall come when He shall change our faith to sight.

Beloved, let us further reflect *how secure is our eternal inheritance* now that Jesus has entered into the heavenly places. Our heaven is secured to us, for it is in the actual possession of our legal representative, who can never be dispossessed of it. Possession is nine points of the law, but it absolutely secures completely our tenure under the gospel. He who possesses a covenant blessing shall never lose it, for the covenant cannot be changed, nor its gifts withdrawn. We are heritors of the heavenly Canaan by actual hold and sure title, for our legal representative, appointed by the highest court of judicature, has entered into possession and actual occupancy of the many mansions of the great Father's house. He has not merely taken possession, but He is making all ready for our reception and eternal inhabitation. A man who enters a house and claims it, if he has any question about his rights, will not think of preparing it for the inhabitants, he will leave any expenditure of that kind till all doubts are cleared up; but our good Lord has such possession of the city of the new Jerusalem for us, that He is daily preparing it for us, that where He is we may be also. If I could send to heaven some mere human being like myself to hold my place for me till my arrival, I should fear that my friend might lose it: but since my Lord, the King of heaven and the Master of angels, has gone thither to represent all his saints and claim their places for them, I know that my portion is secure. Rest content, beloved, and sing for joy as the apostle's heart did when he wrote, " n whom also we have obtained an inheritance."

Further, if Jesus has gone into the glory, *how successful must our prayers be.* You send a petition to court, and you hope for its success, for it is drawn up in proper style, and it has been countersigned by an influential person; but when the person who has backed your plea for you is himself at court, to take the petition and present it there, you feel safer still. To-day our prayers do not only receive our Saviour's imprimatur, but they are presented by His own hand, as His own requests. "Seeing then that we have a great high priest, that is passed into the heavens, Jesus the Son of God," "let us come boldly unto the throne of grace, that we may obtain mercy, and find grace to help in time of need." No prayer which Jesus urges can ever be dismissed unheard, that case is safe for which He is advocate.

> "Look up, my soul, with cheerful eye,
> See where the great Redeemer stands;
> The glorious Advocate on high,
> With precious incense in His hands.
>
> He sweetens every humble groan,
> He recommends each broken prayer;
> Recline thy hope on Him alone,
> Whose power and love forbid despair."

Once more, t ough I feel this theme might detain us long, we must leave it, and remark further that, as we consider Christ ascended, our hearts burn within us at the thought that *He is the type of all His people.* As He was, so are we also in this world; and as He is, so shall we also be. To us also there remain both a resurrection and an ascension. Unless the Lord come very speedily, we shall die as He did, and the sepulchre shall receive our bodies for awhile; there is for us a tomb in a garden, or a rest in the Machpelah of our fathers. For us there are winding-sheets and grave clothes; yet like our Lord we shall burst the bonds of death, for we cannot be holden of them. There is a resurrection morning for us, because there was a rising again for Him. Death could as soon have held the Head as the members; the prison doors once taken away, post and bar and all, the captives are set free. Then when we have risen from the dead at the blast of the archangel's trumpet, we shall ascend also, for is it not written that we shall be caught up together with the Lord in the air, and so shall be for ever with the Lord? Have courage, brother; that glittering road up to the highest heavens, which Christ has trodden, you too must tread; the triumph which He enjoyed shall be yours in your measure. You too, shall lead your captivity captive, and amidst the acclamations of angels you shall receive the "well done" of the ever-blessed Father, and shall sit with Jesus on His throne, even as He has overcome and sits with the Father upon His throne.

I have rather given you suggestions for meditation than the meditations themselves. May the Holy Spirit bless them to you; and as you in imagination sit down on Olivet and gaze into the pure azure, may the heavens open to you, and, like Stephen, may you see the Son of Man at the right hand of God.

II. Let us advance to the second point, and dwell upon it very briefly—THE TRIUMPH OF THE ASCENSION. Psalmists and apostles have delighted to speak upon our Lord's triumphal ascension to the hill of the Lord. I shall not attempt to do more than refer to what they have said. Call to your minds how the Psalmist in vision saw the Saviour's ascension, and, in the twenty-fourth Psalm, represented the angels as saying: "Lift up your heads, O ye gates; and be ye lift up, ye everlasting doors; and the King of glory shall come in. Who is this King of glory? The Lord strong and mighty, the Lord mighty in battle." The scene is described in rich poetic imagery of the most sublime kind, and it evidently teaches us that when our Saviour left the sight of mortals, He was joined by bands of spirits, who welcomed Him with acclamations and attended Him in solemn state as He entered the metropolis of the universe. The illustration which has usually been given is, I think, so good that we cannot better it. When generals and kings returned from war, in the old Roman ages, they were accustomed to celebrate a triumph; they rode in state through the streets of the capital, trophies of their wars were carried with them, the inhabitants crowded to the windows, filled the streets, thronged the house-tops, and showered down acclamations and garlands of flowers upon the conquering hero as he rode along. Without being grossly literal, we may conceive some such a scene as that attending our Lord's return to the celestial seats. The sixty-eighth Psalm is to the same effect: "The chariots of God are twenty thousand, even thousands of angels: the Lord is among them, as in Sinai, in the holy place. Thou hast ascended on high, Thou hast led captivity captive: Thou hast received gifts for men; yea, for the rebellious also, that the Lord God might dwell among them." So also in Psalm forty-seven: "God is gone up with a shout, the Lord with the sound of a trumpet." Angels and glorified spirits saluted our returning Champion; and, leading captivity captive, He assumed the mediatorial throne amidst universal acclamations. "Having spoiled principalities and powers, He made a show of them openly, triumphing over them in it."

Our Lord's ascension was a triumph over *the world.* He had passed through it unscathed by its temptations; He had been solicited on all hands to sin, but His garments were without spot or blemish. There was no temptation which had not been tried upon Him, the quivers of the earth had been emptied against Him, but the arrows had glanced harmlessly from His armour of proof. They had persecuted Him relentlessly; He had been made to suffer all that cruel scorn could invent, but He came forth from the furnace with not the smell of fire upon Him. He had endured death itself with love unquenched and courage invincible. He had conquered by enduring all. As He rose He was infinitely beyond their reach; though they hated Him no less than before, He had been forty days amongst them, and yet no hand was outstretched to arrest Him. He had shown himself openly in divers places, and yet not a dog dare move his tongue. In the clear air, from far above the hills of Salem, He who was once tempted in the desert, looked down upon the kingdoms of the earth, which had been shown Him by Satan as the price of sin, and reserved them all as His own by right of merit. He rises above all, for He is superior to all. As the world could not injure His character by its temptations, so no longer could it touch His person by its malice. He has defeated altogether this present evil world.

There, too, He led captive *sin*. Evil had assailed Him furiously, but it could not defile Him. Sin had been laid upon Him, the weight of human guilt was borne upon His shoulders, it crushed Him down, but He rose from the dead, He ascended into heaven, and proved that He had shaken off the load, and left it buried in His sepulchre. He has abolished the sins of His people; His atonement has been so efficacious that no sin is upon Him, the Surety, and certainly none remains upon those for whom He stood as substitute. Though once the Redeemer stood in the place of the condemned, He has so suffered the penalty that He is justified now, and His atoning work is finished for ever. Sin, my brethren, was led captive at our Immanuel's chariot-wheels when He ascended.

Death also was led in triumph. Death had bound Him, but He snapped each fetter and bound death with His own cords.

> "Vain the stone, the watch, the seal,
> Christ has burst the gates of hell;
> Death in vain forbids His rise,
> Christ hath opened Paradise.
>
> Lives again our glorious King!
> 'Where O death, is now thy sting?'
> Once He died our souls to save;
> 'Where's thy victory, boasting grave?'"

Our Saviour's ascension in that same body which descended into the lower parts of the earth, is so complete a victory over death, that every dying saint may be sure of immortality, and may leave his body behind without fear that it shall for ever abide in the vaults of the grave.

So, too, *Satan*, was utterly defeated! He had thought that he should overcome the seed of woman when he bruised His heel, but lo! as the conqueror mounts aloft, He breaks the dragon's head beneath His feet. See ye not the celestial coursers as they drag the war chariot of the Prince of the house of David up the everlasting hills! He comes who has fought the prince of darkness! Lo! He has bound him in iron fetters. See how He drags him at His chariot wheels, amidst the derision of all those pure spirits who retained their loyalty to the almighty King! Oh, Satan! thou wast worsted then! Thou didst fall like lightning from heaven when Christ ascended to His throne.

Brethren in Christ, *everything that makes up our captivity Christ has led captive*. Moral evil He has defeated, the difficulties and trials of this mortal life He has virtually overcome. There is nothing in heaven, or earth, or hell, that can be thought to be against us which now remaineth; He hath taken all away. The law He hath fulfilled; its curse He hath removed: the handwriting against us, He hath nailed to His cross. All foes of ours He hath made a show of openly. What joy there is to us in this triumph! What bliss to be interested in it by the gift of faith in him!

III. We may now turn to consider THE GIFTS OF THE ASCENSION. Our Lord ascended on high, and gave gifts to men. What were these gifts which He both received from God and gave to men? Our

text says that He ascended that He might fill all things. I do not think this alludes to His omnipresence—in that respect He does fill all things; but allow me to explain, as I receive it, the meaning of the passage, by a very simple figure. Christ descended into the lowest parts of the earth, and thereby He laid the foundations of the great temple of God's praise: He continued in His life labouring, and thereby He built the walls of His temple: He ascended to His throne, and therein He laid the topstone amidst shoutings. What remained then? It remained to furnish it with inhabitants, and the inhabitants with all things necessary for their comfort and perfection Christ ascended on high that He might do that. In that sense the gift of the Spirit fills all things, bringing in the chosen and furnishing all that is necessary for their complete salvation. The blessings which come to us through the ascension, are "for the perfecting of the saints, for the work of the ministry, for the edifying of the body of Christ: till we all come in the unity of the faith, and of the knowledge of the Son of God, unto a perfect man, unto the measure of the stature of the fulness of Christ."

Observe next, that these filling blessings of the ascension are *given to all the saints*. Does not the first verse of our text say: "Unto every one of us is given grace according to the measure of the gift of Christ." The Holy Spirit is the particular benediction of the ascension, and the Holy Spirit is in measure given to all truly regenerated persons. You have all, my brethren, some measure of the Holy Spirit; some more; some less: but whatever you have of the Holy Spirit comes to you, because Christ, when He ascended up on high, received gifts for men, that the Lord God might dwell among them. Every Christian having the gift of God in his measure, is bound to use it for the general good; for in a body no joint or member exists for itself, but for the good of the whole. You, brother, whether you have much grace or little, must, according to the effectual working in you, supply your part to the increase of the body unto the edifying of itself in love. See that ye regard your gifts in this light; trace them to Christ, and then use them for the object for which He designed them.

But to some persons the Holy Spirit is given more largely. As the result of the ascension of Christ into heaven the church received apostles, men who were selected as witnesses because they had personally seen the Saviour—an office which necessarily dies out, and properly so, because the miraculous power also is withdrawn. They were needed temporarily, and they were given by the ascended Lord as a choice legacy. Prophets, too, were in the early church. They were needed as a link between the glories of the old and new covenant; but each prophetic gift came from the Spirit through the Redeemer's ascent to glory. There remains rich gifts among us still, which I fear we do not sufficiently prize. Among men God's richest gifts are men of high vocation, separated for the ministry of the gospel. From our ascended Lord came all true *evangelists;* these are they who preach the gospel in divers places, and find it the power of God unto salvation; they are founders of churches, breakers of new soil, men of a missionary spirit, who build not on other men's foundations, but dig out for themselves. We need many such deliverers of the good news where as yet the message has not been heard. I scarcely know of any greater blessing to the church than the sending forth of earnest, indefatigable, anointed men of God, taught of the Lord to be winners of souls. Who among us can estimate the value of George Whitefield to the age in which he lived? Who shall ever calculate the price of a John Williams or a William Knibb? Whitefield was, under God, the salvation of our country, which was going down straight to Pandemonium; Williams reclaimed the islands of the sea from cannibalism, and Knibb broke the negro's chains. Such evangelists as these are gifts beyond all price. Then come the *pastors and teachers* doing one work in different forms. These are sent to feed the flock; they abide in one place, and instruct converts which have been gathered —these also are invaluable gifts of the ascension of Jesus Christ. It is not given unto all men to be pastors, nor is it needed; for if all were shepherds, where were the flock? Those to whom this grace is especially given are fitted to lead and instruct the people of God, and this leading is much required. What would the church be without her pastors? Let those who have tried to do without them be a warning to you.

Wherever you have pastors or evangelists they exist for the good of the church of God. They ought to labour for that end, and never for their own personal advantage. Their power is their Lord's gift, and it must be used in His way.

The point I want to come at is this. Dear friends since we all, as believers, have some measure of the Spirit, let us use it. Stir up the gift that is in thee. Be thou not like to him in the parable who had but one talent and hid it in a napkin. Brother, sister, if thou be in the body the least known joint, rob not the body by indolence or selfishness, but use the gift thou hast in order that the body of Christ may come to its perfection. Yet since thou hast not great personal gifts, serve the church by praying the Lord who has ascended to give us more evangelists, pastors and teachers. He alone can give them; any that come without Him are impostors. There are some prayers you must not pray, there are others you may pray, but there are a few you must pray. There is a petition which Christ has commanded us to offer, and yet I very seldom hear it. It is this one. "Pray ye therefore the Lord of the harvest, that He will send forth labourers into His harvest." We greatly lack evangelists and pastors. I do not mean that we lack muffs, who occupy the pulpits and empty pews. I believe the market has for many years been sufficiently supplied therewith; but we lack men who can stir the heart, arouse the conscience, and build up the church. The scatterers of flocks may be found everywhere; the gatherers of them, how many have we of such? Such a man at this day is more precious than the gold of Ophir. The Queen can make a bishop of the Established Church, but only the ascended Lord can send a bishop to the true church. Prelates, popes, cardinals, vicars, prebends, canons, deans, the Lord has nothing to do with. I see not even the name of them in His word, but the very poorest pastor whom the Lord ordains is a gift of His ascending glory. At this moment we are deploring that in the mission field our good men are grey. Duff, Moffat, and the like, are passing from the stage of action. Where are their successors? I was almost about to say, Echo answers, Where? We want evangelists for India, for China, for all the nations of the earth; and though we have many godly fathers among us, who are in-structors in the faith, yet have we in all our pastorates few. of eminence, who could be mentioned in the same day as the great Puritanic divines. If the ministry should become weak and feeble among us, the church richly deserves it, for this, the most important part of her whole organisation has been more neglected than anything else. I thank God this church has not only prayed for ministers, but has proved the sincerity of her prayer by helping such as God has called, by affording them leisure and assistance for understanding the way of God more perfectly. We have thought that Christ's gifts were valuable enough for us to treasure up and improve them. Our College has now received and sent forth, in the name of Jesus, more than two hundred ministers of the word. Look around you and see how few churches care to receive the ascension gifts of Christ, and how few pastors encourage young men to preach. I read the other day, with unutterable horror, the complaint that our churches were like to have too many ministers; an almost blasphemous complaint, impugning the value of Christ's ascension gifts. O that God would give us ten times the number of men after His own heart, and surely there would be then great lack of more! But there are too many, say they, for the present pulpits. Oh, miserable soul! is it come to this, that a minister of Christ must have a pulpit ready to hand? Are we all to be builders on other men's foundations? Have we none among us who can gather their own flocks? In a three-million city like this can any man say that labourers for Christ are too many? Loiterers are too many, doubtless; and when the church drives out the drones, who shall pity them? While there remain hundreds of towns and villages without a Baptist church, and whole districts of other lands without the gospel, it is idle to dream that of evangelists and teachers we can have too many. No man is so happy in his work as he who presides over a flock of his own gathering, and no pastor is more beloved than he who raised from ruin a destitute church and made it to become a joy and praise in the earth. Pray the Lord to send true pastors and true evangelists. Christ procured them by His ascension. Let us not forget this. What! shall it be thought that the blessings of the crucifixion are worth the having, and the blessings of the resurrection worth receiving, but the blessings of the ascension are to be regarded with indifference or even with suspicion? No; let us prize the gifts which God gives by His son, and when He sends us evangelists and pastors, let us treat them with loving respect. Honour Christ in every true minister; see not so much the man as his Master in him. Trace all gospel success to the ascended Saviour. Look to Christ for more successful workers. As they come receive them from His hands, when they come treat them kindly as His gifts, and daily pray that the Lord will send to Zion mighty champions of the faith.

IV. We shall conclude by noticing THE BEARING OF OUR LORD'S ASCENSION UPON SINNERS.

We will utter a few words, but full of comfort. Did you notice in the sixty-eighth Psalm the words: "He received gifts for men; *yea, for the rebellious also*"? When the Lord went back to His throne He had thoughts of love towards rebels still. The spiritual gifts of the church are for the good of the rebels as well as for the building up of those who are reconciled. Sinner, every true minister exists for thy good, and all the workers of the church have an eye to you.

There are one or two promises connected with our Lord's ascension which show His kindness to you: "I, if I be lifted up from the earth, will draw all men unto Me." An ascended Saviour draws you—run after Him. Here is another word of His: "He is exalted on high." To curse? No; "to give repentance and remission of sins." Look up to the glory into which He has entered; ask for repentance and remission. Do ye doubt His power to save you? Here is another text: "He is able also to save them to the uttermost that come unto God by Him, seeing He ever liveth to make intercession for them." Surely He has gone to heaven for you as well as for the saints. You ought to take good heart, and put your trust in Him at this happy hour.

How dangerous it will be to despise Him! They who despised Him in His shame perished. Jerusalem became a field of blood because it rejected the despised Nazarene. What will it be to reject the King, now that He has taken to Himself His great power? Remember, that this same Jesus who is gone up to heaven, will so come in like manner as He was seen to go up into heaven. His return is certain, and your summons to His bar equally certain; but what account can you give if you reject Him? O come and trust Him this day. Be reconciled to Him lest He be angry, and ye perish from the way while His wrath is kindled but a little. The Lord bless you, and grant you a share in His ascension. Amen, and Amen.

GRIEVING THE HOLY SPIRIT

"And grieve not the Holy Spirit of God, whereby ye are sealed unto the day of redemption."—Ephesians iv. 30.

THERE is something very touching in this admonition, "Grieve not the Holy Spirit of God." It does not say, "Do not make Him angry." A more delicate and tender term is used—"Grieve Him not." There are some men of so hard a character, that to make another angry does not give them much pain; and indeed, there are many of us who are scarcely to be moved by the information that another is angry with us; but where is the heart so hard, that it is not moved when we know that we have caused others grief?—for grief is a sweet combination of anger and of love. It is anger, but all the gall is taken from it. Love sweetens the anger, and turns the edge of it, not against the person, but against the offence. We all know how we use the two terms in contradistinction the one to the other. When I commit any offence, some friend who hath but little patience suddenly snaps asunder his forbearance and is angry with me. The same offence is observed by a loving father, and he is grieved. There is anger in his bosom, but he is angry and he sins not, for he is angry against my sin; and yet there is love to neutralize and modify the anger towards me. Instead of wishing me ill as the punishment of my sin, he looks upon my sin itself as being the ill. He grieves to think that I am already injured, from the fact that I have sinned. I say this is a heavenly compound, more precious than all the ointment of the merchants. There may be the bitterness of myrrh, but there is all the sweetness of frankincense in this sweet term "to grieve." I am certain, my hearers, I do not flatter you when I declare that I am sure that the most of you would grieve if you thought you were grieving anyone else. You, perhaps, would not care much if you had made any one angry without a cause; but to grieve him, even though it were without a cause and without intention, would nevertheless cause you distress of heart, and you would not rest until this grief had subsided, till you had made some explanation or apology, and had done your best to allay the smart and take away the grief. When we see anger in another, we at once begin to feel hostility. Anger begets anger; but grief begets pity, and pity is next akin to love; and we love those whom we have caused to grieve. Now, is not this a very sweet expression—"Grieve not the Holy Spirit"? Of course, the language is be to understood as speaking after the manner of men. The Holy Spirit of God knoweth no passion or suffering; but nevertheless, His emotion is here described in human language as being that of grief. And is it not, I say, a tender and touching thing, that the Holy Spirit should direct His servant Paul to say to us, "Grieve not the Holy Spirit," do not excite His loving anger, do not vex Him, do not cause Him to mourn? He is a dove; do not cause Him to mourn, because you have treated Him harshly and ungratefully. Now, the purport of my sermon, this morning, will be to exhort you not to grieve the Spirit; but I shall divide it thus:—first, I shall discourse *upon the love of the Spirit;* secondly, *upon the seal of the Spirit;* and then, thirdly, *upon the grieving of the Spirit.*

I. The few words I have to say UPON THE LOVE OF THE SPIRIT will all be pressing forward to my great mark, stirring you up not to grieve the Spirit; for when we are persuaded that another loves us, we find at once a very potent reason why we should not grieve Him. The love of the Spirit!—how shall I tell it forth? Surely it needs a songster to sing it, for love is only to be spoken of in words of song. The love of the Spirit!—let me tell you of His early love to us. He loved us without beginning. In the eternal covenant of grace, as I told you last Sabbath, He was one of the high contracting parties in the divine contract, whereby we are saved. All that can be said of the love of the Father, of the love of the Son, may be said of the love of the Spirit—it is eternal, it is infinite, it is sovereign, it is everlasting; it is a love which cannot be dissolved, which cannot be decreased, a love which cannot be removed from those who are the objects of it. Permit me, however, to refer you to His acts, rather than His attributes. Let me tell you of the love of the Spirit to you and to me. Oh, how early was that love which He manifested towards us, even in our childhood! My brethren, we can well remember how the Spirit was wont to strive with us. We went astray from the womb speaking lies, but how early did the Spirit of God stir up our conscience, and solemnly correct us on account of our youthful sins. How frequently since then has the Spirit wooed us! How often under the ministry has He compelled our hearts to melt, and the tear has run down our cheeks, and He has sweetly whispered in our ear, "My son, give Me thy heart; go to thy chamber, shut thy door about thee, confess thy sins, and seek a Saviour's love and blood." Oh,—but let us blush to tell it—how often have we done despite to Him! When we were in a state of unregeneracy, how we were wont to resist Him! We quenched the Spirit; He strove with us, but we strove against Him. But blessed be His dear name, and let Him have everlasting songs for it, He would not let us go! We would not be saved, but He would save us. We sought to thrust ourselves into the fire, but He sought to pluck us from the burning. We would dash ourselves from the precipice, but He wrestled with us and held us fast; He would not let us destroy our souls. Oh, how we illtreated Him, how we did set at nought His counsel! How did we scorn and scoff Him; how did we despise the ordinance which would lead us to Christ! How did we violate that holy cord which was gently drawing us to Jesus and His cross! I am sure, my brethren, at the recollections of the persevering struggles of the Spirit with you, you must be stirred up to love Him. How often did He restrain you from sin, when you were about to plunge headlong into a course of vice! How often did He constrain you to good, when you would have neglected it! You, perhaps, would not have been in the way at all, and the Lord would not have met you, if it had not been for that sweet Spirit, who would not let you become a blasphemer, who would not suffer you to forsake the house of God, and would not permit you to become a regular attendant at the haunts of vice, but checked you, and held you in, as it were, with bit and bridle. Though you were like a bullock, unaccustomed to the yoke, yet He would not let you have your way. Though you struggled against Him, yet He would not throw the reins upon your neck, but He said, "I will have him, I will have him against his will; I will change his heart, I will not let him go till I have made him a trophy of My mighty power to save." And then think my brethren of the love of the Spirit after that—

"Dost mind the time, the spot of land,
Where Jesus did thee meet?
Where He first took thee by the hand,
Thy Bridegroom's love—how sweet!"

Ah, then, in that blest hour, to memory dear, was it not the Holy Spirit who guided you to Jesus? Do you remember the love of the Spirit, when, after having quickened you, He took you aside, and showed you Jesus on the tree? Who was it that opened your blind eye to see a dying Saviour? Who was it that opened your deaf ear to hear the voice of pardoning love? Who opened your clasped and palsied hand to receive the tokens of a Saviour's grace? Who was it that brake your hard heart and made a way for the Saviour to enter and dwell therein? Oh! it was that precious Spirit, that self-same Spirit, to whom you had done so much despite, whom in the days of your flesh you had resisted! What a mercy it was that He did not say, "I will swear in My wrath that they shall not enter into My rest, for they have vexed Me, and I will take My everlasting flight from them"; or thus, "Ephraim is joined unto idols, I will let him alone!" And since that time, my brethren, how sweetly has the Spirit proved His love to you and to me. It is not only in His first strivings, and then His divine quickenings; but in all

the sequel, how much have we owed to His instruction. We have been dull scholars with the word before us, plain and simple, so that he that runs may read, and he that reads may understand, yet how small a portion of His Word has our memory retained; how little progress have we made in the school of God's grace! We are but learners yet, unstable, weak, and apt to slide, but what a blessed instructor we have had! Has He not led us into many a truth, and taken of the things of Christ and applied them unto us? Oh! when I think how stupid I have been, I wonder that He has not given me up. When I think what a dolt I have been, when He would have taught me the things of the kingdom of God, I marvel that He should have had such patience with me. Is it a wonder that Jesus should become a babe? Is it not an equal wonder that the Spirit of the living God should become a teacher of babes? It is a marvel that Jesus should lie in a manger; is it not an equal marvel that the Holy Spirit should become an usher in the sacred school, to teach fools, and make them wise? It was condescension that brought the Saviour to the cross, but is it not equal condescension that brings the mighty Spirit of grace down to dwell with stubborn, unruly, wild asses' colts, to teach them the mystery of the kingdom, and make them know the wonders of a Saviour's love?

Furthermore, my brethren, forget not how much we owe to the Spirit's consolation, how much has He manifested His love to you in cherishing you in all your sicknesses, assisting you in all your labours; and comforting you in all your distresses. He has been a blessed comforter to me I can testify; when every other comfort failed, when the promise itself seemed empty, when the ministry was void of power, it is then the Holy Spirit has proved a rich comfort unto my soul, and filled my poor heart with peace and joy in believing. How many times would your heart have broken if the Spirit had not bound it up! How often has He who is your teacher become also your physician, has closed the wounds of your poor bleeding spirit, and has bound up those wounds with the court plaister of the promise, and so has stanched the bleeding, and has given you back your spiritual health once more. It does seem to me a marvel that the Holy Ghost should become a comforter, for comforting is, to many minds, but an inferior work in the church, though really it is not so. To teach, to preach, to command with authority, how many are willing to do this because this is honourable work; but to sit down and bear with the infirmities of the creature, to enter into all the stratagems of unbelief, to find the soul a way of peace in the midst of seas of trouble—this is compassion like a God, that the Holy Spirit should stoop from heaven to become a comforter of disconsolate spirits. What! must He Himself bring the cordial? must He wait upon His sick child and stand by his bed? must He make his bed for him in his affliction? must He carry him in his infirmity? must He breathe continually into him His very breath? Doth the Holy Spirit become a waiting servant of the church? Doth He become a lamp to enlighten? and doth He become a staff on which we may lean? This, I say, should move us to love the Holy Spirit, for we have in all this abundant proofs of His love to us.

Stay not here, beloved, there are larger fields yet beyond, now that we are speaking of the love of the Spirit. Remember how much He loves us when He helpeth our infirmities. Nay, not only doth He help our infirmities, but when we know not what to pray for as we ought He teacheth us how to pray, and when "we ourselves groan within ourselves," then the Spirit Himself maketh intercession for us with groanings which cannot be uttered—groans as we should groan, but more audibly, so that our prayer, which else would have been silent, reaches the ears of Christ, and is then presented before His Father's face. To *help* our infirmities is a mighty instance of love. When God overcomes infirmity altogether, or removes it, there is something very noble, and grand, and sublime in the deed; when He permits the infirmity to remain and yet works with the infirmity, this is tender compassion indeed. When the Saviour heals the lame man you see His Godhead, but when He walketh with the lame man, limping though his gait may be; when He sitteth with the beggar, when He talketh with the publican, when He carrieth the babe in His bosom, then this helping of infirmities is a manifestation of love almost unequalled. Save Christ's bearing our infirmities upon the tree, and our sins in His own body, I know of no greater or more tender instance of divine love than when it is written, "Likewise the Spirit also helpeth our infirmities." Oh, how much you owe to the Spirit when you have been on your knees in prayer! You know, my brethren, what it is to be dull and lifeless there; to groan for a word, and yet you cannot find it; to wish for a word, and yet the very wish is languid; to long to have desires, and yet all the desire you have is a desire that you may be able to desire. Oh, have you not sometimes, when your desires have been kindled, longed to get a grip at the promise by the hand of faith? "Oh," you have said, "if I could but plead the promise, all my necessities would be removed, and all my sorrows would be allayed," but, alas, the promise was beyond your reach. If you touched it with the tip of your finger, you could not grasp it as you desired, you could not plead it, and therefore you came away without the blessing. But when the Spirit has helped our infirmities how have we prayed! Why, there have been times when you and I have so grasped the knocker of the gate of mercy, and have let it fall with such tremendous force, that it seemed as if the very gate itself did shake and totter; there have been seasons when we have laid hold upon the angel, have overcome heaven by prayer, have declared we would not let Jehovah Himself go except He should bless us. We have, and we say it without blasphemy, moved the arm that moves the world. We have brought down upon us the eyes that look upon the universe. All this we have done, not by our own strength, but by the might and by the power of the Spirit; and seeing He has so sweetly enabled us, though we have so often forgotten to thank Him: seeing that He has so graciously assisted us, though we have often taken all the glory to ourselves instead of giving it to Him, must we not admire His love, and must it not be a fearful sin indeed to grieve the Holy Spirit by whom we are sealed?

Another token of the Spirit's love remains, namely, His indwelling in the saints. We sing in one of our hymns,—

"Dost thou not dwell in all the saints?"

We ask a question which can have but one answer. He does dwell in the heart of all God's redeemed and blood-washed people. And what a condescension is this, that He whom the heaven of heavens cannot contain, dwells in thy breast, my brother. That breast often covered with rags, may be a breast often agitated with anxious care and thought, a breast too often defiled with sin, and yet He dwells there. The little narrow heart of man, the Holy Spirit hath made His palace. Though it is but a cottage, a very hovel, and all unholy and unclean, yet doth the Holy Spirit condescend to make the heart of His people His continual abode. Oh, my friends, when I think how often you and I have let the devil in, I wonder the Spirit has not withdrawn from us. The final perseverance of the saints is one of the greatest miracles on record; if fact, it is the sum total of miracles. The perseverance of a saint for a single day is a multitude of miracles of mercy. When you consider that the Spirit is of purer eyes than to behold iniquity, and yet He dwells in the heart where sin often intrudes, a heart out of which comes blasphemies, and murders, and all manner of evil thoughts and concupiscence, what if sometimes He is grieved, and retires and leaves us to ourselves for a season? It is a marvel that He is there at all, for He must be daily grieved with these evil guests, these false traitors, these base intruders who thrust themselves into that little temple which He had honoured with His presence, the temple of the heart of man. I am afraid, dear friends, we are too much in the habit of talking of the love of Jesus, without thinking of the love of the Holy Spirit. Now I would not wish to exalt one person of the Trinity above another, but I do feel this, that because Jesus Christ was a man, bone of our bone, and flesh of our flesh, and therefore there was something tangible in Him that can be seen with the eyes, and handled with the hands, therefore we more readily think of Him, and fix our love on Him, than we do upon the Spirit. But why should it be? Let us love Jesus with all our hearts, and let us love the Holy Spirit too. Let us have songs for Him, gratitude for Him. We do not forget Christ's cross, let us not forget the Spirit's operations. We do not forget what Jesus has done for us, let us always remember what the Spirit does in us. Why, you talk of the love, and grace, and tenderness, and faithfulness of Christ, why do you not say the like of the Spirit? Was ever love like His, that He should visit us? Was ever mercy like His, that He should bear with our ill manners, though constantly repeated by us? Was ever faithfulness like His, that multitudes of sins cannot drive him away? Was ever power like His, that overcometh all our iniquities, and yet leads us safely on, though hosts of foes within and without would rob us of our Christian life?

"Oh, the love of the Spirit I sing,
By whom is redemption applied."

And unto His name be glory for ever and ever.

II. This brings me to the second point. Here we have another reason why *we should not grieve the Spirit*. IT IS BY THE HOLY SPIRIT WE ARE SEALED. "By whom we are sealed unto the day of redemption." I shall be very brief here. The Spirit Himself is expressed as the seal, even as He Himself is directly said to be the pledge of our inheritance. The sealing, I think, has a three-fold meaning. It is a sealing of *attestation* or confirmation. I want to know whether I am truly a child of God. The Spirit itself also beareth witness with my spirit that I am born of God. I have the writings, the title-deeds of the inheritance that is to come—I want to know whether those are valid, whether they are true, or whether they are mere counterfeits written out by that old scribe of hell, Master Presumption and Carnal Security. How am I to know? I look for the seal. After that we have believed on the Son of God, the Father seals us as His children, by the gift of the Holy Ghost. "Now He which hath anointed us is God, who also hath sealed us, and given the earnest of the Spirit in our hearts." No faith is genuine which does not bear the seal of the Spirit. No love, no hope can ever save us, except it be sealed with the Spirit of God, for whatever hath not His seal upon it is spurious. Faith that is unsealed may be a poison, it may be presumption; but faith that is sealed by the Spirit is true, real, genuine faith. Never be content, my dear hearers, unless you are sealed, unless you are sure, by the inward witness and testimony of the Holy Ghost, that you have been begotten again unto a lively hope by the resurrection of Jesus Christ from the dead. It is possible for a man to know infallibly that he is secure of heaven. He may not only hope so, but he may know it beyond a doubt, and he may know it thus,—by being able with the eye of faith to see the seal, the broad stamp of the Holy Spirit set upon His own character and experience. It is a seal of attestation.

In the next place, it is a sealing of *appropriation*. When men put their mark upon an article, it is to show that it is their own. The farmer brands his tools that they may not be stolen. They are his. The shepherd marks his sheep that they may be recognized as belonging to his flock. The king himself puts his broad arrow upon everything that is his property. So the Holy Spirit puts the broad arm of God upon the hearts of all His people. He seals us. "Thou shalt be mine," saith the Lord, "in the day when I make up My jewels." And then the Spirit puts God's seal upon us to signify that we are God's reserved inheritance—His peculiar people, the portion in which His soul delighteth.

But, again, by sealing is meant *preservation*. Men seal up that which they wish to have preserved, and when a document is sealed it becomes valid henceforth. Now, it is by the Spirit of God that the Christian is sealed, that he is kept, he is preserved, sealed unto the day of redemption—sealed until Christ comes fully to redeem the bodies of His saints by raising them from the dead, and fully to redeem the world by purging it from sin, and making it a kingdom unto Himself in righteousness. We shall hold on our way; we shall be saved. The chosen seed cannot be lost, they must be brought home at last, but how? By the sealing of the Spirit. Apart from that they perish; they are undone. When the last general fire shall blaze out, everything that has not the seal of the Spirit on it shall be burned up. But the men upon whose forehead is the seal shall be preserved. They shall be safe, "amid the wreck of matter, and the crash of worlds." Their spirits, mounting above the flames, shall dwell with Christ eternally, and with that same seal in their forehead upon Mount Zion, they shall sing the everlasting song of gratitude and praise. I say this is the second reason why we should love the Spirit and why we should not grieve Him.

III. I come now to the third part of my discourse, namely, THE GRIEVING OF THE SPIRIT. How may we grieve Him,—what will be the sad result of grieving Him—if we have grieved Him, how may we bring Him back again? *How may we grieve the Spirit?* I am now, mark you, speaking of those who love the Lord Jesus Christ. The Spirit of God is in your heart, and it is very, very easy indeed to grieve Him. Sin is as easy as it is wicked. You may grieve Him by impure thoughts. He cannot bear sin. If you indulge in lascivious expressions, or if even you allow imagination to dote upon any lascivious act, or if your heart goes after covetousness, if you set your heart upon anything that is evil, the Spirit of God will be grieved, for thus I hear Him speaking of Himself. "I love this man, I want to have his heart, and yet he is entertaining these filthy lusts. His thoughts, instead of running after me, and after Christ, and after the Father, are running after the temptations that are in the world through lust." And then His Spirit is grieved. He sorrows in His soul because He knows what sorrow these things must bring to our souls. We grieve Him yet more if we indulge in outward acts of sin. Then is He sometimes so grieved that He takes His flight for a season, for the dove will not dwell in our hearts if we take loathsome carrion in there. A cleanly being is the dove, and we must not strew the place which the dove frequents with filth and mire, if we do He will fly elsewhere. If we commit sin, if we openly bring disgrace upon our religion, if we tempt others to go into iniquity by our evil example, it is not long before the Holy Spirit will begin to grieve. Again, if we neglect prayer, if our closet door is cobwebbed, if we forget to read the Scriptures, if the leaves of our Bible are almost stuck together by neglect, if we never seek to do any good in the world, if we live merely for ourselves and not to Christ, then the Holy Spirit will be grieved, for thus He saith, "They have forsaken Me, they have left the fountain of waters, they have hewn unto themselves broken cisterns." I think I now see the Spirit of God grieving, when you are sitting down to read a novel and there is your Bible unread. Perhaps you take down some book of travels, and you forget that you have got a more precious book of travels in the Acts of the Apostles, and in the story of your blessed Lord and Master. You have no time for prayer, but the Spirit sees you very active about worldly things, and having many hours to spare for relaxation and amusement. And then He is grieved because He sees that you love worldly things better than you love Him. His spirit is grieved within Him; take care that He does not go away from you, for it will be a pitiful thing for you if He leaves you to yourself. Again, ingratitude tends to grieve Him. Nothing cuts a man to the heart more, than after having done his utmost for another, he turns round and repays him with ingratitude or insult. If we do not want to be thanked, at least we do love to know that there is thankfulness in the heart upon which we have conferred a boon, and when the Holy Spirit looks into our soul and sees little love to Christ, no gratitude to Him for all He has done for us, then is He grieved.

Again, the Holy Spirit is exceedingly grieved by our unbelief. When we distrust the promise He hath given and applied, when we doubt the power or the affection of our blessed Lord, then the Spirit saith within Himself—"They doubt My fidelity; they distrust My power; they say Jesus is not able to save unto the uttermost"; thus again is the Spirit grieved. Oh, I wish the Spirit had an advocate here this morning, that could speak in better terms than I can. I have a theme that overmasters me, I seem to grieve for Him; but I cannot make you grieve, nor tell out the grief I feel. In my own soul I keep saying,

"Oh, this is just what you have done—you have grieved Him." Let me make a full and frank confession even before you all. I know that too often, I as well as you have grieved the Holy Spirit. Much within us has made that sacred dove to mourn, and my marvel is, that He has not taken His flight from us and left us utterly to ourselves.

Now suppose the Holy Spirit is grieved, what is the effect produced upon us? When the Spirit is grieved first, He bears with us. He is grieved again and again, and again and again, and still He bears with it all. But at last, His grief becomes so excessive, that He says, "I will suspend My operations; I will begone; I will leave life behind Me, but My own actual presence I will take away." And when the Spirit of God goes away from the soul and suspends all His operations, what a miserable state we are in. He suspends His instructions; we read the Word, we cannot understand it; we go to our commentaries, they cannot tell us the meaning; we fall on our knees and ask to be taught, but we get no answer, we learn nothing. He suspends His comfort; we used to dance, like David before the ark, and now we sit like Job in the ash-pit, and scrape our ulcers with a potsherd. There was a time when His candle shone round about us, but now He is gone; He has left us in the blackness of darkness. Now, He takes from us all spiritual power. Once we could do all things; now we can do nothing. We could slay the Philistines, and lay them heaps upon heaps, but now Delilah can deceive us, and our eyes are put out and we are made to grind in the mill. We go preaching, and there is no pleasure in preaching, and no good follows it. We go to our tract distributing, and our Sunday-school, we might almost as well be at home. There is the machinery there, but there is no love. There is the intention to do good, or perhaps not even that, but alas! there is no power to accomplish the intention. The Lord has withdrawn Himself, His light, His joy, His comfort, His spiritual power, all are gone. And then all our graces flag. Our graces are much like the flower called the *Hydrangia*, when it has plenty of water it blooms, but as soon as moisture fails, the leaves drop down at once. And so when the Spirit goes away, faith shuts up its flowers; no perfume is exhaled. Then the fruit of our love begins to rot and drops from the tree; then the sweet buds of our hope become frostbitten, and they die. Oh, what a sad thing it is to lose the Spirit. Have you never, my brethren, been on your knees and have been conscious that the Spirit of God was not with you, and what awful work it has been to groan, and cry, and sigh, and yet go away again, and no light to shine upon the promises, not so much as a ray of light through the chink of the dungeon. All forsaken, forgotten, and forlorn, you are almost driven to despair. You sing with Cowper:—

"What peaceful hours I once enjoyed,
   How sweet their memory still!
But they have left an aching void,
   The world can never fill.

Return, Thou sacred dove, return,
   Sweet messenger of rest,
I hate the sins that made Thee mourn,
   And drove Thee from my breast.

The dearest idol I have known,
   Whate'er that idol be,
Help me to tear it from its throne,
   And worship only Thee."

Ah! sad enough it is to have the Spirit drawn from us. But, my brethren, I am about to say something with the utmost charity, which, perhaps, may look severe, but, nevertheless, I must say it. The churches of the present day are very much in the position of those who have grieved the Spirit of God; for the Spirit deals with churches just as it does with individuals. Of these late years how little has God wrought in the midst of His churches. Throughout England, at least some four or five years ago, an almost universal torpor had fallen upon the visible body of Christ. There was a little action, but it was spasmodic; there was no real vitality. Oh! how few sinners were brought to Christ, how empty had our places of worship become; our prayer-meetings were dwindling away to nothing, and our church meetings were mere matters of farce. You know right well that this is the case with many London churches to this day; and there be some that do not mourn about it. They go up to their accustomed place, and the minister prays, and the people either sleep with their eyes or else with their hearts, and they go out, and there is never a soul saved. The pool of baptism is seldom stirred; but the saddest part of all is this, the churches are willing to have it so. They are not earnest to get a revival of religion. We have been doing something, the church at large has been doing something. I will not just now put my finger upon what the sin is, but there has been something done which has driven the Spirit of God from us. He is grieved, and He is gone. He is present with us here, I thank His name, He is still visible in our midst. He has not left us. Though we have been as unworthy as others, yet has He given us a long outpouring of His presence. These five years or more, we have had a revival which is not to be exceeded by any revival upon the face of the earth. Without cries or shoutings, without fallings down or swooning, steadily God adds to this church numbers upon numbers, so that your minister's heart is ready to break with very joy when he thinks how manifestly the Spirit of God is with us. But brethren, we must not be content with this; we want to see the Spirit poured out on all churches. Look at the great gatherings that there were in St. Paul's, and Westminster Abbey, and Exeter Hall, and other places, how was it that no good was done, or so very little? I have watched with anxious eye, and I have never from that day forth heard but of one conversion, and that in St. James' Hall, from all these services. Strange it seems. The blessing may have come in larger measure than we know, but not in so large a measure as we might have expected, if the Spirit of God had been present with all the ministers. Oh, would that we may live to see greater things than we have ever seen yet. Go home to your houses, humble yourselves before God, ye members of Christ's church, and cry aloud that He will visit His church, and that He would open the windows of heaven and pour out His grace upon His thirsty hill of Zion, that nations may be born in a day, that sinners may be saved by thousands—that Zion may travail and may bring forth children. Oh! there are signs and tokens of a coming revival. We have heard but lately of a good work among the Ragged School boys of St. Giles's, and our soul has been glad on account of that; and the news from Ireland comes to us like good tidings, not from a far country, but from a sister province of the kingdom. Let us cry aloud to the Holy Spirit, who is certainly grieved with His church, and let us purge our churches of everything that is contrary to His Word and to sound doctrine, and then the Spirit will return, and His power shall be manifest.

And now, in conclusion, there may be some of you here who have lost the visible presence of Christ with you; who have in fact so grieved the Spirit that He has gone. It is a mercy for you to know that the Spirit of God never leaves His people finally; He leaves them for chastisement, but not for damnation. He sometimes leaves them that they may get good by knowing their own weakness, but He will not leave them finally to perish. Are you in a state of backsliding, declension, and coldness? Hearken to me for a moment, and God bless the words. Brother, stay not a moment in a condition so perilous; be not easy for a single second in the absence of the Holy Ghost. I beseech you use every means by which that Spirit may be brought back to you. Once more, let me tell you distinctly what the means are. Search out for the sin that has grieved the Spirit, give it up, slay that sin upon the spot; repent with tears and sighs; continue in prayer, and never rest satisfied until the Holy Ghost comes back to you. Frequent an earnest ministry, get much with earnest saints, but above all, be much in prayer to God, and let your daily cry be, "Return, return, O Holy Spirit return, and dwell in my soul." Oh, I beseech you be not content till that prayer is heard, for you have become weak as water, and faint and empty while the Spirit has been away from you. Oh! it may be there are some here this morning with whom the Spirit has been striving during the past week. Oh yield to Him, resist Him not; grieve Him not, but yield to Him. Is he saying to you now "Turn to Christ?" Listen to Him, obey Him, He moves you. Oh, I beseech you, do not despise Him. Have you resisted Him many a time, then take care you do not again, for there may come a last time when the Spirit may say, "I will go unto my rest, I will not return unto Him, the ground is accursed, it shall be given up to barrenness." Oh! hear the word of the gospel, ere ye separate, for the Spirit speaketh effectually to you now in this short sentence—"Repent and be converted everyone of you, that your sins may be blotted out when the times of refreshing shall come from the presence of the Lord," and hear this solemn sentence, "He that believeth in the Lord Jesus, and is baptized, shall be saved; but he that believeth not shall be damned." May the Lord grant that we may not grieve the Holy Spirit. Amen.

THE CHILD OF LIGHT AND THE WORKS OF DARKNESS

"Have no fellowship with the unfruitful works of darkness, but rather reprove them."—Ephesians v. 11.

SINS, especially the grosser vices, are "works of darkness." They delight in concealment, they are not fit to be seen, they flourish in the darkness of the unrenewed heart, they are most fully maintained in the ignorance of a soul that is without the knowledge of the ever-blessed God. They are also works of darkness, because those who follow them have a sad life of it, after all; they are not only dark as to knowledge, but they are dark as to comfort as well. There is no true light, no real joy, in sin: "The wages of sin is death." And they are works of darkness, too, because they tend to further darkness; the man who pursues them goes from blackness to a deeper blackness, and in the end his portion will be darkness unbroken by a ray of hope, "the blackness of darkness for ever."

You know that darkness stands for the powers of evil, as light is the fit emblem of the holiness of God, and of his infinite goodness and purifying grace. Well, now, whether we who are the children of light are busy or not, it is quite certain that children of darkness work. They are always working; there is no cessation in their activity. Master Latimer used to say that the most diligent bishop in England was the devil, for whoever did not visit his diocese the devil was always visiting his people. His plough never rusts in the furrow, his sword never rests in its scabbard. The powers of darkness cannot be blamed for their slothfulness; is there ever a moment in which they are not busy and active? Lukewarmness never steals over the powers of darkness. The work of the night goes on horribly, there is no pause to it; therefore, let us who are of the day work, too. God help us to counteract the working of the silent, hidden leaven of sin by our own struggling to produce in the world a better tone of thought and feeling, and by spreading the knowledge of God's grace, and everything which will increase reverence to God and love to men!

The text speaks of the works of darkness, and it calls them "unfruitful." So they are; for sin is sterile. It produces its like, and multiplies itself; but as for any fruit that is good, any fruit that can elevate and benefit men, any fruit which God can accept, and which you and I ought to desire, sin is barren as the desert sand. Nothing good can come of it. Every now and then, we hear it said, "Well, you know, on this occasion, we must set aside the higher laws of equity, because just now it is imperatively necessary that such and such a policy should be pursued." But it is never right either for an individual or for a nation to do wrong; and the most fruitful policy for men and for nations is to do that which will bear the light. The works of the light are fruitful works, rich and sweet, and fit to be gathered, pleasant to God and profitable to men; but the works of darkness are fruitless, they come to nothing, they produce no good result. They are like the apples of Sodom, which may appear fair to the eye, but he that plucks them shall find that he has nothing but ashes in his hand. O you who are performing works of darkness, know that no good fruit will come of all your work! You can have nothing that is worth having as the result of all your toil.

My text, which I have just introduced to you by these few remarks, demands our attention as a great practical lesson to Christians: "Have no fellowship with the unfruitful works of darkness, but rather reprove them." Those works of darkness which are horrible and unmentionable, you cannot have fellowship with them. They produce an evil very potent to all mankind; of course, you will avoid them, pass not by them, and flee from them; but you must also keep clear of those works of darkness which apparently seem to be colourless, and to produce no particularly evil effect. You, as a Christian man, have to live a solemn, earnest, serious life. To you,—

"Life is real, life is earnest;"

and there are works of darkness which do not seem to be as bad as others, but are simply frivolous, foolish, and time-wasting, have no fellowship with them. These unfruitful works of darkness are to be avoided by you as much as those which are most defiling. Hear this, ye Christian men, and God help you to obey the command!

In coming to the consideration of our text, let us enquire, first, *What is forbidden?* Fellowship with "the unfruitful works of darkness." Secondly, let us ask, *What is commanded?* "Reprove them;" and thirdly, let us consider, *Why are we thus to act?*

I. First, then, WHAT IS FORBIDDEN? "Have no fellowship with the unfruitful works of darkness." We can have fellowship with them in a great number of ways.

Notice that the text does not say, "Have no fellowship with wicked men; have no dealings with men who are not converted;" for then we must needs go out of the world. Many of us are obliged to earn our daily bread in the midst of men whom we certainly would not choose for our companions. Many of you, I know, are forced every day to hear language which is disgusting to you; and you are brought into contact with modes of procedure which sadden your gracious spirits. Our Saviour does not pray that you should be taken out of the world, but that you should be preserved from the evil of it. If you are what you profess to be, you are the salt of the earth; and salt is not meant to be kept in a box, but to be well rubbed into the meat to keep it from putrefaction. We are not to shut ourselves up as select companies of men seeking only our own edification and enjoyment, but it is intended that we should mingle with the ungodly so far as our duties demand. We are forced to do so; it is the Lord's intent that we should, so that we may act as salt among them. God grant that the salt may never lose its savour, and that the unsavoury world may never destroy the pungency of the piety of God's people! With evil men, then, we must have some kind of fellowship, but with their works we are to have no fellowship. In order to avoid this evil, let us see what is here forbidden. "Have no fellowship with the unfruitful works of darkness."

And first, dear friends, we have fellowship with the unfruitful works of darkness *by personally committing the sins so described.* "Be not deceived; God is not mocked." After all, a man must be judged by his life. If you do that which is holy and righteous and gracious, you have fellowship with the holy and the righteous and the gracious; but if you do that which is unclean and dishonest, you have fellowship with the unclean and the dishonest. The Lord will, at the last, put us among those whom we are most like; in that day when he shall separate the people gathered before him as a shepherd divideth the sheep from the goats, the sheep will be put with the sheep, and the goats with the goats. If you have lived like the wicked, you will die like the wicked, and be damned like the wicked. It is only those who live the life of the righteous who can hope that they shall die the death of the righteous. I, who preach to you with all my heart the doctrine of the grace of God, do, nevertheless, just as boldly remind you that the grace of God brings forth fruit in the life; and where it is really in the heart, there will be in the life that which betokens its presence. If you and I are drunkards, if we can do a dishonest action, if we are guilty of falsehood, if we are covetous (I need not go over the list of all those evil things), then we belong to the class of men who delight in such practices, and with them we must go for ever. We are having fellowship with them by doing as they do, and we shall have an awful fellowship with them at the last by suffering as they shall suffer. God make us holy, then! The very name of Jesus signifies that He will save His people *from* their sins, and He saves them from their sins by their ceasing to commit those sins that others do. His own word is, "Be ye holy, for I am holy." "Be ye clean that bear the vessels of the Lord." Nothing more dishonours Him than to have a following of unclean men—men who refuse to be washed, and resolve not to quit their old sins. Great sinners, ay, the biggest sinners out of hell, are welcome to come to Christ in order to be cleansed from their sin, and set free from it. He keeps a hospital wherein He receives the most sick of all the sick, but it is that He may heal them; and if men do not wish to be healed, but count the marks of their disease to be beauty-spots, if they love their sins, and hug them to their bosoms, then thus saith the Lord to them, "Ye shall die in your sins." God save all His professing people from this form of fellowship with the works of darkness!

Next, we can have fellowship with the unfruitful works of darkness *by teaching wrong-doing, either by plain word or by just inference.* Any man whose teaching tends towards unholiness, who directly or indirectly, either by overt phrase or by natural inference, leads another man into sin, is *particeps criminis*, a partaker of the crime. If you teach your children what they ought never to learn, if you teach your fellow-workmen what they had better never know, and if they improve upon your lessons, and go much farther than you ever meant that they should, if they proceed from folly to crime, you are a partaker of their sins, you have fellowship with the unfruitful works of darkness. And, believe me, there is nothing more awful than for any minister of Christ to have fellowship with the unfruitful works of darkness by keeping back any part of the truth, by withholding any of the precepts of God's Word, or by denying the terrible and eternal consequences of sin. There is nothing more dreadful than the end of such a man must be; I think that I would sooner die, and be judged of God as a murderer of men's bodies, than have to go before the judgment seat charged with being the murderer of their souls, through having kept back helpful truth, or insinuated destructive and erroneous doctrines. Yes, we can easily have fellowship with the unfruitful works of darkness in that way.

Further, there are some who will have fellowship with the unfruitful works of darkness *by constraining, commanding, or tempting others to sin.* How much harm is often done in this respect by want of thought! What you do by another, you do yourself. If you command another to do for you what you know to be wrong,—I will not say that the other is right in the compliance,—but I will say that you are wrong in having given the command. Let fathers, let masters, let mistresses, see to it that they never command others to do what God has not commanded them to do.

Sometimes, it is not actually a command that you give, but you put the person into such a position of temptation and trial, that the probabilities are that that person will do wrong; and if it be so, in the sight of God, you will have to share the guilt of that wrong. When a master pays his servant less wages than he ought to have,—if that servant commits a theft, I condemn the theft, but I cannot clear the master who put the man into a position in which he must have been sorely tempted to take something more to make up that of which he had been defrauded. I do not excuse the theft by him who committed it; but still I cannot screen the one who put the other where in all probability, he would be driven to commit a dishonest act. If I place a man in a position where it is most probable, seeing that human nature is what it is, that he will commit a sin, if I have wantonly put him there, or put him there for my own profit and gain, I shall be a partaker of the sin if he falls. If you are a nurse girl, and you take those little children, and set them on the edge of the cliff, letting them go to the very brink of it, and they fall over, you cannot clear yourself of blame in the matter. It may be that you told the children not to go too close to the edge; but then you put them where you might be morally certain that, as children, they would go there, and you are responsible for all that happens to them. So, if I set another in a place where I might be able to stand myself, but might be pretty sure that he could not, I shall be a partaker of his sin. "Well, I drink my glass of wine," says one. Yes, and apparently it does you no harm whatever; you have never been excited by it, and you feel grateful for it; but there is another man who could not do as you have done without becoming a drunkard, and by your example he is made a drunkard, and helped to remain so. The practice may be safe enough for you; but if it is ruinous to him, take heed lest you be a partaker of his unfruitful works of darkness. It will require great care, and some self-denial, so to act towards others that we can say when we go to bed at night, " If any man has done a wrong thing to-day, it is not because I have set him the example." Oh, that we might all repent of other people's sins! Did you ever repent of them? "I have had enough to do to repent of my own sins," says one. But these sins of which I am speaking are your own, as well as other people's; if you have led others into the way of committing the sin, or have put any pressure upon them to lead them to commit sin, you are having fellowship with the unfruitful works of darkness.

Sometimes, men get to be partakers of other's sins *by provoking them.* When fathers provoke their children to anger, who has the chief blame of that sin? Surely the father has. And when, sometimes, persons purposely play upon the infirmities of others to provoke them, are they not more to blame than the offenders? I am sure that it is so. I have known some try to draw others out when they have known their propensity to go beyond the truth; they have, for mirth's sake, led them on, and tempted them to lie. Who is the greater sinner of the two in such a case as that? I am no casuist, and shall not attempt to weight actions; but I am able to say this most assuredly, that, if you provoke another to anger, that anger is in part your sin; if you wantonly incite another to sin by daring him to do it, or by any other method of tempting him to do wrong, you

yourself shall share the accusation at the last great day.

Further, friends, we can be partakers of the unfruitful works of darkness *by counselling them.* There are some men who will not do the wrong things themselves, but they will give evil advice to others, and so lead them into iniquity. We have known persons act the part of the cat with the monkey; they have used some other hand to draw the chestnuts from the fire. They were not themselves burned, but then they really did the deed by their agents. Theirs was the advice, theirs the wit, theirs the shrewd hardheadedness by which the evil was done; and though they did not appear in the transaction, yet God saw them, and He will reckon with them in the day of account.

I feel very jealous of myself when I have to give advice; and that experience often falls to my lot. A person will plead, "Well, if I do right in such a case as this, I shall remain in poverty, or I shall lose my situation. If I follow out my conscientious convictions to the full, who is to provide for me?" And, you know, the temptation is to feel, "Well, now, really we must not be too severe in our judgment upon this poor soul; can we not agree with the evident wish of the person asking the advice, moderate the law of God, or in some way make a loophole, and say, 'Well, it will not be right; but still, you see, *under the circumstances,* ——.'" Now, I never dare do that, because, if wrong be done, and I have counselled it, I shall be a partaker in the wrong. You who are called to give advice to others—as many of you may be by reason of your age and experience,—always give straight advice; never let any mean learn *policy* from you. Of all things in this world, that which often commends itself to certain "prudent" men, but which, nevertheless, never ought to commend itself to Christian men, is the idea of doing a little evil in order to obtain a great good; in fact, believing ourselves to be wiser than the commands of God, and imagining that strict truth and probity and integrity would, after all, not be the best thing for men, even though God has so ordained. Do let us so guide others that we shall have no fellowship with the unfruitful works of darkness.

But we may have fellowship with the unfruitful works of darkness *by consenting to them, and conniving at them.* For instance, you live in a house where there is a great deal of evil going on, and you yourself keep clear of it. So far so good; but you never protest against it, you have been altogether silent about it. "Mum," has been the word with you; and, sometimes, when they come home from a place of ill resort, and they tell you about the "fun" they have had, you laugh with the rest, or if you do not laugh, at any rate you have not decidedly expressed your disapproval. You do disapprove of the evil; in secret, you even pray against it; but nobody knows that it is so, the wrongdoers especially are not aware that it is so; in fact, they fancy that, as they treat leniently your pursuit of religion, though they think it cant, so you treat leniently their pursuit of sin, though in your heart of hearts you believe that pursuit to be evil. Our Lord commands us to clear ourselves of all conniving at sin, —not with harshness, not with denunciation, and in an unkind spirit,—but with a mild, gentle, but still powerful, honest rebuke. We must say, especially if we are parents, or masters, or persons having much influence with others, "Oh, do not this abominable thing! I cannot have any share in this evil, even by silently tolerating it. How I wish that you would give it up! I entreat you, come out of this Sodom; escape for your lives!" A few more loving home testimonies for God, and who can tell but that the husband may be converted, and the son may be led to the Saviour? But for want of this personal witness-bearing among Christians, I am afraid that the Church of God comes to be paralyzed, and much of her power and usefulness is taken from her. Do not let us connive or wink at sin in any case whatever.

Far be it from us also ever to have fellowship with the unfruitful works of darkness *by commending or applauding sin, or seeming to agree with it.* We must let all men know that, whatever they may do which has about it an ill savour, it has an ill savour to us, and we cannot endure it, but must ever protest against it, lest we be partakers of the sin of others. O dear friends, I believe that the great lack of the church just now is holiness! The great want of the church is non-conformity; I mean, nonconformity to the world. We must endeavour to bring back the strictness of the Puritan times, and somewhat more. Everybody is so liberal and takes such latitude, nowadays, that in some quarters it is impossible to tell which is the church and which is the world. I have even heard some ministers propose that there should be no church distinct from the congregation, but that everybody should be a church-member, without the slightest examination, or even a profession of conversion. It is supposed that people are now so generally good that we may take them indiscriminately, and that they will make a church quite good enough for the Lord Jesus Christ! Ah, me! that is not according to Christ's mind, and that is not Christ's teaching. God's call to this age, as to all that went before, is, "Come out from among them, and be ye separate, saith the Lord, and touch not the unclean thing; and I will receive you, and will be a Father unto you, and ye shall be my sons and daughters, saith the Lord Almighty." Bear your protest, my brethren and my sisters, against everything that is unrighteous and unholy, everything that is not Godlike and Christlike, and let your lives be such that men shall not need to ask to whom you belong, whether to God or to the devil, but they shall see at once that you are the people of the ever-living and blessed God.

This, then, is what is forbidden: "Have no fellowship with the unfruitful works of darkness."

II. The time flies so fast, that I can only very briefly answer the second question, WHAT IS COMMANDED? "Reprove them." Our life's business in the world comprehends this among our other Christian duties, the reproving of the unfruitful works of darkness.

First, *we are to rebuke sin.* I find that the word which is here rendered "reprove" is that which is used concerning the Holy Spirit: "When He is come, He will reprove the world of sin, of righteousness, and of judgment." We are, therefore, so to live as to let light in upon men's consciences, that we may rebuke them for their sin.

But we are also to try to let the sinners themselves see the sinfulness of their sin, to let the light in upon the sin, and, by God's grace, so to reprove them as *to convict them of sin,* to make them feel, from the testimony of God's people, that sin is an evil and a bitter thing, and that their course of conduct is that evil thing. The light has come into the world on purpose that the darkness may know that it is darkness, and that God's light may overcome and disperse

it. We are not to quench our light and mingle with others who are in the dark; but to unveil our lamps, and let the light that is in them so shine that the darkness shall thereby be reproved. I do not say, brothers and sisters, that we are to go through the world wearing surly faces, looking grim as death, perpetually promulgating the law, and saying, "Thou shalt not do this, and thou shalt not do that;" but, cheerful as we must be with the love of God in our hearts, we shall prove to men that the freest and the happiest life is a life of holiness, a life of consecration to God, and that, together with the faithful testimony of our lips, shall be a reproving of the sin that is in the world. The very existence of a true believer is the reproof of unbelief; the existence of an honest man is the reproof of knavery; the existence of a godly man is the best reproof of ungodliness; but when that existence is backed up by verbal testimony, and by a consistent example, then the command in the text is fulfilled, for we are reproving the unfruitful works of darkness.

III. Thirdly, let us ask, WHY ARE WE TO ACT THUS? Why are we sent into the world, dear friends, to reprove sin, and not to follow in its track? The reasons are given in this very chapter.

First, *because we are God's dear children, and therefore we must be imitators of him.* Thou, a child of God, and having fellowship with the unfruitful works of darkness? Thou, a child of God, imitating the lost and fallen world? Thou, a child of God, submitting to the influences of the devil, and his filthy crew? Far be it from thee; ask thy Father to make thee holy as He is holy. To that end wast thou born and sent into the world; entreat thy Father to help thee to fulfil the very purpose of thy being.

Next, remember that *we who are believers have an inheritance in the kingdom of God.* We are heirs of God, joint-heirs with Jesus Christ. Well, then, shall we have fellowship with those who have no inheritance in this kingdom? Remember what we read just now: "For this ye know, that no whoremonger, nor unclean person, nor covetous man, who is an idolater, hath any inheritance in the kingdom of Christ and of God." And wilt thou, who hast a part in this inheritance, make common lot with such people? Oh, be it far from thee! Heir of glory, wilt thou be a companion of the heirs of wrath? Joint-heir with Christ, wilt thou sit on the drunkard's bench, or trill an unclean song with the profane? Are their places of amusement fit for thee to frequent? Are their dens of iniquity haunts for thee? Up and away from the dwellings of these wicked men, lest thou be destroyed in their destruction!

A little further down in the chapter, in the seventh and eighth verses, we read: "Be not ye therefore partakers with them. For *ye were sometimes darkness, but now are ye light in the Lord.*" What! has a marvellous conversion happened to you? Have you been turned from darkness to light? Are you really new creatures in Christ Jesus, or is it all a lie? For, if indeed you have been twice-born, if you have had a resurrection from among the dead, if a second creation has been wrought in you, how can you go and live with these dead men, and mingle with these who know not the life of God? Unless your profession is nothing but a farce or a fraud, grace will so constrain you that you must come out, and refuse to have fellowship with the unfruitful works of darkness.

The text describes these works as being unfruitful,

and you read in the ninth verse, "*The fruit of the Spirit is in all goodness and righteousness and truth.*" Now, if you are to bear the fruits of the Spirit, what fellowship can you have with the unfruitful works of darkness? The two things are opposed to one another. You fruit-bearing trees, are you going to join in affinity with these cumber-grounds that soon must be cut down, and cast into the fire? What! will you interlace your vine branches with these fig trees that have leaves upon them, but no fruit, and upon which no fruit will ever grow, for they are under the curse of God? No, it must not be so. People of God, serve Him, and come away from those who render Him no service, but who rather seek to pull down His holy temple, and to destroy His name and influence from among the sons of men!

The apostle gives us one more reason why we should have no fellowship with the unfruitful works of darkness: "*for it is a shame even to speak of those things which are done of them in secret.*" What! shall we have fellowship with things of which we are ashamed even to speak? Yet I have to say it, and to say it to my own sorrow and horror, I have known professors to have fellowship with things that I dare not even think of now. They have been found out at length; some of them were never found out till after they were dead. What a life to lead,—to sit with God's people at the communion table, to talk even to others about the way of salvation, yet all the while living in the practice of secret sin! Why, surely, it were better to get into prison at once than to be always afraid of being apprehended; to go up and down the world making a profession of religion, and yet to be acting a lie all the while, and living in constant fear of being found out! Whatever sin we may fall into, God save us from hypocrisy, and make us honest and straightforward in all things! Shall we, then, go and have fellowship with things of which we should be ashamed even to speak? God forbid!

I am afraid that I am speaking many truths that you will regard as having nothing in them that is comfortable to you; but, brothers and sisters, can I help it? Can it be avoided? If we are to make full proof of our ministry, and preach all the truth to you, must we not take every passage of God's Word, whether it be of rebuke or of comfort, in its due season? To myself, the effect of thinking over this subject is just this. I have cried, "Lord, have mercy upon me." I have fled again to the cross of Christ. I have sought anew for an anointing of the Holy Spirit that I might not in anything have fellowship with the unfruitful works of darkness; and if my discourse has that effect upon you, it will do you great service. Oh, do ask the Lord to make our outward lives more thoroughly pure and true! Give me a little church of really gracious, devoted, upright, godly men, and I will be glad to minister to them, and I shall expect God to bless them. But give me a large church consisting of thousands,—if there are in it many whose lives, if they were known, would disgust a man of God, and whose lives, being known to the Spirit of God, are a grief to Him, why, then the blessing must be withheld! We may preach our hearts out, and wear ourselves to death in all kinds of holy service; but, with an Achan in the camp, Israel cannot win the victory. I beseech you, therefore, search and look. One pair of eyes, two pairs of eyes, in the pastorate, and the eyes of the elders and deacons of the church, can never suffice to watch over such a company as this is. The Lord watch over you, and may you have a mutual oversight of one another; and above all, may each one exercise daily watchfulness over his own heart and life! Thus, beloved brethren and sisters in Christ, I leave the text with you, praying God to bless it: "Have no fellowship with the unfruitful works of darkness, but rather reprove them."

Now, if any here are living in fellowship with those unfruitful works of darkness, I pray them to escape for their lives from them. May they fly to Christ, who alone can save them; and when they have once found healing through His wounds, and life through His death, then let them pray to be kept from all sin, that they may lead a holy and gracious life to the glory of Him who has washed them in His own most precious blood. The Lord send a blessing, for His dear Son's sake! Amen.

ALWAYS, AND FOR ALL THINGS

"Giving thanks always for all things unto God and the Father in the name of our Lord Jesus Christ."—Ephesians v. 20.

THE position of our text in the Epistle is worthy of observation. It follows the precept with regard to sacred song, in which believers are bidden to speak to themselves and one another in psalms and hymns and spiritual songs, singing and making melody in their hearts to the Lord. If they cannot be always singing they are always to maintain the spirit of song. If they must of necessity desist at intervals from outward expressions of praise, they ought never to refrain from inwardly giving thanks. The apostle having touched upon the act of singing in public worship, here points out the essential part of it, which lies not in classic music and thrilling harmonies but in the melody of the heart. Thanksgiving is the soul of all acceptable singing.

Note also that this verse immediately precedes the apostle's exhortations to believers concerning the common duties of ordinary life. The saints are to give thanks to God always, and then to fulfil their duties to their fellow men. The apostle writes, "Submitting yourselves one to another in the fear of God," and then he adds the various branches of holy walking which belong to wives and to husbands, to children and to parents, to servants and to masters; so that it would seem that thanksgiving is the preface to a holy life, the foundation of obedience, the vestibule of sanctity. He who would serve God must begin by praising God, for a grateful heart is the mainspring of obedience. We must offer the salt of gratitude with the sacrifice of obedience; our lives should be anointed with the precious oil of thankfulness. As soldiers march to music, so while we walk in the paths of righteousness we should keep step to the notes of thanksgiving. Larks sing as they mount, so should we magnify the Lord for His mercies while we are winging our way to heaven.

My text is a very appropriate one for this cold morning, when wind and snow conspire against our comfort. Let it peep up like the golden cup of the crocus out of the wintry waste. When the weather is unusually dull and dreary we should resolve to set a stout heart against the pelting storm, and determine that if we shiver in body we will at least be warm in heart. Our thanksgiving is not a swallow which is gone with the summer. The birds within our bosom sing all the year round, and on such a morning as this their song is doubly welcome. The fire of gratitude will help to warm us—heap on the big logs of loving memories. No cold shall freeze the genial current of soul, our praise shall flow on when brooks and rivers are bound in chains of ice. Let us see which among us can best rejoice in the Lord in ill weathers.

This morning I shall ask you to think over *the pleasant duty prescribed;* then I shall lead you to think of *its spiritual prerequisites,* or what is necessary to help a man to give thanks always for all things; and we will close by dwelling upon *the eminent excellencies of the duty,* or rather of the privilege which is here described.

I. First, let us think of the PLEASANT DUTY which is here both prescribed and described. Think *what it is—giving thanks.* By this is meant the emotion of gratitude and the expression of it either by song, by grateful speech, by the thankful look, which means far more than words can express, or by any other method. We have sometimes been so overcome by the devout emotion of gratitude to God for His mercy that we could not help but weep; and strange it is that the same sluices which furnish vent for our sorrows also supply a channel for the overflow of our joys. We may weep to God's praise if we feel it to be most natural. We are to give thanks in our spirit, feeling not only resigned, acquiescent, and content, but grateful for all that God does to us and for us. We are bound to show this gratitude by our actions, for obedience is at once the most sincere and the most acceptable method of giving thanks. To go about irksome and laborious duty cheerfully is to thank God; to bear sickness and pain patiently, because it is according to His will, is to thank God; to sympathize with suffering saints for love of Jesus is to bless God; and to love the cause of God, and to defend it for Christ's sake, is to thank God. The angels, when they praise God, not only sing "Hallelujah, hallelujah," but they obey, "doing His commandments, hearkening to the voice of His word." We must give thanks to God in every shape that shall be expressive of our hearts and suitable to the occasion; and although changing the mode, we may thus continue without cessation to give thanks unto God, even the Father.

Beloved, after all it is but a light thing to render to our heavenly Father our poor thanks, after He has given us our lives, maintained us in being, saved us our souls through the precious redemption of Jesus Christ, given us to be His children, and made us heirs of eternal glory. What are our thanks in the presence of all these priceless favours? Why, if we gave our God a thousand lives, and could spend each one of these in a perpetual martyrdom, it were a small return for what He has bestowed upon us; but to give Him thanks is the least we can do, and shall we be slack in that? He gives us breath, shall we not breathe out His praise? He fills our mouth with good things, shall we not speak well of His name?

"Words are but air and tongues but clay,
And His compassions are divine."

Shall we fail even with words and tongues? God forbid. We will praise the name of the Lord, for His mercy endureth for ever. None of us will say, "I pray Thee have me excused." The poorest, weakest, and least-gifted person can give thanks. The work of thanksgiving does not belong to the man of large utterance, for he who can hardly put two words together can give thanks; nor is it confined to the man of large possessions, for the woman who had but two mites—which make a farthing—gave substantial thanks. The smoking flax may give thanks that it is not quenched, and the bruised reed may give thanks that it is not broken. Even the dumb may give thanks, their countenance can smile a psalm; and the dying can give thanks, their placid brow beaming forth a hymn. No Christian therefore can honestly say, "I am unable to exercise the delightful privilege of giving thanks." We may one and all at this moment give thanks unto God our Father. Brethren, let us do so.

Now, as we have considered what it is we are to do, let us notice *when* we are to do it, for the pith of the precept lies very much in the two "alls" which are in the text—"always for all things." We are to give thanks *always.* To give thanks sometimes is easy enough; any mill will grind when the wind blows. Brethren, we scarcely need exhorting to do this when the wine and oil increase, for we cannot help it. There are glad days when, if we did not thank God, we should be something worse than fallen men, and should be only fit to be compared with devils. Anyone can give God thanks when the harvests are plentiful, the stalls full of fat cattle, and the meadows covered with increasing herds. When the fig-tree blossoms and the fruit is in the vines, when the labour of the olive fails not, and the fields yield abundance of meat, then it is but natural to give thanks. When health enjoys life, and wealth adorns it, who will not say, "I thank God"? When the wind blows soft on the merchant's cheek and wafts home his argosies of treasure, how can he do other than say that God is good? But, to give thanks to God always is another matter; to bless the Lord in all winds and weathers, and praise Him for losses and pains, this is a work of quite another character.

"O," say you, "we cannot be always praising God with our lips." I have already said that, and explained that vocal thanksgiving is not essential. Perhaps the most doubtful form of praising God is that which is performed by the tongue, and the most sure and truthful way of giving thanks is that which is found in the actions of common life. But we are to be always praising God under some shape or other; the heart is always to be full of gratitude. At all times of the day we should be grateful,—our first waking thought should be "Bless the Lord"; our last, ere we drop to sleep, should be "Praised be the God of love, who gives a pillow for my weary head." At all times of life we should give thanks: in youth we should praise God, for godly parents and for early grace; in our mid-life we should give thanks for strength, for household joys, and experience of the divine lovingkindness; and, certainly, in those maturer days, when the head, like the golden grain, bows down with ripeness, the aged saint should commence the employment of heaven, and should be always giving thanks. We should give God thanks when our wealth increases, and also when it melts away, when it flows in and when it ebbs out,—we must bless Him in success, and also in disaster. We must give Him thanks when health departs, thanks when, by gradual decay, the tabernacle falls about our ears, and thanks, in those expiring moments, when the sigh of earth is hushed by the song of heaven.

It is easy to stand here and tell you this, but I have not always found it easy to practise the duty, this I confess to my shame. When suffering extreme pain some time ago, a brother in Christ said to me, "Have you thanked God for this?" I replied that I desired to be patient, and would be thankful to recover. "Ah, but," said he, "'in everything give thanks,' not after it is over, but while you are still in it, and, perhaps, when you are enabled to give thanks for the severe pain, it will cease." I believe that there was much force in that good advice. It may have sounded rather strange at the time, yet, if there is grace in our hearts, we acknowledge the correctness of it; we struggle after the holy joy of heart which it depicts, and at last, by God's grace, are able to attain to it, so as to give thanks unto God unceasingly. We shall never come to a time in which we shall say: "I will thank God no more." No. No. A thousand times NO; we could sooner cease to live than to give thanks. This solemn determination enables believers to play the man right gloriously. Was not it grand on Job's part to say—"The Lord gave, and the Lord hath taken away, blessed be the name of the Lord," even when he had rent his mantle and shaved his head for grief? Was not it noble on the part of Paul and Silas, when they were thrust into the inner dungeon, to sing praises there? None of us know how foul the air was in an inner Roman dungeon, how full of fever the dismal vault, how dank the dripping walls, how foul the stony floor; yet, here were two poor creatures who had been beaten till their backs were bleeding, fastened in the stocks, probably made to lie upon their backs upon the floor, and yet, at midnight, they sang praises unto God so loudly, that the prisoners heard them. This it is to praise God aright, to bless Him in the dead of night, to bless Him with bleeding back, to bless Him with feet in the stocks! Oh, to feel that nothing in this life, and nothing in death, shall make us cease to bless the Lord while thought and being last! This is grace indeed!

The text next tells us the *wherefore* of our gratitude —"Giving thanks always *for all things* unto God." "For all things"—whatever may happen to us. For the things which are of greatest moment we should always be grateful: for the new birth, for pardon of sin, for the indwelling of the Holy Ghost, for all covenant mercies, for all the blessings of the cross, and of the crown. Dear friends, a Christian has infinite cause for gratitude. When I first looked to Christ and was lightened, I thought that if I never received another mercy except that one of being delivered from my load of guilt, I would praise God, if He would but let me, for ever and ever. To have the feet taken out of the miry clay, and to feel them set on the rock of ages, is a subject for eternal gratitude. But you have not received one spiritual mercy only, beloved brother, nor two, nor twenty; you have had them strewn along your path in richest profusion; the stars above are not more numerous, nor the sands beneath more innumerable. Every hour, yea, every moment has brought a favour upon its wings. Look downward and give thanks, for you are saved from hell; look on the right hand and give thanks, for you are enriched with gracious gifts; look on the left hand and give thanks, for you are shielded from deadly ills; look above you and give thanks, for heaven awaits you.

Nor is it alone for great and eternal benefits, but even for minor and temporary benefits we ought to give thanks. There ought not to be brought into the house a loaf of bread without thanksgiving; nor should we cast a coal upon the fire without gratitude. We eat like dogs if we sit down to our meals without devoutly blessing God. We live like serpents if we never rise to devout recognition of the Lord's kindness. We ought not to put on our garments without adoring God, or take them off to rest in our beds without praising Him. Each breath of air should inspire us with thanks, and the blood in our veins should circulate gratitude throughout our system. Oh, how sacred would our temporal mercies be to us if we were always thanking God for them! Instead of that, we too often complain because we have not somewhat more. We have a position which, in God's sight, is the best for us. We could not have been better off than we are now, all things being considered, eternal things as well as present things; and yet we murmur and groan as though God had dealt hardly with us. The worst of all is that sometimes the poorest are the most thankful, those dear souls that are always sick and never have a waking moment free from pain are often the happiest and most grateful, while persons with wealth, health, and strength, and surrounded by every comfort, are often of such a crooked disposition that they complain they know not why, and are most disagreeable companions. God save you who are His saints from ever falling into a murmuring spirit; it is clean contrary to what God can approve of. Give thanks always for all things. Whenever the salt is put on the table let us see in it a lesson to us to season our conversation with thanks, of which salt we cannot use too much.

We ought also to thank God for the mercies which we do not see, as well as for those which are evident. We receive, perhaps, ten times as many mercies which escape our notice as those which we observe—mercies which fly by night on soft wings, and bless us while we sleep. You have heard, perhaps, of a Puritan who met his son, each one of them travelling some ten or twelve miles to meet the other; and the son said to his father, "Father, I am thankful to God for a very remarkable providence which I have had on my journey here. My horse has stumbled three times, with me, and yet I am unhurt." The Puritan replied "My dear son, I have to thank God for an equally remarkable providence on my way to you, for my horse did not once stumble all the way." If we happen to be in an accident by railway we feel so grateful that our limbs are not broken; but should we not be thankful when there is no accident? Is not that the better thing of the two? If you were to fall into poverty, and some one were to restore you to your former position in trade, you would be very grateful; should you not be grateful that you have not fallen into poverty? Bless God for His unknown benefits; extol Him for favours which you do not see, always giving thanks to God for all things.

Still this is easy; the difficult point is to give thanks to Him for the bitter things, for the despised blessings, for the love tokens which come to us from Him in black envelopes, for those benefits which travel to us *via crucis*, by the way of the cross, which are generally the most heavily laden wagons that ever come from our Father's country. We are to give thanks for the dark things, the cutting things, the things which plague and vex us, and disquiet our spirits, for these are among the *all things* for which we ought to praise and bless God. Doubtless, if our eyes were opened, like those of Elijah's servant, we should see our trials to be amongst our choicest treasures. If we exercise the far seeing eye of faith and not the dim eyes of sense, we shall discover that nothing can be more fatal to us than to be without affliction, and that nothing is more beneficial to us than to be tried as with fire. Therefore we will glory in tribulations also; we will bless and magnify the name of the Lord that He leads us through the wilderness that He may prove us, and that He may fit us for dwelling by-and-by in the promised land. "Giving thanks always for all things." I should like to be towards God of the mind that John Bradford was towards Queen Mary. When reviled as a rebel, that saint and martyr said, "I have no quarrel with the queen. If she release me I will thank her, if she imprison me I will thank her, if she burn me I will thank her." We should say of the Lord, "Let Him do what seemeth Him good; if He will give us health we will thank Him, if He will send us sickness we will thank Him. If He indulges us with prosperity or if He tries us with affliction, if the Holy Spirit will but enable us, we will never cease to praise the Lord as long as we live." Augustine tells us that the early saints when they met each other would never separate without saying, "Deo gratias! thanks be to God." Frequently their conversation would be about the persecutions which raged against them, but they finished their conversation with "Deo gratias!" Sometimes they had to tell of dear brethren devoured by the beasts in the amphitheatre, but even then they said "Deo gratias!" Frequently they mourned the uprise of heresy, but this did not make them rob the Lord of His "Deo gratias." So should it be with us all the day long. The motto of the Christian should be "Deo gratias!" "Giving thanks always for all things."

But the text has another word which is important —*to whom* is this gratitude to be rendered? "Giving thanks for all things *to God the Father.*" To God. To man we are bound to render thanks in proportion as he benefits us. God does not require that in order to be grateful to Him we should be ungrateful to our fellow men. To keep the first table it is never needful to break the second. Gratitude to parents and friends is but gratitude to God, if it be properly rendered with a view to the highest benefactor. To neglect the lower would be to spoil the higher gratitude. Yet we should never end with gratitude to men: that were to thank the clouds for rain, instead of blessing the Lord who sends both clouds and showers. Remember, that if you have benefactors, God inclined their hearts towards you. Give thanks to God for He is good, and doeth good. Give thanks to God; let not your gratitude stop short of the source from which the streams of mercy come.

Think of the Lord also under the relation which the text sets before you, namely, as the Father—as your Father. Remember, that as the Father, God is the Creator; it is He that made us, and not we ourselves; as the Father, He is the Sustainer and Preserver of men; as the Father, He has elected His people, for it is the Father who hath chosen His people in Christ Jesus; and, as the Father, He is the Progenitor of the spiritual seed, for He hath begotten us again unto a lively hope by the resurrection of Jesus Christ from the dead. Think of God the Father in

those varied capacities and you will have so many reasons for giving thanks always unto Him. Never give thanks to the Lord Jesus Christ in such a way as to dishonour the Father. You owe much to Jesus, but Jesus did not make the Father gracious to you, since "the Father Himself loveth you," Jesus is the gift of His Father's love and not the cause of it. Bless the Father, then, and, give honour and praise unto Him who hath made us meet to be partakers of the inheritance of the saints in light. There is an old Jewish tradition, that when God had made this world, and the six days' work was over, He called the angels to behold it, and it was so very beautiful that they sang for joy. Then the Lord asked them what they thought of this work of His hands. One of them replied, that it was so vast and so perfect that there should be created a clear, loud, melodious voice, which should fill all the quarters of the world with its sweet sound, and, both by day and night, offer thanksgiving to the Creator for His incomparable blessings. We ought to be of the same mind as the angel, not that there is a defect in creation, but that everywhere in creation intelligent beings should be that voice of ceaseless song which the angel desired.

Once more, in describing this duty the text tells us *how* to give thanks, namely, "*in the name of our Lord Jesus Christ.*" Now here we have directions to present our praises always through the Mediator. Jesus, our great High Priest, stands between us and God; we are to put our thanks into His sacred hand, that He may present them before the Father with something of His own, "not to our loss," even with His precious merit which shall sweeten all. But the text means more than that; we are to give thanks to the Father *in the name* of Jesus, that is, because Jesus bids us to do so, and we are commanded and commissioned by Christ; we have His example as well as His precept for blessing God for all things. I think the text means more than this—we are to give thanks to God in the name of Jesus, as though we did it in Jesus' stead: as though we stood where Jesus once stood, when He said on earth, "I thank thee, O Father." You Christian people are sent into the world as Christ was sent into the world; now Christ's office was to glorify God: and such is your office for His sake and in His name. Bethink you, how would Jesus have given thanks, how would He have praised God? In what sort of spirit would the ever adorable Son, whose meat and drink it was to serve His Father, have praised God? After that fashion, and in that same way, you are to give thanks unto God and the Father. It is a high position for a poor son of man to occupy, but if the Lord has called you to it by His grace, be not slack in the performance of the heavenly service.

The day will come when we shall fulfil our text in the widest sense, for then we shall give thanks to God, at the winding up of the drama of human history, for everything that has happened, from the fall even to the destruction of the wicked. We may not be able to do so now. Our eye sees the gigantic evil, and does not see the overruling good which, like a boundless sea, rolls over all: the dreadful mysteries of evil make us tremble as we think of them; but the day may come when, with the Lord Jesus, we may not only bless God for electing love, but may even say, "I thank Thee, O Father, Lord of heaven and earth, that Thou hast hid these things from the wise and prudent." The day may come when even the darkest side of the divine decrees, and the profoundest depths of the divine action, shall cause us to adore with gratitude, and when even that which can least be understood in providence shall no longer be the subject of awe-struck wonder, but of unspeakable delight. We shall trace the line of perfection along the course of the divine decrees and workings, and though the way of the Lord may have seemed to us to be inscrutable, we shall then adore Him for that wondrous display of all His attributes—His justice, His love, His truth, His faithfulness, His omnipotence—which shall blaze forth with tenfold splendour. In heaven we shall give thanks unto God always for *all* things, without exception and throughout eternity we shall magnify His holy name, through Jesus Christ our Lord. Let us do it as best we can to-day, God's Spirit helping us. Thus I have expounded the duty itself.

II. Now, briefly, let me speak to you upon THE SPIRITUAL PREREQUISITES which are necessary for the performance of this very pleasant work. And be it remembered solemnly, that no man can give thanks always to God, through Jesus Christ, till He has *a new heart*. The old heart is an ungrateful one, and even if a man should try with an unrenewed nature to give thanks to God, it would be like the impossible supposition of the dead struggling to make themselves alive, which cannot be. The old heart is a putrid fountain, it cannot send forth sweet streams; it is opposed to God, and it cannot bless Him in a way that He can accept. Looking at this fair and lovely duty, I would say to all who wish to practise it, "ye must be born again": unless you are made new creatures in Christ Jesus, you never can give thanks to God always for all things.

And next, I would remind you that in order to perform this duty aright a man *must have a sense of God*. To give thanks to God aright a man must believe that there is a God; he must go further than that, he must feel that God is the author of the good things which he receives; and to give thanks always he must advance yet further and believe that even in seeming evil love is at work. He must also come to believe in God as present to hear his thanks, or he will soon tire of presenting them. "Thou God seest me" must be printed on the newborn heart, or else there will be no constant giving of thanks to God. Let me ask thee, dear friend, thou believest in God, and thou doest well, but hast thou done better than the devils who also believe in God? They tremble: hast thou gone as far as that? There are some who have not. Devils cannot, however, love God and give Him thanks: hast thou gone beyond the trembling of a devil up to the giving of thanks and the adoration of a truly loving heir of heaven? Answer that question,—is God as real to thee as thy wife or child? as real as thyself? He must be so, and thou must know Him to be ever present with thee or else thou wilt never continue praising Him.

A man who gives thanks to God always for all things, must have *a sense of complete reconciliation to God*. You cannot bless God till you have heard Him say, "I have blotted out thy sins like a cloud, and like a thick cloud thy transgressions." Lean and false are the thanks which come from an unforgiven heart. A soul condemned for its unbelief is not a soul that can be accepted for its gratitude, it cannot be condemned for one thing and accepted for another. As I came here, this morning put me very joyfully in mind of another morning many years ago, which was, as to snow and cold, precisely like it. I remem-

ber when the family to which I belonged felt unable to go up to the house of God, for the snow was deep and falling heavily as it is now, when I also was unable to go up to the place of worship where our household usually attended, and, by reason of the snow was drifted into the little Methodist chapel where I heard of Jesus and found peace with God. I have learned to bless His name since then; but before then, though I could have sung as others sing, there was no giving thanks unto God by Jesus Christ in my heart. I wondered as I came along, whether God might not lead to this house some one whom He would bring to Himself this morning, to whom this cold day should become as memorable as that day of snow was to me. That morning in that Methodist Chapel there was a good work done, for though there were but few of us, one at least was called, and that one God has made the spiritual parent of many thousands of His children. I am surprised to find this house so full to-day, it is clear proof that you love to hear the gospel, and it encourages me to hope that there may be one here whom God shall make eminently useful when He has saved him. This we shall be sure of, whoever it may be, if he be reconciled to God by the death of God's dear Son, he will give thanks to God indeed and of a truth; if nobody else does so, he will from this day forward sing:

> "I will praise Thee every day
> Now Thine anger's turned away;
> Comfortable thoughts arise
> From the bleeding sacrifice."

We cannot give thanks to God through Jesus Christ except we have *accepted the Mediator*. All the thanks commanded in the text are to come up to God *through Jesus Christ*. If we reject Him, or if we associate Him as a Mediator with somebody else, we have gone contrary to God's way, and we cannot praise God. Virgins and saints and martyrs must never be made rivals to Jesus.

To praise God, even the Father, does it not strike you that we must *feel the spirit of adoption*? Who could praise a person as father whom he does not recognize as father? but he who feels—"Yes, I am the Lord's child, erring though I be, and my heart saith Abba"; he can praise God indeed.

To the fullest performance of this duty there must be *a subordination of ourselves to the will of God*. We must not desire to have our own way; we must be content to say, "Not my will, but Thine be done." I cannot give thanks to God always for all things till my old self is put down. While self rules, the hungry horseleech is in the heart, and that is fatal to gratitude. Self and discontent are mother and child. But when thou sayest in thine heart, "I am perfectly resigned to the will of God, my will consents to His will," then shall thy praise be as the continual sacrifice, and thy thanksgiving shall smoke before Him as incense.

III. I only want your attention a few minutes more while I speak upon THE EMINENT EXCELLENCIES of continually giving thanks to God, even the Father.

And the first excellency is, *it honours God*. A thankful spirit glorifies the Most High. "Whoso offereth praise glorifieth Me," saith the Lord. We might have imagined that whether we grumbled or complained it would make no difference to God. It would be of no consequence to any one of us what might be the opinion of a little community of ants about us, but God is infinitely more superior to us than we are to emmets; yet He considers that our praising and blessing Him renders glory to His name. Let us render it to Him then without stint. There is no higher commendation for any course of action or for any virtue to a Christian man than to tell him that it will honour God. Will it dishonour God? He will shrink from it though mines of gold should tempt him. Will it honour God? The believer rushes forward to it though floods and flames lies in his way? A grateful spirit is a blessed and yet a cheap way of honouring God, for it brings to us its own return. Like mercy, it is "twice blessed," it blesses us in the giving and honours God in the receiving. Let the Christian see to it that he abounds in it. Obedience to our text will tend to *check us from sin :* "Giving thanks always for all things." Very well; then there are some places that we must not enter, for it would be blasphemous to be giving thanks there. There are some things which I must not do, for I could not give God thanks for them. Suppose I have ground down the poor, how can I give God thanks for the miserable shillings which are the blood of these men. Suppose I have gained my living by an evil trade, how can I give thanks to God for the gold as I hear it chink in my bag? Suppose every day my prosperity brings misery to others, how can I give thanks for it? To give thanks for the fruit of sin were practically to blaspheme the thrice holy God. Oh, no; if the Christian is always to give thanks, he must always be where he can give thanks; and if he is to give God thanks for all things, he must not touch that which he cannot give God thanks for. I must never grasp the fruit of covetousness, the gain of dishonesty, the profit of Sabbath breaking, the result of oppression; for if I do, I have that for which I may weep and howl before God, but certainly not that for which I can give Him thanks. Brethren, I say, that if we looked well to our text, it would, by the power of God's Holy Spirit, restrain us from sin.

But one of the truest excellencies of a spirit of perpetual thanksgiving is this, that *it calms us when we are glad and it cheers us when we are sorrowful*— a double benefit; it allays the feverish heat at the same time that it mitigates the rigorous cold. If a man be rich, and God has given him a thankful spirit, he cannot be too rich. If he will give thanks to God, he may be worth millions, and they will never hurt him; and, on the other hand, if a man has learned to give thanks to God, and he becomes poor, he cannot be too poor, he will be able to bear up under the severest penury. The rich man should learn to find God in all things; the poor man should learn to find all things in God, and there is not much difference when you come to the bottom of these two causes. One child of God will be as grateful and as happy, as blessed and as rejoicing, as another, if he be but satisfied still to give God thanks. There is no overcoming a man who has climbed into this spirit. "I will banish you," said a persecutor of the saints. "But you cannot do that," said he, "for I am at home everywhere where Christ is," "I shall take away all your property," said he. "But I have none," said the other, "and if I had you could not take away Christ from me, and as long as He is left I shall be rich." "I will take away your good name," cried the persecutor. "That is gone already," said the Christian, "and I count it joy to be counted the off-scouring of all things for Christ's sake." "But I will put you in prison." "You may do as you please, but I shall be always free, for where Christ is there is liberty."

"But I shall take away your life," said he. "Aye, well," said the other, "then I shall be in heaven, which is the truest life, so that you cannot hurt me." This was a brave defiance to throw down at the feet of the foe. It is not in the power of the enemy to injure the man of God when once self is dethroned and the heart has learned to be resigned to the will of God. O, ye are great, ye are strong, ye are rich, ye are mighty, when you have bowed yourselves to the will of the Most High! Stoop that you may conquer, bow that you may triumph, yield that you may get the mastery. It is when we are nothing that we are everything—when we are weak we are strong, when we have utterly become annihilated as to self, and God is all in all, it is then that we are filled with all the fulness of God. May the Holy Ghost conduct us into this spirit of perpetual thankfulness.

One thing I am sure of, that the more we have of this, *the more useful we shall assuredly become.* Nothing has had a greater effect upon the minds of thoughtless men, than the continued thankfulness of true Christians. There are sick beds which have been more fruitful in conversions than pulpits. I have known women confined to their chambers by the space of twenty years together, whose remarkable cheerfulness of spirit has been the talk of the entire district, and many there have been who have called to see poor Sarah in her cottage, knowing that she has scarce been a single day without distressing pain, and have heard her voice, and looked into that dear smiling face and have learned the reality of godliness. The bedridden saint has been a power throughout all the district, and many have turned to God, saying, "What is this which enables the Christian to give thanks always to God?" Beloved, our crusty tempers and sour faces will never be evangelists. They may become messengers of Satan, but they will never become helpers of the gospel. To labour to make other people happy is one of the grand things a Christian should always try to do. In little things we ought not to be everlastingly worrying, fidgeting, finding little difficulties and spying out faults in others. I believe that to a faulty man everybody is faulty; but there are better people in the world than you have dreamed of, sir, and when you are better you will find them out. If you were always grateful to God, you would thank Him that people are as good as they are; if you would be thankful when you meet even with bad people, thankful that they are not worse than they are, and try to get hold of the best points in them, and not their worst points, you would be much more likely to gain your purpose, if your purpose be to glorify God by doing them good. If you want to catch flies, try honey: they will be more readily caught with that than with vinegar, at least if they are human flies. Put into your speech love rather than bitterness, and you will prevail. There are times when you must speak with all the sternness of an Elias. There are proper seasons when there must be no holding back of the most terrible truth; but, for all that, let the general current of your life, the natural outflow of your entire being, be a thankfulness to God which makes you loving towards men. I am sure in this way, when you come to speak of Jesus, you will get a more attentive ear, and when you tell your experience you will recommend the gospel by your own conversation.

Beloved, the Lord give us evermore a thankful spirit, and, when we talk to each other, let it not be our habit as it is ordinarily with Englishmen—to complain of this and of that, but let us thank God and testify of His goodness. I have heard that farmers are greatly given to grumbling; well, if they are more apt at complaining than tradespeople are, they are very far gone in it, for generally wherever I go I hear that trade is bad—it always has been ever since I have been in London, and commerce has been constantly going to ruin. I have known some who have lost money every month, and yet are richer every year. How is this? Had not we better change our way of talking, and dwell not upon our miseries but our mercies? Let us speak much of what God has given rather than of that which He has in love withheld from us; blessing Him rather than speaking ill of our neighbours, or complaining of our circumstances.

But, alas! there are some to whom I speak who will never undertake this duty till, as I have already said, they have new hearts and right spirits, and have become reconciled to God by Jesus Christ. Now, to you, this one word: You are guilty and must be punished, unless you find forgiveness. There is before you this morning an altar of sacrifice in the person of Jesus Christ. There are four horns to the altar, looking either way, and whosoever touches the horns of this altar shall live, and live for ever. Jesus Christ is the great altar of sacrifice, a touch of Him at this moment will save thee. It is the whole gospel—believe, trust and live, for "whosoever believeth that Jesus is the Christ is born of God"—whosoever trusteth in Christ shall be saved. Come to the altar, where His blood was spilt; come, now, and lay your hands upon its horn —you can but perish there: nay, I must correct myself, you *cannot* perish there, you must perish anywhere else! Come, then, and rest in Jesus, and the Lord bless you for His dear name's sake. Amen.

THE MATCHLESS MYSTERY

" For we are members of His body, of His flesh, and of His bones."—Ephesians v. 30.

I DO not hesitate to say that this is one of the most wonderful texts in the whole compass of revelation. It sets forth the mystery of mysteries, the very pith and marrow of the loftiest divinity. It is fitted rather to be the theme for a hundred elaborate discourses than for one brief homily. Most assuredly it is a deep that knows no sounding, an abyss where thought plunges into never-ending contemplations. He who handles it had need, first of all, to be filled with all the fulness of God. Hence we feel incapable of dealing with it as it should be dealt with ; it is all too great and vast for us, we can no more hope to compass it than a child can hold an ocean in his hand. Beloved, it is a text that must not be looked upon with the eyes of cold, theological orthodoxy, which might make us content to say, " Yes, that is a great and important truth," and there leave it. It is a text to be treated as the manna was that fell from heaven ; namely, to be tasted, to be eaten, to be digested, and to be lived upon from day to day. It is a text for the quietude of your meditation, when you can sit still and turn it over, and, like Mary, ponder it in your hearts. Long and loving should be your gaze upon the facets of this diamond of truth, this Koh-i-noor of revelation. It is a golden sentence fitted for those choice hours when the King brings us into His banqueting house, and His banner over us is love ; when the distance between earth and heaven has become less and less, till it scarce exists—those halcyon times when all is rest round about us, because He who is our rest enables us to lean upon His bosom and to feel His heart of love beating true to us.

I ask you, O my brethren, therefore, as though you were quite alone in your own chamber, to pray for that frame of mind which is suitable to the subject, and to pray for me that I may be placed in that condition of heart which shall best enable me to speak upon it. We need our thoughts to be focused before they can reveal to us the great sight before us. Get to the place where Mary sat at Jesus' feet, and then will this text sound like music in your ears. Without any accompaniment of exposition from me, it will have all heaven's music in it : "We are members of His body, of His flesh, and of His bones." Sevenfold will be the happiness of the spirit which knows how to sit down and to taste of the marrow and the fatness, to drink of the " wine on the lees well refined," which are to be found in this inspired declaration.

Ere I preach upon it, there is one thing which it is necessary for us to do. They have a way in Scotland, before the communion, of "fencing the tables " ; that is to say, warning all those who have no right to come to the table to avoid the sin of unlawful intrusion, and so of eating and drinking condemnation unto themselves. They help the hearers to self-examination, lest they should come thoughtlessly and participate in that which does not belong to them. Now, my text is like a table of communion richly loaded, and far hence be ye to whom it does not belong, except ye learn the sacred way of coming in by the door into this sheepfold, where the pasture is so rich and green. If ye come by Christ the way, come and welcome ; if ye rest in Him, if His dear wounds are the fountains of your life, and if His atoning sacrifice is your soul's only peace, come and welcome ; for of you, and such as you, and all of us who are trusting in Jesus, it may be truly said, " We are members of His body, of His flesh, and of His bones." But if not believers in Him, this heavenly verse has nothing to do with you. It is " the children's bread " ; it belongs only to the children. It is Israel's manna ; it falls for Israel. It is the stream which leaps from Israel's smitten rock, and flows neither for Edom, nor for Amalek, but for the chosen seed alone.

Look back, then, to the beginning of the epistle, and see of whom the apostle was speaking when he said " we." This little word " we " is like the door of Noah's ark, it shuts out and shuts in. Does it shut us out or in ?

Now, the apostle wrote his epistle to those of whom he said, " Blessed be the God and Father of our Lord Jesus Christ, who hath blessed us with all spiritual blessings in heavenly places in Christ, according as He hath chosen us in Him before the foundation of the world, that we should be holy and without blame before Him in love." Answer thou this question, thou who wouldst enjoy this text, Hast thou made thy calling and election sure ? Has that matter ever been decided in thy spirit after honest search and inquiry into the grounds of thy confidence ? Hast thou been led to choose thy God, for if so thy God had long ago chosen thee, and that matter is ascertained beyond all question, and out of it springs the undoubted assurance that you are one with Him, since of all whom He has chosen it is true, "We are members of His body, of His flesh, and of His bones."

The apostolic description is before you, I pray you read on : "Having predestinated us into the adoption of children by Jesus Christ to Himself, according to the good pleasure of His will." Knowest thou anything about adoption ? Hast thou been taken out of the family of Satan and enrolled in the family of God ? Hast thou the Spirit of adoption in thee ? Does thy soul cry "Abba, Father," at the very thought of God ? Art thou an imitator of God as a dear child ? Dost thou feel that thy nature has been renewed, so that, whereas thou wast a child of wrath, even as others, thou hast now become a child of God ? Judge, I pray thee, and discern concerning these things, for on thine answer to this question depends thy condition before God, thy union with Christ, or thy separateness from Him.

Note, still, the apostle's words as you read on, "To the praise of the glory of His grace, wherein He hath made us accepted in the beloved." Dear hearer, dost thou know the meaning of those last words, "Accepted in the beloved" ? Thou canst never be accepted in thyself ; thou art sinful, and undone, and unworthy ; but hast thou come and cast thyself upon the work, the blood, and the righteousness of Jesus, and art thou therefore accepted, "Accepted in the beloved" ? Hast thou ever enjoyed a sense of acceptance, so that thou couldst draw near to God, as no longer a servant beneath the curse, but a son beneath the blessing ? If so, come and welcome to the text ; it is all thine own.

But note the next verse :—" In whom we have redemption through His blood." Oh, dear hearers, do you know the blood ? I do not care what else you know if you do not know the blood ; nor do I much mind what else you do not know. You may differ very widely in doctrine from some of the truths which I think I have learned from the word of God, but do you know the blood ? Were you ever washed in it ? Have you seen it sprinkled over-head and on the side-posts of the house wherein you dwell, so that the destroying angel passes you by ? Is the blood of Christ the life-blood of your hope ? God save me from preaching, and you from believing in a bloodless theology. It is a dead theology. Take Christ away, take the atonement by a substitutionary sacrifice away, and what is there left ? But, oh, if we in very deed have redemption through His blood, then we are "members of His body, of His flesh, and of His bones."

The apostle adds, "The forgiveness of sins, according to the riches of His grace." And here, again, I press home the question upon the consciences of the members of this church, and upon the members of every professing church of Christ— Have you tasted forgiveness ? Have you felt the burden of sin ? Have you gone with that burden to the foot of the cross ? Has the Heavenly Father ever said to you, "Thy sins are forgiven thee" ? Do you believe in the forgiveness of sins, and that in reference to yourselves ? Oh, do not be satisfied unless you do. Do not be put off with a bare hope that perhaps your sin is forgiven you, but struggle after that blessed full assurance which is able to say—

> "Oh, how sweet to view the flowing
> Of my Saviour's precious blood,
> With divine assurance knowing
> He has made my peace with God ! "

And if you do so know, possess, and enjoy the forgiveness of sins, then are you "members of His body, of His flesh, and of His bones."

Oh, how this last sentence concerning pardon and rich grace seems to cheer my soul ! If none might come but those who never sinned, my guilty soul could never venture near the Lord. If none might come but those who have committed little sin, then must I be debarred. But it is "the forgiveness of sins " on a grand scale. Let me read the words : "The forgiveness of sins, according to the riches of His grace." So it is great forgiveness, the forgiveness of great sin, because of great love. O beloved hearer, great sinner as you have been, yet if you are "accepted in the Beloved," and have "redemption through His blood," then all that is in the text belongs to you ; so I will keep you waiting in the vestibule no longer, but set the door wide open, saying, "Come in, thou blessed of the Lord. Wherefore standest thou without ? " I pray the Holy Ghost to help you to come in to this high festival, give you a sacred appetite, and enable you now to appreciate the extraordinary sweetness of the words before us.

First, I shall try and expound—and it must be but feebly—what the text means, and, secondly, what the text secures.

I. First, WHAT DOES THE TEXT MEAN ? "We are members of His body, of His flesh, and of His bones." Read it in the light of the second chapter of the book of Genesis, for it is evident that there is a distinct allusion to the creation of Eve. The very words of Adam are quoted, and we are mentally conducted to that scene in the garden of Eden when the first man gazed upon the first woman, created to be his dear companion and helpmeet. What did Adam mean when he used these words ? for the great husband of our souls must mean the same, only in a more spiritual and emphatic sense.

And, first, there was meant here similarity of nature. Adam looked at Eve, and he did not regard her as a stranger, as some creature of a different genus and nature ; but he said, "She is bone of my bones, and flesh of my flesh." He meant that she was of the same race, a participant in the same nature ; he recognised her as a being of the same order as himself. Now, that is a low meaning of the text, but it is one meaning. Brethren, beloved, think of this truth for a moment. Jesus, the Son of God, counted it not robbery to be equal with God. "Without Him was not anything made that was made." He is "very God of very God." Yet He deigned for love of us to take upon Himself our nature, and He did it completely, so that He assumed the whole of human nature, apart from its sin ; and in that respect we may say of ourselves—that we are "bone of His bone, and flesh of His flesh." The very nature which we wear on earth Christ Jesus once carried about among us, and at last carried aloft to heaven. You believe in His Godhead, take heed never to commingle His Godhead and His humanity. Remember, Christ was not a deified man, neither was He a humanized God. He was perfectly God, and at the same time perfectly man, made like unto His brethren in all things. Dwell for a moment upon this truth, for the text sets it forth. Born of a human mother, and swaddled like another child, He was from His birth as perfectly human even as you are. In nothing did He differ from you except in this, that He never wandered from God and broke His commands, and He was not defiled with that hereditary taint of original sin which dwelleth in you by nature. The like depressions to those which sadden your spirit He knew; the temptations of your nature assailed Him; men and devils both sought to influence Him. He was amenable to all the external physical arrangements of the globe. On Him the shower pelted down, and wetted His garments; and on Him the burning sun poured forth its undiminished heat. Upon His sacred person on the lone mountain-side, the dews descended till His head was wet with them, and His locks with the drops of the night. For Him there were poverty, and hunger, and thirst, reproach, slander, and treachery. For Him the sea tossed the barque as it will for you; and for Him the land yielded thorn and thistle, as it does to you. He suffered, He ate, He toiled, He rested, He wept, and He rejoiced, even as you do, sin alone excepted. A real kinsman was He, not in fiction, but in substantial reality. Are you man? Jesus was a man. Do not doubt it. Do not look at your Lord as standing up there on a pinnacle of superior nature, where you cannot come near Him, but view Him as your own flesh and blood, "a brother born for adversity." For so He is. He comes to you and says, "Handle Me and see. A spirit hath not flesh and bones as you see Me have." He invites your faith to look at the prints of the nails, and the scar of the spear-thrust. Did He not, after He had risen from the dead, prove His True humanity by eating a piece of a broiled fish and of a honeycomb? And that same humanity has gone to heaven. The clouds received it out of our sight, but it is there.

> "A Man there was, a real Man,
> Who once on Calvary died;
> And streams of blood and water ran
> Down from His wounded side."

That same blest man exalted sits high on His Father's throne. Believe this, and you will see how He is bone of your bone, and flesh of your flesh.

And then recollect that, as His nature is as yours, so, in another sense, He has made your nature as His; for you are born again, and gifted with a higher life. You were carnal; He has now made you spiritual. You could not drink of His cup, or be baptized with His baptism, till His Spirit had come upon you. But now ye are made "partakers of the divine nature,"—strong words, but scriptural: "partakers of the divine nature, having escaped the corruption that is in the world through lust." "For as ye have borne the image of the earthy Adam, ye shall also bear the image of the heavenly." Now you, as spiritual men, cry out to God in prayer, and so did He when He was here. Now you are in an agony as you strive with God, and so was He, but the bloody sweat is a part of His substitutionary work, in which He trod the wine-press alone. His meat and drink was to do the will of Him that sent Him, and it is yours, I trust; at any rate, it should be if you are your Lord's. He lived for God; He lived and died for love of men; and that same love of God and man, though in a feebler measure, burns within your heart. You are, there-

fore, now made by His grace to participate in His moral and spiritual nature, and you will never be satisfied till you awake in His likeness. But you will awake in His likeness, so that when He sees you and you see Him, then shall be abundantly manifest to you that you are a member "of His body, of His flesh, and of His bones":—

> "Such was Thy grace, that for our sake
> Thou didst from heaven come down,
> Thou didst of flesh and blood partake,
> In all our sorrows ONE.
>
> Ascended now, in glory bright,
> Still ONE with us Thou art;
> Nor life, nor death, nor depth, nor height,
> Thy saints and Thee can part.
>
> Oh, teach us, Lord, to know and own
> This wondrous mystery,
> That Thou with us art truly ONE,
> And we are ONE with Thee!
>
> Soon, soon shall come that glorious day,
> When, seated on Thy throne,
> Thou shalt to wondering worlds display,
> *That Thou with us art ONE!*"

Similarity of nature, then, is the first meaning of the text.

Regard, I pray you, brethren, with much solemn attention, a higher step of the ladder. It signifies *intimate relationship*, for I hardly think that Adam would have said quite so strongly, "She is bone of my bones, and flesh of my flesh," if he had thought that the woman would disappear, or would become the wife of another. It was because she was to be his helpmeet, and they were to be joined together in bonds of the most intimate communion, that therefore he said, "Not only is she of the same bone and flesh as I am, but she is bone of *my* bones, and flesh of *my* flesh. She is related to me." What a near and dear and loving relationship marriage has bestowed upon us! It is a blessing for which good men dwelling with affectionate wives praise God every day they live. Marriage and the Sabbath are the two choice boons of primeval love that have come down to us from Paradise, the one to bless our outer and the other our inner life. Oh, the joy, the true, pure, elevated peace and joy which many of us have received through that divinely ordained relationship! We cannot but bless God every time we repeat the dear names of those who are now parts of ourselves. Marriage creates a relationship which ends only when death doth us part. It may be dissolved. Alas, sin enters even here! A dark crime may be committed, but, with the exception of that, it is for life—for better, for worse; only the mortal stroke can part. Now think of it. As is your relation, O woman, to your husband, and as is your relation, O man, to your wife, such is the relation which exists between you, as a believer in Jesus, and Christ Jesus your Lord. It is the nearest, dearest, closest, most intense, and most enduring relationship that can be imagined. I love and bless God for ever declaring that His relationship to us may be likened to that of a father or a mother to a child. Did you ever hear those words without tears—(I think I never did) —"Can a woman forget her sucking child, that she should not have compassion on the son of her womb? Yea, they may forget; yet will not I forget thee." And yet there is a closer intimacy, somehow, in the relationship which is declared in the text, because there is a kind of equality between the married ones, tempered by that headship of which the apostle speaks, and which we delight to recognize in our beloved Lord towards ourselves. The child cannot, while it is yet a babe, at any rate, enter into its mother's feelings; it is far below the mother; but the wife communes with her husband, she is lifted up to his level; she is made a partaker of his cares and sorrows, of his joys and his successes, and the intimacy arising out of their conjugal union is of the closest kind. Now—again I say it, and I cannot open it up further than to say it—such is the relationship between the believer's soul and the Lord Jesus. Well did the spouse break out with the rapturous language which forms the first word of the song— "Let him kiss me with the kisses of his mouth, for his love is better than wine," as if she did not need to describe her relationship, but longed to enjoy the sweets of it. My brother, I pray you may so enjoy it; that now, if you be poor in this world, if you be an orphan, if you be almost a lone one in this great city, you may feel, "No longer am I an orphan, no longer am I alone. My Maker is my husband. The Lord of Hosts is His name, and my redeemer the Mighty One of Israel; and from this day forth will I rejoice that I am bone of His bones, and flesh of His flesh." Similarity of nature, and closeness of relationship, are evidently in the text.

But I clearly see another and deeper meaning. It meant, from Adam's lips, *mysterious extraction.* I will not make bold to say that he knew what had occurred to him in his sleep. He might not have known all, but he seems to have had a mystic enlightenment which made him guess what had occurred—at least the words seem to me to have that ring in them. "She is bone of my bones"— for a bone had been taken from him, "and flesh of my flesh," for out of him had she been taken. He seems to have known that somehow or other she sprang of him. Whether he knew it or not, Christ knows right well the origin of His spouse. He knew where His church came from. There is the mark in His side still: there is the memorial in the palms of His hands and on His feet. Whence came this new Eve, this new mother of all living? Whence came this spouse of the second Adam? She came of the second Adam. She was taken from his side, full near his heart. Have you never read, "Except a corn of wheat fall into the ground and die, it abideth alone; but if it die, it bringeth forth much fruit"? Had Jesus never died, He would have been made to abide alone as to any who could be helpmeets for Him, and could enter into fellowship with Him; but, inasmuch as He has died, He has brought forth much fruit, and His church has sprung from Him, and in that sense she is bone of His bones, and flesh of His flesh. What mean I by the church? says one. I mean by the church all the people of God, all the redeemed, all believers, as I explained at the commencement. Think you I mean by the church the harlot of the seven hills? God forbid that Christ should have fellowship with her! How can He so much as look upon her except with horror? Means He by the church the politically supported corporation that men call a church now-a-days? Nay, but the spiritual, the quickened, the living, the believing, the holy people, wherever they may be, or by whatsoever name they may be called. These are they that sprang of Christ, even as Levi from the loins of Abraham. They live because they receive life from Him, and at this day they are dead in themselves,

and their life is hid with Christ in God. So the text leads us to a deep meditation as to mysterious extraction.

But I find the time goes too swiftly for me, and I must observe next that I am sure that in the text there is more than this. There is, in the fourth place, *loving possession.* He said, "She is bone of my bones, and flesh of my flesh"; he felt she was his own, and belonged solely to him. Of anything there might be in the garden, Adam was but owner in the second degree; but when he saw her, he felt she was all his own. By bonds and ties which did not admit of dispute, his bone and his flesh was she. Now, beloved, at this moment let this thought dance through your soul: you belong to Jesus, altogether you belong to Jesus. Let not your love go forth to earthly things, so soiled and dim; but send it all away, up to Him to whom you belong; aye, send it all to Him. "Set not your affection upon things on the earth," but set it all upon things above, for you belong wholly to your Lord. All that there is of your spirit, soul, and body, the treble kingdom of your nature, Christ has purchased by His blood. It were a dark thought to cross a man's mind, that His spouse belonged in part to some other. It could not be. And will you provoke your Lord to jealousy? Will you suffer it to seem so by your actions or your words? Nay, rather say to-night anew,

> " 'Tis done, the great transaction's done:
> I am my Lord's, and He is mine.
> He drew me, and I followed on,
> Charmed to confess the voice divine.
>
> High heaven, that heard the solemn vow,
> That vow renewed shall daily hear,
> Till in life's latest hour I bow,
> And bless in death a bond so dear."

"For ye are not your own, ye are bought with a price." "We are members of His body, of His flesh, and of His bones." We belong entirely unto Him.

And to close this exposition—this skimming of the surface, rather—there is one more matter, and this is the very essence of the meaning. A *vital union* exists between us and Christ. When the apostle was showing that we were one with Christ, as the wife is with the husband, he felt that the metaphor, though it set forth much, did not set forth all. He would have us know that we are more closely knit to Jesus than is a woman to her husband; for they are, after all, separate individualities, and they may act, and too often do so, far too distinctly for themselves. But here he puts it, "We are members of His body." Now, here is a vital union, the closest imaginable. It is not unity; it is identity. It is more than being joined to; it is being made a part of, and an essential part of the whole. Do you think I strain the text, and go beyond the fact? Listen to this word. The apostle, in speaking of the church, said, concerning Christ, that the church was His body, "the fulness of Him that filleth all in all." And note the majesty of that speech—that the church should be the fulness of Christ. Now, Christ, without His fulness, is evidently not full: He must have His people; they are essential to Him. The idea of a Saviour is lost, apart from the saved. He is a head without a body if there be no members. What without His people is Jesus but a king without subjects, and a shepherd without a flock? It is essential to any true thought of Christ, that you think of His people. They must come in. They are one with Him in every true view of Jesus Christ our Lord.

How we are one with Him ! Ah, brethren, much might be said, but I fear little would be explained by words. I want you to feel it, and to be comforted by the fact of the vital union of Jesus and His saints. Have you never heard Him say to you—

> " I feel at my heart all Thy sighs and Thy groans,
> For Thou art most near me, my flesh and my bones.
> In all Thy distresses Thy head feels the pain,
> They all are most needful, nor one is in vain " ?

Oh, do get to know this, you tried and tempted ones, you poor poverty-stricken people of God, you who could not help coming here to-night, wet as it was, because you must have spiritual meat, you were so hungry after your Lord. Oh, do get this morsel now, and feed on it. You are one with Him. You were "buried in Him in baptism unto death," wherein also you have risen with Him. You were crucified with Him upon the cross ; you have gone up into heaven with Him, for He has raised us up together, and made us sit together in the heavenly places in Christ Jesus. And surely you shall be actually in your very person with Him where He is, that you may behold His glory. You are one with Him.

Now, tie up these five truths like five choice flowers in a nosegay. Blend them like sweet spices, and let them be a bundle of camphire and a cluster of myrrh, to lie all night upon your bosom, to give you rest and to sweeten your repose. There is between you and your Lord a similarity of nature, and an intimate relationship ; you have a mysterious extraction from Him, and He has a loving possession of you, and a vital union with you.

Come, now, we must only have a few minutes to catch some of the juice that will flow out of these clusters of Eshcol while we tread them for a moment, just to show what the wines of the kingdom are like. WHAT DOES THE TEXT SECURE ?

First, it seems to me, that the text secures the eternal safety of every one who is one with Christ. You know the figure we often use, that when a man's head is above water you cannot drown his feet ; and as long as my Head is in glory, though I be but the sole of His foot, and only worthy to be trodden in the mire, how can ye drown me ? Is it not written, " Because I live ye shall live also "— all of you who are one with Him ? The idea of Christ losing members of His body is to me grotesque, and at the same time ghastly. Does He change His members like some aquatic creatures which shoot their limbs and get fresh joints ? I trow it is not so with Christ, the second Adam. Will He lose His members ? Can He lose *one* member ? Then can He lose *all* ?

> " If ever it should come to pass
> That sheep of Christ could fall away,
> My fickle, feeble soul, alas,
> Would fall a thousand times a day."

But herein lies our safety ; " I give unto My sheep eternal life, and they shall never perish ; neither shall any pluck them out of My hand." I know that some have perverted this blessed truth into the wicked lie that the Christian man may live as he likes, and yet be safe. No such doctrine is to be found between the covers of that book ; the doctrine of the safety of the saints is far other than that. It is that the renewed man shall live as God likes, shall persevere in holiness and hold on his way, until he arrives at the blessed perfection of his Lord, changing from glory to glory into that image which he shall reach and possess for ever. I see—I pity those who do not see it, but I will not blame—I see, I think, strong reason for believing in the security of every soul which is one with Christ.

But, next, I see here a very sweet thought. If I am one with Christ, then I certainly enjoy, above all things, His love. Last Saturday week in the evening I was trying to turn over this text to preach to you from it in the morning ; but I was wrung with bitter pains which made me feel that I should not preach, and kept me wearily waiting through the night watches. But do you know what comforted me very much about the text ? It was that sentence which is a near neighbour of it : " No man ever yet hated his own flesh." I seized upon that, and my sad heart cried out, " Surely the Man Christ Jesus never yet hated His own flesh." If we are members of His body, of His flesh, and of His bones, He may chasten, He may correct, and lay on heavy strokes, and give sharp twinges, and make us cry out ; He may even thrust us in the fire, and heat the furnace seven times hotter ; but He never can neglect and abhor His own flesh. Still is there love in His heart. I hate no part of my body, not even when it aches. I hate it not, but love it still ; it is a part of myself ; and so doth Jesus love His people. And you, poor sinners, who feel that you are not worthy to be called His people, nevertheless His love goes out to you, despite your imperfections. Having loved His own, which were in the world, He loved them to the end, and He has left it upon record, " As My Father hath loved Me, even so have I loved you. Continue ye in My love."

Another most enchanting thought also arises from our subject. The apostle goes on to say, " No man ever yet hated his own flesh, but nourisheth and cherisheth it, even as the Lord the church." Oh, those two words, " nourisheth it." Are you living in a district where you do not get the gospel ? Well, then, go to the gospel's Lord and say to Him, " Lord, hate not Thine own flesh, but nourish me." Have you been for a while without visits from Christ ? have you lost the light of His countenance ? Do not be satisfied with nourishing : go further and plead for cherishing. Ask for those love tokens, for those gentle words, for those secret blandishments, known to saints, and to none but saints, for " the secret of the Lord is with them that fear Him, and He will show them His covenant." Go and ask for both these forms of love, and you shall be nourished and cherished. The good husband does not merely bring so much bread and meat into the house and fling it down, saying, " There, that will nourish you." Oh, not so, but there are tender words and kindly acts, by which He cherishes as well as nourishes. And your Lord will not only give you bread to eat which the world knows not of, but He will give it you according to His loving-kindness and the multitude of His tender mercies : for He maketh us to lie down in green pastures, He leadeth us beside the still waters, gently guiding as a shepherd conducts His flock. Rejoice, then, that your nourishing and your cherishing are secure.

I will not keep you longer when I have said this much. If we are members of His body, of His flesh, and of His bones, then He will one day present us to Himself, " without spot, or wrinkle, or any such thing," for the whole body must be so presented. Alas, our spots are many, and sadly mar our beauty ! Brethren, I love not to think little of my spots. I wish I had not even a speck. Alas, our wrinkles ! Let us not talk lightly of them. It is most sad that on the Beloved's darling there should be a solitary blot. It is the worst wrinkle of all when a man does not see his own wrinkles, and when he does not mourn over them. But spots and wrinkles there are. I hope we do not say, " Yes, they are there," and then add, " And they must be there." No, beloved, they ought not to be there : there ought to be no sin in us. If there be a sin which ought to be upon us, why it is clear it is no sin. A thing that ought to be is not a sin. If we served our Master as He deserves to be served, we should never sin, but our lives would be perfect ; and therefore it is our daily burden that the spots and wrinkles still will show; and this is our consolation, that He will one day present us to Himself, holy and without blemish, " not having spot or wrinkle, or any such thing."

> " Oh, glorious hour, oh, blest abode ;
> I shall be near, and like my God.
> Nor spot nor wrinkle shall remain,
> His perfect image to profane."

It will be a blessed thing indeed to have attained to this, to wear the image of the heavenly, and be perfect even as our Bridegroom is perfect.

Then, remember, all the glory Christ has we shall share in. You cannot honour a warrior who returns from the wars, and say to him, " Great general, we honour your head." Oh, no ; he who fought his country's battles, and won the victory, when he was honoured was altogether honoured as a man. And when the Master at the last shall have finished all His work, and the whole battle that He undertook being finished, and the victory gained, He enters perfectly into His joy, we shall enter into the joy of our Lord. Does He sit upon a throne ? He has said we shall sit upon His throne. Has He triumphed ? We shall bear the palm branch, too. Whatever He has we shall share. Are we not heirs of God, joint heirs with Jesus Christ ? My soul feels ready to leap right away from this body at the thought of the glory that shall be revealed in us—not in Paul and Peter only, but in us. Poor things, poor things, that struggle hard each day with infirmities and trials, ye shall be with Him where He is, and shall behold His glory for ever. " So shall we ever be with the Lord. Wherefore comfort one another with these words."

> " Since Christ and we are one,
> Why should we doubt or fear ?
> If He in heaven hath fixed His throne,
> He'll fix His members there."

In this spirit come ye to the communion table, and find your Master there. But oh, if you are not resting in Him, if the blood was never upon you, you are condemned already, because you have not believed on the Son of God ; and I pray that your bed may be cold and hard as a stone to you to-night, and your eyes may forget to sleep, and your heart may know no rest till you have said, " I will arise, and go to my Father, and will say unto Him, Father, I have sinned." Then take with you Jesus as a mediator, and draw nigh to the throne of grace. Go, plead His blood and merits, and you shall live ; and then you, too, shall be able to join with the saints who say, " We are members of His body, of His flesh, and of His bones." Amen. Amen.

THE SHIELD OF FAITH

"Above all, taking the shield of faith, wherewith ye shall be able to quench all the fiery darts of the wicked."—Ephesians vi. 16.

LIKE the Spartans, every Christian is born a warrior. It is his destiny to be assaulted; it is his duty to attack. Part of his life will be occupied with defensive warfare. He will have to defend earnestly the faith once delivered to the saints; he will have to resist the devil; he will have to stand against all his wiles; and having done all, still to stand. He will, however, be but a sorry Christian if he acteth only on the defensive. He must be one who goes against his foes, as well as stands still to receive their advance. He must be able to say with David, " I come against thee in the name of the Lord of hosts, the God of the armies of Israel whom thou hast defied." He must wrestle not with flesh and blood, but against principalities and powers. He must have weapons for his warfare —not carnal—but "mighty through God to the pulling down of strongholds." He must not, I say, be content to live in the stronghold, though he be then well guarded, and munitions of stupendous strength his dwelling place may be; but he must go forth to attack the castles of the enemy, and to pull them down, to drive the Canaanite out of the land. Now, there are many ways in which the Christian may to a great degree forget his marshal character. And alas! there are not a few who, if they be Christians at all, certainly know but very little of that daily warfare to which the Captain of our salvation calleth His disciples. They will know most of fighting who cleave closest to king David; who are willing not merely to be with him when he is in Saul's court with his fingers amid the strings of the harp, going in and out before the people, and behaving discreetly, so that "all Israel and Judah loved David because he went out and came in before them;" but men who are willing to go with David into the cave of Adullam when he is outlawed, when his character has become a stench in the nostrils of every proud hypocrite, and when Saul the king—in his day the representative of that worldly religion which is not of God, but standeth in the strength of man—when he hunteth David to seek his life. Thus the men who are willing to follow Christ in the midst of an ungodly and perverse generation, to come right out from it and be separate; their life will have to be like the life of the men of Naphtali, who hazarded their lives unto the death in the high places of the field. You will remember that Jonathan, one of the sweetest characters in the word of God, is one of whom after all there is little to be said. His life was inglorious from the very time that he forsook David, and his death was amongst the slain of the Philistians upon the dewless mountains of Gilboa. Alas, poor Jonathan, he could give David his bow, but he could not draw the bow for David; he could give David his garments, even to his armour, but he could not put on the armour for David. The attraction of his father's court was too much for him, and there he stayed. In that Book of the Chronicles, where the Holy Ghost has recorded the names of the mighty men that were with David in Adullam, we find not the name of Jonathan. We find the names of those who broke through the Philistines to give David a drink of the water of the well of Bethlehem; we find the name of the man who went down into the pit in the time of winter and smote the lion; but Jonathan has not the honour to stand recorded in the list of the great host which was like the host of God. And there are Christians of that kind nowaday. They have a soft religion—a religion which shuns opposition, a reed-like religion which bows before every blast, unlike that cedar of godliness which standeth aloft in the midst of the storm, and claps its boughs in the hurricane for very joy of triumph, though the earth be all in arms abroad. Such men, like those who shunned David in Adullam, lack the faith that shares the glory. Though saved, yet their names shall not be found written among the mighty men who for our Great Commander's sake are willing to suffer the loss of all things and to go forth without the camp bearing His reproach. Those Christians too, who, having come clean out from the world, are diligently engaged in building up the Church, will have to fight more than others who are rather built up than builders. You remember, in Nehemiah's day, how the Jews wrought in their work when they built the walls of Jerusalem. With one hand they held the trowel, and in the other they held a weapon. "The builders, every one had his sword girded by his side and so builded." Moreover there were master masons along the wall, and the labourers all actually engaged, yet here and there you might see a sentinel ready to sound the trumpet so that the workmen might prove warriors, rush to the fray, and drive away their foes. Be you but very diligent in doing good to the Church of Christ, and you shall soon have reason to defend your cause. Do you but serve your Master zealously and diligently, and let but the Lord's blessing rest upon your labours, the Lord's blessing will entail Satan's curse, the smile of God will necessarily incur the frown of man. According to your nonconformity to the world, your daring to be singular—when to be singular is to be right,—according to your diligence in building up the walls of Jerusalem, you shall be compelled to recognize your soldierly character. To you the text shall come with greater emphasis than to more cowardly souls. "Above all, take the shield of faith wherewith ye shall be able to quench all the fiery darts of the wicked."

Having treated the character of the persons who will most require the shield provided in the text, let us proceed at once to discuss the words before us. We will do so thus. First, let us *expound the comparison;* secondly, *enforce the exhortation;* and thirdly *propound it as a word of comfort to any trembling sinners who are now specially attacked with the fiery darts of the wicked.*

I. First, then, let us EXPOUND THE METAPHOR. Faith is here compared to a shield. There are four or five particulars in which we may liken faith to a shield.

The natural idea which lies upon the very surface of the simile is, that faith, like a shield, *protects us against attack.* Different kinds of shields were used by the ancients, but there is a special reference in our text to the large shield which was sometimes employed. I believe the word which is translated "shield," sometimes signifies a door, because their shields were as large as a door. They covered the man entirely. You remember that verse in the Psalms which exactly hits the idea, "Thou Lord wilt bless the righteous, with favour wilt thou compass Him as with a shield." As the shield enveloped the entire man, so we think faith envelops the entire man, and protects him from all missiles wherever they may be aimed against him. You will remember the cry of the Spartan mother to her son when he went out to battle. She said, "Take care that you return with your shield, or upon it." Now, as she meant that he could return upon his shield dead, it shows that they often employed shields which were large enough to be a bier for a dead man, and consequently quite large enough to cover the body of a live man. Such a shield as that is meant in the text. That is the illustration before us. Faith protects the whole man. Let the assault of Satan be against the head, let him try to deceive us with unsettled notions in theology, let him tempt us to doubt those things which are verily received among us; a full faith in Christ preserves us against dangerous heresies, and enables us to hold fast those things which we have received, which we have been taught, and have learned, and have made our own by experience. Unsettledness in notion generally springs from a weakness of faith. A man that has strong faith in Christ, has got a hand that gets such a grip of the doctrines of grace, that you could not unclasp it, do what you would. *He* knows what he has believed. *He* understands what he has received. *He* could not and would not give up what he knows to be the truth of God, though all the schemes that men devise should assail him with their most treacherous art. While faith will guard the head, it will also guard the heart. When temptation to love the world comes in, then faith holds up thoughts of the future and confidence of the reward that awaits the people of God, and enables the Christian to esteem the reproach of Christ greater riches than all the treasures of Egypt, and so the heart is protected. Then when the enemy makes his cut at the sword-arm of a Christian, to disable him, if possible, from future service, faith protects the arm like a shield, and he is able to do exploits for his Master, and go forth, still conquering, and to conquer, in the name of Him that hath loved us. Suppose the arrow is aimed at his feet, and the enemy attempts to make him trip in his daily life—endeavours to mislead him in the uprightness of his walk and conversation. Faith protects his feet, and he stands fast in slippery places. Neither does his foot slip, nor can the enemy triumph over him. Or suppose the arrow is aimed at the knee, and Satan seeks to make him weak in prayer, and tells him that God will shut out his cry, and never listen to the voice of his supplication; the faith protects him, and in the power of faith, with confidence, he has access to God, and draws near unto His mercy-seat. Or let the arrow be aimed at his conscience, and let it be winged with the remembrance of some recent sin; yet faith protects the conscience, for its full assurance of atonement quenches the fiery darts with that delightful text, "The blood of Jesus Christ His Son cleanseth us from all sin." So there is no part of a man which is not secure. Although Satan will certainly attack him in every direction, yet, let him come where he will.

> "He that hath made his refuge God,
> Shall find a most secure abode."

Nor does faith only protect the whole man, but if you will think for a moment you will see that the apostle suggests the idea that *it protects his armour too*. After recounting various pieces, he says, "Above all." The man of God is to put on the girdle and the breast-plate, and he is to be shod, and he is to wear his helmet. But though tnese are all armour, yet faith is an armour for his armour; it is not only a defence for him, but a defence for his defences. Thus faith not only shields the man, but shields his graces too. You may easily perceive how this is. Satan sometimes attacks our sincerity; he tries to cut the girdle of truth which is about our loins. But faith enables us to be all sincere; like Moses who forsook Egypt, not fearing the wrath of the king, and refused to be called the son of Pharaoh's daughter. Then the enemy will often make an attack against our righteousness, and try to batter our breas plate. Yet doth faith come in and enable us like Joseph to exclaim, "How can I do this great wickedness and sin against God." Or like Job we cry, "Till I die I will not remove mine integrity from me." Or like David we can cry, even in tne worst of slanders, "Thou Lord that delivered me out of the jaw of the lion, and out of the paw of the bear, will deliver me out of the hand of this Philistine." You see how faith guards the breastplate and protects the girdle. All our virtues are unable to live of themselves, they need grace to preserve them, and that grace is given us through faith. Are you meek? cover your meekness with faith, or else you will give way to a hasty speech. Are you full of decision? let your decision be shielded with confidence in God, or else your decision may waver, and your firmness may give way. Have you the spirit of love and gentleness? take care that you have the shield of faith, or your gentleness may yet turn to anger and your love be changed to bitterness. We must protect our graces with faith as well as the nature they adorn. It is not simply the head, but the helmet; not the feet merely, but the shoes; not the loins, but the girdle;—all must be shielded and secure by this all-covering, all-triumphant shield of faith.

In the second place, let me suggest, that faith like a shield *receives the blows which are meant for the man himself*. Some Christians think that faith would enable them to escape blows,—that if they had faith everything would be quiet, everything would be peaceful and calm. I know how young Christians imagine this. They think as soon as ever they have come out of their first convictions of their own sinfulness and found the Saviour, oh! now they are going to ride softly to heaven, singing all the way. What did they put their armour on at all for if there were to be no battles? What have they put their hand to the plough for if they are not to plough to the end of the furrow and often to wipe the sweat from their face through their hard toil? Why enlist, young men, if you are not wanted to fight? What is the good of a fair-weather soldier,—one who stays at home to feed at the public expense? No! let the soldier be ready when war comes; let him expect the conflict as a part and necessary consequence of his profession. But be armed with faith, it receives the blows. The poor shield is knocked and hammered and battered like a pent-house exposed in the time of storm; blow after blow comes rattling upon it, and though it turns death aside yet the shield is compelled itself to hear the cut and the thrust. So must our faith do—it must be cut at, it must bear the blows. Some people, instead of using the shield of faith to bear the blow, use the skulking place of cowards. Ashamed of Christ they make no profession of him, or having professed Christ, ashamed of the profession, they hide themselves by deserting their colours, by conformity to the world. Perhaps they are even called to preach the gospel, but they do it in so quiet and gentle a way, like men that wear soft raiment, and ought to be in kings' houses. Unlike John the Baptist, they are "reeds shaken with the wind." Of them no one saith anything ill, because they have done no ill to Satan's kingdom. Against them Satan never roars —why should he! He is not afraid of them, therefore he need not come out against them. "Let them alone," saith he, "thousands such as these will never shake my kingdom." But this is not to use the shield of faith; this, I repeat it, is to use the skulking-places of an ignoble cowardice. Others use the shield of presumption, they think it is right with them when it is not, but so they are proof, not against the attacks of Satan, but against the weapons of our spiritual warfare. Seared in their conscience as with a hot iron they fear not the rebukes of God's law. Deadened even to the voice of love they bow not before the invitations of Christ; they go on their way caring for none of those things; presumption has made them secure. Some people have no blows to suffer. Their shield lets them go through the world quietly, saying, "Peace, peace, where there is no peace." But only uplift the shield of faith, bearing the blood-red escutcheon of the cross, and there are plenty of the knights of hell who are ready to unhorse you. On, champion, on! in the name of Him that is with you. No lance can pierce that shield; no sword shall ever be able to cut through it; it shall preserve you in all battle and in all strife; you shall bring it home yourself, through it you shall be more than conqueror. Faith, then, is like a shield, because it has to bear the blows.

Thirdly, faith is like a shield, because it hath good need to be *strong*. A man who has some pasteboard shield may lift it up against his foe, the sword will go through it and reach his heart. Or perhaps in the moment when the lance is in rest, and his foe is dashing upon him, he thinks that his shield may preserve him, and lo it is dashed to shivers and the blood gushes from the fountain and he is slain. He that would use a shield must take care that it be a shield of proof. He that hath true faith, the faith of God's elect, hath such a shield that he will see the scimitars of his enemies go to a thousand shivers over it every time they smite the bosses thereof. And as for their spears, if they but once come in contact with this shield, they will break into a thousand splinters, or bend like reeds when pressed against the wall,—they cannot pierce it, but they shall themselves be quenched or broken in pieces. You will say, how then are we to know whether our faith is a right faith, and our shield a strong one? One test of it is, it must be all of a piece. A shield that is made of three or four pieces in this case will be of no use. So your faith must be all of a piece; it must be faith in the finished work of Christ; you must have no confidence in yourself or in any man, but rest wholly and entirely upon Christ, else your shield will be of no use. Then your faith must be of heaven's forging or your shield will **certainly fail you; you must have** the faith of God's elect which is of the operation of the Holy Spirit who worketh it in the soul of man. Then you must see to it that your faith is that which rests only upon truth, for if there be any error or false notion in the fashioning of it, that shall be a joint in it which the spear can pierce. You must take care that your faith is agreeable to God's word, that you depend upon true and real promises, upon the sure word of testimony and not upon the fictions and fancies and dreams of men. And above all, you must mind that your faith is fixed in the person of Christ, for nothing but a faith in Christ's divine person as "God over all, blessed for ever," and in His proper manhood when as the Lamb of God's passover He was sacrificed for us—no other faith will be able to stand against the tremendous shocks and the innumerable attacks which you must receive in the great battle of spiritual life. Look to your shield, man. Not so fast there with that painted God! Not so fast there with that proud heraldic symbol which has no strength in it. See to thy shield. See if it be like the shields of Solomon which were borne before the king, each one made of gold. Or at least let them be like the shields of Rehoboam, every one of the best brass, so that there be found no wooden shield in thy hand which may be dashed in pieces when most thou needest its help.

But to pass on—for we must not pause long on any one particular—faith is like a shield because it is of no use except it be *well handled*. A shield needs handling, and so does faith. He was a silly soldier who, when he went into the battle, said he had a shield but it was at home. So there be some silly professors who have a faith, but they have not got it with them when they need it. They have it with them when there are no enemies. When all goeth well with them, then they can believe; but just when the pinch comes their faith fails. Now there is a sacred art in being able to handle the shield of faith. Let me explain to you how that can be. You will handle it well if you are able to quote the *promises* of God against the attacks of your enemy. The devil said "One day you shall be poor and starve." "No," said the believer, handling his shield well, "He hath said 'I will never leave thee, nor forsake thee;'" "bread shall be given thee and thy water shall be sure." "Aye," said Satan, "but thou wilt one day fall by the hand of the enemy." "No," said faith, "for I am persuaded that He that hath begun a good work in me will perform it until the day of Jesus Christ." "Aye," said Satan, "but the slander of the enemy will overturn you." "No," said faith, "He maketh the wrath of man to praise Him; the remainder of wrath doth He restrain." "Aye," said Satan, as he shot another arrow, "you are weak." "Yes," said faith, handling his shield, "but 'My strength is made perfect in weakness.' Most gladly therefore will I rather glory in my infirmities, that the power of Christ may rest upon me." "Aye," said Satan, "but thy sin is great." "Yes," said faith, handling the promise, "but He is able to save to the uttermost them that come unto God by Him." "But," said the enemy again, drawing his sword and making a tremendous thrust, "God hath cast thee off." "No," said faith, "He hateth putting away; He does not cast off His people, neither doth He forsake His heritage." "But I will have thee, after all," said Satan. "No," said faith, dashing the bosses in the enemy's jaws, "He hath said, 'I give unto My sheep

eternal life, and they shall never perish, neither shall any pluck them out of My hand.'" This is what I call handling the shield.

But there is another way of handling it, not merely with the promises, but with the *doctrines*. "Ah," says Satan, "what is there in thee that thou shouldst be saved? Thou art poor, and weak, and mean, and foolish!" Up came faith, handling the shield doctrinally, this time, and said, "God hath chosen the base things of this world, and things which are despised hath God chosen, yea, and things which are not, to bring to nought the things that are"; for "not many wise men after the flesh, not many mighty, not many noble are called." "Hath not God chosen the poor of this world, rich in faith, and heirs of the kingdom which He hath promised to them that love Him?" "Aye," said he, "if God should have chosen you, yet after all you may certainly perish!" And then, Christian handling his shield of faith doctrinally again, said, "No, I believe in the final perseverance of the saints, for is it not written, 'the righteous shall hold on His way, and he that hath clean hands shall wax stronger?'" "Those that thou gavest Me I have kept, and none of them is lost," and so forth. So by well understanding the doctrines of grace, there is not a single doctrine which may not in its way minister to our defence against the fiery darts of the wicked. Then, the Christian soldier ought to know how to handle the shield of faith according to the rules of observation. "Aye," saith the enemy, "thy confidence is vain, and thy hope shall soon be cut off." "No," saith faith, "I have been young and now am old, yet have I not seen the righteous forsaken?" "Yes, but thou hast fallen into sin, and God will leave thee." "No," saith faith, "for I saw David, and he stumbled, but yet the Lord surely brought him out of the horrible pit, and out of the miry clay." To use this shield in the way of observation, is very profitable when you mark the way whereby God has dealt with the rest of His people; for as He deals with one, so He will deal with the rest, and you can throw this in the teeth of your enemy. "I remember the ways of God. I call to remembrance His deeds of old. I say hath God cast off His people, hath He forsaken one of His chosen? And since He has never done so, I hold up my shield with great courage, and say He never will; He changes not; as He has not forsaken any, He will not forsake me."

Then there is another way of handling this shield, and that is *experimentally*. When you can look back, like the Psalmist, to the land of Jordan and of the Hermonites, from the hill Mizar, when you can return to those days of old, and call to remembrance your song in the night, when your spirit can say, "Why art thou cast down, O my soul, why art thou disquieted within me. Hope thou in God, for I shall yet praise Him." Why, brethren, some of us can talk of deliverances so many, that we know not where to end, scarcely do we know where to begin. Oh! what wonders has God done for us as a Church and people! He has brought us through fire and through water. Men did ride over our heads, but hitherto all things have worked together for our good. His glory has appeared amidst all the villanies and slanders of men to which we have been exposed. Let us handle our shield then, according to the rules of past experience, and when Satan tells us that God will fail us at the last, let us reply, "Now thou liest, and I tell it to thee to thy face, for what our God was in the past, He will be in the present, and in the future, and so on even to the end." Young soldiers of Christ, learn well the art of handling your shield.

Lastly for the matter of the figure. The shield in olden times was an emblem of the warrior's honour, and more especially in later days than those of Paul. In the age of chivalry, the warrior carried his escutcheon upon his shield. Now, faith is like a shield, because it carries the Christian's glory, the Christian's coat of arms, the Christian's escutcheon. And what is the Christian's coat of arms? Well, good Joseph Irons used to say it was a cross and a crown, with the words "No cross, no crown"—a most blessed coat of arms too. But methinks the Christian's best coat of arms is the cross of his Saviour—that blood-red cross; always stained, yet never stained; always dyed in blood, yet always resplendent with ruby brightness; always trodden on, yet always triumphant; always despised, yet always glorified; always attacked, yet always without resistance, coming off more than conquerer. Some of the old Reformers used to have an anvil for their coat of arms, and a significant one too, with this motto, "The anvil hath broken many hammers." By which they meant that they stood still, and just let men hammer at them till their hammers broke of themselves. Another old coat of arms with some of the Reformers, was wont to be a candle with a great many enemies all puffing to blow it out, and though they all blew as hard as they could, yet the candle did but burn the brighter. Out of darkness came light, and from all their attacks, the light grew stronger. This morning put thy coat of arms upon thy shield, and lift it up. Let that blood-red cross be your choice; then when thy battle is over, they will hang thy escutcheon up in heaven; and when the old heraldries have gone, and the lions, and tigers, and griffins, and all manner of strange things have vanished from remembrance, that cross and thy old shield indented with many a blow, shall be honourable with many a triumph before the throne of God. Above all things, then, take the shield of faith.

II. I now leave the expounding of the figure in haste, and pass on to ENFORCE THE EXHORTATION. "Above all taking the shield of faith."

If you sent a servant upon an errand, and you said to him, "Get so-and-so, and so-and-so, and so-and-so, but above all now see to such-and-such a thing"; he would not understand that he ought to neglect any, but he would perceive that there was some extra importance attached to one part of his mission. So let it be with us. We are not to neglect our sincerity, our righteousness, or our peace, but above all, as the most important we are to see to it that our faith is right, that it be true faith, and that it covers all our virtues from attack. The necessity of true faith is clearly explained by the text. Faith is here said to have a quenching power. The ancients were wont to use small arrows, perhaps light cane arrows, which were tinged with poison. They would be called fiery darts, because they no sooner touched the flesh or even grazed the skin than they left a fiery poison in the veins. Sometimes too they employed darts which were tipped with tow that had been dipped in some inflammable spirit, and were blazing as they flew through the air in order to set the tents of their antagonists on fire, or burn down houses in besieged cities. Now faith has a quenching power; it sees the temptation or the blasphemy, or the insinuation coming against it with poison and with fire in it to take away its life or to burn up its

comforts. Faith catches the dart, not only receives it, but takes away its sting, and quenches its fire. Oh it is wonderful how God sometimes enables His people to live in the midst of temptations and tribulations as though they had none of them. I believe that some of the martyrs when they were burning in the fire suffered hardly any pain, because the joy and peace which God gave them delivered them from the vehement heat. This I know. There are times when everybody is speaking well of some of us, and we are wretched by reason of the world's fawnings. We do not want to be called "Son of Pharaoh's daughter." And yet there are other times when, though every one speaks ill, our peace is like a river, and our righteousness like the waves of the sea. Truly at such times we can say, "Now I am in my proper place; this is where I should be—outside the camp, bearing the reproach of Christ." The praise of man is deadly and damnable; his censure is goodly and godlike. Let it come; it cannot dishonour, it does but ennoble. Thus does it often happen that faith quenches the fire of attack, nay, more, turns the attack into comfort, extracts honey from the nettle, and sweets of joy from the wormwood and the gall. "Above all, take the shield of faith."

Another commendation which the text gives is this—that faith alone, out of all the pieces of armour, is able to quench all the darts. The helmet can only keep off those that are aimed against the head. The foot is only and alone protected by the sandals, the breast alone is guarded by the breastplate, but faith protects against all attacks. Have all other virtues, but most of all have faith, for faith is the Catholica, it is the cure-all, it is the universal remedy, it is good not only for the heat of fever, but for the shaking of ague. It is good for everything,—good for the timid to make them strong, good for the rash to make them wise; it is good for those who are desponding to make them brave, and good for those who are too daring, to make them discreet. There is no respect in which faith is not useful to us, therefore, whatever you leave out, see to your faith; if you forget all besides, be careful above all that ye take the shield of faith.

And then, again, we are told above all to take the shield of faith, because faith preserves from all sorts of enemies. The fiery darts of the wicked? Does that refer to Satan? Faith answers him. Does it refer to wicked men? Faith resists them. Does it refer to one's own wicked self? Faith can overcome that. Does it refer to the whole world? "This is the victory that overcometh the world, even our faith." It matters not who the enemy may be; let the earth be all in arms abroad, this faith can quench all the fiery darts of the wicked. Above all then, take the shield of faith. I know there are some ministers who seem to teach doubting as a duty. I cannot; I dare not. Above all, take the shield of faith. You know in the old Grecian contests the aim of the enemy was to get near enough to push aside the shield, and then to stab under the armour. And that is what Satan wants to do. If he can knock aside the shield and get under it, then he can stab us mortally. Take care of your shield. Do not live in perpetual unbelief. Be not always cast down. Pray unto thy God till thou canst say—"I know whom I have believed, and am persuaded that He is able to keep that which I have committed unto Him." Oh! the old saints were not always doubting. "My beloved is mine, and I am His," said Solomon. David said— "Say unto my soul, I am thy salvation." "The

Lord is my salvation." "The Lord is my shepherd." Job too could say, "I know that my Redeemer liveth." Paul could speak very confidently in full many places. And why should we be content to say—"I hope, I trust,"—when they said they knew, and were persuaded—all was well between God and their souls? Let it be so with us. Unbelief dishonours us, weakens us, destroys our comforts, prevents our usefulness. Faith will make us happy, and make us useful, and what is best of all, it will enable us to honour God on earth, and to enjoy His presence while yet we are in the low-lands of this present world.

III. Lastly, I have a word or two to say by way of conclusion to some POOR SINNER WHO IS COMING TO CHRIST, BUT WHO IS GREATLY VEXED WITH THE FIERY DARTS OF THE WICKED ONE.

You remember how John Bunyan in his *Pilgrim's Progress* represents Christiana and Mercy and the children coming to knock at the gate. When they knocked, the enemy who lived in a castle hard by sent out a big dog, which barked at them at such a rate that Mercy fainted, and Christiana only dared to knock again, and when she obtained entrance, she was all in a tremble. At the same time hard by in the castle there were men who shot fiery darts at all who would enter; and poor Mercy was exceedingly afraid because of the darts and the dog. Now, it generally happens that when a soul is coming to Christ the devil will dog him. As sure as ever he feels his need of a Saviour and is ready to put his trust in Christ, it will be true of him as of the poor demoniac child;—as he was a coming, the devil threw him down and tear him. Now, poor tempted sinner, there is nothing that can bring joy and peace into your heart but faith. Oh, that you may each grace this morning to begin to use this shield. "Ah, sir, say you, I have been looking within and I cannot see anything that is good; I have been looking to my experiences and I am afraid I have never felt as So-and-so did." That is the way to ruin yourself. Did you ever hear of a man who in cold winter's weather got warm by rolling on the ice, and saying, "I don't feel any heat as some people do." No, because he is looking in the wrong place to get the heat. If you expect to get anything in yourself you expect more than Paul ever got, for he said after he had long known his Master, "I know that in me—(that is, in my flesh)—there dwelleth no good thing." "Oh, sir," you reply again, "I find I am willing to do a great many things, but I cannot; and when I would be what I should be, I find a resistance somewhere within my own breast." Well, and what of that? Even so did the apostle: "When I would do good, evil is present with me." The fact is you have no business to look there. These things are not shields against Satan. What cares he for your experiences? Were they never so good he would still roar at you. What he is afraid of is your faith. Throw down these things, then, which only encumber you and expose you, and lay your breast bare to his attacks, and take up the shield of faith. What has Satan said to you? "You are too great a sinner to be saved." Well, quote this text, "Him that cometh unto Me, I will in nowise cast out." I had a lesson this week in the case of a good Christian man, who through feebleness of mind has fallen at last into the deepest despair. I never met with a person in such awful despair as he was, and you cannot tell how it puzzled me to give him any sort of comfort; indeed, I failed

after all. He said, "I'm too big a sinner to be saved." So I said, "But the blood of Jesus Christ His Son cleanseth us from all sin." "Aye," said he, "but you must remember the context, which says, "if we walk in the light, as He is in the light, we have fellowship one with another, and the blood of Jesus Christ His Son cleanseth us from all sin." Now, I do not walk in the light," said he; "I walk in the dark, and I have no fellowship with the people of God now, and therefore it does not apply to me." "Well," I said, "but He is able to save to the uttermost them that come unto God by Him." "That is the only text," he said, "I never can get over, for it says 'to the uttermost,' and I know I cannot have gone beyond that, and still it does not yield me comfort." I said, but God asketh nothing of you but that you will believe Him; and you know if you have ever so feeble a faith you are like a child—the feeble hand of a child can receive; and that is the mark of a Christian, —"of His fulness have all we received"—and if you only receive with your hand, that is enough. "Aye, said he, "I have not the hand—I have not the hand of faith." "Very well," I said, "you have the mouth of desire; you can ask, if you cannot receive with the hand." "No," said he, "I have not; I do not pray, I cannot pray; I have not the mouth of desire." "Then," I said, "all that is wanted is an empty place, a vacuum, so that God can put it in." "Ah," Sir, said he, "you have got me there! I have a great deal of vacuum; I have an aching void—a vacuum. If ever there was an empty sinner in this world, I am one." "Well," I said, "Christ will fill that vacuum; there is a full Christ for empty sinners." Let me now say the same to you as I said to that poor man. All God wants is a vacuum. You have got a vacuum. This is not much to have; simply to be empty, to be pumped dry, to have nothing at all in you. But then, "He filleth the hungry with good things, and the rich He sendeth empty away." All that is wanted is to be down there on the ground. It is not hard work. It is not to sit up, nor to stand up, nor to kneel, but to lie there at His feet; and when He sees the soul flat on its face before Him, He will have mercy upon him,

Now, soul, for that shield of faith. Say to Satan, "In the name of God I dare believe." "Thou art a great sinner," says he. "Yes, but I believe He is a great Saviour." "But thou hast sinned beyond all hope." "No, there is forgiveness with Him, that He may be feared." But he says, "You are shut out." "No," say you, "though He slay me, yet will I trust Him." "But your disease is of long standing." Aye, but say you, "If I but touch the hem of His garment, I shall be clean." But saith Satan again, "How dare you? would you have the impudence?" "Well," say you, "if I perish I will trust Christ, and I will perish only there." Have it in your soul fixed, that in the teeth of everything you will trust Christ,— that be you such a sinner or no, still you will trust Christ,—that whether Satan's accusations be true or false, you mean to have done answering them and simply trust Christ. Ah, soul, then thou shalt have such joy and peace that nothing shall be like it. O that thou wouldst believe on Jesus *now!* Leave thy feelings, leave thy doings and thy willings, and trust Christ. "I dare not," saith one. Dare it, man, dare it! you cannot do wrong for He commands you. This is the commandment, that ye believe on Jesus Christ whom He hath sent. "Oh, but I may be lost even if I do." You will be lost if you do not, for "he that believeth not shall be damned." "But I am afraid of being condemned if I were to believe." "He that believeth not is condemned already." You are like the poor lepers at the gate; you are dying, and you say, "Let us fall to the Syrians: if they kill us we can but die, and if they save us alive we shall live." Say you, as Benhadad did concerning king Ahab, "We have heard that the kings of Israel are merciful kings, but let us put ropes upon our heads, and go out to the king of Israel: peradventure he will save thy life." So say thou to God, "I have heard that Thou art merciful; if there is a wretch out of hell that deserves to be in it, I am that sinner—if there is one that now feels that earth is provoked against him, and the ground says, swallow him up; and heaven is provoked against him, and cries, let the lightning flash destroy him; and the sea says, drown him; and the stars say, smite him with pestilence; and the sun says, scorch him; and the moon says, let him be blasted; and the mildew says, let me devour his crops; and fever says, let me cut off the thread of his life,—if there be such a wretch out of hell, I am he."—yet, say, but to God, "I believe in Thy mercy, I believe in Thy promise, I believe in Thy Son Jesus, I believe in His precious blood, and here I am, do with me as seemeth good in Thy sight," —say but this and thou shalt have mercy, and pardon, and peace. My dear hearers, shall I say this for myself and not for you? Nay, but may God grant that many a score of you this morning may be led to put your trust in Him who has said, "They that trust in Me shall never be confounded."

THE PERSEVERANCE OF THE SAINTS

"Being confident of this very thing, that He which hath begun a good work in you will perform it until the day of Jesus Christ."—Philippians i. 6.

THE dangers which attend the spiritual life are of the most appalling character. The life of a Christian is a series of miracles. See a spark living in mid-ocean, see a stone hanging in the air, see health blooming in a lazar-house, and the snow-white swan among rivers of filth, and you behold an image of the Christian life. The new nature is kept alive between the jaws of death, preserved by the power of God from instant destruction; by no power less than divine could its existence be continued. When the instructed Christian sees his surroundings, he finds himself to be like a defenceless dove flying to her nest, while against her tens of thousands of arrows are levelled. The Christian life is like that dove's anxious flight, as it threads its way between the death-bearing shafts of the enemy, and by constant miracle escapes unhurt. The enlightened Christian sees himself to be like a traveller, standing on the narrow summit of a lofty ridge; on the right hand and on the left are gulfs unfathomable, yawning for his destruction; if it were not that by divine grace his feet are made like hind's feet, so that he is able to stand upon his high places, he would long ere this have fallen to his eternal destruction. Alas! my brethren, we have seen too many professors of religion thus fall. It is the great and standing grief of the Christian church, that so many in her midst become apostates. It is true they are not truly of her, but before hand it is not possible for her to know this. Not a few of her brightest stars have been swallowed up of night. Those who bid fairest to be fruitful trees in Christ's vineyard, have turned out to be cumberers of the ground, or very upas trees, dripping poison on all around. The young Christian, therefore, if he be observant, fears lest after putting on his burnished harness, amid the congratulations of friends, he may return from the battle ingloriously defeated. He does not pride himself because, like some gallant knight, he puts on his glittering harness; but as he buckles on his helmet, and grasps his sword, he fears lest he should be brought back into the camp with his scutcheon marred and his crest trailed in the dust. To such a one, conscious of spiritual perils, and fearful lest he should be overcome by them, the doctrine of the text will afford richest encouragement. If we are helped to set forth the doctrine of the final perseverance of the saints, so as to commend the truth to your understandings, and confirm it upon your souls, we shall be glad at heart, because the truth will make you glad, and strong, and thankful.

Without further preface, we shall *expound the apostle's words*, in order to show in detail the matter of his confidence; we shall then, in the second place, *support that confidence by further arguments*; and then, thirdly, we shall seek to *draw out certain excellent uses from the doctrine* which the text undoubtedly teaches.

I. First, let us EXPOUND THE APOSTLE'S OWN WORDS.

He speaks of *a good work* commenced in "all the saints in Christ Jesus which are at Philippi." By this he intended the work of grace in the soul which is of the operation of the Holy Ghost. This is eminently a good work, since it works nothing but good in the heart that is the subject of it. To bring a man from darkness into light is good, to deliver him from the bondage of his natural corruption, and make him the Lord's free man, must be good; it is good for himself, it is good for society, it is good for the church of God, it is good for the glory of God Himself. It is so good a thing, that he who receives it becomes the heir of all good, and moreover, the advocate and author of further good. This good is the best that a man can receive. To make a man healthy in body and wealthy in estate, to educate his mind and train his faculties, all these are good, but in comparison with the salvation of the soul, they sink into insignificance. The work of sanctification is a good work in the highest possible sense, since it influences a man by good motives, sets him on good works, introduces him among good men, gives him fellowship with good angels, and in the end makes him like unto the good God Himself. Moreover, the inner life is a good work, because it springs and originates from the pure goodness of God. As it is always good to show mercy, so it is pre-eminently good on God's part to work upon sinful and fallen men, so as to renew them again after the image of Him that created them. The work of grace has its root in the divine goodness of the Father, it is planted by the self-denying goodness of the Son, and it is daily watered by the goodness of the Holy Spirit; it springs from good and leads to good, and so is altogether good. The apostle calls it a "*work*," and, in the deepest sense, it is indeed a work to convert a soul. If Niagara could suddenly be made to leap upward instead of for ever dashing downward from its rocky height, it were not such a miracle as to change the perverse will and the raging passions of men. To wash the Ethiop white, or remove the leopard's spots, is proverbially a difficulty, yet these are but surface works; to renew the very core of manhood, and tear sin from its hold upon man's heart, this is not alone the finger of God, but the baring of his arm. Conversion is a work comparable to the making of a world. He only who fashioned the heavens and the earth could create a new nature. It is a work that is not to be paralleled, it is unique and unrivalled, seeing that Father, Son, and Spirit, must all co-operate in it; for to implant the new nature in the Christian, there must be the decree of the Eternal Father, the death of the ever-blessed Son, and the fulness of the operation of the adorable Spirit. It is a work indeed. The labours of Hercules were but trifles compared with this; to slay lions and hydras, and cleanse Augean stables—all this is child's play compared with renewing a right spirit in the fallen nature of man.

Observe that the apostle affirms that this good work was *begun by God*. He was evidently no believer in those remarkable powers which some theologians ascribe to free will; he was no worshipper of that modern Diana of the Ephesians. He declares that the good work was begun by God, from which I gather that the faintest gracious desire which ultimately blossoms into the fragrant flower of earnest prayer and humble faith, is the work of God. No, sinner, thou shalt never be beforehand with God! The first step towards ending the separation between the prodigal son and his father is taken by the father, not by the son. Midnight never seeks the sun; long would it be ere darkness found within itself the germs of light; long ages might revolve before Hades should develop the seeds of heaven, or Gehenna discover in its fires the elements of everlasting glory; but till then it shall never happen that corrupt nature shall educe from itself the germs of the new and spiritual life, or sigh after holiness and God. I have heard lately to my deep sorrow, certain preachers speaking of conversions as being developments. Is it so, then, that conversion is but the development of hidden graces within the human soul? It is not so; the theory is a lie from top to bottom. There lies within the heart of man no grain or vestige of spiritual good. He is to all good alien, insensible, dead, and he cannot be restored to God except by an agency which is altogether from without himself and from above. If you could develop what is in the heart of man, you would produce a devil, for that is the spirit which worketh in the children of disobedience; develop that carnal mind which is enmity against God, and cannot by any possibility be reconciled to Him, and the result is hell. The fact is, that the divine life has departed from the natural man; man is dead in sin, and life must come to him from the Giver of life, or he must remain dead for evermore. The work that is in the soul of a true Christian is not of his own beginning, but is commenced by the Lord.

It is implied in the text further, that *He who began the work must carry it on*. "He which hath begun a good work in you will perform it," will complete it, will finish it, as the margin puts it. The apostle does not say as much, but still it is in the run of the sense, if not of the words, that God must perform it, or else it never will be performed. Along the road from sin to heaven, from the first leaving of the swine trough right up to the joyful entrance into the banquet, and the music and dancing of glorified spirits, every step we must be enabled to take by divine grace. Every good thing that is in a Christian, not merely begins, but progresses and is consummated by the fostering grace of God, through Jesus Christ. If my finger were on the golden latch of paradise, and my foot were on its jasper threshold, I should not take the last step so as to enter heaven unless the grace which brought me so far should enable me fully and fairly to complete my pilgrimage. Salvation is God's work, not man's. This is the theology which Jonah learned in the great fish college, in the university of the great deep, to which college it would be a good thing if many of our divines in these days could be sent, for human learning often puffeth up with the idea of human sufficiency: but he that is schooled and disciplined in the college of a deep experience, and made to know the vileness of his own heart, as he peers into its chambers of imagery, will confess that from first to last salvation is not of him that willeth, nor of him that runneth, but of God that showeth mercy.

But the apostle's main drift in the verse is that this good work which is begun in believers by God, which can only be further performed by God, *most certainly will be so carried on*. You observe he declares himself to be confident of this truth. Why did Paul need to write so positively, "being confident of this very thing"? Surely, as an inspired man, he might simply have written, "He which hath begun a good work in you!" but he gives us over an[1] above the inspiration of the Holy Ghost, the confidence which had been wrought in him as the result of his own personal faith. He had been himself very graciously sustained, and he had been favoured personally with such clear views of the character of God, and of the Lord Jesus Christ, that he felt quite confident that God would not leave His work unfinished. He felt in his own mind that whatever anybody else might affirm, he was fully assured, and would stand to the truth and defend it with all his might, that He which hath begun a good work in His people will surely finish it in due season. Indeed, dear friends, in the apostle's words there is good argument. If the Lord began the good work, why should He not carry it on and finish it? If He stays His hand, what can be the motive? When a man commences a work, and leaves it half complete, it is often from want of power; men say of the unfinished tower, "This man began to build, and was not able to finish." Want of forethought, or want of ability, must have stayed the work; but can you suppose Jehovah, the Omnipotent, ceasing from a work because of unforeseen difficulty which He is not able to overcome? He seeth the end from the beginning, He is almighty; His arm is not shortened; nothing is too hard for Him. It were a base reflection upon the wisdom and power of God, to believe that He has entered upon a work which He will not in due time conduct to a happy conclusion. God did not begin the work in any man's soul wit out due deliberation and council. From all eternity He knew the circumstances in which that man would be placed, though He foresaw the hardness of the human heart and the fickleness of human love. If then He deemed it wise to begin, how can it be supposed that He shall change and amend His resolve? There can be no conceivable reason with God for leaving off such a work; the same motive which dictated the commencement, must be still in operation, and He is the same God; therefore, there must be the same result, namely, His continuing to do what He has done. Where is there an instance of God's beginning any work and leaving it incomplete? Show me for once a world abandoned and thrown aside half formed; show me a universe cast off from the Great Potter's wheel, with the design in outline, the clay half hardened, and the form unshapely from incompleteness. Direct me, I pray you, to a star, a sun, a satellite—nay, I will challenge you on lower ground: point me out a plant, an emmet, a grain of dust that hath about it any semblance of incompleteness. All that man completes, let him polish as he may—when it is put under the microscope, is but roughly finished, because man has only reached a certain stage, and cannot get beyond it; it is perfection to his feeble optics, but it is not absolute perfection. But all God's works are finished with wondrous care; He as accurately fashions the dust of a butterfly's wing, as those mighty orbs that gladden the silent night. Yet, my brethren, some would persuade us that this great work of the salvation of souls is begun by God, and then deserted and left incomplete, and that there will be spirits lost for ever upon whom the Holy Ghost once exerted His sanctifying power, for whom the Redeemer shed His precious blood, and whom the eternal Father once looked upon with eyes of complacent love. I believe no such thing. The repetition of such beliefs curdles my blood with horror; they sound so like to blasphemy. Nay, where the Lord begins He will complete; and if He puts His right hand to any work, He will not stay until the work is done, whether it be to smite Pharaoh with plagues, and at last to drown His chivalry in the Red Sea, or to lead His people through the wilderness like sheep, and bring them in the end into the land that floweth with milk and honey. In nothing doth Jehovah turn from His intent. "Hath He said, and shall He not do it? Hath He purposed it, and shall it not come to pass?" He is God and changeth not, and therefore the sons of Jacob are not consumed. There is a world of argument in the quiet words which the apostle uses. He is confident, knowing what he does of the character of God, that He which hath begun a good work in His saints will perform it until the day of Christ.

Notice *the time* mentioned in the text—the good work is to be perfected in the day of Christ; by which we suppose is intended the second coming of our Lord. The Christian will not be perfected until the Lord Christ shall descend from heaven with a shout, with the trump of the archangel, and the voice of God. But how say ye concerning those who have died before His coming? How is it with them? I answer, their souls are doubtless perfect and made mete to be partakers of the inheritance of the saints in light; but Holy Scripture does not regard a man as perfect when the soul is perfected, it regards his body as being a part of himself; and as the body will not rise again from the grave till the coming of the Lord Jesus, when we shall be revealed in the perfection of our manhood, even as He will be revealed, that day of the second coming is set as the day of the finished work which God hath begun, when, without spot or wrinkle or any such thing, body, soul, and spirit, shall see the face of God with acceptance, and for ever and ever rejoice in the pleasures which are at God's right hand. This is what we are looking forward to, that

God who taught us to repent, will sanctify us wholly; that He who made the briny tear to flow will wipe every tear from the selfsame eye; that He who made us gird ourselves with the sackcloth and the ashes of penitence, will yet gird us with the fair white linen which is the righteousness of the saints; He who brought us to the cross will bring us to the crown; He who made us look upon Him whom we pierced and mourn because of Him, will cause us to see the King in His beauty, and the land that is very far off. The same dear hand that smote and afterwards healed, will in the latter days caress us; He who looked upon us when we were dead in sin, and called us into spiritual life, will continue to regard us with favour till our life shall be consummated in the land where there is no more death, neither sorrow no sighing. Such is the truth which the text evidently teaches us.

One remark I here feel bound to make, though it is running somewhat from the theme. It is this: I marvel beyond measure at those of our Christian brethren who hold the doctrine of the final perseverance, and yet remain in the Anglican church, because their so remaining is utterly inconsistent with such a belief. You will say, "How? Is not the doctrine of final perseverance taught in the Articles?" Undoubtedly it is; but it is a flat contradiction to what is taught in the catechism. In the catechism, and in parts of the liturgy, we are distinctly taught that children are born again and made members of Christ in baptism. Now, to be regenerated, or born again, is surely the beginning of a good and divine work in the soul; and then, according to this text, and according to the doctrine of final perseverance, such a divine work being begun, will most certainly be performed until the day of Christ. Now, no one will be so foolhardy as to assert that the good work which, according to the Prayer-book is begun in an infant at its so-called baptism, is beyond all question perfected in the day of Christ; for, alas! we see these regenerated people drunk, lying, swearing; we have them in prison, convicted of all kinds of crimes; we have even known them to be hanged. If I were an evangelical clergyman, and believed in the doctrine of final perseverance, I must at once renounce a church which teaches a lie so intolerable as that, that there is a work of grace begun on an unconscious infant in every case when water is sprinkled from priestly hands. No such work is begun, and consequently no such work is carried on; the whole business of infant baptism, as practised in the Anglican Episcopal Church, is a perversion of Scripture, an insult to God, a mockery of truth, and a deceiving of the souls of men. Let all who love the Lord, and hate evil, come out of this more and more apostatising church, lest they be partakers of the plague which will come upon her in the day of her visitation.

II. Secondly, WE SHALL SHOW FURTHER GROUND FOR OUR BELIEF IN THE DOCTRINE OF THE FINAL PERSEVERANCE OF THE SAINTS.

Our first ground shall be *the express teaching of Holy Scripture.* But, my dear friends, to quote all the scriptural passages which teach that the saints shall hold on their way, would be to quote a large proportion of the Bible, for, to my mind, Scripture is saturated through and through with this truth; and I have often said that if any man could convince me that Scripture did not teach the perseverance of believers, I would at once reject Scripture altogether as teaching nothing at all, as being an incomprehensible book, of which a plain man could make neither head nor tail, for this seems to be of all doctrines the one that lies most evidently upon the surface. Take the ninth verse of the seventeenth chapter of the book of Job, and hear the testimony of the patriarch: "The righteous also shall hold on his way, and he that hath clean hands shall be stronger and stronger." Not "the righteous shall be saved, let him do what he will" —that we never believed, and never shall, but "the righteous shall hold on his way"—his way of holiness, his way of devotion, his way of faith—he shall hold to that, and he shall make a growth meanwhile, for he that hath clean hands shall add "strength to strength," as the Hebrews hath it, or, as we put it, "shall be stronger and stronger." In the one hundred and twenty-fifth Psalm, read the first and second verses, "They that trust in the Lord," that is the especial description of a believer, "shall be as mount Zion, which cannot be removed, but abideth for ever. As the mountains are round about Jerusalem, so the Lord is round about His people from henceforth even for ever." Here are two specimen ears pulled out of those rich sheaves which are to be found in the Old Testament. As for the New Testament, how peremptory are the words of Christ in the tenth of John, twenty-eighth verse, "I give unto them eternal life" —not life temporal which may die—"and they shall never perish, neither shall any man pluck them out of My hand. My Father, which gave them Me, is greater than all; and no man is able to pluck them out of My Father's hand." The apostle tells us, eleventh Romans, twenty-ninth verse, that "the gifts and calling of God are without repentance;" that is, whatever gifts the Lord gives, He never repents of having given them so as to take them back again; and whatever calling He makes of any man, He never retracts it, but He stands to it still. There is no playing fast and loose in divine mercy; His gifts and calling are without repentance. Following that terrible passage, in the sixth of Hebrews, which has raised so many questions, you find the apostle, who seems at first sight to have taught that believers might turn away, you find him in the ninth and tenth verses disclaiming any such idea: "Beloved," says he, "we are persuaded better things of you, and things that accompany salvation, though we thus speak. For God is not unrighteous to forget your work and labour of love, which ye have showed toward His name, in that ye have ministered to the saints, and do minister." The apostle Peter, who is in no way given to administer too much comfort to the saints, but deals very sternly with hypocrisy, has put it very strongly in the first chapter of his epistle, at the fifth verse, where he says of all the elect according to the foreknowledge of God, that they are "kept by the power of God through faith unto salvation ready to be revealed in the last time." Brethren, the fifty-fourth of Isaiah, which I read in your hearing this morning, with many more to the same effect, are scarcely to be understood if it be true that God's children may be cast away, and that God may forsake those whom He did foreknow. Yonder Bible seems to be disembowelled, and stripped of its life, if the unchanging love of God be denied. The word of God is laid on the threshing-floor, and the chaff alone is gathered, and the wheat is cast away, if you take out of it its constant and incessant teaching that the "path of the just is as the shining light, that shineth more and more unto the perfect day."

But further, in addition to the express testimonies of Scripture, we have to support this doctrine *all the*

attributes of God for if those who have believed in Christ are not saved, then surely all the attributes of God are in peril; if He begins and doth not finish His work, all the parts of His character are dishonoured. Where is His wisdom? Why did He begin that which He did not intend to finish? Where is His power? Will not evil spirits always say, "that He *could not* do what He did not do"? Will it not be a standing jeer throughout the halls of hell that God commenced the work and then stayed from it? Will they not say that the obstinacy of man's sin was greater than the grace of God, that the adamant of the human heart was too hard for God to dissolve? Would there not be a slur at once cast upon the omnipotence of grace? And what shall we say of the immutability of God, if He casts away those whom He loves—how shall we think that He doth not change? How will the human heart ever be able to look upon Him again as immutable if after loving He hateth? And, my brethren, where will be the faithfulness of God to the promises which He has made over and over again, and signed and sealed with oaths by two immutable things, wherein it was impossible for God to lie? Where will be His grace if He casts away those that trust in Him, if after having tantalised us with sips of love He shall not bring us to drink from the fountain head? It is all in vain for us henceforth to trust if His promise can be forgotten and His mind can be turned. Henceforth we need not talk of Ebenezers in the past as though they comforted us for the future, if the Lord doth cast away His children; for the past is no guarantee whatever as to what He may do in days to come. But the veracity of God to His promise, the faithfulness of God to His purpose, the immutability of God in His character, and the love of God in His essence, all these go to prove that He cannot and will not leave the soul that He has looked upon in mercy until the great work is done.

Further, how can it be that the righteous should, after all, fall from grace, and perish, if you recollect *the doctrine of the atonement?* The doctrine of atonement, as we hold it, and believe it to be in Scripture, is this—that Jesus Christ rendered to divine justice a satisfaction for the sins of His people; that He was punished in their room, and place, and stead. Now if He were so, and I do not believe any other atonements worth the turn of a finger, if He was really our satisfactory vicarious sacrifice, then how could the Child of God be cast into hell? Why should He be cast there? His sins were laid on Christ, what is to condemn him? Christ has been condemned in his stead. In the name of everlasting justice, which must stand, though heaven and earth should rock and reel, how can a man for whom Christ shed His blood be held as guilty before God, when Christ took his guilt and was punished in his stead? He who believes, must surely be ultimately brought to glory, the atonement requires it; and since he cannot come to glory without persevering in holiness, he must so persevere, or else the atonement is a thing that has no efficacy and force.

The doctrine of *justification*, in the next place, proves this. Every man that believes in Jesus is justified from all things, from which he could not be justified by the law of Moses. The apostle Paul regards a man who is justified as being completely set free from the possibility of accusation. Have you not the rolling thunder of the apostle's holy boasting still in your ears: "Who shall lay anything to the charge of God's elect?" If nothing can be laid to their charge, if there be no accuser, who is he that condemneth? If God considers believers just and righteous through the righteousness of His dear Son, if they put on His wondrous mantle, the fair white linen of a Saviour's righteousness, where is there room for anything to be brought against them by which they can be condemned? and if not accused, nor condemned, they must hold on their way, and be saved.

Further still, my brethren, *the intercession of Christ in heaven* is a guarantee for the salvation of all who trust Him. Remember Peter's case: "Simon, Simon, behold, Satan hath desired to have you that he may sift you as wheat; but I have prayed for thee, that thy faith fail not:" and the prayer of Christ preserved Peter, and made him weep bitterly after he had fallen into sin. The like prayer of our ever watchful Shepherd is put up for all His chosen; day and night He pleads, wearing the breastplate as our great High Priest before the throne; and if He pleads for His people, how shall they perish unless indeed His intercession has lost its authority?

Moreover, do you not remember that every believer is said to be "*one with Christ*"? "For ye are members of His body," saith the apostle, "of His flesh, and of His bones." And is your imagination so depraved that you can picture Christ, the Head, united to a body in which the members frequently decay—hand and foot, and eye, perhaps rotting off so as to need fresh members to be created in their stead? The metaphor is too atrocious for me to venture to enlarge upon it. "Because I live ye shall live also," is the immortality that covers every member of the body of Christ. No fear that the righteous should turn back to sin, and give themselves up to their old corruptions, for the holiness that is in Christ by the vital energy of the Holy Spirit, penetrates the entire system of the spiritual body, and the least member is preserved by the life of Christ.

Once more, *the inner life of the Christian* is a guarantee that he shall not go back into sin. Take such passages as these, "Being born again, not of corruptible seed, but of incorruptible, by the word of God, which liveth and abideth for ever." 1 Peter i. 23. Now, if this seed be incorruptible, and liveth, and abideth for ever, how say some among you that the righteous become corrupt, and fall from grace? Hear the Master: "The water that I shall give him shall be in him a well of water springing up into everlasting life." How say you then that this water which Jesus gives dries up and ceases to flow? Hear Him yet again: "As the living Father hath sent Me, and I live by the Father: so he that eateth Me, even he shall live by Me. . . . He that eateth of this bread shall live for ever." John vi. 47, 58. The life which Jesus implants in the heart of His people is allied to His own life: "For ye are dead, and your life is hid with Christ in God." "When He who is your life shall appear, then shall ye also appear with Him in glory." The Holy Ghost dwells in us. "Know ye not that your bodies are temples of the Holy Ghost?" O beloved, God Himself shall as soon die as the Christian, since the life of God is but eternal, and that is the life which Christ has given to us: "I give unto My sheep *eternal* life, and they shall never perish neither shall any pluck them out of My hand."

I leave the doctrine with your understandings, the word of God being in your hands, and may the Spirit of God put it beyond a doubt in your souls that it is even so. Remember, it is not the doctrine that every man that believeth in Christ shall be saved, let him do as he listeth, but it is this doctrine: that each man believing in Jesus shall receive the spirit of holiness, and shall be led on in the way of holiness from strength to strength until he cometh unto the perfection which God will work in us at the coming of His own dear Son.

III. Lastly, we have to DRAW CERTAIN USEFUL INFERENCES from this doctrine.

One of the first is this: there is much in this truth *by way of comfort* to a child of God who to-day walks in darkness and sees no light. You know that sometime ago the Lord revealed Himself to you; you remember times when the promises were peculiarly sweet, when the person of Christ was revealed to your spiritual vision in all its glory; then, beloved, if some temporary depression of spirit should just now overwhelm you, if some heavy personal trial should pass over you, hear you the words, "I am the Lord, I change not." Believe that if He hides His face, He loves you still. Do not judge Him by the outward providences, judge Him by the teaching of His word. Do as the bargemen do on the canals, when they push backwards to drive their boat forwards. Take comfort from the past; snatch firebrands of comfort from the altars of yesterday to enkindle the sacrifices of to-day.

"Determined to save, He watched o'er your path,
When Satan's blind slave, you sported with death:
And can He have taught you to trust in His name,
And thus far have brought you to put you to shame?"

This doctrine should suggest to every Christian *the need of constant diligence*, that he may persevere to the end. "What," saith one, "is that an inference from the doctrine? I should have thought the very reverse, for if the believer is to hold on his way, what need of diligence?" I reply, that the misunderstanding lies with the objector. If the man is to be kept in holiness till life's end, surely there is need that he should be kept in holiness; and the doctrine that he shall be so kept is one of his best means of producing the desired result. If any of you should be well assured that, in a certain line of business, you would make a vast sum of money, would that confidence lead you to refuse that business, would it lead you to lie in bed all day, or to desert your post altogether? No, the assurance that you would be diligent and would prosper would make you diligent. I will borrow a metaphor from the revelries of the season, such as Paul aforetime borrowed from the games of Greece—if any rider at the races should be confident that he was destined to win, would that make him slacken speed? Napoleon believed himself to be the child of destiny, did that freeze his energies? To show you that the certainty of a thing does not hinder a man from striving after it, but rather quickens him, I will give you an anecdote of myself: it happened to me when I was but a child of some ten years of age, or less. Mr. Richard Knill, of happy and glorious memory, an earnest worker for Christ, felt moved, I know not why, to take me on his knee, at my grandfather's house, and to utter words like these, which were treasured up by the family, and by myself especially, "This child," said he, "will preach the gospel, and he will preach it to the largest congregations of our times." I believed his prophecy, and my standing here to-day is partly occasioned by such belief. It did not hinder me in my diligence in seeking to educate myself because I believed I was destined to preach the gospel to large congregations; not at all, but the prophecy helped forward its own fulfilment; and I prayed, and sought, and strove, always having this Star of Bethlehem before me, that the day should come when I should preach the gospel. Even so the belief that we shall one day be perfect, never hinders any true believer from diligence, but is the highest possible incentive to make a man struggle with the corruptions of the flesh and seek to persevere according to God's promise. "Well, but," saith one, "if God guarantees final perseverance to a man, why needs he pray for it?" Sir, how dare he pray for it if God had not guaranteed it? I dare not pray for what is not promised, but as soon as ever it is promised I pray for it; and when I see it in God's word I labour for it. "Say what you will," saith one, "you are inconsistent." Ah, well, my dear friend, we are bound to explain as best we can, but we are not bound to give understanding to those who have none; it is hard trying to make things appear aright to eyes that squint. It will sometimes happen that people cannot see truths which they do not particularly want to see; but the practical is the main thing: and I hope it shall be ours by practical argument, to prove that while those who think that they can fall from grace run awful risks, and do fall, those who know they cannot, if they have truly believed, yet seek to walk with all carefulness and circumspection. I would seek to live as if my salvation depended on myself, and then go back to my Lord, knowing that it does not depend on me in any sense at all. We would live as the opposite doctrine is *supposed* to make men live, which is exactly as the Calvinistic doctrine actually does make men live—namely, with earnestness of purpose, and with gracious gratitude to God, which is, after all, the mightiest influence; gratitude to God for having secured our salvation through Jesus Christ our Lord.

Another matter drawn from the text is this: let us *learn from the text how to persevere.* Brethren, you will observe that the apostle's reason for believing that the Philippians would persevere was not because they were such good and earnest people, but because God had begun the work. So our ground for holding on must be our resting in God. There is a dear brother sitting here this morning, a member of this church, who was once a member of another denomination of Christians. One night, when he was quite young, and lately converted, he knelt down to pray, and he felt himself cold and dead, and did not pray many minutes, but went to bed. No sooner had he laid down than a horror of darkness came over him, and he said to himself, "I have fallen from grace." Dear good soul as he was and is, he rose from his bed, began to pray, but got no better; and at five o'clock in the morning, away he went to his class leader, began knocking at the door and shouting to awaken him. "What do you want?" said the class leader, as he opened the window. The reply was, "Oh, I have fallen from grace." "Well," said the class leader, "if you have fallen from grace, go home and trust in the Lord." "And," said my friend, "I have done so ever since." Yes, and if he had known the great truth before, he would not have been taken up with such nonsense as that of having fallen from grace. "Fallen from grace! then go and simply trust in the Lord." Aye, and this is what we must all do, fallen or not; we must not trust within, but always rely on

that dear Christ who died on the cross. Lord, if I am not a saint, and I often fear I have nothing to do with saintship, yet, Lord, I am a sinner, and thou hast died to save sinners, and I will cling to that. O precious blood, if I never did experience thy cleansing power; if, up till now, I have been in the gall of bitterness and the bonds of iniquity, yet there stands the grand old gospel of the cross, "He that believeth and is baptized shall be saved." Lord, I believe to-day if I never did before; help thou mine unbelief. This is the true theory of perseverance; it is to persevere in being nothing, and letting Christ be everything; it is to persevere in resting wholly and simply in the power of the grace which is in Christ Jesus.

Lastly, *this doctrine has a voice to the unconverted.* I know it had to me. If anything in this world first led me to desire to be a Christian, it was the doctrine of the final perseverance of the saints. I had seen companions of my boyhood, somewhat more advanced than myself, who were held up to me as patterns of all that was excellent. I had seen them apprenticed in large towns, or launching out in business for themselves, and soon their moral excellences were swept away. Instead of being patterns, they came to be persons against whom the young were warned for their supremacy in vice. This thought occurred to me: "That may also be my character in years to come; is there any way by which a holy character can be ensured for the future? is there any way by which a young man by taking heed may be kept from uncleanness and iniquity?" And I found that if I put my trust in Christ, I had the promise that I should hold on my way, and grow stronger and stronger; and though I feared I might never be a true believer, and so get the promise fulfilled to myself, for I was so unworthy, yet the music of it always charmed me. "Oh, if I could but come to Christ and hide myself like a dove in His wounds, then I should be safe. If I could but have Him to wash me from my past sins, then His Spirit would keep me from future sin, and I should be preserved to the end." Does not this attract you? Oh, I hope there may be some who will be allured by such a salvation as this. We preach no rickety gospel which will not bear your weight; it is no chariot whose axles will snap, or whose wheels will be taken off. This is no foundation of sand that may sink in the day of the flood. Here is the everlasting God pledging Himself by covenant and oath, and He will write His law in your heart, that you shall not depart from Him; He will keep you, that you shall not wander into sin, and if for awhile you stray, He will restore you again to the paths of righteousness. O young men and maidens, turn in hither! cast in your lot with Christ and His people. Trust him, trust him, trust him, and then shall this precious truth be yours, and the experience of it be illustrated in your life:—

> "My name from the palms of His hands
> Eternity will not erase;
> Impressed on His heart it remains
> In marks of indelible grace.
> Yes, I to the end shall endure,
> As sure as the earnest is given;
> More happy, but not more secure,
> Are the glorified spirits in heaven."

THE MINISTER'S PLEA

"Through your prayer, and the supply of the Spirit of Jesus Christ."—Philippians i. 19

THE apostle was in prison, in great jeopardy of his life; he was much troubled by many who had begun to preach Jesus Christ, but did not preach Him in a proper spirit: he was also often depressed by that which came daily upon him, the care of all the churches: yet, while he looked in the face the evils which surrounded him, he was able to see beyond them, and to believe that the consequences of all his trials would be real and lasting good. He felt sure that it was a good thing for him to be in prison; that it would be a good thing even if he had to die there; that it was well that many were preaching Christ, even though some did it of ill-will, for Christ was preached, and the result could not be evil; and that the troubles and trials of the churches were good, for somehow or other they would be overruled for God's glory. Let us learn from Him to look at the end as well as at the beginning of things. The bud of our present trouble may have no beauty in it, but fair will be the flower which will ultimately develop from it. The clouds hang heavily above our heads, but let us not, like little children, be alarmed at their blackness, but remember that they are—

"Big with mercy and will break
With blessings on our head."

Whatsoever happeneth to the true servant of the Lord will turn out for the furtherance of the gospel; therefore will we rejoice in tribulations, and accept God's will, whatever it may be.

But observe that the apostle did not expect that good would arise out of everything apart from prayer. He believed that it would be through the prayer of his beloved friends at Philippi, and the supply of the Spirit, that everything which happened to him would work to promote his salvation, his spiritual advantage and his success as a minister of Christ. He looked for the transformation of the evil into good by that sacred alchemy of heaven which can transmute the basest metal into purest gold, but he did not expect this to happen apart from the ordained methods and ordinary institutions of grace; he counted upon the result because he saw two great agents at work, namely, prayer and the supply of the Spirit. Whoever else may be foolish enough to look for effects apart from causes, the apostle was not of their mind.

This morning, my sermon will be mainly upon my own behalf, and on the behalf of my brethren in the ministry. We ought sometimes to have a sermon for ourselves, for we preach a great many for others; and we may the more boldly become pleaders on our own account, inasmuch as what we ask for is really intended for the profit of our people, and for the good of Christ's cause.

My real subject will be, "Brethren, pray for us." The end which I shall drive at will be to excite you to be much in prayer, both for myself and all ministers of Christ Jesus, that so everything that is occurring abroad, and happening personally to any one of us, may be turned to the best account, "Through your prayer, and the supply of the Spirit."

Let us speak, first of all, upon *the prayer of the church*; and then concerning *the supply of the Spirit*. The two matters are closely connected, and cannot be separated.

I. THE PRAYER OF THE CHURCH. The apostle evidently expected to be prayed for. He had the fullest confidence that his brethren at Philippi were praying for him. He does not ask for their prayers so much as assume that he is already receiving them. And truly I wish that all pastors could always, without doubt, assume that they enjoyed the perpetual prayers of those under their charge. Some of us are very rich in this respect, and this is our joy and comfort, the reward of our labour and the strength of our hands. We have abundant evidence that we live in the hearts of our people; but I am afraid that there are many of my brother ministers who are sad because they hear not their people's loving intercessions, weak because they are not prayed for, and unsuccessful because they have not so gained their people's affections that they are borne upon their hearts at the mercy seat. Unhappy is that minister who dares not take it for granted that His people are praying for him.

Paul exceedingly valued the prayers of the saints. He was an apostle, but he felt he could not do without the intercessions of the poor converts at Philippi. He valued Lydia's prayers and the prayers of her household; he valued the jailer's prayer, and the prayers of his family; he desired the prayers of Euodias and Syntyche, and Clement, and the rest—the most of them, probably, persons of no great social standing, as the world has it—yet he valued their supplications beyond all price, and was as grateful for their prayers as for those temporal gifts whereby the Philippians had again and again ministered to his necessities. If the apostle thus felt indebted to the pleadings of the brethren, how much more may we, who are so far inferior to him!

He expected great results from the prayers of the church. That is certain from the text. He expected evil to be turned to good, and himself to be helped onward in the divine life. Beloved, my heart has no deeper conviction than this, that prayer is the most efficient spiritual agency in the universe, next to the Holy Ghost. He is omnipotent, and doeth as He wills; but next to the omnipotence of the in-dwelling Spirit is the potence of prayer. "Ask, and ye shall receive; seek, and ye shall find; knock, and it shall be opened to you": this great charter of the church of Jesus Christ confers upon her powers which are almost, if not quite, omnipotent; and if a church will but pray, it shall set in motion the second most potent agent under heaven. The apostle knew the power of prayer, and we know it too, and hope to prove it more and more.

Paul expected the people at Philippi to be praying for him all the more, because his troubles were just then more heavy than usual. He was sure that this would excite their sympathy, and so make them plead more eagerly. Truly, if ever there were times when the people of God should pray for their ministers, these are the times, for the minister of Christ is beset by legions of evils of all kinds, and has to cut his way through perpetual opposition. The church is sailing now like a vessel in the Arctic Sea when the frost is setting in and is turning the sea into plates of iron, and each wave into an iceberg, to block up the vessel's path. These are evil days, almost beyond any age that has gone before, and therefore we may exhort the church to pray more importunately, because her prayers are more than ever needed.

Plunging into the middle of my subject. I would say, first, that *ministers may justly claim the prayers of their brethren*. Every Christian should be prayed for; we have each a claim upon the other for loving intercession. The members of the body of Christ should have a care for one another, but especially should the minister receive the prayers of his flock. I have sometimes heard *his duties* called arduous, but that word is not expressive enough. The works in which he is occupied lie quite out of the region of human power. The minister is sent to be God's messenger for the quickening of the dead. What can he do in it? He can do nothing whatever unless the Spirit of God be with him through the prayer of his brethren. He is sent to bring spiritual food to the multitude, that is to say, he is to take the loaves and fishes, and with them, few as they are, he is to feed the thousands. An impossible commission! He cannot perform it. Apart from divine help, the enterprise of a Christian minister is only worthy of ridicule. Apart from the power of the Eternal Spirit, the things which the preacher has to do are as much beyond him as though he had to weld the sun and moon into one, light up new stars, or turn the Sahara into a garden of flowers. We have a work to do concerning which we often cry, "Who is sufficient for these things?" and if we be put to this work but have not your prayers, and in consequence have not the supply of the Spirit, we are of all men the most miserable.

Remember also that in addition to extraordinary duties the minister is burdened by remarkable *responsibilities*. All Christians are responsible for their gifts and opportunities, but peculiar responsibilities cluster around the preacher of the Word. "If the watchman warn them not, they shall perish; but their blood will I require at the watchman's hands." When I look at Paul labouring night and day, weeping, praying, pleading, pouring out his soul in his ministry, I feel his example to be so high that I cannot attain unto it, and yet I shall never feel satisfied with anything below that standard. The responsibilities resting upon one minister are the same as those which press upon another, in proportion to his sphere and capacity of service. Oh, unhappy men, if we be found unfaithful!—of criminals the chief, murderers of immortal souls; if we have not preached the pure gospel, we shall be wholesale poisoners of the bread of men, the bread which their souls require. We, if we be not true to God, are the choice servants of Satan. Judas himself was not more the son of perdition than the man who calls himself an ambassador for Christ, and yet dares to be unfaithful to the souls of men. Brethren, we claim your prayers by the solemnity of the responsibility which rests upon us.

Remember, too—what I think is not often noticed —that every true minister of Christ, who is sent to men's souls, has an *experience* singular and by itself. A physician who has to treat the diseases incident to our flesh need not have personally suffered from the sicknesses with which he deals; but a physician of souls never handles a wound well unless he has felt a like wound himself. The true shepherds, who really feed the sheep, must themselves have gone through the experiences of the flock. Did you ever read the life of Martin Luther? Then you must have remarked the mental storms and spiritual convulsions which shook the man. He could not have been so influential with his fellow-men if he had not felt within himself a sort of aggregation of all their sorrows and their struggles. Thou canst not bring forth God's living word to others till first thou hast eaten the roll, and it has been in thine own bowels like gall for bitterness, and yet at times like honey for sweetness. Every successful husbandman in the Lord's vineyard must first have been a partaker of the fruit, yea, and of each kind of fruit too. Hence it often happens, that to comfort yonder desponding heart we must have been ourselves despondent; to console yonder downcast, despairing spirit, we must have been despairing too; to direct the perplexed we must ourselves have been in dilemma. To ride the whirlwind, and come as God's messenger to the help of those who are in the storm, we must have ourselves been tossed with tempest and not comforted. David could not have written his psalms, which, as in a mirror, reflect all changes of the human mind, if he had not himself been the epitome of the lives of all men; and in proportion as God qualifies His minister really and effectually to feed the souls of His people, that minister must go through the whole of their experience; and I ask you whether in such a case he does not claim, and should not have, the prayers of the church of God.

Remember, too, that the *temptations* of those who serve God in the public ministry are subtle, numerous, and withal peculiar. Do you suppose that a man attracts thousands to listen to him, that he conducts large agencies successfully, that he wins souls to Christ, and edifies the household of faith, and that the temptation to pride never crosses his soul? Have you not seen men who have been set upon a pinnacle of eminence, and their heads have been turned, and they have fallen, to their own disgrace, and to the church's sorrow? Do you wonder at it? If you do, you know not what is in men. And do you wonder that ministers are often tempted to grow formal in service? Here, so many times in the year, must I come and speak to you, whether I am fit to do so or not. How can I be always alike zealous, when even the weather has an effect upon nerve and brain? Are you always earnest in your hearing? Do you wonder, therefore, that sometimes the preacher does not find it easy to be earnest in his speaking; and yet he would loathe himself if he dared speak to you what he did not feel, and would think himself accursed if he dared to preach with cold and chilly lips those matchless truths which have been bedewed by the bleeding heart of Jesus. We, who would instruct others, must keep up our spiritual life to a high point; and yet the temptation is, from our familiarity with holy things, to become mechanical in our service, and to lose the freshness and ardour of our first love. I might instance many temptations which are peculiar to us, but the recital might be of no benefit to you: suffice it to say that there are such, and if by your choice you place any man, in the name of God, in a place where he is so peculiarly assailed by the enemy, you will not be so ungenerous as to leave him without the perpetual support of your extraordinary prayer. Fail not your standard-bearer; but form around him a bodyguard of valiant intercessors.

And then, mark you, if any man shall lead the

way in the church of God, he will be the main object of the *assaults* of the enemy. The private Christian will have some persecution, but the minister must expect far more. His words will be misrepresented and tortured into I know not what of evil, and his actions will be the theme of slander and falsehood. If he shall speak straight out and boldly, fearless of man, and only fearful lest he should grieve his God, he will stir the kennels of hell, and make all the hounds of Satan howl at his heels; and he may count himself happy if he shall do so, for who is he that wants to be on good terms with this evil generation, which cares nothing whatever for God's truth, but sets up, for its own church, a church which has made a league with Antichrist, and a compromise between the gospel and idolatry, so that it may drag down this nation into the deeps of Romanism! I say, who cares to have honour from this adulterous generation? And yet, if a man once dares to provoke its wrath by his faithfulness, he needs the prayers of those who believe with him, that he may be sustained. Many are the archers who sorely shoot at us and grieve us; pray ye, therefore, that our bow may abide in strength, and that the arms of our hands may be made strong by the Mighty God of Jacob.

One plea more, and I will not further add to the points of my argument. Amongst the worst trials of the ministry are the *discouragements* of it. I do not just now refer to discouragements from the outside world—we expect opposition from that quarter, and are not discouraged by it. If the world hate us, we know that it hated the Lord before it hated us. But our saddest discouragements arise from within the church and congregation. There are those whom we hoped to see converted, who go back to their old sins and disappoint us, and others who are a little impressed relapse into their natural indifference. There are those who are, we hope, right at heart, who nevertheless live inconsistently; for many walk so far from Jesus that they pierce us with sorrow. And then there are others who profess great things, and unite themselves with the church of God, of whom I have told you often, and now tell you even weeping, that they are the enemies of the cross of Christ. They shame us; they make the world to say, "Is this your religion?" They open the mouths of atheists and infidels and ungodly men of all sorts, against the precious Christ Himself, so that He is wounded in the house of His friends, and put to an open shame by those who ought rather to have laid down their lives to promote His cause and kingdom. Oh, if you be called of the Lord to shepherd His flock, and if you bear in your bosom the church of God, and the cause of Christ, and live for it with all your heart and soul, you shall not live many days without many heart-breaking trials, and you will greatly need the supply of the Spirit in answer to the prayers of the people of God!

Now, having stated the case, and pleaded not for myself only but for all my brethren, let me say, next, that *the prayers which are wanted are the prayers of the entire church.* From some other labour some of you might be exempted, but from this service not a single one can be excused. "*Your* prayer," says the apostle, and he means the prayer of all the faithful. My brother, my fellow-worker, you of the Sunday-school, you of the Evangelistic Society, you who visit from house to house, I want your prayer, my brother; you can sympathise with us; you know something of this way; you can, therefore, bear us up with hands

that have been exercised in the same warfare. We want your prayers also, you who are not workers in any public capacity, you who feel you have not the ability or the opportunity. If there be such among us, you ought to pray doubly for those who are working, and so in some measure make amends for your own lack of energy. If you feel laid aside from actual service yourselves, so that you have to abide by the stuff, let your prayers go up doubly for those who go down to the battle. Hold up their hands, I pray you, if you can do nothing else.

We ask the prayers of all who profit by our ministry. If you feed upon the word, pray to God that we may feed others also. If your hearts are ever made glad within you by the word we speak, do plead for us that we may have the power of God resting upon us yet further. If you do not profit we have an equal claim upon you. We beseech you pray that you may profit. If we are not suited to teach you, pray the Lord to make us suitable. If you discover some lack or deficiency which mars our ministry, do not unkindly go and speak of it everywhere, but tell the Lord about it. You will be doing more good, and acting more after the mind of Christ; and—who knows? —the very ministry which is flat and unprofitable to you now may yet become a great blessing to you when you have prayed concerning it.

Some of you are our spiritual children, begotten unto God by us; and surely we hardly need take you by the hand and say, "Brethren, children, pray for us." There is between us and you a tie which neither life nor death can break. We shall recognise it in eternity. When fathers, and mothers, and husbands, and wives will find all human relationship forgotten, the relationship which exists between the spiritual father and his children shall last on. Therefore, as you feel the tie, yield to its gentle persuasions, and let your pastor have a very warm place in your prayers.

You, aged men and matronly women, you of experience, you of power with God, you who are mighty in your private wrestlings, we want your prayers; and you young Christians with your new-born zeal, in the freshness and vigour of your spiritual life, we want your entreaties too. My little children, you who have been added to the church while yet you are boys and girls, there are no intercessions more precious than yours. Do not forget your minister when you say, "Our Father which art in heaven." God will hear the petitions of little children who love Him.

As for those who are not, and could not be here this morning, my voice will reach them through the press, and therefore let me say to them—You cannot come up to the house of God, but are appointed to lie tossing upon the bed of pain; and yet from you also we ask intercessory prayer. You are especially set to do this service for the church; if you cannot appear in the public assembly, you may in secret wrestlings bring down power upon that assembly. Ye keep the watches of the weary night when pain forbids your eyelids to find rest; let each weary hour be cheered for yourselves, and enriched for us by prayers for the church of God and prayers for us. Perhaps to this end some among the saints are always sick, that warders for the hours of night may not be wanting; the sleepless sufferers change guard before the mercy seat, lest perchance there should be an hour in the night unhallowed by a prayer, in which the world should pass away beneath the unrestrained wrath of God. Prayer must be kept up like the quenchless fire on Israel's altar. We must belt and girdle the world with prayer, and the sick ones are they to whom much of the sacred work is allotted. I believe in the efficacy of united prayer, but each one must pray. There would be no clouds unless the drop of dew from each blade of grass were exhaled by the sun. Each drop ascending in vapour falls again in the blessed shower which removes the drought. So the grace that trembles upon each one of you, my brethren, must exhale in prayer, and a blessing will come down upon the church of God.

Let me suggest for a moment, in passing on, that the prayers of God's people ought to go up for the minister in many forms. I think it should be daily work. I was pleased to hear one of our brethren say the other day, what I am sure was true, and true of a great many beside himself, that he never did pray for himself without praying for me; that he never bowed his knee, morning or night, without remembering the work carried on in this place. It ought to be so with us all.

Besides that, if we expect a blessing on our families through the ministry, we should, as a family, ask God to bless that ministry. When we come around the family altar, amongst the petitions never to be forgotten should be this—that he who is set to feed our souls may himself receive the bread of heaven.

Then there are our prayer-meetings, our public gatherings for intercession. Ah, beloved! I may well glory in our prayer-meetings, for I know not where the like have been found continuously, year after year. Still, though I may glory, I am not sure that all of you could; for as I look around upon you to-day I cannot help remarking that I see some faces on the Sabbath which I have never had the pleasure of seeing on the Monday evening; or, if ever I did, I remember it very well, because it has not been so common an occurrence that it is likely to slip out of my mind. I know there are some who could not come, and would be neglecting family duties if they did; their duty and their calling keep them from it. At the same time, there are others to whom a gentle hint may be serviceable. Forsake not the assembling of yourselves together for earnest prayer, as the manner of some is.

Beside the prayer meetings, there ought to be meetings very frequently of Christian friends who gather by appointment for this very purpose. When they come together, professors often waste time in idle talk which would be used to great profit if they spent it in prayer. When two Christians meet together for united prayer, amongst their other supplications should be one that the Lord would bless throughout all England the preaching of the gospel of Jesus. Oh, dear friends, we want more than anything else to have the gospel preached with power. God forbid we should criticize severely those who may be doing their best, but how much preaching is utterly powerless. We want a telling ministry; we want a ministry which cuts like a two-edged sword and goes through into the very heart. God send us thousands of men armed with His Spirit's own sword, endowed with the muscle of grace, and gifted with manliness to use the celestial weapon. Pray for such often, not at set times only, but at all convenient seasons.

And here, let me remark, should there not be especial prayer by each Christian for his own minister before every service, before going up to the house of the Lord, and when he arrives there? Many people have a habit of looking into their hats to see the name of the maker whenever they get inside a place of worship; they are themselves the best judges whether it is not a piece of Pharisaic formalism or fashionable hypocrisy. There is a formalism about it, and we are the very last to care about outward forms; still, what can be a better beginning for a service than secret prayer? Then, during the service, how much of prayer there should be for the preacher: "Lord, help him to speak the truth outright, and put Thy power into it to send it home to the hearts and consciences of the hearers." It is well to pick out some one in the congregation, and pray, "Lord, bless the word to him." You would often find God hearing you in that respect. Then, after the whole service is done, what can be better than to rake in with earnest prayer the good seed which has already been sown.

I must not keep you longer on this point. Suffice it to add that the prayers of the church of God must always be true prayers to be good for anything, and if they are true prayers, they will be attended with consistent lives. The man who says, "I pray for the church and pray for the minister," and then is a thief in his business, or is guilty of some secret vice—why, he is pulling down, not building up. Can unclean hands ever be acceptable in prayer? Consistent living there must be, or prayer will be a vanity of vanities. And there must be consistent effort too. If I want God to bless the church, I must try to bless it myself, by the gift of my substance, by the consecration of my talents, by the laying out of my time for the glory of God; for to pray one way and to act another is to be a hypocrite; and when the wheel sticks in the mire, to pray to God to help the cart out of it, and never to put my shoulder to the wheel, is to mock the Most High. We must act as well as pray. And we must believe as well as act. We must have faith in the gospel, and faith in prayer; and if, beloved friends, such prayer as this shall go up from this church, we shall continue to enjoy the prosperity we have had for many years, and we may hopefully look for an increase of it; though sometimes I must confess I can hardly look for an increase, for God has blessed us so much that we have rejoiced and wondered as we have seen that His hand is stretched out still.

II. The apostle has put in connection with your prayer THE SUPPLY OF THE SPIRIT. "The Spirit of Jesus Christ" does he not say? Yes, because the Spirit we want is the Spirit that rested upon Jesus Christ, the spirit which gave power to His ministry, for he said, "The Spirit of the Lord is upon Me." That same Spirit we need, even the Spirit who represents Christ on earth; for Jesus is gone but the Comforter abides with us as His vicegerent; He moves at Jesus Christ's will, and operates upon human thought and heart and will, subduing all to God. Now the Holy Spirit is essential to every true minister. We must have it. A preacher may save souls without being learned; it is a pity but what he should possess a good education, but he can be useful without it. The preacher can save souls without eloquence; it is well if he be fluent, but even stammering lips may convey the life-message from God. But the man of God is nothing without the Spirit of God. It is the *sine quâ non* of a ministry from God that it should be in the power of the Spirit. For the preacher must be himself first taught of the Spirit, else how shall he speak? And being taught, he must be led as to which shall be the proper theme for each occasion, for much of the power of true ministry lies in the fitness of the word to the case of the hearer, so that the hearer perceives that his experience is known and is met at the time by the ministry. The Spirit of God must teach us the truth, and then guide us as to which truth is to be spoken. Then the Holy Spirit must inflame the minister. The man who never takes fire, how is he sent of God? He who never glows and burns, what knows he of the baptism of the Holy Ghost, which is also the baptism of fire? Pray, therefore, for the supply of the Spirit. Without the Spirit every ministry lacks that subtle—I was about to say indescribable—something which is known by the name of *unction*. Nobody here can tell what unction is. He knows that the Spirit of God gives it, and he knows when it is in a discourse and when it is absent. Unction is, in fact, the power of God. There is an old Romish story, that a certain famous preacher was to preach on a certain occasion, but he missed his way and was too late, and the devil knowing of it put on the appearance of the minister, took his place, and preached a sermon to the people, who supposed they were listening to the famous divine whom they had expected. The devil preached upon hell, and was very much at home, so that he delivered a marvellous sermon, in which he exhorted persons to escape from the wrath to come. As he was finishing his sermon, in came the preacher himself, and the devil was obliged to resume his own form. The holy man then questioned him, "How dare you preach as you have done, warning men to escape from hell?" "Oh," said the devil, "it will do no hurt to my kingdom, for I have no unction." The story is grotesque, but the truth is in it. The same sermon may be preached and the same words uttered, but without unction there is nothing in it. The unction of the Holy One is true power; therefore, brethren, we need your prayers that we may obtain the supply of the Spirit upon our ministry; for otherwise it will lack unction, which will amount to lacking heart and soul. It will be a dead ministry, and how can a dead ministry be of any service to the people of God?

The supply of the Spirit is essential to the edification of the church of God. What if the ministry should be the best that ever was produced, its outward form and fashion orthodox and ardent? what if it should be continued with persevering consistency? yet the church will never be built up without the Holy Ghost. To build up a church, life is needed: we are living stones of a living temple. Where is the life to come from but from the breath of God? To build up a church there is needed light, but where is the light to come from but from Him who said "Let there be light"? To build up a church there is needed love, for this is the cement which binds the living stones together; but whence comes true genuine love but from the Spirit, who sheds abroad in the heart the love of Jesus! To build up a church we must have holiness, for an unholy church would be a den for the devil, and not a temple for God; but whence cometh holiness but from the Holy Spirit? There must be zeal too, for God will not dwell in a cold house; the church of God must be warm with love; but whence cometh the fire except it be the fire from heaven. We must have the Holy Ghost, for to build up a church there must be joy; a joyous temple God's temple must always be; but the Spirit of God alone produces the fruit of heavenly joy. There must be spirituality in the members, but we cannot have a spiritual people if the Spirit of God Himself be not here. For the edification of the saints, then, we must have beyond everything else the supply of the Spirit.

And, O brethren, we must have it for the salvation of sinners. Here comes the tug of war indeed. Who can enlighten the blind eye? who can bring spiritual hearing into the deaf ear? yea, who can quicken the dead soul, but the eternal, enlightening, quickening Spirit? There it lies before us, a vast valley, full of bones. Our mission is to raise them from the dead. Can we do it? No, by no means, of ourselves; yet are we to say to those dry bones, "Live." Brethren, our mission is absurd, it is worthy of laughter, unless we have your prayers and the supply of the Spirit with us; and if we have those, the bones shall come to their bones, the skeleton shall be fashioned, the flesh shall clothe the bony fabric, the Holy Ghost shall blow upon the inanimate body, and life shall be there, and an army shall throng the charnel house. Let us but invoke the Spirit and go forth to minister in His might, and we shall do marvels yet, and the nation, and the world itself, shall feel the power of the gospel of Jesus. But we must have the Spirit.

And, oh! we must have the Spirit of God just now, I am sure. It is essential to the progress of the gospel, and to the victory of the truth. At this moment the gospel is on its trial. It has had its trials before, and has come out of them like gold from the furnace, purified by the heat; but just now they are telling us on all hands that the old-fashioned gospel is effete. I have found myself dubbed in the public prints by the honourable title of *Ultimus Puritanorum*, the last of the Puritans, the last preacher of a race that is nearly extinct, the mere echo of a departed creed, the last survivor of a race of antiquated preachers. Ah, my brethren, it is not so! They come, they come, a mighty band, to bear on the truth to future ages, and even yet there are among us men who hold the truth and preach it. Yet everywhere we encounter the sneer of the servants of error. They dress themselves out in many colours, in blue, and scarlet, and fine linen, and I know not what; and they tell us that the day of our stern, gaunt religion has gone by. Then your wise men, the philosophers, the men of thought, the men of culture, they sneer at us. Such preaching of the gospel as ours might have done for two hundred years ago—might even, perhaps, have sufficed for Whitefield and Wesley, and the Methodists who followed at their heels; but now, in this enlightened nineteenth century, we do not want any more of it. From this insult we make our appeal to the God of heaven. O God, the God of Israel, avenge Thine own truth. O Thou whose mighty hammer can yet break rocks in pieces, Thou hast not changed Thine hammer; smite, and make the mountains fall before Thee. O Thou whose sacred fire burns in Thy word, for ever the same flame, Thou hast forbidden us to offer strange fire upon Thine altar; and we have not done so, but kept the faith and held the truth. Own it, we beseech Thee, and prove that it is the gospel of the blessed God. Let the sacrifice that is now before Thee in the midst of this great nation be consumed with the flame from heaven, and let the God that answereth by fire be God. The fact is, the church only lives in the esteem of men by what she does. If she does not convert sinners she has not a reason for existing. The proof of the gospel is not to be found in theories and problems, and propositions in catechisms or creeds, or even in scriptural texts alone; the proof of the gospel lies in what it does; and if it does not raise the depressed, if it does not save the sinful, if it does not send light into the dark places of the earth, in fact, if it does not make sinners into saints, and transform the nature of men, Thou let it be thrown on a dunghill, or cast away, for if the salt have lost its savour it is thenceforth good for nothing. But we cry to God that the savour of our salt may continue in all its pungency, and penetrating and preserving power. I ask you to pray that it may be so—that God will bring to the front the old gospel, the doctrines of Whitefield and Calvin and Paul, the old gospel of Christ, and once for all by a supernatural working of the Holy Spirit give an answer to those who, in this age of blasphemy and of rebuke, are reviling the gospel of the living God, and would have us cast it behind our backs. By the name of Him who never changes, our gospel shall never change: by the name of Christ who is gone to heaven, we have nothing to preach but Christ and Him crucified: by the name of the Eternal Spirit who dwells in us, we know nothing but what the Holy Ghost has revealed. To your knees, my brethren, to your knees, and win for us the victory. Feeble as we are, and unable as we are to cope with our antagonists in any other field but this, we will vanquish them by the power of prayer through the supply of the Spirit of God.

With you I leave it, my own beloved friends. Through your prayers and the supply of the Spirit all will be well. Amen.

"FOR EVER WITH THE LORD"

"To be with Christ; which is far better."—Philippians i.23.

THE apostle was confined in the guard-room of the Prætorium. It is very probable that he had a soldier chained to his right hand, and another to his left, and it is very possible that this position suggested to him the expression, "I am in a strait betwixt two." He was literally held by two forces, and he was mentally in the same condition, exercised with two strong desires, influenced by two master passions, and he did not know to which he should yield. He says, "Between the two I am in perplexity," or, as some render it, "I am straitened by the pressure of the two things." Picture yourself sitting in a gloomy dungeon, a captive in the hands of the cruel tyrant Nero, and under the supervision of the infamous præfect Tigellinus, the most detestable of all Nero's satellites. Conceive yourself as expecting soon to be taken out to death—perhaps to such a horrible death as the refined cruelty of the monster had often devised—as, for instance, to be smeared over with bituminous matter and burned in the despot's garden, to adorn a holiday. What would be your feelings? If you were not a Christian I should expect you to tremble with the fear of death, and even if you were a believer, I should not marvel if the flesh shrunk from the prospect. Paul was an utter stranger to any feeling of the kind. He had not the slightest dread of martyrdom. He calls his expected death a departure, a loosing of the cable which holds his ship to the shore, and a putting forth upon the main ocean. So far from being afraid to die, he stands fully prepared, he waits patiently, and even anticipates joyfully the hour when his change shall come. On the other hand, I can readily imagine that amidst the miseries of a wretched prison, subject to frequent insults from a rude soldiery, you might be seized with a desire to escape from life. Good men have felt the power of that feeling. Elijah said, "Let me die; I am no better than my fathers." Job sighed to be hidden in the grave, and oftentimes under far less afflictions than those which vexed the apostle, good men have said, "Would God this life were at an end, and these miseries over; I am a-weary, I am a-weary; when will death release me?" I see nothing of that feeling in the apostle; he is not restive under the chain; there is not a trace of impatience about him. He admits, and joyfully admits it, that to be with Christ is far better; but upon consideration he sees reasons for his remaining here, and therefore he cheerfully submits to whatever may be the Lord's will. He does not choose.

his mind is so wrapt up with God, and free from self, that he cannot choose. What a blessed state of heart to be in! One might be willing to wear Paul's chain on the wrist to enjoy Paul's liberty of mind. He is a freeman whom the Lord makes free, and such a man Nero himself cannot enslave. He may confine him in the military prison, but his soul walks at liberty through the earth, yea, and climbs among the stars. Paul, instead of being either weary of life or afraid of death, sits down and coolly considers his own case, as calmly indeed as if it had been the case of some one else. Do you observe how he weighs it? He says, to depart and to be with Christ is, in itself considered, far better, he therefore desires it: but looking round upon the numerous churches which he had formed, which in their feebleness and exposure to many perils needed his care, he says, on the other hand, "To abide in the flesh is more needful for you." He holds the balance with unquivering hand, and the scales quietly vibrate in equilibrium: one rises and then the other, gently swaying his heart by turns. He is in a strait, a blessed strait betwixt two, and he does not say that he knew not which of two things to avoid, or which to deprecate, but his mind was in such a condition that either to live or to die seemed equally desirable, and he says, "What I shall choose I wot not." It is a poor choice, to choose to live in a dungeon, and an equally poor business, as men judge it, to choose to die, but the apostle regards both of them as choice things, so choice that he does not know which to select. He deliberates as coolly and calmly as if he were not at all concerned about it: and indeed it is fair to say he was not at all concerned about it, he was moved by a higher concern than any which had to do with himself, for his main object was the glory of God. He desired the glory of God when he wished to be with Christ, he desired the same when he was willing to remain with Christ's people, and to labour on.

His mind, as we have seen, hung in an equilibrium between two things, but he is clear enough upon one matter, namely, that considering his own interests only, it would greatly increase his happiness to depart and to be with Christ. He had said the same before, when he declared that, "To die is gain." He had no doubt that to be loosed from the body and suffered to fly away to Jesus, would be a great boon to him. Of that assurance we will now speak.

I. The first thing to which I shall call your attention is THE APOSTLE'S CERTAINTY CONCERNING THE

DISEMBODIED STATE:—"Having a desire to depart, and to be with Christ; which is far better." Now, the apostle was an eminently conscientious man. At the time when he was a Jewish teacher, whatever else he might not be, he was very conscientious—he verily thought that he did God service in persecuting the Christians; and throughout the whole of his subsequent career, in every incident of his history we mark him as pre-eminently a man guided by conscience. If he believed a thing to be right, he attended to it ; and if anything struck him as being wrong, he could not be persuaded to countenance it. He would not do or say that which he did not fully believe to be right and true. It is a grand thing to meet with a witness of this order, for his testimony can be relied on. What such a man affirms we may be quite certain is correct, so far as he knows.

And withal, the apostle was eminently cool. He was a man of well-balanced reason. I should think that logic greatly preponderated amongst his faculties. John has a warm and glowing heart, and one does not wonder that he is rather a warm lover of Jesus than a systematic unfolder of doctrine; Peter is impulsive, and when he writes he writes with force, but it is not the force of reasoning. Paul is calm, collected; you never find him excited beyond the bounds of reason. He is as orderly, correct, and argumentative as a Grecian sage. He is enthusiastic to a white heat, but withal he still holds himself well in hand. The coursers of his imagination can outstrip the wind; but he always holds the reins with a strong hand, and knows how to turn them, or to make them stand still at his pleasure. It is a great thing to receive the testimony of a man who is both conscientious to tell what he believes to be true, and calm and logical to form a clear judgment as to what is really fact.

Now this man, Paul, was convinced that there is a future state for believers, he was quite sure about it, and he believed it to be a future conscious state, which commenced the moment they died, and was beyond measure full of blessedness. He did not believe in purgatorial fires through which believers' souls must pass; much less did he believe the modern and detestable heresy which some have broached, that like the body the soul of the saint dies until the resurrection; but he was wont to speak of being "absent from the body and present with the Lord," and here he speaks about departing not to sleep or to lie in the cold shade of oblivion till the trumpet should arouse him, but to depart and immediately to be with Christ, which is far better. What had made this very conscientious and very collected man come to this conclusion? I suppose he would have replied first, that he had been converted by a sight of the Lord Jesus Christ. On the road to Damascus, while desperately set against the religion of Jesus, the Lord Himself had appeared to him, so that he had seen Jesus with his own eyes, and had heard Him speak. About that sight and sound he had no question; he was sure that he had seen the Lord Jesus and heard His voice. He was so certain of this that he was led to give up his position in society, which was a very elevated one, to lose his repute, which he greatly valued, to be rejected by his countrymen, whom he loved with more than ordinary patriotism, and to run continual risk of death for the sake of the·truth to which he was a witness. He was content to be made the offscouring of all things for the love of that once despised Saviour, who, out of the windows of heaven, had looked down upon him in mercy. Now, he was quite sure that Jesus Christ came from somewhere, and went back to some place or other. He felt sure that there must be a place where the man Jesus Christ dwelt, and he felt quite certain that wherever that might be it would be a place of happiness and glory. Recollecting the prayer of the Lord Jesus, which John had recorded, "Father, I will that they also whom Thou hast given Me be with Me where I am, that they may behold My glory," he was quite certain that as soon as saints died they would be where their glorious Lord Jesus was, and would share His honours.

Remember, also, that this judicious and truthful witness tells us that he had on other occasions distinct evidence of the disembodied state. He informs us that he was caught up into the third heaven, and there heard things which it was not lawful for a man to utter. He observes that he does not understand how he went there, but of the fact he is quite sure. His body was here on earth still alive, and yet his spirit was caught away into heaven; the question with him was, whether he was in the body or out of the body, and I dare say his metaphysical mind often tried to untie that knot. His soul must have remained in the body to keep the body alive, and if so, how could it go up to heaven; and yet into heaven he was quite clear that he had entered. At last the apostle came to the conclusion that whether in the body or out of the body he could not tell, but God knew. This, however, he was sure of, that he had been caught up into paradise, or the third heaven, and therefore there was a paradise; he had heard words which it was not possible for him to utter, therefore there was a place where glorious words were to be heard, and glorious words to be said, and he was quite sure, not merely as a matter of belief, but as a matter of observation, that there was a place into which disembodied spirits go, where they are with Jesus, their Lord, which is far better. It is clear that it would not be far better for a saint to die and sleep till the resurrection than it would be to work on here. It would be evidently by far a better thing for saints to continue in life till Christ came, than to lie dormant in oblivion; yet he says it is far better for them to depart, and the ground of his judgment lies in the fact that there is a place of real happiness, of intense joy, where it is far better for the disembodied spirit to be than for it to remain here in the body. About this Paul expressed no sort of doubt. There was such a state; it was a state of great joy, so that even to him who was one of the greatest apostles, the most useful of the saints, and the most honoured, with his Master's blessing—even to him to depart and to be with Christ, would be far better.

I want you also to notice that he does not express any sort of doubt about his own entrance into a state of felicity so soon as he should depart. He does not say, as I am afraid some here would have done, " It would be far better, certainly, for me to die if I were sure I should then be with Christ." Oh, no; he had risen above such hesitation. Dear brethren, it is a wretched state to be in to be saying, "It would be sweet for me to depart if, indeed, these glories were for me." He had got beyond all doubt as to whether eternal bliss would be his; he was sure of that, and why are we not sure, too? Why do we hesitate where he spoke so confidently? Had Paul something to ground his confidence upon which we have not? Do you suppose that Paul reckoned he should be saved because of his abundant labours, his earnest ministry, and his great successes? Far from it; know ye not what he himself said, "God forbid that

I should glory save in the cross of our Lord Jesus Christ"? As for anything that he had ever done, he declared that he trusted to be found in Christ, not having his own righteousness, which was of the law, but the righteousness which is of God by faith. Now, where Paul built we build, if we build aright; our hope is founded upon the righteousness of Christ, upon the grace of God, upon the promise of our heavenly Father. Well, I dare to say it, he, the chief of the apostles, had not a solitary grain of advantage over any one of us as to the basis and essence of his hope. Mercy, grace, atoning blood, the precious promise; these alone he built on, for other foundation can no man lay. If Paul was sure of eternal bliss, I would be sure of it too; nay, I am; are you, beloved? Are you equally as sure of being with Christ as Paul was? You should be, for you have the same reason for certainty as the apostle had, if indeed you are believing in the Lord Jesus. God is not a God of perhapses, and ifs, and buts, but he is a God of shalls and wills, of faithful truth and everlasting verities. "He that believeth on Him is not condemned." "There is, therefore, now no condemnation to them that are in Christ Jesus." "He that believeth and is baptized, shall be saved." "Who shall lay anything to the charge of"—what? Paul, the apostle? No, but "of God's elect"? Of all of them, of any one of them whom you shall please to select, however humble, however obscure, they are all safe in Jesus. He is made sin for us that we might be made the righteousness of God in Him, and we may, each one of us, cry, "I know whom I have believed, and am persuaded that He is able to keep that which I have committed to Him until that day," So much, then, concerning the apostle's certainty as to the disembodied state, its happiness, and his own possession of it before long.

II. It is very interesting to notice THE APOSTLE'S IDEA OF THAT STATE. He says, "To be with Christ." It is a one-sided idea, and it is almost a one-worded description of it. "To be with Christ." I have no doubt Paul had as enlarged ideas as to what the state of disembodied spirits would be as the most intelligent and best read Christian that ever lived. I have no doubt he would have said, "Yes, there is fellowship among the saints: we shall sit down with Abraham, and Isaac, and Jacob in the kingdom of heaven: it will be certainly as true in heaven as it is on earth that we have fellowship one with another." I have no doubt, he believed that heaven was a place of a far clearer knowledge than any we possess below: he said so once—"Here I know in part, but there shall I know even as I am known." Some Christians have entertained the idea that they shall gaze upon the various works of God in distant parts of His universe, and enjoy infinite happiness in beholding the manifold wisdom of God—very possible, and if it will conduce to their happiness—very probable. Perhaps Paul believed all that, but we do not know whether he did or not. Here it is plain that he gives us only one idea. He was a man of great mind and much information, but here he gives us only one idea—for my part, one that perfectly satisfies me, and I think one which charms and fills to overflowing the heart of every believer. He describes the disembodied state as "to be with Christ." A very exclusive idea! No, a very inclusive idea—for it takes in all the heaven which the largest mind can conceive. It does seem to omit a great many things, but I dare say Paul felt that they were such trifles that it did not matter about forgetting them.

Being with Christ is so great a thing that he mentioned it alone. I think he did this first, because his love was so concentrated upon Christ that he could think of nothing else in connection with going away to heaven. There is a wife here, perhaps, and her husband has accepted an appointment in India. He has been long away, and the years of his forced absence have been weary to her. She has had loving messages from him and kind letters, but often has she sighed, and her heart has looked out of the windows towards the east, yearning for his return; but now she has received a letter entreating her to go out to her husband, and without hesitation has resolved to go. Now, if you ask her what she is going to India for, the reply will be, "I am going to my husband." But she has a brother there. Yes, she will see him, but she does not tell you that; her great thought is that she is going to her husband. She has many old friends and companions there, but she is not drawn to the far-off land by desire for their company, she crosses the sea for the sake of her beloved. But her husband has a handsome estate there, and he is wealthy, and has a well-furnished house and many servants. Yes, but she never says, "I am going out to see my husband's home," or anything of that kind. She is going to her husband. That is the all-absorbing object. There may be other inducements to make the voyage, but to be with her beloved is the master object of her journey. She is going to the man she loves with all her soul, and she is longing for the country, whatever that country may be, because he is there. It is so with the Christian, only enhanced in a tenfold degree. He does not say, "I am going to the songs of angels, and to the everlasting *chorales* of the sanctified," but, "I am going to be with Jesus." It would argue unchastity to Christ if that were not the first and highest thought. To come back to the figure—and it is one which Christ Himself would approve of, for He continually uses the metaphor of marriage in relation to Himself and the soul—if that woman did regard as the first thing in that journey out to the East, the sight of some other person, or the mere enjoyment of wealth and possessions, it would argue that she had little love to her husband, that she was not such a wife as she ought to be. And if it could be so that the Christian should have some higher thought than being with Christ, or some other desire worth mentioning in the same day with it, it would look as if he had not presented himself as a chaste virgin to Christ, to be His and His alone. I see, therefore, why Paul calls the disembodied state a being with Christ, because his love was all with his Lord.

And, no doubt, there was this further reason amongst others—he was persuaded that heaven could not be heaven if Christ was not there. Oh, to think of heaven without Christ! It is the same thing as thinking of hell. Heaven without Christ! It is day without the sun; existing without life, feasting without food, seeing without light. It involves a contradiction in terms. Heaven without Christ! Absurd. It is the sea without water, the earth without its fields, the heavens without their stars. There cannot be heaven without Christ. He is the sum total of bliss; the fountain from which heaven flows, the element of which heaven is composed. Christ is heaven and heaven is Christ. You shall change the words and make no difference in the sense. To be where Jesus is is the highest imaginable bliss, and bliss away from Jesus is inconceivable to the child of

God. If you were invited to a marriage feast, and you were yourself to be the bride, and yet the bridegroom were not there—do not tell me about feasting. In vain they ring the bells till the church tower rocks and reels, in vain the dishes smoke and the red wine sparkles, in vain the guests shout and make merry; if the bride looks around her and sees no bridegroom, the dainties mock her sorrow and the merriment insults her misery. Such would a Christless heaven be to the saints. If you could gather together all conceivable joys, and Christ were absent, there would be no heaven to His beloved ones. Hence it is that heaven is to be where Christ is.

To dwell with Christ, to feel His love,
Is the full heaven enjoyed above;
And the sweet expectation now,
Is the young dawn of heaven below.

And, beloved, just to be with Christ is heaven—that bare thing. Excuse my using such words; I only want to make the sense the stronger. That bare thing, just to be with Christ is all the heaven a believer wants. The angels may be there or not, as they will, and the golden crowns and harps present or absent as may be, but if I am to be where Jesus is, I will find angels in His eyes, and crowns in every lock of His hair; to me the golden streets shall be my fellowship with Him, and the harpings of the harpers shall be the sound of His voice. Only to be near Him, to be with Him—this is all we want. The apostle does not say, "to be in heaven; which is far better": no, but, "to be with Christ; which is far better," and he adds no description; he leaves the thoughts just as they are, in all their majestic simplicity. "To be with Christ; which is far better."

But what is it to be with Christ, beloved? In some sense we are with Christ now, for He comes to us. We are no strangers to Him. Even while we are in this body we have communion with Jesus; and yet it must be true that a higher fellowship is to come, for the apostle says, that while we are present in the body we are absent from the Lord. There is a sense in which, so long as we are here, we are absent from the Lord; and one great saint used to say upon his birthday that he had been so many years in banishment from the Lord: to abide in this lowland country, so far from the ivory palaces, is a banishment at the very best. All that we can see of Christ here is through a glass darkly; face to face is true nearness to Him, and that we have not reached as yet.

What will it be, then, to be with Christ? Excuse me if I say it will be, first of all, exactly what it says, namely, to be with Him. I must repeat that word—it is heaven only to be with Him. It is not merely what comes out of being with Him, His company itself is heaven. Why, even to have seen Jesus in His flesh was a privilege:—

"I think when I read that sweet story of old,
    When Jesus was here among men,
How He took little children like lambs to His fold,
    I should like to have been with Him then.
I wish that His hands had been placed on my head,
    That His arms had been thrown around me,
And that I might have seen His kind look when He said,
    'Let the little ones come unto me.'"

I think I should have found a little heaven in gazing on that blessed form. But our text speaks of a different sort of being with Him, for there were people near Him here in body who were a long way off from Him in spirit. The text speaks of being with Him in the spirit when the soul shall have shaken itself loose of the flesh and blood, and left all its slough behind it, and gone right away, to bask in the glory of Jesus, to participate in the nature of Jesus: and, best of all, to abide near to His person, with the God-man Mediator, who is Lord of all.

Still, there will flow out of that nearness the following things among many others. We shall enjoy, first of all, a clearer vision of Him. Oh, we have not seen Him yet! Our views of Him are too dim to be worth calling sights. The eyes of faith have looked through a telescope and seen Him at a distance, and it has been a ravishing vision; but when the eyes of the soul shall really see Him—Him, and not another, Him for ourselves, and not another for us, oh, the sight! Is not the thought of it a burning coal of joy? The sight of His very flesh will charm us, His wounds still fresh, the dear memorials of His passion still apparent. The perception of His soul will also delight us, for our soul will commune with His soul, and this is the soul of communion. The sight of His Godhead, so far as created spirit can see it, will also ravish us with joy.

And then we shall have a brighter knowledge of Him. Here we know in part—we know the names of His offices, we know what He has wrought, we know what He is working for us; but there those offices will shine in their splendour, and we shall see all that He did for us in its real weight and value; we shall comprehend then the height and depth, and know the love of Christ which passeth knowledge, as we do not know it at this hour.

And with that will come a more intimate intercourse. Our soul will lean her head on Jesus' bosom, our heart will get into His heart and hide herself in His wounds. What must it be to speak to Him as our soul will speak to Him, as our spirit nature will commune with His inmost nature, His spirit speaking to our spirits, without a veil between! We shall not see Him looking down from the windows, but we shall rest in His arms, in a far more intimate intercourse than any we can enjoy this side the grave. To-day I see Him through the grating of my prison-windows, and my heart is ready to leap out of my body; what will it be when His left hand shall be under my head, and His right hand shall embrace me?

And then, beloved, when we shall be with Him it will be unbroken fellowship. There will be no sin to blind our eyes to His charms, or to entice us away from His love. Blessed be God, there will be no Monday mornings to recall us to the world, but our sacred Sabbath will last on for ever. Doubts, backslidings, and spiritual chills will then be gone for ever. No more shall we cry, "Saw ye Him whom my soul loveth?" but we shall hold Him, and never let Him go. There will be no need even for the spirit to fall asleep, and so suspend its joy; it will find its true rest in constant communion with Jesus. It is possible to live in fellowship with Jesus here always; possible but, oh, how few ever reach it! but there we shall all have reached it, the very lowest amongst us, and we shall be with the Lord for ever.

And then we shall have a sight of His glory, and though I put this after a sight of Himself, yet, remember, our Lord thinks much of it. He prayed, "Father, I will that they also whom Thou hast given Me be with Me where I am, that they may behold My glory." We have seen something of His shame, and have been partakers in the reproach that is poured upon His gospel; but we shall see Him then with silver sandals on the feet that once were mired by the clay of earth, and a crown of gold upon the once thorn-pierced brow. We shall see Him where His hands shall gleam as with gold rings set with beryl, and look no more like a malefactor's hand nailed to the cruel wood. Then shall we say—

> His body's like bright ivory
> With sapphires overlaid,
> His limbs like marble pillars
> In golden sockets stayed.

Then looking on His face we shall understand Solomon's Song, when he said, "His countenance is as Lebanon, excellent as the cedars; His voice is most sweet, yea, He is altogether lovely." One would wish to leap right away out of this body to behold Him in His glory.

And then, beloved, we shall share in the glory too, for His joy will be our joy, His honour will be our honour. Our spirits which wrestled hard here below, and had to strive against a thousand outward enemies, and inward doubts and fears, will then be all light, and joysome, and gladsome, full of the life of God, and beaming with ecstatic bliss. The Lord grant us to know this in due season, and so we shall if, indeed, we are believers in Jesus. So you see Paul's one idea was that he should be with Jesus; that was all; he cared little for anything else.

III. Very briefly, let us consider THE APOSTLE'S ESTIMATE OF THIS DISEMBODIED STATE. He says, "To be with Christ; *which is far better.*" Now, the Greek has a triple comparative. We could not say "far more better" in our language, but that would be a fair translation. We will therefore read, "It is far rather preferable," or it is much better to be with Christ away from the body, than it would be to abide here. Now, you must recollect that Paul does not claim for the disembodied state that it is the highest condition of a believer, or the ultimate crown of his hopes. It is a state of perfection so far as it goes; the spirit is perfect, but the entire manhood is not perfect while the body is left to moulder in the tomb. One half of the saint is left behind in the grave; corruption, earth, and worms have seized upon it, and the grand concluding day of our manifestation can only come when the redemption of the body is fully achieved. The fulness of our glory is the resurrection, for then the body will be united to our spirit, and perfected with it. At present the saints who are with Jesus are without their bodies, and are pure spirits; their humanity is in that respect maimed; only half their manhood is with Jesus; yet even for that half of the manhood to be with Christ is far better than for the whole of their being to be here in the best possible condition. Now, the apostle does not say, that to be with Christ is far better than to be here, and to be rich, young, healthy, strong, famous, great, or learned: Paul never thinks of putting those petty things into contrast with being with Christ. He had got above all that. There was he sitting chained in the dungeon, the poorest man in the emperor's dominions, and often, I have no doubt —for he was getting on to be "such an one as Paul the aged," and wrote particularly about an old cloak he had left at Troas—often he felt rheumatic pains shooting through him; and he did not find this life to have many attractions of wealth or ease, though he might have had them if he had chosen them as his portion. He had given them all up, and counted them as insignificant trifles, not to be mentioned at all, for Jesus' sake. He is not speaking of the low joys of this world; he is far above such considerations; but he does mean that to be with Christ is infinitely superior to all the joys of Christians. Anything that the most of Christians know about Christ and heavenly joys and heavenly things is very poor compared with being with Christ. But he meant more than that; he meant that the highest joys which the best taught believer can here possess are inferior to being with Christ. For, let me say, Paul was no obscure believer; he was a leader among the followers of Christ. Could he not say, "Thanks be unto God, who always maketh us to triumph in every place"? He knew the graces of the Holy Spirit, he had them abundantly; he was head and shoulders above the tallest Christian here; he had the highest experience of any man out of heaven, and it was that which he contrasted with being with Christ, and he said that the most that he could get here of heavenly things was not to be compared with being with Christ. That was far, far, far better. And truly, brethren, so it is. Thanks be to God for all the mercies of the pilgrimage, for all the dropping manna and the following stream; but oh, the wilderness with all its manna, is nothing compared with the land that floweth with milk and honey. Let the road be paved with mercy, it is not so sweet as the Father's house of the many mansions to which it leads. It is true that in the battle our head is covered, the wings of angels oft protect us, and the Spirit of God Himself nerves our arm to use the sword; but who shall say that the victory is not better than the battle? The warrior who has won the most of victory will tell you that the gladdest day will be when the sword rattles back into the scabbard, and the victory is won for ever. Oh, the wooing of Christ and the soul, this is very sweet: the rapturous joys we have had in the love-making between Christ and us, we would not exchange with emperors and kings, even if they offered us their crowns; but the marriage day will be better far, the glorious consummation of our soul's highest desire, when we shall be with our Well-beloved where He is. Far better, said the apostle, and he meant it; far better it is.

He did not say—and I want you to notice this again—though he might have said it, "We shall be better in condition; no poverty there, no sickness there"; he did not say, "We shall be better in character"; he might have said it: there will be no sin, no depravity, no infirmity, no temptation there. He did not say, "We shall be better in employment," though surely it will be better to wait on the Master, close at His hand, than to be here amongst sinners and often amongst cold-hearted saints. He did not say, "We shall have better society there," though, truth to tell, it will be better to be with the perfect than with the imperfect. Neither did he say we should see fairer sights there, though we shall see the city that hath foundations of jasper, whose light is the light of the Lamb's own presence. But he did say, "To be with Christ." He summed it up there. The bare being with Christ would be far better. And so it will be. Our spirit longs for it.

Yet mark you, for all that, he said he felt a pull the other way. He had a twitch towards stopping on earth, as well as a pull towards going to heaven, for he said, "To abide in the flesh is more needful for you." How I love Paul for thinking of the churches here when he had got heaven before him. Anthony Farindon says it is like a poor beggar woman outside the door, and she carries a squalling child, and some one says, "You may come in and feast, but you must leave the babe outside"; and she is very hungry, and she wants the feast; but she does not like to leave the babe, and so she is in a strait betwixt two. Or, he says again, it is like a wife who has children at home, five or six little ones, and her husband is on a journey, and suddenly there comes a letter which says that he wants her, and she must go to him, but she may do as she thinks best. She desires to go to her husband, but who will take care of the last little babe, and who is to see to all the rest? and so she is in a strait betwixt two. She loves him and she loves them. So stood the apostle, and oh! it is blessed to think of a man having such a love for Christ that for Christ's sake he loves poor souls well enough to be willing to stop out of heaven awhile. "Oh," says he, "it is all gain for me to go to heaven; for me to die is far better; yet there are some poor sinners who need to be called, some poor trembling saints to be comforted, and I do not know which is the best"; and the apostle stands puzzled; he does not know which it shall be. There we leave him. May we get into the same blessed embarrassment ourselves.

The last word shall be this. Concerning our beloved friends gone from us, we do not sorrow as those who are without hope; what is more, we do not sorrow at all. If we chance to sorrow, it is for ourselves, that we have lost their present company, but as for them it is far better with them; and if the lifting of our little finger could bring them back again, dear as they are to us, we would not be so cruel as to subject them again to the troubles of this stormy sea of life. They are safe landed. We will go to them, we would not have them return to us.

Then, with regard to ourselves, if we have believed in Jesus we are on our journey home, and all fear of death is now annihilated. You notice the apostle does not say anything at all about death, he did not think it worth mentioning; in fact, there is no such thing to a Christian. I have heard of people being afraid of the pains of death. There are no pains of death: the pain is in life. Death is the end of pain. It is all over. Put the saddle on the right horse. Do not blame death for what he does not do. It is life that brings pain: death to the believer ends all evil. Death is the gate of endless joy, and shall we dread to enter there? No, blessed be God, we will not.

And this points us to the fountain of bliss while we are here, for if heaven is to be with Christ, then the nearer we get to Christ here, the more we shall participate in that which makes the joy of heaven. If we want to taste heaven's blessed dainties while here below, let us walk in unbroken fellowship with Him —so we shall get two heavens, a little heaven below, and a boundless heaven above, when our turn shall come to go home. Oh, I wish you were all on the way to being with Christ. If you do not go to be with Christ, where can you go? Answer that question, and go to Jesus now by humble faith, that afterwards He may say, "Come; ye did come on earth, now come again, ye blessed of My Father, inherit the kingdom prepared for you from before the foundation of the world."

OUR LORD IN THE VALLEY OF HUMILIATION

"And being found in fashion as a man, He humbled Himself, and became obedient unto death, even the death of the cross."
—Philippians ii. 8.

PAUL wishes to unite the saints in Philippi in the holy bands of love. To do this, he takes them to the cross. Beloved, there is a cure for every spiritual disease in the cross. There is food for every spiritual virtue in the Saviour. We never go to Him too often. He is never a dry well, or a vine from which every cluster has been taken. We do not think enough of Him. We are poor because we do not go to the gold country which lieth round the cross. We are often sad because we do not see the bright light that shines from the constellation of the cross. The beams from that constellation would give us instantaneous joy and rest, if we perceived them. If any lover of the souls of men would do for them the best possible service, he would constantly take them near to Christ. Paul is always doing so; and he is doing it here.

The apostle knew that to create concord, you need first to beget lowliness of mind. Men do not quarrel when their ambitions have come to an end. When each one is willing to be least, when everyone desires to place his fellows higher than himself, there is an end to party spirit; schisms and divisions are all passed away. Now, in order to create lowliness of mind, Paul, under the teaching of the Spirit of God, spoke about the lowliness of Christ. He would have us go down, and so he takes us to see our Master going down. He leads us to those steep stairs down which the Lord of glory took His lowly way, and he bids us stop while, in the words of our text, he points us to the lowly Christ: "Being found in fashion as a man, He humbled Himself, and became obedient unto death, even the death of the cross."

Before Paul thus wrote, he had indicated in a word or two, the height from which Jesus originally came. He says of Him, "Who, being in the form of God, thought it not robbery to be equal with God." You and I can have no idea of how high an honour it is to be equal with God. How can we, therefore, measure the descent of Christ, when our highest thoughts cannot comprehend the height from which He came? The depth to which He descended is immeasurably below any point we have ever reached; and the height from which He came is inconceivably above our loftiest thought. Do not, however, forget the glory that Jesus laid aside for a while. Remember that He is very God of very God, and that He dwelt in the highest heaven with His Father; but yet, though He was thus infinitely rich, for our sakes He became poor, that we, through His poverty, might be rich.

The apostle, having mentioned what Jesus was, by another stroke of his pen reveals Him in our human nature. He says concerning Him that, "He made Himself of no reputation, and took upon Him the form of a servant, and was made in the likeness of men." A great marvel is that Incarnation, that the eternal God should take into union with Himself our human nature, and should be born at Bethlehem, and live at Nazareth, and die at Calvary on our behalf.

But our text does not speak so much of the humiliation of Christ in becoming man, as of His humiliation after He took upon Himself our nature. "Being found in fashion, as a man, He humbled Himself." He never seems to stop in His descent until He comes to the lowest point, obedience unto death, and that death the most shameful of all, "even the death of the cross." Said I not rightly, that, as you cannot reach the height from which He came, you cannot fathom the depth to which He descended? Here, in the immeasurable distance between the heaven of His glory and the shame of His death, is room for your gratitude. You may rise on wings of joy, you may dive into depths of self-denial; but in neither case will you reach the experience of your divine Lord, who thus, for you, came from heaven to earth, that He might take you up from earth to heaven.

Now, if strength be given me for the exercise, I want to guide you, first, while we *consider the facts of our Lord's humiliation ;* and, secondly, when we have considered them, I want you *practically to learn from them some useful lessons.*

I. First of all, CONSIDER THE FACTS OF OUR LORD'S HUMILIATION.

Paul speaks first of *the point from which He still descends :* "Being found in fashion as a man, He humbled Himself." My gracious Lord, Thou hast come far enough already; dost Thou not stop where Thou art? In the form of God, Thou wast; in the form of man, Thou art. That is an unspeakable stoop. Wilt Thou still humble Thyself? Yes, says the text, "Being found in fashion as a man, He humbled Himself." Yet, surely one would have thought that He was low enough. He was the Creator, and we see Him here on earth as a creature; the Creator, who made heaven and earth, without whom was not anything made that was made, and yet He lieth in the virgin's womb; He is born; and He is cradled where the horned oxen feed. The Creator is also a creature. The Son of God is the Son of man. Strange combination! Could condescension go farther than for the Infinite to be joined to the infant, and the Omnipotent to the feebleness of a new-born babe?

Yet, this is not all. If the Lord of life and glory must needs be married to a creature, and the High and Mighty One must take upon Himself the form of a created being, yet why does He assume the form of man? There were other creatures, brighter than the stars, noble spiritual beings, seraphim and cherubim, sons of the morning presence-angels of the eternal throne; why did He not take their nature? If He must be in union with a creature, why not be joined to the angels? But, "He took not on Him the nature of angels; but He took on Him the seed of Abraham." A man is but a worm, a creature of many infirmities. On his brow death has written with his terrible finger. He is corruptible, and he must die. Will the Christ take that nature upon Him, that He too, must suffer and die? It was even so; but when He had come so far, we feel as if we must almost put ourselves in the way to stop Him from going farther. Is not this stoop low enough? The text says that it was not, for, "Being found in fashion as a man, He humbled Himself," even then.

What will not Christ do for us who have been given to Him by His Father? There is no measure to His love; you cannot comprehend His grace. Oh, how we ought to love Him, and serve Him! The lower He stoops to save us, the higher we ought to lift Him in our adoring reverence. Blessed be His name, He stoops, and stoops, and stoops, and, when He reaches our level, and becomes man, He still stoops, and stoops, and stoops lower and deeper yet: "Being found in fashion as a man, He humbled Himself."

Now let us notice, next, *the way in which He descended after He became a man :* "He humbled Himself." We must assume that He has stooped as low as our humanity; but His humanity might have been, when born, cradled daintily. He might have been among those who are born in marble halls, and clothed in purple and fine linen; but He chose not so. If it had pleased Him, He might have been born a man, and not have been a child; He might have leaped over the period of gradual development from childhood to youth, and from youth to manhood; but He did not so. When you see Him at home at Nazareth, the apprenticed son, obedient to His parents, doing the little errands of the house, like any other child, you say, as our text says, "He humbled Himself." There He dwelt in poverty with His parents, beginning His life as a workman's boy, and I suppose, running out to play with youthful companions. All this is very wonderful. The apocryphal gospels represent Him as having done strange things while yet a child; but the true Gospels tell us very little of His early days. He veiled His Godhead behind His childhood. When He went up to Jerusalem, and listened to the doctors of the law, though He astonished them by His questions and answers, yet He went home with His parents, and was subject to them, for, "He humbled Himself." He was by no means pushing and forward, like a petted and precocious child. He held Himself in, for He determined that, being found in fashion as a man, He would humble Himself.

He grew up, and the time of His appearing unto men arrived; but I cannot pass over the thirty years of His silence without feeling that here was a marvellous instance of how He humbled Himself. I know young men who think that two or three years' education is far too long for them. They want to be preaching at once; running away, as I sometimes tell them, like chickens with the shell on their heads. They want to go forth to fight before they have buckled on their armour. But it was not so with Christ; thirty long years passed over His head, and still there was no Sermon on the Mount. When He did show Himself to the world, see how He humbled Himself. He did not knock at the door of the high priests, or seek out the eminent Rabbis and the learned scribes; but He took for His companions fishermen from the lake, infinitely His inferiors, even if we regarded Him merely as a man. He was full of manly freshness and vigour of mind; and they were scarcely able to follow Him, even though He moderated His footsteps out of pity for their weakness. He preferred to associate with lowly men, for He humbled Himself.

When He went out to speak, His style was not such as aimed at the gathering of the *élite* together; He did not address a few specially cultured folk. "*Then drew near unto Him all the scribes and Pharisees for to hear Him.*" Am I quoting correctly? Nay, nay: "*Then drew near unto Him all the publicans and sinners for to hear Him.*" They made an audience with which He was at home; and when they gathered about Him, and when little children stood to listen to Him, then He poured out the fulness of His heart, for He humbled Himself. Ah, dear friends, this was not the deepest humiliation of the Lord Jesus! He allowed the devil to tempt Him. I have often wondered how His pure and holy mind, how His right royal nature could bear conflict with the prince of darkness, the foul fiend, full of lies. Christ allowed Satan to put Him to the test, and spotless purity had to bear the nearness of infamous villainy. Jesus conquered; for the prince of this world came, and found nothing in Him; but He humbled Himself when, in the wilderness, on the pinnacle of the temple, and on the exceeding high mountain, He allowed the devil thrice to assail Him.

Personally, in His body, He suffered weakness, hunger, thirst. In His mind, He suffered rebuke, contumely, falsehood. He was constantly the Man of sorrows. You know that, when the head of the apostate church is called "the man of sin," it is because it is always sinning; and when Christ is called "the Man of sorrows," it is because He was always sorrowing. How wonderful is it that He should humble Himself so as to be afflicted with the common sorrows of our humanity; yet it was even so! "Being found in fashion as a man," He consented even to be belied, to be called a drunken man and a wine-bibber, to have His miracles ascribed to the help of Beelzebub, to hear men say, "He hath a devil, and is mad; why hear ye Him?"

"He humbled Himself." In His own heart there were, frequently, great struggles; and those struggles drove Him to prayer. He even lost consciousness of God's presence, so that He cried in sore anguish, "My God, My God, why hast Thou forsaken Me?" All this was because still He humbled Himself. I do not know how to speak to you upon this great subject; I give you words; but I pray the Holy Spirit to supply you with right thoughts about this great mystery. I have already said that it was condescension enough for Christ to be found in fashion as a man; but after that, He still continued to descend the stairway of condescending love by humbling Himself yet more and more.

But notice, now, *the rule of His descent;* it is worth noticing: "He humbled Himself, and became obedient." I have known persons try to humble themselves by will-worship. I have stood in the cell of a monk, when he has been out of it, and I have seen the whip with which he flagellated himself every night before he went to bed. I thought that it was quite possible that the man deserved all he suffered, and so I shed no tears over it. That was his way of humbling himself, by administering a certain number of lashes. I have known persons practise voluntary humility. They have talked in very humble language, and have decried themselves in words, though they have been as proud as Lucifer all the while. Our Lord's way of humbling Himself was by obedience. He invented no method of making Himself ridiculous; He put upon Himself no singular garb, which would attract attention to His poverty; He simply obeyed His Father; and, mark you, there is no humility like obedience: "To obey is better than sacrifice, and to hearken than the fat of rams." To obey is better than to wear a special dress, or to clip your words in some peculiar form of supposed humility. Obedience is the best humility, laying yourself at the feet of Jesus, and making your will active only when you know what it is God's will for you to do. This is to try to be truly humble.

In what way, then, did the Lord Jesus Christ in His life obey? I answer,—there was always about Him the spirit of obedience to His Father. He could say, "Lo, I come: in the Volume of the Book it is written of Me, I delight to do Thy will, O My God: yea, Thy law is within My heart." He was always, while here, subservient to His Father's great purpose in sending Him to earth; He came to do the will of Him that sent Him, and to finish His work. He learned what that will was partly from Holy Scripture. You constantly find Him acting in a certain way "that the Scripture might be fulfilled." He shaped His life upon the prophecies that had been given concerning Him. Thus He did the will of the Father.

Also, there was within Him the Spirit of God, who led and guided Him, so that He could say, "I do always those things that please the Father." Then, He waited upon God continually in prayer. Though infinitely better able to do without prayer than we are, yet He prayed much more than we do. With less need than we have, He had a greater delight in prayer than we have; and thus He learned the will of God as man, and did it, without once omitting, or once transgressing in a single point.

He did the will of God also, obediently, by following out what He knew to be the Father's great design in sending Him. He was sent to save, and He went about saving, seeking and saving that which was lost. Oh, dear friends, when we get into unison with God, when we wish what He wishes, when we live for the great object that fills God's heart, when we lay aside our wishes and whims, and even our lawful desires, that we may do only the will of God, and live only for His glory, then we shall be truly humbling ourselves!

Thus, I have shown you that Jesus did descend after He became man; and I have pointed out to you the way and the rule of His descending. Now, let us look, with awe and reverence, at *the abyss into which He descended.* Where did He arrive, at length, in that dreadful descent? What was the bottom of the abyss? It was death: "He humbled Himself, and became obedient unto death, even the death of the cross." Our Lord died willingly. You and I, unless the Lord should come quickly, will die, whether we are willing or not: "It is appointed unto men once to die." He needed not to die, yet He was willing to surrender His life. He said, "I have power to lay it down, and I have power to take it again. This commandment have I received of My Father." He died willingly; but, at the same time, He did not die by His own hand; He did not take His own life as a suicide; He died obediently. He waited till His hour had come, when He was able to say, "It is finished," then He bowed His head, and gave up the ghost. He humbled Himself, so as willingly to die.

He proved the obedience of His death, also, by the meekness of it, as Isaiah said, "As a sheep before her shearers is dumb, so He openeth not His mouth." He never spoke a bitter word to priest or scribe, Jewish governor or Roman soldier. When the women wept and bewailed, He said to them, "Daughters of Jerusalem, weep not for Me, but weep for yourselves, and for your children." He was all gentleness; He had not a hard word even for His murderers. He gave Himself up to be the Sin-bearer, without murmuring at His Father's will, or at the cruelty of His adversaries. How patient He was! If He says, "I thirst," it is not the petulant cry of a sick man in his fever; there is a royal dignity about Christ's utterance of the words. Even the "Eloi, Eloi, lama sabachthani," with the unutterable gall and bitterness it contains, has not even a trace of impatience mingled with it.

Oh, what a death Christ's was! He was obedient in it, obedient not only till He came to die, but obedient in that last dread act. His obedient life embraced the hour of His departure.

But, as if death were not sufficiently humbling, the apostle adds, "even the death of the cross." That was the worst kind of death. It was a violent death. Jesus fell not asleep gently, as good men often do, whose end is peace. No, He died by murderous hands. Jews and Gentiles combined, and with cruel hands took Him, and crucified and slew Him. It was, also, an extremely painful death of lingering agony. Those parts of the body in which the nerves were most numerous, were pierced with rough iron nails. The weight of the body was made to hang upon the tenderest part of the frame. No doubt the nails tore their cruel way through His flesh while He was hanging on the tree. A cut in the hand has often resulted in lockjaw and death; yet Christ's hands were nailed to the cross. He died in pain most exquisite of body and of soul. It was, also, a death most shameful. Thieves were crucified with Him; His adversaries stood and mocked Him. The death of the cross was one reserved for slaves and the basest of felons; no Roman citizen could be put to death in such a way as that, hung up between earth and heaven, as if neither would have Him, rejected of men and despised of God. It was, also, a penal death. He died, not like a hero in battle, nor as one who perishes while rescuing his fellow-men from fire or flood; he died as a criminal. Upon the cross of Calvary He was hung up. It was an accursed death, too. God Himself had called it so: "Cursed is every one that hangeth on a tree." He was made a curse for us. His death was penal in the highest sense. He "bare our sins in His own body on the tree."

I have not the mental, nor the physical, nor the spiritual strength to speak to you aright on such a wondrous topic as that of our Lord in the Valley of Humiliation. There have been times with me when I have only wanted a child's finger to point me to the Christ, and I have found enough in a sight of Him without any words of man. I hope that it is so with you to-night. I invite you to sit down, and watch your Lord, obedient unto death, even the death of the cross. All this He did that He might complete His own humiliation. He humbled Himself even to this lowest point of all, "unto death, even the death of the cross."

II. If you have this picture clearly before your eyes, I want you, in the second place, to PRACTICALLY LEARN SOME LESSONS FROM OUR LORD'S HUMILIATION.

The first is, learn to have *firmness of faith* in the atoning sacrifice. If my Lord could stoop to become man; and if, when He had come as low as that, He went still lower, and lower, and lower, until He became obedient unto death, even the death of the cross, I feel that there must be a potency about that death which is all that I can require. Jesus by dying has vindicated law and justice. Look, brethren, if God can punish sin upon His own dear Son, it means far more than the sending of us to hell. Without shedding of blood there is no remission of sin; but His blood was shed, so there is remission. His wounds let out His life blood; one great gash opened the way to His heart; before that, His whole body had become a mass of dripping gore, when, in the garden, His sweat was as it were great drops of blood falling to the ground. My Lord, when I study Thy sacrifice, I see how God can be "just, and the Justifier of Him

which believeth in Jesus." Faith is born at the cross of Christ. We not only bring faith to the cross, but we find it there. I cannot think of my God bearing all this grief in a human body, even to the death on the cross, and then doubt. Why, doubt becomes harder than faith when the cross is visible! When Christ is set forth evidently crucified among us, each one of us should cry, "Lord, I believe, for Thy death has killed my unbelief."

The next lesson I would have you learn from Christ's humiliation is this, cultivate a great *hatred of sin*. Sin killed Christ; let Christ kill sin. Sin made Him go down, down, down; then pull sin down, let it have no throne in your heart. If it *will* live in your heart, make it live in holes and corners, and never rest till it is utterly driven out. Seek to put your foot upon its neck, and utterly kill it. Christ was crucified; let your lusts be crucified: and let every wrong desire be nailed up, with Christ, upon the felon's tree. If, with Paul, you can say, "God forbid that I should glory, save in the cross of our Lord Jesus Christ, by whom the world is crucified unto me, and I unto the world;" with Him you will also be able to exclaim, "From henceforth let no man trouble me: for I bear in my body the marks of the Lord Jesus." Christ's branded slave is the Lord's freeman.

Learn another lesson, and that is, *obedience*. Beloved, if Christ humbled Himself, and became obedient, how obedient ought you and I to be! We ought to stop at nothing when we once know that it is the Lord's will. I marvel that you and I should ever raise a question or ask a moment's delay in our obedience to Christ. If it be the Lord's will, let it be done, and done at once. Should it rend some fond connection, should it cause a flood of tears, let it be done. He humbled Himself, and became obedient. Would obedience humble me? Would it lower me in man's esteem? Would it make me the subject of ridicule? Would it bring contempt upon my honourable name? Should I be elbowed out of the society wherein I have been admired, if I were obedient to Christ? Lord, this is a question not worth the asking! I take up Thy cross right joyfully, asking grace to be perfectly obedient, by the power of Thy Spirit.

Learn next, another lesson, and that is, *self-denial*. Did Christ humble Himself? Come, brothers and sisters, let us practise the same holy art. Have I not heard of some saying, "I have been insulted; I am not treated with proper respect. I go in and out, and I am not noticed. I have done eminent service, and there is not a paragraph in the newspaper about me." Oh, dear friend, your Master humbled Himself, and it seems to me that you are trying to exalt yourself! Truly, you are on the wrong track. If Christ went down, down, down, it ill becomes us to be always seeking to go up, up, up. Wait till God exalts you, which He will do in His own good time. Meanwhile, it behoves you, while you are here, to humble yourself. If you are already in a humble position, should you not be contented with it; for He humbled Himself? If you are now in a place where you are not noticed, where there is little thought of you, be quite satisfied with it. Jesus came just where you are; you may well stop where you are: where God has put you. Jesus had to bring Himself down, and to make an effort to come down to where you are. Is not the Valley of Humiliation one of the sweetest spots in all the world? Does not the great geographer of the heavenly country, John Bunyan, tell us that the

Valley of Humiliation is as fruitful a place as any the crow flies over, and that our Lord formerly had His country house there, and that He loved to walk those meadows, for He found the air was pleasant? Stop there, brother. "I should like to be known," says one. "I should like to have my name before the public." Well, if you ever had that lot, if you felt as I do, you would pray to be unknown, and to let your name drop out of notice; for there is no pleasure in it. The only happy way seems to me, if God would only let us choose, is to be known to nobody, but just to glide through this world as pilgrims and strangers, to the land where our true kindred dwell, and to be known there as having been followers of the Lord.

I think that we should also learn from our Lord's humiliation to have *contempt for human glory.* Suppose they come to you, and say, "We will crown you king!" you may well say, "Will you? All the crown you had for my Master was a crown of thorns; I will not accept a diadem from you." "We will praise you." "What, will you praise me, you who spat in His dear face? I want none of your praises." It is a greater honour to a Christian man to be maligned than to be applauded. Aye, I do not care where it comes from, I will say this; if he be slandered and abused for Christ's sake, no odes in his honour, no articles in his praise, can do him one-tenth the honour. This is to be a true knight of the cross, to have been wounded in the fray, to have come back adorned with scars for His dear sake. O despised one, look upon human glory as a thing that is tarnished, no longer golden; but corroded, because it came not to your Lord.

And, O beloved, I think, when we have meditated on this story of Christ's humbling Himself, we ought to feel our *love to our Lord* growing very vehement! We do not half love Him as we ought. When I read the sentences of Bernard, half Romanist, but altogether saint, I feel as if I had not begun to love my Lord; and when I turn over Rutherford's letters, and see the glow of his heart toward his divine Master, I could smite on my breast to think that I have such a heart of stone where there ought to be a heart of flesh. If you hear George Herbert sing his quaint, strange poetry, suffused with love for his dear Lord, you may well think that you are a tyro in the school of love. Aye, and if you ever drink in the spirit of McCheyne, you may go home, and hide your head, and say, "I am not worthy to sing,—

"'Jesus, lover of my soul,'

for I do not return His love as I ought to do." Come, seek His wounds, and let your hearts be wounded. Come, look to His heart that poured out blood and water, and give your heart up to Him. Put your whole being now among the sweet spices of His all-sufficient merit, set all on fire with burning affection, and let the fragrance of it go up like incense before the Lord.

Lastly, let us be inflamed with a strong *desire to honour Christ.* If He humbled Himself, let us honour Him. Every time that He seems to put away the crown, let us put it on His head. Every time we hear Him slandered,—and men continue to slander Him still,—let us speak up for Him right manfully.

"Ye that are men, now serve Him,
  Against unnumbered foes;
Your courage rise with danger,
  And strength to strength oppose."

Do you not grow indignant, sometimes, when you see how Christ's professed Church is treating Him, and His truth? They are shutting Him out still, till His head is wet with dew, and His locks with the drops of the night. Proclaim Him King in the face of His false friends. Proclaim Him, and say that His Word is infallibly true, and that His precious blood alone can cleanse from sin. Stand out the braver because so many Judases seem to have leaped up from the bottomless pit to betray Christ again. Be you firm and steadfast, like granite walls, in the day when others turn their backs, and fly, like cravens.

The Lord help you to honour Him who humbled Himself, who became obedient unto death, even the death of the cross! May He accept these humble words of mine, and bless them to His people, and make them to be the means of leading some poor sinner to come and trust in Him! Amen.

THE EXALTATION OF CHRIST

"Wherefore God also hath highly exalted Him, and given Him a name which is above every name: That at the name of Jesus every knee should bow, of things in heaven, and things in earth, and things under the earth; And that every tongue should confess that Jesus Christ is Lord, to the glory of God the Father."—Philippians ii. 9—11.

I ALMOST regret this morning that I have ventured to occupy this pulpit, because I feel utterly unable to preach to you for your profit. I had thought that the quiet and repose of the last fortnight had removed the effects of that terrible catastrophe; but on coming back to the same spot again, and more especially, standing here to address you, I feel somewhat of those same painful emotions which wellnigh prostrated me before. You will therefore excuse me this morning, if I make no allusion to that solemn event, or scarcely any. I could not preach to you upon a subject that should be in the least allied to it. I should be obliged to be silent if I should bring to my remembrance that terrific scene in the midst of which it was my solemn lot to stand. God shall overrule it doubtless. It may not have been so much by *the malice* of men, as some have asserted; it was perhaps simple wickedness—an intention to disturb a congregation; but certainly with no thought of committing so terrible a crime as that of the murder of those unhappy creatures. God forgive those who were the instigators of that horrid act! They have my forgiveness from the depths of my soul. *It shall not stop us, however;* we are not in the least degree daunted by it. I shall preach there again yet; aye, and God shall give us souls there, and Satan's empire shall tremble more than ever. "God is with us; who is he that shall be against us?" The text I have selected is one that has comforted me, and in a great measure, enabled me to come here to-day—the single reflection upon it had such a power of comfort on my depressed spirit. It is this:— "Wherefore God also hath highly exalted Him, and given Him a name which is above every name: That at the name of Jesus every knee should bow, of things in heaven, and things in earth, and things under the earth; And that every tongue should confess that Jesus Christ is Lord, to the glory of God the Father."—Philippians ii. 9—11.

I shall not attempt to preach upon this text; I shall only make a few remarks that have occurred to my own mind; for I could not preach to-day; I have been utterly unable to study, but I thought that even a few words might be acceptable to you this morning, and I trust to your loving hearts to excuse them. Oh, Spirit of God, magnify Thy strength in Thy servant's weakness, and enable him to honour His Lord, even when his soul is cast down within him.

When the mind is intensely set upon one object, however much it may by divers calamities be tossed to and fro, it invariably returns to the place which it had chosen to be its dwelling place. Ye have noticed in the case of David. When the battle had been won by his warriors, they returned flushed with victory. David's mind had doubtless suffered much perturbation in the mean time; he had dreaded alike the effects of victory and defeat; but have you not noticed how his mind in one moment returned to the darling object of his affections? "Is the young man Absalom safe?" said he, as if it mattered not what else had occurred, if his beloved son were but secure! So, beloved, is it with the Christian. In the midst of calamities, whether they be the wreck of nations, the crash of empires, the heaving of revolutions, or the scourge of war, the great question which he asks himself, and asks of others too, is this—Is Christ's kingdom safe? In his own personal afflictions his chief anxiety is,—Will God be glorified, and will His honour be increased by it? If it be so, says he, although I be but as smoking flax, yet if the sun is not dimmed I will rejoice; and though I be a bruised reed, if the pillars of the temple are unbroken, what matters it that my reed is bruised? He finds it sufficient consolation, in the midst of all the breaking in pieces which he endures, to think that Christ's throne stands fast and firm, and that though the earth hath rocked beneath *his* feet, yet Christ standeth on a rock which never can be moved. Some of these feelings, I think, have crossed our minds. Amidst much tumult and divers rushings to and fro of troublous thoughts our souls have returned to the darling object of our desires, and we have found it no small consolation after all to say, "It matters not what shall become of us: God hath highly exalted *Him*, and given *Him* a name which is above every name: That at the name of *Jesus* every knee should bow."

This text has afforded sweet consolation to every heir of heaven. Allow me, very briefly, to give you the consolations of it. *To the true Christian there is much comfort in the very fact of Christ's exaltation.* In the second place, *there is no small degree of consolation in the reason of it.* "*Wherefore*, also, God hath highly exalted Him;" that is, because of His previous humiliation. And thirdly, there is no small amount of really divine solace in the thought of *the person who has exalted Christ.* Wherefore *God also*"—although men despise Him and cast Him down—"God also hath highly exalted Him."

I. First, then, IN THE VERY FACT OF CHRIST'S EXALTATION THERE IS TO EVERY TRUE CHRISTIAN A VERY LARGE DEGREE OF COMFORT. Many of you who have no part nor lot in spiritual things, not having love to Christ, nor any desire for His glory, will but laugh when I say that this is a very bottle of cordial to the lip of the weary Christian, that Christ, after all, is glorified. To you it is no consolation, because you lack that condition of heart which makes this text sweet to the soul. To you there is nothing of joy in it; it does not stir your bosom; it gives no sweetness to your life; for this very reason, that you are not joined to Christ's cause, nor do you devoutly seek to honour Him. But the true Christian's heart leapeth for joy, even when cast down by divers sorrows and temptations, at the remembrance that Christ is exalted, for in that he finds enough to cheer his own heart. Note here, beloved, that the Christian has certain features in his character which make the exaltation of Christ a matter of great joy to him. First, he has in his own opinion, and not in his own opinion only, but in reality, a *relationship to Christ*, and therefore he feels an interest in the success of his kinsman. Ye have watched the father's joy, when step by step his boy has climbed to opulence or fame; ye have marked the mother's eye, as it sparkled with delight when her daughter grew up to womanhood, and burst forth in all the grandeur of beauty. Ye have asked why they should feel such interest; and ye have been told, because the boy was his, or the girl was hers. They delighted in the advancement of their little ones, because of their relationship. Had there been no relationship, they might have been advanced to kings, emperors, or queens, and they would have felt but little delight. But from the fact of kindred, each step was invested with a deep and stirring interest. Now, it is so with the Christian. He feels that Jesus Christ, the glorified "Prince of the kings of the earth," is his brother. While he reverences Him as God, he admires Him as the man-Christ, bone of his bone, and flesh of his flesh, and he delights, in his calm and placid moments of communion with Jesus, to say to Him, "O Lord, thou art my brother." His song is, "My beloved is mine, and I am His." It is his joy to sing—

"In ties of blood with sinners one,"

Christ Jesus is; for He is man, even as we are; and He is no less and no more man than we are, save only sin. Surely, when we feel we are related to Christ, His exaltation is the source of the greatest joy to our spirits; we take a delight in it, seeing it is one of our family that is exalted. It is the Elder Brother of the great one family of God in heaven and earth; it is the Brother to whom all of us are related.

There is also in the Christian not only the feeling of relationship merely, but there is a feeling of *unity in the cause*. He feels that when Christ is exalted, it is himself exalted in some degree, seeing he has sympathy with his desire of promoting the great cause and honour of God in the world. I have no doubt that every common soldier who stood by the side of the Duke of Wellington felt honoured when the commander was applauded for the victory; for said he, "I helped him, I assisted him; it was but a mean part that I played; I did but maintain my rank; I did but sustain the enemy's fire; but now the victory is gained, I feel an honour in it, for I helped, in some degree, to gain it." So the Christian, when he sees his Lord exalted, says, "It is the Captain that is exalted, and in His exaltation all His soldiers share. Have I not stood by His side? Little was the work

I did, and poor the strength which I possessed to serve Him; but still I aided in the labour;" and the commonest soldier in the spiritual ranks feels that he himself is in some degree exalted when he reads this—"Wherefore God also hath highly exalted Him, and given Him a name which is above every name:" a renown above every name—"that at the name of Jesus every knee should bow."

Moreover, the Christian knows not only that there is this unity in design, but that there is *a real union* between Christ and all His people. It is a doctrine of revelation seldom descanted upon, but never too much thought of—the doctrine that Christ and His members are all one. Know ye not, beloved, that every member of Christ's church is a member of Christ Himself? We are "of His flesh and of His bones," parts of His great mystical body; and when we read that our Head is crowned, O rejoice, ye members of His, His feet or His hands, though the crown is not on you, yet being on your Head, you share the glory, for you are one with Him. See Christ yonder, sitting at His Father's right hand! Believer! He is the pledge of thy glorification; He is the surety of thine acceptance; and, moreover, He is thy representative. The seat which Christ possesses in heaven He has not only by His own right, as a person of the Deity, but He had it also as the representative of His whole church, for He is their forerunner, and He sits in glory as the representative of every one of them. O rejoice, believer, when thou seest Thy Master exalted from the tomb, when thou beholdest Him exalted up to heaven. Then, when thou seest Him climb the steps of light, and sit upon His lofty throne, where angels' ken can scarcely reach Him—when thou hearest the acclamations of a thousand seraphs—when thou dost note the loud pealing choral symphony of millions of the redeemed; think, when thou seest Him crowned with light—think that thou art exalted too in Him, seeing that thou art a part of Himself. Happy art thou if thou knowest this, not only in doctrine, but in sweet experience too. Knit to Christ, wedded to Him, grown into Him, parts and portions of His very self, we throb with the heart of the body; when the head itself is glorified we share in the praise; we feel that His glorification bestows an honour upon us. Ah! beloved, have you ever felt that unity to Christ? Have you ever felt a unity of desire with Him? If so, you will find this rich with comfort; but if not—if you know not Christ—it will be a source of grief rather than a pleasure to you that He is exalted, for you will have to reflect that He is exalted to crush you, exalted to judge you and condemn you, exalted to sweep this earth of its sins, and cut the curse up by the roots, and you with it, unless you repent and turn unto God with full purpose of heart.

There is yet another feeling, which I think is extremely necessary to any very great enjoyment of this truth, that Christ is exalted. It is a feeling of *entire surrender of one's whole being to the great work of seeking to honour Him.* Oh! I have striven for that: would to God I might attain unto it! I have now concentrated all my prayers into one, and that one prayer is this, that I may die to self, and live wholly to Him. It seems to me to be the highest stage of man—to have no wish, no thought, no desire but Christ—to feel that to die were bliss, if it were for Christ—that to live in penury and woe, and scorn, and contempt, and misery, were sweet for Christ—to feel that it did not matter what became of one's self, so that one's Master was but exalted—to feel that though, like a sear leaf, you are blown in the blast, you are quite careless whither you are going, so long as you feel that the Master's hand is guiding you according to His will. Or rather to feel that though like the diamond you must be cut, that you care not how sharply you may be cut, so that you may be made fit to be a brilliant in *His* crown; that you care little what may be done to you, if you may but honour *Him.* If any of you have attained to that sweet feeling of self-annihilation, you will look up to Christ as if He were the sun, and you will say of yourself, "O Lord, I see Thy beams; I feel myself to be not a beam from Thee—but darkness, swallowed up in Thy light. The most I ask is, that Thou wouldst live in me, that the life I live in the flesh may not be my life, but Thy life in me, that I may say with emphasis, as Paul did, 'For me to live is Christ.'" A man that has attained to this, never need care what is the opinion of this world. He may say, "Do you praise me? Do you flatter me? Take back your flatteries; I ask them not at your hands; I sought to praise my Master; ye have laid the praises at my door; go, lay them at *His*, and not at mine. Do ye scorn me? Do ye despise me? Thrice happy am I to bear it, if ye will not scorn and despise *Him!*" And if ye will, yet know this, that He is beyond your scorn; and, therefore, smite the soldier for his Captain's sake; ay, strike, strike; but the King ye cannot touch—He is highly exalted—and though ye think ye have gotten the victory, ye may have routed one soldier of the army, but the main body is triumphant. One soldier seems to be smitten to the dust, but the Captain is coming on with His victorious cohorts, and shall trample you, flushed with your false victory, beneath His conquering feet. As long as there is a particle of selfishness remaining in us, it will mar our sweet rejoicing in Christ; till we get rid of it, we shall never feel constant joy. I do think that the root of sorrow is self. If we once got rid of that, sorrow would be sweet, sickness would be health, sadness would be joy, penury would be wealth, so far as our feelings with regard to them are concerned. *They* might not be changed, but *our feelings* under them would be vastly different. If you would seek happiness, seek it at the roots of your selfishness; cut up your selfishness, and you will be happy. I have found that whenever I have yielded to the least joy when I have been praised, I have made myself effeminate and weak; I have then been prepared to feel acutely the arrows of the enemy; but when I have said of the praises of men, "Yes, what are ye? worthless things!"—then I could also say of their contempt—"Come on! come on! I'll send you all where I sent the praises: you may go together, and fight your battles with one another; but as for me, let your arrows rattle on my mail—they must not, and they shall not, reach my flesh." But if you give way to one you will to another. You must seek and learn to live wholly on Christ—to sorrow when you see *Christ* maligned and dishonoured, to rejoice when you see *Him* exalted, and then you will have constant cause for joy. Sit down now, O reviled one, poor, despised, and tempted one; sit down, lift up thine eyes, see Him on His throne, and say within thyself, "Little though I be, I know I am united to Him; He is my love, my life, my joy; I care not what happens, so long as it is written, 'The Lord reigneth.'"

II. Now, briefly upon the second point. Here also is the very fountain and well-spring of joy, in

THE REASON OF CHRIST'S EXALTATION. "Wherefore God also hath highly exalted Him." Why? Because," He being in the form of God, thought it not robbery to be equal with God: But made Himself of no reputation, and took upon Him the form of a servant, and was made in the likeness of men: And being found in fashion as a man, He humbled Himself, and became obedient unto death, even the death of the cross. Wherefore God also hath highly exalted Him." This of course relates to the manhood of our Lord Jesus Christ. As God, Christ needed no exaltation; He was higher than the highest, "God over all, blessed for ever." But the symbols of His glory having been for a while obscured, having wrapped His Godhead in mortal flesh, His flesh with His Godhead ascended up on high, and the man-God, Christ Jesus, who had stooped to shame, and sorrow, and degradation, was highly exalted, "far above all principalities and powers," that He might reign Prince-regent over all worlds, yea, over heaven itself. Let us consider, for a moment, that depth of degradation to which Christ descended; and then, my beloved, it will give you joy to think, that for that very reason His manhood was highly exalted. Do you see that man—

> "The humble Man before his foes,
> The weary Man and full of woes?"

Do you mark Him as He speaks? Note the marvellous eloquence which pours from His lips, and see how the crowds attend Him? But do you hear, in the distance, the growling of the thunders of calumny and scorn? Listen to the words of His accusers. They say He is "a gluttonous man and a winebibber, a friend of publicans and sinners;" "He has a devil, and is mad." All the whole vocabulary of abuse is exhausted by vituperation upon Him. He is slandered, abused, persecuted! Stop! Do you think that He is by this cast down, by this degraded? No, for this very reason: "*God hath highly exalted Him.*" Mark the shame and spitting that have come upon the cheek of yonder Man of sorrows! See His hair plucked with cruel hands; mark ye how they torture Him and how they mock Him. Do you think that this is all dishonourable to Christ? It is apparently so; but list to this: "He became obedient," and therefore "*God hath highly exalted Him.*" Ah! there is a marvellous connection between that shame and spitting, and the bending of the knee of seraphs; there is a strange yet mystic link which unites the calumny and the slander with the choral sympathies of adoring angels. The one was, as it were, the seed of the other. Strange that it should be, but the black, the bitter seed brought forth a sweet and glorious flower which blooms for ever. He suffered and He reigned; He stooped to conquer, and He conquered for He stooped, and was exalted for He conquered. Consider Him further still. Do you mark Him in your imagination nailed to yonder cross! O eyes! ye are full of pity, with tears standing thick! Oh! how I mark the floods gushing down His cheeks! Do you see His hands bleeding, and His feet too, gushing gore? Behold Him! The bulls of Bashan gird Him round, and the dogs are hounding Him to death! Hear Him! "Eloi, Eloi, lama sabachthani?" The earth startles with affright. A God is groaning on a cross! What! Does not this dishonour Christ? No; it honours Him! Each of the thorns becomes a brilliant in His diadem of glory; the nails are forged

into His sceptre, and His wounds do clothe Him with the purple of empire. The treading of the wine-press hath stained His garments, but not with stains of scorn and dishonour. The stains are embroideries upon His royal robes for ever. The treading of that wine-press hath made His garments purple with the empire of a world; and He is the Master of a universe for ever. O Christian! sit down and consider that Thy Master did not mount from earth's mountains into heaven, but from her valleys. It was not from heights of bliss on earth that He strode to bliss eternal, but from depths of woe He mounted up to glory. Oh! what a stride was that, when, at one mighty step from the grave to the throne of The Highest, the man Christ, the God, did gloriously ascend. And yet reflect! He in some way, mysterious yet true, was exalted because He suffered. "Being found in fashion as a man, he humbled Himself, and became obedient unto death, even the death of the cross. Wherefore God also hath highly exalted Him, and given Him a name which is above every name." Believer, there is comfort for thee here, if thou wilt take it. If Christ was exalted through His degradation, so shalt thou be. Count not thy steps to triumph by thy steps upward, but by those which are seemingly downward. The way to heaven is down-hill. He who would be honoured for ever must sink in his own esteem, and often in that of his fellow-men. Oh! think not of yon fool who is mounting to heaven by his own light opinions of himself and by the flatteries of his fellows, that he shall safely reach Paradise; nay, that shall burst on which he rests, and he shall fall and be broken in pieces. But he who descends into the mines of suffering, shall find unbounded riches there; and he who dives into the depths of grief, shall find the pearl of everlasting life within its caverns. Recollect, Christian, that thou art exalted when thou art disgraced; read the slanders of thine enemies as the plaudits of the just; count that the scoff and jeer of wicked men are equal to the praise and honour of the godly; their blame is censure, and their censure praise. Reckon too, if thy body should ever be exposed to persecution, that it is no shame to thee, but the reverse; and if thou shouldst be privileged, (and thou mayest) to wear the blood-red crown of martyrdom, count it no disgrace to die. Remember, the most honourable in the church are "the noble army of martyrs." Reckon that the greater the sufferings they endured, so much the greater is their "eternal weight of glory;" and so do thou, if thou standest in the brunt and thick of the fight, remember that thou shalt stand in the midst of glory. If thou hast the hardest to bear, thou shalt have the sweetest to enjoy. On with thee, then—through floods, through fire, through death, through hell, if it should lie in thy path. Fear not. He who glorified Christ because He stooped shall glorify thee; for after He has caused thee to endure awhile, He will give thee "a crown of life which fadeth not away."

III. And now, in the last place, beloved, here is yet another comfort for you. THE PERSON who exalted Christ is to be noticed. "GOD also hath highly exalted Him." The emperor of all the Russias crowns himself: he is an autocrat, and puts the crown upon his own head: but Christ hath no such foolish pride. Christ did not crown Himself. "GOD also hath highly exalted Him." The crown was put upon the head of Christ by God; and there is to me a very sweet reflection in this,—that the hand that put the crown on Christ's head, will one day put the crown on ours;—that the same Mighty One who crowned Christ, "King of kings, and Lord of lords," will crown us, when He shall make us "Kings and priests unto Him for ever." "I know," said Paul, "there is laid up for me a crown of glory which fadeth not away, which God, the righteous judge, shall give me in that day."

Now, just pause over this thought—that Christ did not crown Himself, but that His Father crowned Him; that He did not elevate Himself to the throne of majesty, but that His Father lifted Him there, and placed Him on His throne. Why, reflect thus: Man never highly exalted Christ. Put this then in opposition to it.—"*God* also hath highly exalted Him." Man hissed Him, mocked Him, hooted Him. Words were not hard enough—they would use stones. "They took up stones again to stone Him." And stones failed; nails must be used, and He must be crucified. And then there comes the taunt, the jeer, the mockery, whilst He hangs languishing on His death-cross. Man did not exalt Him. Set the black picture there. Now put this, with this glorious, this bright scene, side by side with it, and one shall be a foil to the other. *Man* dishonoured Him; "*God* also exalted Him." Believer, if all men speak ill of thee, lift up thy head, and say, "Man exalted not my Master; I thank Him that He exalts not me. The servant should not be above his master, nor the servant above his lord, nor He that is sent greater than He that sent him."

"If on my face for His dear name,
  Shame and reproach shall be;
I'll hail reproach and welcome shame,
  For He'll remember me."

God will remember me, and highly exalt me after all, though man casts me down.

Put it, again, in opposition to the fact, that Christ did not exalt Himself. Poor Christian! *you* feel that you cannot exalt yourself. Sometimes you cannot raise your poor depressed spirits. Some say to you, "Oh! you should not feel like this." They tell you, "Oh! you should not speak such words, nor think such thoughts." Ah! "the heart knoweth its own bitterness, and a stranger intermeddleth not therewith,"—ay, and I will improve upon it, "nor a friend either." It is not easy to tell how another ought to feel and how another ought to act. Our minds are differently made, each in its own mould, which mould is broken afterwards, and there shall never be another like it. We are all different, each one of us; but I am sure there is one thing in which we are all brought to unite in times of deep sorrow, namely, in a sense of helplessness. We feel that we cannot exalt ourselves. Now remember, our Master felt just like it. In the 22nd Psalm, which, if I read it rightly, is a beautiful soliloquy of Christ upon the cross, He says to Himself, "I am a worm, and no man." As if He felt Himself so broken, so cast down, that instead of being more than a man, as He was, He felt for awhile less than man. And yet, when He could not lift finger to crown Himself, when He could scarce heave a thought of victory, when His eye could not flash with even a distant glimpse of triumph,—then His God was crowning Him. Art thou so broken in pieces, Christian? Think not that thou art cast away for ever; for "God also hath highly exalted Him" who did not exalt Himself; and this is a picture and prophecy of what He will do for thee.

And now, beloved, I can say little more upon this text, save that I bid you now for a few minutes meditate and think upon it. Oh! let your eyes be lifted up; bid heaven's blue veil divide; ask power of God—I mean spiritual power from on high, to look within the veil. I bid you not look to the streets of gold, nor to the walls of jasper, nor to the pearly-gated city. I do not ask you to turn your eyes to the white-robed hosts, who for ever sing loud hallelujahs; but yonder, my friends, turn your eyes,

"There, like a man, the Saviour sits:
  The God, how bright He shines;
And scatters infinite delight
  On all the happy minds."

Do you see Him?

"The head that once was crowned with thorns,
  Is crowned with glory now;
A royal diadem adorns
  That mighty Victor's brow.

No more the bloody crown,
  The cross and nails no more:
For hell itself shakes at His frown,
  And all the heavens adore."

Look at Him! Can your imagination picture Him? Behold His transcendent glory! The majesty of kings is swallowed up; the pomp of empires dissolves like the white mist of the morning before the sun; the brightness of assembled armies is eclipsed. He in Himself is brighter than the sun, more terrible than armies with banners. See Him! See Him! Oh! hide your heads, ye monarchs; put away your gaudy pageantry, ye lords of this poor narrow earth! His kingdom knows no bounds; without a limit His vast empire stretches out itself. Above Him all is His; beneath Him many a step are angels, and they are His; and they cast their crowns before His feet. With them stand His elect and ransomed, and *their* crowns too are His. And here upon this lower earth stand His saints, and they are His, and they adore Him; and under the earth, among the infernals, where devils growl their malice, even there is trembling and adoration; and where lost spirits, with wailing and gnashing of teeth for ever lament their being, even there, there is the acknowledgement of His Godhead, even though the confession helps to make the fire of their torments. In heaven, in earth, in hell, all knees bend before Him, and every tongue confesses that He is God. If not now, yet in the time that is to come this shall be carried out, that every creature of God's making shall acknowledge His Son to be "God over all, blessed for ever. Amen." Oh! my soul anticipates that blessed day, when this whole earth shall bend its knee before its God willingly! I do believe there is a happy era coming, when there shall not be one knee unbent before my Lord and Master. I look for that time, that latter-day glory, when kings shall bring presents, when queens shall be the nursing mothers of the church, when the gold of Sheba and the ships of Tarshish, and the dromedaries of Arabia shall alike be His, when nations and tribes of every tongue shall

"Dwell on His name with sweetest song,
  And infant voices shall proclaim
Their early blessings on His name."

Sometimes I hope to live to see that all-auspicious era —that halcyon age of this world, so much oppressed with grief and sorrow by the tyranny of its own habitants. I hope to see the time, when it shall be said, "Shout, for the great Shepherd reigns, and His unsuffering kingdom now is come"—when earth shall be one great orchestra of praise, and every man shall sing the glorious hallelujah anthem of the King of kings. But even now, while waiting for that era, my soul rejoices in the fact, that every knee does virtually bow, though not willingly, yet really. Does the scoffer, when he mouths high heaven, think that he insults God? He thinks so, but his insult dies long ere it reaches half-way to the stars. Does he conceive, when in his malice he forges a sword against Christ, that his weapon shall prosper? If he does, I can well conceive the derision of God, when He sees the wildest rebel, the most abandoned despiser, still working out His great decrees, still doing that which God hath eternally ordained, and in the midst of his wild rebellion still running in the very track which in some mysterious way from before all eternity had been marked as the track in which that being should certainly move. "The wild steeds of earth have broken their bridles, the reins are out of the hands of the charioteer"—so some say; but they are not, or if they are, the steeds run the same round as they would have done had the Almighty grasped the reins still. The world has not gone to confusion; chance is not God; God is still Master, and let men do what they will, and hate the truth we now prize, they shall after all do what God wills, and their direst rebellion shall prove but a species of obedience, though they know it not.

But thou wilt say, "Why dost Thou yet find fault; for who hath resisted such a will as that?" "Nay, but O man, who art thou that repliest against God? Shall the thing formed say to Him that formed it, why hast Thou made me thus? Hath not the potter power over the clay, of the same lump to make one vessel unto honour, and another unto dishonour? What if God, willing to show His wrath, and to make His power known, endured with much longsuffering the vessels of wrath fitted to destruction: and that He might make known the riches of His glory on the vessels of mercy, which He had afore prepared unto glory." Who is he that shall blame Him? Woe unto him that striveth with his Maker! He is God —know that, ye inhabitants of the land; and all things, after all, shall serve His will. I like what Luther says in his bold hymn, where, notwithstanding all that those who are haters of predestination choose to affirm, he knew and boldly declared, "He everywhere hath sway, and all things serve His might." Notwithstanding all they do, there is God's sway, after all. Go on, reviler! God knoweth how to make all thy revilings into songs! Go on, thou warrior against God, if thou wilt; know this, thy sword shall help to magnify God, and carve out glory for Christ, when thou thoughtest the slaughter of His church. It shall come to pass that all thou dost shall be frustrated; for God maketh the diviners mad, and saith, "Where is the wisdom of the scribe? Where is the wisdom of the wise?" Surely, "Him hath God exalted, and given Him a name which is above every name."

And now, lastly, beloved, if it be true, as it is, that Christ is so exalted that He is to have a name above every name, and every knee is to bow to Him, will we not bow our knees this morning before His Majesty? You must, whether you will or no, one day bow your knee. O iron-sinewed sinner, bow thy knee now! Thou wilt have to bow it, man, in that day when the lightnings shall be loosed, and the thunders shall roll in wild fury: thou wilt have to bow thy knee then. Oh! bow it now! "Kiss the Son, lest He be angry, and ye perish from the way, when His wrath is kindled but a little." O Lord of hosts! bend the knees of men! Make us all the willing subjects of Thy grace, lest afterward, we should be the unwilling slaves of Thy terror; dragged with chains of vengeance down to hell. O that now those that are on earth might willingly bend their knees lest in hell it should be fulfilled, "Things under the earth shall bow the knee before Him."

God bless you, my friends; I can say no more but that. God bless you, for Jesus' sake! Amen.

"YOUR OWN SALVATION"

"Your own salvation."—Philippians ii. 12.

WE select the words, "*your own salvation,*" as our text this morning, not out of any singularity, or from the slightest wish that the brevity of the text should surprise you; but because our subject will be the more clearly before you if only these three words are announced. If I had nominally taken the whole verse I could not have attempted to expound it without distracting your attention from the topic which now weighs upon my heart. O that the divine Spirit may bring home to each one of your minds the unspeakable importance of "your own salvation"!

We have heard it said by hearers that they come to listen to us, and we talk to them upon subjects in which they have no interest. You will not be able to make this complaint to-day, for we shall speak only for "your own salvation"; and nothing can more concern you. It has sometimes been said that preachers frequently select very unpractical themes. No such objection can be raised to-day, for nothing can be more practical than this; nothing more needful than to urge you to see to "your own salvation." We have even heard it said that ministers delight in abstruse subjects, paradoxical dogmas, and mysteries surpassing comprehension; but, assuredly, we will keep to plain sailing this morning. No sublime doctrines, no profound questions shall perplex you; you shall only be called on to consider "your own salvation": a very homely theme, and a very simple one, but for all that, the most weighty that can be brought before you. I shall seek after simple words also, and plain sentences, to suit the simplicity and plainness of the subject, that there may be no thought whatever about the speaker's language, but only concerning this one, sole, only topic, "your own salvation." I ask you all, as reasonable men who would not injure or neglect yourselves, to lend me your most serious attention. Chase away the swarming vanities which buzz around you, and let each man think for himself upon his "own salvation." Oh, may the Spirit of God set each one of you apart in a mental solitude, and constrain you each one, singly, to face the truth concerning his own state! Each man apart, each woman apart; the father apart, and the child apart: may you now come before the Lord in solemn thought, and may nothing occupy your attention but this: "your own salvation."

I. We will begin this morning's meditation by noting THE MATTER UNDER CONSIDERATION—*Salvation!*

Salvation! a great word, not always understood, often narrowed down, and its very marrow overlooked. Salvation! This concerns every one here present. We all fell in our first parent; we have all sinned personally; we shall all perish unless we find salvation. The word salvation contains within it *deliverance from the guilt of our past sins.* We have broken God's law each one of us, more or less flagrantly; we have all wandered the downward road, though each has chosen a different way. Salvation brings to us the blotting out of the transgressions of the past, acquittal from criminality, purging from all guiltiness, that we may stand accepted before the great Judge. What man in his sober senses will deny that forgiveness is an unspeakably desirable blessing!

But salvation means more than that: it includes *deliverance from the power of sin.* Naturally we are all fond of evil, and we run after it greedily; we are the bondslaves of iniquity, and we love the bondage. This last is the worst feature of the case. But when salvation comes it delivers the man from the power of sin. He learns that it is evil, and he regards it as such, loathes it, repents that he has ever been in love with it, turns his back upon it, becomes, through God's Spirit, the master of his lusts, puts the flesh beneath his feet, and rises into the liberty of the children of God. Alas! there are many who do not care for this: if this be salvation they would not give a farthing for it. They love their sins; they rejoice to follow the devices and imaginations of their own corrupt hearts. Yet be assured, this emancipation from bad habits, unclean desires, and carnal passions is the main point in salvation, and if it be not ours, salvation in its other branches is not and cannot be enjoyed by us. Dear hearer, dost thou possess salvation from sin? hast thou escaped the corruption which is in the world through lust? If not, what hast thou to do with salvation? To any right-minded man deliverance from unholy principles is regarded as the greatest of all blessings. What thinkest thou of it?

Salvation includes *deliverance from the present wrath of God* which abides upon the unsaved man every moment of his life. Every person who is unforgiven is the object of divine wrath. "God is angry with the wicked every day. If He turn not, He will whet His sword." "He that believeth not is condemned already, because he hath not believed in the name of the only begotten Son of God." I frequently hear the statement that this is a state of probation. This is a great mistake, for our probation has long since passed. Sinners have been proved, and found to be unworthy; they have been "weighed in the balances," and "found wanting." If you have not believed in Jesus, condemnation already rests upon you: you are reprieved awhile, but your condemnation is recorded. Salvation takes a man from under the cloud of divine wrath, and reveals to him the divine love. He can then say, "O God, I will praise Thee, though Thou wast angry with me, Thine anger is turned away, and Thou comfortest me." Oh, it is not hell hereafter which is the only thing a sinner has to fear, it is the wrath of God which rests upon him now. To be unreconciled to God now is an awful thing; to have God's arrow pointed at you as it is at this moment, even though it fly not from the string as yet, is a terrible thing. It is enough to make you tremble from head to foot when you learn that you are the target of Jehovah's wrath: "He hath bent His bow, and made it ready." Every soul that is unreconciled to God by the blood of His Son is in the gall of bitterness. Salvation at once sets us free from this state of danger and alienation. We are no longer the "children of wrath, even as others," but are made children of God and joint heirs with Christ Jesus. What can be conceived more precious than this?

And then, we lastly receive that part of salvation which ignorant persons put first, and make to be the whole of salvation. In consequence of our being delivered from the guilt of sin, and from the power of sin, and from the present wrath of God, we are *delivered from the future wrath of God.* Unto the uttermost will that wrath descend upon the souls of men when they leave the body and stand before their Maker's bar, if they depart this life unsaved. To die without salvation is to enter into damnation. Where death leaves us there judgment finds us; and where judgment finds us eternity will hold us for ever and ever. "He which is filthy, let him be filthy still," and he that is wretched as a punishment for being filthy, shall be hopelessly wretched still. Salvation delivers the soul from going down into the pit of hell. We, being justified, are no longer liable to punishment, because we are no longer chargeable with guilt. Christ Jesus bore the wrath of God that we might never bear it. He has made a full atonement to the justice of God for the sins of all believers. Against him that believeth there remaineth no record of guilt; his transgressions are blotted out, for Christ Jesus hath finished transgression, made an end of sin, and brought in everlasting righteousness. What a comprehensive word then is this—"salvation"! It is a triumphant deliverance from the guilt of sin, from the dominion of it, from the curse of it, from the punishment of it, and ultimately from the very existence of it. Salvation is the death of sin, its burial, its annihilation, yea, and the very obliteration of its memory; for thus saith the Lord: "their sins and their iniquities will I remember no more."

Beloved hearers, I am sure that this is the weightiest theme I can bring before you, and therefore I cannot be content unless I see that it grasps you and holds you fast. I pray you give earnest heed to this most pressing of all subjects. If my voice and words cannot command your fullest attention, I could wish to be dumb, that some other pleader might with wiser speech draw you to a close consideration of this matter. Salvation appears to me to be of the first importance, when I think of what it is in itself, and for this reason I have at the outset set it forth before your eyes; but you may be helped to remember its value if you consider that God the Father thinks highly of salvation. It was on His mind or ever the earth was. He thinks salvation a lofty business, for He gave His Son that He might save rebellious sinners. Jesus Christ, the only Begotten, thinks salvation most important, for He bled, He died to accomplish it. Shall I trifle with that which cost Him His life? If He came from heaven to earth, shall I be slow to look from earth to heaven? Shall that which cost the Saviour a life of zeal, and a death of agony, be of small account with me? By the bloody sweat of Gethsemane, by the wounds of Calvary, I beseech you, be assured that salvation must be worthy of your highest and most anxious thoughts. It could not be that God the Father, and God the Son, should thus make a common sacrifice: the one giving His Son and the other giving Himself for salvation, and yet salvation should be a light and trivial thing. The Holy Ghost thinks it no trifle, for He condescends to work continually in the new creation that He may bring about salvation. He is often vexed and grieved, yet He continues still His abiding labours that He may bring many sons unto glory. Despise not what the Holy Ghost esteems, lest thou despise the Holy Ghost Himself. The sacred Trinity think much of salvation; let us not neglect it. I beseech you who have gone on trifling with salvation, to remember that we who have to preach to you dare not trifle with it. The longer I live the more I feel that if God do not make me faithful as a minister, it had been better for me never to have been born. What a thought that I am set as a watchman to warn your souls, and if I warn you not aright, your blood will be laid at my door! My own damnation will be terrible enough, but to have your blood upon my skirts as well—! God save any one of His ministers from being found guilty of the souls of men. Every preacher of the gospel may cry with David, "Deliver me from bloodguiltiness, O God, thou God of my salvation."

Bethink you, O careless hearers, that God's church does not consider salvation to be a little matter? Earnest men and women, by thousands, are praying day and night for the salvation of others, and are labouring, too, and making great sacrifices, and are willing to make many more, if they may by any means bring some to Jesus and His salvation. Surely, if gracious men, and wise men, think salvation to be so important, you who have hitherto neglected it ought to change your minds upon the matter, and act with greater care for your own interests.

The angels think it a weighty business. Bowing from their thrones, they watch for repenting sinners; and when they hear that a sinner has returned to his God, they waken anew their golden harps and pour forth fresh music before the throne, for "there is joy in the presence of the angels of God over one sinner that repenteth." It is certain also that devils think salvation to be a great matter, for their arch-leader goeth about seeking whom he may devour. They never tire in seeking men's destructon. They know how much salvation glorifies God, and how terrible the ruin of souls is; and, therefore they compass sea and land, if they may destroy the sons of men. Oh, I pray you, careless hearer, be wise enough to dread that fate which your cruel enemy, the devil, would fain secure for you! Remember, too, that lost souls think salvation important. The rich man, when he was in this world, thought highly of nothing but his barns, and the housing of his produce; but when he came into the place of torment, then he said: "Father Abraham, send Lazarus to my father's house: for I have five brethren; that he may testify unto them, lest they also they come into this place of torment." Lost souls see things in another light than that which dazzled them here below; they value things at a different rate from what we do here, where sinful pleasures and earthly treasures dim the mental eye. I pray you then, by the blessed Trinity, by the tears and prayers of holy men, by the joy of angels and glorified spirits, by the malice of devils and the despair of the lost, arouse yourselves from slumber, and neglect not this great salvation!

I shall not depreciate anything that concerns your welfare, but I shall steadfastly assert that nothing so much concerns any one of you as salvation Your health by all means. Let the physician be fetched if you be sick; care well for diet and exercise, and all sanitary laws. Look wisely to your constitution and its peculiarities; but what matters it, after all, to have possessed a healthy body, if you have a perishing soul? Wealth, yes, if you must have it, though you shall find it an empty thing if you set your heart upon it. Prosperity in this world, earn it if you can do so fairly, but "what shall it profit a man, if he shall gain the whole world, and lose his own soul?" A golden coffin will be a poor compensation for a damned soul. To be cast away from God's presence, can that misery be assuaged by mountains of treasure? Can the bitterness of the second death be sweetened by the thought that the wretch was once a millionaire, and that his wealth could affect the politics of nations? No, there is nothing in health or wealth comparable to salvation. Nor can honour and reputation bear a comparison therewith. Truly they are but baubles, and yet for all that they have a strange fascination for the sons of men. Oh, sirs, if every harpstring in the world should resound your glories, and every trumpet should proclaim your fame, what would it matter if a louder voice should say, "Depart from me, ye cursed, into everlasting fire, prepared for the devil and his angels"? Salvation! *salvation!* salvation! Nothing on earth can match it, for the merchandise of it is better than silver, and the gain thereof than fine gold. The possession of the whole universe would be no equivalent to a lost soul for the awful damage it has sustained and must sustain for ever. Pile up the worlds, and let them fill the balance: aye, bring as many worlds as there are stars, and heap up the scale on the one side; then in this other scale place a single soul endowed with immortality, and it outweighs the whole. Salvation! nothing can be likened unto it. May we feel its unutterable value, and therefore seek it till we possess it in its fulness!

II. But now we must advance to a second point of consideration, and I pray God the Holy Spirit to press it upon us, and that is, WHOSE MATTER IS IT? We have seen what the matter is—salvation; now, consider whose is it. "*Your own* salvation." At this hour nothing else is to occupy your thoughts but this intensely personal matter, and I beseech the Holy Spirit to hold your minds fast to this one point.

If you are saved it will be "your own salvation," and you yourself will enjoy it. If you are not saved, the sin you now commit is your own sin, the guilt your own guilt. The condemnation under which you live, with all its disquietude and fear, or with all its callousness and neglect, is your own—all your own. You may share in other men's sins, and other men may become participators in yours, but a burden lies on your own back which no one besides can touch with one of his fingers. There is a page in God's Book where your sins are recorded unmingled with the transgressions of your fellows. Now, beloved, you must obtain for all this sin a personal pardon. or you are undone for ever. No other can be washed in Christ's blood for you; no one can believe and let his faith stand instead of your faith. The very supposition of human sponsorship in religion is monstrous. You must yourself repent, yourself believe, yourself be washed in the blood, or else for you there is no forgiveness, no acceptance, no adoption, no regeneration. It is all a personal matter through and through: "your own salvation" it must be, or it will be your own eternal ruin.

Reflect anxiously that you must personally die. No one imagines that another can die for him. No man can redeem his brother or give to God a ransom. Through that iron gate I must pass alone, and so must you. Dying will have to be our own personal business; and in that dying we shall have either personal comfort or personal dismay. When death is past, salvation is still our "own salvation;" for if I am saved, *mine* "eyes shall see the king in His beauty: they shall behold the land that is very far off." Mine eyes shall see Him, and not another on my behalf. No brother's head is to wear your crown; no stranger's hand to wave your palm; no sister's eye to gaze for you upon the beatific vision, and no sponsor's heart to be filled as your proxy with the ecstatic bliss. There is a personal heaven for the personal believer in the Lord Jesus Christ. It must be if you possess it, "your own salvation." But if you have it not, reflect again, that it will be your own damnation. No one will be condemned for you; no other can bear the hot thunderbolts of Jehovah's wrath on your behalf. When you shall say, "Hide me, ye rocks! Conceal me, O mountains!" no one will spring forward, and say, "You can cease to be accursed, and I will become a curse for you." A Substitute there is to-day for every one that believeth —God's appointed Substitute, the Christ of God; but if that substitution is not accepted by you, there can never be another; but there remains only for you a personal casting away to suffer personal pangs in your own soul and in your own body for ever. This, then, makes it a most solemn business. Oh, be wise, and look well to "your own salvation."

You may be tempted to-day, and very likely you are to forget your own salvation by thoughts of other people. We are all so apt to look abroad in this matter, and not to look at home. Let me pray you to reverse the process, and let everything which has made you neglect your own vineyard be turned to the opposite account, and lead you to begin at home, and see to "your own salvation." Perhaps you dwell among the saints of God, and you have been rather apt to find fault with them, though for my part I can say these are the people I desire to live with and desire to die with: "thy people shall be my people, and thy God my God." But, oh, if you live among the saints, ought it not to be your business to see to "your own salvation"? See that you are truly one of them, not written in their church-book merely, but really graven upon the palms of Christ's hands; not a false professor, but a real possessor; not a mere wearer of the name of Christ, but a bearer of the nature of Christ. If you live in a gracious family be afraid lest you should be divided from them for ever. How could you endure to go from a Christian household to the place of torment? Let the anxieties of saints lead you to be anxious. Let their prayers drive you to prayer. Let their example rebuke your sin, and their joys entice you to their Saviour. Oh, see to this! But perhaps you live most among ungodly men, and the tendency of your converse with the ungodly is to make you think as they do of the trifles and vanities, and wickednesses of this life. Do not let it be so; but, on the contrary, say, "O God, though I am placed among these people, yet gather not my soul with sinners, nor my life with bloody men. Let me avoid the sins into which they fall, and the impenitence of which they are guilty. Save me, I pray Thee, O my God, save me from the transgressions which they commit."

Perhaps to-day some of your minds are occupied with thoughts of the dead who have fallen asleep. There is a little one unburied at home, or there is a father not yet laid in the grave. Oh, when you weep for those who have gone to heaven, think of "your own salvation," and weep for yourselves, for you have parted with them for ever unless you are saved. You have said, "Farewell" to those beloved ones, eternally farewell, unless you yourselves believe in Jesus. And if any of you have heard of persons who have lived in sin and died in blasphemy, and are lost, I pray you think not of them carelessly lest you also suffer the same doom: for what saith the Saviour: "Suppose ye that these were sinners above all the sinners?" "I tell you, Nay: but, except ye repent, ye shall all likewise perish." It seems to me as if everything on earth, and everything in heaven, and everything in hell, yea, and God Himself, calls upon you to seek "your own salvation," first, and foremost, and above all other things.

It may be profitable to mention some persons upon whom this theme needs much pressing. I will begin at home. There is great need to urge this matter upon official Christians, such as I am, such as my brethren, the deacons and elders, are. If there are any persons who are likely to be deceived, it is those who are called by their office to act as shepherds to the souls of others. O my brethren! it is so easy for me to imagine I am a minister, and have to deal with holy things, that therefore I am safe. I pray I may never fall into that delusion, but may always cling to the cross, as a poor, needy sinner resting in the blood of Jesus. Brother ministers, co-workers, and officials of the church, do not imagine that office can save you. The son of perdition was an apostle, greater than we are in office, and yet at this hour he is greater in destruction. See to it, ye that are numbered amongst the leaders of Israel, that you yourselves be saved.

Unpractical doctrinalists are another class of persons who need to be warned to see to their own salvation. When they hear a sermon, they sit with their mouths open, ready to snap at half a mistake. They make a man an offender for a word, for they conclude themselves to be the standards of orthodoxy, and they weigh up the preacher as he speaks, with as much coolness as if they had been appointed deputy judges for the Great King Himself. O sir, weigh yourself! It may be a great thing to be sound in the head, in the faith, but it is a greater thing to be sound in the heart. I may be able to split a hair between orthodoxy and heterodoxy, and yet may have no part nor lot in the matter. You may be a very sound Calvinist, or you may happen to think soundness lies in another direction; but, oh, it is nought, it is less than nought, except your souls feel the power of the truth, and ye yourselves are born again. See to "your own salvation," O ye wise men in the letter, who have not the Spirit.

So, too, certain persons who are always given to curious speculations need warning. When they read the Bible it is not to find whether they are saved or no, but to know whether we are under the third or fourth vial, when the millennium is going to be, or what is the battle of Armageddon. Ah, sir, search out all these things if thou hast time and skill, but look to thine own salvation first. The book of Revelation, blessed is he that understands it, but not unless, first of all, he understands this, "He that believeth and is baptized shall be saved." The greatest doctor in the symbols and mysteries of the Apocalypse shall be as certainly cast away as the most ignorant, unless he has come to Christ, and rested his soul in the atoning work of our great Substitute.

I know some who greatly need to look to their own salvation. I refer to those who are always criticizing others. They can hardly go to a place of worship but what they are observing their neighbour's dress or conduct. Nobody is safe from their remarks, they are such keen judges, and make such shrewd observations. Ye faultfinders and talebearers, look to "your own salvation." You condemned a minister the other day for a supposed fault, and yet he is a dear servant of God, who lives near his Master; who are you, sir, to use your tongue against such a one as he? The other day a poor humble Christian was the object of your gossip and your slander, to the wounding of her heart. Oh, see to yourself, see to yourself. If those eyes which look outward so piercingly would sometimes look inward they might see a sight which would blind them with horror. Blessed horror if it led them to turn to the Saviour who would open those eyes afresh, and grant them to see His salvation.

I might also say that in this matter of looking to personal salvation, it is necessary to speak to some who have espoused certain great public designs. I trust I am as ardent a Protestant as any man living, but I know too many red-hot Protestants who are but little better than Romanists, for though the Romanists of old might have burnt them, they would certainly withhold toleration from Romanists to-day, if they could; and therein I see not a pin to choose between the two bigots. Zealous Protestants, I agree with you, but yet I warn you that your zeal in this matter will not save you, or stand in the stead of personal godliness. Many an orthodox Protestant will be found at the left hand of the Great Judge. And you, too, who are for ever agitating this and that public question, I would say to you, "Let politics alone till your own inward politics are settled on a good foundation." You are a Radical Reformer, you could show us a system of political economy which would right all our wrongs and give to every man his due; then I pray you right your own wrongs, reform yourself, yield yourself to the love of Jesus Christ, or what will it signify to you, though you knew how to balance the affairs of nations, and to regulate the arrangement of all classes of society, if you yourself shall be blown away like chaff before the winnowing fan of the Lord. God grant us grace, then, whatever else we take up with, to keep it in its proper place, and make our calling and election sure.

III. And now, thirdly, and oh, for grace to speak aright, I shall try to ANSWER CERTAIN OBJECTIONS. I think I hear somebody say, "Well, but don't you believe in *predestination*? What have we to do with looking to our own salvation? Is it not all fixed?" Thou fool, for I can scarce answer thee till I have given thee thy right title; was it not fixed whether thou shouldst get wet or not in coming to this place? Why then did you bring your umbrella? Is it not fixed whether you shall be nourished with food to-day or shall go hungry? Why then will you go home and eat your dinner? Is it not fixed whether you shall live or not to-morrow; will you, therefore, cut your

throat? No, you do not reason so wickedly, so foolishly from destiny in reference to anything but "your own salvation," and you know it is not reasoning, it just mere talk. Here is all the answer I will give you, and all you deserve.

Another says, "I have a difficulty about this looking to our own salvation. Do you not believe in *full assurance*? Are there not some who know that they are saved beyond all doubt?" Yes, blessed be God, I hope there are many such now present. But let me tell you who these are not. These are not persons who are afraid to examine themselves. If I meet with any man who says, "I have no need to examine myself any more, I know I am saved, and therefore have no need to take any further care," I would venture to say to him, "Sir, you are lost already. This strong delusion of yours has led you to believe a lie." There are none so cautious as those who possess full assurance, and there are none who have so much holy fear of sinning against God, nor who walk so tenderly and carefully as those who possess the full assurance of faith. Presumption is not assurance, though, alas! many think so. No fully assured believer will ever object to being reminded of the importance of his own salvation.

But a third objection arises. "This is very *selfish*," says one. "You have been exhorting us to look to ourselves, and that is sheer selfishness." Yes, so you say; but let me tell you it is a kind of selfishness that is absolutely needful before you can be unselfish. A part of salvation is to be delivered from selfishness, and I am selfish enough to desire to be delivered from selfishness. How can you be of any service to others if you are not saved yourself? A man is drowning. I am on London Bridge. If I spring from the parapet and can swim, I can save him; but suppose I cannot swim, can I render any service by leaping into sudden and certain death with the sinking man? I am disqualified from helping him till I have the ability to do so. There is a school over yonder. Well, the first enquiry of him who is to be the master must be, "Do I know myself that which I profess to teach?" Do you call that enquiry selfish? Surely it is a most unselfish selfishness, grounded upon common sense. Indeed, the man who is not so selfish as to ask himself, "Am I qualified to act as a teacher?" would be guilty of gross selfishness in putting himself into an office which he was not qualified to fill. I will suppose an illiterate person going into the school, and saying, "I will be master here, and take the pay," and yet he cannot teach the children to read or write. Would he not be very selfish in not seeing to his own fitness? But surely it is not selfishness that would make a man stand back and say, "No, I must first go to school myself, otherwise it is but a mockery of the children for me to attempt to teach them anything." This is no selfishness, then, when looked at aright, which makes us see to our own salvation, for it is the basis from which we operate for the good of others.

IV. Having answered these objections, I shall for a minute attempt to RENDER SOME ASSISTANCE to those who would fain be right in the best things.

Has the Holy Spirit been pleased to make any one here earnest about his own salvation? Friend, I will help you to answer two questions. Ask yourself, first, "Am I saved?" I would help thee to reply to that very quickly. If you are saved this morning, you are the subject of a work within you, as saith the text, "Work out your own salvation; for it is God which worketh in you." You cannot work it *in*, but when God works it in you work it *out*. Have you a work of the Holy Ghost in your soul? Do you feel something more than unaided human nature can attain unto? Have you a change wrought in you from above? If so, you are saved. Again, does your salvation rest wholly upon Christ? He who hangs anywhere but upon the cross, hangs upon that which will deceive him. If thou standest upon Christ, thou art on a rock; but if thou trustest in the merits of Christ in part, and thy own merits in part, then thou hast one foot on a rock but another on the quicksand; and thou mightest as well have both feet on the quicksand, for the result will be the same.

> "None but Jesus, none but Jesus
> Can do helpless sinners good."

Thou art not saved unless Christ be all in all in thy soul, Alpha and Omega, beginning and ending, first and last. Judge by this, again: if you are saved, you have turned your back on sin. You have not left off sinning—would to God we could do so— but you have left off loving sin; you sin not wilfully, but from infirmity; and you are earnestly seeking after God and holiness. You have respect to God, you desire to be like Him, you are longing to be with Him. Your face is towards heaven. You are as a man who journeys to the Equator. You are feeling more and more the warm influence of the heavenly heat and light. Now, if such be your course of life, that you walk not after the flesh, but after the Spirit, and bring forth the fruits of holiness, then you are saved. May your answer to that question be given in great honesty and candour to your own soul. Be not too partial a judge. Conclude not that all is right because outward appearances are fair. Deliberate before you return a favourable verdict. Judge yourselves that ye be not judged. It were better to condemn yourself and be accepted of God, than to acquit yourself and find your mistake at the last.

But suppose that question should have to be answered by any here in the negative (and I am afraid it must be), then let those who confess that they are not saved hear the answer to another enquiry: "How can I be saved?" Ah, dear hearer, I have not to bring a huge volume nor a whole armful of folios to you, and to say, "It will take you months and years to understand the plan of salvation." No, the way is plain, the method simple. Thou shalt be saved within the next moment if thou believest. God's work of salvation is, as far as its commencement and essence is concerned, instantaneous. If thou believest that Jesus is the Christ, thou art born of God now. If thou dost now stand in spirit at the foot of the cross, and view the incarnate God suffering, bleeding, and dying there, and if as thou dost look at Him, thy soul consents to have Him for her Saviour, and casts herself wholly on Him, thou art saved. How vividly there comes before my memory this morning the moment when I first believed in Jesus! It was the simplest act my mind ever performed, and yet the most wonderful, for the Holy Spirit wrought it in me. Simply to have done with reliance upon myself, and have done with confidence in all but Jesus, and to rest alone, my undivided confidence in Him, and in what He had done. My sin was in that moment forgiven me, and I was saved, and may it all be so with you, my friend, even with you if you also trust the Lord Jesus. "Your own salvation" shall be secured by that one simple act of faith; and henceforward, kept by the power of God through faith unto salvation, you shall tread the way of holiness, till you come to be where Jesus is in everlasting bliss. God grant that not a soul may go out of this place unsaved. Even you, little children, who are here, you youngsters, you young boys and girls, I pray that you may in early life attend to "your own salvation." Faith is not a grace for old people only, nor for your fathers and mothers only; if your little hearts shall look to Him who was the holy child Jesus, if you know but little yet, if you trust Him, salvation shall be yours. I pray that to you who are young, "your own salvation" may become, while you are yet in your youth, a matter of joy, because you have trusted it in the hands of your Redeemer.

Now I must close: but one or two thoughts press me. I must utter them ere I sit down I would anxiously urge each person here to see to this matter of his own salvation. Do it, I pray you, and in earnest, for no one can do it for you. I have asked God for your soul, my hearer, and I pray I may have an answer of peace concerning you. But unless you also pray, vain are my prayers. You remember your mother's tears. Ah! you have crossed the ocean since those days, and you have gone into the deeps of sin, but you recollect when you used to say your prayers at her knee, and when she would lovingly say "Amen," and kiss her boy and bless him, and pray that he might know his mother's God. Those prayers are ringing in the ears of God for you, but it is impossible that you can ever be saved unless it is said of you, "Behold, he prayeth." Your mother's holiness can only rise up in judgment to condemn your wilful wickedness unless you imitate it. Your father's earnest exhortations shall but confirm the just sentence of the Judge unless you hearken to them, and yourselves consider and put your trust in Jesus. Oh! bethink you each one of you, there is but one hope, and that one hope lost, it is gone for ever. Defeated in one battle, a commander attempts another, and hopes that he may yet win the campaign. Your life is your one fight, and if it be lost it is lost for aye. The man who was bankrupt yesterday commences again in business with good heart, and hopes that he may yet succeed: but in the business of this mortal life, if you are found bankrupt, you are bankrupt for ever and ever. I do therefore charge you by the living God, before whom I stand, and before whom I may have to give an account of this day's preaching ere another day's sun shall shine, I charge you see to your own salvation. God help you, that you may never cease to seek unto God till you know by the witness of the Spirit that you have indeed passed from death unto life. See to it now, *now*, NOW, NOW. This very day the voice of warning comes to certain of you from God, with special emphasis, because you greatly need it, for your time is short. How many have passed into eternity during this week! You may yourself be gone from the land of the living before next Sabbath-day. I suppose, according to the calculation of probabilities, out of this audience there are several who will die within a month. I am not conjecturing now, but according to all probabilities these thousands cannot all meet again, if all have a mind to do so. Who then among us will be summoned to the unknown land? Will it be you, young woman, who have been laughing at the things of God? Shall it be yonder merchant, who has not time enough for religion? Shall it be you, my foreign friend, who have crossed the ocean to take a holiday? Will you be carried back a corpse? I do conjure you bethink yourselves, all of you. You who dwell in London will remember years ago when the cholera swept through our streets, some of us were in the midst of it, and saw many drop around us, as though smitten with an invisible but deadly arrow. That disease is said to be on its way hither again; it is said to be rapidly sweeping from Poland across the Continent, and if it come and seize some of you, are you ready to depart? Even if that form of death do not afflict our city, as I pray it may not, yet is death ever within our gates, and the pestilence walketh in darkness every night, therefore consider your ways. Thus saith the Lord, and with His word I conclude this discourse: "Prepare to meet thy God, O Israel."

BELIEVERS—LIGHTS IN THE WORLD

"Do all things without murmurings and disputings: that ye may be blameless and harmless, the sons of God, without rebuke, in the midst of a crooked and perverse nation, among whom ye shine as lights in the world; holding forth the word of life; that I may rejoice in the day of Christ, that I have not run in vain, neither laboured in vain."—Philippians ii. 14-16.

WE shall be very far from the truth if we suppose that Christian precepts have suffered any degeneration of meaning. If we imagine that the precepts of the gospel were more stern in apostolic times than in these later ages, we labour under a very gross and dangerous delusion. Fresh from the abominations of heathenism, the early converts would naturally be placed under the mildest rules, rather than the more severe. If the gospel could have known a change, the apostle would have given its easiest precepts at the first, and then in these better days, the whole revelation would have been brought out, and more stringent precepts would have been proclaimed. Since, however, it is contrary to the genius of the gospel to be progressive in its revelation, since it was all revealed at once, we must never imagine that the precepts given by Paul may be toned down and diluted to suit the present age. I say again, brethren, if these men, fresh from the foul Stygian ditch of heathen abomination and lasciviousness, were nevertheless exhorted to the greatest sublimity of holiness, much more is it incumbent upon us to arrive at a very high state of Christian perfection, and walk very near to God, and be very close imitators of Christ. May God help us to hear this morning, the address which Paul gave to the Church in Philippi; may we feel its full force in our consciences, and embody its full meaning in our lives.

The apostle says, *"Do all things,"*—by which he seems to teach the activity of the Christian Church, for the Christian religion is not mere thinking or feeling, but doing and working for God. *"Do all things without murmurings,"* without murmuring at *God's providence*—which was a common vice of the heathen, who, on their tombstones often recorded their protest against God for having removed their darlings, and upbraided Him as cruel and unkind for taking away their relatives. "Do all things without murmurings *against one another."* Let your love be so hearty and sincere, that ye do not envy your richer or more talented brethren. Let there be no low whispers travelling through your assemblies against those who ought to be esteemed among you. Whatever ye do, let no murmuring be mixed with it, but labour with delight, and suffer with patience. Let there be no murmurings even against *the ungodly world.* If they be unjust, bear their injustice in silence; be not always offering complaints; there are a thousand things which ye might speak of, but it is better that like Aaron ye should hold your peace. To suffer in silence shall dignify you and make you greater than ordinary manhood, for then you shall

become like Him, who before His accusers opened not His mouth.

The apostle continues, do all things without *"disputings."* Dispute not with God; let Him do what seemeth Him good. Dispute not with your fellow Christians, raise not railing accusations against them. When Calvin was told that Luther had spoken ill of him, he said, "Let Luther call me devil if he please, I will never say of him but that he is a most dear and valiant servant of the Lord." Raise not intricate and knotty points by way of controversy. Remember, you have adversaries upon whom to use your swords, and therefore there is little need that you should turn their edges by dashing at the armour of your fellows. Dispute not even with the world. The heathen philosophers always sought occasions for debate; be it yours to testify what God has told you, but court not controversy. Be not ashamed to contend earnestly for the faith once delivered to the saints, but never do it in a spirit of mere debating, never because you wish to gain a victory, but only because ye would tell out what God hath bidden ye reveal.

"That ye may be blameless." Men *will* blame you, but you must seek as Christians to lead lives that give no occasion for blame. Like Daniel, compel them to say of you, "We shall not find any occasion against this Daniel, except we find it against him concerning the law of his God." Erasmus writes of his great adversary Luther, "Even Luther's enemies cannot deny but that he is a good man." Brethren, force this encomium from an unwilling world. Live so that as in Tertullian's age, men may say as they did in his time, "Such-and-such a man is a good man, even though he be a Christian." The heathens thought the Christians the worst of men, but were compelled to confess them to be the best, even though they were Christians. "Be ye blameless *and harmless,"* says the apostle. The Greek word might be translated "hornless," as if ye were to be creatures not only that *do* no harm, but *could* not do any; like sheep that not only *will not* devour, but *cannot* devour, for it were contrary to their nature; for they have no teeth with which to bite, no fangs with which to sting, no poison with which to slay. If ye carry arrows let them be dipped in love; if ye bear a sword let it be the sword of the Spirit, which is the word o God; but otherwise, be ye everywhere, even among those that would harm you, "holy, harmless, undefiled, separate from sinners." *"As the sons of God,"* the apostle goes on to say, as if the dignity of our relationship should beget in us an equally dignified

deportment. "Remember," saith the old philosopher—"Remember, O Antigonus, that thou art a king's son!" Remember, O Christian, that thou art a son of the King of kings—even God Himself. Soil not the fingers which are soon to sweep celestial strings; let not those eyes become the windows of lust which are soon to see the King in His beauty—let not those feet be defiled in miry places, which are soon to walk the golden streets—let not those hearts be filled with pride and bitterness which are soon to be filled with heaven, and to overflow with ecstatic joy. As "the sons of God," remember that the eyes of all are upon you; more is expected from you than from other men, because ye have a higher pedigree, for ye are descended from the very Highest Himself, and therefore should be the highest and best in the world. The apostle then adds, "*without rebuke.*" Men whom the world cannot rebuke. Men who can stand right straight up, and defy their enemies to find any real fault in them, who can say without any Phariseeism, as Job did, "Lord, thou knowest that I am not wicked." My brethren, I would ye were such that men must lie before they can revile you; I would have you men upon whose snow-white garments filth will not stick—who may be, and must be slandered, but cannot be really rebuked. O beloved, to use Paul's own words, "Be ye sons of God without rebuke, in the midst of a crooked and perverse nation."

I have expounded the address of Paul, permit me to remind you, that all the while he is telling us to do this as the means to an end—and what is the end? why, that we may "shine as lights in the world in the midst of a crooked and perverse nation." . The means themselves are precious; to be "holy, harmless, and undefiled," is a glorious matter of itself, but when such a bright thing becomes but a means, how excellent must the end be! How desirable that you and I, and each one of us who have named the name of Jesus, should "shine as lights in the world, holding forth the word of life!"

This brings me to the subject which I want to impress upon your hearts this morning. I would that every believer here, whether member of this Church or of any of the part of Christ's family, might see to it, that henceforth he should shine as a light in the midst of the darkness of this world, giving light to those that come within the range of his influence. There seems to me to be four things about which I may well speak. First, here is *publicity required*—they cannot shine without it; here is, secondly, *usefulness intended ;* here is, thirdly, *position indicated*—they are "in the midst of a crooked and perverse nation;" and here is, fourthly, *an argument suggested*, that in the day of Christ I may rejoice that I have not run in vain, neither laboured in vain.

I. First then, here is A MEASURE OF PUBLICITY REQUIRED.

You will note the text says they are to be *lights.* Now how they can be lights without being seen, and of what use they would be if they could be unseen lights, I cannot tell. But then, they are to *shine*, and how can they shine unless there be some radiance proceeding from them, and how this if they live in secret, and if they are never understood to be Christians at all? But then, where does the text say they are to shine as lights?—in their house? No, "*in the world.*" True they are to be lights in their own family; but moreover if they come up to the full standard of what they should be, they are to be lights *in the world*. These three words—lights, lights shining, and lights in the world, most positively teach that a Christian must have some degree of publicity, and that it is hardly possible for him to carry out his true character if he lives in such retirement and secrecy as never to be known to be a Christian. Some timid hearts there be, some gentle spirits, that shun altogether the exposure of their religion; they quote Nicodemus as if they did not know that Nicodemus is rather a beacon than an example. I would be far from crushing a tender spirit, far from laughing at the nervousness which may keep a man in the back rank when he ought to stand in the fore-front of the battle; but if I should by some Scriptural remarks lead Christians to see that they are not to be always seeking retirement, but that they must stand out and avow the Master, and if I can persuade the gentle spirit to bear its willing witness to Christ, thrice happy shall I be. Pharisees of old courted publicity. They could not give away one halfpenny in the street but they must sound a trumpet that everybody might see their splendid charity. They could not pray in their closet, but they must seek some corner of the street that every passer-by might hold up his hands in amazement at the man who was so good that he prayed even in the street. The world has found this trick out; we usually say of ladies, when we find them working out at parties, that they do not work at home; and we should surely think of people who pray in the streets that they pray nowhere else, and of persons who show their charity publicly that they show all that they have to show. Ostentatious religion nowadays is soon discovered and detected. But while we must be warned against the pride of the Pharisee, we must take care that we run not into another extreme. "Am I always to serve God by stealth? Am I never to speak a good word for Christ lest somebody should say I am proud?" Your own conscience will be your guide in that matter. If you detect in yourself any desire to glorify yourself, then you are wrong in making your religion public at all. Plainly, if you discover that you are keeping back in order to get an easier path for yourself, then you are grievously wrong in seeking to hide your religion. If it be for God's honour for you to publish on the house-tops what He has told you in the closet, do it; and if it be for Christ's honour to do only in the closet that which another man would do in the street, do it. Your conscience will always teach you, if it be an enlightened conscience, when you might act ostentatiously, and when on the other hand you would be cowardly. I think there is no difficulty in steering between this Scylla and Charybdis. Any man with a little wisdom will soon discern what he ought to do. But do not, I pray you, make the Pharisee's pride an excuse for your cowardice; never say, "I do not like to make a profession because there are so many hypocrites!" the more reason why *you* should make a profession that there may be some honest ones. Do not say, "Oh, I would not for fear people should think I am proud!" Why should you look at the fear of man which bringeth a snare; is it not yours to obey God rather than man?

I cannot understand Christ's words, "Ye are a city set on a hill which cannot be hid"; nor these, "Let your light so shine before men, that they may see your good works, and glorify your Father which is in heaven"; nor these, "He that with his mouth confesseth, and with *his* heart believeth on the Lord Jesus Christ shall be saved."—I cannot understand these passages, if you are never to avow your faith, but keep your religion hidden up in a secret place, and go to heaven by stealth. How much of publicity then, do we really think is necessary in a Christian? It is becoming that *he should make a public avowal of his faith;* he should come out from among the world and declare himself to be on the Lord's side. There is an ordinance which God has Himself ordained, which is the proper way in which to make this profession— to be baptized in water, in the name of the Father, and of the Son, and of the Holy Ghost; thus openly being buried in water to show our death to the world, and rising out of the water to show that we hope to live a new life as the result of the resurrection of Christ from the dead. If you should differ as to the form in which this profession is to be made, yet the profession should be made. If you would be honest and true, you must in answer to the Master's summons, "Who is on the Lord's side?" come out and say, "Here am I, Lord, I am Thy servant, and I would serve Thee even to the end." You should also be *associated constantly with Christian people.* The one act of profession is not enough, it should be continued by union with some visible church of Christ. We find in the apostle's days that those who were converted were added to the Church. It is written, "They first gave their own selves to the Lord, and unto us by the will of God." Christianity requires you to unite yourselves with those who are united to Christ. If the Church of Christ be the spouse of Jesus, you should seek to be a member of her visibly as well as invisibly; especially you that are lately converted, for your presence in the Church is for your good, and much for the Church's comfort. The man that was healed stood with Peter and John; and it is written, when they saw the man that was healed standing with Peter and John, they could say nothing against them. The gathering together of the converts to sustain the minister is a very great help in the propagation of the truth as it is in Jesus. Beside this association with Christians, there should be *a daily carrying out of your Christianity in your life.* It is not all that we *say* that shines; that may be only a flash, a sparkle, a display of fireworks, but it is our daily acting which is the true shining out of Christ within. Let the servant prove her Christianity by being more attentive than any other. Let the master prove His by being more generous than any other master; let the rich man shine in his liberality; let the poor man shine in his patience; let each in every sphere seek to excel those who are not in Christ, that so everyone may prefer us in our position to the worldling in the same office, and take knowledge of us that we have been with Jesus and have learned of Him. But to shine as lights, we must add *the open testimony of our words.* I will not give a rusty nail for your religion if you can be quiet about it; I do not believe you have any; that which is nearest to the heart is generally most on the tongue. You must be constantly bearing your witness by the word of your mouth for Christ, seeking to teach the ignorant, to warn the careless, to reclaim the backsliding, and to bring the wanderers to the cross. You will have many opportunities in the sphere in which you move, avail yourself of them all, so shall you shine as a light in the *world ;* and there are times when you cannot shine without *a very bold and stern decision for Christ.* When the old Roman senator, in the days of Vespasian, was told by the emperor that he might go into the senate-house but he must hold his tongue, he answered, "I, being a senator, feel impelled to go into the senate-house, and being in the senate it is the part of a senator to speak what his conscience dictates." "Then," said Vespasian, "if you speak you will die." "Be it known to thee, O emperor," said he, "that I never hoped to be immortal, nor did I ever wish to live when I might not speak my mind." Brave Roman! We must have brave Christians, too, who say, "Being a Christian, it is mine to speak, and if that should cost me all I have, and life itself, I never thought myself immortal, and I wish to die when I may not speak out that which God has written in my heart." There are times, I say, when if we should falter, or delay, we become traitors at once; beware ye in these "crises of your being," that promptly ye follow your Lord.

So much of publicity I think is needed then—an open profession, a constant association with the Christian Church, a perpetual living out of godliness, an open declaration of the same, and a deliberate decision when occasion shall present itself. Look ye sirs, Christians are *soldiers.* If our soldiers were to take it into their heads that they ought never to be seen, a pretty pass things would come to; what were the soldiers worth when they shunned parade and dreaded battle? Take off your regimentals and be packing sirs! We want not men who must always be skulking behind a bush, and dare not show themselves to friend or foe. Christians are *runners* too, and what sort of runners are men who run in the dark? Not so saith the apostle; he says, we are "encompassed about by so great a cloud of witnesses," and therefore bids us "lay aside every weight, and the sin that doth so easily beset us." What! a running match and no spectators! Ave Imperator! The champion salutes thee! He prays thee to dismiss the spectators. Conscript Fathers, leave your seats, and ye knights of the empire retire from the race. Ye common herd retire, or put your fingers to your eyes, here comes a runner who is so dainty that he cannot be looked at, a swift-footed racer who must be scrutinized by no vulgar eye or he will faint and lose the crown. Ha! ha! ha! ha! the mob laugh. "Ah!" say they, "these are not the men to make a Roman holiday, these timid fools had better play with babes in the nursery, they are not fit to consort with men." What think ye of Christians who must have the stadium cleared before they can enter the course. Rather, O sons of God, defy all on-lookers. Crowd the seats and look on, ye angels, and men, and devils too, and see what ye will. What mattereth it to the Christian, for he is looking unto Jesus, he runneth not for you but for the reward, and whether ye look or look not, his zeal and earnestness are still the same, for Christ is in him and run he must, look on who will.

II. Secondly, here is in the text, USEFULNESS.

"Well," saith one, "if I were known to be a Christian what use would it be?" We will soon show you; one remark, however, I will make; the better Christian you are the more public you will be, but the less will be thought *of you.* You have noticed at night a star, it is only a little spark comparatively, but still it is very bright, and everybody says, "Do you see that star?" Yes, but there is a moon, why does not everybody say, "Look, what a beautiful moon?" But they notice the star first, because it is not usual to see stars so brilliant. By-and-by, of a moonlight night, you will hear people say, "What a lovely moon!" Now, in the daylight people do not say, "What a lovely sun!" No. "What a lovely landscape! What a beautiful view!

Look at the tints of those trees now the sun is shining!" Just so the little Christian is like a star, bright in his little sphere. Others are like the moon, they excite admiration and attention to themselves; but a full-grown Christian, who should be perfectly conformed to the image of Christ, though giving more light than either the moon or the star, would not be half so much looked at, for men would be looking at what he shed light upon rather than upon him; they would look to the doctrine that he taught rather than to how he taught it; they would be looking rather at the lesson of his life than at the life itself. So that if I should urge you to more and more publicity, it will not be for your sake, but that you may be more and more forgotten, while the truth is the more clearly seen.

But what is the use of lights, what is the use of Christians as lights? The answer is manifold. We use lights to *make manifest*. A Christian man should so shine in his life, that those who come near him can see their own character in his life, can see their sins, can see their lost estate; he should so live that a person could not live with him a week without knowing the gospel. His conversation should be such that all who are about him should perfectly understand the way to heaven; things that men will not see and cannot see without him, should be very clear wherever he is. Men sometimes read their Bibles, and they do not understand the Bible because they want light. Like Philip, we should be willing to sit in the chariot and instruct the passer-by, making manifest the meaning of God's word, the power of God's word, the way of salvation, the life of godliness, and the force of truth. May I ask each one of you, have you made men understand the gospel the better? "Ah," says one, "I left that to the minister." Then you have neglected your duty; repent of your great sin, and ask God now to help you to be making manifest to all persons who come near you their sin and the Saviour. The next use of a light is *to guide*. The mariner understands this. When our sailors, some years ago had a Nore light, they thought they were getting on marvellously, but when they had the Mouse, the Maplin, the Swin Middle, and all the other lights on the sands, they soon found navigation much easier than it had been before. Every Christian should light some part of the voyage of life, and there should not be a channel without its light. Blessed pole star! how many a slave hast thou guided from the swamps and whips of the South up to the country of the free. Blessed art thou, O Christian too, if thy light has led some soul to Jesus, to the land of the free, where the slave can never wear his fetters again. I hope that you have often, when men have scarcely known it, pointed them the way to Christ, by saying, "Behold the Lamb of God."

Lights are also used for *warning*. On our rocks and shoals a lighthouse is sure to be erected. Christian men should know that there are plenty of false lights shown everywhere in the world. The wreckers of Satan are always abroad, tempting the ungodly to sin under the name of pleasure; they hoist the wrong light, be it yours and mine to put up the true light upon every dangerous rock, to point out every sin, and tell what it leads to, that so we may be clear of the blood of all men, shining as lights in the world.

Lights also have a very *cheering* influence, and so have Christians. Late one night we had lost our way in a park not far from the suburbs of London, and we were walking along and wondering where we were. We said, "There is a light over there," and you cannot tell what a source of comfort that candle in a cottage window proved to us. I remember riding in a third class carriage. crowded full of people, on a dark night, when a woman at the end of the carriage struck a match and lit a candle; with what satisfaction everybody's face was lit up, as all turned to see it. A light really does give great comfort; if you think it does not, sit in the dark an hour or two. A Christian ought to be a comforter; with kind words on his lips, and sympathy in his heart, he should have a cheering word for the sons of sorrow.

Light, too, also has its use in *rebuking sin*. I think our street gas-lamps are the best police we have; if those lamps were out we should need ten times the numbers of watchers, and there would be far more crimes. Why is it that thieves do not like the light?—because their dark deeds can only be done in darkness. And how is it ungodly men do not like Christians? Why, because they rebuke them; and just as lights tend to make a city safe and stop robberies and crime, so Christian men when they are in sufficient numbers to act upon the commonwealth, will make crime less common; certainly they will compel it to hide its deformity under the shadows of night, whereas, before it might have walked in the blaze of day with approbation. But the Christian is a light in a very peculiar sense, he is a *light with life in it*. Turn the lanthorn upon that dead man's face: you can see it cold and white, like the chiselled marble. Shoot the light right into his eye; he does not see; you cannot make him live by the power of any human light. But the believer is God's lanthorn, full of the Holy Ghost—and it happeneth often that through our testimony God shooteth into the eyes of the dead a light which makes them live, so that the darkness of Hades gives way to the brightness of glory, and the midnight darkness of the spirit is made to fly before the rising Sun of Righteousness.

We have dwelt long enough upon the uses of these lights, and I may only say, in concluding that point, I wonder what is the good of a Christian, who is not thus useful to the world? He has a treasure, but he hoards it. What is the good of misers while they live? They are like swine which only eat—they are of no service till they die. Then they are cut up, and their estates are pulled into pieces, and perhaps some good may be gotten by those who get a flitch or rasher from them. Vile is the wretch who hoards gold, but what is he who hoards bread. The world is starving, and they hoard the bread of life. It is like manna—it breeds worms, and they cannot eat it themselves, but they will not give it to others. A religion that is no blessing to others, is no blessing to me—I am just laying up for myself a mass of putridity; it will never do my soul good, or else it would have compelled me to do good to others. But they are hoarding water, the living water; they are damming up the stream to keep enough for themselves, and what is it doing? It is covered with rank weeds; it breeds miasma; it turns foul; all manner of loathsome creatures are in it. They are more foolish still, they are trying to hoard up the light, as if they would have any the less if they let others have it. Hoard up light as if there were only a scant supply. Infamous! Diabolical! I wish there were a stronger word than that, "If any man love not the Lord Jesus Christ, let him be Anathema Maran-atha," says Paul. And I question whether that dreadful anathema does not include within it those who do not love souls, and therefore prove they do not love Christ; for if they loved Christ they must love sinners; if they loved Jesus they must seek to extend His kingdom, and to let Him see of the travail of His soul.

III. But time waits not for me, and I must proceed to touch with brevity upon the third point—POSITION INDICATED.

"But," says one, "I cannot shine, it is of no use talking about it, I am not in a position to do any good." The apostle anticipates you, he says "in the midst of a crooked and perverse nation." "If I were to remove from this," says one, "I might serve the Lord's cause, but I cannot where I am." But, dear friend, you are not to get out of it, you are to speak for your Lord where you are. In the midst of that crooked and perverse nation you are to shine as lights in the world. Your position teaches you three things. First of all, it should be *an incentive to you*; the worse the people are among whom you live, the more need have they of your exertions; if they be crooked, the more necessity that you should set them straight: and if they be perverse, the more need have you to turn their proud hearts to the truth. The worse your position is, the more thankful you ought to be that you are in it. Where should the physician be but where there any many sick? Where is honour to be won by the soldier but in the hottest fire of the battle? Do not blame your position if you are an unprofitable servant, but lay the blame upon yourself. If you find it hard to do good where you are, it will be harder anywhere else. As the bird that wandereth from her nest so is the man that wandereth from his place. Lazy workmen find fault with their tools and employers. If you transplant a tree to make it produce more fruit, you may possibly succeed, but there are nine chances to one that you will kill it altogether.

Again, as you are in such a position, let it *administer a caution* to you. They are a crooked nation and perverse, do not wonder therefore if they hate your light and try to blow it out. Be the more anxious not to give them any unnecessary offence. Let your goodness be the only fault they can find in you. Ask the Lord to keep your lamp well trimmed for you; beseech Him to protect it from their malicious breath. Be the more anxious to cultivate a close acquaintance with Christ, because a crooked nation would decoy you from Him. Do not try to please men; make not the opinion of this generation your rule, for it is very crooked, and if you travel one way you will not please them unless you turn the other way and then turn again to humour their crooks. One is often amused to find one's self publicly abused for doing the very thing, the opposite of which one was abused for the week before; and sometimes in the same newspaper article you will nowadays catch the writer first falling foul with you for doing one thing, and then falling foul with you for not doing it again. It is a crooked and perverse nation: the man who tries to please man shall find himself in a labyrinth of the most mazy kind; he shall be a wretched time-server all his life, and a detestable hypocrite even to his death. Such a man, to use a rustic simile, is like a toad under a harrow, he will have to be crawling continually to escape the spikes on the right and iron teeth on the left, and he will probably die a miserable death with the iron in his soul at the last. Be cautious, but be particularly cautious against excessive caution. Please the Lord, and let men please themselves.

Once more, while the eyes of perverse men should be an incentive and a caution to you, do not forget the *rich consolation* afforded by the fact that all the saints have endured the like trial. Are you in the midst of a crooked people? So was Paul; so the Church at Philippi; so all the saints. Remember that as they won their crowns in a strife which was none of their choosing, so must you. They were not carried on beds of down to heaven, and you must not expect to travel more easily than they. They had to hazard their lives unto the death in the high places of the field, and you shall not be crowned till you also have endured hardness as a good soldier of Jesus Christ. The road of your pilgrimage will not be smooth if it be the way of apostles and prophets. Soft raiment, delicate nursing, dainty feeding, and luxurious ease, belong to the palaces of earth, but not to the company without the camp who bear their Lord's reproach. I charge ye, O servants of the Lord, and you who are members of this church especially, stand fast, wait, watch, and wrestle. Be stedfast, unmovable, always abounding in the work of the Lord.

IV. To conclude, there is an ARGUMENT SUGGESTED.

It is a very affectionate and touching one which I mean to take the liberty of applying to you, my beloved flock. "That I may not run in vain, nor labour in vain in the day of Christ." The apostle was the founder of the Church at Philippi; he had watched over them with all the anxiety of one who had planted and watered, and who looked for the increase. He therefore appealed to the affection which he knew they had for him. "I have run," argues the apostle, "with all men looking on and gazing, many of them hating and scoffing. I have run with all my might; would you have me run in vain? I have laboured, I have laboured more than they all," the apostle could say, "would ye have me labour for nought?" He knew the answer they would give him would be, "No, beloved Paul, we would see thee win the prize for which thou didst run, and reap the fruit for which thou didst labour." "Well," argues the apostle, "but I cannot, except ye shine as lights in the world; ye disappoint my hopes, ye snatch the prize from my grasp, ye fill me with anguish, if ye be not holy, heavenly-minded witnesses for Christ." I use the same argument with you; to the stranger here to-day it will have no force, but with many of you I know it will be an argument of power. How many out of this congregation first learned of Jesus from my lips. A multitude of you were brought to Christ through the preaching of the word here, or in Park Street, or the Surrey Gardens, or Exeter Hall. The word was feebly preached in rough language then as now,—but God owned it,—not to tens nor twenties, but to hundreds, aye, to thousands of you, and not to you only, but to people in every land and of every kindred. The Lord hath made my spiritual children so many as the stars of heaven for multitude. I rejoice, yea, I must rejoice, when I hear continually of the multitudinous conversions which are wrought by the Holy Ghost through the sermons both printed and preached. God is with us, and He does not let one word fall to the ground. But what if you, as a church, should be idle! What if your lives should be unholy! What if you should want zeal and faith to testify for Christ!

What then! My best expectations are defeated, my life has been a failure, and all that I have done falls to the ground. I have thought it in my heart, and I earnestly pray to my God that it may come to pass that here, as in a barracks, a great army may find its constant lodging place, that afterwards the Lord may pour you out like a vast conquering host, upon all parts of the world, to teach and testify, and live and labour, and speak for Christ. Surely, my brethren, you would desire this yourselves. I pray for it, you will unite in desiring it and praying for it with me.

It has happened of late, especially to me, to see God's hand very visible. Never in my experience have I seen so much spiritual activity as just now, and while it is true of all sections of the Christian Church, it has been peculiarly so of that section over which it is my lot to preside. The sermons have been now for eight years scattered in English, Welsh, French, Dutch, German, Swedish—in fact, in all Protestant languages. At first there were many conversions—there are still. Next I find that those who were regular subscribers to the sermons begin to receive the doctrine of the preacher. The converts to Christ grow and get clear views of truth. Even in the point of baptism there are great numbers who are convinced that it is most Scriptural that believers only should be baptized. Very many have come here, and in the pool beneath, I have baptized them into the name of Christ. Our denomination does not increase. I am not very anxious that it should, for as it stands at present I have no great love for it; but our principles are spreading marvellously, and in this I must rejoice. As the result of this I have constantly letters like this, "Sir, I live in a village where the gospel is not preached, there is a Church, it is true, but we have a Puseyite clergyman; cannot you do something for us. You have many young men training for the ministry, could you not send a friend to preach in my drawing-room?" Then comes another—"Sir, the chapel has been shut up in our village a long time, could you not come and help us?" Then there are many of this kind: two Christian men write up, wishing to be baptized into Christ—they come, they go back, within a month there are four more from the same village—they go back, and I almost forget them, but they do not forget me; soon, the whole six will write a letter—this is a common thing—they say, "Could not we be formed into a Church? we will find a room—send some one to preach to us?" This happens every week, and your minister feels that as long as ever he has a man, he will say, "I will do it for you;" and as long as he has any money of his own he will say, "Oh, yes, I will do it for you;" but every now and then he wishes that he had some who would stand by him in larger attempts. Cheerfully you give week after week for the support of our young ministers, and I

think our friends will continue to do this. At any rate the Lord will provide, and friends far away may be moved to assist us. I want still more aid, for the field is ripe and we want more harvest men to reap it. It grows, the thing grows, every day it increases, it started but as a little flake of snow, and now like an avalanche it sweeps the Alps' sides bare before its tremendous force. I would not now that ye should prove unworthy of the day in which ye live, or the work to which God has called us as a Church. Four Churches of Christ have sprung of our loins in one year, and the next year shall it not be the same, and the next, and the next, if the Holy Ghost be with us, and He has promised to be with us if we be with Him.

Now, in regard to the particular effort at Wandsworth, for which a collection is to be made. When I was sore sick some three years or more ago, I walked about to recover strength, and walking through the town of Wandsworth, I thought "How few attend a place of worship here. Here are various churches, but there is ample room for one of our own faith and order; something must be done." I thought "If I could start a man here preaching the word, what good might be done." The next day, some four friends from the town called to see me, one a Baptist, and the three others were desirous of baptism, "Would I come there and form a church?" We took the large rooms at a tavern, and preaching has been carried on there ever since. Beginning with four, the church has increased to one hundred and fifty. I have greatly aided the interest by going there continually and preaching and helping to support the minister. Now, a beautiful piece of ground has been taken, and a chapel is to be erected, and I firmly believe there will be a very strong cause raised. We have many rising churches, but this one has just come to such a point, that a house of prayer is absolutely needed. I should not have asked you for this aid so soon, but the rooms in which they worship are now continually used for concerts on Saturday evenings, and are not altogether agreeable on the Sunday. I would just as soon worship in one place as another, for my own part, but I see various difficulties are now in the way, which a new chapel will remove. I hope you will help them in so doing, help me in the earnest effort of my soul to hold forth the word of life, and to let Christ's kingdom come and His will be done.

You that feel no desire to honour the Master—you that care nothing for the spread of His kingdom—you that are satisfied to hold your heads down, and not boast and glory in Him—stand back and assist us not; but you who would help His kingdom—you who love His name—you who are the debtors of His grace—help the cause everywhere, and help it this day. For Christ's sake I ask it of you, and you will not deny me.

A BUSINESS-LIKE ACCOUNT

"But what things were gain to me, those I counted loss for Christ. Yea doubtless, and I count all things but loss for the excellency of the knowledge of Christ Jesus my Lord: for whom I have suffered the loss of all things, and do count them but dung, that I may win Christ, and be found in Him, not having mine own righteousness, which is of the law, but that which is through the faith of Christ, the righteousness which is of God by faith."—Philippians iii. 7–9.

OUR Saviour's advice to those who wished to be His disciples was "Count the cost." He did not wish to entice any man to enlist in His army by keeping him in ignorance as to the requirements of His service. Again and again He tested professed converts Himself, and He frequently exhorted men to try themselves, lest they should begin a profession and be unable to maintain it.

True religion is a matter of enthusiasm, but at the same time its truths and precepts can endure the severest examination. The exercise of our judgments upon the gospel is invited, yea required. It is true that many persons are brought to Christ in earnest assemblies, where they are addressed in fervent language; but yet a man may sit down in his study or his counting house with his pen in his hand, and in the coolest possible manner he may calculate, and, if under the Holy Spirit's guidance he shall be led to calculate truthfully, he will come to the conclusion that the cause of the Lord Jesus is worthiest and best. Do not imagine, as some do, that religion consists in a wild fanaticism which never considers, calculates, judges, estimates, or ponders; for such an imagination will be the reverse of truth. Ardour, fervour, enthusiasm, these are desirable, and we cannot well have too much of them; but at the same time, as I have already said, we can justify our attachment to Christ by the calmest logic, by the most patient consideration. We may make a lengthy and deliberate estimate, taking both things temporal and things eternal into review, and yet we may challenge all gainsayers while we declare that it is the wisest and the best thing in all the world to be a disciple of Jesus Christ.

In our text the apostle gives us the word "count" three times over. He was skilled in spiritual arithmetic, and very careful in his reckoning. He cast up his accounts with caution, and observed with a diligent eye his losses and his gains. In his reckoning he does not ignore any losses that may be supposed to be sustained, or really may be sustained; and he does not, on the other hand, for a moment forget that blessed gain for which he counts it worth while to suffer surprising loss. Paul here seems to be in a mercantile frame of mind, adding and subtracting, counting and balancing, with much quiet and decision of mind. I commend the text to business men; I invite them to follow the apostle's example, to use their best judgments upon eternal things, to sit down, take out their pen and figure as he did, and make out estimates and calculations as to themselves and Christ, their own works and the righteousness of faith.

The subject this morning will be, first, *the apostle's calculations ;* and secondly, *our own :* the object being in the second part to put questions to ourselves as to whether we estimate things after the apostolic fashion.

I. First, then, let us consider THE APOSTLE'S CALCULATIONS. Looking at the text, you will notice that he made three distinct countings; they all came to much the same thing, with this difference, that each one as it succeeded its fellow was more emphatic in its result: the result was the same, but it was more and more forcibly expressed.

And, first, we have his *counting at the outset of his Christian life.* When he became a believer, he says of himself, "what things were gain to me, thóse I counted loss for Christ." That is to say, at the first and earliest period when, from being Saul, the Rabbi, the intense Pharisee, he became Paul, the convert, and the preacher of the faith which once he destroyed, those things which to himself had seemed very splendid gains all dissolved into one great loss. At that time he says he made a calculation and formed a deliberate opinion that what had appeared to him to be most advantageous was really, so far as Christ was concerned, a positive disadvantage and hindrance to him—the gains were a loss.

Now, you will notice that in this first calculation he dwelt upon the separate items, noting each with great distinctness. The list of the things whereof he might glory in the flesh reads like a catalogue. "Circumcised the eighth day, of the stock of Israel, of the tribe of Benjamin, an Hebrew of the Hebrews; as touching the law, a Pharisee; concerning zeal, persecuting the church; touching the righteousness which is in the law, blameless." These are the things which were gains to him, and the list is very comprehensive, beginning at his birth and circumcision and running right on to the date of his conversion. He dwells with a high degree of interest upon the items of his Jewish advantages: they had been as precious pearls to him once, and while he freely renounces them, he yet remembers that they were once dear as the apple of his eye. They had been his pride, his patent of nobility, and his daily boast. He felt himself to be in these respects far in advance of the most of mankind, and second to none, even of his favoured race, for even now, he says, " If any other man thinketh that he hath whereof he might trust in the flesh, I more." "Circumcised the eighth day":—the rite which introduced him to the outward covenant of Abraham had been performed exactly when ordained by the law. He was not one who had been circumcised as proselytes were, late in life, nor at an irregular season on account of ill health, travelling, or parental neglect; but to the moment as the Mosaic ritual required he had as a babe been received into the congregation of Israel. Next, he was of "the stock of Israel," he was not one who had been converted to the Israelitish faith, nor a descendant of Gibeonites or of proselyted parents, but he was of the pure stock of Israel, descended by a clear line, which probably he was able genealogically to trace, from that Israel who was a prevailing prince with God. He was proud of this descent, and well he might be, for every Jew is of noble lineage. Speak of ancient families who can match the seed of Israel! Theirs is the best blood in the universe, if one blood be better than another.

Paul also boasted that he was "of the tribe of Benjamin": the tribe which Moses called the beloved of the Lord, the tribe within whose canton the temple stood: the tribe which was descended from the beloved wife of Jacob, even Rachel, and not from the sons of either of the bondwomen. The tribe of Benjamin was that from which the first king of Israel was chosen, and he bore the same name as that by which Paul had been known among his Jewish brethren. Paul was, therefore, of the very choicest branch of that vine which the Lord Himself brought out of Egypt.

He next adds that he was a "Hebrew of the Hebrews"; he was the cream of the cream, the very pick and choice out of the choice nation and the elect people. If there was any benefit to be had by being of the seed of Abraham, the Hebrew, he had all that benefit in the highest possible degree. Then he had appended to all the advantages of birthright and of nationality that of entering into a peculiar sect, the most orthodox, the most devout—for "as touching the law he was a Pharisee," and belonged to the sect which attached importance to the minutest details of the law, and tithed its mint and its anise, and its cummin. What more could he be? He was a Jesuit among the Catholics, one who went to the extreme among extremists, one of those initiated into the innermost secrets of the faith. Then, as to personal character, he felt that here in his natural state he had something which was gain, for he was so full of zeal that those who appeared to speak against the law of Moses by declaring the gospel were counted as his enemies, whom he hunted down with all his might—"concerning zeal, persecuting the church." This he had done in all honesty of purpose as the result of his thorough self-righteousness. He finishes by saying that he himself was as to every detail of the law, every little point of ritual, and every particular rubric, altogether blameless. This was no small thing to say, but he spake no more than the truth. These things all put together are what he counted gains (for the Greek word is in the plural), and I think he dwells somewhat lingeringly upon each separate point, as very well he might, for they had been very dear to him in former days, and these privileges were in themselves things of no mean worth.

But now, what was to be set on the other side? Here is a long list on one side, what is to be placed *per contra*? He says, "What things were gain to me, those I counted loss *for Christ*." What! What! Nothing on the other side but one item! One? One only? and yet there were so many privileges on the other side! There was but one name, one person in that scale, while in the other there were so many advantages! Why, one begins to think that the calculation will soon come to an end in favour of Saul's Israelitish descent, and the rest of it: but not so, the one outweighed the many. Here I want you to notice that Paul does not say that those he counted loss for Christianity, or for the church, or for the orthodox faith. There would have been truth in such a statement, but the centre of the truth lies here—he counted these things *for Christ*, that is, for the Lord Jesus Christ Himself. He thought of that divine One, blessed be His name, that Brother of our souls who was born at Bethlehem, the Kinsman, Redeemer of His people; Christ, the living, loving, bleeding, dying, buried, risen, ascended, glorified Christ; this was the glorious Person whom he placed on the other side of the balance-sheet. And now see the result. He says, "What things were gain to me, those I counted loss." A singular result. Not only that after putting the one under the other, and making a subtraction, he found that all his carnal advantages were less than Christ; but, far more than this, he found those gains actually transformed into a loss. They were not a *plus* on that side to stand in proportion to the *plus* on this side; but they were turned into a *minus* of actual deficit. He felt that his fleshly advantages, when he came to look at them in regard to Christ were disadvantages, and what he had reckoned to be gains operated rather against him than for him when he began to know Christ. My brethren, he does not mean that to be a "Hebrew of the Hebrews" was in itself a loss; nor that to be of the stock of Israel was a loss, for there was a natural advantage about all this. "What advantage then hath the Jew?" saith he in another place, and he replies, "Much every way:" but he meant that with respect to Christ those things which were naturally an advantage became a disadvantage, because their tendency had been to keep him from trusting Christ, and their tendency still was to tempt him away from simple faith in Jesus. "Alas!" he seemed to say to himself, "it was because I gloried that I was of the stock of Israel that I rejected the Christ of God; it was because I boasted that as touching the law I was blameless that therefore I refused to accept the glorious righteousness of Jesus Christ by faith. These

advantages were scales upon my eyes to keep me from seeing the beauty of my Lord; these privileges were stumbling blocks in my way to prevent my coming as a poor, humble, needy sinner and laying hold on the atoning sacrifice of Jesus." My brethren, it is a grand thing to have led a virtuous life: it is a matter for which to praise God to have been kept in the very centre of the paths of morality; but this blessing may by our own folly become a curse to us if we place our moral excellences in opposition to the righteousness of our Lord Jesus, and begin to dream that we have no need of a Saviour. If our character is in our own esteem so good that it makes a passable garment for us, and therefore we reject the robe of Christ's righteousness, it would have been better for us if our character had been by our own confession a mass of rags, for then we should have been willing to be clothed with the vesture which divine charity has prepared. Yea, better, so far as this matter is concerned, to be like the open sinner, who will not readily be tempted that way, because he is too foul, too bankrupt to pretend to be righteous before God. I say again, he does not say that these things are not advantages, but that *for Christ*; and when he comes to look at them in the light of Christ, he regards them as being a loss rather than a gain. If I had this day a righteousness of my own, yet would I fling it to the winds to lay hold of the righteousness of Christ, fearing all the while lest so much as the smell of it should cling to my hand. Had I never sinned in one solitary open sin, and if but one secret transgression of my heart had ever been committed, yet would I loathe my righteousness as filthy rags, and only tremble lest my proud spirit should be so foolish as to cling to such a useless thing. Adam fell through one sin, and lost Paradise, and lost us all; so that one sin suffices to curdle the purest righteousness into utter sourness. Away, then, with the very shadow of self and legal righteousness.

But let us now proceed to notice that Paul gives us *his second calculation, which is his estimate for the time then present.* "Yea doubtless," saith he, "and I count"—not "I counted," as he said before, but "I count all things but loss for the excellency of the knowledge of Christ Jesus my Lord." We are always anxious to hear what a man has to say about a thing after he has tried it. It is all very well to begin with eagerness, but how does the venture answer after a trial? After twenty years or more of experience Paul had an opportunity of revising his balance-sheet, and looking again at his estimates, and seeing whether or not his counting was correct. What was the issue of his latest search? How do matters stand at his last stock-taking? He exclaims with very special emphasis, "Yea doubtless, and I count all things but loss for the excellency of the knowledge of Christ Jesus my Lord." The two words, "yea doubtless," are a very strong affirmation. He is speaking very positively as to his present confirmed assurance and established judgment. Look at him then, again, making his estimate to-day, after he has been for some time in the divine life, and has been made to suffer as the result of his earnest service. You perceive that he has not forgotten the things that *were* gains, for, as we have already seen, he has given us a detailed list of them. On this second occasion he does not repeat the catalogue, partly because there was no need for it, and partly because he cares less for each item, and mainly because for fear anything should have been omitted he succinctly sums up the whole by saying, "all things." He as good as says —yea, doubtless, and I counted as loss all the advantages of birth, nationality, and self-righteousness, which once I reckoned to be gains. If I have left out anything whereof as an Israelite I might have gloried, I beg you to insert it in the list, for I mean that all should be included when I say that I count all things but loss for Christ's sake.

So you see he has not altered the original summary he has even made it more comprehensive, but he stands to the same estimate as ever: the gain is still "but loss"; only we perceive that now he dwells longer and evidently with greater delight of expression upon the other side, for now he uses not barely the word "Christ," but the fuller expression, "for the excellency of the knowledge of Christ Jesus my Lord." Now he has come to *know* the Christ in whom before he trusted. He spoke of Him before as one for whom he counted gain as loss, but now he perceives so great an excellency in Him that even to know Him he reckons to be a super-eminent blessing. Our divine Lord is better loved as He is better known. The closer our inspection the greater is the manifest excellency of His character.

The words used by the apostle show us the points upon which he had the fullest knowledge. He knew the Lord as *Christ*, or as the Messiah, sent and anointed of the Father. He understood more fully than at the first the fulness, power, and exceeding efficacy of the anointing of our Lord which he had received above his fellows. He saw Him to be the woman's promised seed, the coming one, the promised light of Israel, the ordained Price and Saviour of the sons of men, and he saw all His qualifications for this wonderful character. He perceived His anointing as prophet and King. He delighted to see the Spirit of the Lord resting upon Him, and descending from Him to His people, as the sacred oil from the head of Aaron distilled to the skirts of His garments. He saw great excellency in the knowledge of the Lord's anointed, whose garments smell of myrrh, and aloes, and cassia; but this was not all, for he proceeds to call Him *Jesus*, Christ Jesus. "Thou shalt call His name Jesus; for He shall save His people from their sins." Paul knew Him as the anointed Saviour, yea, as the actual Saviour who had saved him: saved him from the madness of his blasphemy and persecution, saved him from all his past guilt, saved him and made him to be an instrument of the salvation of others. He delights in the title of Saviour, as we all do who know the Savour of it. How sweetly musical is the name of Jesus; how fragrant is it even as ointment poured forth. Excellent indeed is the knowledge of our Lord in this character.

How delicious is the apostle's next word, "*my Lord;*" not merely the Lord, but "my Lord." His knowledge was an appropriating knowledge. He knew the Redeemer as anointed for him, as saving him, as Lord over all for him, and now as Lord to him. The honey of the sentence lies in that word "*my.*" I do not know how it seems to your hearts, but to me it is one of the sweetest words than can possibly be used by mortal lip, "the knowledge of Christ Jesus *my Lord.*" Whether He is your Lord or not, yet is He surely mine, whether He be accepted as Lord by the sons of men or not, yet is He joyfully owned as Lord to me and Master of my spirit, sole monarch of my whole nature,—"Christ Jesus my Lord." You see, then, how truly, fully, practically, and personally he knew the Lord Jesus.

The text implies that he knew Him *by faith*. He had seen Him after the flesh, but in that he did not glory, for he had now come to value only the things of faith, desiring mainly that the righteousness which is of God by faith might be imputed unto him. He believed, and hence he knew. There is no knowledge so gracious as the knowledge of faith, for a man may know a great deal in a natural way and yet perish, but that which comes of faith is saving. If a man only knows Christ in the head, but does not trust Him with the heart, what is the good of his knowledge? It will rather ruin than save him. So to know the Lord Jesus Christ as to lean your soul's full weight upon Him, so to know Him as to experience peace because you trust in Him, so to know Him as to feel that you can rest in Him more and more, from day to day, because He is all your salvation and all your desire,—this is to know Him indeed! But Paul also knew the Lord by *experience*, for he speaks of knowing Him and "the power of His resurrection." This is excellent knowledge indeed, when the power of a fact is realized within and shown in the life. When we are raised from the death of our sin, and feel that we are so, then is our knowledge of the risen Christ excellent indeed. When we feel a new life within us, quickening us unto spiritual things, and know that this springs from the resurrection of our Lord, and is wrought in us according to the mighty power which raised Jesus Christ from the dead, then indeed can we rejoice in the excellency of the knowledge of Christ Jesus our Lord.

More than that, Paul knew something of Christ, and was aiming to know more, by *a growing likeness to Him :* "that I may know Him, and the fellowship of His Sufferings, being made conformable unto His death." He had entered, in some measure, into his Master's sufferings, he had been persecuted and despised of men, and for much the same reason as his Master. He had, in a degree, felt Christ's motives, Christ's love for man, Christ's zeal for God, Christ's self sacrifice, Christ's readiness to die on behalf of the truth. This is an excellent knowledge indeed, and Paul might well esteem it as far more precious than all legal privileges. He spoke of it as super-eminent knowledge, for such is his meaning, and he reckoned it to be beyond all price. Beloved, there is no knowledge in the world which can be compared with such a knowledge of Christ Jesus as I have tried to describe just now, for it is a knowledge which concerns the highest conceivable object—even the Son of God. To know the science of nature, to be familiar with rocks, to read the stars, to comprehend all things else, is a comparative trifle when we consider what it is to know God in the person of the Lord Jesus. He in whom dwelleth all the fulness of the Godhead bodily is most worthy to be known, and angels and principalities unite with all the saints in thinking so. One truth about Christ is more precious than the total of all other knowledge! This is a knowledge which no man hath except it be given him by the Holy Spirit and hence its excellence. We may say to all, who know Christ, "Flesh and blood hath not revealed this unto thee." Divinely taught must he be who has learned Christ. This science cannot be acquired in the schools, nor imparted by learned professors, nor even gathered by years of diligent research: to the heart, renewed by the Holy Ghost, the Lord Jesus must be revealed by the Spirit Himself, for no man can say that Jesus Christ is Lord but by the Holy Ghost. That must needs be a superlative knowledge which requires in each case to be communicated by God Himself.

If you would see the excellency of this knowledge look at its effects. Some knowledge puff up, but this knowledge makes us humble, and the more we have of it the less are we in our own esteem. This knowledge sanctifies, purges, and delivers from the love of sin. It saves the soul,—saves it from present sin and from eternal woe. This knowledge elevates the motives, sweetens the feelings, and gives nobility to the entire life: for the man who knows Christ lives after a loftier order of life than those who are ignorant of Him. This knowledge indeed, beloved is excellent, because it never can be lost; it is a knowledge which will continue to progress, even in eternity. The most of the subjects which mortals study here will be forgotten in the world to come; the profoundest of them will be too trifling to be pursued amid angelic thrones. The honours of classical and mathematical attainments will shine but dimly admidst the glories of heaven, but the knowledge of Christ Jesus will still be priceless, and it will cause those who possess it to shine as the sun. He that knoweth Christ shall go on to sit at His feet and still to learn, and as he learns he will tell to principalities and powers the manifold wisdom of God in the person of Jesus Christ. See ye, then, beloved, that the apostle for the sake of the knowledge of Christ Jesus his Lord still counted all the things that he had once gloried in to be but loss. This was his calculation when he was writing. It was not merely the estimate of his younger days, but it was his present renewed and confirmed judgment. My friends, is it ours?

The great apostle gives us a third counting, which may be regarded as *his life estimate ;* not of the past only, nor of the present merely, but of the past and present inclusively. Here it is "For whom I have suffered the loss of all things, and do count them but dung, that I may win Christ, and be found in Him." Here, beloved, you see that his estimate sets out with actual test and practical proof. He is sitting down, I suppose, in the guard room of the Prætorium at Rome, where he was a prisoner; the chains are on his wrist, and if he likes he needs no blotting paper, but may powder his writing with the rust of his fetters. He has nothing in all the world; he has lost all his old friends; his relations disown him, his countrymen abhor him, and even his Christian brethren often distress him. No man made the Jew gnash his teeth more maliciously than did the name of Saul of Tarsus, who was adjudged to be the vilest of renegades. He has lost caste, and lost all ground of glorying, he has no longer a righteousness of his own wherein to glory, but he is stripped of every rag of legal hope: Christ is his all, and he has nothing else. He has no worldly property, he has no provision for his commonest needs, and most true are his words as he writes—"For whom I have suffered the loss of all things." Let us enter the prison and put a personal question to the good man. Paul, your faith has brought you to absolute penury and friendlessness: what is your estimate of it now? Theory is one thing, but does practice bear it out? The sea looks smooth as glass, but seafaring is pleasanter to talk of than practice. The embarking was a fine spectacle, but what think you of a sea voyage when the storm rages? How now, Paul? "Well," saith he, "I confess I have suffered the loss of all things." And do you deeply regret it, Paul? "Regret it," saith he, "regret the loss of my Phariseeism, my circum-

cision, my Israelitish dignity? Regret it! No," he says, "I am glad that all these are gone, for I count it to be a deliverance to be rid of them."

In his first and second countings he called his former gains loss, but now he sets them down as "dung." He could not use a stronger word: he calls all his boastings in the flesh mere offal—something to get rid of, and no loss when it is gone, but rather a subject for congratulation that it is removed from him. The word signifies that which is worthless, and is used to express the lees and dregs of wine, the settlement which a man finds in his cup, and drains out upon the ground when he has drank his liquor, the refuse of fruit, the dross of metals, and the chaff and stubble of wheat. In fact, the root of the word signifies things cast to dogs,—dog's meat, bones from the plates, crumbs and stale pieces brushed from the table, and such things as one is anxious to be rid of. The apostle puts down the whole of the fine things which he had enumerated as no better than dung. "Of the stock of Israel, of the tribe of Benjamin, an Hebrew of the Hebrews," he shakes out the whole lot for the dogs, and is glad to be rid of it all for Christ's sake. It reminds me of a ship in a storm. When the captain leaves the harbour he has a cargo on board of which he takes great care, but when a tremendous wind is blowing and the ship labours, being too heavily laden, and there is great fear that she will not outride the storm, see how eagerly the sailors lighten the ship. They bring up from the hold with all diligence the very things which before they prized, and they seem rejoiced to heave them into the sea. Never men more eager to get than these are to throw away. There go the casks of flour, the bars of iron, the manufactured goods: overboard go valuable bales of merchandise; nothing seems to be worth keeping. How is this? Are not these things good? Yes, but not good to a sinking ship. Anything must go to save life, anything to outride the storm. And so the apostle says that in order to win Christ and to be found in Him he flung the whole cargo of his beloved confidences over, and was as glad to get rid of them as if they were only so much dung. This he did to win Christ, and that fact suggests another picture: an English war ship of the olden times is cruising the ocean, and she spies a Spanish galleon in the distance laden with gold from the Indies. Captain and men are determined to overtake and capture her, for they have a relish for prize-money; but their vessel sails heavily. What then? If she will not move because of her load they fling into the sea everything they can lay their hands on, knowing that if they can capture the Spanish vessel the booty will make amends for all they lose and vastly more. Do you wonder at their eagerness to lose the little to gain the great? Sailor, why cast overboard those useful things? "Oh," says he, "they are nothing compared with that prize over yonder. If we can but get side by side and board her we will soon make up for all that we now throw into the sea." And so it is with the man who is in earnest to win Christ and to be found in Him. Overboard go circumcision and Phariseeism, and the blamelessness touching the law, and all that, for he knows that he will find a better righteousness in Christ than any which he forgoes, yea, find everything in Christ which he now for his Lord's sake counts but as the slag of the furnace.

Now, beloved, notice how much nearer Paul had got to Christ than he was before, for in his second estimate he spoke of knowing Him, but now he speaks of *winning* Him for his own. The word meant and should have been translated "gain," "that I may gain Christ," for the apostle keeps to the mercantile figure all the way through, and means that I may gain Christ, and know Him as my own, that I may have Him and hold Him, and sing with the spouse "My beloved is mine." For this cause we may wisely count all things but dung, that we may have the Lord Jesus in everlasting possession.

Then Paul adds "and be found in Him." He longs to be hidden in Jesus, and to abide in Him as a bird in the air, or a fish in the sea; he pants to be one with Christ, and so to be in Him as a member is in the body. He desires to get into Christ as a fugitive shelters himself in his hiding place; he aspires to be so in Christ as never to come out of Him; so that whenever any one looks for him he may find him in Jesus, and that when the Great Judge of all calls for him at the last great day he may find him in Christ. It would be ill to be found where Adam was, shivering under the trees of the garden with his fig-leaves on; but to be found beneath the tree of life, wearing the robe of God's righteousness, this will be bliss indeed. We are lost out of Christ, but we are found in Him. Once met with by the Great Shepherd, we are found *by* Him, but when safely folded in His love, we are found *in* Him.

Do notice how Paul sticks to what he began with, namely, the unrobing himself of his boastings in the flesh and his arraying himself with Christ. He desires to be found in Christ, but he adds, "not having mine own righteousness, which is of the law." No, he will have nothing to do with that; he has already despised it as loss, and thrown it overboard as dross, and now he will not have it or call it his own at all. It is strange for a man to say "not having my own," but he does say so he: disowns his own righteousness as eagerly as other men disown their sins, and he highly esteems the righteousness which Christ has wrought out for us, which becomes ours by faith. He calls it "the righteousness which is of God by faith," and he sets great store by it; yea, it is all he desires. My brethren, this is the thing we ought to be seeking after, to be more and more conscious that we have Christ, to abide in Him more continually, to be more like Him, even in His sufferings and in His death, and to feel the full power of His resurrection-life within ourselves. May God grant us grace to do this, and the more we do it the more we shall coincide with the apostle in his slight esteem for all things else. This matter is like a balance, if one scale goes down, the other must go up. The weightier Christ's influence, the lighter will be the world and self-righteousness: and when Christ is all in all, then the world and self will be nothing at all.

II. I shall not weary you, I hope, by taking a few minutes for the last head, which is OUR OWN CALCULATIONS.

First, *do we join in Paul's earliest estimate?* At the outset of his spiritual life he saw all his own natural advantages and excellences, and he counted them loss for Christ. Every true Christian here remembers, the time he also counted all wherein he had formerly trusted to be of no value whatever, and betook himself to Jesus. But perhaps I speak to some who have never done so. You are at this time, my friend, still confident that you never did anybody any harm; that your life has been amiable and upright; that you have been just, charitable, and kind;

and that all this certainly qualifies you for heaven. You count your natural virtues to be of great gains. I spoke but three days ago to an old man, more than eighty, and when he told me of his great age I said, "I hope that when you die you will go to heaven. "Ah master," says he, "I never did anything why I should go anywhere else." There are multitudes who believe that creed, they do not speak it out quite so plainly as the aged peasant did, but they mean it all the same. Ah, dear friends, you must be brought out of that delusion, and all these moral excellences and virtues must be loss to you that Christ's righteousness may be your only gain. May the Holy Spirit teach you this distasteful truth. I wish your heart would sing—

"No more, my God, I boast no more
Of all the duties I have done;
I quit the hopes I held before,
To trust the merits of Thy Son.

"Yes, and I must and will esteem
All things but loss for Jesus' sake:
O may my soul be found in Him,
And of His righteousness partake."

You will never be saved till you lose all your legal hopes.

Now secondly, after years of profession which many of you have made, *do you still continue in the same mind and make the same estimate?* I have known, I am sorry to say, some professors who have by degrees settled down upon something other than Christ. Beloved, are you resting now upon your years of manifest improvement since conversion? Are you beginning to depend upon the regularity of your attendance at the means of grace, upon your private prayer, upon what you have given, or upon your preaching, or anything else? Ah, it will not do. We must continue to stand where we stood at first, saying, "Yea doubtless, and I count all things but loss for the excellency of the knowledge of Christ Jesus my Lord." Come now, Christian, if you could go back, would you begin at the cross? If you could retrace your steps, would you begin again by resting upon Christ and by taking Him to be your all in all? I will tell you my answer,—I have no other foundation upon which I could begin, I must rest on my Lord.

"To whom or whither should I go
If I should turn from Thee?"

Lone refuge of my spirit, sole port of my poor labouring barque, to Thee I fly to-day, if never I did so before; or if before, to Thee I fly anew. Say you, so brothers and sisters? I am sure you do.

Now, again, you cannot join Paul in the third calculation and say, "For whom I have suffered the loss of all things"; but still I must put it to you—*do you think you could have suffered the loss of all things if it had been required of you for Christ's sake?* If it had come to this, that you must be banished or renounce your Saviour, would you go into banishment? If the alternative were the spoiling of your goods, would you let all go rather than renounce your Lord? Your forefathers did so, and what the Spirit wrought in them I doubt not He would have wrought in you, had the times been of a severer character. But I will put you a more practical question. Since you have not had to suffer the loss of all things, do you hold all things at God's disposal? Are you ready to part with comfort and honour for Him? Can you take up the social cross and join with the most despised sect for the truth's sake? Can you lose the respectability which attaches to popular creeds, and can you cast in your lot with the despised Redeemer, when religion no more walks in her silver slippers, but travels barefooted through the mire? Can you be content to share with the "despised and rejected of men?" If you can, then you could also suffer the loss of all things; but see to it that it be indeed so.

Let me ask another question. You have not suffered the loss of all things, but seeing God has left your worldly comforts to you, *have you used all things for His sake*? Have you given to His cause all that cause might fairly ask? I hope you can say, "Yes, I hope I have, and, as the world judges, vastly more, for I have said in my soul—

"And if I must make some reserve,
And duty did not call,
I love my God with zeal so great
That I would give Him all."

Well, then, you also may make your estimate as the apostle did: though you have not had practically to endure the loss of all things, yet you do count them but dung for Christ's sake.

But one thing more. Beloved, if Christ be so to you that all things else in comparison to Him are dross and dung, *do you not want Him for your children*? Do you not desire Him for your friends? Do you not wish all your kinsfolk to have Him? Whatever a man values for himself he values for others. You want your boy to follow your trade if you believe it to be a very good one. You desire to see your children well placed in life, but what position in life can be equal to being found in Christ? and what winnings under heaven can be compared with winning Christ. You may judge your own sincerity by the measure of your desire for the salvation of others, and I earnestly entreat you be not backward to tell to others the excellency of the knowledge of Christ Jesus your Lord, and be not slow to impress upon them the absolute necessity of being found in Him. Loathe the idea of having a righteousness of your own, but grasp with all your faith the righteousness of Jesus Christ. I commend to you Christians that you give your whole selves to Christ, that from this day forward ye serve Him, spirit, soul and body, for after all there is nothing worth living for, nothing worth even giving a single tear for if you lose it, nor worth a smile if you gain it, save only that which comes from Christ, and can be used for Christ, and is found in Christ. Christ is all. May He be so to you. Amen.

THE PRICELESS PRIZE

"That I may win Christ."—Philippians iii. 8.

THE very high value that the apostle Paul set upon the Saviour is most palpable when he speaks of *winning* Him. This shows that the Saviour held the same place in Paul's esteem as the crown did in the esteem of the runner at the Olympic games. To gain that crown, the competitor strained every nerve and sinew, feeling as though he were content to drop down dead at the goal if he might but win it. Paul felt that, were he to run with all his might, if that were the way of winning Christ, were he to strain soul and body to win Him, He would be well worth the effort. He shows his value of Christ by speaking of Him as the prize he panted to win. He uses the very same word which the soldier would use concerning the victory, when, with garments rolled in blood, amidst confused noise and clouds of smoke, he counts all things but little if he may but hear the shout of triumph. So Paul, regarding Christ as more glorious and excellent than mountains of prey, considered such a prize to be worth all the fighting, even though he should agonize and sweat with blood. He would be well worth dying to win. I take it that he speaks of Christ here as though he felt that He was the very climax of his desire, the summit of his ambition. If he might but get Christ, he would be perfectly satisfied; but if he could not get Him, whatever else he might have, he would still remain unblessed.

I would to God that you all felt the same. I wish that the ambition of every one of my fellow-creatures here assembled—and, indeed, the wide world over,—were this, that they might win Christ. Oh, if they did but know His preciousness; if they did but understand how happy and how blessed He makes those to be who gain Him, they, too, would give up everything else for this one desire,—that they may win Christ. I hope that, perhaps, a few words of mine may be blessed of God the Spirit to stir up such a desire in the hearts of the congregation now assembled here. How then shall I begin?

I. WHILE YOU HAVE NOT CHRIST, YOU ARE IN A VERY ILL CONDITION,—SHOULD NOT THIS MAKE YOU LONG FOR HIM?

Consider, my dear hearer, thou who art Christless to-night, *what thou art, and where thou art*. Thou art a sinner,—that thou knowest. Without Christ thou art an unpardoned sinner, a condemned sinner, and ere long thou wilt be a sinner judged, sentenced, and cast into hell! Dost thou not know that? Thou art a diseased sinner. Sin is the leprosy which is in thee; and without Christ, thou art sick without a physician. For thee there is no balm in Gilead, no physician there. Thy sickness is mortal. It will certainly be thy ruin, for thou hast no Saviour. Thou art a mortal man; thou canst not doubt it. Thou wilt soon die; and canst thou tell what it will be to die without Christ? Hast thou ever formed an idea of what it will be to pass into the realm of separate spirits with no rod to lean on, and no staff to comfort thee in the dark valley? Man, thou art an immortal being; thou knowest *that*, too. Thou wilt not cease to be when thou diest. Thou wilt live again; and what will it be to live again without Christ? It will be to live the life of a condemned spirit, withered by the wrath of God, scathed by the lightning of divine justice! Canst thou think of that without dismay?

"Sinner, is thy heart at rest?
Is thy bosom void of fear?
Art thou not by guilt oppress'd?
Speaks not conscience in thy ear?

Can this world afford thee bliss?
Can it chase away thy gloom?
Flattering, false, and vain it is;
Tremble at the worldling's doom."

Why, even now. man, I think I can see thee. Thou art like the ship upon the lake of Gennesareth, tempest-tossed. The winds howl about her, every timber creaks, the sail is rent to ribands, and the mast is going by the board; and for thee there is no Saviour to come and walk the billows, and to say, "It is I; be not afraid!" At the helm of thy ship there sleeps no Saviour who can arise, and say to the waves. "Peace, be still!" Thou art a ship in a storm, with none to rescue thee, seeing that thou hast no Saviour. The devil has scuttled thee. There are holes bored through and through thy spirit's hope and confidence, and it will go down before long in depths of unutterable woe.

I think I see thee again. Thou art like Lazarus in the grave, and by this time thou art foul and noxious, for thou hast been dead these thirty or forty years, and that death has festered into putrid corruption. Yes, there thou art, and thou hast no Christ to say, "Roll away the stone." Thou hast no Christ to say, "Lazarus, come forth!" no Saviour to bid thy friends loose thee, and let thee go! I think I see thee yet again. Thou hast been singing of the dying thief. We often sing of him: and thou wilt die as the thief died, only—only there will be no Christ hanging on the cross, from whom thou shalt hear the words, "This day shalt thou be with Me in paradise."

Unto what shall I liken thee, and wherewith shall I compare thee? A soul without Christ! Why, it were better for thee, man, that thou hadst never been born if thou shalt continue so! Thou wouldst be better off with the mill-stone about thy neck, and cast into the sea, if that would make an end of thee; thou wert happier far than thou art now without Christ, for without Christ thou art without God, and without hope in the world. Thou art a sheep lost on the mountains, and no Shepherd to find thee; a soul wandering in the blackness of darkness, and no lamp to guide thy wandering footsteps; and soon thou wilt be a desolate spirit. without a ray of comfort, without a home, shut out in the blackness of darkness for ever! Does not that make thee long for Christ? It would, if I could make thee feel what I can only say. I can only deal with your outward ears, my Master must deal with your hearts; and I do pray Him, by His almighty Spirit, to make you feel so wretched without Christ that you will not dare to sleep to-night until you have sought Him. and laid hold upon Him, and said to Him, "I will not let Thee go, except Thou bless me "

O ye souls out of Christ, I could, with half a moment's thought, stop and burst into tears, and say no more; but I must command myself, for I must speak to you; and I do pray you, by the living God, unless you are beside yourselves, if you have any love to your own souls, fly to Christ; seek the Lord; try to lay hold upon Him, for as you now are, your position is perilous in the extreme!

"Come, guilty souls, and flee away
Like doves to Jesu's wounds;
This is the welcome gospel-day,
Wherein free grace abounds.

God loved the church, and gave His Son
To drink the cup of wrath;
And Jesus says He'll cast out none
That come to Him by faith."

II. We will now change the strain, but not the object. Remember, that ALL THE THINGS IN THE WORLD ARE VAIN WITHOUT CHRIST.

The world's goods, its substance, its riches, its pleasures, its pomp, its fame, *what are all these without Christ?* They are a painted pageantry to go to hell in! They are a mockery to an immortal spirit. They are a *mirage* of the wilderness, deluding the traveller, but not yielding to his desires one substantial drop of joy. There have been those in this world who have tried it, and they say, "It sounds, it sounds, it sounds, because it is empty and hollow as a drum." It is—

"False as the smooth, deceitful sea,
And empty as the whistling wind."

There is nothing in it all.

"Honour's a puff of noisy breath,
And gain a heap of yellow clay."

And what is even power itself but anxiety and care? Solomon knew the world at its best, and his verdict upon her was, "Vanity of vanities, saith the Preacher, vanity of vanities; all is vanity." Without Christ, sinner, you will find the world to be unsatisfactory. When you have tried it at its best, you will turn from it, and say, "I have been deceived! I have eaten the wind, and I am not satisfied. I am like one that feasteth in a dream, and waketh, and, lo! he is hungry." Without Christ, you will not even find this world to be comfortable. Perhaps there are none so unhappy as those who are surrounded with what we think to be the means of happiness. I know this, if I had to find the extreme of wretchedness, I should not go to the dens of poverty, but I should go amongst men surrounded with the trappings of wealth, and find you hearts broken with anguish, and spirits wrung with griefs which they could not tell. Oh, yes! the world is a heap of chaff; the only solid treasure is to be found in Christ; and if you neglect Him, you neglect all that is worth the having.

Besides, *all this world must soon pass away.* See how it melts! Or, if it melts not from you, you must melt from it. There, down goes the ship; she floated gaily but an hour before, but she foundered, and she is gone; and now, merchant, what wilt thou do? Thy vessel has gone down with all thy treasure on board, and thou art left penniless! Oh, happy are they who lay up their treasure in Christ, for no shipwreck need they fear! But, oh!—

"This world's a dream, an empty show,"—

which cannot satisfy an immortal soul.

Further than this, let me remind you, my dear hearer, that *if you have not Christ, nothing else will avail for you.* A profession of religion will only be a sort of respectable pall to throw over the corpse of your dead soul. Nay, a profession of religion, if you have not Christ in it, will be a swift witness against you to condemn you. What right have you to profess to be a follower of Christ, unless Christ be in you the hope of glory? And to have listened to the ministry of the Word will be of no use to you if you do not get Christ. Alas! alas! what can our poor sermons do? Our prayers, our hymns,—what are they all? They are wasted breath unless you get Christ. Ah! and what will your baptism be, and what will the Lord's supper be, unless by faith you grasp a Saviour? These ordinances, though ordained of God

Himself, are wells without water, and clouds without rain, unless they get us Christ, who is the sum and substance of them all. It will be of no use to you that you were regular in your private prayers, that you were good to the poor, that you were generous to the church, that you were constant in your attendance upon the outward means of grace. I say, as I said before, that all these are but a painted pageantry for your soul to go to hell in, except you have Christ. You may as surely go down to the pit by the religious road as by the irreligious. If you have not Christ, you have not salvation, whatever else you may have.

"Give me Christ, or else I die,"—

should be your daily and nightly prayer; for all else must destroy you if you have not a Saviour.

And let me tell thee, dear hearer, that thy repentance, if it does not lead thee to Christ, will need to be repented of; and thy faith, if it be not based upon His atoning sacrifice, is a faith that is not the faith of God's elect; and all thy convictions of sin— all the visions that have scared thee, all the fears that have haunted thee,—will only be a prelude to something worse, unless thou gettest Christ. There is one door, and if thou goest not through that, climbing up some other way, though it be never so tedious, will not answer thy turn. Thou must even go down to hell after all thine efforts, all thy repentings, all thy believings, unless thy soul can say—

> "My hope is built on nothing less
> Than Jesu's blood and righteousness;
> I dare not trust the sweetest frame,
> But wholly lean on Jesu's name:
>   On Christ, the solid rock, I stand;
>   All other ground is sinking sand."

Oh, how this ought to make you long for Christ, when you think that everything else is but a bauble when compared with Him; and bethink you what a state you are in as long as you are destitute of Him!

III. I must not tarry, so let me remind you, my dear hearer, though you cannot possibly know how anxious I am to speak so that you may feel what I say, that NOTHING CAN MAKE AMENDS TO YOU FOR LOSING CHRIST.

I know how it is with some of you. *You say you cannot afford to follow Christ.* Your trade—your wicked trade, you would have to give that up; for it happens to be an ungodly calling. Well, now, friend, let me take thee by the button-hole a minute. Which hadst thou better be, a beggar and go to heaven, or a duke and go to hell? Come, now, which hadst thou better do, go to heaven with an empty pocket or go down to the pit with a full one? Ah, ye who worship Mammon, I know how you will answer; but you who have souls above earth, I hope you will reply, "Nothing in the form of wealth will compensate us for losing our souls." Men have been known, on their dying beds, to have their money-bags brought to them, and they have put them to their hearts, and have said, "This won't do," and they have taken up another, and put it to their palpitating hearts, and said again, "This won't do." Ah, no, it cannot cure a heart-ache; what can it do for a soul in eternity? Is it not a painful thing to attend upon some men who die rich in ill-gotten gain? What are they the better for their wealth? They only have it said of them, "He died worth so much"; that is all, but they sleep in the same earth, and the same worms devour them. There is more fighting over their graves, and more joy because they are gone, among the heirs who divide the plunder, while, oftentimes, the poor man has the honest tears of his children shed upon a coffin which they have had to contribute to purchase out of their little savings, and the grave itself has been prepared by the charity of some who found in their father's character the only patrimony which he had to bequeath. Oh, may God grant you grace to perceive that all the riches you can ever get would never make up for losing Christ!

Some lose Christ for the sake of fame. It is not a fashionable thing to be a Christian. To be a Christian after the world's sort, I grant you, is; but after the sort of the New Testament, it is not; and many say, "Well, it is not fashionable," and they bend to the fashion; and many do the same in another way, for young men are laughed out of going to the house of God, and young women are decoyed from attending the means of grace by the laughter, and jeers, and jokes of their companions. Remember that they can laugh you into hell, but they can never laugh you out again; and that, though their jokes may shut the door, their jokes can never open that door again. Oh, is this all? Will you sell your souls to escape from a fool's laughter? Then, what a fool you must be yourself! What, are you so thin-skinned that you cannot bear to be questioned, or to be asked whether you are a follower of the Lord Jesus? Ah, sir, you shall have that thin skin of yours tormented more than enough in the world to come, when *shame*, which you dread so much, shall be your everlasting portion! O soul, how canst thou sell Christ for the applause of men? How canst thou give Him up for the laughter of fools?

Some give Jesus Christ up for the pleasures of the world, but can the giddy dance for a few minutes of this life be worth the torments of the world to come? Oh, weigh, like wise men,—as merchants weigh their goods against the gold,—I pray you, weigh your souls against the pleasures of this world. Oh, where is the pleasure? Even Tiberius, in his desert island, when he had ransacked the world to find a new joy, could not, if he could give us all the mirth he knew, tell us of anything that would be worth the casting away of the soul. This pearl is too priceless for the world to attempt to purchase it. I pray you, be wise enough to see that nothing can compensate you for this loss, and do seek Jesus, and may you find Him to-night!

IV. A fourth observation, upon which I shall not enlarge, is this,—DEPEND UPON IT, THAT WHATEVER YOU LOSE FOR CHRIST'S SAKE WILL BE A BLESSED LOSS FOR YOU.

Gregory Nazianzen, a foremost father of the Christian Church, rejoiced that he was well versed in the Athenian philosophy; and why do you think he rejoiced in that? Because he had to give it all up when he became a Christian; and, said he, "I thank God that I had a philosophy to throw away." He counted it no loss, but a gain, to be a loser of such learned lumber when he found a Saviour. Says an old divine, "Who would refuse to give up a whole sky full of stars if he could buy a sun therewith, and who would refuse to give up all the comforts of this life if he could have Christ at so goodly a price?" That grand old Ignatius, one of the earliest of the Church fathers, said, "Give me burning, give me hanging, give me all the torments of hell; if I may but get my Saviour, I would fain be content to bear them all as a price." And so might we. Did I not tell you of the martyrs sitting and singing in old Bonner's damp coal-hole, and one of them writing, "There are six brave companions with me in this paradise, and we do sit and sing in the dark all day"? Ah, yes, they were no losers. Did not Rutherford say, when he declared that he had but one eye, and his enemies had put that out,—for that one eye was the preaching of the gospel, and eye to the glory of God,—and his enemies had made him silent in Aberdeen, so that he used to weep over his dumb and silent Sabbaths,— yet did he not say, "But how mistaken they are! They thought they sent me to a dungeon, but Christ has been so precious to me that I thought it to be the king's parlour, and the very paradise of God"? And did not Renwick say that, oftentimes, when he had been out among the bogs on the Scotch mountains, hunted over the mosses, with the stars of God looking down upon the little congregation, that they had had more of God's fellowship than bishops had ever had in cathedrals, or than they themselves had ever had in their kirks, when, in brighter days, they had worshipped God in peace? The dragoons of Claverhouse, and the uniformity of Charles II were incapable of quenching the joy of our Puritanic and Covenanting forefathers. Their piety drew its mirth from deeper springs than kings could stop, or persecution could dry up. The saints of Christ have given Christ their all, and when they have given all, they have felt that they were the richer for their poverty, the happier for their sorrows; and when they have been in solitude for Christ, they have felt that they have had good company, for He has been with them to be their strength and their joy. You may have Christ at what price you will, but you will make a good bargain of it. I charge thee, my dear hearer, if it should come to this, that thou shouldst have to sell thy house and thy home, if the wife of thy bosom should become thine enemy, if thy children should refuse to know their own father, or to look him in the face, if thou shouldst be banished from thy country, if there should be a halter for thy neck, and no grave for thy body, thou wouldst make a good bargain in taking up my Lord and Master; for, oh! He will own you in the day when men disown you; and in the day when He cometh, there shall be none so bright as those who have suffered for Him.

> "And they who, with their Leader,
> Have conquer'd in the fight,
> For ever and for ever
> Are clad in robes of white."

Yes, if you suffer with Him, you shall also be glorified together. God grant you grace to feel this to be true, and to make any sacrifice so long as you can but "win Christ, and be found in Him."

V. IF EVER YOU DO GET CHRIST, YOU WILL FIND HIM ALL GAIN, AND NO LOSS.

The apostle says, "That I may *win Christ*." It is all winning, and no losing. Why, *if you get Christ, you will get life*. Does He not give life and immortality to those that have Him? Yea, saith He, "he that believeth in Me, though he were dead, yet shall he live." *If you get Christ, you will get light*. He said, "I am the light of the world: he that followeth Me shall not walk in darkness." The Sun of righteousness shall arise upon you. *Get Christ, and you shall get health*; your soul shall leave her sicknesses with Him who bore her sickness in the days of His flesh. *Get Christ, and you shall get riches*; "the unsearchable riches of Christ." You may be poor, perhaps, out-

wardly; but you shall be rich yourselves, and be able to make many others rich,—rich in faith, giving glory to God. Get Christ, and prosperity shall not hurt you; your feet shall be like hinds' feet, to stand upon your high places. Get Christ, and He will turn your bitter Marahs into sweet Elims. He is the tree which, when put into the brackish water, makes it sweet to the taste. Affliction is no longer affliction when Christ is with us. Then the furnace glows, not with heat alone, but with a golden radiance, a present glory, when Christ treads the burning coals.

Get Christ, beloved, and you have got all your soul can wish for. Now may you stretch your capacious powers to the utmost, and, with a holy covetousness, and a sacred greediness, desire all you can. You may open your mouth wide, for Christ will fill it. You may enlarge your desires, but the infinite riches of Christ will satisfy them at their largest and widest stretch. Get Christ, and you have heaven on earth, and shall have heaven for ever. Get Christ, and angels shall be your servitors; the wheels of providence shall grind for your good; the chariot of God, which brings on the events prophesied in apocalyptic vision, shall bring only joy and peace to you; and you shall hear it said, both in time and in eternity,—

"'Tis with the righteous well."

Get Christ, and you have nothing to fear, and everything to hope for. Get Christ, and sin is buried in the Red Sea of Jesu's blood, while you are arrayed in the spotless righteousness of the Lord Jesus Christ,— Jehovah Tsidkenu Himself. Get Christ, and—what more shall I say? Then may you swim in seas of bliss, then may you walk Elysian fields of holy joy even here on earth. Get Christ, and you need not envy the angels. Get Christ, and you may count yourselves to be raised up together, and made to sit together in heavenly places with Him.

Surely all this ought to make the sinner's mouth water to get Christ! It ought to make his heart ache till he gets Christ. It ought to set his soul a-hungering and a-thirsting till he gets Jesus. It ought to make him resolve that he will not be kept back till at last he gets a firm hold upon the Crucified.

VI. My last remark shall be this, WE SHALL UNDERSTAND ALL THIS A GREAT DEAL BETTER VERY SOON.

There is a curtain, but it is lifting, it is lifting, it is lifting; and when it is lifted, what do I see? The spirit world! 'Tis death that lifts the curtain; and when it is lifted, these present things will vanish, for they are but shadows. The world of eternity and reality will then be seen. I would summon a jury of the spirits that have passed that curtain, and they would not be long debating about the question whether Christ is worth the winning. I care not where you select them from,—whether from among the condemned in hell, or from among the beatified in heaven. Let them sit,—let even *those who are in hell* sit, and judge upon the matter, and if they could for once speak honestly, they would tell you that it is a dreadful thing to despise Christ; now that they have come to see things in a true light,—now that they are lost for ever, for ever, for ever,—now that they are crushed with knowledge and feeling which have come too late to be profitable,—now they wish that they had listened to the ministrations of truth, to the proclamations of the gospel. If they could have a sane mind back again, they would shriek, "Oh, for one more Sabbath! Oh, to listen once more to an honest preacher, though his words might be clumsy and uncouth! Oh, to hear a voice once more say, 'Come to Jesus while the day of mercy lasts!' Oh, to be once more pressed to come to the marriage-feast,—once more bidden to look to Jesus and to live!" I tell you, sirs, some of you who make so light of Sundays, and think preaching is but a pastime, so that you come here to hear us as you would go to hear some fiddler on a week-night,—I tell you, sirs, the lost in hell reckon these things at a very different rate, and so will you ere long, when another preacher, with skeleton fingers, shall talk to you upon your death-bed. Ah! then you will see that we were in earnest, and you were the players, and you will comprehend that what we said to you demanded earnest, immediate attention, though, alas! you would not give it, and so played false to your own soul, and

committed spiritual suicide, and went your way like a bullock to the slaughter, to be the murderers of your own spirits!

But suppose I summoned a jury of bright spirits from heaven? Ah! they would not need to consider, but I am sure they would unanimously say to you, if they might, "Seek ye the Lord while He may be found; seek the Lord and His strength; seek the Lord and His face evermore; put your trust in Jesus, for He is sweet beyond all sweetness." May you do this, and may you sing,—

> "Oh! spread Thy savour on my frame,
>   No sweetness is so sweet;
> Till I get up to sing Thy name
>   Where all Thy singers meet."

Pray that prayer. Ask Him to save you, and may the Lord bless you, for Jesus' sake! Amen.

THE POWER OF HIS RESURRECTION

"That I may know Him, and the power of His resurrection."—Philippians iii. 10.

PAUL, in the verses before the text, had deliberately laid aside his own personal righteousness. "But what things were gain to me, those I counted loss for Christ: for whom I have suffered the loss of all things, and do count them but dung, that I may win Christ, and be found in Him, not having mine own righteousness, which is of the law." It is insinuated in these days that a belief in the righteousness of faith will lead men to care little for good works, that it will act as a sedative to their zeal, and therefore they will exhibit no ardour for holiness. The very reverse is seen in the case of the apostle, and in the case of all who cast aside the righteousness of the law, that they may be clothed with that righteousness "which is through the faith of Christ, the righteousness which is of God by faith." Paul made a list of his advantages as to confidence in the flesh, and they were very great; but he turned his back upon them all for Christ's sake; but accepting Christ to be everything to him, did he, therefore, sit down in self-content, and imagine that personal character was nothing? By no manner of means. A noble ambition fired his soul: he longed to know Christ, and the power of His resurrection, and the fellowship of His sufferings, being made conformable unto His death; if by any means he might attain unto the resurrection from the dead. He became a holy walker, and a heavenly runner, because of what he saw in Christ Jesus. Be you sure of this, that the less you value your own righteousness, the more will you seek after true holiness; the less you think of your own beauty the more ardently will you long to become like the Lord Jesus. Those who dream of being saved by their own good works are usually those who have no good works worth mentioning; while those who sincerely lay aside all hope of salvation by their own merits are fruitful in every virtue to the praise of God. Nor is this a strange thing; for the less a man thinks of himself, the more he will think of Christ, and the more will he aim at being like Him. The less esteem he has of his own past good works, the more earnest will he be to show his gratitude for being saved by grace through the righteousness of Christ. Faith works by love, and purifies the soul, and sets the heart a running after the prize of our high calling in Christ Jesus; hence it is a purifying and active

principle, and by no means the inert thing which some suppose it to be.

What, then, was the great object of the apostle's ardour? It was "that I may know Him, and the power of His resurrection." Paul already knew the Lord Jesus by faith; he knew so much of Him as to be able to teach others. He had looked to Jesus, and known the power of His death; but he now desired that the vision of his faith might become still better known by experience. You may know a man, and have an idea that he is powerful; but to know him and his power over you is a stage further. You may have read of a man so as to be familiar with his history and his character, and yet you may have no knowledge of him and of his personal influence over yourself. Paul desired intimate acquaintance with the Lord Jesus, personal intercourse with the Lord to such a degree that he should feel His power at every point, and know the effect of all that He had wrought out in His life, death, and resurrection. He knew that Jesus died, and he aspired to rehearse the history in his own soul's story: he would be dead with Him to the world. He knew that Jesus was buried, and he would fain be "buried with Him in baptism unto death." He knew that Jesus rose, and his longing was to rise with Him in newness of life. Yes, he even remembered that his Lord had ascended up on high, and he rejoiced to say, "He hath raised us up together, and made us sit together in heavenly places in Christ Jesus." His great desire was to have reproduced in himself the life of Jesus, so as to know all about Him by being made like Him. The best Life of Christ is not by Canon Farrar, or Dr. Geikie: it is written in the experience of the saint by the Holy Ghost.

I want you to observe, at the very outset, that all Paul desired to know was always in connection with our Lord Himself. He says, "That I may know HIM, and the power of His resurrection." Jesus first, and then the power of His resurrection. Beware of studying doctrine, precept, or experiences apart from the Lord Jesus, who is the soul of all. Doctrine without Christ will be nothing better than His empty tomb; doctrine with Christ is a glorious high throne, with the King sitting thereon. Precepts without Christ are impossible commands; but precepts from the lips of Jesus have a quickening effect upon the heart. Without Christ you can do nothing; but, abiding in Him, you bring forth much fruit. Always let your preaching and your hearing look towards the personal Saviour. This makes all the difference in preaching. Ministers may preach sound doctrine by itself, and be utterly without unction; but those who preach it in connection with the person of the blessed Lord have an anointing which nothing else can give. Christ Himself, by the Holy Ghost, is the savour of a true ministry.

This morning we will confine our thoughts to one theme, and unite with the apostle in a strong desire to know our Lord in connection with *the power of His resurrection.* The resurrection of the Lord Jesus was in itself a marvellous display of power. To raise the dead body of our Lord from the tomb was as great a work as the creation. The Father, the Son, and the Holy Spirit, each one wrought this greatest miracle. I need not stay to quote the texts in which the resurrection of our Lord is ascribed to the Father, who brought again from the dead that great Shepherd of the sheep; nor need I mention Scriptures in which the Lord is said to have been quickened by the Holy Spirit; nor those instances in which that great work is ascribed to the Lord Jesus Himself; but assuredly the sacred writings represent the divine Trinity in Unity as gloriously co-operating in the raising again from the dead the person of our Lord Jesus Christ. It was, however, a special instance of our Lord's own power. He said, "Destroy this temple, and in three days I will raise it up." He also said, concerning His life, "I have power to lay it down, and I have power to take it again." I do not know whether I can convey my own thought to you; but what strikes me very forcibly is this—no mere man going to his grave could say, "I have power to take my life again." The departure of life leaves the man necessarily powerless: he cannot restore himself to life. Behold the sacred body of Jesus, embalmed in spices, and wrapped about with linen; it is laid within the sealed and guarded tomb; how can it come forth to life? Yet Jesus said, "I have power to take My life again"; and He proved it true. Strange power! That spirit of His, which had travelled through the underlands, and upwards to the eternal glory, had power to return, and to re-enter that holy thing which had been born of the virgin, and to revivify that flesh which could not see corruption. Behold the dead and buried One makes Himself to live! Herein is a marvellous thing. He was master over death, even when death seemed to have mastered Him: He entered the grave as a captive, but left it as a conqueror. He was compassed by the bonds of death, but He could not be holden of them; even in His cerements He came to life; from those wrappings He unbound Himself; from the close-fastened tomb He stepped into liberty. If, in the extremity of His weakness, He had the power to rise out of the sepulchre, and come forth in newness of life, what can He not now accomplish?

I do not think, however, that Paul is here thinking so much of the power displayed in the resurrection, as of the power which comes out of it, which may most properly be called, "the power of His resurrection." This the apostle desired to apprehend and to know. This is a very wide subject, and I cannot encompass the whole region; but many things may be said under four heads. The power of our Lord's resurrection is *an evidencing power, a justifying power, a life-giving power, and a consoling power.*

I. First, the power of our Lord's resurrection is AN EVIDENCING POWER. Here I shall liken it to a seal which is set to a document to make it sure. Our Lord's resurrection from the dead was *a proof that He was the Messiah,* that He had come upon the Father's business, that He was the Son of God, and that the covenant which Jehovah had made with Him was henceforth ratified and established. He was "declared to be the Son of God with power, according to the spirit of holiness, by the resurrection from the dead." Thus said Paul at Antioch: "The promise which was made unto the fathers, God hath fulfilled the same unto us their children, in that He hath raised up Jesus again"; as it is also written in the second psalm, "Thou art My Son, this day have I begotten Thee." Nobody witnessing our Lord's resurrection could doubt His divine character, and that His mission upon earth was from the eternal God. Well did Peter and John declare that it was the Prince of life that God had raised from the dead. Our Lord had given this for a sign unto the cavilling Pharisees, that as Jonah lay in the deep till the third day, and then came forth, even so would He Himself lie in the heart of the earth till the third day, and then arise from the dead. His rising proved that He was sent of God, and that the power of God was with Him. Our Lord had entered into a covenant with the Father before all worlds, wherein He had on His part engaged to finish redemption and make atonement for sin. That He had done this was affirmed by His rising again from the dead: the resurrection was the attestation of the Father to the fulfilment on the part of the Second Adam of His portion in the eternal covenant. His blood is the blood of the everlasting covenant, and His resurrection is the seal of it. "Christ was raised from the dead by the glory of the Father" as the witness of the Eternal God to the glory of the Son.

So much is the resurrection the proof of our Lord's mission, that it falls to the ground without it. If our Lord Jesus had not risen from the dead, our faith in Him would have lacked the corner-stone of the foundation on which it rests. Paul writes most positively: "If Christ be not risen, then is our preaching vain, and your faith is also vain." He declares that the apostles would have been found false witnesses of God, "Because," says he, "we have testified of God that He raised up Christ: whom He raised not up, if so be that the dead rise not." "If Christ be not raised, your faith is vain; ye are yet in your sins." The Resurrection of Jesus is the key-stone of the arch of our holy faith. If you take the resurrection away, the whole structure lies in ruins. The death of Christ, albeit that it is the ground of our confidence for the pardon of sin, would not have furnished such a foundation had He not risen from the dead. Were He dead still, His death would have been like the death of any other person, and would have given us no assurance of acceptance. His life, with all the beauty of its holiness, would have been simply a perfect example of conduct, but it could not have become our righteousness if His burial in the tomb of Joseph had been the end of all. It was essential for the confirmation of His life-teaching and His death-suffering that He should be raised from the dead. If He had not risen, but were still among the dead, you might well tell us that we preach to you a cunningly devised fable. See, then, the power of

His resurrection: it proves to a demonstration the faith once delivered to the saints. Supported by infallible proofs, it becomes itself the infallible proof of the authority, power, and glory of Jesus of Nazareth, the Son of God.

I beg you further to notice that *this proof had such power about it to the minds of the apostles, that they preached with singular boldness.* These chosen witnesses had seen the Lord after His resurrection; one of them had put his finger into the print of the nails, and others had eaten and drunk with Him: they were sure that they were not deceived. They knew that He was dead, for they had been present at His burial: they knew that He lived again, for they had heard Him speak, and had seen Him eat a piece of a broiled fish and of an honeycomb. The fact was as clear to them as it was wonderful. Peter and the rest of them without hesitation declared, "This Jesus hath God raised up, whereof we all are witnesses." They were sure that they saw the man who died on Calvary alive again, and they could not but testify what they had heard and seen. The enemies of the faith wondered at the boldness with which these witnesses spake; theirs was the accent of conviction, for they testified what they knew of a surety. They had no suspicion lurking in the background; they were sure that Jesus had risen from the dead, and this unquestionable certainty made them confident that He was indeed the Messiah and the Saviour of men. The power of this fact upon those who believe it is great; but upon those who saw it as eye-witnesses it must have been inconceivably mighty. I wonder not that they defied contradiction, persecution, and even death. How could they disbelieve that of which they were so certain? How could they withhold their witness to a fact which was so important to the destiny of their fellow-men? In the apostles and the first disciples we have a cloud of witnesses to a fact more firmly attested than any other recorded in history; and that fact is the witness to the truth of our religion. Honest witnesses, in more than sufficient number, declare that Jesus Christ, who died on Calvary, and was buried in the tomb of Joseph of Arimathæa, did rise again from the dead. In the mouth of many witnesses the fact is established; and this fact established, proves other blessed facts.

If the cloud of witnesses might not seem sufficient in itself, I see that cloud tinged with crimson. Reddened as by the setting sun, the cloud of witnesses in life becomes *a cloud of martyrs in death.* The disciples were put to cruel deaths asserting still the fact that Jesus had risen from the grave. They and their immediate followers, nothing doubting, "counted not their lives dear to them" that they might bear witness to this truth. They suffered the loss of all things, were banished, and were accounted the offscouring of all things; but they could not, and would not, contradict their faith. They were nailed to a cross, or bound to a stake to be burned; but the enthusiasm of their conviction was never shaken. Behold an array of martyrs reaching on through the centuries! Behold how they are all sure of the gospel, because sure of their Lord's endless life! Is not this a grand evidence of "the power of His resurrection"? The Book of Martyrs is a record of that power.

The resurrection of Christ casts a side-light upon the gospel by *proving its reality and literalness.* There is a tendency in this generation to spirit away the truth, and in the doing thereof to lose both the truth and its spirit. In these evil days fact is turned into myth, and truth into opinion. Our Lord's resurrection is a literal fact: when He rose from the dead He was no spectre, ghost, or apparition; but as He was a real man who died the cruel death of the cross, so He was a real man who rose again from the dead, bearing in His body the marks of the crucifixion. His appearance to His familiar companions was to them no dream of the night, no fevered imagination of enthusiastic minds: for He took pains to make them sure of His real presence, and that He was really among them in His proper person.

> "A Man there was, a real Man,
> Who once on Calvary died,
> That same blest Man arose from death:
> The mark is in His side!"

There was as much reality about the rising of our Lord as about His death and burial. There is no fiction here. This literal fact gives reality to all that comes from Him and by Him. Justification is no mere easing of the conscience, it is a real arraying of the soul in righteousness: adoption into the family of God is no fancy, but brings with it true and proper sonship. The blessings of the gospel are substantial facts, and not mere theological opinions. As the resurrection of the Lord Jesus Christ from the dead was a plain visible matter of fact, so are the pardon of sin and the salvation of the soul matters of actual experience, and not the creatures of religious imagination.

Brethren, such is the evidencing power of the resurrection of Christ, that *when every other argument fails your faith, you may find safe anchorage in this assured fact.* The currents of doubt may bear you towards the rocks of mistrust; but when your anchor finds no other hold, it may grip the fact of the resurrection of Christ from the dead. This must be true. The witnesses are too many to have been deceived; and their patient deaths on account of their belief proved that they were not only honest men, but good men, who valued truth more than life. We know that Jesus rose from the dead; and, whatever else we are forced to question, we have no question on that score. We may be tossed about upon the sea in reference to other statements, but we step to shore again, and find terra firma in this unquestionable, firmly-established truth: "The Lord is risen indeed." Oh, that any of you who are drifting may be brought to a resting-place by this fact! If you doubt the possibility of your own pardon, this may aid you to believe, for Jesus lives. I read the other day of one who had greatly backslidden, and grievously dishonoured his Lord; but he heard a sermon upon the resurrection of Christ from the dead, and it was life to him. Though he had known and believed that truth before, yet he had never realized it vividly. After service he said to the minister, "Is it so, that our Lord Jesus has really risen from the dead, and is yet alive? Then He can save me." Just so. A living Christ can say assuredly to you, "Thy sins be forgiven thee." He is able now to breathe into you the life eternal. The Lord is risen indeed: in this see the evidence of His power to save to the uttermost. From this first solid stone of the resurrection, you may go, step by step, over the stream of doubt, till you land on the other side, fully assured of your salvation in Christ Jesus.

Thus, you see, there is an evidencing power in the

resurrection of our Lord Jesus Christ. I pray that you may feel it now. You cannot have too much holy confidence. You cannot be too sure. He that died for you is alive, and is making intercession for sinners. Believe that firmly, and realize it vividly, and then you will be filled with rest of heart, and will be bold to testify in the name of your Lord. The timid by nature will become lion-like in witnessing when the resurrection has borne to them overwhelming evidence of their Redeemer's mission and power.

II. We will dwell next upon THE JUSTIFYING POWER OF HIS RESURRECTION. Under the first head I compared the resurrection to a seal; under this second head I must liken it to a note of acquittance, or a receipt. Our Lord's rising from the dead was a discharge in full, from the High Court of Justice, from all those liabilities which He had undertaken on our behalf.

Observe, first, that *our Lord must have fully paid the penalty due to sin.* He was discharged because He had satisfied the claim of justice. All that the law could possibly demand was the fulfilment of the sentence, "The soul that sinneth, it shall die." There is no getting away from that doom: life must be taken for sin committed. Christ Jesus is our substitute and sacrifice. He came into the world to vindicate the law, and He has achieved it by the offering of Himself. He has been dead and buried, and He has now risen from the dead because He has endured death to the full, and there remaineth no more to be done. Brethren, consider this, and let your hearts be filled with joy: the penalty which has come upon you through breaches of the law is paid. Yonder is the receipt. Behold the person of your risen Lord! He was your hostage till the law had been honoured and divine authority had been vindicated: that being done, an angel was sent from the throne to roll back the stone, and set the hostage free. All who are in Him—and all are in Him who believe in Him—are set free by His being set free from the prison-house of the sepulchre.

> "He bore on the tree the ransom for me,
> And now both the sinner and Surety are free."

Our Lord has blotted out the record which was against us, and that in a most righteous way. Through the work of Jesus, God is just, and the justifier of him that believeth. Jesus died for our sins, but rose again for our justification. As the rising of the sun removes the darkness, so the rising of Christ has removed our sin. The power of the resurrection of Christ is seen in the justifying of every believer; for the justification of the Representative is the virtual justification of all whom He represents.

When our Lord rose from the dead, it was certified that *the righteousness, which He came to work out, was finished.* For what remained to be done? All was accomplished, and therefore He went up unto His Father's side. Is He toiling there to finish a half-accomplished enterprise? Nay, "This man, after He had offered one sacrifice for sins for ever, sat down on the right hand of God." Our righteousness is a finished one, for Jesus quits the place of humiliation, and rises to His reward. He cried upon the cross, "It is finished!" and His word was true. The Father endorsed His claim by raising Him from the dead. Put on, therefore, O ye faithful, this matchless robe of perfect righteousness! It is more than royal, it is divine. It is for you that this best robe is provided.

Wear it, and be glad. Remember that in Christ Jesus you are justified from all things. You are, in the sight of God, as righteous as if you had kept the law; for your covenant Head has kept it. You are as justified as if you had been obedient unto death; for He has obeyed the law on your behalf. You are this day justified by Christ who is "the end of the law for righteousness to every one that believeth." Because He is delivered from the tomb, we are delivered from judgment, and are sent forth as justified persons. "Therefore, being justified by faith, we have peace with God." Oh, that a deep peace, profound as the serenity of God, may fall upon all our hearts as we see Jesus risen from the dead!

His resurrection did not only prove our pardon and our justification, but *it proved our full acceptance.* "He hath made us accepted in the Beloved." Christ is never separated from His people, and therefore whatever He is, they are in Him. He is the Head: and as is the Head, such are the members. I will suppose that a dead body lies before us. See, the head comes to life; it opens its eyes; it lifts itself; it rises from the ground; it moves to the table. I need not tell you that the arms, the feet, and the whole body must go with the head. It cannot be that there shall be a risen head, and yet the members of the body shall still be dead. When God accepted Christ my Head, He accepted *me ;* when He glorified my Head, He made me a partaker of that glory through my Representative. The infinite delight of the Father in His Only-begotten is an infinite delight in all the members of His mystical body. I pray that you may feel the power of His resurrection in this respect, and become flooded with delight by the conviction that you are accepted, beloved, and delighted in by the Lord God. The resurrection will make your heart dance for joy if you fully see the pardon, justification, and acceptance which it guarantees to you. Oh, that the Holy Spirit may now take of the things of Christ's resurrection, and apply them to us with justifying power!

III. Thirdly, let us now notice THE LIFE-GIVING POWER OF THE RESURRECTION OF CHRIST. This will be seen if we perceive that *our Lord has life in Himself.* I showed you this just now, in the fact that He raised Himself from the dead. He took up the life which He laid down. He only hath immortality, essential and underived. Remember how He said, "I am the resurrection and the life." Do not say, "I believe in Christ, and desire life." You have it. Christ and life are not two things. He says, "I am the resurrection and the life." If you have Jesus Christ, you have the resurrection. Oh, that you might now realize what power lies in Him who is the resurrection and the life! All the power there is in Christ is there for His people. "It pleased the Father that in Him should all fulness dwell," and "of His fulness have all we received." Christ has a life in Himself, and He makes that life to flow into every part of His mystical body, according to His own word, "Because I live, ye shall live also." Triumph, therefore, that you possess as a believer this day that same life which is inherent in the person of your glorious covenant Head.

Moreover, *our Lord has power to quicken whom He will.* If the Lord Jesus Christ will this morning speak to the most clay-cold heart in this assembly, it will glow with heavenly life. If the salvation of souls depended upon the preacher, nobody would be saved;

but when the preacher's Master comes with him, however feeble his utterance, the life flashes forth, and the dead are raised. See how the dry bones come together! Behold how, at the coming of the divine wind, they stand upon their feet an exceeding great army! Our risen Redeemer is the Lord and Giver of life. What joy to Christian workers is found in the life-giving power of the resurrection! The warrant of Jesus will run through the domain of death and set dead Lazarus free. Where is He this morning? Lord, call Him!

This life, whenever it is imparted, is new life. In reading the four evangelists, have you never noticed the difference between Jesus after resurrection and before? A French divine has written a book entitled "The Life of Jesus Christ in Glory." When I bought it, I hardly knew what the subject might be; but I soon perceived that it was the life of Jesus on earth after He was risen from the dead. That was, indeed, a glorious life. He feels no more suffering, weakness, weariness, reproach, or poverty: He is no more cavilled at or opposed by men. He is in the world, but He scarcely seems to touch it, and it does not at all touch Him. He was of another world, and only a temporary sojourner on this globe, to which He evidently did not belong. When we believe in Jesus, we receive a new life, and rise to a higher state. The spiritual life owes nothing to the natural life: it is from another source, and tends in another direction. The old life bears the image of the first and earthy Adam; the second life bears the image of the second and heavenly Adam. The old life remains, but becomes to us a kind of death: the new life which God gives is the true life, which is part of the new creation, and links us to the heavenly and divine. To this, I say, the old life is greatly opposed; but that evil life gets not the upper hand. Wonderful is the change wrought by the new birth! Faculties that were in you before are purged and elevated; but, at the same time, new spiritual faculties are conferred, and a new heart and a right spirit are put within us. Wonder at this—that the risen Christ is able to give us an entirely new life. May you know, in this respect, the power of His resurrection! May you know the peace, the repose, the power of your risen Lord! May you, like Him, be a stranger here, soon expecting to depart unto the Father! Before His death our Lord was straitened, because His work was unaccomplished: after His death He was at ease, because His work was done. Brethren, we may enter into His rest, for we are complete in Him! We are working for our Lord, as He was for His Father during the forty days; but yet the righteousness in which we are accepted is finished, and therefore we find rest in Him.

Once more, *the resurrection of Christ is operating at this present time with a quickening power on all who hear the Word aright.* The sun is, to the vegetable world, a great quickener. In this month of April he goes forth with life in his beams, and we see the result. The buds are bursting, the trees are putting on their summer dress, the flowers are smiling, and even the seeds which lie buried in the earth are beginning to feel the vivifying warmth: they see not the lord of day, but they feel his smile. Over what an enormous territory is the returning sun continually operating! How potent are his forces when he crosses the line and lengthens the day! Such is the risen Christ. In the grave He was like the sun in his winter solstice, but He crossed the line in His resurrection; He has brought us all the hopes of spring, and is bringing us the joys of summer. He is quickening many at this hour, and will yet quicken myriads. This is the power with which the missionary goes forth to sow; this is the power in which the preacher at home continues to scatter the seed. The risen Christ is the great harvest-producer. By the power of His resurrection men are raised from their death in sin to eternal life.

I said eternal life, for *wherever Jesus gives life, it is everlasting life.* "Christ being risen from the dead, dieth no more; death hath no more dominion over Him"; and as we have been raised in the likeness of His resurrection, so are we raised into a life over which death has no more dominion. We shall not die again, but the water which Jesus gives us shall be in us a well of water springing up into everlasting life.

I wish I could venture further to unveil this secret force, and still more fully reveal to you the power of our Lord's resurrection. It is the power of the Holy Ghost; it is the energy upon which you must depend when teaching or preaching; it must all be "according to the working of His mighty power, which He wrought in Christ, when He raised Him from the dead." I want you to feel that power to-day. I would have you feel eternal life throbbing in your bosoms, filling you with glory and immortality. Are you feeling cast down? Are your surroundings like those of a charnel-house? When you return will you seem to go home to endure the rottenness and corruption of profanity and lewdness? Your remedy will lie in eternal life flooding you with its torrents, and bearing you above these evil influences. May you not only have life, but have it more abundantly, and so be vigorous enough to throw off the baneful influences of this evil world!

IV. The last point is THE CONSOLING POWER OF THE RESURRECTION OF CHRIST.

This consoling power should be felt *as to all departed saints.* We are often summoned to the house of mourning in this church; for we seldom pass a week without one or two deaths of beloved ones. Here is our comfort—Jesus says, "Thy dead men shall live, together with My dead body shall they arise."

"As the Lord our Saviour rose
So all His followers must."

He is the first-fruits from among the dead. The cemeteries are crowded, precious dust is closely heaped together; but as surely as Jesus rose from the tomb of Joseph, all those who are in Him shall rise also. Though bodies may be consumed in the fire, or ground to powder, or sucked up by plants, and fed upon by animals, or made to pass through ten thousand changeful processes, yet difficulties there are none where there is a God. He that gave us bodies when we had none, can restore those bodies when they are pulverized and scattered to the four winds. We sorrow not as those that are without hope. We know where the souls of the godly ones are: they are "for ever with the Lord." We know where their bodies will be when the clarion blast shall wake the dead, and the sepulchre shall give up its spoils. Sweet is the consolation which comes to us from the empty tomb of Jesus. "God hath both raised up the Lord, and will also raise up us by His own power."

Here, too, is comfort in our inward deaths. In order that we should know the resurrection of Christ, we must be made conformable unto His death. Have we not to die many deaths? Have you ever felt the sentence of death in yourself that you might not trust in yourself? Have you not seen all your fancied beauty decay, and all your strength wither "like the leaves of the forest when autumn has blown"? Have not all your carnal hopes perished, and all your resolves turned to dust? If any of you are undergoing that process to-day, I hope you will go through with it, till the sword of the Spirit has slain you; for you must die before you can be raised from the dead. If you are undergoing the process of crucifixion with Christ, which means a painful, lingering death within, remember that this is the needful way to resurrection. How can you know your Lord's resurrection except by knowing His death? You must be buried with Him to rise with Him. Is not this sweet consolation for a bitter experience?

I think there is here great consolation for *those of us who mourn because the cause of Christ seems to be in an evil case.* I may say to the enemy, "This is your hour, and the power of darkness." Alas! I cry with the holy woman, "They have taken away my Lord, and I know not where they have laid Him!" In many a pulpit the precious blood no longer speaks. They have taken the heart out of the doctrine of propitiation, and left us nothing but the name of it. Their false philosophy has overlaid the gospel, and crushed out its life, so far as they are concerned. They boast that we are powerless: our protest is despised, error shows her brazen forehead, and seizes the strongholds of truth. Yet we despair not; nay, we do not even fear. If the cause of Christ were dead and buried, and the wise men had fixed the stone, and set their seal, and appointed their guards, yet, at the appointed hour, the Lord's truth would rise again. I am not uneasy about ultimate issues. The mischief for the time being grieves me; but the Lord will yet avenge His own elect, which cry day and night unto Him. Jesus must live if they kill Him; He must rise if they bury Him: herein lieth our consolation.

This truth affords choice consolation *to persecuted saints.* In Paul's day to be a Christian was a costly matter. Imprisonment was the lightest of their trials: stripes and tortures of every kind were their portion. "Christians to the lions!" was the cry heard in the amphitheatre; and nothing pleased the people better, unless it was to see saints of God smeared with pitch from head to foot, and set on fire. Did they not call themselves the lights of the world? Such were the brutal pleasantries of the Romans. Here was the backbone of saintly comfort —they would rise again and share in the glory of their Lord for ever. Though they might find a living grave between a lion's jaws, they would not be destroyed: even the body would live again, for Jesus lived again, even the Crucified One in whom they trusted.

My brethren, my text is like a honeycomb dripping with honey. It has in it comfort for the ages to come. *There will be a living issue for these dead times.* Do you see that train steaming along the iron way? See, it plunges into a cavern in yonder hill! You have now lost sight of it. Has it perished? As on an angel's wing, you fly to the top of the hill, and you look down on the other side. There it comes steaming forth again from the tunnel, bearing its living freight to its destined terminus. So, whenever you see the church of God apparently plunging into a cavern of disaster or a grave of defeat, think not that the spirit of the age has swallowed it up. Have faith in God! The truth will be uppermost yet.

"The might with the right,
And the right with the might shall be:
And, come what there may
To stand in the way,
That day the world shall see."

The opposition of men might have proved a dark den in which the cause of God should have been hopelessly buried; but in the resurrection of our Lord we see a cavern turned into a tunnel, and a way pierced through death itself. "Who art thou, O great mountain?" The Alps are pierced; God's way is made clear; He triumphs over all difficulties. "The glory of the Lord shall be revealed, and all flesh shall see it together: for the mouth of the Lord hath spoken it."

That is my close. I desire that you should feel resurrection power. We have many technical Christians, who know the phrases of godliness, but know not the power of godliness. We have ritualistic Christians, who stickle for the outward, but know not the power. We have many moral religionists, but they also know not the power. We are pestered with conventional, regulation Christians. Oh, yes, no doubt we are Christians; but we are not enthusiasts, fanatics, nor even as this bigot. Such men have a name to live, and are dead. They have a form of godliness, but deny the power of it. I pray you, my hearers, be not content with a truth till you feel the force of it. Do not praise the spiritual food set before you, but eat of it till you know its power to nourish. Do not even talk of Jesus till you know His power to save. God grant that you may know the powers of the world to come, for Jesus' sake! Amen.

ONWARD!

"Brethren, I count not myself to have apprehended: but this one thing I do, forgetting those things which are behind, and reaching forth unto those things which are before, I press toward the mark for the prize of the high calling of God in Christ Jesus."—Philippians iii. 13, 14.

SO far as his acceptance with God is concerned a Christian is complete in Christ as soon as he believes. Those who have trusted themselves in the hands of the Lord Jesus are saved: and they may enjoy holy confidence upon the matter, for they have a divine warrant for so doing. "There is therefore now no condemnation to them that are in Christ Jesus." To this salvation the apostle had attained. But while the work of Christ for us is perfect, and it were presumption to think of adding to it, the work of the Holy Spirit in us is not perfect, it is continually carried on from day to day, and will need to be continued throughout the whole of our lives. We are being "conformed to the image of Christ," and that process is in operation, as we advance towards glory. The condition in which a believer should always be found is that of progress: his motto must be, "Onward and upward!" Nearly every figure by which Christians are described in the Bible implies this. We are plants of the Lord's field, but we are sown that we may grow—"First the blade, then the ear, then the full corn in the ear." We are born into the family of God; but there are babes, little children, young men, and fathers in Christ Jesus; yea, and there are a few who are perfect or fully developed men in Christ Jesus. It is a growth evermore. Is the Christian described as a pilgrim? He is no pilgrim who sits down as if rooted to the place. "They go from strength to strength." The Christian is compared to a warrior, a wrestler, a competitor in the games: these figures are the very opposite of a condition in which nothing more is to be done. They imply energy, the gathering up of strength, and the concentration of forces, in order to the overthrowing of adversaries. The Christian is also likened to a runner in a race, and that is the figure now before us in the text. It is clear that a man cannot be a runner who merely holds his ground, contented with his position: he only runs aright who each moment nears the mark. Progress is the healthy condition of every Christian man; and he only realizes his best estate while he is growing in grace, "adding to his faith virtue," "following on to know the Lord," and daily receiving grace for grace out of the fulness which is treasured up in Christ Jesus.

Now, to this progress the apostle exhorts us—nay, he does more than exhort, he allures us. He stands among us; he does not lecture us *ex cathedra*, standing like a learned master far above his disciples, but he puts himself on our level, and though not a whit behind the very chief of the apostles, he says, "Brethren, I count not myself to have apprehended." He does not give us the details of his own imperfections and deficiencies, but in one word he confesses them in the gross, and then declares that he burned with eager desire for perfection, so that it was the one passion of his soul to press onward towards the great goal of his hopes, the prize of his high calling in Christ Jesus. We cannot desire to have a better instructor than a man who sympathizes with us because he humbly considers himself to be of the same rank as ourselves. Teaching us to run, the apostle himself runs; wishing to fire our holy ambition, he bears testimony to that same ambition flaming within his own spirit. I desire so to speak from this text that every believer may pant for progress in the divine life.

Paul's statements in the text call us to look at him under four aspects: first, as *forming a just estimate of his present condition*—"Brethren, I count not myself to have apprehended;" secondly, as *placing his past in its proper position*—"forgetting the things which are behind;" thirdly, as *aspiring eagerly to a more glorious future*—"reaching forth unto those things which are before;" and fourthly, as *practically putting forth every exertion to obtain that which he desired*—"I press toward the mark for the prize of the high calling of God in Christ Jesus."

First, admire our apostle as PUTTING A JUST ESTIMATE UPON HIS PRESENT CONDITION.

He was not one of those who consider the state of the believer's heart to be a trifling matter. He was not indifferent as to his spiritual condition. He says, "I count,"—as if he had taken stock, had made a careful estimate, and had come to a conclusion. He is not a wise man who says, "I am a believer in Christ, and therefore it little matters what are my inward feelings and experience." He who so speaks should remember that keeping the heart with all diligence is a precept of inspiration, and that a careless walk usually comes to a very sorrowful ending. The

apostle did take account; but when he had done so he was dissatisfied: "I count not myself to have apprehended." Nor was that dissatisfaction to be regretted: it was a sign of true grace, a conclusion which is always arrived at when saints judge themselves rightly. Most weighty is that word of Chrysostom, "He who thinks he has obtained everything, hath nothing." Had Paul been satisfied with his attainments he would never have sought for more. Most men cry "hold," when they think they have done enough. The man who could honestly write, "I press forward," you may be quite sure was one who felt that he had not yet apprehended all that might be gained. Self-satisfaction rings the death-knell of progress. There must be a deep-seated discontent with present attainments, or there will never be a striving after the things which are yet beyond.

Now, beloved, remark, that the man who in our text tells us that he had not apprehended was a man vastly superior to any of us. Among them that were born of women there has never lived a greater than Paul the apostle; in sufferings for Christ a martyr of the first class; in ministry for Christ an apostle of foremost degree. Where shall I find such a man for revelations? for he had been caught up into the third heaven, and heard words which it was not lawful for him to utter. Where shall I find his match for character? a character splendidly balanced, as nearly approximating to that of his divine Master as we may well expect to see in mortal men. Yet, after having duly considered the matter, this notable saint said, "I count not myself to have apprehended." Shame, then, on any of us poor dwarfs if we are so vain as to count that we have apprehended! Shame upon the indecent self-conceit of any man who congratulates himself upon his own spiritual condition, when Paul himself said, "Not as though I had already attained, either were already perfect." The injury which self-content will do a man it would be hard to measure, it is the readiest way to stunt him, and the surest method to keep him weak. I should be sorry indeed if I should be addressing one who imagines that he has apprehended, for his progress in grace is barred from this time forth. The moment a man says, "I have it," he will no longer try to obtain it; the moment he cries, "It is enough," he will not labour after more.

Yet, brethren, far too often of late have I come across the path of those who speak as if they have apprehended,—brethren whose own lips praise them, who descant upon their own fulness of grace, with an unction rather too unctuous for my taste. I am not about to condemn them; I cannot say I am not about to censure them, for I intend to do so, from a deep sense of the necessity that they should be censured. These friends assure us that they have reached great heights of grace, and are now in splendid spiritual condition. I should be very glad to know that it is so, if it were true; but I am grieved to hear them act as witnesses for themselves, for then I know that their witness is not true; if it were so, they would be the last men to publish it abroad. There are brethren abroad, whose eminent graciousness is not very clear to others, but it is very evident to themselves; and equally vivid is their apprehension of the great inferiority of most of their brethren. They talk to us, not as men of like passions with ourselves and brethren of the same stock, but as demigods, thundering out of the clouds, giants discoursing to the little men around them. If it be true that they are so superior, I rejoice, yea, and will rejoice; but my suspicion is, that their glorying is not good, and that the spirit which they manifest will prove a snare to them. I meet, I say, sometimes with brethren who feel contented with their spiritual condition. They do not ascribe their satisfactory character to themselves, but to the grace of God; but for all that, they do feel that they are what they ought to be, and what others ought to be but are not. They see in themselves a great deal that is good, very much that is commendable, and a large amount of excellence, which they can hold up for the admiration of others. They have reached the "higher life," and are wonderfully fond of telling us so, and explaining the phenomena of their self-satisfied condition. Though Paul was compelled to say, " In me, that is, in my flesh, there dwelleth no good thing," their flesh appears to be of a better quality: whereas he had spiritual conflicts, and found that without were fightings, and within were fears, these very superior persons have already trodden Satan under their feet, and reached a state in which they have little else to do but to divide the spoil. Now, brethren, whenever we meet with persons who can congratulate themselves upon their personal character, or whenever we get into the state of self-content ourselves, there is an ill savour about the whole concern. I do not know what impression it makes upon you, but whenever I hear a brother talk about himself, and how full he is of the Spirit of God, and all that, I am distressed for him. I think I hear the voice of that stately professor, who said, "God, I thank Thee that I am not as other men are." I feel that I would prefer to listen to that other man, who said, "God be merciful to me a sinner," and went down to his house justified rather than the other. When I hear a man crow about himself, I think of Peter's declaration—"Though all men should deny Thee, yet will not I," and I hear another cock crow. Self-complacency is the mother of spiritual declension. David said, "My mountain standeth firm: I shall never be moved;" but ere long the face of God was hidden and he was troubled. In the presence of a professor who is pleased with his own attainments, one remembers that warning text: "Let him that thinketh he standeth, take heed lest he fall." Great I! great I! wherever thou art, thou must come down. Great I is always opposed to great Christ. John the Baptist knew the truth when he said, ''He must increase, but I must decrease." There is no room in this world for God's glory and man's glory. He who is less than nothing, magnifies God; but he "who is rich, and increased in goods, and hath need of nothing," dishonours God, and he himself "is naked and poor and miserable."

Furthermore, we have observed that the best of men do not talk of their attainments; their tone is self-depreciation, not self-content. We have known some eminently holy men, who are now in heaven, and in looking back upon their lives we note that they were never conscious of being what we all thought them to be. Everybody could see their beauty of character except themselves. *They* lamented their imperfections while *we* admired the grace of God in them. I remember a minister of Christ, now with God—I will not mention his name—if I did, it would be familiar to your ears as household words; it was proposed by some of us, when he left the ministry in his old age, that we should hold a meeting to bid him farewell, and testify our esteem for him. It was my duty to propose the fraternal act, but I hesitated as I saw the blush mantle his cheek, and I paused when

he rose and besought us never to think of such a thing, for he felt himself to be one of the most unworthy of all the servants of the Lord. Every man of the associated ministers that day assembled, felt that our venerable friend was by far the superior of us all, and yet his own estimate of himself was lowliest of the lowly. He had sacrificed much, but I never heard him speak of his sacrifices; he lived in habitual fellowship with God, but I never heard him declare it, much less glory in it. Shallow streams brawl and babble, but deep waters flow on in silence. Of all the departed saints whom it has been my lot to esteem highly in love for their works' sake, I do not remember one who dared to praise himself, though I can recollect several poor little spiritual babes who did so to their own injury. If ever true saints speak of what God has done by them, they do it in such a modest way that you might think they were talking of some one five hundred miles away, rather than of themselves. They have scrupulously laid all their crowns at the Saviour's feet, not in word only, but in spirit. When I remember these sacred names of the great departed, I feel it hard to have patience with the unspiritual, unholy boastings of personal holiness and high spirituality, which are getting common in these days. Drums make much noise, but we know by observation that it is not their fulness which makes the sound.

Again, we have noticed that we ourselves, in our own holiest moments, do not feel self-complacent. Whenever we get near to God, and really enter into fellowship with Him, the sensations we feel are the very reverse of self-congratulation. Job, in this, was the type of every believing man. Till he saw God he spoke up for his own innocence, and defended himself against the charges of his friends; but when the Lord revealed Himself to him, he said, " Mine eye seeth *Thee*, therefore I abhor myself and repent in dust and ashes." We never see the beauty of Christ without at the same time perceiving our own deformity. When we neglect prayer and self-examination we grow mighty vain fellows, but when we live near to God in private devotion and heart-searching, we put off our ornaments from us. In the light of God's countenance we perceive our many flaws and imperfections, and instead of saying, " I am clean," we cry out, "Woe is me, for I am a man of unclean lips." Now if this be our own experience we infer from it that those who think well of themselves must know little of that revealing light which humbles all who dwell in it.

My observation of personal character has been somewhat wide, and I cannot help bearing my testimony that I am greatly afraid of men who make loud professions of superior sanctity. I have had the misfortune to have known, on one or two occasions, superfine brethren, who were, in their own ideas, far above the rest of us, and almost free from human frailties. I confess to have felt very much humbled by their eminent goodness until I found them out: they talked of complete sanctification, of a faith which never staggered, of an old nature entirely dead, until I wondered at them; but I wondered more when I found that all the while they were rotten at the core, were negligent of common duties while boasting of the loftiest spirituality, and were even immoral while they condemned others for comparative trifles. I have now become very suspicious of all who cry up their own wares. I had rather have a humble, timid, fearful, watchful, self-depreciating Christian to be my companion, than any of the religious exquisites who crave our admiration. These great-winged eagles who fly so loftily will, I fear, turn out to be unclean birds. The excessive verdure of a superfinely flourishing religiousness often covers a horrible bog of hypocrisy.

Let me add, once more, that whatever shape self-satisfaction may assume—and it bears a great many—it is at bottom nothing but a shirking of the hard-ship of Christian soldierhood. The Christian soldier has to fight with sins every day, and if he be a man of God, and God's Spirit is in him, he will find he wants all the strength he has, and a great deal more, to maintain his ground and make progress in the divine life. Now, self-contentment is a shirking of the battle, I do not care how it is come by. Some people shirk watchfulness, repentance, and holy care, by believing that the only sanctification they need is already theirs by imputation. They use the work of the Lord Jesus *for* them as though it could thrust away the necessity of the Spirit's work *in* them. Personal holiness they will not hear of: it is legal. If they come across such a text as "Without holiness no man shall see the Lord;" or, "Be not deceived, God is not mocked, whatsoever a man soweth that shall he also reap," they straightway force another meaning upon it, or else forget it altogether. Another class believe that they have perfection in the flesh, while a third attain to the same complacent condition by the notion that they have overcome all their sins by believing that they have done so; as if believing your battles to be won was the same thing as winning them. This, which they call faith, I take the liberty to call a lazy, self-conceited presumption; and though they persuade themselves that their sins are dead, it is certain that their carnal security is vigorous enough, and highly probable that the rest of their sins are only keeping out of the way to let their pride have room to develop itself to ruinous proportions.

You can reach self-complacency by a great many roads. I have known enthusiasts reach it by sheer intoxication of excitement, while Antinomians come at it by imagining that the law is abolished, and that what is sin in others is not sin in saints. There are theories which afford an evil peace to the mind by throwing all blame of sin upon fate, and others which lower the standard of God's demands so as to make them reachable by fallen humanity. Some dream that a mere dead faith in Jesus will save them, let them live as they list; and others that they are already as good as need be.

Many have fallen into the same condition by another error, for they have said, "Well, we cannot conquer all sin, and therefore we need not aim at it. Some of our sins are constitutional, and will never be got rid of." Under these evil impressions they sit down and say, "It is well, O soul, thou art in an excellent condition; sit still and take thine ease, there is little more to be done, there is no need to attempt more." All this is evil to the last degree.

I have used few theological terms, because it does not matter how we get to be self-satisfied, whether by an orthodox or a heterodox mode of reasoning; it is a mischievous thing in any case. The fact is, my brother, the Lord calls us to this high calling of con-tending with sin within and without until we die; and it is of no use our mincing the matter, we must fight if we would reign; our sins will have to be contended with till our dying day, and probably we shall have to fight upon our death-bed. Therefore, every day we are bound to be upon our watch-tower against sin around and within us. It is of no use our deluding ourselves with pretty theories, which act only as spiritual opium to cause unhealthy dreams. Sin is a real thing with each one of us, and must be daily wrestled with; there is an evil heart of unbelief within us, and the devil without us, and we must watch, and pray, and cry mightily, and strive, and struggle, and own that we have not yet apprehended. If we dream that we are at the goal already, we shall stop short of the prize. The full soul loatheth the honeycomb; a man full of self, cares for nothing more. Shake off these slothful bands, my brethren; quit you like men—be strong. You are as weak as others, and as likely to sin; watch, therefore, and pray, lest ye enter into temptation.

What is it, at bottom, that makes men contented with themselves? It may be, first of all, a forgetful-ness of the awful holiness of the law of God. If the law of the ten commandments is to be read only as its letter runs, I could imagine a man's judging himself and saying, "I have apprehended;?" but when we know that the law is spiritual, how can we be self-complacent? My dear brother, if thou thinkest thou hast reached its perfect height, I ask thee to hear these words: "Thou shalt love the Lord thy God with all thy heart, with all thy soul, with all thy mind, and with all thy strength, and thy neighbour as thyself." Canst thou say, in the sight of a heart-searching God, "I have fulfilled all that"? If you can, I am staggered at you, and think you the victim of a strong delusion, which leads you to believe a lie.

Brethren who can take delight in themselves must have lost sight of the heinousness of sin. The least sin is a desperate evil, an assault upon the throne of God, an insult to the majesty of heaven. The simple act of plucking the forbidden fruit cost us Paradise. There is a bottomless pit of sin in every transgression, a hell in every iniquity. If we keep clear of sins of action, and if our tongue be so bridled that we avoid every hasty and unadvised speech, yet do we not know that our thoughts and imaginations, our looks and longings of heart, have in them an infinity of evil? If, after having learned that sin can only be washed out by the death of the Son of God, and that even the flames of hell cannot make atonement for a single sin, a man can then say, "I am content with myself," it is to be feared that he has made a fatal mistake as to his own character.

Is there not a failure, in such cases, to understand the highest standard of Christian living? If we measure ourselves among ourselves, there are many believers here who might be pretty well satisfied. You are as generous as other Christians are, con-sidering your income. You are as prayerful as most other professors, and as earnest in doing good as any of your neighbours; if you are worldly, yet not more worldly than most professors, nowadays, and so you judge yourself not to be far below the standard. But what a standard! Let us seek a better. Brethren, it is a very healthy thing for us who are ministers to read a biography like that of M'Cheyne. Read that through, if you are a minister, and it will burst many of your wind-bags. You will find yourselves collapse most terribly. Take the life of Brainerd amongst the Indians, or of Baxter in our own land. Think of the holiness of George Herbert, the devoutness of Fletcher, or the zeal of Whitefield. Where do you find yourself after reading their lives? Might you not peep about to find a hiding-place for your insignificance? When we mix with dwarfs we think ourselves giants, but in the presence of giants we become dwarfs. When we think of the saints departed, and remember their patience in suffering, their diligence in labour, their ardour, their self-denial, their humility, their tears, their prayers, their midnight cries, their intercession for the souls of others, their pouring out their hearts before God for the glory of Christ, why, we shrink into less than nothing, and find no word of boasting on our tongue. If we survey the life of the only perfect One, our dear Lord and Master, the sight of His beauty covers our whole countenance with a blush. He is the lily, and we are the thorns. He is the sun, and we are as the night. He is all good, and we are all ill. In His presence we bow in the dust, we confess our sin, and count ourselves unworthy to unloose His shoelatchets.

It is to be feared that there is springing up in some parts of the Christian church a deceitful form of self-righteousness, which leads even good people to think too highly of themselves. It is a fashionable form of fanaticism, very pleasing to the flesh, very fascinating, and very deadly. Many, I fear, are not really living so near to God as they think they are, neither are they as holy as they dream. It is very easy to frequent Bible readings, and conferences, and excited public meetings, and to fill one's self with the gas of self-esteem. A little pious talk with a sort of Christians who always walk on high stilts will soon tempt you to use the stilts yourself; but indeed, dear brother, you are a poor, unworthy worm and a nobody, and if you get one inch above the ground, you get just that inch too high. Remember, you may think yourself to be very strong in a certain direction, because you do not happen to be tried on that point. Many of us are exceedingly good tempered when nobody provokes us. Some are wonderfully patient, because they have a sound constitution, and have no racking pains to endure; and others are exceedingly generous because they have more money than they want. A ship's seaworthiness is never quite certain till she has been out at sea. The grand thing will be to be sound before the living God in the day of trial. I pray every believer here to get off the high horse, and to remember that he is "naked and poor and miserable" apart from Christ, and only in Jesus Christ is he anything, and that if he thinketh himself to be something when he is nothing, he deceiveth himself, but does not deceive God.

II. In the second place, look at Paul as PLACING THE PAST IN ITS TRUE LIGHT. He says, "Forgetting those things which are behind." What does he mean? Paul does not mean that he forgot the mercy of God which he had enjoyed; far from it. Paul does not mean that he forgot the sins which he had committed; far from it, he would always remember them to humble him. We must follow out the figure which he is using and so read him. When a man ran in the Grecian games, if he had run half way, and passed most of his fellows, and had then turned to look round and to rejoice over the distance which he had already covered, he would have lost the race. Suppose he had commenced singing his own praises, and said, "I have come down the hill, along the valley, and up the rising ground on this side. See, there are one, two, three, four, five, six runners far behind me." While thus praising himself he would lose the race. The only hope for the racer was to forget all that was behind, and occupy his entire thoughts with the piece of ground which lay in front. Never mind though you have run so far, you must let the space which lies between you and the goal engross all your thoughts and command all your powers. It must be so with regard to all sins which we have overcome. Perhaps at this moment you might honestly say, "I have overcome a very fierce temper," or, "I have bestirred my naturally indolent spirit." Thank God for that. Stop long enough to say, "Thank God for that," but do not pause to congratulate yourselves as though some great thing had been done, for then it may soon be undone. Perhaps the very moment you are rejoicing over your conquered temper it will leap back upon you, like a lion from the covert, and you will say, "I thought you were dead and buried, and here you are roaring at me again." The very easiest way to give resurrection to old corruptions is to erect a trophy over their graves; they will at once lift up their heads and howl out, "We are alive still." It is a great thing to overcome any sinful habit, but it is needful to guard against it still, for you have not conquered it so long as you congratulate yourself upon the conquest. In the same light we must regard all the grace we have obtained. I know some dear friends who are mighty in prayer, and my soul rejoices to join in their supplications; but I should be sorry indeed to hear them praise their own prayers. We love yonder brother for his generosity, but we hope he will never tell others that he is liberal; yonder dear friend is very humble, but if he were to boast of it, there would be an end of it. Self-esteem is a moth which frets the garments of virtue. Those flies, those pretty flies of self-praise, must be killed, for if they get into your pot of ointment they will spoil it all. Forget the past; thank God who has made you pray so well; thank God who has made you kind, gentle, or humble; thank God who has made you give liberally; but forget it all and go forward, since there is yet very much land to be possessed!

And so with all the work for Jesus which we have done. Some people seem to have very good memories as to what they have performed. They used to serve God wonderfully when they were young! They began early and were full of zeal! They can tell you all about it with much pleasure. In middle life they wrought marvels, and achieved great wonders; but now they rest on their oars, they are giving other people an opportunity to distinguish themselves— their own heroic age is over. Dear brother, as long as ever you are in this world forget what you have already done, and go forward to other service! Living on the past is one of the faults of old churches. We, for instance, as a church, may begin to congratulate ourselves upon the great things God has done by us, for we shall be sure to put it in that pretty shape, although we shall probably mean the great things we have done ourselves. After praising ourselves thus we shall gain no further blessing, but shall decline by little and little. The same is true of denominations. What acclamations are heard when allusion is made to what our fathers did! Oh, the name of Carey, and Knibb, and Fuller! We Baptists think we have nothing to do now but to go upstairs and go to bed, for we have achieved eternal glory through the names of these good men; and as for our Wesleyan friends, how apt they are to harp upon Wesley, Fletcher, Nelson, and other great men! Thank God for them: they were grand men; but the right thing is to forget the past, and pray for another set of men to carry on the work. We should never be content, but, "On, on, on," should be our cry! When they asked Napoleon why he continually made wars, he said, "I am the child of war; conquest has made me what I am, and conquest must maintain me." The Christian church is the child of spiritual war; she only lives as she fights, and rides forth conquering and to conquer. God deliver us from the self-congratulatory spirit, however it may come, and make us long and pine after something better!

III. And now the third point. Paul, having put the present and past into their right places, goes on to the future, ASPIRING EAGERLY TO MAKE IT GLORIOUS; for he says, "reaching forth unto those things which are before." Does he not here give us the picture of a runner? He reaches forth. The man, as he speeds, throws himself forward, almost out of the perpendicular. His eye is at the goal already. His hand is far in advance of his feet, the whole body is leaning forward; he runs as though he would project himself to the end of the journey before his legs can carry him there. That is how the Christian should be; always throwing himself forward after something more than he has yet reached, not satisfied with the rate at which he advances, his soul always going at twenty times the pace of the flesh. John Bunyan gives us a little parable of a man on horseback. He is bidden by his master to ride in a hurry to fetch the physician. But the horse is a sorry jade. "Well," saith Bunyan, "but if his master sees that the man on the horse's back is whipping and spurring, and pulling the bridle, and struggling with all his might, he judges that the man would go if he could." That is how the Christian should always be, not only as devout, earnest, and useful as he can be, but panting to be a great deal more so, spurring this old flesh and striving against this laggard spirit if perchance he can do more. Brethren, we ought to be reaching forward to be like Jesus. Never may we say, "I am like so-and-so, and that is enough." Am I like Jesus, perfectly like Jesus? If not, away, away, away from everything I am or have been; I cannot rest until I am like my Lord. The aim of the Christian is to be perfect: if he seeks to be anything less than perfect, he aims at an object lower than that which God has placed before him. To master every sin, and to have and possess and exhibit every virtue,— this is the Christian's ambition. He who would be a great artist must not follow low models. The artist must have a perfect model to copy; if he does not reach to it, he will reach far further than if he had an inferior model to work by. When a man once realizes his own ideal, it is all over with him. A great painter once had finished a picture, and he said to his wife with tears in his eyes, "It is all over with me, I shall never paint again, I am a ruined man." She enquired, "Why"? "Because," he says, "that painting contents and satisfies me; it realizes my idea of what painting ought to be, and therefore I am sure my power is gone, for that power lies in having ideals which I cannot reach, something yet beyond me which I am striving after." May none of us ever say, "I have reached my ideal, now I am what I ought to be, there is nothing beyond me." Perfection, brethren, absolute perfection, may God help us to strive after it! That is the model, "Be ye perfect, even as your Father which is in heaven is perfect." "Shall we ever reach it?" says one. Thousands and millions have reached it; there they are before the throne of God, their robes are washed and made white in the blood of the Lamb; and we shall possess the same, only let us be struggling after it by God's good help. Let every believer be striving, that in the details of

common life, in every thought, in every word, in every action, he may glorify God. This ought to be our object; if we do not reach it, it is that which we must press for,—that from morning light to evening shade we shall live unto God. Whether we eat or drink, or whatsoever we do, we should do all in the name of the Lord Jesus. This is what we are to seek after, praying always in the Holy Ghost to be sanctified wholly, spirit, soul, and body. "It is a wonderfully high standard," says one. Would you like me to lower it, brother? I should be very sorry to have it lowered for myself. If the highest degree of holiness were denied to any one of us, it would be a heavy calamity. Is it not the joy of a Christian to be perfectly like his Lord? Who would wish to stop short of it? To be obliged to live under the power of even the least sin for ever, would be a horrible thing! No, we never can be content short of perfection; we will reach forward towards that which is before.

IV. And now the apostle is our model, in the fourth place, because he PUTS FORTH ALL HIS EXERTIONS TO REACH THAT WHICH HE DESIRES. He says, "This one thing I do," as if he had given up all else, and addicted himself to one sole object—to aim to be like Jesus Christ. There were many other things Paul might have attempted, but he says, "this one thing I do." Probably Paul was a poor speaker: why did not he try to make himself a rhetorician? No; he came not with excellency of speech. But you tell me Paul was busy with his tent-making. I know he was; what with tent-making, preaching, and visiting, and watching night and day, he had more than enough to do, but all these were a part of his pursuit of the one thing, he was labouring perfectly to serve his Master, and to render himself up as a whole burnt-offering unto God. I invite every soul that has been saved by the precious blood of Christ, to gather up all its strength for this one thing, to cultivate a passion for grace, and an intense longing after holiness. Ah, if we could but serve God as God should be served, and be such manner of people as we ought to be in all holy conversation and godliness, we should see a new era in the church. The greatest want of the church at this day is holiness.

Why did Paul pursue holiness with such concentrated purpose? Because he felt God had called him to it. He aimed at the prize of his high calling. God had elected Paul to be a champion against sin. Selected to be Jehovah's champion, he felt that he must play the man. Moreover, it was "God in Christ Jesus" who made the choice, and as the apostle looked up and saw the mild face of the Redeemer, and marked the thorn-crown of the King of Sorrows, he felt he must overcome sin, and, though he had not yet apprehended, yet he felt he must press forward till he had apprehended that to which God in Christ had called him.

Moreover, the apostle saw his crown, the crown of life that fadeth not away, hanging bright before his eyes. What, said he, shall tempt me from that path of which yon crown is the end? Let the golden apples be thrown in my way; I cannot even look at them, nor stay to spurn them with my feet. Let the sirens sing on either side, and seek to charm me with their evil beauty, to leave the holy road; but I must not, and I will not. Heaven! Heaven! Heaven! is not this enough to make a man dash forward in the road thither? The end is glorious, what if the running be laborious? When there is such a prize to be had, who will grudge a struggle? Paul pressed forward towards the mark for the prize of his high calling in Christ Jesus. He felt he was a saved man, and he meant through the same grace to be a holy man. He longed to grasp the crown, and hear the "Well done, good and faithful servant," which his Master would award him at the end of his course. Brethren and sisters, I wish I could stir myself and stir you to a passionate longing after a gracious, consistent, godly life, yea, for an eminently, solidly, thoroughly devoted and consecrated life. You will grieve the Spirit if you walk inconsistently; you will dishonour the Lord that bought you; you will weaken the church; you will bring shame upon yourself. Even though you be "saved so as by fire," it will be an evil and a bitter thing to have in any measure departed from God. But to be always going onward, to be never self-satisfied, to be always labouring to be better Christians, to be aiming at the rarest sanctity, this shall be your honour, the church's comfort, and the glory of God. May the Lord help you to perfect holiness in the fear of God. Amen.

CITIZENSHIP IN HEAVEN

"For our conversation is in heaven; from whence also we look for the Saviour, the Lord Jesus Christ."—Philippians iii. 20.

THERE can be no comparison between a soaring seraph and a crawling worm. Christian men ought so to live that it were idle to speak of a comparison between them and the men of the world. It should not be a comparison but a contrast. No scale of degrees should be possible; the believer should be a direct and manifest contradiction to the unregenerate. The life of a saint should be altogether above, and out of the same list as the life of a sinner. We should compel our critics not to confess that moralists are good, and Christians a little better; but while the world is darkness, we should manifestly be light; and while the world lieth in the Wicked One, we should most evidently be of God, and overcome the temptations of that Wicked One. Wide as the poles asunder, are life and death, light and darkness, health and disease, purity and sin, spiritual and carnal, divine and sensual. If we were what we profess to be, we should be as distinct a people in the midst of this world, as a white race in a community of Ethiopians; there should be no more difficulty in detecting the Christian from the wordling than in discovering a sheep from a goat, or a lamb from a wolf. Alas! the Church is so much adulterated, that we have to abate our glorying, and cannot exalt her character as we would. "The precious sons of Zion, comparable to fine gold, how are they esteemed as earthen pitchers, the work of the hands of the potter!" O for the time when "our conversation shall be in heaven," and the ignoble life of the man, whose god is his belly and whose end is destruction, shall be rebuked by our unworldly, unselfish character. There should be as much difference between the worldling and the Christian as between hell and heaven, between destruction and eternal life. As we hope at last that there shall be a great gulf separating us from the doom of the impenitent, there should be here a deep and wide gulf between us and the ungodly. The purity of our character should be such that men must take knowledge of us that we are of another and superior race. God grant us more and more to be most clearly a chosen generation, a royal priesthood, a holy nation, a peculiar people, that we may shew forth the praises of Him who has called us out of darkness into His marvellous light.

Brethren, to-night I exhort you to holiness, not by the precepts of the law: not by the thunderings from Sinai; not by the perils or punishments which might fall upon you if you are unholy; but by the privileges to which you have been admitted. Gracious souls should only be urged by arguments from grace. Whips are for the backs of fools, and not for heirs of heaven. By the honourable citizenship which has been bestowed upon you, I shall beseech you to let your conversation be in heaven, and I shall urge that most prevailing argument, that the Lord Jesus Christ cometh, and therefore we should be as men that watch for our Lord, diligently doing service unto Him, that when He cometh He may say unto us, "Well done, good and faithful servants." I know that the grace which is in you will freely answer to such a plea.

Our text, I think, might be best translated thus —"Our citizenship is in heaven." The French translation renders it, "As for us, our burgess-ship is in the heavens." Doddridge paraphrases it, "But we converse as citizens of heaven, considering ourselves as denizens of the New Jerusalem, and only strangers and pilgrims upon earth."

I. The first idea which is suggested by the verse under consideration is this: if our citizenship be in heaven, then WE ARE ALIENS HERE; we are strangers and foreigners, pilgrims and sojourners in the earth, as all our fathers were. In the words of Sacred Writ "Here we have no continuing city," but "we desire a better country, that is an heavenly." Let us illustrate our position. A certain young man is sent out by his father to trade on behalf of the family: he is sent to America, and he is just now living in New York. A very fortunate thing it is for him that his citizenship is in England; that, though he lives in America and trades there, yet he is an alien, and does not belong to that afflicted nation; for he retains his citizenship with us on this side the Atlantic. Yet there is a line of conduct which is due from him to the country which affords him shelter, and he must see to it that he does not fail to render it. Since we are aliens, we must remember to behave ourselves as aliens should, and by no means come short in our duty. We are affected by the position of our temporary country. A person trading in New York or Boston, though a freeman of the city of London, will find himself very much affected by the trade of the Dis-United States; when the merchants of his city suffer, he will find himself suffering with them, the fluctuations of their money-market will affect his undertakings, and the stagnation of commerce will slacken his progress; but if prosperity should happily return, he will find that when the coffers of their merchants are getting full, his will be the better; and the happy development of trade will give buoyancy to his own ventures. He is not of the nation, and yet every trembling of the scale will affect him; he will prosper as that nation prospers, and he will suffer as that nation suffers; that is to say, not as a citizen, but as a trader. And so we in this country find that though we are strangers and foreigners on earth, yet we share all the inconveniences of the flesh. No exception is granted to us from the common lot of manhood. We are born to trouble, even as others, and have tribulation like the rest. When famine comes we hunger; and when war rages we are in danger; exposed to the same clime, bearing the same burning heat, or the same freezing cold; we know the whole train of ills, even as the citizens of earth know them. When God in mercy scatters liberally with both His hands the bounties of His providence, we take our share, though we are aliens, yet we live upon the good of the land, and share the tender mercies of the God of Providence. Hence we have to take some interest in it; and the good man, though he be a foreigner, will not live even a week in this foreign land without *seeking to do good* among the neighbours with whom he dwells. The good Samaritan sought not only the good of the Samaritan nation, but of the Jews. Though there was no sort of kinship among them (for the Samaritans were not, as we have often heard erroneously said, first cousins or relations to the Jews; not a drop of Jewish blood ever ran in the Samaritans' veins; they were strangers brought from Assyria; they had no relation to Abraham whatever) yet the good Samaritan, finding himself travelling between Jericho and Jerusalem, did good to the Jew, since he was in Judea. The Lord charged His people by His servant Jeremiah, "Seek the peace of the city whither I have caused you to be carried away captives, and pray unto the Lord for it: for in the peace thereof shall ye have peace." Since we are here, we must seek the good of this world. "To do good and to communicate forget not." "Love ye your enemies, and do good, and lend, hoping for nothing again; and your reward shall be great, and ye shall be the children of the Highest: for He is kind unto the unthankful and to the evil." We must do our utmost while we are here to bring men to Christ, to win them from their evil ways, to bring them to eternal life, and to make them, with us citizens of another and a better land; for, to tell the truth, we are here as recruiting sergeants for heaven; here to give men the enlisting money, to bind upon them the blood-red colours of the Saviour's service, to win them to King Jesus, that, by-and-bye, they may share His victories after having fought His battles.

Seeking the good of the country as aliens, we must also remember that it behoves aliens to *keep themselves very quiet.* What business have foreigners to plot against the government, or to intermeddle with the politics of a country in which they have no citizenship? An Englishman in New York had best be without a tongue just now; if he should criticize the courage of the generals, the accuracy of their despatches, or the genius of the President, he might meet with rather rough usage. He will be injudicious indeed, if he cannot leave America to the Americans. So, in this land of ours, when you and I are strangers, we must be orderly sojourners, submitting ourselves constantly to those that are in authority, leading orderly and peaceable lives, and, according to the command of the Holy Ghost through the apostle, "honouring all men, fearing God, honouring the king"; "submitting ourselves to every ordinance of man for the Lord's sake." I cannot say that I delight in political Christians; I fear that party-strife is a serious trial to believers, and I cannot

reconcile our heavenly citizenship with the schemes of the hustings and the riot of the polling-booth. You must follow your own judgment here, but for my part, I am a foreigner even in England, and as such, I mean to act. We are simply passing through this earth, and should bless it in our transit, but never yoke ourselves to its affairs. An Englishman may happen to be in Spain—he wishes a thousand things were different from what they are, but he does not trouble himself much about them: says he, "If I were a Spaniard I would see what I could do to alter this government, but, being an Englishman, let the Spaniards see to their own matters. I shall be back to my own country by-and-bye, and the sooner the better." So with Christians here; they are content very much to let the potsherds strive with the potsherds of the earth; their politics concern their own country, they do not care much about any other; as *men* they love liberty, and are not willing to lose it even in the lower sense; but, spiritually, their politics are spiritual, and as citizens they look to the interest of that divine republic to which they belong, and they wait for the time when, having patiently borne with the laws of the land of their banishment, they shall come under the more beneficent sway of him who reigns in glory, the King of kings, and Lord of lords. If it be possible, as much as lieth in you, live peaceably with all men, and serve your day and generation still, but build not your soul's dwelling place here, for all this earth must be destroyed at the coming of the fiery day.

Again, let us remember that as aliens *we have privileges as well as duties.* The princes of evil cannot draft us into their regiments; we cannot be compelled to do Satan's work. The king of this world may make his vassals serve him, but he cannot raise a conscription upon aliens. He may order out his troops to this villany, or to that dastard service, but the child of God claims an immunity from all the commands of Satan; let evil maxims bind the men that own their sway, we are free, and own not the prince of the power of the air. I know that men of this world say we must keep up appearances; we must be respectable; we must do as others do; we must swim with the tide; we must move with the crowd; but not so the upright believer: "No," says he, " do not expect me to fall in with your ways and customs; I am in Rome, but I shall not do as Rome does. I will let you see that I am an alien, and that I have rights as an alien, even here in this foreign land. I am not to be bound to fight your battles, nor march at the sound of your drums." Brethren, we are soldiers of Christ; we are enlisted in *His* army; and as aliens here, we are not to be constrained into the army of evil. Let lords and lands have what masters they will, let us be free, for Christ is our Master still. The seventy thousand whom God has reserved, will not bow the knee to Baal. Be it known unto thee, O world, that we will not serve thy gods, nor worship the image which thou hast set up. Servants of God we are, and we will not be in bondage unto men.

As we are free from the conscription of the State, we must remember, also, that we are *not eligible to its honours.* I know you will say that is not a privilege; but it is a great boon if looked at aright. An Englishman in New York is not eligible for the very prickly throne of the President; I suppose he could not well be made a governor of Massachusetts or any other State, and, indeed, he may be well content to renounce the difficulties and the honour too. So also, the Christian man here is not eligible to this world's honours. It is a very ill omen to hear the world clap its hands, and say "Well done" to the Christian man. He may begin to look to his standing, and wonder whether he has not been doing wrong when the unrighteous give him their approbation. "What, did I do wrong," said Socrates, "that yonder villain praised me just now?" And so may the Christian say, "What, have I done wrong, that So-and-so spoke well of me, for if I had done right he would not; he has not the sense to praise goodness, he could only have applauded that which suited his own taste." Christian men, ye must never covet the world's esteem; the love of this world is not in keeping with the love of God. "If any man love the world the love of the Father is not in him." Treat its smiles as you treat its threats, with quiet contempt. Be willing rather to be sneered at than to be approved, counting the cross of Christ greater riches than all the treasures of Egypt. O harlot world, it were a sad dishonour to be thy favorite. Tire they head and paint thy face, thou Jezebel, but thou art no friend of ours, nor will we desire thy hollow love. The men of this world were mad to raise us to their seats of honour, for we are aliens and citizens of another country. When the Pope sent a noted Protestant statesman a present of some silver goblets, he returned them with this answer—"The citizens of Zurich compel their judges to swear twice in the year that they will receive no presents from foreign princes, therefore take them back." More than twice in the year should the Christian resolve that he will not accept the smiles of this world, and will do no homage to its glory. "We fear the Greeks even when they bear gifts." Like the Trojans of old, we may be beguiled with presents even if unconquered in arms. Forswear then the grandeur and honour of this fleeting age. Say in life, what a proud cardinal said in death, "Vain pomp and glory of the world, I hate ye." Pass through Vanity-Fair without trading in its vanities; crying, in answer to their "What will ye buy?"—"We buy the truth." Take up the pilgrim's song and sing it always—

"The things eternal I pursue,
    And happiness beyond the view
        Of those who basely pant
    For things by nature felt and seen;
    Their honours, wealth, and pleasures mean,
        I neither have nor want.

Nothing on earth I call my own:
    A stranger to the world unknown,
        I all their goods despise;
    I trample on their whole delight,
    And seek a country out of sight,—
        A country in the skies."

Furthermore, as aliens, *it is not for us to hoard up this world's treasures*. Gentlemen, you who know the exchange of New York, would you hoard up any extensive amount of Mr. Chase's green backed notes? I think not. Those stamps which officiate in the States in lieu of copper coinage I should hardly desire to accumulate; perhaps the fire might consume them, or if not, the gradual process of wear and tear which they are sure to undergo might leave me penniless ere long. "No, sir," says the British trader, "I am an alien; I cannot very well accept payment in these bits of paper, they are very well for you; they will pass current in your state, but my riches must be riches in England, for I am going there to live directly; I must have solid gold, old English sovereigns, nothing else but these can make me rich." Brethren, so it is with us. If we are aliens, the treasures of this world are like those bits of paper, of little value in our esteem; and we should lay up our treasure in heaven, "where neither moth nor rust doth corrupt, and where thieves do not break through nor steal." The money of this world is not current in Paradise; and when we reach its blissful shore, if regret can be known, we shall wish that we had laid up more treasure in the land of our fatherhood, in the dear fatherland beyond the skies. Transport thy jewels to a safer country than this world; be thou rich toward God rather than before men. A certain minister, collecting for a chapel, called upon a rich merchant who generously gave him fifty pounds. As the good man was going out with sparkling eye at the liberality of the merchant, the tradesman opened a letter, and he said, "Stop a minute, I find by this letter I have lost this morning a ship worth six thousand pounds." The poor minister trembled in his shoes, for he thought the next word would be, "Let me have the fifty pound cheque back." Instead of it, it was "Let me have the cheque back a moment," and then taking out his pen he wrote him a cheque for five hundred pounds. "As my money is going so fast, it is well," said he, "to make sure of some of it, so I will put some of it in God's bank." The man, you doubt not, went his way astonished at such a way of dealing as this, but indeed that is just what a man should do, who feels he is an alien here, and his treasure is beyond the sky.

"There is my house and portion fair;
    My treasure and my heart are there,
        And my abiding home:
    For me my elder brethren stay,
    And angels beckon me away,
        And Jesus bids me come."

II. It is our comfort now to remind you that although aliens *on earth*, WE ARE CITIZENS IN HEAVEN.

What is meant by our being citizens in heaven? Why, first that *we are under heaven's government*. Christ the king of heaven reigns in our hearts; the laws of glory are the laws of our consciences; our daily prayer is, "Thy will be done on earth, as it is in heaven." The proclamations issued from the throne of glory are freely received by us, the decrees of the Great King we cheerfully obey. We are not without law to Christ. The Spirit of God rules in our mortal bodies, grace reigns through righteousness, and we wear the easy yoke of Jesus. O that He would sit as king in our hearts, like Solomon upon his throne of gold. Thine are we, Jesus, and all that we have; rule thou without a rival.

As citizens of the New Jerusalem, *we share heaven's honours*. The glory which belongs to beatified saints belongs to us, for we are already sons of God, already princes of the blood imperial; already we wear the spotless robe of Jesu's righteousness; already we have angels for our servitors, saints for our companions, Christ for our brother, God for our Father, and a crown of immortality for our reward. We share the honours of citizenship, for we have come to the general assembly and Church of the firstborn, whose names are written in heaven. "Beloved, now are we the sons of God, and it doth not yet appear what we shall be: but we know that, when He shall appear, we shall be like Him; for we shall see Him as He is."

As citizens, *we have common rights in all the property of heaven.* Those wide extensive plains we sung of just now are ours; ours yon harps of gold and crowns of glory; ours the gates of pearl and walls of chrysolite; ours the azure light of the city that needs no candle nor light of the sun; ours the river of the water of life, and the twelve manner of fruits which grow on the trees planted at the side thereof; there is nought in heaven that belongeth not unto us, for our citizenship is there. "Things present, nor things to come ; all are ours; and we are Christ's; and Christ is God's."

And as we are thus under heaven's government, and share its honours and partake of its possessions, so we to-day *enjoy its delights.* Do they rejoice over sinners that are born to God—prodigals that have returned? So do we. Do they chant the glories of triumphant grace? We do the same. Do they cast their crowns at Jesu's feet? Such honours as we have, we cast there too. Do they rejoice in Him? So also do we. Do they triumph, waiting for His second advent? By faith we triumph in the same. Are they to-night singing "Worthy the Lamb?" We also have sung the same tune, not to such glorious notes as theirs, but with as sincere hearts; with minstrelsy not quite so splendid, but we hope as sincere, for the Spirit gave us the music which we have, and the Spirit gave them the thunders of their acclamations before the throne. "Our citizenship is in heaven."

Brethren, we rejoice to know also that as the result of our being citizens, or rather I ought to have said as the cause of it, our *names are written in the roll* of heaven's free-men. When, at last, the list shall be read, our names shall be read too; for where Paul and Peter, where David and Jonathan, where Abraham and Jacob shall be found, we shall be found too; numbered with them we were in the divine purpose, reckoned with them we were in the purchase on the cross, and with them shall we sit down for ever at the tables of the blessed. The small and the great are fellow-citizens and of the same household. The babes and the perfect men are recorded in the same great registry, and neither death nor hell can erase a single name.

Our citizenship then is in heaven. We have not time to extend that thought. John Calvin says of this text, "It is a most abundant source of many exhortations, which it were easy for any one to elicit from it. We are not all Calvins; but even to our smaller capacities, the subject appears to be one not readily exhausted, but rich with unfathomable joy.

III. We must now come to our third point, which is, OUR CONVERSATION IS IN HEAVEN, our walk and acts are such as are consistent with our dignity *as citizens of heaven.* Among the old Romans, when a dastardly action was proposed it was thought a sufficient refusal to answer "Romanus sum,—I am a Roman." Surely it should be a strong incentive to every good thing if we can claim to be freemen of the Eternal City. Let our lives be conformed to the glory of our citizenship. In heaven they are holy, so must we be,—so are we if our citizenship is not a mere pretence. They are happy, so must we be rejoicing in the Lord always. In heaven they are obedient, so must we be, following the faintest monitions of the divine will. In heaven they are active, so should we be, both day and night praising

and serving God. In heaven they are peaceful, so should we find a rest in Christ and be at peace even now. In heaven they rejoice to behold the face of Christ, so should we be always meditating upon Him, studying His beauties, and desiring to look into the truths which He has taught. In Heaven they are full of love, so should we love one another as brethren. In heaven they have sweet communion one with another, so should we, who though many, are one body, be every one members one of the other. Before the throne they are free from envy and strife, ill-will, jealousy, emulation, falsehood, anger, so should we be: we should, in fact, seek while we are here to keep up the manners and customs of the good old fatherland, so that, as in Paris, the Parisian soon says, "There goes John Bull," so they should be able to say in this land, "There goes a heavenly citizen, one who is with us, and among us, but is not of us." Our very speech should be such that our citizenship should be detected. We should not be able to live long in a house without men finding out what we are. A friend of mine once went across to America, and landing I think at Boston, he knew nobody, but hearing a man say, when somebody had dropped a cask on the quay, "Look out there, or else you will make a Coggeshall job of it." He said, "You are an Essex man I know, for that is a proverb never used anywhere but in Essex: give me your hand"; and they were friends at once. So there should be a ring of true metal about our speech and conversation, so that when a brother meets us, he can say "You are a Christian, I know, for none but Christians speak like that, or act like that." "Thou also wast with Jesus of Nazareth, for thy speech bewrayeth thee." Our holiness should act as a sort of freemasonry by which we know how to give the grip to the stranger, who is not a real stranger, but a fellow-citizen with us, and of the household of faith. Oh! dear friends, wherever we wander, we should never forget our beloved land. In Australia, on the other side the world, or in the Cape of Good Hope, or wherever else we may be exiled, surely every Englishman's eye must turn to this fair island; and with all her faults, we must love her still. And surely let us be where we may, our eyes must turn to heaven; the happy land unstained by shadow of fault; we love her still, and love her more and more, praying for the time when our banishment shall expire, and we shall enter into our fatherland to dwell there for ever and ever. Shenstone says, "The proper means of increasing the love we bear our native country, is to reside some time in a foreign land." Sure am I that we who cry, "Woe is me, for I dwell in Mesech, and sojourn in the tents of Kedar!" are sure to add "Oh, that I had wings like a dove, for then would I fly away, and be at rest."

IV. The text says, "Our conversation is in heaven," and I think we may read it, as though it said, "OUR COMMERCE IS IN HEAVEN." We are trading on earth, but still the bulk of our trade is with heaven. We trade for trinkets in this land, but our gold and silver are in heaven. We commune with heaven, and how? Our trade is with heaven by *meditation ;* we often think of God our Father, and Christ our Brother; and, by the Spirit, the Comforter, we are brought in contemplative delight, to the general assembly and Church of the firstborn, whose names are written in heaven. Brethren, do not our *thoughts* sometimes burn within us, when we trade with that blessed land. When I have sent the ships of understanding and consideration to that land of Ophir, which is full of gold, and they have come back again laden with all manner of precious things, my thoughts have been enriched, my soul has longed to journey to that good land. Black and stormy art thou, O sea of death, but I would cross thee to reach that land of Havilah, which hath dust of gold. I know that he who is a Christian will never have his mind long off that better land. And do you know we sometimes trade with heaven in our *hymns?* They tell us of the Swiss soldiery in foreign countries, that there is a song which the band is forbidden to play, because it reminds them of the cowbells of their native hills. If the men hear it, they are sure to desert, for that dear old song revives before their eyes the wooden chalets and the cows, and the pastures of the glorious Alps, and they long to be away. There are some of our hymns that make us homesick, until we are hardly content to stop, and therefore, well did our poet end his song,

> " Filled with delight, my raptured soul,
> Can here no longer stay.
> Though Jordan's waves around us roll,
> Fearless we launch away."

I feel the spirit of Wesley, when he said—

> "O that we now might see our guide!
> O that the word were given!
> Come, Lord of hosts, the waves divide,
> And land us all in heaven."

In times of high, hallowed, heavenly harmony of praise, the songs of angels seem to come astray, and find their way down to us, and then our songs return with them, hand in hand, and go back to God's throne, through Jesus Christ.

We trade with heaven, I hope, too, not only thus by meditation, and by thought, and by song, but *by hopes and by loves.* Our love is toward that land. How heartily the Germans sing of the dear old fatherland; but they cannot, with all their Germanic patriotism, they cannot beat the genial glow of the Briton's heart, when he thinks of his fatherland too. The Scotchman, too, wherever he may be, remembers the land of "brown heath and shaggy wood." And the Irishman, too, let him be where he will, still thinks the "Emerald Isle" the first gem of the sea. It is right that the patriot should love his country. Does not our love fervently flame towards heaven? We think we cannot speak well enough of it, and indeed here we are correct, for no exaggeration is possible. When we talk of that land of Eshcol, our mouths are watering to taste its clusters; already, like David, we thirst to drink of the well that is within the gate; and we hunger after the good corn of the land. Our ears are wanting to have done with the discords of earth, that they may open to the harmonies of heaven; and our tongues are longing to sing the melodious sonnets, sung by flaming ones above. Yes, we do love heaven, and thus it is that we prove that our commerce is with that better land.

Brethren, just as people in a foreign land that love their country always are glad to have plenty of letters from the country, I hope we have much *communication with the old fatherland.* We send our prayers there as letters to our Father, and we get His letters back in this blessed volume of His word. You go into an Australian settler's hut, and you find a newspaper. Where from, sir? A gazette

from the south of France, a journal from America? Oh no, it is a newspaper from England, addressed to him in his old mother's handwriting, bearing the postage stamp with the good Queen's face in the corner; and he likes it, though it be only a newspaper from some little pottering country town, with no news in it; yet he likes it better, perhaps, than the "Times" itself, because it talks to him about the village where he lived, and consequently touches a special string in the harp of his soul. So must it be with heaven. This book, the Bible, is the newspaper of heaven, and therefore we must love it. The sermons which are preached are good news from a far country. The hymns we sing are notes by which we tell our Father of our welfare here, and by which He whispers into our soul His continued love to us. All these are and must be pleasant to us, for our commerce is with heaven. I hope, too, we are sending a good deal home. I like to see our young fellows when they go out to live in the bush, recollect their mother at home. They say "She had a hard struggle to bring us up when our father died, and she scraped her little together to help us to emigrate." John and Tom mutually agree, "the first gold we get at the diggings we will send home to mother." And it goes home. Well, I hope you are sending a great many things home. Dear friends, I hope as we are aliens here, we are not laying up our treasure here, where we may lose it, but packing it off as quickly as we can to our own country. There are many ways of doing it. God has many banks; and they are all safe ones. We have but to serve His Church, or serve the souls which Christ has bought with His blood, or help His poor, clothe His naked, and feed His hungry, and we send our treasures beyond sea in a safe ship, and so we keep up our commerce with the skies.

V. Time has gone; those clocks will strike when they ought not. There is a great reason why we should live like aliens and foreigners here, and that is, CHRIST IS COMING SOON. The early Church never forgot this. Did they not pant and thirst after the return of their ascended Lord? Like the twelve tribes, day and night they instantly watched for Messiah. But the Church has grown weary of this hope. There has been so many false prophets who tell us that Christ is coming, that the Church thinks He never will come; and she begins to deny, or to keep in the background the blessed doctrine of the second advent of her Lord from heaven. I do not think the fact that there have been many false prophets should make us doubt our Lord's true word. Perhaps the very frequency of these mistakes may show that there is truth at the bottom. You have a friend who is ill, and the doctor says he cannot last long; he must die; you have called a great many times expecting to hear of his departure, but he is still alive; now the frequent errors of the physicians do not prove that your friend will not die one of these days, and that speedily too. And so, though the false prophets have said, "Lo, here," and "Lo, there," and yet Christ has not come, that does not prove that His glorious appearing will never arrive. You know I am no prophet. I do not know anything about 1866; I find quite enough to do to attend to 1862. I do not understand the visions of Daniel or Ezekiel; I find I have enough to do to teach the simple word such as I find in Matthew, Mark, Luke, and John, and the Epistles of Paul. I do not find many souls have been converted to God by exquisite dissertations about the battle of Armageddon, and all those other fine things; I have no doubt prophesyings are very profitable, but I rather question whether they are so profitable to the hearers, as they may be to the preachers and publishers. I conceive that among religious people of a certain sort, the abortive explanations of prophecy issued by certain doctors gratify a craving which in irreligious people finds its food in novels and romances. People have a panting to know the future; and certain divines pander to this depraved taste, by prophesying for them, and letting them know what is coming by-and-bye. I do not know the future, and I shall not pretend to know. But I do preach this, because I know it, that *Christ will come*, for He says so in a hundred passages. The Epistles of Paul are full of the advent, and Peter's too, and John's letters are crowded with it. The best of saints have always lived on the hope of the advent. There was Enoch, he prophesied of the coming of the Son of Man. So there was another Enoch who was always talking of the coming, and saying, "Come quickly." I will not divide the house to-night by discussing whether the advent will be pre-millennial or post-millennial, or anything of that, it is enough for me that *He will come*, and "in such an hour as ye think not, the Son of Man will come." To-night He may appear, while here we stand; just when we think that he will not come, the thief shall break open the house. We ought, therefore, to be always watching. Since the gold and silver that you have will be worthless at His advent; since your lands and estates will melt to **smoke** when He appeareth; since, **then** the righteous shall be rich, and the godly shall be great, lay not up your treasure here, for it may at any time vanish, at any time disappear, for Christ may at any moment come.

I think the Church would do well to be always living as if Christ might come to-day. I feel persuaded she is doing ill if she works as if He would not come till 1866, because He may come before, and He may come this moment. Let her always be living as if He would come *now*, still acting in her Master's sight, and watching unto prayer. Never mind about the last vials, fill your own vial with sweet odours and offer it before the Lord. Think what you like about Armageddon, but forget not to fight the good fight of faith. Guess not at the precise era for the destruction of Antichrist, go and destroy it yourself, fighting against it every day; but be looking forward and hastening unto the coming of the Son of Man; and let this be at once your comfort and excitement to diligence—that the Saviour will soon come from heaven.

Now, I think you foreigners here present—and I hope there are a great many true aliens here—ought to feel like a poor stranded mariner on a desolate island, who has saved a few things from the wreck and built himself an old log hut, and has a few comforts round about him, but for all that he longs for home. Every morning he looks out to sea, and wonders when he shall see a sail; many times while examining the wide ocean to look for a ship, he has clapped his hands, and then wept to find he was disappointed; every night he lights his fire that there may be a blaze, so that if a ship should go by, they may send relief to the stranded mariner. Ah! that is just the way we ought to live. We have heard of one saint who used to open his window every morning when he woke, to see if Christ had come; it might be fanaticism, but better to be enthusiastic than to mind earthly things. I would have us look out each night and light the fire of prayer, that it may be burning in case the ships of heaven should go by, that blessings may come to us poor aliens and foreigners who need them so much. Let us wait patiently till the Lord's convoy shall take us on board, that we may be carried into the glories and splendour of the reign of Christ, let us always hold the log-hut with a loose hand, and long for the time when we shall get to that better land where our possessions are, where our Father lives, where our treasures lie, where all our brethren dwell. Well said our poet—

"Blest scenes, through rude and stormy seas
      I onward press to you."

My beloved friends, I can assure you it is always one of the sweetest thoughts I ever know, that I shall meet with you in heaven. There are so many of you members of this Church, that I can hardly get to shake hands with you once in a year; but I shall have plenty of time then in heaven. You will know your pastor in heaven better than you do now. He loves you now, and you love him. We shall then have more time to recount our experience of divine grace, and praise God together, and sing together, and rejoice together concerning Him by whom we were helped to plant, and sow, and through whom all the increase came.

"I hope when days and years are past,
    We all shall meet in heaven,
  We all shall meet in heaven at last,
    We all shall meet in heaven."

But we shall not all meet in glory; not all, unless you repent. Some of you will certainly perish, unless you believe in Christ. But why must we be divided? Oh! why not all in heaven? "Believe in the Lord Jesus Christ, and thou shalt be saved." "He that believeth and is baptized shall be saved, but he that believeth not shall be damned." Trust Christ, sinner, and heaven is thine, and mine, and we are safe for ever. Amen.

THE WATCHWORD FOR TO-DAY:
"STAND FAST"

"For our conversation is in heaven; from whence also we look for the Saviour, the Lord Jesus Christ: who shall change our vile body, that it may be fashioned like unto His glorious body, according to the working whereby He is able even to subdue all things unto Himself. Therefore, my brethren dearly beloved and longed for, my joy and crown, so stand fast in the Lord, my dearly beloved."—Philippians iii. 20, 21; iv. 1.

EVERY doctrine of the Word of God has its practical bearing. As each tree beareth seed after its kind, so doth every truth of God bring forth practical virtues. Hence you find the apostle Paul very full of *therefores*—his therefores being the conclusions drawn from certain statements of divine truth. I marvel that our excellent translators should have divided the argument from the conclusion by making a new chapter where there is least reason for it.

Last Lord's day I spoke with you concerning the most sure and certain resurrection of our Lord Jesus: now there is a practical force in that truth, which constitutes part of what is meant by "the power of His resurrection." Since the Lord has risen, and will surely come a second time, and will raise the bodies of His people at His coming, there is something to wait for, and a grand reason for steadfastness while thus waiting. We are looking for the coming of our Lord and Saviour Jesus Christ from heaven, and that He shall "fashion anew the body of our humiliation, that it may be conformed to the body of His glory;" therefore let us stand fast in the position which will secure us this honour. Let us keep our posts until the coming of the great Captain shall release the sentinels. The glorious resurrection will abundantly repay us for all the toil and travail we may have to undergo in the battle for the Lord. The glory to be revealed even now casts a light upon our path, and causes sunshine within our hearts. The hope of this happiness makes us even now strong in the Lord, and in the power of His might.

Paul was deeply anxious that those in whom he had been the means of kindling the heavenly hope might be preserved faithful until the coming of Christ. He trembled lest any of them should seem to draw back, and prove traitors to their Lord. He dreaded lest he should lose what he hoped he had gained, by their turning aside from the faith. Hence he beseeches them to "stand fast." He expressed in the sixth verse of the first chapter his conviction that He who had begun a good work in them would perform it, but his intense love made him exhort them, saying, "Stand fast in the Lord, my dearly beloved." By such exhortations final perseverance is promoted and secured.

Paul has fought bravely; and in the case of the Philippian converts he believes that he has secured the victory, and he fears lest it should yet be lost. He reminds me of the death of that British hero, Wolfe, who on the heights of Quebec received a mortal wound. It was just at the moment when the enemy fled, and when he knew that they were running, a smile was on his face, and he cried, "Hold me up. Let not my brave soldiers see me drop. The day is ours. Oh, do keep it!" His sole anxiety was to make the victory sure. Thus warriors die, and thus Paul lived. His very soul seems to cry, "We have won

the day. Oh, do keep it!" O my beloved hearers, I believe that many of you are "in the Lord," but I entreat you to "stand fast in the Lord." In your case, also, the day is won; but oh, do keep it! There is the pith of all I have to say to you this morning: may God the Holy Spirit write it on your hearts! Having done all things well hitherto, I entreat you to obey the injunction of Jude, to "keep yourselves in the love of God," and to join with me in adoring Him who alone is able to keep us from falling, and to present us faultless before His presence with exceeding great joy. Unto Him be glory for ever. Amen.

In leading out your thoughts I will keep to the following order:—

First, it seems to me from the text that *the apostle perceived that these Philippian Christians were in their right place*; they were "in the Lord," and in such a position that he could safely bid them "stand fast" in it. Secondly, *he longed for them that they should keep their right place*—"Stand fast in the Lord, my dearly beloved"; and then, thirdly, *he urged the best motives for their keeping their place*. These motives are contained in the first two verses of our text, upon which we will enlarge further on.

I. Paul joyfully perceived that HIS BELOVED CONVERTS WERE IN THEIR RIGHT PLACE. It is a very important thing indeed that we should begin well. The start is not everything, but it is a great deal. It has been said by the old proverb, that "Well begun is half done"; and it is certainly so in the things of God. It is vitally important to enter in at the strait gate; to start on the heavenly journey from the right point. I have no doubt that many slips and falls and apostasies among professors are due to the fact that they were not right at first; the foundation was always upon the sand, and when the house came down at last, it was no more than might have been expected. A flaw in the foundation is pretty sure to be followed by a crack in the superstructure. Do see to it that you lay a good foundation. It is even better to have no repentance than a repentance which needs to be repented of: it is better to have no faith than a false faith: it is better to make no profession of religion than to make an untruthful one. God give us grace that we may not make a mistake in learning the alphabet of godliness, or else in all our learning we shall blunder on and increase in error. We should early learn the difference between grace and merit, between the purpose of God and the will of man, between trust in God and confidence in the flesh. If we do not start aright, the further we go the further we shall be from our desired end, and the more thoroughly in the wrong shall we find ourselves. Yes, it is of prime importance that our new birth and our first love should be genuine beyond all question.

The only position, however, in which we can begin aright is to be "in the Lord." This is to begin as we may safely go on. This is the essential point. It is a very good thing for Christians to be in the church; but if you are in the church before you are in the Lord you are out of place. It is a good thing to be engaged in holy work; but if you are in holy work before you are in the Lord you will have no heart for it, neither will the Lord accept it. It is not essential that you should be in this church or in that church; but it is essential that you should be "in the Lord": it is not essential that you should be in the Sabbath-school, nor in the Working Meeting, nor in the Tract Society; but it is essential to the last degree that you should be in the Lord. The apostle rejoiced over those that were converted at Philippi because he knew that they were in the Lord. They were where he wished them to remain, therefore he said, "Stand fast in the Lord."

What is it to be "in the Lord"? Well, brethren, *we are in the Lord vitally and evidently when we fly to the Lord Jesus by repentance and faith*, and make Him to be our refuge and hiding-place. Is it so with you? Have you fled out of self? Are you trusting in the Lord alone? Have you come to Calvary, and beheld your Saviour? As the doves build their nests in the rock, have you thus made your home in Jesus? There is no shelter for a guilty soul but in His wounded side. Have you come there? Are you in Him? Then keep there. You will never have a better refuge; in fact, there is no other. No other name is given under heaven among men whereby we must be saved. I cannot tell you to stand fast in the Lord, unless you are there: hence my first enquiry is—Are you in Christ? Is He your only confidence? In His life, His death, and His resurrection do you find the grounds of your hope? Is He Himself all your salvation, and all your desire? If so, stand fast in Him.

Next, these people, in addition to having fled to Christ for refuge, were now *in Christ as to their daily life*. They had heard Him say, "Abide in Me"; and therefore they remained in the daily enjoyment of Him, in reliance upon Him, in obedience to Him, and in the earnest copying of His example. They were Christians, that is to say, persons upon whom was named the name of Christ. They were endeavouring to realize the power of His death and resurrection as a sanctifying influence, killing their sins and fostering their virtues. They were labouring to reproduce His image in themselves, that so they might bring glory to His name. Their lives were spent within the circle of their Saviour's influence. Are you so, my dear friends? Then stand fast. You will never find a nobler example; you will never be saturated with a diviner spirit than that of Christ Jesus your Lord. Whether we eat or drink, or whatsoever we do, let us do all in the name of the Lord Jesus, and so live in Him.

These Philippians had, moreover, realized that they were *in Christ by a real and vital union with Him*. They had come to feel, not like separated individualities, copying a model, but as members of a body made like to their Head. By a living, loving, lasting union they were joined to Christ as their covenant Head. They could say, "Who shall separate us from the love of God which is in Christ Jesus our Lord?" Do you know what it is to feel that the life which is in you is first in Christ, and still flows from Him, even as the life of the branch is mainly in the stem "I live; yet not I, but Christ liveth in me." This is to be in Christ. Are you in Him in this sense? Forgive my pressing the question. If you answer me in the affirmative, I shall then entreat you to "stand fast" in Him. It is in Him, and in Him only, that spiritual life is to be sustained, even as only from Him can it be received. To be engrafted into Christ is salvation; but to abide in Christ is the full enjoyment of it. True union to Christ is eternal life. Paul, therefore, rejoiced over these Philippians, because they were joined unto the Lord in one spirit.

This expression is very short, but very full. "In Christ." Does it not mean that we are in Christ as the birds are in the air which buoys them up, and enables them to fly? Are we not in Christ as the fish are in the sea? *Our Lord has become our element*, vital, and all surrounding. In Him we live, and move, and have our being. He is in us, and we are in Him. We are filled with all the fulness of God, because in Christ doth all fulness dwell, and we dwell in Him. Christ to us is all; He is in all; and He is all in all! Jesus to us is everything in everything. Without Him we can do nothing, and we *are* nothing. Thus are we emphatically in Him. If you have reached this point, "stand fast" in it. If you dwell in the secret place of the tabernacles of the Most High, abide under the shadow of the Almighty. Do you sit at His table, and eat of His dainties? Then prolong the visit, and think not of removal. Say in your soul—

> "Here would I find a settled rest,
>   While others go and come;
> No more a stranger, or a guest,
>   But like a child at home."

Has Jesus brought you into His green pastures? Then lie down in them. Go no further, for you will never fare better. Stay with your Lord, however long the night, for only in Him have you hope of morning.

You see, then, that these people were where they should be—in the Lord, and that this was the reason why the apostle took such delight in them. Kindly read the first verse of the fourth chapter, and see how he loves them, and joys over them. He heaps up titles of love! Some dip their morsel in vinegar, but Paul's words were saturated with honey. Here we not only have sweet words, but they mean something: his love was real and fervent. The very heart of Paul is written out large in this verse—"Therefore, my brethren dearly beloved and longed for, my joy and crown, so stand fast in the Lord, my dearly beloved." Because they were in Christ, therefore first of all they were Paul's *brethren*. This was a new relationship, not earthly, but heavenly. What did this Jew from Tarsus know about the Philippians? Many of them were Gentiles. Time was when he would have called them dogs, and despised them as the uncircumcised; but now he says, "My brethren." That poor word has become very hackneyed. We talk of brethren without particularly much of brotherly love; but true brothers have a love for one another which is very unselfish and admirable, and so there is between real Christians a brotherhood which they will neither disown, nor dissemble, nor forget. It is said of our Lord, "For this cause He is not ashamed to call them brethren"; and surely they need never be ashamed to call one another brethren. Paul, at any rate, looks at the jailor, that jailor who had set his feet in the stocks, and he looks at the jailor's family, and at Lydia, and many others; in fact, at the whole company that he had gathered at Philippi, and he salutes them lovingly as " My brethren." Their names were written in the same family register because they were in Christ, and therefore had one Father in heaven.

Next, the apostle calls them "my *dearly beloved*." The verse almost begins with this word, and it quite finishes with it. The repetition makes it mean, "My doubly dear ones." Such is the love which every true servant of Christ will have for those who have been begotten to the faith of Christ by his means. Oh, yes, if you are in Christ His ministers must love you. How could there be a lack of affection in our hearts towards you, since we have been the means of bringing you to Jesus? Without cant or display we call you our "dearly beloved."

Then the apostle calls them his "*longed for*," that is, his most desired ones. He first desired to see them converted; after that he desired to see them baptized; then he desired to see them exhibiting all the graces of Christians. When he saw holiness in them he desired to visit them and commune with them. Their constant kindness created in him a strong desire to speak with them face to face. He loved them, and desired their company, because they were in Christ. So he speaks of them as those for whom he longed. His delight was in thinking of them and in hoping to visit them.

Then he adds, "My joy and crown." Paul had been the means of their salvation, and when he thought of that blessed result he never regretted all that he had suffered: his persecutions among the Gentiles seemed light indeed since these priceless souls were his reward. Though he was nothing but a poor prisoner of Christ, yet he talks in right royal style: they are his crown. They were his *stephanos*, or crown given as a reward for his life-race. This among the Greeks was usually a wreath of flowers placed around the victor's brow. Paul's crown would never fade. He writes as he felt the amaranth around his temples; even now he looks upon the Philippians as his chaplet of honour; they were his joy and his crown; he anticipated, I do not doubt, that throughout eternity it would be a part of his heaven to see them amid their blessedness, and to know that he helped to bring them to that felicity by leading them to Christ. O beloved, it is indeed our highest joy that we have not run in vain, neither laboured in vain: you who have been snatched as "brands from the burning," and are now living to the praise of our Lord Jesus Christ, you are our prize, our crown, our joy.

These converts were all this to Paul simply because they were "in Christ." They had begun well, they were where they should be, and he therefore rejoiced in them.

II. But secondly, it was for this reason that HE LONGED THAT THEY SHOULD KEEP THERE. He entreated them to stand fast. "So stand fast in the Lord, my dearly beloved." The beginning of religion is not the whole of it. You must not suppose that the sum of godliness is contained within the experience of a day or two, or a week, or a few months, or even a few years. Precious are the feelings which attend conversion; but dream not that repentance, faith, and so forth, are for a season, and then all is done, and done with. I am afraid there are some who secretly say, "Everything is now complete; I have experienced the necessary change, I have been to see the elders and the pastor, and I have been baptized, and received into the church, and now all is right for ever." That is a false view of your condition. In conversion you have started in the race, and you must run to the end of the course. In your confession of Christ you have carried your tools into the vineyard, but the day's work now begins. Remember, "He that shall endure unto the end, the same shall be saved." Godliness is a life-long business. The working out of the salvation which the Lord Himself works in you is not a matter of certain hours, and of a limited period of life. Salvation is unfolded throughout all our sojourn here. We continue to repent and to believe, and even the process of our conversion continues as we are changed more and more into the image of our Lord. Final perseverance is the necessary evidence of genuine conversion.

In proportion as we rejoice over converts we feel an intense bitterness when any disappoint us, and turn out to be merely temporary camp-followers. We sigh over the seed which spring up so speedily, but which withers so soon because it has neither root nor depth of earth. We were ready to say—"Ring the bells of heaven"; but the bells of heaven did not ring because these people talked about Christ, and said they were in Christ; but it was all a delusion. After a while, for one reason and another, they went back; "they went out from us, but they were not of us; for if they had been of us, they would no doubt have continued with us: but they went out, that they might be made manifest that they were not all of us." Our churches suffer most seriously from the great numbers who drop out of their ranks, and either go back to the world, or else must be pursuing a very secret and solitary path in their way to heaven, for we hear no more of them. Our joy is turned to disappointment, our crown of laurel becomes a circle of faded leaves, and we are weary at the remembrance of it. With what earnestness, therefore, would we say to you who are beginning the race, "Continue in your course. We beseech you turn not aside, neither slacken your running, till you have won the prize!"

I heard an expression yesterday which pleased me much. I spoke about the difficulty of keeping on. "Yes," answered my friend, "and it is harder still to keep on keeping on." So it is. There is the pinch. I know lots of fellows who are wonders at the start. What a rush they make! But then there is no stay in them; they soon lose breath. The difference between the spurious and the real Christian lies in this staying power. The real Christian has a life within him which can never die, an incorruptible seed which liveth and abideth for ever; but the spurious Christian begins after a fashion, but ends almost as soon as he begins. He is esteemed a saint; but turns out a hypocrite. He makes a fair show for a while, but soon he quits the way of holiness, and makes his own damnation sure. God save you, dear friends, from anything which looks like apostasy. Hence I would with all my might press upon you these two most weighty words: "Stand fast."

I will put the exhortation thus—"Stand fast *doctrinally*." In this age all the ships in the waters are pulling up their anchors; they are drifting with the tide; they are driven about with every wind. It is your wisdom to put down more anchors. I have taken the precaution to cast four anchors out of the stern, as well as to see that the great bower anchor is in its proper place. I will not budge an inch from the old doctrine for any man. Now that the cyclone is triumphant over many a bowing wall and tottering fence, those who are built upon the one foundation must prove its value by standing fast. We will hearken to no teaching but that of the Lord Jesus. If you see a truth to be in God's word, grasp it by your faith; and if it be unpopular, grapple it to you as with hooks of steel. If you are despised as a fool for holding it, hold it the more. Like an oak, take deeper root, because the winds would tear you from your place. Defy reproach and ridicule, and you have already vanquished it. Stand fast, like the British squares in the olden times. When fierce assaults were made upon them every man seemed transformed to rock. We might have wandered from the ranks a little in more peaceful times, to look after the fascinating flowers which grow on every side of our march; but, now we know that the enemy surrounds us, we keep strictly to the line of march, and tolerate no roaming. The watchword of the host of God just now is—"Stand fast!" Hold you to the faith once delivered to the saints. Hold fast the form of sound words, and deviate not one jot or tittle therefrom. Doctrinally stand fast!

Practically, also, abide firm in the right, the true, the holy. This is of the utmost importance. The barriers are broken down; they would amalgamate church and world: yes, even church and stage. It is proposed to combine God and devil in one service; Christ and Belial are to perform on one stage. Surely now is the time when the lion shall eat straw like the ox, and very dirty straw too. So they say; but I repeat to you this word, "Come out from among them, and be ye separate, and touch not the unclean thing." Write "holiness unto the Lord" not only on your altars, but upon the bells of the horses; let everything be done as before the living God. Do all things unto holiness and edification. Strive together to maintain the purity of the disciples of Christ; and take up your cross, and go without the camp bearing His reproach. If you have already stood apart in your decision for the Lord, continue to do so. Stand fast. In nothing moved by the laxity of the age, in nothing affected by the current of modern opinion, say to yourself, "I will do as Christ bids me to the utmost of my ability. I will follow the Lamb whithersoever He goeth." In these times of worldliness, impurity, self-indulgence, and error, it becomes the Christian to gather up his skirts and keep his feet and his garments clean from the pollution which lies all around him. We must be more Puritanic and precise than we have been. Oh, for grace to stand fast!

Mind also that you stand fast *experimentally*. Pray that your inward experience may be a close adhesion to your Master. Do not go astray from His presence. Neither climb with those who dream of perfection in the flesh, nor grovel with those who doubt the possibility of present salvation. Take the Lord Jesus Christ to be your sole treasure, and let your heart be ever with Him. Stand fast in faith in His atonement, in confidence in His Divinity, in assurance of His Second Advent. I pine to know within my soul the power of His resurrection, and to have unbroken fellowship with Him. In communion with the Father and the Son let us stand fast. He shall fare well whose heart and soul, affections and understanding are wrapped up in Christ Jesus, and in none beside. Concerning your inward life, your secret prayer, your walk with God, here is the watchword of the day—"Stand fast."

To put it very plainly, "Stand fast *in the Lord*," *without wishing for another trust*. Do not desire to have any hope but that which is in Christ. Do not entertain the proposition that you should unite another

confidence to your confidence in the Lord. Have no hankering after any other fashion of faith except the faith of a sinner in his Saviour. All hope but that which is set before us in the gospel, and brought to us by the Lord Jesus is a poisoned delicacy, highly coloured, but by no means to be so much as tasted by those who have been fed upon the bread of heaven. What need we more than Jesus? What way of salvation do we seek but that of grace? What security but the precious blood? Stand fast; and wish for no other rock of salvation save the Lord Jesus.

Next, stand fast *without wavering in our trust*. Permit no doubt to worry you. Know that Jesus can save you, and, what is more, know that He has saved you. So commit yourself to His hands, that you are as sure of your salvation as of your existence. The blood of Jesus Christ this day cleanseth us from all sin; His righteousness covers us, and His life quickens us into newness of life. Tolerate no doubt, mistrust, suspicion, or misgiving. Believe in Christ up to the hilt. As for myself, I will yield to be lost for ever if Jesus does not save me. I will have no other string to my bow, no second door of hope, or way of retreat. I could risk a thousand souls on my Lord's truth and feel no risk. Stand fast, without wishing for another trust, and without wavering in the trust you have.

Moreover, stand fast *without wandering into sin*. You are tempted this way and that way: stand fast. Inward passions rise: lusts of the flesh rebel; the devil hurls his fearful suggestions; the men of your own household tempt you: stand fast. Only so will you be preserved from the torrents of iniquity. Keep close to the example and spirit of your Master; and having done all, still stand.

As I have said, stand fast without wandering, so next I must say stand fast *without wearying*. You are a little tired. Never mind, take a little rest and brush up again. "Oh," you say, "this toil is so monotonous." Do it better, and that will be a change. Your Saviour endured His life and labour without this complaint, for zeal had eaten Him up. "Alas!" you cry, "I cannot see results." Never mind; wait for results, even as the husbandman waiteth for the precious fruits of the earth. "Oh, sir, I plod along and make no progress." Never mind, you are a poor judge of your own success. Work on, for in due season you shall reap if you faint not. Practise perseverance. Remember that if you have the work of faith and the labour of love, you must complete the trio by adding the patience of hope. You cannot do without this last. "Be ye steadfast, unmoveable, always abounding in the work of the Lord, forasmuch as ye know that your labour is not in vain in the Lord." I am reminded of Sir Christopher Wren, when he cleared away old St. Paul's to make room for his splendid pile. He was compelled to use battering rams upon the massive walls. The workmen kept on battering and battering. An enormous force was brought to bear upon the walls for days and nights, but it did not appear to have made the least impression upon the ancient masonry. Yet the great architect knew what he was at: he bade them keep on incessantly, and the ram fell again and again upon the rocky wall, till at length the whole mass was disintegrating and coming apart; and then each stroke began to tell. At a blow it reeled, at another it quivered, at another it moved visibly, at another it fell over amid clouds of dust. These last strokes did the work. Do you think so? No, it was the combination of blows, the first as truly as the last.

Keep on with the battering-ram. I hope to keep on until I die. And, mark you, I may die and I may not see the errors of the hour totter to their fall, but I shall be perfectly content to sleep in Christ, for I have a sure expectation that this work will succeed in the end. I shall be happy to have done my share of the work, even if I personally see little apparent result. Lord, let Thy work appear unto Thy servants, and we will be content that Thy glory should be reserved for our children. Stand fast, my brethren, in incessant labours, for the end is sure.

And then, in addition to standing fast in that respect, stand fast *without warping*. Timber, when it is rather green, is apt to go this way or that. The spiritual weather is very bad just now for green wood: it is one day damp with superstition, and another day it is parched with scepticism. Rationalism and Ritualism are both at work. I pray that you may not warp. Keep straight; keep to the truth, the whole truth, and nothing but the truth; for in the Master's name we bid you "Stand fast in the Lord."

Stand fast, for there is great need. Many walk of whom I have told you often, and now tell you even weeping, that they are the enemies of the cross of Christ.

Paul urged them to stand fast because, even in his own case, spiritual life was a struggle. Even Paul said, "Not as though I had already attained." He was pressing forward; he was straining with all energy by the power of the Holy Ghost. He did not expect to be carried to heaven on a feather-bed; he was warring and agonizing. You, beloved, must do the same. What a grand example of perseverance did Paul set to us all! Nothing enticed him from his steadfastness. "None of these things move me," said he, "neither count I my life dear unto me." He has entered into his rest, because the Lord his God helped him to stand fast, even to the end. I wish I had power to put this more earnestly, but my very soul goes forth with it. "Stand fast in the Lord, my dearly beloved."

III. Thirdly, THE APOSTLE URGED THE BEST MOTIVES FOR THEIR STANDING FAST.

He says, "Stand fast *because of your citizenship*." Read the twentieth verse; "For our citizenship is in heaven." Now, if you are what you profess to be, if you are in Christ, you are citizens of the New Jerusalem. Men ought to behave themselves according to their citizenship, and not dishonour their city. When a man was a citizen of Athens, in the olden time, he felt it incumbent upon him to be brave. Xerxes said, "These Athenians are not ruled by kings: how will they fight?" "No," said one, "but every man respects the law, and each man is ready to die for his country." Xerxes soon had to know that the like obedience and respect of law ruled the Spartans, and that these, because they were of Sparta, were all brave as lions. He sends word to Leonidas and his little troop to give up their arms. "Come and take them," was the courageous reply. The Persian king had myriads of soldiers with him, while Leonidas had only three hundred Spartans at his side; yet they kept the pass, and it cost the eastern despot many thousand of men to force a passage. The sons of Sparta died rather than desert their post. Every citizen of Sparta felt that he must stand fast: it was not for such a man as he to yield. I like the spirit of Bayard, that "knight without fear and without reproach." He knew not what fear meant. In his last battle, his spine was broken, and he said to those around him, "Place me up against a tree, so that I may sit up and die with my face to the enemy." Yes, if our backs were broken, if we could no more bear the shield or use the sword, it would be incumbent upon us, as citizens of the New Jerusalem, to die with our faces towards the enemy. We must not yield, we dare not yield, if we are of the city of the great King. The martyrs cry to us to stand fast; the cloud of witnesses bending from their thrones above beseech us to stand fast; yea, all the hosts of the shining ones cry to us "Stand fast." Stand fast for God, and the truth, and holiness, and let no man take your crown.

The next argument that Paul used was *their outlook*. "Our conversation is in heaven; from whence also we look for the Saviour, the Lord Jesus Christ." Brethren, Jesus is coming. He is even now on the way. You have heard our tidings till you scarcely credit us; but the word is true, and it will surely be fulfilled before long. The Lord is coming indeed. He promised to come to die, and He kept His word: He now promises to come to reign, and be you sure that He will keep His tryst with His people. He is coming. Ears of faith can hear the sound of His chariot wheels; every moment of time, every event of providence is bringing Him nearer. Blessed are those servants who shall not be sleeping when He comes, nor wandering from their posts of duty; happy shall they be whom their Lord shall find faithfully watching, and standing fast in that great day!

To us, beloved, He is coming, not as Judge and Destroyer, but as *Saviour*. We look for the Saviour, the Lord Jesus Christ. Now, if we do look for Him, let us "stand fast." There must be no going into sin, no forsaking the fellowship of the church, no leaving the truth, no trying to play fast and loose with godliness, no running with the hare and hunting with the hounds. Let us stand so fast in singleness of heart that, whenever Jesus comes, we shall be able to say, "Welcome, welcome, Son of God!"

Sometimes I wait through the weary years with great comfort. There was a ship some time ago outside a certain harbour. A heavy sea made the ship roll fearfully. A dense fog blotted out all buoys and lights. The captain never left the wheel. He could not tell his way into the harbour, and no pilot could get out to him for a long time. Eager passengers urged him to be courageous and make a dash for the harbour. He said "No; it is not my duty to run so great a risk. A pilot is required here, and I will wait for one if I wait a week." The truest courage is that which can bear to be charged with cowardice. To wait is much wiser than when you cannot hear the fog-horn and have no pilot yet to steam on and wreck your vessel on the rocks. Our prudent captain waited his time, and at last he espied the pilot's boat coming to him over the boiling sea. When the pilot was at his work the captain's anxious waiting was over. The Church is like that vessel, she is pitched to and fro in the storm and the dark, and the Pilot has not yet come. The weather is very threatening. All around the darkness hangs like a pall. But Jesus will come, walking on the water, before long; He will bring us safe to the desired haven. Let us wait with patience. Stand fast! Stand fast! for Jesus is coming, and in Him is our sure hope.

Further, there was another motive. *There was an expectation*. "He shall change our vile body," or rather, "body of our humiliation." Only think of it, dear friends! No more headaches or heartaches, no more feebleness and fainting, no more inward tumour or consumption; but the Lord shall transfigure this body of our humiliation into the likeness of the body of His glory. Our frame is now made up of decaying substances, it is of the earth earthy. "So to the dust return we must." This body groans, suffers, becomes diseased, and dies: blessed be God, it shall be wonderfully changed, and then there shall be no more death, neither sorrow nor crying, neither shall there be any more pain. The natural appetites of this body engender sad tendencies to sin, and in this respect it is a "vile body." It shall not always be so; the great change will deliver it from all that is gross and carnal. It shall be pure as the Lord's body! Whatever the body of Christ is now, our body is to be like it. We spoke of it last Sunday, you know, when we heard Him say, "Handle Me." We are to have a real, corporeal body as He had for substance and reality; and, like His body, it will be full of beauty, full of health and strength; it will enjoy peculiar immunities from evil, and special adaptations for good. That is what is going to happen to me and to you; therefore let us stand fast. Let us not wilfully throw away our prospects of glory and immortality. What! Relinquish resurrection? Relinquish glory? Relinquish likeness to the risen Lord? O God, save us from such a terrible piece of apostasy! Save us from such immeasurable folly! Suffer us not to turn our backs in the day of battle, since that would be to turn our backs from the crown of life that fadeth not away.

Lastly, the apostle urges us to stand fast because of *our resources*. Somebody may ask, "How can this body of ours be transformed and transfigured until it becomes like the body of Christ?" I cannot tell you anything about the process; it will all be accomplished in the twinkling of an eye, at the last trump. But I can tell you by what power it will be accomplished. The Omnipotent Lord will lay bare His arm, and exercise His might, "according to the working whereby He is able even to subdue all things unto Himself." O brethren, we may well stand fast since we have infinite power at our backs. The Lord is with us with all His energy, even with His all-conquering strength, which shall yet subdue all His foes. Do not let us imagine that any enemy can be too strong for Christ's arm. If He is able to subdue all things unto Himself, He can certainly bear us through all opposition. One glance of His eye may wither all opposers, or, better still, one word from His lips may turn them into friends. The army of the Lord is strong in reserves. These reserves have never yet been fully called out. We, who are in the field, are only a small squadron, holding the fort; but our Lord has at His back ten thousand times ten thousand who will carry war into the enemy's camp. When the Captain of our salvation comes to the front, He will bring His heavenly legions with Him. Our business is to watch until He appears upon the scene, for when He comes, His infinite resources will be put in marching order. I like that speech of Wellington (who was so calm amid the roar of Waterloo), when an officer sent word, "Tell the Commander-in-Chief that he must move me, I cannot hold my position any longer, my numbers are so thinned." "Tell him," said the great general, "He *must* hold his place. Every Englishman to-day must die where he stands, or else win the victory." The officer read the command to stand, and he did stand till the trumpet sounded victory. And so it is now. My brethren, we must die where we are rather than yield to the enemy. If Jesus tarries we must not desert our posts. Wellington knew that the heads of the Prussian columns would soon be visible, coming in to ensure the victory; and so by faith we can perceive the legions of our Lord approaching: in serried ranks His angels fly through the opening heaven. The air is teeming with them. I hear their silver trumpets. Behold, He cometh with clouds! When He cometh He will abundantly recompense all who stood fast amid the rage of battle. Let us sing, "Hold the fort, for I am coming."

JOY, A DUTY

"Rejoice in the Lord alway: and again I say, Rejoice."—Philippians iv. 4.

THERE is a marvellous medicinal power in joy. Most medicines are distasteful; but this, which is the best of all medicines, is sweet to the taste, and comforting to the heart. We noticed, in our reading, that there had been a little tiff between two sisters in the church at Philippi;—I am glad that we do not know what the quarrel was about; I am usually thankful for ignorance on such subjects;—but, as a cure for disagreements, the apostle says, "Rejoice in the Lord alway." People who are very happy, especially those who are very happy in the Lord, are not apt either to give offence or to take offence. Their minds are so sweetly occupied with higher things, that they are not easily distracted by the little troubles which naturally arise among such imperfect creatures as we are. Joy in the Lord is the cure for all discord. Should it not be so? What is this joy but the concord of the soul, the accord of the heart, with the joy of heaven? Joy in the Lord, then, drives away the discords of earth.

Further, brethren, notice that the apostle, after he had said, "Rejoice in the Lord alway," commanded the Philippians to be careful for nothing, thus implying that joy in the Lord is one of the best preparations for the trials of this life. The cure for care is joy in the Lord. No, my brother, you will not be able to keep on with your fretfulness; no, my sister, you will not be able to weary yourself any longer with your anxieties, if the Lord will but fill you with His joy. Then, being satisfied with your God, yea, more than satisfied, overflowing with delight in Him, you will say to yourself, "Why art thou cast down. O my soul? and why art thou disquieted in me? hope thou in God: for I shall yet praise Him for the help of His countenance." What is there on earth that is worth fretting for even for five minutes? If one could gain an imperial crown by a day of care, it would be too great an expense for a thing which would bring more care with it. Therefore, let us be thankful, let us be joyful in the Lord. I count it one of the wisest things that, by rejoicing in the Lord, we commence our heaven here below. It is possible so to do, it is profitable so to do, and we are commanded so to do.

Now I come to the text itself, "Rejoice in the Lord alway: and again I say, Rejoice."

I. It will be our first business at this time to consider THE GRACE COMMANDED, this grace of joy; "Rejoice in the Lord," says the apostle.

In the first place, *this is a very delightful thing.* What a gracious God we serve, who makes delight to be a duty, and who commands us to rejoice! Should we not at once be obedient to such a command as this? It is intended that we should be happy. That is the meaning of the precept, that we should be cheerful; more than that, that we should be thankful; more than that, that we should rejoice. I think this word "rejoice" is almost a French word; it is not only joy, but it is joy over again, re-joice. You know *re* usually signifies the re-duplication of a thing, the taking it over again. We are to joy, and then we are to re-joy. We are to chew the cud of delight; we are to roll the dainty morsel under our tongue till we get the very essence out of it. "Rejoice." Joy is a delightful thing. You cannot be too happy, brother. Nay, do not suspect yourself of being wrong because you are full of delight. You know it is said of the divine wisdom, "Her ways are ways of pleasantness, and all her paths are peace." Provided that it is joy in the Lord, you cannot have too much of it. The fly is drowned in the honey, or the sweet syrup into which he plunges himself; but this heavenly syrup of delight will not drown your soul, or intoxicate your heart. It will do you good, and not evil, all the days of your life. God never commanded us to do a thing which would really harm us; and when He bids us rejoice, we may be sure that this is as delightful as it is safe, and as safe as it is delightful. Come, brothers and sisters, I am inviting you now to no distasteful duty when, in the name of my Master, I say to you, as Paul said to the Philippians under the teaching of the Holy Spirit, "Rejoice in the Lord alway: and again I say, Rejoice."

But, next, *this is a demonstrative duty :* "Rejoice in the Lord." There may be such a thing as a dumb joy, but I hardly think that it can keep dumb long. Joy! joy! Why, it speaks for itself! It is like a candle lighted in a dark chamber; you need not sound a trumpet, and say, "Now light has come." The candle proclaims itself by its own brilliance; and when joy comes into a man, it shines out of his eyes, it sparkles in his countenance. There is a something about every limb of the man that betokens that his body, like a well-tuned harp, has had its strings put in order. Joy—it refreshes the marrow of the bones; it quickens the flowing of the blood in the veins; it is a healthy thing in all respects. It is a speaking thing, a demonstrative thing; and I am sure that joy in the Lord ought to have a tongue. When the Lord sends you affliction, sister, you generally grumble loudly enough; when the Lord tries you, my dear brother, you generally speak fast enough about that. Now when, on the other hand, the Lord multiplies His mercies to you, do speak about it, do sing about it. I cannot recollect, since I was a boy, ever seeing in the newspapers columns of thankfulness and expressions of delight about the prosperity of business in England. It is a long, long time since I was first able to read newspapers—a great many years now; but I do not recollect the paragraphs in which it was said that everybody was getting on in the world.

and growing rich; but as soon as there was any depression in business, what lugubrious articles appeared concerning the dreadful times which had fallen upon the agricultural interest and every other interest! Oh, my dear brethren, from the way some of you grumble, I might imagine you were all ruined if I did not know better! I knew some of you when you were not worth twopence, and you are pretty well-to-do now; you have got on uncommonly well for men who are being ruined! From the way some people talk, you might imagine that everybody is bankrupt, and that we are all going to the dogs together; but it is not so, and what a pity it is that we do not give the Lord some of our praises when we have better times! If we are so loud and so eloquent over our present woes, why could we not have been as eloquent and as loud in thanksgiving for the blessings that God formerly vouchsafed to us? Perhaps the mercies buried in oblivion have been to heaven, and accused us to the Lord, and therefore He has sent us the sorrows of to-day. True joy, when it is joy in the Lord, must speak; it cannot hold its tongue, it must praise the name of the Lord.

Further, *this blessed grace of joy is very contagious.* It is a great privilege, I think, to meet a truly happy man, a graciously happy man. My mind goes back at this moment to that dear man of God who used to be with us, years ago, whom we called "Old Father Dransfield." What a lump of sunshine that man was! I think that I never came into this place, with a heavy heart, but the very sight of him seemed to fill me with exhilaration, for his joy was wholly in his God! An old man and full of years, but as full of happiness as he was full of days; always having something to tell you to encourage you. He constantly made a discovery of some fresh mercy for which we were again to praise God. O dear brethren, let us rejoice in the Lord, that we may set others rejoicing! One dolorous spirit brings a kind of plague into the house; one person who is always wretched seems to stop all the birds singing wherever he goes; but, as the birds pipe to each other, and one morning songster quickens all the rest, and sets the groves ringing with harmony, so will it be with the happy cheerful spirit of a man who obeys the command of the text, "Rejoice in the Lord alway." This grace of joy is contagious.

Besides, dear brethren, *joy in the Lord is influential for good.* I am sure that there is a mighty influence wielded by a consistently joyous spirit. See how little children are affected by the presence of a happy person. There is much more in the tone of the life than there is in the particular fashion of the life. It may be the life of one who is very poor, but oh, how poverty is gilded by a cheerful spirit! It may be the life of one who is well read and deeply instructed; but, oh, if there be a beauty of holiness, and a beauty of happiness added to the learning, nobody talks about "the blue stocking" or "the book-worm" being dull and heavy. Oh, no, there is a charm about holy joy! I wish we had more of it! There are many more flies caught with honey than with vinegar; and there are many more sinners brought to Christ by happy Christians than by doleful Christians. Let us sing unto the Lord as long as we live; and, mayhap, some weary sinner, who has discovered the emptiness of sinful pleasure, will say to himself, "Why, after all, there must be something real about the joy of these Christians; let me go and learn how I may have it." And when he comes and sees it in the light of your gladsome countenance, he will be likely to learn it, God helping him, so as never to forget it. "Rejoice in the Lord alway," says the apostle, for joy is a most influential grace, and every child of God ought to possess it in a high degree.

I want you to notice, dear friends, that *this rejoicing is commanded*. It is not a matter that is left to your option; it is not set before you as a desirable thing which you can do without, but it is a positive precept of the Holy Spirit to all who are in the Lord: "Rejoice in the Lord alway." We ought to obey this precept because joy in the Lord makes us like God. He is the happy God; ineffable bliss is the atmosphere in which He lives, and He would have His people to be happy. Let the devotees of Baal cut themselves with knives and lancets, and make hideous outcries if they will; but the servants of Jehovah must not even mar the corners of their beard. Even if they fast, they shall anoint their head, and wash their face, that they appear not unto men to fast, for a joyous God desires a joyous people.

You are commanded to rejoice. brethren, because this is for your profit. Holy joy will oil the wheels of your life's machinery. Holy joy will strengthen you for your daily labour. Holy joy will beautify you, and, as I have already said, give you an influence over the lives of others. It is upon this point that I would most of all insist, we are commanded to rejoice in the Lord. If you cannot speak the gospel, live the gospel by your cheerfulness; for what is the gospel? Glad tidings of great joy; and you who believe it must show by its effect upon you that it is glad tidings of great joy to you. I do believe that a man of God—under trial and difficulty and affliction, bearing up, and patiently submitting with holy acquiescence, and still rejoicing in God— is a real preacher of the gospel, preaching with an eloquence which is mightier than words can ever be, and which will find its secret and silent way into the hearts of those who might have resisted other arguments. Oh, do, then, listen to the text, for it is a command from God, "Rejoice in the Lord alway!"

May I just pause here, and hand this commandment round to all of you who are members of this church, and to all of you who are truly members of Christ? You are bidden to rejoice in the Lord alway; you are not allowed to sit there, and fret, and fume; you are not permitted to complain and groan. Mourner, you are commanded to put on beauty for ashes, and the oil of joy for mourning. For this purpose your Saviour came, the Spirit of the Lord is upon Him for this very end, that He might make you to rejoice. Therefore, sing with the prophet, "I will greatly rejoice in the Lord, my soul shall be joyful in my God; for He hath clothed me with the garments of salvation, He hath covered me with a robe of righteousness, as a bridegroom decketh himself with ornaments, and as a bride adorneth herself with her jewels."

II. Now we come to the second head, on which I will speak but briefly; that is, THE JOY DISCRIMINATED: "Rejoice *in the Lord*."

Notice *the sphere of this joy:* "Rejoice in the Lord." We read in Scripture that children are to obey their parents "in the Lord." We read of men and women being married "only in the Lord." Now, dear friends, no child of God must go outside that ring, "in the Lord." There is where you are,

where you ought to be, where you must be. You cannot truly rejoice if you get outside that ring; therefore, see that you do nothing which you cannot do "in the Lord." Mind that you seek no joy which is not joy in the Lord; if you go after the poisonous sweets of this world, woe be to you. Never rejoice in that which is sinful, for all such rejoicing is evil. Flee from it; it can do you no good. That joy which you cannot share with God is not a right joy for you. No; "in the Lord" is the sphere of your joy.

But I think that the apostle also means that *God is to be the great object of your joy:* "Rejoice in the Lord." Rejoice in the Father, your Father who is in heaven, your loving, tender, unchangeable God. Rejoice, too, in the Son, your Redeemer, your Brother, the Husband of your soul, your Prophet, Priest, and King. Rejoice also in the Holy Ghost, your Quickener, your Comforter, in Him who shall abide with you for ever. Rejoice in the one God of Abraham, of Isaac, and of Jacob; in Him delight yourselves, as it is written, "Delight thyself also in the Lord; and He shall give thee the desires of thine heart." We cannot have too much of this joy in the Lord, for the great Jehovah is our exceeding joy. Or if, by "the Lord" is meant the Lord Jesus, then let me invite, persuade, command you to delight in the Lord Jesus, incarnate in your flesh, dead for your sins, risen for your justification, gone into the glory claiming victory for you, sitting at the right hand of God interceding for you, reigning over all worlds on your behalf, and soon to come to take you up into His glory that you may be with Him for ever. Rejoice in the Lord Jesus. This is a sea of delight; blessed are they that dive into its utmost depths.

Sometimes, brethren and sisters, you cannot rejoice in anything else, but you can rejoice in the Lord; then, rejoice in Him to the full. Do not rejoice in your temporal prosperity, for riches take to themselves wings, and fly away. Do not rejoice even in your great successes in the work of God. Remember how the seventy disciples came back to Jesus, and said, "Lord, even the devils are subject unto us through Thy name," and He answered, "Notwithstanding in this rejoice not, that the spirits are subject unto you; but rather rejoice, because your names are written in heaven." Do not rejoice in your privileges; I mean, do not make the great joy of your life to be the fact that you are favoured with this and that external privilege or ordinance, but rejoice in God. He changes not. If the Lord be your joy, your joy will never dry up. All other things are but for a season; but God is for ever and ever. Make Him your joy, the whole of your joy, and then let this joy absorb your every thought. Be baptized into this joy; plunge into the deeps of this unutterable bliss of joy in God.

III. Thirdly, let us think of THE TIME APPOINTED for this rejoicing: "Rejoice in the Lord *alway*."

"Alway." Well, then, that begins at once, certainly; so let us now begin to rejoice in the Lord. If any of you have taken a gloomy view of religion, I beseech you to throw that gloomy view away at once. "Rejoice in the Lord alway," therefore, rejoice in the Lord now. I recollect what a damper I had, as a young Christian, when I had but lately believed in Jesus Christ. I felt that, as the Lord had said, "He that believeth in Me hath everlasting life," I, having believed in Him, had everlasting life, and I said so, with the greatest joy and delight and enthusiasm, to an old Christian man; and he said to me, "Beware of presumption! There are a great many who think they have eternal life, but who have not got it," which was quite true; but, for all that, is there not more presumption in doubting God's promise than there is in believing it? Is there any presumption in taking God at His word? Is there not gross presumption in hesitating and questioning as to whether these things are so or not? If God says that they are so, then they are so, whether I feel that they are so or not; and it is my place, as a believer, to accept God's bare word, and rest on it. "We count cheques as cash," said one who was making up accounts. Good cheques are to be counted as cash, and the promises of God, though as yet unfulfilled, are as good as the blessings themselves, for God cannot lie, or make a promise that He will not perform. Let us, therefore, not be afraid of being glad, but begin to be glad at once if we have hitherto taken a gloomy view of true religion, and have been afraid to rejoice.

When are we to be glad? "Rejoice in the Lord alway"; that is, *when you cannot rejoice in anything or anyone but God.* When the fig-tree does not blossom, when there is no fruit on the vine and no herd in the stall, when everything withers and decays and perishes, when the worm at the root of the gourd has made it to die, then rejoice in the Lord. When the day darkens into evening, and the evening into midnight, and the midnight into a sevenfold horror of great darkness, rejoice in the Lord; and when that darkness does not clear, but becomes more dense and Egyptian, when night succeedeth night, and neither sun nor moon nor stars appear, still rejoice in the Lord alway. He who uttered these words had been a night and a day in the deep, he had been stoned, he had suffered from false brethren, he had been in peril of his life, and yet most fittingly do those lips cry out to us, "Rejoice in the Lord alway." Ay, at the stake itself have martyrs fulfilled this word; they clapped their hands amid the fire that was consuming them. Therefore, rejoice in the Lord when you cannot rejoice in any other.

But also take care that you *rejoice in the Lord when you have other things to rejoice in.* When He loads your table with good things, and your cup is overflowing with blessings, rejoice in *Him* more than in *them.* Forget not that the Lord your Shepherd is better than the green pastures and the still waters, and rejoice not in the pastures or in the waters in comparison with your joy in the Shepherd who gives you all. Let us never make gods out of our goods; let us never allow what God gives us to supplant the Giver. Shall the wife love the jewels that her husband gave her better than she loves him who gave them to her? That were an evil love, or no love at all. So, let us love God first, and rejoice in the Lord alway when the day is brightest, and multiplied are the other joys that He permits us to have.

"Rejoice in the Lord alway." That is, *if you have not rejoiced before, begin to do so at once;* and *when you have long rejoiced, keep on at it.* I have known, sometimes, that things have gone so smoothly that I have said, "There will be a check to this prosperity; I know that there will. Things cannot go on quite so pleasantly always."

"More the treacherous calm I dread
Than tempests lowering overhead."

One is apt to spoil his joy by the apprehension that there is some evil coming. Now listen to this: "He shall not be afraid of evil tidings: his heart is fixed, trusting in the Lord." "Rejoice in the Lord alway." Do not anticipate trouble. "Sufficient unto the day is the evil thereof." Take the good that God provides thee, and rejoice not merely in it, but in Him who provides it. So mayest thou enjoy it without fear, for there is good salt with that food which is eaten as coming from the hand of God.

"Rejoice in the Lord alway." That is, *when you get into company, then rejoice in the Lord.* Do not be ashamed to let others see that you are glad. *Rejoice in the Lord also when you are alone.* I know what happens to some of you on Sunday night. You have had such a blessed Sabbath, and you have gone away from the Lord's table with the very flavour of heaven in your mouths; and then some of you have had to go home where everything is against you. The husband does not receive you with any sympathy with your joy, or the father does not welcome you with any fellowship in your delight. Well, but still, "Rejoice in the Lord *alway.*" When you cannot get anybody else to rejoice with you, still continue to rejoice. There is a way of looking at everything which will show you that the blackest cloud has a silver lining. There is a way of looking at all things in the light of God, which will turn into sweetness that which otherwise has been bitter as gall. I do not know whether any of you keep a quassia cup at home. If you do, you know that it is made of wood, and you pour water into the bowl, and the water turns bitter directly before you drink it. You may keep this cup as long as you like, but it always embitters the water that is put into it. I think that I know some dear brethren and sisters who always seem to have one of these cups handy. Now, instead of that, I want you to buy a cup of another kind that shall make everything sweet, whatever it is. Whatever God pleases to pour out of the bowl of providence shall come into your cup, and your contentment, your delight in God, shall sweeten it all. God bless you, dear friends, with much of this holy joy!

IV. So now I finish with the fourth head, which is this, THE EMPHASIS LAID ON THE COMMAND: "Rejoice in the Lord alway: *and again I say, Rejoice.*" What does that mean, "Again I say, Rejoice"?

This was, first, *to show Paul's love for the Philippians.* He wanted them to be happy. They had been so kind to him, and they had made him so happy, that he said, "Oh, dear brethren, do rejoice; dear sisters, do rejoice. I say it twice over to you, 'Be happy, be happy,' because I love you so well that I am anxious to have you beyond all things else to rejoice in the Lord alway."

I also think that, perhaps, he said it twice over to suggest the *difficulty of continual joy.* It is not so easy as some think always to rejoice. It may be for you young people, who are yet strong in limb, who have few aches and pains, and none of the infirmities of life. It may be an easy thing to those placed in easy circumstances, with few cares and difficulties; but there are some of God's people who need great grace if they are to rejoice in the Lord always; and the apostle knew that, so he said, "Again I say, Rejoice." He repeats the precept, as much as to say, "I know it is a difficult thing, and so I the more earnestly press it upon you. Again I say, Rejoice."

I think, too, that he said it twice over *to assert the possibility of it.* This was as much as if he had said, "I told you to rejoice in the Lord always. You opened your eyes, and looked with astonishment upon me; but, 'Again I say, Rejoice.' It is possible, it is practicable; I have not spoken unwisely. I have not told you to do what you never can do; but with deliberation I write it down, 'Again I say, Rejoice.' You can be happy. God the Holy Ghost can lift you above the down-draggings of the flesh, and of the world, and of the devil; and you may be enabled to live upon the mount of God beneath the shinings of His face. 'Again I say, Rejoice.'"

Do you not think that this was intended also *to impress upon them the importance of the duty*? "Again I say, Rejoice." Some of you will go and say, "I do not think that it matters much whether I am happy or not, I shall get to heaven, however gloomy I am, if I am sincere." "No," says Paul, "that kind of talk will not do; I cannot have you speak like that. Come, I must have you rejoice, I do really conceive it to be a Christian's bounden duty, and so, 'Again, I say, Rejoice.'"

But do you not think, also, that Paul repeated the command *to allow of special personal testimony*? "Again, I say, Rejoice. I, Paul, a sufferer to the utmost extent for Christ's sake, even now an ambassador in bonds, shut up in a dungeon. I say to you, Rejoice." Paul was a greatly-tried man, but he was a blessedly happy man. There is not one of us but would gladly change conditions with Paul, if that were possible, now that we see the whole of his life written out; and to-night, looking across the ages, over all the scenes of trouble which he encountered, he says to us, "Brethren, rejoice in the Lord alway: and again I say, Rejoice."

Did you ever notice how full of joy this Epistle to the Philippians is? Will you spare me just a minute while I get you to run your eyes through it, to observe what a joyful letter it is? You notice that, in the first chapter, Paul gets only as far as the fourth verse when he says, "Always in every prayer of mine for you all making request with joy." Now he is in his right vein: he is so glad because of what God has done for the Philippians that, when he prays for them, he mixes joy with his prayer. In the eighteenth verse, he declares that he found joy even in the opposition of those who preached Christ in order to rival him. Hear what he says: "The one preach Christ of contention, not sincerely, supposing to add affliction to my bonds: but the other of love, knowing that I am set for the defence of the gospel. What then? Notwithstanding, every way, whether in pretence, or in truth, Christ is preached; and I therein do rejoice, yea, and will rejoice." And he does not finish the chapter till, in the twenty-fifth verse, he declares that he had joy even in the expectation of not going to heaven just yet, but living a little longer to do good to these people: "And having this confidence, I know that I shall abide and continue with you all for your furtherance and joy of faith; that your rejoicing may be more abundant in Jesus Christ for me by my coming to you again." You see it is joy, joy, joy, joy. Paul seems to go from stave to stave of the ladder of light, as if he were climbing up from Nero's dungeon into heaven itself by way of continual joy. So he writes, in the second verse of the second chapter, "Fulfil ye my joy, that ye be likeminded, having the same love, being of one accord, of one mind." When he gets to the sixteenth verse, he says, "That I may rejoice in the day of Christ that I have not run in vain, neither laboured in vain."

But I am afraid that I should weary you if I went through the Epistle thus, slowly, verse by verse. Just notice how he begins the third chapter: "Finally, my brethren, rejoice in the Lord." The word is sometimes rendered "farewell." When he says, "Rejoice," it is the counterpart of "welcome." We say to a man who comes to our house, "Salve," "Welcome." When he goes away, it is our duty, to "speed the parting guest," and say, "Farewell." This is what Paul meant to say here. "Finally, my brethren, fare you well in the Lord. Be happy in the Lord. Rejoice in the Lord." And I do not think that I can finish up my sermon better than by saying on this Sabbath night, "Finally, my brethren, fare you well, be happy in the Lord."

"Fare thee well! and if for ever,
      Still for ever, fare thee well."

May that be your position, so to walk with God that your fare shall be that of angels! May you eat angels' food, the manna of God's love! May your drink be from the rock that flows with a pure stream! So may you feed and so may your drink until you come unto the mount of God, where you shall see His face unveiled, and standing in His exceeding brightness, shall know His glory, being glorified with the saved. Till then, be happy. Why, even—

"The thought of such amazing bliss,
      Should constant joys create."

Be happy. If the present be dreary, it will soon be over. Oh, but a little while, and we shall be transferred from these seats below to the thrones above! We shall go from the place of aching brows to the place where they all wear crowns; from the place of weary hands to where they bear the palm branch of victory; from the place of mistake and error and sin, and consequent grief, to the place where they are without fault before the throne of God, for they have washed their robes, and made them white in the blood of the Lamb. Come, then, let us make a solemn league and covenant together in the name of God, and let it be called, "The Guild of the Happy"; for the—

"Favourites of the Heavenly King
      May speak their joys abroad";

nay, they *must* speak their joys abroad; let us endeavour to do so always, by the help of the Holy Spirit. Amen and Amen.

PRAYER, THE CURE FOR CARE

"Be careful for nothing; but in every thing by prayer and supplication with thanksgiving let your requests be made known unto God. And the peace of God, which passeth all understanding, shall keep your hearts and minds through Christ Jesus."—Philippians iv. 6, 7.

WE have the faculty of forethought; but, like all our faculties, it has been perverted, and it is often abused. It is good for a man to have a holy care, and to pay due attention to every item of his life; but, alas! it is very easy to make it into an unholy care, and to try to wrest from the hand of God that office of providence which belongs to Him and not to ourselves. How often Luther liked to talk about the birds, and the way God cares for them! When he was full of his anxieties, he used constantly to envy the birds because they led so free and happy a life. He talks of Dr. Sparrow, and Dr. Thrush, and others that used to come and talk to Dr. Luther, and tell him many a good thing. You know, brethren, the birds out in the open yonder, cared for by God, fare far better than those that are cared for by man. A little London girl, who had gone into the country, once said, "Look, mamma, at that poor little bird; it has not got any cage!" That would not have struck me as being any loss to the bird; and if you and I were without our cage, and the box of seed, and glass of water, it would not be much of a loss if we were cast adrift into the glorious liberty of a life of humble dependence upon God. It is that cage of carnal trust, and that box of seed that we are always labouring to fill, that makes the worry of this mortal life; but he who has grace to spread his wings and soar away, and get into the open field of divine trustfulness, may sing all the day, and ever have this for his tune,—

"Mortal, cease from toil and sorrow;
God provideth for the morrow."

Here, then, is the teaching of the text: "Be careful for nothing." The word "careful" does not now mean exactly what it did when the Bible was translated; at least, it conveys a different meaning to me from what it did to the translators. I would say that we should be careful. "Be careful," is a good lesson for boys and young people when they are starting in life; but, in the same sense in which the word "care-ful" was understood at the time of the translators, we must not be careful, that is, full of care. The text means, be not anxious; be not constantly thinking about the needs of this mortal life. I will read it again, stretching the word out a little, and then you will get the meaning of it: "Be care-ful for nothing." Oh, that God might teach us how to avoid the evil which is here forbidden, and to live with that holy carelessness which is the very beauty of the Christian life, when all our care is cast on God, and we can joy and rejoice in His providential care of us!

"Ah!" says somebody, "I cannot help caring." Well, the subject to-night is to help you to leave off caring; and, first, consider here *the substitute for care*. Be careful for nothing, but be prayerful for everything; that is the substitute for care, "prayer and supplication." Secondly, note *the special character of this prayer*, which is to become the substitute for anxiety: "In every thing by prayer and supplication with thanksgiving let your requests be made known unto God." And then I hope we shall have a few minutes left in which to consider *the sweet effect of this prayer*: "The peace of God, which passeth all understanding, shall keep your hearts and minds through Christ Jesus."

I. To begin, then, here is, first, THE SUBSTITUTE FOR CARE.

I suppose it is true of many of us that *our cares are manifold*. If you once become careful, anxious, fretful, you will never be able to count your cares, even though you might count the hairs of your head. And cares are apt to multiply to those who are careful; and when you are as full of care as you think you can be, you will be sure to have another crop of cares growing up all around you. The indulgence of this ill habit of anxiety leads to its getting dominion over life, till life is not worth living by reason of the care we have about it. Cares are manifold; therefore let your prayers be as manifold. Turn into a prayer everything that is a care. Let your cares be the raw material of your prayers; and, as the alchemists hoped to turn dross into gold, so do you, by a holy alchemy, actually turn what naturally would have been a care into spiritual treasure in the form of prayer. Baptize every anxiety into the name of the Father, and of the Son, and of the Holy Ghost, and so make it into a blessing.

Have you a care to get? Take heed that it does not get you. Do you wish to make gain? Mind you do not lose more than you gain by your gains. I beseech you, have no more care to gain than you dare turn into a prayer. Do not desire to have what you dare not ask God to give you. Measure your desires by a spiritual standard, and you will thus be kept from anything like covetousness. Cares come to many from their losses; they lose what they have gained. Well, this is a world in which there is the tendency to lose. Ebbs follow floods, and winters crush out summer flowers. Do not wonder if you lose as other people do; but pray about your losses. Go to God with them; and instead of fretting, make them an occasion for waiting upon the Lord, and saying, "The Lord gave, and the Lord hath taken away; blessed be the name of the Lord. Show me wherefore Thou contendest with me, and deliver Thy servant, I pray Thee, from ever complaining of Thee whatever Thou dost permit me to lose!"

Perhaps you say that your care is neither about your gainings nor your losings, but even about your daily bread. Ah, well, you have promises for that, you know! The Lord has said, "So shalt thou dwell in the land, and verily thou shalt be fed." He gives you sweet encouragement when He says that He clothes the grass of the field, and shall He not much more clothe you, O ye of little faith? And the Lord Jesus bids you consider the fowls of heaven, how they sow not, neither do they gather into barns, and yet your heavenly Father feedeth them. Go, then, to your God with all your cares. If you have a large family, a slender income, and much ado to make ends meet, and to provide things honest in the sight of all men, you have so many excuses for knocking at God's door, so many more reasons for being often found at the throne of grace. I beseech you, turn them to good account. I feel free to call upon a friend when I really have some business to do with him; and you may be bold to call upon God when necessities press upon you. Instead of caring for anything with anxious care, turn it at once into a reason for renewed prayerfulness.

"Ah!" says one, "but I am in perplexity; I do not know what to do." Well, then, dear friend, you should certainly pray when you cannot tell whether it is the right hand road, or the left hand, or straight on, or whether you should go back. Indeed, when you are in such a fog that you cannot see the next lamp, then is the time that you must pray. The road will clear before you very suddenly. I have often had to try this plan myself; and I bear witness that, when I have trusted to myself, I have been a gigantic fool, but when I have trusted in God, then He has led me straight on in the right way, and there has been no mistake about it. I believe that God's children often make greater blunders over simple things than they do over more difficult matters. You know how it was with Israel, when those Gibeonites came, with their old shoes and clouted, and showed the bread that was mouldy, that they said they took fresh out of their ovens. The children of Israel thought, "This is a clear case; these men are strangers, they have come from a far country, and we may make a league with them." They were certain that the evidence of their eyes proved that these were no Canaanites, so they did not consult God; the whole matter seemed so plain that they made a league with the Gibeonites, which was a trouble to them ever afterwards. If we would in everything go to God in prayer, our perplexities would lead us into no more mistakes than our simplicities; and in simple things and difficult things we should be guided by the Most High.

Perhaps another friend says, "But I am thinking about the future." Are you? Well, first, I beg to ask you what you have to do with the future. Dost thou know what a day will bring forth? You have been thinking about what will become of you when you are old; but are you sure that you ever will be old? I did know one Christian woman who used to worry herself about how she would get buried. That question never troubled me; and there are many other matters about which we need not worry ourselves. You can always find a stick with which to beat a dog; and, if you want a care, you can generally find a care with which to beat your own souls; but that is a poor occupation for any of you. Instead of doing that, turn everything that might be a subject of care into a subject of prayer. It will not be long before you have a subject of care, so you will not be long without a subject of prayer. Strike out that word "care," and just write in the stead of it this word "prayer"; and then, though your cares are manifold, your prayers will also be manifold.

Note, next, dear friends, that *undue care is an intrusion into God's province.* It is making yourself the father of the household instead of being a child; it is making yourself the master instead of being a servant, for whom the master provides his rations. Now, if, instead of doing that, you will turn care into prayer, there will be no intrusion, for you may come to God in prayer without being charged with pre-sumption. He invites you to pray; nay, here, by His servant, He bids you "in every thing by prayer and supplication with thanksgiving let your requests be made known unto God."

Once more, *cares are of no use to us, and they cause us great damage.* If you were to worry as long as you wished, you could not make yourself an inch taller, or grow another hair on your head, or make one hair white or black. So the Saviour tells us; and He asks, if care fails in such little things, what can care do in the higher matters of providence? It cannot do anything. A farmer stood in his fields, and said, "I do not know what will happen to us all. The wheat will be destroyed if this rain keeps on; we shall not have any harvest at all unless we have some fine weather." He walked up and down, wringing his hands, and fretting, and making his whole household uncomfortable; but he did not produce one single gleam of sunlight by all his worrying, he could not puff any of the clouds away with all his petulant speech, nor could he stay a drop of rain with all his murmurings.

What is the good of it, then, to keep gnawing at your own heart, when you can get nothing by it? Besides, it weakens our power to help ourselves, and especially our power to glorify God. A care-full heart hinders us from judging rightly in many things. I have often used the illustration (I do not know a better) of taking a telescope, breathing on it with the hot breath of our anxiety, putting it to our eye, and then saying that we cannot see anything but clouds. Of course we cannot, and we never shall while we breathe upon it. If we were but calm, quiet, self-possessed, we should do the right thing. We should be, as we say, "all there" in the time of difficulty. That man may expect to have presence of mind who has the presence of God. If we forget to pray, do you wonder that we are all in a fidget, and a worry, and we do the first thing that occurs to us, which is generally the worst thing, instead of waiting till we saw what should be done, and then trustfully and believingly doing it as in the sight of God? Care is injurious; but if you only turn this care into prayer, then every care will be a benefit to you.

Prayer is wonderful material for building up the spiritual fabric. We are ourselves edified by prayer; we grow in grace by prayer; and if we will but come to God every moment with petitions, we shall be fast-growing Christians. I said to one this morning, "Pray for me, it is a time of need;" and she replied, "I have done nothing else since I woke." I have made the same request of several others, and they have said that they have been praying for me. I felt so glad, not only for my own sake who had received benefit from their prayers, but for their sakes, because they are sure to grow thereby. When little birds keep flapping their wings, they are learning to fly. The sinews will get stronger, and the birds will quit the nest before long; that very wing-clapping is an education, and the attempting to pray, the groaning, the sighing, the crying, of a prayerful spirit, is itself a blessing. Leave off, then, this endamaging habit of care, and take to this enriching habit of prayer. See how you will thus make a double gain; first, by avoiding a loss, and secondly, by getting that which will really benefit you and others, too.

Then, again, *cares are the effect of forgetfulness of Christ's closeness to us.* Did you notice how the context runs? "The Lord is at hand. Be careful for nothing." The Lord Jesus Christ has promised to come again, and He may come to-night; at any moment He may appear. So Paul writes, "The Lord is at hand. Be careful for nothing; but in every thing by prayer and supplication with thanksgiving let your requests be made known unto God." Oh, if we we could but stand on this earth as upon a mere shadow, and live as those who will soon have done with this poor transient life, if we held every earthly thing with a very loose hand, then we should not be caring, and worrying, and fretting, but we should take to praying, for thus we should grasp the real, and the substantial, and plant our feet upon the invisible, which is, after all, the eternal! Oh, dear friends, let the text, which I have read to you over and over again, now drop into your hearts as a pebble falls into a mountain tarn, and as it enters let it make rings of comfort upon the very surface of your soul!

II. Now we want to look into the text a little more closely to see, in the second place, THE SPECIAL CHARACTER OF THIS PRAYER. What sort of prayer is that which will ease us of care?"

Well, first, it is *a prayer which deals with every-thing.* "In every thing" "let your requests be made known unto God." You may pray about the smallest thing and about the greatest thing; you may not only pray for the Holy Spirit, but you may pray for a new pair of boots. You may go to God about the bread you eat, the water you drink, the raiment you wear, and pray to Him about everything. Draw no line, and say, "So far is to be under the care of God." Dear me, then, what are you going to do with the rest of life? Is that to be lived under the withering blight of a sort of atheism? God forbid! Oh, that we might live in God as to the whole of our being, for our being is such that we cannot divide it! Our body, soul, and spirit are one, and while God leaves us in this world, and we have necessities which arise out of the condition of our bodies, we must bring our bodily necessities before God in prayer. And you will find that the great God will hear you in these matters. Say not that they are too little for Him to notice; everything is little in comparison with Him. When I think of what a great God He is, it seems to me that this poor little world of ours is just one insignificant grain of sand on the seashore of the universe, and not worth any notice at all. The whole earth is a mere speck in the great world of nature; and if God condescends to consider it, He may as well stoop a little lower, and consider us; and He does so, for He says, "Even the very hairs of your head are all numbered." Therefore, in everything let your requests be made known unto God.

The kind of prayer that saves us from care is *prayer that is repeated:* "In every thing by prayer and supplication." Pray to God, and then pray again: "by prayer and supplication." If the Lord does not answer you the first time, be very grateful that you have a good reason for praying again. If He does not grant your request the second time, believe that He loves you so much that He wants to hear your voice again; and if He keeps you waiting till you have gone to Him seven times, say to yourself, "Now I know that I worship the God of Elijah, for Elijah's God let him go again seven times before the blessing was given." Count it an honour to be permitted to wrestle with the angel. This is the way God makes His princes. Jacob had never been Israel if he had obtained the blessing from the angel at the first asking; but when he had to keep on wrestling till he prevailed, then he became a prince with God. The prayer that kills care is prayer that is continued and importunate.

Next, it is *intelligent prayer:* "Let your requests be made known unto God." I heard of a Mohammedan who spent, I think, six hours in prayer each day; and lest he should go to sleep, when on board a boat, he stood upright, and only had a rope stretched across, so that he might lean against it, and if he slept, he would fall. His object was to keep on for six hours with what he called prayer. "Well," I said to one who knew him, and who had seen him on board his dahabieh on the Nile, "What sort of prayer was it?" "Why," my friend replied, "he kept on repeating, 'There is no God but God, and Mohammed is the prophet of God,' the same thing over, and over, and over again." I said, "Did he ask for anything?" "Oh, no!" "Was he pleading with God to give him anything?" "No, he simply kept on with that perpetual repetition of certain words, just as a witch might repeat a charm." Do you think there is anything in that style of praying? And if you go on your knees, and simply repeat a certain formula, it will be only a mouthful of words. What does God care about that kind of praying? "Let your requests be made known unto God." That is true prayer. God does know what your requests are; but you are to pray to Him as if He did not know. You are to make known your requests, not because the Lord does not know, but perhaps because you do not know; and when you have made your requests known to Him, as the text tells you, you will more clearly have made them known to yourself. When you have asked intelligently, knowing what you have asked, and knowing why you have asked it, you will perhaps stop, and say to yourself, "No, I must not, after all, make that request." Sometimes, when you have gone on praying for what God does not give you, it may be that there will steal over your mind the conviction that you are not on the right track; and that result of your prayer will in itself do you good, and be a blessing to you.

But you are to pray, making your requests known unto God. That is, in plain English, say what you want; for this is the true prayer. Get alone, and tell the Lord what you want; pour out your heart before Him. Do not imagine that God wants any fine language. No, you need not run upstairs for your prayer-book, and turn to a collect; you will be a long time before you will find any collect that will fit you if you are really praying. Pray for what you want just as if you were telling your mother or your dearest friend what your need is. Go to God in that fashion, for that is the real prayer, and that is the kind of prayer that will drive away your care.

So, dear friends, again, the kind of prayer that brings freedom from care is *communion with God.* If you have not spoken to God, you have not really prayed. A little child has been known (I daresay your children have done it) to go and put a letter down the grating of a drain; and of course there was never any reply to a letter posted in that way. If the letter is not put into the post-box, so that it goes to the person to whom it is addressed, what is the use of it? So, prayer is real communication with God. You must realize that He is, and that He is the Rewarder of them that diligently seek Him, or else you cannot pray. He must be a reality to you, a living reality; and you must believe that He does hear prayer, and then you must speak with Him, and believe that you have the petition that you ask of Him, and so you shall have it. He has never yet failed to honour believing prayer. He may keep you waiting for a while; but delays are not denials, and He has often answered a prayer that asked for silver by giving gold. He may have denied earthly treasure, but He has given heavenly riches of ten thousand times the worth, and the suppliant has been more than satisfied with the exchange. "Let your requests be made known unto God." I know what you do when you are in trouble: you go to your neighbour, but your neighbour does not want to see you quite so often about such business. Possibly you go to your brother; but there is a text that warns you not to go into your brother's house in the day of your calamity. You may call on a friend too often when you are hard up; he may be very pleased to see you till he hears what you are after; but if you go to your God, He will never give you the cold shoulder, He will never say that you come too often. On the contrary, He will even chide you because you do not come to Him often enough.

There is one word which I passed over just now because I wanted to leave it for my last observation on this point: "By prayer and supplication *with thanksgiving* let your requests be made known unto God." Now what does that mean? It means that the kind of prayer that kills care is *a prayer that asks cheerfully, joyfully, thankfully*. "Lord, I am poor; let me bless Thee for my poverty, and then, O Lord, wilt Thou not supply all my needs?" That is the way to pray. "Lord, I am ill; I bless Thee for this affliction, for I am sure that it means some good thing to me. Now be pleased to heal me, I beseech Thee!" "Lord, I am in a great trouble; but I praise Thee for the trouble, for I know that it contains a blessing though the envelope is black-edged; and then, Lord, help me through my trouble!" That is the kind of prayer that kills care: "supplication with thanksgiving." Mix these two things well; one drachm,—no, two drachms of prayer, prayer and supplication, then one drachm of thanksgiving. Rub them well together, and they will make a blessed cure for care. May the Lord teach us to practise this holy art of the apothecary!

III. I finish with this third point, THE SWEET EFFECT OF THIS PRAYER: "And the peace of God, which passeth all understanding, shall keep your hearts and minds through Christ Jesus."

If you can pray in this fashion, instead of indulging evil anxiety, the result will be that an *unusual peace* will steal over your heart and mind, unusual, for it will be "the peace of God." What is God's peace. The unruffled serenity of the infinitely-happy God, the eternal composure of the absolutely well-contented God. This shall possess your heart and mind. Notice how Paul describes it: "The peace of God, which passeth all understanding." Other people will not understand it; they will not be able to make out how you can be so quiet. What is more, you will not be able to tell them; for if it surpasses all understanding, it certainly passes all expression; and what is even more wonderful, you will not understand it yourself.

It will be such a peace that it will be to you *unfathomable and immeasurable*. When one of the martyrs was about to burn for Christ, he said to the judge who was giving orders to fire the pile, "Will you come and lay your hand on my heart?"

The judge did so. "Does it beat fast?" enquired the martyr. "Do I show any signs of fear?" "No," said the judge. "Now lay your hand on your own heart, and see whether you are not more excited than I am." Think of that man of God, who, on the morning he was to be burned, was so soundly asleep that they had to shake him to wake him; he had to get up to be burned, and yet knowing that it was to be so, he had such confidence in God that he slept sweetly. This is "the peace of God, which passeth all understanding." In those old Diocletian persecutions, when the martyrs came into the amphitheatre to be torn by wild beasts, when one was set in a red-hot iron chair, another was smeared with honey, to be stung to death by wasps and bees, they never flinched. Think of that brave man who was put on a gridiron to be roasted to death, and who said to his persecutors, "You have done me on one side; now turn me over to the other." Why this peace under such circumstances? It was "the peace of God, which passeth all understanding." We do not have to suffer like that nowadays; but if it ever comes to anything like that, it is wonderful what peace a Christian enjoys. After there had been a great storm, the Master stood up in the prow of the vessel, and said to the winds, "Be still," and "there was a great calm," we read. Have you ever felt this? You do feel it to-night if you have learnt this sacred art of making your requests known unto God in everything, and the peace of God which passeth all understanding is keeping your hearts and minds through Jesus Christ.

This blessed peace keeps our hearts and minds; it is *a guardian peace*. The Greek word implies a garrison. Is it not an odd thing that a military term is used here, and that it is peace that acts as a guard to the heart and to the mind? It is the peace of God that is to protect the child of God; strange but beautiful figure! I have heard that fear is the housekeeper for a Christian. Well, fear may be a good guardian to keep dogs out; but it has not a full cupboard. But peace, though it seems weakness, is the essence of strength; and, while it guards, it also feeds us, and supplies all our needs.

It is also *a peace which links us to Jesus*: "The peace of God which passeth all understanding, shall keep your hearts and minds,"—that is, your affections and your thoughts, your desires and your intellect; your heart, so that it shall not fear; your mind, so that it shall not know any kind of perplexity; —"the peace of God shall keep your hearts and minds through Jesus Christ." It is all "through Christ Jesus," and therefore it is doubly sweet and precious to us.

O my dear hearers, some of you come in here on Thursday nights, and you do not know anything about this peace of God, and perhaps you wonder why we Christian people make such a fuss about our religion. Ah, if you knew it, you would perhaps make more fuss about it than we do; for if there were no hereafter,—and we know that there is,—yet the blessed habit of going to God in prayer, and casting all our care upon Him, helps us to live most joyfully even in this life. We do not believe in secularism; but if we did, there would be no preparation for the earthly life like this living unto God, and living in God. If you have a sham god, and you merely go to church or chapel, and carry your prayer-book or your hymn-book with you, and therefore think you are Christians, you are deceiving yourselves; but if you have a living God, and you have real fellowship with Him, and constantly, as a habit, live beneath the shadow of the wings of the Almighty, then you shall enjoy a peace that shall make others wonder, and make you yourself marvel, too, even "the peace of God, which passeth all understanding." God grant it to you, my beloved hearers, for Christ's sake! Amen.

THE PEACE OF GOD

"And the peace of God, which passeth all understanding, shall keep your hearts and minds through Christ Jesus."—Philippians iv. 7.

"PEACE" is a heavenly word. When at the advent of our Lord angels came to sing among men a midnight sonnet their second note was "Peace on earth." Would God the shining ones would chant that song again till yonder Balkans heard the strain, and shook off the sulphurous cloud which now hangs around them. Those who have ever seen war, or even come near the trail of its bloody march, will be thankful to God for peace. I am almost of his mind who said that the worst peace is preferable to the very best war that was ever waged, if best there can be where all is bad as bad can be. Peace is most pleasant when religion sits beneath its shade, and offers her joyful vows to heaven. How grateful we ought to be that we can meet together to worship God after that form which best satisfies our consciences without any fear of being hunted down by the authorities of the land. We have no watchman on the hill tops looking out for Claverhouse's dragoons. We put none at the front door of our conventicle to watch lest the constable should come to take off worshipper and minister, that they may suffer imprisonment or fine. We worship God in unlimited liberty, and we ought to be exceedingly glad of the privilege, and infinitely more grateful for it than we are. Do we not sit every man under his own vine and fig tree, none making us afraid? Blessed is the land in which we dwell, and blessed are the days in which we live, when in all peace and quietness we worship God in public and sing His high praises as loudly as we please. Great God of peace, Thou hast given us this peace, and in remembrance of our hunted forefathers we bless Thee with our whole hearts!

We have met to-night for the purpose of hearing the gospel of peace, and many of us are afterwards coming to that sacred festival which celebrates peace, and is to all time the memorial of the great peace-making between God and man. And yet it may be that even all believers here are not quite at peace. Possibly you did not leave your family in peace this afternoon. Jars occur even among loving hearts. Alas! even Sabbaths are sometimes disturbed, for evil tempers cannot be bound over to keep the peace, but are riotous even on this sweet restful day. Do Christian men ever permit angry feelings to rise within them? If they do, I am sure that even in coming away from home to the house of God, they come with a disturbed mind. Ah, how insignificant a matter will mar our peace of mind: some little thing that happened in getting to your pew—some trifling incident even while you are in it, waiting for worship to begin, may, like dust in your eye, cause you the greatest distress. Such poor creatures are we that we may lose our peace of mind even by a word or a look. Peace, in the form of perfect calm and serenity, is a very delicate and sensitive thing, and needs more careful handling than a Venice glass. It is hard for the sea of our heart to remain long in a smooth and glassy state, it may be rippled and ruffled by an infant's breath. Perhaps, too, some of my brothers and sisters here have not been walking near to God; and if so their peace will not be perfect. It may be, my brother, that during the week you have back-slidden somewhat from your true standing; and if so, your heart is troubled, and your peace has fled. Your heart is troubled, and though you are believing in Christ for salvation, and are therefore safe, yet for all that your inward rest may be broken; therefore would I turn the text into a prayer, and pray for myself and for every believer in Jesus Christ—that the peace of God which passeth all understanding may now keep our hearts and minds through Christ Jesus. May you all know the text by experience. He who wrote it had felt it; may we who read it feel it too. Paul had oftentimes enjoyed the brightness of peace in the darkness of a dungeon, and he had felt living peace in prospect of a sudden and cruel death. He loved peace, preached peace, lived in peace, died in peace, and behold he hath entered into the fruition of peace, and dwells in peace before the throne of God.

Looking at the text, and thinking how we might handle it best to our profit, I thought we would notice first of all *the unspeakable privilege*—"the peace of God, which passeth all understanding." Then, secondly, I thought that we might gather, from its connection, *the method of coming at it*; for the preceding sentences are linked on to our text by the word "and," which is not an incidental conjunction, but is placed there with a purpose. Paul means to say that if we do what he bids us do in the fourth, fifth, and sixth verses, then the peace of God shall keep our hearts and minds. When we have looked at that matter for a few minutes, I shall want your careful attention, in the third place, to *the power of its operation*—for the peace of God "*shall* keep your hearts and minds"; and then we shall close, in the fourth place, by noticing *the sphere of its action*, namely "in Christ Jesus": the word should have been "in" rather than "through"—"shall keep your hearts and minds in Christ Jesus." May the Holy Spirit, who is the spirit of peace, now lead us into the centre and secret of our text.

I. First, then, here is AN UNSPEAKABLE PRIVILEGE —one of which it is very hard to speak, because it passeth all understanding, and therefore, you may be sure, it must pass all description. It is one of those things which can be more readily experienced than explained. Good Joseph Stennett was right when he spoke of those who

> "Draw from heaven that sweet repose
> Which none but he that feels it knows."

We may talk about inward rest, and dilate upon the peace of God, and select the most choice expressions to declare the delicacy of its enjoyment, but we cannot convey to others the knowledge at second hand; they must feel it, or they cannot understand it. If I were speaking to little children I would illustrate my point by the story of the boy at one of our mission stations who had a piece of loaf sugar given him one day at school. He had not before tasted such essence of sweetness, and when he went home to his father, he told him that he had eaten something which was wonderfully sweet. His father said, "Was it as sweet as such a fruit?" "It was far sweeter than that." "Was it as sweet as such and such a food?" which he mentioned. "It was much sweeter than that. But father," said he, "I cannot tell you." He rushed out of the house back to the mission house, begged a piece of sugar, got it, and brought it back, and said, "Father, taste and see, and then you will know how sweet it is." So I venture to use that simple illustration and say, "O taste and see that the peace of God is good," for in very deed it surpasseth all the tongues of men and of angels to set it forth.

What is the peace of God? I would describe it first by saying it is, of course, *peace with God*, peace of conscience, actual peace with the Most High through the atoning sacrifice. Reconciliation, forgiveness, restoration to favour there must be, and the soul must be aware of it: there can be no peace of God apart from justification through the blood and righteousness of Jesus Christ received by faith. A man conscious of being guilty can never know the peace of God till he becomes equally conscious of being forgiven. When his consciousness of pardon shall become as strong and vivid as his consciousness of guilt had been, then will he enter into the enjoyment of the peace of God which passeth all understanding. Dear brothers and sisters in Christ—you that have believed in Jesus—there is perfect peace between you and God now: "Therefore being justified by faith, we have peace with God." Your sin was the ground of the quarrel; but it has gone, it has ceased to be, it is blotted out, it is cast into the depth of the sea. As far as the east is from the west, so far hath He removed our transgressions from us. Our divine scapegoat has carried our iniquities into the wilderness. Our Lord and Master has finished transgression, made an end of sin, and brought in everlasting righteousness. The cause of offence is gone, and gone for ever: Jesus hath taken our guilt, hath suffered in our stead, hath made full compensation to the injured law, and vindicated justice to the very highest; and now there is nothing which can excite the anger of God towards us, for our sin is removed, and our unrighteousness is covered. We are reconciled to God by Christ Jesus, and accepted in the Beloved.

Now this actual reconciliation brings to the heart a profound sense of peace. O that all of you possessed it now! O that those who know it knew it more fully! Remember, O soul, if Christ did indeed suffer in your stead and was made a curse for thee, justice can never require at thy hands the penalty which thy Surety has discharged: for this would be to dishonour His sacrifice by making it of none effect. If Jesus stood as thy Substitute, and bore what God required as the vindication of His law, then thou art clear, beyond all hazard, clear for ever, saved in the Lord with an everlasting salvation. If it were not so, why was there a Substitute permitted? Did God design to tantalize mankind by permitting an ineffectual substitution? What did that Substitute accomplish after all if He did not save those for whom He died? What meaning is there in the gospel if it does not reveal an effectual atonement? But truly the Lord Jesus was made sin for us, and the chastisement of our peace was upon Him, and by His stripes we are saved. Here the soul rests: at the foot of the cross it finds a peace it never could have found elsewhere. I hope that many of you are now able to sing.

> "Jesus was punish'd in my stead,
> Without the gate my Surety bled
>   To expiate my stain:
> On earth the Godhead deign'd to dwell,
> And made of infinite avail
>   The sufferings of the Man.

> "And was He for such rebels given?
> He was; the Incarnate King of Heaven
>   Did for His foes expire:
> Amazed, O earth, the tiding shear;
> He bore, that we might never bear
>   His Father's righteous ire."

There take your fill of peace, for by this sacrifice a covenant of peace is now established between you and your God, and it is sealed by atoning blood.

"The peace of God, which passeth all understanding" also takes a second form, namely, that of *a consequent peace in the little kingdom within*. When we know that we are forgiven and that we are at peace with God things within us come to a sudden and delightful change. By nature everything in our inner nature is at war with itself: it is a cage of evil beasts all rending and devouring each other. Man is out of order: out of order with God, with the universe, and with himself. The machinery of manhood has fallen into serious disorder; its cogs and wheels do not work in due harmony, but miss their touch and stroke. The passions, instead of being ruled by reason, often demand to hold the reins; and reason, instead of being guided by the knowledge which God communicates by His word, chooses to obey a depraved imagination, and demands to become a separate power and to judge God Himself. There is not a faculty of our nature which is not in rebellion against God, and consequently in a state of confusion with regard to the rest of our system. A cruel internal war often rages among our mental powers, animal instincts, and moral faculties, causing distress, fear and unhappiness. There is no cure for this but restoring grace. O man, you cannot get your heart right, you cannot get your conscience right, you cannot get your understanding right, you cannot bring your various powers to their bearings and make them act in true harmony till first you are right with God. The King must occupy the throne, and then the estate of Mansoul will be duly settled, but till the chief authority has due eminence rebellion and riot will continue. When the Lord breathes peace into a man, and the Holy Spirit descends like a dove to dwell within the soul, then is there quiet: where all was chaos order appears, the man is created anew, and becomes a new creature in Christ Jesus; and though rebellious lusts still try to get the mastery, yet there is now a ruling power which keeps the man in order so that within him there is "the peace of God, which passeth all understanding."

This leads on to *peace in reference to all outward circumstances* by reason of our confidence that God ordereth them all rightly, and arranges them all for our good. The man who believes in Jesus and is reconciled to God has nothing outside of him that he needs to fear. Is he poor? He rejoices that Christ makes poor men rich. Does he prosper? He rejoices that there is grace to sanctify his prosperity lest it become intoxicating to him. Does there lie before him a great trouble? He thanks God for His promise that as his day his strength shall be. Does he apprehend the loss of friends? He prays that the trial may be averted, for he is permitted so to pray, even as David begged for the life of his child; but, having so done, he feels sure that God will not take away an earthly friend unless it be with kind intent to gather up our trust and confidence more fully to Himself. Does there lie before him the prospect of speedy death? The hope of resurrection gives peace to his dying pillow. He knows that his Redeemer lives, and he is content to let his body sleep in the dust awhile. Is he reminded by Scripture of a day of judgment when all hearts shall be revealed? He has peace with regard to that dread mystery and all that surrounds it, for he knows whom he has believed, and he knows that He will protect him in that day. Whatever may be suggested that might alarm or distress the believer, deep down in his soul he cannot be disturbed, because he sees his God at the helm of the vessel holding the rudder with a hand which defies the storm. This is peculiarly advantageous in days like these when all things wear a dreary aspect. The storm signals are flying, the clouds are gathering, flashes of lightning and grumblings of distant thunder are around us. If you read the papers, wars and rumours of wars are incessant; your eyes light upon narratives of famine and drought; you see distress here, slackness of business there, and poverty and starvation in many places, and the fear creeps over you that there are dark days yet to come, and seasons in which faces will grow pale and hands hang heavy. Brethren, it is for the believer in such a case to feel no dismay, for our God is in the heavens, and He doth not forsake the throne; His purposes will be fulfilled and good will come out of evil, for at this very moment God sitteth in the council-chambers of kings, and ordereth all things according to the counsel of His will. We are not children whose father has gone to sea and left them at home without a guardian. We read just now the words, "I will not leave you comfortless: I will come to you," and we believe that gracious word. God is most near us, and we are most safe. Though we cannot see the future, and do not wish to pry between the folded leaves of the book of destiny, we are absolutely certain that nothing is written upon the unopened page of the future which can contradict the divine faithfulness so conspicuous in the past. We are sure that all things work together for good to them that love God, to them that are the called according to His purpose, and therefore our soul as to all external circumstances casts anchor and enjoys the peace of God, which passeth all understanding.

Nor is this all. God is pleased to give to His people peace *in reference to all His commands.* While the soul is unregenerate it rebels against the mind and will of God. If God forbids, the unrenewed heart longs for the forbidden thing. If God commands, the natural mind, for that very reason, refuses to do it. But when the change takes place, and we are reconciled to God by the death of His Son, then, beloved, we drop into the same line with God, and our deepest desire is to abide in full harmony with Him. His will becomes our delight, and our only sorrow is that we cannot be perfectly conformed to it. There is no precept of God which is grievous to a gracious heart. His statutes are our songs in the house of our pilgrimage. We also feel perfect peace *with regard to God's providential doings,* because we believe that they are helping us to arrive at conformity with Him, and that is just what we want. Oh that we could never have a thought or wish henceforth that would be disagreeable to the Lord. We now love Him, we love His ways, we love His people, we love His word, we love His day, we love His promises, we love His precepts—we are altogether agreed with Him through His rich grace; and in this sense we have a peace towards God which passeth all understanding.

What a wonderful description that is of this peace —*it "passeth all understanding."* It is not only beyond a common understanding, but it passeth *all* understanding. Some have said it means that the ungodly man cannot understand it; that statement is true, but it is not a tithe of the whole meaning, for even he who enjoys it cannot understand it. It is deeper, it is broader, it is sweeter, it is more heavenly than the joyful saint himself can tell. He enjoys what he cannot understand. What a mercy that such a thing is possible, for otherwise our joys would be narrow indeed! Reason has limits far narrower than joy.

Truly this peace is hid from the eyes of the ungodly and the unbelieving; it is far above, out of their sight. Now, there are kinds of peace in the world which the ungodly man can understand. There were the Stoics, who schooled themselves to apathy; they would not feel, and so they attained a senseless peace: their secret is easily discovered, it does not pass understanding. Many a Red Indian has been as stolid as the greatest Stoic, and has, perhaps, surpassed him, in hardening himself so that he would not groan if pierced with arrows or burned with fires. Some men have had such mastery over themselves that it has seemed a matter of perfect indifference whether they suffered pain or not. But Christianity does not teach us Stoicism, nor does it point in that direction; it cultivates tenderness, and not insensibility. Its influence tends to make us sensitive rather than callous, and it gives us a peace consistent with the utmost delicacy of feeling, yea, with a sensitiveness more intense than other men know, since it makes our conscience more tender, and causes the mind to be deeply distressed by the slightest frown of heaven. Our peace is not the peace of apathy, but one of a far nobler sort. Others have aimed at the peace of levity, which the world can readily understand. They count it one of the wisest things to drive dull care away, and whatever happens of ill they drown reflection in the flowing bowl and laugh over it—making mirth when misery devours their souls. Christians do not attempt to get rid of the trials of life in that fashion. The world, therefore, cannot understand the believer's peace, since he is neither apathetic nor frivolous.

Whence comes this peace? The jaunty answer of many a worldling is, "Oh, it comes from some fanatical delusion." But, indeed, we are not deluded. The grounds of a Christian's peace are rational, logical, and well grounded. They are to be justified by common sense. A person who has been in debt, and who is still in debt, ought not to be at peace; but suppose a man is found to be perfectly at his ease, who can blame him if he can say, "I have a right to be so, for my debt is paid"? No one can challenge such an argument. He who believes that Christ Jesus suffered in his stead that which was due to God's justice, has a rational argument for being at peace which he may plead anywhere he pleases. God has forgiven for Christ's sake all his iniquity, why should he not be at peace? And if it be indeed so—that the Christian has become the child of God, ought he not to be at peace? If God his Father rules all things for his good, ought he not to be at peace? If for him there remains no hazard of eternal death—if for him there is prepared no glorious resurrection, and if he is ultimately to shine with Christ in eternal glory, why should not the man have peace? It is far more difficult, I should think, rationally to blame him for his happiness than it would be to justify him if he were in alarm. We are not victims of delusion, but speak the w rds of truth and soberness when we claim to be the most favoured of mankind; the folly and the fanaticism lie with those who neglect God and eternity, and make a mock at sin.

Hence the worldling does not understand our peace, and frequently sneers at it because he is puzzled by it. Even the Christian is sometimes surprised at his own peacefulness. I know what it is to suffer from terrible depression of spirit at times; yet at the very moment when it has seemed to me that life was not worth one single bronze coin, I have been perfectly peaceful with regard to all the greater things. There is a possibility of having the surface of the mind lashed into storm while yet down deep in the caverns of one's inmost consciousness all is still: this I know by experience. There are earthquakes upon this earth, and yet our globe pursues the even tenor of its way, and the like is true in the little world of a believer's nature. Why, sometimes the Christian will feel himself to be so flooded with a delicious peace that he could not express his rapture. He is almost afraid to sing, lest even the sound of his voice should break the spell; but he says to himself,

"Come, then, expressive silence, muse His praise."

Satan has breathed a whisper into the mind—"It is too good to be true;" but the spirit, firmly believing in the truthfulness of God, has repelled the insinuation, and rested, in the faithfulness of God. in the eternal covenant, in the finished work of Christ, in the love of God manifested towards His people in Christ Jesus. This is the peace of God. "So He giveth His beloved sleep." It is a rest with an emphasis, rest in Jesus' sense when He said, "Come unto Me. all ye that labour and are heavy laden, and I will give you rest"—rest in the most golden sense that we can ever give to the word. and much more. It passeth understanding. but it does not surpass experience. Do you know it? Pray answer the question each one for himself, for I must come back to where I started from. It is not to be described: it must be tested to be known.

II. Now, I must, in the second place, with very much brevity, indicate, beloved friends, HOW THIS PEACE IS TO BE OBTAINED.

Now. mark you, the apostle was addressing himself only to believers in the Lord Jesus, and I must beg you to take heed to the limitation. I am not now addressing myself to the ungodly: I speak to Christians alone. You are always at peace with God. though you do not always enjoy the sense of it; but if you wish to realize it, how are you to do so? The connection tells you. In the fourth verse Paul says "Rejoice in the Lord alway; and again I say. Rejoice." If you want to have peace of mind make God your joy, and place all your joy in God. You cannot rejoice in yourself, but you ought to rejoice in God. You cannot always rejoice in your circumstances, for they greatly vary, but the Lord never changes. "Rejoice in the Lord alway." If you have rejoicing in earthly things you must indulge it moderately; but rejoicing in the Lord may be used without the possibility of excess, for the apostle adds, "Again I say. Rejoice"— rejoice, and rejoice again. Delight yourselves in the Lord. Who has such a God as you have? "Their rock is not as our Rock, our enemies themselves being judges." Who has such a Friend, such a Father, such a Saviour. such a Comforter as you have in the Lord your God? To think of God as our exceeding joy is to find "the peace of God, which passeth all understanding."

Go on to the fifth verse, where the apostle says, "Let your moderation be known unto all men"; that is to say, While all your joy is in God deal with all earthly things on the principle of caution, If any man praises you, do not exult; if, on the contrary, you are censured, do not let your spirit sink. If you have prosperity, thank God for it, but do not be sanguine that it will continue. If property be yours, take it, but do not let it become your treasure or the chief consideration of your mind. Do you suffer adversity? Pray God to help you, but do not be so cast down as to despair. Drink of earthly cups by sips; do not be foolish like the fly which drowns itself in sweets. Use the things of time as not abusing them. Do not wade far out into the dangerous sea of this world's comfort. Take the good that God provides you, but say of it, "It passeth away," for indeed it is but a temporary supply for a temporary need. Never suffer your goods to become your god. Rejoice in God alone, and as for all else, come or go, rise or fall, let it neither distress you nor make you exult. Take matters quietly and calmly, and if you do that you will have peace. If you idolize any earthly good your peace will depart, but keep the world under your feet, and the peace of God shall keep your heart and mind.

Three rules are then added by the apostle, which you will be sure to recollect. He tells us to be careful for nothing, to be prayerful for everything. and to be thankful for anything. Anyone who can keep these three rules. with the other two. will be quite sure to have a peaceful mind. "Be careful for nothing": that is—leave your care with God. Having done your best to provide things honest in the sight of all men, take no distressing, disturbing. anxious thought about anything, but cast your burden on the Lord. Then pray about everything, little as well as great, joyous as well as sad. "In everything by prayer and supplication let your requests be made known unto God." That which you pray over will have the sting taken out of it if it be evil, and the sweetness of it will be sanctified if it be good. The tribulation which you pray over will become bearable, even if it be not changed into a subject for rejoicing. A trouble prayed over is a dead lion with honey in the carcase.

And then we are bidden to be thankful for anything, for the apostle says, "In every thing with thanksgiving let your requests be made known unto God." Thankfulness is the great promoter of peace; it is the mother and nurse of restfulness. Doubtless, our peace is often broken because we receive mercies from God without acknowledging them: neglected praises sour into unquiet forebodings. If we render to the Lord the fragrant incense of holy gratitude we shall find our soul perfumed with the sweet peace of God.

Take those five things, then, as the connection sets them before you. Pile up all your joy into the sacred storehouse of your God, and be glad in the Lord. Next, leave, as much as you can, the things of this world alone; touch them with a light finger— "Let your moderation be known unto all men." And then pray much, care for nothing, and bless God from morning to night. In such an atmosphere shall peace grow as rare flowers and fruits bloom beneath sunny skies in well-watered gardens. May the Holy Spirit work these things in us and cause us to rest.

III. This brings me to the third point of our subject to-night, which was THE OPERATION OF THIS BLESSED PRIVILEGE UPON OUR HEARTS.

It is said that the peace of God will keep our hearts and minds. The Greek word is *phroureo*, which signifies keeping guard, keeping as with a garrison: so completely and so effectually does the peace of God keep our hearts and minds. Look, then: our *hearts* want keeping, keeping from sinking, for our poor spirits are very apt to faint, even under small trials. They also want keeping from wandering, for how soon are they beguiled! What feeble charms are able to attract us away from the altogether lovely One! Our hearts need keeping up, and keeping right. The way to keep the heart, according to the text, is to let it be filled with the peace of God which passeth all understanding. A quiet spirit, calm, restful, happy, is one that will neither sink nor wander: how can it? If the peace of God be in you, what can cause you distress? You will be like those great buoys moored out at sea, which cannot sink; it matters not what storms may be raging, they always rise above all. Our souls, moored fast and rendered buoyant with peace, will be as fixed marks whereby others may know their way. Moreover, a man who has his heart full of peace is not likely to wander, for he says to himself, "Why should I wander? Where can such sweetness be found as I have tasted in my Lord? Why should I seek elsewhere?" The best way to keep a person in your service is to make it worth his while to stop; and if he is so happy and so content that he feels he could not better himself, you are likely to retain him for many a long day. Now, our Lord and Master has made His service such that we could not better ourselves. When He said to some of His servants, "Will ye also go away?" they said, "To whom shall we go?" Ah, indeed! to whom could we go? Eyes, will you leave the light for the thick darkness? Ears, will ye turn away from the music of Jesus' voice? Heart, wilt thou leave a faithful lover for a deceiver? Understanding, wilt thou go abroad after novelties when thou hast found the old, sure, satisfactory truth? Conscience, wilt thou burden thyself again with thy former load? When thou art so perfectly satisfied with the work and person of Christ, wilt thou not stay where thou art? Oh yes, the heart is held with bands as strong as they are tender when it is full of the peace of God which passeth understanding. You young people get tempted, I know, and who among us does not? And the world has many charms for you. I recommend you, therefore, to pray the Lord to maintain your happiness in Christ, your joy in the Lord, for if you get out of heart with regard to your Lord and Master, it may be the devil may catch you when you are bad-tempered and cross-grained towards your great Lord and entice you

away from your allegiance; but if your heart is always peaceful you will have a strength about you with which to resist the suggestions of the evil one. Rivets of peace are good fastenings for Christian loyalty. It is a very serious thing for a Christian to be in an uncomfortable state, for he is then weak in an important point. "Comfort ye, comfort ye, My people," are God's words to His prophets, because He knows that when we lose comfort, or lose peace, we lose one of the most valuable pieces of armour of which our panoply is composed.

But the text also adds that this will keep our *mind* as well as our heart. Now in all ages we find that the minds of Christian have been apt to be disturbed and vexed upon vital truths. I think sometimes that this is the worst age for error which has ever darkened the world. I get distressed and bowed to the earth as I see the treachery of ministers, professed ministers of Christ, who deny the inspiration of Scripture and lay the axe at the very root of all the doctrines which we hold dear, while yet they continue to occupy Christian pulpits. For when I look back all through history I find it was always so. From the days of Judas Iscariot until now there have been traitors and there have been men of ready speech and of quick thought who have used both fair speech and subtle thought to turn away simple minds from the gospel, insomuch that they would deceive, if it were possible, the very elect. But why are not the elect deceived? As a rule it is because they find such peace—such perfect peace in the truths which they have received, that deceivers vainly attempt to entice them away from it. "Ah," cries the restful believer, "I cannot give up the gospel. It is my life, my strength, my solace, my all. It was the comfort of my dying mother, and it remains the mainstay of my aged father. It was that which brought me to a Saviour's feet and gives me grace to remain there. It has helped me in the hour of trial again and again. I feel I want its consolations, and therefore I can never part with it." And so he grows indignant with the man who casts a doubt thereon, especially if he be of the clerical order, and a pretender to the Christian ministry. Brethren, we cannot move one single inch from the truth which we have been taught by the Holy Ghost in our soul, and it is only such truth as that which can bring into the heart the peace of God which passeth understanding. When the Lord has brought His own truth into our minds by His own power and made the sweet savour of it to pervade our frame, and given us to drink thereof till we have been filled with joy and peace unutterable, we cannot, then, depart from it. Truth taught us by man we may forget, but that which the Holy Ghost engraves upon the inmost heart we cannot depart from. So help us God, we *must* stand to it, even if we die for it.

And what are the inventions they offer us instead of the choice things of the covenant of peace? They are trifles light as air. If they were true they would not be worth propagating: they might be left among the minor matters which are of no practical value to the sons of men. They bring us no new grounds of solid peace or fresh discovered arguments for holy joy. The negative theology promises no blessings to mankind; it is an empty-handed plunderer, robbing us of every solace, but offering nothing in return. If modern thought could be proved to be true the next thing that ought to be done would be to hang the world in sackcloth, because such vanity of vanities has taken the place of the delightful truth which one gladdened the hearts of men. It were the saddest of all facts if we were assured that the doctrines of grace are after all a fiction. But they are not so. They cannot be: they bear their own witness within themselves. Some of us can speak about them as Christian replied to Atheist, when Atheist said, "Go back: go back!" Christian's reply was, "We are seeking the Celestial City." "Oh," said Atheist, "but I have gone farther than any of you, and I can tell you that there is no such place. I have met with many learned men who have studied the whole matter, and it is all a delusion. Go back: go back." Then Christian said, "What! No Celestial City? Did we not see it from the top of Mount Clear, when we were with the shepherds and looked through the telescopic glass?" So we say—No atonement? Have we not felt the peace with which it soothes the conscience? No regeneration? Are we not ourselves the living evidence that men are made new creatures in Christ Jesus? No answers to prayer? Surely we are not sane men at all, and our senses have failed us. No final perseverance? What then has kept us to this day? No work of the Holy Ghost? What? Are we asleep? Is even our existence a delusion? No, as we rub our eyes we feel that we have not been dreaming, but we feel sure that some other people are dozing and doting, and we pray that God in mercy may end their dream, and bring them to know those glorious and substantial verities which fill us with the peace of God which passeth all understanding, and in so doing keep our hearts and minds. We are bound to the cross for ever, nailed to the wood with Christ for ever. The blood-red colours of the atonement are fastened to our masthead, to fly there till our vessel sinks, if sink it must, but never to be struck, though man or devil, priest or philosopher, fire hot shot into our vessel. We dare not change, but stand faithful to that which Jesus has taught us, at whose feet we sat in our youth, and who continues to teach us still. His peace keeps our heart and mind, and therefore we will with heart and mind keep His truth come what may.

IV. Lastly, let us observe THE SPHERE OF ITS ACTION.

The text says, "In Christ Jesus." Now, beloved, I beg you to note this with interest. The apostle never mentions the name of Jesus too often. You cannot say that he drags it in, but he mentions it as often as ever he can, for he delights in the sound of it. "In Christ Jesus." These words touch every point of our text all the way through. Are we speaking of ourselves? We are in Christ Jesus. Our faith has realised our union with His sacred Person. He is our Head, and we are His members: He is the Corner-stone, and we are built upon Him. There is nothing about ourselves worth thinking of apart from Him: and it will be well if we dismiss the thought.

Then if we dwell upon the peace of God, we still think of our Lord Jesus, for it is all in Him. No peace is to be found out of Christ. No peace can warm our heart while we forget Christ. "He is our peace." Never go, dear brethren and sisters, for your peace to the law or to your own experience, to your own past achievements, or even to your faith. All your peace is in Jesus.

And then our hearts and our minds, mentioned in the text, must all be in Jesus: the heart loving Him, and loved of Him: the mind believing Him, resting in Him, using its faculties for Him,—all in Him. If I leave that last thought with you it will be the best ending for my sermon: namely, that to get peace, and to get your hearts and minds kept, the grand necessity is to be in Christ—in your dying, risen, reigning Lord. Let Him be upon your thoughts now and always. His table is now spread, come hither to commune with Him. Come hither with your Master, to see your Master, and to eat His flesh, and drink His blood, after a spiritual fashion, at His own table.

A word to you who do not know our Lord. How I wish you did know Him. You can never possess peace till you possess Christ. What a blessed beginning of Sabbaths it would be to your souls if you were to seek Christ to-night. You have not far to go to find Him. He is not far from any of us. Cover your eyes and breathe a prayer to Him. Stand behind one of the columns outside, or get into the street and let you heart say, "Saviour, I want peace, and peace I can never have till I have found Thee. Behold, I trust Thee. Manifest Thyself to me at this moment and say unto my soul, 'I am thy salvation.'" God grant you may so pray. It seems to me very wonderful that we should need to persuade men to think of their own interests, and to care for their own selves. In other things they are always sharp enough to look after what they call "number one," but when it comes to the most solemn concern, the greatest blessing, and the purest happiness that can be had, they are so foolish as to let all things else attract them more than the Lord Jesus. The Lord save you all for His infinite mercy's sake. Amen.

CONTENTMENT

"For I have learned, in whatsoever state I am, therewith to be content."—Philippians iv. 11.

THE apostle Paul was a very learned man, but not the least among his manifold acquisitions in science was this—he had learned to be content. Such learning is far better than much that is acquired in the schools. Their learning may look studiously back on the past, but too often those who cull the relics of antiquity with enthusiasm, are thoughtless about the present, and neglect the practical duties of daily life. Their learning may open up dead languages to those who will never derive any living benefit from them. Far better the learning of the apostle. It was a thing of ever-present utility, and alike serviceable for all generations, one of the rarest, but one of the most desirable accomplishments. I put the senior wrangler, and the most learned of our Cambridge men in the lowest form, compared with this learned apostle; for this surely is the highest degree in *humanities* to which a man can possibly attain, to have learned in whatsoever state he is, to be content. You will see at once from reading the text, upon the very surface, that contentment in all states is not a natural propensity of man. Ill weeds grow apace; covetousness, discontent, and murmuring, are as natural to man as thorns are to the soil. You have no need to sow thistles and brambles; they come up naturally enough, because they are indigenous to earth, upon which rests the curse; so you have no need to teach men to complain, they complain fast enough without any education. But the precious things of the earth must be cultivated. If we would have wheat, we must plough and sow; if we want flowers, there must be the garden, and all the gardener's care. Now, contentment is one of the flowers of heaven, and if we would have it, it must be cultivated. It will not grow in us by nature; it is the new nature alone that can produce it, and even then we must be specially careful and watchful that we maintain and cultivate the grace which God has sown in it. Paul says, "I have *learned* to be content;" as much as to say he did not know how at one time. It cost him some pains to attain to the mystery of that great truth. No doubt he sometimes thought he had learned, and then broke down. Frequently too, like boys at school, he had his knuckles rapped; frequently he found that it was not easy learning this task, and when at last he had attained unto it, and could say, "I have learned, in whatsoever state I am, therewith to be content," he was an old grey-headed man upon the borders of the grave, a poor prisoner shut up in Nero's dungeon at Rome.

We, my brethren, might well be willing to endure Paul's infirmities, and share the cold dungeon with him, if we too might by any means attain unto such a degree of contentment. Do not indulge, any of you, the silly notion that you can be contented without *learning*, or learn without discipline. It is not a power that may be exercised naturally, but a science to be acquired gradually. The very words of the text might suggest this, eve if we did not know it from experience. We need not be taught to murmur, but we must be taught to acquiesce in the will and good pleasure of the Lord our God.

When the apostle had uttered these words, he immediately gave a commentary upon them. Read the 12th verse, "I know both how to be abased, and I know how to abound; everywhere and in all things I am instructed both to be full and to be hungry, both to abound and to suffer need."

Notice first, that the apostle said he knew how to be *abased*. A wonderful knowledge this. When all men honour us, then we may very well be content; but when the finger of scorn is pointed at us, when our character is held in ill repute, and men hiss us by the wayside, it requires much gospel knowledge to be able to endure that with patience and with cheerfulness. When we are increasing, and growing in rank, and honour, and human esteem, it is easy work to be contented; but when we have to say with John the Baptist, "*I* must decrease," or when we see some other servant advanced to our place, and another man bearing the palm we had longed to hold, it is not easy to sit still, and without an envious feeling cry with Moses, "Would to God that all the Lord's servants were prophets." To hear another man praised at your own expense, to find your own virtues made as a foil to set forth the superior excellence of some new rival—this, I say, is beyond human nature, to be able to bear it with joy and thankfulness, and to bless God. There must be something noble in the heart of the man who is able to lay all his honours down as willingly as he took them up, when he can as cheerfully submit himself to Christ to humble him, as to lift him up and seat him upon a throne. And yet, my brethren, we have not any one of us learned what the apostle knew, if we are not as ready

to glorify Christ by shame, by ignominy and by reproach, as by honour and by esteem among men. We must be ready to give up everything for Him. We must be willing to go downwards, in order that Christ's name may ascend upwards, and be the better known and glorified among men. "I know how to be abased," says the apostle.

His second piece of knowledge is equally valuable, "I know how to *abound*." There are a great many men that know a *little* how to be abased, that do not know *at all* how to abound. When they are put down into the pit with Joseph, they look up and see the starry promise, and they hope for an escape. But when they are put on the top of a pinnacle, their heads grow dizzy, and they are ready to fall. When they were poor they used to battle it, as one of our great national poets has said—

> "Yet many things, impossible to thought,
> Have been by Need to full perfection brought.
> The daring of the soul proceeds from thence,
> Sharpness of Wit, and active Diligence;
> Prudence at once and Fortitude it gives;
> And, if in patience taken, mends our lives."

But mark the same men after success has crowned their struggles. Their troubles are over; they are rich and increased with goods. And have you not often seen a man who has sprung up from nothing to wealth, how purse-proud he becomes, how vain, how intolerant? Nobody would have thought that man ever kept a shop; you would not believe that man at any time ever used to sell a pound of candles, would you? He is so great in his own eyes, that one would have thought the blood of all the Cæsars must flow in his veins. He does not know his old acquaintances. The familiar friend of other days he now passes by with scarce a nod of recognition. The man does not know how to abound; he has grown proud; he is exalted above measure. There have been men who have been lifted up for a season to popularity in the Church. They have preached successfully, and done some mighty work. For this the people have honoured them, and rightly so. But then they have become tyrants; they have lusted after authority; they have looked down contemptuously upon everybody else, as if other men were small pigmies, and they were huge giants. Their conduct has been intolerable, and they have soon been cast down from their high places, because they did not know how to abound. There was once a square piece of paper put up into George Whitfield's pulpit, by way of a notice, to this effect:—"A young man who has lately inherited a large fortune, requests the prayers of the congregation." Right well was the prayer asked, for when we go up the hill we need prayer that we may be kept steady. Going down the hill of fortune there is not half the fear of stumbling. The Christian far oftener disgraces his profession in prosperity than when he is being abased. There is another danger—the danger of growing *worldly*. When a man finds that his wealth increases, it is wonderful how gold will stick to the fingers. The man who had just enough, thought if he had more than he required he would be exceedingly liberal. With a shilling purse he had a guinea heart, but now with a guinea purse he has a shilling heart. He finds that the money adheres, and he cannot get it off. You have heard of the spider that is called a "money spinner," I do not know why it is called so, except that it is one of the sort of spiders you cannot get off your fingers; it gets on one hand, then on the other hand, then on your sleeve; it is here and there; you cannot get rid of it unless you crush it outright: so is it with many who *abound*. Gold is a good thing when put to use—the strength, the sinews of commerce and of charity—but it is a bad thing in the heart, and begets "foul-cankering rust." Gold is a good thing to stand on, but a bad thing to have about one's loins, or over one's head. It matters not, though it be precious earth with which a man is buried alive. Oh, how many Christians have there been who seemed as if they were destroyed by their wealth! What leanness of soul and neglect of spiritual things have been brought on through the very mercies and bounties of God! Yet this is not a matter of necessity, for the apostle Paul tells us that he knew how to abound. When he had much, he knew how to use it. He had asked of God that he might be kept humble—that when he had a full sail he might have plenty of ballast—that when his cup ran over he might not let it run to waste—that in his time of plenty he might be ready to give to those that needed—and that as a faithful steward he might hold all he had at the disposal of his Lord. This is divine learning. "I know both how to be abased, and I know how to abound." The apostle goes on to say, "everywhere and in all things I am instructed both to be full and to be hungry." It is a divine lesson, let me say, to know how to be full; for the Israelites were full once, and while the flesh was yet in their mouth the wrath of God come upon them. And there have been many that have asked for mercies, that they might satisfy their own heart's lusts; as it is written, "the people sat down to eat and drink, and rose up to play." Fulness of bread has often made fulness of blood, and that has brought on wantonness of spirit. When men have too much of God's mercies—strange that we should have to say this, and yet it is a great fact when men have much of God's providential mercies, it often happens that they have but little of God's grace, and little gratitude for the bounties they have received. They are full, and they forget God; satisfied with earth, they are content to do without heaven. Rest assured, my dear hearers, it is harder to know how to be full than it is to know how to be hungry. To know how to be hungry is a sharp lesson, but to know how to be full is the harder lesson after all. So desperate is the tendency of human nature to pride and forgetfulness of God! As soon as ever we have a double stock of manna, and begin to hoard it, it breeds worms and becomes a stench in the nostrils of God. Take care that you ask in your prayers that God would teach you how to be full.

The apostle knew still further how to experience the two extremes of fulness and hunger. What a trial that is! To have one day a path strewn with mercies, and the next day to find the soil beneath you barren of every comfort. I can readily imagine the poor man being contented in his poverty, for he has been inured to it. He is like a bird that has been born in a cage, and does not know what liberty means. But for a man who has had much of this world's goods, and thus has been full, to be brought to absolute penury, he is like the bird that once soared on highest wing but is now encaged. Those poor larks you sometimes see in the shops, always seem as if they would be looking up, and they are constantly pecking at the wires, fluttering their wings, and wanting to fly away. So will it be with you unless grace

prevent it. If you have been rich and are brought down to be poor, you will find it hard to know "how to be hungry." Indeed, my brethren, it must be a sharp lesson. We complain sometimes of the poor, that they murmur. Ah! we should murmur a great deal more than they do, if their lot fell to us. To sit down at the table, where there is nothing to eat, and five or six little children crying for bread, were enough to break the father's heart. Or for the mother, when her husband has been carried to the tomb, to gaze round on the gloom-stricken home, press her new-born infant to her bosom, and look upon the others, with widowed heart remembering that they are without a father to seek their livelihood. Oh! it must need much grace to know how to be hungry. And for the man who has lost a situation, and has been walking all over London—perhaps a thousand miles—to get a place, and he cannot get one, to come home, and know that when he faces his wife, her first question will be "Have you brought home any bread?" "Have you found anything to do?" and to have to tell her "No; there have been no doors open to me." It is hard to prove hunger, and bear it patiently. I have had to admire, and look with a sort of reverence on some of the members of this Church, when I have happened to hear afterwards of their privations. They would not tell anyone, and they would not come to me; but they endured their pangs in secret, struggled heroically through all their difficulties and dangers, and came out more than conquerors. Ah! brothers and sisters, it looks an easy lesson when you come to see it in a book, but it is not quite so easy when you come to put it in practice. It is hard to know how to be full, but it is a sharp thing to know how to be hungry. Our apostle had learned both—both how to abound, and to suffer need.

Having thus expounded to you the apostle Paul's own commentary, in enlarging upon the words of my text, let me return to the passage itself. You may now ask by what course of study did he acquire this peaceful frame of mind? And of one thing we may be quite certain, it was by no stoic process of self-government, but simply and exclusively *by faith in the Son of God*.

You may easily imagine a nobleman whose home is the abode of luxury, travelling through foreign parts for purposes of scientific discovery, or going forth to command some military expedition in the service of his country. In either case he may be well content with his fare, and feel that there is nothing to repine at. And why? because he had no right to expect anything better; not because it bore any comparison with his rank, his fortune, or his social position at home. So our apostle. He had said "Our conversation or citizenship is in heaven." Travelling through earth as a pilgrim and stranger e was content to take travellers fare. Or entering the battle field, he had no ground of complaint that perils and distresses should sometimes encircle his path, while at other times a truce gave him some peaceful and pleasing intervals.

Again, adverting to the text, you will notice that the word "*herewith*" is written in italics. If therefore we do not omit it, we need not lay upon it a heavy stress in the interpretation. There is nothing in hunger, or thirst, or nakedness, or peril, to invite our contentment. If we are content under such circumstances, it must be from higher motives than our condition itself affords. Hunger is a sharp thorn when in the hands of stern necessity. But hunger may be voluntarily endured for many an hour when conscience makes a man willing to fast. Reproach may have a bitter fang, but it can be bravely endured, when I am animated by a sense of the justice of my cause. Now Paul counted that all the ills which befel him were just incident to the service of his Lord. So for the love he bears to the name of Jesus, the hardships of servitude or self-mortification sat lightly on his shoulders, and were brooked cheerily by his heart.

There is yet a third reason why Paul was content. I will illustrate it. Many an old veteran takes great pleasure in recounting the dangers and sufferings of his past life. He looks back with more than contentment, oftentimes with self-gratulation, upon the terrible dangers and distresses of his heroic career. Yet the smile that lights his eye, and the pride that sits on his lofty wrinkled brow as he recounts his stories, were not there when he was in the midst of the scenes he is now describing. It is only since the dangers are past, the fears have subsided, and the issue is complete, that his enthusiasm has been kindled to a flame. But Paul stood on vantage ground here "*In all these things*," said he, "we are more than conquerors." Witness his voyage toward Rome. When the ship in which he sailed was caught and driven before a tempestuous wind; when darkness veiled the skies; when neither sun nor stars in many days appeared; when hope failed every heart;— he alone bore up with manly courage. And why? The angel of God stood by him, and said, Fear not. His faith was *predestinarian*, and as such, he had as much peaceful contentment in his breast while the tribulation lasted as when it had closed.

And now I want to commend the lesson of my text very briefly to the *rich*, a little more at length to the *poor*, and then with sympathy and counsel to the *sick*—those who are sore-tried in their persons by suffering.

First, to the RICH. The apostle Paul says, "I have learned, in whatsoever state I am, therewith to be content." Now some of you have, as far as your circumstances are concerned, all that the heart can wish. God has placed you in such a position that you have not to toil with your hands, and in the sweat of your face gain a livelihood. You will perhaps think that any exhortation to you to be contented is needless. Alas! my brethren, a man may be very discontented though he be very rich. It is quite as possible for discontent to sit on the throne, as it is to sit on a chair—a poor broken-backed chair in a hovel. Remember that a man's contentment is in his mind, not in the extent of his possessions. Alexander, with all the world at his feet, cries for another world to conquer. He is sorry because there are not other countries into which he may carry his victorious arms, and wade up to his lions in the blood of his fellow men, to slake the thirst of his insatiable ambition. To you who are rich, it is necessary that we give the same exhortation as to the poor: "learn to be content." Many a rich man who has an estate is not satisfied, because there is a little corner-piece of ground that belongs to his neighbour, like Naboth's vineyard that the king of Israel needed that he might make a garden of herbs hard by his palace. "What matters it," says he, "though I have all these acres, unless I can have Naboth's vin·yard?" Surely a king should have been ashamed to crave that paltry half-acre of a poor man's patrimony. But yet so it is; men with vast estates, which they are scarcely

able to ride over, may have that old horse-leech in their hearts, which always cries, "Give, give! more, more!" They thought when they had but little, that if they had ten thousand pounds it would be enough. They have it: they want twenty thousand pounds. When they have that, they still want more. Yes, and if you had it, it would be "A trifle more!" So would it continually be. As your possessions increased, so would the lust of acquiring property increase. We must, then, press upon the rich this exhortation: "Learn in your state, therewith to be content."

Besides, there is another danger that frequently awaits the rich man. When he has enough wealth and property, he has not always enough honour. If the queen would but make him a justice of the peace for the county, how glorious would my lord become! That done, he will never be satisfied till he is a knight; and if he were a knight, he would never be content until he became a baron; and my lord would never be satisfied till he was an earl; nor would he even then be quite content unless he could be a duke: nor would he be quite satisfied I trow then, unless there were a kingdom for him somewhere. Men are not easily satisfied with honour. The world may bow down at a man's feet; then he will ask the world to get up and bow again, and so keep on bowing for ever; for the lust of honour is insatiate. Man must be honoured, and though king Ahasuerus make Haman the first man in the empire, yet all this availeth nothing, so long as Mordecai in the gate doth not bow down to my lord Haman. Oh! learn, brethren, in whatever state you are, therewith to be content.

And here let me speak to the elders and deacons of this church. Brethren, learn to be content with the office you hold, not envious of any superior honour to exalt yourselves. I turn to myself. I turn to the ministry, I turn to all of us in our ranks and degrees in Christ's Church: we must be content with the honour God is pleased to confer upon us; nay, let us think nothing of honour, but be content to give it all up, knowing that it is but a puff of breath after all. Let us be willing to be the servants of the Church, and to serve them for nought, if need be even without the reward of their thanks, may we but receive at last the right good sentence from the lips of the Lord Jesus Christ. We must learn, in whatever state we are, therewith to be content.

At a little more length I have to counsel the POOR. "I have learned," says the apostle, "in whatever state I am, therewith to be content."

A very large number of my present congregation belong to those who labour hard, and who, perhaps, without any unkindly reflection, may be put down in the catalogue of the poor. They have enough— barely enough, and sometimes they are even reduced to straitness. Now remember, my dear friends, you who are poor, there are two sorts of poor people in the world. There are the Lord's poor, and there are the devil's poor. As for the devil's poor: they become pauperized by their own idleness, their own vice, their own extravagance. I have nothing to say to them to-night. There is another class, the Lord's poor. They are poor through trying providences, poor, but industrious,—labouring to find all things honest in the sight of all men, but yet they still continue through an inscrutable providence to be numbered with the poor and needy. You will excuse me, brothers and sisters, in exhorting you to be contented; and yet why should I ask excuse, since it is but a part of my office to stir you up to everything that is pure and lovely, and of good report? I beseech you, in your humble sphere, cultivate contentment. Be not idle. Seek, if you can, by superior skill, steady perseverance, and temperate thriftiness, to raise your position. Be not so extravagant as to live entirely without care or carefulness; for he that provideth not for his own household with careful forethought, is worse than a heathen man and a publican; but at the same time, be contented; and where God has placed you, strive to adorn that position, be thankful to Him, and bless His name. And shall I give you some reasons for so doing?

Remember, that if you are poor in this world so was your Lord. A Christian is a believer who hath fellowship with Christ; but a poor Christian hath in his poverty a special vein of fellowship with Christ opened up to him. *Your* Master wore a peasant's garb, and spoke a peasant's brogue. His companions were the toiling fishermen. He was not one who was clothed in purple and fine linen, and fared sumptuously every day. He knew what it was to be hungry and thirsty, nay, He was poorer than you, for He had not where to lay His head. Let this console you. Why should a disciple be above his Master, or a servant above his Lord? In your poverty, moreover, you are capable of communion with Christ. You can say, "Was Christ poor? Now can I sympathize with Him in His poverty. Was He weary, and did He sit thus on the well? I am weary too, and I can have fellowship with Christ in that sweat which He wiped from His brow." Some of your brethren cannot go the length you can; it were wrong of them to attempt to do it, for voluntary poverty is voluntary wickedness. But inasmuch as God hath made you poor, you have a facility for walking with Christ, where others cannot. You can go with Him through all the depths of care and woe, and follow Him almost into the wilderness of temptation, when you are in your straits and difficulties for lack of bread. Let this always cheer and comfort you, and make you happy in your poverty, because your Lord and Master is able to sympathize as well as to succour.

Permit me to remind you again, that you should be contented, because otherwise you will belie your own prayers. You kneel down in the morning, and you say, "Thy will be done!" Suppose you get up and want your own will, and rebel against the dispensation of your heavenly Father, have you not made yourself out to be a hypocrite? the language of your prayer is at variance with the feeling of your heart. Let it always be sufficient for you to think that you are where God put you. Have you not heard the story of the heroic boy on board the burning ship? When his father told him to stand in a certain part of the vessel, he would not move till his father bade him, but stood still when the ship was on fire. Though warned of his danger he held his ground. Until his father told him to move, there would he stay. The ship was blown up, and he perished in his fidelity. And shall a child be more faithful to an earthly parent than we are to our Father, who is heaven? He has ordered everything for our good, and can He be forgetful of us? Let us believe that whatever He appoints is best; let us choose rather His will than our own. If there were two places, one a place of poverty, and another a place of riches and honour, if I could have my

choice, it should be my privilege to say, "Nevertheless, not as I will, but as Thou wilt."

Another reflection suggests itself. If you **are** poor you should be well content with your position, because, depend upon it, it is the fittest for you. Unerring wisdom cast your lot. If you were rich, you would not have so much grace as you have now. Perhaps God knew, that did He not make you poor, He would never get you to heaven at all; and so He has kept you where you are, that He may conduct you thither. Suppose there is a ship of large tonnage to be brought up a river, and in one part of the river there is a shallow, should some one ask, "Why does the captain steer his vessel through the deep part of the channel?" His answer would be, "Becasue I should not get it into harbour at all if I did not take it by this course." So, it may be, you would remain aground and suffer shipwreck, if your Divine Captain did not always make you trace the deepest part of the water, and make you go where the current ran with the greatest speed. Some plants die if they are too much exposed; it may be that you are planted in some sheltered part of the garden where you do not get so much sun as you would like, but you are put there as a plant of His own righteous planting, that you may bring forth fruit unto perfection. Remember this, had any other condition been better for you than the one in which you are, God would have put you there. You are put by Him in the most suitable place, and if you had had the picking of your lot half-an-hour afterwards, you would have come back and said, "Lord, choose for me, for I have not chosen the best after all." You have heard, perhaps, the old fable in Æsop, of the men that complained to Jupiter, of their burdens, and the god in anger bade them every one get rid of his burden, and take the one he would like best. They all came and proposed to do so. There was a man who had a lame leg, and he thought he could do better if he had a blind eye; the man who had a blind eye thought he could do better if he had to bear poverty and not blindness, while the man who was poor thought poverty the worst of ills; he would not mind taking the sickness of the rich man if he could but have his riches. So they all made a change. But the fable saith that within an hour they were all back again, asking that they might have their own burdens, they found the original burden so much lighter than the one that was taken by their own selection. So would you find it. Then be content; you cannot better your lot. Take up your cross; you could not have a better trial than you have got; it is the best for you; it sifts you the most; it will do you the most good, and prove the most effective means of making you perfect in every good word and work to the glory of God.

And surely, my dear brethren, if I need to add another argument why you should be content, it were this: whatever your trouble, it is not for long; you may have no estate on earth, but you have a large one in heaven, and perhaps that estate in heaven will be all the larger by reason of the poverty you have had to endure here below. You may have scarcely a house to cover your head, but you have a mansion in heaven,—a house not made with hands. Your head may often lie without a pillow, but it shall one day wear a crown. Your hands may be blistered with toil, but they shall sweep the strings of golden harps. You may have to go home often to a dinner of herbs, but there you shall eat bread in the kingdom of God, and sit down at the marriage supper of the Lamb.

> "The way may be rough, but it cannot be long,
> So we'll smooth it with hope and cheer it with song."

Yet a little while, the painful conflict will be over. Courage, comrades, courage,—glittering robes for conquerors. Courage, my brother, courage, thou mayest sooner become rich than thou dreamest of; perhaps there is e'en now, but a step between thee and thine inheritance. Thou mayest go home, peradventure, shivering in the cold March wind; but ere morning dawneth thou mayest be in thy Master's bosom. Bear up with thy lot then, bear up with it. Let not the child of a king, who has an estate beyond the stars, murmur as others. You are not so poor after all, as they are who have no hope; though you seem poor, you are rich. Do not let your poor neighbours see you disconsolate, but let them see in you that holy calmness, that sweet resignation, that gracious submission, which makes the poor man more glorious than he that wears a coronet, and lifts the son of the soil up from his rustic habitation, and sets him among the princes of the blood-royal of heaven. Be happy, brethren, be satisfied and content. God will have you to learn, in whatever state you may be, therewith to be content.

And now just one or two words to SUFFERERS. All men are born to sorrow, but some men are born to a double portion of it. As among trees, so among men, there are different classes. The cypress seems to have been created specially to stand at the grave's head and be a weeper; and there are some men, and some women, that seem to have been made on purpose that they might weep. They are the Jeremiahs of our race; they do not often know an hour free from pain. Their poor weary bodies have dragged along through a miserable life, diseased, perhaps, even from their birth, suffering some sorrowful infirmity that will not let them know even the gaiety and the frolic of youth. They grow up to mourning, and each year's suffering drives its ploughshare deeper into their brows, and they are apt—and who can blame them?—they are apt to murmur, and they say, "Why am I thus? I cannot enjoy the pleasures of life as others can; why is it?" "Oh!" says some poor sister, "consumption has looked on me; that fell disease has blanched my cheek. Why should I have to come, scarcely able to breathe, up to the house of God, and after sitting here, exhausted with the heat of this crowded sanctuary, to retire to my home, and prepare to engage in daily labour much too heavy for me; my very bed not yielding me repose, and my nights scared with visions and affrighted with dreams?—why is this?" I say if these brothers and sisters mourn, we are not the men to blame them, because, when we are sick, we brook it ill, and murmur more than they. I do admire patience, because I feel myself so incapable of it. When I see a man suffering, and suffering bravely, I often feel small in his presence. I wonder, yea, I admire and love the man who can bear pain, and say so little about it. We who are naturally healthy and strong, when we do suffer, we can hardly endure it. Cæsar pules like a sick girl, and so do some of the strongest when they are brought down; while those who are always enduring suffering bear it likes heroes,—martyrs to pain, and yet not uttering a complaint. There was good John Calvin, all his life long a victim of sickness; he was a complication of diseases. His visage, when he was a young man, as may be judged of from the different portraits of him, exhibited the signs of decay; and though he lived a long while, he seemed as if he was always going to die to-morrow. In the deepest of his agony, suffering from severe spinal pains and acute disease, the only cry he was ever known to utter was, "*Domine usquequo?* How long, Lord? how long, Lord?" A more repining expression than that he never used. Ah! but we get kicking against the pricks, murmuring and complaining. Brothers and sisters, the exhortation to you is to be content. Your pains are sharp, yet "his strokes are fewer than your crimes, and lighter than your guilt." From the pains of hell Christ has delivered you. Why should a living man complain? As long as you are out of hell, gratitude may mingle with your groans.

Besides, remember that all these sufferings are less than his sufferings. "Canst thou not watch with thy Lord one hour?" He hangs upon the tree with a world's miseries in His bowels; cannot you bear these lesser miseries that fall on you? Remember that all these chastenings work for your good; they are all making you ready; every stroke of your Father's rod is bringing you nearer to perfection. The flame doth not hurt thee; it only refines thee, and takes away thy dross. Remember too, that thy pain and sickness have been so greatly blessed to thee already, that thou never oughtest to rebel. "Before I was afflicted I went astray, but now I have kept Thy word." You have seen more of heaven through your sickness, than you ever could have seen if you had been well. When we are well, we are like men in a clay hut, we cannot see much light; but when disease comes and shakes the hut, and dashes down the mud, and makes the wattles in the wall tremble, and there is a crevice or two, the sunlight of heaven shines through. Sick men can see a great deal more of glory than men do when they are in health. This hard heart of ours, when it is undisturbed, waxes gross. When the strings of our harp are all unstrung, they make better music than when they are best wound up. There are some heaven-notes that never come to us but when we are shut up in the darkened chamber. Grapes must be pressed before the wine can be distilled. Furnace work is necessary to make us of any use in the world. We should be just the poorest things that can be, if we did not sometimes get sick. Perhaps, you that are frequently tried and frequently pained, would have been scarcely worth anything in the vineyard of Christ, if it had not been for this trial of your faith. You have sharp filing, but if you had not been well filed, you would not have been an instrument fit for the Master's use, you would have grown so rusty. If He had kept you always free from suffering, you would have been often lacking those sweet cordials which the Physician of souls administers to His fainting patients.

Be content, then; but I feel as if I hardly must say it, because I am not sick myself. When I came to you once, from the chamber of suffering, pale, and thin, and sick, and ill, I remember addressing you from that text, that was blessed to some far away in America,—"If needs be ye are in heaviness through manifold temptations." Then I think I might very justly have said to you, "In whatsoever state you are, be content;" but now that I am not suffering myself, I do not feel as if I can say it so boldly as I could then. But nevertheless, be it so, brothers and sisters; try if you can and imitate this beloved apostle Paul. "I have learned in whatsoever state I am, therewith to be content."

Before I dismiss you there is this one other sentence. You that love not Christ, recollect that you are the most miserable people in the world. Though you may think yourselves happy, there is no one of us that would change places with the best of you. When we are very sick, very poor, and on the borders of the grave, if you were to step in and say to us "Come, I will change places with you; you shall have my gold, and my silver, my riches, and my health," and the like, there is not one living Christian that would change places with you. We would not stop to deliberate, we would give you at once our answer—"No, go your way, and delight in what you have; but all your treasures are transient, they will soon pass away. We will keep our sufferings, and you shall keep your gaudy toys." Saints have no hell but what they suffer here on earth; sinners will have no heaven but what they have here in this poor troublous world. We have our sufferings here and our glory afterwards; you may have your glory here, but you will have your sufferings for ever and ever. God grant you new hearts, and right spirits, a living faith in a living Jesus, and then I would say to you as I have said to the rest—man, in whatsoever state you are, be content.

ALL-SUFFICIENCY MAGNIFIED

"I can do all things through Christ which strengtheneth me."—Philippians iv. 13.

THE former part of the sentence would be a piece of impudent daring without the latter part to interpret it. There have been some men who, puffed up with vanity, have in their hearts said, "I can do all things." Their destruction has been sure, and near at hand. Nebuchadnezzar walks through the midst of the great city; he sees its stupendous tower threading the clouds; he marks the majestic and colossal size of every erection, and he says in his heart, "Behold this great Babylon which I have builded. 'I can do all things.'" A few hours and he can do nothing except that in which the beast excels him; he eats grass like the oxen, until his hair has grown like eagle's feathers, and his nails like birds' claws. See, too, the Persian potentate; he leads a million of men against Grecia, he wields a power which he believes to be omnipotent; he lashes the sea, casts chains upon the wave, and bids it be his slave. Ah, foolish pantomime.—"I can do all things!" His hosts melt away, the bravery of Grecia is too much for him; he returns to his country in dishonour. Or, if you will take a modern instance of a man who was born to rule and govern, and found his way upwards from the lowest ranks to the highest point of empire, call to mind Napoleon. He stands like a rock in the midst of angry billows; the nations dash against him and break themselves; he himself puts out the sun of Austria, and bids the star of Prussia set; he dares to proclaim war against all the nations of the earth, and believes that he himself shall be a very Briarius with a hundred hands attacking at once a hundred antagonists. "I can do all things," he might have written upon his banners. It was the very note which his eagles screamed amid the battle. He marches to Russia; he defies the elements; he marches across the snow and sees the palace of an ancient monarchy in flames. No doubt as he looks at the blazing Kremlin, eh thinks, "I can do all things." But thou shalt come back to thy country alone; thou shalt strew the frozen plains with men; thou shalt be utterly wasted and destroyed. Inasmuch as thou hast said, "*I propose and dispose too,*" lo! Jehovah disposes of thee, and puts thee from thy seat, seeing thou hast arrogated to thyself omnipotence among men. And what shall we say to our apostle, little in stature, stammering in speech, his personal presence weak, and his speech contemptible, when he comes forward and boasts, "I can do all things?" O impudent presumption! What canst thou do, Paul? The leader of a hated sect, all of them doomed by an imperial edict to death! Thou, thou, who darest to teach the absurd dogma that a crucified man is able to save souls, that He is actually king in heaven and virtually king in earth! Thou sayest, "I can do all things." What! has Gamaliel taught thee such an art of eloquence, that thou canst baffle all that oppose thee! What! have thy sufferings given thee so stern a courage that thou art not to be turned away from the opinions which thou hast so tenaciously held? Is it in thyself thou reliest? No, "I can do all things," saith he, "through Christ which strengtheneth me." Looking boldly around him, he turns the eye of his faith humbly towards his God and Saviour, Jesus Christ, and dares to say, not impiously, nor arrogantly, yet with devout reverence and dauntless courage, "I can do all things through Christ which strengtheneth me."

My brethren, when Paul said these words, he meant them. Indeed, he had to a great measure already proved the strength, of which he now asserts the promise. Have you never thought how varied were the trials, and how innumerable the achievements of the apostle Paul? Called by grace in a sudden and miraculous manner, immediately—not consulting with flesh and blood—he essays to preach the gospel he has newly received. Anon, he retires a little while, that he may more fully understand the Word of God; when from the desert of Arabia, where he has girded his loins and strengthened himself by meditation and personal mortification, he comes out, not taking counsel with the apostles, or asking their guidance or their approbation; but at once, with singular courage, proclaiming the name of Jesus, and protesting that he himself also is an apostle of Christ. You will remember that after this, he undertook many difficult things; he withstood Peter to the face—no easy task with a man so bold and so excellent as Peter was; but Peter might be a time-server: Paul never. Paul rebukes Peter even to the face. And then mark his own achievements, as he describes them himself, "In labours more abundant, in stripes above measure;" "in prisons more frequent, in deaths oft. Of the Jews five times received I forty stripes save one. Thrice was I beaten with rods, once was I stoned, thrice I suffered shipwreck, a night and a day I have been in the deep; in journeyings often, in perils of waters, in perils of robbers, in perils by mine own countrymen, in perils by the heathen, in perils in the city, in perils in the wilderness, in perils in the sea, in perils among false brethren; In weariness and painfulness, in watchings often, in hunger and thirst, in fastings, in cold and nakedness. Beside those things that are without, that which cometh upon me daily, the care of all the churches." Ah! bravely spoken, beloved Paul. Thine was no empty boast. Thou hast indeed, in thy life, preached a sermon upon the text. "I can do all things through Christ which strengtheneth me."

And now, my dear friends, looking up to Christ which strengtheneth me, I shall endeavour to speak of my text under three heads. First, *the measure of it*; secondly, *the manner of it*; and thirdly, the *message of it*.

I. As for THE MEASURE OF IT. It is exceeding broad; for it says, "I can do all things." We cannot, of course, mention "all things," this morning; for the subject is illimitable in its extent. "I can do all things through Christ which strengtheneth me."

But let me notice that Paul here meant that he could *endure all trials*. It matters not what suffering his persecutors might put upon him; he felt that he was quite able through divine grace to bear it; and no doubt though Paul had seen the inside of almost every Roman prison, yet he had never been known to quake in any one of them; though he understood well the devices which Nero had invented to put torment upon Christians; though he had heard doubtless in his cell of those who were smeared with pitch and set on fire in Nero's gardens to light his festivities; though he had heard of Nero's racks and chains and hot pincers, yet he felt persuaded that rack and pincers, and boiling pitch, would not be strong enough to break his faith. "I can endure *all* things," he says, "for Christ's sake." He daily expected that he might be led out to die, and the daily expectation of death is more bitter than death itself; for what is death? It is but a pang, and it is over. But the daily expectation of it is fearful. If a man fears death, he feels a thousand deaths in fearing one. But Paul could say, "I die daily;" and yet he was still stedfast and immovable in the hourly expectation of a painful departure. He was ready to be offered up, and made a sacrifice for his Master's cause. Every child of God by faith may say, "I can suffer all things." What though to-day we be afraid of a little pain? Though perhaps the slightest shooting pang alarms us, yet I do not doubt, if days of martyrdom should return, the martyr-spirit would return with martyrs' trials; and if once more Smithfield's fires needed victims, there would be victims found innumerable —holocausts of martyrs would be offered up before the shrine of truth. Let us be of good courage under any temptation or suffering we may be called to bear for Christ's sake; for we can suffer it all through Christ who strengtheneth us.

Then Paul meant also that he could *perform all duties*. Was he called to preach? He was sufficient for it, through the strength of Christ; was he called to rule and govern in the churches—to be, as it were, a travelling over-looker and bishop of the flock? He felt that he was well qualified for any duty which might be laid upon him, because of the strength which Christ would surely give. And you, too, my dear brother, if you are called this day to some duty which is new to you, be not behind the apostle, but say, "I can do all things through Christ which strengtheneth me." I have seen the good man dis-

appointed in his best hopes, because he hath not won the battle in the first charge, laying down his arms and saying, "I feel that I can do no good in this world; I have tried, but defeat awaits me; perhaps it were better that I should be still and do no more." I have seen the same man too for a while lie down and faint, because, said he, "I have sown much, but I have reaped little; I have strewed the seed by handfuls, but I have gathered only here and there an ear of precious grain." O be not a craven: play the man. Christ puts His hand upon thy loins to-day, and He saith, "Up and be doing;" and do thou reply, "Yea, Lord, I *will* be doing, for I can do all things through Christ which strengtheneth me." I am persuaded there is no work to which a Christian can be called for which he will not be found well qualified. If his Master should appoint him to a throne, he would rule well; or should He bid him play the menial part he would make the best of servants: in all places and in all duties the Christian is always strong enough, if the Lord his God be with him. Without Christ he can do nothing, but with Christ he can do all things.

This is also true of the Christian's inward *struggles with his corruptions*. Paul I know once said, "O wretched man that I am, who shall deliver me from the body of this death." But Paul did not stay there; his music was not all in a minor key; right quickly he mounts the higher chords, and sings, "But thanks be to God who giveth us the victory through our Lord Jesus Christ." I may be addressing some Christians who have naturally a very violent temper, and you say you cannot curb it. "You can do all things through Christ which strengtheneth us." I may be speaking to another who has felt a peculiar weakness of disposition, a proneness to be timid, and yielding. My brother, you shall not disown your Lord, for through Christ that strengtheneth thee, the dove can play the eagle, and thou who art timid as a lamb can be mighty and courageous as a lion. There is no weakness or evil propensity which the Christian cannot overcome. Do not come to me and say, "I have striven to overcome my natural slothfulness, but I have not been able to do it." I do avow, brother, that if Christ hath strengthened you, you can do it. I don't believe there exists anywhere under heaven a more lazy man than myself naturally; I would scarce stir if I had my will; but if there be a man under heaven who works more than I do, I wish him well through his labours. I have to struggle with my sloth, but through Christ who strengtheneth me, I overcome it. Do not say thou hast a physical incapacity for strong effort; my brother, thou hast not; thou canst do all things through Christ who strengtheneth thee. A brave heart can master even a sluggish liver. Often do I find brethren who say, "I hope I am not too timid or too rash in my temper, or that I am not idle; but I find myself inconstant, I cannot persevere in anything." My dear brother, thou canst. You can do all things through Christ who strengtheneth you. Do not sit down and excuse yourself by saying, "Another man can do this, but I cannot; the fact is, I was made with this fault, it was in the mould originally, and it cannot be got rid of; I must make the best I can of it." You can get rid of it, brother; there is not a Hittite or a Jebusite in all Canaan that you cannot drive out. You can do nothing of yourself, but Christ being with you, you can make their high walls fall flat even as the walls of Jericho.

You can go upon the tottering walls and slay the sons of Anak, and although they be strong men, who like the giants had six toes on each foot and six fingers on each hand, you shall be more than a match for them all. There is no corruption, no evil propensity, no failing that you cannot overcome, through Christ which strengtheneth you. And there is no temptation to sin from without which you cannot also overcome through Christ which strengtheneth you. Sitting one day this week with a poor aged woman who was sick, she remarked that oftentimes she was tempted by Satan; and sometimes she said, "I am a little afraid, but I do not let other people know, lest they should think that Christ's disciples are not a match for Satan. Why, sir," said she, "he is a chained enemy, is he not? He cannot come one link nearer to me than Christ lets him; or when he roars never so loudly I am not afraid with any great fear of him, for I know it is only roaring—he cannot devour the people of God." Now, whenever Satan comes to you with a temptation, or when your companions, or your business, or your circumstances suggest a sin, you are not timidly to say, "I must yield to this; I am not strong enough to stand against this temptation." You are not in yourself, understand that; I do not deny your own personal weakness; but through Christ, that strengtheneth you, you are strong enough for all the temptations that may possibly come upon you. You may play the Joseph against lust; you need not play the David; you may stand steadfast against sin—you need not to be overtaken like Noah—you need not be thrown down to your shame, like Lot. You *may* be kept by God, and you *shall* be. Only lay hold on that Divine strength, and if the world, the flesh, and the devil, should beleaguer and besiege you day after day, you shall stand not only a siege as long as the siege of old Troy, but seventy years of siege shall you be able to stand, and at last to drive your enemies away in confusion, and make yourselves rich upon their spoils. "I can do all things through Christ which strengtheneth me."

Though I despair of explaining the measure of my text, so as to classify even the tenth part of all things, let me make one further attempt. I have no doubt the apostle specially meant that he found himself able to serve God in every state. "I know how to be abased, and I know how to abound: everywhere and in all things I am instructed to be full and to be hungry, both to abound and to suffer need." Some Christians are called to sudden changes, and I have marked many of them who have been ruined by their changes. I have seen the poor man exceedingly spiritual-minded; I have seen him full of faith with regard to Divine Providence, and living a happy life upon the bounty of his God, though he had but little. I have seen that man acquire wealth, and I have marked that he was more penurious; that he was, in fact, more straitened than he was before; he had less trust in God, less liberality of soul. While he was a poor man he was a prince in a peasant's garb; when he became rich, he was poor in a bad sense—mean in heart with means in hand. But this need not be. Christ strengthening him, a Christian is ready for all places. If my Master were to call me this day from addressing this assembly to sweep a street-crossing, I know not that I should feel very contented with my lot for awhile; but I do not doubt that I could do it through Christ that strengthened me. And you, who may have to follow some very humble occupation, you have had grace enough to follow it, and to be happy in it, and to honour Christ in it. I tell you, if you were called to be a king, you might seek the strength of Christ, and say in this position too, "I can do all things through Christ which strengtheneth me." You ought to have no choice as to what you shall be. The day when you gave yourself up to Christ, you gave yourself up wholly to Him, to be His soldier, and soldiers must not be choosers; if they are called to lie in the trenches, if they are bidden to advance under a galling fire, they must do it. And so must you, feeling that whether He bid you do one thing or another, in all states and in all circles, you can do what God will have you do, for through Him you can do all things.

To conclude upon this point, let me remind you that you can do all things with respect to all worlds. You are here in this world, and can do all things in respect to this world. You can enlighten it; you can play the Jonah in the midst of this modern Nineveh; your own single voice may be the means of creating a spiritual revival. You can do all things for your fellow-men. You may be the means of uplifting the most degraded to the highest point of spiritual life; you can doubtless, by resisting temptation, by casting down high looks, by defying wrath, by enduring sufferings; you can walk through this world as a greater than Alexander, looking upon it all as being yours, for your Lord is the monarch of it. "You can do all things." Then may you look beyond this world into the world of spirits. You may see the dark gate of death; you may behold that iron gate, and hear it creaking on its awful hinges; but you may say, "I can pass through that; Jesus can meet me; He can strengthen me, and my soul shall stretch her wings in haste, fly fearless through death's iron gate, nor fear the terror as she passes through. I can go into the world of spirits, Christ being with me, and never fear. And then look beneath you. There is hell, with all its demons, your sworn enemy. They have leagued and banded together for your destruction. Walk through their ranks, and as they bite their iron bonds in agony and despair, say to them as you look in their face, "I can do all things;" and if loosed for a moment Diabolus should meet you in the field, and Apollyon should stride across the way, and say, "I swear by my infernal den that thou shalt come no further, here will I spill your soul,"—up at him! Strike him right and left, with this for thy battle-cry, "I can do all things," and in a little while he will spread his dragon wings and fly away. Then mount up to heaven. From the lowest deeps of hell ascend to heaven; bow your knee before the eternal throne; you have a message; you have desires to express and wants to be fulfilled, and as you bend your knee, say, "O God, in prayer I can prevail with Thee; let me wonder to tell it; I can overcome heaven itself by humble, faithful prayer." So you see in all worlds—this world of flesh and blood, and the world of spirits, in heaven and earth and hell—everywhere the believer can say, "I can do all things through Christ which strengtheneth me."

II. Thus have I discussed the first part of our subject—the measure; I shall now talk for awhile upon THE MANNER.

How is it that Christ doth strengthen His people? None of us can explain the mysterious operations of the Holy Spirit; we can only explain one effect by another. I do not pretend to be able to show how Christ communicates strength to His people by the mysterious inflowings of the Spirit's energy; let me rather show what the Spirit does, and how these acts of the Spirit which He works for Christ tend to strengthen the soul for "all things."

There is no doubt whatever that Jesus Christ makes His people strong by strengthening their faith. It is remarkable that very many poor timid and doubting Christians during the time of Mary's persecution were afraid when they were arrested that they should never bear the fire; but a singular circumstance is, that these generally behaved the most bravely, and played the man in the midst of the fire with the most notable constancy. It seems that God gives faith equal to the emergency, and weak faith can suddenly sprout, and swell, and grow, till it comes to be great faith under the pressure of a great trial. Oh! there is nothing that braces a man's nerves like the cold winter's blast; and so, doubtless, the very effect of persecution through the agency of the Spirit going with it, is to make the feeble strong.

Together with this faith it often happens that the Holy Spirit also gives a singular firmness of mind—I might almost call it a celestial obstinacy of spirit. Let me remind you of some of the sayings of the martyrs, which I have jotted down in my readings. When John Ardley was brought before Bishop Bonner, Bonner taunted him, saying, "You will not be able to bear the fire; that will convert you; the faggots will be sharp preachers to you." Said Ardley, "I am not afraid to try it; and I tell thee, Bishop, if I had as many lives as I have hairs on my head, I would give them all up sooner than I would give up Christ." That same wicked wretch held the hand of poor John Tomkins over a candle, finger by finger, saying to him, "I'll give thee a taste of the fire before thou shalt come there;" and as the finger cracked and spurted forth, Tomkins smiled, and even laughed in his tormentor's face, being ready to suffer as much in every member as his fingers then endured. Jerome tells the story of a poor Christian woman, who being on the rack, cried out to her tormentors as they straitened the rack and pulled her bones asunder, "Do your worst; for I would sooner die than lie." It was bravely said. Short, pithy words; but what a glorious utterance! what a comment! what a thrilling argument to prove our text! Verily, Christians *can* do all things through Christ who strengtheneth them.

And not only does He thus give a sort of sacred tenacity and obstinacy of spirit combined with faith; but often Christians anticipate the joys of heaven, just when their pangs are greatest. Look at old Ignatius. He is brought into the Roman circus, and after facing the taunts of the emperor and the jeers of the multitude, the lions are let loose upon him, and he thrusts his arm into a lion's mouth, poor aged man as he is, and when the bones were cracking, he said, "Now I begin to be a Christian." Begin to be a Christian: as if he had never come near to his Master till the time when he came to die. And there was Gordus, a martyr of Christ, who said when they were putting him to death, "I pray you do not spare any torments, for it will be a loss to me hereafter if you do; therefore inflict as many as you can." What but the singular joy of God poured down from heaven—what but some singular vials of intense bliss could have made these men almost sport with their anguish? It was remarked by early Christians in England, that when persecution broke out in Luther's days, John and Henry, two Augustine monks,—the first who were put to death for Christ in Germany—died singing. And

Mr. Rogers, the first put to death in England for Christ, died singing too—as if the noble army of martyrs marched to battle with music in advance. Why, who would charge in battle with groans and cries? Do not they always sound the clarion as they rush to battle, "Sound the trumpet, and beat the drums, now the conquering hero comes," indeed—comes face to face with death, face to face with pain; and surely they who lead the van in the midst of such heroes should sing as they come to the fires. When good John Bradford, our London martyr, was told by his keeper, that he was to be burned on the morrow, he took off his cap and said, "I heartily thank my God;" and when John Noyes, another martyr, was just about to be burned, he took up a faggot, and kissed it, and said, "Blessed be God that He has thought me worthy of such high honour as this;" and it is said of Rowland Taylor, that when he came to the fire he actually, as I think Fox says in his *Monuments*, "fetched a frisk, by which he means, he began to dance when he came to the flames, at the prospect of the high honour of suffering for Christ.

But in order to enable His people to do all things, Christ also quickens the mental faculties. It is astonishing what power the Holy Spirit can bestow upon the mind of men. You will have remarked, I do not doubt, in the controversies which the ancient confessors of the faith have had with heretics and persecuting kings and bishops, the singular way in which poor illiterate persons have been able to refute their opponents. Jane Bouchier, our glorious Baptist martyr, the maid of Kent, when she was brought before Cranmer and Ridley, was able to non plus them entirely; of course we believe part of her power lay in the goodness of the subject, for if there be a possibility of proving infant baptism by any text in the Bible, I am sure I am not aware of the existence of it; Popish tradition might confirm the innovation, but the Bible knows no more of it than the baptism of bells and the consecration of horses. But, however, she answered them all with a singular power—far beyond what could have been expected of a countrywoman. It was a singular instance of God's providential judgment that Cranmer and Ridley, two bishops of the Church who condemned this Baptist to die, said when they signed the death-warrant, that burning was an easy death, and they had themselves to try it in after days; and that maid told them so. She said, "I am as true a servant of Christ as any of you; and if you put your poor sister to death, take care lest God should let loose the wolf of Rome on you, and you have to suffer for God too." How the faculties were quickened, to make each confessor seize every opportunity to avail himself of every mistake of his opponent, and lay hold of texts of Scripture, which were as swords to cut in pieces those who dared to oppose them, is really a matter for admiration.

Added to this, no doubt, also, much of the power to do all things lies in the fact, that the Spirit of God enables the Christian to overcome himself. He can lose all things, because he is already prepared to do it; he can suffer all things, because he does not value his body as the worldling does; he can be brave for Christ, because he has learned to fear God, and therefore has no reason to fear man. A healthy body can endure much more fatigue, and can work much more powerfully than a sick body. Now, Christ puts the man into a healthy state, and he is prepared for long injuries, for hard duties, and for stern privations.

Put a certain number of men in a shipwreck; the weak and feeble shall die, those who are strong and healthy, who have not by voluptuousness become delicate, shall brave the cold and rigours of the elements, and shall live. So with the quickened yet feeble professor; he shall soon give way under trial; but the mature Christian, the strong temperate man, can endure fatigues, can perform wonders, can achieve prodigies, because his body is well disciplined, and he has not permitted its humours to overcome the powers of the soul.

But observe that our text does not say, "I can do all things through Christ, which *has* strengthened me;" it is not past, but present strength that we want. Some think that because they were converted fifty years ago they can do without daily supplies of grace. Now the manna that was eaten by the Israelites when they came out of Egypt must be renewed every day, or else they must starve. So it is not your old experiences, but your daily experiences; not your old drinkings at the well of life, but your daily refreshings from the presence of God that can make you strong to do all things.

III. But I come now to the third part of my discourse, which is THE MESSAGE OF THE TEXT. "I can do all things through Christ which strengtheneth me."

Three distinct forms of the message: first, a message of encouragement to those of you who are doing something for Christ, but who begin to feel painfully your own inability. Cease not from God's work, because you are unable to perform it of yourself. Let it teach you to cease from yourself, but not from your work. "Cease ye from man, whose breath is in his nostrils," but cease not to serve your God; but the rather in Christ's strength do it with greater vigour than before. Remember Zerubbabel. A difficulty is in his path, like a great mountain; but he cries, "Who art thou, great mountain? Before Zerubbabel thou shalt become a plain." If we did but believe ourselves great things, we should do great things. Our age is the age of littleness, because there is always a clamour to put down any gigantic idea. Every one praises the man who has taken up the idea and carried it out successfully; but at the first he has none to stand by him. All the achievements in the world, both political and religious, at any time, have been begun by men who thought themselves called to perform them, and believed it possible that they should be accomplished. A parliament of wise-acres would sit upon any new idea—sit upon it indeed —yes, until they had destroyed it utterly. They would sit as a coroner's inquest, and if it were not dead they would at least put it to death while they were deliberating thereon. The man who shall ever do anything is the man who says, "This is a right thing; I am called to do it; I *will* do it. Now, then, stand up all of you—my friends or my foes, whichever you will; it is all the same; I have God to help me, and it must and shall be done." Such are the men that write their records in the annals of posterity; such the men justly called great, and they are only great because they believed they could be great—believed that the exploits could be done. Applying this to spiritual things, only believe, young man, that God can make something of you; be resolved that you will do something somehow for Christ, and you will do it. But do not go drivelling through this world, saying, "I was born little;" of course you were, but were you meant to be little, and with the feebleness of a child all your days do little or nothing? Think so, and you will be little as long as you live, and you will die little, and never achieve anything great. Just send up a thought of aspiration, oh thou of little faith. Think of your dignity in Christ—not of the dignity of your manhood, but the dignity of your degenerated manhood, and say, "Can I do all things, and yet am I to shrink first at this, then at that, and then at the other?" Be as David, who, when Saul said, "Thou art not able to fight with this Goliath," replied, "Thy servant slew both the lion and the bear, and this uncircumcised Philistine shall be as one of them;" and he put his stone into the sling and ran cheerfully and joyously, so Goliath fell; and he returned with the bloody dripping head. You know his brothers said at first, "Because of thy pride and the naughtiness of thy heart, to see the battle art thou come." All our elder brethren say that to us if we begin anything. They always say it is the naughtiness of our heart and our pride. Well, we don't answer them; we bring them Goliath's head, and request them to say whether that is the effect of our pride and the naughtiness of our heart. We wish to know whether it would not be a blessed naughtiness that should have slain this naughty Philistine. So do you my dear brothers and sisters. If you are called to any work, go straight at it, writing this upon your escutcheon, "I can do all things through Christ which strengtheneth me; and I will do what God has called me to do, whether I am blessed or whether I am left alone."

A second lesson is this—Take heed, however, that you get Christ's strength. You can do nothing without that. Spiritually in the things of Christ you are not able to accomplish even the meanest thing without Him. Go not forth to thy work therefore till thou hast first prayed. That effort which is begun without prayer will end without praise. That battle which commences without holy reliance upon God, shall certainly end in a terrible rout. Many men might be Christian victors, if they had known how to use this all prevailing weapon of prayer; but forgetting this they have gone to the fight and they have been worsted right easily. O be sure Christian that you get Christ's strength. Vain is eloquence, vain are gifts of genius, vain is ability, vain are wisdom and learning; all these things may be serviceable when consecrated by the power of God, but apart from the strength of Christ they shall all fail you. If you lean upon them they shall all deceive you. You shall be weak and contemptible, however rich or however great you may be in these things, if you lack the all sufficient strength.

Finally, the last message that I have is this: Paul says, in the name of all Christians, "I can do all things through Christ which strengtheneth me." I say, not in Paul's name only, but in the name of my Lord and Master Jesus Christ, How is it that some of you are doing nothing? If you could do nothing you might be excused for not attempting it; but if you put in the slightest pretence to my text, you must allow my right to put this question to you. You say, "I can do all things;" in the name of reason I ask why are you doing nothing? Look what multitudes of Christians there are in the world; do you believe if they were all what they profess to be, and all to work for Christ, there would be the long degrading poverty, the ignorance, the heathenism, which is to be found in this city? What cannot one individual accomplish? What could be done therefore by the tens of thousands of our churches? Ah professors! you will have much to answer for with regard to the souls of your fellow men. You are sent by God's providence to be as lights in this world; but you are rather dark lanterns than lights. How often are you in company, and you never avail yourself of an opportunity of saying a word for Christ? How many times are you thrown in such a position that you have an excellent opportunity for rebuking sin, or for teaching holiness, and how seldom do you accomplish it? An old author named Stuckley writing upon this subject, said, "There were some professed Christians who were not so good as Balaam's ass; for Balaam's ass once rebuked the mad prophet for his sin; but there were some Christians who never rebuked any one all their lives long. They let sin go on under their very eyes, and yet they did not point to it; they saw sinners dropping into hell, and they stretched not out their hands to pluck them as brands from the burning; they walked in the midst of the blind, but they would not lead them; they stood in the midst of the deaf, but they would not hear for them; they were where misery was rife, but their mercy would not work upon the misery; they were sent to be saviours of men, but by their negligence they became men's destroyers. "Am I my brother's keeper?" was the language of Cain. Cain hath many children even at this day. Ye *are* your brother's keeper. If you have grace in your heart, you are called to do good to others. Take care lest your garments be stained and sprinkled with the blood of your fellow men. Mind, Christians, mind, lest that village in which you have found a quiet retreat from the cares of business, should rise up in judgment against you, to condemn you, because, having means and opportunity, you use the village for rest, but never seek to do any good in it. Take care, masters and mistresses, lest your servant's souls be required of you at the last great day. "I worked for my master; he paid me my wages, but he had no respect for his greater Master, and never spoke to me, though he heard me swear, and saw me going on in my sins." Mind, I speak, sirs, to some of you. I would I could thrust a thorn into the seat where you are now sitting, and make you spring for a moment to the dignity of a thought of your responsibilities. Why, sirs, what has God made you for? What has He sent you here for? Did He make stars that should not shine, and suns that should give no light, and moons that should not cheer the darkness? Hath He made rivers that shall not be filled with water, and mountains that shall not stay the clouds? Hath He made even the forests which shall not give a habitation to the birds; or hath He made the prairie which shall not feed the wild flocks? And hath He made thee for nothing? Why, man, the nettle in the corner of the churchyard hath its uses, and the spider on the wall serves her Maker; and thou, a man in the image of God, a blood-bought man, a man who is in the path and track to heaven, a man regenerated, twice created,—art thou made for nothing at all but to buy and to sell, to eat and to drink, to wake and to sleep, to laugh and to weep, to live to thyself? Small is that man who holds himself within his ribs; little is that man's soul who lives within himself; aye, so little that he shall never be fit to be a compeer with the angels, and never fit to stand before Jehovah's throne.

I am glad to see so large a proportion of men here. As I always have a very great preponderance of men —therefore, I suppose I am warranted in appealing to you,—are there not here those who might be speakers for God, who might be useful in His service? The Missionary Societies need you, young men. Will you deny yourselves for Christ? The ministry needs you—young men who have talents and ability. Christ needs you to preach His Word. Will you not give yourselves to Him? Tradesmen! Merchants! Christ needs you, to alter the strain of business and reverse the maxims of the present day—to cast a healthier tone into our commerce. Will you hol yourselves back? The Sabbath-school needs you; a thousand agencies require you. Oh! if there is a man here to-day that is going home to his house, and when he gets there will say this afternoon—"Thank God I have nothing to do;" and if to-morrow when you come home from your business, you say, "Thank God I have no connexion with any church; I have nothing to do with the religious world; I leave that to other people; I never trouble myself about that," —you need not trouble yourself about going to heaven; you need not trouble yourself about being where Christ is, at least until you can learn that more devoted lesson. "The love of Christ constraineth me; I must do something for Him; Lord, show me what Thou wouldst have me to do, and I will begin this very day, for I feel that through Thee, Christ strengthening me, I can do all things."

God grant the sinner power to believe on Christ— power to repent—power to be saved; for Christ strengthening him, even the poor lost sinner, "can do all things,"—things impossible to fallen nature can he do, by the enabling of the Spirit and the power of Christ resting on him.

FILLING THE EMPTY VESSELS

"But My God shall supply all your need, according to His riches in glory by Christ Jesus."—Philippians iv. 19.

VERY beautiful, to my mind, is the sight of "Paul the aged" immured in his prison at Rome, likely by-and-by to be put to death, but calm, quiet, peaceful, and joyful. Just now he is so happy that a gleam of sunlight seems to light up his cell, and his face shines like that of an angel. He is exceedingly delighted because he has been, in his deep poverty, kindly remembered by the little church at Philippi, and they have sent him a contribution. See how cheerful the man is—I was about to say, how contented: but I drop the word because it falls far short of the mark. He is far more happy than Cæsar overhead in the palace. He is charmed with the love which has sent him this relief. Probably the gift does not come to very much, if estimated in Roman coin: but he makes a great deal of it, and sits down to write a letter of thanks abounding in rich expressions like these:—"I have all things, and abound: I am full, having received of Epaphroditus the things which were sent from you." His heart was evidently greatly touched: for he says, "I rejoiced in the Lord greatly, that now at the last your care of me hath flourished again." See how little a gift may make a good man glad! Is it not worth while to be free with our cups of cold water to the prophets of the Lord? Instead of a little money, the brethren and sisters at Philippi receive a boundless blessing, and are enriched by the fervent prayers of the apostle. Hear how earnestly Paul invokes benedictions on the heads of his benefactors. Is it not a blessed state of mind which enables a heart so soon to be full to overflowing? Some would grumble over a roasted ox, and here is Paul rejoicing over a dinner of herbs.

So great was the disinterestedness of Paul that there was nothing of selfishness about his joy. He did not speak in respect of want, for he knew how to suffer need without complaint; but he looked upon the kindly contribution as a fruit of the grace of God in the Philippians: a generous proof that they were lifted out of heathen selfishness into Christian love. There was little enough of kindness in the old Roman and Greek world into which Paul went preaching the gospel. Those were times of great hardness of heart, even to cruel heartlessness. There was no sort of provision for the poor. If a man was poor, why, that was his own look out, and he might starve and die. You know how hardened the people had become through the fights in the amphitheatre, so that the sight of blood produced a fierce delight in their brutal bosoms, and human suffering was to them rather a thing to be rejoiced in than to be prevented. There might be here and there a tender hand that gave an obolus to the poor, but, for the most part, charity was dead. The voluptuaries of that most degenerate age planned no hospitals and built no orphanages: they were too intent upon their gladiators and their mistresses. Self was lord paramount in Cæsar's court, and all over Roman realms. But here are people at Philippi thinking about one who had preached the gospel to them, and who is now suffering. They are moved by a new principle: love to God in Christ Jesus has created love to the man whose word has changed them. They will not abandon him: they will out of their own slender means cheer his sad condition. There were churches that had no such bowels of mercy: alas, that so early in the gospel-day holy charity should be so rare! There were people whom Paul had blessed greatly, who even quarrelled about him, and denied that he was an apostle of Christ; but not so the beloved church at Philippi. They had again and again ministered to his necessities, and Paul now rejoices in them again because he delights to see another instance of the transforming power of the grace of God upon character, so that those who were once selfish now rejoiced, unprompted and unasked, to send their offering to him. Was Lydia at the bottom of that subscription? I should not wonder: we know that she was open-hearted. Did the jailer add his full share? I feel sure of it, for in the prison he courteously entertained the apostle. These were a generous people, and Paul is happy in thinking of them. I may here dare to say that I also have had the like joy over many of you when I have seen how freely you have given of your substance to the work of the Lord. It would be unfair if I withheld commendation for liberality from many now before me. You have rejoiced my heart by your gifts to the cause of God. You have given up to the measure of your means, and some of you beyond what we could have asked of you. The gospel has taught you this. To God be glory that it is so. Continue in the same spirit, that none may rob me of this joy.

The apostle makes to them an assurance in the following verses that they shall be abundantly repaid for all that they have done. He says to them, "*You have helped me; but my God shall supply you.* You have helped me in *one* of my needs—my need of clothing and of food: I have other needs in which you could not help me; but my God shall supply *all your need.* You have helped me, some of you, out of your deep poverty, taking from your scanty store: but my God shall supply all your need *out of his riches* in glory. You have sent Epaphroditus unto me with your offering. Well and good: he is a most worthy brother, and a true yoke-fellow; but for all that God shall send a better messenger to you, for he shall supply all your needs *by Christ Jesus.*" He seems to me to make a parallel of his needs with theirs, and of his supplies from them with their supplies from the Lord. He would seem to say,—Just as God has through you filled me up, so shall he by Christ fill you up. That is a translation of the Greek which most nearly touches the meaning,—"My God shall *fill up* all your need according to His riches in glory by Christ Jesus."

Will you allow me to make a break here for one instant? I read you just now the story of the prophet's widow whose children were about to be taken for a debt, and how the oil was multiplied in the vessels which she borrowed, until there was enough to discharge the debt, and sufficient surplus for herself and children to live upon. Now kindly take that picture, and join it on to this, and we have here, first, *the empty vessels.* Set them out in a row, "all your need." Secondly, *who will fill them up?*—"My God shall fill up all your need." Thirdly, *after what fashion will He do it?*—"According to His riches in glory." Fourthly, *by what means will He do it?*—"By Christ Jesus." Keep the widow and the vessels before you, and let us see the miracle worked over again on a grand scale in our own houses and hearts. May the Holy Spirit make the sight refreshing to our faith.

I. So, then, we will begin our discourse this evening by asking you to SET OUT THE EMPTY VESSELS. "My God shall supply all your need." Bring forth your vessels, even empty vessels not a few. "All your need."

I do not suppose that you are under any great obligation to go out to-night and borrow other people's needs, for you have enough of your own at home—*needs many, and needs varied.* Very well, set them out. Hide none of them away, but put them down one after another, in a long row, all of them. There are needs for your body, needs for your soul; needs for yourselves, needs for your families; needs for the present, needs for the future; needs for time, needs for eternity; needs for earth, needs for heaven. Your needs are as many as your moments; as many as the hairs of your head. I suppose it would be useless for me to attempt a catalogue of them: however carefully we made the list we should have to add a host of sundries altogether unmentionable until circumstances suggested them. I could hardly tell you all my own needs, but I know that they are enormous, and increasing with my years. I have needs as a man, as a husband, as a father, as a citizen, as a Christian, as a pastor, as an author—in fact, every position I take up adds to my needs. If I went through my own personal bill of requests I should fill a document like the roll mentioned in the Old Testament, written within and without; and hardly then could I enumerate all my own demands upon the Bank of Heaven. But if I then attempted to take all the thousands that are gathered beneath this roof, and to let each man state his particular wants, where would the computation end? The sands upon the sea-shore are not more innumerable. Dear! dear! we should want a library larger than the Bodleian to hold all the books which could be written of all the needs of the needy congregation now before me. Well, I am not sorry for it, for here is so much the more room for the Lord to work His miracles of bountiful grace. Sometimes, when I have been in need for the work of the Orphanage and the College, and such like things—and these times have occurred—I do solemnly assure you that I have felt a wonderful joy in my spirit. I have watched the ebb of the funds till nearly everything has been gone, and then I have joyfully said to myself, "Now for it! The vessels are empty; now I shall see the miracle of filling them." What wonders the Lord has wrought for me I cannot now tell you in detail; but many of you who have been my faithful helpers know how hundreds and even thousands of pounds have poured in from our great Lord in the moment of necessity. It will always be the same, for the Lord God is the same. Until the funds run low we cannot expect to see them replenished: but when they get low, then will God come and deal graciously with us. Money is, however, our smallest want; we need grace, wisdom, light, and comfort; and these we shall have. All our needs are occasions for blessing. The more needs you have the more blessing you will get. God has promised to fill up all your needs. That is, all your empty vessels will be filled, and therefore the more the merrier. What! the more in need the better? Yes, I would have your faith believe that strange statement: your poverty shall thus be your riches, your weakness your strength, your abasement your exaltation. Your extremity shall be an opportunity that God will use to show the riches of His grace; to your utter exhaustion He will draw near with all the fulness of His inexhaustible grace, and He will replenish you till your cup runs over. He will fill up all your empty vessels. Be not slow to fetch them out from holes and corners, and place them before the Lord, however many they may be. Weep not over the empty jars, but place them out in rows in full expectation of their being filled to the brim.

These empty vessels of yours are, some of them, I have no doubt, *very large, and they even grow larger*. Most of our wants grow upon us. You still pray, "Give us this day our daily bread;" but the one loaf which was a large answer to the prayer when you were single, would not go far at your table now: the quarterns vanish like snow in the sun. You wanted faith fifty years ago, but you want more now, do you not? for you have more infirmities, and perhaps more trials, than in your younger days. I know that, apart from my loving Lord, I am much more needy now than I ever was before. Whatever a man requires in the things of God, usually the older he grows, and the more experience he has, the more he wants it, and the more of it he wants. He needs more love than he had when he was younger, more patience, more resignation, more humility, more charity, more wisdom, more holiness. He desires more faith, and a brighter hope. He wants in prospect of death especially, more courage, and more bold, simple, child-like confidence in his Saviour. Why, some of us have wants that could not be supplied if we could turn the stars to gold and coin them and pay them away: these could not touch the hunger of the heart and soul. The world itself would be but a mouthful for our spirits' necessity—a drop in the bucket. I know some saints that have grown to be so deeply in debt to their Lord, and to His Church, and to the world, that they are over head and ears in it—hopelessly involved in boundless obligation. How can we meet the demands upon us? Our responsibilities are overwhelming. All that some of us have made by our lifelong trading is a bigger stock of wants than ever we had before. The vacuum within our spirit expands and enlarges, and we cry out, "More knowledge of the Scriptures; more of Christ; more of grace; more of God; more of the Holy Ghost; more power to serve God." Our oil-vessels would each one hold a sea: and even these are expanding. We want more and more, and the mercy is that the text before us keeps pace with the growth—"My God shall supply all your need:" this includes the big needs as well as the little ones; it comprehends all that can be as well as all that is; it warrants us that our growing needs shall all be supplied. Let the vessels expand to their utmost, "Yet my God," says Paul, "shall fill up all those needs of yours."

Certain of our needs, again, are of this extraordinary kind, that *if they were filled up to-night they would be empty to-morrow morning*. Some of our necessities are fresh every morning; the crop is a daily one, it springs up every moment. The grace I had five minutes ago will not serve me now. Yesterday I may have possessed great love, great faith, great courage, great humility, great joy; but I need these to-day also, and none can give them to me but my Lord. You had great patience under your last trial. Yes, but old patience is stale stuff. You must grow more of that sweet herb in your garden; for the trial that is now coming can only be sweetened by the herb content, newly gathered from the garden of your heart and mixed with the bitter water of your afflictions. Our condition apart from our God may be compared to those fabled vessels that we read of in mythology that were so full of holes that, though the fifty daughters of Danaus laboured hard to fill them up, they could never accomplish the task. You and I are such leaky vessels that none but God can ever fill us; and when we are filled none but God can keep us full. Yet so the promise stands, "My God shall supply all your need": all the vessels shall be filled and shall be kept full.

We have certain needs, dear friends, that are *very pressing*, and perhaps most clamorous at this moment. Some wants are urgent: they must be supplied, and supplied speedily, or we shall perish with hunger, or die of sickness, or wither up in despair. Here let me add a caution: I dare not tell you that God will supply all the needs of everybody, for this promise is to the children of God, and in its most emphatic sense it is only to a certain class even among them. Those persons who profess to be Christians, and when they were well-to-do never helped anybody else, I think the Lord will let them pinch a bit, and know what a condition of poverty is like that they may become more sympathetic with the poor. I have known good stewards, and the Lord has sent them more, for they have dealt well with what they had: they have given away their substance by shovelfuls, and the Lord has sent it back by cartloads, and entrusted them with more. Others who have been bad stewards, and have not served their Master well, have lost what they had, and have come to penury. Let us hope that their substance has gone to somebody that will use it better; but meanwhile they have to pinch, and deservedly so. But, remember, the apostle is speaking to people of a very different character from that. He is speaking to the Philippians, and I think that there is point in that pronoun, "My God shall supply all *your* need." You have been generous in helping the Lord's servant, and the Lord will repay you. Up to the measure of your ability you have served His church and helped to carry on His work in the world, and therefore God will supply all *your* need. This is not spoken to hoarding Judas, but to the generous who had voluntarily yielded of their substance when a fit opportunity was given them. Will any of you bring your need to God and test Him by like conduct? Remember that old promise of His, "Bring ye all the tithes into the storehouse, that there may be meat in mine house, and prove me now herewith, saith the Lord of hosts, if I will not open you the windows of heaven, and pour you out a blessing, that there shall not be room enough to receive it." There is that scattereth and yet increaseth. Give, and it shall be given unto you. Oh yes, our gracious God will fill all the vessels at once, if time presses! If your needs urgently require to be filled bring them to Him.

I began by saying that few of us had any great call to borrow other people's empty pots; *yet there are some of us whose main anxiety is about the vessels that we have borrowed.* We want more oil than others for this very reason, that we care for others. Certain of us have been called to a life which intertwists itself with many lives; we have been led by grace and providence to take upon ourselves the wants of thousands. Every genuine warm-hearted Christian does this more or less. We try to make other men's needs our own needs, by working for the poor, the ignorant, the sick, the helpless. You that care for our orphan children may well join with me in prayer that the Lord will fill up all those empty vessels not a few, which we have borrowed of poor widows. Think of my hundreds of borrowed vessels in the Orphanage, and of the number in the College. Blessed be the Lord my God, He will fill up all these. Those whom we try to help in different ways, especially those we try to lead to the Saviour, are like the woman's borrowed vessels, and they are not a few. You have made their spiritual needs your own, you have come before God to pray for them as for your own soul, and you shall be heard. You have talked to your neighbours and laid yourself out for their good as if your own eternal destiny were in their stead: rest you fully assured that the Lord that filled the borrowed pots in Elisha's day will also supply your borrowed needs. "My God will fill up all your needs." It is a blessed word. Bring out your vessels, and see if it be not true.

I should like to see every Christian here setting out all his vessels in rows at once, whatever they may be. Do not put your cares away in the back room and say, "I shall draw them out to-morrow and begin worrying over them." Instead of that, while the oil is flowing, bring them here before the Lord, that the oil may have free course, and find suitable storage. Would you limit the miracle? Have you one forgotten want? Make haste with it! Still the oil is multiplying. Come one! Come all! Arrange your vessels; and the Lord will fill up your needs by His grace, and fill your mouths with a song.

II. Secondly, let us enquire, WHO IS TO FILL THESE VESSELS? Paul says, "*My God will supply all your need.*"

"*My God!*" Oh, that is grand! It were foolish talking if any other name were mentioned. God can supply all the needs of His people, for He is All-sufficient; but nobody else can. He can do it alone without help; for nothing is too hard for the Lord. He is able to number the myriads of His creatures and attend to the commissariat of them all, so that not one of them shall lack: "He calleth them all by their names, by the greatness of His power not one faileth." "They that wait upon the Lord shall not want any good thing." As for thee, dear brother, "trust in the Lord and do good, so shalt thou dwell in the land, and verily thou shalt be fed." He that promises to fill up all thy empty vessels is one who can do it: there is no bound to the goodness and power of God.

Then, notice that sweet word which Paul has put before the glorious word "God." He writes,—"*My* God." As Paul looked at the money which the Philippians had sent him, and perhaps at the warm garments that should cover him in the cold, damp jail, he cried, "See how *my* God has supplied *me!*" And then he says, "*My* God shall supply *you.*" This same God, Paul's God—"shall fill up all your need." Wonderfully had God protected Paul from the malice of those who sought for his life. Very wonderfully had he been carried by divine power through unparalleled labours, so that he had been made to triumph in every place in the preaching of the gospel; and thus he had learned from day to day to get a firmer grip of his God, and say, "My God!" with more and more emphasis. Jehovah was not to Paul the unknown God, but "My God." With God he dwelt, and in Him he reposed all his cares. This same God is our God. Think of that, poor friend, in your hour of need. Think of that, you afflicted widow-woman: you have Paul's God to go to. Think of that, dear child of God in trouble: you have the same God as Paul had, and He is as much yours as He was Paul's. His arm has not waxed short, neither has His heart grown hard towards any of His children. "My God," says Paul, "who is also your God, will supply all your need."

Who is this God that will supply all our needs? Paul's God, remember, was and is *the God of providence*, and what a wonderful God that is! We speak as if we were some very important part of the universe, but really, what are we? Our little island can scarcely be found upon the globe till you hunt for it; what a tiny speck this congregation must be. But God supplies the wants of all the millions of mankind. "Mankind," I said: but I ought to have included all the other creatures, too;—the myriads of herrings in the sea, the multitudes of birds that sometimes darken the sun in their migrations, the countless armies of worms and insects, strangely supplied we know not how; and yet "your heavenly Father feedeth them." Is that all the sphere of His providence? No; far from it. I suppose that this round world of ours is but one apple in the orchard of creation, one grain of dust in the corner of God's great palace. But all yon orbs, with all the living things that may be peopling every star, he supplies. And how? "He openeth His hand and supplieth the want of every living thing." See how easy to Him is this universal provision; He doth but open His hand and it is done. This is the God that will supply all your need. He calleth the stars by name. He leadeth out Arcturus with his sons. He looseth the bands of Orion. He doeth great things without number; and shall He not feed and clothe you, O ye of little faith? Yes, be ye sure of this, the God of providence shall supply all your needs for this life and its surroundings.

If that suffice you not, let me remind you that this God is _the God of grace_, for Paul above all men counted grace to be his treasure: his God was the God of grace. Chiefly He is the God who gave His Son to bleed and die for men. Oh, stand at Calvary and see God's great sacrifice—the gift of His only-begotten Son; and when you have marked the wounds of the Well-beloved and seen Jesus die, answer me this question—" He that spared not His own Son, but delivered Him up for us all, how shall He not with Him also freely give us all things?" What will He deny us who has given up the best jewel that He had, the glorious One that heaven could not match? There was never the like of Jesus, and yet He bowed His head to die on our behalf. Oh, my dear, dear friends, if you are anxious to-night and vexed with many cares, do think of that. It is the God and Father of our Lord and Saviour Jesus Christ who says that He will fill up all your need. Do you doubt Him? can you? dare you distrust Him?

Now, take a flight above this present cloud-lane and behold _the God of heaven_. Think of what God is up yonder.

"Beyond, beyond this lower sky,
Up where eternal ages roll,
Where solid pleasures never die,
And fruits immortal feast the soul."

Behold the splendour of God! Gold in heaven is of no account: the streets of that city are all of pure gold like unto transparent glass. The riches and the merchandise of nations are but as rags and rottenness compared with the commonest utensils of God's great house above. There they possess inexhaustible treasures and everything that is precious; for the walls of the New Jerusalem are described as made of twelve manner of precious stones, as if these stones were so common in Immanuel's land that they built the walls therewith. The gates are each one a pearl. What pearls are those! Is God thus rich? inconceivable, incalculable rich, so that He clothes the very grass of the field more gloriously than Solomon clothed himself? What am I at to be of a doubtful mind? Is He my Father, and will He let me suffer want? What! I starving and my Father owning heaven? No, no.

"He that has made my heaven secure,
Will here all good provide;
While Christ is rich, can I be poor?
What can I want beside?"

My precious text is one which, years ago, when we built the Orphanage, I caused to be cut on one of the pillars of the entrance. You will notice it inside the first columns on either side whenever you go there. "My God shall supply all your need according to His riches in glory by Christ Jesus." This I took for the foundation of the Institution, and set my seal to it as true. And it has been so. Time would fail me if I were to tell how often God has interposed there for His numerous family—those children that are cast upon the divine Fatherhood. He has honoured His own promise and our faith, and I believe He always will. There on the fore-front of the Orphanage stands also the word—"The Lord will provide." You shall see whether it be not so. As long as that place stands my God shall supply our need, and it shall be a standing encouragement to us all. Think of the far more extensive orphanage of our brother Müller, of Bristol, with those two thousand five hundred children living simply through prayer and faith, and yet as abundantly supplied as the Queen in her palace. Nothing is wanting where God is the Provider. The Lord will supply without fail; let us trust without fear. Go and plead this promise with the Lord your God and He will fulfil it to you as well as to the rest of His saints.

III. Now, thirdly, let us enquire IN WHAT STYLE WILL GOD SUPPLY HIS PEOPLE'S NEEDS?

He will do it in such style _as becomes His wealth_—"_according to His riches._" There are several ways of doing most things. There is more than one way of giving a penny to a beggar. You can throw it at him, if you like; or pitch it in the mud as if you threw a bone to a dog; or you may hand it to him in a sort of huff as if you said, "Take it, and be off with you;" or you may drag the coin out of your pocket as unwillingly as if you were losing your eye-tooth. There is yet another way of doing it, namely that which makes the copper turn to gold, by a courteous kindness which expresses sympathy with the poor creature's need. Always give good things in the best way; for your heavenly Father does so.

Now, how does God supply His children? Stingily, miserably, grudging them every penny-worth? Certainly not! I hope that it was never your misery to dine with a grudging man who watched every mouthful that went down your throat as if there was so much the less for him. Why, when one does eat, at whatever table it may be, if it is the commonest fare, one likes a welcome. It is the welcome which makes the covenant invitation so sweet, when you hear the exhortation, "Eat, O friends; drink, yea, drink abundantly, O beloved." One enjoys the welcome of a heart which does all it can: like the Scotchwoman at a great communion meeting when there was nobody to take the people in,—"Come in," said she: "come in; I have room for ten of you in my house, and I have room for ten thousand of you in my heart. Come along with you. Nobody so welcome as you that have been sitting at my Master's table with me." How then does God dispense his favours? How does He fill up the vessels? The way He does it is not according to our poverty, nor according to our desert, "but according to His riches." He gives like a king. Brethren, I must correct myself:—He gives as a God, and as only God can give, according to His own Godlike riches.

Nay, that is not all. He will do it in a style _consistent with His present glory_. It is "according to His riches _in glory_," which means that, as rich as God is in glory so rich is He in giving. He never demeans Himself in the mercies that He gives. He gives according to His rank, and that is the highest conceivable. He gives _so as to bring Him new glory_. I never heard of one of His children receiving a great blessing from Him, and then saying that it did not glorify God to bestow it. No, no. The more He gives the more glorious He is in the eyes of men; and He delights to give, that His glory may be seen, and that the riches of His manifested glory may be increased. Withholding would not enrich the Lord of heaven; rather would it impoverish Him in glory But giving enriches Him with more revealed glory, and He therefore delights to scatter His bounty.

The fact is, brethren, *God gives gloriously.* The calculations of God—did you ever think of them? Well, let me say that He always calculates so as to leave something to spare, by which to illustrate the infinity of His goodness. I know that it is so. He does not give us just as much light as our eyes can take in, but He floods the world with splendour till we shade our eyes amidst the blaze of noon. After this fashion did His only-begotten Son feed the thousands when He multiplied bread and fish for them to eat. We read that "they did all eat"; no doubt they were hungry enough to do a great deal of that sort of labour. So far so good: but it is added "and were filled." It takes a good deal to fill men who have come a long way into the country and have had nothing to eat for a whole day. But they *were* filled, fainting and famished though they had been. Yes; but do not stop there:—"And they took up of the fragments twelve baskets full." The Lord always has baskets full of leavings remaining for the waiters. He will be sure to fill all your needs till you have no other need remaining, and have provision on hand for needs not yet arrived. Will the day ever come when we shall say, "Bring yet another need for God to fill," and the answer will be, "I have no more needs"? Then the oil of grace will stay; but it never will till then. Nay, according to what I have said, it will not stop then, but it will go on flowing and flowing, and flowing and flowing, world without end, "according to His riches in glory by Christ Jesus."

The Lord will give enough, enough for all time, enough *of* all, enough *for* all, and more than enough. There shall be no real need of any believer but what the Lord will fill it full, and exceed it. It is a wonderful expression "filled with all the fulness of God"; it pictures our being in God and God in us. One has illustrated it by taking a bottle, holding it in the sea, and getting it right full,—there is the sea in the bottle. Now, throw it right into the waves, and let it sink, and you have the sea in the bottle and the bottle in the sea. So God enters into us, and as we cannot hold more, He makes us enter into Himself. Into the very fulness of Christ are we plunged. What more can the amplest imagination conceive, or the hungriest heart desire? Thus God will supply our needs. Well may you fill others, who are yourselves so filled by God. Well may you serve His cause with boundless generosity when the infinite liberality of God is thus ensured to you.

IV. Lastly, let us notice BY WHAT MEANS THE LORD FILLS OUR NEEDS? It is "by Christ Jesus." Does God supply all His people's needs by Christ Jesus?

Yes, first, *by giving them Christ Jesus,* for there is everything in Christ Jesus. Christ is all. The man who has Christ has all things, as saith the apostle, "All things are yours; for ye are Christ's; and Christ is God's." You will never have a spiritual want which is not supplied in Christ. If you need courage He can create it. If you need patience He can teach it. If you need love, He can inspire it? You want washing, but there is the fountain. You require a garment, but there is the robe of righteousness. You would have great wants if you went to heaven without Christ, but you shall not go there

without Him: even there He shall supply you with everything. He it is that prepares your mansion, provides your wedding-dress, leads you to His throne, and bids you sit there with Him for ever. God will supply your eternal needs by giving you Christ.

Moreover, all things shall come to you *by virtue of Christ's merit.* You deserve no good thing, but He deserves it and He says, "Set it to my poor servant's account." You may use Christ's name at the Bank of Heaven freely, for though God might not give His favour to you, He will always give it to His dear, dying, risen, pleading Son. When Jesus' name is quoted all things are yielded by the Father. God will give you all things by Christ: therefore do not go to anybody else after those things. If you have begun in the Spirit do not attempt to be perfected by the flesh. If your only hope is in what Christ has done, stick to that, and add nothing to it. Be this your motto:—

"None but Jesus! None but Jesus!"

Jesus is our all. We are complete in Him. We need no *addenda* to the volume of His love. Christ, and Christ alone, shall supply all your need—all your fresh springs are in Him. "It pleased the Father that in Him should all fulness dwell; and of His fulness have all we received, and grace for grace."

Now, once more, I would to God that some poor soul here that has no faith—that has no good thing about him—would, nevertheless, look over his house and see whether he has not an empty vessel somewhere. All that Christ wants of you, poor sinner, is that you should be empty and come and let Him fill you with His grace. Come along with you, just as you are! Bring no good works, no prayers, no anything: but come with all your sins, and follies, and failures, which you may look upon as so many empty pots. Come to Jesus for everything. "But I have scarce a sense of need," say you. Come to Him for that too. You must be very needy to be in want of *that.* Come and get it of Him. I tell you, soul, you do not want a halffarthing's worth of your own; for what you think you have will only keep you back from Jesus. Come in all your poverty—a beggar, a king of beggars, come and be made rich by Jesus. You that have not a rag to cover your sin with; you that are only fit to be put into the devil's dust bin, and thrown away as worthless: come along with you! My Lord Jesus is ready to receive those that Satan himself flings away. If you are such that you cannot find anything in yourself that is desirable, and even your old companions who once cheered you on now think you too mean for them; yet come into my Master's company, for "this Man receiveth sinners." Come with your beggary and bankruptcy: you cannot dig, but to beg be not ashamed, for "My God will supply all your need according to His riches in glory by Christ Jesus."

As for you that have not trusted my Lord, and boast that you can do very well without Him, I suppose I must leave you to fight your own way. You declare that you will carry on your own business, and will not be dependent upon God, nor fall into any fanatical ideas, as you are pleased to call them. *But we shall see.* Already we see that the youths do faint and are wearied, and the young men utterly fall. We see that the young lions do lack and suffer hunger, and also that the best-laid plans of wisest men go oft awry, and they that have felt assured that they could fight their own way—even they have come to terrible failure. We shall see how you fare. They that mount up with wings as eagles and are proud and vainglorious, even these go down to destruction so that no flesh hath whereof to glory. As for me, let me wait upon the Lord God and live by faith in Him. Is it not better to drink of life out of the deep, inexhaustible fulness of God than to go for ever pumping and pumping at your own shallow cisterns which hold no water? Self-reliance may be well enough, but God-reliance eclipses it as the sun outshines the stars. "Oh, rest in the Lord, and wait patiently for Him." "Trust in the Lord, and do good; so shalt thou dwell in the land, and verily thou shalt be fed." "He shall cover thee with His feathers, and under His wings shalt thou trust: His truth shall be thy shield and buckler." There is a God, and those who love Him and trust Him and serve Him know that He is a good Master. Job was slandered by the devil when he came and said, "Does Job serve God for nought?" He insinuated that Job made a good thing out of his religion and was moved by selfish motives. It was a great falsehood, and yet, in a certain sense, it is true. If anybody says the same of you, admit that it is true;

own that you do make a fine thing out of your religion. God will not let you serve Him for nought; you shall never have to ask the question "What profit is there if we serve God?" You shall have His peace, His love, His joy, His supplies, according to His riches in glory by Christ Jesus. You shall know that in keeping His commandments there is great reward.

Believer, you shall have everything through Christ and nothing without Him He that trusts not the Saviour, and prays not to Him, shall be like Gideon's fleece—when all around it was wet the fleece was dry; but the man who trusts God and blesses His name shall be like Gideon's fleece, when all around was dry it was full of moisture. God will not hear a man's prayers except through Christ Jesus, but if that name be mentioned the gates of heaven fly open. God withholds no real good from the man of God who is in Christ. But our plea must be Jesus first, and Jesus last, and Jesus in the midst. We must present the bleeding Lamb before God each morning and each night. I pray you seek no mercy of God apart from Christ, but lay hold upon God in Christ; and you have enough for all your need. May God the Holy Spirit cause you to abide in Christ Jesus for His name's sake. Amen.

A NEW YEAR'S WISH

"But my God shall supply all your need according to His riches in glory by Christ Jesus."—Philippians iv. 19.

THE Philippians had several times sent presents to Paul, to supply his necessities. Though they were not themselves rich, yet they made a contribution, and sent Epaphroditus with it, "an odour of a sweet smell, a sacrifice acceptable, well pleasing to God." Paul felt very grateful: he thanked God, but he did not forget also to thank the donors; he wished them every blessing, and he did as good as say, "You have supplied my need, and my God shall supply yours. You have supplied my need of temporal food and raiment out of your poverty; my God shall supply *all* your need out of His riches in glory." "As," he says, in the eighteenth verse, "I have all and abound: I am full," "so," he adds, "'my God shall supply all your need.' You have sent what you gave me by the hand of a beloved brother, but God will send a better messenger to you, for He will supply all your need 'by Christ Jesus.'" Every single word sounds as if he had thought it over, and the Spirit of God had guided him in his meditation, so that he should to the fullest extent wish them back a blessing similar to that which they had sent to him, only of a richer and more enduring kind.

Now, on this New Year's Day I would desire, somewhat in the spirit of Paul, to bless those of you who have supplied, according to your abilities, the wants of God's work in my hands, and have given, even out of your poverty, to the cause of God, according as there has been need. I count myself to be personally your debtor though your gifts have been for the students, and the orphans, and the colporteurs, and not for myself. In return for your kindness, after the manner of His gracious love, "my God shall supply all your need, according to His riches in glory by Christ Jesus."

This verse is particularly sweet to me, for, when

we were building the Orphanage, I foresaw that, if we had no voting, and no collecting of annual subscriptions, but depended upon the goodness of God, and the voluntary offerings of His people, we should have times of trial, and therefore I ordered the masons to place upon the first columns of the Orphanage entrance these words, "My God shall supply all your need, according to His riches in glory by Christ Jesus." The text therefore is cut in stone upon the right hand and upon the left of the great archway. There stands this declaration of our confidence in God; and as long as God lives, we shall never need to remove it, for He will certainly supply the needs of His own work. While we serve Him, He will furnish our tables for us.

I. The text might suggest to us a field of gloomy thought, if we wished to indulge the melancholy vein, for it speaks of "all your need." So, first, behold A GREAT NECESSITY: "*all your need*." What a gulf! What an abyss! "*All your need*." I do not know how many believers made up the church at Philippi, but the need of one saint is great enough; what must many need? It would not be possible to tell the number of God's children on earth, but the text comprehends the need of the whole chosen family, "*all your need*." We will not ask you to reckon up the wonderful draught upon the divine exchequer which must be made by all the needs of all the saints who are yet on earth: but please think of your own need; that will be more within the compass of your experience and the range of your meditation. May the Lord supply your need and *all* your need!

There is *our temporal need*, and that is no little matter. If we have food and raiment, we should be therewith content; but there are many of God's people to whom the mere getting of food and raiment is a wearisome toil; and what with household cares, family trials, sickness of body, losses in business, and sometimes the impossibility of obtaining suitable labour, many of God's saints are as hard put to it as Elijah was when he sat by the brook Cherith. If God did not send them their bread and meat in a remarkable manner, they would surely starve ; but their bread shall be given them, and their water shall be sure. "My God shall supply all your need." You have, perhaps, a large family, and your needs are therefore greatly increased, but the declaration of the text includes the whole of your needs personal and relative.

After all, our temporal needs are very small compared with *our spiritual needs*. A man may, with the blessing of God, pretty readily provide for the wants of the body, but who shall provide for the requirements of the soul ? There is need of perpetual pardon, for we are always sinning ; and Jesus Christ's blood is always pleading for us, and cleansing us from sin. Every day there is need of fresh strength to battle against inward sin ; and, blessed be God, it is daily supplied, so that our youth is renewed like the eagle's. As good soldiers of Jesus Christ, we need armour from head to foot, and even then we do not know how to wear the armour, or how to wield the sword, unless He who gave us these sacred implements shall be always with us. Warring saint, God will supply all your need by His presence and Spirit. But we are not merely warriors, we are also workers. We are called, many of us, to important spheres of labour (and, indeed, let no man think his sphere unimportant), but here also our hands shall be sufficient for us, and we shall accomplish our life-work. You have need to be helped to do the right thing, at the right time, in the right spirit, and in the right manner ; your need, as a Sunday-school teacher, as an open-air preacher, and especially as a minister of the gospel, will be very great ; but the text meets all your requirements, "My God shall supply all your need." Then comes our need in suffering, for many of us are called to take our turn in the Lord's prison-house. Here we need patience under pain, and hope under depression of spirit. Who is sufficient for furnace-work ? Our God will supply us with those choice graces and consolations which shall strengthen us to glorify His name even in the fires. He will either make the burden lighter, or the back stronger ; He will diminish the need, or increase the supply.

Beloved, it is impossible for me to mention all the forms of our spiritual need. We need to be daily converted from some sin or other, which, perhaps, we have scarcely known to be sin. We need to be instructed in the things of God, we need to be illuminated as to the mind of Christ, we need to be comforted by the promises, we need to be quickened by the precepts, we need to be strengthened by the doctrines. We need, oh, what do we *not* need ? We are just a bag of wants, and a heap of infirmities. If any one of us were to keep a *want-book*, as I have seen the tradesmen do, what a huge folio it would need to be ; and it might be written within and with-out, and crossed and re-crossed, for we are full of wants from the first of January to the end of December ; but here is the mercy, " My God shall supply all your need." Are you put in high places ? Have you many comforts ? Do you enjoy wealth ? What need you have to be kept from loving the world, to be preserved from wantonness and pride, and the follies and fashions of this present evil world.

My God will supply your need in that respect. Are you very poor? Then the temptation is to envy, to bitterness of spirit, to rebellion against God. "My God shall supply all your need." Are you alone in the world? Then you need the Lord Jesus to be your Companion; and your Companion He will be. Have you many around you? Then you have need of grace to set them a good example, to bring up your children and manage your household in the fear of God. "My God shall supply all your need." You have need, in times of joy, to be kept sober and steady; you have need, in times of sorrow, to be strong and quit yourselves like men; you have needs in living, and you will have needs in dying, but your last need shall be supplied as surely as your first. "My God shall supply *all* your need."

Come, then, brethren, and look down into this great gulf of need, and exultingly say, "O Lord, we thank Thee that our needs are great, for there is the more room for Thy love, Thy tenderness, Thy power, Thy faithfulness, to fill the chasm."

That first thought, which I said might be a gloomy one, has all the dreariness taken out of it by four others equally true, but each of them full of good cheer. The text not only mentions *a great necessity*, but it mentions also *a great Helper*: "My God;" next, *a great supply*: "My God shall supply all your need;" thirdly, *an abundant store* out of which to draw the gift: "according to His riches in glory;" and lastly, *a glorious channel* through which the supply shall come: "by Christ Jesus."

II. So, for our enormous wants here is A GREAT HELPER: "*My God* shall supply all your need."

Whose God is that? Why, Paul's God. That is one of the matters in which the greatest saints are no better off than the very least, for though Paul called the Lord "My God," He is my God too. My dear old friend who sits yonder, and has nothing but a few pence in all the world, can also say, "and He is my God too. He is my God, and He is as much my God if I am the meanest, most obscure, and weakest of His people, as He would be my God if I were able, like Paul, to evangelize the nations." It is, to me, delightful to think that *my God is Paul's God*, because, you see, Paul intended this; he meant to say, "You see, dear brethren, my God has supplied all my wants; and as He is your God, He will supply yours." I have been in the Roman dungeon in which Paul is said to have been confined, and a comfortless prison indeed it is. First of all you descend into a vaulted chamber, into which no light ever comes except through a little round hole in the roof; and then, in the middle of the floor of that den, there is another opening, through which the prisoner was let down into a second and lower dungeon, in which no fresh air or light could possibly come to him. Paul was probably confined there. The dungeon of the Prætorium in which he was certainly immured is not much better. Paul would have been left well nigh to starve there, but for those good people at Philippi. I should not wonder but what Lydia was at the bottom of this kind movement, or else the jailor. They said, "We must not let the good apostle starve;" and so they made up a contribution, and sent him what he wanted; and when Paul received it he said, "My God has taken care of me. I cannot make tents here in this dark place so as to earn my own living, but my Master still supplies my need; and even so, when you are in straits, will He supply you."

"*My God*. It has often been sweet to me, when

I have thought of my orphan children, and money has not come in, to remember Mr. Müller's God, and how he always supplied the children at Bristol. His God is my God, and I rest upon Him. When you turn over the pages of Scripture, and read of men who were in sore trouble, and were helped, you may say, "Here is Abraham, he was blessed in all things, and Abraham's God will supply all my need, for He is *my* God. I read of Elijah, that the ravens fed him; I have Elijah's God, and He can command the ravens to feed me if He pleases." The God of the prophets the God of the apostles, the God of all the saints that have gone before us, "this God is our God for ever and ever." It seems to be thought by some that God will not work now as He used to do. "Oh, if we had lived in miraculous times," they say, "then we could have trusted Him! Then there was manifest evidence of God's existence, for He pushed aside the laws of nature, and wrought for the fulfilment of His promises to His people." Yet that was a rather coarser mode of working than the present one, for now the Lord produces the same results without the violation of the laws of nature. It is a great fact that, without the disturbance of a single law of nature, prayer becomes effectual with God; and God being enquired of by His people to do it for them, does fulfil His promise, and supply their needs. Using means of various kinds, He still gives His people all things necessary for this life and godliness. Without a miracle, He works great wonders of loving care, and He will continue so to do.

Beloved, *is the God of Paul your God?* Do you regard Him as such? It is not every man who worships Paul's God. It is not every professing Christian who really knows the Lord at all, for some invent a deity such as they fancy God ought to be. The God of Paul is the God of the Old and New Testament,—such a God as we find there. Do you trust such a God? Can you rest upon Him? "There are such severe judgments mentioned in Scripture." Yes, do you quarrel with them? Then you cast Him off; but if, instead thereof, you feel, "I cannot understand Thee, O my God, nor do I think I ever shall, but it is not for me, a child, to measure the infinite God, or to arraign at my bar, and say to Thee, 'Thus shouldst Thou have done, and thus oughtest Thou not to have done.' Thou sayest, 'Such am I,' and I answer, 'Such as Thou art, I love Thee, and I cast myself upon Thee, the God of Abraham, of Isaac, and of Jacob, the God of Thy servant Paul. Thou art my God, and I will rest upon Thee.'" Very well, then, He will "supply all your need, according to His riches in glory by Christ Jesus." Just think of that for a minute.

If *He* will supply you, you will be supplied indeed, for God is infinite in capacity. He is infinitely wise as to the manner of His actions; and infinitely powerful as to the acts themselves. He never sleeps nor tires; He is never absent from any place, but is always ready to help. Your needs come, perhaps, at very unexpected times; they may occur in the midnight of despondency or in the noonday of delight, but God is ever near to supply the surprising need. He is everywhere present and everywhere omnipotent, and He can supply all your need, in every place, at every time, to the fullest degree.

"Remember that Omnipotence has servants everywhere;"—

and that, whenever God wishes to send you aid, He can do it without pausing to ask, "How shall it be done?" He has but to will it, and all the powers of heaven and earth are subservient to your necessity. With such a Helper, what cause have you to doubt?

III. The next point in the text is, A GREAT SUPPLY. "My God shall *supply* all your need."

Sometimes we lose a good deal of the meaning of Scripture through the translation; in fact, nothing ever does gain by translation except a bishop. The present passage might be rendered thus, "My God will fill to the full all your need." The illustration which will best explain the meaning is that of the woman whose children were to be sold by her creditor to pay the debts of her late husband. She had nothing to call her own except some empty oil-jars, and the prophet bade her set these in order, and bring the little oil which still remained in the cruse. She did so, and he then said to her, "Go among your neighbours, and borrow empty vessels, not a few." She went from one to another till she had filled her room full of these empty vessels, and then the prophet said, "Pour out." She began to pour out from her almost empty cruse; and, to her surprise, it filled her largest oil-jar. She went to another, and filled that, and then another and another. She kept on filling all the oil-jars, till at last she said to the prophet, "there is not a vessel more." Then the oil stayed, but not till then. So will it be with your needs. You were frightened at having so many needs just now, were you not? But now be pleased to think you have them, for they are just so many empty vessels to be filled. If the woman had borrowed only a few jars, she could not have received much oil; but the more empty vessels she had, the more oil she obtained. So, the more wants and the more needs you have, if you bring them to God, so much the better, for He will fill them all to the brim, and you may be thankful that there are so many to be filled. When you have no more wants—but oh, when will that be?—then the supply will be stayed, but not till then.

How gloriously God gives to His people! We wanted pardon once: He washed us, and He made us whiter than snow. We wanted clothing, for we were naked. What did He do? Give us some rough dress or other? Oh, no! but He said, "Bring forth the best robe, and put it on him." It was a fortunate thing for the prodigal that his clothes were all in rags, for then he needed raiment, and the best robe was brought forth. It is a grand thing to be sensible of spiritual needs, for they will all be supplied. A conscious want in the sight of God,—what is it but a prevalent request for a new mercy? We have sometimes asked Him to comfort us, for we were very low; but when the Lord has comforted us, He has so filled us with delight that we have been inclined to cry with the old Scotch divine, "Hold, Lord, hold! It is enough. I cannot bear more joy. Remember I am only an earthen vessel." We, in relieving the poor, generally give no more than we can help, but our God does not stop to count His favours, He gives like a king. He pours water upon him that is thirsty, and floods upon the dry ground.

IV. We must pass on to the next thought, and consider for a minute or two THE GREAT RESOURCES out of which this supply is to come: "My God shall supply all your need, *according to His riches in glory.*" The preacher may sit down now, for he cannot compass this part of the text. God's riches in glory are beyond all thought.

Consider *the riches of God in nature;* who shall

count his treasures? Get away into the forests; travel on league after league among the trees which cast their ample shade for no man's pleasure, but only for the Lord. Mark on lone mountain-side and far-reaching plain the myriads of flowers whose perfume is for God alone. What wealth each spring and summer is created in the boundless estates of the great King! Observe the vast amount of animal and insect life which crowds the land with the riches of divine wisdom, for "the earth is the Lord's, and the fulness thereof." Look towards the sea; think of those shoals of fish, so countless that, when only the fringe of them is touched by our fishermen, they find enough food to supply a nation. Mark, too, the sunken treasures of the ocean, which no hand gathereth but that of the Eternal. If you would see the wealth of the Creator, cast your eye to the stars; tell ye their numbers if ye can. Astronomy has enlarged our vision, and made us look upon this world as a mere speck compared with innumerable other worlds that God has made; and it has told us that, probably, all the myriads of worlds that we can see with the telescope are a mere fraction of the countless orbs which tenant infinite space. Vast are God's riches in nature. It needs a Milton to sing, as he sang in *Paradise Lost*, the riches of the creating God.

The riches of God in providence are equally without bound. He saith to this creature, "Go," and he goeth, and to another, "Do this," and he doeth it, for all things do His bidding. Think of *the wealth of God in grace*. There nature and providence stand eclipsed, for we have the fountain of eternal love, the gift of an infinite sacrifice, the pouring out of the blood of His own dear Son, and the covenant of grace in which the smallest blessing is infinite in value. The riches of His grace! "God is rich in mercy,"—rich in patience, love, power, kindness, rich beyond all conception.

Now your needs shall be supplied according to the riches of nature, and the riches of providence, and the riches of grace; but this is not all; the apostle chooses a higher style, and writes "according to *His riches in glory*." Ah, we have never seen God in glory! That were a sight our eyes could not at present behold. Christ in His glory, when transfigured upon earth, was too resplendent a spectacle even for the tutored eyes of Peter, and James, and John.

"At the too-transporting light,"—

darkness rushed upon them, and they were as men that slept. What God is in His glory do ye know, ye angels? Does He not veil His face even from you lest, in the excessive brightness of His essence, even you should be consumed? Who amongst all His creatures can tell the riches of His glory, when even the heavens are not pure in His sight, and He charges His angels with folly?

"His riches in glory." It means not only the riches of what He has done, but the riches of what He could do; for if He had made hosts of worlds, He could make as many myriads more, and then have but begun. The possibilities of God omnipotent, who shall reckon? But the Lord shall supply all your need according to such glorious possibilities. When a great king gives according to his riches, then he does not measure out stinted alms to beggars, but he gives *like a king*, as we say; and if it be some grand festival day, and the king is in his state array, his largesse is on a noble scale. Now, when God is in His glory, bethink you, if you can, what must be the largesse that He distributes,—what the treasures that He brings forth for His own beloved! Now, "according to His riches in glory," He will supply all your needs. After that, dare you despond? O soul, what insanity is unbelief! What flagrant blasphemy is doubt of the love of God! He must bless us; and, blessed by Him, we must be blest indeed. If He is to supply our needs "according to His riches in glory," they will be supplied to the full.

V. Now let us close our meditation by considering THE GLORIOUS CHANNEL by which these needs are to be supplied: "According to His riches in glory *by Christ Jesus*."

You shall have all your soul's wants satisfied, but you must go to Christ for everything. "By Christ Jesus." That is the fountain-head where the living waters well up. You are not to keep your wants supplied by your own care and fretfulness. "Consider the lilies, how they grow." You are to be enriched "by Christ Jesus." You are not to have your spiritual wants supplied by going to Moses, and working and toiling as if you were your own saviour, but by faith in Christ Jesus. Those who will not go to Christ Jesus must go without grace, for God will give them nothing in the way of grace except through His Son. Those who go to Jesus the most shall oftenest taste of His abundance, for through Him all blessings come. My advice to myself and to you is that we abide in Him; for, since that is the way by which the blessing comes, we had better abide in it. We read of Ishmael that he was sent into the wilderness with a bottle, but Isaac dwelt by the well Lahai-roi, and it is wise for us to dwell by the well Christ Jesus, and never trust to the bottles of our own strength. If you wander from Christ Jesus, brother, you depart from the centre of bliss.

All this year I pray that you may abide by the well of this text. Draw from it. Are you very thirsty? Draw from it, for it is full; and when you plead this promise, the Lord will supply all your need. Do not cease receiving from God for a minute. Let not your unbelief hinder the Lord's bounty, but cling to this promise, "My God shall supply all your need, according to His riches in glory by Christ Jesus." I know not how to wish you a greater blessing. If you are enabled by the Holy Spirit to realize it, you will enjoy what I earnestly wish for you, namely,—

A HAPPY NEW YEAR.

THE HOPE LAID UP IN HEAVEN

"For the hope which is laid up for you in heaven, whereof ye heard before in the word of the truth of the gospel."—Colossians i. 5.

THREE graces should be always conspicuous in Christians—faith, love, and hope. They are each mentioned by Paul in the opening verses of the epistle from which our text is taken. These lovely graces should be so conspicuous in every believer as to be spoken of, and consequently heard of even by those who have never seen us. These flowers should yield so sweet a perfume that their fragrance may be perceived by those who have never gazed upon them. So was it with the saints at Colosse. Paul says, "We give thanks to God and the Father of our Lord Jesus Christ, praying always for you, since we *heard* of your *faith* in Christ Jesus, and of the *love* which ye have to all the saints, for the *hope* which is laid up for you in heaven." May our characters be such as can be reported of without causing us to blush; but that can never be the case if these essential virtues are absent. If these things be in us and abound we shall not be barren or unfruitful, but if they be lacking we are as withered branches. We should, therefore, be rich in faith, which is the root of every grace; and to this end we should daily pray, "Lord, increase our faith." We should strive to be full even to overflowing with love, which is of God, and makes us like to God; and we should also abound in hope, even that heavenly hope which causeth a man to purify himself in readiness for the inheritance above. See ye to it that neither of these three divine sisters are strangers to your souls, but let faith, hope, and love take up their abode in your hearts.

Note, however, the special character of each of these graces as it exists in the Christian. It is not every faith and love that will serve our turn, for of all precious things there are counterfeits. There is a kind of *faith* in all men, but ours is *faith in Christ Jesus*, faith in Him whom the world rejects, whose cross is a stumblingblock, and whose doctrine is an offence. We have faith in the Man of Nazareth, who is also the Son of God, faith in Him who having made atonement by His own blood once for all, is now exalted to His Father's right hand. Our confidence is not placed in ourselves, nor in any human priest nor in the traditions of our fathers, nor in the teachings of human wisdom, but alone in Christ Jesus. This is the faith of God's elect.

The *love* of Christians, too, is also special, for while a Christian man is moved by universal benevolence and desires to do good unto all men, yet he has a special love *unto all the saints*, and these the world loves not, because it loves not their Lord. The true believer loves the persecuted, the misrepresented, and despised people of God for Christ's sake. He loves them all, even though he may think some of them to be mistaken in minor matters; he has love to the babes in grace as well as to the grown saints, and love even to those saints whose infirmities are more manifest than their virtues. He loves them not for their station, or for their natural amiability, but because Jesus loves them, and because they love Jesus. You see the faith is in Christ Jesus, but the love extends beyond Christ Himself to all those who are in union with Him: while hope takes a still

wider sweep, and includes the eternal future in its circuit; thus do our graces increase in range as well as in number.

Our *hope*, too, upon which we are to speak this morning, is special, because it is a hope which is laid up for us in heaven; a hope, therefore, which the worldling cares not one whit about. He hopes that to-morrow may be as this day, and yet more abundant, but he cares nothing for the land where time has ceased to flow. He hopes for riches, or he hopes for fame; he hopes for long life and prosperity; he hopes for pleasure and domestic peace; the whole range of his hope is within the compass of his eye: but our hope has passed beyond the sphere of sight, according to the word of the apostle, "What a man seeth, why doth he yet hope for? But if we hope for that we see not, then do we with patience wait for it." Ours is a hope which demands nothing of time, or earth, but seeks its all in the world to come. It is of this hope that we are about to speak. May the Holy Spirit lead us into a profitable meditation upon it.

The connection of our text seems to be this: the apostle so much rejoiced when he saw the saints at Colosse possessing faith, love, and hope, that he thanked God and prayed about them. He saw these seals of God upon them, these three tokens that they were a really converted people, and his heart was glad. All the faithful ministers of Christ rejoice to see their people adorned with the jewels of faith, and love, and hope; for these are their ornament for the present, and their preparation for the future. This I believe to be the connection, but yet from the form of the language it is clear that the apostle intended to state that their love to the saints was very much produced in them by the hope which was laid up in heaven. You notice the word "for," which stands there: "The love which ye have to all the saints for," or *on account of*, or *because of*, "the hope which is laid up for you in heaven." There can be no doubt that the hope of heaven tends greatly to foster love to all the saints of God. We have a common hope, let us have a common affection: we are on our way to God, let us march in loving company; we are to be one in heaven, let us be one on earth. One is our Master and one is our service; one is our way and one is our end; let us be knit together as one man. We all of us expect to see our Well-beloved face to face, and to be like Him; why should we not even now love all those in whom there is anything of Christ? Brethren, we are to live together for ever in heaven: it is a pity we should quarrel. We are for ever to be with Jesus Christ, partakers of the same joy, of the same glory, and of the same love; why should we be scant in our love to each other? On the way to Canaan we have to fight the same enemy, to publish the same testimony, to bear the same trials, and to fly to the same Helper: therefore let us love one another. It were not difficult to show that the hope which is laid up in heaven should be productive of love among the saints on earth. This connection of my text with the clause immediately before it does not at all prevent its being regarded in the sense which I first mentioned, namely, that it was a subject for joy with the apostle that the Colossians had faith and love and hope; for he would rejoice none the less because their faith was fostered by their hope. It commendeth these sweet graces, that they are so wonderfully intertwisted with each other and dependent upon one another. There would be no love to the saints if there were not faith in Christ Jesus, and if there were not faith in Christ Jesus there would be no hope laid up in heaven. If we had no love it would be certain that we had no true faith, and if we had no hope, faith would be assuredly absent. If we entertain one of the graces we must receive her sisters, for they cannot be separated. Here are three brilliants set in the same golden setting, and none must break the precious jewel. "Now abideth faith, hope and love, these three," and blessed is he who hath them abiding in his own heart.

Now we will let faith and love stand by for a little while, and we will talk about hope, the hope mentioned in our text, the hope which is laid up for you in heaven. First, *it is a very marvellous hope;* secondly, *it is a very secure hope;* and thirdly, *it is a very powerfully influential hope.* May the Holy Ghost bless these three thoughts to us all.

I. First, then, we speak of our hope which is laid up for us in heaven as A VERY MARVELLOUS HOPE, and it is so, if we only consider that *it is a great act of grace that sinners should have a hope at all.* That when man had broken his Maker's law there should remain a hope for him is a thought which should make our hearts leap with gratitude. Do you not recollect when you felt it to be so? When sin lay heavily upon your conscience Satan came and wrote over the lintel of your door, "No HOPE," and the grim sentence would have stood there to this day had not a loving hand taken the hyssop, and by a sprinkling of precious blood removed the black inscription. "Wherefore remember that at that time ye were without Christ, having no hope, and without God in the world." That was our condition once; and it is a marvellous thing that it should be thoroughly changed, and that assurance should have taken the place of despair. In our carnal estate many false hopes, like will-o'-the-wisps, danced before us, deceived us, and led us into bogs of presumption and error, but we really had no hope. This is a dreadful condition for a man to be in: it is, indeed, the very worst of all; never in the storm so terrible as when in the howling of the winds the man distinctly hears the words "*No hope.*" Yet into the thick darkness of NO HOPE we once steered our course, and each time we tried to rely upon good works, outward ceremonies, and good resolutions, we were disappointed anew, and the words rung into our souls with dread monotony, "No hope, no hope," until we were fain to lie down and die. Now, sinners though we be, we have a hope. Ever since by faith we looked to Jesus on the cross, a hope full of glory has taken possession of our hearts. Is not this a marvellous thing?

More marvellous still is it *that our hope should venture to be associated with heaven.* Can there be heaven for such as we are? It seems almost presumptuous for a sinner who so richly deserves hell even to lift up his eyes towards heaven. He might have some hope of purgatory, if there were such a region, but a hope of heaven, is not that too much? Yet, brethren, we have no fear of hell or of purgatory now, but we expect to taste the joys laid up in heaven. There is no purgatory for anyone, and there is no hell for saints, heaven awaits all believers in Jesus. Our hope is full of glory, for it has to do with the glory of Christ, whom we hope to behold. Dost thou expect then, thou who wast black with lust, that thou shalt sit among the angels? "Aye, that I do," saith the believer, "and nearer to the throne than they." And thou who hast plunged into every form of uncleanness, dost thou expect to see God, for none but the pure in heart can behold Him? "Aye, that I do," saith he, "and not only to see Him, but to be like His Son, when I see Him as He is." What a divine hope is this. Not that we shall sit down on heaven's doorstep, and hear stray notes of the songs within, but that we shall sing with the happy band; not that we shall have an occasional glance within the gates of pearl, and feel our hearts hankering after the unutterable joys within the sacred enclosure, but we shall actually and personally enter into the halls of the palace, and see the King in His beauty in the land which is very far off. This is a brave hope, is it not? Why, she aspireth to all that the best of saints have received, she looketh for the same vision of glory, the same ecstasy of delight; she even aspireth to sit upon the throne of Christ, according to the promise, "To him that overcometh will I grant to sit with Me in My throne, even as I also overcame, and am set down with My Father in His throne." Hope reckons to be among the overcomers, and to partake in their enthronement. This is marvellous hope for a struggling believer to entertain; yet it is not presumption, but confidence warranted by the word of God. Is not this a miracle of love that such poor creatures as ourselves should be enabled thus to hope in God?

This hope is the more marvellous because *it is so substantial.* In our text the apostle scarcely seems to be speaking of the grace of hope, since that can hardly be said to be laid up in heaven, but dwells in our bosoms: he rather speaks of the *object* of hope, and yet it is clear than in his mind the grace of hope as well as the object must have been intended, because that which is laid up in heaven is not a hope except to those who hope for it; it is clear that no man has a hope laid up in heaven, unless he has hope within himself. The truth is that the two things—the grace of hope and its object—are here mentioned under one term, which may be intended to teach us that when hope is wrought in the heart by the Holy Ghost, it is the thing hoped for, even as faith is the thing believed, because it realizes and secures it. Just as faith is the substance of things hoped for, and the evidence of things not seen, so is hope the substance of the thing it expects, and the evidence of the thing it cannot see. Paul in this case, as in many others, uses language rather according to the theological sense which he would convey than according to the classical usage of the Greek tongue. The words of a heathen people must be somewhat strained from their former use if they are to express divine truth, and Paul does thus stretch them to their utmost length in this case. The hope of the true believer is so substantial that Paul even speaks of it as though it were the thing itself, and were laid up in heaven. Many a man hath a hope of wealth, but that hope is a different thing from being wealthy. There is many a slip 'twixt the cup and the lip, saith the old proverb, and how true it is! A man may have a hope of old age, yet he may never reach even middle life, and thus it is clear that the hope of long life is not in itself longevity; but he that hath the divine hope which grows out of faith and love hath a hope which shall never be disappointed, so that the apostle speaks of it as being identical with the thing hoped for, and describes it as laid up in heaven. What a marvellous hope is this which long before its realization is treated as a matter of actual attainment, and spoken of as a treasure reserved in the coffers of heaven!

One marvellous point about our hope is this, that *it is the subject of divine revelation*. No one could ever have invented this hope, it is so glorious as to baffle imagination. The prince of dreamers could never have dreamed it, nor the master of the art of logic have inferred it by reason: imagination and understanding are both left upon the ground, while the Bible idea of heaven soars upward like a strong-winged angel. The eternal hope had to be revealed to us; we should never have known it else, for the apostle says, "Whereof ye heard before in the word of the truth of the gospel." That a sinful man should have a hope of enjoying the perfect bliss of Paradise is a thing not to be thought of, were it not that the Lord hath promised it. I say again, imagination's utmost stretch had never reached to this, neither could we have had the presumption to suppose that such a bliss could be in store for men so unworthy and undeserving, had we not been assured thereof by the word of God. But now the word of God hath opened a window in heaven and bidden us look therein and hope for the time when we shall drink of its living fountains of water, and go no more out for ever.

This is marvellous, and it is even more marvellous to think that *this hope came to us simply by hearing*. "Whereof ye heard before in the word of the truth of the gospel." "Faith cometh by hearing," and hope comes by faith; and so the divine hope of being in heaven came to us by hearing,—not by working, not by deserving, not by penance and sacrifice, but simply by hearkening diligently unto the divine word, and believing unto life. We heard that the pierced hand of Jesus had opened the kingdom of heaven to all believers, and we believed, and saw a way of entrance into the holiest by His blood. We heard that God had prepared for them that love Him joys indescribable, and we believed the message, trusting in His Son. Our confidence is in the word which we have heard, for it is written, "Hear and your soul shall live"; and we find that by hearing our confidence is strengthened, and our heart filled with inward assurance and joyful expectation, therefore do we love the word more and more. Will we not prize to the uttermost that sacred word which has brought us such a hope? Yes, that we will: till we exchange hearing for seeing, and the message of Jesus for Jesus Himself, we will always lend a willing ear to the testimony of Jesus.

This hope is marvellous, once more, because *the substance of it is most extraordinary*. Brethren, what is the hope which is laid up for us in heaven? It would need many a sermon to bring out all the phases of delight which belong to that hope. It is the hope of *victory*, for we shall overcome every foe, and Satan shall be trodden under our feet. A palm of victory is prepared for our hands, and a crown for our heads. Our life struggle shall not end in defeat, but in complete and eternal triumph, for we shall overcome through the blood of the Lamb.

Nor do we hope for victory only: but in our own persons we shall possess *perfection*. We shall one day cast off the slough of sin, and shall be seen in the beauty of our new-born life. Truly, "it doth not yet appear what we shall be," but when we think of the matchless character of our Lord Jesus, we are overjoyed by the assurance that "we shall be like Him." What an honour and a bliss for the younger brethren to be like the firstborn! To what higher honour could God Himself exalt us? I know not of aught which could surpass this. Oh, matchless joy to be as holy, harmless and undefiled as our own beloved Lord! How delightful to have no propensity to sin remaining in us nor trace of its ever having been there; how blissful to perceive that our holy desires and aspirations have no weakness or defect remaining in them. Our nature will be perfect and fully developed, in all its sinless excellence. We shall love God, as we do now, but oh how much more intensely! We shall rejoice in God, as we do now, but oh what depth there will be in that joy! We shall delight to serve Him, as we do now, but there will then be no coldness of heart, no languor of spirit, no temptation to turn aside. Our service will be as perfect as that of angels. Then shall we say to ourselves without fear of any inward failure, "Bless the Lord, O my soul, and all that is within me bless His holy name." There will be no recreant affection then; no erring judgment, no straying passion, no rebellious lust; there will remain nothing which can defile, or weaken, or distract. We shall be perfect, altogether perfect. This is our hope—victory over evil and perfection in all that is good. If this were all our hope it would be marvellous, but there is more to be unfolded.

We expect to enjoy *security* also from every danger. As there will be no evil in us, so there will be none around us or about us to cause us alarm. No temporal evil, such as pain, bereavement, sorrow, labour, or reproach shall come near us: all will be security, peace, rest, and enjoyment. No mental evil will intrude upon us in heaven; no doubts, no staggering difficulties, no fears, no bewilderments will cause us distress. Here we see through a glass darkly, and we know in part, but there shall we see face to face, and know even as we are known. Oh, to be free from mental trouble! What a relief will this be to many a doubting Thomas! This is a marvellous hope. And then no spiritual enemy will assail us, no world, no flesh, no devil will mar our rest above. What will you make out of it, ye tried ones? Your Sabbaths are very sweet now on earth, but when they are over you have to return to yon cold world again; but there your Sabbath shall never end, and your separation from the wicked will be complete. It will be a strange sensation for you to find no Monday morning, no care to be renewed, no toil to be encountered, no harness to be buckled on afresh; above all, no sin to be dreaded, no temptation to be escaped. Heaven is so peaceful that the storms of earth are there unknown, the stirrings of the flesh are never felt, and the howlings of the dog of hell are never heard. There all is peace and purity, perfection and security for ever.

With this security will come perfect *rest*: "Yea, saith the Spirit, for they rest from their labours." Heavenly rest is quite consistent with *continual service*, for, like the angels, we shall rest on the wing, and find it rest to serve God day and night. But there you shall not toil till the sweat bedews your face, neither shall the sun smite you, nor any heat. No weary limb nor fevered brain shall follow upon the blessed service of the glory-land. It is a paradise of pleasure, and a palace of glory; it is a garden of supreme delights, and a mansion of abiding love; it is an everlasting *sabbatismos*, a rest which never can be broken, which evermore remaineth for the people of God; it is a kingdom where all are kings, an inheritance where all are heirs. My soul panteth for it. Is not this a charming hope? Did I not say well when I declared it to be marvellous?

Nor is this all, brethren, for we expect to enjoy in heaven, a *happiness* beyond compare. Eye hath not seen it, nor ear heard it, nor hath the heart conceived it; it surpasses all carnal joy. We know a little of it, for the Lord hath revealed it unto us by the Spirit, who searcheth all things, even the deep things of God; yet what we know is but a mere taste of the marriage feast: enough to make us long for more, but by no means sufficient to give us a complete idea of the whole banquet. If it be so sweet to preach about Christ, what must it be to see Him and be with Him? If it be so delightful to be ravished by the music of His name, what must it be to lie in His bosom? Why, if these few clusters of Eshcol which are now and then brought to us are so sweet, what will it be to abide in the vineyard, where all the clusters grow? If that one bucketful from the well of Bethlehem tasted so sweetly that we scarce dared to drink it, but poured it our before the Lord as a thankoffering, what a joy will it be to drink at the well-head without stint for ever? O to be eternally at the right hand of God, where there are pleasures for evermore!

This is our hope, and yet there is more, for we have the hope of everlasting *fellowship* with Christ. I would give ten thousand worlds, if I had them, to have one glimpse of that dear face, which was marred with sorrow for my sake; but to sit at my Lord's feet and look up into His countenance, and hear His voice, and never, never grieve Him, but to participate in all His triumphs and glories for ever and for ever, —what a heaven will this be? Then shall we have fellowship with all His saints, in whom He is glorified, and by whom His image is reflected; and thus shall we behold fresh displays of His power and beamings of His love. Is not this surpassing bliss? Said I not well when I declared that ours is a marvellous hope? Had I eloquence and could pile on goodly words, and could a poet assist me with his sweetest song, to tell of the bliss and joy of the eternal world, yet must preacher and poet both confess their inability to describe the glory to be revealed in us. The noblest intellect and the sweetest speech could not convey to you so much as a thousandth part of the bliss of heaven.

There I leave the first head. It is a very marvellous hope.

II. Secondly, let us remark that IT IS A MOST SECURE HOPE. It is so according to the text, because *it is laid up* or secured. The recent calamities which have occurred in connection with the Glasgow City Bank will make business men very careful where they lay up their treasures; but no one can entertain any fear of the safety of that which God Himself takes under His charge. If your hope is laid up with Him it becomes sinful to doubt its security. It is "laid up," the text says, and this means that it is hidden in a safe place like a treasure which is well secured. We find it hard to lay up our valuables safely in this world because thieves break through and steal; the iron safe, the strong room, and all sorts of inventions are employed to preserve them from felonious grip; but when God becomes the guardian of our treasure He lays it up where none can touch it, and neither man nor devil can steal it. Our hope is laid up just as crowns and wreaths were laid up at the Grecian games for those who gained them: no one could snatch them away from their rightful owners, but the rewards were safely retained for the winners, to be distributed when the contest was over. You see not as yet your hope, beloved, but it is laid up: it is hidden with Christ in God, and made as safe as the throne of God Himself.

Notice the next word, it is laid up *"for you."* It is something to have your hope laid up, but it is much better to have it laid up for yourself. "Laid up *for you"*; that is, for you whose faith is in Christ Jesus, and who have love to all the saints. There is a crown in heaven which will never be worn by any head but yours; there is a harp in glory that never will be touched by any finger but yours. Make no mistake about it; it is laid up in heaven *for you*, "reserved in heaven *for you*, who are kept by the power of God, through faith unto salvation." "For *you*";— "Fear not, little flock; for it is your Father's good pleasure to give *you* the kingdom." Lay the stress there, and get honey out of it. "Laid up for *you*."

Where is it laid up? The next word tells us. "Laid up for you *in heaven*," "where," says the Saviour as though he were expounding the text, "neither moth nor rust doth corrupt." This means that no process of decay will cause your treasure to become stale and worn out; no secret moth will eat the garments of heaven's courtiers, and no rust will tarnish the brightness of their crowns. Our Lord adds, "Nor do thieves break through nor steal." We cannot imagine a burglar's breaking through the walls of heaven. We could not imagine Satan himself undermining the bastions of the New Jerusalem, or leaping over the bulwarks which guard the city of the Great King. If your hope is laid up in heaven it must be perfectly safe. If your hope lies in the bank, it may break; if it lies in an empire it may melt away; if it lies in an estate, the title-deeds may be questioned; if it lies in any human creature, death may bereave you; if it lies in yourself, it is deceitful altogether: but if your hope is laid up in heaven, how secure it is. Be glad, and bless the Lord.

To show how secure is our hope, the apostle tells us that we have an indisputable certificate and guarantee for it. He says, "We heard of it in the word of the truth of the gospel." Notice these three emphatic words—"In *the word* of *the truth* of *the gospel*." First, "In the word." What word is that? Man's word? Man's words are so much wind. But this is God's word, the same word that made heaven and earth, a word of power which cannot fail and of truth which cannot lie. You first hear of this blessed hope through the word of God, and that word is the best of evidence. You know how a person will say, "My word for it"—here you have God's word for it. We take a good man's word freely: and will we not take God's word much more readily? You have the word of God for the sure hope that believers in Christ Jesus shall be blessed for ever: is not this security enough?

Our text goes on to say, "the word *of the truth*": so, then, it is not a word of guess, conjecture, or of probable inference, but of infallible truth. My brethren of the modern school, my wise brethren, have a word of excogitation, and outcome, and development; but the word the apostle preached was "the word of *the truth*"—something positive, dogmatic, and certain. Ugly as the word may sound, the Lord grant that we may never be ashamed of the thing *called* dogmatism nowadays, which is none other than faith in God's truth. We believe the word of God not only to be true, but to "the word of *the* truth." "Let God be true and every man a liar." There may be other true things in the world, but God's word is the essence of truth, *the* truth beyond all things else that may be true, for He hath said, "Heaven and earth shall pass away, but My word shall never pass away." The apostle saith in another place, "All flesh is as grass, and all the glory of man as the flower of grass. The grass withereth, and the flower thereof falleth away; but the word of the Lord endureth for ever. And this is the word which by the gospel is preached unto you."

Note the next word, "The word of the truth of *the gospel*," or of the good news. That is to say, the sum and substance of the good news is to be found in this glorious hope. If you extract the essence of the gospel, and get *the* truth, which is the central germ of the glad tidings, you come at that blessed hope most sure and steadfast, which entereth into that within the veil.

Now, then, before your God-created hope can fail the word of God will have to be broken, but the word of God cannot be broken: the truth will have to fail, but the truth abideth for ever, and is by force of its own nature eternal; and the gospel will have to be disproved, but that cannot be, since the glory of God is made to hang upon it. Ye have heard it, then, "in the word of the truth of the gospel," what better assurance do you need? Hold to it and rejoice in it, and you shall never be ashamed of your hope.

III. I close by saying that IT IS A MOST POWERFULLY INFLUENTIAL HOPE. Brethren, I have already said to you that this hope is *the parent and nurse of love*, because the text says, "The love which ye have to all the saints for the hope which is laid up for you in heaven." Now, that is no trifling fountain of action which leads believing hearts to love, since love is always a working grace. Oh, for more love in this distracted world. Whatsoever in this world promotes Christian love is to be admired, and since the hope that we shall be for ever together before the throne of God lifts us above the little disagreements of society, and makes us affectionate to each other, it is a thing to cultivate with care.

Love is one part of the powerful operation of hope upon ourselves, but *hopefulness affects others also.* Where the hopefulness of saints is conspicuous, it leads ministers and gracious people to give thanks to God. Paul says, "We give thanks to God and the Father, praying always for you since we heard of your hope." I do not know a greater delight that a minister can have than the thought of all his people entering the bliss of heaven, and of his meeting them all there. We hardly have time to know each other here below; we have loved each other in the Lord, and we have striven together in the service of God, and some of us are old fellow-soldiers now, after many years of Christian warfare. how pleasant it will be to dwell together above world without end! Some have gone home whom we dearly loved, and

would almost have detained if we could; and there are others among us who in the order of nature will soon be translated; happy are we because we cannot long be separated. The age of some among us prophesies their speedy departure, and foreshadows that they will soon go over to the majority: but it is a most blessed reflection that all of us who are in Christ shall meet together above. We shall have ample room and verge enough for fellowship when we have reached eternity, and what will our joy be then! Perhaps some of you will say to me when we converse in heavenly language,—"You remember talking to us concerning the blessed hope on that fine Lord's-day morning, but you did not know much about it. We said then, 'The half has not been told us'; but now we perceive you did not tell us the one-hundredth part. Still we were glad to share in the joy of what little we did know, and in the blessed hope of knowing so much more." Oh yes, dear friends, because the hope of heaven in us helps to make other people thank God on our account, it is a sweet grace and mightily influential, and the more we have of it the better.

Moreover, hearing of their hope, *led the apostle to pray*, and if you will follow me in reading the words which succeed the text, you will see what he desired for his friends at Colosse. In the ninth verds you will see what he prayed for. He says, "For this cause we also, since the day we heard it, do not cease to pray for you, and to desire that ye might be filled with the knowledge of His will in all wisdom and spiritual understanding." Having believed in Jesus, and loving His people, you are going to heaven; and so Paul says "I desire that you be filled with the knowledge of His will," and well may he so desire, since to do that will is the joy and business of heaven. Is not our prayer, "Thy will be done on earth as it is in heaven"? Brethren, let us learn the will of the Lord now, and so be educated for the skies. Here we are to go through our apprenticeship, that we may be able to take up our freedom as citizens of the New Jerusalem. Here we are at school, preparing to take our degree above among the instructed saints of God. Are we to enter heaven ignorant of what the will of the Lord is? Surely we ought to know something of the ways of the place, something of the rules of the court. This part of our life below is intended to be a prelude to our life above, a preparation for perfection. Here below we undergo the tuning of the instruments. It is not meet that there should be discordant scrapings and screwings of strings in heaven. No, let us do all that here. Let us have our harps tuned below, so that when we reach the orchestra of the skies we may take our right place, and drop into the right note directly. A good hope should make you eager to know the will of the Lord. It should purify you even as Christ is pure, and make you anxious to begin the perfect service of heaven while yet you linger below.

Then the apostle prays "that ye might walk worthy of the Lord unto all pleasing." Is it not fit that you who are to rise to Enoch's heaven should walk as he did, and have this testimony that you please God? You are going to dwell at God's right hand, where there are pleasures for evermore, would not you wish to do all you can to please your Lord before you see Him? You are a son of a king: you have not put on your glittering array as yet; your crown is not yet on your head; but surely you wish to behave yourself as becometh one who is fore-ordained for so much honour and glory. If a son is in a distant country and is coming home, he begins to think "What can I take home? What can I do to please the beloved father whom I am soon to see?" Begin, beloved, to see what you can do to please God, because you are so soon to enter into His pleasure, and dwell with those that wear white robes, "for they are worthy."

Next he says, "Being fruitful in every good work." Why, if there is to be such a rich reward of grace, let us bear all the gracious fruit we can, and if the time of working is so soon to be over, let us be instant in every holy labour while yet the season is with us. Who wants to go into heaven empty-handed? Who wishes to spend the time of his sojourning here in idleness? Oh no; let us seek to be fruitful to the glory of God that so we may have an abundant entrance into the kingdom.

The apostle further adds, "Increasing in the know-ledge of God." If I am going to dwell with God, let me know something of Him; let me search His word and see how He has revealed Himself; let me endeavour to have fellowship with Him and His Son Jesus that I may know Him. How can I enter heaven as a total stranger to Him who is the king of it? Is not the knowledge of God as needful as it is desirable? Those who have a good hope of heaven will not rest without knowing the Lord, from the least even to the greatest of them. If anyone were to make you a present of a great estate, no matter in what country it might be situated, you would feel an interest in the land and its neighbour-hood, and before nightfall you would be found en-quiring about the place. No matter how rustic the neighbourhood or remote the locality, you would set your thoughts towards it if you knew the estate to be yours. As a usual thing, one of the driest docu-ments in all the world is a rich man's will. If you have ever heard one read you will know how it proses on and on in that rigmarole fashion dear to lawyers: but if you are present when it is read to the family, please notice how "my son John's" eyes clear up when it comes to the clause which concerns himself,

and how even the aged countenance of "my faithful servant Jane" brightens when her small legacy is mentioned. Everyone is on the alert when his own interests are affected. Even so he that hath a hope in heaven and an interest in Christ's great testament, will at once take an interest in divine things, and will desire to increase in the knowledge of God.

Once again, the apostle says, "strengthened with all might, according to His glorious power, unto all patience and longsuffering with joyfulness." A hope of heaven is a mighty strengthener for bearing the ills of life and the persecutions of the adversary. "It will soon be over," says a man who looks for heaven, and therefore he is not over-weighted with grief. "It is an ill lodging," said the traveller, "but I shall be away in the morning." Well may we be strengthened with all might by the hope of heaven: it is but reason that the exceeding weight of glory should cast into the shade this light affliction, which is but for a moment.

You will say, "But have you not wrought this part of the chapter into your subject without any warrant?" No. Here is my warrant in the next verse: "Giving thanks unto the Father, which has made us meet to be partakers of the inheritance of the saints in light." I have been following the evi-dent track of the apostle's thoughts. The Lord gives us a hope of glory, and then He gives us a meetness for it, and that meetness is largely wrought in us by the Holy Spirit through the instrumentality of our hope. Cultivate, then, your hope, dear brethren. Make it to shine so plainly in you that your minister may hear of your hopefulness and joy; cause observers to take note of it, because you speak of heaven, and act as though you really expected to go there. Make the world know that you have a hope of heaven: make worldlings feel that you are a believer in eternal glory, and that you hope to be where Jesus is. Often surprise them as they see what they call your simplicity, but what is in truth only your sincerity, while you treat as matter of fact the hope laid up for you in heaven. The Lord grant it for Jesus Christ's sake. Amen.

SPIRITUAL KNOWLEDGE AND ITS PRACTICAL RESULTS

"For this cause we also, since the day we heard it, do not cease to pray for you, and to desire that ye might be filled with the knowledge of His will in all wisdom and spiritual understanding; that ye might walk worthy of the Lord unto all pleasing, being fruitful in every good work, and increasing in the knowledge of God."—Colossians i. 9, 10.

FOR the church that was at Colosse Paul gave hearty thanks to God for many most important blessings, especially for their faith, their love, and their hope. It would be a very useful exercise to our hearts if we would often give thanks to God for the gifts and graces which we discover in our Christian brethren. I am afraid we are more inclined to spy out their faults, and to suppose that we deplore them, than we are to discern the work of the Holy Spirit in them, and from the bottom of our hearts to give thanks to God for them. Paul felt encouraged by what he saw in the Colossian believers to pray to God to enrich them yet further. It should be our desire that our best brethren should be better, and that

those who are most like Jesus should be still more completely conformed to His image. We cannot more wisely show our love to our friends than by first acknowledging the grace which is in them, and then by praying that God may give them more. Paul, as with an eagle eye, surveyed the church at Colosse, which he loved so well, and he noted that it was somewhat lacking in knowledge. The Colossian brotherhood differed considerably from the church at Corinth, which abounded in talent, and was enriched with all knowledge. The Colossians had fewer gifted brethren among them who could act as teachers, and, though this was no fault of theirs, it impoverished them in the matter of knowledge, and as Paul would not have them come behind in any desirable attainment, he therefore prayed for them that they might be filled with knowledge in all wisdom and spiritual understanding. If you read this epistle through, you will observe that Paul frequently alludes to knowledge and wisdom. To the point in which he judged the church to be deficient he turned his prayerful attention. He would not have them ignorant. He knew that spiritual ignorance is the constant source of error, instability, and sorrow; and therefore he desired that they might be soundly taught in the things of God. Not that they were destitute of saving knowledge already, for he says in the sixth verse that they "knew the grace of God in truth," and that they had brought forth fruits meet for salvation; but saving knowledge, though it be the most essential attainment, is not the only knowledge which a Christian should seek after. He longs to be useful as well as to be safe. Being himself delivered out of darkness he strives to bring others into the marvellous light of grace. Paul would have his brethren thoroughly furnished for sacred service, knowing the will of the Lord themselves, and able to teach others. He desired for them that they might possess comforting knowledge, strengthening knowledge, edifying knowledge, sanctifying knowledge, directing knowledge; so that they might be ready for all the trials, duties, and labour of life.

Upon this subject I am led to make four observations, and to enlarge upon each of them. May the Holy Spirit by this discourse build us up in the knowledge of God.

I. My first subject is THE GREAT VALUE OF INTERCESSORY PRAYER; for as soon as Paul felt his heart burning with love to the saints at Colosse, and had heard of the work of the Spirit among them, he began to show his love by lifting up his heart in prayer for them. He did that for them which he knew would bless them.

Notice, that intercessory prayer is a very *important part of the work of Christians for one another*. We are not sent into the world to live unto ourselves, but we are members of one body, and each member is expected to contribute to the health and the comfort of the whole. It is true we cannot all preach, but we can all pray; we cannot all distribute alms from our substance, but we can all offer prayer from our hearts. In temporal things we may not be able to enrich the church for lack of substance; but if we fail to bless the church by our prayers it will be for lack of grace. Whatever you fail in, dearly beloved,—and I pray that you may in nothing come behind,—yet do not fail in prayer for all the saints, that every blessing may abound towards them.

Intercessory prayer is to be esteemed as an *invaluable proof of love*, and as the creator of more love. The man who will truly pray for me will certainly forgive me readily if I offend him; he will relieve me if I am in necessity; and he will be prepared to assist me if I am engaged in a service too hard for me. Give us your earnest prayers, and we know that we live in your hearts. How sweet it is to be permitted thus to manifest our love to one another! When our hand is palsied we can still pray; when our eye grows dim we can see to pray; when by sickness we are altogether laid aside we can still pray; and when we meet with cases in which we are unable to help, and yet are moved with sympathy for a brother, our sympathy

can always find one open channel, for we can pray, and by prayer call in the aid of one whose help is effectual. Therefore, by your love to your Lord, and to all those who are in Him, I beseech you abound in intercessory prayer, as the apostle did.

Intercessory prayer, again, is most valuable, because it is an *infallible means of obtaining the blessings* which we desire for our friends. It is not in vain that we ask, for it is written, " Everyone that asketh receiveth." It is not in vain that we interceded for others, for the Lord delights to answer such petitions. The unselfish devotion which pleads as eagerly for others as for itself is so pleasing to the Lord that He puts great honour upon it. If we desire any blessing for our friends our best course is to pray: even if we would have them to be filled with knowledge in all wisdom our safest course is to pray that it may be so. Of course, we must not forget to instruct them and to aid them in their own studies as far as lieth in our power, for every honest prayer supposes the use of all proper means; but the instruction which we offer will be of no service unless we first bring down the blessing of God upon it, that thereby our friends may be made willing to learn, and may receive the truth not as the word of man, but as from the Lord Himself. None but spiritual teaching will nourish spiritual life. The Holy Ghost must teach divine truth to the heart, or it will never be truly known. Whatsoever thou wisely desirest for thy friend go about to get it for him, but hasten first to the throne of grace. If thou wouldst have thy friend converted, if thou wouldst have him strengthened, if thou wouldst have him taught of God, if thou wouldst have him quickened to a nobler life, and elevated to a higher consecration, do him this great service—take his case before the Lord in prayer; and in so doing thou hast gone the wisest way to work to enrich him.

Note, brethren, for I am keeping to my text closely, that such intercessory prayer will be all the more valuable if it is our *immediate resort*. The apostle says, " Since the day we heard it, we do not cease to pray for you." He began to pray at once. Whenever you perceive the work of the Spirit in any heart, pray at once, that the holy change may proceed with power. Whenever you discover any lack in a brother begin on the day you hear of it to pray that his lack may be supplied. There should be no delaying of prayer. " He gives twice who gives quickly " is a human proverb, but I believe that when we pray speedily we shall often find that God in answering quickly gives us a double blessing. Usually he shall win worldly riches who is the most diligent in the pursuit of them, and assuredly he shall be richest towards God who is most diligent in supplication. Linger not a minute, speed thee to the mercy-seat. Now is the accepted time; the Lord waits to be gracious to thee. The Lord indicates to thee what thy prayer shall be by the news which thou hast just heard of thy friend; therefore, bring his case at once before the throne of grace. Divine providence has brought the needful subject for prayer under thy notice; therefore, this day begin to pray about it.

Our prayers will be all the more valuable if they are *incessant as well as immediate*. "We cease not," said Paul, "to pray for you since the day we heard it." "Oh," says one, "was Paul always praying for the Colossians from the day he heard of their welfare ? It may have been months and years ; did he never cease to pray ? " I answer, he was always praying for them in the sense which he explains : he adds, " and to desire." Now, desire is the essence of prayer ; in fact, desire is the kernel of prayer, and the vocal expressions which we call by the name of prayer are often but its shell ; inward desire is the life, the heart, the reality of prayer. Though you cannot always be speaking in prayer, you can always be desiring in prayer. The miser is always desiring riches, though he is not always talking about his gold and silver ; and the man who loves his fellow-men, and desires their profit, is really always praying for their benefit, though he is not always lifting up his voice in supplication. " Since the day we heard it," saith Paul, " we do not cease to pray for you." The act of prayer is blessed, the habit of prayer is more blessed, but the spirit of prayer is the most blessed of all ; and it is this that we can continue for months and years. The act of prayer must, from force of circumstances, be sometimes stayed ; but the habit of prayer should be fixed and unvarying ; and the spirit of prayer, which is fervent desire, should be perpetual and abiding. We can hardly realize the value to the church and to the world of that intercessory prayer which ceases not day nor night, but without fail ascends before the Lord from the whole company of the faithful, as the incense ascended from the altar.

Dear friends, our intercessory prayer will be all the more precious if it is an *intense expression unto God*. I suppose that by the use of the word " desire " here, the apostle not only explains how he continued to pray, but in what manner he prayed —with " desire." Remember how our Lord puts it—" with desire have I desired to eat this passover with you before I suffer." I wish we could always say " with desire have I desired in prayer. I did not repeat a merely complimentary benediction upon my friends, but I pleaded for them as for my life ; I importuned with God ; I offered an effectual inwrought prayer, which rose from the depths of my heart to the heights of heaven, and obtained an audience with God." Fervency is a great essential for victorious prayer. God grant us to be importunate, for then we shall be invincible.

One more observation, and I have done with this. Intercessory prayer is increased in value when it is not from one person alone, but is offered in *intimate union with other saints*. Paul says, " We also," not " I only," but " We also, since the day *we* heard it, cease not." If two of you agree as touching anything concerning the kingdom, you have the blessing secured to you by a special promise of God. Remember how Abraham prayed for the cities of the plain, but succeeded not until Lot also added his supplication for Zoar. Then the little city was spared. I compare Abraham's intercession to a ton weight of prayer, and poor Lot's I can hardly reckon to have been more than half an ounce, but still that half ounce turned the scale. So here is Paul, and with him is youthful Timothy, who, compared with Paul, is inconsiderable ; yet Paul's prayer is all the more effectual because Timothy's prayer is joined with it. Our Lord sent out His servants by two and two, and it is well when they come back to Him in prayer two and two. I commend to you, brethren and sisters, the habit of frequent prayer together. When a Christian friend drops

in, his visit will perhaps end in mere talk unless you secure its spiritual profit by at least a few minutes spent in united prayer. I frequently during the day, when a friend comes in upon the Master's business, say, " Let us pray before you go," and I always find the request is welcomed. Such prayers do not occupy much time, and if they did, it might be well spent ; but such united supplications oil the wheels of life's heavy wain, and cause it to move with less of that creaking which we too often hear. " I alone " is certainly a good word in prayer ; but " we also " is a better one. Let us link hands and intercede for our brethren and the whole church of God.

Thus have I expatiated upon the excellences which increase the value of intercessory prayer. Use much this heavenly art. It is effectual for ten thousand ends. It turneth every way to bless the church. Brethren, pray for us, pray for all saints, pray for all sinners, and by so doing you will be the benefactors of your age.

II. Our second observation from the text is this—we learn here THE PRECIOUSNESS OF SPIRITUAL KNOWLEDGE ; for all this earnest, ceaseless prayer is offered for this end, " That ye might be filled with the knowledge of His will in all wisdom and spiritual understanding." Here let us speak of the usefulness and blessedness of that spiritual knowledge for which the apostle and his friend cried incessantly unto the Lord.

First, consider the *men* for whom this knowledge is desired. They are saints and faithful brethren, of whom we read that they "knew the grace of God in truth," and were " bringing forth fruit " unto God. For those who know the Lord already we must no cease to pray. They are not beyond the need of our prayers while they are in this life. We may pray for those who know nothing of the Lord, that He would open their blind eyes ; but even those who have been taught of God already are in need of our supplications that they may learn yet more. We have great encouragement to pray that they may be filled with all knowledge, since the Lord has already done so much for them. We dare not say in this case that a little knowledge is a dangerous thing, for a little knowledge of the things of God may suffice to save the soul ; but knowledge is a most desirable thing for those who have that little knowledge. Pray therefore for them. Let not your prayers plead only and altogether for the unconverted, but entreat for our young converts that they may be further edified. It will be an ill day when we are so engaged in seeking lost sheep that we forget the lambs. It would be very mischievous for us to neglect our work at home in order to carry on warfare with the adversary abroad. No, let us cry to God daily in prayer that the stones lately quarried may be built up upon the one foundation, and embedded in the walls of the church of God unto eternal glory. We desire life for the dead, health for the living, and maturity for the healthy. For the deeper instruction of our younger brethren let us pray.

Of this desirable knowledge, what is the *measure* ? We desire for them " that they may be filled with the knowledge of His will." " Filled "—this is grand scholarship, to have the mind, and heart, and the whole of our manhood filled with knowledge. Paul would not have a believer ignorant upon any point : he would have him filled with knowledge for when a measure is full of wheat there is no room for chaff. True knowledge excludes error. The men that go after false doctrine are usually those who know little of the word of God ; being untaught they are unstable, ready to be blown about with every wind of doctrine. If you leave empty spots in your minds unstored with holy teaching, they will be an invitation to the devil to enter in and dwell there. Fill up the soul, and so shut out the enemy. Paul desired the Colossian saints to be filled—filled up to the brim with the knowledge of God's will. Brethren, we would have you know all that you can know of God's truth. Rome flourishes by man's ignorance, but the New Jerusalem rejoices in light. No knowledge of the revealed will of God can ever do you any harm if it be sanctified. Do not be afraid of what they call "high doctrines," or the "deep things of God." They tell us that those things are secrets, and therefore we ought not to pry into them. If they are secrets, there is no fear that anybody can pry into them ; but the truths revealed in the word are no longer secrets, seeing that they are revealed to us by the Spirit of God, and as far as they are revealed it should be our desire to understand them, so as to be filled with the knowledge of them.

Let us try to know divine truth more and more intimately. You know a man, for you pass him in the streets with a nod ; you know another man far better, for you lodge in the same house with him ; you know him best of all when you have shared his trouble, partaken in his joy, and have, in fact, had fellowship with him by blending your two lives in one common stream of friendship. When you learn a spiritual truth endeavour to know it out and out ; to know its foundation and upbuilding ; to know it by the application of the Spirit to your own soul so that you are filled with it. You may have knowledge in the brain, but it may not run into your spirit, so as to penetrate, and permeate, and saturate your spirit, till you are filled there with. Oh, to get the gospel into one's entire nature, and to be like the waterpots of Cana, filled up to the brim ! Lord, fill Thy children with the knowledge of Thy will !

This makes me notice what the *matter* of this knowledge is ; "filled with the knowledge of His will." What is that ? It means the revealed will of God. Paul would have the Colossians know what the Lord has revealed, as far as human mind could grasp it, whether it were doctrine, precept, experience, or prophecy. How well it is to know the preceptive will of God. Our prayer should daily be, "Lord, what wilt Thou have me to do ?" Lord, teach me what is sin, and what is righteousness, that I may discern things which are excellent. Whereas there are questions in the church of God itself upon what the will of the Lord is, Lord help me not to care to know what is the will of this learned doctor, or what is the will of a certain assembly, but what is the Lord's will. "To the law and to the testimony," this is our touchstone. Our desire is to be filled with the knowledge of the Lord's will so as to do it without fail. Especially would we know the will of God, as it constitutes the gospel ; for Jesus says, "This is the will of Him that sent Me, that every one which seeth the Son, and believeth on Him, may have everlasting life." Oh, to know His will in that respect most clearly, so as to go and tell it out on all sides, that men may know the way of life, and may be led into it by our word ! Once more we read in 1 Thessalonians iv. 3 : "This is the will of God, even your sanctification." Oh, to be filled with the knowledge of the Lord's will till you know what sanctification means, and exhibit it in your daily life ! It is yours to teach men what God means by holiness. Your mission is not fulfilled, and the will of God is not accomplished unless you are sanctified. This it is with which we need to be filled.

Know anything, know everything that is worth knowing. "That the soul be without knowledge is not good." Never attempt to run side by side with the agnostic whose glory it is that he knows nothing ; but let it be your delight to know all that can be learned out of the Book of the Lord, by the teaching of the Holy Ghost. Concentrate your faculties upon the will of God. Here dive into the deeps and climb up to the heights, and be afraid of nothing ; ask the Holy Spirit to saturate you with truth, as Gideon's fleece was wet with the dew of heaven, as the golden pot was filled with manna, or as Jordan is filled in the time of harvest, when it overfloweth all its banks.

Still we have not done, for we must now notice the *manner* as well as the matter of this knowledge : "in all wisdom and spiritual understanding." Wisdom is better than knowledge, for wisdom is knowledge rightly used. Knowledge may find room for folly, but wisdom casts it out. Knowledge may be the horse, but wisdom is the driver. When a man hath knowledge it is like the corn which is laid in the barn ; but wisdom is the fine flour prepared for food. We want Christian people not only to know, but to use what they know. Happy is he who knows what to do at the right time ! Many people are very knowing half an hour after it is too late ; but to be filled with wisdom is to be able at once to apply knowledge rightly in difficult cases. Wisdom enables you to bring your knowledge practically to bear upon life, to separate between the precious and the vile, to deal with your fellow Christians in their different conditions, and to deal with sinners and those that are without. You need wisdom so to conduct your affairs that nothing therein shall scandalize the weak, or bring dishonour upon the name of Christ ; for knowledge will not suffice for this. Knowledge is the blade, wisdom is the full corn in the ear. Knowledge is the cloth, but wisdom is the garment. Knowledge is the timber, but wisdom hath builded her house. May all our knowledge be sanctified by grace and attended with the guidance of the Spirit that we may become wise to know what the will of the Lord is.

"All wisdom," saith the apostle—many-handed wisdom, wisdom of all sorts, wisdom that will serve you in the shop, wisdom that will be useful in the counting-house, wisdom that will aid the church of God, and wisdom that will guide you if you are cast among the vilest of mankind. May you "be filled with knowledge in all wisdom."

But that wisdom which operates without must be attended by a spiritual understanding which is powerful within. I hardly know how to explain this : it is an inward knowledge of truth, the knowledge of the inward parts of things. It is a spiritual discernment, taste, experience, and reception of truth, whereby the soul feeds upon it, and takes it into herself. We know many men who know much but understand nothing. They accept implicitly what they are taught, but they have never considered it, weighed it, estimated it, found out the roots of it, or seen the heart of it. Oh, to have in the church men full of spiritual understanding ! These can say that they have tasted and handled the good word of life, and have proved and tested the truth as it is in Jesus. You know how it was with the sacrifices of old : a man who was poor brought turtle-doves or pigeons, and of these we read of each bird, " The priest shall cleave it with the wings thereof, but shall not divide it asunder " : but a man who was rich in Israel brought a bullock or a sheep, and this offering was not only cleft down the middle, but further divided, and the fat and the " inwards " are mentioned in detail. The poorer sacrifice represents the offering of the uninstructed ; they have never rightly divided the word of God, and know not its fulness of meaning ; but the man who is rich in grace is comparable to him who brought his bullock ; for he can enter into detail and see the secret meanings of the Word. There is a deep which lieth under, and he that is taught of the Lord shall find it. " The secret of the Lord is with them that fear Him ; and He will show them His covenant " ; and blessed are they that are taught of the Lord so as to read the mystery of His grace !

Here, then, is a grand petition for us. To go back to our first head, let our intercessory prayers go up for all our brethren. Lord, teach them Thy word. Let them know Thy book from cover to cover, and let the truths therein revealed enter into them until they are filled to the brim : then grant Thou them the skill to use in daily life the knowledge which Thy Spirit has imparted, and may they more and more in their inmost souls be guided into all truth, that they may comprehend with all saints what are the heights, and depths, and know the love of Christ which passeth knowledge.

III. Now, thirdly, let us see in the text a lesson concerning THE PRACTICAL RESULT OF SPIRITUAL KNOWLEDGE. Paul prays for his friends " that ye might be filled with the knowledge of His will in all wisdom and spiritual understanding ; that ye might walk worthy of the Lord unto all pleasing." See, see the drift of his prayer—" that ye may walk." Not that ye might talk, not that ye might sit down and meditate, and enjoy yourselves, but " that ye might walk." He aims at practical results.

He desires that the saints may be instructed so that they may *walk according to the best model.* By walking worthy of the Lord Jesus we do not understand in any sense that He expected them to possess such worthiness as to deserve to walk with the Lord ; but he would have them live in a manner that should be in accordance with their communion with Christ. You would not have a man walk with Christ through the streets to-day clothed in motley garments, or loathsome with filth : would you ? No, if a man be a leper, Christ will heal him before He will walk with him. Let not a disciples walk so as to bring disgrace upon his Lord ! When you walk with a king, you should be yourself royal in gait ; when you commune with a prince you should not act the clown. Dear friends, may you know so much of Jesus that your lives shall become Christ-like, fit to be put side by side with the character of Jesus, worthy of your perfect Lord. This is a high standard, is it not ? It is always better to have a high standard than a low one, for you will never go beyond that which you set up as your model. If you get a low standard you will fall below even that. It is an old proverb, " He that aims at the moon will shoot higher than he that aims at a bush." It is well to have no lower standard than the desire to live over again the life of the Lord Jesus—a life of tenderness, a life of self-sacrifice, a life of generosity, a life of love, a life of honesty, a life of holy service, a life of close communion with God. Mix all virtues in due proportion, and that is the life of Jesus towards which you must press forward with all your heart.

Next, the apostle would have us get knowledge in order that we may so live as to *be pleasing to our best friend*—" worthy of the Lord unto all pleasing." Is not that beautiful ? To live so as to please God in all respects ! Some live to please themselves, and some to please their neighbours, and some to please their wives, and some to please their children, and some live as if they wished to please the devil ; but our business is to please Him in all things whose servants we are. Without faith it is impossible to please Him ; so away with unbelief ! Without holiness no man shall see Him, much less please Him ; therefore let us follow after holiness, and may the Lord work it in us. " Unto all pleasing "—so that we may please God from the moment we rise in the morning to the time when we lie down, aye, and please Him even when we are asleep : that we may eat and drink so as to please Him ; that we may speak and think so as to please Him ; that we may go or stay so as to please Him ; that we may rejoice or suffer so as to please Him—" walking worthy of the Lord unto all pleasing." Oh, blessed man, whose life is pleasing to God in all respects ! The apostle Paul desires that we may be filled with knowledge to this very end. If I do not know the will of God how can I do the will of God ? At least, how can there be anything pleasing to God which is ignorantly done without an intent to do His will ? I fear that many children of God grieve their heavenly Father much through sins of ignorance —an ignorance in which they ought not to remain a single day. Be it clearly understood that sins of ignorance are truly sins. They have not about them the venom and the aggravation which are found in sins against light and knowledge, but still they are sins ; for the measure of our duty is not our light, but the law of God itself. If a man pleads that he follows his conscience, yet this will not excuse his wrong-doing if his conscience is an unenlightened conscience, and he is content to keep it in the dark. You are to obey the will of the Lord : that will is the standard of the sanctuary. Our conscience is often like a deficient weight, and deceives us ; be it ours to gather a clear knowledge of the word, that we may prove what is that perfect and acceptable will of God. The law makes no allowances for errors committed through false weights ; when a man says, " I thought my weights and measures were all right," he is not thereby excused. The law deals with facts, not with men's imaginations ; the weights must actually be correct, or the penalty is exacted ; so is it with conscience, it ought to be instructed in the knowledge of the divine will, and if it is not so, its faultiness affords no justification for evil. Hence the absolute necessity of knowledge in order to true holiness. God grant us grace to know His will, and then to obey it " unto all pleasing."

Look at the text again—" That ye might walk

worthy of the Lord unto all pleasing, being fruitful." Paul would have us *producing the best fruit.* Without knowledge we cannot be fruitful; at least in the points whereof we are ignorant we must fail to bring forth fruit. Therefore would He have us to be right well taught, that we may abundantly produce fruit unto God's glory. He says, "fruitful in every good work"; and this means much. He desires us to be as full of good works as we can hold. Some are hindered in this because they do not know how to set about holy service. How can a man be fruitful as a preacher if he does not know what to preach? True, he may preach the elementary doctrine of the cross, but even that he will be apt to set forth in a blundering manner. For certain, a man cannot teach what he does not know. The zealous, but untaught man, would be much more fruitful if he had a clearer understanding of divine things. In daily life, if in knowledge you are ignorant as to the things of God, you will be ready to become the prey of any false teacher who may chance to pick you up. In hundreds of ways ignorance will make you run risks, lose opportunities of usefulness, and fall into dangerous mistakes. Knowledge is food to the true heart, and strengthens it for the Lord's work. Oh, to have knowledge placed like good soil around the roots of the soul, to fertilize the mind, that thus the clusters of usefulness may be as large as those of Eshcol: beautiful, plentiful, sweet, and full. May our Lord, the King of Israel, to whom the vineyard belongs, receive an abundant reward for all His labour for the vines which He has planted.

There is another note in this verse which I beg you to notice. Paul would have them cultivate *a comprehensive variety of the best things.* He says— "Fruitful in *every* good work." Here is room and range enough—"in every good work." Have you the ability to preach the gospel? Preach it! Does a little child need comforting? Comfort it! Can you stand up and vindicate a glorious truth before thousands? Do it! Does a poor saint need a bit of dinner from your table? Send it to her. Let works of obedience, testimony, zeal, charity, piety, and philanthropy all be found in your life. Do not select big things as your special line, but glorify the Lord also in the littles—"fruitful in every good work." You never saw in nature a tree which yielded all sorts of fruit, and you never will. I have seen a tree so grafted that it produced four kinds of fruit at one time, but I remarked that it was a poor business in reference to two of the varieties; for one of the grafts, more natural than the others to the parent stem, drew off the most of the sap, and flourished well, but robbed the other branches. The second sort of fruit managed to live pretty fairly, but not so well as it would have done on its own stem. As for the third and fourth, they were mere attempts at fruit of the smallest size. This tree was shown to me as a great curiosity; it is not likely that practical gardeners will be encouraged by the experiment. But what would you think of a tree upon which you saw grapes, and figs, and olives, and apples, and all other good fruits growing at one time? This is the emblem of what instructed believers will become: they will produce all sorts of goodness and graciousness to the honour of their heavenly Father. I have no doubt that you will naturally abound most in certain good works for which you have the largest capacity, but still nothing ought to come amiss to you. In the great house of the church we want servants who will not be simply cooks or housemaids, but general servants, maids of all-work, prepared to do anything and everything. I have known persons in household employment in England who would not do a turn beyond their special work to save their masters' lives: these are a sort of servants of whom the fewer the better. In India this is carried to a ridiculous extreme. The Hindoo water-bearer will not sweep the house, nor light a fire, nor brush your clothes—he will fetch water, and nothing else: you must, therefore, have a servant for each separate thing, and then each man will do his own little bit, but he will not go an inch beyond. When we enter into Christ's church we should come prepared to wash the saints' feet, or bear their burdens, or bind up their wounds, or fight their foes, or act as steward, or shepherd, or nurse. It has been well said that if two angels in heaven were summoned to serve the Lord, and there were two works to be done, an empire to be ruled, or a crossing to be swept, neither angel would have a choice as to which should be appointed him, but would gladly abide the will of the Lord. Let us be equally prepared for anything, for everything by which fruit can be produced for the Well-beloved.

Why is it that some are not fruitful in this comprehensive way? Because they are not filled with knowledge in all wisdom. When a man says, "You ask me to do the lowest work! Don't you know that I am a man of remarkable ability who should have higher work to do?" I venture to assert that he is an ignorant man. Self-assertion is ignorance on horseback. You have probably read of a certain renowned corporal in the American service a century ago. A general as he rode along saw a body of men endeavouring to lift timber. They were short-handed, and the work lagged, but their famous corporal stood by ordering them about at a magnificent rate. The general passed and said, "Why don't you lend them help and put your shoulder to it?" "Why, sir," said the great little officer, "how can you think of such a thing? Do you know who I am? I am a corporal!" The general got off his horse, pulled off his coat, and helped to move the timber, and by his judicious help the the soldiers achieved their task. Then he turned to the high and mighty gentleman and said, "Mr. Corporal, next time you want a man to do such work as this you can send for me: I am General Washington." Just so the Lord Jesus Christ if He were here would gladly do a thousand things which His poor little servants are too great to touch. I know you, dear brother, you are too experienced, too old, too learned to help the Sunday-school! I know you are too respectable to give away a tract! Pray get out of such ignorant ways of thinking, and ask to be useful in all possible ways. If you have done a little, do much; if you have done much, do more; and when you have done more, ask for grace to proceed to the highest possible degree of usefulness for your Lord.

IV. And now, fourthly, notice THE REFLEX ACTION OF HOLINESS UPON KNOWLEDGE. We have only a few moments left; let my few words sink into your hearts. "Fruitful in every good work"— what then? "increasing in the knowledge of God." Look at that. It seems, then, that *holiness is the road to knowledge.* God has made it so. If any man will do His will he shall know of the doctrine. If you read and study, and cannot make out the it may be, in the doing of it, you shall discover the secret. Holiness of heart shall increase the illumination of your mind.

Will you kindly observe that *this knowledge rises in tone?* for Paul first prayed that they " might be filled with the knowledge of God's will " ; but now he implores for them an increase in the knowledge of God Himself. Oh, blessed growth, first to know the law, and then to know the Law-giver ! first to know the precept, and then to know the mouth from which it comes ! This is the height of knowledge, to see Christ and know the Father, and learn how to say from the heart, " Truly our fellowship is with the Father, and with His Son Jesus Christ."

I would call your willing attention to another thought. The apostle, if he is to be judged according to his outward language, often utters impossible things, and yet his every sentence is not only full of deep meaning, but is strictly correct. Notice his language here : in the ninth verse he says, " that ye might be filled with the knowledge of His will." Can anything go beyond this ? The vessel is filled right up to the brim, what can it have more ? Yet the apostle says, " increasing in the knowledge of God." What can that mean ? If the mind is full to the brim, how can it receive more ? If the man is full of knowledge, how can his knowledge increase ? Can there be any increase after that ? I propose to you the riddle. Here is the answer of it : Make the vessel larger, and then there can be an increase. This solution of the difficulty requires no great wit to discover it. So that Paul plainly teaches us here

meaning of Scripture, get up and do something, and that, if we have so increased in knowledge as to be full, *he would have us increased in capacity to know yet more ;* he would have our manhood enlarged, our powers of reception increased, that we might grow from being children to be young men, and from young men to be fathers, and so may be filled— filled, always filled with all the fulness of God ! The Lord grant unto us to perceive with humility, that if we are already full of knowledge, we can still advance, for we " have not yet attained." Let no man think that he can go no further. " There is," says Augustine, " a certain perfection according to the measure of this life, and it belongs to that perfection that such a perfect man should know that he is not yet perfect." To that I heartily subscribe. There is a certain fulness to be found in this life according to the measure of a man, and it belongs to that fulness that the man should know that he can yet increase in knowledge. Holy Bernard says " he is not good at all who doth not desire to be better." I also subscribe to that saying. Some might become good if they were not puffed up with the fancy of their own perfection. Others are somewhat commendable, but will never grow because they judge themselves to be full-grown already. I would have you filled, and yet have room for more : filled with all knowledge, filled with all holiness, filled with the indwelling Spirit, filled with God, and yet increasing in knowledge, in holiness, in likeness to God, and in all good things evermore to His glory. The Lord add His blessing for Jesus' sake. Amen.

SPECIAL THANKSGIVING TO THE FATHER

"Giving thanks unto the Father, which hath made us meet to be partakers of the inheritance of the saints in light: who hath delivered us from the power of darkness, and hath translated us into the kingdom of His dear Son."—Colossians i. 12, 13.

THIS passage is a mine of riches. I can anticipate the difficulty in preaching and the regret in concluding we shall experience this evening because we are not able to dig out all the gold which lies in this precious vein. We lack the power to grasp and the time to expatiate upon that volume of truths which is here condensed into a few short sentences.

We are exhorted to "give thanks unto the Father." This counsel is at once needful and salutary. I think, my brethren, we scarcely need to be told to give thanks unto the Son. The remembrance of that bleeding body hanging upon the cross is ever present to our faith. The nails and the spear, His griefs, the anguish of His soul, and His sweat of agony, make such tender touching appeals to our gratitude— these will prevent us always from ceasing our songs, and sometimes fire our hearts with rekindling rapture in praise of the *Man* Christ Jesus. Yes, we *will* bless Thee, dearest Lord; our souls are all on fire. As we survey the wondrous cross, we cannot but shout—

"O for this love let rocks and hills
Their lasting silence break,
And all harmonious human tongues
The Saviour's praises speak."

It is in a degree very much the same with the Holy Spirit. I think we are compelled to feel every day our dependence upon His constant influence. He abides with us as a present and personal Comforter

and Counsellor. We, therefore, do praise the Spirit of Grace, who hath made our heart His temple, and who works in us all that is gracious, virtuous, and well-pleasing in the sight of God. If there be any one Person in the Trinity whom we are more apt to forget than another in our praises, it is God the Father. In fact there are some who even get a wrong idea of Him, a slanderous idea of that God whose name is LOVE. They imagine that love dwelt in Christ, rather than in the Father, and that our salvation is rather due to the Son and the Holy Spirit, than to our Father God. Let us not be of the number of the ignorant, but let us receive this truth. We are as much indebted to the Father as to any other Person of the Sacred Three. He as much and as truly loves us as any of the adorable Three Persons. He is as truly worthy of our highest praise as either the Son or the Holy Spirit.

A remarkable fact, which we should always bear in mind, is this: in the Holy Scriptures most of the operations which are set down as being the works of the Spirit, are in other Scriptures ascribed to God the Father. Do we say it is God the Spirit that quickens the sinner who is dead in sin? it is true; but you will find in another passage it is said, "The Father quickeneth whom He will." Do we say that the Spirit is the sanctifier, and that the sanctification of the soul is wrought by the Holy Ghost? You will find a passage in the opening of the Epistle of St. Jude, in which it is said, "Sanctified by God the Father."

Now, how are we to account for this? I think it may be explained thus. God the Spirit cometh from God the Father, and therefore whatever acts are performed by the Spirit are truly done by the Father because He sendeth forth the Spirit. And again, the Spirit is often the instrument—though I say not this in any way to derogate from His glory—He is often the instrument with which the Father works. It is the Father who says to the dry bones, live; it is the Spirit, who, going forth with the divine word, makes them live. The quickening is due as much to the word as to the influence that went with the word; and as the word came with all the bounty of free grace and good-will from the Father, the quickening is due to Him. It is true that the seal on our hearts is the Holy Spirit; He is the seal, but it is the Eternal Father's hand that stamps the seal; the Father communicates the Spirit to seal our adoption. The works of the Spirit are, many of them, I repeat it again, attributed to the Father, because He worketh in, through, and by the Spirit.

The works of the Son of God, I ought to observe are every one of them in intimate connection with the Father. If the Son comes into the world, it is because the Father sends Him; if the Son calls His people, it is because His Father gave this people into His hands. If the Son redeems the chosen race, is not the Son Himself the Father's gift, and doth not God send His Son into the world that we may live through Him? So that the Father, the great Ancient of Days, is ever to be extolled; and we must never omit the full homage of our hearts to Him when we sing that sacred doxology,

"Praise Father, Son, and Holy Ghost."

In order to excite your gratitude to God the Father to-night, I propose to dilate a little upon this passage as God the Holy Spirit shall enable me. If you will look at the text, you will see two blessings in it. The first has regard to *the future*; it is a meetness for the inheritance of the saints in light. The second blessing, which must go with the first, for indeed it is the cause of the first, the effective cause, has relation to *the past*. Here we read of our deliverance from the power of darkness. Let us meditate a little upon each of these blessings, and then, in the third place, I will endeavour to show *the relation which exists between the two.*

I. The first blessing introduced to our notice is this—"God the Father has made us meet to be partakers of the inheritance of the saints in light." It is a PRESENT BLESSING. Not a mercy laid up for us in the covenant, which we have not yet received, but it is a blessing which every true believer already has in his hand. Those mercies in the covenant of which we have the earnest now while we wait for the full possession, are just as rich, and just as certain as those which have been already with abundant loving kindness bestowed on us; but still they are not so precious in our enjoyment. The mercy we have in store, and in hand, is after all, the main source of our present comfort. And oh what a blessing this! "Made meet for the inheritance of the saints in light." The true believer is fit for heaven; he is meet to be a partaker of the inheritance—and that now, at this very moment. What does this mean? Does it mean that the believer is perfect; that he is free from sin? No, my brethren, where shall you ever find such perfection in this world? If no man can be a believer but the perfect man, then what has the

perfect man to believe? Could he not walk by sight? When he is perfect he may cease to be a believer. No, brethren, it is not such perfection that is meant, although perfection is implied, and assuredly will be given as the result. Far less does this mean that we have a right to eternal life from any doings of our own. We have a fitness for eternal life, a meetness for it, but we have no desert of it. We deserve nothing of God even now, in ourselves, but His eternal wrath and His infinite displeasure. What, then, does it mean? Why, it means just this: we are so far meet that we are accepted in the Beloved, adopted into the family, and fitted by divine approbation to dwell with the saints in light. There is a woman chosen to be a bride; she is fitted he may be married, fitted to enter into the honourable state and condition of matrimony; but at present she has not on the bridal garment, she is not like the bride adorned for her husband. You do not see her yet robed in her elegant attire, with her ornaments upon her, but you know she is fitted to be a bride, she is received and welcomed as such in the family of her destination. So Christ has chosen His Church to be married to Him; she has not yet put on her bridal garment, and all that beautiful array in which she shall stand before the Father's throne, but notwithstanding, there is such a fitness in her to be the bride of Christ, when she shall have bathed herself for a little while, and lain for a little while in the bed of spices—there is such a fitness in her character, such a grace-given adaption in her to become the royal bride of her glorious Lord, and to become a partaker of the enjoyments of bliss—that it may be said of the church as a whole, and of every member of it, that they are "meet for the inheritance of the saints in light."

The Greek word, moreover, bears some such meaning as this, though I cannot give the exact idiom, it is always difficult when a word is not used often. This word is only used twice, that I am aware of, in the New Testament. The word may be employed for "suitable," or, I think, "sufficient." "He hath made us meet"—sufficient—"to be partakers of the inheritance of the saints in light." But I cannot give my idea without borrowing another figure. When a child is born, it is at once endowed with all the faculties of humanity. If those powers are awanting at first, they will not come afterwards. It has eyes, it has hands, it has feet, and all its physical organs. These of course are as it were embryo. The senses though perfect at first, must be gradually developed, and the understanding gradually matured. It can see but little, it cannot discern distances; it can hear, but it cannot hear distinctly enough at first to know from what direction the sound comes; but you never find a new leg, a new arm, a new eye, or a new ear growing on that child. Each of these powers will expand and enlarge, but still there is the whole man there at first, and the child is *sufficient* for a man. Let but God in His infinite providence cause it to feed, and give it strength and increase, it has *sufficient* for manhood. It does not want either arm or leg, nose or ear; you cannot make it grow a new member; nor does it require a new member either; all are there. In like manner, the moment a man is regenerated, there is every faculty in his new creation that there shall be, even when he gets to heaven. It only needs to be developed and brought out: he will not have a new power, he will not have a new grace, he will have those which he had before, developed and brought out. Just as we are told by the careful observer, that in the acorn there is in embryo every root and every bough and every leaf of the future tree, which only requires to be developed and brought out in their fulness. So, in the true believer, there is a sufficiency or meetness for the inheritance of the saints in light. All that he requires is, not that a new thing should be implanted, but that that which God has put there in the moment of regeneration, shall be cherished and nurtured, and made to grow and increase, till it comes unto perfection and he enters into "the inheritance of the saints in light." This is, as near as I can give it to you, the exact meaning and literal interpretation of the text as I understand it.

But you may say to me, "In what sense is this meetness or fitness for eternal life the work of God the Father? Are we already made meet for heaven? How is this the Father's work?" Look at the text a moment, and I will answer you in three ways.

What is heaven? We read it as an *inheritance.* Who are fit for an inheritance? Sons. Who makes us sons? "Behold what manner of love *the Father* hath bestowed upon us, that we should be called the sons of God." A son is fitted for an inheritance. The moment the son is born he is fitted to be an heir. All that is wanted is that he shall grow up and be capable of possession. But he is fit for an inheritance at first. If he were not a son he could not inherit as an heir. Now, as soon as ever we become sons we are meet to inherit. There is in us an adaptation, a power and possibility for us to have an inheritance. This is the prerogative of the Father, to adopt us into His family, and to "beget us again unto a lively hope by the resurrection of Jesus Christ from the dead." And do you not see, that as adoption is really the meetness for inheritance, it is the Father who hath "made us meet to be partakers of the inheritance of the saints in light?"

Again, heaven is an inheritance; but whose inheritance is it? It is an inheritance of the *saints.* It is not an inheritance of sinners, but of saints—that is, of the holy ones—of those who have been made saints by being sanctified. Turn then, to the Epistle of Jude, and you will see at once who it is that sanctifies. You will observe the moment you fix your eye upon the passage that it is God the Father. In the first verse you read, "Jude, the servant of Jesus Christ, and brother of James, to them that are sanctified by God the Father." It is an inheritance for saints; and who are saints? The moment a man believes in Christ, he may know himself to have been truly set apart in the covenant decree; and he finds that consecration, if I may so speak, verified in his own experience, for he has now become "a new creature in Christ Jesus," separated from the rest of the world, and then it is manifest and made known that God has taken him to be His son for ever. The meetness which I must have, in order to enjoy the inheritance of the saints in light, is my becoming a son. God hath made me and all believers sons, therefore we are meet for the inheritance; so then that meetness has come from the Father. How meetly therefore doth the Father claim our gratitude, our adoration and our love!

You will however observe, it is not merely said that heaven is the inheritance of the saints, but that it is "the inheritance of the saints *in light.*" So the saints dwell in light—the light of knowledge, the light of purity, the light of joy, the light of love, pure ineffable love, the light of everything that is glorious and ennobling. There they dwell, and if I am to appear meet for that inheritance, what evidence must I have? I must have light shining into my own soul. But where can I get it? Do I not read that "every good gift and every perfect gift is from above, and cometh down"—yea verily, but from whom? From the Spirit? No—"from the Father of lights, with whom is no variableness, neither shadow of turning." The preparation to enter into the inheritance in light is light; and light comes from the Father of lights: therefore, my meetness, if I have light in myself, is the work of the Father, and I must give Him praise. Do you see then, that as there are three words used here—"the *inheritance* of the *saints* in *light*," so we have a threefold meetness? We are adopted and made sons. God hath sanctified us and set us apart. And then, again, He hath put light into our hearts. All this, I say, is the work of the Father, and in this sense, we are "meet to be partakers of the inheritance of the saints in light."

A few general observations here. Brethren, I am persuaded that if an angel from heaven were to come to-night and single out any one believer from the crowd here assembled, there is not one believer that is unfit to be taken to heaven. You may not be ready to be taken to heaven now; that is to say, if I foresaw that you were going to live, I would tell you you were unfit to die, in a certain sense. But were you to die in your pew, if you believe in Christ, you are fit for heaven. You have a meetness even now which would take you there at once, without being committed to purgatory for a season. You are even now fit to be "partakers of the inheritance of the saints in light." You have but to gasp out your last breath and you shall be in heaven, and there shall not be one spirit in heaven more fit for heaven than you, nor one soul more adapted for the place than you are. You shall be just as fitted for its element as those who are nearest to the eternal throne.

Ah, this makes the heirs of glory think much of God the Father. When we reflect, my brethren, upon our state by nature, and how fit we are to be fire-brands in the flames of hell—yet to think that we are this night, at this very moment if Jehovah willed it, fit to sweep the golden harps with joyful fingers, that this head is fit this very night to wear the everlasting crown, that these loins are fit to be girded with that fair white robe throughout eternity, I say, this makes us think gratefully of God the Father; this makes us clap our hands with joy, and say, "Thanks be unto God the Father, who hath made us meet to be partakers of the inheritance of the saints in light." Do ye not remember the penitent thief? It was but a few minutes before that he had been cursing Christ. I doubt not that he had joined with the other, for it is said, "*They* that were crucified with Him reviled Him." Not one, but both; *they* did it. And then a gleam of supernatural glory lit up the face of Christ, and the thief saw and believed. And Jesus said unto him, "Verily I say unto thee this day," though the sun was setting, "*this day* shalt thou be with Me in Paradise." No long preparation required, no sweltering in purifying fires. And so shall it be with us. We may have been in Christ Jesus to our own knowledge but three weeks, or we may have been in Him for ten years, or three-score years and ten—the date of our conversion makes no difference in our meetness for heaven, in a certain sense. True indeed the older we grow the more grace we have tasted, the riper we are becoming, and the fitter to be housed in heaven; but that is in another sense of the word,—the Spirit's meetness which He gives. But with regard to that meetness which the Father gives, I repeat, the blade of corn, the blade of gracious wheat that has just appeared above the surface of conviction, is as fit to be carried up to heaven as the full-grown corn in the ear. The sanctification wherewith we are sanctified by God the Father is not progressive, it is complete at once; we are now adapted for heaven, now fitted for it, and we shall be by-and-bye completely ready for it, and shall enter into the joy of our Lord.

Into this subject I might have entered more fully; but I have not time. I am sure I have left some knots untied, and you must untie them if you can yourselves; and let me recommend you to untie them on your knees—the mysteries of the kingdom of God are studied much the best when you are in prayer.

II. The second story is A MERCY THAT LOOKS BACK. We sometimes prefer the mercies that look forward, because they unfold such a bright prospect.

"Sweet fields beyond the swelling flood."

But here is a mercy that looks backward; turns its back, as it were, on the heaven of our anticipation, and looks back on the gloomy past, and the dangers from which we have escaped. Let us read the account of it—"Who hath delivered us from the power of darkness, and hath translated us into the kingdom of His dear Son." This verse is an explanation of the preceding, as we shall have to show in a few minutes. But just now let us survey this mercy by itself. Ah! my brethren, what a description have we here of what manner of men we used to be. We *were* under "the power of darkness." Since I have been musing on this text, I have turned these words over and over in my mind—"the power of darkness!" It seems to me one of the most awful expressions that man ever attempted to expound. I think I could deliver a discourse from it, if God the Spirit helped me, which might make every bone in your body shake. "The power of darkness!" We all know that there is a *moral* darkness which exercises its awful spell over the mind of the sinner. Where God is unacknowledged the mind is void of judgment. Where God is unworshipped the heart of man becomes a ruin. The chambers of that dilapidated heart are haunted by ghostly fears and degraded superstitions. The dark places of that reprobate mind are tenanted by vile lusts and noxious passions, like vermin and reptiles, from which in open daylight we turn with disgust. And even *natural* darkness is tremendous. In the solitary confinement which is practised in some of our penitentaries the very worst results would be produced if the treatment were prolonged. If one of you were to be taken to-night and led into some dark cavern, and left there, I can imagine that for a moment, not knowing your fate, you might feel a child-like kind of interest about it;—there might be, perhaps, a laugh as you found yourselves in the dark; there might for the moment, from the novelty of the position, be some kind of curiosity excited. There might, perhaps, be a flush of silly joy. In a little time you might endeavour to compose yourself to sleep; possibly you might sleep; but if you should awake, and still find yourself down deep in the bowels of earth, where never a ray of sun or candle light could reach you; do you know the next feeling that would come over you? It would

be a kind of idiotic thoughtlessness. You would find it impossible to control your desperate imagination. Your heart would say, "O God I am alone, alone, alone, in this dark place." How would you cast your eyeballs all around, and never catching a gleam of light, your mind would begin to fail. Your next stage would be one of increasing terror. You would fancy that you saw something, and then you would cry, "Ah! I would I could see something, were it foe or friend!" You would feel the dark sides of your dungeon. You would begin to "scribble on the walls," like David before king Achish. Agitation would seize hold upon you, and if you were kept there much longer, delirium and death would be the consequence. We have heard of many who have been taken from the penitentiary to the lunatic asylum; and the lunacy is produced partly by the solitary confinement, and partly by the darkness in which they are placed. In a report written by the Chaplain of Newgate, there are some striking reflections upon the influence of darkness in a way of *discipline*. Its first effect is to shut the culprit up to his own reflections, and make him realize his true position in the iron grasp of the outraged law. Methinks the man that has defied his keepers, and come in there cursing and swearing, when he has found himself alone in darkness, where he cannot even hear the rattling of carriages along the streets and can see no light whatever, is presently cowed; he gives in, he grows tame. "The power of darkness" literally is something awful. If I had time, I would enlarge upon this subject. We cannot properly describe what "the power of darkness" is, even in this world. The sinner is plunged into the darkness of his sins, and he sees nothing, he knows nothing. Let him remain there a little longer, and that joy of curiosity, that hectic joy which he now has in the path of sin, will die away, and there will come over him a spirit of slumber. Sin will make him drowsy, so that he will not hear the voice of the ministry, crying to him to escape for his life. Let him continue in it, and it will by-and-bye make him spiritually an idiot. He will become so set in sin, that common reason will be lost on him. All the arguments that a sensible man will receive, will be only wasted on him. Let him go on, and he will proceed from bad to worse till he acquires the raving mania of a desperado in sin; and let death step in, and the darkness will have produced its full effect; he will come into the delirious madness of hell. Ah! it needs but the power of sin to make a man more truly hideous than human thought can realize, or language paint. Oh "the power of darkness!"

Now, my brethren, all of us were under this power once. It is but a few months—a few weeks with some of you—since you were under the power of darkness and of sin. Some of you had only got as far as the curiosity of it; others had got as far as the sleepiness of it; a good many of you had got as far as the apathy of it; and I do not know but some of you had got almost to the terror of it. You had so cursed and swore; so yelled ye out your blasphemies, that you seemed to be ripening for hell; but, praised and blessed be the name of the Father, He has "translated you from the power of darkness, into the kingdom of His dear Son."

Having thus explained this term, "the power of darkness," to show you what you were, let us take the next word, "and hath translated us." What a singular word this—"translated"—is. I dare say you think it means the process by which a word is interpreted, when the sense is retained, while the expression is rendered in another language. That is one meaning of the word "translation," but it is not the meaning here. The word is used by Josephus in this sense—the taking away of a people who have been dwelling in a certain country, and planting them in another place. This is called a translation. We sometimes hear of a bishop being translated or removed from one see to another. Now, if you want to have the idea explained, give me your attention while I bring out an amazing instance of a great translation. The children of Israel were in Egypt under taskmasters that oppressed them very sorely, and brought them into iron bondage. What did God do for these people? There were two millions of them. He did not temper the tyranny of the tyrant; He did not influence his mind, to give them a little more liberty; but He translated His people; He took the whole two millions bodily, with a high hand and outstretched arm, and led them through the wilderness, and translated them into the kingdom of Canaan; and there they were settled. What an achievement was that, when, with their flocks and their herds, and their little ones, the whole host of Israel went out of Egypt, crossed the Jordan, and came in to Canaan! My dear brethren, the whole of it was not equal to the achievement of God's powerful grace, when He brings one poor sinner out of the region of sin into the kingdom of holiness and peace. It was easier for God to bring Israel out of Egypt, to split the Red Sea, to make a highway through the pathless wilderness, to drop manna from heaven, to send the whirlwind to drive out the kings; it was easier for Omnipotence to do all this than to translate a man from the power of darkness into the kingdom of His dear Son. This is the grandest achievement of Omnipotence. The sustenance of the whole universe, I do believe, is even less than this—the changing of a bad heart, the subduing of an iron will. But thanks be unto the Father, He has done all that for you and for me. He has brought us out of darkness; He has translated us, taken up the old tree that has struck its roots never so deep—taken it up, blessed be God, roots and all, and planted it in a goodly soil. He had to cut the top off, it is true—the high branches of our pride; but the tree has grown better in the new soil than it ever did before. Who ever heard of moving so huge a plant as a man who has grown fifty years old in sin? Oh! what wonders hath our Father done for us! He has taken the wild leopard of the wood, tamed it into a lamb, and purged away its spots. He has regenerated the poor Ethiop—oh, how black we were by nature—our blackness was more than skin deep; it went to the centre of our hearts; but blessed be His name, He hath washed us white, and is still carrying on the divine operation, and He will yet completely deliver us from every taint of sin, and will finally bring us into the kingdom of His dear Son. Here, then, in the second mercy, we discern from what we were delivered, and how we were delivered—God the Father hath "translated" us.

But where are we now? Into what place is the believer brought, when he is brought out of the power of darkness? He is brought into the kingdom of God's dear Son. Into what other kingdom would the Christian desire to be brought? Brethren, a republic may sound very well in theory, but in spiritual matters, the last thing we want is a republic. We want a kingdom. I love to have Christ an absolute monarch in the heart. I do not want to have a doubt about it. I want to give up all my liberty to Him, for I feel that I never shall be free till my self-control is all gone; that I shall never have my will truly free till it is bound in the golden fetters of His sweet love. We are brought into a kingdom—He is Lord and Sovereign, and He has made us "kings and priests unto our God," and we shall reign with Him. The proof that we are in this kingdom must consist in our obedience to our King. Here, perhaps, we may raise many causes and questions, but surely we can say after all, though we have offended our King many times, yet our heart is loyal to Him. "Oh, Thou precious Jesus! we would obey Thee, and yield submission to every one of Thy laws; our sins are not wilful and beloved sins, but though we fall we can truly say, that we would be holy as Thou art holy, our heart is true towards Thy statutes; Lord, help us to run in the way of Thy commandments."

So, you see, this mercy which God the Father hath given to us, this second of these present mercies, is, that He hath "translated us out of the power of darkness into the kingdom of His dear Son." This is the Father's work. Shall we not love God the Father from this day forth? Will we not give Him thanks and sing our hymns to Him, and exalt and triumph in His great name?

III. Upon the third point, I shall be as brief as possible; it is to SHOW THE CONNECTION BETWEEN THE TWO VERSES.

When I get a passage of Scripture to meditate upon, I like, if I can, to see its drift, then I like to examine its various parts, and see if I can understand each separate clause; and then I want to go back again, and see what one clause has to do with another. I looked and looked again at this text, and wondered what connection there could be between the two verses. "Giving thanks unto God the Father, who hath made us meet to be partakers of the inheritance of the saints in light." Well, that is right enough; we can see how this is the work of God the Father, to make us meet to go to heaven. But has the next verse, the 13th, anything to do with our meetness?" —"Who hath delivered us from the power of darkness, and hath translated us into the kingdom of His dear Son." Well, I looked it over, and I said I will read it in this way. I see the 12th verse tells me that the inheritance of heaven is the inheritance of light. Is heaven light? Then I can see my meetness for it as described in the 13th verse.—He hath delivered me from the power of darkness. Is not that the same thing? If I am delivered from the power of darkness, is not that being made meet to dwell in light? If I am now brought out of darkness into light, and am walking in the light, is not that the very meetness which is spoken of in the verse before? Then I read again. It says they are saints. Well, the saints are a people that obey the Son. Here is my meetness then in the 13th verse, where it says "He hath translated me from the power of darkness into the kingdom of His dear Son." So that I not only have the light, but the sonship too, for I am in "the kingdom of His dear Son." But how about the inheritance? Is there anything about that in the 13th verse? It is an inheritance; shall I find anything about a meetness for it there? Yes, I find that I am in the kingdom of His dear Son. How came Christ to have a kingdom? Why, by inheritance. Then it seems I am in His inheritance; and if I am in His inheritance here, then I am meet to be in it above, for I am in it already. I am even now part of it and partner of it, since I am in the kingdom which He inherits from His Father, and therefore there is the meetness.

I do not know whether I have put this plainly enough before you. If you will be kind enough to look at your Bible, I will just recapitulate. You see, heaven is a place of light; when we are brought out of darkness, that, of course, is the meetness for light. It is a place for sons; when we are brought into the kingdom of God's dear Son, we are of course made sons; so that there is the meetness for it. It is an inheritance; and when we are brought into the inherited kingdom of God's dear Son, we enjoy the inheritance now, and consequently are fitted to enjoy it for ever.

Having thus shown the connection between these verses, I propose now to close with a few general observations. I like so to expound the Scripture, that we can draw some practical inferences from it. Of course the first inference is this: let us from this night forward never omit God the Father in our praises. I think I have said this already six times over in the sermon. Why I am repeating it so often, is that we may never forget it. Martin Luther said he preached upon justification by faith every day in the week, and then the people would not understand. There are some truths, I believe, that need to be said over and over again, either because our silly hearts will not receive, or our treacherous memories will not hold them. Sing, I beseech you, habitually, the praises of the Father in heaven, as you do the praises of the Son hanging upon the cross. Love as truly God, the ever-living God, as you love Jesus the God-man, the Saviour who once died for you. That is the great inference.

Yet another inference arises. Brothers and sisters, are you conscious to-night that you are not now what you once were? Are you sure that the power of darkness does not now rest upon you, that you love divine knowledge, that you are panting after heavenly joys? Are you sure that you have been "translated into the kingdom of God's dear Son?" Then never be troubled about thoughts of death, because, come death whenever it may, you are meet to be a "partaker of the inheritance of the saints in light." Let no thought distress you about death's coming to you at an unseasonable hour. Should it come to-morrow, should it come now, if your faith is fixed on nothing less than Jesu's blood and righteousness, you shall see the face of God with acceptance. I have that consciousness in my soul, by the witness of the Holy Spirit, of my adoption into the family of God, that I feel that though I should never preach again, but should lay down my body and my charge together, ere I should reach my home, and rest in my bed, "I know that my Redeemer liveth," and more, that I should be a "partaker of the inheritance of the saints in light." It is not always that one feels that; but I would have you never rest satisfied till you do, till you know your meetness, till you are conscious of it; until, moreover, you are panting to be gone, because you feel that you have powers which never can be satisfied short of heaven—powers which heaven only can employ.

One more reflection lingers behind. There are some of you here that cannot be thought by the utmost charity of judgment, to be "meet for the inheritance of the saints in light." Ah! if a wicked man should go to heaven without being converted, heaven would be no heaven to him. Heaven is not adapted for sinners; it is not a place for them. If you were to take a Hottentot who has long dwelt at the equator up to where the Esquimaux are dwelling, and tell him that you would show him the aurora, and all the glories of the North Pole, the poor wretch could not appreciate them; he would say, "It is not the element for me; it is not the place where I could rest happy!" And if you were to take, on the other hand, some dwarfish dweller in the north, down to the region where trees grow to a stupendous height, and where the spices give their balmy odours to the gale, and bid him live there under the torrid zone, he could enjoy nothing; he would say, "This is not the place for me, because it is not adapted to my nature." Or if you were to take the vulture, that has never fed on anything but carrion, and put it into the noblest dwelling you could make for it, and feed it with the daintiest meals, it would not be happy because it is not food that is adapted for it. And you, sinner, you are nothing but a carrion vulture; nothing makes you happy but sin; you do not want too much psalm singing, do you? Sunday is a dull day to you; you like to get it over, you do not care about your Bible; you would as soon there should be no Bible at all. You find that going to a meeting-house or a church is very dull work indeed. Oh then you will not be troubled with that in eternity; do not agitate yourself. If you love not God, and die as you are, you shall go to your own company, you shall go to your jolly mates, you shall go to your good fellows, those who have been your mates on earth shall be your mates for ever, but you shall go to the Prince of those good fellows, unless you repent and be converted. Where God is you cannot come. It is not an element suited to you. As well place a bird at the bottom of the sea, or a fish in the air, as place an ungodly sinner in heaven. What is to be done then? You must have a new nature. I pray God to give it to you. Remember if now you feel your need of a Saviour, that is the beginning of the new nature. "Believe on the Lord Jesus Christ;" cast yourselves simply on Him, trust in nothing but His blood, and then the new nature shall be expanded, and you shall be made meet by the Holy Spirit's operations to be a "partaker of the inheritance of the saints in light." There is many a man who has come into this house of prayer, many a man is now present, who has come in here a rollicking fellow, fearing neither God nor devil. Many a man has come from the ale house up to this place. If he had died then, where would his soul have been? But the Lord that very night met him. There are trophies of that grace present here to-night. You can say, "Thanks be to the Father, who hath brought us out of the power of darkness, and translated us into the kingdom of His dear Son." And if God has done that for some, why cannot He do it for others? Why need you despair, O poor sinner? If thou art here to-night, the worst sinner out of hell, remember, the gate of mercy stands wide open, and Jesus bids thee come. Conscious of thy guilt, flee, flee to Him. Look to His cross, and thou shalt find pardon in His veins, and life in His death.

ALL FULNESS IN CHRIST

"For it pleased the Father that in Him should all fulness dwell."—Colossians i. 19.

THE preacher is under no difficulties this morning as to the practical object to be aimed at in his discourse. Every subject should be considered with an object, every discourse should have a definite spiritual aim; otherwise we do not so much preach as play at preaching. The connection plainly indicates what our drift should be. Read the words immediately preceding the text, and you find it declared that our Lord Jesus is in all things to have the pre-eminence. We would seek by this text to yield honour and glory to the ever-blessed Redeemer, and enthrone Him in the highest seat in our hearts. O that we may all be in an adoring frame of mind, and may give Him the pre-eminence in our thoughts, beyond all things or persons in heaven or earth. Blessed is he who can do or think the most to honour such a Lord as our Immanuel. The verse which succeeds the text, shows us how we may best promote the glory of Christ, for since He came into this world that He might reconcile the things in heaven and the things in earth to Himself, we shall best glorify Him by falling in with His great design of mercy. By seeking to bring sinners into a state of reconciliation with God, we are giving to the great Reconciler the pre-eminence. Our gospel shall be the gospel of reconciliation on this occasion. May the reconciling word come home by the power of Christ's Spirit to many, so that hundreds of souls may from this day forth glorify the great Ambassador who has made peace by the blood of His cross.

The text is a great deep, we cannot explore it, but we will voyage over its surface joyously, the Holy Spirit giving us a favourable wind. Here are plenteous provisions far exceeding those of Solomon, though at the sight of that royal profusion, Sheba's queen felt that there was no more spirit in her, and declared that the half had not been told her.

It may give some sort of order to our thoughts if they fall under four heads. *What* is here spoken of —"all fulness." *Where* is it placed—"*in Him*," that is, in the Redeemer. We are told *why*, because "it pleased the Father;" and we have also a note of time, or *when*, in the word "dwell." "It pleased the Father that in Him should all fulness dwell." Those catch words, *what, where, why,* and *when,* may help you to remember the run of the sermon.

I. First, then, let us consider the subject before us, or WHAT—"It pleased the Father that in Him should *all fulness* dwell." Two mighty words; "*fulness,*" a substantial, comprehensive, expressive word in itself, and "*all,*" a great little word including everything. When combined in the expression, "*all fulness,*" we have before us a superlative wealth of meaning.

Blessed be God for those two words. Our hearts rejoice to think that there is such a thing in the universe as "all fulness," for in the most of mortal pursuits utter barrenness is found. "Vanity of vanity, all is vanity." Blessed be the Lord for ever that He has provided a fulness for us, for in us by nature there is all emptiness and utter vanity. "In me, that is, in my flesh, there dwelleth no good thing." In us there is a lack of all merit, an absence of all power to procure any, and even an absence of will to procure it if we could. In these respects human nature is a desert, empty, and void, and waste, inhabited only by the dragon of sin, and the bittern of sorrow. Sinner, saint, to you both alike these words, "all fulness," sound like a holy hymn. The accents are sweet as those of the angel-messenger when he sang, "Behold, I bring you glad tidings of great joy." Are they not stray notes from celestial sonnets? "All fulness!" You, sinner, are all emptiness and death; you, saint, would be so if it were not for the "all fulness" of Christ of which you have received; therefore both to saint and sinner the words are full of hope. There is joy in these words to every soul conscious of its sad estate, and humbled before God.

I will ring the silver bell again, "all fulness," and another note charms us; it tells us that Christ is substance, and not shadow, fulness, and not foretaste. This is good news for us, for nothing but realities will meet our case. Types may instruct, but they cannot actually save. The patterns of the things in the heavens are too weak to serve our turn, we need the heavenly things themselves. No bleeding bird nor slaughtered bullock, nor running stream, nor scarlet wool and hyssop, can take away our sins.

"No outward forms can make me clean,
The leprosy lies deep within."

Ceremonies under the old dispensation were precious because they set forth the realities yet to be revealed, but in Christ Jesus we deal with the realities themselves, and this is a happy circumstance for us; for both our sins and our sorrows are real, and only substantial mercies can counteract them. In Jesus, we have the substance of all that the symbols set forth. He is our sacrifice, our altar, our priest, our incense, our tabernacle, our all in all. The law had "the shadow of good things to come," but in Christ we have "the very image of the things." Heb. x. 1. What transport is this to those who so much feel their emptiness that they could not be comforted by the mere representation of a truth, or the pattern of a truth, or the symbol of a truth, but must have the very substance itself! "The law was given by Moses, but grace and truth came by Jesus Christ." John i. 16.

I must return to the words of the text again, for I perceive more honey dropping from the honeycomb. "All fulness" is a wide, far-reaching, all-comprehending term, and in its abundant store it offers another source of delight. What joy these words give to us when we remember that our vast necessities demand a fulness, yea, "*all fulness*" before they can be supplied! A little help will be of no use to us, for we are altogether without strength. A limited measure of mercy will only mock our misery. A low degree of grace will never be enough to bring us to heaven, defiled as we are with sin, beset with dangers, encompassed with infirmities, assailed by temptations, molested with afflictions, and all the while bearing about with us "the body of this death." But "all fulness," ay, that will suit us.

Here is exactly what our desperate estate demands for its recovery. Had the Saviour only put out His finger to help our exertions, or had He only stretched out His hand to perform a measure of salvation's work, while He left us to complete it, our soul had for ever dwelt in darkness. In these words, "all fulness," we hear the echo of His death-cry, "It is finished." We are to bring nothing, but to find all in Him, yea, the fulness of all in Him: we are simply to receive out of His fulness grace for grace. We are not asked to contribute, nor required to make up deficiencies, for there are none to make up—all, all is laid up in Christ. All that we shall want between this place and heaven, all we could need between the gates of hell, where we lay in our blood, to the gates of heaven, where we shall find welcome admission, is treasured up for us in the Lord Christ Jesus.

> "Great God, the treasures of Thy love
> Are everlasting mines,
> Deep as our helpless miseries are,
> And boundless as our sins."

Did I not say well that the two words before us are a noble hymn? Let them, I pray you, lodge in your souls for many days; they will be blessed guests. Let these two wafers, made with honey, lie under your tongue; let them satiate your souls, for they are heavenly bread. The more you bemoan your emptiness the sweeter these words will be; the more you feel that you must draw largely upon the bank of heaven, the more will you rejoice that your drafts will never diminish the boundless store, for still will it retain the name and the quality of "all fulness."

The expression here used denotes that there is in Jesus Christ the fulness of the Godhead; as it is written, "In Him dwelleth all the fulness of the Godhead bodily." When John saw the Son of Man in Patmos, the marks of Deity were on Him. "His head and His hairs were white like wool, as white as snow"—here was His eternity; "His eyes were as a flame of fire"—here was His omniscience; "Out of His mouth went a sharp two-edged sword"—here was the omnipotence of His word; "And His countenance was as the sun shineth in His strength"—here was His unapproachable and infinite glory. He is the Alpha and Omega, the beginning and the end, the first and the last. Hence nothing is too hard for Him. Power, wisdom, truth, immutability, and all the attributes of God are in Him, and constitute a fulness inconceivable and inexhaustible. The most enlarged intellect must necessarily fail to compass the personal fulness of Christ as God; therefore we do no more than quote again that noble text: "In Him dwelleth all the fulness of the Godhead bodily; and ye are complete in Him."

Fulness, moreover, dwells in our Lord not only intrinsically from His nature, but as the result of His mediatorial work. He achieved by suffering as well as possessed by nature a wondrous fulness. He carried on His shoulders the load of our sin; He expiated by His death our guilt, and now He has merit with the Father, infinite, inconceivable, a fulness of desert. The Father has stored up in Christ Jesus, as in a reservoir, for the use of all His people, His eternal love and His unbounded grace, that it may come to us through Christ Jesus, and that we may glorify Him. All power is put into His hands, and life, and light, and grace, are to the full at His disposal. "He shutteth and no man openeth, He openeth and no man shutteth." He has received

gifts for men; yea, for the rebellious also. Not only as the Mighty God, the Everlasting Father, is He the possessor of heaven and earth, and therefore filled with all fulness, but seeing that as the Mediator He has finished our redemption, "He is made of God unto us wisdom, and righteousness, and sanctification, and redemption." Glory be to His name for this double fulness.

Turn the thought round again, and remember that all fulness dwells in Christ *towards God and towards men*. All fulness towards *God*—I mean all that God requires of man; all that contents and delights the eternal mind, so that once again with complacency He may look down on His creature and pronounce him "very good." The Lord looked for grapes in His vineyard, and it brought forth wild grapes, but now in Christ Jesus the great Husbandman beholds the true vine which bringeth forth much fruit. The Creator required obedience, and He beholds in Christ Jesus the servant who has never failed to do the Master's will. Justice demanded that the law should be kept, and, lo, Christ is the end of the law for righteousness to everyone that believeth. Seeing that we had broken the law, justice required the endurance of the righteous penalty, and Jesus has borne it to the full, for He bowed His head to death, even the death of the cross. When God made man a little lower than the angels, and breathed into his nostrils the breath of life, and so made him immortal, He had a right to expect singular service from so favoured a being—a service perfect, joyful, continuous; and our Saviour has rendered unto the Father that which perfectly contents Him; for He cries, "This is My beloved Son in whom I am well pleased." God is more glorified in the person of His Son than He would have been by an unfallen world. There shines out through the entire universe a display of infinite mercy, justice, and wisdom, such as neither the majesty of nature nor the excellence of providence could have revealed. His work in God's esteem is honourable and precious; for His righteousness sake, God is well pleased. The Eternal mind is satisfied with the Redeemer's person, work, and sacrifice; for "unto the Son, He saith, Thy throne, O God, is for ever and ever: a sceptre of righteousness is the sceptre of Thy kingdom. Thou hast loved righteousness, and hated iniquity; therefore God, even Thy God, hath anointed Thee with the oil of gladness above Thy fellows." Hebrews i. 8, 9.

What unspeakable consolations arise from this truth, for, dear brethren, if we had to render to God something by which we should be accepted, we should be always in jeopardy; but now since we are "accepted in the Beloved," we are safe beyond all hazard. Had we to find wherewithal we should appear before the Most High God, we might still be asking, "Shall I come before Him with burnt-offerings, with calves of a year old? Will the Lord be pleased with thousands of rams, or with ten thousands of rivers of oil?" But now hear the voice which saith, "Sacrifice and offering and burnt offerings and offering for sin thou wouldest not, neither hadst pleasure therein:" we hear the same divine voice add, "Lo, I come to do Thy will," and we rejoice as we receive the witness of the Spirit, saying, "By the which will ye are sanctified through the offering of the body of Jesus Christ once for all," for henceforth is it said, "Their sins and iniquities will I remember no more for ever."

The all-fulness of Christ is also *man-ward*, and that in respect of both the sinner and the saint. There is a fulness in Christ Jesus which the seeking sinner should behold with joyfulness. What dost thou want, sinner? Thou wantest all things, but Christ is all. Thou wantest power to believe in Him—He giveth power to the faint. Thou wantest repentance—He was exalted on high to give repentance as well as remission of sin. Thou wantest a new heart: the covenant runs thus, "A new heart also will I give them, and a right spirit will I put within them." Thou wantest pardon—behold His streaming wounds, wash thou and be clean. Thou wantest healing: He is "the Lord that healeth thee." Thou wantest clothing—His righteousness shall become thy dress. Thou wantest preservation—thou shalt be preserved in Him. Thou wantest life, and He has said, "Awake, thou that sleepest, and arise from the dead, and Christ shall give thee life." He is come that we might have life. Thou wantest —but indeed, the catalogue were much too long for us to read it through at this present, yet be assured though thou pile up thy necessities till they rise like Alps before thee, yet the all-sufficient Saviour can remove all thy needs. You may confidently sing—

> "Thou, O Christ, art all I want,
> More than all in Thee I find."

This is true also of the saint as well as the sinner. O child of God, thou art now saved, but thy wants are not therefore removed. Are they not as continuous as thy heart-beats? When are we not in want, my brethren? The more alive we are to God, the more are we aware of our spiritual necessities. He who is "blind and naked," thinks himself to be "rich and increased in goods," but let the mind be truly enlightened, and we feel that we are completely dependent upon the charity of God. Let us be glad, then, as we learn that there is no necessity in our spirit but what is abundantly provided for in the all-fulness of Jesus Christ. You seek for a higher platform of spiritual attainments, you aim to conquer sin, you desire to be plentiful in fruit unto His glory, you are longing to be useful, you are anxious to subdue the hearts of others unto Christ; behold the needful grace for all this. In the sacred armoury of the Son of David behold your battle-axe and your weapons of war; in the stores of Him who is greater than Aaron see the robes in which to fulfil your priesthood; in the wounds of Jesus behold the power with which you may become a living sacrifice. If you would glow like a seraph, and serve like an apostle, behold the grace awaiting you in Jesus. If you would go from strength to strength, climbing the loftiest summits of holiness, behold grace upon grace prepared for you. If you are straitened, it will not be in Christ; if there be any bound to your holy attainments, it is set by yourself. The infinite God Himself gives Himself to you in the person of His dear Son, and He saith to you, "All things are yours." "The Lord is the portion of your inheritance and of your cup." Infinity is ours. He who gave us His own Son has in that very deed given us all things. Hath He not said, "I am the Lord thy God, which brought thee out of the land of Egypt; open thy mouth wide, and I will fill it"?

Let me remark that this is not only true of saints on earth, but it is true also of saints in heaven, for all the fulness of the church triumphant is in Christ as well as that of the church militant. They are nothing even in heaven without Him. The pure river of the water of life of which they drink, proceedeth out of the throne of God and of the Lamb. He hath made them priests and kings, and in His power they reign. Those snowy robes were washed and made white in His blood. The Lamb is the temple of heaven (Rev. xxi. 22), the light of heaven (Rev. xxi. 23), His marriage is the joy of heaven (Rev. xix. 7), and the song of Moses, the servant of God, and the song of the Lamb, is the song of heaven (Rev. xv. 3). Not all the harps above could make a heavenly place if Christ were gone; for He is the heaven of heaven, and filleth all in all. It pleased the Father that for all saints and sinners all fulness should be treasured up in Christ Jesus.

I feel that my text overwhelms me Men may sail round the world, but who can circumnavigate so vast a subject as this? As far as the east is from the west so wide is its reach of blessing.

> "Philosophers have measured mountains,
> Fathomed the depths of seas, of states, and kings,
> Walked with a staff to heaven, and traced fountains.
> But there are two vast spacious things,
> The which to measure it doth more behove:
> Yet few there are that sound them: Grace and Love."

Who is he that shall be able to express all that is meant by our text? for here we have "all" and "fulness"—all in fulness and a fulness in all. The words are both exclusive and inclusive. They deny that there is any fulness elsewhere, for they claim all for Christ. They shut out all others. "It pleased the Father that *in Him* should *all* fulness dwell." Not in you, ye pretended successors of the apostles, can anything dwell that I need. I can do well enough without you; nay, I would not insult my Saviour by trading with you, for since "all fulness" is in Him, what can there be in you that I can require? Go to your dupes who know not Christ, but those who possess the exceeding riches of Christ's grace bow not to you. We are "complete in Christ" without you, O hierarchy of bishops; without you, ye conclave of cardinals; and without you, O fallible Infallible, unholy Holiness of Rome. He who has all in Christ would be insane indeed if he looked for more, or having fulness craved for emptiness. This text drives us from all confidence in men, ay, or even in angels, by making us see that everything is treasured up in Jesus Christ. Brethren, if there be any good in what is called catholicism, or in ritualism, or in the modern philosophical novelties, let religionists have what they find there; we shall not envy them, for they can find nothing worth having in their forms of worship or belief but what we must have already in the person of the all-sufficient Saviour. What if their candles burn brightly, the sun itself is ours! What if they are successors of the apostles, we follow the Lamb Himself whithersoever He goeth! What if they be exceeding wise, we dwell with the Incarnate Wisdom Himself! Let them go to their cisterns, we will abide by the fountain of living water. But indeed there is no light in their luminaries, they do but increase the darkness; they are blind leaders of the blind. They put their sounding emptinesses into competition with the all-fulness of Jesus, and preach another gospel which is not another. The imprecation of the apostle be upon them. They add unto the words of God, and He shall add to them its plagues.

While the text is exclusive it is also inclusive. It

shuts in everything that is required for time and for eternity for all the blood-bought. It is an ark containing all good things conceivable, yea, and many that are as yet inconceivable; for by reason of our weakness we have not yet conceived the fulness of Christ. Things which ye yet have not asked nor even thought, He is able to give you abundantly. If you should arrive at the consecration of martyrs, the piety of apostles, the purity of angels, yet should you never have seen or be able to think of anything pure, lovely, and of good report, that was not already treasured up in Christ Jesus. All the rivers flow into this sea, for from this sea they came. As the atmosphere surrounds all the earth, and all things live in that sea of air, so all good things are contained in the blessed person of our dear Redeemer. Let us join to praise Him. Let us extol Him with heart and voice, and let sinners be reconciled unto God by Him. If all the good things are in Him which a sinner can require to make him acceptable with God, then let the sinner come at once through such a mediator. Let doubts and fears vanish at the sight of the mediatorial fulness. Jesus must be able to save to the uttermost, since all fulness dwells in Him. Come, sinner, come and receive Him. Believe thou in Him and thou shalt find thyself made perfect in Christ Jesus.

> "The moment a sinner believes,
> And trusts in his crucified God,
> His pardon at once he receives,
> Redemption in full through His blood."

II. Having thus spoken of *what*, we now turn to consider WHERE.

"It pleased the Father that *in Him* should all fulness dwell." Where else could all fulness have been placed? There was wanted a vast *capacity to contain* "all fulness." Where dwells there a being with nature capacious enough to compass within himself all fulness? As well might we ask, "Who hath measured the waters in the hollow of His hand, and meted out heaven with the span, and comprehended the dust of the earth in a measure, and weighed the mountains in scales, and the hills in a balance?" To Him only could it belong to contain "all fulness," for He must be equal with God, the Infinite. How suitable was the Son of the Highest, who "was by Him, as one brought up with Him," to become the grand storehouse of all the treasures of wisdom, and knowledge and grace, and salvation. Moreover, there was wanted not only capacity to contain, but *immutability to retain* the fulness, for the text says, " It pleased the Father that in Him should all fulness *dwell*," that is, abide, and remain, for ever. Now if any kind of fulness could be put into us mutable creatures, yet by reason of our frailty we should prove but broken cisterns that can hold no water. The Redeemer is Jesus Christ, the same yesterday, to-day, and for ever: therefore was it meet that all fulness should be placed in Him. "The Son abideth ever." "He is a priest for ever after the order of Melchisedec." "Being made perfect He became the author of eternal salvation unto all them that obey Him." "His name shall endure for ever: His name shall be continued as long as the sun: and men shall be blessed in Him: all nations shall call Him blessed."

Perhaps the sweetest thought is, that the "all fulness" is fitly placed in Christ Jesus, because in Him there is a *suitability to distribute it*, so that we may *obtain* it from Him. How could we come to God Himself for grace? for "even our God is a consuming fire." But Jesus Christ while God is also man like ourselves, truly man, of a meek lowly spirit, and therefore easily approachable. They who know Him, delight in nearness to Him. Is it not sweet that all fulness should be treasured up in Him who was the friend of publicans and sinners: and who came into the world to seek and to save that which was lost? The Man who took the child up on His knee and said, "Suffer the little children to come unto Me," the Man who was tempted in all points like as we are, the Man who touched the sick, nay, who "bore their sicknesses," the Man who gave His hands to the nails, and His heart to the spear; that blessed Man, into the print of whose nails his disciple Thomas put his finger, and into whose side he thrust his hand; it is He, the incarnate God, in whom all fulness dwells. Come, then, and receive of Him, ye who are the weakest, the most mean, and most sinful of men. Come at once, O sinner, and fear not.

> "Why art thou afraid to come,
> And tell Him all thy case?
> He will not pronounce thy doom,
> Nor frown thee from His face.
> Wilt thou fear Immanuel?
> Or dread the Lamb of God,
> Who, to save thy soul from hell,
> Has shed His precious blood?"

Let it be noted here, however, very carefully, that while fulness is treasured up in Christ, it is not said to be treasured up in the doctrines of Christ; though they are full and complete, and we need no other teaching when the Spirit reveals the Son in us; nor is it said to be treasured up in the commands of Christ, although they are amply sufficient for our guidance; but it is said, "It pleased the Father that *in Him*," in His person, "should all fulness dwell." In Him, as God incarnate, dwelleth "all the fulness of the Godhead *bodily*;" not as a myth, a dream, a thought, a fiction, but as a living, real personality. We must lay hold of this. I know that the fulness dwells in Him officially as Prophet, Priest, and King —but the fulness lies not in the prophetic mantle, nor in the priestly ephod, nor in the royal vesture, but in the person that wears all these. "It pleased the Father that *in Him* should all fulness dwell." You must get to the very Christ in your faith, and rest alone in Him, or else you have not reached the treasury wherein all fulness is stored up. All fulness is in Him radically; if there be fulness in His work, or His gifts, or His promises, all is derived from His person, which gives weight and value to all. All the promises are yea and amen *in Christ Jesus*. The merit of His death lies mainly in His person, because He was God who gave Himself for us, and His own self bare our sins in His own body on the tree. The excellence of His person gave fulness to His sacrifice. Hebrews i. 3. His power to save at this very day lies in His person, for "He is able to save to the uttermost them that come unto God by Him, *seeing he ever liveth to make intercession for them*." I desire you to see this, and feel it; for when your soul clasps the pierced feet of Jesus, and looks up into the face more marred than that of any man, even if you cannot understand all His works and offices, yet if you believe in Him, you have reached the place wherein all fulness dwells, and of His fulness you shall receive.

Beloved, remember our practical aim. Praise His person, ye saints! Be ye reconciled to God through His person, ye sinners! Ye angels, lead us in the song! Ye spirits redeemed by blood, sing, "Worthy is the Lamb that was slain," and our hearts shall keep tune with yours, for we owe the same debt to Him. Glory be unto the person of the blessed Lamb. "Blessing, and glory, and wisdom, and thanksgiving, and honour, and power, and might, be unto our God for ever and ever." Would God we could see Him face to face, and adore Him as we would. O sinners, will you not be reconciled to God through Him, since all fulness is in Him, and He stoops to your weakness, and holds forth His pierced hands to greet you? See Him stretching out both His hands to receive you, while He sweetly woos you to come to God through Him. Come unto Him. O come with hasty steps, ye penitents; come at once, ye guilty ones! Who would not be reconciled unto God by such a One as this, in whom all fulness of grace is made to dwell?

III. The third question is, WHY? "It pleased the Father." That is answer enough. He is a sovereign, let Him do as He wills. Ask the reason for election, you shall receive no other than this, "Even so, Father, for so it seemed good in Thy sight." That one answer may reply to ten thousand questions. It is the Lord, let Him do what seemeth Him good. Once "it pleased the Father to bruise Him," and now "it pleased the Father that in Him should all fulness dwell." Sovereignty may answer the question sufficiently, but harken! I hear justice speak, she cannot be silent. Justice saith there was no person in heaven or under heaven so meet to contain the fulness of grace as Jesus.

None so meet to be glorified as the Saviour, who "made Himself of no reputation, and took upon Himself the form of a servant, and being found in fashion as a man, humbled Himself, and became obedient to death, even the death of the cross." It is but justice that the grace whch He has brought to us should be treasured up in Him. And while justice speaks wisdom will not withhold her voice. Wise art thou, O Jehovah, to treasure up grace in Christ, for to Him men can come; and to Him coming, as unto a living stone, chosen of God and precious, men find Him precious also to their souls. The Lord has laid our help in the right place, for He has laid it upon One that is mighty, and who is as loving as He is mighty, as ready as He is able to save. Moreover, in the fitness of things the Father's pleasure is the first point to be considered, for all things ought to be to the good pleasure of God. It is a great underlying rule of the universe that all things were created for God's pleasure. God is the source and fountain of eternal love, and it is but meet that He should convey it to us by what channel He may elect. Bowing, therefore, in lowly worship at His throne we are glad that in this matter the fulness dwells where it perpetually satisfies the decree of heaven. It is well that "it pleased the Father."

Now, brethren, if it pleased the Father to place all grace in Christ, let us praise the elect Saviour. What pleases God pleases us. Where would you desire to have grace placed, my brethren, but in the Well-beloved? The whole church of God is unanimous about this. If I could save myself I would not; I would think salvation to be no salvation if it did not glorify Jesus. This is the very crown and glory of being saved, that our being saved will bring honour to Christ. It is delightful to think that Christ will have the glory of all God's grace; it were shocking if it were not so. Who could bear to see Jesus robbed of His reward? We are indignant that any should usurp His place, and ashamed of ourselves that we do not glorify Him more. No joy ever visits my soul like that of knowing that Jesus is highly exalted, and that to Him "every knee shall bow and every tongue confess that Jesus Christ is Lord, to the glory of God the Father." A sister in Christ, in her kindness and gratitude, used language to me the other day which brought a blush to my cheek, for I felt ashamed to be so undeserving of the praise. She said, "Your ministry profits me because you glorify Christ so much." Ah, I thought, if you knew how I would glorify Him if I could, and how far I fall below what I fain would do for Him, you would not commend me. I could weep over the best sermons I have ever preached because I cannot extol my Lord enough, and my conceptions are so low, and my words so poor. Oh, if one could but attain really to honour Him, and put another crown upon His head, it were heaven indeed! We are in this agreed with the Father, for if it pleases Him to glorify His Son, we sincerely feel that it pleases us.

Ought not those who are yet unrenewed, to hasten to be reconciled to God by such a Redeemer? If it pleases the Father to put all grace in Christ, O sinner, does it not please you to come and receive it through Christ? Christ is the meeting-place for a sinner and his God. God is in Christ, and when you come to Christ, God meets you, and a treaty of peace is made between you and the Most High. Are you not agreed with God in this—that Christ shall be glorified? Do you not say, "I would glorify Him by accepting this morning all His grace, love, and mercy"? Well, if you are willing to receive Jesus, God has made you willing, and therein proved His willingness to save you. He is pleased with Christ; are you pleased with Christ? If so, there is already peace between you and God, for Jesus "is our peace."

IV. We must close by dwelling upon the WHEN. When is all fulness in Jesus? It is there in all time, past, present, and to come. "It pleased the Father that in Him should all fulness dwell." Fulness, then, was in Christ of old, is in Christ to-day, will be in Christ for ever. Perpetuity is here indicated; all fulness was, is, shall be in the person of Jesus Christ. Every saint saved under the old dispensation found the fulness of his salvation in the coming Redeemer; every saint saved since the advent is saved through the selfsame fulness. From the streaming fount of the wounds of Christ on Calvary, redemption flows evermore; and as long as there is a sinner to be saved, or one elect soul to be ingathered, Christ's blood shall never lose its power, the fulness of merit and grace shall abide the same.

While the expression "dwell" indicates perpetuity, does not it indicate constancy and accessibility? A man who dwells in a house is always to be found there, it is his home. The text seems to me to say that this fulness of grace is always to be found in Christ, ever abiding in Him. Knock at this door by prayer, and you shall find it at home. If a sinner anywhere is saying, "God be merciful to me!" mercy has not gone out on travel, it dwells in Christ both night and day; it is there now at this moment. There is life in a look at the crucified One, not at certain canonical hours, but at any hour, in any place, by any man who looks. "From the end of the earth will I cry unto Thee, when my heart is overwhelmed," and my prayer shall not be rejected. There is fulness of mercy in Christ to be had at any time, at any season, from any place. It pleased the Father that all fulness should permanently abide in Him as in a house whose door is never shut.

Above all, we see here *immutability*. All fulness dwells in Christ—that is to say, it is never exhausted nor diminished. On the last day wherein this world shall stand before it is given up to be devoured with fervent heat, there shall be found as much fulness in Christ as in the hour when the first sinner looked unto Him and was lightened. O sinner, the bath that cleanses is as efficacious to take out spots to-day as it was when the dying thief washed therein. O thou despairing sinner, there is as much consolation in Christ to-day as when He said to the woman, "Thy sins are forgiven thee, go in peace." His grace has not diminished. He is to-day as great a Saviour as when Magdalen was delivered from seven devils. Till time shall be no more He will exercise the same infinite power to forgive, to renew, to deliver, to sanctify, to perfectly save souls.

Shall not all this make us praise Christ, since all fulness is permanent in Him? Let our praises abide where the fulness abides. "All Thy works praise Thee, O God, but Thy saints shall bless Thee"; yea, they shall never cease their worship, because Thou shalt never abate Thy fulness. This is a topic upon which we who love Christ, are all agreed. We can dispute about doctrines, and we have different views upon ordinances; but we have all one view concerning our Lord Jesus. Let Him sit on a glorious high throne. When shall the day dawn that He shall ride through our streets in triumph? When shall England and Scotland, and all the nations become truly the dominions of the great King? Our prayer is that He may hasten the spread of the gospel, and His own coming, as seemeth good in His sight. O that He were glorious in the eyes of men!

And surely if all fulness abides perpetually in Christ, there is good reason why the unreconciled should this morning avail themselves of it. May the blessed Spirit show thee, O sinner, that there is enough in Jesus Christ to meet thy wants, that thy weakness need not keep thee back, nor even the hardness of thy heart, nor the inveteracy of thy will; for Christ is able even to subdue all things to Himself. If you seek Him he will be found of you. Seek Him while He may be found. Leave not the seat until your soul is bowed at His feet. I think I see Him; cannot your hearts picture Him, glorious to-day, but yet the same Saviour who was nailed like a felon to the cross for guilty ones? Reach forth thy hand and touch the silver sceptre of mercy which He holds out to thee, for those who touch it live. Look into that dear face where tears once made their furrows, and grief its lines; look, I say, and live. Look at that brow radiant with many a glittering gem, it once wore a crown of thorns; let His love melt you to repentance. Throw yourself into His arms now, feeling, "If I perish I will perish there. He shall be my only hope." As the Lord liveth, before whom I stand, there shall never be a soul of you lost who will come and trust in Jesus. Heaven and earth shall pass away, but this word of God shall never pass away. "He that believeth and is baptized shall be saved." God has said it; will He not do it? He has declared it, it must stand fast. "Whosoever believeth in Him shall not perish, but have everlasting life." O trust ye Him! I implore you by the mercy of God, and by the fulness of Jesus, trust Him now, this day! God grant you may, for Christ's sake. Amen.

STAND FAST

"Be not moved away from the hope of the gospel."—Colossians i. 23.

I THINK this morning we showed pretty plainly that many a soul has a great struggle to attain to the hope of the gospel. Not without hand-to-hand fighting do many hearts lay hold on Christ and eternal life. Conscience often sets up a *chevaux de frise* around the hill of Calvary, and thus cuts off the convinced sinner from approaching his Saviour. Doubts and fears, the Black Watch of evil, drive back the coming ones, and worry those who would fain hide in the Rock of Ages. Satan summonses all his hosts to push men back from the cross that they may not come to Christ and live. But, brethren, the battle does not end when by a desperate rush a man has come to Christ. In many it assumes a new form; the enemy now attempts to drag the trembler from his refuge, and eject him from his stronghold. It is difficult to get at the hope of the gospel; but quite as difficult to keep it so as not to be moved away from it. If Satan spends great power in keeping us from the hope, he uses equal force in endeavouring to drag us away from it, and equal cunning in endeavouring to allure us from it. Hence the apostle tells us not to be moved away from the hope of the gospel: the exhortation is needful in presence of an imminent danger. Do not think that in the moment when you believe in Christ the conflict is over, or you will be bitterly disappointed. It is then that the battle renews itself, and every inch of the road swarms with foemen. Between here and heaven you will always have to fight more or less, and frequently the severest struggle will be at a time when you are least prepared for it. There may be smooth passages in your career, and you may for a while be like your Saviour in the wilderness, of whom it is said, "Then the devil departed from Him, and angels came and ministered unto Him"; but you may not therefore cry, "My mountain standeth firm, I shall never be moved"; for fair weather may not outlast a single day. Do not grow secure, or carnally presumptuous. There is but a short space between one battle and another in this world. It is a series of skirmishes even when it does not assume the form of a pitched battle. He that would win heaven must fight for it. He that would take the new Jerusalem must scale it, and if he has the wit to take Jacob's ladder and set it against the wall and climb up that way, he will win the city. "The kingdom of heaven suffereth violence, and the violent take it by force." At this time our subject is not the winning, but the wearing; not the taking, but the holding of the fort: "Be not moved away," you that have come to it, "Be not moved away from the hope of the gospel."

I. First, BE NOT MOVED AWAY FROM THE SUBJECT OF THAT HOPE so as to give up any part of the hope which is revealed to you by the gospel. What is your hope?

First, it is the hope of *full salvation*—the hope that, inasmuch as you have believed in Jesus Christ, you are free from all condemnation at the present moment, and shall be free from all condemnation in the future as to all your sins; and that, in addition to this, He that takes away the condemnation of sin will also destroy the power of it over you. You have this hope—that being made to love righteousness you shall be enabled to walk in obedience, and "to perfect holiness in the fear of the Lord." Your hope is that one day you shall be presented holy, unblameable, and unreproveable in the sight of the great Father. You shall one day be presented "without spot or wrinkle, or any such thing," cleansed from all guilt, and cleansed from all tendency to sin and to corruption, and made like unto the perfect creature of God when first it comes from His hands. Oh, this is a blessed hope! "He that hath this hope in him purifieth himself, even as Christ is pure." We hope that we shall be like unto Christ Himself, and that the glory of His holiness shall be our glory, and we shall see His face, and His name shall be in our foreheads, and we shall be without fault before the throne of God. Now, never give that up: never allow a particle of it to be diminished. God means all that He has said, and more rather than less. Let no man debase the currency of heaven or clip the coin of the realm of the Great King. The first part of it—hold to it, that the Lord Jesus Christ has cleansed you from all the guilt and penalty of sin, so that not a speck remains to accuse or condemn you. Hold to it, moreover, that if He has once washed you, you shall not need to wash again in that fountain filled with blood, for "he that is washed needeth not except to wash his feet"; and that washing shall be given to him by the condescending hands of Christ. The water shall be a second cure of that which the blood has already cleansed and removed. The blood-washing has removed all guilt, and prevented all possibility that sin shall have dominion over you. Complete forgiveness and full justification are proofs that through your Lord's endurance of the death-penalty you are no more under the law, but under grace. My soul rejoices to-night in perfect pardon. I will not take off a corner of it, so as to allow that the smallest charge can lie against us. We are complete in Christ. He that believeth in Him is justified from all things.

> "Here's pardon for transgressions past,
> It matters not how black their cast;
> And, oh! my soul, with wonder view:
> For sins to come here's pardon too!"

All pardon is provided in the one great sacrifice offered by our bleeding Lord, who has now gone into the heavens to plead the merit of His blood. Never take off a fraction from that other part of full salvation, namely, the possibility and the absolute certainty that every sinful tendency now in your nature shall be utterly destroyed. There shall remain in you no root of bitterness, no scar of evil, no footprint of iniquity. There shall be no tinder in your soul upon which the sparks of temptation can fall, so as to live and make a flame; and when the prince of this world cometh he shall find nothing in you. Then you shall

enter into your rest eternal; for God keeps not His ripe wheat in the field, but takes it home when it is once fit to be gathered into the garner. This is your hope through the gospel: be not moved away from it.

In connection with this there is the hope of *final perseverance*. I confess that to me it is one of the most attractive doctrines of God's word, that "the righteous shall hold on his way, and he that hath clean hands shall be stronger and stronger." For I am "confident of this very thing, that He which hath begun a good work in you will perform it until the day of Jesus Christ." "I give unto My sheep eternal life, and they shall never perish; neither shall any pluck them out of My hand." "He that believeth in Him is not condemned." "He that liveth and believeth in Me shall never die." There are many assurances to this effect, and if anything definite is taught in Scripture, I am confident that this is among the plainest of such teachings. I beseech you, do not shun this doctrine as though it would lead you into the least presumption if properly understood. Its legitimate effect is the very reverse of carelessness. If it be true that, once enlisted in this army of the Lord, you must and shall fight until you are a conqueror, then there is no temptation to lay down the sword for a while in the hope of taking it up again at a more convenient season. If, as some say, you may be Christ's soldier to-day and desert to-morrow, and then be enlisted again,—if it be indeed true that a man may be regenerated and then lose the divine life, and upon repentance be re-generated and re-re-re-re-re-regenerated I know not how many times, I am not aware that this novelty is hinted at in my unrevised New Testament. There I read of being "born again," but not of being born again and again and again and again and again and again—I say I cannot find a trace of this in the Bible. On the other hand, I find that if the one regeneration fails, which is impossible, there would remain nothing else to be done. God's best work is broken down, and He will never try it again. He has said, "It is impossible for those who were once enlightened, and have tasted of the heavenly gift, and were made partakers of the Holy Ghost, and have tasted the good word of God, and the powers of the world to come, if they shall fall away, to renew them again unto repentance; seeing they crucify to themselves the Son of God afresh, and put Him to an open shame. For the earth which drinketh in the rain that cometh oft upon it, and bringeth forth herbs meet for them by whom it is dressed, receiveth blessing from God: but that which beareth thorns and briers is rejected, and is nigh unto cursing; whose end is to be burned." You cannot re-salt the salt if it has once lost its savour. If, then, grace does utterly depart, which I believe to be impossible, there remains no hope for such a one. God's supreme effort, according to that theory, has been made and failed. Now, there is nothing for it but that the land which has received the dew of heaven, and brought forth no fruit, is nigh unto cursing, whose end is to be burned. "But, beloved, we are persuaded better things of you, and things that accompany salvation, though we thus speak." We have but made the supposition to show you the danger, upon whose brink you stand, and over whose verge you would slide if grace did not prevent. If you indeed believe in Christ Jesus, set this to your seal, that He will keep you to the end. Whatsoever happens, "I am persuaded that neither things present, nor things to come, nor height, nor depth, nor any other creature, shall be able to separate us from the love of God which is in Christ Jesus our Lord." For dear life hold on to the hope of final preservation; for there is a purifying, encouraging, stimulating power about that precious truth. "He keepeth the feet of His saints:" "be not moved away from the hope of the gospel."

We have a hope beyond this; for we believe that we shall experience *the resurrection*. Though they fall down and men call them corpses, they are precious in the sight of the Lord, and the grave shall be a refining pot, out of which the pure metal of our purified body shall come forth. At the word of the Lord the dry bones shall live; they shall be clothed with flesh, and skin shall come upon them, if after that fashion the body is to be raised. But, if not—if the body is to assume another form, and we are to be made like unto a glory which as yet we cannot comprehend, then we may be sure of this—that we shall so rise that mortality shall put on immortality, and corruption shall give place to incorruption. In any case, our bodies shall rise again. The grace of God secures the bodies as well as the souls of the saints. Christ bought not the half of a man, but the whole trinity of our manhood is His redeemed inheritance: spirit, soul, and body shall dwell for ever with Him, for He has redeemed our undivided manhood. Never give up that hope either concerning yourselves or your friends. Let nothing shake your confidence in the resurrection; let no philosophical explanation fritter it away. No other historical fact is so well attested as the resurrection of Christ, and that is the very corner-stone of our confidence. "For if the dead rise not, then is not Christ raised: and if Christ be not raised, your faith is vain; ye are yet in your sins. Then they also which are fallen asleep in Christ are perished. If in this life only we have hope in Christ, we are of all men most miserable. But now is Christ risen from the dead, and become the firstfruits of them that slept." Often and often when I am sore beset with devilish temptations and insinuations as to the eternal hope of my soul and body, I fly to this,—Jesus Christ did rise from the dead, and, inasmuch as He rose from the dead, He has come back to tell us that there is another world, and that not only our souls but our bodies shall inherit a far more blessed condition than this present one. Hold on to this hope of the gospel, and never let it go.

> "The Lord is risen: He liveth,
> The Firstborn from the dead.
> To Him the Father giveth
> To be creation's Head.
> O'er all for ever reigning,
> Of death He holds the keys;
> And hell—His might constraining—
> Obeys His high decrees.
>
> Flies now the gloom that shaded
> The vale of death to me;
> The terrors that invaded
> Are lost, O Christ, in Thee!
> The grave, no more appalling,
> Invites me to repose;
> Asleep in Jesus falling,
> To rise as Jesus rose."

Then, remember, you have the hope of *the second advent;* if Jesus comes before you die you will meet Him—gladly meet and welcome the Son of God upon this earth. You shall be changed so that you shall be fit to inherit the incorruptible glories of the skies. You shall see your Redeemer when He stands in the latter day upon the earth. As Job said, "In my flesh shall I see God, whom my eyes shall see for myself, and not another." Have joy, then, at every thought of your Master's coming. Do not put it among dark prophecies or doubtful dreams. It is a clearly revealed truth that Jesus will come again and take His people up to their eternal home; "Wherefore comfort one another with these words," and be not moved away from that hope of the gospel, which lies so sweetly in the second advent of our Lord Jesus Christ.

And, once more, we have this hope—that when we have passed through all that concerns time and are in eternity, that shoreless, bottomless sea, there remains for us no fear or dread; but we shall be *"for ever with the Lord."* I notice that certain of those who deny the eternity of future punishment are ready, for the sake of their notion, to pull down the battlements of heaven itself, and to make the joy of saints to be as short as the misery of sinners. I, for one, will not pawn heaven in that fashion, to make sin cheap for the wilfully impenitent. Once landed on that eternal shore, there are no storms to dread or hurricanes to fear for these frail barks of ours. There shall not a wave of trouble roll across our peaceful spirits when once we cast anchor in the "Fair Havens," in the port of peace for ever. Be not dismayed as though there would be an after-probation, or a purgatory, or a *limbus patrum*, or any of those pretty places that have filled priests' pockets so long, and are now being newly vamped and produced by our proud thinkers as an aid to their pretty speculations. We will have no purgatory under any form, it is the larder of priests, and the refuge of heresy-mongers; but there is not a word of it in God's book. We stand to the text—"So shall we be for ever with the Lord." "The righteous shall go away into life eternal." There is "an inheritance incorruptible, and undefiled, and that fadeth not away, reserved in heaven for you." "Him that overcometh will I make a pillar in the temple of My God, and he shall go no more out: and I will write upon him the name of My God, and the name of the city of My God, which is New Jerusalem, which cometh down out of heaven from My God: and I will write upon him My new name." "They shall hunger no more, neither thirst any more; neither shall the sun light on them, nor any heat. For the Lamb which is in the midst of the throne shall feed them, and shall lead them unto living fountains of waters: and God shall wipe away all tears from their eyes." "Be not moved away from the hope of the gospel," as to the objects of that hope.

II. But now, secondly, I charge you, beloved, before God, that ye BE NOT MOVED AWAY FROM THE HOPE OF THE GOSPEL AS TO THE GROUND OF THAT HOPE. And what is the ground of that hope?

The ground of that hope is, first, *the rich, free, sovereign grace of God*, because He has said, "I will have mercy on whom I will have mercy, and I will have compassion on whom I will have compassion." The Lord claims for Himself the prerogative of mercy, and as He can exercise it without the violation of His justice through the atoning sacrifice of Christ, we joy and rejoice in the fact that men are not saved because of any natural goodness of disposition, or because of anything that they have done, or ever shall do. The children being not yet born, neither having done good nor evil, the divine decree stood fast fixed in the sovereign will and immutable counsels of Jehovah, and it is a good ground of hope for the very chief of sinners. If He has saved the dying thief,—if He has saved the adulterer,—if He has saved even the murderer, why should He not save me? He can if He will, and He is exceeding gracious, and infinite in compassion, willing not the death of any, but that all should come to repentance. It is in the mercy of our God that all our hopes begin, and the cause of that mercy is itself. The reason of divine love is divine love. Because God is gracious therefore He bestows His grace upon the undeserving and the lost. Be not moved away from this.

The ground of our salvation is, next, *the merit of Christ*—what Christ is—what Christ has done—what Christ has suffered. This is the ground upon which God saves the sons of men. Even Cardinal Bellarmin, the mighty opponent of Luther—perhaps the best opponent that he had, whose eyes saw much of gospel light, once said this, that albeit that good works are necessary unto salvation, yet, inasmuch as no man can be sure that he has performed as many good works as will save him, it is, upon the whole, safest to trust alone in the merits and sufferings of Christ. Cardinal! the safest way suits me. If that be the best and safest, what better do any of us want? Where is the rest for our soul if the ground of our hope is to be what we are, or what we do, or what we feel? But when we fall back upon the finished work of Jesus Christ and believe in Him whom God has set forth to be a propitiation for sin, and not for ours only, but for the sins of the whole world,—I say, when we fall back on Him, then we have something solid to rest upon. Our eyes cannot bear to look into eternity so long as we cling in the least degree to human merit; but when it is all put aside, and we look to Him bleeding yonder on the cross, then is there a "peace that passeth all understanding," filling our hearts by Christ Jesus. Brethren, if a man were to live in good works without a single sin for ten thousand years, he would be well recompensed for that by half-and-hour of heaven. How, then, can we expect to merit eternal bliss by any works of ours? Ah, no; the hope were vanity. Heaven is too precious a thing to be purchased by anything that we can by any possibility do; but it is not too great to be purchased by the blood of Christ; and when we come to His atonement our anchor holds abidingly. "Be not moved away from the hope of the gospel."

Another ground of our hope is this,—that *God has solemnly pledged* that "whosoever believeth in Christ shall not perish, but shall have everlasting life." If, then, we do really and in very deed believe in Jesus Christ and rest on Him, we cannot perish, for God cannot contradict Himself. Thus it is written: hear it and accept it,—"He that believeth and is baptized shall be saved." Those of us, then, who do trust the Saviour, and Him only, and have made confession of that trust in His own appointed way, know of a surety that God's eternal veracity is staked upon our salvation. It is not possible that the Lord should cast away a believer. Is it not written, "The just shall live by faith"? We live because we believe in the ever living One. "He that believeth in Him hath everlasting life." Be not moved away from this gospel hope, which God that cannot lie has set before us.

"The covenant of the King of kings
Shall stand for ever sure;
Beneath the shadow of His wings
His saints repose secure."

Another ground of our hope is *the immutability of God.* God changes not, and therefore the sons of Jacob are not consumed. The immutability of Christ also confirms our hope; for He is "the same yesterday, and to-day, and for ever." The unchanging power of His blood is a tower of strength to our faith.

"Dear dying Lamb, Thy precious blood
Shall never lose its power,
Till all the ransomed Church of God
Be saved to sin no more."

If God be immutable, then those that believe in Him have an immutable hope: be sure that you never cast it away.

But, once again, our hope of the gospel is grounded in *the infallibility of Scripture.* The Papist has an infallible pope, but we have an infallible Bible. If that which is spoken in this Book be not true, neither is our hope sure. If these things be questionable, our confidence is questionable; but if this word of God abides fast for ever and ever, though heaven and earth should pass away, then he that believes and builds on this infallible truth may rejoice and stand fast. I beseech you, "be not moved away from the hope of the gospel."

III. So far have I come with all my heart and soul, and I believe that you, dear friends, the members of this church at any rate, have accompanied me therein. Now let us consider HOW WE MAY BE MOVED AWAY FROM THE HOPE OF THE GOSPEL unless grace be given to prevent us.

We may be moved from the hope of the gospel in the following ways. Sometimes by *a conceit of ourselves.* You may get off the ground of confidence in free grace to think, "Now I am somebody. Have not I prayed at the prayer-meeting? Did not friends say that they were edified by it? Have not I preached a wonderful sermon? Am I not generous? Have not I given large sums to the church and to the poor? Am I not somebody?" Ah! you and the devil together can make a fine tale about that, and I have no doubt that he tells you you will very greedily suck in, for we like to be praised, and, though the praise comes from Satan himself, it is welcome to our proud flesh. Well, whenever we get to think we are somebody, we are moved away from the hope of the gospel. Jesus Christ came into the world to save sinners. Somebody says, "But I am not one." Ah! then He did not come to save you. "Do you say I was a sinner once, but I have grown so perfect that I do not sin now." Don't you? Then you are removed from that hope which belongs to those who confess and lament their sins. You un-Christianize yourself as soon as you strike your name out of the list of sinners who are saved by the Saviour's grace. You are a sinner and Christ died to save you, but do not be moved away from the hope of the gospel by a vain notion that you are no longer sinful. Christ came not to heal the whole, but those who are sick.

Do not be moved away, on the other hand, by *despondency.* Satan does not mind which way you get off the rock, whether it is by jumping up or by jumping down. It is all the same to him, so long as you leave the rock of your salvation. Many there are that go up in a balloon of conceit, while others are ready to roll down the steeps of despondency and despair. But be not moved away from the hope of the gospel either one way or the other. The least sin ought to make you humble, but the greatest sin ought not to make you despair. If you are even now as big a sinner as any fifty men rolled into one, Christ can save you readily,—nay, has saved you if you put your trust in Him. But, on the other hand, if you presume that you are not guilty, or despairingly say, "I am guilty, but I dare not believe that He can forgive me," you are in either case moved away from the hope of the gospel. May eternal mercy keep you hourly penitent and believing; for repentance and faith walk on either side of a Christian till he enters the pearly gate.

You may be moved away from the hope of the gospel also by *false teaching*. If, for instance, you do not believe Christ to be "Light of light, very God of very God," you have moved away from our hope, which depends upon His Godhead. If you think that the priest can save you, you are moved away from the one only Priest before whom all other priests must let their censers die out into blackness. He alone can save you. If you listen to any teaching which puts your working or your doing into the place of Christ, you are drinking in error, and you will be removed from the hope of your calling, which is free grace, received by faith, which is in Christ Jesus our Lord.

You can be removed from the hope of your calling by *hoping to live by feelings*. Ah! there are many Christians who get tempted that way. They feel so happy, and that is the reason why they believe that they are saved. That is not the reason why I believe I am saved. I am saved because I trust Christ, and if I were as miserable as misery itself I should be just as truly saved as if I were as happy as heaven itself. It is faith that does it, not feeling. Faith is precious, feeling is fickle. Believing, we stand firm, but by feeling we are tossed about. True feeling follows faith, and as such is valuable; but faith is the root, and the life of the tree lies there, and not in the boughs and leaves, which may be taken away, and yet the tree will survive. Some have very joyous feelings; they swim in trances and deliriums, and yet they are all wrong. Rest you on Christ, whether it is bright day or dark night with you: though He slay you, trust in Him,—as much trust in Him as if He pressed you to His bosom. Faith must abide, though joy depart. If your feelings are down in the dust,— if you feel as though you could not hold up your head or look towards heaven, never mind that, but cling to the promise, feel what you may. Believe in the Lord Jesus Christ, who came into the world to save sinners, and good feelings will follow by-and-by; but, just now, your first business is this—"He that believeth in Him is not condemned." "He that believeth in Him hath everlasting life." Stand you to that hope of the gospel.

Many are moved away from the hope of their calling by *a dazzle of intellect*. They are content simply to believe in Jesus till they meet some fine man, a thinker with a big forehead and a large box which ought to be full of brains. We have not been inside to see what is there, but the preacher talks much of his thought and culture. He tells you that you are behind the age,—that a faith which believes God might do very well for the times of Cromwell and the roundhead Puritans, but that, nowadays, we are far in advance of all that kind of thing. Whenever a brother dazzles you like that, let him dazzle. Let him shine as much as he likes; but, as for you, tell him that he who has once looked the sun in the face is not to be dazzled by a glow-worm. Go back to your bank, and dazzle your brother worms, but you

cannot dazzle me! A man who once has come to know Christ experimentally, and lives by faith upon the Son of God, may, if he likes, read all your essays and reviews, and all the articles in your quarterlies which ridicule the power of faith whether in living or in dying, and he will say when he has read them all through, "This is all they know about it." I daresay that if a horse were to write a book he would tell us that roast beef is exceedingly bad food to eat. "Well," we should say, "that is a very natural opinion for a horse. Let him keep to his oats and his hay." And when a man says that there is no power in prayer, he shows that he does not know anything about praying. Let him keep to what he does know and hold his tongue about what he does not know. He says that it cannot be so. "Ah," say we, "but it is so"; and when we have tasted and handled it and known it, there is no dazzling us out of it by a sense of the great man's superiority of mind. I have often thought that those who cry up their own learning must have wonderfully little of it, for I have jotted down in my pocket-book that I never saw the Bank of England send its bullion anywhere with a number of bells upon the cart to say, "Here is bullion coming along." But I have noticed that every dustman does that. When I hear the bells ringing so much about "culture," I say to myself, "Dust oh!" If they had real diamonds on board they would hold their tongues about them. At any rate, dust or diamonds, the load in these men's carts is nothing to us, we have a more sure word of testimony to which our experience has set its seal. We have believed in Christ Jesus and found salvation, and by God's grace we will not be moved away from the hope of our calling.

Lastly, be not moved away by *persecution*, or by *sneers*, or by *ridicule*. The persecution of this present day is a small thing compared with what our forefathers suffered. Look at that picture of the amphitheatre by Doré. All is over. Every seat is empty. The stars, like the eyes of God, are looking down upon the arena. There lie the bodies of the saints, and there are the tigers and the lions prowling over the sanded floor, tearing the carcases which they have slain. But the painter pictures a vision of angels, descending from over the uttermost parapet of the amphitheatre; they are tenderly watching over those precious bodies for they have triumphed, and from the mouths of the beasts they have gone to the thrones of the angels. Only hold you fast where the saints held fast at the first, "in nothing terrified by your adversaries." No more mind the advance of learning than they dreaded the universality of ignorance. We have to fight with both the ignorance of this world and the wisdom of it, too; "But the foolishness of God is wiser than man, and the weakness of God is stronger than man." How readily shall the divine wisdom and power make an end of learned babblings. Be not moved away from the hope of your calling. "Cast not away your confidence," which hath great recompense of reward. Be like the Grecian youth who took his shield to battle, let it be your glory and your defence. We would say to you what the Spartan mother said to her son: "Come back with your shield, or on it." Come back with the gospel with it strapped upon your arm like a golden shield, or, if you die, may it become your bier, and may you be borne home upon it as a steadfast believer in Christ; but never be moved away from the hope of your calling, for so would your shield be vilely cast away.

III. Lastly, WHY IS IT THAT WE CANNOT BE MOVED

AWAY FROM THE HOPE OF THE GOSPEL? What would follow if we were?

Well, first, we will not be moved away from the hope of our calling, for *there is nothing better to take its place*. A man would not think of going to Australia if he heard that the wages were less there than here, and the expense of living greater, and that the people were poorer. "No," he would say, "I shall not jump out of the frying-pan into the fire. I shall certainly stop where I am rather than go farther and fare worse." Well, we are just of that mind. We do not see how we could improve ourselves. Jonathan Edwards, in one of his treatises, speaks somewhat to this effect: "If any man can prove this form of the gospel to be untrue and a mere dream, the very best thing that he can do is to sit down and weep for ever to think that he has disproved the brightest hope that ever shone upon the eyes of men." And that is so. To have the glorious hope that, believing in Christ, we are saved, is such a blessedness and such a joy that nothing can compare with it. Where are the fields that can tempt away the sheep of Christ? Where is the shepherd that can vie with Him? Where is the light that is brighter than this eternal sun? Oh! ye tempt us with your rattles like children, but having become men we despise them. What have you to offer of truth, of hope, of comfort, of joy, equal to what we possess? Let us each one sing our answer to the tempter,—

"Thou only Sovereign of my heart,
   My refuge, my almighty Friend,
And can my soul from Thee depart,
   On whom alone my hopes depend?

"Let earth's alluring joys combine,
   While Thou art near, in vain they call;
One smile, one blissful smile of Thine,
   My dearest Lord, outweighs them all.

"Thy name, my inmost powers adore,
   Thou art my life, my joy, my care;
Depart from Thee! 'tis death—'tis more,
   'Tis endless ruin, deep despair!"

Remember, too, that if we are moved away from the hope of our calling *we shall soon be in bondage*. A man may be as merry as a lark if he believes in Christ for salvation; but let him leave that and before long he will be as dull as an owl. What is there that can give us joy apart from Christ? Are we not bound in chains of doubt when once we leave the way of sovereign grace through believing in Christ? If we are moved away from the hope of our calling we cannot grow. A tree that is frequently moved usually dies; but growth there cannot be; and a man who begins in the spirit, and hopes to be made perfect by the flesh,—begins in free grace and then gets tagging on his own works,—begins by trusting in Christ and then makes confession to a priest,—rests in the precious blood, and then dabbles in sacraments, and hopes to find salvation there; he can never grow in grace. He is wherried about with every oar. Every tide of doctrine puts him up stream or down stream. He can make no progress. And what good can such a man do? He cannot influence others beneficially, for he teaches one thing to-day, and another to-morrow. He says that God has saved him, and the next day he doubts it. He says that the atonement is full and free, and to-morrow he says that penance is to be performed. He cannot bless others, he does not himself know the way to blessing.

Besides, if we were moved away from the hope of our calling, what mean, miserable wretches we should be, for we should have *deserted our Saviour*. I wonder where I could hide my dishonourable head if I once came here to preach to you salvation by the works of the flesh and not by the grace of God. I hope that you would hiss me from the platform, and I hope that you will so serve everybody that shall succeed me when I am gone who shall preach to you any other gospel than that ye have received. Hold fast with all your might right solemnly to the grand old faith, for if you do not, in rejecting that way of salvation you reject yourselves. What did Christ die for, if we can be saved in some other way? Why did He pour out His blood if there is a cheaper method to win the skies? Why did He go down into the depths of death-shade, if you can force your way to heaven by your own endeavours without Him? No, no: we will stand fast where we now are, resting only and alone upon Jesus Christ our Saviour.

For us to leave the plan of salvation—and with this I close—is something like a soldier entrenched in an impregnable fortress accepting an invitation to come out of it. You remember how the black monarch who had been so much run after in England, said that our soldiers ought to come out of the entrenchments. They were rats, he said, to hide behind earthworks. If they would only come out, he would destroy them; but our soldiers were wise enough not to venture into the open until the proper time. So the world, the flesh, the devil, and error say, "Come out! Come out: You talk about an infallible Scripture and an almighty Saviour, and a simple faith in Him. Come out and fight us fairly on the level." Yes, but we do not see it, and we shall never attempt it. We are like the little coney, of whom Solomon speaks. He hid himself among the rocks, and the sportsman, I have no doubt, said, "Why don't you come out, little coney? Come, and let me be your friend." But the coney, though he was feeble, was wise, and he hid himself in the rock all the more, because a stranger invited him out. Do you the same when Satan cries, "Come away and be free. Be a man. Do not be always trusting in authority." "No," say you, "I shall keep where I am." As I was riding along in the south of France one day I saw a pair of fine birds overhead. The driver called out in the French tongue, "Eagles!" Yes; and there was a man below with a gun, who was wishful to get a nearer acquaintance with the eagles, but they did not come down to oblige him. He pointed his rifle at them, but his shots did not reach half way, for the royal birds kept above. The higher air is the fit dominion for eagles. Up there is the eagle's play-ground, where he plays with the callow lightnings. Up above the smoke and clouds he dwells. Keep there, eagles! Keep there! If men can get you within range, they mean no good to you. Keep up, Christians. Keep up in the higher element, resting in Jesus Christ, and do not come down to find a perch for yourself among the trees of philosophy.

Whatever we do let us never leave the way of truth, of peace, of safety. We are going along the king's highway, and the thieves on the side of the road say, "Come off the highway: it is so dull and monotonous. Come into the woods; we will show you fair flowers, and ferny dells, and quiet caves. Come, listen to the birds that sing all day and all night too. Come quick with us." We heed you not: he that travels along the king's highway is under the king's protection; but he that wanders into the dark mountains and lonesome woods may take care of himself. We shall do as we have done—follow the way that leads from the banishment—the way of trusting in the Saviour and in Him alone.

As you hold to the faith, so may God bless and enrich you. As with simple heart you plod along the road that leads to heaven by the righteousness of the Son of God, may the Lord be with you and comfort you. But if you turn back, woe unto you! A curse will fall upon you in that day of shame and crime!

The Lord keep you that you may keep the faith. Amen.

CHRIST IN YOU

"Christ in you, the hope of glory."—Colossians i. 27.

THE gospel is the grand secret: the mystery of mysteries. It was hidden from ages and from generations, but is now made manifest to the saints. To the mass of mankind it was utterly unknown; and the chosen people, who saw something of it, only perceived it dimly through the smoke of sacrifices and the veil of types. It remained a mystery which wit could not guess nor invention unravel; and it must for ever have continued a secret had not God in His infinite mercy been pleased to reveal it by the Holy Ghost. In a still deeper sense it is even yet a hidden thing unless the Spirit of God has revealed it to us individually, for the revelation of the gospel in the word of God does not of itself instruct men unto eternal life: the light is clear enough, but it availeth nothing till the eyes are opened. Each separate individual must have Christ revealed to him and in him by the work of the Holy Ghost, or else he will remain in darkness even in the midst of gospel day. Blessed and happy are they to whom the Lord has laid open the divine secret which prophets and kings could not discover, which even angels desired to look into.

Brethren, we live in a time when the gospel is clearly revealed in the word of God, and when that word has its faithful preachers lovingly to press home its teachings, let us take care that we do not despise the mystery which has now become a household word. Let not the commonness of the blessing cause us to undervalue it. You remember how in the wilderness the Israelites fed upon angels' food until they had enjoyed it so long, so constantly, and so abundantly that in their wicked discontent they called it "light bread." I fear me that many in these times are cloyed with the gospel like those who eat too much honey. They even venture to call the heavenly word "common-place," and talk as if it were not only "the old, old story," but a stale story too. Are not many hungering after novelties, longing for things original and startling, thirsting after the spiritual dram-drinking of sensational preaching, dissatisfied with Christ crucified, though He is the bread which came down from heaven? As for us, let us keep clear of this folly, let us rest content with the old food, praying from day to day, "Lord, evermore give us this bread." May it never happen to us unto the Jews of the apostle's time, who refused utterly the word of life; so that the truth became to them a stumbling-block, and those who preached it were compelled to turn to the Gentiles. If we despise the heavenly message we cannot expect to fare better than they did: let us not incur the danger of refusing Him that speaks from heaven. If there be life, rejoice in it; if there be light, walk in it; if there be love, rest in it. If the Lord God Almighty has at length set open the treasures of His grace, and put eternal bliss within your reach, stretch out the hand of faith, and be enriched thereby. Turn not your backs upon your God, your Saviour; for in so doing you will turn your backs on eternal life and heaven. God grant that none of you may do this.

In our text we have in a few words that great mystery with which heaven did labour as in travail, that mystery which is to transform this poor world into new heavens and a new earth; we have it, I say, all in a nutshell in the seven words of our text: the riches of the glory of this mystery may here be seen set out to open view—"Christ in you, the hope of glory."

By the assistance of the divine Spirit, I shall speak upon this mystery in three ways: *The essence of it is "Christ"; the sweetness of it is "Christ in you";* and *the outlook of it is "the hope of glory."* The words read like a whole body of divinity condensed into a line,—"Christ in you, the hope of glory."

I. The eternal mystery of the gospel, THE ESSENCE OF IT IS CHRIST. I hardly know what is the antecedent to the word "which" here: whether it is "mystery," or "riches," or "glory"; and I do not greatly care to examine which it may be. Any one of the three words will be suitable, and all three will fit best of all. If it be "the mystery," Christ is that mystery: "Without controversy great is the mystery of godliness: God was manifest in the flesh." If it be the word "glory," beyond all question our Lord Jesus wears a "glory as of the Only-begotten of the Father, full of grace and truth." Is He not "the brightness of the Father's glory"? If we take the word "riches," ye have often heard of "the unsearchable riches of Christ," for in Him dwelleth all the fulness of the Godhead bodily. Oh, the riches of the grace of God which it hath pleased the Father to impart unto us in Christ Jesus! Christ is the "mystery," the "riches," and the "glory." He is all this; and blessed be His name, He is all this among us poor Gentiles who at first were like dogs, scarce accounted worthy to eat the crumbs from under the children's table, and yet we are now admitted into the children's place, and made heirs of God, joint-heirs with Christ Jesus. Riches of glory among the Gentiles would have sounded like a mockery in the first ages, and yet the language is most proper at this day, for all things are ours in Christ Jesus the Lord.

The essence of this mystery is *Christ Himself.* In these days certain would-be-wise men are laboriously attempting to constitute a church without Christ, and to set forth a salvation without a Saviour; but their Babel building is as a bowing wall and a tottering fence. The centre of the blessed mystery of the gospel is *Christ Himself in His person.* What a wonderful conception it was that ever the infinite God should take upon Himself the nature of man! It never would have occurred to men that such a condescension would be thought of. Even now that it has been done it is a great mystery of our faith. God and man in one person is the wonder of heaven, and earth, and hell. Well might David exclaim, "What is man, that Thou art mindful of him? and the son of man, that Thou visitest him?" The first thought of the incarnation was born in the unsearchably wise mind of God. It needed omnipotent omniscience to suggest the idea of "Immanuel, God with us." Think of it! The Infinite an infant, the Ancient of days a child, the Ever Blessed a man of sorrows and acquainted with grief! The idea is original, astounding, divine. Oh, that this blending of the two natures should ever have taken place! Brethren, the heart of the gospel throbs in this truth. The Son of the Highest was born at Bethlehem, and at His birth, ere He had wrought a deed of righteousness or shed a drop of blood, the angels sang, "Glory to God in the highest, on earth peace, good will toward men," for they knew that the incarnation had within itself a wealth of good things for men. When the Lord Himself took our manhood it meant inconceivable benediction to the human race. "Unto us a child is born, unto us a son is given," and in that child and son we find our salvation. God in our nature can mean for us nothing but joy. How favoured is our race in this respect! What other creature did the Lord thus espouse? We know that He took not up angels, but He took up the seed of Abraham; He took upon Him human nature, and now the next being in the universe to God is man. He who was made a little lower than the angels for the suffering of death is this day crowned with glory and honour, and made to have dominion over all the works of Jehovah's hands. This is the gospel indeed. Do not sinners begin to hope? Is there one in your nature who is "Light of lights, very God of very God," and do you not perceive that this must mean good to you? Does not the "word made flesh" dwelling among men arouse hope in your bosoms, and lead you to believe that you may yet be saved? Certainly, the fact of there being such an union between God and man is the delight of every regenerated mind.

Our Lord's person is at this day constituted in the same manner. He is still God and man; still He can sympathize with our manhood to the full, for He is bone of our bone and flesh of our flesh; and yet He can help us without limit, seeing He is equal with the Father. Though manifestly divine, yet Jesus is none the less human; though truly man, He is none the less divine; and this is a door of hope to us, a fountain of consolation which never ceases to flow.

When we think of our Lord we remember with His person *the glorious work which He undertook and finished on our behalf.* Being found in fashion as man He humbled Himself and became obedient unto death, even the death of the cross. He took upon Himself the form of a servant, and was made in the likeness of sinful flesh, because we had failed in our service, and could not be saved unless another did suit and service on our behalf. The heir of all things girded Himself to be among us as one that serveth. What service His was! How arduous! how humble! how heavy! how all-consuming! His was a life of grief and humiliation, followed by a death of agony and scorn. Up to the cross He carried all our load,

and on the cross He bore, that we might never bear, His Father's righteous wrath. Oh, what has not Christ done for us? He has cast our sins into the depths of the sea; He has taken the cup which we ought to have drunk for ever, and He has drained it dry, and left not a dreg behind. He has redeemed us from the curse of the law, being made a curse for us; and now He has finished transgression, made an end of sin, and brought in everlasting righteousness, and gone up to His Father's throne within the veil, bearing His divine oblation, and making everything right and safe for us, that by-and-by we may follow Him, and be with Him where He is. Oh yes, brethren, Christ's person and finished work are the pillars of our hope. I cannot think of what He is, and what He has done, and what He is doing, and what He will yet do, without saying, "He is all my salvation and all my desire."

My brethren, every one of *our Lord's offices* is a well-spring of comfort. Is He prophet, priest, and king? Is He friend? Is He brother? Is He husband? Is He head? Every way and everywhere we lean the weight of our soul's great business upon Him, and He is our all in all. Besides, there is this sweet thought, that He is *our representative.* Know ye not that of old He was our covenant head, and stood for us in the great transactions of eternity? Like as the first Adam headed up the race, and stood for us —alas, I must correct myself—*fell* for us, and we fell in him; so now hath the second Adam taken up within Himself all His people and stood for them, and kept for them the covenant, so that now it is ordered in all things and sure, and every blessing of it is infallibly secured to all the seed. Believers must and shall possess the covenanted inheritance because Jesus represents them, and on their behalf have taken possession of the estate of God. Whatever Christ is His people are in Him. They were crucified in Him, they were dead in Him, they were buried in Him, they are risen in Him; in Him they live eternally, in Him they sit gloriously at the right hand of God, "who has raised us up together, and made us sit together in the heavenly places in Christ Jesus." In Him we are "accepted in the Beloved," both now and for ever; and this, I say, is the essence of the whole gospel. He that preaches Christ preaches the gospel; he who does not preach Christ, preaches no gospel. It is no more possible for there to be a gospel without Christ than a day without the sun, or a river without water, or a living man without a head, or a quickened human body without a soul. No, Christ Himself is the life, soul, substance, and essence of the mystery of the gospel of God.

Christ Himself, again I say, and no other. I have been trying to think what we should do if our Lord were gone. Suppose that a man has heard of a great physician who understands his complaint. He has travelled a great many miles to see this celebrated doctor; but when he gets to the door they tell him that he is out. "Well," says he, "then I must wait till he is in." "You need not wait," they reply, "his assistant is at home." The suffering man, who has been often disappointed, answers, "I do not care about his assistant, I want to see the man himself: mine is a desperate case, but I have heard that this physician has cured the like; I must, therefore, see *him.* No assistants for me." "Well," say that, "he is out; but there are his books: you can see his books." "Thank you," he says, "I cannot be content with his books I want the living man and nothing less. It is to him that I must speak, and from him I will receive instructions." "Do you see that cabinet?" "Yes." "It is full of his medicines." The sick man answers, "I dare say they are very good, but they are of no use to me without the doctor: I want their owner to prescribe for me, or I shall die of my disease." "But see," cries one, "here is a person who has been cured by him, a man of great experience, who has been present at many remarkable operations. Go into the inquiry-room with him, and he will tell you all about the mode of cure." The afflicted man answers, "I am much obliged to you, but all your talk only makes me long the more to see the doctor. I came to see *him*, and I am not going to be put off with anything else. I must see the man himself, for myself. He has made my disease a speciality; he knows how to handle my case, and I will stop till I see *him*." Now, dear friends, if you are seeking Christ, imitate this sick man, or else you will miss the mark altogether. Never be put off with books, or conversations. Be not content with Christian people talking to you, or preachers preaching to you, or the Bible being read to you, or prayers being offered for you. Anything short of Jesus will leave you short of salvation. You have to reach Christ, and touch Christ, and nothing short of this will serve your turn. Picture the case of the prodigal son when he went home. Suppose when he reached the house the elder brother had come to meet him. I must make a supposition that the elder brother had sweetened himself, and made himself amiable; and then I hear him say, "Come in, brother; welcome home!" But I see the returning one stand there with the tears in his eyes, and I hear him lament, "I want to see my father. I must tell *him* that I have sinned and done evil in his sight." An old servant whispers, "Master John, I am glad to see you back. Be happy, for all the servants are rejoiced to hear the sound of your voice. It is true your father will not see you, but he has ordered the fatted calf to be killed for you; and here is the best robe, and a ring, and shoes for your feet, and we are told to put them upon you." All this would not content the poor penitent. I think I hear him cry —"I do not despise anything my father gives me, for I am not worthy to be as his hired servant; but what is all this unless I see *his* face, and know that he forgives me? There is no taste in the feast, no glitter in the ring, no fitness in the shoes, no beauty in the robe unless I can see my father and can be reconciled to him." Do you not see that in the case of the prodigal son the great matter was to get his head into his father's bosom, and there to sob out "Father, I have sinned"? The one thing needful was the kiss of free forgiveness, the touch of those dear, warm, loving lips, which said, "My dear child, I love you, and your faults are blotted out." That was the thing that gave his soul rest and perfect peace; and this is the mystery we come to preach to you—God Himself drawing near to you in Christ Jesus, and forgiving you all trespasses. We are not content to preach unless Jesus Himself be the theme. We do not set before you something about Christ, nor something that belongs to Christ, nor something procured by Christ, nor somebody that has known Christ, nor some truth which extols Christ; but we preach Christ crucified. We preach not ourselves, but Christ Jesus the Lord; and we say to you, never be content till you clasp the Saviour in your arms as Simeon did in the temple. That venerable saint did not pray to depart in peace while he only saw the child in Mary's bosom;

but when he had taken the dear one into his own arms, then he said, "Lord, now lettest Thou Thy servant depart in peace." A personal grasp of a personal Christ, even though we only know Him as an infant, fills the heart to the full; but nothing else will do it.

I go a little farther still. As it must be Christ Himself, and none other, it must also be *Christ Himself rather than anything which Christ gives*. I was thinking the other day how different Christ is from all the friends and helpers that we have. They bring us good things, but Jesus gives us Himself. He does not merely give us wisdom, righteousness, sanctification, and redemption; but He Himself is made of God all these things to us. Hence we can never do without Him. When very ill you are pleased to see the doctor; but when you are getting well you say to yourself, "I shall be glad to see the back of the good man, for that will be a sure sign that I am off the sick list." Ah, but when Jesus heals a soul he wants to see Jesus more than ever. Our longing for the constant company of our Lord is the sign that we are getting well: he who longs for Jesus to abide with him for ever is healed of his plague. We never outgrow Christ; but we grow to need Him more and more. If you eat a meal you lose your appetite, but if you feed upon Christ you hunger and thirst still more after Him. This insatiable desire after Him is not a painful hunger, but a heavenly, pleasant hunger which grows upon you the more its cravings are gratified. The man who has little of Christ can do with little of Christ; but he that gets more of Christ pines for a yet fuller supply. Suppose a wise man were to instruct you: you would learn all he had to teach and then say, "Let him go on and teach somebody else;" but when Jesus teaches we discover so much of our own ignorance that we would fain keep Him as our life-tutor. When our Lord taught the two disciples on the road to Emmaus, He opened the Scriptures and He opened their minds until their hearts burned within them. What next? Shall the divine teacher pass on? No, no; they constrain Him, saying "Abide with us: it is toward evening, and the day is far spent." The more He taught them the more they wished to be taught. This is ever the way with Christ: He is growingly dear, increasingly necessary. Oh my brothers, you cannot do without Him. If you have your foot upon the threshold of pure gold, and your finger on the latch of the gate of pearl, you now need Christ more than ever you did. I feel persuaded that you are of Rutherford's mind, when he cried to have his heart enlarged till it was as big as heaven, that he might hold all Christ within it; and then he felt that even this was too narrow a space for the boundless love of Jesus, since the heaven of heavens cannot contain Him, and so he cried out for a heart as large as seven heavens, that he might entertain the Well-beloved. Truly, I am content with what God has given me in all points, save that I long for more of Christ. I could sit down happy if I knew that my portion in the house and in the field would never grow; but I am famished to have more of my Lord. The more we are filled with Christ, the more we feel our own natural emptiness: the more we know of Him, the more we long to know Him. Paul, writing to the Philippians, when he had been a Christian for many a year, yet says, "That I may know Him." Oh, Paul, do you not know Christ yet? "Yes," says he, and "No": for he knew the love of Christ, but felt that it surpassed all knowledge. "All the rivers run into the sea, yet the sea is not full": this is not our case in one respect, and yet it is in another, for all the streams of grace and love and blessedness flow into our souls, and we are full; yet, being full, we are longing for more. Not Thy gifts, Lord, but Thyself: Thou art the desire of our hearts.

Christ alone is enough. Mark this. Nothing must be placed with Christ as if it were necessary to Him. Some hold a candle to the sun by preaching Christ and man's philosophy, or their own priestcraft. When the blessed rain comes fresh from heaven they would fain perfume it with their own dainty extract of fancy. As for God's blessed air fresh from the eternal hills, the dream that it cannot be right unless by scientific experiments they load it with their own smoke and cloud. Come, clear out, let us see the sun! We want not your rushlights. Away with your gauzes and your fineries, let the clear sunlight enter! Let the holy water drop from heaven; we want not your scented essences. Out of the way, and let the fresh air blow about us. There is nothing like it for the health and strength of the soul. We rejoice in Christ and nothing else but Christ: Christ and no priestcraft; Christ and no philosophy; Christ and no modern thought; Christ and no human perfection. Christ, the whole of Christ, and nothing else but Christ: here lies the mystery of the gospel of the grace of God.

Brethren, what else but Christ can satisfy the justice of God? Look around you when a sense of sin is on you, and the dread tribunal is before your eyes: what can you bring by way of expiation but Christ? What can you bring with Christ? What dare you associate with His blood and merits? Oh, my God, nothing will content Thee but Thy Son, Thy Son alone. What else can quiet conscience? Some professors have consciences as good as new, for they have never been used; but he that has once had his conscience thoroughly exercised and pressed upon with all the weight of sin till he has felt as if it were better for him not to be than to be guilty before God—that man acknowledges that nothing but Christ will ever quiet his agonized heart. See the bleeding Lamb, and you will be pacified! See the exalted Lord pleading His righteousness before the throne; and conscience is even as a weaned child; and all the storm within the spirit is hushed into a great calm. What else will do to live with but Christ? I do not find in times of pain and depression of spirit that I can keep up upon anything but my Lord. The mind can feed at other times on pretty kickshaws and fine confectionary such a certain divines serve out in the form of orations and essays, and the like; but when you are sore sick your soul abhors all manner of earthly meat, and nothing will stay on the stomach but the bread of heaven, even the blessed Christ of God. Think also, when you come to die, what else will do but Christ? Oh, I have seen men die with heaven in their eyes, the eternal Godhead seeming to transfigure them, because they rejoiced in Christ; but a death-bed without Christ, it is the darkening twilight of eternal night: it is the gloomy cave which forms the entrance of the land of darkness. Do not venture on life or death without Jesus, I implore you. "None but Christ, none but Christ," this has been the martyr's cry amidst the fire; let it be ours in life and death.

II. Secondly, we are to consider THE SWEETNESS OF THIS MYSTERY, WHICH IS CHRIST IN YOU. This is a grand advance. I know that there are a great many fishermen here this morning, and I heartily welcome them. When you are out at sea you like to know that there are plenty of fish in the sea all round your boats. It is a fine thing to get in among the great shoals of fish. Yes, but there is one thing better than that. Fish in the sea are good; but the fish in the boat are the fish for you. Once get them in the net, or better still, safe into the vessel, and you are glad. Now Christ in heaven, Christ free to poor sinners is precious, but Christ here in the heart is most precious of all. Here is the marrow and fatness. Christ on board the vessel brings safety and calm. Christ in your house, Christ in your heart, *Christ in you;* that is the cream of the matter, the honey of the honeycomb. Gold is valuable, but men think more of a pound in their pockets than of huge ingots in the Bank-cellar. A loaf of bread is a fine thing, but if we could not eat it, and so get it within us, we might die of starvation. A medicine may be a noble cure, but if it is always kept in the phial, and we never take a draught from it, what good will it do us? Christ is best known when He is Christ *in you.* Let us talk about that a little.

Christ in you—that is, first, *Christ accepted by faith.* Is it not a wonderful thing that Christ Jesus should ever enter into a man? Yes, but I will tell you something more wonderful, and that is, that He should enter in by so narrow an opening as our little faith. There is the sun; I do not know how many thousands of times the sun is bigger than the earth, and yet the sun can come into a little room or a close cell; and what is more, the sun can get in through a chink. When the shutters have been closed I have known him come in through a little round hole in them. So Christ can come in through a little faith —a mere chink of confidence. If you are such a poor believer that you can hardly think of assurance or confidence, yet if you do trust the Lord, as surely as the sun comes in by a narrow crack, so will Christ come into your soul by the smallest opening of true faith. How wise it will be on your part when you see your Lord's sunny face shining through the lattices to say, "I am not going to be satisfied with these mere glints and gleams, I would fain walk in the light of His countenance. Pull up those blinds; let the heavenly sun shine in, and let me rejoice in its glory." Grow in faith, and enlarge your receiving power till you take in Christ, into your inmost soul by the Holy Spirit; for it is Christ in you by faith that becomes the hope of glory.

By Christ in you we mean *Christ possessed.* You see nothing is so much a man's own as that which is within him. Do you tell me that a certain slice of bread is not mine, and that I have no right to it? But I have eaten it, and you may bring a lawsuit against me about that bread if you like, but you cannot get it away from me. That question is settled; that which I have eaten is mine. In this case possession is not only nine points of the law, but all the points. When a man gets Christ into him, the devil himself cannot win a suit against him to recover Christ; for that matter is settled beyond question. Christ in you is yours indeed. Men may question whether an acre of land or a house belongs to me; but the meat I ate yesterday is not a case of property which Chancery or any other court can alter. So, when the believer has Christ in him, the law has no more to say. The enclosure made by faith carries its own title-deeds with it.

It means, too, *Christ experienced* in all His power.

There may be a valuable medicine that works like magic to expel a man's pains, and cure his dieases; but it is of no efficacy till it is within him! When it commences to purify his blood, and to strengthen his frame, he is in a fair way to know it without depending upon the witness of others. Get Christ in you, curing your sin, Christ in you filling your soul with love to virtue and holiness, bathing your heart in comfort and firing it with heavenly aspirations,—then will you know the Lord. Christ believed in, Christ possessed, Christ experienced, Christ in you, this is worth a world.

Moreover, Christ in us is *Christ reigning*. It reminds me of Mr. Bunyan's picture of Mansoul, when the Prince Immanuel laid siege to it, and Diabolus from within the city tried to keep him out. It was a hard time for Mansoul then; but when at last the battering rams had broken down the gates, and the silver trumpets sounded, and the prince's captains entered the breach, then on a day the prince himself did ride down the city's streets, while liberated citizens welcomed him with all their hearts, hung out all their streamers, and made the church towers rock again as the bells rang out merry peals, for the king himself was come. Up to the castle of the heart he rode in triumph, and took his royal throne to be henceforth the sole lord and king of the city. Christ in you is a right royal word. Christ swaying His sceptre from the centre of your being, over every power and faculty, desire and resolve, bringing every thought into captivity to Himself, oh, this is glory begun, and the sure pledge of heaven. Oh for more of the imperial sovereignty of Jesus! it is our liberty to be absolutely under His sway.

Yes, and then Christ in you is *Christ filling you*. It is wonderful when Christ once enters into a soul, how by degrees He occupies the whole of it. Did you ever hear the legend of a man whose garden produced nothing else but weeds, till at last he met with a strange foreign flower of singular vitality. The story is that he sowed a handful of this seed in his overgrown garden, and left it to work its own sweet way. He slept and rose, and knew not how the seed was growing till on a day he opened the gate and saw a sight which much astounded him. He knew that the seed would produce a dainty flower and he looked for it; but he had little dreamed that the plant would cover the whole garden. So it was: the flower had exterminated every weed, till as he looked from one end to the other from wall to wall he could see nothing but the fair colours of that rare plant, and smell nothing but its delicious perfume. Christ is that plant of renown. If He be sown in the soil of your soul, He will gradually eat out the roots of all ill weeds and poisonous plants, till over all your nature there shall be Christ in you. God grant we may realize the picture in our own hearts, and then we shall be in Paradise.

It may sound strange to add that Christ in you *transfigures the man till he becomes like Christ Himself*. You thrust a bar of cold, black iron into the fire, and keep it there till the fire enters into it. See, the iron is like fire itself—he that feels it will know no difference. The fire has permeated the iron, and made it a fiery mass. I should like to have seen that bush in Horeb before which Moses put off his shoes. When it was all ablaze it seemed no longer a bush, but a mass of fire, a furnace of pure flame. The fire had transfigured the bush. So it is with us when Christ enters into us: He elevates us to a nobler state; even, as Paul saith "I live, yet not I, but Christ lives in me." Jesus sanctifies us wholly, spirit, soul, and body, and takes us to dwell with Him in the perfect state above.

Christ in you,—how can I explain it? We are the little graft and He is the strong and living stem. We are laid to Him, bound to Him, sealed to Him, and when there is nothing between the new shoot and the old tree, at last the sap flows into the graft, and the graft and the tree are one. Ye know right well how Christ enters into us and becomes our life.

Christ in you means power in you. A strong man armed keeps his house till a stronger than he comes, and when the stronger enters the first tenant is ejected by the power of the new comer, and kept out by the same means. We were without strength till Christ came, and now we war with principalities and powers, and win the victory.

Christ in you! Oh, what blisss! what joy! The Bridegroom is with us, and we cannot fast: the King is with us, and we are glad. When King Charles went to live at Newmarket it is said that a most poverty-stricken village became a wealthy place, truly when Christ comes to dwell in our hearts our spiritual poverty suddenly turns to blessed wealth.

Christ in you! What a wonder it is that He should deign to come under our roof! Lift up your heads, O ye gates, and be ye lifted up, ye everlasting doors, that the King of glory may come in. See the honour which His entrance brings with it! He glorifies the place where His foot rests even for a moment. If Jesus doth but enter into your heart, His court comes with Him: honour, and glory, and immortality, and heaven, and all other divine things follow where He leads.

"Oh, says one, " I wish He would come and dwell in me." Then, be humble, for He loves to dwell with him that is humble and of a contrite spirit. Next, be clean; for if they must be clean that bear God's vessels, much more they that have Christ Himself in them. Next, be empty; for Christ will not live amid the lumber of self, and pride, and carnal sufficiency. Learn abundantly to rejoice in Christ, for he who welcomes Christ will have Him always for a guest. Jesus never tarries where He is not desired. If His welcome is worn out, away He goes. Oh, desire and delight in Him; hunger and thirst after Him; for Christ delights to dwell with an eager people, a hungry people, a people who value Him, and cannot be happy without Him.

Surely I have said enough to make you feel that the sweetness of true godliness lies in having Christ in you.

III. Thirdly, we are to consider that THE OUTLOOK OF ALL THIS IS "CHRIST IN YOU THE HOPE OF GLORY." Last Sunday morning, as best I could in my feebleness, I spoke to you about the time when this earthly house of our tabernacle shall be dissolved, when we shall find that we have a building of God, a house not made with hands, eternal in the heavens; but this morning's text goes a little farther: it speaks of glory, which is a hope for soul as well as body. Why glory! Glory? Surely that belongs to God only. To Him alone be glory. Yes, but Christ has said, "Father, I will that they also whom Thou hast given Me be with Me where I am, that they may behold My glory"; and He also says, "And the glory which Thou hast given Me I have given them." Think of it. Glory for us poor creatures! Glory for you, sister; glory for me! It seems a strange thing that a sinner should ever have anything to do with glory when he deserves nothing but shame. We are neither kings nor princes, what have we to do with glory? Yet glory is to be our dwelling, glory our light, glory our crown, glory our song. The Lord will not be content to give us less than glory. Grace is very sweet: might we not be content to swim for ever in a sea of grace? But no, our Lord "will give grace and glory."

> "All needful grace will God bestow,
> And crown that grace with glory too."

We shall have glorified bodies, glorious companions, a glorious reward, and glorious rest.

But how know we that we shall have glory Why, first, He that has come to live in our hearts, and reigns as our bosom's Lord, makes us glorious by His coming. His rest is glorious: the place of His feet is glorious. He must mean some great thing towards us, or He would never dwell in us. I saw a fine carriage stopping the other day at a very humble hovel; and I thought to myself, "that carriage is not stopping there to collect rent, or to borrow a broom." Oh, no; that lady yonder is calling round and visiting the poor, and I doubt not she has taken in some nourishment to an invalid. I hope it was so: and I am sure my Lord Jesus Christ's carriage never stops at my door to get anything out of me: whenever He comes He brings countless blessings with Him. Such a one as He is, God over all, blessed for ever, it cannot be that He took our nature, unless with high designs of love unsearchable. Thus we nourish large expectations upon the food of solid reason. I am sure our Lord Jesus would never have done so much if He had not meant to manifest the immeasurable breadth and length of a love which is beyond imagining. What He has done already surprises me even to amazement. I think nothing can appear strange or hard to believe, let Him do what He may in the future. If the Scriptures tell me my Lord is going to fill me with His own glory, and to set me at His own right hand, I can believe it. He who went to the cross for me will never be ashamed of me: He who gave me Himself will give me all heaven and more: He that opened His very heart to find blood and water to wash me in, how shall He keep back even His kingdom from me? O sweet Lord Jesus, thou art indeed to us the hope, the pledge, the guarantee of glory. Friend, do you not feel that Christ in you is the dawn of heaven?

Besides this, Christ is He that has entered into covenant with God to bring His people home to glory; He has pledged Himself to bring every sheep of His flock safe to His Father's right hand, and He will keep his engagement, for He never failed of one covenant promise yet.

Moreover, this we do know, that the Christ who is come to live with us will never be separated from us. If He had not meant to stop He would not have entered our heart at all. There was nothing to tempt Him to come, and if in soverign grace He deigned to live in the poor cottage of our nature, then, brethren, He knew what He was about: He had counted the cost, He had foreseen all the evil that would be in us and about us, and when He came, He came with the intent to stay. Someone asked another the other day, "What persuasion are you of?" and the answer was, "I am persuaded that neither life, nor death, nor things present, nor things to come, shall separate us from the love of God which is in Christ Jesus our Lord." Are not you of that persuasion, brother? If so, you can see how Christ in you is the hope of glory.

Why, look ye, sirs, Christ in you is glory. Did we not show that just now? "Lift up your heads, O ye gates, and be ye lifted up, ye everlasting doors, that the King of glory may come in!" You have heaven in having Christ, for Christ is the biggest part of heaven. Is not Christ the soul of heaven, and having Him you have glory? What is more, having gotten Christ, Christ's glory and your glory are wrapped up together. If Christ were to lose you, it would be a great loss to you, but a greater loss to Him. If I can perish with Christ in me, I shall certainly be a fearful loser, but so will He, for where is His honour, where His glory if a believer perishes? His glory is gone if one soul that trusts in Him is ever cast away. Wherefore comfort yourselves with this word, Christ in you means you in glory, as sure as God lives. There is no question about that. Go your ways and rejoice in Christ Jesus, and let men see who it is that lives in you. Let Jesus speak through your mouth, and weep through your eyes, and smile through your face: let Him work with your hands and walk with your feet, and be tender with your heart. Let Him seek sinners through you; let Him comfort saints through you; until the day break and the shadows flee away.

WORK IN US AND WORK BY US

"Whereunto I also labour, striving according to His working, which worketh in me mightily."—Colossians i. 29.

THE apostle Paul could very truthfully assert that he laboured and agonized. When the Holy Spirit had anointed the apostles, they all became ardent enthusiasts for the spread of the Redeemer's kingdom. Having the whole world committed to them that they might enlighten it, they laboured most ardently each one in his sphere to spread abroad the truth of the gospel; but the apostle of the Gentiles laboured more abundantly than they all. Into how many countries did he carry the testimony of Christ! How often did he cross the sea, traverse mountains, and ford rivers! One sees in his career something more than an ordinary Christian life; he was so indefatigable in service, that surely nothing beyond could have been possible to humanity, even under the help of God. His public labours were not only abundant, but they were the cause of of continual inward conflict. He never preached a sermon, wrote epistle, or attempted a work, without earnest prayer and soul-consuming zeal. Night and day with tears, he said of a certain church that he had laboured for its good. He was a man so whole hearted and intense in all that he did, that we ought to remember not merely the amount of his labours, but the way in which he wore out himself by the intensity of his zeal in them. Probably never man led a more intensely ardent life than he. Moreover, added to all this, he carried a weight of care enough to crush him; for there came upon him the care of all the churches—to plant them, to defend them against rising errors, to prevent schisms from dividing the flock, to lead on the converts from grace to grace, to instruct them, and to present every one perfect before God. The burden resting upon the apostle was greater than the cares of an empire; and then, as if to complete the whole, he was called to suffer persecution of which he has given us a list, which as we read it makes us shudder that one man should have endured so much, and makes us also glory in humanity that it should be possible that so much should be borne and done for God by a single individual.

Yet, note it well, the apostle takes no honour to himself, but humbly ascribes whatever he had done or suffered entirely to his Lord. He declares that he laboured and agonized, but he confesses that it was through the work of the Lord Jesus Christ, who mightily by the Holy Spirit wrought in him. In another place, when he had mentioned his abundant labours, he added, "Yet not I, but the grace of God which was with me." He remembered where to put the crown; he took care not to steal an atom of the glory for himself, but he ascribed all to the power of Him who loved him and gave Himself for him. Let us imitate the apostle in these two things. My brethren, let us live, while we live, a life of energy, but let us at the same time confess, when we have done all, that we are unprofitable servants; and if there be any glory and any praise resulting from the work which we achieve, let us be careful to lay it all at the Redeemer's feet.

The doctrine of the text upon which I intend to preach, this morning, as I may be enabled, is this, it is clear from what Paul has here said that the work of Christ in us and for us does not exempt us from work and service, nor does the Holy Spirit's work supersede human effort, but rather excites it. Paul speaks of an inner work, a mighty work wrought in him, but he also declares, "whereunto I also labour, striving." So that the doctrine of the work of the Holy Spirit is not intended in any degree to lull our minds into sloth, but wherever the Holy Spirit works He makes men work; He worketh in us to will and to do of His own good pleasure, that we also may work out our own salvation with fear and trembling. I shall try to illustrate this truth in the two respects, first, in reference to *a man's own salvation ;* and secondly, in the matter of *the Christian man's ministry for the salvation of others.* The work of the Holy Spirit does not supersede Christian effort in either case.

I. First, then, IN THE BELIEVER'S SALVATION.

We believe, each one of us, and we have scriptural warrant for it, that if any man be saved, the work within his soul is entirely wrought by the Holy Ghost. Man is dead in sin, and the dead cannot raise themselves from the grave. Quickening and spiritual resurrection must be accomplished by divine power. Man must be born again, and this birth must be affected by divine power, for unless a man be born from above, he cannot see the kingdom of God. As the commencement of salvation is dependent upon the Holy Spirit, so is the carrying of it on. "Without Me ye can do nothing," is Christ's testimony. We shall never persevere except as grace shall keep us from falling, nor may we hope to be presented faultless before the august presence except as the Holy Spirit shall sanctify us from day to day,

and make us meet to be partakers of the inheritance of the saints in light. I trust, my brethren, I need not do more than assert this doctrine in your hearing, since you know how continually we insist upon it, and our trumpet never gives an uncertain sound as to the great truth that God worketh all our works in us, and that salvation is of the Lord from first to last. But at this present we intend to insist upon this further truth that the working of the Holy Spirit in us does not exempt the believer from the most energetic labour, but rather necessitates his doing all that lieth in him.

To enforce this we remark, first, that *the Christian life is always described as a thing of energy.* Sometimes we read of it as a pilgrimage. That master allegorist, John Bunyan, has not pictured Christian as carried to heaven while asleep in an easy chair. He makes Christian lose his burden at the cross-foot, he ascribes the deliverance of the man from the burden of his sin entirely to the Lord Jesus, but he represents him as climbing the Hill Difficulty; ay, and on his hands and knees too, Christian has to descend into the Valley of Humiliation, and to tread that dangerous pathway through the gloomy horrors of the Shadow of Death. He has to be urgently watchful to keep himself from sleeping in the Enchanted Ground. Nowhere is he delivered from the necessities incident to the way, for even at the last he fords the black river, and struggles with its terrible billows. Effort is used all the way through, and you that are pilgrims to the skies will find it to be no allegory, but a real matter of fact; your soul must gird up her loins; you need your pilgrim's staff and armour, and you must foot it all the way to heaven, contending with giants, fighting with lions, and combating Apollyon himself.

Our life is in Scripture represented as a race which is even sterner work than pilgrimage. In such foot-races as were witnessed among the Greeks, in every case the man spent all the strength there was in him, and underwent a training beforehand, that he might be fit for the contest. It sometimes happened, and indeed not seldom, that men fell dead at the winning-post, through their extreme exertions. Running to heaven is such running as that, we are to strain every nerve. We shall require all the power we have, and more in order to win that incorruptible crown which now glitters before the eye of our faith. If we are so to run that we may obtain, we shall have no energy to spare, but shall spend it all in our heavenly course.

Not unfrequently the apostle compares our spiritual life to a boxing match, and the terms in the original Greek if they were translated into pure vernacular English, would remind us very much of a boxing ring and of the place where wrestlers strive for the mastery. To wit, in that notable passage, "I keep under my body," we are told by scholars that the Greek word alludes to the getting of the antagonist's head under the arm, and dealing it heavy blows. So the flesh must be mortified. Now the wrestlers in the Greek and Roman games strained every muscle and sinew, there was no part of the body that was not brought into action to overthrow their adversary. For this they agonized till often blood would spurt from the nostrils, and veins would burst. Such a spiritual sense must be the agony of a Christian if he is to overcome temptation, and subdue the power of sin. Ah brethren! it is no child's play to win heaven. Saved, as I repeat it, through the power of Christ's blood and with the energy of His Holy Spirit within us, yet we have no time to loiter, no space in which to trifle; we must labour, striving according to His working who worketh in us mightily. All the figures which represent the Christian life imply the most energetic exertion.

Secondly, be it remarked *that there is no illustration used in Scripture to set forth the heavenly life, which allows the supposition that in any case heaven is won by sloth.* I do not remember ever finding in Scripture the life of the Christian described as a slumber. To the sluggard I find a warning always; thorns and thistles in his garden, and rags and disease in his person. "The hand of the diligent maketh rich." There may be occasional opportunities by which even idle men may become wealthy, but such spiritual wealth I have never heard of. I find that wherever the Spirit of God comes upon men, He never leaves a saved man effortless or fruitless, but as soon as He descends upon him, according to his capacity he begins to work out his own salvation. Remember the question of the inspired writer, "Likewise also was not Rahab the harlot justified by works, when she had received the messengers, and had sent them out another way?" Her faith saved her; and though it was very weak and very ignorant faith, it made her work, and therefore she hid the spies to save their lives. Look at the dying thief, with his hands and feet fastened to the wood, and ready to expire, yet he rebuked the reviling malefactor, thus doing all he possibly could for his Lord, in whom he trusted for salvation, what more could he have done? It may be said of him, "He hath done what he could." It shall be well if as much can be said for us. No brethren, you cannot be carried to heaven on "flowery beds of ease." You must fight if you would reign, you must stem the flood, you must breast the waves if you mean to reach the further shore. Grace will help you, else were the work an impossibility; but even with the aid of grace you are not permitted to slumber into glory, nor sleep your way to the celestial throne. You must be up and doing, watching diligently, lest any man fail of the grace of God. The trumpet sounds, and not the dulcimer, the call is to conflict, not to feasting.

I would next bid you note, dear friends, that *it is natural it should be so;* it is unavoidable in the nature of things, that when the Holy Spirit comes He should not beget a spirit of slumber, but awaken us to diligent action. It is natural, I say, because one of the first results of the Holy Spirit's entrance into a man's heart is to let him see his sin and his danger. If I feel myself guilty, and perceive that God is angry with me, and that I shall be cast by-and-by into the lake of fire, what is the inevitable result? Shall I not hear a voice crying, "Escape for thy life! Look not behind thee! Stay not in all the plain"? Wherever the Holy Ghost works a sense of sin, the sinner is constrained to cry, "What must I do to be saved?" Never does the Spirit effectually show a man his sin, and then leave him to fold his arms and ask for "a little more sleep and a little more slumber." No, the awakened soul exclaims, "I am guilty, I am accursed of God. How can I escape? Lord help me, help me now to find rest if rest is to be found!" Then the Holy Spirit further reveals to us the excellence of the salvation of Christ, the happiness of those who rest in Jesus, the future reward of such as serve God on earth. And what is the result? The enlightened soul cries, "I fain would find this pearl of great price,

I fain would be enriched by an interest in Christ, I too, would, with the blessed, take my everlasting heritage." See you not then that the Holy Ghost cannot make a man appreciate salvation without at the same time creating a desire to gain it, out of which arises prayer for the promised blessing? After a man has found Christ to the pardon of his sin, the Holy Spirit is pleased to endear Christ more and more to him. It is the office of the Spirit to take of the things of Christ and show them to us. Now, my brethren, you know very well that whenever you have a sight of the preciousness of Christ, you are moved at once to glorify Him. Do you not cry—

"Oh, for this love let rocks and hills
Their lasting silence break,
And all harmonious human tongues
The Saviour's praises speak"?

I know it is so. It is because we think so little of Christ that we do so little for Him; but when Christ is brought with vivid power home to the mind, then at once we cry, "Lord, what wouldst Thou have me to do?" and we bestir ourselves to honour Him.

Brethren, the fact that the Holy Spirit is working in a man, never can be a reason for his not working; on the contrary, the moment a man perceives that the Spirit is helping him, he is encouraged diligently to labour. "Why," saith he, "*my* work may fail, but if it be the Spirit's work it cannot fail." I bow my knee in prayer, and if I believe that all acceptable prayer is wrought in me by the Holy Spirit, I am fully assured that God will not refuse to grant what He Himself by His Spirit suggests to me to ask. If the Holy One of Israel Himself breaks my heart and leads me to long after a Saviour, surely he does not intend to tantalize me; He will continue His work till He has saved me. Thus encouraged, a man is certain to give diligence to make his calling and election sure. Moreover every intelligent man feels that if he does not work when the Spirit of God is working in him, he is dishonouring that Divine Person, and is running the solemn peril of committing the sin against the Holy Ghost which shall never be forgiven him. He feels that if he should be slothful that text would condemn him, "How shall we escape if we neglect so great salvation?" Neglect, mere neglect, nobody ever gets to heaven by it; but ah, how many perish by that alone!

To conclude this point, *it is most certain that all saving acts must be performed by the man himself.* Faith is the gift of God, but the Holy Ghost never believed for anybody; it is not His office to believe. The sinner must believe. Repentance is the work of the Holy Spirit, but the Holy Ghost never repented. What had He to repent of? He has done no ill. It cannot be possible to Him to repent for us. Nay, we ourselves must repent. My brethren, this is self-evident to every candid mind. There must be in every man a personal faith, and a personal repentance; and though these are wrought in him by the Holy Spirit, yet they are his own acts; they cannot be the acts of anybody else, or else the man has not believed, and has not repented, and there is no life in him. Right on to the end of the Christian life all those acts which bring us into communion with God are our own. For instance, the Holy Ghost helps men to pray. He helps their infirmities. But *they* pray; *they themselves* pray. Prove to me that the man does not himself pray, and I will be bold to tell you that he is not saved. The intercession of Christ is prevalent, but it will not save those who live and die without praying for themselves. True desires after God must be your own desires. The desire is wrought in you, but still it is yours. And the expression of that desire is helped by the teaching of the Spirit, but still it is your own expression, or else what are you but a dead soul? There must be a voluntary putting forth on your part of the life which is quickened in you by the Spirit. This is so plain as to be self-evident.

Note again, if we were not made active, but are simply acted on by the Holy Ghost, there is a reduction of manhood to materialism. If the man does not believe nor pray, and if spiritual acts are not a man's own acts, but the acts of another in him, then what is the man? There is no moral good or moral evil in a work which is not my own—I mean no moral good or evil to me. A work which I do not myself perform may be creditable or discreditable to somebody else, it is neither to me. Take an illustration. In the Square of St. Mark, at Venice, at certain hours the bell of the clock is struck by two bronze figures as large as life, wielding hammers. Now, nobody ever thought of presenting thanks to those bronze men for the diligence with which they have struck the hours; of course, they cannot help it, they are wrought upon by machinery, and they strike the hours from necessity. Some years ago a stranger was upon the top of the tower, and incautiously went too near one of these bronze men; his time was come to strike the hour, he knocked the stranger from the battlement of the tower and killed him; nobody said the bronze man ought to be hanged; nobody ever laid it to his charge at all. There was no moral good or moral evil, because there was no will in the concern. It was not a moral act, because no mind and heart gave consent to it. Am I to believe that grace reduces men to this? I tell you, sirs, if you think to glorify the grace of God by such a theory, you know not what you do. To carve blocks, and move logs, is small glory, but this is the glory of God's grace, that without violating the human will, He yet achieves His own purposes, and treating men as men, He conquers their hearts with love, and wins their affections by His grace.

I warn any here present, who imagine that man is a merely passive being in salvation, against putting their theory in practice. I am alarmed for you if you say, "God will save me if He so decrees, and therefore I will sit still and wait." My hearer, I am afraid for you, you are neglecting the great salvation, and I again remind you of the warning: "How shall we escape if we neglect so great salvation?" I confess, I have no hope for you. But on the contrary, if you cry, "Lord, save, or I perish," I have good hope of you, you shall not perish, the Spirit of God is working in you these desires and this longing and seeking. Whosoever calleth upon the name of the Lord shall be saved. I pray you check not your aspirations. Quench not the Spirit. Led and guided by His mighty working, come to the foot of Christ's cross; trust alone to Him, and a voice shall sound in your heart, "Thy sins which are many, are all forgiven thee." God grant it may be so.

II. We shall now turn to the second part of our subject, in reference to THE MINISTRY OF THE SAINTS FOR THE CONVERSION OF OTHERS.

The Holy Spirit alone can convert a soul. All the ministries in the world put together, be they what they may, are utterly powerless for the salvation of a single soul apart from the Holy Ghost. "Not by might nor by power, but by My Spirit saith the Lord." But wherever the Holy Spirit works, as a general rule (so general that I scarcely know an exception), it is in connection with the earnest efforts of Christian men.

This is clear, first, from *the example of the text.* The apostle Paul certifies that the salvation of souls is the sole work of Christ, but he declares that he laboured, and the next word he adds "striving," or as in the Greek, "agonizing." Though the Spirit did the work, it was in connection with the apostle's labour and agony for souls. Now, my brethren labouring implies abundant work. No man can be said to labour who only does half an hour's work in a day. A man who is a thorough labourer makes long hours, and is ever at it. The apostle Paul was this. The winning of souls was not a piece of by-play with him; it was his one object, to which he consecrated everything. He was "in labours more abundant." In the morning he sowed his seed, and in the evening he withheld not his hand. If we are to have souls saved we must do the same. No tradesman expects his shop to prosper who has it open only one hour a day, and you must not expect to be soul-winners if you only now and then seek to be such. There must be, as far as time and capacity allow, the consecration of yourselves to this work, even to an abundance of effort.

Labour, again, means hard work. It is not trifling. He is no labourer who takes the spade to play with it as a little child upon the sand. He that labours works till the sweat streams from his face; and he that would win souls will find that, though it is all of the Holy Spirit, yet it involves on his part the sternest form of spiritual work. Baxter used to say if any minister found his ministry easy, he would find it hard to answer for it at the day of judgment; and I add, if any one of you teaching in your classes, or officiating in any form of Christian work, find it easy, you will find it hard to give an account of your stewardship at the Lord's coming.

The labour must be personal labour, for no man is a labourer who does it through his servants. He may be an employer, and in a certain sense he may be said to do the work, but he cannot say, "I labour." The apostle performed personal work. Ah! brethren, the power of the church very much lies under God in the personal influence of her members. On this platform I feel that I am a long way off from you. I wish I could devise some mode of speech by which I could thrust my hand into your hearts and get my soul to pulsate close by yours to make you feel what I feel. Between the pulpit and the pew there is too often a great gulf fixed. But you who get your friends into the parlour, and talk concerning eternal things, you have a fine opportunity. Your personal influence then bears with mighty force upon the person with whom you are speaking, and you may hope that a blessing will be the result. Learn ye from your adversaries. What is the strength of the shavelings of Rome? What but their conversing with men and women by themselves at the confessional? Who could not prevail with such an instrument? We, with nobler ends and aims, must use personal private intercourse in all honest earnestness to bring men to repentance, to faith, and to the foot of the cross.

My brethren, I do not believe that even this will suffice. Abundant Christian work, and hard Christian work, and personal Christian work, must have combined with it inward soul conflict. If your soul never breaks for another, you will not be the means of breaking that other's heart; but when it comes to this, "I must have that soul saved, I cannot bear the thought that it should be cast away"—you are near winning that soul. Suppose it be your child, your unconverted husband, or your brother, and you are enabled to say in yourself, "I have continual heaviness for my kinsmen according to the flesh," so that you could almost sacrifice your own soul if they might but be saved; when it comes to tears the Lord will not deny you. My brother, when your heart breaketh with love to souls, they shall be yours. But there must be conflicts. I pity that minister whose life is one of uninterrupted spiritual ease. What, can we see ye backslide and not weep till ye come back to the cross? Can I know that among these thousands who are listening to my voice, perhaps half are dead in trespasses and sins, and can I be insensible as a marble statue? Then God have mercy upon me as well as upon you! Unhappy souls to be entrusted to the care of one so utterly unfit for such a service. No, the heart must be stirred, there must be an anguishing and yearning for souls. They tell us that in the sea certain waves rise from the bottom, and these cause the ground swells and the breakers. There must be great ground swells of desire within us that souls may, by some means, be delivered from the wrath to come; and where these deep heart-searchings are found there must be conversions. Where these four things, of which we have spoken, are the result of the Holy Ghost working in any of you, it is as certain that souls will be saved as that spring will follow when the sun returns from his southern tropic.

We must further note that *this is plain from the work itself.* For, brethren, souls are not converted as a rule without previous prayer for them on the part of some one or other. Well, then, we must be stirred up to prayer, and the praying which God hears is not that of people half asleep. The petitions which pierce the ears of God are not those that fall from careless lips, they must come from your heart or they will never go to His heart. The importunate pleader prevails with heaven. Souls are saved instrumentally through teaching, but the teaching which saves souls is never cold, dead teaching. God may occasionally bless such words, for He doeth great wonders, but as a rule the teaching that convinces and enlightens is earnest and enthusiastic. We have heard of a traveller who, journeying onward, met with one who said, "Sir, the night is dark, and I should not advise you to go on to the river, for the bridge is broken in the middle, you will be in the stream before you know it." This was said in so careless a tone that the traveller went on. He was met sometime afterwards, fortunately for him, by another who again warned him; "The bridge is broken! don't go on, you will be sure to lose your life if you attempt it. You cannot ford the stream and the bridge is broken." The traveller replied, "Why, I have been told that tale before, but the man who told me it spoke in such a tone that I could see through him, I knew it was all a hoax." "Oh, but sir," said the other, "it is true! I have but now escaped myself. I am sure it is true!" "But," said the traveller, "I am not so easily scared." "Well, then," said the other, "I beseech you once again do not go on, for you will perish," and rushing up to him he said, "I

will not let you go." He grasped him and held him fast. "Now," said the other, "I believe you have spoken the truth, and I will turn with you." So there are some who warn souls of their danger in such a careless tone, that they create an unbelief which many an earnest tongue will not be able to dispel. But if you get hold of the soul and say to it, "I will not let thee perish"; if you say to your friends as Whitefield would say to his congregation, "If you perish it shall not be for want of praying for, it shall not be for want of weeping over; if you are damned it shall not be because my heart was cold towards you," you will win them, they will be led to believe from your earnestness. Who knows how many your earnest spirit may bring to Jesus? Praying and teaching if effectual must be earnest, and hence when the Spirit comes to save the sons of men He always gives us earnest praying men and earnest teachers.

But, brethren, teaching is not all. We must come to persuasion with men, and that persuasion must be very persevering. Certain men we must dog day after day with our entreaties. Some souls will not come with one invitation, they must therefore be plied with many. I remember a minister who went to see a dying labourer, and the man growled from his bed, "Tell him to begone—I want none of the like of him to disturb me." He called again, and received the same rude answer. He called again, and went half-way up the stairs; he heard an oath, and would not intrude. He continued to call till he had numbered twenty times, and the twenty-first time the man said, "Well, as you are so set on it, you may come in," and he did go in, and that soul was won for God. Humanly speaking where had that man been but for persevering zeal? When the Lord means to save men by you, He will give you perseverance in seeking them, He will work in you mightily by His Spirit; you will feel a determination, that twist and turn as they may with indefatigable earnestness of self-destruction, you will still pursue them if by any means you may prevent their everlasting misery.

Earnest zeal is a natural result of the Holy Spirit's working upon the souls of men. Whenever the Spirit of God comes, He sanctifies in men the natural instinct which leads them to wish others to be like themselves. Whether a man be bad or good, He seeks to make others like Himself; the Holy Ghost lays hold of this, and constrains Christians to desire to bring others to their state of mind. This done, He arouses in the Christian mind the commendable principle of love to our fellow men. Having experienced the blessedness of salvation for ourselves, we desire to see others enjoying like happiness. The patriot's bosom glows with the same passion as before, but now it is refined and purified, and he prays for his nation that not only it may be free, but that the Spirit of God may make it free indeed.

The Holy Spirit bestirs in us the impulse of gratitude. "Has Christ saved me?" then the man exclaims, "I will live for Him." The Spirit gives impetus to that suggestion, and we resolve that since Jesus has loved us so, we will give to Him all that we are, and all that we have.

In addition to this, the Holy Spirit sanctifies many other natural emotions, such for instance as that which we sometimes call the *esprit de corps*, by which men are moved to desire the prosperity of the community to which they belong. The Holy Spirit makes us feel one with Christ's church, and we ardently desire her success. A holy emulation as to which shall serve the Master most runs through our ranks, not that *we* may get honour, but that we may honour *Him*. We cannot endure it that our brethren should go to the war and we sit still. We begin to be afraid lest the denunciation should go forth against us, "Curse ye Meroz, said the angel of the Lord, curse ye bitterly the inhabitants thereof; because they came not to the help of the Lord, to the help of the Lord against the mighty." Inspired by such feelings we rush to the fight that we may rescue souls for Christ.

Then the Spirit in some men, I pray it may be in your case, my dear friends, sheds abroad the love of Christ at such a rate that the soul is all on fire to exalt Christ. Nay, in some He has made this sacred passion to eat them up till they have been consumed with holy zeal. Like men inspired, like ancient apostles, certain choice spirits have lived the life of Christ on earth with an awful vehemence of enthusiasm. Wherever such men are raised up, God is about to save souls. Whenever you listen to a man who is carried away by an all-consuming desire for the glory of God, you may conclude that he is the instrument of God to thousands; his lips shall feed many, he shall be the spiritual progenitor of tribes of believers. Thus where the Spirit of God comes, energy is evinced and souls are saved; but we do not find it otherwise.

I would have you notice, once more, that *the whole history of the church confirms what I have stated.* When the Holy Spirit descended, there were two signs of His presence; the one was a rushing mighty wind, the other was the tongue of fire. Now if the Holy Spirit intended to do all the work Himself, without using us as earnest instruments, the first emblem would have been stagnant air; and the next might have been a mass of ice, or what you will, but certainly not the tongue of fire. The first emblem was not only wind, but it was a mighty wind, and not only that, but a rushing mighty wind, as if to show us that He intended to set every spiritual sail in the most rapid motion; and as birds are drifted before the gale, so would He impel His people forward with His mighty influences. The other emblem was fire, a consuming, devouring, imperial element. May we be baptized in the Holy Ghost, and in fire, so shall we know what is meant by the symbol. Our Lord's commencement of the gospel ministry was signalized by vehemence. Here is His own experience, "From the days of John the Baptist until now the kingdom of heaven suffereth violence, and the violent take it by force." Christ's ministry and life was notably earnest, he was clad with zeal as with a cloak. His apostles also were men so vehement, that in their earliest deliverances they were thought to be drunken with wine. Every era of the church's prosperity has been marked by this same holy violence. Hear Chrysostom speak, he is no player upon a goodly instrument, he gives forth no dulcet tones for gentle ears. Listen to his denunciation of the Empress Eudoxia! Hear how he denounces the sins of the times! How vehemently he calls upon men to escape for their lives because of coming judgment! Listen to Augustine, his vehement tones you will not soon forget. Turn to the notable era of the Reformation. The men who wrought the Reformation were no dullards, no men of polite speech, of elegant chillinesses and dainty sentences. Luther was a type of them all, vehement to the extreme of vehemence.

I say not that their natural violence was the power which wrought the Reformation, but that the Holy Ghost made their hearts vehement, and so they wrought marvels. And we, dear brethren, if we are to see in these days a genuine revival of religion, worthy of the name, must return to the old enthusiasm which once made the church fair as the moon, clear as the sun, and terrible as an army with banners. O that we may live to see it, and the Lord's name shall be glorified!

The conclusion of the whole matter is just this. Let us combine the two things of which we have spoken. Dear brethren, let us rely upon the Holy Ghost, and the Holy Ghost only. Let us not go a warfare at our own charges. Let us believe that without the Lord nothing good can be done. But let us rest assured that Jesus is never absent where He gives the spirit of prayer, as He has given to this church; and that He never deserts those to whom He vouchsafes holy zeal for His kingdom, such as He has bestowed on many here present. Let us be encouraged by His presence. Gideon, when he obtained the token of the fleece wet with dew, and when by night he heard the story of the barley cake that overturned the tents of Midian, did not straightway go to his home and renounce the enterprise, because God was with him. No, but on the contrary, thus encouraged he gathered together his three hundred valiant men in the darkness of the night, they broke the pitchers, bade the torches shine, and shouted the watchword, "The sword of the Lord and of Gideon! The sword of the Lord and of Gideon!" Even so be it with us at this hour. Knowing that God the Holy Ghost is with us, let us lift the cry amid the midnight of our age, "The sword of the Lord and of His Son Jesus!" and we shall see what God will do, for He will surely put to flight the armies of the aliens, and get to Himself renown.

But, brethren, let us combine with this confidence in the Holy Spirit, the most earnest effort on the part of every one to do all he can. I have a scene before my mind's eye at this moment; I see in this church and neighbourhood the counterpart of the mountain side when the multitude were fainting for lack of bread. They must be fed, Christ willed it. The disciples must bring their barley loaves and fishes— what were they among so many? Christ must break and multiply. The disciples must receive from His hand, they must then go among the many, the fifties and the hundreds, and break the bread that Christ had blessed, for the hungry must be fed; not only men, but women and children must be satisfied. Behold, my brethren, this great city hungry and faint, and ready to die. Bring hither, all ye disciples of Christ, your loaves and fishes—I mean not to me but to the Master. What you have of ability, however slender, bring it out. Christ will not begin to multiply till you have brought forth all you have. Miracles are not to be expected till nature is brought to a *nonplus*. Bring out, then, whatever of talent or grace you have, consecrate all to Jesus, and then as He begins to multiply stand ready as your Master's servants to wait upon the crowd; and if they push and clamour, yet weary not, break still the bread till every soul shall have been supplied. Go on, go on, and do not say the toil is hard, it is so blessed to do good to others. It is thrice blessed, nay, sevenfold blessed, to turn a sinner from the error of his ways, and save a soul from death. Nay, weary not, though you have been so long at it that your spirit is faint.

My brother, your physical frame is weary, but be of good cheer. Do ye not hear them? Hearken, I pray you! Up yonder, there are angels bending from their thrones, and I think I hear them say, "How blest a work to feed the hungry, and those men how honoured to be permitted to hand round the Master's precious gift! Do they not whisper, "We would fain be with them"? One bright spirit thinks he would exchange his crown with the meanest of the disciples, if he might share the service of gospel teaching. Might they not envy you; those blessed harpers upon the sea of glass, because you can do what they cannot; you can tell of Jesus, you can fetch in the prodigals, you can find the lost jewels for the Master's crown!

I charge you, my brethren, by the living God, unless your religion be hypocrisy, help me this month, help my brethren the elders and deacons, help us every one of you. By the blood that bought you, if ye be indeed redeemed; by the Holy Ghost that is in you, except ye be reprobates; by everything that God in lovingkindness has done for you, I charge you come to the help of the Master in this the hopeful hour. So may the Lord do unto you as you shall deal with us this day. If you shall indeed consecrate yourselves to Him, and serve Hm, may He enrich you with the increase of God, and may the peace of God that passeth all understanding keep your hearts and minds; but if ye refuse your service, the Lord shall judge you. He that knoweth his Master's will and doeth it not, shall be beaten with many stripes.

LIFE AND WALK OF FAITH

" As ye have therefore received Christ Jesus the Lord, so walk ye in Him."—Colossians ii. 6.

OUR nature is fond of change. Although man was made in the image of God at first, it is plain enough that any trace of immutability which he may once have possessed has long ago departed. Man, unrenewed, could he possess the joys of heaven, would in time grow weary of them, and crave for change. When the children of Israel in the wilderness were fed on angels' food, they murmured for variety, and groaned out, " Our soul loatheth this light bread." It is little wonder, then, that we need cautions against shifting the ground of our hope and the object of our faith. Another evil principle will co-work with this love of change in our hearts, and produce much mischief—our natural tendency to build up our own works. For a time that pernicious habit is cured by conviction of sin. The law, with its sharp axe, cuts down the lofty cedar of fleshly confidence, and withers all its vendure ; but, since the root still remains, at the very scent of water it sprouts again, and there is good need to set the axe going with all its former edge and weight. When we think legality quite dead, it revives, and, linking hands with our love of change, it tempts us to forsake our simple standing upon Christ, the Rock of Ages, and urges us to advance to a something which it decorates before our eyes with fancied colours, and makes out to our feeble understandings to be better or more honourable to ourselves. Though this will certainly be again beaten down in a Christian, for he will meet trouble after trouble when once he goeth astray from his first path, yet again the old secret desire to be something, to do something, to have some little honour by performing the works of the law, will come in, and we shall have need to hear the voice of wisdom in our hearts saying to us, " As ye have received Christ Jesus the Lord, so walk ye in Him ; " persevere in the same way in which ye have begun, and, as at the first Christ Jesus was the source of your life, the principle of your action, and the joy of your spirit, so let Him be the same even till life's end, the same when you walk through the valley of the shadow of death, and enter into the joy and the rest which remains for the people of God.

In trying to teach this very useful, though simple lesson, I shall, in the plainest possible language, first of all talk a little of the text by way of exposition ; then, secondly, by way of advocacy ; and then, thirdly, by way of application.

I. Oh that the gracious Spirit, who alone can lead us into all truth, would aid me while I endeavour to open up this verse BY WAY OF EXPOSITION.

In expounding the text, we readily break it up into two parts : here is the life of faith—receiving Christ Jesus the Lord ; here is, secondly, the walk of faith—so walk ye in Him.

1. The Holy Spirit here reveals to us the life of faith—the way by which you and I are saved, if saved at all. Remark, carefully, that it is represented as receiving. Now the word receiving implies the very opposite of anything like merit. Merit is purchasing ; merit might be called making by labour, or winning by valour ; but receiving is just the accepting of a thing as a gift. The eternal life which God gives His people is in no sense whatever the fruit of their exertions ; it is the gift of God. As the earth drinks in the rain, as the sea receives the streams, as night accepts light from the stars, so we, giving nothing, partake freely of the grace of God. The saints are not by nature wells, or streams, they are but cisterns into which the living water flows. They are but as the empty vessel ; sovereign mercy puts them under the conduit-pipe, and they receive grace upon grace till they are filled to the brim. He that talks about winning salvation by works ; he that thinks he can earn it by prayers, by tears, by penance, by mortification of the flesh, or by zealous obedience to the law, makes a mistake ; for the very first principle of the divine life is not giving out, but receiving. It is that which comes from Christ into me which is my salvation ; not that which springs out of my own heart, but that which comes from the divine Redeemer and changes and renews my nature. It is not what I give out, but what I receive, which must be life to me.

The idea of receiving, again, seems to imply in it a sense of realization, making the matter a reality. One cannot very well receive a shadow ; we receive that which is substantial. Gold, silver, precious stones—such things we can receive ; estates, riches, bread, water, food, raiment—all these are things which are substances to us, and therefore it becomes possible for us to receive them. We do not receive a dream ; we do not receive, again I say, a shadow ;

we do not speak of receiving a spectre ; we do not receive a phantom. There is something real in a thing that is received. Well now so is it also in the life of faith ; we realize Christ. While we are without faith, Christ is a name to us, a person that may have lived a long while ago, so long that His life is only a history to us now ! By an act of faith Christ becomes a real person in the consciousness of our heart, as real to us as our own flesh, and blood, and bones, and we speak of Him and think of Him as we would of our brother, our father, our friend. Our faith gives a substance to the history and idea of Christ, puts real solidity into the spirit and name of Christ, and that which to the worldly man is but a phantom, a thing to hear about, and talk about, becomes to us a thing to taste, and handle, to lay hold upon, and to receive as real and true. I know, ye that are unconverted, that ye think all these things an idle tale ; but you that are saved, you who have received Christ, you know that there is substance here, and shadow everywhere else. This has become to you the one grand reality, that God is in Christ reconciling you unto Himself.

But receiving means also a third thing, that is *getting a grip of it, grasping it*. The thing which I receive becomes my own. I may believe it to be real, but that is not receiving it. I may believe, also, that if I ever do get it it must be given to me, and that I cannot earn it for myself, but still that is not receiving it. Receiving is the *bona fide* taking into my hand and appropriating to myself as my own property that which is given to me. Now this is what the soul doth when it believes in Christ. Christ becomes *my* Christ ; His blood cleanses my sin, and it is cleansed ; His righteousness covers me, and I am clothed with it ; His Spirit fills me, and I am made to live by it. He becomes to me as much mine as anything that I can call my own ; nay, what I call my own here on earth is not mine ; it is only lent to me, and will be taken from me ; but Christ is so mine, that neither life, nor death, nor things present, nor things to come, shall ever be able to rob me of Him. Oh ! I hope, dear friends, you have that blessed appropriating faith which says, " Yes, He is not another man's Christ, He is my Christ," I hope you can look into His face to-day and say, " *My* beloved, who loved *me*, and gave Himself to *me*." I hope you do not talk of these things as I might talk of my lord So-and-So's park, and admire its beauties, while I myself have no right to one acre of the many thousands within the park-fence ; but I trust, on the other hand, you can say—" The blessings and promises of the Lord my God are all my own ; whatever I read of in the covenant of grace that is good, that is comely, that is desirable, I have heard a voice say in my ears, ' Lift up now thine eyes, and look to the north, and the south, to the east, and the west— all this have I given *thee* to be thy possession for ever and ever by a covenant of salt.' " Now put these three things together, and I think you have the idea of receiving Christ. To receive Him is to have Him as the result of God's free gift ; to realize Him ; and then to appropriate Him to yourselves.

The word " receive " is used in some ten or a dozen senses in holy Scripture ; five of them will suffice my purpose just now. To receive is often used for *taking*. We read of receiving a thousand shekels of silver, and of receiving money, garments, olive-yards, sheep, and oxen. Perhaps in this sense we understand the words of the Master—" No man can receive anything unless it be given him from above," and that other sentence—" To as many as received Him, to them gave He power to becomes the sons of God." We take Christ into us—to return to my old simile—as the empty vessel takes in water from the stream ; so we receive Christ. The love, life, merit, nature, and grace of Jesus freely flow into us, as the oil into the widow's vessels. But the word is also used in Scripture to signify *holding that which we take in* ; indeed, a vessel without a bottom could hardly be said to receive water. I do not suppose any one would talk of a sieve receiving water, except in a mock sense. But the life of faith consists in holding within us that which Christ hath put into us, so that Jesus Christ is formed in us the hope of glory. By faith it comes in ; by faith it is kept in ; faith gives me what I have ; faith keeps what I have ; faith makes it mine ; faith keeps it mine ; faith gets hold of it with one hand, and then clasps it with both hands with a grasp that neither death nor life can loose. Then, receiving sometimes means in Scripture simply *believing*. " He came unto His own and His own received Him not." We read of receiving false prophets, that is, believing them. Now, to receive Christ is to believe Him. He says, " I can save you." —I receive that. He says, " I will save you."—I receive that. He says, " Trust Me and I will make you like Myself."—I receive that. Whatever Jesus says, I believe Him, and receive Him as true. I make His word so true to myself that I act upon it as being true, and regard it not as a word that may possibly be true, but which must be true, even if heaven and earth should pass away. This is receiving Christ— believing what He has said. Receiving, also, often signifies in Scripture *entertaining*. Thus the barbarous people at Melita received Paul and his companions kindly, and kindled a fire. Ah ! after we have once found all in Christ to be our own, and have received Him into ourselves by faith, then we entreat the Lord to enter our hearts and sup with us. We give Him the best seat at the table of our souls ; we would feast Him on the richest dainties of our choicest love. We ask Him to abide with us from morn till eve ; we would commune with Him every day, and every hour of the day. We entertain Him ; we have a reception-chamber in our hearts, and we receive Christ. And then once again, receiving in Scripture often signifies *to enjoy*. We hear of receiving a crown of life which fadeth not away ; that is, enjoying it, enjoying heaven, and being satisfied with all its bliss. Now, dear friends, when we receive Christ, there is intended in this an enjoying of it. I am only now talking of the simplicities of our faith, but I do want to make them very personal to you. Are you thus enjoying Christ ? If you had a crown you would wear it ; you have a Christ—feed on Him. If you were hungry and there were bread on the table, you would eat. Oh ! eat and drink, beloved, of your Lord Jesus Christ. If you have a friend, you enjoy his company : you have a friend in Christ ; Oh ! enjoy His conversation. Do not leave Him, like a bottle of cordial for the fainting, sealed up from us ; let Him not be as some choice dainty all untasted, while you are hungry. Oh ! receive Christ, for this is the very heaven and rest of the soul. His flesh is meat indeed, His blood is drink indeed. Never did angels taste such divine fare. Come hither saints and satiate yourselves in Him. To take Him into one's self, to hold Him there, to believe every word He says, to entertain Him in our hearts, and to enjoy the luscious sweetness which He must confer upon all those who have eaten His flesh, and have been made to drink of His blood—this is to receive Christ.

But we have not brought out the real meaning of this life of faith yet till we dwell upon another word. As ye have received. Received what ? Salvation may be described as the blind receiving sight, the deaf receiving hearing, the dead receiving life ; but beloved, beloved, here is a thought here—oh that you may get hold of it ! We have not only received these things, but we have received CHRIST. " As ye have received *Christ Jesus the Lord.*" Do you catch it ? It is true that He gave us life from the dead ? He gave us pardon of sin ; He gave us imputed righteousness. These are all precious things, but you see we are not content with them ; we have received *Christ Himself.* The Son of God has been poured out into us, and we have received Him, and appropriated Him. Mark, I say, not merely the blessings of the covenant, but *Himself* ; not merely the purchase of His blood, but He Himself from whose veins the blood hath flowed has become ours ; and every soul that hath eternal life is this day a possessor of Christ Jesus the Lord. Now we will put this, also, personally to you. Have I received *Christ*, that is the *anointed* ? My soul, hast thou seen Christ as the anointed of the Father in the divine decree to execute His purposes ? Hast thou seen Him coming forth in the fulness of time wearing the robes of His priesthood, the anointed of the Father ? Hast thou seen Him standing at the altar offering Himself as a victim, an anointed priest, anointed with the sacred oil by which God has made him a priest for ever after the order of Melchisedec ? My soul, hast thou seen Jesus going within the veil and speaking to thy Father and to His Father as one whom the Father has accepted, of whom we can speak, in the language of David, as our shield and God's anointed ? Oh ! it is a delight indeed to receive Christ not as an unsent prophet, not as a man who came of his own authority, not as a teacher who spoke his own word, but as one who is *Christos*, the anointed, the anointed of God, ordained of the Most High, and therefore most certainly acceptable, as it is written, " *I* have laid help upon One that is mighty ; *I* have exalted One chosen out of the people. It pleased the *Father* to bruise Him ; *He* hath put Him to grief." Delightful is the contemplation of Christ under that aspect ! Soul, dost thou thus receive the Messias of God ? But the text says, " Christ *Jesus.*" Now Jesus means a Saviour. *Christ* is His relation to God, *Jesus* His relation to me. Have I received Christ in His relationship to me as a Saviour ? My soul, has Christ saved thee ? Come, no " ifs " and " ans " about it. Hast thou received Him as thy Saviour ? Couldst thou say in that happy day when thy faith closed with Him, " Yes, Jesus, Thou hast saved me ! " Oh ! there are some professors of religion who do not seem to have received Christ as *Jesus.* They look upon Him as One who may help them to save themselves, who can do a great deal for them, or may begin the work but not complete it. Oh ! beloved, we must get a hold of Him as One that has saved us, that has finished the work. What, know ye not that ye are this day whiter than the driven snow because His blood has washed you ? Ye are this day more acceptable to God than unfallen angels ever were, for ye are clothed in the perfect righteousness of a divine one. Christ has wrapped you about with His own righteousness : you are saved ; you have received

Him as God's anointed, see that you receive Him as Jesus your Saviour.

Then, again, it is clear that saving faith consisteth also in receiving Him *as He is in Himself, as the divine Son.* " Ye have received Christ Jesus *the Lord.*" Those who say they cannot believe in His Deity have not received Him. Others theoretically admit Him to be divine, but He is never a subject of confidence as such ; *they* have not received Him. But I trust I speak to many hundreds this morning who willingly accept His Godhead, and say, " I entertain no doubt about His Deity, and, moreover, on that I risk my soul ; I do take Him into my heart as being God over all, blessed for ever, Amen ; I kiss His feet while I see His humanity ; but I believe that, since those feet could tread the waters, He is divine. I look up to His hands, and as I see them pierced I know that He is human ; but as I know that those hands multiplied the loaves and fishes till they fed five thousand, I know that He is divine. I look upon His corpse in the tomb, and I see that He is man ; I see Him in the resurrection, and I know that He is God. I see Him on the cross, suffering, and I know that He is bone of my bone, and flesh of my flesh ; but I hear a voice which saith, ' Let all the angels of God worship Him ' ; ' Thy throne, O God, is for ever and ever ' ; and I bow before Him and say, ' O Lord, Thou Son of God and Son of Mary, I receive Thee as Christ Jesus *the Lord.*' "

Now this is all very plain talking you will say ; and I remind you that souls are saved by very plain truths, and the dealings of men's souls with Christ are not carried on in learned or metaphysical terms. We do believe, and so take Christ Jesus, the Lord in us, and by that act of faith, without any doing of our own, we are completely saved.

I shall only make this further remark here, that the apostle speaks of this *as a matter of certainty*, and goes on to argue from it. Now we do not argue from a supposition. I must have you clear, dearly beloved in the Lord, that this is a matter of certainty *to you.* We can hardly get to the next point unless you can say, " I have received Jesus." The verse runs, " As or since *ye have* received Christ Jesus the Lord so walk ye in Him." We must not alter it into, " Since *I hope* I have," " Since *I trust* I have." Ye either have or have not ; if ye have not, humble yourselves under the mighty hand of God, and cry to Him for His great gift ; but if you have, O dear friends, do not let it be a question with you, but say, " Yes, yes, yes, I can say, once for all, I have received Him ; poor, weak, and worthless though I am, I do put my humble seal to the fact that God is true, and I trust in Him who is able to save unto the uttermost them that come unto God by Him." This is the life of faith.

2. Now, in expounding the text, our second point was *the walk of faith.* " Since ye have received Him, walk in Him." Walk implies, first of all, *action.* Do not let your reception of Christ be a mere thing of thought to you, a subject only for your chamber and your closet, but act upon it all. If you have really received Christ, and are saved, act as if you were saved, with joy, with meekness, with confidence, with faith, with boldness. Walk in Him ; do not sit down in indolence, but rise and act in Him. Walk in Him ; carry out into practical effect that which you believe. See a man who has received an immense fortune, his purse is bursting, and his caskets are heavy ; what does he do ? Why, he behaves like a rich man ; he sees a luxury which pleases him,

and he buys it ; there is an estate he desires, and he purchases it ; he acts like a rich man. Beloved brethren, you have received Christ—act upon it. Do not play the beggar now that boundless wealth is conferred upon you. Walking, again, implies *perseverance*, not only being in Christ to-day, that would be standing in Him and falling from Him : but being in Him to-morrow, and the next day, and the next, and the next, and the next ; walking in Him all your walk of life. I remember Matthew Henry, speaking about Enoch walking with God, says he did not only take a turn or two up and down with God, and then leave Him, but he walked with God four hundred years. This implies perseverance. You have received Christ—persevere in receiving Him ; you have come to trust Him—keep on trusting Him ; you hang about His neck as a poor, helpless sinner—remain hanging there ; in other words abide in Him. Walking implies *habit*. When we speak of a man's walk and conversation, we mean his habits, the constant tenor of his life. Now, dear friends, if you and I sometimes enjoy Christ, and then forget Him ; sometimes say He is ours, and anon loose our hold, that is not a habit ; we do not *walk* in Him. But if you have received Him, let it be your habit to live upon Him ; keep to Him ; cling to Him ; never let Him go, but live and have your being in Him. This walking implies *a continuance*. There is no notice given in the text of the suspension of this walking, but there must be a continual abiding in Christ. How many Christians there are who think that in the morning and evening they ought to come into the company of Christ, and then they may be in the world all the day. Ah ! but we ought always to be in Christ, that is to say, all the day long, every minute of the day ; though worldly things may take up some of my thoughts, yet my soul is to be in a constant state of being in Christ ; so that if I am caught at any moment, I am in Him ; at any hour if any one should say to me, " Now are you saved ? " I may be able still to say, " Yes." And if they ask me for an evidence of it, I may, without saying so, prove it to them by the fact that I am acting like a man who is in Christ, who has Christ in him, has had his nature changed by receiving Christ's nature, and has Christ to be his one end and aim. I suppose, also, that walking signifies *progress*. So walk ye in Him ; proceed from grace to grace, run forward until you reach the uttermost limit of knowledge that man can have concerning our Beloved. " As ye have received Him, walk in Him."

But now I want you to notice just this ; it says, " Walk ye *in Him*." Oh ! I cannot attempt to enter into the mystery of this text—" Walk *in* Him ! " You know if a man has to cross a river, he fords it quickly and is out of it again at once, but you are to suppose a person walking *in* a certain element always, in Christ. Just as we walk in the air, so am I to walk in Christ ; not sometimes, now and then coming to Him and going away from Him, but walking in Him as my element. Can you comprehend that ? Not a soul here can make anything out of that but the most silly jargon, except the man who having received the inner spiritual life, understandeth what it is to have fellowship with the Father and with His Son Jesus Christ. Dear friends, in trying to open up that point just for a moment, let us notice what this walking in Christ must mean. As Christ was at first when we received Him *the only ground of our faith* ; so as long as we live, we are to stand to

the same point. Did you not sing the other day when you first came to Him—

" I'm a poor sinner and nothing at all,
But Jesus Christ is my all in all ? "

Well, that is how you are to continue to the end. We recommence our faith with—

" Nothing in my hand I bring,
Simply to the cross I cling."

When thou art hoary with honours, when thou art covered with fame, when thou hast served thy Master well, still come in just the same way with—

" A guilty weak and helpless worm,
On Christ's kind arms I fall,
He is my strength and righteousness,
My Jesus and my all."

Let not your experience, your sanctification, your graces, your attainments, come in between you and Christ, but just as you took Him to be the only pillar of your hope at first, so let Him be even to the last. You received Christ, as *the substance of your faith*. The infidel laughed at you, and said you had nothing to trust to ; but your faith made Christ real to you. Well, now, just as the first day when you came to Jesus you no more doubted the reality of Christ than you did your own existence, so walk ye in Him. Well can I recollect that first moment when these eyes looked to Christ ! Ah ! there was never anything so true to me as those bleeding hands, and that thorn-crowned head. I wish it were always so, and indeed it ought to be. As ye have received Christ really, so keep on realizing and finding substance in Him. And that day, beloved, Christ became to us *the joy of our souls*. Home, friends, health, wealth, comforts—all lost their lustre that day when He appeared, just as stars are hidden by the light of the sun. He was the only Lord and giver of life's best bliss, the only well of living water springing up unto everlasting life. I know that the first day it mattered not to me whether the day itself was gloomy or bright. I had found Christ ; that was enough for me. He was my Saviour ; He was my all. I do think that that day I could have stood upon the faggots of Smithfield to burn for Him readily enough. Well, now, just as you received Him at first as your only joy, so receive Him still, walking in Him, making Him the source, the centre, aye, and the circumference too of all your soul's range of delight, having your all in Him. So, beloved, that day when we received Him, we received Him as *the object of our love*. Oh ! how we loved Christ then ! Had we met Him that day, we would have broken the alabaster box of precious ointment, and poured it upon His head ; we would have washed His feet with our tears, and wiped them with the hairs of our head. Ah ! Jesus, when I first received Thee, I thought I should have behaved far better than I have ; I thought I would spend and be spent for Thee, and should never dishonour Thee or turn aside from my faith, and devotedness, and zeal ; but ah ! brethren, we have not come up to the standard of our text—walking in Him as we have received Him. He has not been by us so well beloved as we dreamed He would have been.

I take it then to be the meaning of our text, as Christ Jesus the Lord was at the first All-in-All to you, so let Him be while life shall last.

II. I shall be very brief upon THE ADVOCACY

OF THIS PRINCIPLE, for surely you need no urgent persuasion to cleave unto such a Lord as yours.

In advocating this principle, I would say, first of all, suppose, my brethren, you and I having been so far saved by Christ, should now begin to walk in some one else, what then ? Why, *what dishonour to our Lord*. Here is a man who came to Christ and says he found salvation in Him, but after relying upon the Lord some half-a-dozen years, he came to find it was not a proper principle, and so now he has begun to walk by feelings, to walk by sight, to walk by philosophy, to walk by carnal wisdom. If such a case could be found, what discredit would it bring upon our Holy Leader and Captain. But I am certain no such instance will be found in you, if you have tasted that the Lord is gracious. Have you not up till now found your Lord to be a compassionate and generous friend to you, and has not simple faith in Him given you all the peace your spirit could desire ? I pray you, then, unless you would stain His glory in the dust, as you have received Christ, so walk in Him.

Besides, *what reason have you to make a change ?* Has there been any argument in *the past* ? Has not Christ proved Himself all-sufficient ! He appeals to you to-day—"Have I been a wilderness unto you ?" When your soul has simply trusted Christ, have you ever been confounded ? When you have dared to come as a guilty sinner and believed in Him, have you ever been ashamed ? Very well, then, let the past urge you to walk in Him. And as for *the present*, can that compel you to leave Christ ? Oh ! when we are hard beset with this world or with the severer trials within the Church, we find it such a sweet thing to come back and pillow our head upon the bosom of our Saviour. This is the joy we have to-day, that we are in Him, that we are saved in Him, and if we find this to-day to be enough, wherefore should we think of changing ! I will not forswear the sunlight till I find a better, nor leave my Lord until a brighter Lover shall appear ; and, since this can never be, I will hold Him with a grasp immortal, and bind His name as a seal upon my arm. As for *the future*, can you suggest anything which can arise that shall render it necessary for you to tack about, or strike sail, or go with another captain in another ship ? I think not. Suppose life to be long—He changes not. Suppose you die ; is it not written that " neither death, nor life, nor things present, nor things to come, shall be able to separate us from the love of God, which is in Christ Jesus our Lord ! " You are poor ; what better than to have Christ who can make you rich in faith ? Suppose you are sick ; what more do you want than Christ to make your bed in your sickness ? Suppose you should be maltreated, and mocked at, and slandered for His sake—what better do you want than to have Him as a friend who sticketh closer than a brother ? In life, in death, in judgment, you cannot conceive anything that can arise in which you would require more than Christ bestows.

But, dear friends, it may be that you are tempted by something else to change your course for a time. Now what is it ? Is it the wisdom of this world, the cunning devices and discoveries of man ? Is it that which our apostle mentions as philosophy ? The wise men of the world have persuaded you to begin questions ; they have urged you to put the mysteries of God to the test of common sense, reason, and so forth, as they call it, and not lean on the in-spiration of God's Word. Ah ! well, beloved, it is wisdom, I suppose, which philosophy offers you, Well, but have you not that in Christ, in whom are hid all the treasures of widsom and knowledge ? You received Christ at first, I thought, as being made of God unto you wisdom, and sanctification, and righteousness, and so on ; well, will you cast Him off when you have already more than all the wisdom which this philosophy offers ?

Is it *ceremonies* that tempt you ? Has the priest told you that you ought to attend to these, and then you would have another ground of confidence ? Well, but you have that in Christ. If there is anything in the circumcision of the Jews, you have that, for you are circumcized in Him. If there be anything in baptism, as some think that to be a saving ordinance, you have been buried with Him in baptism ; you have that. Do you want life ? your life is hid with Him. Do you want death ? You are dead with Christ, and buried with Him. Do you want resurrection ? He hath raised you up with Him. Do you want heaven ? He hath made you sit together in heavenly places in Him. Getting Christ, you have all that everything else can offer you ; therefore be not tempted from this hope of your calling, but as ye have received Christ, so walk in Him.

And then, further, do you not know this ? that your Jesus is the Lord from heaven ? *What can your heart desire* beyond God ? God is infinite ; you cannot want more than the infinite. " In Him dwelleth all the fulness of the Godhead bodily." Having Christ you have God, and having God you have everything. Well might the apostle add to that sentence, " And ye are complete in Him " ! Well, then, if you are complete in Christ, why should you be beguiled by the bewitcheries of this world to want something besides Christ ? If resting upon Him, God is absolutely yours, and you are, therefore, full to the brim with all that your largest capacity can desire, oh ! wherefore should you thus be led astray, like foolish children, to seek after another confidence and another trust ? Oh ! come back, thou wanderer ; come thou back to this solid foundation, and sing once again with us—

" On Christ the solid rock I stand
All other ground is sinking sand."

III. And now, last of all, a few words BY WAY OF APPLICATION.

" So walk ye in Him." One of the first applications shall be made with regard to some who complain of a want of communion, or rather, of those of whom WE ought to complain, since they injure us all by their distance from Christ. There are some of you never have much communion with Christ. You are members of the Church, and very decent people, I dare say, in your way ; but you do not have communion with Christ. Ask some professors—" Do you ever have communion with Christ ? " They would be obliged to say—" Well, I do not know that my life is inconsistent ; I do not think anybody could blame me for any wrong act towards my fellow-man ; but if you come to that, whether I have ever had communion with Christ, I am compelled to say that I have had it now and then, but it is very seldom ; it is like the angels' visits, few and far between." Now, brethren, you have received Christ, have you not ? Then the application of the principle is, as you have received Him, so walk in Him. If it were worth while for you to come to Him at first, then it is worth while for you always to keep to Him. If it were really a safe thing for you to come to Him and say, " Jesus, Thou art the way," then it is a safe thing for thee to do now ; and if that was the foundation of blessedness to thee, to come simply to Christ, then it will be the fountain of blessedness to thee to do the same now. Come, then, to Him *now*. If thou wert foolish in trusting Him at the first, then thou art wise in leaving off doing so now. If thou wert wise, however, in approaching to Christ years gone by, thou art foolish in not standing by Christ now. Come, then, let the remembrance of thy marriage unto the Lord Jesus rebuke thee ; and if thou hast lost thy fellowship with Jesus, come again to His dear body wounded for thy sake, and say, " Lord Jesus, help me frⁿm this time forth as I have received Thee, day by day to walk in Thee."

There are many of you who complain of *a want of comfort*. You are not so comfortable as you would like to be, and why ? Why you have sinned. Yes, yes, but how did you receive Christ. As a saint ? " No, no," say you, " I came to Christ as a sinner." Come to Him as a sinner now, then. " Oh ! but I feel so guilty." Just so, but what was your hope at first ? Why, that guilty though you were, He had made an atonement, and you trusted in Him. Well, you are guilty still ; do the same as you did at first ; walk in Him, and I cannot imagine a person without comfort who continually makes this the strain of his life, to rest on Christ as a poor sinner, just as he did at first. Why, Lord, Thou knowest the devil often says to me, " Thou art no saint." Well then if I be not a saint, yet I am a sinner, and it is written " Jesus Christ came into the world to save sinners." Then

" Just as I am, and waiting not,
To rid my soul of one foul spot,
To Him whose blood can cleanse each blot,
O Lamb of God, I come, I come."

Why, you cannot help having comfort if you walk with your Surety and Substitute as you did at the first, resting on Him, and not in feelings, nor experience, nor graces, nor anything of your own ; living and resting alone on Him who is made of God unto you all that your soul requires.

There is yet another thing. There are many Christians whose lives really *are not consistent*. I cannot understand this if they are walking in Christ ; in fact, if a man could completely walk in Christ he would walk in perfect holiness. We hear an instance, perhaps, of a little shopkeeper who puffs and exaggerates as other shopkeepers do—he does not exactly tell a lie, but something very near it. Now I want to know whether that man was walking in Christ when he did that. If he had said to himself, " Now I am in Christ," do you think he would have done it ? We hear of another who is constantly impatient, always troubled, fretting, mournful. I want to know whether that man is really walking in Christ as he walked at first, when he is doubting the goodness, the providence, the tenderness of God. Surely he is

not. I have heard of hard-hearted professors who take a Christian brother by the throat with " Pay me what thou owest." Do you think they are walking in Christ when they do that ? We hear of others when their brothers have need, shut up the bowels of their compassion ; are mean and stingy ; are they walking in Christ when they do that ? Why, if a man walks in Christ, then he so acteth as Christ would act ; for Christ being in him, his hope, his love, his joy, his life, he is the reflex of the image of Christ ; he is the glass into which Christ looks ; and then the image of Christ is reflected, and men say of that man, " He is like his Master ; he lives in Christ." Oh ! I know, dear brethren, if we lived now as we did the first day we came to Christ, we should live very differently from what we do. How we felt towards Him that day ! We would have given all we had for Him ! How we felt towards sinners that day ! Lad that I was, I wanted to preach, and

" Tell to sinners round,
What a dear Saviour I have found."

How we felt towards God that day ! When we were on our knees what pleading there was with Him, what a nearness of access to Him in prayer ! Oh ! how different ; how different with some now ! This world has with rude hand brushed the bloom from the young fruit. Is it true that flowers of grace, like the flowers of nature, die in the autumn of our piety ? As we all get older, ought we to be more worldly ? Should it be that our early love, which was the love of our espousals, dies away ? Forgive, O Lord, this evil, and turn us anew unto Thee.

" Return, O holy Dove ! return,
Sweet messenger of rest !
We hate the sins that made Thee mourn,
And drove Thee from our breast.

The dearest idol we have known,
Whate'er that Idol be,
Help us to tear it from Thy throne,
And worship only Thee.

So shall our walk be close with God,
Calm and serene our frame ;
So purer light shall mark the road
That leads us to the Lamb."

" As ye have received Him, walk in Him," and if ye have not received Him, oh ! poor sinner, remember He is free and full, full to give thee all thou needest, and free to give it even to thee. Let the verse we sung be an invitation to thee :—

" This fountain, though rich, from charge is quite clear ;
The poorer the wretch, the welcomer here :
Come, needy and guilty ; come, loathsome and bare ;
Though leprous and filthy, come just as you are.

Trust in God's anointed—that is receive Him—and then, having trusted Him, continue still to trust Him. May His Spirit enable you to do it, and to His name shall be glory for ever and ever.

"AS" AND "SO"

"As ye have therefore received Christ Jesus the Lord, so walk ye in Him."—Colossians ii. 6.

THIS is a very simple text, yet no human being has ever discovered its full meaning. It is a great deep; happy are they who know how to dive into its depths, and to swim at ease in its lengths and breadths. Blessed are they who continually obey the exhortation which it contains, "As ye have therefore received Christ Jesus the Lord, so walk ye in Him."

The text divides itself into faith and practice. "Ye have received Christ Jesus the Lord," there is your faith. "Walk ye in Him," that is to be your daily practice. The text also contains a model for that practice in the "as" and the "so" which are its cardinal points: "*As* ye have received Christ Jesus the Lord, *so* walk ye in Him." What we have done suggests the way in which we are to do what still lies before us: "As ye have received . . . so walk."

I. Notice in the text, first, THE FACT STATED: "Ye have received Christ Jesus the Lord."

Whatever else you have done or have not done, *you have received Christ.* The act of faith was the putting out of your empty hand to receive all the fulness of the Godhead in receiving Christ. There are some precious experiences to which you have not yet attained, some lofty heights to which you have not yet climbed, but you "*have* received Christ Jesus the Lord." That is the distinguishing mark of all true Christians. Though you may not all belong to the same denomination, yet without a single exception this is true concerning you, whether you are old or young, whether you are well-instructed or ill-taught, whether you are full of faith or are troubled with many a doubt and many a fear, you "have received Christ Jesus the Lord."

There is nothing in this fact to cause you one boastful thought. You have *received ;* that is what emptiness does in order that it may be filled, that is what hunger does in order that its cravings may be satisfied, that is what the beggar in the street does when he craves and obtains alms. There is nothing whereof you can glory in the fact that you have received, for I may further remind you that even your very receiving you have received. The faith by which you received Christ was as much the gift of God to you as was the Christ upon whom your faith was fixed. You know that it is so, and therefore you also know that boasting is for ever excluded from the fact that you are saved. You have received Christ Jesus, that is all. I hope you prize the gift, and praise the Giver; I trust that you often cry, with the apostle Paul, "Thanks be unto God for His unspeakable gift"; and that your soul makes her boast in the Lord concerning the Saviour whom you have received, but no other boasting is permissible even for a moment.

I remind you once more, beloved, that *you have received* CHRIST. It is true that you have received His doctrines, and that you still believe them. It is true that you have received His precepts, and that you have obeyed them, though, alas! your obedience has been far from perfect. It is true that you have received His ordinances, and that you have

conformed to them by being baptized on profession of your faith in Him, and by sitting down with your fellow-believers at His table. But, after all, the main point is that you have received Jesus Christ Himself. Every word that He has spoken is sweeter than honey and the honeycomb, but sweeter far are the lips with which He uttered those words. Every command of His is to be esteemed more highly than the finest of fine gold, but as for the King who gave those commands, "He is altogether lovely." Human language cannot describe Him, and yet you have received Him, His very self; you have received Him into your hearts, to dwell there as your sole Lord and Master. You have received Him as your life, for you live through Him; and you receive Him day by day as the Bread of life upon which your soul feeds, and as the Water of life which quenches the thirst of your soul. You have not merely received His offices, His gifts, His grace, His promises, but you have received Him. He is the centre of your confidence, the target of your hopes.

The text says that you have received "Christ Jesus the Lord." Here are three out of His many names; and first, beloved, you have received Him as *Christ,* the Anointed of God. You see in Him no amateur Saviour, uncommissioned; but one sent by the Father, the authorized Representative of the Most High, the Christos, the Messias, the Sent One, who could rightly apply to Himself the ancient promise, "The Spirit of the Lord is upon Me, because He hath anointed Me to preach the gospel to the poor; He hath sent Me to heal the broken-hearted, to preach deliverance to the captives, and recovering of sight to the blind, to set at liberty them that are bruised, to preach the acceptable year of the Lord." Christ came to this world because the Father sent Him; He said to the Jews, "I came down from heaven, not to do Mine own will, but the will of Him that sent Me." He lived and died here because it pleased the Father for Him to do so, and He is still appointed by the Father to distribute unnumbered gifts to His people. "It pleased the Father that in Him should all fulness dwell." You believe that upon Christ the Spirit rests without measure, that He is anointed with the oil of gladness above His fellows, and in receiving Him as the anointed One, you also have an unction from the Holy One, and therefore you also are anointed to be kings and priests unto God. So you have received Him as Christ, the Anointed.

But you have also received Him as *Jesus,* and you love that charming name. No hymn more truly expresses your feelings than that one by John Newton which begins,—

"How sweet the name of Jesus sounds
In a believer's ear!
It soothes his sorrows, heals his wounds,
And drives away his fear."

You sing also, with Bernard of Clairvaux,—

"Jesus, the very thought of Thee
With sweetness fills my breast;
But sweeter far Thy face to see,
And in Thy presence rest."

Nor voice can sing, nor heart can frame,
   Nor can the memory find,
A sweeter sound than Thy blest name,
   O Saviour of mankind!"

You received Him as your Saviour, and therefore He has saved you from the penalty of sin, and He will also save you from the dominion and power of sin. If you are saved, you are saved entirely through Jesus; and you do not need, and you do not desire any other Saviour. You look to Jesus for all that can be comprehended in the word salvation. His name means Saviour, and you have found Him to be a Saviour to you. So you have received the anointed Saviour, Christ Jesus.

And you have received Him as *the Lord*. You have not accepted Him as merely one of many anointed prophets, nor as a man sent from God, as John the Baptist was, but you worship Him as the Lord; and oh, how blessed it is to adore the Son of God! We cannot make any terms of peace with those who deny the Deity of Christ, nor ought they to want to be at peace with us; for if Christ is not the Son of God, we are idolaters; and if He is, they are not Christians. There is a great gulf between us and them, and we do not hesitate for a moment to say on which side of that gulf we stand. That same Jesus who was nailed to the tree is to us both Lord and Christ. By faith, we put our finger into the print of the nails, and our hand into His pierced side, and never questioning the fact that He is truly man, we rejoice to say to Him, as Thomas did, "My Lord and my God." Jesus Christ is indeed to us "very God of very God." This being so, we have received Him as our Lord to rule and govern us. In spiritual matters He is our only King, we own no master save Him who is *The* Master, of whom Martha said to her sister Mary, "The Master is come, and calleth for thee." No teacher has any right to impart to us any instruction except that which He has received from the only infallible Teacher. "He is the Head of the body, the Church," and we recognize no other headship; but we joyfully acknowledge that He is our sovereign Lord in the spiritual realm. He is the absolute monarch of our soul. He is that perfect Husband who is the true Head of His mystical body, the Church; oh, that we more fully carried out, practically, in every thought, and wish, and action of our entire life, all that is implied in receiving Jesus Christ as Lord!

Beloved friends, as I look round upon you all, and gaze into your faces, this question rushes from my heart to my lips,—Have all of you received Christ Jesus the Lord? Alas! I am sorrowfully persuaded that there are some of you who have not received Him. He has knocked again and again, with that pierced hand of His, at the door of your heart, but you have not let Him in. This fountain of the Water of life has flowed close to your feet, yet you have not drunk of it. Christ has been set before you as the Bread of life sent down from heaven, but you have not eaten of Him; you have refused Him even until now. "Nay," say you, "you are too severe in charging us with having refused Christ, for we have not done that." Well, it seems to me that this is just what you have done; but I will put it more softly, and say that, at any rate, you have not received Him. You have put Him off to a more convenient season, which will probably never come to you. O poor souls, poor souls, how sad is your state in not having received Christ Jesus the Lord! Leaving out heaven and eternity for the moment, and speaking only of to-day, how wretched you must be in not having received Christ! When I see a man who has never seen the sun, I pity Him, but not as I pity you who have never seen the Sun of Righteousness. If I heard of a child who had never known a father's love, and who had never looked up with affection into a mother's face, I should pity that poor orphan, but not as much as I pity you who are living without a Saviour. If I knew a man who had never known what health was, but who, from the day of His birth, was always sickly, and bowed down with pain and infirmity, I should pity him, but not as I pity you who are sick unto death, yet who will not accept healing from the great Physician. May God look down upon you now, not only with pity, as He always does, but also in the power of His almighty grace, and turn the heart of stone to flesh, and lead you to receive Christ Jesus as Lord! That is all you have to do,—to receive Jesus, as the parched earth receives the refreshing showers, and as the wilted lilies receive the reviving rain-drops, and lift up their drooping heads again. That is all you have to do,—to receive Jesus. A child can receive; the feeblest can receive; aye, one lying at the point of death, the sick man dying of fever may receive the cooling draught that is put to his lips. This is all that is asked of you,—that you will receive Christ Jesus the Lord. Oh, that you would all receive Him now! God grant that it may be so, and He shall have the praise.

II. Now, secondly, notice THE COUNSEL GIVEN: "so walk ye in Him." The text not only reminds us of what we have done, but it also tells us what we are now to do.

Brethren and sisters in Christ, it is not easy to decide whether this counsel is to be regarded as a permission or as a precept: "so walk ye in Him." Taking them either way, the words are a sweet morsel in my mouth; yet I think I prefer to regard them as a permission. Suppose I had been to Jesus as a poor sinner, and that He had saved me; but that He had then said to me, "There, you are saved, so go your way; you have been a prodigal, but you are forgiven; you have shoes on your feet, a ring on your finger, and the best robe to cover your nakedness; now go and do what you can for yourself;"—well, it would have been infinite mercy that would have welcomed me, and pardoned me; but how much more gracious and tender is the Lord's message, "Come, my child, take up your abode with Me, and wander away no more." It is thus that God speaks to all who have believed in Jesus, "You have received Jesus Christ the Lord, so now you may walk in Him, and you may always walk in Him. What He was to you at the first, He may be to you still, and He may be to you for ever and ever. Did you at the first eat Him as the Bread of life to your soul? Then go on still eating Him. Did you spiritually drink of Him as the Water of life? Then still drink of Him. He is yours for ever, so continue to draw from His fulness all that you need. As you have received Him, so keep on receiving Him." Surely, this is a most gracious permission as well as a very precious precept.

"Walk in Him." Does not this mean, first, look upon Jesus Christ as your Way to heaven, and walk in Him? Look upon Him as your Forerunner, and follow Him. Look upon Him as your Companion, and lean upon Him. Look upon Him as your delight, and live in Him, abide in Him. The expression,

"Walk in Him," implies action and progress. Let your whole life be practically governed by your union with Christ, let your actions speak of your fellowship with Him. But walking also means progress, so do not stand still in Christ, but go on to know more and more of Him, make advances in the Christian life, "grow in grace, and in the knowledge of our Lord and Saviour Jesus Christ." There is also something of the idea of permanence in the precept, "Walk ye in Him." It means, go nowhere else, but continue in Him, let your ordinary life and your common conversation indicate your closeness of communion with Him.

"Walk ye in Him." I trust that at least some of us know what it is to "walk in Him." Though we could not tell to others all that it means, yet it is a blessed fact in our experience; and we intend, by God's grace, to "walk in Him" as long as we live. I think this is what walking in Him means,—to wake up in the morning, and to have our first thoughts full of the Saviour; to seek His guidance and blessing in everything that is to happen to us during the day; to go down to our morning meal with our heart's affection fixed upon Jesus; to go off to the business or the workshop in the full consciousness that He is going with us; when our hands are busy, and our mind is occupied with our trading or our working, still realizing that our heart is with our Beloved in the secret place where none can follow us; and so, as the hours run on, through the noontide heat Christ is our shade and shelter, in the cool of the evening His company is our supreme delight, and then, as we retire to our beds, our last thought being—

"How sweet to rest
For ever on our Saviour's breast!"

Christian, this ought to be your way of living; and if you are right with God, this is the way in which you actually do live. You "walk in Him." What a lovely garden! What a delightful place! The air is balmy, the scenery all around is charming; there is nothing to distract, or disturb, or disgust, but everything to delight, and gratify, and satiate the spirit; so "walk in Him." Climb to every lofty hill of His infinite love, explore the deepest recesses of His eternal purposes so far as they are accessible to mortal man; and in this way, "as ye have received Christ Jesus the Lord, so walk ye in Him."

III. Notice, thirdly, THE MODEL WHICH IS PRESENTED TO US IN THE TEXT: "As ye have therefore received Christ Jesus the Lord, so walk ye in Him." The two emphatic words are "as" and "so." We are to walk in Christ Jesus as we received Him.

There is great safety in going back to first principles. To make sure of being in the right way, it is well to look back to the gate by which we entered the way. You know how, in ordinary life, in the matter of mutual love, we often look back upon the early days of that experience as the sweetest. Not long ago, I heard a good man, whose time had been very fully occupied in business, so that for many a year he had scarcely been able to have a holiday, say that, when at last he did manage to take one with his wife, it was like his honeymoon. You recollect also how the Lord said to Israel, "I remember thee, the kindness of thy youth, the love of thine espousals, when thou wentest after Me in the wilderness." God likes us to go back in thought to the time when we began with Him, and I want to take you who are

Christians back to your first love of God. Perhaps, with some of you, religion has beome a very mechanical sort of thing; you have become stereotyped in your religious observances. You need to go back to the place where you first received Christ Jesus the Lord, and there refurbish your faith and love, and all your other graces.

So I ask you, how did you receive Christ? Possibly, your first answer is, "I received Him in the depth of sorrow and humiliation of soul. I had been broken in pieces by the great plough of the law, and was rent and torn asunder by my own consciousness of guilt. I lay before the cross, moaning and roaring like a wounded beast, and in my extremity I received Christ as being the very Saviour that I needed. I felt myself to be less than nothing, and I took Him to be my All-in-all. Shivering in my nakedness through sin, I took His righteousness as my perfect covering. Famished to death, I took Him to be both my life and the food of that life. I grasped Christ in my despair at finding there was nothing else to which I could cling. Out of the great deeps of my soul's distress, I cast myself upon His mercy, saying,—

" 'I can but perish if I go,
I am resolved to try;
For if I stay away, I know
I must for ever die.' "

Our daily walk in Christ must be very much like that; not exactly so, for there should be no unbelief in it. As for myself, I must confess that I never realize Christ's preciousness so much as when I feel myself still to be, apart from Him, an undeserving, ill-deserving, hell-deserving sinner. Sometimes, when our Lord gives us sweet enjoyments, we make too much of them by letting them come between Himself and our souls; and when the Holy Spirit bestows upon us certain graces, we think we are very fine fellows, and carry our heads aloft very proudly, instead of giving all the glory to His holy name. Now, if we ever act like that, we may rest assured that, as we go up in our own estimation, Christ will go down, and that would be a sorry thing indeed. Grow in grace, but not in self-esteem. Have more faith, but do not boast of having it. Be full of zeal, but not of conceit concerning it. Be as holy as it is possible for you to become, but do not prate and brag about your holiness, as some have done. Be not like those who push with horn and with shoulder the weak ones of the flock because they have not attained to such heights as these strong ones profess to have reached; though, possibly, the feebler and humbler ones are really nearer to God than the boasters are. Lie low, brother; lie low, sister; for what the old Essex ploughman used to tell me is true, "If you are one inch above the ground, you are just that inch too high." So lie low, and thus continue to walk in Christ, yourself being nothing, and Christ being everything. You know that, if you get to be something, Christ cannot then be everything to you; but if you are still nothing, and less than nothing in your own estimation, as you sink in self-esteem, your Lord will rise to His right position in your sight, and so you will be walking humbly in Him as you ought.

Think again how you received Christ. When you really did lay hold of Him by faith, I am sure that you received Him with great certainty. There was no mockery, no sham about your reception of Christ. You were a lost sinner, and you were pointed to the only Saviour, and you did really and truly look unto Him who said, "Look unto Me, and be ye saved."

Whatever else there was in your look, there was intense earnestness in it; there was no pretence or affectation about it, it was very real. Is all your religion as real as that first faith-look at Jesus was? Do you walk in Him as truly and as decidedly as you did that first day? My dear brother, do you never pray sham prayers? My dear sister, do you never sing sham praises? Is there not a very great risk of our making our religion into a mere shell with no life in it? May God save us from everything that would be such a sham as that, and make us as sincere in our walk in Christ as we were in our first reception of Him! I know that I was most anxious to be certain that I had really believed in Jesus to the saving of my soul. I was not satisfied with just one look at Jesus, but I looked, and looked, again and again, with a holy anxiety lest I might possibly have been mistaken, and not really have trusted Christ as my Saviour. I wish we had more of that sacred anxiety concerning our walking in Christ.

We were not only very sincere in our early repentance and faith, but *our reception of Christ was very vital.* Salvation was to us a matter of life or death; it was not something *about* which we were only slightly concerned. It would be well if we manifested a similar vitality about our daily walk in Christ. There are some professors, whom I know, who do not seem to me to be alive much above their ankles; they have not sufficient vitality to reach up to their knees, so as to make them mighty in prayer. They are alive, I hope, but they remind me very vividly of a remarkable but gruesome picture of the resurrection that I once saw. There were skeletons coming out of the graves, with the bones only partly covered with flesh. One man had a head without any eyes in it; another was stretching out an arm that was all bone; and the rest of the figures in the picture were of a similar character. It was a strange conception on the part of the painter, yet I fear it was only too true a representation of the spiritual state of many nominal Christians. I hope they are really rising from among the dead, but they have not risen yet into fulness of life. Many professors appear to have a very low vitality, if they are alive at all. Their hearts are hard and horny, their consciences unsensitive; sin does not shock them as it shocks the young convert. He is startled and alarmed at the very appearance of evil, but they have become so callous that they walk, unconcerned, among scenes that ought to break their hearts. May the Lord save you, beloved brethren and sisters in Christ, from all such callousness as that! May you have the same tender sensitiveness to sin that you had when you received Christ Jesus the Lord; and as you welcomed Him then with a warm, loving, overflowing emotion, so may you walk in Him, all your days, as one who is alive from the dead, thoroughly alive, with all your powers and faculties in active exercise, and your whole soul brimming over with love to Him!

Did you not also, beloved, *receive Christ very eagerly?* Have you ever helped to feed a man who had long been without food? If so, you know that it is a great treat to see how eagerly he eats. He does not pick over the meat to see if it is well done; it is all well done to him. He does not leave a scrap of food upon the plate, and he looks round to see if there is any more that he can beg. It was in such a fashion that we feasted upon Christ when we first received Him. We had been for months, perhaps even for years, longing with a great heart-ache to find the Saviour; and when we did find Him, and began to feast upon Him, we thought we never could have enough of Him. Do you recollect how eager you were, in those days, to go where you could hear the gospel? You went to a place which was so crowded that you could not get a seat; but you did not mind standing in the aisle, and you did not feel tired then. But now you want a nice soft cushion to sit on, and a hassock for your feet, and you are weary long before the sermon is finished. In those early days, you would have tramped many miles to hear about Jesus Christ, and even if the preacher's language was somewhat rough and uncouth, what cared you for that so long as he faithfully preached Jesus Christ and Him crucified? That is the way in which we should eagerly walk in Christ still, feeling that we can never have too much of His company, longing to be often where He meets with His people, delighting in His worship, charmed with everything He says and does. We received Christ eagerly, so let us walk in Him with the same eagerness and earnestness.

Many of us also *received Christ very resolutely.* I know that I asked the question, over and over again, "Shall I go to Him?" and at last, when I was almost driven to despair, I cried, "I must, I will,—

"' I'll go to Jesus, though my sin
Hath like a mountain rose;
I know His courts, I'll enter in,
Whatever may oppose.' "

That was how many of us received Christ Jesus the Lord. There were difficulties in our way, but we overcame them, for we were determined to be saved if it was possible. What sacred doggedness, what holy pertinacity will a soul bestow when it is resolved on being saved! Hunger will make a man break through stone walls and iron bars, but a soul that is hungering and thirsting after Christ does not know that there are any walls or bars, so overpowering is its eagerness to get to Him. It was with such eagerness as this that we received Christ Jesus the Lord; are we just as eager to walk in Him? I know that some of you are sorely tempted; are you standing fast? Are you standing up for Jesus as you used to do when you first knew Him? Are you firm as a rock in your resistance to everything that is opposed to Him and to His truth! You ought to be; your song should still be that one of which you were so fond in those early days,—

"Through floods and flames, if Jesus lead,
I'll follow where He goes."

A lion-like spirit was in you then; you would gladly have gone to prison for Christ's sake, or even to death if He had required it. If somebody had told me, when I was converted, that I should have to go to prison, and lie there for twelve years, as John Bunyan did, if I became a Christian, I verily believe that I should have leaped for joy at the prospect of so high an honour. To be a martyr for the truth's sake,—the prospect looked glorious; the ruby crown glowed in the sunshine of our ardent anticipation, and we envied those who had been privileged to wear it. It was so then; but, beloved, is it so now? Can you cleave to Christ as tenaciously now as you did then? Can you bear to be in ill repute for His sake? Can you rejoice in being scoffed at because you are a Christian as you did when you received Christ Jesus the Lord? If you cannot, blush and be ashamed; and from henceforth pray that, with the same undaunted courage and determination with which you received Him, you may continue to walk in Him.

I will not weary you by multiplying words, but I must ask whether you do not recollect *how joyfully you received Christ.* Ah, you cannot forget that; for in proportion to your sorrow before, was your joy when you accepted Christ as your Saviour. No wonder you sang,—

> "Happy day, happy day,
> When Jesus washed my sins away!"

We are not surprised that Miriam and the women went out with timbrels and with dances when Pharaoh and all his host were drowned in the Red Sea, and we do not marvel at Miriam's jubilant song, "Sing ye to the Lord, for He hath triumphed gloriously," for our soul took a timbrel, and our feet danced before the Lord, as we sang unto Him who had triumphed so gloriously for us. As I go back, and remind you of those early joys, I ask you again whether you are as joyous now as you were then; you ought to be a great deal more joyous, for you have had so much more cause to praise the Lord than you had then. Come, brothers and sisters, let us go again to Jesus as we went to Him at the first; let us go as poor, guilty, needy sinners, to Jesus Christ upon the cross, just as though we had never gone before. If we do so, I can tell you what the consequence will be, just as it was at the first. As we

> "View the flowing
> Of our Saviour's precious blood,
> With divine assurance knowing
> He hath made our peace with God,"

we shall feel as though we were young converts once again. We may be getting old and grey, and perhaps cold as well as grey, but we shall become like little children again, and we shall shout "Hosanna! Hosanna! Hosanna!" as the Son of David rides in triumph down the streets of our soul. Oh, that it may be so with many of us here! It ought to be so, and it will be so, if you walk in Christ Jesus the Lord as you received Him in the hour of your conversion.

I will close my discourse when I have just reminded you that, when we received Christ Jesus the Lord, *we received the whole of Him.* We took Him for all that we knew of Him, and we found that He was much more than we then thought He was; but we did not pick and choose, and say, "We will have His pardon, but we will not have His sanctification." We took the many-sided Christ, the Christ of many glorious characters, the Christ of ten thousand times ten thousand beauties; we took Christ to teach us, Christ to lead us, Christ to feed us, Christ to cheer us,

Christ for us to obey, and Christ for us to delighti n; we took a whole Christ. And then we gave Him our whole selves. We said, "Lord, take us, body, soul, and spirit;" we prayed that the sacrifice might be bound with cords to the horns of the altar for ever. We made no bargains with Him; we gave the freehold of our souls to Jesus, and of our bodies too, and we only asked that we might not have a pulse beating except for Him, or our lungs heaving except as He was our very life. And we took Christ—at least I know I did,—for better or worse, in health or in sickness, to have and to hold so that even death should never part us. We put our hand in His, and asked Him to take us, and keep us for ever; and we took Him, and said, "We will hold to Thee, and will not let Thee go." Since then, there has been many a tug from Satan, who has tried to drag us away from Christ, or to make us think that Christ was going away from us; but we have managed to hold to Him to this hour. Perhaps you feel as though you had only got a hold of the hem of His garment; if so, try to get a firmer hold of Him; grasp Him, hold Him by the feet, throw your arms about Him, and tell Him that, without a smile from Him, your spirit cannot rest. Tell Him that you are sick of love, and want His presence, and must have it; and beg Him, by the roes and by the hinds of the field, to come to you. Say unto Him, "My Lord, if Thou dost love me, come and show Thy love. If, indeed, there be between Thee and me a union of an eternal nature, come to me. Be not strange to Thine own flesh; but be now as Thou wast of old. Come to me again and let Thy left hand be under my head while Thy right hand doth embrace me." Oh, for more of these blessed hungerings and longings! Beloved, we will never let Christ go. We took Him for ever, and we will hold Him for ever; and, blessed be His name, He will hold us for ever. We are in His hand, and none can pluck us thence. There shall we be when earth and heaven are in a blaze; there shall we be when He shall sit upon His judgment-seat; and there shall we be world without end. Amen.

I leave this sermon with God's people, but I cannot help adding that I do earnestly pray that all of you may receive Christ Jesus the Lord. Oh, come to Him to-night! He is willing that you should have Him, and every soul that wills to have Christ may have Him; for "the Spirit and the bride say, Come. And let him that heareth say, Come. And let him that is athirst come. And whosoever will, let him take the water of life freely." Amen, and Amen.

LIFE AND PARDON

"And you, being dead in your sins and the uncircumcision of your flesh, hath He quickened together with Him, having forgiven you all trespasses."—Colossians ii. 13.

THE teaching of this verse is much the same as that in preceding verses; but the apostle does not hesitate to dwell again and again upon the important matters of quickening and forgiveness. These lie in the foundation. Ministers of Christ cannot too often go over the essential points: their hearers cannot too often hear vital truths. Our frail memories and dull understandings require line upon line, precept upon precept, in reference to fundamental truths: our apprehension of them is far too feeble, and can never be too vivid.

To find instances of the work of God in quickening souls and in pardoning sins, Paul does not look far afield. In the text he says, "*And you,*" and, according to the Revised Version, he repeats the word further on, and the passage runs thus, "You, being dead through your trespasses and the uncircumcision of your flesh, *you, I say,* did He quicken together with Him." He points personally to the saints at Colosse. We are not about to consider a prophecy to be fulfilled in the millennium, neither are we speaking of matters which concern the unknown dwellers in the moon. No; the theme belongs to you, to you, I say, if indeed you be the people of God. You are specimens of the divine work: *you* hath He quickened, *you* hath He pardoned. It is profitable for us to be engaged upon matters which concern us. I shall speak to you of those things which I have tasted and handled of the good word of life, and it is my firm belief that, to the most of you, these matters are familiar in your mouths as household words. If not, I grieve over you. Let none of us be content unless the works of the Holy Spirit are manifest in us. What boots it to me if another man receive life and pardon, if I am cast for death, and he still under condemnation? Press forward, my beloved, to a personal enjoyment of these chief blessings of the covenant of grace—life in Jesus, forgiveness through His blood. Let every part of the sermon have a finger pointed at yourselves. Hear it speak to you, even to you.

In the text we have the conjunction of two things—quickening and forgiveness. We will consider these things in connection with each other. Their order it may be difficult to lay down: in the text they are described as if they were the same thing. Which comes first, the impartation of the new life, or the blotting out of sin? Is not pardon first? Doth God pardon a dead man? How can He give the life which is the proof of pardon to the man who is not forgiven? On the other hand, if a man has not spiritual life sufficient to make him feel his guilt, how can he cry for pardon? And if it be unsought, how shall it be received? A man may be spiritually alive so as to be groaning under the pollution and the burden of sin, and yet he may not have received by faith the remission of sins. In the order of our experience, the reception of life comes before the enjoyment of pardon. We are made to live spiritually, and so we are made to repent, to confess, to believe, and to receive forgiveness. First, the life which sighs under sin, and then the life which sings concerning pardon. Misery is first felt, and then mercy is received.

Following the line of experience, we shall notice concerning the favoured ones of God, *what they were :* "You, being dead in your sins and the uncircumcision of your flesh." Secondly, we shall note *what has been done in them :* "Hath he quickened together with Him"; and then, thirdly, *what He hath done for them :* "Having forgiven you all trespasses." May the Holy Ghost lead us into these truths, and give us the life of God and the rest of faith!

I. First, then, consider WHAT THEY WERE. Beloved, they were all by nature children of wrath, even as others. There is no distinction in the condition of natural men before the law. We all fell in Adam. We are all gone out of the way, and have all become unprofitable. Any difference which now exists has been made by divine grace; but by nature we are all in the same condemnation, and all tainted by the same depravity.

Where were we when the Lord first looked on us? Answer.—We were *dead according to the sentence of the law.* The Lord had said, "In the day that thou eatest thereof thou shalt surely die"; and Adam did die the moment that he ate of the forbidden fruit, and his posterity died in him. What is death natural? It is the separation of the body from the soul, which is its life. What is death spiritual? It is the separation of the soul from God, who is its life. It had been the very life of Adam to be united to God; and when he lost his union of heart with God, his spirit underwent a dreadful death. This death is upon each one of us by nature. Above this comes in the dreadful fact, that "He that believeth not is condemned already." The position of every unbeliever is that of one who is dead by law. As far as the liberties, and privileges, and enjoyments of heavenly things are concerned, he is written among the dead. His name is registered among the condemned. Yet, beloved, while we are under the sentence of death, the Lord comes to us in almighty grace, and quickens us into newness of life, forgiving us all trespasses. Are you trembling because of your condemned condition under the law? Do you recognize the tremendous truth that death is the sure and righteous result of sin? Then to you, even to you, the life-giving, pardoning word is sent in the preaching of the everlasting gospel. Oh that you may believe, and so escape from condemnation!

These favoured people were *dead through the action of their sin.* Sin stupefies and kills. Where it reigns, the man is utterly insensible to spiritual truth, feeling, and action; he is dead to everything that is holy in the sight of God. He may have keen moral perceptions, but he has no spiritual feelings. Men differ widely as to their moral qualities; all men are not alike bad, especially when measured in reference to their fellow-men; some may even be excellent and praiseworthy, viewed from that standpoint. But to *spiritual* things all men are alike dead. Look at the multitude of our hearers; to what purpose do we preach to them? You may declare the wrath of God against the godless, but what do they care? You may speak of Jesus' love to the lost; how little it affects them! Sin is not horrible, and salvation is not precious, to them. They may not controvert your teaching; but they have no sensible apprehension of truth; it does not come home to them as a matter of any consequence. Let eternal things drift as they may, they are perfectly content so long as they can answer those three questions—"What shall we eat? what shall we drink? and wherewithal shall we be clothed?" No higher question troubles their earth-bound minds. They may entertain some liking towards theological study and Bible-teaching, as a matter of education; but they do not view the truths revealed in Scripture as matters of overwhelming importance. They trifle; they delay; they set on one side the things which make for their peace. Their religion has no influence upon their thoughts and actions: they are dead. Sin has slain them. I see them mingled with this great congregation like corpses sitting upright among the living. I look out upon the masses of this vast city and upon the innumerable hosts of populous countries, and I see a measureless cemetery, a dread domain of death; a region without life.

One point must be noticed here, which makes this spiritual death the more terrible: *they are dead, but yet responsible.* If men were literally dead, they were incapable of sin; but the kind of death of which we speak involves a responsibility none the less, but all the greater. If I say of a man that he is such a liar that he cannot speak the truth, do you therefore think him blameless? No; but you judge him to be all the more worthy of condemnation because he has lost the very sense which discerns between a truth and a lie. If we say of a certain man, as we have had to do, "He is a rogue ingrained; he is so tricky that he cannot deal honestly, but must always be cheating"; do you therefore excuse his fraud, and pity him? Far from it. His inability is not physical, but moral inability, and is the consequence of his own persistence in evil. The law is as much binding upon the morally incapable as upon the most sanctified in nature. If, through a man's own perversity, he wills to reject good and love evil, the blame is with himself. He is said to be dead in sin, not in the sense that he is irresponsible, but in the sense that he is so evil that he will not keep the law of God. If a man were brought tomorrow before the Lord Mayor, and he were accused of theft; suppose he should say, "My lord, I ought to be set free, for I am such a rascal that I cannot see an article in a shop but what my fingers itch to lay hold upon it"; would not the judge give such a worthless person all the more punishment? O sinners, dead in sin, you are not so dead as thereby to be free from the guilt of breaking God's command, and rejecting Christ; but you heap upon yourselves mountains of guilt every day that you abide in this condition.

The ungodly are so dead as to be careless as to their state. Indeed, all gracious things are despised of them. Sometimes they attend religious services; but they get angry if the preacher presses them too hard. I have known them vow that they will never hear the man again because he is so personal. Pray, sirs, what is a preacher to be but personal? If he shoots, is he to have no target, and take no aim? What is our very office and business for, but to deal personally with you about your sins? In ungodly men there is an utter recklessness as to their condition before God. They know that they may die, they know that if they die they will be lost; but they try to forget these facts. The ostrich is said to bury its head in the sand so as not to see the hunter, and then to fancy that it is safe. Thus do men fancy that, by forgetting the danger, they escape it. Some of you have lived in carelessness until grey hairs are on your head. Will you still risk your souls? Alas, you look more anxiously after a battered sixpence, which you miss from your pocket, than after your immortal soul! If you miss a ring from your finger while sitting here, you are more concerned about it than about your eternal destiny. How foolish! How dead are you to all just judgment and prudence! It is your soul, your own soul, your only soul, your never-dying soul, to which we beg you to pay attention, and yet you can hardly have patience with us. If a prisoner in the condemned cell had no sort of care whether he should be set free or hanged, but could even joke about the scaffold and the executioner, you would feel that only by an extreme act of mercy could such a person be pardoned. Nay, if he cares nothing for the penalty, let him bear it: so man would say, and there would be justice in it. Yet God spake not so in reference to some of us; for while we were in a condition of callousness the grace of God came to us, and by quickening us, gave us to be anxious, and led us to pray.

The text adds that we were *dead in the uncircumcision of our flesh.* I need not dwell upon the external figure here employed; its meaning is clear enough. The uncircumcision of our flesh means that we were not in covenant with God; it shows also the abiding of our filthiness upon us; the willingness of our souls to be aliens from the commonwealth of Israel, without God in the world. This is where we were in the uncircumcision of our flesh; and yet the **grace** of God found us out. Oh, I could paint the man! He is anxious about this world, but what cares he for the world to come? He is a master of his own trade, and he prospers in it; but for his God, and His service, he spares not an hour's consideration. He cries, "The covenant of grace, what is that?" And he turns on his heel, like Pilate, when he had said, "What is truth?" As to having any sense of the constant presence of God, and his deep indebtedness to God, and of the sweetness of being pardoned, and the bliss of enjoying the love of God, and walking with God, he has no notion, or, at best, he cries, "Oh, yes, that is all very fine for those who have nothing else to do; let them find delight in it if they can!" To him God is nothing, heaven is nothing, hell less than nothing. He passes by Calvary itself, where God in human flesh is bleeding out redemption, and it is nothing to him. The wail from the cross he never hears, though it asks him this question—"Is it nothing to you, all ye that pass by? behold, and see if there be any sorrow like unto My sorrow!" What cares he for the wounds of his soul's best Lover? He has no concern about any purchase made by the Redeemer, or of any death especially on his behalf, or any resurrection with Christ which he may hope to enjoy. The man is dead to faith, and glory, and immortality. The low and the grovelling charm him, but the pure and the noble find him dead to their claims. Yet to such, even to such, does sovereign grace approach. Unbought, unsought, it cometh according to that word of Scripture, "I am found of them that sought Me not."

Again, spiritually the ungodly are *dead, and utterly incapable of obtaining life for themselves.* Could any of you, with the utmost diligence, create life, even the lowest form of it? To a man who is dead, could you impart life? You might galvanize his limbs into a kind of motion; but real life, the pulsing of the heart, the heaving of the lungs, could you create it? You know you cannot! Much less can the dead man himself create life within himself. The man without Christ is utterly unable to quicken himself. We are "without strength," unable to do anything as of ourselves, and while we are in this condition grace comes to us.

Alas, there remains one more point! Man may be described as *dead and becoming corrupt.* After a while the dead body shows symptoms of decay: this is vice in its beginning. Leave the corpse where it is, and it will become putrid, polluting the air, and disgusting every sense of the living. "Bury my dead out of my sight," is the cry of the most affectionate mother or wife. And so it is with many ungodly men. Some of them are restrained from the grosser vices, just as Egyptian bodies were, by spices, preserved from rottenness. By example, by instruction, by fear, by surroundings, many are kept from the more putrid sins, and therefore are not so obnoxious to society. Towards God they are dead as ever; but towards man they are no more objectionable than the mummies in yonder cases in the British Museum. But this embalming of the dead with spices of morality, has not been carried out with hosts of those around us. They rot above ground: their blasphemies pollute the air, their lewdness infects our streets, their revelry makes night hideous. The tendency of dead flesh is towards the corruption which shows itself in loathesome actions. The mercy is, that where even this has taken place, where the foul worm of vice has begun its awful work, in drunkenness, in blasphemy, in dishonesty, or in uncleanness of life—even there the quickening Spirit can come. As life came to Lazarus, who had been dead four days, so can spiritual life come to those who have fallen into the noisomeness of open transgression. Leaving this painful matter, let us be filled with deep humility; for such were we in days not long since: but let us also be filled with hope for others; for He who quickened us can do the same for them.

II. And now, secondly, WHAT HAS BEEN DONE IN US? What hath God wrought?

We have been quickened. To tell you, exactly, how quickening is worked in us, is quite beyond my power. The Holy Spirit comes to a man when he is dead in sin, and He breathes into him a new and mysterious life. We do not know how we receive our natural life: how the soul comes into the body we know not. Do you suppose that spiritual life in its beginning will be less mysterious? Did not our Lord say, "The wind bloweth where it listeth, and thou hearest the sound thereof, but canst not tell whence it cometh, and whither it goeth: so is every one that is born of the Spirit"? Thou knowest not the way of the Spirit, nor how He breathes eternal life. We know, however, that as soon as life comes, our first feeling is one of pain and uneasiness. In the case of persons who have been nearly drowned, when they begin to revive they experience very unpleasant sensations. Certainly the parallel holds good in spiritual things. Now, the man sees sin to be an exceeding great evil. He is startled by the discovery of its foulness. He was told all about it, and yet he knew nothing to purpose; but now sin becomes a load, a pain, a horror. As dead, he felt no weight; but as quickened, he groans beneath a load. Now he begins to cry, "O wretched man that I am! who shall deliver me?" Now the angels see him on his knees in private. Behold, he prayeth! "God be merciful to me a sinner," is his hourly sigh. Now, also, he begins to struggle against his evil habits: he addicts himself to Bible reading, to praying, and to hearing the word of God. He is for a while desperately earnest. Alas, he goes back to his old sin! Yet he cannot rest: again he seeks the Lord. With some men a large part of their early spiritual life has been taken up with agonizing strivings and painful endeavours to free themselves from the chains of sin. They have had to learn their weakness by their failures; but the grace of God has not failed. Some, even for years after their conviction by the Spirit of God, have had no comfortable sense of pardon, but very much conflict with sin: yet, still, the life of God has never been utterly quenched within them. Their struggles have proved that the heavenly germ was alive, and was painfully resisting the forces of evil. Men themselves act as if they tried to put out the light which grace has kindled; but they cannot effect their purpose. When once they have been disturbed in their nest, the Lord has not allowed them to settle down in it again. Their once sweet sin has become bitter as wormwood to them. We have known men under conviction go further into sin to drown their convictions; just as a whale, when harpooned, will dive into the depths. But they come up again, and again are wounded: they cannot escape. In the biography of a man of God, who in his early days was a terrible drunkard, we find that, in struggling against intoxication, he was frequently beaten; and there appears in his diary a long blank of which he says, "Four years and a half elapsed, and no account rendered! What can have been the cause of this chasm? Sin! Yes, sin of the blackest dye, of the deepest ingratitude to the Father of mercies!" The wanderer was restless and unhappy in sin. The life within was, like Jonah, thrown into the depths of the sea; but it hated its condition, and struggled to rise out of it. God will not leave the life He has given, even under the worst conditions.

But quickening leads to far more than this. By-and-by the new life exercises its holy senses, and is more clearly seen to be life. The man begins to see that his only hope is in Christ, and he tries humbly to hide himself beneath the merit of the Lord Jesus. He does not dare to say, "I am saved," but he deeply feels that if ever he is saved it must be through the blood and righteousness of the Lord Jesus. Now also he begins to pray, pleading the precious blood; now he hopes, and his hope looks only through the windows of his Lord's wounds. He looks for mercy only through the atoning sacrifice. By-and-by he comes to trust that this mercy has really come to him, and that Jesus had him on His heart when He suffered on the tree. By a desperate effort he throws himself on Christ, and determines to lie at His feet, and, if he must perish, to perish looking unto Jesus. This is a glorious resolve. See him after a while as he rises up into peace, and joy, and consecration! His life now being joined to that of his Lord, he rejoices that he is never to be separated from Him. I think I hear him say, "I see it all now. The Lord Jesus bore my sin and carried it away. I died because He died. I live because He lives. The Lord accepts me, because He accepts His Son, and thus I am 'accepted in the Beloved.'"

Henceforth the quickened man tries to live for Christ, out of gratitude; this is the nature of the life he has received. He strives to grow up into Christ, and to become like his Lord in all things. Henceforth he and his Lord are linked together in an everlasting union, and the cause of Jesus is the one thing for which he lives, and for which he would be content to die. Blessed be God, I am not talking any new things to you: you know what I mean. For these forty years have I felt these things, and many of you have felt them longer still. At first the struggling life within you revealed to you nothing but your darkness; but now you see Jesus, and see yourselves alive in Him with a life eternal and heavenly. Blessed be the Lord who hath raised Jesus from the dead, and hath quickened us in Him and with Him!

III. Now we come to the third point, upon which I pray for a renewed unction from the Holy One. Let us consider, in the last place, WHAT HAS BEEN DONE FOR US: "Having forgiven you all trespasses." Believing in Christ Jesus, I am absolved. I am clear, I am clear before the Lord. "There is therefore now no condemnation to them which are in Christ Jesus." This is the most joyful theme that I can bring before you. And I want you to notice, first, that *pardon is a divine act.* "Having forgiven all trespasses." Who does that? Why, He that quickened you. I showed just now that none could quicken a dead man but God only; for the giving of life is an act which is exclusively the Lord's own: and the same God who gives us spiritual life also grants us pardon from His throne. He sovereignly dispenses pardons. We need not go to any human priest to seek absolution, for we may go at once to God who alone hath sovereign right to execute the death-sentence or to pardon the offender. He alone can grant it with sure effect. If any man should say, *absolvo te* (I absolve thee), I would take it for what it was worth, and its worth would not be much. But if HE saith it, who is the Law-giver, and the supreme King; if HE saith it, against whom I have offended, then am I happy indeed. Glory be to His name, who is a God ready to pardon! What bliss I have received in receiving forgiveness from God! Oh, my hearer, if you have done wrong to your fellow-man, ask his forgiveness, as you are bound to do; and if you get it, be thankful, and feel as if a weight were removed from your conscience. But, after all, what is this compared with being forgiven all trespasses by God Himself? This can calm the ruffled sea of the soul; yea, still its fiercest tempest. This can make you sleep at nights, instead of tossing to and fro upon a pillow, which conscience turns to stone beneath your aching head. This gives the gleaming eye, the beaming face, the bounding heart. This brings heaven down to earth, and lifts us near to heaven. The Lord hath blotted out our sins, and thus He has removed the bitterest fountain of our sorrows. Pardon from God is a charter of liberty, a testament of felicity.

God's pardon is a gift most free. Look at the text, and note that this pardon comes to persons who are dead in sin. They were utterly unworthy, and did not even seek mercy. The Lord who comes to men when they are dead in sin, comes to quicken them and to pardon them; not because they are ready, but because HE is ready. Hearken, O man! If in thy bosom there is at this moment a great stone instead of a heart of flesh; if thou art paralyzed as to all good things; if there is only enough life in thee to make thee feel thy terrible incapacity for holiness and fellowship with God, yet God can pardon thee, even as thou art, and where thou art. We were in that condition, my brethren, when the Lord came to us in love. "When we were yet without strength, in due time Christ died for the ungodly." We saw that Jesus died, we believed in Him as able to save, and we received the forgiveness of sins. Forgiveness is free. The Lord looks for no good thing in the sinner; but He gives him every good thing. O my hearer, if the Lord looked for good in thee, He could not find it. He looks for nothing thou canst do, and nothing thou canst feel, and nothing thou canst resolve to do or feel; but He shows mercy because He delighteth in mercy. He passes by iniquity, transgression, and sin, because it is His nature to be gracious. The cause of divine pardon is in God Himself, and in His dear Son. It is not in thee, O sinner! Being dead in the uncircumcision of thy flesh, what canst thou do? He quickens thee and He pardons thee; yea, He is all in all to thee. Wonders of grace! When I get upon this subject I do not need to give you illustrations, nor to find out choice phrases; the glorious fact stands forth in its own native beauty: infinite pardon from an infinite God, given because of His own mercifulness and the merit of His beloved Son, and not because of anything whatsoever in the man whom He pardons. "But the man repents," says one. Yes, I know; but God gives him repentance. "But he confesses sin." Yes, I know it; for the Lord leads him to acknowledge his trespasses. All and everything which looks like a condition of pardon, is also given by the free and sovereign grace of God, and given freely, without money and without price.

I want you to notice *how universal is this pardon* in reference to all sin: "Having forgiven you *all* trespasses." Consult your memory, and think of all your trespasses, if you dare. That one black night! Has it left a crimson spot, indelible, never to be concealed? In many instances one special sin breeds more distress than a thousand others. That crime has left a deeper scar than any other. In vain you cry, "Out, hideous spot!" Should you wash that hand, it would incarnadine ten thousand Atlantics, and yet it would remain a scarlet spot, never to be erased for ever. No process known to men can wash out the stain. But God's infinite mercy can put away that hideous, unmentionable crime, and it shall be as though it had never been. Possibly, however, you do not so much remember any one transgression as the whole heap of them. Certainly, a multiplicity of minor sins heaped together tower upward like a great Alp, although no one offence may seem so notable as to demand mention. We have sinned every day, and every hour, and almost every moment of every hour: how numberless our transgressions! Our sins of omission are beyond all compute. But all these, too many for you to remember, too many for me to number, are forgiven to the man in Christ: "Having forgiven you all trespasses"—all, not one excepted. Thou hast sins not yet known and confessed—but they are forgiven; for the blood cleanseth from all sin.

I should like to help your memory by reminding you of your sins before conversion. Blessed is he whose sin is covered. One does not wish to uncover it. "Lord, remember not the sins of my youth, nor my transgressions." The child of God, who has long been rejoicing in faith, has need to pray *that;* for our sins may vex our bones long after they have been removed from our consciences: the consequences of a sin may fret us after the sin itself is forgiven.

Then think of your sins after conviction. You were struck down on a certain day with a great sense of sin, and you hurried home and cried upon your knees, "O God, forgive me!" Then you vowed you would never do the like again; but you did. The dog returned to his vomit. You began to attend a place of worship, you were very diligent in religious duties; but on a sudden you went back to your old companions, and your old ways. If your sin was drink, you thought you had mastered it, and could be very moderate; but a fierce thirst came upon you, which you could not resist, and you were soon as drunken as ever. Remember this with shame. Or it may have been a more deliberate backsliding; and deliberation greatly adds to the sin of sins. Without being particularly tempted, you began to hanker after your old pleasures, and almost to despise yourself for having denied yourself their indulgence. I know a man who was present at a prayer-meeting and was so wrought upon that he prayed; but afterwards he said that he would never go into such a place again, for fear he should again be overcome. Think of being afraid to be led aright: ashamed to go to heaven! Ah friends, we have been bullocks unaccustomed to the yoke, dogs that have slipped their collars, horses that have kicked over the traces. Sins after conviction, as doing despite to divine love, are very grievous trespasses. Like the moth, you had your wings singed in the candle, and yet you flew back to the flame: if you had perished in it, who could have pitied you? Yet, after such folly, the Lord had mercy on you: "Having forgiven you all trespasses."

A still worse set of sins must be remembered, sins after conversion, sins after you have found peace with God, after you have enjoyed high fellowship with Jesus. O brothers and sisters, these are cruel wounds for our Lord! These are evils which should melt us to tears even to hear of them. What! pardoned and then sin again! Beloved of the Lord, and still rebelling! You sang so sweetly,

"Thy will be done; Thy will be done,"

and then went home and murmured! You talked to others about evil temper, and yet grew angry. You are old and experienced, and yet no boy could have been more imprudent! O God, we bless Thee for the morning and the evening lamb; for Thy people need the sacrifice perpetually! We need a morning sacrifice, lest the night have gathered aught of evil; and we require an evening sacrifice for the sins of the day.

Dwell for a while upon the large blessing of the text. Whatever your sins may have been, if you are a believer in the Lord Jesus Christ, God has quickened you together with Him, and has forgiven you all trespasses. *He pardons most effectually.* Ask God about your sins, and He says, "Their sins and their iniquities will I remember no more!" If God Himself does not remember them, they are most effectually removed. Ask Holy Scripture where they are, and Hezekiah tells you, "Thou hast cast all my sins behind Thy back." Where is that? God sees everything and everywhere, and therefore everywhere is before His face; if, therefore, He casts our sins behind His back, He throws our sins into "the nowhere": they cease to exist. "In those days, saith the Lord, the iniquity of Israel shall be sought for, and there shall be none; and the sins of Judah, and they shall not be found." Surely this is enough to set all the bells of your heart a-ringing.

Remember, also, dear friends, that *this pardon is most perfect.* He does not commute the punishment but He pardons the crime. He does not pardon and then confine for life, nor pardon to-day and punish to-morrow: this were not worthy of God. The pardon is given, and never revoked: the deed of grace is done, and it can never be undone. God will not remember the sin which He has blotted out, nor condemn the offender whom He has absolved. O believer, the Lord so fully absolves thee, that all thy sin, which might have shut thee out of heaven, shall not even hinder thy way thither! All that sin of thine, which might have filled thee with despair shall not even fill thee with dismay. The Lord shall wipe the tear from thine eyes, as He has washed the sin from thy person. Even the very stain of sin shall be removed. Remember what He says of scarlet and crimson sins. Does He say, "I will wash them so that nothing shall remain beyond a pale red"? Does He say, "I will wash them till nothing shall remain but a slight rosy tint"? No; He says, "They shall be as wool: I will make them white as snow." The Almighty Lord will do His work of remission in an absolutely perfect style, and not a shadow of a spot shall remain.

Here is a point that I must dwell upon for a moment, namely, that *this pardon shall be seen to be perfectly consistent with justice.* If I were pardoned, and felt that God had weakened the foundations of His moral government by winking at evil, I should feel insecure in my pardoned state, and should have no rest. If the justice of God were in the least infringed by my forgiveness, I should feel like a felon towards the universe, and a robber of God. But I bless God that He pardons sin in strict connection with justice. Behold the costly system by which this was effected. He Himself came hither in the person of His dear Son; He Himself became man, and dwelt among us; He Himself took the load of His people's sin; He bare the sin of many, and was made a curse for us. He put away both sin and the curse by His wondrous sacrifice. The marvel of heaven and earth, of time and eternity, is the atoning death of Jesus Christ. This is the mystery that brings more glory to God than all creation, and all providence. How could it be that He should be slain for sinners, the just for the unjust, to bring us to God? To finish transgression, and make an end of sin, was a labour worthy of His Godhead, and Christ has perfectly achieved it by His sufferings and death. You had no fiction before you when, just now, you sang concerning Him,

"Jesus was punished in my stead,
Without the gate my Surety bled
To expiate my stain:
On earth the Godhead deigned to dwell,
And made of infinite avail
The sufferings of the Man."

Now are we justly forgiven; and the throne of God is established. By His death as our Substitute our Lord Jesus has set forth the righteous severity of God as well as His boundless mercy. To us justice and mercy seemed opposed, but in Jesus we see them blended. We bless the Lord for His atoning sacrifice, and feel an infinite satisfaction in the fact that none can dispute the validity of a pardon which comes to us signed by the hand of the eternal King, and counter-signed by the pierced hand of Him who bare our sins in His own body on the tree, and gave for those sins a complete vindication of the law which we had broken.

Note well the last consideration upon this point of the forgiveness of all trespasses. It ought to make you feel unutterably happy. Henceforth, *your pardon is bound up with the glory of Christ.* If your pardon does not save you, then Christ is no Saviour. If, resting in Him, your sin is not forgiven, then He undertook a fruitless errand when He came to save His people from their sins. Every drop of Christ's blood demands the eternal salvation of every soul that is washed in it. The Godhead and manhood of Christ, and all the glory of His mediatorship, stand up and claim for every believer that he shall be delivered from sin. What! did He bear sin, and shall *we* bear it? Nay: if the Lord hath found in Him a ransom, His redeemed are free. Since to save me, who was once dead in sin and in the uncircumcision of my flesh, has become the glory of Christ, I am sure I shall be saved, for He will not tarnish His own name. O believer, to bring you home without spot, or wrinkle, or any such thing, has become the ambition of your Saviour, and He shall not fail nor be discouraged. He will neither lose His life-work, nor His death throes. God forbid! And yet this must be, unless you who are quickened together with Him, shall be found at the last without fault before the throne of God.

Now, let us just think of this: *we are forgiven.* I

do not mean all of you; for if you are out of Christ, you have no part in this grand absolution. May the Lord have mercy upon you, quicken you to-day and bring you to Christ! But as many as are trusting in Christ, and so are living in union with Him, *are forgiven*. A person who has been condemned by the law, and then has received a free pardon, walks out of the prison, and goes where he pleases. There is a policeman. Does he fear him? No, he has a free pardon, and the policeman cannot touch him. But there are a great many persons who know him, and know him to be guilty. That does not matter; he has a free pardon, and nobody can touch him. He cannot be tried again, however guilty he may have been; the free pardon has wiped the past right out. Now, to-day, child of God, thou beginnest anew; thou art clean, for He has washed thee, and has done the work right well. We have washed our robes and made them white in the blood of the Lamb,

therefore shall we be before the throne of God, and praise Him. What could we do less than praise Him day and night? When shall we ever stop? When we are in His temple, free from all danger of future sin and trial, we will for ever praise Him who hath forgiven us all trespasses. I charge you, let us meet in heaven, all of us. Some have dropped in here this morning from all parts of the country, and from America, and we may never meet again on earth. Let us meet around the throne in heaven, and sing "unto Him that loved us, and washed us from our sins in His own blood." God grant that we may. Who wants to be left out? Is there one person here who would like to be shut out in that day? I pray you, enter in at once.

> "Come guilty souls, and flee away
> Like doves to Jesus' wounds;
> This is the welcome gospel-day,
> Wherein free grace abounds."

CHRIST TRIUMPHANT

"And having spoiled principalities and powers, He made a show of them openly, triumphing over them in it."—Colossians ii. 15.

TO the eye of reason the cross is the centre of sorrow and the lowest depth of shame. Jesus dies a malefactor's death. He hangs upon the gibbet of a felon and pours out His blood upon the common mount of doom with thieves for His companions. In the midst of mockery, and jest, and scorn, and ribaldry, and blasphemy, He gives up the ghost. Earth rejects Him and lifts Him from her surface, and heaven affords Him no light, but darkens the mid-day sun in the hour of His extremity. Deeper in woe than the Saviour dived, imagination cannot descend. A blacker calumny than was cast on Him satanic malice itself could not invent. He hid not His face from shame and spitting; and what shame and spitting it was! To the world the cross must ever be the emblem of shame: to the Jew a stumbling-block, and to the Greek foolishness. How different however is the view which presents itself to the eye of faith. Faith knows no shame in the cross, except the shame of those who nailed the Saviour there; it sees no ground for scorn, but it hurls indignant scorn at sin, the enemy which pierced the Lord. Faith sees woe, indeed, but from this woe it marks a fount of mercy springing. It is true it mourns a dying Saviour, but it beholds Him bringing life and immortality to light at the very moment when His soul was eclipsed in the shadow of death. Faith regards the cross, not as the emblem of shame, but as the token of glory. The sons of Belial lay the cross in the dust, but the Christian makes a constellation of it, and sees it glittering in the seventh heaven. Man spits upon it, but believers, having angels for their companions, bow down and worship Him who ever liveth though once He was crucified. My brethren, our text presents us with a portion of the view which faith is certain to discover when its eyes are anointed with the eye-salve of the Spirit. It tells us that the cross was Jesus Christ's field of triumph. There He fought, and there He conquered, too. As a victor on the cross He divided the spoil Nay, more than this; in our text the cross is spoken of as being Christ's triumphal chariot in which He rode when He led captivity captive, and received gifts for men.

Calvin thus admirably expounds the last sentence of our text:—"The expression in the Greek allows, it is true, of our reading—*in Himself*; the connection of the passage, however, requires that we read it otherwise; for what would be meagre as applied to Christ, suits admirably well as applied to the cross. For as He had previously compared the cross to a signal trophy or show of triumph, in which Christ led about His enemies, so He now also compares it to a triumphal car in which He showed Himself in great magnificence. For there is no tribunal so magnificent, no throne so stately, no show of triumph so distinguished, no chariot so elevated, as is the gibbet on which Christ has subdued death and the devil, the prince of death; nay, more, has utterly trodden them under His feet."

I shall this morning, by God's help, address you upon the two portions of the text. First, I shall endeavour to describe *Christ as spoiling His enemies on the cross*; and having done that I shall lead your imagination and your faith further on to see *the Saviour in triumphal procession upon His cross*, leading His enemies captive, and making a shew of them openly before the eyes of the astonished universe.

I. First, our faith is invited this morning to behold CHRIST MAKING A SPOIL OF PRINCIPALITIES AND POWERS. Satan, leagued with sin and death, had made this world the home of woe. The Prince of the power of the air, fell usurper, not content with his dominions in hell, must need invade this fair earth. He found our first parents in the midst of Eden; he tempted them to forego their allegiance to the King of heaven; and they became at once his bondslaves—bondslaves for ever, if the Lord of heaven had not interposed to ransom them. The voice of mercy was heard while the fetters were being rivetted upon their feet, crying, "*Ye shall yet be free!*" In the fulness of time there shall come One who shall bruise the serpent's head, and shall deliver His prisoners from the house of their bondage. Long did the promise tarry. The earth groaned and travailed in its bondage. Man was Satan's slave, and heavy were the clanking chains which were upon his soul. At last, in the fulness of time, the Deliverer came forth, born of a woman. This infant conqueror was but a span long. He lay in the manger—*He* who was one day to bind the old dragon and cast him into the bottomless pit, and set a seal upon him. When the old serpent knew that his enemy was born, he conspired to put him to death; he leagued with Herod to seek the young child that he might destroy Him. But the providence of God preserved the future conqueror; He went down into Egypt, and there was He hidden for a little season. Anon, when He had come to fulness of years, He made His public advent, and began to preach liberty to the captives, and the opening of the prison to them that were bound. Then Satan again shot forth his arrows, and sought to end the existence of the woman's seed. By divers means he sought to slay Him before His time. Once the Jews took up stones to stone Him; nor did they fail to repeat the attempt. They sought to cast Him down from the brow of a hill headlong. By all manner of devices they laboured to take away His life, but His hour was not yet. Dangers might surround Him, but He was invulnerable till the time was come. At last the tremendous day arrived. Foot to foot the conqueror must fight with the dread tyrant. A voice was heard in heaven, "This is your hour, and the power of darkness." And Christ Himself exclaimed, "Now is the crisis of this world; now must the prince of darkness be cast out." From the table of communion the Redeemer arose at midnight, and marched forth to the battle. How dreadful was the contest! In the very first onset the mighty conqueror seemed Himself to be vanquished. Beaten to the earth at the first assault, He fell upon His knees and cried, "My father, if it be possible let this cup pass from Me." Revived in strength, made strong by heaven, He no longer quailed, and from this hour never did He utter a word which looked like renouncing the fight. From the terrible skirmish all red with bloody sweat, He dashed into the thick of the battle. The kiss of Judas was, as it were, the first sounding of the trumpet; Pilate's bar was the glittering of the spear; the cruel lash was the crossing of the swords. But the cross was the centre of the battle; there, on the top of Calvary, must the dread fight of eternity be fought. Now must the Son of God arise, and gird His sword upon His thigh. Dread defeat or glorious conquest awaits the Champion of the church. Which shall it be? We hold our breath with anxious suspense while the storm is raging. I hear the trumpet sound. The howlings and yells of hell rise in awful clamour. The pit is emptying out its legions. Terrible as lions, hungry as wolves, and black as night, the demons rush on in myriads. Satan's reserved forces, those who had long been kept against this day of terrible battle, are roaring from their dens. See how countless are their armies, and how fierce their countenances. Brandishing his sword the arch fiend leads the van, bidding his followers fight neither with small nor great, save only with the King of Israel. Terrible are the leaders of the battle. Sin is there, and all its innumerable offspring, spitting forth the venom of asps, and infixing their poison-fangs in the Saviour's flesh. Death is there upon his pale horse, and his cruel dart rends its way through the body of Jesus even to His inmost heart. He is "exceeding sorrowful, even unto death." Hell comes, with all its coals of juniper and fiery darts. But chief and head amongst them is Satan; remembering well the ancient day when Christ hurled him from the battlements of heaven, he rushes with all his malice yelling to the attack. The darts shot into the air are so countless that they blind the sun. Darkness covers the battle-field, and like that of Egypt it was a darkness which might be felt. Long does the battle seem to waver, for there is but one against many. One man—nay, tell it, lest any should misunderstand me, one *God* stands in battle array against ten thousands of principalities and powers. On, on they come, and He receives them all. Silently at first He permits their ranks to break upon Him, too terribly enduring hardness to spare a thought for shouting. But at last the battle-cry is heard. He who is fighting for His people begins to shout, but it is a shout which makes the church tremble. He cries, "I thirst." The battle is so hot upon Him, and the dust so thick that He is choked with thirst. He cries, "I thirst." Surely, now, He is about to be defeated? Wait awhile; see ye yon heaps; all these have fallen beneath His arm, and as for the rest fear not the issue. The enemy is but rushing to His own destruction. In vain His fury and His rage, for see the last rank is charging, the battle of ages is almost over. At last the darkness is dispersed. Hark how the conqueror cries, "It is finished." And where are now His enemies? They are all dead. There lies the king of terrors, pierced through with one of his own darts! There lies Satan with his head all bleeding, broken! Yonder crawls the broken-backed serpent, writhing in ghastly misery! As for sin, it is cut in pieces, and scattered to the winds of heaven! "*It is finished*," cries the conqueror, as He came with dyed garments from Bozrah, "I have trodden the wine-press alone, I have trampled them in My fury, and their blood is sprinkled on My garments."

And now He proceeds to *divide the spoil*.

We pause here to remark that when the spoil is divided it is a sure token that the battle is completely won. The enemy will never suffer the spoil to be divided among the conquerors as long as he has any strength remaining. We may gather from our text of a surety, that Jesus Christ had totally routed, thoroughly defeated once for all, and put to retreat all His enemies, or else He would not have divided the spoil.

And now, what means this expression of Christ dividing the spoil? I take it that it means, first of all, that *He disarmed all His enemies*. Satan came against Christ; he had in his hand a sharp sword called the Law, dipped in the poison of sin, so that every wound which the law inflicted was deadly. Christ dashed this sword out of Satan's hand, and there stood the prince of darkness unarmed. His helmet was cleft in twain, and his head was crushed as with a rod of iron. Death rose against Christ. The Saviour snatched his quiver from him, emptied out all his darts, cut them in two, gave Death back the feather end, but kept the poisoned barbs from him, that he might never destroy the ransomed. Sin came against Christ; but sin was utterly cut in pieces. It had been Satan's armour bearer, but its shield was cast away, and it lay dead upon the plain. Is it not a noble picture to behold all the enemies of Christ? —nay, my brethren, all your enemies, and mine, totally disarmed? Satan has nothing left him now wherewith he may attack us. He may attempt to injure us, but wound us he never can, for his sword and spear are utterly taken away. In the old battles, especially among the Romans, after the enemy had been overcome, it was the custom to take away all their weapons and ammunition; afterwards they were stripped of their armour and their garments, their hands were tied behind their backs, and they were made to pass under the yoke. Now, even so hath Christ done with sin, death, and hell; He hath taken their armour, spoiled them of all their weapons, and made them all to pass under the yoke; so that now they are our slaves, and we in Christ are conquerors of them who were mightier than we.

I take it this is the first meaning of dividing the spoil—total disarming of the adversary.

In the next place, when the victors divide the spoil they carry away not only the weapons but all the treasures which belong to their enemies. They dismantle their fortresses, and rifle all their stores, so that in future they may not be able to renew the attack. Christ hath done the like with all His enemies. Old Satan had taken away from us all our possessions. Paradise, Satan had added to his territories. All the joy, and happiness, and peace of man, Satan had taken—not that he could enjoy them himself, but that he delighted to thrust us down into poverty and damnation. Now, all our lost inheritances Christ hath gotten back to us. Paradise is ours, and more than all the joy and happiness that Adam had, Christ hath brought back to us. O robber of our race, how art thou spoiled and carried away captive! Didst thou despoil Adam of his riches? The second Adam hath rent them from thee! How is the hammer of the whole earth cut asunder and broken, and the waster is become desolate. Now shall the needy be remembered, and again shall the meek inherit the earth. "Then is the prey of a great spoil divided, the lame take the prey."

Moreover, when victors divide the spoil, it is usual to take away all the ornaments from the enemy, the crowns and the jewels. Christ on the cross did the like with Satan. Satan had a crown on his head, a haughty diadem of triumph. "I fought the first Adam," he said; "I overcame him, and here's my glittering diadem." Christ snatched it from his brow in the hour when He bruised the serpent's head. And now Satan cannot boast of a single victory, he is thoroughly defeated. In the first skirmish he vanquished manhood, but in the second battle manhood vanquished him. The crown is taken from Satan. He is no longer the prince of God's people. His reigning power is gone. He may tempt, but he cannot compel; he may threaten, but he cannot subdue; for the crown is taken from his head, and the mighty are brought low. O sing unto the Lord a new song, all ye His people, make a joyful noise unto Him with psalms, all ye His redeemed; for He hath broken in sunder the gates of brass, and cut the bars of iron, he hath broken the bow and cut the spear in sunder, He hath burned the chariots in the fire, He hath dashed in pieces our enemies, and divided the spoil with the strong.

And now, what says this to us? Simply this. If Christ on the cross hath spoiled Satan, let us not be afraid to encounter this great enemy of our souls. My brethren, in all things we must be made like unto Christ. We must bear our cross, and on that cross we must fight as he did with sin, and death and hell. Let us not fear. The result of the battle is certain, for as the Lord our Saviour hath overcome once even so shall we most surely conquer in Him. Be ye none of you afraid with sudden fear when the evil one cometh upon you. If he accuse you, reply to him in these words:—"Who shall lay anything to the charge of God's elect?" If he condemn you, laugh him to scorn, crying:—"Who is he that condemneth? It is Christ that died, yea rather hath risen again." If he threaten to divide you from Christ's love, encounter him with confidence:—"I am persuaded that neither things present nor things to come, nor height nor depth, nor any other creature shall be able to separate us from the love of God which is in Christ Jesus your Lord." If he let loose your sins upon you dash the hell-dogs aside with this:—"If any man sin we have an advocate with the Father, Jesus Christ the righteous." If death should threaten you, shout in his very face:—"O death! where is thy sting; O grave! where is thy victory." Hold up the cross before you. Let that be your shield and buckler, and rest assured that as your master not only routed the foe but afterwards took the spoil, it shall be even so with you. Your battles with Satan shall turn to your advantage. You shall become all the richer for your antagonists. The more numerous they shall be, the greater shall be your share of the spoil. Your tribulation shall work patience, and your patience experience, and your experience hope—a hope that maketh not ashamed. Through this much tribulation shall you inherit the kingdom, and by the very attacks of Satan shall you be helped the better to enjoy the rest which remaineth to the people of God. Put yourselves in array against sin and Satan. All ye that bend the bow shoot at them, spare no arrows, for your enemies are rebels against God. Go ye up against them, put your feet upon their necks, fear not, neither be ye dismayed, for the battle is the Lord's and He will deliver them into your hands. Be ye very courageous, remembering that you have to fight with a stingless dragon. He may hiss, but his teeth are broken and his poison fang extracted. You have to do battle with an enemy already scarred by your Master's weapons. You have to fight with a naked enemy. Every blow you give him tells upon him, for he has nothing to protect him. Christ hath stripped him naked, and divided his armour, and left him defenceless before his people. Be not afraid. The lion may howl, but rend you in pieces he never can. The enemy may rush in upon you with hideous noise and terrible alarms, but there is no real cause for fear. Stand fast in the Lord. Ye war against a king who hath lost his crown; ye fight against an enemy whose cheek-bones have been smitten, and the joints of whose loins have been loosed. Rejoice, rejoice ye in the day of battle, for it is for you but the beginning of an eternity of triumph.

I have thus endeavoured to dwell upon the first part of the text, Christ on the cross divided the spoil, and He would have us do the same.

II. The second part of our text refers not only to the dividing of the spoil, but to THE TRIUMPH. When a Roman general had performed great feats in a foreign country, his highest reward was that the senate should decree him a triumph. Of course there was a division of spoil made on the battle-field, and each soldier, and each captain took his share; but every man looked forward rapturously to the day when they should enjoy the public triumph. On a certain set day the gates of Rome were thrown open; the houses were all decorated with ornaments; the people climbed to the tops of the houses, or stood in great crowds along the streets. The gates were opened, and by-and-bye the first legion began to stream in with its banners flying, and its trumpets sounding. The people saw the stern warriors as they marched along the street returning from their blood-red fields of battle. After one half of the army had thus defiled, your eye would rest upon one who was the centre of all attraction: riding in a noble chariot drawn by milk-white horses, there came the conqueror himself, crowned with the laurel crown and standing erect. Chained to his chariot were the kings and mighty men of the regions which he had conquered. Immediately behind them came part of the booty. There were carried the ivory and the ebony, and the beasts of the different countries which he had subdued. After these came the rest of the soldiery, a long, long stream of valiant men, all of them sharing the triumphs of their captain. Behind them came banners, the old flags which had floated aloft in the battle, the standards which had been taken from the enemy. And after these. large painted emblems of the great victories of the warrior. Upon one there would be a huge map depicting the rivers which he had crossed, or the seas through which his navy had found their way. Everything was represented in a picture, and the populace gave a a fresh shout as they saw the memorial of each triumph. And then, behind. together with the trophies, would come the prisoners of less eminent rank. Then the rear would be closed with sound of trumpet, adding to the acclamation of the throng. It was a noble day for old Rome. Children would never forget those triumphs; they would estimate their years from the time of one triumph to another. High holiday was kept. Women cast down flowers before the conqueror, and he was the true monarch of the day.

Now, our apostle had evidently seen such a triumph, or read of it, and he takes this as a representation of what Christ did on the cross. He says, "Jesus made a show of them openly, triumphing over them in it." Have you ever thought that the cross could be the scene of a triumph. Most of the old commentators can scarcely conceive it to be true. They say, "This must certainly refer to Christ's resurrection and ascension." But, nevertheless, so saith the Scripture, even on the cross Christ enjoyed a triumph. Yes! while those hands were bleeding the acclamations of angels were being poured upon His head. Yes, while those feet were being rent with the nails, the noblest spirits in the world were crowding round Him with admiration. And when upon that blood-stained cross He died in agonies unutterable, there was heard a shout such as never was heard before for the ransomed in heaven, and all the angels of God with loudest harmony chanted His praise. Then was sung, in fullest chorus, the song of Moses, the servant of God and of the Lamb, for He had indeed cut Rahab and sorely wounded the dragon. Sing unto the Lord, for He hath triumphed gloriously. The Lord shall reign for ever and ever, King of Kings, and Lord of Lords.

I do not feel able, however, this morning, to work out a scene so grand. and yet so contrary to everything that flesh could guess as a picture of Christ actually triumphing on the cross—in the midst of His bleeding, His wounds, and His pains, actually being a triumphant victor, and admired of all. I choose, rather, to take my text thus: the cross is the ground of Christ's ultimate triumph. He may be said to have really triumphed there, because it was by that one act of His, that one offering of Himself, that He completely vanquished all His foes, and for ever sat down at the right hand of the Majesty in the heavens. In the cross, to the spiritual eye, every victory of Christ is contained. It may not be there in fact, but it is there virtually; the germ of His glories may be discovered by the eye of faith in the agonies of the cross.

Bear with me while I humbly attempt to depict the triumph which now results from the cross.

Christ has for ever overcome all His foes, and divided the spoil upon the battle field, and now, even at this day is He enjoying the well-earned reward and triumph of His fearful struggle. Lift up your eyes to the battlements of heaven, the great metropolis of God. The pearly gates are wide open, and the city shines with her bejewelled walls like a bride prepared for her husband. Do you see the angels crowding to the battlements? Do you observe them on every mansion of the celestial city, eagerly desiring and looking for something which has not yet arrived? At last, there is heard the sound of a trumpet, and the angels hurry to the gates—the vanguard of the redeemed is approaching the city. Abel comes in alone, clothed in a crimson garb, the herald of a glorious army of martyrs. Hark to the shout of acclamation! This is the first of Christ's warriors, at once a soldier and a trophy, that have been delivered. Close at his heels there follow others, who in those early times had learned the coming Saviour's fame. Behind them a mighty host may be discovered of patriarchial veterans, who have witnessed to the coming of the Lord in a wanton age. See Enoch still walking with his God, and singing sweetly—"Behold the Lord cometh with ten thousands of His saints." There too is Noah, who had sailed in the ark with the Lord as his pilot. Then follow Abraham, Isaac, and Jacob, Moses, and Joshua, and Samuel, and David, all mighty men of valour. Hearken to them as they enter! Every one of them waving his helmet in the air, cries, "Unto Him that loved us, and washed us from our sins in His blood, unto Him be honour, and glory, and dominion, and power, for ever and ever." Look, my brethren, with admiration upon this noble army! Mark the heroes as they march along the golden streets, everywhere meeting an enthusiastic welcome from the angels who have kept their first estate. On, on they pour, those countless legions—was there ever such a spectacle? It is not the pageant of a day, but the "show" of all time. For four thousand years, on streams the army of Christ's redeemed. Sometimes there is a short rank, for the people have been often minished and brought low; but, anon, a crowd succeeds, and on, on, still on they come, all shouting, all praising Him who loved them and gave Himself for them. But see, *He* comes! I see His immediate herald. clad in a garment of camel's hair, and a leathern girdle about his loins. The Prince of the house of David is not far behind. Let every eye be open. Now, mark, how not only angels, but the redeemed crowd the windows of heaven! He comes! He comes! It is Christ Himself! Lash the snow-white coursers up the everlasting hills; "Lift up your heads, O ye gates, and be ye lifted up ye everlasting doors, that the King of glory may come in." See,

He enters in the midst of acclamations. It is He! but He is not crowned with thorns. It is He! but though His hands wear the scar, they are stained with blood no longer. His eyes are as a flame of fire, and on His head are many crowns, and He hath on His vesture and on His thigh written, KING OF KINGS AND LORD OF LORDS. He stands aloft in that chariot which is "paved with love for the daughters of Jerusalem." Clothed in a vesture dipped in blood, He stands confessed the emperor of heaven and earth. On, on He rides, and louder than the noise of many waters and like great thunders are the acclamations which surround Him! See how John's vision is become a reality, for now we can see for ourselves and hear with our ears the new song, whereof he writes, "They sung a new song, saying, Thou art worthy to take the book, and to open the seals thereof: for Thou wast slain, and hast redeemed us to God by Thy blood out of every kindred, and tongue, and people, and nation; and hast made us unto our God kings and priests: and we shall reign on the earth. And I beheld, and I heard the voice of many angels round about the throne and the beasts and the elders: and the number of them was ten thousand times ten thousand, and thousands of thousands; saying with a loud voice, worthy is the Lamb that was slain to receive power, and riches, and wisdom, and strength, and honour, and glory, and blessing. And every creature which is in heaven, and on the earth, and under the earth, and such as are in the sea, and all that are in them, heard I saying, blessing, and honour, and glory, and power, be unto Him that sitteth upon the throne, and unto the Lamb for ever and ever. And the four beasts said, amen. And the four and twenty elders fell down and worshipped Him that liveth for ever and ever." But who are those at His chariot's wheels? Who are those grim monsters that come howling in the rear? I know them. First of all there is the arch enemy. Look to the old serpent, bound and fettered, how he writhes his ragged length along! his azure hues all tarnished with trailing in the dust, his scales despoiled of their once-vaunted brightness. Now is captivity led captive, and death and hell shall be cast into the lake of fire. With what derision is the chief of rebels regarded. How is he become the object of everlasting contempt. He that sitteth in the heavens doth laugh, the Lord doth have him in derision. Behold how the serpent's head is broken, and the dragon is trampled under foot. And now regard attentively yon hideous monster, *Sin*, chained hand in hand with his satanic sire. See how he rolls his fiery eye-balls, mark how he twists and writhes in agonies. Mark how he glares upon the holy city, but is unable to spit his venom there, for he is chained and gagged, and dragged along an unwilling captive at the wheels of the victor. And there, too, is old Death, with his darts all broken and his hands behind him—the grim king of terrors, he too is a captive. Hark to the songs of the redeemed, of those who have entered into Paradise, as they see these mighty prisoners dragged along! "Worthy is He," they shout, "to live and reign at His Almighty Father's side, for He hath ascended up on high, He hath led captivity captive, and received gifts for men."

And now behind Him I see the great mass of His people streaming in. The apostles first arrive in one goodly fellowship hymning their Lord; and then their immediate successors; and then a long array of those who through cruel mockings and blood, through flame and sword, have followed their Master. These are those of whom the world was not worthy, brightest among the stars of heaven. Regard also the mighty preachers and confessors of the faith, Chrysostom, Athanasius, Augustine, and the like. Witness their holy unanimity in praising their Lord. Then let your eye run along the glittering ranks till you come to the days of Reformation. I see in the midst of the squadron, Luther, and Calvin, and Zwingle, three holy brothers. I see just before them Wickliffe, and Huss, and Jerome of Prague, all marching together. And then I see a number that no man can number, converted to God through these mighty reformers, who now follow in the rear of the King of kings and Lord of lords. And looking down to our own time I see the stream broader and wider. For many are the soldiers who have in these last times entered into their Master's triumph. We may mourn their absence from *us*, but we must rejoice in their presence with the *Lord*. But what is the unanimous shout, what is the one song that still rolls from the first rank to the last? It is this: "Unto Him that loved us, and washed us from our sins in His own blood, to Him be glory and dominion for ever and ever!" Have they changed the tune? Have they supplanted His name by another? Have they put the crown on another head, or elevated another hero into the chariot? Ah, no: they are content still to let the triumphant procession stream along its glorious length; still to rejoice as they behold fresh trophies of His love, for every soldier is a trophy, every warrior in Christ's army is another proof of His power to save, and His victory over death and hell.

I have not time to enlarge further, or else I might describe the mighty pictures at the end of the procession; for in the old Roman triumphs, the deeds of the conqueror were all depicted in paintings. The towns he had taken, the rivers he had passed, the provinces he had subdued, the battles he had fought, were represented in pictures and exposed to the view of the people, who with great festivity and rejoicing, accompanied him in throngs, or beheld him from the windows of their houses, and filled the air with their acclamations and applauses. I might present to you first of all the picture of hell's dungeons blown to atoms. Satan had prepared deep in the depths of darkness a prison-house for God's elect; but Christ has not left one stone upon another. On the picture I see the chains broken in pieces, the prison doors burnt with fire, and all the depths of the vasty deep shaken to their foundations. On another picture I see heaven open to all believers; I see the gates that were fast shut heaved open by the golden lever of Christ's atonement. I see on another picture, the grave despoiled; I behold Jesus in it, slumbering for awhile, and then rolling away the stone and rising to immortality and glory. But we cannot stay to describe these mighty pictures of the victories of His love. We know that the time shall come when the triumphant procession shall cease, when the last of His redeemed shall have entered into the city of happiness and of joy, and when with the shout of a trumpet heard for the last time, He shall ascend to heaven, and take His people up to reign with God, even our Father, for ever and ever, world without end.

Our only question, and with that we conclude, is, have we a good hope through grace that we shall march in that tremendous procession? Shall we pass under review in that day of pomp and glory? Say, my soul, shalt thou have an humble part in that glorious pageant? Wilt thou follow at His chariot wheels? Wilt thou join in the thundering hosannas? Shall thy voice help to swell the everlasting chorus? Sometimes, I fear it shall not. There are times when the awful question comes—what if my name should be left out when He should read the muster-roll? Brethren, does not that thought trouble you? But yet I put the question again. Can you answer it? Will you be there—shall you see this pomp? Will you behold Him triumph over sin, death, and hell at last? Canst thou answer this question? There is another, but the answer will serve for both —dost thou believe on the Lord Jesus Christ? Is He thy confidence and thy trust? Hast thou committed thy soul to His keeping? Reposing on His might canst thou say for thine immortal spirit—

> "Other refuge have I none,
> Hangs my helpless soul on Thee."

If thou canst say that, thine eyes shall see Him in the day of His glory; nay, thou shalt share His glory, and sit with Him upon His throne, even as He has overcome and sits down with His Father upon His throne. I blush to preach as I have done this morning on a theme far beyond my power; yet I could not leave it unsung, but, as best I might, sing it. May God enlarge your faith, and strengthen your hope, and inflame your love, and make you ready to be made partakers of the inheritance of the saints in light, that when He shall come with flying clouds on wings of wind, ye may be ready to meet Him, and may with Him ascend to gaze for ever on the vision of His glory.

May God grant this blessing, for Christ's sake. Amen.

A WARNING TO BELIEVERS

"Let no man beguile you of your reward."—Colossians ii. 18.

THERE is an allusion here to the prize which was offered to the runners in the Olympic games, and at the outset it is well for us to remark how very frequently the Apostle Paul conducts us by his metaphors to the racecourse. Over and over again he is telling us so to run that we may obtain, bidding us strive, and at other times to agonize, and speaking of wrestling and contending. Ought not this to make us feel what an intense thing the Christian life is—not a thing of sleepiness or haphazard, not a thing to be left now and then to a little superficial consideration? It must be a matter which demands all our strength, so that when we are saved there is a living principle put within us which demands all our energies, and gives us energy over and above any that we ever had before. Those who dream that carelessness will find its way to heaven have made a great mistake. The way to hell is neglect, but the way to heaven is very different. " How shall we escape if we neglect so great salvation ? " A little matter of neglect brings you to ruin, but our Master's words are " *Strive* to enter in at the straight gate, for many, I say unto you, shall seek "—merely seek—" to enter in, and shall not be able." Striving is wanted more than seeking. Let us pray that God the Holy Spirit would always enable us to be in downright, awful earnest about the salvation of our souls. May we never count this a matter of secondary importance, but may we seek first, and beyond everything else, the kingdom of God and His righteousness. May we lay hold on eternal life ; may we so run that we may obtain.

I would press this upon your memories because I do observe it in myself as well as in my fellow-Christians, that we are often more earnest about the things of this life than we are about the things of the life to come. We are all impressed with the fact that in these days of competition, if a man would not be run over and crushed beneath the wheels of the Juggernaut of poverty, he must exert himself. No man seems now able to keep his head above water with the faint-swimmer strokes which our forefathers used to give. We have to strive, and the bread that perisheth hath to be laboured for. Shall it be that this poor world shall engross our earliest thoughts and our latest cares, and shall the world to come have only now and then a consideration ? No ; may we love our God with all our heart, and all our soul, and all our strength, and may we lay our body, soul, and spirit upon the alter of Christ's service, for these are but our reasonable sacrifice to Him.

Now the apostle in the text before us gives us a warning, which comes to the same thing, however it is interpreted ; but the passage is somewhat difficult of rendering, and there have been several meanings given to it. Out of these things are three meanings which have been given of the text before us which are worthy of notice. " Let no man beguile you of your reward." The Apostle, in the first place, may mean here :—

I. LET NO MAN BEGUILE ANY OF YOU who profess to be followers of Christ *of the great reward that will await the faithful at the last.*

Now, my brethren, we have, many of us, commenced the Christian race, or we profess to have done so, but the number of the starters is far greater than the number of the winners. " They that run in a race run all, but one receiveth the prize." " Many are called, but few are chosen." Many commence, apparently, in the Christian career, but after a while, though they did run well, something hinders them that they do not obey the truth, and they go out from us because they were not of us, for if they had been of us, doubtless they would have continued with us. Now we may expect, now that we have commenced to run, that *some will come and try to turn us out of the racecourse openly*—not plausibly and with sophistry, but with an open and honest wickedness. Some will tell us plainly that there is no reward to run for, that our religion is all a mistake, that the pleasures of this world are the only things worth seeking, that there are delights of the flesh and the lusts thereof, and that we should do well to enjoy them. We shall meet the Atheist with his sneer and with his ringing laugh. We shall meet with all kinds of persons who will to our faces tell us to turn back, for there is no heaven, there is no Christ, or, if there be, it is not worth our while to take so much trouble to find Him. Take heed of these people. Meet them face to face with dauntless courage. Mind not their sneers. If they persecute you only, reckon this to be an honour to you, for what is persecution but the tribute which wickedness pays to righteousness, and what is it, indeed, but the recognition of the seed of the woman when the seed of the serpent would fain bite his heel ?

But the Apostle does not warn you so much against those people who openly come to you in this way. He knows that you will be on the alert against them. He gives a special warning against some others who would beguile you ; that is to say, *who will try to turn you out of the right road, but who will no tell you that they mean to do so.* They pretend that they are going to show you something better than what you have, to teach you something that you knew not before, some improvement upon what you have hitherto learned. In Paul's day there were some who took off the intention of the Christian from the worship of God to the worship of angels. "Angels," said they, "these are holy beings ; they keep watch over you ; you should speak of them with great respect"; and then when they grew bolder, they said, "You should ask their protection "; and then after a while they said, "You should worship them ; you should make them intermediate intercessors "; and so, step by step, they went on and established an old heresy which lasted for many years in the Christian Church, and which is not dead even now, and thus the worship of angels crept in.

And nowadays you will meet with men who will say, "That bread upon the Table—why, it represents the body of Jesus Christ to you when you come to the Lord's Supper ; therefore, you ought to treat that bread with great respect." By and bye they will get a little bolder, and then they say, "As it represents Christ, you may worship it, pay it respect as if it were Christ." By and bye it will come to this, that you must have a napkin under your chin, lest you should drop a crumb ; or it will be very wicked if a drop of the sacred wine should cling to your moustache when you drink ; and there will be. the directions which are given in some of the papers coming out from the High Church party— absurdities which are only worthy of the nursery— about the way in which the holy bread is to be eaten, and the holy wine is to be drunk—bringing in idolatry, sheer, clear idolatry, under the pretence of improving upon the too bare simplicity of the worship of Christ. Have a care of the very first step, I pray you.

Or, perhaps, it may come to you in another shape. One will say to you, "The place in which you worship —is it not very dear to you ? That seat where you have been accustomed to sit and listen, is it not dear ?" and your natural instincts will say, "Yes." Then it will go a little farther. "That place is holy ; it ought never to be used for anything but worship." Then a little farther it will be, "Oh ! that is the house of God," and you will come to believe that, contrary to the words which you know are given to you of the Holy Ghost, that God dwelleth not in temples made with hands ; that is to say, in these buildings, and you will get by degrees to have a worship of places, and a worship of days, and a worship of bread, and a worship of wine, And then it will be said to you, "Your minister, has he not often cheered you ? Well then, you should reverence him ; call

him 'Reverend.'" Go a little farther, and you will call him "Father "; yet a little farther, and he will be your confessor ; get a little farther and he will be your infallible Pope. It is all step by step it is done. The first step seems to be very harmless indeed. Indeed, it is a kind of voluntary humility. You look as if you were humbling yourselves, and were paying reverence to these things for God's sake, whereas the object is to get you to pay reverence to them, instead of to God, and here the Apostle's words come in, "Let no man beguile you of your reward." They will often attack you in that insidious manner by setting up other objects of reverence besides those which spiritual men worship.

So, too, they will by slow degrees try to *insinuate a different way of living from that which is the true life of the Christian.* You who have believed in Jesus are saved ; your sins are forgiven you for His name's sake. You are accustomed to go to Jesus Christ constantly to receive that washing of the feet of which He spake to Peter when He said, "He that is washed needeth not except to wash his feet, for he is clean every whit." You go to Him with "Forgive us our trespasses as we forgive them that tresspass against us." But there will be some who will come in and tell you that to live in that way by a simple faith in Jesus Christ is not, perhaps, the best way. Could you not get a little farther ? Could you not lead the life of those recluses who mortify the flesh in such a way that at at last they come to have no sins, but commence to be perfect in themselves ? Could you not begin, at least in some degree, to commit your soul's care to some priest, or to some friend, and instead of making every place holy and every day a holy day, would it not be well to fast on such and such days in the week, to scrupulously observe this rule, and the other rule, and walk by the general opinion of the ancient Church, or by the Anglicanum Directorium, or some one of those books which profess to show how they used to do it a thousand years ago ? All this may have a great show of wisdom, and antiquity, and beauty ; there may be a semblance of everything that is holy about it, and names that should never be mentioned without reverence may be appended to it all, but listen to the Apostle as he saith, "Beware lest any man beguile you of your reward," for if they get you away from living upon Christ as a poor sinner from day to day by simple confidence in Him, they will beguile you of your reward.

There is another party who will seek to beguile you of your reward *by bringing in speculative notions instead of the simple truths of God's word.* There is a certain class of persons who think that a sermon must be a good one when they cannot understand it, and who are always impressed with a man whose words are long ; and if his sentences are involved they feel, poor souls, that because they do not know what he is talking about, there is no doubt that he is a very wise and learned man ; and after a while when he does propound something that they can catch at, though it may be quite contrary to what they have learned at their mother's knee or from their father's Bible, yet they are ready to be led off by it. There are many men now-a-days who seem to spend their time in nothing else but in spinning new theories, and inventing new systems, gutting the gospel, taking the very soul and bowels out of it, and leaving there nothing but the mere skin and outward bones. The life and marrow of the gospel is being taken away by their learning, by their philosophies, by their refinements, by their bringing everything down to the test of this wonderfully enlightened nineteenth century, to which we are all, I suppose, bound to defer. But a voice comes to us, " Let no man beguile *you* of your reward." Stand fast to the old truths ; they will outlast all these philosophies. Stand fast to the old way of living ; it will outlast all the inventions of men. Stand fast by Christ, for you want no other object of worship but Himself.

The Apostle gives us this warning, " Let no man beguile you of your reward," reminding us that these persons are very likely to beguile us. They will beguile us *by their character.* Have I not often heard young people say of such and such a preacher who preaches error, " But he is so good a man." That is nothing to the point. " Though we or an angel from heaven preach any other gospel unto you than that which we have preached unto you, let him be accursed." If the life of the man should be blameless as the life of Christ, yet if he preach to you other than the gospel of Jesus Christ, take no heed of him ; he weareth but the sheep's clothing, and is a wolf after all. Some will plead, " But such and such a man is so eloquent." Ah ! brethren, may the day never come when your faith shall stand in the words of men. What is a ready orator, after all, that he should convince your hearts ? Are there not ready orators caught any day for everything ? Men speak, speak fluently, and speak well in the cause of evil, and there are some that can speak much more fluently and more eloquently for evil than any of our poor tongues are ever likely to do for the right. But words, words, words, flowers of rhetoric, oratory—are these the things that saved you ? Are ye so foolish that having begun in the Spirit by being convinced of your sins, having begun by being led simply to Christ, and putting your trust in Him—are you now to be led astray by these poetic utterances and flowery periods of men ? God forbid ! Let nothing of this kind beguile you.

Then there will be added to these remarks that the man is not only very good and very eloquent, but *that he is very earnest—he seems very humble-minded.* Yes, and of old they wore rough garments to deceive, and in the connection of the text we find that those persons were noted for their voluntary humility and their worship of angels. Satan knows very well that if he comes in black he will be discovered, but if he puts on the garb of an angel of light, then men will think he comes from God, and so will be deceived. " By their fruits ye shall know them." If they give you not the gospel, if they exalt not Christ, if they bear not witness to salvation through the precious blood, if they do not lift up Jesus Christ as Moses lifted up the serpent in the wilderness, have nothing to do with them, speak as they may. " Let no man beguile you of your reward." Though it should happen to be your relative, one whom you love, one who may have many claims on your respect otherwise—let no man, let no man, however plausible may be his speech or eminent his character, beguile you of your reward.

Recollect, you professors, you lose the reward if *you lose the road to the reward.* He that runs may run very fast, but if he does not run in the course, he wins not the prize. You may believe false doctrine with great earnestness, but you will find it false for all that. You may give yourself up indefatigably to the pursuit of the wrong religion, but it will ruin your souls. A notion is abroad that if you are but earnest and sincere, you will be all right. Permit me to remind you that if you travel never so earnestly to the north, you will never reach the south, and if you earnestly take prussic acid you will die, and if you earnestly cut off a limb you will be wounded. You must not only be earnest, but you must be right in it. Hence is it necessary to say, " Let no man beguile you of your reward." " I bear them witness," said the Apostle, " that they had a zeal for God, but not according to knowledge, but went about to establish their own righteousness, and have not submitted themselves to the righteousness of God." Oh ! may we not be beguiled, then, so as to miss the reward of heaven at the last !

But I must pass on, especially as the light fails us this evening ; I hope it is prognostic of a coming shower. Here is a second rendering which may be given to the text :—

II. LET NO MAN DOMINEER OVER YOU.

This rendering, or something analogous to it, is in the French translation. One of the great expositors in his commentary upon this passage refers it to the judges at the end of the course, who sometimes would give the reward to the wrong person, and the person who had really run well might thus be deprived of his reward. Now, however close a man may be to Christ, the world, instead of honouring him for it, will, on the contrary, censure and condemn him, and hence the Apostle's exhortation is, " Let no man domineer over you."

And, my brethren, I would earnestly ask you to remember this first *as to your course of action.* If you conscientiously believe that you are right in what you are doing, study very little who is pleased or who is displeased. If you are persuaded in your own soul that what you believe and what you do are acceptable to God, whether they are acceptable to man or not is of very small consequence. You are not man's servant, you do not look to man for your reward, and, therefore, you need not care what man's opinion may be in this matter. Be just and fear not. Tread in the footsteps of Christ, follow may. Live not on the breath of men. Let not their applause make you feel great, for perhaps then their censure will make you faint. Let no man in this respect domineer over you, but let Christ be your Master, and look to His smile.

So not only with regard to your course of action, *but also with reference to your confidence,* let no man domineer over you. If you put your trust in Jesus Christ, there are some who will say it is presumption. Let them say it is presumption. " Wisdom is justified of all her children," and so shall faith be. If you take the promise of God and rest upon it, there will be some who will say that you are hare-brained fanatics. Let them say it. They that trust in Him shall never be confounded. The result will honour your faith. You have but to wait a little while, and, perhaps, they that now censure you will have to hold up their hands in astonishment, and say with you, " What hath God wrought ? " Your confidence in Christ, especially, my dear young friend, I trust does not depend upon the smile of your relatives. If it did, then their frown might crush it. Walk with your Saviour in the lowly walk of holy confidence, and let not your faith rest in man, but in the smile of God.

Let no man domineer over you, again, *by judging your motives.* Men will always give as bad a reason as they can for a good man's actions. It seems to be innate in human nature never to give a man credit for being right if you can help it, and often tender minds have been greatly wounded when they have been misrepresented, and their actions have been imputed to sinister and selfish motives, when they have really desired to serve Christ. But do not let your heart be broken about that. You will appear before the judgment-seat of Christ : do not care about these petty judgment-seats of men. Go on with your Master's work dauntlessly and fearlessly. Let them say, as David's brethren said of him, " Because of thy pride and the naughtiness of thy heart to see the battle, art thou come." Go you and get Goliath's head, and bring it back, and that shall be the best answer to these sneering ones. When they see that God is with you, and that He has given you the triumph, you shall have honour, even in the eyes of those who now ridicule you. I think sometimes the Christian should have very much the same bravado against the judgment of men as David had when Michal, the daughter of Saul, came out and said, " How glorious was the king of Israel to-day, who uncovered himself to-day in the eyes of the housemaids of his servants," and he said, " It was before the Lord, and I will yet be more vile than thus." Let your eyes be to God, and forget the eyes of men. Live so that, whether they know what you do, or do not know, you will not care, for your conduct will bear the blaze of the great Judgment Day, and, therefore, the criticisms of earth do not affect you. Let no man domineer over you.

So may I put it in another light—*let no man sway your conscience so as to lead you.* I am always anxious, my dear hearers, that, whatever respect I may ever win from you—and I trust I may have your esteem and your affection—yet that you will never believe a doctrine simply because I utter it, but unless I can confirm it from the word of God, away with it. If it be not according to the teaching of the Lord and Master, I beseech you follow me not. Follow me only as far as I follow Christ. And so with every other man. Let it be God's truth, God's word, the Holy Spirit's witness to that word in your soul, that you are seeking after, but rest, I pray you, never short of that, for if you do your faith must stand merely in the wisdom of men, and when the man who helped you to believe is gone, perhaps your faith may be gone too, when most you need its comforting power. No ; let no man domineer over you, but press forward in the Christian race, looking unto Jesus, and looking unto Jesus only.

But now a third meaning belongs to the text. A happy circumstance it is, this dark night, that the preacher does not need to use his manuscript, for if he did his sermon must certainly come to an end now. But here is this point, " Let no man beguile you of your reward." It may mean this :—

III. LET NO MAN ROB YOU OF THE PRESENT REWARD WHICH YOU HAVE IN BEING A CHRISTIAN.

Let no man deprive you of the present comfort which your faith should bring to you. Let me just for a few minutes have your attention while I speak upon this. Dear brethren, you and I, if we are believers in Christ, are this day completely pardoned. There is no sin in God's book against us. We are wholly and completely justified. The righteousness of Jesus Christ covers us from head to foot, and we stand before God as if we had never sinned. Now let no man rob you of this reward. Do not be tempted by anything that is said to doubt the completeness of a believer in Christ. Hold this, and, as you hold it, enjoy it. Do not let the man, yourself, whom you have most to fear, beguile you. Even though conscience should upbraid you, and you should have many grave reasons for doubt, as you imagine, yet if you believe in Jesus, stand to it—" There is, therefore, now no condemnation to me, for I am in Christ Jesus ; he that believeth on Him is not condemned ; I have believed, and am not condemned, neither will He permit condemnation to be thundered against me, for Christ has borne my sin for me, and I am clear in Him." Let no man beguile you of the reward of feeling that you are complete in Christ.

Further, you who have believed in Jesus Christ *are safe in Christ.* Because He lives, you shall live also. Who shall separate us from the love of God which is in Christ Jesus our Lord ? He has said, " I give unto My sheep eternal life, and they shall never perish, neither shall any pluck them out of My hand." Now there are some who will tell you that you are not safe, and that it is dangerous for you to believe that you are. Let no man beguile you of this reward. You are saved. If you are believing on Him, He will keep you, and you may sing, " Now unto Him that is able to keep us from falling, and to present us faultless before His presence with exceeding great joy, unto Him be glory." Hold to that blessed truth that you are in Jesus—safe in Jesus Christ.

There is a third blessed truth, that not only are you pardoned and safe in Christ, but you are accepted at this moment in the Beloved. Your acceptance with God does not rest upon anything in you. You are accepted because you are in Christ, accepted for Christ's sake. Now sometimes you will get robbed of this reward if you listen to the voice which says, " Why, there is sin in you still ; your prayers are imperfect ; your actions are stained." Yes, but let no man beguile you of this conviction that, sinner as you are, you are still accepted in Christ Jesus.

The Lord grant that you may feel this within, and let no man beguile you of your reward as long as you live. May you live and die in the enjoyment of it, beloved, for Christ's sake. Amen.

FOLLOWING THE RISEN CHRIST

" If ye then be risen with Christ, seek those things which are above, where Christ sitteth on the right hand of God. Set your affection on things above, not on things on the earth."—Colossians iii. 1, 2.

THE resurrection of our divine Lord from the dead is the corner-stone of Christian doctrine. Perhaps I might more accurately call it the key-stone of the arch of Christianity, for if that fact could be disproved the whole fabric of the gospel would fall to the ground. If Jesus Christ be not risen then is our preaching vain, and your faith is also vain ; ye are yet in your sins. If Christ be not risen, then they which have fallen asleep in Christ have perished, and we ourselves, in missing so glorious a hope as that of resurrection, are of all men the most miserable.

Because of the great improtance of His resurrection, our Lord was pleased to give many infallible proofs of it, by appearing again and again in the midst of His followers. It would be interesting to search out how many times He appeared ; I think we have mention of some sixteen manifestations. He showed Himself openly before His disciples, and did eat and drink with them. They touched His hands and His side, and heard His voice, and knew that it was the same Jesus that was crucified. He was not content with giving evidence to the ears and to the eyes, but even to the sense of touch He proved the reality of His resurrection. These appearances were very varied. Sometimes He gave an interview to one alone, either to a man, as to Cephas, or to a woman, as to Magdalen. He conversed with two of His followers as they went to Emmaus, and with the company of the apostles by the sea. We find Him at one moment amongst the eleven when the doors were shut for fear of the Jews, and at another time in the midst of an assembly of more than five hundred brethren, who years after were most of them living witnesses to the fact. They could not all have been deceived. It is not possible that any historical fact could have been placed upon a better basis of credibility than the resurrection of our Lord from the dead. This is put beyond all dispute and question, and of purpose is it so done, because it is essential to the whole Christian system.

For this same cause the resurrection of Christ is commemorated frequently. There is no ordinance in Scripture of any one Lord's-day in the year being set apart to commemorate the rising of Christ from the dead, for this reason, that every Lord's-day is the memorial of our Lord's resurrection. Wake up any Lord's-day you please, whether in the depth of winter, or in the warmth of summer, and you may sing :—

> " To-day He rose and left the dead,
> And Satan's empire fell ;
> To-day the saints His triumph spread,
> And all His wonders tell."

To set apart an Easter Sunday for special memory of the resurrection is a human device, for which there is no Scriptural command, but to make every Lord's-day an Easter Sunday is due to Him who rose early on the first day of the week. We gather together on the first rather than upon the seventh day of the week, because redemption is even a greater work than creation, and more worthy of commemoration, and because the rest which followed creation is far outdone by that which ensues upon the completion of redemption. Like the apostles, we meet on the first day of the week, and hope that Jesus may stand in our midst, and say, " Peace be unto you." Our Lord has lifted the Sabbath from the old and rusted hinges whereon the law had placed it long before, and set it on the new golden hinges which His love has fashioned. He hath placed our rest-day, not at the end of a week or toil, but at the beginning of the rest which remaineth for the people of God. Every first day of the week we should meditate upon the rising of our Lord, and seek to enter into fellowship with Him in His risen life.

Never let us forget that all who are in Him rose from the dead in His rising. Next in importance to the fact of the resurrection is the doctrine of the federal headship of Christ, and the unity of all His people with Him. It is because we are in Christ that we become partakers of everything that Christ did— we are circumcised with Him, dead with Him, buried with Him, risen with Him, because we cannot be separated from Him. We are members of His Body, and not a bone of Him can be broken. Because that union is most intimate, continuous, and indissoluble, therefore all that concerns Him concerns us, and as He rose so all His people have arisen in Him.

They are risen in two ways. First, representatively. All the elect rose in Christ in the day when He quitted the tomb. He was justified, or declared to be clear of all liabilities on account of our sins, by being set free from the prison-house of the tomb. There was no reason for detaining Him in the sepulchre, for He had discharged the debts of His people by dying ' unto sin once.' He was our hostage and our representative, and when He came forth from His bonds we came forth in Him. We have endured the sentence of the law in our Substitute, we have lain in its prison, and even died under its death-warrant, and now we are no longer under its curse. " Now if we be dead with Christ, we believe that we shall also live with Him : knowing that Christ being raised from the dead no more ; death hath no more dominion over Him. For in that He died, He died unto sin once : but in that He liveth, He liveth unto God."

Next to this representative resurrection comes our spiritual resurrection, which is ours as soon as we are led by faith to believe in Jesus Christ. Then it may be said of us, " And you hath He quickened who were dead in trespasses and sins."

The resurrection blessing is to be perfected by-and-by at the appearing of our Lord and Saviour, for then our bodies shall rise again, if we fall asleep before His coming. He redeemed our manhood in its entirety, spirit, soul, and body, and He will not be content until the resurrection which has passed upon our spirit shall pass upon our body too. These dry bones shall live ; together with his dead body they shall rise.

> " When He arose ascending high,
> He showed our feet the way ;
> Up to the Lord our flesh shall fly
> At the great rising day."

Then shall we know in the perfection of our resurrection beauty that we are indeed completely risen in Christ, and " as in Adam all die, so in Christ shall all be made alive."

This morning we shall only speak of our fellowship with Christ in His resurrection as to our own spiritual resurrection. Do not misunderstand me as if I thought the resurrection to be only spiritual, for a literal rising from the dead is yet to come ; but our text speaks of spiritual resurrection, and I shall therefore endeavour to set it before you.

I. First, then, LET US CONSIDER OUR SPIRITUAL RISING WITH CHRIST : " If ye then be risen with Christ." Though the words look like a supposition they are not meant to be so. The apostle casts no doubt, and raises no question, but merely puts it thus for argument's sake. It might just as well be read, " Since ye then are risen in Christ." The " if " is used logically, not theologically : by way of argument, and not by way of doubt. All who believe in Christ are risen with Christ. Let us meditate on this truth.

For, first, we were " dead in trespasses and sins," but having believed in Christ *we have been quickened by the Holy Ghost*, and we are dead no longer. There we lay in the tomb, ready to become corrupt ; yea, some of us were corrupt, the marks of the worm of sin were upon our character, and the foul stench of actual sin arose from us. More or less according to the length of time in which we abode in that death, and according to the circumstances with which we were surrounded, death wrought in us corruption. We lay in our death quite unable to raise ourselves therefrom ; ours were eyes that could not see, and ears that could not hear ; a heart that could not love ; and a withered hand that could not be stretched out to give the touch of faith. We were even as they that go down into the pit, as those that have been long dead : only in this we were in a worse plight than those actually dead, for we were responsible for all our omissions and inabilities. We were as guilty as if we had power, for the loss of moral power is not the loss of moral responsibility ; we were, therefore, in a state of spiritual death of the most fearful kind. The Holy Spirit visited us and made us live. We remember the first sensation of life, some of us—how it seemed to tingle in our soul's veins with pain sharp and bitter ; just as drowning persons when life is coming back to them suffer great pain ; so did we. Conviction was wrought in us and confession of sin, a dread of judgment to come and a sense of present condemnation ; but these were tokens of life, and that life gradually deepened and opened up until the eye was opened—we could see Christ, the hand ceased to be withered, and we stretched it out and touched His garment's hem ; the feet began to move in the way of obedience, and the heart felt the sweet glow of love within. Then the eyes, not content with seeing, fell to weeping ; and afterwards, when the tears were wiped away, they flashed and sparkled with delight. Oh, my brethren, believers in Jesus, you are not spiritually dead any longer ; on Christ you have believed, and that grand act proves that you are no more dead. You have been quickened by God according to the working of His mighty power, which He wrought in Christ when He raised Him from the dead, and set Him at His own right hand in the heavenlies. Now, beloved, you are new creatures, the produce of a second birth, begotten again in Christ Jesus unto newness of life. Christ is your life ; such a life as you never knew before, nor could have known apart from Him. If ye then be risen with Christ ye walk in newness of life, while the world abideth in death.

Let us advance another step : we are risen with Christ, and therefore *there has been wrought in us a wonderful change*. When the dead shall rise they will not appear as they now are. The buried seed rises from the ground, but not as a seed, for it puts forth green leaf, and bud, and stem, and gradually develops expanding flower and fruit, and even so we wear a new form, for we are renewed after the image of Him that created us in righteousness and holiness.

I ask you to consider the change which the Spirit of God has wrought in the believer : a wonderful change indeed ! Before regeneration our soul was as our body will be when it dies ; and we read that " it is sown in corruption." There was corruption in our mind and it was working irresistibly towards every evil and offensive thing. In many the corruption did not appear upon the surface, but it worked within ; in others it was conspicuous and fearful to look upon. How great the change ! For now the power of corruption within us is broken, the new life has overcome it, for it is a living and incorruptible seed which liveth and abideth for ever. Corruption is upon the old nature, but it cannot touch the new, which is our true and real self. Is it not a great thing to be purged of the filthiness which would have ultimately brought us down to Tophet where the fire unquenchable burns, and the worm undying feeds upon the corrupt ?

Our old state was further like that which comes upon the body at death ; because it was in a state of dishonour. You know how the apostle saith of the body, " It is sown in dishonour " ; and certainly no corpse weareth such dishonour as that which rests upon a man who is dead in trespasses and sins. Why, of all things in the world that deserve shame and contempt, a sinful man is certainly the most so. He despises His Creator, he neglects his Saviour, he chooses evil instead of good, and puts the light from him because his deeds are evil, and therefore he prefers the darkness. In the judgment of all pure spirits a sinful man is a dishonourable man. But oh how changed is man when the grace of God works within him, for then he is honourable. " Behold, what manner of love the Father hath bestowed upon us, that we should be called the sons of God." What an honour is this ! Heaven itself contains not a more honourable being than a renewed man. Well may we cry with David, " What is man, that Thou art mindful of him ? and the son of man, that Thou visitest him ? " But when we see man, in the person of Jesus, made to have dominion over all the works of God's hands, and know that Jesus hath made us kings and priests unto God, we are filled with amazement that God should so exalt us. The Lord Himself has said, " Since thou wast precious in My sight, thou hast been honourable, and I have loved thee." " Unto you therefore which believe He is an honour," for so the original text may run. A precious Christ makes us precious : such honour have all the saints.

When a body is buried, we are told by the apostle again that it is " sown in weakness." The poor dead frame cannot lay itself down in its last bed, friendly hands must place it there ; even so we were utter weakness towards all good. When we were the captives of sin we could do nothing good, even as our Lord said, " Without Me ye can do nothing." We were incapable of even a good thought apart from Him. But " when we were yet without strength, in due time Christ died for the ungodly " ; and now we know Him and the power of His resurrection. God hath given us the spirit of power and of love ; is it not written, " As many as received Him, to them gave He power to become the sons of God, even to them that believe on His name " ?

What an amazing power is this ! Now we " taste of the powers of the world to come," and we are " strengthened with all might, according to His glorious power, unto all patience and longsuffering with joyfulness." Faith girds us with a divine power, for " all things are possible to him that believeth," and each believer can exclaim, without boasting, " I can do all things through Christ which strengtheneth me." Is not this a marvellous change which the spiritual resurrection has wrought upon us ? Is it not a glorious thing, that God's strength should be perfect in our weakness ?

The great change mainly concerns another point. It is said of the body, " It is sown a natural body, it is raised a spiritual body." Aforetime we were natural men and discerned not the things that be of the Spirit of God. We minded earthly things and were moved by carnal lustings after the things which are seen ; but now through divine grace a spirit had been created in us which feeds on spiritual bread, lives for spiritual objects, is swayed by spiritual motives and rejoices in spiritual truth. This change from the natural to the spiritual is such as only God Himself could have wrought, and yet we have experienced it. To God be the glory. So that by virtue of our rising in Christ we have received life and have become the subjects of a wondrous change,—" old things are passed away ; behold, all things are become new."

In consequence of our receiving this life and undergoing this change *the things of the world and sin become a tomb to us*. To a dead man a sepulchre is as good a dwelling as he can want. You may call it his bedchanber, if you will ; for he lies within it as unconscious as if he were in slumber. But the moment the dead man lives, he will not endure such a bedchamber ; he calls it a dreary vault, a loathsome dungeon, an unbearable charnel, and he must leave it at once. So when you and I were natural men, and had no spiritual life, the things of this life contented us ; but it is far otherwise now. A merely outward religion was all that we desired ; a dead form suited a dead soul. Judaism pleased those who were under its yoke, in the very beginning of the gospel ; new moons and holy days and traditional ordinances, and fasting and feasting were great things with those who forgot their resurrection with Christ. All those things make pretty furniture for a dead man's chamber ; but when the eternal life enters the soul these outward ordinances are flung off, the living man rends off his grave clothes, tears away his cerements, and demands such garments as are suitable for life. So the apostle in the chapter before our text tells us to let no man spoil us by the traditions of men and the inventions of a dead ritualism, for these things are not the portion of renewed and spiritual men.

So, too, all merely carnal objects become as a grave to us, whether they be sinful pleasures or selfish gains. For the dead man the shroud, the coffin, and the vault are suitable enough ; but make the corpse alive again, and he cannot rest in the coffin ; he makes desperate struggles to break it up. See how by main force he dashes up the lid, rends off his bandages, and leaps from the bier. So the man renewed by grace cannot abide sin, it is a coffin to him : he cannot bear evil pleasures, they are as a shroud ; he cries for liberty. When resurrection comes the man uplifts the hillock above his grave, and scatters monument and head-stone, if these are raised above him. Some souls are buried under a mass of self-righteousness, like wealthy men on whom shrines of marble have been heaped ; but all these the believer shakes off, he must have them away, he cannot bear those dead works. He cannot live otherwise than by faith ; all other life is death to him. He must get out of his former state ; for as a tomb is not a fit place for a living man, so when we are quickened by grace the things of sin, and self, and carnal sense become dreary catacombs to us, wherein our soul feels buried, and out of which we must arise. How can we that are raised out of the death of sin live any longer therein ?

And, now, beloved, *we are at this time wholly raised from the dead* in a spiritual sense. Let us think of this, for our Lord did not have His head quickened while His feet remained in the sepulchre ; but He rose a perfect and entire man, alive throughout. Even so have we been renewed in every part. We have received, though it be but in its infancy, a perfect spiritual life : we are perfect in Christ Jesus. In our inner man our eye is opened, our ear is awakened, our hand is active, our foot is nimble : our every faculty is there, though as yet immature, and needing development, and having the old dead nature to contend with.

Moreover, and best of all, we are so raised that *we shall die no more*. Oh, tell me no more the dreary tale that a man who has received the divine life may yet lose grace and perish. With our Bibles in our hands we know better. " Christ being raised from the dead dieth no more, death hath no more dominion over Him," and therefore he that hath received Christ's life in him shall never die. Hath he not said, " He that believeth in Me, though he were dead yet shall he live ; and whosoever liveth and believeth in Me shall never die " ? This life which He has given us shall be in us " a well of water, springing up into everlasting life." He has Himself said, " I give unto My sheep eternal life, and they shall never perish, neither shall any pluck them out of My hand." On the day of our quickening we bid farewell to spiritual death, and to the sepulchre wherein we slept under sin's dominion. Farewell, thou deadly love of sin ; we have done with thee ! Farewell, dead world, corrupt world ; we have done with thee ! Christ has raised us. Christ has given us eternal life. We forsake for ever the dreary abodes of death, and seek the heavenly places. Our Jesus lives, and because He lives we shall live also, world without end.

Thus I have tried to work out the metaphor of resurrection, by which our spiritual renewal is so well set forth.

II. We are urged by the apostle to use the life which we have received, and so, secondly, LET US EXERCISE THE NEW LIFE IN SUITABLE PURSUITS. " If ye then be risen with Christ, seek those things which are above." Let your actions be agreeable to your new life.

First, then, *let us leave the sepulchre*. If we are quickened, our first act should be to leave the region of death. Let us quit the vault of a merely outward religion, and let us worship God in spirit and in truth. Let us have done with priestcraft, and all the black business of spiritual undertaking, and let the dead bury their dead ; we will have none of it. Let us have done with outward forms, and rites, and ceremonies, which are not of Christ's ordaining, and let us know nothing save Christ crucified ; for that which is not of the living Lord is a mere piece of funeral pomp, fit for the cemeteries of formalists, whose whole religion is a shovelling in of dust on coffin-lids. " Earth to earth, ashes to ashes, dust to dust." " That which is born of the flesh is flesh."

Let us also quit the vault of carnal enjoyments, wherein men seek to satisfy themselves with provision for the flesh. Let us not live by the sight of the eye, not by the hearing of the ear. Let us not live for the amassing of wealth, or the gaining of fame, for these ought to be as dead things to the man who is risen in Christ. Let us not live for the world which we see, nor after the fashion of men to whom this life is everything. Let us live as those that have come out of the world, and who, though they are in it, are no more of it. Let us be unmindful of the country from whence we came out, and leave it, as Abraham did, as though there were no such country, henceforth dwelling with our God, sojourners with Him, seeking " a city which hath foundations, whose builder and maker is God." As Jesus Christ left behind Him all the abodes of death, let us do the same.

And, then, let us *hasten to forget every evil, even as our Lord hastened to leave the tomb.* How little a time, after all, did He sojourn among the dead. He must needs lie in the heart of the earth three days, but He made them as short as possible, so that it is difficult to make out the three days at all. They were there, for there were fragments of each period, but surely never were three days so short as Jesus made them. He cut them short in righteousness, and being loosed from the pains of death, He rose early, at the very break of day. At the first instant that it was possible for Him to get away from the sepulchre consistently with the Scriptures He left the napkin and the grave-clothes, and stood in the garden, waiting to salute His disciples. So let it be with us ; there should be no lingering, no loitering, no hankering after the world, no clinging to its vanities, no making provision for the flesh. Up in morning early, oh ye who are spiritually quickened ! Up in the morning early, from your ease, your carnal pleasure, your love of wealth and self, and away out from the dark vault into a congenial sphere of action : " If ye then be risen with Christ, seek those things which are above."

To pursue the analogy : when our Lord had left the tomb thus early He spent a season on earth among His disciples, *and we are to pass the time of our sojourning here on earth, as His was passed, in holy service.* Our Lord reckoned that He was on the move from earth as soon as He rose. If you remember, He said, " I ascend unto My Father, and your Father." He did not say, " I shall ascend," as though He looked at it as a future thing ; but He said, " I ascend," as if it were so quickly to be done that it was already doing. Forty days He stayed, for He had forty days' work to do ; but He looked upon Himself as already going up into heaven. He had done with the world, He had done with the grave, and now He said, " I ascend to My Father, and your Father." We also have our forty days to tarry here ; the period may be longer or shorter as the providence of God ordains, but it will soon be over, and the time of our departure will come. Let us spend our risen life on earth as Jesus spent His,—in a greater seclusion from the world and in greater nearness to heaven than ever. Our Lord occupied Himself much in testimony, manifesting Himself, as we have already seen, in divers ways, to His friends and followers. Let us also manifest the fruits of our risen life, and bear testimony to the power of God. Let all men see that you are risen. So live that there can be no more doubt about your spiritual resurrection than there was about Christ's literal resurrection. Do not publish to the world your own virtues that you may be honoured among them ; yet " let your light so shine before men, that they may see your good works, and glorify your Father which is in heaven." Put your possession of the new life beyond question, so that when you have gone home your friends and acquaintances may say— " He was a living child of God, for we felt the power of his life ; he was a changed man, for we saw the renewing." Jesus spent His risen life also in comforting His saints. He said, " Peace be unto you." He spoke to one and another—to the Marys, to poor Peter who denied Him, and to all the assembled company, cheering them and preparing them for their future career. He spent those forty days in setting everything in order in His kingdom, arranging as to what would be when He should be taken up, and leaving His last commission to His followers that they should " go into all the world and preach the gospel to every creature." Beloved, let us also spend the time of our sojourning here in the fear of God, worshipping Him, serving Him, glorifying Him, endeavouring to set everything in order for the extension of our Master's kingdom, for the comforting of His saints, for the accomplishment of His sacred purposes.

But now I have led you up so far, I want to go further and rise higher. May the Lord help us. *Let our minds ascend to heaven in Christ.* Even while our bodies are here we are to be drawn upward with Christ ; attracted to Him, so that we can say, " He hath raised us up together, and made us sit together in heavenly places in Christ Jesus." Our text saith, " Seek those things which are above where Christ sitteth on the right hand of God " ; what is this but rising to heavenly pursuits ? Jesus has gone up ; let us go up with Him. As to these bodies, we cannot as yet ascend, for they are not fit to inherit the kingdom of God ; yet let our thoughts and hearts mount up and build a happy rest on high. Let not a stray thought alone ascend like one lone bird which sings and mounts the sky ; but let our whole mind, soul, spirit, heart, arise as when doves fly as a cloud. Let us be practical, too, and in very deed seek the things that are above : seek them because we feel we need them ; seek them because we greatly prize them ; seek them because we hope to gain them ; for a man will not heartily seek for that which he hath no hope of obtaining. The things which are above which we are even now to seek are such as these ; let us seek heavenly communion, for we are no more numbered with the congregation of the dead, but we have fellowship in Christ's resurrection, and with all the risen ones. " Truly our fellowship is with the Father and with His Son Jesus Christ," and " our conversation is in heaven." Let us seek to walk with the living God, and to know the fellowship of the Spirit.

Let us seek heavenly graces ; for " every good gift and every perfect gift is from above." Let us seek more faith, more love, more patience, more zeal ; let us labour after greater charity, greater brotherly kindness, greater humbleness of spirit. Let us labour after likeness to Christ, that He may be the firstborn among many brethren. Seek to bear the image of the heavenly, and to wear those jewels which adorn heavenly spirits.

Seek also heavenly objects. Aim at the glory of God in everything. You have to labour and toil in this world, for you are yet in the body ; take care to use worldly things to God's glory. Exercise your privileges and fulfil your duties as men, and as Englishmen, as before God, not minding the judgment of men. Wherein you mingle with the sons of men, take heed that you descend not to their level, nor act from their motives. You are not to seek your your own selfish ends, or the aggrandizement of a party, but to promote the general good, and the interests of truth, righteousness, peace, and purity. Sanctify everything by the love of God and your neighbour. Seek no party ends, but things which are pure, and honest, and of good report. Descend not to the falsehood, the trickery, the policy which are from beneath ; but honestly, sincerely, righteously, ever seek to live as those who are alive from the dead.

"Seek those things which are above," that is, heavenly joys. Oh seek to know on earth the peace of heaven, the rest of heaven, the victory of heaven, the service of heaven, the communion of heaven, the holiness of heaven : you may have foretastes of all these ; seek after them. Seek, in a word, to be preparing for the heaven which Christ is preparing for you. You are soon to dwell above ; robe yourselves for the great festival. Your treasure is above, let your hearts be with it. All that you are to possess in eternity is above, where Christ is ; rise, then, and enjoy it. Let hope anticipate the joys which are reserved, and so let us begin our heaven here below. If ye then be risen with Christ, live according to your risen nature, for your life is hid with Christ in God.

What a magnet to draw us towards heaven should this fact be,—that Christ sitteth at God's right hand. Where should the wife's thoughts be when her husband is away but with the absent and beloved one ? You know, brethren, it is not otherwise with us ; the objects of our affection are always followed by our thoughts. Let Jesus, then, be as a great loadstone, drawing our meditations and affections towards Himself. He is *sitting*, for His work is done ; as it is written, " This Man, when He had offered one sacrifice for sins for ever, sat down at the right hand of God." Let us rise and rest with Him. He is sitting on a throne. Observe His majesty, delight in His power, and trust in His dominion. He is sitting at the right hand of God in the place of honour and favour. This is a proof that we are beloved and favoured of God, for our representative has the choicest place, at God's right hand. Let your hearts ascend and enjoy that love and favour with Him. Take wing, my thoughts, and fly away to Jesus. My soul, hast thou not often said, " Woe's me that I dwell in Meshech, and tabernacle in the tents of Kedar : oh that I had wings like a dove, that I might flee away and be at rest " ? Now, then, my soul, here are wings for thee. Jesus draws thee upward. Thou hast a right to be where Jesus is, for thou art married to Him ; therefore let thy thoughts abide with Him, rest in Him, delight in Him, rejoice in Him, and yet again rejoice. The sacred ladder is before us ; let us climb it until by faith we sit in the heavenlies with Him.

May the Spirit of God bless these words to you.

III. Thirdly, inasmuch as we are risen with Christ, LET THE NEW LIFE DELIGHT ITSELF IN SUITABLE OBJECTS. This brings in the second verse : " Set your affection on things above, not on things on the earth." " Set your affection." These words do not quite express the meaning, though they are as near it as any one clause could well come. We might render it thus : " Have a relish for things above " ; or, " study industriously things above " ; or, " set your mind on things above, not on things on the earth." That which is proper enough for a dead man is quite unsuitable for a risen one. Objects of desire which might suit us when we were sinners are not legitimate nor worthy objects for us when we are made saints. As we are quickened we must exercise life, and as we have ascended we must love higher things than those of earth.

What are these " things above " which we should set our affection upon ? I ask you now to lift your eyes above yon clouds and this lower firmament is the residence of God. What see you there ? First, there is *God Himself*. Make Him the subject of your thoughts, your desires, your emotions, your love. " Delight thyself also in the Lord, and He will give thee the desires of thine heart." " My soul, wait thou only upon God, for my expectation is from Him." Call Him " God my exceeding joy." Let nothing come between you and your heavenly Father. What is all the world if you have not God, and when you once have God, what matters it though all the world be gone ? God is all things, and when thou canst say " God is mine," thou art richer than Crœsus. O to say, " Whom have I in heaven but Thee ? and there is none upon earth that I desire beside Thee." O to love God with all our heart, and with all our soul, and with all our mind, and with all our strength : that is what the law required, it is what the gospel enables us to render.

What see I next ? I see *Jesus*, who is God, but yet is truly man. Need I press upon you, beloved, to set your love upon the Well-beloved ? Has He not won your heart, and doth He not hold it now as under a mighty spell ? I know you love Him. Fix your mind on Him then. Often meditate upon His divine person, His perfect work, His mediatorial glory, His second coming, His glorious reign, His love for you, your own security in Him, your union with Him. Oh let these sweet thoughts possess your breasts, fill your mouths, and influence your lives. Let the morning break with thoughts of Christ, and let your last thought at night be sweetened with His presence. Set your affection upon Him who has set His affection upon you.

But what next do I see above ? I see *the new Jerusalem*, which is the mother of us all. I see the church of Christ triumphant in heaven, with which the church militant is one. We do not often enough realize the face that we are come into the general assembly and church of the firstborn, whose names are written in heaven. Love all the saints, but do not forget the saints above. Have fellowship with them, for we make but one communion. Remember those :—

" Who once were mourning here below,
  And wet their couch with tears,
Who wrestled hard, as we do now,
  With sins, and doubts, and fears."

Speak with the braves who have won their crowns, the heroes who have fought a good fight, and now rest from their labours, waving the palm. Let your hearts be often among the perfected, with whom you are to spend eternity.

And what else is there above that our hearts should love but *heaven itself* ? It is the place of holiness ; let us so love it that we begin to be holy here. It is the place of rest ; let us so delight in it that by faith we enter into that rest. O my brethren, you have vast estates which you have never seen ; and methinks if I had an estate on earth which was soon to be mine I should wish to take a peep over the hedge now and then. If I could not take possession, I should like to see what I had in reversion. I would make an excuse to pass that way and say to any who were with me, " That estate is going to be mine before long." In your present poverty console yourselves with the many mansions. In your sickness delight much in the land where the inhabitants shall no more say, " I am sick." In the midst of depression of spirit comfort your heart with the prospect of unmixed felicity.

> " No more fatigue, no more distress,
> Nor sin nor death shall reach the place ;
> No groans to mingle with the songs
> Which warble from immortal tongues."

What ! Are you fettered to earth ? Can you not project yourself into the future ? The stream of death is narrow ; cannot your imagination and your faith leap over the brook to stand on the hither shore awhile and cry, " All is mine, and mine for ever. Where Jesus is there shall I be : where Jesus sits there shall I rest :

> ' Far from a world of grief and sin,
> With God eternally shut in " ?

" Set your affection on things above." Oh to get away at this present time from these dull cares which like a fog envelop us ! Even we that are Christ's servants, and live in His court, at times feel weary, and droop as if His service were hard. He never means it to be a bondage, and it is our fault if we make it so. Martha's service is due, but she is not called to be *cumbered* with much serving ; that is her own arrangement : let us serve abundantly, and yet sit with Mary at the Master's feet. You who are in business, and mix with the world by the necessity of your callings, must find it difficult to keep quite clear of the down-dragging influences of this poor world ;

it will hamper you if it can. You are like a bird, which is always in danger when it alights on the earth. There are lime-twigs, and traps, and nets, and guns, and a poor bird is never safe except upon the wing and up aloft. Yet birds must come down to feed, and they do well to gather their meal in haste, and take to their wings again. When we come down among men we must speedily be up again. When you have to mix with the world, and see its sin and evil, yet take heed that you do not light on the ground without your Father : and then, as soon as ever you have picked up your barley, rise again, away, away, for this is not your rest. You are like Noah's dove flying over the waste of waters, there is no rest for the sole of your feet but on the ark with Jesus. On this resurrection-day fence out the world, let us chase away the wild boar of the wood, and let the vines bloom, and the tender grapes give forth their good smell, and let the Beloved come and walk in the garden of our souls, while we delight ourselves in Him and in His heavenly gifts. Let us not carry our burden of things below on this holy day, but let us keep it as a Sabbath unto the Lord. On the Sabbath we are no more to work with our minds than with our hands. Cares and anxieties of an earthly kind defile the day of sacred rest. The essence of Sabbath-breaking lies in worry, and murmuring and unbelief, with which too many are filled. Put these away, beloved, for we are risen with Christ, and it is not meet that we should wander among the tombs. Nay, rather let us sing unto the Lord a new song, and praise Him with our whole soul.

CHRIST OUR LIFE—SOON TO APPEAR

" When Christ, who is our life, shall appear, then shall ye also appear with Him in glory."—Colossians iii. 4.

MY discourse on Sabbath mornings is very frequently the gathering up of the thoughts and experiences of the week—a handful of barley which I have gleaned among the sheaves ; but I could not thrust upon you this morning the poverty-stricken productions of my own insufferable dulness of brain, weariness of heart, and sickness of spirit during this week, for this were a sure method of making you partakers of my misery. I have wandered through a wilderness, but I will not scatter handfuls of the hot sand among you. I have traversed the valley of the shadow of death, but I will not repeat the howlings of Apollyon. This day of rest is appointed for a far better purpose.

Scarcely knowing how to fulfil the appointed service of this morning, I sit me down and remember the ancient minstrel, who, when the genius of song had for a time departed from him, was nevertheless called upon to discourse sweet music. What could he do but lay his fingers among the strings of his harp, and begin some old accustomed strain. His fingers, and his lips moved at first mechanically ; the first few stanzas dropped from him from mere force of habit, and fell like stones without life or power, but by and by, he struck a string which woke the echoes of his soul, a note fell on his heart like a blazing torch, and the smouldering fire within his soul suddenly flamed up ; the heaven-born muse was with him, and he sang as in his better times. So may it be my happy lot this morning : placing my fingers on the strings which know so well the

name of Jesus, and beginning to discourse upon a theme which so constantly has made these walls to ring, although at first insipid periods try your patient ears, yet shall they nevertheless lead to something that may kindle in you hope, and joy, and love, if not rapture and delight. O for the wings of eagles to bear our souls upward towards the throne of our God. Already my heart warms with the expectation of a blessing ! Does the earth feel the rising of the sun before the first bright beams gild the east ? Are there not sharp-witted birds, which know within themselves that the sunbeams are on the road, and therefore begin right joyously to wake up their fellows to tell them that the morning cometh leaping over the hills ? Certain hopeful, joyful thoughts have entered within our heart, prophetic of the Comforter's divine appearing, to make glad our souls. Does not the whole earth prophecy the coming of the happy days of spring ? There are certain little bulbs that swell, and flowers that peep from under the black mould, and say, " We know what others do not know, that the summer's coming, coming very soon " ; and surely there are rising hopes within us this morning, which show their golden flowers above our heaviness, and assure us with joyful accents, that Christ is coming to cheer our hearts yet again. Believer, you shall once again behold His comfortable presence ; you shall no longer cry unto Him out of the depths, but your soul shall lean upon His arm, and drink deep of His love. Beloved, I proceed in the hope that the gracious Lord will favour His most unworthy servant, and in His own mercy fulfil our best expectations.

Our text is a very simple one, and bears upon its surface four thoughts; namely, that *Christ is our life*; that, secondly, *Christ is hidden, and so is our life*; that, thirdly, *Christ will one day appear*; and, fourthly, that *when He appeareth we also shall appear with Him in glory.*

I. The first most precious and experimental doctrine lies in these words, "CHRIST WHO IS OUR LIFE."

We hardly realize that we are reading in Colossians when we meet with this marvellously rich expression. It is so like John's way of talking. See his opening words in his gospel, "In Him was life, and the life was the light of men." Remember how he reports the words at Lazarus' tomb, "I am the resurrection and the life." How familiarly he speaks of the Lord Jesus under the same character in his first epistle: "That which was from the beginning, which we have heard, which we have seen with our eyes, which we have looked upon, and our hands have handled, of the Word of life; for *the life* was manifested, and we have seen it, and bear witness, and shew unto you that eternal life which was with the Father, and was manifested unto us." How close John cleaves to Jesus! He does not say, as the preacher of this morning will—Christ is the food of our life, and the joy of our life, and the object of our life, and so on, no, but "Christ *is* our life." I think that Peter or James would have said, "He is the *strength* or guide of our life," but John must needs put his head right into the Saviour's bosom, he cannot talk at a distance, or whisper from a second seat, but his head must go sweetly down upon the Saviour's heaving bosom; he must feel himself in the closest, nearest possible contact with his Lord; and so he puts it, "The Life was manifested," getting to the very pith and marrow of it at once. Paul has somewhat of the same loving spirit, and if not entitled to be called "that disciple whom Jesus loved," the angel might well have addressed him as he did Daniel, "O man, greatly beloved." Hence, you see, he leaps at once into the depths of the truth, and delights to dive in it. Whereas others, like the Israelites, stand outside the bound which surrounds the mount, he, like Moses, enters into the place where God is, and beholds the excellent glory. We, I fear, must compass this holy truth round about, before we can fully enter into it. Blessed is it to wait at the doors of such a truth, though better far to enter in. Let it be understood that it is not natural but spiritual life of which the text treats, and then we shall not mislead the ignorant.

1. *Christ is the source of our life.* "For as the Father raiseth up the dead, and quickeneth them; even so the Son quickeneth whom He will." Our Lord's own words are—"Verily, verily, I say unto you, he that heareth My word, and believeth on Him that sent Me, hath everlasting life, and shall not come into condemnation; but is passed from death unto life. Verily, verily, I say unto you, the hour is coming, and now is, when the dead shall hear the voice of the Son of God; and they that hear shall live." Four verilies, as if to show the importance of the truth here taught to us. We are dead in sin. That same voice which brought Lazarus out of the tomb, brings us out of our grave of sin. We hear the word of God, and we live according to the promise—"Awake thou that sleepest, and arise from the dead, and Christ shall give thee light." (Eph. v. 14.) Jesus is our Alpha, as well as our Omega: He is the Author of our faith, as well as its finisher. We should have been to this day dead in trespasses and sins, if it had not been said, "And you hath He quickened." It is by *His* life that we live; He gives us the living water, which is in us a well of water springing up unto everlasting life.

2. *Christ is the substance of our spiritual life.*

What is life? The physician cannot discover it; the anatomist hunts in vain for it, through flesh, and nerve, and brain. Be quick, sir! with that scapel of yours; "life's just departed," men say; cut quick to the heart, and see if you cannot find, at least, some lingering footprint of the departed thing called life. Subtle anatomist, what hast thou found? Look at that brain—what canst thou see there but a certain quantity of matter strangely fashioned? Canst thou discover what is life? It is true that somewhere in that brain and in that spinal cord it dwells, and that heart with its perpetual pumpings and heavings has something or other to do with it, but where is the substance, the real substance of the thing called life? Ariel's wings cannot pursue it—it is too subtle. Thought knows it but cannot grasp it; knows it from its being like itself, but cannot give a picture of it, nor represent what it is. In the new nature of the Christian there is much mystery, but there is none as to what is its life; if you could cut into the centre of the renewed heart you would find sure footprints of divine life, for you would find love to Jesus, nay, you would find Christ Himself there. If you walk in search of the springs of the sea of the new nature, you will find the Lord Jesus at the fount of all. "All my springs are in Thee," said David. Christ creates the life-throbs of the believer's soul, He sends the life-floods through the man according to His own will. If you could penetrate the brain of the believer you would find Christ to be the central thought moving every other thought, and causing every other thought to take root and grow out of itself; you would find Christ to be the true substance of the inner life of the spiritual nature of every soul quickened by the breath of heaven's life.

3. *Christ is the sustenance of our life.* What can the Christian feed upon but Jesus' flesh and blood? As to his natural life he needs bread, but as to his spiritual life, of which alone we are now speaking, he has learned that "man shall not live by bread alone, but by every word which proceedeth out of the mouth of God shall man live." "This is the bread which cometh down from heaven, that a man may eat thereof, and not die. I am the living bread which came down from heaven; if any man eat of this bread, he shall live for ever; and the bread that I will give is My flesh, which I will give for the life of the world." We cannot live on the sand of the wilderness, we want the manna which drops from on high; our skin bottles of creature confidence cannot yield us a drop of moisture, but we drink of the rock which follows us, and that rock is Christ. O wayworn pilgrims in this wilderness of sin, you never do get a morsel, much less a meal, to satisfy the craving hunger of your spirits, except ye find it in Christ Jesus. When you feed on Him your soul can sing, "He hath satisfied my mouth with good things, so that my youth is renewed like the eagle's," but if you have Him not, your

bursting wine vat and your well filled barn can give you no sort of satisfaction; rather you lament over them in the words of wisdom, "Vanity of vanities, all is vanity!" O how true are Jesus' own words, "For My flesh is meat indeed, and My blood is drink indeed. He that eateth My flesh, and drinketh My blood, dwelleth in Me, and I in him. As the living Father hath sent Me, and I live by the Father: so he that eateth Me, even he shall live by Me."

Christ is the solace of our life. Noah's ark had but one window, and we must not expect more. Jesus is the only window which lets light into the Christian's spirit when he is under sharp affliction. Kirke White's picture of his midnight voyage, when one star alone of all the train could guide the mariner's foundering bark to the port of peace, is a faint but truthful representation of the Christian's life in its hour of peril. Paul says that during his disastrous voyage "neither sun nor stars for many days appeared, and no small tempest lay on them, and all hope that they should be saved was taken away, but then, the angel of God stood at his side"; and even so will the Lord appear to His saints in their extremities, and be their joy and safety. And, brethren, if Christ appear, what mattereth it where we are?

"Midst darkest shades if He appear
My dawning is begun;
He is my soul's bright morning star,
And He my rising sun."

Do not talk of poverty! Our tents are the curtains of Solomon, and not the smoke-dried skins of Kedar, when Christ is present. Speak not of want! There are all manner of precious fruits laid up for my beloved when He cometh into my cot. Speak not of sickness! my soul is no longer sick except it be of love, but full of holy health when once the Sun of Righteousness hath risen with healing beneath His wings. Christ is the very soul of my soul's life. His loving kindness is better than life! There is nothing in life worth living for but Christ. "Whom have I in heaven but Thee, and there is none upon earth that I desire beside Thee!" The rest is mere skim milk and curds fit to be given to the swine, but Christ is the cream; all else is but the husk and bran, and coarse gritty meal; the Lord Jesus is the pure flour. All that remaineth is the chaff; fan it, and the wind shall carry it away, or the fire shall burn it, and little shall be the loss; Christ is the golden grain, the only thing worth having. Life's true life, the true heart's blood, the innermost fount of life is in Jesus.

To the true Christian, *Christ is the object of his life.* As speeds the ship towards the port, so hastes the believer towards the haven of his Saviour's bosom. As flies the arrow to its goal, so flies the Christian towards the perfecting of his fellowship with Christ Jesus. As the soldier fights for his captain, and is crowned in his captain's victory, so the believer contends for Christ, and gets his triumph out of the triumphs of his Master. "For him to live is Christ"; —at least, it is this he seeks after, and counts that all life apart from this is merely death in another form. That wicked flesh of his, that cumbrous clay, those many temptations, that Satanic trinity of the world, the flesh, and the devil, all these mar his outward actions; but if he could be what he would be, he would stand like the bullock at Christ's altar to be slaughtered, or march forward like a bullock in Christ's furrow to plough the blood-bought field. He desires that he may not have a hair of his head unconsecrated, nor heave one breath which is not for his Saviour, nor speak one word which is not for the glory of his Lord. His heart's ambition is to live so long as he can glorify Christ better on earth than in heaven, and to be taken up when it shall be better for him and more honourable for his Master that he should be with Jesus where He is. As the river seeks the sea, so, Jesus, seek I Thee! O let me find Thee and melt my life into Thine for ever!

It follows from all this, that *Christ is the exemplar of our life.* A Christian lays the life of Christ before him as the schoolboy put his copy at the top of the page, and he tries to draw each line, down-stroke and up-stroke, according to the hand-writing of Christ Jesus. He has the portrait of Christ before him as the artist has in his studio his Greek sculptures, busts and torsos; he knows that there is all the true anatomy of virtue in Christ. If he wants to study life, he studies from Christ; or, if he would closely learn the beauties of the antique, he studies from the Saviour, for Christ is ancient and modern, antique and living too, and therefore God's artists in their life-sculpture keep to the Saviour, and count that if they imitate every vein, and fetch out every muscle of their great copy, they shall then have produced the perfection of manhood. I would give nothing for your religion if you do not seek to be like Christ; where there is the same life within, there will, there must be, to a great extent, the same developments without. I have heard it said, and I think I have sometimes noticed it, that husbands and wives who are truly knit together in near and dear conjugal affection, grow somewhat like each other in expression, if not in feature. This I well know, that if the heart is truly wedded to the Lord Jesus, and lives in near fellowship with Him, it must grow like Him. Grace is the light, our loving heart is the sensitive plate, Jesus is the person who fills the lens of our soul, and soon a heavenly photograph of His character is produced. There will be a similarity of spirit, temper, motive, and action; it will not be manifest merely in great things but in little matters too, for even our speech will bewray us.

Thus you see after all, I have only been wading along the banks, or at best conducting you up to the knees in the gently flowing stream of my text. Experience must lead you further, for there is a great deep here; Paul could perceive it, for *he* does not say as I have been saying, "Jesus is the source of our life, the substance of our life, the solace of our life, the object of our life, the exemplar of our life"; but he says, "Christ *is* our life," and so He is indeed. Just as we have a natural life of which we know so little, so we have a spiritual life which is more mysterious far, and of that we know beyond its effects and operations little more than this, that Christ *is* that life, that when we get Christ we have eternal life, that if we have life it is only because we have Christ in us, the hope of glory.

I must pause a minute here, just to say that what is true concerning our spiritual life, *now*, is *equally true of our spiritual life in heaven*. Different as are the circumstances of the life in heaven and the life on earth, yet as to real essence there is only one life in both places. Saints in heaven live by precisely the same life which makes them live here. Spiritual life in the kingdom of grace and in the kingdom of glory is the same, only here it is uneducated spiritual life, there it is educated and trained ; here it is undeveloped, it is the babe, the child, there it is developed, manifested, perfected ; but in very deed the life is precisely the same. Saints need not to be born again after once being regenerate. You who have been born again, have now within you the life which will last on throughout eternity ; you have the very same vital spark of heavenly flame which will burn in glory, world without end.

It will be no digression if we here remark, that as we have eternal life in having Christ, this *marks our dignity.* " Christ our life ! " Why, this cannot be said of princes or kings ! What is their life ? Talk of blue blood and pedigree, and so on, here is something more, here is *God's own Son, our life !* You cannot say this of angels. Bright spirits ! your songs are sweet and your lives are happy, but Christ is not your life ! Nay this cannot be asserted of archangels. Gabriel ! thou mayest bend thyself before God's throne, and worship Him in praise too high for me, but thou canst not boast what I can surely claim, that Christ is my life ! Even those mysterious presence-angels of whom we read in Ezekiel and Revelation, called the four living creatures, though they seem to bear up the moving throne of deity, creatures who appear to be an embodiment of divine power and glory, yet even of these it is not written that Christ is their life. Here in men, redeemed, elect, favoured men rise to a supernatural height, for they can say what no spirits but those redeemed by blood may venture to assert, " Christ is our life." Does not this account for *Christian holiness ?* How can a man live in sin if Christ is his life ? Jesus dwell in him and he continue in sin ? Impossible ! Can he sin without his life ? He *must* do so if he sins, because Christ cannot sin, and Christ is his life. Why, if I see the saint never so self-denying, never so zealous, never so earnest, never so like his Lord, it is no wonder now, when I understand that Christ is his life.

See *how secure* the Christian is. No dagger can reach his life, for it is hidden beyond the skies. No temptation, no hellish blast, no exhalation from the Stygian pits of temptation can ever with burning fever or chill consumption waste the life of the Christian spiritually. No, it is hid with Christ, it *is* Christ, and unless Christ dies, the Christian's life dies not. Oh how safe, how honoured, how happy is the Christian !

But we may not linger longer, time warns us to proceed. There is much more than ever we shall be able to bring out. Let down your buckets, here is a deep well ; I hope you have something to draw with. You that have life within have. You that have not, may look down the well and see the darkness, or the reflection of the water, but you cannot reach the cooling flood. It is only you who can draw, who can know the excellence of this living water. I pray the Lord help you to drink to the full and draw again, for there is no fear of ever draining the inexhaustible fulness of this deep truth of God.

II. Now, as our Lord Jesus has not yet appeared in His glory, OUR LIFE IS THEREFORE HIDDEN.

" The earnest expectation of the creature waiteth for the manifestation of the sons of God," but as yet they are unknown and unmanifested. The major part of the believer's life is not seen at all, and never can be by the unspiritual eye. Where is Christ ?

To the worldling at the present moment there is no such person as Christ ; he says, " I cannot see Him, touch Him, hear Him. He is beyond all cognizance of my senses, I do not believe in Him." Just such is spiritual life to the unbeliever. You must not expect because you are a Christian that unbelievers will begin to admire you, and say, " What a mystery ! This man has a new life in him, what an admirable thing, what a desirable possession, we wish we partook of the same." Nothing of the kind. They do not know that you have such a life at all. They can see your outward actions, but your inward life is quite out of reach of their observation. Christ is in heaven to-day, He is full of joy ; but the world does not know His joy ; no worldly heart is boasting and rejoicing because Christ is glad in heaven. Christ to-day is pleading before the Father's throne, but the world does not see Christ's engagements ; Christ's occupations are all hidden from carnal eyes. Christ at this present moment reigns, and has power in heaven, and earth, and hell ; but what does the worldly man see of it ? Jesus has fellowship with all His saints everywhere, but what does the ungodly discern ? I might stand and preach until midnight concerning my Lord, but all that men who are unconverted would gain would be to hear what I have to tell, and then to say, " Perhaps it is true," but they could not possibly discern it, the thing is beyond the cognizance of sense. So is our spiritual life. Beloved, you may reign over sin, but the sinner does not comprehend your being a king. You may officiate as a priest before God, but the ungodly man does not perceive your priesthood and your worship. Do not expect Him to do so ; your labour is lost if you try by any way to introduce him to these mysteries, except by the same door through which you came yourself. I never try to teach a horse astronomy ; and to teach an unconverted man spiritual experience would be a folly of the same sort. The man who knows nothing of our inner life takes up " Pilgrim's Progress," and he says, " Yes, it is a very wonderful allegory." It is, sir, but unrenewed minds know nothing about it. When we have sometimes read explanations of the Pilgrim's Progress, we could not but detect that the writer of the explanation had need to have had it explained to himself ; he could describe the shell, but the kernel of the nut was far beyond his reach ; he had not learned to crack the shell, and to feed upon the meat. Now it must be so, it must be so, if Christ is our life ; Christ has gone away and cannot be seen ; it must be so that the greater proportion of the spiritual life must be for ever a secret to all but spiritual men. But then there is a part which men do see, and that I may liken to Christ when He was on earth : Christ seen of men and angels. What did the world do with Christ as soon as they saw Him ? Set Him in the chair of state and fall down and worship His absolute perfection ? No, not they : " He was despised and rejected of men, a Man of sorrows and acquainted with grief." Outside of the camp was His place ; cross-bearing was for Him the occupation, not of one day, but of every day. Did the world yield Him solace and rest ? Foxes, ye have your holes, ye birds of the air, ye have your nests, but the Son of man had not where to lay His head. Earth could afford Him no bed, no house, no shelter ; at last it cast Him out for death, and crucified Him, and then would have denied Him a tomb, if one of

His disciples had not begged His body. Such you must expect to be the lot of the part of your spiritual life which men can see ; as soon as they see it to be spiritual life, they will treat it as they treated the Saviour. They will despise it, " Sure ! " say they, " pretty fancies, fine airs, nice ideas." You expect them to give you comfort, do you—worldlings to give you comfort ! Do you think that Christ will have anywhere to lay His head in this world to-day any more than He had one thousand eight hundred years ago ? You go about to find what God gives the foxes and the birds, but what He never meant to give to you in this world, a place whereon to lay your head. Your place to lay your head is up yonder on your Saviour's bosom, but not here. You dream that men will admire you, that the more holy you are and the more Christ-like you are, the more peaceable people will be toward you. My dear friends, you do not know what you are driving at. " It is enough for the disciple that he be as his Master, and the servant as his Lord. If they have called the Master of the house Beelzebub, how much more shall they call them of His household ? " I believe if we were more like Christ we should be much more loved by His friends, and much more hated by His enemies. I do not believe the world would be half so lenient to the Church, nowadays, if it were not that the Church has grown complacent to the world. When any of us speak up boldly, mercenary motives are imputed to us, our language is turned upside down, and we are abhorred of men. We get smooth things, brethren, because I am afraid we are too much like the prophets who prophesied peace, peace, where there was no peace. Let us be true to our Master, stand out and come out and be like Him, and we must expect the same treatment which He had ; and if we receive it we can only say, This is what I expected ;—

> " Tis no surprising thing
>   That we should be unknown ;
> The Jewish world knew not their King,
>   God's everlasting Son."

III. CHRIST WILL APPEAR. The text speaks of it as a fact to be taken for granted. " When Christ, who is our life, shall appear." It is not a matter of question in the Christian church whether Christ will appear or not. Has not Christ appeared once ? Yes, after a certain sort. I remember reading a quaint expression of some old divine, that the book of Revelation might quite as well be called an Obvelation, for it was rather a hiding than a revealing of things to come. So, when Jesus came, it was hardly a revealing, it was a hiding of our Lord. It is true that He was " manifest in the flesh," but it is equally true that the flesh shrouded and concealed His glory. The first manifestation was very partial ; it was Christ seen through a glass, Christ in the mist of grief, and the cloud of humiliation. Christ is yet to appear in the strong sense of the word " appearing " ; He is to come out and shine forth. He is to leave the robes of scorn and shame behind, and to come in the glory of the Father and all His holy angels with Him. This is the constant teaching of the word of God, and the constant hope of the Church, that Christ will appear. A thousand questions at once suggest themselves : How will Christ appear ? When will Christ appear ? Where will Christ appear ? and so on. What God answers we may enquire, but some of our questions are mere impertinence. How will Christ appear ? I believe Christ will appear in person. Whenever I think of the second coming, I never can tolerate the idea of a spiritual coming. That always seems to me to be the most transparent folly that can possibly be put together, because Christ cannot come spiritually, He always is here : " Lo ! I am with you alway, even unto the end of the world." Christ's spiritual coming never can be that which is spoken of in Scripture, as the day of our release. I sometimes say to brethren, " Do you think if Christ were to come spiritually now, we should observe the ordinances better ? " " Yes, certainly." " Do you think, for instance, the ordinance of the Lord's Supper would be better attended to ? " " Yes, no doubt it would." Yes, but then this proves that this is not the coming which the Bible speaks of, because it is expressly said of the Lord's Supper, that we are to do it in remembrance of Him, till He come. A spiritual coming would make us do it more zealously ; there must be another form of coming which would justify our giving up the supper altogether, and that must be of a personal character, for then, and then only, might the Supper properly cease. We shall not need to have a supper to remind us of the Person, when the Person Himself shall be present in our midst reigning and triumphant in His Church. We believe in a personal reign and coming of our Lord Jesus Christ. But how will He come ? He will doubtless come with great splendour ; the angels of God shall be His attendants. We gather from Scripture, that He will come to reign in the midst of His people, that the house of Israel will acknowledge Him as King, yea, that all nations shall bow down before Him, and kings shall pay Him homage. None shall be able to stand against Him. " Those that pierced Him shall wail because of Him." He will come to discern between the righteous and the wicked, to separate the sheep from the goats. He will come graciously to adjudge His people their reward according to their works. He will give to those who have been faithful over a few things to be rulers over many things ; and those who have been faithful over many things shall be rulers over many cities. He will come to discern between the works of His people ; such as are only wood, hay, and stubble, will be consumed ; such as are gold and silver, and precious stones, will stand the fire. He will come to condemn the wicked to eternal punishment, and to take His people up to their everlasting mansions in the skies. We look for such a coming, and without entering into minute details, drawing charts, and painting pictures, we are content to believe that He is coming in His glory, to show Himself to be what He ever was—King of kings, and Lord of lords, God over all, blessed for ever ; to be adored and worshipped, and no more to be despised and rejected of men. When will He come ? That is a question which unbelief asks with a start. Faith replies, " It is not for you to know the times and seasons ; of that day and of that hour knoweth no man." Some simpleton says, " But we may know the week, month, or year." Do not trifle with God's word and make a fool of yourself, because you must know that the expression means that you do not know anything about the time at all, and never will know. Christ will come in a time when we look not for Him, just perhaps when the world and the Church are most asleep, when the wise and the foolish virgins have alike fallen into a deep slumber ; when the stewards shall begin to beat their fellow-servants, and to drink, and to be drunken ; at midnight, or perhaps not till cock-crowing, He will come like a thief, and the house shall be suddenly broken up ; but come He will, and that is enough for you and for me to know ; and when He cometh we shall appear, for as *He* shall appear, *we* shall also appear with Him in glory.

IV. The fourth thought is, THAT WHEN CHRIST SHALL APPEAR, WE ALSO SHALL APPEAR.

Do you ever feel like those lions in the Zoological Gardens, restlessly walking up and down before the bars of their cage, and seeming to feel that they were never meant to be confined within those narrow limits ? Sometimes they are for thrusting their heads through the bars, and then for dashing back and tearing the back of their dungeon, or for rending up the pavement beneath them, as if they yearned for liberty. Do you ever feel like that ? Does your soul ever want to get free from her cage ? Here is an iron bar of sin, of doubt, and there is another iron bar of mistrust and infirmity. Oh ! if you could tear them away, could get rid of them all, you would do something for Christ—you would be like Christ. Oh ! if you could but by some means or other burst the bands of this captivity ! but you cannot, and therefore you feel uneasy. You may have seen an eagle with a chain upon its foot, standing on a rock—poor unhappy thing ! it flaps its wings—looks up to the sun—wants to fly right straight ahead at it and stare the sun out of countenance—looks to the blue sky, and seems as if it could sniff the blue beyond the dusky clouds, and wants to be away ; and so it tries its wings and dreams of mounting—but that *chain*, that *cruel chain*, remorselessly holds it down. Has not it often been so with you ? You feel, " I am not meant to be what I am, I am sure I am not ; I have a something in me which is adapted for something better and higher, and I want to mount and soar, but that chain—that dragging chain of the body of sin and death will keep me down." Now it is to such as you that this text comes, and says to you, " Yes, your present state is not your soul's true condition, you have a hidden life in you ; that life of yours pants to get out of the bonds and fetters which control it, and it shall be delivered soon, for Christ is coming, and when Christ shall appear you shall appear,—the same appearance that belongs to Him belongs to you. He shall come, and then your day of true happiness, and joy, and peace, and everything that you are panting for, and longing for, shall certainly come too." I wonder whether the little oak inside the acorn—for there is a whole oak there, and there are all the roots, and all the boughs, and everything inside that acorn—I wonder whether that little oak inside the acorn ever has any premonition of the summer weather that will float over it a hundred years hence, and of the mists that will hang in autumn on its sere leaves, and of the hundreds of acorns which itself will cast, every autumn, upon the earth, when it shall become in the forest a great tree. You and I are like that acorn ; inside of each of us are the germs of great things. There is the tree that we are to be—I mean there is the spiritual thing we are to be, both in body and soul even now within us, and sometimes here below, in happy moments, we get some inklings of what we are to be ; and then how we want to burst the shell, to get out of the acorn and to be

the oak ! Aye, but stop. Christ has not come, Christian, and you cannot get out of that till the time shall come for Jesus to appear, and then shall you appear with Him in glory. You will very soon perceive in your rain-water, certain ugly little things which swim and twist about in it, always trying if they can to reach the surface and breathe through one end of their bodies. What makes these little things so lively, these innumerable little things like very small tadpoles, why are they so lively ? Possibly they have an idea of what they are going to be. The day will come when all of a sudden there will come out of the case of the creature that you have had swimming about in your water, a long-legged thing with two bright gauze-like wings, which will mount into the air, and on a summer's evening will dance in the sunlight. It is nothing more nor less than a gnat ; you have swimming there a gnat in one of its earliest stages. You are just like that ; you are an undeveloped being ; you have not your wings yet, and yet sometimes in your activity for Christ, when the strong desires for something better are upon you, you leap in foretaste of the bliss to come. I do not know what I am to be, but I feel that there is a heart within me too big for these ribs to hold, I have an immortal spark which cannot have been intended to burn on this poor earth, and then to go out ; it must have been meant to burn on heaven's altar. Wait a bit, and when Christ comes you will know what you are. We are in the chrysalis state now, and those who are the liveliest worms among us grow more and more uneasy in that chrysalis state. Some are so frozen up in it that they forget the hereafter, and appear content to remain a chrysalis for ever. But others of us feel we would sooner not be than be what we now are for ever, we feel as if we must burst our bonds, and when that time of bursting shall come, when the chrysalis shall get its painted wings and mount to the land of flowers, then shall we be satisfied. The text tells us—" When Christ, who is our life, shall *appear* "—when He comes out in all His glory—" we also shall appear with Him in glory." If you would like these gracious promises drawn out into detail with regard to the body, you may listen to just such words as these. " It is sown a soulish body, it is raised a spiritual body. The first man is of the earth earthy, the second man is the Lord from heaven. As is the earthy, such are they also that are earthy ; as is the heavenly, such are they also that are heavenly." Whatever Christ's body is in heaven, our body is to be like it ; whatever its glory and strength and power, our vile body is to be fashioned like unto His glorious body. As for our soul, whatever of absolute perfection, whatever of immortal joy Christ possesses we are to possess that ; and as for honour, whatever of esteem and love Christ may have from intelligent beings, we are to share in the same ; and as for position before God, whatever Christ has, we are to stand where He stands. Are His enemies put to confusion ? So are ours. Do all words discern His glory ? they shall discern ours too. Is all dishonour wiped away from Him ? so shall it be from us. Do they forget for ever the shame and spitting, the cross and the nails ? so shall they in our case. Is it for ever " Glory, and honour, and power, and dominion, and bliss without end ? " so shall it be in our case. Let us comfort one another, therefore, with these words, and look up out of our wormhood and our chrysalis state, to that happier and better day when we shall be like Him, for we shall see Him as He is.

All this has nothing to do with a great many of you. You will die, but you will never rise like Christ. You will die, *and you will die.* Why did I say " and you will die ? " Why, because you will have to feel the second death, and that second death, mark you, is as much more tremendous than the first as the trumpet of the angel is more terrible than the voice of the preacher can be this morning. Oh I would that Christ were your life, but you are dead, and God will say of you one of these days as Abraham said of Sarah, " Bury the dead out of my sight," and you must be put out of His sight as an obnoxious putrid thing. Oh that He would quicken you this day ! " There is life," says the hymn, " in a look at the crucified One." God help you to exercise one look at that Christ of whom I spoke, and then you shall join with the rest of His people in saying, " Christ is our life."

May God bless these feeble words of mine, and own them because of their weakness, the more to illustrate His own grace and power, for Jesus' sake. Amen.

CHRIST IS ALL

" Christ is all, and in all."—Colossians iii. 11.

THE apostle was arguing for holiness. He was earnestly contending against sin and for the maintenance of Christian graces, but he did not, as some do, who would like to be thought preachers of the gospel, resort to reasons inconsistent with the gospel of free grace. He did not bring forward a single legal argument ; he did not say, " This do, and ye shall merit reward " ; or, " This do not, and ye shall cease to be the beloved of the Lord." He knew that he was writing to believers, who are not under the law but under grace, and he therefore used arguments fetched from grace, and suitable to the character and condition of " the elect of God, holy and beloved." He fed the flame of their love with suitable fuel, and fanned their zeal with appropriate appliances.

Observe in this chapter that he begins by reminding the saints of their having risen with Christ. If they indeed have risen with Him, he argues that they should leave the grave of iniquity and the grave-clothes of their sins behind, and act as those who are endowed with that superior life, which accounts sin to be death and corruption. He then goes on to declare that the believer's life is in Christ, " for ye are dead, and your life is hid with Christ in God." He infers holiness from this also. Shall those who have Christ for their life defile themselves with guilt ? Is it not inevitable that, if the Holy One of Israel be in them as their life, their life should be fraught with everything that is virtuous and good ? And then he brings forward the third argument, that in the Christian church Christ is the only distinguishing mark. In the new birth we are created in the image of Jesus, the second Adam, and in consequence all the distinctions that appertain to the old creation are rendered valueless ; " there is neither Greek nor Jew, circumcision nor uncircumcision, Barbarian, Scythian, bond nor free : but Christ is all, and in all " ; the argument from this fact being, that since the only abiding distinction in the new creation is Christ, we should take care that His image is most clearly stamped upon us, so that we may not only confess with our tongues that we are Christians, but our conversation and our entire character shall bespeak us to be such. As you may recognise the Jew by his physiognomy, the Greek by his gracefulness, and the barbarian by his uncouthness, so should the Christian be known by his Christliness, by the light, love, and life of Christ streaming forth from him. This is the seal of God which is set upon the forehead of the faithful, and this is the mark of election which is in due season graven in the right hand of all the elect.

Now, as the only distinction which marks the Christian from other men, and the only essential distinction in the new world of grace, is Christ, we are led to see beneath this fact a great underlying doctrine. In the realm of grace, things are what they seem. Christ is apparently all, because He is actually all. The fact of a man's possessing Christ is all in all in the church, because in very deed Christ is all in all. All that is real in the Christian, all that is holy, heavenly, pure, abiding, and saving, is of the Lord Jesus. This great granite fact lies at the basis of the whole Christian system. Christ is really and truly all in all in His Church, and in each individual member of it.

We shall, this morning, in trying to open up this precious subject, by the help of the Divine Spirit, first, notice *by whom this truth is recognised ;* secondly, we shall consider *what this truth includes ;* thirdly, *what it involves ;* and fourthly, *what it requires of us ;* for if you observe, the text is followed by a " Therefore " ; there is a conclusion logically drawn from it.

I. First, then, BY WHOM IS THIS TRUTH RECOGNISED ? Paul does not say that Christ is all in all to all men, but he tells us that there is a new creation, in which the man is " renewed in knowledge after the image of Him that created him," where all national and ceremonial distinctions cease, and Christ is all and in all. It is not to every man that Christ is all and in all. Alas ! there are many in this world to whom Christ is nothing ; He scarcely enters into their thoughts. Some of the baser sort only use His name to curse by ; and as to many others, if they have a religion, it is a proud presumption which excludes a Saviour. The creed of the self-righteous has no room in it for the sinner's Saviour ; the justifier of the ungodly is nothing to them. The worldly, the frivolous, the unchaste, the licentious, these do not permit themselves to think of the Holy Redeemer. Perchance some such are now present, and though they will hear about Him this morning, and of nothing else but Him, they will say, " what a weariness it is," and be glad when the discourse in ended. Jesus is a root out of a dry ground to multitudes, to them He hath no form nor comeliness, and in Him they see no beauty that they should desire Him. Ah, what will they do when He is revealed in the glory of His power ? They thought it nothing to them as they passed by His cross, but they will not be able to despise Him as they stand convicted before His throne. O ye who make Jesus nothing, kiss the Son lest He be angry, and ye perish from the way, when His wrath is kindled but a little. Without Christ, you are to-day without peace, and will be for ever without hope! Nothing remains for Christless souls at the last, but a fearful looking-for of judgment and of fiery indignation. I could well pause here, and say, let us pray for those who are unbelievers, and so are living without a Saviour, that they may not remain any longer in this state of condemnation.

There are others in this world to whom Christ is something, but not much. They are anxious to save themselves, but since they must confess some imperfections, they use the merits of Christ as a sort of makeweight for their slight deficiencies. Their robe is almost long enough, and by adding a little fringe of the Redeemer's grace it becomes all they can wish. To say prayers, to go to church, to take the sacrament, to observe Good Friday, these are the main reliances of many a religionist, and then if the coach sticks a little in a deeper rut than usual, they call in the help of the Lord Jesus, and hope that He will put His shoulder to the wheel. They commonly say, "Well, we must do our best, then Christ will be our Saviour, and God is very merciful." They allow the blessed and all-sufficient work and sacrifice of the Saviour to fill up their failures; and imagine that they are extremely humble in allowing so much as that. Jesus is to them a stopgap, and nothing more. I know not whether the condition of such people is one whit more desirable than that of those to whom Jesus is nothing at all, for this is a vile contempt and despising of Christ indeed, to think that He came to help you to save yourselves, to dream that He is a part Saviour, and will divide the work and honour of salvation with the sinner. Those who yoke the sinner and the Saviour together, as each doing a part, rob Christ of all His glory; and this is robbery indeed, to pilfer from the bleeding Lamb of God the due reward of His agonies. "He trod the winepress alone, and of the people there was none with Him." In the work of salvation Jesus stands alone. Salvation is of the Lord. If Christ is not all to you He is nothing to you. He will never go into partnership as a part Saviour of men. If He be something He must be everything, and if He be not everything He is nothing to you.

There are many who, unconsciously to themselves, think Jesus Christ to be much, but yet they do not understand that He is all in all. I allude to many seeking souls, who say, "I would put my trust in Jesus this morning, but I do not feel as I ought." I see, thou thinkest that there is at least a little of thy feeling to be added to the Saviour's work ere it can avail for thee. "But I am not as penitent as I should be, and, therefore, I cannot rest in Jesus." I see, thy penitence is to add the topstone to the Saviour's yet unfinished work. Perhaps it is one of the hardest works in the world, so hard as to be impossible except to the Holy Spirit Himself, to drive a man away from the idea that he is to do something, or to be something, in order to his own salvation. Sinner, thou art the emptiness, and Christ the fulness; thou art the filthiness, and He the cleansing; thou art nothing, and He is all in all; and the sooner thou consentest to this the better. Have done with saying, "I would come to the Saviour if this, and if that," for this quibbling will

delude, delay, and destroy thee. Come as thou art, just now, even at this moment, for Christ is not almost all, but all in all.

There are some, too, who think that Christ is all in some things, but they have not yet seen the full teaching of the text; for it saith: "Christ is all, and in all." "He is all," say they, "in justification; He it is that pardons all our sins and covers us with His righteousness, but as to our sanctification, surely, we are to effect that ourselves; and as to our final perseverance, it must depend wholly upon our own watchfulness. Are we not in jeopardy still? Are there not some points which depend upon our own virtue and goodness?" Beloved, God forbid I should say a word against the most earnest watchfulness, against the most diligent endeavours, but I beseech you do not place them in a wrong position, or speak as though the ultimate salvation of the believer were based upon such shifting sand. We are saved in Christ. We are complete in Him. We are sanctified in Christ Jesus: "And He is made of God unto us wisdom, righteousness, sanctification, and redemption." Christ is all, not in my justification only, but in my sanctification too. He is all, not only in the first steps of my faith, but in the last. "He is Alpha and Omega; He is the beginning and the ending, saith the Lord." There is no point between the gates of hell and the gates of heaven where a believer shall have to say, "Christ fails me here, and I must rely upon my own endeavours. From the dunghill of our corruption up to the throne of our perfection there is no point left to hazard, or set aside for us to supply; our salvation has Christ to begin with, Christ to go on with, and Christ to finish with, and that in all points, at all times, for every man of woman born that ever shall be saved. There is no point in which the creature comes in to claim merit, or to bring strength, or to make up for that which was lacking. "Christ is all, and in all." The saints are "perfect in Christ Jesus." He said, "it is finished," and finished it is. He is not the author of our faith only, but the finisher of it too. He is all in all, and man is nothing at all.

This is a truth which every believer has recognised. There are a great many differences among believers, but there is no difference as to this essential point. Unhappily, the Christian church has been divided into sections, but those divisions do not affect our agreement upon this one point, that Christ is all. It is no uncharity if I say that the man who does not accept this is no Christian, nor is it too wide a liberality to affirm that every man who is sound in heart upon this point is most certainly a believer. He who trusts alone in Christ, who submits to Him as his sole Teacher, King, and Saviour, is already a saved man; but he who gives not Christ the glory, though he should speak with the tongues of men and of angels, though he should have the gift of prophecy, and all knowledge, and though he should have all faith, and could remove mountains, and he should appear to have all virtue, yet he is no Christian if Christ be held in light esteem by him, or be anything less than all in all; for in the new creation this one thing stands as the mark of the newly created, that "Christ is all, and in all" to them, whatever He may be to others.

II. Having thus shown where this truth is recognised, we pass on to notice WHAT THIS TRUTH INCLUDES.

It was the advice of an aged tutor to a young

student not to take too magnificent a text. I have sounded that warning in my own ears this morning. This little text is yet one of the greatest in the whole Bible, and I feel lost in its boundless expanse. It is like one of those rare gems which are little to look upon, and yet he who carries them bears the price of empires in his hand. It would not be within the compass of arithmetic to set down the value of this sapphire text. I might as soon hope to carry the world in my hand as to grasp all that is contained in these few words. I cannot navigate so huge a sea, my skiff is too small, I can only coast along the shore. Who can compress " all things " into a sermon ? I will warrant you that my discourse this morning will be more remarkable for its omissions than for what it contains, and I shall hope indeed that every Christian here will be remarking upon what I do not say ; for then I shall have done much good in exciting meditations and reflections. If I were to try to tell you all the meaning of this boundless text, I should require all time and eternity, and even then all tongues, human and angelic, could not avail me to compass the whole. We will swim in this sea though we cannot fathom it, and feast at this table though we cannot reckon up its costliness.

1. According to the connection, Christ is all by way of *national distinction, subject for glorying, and ground for custom.* Observe, " there is neither Greek nor Jew, circumcision nor uncircumcision, Barbarian, Scythian, bond nor free," in the new creation, but " Christ is all, and in all." In the new world there is no difference between Jew and Gentile ; barbarian simplicity and Greek cultivation are as nothing. I suppose as long as we are in the flesh we shall set some store by our nationality, and like Paul shall somewhat glory that we were free born : but surely the less of this the better. Within the gates of the Christian church we are cosmopolitan, or rather we are citizens of the New Jerusalem only. As a man, I rejoice that I am an Englishman, but not with the same holy joy which fills me when I remember that I am a Christian. When I meet another man who fears God, I do not want him to think me an Englishman, nor do I desire to regard him as an American, a Frenchman, or a Dutchman ; for we are no longer strangers and foreigners but fellow-citizens. If any man be a Christian and a foreigner after the flesh, he is yet in spirit ten thousand times more allied to me than if he were an Englishman and an unbeliever. Greatly is it to be deplored whenever the convulsions of nations drag Christian men into opposition to one another on the ground of politics. One part of the body of Christ cannot be at war with another. It is a shameful thing whenever we suffer our earthly nationality to dominate over our heavenly citizenship. Queen Victoria and President Grant are well enough in their places, but King Jesus is Lord of all ; we are above all things subjects of His Imperial Highness the Prince of Peace. Nobody comes into the church as a Jew or a Gentile, nor does he remain there as a Greek or a Scythian, whatever he may have been before ; when he becomes a Christian, Christ is all. Earthly distinctions of rank, if they still exist, as they must while we are in this world, are brought to a minimum within the church, they are almost obliterated, and what remains is sanctified to sacred ends.

Christ is all in the church by way of glorying. The Greek said, " The Hellenes are a race of heroes ;

remember Sparta and Athens. Are we not foremost in civilisation, and were we not chief in war ? Who set bounds to the Persian tyrant, and bade the boastful monarch bite the dust ? We hold our heads erect when we think of Marathon and Salamis." But when the Greek joined the Christian church, he forgot his national boastings, and henceforth gloried only in the cross of Him whose single arm defeated the hosts of Satan, and led captivity captive. The Jew when despised returned scorn for scorn, and said to Greek and Roman, " You may speak of Marathon, but I sing of the Red Sea ; you may boast of Persia broken, but I tell of Egypt vanquished ; mine are the glories of the Lord of Hosts in the far off ages. We were a people when you were as yet unknown, and we are the chosen favourites of Jehovah." The moment the Jew sat down at the gospel supper, he laid aside his hereditary pride and bigotry, and recognised the fact that the Greek was as much a brother as the believing Hebrew at his side. So the Scythian, when he came into the Christian church, was no longer a Barbarian, he spoke the language of Canaan as correctly as his Grecian fellow Christian. The slave no sooner breathed the air of the Christian church than his shackles fell from off him. He might be a slave at home with his master, but he was no slave there. While the freeman, though he had been born free, or with a great price had obtained his freedom, never in the Christian church looked down upon the slave. Bond and free were one in Christ Jesus. Nobody had any personal ground for glory ; neither race, nor pedigree, nor rank, nor position, were of any account, but Christ was all. " *Christianus sum*," I am a Christian, was and is the universal glorying of all saints.

This at the same time obliterated all their sinful national customs. The Greek said originally, " I may certainly indulge in this vice, because the Lacedæmonians have always observed this custom " ; and the Jew, perhaps, might have said, " I will eat nothing common or unclean, neither will I consort with Gentiles, because our fathers did not so." The Barbarian said, " I cannot submit to the laws of civilised life ; my father ranged the desert " ; and the Scythian said, " I shall rob, and pillage, and kill, for I am a wild man ; why should I not ? Did not my fathers do so from generation to generation ? " When the various tribes came into the Christian church, down went all separating and evil customs at once. What hath Christ said ? What hath Christ done ? What hath He bidden us ? These are law to us and nothing else.

Thus the distinctions of race, the gloryings of the nationality, and the habitudes and customs of various nations, all sank into nothing, for Jesus Christ in the Christian church became all in all. That, I doubt not, is the meaning of the text in its connection. Christ all and in all by way of distinction.

2. Secondly, Christ is all in all to us in another threefold way—*to God, before our enemies, within ourselves.* Happy art thou, O child of God, that in all thy relationships to the Great Judge of all the earth, Christ is all in all to thee. Thou needest a mediator to stand between thee and God ; Christ is that. Thou wantest a High Priest to present with his own sacrifice thy prayers and praises ; Christ is that. Thou wantest a representative to stand at all times before God, an intercessor to plead for thee, one who shall be a daysman, akin to thee and

akin to God, who can put His hand upon both; Christ is that to thee. Whenever God looks upon thee in Christ, He sees in thee all that ought to be there. Did He look upon thee apart from Christ, He would see in thee nothing He could commend : but thou art " accepted in the Beloved." Even the omniscient eye of God detects nothing for which to condemn the soul which is covered with the righteousness of Christ. " Who shall lay anything to the charge of God's elect ? It is God that justifieth." Without spot, or wrinkle, or any such thing, is the. entire church as seen in the person of Christ Jesus, her Representative and Head. Christ is all for us before the throne of God.

But, alas ! we need some one to stand between us and our enemies. There is Satan ; how shall I meet him ? He will accuse me ; who shall plead my cause ? Christ is all in all for that. Whatever fiery darts Satan may shoot, Christ is the shield that can quench those darts. If Satan tempt me, Christ shall plead for me before the temptation comes. Whenever I have to contend with Satan, this is the weapon with which I should arm myself. If I reason with him, if I bring forward any strength of my own to oppose him, he may well say to me : " Jesus I know, but who art thou ? " But if I bring Jesus into the conflict, and wield the merit of His blood, and the faithfulness of His promise, the destroying angel cannot overcome the sprinkled blood. We overcome through the blood of the Lamb. Christ Jesus is both shield and sword to us, armour and weapons of war.

So in our conflict with the world. Whatever trials you have, my dear brother, Christ is all in all to meet them. Are you poor ? He will make you rich in your poverty by His consoling presence. Arc you sick ? He will make your bed in your sickness, and will so make your sick-bed better than the walks of health. Are you persecuted ? Be it for His sake, and you may even leap for joy. Are you oppressed ? Remember how He also was oppressed and afflicted ; and you will have fellowship with Him in His sufferings. Amidst all the vicissitudes of this present life, Christ is all that the believer wants to bear him up, and bear him through. No wave can sink the man who clings to this life-buoy ; he shall swim to glory on it.

So, too, *within myself* Christ is all. If I look into the chambers of my inner nature, I see all manner of deficiencies and deformities, and I may well be filled with dismay ; but when I see Christ there, my heart is comforted, for He will both destroy the works of the devil, and perfect that which He has begun in me. I am a sinner, but my heart rests on its Saviour ; I am burdened with this body of sin and death, but behold my Saviour is formed in me the hope of glory. I am by nature an heir of wrath, even as others, but I am born into the second Adam's household, and therefore I am beloved of the Most High, and a joint-heir with Christ. Is there Christ in thy heart, beloved ? Then everything that is there that would make thee sorrow may also suggest to thee a topic for joy. The saint is grieved to think that he has sin to confess, but he is glad to think that he is enabled to confess sin. The saint is vexed that he should have so much infirmity, yet he glories in infirmity because the power of Christ doth rest upon him. He is grieved day by day to observe his wanderings, but he is also rejoiced to see how the Good Shepherd follows him and restores his soul. So that all the evils and short-comings in me which make me weep, also make me glad when Jesus is seen within. For all I see within myself lacking or sinful, I see a sufficient remedy in Christ, who is all in all.

Thus I have given you a second way of meditating upon our text. Christ is not only all by way of distinction, but He is all to God, all between ourselves and our enemies, and all within ourselves.

3. We may see another phase of the same meaning if we take a third division. Christ is all *for* us, He is all *to* us, He is all *in* us.

Christ is all *for* us, the surety, the substitute in our stead to bear our guilt ; " For the Lord hath laid on Him the iniquity of us all." " The chastise-ment of our peace was upon Him." " He hath made Him to be sin for us who knew no sin, that we might be made the righteousness of God in Him." He is also the worker standing in our place to fulfil all righteousness for us. He is the end of the law for righteousness to every one that believeth. All that God requires us to be, Christ is for us. He has not presented to God a part of what was done, but has to the utmost farthing paid all that His people owed. Acting as our forerunner in heaven, He has taken possession of our inheritance, and as our surety He secures to us our entrance there. *For* us all Jesus is all.

And this day He is all *to* us. We trust wholly in Him. I often question myself upon many Christian graces, but there is one thing I never can doubt about, and that is I know I have no other hope but in the blood and righteousness of Jesus Christ. If a soul can perish relying with all its power upon the finished work of the Saviour, then I shall perish ; but if saving faith be an entire reliance upon Him whom God hath sent forth to be a propitiation for sin, then I can never perish until God's word be broken. Can you not say that, dear brethren, and will it not yield you comfort ? Have you anything else you could trust to ? Have you one good work that you could rely upon ? Is there a prayer you have ever offered, an emotion you have ever felt, that you would dare to use as a buttress, or as in some degree a prop, to your hope of salvation ? I know you reply, " I have nothing, nothing, nothing, nothing ; but Christ my Saviour is all my salvation and all my desire, and I abhor the very idea of putting anything side by side with Him as a ground of my dependence before God." Oh, then, assuredly you have the mark of Christ's sheep, for to all of them Christ is all.

I said also that Christ is all *in* us, and so He is. Whatever there is in us that is not of Christ and the work of His Spirit, will have to come out of us, and blessed be the day in which it is ejected. If I am growing and advancing, but it is a growth in the flesh and an advance in self, it is a spurious fungus growth ; and, like Jonah's gourd, it will perish in a night. Wood, hay, stubble, are quick building, but they are also quick burning ; only that which belongs to " Christ formed in me the hope of glory," will prove to be gold, silver, precious stones ; this may seem slow building, but it will abide the fire. O Christian, pray much and labour much to have Christ in thee, for He is all that is worth having in thee. He is only the husk of a Christian who has not the precious kernel of Christ in his heart. Christ on the cross saves us by becoming Christ in the heart. Jesus is indeed all for us, all to us, all in us.

4. Shift the kaleidoscope, and take the same truth in another way. *Christ is the channel of all, the pledge of all, the sum of all.*

The *channel* of all. All love and mercy flow from God through Christ the Mediator. We get nought apart from Him. "No man cometh unto the Father but by Me." Other conduits are dry, but this channel is always full. "He is able to save them to the uttermost that come unto God by Him, seeing He ever liveth to make intercession for them."

Christ is the *pledge* of all. When God gave us Christ, He did as much as say, "I have given you all things." "He that spared not His own Son, but freely delivered Him up for us all, how shall He not with Him also freely give us all things?" He is a covenant to us, the title-deeds of the promised rest.

And, indeed, Christ is not only the channel of all, and the pledge of all, but the apostle says He is all; so I take it He is *the sum* of all. If you are going to travel on the Continent, you need not carry a bed with you, nor a house, nor a table, nor medicine, nor food; if you only have gold in your purse, you have these condensed. Gold is the representative of everything it can buy, it is a kind of universal talisman, producing what its owner wishes for. I have never yet met with a person in any country who did not understand its meaning. "Money answereth all things," says the wise man, and this is true in a limited sense; but he that has Christ, has indeed all things: he has the essence, the substance of all good. I have only to plead the name of Jesus before the Father's throne, and nothing desirable shall be denied me. If Christ is yours, all things are yours. God, who gave you Christ, has in that one gift summed up the total of all you will want for time and for eternity, to obliterate the sin of the past, to fulfil the needs of the present, and to perfect you for all the work and bliss of the future.

5. Once more let us view our text in another light. *Christ is all we need, all we desire, and all of good that we can conceive.* He is all I need. Jesus is the living water to quench my thirst, the heavenly bread to satisfy my hunger, the snow-white robe to cover me, the sure refuge, the happy home of my soul, my meat and my medicine, my solace and my song, my light and my delight.

He is all I *desire*, and when most covetous I only covet more of His presence; when most ambitious, it is my ambition to be like Him; when most insatiable in desire, I only long to be with Him where He is. He is all I can *conceive* of good. When my imagination stretches all her wings to take a flight into realms beyond where the eagle's wing hath been, yet even then she reacheth not the height of the glory which Christ Jesus hath promised her; she cannot conceive with her most expanded powers of anything more rich and precious than Christ, her Christ, herself Christ's, and Christ all her own. Oh, if you want to know what heaven is, know what Christ is, for the way to spell heaven is with those five letters that make up the word Jesus. When you get Him He shall be all to you that your glorified body shall need, and all your glorified spirit can conceive. O precious Christ, Thou art all in all.

III. I have shown you then, in a very hurried way, what it is that this truth includes; now, with greater brevity still, WHAT DOES THIS TRUTH INVOLVE? It involves a great many things. First,

it involves the glory and excellence of Christ. Of whom else could it be said that He is all in all? There are many things in this world that are good, but there is nothing that is good for everything. Some plants may be a good medicine, but not a good cordial; the plant of renown is good every way. Good clothing is not able to stay your hunger, but Christ the bread of heaven is also the Father's best robe. You cannot expect any finite thing to be good for all things, but Christ is infinite goodness. This tree of life bears all manner of fruits, and the leaves are for the healing of the nations. He is strength and beauty, safety and sanctity, peace and plenty, healing and help, comfort and conquest, life here, and life for ever. Glory be to the Lord Jesus Christ! What can He be less than God, if He be all? "All." Is it not a synonyme for God? We say there cannot be two Gods, because the one God is everywhere, and fills all space; and who then can He be who is called "all in all," but "very God of very God"? Worship Him, my brethren, with all your hearts, rejoice in Him, bless Him from day to day. Let not the world think you poor who are so rich in Him. Never suffer men to think you unhappy, who have perfect happiness in the ever-blessed Immanuel.

See, in the next place, the safety and the blessedness of the believer. Christ is all; but the believer can add, "And Christ is mine." Then the believer has all things—all that he *will* want, as well as all he does want. No emperor that has not Christ is half as rich as he that has Christ and is a beggar. He that hath Christ, being a pauper, hath all things; and he that hath not Christ, possessing a thousand worlds, possesses nothing for real happiness and joy. Oh, the blessedness of the man who can say, "Christ is mine." On the other hand, see the wretchedness of the man who has not the Saviour: for if Christ is all, you who believe not on Him are devoid of all, in being destitute of Christ. But you say, "I try my best, I attend public worship, I do a great deal that is good"; you have nothing if you have not Christ. Do not flatter yourself that you are getting on and adding goods to goods in spiritual things; if you have not a Saviour you are naked and poor and miserable; you are without all if you are without Christ, who is all. The Christain, then, is rich, but everyone who is destitute of Christ is poor to the extreme of poverty.

See, too, in the truth before us a rebuke for the doubts of many seekers. They will say, "I have not this, I have not that." Suppose thou hast it not, Christ has it, if it be good for anything. "I would fain cast myself upon the mercy of God in Christ this day, but,"—Ah, away with thy "buts." What dost thou want? "I want true belief," saith one. Come to Christ for it then. "I want a broken heart," says another. If you cannot come with a broken heart to Christ, come for a broken heart.

"True belief, and true repentance,
  Every grace that brings us nigh,
    Without money,
  Come to Jesus Christ and buy."

We have an old proverb about the folly of taking coals to Newcastle; but what folly must that be which makes a man think that he can take something to Christ, when Christ is all. Come, come, come, come to Him, poor sinner, and let Him be all in all to thee. Simply rely upon Him and be at peace.

How this, again, rebukes the coldness of saints.

If Christ be all in all, then how is it we love Him so little ? If He be so precious, how is it we prize Him so little ? Oh ! my dull, dead, cold heart, what art thou at ? Art thou harder than adamant, and baser than brutish, that thou art not much more moved with ardour and fervent affection towards such a Lord as this ? Christ is all, my brethren, yet look how little we offer to Him—of our substance how scant a portion—of our time how slender a part —of our talents how small a parcel ! God stir us to holy fervency, that if Christ be all for us, we may be all for Christ. May we lay ourselves out without reservation to the utmost stretch of our power, asking fresh strength from Him, that we may do all that can be done by mortal men, and that all may be done with us by God, that He shall see it to be compatible with His glory to do.

Again, by our text another lesson is furnished us. We learn here how to measure young converts. We ought not to expect them to be philosophers or divines ; Christ is all. If they know Christ, and are resting in Him, we are bound to say, " Come, and welcome." Be they poor, be they unlettered, if Jesus Christ be formed in their hearts, even though we can see Him there only as a dim outline, we are to open wide the gate, and receive them as Jesus received us.

Here is a measure, too, by which to measure ministers. The fashion of the world is to admire him most who shall speak most rhetorically. Accursed be the day in which oratory was tolerated in the Christian pulpit. It has been the bane and plague of the church of God. This labour after flowery speech, this seeking after polished periods and gaudy sentences, what is it but a pandering to the world, and a prostitution of the ministry of reconciliation. Had men learned what the apostle meant when he said, " I brethren, came not with excellency of speech or of wisdom," they would have preached far otherwise than they have done. We should strive to speak the gospel simply from our hearts, and then men's hearts will be impressed with the truth. Alas, this toying with fair words, and seeking after pleasing expressions, this dressing up of truth in the flaunting finery of falsehood, degrades rather than adorns the gospel, and it has done incalculable damage to souls, and to the advance of truth. Measure ministers by this, What is there of Christ about them ? That ministry which hath no savour of Christ in it, be it what it may, is a ministry which the Lord will not own, and that you ought not to own ; it is not God-sent, and ought not to be received by you. Give me Christ Jesus, though the speech in which He be set forth be of the most uncouth kind, rather than the choicest inventions of the most ingenious thinkers, from which Jesus Christ is absent, or in which He is not exalted.

Brother, this will also help you to estimate your own devotions. You came to the communion table the other day, but you did not enter into fellowship with Christ. Ah ! then there was a lost opportunity. You were in your closet this morning in prayer, but you did not plead the name of Jesus. Ah ! then again there was a lost season of devotion. You are a Bible reader, and your eye glances over the holy words, but you do not see Jesus in each page ; then your reading has failed. You have been giving to the poor of late ; but have you done it for Christ's sake ? You have sought to win souls :

have you done it in Christ's strength ? If Jesus be absent, you have offered a sacrifice from which the heart is gone ; and among the Romans, no omen was supposed to be so damaging as the absence of the heart from the sacrifice. No Christ, then there can be no acceptance, but a fulness of Christ proves a fulness of acceptance with God.

IV. There are many other things which I could have said, but time has failed me, and therefore I must close by noticing WHAT THIS TRUTH REQUIRES OF US. Christ is all in all ; therefore " put on, as the elect of God, holy and beloved, bowels of mercies, kindness, humbleness of mind, meekness, longsuffering." The exhibition of the Christ-life in the saints is the legitimate inference from the fact that Christ is all to them. If Christ is all, and yet I being a Christian am not like Christ, my Christianity is a transparent sham, I am nothing but a base pretender, and my outward religiousness is a pompous pageantry for my soul to be carried to hell in—nothing more. It is a gilded coffin for a lifeless spirit. I shall perish with a double destruction if I have dared to profane the name of Christ by taking it upon me, when I have not the essence of the Christian religion within me. Orthodoxy, though it be of the most assured sort, is vanity of vanities, unless there be with it an orthodoxy of life : and experience, whatever man may say about it, is but a dream, a fiction of his own imagining, if it does not display itself in shaking off the sins of the flesh, and putting on the adornments of holiness. O brethren, these are searching things to every one of us. Who amongst us lives as he should at home ? Could you bear that the angel who visits your house should publish before that great cloud of witnesses all that he has seen there ? In your shops, in your businesses, you professors, are you always upright and straightforward as Christians should be ! You merchants on the Exchange, are not some of you, who profess to be Christians, as greedy and as overreaching as others ? I charge you, if you have any respect for Christ, lay down His name if you will not endeavour to honour it. You will be lost, you covetous money-grubbers, you earth-scrapers, who live only for this world, you will be lost ; you need not doubt of that, you will be lost sure enough ; but why need you make the assurance of your condemnation doubly sure by the base imposture of calling yourselves Christians. Meanwhile, let the Ethiopian call himself white, if he will ; let the leopard declare that he has no spots ; these things shall not matter ; but the falsehood of a man who lives without Christ, while calling himself a Christian, brings such dishonour upon Him who was nailed to the tree, and whose religion is that of holiness, that I beseech you, by the living God, give up your profession, if you do not endeavour to make it true. If you are not living as you should, do not pretend to be what you are not. Seek ye unto God, that the life of Christ being in you, you may manifest it in your conversation.

Without Christ ye are nothing, though ye be baptised, though ye be members of churches, though ye be highly esteemed as deacons, elders, pastors. Oh, then, have Christ everywhere in all things, and constrain men to say of you, " To that man Christ is all in all : I have marked him ; he has been with Jesus, he has learned of Him, for he acts as Jesus did. God grant a blessing on these words, for Christ's sake. Amen.

DIVINE FORGIVENESS ADMIRED AND IMITATED

" Forbearing one another, and forgiving one another, if any man have a quarrel against any : even as Christ forgave you, so also do ye."—Colossians iii. 13.

TO whom is this exhortation addressed ? The apostle speaketh thus in the twelfth verse : " Elect of God, holy and beloved." Here are three particulars. They are, first of all, " elect of God," that is to say, chosen according to His eternal purpose. They are made choice ones by being thus chosen. Next, they are sanctified by the Spirit of God, and are, therefore, called " holy " : this holiness appertaining to their persons and their pursuits, their calling and their conversation. When the Spirit of God has fully done His work He sheds abroad in their hearts the love of God, so that experimentally they feel themselves to be " beloved." To abide in the love of God is the fruit of election, and the result of holiness. If any of you can with humble confidence claim these three titles, " elect of God, holy and beloved," you are among the most favoured of all mankind : of you the Father hath made a special choice, in you His Holy Spirit has wrought a special work, and you possess within your souls the special joy of living in the love of God. " Elect of God, holy and beloved " : it is as you enjoy these three things that you will find it easy to carry out the precept which is now set before you, " Forbearing one another, and forgiving one another, if any man have a quarrel against any : even as Christ forgave you, so also do ye."

Note in our text, before we proceed to the full discussion of it, what an honour this scripture puts upon our Lord Jesus Christ. In Ephesians iv. 32 a similar precept is placed in a rather different form ; for it runs thus : " Even as God for Christ's sake hath forgiven you." Here, as if to show the true and proper equality of the Christ with God, it is written, " Even as Christ forgave you." In the Revised Version they read, " even as the Lord forgave you " ; but they place in the margin, " Many ancient authorities read *Christ*." In that case we see that Lord and Christ were interchangeable terms when those ancient authorities were alive. None can forgive sins but God only. He alone forgives against whom the sin is committed. Sin, therefore, being against Christ, and Christ being able to forgive it, we see that He is exalted on high to give remission of sins. He shares in the high and royal prerogative of God, seeing He is able to forgive sin.

Doth not this expression seem to say that albeit the apostle and other inspired writers had many things to write of, yet one thing was always upon their hearts, namely, to honour their Lord ? Is not this a proof of how thoroughly they were under the influence of the Spirit of God, of whom Jesus said, " He shall glorify Me " ? Whatever He is teaching, whatever duty He is enforcing, whatever promise He is delivering, He taketh care so to do it that the Lord Jesus Christ is exalted in the hearts of His people thereby. Let us in our hearts adore the anointed One, Christ Jesus of Nazareth, the Son of God, and never let us hesitate to honour the Son even as we honour the Father. Let us as penitents adore the pardoning Saviour, seeing He hath power to forgive sins, and hath cleansed the myriads of His redeemed from all their iniquities.

But brethren, while this gives glory to Christ, what a weight is lent to the precept, since it is supported by the example and the authority of our divine Lord : " Even as Christ forgave you, so also do ye." What a model is set before us ! How perfect is that spirit of love which we are to manifest ! Even as Christ forgave us we are bidden to forgive others ; what nobler pattern could have been chosen ? Surely he that trifles with this precept, or thinks it one that is left to our option to obey or to neglect, cannot rightly know the dignity of the Christ in whose pierced hand this law is held forth before our eyes. Depend upon it, this command so wondrously linked with the Person of the pardoning Christ is of no common importance. If the law given by Moses was so solemnly binding, what shall we say of this law which is embodied in the life of the Lord Jesus ? Surely I shall scarcely need to plead with you, who are his disciples, that you give your heart's best attention to such teaching. Your Lord Himself stands before you ; you remember how He forgave you all your trespasses, and I am sure you will give earnest heed to His exhortation to forgive. May the dove-like Spirit now brood over this assembly, and create love in all our bosoms.

Two things are to be done. First, let us *study the pattern of forgiveness* here set before us ; and then, secondly, let us *copy it for ourselves* in our forgiveness of those who trespass against us.

I. Carefully STUDY THE PATTERN OF FORGIVENESS set before us in the text. " Even as Christ forgave you, so also do ye." *What is this forgiveness of Christ ?* You know how He exhibited it in His daily life. He was much tried, but He was never provoked to wrath. Both by friends and by enemies He was made to suffer, yet He neither accused the one nor the other to His great Father. He never reviled those who reviled Him, but patiently yielded to their malice, giving His back to the smiters, and His cheeks to them that plucked off the hair. His disciples He gently rebuked, but He never spake to them in anger. A life of forgiveness was crowned by His dying prayer for His persecutors, " Father, forgive them ; for they know not what they do." He loved His enemies ; He lived for His enemies ; He died for His enemies. He was incarnate gentleness, the mirror and paragon of forgiveness.

Observe, that He forgave offences most great and grievous. It was a horrible thing that when the Lord Jesus came into the world moved by pure love, He was not welcomed, but Herod sought to slay the young child. Afterwards, when He appeared publicly among men, the Jews took up stones to stone Him. He was treated with contumely ; His miracles were ascribed to the devil, and His holy and unspotted character was traduced by His being called a drunken man and a winebibber. He was the firstborn of the lord of the vineyard ; but when the husbandmen saw Him, they said, " This is the heir ; come, let us kill Him, and the inheritance shall be our's." You know with what scornful cruelty they treated him in the hour of His passion. What could the malice of hell have invented more contemptuous and cruel than that which men used towards the Well-Beloved ? Had He been the basest of beings, His sufferings would have been too cruel. Men did all they could against Him. Say not that *you* have never thus transgressed. Oh, sirs, we also have crucified Him ; for our sins were laid upon Him by Jehovah. We also must confess, " He was despised, and we esteemed Him not." There was a time when we, who are now His followers, once " hid as it were our faces from Him." He called us, but we gave Him no answer ; He wooed us, but we were blind to His beauties. We can never remember this without deep emotions of regret. We used no other friend so ill. We crucified Him and slew Him, as far as we were able to do it, by our rejection of His love ; and yet He has forgiven us. He is ready to forgive all such as seek His face. Oh, the splendour of that love which blots out sins like ours ! What a flood of grace is this which rises above the tops of the mountains of our sins, and covers them for ever. It mattereth not how black or crimson our transgressions may have been, the moment we come to Jesus He makes us whiter than snow. He puts away the most horrible of offences, the most glaring of transgressions, in a moment ; He says, " I forgive thee ; go, and sin no more " ; and we, there and then, receive a perfect pardon. I would that all of you who have never sought that grace would be induced by this blessed fact to come with all your sins about you, and receive immediate absolution from the hand of your Lord.

Remember, also, to increase your wonderment at His forgiveness, that these offences which were committed against Christ were altogether wanton and unprovoked. He could demand of His adversaries, " For which of those works do ye stone me ? " Towards no man had He acted unjustly or even harshly. He had been all tenderness and lowliness in every place towards all sorts of men, and yet certain men became incensed against Him because of His goodness. Did they refuse to love Him because He was altogether lovely ? Did they despise Him because He was so truly great? Such is the depravity of the human heart that the very virtues of Christ provoked the hostility of men. What has my Lord Christ ever done against any of you ? Wherefore do ye refuse Him ? I have heard many a man say,“ If I had done anything whatever to provoke this ill-will I could account for it, but they persecute me wrongfully." It was pre-eminently so in the case of our Lord, who says in the Psalm, " They hated me without cause." Yet He forgave this wanton malice. He continues to forgive such causeless wrong. With His own blood He blots out horrible insults against His person, His people, His gospel, and His love. Even you who oppose His kingdom and refuse His service, shall be at once forgiven if you will bow your hearts before Him and accept that rich mercy which His hand is is so ready to bestow. See what a pattern is here of the passing-by of the greatest and most malicious offences ! How can hatred live in the presence of such love ?

This pardon Christ has shown to the most un-worthy persons. Of all that He forgave when He was below none deserved such kindness ; in fact, to talk of deserving forgiveness is a contradiction in terms. Certainly in me, and I have no doubt in you, my brothers and sisters, who have tasted of His infinite mercy, there was no pretence of claim to His mercy in our cases. If He had left us in our sin, if He had passed us by and allowed us to perish, what complaint could we have brought against Him ? Since He loved us and forgave us, it must have been because of something within Himself ; it could not have been from anything in us. We are unworthy, but He is gracious ; and herein He teaches us to pardon the most provoking and worthless of those who trespass against us.

Be it never forgotten that He always had the power to have executed vengeance upon any one of us if He had pleased so to do. Some men pardon because they cannot punish ; they are too weak to execute vengeance, and therefore they refrain from it. Half the forgiveness in the world comes rather from a feeble hand than from a forgiving heart ; but the Christ could have crushed His adversaries in a moment if He had willed it, and yet He freely forgave. When they said, " Come down from the cross,"—suppose He had instantly loosed the nails and leaped among them, where had they been ? They would have begged the rocks to fall upon them, and the mountains to cover them from His face, if He had but manifested the glory of His power : but He was not provoked to leave the cross, or to break the silence of His passion by so much as a rebuke. Mercy was stored like honey in His heart, and pardon dropped its sweetness from His lip. The Lord has been greatly long-suffering with ourselves when a breath might have destroyed us. We might easily have been destroyed in accidents which befell us, or we might have died in our various sicknesses, and so have sunk to the lowest hell ; but instead of slaying us, our Lord even interposed to spare us,—to spare us when our life was rebellion. When He could so easily have blotted out our lives, He did not so, but in boundless mercy blotted out our sins. Let us magnify His amazing grace, and imitate it in our lives.

I want you for a moment to consider the question, *How did He forgive?* The manner of our Lord's forgiveness is as noteworthy as the pardon itself. The Lord Jesus came and pardoned us when that act of grace was unsolicited : before we had thought of mercy He had thoughts of mercy towards us. I remember reading in one of our magazines a story of a city missionary who discovered a poor girl who had wandered from the ways of virtue, and sought to restore her to a better life. He spoke with her till she became somewhat tender of heart. He enquired about her family, and learned that she had once enjoyed a happy home, and had known a tender father's love. " But he would never look at me now," said she ; " I am sure he never would ; I am such a degraded creature that I could not venture near his door." " Have you never written to him ? " " No, I could not write to him ; it would be of no use ; I could not expect him to send me an answer, and it would break my heart to be refused." " We will try," said the good man, " we will write to him." He wrote to the father, and the next post brought back an answer, with the word, " Immediate," written upon the envelope. The sum of the letter enclosed within was, " Ready to forgive." She was taken to her father; she was soon locked in his embrace; all was forgiven; the wanderer was restored. Notice, that her father had been praying for her night and day ever since she left his roof, and he had longed to receive her to his home again. Her seeking his forgiveness did not cause it; it was in his heart long before; and no doubt it was because of his cries and tears that God in mercy touched his girl's heart, and brought her home. O sinner, before thou thinkest of Christ He has thoughts of love towards thee. He says, "I have blotted out, as a thick cloud, thy transgressions, and, as a cloud, thy sins: return unto Me; for I have redeemed thee." The forgiveness is first, and the returning to the Lord is urged as consequence of that forgiveness. Pardon is not first in the matter of our personal experience, but it is first as matter of fact with God. Oh! the mercy of the Lord Christ, that before we know our sin He has made atonement for it by His own precious blood.

The Lord Jesus Christ is to be held up as an example of pardoning love for the true and hearty way in which He forgives sin. Forgiveness when it comes from human lips in measured, studied phrase, is not worth the having; for the heart is not in it, or it would be more free and joyful. The Lord Jesus Christ absolves sinners with all His heart: He never acts in a cold, formal manner. Never does He outwardly forgive and in secret retain His wrath; but wholly, entirely, joyfully, He puts away the sin of those He forgives, and puts it away for ever. When He forgives He forgives the whole of our faults, follies, failures, and offences. There is a certain solidarity about sin, so that it makes up one lump. I read the other day of a certain theologian speaking of Christ having put away original sin while He left actual sin. Nonsense! Sin is one and indivisible. Iniquity is not to be done up in separate parcels. The sin, the iniquity of men, is spoken of in the Bible as one thing. Although we sin multitudes of times the various streams all flow into one sea of evil: when sin is forgiven all sin is put away; not a shred, nor fragment, nor particle remains. The Lord Jesus drowns all the hosts of sin in the depths of the sea, and the whole of our guilt is swallowed up for ever. This is great forgiveness, indeed. Glory be to Him who gives it! Let us follow Him in His truth and heartiness.

This forgiveness, again, is given by the Lord Jesus Christ in the completest possible manner. He keeps no back reckonings; He retains no reserves of anger. He so forgives that He forgets. That is the wonder of it: He says, "I will not remember thy sins." He casts them behind His back; they are wholly and completely gone from His observation or regard. Alas, such is poor human nature, that even fathers, when they have forgiven a wayward child, will, perhaps, throw the offence in his teeth years after, when he again offends; but it is never so with Christ. He says, "Thy sins shall not be mentioned against thee any more for ever." He has done with the sins of His people in so effectual a way that not a whisper concerning them shall ever come from His mouth so as to grieve them. They will themselves remember their sins with deep repentance; but the Lord will never challenge them on account of their past rebellions. Blessed be the name of Christ for such complete forgiveness as this.

The Lord Jesus Christ forgives His people in a continuous manner. He forgave us long ago: He still forgives us. He does not forgive and afterwards accuse; His forgiveness is eternal; it is not a reprieve He gives to you, believing ones, but a free pardon, under the King's hand and seal, which shall effectively protect you from accusation and punishment. "In those days, and in that time, saith the Lord, the iniquity of Israel shall be sought for, and there shall be none; and the sins of Judah, and they shall not be found: for I will pardon them whom I reserve." He hath finished transgression, made an end of sin, and brought in everlasting righteousness. Send to hell a pardoned sinner! It were a contradiction to the very nature of God. Condemn those for whom Jesus died! Why, the apostle mentions that death as a conclusive answer to the challenge, "Who is He that condemneth? It is Christ that died, yea rather, that is risen again, who is even at the right hand of God, who also maketh intercession for us." How shall He intercede for us and yet accuse us? It is impossible for Christ to be both Redeemer and Condemner to the same persons. So perfect is His pardon that our sin has ceased to be; He hath put away sin for ever by the sacrifice of Himself.

Greatly do I admire the very gracious way in which that pardon is given. Some people offer forgiveness in an ungracious way; they make it appear that they are coming down from such awful heights when they forgive a fellow-mortal. In great dignity they march down in state from their own splendid innocence to the poor brother who has done them a wrong; as good as saying, "I will condescend to do this, though it is an awful stoop for such an angelic being as I am." You never feel that about the Christ, for He places His pardon down so low that He seems to say, "Receive my mercy, I beg you to receive it." He speaks as if He were favoured by a sinner's accepting His forgiveness. He humbles Himself, and never scalds a sinner with scornful pity. Though the Christ condescends more than all the condescensions of all men put together, "for worms were never raised so high above their meanest fellow-worms," yet the condescension is so real and royal that there is no ostentation in it; He is to the manner born; He condescendeth naturally, like condescension's own self. Some are proudest when they stoop; but Jesus graciously seemeth to put Himself on a level with us, aye, and even to go lower than we are, that He may lift us up. Admire as much the way in which Christ forgives as the forgiveness which He bestows. It breaks my heart to think what a loving Christ He was to me when I sought His forgiveness. Truly "He giveth liberally, and upbraideth not": He frowned and thundered when I looked to my own righteousness, but when I turned to His gospel of free grace I had from Him not even a hard word, but He was all love and tenderness to me, the chief of sinners.

Above all, the greatness of His forgiveness is seen in the fact that the offence had brought great trouble into the world, and He bore that trouble. The sinner, by his wrong doing, had subjected himself to great loss and calamity. Now, when we forgive a person who has done us a wrong we say, "I freely forgive you, but you have involved yourself in certain consequences which you will have to bear, and out of these I cannot help you." Our blessed Master seemed to say, "Sinner, thou hast sinned thyself under the curse of God, thou hast sinned thyself into misery and into death, and as the proof that I do freely forgive thee I will take all this suffering and this death upon Myself. Thou hast done the wrong wantonly and wickedly, but I will bear the consequences. Thou hast knotted the whips, they shall scourge My shoulders ; thou hast sharpened the nails, they shall pierce My hands and feet ; thou hast put thyself under curse and penalty, I will bear the curse of death that thou mayst be free." Was there ever mercy like this ? Do not all who know this love accept it gladly ? Sinner, do you not know this ? Have you never heard about it ? Know you not that the Lord, even Jesus, the Son of God, is able to forgive you all your trespasses, that it will be a joy to His heart to do so, and to do it at once ? Oh, that before that clock shall strike again you may be able to say, " There is therefore now no condemnation, for Christ has put away my sin." This is not according to the manner of men ; it is Godlike : it is a sure proof that Jesus is the Son of God, for who could act like this but One who is Himself the Son of God ?

Thus have I set before you, in my poor way, this great forgiveness, and the manner of it. I trust you have had an experience of it. Assuredly we all need such forgiveness : do any of you deny it ? May the Holy Spirit open your blind eyes, and melt your hearts. According to the text, those who have received pardon know that they have it ; for Paul speaks positively,—" Even as Christ forgave you " ; as if it were a matter of fact well known among the people of God. There is a theory abroad that we may be forgiven and not know it ; that Jesus may forgive, and we may never discover it until we come unto our dying moments. That is a wretched kind of gospel ; but by the true gospel we may know we are forgiven, and be sure of it ; surer than if we saw, written by the autograph of Christ, the words— " I have forgiven thee." The eyes may deceive, but the witness of the Spirit of God within the heart can never delude us. If thou believest that Jesus is the Christ, and if thou art resting alone on Him, thy sins, which are many, are forgiven thee ; " for the blood of Jesus Christ, His Son, cleanseth us from all sin." Knowing that we are forgiven by Christ, let us be clear and decided in our forgiveness of others : not in word only, but in deed and in truth, let us exhibit a forbearing spirit.

II. You see your example. Our second word is, COPY IT FOR YOURSELVES. If the Holy Spirit enables you to write according to this copy, you will have the approval of the Lord resting upon you. See how large and clear the letters ! It will be no small success if you can reproduce them. " Even as Christ forgave you " ; the imitation should be as exact as possible. Mark the " even," and the " so," and endeavour to keep touch with your gracious Lord.

Notice, however, in the text, that this precept concerning the imitation of Christ in forgiveness is *universally applicable.* The text is not long, but see how unqualified is its range. " Forbearing one another, and forgiving one another, if any man have a quarrel against any." You see it is not put that superiors are to forgive inferiors ; or, on the other hand, that the less are to forgive the greater ; but the circle of the command includes the whole : it is, " forbearing one another." The rich are to be forbearing to the poor, the poor are to be forbearing to the rich ; the elderly man is to forgive the junior

for his imprudence, the junior is to bear with the petulance and slowness of the elder. It is an all-round business, implying that one of these days I shall have to forgive you, and you will have to forgive me. Personally, I tax your forbearance to put up with me ; and I need not say that sometimes I have need to exercise forbearance towards one and another in so large a church. We have all our own angles and edges, and these are apt to come into contact with others. We are all pieces of one puzzle, and shall fit in with each other one day, and make a complete whole ; yet just now we seem misshapen and unfitting. Our corners need to be rounded. Sometimes they are chipped off by collision with somebody else ; and that is not comfortable for the person with whom we collide. Like pebbles in the river of the water of life, we are wearing each other round and smooth, as the living current brings us into communion : everybody is polishing and being polished, and in the process it is inevitable that some present inconvenience should be sustained ; but nobody must mind it, for it is part of a great process by which we shall all come into proper shape, and be made meet for endless fellowship.

" Forbearing one another, and forgiving one another " : you see it has two sides. " Ah," says one, " I cannot understand it ; people ought to be far more forbearing to me." Just so ; but the first point is that you should be forgiving towards them. What numbers of church members think that the duties of a church are all one-sided. " I was ill, and nobody came to see me." " Did you send for anybody to see you ? " " No, I did not." Brother, before you find fault, remember your own fault ; you have violated the command, " Is any sick among you ? let him call for the elders of the church." " But nobody exhibits Christian love," says one. Is that true of yourself ? I have noticed that the man who says that love is dead is usually rather short of love himself. How very different the church looks to different eyes : one sees a thousand virtues to admire, and another a world of evil to expose. One gratefully cries, " When I was ill, the dear brethren came to see me so often that I had even to ask them not to stay very long." Another grumbles, " I might have laid there a month, and nobody would ever have come near me." We understand the reason for this difference : the tone of the speech is the key to the riddle. As a rule, with what measure we mete it is measured to us again. I do not find Christ's people to be one half so faulty as I am myself. I meet with many Christians whom I think it an honour to know, and commune with ; and those of another sort are useful to me as warnings, and as fields for exercising my graces. The forgiveness and the forbearance are needed all round, and must both give and take. By the sweet love of Jesus, let us not fail in this business.

Let me say here that this matter is an absolutely essential one,—*this forbearance and this forgiveness are vital.* Be not deceived ; God is not mocked : no man is a child of God who has not a likeness to God ; and no man is forgiven who will not himself forgive. In the Middle Ages a certain baron had a feud with another nobleman, and determined to avenge himself for some insult, real or imaginary. His enemy was to pass by the castle with a small retinue, and therefore the baron determined to waylay him and kill him, or, at least, to punish him severely, and exact a ransom. A holy man who lived in the castle begged and entreated the baron to forbear from bloodshed, and make peace ; but for some time he pleaded in vain. The baron would not be appeased, but swore that he would be avenged of his adversary. So this godly man begged one favour of him, namely, that he would come with him into the chapel and offer prayer before he sallied forth. They knelt together in prayer, and ere they rose the saintly man said, " My lord, repeat after me the Lord's Prayer." He went on saying word by word, as the other did, till he came to that, " Forgive us our trespasses, as we forgive them that trespass against us "; but there the good man stopped, and said, " I charge you not to say this unless you really mean it ! Do not mock the Lord. You may not go out and fight if you thus speak with God. You will have to appear before God and be judged for your sins, for you will not be forgiven if you do not forgive. Choose, then, either to utter this prayer ·and forgive, and be saved ; or to refuse the prayer, and go forth to battle and be lost." The baron paused and bit his lip, but at last his better spirit prevailed, and he cried, " I cannot renounce my hope of heaven ; I cannot renounce my hope of forgiveness ; therefore my enemy shall pass by my castle in safety, and I will say, ' Forgive us our trespasses, as we forgive them that trespass against us.' " Do not attempt to deceive God. If you must lie and cheat, practise your impositions upon your fellow-men, but do not imagine that you can flatter your Maker or deceive the Omniscient One. If you will not forgive, say so, and expect eternal perdition ; but if you profess to be a Christian obey this great and essential precept, and forgive as Christ forgave you. Be honest, be straight with God, for He will be honest and straight with you ; but if you cannot and will not forgive, then look forward to a portion with the tormentors ; for even ᵗhe loving Jesus says, " Neither shall my heavenly Father forgive you."

In urging you to this copying of Christ, let me notice that this forgiveness of those who offend against us is *gloriously ennobling*. We are not asked to perform a duty which will in the least degrade us. Revenge is paltry, forgiveness is great-minded. Was not David infinitely greater than Saul, when he spared his life in the cave, and when he would not smite him as he lay asleep on the battle-field ? Did not the king humble himself before David when he perceived his forbearance ? If you would be the greatest among men, bear injuries with the greatest gentleness ; if you would win the noblest of conquests, subdue yourself. To win a battle is a little thing if it be fought out with sword and gun ; but to win it in God's way, with no weapons but love, and patience, and forgiveness, this is the most glorious of victories. Blessed is that man who is more than a conqueror, because he inflicts no wounds in the conflict, but overcomes evil with good. In the process of such a conquest the warrior is himself a gainer. A nation in fighting, even if it wins the campaign, has to suffer great expense and loss of life ; but he that overcomes by love is the better and stronger man through what he has done. He comes out of the conflict not only victor over his adversary, but victor over sin within himself, and all the readier for future war against evil. He glorifies God and himself becomes strong in grace. Nothing is more glorious than love. Your Master, who is King of kings, set you an example of gaining glory by enduring

wrong : if you would be knights of His company, imitate His graciousness.

Notice that this imitation of Christ is *logically appropriate to you all*. Brothers, if Christ has forgiven you, the parable we read just now shows that it is imperative that you should forgive your fellows. If our Lord has forgiven us our ten thousand talents, how can we take our brother by the throat for the hundred pence, and say, " Pay me what thou owest "? If we are indeed members of Christ, should we not be like our Head ? If we profess to be His servants, are we to pretend to a dignity greater than our Master, who washed His disciples' feet ? If He forgave so freely, how dare we call ourselves His brethren if our spirit is hard and malice lingers within us ?

I say, to conclude, that this copying of Christ is *most forcibly sustained by the example given in the text*. We are to forbear and to forgive ; " Even as Christ forgave you, so also do ye." I have heard it said, " If you pass by every wanton offence, and take no notice of it, you will come to be despised, and regarded as a person of mean spirit : your honour demands vindication." When Christ forgave you, did His honour suffer by that forgiveness ? You transgressed most wickedly, and yet He forgave you ; do you regard Him as less honourable because of that readiness to pass by offences ? Far from it : it is His glory to forgive. The hallelujahs of saints, and the songs of angels are sent up to His throne the more heartily because of the richness of His grace, and the freeness of His mercy. Dishonour indeed ! What pride it is on the part of such poor creatures as we are to talk about our honour ! Where is the honour of revenge ? It is a dishonourable thing to put yourself on the level of him who injures you. A heathen philosopher used to say, " If an ass kicks you, is it necessary for the maintenance of your honour to kick that ass again ? " That speech looks like a noble one, but yet it is too much flavoured with contempt. When you speak, or even think, of another who has wronged you as though he were only worthy to be regarded as a beast, you are not right in spirit, a degree of evil remains in your heart. Think of the offender without contempt, as well as without resentment. Believe he is a brother worth winning. Say, " If he does me an injury, for that very reason I will do him a double service. My only vengeance shall be double love. I will not allow myself even to think hardly of him. I will put the best possible construction on all that he does, and thus show that the spirit of Christ is in me, conquering the spirit of fallen humanity both in me and in him."

Says one, " If we always overlook offences other people may be tempted to do us wrong also." Our text furnishes us with a ready answer to this also. The Lord Jesus Christ forgave you. Have you met anybody who has been tempted to do wrong because the Lord has forgiven you ? He has freely forgiven myriads of poor unworthy sinners, and has that promoted sin ? No. Is it not the very groundwork and cause of holiness in the world, that Jesus is so gracious as to pardon sin ? Why then should your forbearance do harm ? Do not you pretend to be so very wise ; for therein you censure your Master. You are not the ruler of the world. It is not for you to be refraining from good for fear that evil may come of it : attend to your own ways, forgive every one his brother his trespasses, and leave consequences with God.

" Oh, but," says one, " I know several pious persons who are very unforgiving." You do not know any really good man who is of that character. I make bold to say that no man is really good if he has not a forgiving spirit. Unwillingness to forgive is a grievous flaw in anyone's character. But if there were such good people, what have you to do with them ? Is the servant to imitate his fellow-servant, especially in his faults ? The example set before you is, " Even as Christ forgave you." You have nothing to do with either saints or sinners in this matter ; your Lord says to you, " What is that to thee ? Follow thou Me." Perhaps you do not know all the story which you think proves that a good man has been unforgiving ; and if you do know it, you are no judge of others. Mind your own business, and " even as Christ forgave you, so also do ye."

But I hear another one saying, " These persons would not have forgiven *me*." Just so ; but then you are a child of God, you are " elect, holy, and beloved." You are not to lower your standard to that of publicans and sinners. Does not Christ continually say, " What do ye more than others ? Do not even the publicans and the sinners the same ? " " If you love them that love you, what thank have ye ? " But if ye love them that despitefully use you, then blessed are you when men shall persecute you. In that case you have an opportunity of showing your love to your Lord. When Dr. Duff first read to some young Brahmins in the Government school the precept, " Love your enemies, bless them that curse you, do good to them that hate you, and pray for them which despitefully use you," one of the Brahmins cried out with delight, " Beautiful ! Beautiful ! This must have come from the true God. I have been told to love those that love me, and I have not always done *that* ; but to love my enemies is a divine thought." That young man became a Christian under the influence of that precept. Do not darken this light, but be sure to display it in your life, that many may be attracted to Christ by its lustre. Let your goodwill go forth even to the worst of men, for Christ's sake. Forget *their* evil as you behold *His* goodness.

" Well," says one, " I would forgive the fellow, but he does not deserve it." That is why you are to forgive him : if he deserved it, you would be bound to do him the justice which he could claim ; but as he does not deserve it, you have here an appeal to your Christian love. Does not your heavenly Father give good things to the unthankful and to the evil ? Did not Jesus forgive the undeserving when He forgave you ? Does He not overlook our wretched characters when He has mercy upon us ?

I hear one say, " I cannot forgive ! " That is a terrible confession. The apostle of the Gentiles said, " I can do all things through Christ which strengtheneth me." Is not the same strength avail-able for you ? Some persons find forgiving and forgetting to be hard work ; but as you are bound to do it or stop out of heaven, you must cry to God for help, and set about it with determination. If you are indeed a child of God you will soon find the difficulty gone ; indeed forgiveness will become easy to you. To be forgiven is such sweetness that honey is tasteless in comparison with it ; but yet there is one thing sweeter still, and that is to forgive. As it is more blessed to give than to receive, so to forgive rises a stage higher in experience than to be forgiven. To be forgiven is, as it were, the root ; to forgive is the flower. That divine Spirit, who bears witness with our spirit when He breathes peace into us because we are pardoned, beareth yet a higher witness with us when He enables us truly to pardon all manner of trespasses against ourselves. Let it never be said in a Christian church, that fellow-members bear a grudge against one another. I do not know that it is so in your case ; assuredly it should not be so anywhere. Let it not be said of any Christian man, that he is unloving, ready to take offence, apt to bear malice, or quick to anger. Cultivate forbearance till your heart yields a fine crop of it. Pray for a short memory as to all unkindnesses. I bless God that I know a man who finds it easy to forgive and to forget all offences against himself. He takes no credit for so doing, for no one ever offends him in a way which is worth remembering. That man has been reminded again and again of the misbehaviour of unreasonable and unkind men, and he has honestly said, " I had quite forgotten it," He does not claim this forgetfulness as a virtue, for as a matter of fact his memory has become weak in that direction, and he has no desire to strengthen it. He has never tried to recollect unkindnesses, and now by long disuse his memory happily fails him upon such matters. That man has often enjoyed exquisite pleasure in doing good to those who have injured him ; and he can truly say that at this moment he bears no ill-will to any soul upon this earth. He does not think this to be any singular attainment, for his belief is that every follower of Jesus should be of the same mind.

Do you not think the same ? I am sure I do. I heard this man once say of another, " He spoke against me that which was false, but if he had known more of me, he might have said something far worse and have been nearer the truth. Perhaps my false accuser believed what he said, and thought he was doing a right thing in protesting against what he thought was my fault. At any rate, no one can harm my character, unless I do so myself." It is a wise thing to profit by every accusation, whether true or false, by trying to be better. Let us so live as to be able to say, " I am as much at peace with all men as a child new born." Thus shall we wear the mark of the Spirit of God. In a word, my brethren, " Even as Christ forgave you, so also do ye." Amen.

THAT HORRIBLE EAST WIND!

" And let the peace of God rule in your hearts, to the which also ye are called in one body ; and be ye thankful."
Colossians iii. 15.

I DO not know how it is, but during the last two or three days I have been called to sympathize with an amount of sorrow such as I have seldom met with before in so short a space of time. One messenger of misery has followed on the heels of another, each one with heavy tidings. Nor is that all ; for I have also been perplexed with a large amount of sinning, quarrelling, and fault-finding. People are murmuring, grumbling, fretting, and fighting on all sides. So much has this tried me that I feel little fitted to act as comforter, for I need comfort myself. I have endeavoured to cheer others till I have drunk of their cup of sorrow, and put my own mouth out of taste : I have tried to make peace for others till I am half afraid of losing my own ; I have answered the people's grumblings till I am tempted to have a growl or two on my own account. Perhaps I may relieve my own mind by the sermon which I hope to deliver.

I said to one whom I greatly esteem, " I do not know how it is, but everybody seems out of sorts with everybody else just now." His wise answer was, " THE WIND IS IN THE EAST." This fact accounts for a great deal, for

" When the wind is in the east,
'Tis neither good for man nor beast."

This is that ill wind which seems to blow no man any good. Some humanities feel the east wind terribly : it sets their teeth on edge, and they feel that they must bite the first person they meet. I am glad to find some sort of excuse for my fellow-Christians, and if I can find it nowhere but in the east wind, I will make the best I can of it ; but I earnestly hope that the wind may soon blow from another quarter, and not come from the east again till we have had a little respite, and laid in a new stock of patience. If a cutting wind causes despondency, vexation, discontent, and bad temper, may soft gales visit us frequently, and bring us healing in their wings. As fair weather will not last for ever, it will be well to prepare ourselves to breast the blast. It will never do for us to have a religion which can be killed by the wind : we must be made of better stuff than that. Yet this wind is blamed, and I wish therefore that it would take itself off. If I could find a snug corner where the cruel east wind was never felt, I should feel inclined to promote an emigration movement for certain persons whom I will not mention : as for myself, I am afraid that it would not suit me to be altogether screened from the wind, for trials are necessary to one who is called to this ministry. Troubles and east winds will come to the servants of God, and they are sent to do us good ; for perhaps, if we could get our backs against a protecting wall, and sit for ever in the sunshine, with no east wind to interfere with us, we should go to sleep ; or waking, we might come to love this world so well as to be loath to leave it. It would be a horrible thing for any one of us if the south wind should softly breathe upon our cheek, and whisper gently in our ear of long-continued joy to be found on earth ; for then we should be tempted to sit down and say, " Soul, take thine ease. Thou hast at last found a place free from the trials of time ; therefore eat, drink, and be merry, and let the future world care for itself."

When I turn over in my mind the events of the last few days I do not suppose that there is more discord or discontent in the world just now than at any other time ; but it happens that a number of black lines have all found their centre in my person, and my thoughts have had to travel out in all those directions ; all which is trying enough, but all the more so when *the wind is in the east*. It is a coincidence, but the like has happened before. I have had to unravel many tangled skeins in my time, out of love to others : I did not get the threads into a ravel, but people are very fond of bringing me their snarls to disentangle, and when I have a hope of succeeding I try my best. Gladly would I be a peacemaker, but it is much easier to make a snarl than to put it straight again, *especially in the east wind*. I have tried to set things right, and meanwhile I have asked myself, " Is there not a remedy for these mischiefs ? " I feel assured there is such a remedy. Family discomfort, husbands and wives that cannot agree, domestic difficulties, brothers and sisters that fall out, church troubles, members that are not treated kindly by others (not generally the kindest sort of people themselves, I notice), difficulties in business, difficulties in preaching—the world teems with these things *when the wind is in the east*. We meet with many people who cannot earn enough wages, others who do not believe they were ever well treated since they were born ; others, again, who are highly deserving people, but have never yet been appreciated as they should be ; and these all come out in crowds *when the wind is in the east*. Good men become rabid for something new, find fault with old friends, invite debate, and quarrel about nothing ; and this happens most often *when the wind is in the east*.

When this kind of spirit gets among Christian people it is very sad ; but surely there must be a remedy for it. Many nostrums are proposed, many quacks are ready to prescribe this and that form of remedy for troubles and discords, but the results of the east wind are not to be removed in that way : a higher power is needed. I have heard of pills for the earthquake, and medicine for the comet ; but I have no such patent physic for the east wind. All I have to tell you is borrowed from an old Book, in which the wisest prescriptions are to be found, prescriptions so excellent that, if they were followed, the inhabitant would no more say, " I am sick."

This windy night I shall take you to the great Physician of souls, Jehovah-Rophi—the Lord who heals us, who is able to cure all our diseases and to give permanent relief from all evil, so that our spirits shall be at rest. I believe that we have a prescription in this verse which, if it be well attended to, will deliver you out of all troubles, make you sing all your lives long, and help you to travel from earth to heaven, and be all the while as happy as the birds in the air. Here it is—" Let the peace of God rule in your hearts, to the which also ye are called in one body ; and be ye thankful."

If we dissect our text we shall find in it four pieces of advice.

I. First, POSSESS THE PEACE OF GOD—" Let the peace of God rule in your hearts." It cannot rule in your hearts if you have never felt its power ; there-fore, make certain that you are truly reconciled to God by Jesus Christ. Many persons have peace, but, alas, it is false peace ! They have the peace of a soft, gentle, timorous, time-serving character—a mean sort of peace, which, if it hurts no one else, often ruins its possessor. Some have the peace of ignorance, the peace of stupidity, the peace of utter indifference, false peace. These are the followers of those false prophets who cried, " peace, peace," where there was no peace. Woe to the man whose peace of mind is like the deadly smoothness of the current just as it nears the cataract ! Many are at ease in a condition which might make a wise man's hair turn grey in a night. They were never emptied from vessel to vessel, and therefore they are settled upon their lees ; but they shall be poured out to their utter confusion. They think right well of themselves, but already the axe of judgment is lifted against them.

The peace that we need to possess is the peace of God, which means, I think, first, *peace with God.* Oh, what a blessed thing it is to feel that the great cause of quarrel between our fallen spirit and the great Spirit is taken away,—that we are reconciled to God by the death of His Son,—that sin, the great divider, has been cast into the depths of the sea, and that there is established between us and God a happy fellowship ! I hope many of you are at this hour enjoying such peace. If you have it, rejoice in it. If ye, then, be at peace with God, do not perpetually act as if that peace were questionable and doubtful. Do not sigh and cry as if the matter trembled in the balance. If we believe in Jesus Christ, " being justified by faith, we have peace with God through our Lord Jesus Christ." Oh ! the joy of knowing that " as far as the east is from the west, so far hath He removed our transgressions from us," and that therefore they can never return from so immense a distance—yea, never return at all, for the Lord Jesus Christ has cast them into the depths of the sea, and if they be searched for they shall not be found ; yea, they shall not be, saith the Lord. Blessed is that man who hath peace with God through the atoning blood !

Growing out of this there comes, next, a peace with God with regard to all His providences, which can only come through a complete and entire sub-mission to the divine will ; for some there are who are not at peace with God, even about a certain providence that afflicted them years ago. They remain quarrelling with God about the decease of a beloved wife, or child, or mother, and they cannot forgive God for having taken a flower out of His own garden. If they were wise they would not thus rebel, but find in their loving Saviour a recompense for all their losses. Was not that fine of Andromache, when she remembered that she had lost all her relatives except her husband, and, gazing on him with delight, she said

" While my Hector still survives, I see
 My father, mother, brethren, all in thee " ?

Cannot a believer say the same of the Lord Jesus ?

Far be it from us to raise a question about what the providence of God has already done ! It must be right. The point is to keep on submitting to that providence in what is now transpiring. If for the present the will of the Lord should send me poverty, obscurity, pain, weariness, reproach, I must be at peace with God about it all. If the Lord says to me, " Go across the sea, and leave all your friends," I must not delay. If He says, " Preach unwelcome truth, which will make you enemies," I must not hesitate. If He says, " Keep in the house with rheuma-tism," I must not come out of doors. If the Lord says, " Lie on thy back and cough," it is not for me to quarrel with Him, and say it ought not so to be. If He denies us that which we think would make us not only more happy but more useful, it is of no use for us to kick against the pricks. The divine appoint-ment will certainly be fulfilled, and the misery to us will be in struggling against the yoke, in endeavour-ing to have it otherwise than divine love and infinite wisdom have determined it should be. If thou canst not change thy place, change thy mind, till thy mind shall take to thy place, and thou shalt love it. Why, there have been men so helped of God to con-quer self that they have hugged their crosses. I think it is Rutherford who somewhere says that he was half afraid lest he should begin to love his cross better than Christ. That is a fear which will seldom need to cross our minds ; but, oh, we ought to be perfectly satisfied, perfectly content with that which pleases God ! " If this be the Lord's will, it is my will " : such a saying comes from a happy heart ; but if God has one will and we have another, it is clear that the peace of God does not yet rule our hearts. Though forgiven, and though the grand cause of quarrel is gone, yet we are raising minor points of difference, and these gender strife. It is like a great lawsuit that has been decided on all the grand features of the case, and yet here is the plaintiff picking little points, and raising little questions, and getting up fresh litigation. The point with us is to say, " It is all given up. Whatsoever Thou willest, Lord, I will ; or at least I wish to will. I ask for grace that I may will it, because Thou willest it." This voluntary submission to our Father's appointment is the peace of God.

This peace of God is, also, *peace such as God commends*—such as God approves of. That, you know, is first, perfect peace with Himself, and then with all men—certainly with His people, but also with all mankind. " If it be possible, as much as lieth in you, live peaceably with all men." Take heed that ye do not offend ; and if you are offended by others, do not offend in return, but accept the offence in patience ; forgive it and forget it. Forbear, and, when you have done so, forbear, and, when you have done so again, forbear, and, when you have forborne seven times, still forbear. I will not repeat the advice seventy times seven, though if I did, I should not go beyond the measure of forbearance and of forgive-ness which the Lord Jesus would have us display. Be so at peace with God that you feel perfectly at peace with your fellow-men. Whenever I have suffered a grievous wrong, it has been a satisfaction to me to feel that, if my Lord Jesus Christ made atonement for my offences and my wrongs, I can look at His atonement as an atonement for the wrong done to me as well as to God, for He satisfied all parties in that quarrel. Gladly do I say, " Surely, this poor soul may well be forgiven by me, for Thou hast died as the sinners' Substitute." In comparison with my own offences against God I may well look upon this man's offence as less than nothing. What if men should do the worst they can do to us ? What is it ? What if they slay us ? It is but a small loss to a Christian to die. Therefore let us harbour no malice, but feel, " No ; we have entered into the truce of God, and we are the friends of every man that breathes." For my own part, I have a crusade against the devil and all evil ; but the truce of God is upon me with regard to all my fellow-men, and henceforth that peace which was proclaimed at Bethlehem by the angels shall stand for me—" Peace on earth : good will toward men." This is a sweet part of the peace of God ; cultivate it carefully.

But this peace is called the peace of God because *it is peace which God works in the soul.* I think I hear you exclaim, " To have such a peace as that—a perfect consciousnesss of full forgiveness, complete acquiescence in the will of God, perfect forgiveness towards all mankind, and in intense desire to live in perfect peace with all, both saints and sinners— how can I get such a peace within me ? " Ah, indeed, how can you ? It is impossible to unrenewed human nature. Man by nature is worse than any one wild beast, for he is a menagerie. There is lion in him, and there is serpent in him ; there is tiger in him, and there is wolf in him ; there is dog in him, and there is devil in him. He is half beast and half devil through the Fall. I do not caricature him ; his body allies him to the beast, and sin makes him a child of Satan. Mr. Whitefield used so to describe fallen nature, and he was pretty near the mark. How shall this wild beast be taught to love ? Shall the lion eat straw like an ox ? It never will till it leaves off being a lion. It cannot do so; it has not fit teeth for eating straw, nor a fit stomach for digesting grass. It cannot live on straw, like an ox, till God changes it, and gives it an ox-like nature. So it is with us : we need a new nature before we can possess this peace with God. But how is that to be done ? Shall the Ethiopian change his skin ? No ; he cannot do that ; and if he could, it would not equal the miracle which we require. Our default is not skin deep only, it is much more than that. Changing skins is difficult, but changing hearts is impossible except to God. Shall the leopard get rid of his spots ? Well, that is difficult ; but still the task of taking spots out of leopards would be small compared with the miracle of taking evil out of the very core of our wild-beast-like heart, and putting into it the peace of God that makes us love. God only can do it. God's own mighty Spirit must put forth that same energy with which He will raise the dead out of their graves at the resurrection ; for nothing short of creation and resurrection power is able to transmute this beastly, devilish heart of ours into a heart in which the peace of God shall reign supreme. Well is it called the peace of God.

My dear hearer, do you know this peace ? If so you will understand that, *because of its excellence, it is called the peace of God.* It is a Hebraism : for among the Hebrews they called certain mountains that were higher than others the hills of God ; and certain gigantic trees, such as the cedars of Lebanon, were the trees of God that were full of sap. So the peace that is greater than every other peace is called the peace of God—it means the holiest, deepest peace. It is " perfect peace "—peace that nothing disturbs : deep peace—" the peace of God, which passeth all understanding " : solemn peace at which you almost stand in awe—a hush within the soul in which there is heard nothing of discord or of fear, but a stillness reigns like that which was maintained in the Holy of Holies, within the veil, where seraphim were silent above the mercy-seat. " The peace of God " signifies the peace that never ends, everlasting peace ; the peace that will live with us throughout the whole of our mortal sojourn till we come into the land of the immortal.

" There shall I bathe my weary soul
    In seas of heavenly rest,
And not a wave of trouble roll
    Across my peaceful breast."

" The peace of God." Oh, I have known it ! You, too, my brethren, must have known it when the Lord Himself has dwelt within your hearts, and kept all adversaries far away. You have then known days of heaven upon the earth. It has left nothing to wish for except the perpetuation of itself, for you have been satisfied with favour and full of the goodness of the Lord, filled with all the fulness of God, anchored fast, settled, grounded, established.

" My heard is resting, O my God !
    I will give thanks and sing.
My heart is at the secret source
    Of every precious thing."

That is the peace of God.

Win it, dear friends, and wear it. By God's good Spirit enter into this serene haven. Rest in the Lord, and be happy in Him, for He is our peace ! When the Lord and Giver of peace once comes to tarry in your heart let Him rest there ; and charge all about you, by the roes and by the hinds of the field, that they stir not up nor awake your love until He please.

II. But now the second piece of advice that grows out of the text let us consider. If you possess this peace of God, let it occupy the throne : LET THE PEACE OF GOD RULE IN YOUR HEARTS.

In order to their being any peace in the heart, or anywhere else, there must be a ruler. Those people who are for putting down all kings and principalities and powers may bid farewell to peace. Anybody who is inclined to anarchy should read Carlyle's *French Revolution* through with care, and ask himself whether the worst king is not, after all, a deal better than the despotism of the mob, the carnival of misrule, wherein every man doth that which is right in his own eyes, and all eyes love darkness rather than light. Let loose the reigns of government, let everybody be equal to everybody else, and a little bigger than everybody else as well, and you will soon see what confusion ensues. See how it is in a house ! I hear that there was great deliberation over those census-papers in many families to know who was the head of the household ; but I am quite clear that it was not a happy household where that question took long to answer ; for the husband is the head of the wife, and where he is not so, everything is out of order, monstrous, outrageous. Where the head is not the head, the hand is not the hand, the eye is not the eye, the heart is not the heart ; and nothing is itself at all. All is what it should not be, and all is misery. You must have a governing faculty somewhere ; and, within your own soul, if nothing governs, I tell you boldly the devil governs. That man who does not control himself is controlled by the devil, for he must have a master somewhere. We cannot have two masters, but it is quite as certain that we must have one. One power or another will master you. Shall it be your Creator, or His enemy ? your Saviour, or your destroyer ?

It is a blessed gift of grace if a man is enabled by the Holy Spirit to say,—" The peace of God shall rule in my heart." Paul advised this : " Let the peace of God rule in your hearts " : if it is in your hearts at all, it must rule, for it has power to put down all rebellion. You know, when we have a government and a magistracy with power at their back, if a riot arises, we appeal to the lawful power to come and protect us, and put down the uproar. So in our hearts, if we have a master principle, and that master principle is the peace of God, we may warrantably pray, " O Lord, put down this riot. I am tossed to and fro in my heart about my circumstances : I do not like them, and I quarrel with God about them. Come, peace of God ; come, and put down my murmuring. Come and calm my wicked, discontented spirit." Or do I feel some discord in my spirit towards one whom I ought to love ? I must cry, " Come, peace of God. Come, and arrest this bad temper of mine. Handcuff it. Take it off to prison. Give it hard labour and short commons ; bring it down till it is no longer able to rebel as it does. Come, peace of God, and help me in the struggles of my daily life, that I may not break out into anger, and wrath, and malice, and all uncharitableness. Come, peace of God, put forth Thy mighty power over my soul." This is the great remedy for the discord within and the discords without : the grand cure for all distempers of the east wind, and all besides.

Yield yourself to the umpireship of the blessed peace of God, for I find that the Greek word has that force,—" Let the peace of God umpire in your hearts." You know the umpire in the Greek games decided how the runners should run, how the wrestlers should wrestle, and he ruled a contest to be, or not to be, according to the law of the festival. He said, perhaps, that such and such a blow in the fight was a foul blow, and if he said so, there was no questioning him : it was decided. He stood at the winning-point when the runners came in, and he declared a certain swift-footed racer to be the winner. No man ever questioned the dictate of the umpire. His voice ended all debate. He was the man who decided in the games, and whose verdict was never to be disputed. Now, the peace of God is to do the same in our hearts. We ought to be resolved to judge all things by the peace of God. " What ought I to do in this case ? Must I humble myself ? I do not like it, but how ought I to act ? Shall I yield ? " Pride says, " Never ! No, no. Play the man. Never give in." But what does the peace of God say ? It says, " Yield : submit." Christ says, " I say unto you, That ye resist not evil : but whosoever shall smite thee on thy right cheek, turn to him the other also. And if any man will sue thee at the law, and take away thy coat, let him have thy cloke also." Christ decides that it will be good to be a sufferer rather than a revenger. We ought to have the peace of God ruling in our hearts so as to let it decide our course, and lead us to do that which is consistent with our own peace with God. I do not know how you find it, but I know that I cannot afford to be angry. It takes so much that is valuable out of me. I am sure it does. It does a man an immense mischief physically ; to some men it is a dangerous thing to get excited, it even endangers their lives. But, spiritually, I believe that to get into a state of enmity towards anybody is one

of the most grievous diseases which can befall a Christian. In such a case you cannot pray as you did ; you cannot read some passages of Scripture as you did ; you cannot look the Well-beloved in the face, and say, " I am acting in a way that pleases Thee." It is therefore a very serious thing for a believer in the Lord Jesus Christ to break his own peace—serious to himself as well as to those that are round about him. I pray you, therefore, dear friends, let the peace of God decide for you in all trials of temper, and endurings of wrong, and questions which lead to debate and separation. Set peace in the chariot, and let it hold the reins ; for anger will, like Phaeton of old, set the world on fire. Oh, Peace of God, rule thou me !

Pray God that the power of this peace may be constantly upon you. If you lose your peace with God you lose your power to judge under difficulties ; you lose your power of self-control under provocations, you lose the best sovereign that ever held a sceptre. I believe that if a man is walking with God in the light, and enjoying full fellowship with heaven, he may go down into any meeting, however turbulent —into any society, however discordant the elements may be—and yet he will be wise to answer, wise to be silent, wise to do, or wise not to do ; for the peace of God will keep him calm and quiet. Once let the mind be thoroughly disturbed and unhinged before the Lord, and you are weak as another man, and you say that which you will have to unsay, and you do that which you would wish to wipe out with your tears. When rest of soul is gone, hard things are spoken and hard things are done, which would not consort with communion with the tender Lord. Let the peace of God always rule, or otherwise you will not always be safe. Especially let the peace of God rule your affections. Be satisfied that you love God, and that your heart cleaves to God, and does not follow after any other. Be at peace with God as to your heart, and, when that is so, and the affections are dominated by conscious love to God, it is then that you fight the battles of life with comfort to yourself, and with honour to the name of Him to whom you belong.

III. Very briefly, I want, in the third place, to say, STRENGTHEN YOURSELF, dear friend, BY GOD'S SPIRIT, WITH ARGUMENTS, in order that you may let the peace of God rule in your hearts, and may be kept from any breach of that heavenly peace.

Remember, you *can only yourself be happy in heart and healthy in spirit as long as you keep the peace of God.* You are sure to become wretched and unhappy, you are sure to stumble here and there into faults, if that peace of God be gone. As you would be in the best possible trim for walking with God in joy while here below, look to your peace. This is no mean argument ; try to feel the force of it.

And, next, *only thus can the church of God prosper.* I am grieved when I receive members from other churches, who come because they say that they are weary of the incessant bickerings and jealousies which have disturbed their rest. I am sure that there can be no blessing where there is no peace. A house divided against itself cannot stand. A church disputing is a church committing suicide. Many and many a church has come to its death by bleeding inwardly through strife ; otherwise it might have defied the whole world, and hell itself. It is generally the little churches that squabble most : if they cannot excel in anything else, they certainly claim the first rank in quarrelling. A few Christian people get together to serve God, and the devil comes in at once and sets them by the ears : they are good men and true, but Satan bewitches them so that they dispute about nothing at all. Whenever I have to settle a dispute, I always like to have some big, bad thing in it. This I can point out, and we soon agree to set the matter right. When I cannot with microscopes on my eyes find out what it is all about, I find that brothers and sisters are hardest to be reconciled. It is easier to shoot an owl than a gnat. Little differences rankle like tiny thorns, and you cannot get them out of the flesh. Oh, that the Spirit of God would come upon the churches, and turn them into masses of fire ; then they would not fall to pieces through intestine strife ! When souls are being won, when the gospel is being enjoyed, when Christ is being glorified, when the church is marching on, conquering and to conquer through the divine power that is in her, then is there peace within her borders, and her citizens are filled with the finest of the wheat. But once let the life of God run low, and let the Spirit of God depart, then peace departs too. Oh, may God save this church and save all the churches from missing this blessed peace ! Let the peace of God rule in your heart, dear brother, dear sister, for the church's sake.

Remember, next, that *God cannot be glorified unless there is the peace of God in our hearts.* My dear friend, if you are always troubled, and fretting, and anxious, I do not see how you can glorify God to any large extent. Seek more faith, more trust, more confidence, more calm of mind, and you will personally glorify God. I am sure a Christian man who always finds fault with everybody is of little service to the cause and kingdom of our Lord. He who, wherever he goes, acts like a carrion crow, that soars aloft with no other design than finding out where a carcase may be, that he may light upon it,—he, I say, is not a man after God's own heart, neither will he advance the Lord's work among men. When you love your fellow Christians so that their faults are covered by your charity, and you rather admire their excellences than publish their infirmities, then it is that God is glorified by you. A happy, peaceful people of whom men can say, " See how these Christians love one another "—these shine as lights in the world, and the darkness feels their power.

The passage from which our text is taken offers us other reasons. It says this—" *To the which also ye are called.*" You were called to the peace of God. My dear brother, if you are not a peaceful man you have not inherited your true calling. When the Lord called you out from the world, He called you to be a peace-maker. He called you on purpose that the Spirit of peace might be shed abroad in your heart, and that afterwards you might carry that peace with you into your own family and amongst all your neighbours, and spread it everywhere. The Lord Jesus never called a man to be a maker of strife. If a Christian woman, as she calls herself, goes from house to house with tittle-tattle, she was not called by God to do so : of that I am certain. A man goes into his pulpit, and preaches a personal sermon on purpose to empty out his own spleen. God did not call him to that, for God loves not firebrands. The man may have been sent as a messenger from other regions, but certainly not as an ambassador from heaven, when he preaches gall and wormwood. Some seem, wherever they go, to make mischief as

speedily as possible : their mission is contention, whereunto they certainly were not called of God. You who are the true heirs of heaven are called to peace ; seek peace, and pursue it. Wherever you go, labour earnestly to make peace. If you see two boys fighting, make them leave off. If you see two girls in a bad temper, try to make them happy with one another. If you see two people disagree in business, do not back one of them up, and cry, " Go to law with him." but plead for peace and mutual concession. " Blessed are the peace-makers." Whatever you may be in a household, whether father or child, husband or wife, master or servant, son-in-law or mother-in-law, let your soul be seasoned and savoured with that blessed word, " Peace." There is always a war party in England : I fear the Jingo is no foreigner, but the genuine offspring of the British bull-dog. An unconverted Britisher is all for blood, and fire, and glory ; and as the unconverted are the majority among us we remain a fighting nation. Fighting— how we delight in it ! Down with the Afghans, down with the Zulus ! The Boers—destroy them ! We cannot get our fill of glory and honour unless we get knee deep in blood. The policy of peace is voted dishonourable, and so we go from land to land till there is hardly a nation which has not been stained with blood by British hands. How fiercely these English talk : but it is not Christian talk. May the Lord teach us the language of peace. Be you at peace, " whereunto also you were called."

And then, notice next, " *Called in one body.*" There must, therefore, be peace among Christians, because we are called in one body to peace. What would you think of my hand, if it should say, " I will have no peace with the eye. That prying eye looked sharply at me the other day and spied out a spot ; I will put it out " ? We shall not enjoy much prosperity if the members of the body thus disagree. Suppose my foot should say, " I am not going to carry that heavy body about. See what I have to suffer through it at times." Suppose my knee should say, " I will not have it. I have been tortured quite enough with rheumatism ; I will no longer carry that heavy fabric." What will become of me if the members of my body thus fall to quarrelling ? And what is to become of the glory of Christ if His members live in contention ? What is the Head to do if the members who make up His one mystical body have nothing to do but to be striving one against the other ? Oh, no. If you have any differences, end them to-night, I pray you, if you can, even though the east wind is so piercing. If you have unwittingly done anything that grieves others, try to remedy it. Or if others have grieved you, end the matter by sweet and swift forgiveness. Let it be all ended with the east wind. We are called in one body ; therefore let us dwell in hearty peace ; and may God the Holy Spirit, the Lord and Giver of peace, bring us into the peace of God, and keep us there, for thereunto also we are called in one body.

IV. The last point upon which I shall speak is this—to keep yourselves right, OCCUPY YOUR MINDS HEALTHILY. " How ? " say you. The text says, " *Be ye thankful.*" That is the way to keep up our peace with God. " Be thankful." Do not complain, but bless His name for everything. Do not quarrel with Him, but be thankful. Say, " Shall we receive good at the hands of the Lord, and shall we not receive evil ? The Lord gave, and the Lord hath taken away ; blessed be the name of the Lord." That is the way to be at peace with Him—to be thankful at all times. Bless God for your mercies and for your miseries ; bless Him for your gains and for your losses ; bless Him for your enjoyments and pleasures, and also for your aches and pains. Bless Him for every hard thing that comes from Him, for there is as much love in the hard as in the soft ; and God is as kind when He uses the rod as when He gives a kiss. " Be ye thankful ! " Bless Him from morning to night, and all through the night watches. What a mercy to be out of the hospital ! What a mercy to have the use of one's limbs and reasoning powers ! What a mercy to be out of prison ! What a mercy to be out of hell ! " He hath not dealt with us after our sins." Be thankful.

Last Sunday morning when I read this chapter in the great congregation I tried to ring it out as loudly as ever I could ; and I would like to ring it out as with a whole peal of bells now. Set them all ringing a marriage-peal, if you like,—" Be ye thankful ! Be ye thankful ! Be ye thankful ! " Up, ye murmuring ! Up, ye discontented ! " Be ye thankful." Rouse yourselves, ye sullen ones ! You that think you have a heavier load to carry than is meet, and say, like Cain, " My burden is greater than I can bear "—" Be ye thankful ! " All of you, young and old, " Be ye thankful." That is the way to keep up your peace with God, and your peace with your fellow-men.

Well, but it does not mean only, " Be thankful to God," but be ye thankful to your fellow-men. Too many receive all kinds of Christian kindness as a matter of course. They look upon the spontaneous kindness of their brethren as a sort of right. Now that the poor should be helped by Christian generosity is certainly according to Scripture ; but this is an obligation not of debt but of grace. Whatever is done in almsgiving and charity should be gratefully and heartily received. It is an unholy spirit which scarcely has the courtesy to say " thank you." Towards one another we ought to have a thankful spirit. How thankful the child ought to be to his mother and his father ! What a happy home we should have if children recognised the deep debt of obligation that is really due to those who have nursed them and cared for them so long ! How obliged, I think, the husband ought to be to his wife for all her tender kindnesses—those hundred unseen minis-

tries of love ! How grateful, I think, the wife should be to her husband, for all his labours and anxieties ! She receives a thousand things from him which make life comfortable. If we live in mutual gratitude, feeling that we are, each one of us, indebted to all others, how merrily will the household wheels go round, and what families of love we shall all gather around us ! I, of all the people in the world, am most in debt to everybody ; and I feel it deeply and truly. There is hardly a person that I look upon from this pulpit but I owe something to his or her Christian love. Everybody has been kind to me, and I am not unmindful of it. When I have lain upon my bed sick and ill, I have marvelled at the kindness of you all. I wonder why you treat me so lovingly. In all holy work, whether it be College, or Orphanage, you have been my ready helpers, and you are still. I cannot help saying, " God bless you." Surely the wind is changing a point or two : we shall find it blowing from another quarter when we leave this Tabernacle. I feel intense gratitude in my soul towards the dear brethren who surround me, and the sisters that work with me for Christ. You have often made me happy and cheered my spirit by the kind and generous way in which you have worked with me for the Lord, bearing with all my infirmities ; and I believe that it is because I feel thankful that I feel peaceful, and so remain the centre of your unity. I am not inclined to quarrel with anybody : I would sooner run a mile than I would fight for half a minute. There is nobody in the world that I would like to contend with : my heart is full of good wishes to all men. It has been a sort of rule with me to measure a man before I fight him : if he is bigger than I am I know he will beat me, and so I decline battle ; and if he is smaller, and I can easily beat him, it would be cruel and cowardly to do so. Nobody in the world is worth contending against as to our temporal interests. Even necessary law is troublesome and vexatious. Be ye thankful, then ; and if, with thankfulness to God and thankfulness to those around you, you can fill up the day, oh, how happy will the days be ! In the family and in the business God will be glorified ; the church will be sweetened and welded together : we shall see better times, and shall no longer grumble at *the east wind.*

May God bless you !

METHOD AND MUSIC, OR THE ART OF HOLY AND HAPPY LIVING

"And whatsoever ye do in word or deed, do all in the name of the Lord Jesus, giving thanks to God and the Father by Him."—Colossians iii. 17.

IT is always an advantage to have the laws of a kingdom as concise as possible. No one will ever be able to tell how much of litigation and consequent calamity has been caused in this country by the confused condition of our laws. When Napoleon issued his celebrated " Code Napoleon," which is an admirable summary of French law, he conferred upon the empire one of the greatest boons, and proved himself a wise ruler. We want law to be put into such a form that it can be understood, and that its application to divers cases can be discovered at once. In the great moral government of God we have no room to complain in this matter ; the

precepts of holiness are few and comprehensive. First of all, the whole of morality was summed up in ten commands, and written upon two tables ; then, as if this were not concise enough, we have the whole law summarised in two commands, " Thou shalt love the Lord thy God with all thy heart, and thy neighbour as thyself " ; and even this is brought into shorter compass still, for that one word " love " is the essence of all divine law. We, as Christians, find in the text an instance of the terseness, brevity, and clearness of divine precepts. We have here a law applicable to every believer—to every action, word and thought, in every place, under all circumstances; and yet this comprehensive command is expressed in very few words. It is a great advantage to the mechanic to be able to carry with him in a small compass his square or rule, by which he can adjust his materials, discover his errors, design correctly, and estimate his work when finished. Without such a rule, he would be quite at a loss; with it he is ready for work. We have before us a compendious rule of life, a standard of morals, a guide to holiness, which we may carry in our memories without the slightest difficulty; and which, if we have but the will to use it, will be found never to fail us on any occasion. As the mariner's compass or the pole-star to the mariner, so may the text be to us. Here is an infallible directory as to the way of holiness; a judge whose decisions in the matter of righteousness and truth none need distrust.

Read the text over, and then I shall ask you to observe the points in it. " Whatsoever ye do in word or deed, do all in the name of the Lord Jesus, giving thanks to God and the Father by Him." Observe, first, *holy walking described;* in the second part of the verse note *holy music prescribed;* and to enforce the whole text bear with me patiently till we close with the third head, which will be *holy motive inscribed*—inscribed, I trust, upon all our hearts.

I. HOLY WALKING DESCRIBED. " Whatsoever ye do in word or deed, do all in the name of the Lord Jesus."

This rule is not applicable to every person here present; it can only be practised by the regenerate. You must be in Christ before you can do anything in Christ's name. Until your nature is renewed, until you have submitted yourselves unto the righteousness of Christ, until Christ is formed in you the hope of glory, you are not capable of walking after this high and hallowed fashion. " Ye must be born again." The precept demanding your immediate attention is not the precept of this text but another; the words of Peter, in the Acts of the Apostles, are for you, " Repent, and be baptized every one of you in the name of Jesus Christ for the remission of sins, and ye shall receive the gift of the Holy Ghost "; or this, " Believe in the Lord Jesus Christ, and thou shalt be saved." You must begin at the beginning. It will but mislead you if I exhort you to walk as believers before you have received the inner life. The root must be changed before the fruit can be bettered. You need a radical change, my unconverted hearer, and you must have it or perish everlastingly. Do not imagine that any imitation of Christian manners will save you: do not conceive that hanging upon your lifeless branches the semblance of fruits will transform you into a tree of righteousness, the planting of the Lord. Oh! no, the sap within you must be changed, the life of God must be infused into your soul, you must be made one with Christ, or you cannot serve Him. This precept, belongs, therefore, to none of you who have not believed in Christ Jesus, but it belongs to all of you, without exception, who are named by the name of Jesus Christ in truth and sincerity; to all of you who have submitted yourselves to His government, and are trusting in Him for salvation. You will listen, I trust, and give earnest heed to this message from your Beloved.

What then meaneth this, that we are to do everything both in word and deed in the name of the Lord Jesus? Answer: there are six points in which this precept requires reverent care. First, do all *through the office and name of Christ as Mediator.* You as a Christian are bound to offer daily praise; you should often lift up your heart in grateful songs and psalms to God, but see to it that you do all this work of praise in the name of the Lord Jesus. No praise of yours can be sweet with God except it be presented through your great High Priest. Bring therefore your gift of thankfulness to this altar which sanctifieth the giver and the gift, and ever bless God through Jesus Christ. You are also to abound in prayer; it is your vital breath. You cannot flourish as a Christian unless you constantly draw near to God in supplication, but your supplications must always be presented through the name of Jesus Christ. His name gives prevalence to prayer; it is not so much your earnestness or sincerity, as His precious blood, that speaks in the ears of God and intercedes for you. Pray ever then with your eye upon the finished propitiation and the living Intercessor; ever plead the merit of Immanuel, and heaven's gate shall open to you. In addition to your prayers and praises, you are bound to serve Him according to the abilities entrusted to you in teaching the ignorant the way of salvation, in bringing in the unconverted, and in edifying the saints; but remember that your service to God in these respects can only be acceptable as you present it through the name of Jesus Christ. The hand of the Crucified One must offer for you the sweet cane which you have bought with money, and the fat of all your sacrifices. If you could give to God all the wealth that you possess, all the time of your mortal existence, all the talents with which you have been endowed, if you could do this henceforth without a failure, yet if you did not present the offering through Jesus Christ it would be as though you had done nothing; your burnt offerings and whole burnt offerings would have no acceptance with Jehovah, for your sinful nature pollutes them all. How necessary it is then that we should often pause in our holy work, and say, " I am doing this for God, but am I presenting it in the appointed way? If I see aught of merit in what I am doing, I am acting contrary to the gospel rule, and I shall be rejected. I must bring all my work to the High Priest of my profession and offer it through Him."

> " Th' iniquity of all our holy things
> Is cleansed by His blood, which covers all,
> And adds a rich perfume divinely sweet,
> Winning acceptance at the throne of God
> For broken prayers, and faulty songs, and e'en
> For service marr'd with sad infirmities.

Take heed, dear hearer, that thou see the blood sprinkled on thy service for God. Almost all things under the law were sanctified by blood, but all things under the gospel, without exception, must be thus made sweet to God. The atoning sacrifice, the prevalent intercession of the one appointed Mediator, Christ Jesus, must be constantly before our minds in all that we attempt to do for our Lord God. Let us never forget this lest we fail utterly.

A second meaning of this precept is, " Do all *under the authority of the Lord Jesus as your King.*" Say of such-and-such a doubtful or evil action, " This I cannot do; I could not feel that I was authorized to do it by any precept or example of my Lord and Saviour Jesus Christ. This I cannot do, for I should be stepping aside from the allegiance which I owe to Him: therefore this I will not do, be the consequences what they may of loss or of suffering. I am not authorized by Christ to follow this course, neither will I, come fair, come foul." On the other hand, when the act is allowed in Scripture, and only forbidden by the traditions of men, you may safely say, " This I feel that I may do. I see my Master has laid down no restriction, therefore I will submit to no human tradition or regulation. The commands which will-worship would inflict upon me I cast to the wind, for superfluities of pretended holiness are but superfluities of naughtiness." When positive duty is concerned, your language will be, " This action I find that I must do, for I see an express command for it ; therefore it shall be done ; be it difficult, it shall be achieved ; be it impossible, I will wait on Him who enableth faith to remove mountains." O that every Christian were altogether and evermore obedient to heavenly rule. As the planet revolves undeviatingly in its orbit, because with the law imposed upon it there has come forth a constraining and impelling force, so may we also pursue our course of duty, because we have not only heard the divine precept, but feel the sacred energy of the Holy Spirit, leading us in the prescribed path. Brethren, how safe we feel, and how happy in our consciences, if we are certain that we have the authority of the Great King for all our actions ! The business of a Christian upon earth is not an independent one ; he is not acting on his own account, but he is a steward for Christ. What if I compare him to a commission agent who is sent abroad by his firm with full powers from his employer to transact business for the house which he represents ! He is not to trade for himself, but he agrees to do all in the name of the firm which commissions him. He receives his instructions, and all he has to do is to carry them out, his whole time and talent being by express agreement at the absolute disposal of his employers. Now, if this man shall lend himself to an opposition firm, or trade on his own account, he is not true to his engagements, and he has to bear the responsibility of his acts ; but so long as he acts for his firm, and does his best, his course is an easy and safe one. If he follows the instructions of his principals he is eased of all responsibility. Should his trade be profitable or otherwise, he need not be vexed with anxieties, provided he has diligently followed the commands received from home. His acts are authorized from headquarters, and they are, therefore, safe for him ; he falls back on his principals who gave him the commands, and in whose name he acted. Now if we serve ourselves or the world, we must take the consequences of our unfaithfulness, but if we honestly serve the Lord all is clear. When a Christian can say concerning any course of conduct, " I am bidden to do this by Christ Jesus my Lord, I can find chapter and verse to authorise my acts " ; when he can feel that he is working for Christ, and not for himself, with a single eye to the glory of God, and not with sinister aims and selfish motives, then he treads as on a rock, and defies the censures of His enemies. Let us, then, take good heed to our Lord's words, and walk carefully in His commands, for then His authority protects us, and every tongue that rises against us in judgment we shall condemn.

This rule of acting under the authority of Christ is applicable in an emphatic sense to those who are called to special service in the kingdom of Christ. Every man is called to do all the good he can, but some men are set apart to labour in peculiar depart-ments of Christian work, and these should be doubly careful to do all in their Master's name. If a man were sinking through the rotten ice, any one of us would be authorized to do all we could to save him, but the iceman, who is appointed on purpose that he may save life, has a peculiar authority for anything that he takes upon himself to do in the way of rescuing the drowning, for he has the name of the Royal Humane Society at his back. If a ship were stranded and breaking up, and the crew were ready to perish, we are all of us authorized to do all we can to save the shipwrecked, but the men who belong to the lifeboat's appointed crew have a right to come to the fore and take the oars and put out to sea. They are authorised to lead the way in daring and danger. So, my brethren, those of you who have felt the divine call within you, the sacred impulse which compels you to devote yourself to the salvation of your fellow men, you may do it boldly and without apology. Your authority is from Christ, for the Holy Spirit has set you apart for the work. Let no man hinder or dispirit you. Press forward to the front rank in self-denying labour. Call it not impertinence, O ye carping critics, it is but holy courage which brings earnest hearts to the fore. Push to the very front, ye men of God, filled with daring and self-sacrifice, for if others should impute your zeal to evil motives the Lord who reads the heart understand you, and having given you a commission He will not fail to vindicate His faithful servants.

A third sense of the text is important. We should do all *under the sanction of the Lord Jesus as our exemplar*. It is an admirable course for us all to pursue, if when we find ourselves in circumstances of perplexity we ask ourselves the question, " What would Jesus Christ have done if He were in my circumstances ? " The answer to that question is the solution of your difficulty. Whatever He would have done it will be safe enough for you to do. It is certain that He would not have been unbelieving ; equally certain that He would not have done a wrong thing to deliver Himself ; we are also sure that He would not have been impatient, rebellious, or despairing, now would He have grown wrathful or morose. Well then, I know what I must *not* be, it may be possible to learn my positive as well as my negative behaviour from the same guide. I shall be able to discover by turning over the pages of the evangelists some portion of the Saviour's life very like my own ; what He was in that situation I must ask grace that I may be, and I shall certainly be led in the path of wisdom. The royal rule for a Christian is not what is fashionable, for we are not to be conformed to this world ; not what is gainful, for the pursuit of gain would lead us to run greedily in the way of Balaam for reward ; not that which is generally prescribed in society, for full often the prescriptions of society are antagonistic to the teachings of Christ ; not even the conduct of professors, for too many even among them walk as Paul tells us even weeping, as the enemies of the cross of Christ. Alas ! my brethren, the current holiness of the church falls far below the scriptural standard ; neither are the common rules of action among professors such as we could safely follow. A safe example is to be found nowhere but in the life of Jesus Christ Himself ; even the holiest of men are only to be followed so far as they follow Christ, but no further. My brethren, how calm will your hearts be, how serenely will you face your afflictions if you can feel, " I have done nothing but what my Master did before me ; I have sought to tread in the footprints of His pilgrimage ! " Why, you must be safe, you must be accepted if you do as Jesus did ; for never can Christ's example lead a simple soul astray.

" 'Tis always safe for souls to follow on
    Where Christ their Holy Shepherd leads the way."

Furthermore, as we are to do all thorugh the office of Christ as Mediator, within the authority of Christ as King, under the sanction of Christ as Exemplar, so we should do everything *to the glory of the Lord Jesus as our Lord and God.* When the Spanish mariners were traversing the seas upon voyages of discovery, they never touched upon new land, whether an insignificant island or a part of the main continent, without at once setting up the standard of Ferdinand and Isabella, and taking possession of the soil in the name of their Catholic Majesties of Spain. Wherever the Christian goes, his first thought should be to take possession of all hearts in the name of the Lord Jesus, consecrating all opportunities and influences to the Redeemer's service. Such common things as eating and drinking become by the giving of devout thanks consecrated to Christ's name. There is no action which is lawful, however common-place it may be but may be sanctified by the word of God and prayer. If the intense desire of our spirit shall be that we may glorify God as long as we are in this body, we shall find ways and means of accomplishing our object, and the Holy Spirit will help our infirmities. My dear brethren, our soul's desires should be always true to Christ, most chastely faithful so as not to tolerate any carnal motive or self-seeking. How easily do we give place to self-glorification ! How almost insensibly do we expect to receive honour of men ! It is very hard to keep ourselves clear of self-seeking under some form or other, for even self-denial may be used with an object which is the reverse of self-denial. The old philosopher seeing a fop in fine apparel, pointed at him, and said, " that's pride," but he was equally right when seeing certain Spartans who affected to dress meanly, he said, " and that's pride." Pride often stands in the doorway, but it can as readily hide in the corner. There is a pride of self-sacrifice and a pride of apparent humility, which is everyway as haughty vainglory itself. Dear friends, we must live for Christ, cost us what it may of watchfulness ; we must not fail here. We dare not live for a party, or a sect, or even altogether for any one church, however dear to us, for Jesus' sake. We may live for the truth, but only because God is glorified thereby. First and last, midst and everywhere, the constraining thought of Christian life should be " all for Jesus."

" All for the Master, all without reserve,
    All to the utmost of our manhood's might ;
Each pulse, each throb of heart and thrill of nerve,
    Each hour of busy day and silent night."

Beloved, it is delightful to know that Christ is all mine, and I am all Christ's. It is a holy aspiration to desire to enjoy as much of Christ as our nature can receive, and then to exhibit as much of Christ as grace can enable us to reveal. " Everything for Jesus " ; " Christ all and in all Christ," let these be the mottoes of every believer. " Whatsoever ye do in word or deed, do all in the name of the Lord Jesus," aiming ever at His glory.

The fifth point is, do all *in the strength of the Lord Jesus as your helper.* With Him is the residue of the Spirit ; and the Spirit of God is the believer's power. " Without Me ye can do nothing," saith our Lord, and we know the truth of that saying by unwise attempts which have ended in mournful failures ; but let us in future remember this truth practically. Never let us commence a work without seeking strength from on high. We go about Christian service very often as though we felt ourselves quite up to the mark for it ; we pray without asking the preparation of the heart from God ; we sing— ah ! my brethren, how universally is it so—without at all entreating the Holy Spirit to quicken our praises ; and I fear some of us must confess sorrowfully that we preach at times as though the preaching were to be our work and not the work of the Holy Ghost through us. Do not you, as hearers, too often listen to the word as if the mere hearing of it would do you good, or as if the speech of such-and-such a man would be certainly blest to you, instead of waiting upon God beforehand that your going up to the assembly might be profitable to your souls ? Do all in the Master's strength, and how differently everything will be done ! Acknowledge all the time you are at your work that your strength comes from the Lord alone. Never let the thought cross your mind that you as an experienced Christian have a fitness for the work peculiarly your own, so that you can dispense with prayers for divine aid, so necessary to the young ; never imagine that because through long years you have performed a service with acceptance you can therefore now do it without renewed help. This is the way by which we sink into routine, degenerate into religious automata, and become like formalists and hypocrites. This is the way in which the power of God and the vitality of godliness are rendered so rare in the churches. If we do not feel conscious day by day of abiding weakness and consequent need of fresh strength from the Most High, we shall soon cease to be full of grace. Write this upon the tablets of your heart, " All my fresh springs are in Thee," and from this day forward in word and deed do all in the name of the Lord Jesus ; deriving all your spiritual energy from Him.

Sixthly, we should do all in the name of the Lord Jesus, for He *should be the element in which we live.* It is said of the modern Greeks that whatever may be their faults mentally, they are faultless physically, for you never saw a Greek peasant in an ungraceful attitude, however much he might be off his guard and unconscious of your gaze. Gracefulness is a part of the Greek nature. So let the Lord Jesus Christ be so woven and intertwisted into you very self, that you cannot be otherwise than Christlike under any circumstances. Lord, grant us this. It would be a glorious thing to be saturated through and through with the Spirit of Christ, so as to live Christ evermore. That eminent ornithologist, M. Audubon, who produced accurate drawings and descriptions of all the birds of the American Continent, made the perfection of that work the one object of his life. In order to achieve this he had to earn his own living by painting portraits, and other labours ; he had to traverse frozen seas, forests, canebrakes, jungles, prairies, mountains, swollen rivers, and pestilential bogs. He exposed himself to perils of every sort, and underwent hardships of every kind. Now, whatever Audubon was doing, he was fighting his way towards his one object, the production of his history of American birds. Whether he was painting a lady's portrait, paddling a canoe, shooting a racoon, or felling a tree, his one drift was his bird-book. He had said to himself, " I mean to carve my name amongst the naturalists as having produced a complete ornithological work for America," and this resolution ate him up, and subdued his whole life. He accomplished his work because he gave himself wholly to it. This is the way in which the Christian man should make Christ his element. All that he does should be subservient to this one thing, "That I may finish my course with joy, that I may deliver my testimony for Christ, that I may glorify God whether I live or die."

We have thus seen what it is to do all in the name of the Lord Jesus ; let us stop a moment to remind you that this text administers a severe rebuke to many professed Christians. *Too many church-members do nothing in Christ's name.* Since the day when they were baptized into the name of the Father, and of the Son, and of the Holy Ghost, they have done nothing else in that name. Ah, hypocrites ! ah, hypocrites ! God have mercy upon you ! Alas, how many others do but very little in Christ's name ! I noted in a letter, by a certain pastor, not I think given to speak severely, this remark—that he did not think in his own church one in three of the members were doing anything for Christ. I could not speak so sorrowfully as that concerning you ; but I much fear that a large proportion of the strength of this church is not used for the Lord. I believe that there is more used here than in almost any other church, but still there is a great deal of waste steam, a great deal of buried talent, and thereby Jesus is defrauded. I noticed in an American paper an observation made concerning the Baptist churches of North Carolina. A man acquainted with them said, "There are a hundred thousand members reported in the various associations, there are a hundred thousand baptized persons, and seventy-five thousand of them are only ' *baptized dead heads.*' " It is an American term, but I am afraid we shall have to import it, for it is frightfully true that numbers of professors are just so many "baptized dead heads." They are of no use ; they are not working—they are perhaps grumbling—the only sign of life they have ; but they are neither giving of their substance nor laying out any other talents in the cause of Christ. If there be any such present, I pray that this text may be a thorn in your side, and act as a spur to you ; and may you henceforth do all that lies in your power in the name of the Lord Jesus.

The text also rebukes those Christians who do much in the name of some eminent Christian man. I shall not censure any particular denomination, but if the truth censures them, let them hear it. When George Whitefield refused to form a new sect, and said, "Let my name perish, and let Christ's name last for ever," he acted as his Lord would have him. Paul was not crucified for you, neither did Apollos die for you, therefore take none of these names, but let the name of Christ be named among you, and under that name be ye known. Though there is a Lutheran church, it was a good saying of Luther, though couched in rugged words, " I desire above all things that my name should be concealed, and that none be called by the name of Lutheran, but of Christian. What is Luther ? My doctrine is not mine, but Christ's. I was not crucified for any. How comes it to pass, that I, who am but a filthy, stinking bag of worms, that any of the sons of God should be denominated from my name ? Away with these schismatical names ; let us be denominated from Christ, from whom alone we have our doctrine." It shall be well for all churches when they are ruled by the like spirit. Names which indicate their difference of doctrine will probably survive till Christ comes, but the name of men they will do well to discard.

Once more, *what a rebuke is our text to those professors who dishonour the name under which they profess to live !* The Spaniards in America acted so cruelly, and with such a dreadful lust for gold, that when they sent their missionaries to convert the Indians, the Indians wished only to know whether the religion that was taught them was the religion of the Spaniards, for if it was they should like to believe something the very opposite of it ; and if there was no heaven but where the Spaniards went, they would sooner go to hell than be with them. Truly some professors' lives give much the same savour to the Christian religion. Men say, " Are these Christians, these mean, covetous, quarrelsome, domineering, or boastful people ? then we will sooner be infidels than Christians." Out upon you, ye caricatures of godliness. If there be one such here, may his conscience prick him. You have crucified the Lord afresh, and put Him to an open shame. How dreadful will be your punishment if you die in your present state ! Repent of your sin, and ask of God grace to make your profession sincere : and if you will not do this, at least be honest enough to give up your false profession, for you do but degrade but it and yourself. There is no necessity, surely, to add to your innumerable sins, this sin of hypocrisy. What gain you by it ? Nay, sir, if you must serve mammon and the devil, serve them ; but why with supererogation of iniquity must you pretend to serve Christ ?

II. We leave this first point, and find in the second part of the text, HOLY MUSIC PRESCRIBED. " Giving thanks unto God and the Father by Him."

Soldiers march best to battle when the trumpet and drum excite them with enlivening strains ; the mariner brightens his toil by a cheery cry at every pull of the rope ; and it is an excellent thing when Christian men know how to sing as well as to work, and mingle holy music with holy service. The best music of a Christian consists in thankfulness to God. Thanks should be rendered by the believer with all the acts common to men. Our eating, our drinking, our social meetings, our quiet conversings one with another, in all we should give thanks unto God and the Father. This we should do in the labours peculiar to our vocation. Whatever your trade and calling may be, if you cannot sing aloud, you can sing in your hearts while your hands are busy ; you can ring out the praises of God as well to the sound of the hammer on the anvil as to the peal of the organ ; your feet at the sewing machine may beat time to a sacred tune ; you can as well praise God while you crack your whip as when you sing to a Psalm tune. Why not ? If the heart be right you can mount up to the heavens from any place or labour. Whatever your calling may be you shall find some peculiarity in it which shall help you to magnify God, if you will but use a spiritual eye to discover it.

We ought especially to praise God in the exercise of our religion. Whenever the assemblies of God's people meet, there should be much of holy joy. Some people are so afraid of joy, that one might suppose them to labour under the delusion that all who are devout must also be unhappy. If we worshipped Baal, to lance ourselves with knives were most fitting, if we were worshippers of Juggernaut or Kalee, self-inflicted tortures might be acceptable ; if we adored the pope, it might be proper for us to wear a hair shirt and practise flagellation ; but as we worship the ever-blessed God, whose delight is to make His creatures happy, holy happiness is a part of worship, and joy in the Lord one of the accepted graces of the Holy Spirit. Brethren, let us be happy when we praise God. I have noticed with pain the way in which people will get rid, if they can, of happy words out of their hymns. The hundredth Psalm for instance, runs thus :—

> " All people that on earth do dwell,
> Sing to the Lord with cheerful voice,
> Him serve with ——"

What ? Well, they moderniye it into—

> " Him serve with *fear.*"

But, as I believe, the older form is—

> " Him serve with *mirth,* His praise forthtell,
> Come ye before Him and rejoice."

I wonder some other scribe did not cut out the word " cheerful," and put in—

> " Sing to the Lord with *doleful* voice."

In this way the Psalm might have been " improved " until there would not have been a grain of worship left in it. I mean to sing it, " Him serve with *mirth* " ; and with a glad and merry heart will I praise my God. If you are His child, rejoice in your Father's presence ; if you are pardoned, rejoice in the mercy that washed away your sins ; even if you are tried and troubled, yet rejoice that your afflictions are working together for your good. " Rejoice in the Lord always ; and again I say, Rejoice."

The text tells us under what aspect we should regard God when we are thus thanking Him, " Giving thanks unto God and the Father," blessing Him that He stands in that relation to us as well as to the Lord Jesus. The belief in the divine fatherhood will surely make the sons of God happy. It is instructive to observe that thanks are directed to be offered especially to the Father ; I suppose because we are most apt to forget to praise the Father. We love Jesus Christ for dying for us ; we forget not the Holy Spirit because He dwells in us ; but the common idea of the Father is dishonouring to Him. Is He not regarded as all justice, and seldom as the fountain of love ? Now, it is the Father who stands at the back of all in the eternal purpose ; it is the Father who gave the Son to die ; it is the Father who justifies us through the righteousness of Christ, and adopts us into His family. The Father is equally to be loved and worshipped with the Spirit and the Son, and through Jesus Christ we should come to God, the terrible God as He was to us in our ungodliness, and worship Him as the Father now with thankful joy, because of the mercies we have received.

The gist of this second precept is that you stir up your hearts, my dear friends, to the cultivation of a cheerful spirit ; that you excite that cheerful spirit to the use of thankful words, telling to your friends and neighbours the goodness of God to you ; that these words be oftentimes elevated into songs ; that these songs should, as on wings of flame, ascend up to where perfect spirits praise God both day and night. O ye that love the Saviour, do not neglect this, " Whoso offereth praise glorifieth God." Glorify Him, then. This praise, this cheerful spirit wins on others. They, marking how you give thanks, will be attracted to your Saviour and your God, while you will strengthen yourselves also, for " the joy of the Lord is your strength." Despondency and murmuring will hamper you in all your efforts to glorify Christ, but to maintain an inward spring of thanksgiving is one of the best ways to keep yourselves in spiritual health. God help you, then, to carry out both these precepts.

> " Work and praise ! Hearts upraise !
> Drink your fill of joy !
> Happy they who all the day
> Spend in Christ's employ.
> For their song makes them strong,
> Ready for their toil ;
> And their mirth, not of earth,
> Sorrow cannot spoil.

III. A few words upon the third point, namely, HOLY MOTIVE TO BE INSCRIBED upon our hearts to secure obedience. These motives are four. A word on each.

Beloved in Christ, you have received all you have from God the Father through Christ. That you are not in hell is due to His longsuffering ; that you have been spiritually quickened is due to His gracious operation ; that you are pardoned is due to His precious blood. Owing all to Him, what arises in your mind but *gratitude* ? And what is the dictate of gratitude ? Does it not teach you that it is your reasonable service to surrender yourselves to Him who bought you at such a price ? For, ah, what a return it will be, how poor compared with what He has done for you ! If you give your body to be burned for Him, yet He deserveth infinitely more than all the sacrifice of the most painful death to recompense His stoop from the highest throne in glory to the cross of the deepest woe. Let your gratitude compel you to do everything for Jesus.

Reflect, too, that the Wellbeloved for whom I plead to-day is worthy. " Him hath God the Father exalted." Do you demur to that exaltation ? Do you not rather rejoice in it ? Is not that song most true—

> " Worthy is He that once was slain,
> The Prince of Peace that groan'd and died ;
> Worthy to rise, and live, and reign,
> At His Almighty Father's side " ?

Will you deny, then, to Christ that which He is worthy to receive ? He deserves the crowns of angels, and the songs of all the perfected ; will you not give Him the best you have, even your hearts ? I appeal to the *justice* which I trust governs your judgment— should not Jesus Christ be the one object of your life ?

Further, many of us here present have professed to be His disciples. We remember well the day when we were buried with Him in baptism unto death. We voluntarily came forward and we took upon ourselves to be immersed in His name, copying His example and obeying His command. If that act meant anything it meant this, that we professed ourselves to be dead henceforth to the world and risen with Christ. Now, by the profession then made, by the communion then enjoyed, I pray you, my dear brother and sister, whatsoever you do in word or deed, do all in the Master's name. Let not this appeal to your *honour* be forgotten.

Lastly, I need not thus plead with some of you, for your hearts are pleading with you. I know you *love* Him whose name is as ointment poured forth; I know how the tendrils of your heart have entwined themselves about His cross. His person fixes all your love; you are only happy when you are walking in communion with Him; He is the sun of your soul,

without whom you cannot live. Well, then, do what love dictates. Bring forth the alabaster box of ointment, break it, pour the sacred nard upon His head, and if any ask, " Wherefore is this waste ? " say that He is worthy of it, and that you love much because you have had much forgiven. This day bring forth the best that is within your store, the spiced wine of your pomegranate, and set it before your Lord, while Jesus sups with you and you with Him. Again I say arouse yourselves to live at a more vigorous rate, and let the whole of the force and energy that dwells within you, and all that you can borrow from the seventh heaven, be given up to Him who loved you and gave Himself for you. May my Master's blessing be with these words, to all who hear or read them, for Jesus' sake. Amen.

ALL FOR JESUS

" Ye serve the Lord Christ."—Colossians iii. 24.

THE gospel does not barely supply us with directions for holy living but furnishes us with reasons for obedience, and tells us where to find the power to obey. Hence in the commencement of this chapter, before the apostle comes to any practical exhortation, he reminds us of our position and privileges. He bids us remember who and what we are as believers in Christ, that we may act accordingly. We are risen with Christ, and therefore our affection should not be set on earthly things; we are dead to the world, and hence we must not, cannot live in sin. Christ is our life, and therefore we must walk after His example.

The apostle knew right well that the conditions of believers here below are various, and therefore he laid down distinct precepts for each position. Some are masters and others servants, some parents and others children, and in each case the requirements differ; but while he suited the exhortation to each one he proposed a common motive for all; he reminded all believers, whether wives or husbands, children or fathers, servants or masters, that there is another and a better life, whose rewards are worthy of our ambition, whose service should engross all our strength. He bade them have respect to that higher life, for they had been representatively lifted up into the highest heaven in the person of Jesus Christ, and with him their hearts and desires should ever be. He bade them live the life of heaven here below, and order their footsteps, not in accordance with the fleeting things of time, but the enduring realities of eternity. He knew that in so doing the inconveniences of the present would be forgotten in the glories of the future, and the trials of to-day would be more than counterbalanced by the joys of the hereafter.

Our Authorized translation is in the indicative, and states the fact, " Ye serve the Lord Christ." Brethren, is it the fact with each of you ? To how many in this place can it be truly said, " Ye serve the Lord Christ " ? I find it might also, and not incorrectly, be translated in the imperative. " Serve ye the Lord Christ "; in this sense it may be directed to those who have no share in it as a statement of fact. Let us take it in both senses. If we dare to hope that we do serve the Lord Christ, yet let us listen to further exhortation, and serve Him still better; let us thank God for the measure of service

which He has wrought in us, and let us earnestly ask Him to work in us still further to will and to do. But if any of you are not yet included in the sacred band who call Jesus " Master and Lord," then when ye have trusted in His blood, come and yield your whole selves unto Him. If, indeed, ye be redeemed from wrath through Him, I charge you be not disloyal to the obligations under which you are laid, but from this time forth make it your joy to " serve the Lord Christ."

To me my text is one of the most joyful sentences from which I have ever preached. " Ye serve the Lord Christ." What an exaltation for a slave of Satan to become a servant of Christ ! With what exultation do I hail permission to do anything for my Lord. To be blessed by Him, to be enriched with priceless gifts from His bounteous hand,—this is lovingkindness; but to be allowed to render tokens of gratitude in return is sweetest of all. Truly, we may say of this condescension, " Thy gentleness hath made me great." By receiving anything from us the Lord has lifted us as beggars from the dunghill, and set us among princes, even the princes of His people. It is a greater honour to serve Christ in the most menial capacity than to occupy the throne of the Cæsars. I speak of honour, I may also dilate upon the happiness of the service of Jesus ! It is the purest of pleasures. We long to express our affection for Jesus by acts of zeal. Love pants for expression, and is not obedience the tongue of love ? That love is feigned which does not declare itself in some practical form or other, by deeds of kindness, or gifts, or sacrifices, or patient endurance, or hearty praise. Beloved, let us count it an unrivalled honour and an unsurpassed delight to do anything for Jesus. For this service let us be insatiably ambitious, resolved at all costs to show our loyalty to our Prince. To serve us He laid aside His glorious array, and girt about Him the garments of a servant; for us He took a basin and towel and stooped to wash His disciples' feet; for us He became obedient to death, even the death of the cross: now, therefore, in our turn, by all the shame He bore, by all the labour He endured, by all the agonies He suffered, let us serve Him and Him alone for ever.

In handling the subject of Christian service, I shall note three things: first, we serve the Lord

Christ *in the common acts of life*; secondly, we serve Him *in what are usually called religious acts*, and thirdly, we have learned to serve Him, and, I trust, we may do it more and more, *in special acts of direct homage to Himself*.

I. First, then " ye serve the Lord Christ " IN THE COMMON ACTS OF LIFE. The fact that our text was addressed to the lowest rather than to the highest in worldly circumstances is very instructive. Paul has been visiting a family, and he has spoken a word to the wife and a word to the husband, he has paid attention to the children, and given a warning to the father, he has also a message for the master of the house ; but he does not address to either master, mistress, or children, that choice saying which he reserves for servants—" Ye serve the Lord Christ." The Greek word here translated servants, may be rendered " slaves," and though its meaning is not confined to slaves, yet it includes them, and there there were many such in the Christian church in Paul's days,—truly converted men and women, who were still held in bondage according to the cruel Roman law. The apostle goes into the kitchen, the cellar, the field, the wine-press, the stable, and he says to his brethren toiling there—" Ye serve the Lord Christ." He whispers in the ear of the aged man who acts as porter at the door, whom he knows to be a devout believer, and this is the secret which he whispers, " Fear not, brother, for despite thy bonds thou servest the Lord Christ." In those hard days, when Paul wrote from Rome to Colosse, many a slave crept out from Cæsar's household by stealth to listen to his gracious words, and poor workpeople gathered around him, and were converted, and as he felt deep sympathy with them he did not merely admonish them to be honest, industrious, conscientious, and obedient, as many a preacher would have done, but he went further, and cheered them in the performance of their duties by assuring them that they served the Lord Jesus, and of Him they would receive a reward. He knew their sorrows and their provocations, and therefore presented them with a rich consolation and a stimulus. He exhorted them to act " as the servants of Christ, doing the will of God from the heart ; with good will doing service, as to the Lord, and not unto men." This he said to servants, and to no other class in particular. He did not mean thereby that the wife, the husband, the master, and the child might not and did not serve Christ, but he would have us infer that if those did so, whose lot was least distinguished, much more should those do it whose responsibilities and opportunities are so much greater. If my poor servant should serve Jesus, how much more ought I to do it ? If those with the least education and means are bound to serve Him, how much more should those who have ten talents lay out all for His glory ?

My brethren, you see that those to whom Paul spoke were not preachers, nor deacons, nor elders of the church, neither were they magistrates, or persons of influence, they were simple servants, engaged in domestic duties ; but he says of them, " Ye serve the Lord Christ." Though what I have to say bears upon all present, I will keep to the line of thought which this fact naturally suggests.

Those who are in low estate serve the Lord Christ by *a quiet acquiescence in the arrangement of Providence which has placed them where they are.* Every one knows that while the human race exists in its present condition somebody must serve. It is a paradox, but it is also a truth, that if there were no servants we should practically be all servants. There are a thousand offices which, if each person were obliged to perform them for himself, would be exceedingly tedious and unpleasant, but which are now done for us by persons to whom use renders them not at all irksome. As things are at present constituted, there will be poor and there will be rich, there will be servants and there will be masters, and when a man can say, " I have learned in whatsoever state I am therewith to be content, I bow me to the providence of my heavenly Father, that man is in his heart serving the Lord Christ. To stand where the Lord places us and keep our position cheerfully has in it the essence of obedience.

We serve the Lord, next, in service, or in any other form of life, *if we exercise the graces of the Holy Spirit* in the discharge of our calling. The servant who is in all things trustworthy, and neither wastes his employer's time nor goods—the servant who does not watch his master's steps, so as to loiter when he is out of sight, but conscientiously renders a fair day's work for his wage, treating his master as he would wish to be treated if their positions were exchanged ; such an one, exhibiting truthfulness, gentleness, sobriety, honesty, and industry, serves the Lord Christ as much in his labour as if he were an evangelist or an apostle. He does not preach vocally, but his life is a powerful sermon. He is a standing evidence of the power of religion, an argument which logic cannot overthrow, nor the most cunning sophistry confute. Holy living preaches where the minister cannot enter, it preaches from the nursery to a worldly mother, from the shop to a graceless tradesman, from the workroom to a godless employer. Where our words are denied a hearing, your lives will nevertheless win attention. At the first the gospel was very much spread in the noble families at Rome by means of their servants. They noticed how different they were from other servants, and as they observed their conduct they inquired what this new religion was which so much improved them. Christians *were* Christians then : they made their Lord their first and last object, and surrendered their whole lives to His service, and hence they were a power in all places. The poorest and meanest did not think themselves exempt from the sacred duty of spreading the faith ; none, indeed, asked for a discharge in this war. Domestic servants became missionaries to the families in which they resided, and acted as apostles in houses where the apostles could not enter.

We serve Christ in such a position *by displaying the joy of the Lord in our service.* I lay great stress upon this point. Many a soul has been converted to our Lord Jesus by noticing the cheerfulness of poor Christians. If a heathen master had a Christian slave, he noticed how contentedly he accepted his hard toil and hard fare, he saw his countenance beaming with delight, and he even heard him sing for joy. He would naturally want to know the reason of that cheerfulness. Servants had a sorry lot with Roman masters and mistresses ; I have seen some of the mere dogholes in which the slave who kept the door found sleeping-quarters in the gay city of Pompeii, yet from such wretched abodes would rise the voice of psalms and hymns and spiritual songs, and the children would wish to hear them, and the mistresses too. Thus would the truth be spread. The Christian would not join in the general jollity upon heathen festivals, and would be absent from the amphitheatre when all the rest of the family were eager to view the spectacle, but he had a quiet cheerfulness and settled calm of mind which was all his own, and when trouble and distress were in the house he was the general comforter and friend. When he lay sick, and scarce anybody cared for him, he still did not lose heart, and when he was near to die his joy came to a climax, and he breathed out his soul with a song. Such a servant served the Lord most effectually. I hope there are many in this church who in these better days are rendering equally valuable service in households where the name of Jesus is not reverenced. We, too, should be doing the like in the circles in which we move. Our holy cheerfulness should be an invitation to our friends to come to Jesus. We shall never bring men to believe in a Master whose servants are unhappy in His service. To toll a knell as an invitation to a wedding feast is most absurd. When we invite men to the banquet of saving grace let us do it with smiling faces. Beloved, let us mingle with the sternness of our integrity and the solemnity of our life-purpose that cheerfulness and joy which are the most natural and the most attractive ornaments of the Christian character.

The true way to serve the Lord in the common acts of life is to *perform them as unto Himself*; and this can be done with everything which it is lawful to do. God forbid we should maintain, as some do, a broad, unbending distinction between things secular and religious. This wicked age must, forsooth, have its holy places and its holy days. What is this but a confession that most of its buildings are unholy and its days unholy too. Of heaven it is written, " I saw no temple therein," and we get nearest to the heavenly state when all superstitious notions about sacred places and sacred substances shall be swept away once for all. To a man who lives unto God nothing is secular, everything is sacred. He puts on his work-day garment and it is a vestment to him : he sits down to his meal and it is a sacrament ; he goes forth to his labour, and therein exercises the office of the priesthood : his breath is incense and his life a sacrifice. He sleeps on the bosom of God, and lives and moves in the divine presence. To draw a hard and fast line and say, " This is sacred and this is secular," is, to my mind, diametrically opposed to the teaching of Christ and the spirit of the gospel. Paul has said, " I know, and am persuaded by the Lord Jesus, that there is nothing unclean of itself." Peter also saw a sheet let down from heaven in which were all manner of beasts and fourfooted creatures, which he was bidden to kill and eat, and when he refused because they were unclean, he was rebuked by a voice from heaven, saying, " What God hath cleansed that call not thou common." The Lord hath cleansed your houses, my brethren, He has cleansed your bed chambers, your tables, your shops, He has made the bells upon your horses holiness to the Lord, He has made the common pots and pans of your kitchens to be as the bowls before the altar, if ye know what ye are and live according to your high calling. Ye housemaids, ye cooks, ye nurses, ye ploughmen, ye housewives, ye traders, ye sailors, your labour is holy if ye serve the Lord Christ in it, by living unto Him as ye ought to live. The sacred has absorbed the secular, the overarching temple of the Lord covers all your houses and your fields.

My brethren, this ennobles life. The bondsman is henceforth free, he serves not man but God ; the galley-slave tugs the oar for Jesus, the menial ministers to the Lord. This cheers the darkest shades, for now we no longer complain of the hardness of our lot, but we rejoice in it, because we bear all for Jesus, and the burden which we carry is His cross, which He Himself places on our shoulders. This ensures us a reward for all we do. If in our service we receive but little thanks from man, and if after a life of toil find ourselves but scantily furnished for old age, we will not complain, for our recompense is sure, our reward is in the hand of one who never forgets His servants. There is no unrewarded toil in the service of the Lord Christ, even a cup of cold water He remembers. He who serves Christ shall have it said of him at last, " Well done, good and faithful servant," and in the fulness of his Master's joy, into which he shall enter, he shall forget that for a while he lived unremunerated among the sons of men.

Let this stimulate your zeal, my brethren : if you serve the Lord Christ, serve Him well. If you had work to do for her Majesty the Queen you would try to do your best. If she honoured you with her commands you would cheerfully obey them ; how much more should you be aroused to diligence by the call of the Infinite Majesty of Him who bled for you ! Perform your every-day work with a heartiness which nothing else could beget in you. Serve the Lord with gladness, and do all for love of His name.

This I thought most important to bring forward, and though I cannot speak upon it as I would, yet I do earnestly urge all of you to remember that piety shines best around the domestic hearth, and that true religion is always best esteemed by unconverted men when they see it in connection with the commonplace duties of life. They do not care how beautifully you pray at prayer-meetings ; they have very little respect for the excellent addresses you deliver in the Sabbath-school ; but to live godly, soberly, righteously, to make other people happy, to be gentle in temper, to be yielding and forgiving, to be strictly upright and honest in your dealings with your fellow men,—this is what the world will read and recognize, and when they see these things in you, the gospel will be commended to them, and they will be the more likely to listen to the truth as it is in Jesus.

II. Secondly, brethren, we ought to serve the Lord Christ in what we more commonly, but incorrectly, call RELIGIOUS ACTIONS. Every professor of religion should have something to do for Jesus Christ. Though the discipline of our church does not turn out of it every one who is an idler, I almost wish it did. I am afraid such a rule would diminish our numbers, but it would materially quicken our energy. Drones in the hive are of very little use as to honey making ; they are at the bottom of all the quarrels, but they cannot really benefit the community. God save us from being drones. Let every man who is really redeemed by the blood of Jesus have something to do, and do it. I wish I could go round the whole of this company this morning and say, " Brother, do you serve the Lord Christ ? Sister, do you the same ? " but I will ask conscience to be my deputy, and leave your own hearts to answer the question. Brother, sister, do you really serve Christ, or does it amount to this, that you enjoy hearing, you enjoy singing, and so on, but you do nothing for Jesus ? Bestir yourself, dear brother, put out your talent to interest. Your Lord has said, " Occupy till I come." Take heed lest he come and find your talent buried in the earth, your Lord's money rusting and your napkin rotting in the soil. Let each one be serving Christ always according to his ability.

But supposing that we are serving Christ, as we think, it is well to raise a further question : are we with our whole soul serving *Christ*. For mark you, it is very easy to make a mistake here : we may be working in a legal spirit, and so not serving Christ. No doubt many attend to the outward matters of religion that they may win merit, or that they may prepare themselves for the receipt of the divine blessing. I do not wonder at the zeal and earnestness which some people show ; if they hope to get to heaven by their works they ought to be zealous indeed. The legal spirit has a measure of power in it : the lash drives on the slave, the fear of punishment impels man to toil. But from such bondage ye are free, " ye are not under the law, but under grace." Do therefore nothing with the hope of deserving well at the Lord's hands, for this would be serving self. Ye are saved, serve then your Saviour out of gratitude. Work, not to obtain life, but because you have life already, and delight to exercise that life to the honour of Him who gave it. Some, I fear, do not serve Christ in what they do, for they go about it as a part of the general routine of their existence. It is the proper thing to go to a place of worship, therefore they go ; it is generally expected of persons in their station to teach in the Sunday-school, and they do so accordingly ; they reckon that they ought to give a guinea if they see the name of a friend down on the list, therefore they do it. I am afraid that a great deal which is put down as work for Christ is a kind of sleep-walking, done without thought, or heart, or desire to glorify God therein. May the Holy Ghost arouse us out of such mere mechanical acts, and bring us to be in heart and soul the Lord's willing, ardent workers.

Some, I fear, render service in a party spirit. They serve, and they think it is Christ they are serving, but in fact it is their own denomination, or little church. They would be almost vexed to hear of God's being honoured among any other sort of Christians ; they hope there will be a revival, but they would like it to be pretty nearly confined to the walls of their own chapel. They serve a clique, not Christ. Their sympathies never go beyond the particular section of the church to which they belong, and they are rather moved by emulation to see their own opinions dominant than by zeal for the glory of God. Oh, brethren, break those bonds if they hold you. We ought to be zealous for the whole truth, and we ought to labour to increase the number of those Christians who would hold the gospel in its purity, but still let our jealousy for pure religion never degenerate into bigotry ; let us love the whole church more than a part, and Christ best of all.

In more instances still the self-spirit comes in to usurp the place of Jesus. I wonder how large a proportion of our zeal, if it were analysed, could be accounted for by the desire of prominence, the ambition to be thought useful, and the wish to shine among our fellow men. I cannot set up a furnace here and put my own zeal or yours into the crucible just now, but again I ask your conscience to be my deputy to analyse honestly the motive which sways you, and to tell you plainly how far you are serving self and how far you are serving Christ.

We are not always serving Jesus, I fear, when we think we are most doing so, for our main object may be to please our fellow-creatures. Our parents wish us to be active in the church, and therefore we do it. Our friends would not be pleased if we were idle, and therefore we bestir ourselves. From our position we are expected to be engaged in some department of Christian service, and therefore we enter upon it. Brethren, we must rise above this. What we do, whether we teach in the school, or visit the sick, or distribute tracts, or preach the gospel, we must do as unto the Lord alone, and the master motive, which should indeed crush out every other, must be this, " We serve the Lord Christ." Brethren, let others take what they will for their motto, I charge you by the Holy Ghost, write this upon your banners, " We serve the Lord Christ." If any request you to serve this literary coterie or that political faction, or to give your whole attention to some great moral reform, let your answer be, " We serve the Lord Christ." Aid in anything that is good, for whatsoever things are lovely, and of good report, and are for the benefit of mankind, you are bound to countenance, but still your main life-work, your true business, which must absorb your energies and eat you up, is this—" We serve the Lord Christ." They beckon us from this point, crying, " Come over and help us." They call to us from the other corner, " Come and work with us," but our answer must be, " We are an independent brigade, we are already committed to the noblest cause ; we are sworn to a Captain who has no rival ; we are not able to promise ourselves to any one of you, though wherein you do good we are your allies ; Jesus we serve and none else. God forbid that we should glory save in the cross of our Lord Jesus Christ." May God help us to do this evermore !

III. Now I am coming to the last part of my discourse, which to me is the most interesting, and I trust it may be so to you. We serve the Lord Christ IN SPECIAL ACTS DONE TO HIMSELF. I cannot tell how you feel, but I often wish I could do something for my Lord Himself personally. I frequently meet with the kind of souls to whom God has blessed my ministry, and they express their thankfulness to God and their love to me, by aiding the various works committed to my charge, for which I am deeply grateful to them : but now and then a friend says, " I will cheerfully subscribe to your work, but I desire also to show my personal thanks to yourself. What can I do *for you ?*" Now, towards those whom we esteem, this is a natural feeling, and in spiritual things there is a similiar desire towards our divine Benefactor. Our hearts long to offer somewhat to Jesus, distinctly to Jesus Himself. He has gone from us, or we would delight to minister to Him of our substance, to make Him a feast, to furnish Him a chamber, or to wash His feet. How gladly would we lend Him our boat, our colt, our guest chamber, or anything we possess. We would watch His every want, and endeavour to forestall it if He were here ; but He has gone : are we therefore denied the privilege of rendering personal service to Him ? I think not. Let it be our pleasant task now to consider what we can do directly and distinctly *for Him*.

First, we can *adore our Lord*. We can bow at His feet and worship Him as our Lord and our God. We shall do well to exercise our hearts in frequent acts of devotion to the Son of God. I do not mean offering prayers and petitions, excellent as these are, but holy contemplation, meditation, admiration, thanksgiving, and worship of Jesus. Far be it from us to neglect the adoration of any one person of the adorable Trinity in Unity, that were a grievous sin ; but to worship Jesus does not involve forgetfulness of the Father or of the Spirit. Fix your eye on the person of Jesus, view His work on earth, contemplate His holy life and expiatory death. Meditate upon His great love, His dying love, His living love. Follow Him from the tomb to Olivet, and from the mountain's brow to heaven's gate and the right hand of the Father. Pay your homage before His throne, blessing, praising, and adoring Him. We ought not to be satisfied without special acts of personal thanksgiving, in which we exercise our love and reverence for Him who is altogether lovely in our eyes. True, we may be doing nothing for our fellow men while thus occupied, but Jesus is dearer to us than the whole race of men, and it is only His due that we render Him when we bow adoringly at His ever-blessed feet.

Then, brethren, when you have adored Him in secret you should do the like in public by speaking well of Him and extolling Him before others, not so much for their good as for Christ's glory. I must confess I enjoy a sermon best in which I have to speak most of my Beloved. If I have to set Him forth rather than to exhort you, I feel best pleased. There are other things to be done beside, but this is the sweetest task. I love to spend all my preaching time in making Jesus lovely in man's eyes, in lifting Him up on a glorious high throne in the esteem of those who listen to me. Brethren, do this yourselves in your common talk. Make a point of turning the conversation round till it bears on Him. Frequently begin a conversation about Jesus and let men know that you glorify Him. In such special acts of devotion to His person, I pray you abound.

Next, we should *pray for Him*. Do you understand that ? Some do not. The psalmist says, " Prayer also shall be made *for Him* continually." It is very delightful to pray for sinners and pray for saints, but there should be special prayer for Jesus Christ, for the extension of His kingdom, that He may see of the travail of His soul, and that His second advent may speedily arrive. We should pray for the conversion of those who deny His deity, and those who fall into deadly errors as to His substitutionary sacrifice ; we should make earnest supplication for the quickening of the love of Jesus in the hearts of the faithful, and for the turning of the disobedient to the knowledge of the truth. Such prayers should be very frequent with us for His sake, and with an eye to His glory. We pray for this and that, but surely Jesus ought to have a larger measure of our supplications.

Brethren, next to this there should be much *communion with Him*. Methinks I hear some one say, " Is that serving Him ? I call it enjoying Him ! " Yes, I know it is, and you may take it in which way you will, for He says, " If any man serve Me, let him follow Me, and where I am there shall also My servant be." So that you will be sure to be with Him if you serve Him. To be near Him is one of the great essentails of true service. Remember His dying request, " This do in remembrance of Me," and what was that ? Why, it was to observe the Lord's supper, which is the outward and visible sign of communing with Him. If He attaches so much importance to the outward sign, how much more does He value the inner act of fellowship with Himself. The fact is that the head which leans upon His bosom is thereby consecrated to His love, and is rendering Him service. The cheek whereon He imprints the kisses of His mouth is doing Him its best homage while it receives His best favours. Walk not at a distance from Jesus, or ye will grieve Him. Abide in Him, and ye will bring forth fruit to Him.

Let no day pass without a word with Jesus. You are His spouse,—can you live without a loving word from your husband ? You are of His flesh and of His bones,—let unbroken communion be the very habit of your being. Brethren, the Lord's supper is worship rendered to Jesus, and is mainly an act which begins and ends upon Him, you commemorate His death, you set forth His flesh and blood ; your communion and intercourse with Christ are not so much meant to benefit others, as to spend itself upon Him ; therefore attend to it for His sake ; let your eye be fixed upon Him only, and whatever others may think of your raptures and delights in Jesus, however much they may call them emotional and unpractical, do you remain content with having done it unto Him.

Bear with me while I mention other ways in which you may serve Jesus personally. You may do so by *sitting at His feet and learning of Him*, studying the word, and pleading for the Holy Spirit to give you light into its meaning. Martha prepared a feast for Him, and our Lord did not blame her, but He gave Mary the preference who sat at His feet. One in the crowd said concerning Christ, " Blessed is the womb that bare Thee, and the paps that gave Thee suck." To administer to His childhood seemed the highest of earthly favours, but Jesus said, " Yea, rather, blessed are they that hear the word of God, and keep it." Get you that blessing, hear it from His own lips ; study His word, make much of every syllable, try to get at the essential spirit, and do not tarry in the killing letter, and you will then be personally serving Him, for as a teacher He is pleased when we are His attentive pupils. This is a sweet way of pleasing the Lord Christ.

Then, brethren, remember if you would serve Christ personally you must *obey Him*. " Oh," say you, " I did not think that would be a very choice way of serving Him." Listen ! " If ye love Me, keep My commandments." He has chosen obedience as the special pledge and token of our love. You have said, " I wish I could build a chapel, or support a minister or a missionary out of my own purse." I wish you could, but still Jesus has not selected that as the love token, but He has said, " If ye love Me, keep My commandments." Complete, prayerful, habitual obedience to Christ is the very choicest pledge of affection which we can present to our Lord. May infinite mercy help us to present it.

We may do to Christ personal service next by being willing to *bear reproach* for His sake. When you are willing to take upon yourself the defence of a man's character, to throw yourself so completely into him that the reproaches of them that reproach him fall upon you, you have rendered to that man no mean proof of love. Oh, brother, if when they laugh at you for Christ's sake you clap your hands for very glee to be counted worthy to be ridiculed for Him, if you take joyfully the spoiling of your goods, or the slandering of your character, if you know the meaning of this word, " Rejoice ye in that day and leap for joy, for so persecuted they the prophets which were before you," then have you rendered personal service to Him whom you love, and you may sit down and be thankful for having been allowed to drink of His cup and to be baptized with His baptism.

Further, you can show personal kindness to Christ by *caring for His church*. The Lord had forgiven Peter, and Peter no doubt wished to do something to prove his love anew. His Lord somewhat vexed him by three times putting to him the question, "Simon, son of Jonas, lovest thou Me?" and when the disciple had protested his love, the Master said to him, "Feed My sheep," and "Feed My lambs." Go then and teach the little children, and instruct those of riper years. What He has taught you teach you to others, and you will be doing service to Him. He bids you consider it so, for to you who love Him He says, "Feed My sheep."

If you cannot serve with your tongue, there remains another mode of pleasing Jesus. Feed the hungry, clothe the naked, visit the sick, and relieve distress of every kind. "But that is not doing service to Him." I have the best authority for saying that it is, for "Then shall the King say unto them on His right hand, I was an hungred and ye gave me meat, I was thirsty and ye gave me drink. Sick and in prison, and ye visited Me. Inasmuch as ye have done it unto one of the least of these My brethren, ye have done it unto Me." Actual gifts to the poor, and helps afforded to those who need them, are grateful love tokens to the Lord Jesus Christ. Jesus is not here, but His poor saints are. Any saint is an image of Christ, but a poor saint is the express image of Christ; there is a something more about him than about the rich, in which he is even in detail and circumstances more like his Lord. Do ye then to your Lord's own members what ye would have done to Him if He Himself were here.

Still, I think that every now and then for Jesus there ought to be a *little special wastefulness of love*. The woman with her alabaster box of very precious ointment would no doubt gladly have joined with the holy ones who ministered to Him of the substance. I have no doubt she would very gladly have poured water on His feet when He came into the house weary, or she would have waited at the table when He ate. But all this would not have sufficed her ardent love, she wanted to perform an extraordinary act which should be all for Him: she looked out that precious box, she must break that, for she would give Him something which she could not afford to every day, in fact, which she never did attempt to give but once in her life. Brothers and sisters, think of something special you can do for Jesus. Let it cost you something, and if it pinch you, so much the better; it will be sweet to bear a pinch for Him. Think of something that you could not justify in prudence if you had to sit down and talk it over. Do it for Him, not to talk about to others afterwards, nor for others to brazen abroad, but do it for Him: and then if they do publish it you need not be angry, for Jesus said, "Wheresoever this gospel shall be preached in the whole world, there shall also this, that this woman hath done, be told for a memorial of her." Be not ostentatious, but do not be in such a great worry to hide your work for Jesus, for the knowledge of it may do other people good, and lead them to imitate the deed. Still do it unto Jesus only. I cannot suggest what you shall do; and it would be indelicate for me to attempt to do so. Who would think of suggesting to a wife what she should give to her husband as a special private love token. Oh, no! these things are too choice for others to meddle with, they are secrets between the Lord and His elect, suggestions of personal love which cannot come from without. Do you enquire, "What shall I do my Jesus to praise?" Bring forth the choicest that you have, and offer it when your heart is best attuned and readiest for the giving of it. My whole soul thirsts to be often doing this, for I owe all I have and all I am to Jesus, my Lord. Here stands a man before you who has not one single thing in all the world but what he has received from his Lord; who has not a penny but what is lent him, who is clothed by charity and fed by mercy, a pauper by nature, and yet wealthier than a millionaire, because he lives as a gentleman commoner upon the daily bounty of God in Christ Jesus. Here stands before you an unworthy servant of the best of masters, a poor relation of the most generous of householders; happy to be in such a case. Are there other men and women here who owe all to my Lord? If they do, let it be said of them, "Ye serve the Lord Christ." So let it be said of them while they live, and till they die: what better can they desire? For myself, I am resolved by divine grace more fully to yield my whole body, soul, and spirit to Him whose I am, whom I serve. Grace be with you. Amen.

DEGREES OF POWER ATTENDING THE GOSPEL

"For our gospel came not unto you in word only, but also in power, and in the Holy Ghost, and in much assurance; as ye know what manner of men we were among you for your sake.—1 Thessalonians i. 5.

PAUL here claimed two things which are absolutely necessary to success in the Christian ministry. He could call the gospel "*our* gospel," and this is a foremost essential in a sent servant of Jesus Christ. Paul, Silas, and Timothy, here speaking at once, declare the words which they had preached to be their own in a peculiar sense: every true minister must be able to do the same; we must ourselves have been saved before we preach salvation. "I believed, therefore have I spoken," says the Psalmist; "we also believe, and therefore speak," say the whole college of the apostles. Without faith, the religious teacher is a mere pretender unworthy of respect. The Christian minister must, however, not only believe the truth of what he asserts, but he must experimentally enjoy it. The husbandman that laboureth must himself also first be partaker of the fruit. Before Ezekiel delivered to the people the prophecies which were written in the roll, the voice came to him, "Son of man, eat this roll"; and he did not only take it into his mouth, where it was like honey for sweetness, but it descended even into his bowels, and mingled with his innermost self. We must ourselves feel the weight of that burden of the Lord which we proclaim to others, or we shall not be ministers of the apostolic sort, but rather shall be descendants of the hypocritical Pharisees who bound heavy burdens, grievous to be borne, upon other men's shoulders, but were not willing to touch them with so much as one of their fingers. The apostle Paul could with peculiar propriety call the gospel his own ; on the road to Damascus he had singularly experienced its mighty power ; and afterwards, in trials oft, in difficulties many, in experiences varied, in temptations furious, he had made each truth of Scripture his own by having tasted its sweetness, handled its strength, proved its comfort, and tried its power. Do not think of preaching, young man, until you have truth written on your very soul ; as well think of steering the *Great Eastern* across the ocean without knowing the first principles of navigation ; as well think of setting up as an ambassador without your country's sanction, as to dare to intrude yourself into the Christian ministry unless the gospel is first your *own*. No amount of training at Oxford, or Cambridge, or anywhere else, no extent of classical or mathematical teaching can ever make you a minister of Jesus Christ, if you lack the first necessary, namely, a personal interest in salvation by Jesus Christ. What! will you profess to be a physician, while the leprosy is on your own brow ? Will you attempt to stand between the living and the dead when you are yourself devoid of spiritual life ? The priests of old were touched with the blood upon the thumb, the toe, and the ear, to show that they were consecrated everywhere ; and none among us must dare to exercise any office for God among His people till first of all we know the cleansing, quickening, refining, sanctifying power of the blood of the Lord Jesus Christ. It must be *our* gospel before we may so much as think of aspiring to the high and holy office of the gospel ministry. But this alone is not sufficient. The Christian minister, if he would imitate Paul, must be very careful of *his manner of life among the people*. He must be able to say without blushing, " Ye know what manner of men we were among you for your sake." Unselfishness must be our prominent attribute, all must be done for our people's sake ; and then, we must in our lives show the truthfulness of our unselfish professions. O God, how much of grace is wanted that Thy servants may be clear of the blood of all men and make full proof of their ministry. We are not appointed to stand as motionless way-posts to point the way with lifeless accuracy and unsympathizing coldness ; this many have done, and while showing the road have never moved one inch in it themselves : such men shall have terrible judgment at the last. We are appointed to be guides to the pilgrims over the hills of life, and we are bound to attend their footsteps and tread the road ourselves ; clambering up every hill of difficulty and descending every valley of humiliation, crying to the pilgrim band, " Be ye followers of us, even as we are followers of Christ Jesus." It is not for us to say, " Go! " but " Come! " We are not to bid you *do* without first doing ourselves. It is an ill time with the preacher when he is compelled to say, " Do as I say, and not as I do ; " for evil practice will drown the best of preaching. Oh! that holy living, intense earnestness, passionate longing for souls, vehement importunity in prayer, humility and sincerity, may so blend together in our walk and conversation, that having the gospel to be our own, we may be fully fitted for the work of the Christian ministry " for your sake," that you who hear us may not find us unprofitable in the day of the Lord Jesus Christ.

Having said thus much upon the ministry itself, we observe that our text deals mainly with the hearers, and therefore has a voice for you. We shall use the text for two purposes : first, by way of *discrimination ;* and, secondly, for *instruction.*

I. The text suggests, and very strongly too, a thoroughly heart-searching DISCRIMINATION, a mode of testing ourselves by which our election may be proved, or our unregeneracy discovered.

The gospel comes to all who hear it. In our own land, especially among you who constantly attend places of worship, it comes to you all. If I understand Scripture aright, it is the same gospel which comes to the unregenerate as to the regenerate ; and though in some it be " a savour of death unto death," and in others " a savour of life unto life," yet the distinction is not in the gospel but in the way in which it is received or rejected. Some of our brethren who are very anxious to carry out the decrees of God, instead of believing that God can carry them out Himself, always try to make distinctions in their preachings, giving one gospel to one set of sinners, and another to a different class. They are very unlike the old sowers, who, when they went out to sow, sowed among thorns, and on stony places, and by the way-side ; but these brethren, with profounder wisdom, endeavour to find out which is the good ground, and they will insist upon it that not so much as a single handful of invitations may be cast anywhere but on the prepared soil. They are much too wise to preach the gospel in Ezekiel's fashion to the dry bones in the valley while they are yet dead ; they withhold any word of gospel till there is a little quivering of life among the bones, and then they commence operations. They do not think it to be their duty to go into the highways and hedges and bid all, as many as they find, to come to the supper. Oh, no! They are too orthodox to obey the Master's will ; they desire to understand first who are appointed to come to the supper, and then they will invite them ; that is to say, they will do what there is no necessity to do. They have not faith enough, or enough subjugation of will to the supreme commands of the great Master, to do that which only faith dare do, namely, tell the dry bones to live, bid the man with the withered hand stretch out his arm, and speak to him that is sick of palsy, and tell him to take up his bed and walk. It strikes me that refusing to set forth Jesus to all men of every character, and refraining from inviting them to come to Him, is a great mistake. I do not find David suiting his counsels to the ability of men. David gives commands to ungodly men. " Be wise, therefore, O ye kings ; be instructed, ye judges of the earth. Kiss the Son, lest He be angry, and ye perish from the way, while His wrath is kindled but a little." He did not withhold his exhortation because they were such rebels that they would not and could not kiss the king. No! but he told them to do it, whether they could or not. So with the prophets. They boldly say, " Wash you! make you clean! Put away the evil of your doings from before mine eyes ; cease to do evil, learn to do well." One of them absolutely cries, " Make you a new heart and a new spirit," Ezek. xviii. 31 ; and yet, I doubt not, that he was perfectly agreed with that other prophet, who taught the powerlessness of man in those two memorable questions, " Can the Ethiopian change his skin, or the leopard his spots ? " These men did not think that they were to judge of what they were to preach by the degree of power in the hearers ; but they judged by the power which dwells in their God to make the word effectual. As it was with prophets, so was it with apostles ; for Peter cried to the crowd who gathered about the Beautiful Gate of the temple, " Repent ye, therefore and be converted, that your sins may be blotted out." They delivered *the* gospel, the same gospel, to the dead as to the living, the same gospel to the non-elect as to the elect. The point of distinction is not in the gospel, but in its being applied by the Holy Spirit, or left to be rejected of man. The same gospel, it strikes me in the text, came to all, and the point of distinction was farther on, namely, in the operation of that gospel upon the heart.

1. It appears then, in the first place, that to some the gospel comes only *in word*. Even here there are gradations. To some it only comes in word in this fashion, that *they scarcely know what it is all about*. Some of you go to a place of worship because it is a right thing, and you sit down on the seats and sit out an hour-and-a-half or so of penance. When that is done you feel you have performed a very proper act, but you do not know what the talk was all about. It may be said of you, that hearing, you do not hear, for your ears are dull and heavy. You know no more of the divine mind than the men who were with Saul on the road to Damascus, who heard a voice but saw no man. I believe a very large majority of church-goers know no more of what the preaching is about than did Jonathan's lad when he ran after the arrows ; their flight David well understood, " but the lad knew nothing of the matter." Too many are merely the stolid, unthinking slumbering worshippers of an unknown God. In others the word comes in a little better sense, but still in word only. They have it, and *they understand it in theory*, and probably are much pleased with it, especially if it be delivered in a manner which suits their taste, or which commends itself to their understandings. They hear and they do not quite forget. They remember, and are gratified with illustrations, doctrinal truths, and so on : but when you have said that you have said all. The gospel remains in them as certain potent drugs remain in the chemist's drawers, they are there but they produce no effect. The gospel comes to them as an unloaded cannon rumbles into its shed, or as a barrel of gunpowder is rolled into the magazine ; there is no force in it because the fire of God's Spirit is absent. The preacher lashes the air and whips the water, woos the wind, and invites the cloud when he preaches to such as these. They hear, but hear in vain, insensible as steel. To others it comes in a preferable manner, but still only in word. *They are really effected by it ;* the tears stream down their cheeks ; they scarcely know how to sit ; they resolve, if they once get home, they will pray ; they think of amending their lives ; past follies and present dangers come before them, and they are somewhat alarmed ; but the morning cloud is not more fleeting, and the early dew vanishes not sooner than these good things of theirs. They look at their natural face in the glass of the word, but they go away to forget what manner of men they are ; because the emotion felt is produced by the words, and not by the spirit and life of the truth. Why, brethren, men weep at a theatre, and weep far more there than they do in many places of worship ; therefore, merely to weep under a sermon is no sign of having derived profit therefrom. Some of my brethren are very great hands at unearthing the dead, conducting you to the funeral urns of your parents, or reminding you of your departed little ones, and possibly they may be the means of introducing better feelings by this kind of working upon your emotions ; but I am not sure of it—I am afraid that much of the holy water which is spilt from human eyes in our places of worship, is not much more valuable than the holy water at the doors of the Catholic chapels. It is mere eye-water after all, and not heart sorrow. Mere excitement produced by oratory is the world's weapon in attaining its end ; we want something more than that for spiritual purposes : if we could " speak with the tongues of men and of angels," and stir you up to as great an enthusiasm as ever Demosthenes wrought in the Greeks of old, all that would avail nothing if it were only the effect of the preacher's impassioned language and telling manner—the gospel would have come to you " in word only " ; and that which is born of the flesh is flesh, and nothing more.

At this point I may very solemnly ask whether it is not true of some who compose the present congregation that you know the truth only *in word ?* There is a certain class of persons, and some of them are present this morning, who are professional sermon-hearers ; you go one Sunday to hear Mr. A., and then another Sunday to hear Mr. B., and you carry with you your saccharometers—instruments for measuring the quantity of sweetness in each sermon—and you take a gauge of the style and matter of the preacher ; you estimate what blunders he makes, and wherein he could be improved, and you compare or contrast him with somebody else, as if you were tea-factors tasting Souchong and Bohea, or cheesemongers trying Cheddar and American. Some individuals of this order are little better than spiritual vagabonds, without settled habitation or occupation ; who go about from place to place, listening to this and to that, and getting no good whatever ; while as to doing good, the thought never enters their brain. You cannot expect that the gospel will come to you in anything else but as a killing letter, for you go to hear it as merely words. You do not look for fruit : if you see leaves you are quite satisfied. You do not desire a blessing ; if you did, you would receive it. It is at once one of the most wicked and one of the most foolish habits to waste our time in constantly criticising God's word and God's ministers. Well said George Herbert, " Judge not the preacher, he is thy judge." What has thou to do to say of God's ambassador, that his words were not well mouthed ? If God speak by him, God knows who is best to speak for Him ; and if his Master sent the man, beware lest you ill-treat him, lest thou suffer like them of old who ill-treated the ambassadors of David, and drove him to proclaim war against them.

2. According to the text, *there are others to whom the word comes with three accompaniments.* The apostle speaks of " power " and " the Holy Ghost," and " much assurance." I do not think that the word of God comes to many people with all these three things. It comes to a very numerous class with " power " ; to a smaller number with " power

and the Holy Ghost "; to an inner circle of select ones " in the Holy Ghost and in much assurance."

If I have the meaning of this passage, and I am not so certain about it as to dogmatize, it strikes me that there are three degrees of effect produced by the gospel. At any rate, we shall not be wrong in saying that there is sometimes an effect produced by the gospel which may be called " *power*," but which, nevertheless, is not the power which saves. To many of you, my dear hearers, the word of our gospel has come with power upon your *understandings*. You have heard it, weighed it, judged it, and received it as being true and of divine authority. Your understanding has assented to the various propositions which we have proclaimed as doctrines of Christ. You feel that you could not well do otherwise ; these truths agree so well, and are so adapted at once to the ruin of your nature and to its best aspirations, that you do not kick as some do against it. You have been convinced of the authenticity and authority of the gospel by the gospel. Perhaps you have never read " Paley's Evidences," and never studied " Butler's Analogy," but the gospel itself has come to you with sufficient power to be its own witness to you, and your understanding joyfully acknowledges that this is the word of God, and you receive it as such. It has done more than that, it has come with power to the *conscience* of some of you. It has convinced you of sin. You feel now that self-righteousness on your part is folly, and though you may indulge in self-righteousness, yet it is with your eyes open. You do not sin now so cheaply as you once did, for you know a little of the sinfulness of sin. Moreover, you have had some alarms with regard to the ultimate end of sin. The gospel has made you know that the wages of sin will be death. You feel that you cannot dwell with everlasting burnings. Your heart is ill at ease when you think upon the wrath to come. Like Felix, you tremble when you are reasoned with concerning " righteousness and judgment to come," and though you have put it off as yet, and have said, " Go thy way till I have a more convenient season," yet it has come to you so far with a degree of power. More than this, it has had an effect upon your *feelings* as well as upon your conscience. Your desires have been awakened. You have sometimes said, " Oh that I were saved." You have advanced as far at any rate as Balaam, When he said, " Let me die the death of the righteous." Your feelings of hope are excited : you hope that yet you may lay hold of eternal life, and your fears are not altogether dead : you tremble when under the word of God. Natural emotions which look like spiritual ones have been produced in you by the hearing of the word, though as yet the gospel has not come with the Holy Ghost. Beyond all this, the gospel has come with power to some of you *on your lives*. I can look with anxious pleasure upon some of you, because I know the gospel has done you much good though it has not saved you ; though alas ! there are others to whom it has only been for a time as a bit and bridle, but they have afterwards turned aside from it. There are those here who, like the dog, have gone back to their vomit, and, like the sow that was washed, to their wallowing in the mire. We had hope for you once, but we must almost cease to hope. Certain persons rush into drunkenness, after seasons of abstinence, having known the evil of the sin, and having professed to hate it ; the passion has been too strong for them, and they have fallen

again into that deep ditch in which so many of the abhorred of the Lord lie and rot. Oh, may God, in His infinite mercy, bring the gospel with something more than this common power to your souls ! May it come with " the Holy Ghost " as well as with power.

You see we have come up by gradations to some considerable height already, but we now come to a far nobler elevation and speak of saving grace. To many in this house, as at Thessalonica, the word has come " *in the Holy Ghost*." Brethren, I cannot describe to you how it is that the Holy Ghost operates by the word. The work of the Spirit is figured forth by some such mysterious thing as a birth, or as the blowing of the wind. It is a great secret, and therefore not to be expounded. but many of you know its experimentally. The Holy Ghost first of all came to you as a great *quickener*. How He made you live you do not know, but this you know, that what you had not once you now have ; that there burns within you a vital spark of heavenly flame far different from that ordinary spark of life which had been there heretofore. You have now, different feelings, different joys, different sorrows from any you were conscious of before ; because, while you were listening to the letter which killeth, the Spirit of God came with it, and the quickening Spirit made you live with a new, higher, and more blessed life. You have within you Jesus Christ, who is life and immortality. You have heaven begun within your heart. You have passed from death unto life, and shall never come into condemnation. To you the word of God then has come with the Holy Ghost in a quickening sense. Then it entered with an *illuminating* power. It enlightened you as to your sins. What blackness you discovered in your sins when the Holy Spirit once cast a light upon them. Brethren, you had no idea that you were such sinners as you turned out to be. The Holy Ghost startled and astonished you with revelations of that great and fathomless depth of depravity which you found to be surging within your souls. You were alarmed, humbled, cast into the dust. You began, perhaps, to despair, but then the same illumination of the Spirit came in to comfort you, for He then showed you Christ Jesus, the unbounded power of His blood to take away your unbounded sins, His willingness to receive you just as you were, His suitability to your case and to your circumstances ; and as soon as you saw Jesus in the light of the Holy Ghost you looked unto Him and were lightened, and henceforth your face has never been ashamed. So the Spirit of God came to you as light, to dispel your darkness, and give you joy and peace. Since that time you have experienced the Holy Spirit as *comforting* you. Amidst darkest shades He has risen as the sunlight upon your souls. Your burdens have been removed by Him, the blessed Paraclete ! He has brought Christ and the things of Christ to your remembrance. He has opened up to you precious promises. He has cracked the shell and given you to partake of the kernel of the privilege of the covenant of grace. He has broken the bone and satisfied you with marrow and fatness out of the deep things of God. His dove-like wings, whenever they brood over you, bring order out of confusion, and yield kindly comfort in the midst of sorest adversity. You have also felt the Holy Spirit in His *inflaming* energies. He has rested on you when you have heard the word, as the spirit of burning ;

your sin has been consumed by the holy revenge which you felt against it. You have been led to great heights of love to Christ, till you could sing,

> " Had I ten thousand thousand tongues,
> Not one should silent be ;
> Had I ten thousand thousand hearts,
> I'd give them all to Thee."

When the Holy Ghost has blessed the word, your heart has been like the alter of incense with the flame always burning, and a sweet perfume going up, acceptable to the Most High. Beloved, you have also felt the Holy Ghost with the word as a spirit of *rejoicing.* Oh ! the bliss we have sometimes tasted ! I am very frequently heavy in spirit, but oh ! the raptures which my heart has known when the Holy Ghost has shown me my eternal election of God, my standing in Christ Jesus, my completeness and acceptance in the Beloved, my security through the faithfulness of the eternal God. What delights come streaming into the soul when you read of everlasting love, of faithfulness never wavering, of affection never changing, of a purpose standing fast as pillars of brass and firm as the eternal hills. And oh, beloved, what extravagance I was about to say, of joy do we sometimes feel in anticipation of the glory to be revealed. Looking from Nebo's brow we see the landscape down below, but, better than Moses could do, we drink already of the rivers which flow with milk and honey, and pluck ripe fruits from celestial trees. While in communion with Christ Jesus we get the best ante-past of the glory that remaineth. Now this it is to receive the word " in the Holy Ghost." Beloved, I hope we know what this means, and you who do not know it, may a prayer go up from every living soul here, " Lord, let the Holy Spirit go with the preaching of Jesus Christ, and let it be made effectual unto salvation."

Beloved, the highest point in the text is " *much assurance.*" If I understand the passage, it means this : first, that they were fully persuaded of its truthfulness, and had no staggering or blinding doubts about it ; and secondly, that they had the fullest possible conviction of their interest in the truth delivered to them. They were saved, but better still, they knew that they were so. They were clean, but better still, they rejoiced in their purity. They were in Christ, but what is more joyous still, they knew that they were in Christ. They had no doubts as some of you have, no dark suspicions ; the word had come with such blessed demonstration that it had swept every Canaanitish doubt clean out of their hearts. According to Poole, the Greek word here used has in it the idea of a ship at full sail, undisturbed by the waves which ripple in its way. A ship, when the wind is thoroughly favourable, and its full sails are bearing it directly into harbour, is not held back by the surging billows. True, the vessel may rock, but it neither turns to the right hand, nor to the left. Let the billows be as they may, the wind is sufficiently powerful to overcome their contrary motion, and the vessel goes right straight ahead. Some Christians get the gospel in that way. They have not a shadow of a doubt about its being true. They have not even the beginning of a doubt about their interest in it, and therefore they have nothing to do, but with God's strong hand upon the tiller, and the heavenly wind blowing right into the sail, to go right straight on, doing the will of God, glorifying His name. May the

word come to you, dear friends, as it does to so very few ! may it come in " full assurance," as well as in " power," and in " the Holy Ghost ! "

3. I shall leave this first head of the text, when I observe that *this is the way in which God's elect are known.* The apostle says, " Knowing, brethren, beloved, your election of God." Why ? Knowing it not by making a guess about it ; not by questioning you whether you are awakened sinners, whether you are sensible or insensible sinners ; not by waiting to preach the gospel to you when you are prepared to receive the gospel ; but we preached the gospel to you as you were, and we found out who were the elect by this, that the elect of God received the gospel as it came, " in power and in the Holy Ghost, and in much assurance." This is the test of election, the Holy Ghost blessing the word ; and, dear friends, if the Holy Ghost has blessed it to you, you need not want to turn over the mysterious pages of the divine decrees, for your name is there. You have not *my* word for it, but *God's* word for it. He would not have brought you to feel the indwelling life of the Holy Spirit, if He had not from before all worlds ordained you unto eternal life. But, mark you, and this, observe, comes from the ensuing context, *you must give good proof that it is so,* or we cannot say, and even the apostle could not have said, " Knowing, brethren beloved, your election of God." We cannot tell whether the word has come to you in the Holy Ghost, and in much assurance, unless there are the corresponding results. Listen to these words : " And ye became followers of us, and of the Lord, having received the word in much affliction, with joy of the Holy Ghost : so that ye were ensamples to all that believe in Macedonia and Achaia. For from you sounded out the word of the Lord not only in Macedonia and Achaia, but also in every place your faith to God-ward is spread abroad ; so that we need not to speak anything. For they themselves show of us what manner of entering in we had unto you, and how ye turned to God from idols to serve the living and true God ; and to wait for His Son from heaven, whom he raised from the dead, even Jesus, which delivered us from the wrath to come." So you see an imitation of apostolical example, a faith which becomes so known as to sound abroad, a joy which affliction itself cannot damp, and a perseverance which is not to be turned aside by difficulties, a conversion which gives up the dearest idols, and binds us to Christ, and makes us watch and wait for Him—all these are necessary as proofs of the Holy Ghost having been with the word. O beloved, I would have you, the members of this congregation, not only converted, but so converted that there should be no doubt about it. I would love to have you not only Christians, but such fruit-bearing Christians, that it will be to a demonstration certain that you have received the word " in much assurance." Then shall it be equally clear that you are the elect of God. May the Lord grant that the word here may ever be like a powerful magnet thrust into a heap of steel-filings and of ashes, which shall attract all the filings and bring them out. For that is what the gospel is to do—it is to discern between the precious and the vile ; it is to be God's winnowing-fan to separate His elect from those who are left in their ruin ; and it only can do this by the way in which it is received, proving the election of those who receive it " in the Holy Ghost." Thus much by way of discrimination.

II. Have patience for a few minutes only while

we now use the text by way of PRACTICAL INSTRUC-
TION.

It is clear from the text, by way of practical
instruction, that it is not enough to preach the gospel.
Something more is wanted for the conversion of souls
than even that. I have stirred you up very often to
assist me, dear brethren, in training those of our young
men who have been called to preach the gospel, that
they may be more efficient in their ministry, and you
have kindly helped me. But we must ever bear in
mind that though God should privilege us to send out
hundreds of His ministering servants, yet there will
not be a solitary case of conversion wrought by them
alone. We wish to do our best to erect fresh places of
worship for this ever increasing city, and it is a happy
day to me whenever I see the topstone brought out of
a new House of Prayer ; but not one single soul shall
ever be made to rejoice in Christ Jesus by the mere
fact of a place of worship being erected, or of worship
being celebrated therein. We *must* have the energy
of the Holy Ghost. There is the one all important
matter. What is there practical about this ? Why,
then *it becomes more and more imperatively necessary
that we should be much in prayer* to God that the Holy
Ghost would come. We have the spirit of prayerfulness among us as a church. Let me earnestly
entreat you never to lose it. There are certain of
my brethren and sisters here who are never absent
from our great gathering on Monday evening, and
whose prayers have brought down many blessings ;
but it is the part of fidelity for me to say that there are
some of you who might be here if you would, who
seldom favour us with your presence, or let me say,
seldom do yourselves the happiness of waiting upon
God in prayer meetings. You are not the best of our
members ; you will never be the best of them if you
stay away without having a justifiable excuse. I do
not say this to those who I know must be absent ;
and I do not say it to bring women out who ought to
be seeing to their husbands, or to bring men out who
ought to be attending to their shops ; but I say it to
some who might as well be here as not, and would bring
no detriment to themselves whatever by being here :
and I must qualify what I say with this, that I have
less to complain of in this respect than any man in
Christendom, for there is no place that I ever knew or
heard of where the prayer meeting bears so good and
fair a proportion to the Sunday gathering as it does
here. But still, brethren, we want you all to pray.
I would I could see you all ! Oh ! it were a happy
day if we could see this place full on Monday evening.
I do not know why it should not be. It strikes me
that if your hearts were once to get thoroughly warmed
we should fill this house for prayer. And what a
blessing we might expect to receive ! Why, we have
had such a blessing already that we have not room
enough to receive it now ; but still, as the cup begins
to run over, let it run over and over ; there are many
churches in this neighbourhood that can catch the
runnings-over, and may they be profited thereby.
Let us increase our prayings as we increase our
doing. I like that of Martin Luther, when he says,
" I have so much business to do to-day, that I shall
not be able to get through it with less than three
hours' prayer." Now most people would say, " I have
so much business to do to-day that I must only have
three minutes' prayer ; I cannot afford the time."
But Luther thought that the more he had to do the
more he must pray, or else he could not get through
it. That is a blessed kind of logic : may we understand it ! " Praying and provender, hinder no man's
journey." If ye have to stop and pray, it is no more
an hindrance than when the rider has to stop at the
farrier's to have his horse's shoe fastened, for if he
went on without attending to that it may be that ere
long he would come to a stop of a far more serious kind.

Let us learn from the text *our own indebtedness to
to distinguishing and sovereign grace.* You observe,
beloved, that the gospel does not come with the power
of the Holy Ghost to everybody. If, then, it has
come to us, what shall we do but bless and praise the
distinguishing grace which made it so to come to us.
You observe that the distinction was not in the
persons themselves, it was in the way in which the
gospel came. The distinction was not even in the
gospel, but in the attendant Spirit making it effectual.
If you have heard the word with power, it was not,
dear brethren, because you were more ready, because
you were less inclined to sin, or more friendly towards
God. You were an alien, a strange, a foreigner, an
enemy ; you were " dead in trespasses and sins,"
even as others were and are. There was in you,
whatever Papists may say, no grace of congruity to
meet with the grace of Christ. They say that there is
something in man congruous to the grace of God, so
that when saving grace comes to those who have the
grace of congruity they are saved. In me I know
everything was incongruous, everything contrary to
God. There was darkness, and light came ; there
was death, and life entered ; there was hatred, and
love drove it out ; there was the dominion of Satan,
and Christ overcame the traitor.

" Then give all the glory to His holy name,
  To Him all the glory belongs ;
  Be yours the high joy still to sound forth His name,
  And praise Him in each of your songs."

A third practical lesson we will but hint at,
namely, we see that *there are degrees of attainment
even among those who have received the word with
the Holy Ghost. Let us seek for the very highest
degree.* You are not generally satisfied with the bare
necessaries of life, you desire to possess its comforts
and luxuries. I will commend you if you carry this
into spiritual things. Do not be content merely to be
saved, merely to be spiritually alive ; ask to be valiant
for truth. I should feel it a great honour, I hope, to
be the commonest soldier, if called upon to defend my
country, but I must confess I should not like to be in
the ranks always. I should like at least be made a
corporal very soon, and a sergeant as soon as possible ;
and I should grumble wonderfully much if I could
not rise to rank among the commissioned officers.
I should like to be found doing my very best, and I
would reach to the most prominent position if I
might therein serve my country better than in the
ranks. So I think it should be with the Christian.
He is not to seek for honour among men, but, if he can
by getting more grace be more serviceable to his
God and bring more honour to His name; why let him
press forward: Ah, my dear brethren, what business
have you to be sitting still and saying, " It is enough."
The " rest-and-be-thankful " policy is not much
approved of in politics, and in religion it will never
answer. On ! Forward ! Upward ! As the eagle
takes for its motto, " Superior," and still mounts
higher, and higher, and higher, till the young wing
which first trembled at the height has grown into the
strong pinion which makes him companion of the sun
and playmate with the lightnings, so let the Christian

do. If he has learned to "run and not be weary," let him seek to "mount up as on the wings of eagles." Onward, fellow-soldier! Be thou yet more valiant till thy name be written among the first three.

To close, does not this text, as a last practical lesson, show us indirectly *how a privilege may become a curse*? The word of God has come to you all. I suppose there is not one here who has not heard the story of the love of God in Christ Jesus. You have been told many times, that though man has fallen, and offended God, yet the Lord has set forth His suffering Son, Christ Jesus, to be a propitiation for sin, and that through faith in His name, "Whosoever believeth on Him shall never perish." You have been told that God waiteth to be gracious, and that whosoever looks to Christ shall live, whosoever calleth upon the Lord shall be saved. Now, having heard this, whatever some may tell you, we feel bound as in the sight of God, to warn you that if this comes "in word only" to you, it will increase your condemnation. Certain preachers think that the word is not "a savour of death unto death" to any, but it is, it is. Whatever their theories, whatever hyper-Calvinistic theology may say, it is God's word, that it shall be more tolerable for Tyre and Sidon in the day of judgment than it shall be for cities like Capernaum and Bethsaida, which heard the word, and yet repented not. You are not machines ; you are not creatures merely to be acted upon, your are to act as well as to be moved ; and every good word that reaches your ear is written down as a debt against you. There is no declaration of the gospel of Jesus Christ which, if refused, does not leave you more disobedient than you were. Remember how the apostle words it : "Unto them which be disobedient, the stone which the builders disallowed, the same is made the head of the corner, and a stone of stumbling, and a rock of offence, even to them which stumble at the word, being disobedient : whereunto also they were appointed." Now they could not have been disobedient if it was not their duty to obey. No man is disobedient where there is no law. It is, therefore, the duty of every sinner hearing the gospel to believe it, and if he does not, this same stone shall fall upon him and shall grind him to powder. Kiss the Son, therefore, lest He, lest *He* be angry, and ye perish from the way while His wrath is kindled but a little. The same Saviour who blesses will be angry. He who loves His people, grows angry with those who reject Him ; and when His wrath is kindled but a little, woe unto the object of it ! Blessed are all they that trust in Him, and may we be found among that blessed number to the praise and glory of *His* grace, wherein He maketh us to differ according to the appointment of His own divine will. May God bless this assembly for Jesus Christ's sake. Amen.

SOUNDING OUT THE WORD OF THE LORD

"For from you sounded out the word of the Lord not only in Macedonia and Achaia, but also in every place your faith to God-ward is spread abroad ; so that we need not to speak anything."—1 Thessalonians i. 8.

PAUL went to Thessalonica from Philippi with a sore back, but with a sound heart. He went resolved to spend and to be spent for his Lord in that city. On the first three Sabbaths he spake to the Jews in the synagogue, but he soon found that they were obstinately resolved to reject Jesus of Nazareth as the Messiah ; and therefore he directed his attention to the heathen of Thessalonica, and among them he had wonderful success. Large numbers of persons, some of honourable rank, turned from their idols to worship the living God, and he soon gathered about him an enthusiastic people. During his stay at Thessalonica, he pretty nearly wore himself out ; for he had determined that he would accept no help from the people, who appear to have been in great straits at that time. He toiled night and day at his trade of tent-making, and even then could not earn sufficient, and might have failed to maintain existence had not the believers at Philippi sent once and again to assist him. Thus, being affectionately desirous of winning them to Jesus, the apostle was willing to have given unto them, not the gospel of God only, but even his own life. The Lord accepted the cheerful sacrifice, and gave the apostle the reward he sought. The Thessalonians not only received the word with joy of the Holy Ghost, but became zealous in making it known. Their intensity of faith helped to spread the gospel, for their lives were notably affected by it ; and for their earnestness and godliness, they were everywhere talked of. Living in a trading town, to which many went, and from which many came, their singular devotion to the faith of the Lord Jesus became the theme of conversation all over Greece ; and thus enquiry was promoted, and the gospel was sounded out far and wide. In their case, learners speedily because teachers. The Lord Jesus had thus not only given them to drink, but He had made them into a well overflowing, to refresh the thirst of thousands. They had heard the gospel trumpet, and now they had become trumpeters themselves. In their lives the echoes of Paul's preaching were preserved. This was a very happy circumstance for the tried apostle, and greatly cheered his spirit.

These Thessalonians must have been specially gracious people for Paul to praise them so heartily. "As the fining-pot for silver, and the furnace for gold ; so is a man to his praise." Many can bear slander better than they could endure praise. Many, when commended, become puffed up ; but the Thessalonians were in such a happy spiritual condition that Paul could safely speak of them as "ensamples to all that believe in Macedonia and Achaia." That praise was all the more precious because it was not indiscriminate—"not laid on with a trowel," as the proverb puts it. The Thessalonians had faulty ones among them. The best church that ever existed has had in it imperfect members ; and the very virtues of the Thessalonians carried them into certain faults. They were notable for their expectation of the coming of the Lord, and certain of them became fanatical, and ceased from work, because of the speedy approach of the last day. The apostle was obliged to talk to them about this in his two epistles, and even to lay down the rule very strongly—"If any man will not work, neither let him eat." Under whatever pretence men might cease from their daily callings, they were not to be maintained by their brethren. These good people were too ready to be deceived by idle rumours of coming wonders. Even the Thessalonian church had its spots. But, then, there are spots on the sun, and yet we do not speak of it as a dark body, since its light so much preponderates. Grave faults in the Thessalonian church did not prevent our honest apostle from awarding praise where praise was due. When a man is sound at heart, praise does not become an intoxicating wine, but an invigorating tonic. Feeling a modest fear that he does not deserve the warm commendation, the good man is anxious to live up to the character imputed to him. This will be the case, however, only with those whose spiritual life is vigorous.

I entreat you, dear friends, practically to learn from these Thessalonians, by being led to imitate them. May it be truly said of us also, " From you sounded out the word of the Lord ! " It is true even now in a measure ; may it be far more so ! The expression to which I would call your attention is this—" From you *sounded out* the word of the Lord." It reminds us of a trumpet and its far-sounding notes. Having heard the gospel sounding within, they in return sounded it out.

First, let us carefully look at *the trumpeters*. What sort of men are these who make God's word to sound out ? When we have talked about the men, we will look at *their trumpets*, and see how it is that they give forth so telling a sound. Next, we will speak of the need of *such a trumpet-blast just now ;* and close by enquiring *whether we are not called to give forth that trumpet-sound ?*

I. We begin by looking at THE TRUMPETERS. Who are these by whom the word of the Lord is sounded out ? I shall hastily give you a picture of these Thessalonians drawn from Paul's letters to them.

Observe, at the outset, that *they were a people in whom the three cardinal graces were conspicuous.* Kindly look at the third verse : " Remembering without ceasing your work of faith, and labour of love, and patience of hope." The three divine sisters—Faith, Hope, Love—linked hands in their lives. These were with them in their best condition— faith working, love labouring, hope enduring. Faith without works is dead ; faith performing her work with energy is healthily alive. Paul saw the Thessalonian believers to be fulfilling the life-work of a true faith. Nor was faith left to work alone ; but at her right hand was love, sweetening and brightening all. Their love did not consist in words, or in mere amiability of temper ; but it wrought with a will. They threw their whole hearts into the cause of God ; they loved Jesus, and rapturously waited for His appearing ; they loved one another, and shared the sufferings of their leaders in the time of persecution. They exhibited a labour of love : it was not work only, but in intensity it deserved to be called " labour." As for hope—that bright-eyed grace, which looks within the veil, and realizes things not seen as yet— it was peculiarly their endowment—this enabled them to bear with patience their suffering for Christ, whether it lay in false accusation, or in the spoiling of their goods. Thus of them it could be said, " Now abideth faith, hope, charity, these three." Brethren, it is of no use for us to attempt to sound out the word of the Lord, if we have not the spiritual voice-power, which lies in those three graces, which are of first importance. Those precious truths, which faith believes, which love delights in, which hope relies

upon—these are the truths we shall diligently make known. We believe, and therefore speak ; we love, and therefore testify ; we hope, and therefore make known.

Next, I note in these Thessalonian believers, that they were *a people whose election was clear.* Read the fourth verse :—" Knowing, brethren beloved, your election of God." Paul said the same of them in the second epistle (ii. 13) : " We are bound to give thanks alway to God for you, brethren beloved of the Lord, because God hath from the beginning chosen you to salvation, through sanctification of the Spirit and belief of the truth." They were not ashamed to believe the doctrine of election, as some professors are. They rejoiced in having been chosen of God from the beginning. They saw the practical nature of the election, for they perceived that they were chosen unto sanctification. Their lives were such as to prove that they were the Lord's chosen men, for they became choice men. They gave evidence of the secret choice of God by their holy lives. This, I hope, is true of us as a people : we are old-fashioned enough to rejoice in the electing love of God, and free grace has a sweet sound to our ears. If it be so, we ought to bring forth fruits worthy of it. Gratitude for sovereign grace and eternal love should operate upon us mightily. Let the slaves of law go to their tasks with a lash at their backs ; but the chosen of God will serve Him with delight, and do ten times more from love than others from hope of wage. None can show forth the praises of God like those who taste His special love, and know the unutterable sweetness of it.

These trumpeters *had received the word of God themselves in much assurance, and with much power.* Note the fifth verse : " For our gospel came not unto you in word only, but also in power, and in the Holy Ghost, and in much assurance." The apostle also says, in the thirteenth verse of the second chapter, " For this cause also thank we God without ceasing, because, when ye received the word of God which ye heard of us, ye received it not as the word of men, but as it is in truth, the word of God, which effectually worketh also in you that believe." Beloved, it is a poor thing to receive the gospel in word only. Then you say, " Yes, it is true, I believe it " ; and there the matter ends. It is a far different matter to feel the power of the word as it comes from the omnipotent Lord, so as to have your heart broken by it, and then healed by it. To receive the gospel as indisputable, infallible, and divine, is to receive it indeed. To receive it, not because you are of a certain way of thinking, but because it carries conviction with it, and bears you away by its irre- sistible force ; this is to receive it in its power. Beloved, I do not believe a man will spend his life in spreading a doctrine which has never yet mastered his spirit ; but when the truth takes possession of a man, and holds him by force, as a strong man armed keeps his own house, then will he run up his flag, and openly acknowledge the Mighty One who reigns within. He who believes and is sure is the man who will propagate the faith, and desire that others should accept it. What a difference there is between the man who has felt the omnipotence of truth, and another who merely professes to entertain sound opinions ! If the almighty word has carried you captive, you will also hold it fast, and nothing will persuade you either to surrender it or to stifle it.

The Thessalonians were *a people whose constancy*

was proved. They received the word " with much affliction." The apostle says, " For ye, brethren, became followers of the churches of God which in Judæa are in Christ Jesus : for ye also have suffered like things of your own countrymen, even as they have of the Jews." The assault by the mob, recorded in Acts xvii., was, doubtless, only one of their many trials. They remained steadfast, enthusiastic under all their tribulations ; and hence the gospel was sounded out by them. Cowards hold their tongues, but brave men are not to be put down. Having already borne slander, reproach, and misrepresentation of every kind, we are not abashed, but rather are hardened to endurance, and publish our belief more unreservedly than ever. We have nothing to conceal, nothing to fear. Slander can say no more. Wherefore, we the more boldly sound forth the word of God. Brethren, unless you can hold on in rough weather, and bear up under opposition, you will do little in sounding out the word of God. Trumpets must be made of hard metal, and trumpeters must have something of the soldier about them, or little will come of it.

Hence, again, *these people really and lovingly served God.* Look at the ninth verse : " For they themselves shew of us what manner of entering in we had unto you, and how ye turned to God from idols to serve the living and true God." I have no doubt many of these folks had been great devotees of their idols, for it is amazing what idolaters will do for their deities ! At this day the gifts of Hindoos to idol shrines put to shame the offerings given by Christians to their Lord. Have you not heard how they were wont to throw their very lives away beneath the wheels of the chariot of their demongod ? Shall hideous deities of wood and stone command a zeal which is not shown in the service of the living God ? I doubt not that these Thessalonians became as earnest worshippers of the living Jehovah as they had once been earnest votaries of their idols. They turned from idols, but they turned to serve God. They were not turned in opinion only, but in a practical manner. What a pity it is, that to many Christian professors religion is opinion, and conversion a feeling ! Do not many live as if God were a myth, and the service of God a sham ? If God be God, *serve* Him : service is the due of Godhead. Does not the Lord Himself say, " If then I be a father, where is Mine honour ? and if I be a master, where is My fear ? " Oh, that to us the service of the Lord may be a delight, and then it will be as natural to us to sound out the word of the Lord as it is to birds to sing !

For one thing the Thessalonians were peculiarly notable : *they were enthusiastic expectants of the second coming of the Lord Jesus Christ.* Paul says of them, in the tenth verse, that they waited for the Son of God from heaven. They really expected Christ to come, and to come speedily. They even carried this expectation beyond its proper bounds, for they grew impatient of the Lord's apparent delay. Some of their number died, and they laid it to heart as though in their case their hope had failed, insomuch that the apostle wrote : " But I would not have you to be ignorant, brethren, concerning them which are asleep, that ye sorrow not, even as others which have no hope." They would be no losers by death ; for those who remained alive till the advent would have no preference over them which slept. In their case, there was no need to write " of the times

and the seasons," for they well knew that the Lord would come as a thief in the night. They came so to expect the immediate coming of the Lord as to fall into unhealthy excitement about it ; and it was needful for Paul, to prevent their becoming fanatical, to say, " Now we beseech you, brethren, by the coming of our Lord Jesus Christ, and by our gathering together unto him, that ye be not soon shaken in mind, or be troubled, neither by spirit, nor by word, nor by letter as from us, as that the day of Christ is at hand." Paul delighted to see them waiting for the coming of Christ ; but he also prayed, " The Lord direct your hearts into the *patient* waiting for Christ." He wishes rest to the troubled. But this unrest was a virtue carried to excess. We are not, many of us, in danger of exaggeration in that direction. I fear that we are more likely to forget the Lord's coming, or to treat it as an unpractical speculation. If any truth should arouse us, this should do it : yet even the wise virgins, as well as the foolish, are all too apt to slumber and sleep because the Bridegroom delayeth His coming. Hear ye not the midnight cry ? Does not this startle you ? " Behold, the Bridegroom cometh ; go ye out to meet Him." If you hearken to that call, you will be the men to sound out the word of the Lord in every place. If we, as a church and people, are more and more influenced by the expectation of our Lord's appearing, we shall be more eager to spread His gospel. Remember that now He may come at once. Those things of which Paul spoke as hindering His coming have now come and gone. Eighteen centuries and more have passed away since Paul wrote, and the Lord cometh quickly. Rouse, then, yourselves to use all diligence. Proclaim His word, and according to your ability go forth into all the world and preach the gospel to every creature. O ye that look for your Lord, ye are the men who should herald His coming by a clear testimony to His name in every place.

Thus I have given you hints as to what kind of men are likely to sound forth the word of God. Judge ye, my brethren, whether you yourselves have these qualifications. It is my sincere impression that they are to be found in many of you.

II. Secondly, let us notice THEIR TRUMPETS. " From you sounded out the word of the Lord." Their testimony was distinct, clear, resonant, and far-sounding. We may find an illustration in the silver trumpets of the sanctuary which were sounded to gather the people together. Let your trumpets ring out the call to assemble to our Lord Jesus, the true Shiloh, unto whom shall the gathering of the people be. We may further think of the Jubilee trumpet, which early in the morning proclaimed clearance of debts, release from bondage, and restoration to lost heritages. Such are the glad announcements of the gospel ; let us hasten to make them. Trumpets are also blown in time of war : many are the allusions to this in Scripture. Oh, that the church of God may boldly sound the war-trumpet, at this time, against impurity, intemperance, false doctrine, and loose living ! Our Lord has come to send a sword upon earth, in these matters. Oh, that from each one of us the war-blast may be sounded, without fear or hesitation ! Fain would we also earn the name given to the apostles, " They that turn the world upside down " ; for at this present it is wrong-side up. A trumpet is also used simply for musical purposes, and the testimony of the church to her Lord Jesus should be the most melodious sound the ears of man have ever heard.

"How sweet the name of Jesus sounds!"

Oh, to sound forth the glorious name, "with trumpet and sound of cornet," that multitudes might be compelled to hear it! Oh, to make all earth and heaven ring with that dear name! Somebody writing upon this verse compares the sounding forth to the voices of church bells. I will suppose that you are sojourning among the hills, and have almost lost reckoning of the days. How clearly are you told that it is the Sabbath morning, when you hear the sweet voices of the bells from yonder tower, far away! The call comes through the wood, and over the moor, and it seems to say, "Come hither, and worship; for the day of rest has come." Each church should find in its living members its best peal of bells. Every individual, great and little, should give forth his sound : not one should be dumb. Oh, that it were always so ; that everyone would constantly show forth the praises of the Lord! The Lord of hosts is with us ; let us l.ft up the shout of a King. He is all in all to us; let us make Him known. God grant us to realize that we may give a loud fanfare upon the silver trumpets to our coming Prince!

What was the means by which these excellent people made the gospel to sound out ? It was made known by the *remarkable conversions* which happened among them. These men had been idolaters, and had fallen into divers lusts common in those times. Paul's preaching had made a change which none could have looked for. They had been brought to worship the true God, and to look for His Son from heaven, and to walk worthy of their high calling. Everybody asked, "Why, what has happened to these Thessalonians? These people have broken their idols : they worship the one God ; they trust in Jesus. They are no longer drunken, dishonest, impure, contentious." Everybody talked of what had taken place among these converted people. Oh, for the conversions, plentiful, clear, singular, and manifest ; that so the word of God may sound out! Our converts are our best advertisements and arguments. Have you not known a whole town startled by the conversion of one great sinner ? A distinct, clear-cut conversion will often astound an entire parish, and compel the crowd to say, "What is this word of the Lord?" Brethren, may your own conversions, and those of many around you, proclaim aloud the power of the word of God, and the efficacy of faith in the precious blood of Jesus.

The attention commanded by their conversion was further secured by *their unmistakable, unquestionable character.* They became such godly, honest, upright, sober, saintly people, that all who observed them took note of their excellence. They were Christians indeed, for they were Christians in their deeds. Their whole lives were affected by their faith, both at home and abroad. They were so admirable in character that they had become ensamples to those who were already saved. Notice, in the seventh verse, the remarkable expression, "Ye were ensamples to all that believe." It is not so difficult to become an example to the ungodly, for their level is a low one ; but it is a high attainment to become an example to those who fear God. This needs great grace. If even saints may copy from you, you had need write a good hand. The Thessa-

lonians had attained to this, and it was by this that they were able to give such voice to the gospel. Holy living is a grand pulpit. A godly character has a louder voice in it than the most eloquent tongue. Character is our Chrysostom : holiness has a golden mouth. The apostle says that their lives were so complete a publication of the gospel, that he did not need to call attention thereto. He writes, "We need not to speak anything" : as much as to say, "We have only to point to you." Shall I ever feel that I have little need to preach in words, since my people preach far better by their lives ? Yes, there are many cases among you concerning which I might say—There, watch that friend's life, and see what the gospel is : there is no need for me to tell you. Nobody stands, on a summer's day, and points upward, saying, "There is the sun." No, the great light sheds its radiance everywhere, and nobody mistakes him for the moon or a star. Oh, that all of us were of such a character that none should mistake us! Till we have more grace in the heart, and more holiness in the life, we shall lack the greatest means of making the gospel known. We must shine by our works if men are to see our light. Oh, what a sounding forth of the Word will your holy lives be! Without these, all is vain. If the life contradicts the voice, it will be as when a trumpet is stopped up, and then, blow as you may, no sound is heard.

I have no doubt that the Thessalonians added to their character many *earnest efforts* for the spread of the truth. They went about telling what they had heard, believed, and enjoyed. Some of them became preachers of the Word at home, and others went abroad to publish the glad tidings. Jesus would be made known to the poor in the back slums of Thessalonica, and talked of to the sailors on board the vessels, and to the merchants on the quays. Are you, beloved, all of you, making Jesus known ? Are there none of you silent ? Have we not among us some who should now be working in foreign lands ? Have we not in these pews many whose voices should be heard in our streets ? We shall never be as we ought to be till every talent is utilized. We must be all at it, always at it, and at it with all our might. We have not come to this yet. May the love of Christ constrain us thereto!

Meanwhile, it was by *their faith that their teaching was made so clear and forcible.* They were intense believers, so that Paul says, "Your faith to God-ward is spread abroad." They did not half-heartedly teach what they half-heartedly believed. They accepted the teaching of the apostle as being, not the word of man, but the word of God ; and so they spoke with the accent of conviction. Those who heard them felt that they were enfeebled by no doubts, but were filled with full assurance of the eternal verities. Their goods were spoiled, they were themselves brought before magistrates, and yet they stood fast in the faith, and had no secret mistrust. There was no moving them, although the philosophers sneered at them, and the superstitious persecuted them. They stood like rocks amid raging seas. This was as a trumpet for the gospel, giving no uncertain sound. When holy constancy is to the front under reproach and ridicule, the gospel is sounded as with a bugle note, and men are compelled to hear it. Brethren, you possess this confidence. Have it more and more!

May we have among us remarkable conversions,

unquestionable character, earnest effort, and intense faith ; and these will be to us all the trumpet that we need. We need not blow our own trumpets, nor borrow the whistles of politics or amusement ; but the Word of the Lord will by these sound forth all around us. I cannot keep you long upon these points ; my aim is not to fill up the time, but to fill you with an eager desire to sound out the truth of God.

III. Oh, that the Holy Ghost would put fire into my sermon, that its live coals may touch your hearts, while I say that THERE IS NEED, AT THE PRESENT TIME, FOR A TRUMPET BLAST OF THIS KIND.

Brethren, the Word of the Lord ought to be sounded out, *because it is the Word of God*. If it is the word of man, let him spread it as he can ; we are not concerned to help him. The word of man comes from a dying source, and it will return to it ; but the Word of the Lord endureth for ever.

> " Waft, waft, ye winds, His story !
> And you, ye waters, roll,
> Till, like a sea of glory,
> It spreads from pole to pole."

The Word of the Lord is so important, that it should have free course, run, and be glorified. When He gives the word, great should be the company of them that publish it. If you believe the gospel to be the divine word, you dare not withhold it. The stones would cry out if you were silent.

With many of us, *this is a matter of solemn obligation*. The Word of God has been to us life from the dead, deliverance out of bondage, food for our hunger, strength for our weakness, comfort for our sorrow, satisfaction for our hearts. Spread it then.

> " Can ye, whose souls are lighted
> With wisdom from on high,
> Can ye, to men benighted,
> The lamp of life deny ? "

Seeing that God's Word has come to you with power, and has saved you from all evil, you must sound it abroad.

Remember, too, that *this is salvation to the perishing.* Did not one dear brother and deacon, on Monday night, pray to the Lord with great fervour, reiterating these words, "They are perishing, they are perishing, they are perishing ; Lord, save them !"? You believe that men are diseased with sin, and that Christ is the only remedy : will you not tell them the remedy ? You see men dying without hope ; will you not tell them where there is hope as to the hereafter ? You tremblingly feel that for souls to die without accepting the Saviour is eternal woe ; will you not pray them, in Christ's stead, to be reconciled to God ? O sirs, by everything that is terrible in the doom of those who die in unbelief, I charge you, sound out the Word of the Lord ! As you will shortly appear before the judgment-seat of Christ, be clear of the blood of all men. The gospel has power to save to-day, and to save for ever : sound it out.

This a time in which the Word of the Lord is much abused. Many venture to say that it has lost its power, and has proved unsuitable to the age. They tell us that we need something in advance of it. O you that love it, avenge this insult by manifesting its power in your lives, and by sounding out the old gospel with new vigour. By your holy characters, and by your incessant labours, force men to see the power of the divine word. Let its secret power be embodied in your practical consecration, and proclaimed in your incessant witness-bearing. When I wish to speak best, my tongue fails me ; I am a poor advocate. But oh, I pray you, by the glory of the Ever Blessed, which is tarnished by the foul mouths of ungodly men, seek with sevenfold energy to make known Christ crucified, and the way of salvation by faith in Him ! If you have slept until now, " Awake, awake ; put on strength ! " for the enemy is at the gate. I beseech you, now that Christ's crown and throne are assailed by His adversaries, put on your armour, grasp the sword, and stand up for the sacred cause.

At this time *many other voices are clamouring to be heard.* The air is full of din. Men have devised new methods by which to elevate the race, and loud are the voices that proclaim the man-invented nostrums. " Shall we be heard ? " cries one, " if we lift up our voices ? " Yes, if you take the gospel trumpet, you will enforce a hearing. It chanced one evening, when there was a large gathering of friends at the Orphanage, that our boys were sweetly discoursing a hymn-tune upon their bells, the American organ was being played as an accompaniment, and all the gathered company were singing at their best, making a rushing flood of music. Just then I quietly hinted to our friend Mr. Manton Smith to put in a few notes from his silver cornet ; and when he placed it to his lips, and threw his soul into it, the lone man was heard above us all. Bells, organ, voices, everything seemed to yield before that one clear blast of trumpet music. So will it be with the gospel. Only sound it out as God's own word, and let the power of the Holy Ghost go with it, and it will drown all music but its own. At any rate, you will have done your part, and will be no longer responsible, even if men do not hear it, if from your very soul you sound out the word of the Lord.

Need I say more to show you how needful it is that just now we should put a tongue into the heavenly doctrine, and let it proclaim salvation to all lands ?

V. I want, during my last few minutes, to hint to the members of this church, and to those many friends far and near who have so generously associated with me in holy enterprises, that WE ARE THE PEOPLE TO GIVE FORTH THIS SOUND.

It is our duty, first, *because of our position.* Thessalonica was a well-chosen centre, because it was a place of great resort. Ships were always coming into that port and going out again. Whatever was done at Thessalonica would soon be known in all quarters. We are placed in a central position in London. Who does not know the Tabernacle ? Hither the tribes come up, and here the multitudes continually assemble. Friends from the country flock to this spot ; and on the Sabbath-day of summertide persons from all countries are in these pews and aisles. I state the simple truth when I speak of this house as known to some of all nations, and therefore what is done here is done in the heart of England, and in the centre of the world. If you, as a church, can sound forth by your character and exertions the word of God, you are in the fittest place for it. The position demands it of you ; act not unworthily.

Providence has forced us into prominence. We have not desired it ; but we are known and observed by multitudes. If, beloved, we keep the fire burning here, it will be a beacon seen afar. If we are consecrated men and women, we have a great opportunity. If my helpers will see to it that nothing fails in this place, we shall encourage many ; but we shall dispirit thousands unless we carry on the work here with great vigour, the Lord being our helper.

Nor can I forget our numbers. There may have been churches of larger numbers than ours, but I have never heard of them. In this I do not glory, but I dare not conceal from you the anxiety which it causes me. If little is done by such an assembly, it will be a great disgrace to us. I am overwhelmed with the thought of more than five thousand souls united here in church fellowship. Large numbers may be our weakness ; we may become a mere horde of men, without discipline, without unity, without power ; but I trust in the great Lord that it shall not be so. If God has caused us to be as large as almost any other ten churches put together, does He not call upon us to exert ourselves with tenfold energy to spread abroad the gospel of our Lord Jesus Christ ? I am sore burdened with this great host : will you allow it to be a burden ? Will you not make it a joy ? Will all these professed believers make up a crowded hospital ? Shall not this house the rather be a barrack of soldiers ? Shall not our voice be louder for our Lord than if we were but five hundred, instead of five thousand ? How would I plead with you, if I knew how ! Do not make this community a gigantic failure. God grant that, remembering our numbers, we may not be satisfied with a thin and feeble voice for Jesus. Our voice should be as the noise of many waters. Is it so ? Is it so much so as it ought to be ? Oh, for the Spirit of God among us as a rushing mighty wind !

Through our agencies we ought to sound out the word of the Lord very loudly. At this moment you have, by the College, sent out more than seven hundred preachers of the Word, into all countries. Oh, that they were all as faithful as some are ! Many are the churches presided over by those trained in your school of the prophets : pray that the Lord may be with them. Your orphan children are growing up : oh, that they may be a seed to serve the Lord ! Your colporteurs are going from door to door with holy literature. Oh, for the power of God with their laborious efforts ! Your evangelists are heard by tens of thousands ; implore the unction from on high for them. The sermons preached in this place are not only printed in our own tongue, but many of them are translated into other languages, and are widely read. This is no mean agency for good. All this, and much more which I will not speak upon, I mention not to boast thereof, but that we may be humbled under our responsibilities, and may cry to God for His power. All this, if the Holy Ghost be with us, must accomplish great results ; but without Him—and we shall be without Him unless we are a holy, godly, earnest, Christ-loving people—nothing

will be accomplished. Our agencies will become burdens to us, until that which should be the armour of our warfare will become the sepulchre of our life. I feel this more than anyone else, since the very finding and using of funds for so great a work would crush me if the Lord were not my helper.

Beloved, I press home upon you the duty of sounding out the word of God because of *your prayers.* If there be a people under heaven that constantly meet in large numbers to pray, we are that people. Albeit, some of you are lax on this point, I am bound to say that I rejoice in your gatherings for prayer. In this you are my joy and crown. God be praised for it ! But if any cry to God, and then do not work for Him, what hypocrisy it is ! What if we ask Him to save souls, and never lift a finger to spread the gospel ! Is this truthful ? Dare we hang the trumpet on the wall, and then pray, " Lord, let it be blown " ? No. By the honesty of your hearts, set that trumpet to your lips, if you desire its sound to go forth. Give it your very life-breath. Lift up your voice with strength ; lift it up ; be not afraid.

Once more, *you have stood with me in solemn protest* against the declensions of the age. He who knoweth all things knows what this has cost me ; but your love has been a great relief to me in the bitter sorrow. We will have no complicity with error : we will not aid the Philistines in shearing away the locks of the gospel's strength. Having protested, we must justify our position by our lives. We shall be dishonoured unless we have the power of God specially resting upon us : that may be a small thing ; but the truth itself will be dishonoured ; and this we cannot bear. If the gospel be indeed true—and we have no doubt about it— we beseech the God of truth to grant us the sign and seal from heaven by baring His holy arm in our midst. To-day, again, I lay the sacrifice upon the altar, by reasserting the old gospel against the down-grade of the times. The God that answereth by fire, let Him be God ! On you may the tongues of fire descend and rest. May you, who are with me, whether in London or in the utmost parts of the earth, be inflamed with zeal, and fired with love. May the water in the trenches be licked up by the flame, and the whole sacrifice be consumed with heaven's own fire till the people, once deluded by Baal, shall be forced to cry, " Jehovah, He is the God ! Jehovah, He is the God ! " May the substitutionary sacrifice of Christ triumph in the midst of the earth, and become, as it always has been, the truth by which the glory of the Lord shall be revealed. The Lord grant it. Labour, all of you, to secure it.

I have not preached to sinners ; I leave that, for once, to you. I lay on you this burden, that you each one make the word of the Lord to sound out, " so that we need not to speak anything." God grant it may be so, for Jesus' sake ! Amen.

A SUMMARY OF EXPERIENCE AND A BODY OF DIVINITY

" For they themselves show of us what manner of entering in we had unto you, and how ye turned to God from idols to serve the living and true God ; and to wait for His Son from heaven, whom He raised from the dead, even Jesus, which delivered us from the wrath to come."—1 Thessalonians i. 9, 10.

IN Thessalonica the conversions to the faith were remarkable. Paul came there without prestige, without friends, when he was in the very lowest condition ; for he had just been beaten and imprisoned at Philippi, and had fled from that city. Yet it mattered not in what condition the ambassador might be ; God, who worketh mighty things by weak instruments, blessed the word of His servant Paul. No doubt when the apostle went into the synagogue to address his own countrymen he had great hopes that, by reasoning with them out of their own Scriptures, he might convince them that Jesus was the Christ. He soon found that only a few would search the Scriptures and form a judgment on the point ; but the bulk of them refused, for we read of the Jews of Berea, to whom Paul fled from Thessalonica, " These were more noble than those in Thessalonica, in that they received the word with all readiness of mind, and searched the Scriptures daily, whether those things were so." Paul must have felt disappointed with his own countrymen ; indeed, he had often cause to do so. His heart was affectionately warm toward them, but their hearts were very bitter towards him, reckoning him to be a pervert and an apostate. But if he seemed to fail with the Jews, it is evident that he was abundantly successful with the Gentiles. These turned from their idols to serve the living God, and their turning was so remarkable that the Jews charged Paul and Silas with turing the world upside down.

In those days there was a good deal of practical atheism abroad, and therefore the wonder was not so much that men left their idols, as that they turned unto the living God. It became a matter of talk all over the city, and the Jews in their violence helped to make the matter more notorious ; for the mobs in the street and the attack upon the house of Jason all stirred the thousand tongues of rumour. Everybody spoke of the sudden appearance of three poor Jews, of their remarkable teaching in the synagogue, and of the conversion of a great multitude of devout Greeks, and of the chief women not a few. It was no small thing that so many had come straight away from the worship of Jupiter and Mercury to worship the Unknown God, who could not be seen, nor imaged ; and to enter the kingdom of one Jesus who had been crucified. It set all Macedonia and Achaia wondering ; and as with a trumpet-blast it aroused all the dwellers in those regions. Every ship that sailed from Thessalonica carried the news of the strange ferment which was moving the city ; men were caring for religion, and were quitting old beliefs for a new and better faith. Thessalonica, situated on one of the great Roman roads, the centre of a large trade, thus became a centre for the gospel. Wherever there are true conversions there will be more or less of this kind of sounding forth of the gospel. It was especially so at Thessalonica ; but it is truly so in every church where the Spirit of God is uplifting men from the dregs of evil, delivering them from drunkenness, and dishonesty, and uncleanness, and worldliness, and making them to become holy and earnest in the cause of the great Lord. There is sure to be a talk when grace triumphs. This talk is a great aid to the gospel : it is no small thing that men should have their attention attracted to it by its effects ; for it is both natural and just that thoughtful men should judge of doctrines by their results ; and if the most beneficial results follow from the preaching of the word, prejudice is disarmed, and the most violent objectors are silenced.

You will notice that in this general talk the converts and the preachers were greatly mixed up :— " For they themselves show of us what manner of entering in we had unto you." I do not know that it is possible for the preacher to keep himself distinct from those who profess to be converted by him. He is gladly one with them in love to their souls, but he would have it remembered that he cannot be responsible for all their actions. Those who profess to have been converted under any ministry have it in their power to damage that ministry far more than any adversaries can do. " There ! " says the world, when it detects a false professor, " this is what comes of such preaching." They judge unfairly, I know ; but most men are in a great hurry, and will not examine the logic of their opponents ; while many others are so eager to judge unfavourably, that a very little truth, or only a bare report, suffices to condemn both the minister and his doctrine. Every man that lives unto God with purity of life brings honour to the gospel which converted him, to the community to which he belongs, and to the preaching by which he was brought to the knowledge of the truth ; but the reverse is equally true in the case of unworthy adherents. Members of churches, will you kindly think of this ? Your ministers share the blame of your ill conduct if ever you disgrace yourselves. I feel sure that none of you wish to bring shame and trouble upon your pastors, however careless you may be about your own reputations. Oh, that we could be freed from those of whom Paul says, " Many walk, of whom I have told you often, and now tell you even weeping, that they are the enemies of the cross of Christ ; whose end is destruction, whose God is their belly, and whose glory is in their shame, who mind earthly things." When these are in a church they are its curse. The Thessalonians were not such : they were such a people that Paul did not blush to have himself implicated in what they did. He was glad to say that the outsiders " show of us what manner of entering in we had unto you, and how ye turned to God from idols, to serve the living and true God, and to wait for His Son from heaven."

Quitting this line of thought, I would observe that these two verses struck me as being singularly full. Oceans of teaching are to be found in them.

A father of the church in the first ages was wont to cry, " I adore the infinity of Holy Scripture." That remark constantly rises from my lips when I am studying the sacred word. This book is more than a book, it is the mother of books, a mine of truth, a mountain of meaning. It was an ill-advised opinion which is imputed to the Mahommedans at the destruction of the Alexandrian Library, when they argued that everything that was good in it was already in the Koran, and therefore it might well be destroyed. Yet it is true with regard to the inspired word of God, that it contains everything which appertains to eternal life. It is a revelation of which no man can take the measure, it compasses heaven and earth, time and eternity. The best evidence of its being written by an Infinite mind is its own infinity. Within a few of its words there lie hidden immeasurable meanings, even as perfume enough to sweeten leagues of space may be condensed into a few drops of otto of roses.

The first part of my text contains *a summary of Christian experience;* and the second part contains *a body of divinity.* Here is ample room and verge enough. It is not possible to exhaust such a theme.

I. The first part of the text contains A SUMMARY OF EXPERIENCE : "What manner of entering in we had unto you, and how ye turned to God from idols to serve the living and true God, and to wait for His Son from heaven." Here we have in miniature the biography of a Christian man.

It begins, first, with *the entering in of the word,* "What manner of entering in we had unto you." When we preach the word you listen, and, so far, the word is received. This is a very hopeful circumstance. Still, the hearing with the outward ear is comparatively a small matter ; or, at least, only great because of what may follow from it. The preacher feels even with some who listen with attention that he is outside the door ; he is knocking, and he hopes that he is heard within ; but the truth is not yet received, the door remains shut, an entrance is not granted, and in no case can he be content to speak with the person outside the door ; he desires an entrance for the word. All is fruitless until Christ entereth into the heart. I have seen the following : the door has been a little opened, and the man inside has come to look at the messenger, and more distinctly to hear what he may have to say ; but he has taken care to put the door on the chain, or hold it with his hand, for he is not yet ready to admit the guest who is so desirous of entertainment. The King's messenger has sometimes tried to put his foot within when the door has stood a little open, but he has not always been successful, and has not even escaped from a painful hurt when the door has been forced back with angry violence. We have called again and again with our message, but we have been as men who besieged a walled city, and were driven from the gates ; yet we had our reward, for when the Holy Spirit sweetly moved the hard heart the city gates have opened of their own accord, and we have been received joyfully. We have heard the hearty cry, " Let the truth come in ! Let the gospel come in ! Let Christ come in ! Whatever there is in Him we are willing to receive ; whatever He demands we are willing to give ; whatever He offers us we are glad to accept. Come and welcome ! The guest-chamber is prepared. Come and abide in our house for ever ! "

The truth has its own ways of entrance ; but in general it first affects the understanding. The man says, " I see it : I see how God is just, and yet the Justifier of him that believeth in Jesus. I see sin laid on Christ that it may not be laid on me, and I perceive that if I believe in Jesus Christ my sins are put away by His atonement." To many all that is wanted is that they should understand this fundamental truth ; for their minds are prepared of God to receive it. Only make it plain and they catch at it as a hungry man at a piece of bread. They discover in the gospel of our Lord Jesus the very thing for which they have been looking for years, and so the truth enters by the door of the understanding.

Then it usually commences to work upon the conscience, conscience being the understanding exercised upon moral truth. The man sees himself a sinner, discovering guilt that he was not aware of ; and he is thus made ready to receive Christ's pardoning grace. He sees that to have lived without thinking of God, without loving God, without serving God was a great and grievous crime : he feels the offensiveness of this neglect. He trembles ; he consents unto the law that it is good, and he allows that, if the law condemns him, he is worthy to be condemned.

When it has thus entered into the understanding and affected the conscience, the word of God usually arouses the emotions. Fear is awakened, and hope is excited. The man begins to feel as he never felt before. His whole manhood is brought under the heavenly spell ; his very flesh doth creep in harmony with the amazement of his soul. He wonders and dreads, weeps and quivers, hopes and doubts ; but no emotion is asleep ; life is in all. When a tear rises to his eye he brushes it away, but it is soon succeeded by another. Repentance calls forth one after another of these her sentinels. The proud man is broken down ; the hard man is softened. The love of God in providing a Saviour, the unsearchable riches of divine grace in passing by transgression, iniquity, and sin,—these things amaze and overwhelm the penitent. He finds himself suddenly dissolved, where aforetime he was hard as adamant ; for the word is entering into him, and exercising its softening power.

By-and-by the entrance is complete ; for the truth carries the central castle of Mansoul, and captures his heart. He who once hated the gospel now loves it. At first he loves it, hoping that it may be his, though fearing the reverse ; yet owning that if it brought no blessing to himself, yet it was a lovable and desirable thing. By-and-by the man ventures to grasp it, encouraged by the word that bids him lay hold on eternal life. One who in digging his land finds a treasure, first looks about for fear lest some one else should claim it ; anon he dares to examine his prize more carefully, and at length he bears it in his bosom to his own home. So is it with the gospel ; when a man finds it by the understanding, he soon embraces it with his heart ; and, believe me, if it once gets into the heart, the archenemy himself will never get it out again. Oh, that such an entrance with the gospel might commence the spiritual life of all here present who are as yet unsaved.

What comes next ? Well, the second stage is *conversion.* " They themselves show of us what manner of entering in we had unto you, and how *ye turned to God* from idols to serve the living and true God."

There came a turning, a decided turning. The man has come so far in carelessness, so far in sin and unbelief ; but now he pauses, and he deliberately turns round, and faces in that direction to which hitherto he had turned his back. Conversion is the turning of a man completely round, to hate what he loved and to love what he hated. Conversion is to turn to God decidedly and distinctly by an act and deed of the mind and will. In some senses we are *turned ;* but in others, like these Thessalonians, we *turn*. It is not conversion to think that you will turn, or to promise that you will turn, or resolve that you will turn, but actually and in very deed to turn, because the word has had a true entrance into your heart. You must not be content with a reformation ; there must be a revolution : old thrones must fall, and a new king must reign. Is it so with you ?

These Thessalonians turned from their idols. Do you tell me that you have no idols ? Think again, and you will not be quite so sure. The streets of London are full of fetish worship, and almost every dwelling is a joss-house crammed with idols. Why, multitudes of men are worshipping not calves of gold, but gold in a more portable shape. Small circular idols of gold and silver are much sought after. They are very devoutly worshipped by some, and great things are said concerning their power. I have heard the epithet of " almighty " ascribed to an American form of these idols. Those who do not worship gold, may yet worship rank, name, pleasure, or honour. Most worship self, and I do not know that there is a more degrading form of worship than for a man to put himself upon a pedestal and bow down thereto and worship it. You might just as well adore cats and crocodiles with the ancient Egyptians as pay your life's homage to yourselves. No wooden image set up by the most savage tribe can be more ugly or degrading than our idol when we adore ourselves. Men worship Bacchus still. Do not tell me they do not : why, there is a temple to him at every street corner. While every other trade is content with a shop or a warehouse, this fiend has his palaces, in which plentiful libations are poured forth in his honour. The gods of unchastity and vice are yet among us. It would be a shame even to speak of the things which are done of them in secret. The lusts of the flesh are served even by many who would not like to have it known. We have gods many and lords many in this land. God grant that we may see, through the preaching of the gospel, many turning from such idols. If you love anything better than God you are idolaters : if there is anything you would not give up for God it is your idol : if there is anything that you seek with greater fervour than you seek the glory of God, that is your idol, and conversion means a turning from every idol.

But then that is not enough, for some men turn from one idol to another. If they do not worship Bacchus they become teetotalers, and possibly they worship the golden calf, and become covetous. When men quit covetousness they sometimes turn to profligacy. A change of false gods is not the change that will save : we must turn unto God, to trust, love, and honour Him, and Him alone.

After conversion comes *service*. True conversion causes us " to serve the living and true God." To serve Him means to worship Him, to obey Him, to consecrate one's entire being to His honour and glory, and to be His devoted servant.

We are, dear friends, to serve the " living " God. Many men have a dead God still. They do not feel that He hears their prayers, they do not feel the power of His Spirit moving upon their hearts and lives. They never take the Lord into their calculations ; He never fills them with joy, nor even depresses them with fear ; God is unreal and inactive to them. But the true convert turns to the living God, who is everywhere, and whose presence affects him at every point of His being. This God he is to worship, obey, and serve.

Then it is added, to serve the *true* God ; and there is no serving a true God with falsehood. Many evidently serve a false god, for they utter words of prayer without their hearts, and that is false prayer, unfit for the true God, who must be worshipped in spirit and in truth. When men's lives are false and artificial they are not a fit service for the God of truth. A life is false when it is not the true outcome of the soul, when it is fashioned by custom, ruled by observation, restrained by selfish motives, and governed by the love of human approbation. What a man does against his will is not in truth done by himself at all. If the will is not changed the man is not converted, and his religious life is not true. He that serves the true God acceptably does it with delight ; to him sin is misery, and holiness is happiness. This is the sort of service which we desire our converts to render : we long to see rebels become sons. Oh the sacred alchemy of the Holy Spirit, who can turn men from being the slaves of sin to become servants of righteousness !

Carefully notice the order of life's progress : the entering in of the word produces conversion, and this produces service. Do not put those things out of their places. If you are converts without the word entering into you, you are unconverted ; and if professing to receive the word you are not turned by it, you have not received it. If you claim to be converted, and yet do not serve God, you are not converted ; and if you boast of serving God without being converted, you are not serving God. The three things are links which draw on each other.

A fourth matter follows to complete this Christian biography, namely, *waiting*—" To wait for His Son from heaven." That conversion which is not followed up by waiting is a false conversion, and will come to nothing. We wait, dear brethren, in the holy perseverance of faith ; having begun with Christ Jesus our Lord we abide in Him : we trust, and then we wait. We do not look upon salvation as a thing which requires a few minutes of faith, and then all is over ; salvation is the business of our lives. We receive salvation in an instant, but we work it out with fear and trembling all our days. He that is saved continues to be saved, and goes on to be saved from day to day, from every sin and from every form of evil. We must wait upon the Lord, and renew the strength of the life which He has imparted. As a servant waiteth on her mistress, or a courtier upon his king, so must we wait upon the Lord.

This waiting also takes the shape of living in the future. A man who waits is not living on the wages of to-day, but on the recompenses of a time which is yet to come ; and this is the mark of the Christian, that his life is spent in eternity rather than in time, and his citizenship is not of earth but of heaven. He has received a believing expectancy which makes him both watch and wait. He expects that the Lord Jesus will come a second time, and that speedily.

He has read of His going up into heaven, and he believes it ; and he knows that He will so come in like manner as He went up into heaven. For the second advent he looks with calm hope : he does not know when it may be, but he keeps himself on the watch as a servant who waits his lord's return. He hopes it may be to-day, he would not wonder if it were to-morrow, for he is always looking for and hasting unto the coming of the Son of God. The coming of the Lord is his expected reward. He does not expect to be rewarded by men, or even to be rewarded of God with temporal things in this life, for he has set his affection upon things yet to be revealed, things eternal and infinite. In the day when the Christ shall come, and the heavens which have received Him shall restore Him to our earth, He shall judge the world in righteousness, and His people with His truth, and then shall our day break and our shadows flee away. The true believer lives in this near future ; his hopes are with Jesus on His throne, with Jesus crowned before an assembled universe.

The convert has come to this condition, he is assured of his salvation. See how he has been rising from the time when he first held the door ajar ! He is assured of his salvation ; for Paul describes him as one who is delivered from the wrath to come ; and therefore he looks with holy delight to the coming of the Lord Jesus Christ. Once he was afraid of this, for he feared that He would come to condemn him ; but now he knows that when the Lord appears his justification will be made plain to the eyes of all men. "Then shall the righteous shine forth as the sun, in the kingdom of their Father." And so he cries, "Even so, come Lord Jesus !" He would hasten rather than delay the appearing of the Lord. He groans in sympathy with travailing creation for the manifestation of the sons of God. He cries with all the redeemed host for the day of the Saviour's glory. He could not do this were he not abundantly assured that the day would not seal his destruction, but reveal his full salvation.

Here, then, you have the story of the Christian man briefly summed up, and I think you will not find a passage of merely human writing which contains so much in so small a compass. It has unspeakable wealth packed away into a narrow casket. Do you understand it ? Is this the outline of your life ? If it is not, the Lord grant that His word may have an entrance into you this morning, that you may now believe in Jesus Christ, and then wait for His glorious appearing.

II. I shall want you to be patient with me while I very briefly unfold the second half of this great roll. Here even to a greater degree we have *multum in parvo*, much in little ; A BODY OF DIVINITY packed away in a nutshell. "To wait for His Son from heaven, whom He raised from the dead, even Jesus, which delivered us from the wrath to come."

To begin my body of divinity, I see here, first, *the Deity of Christ*. "To wait for His Son." "His Son." God has but one Son in the highest sense. The Lord Jesus Christ has given to all believers power to become the sons of God, but not in the sense in which He, and He alone, is the Son of God. "Unto which of the angels said He at any time, Thou art My Son, this day have I begotten thee ?" "When He bringeth in the First-begotten into the world He saith, Let all the angels of God worship Him." The Eternal Filiation is a mystery into which it is better for us never to pry. Believe it ; but how it

is, or how it could be, certainly it is not for you or for me to attempt to explain. There is one "Son of the Highest," who is "God, of the substance of the Father, begotten before all worlds," whom we with all our souls adore, and own to be most truly God ; doing so especially every time in the benediction we associate Him with the Father and with the Holy Spirit as the one God of blessing.

Side by side with this in this text of mine is *His humanity*. "His Son, whom He raised from the dead." It is for man to die. God absolutely considered dieth not ; He therefore took upon Himself our mortal frame, and was made in fashion as a man ; then willingly for our sakes He underwent the pangs of death, and being crucified, was dead, and so was buried, even as the rest of the dead. He was truly man, "of a reasonable soul, and human flesh subsisting" : of that we are confident. There has been no discussion upon that point in these modern times, but there was much questioning thereon in years long gone ; for what is there so clear that men will not doubt it or mystify it ? With us there is no question either as to His Deity, which fills us with reverence ; or His manhood, which inspires us with joy. He is the Son of God and the Son of Mary. He, as God, is "immortal, invisible" ; and yet for our sakes He was seen of men and angels, and in mortal agony yielded up the ghost. He suffered for our salvation, died upon the cross, and was buried in the tomb of Joseph of Arimathæa, being verily and truly man.

Notice a third doctrine which is here, and that is *the unity of the Divine Person of our Lord ;* for while the apostle speaks of Christ as God's Son from heaven, and as one who had died, he adds, "even Jesus" : that is to say, one known, undivided Person. Although He be God and man, yet He is not two, but one Christ. There is but one Person of our blessed and adorable Lord : "one altogether ; not by confusion of substance, but by unity of Person." He is God, He is man ; perfect God and perfect man ; and, as such Jesus Christ, the one Mediator between God and men. There have been mistakes about this also made in the church, though I trust not by any one of us here present. We worship the Lord Jesus Christ in the unity of His divine Person as the one Saviour of men.

Furthermore, in our text, we perceive a doctrine about ourselves very plainly implied, namely that *men by nature are guilty*, for otherwise they would not have needed Jesus, a Saviour. They were lost, and so He who came from heaven to earth bore the name of Jesus, "for He shall save His people from their sins." It is clear, my brethren, that we were under the divine wrath, otherwise it could not be said, "He hath delivered us from the wrath to come." We who are now delivered were once "children of wrath, even as others." And when we are delivered it is a meet song to sing, "O Lord, I will praise Thee : though Thou wast angry with me, thine anger is turned away, and Thou comfortedst me." We were guilty, else we had not needed a propitiation by the Saviour's death : we were lost, else we had not needed one who should seek and save that which is lost ; and we were hopelessly lost, otherwise God Himself would not have shared our nature to work the mighty work of our redemption. That truth is in the text, and a great deal more than I can mention just now.

But the next doctrine, which is one of the fundamentals of the gospel, is that *the Lord Jesus Christ died for these fallen men.* He could not have been raised from the dead if He had not died. That death was painful, and ignominious ; and it was also substitutionary : " for the transgression of My people was He stricken." In the death of Christ lay the essence of our redemption. I would not have you dissociate His life from His death, it comes into His death as an integral part of it ; for as the moment we begin to live, we, in a sense, begin to die, so the Man of Sorrows lived a dying life, which was all preparatory to His passion. He lived to die, panting for the baptism, wherewith He was to be baptized, and reaching forward to it. But it was especially, though not only, by His death upon the cross that Jesus put away our sin. Without shedding of blood there is no remission of sin. Not even the tears of Christ, nor the labours of Christ could have redeemed us if He had not given Himself for us an offering and a sacrifice. " Die He, or justice must," or man must die. It was His bowing the head and giving up of the ghost which finished the whole work. " It is finished " could not have been uttered except by a bleeding, dying Christ. His death is our life. Let us always dwell upon that central truth, and when we are preaching Christ risen, Christ reigning, or Christ coming, let us never so preach any of them as to overshadow Christ crucified. " We preach Christ crucified." Some have put up their ensign, " We preach Christ glorified " ; and we also preach the same ; but yet to us it seems that the first and foremost view of Jesus by the sinner is as the Lamb of God which taketh away the sin of the world. Therefore do we preach first Christ crucified, while at the same time we do not forget that blessed hope of the child of God, namely, Christ in glory soon to descend from heaven.

The next doctrine I see in my text is *the acceptance of the death of Christ by the Father.* " Where is that ? " say you. Look ! " Whom He raised from the dead." Not only did Jesus rise from the dead, but the Father had a distinct hand therein. God as God gave the token of His acceptance of Christ's sacrifice by raising Him from the dead. It is true, as we sometimes sing,

" If Jesus had not paid the debt,
He ne'er had been at freedom set."

The Surety would have been in prison to this day if He had not discharged His suretyship engagements, and wiped out all the liabilities of His people. Therefore it is written, " He was delivered for our offences, and was raised again for our justification." In His glorious uprising from the dead lies the assurance that we are accepted, accepted in the Beloved : the Beloved being Himself certainly accepted because God brought Him again from the dead.

Further on, we have another doctrine, among many more. We have here the doctrine of *our Lord's resurrection,* of which we spake when we mentioned the acceptance of His offering. Christ is risen from the dead. I pray you, do not think of the Lord Jesus Christ as though He were now dead. It is well to dwell upon Gethsemane, Golgotha, and Gabbatha ; but pray remember the empty tomb, Emmaus, Galilee, and Olivet. It is not well to think of Jesus as for ever on the cross or in the tomb. " He is not here, but He is risen." Ye may " come and see the place where the Lord lay," but He lies there no longer ; He hath burst the bands of death by which He could not be holden ; for it was

not possible that God's holy One could see corruption. The rising of Jesus from the dead is that fact of facts which establishes Christianity upon an historical basis, and at the same time guarantees to all believers their own resurrection from the dead. He is the firstfruits and we are the harvest.

Further, there is here the doctrine of *His ascension :* " to wait for His Son from heaven." It is clear that Jesus is in heaven, or He could not come from it. He has gone before us as our Forerunner. He has gone to His rest and reward ; a cloud received Him out of sight ; He has entered into His glory.

I doubt not our poet is right when he says of the angels—

" They brought His chariot from on high,
    To bear Him to His throne ;
Clapped their triumphant wings and cried,
    ' The glorious work is done ! ' "

That ascension of His brought us the Holy Spirit. He " led captivity captive, and received gifts for men," and He gave the Holy Ghost as the largess of His joyous entry to His Father's courts, that man on earth might share in the joy of the Conqueror returning from the battle. " Lift up your heads, O ye gates ; and be ye lift up, ye everlasting doors ; and the King of glory shall come in," was the song of that bright day.

But the text tells us more : not only that He has gone into heaven, but that *He remains there ;* for these Thessalonians were expecting Him to come " from heaven," and therefore He was there. What is He doing ? " I go to prepare a place for you." What is He doing ? He is interceding with authority before the throne. What is He doing ? He is from yonder hill-top looking upon His church, which is as a ship upon the sea buffeted by many a storm. In the middle watch ye shall see Him walking on the waters ; for He perceives the straining of the oars, the leakage of the timbers, the rending of the sails, the dismay of the pilot, the trembling of the crew ; and He will come unto us, and save us. He is sending heavenly succours to His weary ones ; He is ruling all things for the salvation of His elect, and the accomplishment of His purposes. Glory be to His blessed name !

Jesus is in heaven with saving power, too, and that also is in the text : " His Son from heaven, even Jesus, which delivereth us from the wrath to come." I alter the translation, for it is a present participle in the case of each verb, and should run, " Even Jesus, delivering us from the wrath coming." He is at this moment delivering. " Wherefore also He is able to save them to the uttermost that come unto God by Him, seeing He ever liveth to make intercession for them." He is away in heaven, but He is not divided from us ; He is working here the better because He is there. He has not separated Himself from the service, and the conflict here below ; but He has taken the post from which He can best observe and aid. Like some great commander who in the day of battle commands a view of the field, and continues watching, directing, and so winning the fight, so is Jesus in the best place for helping us. Jesus is the master of legions, bidding His angels fly hither and thither, where their spiritual help is needed. My faith sees Him securing victory in the midst of the earth. My God, my King, Thou art working all things gloriously from Thy vantage ground, and ere long the groans and strifes of battle shall end in Hallelujahs unto the Lord God Omnipotent! Christ's residence in the heavens is clearly in the text.

Here is conspicuously set forth *the second coming,* a subject which might well have occupied all our time,—" To wait for His Son from heaven." Every chapter of this epistle closes with the Second Advent. Do not deceive yourselves, oh ye ungodly men who think little of Jesus of Nazareth! The day will come when you will change your minds about Him. As surely as He died, He lives, and as surely as He lives He will come to this earth again! With an innumerable company of angels, with blast of trumpet that shall strike dismay into the heart of all His enemies, Jesus comes! And when He cometh there shall be a time of judgment, and the rising again of the dead, and " Every eye shall see Him, and they also which pierced Him : and all the kindreds of the earth shall wail because of Him." He may come to-morrow! We know not the times and the seasons ; these things are in the Father's keeping ; but that He comes is certain, and that He will come as a thief in the night to the ungodly is certain too. Lay no flattering unction to your souls as though when He was crucified there was an end of Him ; it is but the beginning of His dealings with you, though you reject Him. " Kiss the Son, lest He be angry, and ye perish from the way, when His wrath is kindled but a little. Blessed are all they that put their trust in Him."

A further doctrine in the text is that *Christ is a deliverer*—"Jesus delivering us from the wrath coming." What a blessed name is this! Deliverer! Press the cheering title to your breast. He delivereth by Himself bearing the punishment of sin. He has delivered, He is delivering, He always will deliver them that put their trust in Him.

But there was something to be delivered from, and that is, *the coming wrath*, which is mentioned here. " Oh," saith one, " that is a long way off, that wrath to come!" If it were a long way off it were wise for you to prepare for it. He is unsafe who will be destroyed most certainly, however distant that destruction may be. A wise man should not be content with looking as an ox doth, as far as his eye can carry him, for there is so much beyond, as sure as that which is seen. But it is not far-off wrath which is here mentioned ; the text saith, " who delivereth us from the wrath coming"; that is, the wrath which is now coming ; for wrath is even now upon the unbelieving. As for those Jews who had rejected Christ, the apostle says of them in the sixteenth verse of the next chapter, " Forbidding us to speak to the Gentiles that they might be saved, to fill up their sins alway : for the wrath is come upon them to the uttermost." The siege of Jerusalem, and the blindness of Israel, are a terrible comment upon these words. " Indignation and wrath, tribulation and anguish, upon every soul of man that doeth evil, of the Jew first, and also of the Gentile." It is said of every one that believeth not in Christ Jesus, that " the wrath of God abideth on him." " God is angry with the wicked every day." This wrath abideth upon some of you. It is the joy of believers that they are delivered from this wrath which is daily coming upon unbelievers, and would come upon themselves if they had not been delivered from it by the atoning sacrifice.

There is evidently in the text the doctrine of *a great division* between men and men. " He hath delivered *us*." All men have not faith, and therefore all men are not delivered from wrath. To-day there is such a division ; the " condemned-already " and the " justified " are living side by side ; but ere long the separation shall be more apparent. While some will go away into everlasting punishment, the people of God will be found pardoned and absolved, and so will be glorified for ever.

Lastly, there is here the doctrine of *assurance.* Some say, " How are you to know that you are saved ? " It can be known ; it ought to be known. " Surely," cries one, "it is presumption to say that you are sure." It is presumption to live without knowing that you are delivered from wrath. Here the apostle speaks of it as a thing well known, that " Jesus delivers us from the wrath coming." He does not say " if," or " perhaps," but he writes that it is so, and therefore he knew it, and we may know it. My brother, you may know that you are saved. " That would make me inexpressibly happy," cries one. Just so, and that is one of the reasons why we would have you know it this day. God saith, " He that believeth in Him hath everlasting life," and therefore the believer may be sure that he has it. Our message is, " He that believeth and is baptized shall be saved ; but he that believeth not shall be damned." God make you to escape that dreadful doom! May you be delivered from the wrath which is coming, for Jesus' sake. Amen.

THREE SIGHTS WORTH SEEING

" For this cause also thank we God without ceasing, because, when ye received the word of God which ye heard of us, ye received it not as the word of men, but as it is in truth, the word of God, which effectually worketh also in you that believe. For ye, brethren, became followers of the churches of God which in Judea are in Christ Jesus : for ye also have suffered like things of your own countrymen, even as they have of the Jews."—1 Thessalonians ii. 13, 14.

PAUL seems very much at home when he is writing to the church at Thessalonica. In his letters to that favoured people he unveils his inmost feelings. He is rather apt to do so when he feels himself quite at ease : for Paul is by no means a man shut up within himself, who is, never at home to any one. When he is battling with an ungrateful people he keeps himself to sharp words and strong arguments ; but when he is writing to a loving, attached, affectionate church, he lets them have the key of his heart, and he lays bare before them his secret emotions. I feel as if we were interviewing Paul to-night—as if we were all sitting in a room with him, and Silas, and Timothy, and were hearing their private conversation. We are come to a round table conference with them, and we are listening to their talk about the ministry which God had committed to them. Even in these two verses we hear of how these holy preachers loved the gospel, told out the gospel, and saw that gospel take hold of their hearer's hearts.

They were not obliged to be reticent about their

own conduct, or their experience with the Thessalonian friends : they were able to tell the story of their transactions with the church of Thessalonica from the very beginning. It is a happy thing to be the pastor of a church where one may wear his heart upon his sleeve. In certain positions prudence demands that we keep ourselvas to ourselves until we know more of the character of those who surround us. This is by no means pleasant ; indeed it is a painful thing to go through life like a man in armour, who scarcely dares to move a single plate of steel, lest somebody should wound him in an unguarded place. One is glad to know that on the face of this earth there is a church where the minister feels himself as much at home as a brother among brethren, and as safe as a father among his sons, since he is not afraid of being misunderstood. It is my joy that for many years I have found such a place of peace, so that I can say with the Shunammite, " I dwell among mine own people." To return to our text : we find the apostle at home, telling out his thoughts in the freest manner. Indeed, he seems to me to show us three sights of the most interesting kind, which it will be pleasing and profitable for us to consider with care. I shall try to speak upon these three things, one after the other.

The first is, *ministers giving thanks.* " For this cause also thank we God without ceasing." Then we have the cause of it, which brings up a second beautiful sight, namely, *hearers receiving the word.* Paul speaks of them thus : " When ye received the word of God which ye heard of us, ye received it not as the word of men, but as it is in truth, the word of God, which effectually worketh also in you that believe." In these words we find a window into the heart of the Thessalonian Christians, and what we see is like a cabinet of jewels. Then we have a third thing which is exceedingly interesting, namely, *new converts exhibiting the family likeness,* turning out to be very like the believers of older churches. Born many miles away from Judea, with a sea dividing them from the first country where the gospel was preached, yet these Thessalonian Gentiles, when converted, looked wonderfully like the converts from among the Jews—" For ye, brethren, became followers of the churches of God which in Judea are in Christ Jesus : for ye also have suffered like things of your own countrymen, even as they have of the Jews."

I. To begin, then : we are asked out to a little social party. We are placed in a corner of a cosy room where we have license and favour to gaze upon MINISTERS GIVING THANKS.

Paul, Silas, and Timothy make up a little meeting. No doubt the Lord is with them, for they form what He has made a quorum. They are within the number to which the promise is made : " Where two or three are gathered together in My name, there am I in the midst of them." These three godly ministers are holding what, if I use a Greek word, I may call a holy eucharistical service—a service of thanksgiving. " For this cause also thank we God without ceasing." It is a pleasant sight to see anybody thanking God ; for the air is heavy with the hum of murmuring, and the roads are dusty with complaints and lamentations. It is a delightful vision to see hard-working, earnest ministers of Christ met together and occupying their time with thanksgiving ; for many waste their hours in speculations, doubtings, and discussions. Let us turn aside and look into their smiling faces !

It will do us good to see who these good men were, and how they came to be in this thankful condition.

And, first, I would remark that *this thankfulness of theirs followed upon sore travail.* It is of no use for you to say, " I shall thank God for a harvest," if you neither plough nor sow. You will have no harvest without labour and patience. " They that sow in tears shall reap in joy " ; but if there be no sowing and no tears there is no promise of any kind of reaping. I have known young preachers envy those who have had many converts, and I do not wonder that they should ; but if they themselves desire to be greatly useful and successful, they must go the same way to work that others have done. In the cause and kingdom of Christ, although the race is not to the swift, it certainly is not to the sluggish ; and although salvation is not of him that willeth nor of him that runneth, it certainly is not of him that does not will and does not run. We may sit and sigh as long as we like, but we shall see no result from lethargy. Dead bees make no honey either in the land of grace or of nature. Neither is anything wrought by merely tucking up your sleeves, and making a brave show. We may plot and we may plan, we may propose and we may expect, but expectations and proposals will fall to the ground like apple-blossoms that have never knit unless we stir ourselves up in the name of God, and throw all the strength we have into the work and faith of labour of love. We shall fail unless we cry for much more strength than nature will yield us. With a vehemence that will not take a denial, we must plead with the Lord until we prevail ; for in this matter " the kingdom of heaven suffereth violence, and the violent taketh it by force." Yes, Paul, and Silas, and Timothy, you would not be sitting together thanking God, if you had not for many a day put your shoulders to the wheel. If you had not laboured night and day, if you had not excercised much labour and travail, and been willing to impart to the people, not only the gospel, but even your own lives also, you would never have rejoiced together in the way you have described. Ministers giving thanks to God are ministers who have worked.

And this work of theirs had been backed by holy living, for the apostle is bold to declare, " Ye are witnesses, and God also, how holily and justly and unblameably we behaved ourselves among you that believe." Brethren, we shall not win success unless we hunt for it by careful lives. You wish to see your Sunday-school class converted. You are anxious to be blest on your tract district. You want to see that little mission-hall crowded, and souls converted. Begin by looking to your own life. As the man is, depend upon it, so will his life-work be. There will not come out of any one of us that which is not in us. You must fill the pitcher, or you cannot go round and fill the cups of those who thirstily ask you for water. That which you would impart of grace or life must be in yourself first ; and when God has wrought it in you, then it shall be yours to work out. The water of life must be placed in you to be a well of living water, springing up, and then the word shall be fulfilled in you— " Out of his belly shall flow rivers of living water." Personal piety is the backbone of success in the service of God. Be you sure of that. Our mistakes and blunders in the work itself usually originate in faults in the closet, faults in the family, faults in our own souls. If we were better, our works would be better. If we walk contrary to God, He will walk contrary to us.

We cannot be too careful of our conduct if we aspire to be used of the Lord. Though the Lord is jealous of all His servants, He is especially jealous of those whom He honours in service. " Be ye clean, that bear the vessels of the Lord." That which He might have passed over in one of His common servants He will not wink at in those whom He largely blesses. Therefore, dear friends, let us remember that rejoicing servants of God must be holy servants of God. They shall not give thanks for the purity of their people unless they have set a holy example themselves. This renders all work for Christ a very solemn thing. May we always think it so, and never go to it in a trifling spirit, but with many cries to the Holy One of Israel that He would make and keep us clean and bright as vessels fit for the Master's use !

You see, dear friends, that these three brethren, who met together, and were thanking God, were men who had worked, and men who had lived holily ; but further notice that, when they congratulated each other, *this mode of expressing their joy by thankfulness prevented their falling into anything like self-laudation*. Neither Paul, nor Silas, nor Timothy, had anything whereof to glory, and they did not meet together either for self-glorification, or for mutual admiration. They glorified God, and thanked Him without ceasing. Let us copy the example of these holy men. Brother, be much in thanking the Lord. If you have had one soul converted by your teaching, thank God. If in your class in the Sabbath-school, or if in your own family at home, you have had one conversion, thank God. I am afraid that we fail in thankfulness. We pray for blessings, and forget to praise for them. We are not grateful enough. I was chiding myself last Tuesday. I think that I selected twenty-eight persons whom I could venture to propose for church-fellowship out of many who came. What a number it was ! I felt when the day was over very weary with the blessed service, and then I chided myself that I had permitted weariness to come in when I should rather have been praising and blessing God. I could not help my weakness, and yet I thought my gratitude ought to have borne me above it. Oh, I recollect the day when I would have given my eyes—aye, given my head—for twenty-eight converts ! I feel that I would sacrifice my all for such a blessing even now. To think that God should send so many in one week, and give me evidence that there are plenty more to follow ! Was not this a delight ? They keep on coming to confess Christ in great numbers still. We ought to be very joyful for this. The whole church should bless God for so many, and pray for more. If it were one soul saved by twenty years' work, we ought to feel that we could dance for joy, and count the service to be as nothing ; but hundreds added to the church should carry us up to the third heaven of delight. As Jacob forgot all his toils when at last he could call the beloved Rachel his own, so should we count nothing hard, laborious, or trying, so long as souls are saved. Oh, to bring souls to God ! Whenever we think of it, or see it done, let us say like these three holy men, " For this cause also thank we God without ceasing."

Notice that *this thankfulness was of a social kind*. " Thank *we* God." They all joined in it. Why, if there was a soul saved anywhere, we ought all to thank God for it ! I hope that over at Walworth Road this week there may be some brought to Christ by their special meetings ; and if they are so brought, glory be to God. What does it matter which church they join ? We hear of God blessing Mr. Moody or somebody else right away in America. Glory be to God for it ! The success of any church is our success. It is all in the family. Let us praise God for it. But some are accustomed to look with a rather jealous eye at God's blessing other denominations, or other prachers, Let us fight against this spirit. O brethren, those of us who have had the most of God's blessing, what a mercy it would be if we were cut out altogether by better and more useful men ! Let our star cease to shine if brighter stars will but shine, and more souls see the blessed light. Do not those of you whom God has blessed feel that you would gladly get out of the way, and leave a clear road for somebody else, if the Lord would use them more than you ? If you do not feel so, I am afraid that the Master will put you out of the way because you are not completely absorbed in His glory. When we are up to the neck in consecration, we are willing to be made nothing of, if God can be glorified thereby. While we cannot be content to see Christ glorified by others and ourselves laid on the shelf, there is a little bit of self left ; and we must try to get rid of it.

At any rate, let us rejoice with those that do rejoice, and triumph in the success of our brethren. Be it ours to make it joint-stock in praising God for all that He works by us all ! What a sweet thing it would be if we oftener met together when God blessed us, and said, " For this cause thank we God " ! We ought all to join in the hallelujahs of the church over souls saved by grace. We must not waste our time in allotting the success to this man, and to that man. Let us at once give all the glory to God. One cries, " It was Timothy that did it." " Oh, no ! " says another, " Silas is the man that brought me to Christ." " Ah ! " says another, " but I like to hear Paul. He is the master-preacher. That young Timothy—why, he is nothing, and Silas is nowhere by the side of Paul." Such comparisons are odious. This kind of talk is evil ; for all God's servants belong to you all, and you must get all the good you can out of them ; but to compare and contrast them is to trifle. Let ministers discourage such vain talk among their people by their hearty love to each other. It is good for God's servants to get together, and to make a common heap of their spoils, and send up a joint thanksgiving for the result of their joint labour. " For this cause thank *we* God without ceasing." Yes, and we do, my brethren ! I can see some here to-night who I know join with me in thanksgiving, as I join heartily with them whenever I think of them. I will bless and praise God for His exceeding mercy in saving souls by them, and by me, and by all His workers.

One thing more is to be noticed : *this was a continual thanksgiving day;* for the apostle says, " For this cause also thank we God *without ceasing*." Our gratitude to God should be as lasting as life, as constant as the bounty to which it bears witness. Our American friends have one Thanksgiving Day in the year, but it was Thanksgiving Day all the year round with Paul and Silas and Timothy when they thought of the Thessalonians. They felt as if they never could leave off thanking God for the Thessalonians, for they knew by sad experience that all churches were not of the same happy kind. There were those Corinthians, for ever quarrelling and thus grieving the apostle. "Never mind." he says, "we will thank God for the Thessalonians." Oh, but there are those Galatians ! They have gone off the line, bewitched by Judaizing teachers. They have wandered into some "modern thought," and left the old orthodox faith. "Yes," says the apostle, "Those Galatians are a burden to me ; but, then, blessed be God for the Thessalonians." So I think we ought to bless God for those that are kept, and for those that are true, and for those that are faithful ; and when our harp is made to hang upon the willows because of part of the work which is barren and unfruitful, yet let us not cease to praise and bless the Lord our God for that part of the work which prospers. Let us magnify Him for those that are brought to know His name. "For this cause also thank we God without ceasing because ye received the word of God."

This spirit of thanksgiving tends to make us stronger and stronger for labour in days to come. Yes, let us sing unto the Lord instead of sighing unto ourselves ! Let us not rob Him of His revenue of praise even in our most desponding moments. "Although my house be not so with God, yet hath He made with me an everlasting covenant ordered in all things and sure." What if Satan does not appear to fall from heaven ? What if the devils do not seem to be subject unto us ? Yet let us rather rejoice because our names are written in heaven. O child of God, fall back upon what the Lord has done, and this shall make you encounter every difficulty with a brave heart ! What the Lord has done is but a token of what He is going to do. Let us hold the fort, and look out for better times. Never let us dream of fainting or retreating. Do not say, "I will give it up because of the Galatians." No, but go at it again because of the Thessalonians. Do not say, "I am worried and wearied with the Corinthians." No, but with your heart full of joy, persevere in your Master's service, because many Thessalonians have received the word, not as the word of man, but as the word of God. Hallelujah, there is still something to sing about ! Bring out the trumpets : we are not yet silenced, nor shall we be while the Lord liveth. The walls of Jericho will be more likely to fall before our trumpets than our tremblings.

So I have painted for you an ancient interior—you can see those three good men singing together to the praise of God as they think of their Thessalonian converts.

Ah, my hearers, you could make some of us very happy ! If you gave your hearts to the Lord, how you would cheer and comfort us ! And some of you that do love the Lord would do us a world of good if you would come and tell us what the Lord has done for your souls. If you have been blessed, do not hide it. If you do, you will rob us of our wages, for our wages come to us very much through our knowing that God has blessed our ministry. Think of this, and treat us fairly and kindly, even as we have sought your good. I, for one, have had such weary times of wolf-hunting that I should be heartily glad to have the quiet joy of watching the young lambs, and noting the growth of the sheep.

Now we leave the ministers, and think of the people.

II. The second sight which we have to look at is, HEARERS RECEIVING THE WORD. Let us keep close to the text. "When ye received the word of God which ye heard of us, ye received it not as the word of men, but as it is in truth, the word of God, which effectually worketh also in you that believe."

Notice, first, *these people received the word of God.* They were willing to hear it ; they were anxious to hear it ; they heard it, and they were attentive in the hearing of it. They lent a willing ear and a ready mind. They did not cavil, and dispute, and question, but they received the word of God. Happy preacher who has such people to deal with ! If we have them not, let us work on till we gather them. Whether they will hear or whether they will forbear, let us tell the people our Lord's message. But if God favours us with receptive hearers, let us be instant in season and out of season. A good bit of soil like that ought to be most diligently ploughed and sown. Thank God, there are, I trust, many here who have received the word of God so far, that they are willing to learn, and anxious to know its meaning, and to feel its power ! Among you our labour is lightened by hope, and cheered with expectation.

But next, *these people had doubly received the word of God ;* at least, the word is twice mentioned in our version. "When ye received the word of God which ye heard of us, ye received it." In the Greek those are two different words altogether. The second "received" might, perhaps, better be read, "accepted." I do not think that I should be straining a point if I read it, "Ye welcomed it." They first received it by eagerly hearing it. They wanted to know what it was all about : they were attentive to it, and wanted to understand it. When they had heard it they rejoiced, and said, "Oh, yes, yes, yes, this is the very thing we want !" They embraced it. That word will do—they *embraced* it. They put their arms around it, and would not let it go. They were hospitable to the gospel, and said, "Come in, thou blessed of the Lord : come and live in our hearts !" They assented and they consented to the word of the Lord. They first appreciated the gospel, and then they apprehended it by faith. They were like the man that was hungry in a foreign land, and he could not make the people quite understand ; but as soon as they brought an article of food which he liked he fell to directly, and made them comprehend that he would be glad of more of that sort of thing. By his hearty reception of what they brought, the hungry man said plainly, "Bring some more of that." So we have a people about us, thank God, that are looking out for the gospel ! They are always willing to hear it if men will but preach it ; and when they do get it they mean business, and feed upon the word with hearty appetite. How glad I am to feed men that will eat ! It is a pleasure indeed. The spiritually hungry welcome heavenly food ; they take it into themselves, and receive it as the bread their souls crave after. Oh, what a mercy it is when sermons are preached which feed souls, and souls hear so as to feed thereon ! It is a happy day when a full Christ and empty sinners meet. Now, I am persuaded, dear friends, that if any of you do not know the gospel—really do not know it—and yet are heavy of spirit and cannot rest, and are unhappy, it will be a very blessed thing for you to find out what the gospel is. I am pretty sure many of you are in such a condition that as soon as you really know that the doctrine proclaimed to you is God's gospel, you will receive it into your very souls, and say, "There is none like it. That is the very thing we have been looking after all our lives." I think I hear one of you say, " I have been hunting after this for years. I did not know that there was anything like it, but it suits me to a turn. It fits me as a key fits a lock: it enters every ward of the lock of my soul as if it were made for me." Brethren, I bear witness that when I received the gospel of Jesus Christ, it seemed to me as if Jesus Christ had made the gospel on purpose for me, and for me only. If there had been nobody else in the world, and Jesus had made a gospel for me only, it could not have been more adapted for me. His gospel exactly suited that poor sinner who, on one snowy morning, looked to him and was lightened. My dear hearer, *you* will find Jesus the very Saviour for you. " But I am an out-of -the-way sinner," cries one. Have you never heard of Him who can have compassion on the ignorant, and on those who are out of the way ? What a wonderful text that is for you—you out-of-the-way ones ! He can have compassion on those that are out of the way. There is a remedy in the gospel for your disease. For the particular shape your malady has taken the Lord has a special eye. His Son, Jesus, has a plaster suited for your peculiar sore, a medicine adapted to your peculiar need. May the Holy Spirit bring you to receive it as these Thessalonians did !

And then, if I may trouble you to look at the text again, you will notice that the word " *it* " is in italics ; and so is the word " *as*." Let me read the text again : " When ye received the word of God which ye heard of us, ye received not the word of men." You see I have left out the " it " and the " as " because they are not really there, though they are correctly added by the translators as giving the meaning of the apostle. Verbally they are not in the text. I take the sense out of its connection, and say that *these Thessalonians received not the word of men*. And I like them for that. Oh, but there were very learned men in those days ! When Paul was on earth, and a little before his day, some of the greatest natural minds that ever existed were in Greece teaching the people. Yet the Thessalonians were in such a state that they received not the word of men. They did not hearken to Plato, or accept Socrates, for there was something about them which made them hunger for more than the philosophers could bring them. God's elect are of that mind. You may know the Lord's sheep by the fact that " a stranger will they not follow: for they know not the voice of strangers." They will not receive the word of man ; it is too light, too chaffy, too frothy for them. You may put it before them in the daintiest guise, illustrate it with poetry, and prove it by the fictions of science, but they cannot feed on such wind. They receive not the word of men ; they will not have it ; they want something more substantial.

To come back to our translation : *they received not the gospel as the word of men*. In these days there are some who receive the gospel, but they receive it as the word of men. This is their spirit— " Yes, I know that such is the view that is held by Mr. Black ; but there is another view held by Mr. White ; and another view is upheld by Professor Gray. All these different ' views ' are supposed to be very much upon a par." Beloved friends, this is not our way ; there is the truth of God, and there is a lie ; and I want you always to feel that there is a solemn difference between the true and the false,

and that no lie is of the truth. " Believe not every spirit, but try the spirits whether they be of God." If one says, " Yes," and the other says, " No," it cannot be that they are both true. Salvation is of grace, or else of works : it cannot be of both. Salvation is the work of God or else of man : it cannot be a joint-stock-company affair. There is truth, and there is error ; and these are opposite the one to the other. Do not indulge yourselves in the folly with which so many are duped—that truth may be error, and error may be truth ; that black is white, and white is black, and that there is a whity-brown that goes in between, which is, perhaps, the best of the whole lot.

There is an essential difference between man's word and God's word, and it is fatal to mistake the one for the other. If you receive even the gospel as the word of man you cannot get the blessing out of it ; for the sweetness of the gospel lies in the confidence of our heart that this is the word of God. You fall back upon Holy Scripture in the grief of an aching heart ; but you cannot rest, however soft the pillow of the promise may seem to be, till you can surely say, " I know that it is of God." If you have even the shadow of a doubt about it, comfort oozes out. The life of comfort flies before doubt, even as love is said to fly out at the window when want comes in at the door. Prick the heart—aye, with but a needle's point—and life will go ; and prick the heart of faith—aye, even with the smallest dobt, and the life of joy is gone ! The joy of faith, and the strength of faith, yea, and the life of faith, are gone when you distrust the word of the Lord !

Are we then infallible ? No, but the Book is. Do we infallibly understand the Book ? No, but the Spirit of God will teach us what He Himself means ; and of those truths which He teaches us we get so firm a grip that we say, " No, no ; I am never going to argue about this any more ! This is proved to my heart and soul beyond all further question. It is woven into my experience. It has stamped itself on my consciousness. It has done that for me which no lie could do. This is the revelation of God, and I will die sooner than I will ever, by any action of mine, permit a doubt to be cast upon it." Brethren, do you accept the word of God as infallible ? Thus have I learned the gospel of Christ. Have you learned it in this fashion ? Then you have received the gospel aright, but not else.

To receive the gospel as the word of man is not to receive the gospel ; but to receive it as a revelation from God, true, sure, infallible, so as to risk your whole soul on it, and to feel that there is no risk—this is to receive the gospel in truth. After this manner we receive it with the deepest reverence ; not as a thing that I am to judge, but as that which judges me ; not as a matter of opinion, but as a sure truth with which I must make my opinion agree. It makes all the difference whether we rule the truth or the truth rules us. The reverent obedience of the understanding to the word of the Lord is a great part of sanctification.

To receive the gospel as the word of God is to receive it with strong assurance. Other things *may* be true, but this *must* be true. Other things may be questioned, but this must be implicitly believed. This gospel of Jesus Christ is of God as surely as you live, and you have not received it at all if you do not know it to be the word of God.

It is to receive it with obedience, because it comes

with authority: to say, "This I must yield to. Other truths I may be master of, but this is master of me. Other truths I may or may not hold—they may not be of sufficient importance for me to bow before them; but this truth has God himself enshrined within it, and therefore I cannot be disobedient to the heavenly vision." With man's statements we are men, but before God's truth we are converted into little children. Is this so with you?

This gospel, if it is received as the word of God, comes with power. Aye, do not let us be misunderstood; the power we mean is by no means a common thing! It is not the force of persuasion, nor the energy of rhetoric; it is divine power—the finger of God. There is still in the world a miraculous force—the divine energy of the Holy Ghost. It does not give us to speak with tongues, neither do we hear it in rushing mighty wind; but it is as unmistakable to those who have it as if it did come with such extraordinary signs. Sometimes a truth has been borne in upon my soul—and I doubt not you can say the same—with inward evidence which is beyond all argument for force and certainty. Though it is not logic, we are more sure than if conquered by reasoning. We prefer it to the demonstrations of mathematics so far as our own assurance is concerned. In my own case, I could not see, but I did more than see: my inner soul without eyes beheld the essential principle of truth. I did not touch it, and yet my inner soul handled it, tasted it, fed on it. It went into the secret spring-head and well-spring of my being, and became one of its first principles. If any man said that the Lord Jesus was not able to save, and that His gospel was not true, I snapped my fingers at him. I could not stop to answer him, because he seemed to be wilfully denying self-evident fact, and there is no answering such folly. For a man to tell me that the gospel is not true, when the Spirit seals it on my heart, is all in vain. He might as well tell me that there was no light when I stood gazing on a landscape in the brightness of the sun, or assure me that there was no such thing as air when the strong north wind was on my cheeks. He might as well tell me that there was no nutriment in food when I had just lost my hunger, and felt refreshed by what I had eaten. There are some things that we have no patience to argue about; we have done with discussion concerning them.

If you do not know spiritual things, ask God to let you know them. But you are out of court as a witness: you cannot prove a negative, nor can your negative disprove our positive. We cannot argue with you who are dead in sin, and have not received as yet spiritual senses. What can you know? Why should we dispute with the blind concerning colours? How can we discuss music with the deaf?

"Oh," says one, "but I do not believe in your spiritual experience!" I did not say you did; on the contrary, I expected you not to believe in it. But what does that prove? Why, only that you have no spiritual perception! That you have not perceived spiritual things is true; but it is no proof that there are none to perceive. The whole case is like that of the Irishman who tried to upset evidence by non-evidence. Four witnesses saw him commit a murder. He pleaded that he was not guilty, and wished to establish his innocence by producing forty persons who did not see him do it. Of what use would that have been? So, if forty people declare that there is no power of the Holy Ghost going with the word, this only proves that the forty people do not know what others do know. If there are four of us that do know it—well, we shall not cease our witness. We receive God's word as the word of God, because it comes to us with that power which effectually worketh in them that believe. It works in us a horror of sin, a detestation of self-confidence, and an aspiration after holy and heavenly things. It works in us love to God and good-will to men. It works in us aspirations after the divine. It works in us victory over evil from day to day; and while it does that, the proof of it is within us. The witness and seal of the truth of the gospel are within our own character and being, and we cannot therefore give up our confidence. People who have come to this pass make glad their ministers. Paul, Silas, and Timothy are all happy men when surrounded by hearers who have received the gospel in all its divine authority and power.

III. Now my time has gone, otherwise my third point would have been a very interesting one. These three men are rejoicing in CONVERTS WHO ARE EXHIBITING A FAMILY LIKENESS.

I only call your attention to the fact that the apostle says, "Ye, brethren, became followers of the churches of God which in Judea are in Christ Jesus." Here are people converted in Judea, and they are of a strongly Jewish type; quite another set of people over at Thessalonica become converted to Christ, and though they are thoroughly of the Greek type, they are very like the converts in Judea. They know nothing about the law of Moses, they have been heathens, worshipping idols; and yet, when they are converted, the strange thing is that they are exceedingly like those Jews over yonder, to whom idolatry was an abomination. Greek believers are like Hebrew believers. They have never spoken to one another, and nobody has been there to tell them the peculiarities of Christians, and yet a family likeness is distinctly visible. Were you never startled with this, that if, in the preaching of the gospel to-day, we were to bring to the Lord Jesus a person of high rank, and another of the very lowest extraction, they have the same experience, and upon the greatest of subjects they talk in the same way? "Oh, but," you say, "they pick up certain phrases." No, no! They differ in speech: the likeness is in heart and character. I frequently meet with converts who have not attended this place of worship more than half-a-dozen times, but they have been converted, and when they come to tell the story of their inner life you would suppose that they had been born and bred among us, and had learned all our ways; for, though they do not use the phrases which we use, yet they say the same things. The fact is, we are all alike lost and ruined, and we are born again in the same way, and we find the Saviour in the same way, and we rejoice in Him when we do find Him after much the same fashion, and express ourselves very much after the same style. Believers differ in many things, and yet they are alike in the main things. There are no two exactly alike in all the family of God, and yet the likeness to the Elder Brother is to be seen more or less in each one.

It is to me one of the evidences of the truth and divine nature of the work of grace in the heart, that if you take a Hottentot in his kraal, and he is converted, and you take a university man, who has won all the degrees of learning, and he is converted, yet you would not know Sambo from the Doctor when they begin to talk about the things of God. The Hottentot's English may be broken, but his theology is sound. The uneducated man's words may limp, but his heart will leap. Ruin, redemption, and regeneration are the chief subjects in every case. When I am talking sometimes with young converts, and they put their statements oddly and ignorantly, I am reminded of Father Taylor, when he was getting old. The old man sometimes lost the thread of his discourse, and whenever he did so, he used to say, "There, I cannot find the end of that sentence, but I am bound for the kingdom! Brethren, I am bound for the kingdom!" Off he went to something else; for though he could not complete the paragraph he was bound for the kingdom. Some brethren and sisters cannot see to the end of their own experience, but they are bound for the kingdom. They cannot put this and that together to make it ship-shape : but you can see that they are bound for the kingdom. There is the same tear of repentance, the same glance of faith, the same thrill of joy, the same song of confidence : each one according to his measure enjoys the same life, if he is indeed bound for the kingdom. The babe is like the man, and the man reminds you of the babe. We are one spirit in Christ Jesus.

I will not enlarge, except to say that it makes us sing for joy when we can see in ourselves a likeness to the children of God. We, too, resemble the early saints in our experiences. Opposition and tribulation come to us in our measure as they did to them. There are the same afflictions, the same persecutions, the same trials, wherever the work of Christ goes on ; but there is the same mighty God to carry on the work of grace, and the same promises of grace to be fulfilled to every believer.

Dear friends, are you believers in the Lord Jesus Christ ? If you are, joy and rejoice with me ; but if you are not, oh, how I wish you were ! Whatever comforts of life you enjoy, you are missing the only thing that makes life worth having. If you are not yet resting on Christ Jesus, you have not yet found out the kernel of the nut. You are boring away at the hard shell of life, and unless you turn to Christ you will die worrying and wearying over the shell, and you will never taste the sweet kernel. If you did but know our Lord Jesus, if you did but trust Him, if you did but find salvation in Him, then you would find that if earth cannot be heaven, it can become marvellously like it. The earnest of our everlasting inheritance may be enjoyed even here. Would God you would seek my Lord and Master, for if you seek Him He will be found of you ! What a pleasure it would be if every one at this time would receive the gospel as the word of God ! Spirit of God, grant that it may be so, for Jesus' sake ! Amen.

SATANIC HINDRANCES

"Satan hindered us."—1 Thessalonians ii. 18.

PAUL, and Silas, and Timothy, were very desirous to visit the Church at Thessalonica, but they were unable to do so for the singular reason announced in the text, namely, "Satan hindered us." *It was not from want of will*, for they had a very great attachment to the Thessalonian brethren, and they longed to look them in the face again. They said to the Thessalonians, "We give thanks to God always for you all, making mention of you in our prayers : remembering without ceasing your work of faith, and labour of love, and patience of hope in our Lord Jesus Christ, in the sight of God and our Father." Their will was overruled as to visiting the Church together, but being anxious for its welfare, they sent Timothy alone to minister for a time in its midst. It was not want of will which hindered them, but want of power. *They were not prevented by God's special providence.* We find on certain occasions that Paul was not allowed to go precisely where his heart would have led him. "They assayed to go into Bithynia : but the Spirit suffered them not." "They were forbidden of the Holy Ghost to preach the word in Asia," but their course was directed towards Troas that they might preach in Europe the unsearchable riches of Christ. They could not, however, trace their absence from Thessalonica to any divine interposition ; it appeared to them to proceed from the great adversary : "Satan hindered them." How Satan did so it would be useless to affirm dogmatically, but we may form a reasonable conjecture. I find in the margin of my pulpit Bible by Bagster, this note, which may probably be correct. "Satan hindered Paul by raising such a storm of persecution against Him at Berea, and other places, that it was deemed prudent to delay his visit till the storm was some-what allayed." Yet I can hardly allow this to have been the only hindrance, for Paul was very courageous, and having a strong desire to visit Thessalonica, no fear of opposition would have kept him away. He did not shun the hottest part of the battle, but like a truly valiant champion, delighted most to be found in the thick of his foes. Possibly the antagonism of the various philosophers whom he met with at Athens, and the heresies at Corinth, from which it seems that this epistle was written, may have called for his presence on the scene of action. He felt that he could not leave struggling Churches to their enemies ; he must contend with the grievous wolves, and unmask the evil ones who wore the garb of angels of light. Satan had moved the enemies of the truth to industrious opposition, and thus the apostle and his companions were hindered from going to Thessalonica. Or it may be that Satan had excited dissensions and discords in the Churches which Paul was visiting, and therefore he was obliged to stop first in one and then in another to settle their differences ; to bring to bear the weight of his own spiritual influence upon the various divided sections of the Church to restore them to unity. Well, whether persecution, or philosophic heresy, or the divisions of the Church, were the outward instruments we cannot tell, but Satan was assuredly the prime mover. You will perhaps wonder why the devil should care so much about Paul and his whereabouts. Why should he take so much interest in keeping these three men from that particular Church ? This leads us to observe what wonderful importance is attached to the action of Christian ministers. Here is the master of all evil, the prince of the power of the air, intently watching the journeying of three humble men ; and apparently far more concerned about their movements than about the doings of Nero or Tiberius. These despised heralds of mercy were his most dreaded foes ; they preached that name which makes hell tremble ; they declared that righteousness against which Satanic hate always vents itself with its utmost power. With malicious glance the arch-enemy watched their daily path, and with cunning hand hindered them at all points. It strikes us that Satan was desirous to keep these apostolic men from the Church of Thessalonica because the Church was young and weak, and he thought that if it was not fostered and succoured by the preaching and presence of Paul he might yet slay the young child. Moreover, he has of old a fierce hatred of the preaching of the gospel, and possibly there had been no public declaration of the truth throughout Thessalonica since Paul had gone, and he was afraid lest the firebrands of gospel truth should be again flung in among the masses, and a gracious conflagration should take place. Besides, Satan always hates Christian fellowship ; it is his policy to keep Christians apart. Anything which can divide saints from one another he delights in. He attaches far more importance to godly intercourse than we do. Since union is strength, he does his best to promote separation : and so he would keep Paul away from these brethren who might have gladdened his heart, and whose hearts he might have cheered ; he would hinder their fraternal intercourse that they might miss the strength which always flows from Christian communion and Christian sympathy.

This is not the only occasion in which Satan has hindered good men : indeed this has been his practice in all ages, and we have selected this one particular incident that some who are hindered by Satan may draw comfort from it, and that we may have an opportunity (if the Spirit of God shall enable us) of saying a good and forceful word to any who count it strange because this fiery trial has happened unto them.

I. Let us open our discourse by observing that IT HAS BEEN SATAN'S PRACTICE OF OLD TO HINDER, WHEREVER HE COULD, THE WORK OF GOD. " Satan hindered us " is the testimony which all the saints in heaven will bear against the arch enemy. This is the witness of all who have written a holy line on the historic page, or carved a consecrated name on the rock of immortality, " Satan hindered us."

In sacred writ, we find Satan interfering to hinder the completeness of *the personal character of individual saints.* The man of Uz was perfect and upright before God, and to all appearance, would persevere in producing a finished picture of what the believer in God should be. Indeed so had he been enabled to live that the arch-fiend could find no fault with his actions, and only dared to impute wrong motives to him. He had considered Job, and he could find no mischief in him ; but then he hinted, " Hast not thou made an hedge about him, and about his house, and about all that he hath on every side ? " Satan sought to turn the life-blessing which Job was giving to God into a curse, and therefore he buffeted him sorely. He stripped him of all his substance. The evil messengers trod upon one another's heels : and their tidings of woe only ceased when his goods were all destroyed and his children had all perished. The poor afflicted parent was then smitten in his bone and in his flesh, till he was fain to sit upon a dunghill and scrape himself with a potsherd. Even then the picture had no blot of sin upon it, the pencil was held with a steady hand by the patient one ; and therefore

Satan made another attempt to hinder his retaining his holy character ; he excited his wife to say, " Wherefore dost thou hold fast thy integrity ? Curse God, and die." This was a great and grievous hindrance to the completion of Job's marvellous career, but, glory be unto God, the man of patience not only overcame Satan, but he made him a steppingstone to a yet greater height of illustrious virtue ; for ye know the patience of Job, and ye would not have known it if Satan had not illuminated it with the blaze of flaming afflictions. Had not the vessel been burnt in the furnace, the bright colours had not been so fixed and abiding. The trial through which Job passed, brought out the lustre of his matchless endurance in submission and resignation to God. Now, just as the enemy of old waylaid and beset the patriarch to hinder his perseverance in the fair path of excellence, so will he do with us. You may be congratulating yourself this morning, " I have hitherto walked consistently ; no man can challenge my integrity." Beware of boasting, for your virtue will yet be tried ; Satan will direct his engines against that very virtue for which you are the most famous. If you have been hitherto a firm believer, your faith will ere long be attacked, if up till now you have been meek as Moses, expect to be tempted to speak unadvisedly with your lips. The birds will peck at your ripest fruit, and the wild boar will dash his tusks at your choicest vines. Oh, that we had among us more eminence of piety, more generosity of character, more fidelity of behaviour ! In all these respects, I doubt not, many have set out with the highest aims and intentions, but alas ! how often have they had to cry, " Satan hindered us ! "

This is not the enemy's only business ; for he is very earnest in endeavouring to hinder *the emancipation of the Lord's redeemed ones.* Ye know the memorable story of Moses : when the children of Israel were in captivity in Egypt, God's servant stood before their haughty oppressor with his rod in his hand, and in Jehovah's name he declared, " Thus saith the Lord, Let My people go, that they may serve Me." A sign was required. The rod was cast upon the ground, and it became a serpent. At this point, Satan hindered. Jannes and Jambres withstood Moses. We read that the magicians did so with their enchantments, whether by devilish arts or by sleight of hand, we need not now enquire : in either case they did the devil service, and they did it well—for Pharaoh's heart was hardened when he saw that the magicians wrought, in appearance, the self-same miracles as Moses. Brethren, take this as a type of Satan's hindrances to the word of the Lord. Christ's servants came forth to preach the gospel ; their ministry was attended with signs and wonders. " My kingdom is shaken," said the prince of evil, " I must bestir myself " ; and straightway he sent magicians to work lying signs and wonders without number. Apocryphal wonders were and are as plentiful as the frogs of Egypt. Did the apostles preach the sacrifice of Christ ?—the devil's apostles preached the sacrifice of the mass. Did the saints uplift the cross ?—the devil's servants upheld the crucifix. Did God's ministers speak of Jesus as the one infallible Head of the Church ?—the devil's servants proclaimed the false priest of Rome as standing in the self-same place. Romanism is a most ingenious imitation of the gospel : it is the magicians " doing so with their enchantments." If you study well the spirit and genius of the great

Antichrist, you will see that its great power lies in its being an exceedingly clever counterfeit of the gospel of the Lord Jesus Christ. As far as tinsel could counterfeit gold, and paste could simulate the gem, and candle-light could rival the sun in its glory, and a drop in the bucket could imitate the sea in its strength, it has copied God's great masterpiece, the gospel of our Lord Jesus Christ ; and to this day, as God's servants scatter the pure gold of truth, their worst enemies are those who utter base coin, on which they have feloniously stamped the image and superscription of the King of kings.

You have another case farther on in history—and all Old Testament history is typical of what is going on around us now. God was about to give a most wonderful system of instruction to Israel and to the human race, by way of type and ceremony, in the wilderness. Aaron and his sons were selected to represent the great High Priest of our salvation, the Lord Jesus Christ. In every garment which they wore there was a symbolical significance ; every vessel of that sanctuary in which they ministered taught a lesson : every single act of worship, whether it were the sprinkling of blood or the burning of incense, was made to teach precious and important truths to the sons of men. What a noble roll was that volume of the book which was unfolded in the wilderness, at the foot of Sinai ! How God declared Himself and the glory of the coming Messiah in the persons of Aaron and his sons ! What then ? With this Satan interfered. Moses and Aaron could say, " Satan hindered us." Korah, Dathan, and Abiram arrogantly claimed a right to the priesthood ; and on a certain day they stood forth with brazen censers in their hands, thrusting themselves impertinently into the office which the Lord had assigned to Aaron and to his sons. The earth opened and swallowed them up alive : true prophecy of what shall become of those who thrust themselves into the office of the priesthood where none but Jesus Christ can stand. You may see the parallel this day. Christ Jesus is the only priest who offers sacrifice of blood, and He brings that sacrifice no more, for having once offered it He has perfected for ever those who are set apart. " This Man, after He had offered one sacrifice for sins for ever, sat down on the right hand of God." Paul, with the strongest force of logic, proves that Christ does not offer a continual sacrifice, but that, having offered it once for all, His work is finished, and He sits down at the right hand of the Father. Now, this doctrine of a finished atonement and completed sacrifice seemed likely to overrun the world—it was such a gracious unfolding of the divine mind, that Satan could not look upon it without desiring to hinder it ; and, therefore, look ye on every hand, and you can see Korah, Dathan, and Abiram, in those Churches which are branches of Antichrist, I mean the Anglican and the Roman. Men to this very day, call themselves " priests," and read prayers from a book in which the rubric runs, " Then shall the priest say——." These arrogate to themselves a priesthood other than that which is common to all the saints : some of them even claim to offer a daily sacrifice, to celebrate an unbloody sacrifice at the thing which they call an altar ; and they claim to have power to forgive sin, saying to sick and dying persons, " By authority committed unto me, I absolve thee from all thy sins." This in England, and this throughout Europe, is the great hindrance to the propagation of the gospel—the priestly pretensions of a set of men who are no priests

of God, though they may be priests of Baal. Thus the ministers of Jesus are made to cry, " Satan hindereth us."

Take another instance of Satanic hatred. When Joshua had led the tribes across the Jordan, they were to attack the various cities which God had given them for a heritage, and from Dan to Beersheba the whole land was to be theirs. After the taking of Jericho, the first contact into which they came with the heathen Canaanites ended in a disastrous defeat to the servants of God. " They fled," it is written, " before the men of Ai." Here again you hear the cry, " Satan hindered us." Joshua might have gone from city to city exterminating the nations, as they justly deserved to be, but Achan had taken of the accursed thing and hidden it in his tent, therefore no victory could be won by Israel till his theft and sacrilege had been put away. Beloved, this is symbolic to the Christian Church. We might go from victory to victory ; our home mission operations might be successful, and our foreign agencies might be crowned with triumph, if it were not that we have Achans in the camp at home. When Churches have no conversions, it is more than probable that hypocrites concealed among them have turned away the Lord's blessing. You who are inconsistent, who make the profession of religion the means of getting wealth, you who unite yourselves with God's people, but at the same time covet the goodly Babylonish garment, and the wedge of gold, you are those who cut the sinews of Zion's strength ; you prevent the Israel of God from going forth to victory. Ah ! little do we know, beloved, how Satan has hindered us. We, as a Church, have had much reason to thank God, but how many more might within these walls have been added to the number of this Church if it had not been for the coldness of some, the indifference of others, the inconsistency of a few, and the worldliness of many more ! Satan hinders us not merely by direct opposition, but by sending Achans into the midst of our camp.

I will give you one more picture. View the building of Jerusalem after it had been destroyed, by the Babylonians. When Ezra and Nehemiah were found to build, the devil was sure to stir up Sanballat and Tobiah to cast down. There was never a revival of religion without a revival of the old enmity. If ever the Church of God is to be built, it will be in troublous times. When God's servants are active, Satan is not without vigilant myrmidons who seek to counteract their efforts.

The history of the Old Testament Church is a history of Satan endeavouring to hinder the work of the Lord. I am sure you will admit it has been the same since the days of the Lord Jesus Christ. When He was on earth Satan hindered Him. He dared to attack Him to His face personally ; and when that failed, Pharisees, Sadducees, Herodians, and men of all sorts hindered Him. When the apostles began their ministry, Herod and the Jews sought to hinder them ; and when persecution availed not, then all sorts of heresies and schisms broke out in the Christian Church : Satan still hindered them. A very short time after the taking up of our Lord, the precious sons of Zion, comparable to fine gold, had become like earthen pitchers, the work of the hands of the potter ; the glory had departed, and the lustre of truth was gone, because by false doctrine, lukewarmness, and worldliness, Satan hindered them. When the Reformation dawned, if God raised up a Luther, the devil brought out an Ignatius Loyola to hinder him. Here in England, if God had His Latimers and His Wickcliffes, the devil had his Gardiners and Bonners. When in the modern reformation Whitefield and Wesley thundered like the voice of God, there were ordained reprobates found to hinder them, to hold them up to opprobrium and shame. Never, since the first hour struck in which goodness came into conflict with evil, has it ceased to be true that Satan hindered us. From all points of the compass, all along the line of battle, in the vanguard and in the rear, at the dawn of day and in the midnight, Satan hindered us. If we toil in the field he seeks to break the plough-shares, if we build the walls he labours to cast down the stones ; if we would serve God in suffering or in conflict—everywhere Satan hinders us.

II.—We shall now, in the second place, INDICATE MANY WAYS IN WHICH SATAN HAS HINDERED US.

The prince of evil is very busy in hindering *those who are just coming to Jesus Christ.* Here he spends the main part of his skill. Some of us who know the Saviour recollect the fierce conflicts which we had with Satan when we first looked to the cross and lived. Others of you, here this morning, are just passing through that trying season : I will address myself to you. Beloved friends, you long to be saved, but ever since you have given any attention to these eternal things you have been the victim of deep distress of mind. Do not marvel at this. This is usual, so usual as to be almost universal. I should not wonder if you are perplexed with the doctrine of election. It will be suggested to you that you are not one of the chosen of God, although your common sense will teach you that it might just as well be suggested to you that you are, since you know neither the one nor the other, nor indeed can know until you have believed in Jesus ; your present business is with the precept which is revealed, not with election which is concealed. Your business is with that exhortation, " Believe on the Lord Jesus Christ, and thou shalt be saved." It is possible that the great fighting-ground between predestination and free-will may be the dry and desert place in which your soul is wandering : now you will never find any comfort there. The wisest of men have despaired of ever solving the mystery of those two matters, and it is not at all probable that you will find peace in puzzling yourself about it. Your business is not with metaphysical difficulty, but with faith in the atonement of the Lord Jesus Christ, which is simple and plain enough. It is possible that your sins now come to your remembrance, and though once you thought little enough of them, now it is hinted to you by Satanic malice that they are too great to be pardoned ; to which, I pray you, give the lie, by telling Satan this truth, that " All manner of sin and blasphemy shall be forgiven unto men." It is very likely that the sin against the Holy Ghost much molests you. You read that whosoever shall speak a word against the Holy Ghost, it shall never be forgiven him. In this, too, you may be greatly tried ; and I wonder not that you are, for this is a most painfully difficult subject. One fact may cheer you—if you repent of your sins, you have not committed the unpardonable offence, since that sin necessitates hardness of heart for ever ; and so long as a man has any tenderness of conscience, and any softness of spirit, he has not so renounced the Holy Spirit as to have lost His presence. It may be that you are the victim of blasphemous thoughts. This very morning, since your have been sitting here,

torrents of the filth of hell have been pouring through your soul. At this be not astonished, for there are some of us who delight in holiness and are pure in heart, who nevertheless have been at times sorely tried with thoughts which were never born in our hearts, but which were injected into them—suggestions born in hell, not in our spirits ; to be hated, and to be loathed, but cast into our minds that they might hinder and trouble us. Now though Satan may hinder thee as he did the child who was brought to Jesus, of whom we read that as he was " a coming, the devil threw him down and tare him," yet do thou come notwithstanding ; for though seven devils were in him, Jesus would not cast the coming sinner out. Even though thou shouldst feel a conviction that the unpardonable sin has fallen to thy lot, yet dare to trust in Jesus ; and, if thou dost do that, I warrant thee there shall be a joy and a peace in believing which shall overcome him of whom we read, that he hath " hindered us."

But I must not stop long on any one point where there are so many. Satan is sure to hinder Christians *when they are earnest in prayer.* Have you not frequently found, dear friends, when you have been most earnest in supplication, that something or other will start across your mind to make you cease from the exercise ? It appears to me that we shake the tree and no fruit drops from it ; and just when one more shake would bring down the luscious fruit, the devil touches us on the shoulder and tells us it is time to be gone, and so we miss the blessing we might have attained. I mean that just when prayer would be the most successful we are tempted to abstain from it. When my spirit has sometimes laid hold upon the angel, I have been painfully conscious of a counter influence urging me to cease from such importunity, and let the Lord alone, for His will would be done ; or if the temptation did not come in that shape yet in some other, to cease to pray because prayer after all could not avail. O brethren, I know if you are much in prayer you can sing Cowper's hymn :—

> " What various hindrances we meet
> In coming to the mercy seat."

The same is true of *Christians when under the promptings of the Spirit of God, or when planning any good work.* You have been prompted sometimes to speak to such a one. " Run, speak to that young man," has been the message in your ear. You have not done it—Satan has hindered you. You have been told on a certain occasion—you do not know how (but believe me, we ought to pay great respect to these inward whispers), to visit such-and-such a person and help him. You have not done it—Satan hindered you. You have been sitting down by the fire one evening reading a missionary report concerning Hindostan, or some district destitute of the truth, and you have thought, " Now I have a little money which I might give to this object " ; but then it has come across you that there is another way of spending it more profitably to your family—so Satan has hindered you. Or you yourself thought of doing a little in a certain district by way of preaching, and teaching, or commencing some new Ragged School, or some other form of Christian effort, but as sure as ever you began to plan it something or other arose, and Satan hindered you. If he possibly can, he will come upon God's people in those times when they are full of thought and ardour, and ready for Christian effort, that he may murder their infant plans and cast these suggestions of the Holy Spirit out of their minds. How often too has Satan hindered us *when we have entered into the work*! In fact, beloved, we never ought to expect a success unless we hear the devil making a noise. I have taken it as a certain sign that I am doing little good when the devil is quiet. It is generally a sign that Christ's kingdom is coming when men begin to lie against you, and slander you, and the world is in an uproar, casting out your name as evil. Oh! those blessed tempests! Do not give me calm weather when the air is still and heavy, and when lethargy is creeping over one's spirit. Lord, send a hurricane, give us a little stormy weather : when the lightning flashes and the thunder rolls, then God's servants know that the Lord is abroad and that His right hand is no longer in His bosom, that the moral atmosphere will get clear, that God's kingdom will come, and His will be done on earth, even as it is in heaven. "Peace, peace, peace," that is the flap of the dragon's wings ; the stern voice which proclaims perpetual war is the voice of the Captain of our salvation. You say, how is this? "Think not that I am come to send peace on earth : I came not to send peace, but a sword. For I am come to set a man at variance against his father, and the daughter against her mother, and the daughter-in-law against her mother-in-law. And a man's foes shall be they of his own household." Peace, physical, Christ does make ; there is to be no strife with the fist, no blow with the sword, but peace, moral, and peace, spiritual, can never be in this world where Jesus Christ is, so long as error is there. But, you know, beloved, that you cannot do any good thing but what the devil will be sure to hinder you. What then! up and at him! coward looks and faint counsels are not for warriors of the cross. Expect fightings and you will not be disappointed. Whitefield used to say that some divines would go from the first of January to the end of December with a perfectly whole skin ; the devil never thought them worth while attacking ; but, said he, let us begin to preach with all our might, and soul, and strength, the gospel of Jesus Christ, and men will soon put a fool's cap on our heads, and begin laughing at us, and ridiculing us : but if so, so much the better. We are not alarmed because Satan hindereth us.

Nor will he only hinder us in working ; he will hinder us *in seeking to unite with one another*. We are about to make an effort, as Christian Churches in London, to come closer together, and I am happy to find indications of success ; but I should not wonder but what Satan will hinder us, and I would ask your prayers that Satan may be put to the rout in this matter, and that the union of our Churches may be accomplished. As a Church ourselves, we have walked together in peace for a long time, but I should not marvel if Satan should try to thrust in the cloven foot to hinder our walking in love, and peace, and unity.

Satan will hinder us *in our communion with Jesus Christ*. When at His table we say to ourselves, "I shall have a sweet moment now," but just then vanity intrudes. Like Abraham, you offer the sacrifice, but the unclean birds come down upon it, and you have need to drive them away. "Satan hindered us." He is not omnipresent, but by his numerous servants he works in all kinds of places, and manages to distract the saints when they would serve the Lord.

III. In the third place THERE ARE TWO OR THREE

RULES BY WHICH THESE HINDRANCES MAY BE DETECTED AS SATANIC.

I think I heard somebody saying to himself this morning, "Yes, I should have risen in the world, and have been a man of money now if it had not been that Satan hindered me." Do not you believe it, dear friend. I do not believe that Satan generally hinders people from getting rich. He would just as soon that they should be rich as poor. He delights to see God's servants set upon the pinnacle of the temple, for he knows the position to be dangerous. High places and God's praise do seldom well agree. If you have been hindered in growing rich, I should rather set that down to the good providence of God which would not place you where you could not have borne the temptation. "Yes," said another, "I had intended to have lived in a certain district and done good, and have not been able to go : perhaps that is the devil." Perhaps it was ; perhaps it was not. God's providence will know best where to place us. We are not always choosers of our own locality : and so we are not always to conclude when we are hindered and disappointed in our own intentions that Satan has done it, for it may very often be the good providence of God.

But how may I tell when Satan hinders me? I think you may tell thus : first, *by the object*. Satan's object in hindering us is to prevent our glorifying God. If anything has happened to you which has prevented your growing holy, useful, humble, and sanctified, then you may trace that to Satan. If the distinct object of the interference to the general current of your life has been that you may be turned from righteousness into sin, then from the object you may guess the author. It is not God who does this, but Satan. Yet know that God does sometimes put apparent hindrances in the way of His own people, even in reference to their usefulness and growth in grace, but then His object is still to be considered : it is to try His saints and so to strengthen them ; while the object of Satan is to turn them out of the right road and make them take the crooked way.

You may tell the suggestions of Satan, again, by *the method* in which they come : God employs good motives, Satan bad ones. If that which has turned you away from your object has been a bad thought, a bad doctrine, bad teaching, a bad motive— that never came from God, that must be from Satan.

Again, you may tell them from *their nature*. Whenever an impediment to usefulness is pleasing, gratifying to you, consider that it came from Satan. Satan never brushes the feathers of his birds the wrong way ; he generally deals with us according to our tastes and likings. He flavours his bait to his fish. He knows exactly how to deal with each man, and to put that motive which will fall in with the suggestions of poor carnal nature. Now, if the difficulty in your way is rather contrary to yourself than for yourself, then it comes from God ; but if that which now is a hindrance brings you gain, or pleasure, or emolument in any way, rest assured it came from Satan.

We can tell the suggestions of Satan, once more, by their season. Hindrances to prayer, for instance, if they are Satanic, come *out of the natural course and relation of human thoughts*. It is a law of mental science that one thought suggests another, and the next the next, and so on, as the links of a chain draw one another. But Satanic temptations do not come in the regular order of thinking ; they dash upon the mind at unawares. My soul is in prayer : it would be unnatural that I should then blaspheme, yet then the blasphemy comes ; therefore it is clearly Satanic, and not from my own mind. If I am set upon doing my Master's will, and presently a recreant thought assails me, that being apart from the natural run of my mind and thoughts, may be at once ejected as not being mine, and may be set down to the account of the devil, who is the true father of it. By these means I think we may tell when Satan hinders, and when it is our own heart, or when it is of God. We ought carefully to watch that we do not put the saddle on the wrong horse. Do not blame the devil when it is yourself, and on the other hand, when the Lord puts a bar in your way, do not say, " That is Satan," and so go against the providence of God. It may be difficult at times to see the way of duty, but if you go to the throne of God in prayer you will soon discover it. " Bring hither the ephod," said David, when he was in difficulty. Say you the same ? Go you to the great High Priest, whose business it is to give forth the oracle ! Lo, upon his breast hangs the Urim and Thummim, and you shall from him find direction in every time of difficulty and dilemma.

IV. Supposing that we have ascertained that hindrances in our way really come from Satan, WHAT THEN ?

I have but one piece of advice, and that is, *go on*, hindrance or no hindrance, in the path of duty as God the Holy Ghost enables you. If Satan hinders you, I have already hinted that this *opposition should cheer you.* " I did not expect," said a Christian minister, " to be easy in this particular pastorate, or else I would not have come here : for I always count it," said he, " to be my duty to show the devil that I am his enemy, and if I do that, I expect that he will show me that he is mine." If you are now opposed and you can trace that opposition distinctly to Satan, congratulate yourself upon it : do not sit down and fret. Why, it is a great thing that a poor creature like you can actually vex the great prince of darkness and win his hate. It makes the race of man the more noble that it comes in conflict with a race of spirits, and stands foot to foot even with the prince of darkness himself. It is a dreadful thing, doubtless, that you should be hindered by such an adversary, but it is most hopeful, for if he were your friend you might have cause to fear indeed. Stand out against him, because *you have now an opportunity of making a greater gain than you could have had had he been quiet.* You could never have had a victory over him if you had not engaged in conflict with him. The poor saint would go on his inglorious way to heaven if he were unmolested, but being molested, every step of his pathway becomes glorious. Our position to-day is like that described by Bunyan, when from the top of the palace the song was heard :—

" Come in, come in,
Eternal glory Thou shalt win."

Now merely to ascend the stairs of the palace, though safe work, would not have been very ennobling ; but when the foemen crowded round the door, and blocked up every stair, and the hero came to the man with the ink-horn, who sat before the door and said, " Write my name down, sir " ; then to get from the lowest step to the top where the bright ones were singing, every inch was glorious. If devils did not oppose my path from earth to heaven, I might travel joyously, peacefully, safely, but certainly without renown ; but now, when every step is contested in winning our pathway to glory, every single step is covered with immortal fame. Press on then, Christian, the more opposition the more honour.

Be in earnest against these hindrances when you consider, again, *what you lose if you do not resist him and overcome him.* To allow Satan to overcome me would be eternal ruin to my soul. Certainly it would for ever blast all hopes of my usefulness. If I retreat and turn my back in the day of battle, what will the rest of God's servants say ? What shouts of derision will ring over the battle-field ! How will the banner of the covenant be trailed in the mire ! Why, we must not, we dare not, play the coward ; we dare not give way to the insinuation of Satan and turn from the Master, for the defeat were then too dreadful to be endured. Beloved, let me feed your courage with the recollection that *your Lord and Master has overcome.* See Him there before you. He of the thorn-crown has fought the enemy and broken his head : Satan has been completely worsted by the Captain of your salvation ; and that victory was representative—He fought and won it for you. You have to contend with a defeated foe, and one who knows and feels his disgrace ; and though he may fight with desperation, yet he fights not with true courage, for he is hopeless of ultimate victory. Strike, then, for Christ has smitten him. Down with him, for Jesus has had him under His foot. Thou, weakest of all the host, triumph thou, for the Captain has triumphed before thee.

Lastly, remember that *you have a promise* to make you gird up your loins and play the man this day. " Resist the devil, and he shall flee from you." Christian minister, resign not your situation ; do not think of sending in your resignation because the Church is divided and because the enemy is making head. Resist the devil. Flee not, but make him flee. Christian young men, you who have begun to preach in the street, or distribute tracts or visit from house to house, though Satan hinders you very much I pray you now redouble your efforts : it is because Satan is afraid of you that he resists you, because he would rob you of the great blessing which is now descending on your head. Resist him, and stand fast. Thou Christian pleading in prayer, let not go thy hold upon the covenant angel now ; for now that Satan hinders thee, it is because the blessing is descending. Thou art seeking Christ, close not those eyes, turn not away thy face from Calvary's streaming tree : now that Satan hinders thee, it is because the night is almost over, and the day-star begins to shine. Brethren, ye who are most molested, most sorrowfully tried, most borne down, yours is the brighter hope : be now courageous ; play the man for God, for Christ, for your own soul, and yet the day shall come when you with your Master shall ride triumphant through the streets of the New Jerusalem, sin, death and hell, captive at your chariot wheels, and you with your Lord crowned as victor, having overcome through the blood of the Lamb. May God bless dear friends now present. I do not know to whom this sermon may be most suitable, but I believe it is sent especially to certain tried saints. The Lord enable them to find comfort in it. Amen.

"FOR EVER WITH THE LORD"

"So shall we ever be with the Lord."—1 Thess. iv. 17.

WE know that these words are full of consolation, for the apostle says in the next verse, "Wherefore comfort one another with these words." The very words it appears were dictated by the Holy Spirit the Comforter, to be repeated by the saints to each other with the view of removing sorrow from the minds of the distressed. The comfort is intended to give us hope in reference to those who have fallen asleep. Look over the list of those, beloved in the Lord, who have departed from you, to your utmost grief, and let the words of our text be a handkerchief for your eyes. Sorrow not as those that are without hope, for they are with the Lord though they are not with you, and by-and-by you shall surely meet them where your Lord is the centre of fellowship for ever and ever. The separation will be very transient ; the reunion will be everlasting. These words are also intended to comfort the saints with regard to themselves, and I pray that they may be a cordial to any who are sick with fear, a matchless medicine to charm away the heartache from all believers. The fact that you bear about a dying body is very evident to some of you by your frequent and increasing infirmities and pains, and this, it may be, is a source of depression of spirits. You know that when a few years are gone you must go the way whence you shall not return ; but be not dismayed, for you shall not go into a strange country alone and unattended. There is a friend that sticketh closer than a brother, who will not fail you nor forsake you ; and, moreover, you are going home ; your Lord will be with you while you are departing, and then you will be ever with Him. Therefore, though sickness warn thee of the near approach of death, be not in the least dismayed ; though pain and weariness should make thy heart and flesh fail, yet doubt not of thy triumph through the Redeemer's blood ; though it should sometimes make thy flesh to tremble when thou rememberest thy many sins and the weakness of thy faith, yet be of good cheer, for thy sins and weakness of faith will soon be removed far from thee, and thou shalt be in His presence where there is fulness of joy, and at His right hand, where there are pleasures for evermore. Comfort yourselves, then, both with regard to those who have gone before and in reference to the thought of your own departure.

Observe that the comfort which the apostle here presents to us may be partly derived from the fact of the resurrection, but not chiefly ; for he does not so much refer to the words "The dead in Christ shall rise," as to these last—" so shall we ever be with the Lord." It is a great truth that you will rise again ; it is a sweeter truth that you will be "ever with the Lord." There is some consolation also in the fact that we shall meet our departed brethren when we all shall be caught up together in the clouds to meet the Lord in the air. Blissful will be the general assembling of the redeemed, never again to be broken up ; the joy of meeting never to part again is a sweet remedy for the bitterness of separation. There is great comfort in it, but the main stress of consolation does not lie even there. It is pleasant to think of the eternal fellowships of the godly above, but the best of all is the promised fellowship with our Lord,—" So shall we ever be with the Lord." Whatever else you draw comfort from, neglect not this deep, clear, and overflowing well of delight. There are other sources of good cheer in connection with the glory to be revealed, for heaven is a many-sided joy ; but still none can excel the glory of communion with Jesus Christ, wherefore comfort one another in the first place, and most constantly, with these words, "So shall we ever be with the Lord."

I shall view our text, in order to our comfort at this time, in three lights. I look upon it, first, as a continuance—we are with the Lord even now, and we ever shall be : secondly, as an advancement—we shall ere long be more fully with the Lord than we are now : and thirdly, as a coherence—for we both are and shall be with Him in a close and remarkable manner.

I. I regard the text as A CONTINUANCE of our present spiritual state—" So shall we ever be with the Lord." To my mind, and I think I am not incorrect in so expounding, the apostle means that nothing shall prevent our continuing to be ever with the Lord ; death shall not separate us, nor the terrors of that tremendous day when the voice of the archangel and the trump of God shall be heard ; by divine plan and arrangement all shall be so ordained that " So shall we ever be with the Lord." By being caught up into the clouds, or in one way or another, our abiding in Christ shall remain unbroken. As we have received Christ Jesus the Lord, so shall we walk in Him, whether in life or in death.

I understand him to mean that we are with the Lord now, and that nothing shall separate us from Him. Even now like Enoch we walk with God, and we shall not be deprived of divine communion. Our fear might be that in the future state something might happen which would become a dividing gulf between us and Christ, but the apostle assures us that it will not be so, there shall be such plans and methods used that " so shall we ever be with the Lord." At any rate, I know that, if this be not the truth here intended, it is a truth worthy to be expounded, and therefore I do not hesitate to enlarge upon it.

We are with the Lord in this life in a high spiritual sense. Read you not, in the epistle to the Colossians, " for ye are dead, and your life is hid with Christ in God " ? Were you not " buried with Him in baptism, wherein also ye are risen with Him through the faith of the operation of God, who hath raised Him from the dead " ? Do you not know what it is to be dead to the world in Him, and to be living a secret life with Him ? Are you not risen with Christ ; aye, and do you not understand in some measure what it is to be raised up together, and made to sit together in the heavenlies in Christ Jesus ? If you are not with Him, brethren, you are not Christians at all, for this is just the mark of the Christian, that he follows with Christ. It is essential to salvation to be a sheep of Christ's fold, nay more, a partaker of Christ's life, a member of His mystical Body, a branch of the spiritual vine. Separated from Him we are spiritually dead : He Himself has said, " If a man abide not in Me, he is cast forth as a branch, and is withered ; and men gather them, and cast them into the fire, and they are burned." Jesus is not far from any one of His people ; nay, it is our privilege to follow Him whithersoever He goeth, and His loving word to us is, " Abide in Me, and I in you." May He enable us sweetly to realize this. We are, dear brethren, constantly with Christ in the sense of abiding union with Him, for we are joined unto the Lord, and are one spirit. Sometimes this union is very sweetly apparent to ourselves ; " We know that we are in Him that is true," and in consequence we feel an intense joy, even Christ's own joy fulfilled in us. For the same reason we are at times bowed down with intense sorrow ; for being in and with Christ we have fellowship with Him in His sufferings, being made conformable with His death : this is such sweet sorrow that the more we experience it the better.

> " Live or die, or work or suffer,
>   Let my weary soul abide,
> In all changes whatsoever,
>   Sure and steadfast by Thy side.
>
> Nothing can delay my progress,
>   Nothing can disturb my rest,
> If I shall, where'er I wander,
>   Lean my spirit on Thy breast."

This companionship is, we trust, made manifest to others by its fruits. It ought always so to be : the life of the Christian should be manifestly a life with Christ. Men should take knowledge of us that we have been with Jesus, and have learned of Him ; they should see that there is something in us which could not have been there if is were not for the Son of God : a temper, a spirit, a course of life, which could not have come by nature but must have been wrought in us through grace which has been received from Him in whom dwells a fulness of grace, even our Lord Jesus Christ. Brethren, if we are what we ought to be, our life is spent in conscious communion, growing out of continued union with the Lord Jesus Christ, and if it be so we have that rich assurance which is written by the beloved John, " If that which ye have heard from the beginning shall remain in you, ye also shall continue in the Son, and in the Father."

We are with Him, dear friends, in this sense too, that His unchanging love is always set upon us, and our love, feeble though it sometimes may be, never quite dies out. In both senses that challenge of the apostle is true, " Who shall separate us from the love of God, which is in Christ Jesus our Lord ? " We can say, " I am my Beloved's, and His desire is towards me " ; and, on the other hand, we also testify, " My Beloved is mine, and I am His." He claims us and we claim Him : He loves us and we love Him. There is a union of heart between us. We are with Him, not against Him ; we are in league with Him, enlisted beneath His banner, obedient to His Spirit. For us to live is Christ : we have no other aim.

He is with us by the continued indwelling of the Holy Ghost, who is with us and shall be in us for ever. His anointing abideth on us, and because of it we abide in Christ Jesus. He has sent us the Comforter to represent Himself, and through that divine Paraclete He continues to be with us, and so even now we are ever with the Lord.

Our Lord has also promised to be with us whenever we are engaged in His work. That is a grand word of encouragement, " Lo, I am with you alway, even unto the end of the world." Think not, therefore, that it will be the first time of our being with Christ when we shall see Him in glory, for even now He manifests Himself unto us as He does not unto the world. Has He not often fulfilled His promise. " Where two or three are gathered together in My name, there am I in the midst of them " ? We have heard the sound of our Master's feet behind us when we have been going on His errands ; we have felt the touch of His hand when we have come to the forefront of the battle for His sake, and we have known that He dwelleth in us by His Spirit, and is with us by the power wherewith He has attended our work, and the deeds which He has wrought by the gospel which we have proclaimed. The Lord Jesus is with His church in her tribulation for His name's sake, and He will ever be so, for He forsaketh not His saints. " Fear not, I am with thee," is as much a word of the Lord under the gospel as in Old Testament times. By the power of His blessed Spirit Jesus abides with us, and through this present dispensation He enables us to be " ever with the Lord."

But, my brethren, the time is coming when we shall die, unless the Lord shall descend from heaven with a shout meanwhile. Assuredly in the article of death we shall still be with the Lord.

> " Death may my soul divide
>   From this abode of clay ;
> But love shall keep me near Thy side
>   Through all the gloomy way."

" Yea, though I walk through the valley of the shadow of death, I will fear no evil : for Thou art with me ; Thy rod and Thy staff they comfort me." This makes dying such delicious work to the people of God, for then especially is Jesus seen to be near. By death they escape from death, and henceforth it is no more death for them to die. When Jesus meets His saints there seems no iron gate to pass through, but in a moment they close their eyes on earth and open them in glory. Beloved, there should be no more bondage through fear of death, since Christ attends His people even in their descent into the tomb, and strengthens them upon the bed of languishing. This has been a great joy to many departing saints. A dying believer, who was attended by an apothecary who was also a child of God, was observed to be whispering to himself while dying, and his good attendant, wishing to know what were his last words, placed his ear against the dying man's lips, and heard him repeating to himself again and again the words, " For ever with the Lord, For ever with the Lord." When heart and flesh were failing, the departing one knew that God was the strength of his life and his portion for ever, and so he chose for his soft, low-whispered, dying song,—" For ever with the Lord."

After death, we shall abide awhile in the separate, disembodied state, and we shall know as to our soul what it is to be still with the Lord ; for what saith the apostle ? " Knowing that when we are absent from the body we are present with the Lord." The dying thief was to be that day with Christ in Paradise, and such shall be our lot as soon as our souls shall have passed out of this tenement of clay into that wondrous state of which we know so little. Our pure spirits shall " come unto Mount Sion, and unto the city of the living God, the heavenly Jerusalem, and to an innumerable company of angels, to the general assembly and church of the firstborn, which are written in heaven, and to God the Judge of all, and to the spirits of just men made perfect, and to Jesus the mediator of the new covenant, and to the blood of sprinkling, that speaketh better things than that of Abel." Who is dismayed when such a prospect opens up before him ?

Aye, and this body which shall fall asleep, though apparently it shall be destroyed, yet shall it not be so, but it shall only slumber awhile, and then awake again and say, " When I awake I am still with Thee." Constantly death is described as sleeping in Jesus : that is the state of the saint's mortal frame through the interregnum between death and resurrection. The angels shall guard our bodies ; all that is essential to complete the identity of our body shall be securely preserved, so that the very seed which was put into the earth shall rise again in the beauty of efflorescence which becomes it : all, I say, that is essential shall be preserved intact, because it is still with Christ. It is a glorious doctrine which is stated by the apostle in the first epistle to the Thessalonians, the fifth chapter, at the ninth and tenth verses, " For God hath not appointed us to wrath, but to obtain salvation by our Lord Jesus Christ, who died for us, that, whether we wake or sleep, we should live together with Him."

In due time the last trump shall sound and *Christ shall come*, but the saints shall be with Him. The infinite providence has so arranged that Christ shall not come without His people, for " Them also that sleep in Jesus shall God bring with Him." The saints shall be with Him in the advent as they are now. Our souls shall hear the shout of victory and join in it ; the voice of the archangel shall be actually heard by all His redeemed, and the trump of God shall be sounded in the hearing of every one of His beloved, for we shall be with Jesus all through that glorious transaction. Whatever the glory and splendour of the second advent, we shall be with Jesus in it. I am not going to give you glimpses of the revealed future, or offer any suggestion as to the sublime history which is yet to be written, but most certainly there is to be a last general judgment, and then we shall be with Christ, assessors with Him at that day. Being ourselves first acquitted, we shall take our seat upon the judgment bench with Him. What saith the Holy Ghost by the apostle—" Do ye not know that the saints shall judge the world ? Know ye not that we shall judge angels ? " The fallen angels, to their shame, shall in part receive the verdict of their condemnation from the lips of men, and thus vengeance shall be taken upon them for all the mischief they have done to the sons of men. Oh, think of it : amidst the terror of the tremendous day you shall be at ease, resting in the love of God, and beholding the glory of Christ, and " so shall you ever be with the Lord."

There is, moreover, to be a reign of Christ. I cannot read the Scriptures without perceiving that there is to be a millennial reign, as I believe, upon the earth, and that there shall be new heavens and new earth, wherein dwelleth righteousness. Well,

whatever that reign is to be, we shall reign also. " And he that overcometh, and keepth my works unto the end, to him will I give power over the nations : and he shall rule them with a rod of iron ; as the vessels of a potter shall they be broken to shivers : even as I received of my Father." " And hast made us unto our God kings and priests : and we shall reign on the earth." He shall reign, but it will be " before His ancients gloriously." We shall be partakers in the splendours of the latter days, whatever they may be, and " so shall we ever be with the Lord."

The particular incident of the text does not exhaust the words, but you may apply them to the whole story of God's own children. From the first day of the spiritual birth of the Lord's immortals, until they are received up into the seventh heaven to dwell with God, their history may be summed up in these words, " So shall we ever be with the Lord." Whether caught up into the clouds or here below on this poor afflicted earth, in paradise or in the renovated earth, in the grave or in the glory, we shall ever be with the Lord. And when cometh the end, and God alone shall reign, and the mediatorial kingdom shall cease, ages, ages, and ages shall revolve, but " so shall we ever be with the Lord." The saints immortal shall be with their covenant Head, and like Him free from sorrow. All tendency to sin shall be gone, and all fear of change or death ; their intimate communion will last on for ever :—

> " Blessed state ! beyond conception !
> Who its vast delights can tell ?
> May it be my blissful portion,
> With my Saviour there to dwell."

I think the text looks like a continuation of what is already begun, only rising to something higher and better. To be with Christ is life eternal : this we have already, and shall continue to have, and " so shall we ever be with the Lord."

II. Secondly, most assuredly, brethren, the text is A GREAT ADVANCEMENT—" So shall we ever be with the Lord."

It is an advancement upon this present state, for however spiritual minded we may be, and however in consequence thereof we may be very near unto our Lord Jesus, yet still we know that while we are present in the body we are absent from the Lord. This life, at its very best, is still comparatively an absence from the Lord, but in the world to come we shall be more perfectly at home. Now we cannot in the highest sense be with Christ, for we must, according to the apostle's phraseology, " depart, and be with Christ ; which is far better " ; but there we shall be for ever beholding His face unveiled. Earth is not heaven, though the believer begins the heavenly life while he is upon it. We are not with Christ as to place, nor as to actual sight, but in the glory-land we shall be.

And it is an advancement, in the next place, upon the present state of the departed, for though their souls are with the Lord yet their bodies are subject to corruption. Still does the sepulchre contain the blessed dust of the fathers of our Israel, or scattered to the four winds of heaven the martyr's ashes are with us still. The glorified saints are not as yet consciously " with the Lord " as to their complete manhood, but when the grand event shall occur of which Paul speaks, the body shall be reanimated. This is our glorious hope. We can say with the patriarch Job—" For I know that my Redeemer liveth, and that He shall stand at the latter day upon the earth : and though after my skin worms destroy this body, yet in my flesh shall I see God : whom I shall see for myself, and mine eyes shall behold, and not another ; though my reins be consumed within me." Know ye not, brethren, that flesh and blood cannot inherit the kingdom of God ? That is, as they are ; but this corruptible must put on incorruption, and this mortal must put on immortality, and then shall the entire manhood, the perfected manhood, the fully developed manhood, of which this manhood is as it were but a shrivelled seed, be in the fullest and divinest sense for ever with the Lord. This is an advancement even upon the present paradisiacal state of departed saints.

And now let us consider what this glorious condition is to which we shall be advanced. We shall be with the Lord in the strongest possible meaning of that language. So with Him that we shall never mind earthly things again, shall have no more to go into city business, or into the workshop, or into the field ; we shall have nought to do but to be engaged for ever with Him in such occupations as shall have no tendency to take us off from communion with Him. We shall be so with Him as to have no sin to becloud our view of Him : the understanding will be delivered from all the injury which sin has wrought in it, and we shall know Him even as we are known. We shall see Him as a familiar friend, and sit with Him at His marriage feast. We shall be with Him so as to have no fear of His ever being grieved and hiding His face from us again. We shall never again be made to cry out in bitterness of spirit, " Oh, that I knew where I might find Him." We shall always know His love, always return it, and always swim in the full stream of it, enjoying it to the full. There will be no lukewarmness to mar our fellowship. He shall never have to say to us, " I would thou wert either cold or hot." There shall be no weariness to suspend our ceaseless bliss : we shall never have to cease from fellowship with Him, because our physical frame is exhausted through the excessive joy of our heart ; the vessel will be strengthened to hold the new wine. No doubts shall intrude into our rest, neither doctrinal doubts nor doubts about our interest in Him, for we shall be so consciously with Him as to have risen ten thousand leagues above that gloomy state. We shall know that He is ours, for His left hand shall be under our head and His right hand shall embrace us, and we shall be with Him beyond all hazard of any remove from Him. The chief blessedness seems to me to lie in this, that we shall be with Him and with Him always. Now we are with the Lord in conscious enjoyment some-times, and then we are away from Him, but there it will be constant, unwavering fellowship. No break shall ever occur in the intimate communion of the saints with Christ. Here we know that our high days and bright Sabbaths, with their sweetest joys, must have their eventides, and then come the work-days with the burden of the week upon them ; but there the Sabbath is eternal, the worship endless, the praise unceasing, the bliss unbounded. " For ever with the Lord." Speak ye of a thousand years of reigning ? What is that compared with " for ever with the Lord " ? The millennium is little compared with " for ever "—a millennium of millenniums would be nothing to it. There can come no end to us and

no end to our bliss, since there can be no end to Him— " because I live, ye shall live also."

" For ever with the Lord "—What will it mean ? I remember a sermon upon this text by a notable preacher, of which the heads were as follows—" For ever life, for ever light, for ever love, for ever peace, for ever rest, for ever joy." What a chain of delights ! What more can heart imagine, or hope desire ? Carry those things in your mind and you will get, if you can drink into them, some idea of the blessedness which is contained in being for ever with the Lord ; but still recollect these are only the fruits, and not the root of the joy. Jesus is better than all these. His company is more than the joy which comes out of it. I do not care so much for " life for ever," nor for " light for ever," as I do for " for ever with the Lord." Oh, to be with Him ! I ask no other bliss, and cannot imagine aught more heavenly. Why, the touch of the hem of His garment healed the sick woman ; the sight of Him was enough to give life to us when we were dead ! What, then, must it be to be with Him actually, consciously, and always ? to be with Him no more by faith, but in very deed with Him for ever ? My soul is ready to swoon away with too much joy as she drinks even in her shallow measure into the meaning of this thought, and I dare not venture further. I must leave you to muse your souls into it, for it needs quiet thought and room for free indulgence of holy imagination till you make your soul to dream of this excess of joy. " Eye hath not seen, nor ear heard, neither have entered into the heart of man, the things which God hath prepared for them that love Him. But God hath revealed them unto us by His Spirit."

> " O glorious hour ! O blest abode !
> I shall be near and like my God ;
> And flesh and sin no more control
> The sacred pleasures of my soul."

We love to think of being with Jesus under the aspect which the text specially suggests to us. We are to be for ever with the Redeemer, not as Jesus the Saviour only, but as *the Lord*. Here we have seen Him on the cross and lived thereby ; we are with Him now in His cross-bearing and shame, and it is well ; but our eternal companionship with Him will enable us to rejoice in Him *as the Lord*. What said our Master in His blessed prayer ? " I will that they also, whom Thou hast given Me, be with Me where I am ; that they may behold My glory." It will be heaven to us to be for ever with Him as the Lord. Oh, how we shall delight to obey Him as our Lord ! How we shall triumph as we see what a lord He is over all the universe ! and what a conqueror He is over all His enemies ! He will be more and more the Lord to us as we see all things put under Him. We shall for ever hail Him as King of kings, and Lord of lords. How we will adore Him there when we see Him in His glory. We do worship Him now, and are not ashamed to believe that the Man of Nazareth is " very God of very God " ; and oh, how His deity will shine upon us with infinite efful-gence when we come to be near Him. Thanks be to His name, we shall be strengthened to endure the sight, and we shall rejoice to see ourselves in the full blaze of His glory. Then shall we see what our poet endeavoured to describe when He said—

> " Adoring saints around Him stand,
> And thrones and powers before Him fall ;
> The God shines gracious through the Man,
> And sheds sweet glories on them all."

We shall be for ever with the Lord, and His Lordship shall be most upon our minds. He has been raised into glory and honour, and is no more able to suffer shame.

> " No more the bloody spear,
> The cross and nails no more ;
> For hell itself shakes at His word,
> And all the heavens adore."

III. Now we come to our third point, and shall consider what, for want of a better word, I entitle A COHERENCE. Those who are acquainted with the Greek language know that the "*with*" here is not *meta*, which signifies being in the same place with a person, but *sun*, which goes very much further, and implies a coherence, the two who are with each other are intimately connected. Let me show you what I mean. We are to be for ever with the Lord : now, the Christian's life is all along like the life of His Lord, and so it is a life with Christ. He was in all things with His brethren, and grace makes us to be with Him. Just hurriedly look at your spiritual experience and your Lord's life, and see the parallel. When you were new born as a Christian you were born as Jesus Christ was, for you were born of the Holy Ghost. What happened after that ? The devil tried to destroy the new life in you, just as Herod tried to kill your Lord : you were with Christ in danger, early and imminent. You grew in stature and in grace, and while yet grace was young, you staggered those who were about you with the things you said, and did, and felt, for they could not understand you ; even thus when He went up to the temple our Lord amazed the doctors who gathered around Him. The Spirit of God rested upon you, not in the same measure, but still as a matter of fact it did descend upon you as it did upon your Lord. You have been with Him in Jordan's stream, and have received the divine acknowledgment that you are indeed the son of God. Your Lord was led into the wilderness to be tempted ; and you too have been tempted of the devil. You have been with the Lord all along, from the first day until now. If you have been by grace enabled to live as you should, you have trodden the separated path with Jesus ; you have been in the world, but not of it, holy, harmless, undefiled, and separate from sinners. Therefore you have been despised ; you have had to take your share of being unknown and misrepresented, because you are even as He was in the world. "Therefore the world knoweth us not, because it knew Him not." As He was here to serve, you have been with Him as a servant, you have carried His yoke and counted it an easy load. You have been crucified to the world with Him : you know the meaning of His cross, and delight to bear it after Him. You are dead to the world with Him, and wish to be as one buried to it. You have already in your measure partaken of His resurrection, and are living in newness of life. Your life-story is still to be like the life-story of your Lord, only painted in miniature. The more you watch the life of Christ the more clearly you will see the life of a spiritual man depicted in it, and the more clearly will you see what the saints' future will be. You have been with Christ in life, and you will be with Him when you come to die. You will not die the expiatory death which fell to His lot, but you will die feeling that " it is finished," and you will breathe out your soul, saying, " Father, into Thy hands I commend my spirit."

Then our Lord went to paradise, and you will go there too. You shall enjoy a sojourn where He spent His interval in the disembodied state. You shall be with Him, and like Him, and then like Him you shall rise when your third morning cometh. " After two days will He revive us : in the third day He will raise us up, and we shall live in His sight." " Thy dead men shall live, together with my dead body shall they arise." You shall also ascend as Christ did. Do you catch the thought ? How did He ascend ? In clouds. " A cloud received Him out of their sight," and a cloud shall receive you. You shall be caught up into the clouds to meet the Lord in the air, and so shall you be ever with the Lord, in the sense of being like to Him, walking with Him in experience, and passing through the like events. That likeness shall continue for ever and ever. Our lives shall run parallel with that of our Lord.

Think then, beloved, we are to be like Christ as to our character : we are to be with the Lord by sharing His moral and spiritual likeness. Conformed to His image, we shall be adorned with His beauty. When the mother of Darius saw two persons entering her pavilion, she being a prisoner bowed to the one whom she supposed to be Alexander. It turned out to be Hyphestion, the King's favourite. Upon discovering that it was Hyphestion the lady humbly begged Alexander's pardon for paying obeisance to the wrong person, but Alexander answered, " You have not mistaken, Madam, for he also is Alexander," meaning that he loved him so much that he regarded him as his other self. Our Lord looks on His beloved as one with Himself, and makes them like Himself. You remember, brethren, how John bowed down before one of his fellow servants, the prophets, in heaven. It was a great blunder to make, but I dare say you and I will be likely to make the same, for the saints are so like their Lord. Know ye not that " we shall be like Him when we shall see Him as He is " ? Christ will rejoice to see them all covered with the glory which His Father has given Him. He will not be ashamed to call them brethren. Those poor people of His, who were so full of infirmity, and mourned over it so much, they shall be so like Him that they shall be at once seen to be His brethren. Where shall such favoured ones be found ?

We shall be with Him in the sense that we shall be partakers of all the blessedness and glory which our adorable Lord now enjoys. We shall be accepted together with Him. Is He the beloved of the Lord ? Does His Father's heart delight in Him, as well it may ? Behold ye also shall be called Hephzibah, for His delight shall be in you. You shall be beloved of the Father's soul. Is He enriched with all manner of blessings beyond conception ? So shall you be, for He has blessed us with all spiritual blessings in Christ Jesus, according as He has chosen us in Him. Is Christ exalted ? Oh, how loftily is He lifted up to sit upon a glorious high throne for ever ! But you shall sit upon His throne with Him and share His exaltation as you have shared His humiliation. Oh, the delight of thus being joint heirs with Christ, and with Him in the possession of all that He possesses. What is heaven ? It is the place which His love suggested, which His genius invented, which His bounty provided, which His royalty has adorned, which His wisdom has prepared, which He Himself glorifies ; in that heaven you are to be with Him for ever. You shall dwell in the King's own palace. Its gates of pearl and streets of gold shall not be too good for you.

You who love Him are to abide for ever with Him, not near Him in a secondary place, as a servant lives at the lodge gate of His master's mansion, but with Him in the self-same palace in the metropolis of the universe.

In a word, believers are to be identified with Christ for ever. That seems to me to be the very life and essence of the text : with Him for ever, that is, identified with Him for ever. Do they ask for the Shepherd ? They cannot behold Him to perfection except as surrounded by His sheep. Will the King be illustrious ? How can that be if His subjects are lost ? Do they ask for the Bridegroom ? They cannot imagine Him in the fulness of joy without His bride. Will the Head be blessed ? It could not be if it were separated from the members. Will Christ be for ever glorified ? How can He be if He shall lose His jewels ? He is a foundation, and what would He be if all His people were not built upon Him into the similitude of a palace ? O brethren, there shall be no Christ without Christians ; there shall be no Saviour without the saved ones ; there shall be no Elder Brother without the younger brethren ; there shall be no Redeemer without His redeemed. We are His fulness, and He must have us with Him. We are identified with Him for ever. Nothing can ever divide us from Him. Oh, joy, joy for ever. Hallelujah !

> " Since Christ and we are one,
> Why should we doubt or fear ?
> If He in heaven hath fix'd His throne,
> He'll fix His members there."

Two or three practical sentences. One word is this—*This " with the Lord " must begin now.* Do you wish to be for ever with the Lord ? You must be with Him by becoming His disciple in this life. None come to be with the Lord hereafter who are not with the Lord here in time. See to it, dear hearers, see to it, lest this unspeakable privilege should never be yours.

Next, every Christian should seek to be more and more with Christ, for *the growth and glory of your life lies there.* Do you want to have heaven below ? Be with Christ below. Do you want to know at once what eternal bliss is ? Know it by living now with the Lord.

The next word is, *how plainly then the way of life is to be with the Lord.* If you want to be saved, sinner, you must be " with the Lord." There is no other way for you. Come near to Him, and lay hold upon Him by faith. Life lies there. Come to Him by a humble, tearful faith. Come at once.

And, lastly, *what must it be to be without the Lord ?* What must it be to be against the Lord ? For it comes to that, " He that is not with Me," saith He, " is against Me." To be for ever without the Lord, banished from His love, and light, and life, and peace, and rest, and joy ! What a loss will this be ! What must it be to be for ever against the Lord ! Think of it : for ever hating Jesus, for ever plotting against Him, for ever gnashing your teeth against Him ; this is hell, this is the infinite of misery, to be against the Lord of love and life, and light. Turn ye from this fatal course. Believe on Him : " Kiss the Son, lest He be angry, and ye perish from the way, when His wrath is kindled but a little. Blessed are all they that put their trust in Him." Amen.

AWAKE! AWAKE!

" Therefore let us not sleep as do others ; but let us watch and be sober."—1 Thessalonians v. 6.

WHAT sad things sin hath done. This fair world of ours was once a glorious temple, every pillar of which reflected the goodness of God, and every part of which was a symbol of good, but sin has spoiled and marred all the metaphors and figures that might be drawn from earth. It has so deranged the divine economy of nature that those things which were inimitable pictures of virtue, goodness, and divine plenitude of blessing, have now become the figures and representatives of sin. 'Tis strange to say, but is strangely true, that the very best gifts of God have by the sin of man become the worst pictures of man's guilt. Behold the flood ! breaking forth from its fountains, it rushes across the fields, bearing plenty on its bosom ; it covers them awhile, and anon it doth subside and leaves upon the plain a fertile deposit, into which the farmer shall cast his seed and reap an abundant harvest. One would have called the breaking forth of water a fine picture of the plenitude of providence, the magnificence of God's goodness to the human race ; but we find that sin has appropriated that figure to itself. The beginning of sin is like the breaking forth of waters. See the fire ! how kindly God hath bestowed upon us that element, to cheer us in the midst of winter's frosts. Fresh from the snow and from the cold we rush to our household fire, and there by our hearth we warm our hands, and glad are we. Fire is a rich picture of the divine influences of the Spirit, a holy emblem of the zeal of the Christian ; but alas ! sin hath touched this, and the tongue is called " a fire " ; " it is set on fire of hell," we are told, and it is so evidently full often, when it uttereth blasphemy and slanders ; and Jude lifts up his hand and exclaims, when he looks upon the evils caused by sin, " Behold how great a matter a little fire kindleth." And then there is sleep, one of the sweetest of God's gifts, fair sleep

> " Tired nature's sweet restorer, balmy sleep."

Sleep God hath selected as the very figure for the blessed. " They that sleep in Jesus," saith the Scripture. David puts it amongst the peculiar gifts of grace : " So He giveth His beloved sleep." But alas ! sin could not let even this alone. Sin did override even this celestial metaphor ; and though God Himself had employed sleep to express the excellence of the state of the blessed, yet sin must have even this profaned, ere itself can be expressed. Sleep is employed in our text as a picture of a sinful condition. " Therefore let us not sleep as do others ; but let us watch and be sober."

With that introduction I shall proceed at once to the text. The " sleep " of the text is *an evil to be avoided.* In the second place, the word " therefore " is employed to show us that there are *certain reasons for the avoiding of this sleep.* And since the apostle speaks of this sleep with sorrow, it is to teach us that there are some, whom he calls "others," *over whom it is our business to lament,* because they sleep, and do not watch, and are not sober.

I. We commence, then, in the first place, by endeavouring to point out the EVIL WHICH THE APOSTLE INTENDS TO DESCRIBE UNDER THE TERM SLEEP. The apostle speaks of "others" who are asleep. If you turn to the original you will find that the word is translated "others" has a more emphatic meaning. It might be rendered (and Horne so renders it,) "the refuse,"—"Let us not sleep as do *the refuse,*" the common herd, the ignoble spirits, those that have no mind above the troubles of earth "Let us not sleep as do the others," the base ignoble multitude who are not alive to the high and celestial calling of a Christian. "Let us not sleep as do the refuse of mankind." And you will find that the word "sleep," in the original, has also a more emphatic sense. It signifies a deep sleep, a profound slumber ; and the apostle intimates, that the refuse of mankind are now in a profound slumber. We will now try if we can explain what he meant by it.

First, the apostle meant, that the refuse of mankind *are in a state of deplorable ignorance.* They that sleep know nothing. There may be merriment in the house, but the sluggard shareth not in its gladness ; there may be death in the family, but no tear bedeweth the cheek of the sleeper. Great events may have transpired in the world's history, but he wots not of them. An earthquake may have tumbled a city from its greatness, or war may have devastated a nation, or the banner of triumph may be waving in the gale, and the clarions of his country may be saluting us with victory, but he knoweth nothing.

> "Their labour and their love are lost,
> Alike unknowing and unknown."

The sleeper knoweth not anything. Behold how the refuse of mankind are alike in this ! Of some things they know much, but of spiritual things they know nothing ; of the divine person of the adorable Redeemer they have no idea ; of the sweet enjoyments of a life of piety they cannot even make a guess ; towards the high enthusiasms and the inward raptures of the Christian they cannot mount. Talk to them of divine doctrines, and they are to them a riddle ; tell them of sublime experiences, and they seem to them to be enthusiastic fancies. They know nothing of the joys that are to come ; and alas ! for them, they are oblivious of the evils which shall happen to them if they go on in their iniquity. The mass of mankind are ignorant ; they know not ; they have not the knowledge of God, they have no fear of Jehovah before their eyes ; but, blind-folded by the ignorance of this world, they march on through the paths of lust to that sure and dreadful end, the everlasting ruin of their souls. Brethren, if we be saints, let us not be ignorant as are others. Let us search the Scriptures, for in them we have eternal life, for they do testify of Jesus. Let us be diligent : let not the word depart out of our hearts ; let us meditate therein both by day and night, that we may be as a tree planted by the rivers of water. "Let us not sleep as do others."

Again, sleep pictures *a state of insensibility.* There may be much knowledge in the sleeper, hidden, stored away in his mind, which might be well developed, if he could but be awakened. But he hath no sensibility, he knoweth nothing. The burglar hath broken into the house ; the gold and silver are both in the robber's hands ; the child is being murdered by the cruelty of him that hath broken in ; but the father slumbereth, though all the gold and silver that he hath, and his most precious child, are in the hands of the destroyer. He is unconscious, how can he feel, when sleep hath utterly sealed his senses ! Lo ! in the street there is mourning. A fire hath just now burned down the habitation of the poor, and houseless beggars are in the street. They are crying at his window, and asking him for help. But he sleeps, and what wots he, though the night be cold, and though the poor are shivering in the blast ? He hath no consciousness ; he feeleth not for them. There ! take the title deed of his estate, and burn the document. There ! set light to his farm-yard ! burn up all that he hath in the field ; kill his horses and destroy his cattle ; let now the fire of God descend and burn up his sheep ; let the enemy fall upon all that he hath and devour it. He sleeps as soundly as if were guarded by the angel of the Lord.

Such are the refuse of mankind. But alas ! that we should have to include in that word "refuse" the great bulk thereof ! How few there are that feel spiritually ! They feel acutely enough any injury to their body, or to their estate ; but alas ! for their spiritual concerns they have no sensation whatever ! They are standing on the brink of hell, but they tremble not ; the anger of God is burning against them, but they fear not ; the sword of Jehovah is unsheathed, but the terror doth not seize upon them. They proceed with the merry dance ; they drink the bowl of intoxicating pleasure ; they revel and they riot ; still do they sing the lascivious song ; yea, they do more than this ; in their vain dreams they do defy the Most High ; whereas, if they were once awakened to the consciousness of their state, the marrow of their bones would melt, and their heart would dissolve like wax in the midst of their bowels. They are asleep, indifferent and unconscious. Do what you may to them ; let everything be swept away that is hopeful, that might give them cheer when they come to die, yet they feel it not ; for how should a sleeper feel anything ? But "Therefore let us not sleep, as do others ; but let us watch and be sober."

Again : the sleeper *cannot defend himself.* Behold yonder prince, he is a strong man, aye, and a strong man armed. He hath entered into the tent. He is wearied. He hath drunken the woman's milk ; he hath eaten her "butter in a lordly dish ; " he casteth himself down upon the floor, and he slumbereth. And now she draweth nigh. She hath with her, her hammer and her nail. Warrior ! thou couldst break her into atoms with one blow of thy mighty arm ; but thou canst not now defend thyself. The nail is at his ear ; the woman's hand is on the hammer and the nail hath pierced his skull ; for when he slept he was defenceless. The banner of Sisera had waved victoriously over mighty foes ; but now it is stained by a woman. Tell it, tell it, tell it ! The man, who when he was awake made nations tremble, dies by the hand of a feeble woman when he sleepeth.

Such are the refuse of mankind. They are asleep ; they have no power to resist temptation. Their moral strength is departed, for God is departed from them. There is the temptation to lust. They are men of sound principle in business matters, and nothing could make them swerve from honesty; but lasciviousness destroyeth them; they are taken like a bird in a snare; they are caught in a trap; they are utterly subdued. Or, mayhap, it is another way that they are conquered. They are men that would not do an unchaste act, or even think a lascivious thought; they scorn it. But they have another weak point, they are entrapped by the glass. They are taken and they are destroyed by drunkenness. Or, if they can resist these things, and are inclined neither to looseness of life nor to excess in living, yet mayhap covetousness entereth into them; by the name of prudence it slideth into their hearts, and they are led to grasp after treasure and to heap up gold, even though that gold be wrung out the veins of the poor, and though they do suck the blood of the orphan. They seem to be unable to resist their passion. How many times have I been told by men, " I cannot help it, sir, do what I may; I resolve, I re-resolve, but I do the same; I am defenceless; I cannot resist the temptation!" Oh, of course you cannot, while you are asleep. O Spirit of the living God! wake up the sleeper! Let sinful sloth and presumption both be startled, lest haply Moses should come their way, and finding them asleep should hang them on the gallows of infamy for ever.

Now, I come to give another meaning to the word " sleep." I hope there have been some of my congregation who have been tolerably easy whilst I have described the first three things, because they have thought that they were exempt in those matters. But sleep signifies also *inactivity*. The farmer cannot plough his field in his sleep, neither can he cast the grain into the furrows, nor watch the clouds, nor reap his harvest. The sailor cannot reef his sail, or direct his ship across the ocean, whilst he slumbereth. It is not possible that on the Exchange, or the mart, or in the house of business, men shall transact their affairs with their eyes fast closed in slumber. It would be a singular thing to see a nation of sleepers; for that would be a nation of idle men. They must all starve; they would produce no wealth from the soil; they would have nothing for their backs, nought for clothing and nought for food. But how many we have in the world that are inactive through sleep! Yes, I say inactive. I mean by that, that they are active enough in one direction, but they are inactive in the right. Oh how many men there are that are totally inactive in anything that is for God's glory, or for the welfare of their fellow creatures! For themselves, they can " rise up early, and sit up late, and eat the bread of carefulness; "—for their children, which is an alias for themselves, they can toil until their fingers ache—they can weary themselves until their eyes are red in their sockets, till the brain whirls, and they can do no more, but for God they can do nothing. Some say that they have no time, others frankly confess that they have no will: for God's church they would not spend an hour whilst for this world's pleasure they could lay out a month. For the poor they cannot spend their time and their attention. They may haply have time to spare for themselves and for their own amusement; but for holy works, for deeds of charity, and for pious acts they declare they have no leisure; whereas, the fact is, they have no will.

Behold ye, how many professing Christians there are that are asleep in this sense! They are inactive. Sinners are dying in the street by hundreds; men are sinking into the flames of eternal wrath; but they hold their arms, they pity the poor perishing sinner, but they do nothing to show that their pity is real. They go to their places of worship; they occupy their well-cushioned easy pew; they wish the minister to feed them every Sabbath; but there is never a child taught in the Sunday-school by them; there is never a tract distributed at the poor man's house; there is never a deed done which might be the means of saving souls. We call them good men; some of them we even elect to the office of deacons; and no doubt good men they are; they are as good as Athony meant to say that Brutus was honourable, when he said, " So are we all, all honourable men." So are we all, all good, if they be good. But these are good, and in some senses good for nothing; for they just sit and eat the bread, but they do not plough the field; they drink the wine, but they will not raise the vine that doth produce it. They think that they are to live unto themselves, forgetting that " no man liveth unto himself, and no man dieth unto himself." Oh, what a vast amount of sleeping we have in all our churches and chapels; for truly if our churches were once awake, so far as material is concerned, there are enough converted men and women, and there is enough talent with them, and enough money with them, and enough time with them, God granting the abundance of His Holy Spirit, which He would be sure to do if they were all zealous—there is enough to preach the gospel in every corner of the earth. The church does not need to stop for want of instruments, or for want of agencies; we have everything now except the will; we have all that we may expect God to give for the conversion of the world, except just a heart for the work, and the Spirit of God poured out into our midst. Oh! brethren, " let us not sleep as the others." You will find the " others " in the church and in the world: " the refuse " of both are sound asleep.

Ere, however, I can dismiss this first point of explanation, it is necessary for me just to say that the apostle himself furnishes us with part of an exposition; for the second sentence, " let us watch and be sober," implies that the reverse of these things is the sleep, which he means. " Let us watch." There are many that never watch. They never watch against sin; they never watch against the temptations of the enemy; they do not watch against themselves, nor against " the lusts of the flesh, the lusts of the eye, and the pride of life." They do not watch for opportunities to do good; they do not watch for opportunities to instruct the ignorant, to confirm the weak, to comfort the afflicted, to succour them that are in need; they do not watch for opportunities of glorifying Jesus, or for times of communion; they do not watch for the promises; they do not watch for answers to their prayers; they do not watch for the second coming of our Lord Jesus. These are the refuse of the world: they watch not, because they are asleep. But let us *watch :* so shall we prove that we are not slumberers.

Again: let us " *be sober.*" Albert Barnes says, this most of all refers to abstinence, or temperance in eating and drinking. Calvin says, not so: this refers more especially to the spirit of moderation in the things of the world. Both are right; it refers to both. There be many that are not sober;

they sleep, because they are not so ; for insobriety leadeth to sleep. They are not sober—they are drunkards, they are gluttons. They are not sober they cannot be content to do a little business—they want to do a great deal. They are not sober—they cannot carry on a trade that is sure—they must speculate. They are not sober—if they lose their property, their spirit is cast down within them, and they are like men that are drunken with wormwood. If on the other hand, they get rich, they are not sober : they so set their affections upon things on earth that they become intoxicated with pride, because of their riches—become purse-proud, and need to have the heavens lifted up higher, lest their heads should dash against the stars. How many people there are that are not sober ! Oh ! I might specially urge this precept upon you at this time, my dear friends. We have hard times coming, and the times are hard enough now. Let us be sober. The fearful panic in America has mainly arisen from disobedience to this command— " Be sober ; " and if the professors of America had obeyed this commandment, and had been sober, the panic might at any rate have been mitigated, if not totally avoided. Now, in a little time you who have any money laid by will be rushing to the bank to have it drawn out, because, you fear that the bank is tottering. You will not be sober enough to have a little trust in your fellow-men, and help them through their difficulty, and so be a blessing to the commonwealth. And you who think there is anything to be got by lending your money at usury will not be content with lending what you have got, but you will be extorting and squeezing your poor debtors, that you may get the more to lend. Men are seldom content to get rich slowly ; but he that hasteth to be rich shall not be innocent. Take care, my brethren—if any hard times should come in London, if commercial houses should smash, and banks be broken—take care to be sober. There is nothing will get us over a panic so well as every one of us trying to keep our spirits up—just rising in the morning, and saying, " Times are very hard, and to-day I may lose my all ; but fretting will not help it ; so just let me set a bold heart against hard sorrow, and go to my business. The wheels of trade may stop ; I bless God, my treasure is in heaven ; I cannot be bankrupt. I have set my affections on the things of God ; I cannot lose those things. There is my jewel ; there is my heart ! " Why, if all men could do that, it would tend to create public confidence ; but the cause of the great ruin of many men is the covetousness of all men and the fear of some. If we could all go through the world with confidence, and with boldness, and with courage, there is nothing in the world that could avert the shock so well. Come, I suppose the shock must ; and there are many men now present, who are very respectable, who may expect to be beggars ere long. Your business is, so to put your trust in Jehovah that you may be able to say, " Though the earth be removed, and though the mountains be carried into the midst of the sea, God is my refuge and strength, a very present help in trouble ; therefore will I not fear ; " and doing that, you will be creating more probabilities for the avoidance of your own destruction than by any other means which the wisdom of man can dictate to you. Let us not be intemperate in business, as are others ; but let us awake. " Let us not sleep "—not be carried away by the somnambulism of the world, for what is better than that? —activity and greed in sheep ; " but let us watch and be sober." Oh, Holy Spirit, help us to watch and be sober.

II. Thus I have occupied a great deal of time in explaining the first point—What was the sleep which the apostle meant ? And now you will notice that the word " therefore " implies that there are CERTAIN REASONS FOR THIS. I shall give you these reasons ; and if I should cast them somewhat into a dramatic form, you must not wonder ; they will the better, perhaps, be remembered. " Therefore," says the apostle, " let us not sleep."

We shall first look at the chapter itself for our reasons. The first reason precedes the text. The apostle tells us that " we are all the children of *the light* and of the day ; *therefore* let us not sleep as do others." I marvel not when, as I walk through the streets after nightfall, I see every shop closed, and every window-blind drawn down ; and I see the light in the upper room significant of retirement to rest. I wonder not that a half an hour later my footfall startles me, and I find none in the streets. Should I ascend the staircase and look into the sleepers placid countenances, I should not wonder ; for it is night, the proper time for sleep. But if some morning at eleven or twelve o'clock, I should walk down the streets and find myself alone, and notice every shop closed, and every house straitly shup up, and hearken to no noise, I should say, " 'Tis strange, 'tis passing strange, 'tis wonderful. What are these people at ? 'Tis day-time, and yet they are all asleep. I should be inclined to seize the first rapper I could find, and give a double knock, and rush to the next door, and ring the bell, and so all the way down the street ; or go to the police station, and wake up what men I found there, and bid them make a noise in the street ; or go for the fire engine, and bid the firemen rattle down the road and try to wake these people up. For I should say to myself, " There is some pestilence here ; the angel of death must have flown through these streets during the night and killed all these people, or else they would have been sure to have been awake." Sleep in the day-time is utterly incongruous. " Well, now," says the apostle Paul, " ye people of God, it is day-time with you ; the Sun of Righteousness has risen upon you with healing in His wings ; the light of God's Spirit is in your conscience ; ye have been brought out of darkness into marvellous light ; for you to be asleep, for a church to slumber, is like a city a bed in the day, like a whole town slumbering when the sun is shining. It is untimely and unseemly."

And now, if you look to the text again, you will find there is another argument. " Let us who are of the day be sober, putting on the breastplate of faith and love." So, then, it seems, it is *war-time ;* and therefore, again, it is unseemly to slumber. There is a fortress yonder, far away in India. A troop of those abominable Sepoys have surrounded it. Blood-thirsty hell-hounds, if they once gain admission, they will rend the mother and her children, and cut the strong man in pieces. They are at the gates : their cannon are loaded ; their bayonets thirst for blood, and their swords are hungry to slay. Go through the fortress, and the people are all asleep. There is the warder on the tower, nodding on his bayonet. There is the captain in his tent, with his pen in his hand and his dispatches before him, asleep at the table. There are soldiers lying down in their tents, ready for the war, but all slumbering. There is not a man to be seen keeping watch ; there is not a sentry there. All are asleep. Why, my friends, you would say, " Whatever is the matter here ? What can it be ? Has some great wizard been waving his wand, and put a spell upon them all ? Or are they all mad ? Have their minds fled ? Sure, to be asleep in war-time is indeed outrageous. Here I take down that trumpet ; go close up to the captains ear and blow a blast, and see if it does not awake him in a moment. Just take away that bayonet from the soldier that is asleep on the walls, and give him a sharp prick with it, and see if he does not awake." But surely, surely, nobody can have patience with people asleep, when the enemy surrounded the walls and are thundering at the gates.

Now, Christians, this is your case. Your life is a life of warfare ; the world, the flesh, and the devil are a hellish trinity, and your poor nature is a wretched mudwork behind which to be intrenched. Are you asleep ? Asleep, when Satan has fire-balls of lust to hurl into the windows of your eyes—when he has arrows of temptation to shoot into your heart—when he has snares into which to trap your feet ? Asleep, when he has undermined your existence, and when he is about to apply the match with which to destroy you, unless sovereign grace prevents ? Oh I sleep not, soldier of the cross I To sleep in war-time is utterly inconsistent. Great Spirit of God forbid that we should slumber.

But now, leaving the chapter itself, I will give you one or two other reasons that will, I trust, move Christian people to awake out of their sleep. " Bring out your dead ! Bring out your dead ! Bring out your dead ! " Then comes the ringing of a bell. What is this ? Here is a door marked with a great white cross. Lord, have mercy upon us ! All the houses down that street seem to be marked with that white death cross. What is this ? Here is the grass growing in the streets ; here are Cornhill and Cheapside deserted ; no one is found treading the solitary pavement ; there is not a sound to be heard but those horse-hoofs, like the hoofs of death's pale horse upon the stones, the ringing of that bell that sounds the death-knell to many, and the rumbling of the wheels of that cart, and the dreadful cry, " Bring out your dead I Bring out your dead I Bring out your dead ! " Do you see that house ? A physician lives there. He is a man who has great skill, and God has lent him wisdom. But a little while ago, whilst in his study, God was pleased to guide his mind, and he discovered the secret of the plague. He was plague-smitten himself, and ready to die ; but he lifted the blessed phial to his lips, and he drank a draught and cured himself. Do you believe what I am about to tell you ? Can you imagine it ? That the man has the prescription that will heal all these people ; he has it in his pocket. He has the medicine which, if once distributed in those streets, would make the sick rejoice, and put that dead man's bell away. And he is asleep I He is asleep I He is asleep I O ye heavens I why do ye not fall and crush the wretch ? O earth I how couldst thou bear this demon upon thy bosom ? Why not swallow him up quick ? He has the medicine ; he is too lazy to go and tell forth the remedy. He has the cure, and is too idle to go out and administer it to the sick and the dying I No, my friends, such an inhuman wretch could not exist I But I can see him here to-day. There are you I You know the world is sick with the plague of sin, and you yourself have been cured by the remedy, which has been provided. You are asleep, inactive, loitering. You do not go forth to

" Tell to others round,
What a dear Saviour you have found."

There is the precious gospel : you do not go and put it to the lips of a sinner. There is the all-precious blood of Christ : you never go to tell the dying what they must do to be saved. The world is perishing with worse than plague : and you are idle I And you are a minister of the gospel ; and you have taken that holy office upon yourself ; and you are content to preach twice on a Sunday, and once on a week-day, and there is no remonstrance within you. You never desire to attract the multitudes to hear you preach ; you would rather keep your empty benches, and study propriety, than you would once, at the risk of appearing over-zealous, draw the multitude and preach the word to them. You are a writer : you have great power in writing ; you devote your talents alone to light literature, or to the production of other things which may furnish amusement, but which cannot benefit the soul. You know the truth, but you do not tell it out. Yonder mother is a converted woman : you have children, and you forget to instruct them in the way to heaven. You yonder, are a young man, having nothing to do on the Sabbath-day, and there is the Sunday-school ; you do not go to tell those children the sovereign remedy that God has provided for the cure of sick souls. The death-bell is ringing e'en now ; hell is crying out, howling with hunger for the souls of men. " Bring out the sinner I Bring out the sinner I Bring out the sinner I Let him die and be damned I " And there are you professing to be a Christian, and doing nothing which might make you the instrument of saving souls—never putting out your hand to be the means in the hand of the Lord, of plucking sinners as brands from the burning I Oh I May the blessing of God rest on you, to turn you from such an evil way, that you may not sleep as do others, but may watch and be sober. The world's imminent danger demands that we should be active, and not be slumbering.

Hark how the mast creaks ! See the sails there, rent to ribbons. Breakers ahead I She will be on the rocks directly. Where is the captain ? Where is the boatswain ? Where are the sailors ? Ahoy there I Where are you ? Here's a storm come on. Where are you ? You are down in the cabin. And there is the captain in a soft slumber. There is the man at the wheel, as sound asleep as ever he can be ; and there are all the sailors in their hammocks. What I and the breakers ahead ? What I the lives of two hundred passengers in danger, and here are these brutes asleep ? Kick them out. What is the good of letting such men as these be sailors, in such a time as this especially ? Why, out with you I If you had gone to sleep in fine weather we might have forgiven you. Up with you, captain I What have you been at ? Are you mad? But hark! the ship has struck; she will be down in a moment. Now you will work, will you? Now you will work, when it is of no use, and when the shrieks of drowning women shall toll you into hell for your most accursed negligence, in not having taken care of them. Well, that is very much like a great many of us, in these times too.

This proud ship of our commonwealth is reeling in a storm of sin; the very mast of this great nation is creaking under the hurricane of vice that sweeps across the noble vessel; every timber is strained, and God help the good ship, or alas! none can save her. And who are her captain and her sailors, but ministers of God, the professors of religion? These are they to whom God gives grace to steer the ship. "Ye are the salt of the earth"; ye preserve and keep it alive, O children of God. Are ye slumbering now? If there were no dens of vice, if there were no harlots, if there were no houses of profanity, if there were no murders and no crimes, oh! ye that are the salt of the earth, ye might sleep; but to-day the sin of London crieth in the ears of God. This behemoth city is covered with crime, and God is vexed with her. And are we asleep, doing nothing? Then God forgive us! But sure, of all the sins He ever doth forgive, this is the greatest, the sin of slumbering when a world is damning—the sin of being idle when Satan is busy, devouring the souls of men. "Brethren, let us not sleep" in such times as these; for if we do a curse must fall upon us, horrible to bear.

There is a poor prisoner in a cell. His hair is all matted over his eyes. A few weeks ago the judge put on the black cap, and commanded that he should be taken to the place from whence he came, and hung by the neck until dead. The poor wretch has his heart broken within him, whilst he thinks of the pinion, of the gallows, and of the drop, and of after-death. Oh! who can tell how his heart is rent and racked, whilst he thinks of leaving all, and going he knoweth not where? There is a man there, sound asleep upon a bed. He has been asleep there these two days, and under his pillow he has that prisoner's free pardon. I would horsewhip that scoundrel, horsewhip him soundly, for making that poor man have two days of extra misery. Why, if I had had that man's pardon, I would have been there, if I rode on the wings of lightning to get at him, and I should have thought the fastest train that ever run but slow if I had so sweet a message to carry, and such a poor heavy heart to carry it to. But that man, that brute, is sound asleep, with a free pardon under his pillow, whilst that poor wretch's heart is breaking with dismay! Ah! do not be too hard with him: he is here to-day. Side by side with you this morning there is sitting a poor penitent sinner; God has pardoned him, and intends that you should tell him that good news. He sat by your side last Sunday, and he wept all the sermon through, for he felt his guilt. If you had spoken to him then, who can tell? He might have had comfort; but there he is now—you do not tell him the good news. Do you leave that to me to do? Ah! sirs, but you cannot serve God by proxy; what the minister does is nought to you; you have your own personal duty to do, and God has given you a precious promise. It is now on your heart.

Will you not turn round to your next neighbour, and tell him that promise? Oh! there is many an aching heart that aches because of our idleness in telling the good news of this salvation. "Yes," says one of my members, who always comes to this place on a Sunday, and looks out for young men and young women whom he has seen in tears the Sunday before, and who brings many into the church, "yes, I could tell you a story." He looks a young man in the face, and says, "Haven't I seen you here a great many times?" "Yes." "I think you take a great interest in the service, do you not?" "Yes, I do; what makes you ask me that question?" "Because I looked at your face last Sunday, and I thought there was something at work with you." "Oh! sir," he says, "nobody has spoken to me ever since I have been here till now, and I want to say a word to you. When I was at home with my mother, I used to think I had some idea of religion; but I came away, and was bound apprentice with an ungodly lot of youths, and have done everything I ought not to have done. And now, sir, I begin to weep, I begin to repent. I wish to God that I knew how I might be saved! I hear the word preached, sir, but I want something spoken personally to me by somebody." And he turns round; he takes him by the hand and says, "My dear young brother, I am so glad I spoke to you; it maks my poor old heart rejoice to think that the Lord is doing something here still. Now, do not be cast down, for you know, 'This is a faithful saying, and worthy of all acceptance, that Christ Jesus came into the world to save sinners.'" The young man puts his handkerchief to his eyes, and after a minute, he says, "I wish you would let me call and see you, sir," "Oh! you may," he says. He talks with him, he leads him onward, and at last by God's grace the happy youth comes forward and declares what God has done for his soul, and owes his salvation as much to the humble instrumentality of the man that helped him as he could do to the preaching of the minister.

Beloved brethren, the Bridegroom cometh! Awake! Awake! The earth must soon be dissolved, and the heavens must melt! Awake! Awake! O Holy Spirit arouse us all, and keep us awake.

III. And now I have no time for the last point, and therefore I shall not detain you. Suffice me to say in warning, there is AN EVIL HERE LAMENTED. There are some that are asleep, and the apostle mourns it.

My fellow sinner, thou that art this day unconverted, let me say six or seven sentences to thee, and thou shalt depart. Unconverted man! unconverted woman! you are asleep to-day, as they that sleep on the top of the mast in time of storm; you are asleep, as he that sleeps when the water-floods are out, and when his house is undermined, and being carried down the stream far out to sea; you are asleep, as he who in the upper chamber, when his house is burning and his own locks are singeing in the fire, knows not the devastation around him; you are asleep—asleep as he that lies under the edge of a precipice, with death and destruction beneath him. One single start in his sleep would send him over, but he knows it not. Thou art asleep this day; and the place where thou sleepest has so frail a support that when once it breaks thou shalt fall into hell: and if thou wakest not till then, what a waking it will be! "In hell he lifted up his eyes, being in torment"; and he cried for a drop of water, but it was denied him. "He that believeth in the Lord Jesus Christ and is baptized, shall be saved; he that believeth not shall be damned." This is the gospel. Believe ye in Jesus, and ye shall "rejoice with joy unspeakable and full of glory."

THE CHRISTIAN'S HELMET

"And for a helmet the hope of salvation."—1 Thess. v. 8.

THE very mention of a helmet may well serve to REMIND EVERY CHRISTIAN HERE THAT HE IS A SOLDIER.

If you were not soldiers, you would not need armour; but being soldiers, you need to be clad from head to foot in armour of proof. I suppose every Christian here knows, as a matter of theory, that he is a Christian soldier, and that he has been enlisted under the banner of the cross, to fight against the powers of darkness until he wins the victory. But we all need to have our memories refreshed upon this matter, for soldiering, in time of war at any rate, is not a very pleasant occupation, and the flesh constantly attempts to give it over. That "we have no abiding city here," is a truth which we all know, and yet the most of us try to make the earth as comfortable for ourselves as if it were to be our abiding residence. We are all soldiers—we know that; but still, too many Christians act as if they could be the friends of the world and the friends of God at the same time. Now, Christian, recollect once for all that you are a soldier. Did you dream, young man, that as soon as you were baptized, and added to the church, the conflict was all over? Ah, it was then but just beginning. Like Cæsar, you then crossed the Rubicon, and declared war against your deadly enemy. You drew your sword then; you did not sheathe it. Your proper note on joining the church is not one of congratulation, as though the victory were won, but one of preparation; for now the trumpet sounds, and the fight begins. You are a soldier at all times, Christian. You ought to sit even at your table as a soldier sits, and you should go out especially into the world as a soldier goes out. Never take off your armour, for if you do, in some unguarded moment you may meet with serious wounds. But *keep your armour ever about you, and be watchful,* for you are always in the midst of enemies wherever you may be; and even when the persons who surround you are your friends, there are still evil spirits unseen of men who watch for your halting; and you must not put up your sword, for you are to wrestle against principalities, and powers, and spiritual wickednesses in high places, against whom you must ever be on the watch. You are a soldier, man; remember that.

Nor are you a soldier in barracks, or at home, but *you are a soldier in an enemy's country.* Your place is either in the trenches or else in the thick of the battle. You who are sick are like soldiers in the trenches. You are patiently hoping and quietly waiting, as it were, upon the ramparts, looking for the time to come. But others of you, out in business, and engaged in the concerns of life, are like soldiers marching in long file to the conflict, like the horsemen dashing on to the front of the battle. More or less, according to your circumstances, you are all exposed to the foe, and that at every period of life.

Where are you, let me ask, but *in the country* of an enemy who never gives any quarter? If you fall, it is death. The world never forgives the Christian; it hates him with a perfect hatred, and it longs to do him ill. Only let the world see you commit half a trip, and they will soon report and magnify it. What might be done by other men without observation, if it were done by a Christian, would be noticed, reported, and misrepresented. The world understands that you are its natural antagonist. Satan perceives in you a representative of his old enemy, the Lord Jesus, and you may rest assured that he will never give you quarter if once he gets an opportunity of destroying you. Mind the enemy, mind the enemy, for he is one of a malicious spirit.

You have to fight with one, too, *who never yet made a truce.* You may come to terms and parley, but the powers of evil never do. *You* may hang out the white flag if you like. The foe may seem for a time as though he gave you credit, but do you never give your foe any credit. He hates you when he seems to love you best. "Dread the Greeks, even when they bring you gifts," said the tradition of old; and let the Christian dread the world most when it puts on its softest speeches. Stand, then, upon your guard, ye warriors of the cross, when least you fear, the cringing foe will come behind you, and stab you, under the pretence of friendship. Your Master was betrayed with a kiss, and so will you be, unless you watch unto prayer.

You have to do with an enemy *who never can make any peace with you, nor can you ever make any peace with him.* If you become at peace with sin, sin has conquered you; and it is imposible, unless you give up the fight, and yield your neck to the everlasting thraldom, that there should ever be peace for so much as a moment. Oh, Christian, see how guarded you ought to be. How needful to be clothed with your armour! How needful to have it of the right kind, to keep it bright, and to wear it constantly! You are a soldier, a soldier in battle, a soldier in the foeman's country, a soldier with a cruel and malicious enemy, who knows neither truce nor parley, and who gives no quarter, but will fight with you till you die. Heaven is the land where your sword should be sheathed; there shall you hang the banner high, but here we wrestle with the foe, and must do so till we cross the torrent of death. Right up to the river's edge must the conflict be waged. Foot by foot, and inch by inch, must all the land to Canaan's happy shore be won. Not a step can be taken without conflict and strife; but once there, you may lay aside your helmet, and put on your crown, put away your sword, and take your palm-branch; your fingers shall no longer need to learn to war, but your hearts shall learn the music of the happy songsters in the skies. This, then, is the first thought —that you are a soldier.

II. But the second thought is—BEING A SOLDIER, LOOK TO YOUR HEAD.

Soldiers, look to your heads. A wound in the head is a serious matter. The head being a vital part, we need to be well protected there. The heart needs to be guarded with the breastplate, but the head needs to be protected quite as much ; for even if a man should be true-hearted, yet if a shot should go through his brain, he would not be worth much as a soldier ; his body would strew the plain. The head must be taken care of. There are a great many Christian people who never have any trouble with their heads at all. There are certain religionists who get their hearts warmed, and then they think that that is enough. Now, give me above everything else a good warm heart ; but, oh, to have that warm heart coupled with a head that is well taken care of. Do you know that a hot head and a hot heart together do a deal of mischief, but with a hot heart and a cool brain you may do a world of service to the Master. Have right doctrine in the head, and then set the soul on fire, and you will soon win the world. There is no standing in that man's way whose head and heart are both right, but to neglect the head has been serious mischief with many Christians. They have been almost powerless for usefulness because they have not taken care of their brains. They have got to heaven, but they have not got many victories on the road, because their brains have been out of order. They have never been able clearly to understand the doctrine ; they have not been able to give a reason for the hope that is in them. They have not, in fact, looked well to the helmet which was to cover their heads.

The text refers us to our head because it speaks of a helmet, and a helmet is of no use to any part except the head. Among other reasons why we should preserve the head in the day of battle, let us give these. *The head is peculiarly liable to the temptations of Satan, of self, and of fame.* It is not easy, you know, to stand on a high pinnacle without the brain beginning to reel ; and if God takes a man and puts him on a high pinnacle of usefulness, he had need to have his head taken care of. If a brother is possessed of a considerable amount of wealth, there is a great danger in that wealth, unless there be a wealth of grace as well as a wealth of gold. If a man is well reported of, his sphere may not be very large, but if everybody praises him, he also will need to have his head well protected, for the little praise, even though it should come from fools, would be too much for a fool. The fining-pot for silver, and praise for the man. If a man can stand commendation, he can stand anything. The severest trial which a Christian has to bear is, probably, the trial which comes from his kind but inconsiderate friends, who would puff him up if they could by telling him what a fine fellow he is. If your friends will not do this, you will probably have a friend within who will do it for you ; and if *you* should forget it, the devil will not. " What a capital sermon you gave us this morning, Mr. Bunyan," said a friend, where John had been preaching. " You are too late," said Bunyan, " the devil told me that before I came out of the pulpit." Yes, and he will be sure to do it ; and hence the need of having a helmet to put on the head ; so that when you are successful, when you are getting on in life, when friends are speaking well of you, you may not get intoxicated with it. Oh, to have a good, cool helmet to put on your brain when it begins to get a little hot with praise, so that you may still stand fast, and not be borne down by

vanity. O Vanity, Vanity, Vanity, how many hast thou slain ! How many who then seemed upon the very brink of greatness have stumbled upon this stumbling-stone ! Men who seemed as though they would enter heaven, but a little bit of honour, some glittering bribe, a golden boon, has turned them asides, and they fell. Take care of your heads, brethren.

And is not *the head liable to attacks from scepticism ?* People who have no brains are not often troubled with doubts, but people who have brains have probably felt that, whether they resolved to use them or not, the brains would use themselves. It is very good of our fathers to tell us not to read dangerous books, very good of them indeed ; but we do read them, for all that ; and though we tell the young folks sometimes not to read this and that heretical treatise, and we wish they would take our advise, yet somehow or other they do get hold of such things, and will ponder them. Brethren, I do believe that, in such times as these, when everything is so free, and when discussion is so common, we must expect that our young fellows will look at a great many things which they had better leave alone, and their heads will be endangered thereby, for the bullets of scepticism threaten to go right through their brains. Well, what then ? As we cannot take Christians out of the way of the bullets, we should give them a helmet to preserve them therefrom. He who has a hope of salvation—a good hope that he is himself saved, a hope that he shall see the face of Christ with joy at last—is not afraid of all the quibbles of scepticism. He may hear them all, and for a moment be staggered by them, as a soldier might be who had a sudden shock or even a wound, but after a while he recovers himself, and feels sound enough to enter into the conflict again. And the Christian can say—

" Let all the forms that men devise
Assail my faith with treacherous art ;
I'd call them vanity and lies,
And bind the gospel to my heart."

It has been very well observed that a man is not often a very thorough democrat after he gets a little money in the savings-bank. Well, I think it is very likely that when a man gets a little stake in his country, he begins to be, just to the nearest merest extent, conservative. As soon as ever a man gets a stake in Christianity, and feels that he has got salvation in Jesus Christ, he gets to be very, very conservative of the old-fashioned truth. He cannot give up the Bible then, because it is a broad land of wealth to him. He cannot give up Christ, for He is *his* Saviour, *his* salvation. He cannot give up a single promise, because that promise is so dear to his own soul. The helmet of salvation, then, will preserve the head in times of scepticism.

The head, again, is very greatly in danger *from the attacks of personal unbelief.* Who among us has not doubted his own interest in Christ ? Happy you who are free from such trouble. But there are seasons with some of us when we turn our title-deeds over, and we are sometimes afraid lest they should not be genuine. There are times when, if we could, we would give a world to know that we are Christ's, for at times we cannot

" Read our title clear
To mansions in the skies."

Well, beloved, this is very dangerous to our heads ; but the man who has got the helmet of a right, sound,

God-given hope of salvation, who has received from God the Holy Spirit a helmet which I am going to describe by-and-by, when these doubts and fears come, they may distress him for a little while, but he knows the smell of gunpowder, and he is not afraid. In the midst of all Satan's accusations, or the uprisings of his old corruptions, or the threatenings of the flesh and of the world, he stands calm and unmoved, because he wears as a helmet the hope of salvation.

Nor are these all the dangers to which the head is exposed. *Some persons are attacked by threatenings from the world.* The world brings down its double-handled sword with a tremendous blow upon the heads of many Christians. " You will suffer the loss of all things for Christ if you are such a fanatic as to do as you do. You will be poor, your children will want bread, your wife will be worse than a widow, if you are such a fool." " Ah," says the Christian, " but I have a hope of salvation," and the blow, when it comes, does not go through his head, but just falls on the helmet, and the world's sword gets blunted. " I can afford to be poor" said Dr. Gill, when one of his subscribers threatened to give up his seat, and would not attend, if the doctor preached such and such a doctrine. So says the Christian, " I can afford to be poor ; I can afford to be despised ; I have in heaven better and more enduring substance." So, by the use of this blessed helmet he is not destroyed by the threatenings of the world.

We want our young people to wear this helmet, too, *because of the errors of the times.* The errors of the times are many. We have to deal, not merely with scepticism, but with superstition. They are tempted on the one side ; they are tempted on the other. This and that you will have cried up. " Lo here," and " Lo there " ; and there will be many misled who are not the people of God. " If it were possible, they would deceive the very elect " ; but the elect are not deceived, because their heads are not vulnerable to these errors, for they wear the hope of salvation, and they are not afraid of all the " ites " or the " isms " in the world. The man knows he is saved. Once get to know Christ personally for yourselves, and that He loved you, and gave Himself for you, and then rejoice that you are forgiven and justified through Him, the world will count you stupid and obstinate ; but you will stand firm, and be able to resist all its sarcasm and its ridicule. He who has made a refuge of Jesus Christ may stand safe, whatever errors may invade the land.

They tell us that the Church of God is in great danger, and that Popery will overspread the land altogether. I believe it will, but that it will overspread the Church of God—no ; I know far better than that. The Church of God never can be in danger. Every man in whom is the life of God would be as ready to die to-morrow for the truth as our forefathers were in the Marian days. Rest assured there would be found men to stand at the burning faggot still if the times required them, and our prisons would not long be without heavenly-minded tenants if the truth needed to be defended by suffering, even unto death. There *is* danger, great danger ; there never was such danger in modern times of Popery overspreading the land as now. But there is no danger to the man who has his helmet on. No, let the arrows fly thick as hail, and let the foes have all political power, and all the *prestige* of antiquity that they may ; a little phalanx of true-hearted Christians will still stand out at the thick of the onslaught, and cut their way to glory and to victory through whole hosts, because their heads are guarded with the heavenly helmet of the hope of salvation. Soldiers, then, take care of your heads. I will say no more on that point.

III. God has provided a covering for your heads, let us therefore now CONSIDER THE HELMET WITH WHICH HE WOULD HAVE YOUR HEADS PROTECTED.

" The hope of salvation " ! This is not the hope I spoke about this morning, for that was the hope that salvation was possible. This helmet is made up of actual hope that, being already saved in Christ Jesus, you should abide unto eternal life. It is a personal hope, founded upon personal conviction, and is wrought in us by the Holy Spirit.

To begin, then, describing this helmet. *Who is its giver ?* You ask our friend the soldier where he gets his regimentals from, and he answers that he gets them from the government stores. He gets his regimentals from Her Majesty, and that is where we must get our helmets from. If any of you construct helmets of hope for yourselves, they will be of no use to you in the day of battle. The true helmet of hope must come from the heavenly arsenal. You must go to the Divine storehouse, for unto God belongeth salvation, and the hope of salvation must be given to you by His free grace. A hope of salvation is not purchasable. Our great King does not sell His armour, but gives it freely to all who enlist. They take the shilling, and accept faith. They trust Christ, and they are enlisted, and then the armour is given them gratis. From head to foot they are arrayed by grace.

Do you ask, *who is the maker of this helmet?* Weapons are valued often according to the maker. A known maker gets his own price for his articles. Armourers of old took much trouble with the ancient helmets, because a man's life might depend upon that very useful means of defence. So we have here the name of God the Holy Ghost upon this helmet. A hope of salvation is the work of God the Holy Spirit in our soul. It is the Spirit who brings us to Jesus, shows us our need of Him, and gives us faith in Him ; and it is that same Spirit who enables us to hope that we shall endure to the end, and enter into eternal life. Be not satisfied with a hope which is natural, but have a hope that is supernatural. Rest not satisfied with that which is made in the workshop of nature ; go not to those who buy and sell for themselves, but go to the blessed Spirit, who giveth freely, and upbraideth not.

Or would you inquire further, *of what metal this helmet is made?* That it is made of hope, we are told ; but it is of the utmost consequence that it be a good hope. Beware of getting a base hope, a helmet made of paltry metal. There were some helmets they used to wear in the olden times which looked very well, but they were of no more use that brown-paper hats ; and when a soldier got into the fight with one of these on, the sword went through his skull. Get a good helmet, one made of the right metal. This is what a Christian's hope is made of— he believes that Christ came into the world to save sinners ; he trusts Christ to save him ; and he hopes that when Christ comes he shall reign with Him— that when the trumpet sounds he shall rise with Christ—and that in heaven he shall have a secure dwelling-place at the right hand of the Father. This hope is made up of proper and fitting deductions from certain truthful statements. That Christ died for *sinners* is true ; that He died to save all who trust in Him is true ; that *I* trust Him is true ; therefore, that I am saved is true ; and, being saved, that I shall inherit all His promises is a matter of course. Some people have a hope, but they do not know where they get it from, nor do they know a reason for it. When some people die, you hear it said, " I hope, I hope he is gone to heaven." Well, I wish he may have gone ; but I dare not say of some that I hope so, because hope must have a reason. An anchor is of no use without its fluke. It must be able to hold fast. It must have—at any rate, the modern anchor—some weight about it with which it can hold to the bottom. Hope must have its fluke, too ; it must have its reason ; it must have its weight. If I say I hope so and so, I am foolish for hoping it, if I have not a reason for hoping. If you were to say you hoped the person sitting next you would give you a thousand pounds, it would be a most absurd hope. You may wish it if you like, but what ground have you for the hope ? But if somebody owes you a thousand pounds, and you have his acknowledgment of the debt, you may then very well say that you hope it will be paid, for you have a legitimate right to expect it. Such is the Christian's hope. God has promised to save those who believe. Lord, I believe Thee ; Thou hast promised to save me, and I hope Thou wilt, I know Thou wilt. The Christian's hope is not a fancy, not a silly desire. It did not spring up in the night, like Jonah's gourd, and it will not wither in a night. The Christian's hope is something that will bear a crack from a club, or a cut from a sharp sword. It is made of good metal. John Bunyan said of a certain sword that it was " a true Jerusalem blade," and I may call this a true Jerusalem helmet, and he that wears it need not fear.

Having shown the metal of which the helmet is made, let me now describe *the strength of the helmet*. It is so strong, that under all sorts of assaults he who wears it is invulnerable. He may stagger under a blow, but he cannot be hurt by it. Recollect what David said. All the troubles in the world set on David once, and began to beat him, and they gave him many terrible blows. They thought they had certainly ruined him ; and David was bleeding, and was full of wounds. He himself half thought he should die, and he tells us himself that he should have fainted, only he had a bottle of cordial with him called faith. He says, " I had fainted if I had not believed." But just at the time when they thought he would faint and die, suddenly the old hero that slew Goliath made all his enemies fly before him as he cried, " Why art thou cast down, O my soul, and why art thou disquieted within me ? Hope thou in God." And he laid about him right and left, as he should. " I shall yet praise Him who is the health of my countenance and my God." " Hope thou in God," Christian. Oh that blessed word HOPE ! You know what the New Zealanders call hope ; they call it in their language " the swimming thought," because it always swims. You cannot drown it ; it always keeps its head above the wave. When you think you have drowned the Christian's hope, up it comes all dripping from the brine, and cries again, " Hope thou in God, for I shall yet praise Him ! " Hope is the nightingale that sings in the night ; faith is the lark that mounts up towards heaven ; but hope is the nightingale that cheers the valley in the darkness. O Christian, be thankful that you have so strong a helmet as this, which can bear all assaults, and can keep you unwounded in the midst of the fray !

This hope of salvation *is a helmet which will not come off*. It is of main importance, you know, to have a helmet that will not be knocked off the first thing in the fight. That is why our policemen are dressed differently from what they used to be, because their hats used to get knocked off the very first thing. So it will be with some people's helmets, if they have a commonplace hope ; but the Christian wears a helmet that he cannot get off anyhow. There was once a good soldier of Jesus Christ ; this soldier happened to be a woman, however, and some women are the best soldiers Christ ever had ; they are His true Amazons. This good woman had been much attacked by a sceptical person ; and when she was very much confounded with some of his knotty questions, she turned round and said to him, " I cannot answer you, sir, but neither can you answer me, for I have something within me that you cannot understand, which makes me feel that I could not give up what I know of Christ for all the world." You see, he could not get her helmet off, and the devil himself cannot drag the Christian's helmet off when he has once got it fairly buckled on. The world can neither give nor take away the hope of a Christian. It comes from God, and He will never withdraw it, for his gifts and calling are without repentance. Once let this helmet be put on, and He will never remove it, but we shall hope on and hope ever, until we shall see His face at the last.

I should like to go round amongst this regiment, as the commanding officers sometimes do, to have a look at you. This helmet is an old-fashioned kind of armour ; and in old days, the lieutenants and other officers, when they went round the regiment, used to look, not only to see that the men had their helmets, but to see that they had oiled them ; for in those times they used to oil their helmets to make them shine, and to keep the various joints, and buckles, and so on, in good order. No rust was ever allowed on the helmets, and it is said that when the soldiers marched out, with their brazen helmets and their white plumes, they shone most brilliantly in the sun. David speaks, you know, of " anointing the shield." He was speaking of a brazen shield which had to be anointed with oil. Now, when God anoints His people's hope, when He gives them the oil of joy, their hope begins to shine bright in the light of the Saviour's countenance, and what a fine array of soldiers they are then ! Satan trembles at the gleaming of their swords ; he cannot endure to look upon their helmets. But some of you do not keep your hope clear ; you do not keep it bright ; it gets rusty out of use, and than ere long it gets to sit uncomfortably upon you, and you get weary with the fight. O Holy Spirit, anoint our heads with fresh oil, and let Thy saints go forth to-night terrible as an army with banners.

Do not let it be overlooked that *the helmet was generally considered to be a place of honour*. The man put his plume in his helmet, he wore his crest frequently there, and in the thick of the fight the captain's plume was seen in the midst of the smoke and dust of battle, and the men pressed to the place where they saw it. Now, the Christian's hope is his honour and his glory. I must not be ashamed of my hope ; I must wear it for beauty and for dignity, and he who has a right good hope will be a leader to others. Others will see it, and will fight with renewed courage ; and where he hews a lane of the foes, they will follow him, even as he follows his Lord and Master, who has overcome, and sits down upon his Father's throne. I hope there are many Christians here who keep their helmets bright, and that there are many more who desire to have such helmets to protect themselves and to grace their profession.

IV. Yet THERE ARE SOME HERE WHO HAVE NO HELMETS. The reason is obvious. They are not Christ's soldiers.

Of course the Lord Jesus does not provide anybody with armour but those in His own service. But Satan knows how to give you a helmet, too. His helmets are very potent ones. Though the sword of the Spirit can go right through them, nothing else can. He can give, and has given some of you, a head-piece that covers your entire skull—a thick head-piece of indifference ; so that no matter what is preached, you do not care. " What do I care ? " say you, and that is your helmet.

Then he puts a piece in the front of the helmet called *a brazen forehead and a brow of brass*. " What do I care ? " That is your cry. Then he takes care to fit the helmet right over your eyes, so that you cannot see ; yea, though hell itself be before you, you do not see it. " What do I care ? " Then he also knows how so to fit the helmet, that it acts as a gag to your mouth, so that you never pray. You can swear through it, but you cannot pray. Still you keep to your old cry, " What do I care ? "

Ah, it is not very likely that any sword of mine will get at your head ! Arguments will not move you, for that is a question that cannot very well be argued—" What do I care ? " It is all very well for you to say that, but oh, I pray God the Holy Spirit to get at your head, notwithstanding that horrible helmet ; for if not, God has a way of dealing with such as you are. When you come to die, you will sing another song ! When you come to lie there upon that bed of sickness, and the grim day of eternity is in view, you will not be able to say quite so gaily as you do now, " What do I care ? " And when the trumpet rings through earth and heaven, and your body starts up from your grave, and you see the great Judge upon His throne, you will not be able to say then, " What do I care ? " Your head will then be bare to the pitiless tempest of divine wrath. Bare-headed, you must be exposed to the everlasting storm that shall descend upon you. And when the great angel binds you up with your fellows in bundles to burn, you will feel then that you are not able to say, " What do I care ? " for cares will come upon you like a wild deluge when you are banished from His presence, and all hope is gone !

Oh, I would you would take off that helmet ! May God grant you grace to unbuckle it to-night, never to put it on again ! Do care. You are not a fool, my friend, are you ? It is only a fool who says, " What do I care ? " *Surely you care about your soul ; surely hell is worth escaping from ; surely heaven is worth winning ; surely that cross on which our Saviour died is worth thinking of ; surely that poor soul of yours is worth caring about !* Do, I pray you, think, and not go hastily on. Oh, may Jesus Christ, who died for such as you are, bring you to trust Him ; and then, unbuckling all that evil armour of " What do I care ? " you will bow before His cross, and kiss His hands, and He will put upon you the golden helmet of a hope of salvation, and you will rise, one of the King's own soldiers, to fight His battles, and win an immortal wreath of everlasting victory. May it be so with every one of us !

REJOICE EVERMORE

" Rejoice evermore."—1 Thessalonians v. 16.

THIS is a sunny precept. When we read it we felt that the time of the singing of birds has come. That joy should be made a duty is a sure token of the blessedness of the New Covenant. Because Jesus has suffered, we are encouraged, commanded, and enabled to rejoice. Only the Man of Sorrows and his chosen apostles can teach for a precept such a word as this—" *Rejoice evermore*." Happy people who can be thus exhorted ! We ought to rejoice that there is a command to rejoice. Glory be unto the God of happiness who bids His children be happy. While musing on this text, I seem carried in spirit to the green woods, and their bowers. As in a dell all blue with hare-bells, where the sun smiles down upon me through the half-born oak leaves, I sit me down, and hear the blessed birds of the air piping out their love-notes : their music saith only this—" *Rejoice evermore*." All that I see, and hear, and feel, surrounds me with garlands of delight ; while the fairest of all the shepherds of Sharon sings to me this delicious pastoral—"*Rejoice evermore*." The very words have breathed spring into my soul, and set my heart a-blossoming. Thus am I also made to be as a daffodil which long has hidden away among the clods, but now at last ventures to uplift her yellow lily, and ring out her golden bell. Who can be sad, or silent, when the voice of the Beloved saith " *Rejoice evermore* " ?

Our apostle speaks of rejoicing as a personal, permanent duty to be always carried out by the people of God. The Lord has not left it to our own option whether we will sorrow or rejoice ; but He has pinned us down to it by positive injunction—" Rejoice evermore." He will have this cloth of gold spread over the whole field of life. He has laid down as first and last, beginning, middle and end—" Rejoice evermore." Some things are to be done at one time, some at another ; but rejoicing is for all times, for ever, and for evermore, which, I suppose, is more than ever, if more can be. Fill life's sea with joy up to high-water mark. Spare not, stint not, when rejoicing is the order of the day. Run out to your full tether ; sweep your largest circle when you use the golden compasses of joy.

Some things being once done are done with, and you need not further meddle with them ; but you have never done with rejoicing. " Rejoice evermore."

Our text is set in the midst of many precepts. Notice how from the fourteenth verse the apostle packs together a number of duties of Christian ministers and church members one towards another. " We exhort you, brethren, warn them that are unruly, comfort the feeble-minded, support the weak, be patient toward all men." All these things are to be done in turn, according as occasion requires ; but " rejoice evermore." You have plenty to do ; but this thing you have always to do. You shall never be able to fold your hands for want of some holy task or other ; but be not worried ; be not fretted by what you have to do ; on the contrary, take up the sacred duties with alacrity, welcoming each one of them, and entering upon them with delight. Rejoice in each one, because you " rejoice evermore." You will have to warn the unruly, and their rebellious tempers will, perhaps, irritate you ; or, if in patience you possess your soul, yet you may grow sad at having so melancholy a duty to perform ; but be not overmuch troubled, even by the grief of injured love. Warn the unruly, but " rejoice evermore." Do not pause in the blessed service of rejoicing when you are called upon to comfort the feeble-minded. There is a danger that the feeble-minded may rob you of your comfort, but let it not be so. In attempting to lift them out of the waters you may, perhaps, be almost drowned yourself ; your deliverance will lie in the sweet word, " Rejoice evermore." You will lose your power both to warn the unruly and to comfort the feeble-minded, if you lose your joy. The joy of the Lord will be your strength in all these matters ; therefore, " rejoice evermore." Close at your hand will lie the weak who want supporting, and you may be half saying to yourselves, " We wish that all God's people were strong, that we might unitedly spend all our strength against the foe, instead of having to use it at home for supporting our own weak soldiery." But be not dejected on that account : while you are supporting the weak, still " rejoice evermore." Your rejoicing will be a great support to the faint ; your ceasing to rejoice will be a terrible confirmation of their sorrow. Lend the feeble a hand, but do not stop your own singing. Does not a mother carry her babe, and sing at the same time ?

As you turn about, you find all men gathering to hinder you, to grieve you, to slander you, or to make use of you for their base purposes. But be not grieved : put up with your poor fellow-creatures since the Lord puts up with you, but do not leave off rejoicing. As you are patient towards all men, let your patience have a flavour of joy in it : however great the provocations that you endure, still " rejoice evermore." As it is written, " With all thy sacrifices thou shalt offer salt," so let it be thy settled purpose with every other duty to offer rejoicing. I am sure, brethren, that we make a very great mistake if we get like Martha—cumbered with much serving ; for that cumbering prevents our serving the Master well. He loves to see those who serve in His house of a cheerful countenance. He wants not slaves to grace His throne. He would have His children wait upon Him with a light in their faces which is the reflection of His own. He would have His joy fulfilled in them, that their joy may be full : it is His royal pleasure that His service should be delight, His worship heaven, His presence glory. Let your hearts be sanctified, but let not your hearts be troubled. Amidst a thousand duties give not way to a single anxiety. While you are desirous to honour God in everything, yet be not overburdened even with the cares of His cause and service, lest you put forth the hand of Uzza to stay the ark of the Lord. The Lord forbade His priests to wear garments that caused sweat, and He will not have any one of us fret and worry about His cause so as to lose our rest in His own self. Wrestle for a blessing, but still " rejoice evermore."

The command to rejoice is set in the midst of duties ; it is put there to teach us how to perform them all.

Also notice that *our text comes after just a flavouring of trouble and bitterness.* Read verse fifteen : " See that none render evil for evil unto any man," Children of God are apt to have evil rendered to them. They may have slanderous reports spread about them : they may be accused of things they never dreamed of : they may be cut to the heart by the ingratitude of those who ought to have been their friends ; but still they are bidden, " rejoice evermore." Even rejoice in the persecution and in the slander. " Blessed are ye, when men shall revile you, and persecute you, and shall say all manner of evil against you falsely, for My sake. Rejoice, and be exceeding glad : for great is your reward in heaven : for so persecuted they the prophets which were before you." So says our Lord. " Rejoice ye," He says, " and be exceeding glad." There is an expression in the Greek that never has been rendered in to English, and never will be—αγαλλιασθε. Old Trapp half puns upon the *agalliasthe* as he says, " dance a galliard." I do not know what a " galliard " was, but I suppose that it was some very joyous kind of dance. Certainly we know of no better way of translating our Lord's words than by—exult, or leap for joy. Even when your good name shall be tarnished by the malice of the wicked, then you are to leap. When are you to be wretched ? Surely despondency is excluded. If slander is to make us dance, when are we to fret ? Suppose some other kind of trial should come upon you, you are still to rejoice in the Lord always. The dearest friend is dead : " rejoice evermore." The sweet babe is sickening, the darling of your household will be taken away : " rejoice evermore." Trade is ebbing out, prosperity is disappearing from you, you may even be brought to poverty ; but, " rejoice evermore." Your health is affected, your lungs are weak, your heart does not beat with regularity, very soon you may be sick unto death ; but, " *rejoice evermore.*" Shortly you must put off this tabernacle altogether ! Token warns you that you must soon close your eyes in death ; but, " rejoice evermore." There is no limit to the exhortation. It is ever in season. Through fire and through water, through life and through death, " rejoice evermore."

Now and then a commentator says that the command of our text must mean that we are to be in the habit of rejoicing, for there must necessarily be intervals in which we do not rejoice. It is to be " constant but intermittent " : so one good man says. I do not know how that can be, though I know what he means. He means that it ought to be the general tenor of our life that we rejoice : yet he evidently feels that there must be black clouds now and then to vary the abiding sunshine. He warns us that there will be broken bits of road where as yet the steam roller has not forced in the granite. But that will not do as an interpretation of the text ; for the apostle expressly says, " Rejoice evermore " ; that is, rejoice straight on, and never leave off rejoicing. Whatever happens, rejoice. Come what may, rejoice. If the worst darkens to the worst—if the night lowers into a sevenfold midnight, yet " *rejoice evermore.*" This carillon of celestial bells is to keep on ringing through the night as well as through the day. " Rejoice, rejoice, ye saints of God at every time, in every place, and under every circumstance. Joy, joy, for ever. Rejoice evermore. In the midst of a thousand duties, amid the surges of ten thousand trials, still rejoice." There is to be about the Christian a constancy of joy.

I am bound to mention among the curiosities of the churches, that I have known many deeply spiritual Christian people who have been afraid to rejoice. Much genuine religion has been "sicklied o'er with the pale cast of thought"! Some take such a view of religion that it is to them a sacred duty to be gloomy. They believe in the holiness of discontent, the sanctity of repining; but they recoil from grateful joy as if it were the devil in the form of an angel of light. One of the commandments of the saints of misery is, "Draw down the blinds on a Sunday." Another is, "Never smile during a sermon: it is wicked." A third precept is, "Never rest yourself, and be sure that you never let anybody else rest for an instant. Why should anybody be allowed a moment's quiet in a world so full of sin? Go through the world and impress people with the idea that it is an awful thing to live." I have known some very good people spoiled for practical usefulness, and spoiled as to being like the Lord Jesus Christ, by their deeply laid conviction that it was wicked to be glad. well do I remember an earnest Christian woman who saw me when I was first converted, full of the joy of the Lord, and joyfully assured of my salvation in Christ Jesus. She seemed distressed at the sight of so much joy. She shook her head. She looked at me with that heavenly-minded pity which these good people usually lay by in store. It seemed to her a dreadful thing that so young a Christian should dare to know whom he had believed. If you had been a Christian a hundred years you might perhaps begin to think it possible that you were saved; but to believe in the Lord Jesus Christ right straight away like a little child, and at once rejoice in His salvation, seemed to this dear old Christian woman to be an act of such shocking temerity that she could only shake her dear head and prognosticate all sorts of horrible things. Since then I have found a great many like her; and when I have seen them shake their heads they have not shaken me half so much as she shook my heart on that first occasion; because I know them now, and I know that there is nothing in that shake of the head after all. The fact is that they ought to shake their heads about themselves for getting into so sad a state while this text stands on the sacred page, "Rejoice evermore." It cannot be a wise and prudent thing to neglect this plain precept of the word. It cannot be an unsafe thing to do what we are commanded to do. It cannot be a wrong thing for a believer to abide in that state of mind which is recommended by the Holy Spirit in words so plain, and so unguarded, "Rejoice evermore."

Oh, dear friends, you may rejoice. God has laid no embargo upon rejoicing; He puts no restriction upon happiness. Do believe it that you are permitted to be happy. Do believe that there is no ordinance of God commanding you to be miserable. Turn this book over and see if there be any precept that the Lord has given you in which He has said, "Groan in the Lord always, and again I say groan." You may groan if you like. You have Christian liberty for that; but, at the same time, do believe that you have larger liberty to rejoice, for so it is put before you. He bids you rejoice, and yet again He says "rejoice." Some of God's sheep dare not go into the Lord's own pasture. It is dark and thick with rich and luscious food; and into that field their Shepherd has already led them. Yet they dream that there is a gate, and that gate is shut, and across it is written this word, "Presumption." They are afraid to feed where God has made the best grass to grow for them because they are afraid of being presumptuous. The fear is groundless, but painfully common. Oh that I could deliver the true believer from this evil influence! If you are believers in the Lord Jesus Christ, everything that there is in Christ is yours. If you are resting in Jesus Christ, though you have only lately begun to trust in Him, the whole covenant of grace with all its infinite supplies belongs to you, and you have the right to partake of that which grace has provided. Jesus invites you to eat and drink abundantly. Beloved in the Lord, the only sin that you can commit at the banquet of love will be to stint yourselves. The feast is spread by a royal hand, and royal bounty bids you come. Hold not back through shame or fear. Come and satiate your souls with goodness. "Eat ye that which is good, and let your soul delight itself in fatness," for so God permits you to do.

But I go a step farther, and that is, that *it is a sin not to rejoice.* I will not say it harshly; I should like to say it as softly and tenderly as it could be put: but it must be said, and I must not take away from the force of it by my tenderness. If it be a command, "Rejoice evermore," then it is a breach of the command not to rejoice evermore. And what is a breach of a command? What is a neglect to obey a precept? Is it not a sin—a sin of shortcoming, though not of transgression? Beloved, why do your faces wear those gloomy colours? Why do you distrust? Why do you mourn? Why are you continually suspicious of the faithfulness of God? Why are you not rejoicing when there is God's word for it, first permitting, and then commanding you? Come, ye unhappy and dolorous professors, question yourselves rather than others. O thou forlorn one, cease to judge those whose eyes flash with exultation. Next time that you meet with a rejoicing Christian, do not begin to chide him, but quietly chide yourself because you do not rejoice. As for you who are swift of foot, I hope that you will not say an unkind word of poor Mephibosheth, who is lame in both his feet, for he is dear to David, and he shall sit at David's table. But, on the other hand, Mephibosheth in his lameness must not grow bitter and censorious, and find fault with Asahel, who is fleet of foot as a young roe, or otherwise it may seem almost too ridiculous. No, no, Heavy-heart, chide not the glad. Glad-heart, deal not roughly with the sorrowful. Bear ye one another's burdens, and share ye one another's joys. If there be any chiding, let it be the chiding of Little-Faith, sorrowfully bemoaning his own weakness of grace. Oh that God would help us to be faithful to our own experiences: then we shall not criticize others, but judge ourselves.

All this by way of introduction.

And now, just for a minute or two, I desire to speak upon THE QUALITY OF THIS REJOICING which is commanded in our text. May the Holy Spirit enable me to set before you the select taste and special quality of a believer's life-long joy! "Rejoice evermore."

Brethren, *this is not a carnal rejoicing.* If it were, it would be impossible to keep it up evermore. There is a joy of harvest; but where shall we find it in winter ? There is a joy of wealth ; but where is this joy when riches take to themselves wings, and fly away ? There is a joy of health ; but that is not with us evermore, for the evil days come and the years of weakness and sorrow. There is a joy in having your children round about you ; sweet are domestic joys, but these last not for ever. At the house of the happiest knocks the hand of death. No : if your joys spring from earthly fountains, those fountains may be dried up, and then your joys are gone. If the foundation of a man's joy be anywhere on earth it will be shaken ; for there is a day coming when the whole earth shall shake, and even now it is far from being a stable thing. Build not on the floods ; and what are outward circumstances but as waves of the changeful sea ? No, beloved, it cannot be carnal joy which is here commanded, since carnal joy in the nature of things cannot be for evermore. I know not that carnal joy is commanded anywhere. Men are permitted to rejoice in the things of this life, but that is the most that we can say. They are forbidden to rejoice too much in these things, for they are as honey, of which a man may soon eat till he is sickened. The joy which God commands is a joy in which it is impossible to go too far. It is a heavenly joy, based upon things which will last for evermore ; or else we could not be bidden to " rejoice evermore."

Again, as this joy is not carnal, so I feel quite sure that *it is not presumptuous.* Some persons ought not to rejoice. Did not the prophet Hosea say, " Rejoice not, O Israel, for joy as other people : for thou hast departed from thy God " ? There are some persons who rejoice, and it would be well if a faithful hand were to dash the cup from their lips. They have never fled to Christ for refuge—they have never been born again—they have never submitted themselves to the righeousness of God, and yet they are at ease in Zion. Ah, wretched ease ! Many are ignorant of their ruin, strangers to the remedy of grace, strangers to the blood that bought redemption ; and yet they rejoice in their own righteousness. They have a joy that has been accumulated through years of false profession, hypocritical formality, and vain pretence. Such as these are not told to " rejoice evermore." There must be sound reasons for rejoicing now, or there can be no reason for rejoicing evermore. If your joy will not bear looking at, have done with it. If, when you run with the footmen of common self-examinations in time of health, they weary you, what will you do when you contend with the black horsemen of dark thought in the hour of death ? The joy that will abide for ever is the joy to be sought after ; but joy which a man cannot justify never ought to be thought of as enduring for " evermore." Is your hope fixed on what Jesus did for sinners on the tree ? Are you really a partaker of the life that is in Him ? Have you been begotten again unto a lively hope by the resurrection of Jesus Christ from the dead ? If so, it is safe for you to rejoice at once ; and it will be equally safe for you to " rejoice evermore." Is it not clear that the rejoicing commanded in our text is not a presumptuous joy, or a carnal joy ?

Again, dear friends, I feel bound to add that *it must not be a fanatical joy.* Certain religious people are of a restless, excitable turn, and never feel good till they are half out of their minds. You would not wonder if their hair should stand bolt upright, like the quills of the fretful porcupine. They are in such a state of mind that they cry " hallelujah " at

anything or nothing, for they feel ready to cry, or shout, or jump, or dance. I do not condemn their delirium, but I am anxious to know what goes with it. Come hither, friend ; let us have a talk. What do you know ? What ? Is it possible that I offend you the moment I seek a reason for the hope that is in you ? Is it so, that you do not know anything of the doctrine of grace ? You were never taught anything ; the object of the institution which enlisted you is not to teach you, but only to excite you. It pours boiling water into you, but it does not feed you with milk. That is a miserable business. We like excitement of a proper kind, and we covet earnestly a high and holy joy, but if our rejoicing does not come out of a clear understanding of the things of God, and if there is no truth at the bottom of it, what does it profit us ? Those who rejoice without knowing why can be driven to despair without knowing why ; and such persons are likely to be found in a lunatic asylum ere long. The religion of Jesus Christ acts upon truthful, reasonable, logical principles : it is sanctified common sense. A Christian man should only exhibit a joy which he can justify, and of which he can say, " There is reason for it." I pray you, take care that you have joy which you may expect to endure for ever, because there is a good solid reason at the back of it. The excitement of animal enthusiasm will die out like the crackling of thorns under a pot ; we desire to have a flame burning on the hearth of our souls which is fed with the fuel of eternal truth, and will therefore burn on for evermore.

I go a little farther, and I say that I believe that this joy which is commanded here, " Rejoice evermore," is *not even that high and divine exhilaration which Christians feel upon special occasions.* We could tell of rapturous ecstasies and sublime joys which, if they be not heaven itself, are so near akin to it, that we would not change them for the place that Gabriel fills when nearest to his Masters' throne. Oh, there are times when God's Elijah, having brought down the fire from heaven, girds up his loins and runs before Ahab's chariot with a divine enthusiasm which onlookers cannot understand. There are moments on the top of the mount when Peter is no fool for saying, " Let us build three tabernacles." It is so good to be there that we would willingly stay in that mount and never come down again to the bustle, and turmoil, and sin of a guilty world. Now, you are not commanded in the text to be always in such a high, exalted, rapturous state of mind as that. " Rejoice evermore,' but you cannot always rejoice at that rate. I have said that you cannot, and I mean it literally. There is a physical impossibility in it. The strain upon the mind would be much too great. We could not live in such a condition of excitement and tension. Sometimes we can swim in the deep waters ; but who can always swim ? We can take to ourselves the wings of eagles, and soar beyond the stars ; but we are not condors, and cannot always fly : we are more like the sparrows which find a house near the altar of God. When we cannot mount as on wings, we think it quite sufficient if we can run without weariness, and walk without fainting. The ordinary joy of the Christian is that which is commanded here : it is not the joy of Jubilee but of every year ; not the joy of harvest but of all the months. " *Rejoice evermore.*" No, Miriam, no, not always the timbrel. Not every day, " Sing unto the Lord, for He hath triumphed gloriously." There is other work for you. No, Moses, not every day,

"Thy right hand, O Lord, hath dashed in pieces the enemy." No, you have other work to do amongst those rebels, quite as honouring to your God and quire as useful as writing Israel's triumphal hymn. No, James and John and Peter, not always on the top of Tabor. Sometimes in the house of death with your Master where the young girl is raised, and sometimes in Gethsemane to keep watch, if you can, while He sweats great drops of blood. You are to "rejoice evermore," but you are not always to be clashing the high-sounding cymbals ; sometimes the softer psaltery must satisfy you hand. All days are not holidays : there was a day when Job lost his cattle and his children, and yet blessed the name of the Lord. All days are not wedding days : there was a day wherein Jacob cried, "All these things are against me." All days are not as the days of heaven upon earth ; and until the day break and the shadows flee away we shall have to bear about a joy that is rather a lamp in the night than a sun in the day—a joy that gladdens us when we are cast down, rather than lifts us up to ecstasy.

I hope that you catch my thought, though I am afraid that I do but dimly put it. This shows you what kind of joy could not be with us always. The joy that can be with us evermore is a part of ourselves, a power of the new nature which God works in us by His own Spirit. It consists in the great cheerfulness of the new-born disposition ; a full conviction that whatever God does is right ; a sweet agreement with the providence of God, let it ordain what it will ; an intense delight in God Himself and in the person of His dear Son ; and consequently a quietness, a calm, a stillness of soul, "the peace of God which passeth all understanding." This holy rejoicing is a drop of the essence of heaven. You have heard of "songs without words" ; such is the joy of the Lord in the soul : a sort of silent song for ever sung within the spirit ; a quiet making of music with every pulse of the heart ; a living psalmody before God with every heaving of the lungs. I hope that you know what it means, or that if you do not, you may soon learn. This is a joy that has no wear and tear about it. You can keep from year to year the even tenor of this way ; for this is the pace for which men's minds were made. "Rejoice evermore." You can live to be as old as Methuselah in this frame ; for this rejoicing will never tear you to pieces. It will conserve you, and act as the salt of your physical, mental, and spiritual man.

Thus much upon the quality of this joy.

Suffer a few words upon THE OBJECT OF THIS REJOICING, in order to help you, dear friends, to indulge it. "Rejoice evermore." Wherewith can we keep this feast ? What are the objects of such a joy as this ?

God helping us, we can always rejoice in God. What a God we have ! "God my exceeding joy," said the Psalmist. "Delight thyself also in the Lord." Every attribute of God, every characteristic of God, is an inexhaustible gold mine of precious joy to every man who is reconciled to God. Delight thyself in God the Father, and His electing love, and His unchanging grace, and His illimitable power, and His transcending glory ; and in thy being His child, and in that providence with which He orders all things for thee. Delight thyself in thy Father God. Delight thyself also in the Son, who is "God with us." God with us or ever the earth was, in the covenant council when He became our surety and

our representative. God with us when His delights were with the sons of men. Delight in Him as man suffering, sympathizing with you. Delight in Him as God putting forth infinite wisdom and power for you. I should need a month in which to give a bare outline of the various points of our Lord's divine and human character which furnish us with objects of joy. Do but think of Him. Do but for a moment consider His love, and if you are at all right in heart it must bring unspeakable pleasure to you.

"Jesus, the very thought of Thee
With sweetness fills my breast."

Then think of the Holy Ghost, and rejoice in Him as dwelling in you, quickening you, comforting you, illuminating you, and abiding with you for ever. Think of the triune God, and be blest.

Then muse upon the covenant of grace ; think of redemption by blood ; think of divine sovereignty and all that has come of it in the form of grace to men. Think of thy effectual calling, thy justification, thy acceptance in the Beloved. Think of thy final perseverance. Think of thy union with the glorious person of the Well-beloved, and of all the life and all the glory that is wrapped up in that surpassing truth. "Rejoice evermore." With such a God you have always a source of joy.

I believe, dear friends, that if we are right-minded every doctrine of the gospel will make us glad, every promise of the gospel will make us glad, every precept of the gospel will make us glad. If you were to go over a list of all the privileges that belong to the people of God, you might pause over each one, and say, "I could rejoice evermore in this if I had nothing else." If ever you fail to rejoice, permit me to exhort you to arouse each one of the graces of the Spirit to its most active exercise. Begin with the first of them—faith. Believe, and as you believe this and that out of the ten thousand blessings which God has promised, joy will spring up in your soul. Have you exercised faith ? then lead out the sister grace of hope. Begin hoping for the resurrection, hoping for the second coming, hoping for the glory which is then to be revealed. What sources of joy are these ! When you have indulged hope, then go on to love, and let this fairest of the heavenly sisters point you to the way of joy. Go on to love God more and more, and to love His people, and to love poor sinners ; and, as you love, you will not fail to rejoice, for joy is born of love ! Love has on her left hand sorrow for the griefs of those she loves, but at her right hand a holy joy in the very fact of loving her fellows ; for he that loves doeth a joyful thing. If you cannot get joy either out of hope, or faith, or love, then go on to patience. I believe that one of the sweetest joys under heaven comes out of the severest suffering when patience is brought into play. "Sweet," says Toplady, "to lie passive in Thy hand, and know no will but Thine." And it is so sweet, so inexpressibly sweet, that to my experience the joy that comes of perfect patience is, under certain aspects, the divinest of all the joys that Christians know this side of heaven. The abyss of agony has a pearl in it which is not to be found upon the mountain of delight. Put patience to her perfect work, and she will bring you the power to rejoice evermore.

I will suppose that you have gone through all this, and that you still say, "I cannot rejoice as I wo uld." Then arise, dear brother, and gird yourself for holy exer_ise. Begin with prayer. Prayer will make the darkening cloud remove; and then you will rejoice. If supplication is over, and you are not rejoicing, then sing a psalm. "Bring hither the minstrel." Often does holy music set the prophet going. Let us sing a song unto the Lord; and if we have no joy in our hearts already, we shall not have sung very many verses before rejoicing will drop on us like the dew which soaks the dry and dusky tents of the Arabians. If neither prayer nor praise will do it, then read the Word. Sit still and meditate on what the Lord has spoken. Go up to the Communion table; gather with the people of God in sweet mutual converse; or go out and preach to sinners. Go to the Sunday-school class, and tell the dear children about Christ. In Christian labour you will joy in the Lord as you would not have rejoiced in Him if you had been idle at home.

At any rate, when you do not rejoice, say to yourself, "Come, heart, this will not do. Why art thou cast down, O my soul?" I have heard of a mother that whenever her children began to cry, and grow fretty, she said, "They must have medicine." She was sure that they were not well. Whenever you begin to fret and worry, say to yourself, "I must take heavenly medicine, for I am not right. The leaves of the Scriptures are for my healing: I will use them for my soul's good. If my heart were right I should rejoice in the Lord, and as I am not rejoicing I must resort to the great Physician."

Brethren, we must rejoice. Why should we not rejoice, since all things are ours? Heaven is ours in the future, and earth is ours in the present. With the past and all its sins blotted out, the future and all its wants provided for by the bounty of an unchanging God, wherefore should we be disquieted? If we are not glad, the stars may rebuke us as they twinkle amid the darkness: the sun may rebuke us for refusing to shine in the light of God. Come, brethren, let us obey the Word that says, "*Rejoice evermore.*"

Lastly, somebody will say, "But why should we rejoice?" What are THE REASONS FOR THIS REJOICING? We ought not to want arguments to persuade us to be happy. The worldling says that "he counts it one of the wisest things to drive dull care away." The child of God may count it the wisest thing to cast his care upon his God. You do not want an argument for rejoicing; but if you did, it is found in the command of your Lord, who says to you, "Rejoice evermore."

Rejoicing wards off temptation. The Christian may be tempted; but little impression is made upon him by the pleasurable bait if he is happy in the Lord. There is a passage in Paul—I forget just now where it is—where he speaks of putting on the armour of light. It is fine poetry as well as solid fact that we wear the armour of light; and part of the meaning is, that we are so surrounded with seraphic joy that nothing can tempt us. The joy which we wear is far superior to any which the evil one can offer us; and so his temptation has lost its power. What can the devil offer the joyous Christian? Why, if he were to say to him, "I will give thee all the kingdoms of the world and the glory thereof, if thou wilt fall down and worship me," the believer would reply to him, "Fiend, I have more than that. I have perfect contentment; I have absolute delight in God. My soul swims in a deep sea of bliss as I think of God." The devil will speedily quit such a man as that; for the joy of the Lord is an armour through which he cannot send the dagger of his temptation.

This joy of the Lord will shut out worldly mirth from the heart. The rejoicing Christian is not the kind of man that wants to spend his evenings in a theatre. "Pooh!" he says, "what can I do there?" You say to the man who has once eaten bread, "I will take you to such a grand feast. I will show you a company of swine all feeding upon husks. Look upon them, see how they enjoy themselves! You shall have as much as you like, and be as happy as they are." He says, "But you do not know me: you do not understand me. I have none of the qualities that link me with swine. I cannot enjoy the things which they enjoy." He that is once happy in God pours contempt upon the sublimest happiness that a worldling can know. It is altogether out of his line. He does not know their mirth, even as they do not know his rejoicing. I suppose that the fish of the sea have joys suitable to their natures. I do not envy them: I am not inclined to dive into their elements. It is so with the children of God; they are not inclined to go after worldly things when they are happy in the Lord. But your miserable professors who simply go to a place of worship because they ought to go, and who are very good because they dare not be anything else, they have no joy in the Lord. They go to the devil for their joy: they openly confess that they must have a bit of pleasure sometimes, and therefore they go to questionable amusements. No wonder that they are found in Satan's court, looking up to him for delights, since they find no rejoicing in the ways of the Lord.

He that rejoices in the Lord always will be *a great encouragement to his fellow Christians.* He comes into the room: you like the very look of his face. It is a half-holiday to look at him; and as soon as ever he speaks he drops a sweet word of encouragement for the weak and afflicted. We have some brethren round about us whose faces always refresh me before preaching. Their words are cheering and strengthening. Those who rejoice in the Lord evermore cannot help perfuming the room where they are with the aroma of their joy. Others catch the blessed contagion of their contentment, and become happy too.

This is the kind of thing that attracts sinners. They used in the old times to catch pigeons and send them out with sweet unguents on their wings: other pigeons followed them into the dovecote for the sake of their perfume, and so were captured. I would that every one of us had the heavenly anointing on our wings, the divine perfume of peace, and joy, and rest; for then others would be fascinated to Jesus, allured to heaven.

God grant that it may be so, for Jesus' sake! Amen.

"PRAY WITHOUT CEASING"

"Pray without ceasing."—1 Thessalonians v. 17.

THE position of our text is very suggestive. Observe what it follows. It comes immediately after the precept, " Rejoice evermore " ; as if that command had somewhat staggered the reader, and made him ask, " How can I always rejoice ? " and, therefore, the apostle appended as answer, " Always pray." The more praying the more rejoicing. Prayer gives a channel to the pent-up sorrows of the soul, they flow away, and in their stead streams of sacred delight pour into the heart. At the same time the more rejoicing the more praying ; when the heart is in a quiet condition, and full of joy in the Lord, then also will it be sure to draw nigh unto the Lord in worship. Holy joy and prayer act and react upon each other.

Observe, however, what immediately follows the text : " In everything give thanks." When joy and prayer are married their first-born child is gratitude. When we joy in God for what we have, and believingly pray to Him for more, then our souls thank Him both in the enjoyment of what we have, and in the prospect of what is yet to come. Those three texts are three companion pictures, representing the life of a true Christian, the central sketch is the connecting link between those on either side. These three precepts are an ornament of grace to every believer's neck ; wear them every one of you, for glory and for beauty. " Rejoice evermore "; " pray without ceasing " ; " in everything give thanks."

But we cannot spare any time for the consideration of the context, but must advance to the precept in hand. Our text though exceedingly short is marvellously full, and we will discuss it under the following heads. We shall ask and answer four questions. *What do these words imply?* Secondly, *What do they actually mean?* Thirdly, *How shall we obey them?* And, fourthly, *Why should* WE *especially obey them?*

I. WHAT DO THESE WORDS IMPLY ? " Pray without ceasing." Do they not imply that *the use of the voice is not an essential. element in prayer?* It would be most unseemly even if it were possible for us to continue unceasingly to pray aloud. There would of course be no oppotrunity for preaching and hearing, for the exchange of friendly intercourse, for business, or for any other of the duties of life ; while the din of so many voices would remind our neighbours rather of the worship of Baal than that of Zion. It was never the design of the Lord Jesus that our throats, lungs, and tongues should be for ever at work. Since we are to pray without ceasing, and yet could not pray with the voice without ceasing, it is clear that audible language is not essential to prayer. We may speak a thousand words which seems to be prayer, and yet never pray ; on the other hand, we may cry into God's ear most effectually, and yet never say a word. In the book of Exodus God is represented as saying to Moses, " Why criest thou unto Me ? " And yet it is not recorded that Moses had uttered so much as a single syllable at that time. It is true that the use of the voice often helps prayer. I find, personally, that I can pray best when alone if I can hear my own voice ; at the same time it is not essential, it does not enter at all into the acceptability, reality, or prevalence of prayer. Silence is as fit a garment for devotion as any that language can fashion.

It is equally clear that *the posture of prayer is of no great importance,* for if it were necessary that we should pray on our knees we could not pray without ceasing, the posture would become painful and injurious. To what end has our Creator given us feet, if He desires us never to stand upon them ? If He had meant us to be on our knees without ceasing, He would have fashioned the body differently, and would not have endowed us with such unnecessary length of limb. It is well to pray on one's knees ; it is a most fitting posture ; it is one which expresses humility, and when humility is truly felt, kneeling is a natural and beautiful token of it, but, at the same time, good men have prayed flat upon their faces, have prayed sitting, have prayed standing, have prayed in any posture, and the posture does not enter into the essence of prayer. Consent not to be placed in bondage by those to whom the bended knee is reckoned of more importance than the contrite heart.

It is clear, too, from the text, that *the place is not essential to prayer,* for if there were only certain holy places where prayer was acceptable, and we had to pray without ceasing, our churches ought to be extremely large, that we might always live in them, and they would have to comprise all the arrangements necessary for human habitations. If it be true that there is some sanctity this side of a brick-wall more than there is on the other side of it, if it be true that the fresh air blows away grace, and that for the highest acceptance we need groined arches, pillars, aisle, chancel, and transept, then farewell, ye green lanes, and fair gardens, and lovely woods, for henceforth we must, without ceasing, dwell where your fragrance and freshness can never reach us. But this is ridiculous ; wherefore I gather that the frequenting of some one particular place has little or nothing to do with prayer ; and such a conclusion is consistent with the saying of Paul upon Mars' Hill, " God that made the world and all things therein, seeing that He is Lord of heaven and earth, dwelleth not in temples made with hands."

" Pray without ceasing." That precept at one stroke *overthrows the idea of particular times* wherein prayer is more acceptable or more proper than at others. If I am to pray without ceasing, then every second must be suitable for prayer, and there is not one unholy moment in the hour, nor one unaccepted hour in the day, nor one unhallowed day in the year. The Lord has not appointed a certain week for prayer, but all weeks should be weeks of prayer : neither has He said that one hour of the day is more acceptable than another. All time is equally legitimate for supplication, equally holy, equally accepted with God, or else we should not have been told to pray without ceasing. It is good to have your times of prayer ; it is good to set apart seasons for special supplication—we have no doubt of that ; but we must never allow this to gender the superstition that there is a certain holy hour for prayer in the **morning,** a specially acceptable hour for prayer in the evening, and a sacred time for prayer at certain seasons of the year. Wherever we seek the Lord with true hearts He is found of us ; whenever we cry unto Him He heareth us. Every place is hallowed ground to a hallowed heart, and every day is a holy day to a holy man. From January to December the calendar has not one date in which prayer is forbidden. All the days are red-letter days, whether Sabbaths or week days they are all accepted times for prayer. Clear, then, is it from the text, that the voice, the posture, the place, the time—none of them enter into the essence of prayer, or else, in this case, we should be commanded to perform an impossibility, which we are quite certain is not after the manner of the Lord our God.

There is one other thing implied in the text, namely, that *a Christian has no right to go into any place where he could not continue to pray.* Pray without ceasing ? Then I am never to be in a place where I could not pray without ceasing. Hence, many worldly amusements without being particularised may be judged and condemned at once. Certain people believe in ready-made prayers, cut and dried for all occasions, and, at the same time, they believe persons to be regenerated in baptism though their lives are anything but Christian ; ought they not to provide prayers for all circumstances in which these, the dear regenerated but graceless sons and daughters of their church, are found ? As, for instance, a pious collect for a young prince or nobleman, who is about to go to a shooting-match, that he may be forgiven for his cruelty towards those poor pigeons who are only badly wounded and made to linger in misery, as also a prayer for a religious and regenerated gentleman who is going to a horserace, and a collect for young persons who have received the grace of confirmation, upon their going to the theatre to attend a very questionable play. Could not such special collects be made to order ? You revolt at the idea. Well, then, have nothing to do with that which you cannot ask God's blessing upon, have nothing to do with it, for if God cannot bless it, you may depend upon it the devil has cursed it. Anything that is right for you to do you may consecrate with prayer, and let this be a sure gauge and test to you, if you feel that it would be an insult to the majesty of heaven for you to ask the Lord's blessing upon what is proposed to you, then stand clear of the unholy thing. If God doth not approve, neither must you have fellowship therewith.

These matters are clearly implied in the precept, " Pray without ceasing."

II. But now, WHAT DOES THIS ACTUALLY MEAN ? If it does not mean we are to be always on our knees, nor always saying prayers, nor always in church or in meeting, and does not mean that we are to consider any day as unfit for praying, what then ? The words mean, first, *a privilege ;* secondly, *a precept*—" Pray without ceasing." Our Lord Jesus Christ in these words assures you that you may pray without ceasing. There is no time when you may not pray. You have here permission given to come to the mercy-seat when you will, for the veil of the Most Holy place is rent in twain from the top to the bottom, and our access to the mercy-seat is undisputed and indisputable. Kings hold their levees upon certain appointed days, and then their courtiers are admitted ; but the King of kings holds a constant levee. The monarch whose palace was in Shushan would have

none approach him unless he sent for them ; but the King of kings has called for all His people, and they may come at all times. They were slain who went in unto the king Ahasuerus, unless he stretched out his sceptre to them ; but our King never withdraws His sceptre, it is always stretched out, and whosoever desires to come to Him may come now, and come at any time. Among the Persians there were some few of the nobility who had the peculiar and special right of an audience with the king at any time they chose. Now, that which was the peculiar right of a very few and of the very great is the privilege of every child of God. He may come in unto the King at all times. The dead of night is not too late for God ; the breaking of the morning, when the first grey light is seen, is not too early for the Most High ; at midday He is not too busy ; and when the evening gathers He is not too weary with His children's prayers. " Pray without ceasing," is, if I read aright, a most sweet and precious permit to the believer to pour out his heart at all times before the Lord. I hear its still small voice saying, " Come to the mercy seat, O my child, whenever thou wilt ; come to the treasury of grace whenever thou desirest—

> " The happy gates of gospel grace
> Stand open night and day."

The doors of the temple of divine love shall not be shut. Nothing can set a barrier between a praying soul and its God. The road of angels and of prayers is ever open. Let us but send out the dove of prayer and we may be certain that she will return unto us with an olive branch of peace in her mouth. Evermore the Lord hath regard unto the pleadings of His servants, and waiteth to be gracious unto them.

Still, however, it is *a precept,* " Pray without ceasing." And what does it mean ? It means a great truth, which I cannot very well convey to you in a few words, and, therefore, must try and bring out under four or five points.

It means, first, *never abandon prayer.* Never for any cause or reason cease to pray. Imagine not that you must pray until you are saved, and may then leave off. For those whose sins are pardoned prayer is quite as needful as for those mourning under a sense of sin. " Pray without ceasing," for in order that you may persevere in grace you must persevere in prayer. Should you become experienced in grace and enriched with much spiritual knowledge, you must not dream of restraining prayer because of your gifts and graces. " Pray without ceasing," or else your flower will fade and your spiritual fruit will never ripen. Continue in prayer until the last moment of your life.

> " Long as they live must Christians pray,
> For only while they pray they live."

As we breathe without ceasing, so must we pray without ceasing. As there is no attainment in life, of health, or of strength, or of muscular vigour which can place a man beyond the necessity of breathing, so no condition of spiritual growth or advance in grace will allow a man to dispense with prayer.

> " Let us pray ! our life is praying ;
> Prayer with time alone may cease :
> Then in heaven, God's will obeying,
> Life is praise and perfect peace."

Never give up praying, not even though Satan should suggest to you that it is in vain for you to cry unto God. Pray in his teeth ; " pray without ceasing." If for awhile the heavens are as brass and your prayer only echoes in thunder above your head, pray on ; if month after month your prayer appears to have miscarried, and no reply has been vouchsafed to you, yet still continue to draw nigh unto the Lord. Do not abandon the mercy-seat for any reason whatever. If it be a good thing that you have been asking for, and you are sure it is according to the divine will, if the vision tarry, wait for it, pray, weep, entreat, wrestle, agonise till you get that which you are praying for. If your heart be cold in prayer, do not restrain prayer until your heart warms, but pray your soul unto heat by the help of the ever-blessed Spirit who helpeth our infirmities. If the iron be hot then hammer it, and if it be cold hammer it till you heat it. Never cease prayer for any sort of reason or argument. If the philosopher should tell you that every event is fixed, and, therefore, prayer cannot possibly change anything, and, consequently, must be folly ; still, if you cannot answer him and are somewhat puzzled, go on with your supplications notwithstanding all. No difficult problem concerning digestion would prevent your eating, for the result justifies the practice, and so no quibble should make us cease prayer, for the assured success of it commends it to us. You know what your God has told you, and if you cannot reply to every difficulty which man can suggest, resolve to be obedient to the divine will, and still " Pray without ceasing." Never, never, never renounce the habit of prayer, or your confidence in its power.

A second meaning is this. *Never suspend the regular offering of prayer.* You will, if you are a watchful Christian, have your times of daily devotion, fixed not by superstition, but for your convenience and remembrance ; just as David, three times a day, and as another saint, seven times a day, sought the Lord : now be sure to keep up this daily prayer without intermission. This advice will not comprehend the whole range of the text, I am not pretending that it does ; I am only mentioning it now as supplementary to other thoughts. " Pray without ceasing " ; that is, never give up the morning prayer, nor the evening prayer, nor the prayer at midday if such has grown to be your habit. If you change the hours and times, as you may, yet keep up the practice of regularly recurring retirement, meditation, and prayer. You may be said to continue in prayer if your habitual devotions be maintained. It would be quite correct for me to say that I know a man who has been always begging ever since I have been in London. I do not think that I ever passed the spot where he stands without seeing him there. He is a blind person, and stands near a church. As long as my recollection serves me he has been begging without ceasing ; of course he has not begged when he has been asleep, he has not begged when he has gone home to his meals, nor did you understand me to have asserted anything so absurd when I said he had begged without ceasing for years. And so, if at those times when it is proper for you to separate yourself from your ordinary labours, you continue perseveringly begging at mercy's throne, it may be with comparative correctness said of you that you pray without ceasing. Though all hours are alike to me, I find it profitable to meet with God at set periods, for these seem to me to be like the winding up of the clock. The clock is to go all day, but there is a time for winding it up ; and the little special

season that we set apart and hedge round about for communion with our God, seems to wind us up for the rest of the day. Therefore, if you would pray without ceasing, continue in the offering of the morning and the evening sacrifice, and let it be perpetually an ordinance with you, that your times of prayer are not broken in upon.

That, however, is only a help, for I must add, thirdly, *between these times of devotion, labour to be much in ejaculatory prayer.* While your hands are busy with the world, let your hearts still talk with God ; not in twenty sentences at a time, for such an interval might be inconsistent with your calling, but in broken sentences and interjections. It is always wrong to present one duty to God stained with the blood of another, and that we should do if we spoiled study or labour by running away to pray at all hours ; but we may, without this, let short sentences go up to heaven, aye, and we may shoot upwards cries, and single words, such as an " Ah," an " Oh," an " O that " ; or, without words we may pray in the upward glancing of the eye or the sigh of the heart. He who prays without ceasing uses many little darts and hand-grenades of godly desire, which he casts forth at every available interval. Sometimes he will blow the furnace of his desires to a great heat in regular prayer, and as a consequence at other times the sparks will continue to rise up to heaven in the form of brief words, and looks, and desires.

Fourthly, if we would pray without ceasing, *we must be always in the spirit of prayer.* Our heart, renewed by the Holy Ghost, must be like the magnetised needle, which always has an inclination towards the pole. It does not always point to that pole, you can turn it aside if you will ; in an iron ship it exhibits serious deflections, under all circumstances it is not exactly true ; but if you put your finger to that needle and force it round to the east, you have only to take away the pressure, and immediately it returns to its beloved pole again. So let your heart be magnetised with prayer, so that if the finger of duty truns it away from the immediate act of prayer, there may still be the longing desire for prayer in your soul, and the moment you can do so, your heart reverts to its beloved work. As perfume lies in flowers even when they do not shed their fragrance upon the gale, so let prayer lie in your hearts.

But, perhaps, the last meaning that I shall give has the most of the truth of the text in it, namely this : *Let all your actions be consistent with your prayers, and be in fact a continuation of your prayers.* If I am to pray without ceasing, it cannot mean that I am always to be in the act of direct devotion ; for the human mind, as at present constituted, needs variety of occupation, and it could not without producing madness or imbecility continue always in the exercise of one function. We must, therefore, change the *modus* or the manner of operation if we are ceaselessly to continue in prayer. We must pursue our prayers, but do it in another manner. Take an instance. This morning I prayed to God to arouse His people to prayerfulness ; very well ; as I came to this house my soul continued to ejaculate, " O Lord, awaken Thy children to prayerfulness." Now, while I am preaching to you and driving at the same point, am I not praying ? Is not my sermon the continuation of my prayer, for I am desiring and aiming at the same thing ? Is it not a continuing to pray when we use the best means towards the obtaining of that which we pray for ? Do you not see my point ? He who prays for his fellow creatures, and then seeks their good, is praying still. In this sense there is truth in that old distich,

" He prayeth best that loveth best
Both man, and bird, and beast."

Loving is praying. If I seek in prayer the good of my fellow creature, and then go and try to promote it, I am practically praying for his good in my actions. If I seek, as I should do, God's glory above everything, then if all my actions are meant to tend to God's glory, I am continuing to pray, though I may not be praying with my thoughts or with my lips. Oh, that our whole life might be a prayer. It can be. There can be a praying without ceasing before the Lord, though there be many pausings in what the most of men would call prayer. Pray then without ceasing, my brother. Let thy whole life be praying. If thou changest the method, yet change not the pursuit ; but continue still to worship, still to adore. This I think to be the meaning of our text,—never altogether abandon prayer ; do not suspend the regular offering of prayer ; be much in earnest ejaculations, be always in the spirit of prayer, and let the whole of your life be consistent with your prayer, and become a part of it.

III. How can we obey these words ? First, let us labour as much as we can to prevent all *sinful* interruptions. "Pray without ceasing." Then if it be impossible to be in the act of prayer always, at least let us be as much as possible in that act ; and let us prevent those interruptions which I mentioned in the early part of my discourse, the interruptions occasioned by our own sin. Let us endeavour to keep clear, as far as we can, of anything and everything in ourselves, or round about us, that would prevent our abounding in supplication. And let us also keep clear of interruptions from the sins of others. Do others forbid us to pray ? Let us not be afraid of their wrath. Remember Daniel, who while he was under the penalty of being cast into a den of lions, yet opened his window towards Jerusalem, and prayed seven times a day as he had done aforetime. Under no threats and for no bribes, let us ever cease to pray. In private let us always pray, and if duty calls us to do so where others observe us, let us so much fear the eye of God that we shall not dare to fear the eye of man.

Let us next avoid all *unnecessary* interruptions of every sort to our prayer. If we know that any matter, from which we can escape, has a tendency to disturb the spirit of prayer within us, let us avoid it earnestly. Let us try, as much as possible, not to be put off the scent in prayer. Satan's object will be to distract the mind, to throw it off the rails, to divert its aim, but let us resolve before God, we will not turn aside from following hard after Him. Sir Thomas Abney had for many years practised family prayer regularly ; he was elected Lord Mayor of London, and on the night of his election he must be present at a banquet, but when the time came for him to call his family together in prayer, having no wish either to be a Pharisee or to give up his practice, he excused himself to the guests in this way,—he said he had an important engagement with a very dear friend, and they must excuse him for a few minutes. It was most true, his dearest friend was the Lord Jesus, and family prayer was an important engagement ; and so he withdrew for awhile to the family altar, and in that

respect prayed without ceasing. We sometimes allow good things to interrupt our prayer, and thus make them evil. Mrs. Rowe observes in one of her letters, that if the twelve apostles were preaching in the town where she lived, and she could never hear them again, if it were her time for private devotion, she would not be bribed our of her closet by the hope of hearing them. I am not sure but what she might have taken another time for her private devotions, and so have enjoyed both privileges, but at the same time, supposing she must have lost the prayer and have only got the preaching in exchange, I agree with her, it would have been exchanging gold for silver. She would be more profited in praying than she would be in hearing, for praying is the end of preaching. Preaching is but the wheat-stalk, but praying is the golden grain itself, and he hath the best who get it.

Sometimes we think we are too busy to pray. That also is a great mistake, for praying is a saving of time. You remember Luther's remark, " I have so much to do to-day that I shall never get through it with less than three hours' prayer." He had not been accustomed to take so much time for prayer on ordinary days, but since that was a busy day, he must needs have more communion with his God. But, perhaps, our occupations begin early, and we therefore say, " How can I get alone with God in prayer ? " It is said of Sir Henry Havelock that every morning when the march began at six, he always rose at four, that he might not miss his time for the reading of the Scripture and communion with his God. If we have no time we must make time, for if God has given us time for secondary duties, He must have given us time for primary ones, and to draw near to Him is a primary duty, and we must let nothing set it on one side. There is no real need to sacrifice any duty, we have time enough for all if we are not idle ; and, indeed, the one will help the other instead of clashing with it. When Edward Payson was a student at College, he found he had so much to do to attend his classes and prepare for examinations, that he could not spend as much time as he should in private prayer ; but, at last, waking up to the feeling that he was going back in divine things through his habits, he took due time for devotion, and he asserts in his diary that he did more in his studies in a single week after he had spent time with God in prayer, than he had accomplished in twelve months before. God can multiply our ability to make use of time. If we give the Lord His due, we shall have enough for all necessary purposes. In this matter seek first the kingdom of God and His righteousness, and all these things shall be added to you. Your other engagements will run smoothly if you do not forget your engagement with God.

We must, dear friends, in order to pray without ceasing, strive against *indolence* in prayer. I believe that no man loves prayer until the Holy Spirit has taught him the sweetness and value of it. If you have ever prayed without ceasing you will pray without ceasing. The men who do not love to pray must be strangers to its secret joy. When prayer is a mechanical act, and there is no soul in it, it is a slavery and a weariness ; but when it is really living prayer, and when the man prays because he is a Christian and cannot help praying, when he prays along the street, prays in his business, prays in the house, prays in the field, when his whole soul is full of prayer, then he cannot have too much of it. He will not be backward in prayer who meets Jesus in it, but he who knows not the Well-beloved will count it a drudgery.

Let us avoid, above all things, *lethargy and indifference* in prayer. Oh, it is a dreadful thing that ever we should insult the majesty of heaven by words from which our heart has gone. I must, my spirit, I must school thee to this, that thou must have communion with God, and if in thy prayer thou dost not talk with God, thou shalt keep on praying till thou dost. Come not away from the mercy-seat till thou hast prayed.

Beloved brother, say unto thy soul, thus—" here have I come to the throne of grace to worship God and seek His blessing, and I am not going away till I have done this ; I will not rise from my knees, because I have spent my customary minutes, but here will I pray till I find the blessing." Satan will often leave off tempting when he finds you thus resolute in prayer. Brethren, we need waking up. Routine grows upon us. We get into the mill-horse way—round, and round, and round the mill. From this may God save us. It is deadly. A man may pray twenty years with regularity, as far as the time goes, and the form goes, and never have prayed a single grain of prayer in the whole period. One real groan fetched from the heart is worth a million litanies, one living breath from a gracious soul is worth ten thousand collects. May we be kept awake by God's grace, praying without ceasing.

And we must take care, dear brethren, again, if we would perform this duty, that we fight against anything like *despair* of being heard. If we have not been heard after six times we must, as Elijah, go again seven times ; if our Peter is in prison, and the church has prayed God to liberate him, and he still is in fetters bound in the inner prison, let us pray on, for one of these days Peter will knock at the gate. Be importunate, heaven's gate does not open to every runaway knock. Knock, and knock, and knock again ; and add to thy knocking asking, and to thy asking seeking, and be not satisfied till thou gettest a real answer.

Never cease from prayer through *presumption ;* guard against that. Feel, O Christian, that you always need to pray. Say not, " I *am* rich and increased in goods, and have need of nothing." Thou art by nature still naked, and poor, and miserable ; therefore, persevere in prayer, and buy of the Lord fine gold, and clean raiment, that thou mayest be rich, and fitly clothed.

Thus I have tried to set before you, beloved, how by resisting presumption and despair, indolence and lethargy, and trying to put aside all sinful and other interruptions, we may pray without ceasing.

IV. Now, very briefly in the last place, WHY SHOULD WE OBEY THIS PRECEPT ? Of course we should obey it because it is of divine authority ; but, moreover, we should attend to it because *the Lord always deserves to be worshipped.* Prayer is a method of worship ; continue, there, always to render to your Creator, your Preserver, your Redeemer, your Father, the homage of your prayers. With such a King let us not be slack in homage. Let us pay Him the revenue of praise continually. Evermore may we magnify and bless His name. His enemies curse Him ; let us bless Him without ceasing. Moreover, brethren, the spirit of love within us surely prompts us to draw near to God without ceasing. Christ is our husband. Is the bride true to her marriage vows if she cares not for her beloved's

company ? God is our Father. What sort of a child is that which does not desire to climb its father's knee and receive a smile from its father's face ? If you and I can live day after day and week after week without anything like communion with God, how dwelleth the love of God in us ? " Pray without ceasing," because the Lord never ceases to love you, never ceases to bless you, and never ceases to regard you as His child.

" Pray without ceasing," for you *want a blessing* on all the work you are doing. Is it common work ? " Except the Lord build the house, they labour in vain that build it." Is it business ? It is vain to rise up early and sit up late, and eat the bread of carefulness, for without God you cannot prosper. You are taught to say, " Give us this day our daily bread,"—an inspired prayer for secular things. Oh, consecrate your seculars by prayer. And, if you are engaged in God's service, what work is there in which you can hope for success without His blessing ? To teach the young, to preach the gospel, to distribute tracts, to instruct the ignorant, do not all these want His blessing ? What are they if that favour be denied ? Pray, therefore, as long as you work.

You are always in *danger of being tempted ;* there is no position in life in which you may not be assaulted by the enemy. " Pray without ceasing," therefore. A man who is going along a dark road where he knows that there are enemies, if he must be alone and has a sword with him, he carries it drawn in his hand, to let the robbers know that he is ready for them. So Christian, pray without ceasing ; carry your sword in your hand, wave that mighty weapon of all-prayer of which Bunyan speaks. Never sheathe it ; it will cut through coats of mail. You need fear no foe if you can but pray. As you are tempted without ceasing, so pray without ceasing.

You need always to pray, for you *always want* something. In no condition are you so rich as not to need something from your God. It is not possible for you to say, " I have all things " ; or, if you can, you have them only in Christ, and from Christ you must continue to seek them. As you are always in need, so beg always at mercy's gate. Moreover, blessings are always waiting for you. Angels are ready with favours that you know not of, and you have but to ask and have. Oh, could you see what might be had for the asking you would not be so slack. The priceless benisons of heaven which lie on one side as yet, oh, did you but perceive that they are only waiting for you to pray, you would not hesitate a moment. The man who knows that his farming is profitable, and that his land brings forth abundantly, will be glad to sow a broader stretch of land another year ; and he who knows that God answers prayer, and is ready still to answer it, will open his mouth yet wider that God may fill it.

Continue to pray, brethren, for even if you should not want prayer yourself there are *others who do*—there are the dying, the sick, the poor, the ignorant, the backsliding, the blaspheming, the heathen at home, and the heathen abroad. " Pray without ceasing," for the enemy works incessantly, and as yet the kingdom has not come unto Zion. You shall never be able to say, " I left off praying, for I had nothing to pray for." This side heaven objects for prayer are as multitudinous as the stars of the sky.

And, now, as I said I would say a word as to why WE ought to pray especially, and that shall close the sermon. Beloved friends, this church ought to pray without ceasing. We have been in years past notable for prayer. If ever a church has prayed it has been this church. I might find many faults with some who hinder prayer, but yet I must say in God's sight I know and feel that there has been living prayer in this church for many years, and hence it is we have had many years of peace and prosperity. We have lacked nothing because we have not lacked prayer. I do not doubt we might have had much more if we had prayed more ; still prayer has been very mighty here. Now, brethren, suppose you had no pastor, suppose the preacher was gone from you, and that the black cloth upon this pulpit was not for a deceased elder of the church but for the preacher himself, you would pray, would you not ? Will you not pray for me, then, while I live ? If you would pray for another to come, will you not pray for me while I am here ? I desire to discharge my office before you in God's sight with all earnestness, but I cannot without your prayers, and as being gone from you, you would lift up many sighs, and you would with prayers ask for a successor, pray for me while I am yet with you. Beloved, you have prayed very earnestly for the pastor when he has been sick, your prayers have been his consolation and his restoration ; will you not pray for him now that he is able to preach the gospel, that his health may be sanctified to God's service, and the ministry of the truth may be mighty in the winning of souls. I ask it of you, I think I might claim it of you. I do beseech you, brethren, pray for us.

Suppose again, dear brethren, there were no conversions in our midst, would you not pray ? And since there are a great many conversions, should that be a reason for leaving off ? Shall we worship God the less because he gives us more ? Instead of one prayer which would go up were there no conversions, there should be ten now that he continues to work salvation among us.

Suppose we were divided, and had many schisms, and jealousies, and bickerings, would not the faithful ones pray in bitterness of spirit ? Will you not pray since there are no divisions, and much Christian love ? Surely, I say again, you will not treat God the worse because he treats you the better. That were foolish indeed.

Suppose we were surrounded to-day with hosts of persecutors, and that error everywhere crept into our midst and did us damage, would you not pray, you who love the Lord ? And now that we live in days of peace, and error, though it prowls around, is kept out of our fold, will you not commune with the Lord all the more ? I will say yet a third time, shall we pray the less because God gives the more ? Oh, no, but the better He is to us the more let us adore and magnify His name.

Just now we need to pray, for some are growing cold, and turning to their old sins. We need to pray, for we are doing much for Christ. Every agency is in full work. We want a *great* blessing upon *great* efforts. We have had such results from prayer as might make a man's ears to tingle who should hear of them for the first time : our history as a church has not been second even to Apostolic history itself : we have seen God's arm made bare in the eyes of all the people, and to the ends of the earth the testimony of this pulpit has gone forth, and thousands have found the Saviour—all in answer to many prayers. Pray, then, without ceasing. O church in the Tabernacle, hold fast that thou hast, that no man take thy crown. Oh, continue to be a praying church that we together, when we shall stand before the judgement-seat of Christ, pastor and people, may not be accused of being prayerless, nor of being slack in the work of the Lord. I earnestly hope all this will tend to make to-morrow's day of prayer more earnest and intense ; but yet more do I pray that at all times all of us may be fervent, frequent, instant, and constant in prayer ; praying in the Holy Ghost, in the name of Jesus.

THE NECESSITY OF GROWING FAITH

" We are bound to thank God always for you, brethren, as it is meet, because that your faith groweth exceedingly, and the charity of every one of you all toward each other aboundeth."—2 Thessalonians i. 3.

LAST Lord's day I tried to say cheering and encouraging words to " Little-faith." I trust that the Holy Spirit, the Comforter, did thereby strengthen some to whom the Saviour said, " O thou of little faith, wherefore didst thou doubt ? " But none of us would desire to remain among the Little-faiths ; we long to press forward in our march to the better land. If we have just started in the heavenly race, it is well ; there are grounds of comfort about the first steps in the right way ; but we are not going to stop at the starting point ; our desire is towards the winning-post and the crown. My prayer at the commencement of this discourse is, that we may each of us rise out of our little faith into the loftier region of assurance, so that those who love us best may be able to say, " We are bound to thank God always for you, brethren, as it is meet, because that your faith groweth exceedingly.

The church of Jesus Christ at Thessalonica did not commence under very propitious circumstances. Remember that oft-quoted text about the Bereans : " These were more noble than those in Thessalonica,

in that they searched the Scriptures daily whether those things were so." That record does not relate to the converts in Thessalonica, but to those Jews who heard Paul preach in the synagogue, and refused to test his teaching by a reference to the Old Testament. They were not a noble sort of people, and yet from among them there were taken by almighty grace a certain company who were led to believe in the true Messiah. Thus they became more noble than even the Bereans ; for we do not hear a church in Berea, neither was an epistle written to the Bereans. Thessalonica received two epistles, bright with hearty commendations. Paul praised the Philippians, but the Thessalonians he praised yet more, thanking God at every remembrance of them, and glorying in them among the churches of God for their patience and faith.

I shall ask you, with your Bibles open, to see whether we cannot account in some measure for this remarkable condition of things. The verse before us is full of thanksgiving to God for the growth of the Thessalonians in faith and in love ; and to my mind it sounds like an echo of the First Epistle to the Thessalonians. The First Epistle is the key and the cause of the Second. Very often a man's success in this place, or in that, will tally with his own condition of heart in relation to that place. As we sow we reap. The grace of God enabled Paul to sow toward the Thessalonians with great hopefulness, and trust, and prayerfulness, and consequently he reaped plentifully.

Observe how (1 Thess. i. 2, 3) Paul began by distinctly recognizing the existence of faith and love in that Church. "We give thanks to God always for you all, making mention of you in our prayers; remembering without ceasing your work of faith, and labour of love, and patience of hope in our Lord Jesus Christ, in the sight of God and our Father." Recognize the root, and then look for the flower. See that faith is in the soul, smile upon it and foster it, and then you may expect that the faith will steadily increase. In our text Paul mentions faith as growing, and love as abounding, while in the next verse he mentions patience, which is the outgrowth of hope— "the patience of hope." He noticed in the Thessalonians the birth of those three divine sisters—faith, hope, and charity. That which he recognised with pleasure he afterwards saw growing exceedingly: those who cherish the seed shall rejoice in the plant. Observe in the children under your care the first blossoms of any good thing, and you shall observe its increase. Despise not the day of small things. When you have learned to recognize faith in its buds, you shall soon see faith in its flowers, and faith in its fruits. Do not overlook feeble grace, or criticize it because it is as yet imperfect; but mark its beginnings with thankfulness, and you shall behold its advance with delight.

In addition to recognizing the beginnings of faith, Paul laboured hard to promote it. Look in the second chapter, and read verses 7, 8, 11, 12:—"But we were gentle among you, even as a nurse cherisheth her children: so being affectionately desirous of you, we were willing to have imparted to you, not the gospel of God only, but also our own souls, because ye were dear unto us. As ye know how we exhorted and comforted and charged every one of you, as a father doth his children, that ye would walk worthy of God, who hath called you unto His kingdom and glory." He threw his whole strength into the work of upholding that church, toiling night and day for it; and consequently he obtained his desire; for still it is true in the husbandry of God, that those who sow, and steep their seed in the tears of earnestness, shall doubtless come again rejoicing, bringing their sheaves with them.

Paul had accompanied his public labours with his private prayers. See how 1 Thessalonians iii. 12 tallies with our text:—"And the Lord make you to increase and abound in love one toward another, and toward all men, even as we do toward you." This was his prayer; and he received exactly what he prayed for. He saw abounding love in each one towards every other. The Lord seemed to have noted the wording of Paul's prayer, and to have answered him according to the letter of his request. If we open our mouth wide, the Lord will fill it. Brethren, what we comfortably recognize in its gracious beginnings, what we labour to increase and what we earnestly guard with prayer, shall in due time be granted to us!

More than this: Paul had gone on to exhort them to abound in love and faith. Look at Chapter iv. verse 9: "As touching brotherly love ye need not that I write unto you: for ye yourselves are taught of God to love one another. And indeed ye do it toward all the brethren which are in all Macedonia: but we beseech you, brethren, that ye increase more and more." Paul did not only quietly pray for the church, but he added his earnest admonitions. He bids them increase more and more; and in response they do increase, so that he says, "Your faith groweth exceedingly." When a man says, "more and more," it is only another way of saying, "exceedingly": is it not so? There was a big heart in Paul towards the Thessalonians. He wanted them to grow in faith and love "more," and then to take another step, and add another "more" to it. The exhortation being given out of a full heart, behold, God has fulfilled it to His servant, and the people have willingly followed up the apostolic precept.

But Paul had added faith to his prayers and his exhortations. Look at chapter v. verses 23, 24, and see if it is not so. "And the very God of peace sanctify you wholly; and I pray God your whole spirit and soul and body be preserved blameless unto the coming of our Lord Jesus Christ. Faithful is He that calleth you, who also will do it." When we are sure that God will do it, it will surely be done. We miss many a blessing because we ask without faith. The apostle believed that he had the petition which he had sought of the Lord; and he received according to his faith. He who can firmly believe shall ere long fervently pour out thanksgiving. The church of Thessalonica, the child of Paul's prayers, the child of his labours, and at last the child of his faith, obtained a remarkable degree of faith, and a singular warmth of love. The Lord give to us who are workers the mind and spirit of Paul, and lead us to follow him in our conduct to others, and then I do not doubt that our good wishes shall be realized. If we are right ourselves, we shall see prosperity in the churches, or classes, or families whose good we seek; and as we feel bound to pray about them, we shall also feel bound to thank God concerning them.

Before I plunge into the sermon, I should like to pause, and ask whether we as Christian men and women are such that Paul could say of us, "We are bound to thank God always for you, brethren, as it is meet, because that your faith groweth exceedingly, and the charity of every one of you all toward each other aboundeth." What think you? Could your pastor bless God for you? Could your nearest and dearest Christian friend feel that he was bound to thank God always for you? If not, why not? Oh that we may rise into such a happy state that we shall be the cause of gratitude in others! It ought to be so; we ought to glorify God, causing men to see our good works, and praise our Father in heaven.

One more question: Do you think we are in such a condition that it would be safe for anybody to praise us? Would it be safe to ourselves for us to be thus commended, and made subjects of thankfulness? It takes a great deal of grace to be able to bear praise. Censure seldom does us much hurt. A man struggles up against slander, and the discouragement which comes of it may not be an unmixed evil; but praise soon suggests pride, and is therefore not an unmixed good. "As the fining-pot for silver, and the furnace for gold; so is a man to his praise." Would it be safe if Paul were here to say good things about you as he did about the

Thessalonians ? Did it not prove that the brethren there were sober, well-established believers ?

Once more, do you ever feel it in your heart to talk like this about your fellow-Christians ? Paul himself was in a fine condition when he could thus extol his brethren. Few men are ready with hearty commendations of others. We are greedy in receiving praise, and niggardly in dispensing it. We seldom speak too kindly of one another. Now and then you hear a person say, " There is no such thing as love in the church at all." I know that gentleman very well, and I never saw any excess of love in *him*. I heard one say, " Brotherly love is all a mockery ; there is no reality in Christian charity " ; and truly he measured his own corn very accurately. Most men would see others better if their own eyes were clearer. When a man honestly feels that his fellow-Christians are for the most part much better than himself, and that he would willingly sit at the feet of many of them, then he is himself in a healthy state. I admire the grace of God in many around me. I see their imperfections as though I did not see them. I am not looking for the thorns, but for the roses ; and I see so many of them that my heart is glad, and in spirit I bless the name of the Lord.

The man who can commend the work of the Lord in others without saying a word about himself, has, by that fact, given himself a good character ; his eyes must have been washed in the fountains of love ; they must have been cleansed from the dust of pride, envy, and self, or he would not have so seen or so spoken. I love the text because it is an instance of a man of great grace, of a man under the inspiration of the Spirit of God, who yet delighted to speak enthusiastically of a church which certainly was far from perfect. I delight in that eye which can be a little blind to faults while it exercises a clear vision in seeing all that is good and praiseworthy towards God.

So, then, we come to our text, and the subject runs thus : for us to grow in faith is *a subject for devout thanksgiving* ; and in the second place, it is *an object for diligent endeavour*. Thirdly, if we greatly grow in faith it will be *the source of other growths* ; for as faith increases, love, patience, and every other virtue, will flourish.

I. For us to grow, and increase in faith is A SUBJECT FOR DEVOUT THANKSGIVING. Paul gives a commendation of the Thessalonian church which is exceedingly warm and hearty. One critic says the words may be regarded as somewhat extravagant, after the mode of the Apostle when he wishes to be emphatic. He writes fervidly : " Your faith groweth exceedingly, and the charity of every one of you all toward each other aboundeth." It is an intense and unreserved commendation. As I have already said, this church was not absolutely perfect ; for, because of the love of every one towards another, and their great kindness towards the poor, certain unworthy persons encroached upon their liberality. To use a very rough word, *cadgers* were multiplied among them, as they always are where generosity abounds. Shame that it should be so. Read chapter iii, verse 11 : " For we hear that there are some which walk among you disorderly, working not at all, but are busybodies." There had been also among them here and there a person of loose life and of sharp business dealings, and to such he spoke in the First Epistle ; but these flies in the pot of ointment did not destroy its sweetness. They were so few comparatively that Paul speaks of the whole body with approbation.

When our faith shall grow and our love abound, it may be proper for a pastor to speak with unrestricted admiration of what the Lord has done.

The blessing of increased faith is of unspeakable value, and therefore should be largely rendered for it. Little faith will save, but strong faith is that which builds up the church, which overcomes the world, which wins sinners, and which glorifies God. Little-faith is slow and feeble, and to suit his pace the whole flock travel softly. Little-faith is a wounded soldier, and has to be carried in an ambulance by the armies of the Lord ; but faith which grows exceedingly, lifts the banner aloft, leads the van, meets hand to hand the foes of our Prince, and puts them to the rout. If we were invoking blessings upon a church we could scarcely ask for a larger boon than that all the brethren might be strong in faith, giving glory to God. Strong-faith ventures into large endeavours for Christ, and hence missions are projected : Strong-faith carries out the projects of holy zeal, and hence daring ideals are turned into facts : Strong-faith is a shield against the darts of error, and hence she is the object of the contempt and hatred of heresy. Strong-faith builds the walls of Zion, and casts down the walls of Jericho. Strong-faith smites the Philistines hip and thigh, and makes Israel to dwell in peace. Oh that the night of Little-faith were over, and that the day of glorious faith would come ! Soon would our young men see visions, and our old men dream dreams, if faith were more among us. When the Son of man cometh shall He find faith in the earth ? At the revival of faith we shall see another Pentecost, with its rushing mighty wind, and its tongues of flame ; but during our lack of faith we still abide in weakness, and the enemy will exact upon us. O God, we beseech thee, make Thy face to shine upon us, cause our faith to grow exceedingly, and out love to abound yet more and more ; then shall there be times of refreshing from the presence of the Lord.

Paul thus fervently gave thanks to God because the blessing came to the church at a remarkably seasonable time. The people of Thessalonica had risen against the church and persecuted it ; thus, without were fightings, but within there were no fears ; for the brethren were firm in faith and fervent in love. The church was subject to constant tribulation ; but its faith grew exceedingly. Has it not often been so with the Lord's people ? Times of cloud and rain have been growing times. Pharaoh dealt hardly with Israel ; but the more he oppressed them, the more they multiplied. The more the Church of God is down-trodden, the more it rises into power and influence. The bush burns and is not consumed ; nay, rather, it flourishes in the flame. I say not that this increase of faith is the immediate effect of persecution, but it is singularly the attendant upon it. God knew that when His poor servants were haled to prison, when they were brought before rulers and kings for His name's sake, and when they were spoiled of their goods, they wanted increased strength, and therefore he gave it to them by growth in faith. As the persecution rose upon them like the deluge, their confidence in God rose above it, like Noah's ark, which rose the higher the deeper the waters became. They stood fast in the day of trial, and became an example to all other churches, whether persecuted or not ; and this because their faith grew exceedingly. Beloved, I pray for each member of this church that your confidence in God may rise from ebb to flood. We need it much just now. This is a time of depression in trade, when many are suffering want, and almost all find their means decreased. We need to be rich in faith, for we are growing poor in pocket. Many children of God cannot find employment wherewith to earn their bread. This is, moreover, a time of abounding vice. Perhaps never in our memories were any of us so shocked as we have been of late by the discoveries of unspeakable abominations. We need that our faith should grow exceedingly, for sin runs down our streets in torrents. It is also a period of grievous departure from the faith once delivered to the saints. Looking back to our younger days, we are amazed at the progress of error. We mourned in those days that men trifled with the doctrines of the gospel ; but what shall we now say, when men deride those doctrines, and mock at them as antiquated fables ? The foundations of the earth are removed, and only here and there will you find a man who beareth up the pillars thereof ; therefore do we need that our faith should be exceedingly steadfast. I charge you, brethren, to be rooted and grounded in faith, seeing the times are evil ! I cannot speak emphatically enough upon the abounding dangers of the times ; they demand of us that we be not of doubtful mind, but that we take firm hold of infallible truth, and endure as seeing Him who is invisible. He that cannot say, " I believe, and am sure," is one born out of due time.

The apostle's commendation was meet and fit, since, if there be any growth in faith, it is the work of God's Spirit. Faith is the gift of God in its beginnings, and it is equally the gift of God in its increase. If thou hast faith as a grain of mustard seed, God gave it thee ; and if thou hast faith as a spreading tree, God has given the increase. The infancy of faith is of God, and so is its perfect manhood. In the natural world we ought as much to admire God's hand in growth as in creation ; for, indeed, the outbursting of spring, the advance of summer, and the maturity of autumn, are all a sort of creation, seen in detail. Even thus the progress of faith reveals the same power as the commencement of faith. If thou dost not look to God for more faith, thou wilt never have more faith : great faith in its strong broad current flows as much from the fountainhead of grace as in its first trickling streamlet of hope in Christ. Let God have all the glory of faith from its Alpha to its Omega. If thou be a strong man in Christ Jesus take heed that thou do not sacrifice to thine own net, nor burn incense to thine own drag, and glorify thine own experience as if thou madest thyself strong and rich in the things of God. We are bound to render all the thanksgiving unto God ; it is meet that it should be so. Look how the apostle puts it : " We are bound to thank God always for you." I like the modesty of that. He does not so much say that he did thank God, though he did do so ; but in deep humility he admits the debt which he could not fully pay. He did not judge his thanksgivings to be sufficient, but owned that he was still under bonds to render more praise. I rejoice to be bound with these bonds, to be bound to thank God every day, and all the day. I wear these golden fetters and count them my best ornaments. " Bind the sacrifice with cords, even with cords to the horns of the altar." I would be bound over, not to keep the peace, but to keep praise for ever. Let the altar of incense be always burning, yea, flaming higher and higher with the sweet spices of love and gratitude. Blessed be God for what He is doing for His people, when He causes their faith to grow ; for it is a blessing so immense, so incalculable, that our praises ought to rise to the height and glory of loud-sounding hallelujahs. Brethren, let us bless God for every good man we know whose faith has grown, for every holy woman whose love in the church is manifest unto all ; and when we have done so, let us turn our eye to God, and say, " Lord, make me such a one that others may glorify in me also ; I am as yet sadly weak and undeveloped ; make me to grow till all Thy image shall be seen in me, and my fellow-Christians shall bless God concerning me." Thus have I set growth in faith before you as a subject for thanksgiving. It is indeed a jewel worth more than both the Indies.

II. In the second place, it is worthy to be AN OBJECT FOR DILIGENT ENDEAVOUR. If you have it not, labour speedily to attain it. As the merchantman seeketh goodly pearls, so seek a growing faith. Covet earnestly the best gifts and the noblest graces. Never be self-satisfied, but cry with Jabez, " Oh that the Lord would bless me indeed, and enlarge my coast."

Why ? Because the proof of faith lies in the growth of faith. If thou hast a dead faith, it will always be the same ; but if thou hast the faith of God's elect, it must grow. If I heard of a child that was born some years ago, and had never grown, I should begin to guess that my friend was entrapping me, and that the child was dead from the birth. Life in its earliest stages is ever attended with growth. Brother, thou must have more faith, or we shall fear that thou hast no faith ; thou must have more love, or else for sure thou hast no love at all. That which does not grow unto God does not live unto God.

We ought to have more faith because God's truth deserves it. It ought to be the easiest thing in the world for us to trust God ; to believe every word of the Lord should be an act to which we need not to be exhorted ; it should be as natural as for the lungs to heave, or the heart to beat. We ought, as children of God, to believe our Father by instinct, even as young eaglets hide under the mother's wing. We ought to exercise faith even as the eye sees, and the ear hears, because thereunto we were created by the Holy Spirit. It should be a necessity of our spiritual existence, that we must and will trust the Lord Jesus Christ yet more and more. I pray that it may be so ; for unbelief is a horrible crime. Have you doubted God ? Have you in any sense mistrusted Him ? Have you limited the Holy One of Israel ? Then continue not the slave of such a sin, but give unto God your heart's confidence from this time henceforth, and for ever.

Moreover, we ought to grow in faith, because it will be so much for our own spiritual health, and strength, and joy. Does Little-faith know what it might be, and do, and enjoy if it could only quit its littleness ? There are many ways of being a Christian, as there are many ways of being an Englishman ; but all are not equally desirable. I may be an Englishman in banishment, or in the workhouse, or in prison ; but I prefer to be an Englishman at home, in health, and at liberty. So you may be a Christian, and be weak, timorous, and sad ; but this is not desirable ; it is better to be a happy, holy, vigorous, useful Christian. As your being an Englishman does not depend on your health or wealth, so neither does your salvation turn upon the strength or joy of your faith ; yet much does depend on it. Why not glorify God on the road to heaven ? Why not have foretastes of it now ? It is not my desire to go through the world in miserable style, singing always—

> " Do I love the Lord or no ?
> Am I His, or am I not ? "

Infinitely do I prefer so to trust God that my peace may be like a river, and my righteousness like the waves of the sea. Look at the difference between Abraham, the Father of the faithful, and his nephew Lot. Lot was righteous, but he was by no means so strong in faith as Abraham, neither was he so great or so happy. Abraham is calm, bold, royal ; Lot is greedy, timid, trembling. Lot, in Sodom, is with difficulty made to run for his life, while Abraham alone with God is interceding for others. Lot escapes from a burning city with the loss of all things, while Abraham dwells peacefully with the Lord who is the possessor of heaven and earth. Abraham's faith makes him rise like some lone Alp till he touches the very heaven of God. It is well to be Lot, but it is infinitely better to be Abraham. Do seek the utmost degree of faith ; for if this be in you and abound, you shall not be barren or unfruitful. Heaven lies that way. More faith, more rest of heart. To grow heavenly we must grow more believing.

The question is, *How* is this to be done ? How is my faith to be made to grow exceedingly ? I have already told you that it is the work of the Holy Spirit ; but still He uses us for the increase of our own faith. If we are to grow in faith, certain evils are to be avoided with scrupulous care. Avoid continual change of doctrine. If you have a tree in your garden and you transplant it often, it will yield you scanty fruit. Those who are everything by turns, and nothing long, are " ever learning, but never able to come to the knowledge of the truth." Unstable as water, they shall not excel. Those brethren who believe this to-day, and that to-morrow, and the other thing the next day, do not believe anything in downright earnest. They cannot grow ; they are not rooted and grounded. Like the moon, they are always changing, and what light they have is cold and sickly. He who can change his religion has none to change. Those who prefer philosophy to Christ never knew Him.

Then, again, if you had a tree, and did not transplant it, but began to dig away the earth from it, removing the ground in which it stood, you would impoverish it, and prevent its fruitfulness. I know certain professors who are giving up the ground which their souls should grow in. One doctrine after another is forsaken, till nothing is held to be important. They do not believe much now, and they are on the line to believe nothing at all. The experiment of the Frenchman who had just brought his horse to live on a straw a day when it died, is being repeated among us, faith literally starved to death. What low diet do some men prescribe for their souls ! Marrow and fatness they do not even smell at ! How can your faith grow when vital truths are abandoned, or held with feeble grasp ? Oh for a band of Puritan believers ! Oh for a troop of spiritiual Ironsides !

Next, a tree cannot grow if it is shut out from sun, and rain, and dew. Without heavenly influences we must be barren. Plant a little tree right under a great oak so that it is always in the shade, and it cannot grow ; clear the big tree away, or the sapling will dwindle to death. Some men's faith cannot grow because it is overshadowed by worldliness, by tolerated sin, by love of riches, by the pride of life, by cares of lower things. The pursuit of Christ crucified must be all-absorbing, or it will be ineffectual. To know what you believe, and to abide steadfast in it, is the way to be robust in faith. Men whose hearts are not in their trades, men who chop and change—these are the men whose names appear in the *Gazette* ; are not many spiritual bankruptcies due to the same cause ?

There are methods which the spiritual husbandman uses to cause faith to grow. First, faith grows by an increase of *knowledge*. Many persons doubt because they are not instructed. Some doubt whether they shall hold on to the end ; they are ignorant of the doctrine of the final perseverance of the saints. Some are in despair because they find evil desires arising in their hearts ; they do not know the teaching of Scripture as to the two natures and the warfare between flesh and spirit. Many think themselves condemned because they cannot wholly keep the law ; they forget that they are justified by faith. A great deal of unbelief vanishes when knowledge, like the morning sun, drives away the mists. Unbelief is an owl of the night, and when the sun rises it hides away in a dark corner. Study the word of God : give your heart to searching it ; seek to get at the inner teaching, and learn the analogy of faith ; practise deep sea-fishery, and you will reach those mysterious truths which are the secret riches of the soul. These truths are much despised now ; but those who rejoice in them will find their faith growing exceedingly.

Better still than mere knowledge, which alone would puff you up, faith grows by *experience*. When a man has tried and proved a thing, then his confidence in it is largely increased. Take a promise and test it, and then you will say, " I know that is so." When you have tested it again, and again, and again, nobody will be able to shake you, for you will say, " I have tasted and handled of this good word ; I have made it my own, and I am not to be driven from it." The experienced Christian is the established Christian. The man who has proved all things is the man who holds fast that which is good. God give grace to increase our faith by knowledge and by experience !

Faith also grows by much *meditation and walking with God*. If you want to believe in a man, you must know him. Half the disputes between Christian people arise from their not knowing one another. There is a hymn of Mr. Sankey's which I venture to alter thus :

> " When we know each other better,
> The mists will roll away."

When we know each other, our suspicions, prejudices, and dislikes will speedily disappear. I am sure it is so with our God. When you walk with Him, when your communion with Him is close and constant, your faith in Him will grow exceedingly. Some of you, I am afraid, do not give five minutes in the day to meditation. You are in too great a hurry for that. In London life men get up in a hurry even as they went to bed in a hurry and slept in a hurry. They swallow their breakfast in a hurry ; they have no time to digest it ; the bell is ringing at the station, and they must hurry to catch the train ; they reach business in a hurry ; they hurry through it, and they hurry to get back from it. Men cannot think, for they have barely time to wink their eyes. As to an hour's meditation and reading the Scriptures, and communing with God, many professors nowadays would think they committed robbery against the god of this world if they took half-an-hour out of his service to give it to fellowship with the world to come. If our faith is to grow exceedingly, we must maintain constant intercourse with God.

Another way of increasing faith is by much *prayer*. Pray for faith and pray with faith ; thus shall thy soul become firm in its reliance on the promises. It is while we wrestle with the angel that we find out our weakness, as the sinew of our thigh shrinks ; but at the same time we prove our God-given strength, since as princes we wrestle with God and prevail. Power from prayer as well as power in prayer is what we want. On our knees we gather strength, till doubting and fearing disappear.

We must be careful to render *obedience to God*. A man cannot trust God while he lives in sin : every act of disobedience weakens confidence in God. Faith and obedience are bound up in the same bundle. He that obeys God, trusts God ; and he that trusts God, obeys God. He that is without faith is without works ; and he that is without works is without faith. Do not oppose faith and good works to one another, for there is a blessed relationship between them ; and if you abound in obedience your faith shall grow exceedingly.

Again, faith grows by *exercise*. The man who uses the little faith he has will get more faith ; but he that says, " I have not enough faith for such and such work," and therefore shrinks back, shall become more and more timid, till at last, like a coward, he runs away. Go forward with thy little faith, and to thy surprise it shall have grown as thou hast advanced. Accomplish much, and then endeavour something more, and something more. I have often used an illustration taken from a person who teaches the art of growing taller. I do not believe in that art : we shall not add a cubit to our stature just yet. But part of this professor's exercise is, that in the morning, when you get up, you are to reach as high as ever you can, and aim a little higher every morning though it be only the hundredth part of an inch. By that means you are to grow. This is so with faith. Do all you can, and then do a little more ; and when you can do that, then do a little more than you can. Always have something in hand that is greater than your present capacity. Grow up to it, and when you have grown up to it, grow more. By many little additions a great house is built. Brick by brick up rose the pyramid. Believe and yet believe. Trust and have further trust. Hope shall become faith, and faith shall ripen to full assurance and perfect confidence in God Most High.

This, then, brethren, is what I commend to you. May God the Holy Ghost help you all to go from faith to faith.

III. Finally, this growing faith becomes THE CENTRE OF OTHER CHRISTIAN GRACES. " Your faith groweth exceedingly, and the charity of every one of you all toward each other aboundeth." A firm faith in gospel verities will make us love one another, for each doctrine of truth is an argument for love. If you believe in God as having chosen His people, you will love His elect ; if you believe in Christ as having made atonement for His people, you will love His redeemed, and seek their peace. If you

believe in the doctrine of regeneration, and know that we must be born again, you will love the regenerate. Whatever doctrine it is that is true, it ministereth toward the love of the heart. I am sure you will find a deep, firm, fervent unity with one another in those that hold the truth in the love of it. If you are not filled with brotherly love, it must be because you are not firmly believing that truth which worketh toward love.

Firmness in the faith ministers toward the unity of the church. The church of Thessalonica did not have a secession, or a split, as some call it : the church at Thessalonica did not divide under the pressure of persecution : they adhered closely to one another, and the more they were hammered, the more they were consolidated. They were welded into one solid mass by the hammer of persecution and the fire of love, and the reason was because they each one held the truth with all firmness. I am always afraid of a church that is made up of mixed elements, when some are Calvinistic, some Arminian, some Baptist and some Pædobaptist. When the minister who holds them together dies, they will disintegrate. When certain reasons that now make them cohere cease to exist, the church will divide like quicksilver, each little bit breaking into smaller bits, and so they will go rolling about in innumerable factions. But given a church that holds the truth firmly, with deep and strong faith, then if the pastor dies, or twenty pastors die, they believe in a Pastor who lives for ever, and whoever comes or does not come, the truth they hold, holds them in living unity. I cannot imagine a greater blessing for you as a church in years to come than for each man and woman to be intelligently established in the truth you have received. Who shall separate the men who are one in Christ by the grip of mighty faith ? I commend firm faith to you with all my heart, as the source of love and the means of unity in years to come.

This faith breeds patience in men, and patience assists love. Truth to tell, God's people are, some of them, a singular tribe. A countryman was accustomed to say that if God had not chosen His people before they were born, He would never have done so afterwards. There is truth in that saying. Therefore if a man loves His fellow-Christian as an act of mere nature, he will often feel himself baffled ; he will say, " They acted very unkindly to me. Who can love people that are so ill-mannered, so ungrateful ? " But when faith is strong, you will say, " What is that to me ? I love them for Christ's sake. If I am to have a reward, it shall come from my Lord Christ. As for God's people, I love them despite their faults ; over the head of the mistaken judgments they form of me, I love all my brethren." The way to make men better is not to be always censuring them, but to love them better. The quickest way to win a sinner, is to love him to Christ ; the quickest way to sanctify a believer is to love him into purity and holiness. Only faith can do this. May faith, therefore, grow exceedingly ; for faith by working patience helps us to bear with others. If there be anything grand, and good, and desirable, anything Christ-like, anything God-like, the way to it is to let your faith grow exceedingly. If this church is to become a missionary church more and more, as I pray God it may, your faith must grow exceedingly. If you are to stand fast as a break-water in these times of departure from the faith once delivered to the saints, your faith must grow exceedingly. If you are to be made a blessing to this wicked city, and shine like a lighthouse over this sea of London, your faith must grow exceedingly. If God has brought you as a church, together with other churches, to the kingdom for such a time as this ; if you are to achieve your destiny, and work for God and glorify His name, your faith must grow exceedingly. The man who is timorous and faint-hearted, let him go home ; he is not fit for the day of battle. The age requires heroes. The chicken-hearted are out of their place in this perilous century. You that know what you know, and believe what you believe, whose tramp is that of fearless warriors, you have a high calling ; fulfil it. You shall see what God will do for you and with you ; and it shall be written in the pages of eternity that at such a time the church grew in its faith, and therefore God used it for His glory. May it be so. May those among us who have no faith be led to Jesus. O believers, try your own faith by speaking to unbelievers as they go away this morning : this afternoon in the Sunday-school, prove your faith by winning your dear children for Christ : try your faith every day in the week by giving sinners no rest until they come to Christ. God bless you each one for His name's sake. Amen.

A LECTURE FOR LITTLE-FAITH

"We are bound to thank God always for you, brethren, as it is meet, because that your faith groweth exceedingly, and the charity of every one of you all toward each other aboundeth."—2 Thessalonians i. 3.

"WE are bound to thank God always for you, brethren, as it is meet." Whether we shall praise God or not, is not left to our opinion. Although the commandment saith not, "Thou shalt praise the Lord," yet praise is God's most righteous due ; and every man, as a partaker of God's bounty, and especially every Christian, is bound to praise God, as it is meet. It is true, we have no authoritative rubric for daily praise; we have no commandment left on record specially prescribing certain hours of song and thanksgiving; but still the law written upon the heart, teacheth us with divine authority that it is right to praise God ; and this unwritten mandate hath as much power and authority about it, as if it had been recorded on the tables of stone, or handed to us from the top of thundering Sinai. The Christian's duty is to praise God. Think not ye who are always mourning that ye are guiltless in that respect ; imagine not that ye can discharge your duty to your God without songs of praise. It is your duty to praise Him. You are bound by the bonds of His love as long as you live to bless His name. It is meet and comely that you should do so. It is not only a pleasurable exercise, but it is the absolute duty of the Christian life to praise God. This is taught us in the text,—" We are bound to thank God always for you, brethren, as it is meet." Let not your harps then hang upon the willows, ye mourning children of the Lord. It is your duty to strike them and bring forth their loudest music. It is sinful in you to cease from praising God ; you are blessed in order that you may bless Him ; and if you do not praise God you are not bringing forth the fruit, which He as the divine husbandman, may well expect at your hands. Go forth then, ye sons of God, and chant His praise. With every morning's dawn lift up your notes of thanksgiving ; and every evening let the setting sun be followed with your song. Girdle the earth with your praises ; surround it with an atmosphere of melody, so shall God Himself look down from heaven and accept your praises as like in kind, though not equal in degree, to the praises of cherubim and seraphim.

It seems, however, that the apostle Paul in this instance exercised praise not for himself but for others, for the church at Thessalonica. If any of you should in ignorance ask the question why it was that Paul should take so deep an interest in the salvation of these saints, and in their growth in faith, I would remind you, that this is a secret known only to the men who have brought forth and nourished children, and therefore love them. The apostle Paul had founded the church at Thessalonica ; most of these people were his spiritual offsprings ; by the words of his mouth, attended by the power of the Spirit, they had been brought out of the darkness into marvellous light ; and they who have had spiritual children, who have brought many sons unto God, can tell you that there is an interest felt by a spiritual father, that is not to be equalled even by the tender affection of a mother towards her babe. " Aye," said the apostle, " I have been tender over you as a nursing father ; " and in another place he says he had " travailed in birth," for their souls. This is a secret not known to the hireling minister. Only he whom God hath Himself ordained and thrust forth into the work, only he who has had his tongue touched with a live coal from off the altar, can tell you what it is to agonize for men's souls before they are converted, and what it is to rejoice with joy unspeakable, and full of glory, when the travail of their souls is seen in the salvation of God's elect.

And now, beloved, having thus given you two thoughts which seemed to me to arise naturally from the text, I shall repair at once to the object of this morning's discourse. The apostle thanks God that the faith of the Thessalonians had grown exceedingly. Leaving out the rest of the text, I shall direct your attention this morning to the subject of growing in faith. Faith hath degrees.

In the first place, I shall endeavour to notice *the inconveniences of little faith ;* secondly, *the means of promoting its growth ;* and thirdly, *a certain high attainment, unto which faith will assurdly grow, if we diligently water and cultivate it.*

I. In the first place, THE INCONVENIENCES OF LITTLE FAITH. When faith first commences in the soul, it is like a grain of mustard seed, of which the Saviour said it was the least of all seeds ; but as God the Holy Spirit is pleased to bedew it with the sacred moisture of His grace, it germinates and grows and begins to spread, until at last it becomes a great tree. To use another figure : when faith commences in the soul it is simply *looking* unto Jesus, and perhaps even then there are so many clouds of doubts, and so much dimness of the eye, that we have need for the light of the Spirit to shine upon the cross before we are able even so much as to see it. When faith grows a little, it rises from looking to Christ to *coming* to Christ. He who stood afar off and looked to the cross by-and-bye plucks up courage, and getting heart to himself, he runneth up to the cross; or perhaps he doth not run, but hath to be drawn before he can so much as creep thither, and even then it is with a limping gait that he draweth nigh to Christ the Saviour. But that done, faith goeth a little farther: it *layeth hold* on Christ; it begins to see Him in His excellency, and appropriates Him in some degree conceives Him to be a real Christ and a real Saviour, and is convinced of His suitability. And when it hath done as much as that, it goeth further; it leaneth on Christ; it leaneth on its beloved; casteth all the burden of its cares, sorrows, and griefs upon that blessed shoulder, and permitteth all its sins to be swallowed up in the great red sea of the Saviour's blood. And faith can then go further still; for having seen and ran towards Him, and laid hold upon Him, and having leaned upon Him, faith in the next place puts in a humble, but a sure and *certain claim* to all that Christ is and to all that He has wrought; and then, trusting alone in this, appropriating all this to itself, faith mounteth to full assurance; and out of heaven there is no state more rapturous and blessed. But, as I have observed at the beginning, faith is but very small, and there are some Christians who never get out of little faith all the while they are here. You notice in John Bunyan's "*Pilgrim's Progress*," how many Little-faith's he mentions. There is our old friend Ready-to-halt, who went all the way to the celestial city on crutches, but left them when he went into the river Jordan. Then there is little Feeble-mind, who carried his feeble mind with him all the way to the banks of the river and then left it, and ordered it to be buried in a dunghill that none might inherit it. Then there is Mr. Fearing, too, who used to stumble over a straw, and was always frightened if he saw a drop of rain, because he thought the floods of heaven were let loose upon him. And you remember Mr. Despondency and Miss Much-afraid, who were so long locked up in the dungeon of Giant Despair, that they were almost starved to death, and there was little left of them but skin and bone; and poor Mr. Feeble-mind, who had been taken into the cave of Giant Slay-good who was about to eat him, when Great-heart came to his deliverance. John Bunyan was a very wise man. He has put a great many of those characters, in his book, because there are a great many of them. He has not left us with one Mr. Ready-to-halt, but he has given us seven or eight graphic characters because he himself in his own time has been one of them, and he had known many others who had walked in the same path. I doubt not I have a very large congregation this morning of this very class of persons. Now let me notice the inconveniences of little faith.

The first inconvenience of little faith is that *while it is very sure of heaven it very seldom thinks so* Little-faith is quite as sure of heaven as Great-faith. When Jesus Christ counts up His jewels at the last day he will take to Himself the little pearls as well as the great ones. If a diamond be never so small yet it is precious because it is a diamond. So will faith, be it never so little, if it be true faith, Christ will never lose even the smallest jewel of his crown. Little-faith is always sure of heaven, because the name of Little-faith is in the book of eternal life.

Little-faith was chosen of God before the foundation of the world. Little-faith was bought with the blood of Christ; aye, and he cost as much as Great-faith. "For every man a shekel" was the price of redemption. Every man, whether great or small, prince or peasant, had to redeem himself with a shekel. Christ has bought all, both little and great, with the same most precious blood. Little-faith is always sure of heaven, for God has begun the good work in him and He will carry it on. God loves him and He will love him unto the end. God has provided a crown for him, and He will not allow the crown to hang there without a head; He has erected for him a mansion in heaven, and He will not allow the mansion to stand untenanted for ever. Little-faith is always safe, but he very seldom knows it. if you meet him he is sometimes afraid of hell; very often that the wrath of God abideth on him. He will tell you that the country on the other side the flood can never belong to a worm so base as he. Sometimes it is because he feels himself so unworthy, another time it is because the things of God are too good to be true, he says, or he cannot think they can be true to such an one as he. Sometimes he is afraid he is not elect; another time he fears that he has not been called aright, that he has not come to Christ aright. Another time his fears are that he will not hold on to the end, that he shall not be able to persevere; and if you kill a thousand of his fears he is sure to have another host by to-morrow; for unbelief is one of those things that you cannot destroy. "It hath," saith Bunyan, "as many lives as a cat"; you may kill it over and over again, but it still lives. It is only one of those ill weeds that sleep in the soil even after it has been burned, and it only needs a little encouragement to grow again. Now Great-faith is sure of heaven, and he knows it. He climbs Pisgah's top, and views the landscape o'er; he drinks in the mysteries of paradise even before he enters within the pearly gates. He sees the streets that are paved with gold; he beholds the wall of the city, the foundations whereof are precious stones; he hears the mystic music of the glorified, and begins to smell on earth the perfumes of heaven. But poor Little-faith can scarcely look at the sun; he very seldom sees the light; he gropes in the valley, and while all is safe he always thinks himself unsafe. That is one of the disadvantages of Little-faith.

Another disadvantage is that *Little-faith, while always having grace enough* (for that is Little-faith's promise, "My grace shall be sufficient for thee") *yet never thinks he has grace enough.* He will have quite enough grace to carry him to heaven; and Great-heart won't have any more. The greatest saint, when he entered heaven, found that he went in with an empty wallet: he had eaten his last crust of bread when he got there. The manna ceased when the children of Israel entered into Canaan; they had none to carry with them there: they began to eat the corn of the land when the manna of the wilderness had ceased. But Little-faith is always afraid that he has not grace enough. You see him in trouble. "Oh!" says he, "I shall never be able to hold my head above water." Blessed be God he never can sink. If you see him in prosperity, he is afraid he shall be intoxicated with pride; that he shall turn aside like Balaam. If you meet him attacked by an enemy, he is scarcely able to say three words for himself, and he lets the enemy exact upon him. If you find him fighting the battle of the Lord Jesus Christ he holds his sword tight enough, good man, but he has not much strength in his arm to bring his sword down with might. He can do but little, for he is afraid that God's grace will not be sufficient for him. Great-faith, on the other hand, can shake the world. What cares he about trouble, trial, or duty?

> " He that helped him bears him through,
> And makes him more than conqueror too."

He would face an army single-handed, if God commanded him; and " with the jawbone of an ass, he would slay heaps upon heaps, and thousands of men." There is no fear of his lacking strength. He can do all things, or can bear all sufferings, for his Lord is there. Come what may, his arm is always sufficient for him; he treads down his enemy, and his cry every day is like the shout of Deborah, " O ! my soul, thou hast trodden down strength." Little-faith treads down strength too, but he does not know it. He kills his enemies, but has not eyesight enough to see the slain. He often hits so hard that his foemen retreat, but he thinks they are there still. He conjures up a thousand phantoms, and when he has routed his real enemies he makes others, and trembles at the phantoms which he has himself made. Little-faith will assuredly find that his garments will not wax old, that his shoes shall be iron and brass, and that as his day is so shall his strength be; but all the way he will be murmuring, because he thinks his garments will grow old, that his feet will be blistered and sore; and he is terrified lest the day should be too heavy for him, and that the evil of the day shall more than counterbalance his grace. Aye, it is an inconvenient thing to have little faith, for little faith perverts everything into sorrow and grief.

Again, there is a sad inconvenience about Little-faith, namely, that *if Little-faith be sorely tempted to sin, he is apt to fall.* Strong-faith can well contest with the enemy. Satan comes along, and says, " All these things will I give thee if thou wilt fall down and worship me." " Nay," we say, " thou canst not give us all these things, for they are ours already." " Nay," says he, " but ye are poor, naked and miserable." " Aye," say we to him, " but still these things are ours, and it is good for us to be poor, good for us to be without earthly goods, or else our Father would give them to us." " Oh," says Satan, " you deceive yourselves; you have no portion in these things; but if you will serve me, then I will make you rich and happy here." Strong-faith says, " Serve thee, thou fiend ! Avaunt ! Dost thou offer me silver ?—behold God giveth me gold. Dost thou say to me, ' I will give thee this if thou disobey ? '—fool that thou art ! I have a thousand times as great wages for my obedience as thou canst offer for my disobedience." But when Satan meets Little-faith, he says to him, " If thou be the Son of God cast thyself down " ; and poor Little-faith is so afraid that he is not a son of God that he is very apt to cast himself down upon the supposition. " There," says Satan, " I will give thee all this if thou wilt disobey." Little-faith says, " I am not quite sure that I am a child of God, that I have a portion among them that are sanctified " ; and he is very apt to fall into sin by reason of the littleness of his faith. Yet at the same time I must observe that I have seen some Little-faiths who are far less apt to fall into sin than others. They have been so

cautious that they dared not put one foot before the other, because they were afraid they should put it awry : they scarcely even dared to open their lips, but they prayed, " O Lord, open Thou my lips " ; afraid that they should let a wrong word out, if they were to speak ; always alarmed lest they should be falling into sin unconsciously, having a very tender conscience. Well, I like people of this sort. I have sometimes thought that Little-faith holds tighter by Christ than any other. For a man who is very near drowning is sure to clutch the plank all the tighter with the grasp of a drowning man, which tightens and becomes more clenched the more his hope is decreased. Well, beloved, Little-faith may be kept from falling, but this is the fruit of tender conscience and not of little faith. Careful walking is not the result of little faith ; it may go with it, and so may keep Little-faith from perishing, but little faith is in itself a dangerous thing, laying us open to innumerable temptations, and taking away very much of our strength to resist them. " The joy of the Lord is your strength " ; and if that joy ceases you become weak and very apt to turn aside. Beloved, you who are Little-faiths, I tell you it is inconvenient for you always to remain so ; for you have many nights and few days. Your years are like Norwegian years—very long winters and very short summers. You have many howlings, but very little of shouting ; you are often playing upon the pipe of mourning, but very seldom sounding the trump of exultation. I would to God you could change your notes a little. Why should the children of a King go mourning all their days ? It is not the Lord's will that you should be always sorrowful. " Rejoice in the Lord always, and again I say rejoice." Oh, ye that have been fasting, anoint your heads and wash your faces, that ye appear not unto men to fast. Oh, ye that are sad in heart, " Light is sown for the righteous, and gladness for the upright in heart." Therefore, rejoice for ye shall praise Him. Say unto yourselves, " Why art thou cast down, O my soul, and why art thou disquieted within me ? Hope thou in God, for I shall yet praise Him, who is the light of my countenance and my God."

II. Having thus noticed the inconveniences and disadvantages of little faith, let me give you A FEW RULES WITH REGARD TO THE WAY OF STRENGTHENING IT. If you would have your little faith grow into great faith, you must *feed it* well. Faith is a feeding grace. It does not ask you to give it the things that are seen, but it does ask you to give it the promise of the things that are not seen, which are eternal. Thou tellest me thou hast little faith. I ask thee whether thou art given to the meditation of God's Word, whether thou hast studied the promises, whether thou art wont to carry one of those sacred things about with thee every day ? Dost thou reply, " No ? " Then, I tell thee, I do not wonder at thine unbelief. He who deals largely with the promises, will, under grace, very soon find that there is great room for believing them. Get a promise, beloved, every day, and take it with you wherever you go ; mark it, learn it, and inwardly digest it. Don't do as some men do—who think it a Christian duty to read a chapter every morning, and they read one as long as your arm without understanding it at all ; but take out some choice text, and pray the Lord during the day to break it up to your mind. Do as Luther says : " When I get hold of a promise," says he, " I look upon it as I would a fruit tree. I think—there hang the fruits above my head, and if I would get them I must shake the tree to and fro." So I take a promise and meditate upon it ; I shake it to and fro, and sometimes the mellow fruit falls into my hand, at other times the fruit is less ready to fall, but I never leave off till I get it. I shake, shake all the day long ; I turn the text over and over again, and at last the pomegranate droppeth down, and my soul is comforted with apples, for it was sick of love. Do that, Christian. Deal much with the promises ; have much commerce with these powders of the merchant : there is a rich perfume in every promise of God ; take it, it is an alabaster box, break it by meditation, and the sweet scent of faith shall be shed abroad in your house.

Again, *prove the promise*, and in that way you will get your faith strengthened. When you are at any time placed in distress, take a promise and see whether it is true. Suppose you are very near lacking bread ; take this promise, " Thy bread shall be given thee, thy water shall be sure." Rise up in the morning when nothing is in the cupboard, and say, " I will see whether God will keep this promise " ; and if He does, do not forget it ; set it down in your book ; make a mark in your Bible against it. Do as the old woman did, who put T and P against the promise, and told her minister that it meant " tried and proved " ; so that when she was again in distress, she could not help believing. Have you been exercised by Satan ? There is a promise that says, " Resist the devil, and he will flee from you." Take that and prove it, and when you have proved it, make a mark against it and say, " This I know is true, for I have proved it to be so." There is nothing in the world that can confirm faith like proof. " What I want," said one, " is facts." And so it is with the Christian. What he wants is a fact to make him believe. The older you grow the stronger your faith ought to become, for you have so many more facts with which to buttress your faith, and compel you to believe in God. Only think of a man who has come to be seventy years of age, what a pile of evidence he could accumulate if he kept a note of all God's providential goodness and all His lovingkindness. You do not wonder when you hear a man, the hairs of whose head are white with the sunlight of heaven, get up and say, " These fifty years have I served God, and He has never forsaken me. I can bear willing testimony to His faithfulness ; not one good thing hath failed of all that the Lord hath promised ; all hath come to pass." Now we, who are young beginners, must not expect that our faith will be as strong as it will be in years to come. Every instance of God's love should make us believe Him more ; and as each promise passes by, and we can see the fulfillment of it at the heels thereof, we must be compelled and constrained to say, that God has kept so many of these promises and will keep them unto the end. But the worst of it is that we forget them all, and so we begin to have grey hairs sprinkled on our heads, and we have no more faith than when we began, because we have forgotten God's repeated answers, and though He has fulfilled the promise we have suffered it to lie buried in forgetfulness.

Another plan I would recommend for the strengthening of your faith, though not so excellent as the last, is to *associate yourselves with godly and much-tried men*. It is astonishing how young believers will get their faith refreshed by talking with old and advanced Christians. Perhaps you are in great doubt and distress ; you run off to an old brother, and you say, " Oh my dear friend, I am afraid I am not a child of God at all, I am in such deep distress ; I have had blasphemous thoughts cast into my heart ; if I were a child of God I should never feel like that." The old man smiles, and says, " Ah ! you have not gone very far on the road to heaven, or else you would know better. Why I am the subject of these thoughts very often. Old as I am, and though I hope I have enjoyed the full assurance for a long time, yet there are seasons when if I could have heaven for a grain of faith, I could not think heaven was mine, for I could not find so much as a grain in me, though it is there." And he will tell you what dangers he has passed, and of the sovereign love that kept him ; of the temptations that threatened to ensnare him, and of the wisdom that guided his feet ; and he will tell you of his own weakness and God's omnipotence ; of his own emptiness, and of God's fulness ; of his own changeableness, and God's immutability ; and if after talking with such a man you don't believe, surely you are sinful indeed ; for " out of the mouth of two witnesses, the whole shall be established," but when there are many such who can bear testimony to God, it would be foul sin indeed if we were to doubt Him.

Another way whereby you may obtain increase of faith is to *labour to get as much as possible free from self*. I have striven with all my might to attain the position of perfect indifference of all men. I have found at times, if I have been much praised in company, and if my heart has given way a little, and I have taken notice of it, and felt pleased, that the very next time I was censured and abused I felt the censure and abuse very keenly, for the very fact that I took the praise rendered me liable to lay hold upon the censure. So that I have always tried, especially of late, to take no more notice of man's praise than of his censure, but to fix my heart simply upon this —I know that I have a right motive in what I attempt to do ; I am conscious that I endeavour to serve God with a single eye to His glory, and therefore it is not for me to take praise from man nor censure, but to stand independently upon the one rock of right doing. Now the same thing will apply to you. Perhaps you find yourself full of virtue and grace one day, and the devil flatters you : " Ah ! you are a bright Christian ; you might join the church now, you would be quite an honour to it ; see how well you are prospering." And unconsciously to yourself you believe the sound of that syren music, and you half believe that really you are growing rich in grace. Well, the next day you find yourself very low indeed in godly matters. Perhaps you fall into some sin, and now the devil says, " Ah ! now you are no child of God ; look at your sins." Beloved, the only way in which you can maintain your faith is to live above the praise of self and the censure of self ; to live simply upon the blood and merits of our Lord Jesus Christ. He who can say in the midst of all his virtues " These are but dross and dung ; my hope is fixed on nothing less than Jesus Christ's finished sacrifice " —such a man, when sins prevail, will find his faith remain constant, for he will say " I once was full of virtue and then I did not trust in myself, and now I have none still do I trust in my Saviour, for change as I may, He changeth not. If I had to depend on myself in the least degree then it would be up and down, up and down ; but since I rely on what Christ has done, since He is the unbuttressed pillar of my hope, then come what may my soul doth rest secure, confident in faith. Faith will never be weak if self be weak, but when self is strong, faith cannot be strong ; for self is very much like what the gardener calls the sucker at the bottom of the tree, which never bears fruit but only sucks away the nourishment from the tree itself. Now, self is that sucker which sucks away the nourishment from faith, and you must cut it up or else your faith will always be little faith, and you will have difficulty in maintaining any comfort in your soul.

But, perhaps, the only way in which most men get their faith increased is by *great trouble.* We don't grow strong in faith on sunshiny days. It is only in strong weather that a man gets faith. Faith is not an attainment that droppeth like the gentle dew from heaven ; it generally comes in the whirlwind and the storm. Look at the old oaks : how is it that they have become so deeply rooted in the earth ? Ask the March winds and they will tell you. It was not the April shower that did it, or the sweet May sunshine, but it was March's rough wind, the blustering month of old Boreas shaking the tree to and fro and causing its roots to bind themselves around the rocks. So must it be with us. We don't make great soldiers in the barracks at home ; they must be made amidst flying shot and thundering cannon. We cannot expect to make good sailors on the Serpentine ; they must be made far away on the deep sea, where the wild winds howl, and the thunders roll like drums in the march of the God of armies. Storms and tempests are the things that make men tough and hardy mariners. They see the works of the Lord and His wonders in the deep. So with Christians. Great-faith must have great trials. Mr. Great-heart would never have been Mr. Great-heart if he had not once been Mr. Great-trouble. Valiant-for-truth would never have put to flight those foes, and have been so valiant, if the foes had not first attacked him. So with us : we must expect great troubles before we shall attain to much faith.

Then he who would have great faith, must *exercise what he has.* I should not like to-morrow to go and shoe horses, or to make horse shoes on an anvil. I am sure my arm would ache in the first hour with lifting the heavy hammer and banging it down so many times. Whatever the time might be, I should not be able to keep time. The reason why the blacksmith's arm does not tire is, because he is used to it. He has kept at it all day long these many years, till there's an arm for you ! He turns up his sleeve and shows you the strong sinew that never tires, so strong has it become by use. Do you want to get your faith strong ? Use it. You lazy lie-a bed Christians, that go up to your churches and chapels, and take your seats, and hear our sermons, and talk about getting good, but never think about doing good ; ye that are letting hell fill beneath you, and yet are too idle to stretch out your hands to pluck brands from the eternal burning ; ye that see sin running down your streets, yet can never put so much as your foot to turn or stem the current, I wonder not that you have to complain of the littleness of your faith. It ought to be little ; you do but little, and why should God give you more strength than you mean to use. Strong faith must always be an exercised faith ; and he that dares not exercise the faith he has shall not have more. " Take away from him the one talent and give it to him that hath, because he did not put it out to usury." In Mr. Whitefield's life, you do not often find him complaining of want of faith ; or if he did, it was when he only preached nine times in a week ; he never complained when he preached sixteen times. Read Grimshaw's life : you do not often find him troubled with despondency when he preached twenty-four times in seven days ; it was only when he was growing a little idle and only preached twelve times. Keep always at it, and all at it, and there is not much fear of your faith becoming weak. It is with our faith as with boys in the winter time. There they go round the fire, rubbing and chafing their hands to keep the blood in circulation, and almost fighting each other to see which shall sit on the fire and get warm. At last the father comes, and says, " Boys, this won't do ; you will never get warm by these artificial means ; run out and do some work." Then they all go out, and they come in again with a ruddy hue in their cheeks, their hands no longer tingle, and they say, " Well, father, we didn't think it half so warm as it is." So must it be with you : you must set to work if you would have your faith grow strong and warm. True, your works won't save you ; but faith without works is dead, frozen to death ; but faith with works groweth to a red heat of fervency and to the strength of stability. Go and teach in the Sunday-school, or go and catch seven or eight poor ragged children ; go and visit the poor old woman in her hovel ; go and see some poor dying creatures in the back streets of our great city, and you will say, " Dear me ! how wonderfully my faith is refreshed just by doing something." You have been watering yourself whilst you were watering others.

Now my last advice shall be this—the best way to get your full strength is to have *communion with Christ.* If you commune with Christ, you cannot be unbelieving. When His left hand is under my head, and His right hand doth embrace me, I cannot doubt. When my Beloved sits at His table, and He brings me into His banqueting house, and His banner over me is His love, then indeed I do believe. When I feast with Him, my unbelief is abashed and hides its head. Speak, ye that have been led in the green pastures, and have been made to lie down by the still waters ; ye who have seen His rod and His staff, and hope to see them even when you walk through the valley of the shadow of death ; speak, ye that have sat at His feet with Mary, or laid your head upon His bosom with the well-beloved John ; have you not found when you have been near to Christ your faith has grown strong, and when you have been far away, then your faith has become weak? It is impossible to look Christ in the face and then doubt Him. When you cannot see Him, then you doubt Him ; but if you live in fellowship with Him, you are like the ewe lambs of Nathan's parable, for you lie in His bosom, and eat from His table, and drink from His cup. You must believe when your Beloved speaks unto you, and says, " Rise up My love, My fair one, and come away." There is no hesitation then ; you must rise from the lowlands of your doubt up to the hills of assurance.

III. And now, in conclusion, there is A CERTAIN HIGH ATTAINMENT TO WHICH FAITH MAY, IF DILIGENTLY CULTIVATED, CERTAINLY ATTAIN. Can a man's faith grow so strong that he will never afterwards doubt at all ? I reply, no. He who has the strongest faith will have sorrowful intervals of despondency. I suppose there has scarcely ever been a Christian who has not, at some time or other, had the most painful doubts concerning his acceptance in the Beloved. All God's children will have paroxysms of doubt even though they may be usually strong in faith. Again, may a man so cultivate his faith that he may be infallibly sure that he is a child of God—so sure that he has made no mistake—so sure that all the doubts and fears which may be thrust upon him may not be able at that time to get an advantage over him ? I answer, yes, decidedly he may. A man may, in this life, be as sure of his acceptance in the Beloved as he is of his own existence. Nay, he not only may, but there are some of us who have enjoyed this precious state and privilege for years ; we do not mean for years together—our peace has been interrupted, we have now and then been subjected to doubts ; but I have known some—I knew one especially, who said that for thirty years he had enjoyed almost invariably a full sense of his acceptance in Christ. " I have had," he said, " very often a sense of sin, but I have had with that a sense of the power of the blood of Christ ; I have now and then for a little time had a great despondency, but still I may say, taking it as a general rule, that for thirty years I have enjoyed the fullest assurance of my acceptance in the Beloved." I trust a large portion of God's people can say that for months and years they have not had to sing.

" Tis a point I long to know."

But they can say, " I know whom I have believed, and am persuaded that He is able to keep that which I have committed to Him." I will try to depict the state of the Christian ; he may be as poor as poverty can make him, but he is rich ; he has no thought with regard to the morrow, for the morrow shall take thought for the things of itself. He casts himself upon the providence of God ; he believes that He who clothes the lilies, and feeds the ravens, will not allow His children to go starving or barefooted. He has but little concern as to his temporal estate ; he folds his arms and floats down the stream of providence singing all the way ; whether he float by mud bank, dark, dreary, and noxious, or by palace fair and valley pleasant, he alters not his position ; he neither moves nor struggles ; he has no will nor wish which way to swim, his only desire being to " lie passive in God's hand, and know no will but His." When the storm flies over his head he finds Christ to be a shelter from the tempest ; when the heat is hot he finds Christ to be the shadow of a great rock in a weary land. He just casts his anchor down deep into the sea, and when the wind blows, he sleeps ; hurricanes may come about his ears, the masts

creak, and every timber seems to be strained and every nail to start from its place, but there he sleeps ; Christ is at the helm ; he says, " My anchor is within the vail, I know it will keep its hold." The earth shakes beneath his feet ; but he says, " Though the earth be removed and mountains be cast into the sea, yet will not we fear, for God is our refuge and strength, and a very present help in time of trouble." Ask him about his eternal interests, and he tells you that his only confidence is in Christ, and that die when he may, he knows he shall stand boldly at the last great day clothed in his Saviour's righteousness. He speaks very confidently though never boastingly ; though he has no time to dance the giddy dance of presumption, he stands firmly on the rock of confidence. Perhaps you think he is proud—ah ! he is a humble man ; he lies low before the cross, but not before you ; he can look you boldly in the face, and tell you that Christ is able to keep that which he has committed to Him. He knows that—

> " His honour is engaged to save
> The meanest of His sheep,
> All that His heavenly Father gave,
> His hands securely keep."

And die when he may he can lay his head upon the pillow of promise, and breathe his life out on the Saviour's breast without a struggle or a murmur, crying—" Victory," in the arms of death ; challenging Death to produce his sting, and demanding of the grave its victory. Such is the effect of strong faith ; I repeat, the weakest in the world, by diligent cultivation may attain to it. Only seek the refreshing influence of the Divine Spirit, and walk in Christ's commandments, and live near to Him ; and ye that are dwarfs, like Zaccheus, shall become as giants ; the hyssop on the wall shall start up into the dignity of the cedar in Lebanon, and ye that fly before your enemies shall yet be able to chase a thousand, and two of you shall put ten thousand to flight. May the Lord so enable His poor little ones so to grow !

As for those of you who have no faith in Christ, let me remind you of one sad thing—namely, that " without faith it is impossible to please God." If thou hast not put thy trust in Christ, then God is angry with thee every day. " If thou turn not He will whet His sword, for He hath bent His bow and made it ready." I beseech thee, cast thyself on Christ ; He is worthy of thy trust ; there is none other to trust to ; He is willing to receive thee ; He invites thee ; He shed His blood for thee ; He intercedes for thee. Believe on Him, for thus His promise runs, " He that believeth and is baptized shall be saved." Do both of these things. Believe on Him, and then profess thy faith in baptism ; and the Lord bless thee, and hold thee to the end, and make thee to increase exceedingly in faith, to the glory of God. May the Lord add His blessing !

JESUS ADMIRED IN THEM THAT BELIEVE

" When He shall come to be glorified in His saints, and to be admired in all them that believe (because our testimony among you was believed) in that day."—2 Thessalonians i. 10.

WHAT a difference between the first and second comings of our Lord ! When He shall come a second time it will be to be glorified and admired, but when He came the first time it was to be despised and rejected of men. He

comes a second time to reign with unexampled splendour, but the first time He came to die in circumstances of shame and sorrow. Lift up your eyes, ye sons of light, and anticipate the change, which will be as great for you as for your Lord ; for now ye are hidden even as He was hidden, and mis-understood even as He was misunderstood when He walked among the sons of men. "We know that, when He shall appear, we shall be like Him ; for we shall see Him as He is." His manifestation will be our manifestation, and in the day in which He is revealed in glory then shall His saints be glorified with Him.

Observe that our Lord is spoken of as coming in His glory, and as at the same time taking vengeance in flaming fire on them that know not God, and that obey not the gospel. This is a note of great terror to all those who are ignorant of God, and wickedly unbelieving concerning His Christ. Let them take heed, for the Lord will gain glory by the overthrow of His enemies, and those who would not bow before Him cheerfully shall be compelled to bow before Him abjectly : they shall crouch at His feet, they shall lick the dust in terror, and at the glance of His eyes they shall utterly wither away, as it is written, they " shall be punished with everlasting destruction from the presence of the Lord, and from the glory of His power." But this is not the main object for which Christ will come, nor is this the matter in which He findeth His chiefest glory, for, observe, He does this as it were by the way, when He comes for another purpose. To destroy the wicked is a matter of necessity in which His spirit takes no delight, for He doth this, according to the text, not so much when He cometh to do it as when He shall come with another object, namely, " To be glorified in His saints, and to be admired in them that believe."

The crowning honour of Christ will be seen in His people, and this is the design with which He will return to this earth in the latter days, that He may be illustrious in His saints and exceedingly magnified in them. Even now His saints glorify Him. When they walk in holiness they do, as it were, reflect His light ; their holy deeds are beams from Him who is the Sun of Righteousness. When they believe in Him they also glorify Him, for there is no grace which pays lowlier homage at the throne of Jesus than the grace of faith whereby we trust Him, and so confess Him to be our all in all. We do glorify our gracious Lord, but, beloved brethren, we must all confess that we do not this as we could desire, for, alas, too often we dishonour Him, and grieve His Holy Spirit. By our want of zeal and by our many sins we are guilty of discrediting His gospel and dishonouring His name. Happy, happy, happy day when this shall no more be possible, when we shall be rid of the inward corruption which now worketh itself into outward sin, and shall never dishonour Christ again, but shall shine with a clear, pure radiance, like the moon on the Passover night, when it looketh the sun full in the face, and then shines upon the earth at her best. To-day we are like vessels on the wheel, but half fashioned, yet even now somewhat of His divine skill is seen in us as His handiwork. Still the unformed clay is in part seen, and much remains to be done ; how much more of the great Potter's creating wisdom and sanctifying power will be displayed when we shall be the perfect products of His hand ! In the bud and germ our new nature brings honour to its Author; it will do far more when its perfection manifests the Finisher. Then shall Jesus be glorified and admired in every one of us when the days of the new creation are ended and God shall usher in the eternal Sabbath by pro-nouncing His grace-work to be very good.

This morning, as God shall help me, I shall speak first of *the special glorification of Christ here intended* : and, secondly, I shall conclude the sermon by calling your attention *to the special considerations which this grand truth suggests*.

I. Let us consider carefully THE SPECIAL GLORIFI-CATION HERE INTENDED.

And the first point to note is *the time*. The text saith, " When He shall come to be glorified in His saints." The full glorification of Christ in His saints will be when He shall come a second time, according to the sure word of prophecy. He is glorified in them now, for He saith, " All Mine are Thine, and Thine are Mine ; and I am glorified in them " ; but as yet that glory is perceptible to Himself rather than to the outer world. The lamps are being trimmed, they will shine ere long. These are the days of preparation before that Sabbath which is in an infinite sense a high day. As it was said of Esther, that for so many months she prepared herself with myrrh and sweet odours before she entered the king's palace, to be espoused of him, even so are we now being purified and made ready for that august day when the perfected church shall be presented unto Christ as a bride unto her husband. John saith of her that shall be " pre-pared as a bride adorned for her husband." This is our night, wherein we must watch, but behold the morn-ing cometh, a morning without clouds, and then shall we walk in a seven-fold light because our Well-beloved hath come. That second advent of His will be His revelation : He was under a cloud here, and men perceived Him not save only a few who beheld His glory ; but when He comes a second time all veils will be removed and every eye shall see the glory of His countenance. For this He waits and His church waits with Him. We know not when the set time shall arrive, but every hour is bringing it nearer to us, therefore let us stand with loins girt, awaiting it.

Note, secondly, *in whom* this glorification of Christ is to be found. The text does not say He will be glorified " by " His saints, but " in His saints." There is a shade of difference, yea, more than a shade, between the two terms. We endeavour to glorify Him now by our actions, but then He will be glorified in our own persons, and character, and condition. He is glorified *by* what we do, but He is at the last to be glorified *in* what we are. Who are these in whom Jesus is to be glorified and admired ? They are spoken of under two descriptions : " in His saints," and " in all them that believe."

In " His saints " first. All those in whom Christ will be glorified are described as holy ones or saints : men and women who have been sanctified, and made pure, whose gracious lives show that they have been under the teaching of the Holy Spirit, whose obedient actions prove that they are disciples of a Holy Master, even of Him who was " holy, harmless, undefiled, and separate from sinners." But, inasmuch as these saints are also said to be believers, I gather that the holiness which will honour Christ at last is a holiness based on faith in Him, a holiness of which this was the root,—that they first trusted in Christ, and then, being saved, they loved their Lord and obeyed Him. Their faith wrought by love and purified their souls, and so cleansed their lives. It is an inner as well as an outer purity, arising out of the living and operative principle of faith. If any think that they can attain to holiness apart from faith in Christ they are as much mistaken as he who should hope to reap a harvest without casting seed into the furrows. Faith is the bulb, and saintship is the delightfully fragrant flower which cometh of it when planted in the soil of a renewed heart. Beware, I pray you, of any pretence to a holiness arising out of yourselves, and maintained by the energy of your own unaided wills ; as well look to gather grapes of thorns or figs of thistles. True saintship must spring from confidence in the Saviour of sinners, and if it doth not it is lacking in the first elements of truth. How can that be a perfect character which finds its basis in self-esteem ? How could Christ be glorified by saints who refuse to trust in Him ?

I would call your attention once again to the second description, " All them that believe." This is enlarged by the hint that they are believers in a certain testimony, according to the bracketed sentence —" because our testimony among you was believed." Now, the testimony of the apostles was concerning Christ. They saw Him in the body, and they bore witness that He was " God manifest in the flesh " ; they saw His holy life, and they bore witness to it ; they saw His death of grief, and they witnessed that " God was in Christ reconciling the world unto Himself " ; they saw Him risen from the dead, and they said, " We are witnesses of His resurrection " ; they saw Him rise into heaven, and they bore witness that God had taken Him up to His right hand. Now, all that believe this witness are saved. " If thou shalt confess with thy mouth the Lord Jesus, and shalt believe in thine heart that God hath raised Him from the dead, thou shalt be saved." All who with a simple faith come and cast themselves upon the incarnate God, living and dying for men, and ever sitting at the right hand of God to make intercession for them,—these are the people in whom Christ will be glorified and admired at the last great day. But inasmuch as they are first said to be saints, be it never forgotten that this faith must be a living faith, a faith which produces a hatred of sin, a faith which renews the character and shapes the life after the noble model of Christ, thus turning sinners into saints. The two descriptions must not be violently rent asunder ; you must not say that the favoured people are sanctified without remembering that they are justified by faith, nor may you say that they are justified by faith without remembering that without holiness no man shall see the Lord, and that at the last the people in whom Christ will be admired will be those holy ones who were saved by faith in Him.

So far, then, we see our way, but now a question arises : *by whom* will Christ be thus glorified and admired ? He shines in His people, but who will see the glory ? I answer first, that His people will see it. Every saint will glorify Christ in Himself, and admire Christ in Himself. He will say, " What a wonder that such a poor creature as I am should be thus perfected ! How glorious is my Lord, who has wrought this miracle upon me ! " Surely our consciousness of having been cleansed and made holy will cause us to fulfil those word of John Berridge which we sang just now :—

> " He cheers them with eternal smile,
> They sing hosannas all the while ;
> Or, overwhelm'd with rapture sweet,
> Sink down adoring at His feet."

This I know, that when I personally enter heaven I shall for ever admire and adore the everlasting love which brought me there. Yes, we will all glorify and admire our Saviour for what He has wrought in us by His infinite grace.

The saints will also admire Christ in one another. As I shall see you and you shall see your brethren and sisters in Christ all perfect, you will be filled with wonderment, and gratitude, and delight. You will be free from all envy there, and therefore you will rejoice in all the beauty of your fellow saints : their heaven will be a heaven to you, and what a multitude of heavens you will have as you will joy in the joy of all the redeemed ! We shall as much admire the Lord's handiwork in others as in ourselves, and shall each one praise Him for saving all the rest. You will see your Lord in all your brethren, and this will make you praise and adore Him world without end with a perpetual amazement of evergrowing delight.

But that will not be all. Besides the blood-bought and ransomed of Christ there will be on that great day of His coming all the holy angels to stand by and look on and wonder. They marvelled much when first He stooped from heaven to earth, and they desired to look into those things, which then were a mystery to them. But when they shall see their beloved Prince come back with ten thousand times ten thousand of the ransomed at His feet, all of them made perfect by having washed their robes and made them white in His blood, how the principalities and powers will admire Him in every one of His redeemed ! How they will praise that conquering arm which has brought home all these spoils from the war ! How will the hosts of heaven shout His praises as they see Him lead all these captives captive with a new captivity, in chains of love, joyfully gracing His triumph and showing forth the completeness of His victory !

We do not know what other races of innocent creatures there may be, but I think it is no stretch of imagination to believe that, as this world is only one speck in the creation of God, there may be millions of other races in the countless worlds around us, and all these may be invited to behold the wonders of redeeming love as manifested in the saints in the day of the Lord. I seem to see these unfallen intelligences encompassing the saints as a cloud of witnesses, and in rapt vision beholding in them the love and grace of the redeeming Lord. What songs ! What shouts shall rise from all these to the praise of the ever blessed God ! What an orchestra of praise will the universe become ! From star to star the holy hymn shall roll, till all space shall ring out the hosannas of wondering spirits. " The Wonderful, the Counsellor, the Mighty God, the Everlasting Father, the Prince of Peace," shall have brought home all the men wondered at, and they with Himself shall be the wonder of eternity.

Then shall Satan and His defeated legions, and the lost spirits of ungodly men, bite their lips with envy and rage, and tremble at the majesty of Jesus in that day. By their confessed defeat and manifest despair they shall glorify Him in His people, in whom they have been utterly overthrown. They shall see that there is not one lost whom He redeemed by blood, not one snatched away of all the sheep His Father gave Him, not one warrior enlisted beneath His banner fallen in the day of battle, but all more than conquerors through Him that loved them. What despair shall seize upon diabolic spirits as they discover their entire defeat ! Defeated in men who were once their slaves ! Poor dupes whom they could so easily beguile by their craftiness,—defeated even in these ! Jesus triumphant by taking the lambs from between the lion's jaws, and rescuing His feeble sheep from their power, will utterly put them to shame in

His redeemed. With what anguish will they sink into the hell prepared for them, because now they hear with anger all earth and heaven and every star ringing with the shout,—Hallelujah, Hallelujah, Hallelujah, for the Lord God omnipotent reigneth, and the Lamb hath conquered by His blood.

You see then that there are enough spectators to magnify Christ in His saints ; and so, fourthly, let us inquire *in what degree* will the Lord Jesus be glorified ? Our answer is, it will be to the very highest degree. He shall come to be glorified in His saints to the utmost, for this is clear from the words, " to be admired." When our translation was made the word " admired " had to ordinary Englishmen a stronger flavour of wonder than it has to us now. We often speak of admiring a thing in the softer sense of loving it, but the real meaning of the English word, and of the Greek also, is *wonder* : our Lord will be wondered at in all them that believe. Those who look upon the saints will feel a sudden wonderment of sacred delight ; they will be startled with the surprising glory of the Lord's work in them ; " We thought He would do great things, but this ! This surpasseth conception ! " Every saint will be a wonder to himself. " I thought my bliss would be great, but not like this ! " All His brethren will be a wonder to the perfected believer. He will say, " I thought the saints would be perfect, but I never imagined such a transfiguration of excessive glory would be put upon each of them. I could not have imagined my Lord to be so good and gracious." The angels in heaven will say that they never anticipated such deeds of grace : they did know that He had undertaken a great work, but they did not know that He would do so much for His people and in His people. The first-born sons of light, used to great marvels from of old, will be entranced with a new wonder as they see the handiwork of Immanuel's free grace and dying love. The men who once despised the saints, who called them canting hypocrites and trampled on them, and perhaps slew them, the kings and princes of the earth who sold the righteous for a pair of shoes, what will they say when they see the least of the Saviour's followers become a prince of more illustrious rank than the great ones of the earth, and Christ shining out in every one of these favoured beings ? For their uplifting Jesus will be wondered at by those who once despised both Him and them.

My next point leads us into the very bowels of the subject ; *in what respects* will Christ be glorified and wondered at ? I cannot expect to tell you one tenth part of it. I am only going to give you a little sample of what this must mean ; exhaustive exposition were quite impossible to me. I think with regard to His saints that Jesus will be glorified and wondered at on account of their number—" a number that no man can number." John was a great arithmetician, and he managed to count up to one hundred and forty-four thousand of all the tribes of the children of Israel ; but that was only a representative number for the Jewish church : as for the church of God, comprehending the Gentile nations, he gave up all idea of computation, and confessed that it is " a number which no man can number." When he heard them sing he says, " I heard a voice like the voice of many waters and like great thunder." There were so many of them that their song was like the Mediterranean sea lashed to fury by a tempest, nay, not one great sea in uproar, but ocean upon ocean, the Atlantic and the Pacific piled upon each other, and the Arctic upon these, and other oceans upon these, layers of oceans, all thundering out their mightiest roar : and such will be the song of the redeemed, for the crowds which swell the matchless hymn will be beyond all reckoning. Behold, and see, ye who laughed at His kingdom, see how the little one has become a thousand ! Now look ye, ye foes of Christ, who saw the handful of corn on the top of the mountains ; see how the fruit thereof doth shake like Lebanon, and they of the city do flourish like grass of the earth. Who can reckon the drops of the dew or the sands on the sea shore ? When they have counted these then shall they not have guessed at the multitude of the redeemed that Christ shall bring to glory. And all this harvest from one grain of wheat, which except it had fallen into the ground and died would have remained alone ! What said the word ? " If it die, it shall bring forth much fruit." Is not the prophecy fulfilled ? Oh beloved, what a harvest from the lone Man of Nazareth ! What fruit from that glorious Man—the Branch ! Men esteemed him stricken, smitten of God and afflicted ; and they made nothing of Him, and yet there sprang of Him (and He as good as dead) these multitudes which are many as the stars of heaven. Is He not glorified and wondered at in them ? The day shall declare it without fail.

But there is quality as well as quantity. He is admired in His saints because they are every one of them proofs of His power to save from evil. My eye can hardly bear, even though it be but in imagination, to gaze upon the glittering ranks of the white-robed ones, where each one outshines the sun, and they are all as if a sevenfold midday had clothed them. Yet all these, as I look at them, tell me, " We have washed our robes,—for they were once defiled. We have made them white,—but this whiteness is caused by the blood of the Lamb." These were heirs of wrath even as others, these were dead in trespasses and sins ; all these like sheep had gone astray and turned every one to his own way ; but look at them and see how He has saved them, washed them, cleansed them, perfected them ! His power and grace are seen in all of them. If your eye will pause here and there you will discover some that were supremely stubborn, whose neck was as an iron sinew, and yet He conquered them by love. Some were densely ignorant, but He opened their blind eyes ; some grossly infected with the leprosy of lust, but He healed them ; some under Satan's most terrible power, but He cast the devil out of them. Oh, how He will be glorified in special cases ! In yon drunkard made into a saint, in yon blasphemer turned into a loving disciple, in yon persecutor who breathed out threatening taught to sing everlastingly a hymn of praise ! He will be exceedingly glorified in such. Brethren, beloved in the Lord, in each one of us there was some special difficulty as to our salvation, some impossibility which was possible with God, though it would have been for ever impossible with us.

Remember, also, that all those saints made perfect would have been in hell had it not been for the Son's atoning sacrifice. This they will remember the more vividly, because they will see other men condemned for the sins with which they also were once polluted. The crash of vengeance upon the ungodly will make the saints magnify the Lord the more as they see themselves delivered. They will each feel,—

" Oh were it not for grace divine,
  That fate so dreadful had been mine."

In each one the memory of the horrible pit whence they were drawn and the miry clay out of which they they were uplifted shall make their Saviour more glorified and wondered at.

Perhaps the chief point in which Christ will be glorified will be—the absolute perfection of all the saints. They shall then be "without spot, or wrinkle, or any such thing." We have not experienced what perfection is, and therefore we can hardly conceive it; our thoughts themselves are too sinful for us to get a full idea of what absolute perfection must be; but, dear brethren, we shall have no sin left in us, for they are "without fault before the throne of God," and we shall have no remaining propensity to sin. There shall be no bias in the will towards that which is evil, but it shall be fixed for ever upon that which is good. The affections will never be wanton again, they will be chaste for Christ. The understanding will never make mistakes. You shall never put bitter for sweet, nor sweet for bitter; you shall be "perfect, even as your Father which is in heaven is perfect": and truly, brethren, He who worketh this in us will be a wonder. Christ will be admired and adored because of this grand result. O mighty Master, with what strange moral alchemy didst Thou work to turn that morose dispositioned man into a mass of love! How didst Thou work to lift that selfish Mammonite up from his hoarded gains to make him find his gain in Thee? How didst Thou overcome that proud spirit, that fickle spirit that lazy spirit, that lustful spirit—how didst Thou contrive to take all these away? How didst Thou extirpate the very roots of sin, and every little rootlet of sin, out of Thy redeemed, so that not a tiny fibre can be found? "The sins of Jacob shall be sought for and they shall not be found, yea, they shall not be, saith the Lord." Neither the guilt of sin nor the propensity of sin,—both shall be gone, and Christ shall have done it, and He will be "glorified in His saints, and admired in them that believe."

This is but the beginning, however. There will be seen in every saint, in that last wondrous day, the wisdom and power and love of Christ in having brought them through all the trials of the way. He kept their faith alive when else it would have died out: He sustained them under trials when else they would have fainted; He held them fast in their integrity when temptation solicited them, and they had almost slipped with their feet. Aye, He sustained some of them in prison, and on the rack, and at the stake, and held them faithful still! One might hardly wish to be a martyr, but I reckon that the martyrs will be the admiration of us all, or rather Christ will be admired in them. However they could bear such pain as some of them did endure for Christ's sake none of us can guess, except that we know that Christ was in them suffering in His members. Eternally will Jesus be wondered at in them as all intelligent spirits shall see how He upheld them, so that neither tribulation, nor distress, nor nakedness, nor famine, nor sword, could separate them from His love. These are the men that wandered about in sheep-skins and goat-skins, destitute, afflicted, tormented, of whom the world was not worthy, but now they stand arrayed as kings and priests in surpassing glory for ever. Verily, their Lord shall be admired in them. Say you not so?

Recollect, dear friends, that we shall see in that day how the blessed Christ, as "Head over all things to His church," has ruled every providence to the sanctification of His people—how the dark days

begat showers which made the plants of the Lord to grow, how the fierce sun which threatened to scorch them to the root, filled them with warmth of love divine and ripened their choice fruit. What a tale the saints will have to tell of how that which threatened to damp the fire of grace made it burn more mightily, how the stone which threatened to kill their faith was turned into bread for them, how the rod and staff of the Good Shepherd was ever with them to bring them safely home. I have sometimes thought that if I get into heaven by the skin of my teeth I will sit down on the glory-shore and bless for ever Him who, on a board, or on a broken piece of the ship, brought my soul safe to land; and surely they who obtain an abundant entrance, coming into the fair havens, like a ship in full sail, without danger of shipwreck, will have to praise the Lord that they thus came into the blessed port of peace: in each case the Lord will be specially glorified and admired.

I cannot stop over this, but I must beg you to notice that as a king is glorious in his regalia, so will Christ put on His saints as His personal splendour in that day when He shall make up His jewels. It is with Christ as it was with that noble Roman matron who, when she called at her friends' houses and saw their trinkets, asked them to come next day to her house, and she would exhibit her jewels. They expected to see ruby, and pearl, and diamond, but she called in her two boys, and said, "These are my jewels." Even so will Jesus instead of emerald and amethyst, and onyx and topaz, exhibit His saints. "These are My choice treasures," saith He, "in whom I will be glorified." Solomon surely was never more full of glory than when he had finished the temple, when all the tribes came together to see the noble structure, and confessed it to be "beautiful for situation, the joy of the whole earth." But what will be the glory of Christ when all the living stones shall be put into their places and His church shall have her windows of agates and her gates of carbuncle, and all her borders of precious stones. Then, indeed, will He be glorified, when the twelve foundations of His new Jerusalem shall be courses of stones most precious, the like of which was never seen.

Now, inasmuch as my text lays special stress upon *believing*, I invite you just for a minute to consider how as believers as well as saints the saved ones will glorify their Lord.

First, it will be wonderful that there should be so many brought to faith in Him: men with no God, and men with many gods, men steeped in ignorance, and men puffed up with carnal wisdom, great men and poor men, all brought to believe in the one Redeemer and praise Him for His great salvation. Will He not be glorified in their common faith? It will magnify Him that these will all be saved by faith, and not by their own merits. Not one among them will boast that he was saved by his own good works, but all of them will rejoice to have been saved by that blessedly simple way of "Believe and live," saved by sovereign grace through the atoning blood, looked to by the tearful eye of simple faith. This, too, shall make Jesus glorious, that all of them, weak as they were, were made strong by faith; all of them personally unfit for battle were yet made triumphant in conflict because by faith they overcame through the blood of the Lamb. All of them shall be there to show that their faith was honoured, that Christ was faithful to His promise, and never allowed them to believe in vain. All of them standing in heavenly places, saved by faith, will ascribe every particle of the glory to the Lord Jesus only :—

" I ask them whence their victory came ?
They, with united breath,
Ascribe their conquest to the Lamb,
Their triumph to His death."

They believed and were saved, but faith taketh no credit to itself ; it is a self-denying grace, and putteth the crown upon the head of Christ, and therefore is it written that He will be glorified in His saints, and He will also be admired in all them that believe.

I have scarcely skirted the subject even now, and time is failing me. I want you to reflect that Jesus will be glorified in the risen bodies of all His saints. Now, in heaven, they are pure spirits, but when He shall come they shall be clothed again. Poor body, thou must sleep awhile, but what thou shalt be at thine awaking doth not yet appear. Thou art now the shrivelled seed, but there is a flower to come of thee which shall be lovely beyond all thought. Though sown in weakness, this body shall be raised in power ; though sown in corruption, it shall be raised in incorruption. Weakness, weariness, pain, and death will be banished for ever ; infirmity and deformity will be all unknown. The Lord will raise up our bodies to be like unto His glorious body. Oh, what a prospect lies before us ! Let us remember that this blessed resurrection will come to us because He rose, for there must be a resurrection to the members because the Head has risen. Oh, the charm of being a risen man perfect in body, soul, and spirit ! All that charm will be due to Christ, and therefore He will be admired in us.

Then let us think of the absolute perfection of the church as to numbers : all who have believed in Him will be with Him in glory. The text saith, He will be " admired in *all* them that believe." Now, if some of those who believe perished He would not be admired in them, but they will all be there, the little ones as well as the great ones. You will be there, you poor feeble folk who when you say " Lord, I believe," are obliged to add " help Thou mine unbelief." He shall be admired in all believers without a single exception, and peradventure there shall be more wonder at the going to heaven of the weak believers than at the stronger ones. Mr. Greatheart, when he comes there will owe his victories to his Master and lay his laurels at His feet ; but fainting Feeblemind, and limping Ready-to-halt with his crutches, and trembling Little-faith, when they enter into rest will make heaven ring with notes of even greater admiration that such poor creeping worms of the earth should win the day by mighty grace. Suppose that one of them should be missing at last ! Stop the harps ! Silence the songs ! No beginning to be merry while one child is shut out ! I am quite certain if as a family we were going to sing our evening hymn of joy and thankfulness, if mother said, " Where is the little mite ? Where is the last one of the family ? " There would be a pause. If we had to say—she is lost, there would be no singing and no resting till she was found. It is the glory of Jesus that as a Shepherd He has lost none of His flock ; as the Captain of Salvation He has brought many sons to glory, and has lost none, and hence He is admired, not in some that believe, nor yet in all but one, but He is " admired in *all* them that believe."

Does not this delight you, you who are weak and trembling, that He will be admired in you ? There is little to admire in you at present, as you penitently confess ; but since Christ is in you now, and will be more fully manifested in you, there will ere long be much to admire. May you partake in the excellence of our divine Lord and be conformed to His likeness that He may be seen in you and glorified in you.

Another point of admiration will be the eternal safety of all His believing people. There they are, safe from fear of harm. Ye dogs of hell, you howled at their heels and hoped to devour them ; but lo, they are clean escaped from you ! What must it be to be lifted above gun-shot of the enemy, where no more watch shall need to be kept, for even the roar of the Satanic artillery cannot be heard ? Oh glorious Christ, to bring them all to such a state of safety, Thou art indeed to be wondered at for ever.

Moreover, all the saints will be so honoured, so happy, and so like their Lord that themselves and everything about them will be themes for never-ending admiration. You may have seen a room hung round with mirrors, and when you stood in the midst you were reflected from every point : you were seen here, and seen there, and there again, and there again, and so every part of you was reflected ; just such is heaven, Jesus is the centre, and all His saints like mirrors reflect His glory. Is He human ? So are they ! Is He the Son of God ? So are they sons of God ! Is He perfect ? So are they ! Is He exalted ? So are they ! Is He a prophet ? So are they, making known unto principalities and powers the manifold wisdom of God. Is He a priest ? So are they ! Is He a King ? So are they, for He hath made us priests and kings unto God, and we shall reign for ever and ever. Look where you will along the ranks of the redeemed, this one thing shall be seen, the glory of Christ Jesus, even to surprise and wonder.

II. I have no time to make those SUGGESTIONS with which I intended to have finished, and so I will just tell you what they would have been.

First, the text suggest that the principal subject for self-examination with us all should be,—Am I a saint ? Am I holy ? Am I a believer in Christ ? Yes or no, for on that yes or no must hang your glorification of Christ, or your banishment from His presence.

The next thing is—observe the small value of human opinion. When Christ was here the world reckoned Him to be a nobody, and while His people are here they must expect to be judged in the same way. What do worldlings know about it ? How soon will their judgment be reversed ! When our Lord shall appear even those who sneered will be compelled to admire. When they shall see the glory of Christ in every one of His people, awe-stricken, they will have nothing to say against us ; nay, not even the false tongue of malicious slander shall dare to hiss out a serpent word in that day. Never mind them, then ; put up with reproach which shall so soon be silenced.

The next suggestion is a great encouragement to enquirers who are seeking Christ ; for I put it to you, you great sinners, if Jesus is to be glorified in saved sinners, would He not be glorified indeed if He saved you ? If He were ever to save such a rebel as you have been, would it not be the astonishment of eternity ? I mean you who are known in the village as Wicked Jack, or known as a common swearer—what if my Master were to make a saint of you ? Bad, raw material ! Yet suppose He transformed you into a precious jewel, and made you to be as holy as God is holy, what would you say of Him? "Say of Him," say you, "I would praise Him world without end." Yes, and you shall do so if you will come and trust Him. Put your trust in Him. The Lord help you to do so at once, and He shall be admired even in you for ever and ever.

Our text gives an exhortation to believers also. Will Jesus Christ be honoured and glorified in all the saints? Then let us think well of them all, and love them all. Some dear children of God have uncomely bodies, or they are blind or deformed, or maimed; and many of these have scanty purses, and it may be the church knows most of them as coming for alms: moreover, they have little knowledge, little power to please, and they are uncouth in manners, and belong to what are called the lowest ranks of society: do not, therefore, despise them, for one day our Lord will be glorified in them. How He will be admired in yonder poor bedridden woman when she rises from the workhouse to sing Hallelujah to God and the Lamb among the brightest of the shining ones. Why, methinks the pain, the poverty, the weakness, and the sorrow of saints below will greatly glorify the Captain of their Salvation as they tell how grace helped them to bear their burdens and to rejoice under their afflictions.

Lastly, brethren, this text ought to encourage all of you who love Jesus to go on talking about Him to others and bearing your testimony for His name. You see how the apostle Paul has inserted a few words by way of parenthesis. Draw the words out of the brackets, and take them home, "Because our testimony among you was believed." Do you see those crowds of idolatrous heathen, and do you see those hosts of saved ones before the throne? What is the medium which linked the two characters? By what visible means did the sinners become saints? Do you see that insignificant looking man with weak eyes? That man whose bodily presence is weak

and whose speech is contemptible? Do you not see his bodkin and needle case? He has been making and mending tents, for he is only a tent-maker. Now, those bright spirits which shine like suns, flashing forth Christ's glory, were made thus bright through the addresses and prayers of that tent-maker. The Thessalonians were heathens plunged in sin, and this poor tent-maker came in among them and told them of Jesus Christ and His gospel; His testimony was believed; that belief changed the lives of his hearers and made them holy, and they being renewed came at length to be perfectly holy, and there they are, and Jesus Christ is glorified in them. Beloved, will it not be a delightful thing throughout eternity to contemplate that you went into your Sunday-school class this afternoon, and you were afraid you could not say much, but you talked about Jesus Christ with a tear in your eye, and you brought a dear girl to believe in His saving name through your testimony. In years to come that girl will be among those that shine out to the glory of Christ for ever. Or you will get away this evening, perhaps, to talk in a lodging-house to some of those poor, despised tramps; you will go and tell one of those poor vagrants, or one of the fallen women, the story of your Lord's love and blood, and the poor broken heart will catch at the gracious word, and come to Jesus, and then a heavenly character will be begun, and another jewel secured for the Redeemer's diadem. Methinks you will admire His crown all the more because, as you see certain stones sparkling in it, you will say, "Blessed be His name for ever: He helped me to dive into the sea and find that pearl for Him," and now it adorns His sacred brow. Now, get at it, all of you! You that are doing nothing for Jesus, be ashamed of yourselves, and ask Him to work in you that you may begin to work for Him, and unto God shall be the glory, for ever and ever. Amen and Amen.

DIVINE LOVE AND ITS GIFTS

"Now our Lord Jesus Christ Himself, and God, even our Father, which hath loved us, and hath given us everlasting consolation and good hope through grace, comfort your hearts, and stablish you in every good word and work."— 2 Thessalonians ii. 16, 17.

THE Thessalonians had been much disturbed by the predictions of divers persons that the day of Christ was at hand. There always have been pretenders to prophetic knowledge, who have fixed dates for the end of the world, and by their fanaticism have driven many into lunatic asylums and disturbed the peace of others; some of this band had worried the saints at Thessalonica. The apostle, after beseeching them not to be soon shaken in mind or troubled by such follies, went on to beg them not to be deceived by forged letters or pretended prophets, and then prayed for them that they might possess abiding consolation, which would keep them calmly persevering in holiness. His prayer is singularly emphatic; he cries to the Lord Jesus Christ Himself, and to God, even our Father, to comfort their hearts, that by such consolations they may be so confirmed that nothing may cause them to decline from any holy enterprise or testimony. Perhaps, during their fright some of them had ceased from service, reckoning it vain to go on with anything when the world was so near its end; therefore, Paul would have them

calmed in spirit that they might diligently persevere in their Christian course. That which frightens us from duty cannot be a good thing; true comfort stablishes us in every good word and work.

It is an ill wind which blows no one any good. We owe to the needless alarms of the Thessalonians this prayer, which, while it was useful for them, is also instructive for us; and I pray that while we look into it we may be led into deep thoughts of the love of God, and not into thoughts only, but into a personal enjoyment of that love, so that this morning the love of God may be shed abroad in our hearts by the Holy Spirit which is given unto us. To hear of the love of God is sweet—to believe it most precious—but to enjoy it is Paradise below the skies; may God grant us a taste thereof this morning.

I shall first call your earnest attention to *the blessed fact* recorded in our text, that "our Lord Jesus Christ Himself, and God, even our Father, hath loved us"; then we will dwell upon *the past manifestations* of that love—"He hath given us everlasting consolation and good hope through grace " : and then we shall dwell for a while upon *the prayer* which Paul based upon this love and its manifestation, " that God would comfort your hearts, and stablish you in every good word and work."

I. First, then, dear brethren, let me ask your hearts, as well as your minds, to consider THIS GLORIOUS FACT : " Our Lord Jesus Christ Himself, and God, even our Father, hath loved us." I cannot help repeating my frequent remark that the love of God is a theme fitter for the solitary contemplation of each person than for public utterance or explanation. It is to be felt, but it never can be uttered. Who can speak of love ? In what language shall we sing its sweetness ? No other word, nor set of words, can utter its meaning. You may go round about and make a long definition, but you have not defined it ; and he who never felt his heart glow with it will remain an utter stranger to it, depict it as you may. Love must be felt in the heart, it cannot be learned from a dictionary. " God hath loved us." I want you not so much to follow what I shall have to say upon that wonderful fact, as to try and think over this thought for yourselves. God hath loved us. Drink into that truth. Take the word, lay it under your tongue, and let it dissolve like a wafer made with honey, till it sweetens all your soul.

God hath *loved* us ? Let me remark that it does not say " He pitied us." That would be true, for " like as a father pitieth his children, so the Lord pitieth them that fear Him." Pity is one degree below love and often leads to it, but it is not love : you may pity a person whom, apart from his sufferings, you would heartily dislike. You cannot endure the man, yet are you sorrowful that he should be so pained. Nor does the text declare that God has had mercy upon us. I could comprehend that, aye, and bless God for ever, because His mercy endureth for ever. It is, to my mind, quite understandable that the good and gracious God should be merciful towards His creatures : but it is a far greater thing that He should *love* them. Love is a feeling vastly more to be valued than mere mercy. Merciful is a man to his beast, but he does not love it ; merciful has many a man been to his enemies, for whom he has had no degree of affection ; but God doth not merely pity us and have mercy upon us, He *loves* us. Neither can this word be bartered for that of benevolence. There is an aspect under which God is love to all His creatures, because He is benevolent and wishes well towards all things that He hath made, but Paul was not thinking of that when he said, " God hath loved *us*, and given *us* everlasting consolation." A mother is not said to be benevolent towards her child, nor a husband coldly benevolent towards his bride : benevolence would be a poor, poor, substitute for love ; love is as infinitely beyond benevolence as the gold of kings in value exceeds the stone of the quarry. We have frequently heard theologians declare that the love of God towards His elect is the love of complacency, and the statement, though perhaps true, is most frosty. One would not like to strike out the word " love," and put in its place the word " complacency." It would be like setting up a globe of ice in the place of the sun. Love glows with sunlight, complacency has at best but cold moonlike beams. No, we must hold to the words, " hath *loved* us." Truly, the Lord has a complacency in His people as He sees them

in Christ, but He has much more than that. He is benevolent towards His people, and towards all creatures, but He is much more than that towards us ; He is merciful, He is pitiful, He is everything that is good, but He is more than that—He " hath *loved* us." You know, mother, how you look upon that dear child of yours as you hold it in your arms. Why, it seems part of yourself. You love it as you love yourself, and your thoughts of it do not differ from your thoughts about your own welfare : the child is intertwisted with your being. Now God also hath united us to Himself by cords of love and bonds of affection, and He thinks of us as He thinks of Himself. I can express this, but I cannot explain it. Even now I feel much more inclined to sit down and weep for joy of heart that God could ever love me, than to try and speak to you. He made the heavens, and I am less than the veriest speck—yet He loves me. It is His eternal arm that has held up the universe in all ages, and I am as a leaf of the forest, green awhile, but soon to grow sere and to be buried with my fellows, yet the Eternal *loves* me, and always will love me. With His great infinite heart He loves me—as a God He loves me, divinely loves me. It is a conquering thought, it utterly overcomes us and crushes us with its weight of joy ; it bows us to the ground and casts us into a swoon of ecstasy when it is realised by the mind. " God, even our Father, hath loved us."

Now, permit the other side of the thought to shine upon your minds, the marvel is not merely that God hath loved, but that He hath loved *us*, so insignificant, so frail, so foolish, let us add—for this increases the marvel—so sinful, and therefore so uncomely, so ungrateful, and therefore so provoking, so wilfully obstinate in returning to old sins again, and therefore so deserving to be abhorred and rejected! I can imagine the Lord's love to the apostles. We can sometimes think of His love to the early saints without any great wonder, and of His love to the patriarchs and to the confessors and the martyrs, and to some eminently holy men whose biographies have charmed us : but that our Lord Jesus Christ, Himself God, even our Father, should have loved *us*, is a world of wonders ! And if I put it into the singular number, and say, " Who loved *me* and gave Himself for *me*," it shall ever stand first of all miracles to my soul's apprehension that I should be the object of divine affection. Dear brethren and sisters, I leave this meditation with you, I cannot speak of it, I beseech you to baptize your souls into it, and to let this one thought overwhelm you this day,—" God, even our Father, hath loved us."

Let me carry your minds onward a little further. Remember that the eternal love of God is the great fountain and source from which proceed all the spiritual blessings which we enjoy. If you stand at the source of a great river like the Thames you see nothing there but a tiny rivulet, the fact being that we do but by courtesy speak of that little brook as the source of the river. It is only a very partial source ; a great river derives its volume of water from a thousand streams, and is sustained by the whole of the watershed along which it flows. The imaginary fountain-head of a river is therefore but a small affair, but suppose the Thames had never borrowed from a single stream in all its course, but welled up at once a full-grown river from some one fountain-head, what a sight it would be ! Now the mercy of God to us in Christ Jesus owes nothing to any other stream, it leaps in all its fulness from the infinite depths of the love of God to us, and if in contemplation you can travel to that great deep, profound and unfathomable, and see welling up all the floods of covenant grace, which afterwards flow on for ever to all the chosen seed, you have before you that which angels wonder at. If it would be marvellous to see one river leap up from the earth full-grown, what would it be to gaze upon a vast spring from which all the rivers of the earth should at once come bubbling up, a thousand of them born at a birth ? What a vision would it be ! Who can conceive it ! And yet the love of God is that fountain from which all the rivers of mercy which have ever gladdened our race—all the rivers of grace in time and of glory hereafter—take their rise. My soul, stand thou at that sacred fountain-head, and adore and magnify for ever and ever " God, even our Father, who hath loved us."

Now please to notice the words of the text, for they are full of instruction : when speaking of this love, the apostle joins our Lord Jesus Christ Himself with " God, even our Father." He honoured the deity of Jesus by speaking of Him side by side, and on terms of equality, with God the Father. But there is more here than this, for the words remind us that our Lord Jesus Christ and God, even our Father, act in holy concert in the matters which concern our welfare. Jesus Christ is the gift of the Father's love to us, but Jesus Himself loved His own, and laid down His life for His sheep. It is true that the Son loves us, but the Father Himself loveth us too. The love of God does not come to us from one person of the blessed Trinity alone, but from all. We ought to make no distinctions by way of preference in the love of either Father, Son, or Holy Ghost. One love dwells in the breast of the undivided Three, we must adore and bless our Lord Jesus Christ and God, even our Father, with equal gratitude.

Still notice that Jesus Christ is here put first, and if the reason be requested, we find it in His meditorial office. He is first to us in our experience. We began our dealings with heaven, not by going to the Father, but to His Son, Jesus Christ. Our Lord has truly said, " No man cometh unto the Father but by Me." All attempts to get to commune with the Father, except through the Son, must be futile. Election by the Father is not first to us, though it stands forth in order of time ; redemption by the Son is our starting point. Not at the throne of sovereignty, but at the cross of dying love, our spiritual life must date its birth. Look to Jesus first, even our Lord Jesus Christ ; and then follow after the Father. I am sure every converted soul here knows that this is the truth, and I would exhort everyone who is seeking salvation, to take care to observe God's order, and remember that the love of the Father will never be perceived by us, nor felt in our hearts, till first of all we go to Jesus Christ, who is the one mediator between God and man.

Note the words of the text again : The love of God to us gives to us the Lord Jesus to be our own Saviour, friend, husband, and Lord. By grace we obtain possession of Jesus Christ—Christ is ours. Observe the word, " Our Lord Jesus Christ." The apostle might have written, " The Lord Jesus Christ " ; but when he was testifying of the great love of God, the article would not have sufficed—he must use a word of possession. Faith looks to Jesus, and finds salvation in that look ; then she grows into assurance, and having used her eyes to look with, she next employs her hands to grasp with. She takes hold of Jesus, and says : " He is all my salvation, He is all my desire, He is my Christ " ; and henceforth assurance speaks not of the Lord Jesus Christ, but of our Lord Jesus Christ. I want you to drink into the love of God this morning from the silver pipe of this thought,—Jesus Christ the Son of the eternal God, who is also a man like yourself, is yours, altogether yours. If you be believers in Him He is from head to foot entirely yours ; in all His offices, in all His attributes, in all that He is, in all that He has done, in all that He is doing, in all that He shall do, He is your Saviour. Though you cannot take Him up in your arms as Simeon did, yet can your faith embrace Him with the like ecstasy, and feel that you have seen God's salvation. Behold what manner of love is revealed in this, that God should give His only Son to us. God commendeth His love to us by this unspeakable gift. Here love has reached its climax. Blessed be the love of God this morning, and for evermore.

Observe that this love displays itself in another shape, for the text goes on to say, " And God, even our Father." He might have said, " God, even the Father." I have no doubt the text does refer to the Father as one person of the blessed Trinity, but it runs thus : " even our Father." A father ! There is music in that word, but not to a fatherless child— to him it is full of sorrowful memories. Those who have never lost a father can scarcely know how precious a relation a father is. A father, who is a father indeed, is very dear ! Do we not remember how we climbed his knee ? Do we not recollect the kisses we imprinted on his cheeks ? Do we not recall to-day with gratitude the chidings of his wisdom and the gentle encouragements of his affection ? We owe, ah ! who shall tell how much we owe to our fathers according to the flesh, and when they are taken from us we lament their loss, and feel that a great gap is made in our family circle. Listen, then, to these words, " Our Father, who is in heaven." Consider the grace contained in the Lord's deigning to take us into the relationship of children, and giving us with the relationship the nature and the spirit of children, so that we say, " Abba, Father." Did you ever lie in bed with your limbs vexed with sore pains, and cry, " Father, pity Thy child ? " Did you ever look into the face of death, and as you thought you were about to depart, cry, " My Father, help me ; uphold me with Thy gracious hand, and bear me through the stream of death ? " It is at such times that we realise the glory of the Fatherhood of God, and in our feebleness learn to cling to the divine strength, and catch at the divine love. It is most precious to think that God is our own Father ! There, now, I cannot talk about it. Upon some themes it would be hard to be silent, but here it is hard to speak. I can but exclaim, " Behold, what manner of love the Father hath bestowed upon us that we should be called the children of God " ; and, having said that, what more remains ?

Before I turn from this gracious and fruitful topic of the love of God, I beg you to notice that it is no new thing, no affair of yesterday. " Our Lord Jesus Christ Himself and God, even our Father, hath loved us " ; He does not tell us when this began, and He could not have done so had He tried. He hath loved us ; loved us when first we came to Him repenting; loved us when we were spending our living with harlots; loved us when we were at the swine trough; loved us when from head to foot we were one mass of defilement. O God, didst Thou love me when I played the rebel—love me when I could blaspheme Thy name? What manner of love is this? Aye, and He loved us ere we had a being; loved us and redeemed us long before we existed; loved us ere this world had sprung out of nothingness; loved us ere the day-star first proclaimed the morning; loved us ere any of the angels had begun to cover their faces with their wings in reverent adoration. From everlasting, the Lord loved His people. Now, again I say, drink into this truth, feed on it; expect us not to expatiate thereon, but contemplate the fact—" Jesus Christ, and God, even our Father, hath loved us."

II. Now we shall turn to the second point, which is THE MANIFESTATIONS OF THIS LOVE. They divide under two heads—" everlasting consolation " and " good hope through grace."

First, God's love has given us everlasting consolation. The Lord found us wretched; when the arrows of conviction were sticking in our hearts we were bleeding to death, and what we wanted, first of all, was to have these wounds staunched; therefore the Lord came to us with consolations. Remember ye not the time when the blood of Jesus Christ flowed warm over your wounds and made them cease to bleed? Have you forgotten the hour when you heard the voice of the Lord saying in the word, " Whosoever believeth in Him is not condemned," and you were enabled to see Jesus Christ as your substitute suffering in your room and stead, and you knew that your sins were forgiven for His name's sake? You have not forgotten that? Well, that was one of the everlasting consolations which He gave you in the time of your distress. Since that day you have had your sorrows, perhaps you have been seldom long without them; but consolation has always followed on the heels of tribulation, and your main consolation has continued to be where it was at the first; you still find the sweetest joy of earth to be looking unto Jesus. When sin rebels you put it down by the self-same grace which overthrew it at the first. Conscience starts and accuses you, and you answer its accusations with that sweet word, " Jesus died for our transgressions, and rose again for our justification." The greatest delight of all is, that this consolation is an everlasting one—other sources of comfort dry up; friends have called to visit you in times of distress, and have suggested pleasant thoughts that have whiled away a mournful hour; but your griefs have returned again, and the passing comfort has been of no further service to you. When a man sees that Jesus Christ took all his sins, and was punished for them, so that the man himself never can be punished again—when he understands that wondrous mystery of substitution, then he gets a consolation which serves him at all times, and in all weathers. Whatever may occur to him he flies to this refuge; and even though he may have fallen into great sin, he knows that the atonement was not made for sham sin, but for real sin; and he resorts again to that same fountain filled with blood, wherein he was once washed, resting fully assured that it will be equal to the washing of him as long as he shall be capable of sin. " Everlasting consolation! " There are some here present who have tried this consolation for forty or fifty years;

dear brethren and sisters, I am sure you do not find it is any the weaker, but on the contrary you understand more of its strength. You are more happy to-day in falling back upon the love of God than you were, and at this moment you feel that in the absence of all other comforts it would suffice you to know that everlasting consolation which is given you in Christ Jesus.

Let us run over for a moment some of our consolations. The first one is, as I have already said, that God hath forgiven us all our transgressions, because Jesus died in our stead. The next consolation is that God loves us, and can never change in His love :—

> " Whom once He loves He never leaves,
> But loves them to the end."

Then we have the grand consolation that the promises of God do not depend upon our faithfulness for their fulfilment but are all stablished and made yea and amen in Christ Jesus. We have this consolation—that our salvation does not depend upon ourselves: as we fell and were lost by the first Adam's unrighteousness, so we have risen and are saved through the second Adam's righteousness, beyond all risk and fear of perishing. We stand upon a firm foundation, not on the shifting sand of creature obedience and faithfulness, but upon the eternal rock of a work which Christ has completed, and over which He sang that joyous pæan,—" It is finished," ere He entered into His rest.

We have also this consolation, that all things work together for good for us who love God and are the called according to His purpose; and again this other consolation, that as long as Christ exists we are as safe, for He has said, " Because I live, ye shall live also." We have this consolation also, that even though we shall sleep in the dust for awhile, yet He hath said it, " I will that they also, whom Thou hast given Me, be with Me where I am; that they may behold My glory." In fact, to tell you all the consolations which God has given us would need many an hour, and fully to enjoy them will occupy your entire lives, for everlasting consolation is not to be spread out before you and done with in the short space of a discourse. Thus much upon one of the first manifestations of divine love.

The next is, He has given us " good hope." Consolation for the present, hope for the future. " Good hope," the hope when days and years are past we all shall meet in heaven; the hope that whatever the future may be, it is full of bliss for us; the hope of immortality for our souls, and of resurrection for our bodies, for when Christ shall come, we also that sleep in Jesus shall come with Him; the hope of reigning with Jesus Christ on earth in the days of His triumph, and reigning with Him for ever and ever in endless felicity. This is our hope, a good hope, for it is based and founded on a good foundation. A fanatic's hope will pass away with the vapours which produced it, but the hope of the true believer is good because it is founded in truth and in grace. " A good hope in grace," is the Greek. If I believed in my own merit, and based my hopes thereon, I should be only self-deceived and blinded, for what merit have I? But if my hope be fixed alone in grace, and that be the sphere in which my consolation and hope are found, then, since God is assuredly gracious, since He has made a covenant of grace with all believers, since He has ratified the covenant by the gift of His own Son, and since He has sworn by

His holiness that He will not lie unto David, a hope founded on His grace is a good hope. Since God will be as good as His word, His hope in grace is good. Here stands the fact : it is written, " He that believeth in the Lord Jesus hath everlasting life." God has covenanted with that man that he shall be saved eternally, and since God cannot lie, the believing man must and shall be saved. Why is it then that some believer's hopes flicker ? Because they get away from a hope in grace, and look towards themselves and their own merits. " Oh," they say, " I have not prayed as I did, I do not feel as I did, therefore, my hope declines." Friend, was your hope founded on your prayers ? was your hope grounded in part upon your feelings ? If so, it may well quiver and tremble ; one of these days it will go down altogether, for the foundation is not able to bear its weight. But if my hope is fixed on this, that God hath promised, and cannot change His promise, I have a good bottom to build on. He will not alter the thing that has gone forth out of His lips : He hath said, " he that believeth and is baptized shall be saved," and He cannot change His own word ; therefore every believer has the promise of eternal life. " But," saith one, " it surprises me to hear you talk so." Does it ? It much more surprises me that I may so speak. It is marvellous to the last degree that God, even our Father, and the Lord Jesus Christ should have given us such a hope as this. I never feel at all astonished at some people's hope when I find that it is this—the hope that if they behave themselves they will get to heaven ; the hope that if they are faithful, God will be faithful. Why ! Any simpleton might have imagined such a hope as that ; but a divine revelation was needed to set before us the great hope of the gospel, and it needs grace-given faith to believe that God will not change nor lie, and, therefore, must save all those who have believed in His Son Jesus Christ. He cannot suffer one of the sheep of Christ to perish, or His promise will be of none effect. " If I believed that," saith one, " it would cause me to lead a careless life." Perhaps it would, but it does not lead true believers to do so ; on the contrary, we feel that if God loves us so, and deals so generously with us, and takes us right away from the whips of Sinai and the covenant of the law, and places us entirely under grace, we love Him as we never loved before, and because of that love sin is hateful to us, and we shun it as a deadly thing ! The law which you think would drive men to holiness has never done it, while the grace which you imagine would lead us to licentiousness binds us with solemn bonds of consecration to serve our God ten times more than before ! Suppose some one were to tell my children that the continuance of my love to them will depend entirely upon their good behaviour. My children would repel the suggestion with indignation. They would answer, " we know better ; you speak falsely ; our father will always love us." Even so the Lord's children know that their Father's love is immutable. For our transgressions, our heavenly Father will visit us with the rod, but never with the sword. He will be angry with us, and chide us, but He will love us just as much when He is angry as He did before ; and as long as ever we are His sons—and that we always must be, for sonship is not a relationship which will ever change—so long will He love us. Do you think that children become disobedient because their relationship is unchangeable ? I never heard of such a thing. They have many reasons for being dis-obedient within their own little wayward hearts, but no child disobeys his father because he always must be his father's child, or because his father loves him. I have heard of one child who said to another, " Come with me, John, and rob an orchard ; your father is so kind he will not beat you if you are found out." The little lad drew himself up, and said, " Do you think because my father is kind to me that, therefore, I will go and vex him ? " This is the holy reasoning of love ; it draws no license from grace, but rather feels the strong constraints of gratitude leading it to holiness. It may be that in unregenerate hearts the love of God, if it could come there, would be turned into an excuse for sin ; but it is not so to us, my brethren. Since the grace of God has made us new creatures in Christ Jesus, the love of God constraineth us not to sin but to walk in holiness all our days. Blessed be His name, then ; we are not ashamed to rejoice that God, even our Father, hath loved us, and given us everlasting consolation and good hope in grace.

III. The last thing is THE PRAYER flowing out of all this. The apostle prays, and we pray this morning, that God would comfort your hearts. This is not spoken of everybody, but of such as believe in the Lord Jesus. It is of the utmost importance that your hearts should be comforted. Cheerfulness, habitual calm, peace of mind, content of spirit,—these ought to be the very atmosphere you breathe ; and Paul thinks it so important that he prays that God Himself, and Christ Himself, may comfort your hearts. I know you have many troubles—how very few are altogether without them ! Some of you are very poor, others suffer heavy losses in business, and exercises of soul, with much trial in the world and in the church. May the good Lord comfort your hearts, speaking not to your ears only, but to your innermost nature. " Let not your heart be troubled, neither let it be afraid." Why, surely, if you believe that God loves you, it ought to make your heart glad ; and if He gives you everlasting consolation you cannot be other wise than happy. I remember well when I was under a sense of sin looking at a dog and wishing I were such as he, that I might die without fear of judgment hereafter, for it seemed so awful a thing to live on for ever as a sinner ; but now, on the other hand, I have sometimes looked at the happiest animals, and I have said to myself, " Ah, but yonder poor creature does not know the love of God, and how thankful I am to God that he has given me the capacity to know Himself." Why, if I could hear of an angel in heaven who did not know the love of God I should pity him. There are kings and mighty emperors who know not the Lord's love, and what poor, pitiable creatures they are. But as for you who rejoice in divine love, I would have you go into the darkest alley if you are forced to live there, and undergo the most wearisome toil if that be your lot—aye, and go home to a per-secuting husband, or a churlish father, and yet hear melodious music ringing in your hearts, for " God, even our Father, which hath loved us, hath given us everlasting consolation and good hope through grace." This is enough to make the wilderness rejoice and blossom as the rose.

The next part of the prayer is that the " Lord would stablish us in every good word and work." I see that the most approved editions of the original have it, " in every good work and word," putting the best first ; and the thought is this, that God would make His people so happy that they would never have an inclination to leave off any good work or word. Depression of spirit often leads to slackness of hand. No doubt many, through sad hearts, have ceased to labour for Christ. A want of gladness has restrained their activity. Now, the apostle would not have any one of us cease from serving God in good works or in good words through a want of consolation. Does God love you ? Do you know it ? How then can you cease from any good work ? Did enemies abuse you for speaking the truth ? Did you say it because you felt you loved God ? Say it again, man ! Say it again ! Did you work in your class without success ? Did you do it because God loved you and you wanted to shew that you loved Him ? Go on, brother ! go on, sister ! success or no success ! God loves you and He has given you everlasting consolation, therefore be stablished in your good work. Have you been accustomed to sing His His praises, and has the devil said, " Leave off ! leave off ! " Have you been accustomed to rebuke sin, and to tell others about the Saviour in your own poor way, and are you getting low in spirit ? Do you doubt your own interest in Christ ? Have you lost the comfort you once enjoyed ? O, dear brother, come back to the old original source of happiness— " Jesus Christ Himself, and God, even our Father, which hath loved us, and given us everlasting consolation and good hope through grace." After refreshing yourself with this blessed truth, you will return with renewed energy to good words and works, and continue in them steadfast, unmoveable, till life's allotted service shall come to a close.

Now and then we become greatly disheartened about the condition of the church. I know I do. I see everywhere Popery spreading, or else rationalism —these rival evils are devouring our country. There is far too little prayerfulness, and too little gospel preaching ; and at times, one is apt to cry out, like Elijah, that no one is left who is faithful to Jehovah— all knees are bowed to Baal ! We must not give way to this feeling, dear friends, for " God, even the Father, hath loved us." When the disciples were too much elated with their success, and came back to Jesus, and said, " Lord, even the devils are subject unto us," Jesus said, " Notwithstanding, in this rejoice not, but rather rejoice because your names are written in heaven." And to-day, when we are depressed with great anxieties, and come back to our Master, and say, " Lord, the devil is getting the upper hand over us " ; He repeats to us the self-same admonition, " Nevertheless do not be depressed about this, but rather rejoice because your names are written in heaven, and your Father hath given you everlasting consolation, and good hope through grace." Stablish your hearts, then, beloved brethren. Be ye " stedfast, unmovable, always abounding in the work of the Lord." Things are not what they seem.

Dark nights are but the prelude to bright days. The rain shall be followed by the clear shining. When truth retreats, she only retires to leap to a greater victory. Though each wave as it comes up upon the shore may die, and you may think that there is no progress, yet the tide is coming in, even Jehovah's tide of everlasting truth which shall cover all the earth. Be not discouraged ! Go to your God. Get away, every man, from your circumstances and from yourselves, and get to your Saviour and your Shepherd ; and there, like sheep in the pasture, lie down to feed ; and then, like sheep obedient to the shepherd, rise up and follow Him whithersoever He goeth. God bless you in this.

Perhaps while I have been preaching, some unconverted person here has been saying—" There is nothing for me." Do you remember, dear friend, what the Syro-Phœnician woman said ? She was called a dog by the Saviour, and that is what you think you are ; but she said, " The dogs eat the crumbs that fall from the master's table." Now, if I called myself a dog, would there be anything in this subject that I might dare to lay hold upon, because, like a crumb, it fell from the table ? Yes. ! It seems to me there is. Evidently God deals with His own people in a way of grace, for it is said, He has " given " us—it is altogether of His free love, and it added— " through grace," or absolute favour. The consolations of the Lord are the gifts of mercy and love ; well, then, if He is gracious to one, why should not He be gracious to another ? And if those who sit at His table were once unclean, and filthy, and depraved, and yet the sovereign grace of God called them and brought them into the banquet of love, why should it not light on me also ? If it is not of him that willeth nor of him that runneth, but of God that showeth mercy, why should He not show mercy to me, whoever I may be ? Why not to me ?

But is there a door through which I can come to the gracious Lord ? Yes, there is, and it is the other crumb in the text, for it begins with " our Lord Jesus Christ." My soul, that is where thou must begin this morning. There is the Lord Jesus Christ. I see Him hanging on the cross bleeding for the sins of others, with hands stretched wide that He may receive sinners to His heart, and that heart has a channel made down to it by the spear, that prayers and tears may find an easy way into His sympathies. Come, my soul, come now, and tell thy case to Jesus. Fellow-sinner, come and confess thy sin to Jesus, and then throw thyself at His feet with this upon thy heart and lips—" If I must perish, I will perish clinging to the cross, declaring to all men that my hope is stayed on Him whom God has set forth to be the propitiation for the sins of man." You will never perish there, sinner. Go there at once, and be safe. God help you for Christ's sake. Amen.

FREE GRACE A MOTIVE FOR FREE GIVING

" Now our Lord Jesus Christ Himself, and God, even our Father, which hath loved us, and hath given us everlasting consolation and good hope through grace, comfort your hearts, and stablish you in every good word and work."— 2 Thessalonians ii. 16, 17.

THE Thessalonian saints had been much persecuted and afflicted, and they had exhibited great faith, insomuch that Paul says, " We ourselves glory in you in the church of God for your patience and faith." As if they had not enough trouble coming from the outside, there sprang up in their midst certain hot-headed teachers who declared that the day of Christ was immediately at hand. The coming of the Lord is the grandest hope of the church, and it is an evidence of the extreme power of error to poison and pervert truth that a hope which is our brightest consolation can be so twisted as to cause the saints to be " shaken in mind " and troubled. So it appears to have been with the Thessalonians. They were perplexed with mysterious rumours, which the zealots probably supported by a misinterpretation of the apostle's own language in his former letter to them. It would appear that they were tempted to leave their regular habits of life : and some of them neglected their business upon the theory that there was no need to attend to it, because the world was so speedily to be at an end. This gave an occasion for " busybodies " to cease from working, and create great disquietude among the more sober members, and therefore Paul wrote them this second letter, with the earnest intent that they might be established in the truth and kept from evil, that disorderly walking might be repressed, and that the church might be at peace. Paul felt that it was of the utmost importance that this honourable church should be at rest, and should not lack consolation, either as to its bitter persecutions or its internal difficulties.

My subject this morning leads me to make this the first point to be dwelt upon—*it is most important that believers should enjoy consolation.* When I have for a while spoken upon that, I would with delight expatiate upon the fact that *this consolation is most freely provided and bestowed in the gospel of our Lord Jesus Christ ;* and it is from this subject that I purpose to draw a practical inference which may help the collection for the hospitals, namely, that the freeness with which *these consolations are given to us should lead us to a holy benevolence towards others who need consolation.*

I. First, then, IT IS OF THE UTMOST IMPORTANCE THAT BELIEVERS SHOULD ENJOY CONSOLATION. We must not say that it does not matter whether we are doubting or believing, whether we are sighing or rejoicing : it does matter a great deal. Every commander knows that if he has not his soldiers in good heart, there may be a great many of them, and they may be well trained for war, but the battle is not likely to be won. Courage is essential to valour. Much depends upon the case in which a man finds himself upon the eve of conflict. If the soldier has no stomach for the fight, as our fore-fathers were wont to say, he will make a sorry display when the tug of war comes on. The Lord delights not to see His people with their heads hanging down like bulrushes, depressed and dismayed. His word to them is, " Be strong ; fear not." He is " the blessed God," and He would have those who know His glorious gospel to live a life of blessedness, that they may the better serve Him. Does not His Spirit say, " Rejoice in the Lord alway : and again I say, Rejoice " ? Has He not given the Comforter, that He may continually console us ? Believers will far better answer the Lord's purpose, and bring more glory to His name, if they are filled with peace and joy in believing, than they will if they yield to despondency ; for the Scripture saith, " the joy of the Lord is your strength."

I am sure that the Lord would have us be of good courage, for its importance is *implied in the very existence of our text.* It is the prayer of an inspired man. Paul wrote not only at the dictate of brotherly love, but under the guidance of the Holy Ghost, when he penned this prayer, " Now our Lord Jesus Christ Himself, and God, even our Father, comfort your hearts, and stablish you in every good word and work." The Holy Spirit moved the man of God to breathe this desire, and to put it on record, that it might be the desire of all good men as long as ever the epistle should be read, and that all Christian men should value consolation, even as it was valued by one who was a tender lover of the flock of Christ. It would be great presumption on our part lightly to esteem that which was a prime matter of concern with so instructed and experienced a teacher as the apostle to the Gentiles.

Paul puts this prayer into a very remarkable shape : to my mind it is expressed in a deeply solemn form, for he writes, " Now our Lord Jesus Christ *Himself.*" Was there need for that word " Himself " ? Does it not make it very emphatic that he seems to call upon the Lord Jesus to give them comfort, not by any intermediate agency, but in His own person and by His own power. It is so essential that we should be comforted that Jesus, even our own Lord Jesus Christ, is entreated Himself to become the consolation of His people. Is not that a weighty matter which leads the reverent heart of Paul thus to plead ? Nor is this all, for he goes on to say, " and God, even our Father " : as if God the Father Himself must undertake the work of cheering His people, so needful was it that they should be at rest. No one else could give them such comfort as they required, but God could do it, and therefore " God, even our Father " must be specially invoked. The prayer is that the Lord Jesus and the Father who are one may join in the most needful work of comforting the hearts of the tried Thessalonian saints. It reminds me of Paul's solemn benediction in the opening of the epistle, " Grace unto you, and peace, from God our Father and the Lord Jesus Christ." This prayer of inspiration, couched in such solemn terms and directed so earnestly to the Lord Jesus Christ Himself, and to God, even our Father, proves the importance and necessity of saints being filled with comfort.

Nor is this the only instance in the epistle where this desire is expressed, for a little further on, in the third chapter, at the sixteenth verse, we have it in other words but with equal forcefulness : " Now the Lord of peace Himself give you peace always by all means." I do not know that in one single sentence there could be compressed a more intense desire that they may be at peace. " The Lord " is invoked, and He is styled " the Lord of peace," that all His divine majesty may be seen, and His peace-making power may be displayed. " The Lord of peace " is entreated to give peace, not by His angels nor by His ministers, nor by His providence, but " Himself " to give peace ; and this is asked for " always," " give you peace always." Peace in the cool of the evening is not enough, it is needed at all parts of the day, in all the days of the year, in every period of life, in every place, and under all circumstances. The wish is expressed with great breadth in the words, " Give you peace always *by all means ":* if it cannot be brought by one means let it be by another, but somehow or other may you enjoy the peace which the Lord alone can create. I cannot imagine that such a prayer as this would have been placed among the Scriptures of truth, which are to be our guide till the Lord cometh, unless it had been of the utmost importance that we should enjoy peace of mind.

The apostle almost hints at one reason for this strong necessity, for in one word he lets us see that it is a vital blessing because *it affects the Christian's heart*. His expression is, "Comfort your hearts." It is well to have a strong hand, how else shall we labour ? It is well to have a firm tread, how else shall we stand ? Yet these are secondary matters as compared with a healthy heart. A disease of the heart is an injury to the whole man. If anything goes amiss at the fountain the streams of life soon feel it. The entire manhood depends upon the heart ; hence the need of comfort for the heart, and the value of the promise " He shall strengthen thine heart." It is a calamity when the springs of action are weakened, and the spirit is made to sink. " The spirit of a man will sustain his infirmity, but a wounded spirit who can bear ? " Touch the flesh where else you will, but spare the brain and the heart, for these are the man so nearly, that he is wounded to the quick when these are hurt. When the spirits begin to sink then the waters have come in, even into the soul. Hence our Lord said to His disciples, " Let not your heart be troubled." However your house may be troubled, however your bodily frame may be troubled, " let not your heart be troubled ; ye believe in God, believe also in Me." Faith upholds the heart, and enables the man to bear up under pressure ; faith, I say, and nothing else. I am sure, dear friends, you will clearly see the need that we should be comforted, because the want of comfort will grievously affect the action of the heart and mar the entire life-force of our being. See ye to it, then, that ye lift up the hands that hang down, and confirm the feeble knees, by saying to them that are of a feeble heart, " Be strong, fear not." Ask that the heart may rejoice in God, for then the roughness of the way and the stress of the weather will be matters of small concern.

Brethren beloved, *this confidence is needful to prevent impatience* and other evils. Possibly it was the lack of comfort which led certain of the Thessalonians to preach the immediate coming of the Lord : their impatience excited the wish, and the wish led on to the assertion. When men lose the present comfort of plain gospel doctrines they are very apt to begin speculating, and in carnal heat foretelling the coming of the Lord. They left that patient waiting which is our duty, for a fevered prophesying which is nowhere encouraged in the word of God. Hence the apostle said to them in the fifth verse of the third chapter, " The Lord direct your hearts into the love of God, and into the patient waiting for Christ." A man does not wait patiently when he is low in spirit and weary at heart. Let a man feel his own heart right with God, and be at peace, and he can quietly wait until Christ comes, even though the Lord shall delay His coming for many a day : but when everything is tossed about, and our hope grows dim, and our fellowship is broken, and our zeal is burning low, we jump at anything which will end the struggle and enable us to avoid further effort. Laziness and despondency lead many to cry, " Why are His chariots so long in coming ? " just as idle workmen long for Saturday night. You think time too long and life too long, for you are not happy where your Lord has placed you, and you are eager to rush out of the field of service into the chamber of rest. This will not do, my brethren, either for you or for me. We must be braced up to further labour. We must receive comfort in our spirit that we may be able patiently to toil on, however long life may be, and however long our Lord may delay ; for if not, if we grow impatient, we may resort to rash fanatical action, as I have already shown you that certain Thessalonians did. Under the idea that the Lord was coming they neglected their daily calling, and became busybodies, gadding about from house to house, and loafing upon others who did not pretend to be quite so spiritual. They were mere star-gazers, looking for the advent with their mouths open and their eyes up-turned, being evermore in grievous danger of falling into a ditch. Paul bade them get to work and eat their own bread, quoting himself as an example, for he had wrought with labour and travail night and day that he might not be chargeable to them.

My friend, if you are growing impatient for the day of the Lord, I pray that comfort of heart may cool you. To-morrow morning take down the shop shutters and sell your goods as if Christ were not coming at all, for should He come you will be all the more fit to meet Him for being engaged in your calling. If I knew that the Lord would come to-morrow I should attend to my regular Monday duties, and on no account leave one of them to go and stand at the window, looking for wonders. Whether the Master comes to-morrow or in a thousand years your wisest course is to follow your calling in His fear and for His sake. We ought to do our work better under the impression that perhaps He may come and find us at it ; but we may not neglect our duty under pretence of His appearing. Of this, however, be sure, you will not patiently wait if you are not happy. You will not go on conscientiously plodding, doing the same work, walking in the same regular way, unless your heart is stayed upon God. You will run after this novelty or that if your mind is not resting in Jesus. Hence the devout prayer of our text that God our Father and our Lord Jesus Christ Himself may comfort our hearts and stablish us in every good word and work.

Once more, I am sure this comfort is eminently desirable, because *it promotes fruitfulness*. The apostle more than hints at this : " Comfort your hearts and stablish you in every good word and work." When we are not happy in the Lord we do not give ourselves heartily to His service. We grow impatient, and then we need the exhortation of the thirteenth verse of the third chapter, " But ye, brethren, be not weary in well doing." If we feel that Jesus is ours, that all things are working for our good, and that eternal glory is secured to us by a sure covenant, we are moved by gratitude to complete consecration, for the love of Christ constraineth us. Doubts and disquietudes take us off from our Master's work, but when He gives us rest we take His yoke upon us cheerfully, and find in it yet further rest unto our souls. When our hearts sing our hands toil, and we cannot do enough for our Redeeming Lord. Right gladly do we present ourselves as living sacrifices to Him who " loved us and gave Himself for us." Thus, too, we are stablished in our work, and bound with fresh bonds to it, so that we delight to labour on till He shall come who shall say, " Well done, good and faithful servant : enter thou into the joy of thy Lord."

So it all comes to this. We, who are constitutionally despondent, must not give way to depression ; we must cry to God to help us by the divine Comforter. We must aim at being cheerful Christians. We have abundant reasons for being cheerful, for the Father Himself loveth us, and hath given us everlasting consolation in Christ Jesus. Do not let us be so unwise, and so ungrateful, as to neglect these consolations of the Spirit. If the table be sumptuously spread why should we be hungry ? If the fountain flows so freely why should we be thirsty ? Moreover, mayhap, if we wear a darksome countenance we may distress the weak ones in the family of God ; it may be that we shall spread the infection of depression among our fellow believers, and this must not be. Let us wear our sackcloth on our loins if we must wear it, but let us not wave it in everybody's face, lest we offend against the generation of the Lord's people. Is it not clear from the Word, brethren, that we shall be damaged if we give way to apprehension and dismay ? Is it not apparent that we are invigorated, equipped, and prepared for our Lord's use when we are strong in the Lord and the power of His might ? Therefore let us breathe earnestly to God the desire that His everlasting consolation may be laid home to our spirits, and that our hearts may be comforted at this moment.

II. We shall now turn to the second point of our meditation, which is this : GOSPEL CONSOLATION IS MOST FREELY BESTOWED. I want, in the chief place, to call your attention to the manner in which all the way through the freeness of divine consolation is set before us by the apostle.

First, observe that the consolations bestowed upon believers are most free because *they are described as a gift.* " Now our Lord Jesus Christ Himself, and God, even our Father, which hath loved us, and hath *given us* everlasting consolation." The old proverb hath it, " Nothing is freer than a gift." Every blessing that we receive from God comes as a gift. We have purchased nothing : what have we to purchase it with ? We have earned nothing : what work did we ever do that could deserve everlasting consolation from the hand of the great Lord ? Comfort in Christ is an absolutely free, spontaneous gift of sovereign grace, given not on account of anything we have done, or ever shall do, but because the Lord has a right to do as He wills His own ; therefore doth He select unto Himself a people, to whom the free gift of His consolation shall be given. If thou hast any comfort at this time, my brother, it is God's gift to thee. If thou dost triumph in God, it is God who hath given thee thy holy joy, therefore bless and praise Him from whom such a boon has come.

The freeness of this gift is seen in every part of it. The consolation given us of God is very complete, but it is as manifestly free as it is evidently perfect. Notice its completeness, I pray you. It covers *the past* with these golden words, " which hath loved us " : as for *the present*, it is enriched with this truth, " hath given us everlasting consolation " ; and as for *the future*, it is glorified with this blessing, " and good hope through grace." Here is a triple comfort, a consolation in three worlds, and under each aspect it is a free favour. He " hath loved us " —why is this ? Come, ye wise men, pry into the ancient past, and tell me why God loved His chosen. Stand and gaze as long as you will into the eternal mind, and say to yourself, why did God make this choice of love ? The sole reply out of the excellent glory falls from Jesus' lips : " Even so Father, for so it seemed good in Thy sight." Shall not the bridegroom elect his own bride ? Shall not the King of kings dispense His favours as He wills ? He hath loved us " from before the foundation of the world " : a love so ancient cannot have been born of any human cause. Eternal love is a flame enfolding itself ; it borrows no fuel from without, but lives upon itself. He says, " I have loved thee with an everlasting love, therefore with lovingkindness have I drawn thee " ; but why that everlasting love we cannot tell. Beloved, by divine love the mysterious past is made to glow with the glory of God : its light is like a stone most precious, even like a jasper stone, clear as crystal. Once when we looked back into the past we saw the blackness of our guilt, and the hole of the pit whence we were digged ; but now we behold a silver stream of mercy flowing from the throne of God and of the Lamb, and we track it to the eternal purpose of love and the covenant of grace. Gaze as you can into light ineffable, but even with the eye of faith all that you can discern in the ages which are past is this word, which hath a splendour about it beyond compare—the word " LOVE." In eternity the Lord loved us. Oh, how free is this ! How much we owe for it ! The past is bright with love, with love most free. As for the *present*, " He hath given us everlasting consolation." We have it now. Christ is His people's Christ to-day : the consolation of Israel even now. The pardon of sin is ours, the perfect righteousness of Christ is ours, life in Christ is ours, union to Christ is ours, marriage to Christ is ours. Glory with Christ shall be ours by-and-by, but even now we have the earnest of it in the Spirit which dwells within us, and shall be with us for ever. All this is assuredly a gift : how could it be otherwise ? We could never have enjoyed this everlasting consolation to-day if free grace and dying love had not brought it to us. Bless, then, the Giver. As for *the future*, what of that ? Dark lower the clouds, and the tempest mutters from afar, and we tremble lest in the end of life, when physical force decays, we may be overtaken with a storm in the article of death ; but this covers all, we have " good hope through grace." The Scriptures of truth have assured us that the great Shepherd will be with us in the valley of death-shade, and that after death there is a resurrection, and that with our risen body we shall behold the King in His beauty when He shall stand in the latter days upon the earth, and we shall in our perfect manhood dwell for ever in His glory. This is so good a hope that it fills all the future with music. This, too, is a gift. There is not a trace of legal claim in it ; it comes not by way of reward, but of divine favour. Thus the past, the present, the future are all rich with the Lord's own generous gifts, and in nothing can we trace a single consolation to anything but free grace.

Lest we should make any mistake about these consolations coming to us most freely, the apostle mentions One from whose hand they come, from whom nothing has ever come in other manner but that of manifest grace. He mentions " *our Lord Jesus Christ Himself.*" Oh it charms me to think that He should comfort me ! When Jesus Christ begins to draw near a man's soul His joy begins ; but when the Lord sets Himself down steadily to console His brethren, I warrant you it is done in heavenly style ; for He will not fail nor be discouraged. He will wash our feet if the weariness be there ; He will give His bosom for a pillow to our head if the pain be there. He hath said, " I will make all his bed in his sickness," so that if the woe comes from disease He will cheer us there. He will anoint our eyes with eye-salve if the eyes are failing, and bind up the broken heart if that be bleeding. Lest we fall He will put underneath us the everlasting arms, and lest we be wounded He will spread over us the shadow of His wing. He will be all to us that He is in Himself : judge ye what that is. His whole being : His godhead in its grandeur, His humanity in its tenderness He hath given to us. He layeth Himself out for us, and be ye sure of this, He will not leave us comfortless, He will come to us. He is such a blessed sympathiser in all grief, such a mighty helper in all distress, that if He come to our succour we may be sure that our deliverance will be accomplished. But, brethren, at the sight of our loving Lord we feel that it would be treason to impute His benefits to any motive but that of grace. Is He not full of grace and truth ? The law came by Moses, not by Jesus. His coming was not to judge and to censure : " God sent not His Son into the world to condemn the world," much less did He send His Son to condemn His people. There will come a day of judgment, but just now the Son of God sits upon His throne to grant pardons, and to give grace to help in times of need : His throne is a throne of grace, and His sceptre is that of love. We know that the comforts of the gospel must be graciously free since they are brought to us by Jesus Christ Himself.

Then the apostle solemnly adds, " and God our Father." There seems to me to be a peculiar touch of sweetness about this. It is not " God the Father " —which notes His relation to Jesus, but our Father, which set forth His relation to us. We love God the Father ; unto the Father be glory for ever and ever : but as " our Father " He comes nearer to us, and gladdens our hearts. Now, a father does not pay wages to his children, his gifts to them are freely bestowed out of the love of his fatherly heart. What father expects to be paid for what he does for his sons and daughters ? Thus we see that the everlasting consolations of the gospel, coming to us because we are the children of God, are quite free from anything which makes them a hire or a debt, and they come to us in the freest possible manner, as spontaneous donations of our great Father, whose delight it is to give good gifts to them that ask Him.

Cannot you look up, you desponding ones, at this moment, and cry, " Our Father " ? Our first hymn greatly refreshed my spirit just now, for I felt very heavy till the Holy Ghost comforted me with it :

" If in my Father's love
I share a filial part,
Send down Thy Spirit, like a dove,
To rest upon my heart."

and felt that I could urge that argument, and in my inmost heart I pleaded it before the Lord :—Oh, if I be indeed Thy child and Thou be a Father to me, then deal with me as with a son, and let me feel Thy Spirit resting within my bosom, that I may know myself to be Thine beyond a doubt. O how sweet to feel the Spirit's witness and to cry, " Abba, Father " ! Now, beloved, the spirit of adoption is never a spirit of bondage or legality : it never boasts of human merit, but its one song is " free grace and dying love." May our Father's free favour make your hearts to sing concerning this, and I know that this will be your strain—

" Behold what wondrous grace
The Father hath bestow'd
On sinners of a mortal race
To call them sons of God ! "

Look at the text again, and you will see how explicit Paul is upon one point. To make us see the freeness of those consolations which come to God's troubled people, he writes it, " Our Lord Jesus Christ Himself, and God, even our Father, which hath loved us." Divine love is the foundation of our consolation. No everlasting consolation could have visited our hearts if the Father and the Son had not loved us. I always feel inclined to sit down when my ministry causes me to come across the great truth of God's love to His people : because it is not so much a truth to speak upon with the tongue as to enjoy in silence in the heart. I can fully understand that God should pity my misery ; I can comprehend God's caring for my weakness ; but I am filled with sacred amazement when I am told that He loves me. Loves me ! What can there be in me for the Holy Ghost to love ! Brother, what can there be in you that Jesus should set His heart on you ? He has made us, and not we ourselves : does the potter fall in love with his own clay ? Will he die to save a broken vessel ? There were other creatures fairer far. Why were angels passed by ? Wonder of wonders that the Lord should love us poor nobodies, defiled with sin, with such evil tempers and such strange natures ; ah, me, with such estranged natures ! which is far worse. That the Lord our God should love us, that Christ should love us so as actually to have died for us, outmiracles all the miracles of His power. Jesus so loved us that He espoused our nature, occupied our dwelling-place, the world ; took our burden of sin, carried our cross, and laid in our grave ! They say that love is blind : I will not say that our Redeemer's love is of that sort, far rather will I say that it must have been wonderfully quick-sighted love to have been able to perceive anything lovable in us. Yet is His love the source and fountain of all our mercies. He hath loved us. Question there can be none that this is free : for love is unpurchasable ; if a man should give all the substance of his house for love it would utterly be condemned. Love goes not in the market, it knows nothing of price, or barter : it must go forth unbribed, unhired, or not at all, in any case ; and far more in the instance of the eternal love of the great Father, and His only begotten Son. Price and purchase for divine love ? Wherein would such an insinuation fall short of blackest blasphemy ?

Yet again, observe that as if the apostle feared that we should get away from this doctrine of grace he added, " He hath given us everlasting consolation and good hope through grace." Some people do not like the sound of that word " grace." It is too Calvinistic. We do not care what you call it, but it is the very best word in the Bible next to the name of God our Saviour. It is from the grace of God that all our hope begins. Man as a rebel can never earn anything but damnation through his own merits : grace must reign, or man must die. Every blessing that can ever come to condemned sinners such as we are must come because God's great love wills it to come, because " He is gracious and full of compassion." All other roads are broken up ; grace alone bridges the chasm, and makes a way for traffic between heaven and earth. Grace reigns in our spiritual comfort, and grace alone; let us glorify God for it.

Everlasting consolation is not a blessing given to us as the result of our own works. This is most clear from the last part of our text, for there it is asked that the Lord may comfort our hearts, not because we are stablished in every good word and work, but that we may be so. All the good works which adorn the Christian character are the result of God's grace, and not the cause of it. Grace is given us in order that we may serve God, not because we do serve God. To make us holy is the object of divine grace, but grace did not wait until it found us holy, or it would never have visited us.

To close this part of the subject I would remark that this is the reason why the consolations which God gives us are *everlasting*. Dwell on that word "everlasting." Do not suffer anyone to fritter away its meaning. You may safely forget that there are certain folks alive who declare that everlasting has not the meaning of endless duration, for it means that or nothing. We have too much personal interest involved in this word to allow it to be toned down into age-lasting or any other miserable sense. We should as soon think that the Bible meant the opposite of what it seems to do as believe that everlasting means something temporary. He has given us everlasting consolation, and the reason why it is everlasting is because it is founded on the grace of God. If it were built upon our merits it would stand upon a foundation of ice or mist; it would rest on a shadow buttressed by a dream : but if God loved us out of pure grace, and if Jesus Christ has given us consolation out of pure love, and if our whole comfort rests upon the sovereign grace of God in Christ Jesus, then there is no reason why it should ever pass away unless God's grace can evaporate, which cannot be, since God changeth not, but must be for evermore the same. Our Lord Jesus changeth not, for He is the "same yesterday, to-day, and for ever." Ah, you high-fliers, who derive a lofty comfort from your feelings, your happy sensations, your holy works, and your belief that sin is dead in you, fly away as much as you can, you will be brought down one of these days ! Like Icarus in the Grecian fable, who flew so high that he melted the wax of his wings and fell, so will it be with all who venture aloft on wings of self-confidence. He who lies humbly at God's feet, conscious of his sin, and mourning over it, and resting for everything upon sovereign grace and free mercy in Christ Jesus, he may keep where he is with safety, for his hope shall never fail him. Let the Lord be magnified for this; He is our rock, and there is no unfaithfulness in Him, and He that resteth in Him shall not be ashamed or confounded world without end.

III. So far have I brought you; now for our closing point, which is a practical one. Since THESE CONSOLATIONS OF GOD'S LOVE HAVE BEEN SO FREELY BESTOWED UPON US THEY SHOULD LEAD US TO A LIFE OF HOLY BENEVOLENCE. We ought to be free in our giving to others, since God has been so free in His giving to us. As He has abounded toward us in infinite liberality we ought to abound towards all with whom we come in contact up to the full measure of our ability, in all love and kindness and mercy.

In every benevolent enterprise Christian men should take a hearty interest. Read that seventeenth verse—

"Comfort your hearts, and stablish you in *every good word and work.*" I am a man, and being a man, everything that concerns men concerns me. I am a Christian man, and as a follower of Christ, the Son of man, everything that can do good to my fellow-men is a matter in which I delight to take my share.

This should be done in direct actions as well as in words. Read—"Stablish you in every good word *and work.*" Certain of the oldest manuscripts run "In every good work and word," and I suppose in our new translation we shall have it so, and very properly too. In this case work is probably first, and word next. Some Christian people think that "word" should be everything and work nothing, but the Scriptures are not of their mind. These professors speak a great deal about what they will do, talk a great deal about what other people ought to do, and a great deal more about what others fail to do ; and so they go on with word, word, word, and nothing else but word. They do not get as far as "work," but the apostle put work first in this case, as much as to say, "whether you talk about it or not, *do it.* Be stablished in every good work even if you do not get so far as being capable of a multiplicity of words." Brethren, let us yoke word and work together : every good thing should command our advocacy and secure our aid to the fun of our ability. Direct practical assistance should be rendered by us all, since our Lord loves not in word only but in deed and in truth.

This should be done without pressure. No one could lay constraint upon God to bless His people, no pressure was put upon Christ to redeem us ; everything as we have shown was spontaneous, sovereign, free. Even so should men give to God out of an overflowing heart. Give to Him as a king giveth to a king. How does a king give ? Why, as he likes, and that is the way to give, to give because you are delighted to give ; not because you feel obliged to do it by being overlooked by others, but out of a royal heart which delights in liberal things. Shall you not do as you will with your own ? How can a gracious heart better please itself than by doing good ? Give as you would give to a king, for we never give our meaner possessions to royal personages ; we give the best we have if we give them anything. Let it be so in all the services that we render to God : let Him have our best, our noblest, our dearest possessions.

The particular case before us this morning is, to my mind, a very important one, and one which should greatly move all generous spirits. In this great city of near upon four millions of inhabitants, the provision of hospital accommodation is small to a painful degree. In those hospitals which will be helped by the collections of to-day, I think there are only 5,531 beds, or about one for 723 persons. Considering the liability of working men to disease and accident, and the great number of the poorer classes, this is a fearfully small preparation for possible necessity. But this is not the worst, for out of these 5,000 beds, as I gather from an admirable paper in *The Lancet*, there are never more than 3,232 in daily use, thus diminishing the supply to an appalling extent. These empty beds are very largely made so by the lamentable fact that the hospitals have not the means of using them. The depression in trade has been felt by our free hospitals to such an extent that they live from hand to mouth in a manner which is not honourable to one of the wealthiest cities in the world. The Hospital Sunday Collection has not yet come up to the proper mark, and it is time for ministers to say so, and instruct their people, who if they knew the need would promptly supply it. *The Lancet* wisely says that if the sermons of to-day could be preached in the hospitals themselves, the collections would be doubled. There are many objections to carrying out the suggestion, but I have no doubt the result would be as anticipated. Suppose me, then, to be preaching in one of the great wards and yourselves to be standing among the beds, I know those poor creatures lying near you writhing in pain, and those others grateful for the relief they have received, would plead much more forcibly than I can. The sight of suffering is the best argument with benevolence. Look at the rows of sick folk and let your heart be touched. As the service could not well be held in the hospital, *The Lancet* suggests that the ministers should spend Saturday in going over a hospital. I could not very well do that, but I have tried in my mind vividly to realize the scene, and I think most of you are quite as able to draw the picture as I am, for you have been there to see for yourselves, and some of you have been there as patients to partake for yourselves in hospital benefits. Picture the wards of mercy, and let every sick person there entreat you to help the funds of these admirable institutions. An exceedingly powerful plea to my mind arises from those empty beds. There they are, two thousand of them! Waiting to be couches of hope to the suffering. Alas, they cannot be filled because there is not the means for providing the people with food and nourishment while they are there. Sorrowful necessity! I cannot endure to think of it. A bed for a sick man rendered useless by some one's meanness! Where is the niggard? Surely he is not here!

It would be even more painful to go to the homes where those persons who ought to occupy those empty beds are pining for the want of the hospital help, waiting the next turn—which turn may find them in the grave—but which turn would come to-morrow morning if funds were forthcoming. Must they lie there till they are beyond the reach of surgical help because the wealthy of this so-called Christian city cannot spare a little from their luxuries to furnish poor sick humanities with nutriment? O that one with a trumpet tongue could speak to our nobles, our merchants, our traders, our gentlemen of leisure, and bid them consider the sick poor. O that they all knew the exquisite luxury of doing good! I would say to employers, will you let these people lie and pine away for want of medical help, many of them your workmen whose strength has been spent in your trades and handicrafts? Pain is crushing them, and provision is made for their help and cure, as far as it can be made, but it is rendered useless by the want of money to bear the expenses of the patients. Is this to be always so? Is this to remain so for another year? Surely it shall not be.

I ask you, dear friends, according as God has entrusted you with this world's wealth, to help the hospitals. I do this with all the greater confidence, because you are believers in the doctrines of free grace. Give freely, for you have received freely. Remember that yesterday and to-day Jews, Catholics, Protestants, people of all sects have heartily joined in this common effort for suffering humanity, and if those who believe in the free grace of God are behind-hand, nay, if they are not among the foremost in the race, it will be the dishonour of the glorious gospel which they profess. The Lord accept your offerings as you now present them! I hear the sound of your gold and silver already, for you are eager in the work of mercy. The collectors are a little too rapid in their work, but I will not restrain them, for it is a fit ending to my discourse that you should hasten to pass from word to work. In so doing may God bless you. Amen.

THE LOVE OF GOD AND THE PATIENCE OF CHRIST

"And the Lord direct your hearts into the love of God, and into the patient waiting for Christ."—2 Thessalonians iii. 5.

FOR the moment, Paul in spirit is coasting the purple shores of the celestial country. With his Thessalonian friends he is making a joyful voyage within hail of Immanuel's land. The sail is bright with the sunlight, and the keel is marking a silver track behind it. The apostle's happy soul has left far in the stern the deceivableness of unrighteousness and the rocks of error. It comes into his heart that he would gladly steer his friends into certain of those lovely creeks which run up far into the inner recesses of the sacred fatherland. Shall he turn the helm that way? He pauses; for the navigation is difficult. One must be greatly expert to thread the streams which descend from the sunny fountains. It is not given even to all saints to follow safely all the windings of the rivers of delight. Paul had been with his brethren to sea in the place where the Lord sank all their transgressions in the depths, and he had been with them in sore affliction when neither sun nor moon appeared, and in all such seafaring he was in his element; but, brave pilot as he was, he could not pretend to penetrate all the richer and rarer experiences which bring elect souls nearest to the heart of the great Father; and therefore, instead of offering to be their pilot, he bowed his head, and prayed, " The Lord direct your hearts into the love of God, and into the patient waiting for Christ."

The special entrance into the goodly land, which the apostle desired for his friends, was one which mere insight, wit, knowledge, or instruction could never give them. If so, he would have directed their minds that way at once. But the perception of the heavenlies is only given to heavenly faculties. The attainments which Paul desired for his friends were not beliefs of the head, but indwellings of the heart. To return to our figure of sailing up the creeks and rivers into the centre of the glorious country—that delicious voyage was only possible to the more refined and spiritual powers of the soul. Those sweet waters could only be navigated by the heart, and the heart itself would need divine direction before it could find the entrance to them. There is a path which the vulture's eye has not seen, and the lion's whelp hath not trodden : only God seeth and knoweth it The Beulah country of spiritual wisdom, especially in its higher reaches, is a matter for personal revelation from God to each one of His own. We are here hopelessly in the dark if we have no light from above ; and even with that light we do but see the difficult nature of our way, and fail to enter upon it, until the light becomes a force, and He whom we desire to know directs our hearts into communion with Himself. Yes, yonder are the radiant coasts, and the rivers of life up which our barque might sail into the centre of "the island of the innocent"; yet our great apostle does not rush into the office of pilot, but humbly acts as intercessor, crying, "The Lord direct your hearts into the love of God."

All this whets our desires ! Who would not wish to go where only choice spirits can enter, and where these can only come as the Lord directs their hearts ?

Paul could give his converts external directions, he could guide his more advanced brethren in the work, walk, and warfare of life ; and he did so with all simplicity and earnestness. He urged them to abound in this grace, and to avoid that folly ; but he felt that this exhortation would be inefficient unless their hearts were touched. Here he felt his own powerlessness, and so he cast the grand matter of heart-work upon the Lord Himself. As the heart naturally baffles all physicians, so spiritually it is far beyond our knowledge. Who among ministers can guide you ? Therefore may "the Lord direct your hearts."

God alone knows the heart, and God alone can rule it : for this ruling Paul makes request. "The Lord direct your hearts." Let us borrow his prayer, and turn it to our own personal use : "*Domine dirige nos.*"

The place for God in reference to the heart is that of supreme director. When the Lord lays His hand on the heart, which is the helm of the ship, then the whole vessel is rightly directed : this, therefore, is what we beseech Him to do. When the Holy Spirit comes into the heart, and takes supreme control of the affections, then the whole life and conversation are after a godly sort. Oh, that He may prove this fact to each one of us ! Some think much of liberty : I long far more to be in perfect subjection to the Lord my God. Oh, how I wish for a Master, a Dictator, a Director ! Oh, that my Lord would take the reins, and bring my every thought into captivity to His own will, henceforth and for ever !

What a heavenly content I feel in yielding myself to the sacred Trinity ! The God who made us may most fitly be called upon to govern us. When we recognize the glory of the whole Godhead, we perceive the perfect suitability of such direction as will come from the Three-One God. Albeit that the Holy Spirit is not mentioned in this verse by name, yet He is mentioned by His operations, for it is the Spirit of God that deals with the hearts of believers. I take rare pleasure in our text because we have the blessed Trinity in unity in these few words, "The Lord "— that is, the Holy Spirit who dwells within believers— "direct your hearts into the love of God (by whom I understand the Father), and into the patient waiting for Christ." May the Trinity in unity work with us, and fulfil in each of us this prayer of the apostle, that our hearts may be directed into the love of God, and into the patient waiting for Christ !

Paul would have his Thessalonian friends advance in a straight line. Our heart is to be as a vessel that is not left to beat about, not to come into harbour by a circuitous route; but is steered directly into the fair haven. May the Spirit of God take us and give us a straight tendency towards the holiest things, and then at once bring us into the love of God, and into the patient waiting for Christ.

But here we must do a little translating or interpreting. Observe in the Revised Version a difference of translation. There we read "into the patience *of* Christ." This is a great improvement upon our former translation ; but, although it is accurate it is not complete : it does not take up the whole of the meaning. In our Authorized Version we have "the patient waiting for Christ," but in its margin we find "into the patience of Christ"; showing that the earlier translators felt that "the patience of Christ" would be a good translation ; and yet, after considering it in all its bearings, they thought that Paul did not quite mean the patience *of Christ*, but that he meant a patience which we exert *towards Christ*. Is there not weight in this ? Does not the context support it ? As the love into which we are do be directed is love to God, so the patience into which we are to be directed must be a patience towards Christ, Our grand old translators expressed this truth by language which may be inaccurate as mere wording, but it is deeply correct as to its sense. Surely Paul did mean "the patience towards Christ which manifests itself in the patient waiting for Christ." If you consider all this, you will see that we have no infant-class lesson in the text before us ! Here are nuts for young men who have cut their wisdom-teeth. May the good Spirit help us to reach the kernels.

Having turned the text over many times, I thought that we might be able to gather up a considerable amount of its real meaning if we thought of it thus : first, *here are two precious things for us to enter into*—the love of God and the patience of Christ ; and, secondly, *here are two eminent virtues to be acquired by us* : the love of God, that is, love to God, and the patience of Christ—the patient waiting for Christ.

I. To begin, then, here are TWO PRECIOUS THINGS FOR US TO ENTER INTO. We cannot enter into them except as the Lord directs our hearts. There is a straight entrance into them, but we do not readily find it. It needs the Holy Spirit to direct our feet along the narrow way which leads to this great blessedness.

The first precious thing which we are to enter is *the love of God*. Beloved, we know the love of God in various ways. Many know it by having heard of it, even as a blind man may thus know the charms of an Alpine landscape. Poor knowledge this ! Others of us have tasted of the love of God, have talked about the love of God, have prayed, and have sung concerning the love of God. All very well, but Paul meant a dove of a brighter feather. To be directed into the love of God is quite another thing from all that we can be told of it. A fair garden is before us. We look over the wall, and are even allowed to stand at the door, while one handeth out to us baskets of golden apples. This is very delightful. Who would not be glad to come so near as this to the garden of heavenly delights ? Yet it is something more to be shown the door, to have the latch lifted, to see the gateway opened, and to be gently directed into the Paradise of God. This is what is wanted— that we may be directed *into* the love of God. Oh, that we may feel something of it while we meditate upon it !

Beloved, we come, when we are taught of the Spirit of God, to *enter into the love of God by seeing its central importance*. We see that the love of God is the source and centre, fountain and foundation of all our salvation, and of all else that we receive from God. At the first we are much taken up with pardoning grace. We are largely engrossed with those royal robes of righteousness with which our nakedness is covered. We are delighted with the viands of the marriage banquet : we eat the fat and we drink the sweet. What else would you expect from starving souls admitted to the abundant supplies of heavenly grace ? Afterwards we begin more distinctly to think of the love that spread the feast, the love that provided the raiment, the love that invited us to the banquet, and gently led us to take our place in it. This does not always come at first ; but I pray that none of us may be long receiving the gifts of love without kissing the hand of love ; that none of us may be content to have had much forgiven without coming and washing the feet of our forgiving Lord with our tears, and declaring our deep and true love to Him. O saved soul, may the Lord fill thee with personal love to that personal Saviour, through whom all blessings come to thee ! Remember, thou hast all good things because God loveth thee ! Remember that every cake of the heavenly manna, every cup of the living water, comes to thee because of His great love wherewith He loved thee. This will put a sweetness into what thou receivest even greater than that which is there intrinsically, sweet though God's mercies be in their own nature and quality. Oh, to enter into God's love by perceiving it to be the well-head of every stream of mercy by which we are refreshed !

If we further enter into the love of God, we see its immeasurable greatness. There is a little word which you have often heard, which I beg to bring before you again—that little word " so." " God *so* loved the world that He gave His only begotten Son, that whosoever believeth in Him should not perish, but have everlasting life." Come, ye surveyors, bring your chains, and try to make a survey of this word " so." Nay, that is not enough. Come hither, ye that make our national surveys, and lay down charts for all nations. Come, ye who map the sea and land, and make a chart of this word " so." Nay, I must go further. Come hither, ye astronomers, that with your optic glasses spy out spaces before which imagination staggers, come hither and encounter calculations worthy of all your powers ! When you have measured between the horns of space, here is a task that will defy you—"God *so* loved the world." If you enter into *that*, you will know that all this love is to you—that while Jehovah loves the world, yet He loves you as much as if there were nobody else in all the world to love. God can pour the infinite love of His heart upon one object, and yet, for all that, can love ten thousand times ten thousand of His creatures just as much. O heir of God, thy store of love is not diminished because the innumerable company of thy brethren share it with thee ! Thy Father loves each child as well as if He had no other. Peer into this abyss of love. Plunge into this sea. Dive into this depth unsearchable. Oh, that God might direct you into the immeasurable greatness of this love !

Neither be thou afraid to enter into this love by remembering its antiquity. Some fight shy of the great truth of the eternal electing love of God ; but to me it is as wafers made with honey. What music lies in that sentence—" Yea, I have loved thee with an everlasting love " ! When this great world, the sun, and moon, and stars, had not yet flashed the morning of their little day, the Lord Jehovah loved His people with an everlasting love. In the divine purposes, which were not of yesterday, nor even of that date of which Scripture speaks as " In the beginning," when the Lord created the heavens and the earth, God loved His own people. He had chosen you, thought of you, provided for you, and made ten thousand forecasts of lovingkindness towards you, or ever the earth was. Beloved believer, you were graven on the hands of Christ even then. Oh, that the Lord would direct you into the antiquity of His love. It shall make you greatly prize that love to think that it had no beginning, and shall never, never have an end.

Again, I pray that we may be directed into the love of God as to *its infallible constancy*. The unchangeable Jehovah never ceases to love His people. It would be a wretched business to be directed into the love of God only to find it a thing of the past. O believing soul, thou hast not to deal with things which once were gems of the mine, but now are dreams of the night. Oh, no ! the love of God abides for ever the same. When thou art in darkness the Lord still sees thee with an eye of love.

> " He saw thee ruined in the fall,
> Yet loved thee notwithstanding all."

When thou wast without strength, " in due time Christ died for the ungodly." Since thou hast known Him He has never varied in His love. When thou hast grown cold He has loved thee ; when thou hast grown cruel He has loved thee. Thou hast grievously provoked Him till He has taken down His rod, and made thee smart ; but He has loved thee in the smiting. With God there is as much love in chastening as in caressing. He never abates in fervour towards His ancient friends. Has He not said, " I am the Lord ; I change not ; therefore ye sons of Jacob are not consumed " ? I pray the Lord to direct us into the immutability of His divine love, for this is a great hold-fast in the day of soul-trouble. When conscious of imperfection, when darkened by the shadow of a great fault, when trembling under apprehension of wrath, it draws you back again if you can feel, " Still my Father is my Father, still will He receive His wandering child, and press His prodigal to His bosom, and rejoice over me, and say, ' This My son was dead, and is alive again.' " O child of God, thy questionings of divine love are grievous to thy God ; but if thou canst learn this truth and be led into it—that He loves thee ever more the same —it will help thee right graciously.

This love we ought to know, and if the Lord will lead us into it we shall know, that it is *omnipresent*. I mean by this, that whatever condition we may be in, the Lord is still active in love towards us. Thou art going across the sea to a far country, but thy Father's love will be as near thee on the blue wave as on the greensward of Old England. Thou hast come out to-night alone : time was when thou didst come to the house of God in company ; but it may be that graves and desertions furnish sad reasons for thy present solitude. Still, thou art not alone, thy Father's love is with thee. Thou art to-night, perhaps, in a very strange part of thy spiritual experience : thou hast not gone this way heretofore. But the road is not new to eternal love. Go where thou mayest, the air is still about thee : go where thou mayest, thy Father's love is all around thee. Higher than thy soarings, deeper than thy sinkings, is all-surrounding love. Thou art going home, perhaps to a bed, from which thou shalt not rise for months. Thou hast no apprehension just now of what lies before thee in the immediate future. It is as well thou shouldst not know. I should be slow to lift the curtain of merciful concealment even if it were in my power to do so. There is no necessity to know details when one or two grand facts provide for all contingencies. Trouble not thyself about the morrow. If thou art to be sick, or if thou art to die, thy Father's love will be with thee still. Therefore go on, and fear not. He cannot, will not, turn away from thee. An omnipresent God means omnipresent love, and omnipotence goes hand in hand with omnipresence. The Lord will show Himself strong on the behalf of them that trust Him. His love, which never fails, is attended by a power that fainteth not, neither is weary. Oh, may the Lord lead you into such love as this ! May the Holy Ghost lead you into the innermost secret of this joy of joys, this bliss unspeakable !

And I would also wish that you may be directed into the love of God as to its *entire agreement with His justice, His holiness, His spotless purity.* I firmly believe that God loves sinners, but I am equally sure that He hates sin. I do believe that He delights in mercy, but I am equally clear that He never dishonours His justice, nor frustrates the sternest threatening of His law. It is our joy that a holy God loves us, and does not find it needful to stain His holiness to save the unclean. We are loved by one so just, so righteous, that He could not pardon us without atonement. Even to-day He will never spare our sins, but He will drive the love of them out of us by chastisement, even as He has washed the guilt of them away by the precious blood of His dear Son. O beloved, we have a holy God, who is determined to make us holy. He would have us love our wives ; and He sets before us a holy model— " Even as Christ also loved the church, and gave Himself for it ; that He might sanctify and cleanse it with the washing of water by the word." All true loves goes towards purification ; and the true love of God goes that way with an invincible current, that can never be turned aside. O believer, thy God loves thee so well that He will not let a darling sin stay in thy heart ; He loves thee so strongly that He will not spare any iniquity in thee. " You only have I known of all the families of the earth ; therefore I will punish you for your iniquities." Out of His pure love He will chasten and refine till He had made us pure and able to abide in fellowship with His perfect nature.

I have thus spoken a little upon a vast theme. I fear it will seem to you mere surface-work ; and yet I pray that it may lead you to deep knowledge of divine things, so that you may apprehend God's love as yours, and then may feel the power, the unction, the savour, which come out of His love, making all your heart as sweet and aromatic as a chamber in which a box of precious ointment has been broken. Oh, that you might be led into the innermost secret of the Lord's love till it shall saturate you, influence you, take possession of you, carry you right away ! The Lord direct you into the love of God.

The second part of the prayer upon which we shall have to dwell is, " *The Lord direct your hearts into the patience of Christ.*" Now, beloved, I have another great sea before me, and who am I that I should act as your convoy over this main ocean ? Here I am lost. I cannot take my bearings. I am a lone speck upon the infinite. I will imitate the wise apostle, and pray, " The Lord direct your hearts into the patience of Christ."

What a patience that was which Jesus exhibited for us in our redemption ! To come from heaven to earth, to dwell in poverty and neglect, and find no room even in the inn ! Admire the patience of Bethlehem. To hold His tongue for thirty years— who shall estimate the wonderful patience of Nazareth and the carpenter's shop ! When He spoke, to be despised and rejected of men, what patience for Him whom cherubim obey ! Oh, the patience of the Christ to be tempted of the devil ! One can hardly tell what patience Christ must have had to let the devil come within ten thousand miles of Him, for He was able to keep him far down in the abyss below His feet. There is not much in a patience which cannot help itself ; but you well know that all the while Christ could have conquered all foes, chased away all suffering, and kept off all temptation ; but for our sakes, as Captain of our Salvation, that He might be made perfect through sufferings, His patience had its perfect work, right on to Gethsemane. Do you need that I tell you this ? Golgotha, with all its woes, its " *lama sabachthani,*" its abysmal griefs, do I need to remind you of the patience of Christ for us when the Lord laid on Him the iniquity of us all ? Patient as a lamb, He opened not His mouth, but stood in omnipotence of patience, all-sufficient to endure. Ye have heard of the patience of Job, but ye have need to enter into the patience of Jesus.

Oh, the patience *within Christ Himself* ! God never seems so like a God as when He divinely rules Himself. I can understand His shaking earth and heaven with His word ; but that He should possess His own soul in patience is far more incomprehensible. Marvel that omnipotent love should restrain omnipotence itself. In the life and death of our Lord Jesus we see almighty patience. He was very sensitive—very sensitive of sin, very sensitive of unkindness, and yet with all that sensitiveness He showed no petulance, but bore Himself in all the calm grandeur of Godhead. He was not quick to resent an ill, but He was patient to the uttermost. As I have said before, there went with His sensitiveness the power at anytime to avenge Himself and deliver Himself, but He would not use it. Legions of angels would have been glad to come to His rescue, but He bowed alone in the garden, and gave Himself up to the betrayer without a word. And all the while He was most tender and graciously considerate of everybody but Himself. He spoke burning words sometimes : His mouth could be like the red lips of a volcano as He poured out the burning love of denunciation upon " scribes and Pharisees, hypocrites " ; but the resentment was never aroused by any injury done to Himself. When He looked that way it was always gentleness : He cried, " Father, forgive them ; for they know not what they do." Oh, the wondrous patience of heaven's own Christ !

Enter into His patience *with us* as well as *for us.* How He put up with each one of us when we would not come to Him! How He wept over us when we neglected Him! How He drew us with constancy of love when we tugged against the cords! And when we came to Him, and since we have been with Him, what patience He has had with our ill-manners! If I had been Christ, I would have discharged such a servant as I have been long ago. Often have I gone to His feet, and cried,

"Dismiss me not Thy service, Lord."

I knew how justly He might have stripped His livery from my back; but He has not done so. Have you not often wondered that He should still love you? He is affianced to you, and He hateth putting away; but is it not marvellous that He keeps His troth with you, and will do so, though you have often defiled yourself, and forgotten Him? Blessed fact, the ring is on *His* finger rather than on yours, and the marriage is as sure as His love He will present you unto Himself, "without spot, or wrinkle, or any such thing," one of these days. But oh! His patience with each one of us. How He has put up with our unbelief, our mistrust, our hard hearts, our indifference, our strange ways! Never lover so kind as He! On our part never return so unworthy. Blessed be the patience of our Best Beloved!

Now, beloved, what is wanted is that we be directed into this patience of Christ. The choicest saints in different ages of the world have studied most the passion of our Lord; and although nowadays we hear from the wise men that it is sensuous to talk about the cross and the five wounds, and so forth, for my part I feel that no contemplation ever does me so much real benefit as that which brings me very near my bleeding Lord. The cross for me! The cross for me! Here is doctrine humbling, softening, melting, elevating, sanctifying. Here is truth that is of heaven, and yet comes down to earth: love that lifts me away from earth even to the seventh heaven. Have you ever read the words of holy Bernard, when his soul was all on fire with love of that dear name of which he so sweetly sang,

"Jesus, the very thought of Thee
With sweetness fills my breast."

Why, Bernard is poet, philosopher, and divine, and yet a child in love. Have you studied Rutherford's letters, and the wondrous things which he says about his own dear Lord? For an hour at glory's gate commend me to heavenly Master Rutherford. Have you never held fellowship with George Herbert, that saintly songster? Hear Him as He cries,

"How sweetly doth *my Master* sound! *My Master!*
"As ambergris leaves a rich scent
Unto the taster,
So do these words a sweet content,
An oriental fragrancy, *My Master!*"

O friends, I can wish you no greater blessing than to be directed into these two things—the love of God, and the patience of your Saviour. Enter both at the same time. You cannot divide them; why should you? The love of God shines best in the patience of the Saviour; and what is the patience of Christ but the love of the Father? "What God hath joined together, let no man put asunder." May the Lord lead us into both of them at this hour and continue upon us the heavenly process all the rest of our lives, in all experiences of sorrow and of rapture and in all moods and growths of our spirit!

II. But now I must ask your attention for the few minutes that remain to me to what is, perhaps, still the real gist of the text: HERE ARE TWO EMINENT VIRTUES TO BE ACQUIRED.

"The Lord direct your hearts into *the love of God.*" Beloved, let the love of God to you flow into your hearts, and abide there till it settles down, and bears on its surface the cream of love to God, yielded by your own heart. The only way to love God is to let God's love to you dwell in your soul till it transforms your soul into itself. Love *to* God grows out of the love *of* God.

Well, now, concerning love to God: if you receive it fully into your souls *it will nourish the contemplative life.* You will want to be alone. You will prefer to sit silently at Jesus' feet, while others wrangle over the little politics of the house. You will give up being busy-bodies, talking in six peoples' houses in an hour: quietude will charm you. You will love no company so much as the society of Him who is the Best and the Most. To be with God in quiet will be your highest enjoyment. You will not say, as some do, "I must have recreation." Contemplation of God is recreation to the child of God. It creates the soul anew; and is not this the truest re-creation? Whenever God's creation in us seems to have grown a little dim, love to God will gender and nourish the contemplative life, and so make us come forth as new creatures, fresh from our Maker's holy hand.

It will also animate the active life if you love God. You will feel that you must yield fruit unto your Lord. Your soul, when full of the love of God, will cry, "I must go after the wanderer; I must care for the poor; I must teach the ignorant." You cannot love God and be lazy. Love to God will stir you up. Contemplation teaches you to sit still, and this is no trifling lesson; but after sitting still, you rise with greater energy to go about the one thing needful, namely, the service of your Lord's love.

Love to God will also arouse enthusiasm. We want more persons in the church who will be a little daring —rash men and women who will do things which nobody else would think of doing, such as will make their prudent friends hold up their hands and say, "How could you? If you had consulted with me, I could have given you many a wise hint as to how it ought to have been done." This has been my lot of late. I have been surfeited with notions as to how I should have acted. Yes, my friend, I know you of old. You have wisdom at your fingers' ends. But let me quietly whisper that you would have done nothing at all; you would have been too anxious to save yourself from trouble. It is an easy thing to tell a man how he ought to have done it; and yet that man perhaps may be suffering intensely for having done bravely a well-meant deed. Instead of your showing sympathy with him, you treat him to the remark, "It might have been done better in another way." There was never a child that was near drowning but what the man that plunged in and drew him out of the river ought to have done it in a better way. He wetted himself too much; he waited too long; or he handled the drowning one too roughly. Alas, for silly criticisms of gracious deeds! If you come to love God with all consuming zeal, you will not be hindered by criticisms. You will testify for Jesus freely, because you cannot help yourself. It has to be done: somebody has to sacrifice himself to do it, and you say to yourself, "Here am I, Lord; send me. At every risk of hazard, send me. For Thy dear love's sake I count it joy to suffer shame or loss. I count it life to suffer death that I may honour Thee." Love to God will arouse enthusiasm.

It will also stimulate holy desire. They that love God can never have enough of Him—certainly never too much. Sometimes they are found pining after Him. When we love the Lord, we chide the laggard hours which keep us from His coming. Time has not wings enough.

> " My heart is with Him on His throne,
>   And ill can brook delay,
> Each moment listening for the voice,
>   ' Rise up, and come away.' "

A heavenly love-sickness sometimes makes God's handmaids swoon ; for they long to see the Beloved face to face, and to be like Him, and to be with Him where He is. The Lord direct your hearts into the love of God in some such fashion as this ; for it will make you sit loose by all things here below. Do you never feel that your wings are growing ? Do you never sigh, " Oh, that I had wings like a dove ! for then would I fly away, and be at rest " ?

And this love, better still, *will transform the character.* It is wonderful what a difference love makes in the person that is possessed with it. A poor timid hen that will fly away from every passer-by, loves its offspring, and when it has its chicks about it, it will fight like a very griffin for its young. And when the love of Christ comes into a timid believer, how it changes Him ! It takes the love of sin away, and implants a sublime nature. God only knows what a mortal man can yet become. Of woman sunken in sin, what saints the Lord has made when He has filled them with His love ! When the sun shines on a bit of glass bottle far away, it flashes like a diamond. A little fleecy vapour in the sky rivals an angel's wing when the sun pours itself upon it. Our Lord can put so much of Himself, by means of His love, into the hearts of His people, that they may be mistaken for Himself. John made a blunder in heaven and fell at the feet of one of his brethren the prophets ; for he had come to be so much like his Lord, that John could hardly tell the one from the other. Had he forgotten that word, " We shall be like Him ; for we shall see Him as He is " ? It doth not yet appear what we shall be, but love is the transfiguring power in the hand of the Holy Spirit. If the heart be directed into the love of Christ, it is on the highway to holiness.

Lastly—I am sorry that time will fly so fast just now—we want our hearts to be directed into *patience towards Christ.* What a subject is this ! Beloved, if our heart is directed into patience towards Christ, we shall suffer in patience for our Lord's sake, and we shall not complain. Those about us will say, " It is wonderful how resigned he seems " ; or, " How gladly she bears grief for love of Christ ! " And if it be the suffering of reproach and scorn for Jesus' sake, if we are directed into the patience of Christ, it will not seem to be any trouble at all. We shall bear it calmly, and in our hearts we shall laugh at those who laugh at us for Jesus' sake.

Yet it is not all patience of suffering that we want. We want the patience of forbearing. We must learn not to answer those who blaspheme. " Bear, and forbear, and silent be." Chew the cud in peace. Put up with such. When reviled, revile not again. The Lord direct your hearts into the patience of Christ. We shall also want the patience of working—

working on when nothing comes of it—pleading on with souls that are not converted—preaching when preaching seems to have no effect—teaching when the children do not care to learn. We need the patience of Christ, who set His face like a flint, and would accomplish His work cost what it may. He never turned aside from it for a moment. The Lord direct our hearts into patient working.

Then there is the patience of watching in prayer—not giving it up because you have not received an answer. What ? Did a friend say she had prayed for seventeen years for a certain mercy, and now meant to ask it no more ? Sister, make it eighteen years, and when you have got to the end of eighteen make it nineteen. May the Lord direct our hearts in to the patience of Christ in prayer ! We long kept Him waiting ; we need not complain if He makes us tarry His leisure. Still believe ; still hope ; still wrestle, until the break of day.

Pray for the patience of waiting His will, saying, " Let Him do what seemeth Him good." Though it be for months, for years, wait on. Christ is glorified by our patience. Depend on it, the best way in which certain of us can extol Him is by letting Him have His way with us. Even though He plunge me into seven boiling caldrons one after the other, I will say : Let Him do what He wills with His own, and I am His own. I am sure that He does not make the furnace one degree too hot. If He means to give His servant ten troubles, let His heavy hand fall even to the tenth, if so He pleases.

We want to be directed into patience towards Christ, and especially in patience in *waiting for His coming.* That, no doubt, is very justly inferred, and so it is put in our translation very prominently : " Patient waiting for Christ." He will come, brothers ; He will come, sisters. It is true the interpreters of the Book of Revelation told us that He was to come three hundred years ago, and there are thousands upon thousands of books in the British Museum which were very dogmatic upon this point, and yet they have all been disproved by the lapse of time. Men were as sure as sure could be that Christ would come just then ; *and He did not,* for He was bound by His word, but not by their interpretation of it. He will come at the appointed hour. To the jots and tittles God's word will stand. He will come to the tick of the clock. We know not when ; we need not ask ; but let us *wait.*

Just now some of you may be, as I am, troubled because the Lord does not yet appear to vindicate His cause ; and there is noise and triumph among the priests of Baal. The Lord direct our hearts into the patience of Christ. It is all right. Clouds gather ; the darkness becomes more dense. The thunder rolls ; friends flee in confusion. What next ? Well, perhaps, before we have hardly time for dread, silver drops of gracious rain may fall, and the sun may break through the clouds, and we may say to ourselves, " Who would have thought it ? '

> " Ye fearful saints, fresh courage take,
>   The clouds ye so much dread
> Are big with mercy, and shall break
>   In blessings on your head."

May the Lord direct each one of us into the patient waiting for Christ !

I am sorry, very sorry, that there are persons here to whom all this must seem a strange lot of talk. They know nothing about it. Dear souls, you cannot at present know anything about it. You must first be born again. A total change of heart must come over you before you can enter into the love of God or the patience of Christ. May that change take place to-night, before you go to sleep ! If the Lord shall lead you to seek His face, this is the way to seek it ; *trust His dear Son.* Lifted on the cross is Jesus Christ, the great Propitiation for sin. Look to Him, and looking alone to Him, you shall be saved. He will give you the new heart and the right spirit with which you shall be enabled to enter into the love of God and the patience of Christ. The Lord direct you at this very hour, for Jesus' sake ! Amen.

FACING THE WIND

"But ye, brethren, be not weary in well doing."—2 Thessalonians iii. 13.

THE Christian church ought to be an assembly of holy men. Its members should all of them be eminently peaceable, honest, upright, gracious, and Christlike. In the main, and in spite of all our failures, I trust these characteristics may be seen in the churches of our Lord Jesus Christ. But, still, from the beginning there has been a mixture. Judas in the sacred college of the twelve apostles seemed to be a prophecy to us that there would be troubles in Israel evermore. It was so in the church at Thessalonica, to which Paul wrote two epistles, part of the last of which we have just been reading ; there was evidently then a class of people who, because of the charity of the Church was very large, imposed upon it, and, under pretence of great spirituality, refused to work, busying themselves instead in doing mischief according to the old adage that

> "Satan finds some mischief still
> For idle hands to do."

We sometimes complain of our churches now. I very greatly question whether an average church of Christ in modern times is not considerably superior to any church that we have read of in the New Testament—certainly very superior to some of them. In the church at Corinth they tolerated a brother who lived in incest. I trust there is no Christian church, at least in our own denomination, that would endure such a thing for an hour. And when this man had been put out by Paul's command, and proved penitent, then the church at Corinth, which was a church that did not believe in ministry, you know, (there is a class of Christians of that sort now, which resembles greatly these Corinthians,) because they had once put him out, refused to receive him again though he was penitent and wanted to return. I scarcely know a Christian church that would refuse to receive into its membership again a brother who had erred if he showed signs of true repentance. The churches of to-day, compared with the early churches of Christ, can say that the grace of God has been extended to us, even as unto them ; and we have no right to be continually crying down the operations of the Holy Spirit in the churches now, by making unfair comparisons between them and the churches of old. They had their faults, as we have ours. They came short in many respects, even as we do. Instead of bringing a railing accusation against churches as they are, the best thing is for everyone of us to do his best in the sight of God to make them what they should be, by seeking our own personal sanctification and endeavouring that the influence of a holy life shall, in our case, help to leaven the rest of the mass.

Paul turns from the consideration of those who had grieved him in the church to speak to the rest of the brethren, and he says to them, " But ye, brethren, be not weary in well doing." In expounding these words we shall, first, notice that our text contains a summary of Christian life ; it is called " well doing." Secondly, we shall see it gives out a very distinct warning against weariness ; and it hints at some of the causes of weariness in the Christian life. In the third place, I shall close the discourse by giving some arguments to meet the reasoning of our soul when, at times, it seems to plead its own weariness as an excuse.

I. First, then, brethren, our text contains A SUMMARY OF CHRISTIAN LIFE. It is " well doing." This is all you have to do—you that have been redeemed by the blood of Jesus and renewed in the spirit of your minds. You have to spend your lives in well doing.

Now this is a very comprehensive term, and we are certain that it includes *the common acts of daily life.* You perceive the apostle had been speaking of some who would not work—" working not at all " he says ; and he commands them that they should labour and should eat their own bread. It is clear, then, from the connection, that the work by which a man earns his daily bread is a part of the well doing to which he is called. It is not alone preaching and praying and going to meetings that are to be commended. These are useful in their place. But well doing consists in taking down the shutters and selling your goods ; tucking up your shirt sleeves and doing a good day's work ; sweeping the carpets and dusting the chairs, if you happen to be a domestic servant. Well doing is attending to the duties that arise out of our relationships in life—attending carefully to them, and seeing that in nothing we are eye-servers and men-pleasers, but in everything are seeking to serve God. I know it is difficult to make people feel that such simple and ordinary things as these are well doing. Sometimes stopping at home and mending the children's clothes does not seem to a mother quite so much " well doing " as going to a prayer-meeting, and yet it may be that the going to a prayer-meeting would be ill-doing if the other duty had to be neglected. It still is a sort of superstition among men that the cobbler's lapstone and the carpenter's adze are not sacred things, and that you cannot serve God with them, but that you must get a Bible and break its back at a revival meeting, or give out a hymn and sing it lustily in order to serve God. Now, far am I from speaking even half a word against all the zeal and earnestness that can be expended in religious engagements. These things ought ye to have done, but the other things are not to be left undone, or to be depreciated in any way whatever. When Peter saw the sheet come down from heaven, you remember, it contained all manners of beasts and creeping things ; God said even of the creeping things that He had cleansed them, and they were not to be counted common ; from which I gather, among a great many other things, that even the most menial of the forms of service—even the commonest actions of life—if they be done as unto the Lord, are cleansed and become holy things, and are by no means to be despised. Do not cry down your church, but make your house also your church. Find fault as you like with vestments, but make your ordinary smock-frock your vestment, and be a priest in it to the living God. Away with superstition ! Kill it by counting every place to be holy, and every day to be holy, and every action that you perform to be a part of the high priesthood to which the Lord Jesus Christ has called every soul that He has washed in His precious blood.

That these common things are well doing is very evident, if you will only think of the result of their being left undone. There is a father, and he thinks that to go to his work—such common work as his—cannot be specially pleasing in God's sight. He means to serve God, and so he stops at home, and he is upstairs in prayer when the factory bell is ringing and he ought to be there. He hears that there is a conference in the morning, so he attends that ; and then he has another period of prayer ; he spends all the week like that ; and then on Saturday night there is nothing for his wife. Now, you see, directly, that he has been ill doing, because it was his duty to provide for his household ; and if a man, being a husband and a father, neglects to find daily food for his wife and little children, all the world cries shame on him. Does not nature itself say, " This man cannot be engaged in well doing " ? It cannot possibly be so. Though at first sight the ordinary toil for daily bread looks to be a very commonplace thing, yet, if you only suppose it to be neglected, the leaving of it out is no commonplace thing, but brings all manner of mischief. Suppose, on the other hand, that the Christian woman were to become so very devout—so ashamed to be like Martha—so certain not to be cumbered with much serving that she would not serve at all in Martha's direction, but always sat still and read and prayed, and meditated, leaving the children unwashed, and nothing done for the household. The husband—perhaps a worldly man—may be driven away from the house by the want of comfort in it, and sent into ill company. He may, indeed, be ruined. You can all see that whatever pretence there might be of well doing about the wife's conduct, it would not, it could not really, be well doing, for the first business of the Christian woman placed in that position is to see to it that her household be ordered aright, even as Christ Jesus would have it. Oh, dear friends, it is an art to balance duties so as never to sacrifice to God one duty stained red with the blood of another duty that you have destroyed in getting this one ready for the sacrifice. Render unto Cæsar the things that be Cæsar's, and unto God the things that be God's. Give to husband and child and to the household the share that is due, and then—I will not say give God the rest, but give God that service and all beside. He would not have you bring robbery for burnt offering, and He will accept that as done to Him which you have as a matter of duty done to others. So, then, common life is included in the term " well doing."

I think also, from the connection, that any one would conclude that *attending to the poor, and doing good to all that are in need*, is included in the term " well doing." The connection seems to say that there were certain persons in the Thessalonian church who had abused Christian charity, living upon it, instead of working and eating their own bread. Now the apostle says, " But ye, brethren, be not weary in well doing." Do not say, as some do, " There are really so many imposters that I shall give nothing at all ; I have been deceived so many times, and have given to persons who have only made a bad use of my gift, that I do not intend to open my purse-strings any more, but shall keep what I have, or lay it out in some other way." " No." says the apostle, " you must not do that ; be not weary in well doing." It is the part of a Christian man to seek as much as lieth in him to do good unto all men, especially to those that are of the household of faith. It is one of Christ's precepts, " Give to him that asketh of thee, and from him that would borrow of thee turn not thou away." A general spirit of generosity to those in need is congruous with the gospel ; the reverse may be suitable to the law with its rigour, but not to the gospel with its noble-hearted love. Christian brother, you must look on the things of others as well as your own things. You must remember those that are in necessity as being yourself also a part of the body of Christ. As much as lieth in you " comfort the feeble-minded, support the weak, be patient towards all men." So we see that within the range of " well doing " is included a kind and tender consideration of all those who are in need.

But, brethren, the circle of " well doing " which is to be the Christian's life, though it makes a wide sweep, includes *the things that are nearer the centre.* " Well doing " means that I love the Lord my God with all my heart,—that I commune with Him,—that I dedicate myself to Him and give all that I have to the extension of His kingdom and to the honouring of His glorious name.

If you want to know what well doing is, I will give you just a few hints and tests. *Everything is well doing that is done in obedience to the divine command* If thou hast God's word for it, it is well doing. Some may call thee imprudent, but it is well doing if thou doest what God bids thee, and it is prudent doing too. In the long run thou shalt find it so. When God says, " Do this," let it be done at once ; that is well doing. And if He say, " Thou shalt not," then well doing will flee from the accursed thing. Let not thine own wisdom and prudence ever fly in the teeth of a positive command of God. When thou art doing what God bids thee, thou art doing well, and thou needest have no difficulty in defending thyself. God will not suffer that man ever to be confounded who makes the will of God to be the law of his life. So may it always be with us.

Taking the first condition for granted, in the next place *everything is well doing that is done in faith.* " Whatsoever is not of faith is sin." That is to say, even though the thing you do is right, if you do not believe it to be right it is not right to you. There are many things that I may do that you must not do, because you do not think it would be right to do them. Therefore you must refrain. Even, I say again, if the thing be not in itself a wrong thing, yet if it *seem* wrong to you, it *will* be wrong to you : there-fore do it not. Paul could eat the meat that had been offered to idols without being troubled in his conscience ; but there were some who thought that if they ate it they would be partakers with the idol. Paul did not think so, and, moreover, he said, " An idol is nothing in the world. Whatsoever is sold in the shambles I eat asking no question for conscience sake." Still " he that doubteth is condemned if he eat " ; if he has his doubts about it, and thinks it should not be, it must not be. He will not be practising the art of well doing if he does that concerning which his conscience raises any scruple. If thou canst say with Scripture warrant, " God permits this and I can do it, feeling that He does permit it," thou art doing well in so doing, not else.

Again, *everything that is done out of love to God is well doing.* Ah, this is a motive that sways no man till he is born again ; but when God, who is love, hath begotten us to His own likeness, then we love God, and love becomes the motive of all our actions. I hope, beloved, this is the mainspring of our doings and goings,—that you would be God's servants or God's ministers because you love God,—that you seek to bear up under poverty or to use with discretion and liberality the riches with which you are entrusted because you love God. If a man love not God, how little there can be of well doing about him, yea, he lacks the very root of it all if he hath not love to God.

Well doing includes doing what we do in the name of the Lord Jesus. How this would stop some professors in a great many actions. Have we not the exhortation. " Whatsoever ye do, in word or deed, do all in the name of the Lord Jesus." If there is anything you cannot do in the name of the Lord Jesus, do it not, for to you it will not be well doing. In the name of the Lord Jesus you may go to your daily labour, for He went to His for thirty years and worked in the carpenter's shop. In the name of the Lord Jesus you may undertake all the duties of your calling, if that calling be a right one ; and if it be not you have no right to be in it at all, but should get out of it directly. You may do in the name of the Lord Jesus all that men should do if you are a saved soul and your heart be right towards Him.

Still further, *well doing includes that which we do in divine strength.* There is no well doing except we get power to do it from the Holy One of Israel. The Spirit of God is the author of all true fruit in the Christian life. Except we abide in Christ and receive the sap of the sacred Spirit from Him, we cannot bring forth fruit, for " without Me," says He, " ye can do nothing." But to work in the divine strength is well doing. Poor and feeble though it be, if I do it out of love to Christ and with the little strength I have, owning that I would not have even that but for His grace, my act is an act of well doing. Even though I have to mourn my failures and mistakes, nevertheless I may feel that with a true heart I am striving to glorify God and that I am surrendering myself to the divine impulses so as to be ready to do everything as unto my Master. Then am I living as a Christian should live in well doing.

Brethren, we are very great at well-wishing, and " if wishes were horses beggars might ride " ; if well-wishes meant anything there would be some very great saints about ; but the practice of a Christian should be to do what he knows should be done—well doing. Well-resolving is a very common habit. Well-suggesting and well-criticizing are tempers of mind familiar to most of us. Some of you could take a high degree in criticizing everybody else that

does anything, and putting your own hands into your pockets and keeping them there. Well-talking also is a great deal more common than well doing. But the Christian life lieth in none of these things. If God has given thee the life of the Spirit, thou wilt not bring forth only buds and blossoms and flowers, but there will be fruit : the fruit of well doing.

So much then concerning that first point.

II. Now let us turn to the second point, which is this. There is A WARNING AGAINST WEARINESS IN WELL DOING. " Is it possible," you say, "that a child of God can ever grow weary of doing well ? " I suppose so, for I remember another text which says, " Let us not be weary in well doing, for in due season we shall reap if we faint not," and the marginal reading of this text itself is " Faint not." I suppose that, blessed as it is to be doing good and to be living unto God, yet while the spirit is willing the flesh is weak, and there is a danger of our getting weary in the most happy exercise.

The first danger is mentioned in the context. There is a tendency to cease from well doing *because of the unworthy receivers of our good deeds.* As I have already said, there were those in the Thessalonian church who received the gifts of the faithful, and who sat still and did nothing that was of any good, but became a pest and nuisance to their neighbours. Now, the natural tendency of others in the church would be to say, " Well, I do not know what others think about it, but I should give no more." " No," says the apostle, " be not weary in well doing." It is bad that that man should make a bad use of thy gifts, but it will be worse still if he should induce thee to harden thy heart. It is a loss, perhaps, to give to a man who wastes, but it will be a greater loss not to give at all. I remember one who spoke on the missionary question one day saying, " The great question is not, ' Will not the heathen be saved if we do not send them the gospel ? ' but ' are we saved ourselves if we do not send them the gospel ? ' " And so it is with regard to Christian gifts. It is not so much a question how far this or that man is benefited or hurt by what we give ; but what about ourselves if we have no bowels of compassion for a brother that is in need ? What about the hardening influence on our own soul if we get at last into this condition, that we say, " I am weary in having done what I have done, because I see to what an ill use it is turned " ? I believe that to be a common temptation of the present age, and I see that all the political economists and the newspaper men almost as good as tell us that it is one of the wickedest things we can ever do to help the poor at all—it is indeed a dreadful thing, unless we do it through that blessed machinery of the poor law, which seems to be the next thing to the kingdom of heaven in their estimation. There seems to me to be, however, a very long distance between them, and I trust that Christian men will continually by their actions bear their protest against the stealing of the believing, Christian, renewed heart against their fellow-men because they seem to pervert the well doing into evil.

We have need of warning again *because idle examples tempt others to idleness.* If there were in the church at Thessalonica some who did not work, well there no doubt be others who would say, " We will do the same. Since that fellow never does a hand's-turn, but only goes about and talks, and makes a good thing of it, why should not I do like-wise ? " " No," says the apostle, " be not weary in well doing. Do not give up your daily work : do not give up any form of service, because others have done so, for you can see, if you look at them, that they turn out to be busybodies. You do not want to become mischief-makers, such as they are : therefore shun their conduct ; avoid it with all your might ; and be not weary in well doing even if you see others, who, apparently, prosper by doing nothing at all."

Again, I think, the apostle would say to us, " Be not weary in well doing *because of unreasonable and wicked men.*" We read about them just now, and I made a remark about them. Whenever anybody gets very earnest for Christ, and lays himself out for God's glory, there is sure to be a little lot of unreasonable and wicked men who get round him. The birds go flying through the orchard, and they do not say a word to one another till they come to a cherry tree where the cherries are very sweet and ripe. Then they all fall to at once and begin to peck away with all their might. So of an ordinary Christian who is doing little for his Master, nobody says much, except, perhaps, " He is a very good respectable man. Never bothers anybody with his religion." But let him become earnest—let his fruits be ripe and sweet before the Lord, and, believe me, more birds than you ever thought were about will come, and they will peck at the ripest fruit ; that which God approves most will be just that which they most violently condemn. If you get into such a case as that, my brother, be not weary of well doing because of your critics. Does it matter, after all, what men think of us ? Are we their servants ? Do we live on the breath of their nostrils ? Do they think that their praises inflate and exalt us ? Do they dream that their censures can make us sleep a wink the less or even ruffle our spirits ? I trust, if we know the Lord aright, we are of the mind of Ann Askew, who, after she had been racked, sat up with every bone out of joint, and, as full of pain as she could live, said to her tormentors,

> " I am not she that list
>   My anchor to let fall,
> For every drizzling mist.
>   My ship's substantial."

And she bore out the storm, and did not intend to cast anchor because of her persecutors. Glory be to God when He shall have delivered you altogether from the bleating of the sheep and from the howling of the wolves too, and make you willing to let your enemies say their say, and say it over again as long as it pleases them, but as for you, your heart is fixed to go on in what you know to be well doing, till thy Master Himself shall say to thee, " Well done ! "

Once more. There is a temptation to cease from well doing, not only because of unreasonable and wicked men outside the church, but, according to the context,—and I am keeping to that,—*because of busybodies inside the church.* Some of these are men : some of them are not. Busybodies there are about everywhere. They do not speak out very distinctly ; they whisper, and they do it with a sigh. Perhaps nothing is said, but there is a shrug of the shoulders. " So and so is an excellent woman. What a wonderful work she is doing for Christ ! " " Well—yes, but—" " Such and such a man ! How greatly God honours him in the winning of souls." " Yes—ah, yes—I *suppose* it is so." That is the style. And then straightway there are ambiguous voices sounding abroad, and depreciating things said ; and I have known some of tender heart that have suffered—I dare not think how much—from the insinuations of idle people who, I hope, did not know the suffering they were causing, or they would have run to give help instead. But there is so much of this thoughtless babblin; of innuendoes even among those who, we trust, are God's people, that if any such are here I would earnestly entreat them to give up that bad business ; and if any brother or sister here has suffered from such people, do not suffer more than you can help, for this idle chatter is not worth a thought. Do not let it prey upon your mind, because—well, there is nothing in it. All the dirt that people can fling will brush off them when it is dry. You do not expect do you, to go to heaven on a grassy path that is mowed and rolled for you every morning, with all the dew swept off ? If you expect that, you will be mistaken. You may even learn something from what these busybodies say about you. It is not true, of course. But, brother, if they had known you better they might have said something worse that was true. They picked a fault where there was none. Well, but you know there are some faults that they do not know, and had not you better amend them lest they should pick those next time ? The eagle eye of envy and malice should even be sanctified to our good, to keep us the more watchful, and to make us the more earnestly seek to be diligent in well doing. Courage ! faint heart ; it will all be over by and by, and we shall be before that judgment-seat where the talk of friends and the threats of foes will go for nothing. We are being examined here by this and that, but what matters the result of the examination ? The Lord weigheth the spirits, and if in those great scales at last we shall, by divine grace, escape from having the sentence pronounced, " Thou art weighed in the balance and found wanting," it will be a theme for everlasting joy. Let us look to that verdict and not care for the praise or blame of men.

III. Now I am going to close by bringing up A FEW ARGUMENTS TO KEEP MY DEAR BRETHREN WITH THEIR FACE TO THE WIND. I want you that are going up hill for Christ, and find the wind blowing very sharp, to set a hard face against a strong wind, and to go right straight on all the same. If you have to fight your way to heaven through every inch of your life, I would encourage you still to keep on. May God's Spirit give you strength to do so !

And, first, you say, " Oh, but this service—keeping your garments always white—is hard work. *Well doing needs so much effort.* I am afraid I shall be weary." Now, I would ask you to remember that when you had just begun business, and you wanted to make a little money, how early you rose in the morning, how many hours you worked in the day ! Why, you that are getting grey now knew that in those days everybody wondered at you, because you threw such strength into everything, you did the work of two or three men. What was all that effort for ? For yourself, was it not ? My dear brother, can you put all those exertions forth for yourself, and cannot you put as much effort for Christ ? That was only for the worldly things ; shall there not be something like that in the spiritual things ? It is enough to shame some people—the way they toil to get on in business, and then the little energy they show in the things of Christ. I used to tell a story of a brother I once knew who, at the prayer-meeting, was accustomed to pray in such a way that I was always sorry when he got up, for nobody could hear him ; and I always thought that he had a very feeble voice. I had indistinctly heard the brother mutter something to God, and I felt that we had better not ask him again, for his voice was so thin. But I stepped into his shop one day ; he did not know that I was there, and I heard him call, " John, bring that half hundred-weight." " Oh," I thought, " there is a very different tone in the business from what there is in the prayer-meeting." It is symbolical of a great many people. They have one voice for the world, and another voice for Christ. What weight they throw into the ordinary engagements, and what little force and weight there is when they come to the things of God ! If that should touch any brother here, I hope he will carefully take it to himself. I am afraid it has to do with a great many of us, and I put it thus—if for the poor things of this world we have often manifested so much vigour, what ought to be expected of us—of us who are under such obligations to divine grace—in the service of such a Master in reference to eternal things.

" But," says one, " such *well doing requires so much self-denial.* I trust I am a Christian, but I sometimes flag because to deny one's self again and again and again, and to lead a life of constant self-denial is, I am afraid, too much for me." Yes, but, dear brother, recollect what Paul bids you remember. He was thinking of the men that went to the boxing matches, and the men that went to the races among the Greeks, how they had to contend for a crown that was only of parsley or laurel ; but weeks and months before they ran they kept under the body, and brought it into subjection, and denied themselves all sorts of things they would have rejoiced in, till they got the muscles well out and by degrees pulled the flesh off their bones to get them into right condition to enter into the arena. Now, saith the apostle, they do it for a corruptible crown, but we for an incorruptible. I am sure the hardships to which some of those champions in the public games put themselves were enough to make the cheek of professors mantle with crimson when they think that the little self-denials of their life are often too severe for them. May God in infinite mercy help us not to be weary in well doing since these stand before us as examples.

" Aye," says one, " but I grow weary because, though I could deny myself, continued *well doing brings such persecution.* I am surrounded by people who have no sympathy with me. On the contrary, if they could stamp out the little spark of spiritual religion that I have in me they would be glad to do it." Now, my dear brethren, be not weary in well doing because of this, but look up yonder. I can see in vision a white-robed throng. Each one bears a palm branch, and together they sing an exultant song of triumph. Who are these that thus wear a ruby crown ?

" These are they who bore the cross,
   Faithful to their Master died,
   Suffered in His righteous cause,
   Followers of the crucified."

Take down Master Fox's Book of Martyrs, and read a dozen pages ; and after that see whether you are able to put yourselves on a par with the saints of old. " Ye have not yet resisted unto blood, striving against sin." Your persecution is only a silly joke or two against you, a bit of frivolous jesting—that is all. These things break no bones. O sirs, ask grace to enable you to rejoice and be exceeding glad when they say all manner of evil against you falsely for Christ's sake. For so persecuted they the prophets that were before you : therefore be not dismayed.

But another says, " No, sir, I could bear anything for Christ, but, do you know, I have been trying to do good to my neighbours. to the children of my class, and to the others ; and I really think that the more I try to do good to people the worse they are, *well doing is followed by so little result.* I have laboured in vain and spent my strength for naught ; and you know, sir, that hope deferred maketh the heart sick. They seem to refuse and reject my message, though I put it very kindly." Now, listen to me, if ever you listened in your life. You must not—you dare not—complain of this, because—and I know you well, there came once to your door One who loved you better than you love these people ; He knocked with a hand that had been pierced for you, and you refused Him admission. He knocked and knocked again, and said, " Open to Me for my head is filled with the dew, and My locks with the drops of the night " ; but you would not open to Him. Then He went His way and you were much worse than before. Sometime you said you would open, but you did not. And by the month together—ah, perhaps I do not exaggerate when I say, by the year together—" that Man of love, the Crucified," came to you again and again and again, and pleaded His wounds and blood with you, and yet you did refuse Him. You have admitted Him now, but no thanks to you ; you would never have done it if He had not put in His hand by the the hole of the door, and then your bowels were moved for Him ; then He came in to your soul, and He is supping with you still. Now, after that, you must never say a word when they shut the door against you. You must say, " This is how I served my Master. It has come back to me again, good measure, but not pressed down or running over. And so I am well content to bear rebuffs for His sake ; since He bore them for me, even from me."

" Still," says one, " I have gone on and on, trying to do good in my sphere ; I have given up, and I desire still to do the same, but I do not appear to get much return, *well doing does not earn much gratitude.* If I had some thanks I would not so much mind. Indeed, I do not seem to be doing good either. If I saw some results I would not be weary." Once more I speak, and then I have done. Dost thou not know that there is One who thus every day bade the showers descend upon the earth ; and when they fell He did not say to the rain-drops, " Fall ye on the root crops of the grateful farmers, and let the Christian men have all the benefit of the shower." No, He sent the clouds and they poured out the rain that fell on the churl's land, and watered his property. To-morrow morning, when the sun rises, it will light the blasphemer's bed, as well as the chamber of the saint, and to-night God lends His moon to those that break His laws with a high hand and defile themselves, as well as to those who go forth on ministries of mercy. He stops neither rain nor sun nor moon, nor makes a star the less to shine, nor sends less of oxygen into the atmosphere, or the less of health in the winds, because man sins. Yet are there whole nations where, when God gives His bounties, idols and images are thanked, and not the gracious Giver. There are other nations where, when God makes the vine to produce its fruit, the people turn it into drunkenness. And when He bids the corn be multiplied they turn it into gluttony and surfeit and pride. Yet doth not He restrain His gifts. Therefore do you keep on still, even as the great well-doer God continues unweariedly to work. He has done good to you and to thousands like you. If you were to stop doing good to men what would you be saying to God ? " Lord, this race does not deserve that Thou shouldest do it any good. Do not any more good." Your conduct in saying that your fellow creatures do not deserve that you should do them any good says, in the most emphatic manner, that you do not think God ought to do them any good ; for, if God should do them good, much more should you who are so much less than He. And if you stop your hand, and say, " It is no use doing any more good," you in effect pray God never to do any more good to your fellow men. That is an inhuman prayer and tempts God. I pray you let not the action which really incarnates such a prayer ever spring from us again.

Come, brother, the Lord Jesus Christ has blotted out our sins, He has bought us with His blood, we belong to Him ; and whatever service He gives us to do He will give us the strength to do it. So let us go back to our work with joy. If we have been grumbling,—if we have complained at all,—let us ask His forgiveness, and buckle our harness on anew, saying, " Master, Thou shalt not find me skulking, but as long as the day lasts, and Thou givest me strength, I will reap in Thy fields, or work in Thy vineyards, according to Thy bidding, thankful for the great honour of being permitted to do anything for Thee and even for having to put up with inconvenience for Thy sake. Seeing that Thou didst endure so much for me, why should I not bear something for Thee ? " You may have to face a gale of wind, but you may face it gaily in the strength of your Lord. Keep on, and keep on keeping on : you shall be more than conquerors through Him that loved you, over all the oppositions of men. Wherefore, be comforted, beloved fellow labourers, and let no brother's heart fail Him because of anything that has happened to him. Let no sister's hands hang down, but " be ye stedfast, unmoveable, always abounding in the work of the Lord, forasmuch as ye know that your labour is not in vain in the Lord." I pray God to lead many others to enlist in this service, but they must first believe in Jesus Christ. When they have so done, then may they also come and share in the blessed warfare, and they shall have their reward. The Lord bless you, for Christ's sake.

THE JEWEL OF PEACE

" Now the Lord of peace Himself give you peace always by all means. The Lord be with you all."—2 Thessalonians iii. 16.

WHEN the heart is full of love it finds the hand too feeble for its desires. Hence it seeks relief in intercession and benediction ; wishing, praying and blessing where it cannot actually effect its loving purpose. The apostle would have done for the Thessalonians all the good that was conceivable had it been in his power, but his wishes far outstripped his abilities, and therefore he betook himself to interceding for them, and to invoking upon them the blessing of the Lord and Master whom he served. Here is a lesson for us in the art of doing good ; as we lengthen the eyesight with the telescope, as we send our words afar by the telegraph, so let us extend our ability to do good by the constant use of intercessory prayer. Parents, when you have done all you can for your children yourselves, be thankful that you may introduce them to a further and greater blessing, by commending them to the care of the great Father in heaven. Friends, do your friends the best possible deed of friendship by asking for them the friendship of God. You who love the souls of men, when you have poured out all your strength on their behalf, bless God that there is still something more which you can do, for by earnest entreaties and supplications you may bring down from on high the effectual energy of the Holy Spirit, who can work in their hearts that which is it not in your power to accomplish. The apostle saw that the Thessalonians were much troubled, and he wrote the most encouraging words to cheer them, but he knew that he could not take the burden from off their hearts, and therefore he turned to the God of all consolation, and prayed Him to give them peace always by all means. The slenderness of our power to bless others will be no detriment to them if it leads us to lay hold upon the eternal strength, for that will bring into the field a superior power to bless, and our infirmity will only make space for the display of divine grace.

Let us look first at *the many-sided blessing* which the apostle invokes—peace ; and then let us note *the special desirableness of it.* Thirdly, let us observe *from whom alone it comes ;* and fourthly, note *the wide sweep of the apostolic prayer.*

I. First, then, let us look at THE MANY-SIDED BLESSING—" The Lord of peace Himself give you peace." Some have thought to restrict the expression to peace within the church, since disorderly members were evidently increasing among the Thessalonians ; but that is a very straitened and niggardly interpretation, and it is never wise to narrow the meaning of God's word. Indeed, such a contracted explanation cannot be borne, for it does not appear that the disorderly persons mentioned in the chapter had as yet created any special disturbance : they had been quietly fattening at the expense of their generous brethren and would not be very eager to quarrel with the rack from which they fed. Although no doubt church quiet is included as one variety of peace, yet it would be a sad dwarfing of the meaning of the Spirit to consider one phase of the blessing to the neglect of the rest. No, the peace here meant is " the deep tranquillity of a soul resting on God," the quiet restfulness of spirit which is the peculiar gift of God, and the choice privilege of the believer. " Great peace have they that love Thy law, and nothing shall offend them."

The peace of the text is a gem with many facets, but in considering its many-sidedness we must remember that its main bearing is *toward God.* The deepest, best, and most worthy peace of the soul is its rest towards the Lord God Himself. I trust we know this, and are enjoying it at this moment. We are no longer afraid of God : the sin which divided us from Him is blotted out, and the distance which it created has ceased to be. The atonement has wrought perfect reconciliation and established everlasting peace. The terrors of God's law are effectually removed from us, and instead thereof we feel the drawings of His love. We are brought nigh by the atoning sacrifice, and have peace with God through Jesus Christ our Lord. We know that all His thoughts to us are thoughts of love, and we bless His name that our thoughts toward Him are no longer those of the slave towards a taskmaster, or of a criminal towards a judge, but those of a beloved child towards a kind and tender father. Fervent love reigns in our hearts, casting out all fear and causing us to joy in God by our Lord Jesus Christ. This is a great blessing. It is surely a choice delight for a man to know that whether he prospers or is afflicted, whether he lives or dies, there is nothing between God and him but perfect amity ; for all that offends has been effectually put away.

Beloved, when the apostle wishes us peace in the words of our text, he no doubt means that our hearts should be at perfect peace, by being placed fully in accord with the will of God ; for, alas, we have known some, who we hope are forgiven and are God's children, who nevertheless quarrel with God very sadly. They are not pleased with what He does, but even complain that He deals hardly with them : they are naughty children, and carry on a sort of sullen contention with their heavenly Father, because He does not indulge them in all their whims and fancies. Now may the Lord of peace put an end to all such grievous warfare of heart in His people. May you love the Lord so well and trust Him so fully that you could not pick a quarrel with Him, even if He smote you and bruised you and broke your bones. Whatever He does is not only to be accepted with submission, but to be rejoiced in. That which pleases Him should please us. Then have we perfect peace when we can magnify and praise the Lord even for the sharp cuts of His rod, and the fierce fires of His furnace. May the Lord bring us into this state, for there is no joy like it ; perfect peace with God is heaven below.

Yea, brethren, we reach a little further than reconciliation and submission, for we come into the enjoyment of conscious complacency. There are men who are at peace with God as to the forgiveness of sins, and in a measure are in accord with His will, but they are not walking carefully in the path of obedience, and so they are missing the sense of divine love. God is their Father, and He loves them, but He hides His face from them ; they walk contrary to Him, and so He walks contrary to them. We cannot consider such a condition to be one of the fullest peace. The truly restful state of mind is enjoyed when the heart and life are daily cleansed by grace, so that there is nothing to grieve the Spirit of God, and therefore the Lord feels it right to favour His child with the light of His countenance in full meridian splendour. O how blessed to bask in the sunlight of Jehovah's love, free from all doubt, and having no more conscience of sin ! In that sense of conscious favour lies the rest of heaven. May the Lord of peace Himself give us this peace.

Peace because sin is forgiven is the sweet fruit of justification—" therefore being justified by faith, we have peace with God." Peace because the heart is renewed and made to agree with the will of God is the blessed result of sanctification, for " to be spiritually minded is life and peace." Peace, because the soul is conscious of being the object of divine love, is a precious attendant upon the spirit of adoption, which is the very essence of peace. Brethren in Christ, may this threefold peace with God be with you always.

Now we look further and note that this peace spreads itself abroad and covers *all things* with its soft light. God is great, and filleth all things, and he who becomes at peace with Him is at peace with all things else. Being reconciled to God, the believer says,—All things are mine, whether things present or things to come ; all are mine, for I am Christ's, and Christ is God's. Behold, the Lord has made us to be in league with the stones of the field, and the beasts of the field are at peace with us. Providence is our pavilion, and angels are our attendants. All things work together for our good, now that we love God and are the called according to His purpose. No longer are we afraid for the terror by night' nor for the arrow that flieth by day, nor for the pestilence that walketh in darkness, nor for the destruction which wasteth at noonday. Behold, the Lord God covereth us with His feathers, and under His wings do we trust ; His truth is our shield and buckler : because we have set our love upon Him He doth deliver us, and He doth set us on high because we have known His name. At peace with the Lord of hosts we are at peace with all the armies of the universe, in alliance with all the forces which muster at Jehovah's bidding. Though we must be at war with Satan, yet even he is chained and made as a slave to accomplish purposes of good contrary to his own will. There is neither in heaven nor earth nor hell anything that we need fear when we are once right with God. Settle the centre, and the circumference is secure : peace with God is universal peace.

This practically shows itself in the Christian's inward peace with regard to *his present circumstances*, be they what they may. Being at peace with God he sees the Lord's hand in everything around him, and is content. Is he poor ? The Lord makes him rich in faith, and he asks not for gold. Is he sick ? The Lord endows him with patience, and he glories in his afflictions. Is he laid aside from the holy service which he so much loves ? He feels that the Lord knows best. If he might be actively engaged in doing God's will he would be very thankful, and run with diligence the race set before him ; but if he must lie in the hospital, and suffer rather than serve, he does not wish to put his own wishes before the will of his Master, but he leaves himself in the Lord's hands, saying, " Lord, do as Thou wilt with me. I am so at peace with Thee that if Thou use me I will bless Thee, and if Thou lay me aside I will bless Thee : if Thou spare my life I will bless Thee, and if Thou bring me down to the grave I will bless Thee ; if Thou honour me among men I will bless Thee, and if Thou make me to be trodden under foot like straw for the dunghill I will still bless Thee : for Thou art everything, and I am nothing, Thou art all goodness and I am sin and emptiness." The soul which thus has perfect peace as to all its personal surroundings is indeed happy ; it is lying down in green pastures beside the still waters.

Blessed be God this peace is mainly to be found *in the soul itself* as to its own thoughts, believings, hopings, expectations, and desires. We have not only peace towards the outer world, but peace within.

After all, happiness and peace lie more within the man than in anything about him. Heaven lies more in the heart than in golden streets, and hell's flame consists rather in man's tortured conscience than in the Tophet fire which the breath of God has kindled. So the peace which Jesus gives is within us ; " the good man is satisfied from himself." Some minds are strangers to peace. How can they have peace, for they have no faith ? They are as a rolling thing before the whirlwind, having no fixed basis, no abiding foundation of belief. These are the darlings of the school of modern thought, whose disciples set themselves as industriously to breed doubt as if salvation came by it. Doubt and be saved is their gospel, and who does not see that this is not the gospel of peace ? Forsooth they are receptive, and are peering about for fresh light, though long ago the Sun of Righteousness has arisen. Such uncertainty suits me not. I must *know* something or I cannot live : I must be sure of something or I have no motive from which to act. God never meant us to live in perpetual questioning. His revelation is not and cannot be that shapeless cloud which philosophical divines make it out to be. There must be something true, and Christ must have come into the world to teach us something saving and reliable ; He cannot mean that we should be always rushing through bogs and into morasses after the will-of-the-wisp of intellectual religion. There is assuredly some ascertainable infallible, revealed truth for common people ; there must be something sure to rest upon. I know that it is so, and declare unto you what I have heard and seen. There are great truths which the Lord has engraven upon my very soul, concerning which all the men on earth and all the devils in hell cannot shake me. As to these vital doctrines, an immovable and unconquerable dogmatism has laid hold upon my soul, and therefore my mind has peace. A man's mind must come to a settlement upon eternal truths by the teaching of the Holy Ghost, or else he cannot know what peace is.

I would ask for every one of my brethren that they may find an anchorage of mind and heart and never leave it. We have been often spoken of as an old-fashioned church, and your minister is said to be *Ultimus Puritanorum*, the last of the Puritans, a man incapable of any thought beyond the limit of the old-fashioned theology. I bless the Lord that it is even so. I am indeed incapable of forsaking the gospel for these new-fangled theories. Down went my anchor years ago : it was a great relief to me when I first felt it grip, and it is a growing joy to me that I know whom I have believed, and am persuaded that He is able to keep that which I have committed to Him. Pretensions to original thought I have never made. I invent nothing, I only tell the old, old story as God enables me. " Ah," said a certain divine to me one day, " it must be very easy to you to preach because you know what you are going to say ; your views are fixed and stereotyped. As for me," he said, " I am always seeking after truth, and I do not know one week what I may preach the next." Thus speak the teachers—do you wonder if the disciples wander into scepticism ? Has the Lord taught the man nothing of sure truth ? Then let him wait till he has received his message. Till he knows the gospel in his own heart experimentally as the power of God unto Salvation let him sit on the penitent form and ask to be prayed for, but never enter a pulpit. What are the churches at to tolerate these sowers of infidelity ? Time was when the fathers in our Israel would have chased from their pulpits those who glory in the unbelief which is their shame. May the Lord of peace Himself give you peace as to your personal beliefs and convictions, and then when you get into deep waters of trial and sorrow you will say, " Ah, I did believe the right doctrine after all. I can feel the grip of my anchor on the things unseen. I have not been deceived. I have not followed cunningly devised fables, for the promise is true and I feel the power of it, it sustains and cheers and comforts. me under all my trials, and I know that it will do so even to my dying hour." May every troubled thinker find the peace of faith and never lose it.

Many minds are for ever restless as to their fears. It is a great thing to know what you tremble at, for when you know what you fear your fear is half gone. The indefinable shape, the mysterious hand which has no arm, but writes upon the wall in strange characters,—the cloudiness of all things dreaded makes the mind more restless. But blessed is the man to whom the Lord has taught His fear, so that he knows what he fears, and does not permit his hopes to be in perpetual eclipse.

Of this many-sided peace we must say something more. The Thessalonian church had been troubled thre ways. They had been *persecuted from without*. That is not a pleasant thing, but the apostle says, " You that are troubled rest with us." Now, when the Lord Jesus Christ says to a persecuted saint, " I am with you : all the evil which is done unto you is done unto Me, and you are bearing it for My name's sake," then, beloved, no persecution can break the peace of the soul, but rather the sufferer rejoices and is exceeding glad that he is counted worthy, not only to believe in Christ, but to suffer for His sake.

Next, the Thessalonian church was annoyed by certain *false teachers*. They did not absolutely teach novel doctrine, but upon a basis of truth they erected an edifice of error. They exaggerated one special truth, and carried its teaching to extravagance. They said, Christ is coming, therefore the day of the Lord is immediately at hand. They belonged to that order of fanatics who are always raving about " the signs of the times," and pretending to know what will happen within the next twenty years. There were impostors of that sort in Paul's day, and there are such impostors now. Believe them not, they can see no more of the future than blind horses. I put them all together as impostors, whether they are preachers or literary hacks, for no man knoweth the future, and no man can tell his fellow about it I care no more for their explanations of prophecy than for the pretended winking of the eyes of the Madonna ; yet they will continue the cheat, and will be saying, one this thing and another that, that this and that wonder shall happen and that terrible judgments shall overwhelm our nation. The apostle would not have the Thessalonians disturbed in their minds by fears about the future. Brethren in Christ, the most terrible fact of the future can be no just cause of alarm to a true believer. The Lord comforts His people, and there is nothing in His plans or purposes which is intended to disquiet them. You may rest assured that if any doctrine in the Bible prevents a godly man from enjoying peace, it must be because he has not yet understood it fully, or else has mistaken its bearing towards himself. Truth must minister peace to true men. All truth, whether doctrinal or prophetic, is on the side of the children of God ; how can it be otherwise ? The apostle tells the Thessalonians not to be disturbed about the coming of Christ. " The Lord be with you all," saith he, and if the Lord be with us, what matters it to us whether He personally comes at once or chooses to delay ? We should be looking for His coming, but not with alarm, for the fact that He has come already is a well-spring of delight. We glory in His first advent, and do not dread the second : since we are already raised up into the heavenly places to sit with Him by faith, what matters it to us whether He is up there or down here, or or whether we are in heaven or on earth, so long as we abide in Him. There may arise, possibly there will arise, wild fanatics who will again spread alarming news about wars and rumours of wars, and select some fatal year as the end of all things. Well, if such things should be, if crowds should go into the wilderness or into the city to look for the coming of Christ, believe them not, but sit ye still in peace and tranquillity of spirit and say, " My soul loves Him and He loves me. He cannot mean ill to me whether He destroys the earth or spares it. Though the heavens pass away and the earth itself melt with fervent heat, my heart is resting in her Lord and knows herself to be secure." Thus the Lord saves His people from the disturbance caused by false teaching.

There were also in the church disorderly characters, people that went about spreading idle tales and gossiping. They would not do anything for a living, and so they set people by the ears. But when the Lord gives a Christian man deep spiritual peace within, he soon puts aside the small nuisances of idle tongues and disorderly deeds. He refuses to be worried. Mosquitoes buzz around every Christian church, and blessed is the man that does not feel their bite or heed their buzzing ; his soul shall dwell at ease. Peace from church troublers is a great blessing, and we ought to praise God for it when we are in the enjoyment of it, for strife within the church, like civil war, is the worst of warfare. O to live in holy love and unbroken concord in reference to all our fellow Christians. May the Lord of peace grant us this.

Thus, you see, the peace which is here spoken of has many sides to it. May you possess it in all its forms, modes, and phases, and may your spirit enter into the peace of God which passeth all understanding.

II. Now, secondly, let us note THE SPECIAL DESIRABLENESS OF PEACE. It is a very great thing for a soul to realize perfect peace, for if it does not do so, it must miss the joy, and comfort, and blessedness of the Christian life. God never meant His children to be like thistledown, wafted about with every breath, nor as a football, hurled to and fro by every foot. He meant us to be a happy, restful, established people. The cattle crop the grass, but they are not fattened till they lie down and ruminate in peace : the Lord makes His people to feed and to lie down in quietness. You do not know the gospel, fear friends, if you have not obtained peace through it ; peace is the juice, the essence, the soul of the gospel. Doctrines are clusters, but you have never trodden them in the wine vat, you have never quaffed the flowing juice of their grapes if you have not

peacefully considered divine truth in the quiet of your heart.

Without peace you cannot grow. A shepherd may find good pasture for his flock, but if his sheep are hunted about by wild dogs, so that they cannot rest, they will become mere skin and bone. The Lord's lambs cannot grow if they are worried and harried ; they must enjoy the rest wherewith the Lord maketh the weary to rest. If your soul is always sighing, and moaning, and questioning its interest in Christ, if you are always in suspense as to what doctrine is true and what is false, if there is nothing established and settled about you, you will never come to the fulness of the stature of a man in Christ Jesus.

Neither without peace can you bear much fruit, if any. If a tree is frequently transplanted you cannot reasonably look for many golden apples upon its boughs. The man who has no root-hold, who neither believes, nor grasps, nor enjoys the gospel, can never know what it is to be steadfast, unmovable, neither will he be always abounding in the work of the Lord.

We know, too, some who, because they have no conscious peace with God, lack all stability, and are the prey of error. That doctrine can soon be driven out of a man's head which affords no light and comfort to his heart. If you derive no sweetness from what you believe, I should not marvel if you soon begin to doubt it. The power of the gospel is its best evidence to the soul ; a man always believes in that which he enjoys. Only make a truth to be a man's spiritual food, let it be marrow and fatness to him, and I warrant you he will believe it. When truth becomes to a proud carnal mind what the manna became to murmuring Israel, namely, light bread that his soul abhorreth, then the puffed up intellect cries after something more pleasing to the flesh ; but to the mind which hungers and thirsts after righteousness the gospel is so soul-satisfying that it never wearies of it.

Brethren, you must have peace for your soul's wealth. What a difference there is between a soul at peace and a soul continually tossed about ! I have seen one man's heart like a country whose hedges are broken down, whose walls are laid level with the ground, where irrigation is neglected, where tilling has ceased, where the vines are untrimmed, where the fields are unploughed, and all because there is a perpetual sound of war in the soul, and the song of peace is never heard. Such a soul may be likened to the Holy Land beneath Turkish rule, where no man has rest, and consequently the highways lie waste, and the gardens are a desert. But I have seen another man's life which has grown up under the influence of holy peace, from whom God has kept back the wandering Arabs of doubt and fear, and to whom He has given a settled government of grace and an establishment in steadfastness and quiet assurance, and, lo, that man has been as the land which floweth with milk and honey. As war spends and peace gathers the riches of the nations, so does inward strife devour us, while spiritual peace makes the soul fat. Even as Palestine when it abounded in corn and wine and oil could nourish Tyre and Sidon, which border thereon, even so does the man who is rich towards God through internal peace become a feeder of other souls, till even they who are but borderers upon Immanuel's land obtain a blessing. Beloved, I would that every Christian knew this soul-enriching peace to the full. I am sorry to meet with so many who " hope " they are believers, and " trust " they are saved, but they are not sure. Ah, brethren, in these matters we must get beyond mere hopes, we must reach to certainties. " If's " and " buts " are terrible in the things which concern the soul and eternity. We must have plain and unquestionable security here, divine security applied to the soul itself by the Holy Ghost. Friend, you are either saved this morning or you are not saved ; either you are in the love of God, or you are not ; either you are secure of heaven, or you are not—one of the two. I beseech you, do not let these things be in jeopardy ; chance anything rather than your soul. Cry mightily to God that you may have these things fixed, certain, positive, beyond all dispute, for then shall your soul enjoy peace with God, and so shall you become strong, useful, and happy.

III. Now, thirdly, we shall get into the very heart of our text while we consider for a minute or two THE SOLE PERSON FROM WHOM THIS PEACE MUST COME—" Now the Lord of peace Himself give you peace." Who is this " Lord of Peace " but the Lord Jesus, the Prince of Peace, born into the world when there was peace all over the world ? It was but a little interval in which the gates of the temple of war were closed, and lo, Jesus came to Bethlehem, and angels sang, " Peace on earth." He came to establish an empire of peace which shall be universal, and under whose influence they shall hang the useless helmet high and study war no more. " The Prince of Peace ! " How blessed is the title ! So was it written of old by Esaias, and Paul, the true successor of Isaiah, changing but a word, now speaks of " The Lord of peace." This is He Who, being in Himself essential peace, undertook to be the Father's great Ambassador, and having made peace by the blood of His cross, ended the strife between man and his offended Maker. This is He Who is our peace, Who hath made Jew and Gentile one, and broken down the middle wall of partition which stood between us. This is the Lord who, when He stood in the midst of His disciples, gave them peace by saying, " Peace be unto you " ; and this is He who in His departure made His last will and testament, and wrote therein this grand legacy—" Peace I leave with you, My peace I give unto you ; not as the world giveth give I unto you." This is that Lord of peace to whom it is part of His nature and office to give peace.

I want to call particular attention to the apostle's words in this place. He does not say " May the Lord of peace send His angel to give you peace." It were a great mercy if He did, and we might be as glad as Jacob was at Mahanaim, when the angels of God met him. He does not even say, " May the Lord of peace send His minister to give you peace." If He did we might be as happy as Abraham when Melchizedec refreshed him with bread and wine. He does not even say, " May the Lord of peace at the communion table, or in reading the word, or in prayer, or in some other sacred exercise give you peace." In all these we might well be as refreshed as Israel was at Elim where wells and palm trees gladdened the tribes ; but he says " the Lord of peace Himself give you peace," as if He alone in His own person could give peace, and as if His presence were the sole means of such a divine peace as He desires.

" The Lord of peace Himself give you peace."

The words are inexpressibly sweet to me. If you will think for a minute you will see that we never do obtain peace except from the Lord Himself. What after all in your worst times will bring you peace ? I will tell you. " This Man shall be the peace." To me it has often afforded great peace to think of His mysterious person. He is a Man tempted in all points like as I am, a Man who knows every grief of the soul and every pain of the body, hence His tender sympathy and power to succour. Have you not often derived peace from that sweet reflection ? You know you have. His person then is a source of peace. And have you not been rested in your soul by meditating upon His death ? You have viewed Him wounded, bleeding, dying on the tree ; and, insensibly to yourself, a wondrous calm has stolen over your heart, and you have felt pacified concerning all things. Yes, Jesus is Himself that bundle of myrrh and spice from which peace flows like a sweet perfume. When He comes very near your heart and lays bare His wounds, and speaks His love home to you, making you feel its divine fervency, when He assures you that you are one with Him, united to Him in an everlasting wedlock, which knows of no divorce—then it is that your soul is steeped in peace. This is an experimental business and no mere words can express it. " The Lord of peace Himself give you peace,"—this, I say, He does mainly by manifesting Himself to the heart of His servants.

Then notice that the text says, " give you peace," not merely offer it to you, or argue with you that you ought to have peace, or show you the grounds of peace, but " give you peace." He has the power to breathe peace into the heart, to create peace in the soul, and lull the spirit into that sweet sleep of the beloved which is the peculiar gift of heaven. " I will give you rest," said He, and He can and will do it.

" The Lord be with you all " : as much as to say, " That is what I mean." I pray that Jesus may be with you, for if He is present you must enjoy peace. Let the sea rage and let every timber of the ship be strained ; yea, let her leak till between each timber there yawns a hungry mouth to swallow you up quick ; yet when Jesus arises He will rebuke the winds and the waves, and there will be a great calm. " It is I, be not afraid," is enough to create peace at once. May you always know this peace which Jesus alone can give.

IV. Now I must conclude with the fourth head, which is consideration of THE SWEEP OF THE PRAYER—" The Lord of peace Himself give you peace always."

What ! always at peace ? Yes, that is what the apostle desires for you. May you have peace given you always. " Well, sir, I feel very happy on Sabbath-days. I have such peace that I wish I could have a week of Sundays." May the Lord Himself give you peace always, on all the week days as well as on the Lord's days. " Truly, I have been very happy of late," says one, " God has prospered us and everyone has been very loving in the family ; but I do not know how I should be if I had an awkward husband and unruly children." Sister, I will tell you what I want you to be—I would have you restful under all circumstances—" The Lord of peace give you peace always." " I enjoy such peace in the prayer-meeting," says one. I want you to have peace in the workshop also. " I do have peace when I get alone with my

Bible," cries another. We pray that you may have equal peace when you are troubled with the ledger, and tired with those unpaid bills, and dull trade, and cross currents of business. You need peace always. Our friends who are commonly called Quakers have, as a rule, set us a fine example of calm, dignified quietness and peace. How undisturbed they generally appear. Whatever they fail in they certainly excel in a certain peacefulness of manner which I hope is the index of calm enjoyed within. Numbers of professors are very fretful, excitable, agitated, hasty, and fickle. It should not be so, brethren; you ought to have more weight about you, more grace, more solidity. Your souls affairs are all right, are they not? All is right for ever, everything is signed, sealed, and delivered; the the covenant is ordered in all things and sure, and everything is in divine hands for our good. Well, then, why not let us be as happy as the angels are? Why are we troubled? Is there anything worth shedding a tear for now that all is well for eternity? Our want of peace arises from the fact that we have not realized the fulness of our text. "The Lord of peace Himself give you peace always." He can always give you peace, for he never changes; there is always the some reason for peace; you may always go to Him for peace, and He is always ready to bestow it. Oh that we might always possess it.

Notice, again, it is written—"May the Lord of peace give you peace always *by all means.*" Can He give us peace by all means? I know He can give us peace by some means, but can all means be made subservient to this end? Some agencies evidently work towards peace, but can He give us peace by opposing forces? Yes, certainly: He can give peace by the bitter as well as by the sweet, peace by the storm as well as by the calm, peace by loss as well as by gain, peace by death as well as by life. For, notice there are two grand ways of giving us peace: and one is by taking away all that disquiets us. Here is a man who frets because he does not make money, or because he has lost much of his wealth. Suppose the Lord takes away from him all covetousness, all greed of gain, all love of the world —is he not at once filled with peace? He is at peace not because he has more money, but because he has less of grasping desire. Another man is very ambitious, he wants to be somebody, he must be great, and yet he never will be, and therefore he is restless. Suppose the grace of God should humble him and take away his lofty aspirations, so that he only wishes to be and to do what the Lord wills. Do you not see how readily he rests? Another man has an angry temper, and is soon put out: the Lord does not alter the people that are round about him, but he changes the man himself, makes him quiet, ready to forgive, and of a gentle spirit. What peace the man now feels! Another person has had an envious eye—he did not like to see others prosper, and if others were better off than himself he always thought hardly of them. The Lord wrings that bitter drop of envy out of his heart, and now see how peaceful he is—he is glad to see others advanced, and if he is tried himself it helps to make him happy to think that others are more favoured. It is a great blessing when the Lord removes the disturbing elements from the heart. Even curiosity may be a source of unrest. Many are a great deal worried by curiosity. I have sometimes wanted to know why the Lord does this and that with me. Blessed be His name, I am

resolved not to question Him any more in that fashion. Somebody prayed the other day that I might see the reason why the Lord has lately afflicted me. I hope the brother will not pray that any more, for I do not want to know the Lord's reasons—why should I? I know He has done right, and I will not dishonour Him by catechizing Him and wanting Him to explain Himself to a poor worm. This is where the mischief has been with most of us, that we have wanted to see how this and that can be right. Why should we? If God conceals a thing let us be anxious to keep it concealed. A servant was passing through a street with a dish that was curiously covered. There met him a fellow who said, " I am most anxious to know what thy lord has put in that dish, for he has so carefully covered it." But the servant said, " Therefore shouldst thou not desire to know, for seeing my lord has so carefully covered it, it is clear that it is no business of thine." So whenever a providence puzzles you take it as a sign that the Lord does not mean you to understand it, and be content to take it upon faith. When curiosity and other restless things are gone peace is enjoyed.

Then the Lord has ways of giving us peace by making discoveries of Himself. Some of you do not know as yet the things which would give you peace. For instance, if you did but know that He loved you from before the foundation of the world, and that whom once He loves He never leaves, you who are now afraid that you have fallen from grace would obtain strong consolation. Aye, and if you understood the grand doctrine of the divine decree, and saw that the Lord will not fail nor be discouraged, nor turn aside from one jot or tittle of His purpose, then you would see how you, poor insignificant believers though you be, are one stitch in the great fabric that must not be suffered to drop, or else the whole fabric will be marred. You would understand how the eternal purpose ordered in wisdom, and backed up with sovereign power, guarantees your salvation as much as it does the glory of God, and so you would have peace.

Many a soul has not the peace it might have, because it does not fully understand the atoning blood. The great doctrine of substitution is not seen in all its length and breadth by some minds. But when they come to see Christ standing in the place of His chosen, made sin for them, and the chosen standing in Christ's place, "the righteousness of God in Him," then will their peace be like a river. The grand truth of the union of the saints with Christ, if it be once understood, what a means of peace it is! He that believeth in Christ is one with Him, a member of His body, of His flesh, and of His bones, one with Christ by eternal and indissoluble union, even as the Father is one with the Son. If this be known, together with the doctrine of the covenant, the attribute of immutability, the eternal purpose, and the marriage union between Christ and His elect, deep peace must be enjoyed, like the calm of heaven, like the bliss of immortality.

But there are some to whom this peace cannot come, some concerning whom the Lord saith, "What hast thou to do with peace?" "There is no peace, saith my God, unto the wicked." Your works, your prayers, your repentances, none of these can bring you peace. As for the world and the pleasures thereof, they are destructive to all hope of peace. Come ye this day and believe in the great sacrifice which God Himself has prepared in the person of His crucified

Son. Come, look into Emmanuel's face, and read where peace is to be found. Come to the great gash in Jesus' side, and see the cleft of the rock where God's elect abide in peace. Trust in Jesus and you shall begin a peace which shall widen and deepen into the peace of God which passeth all understanding, which shall keep your hearts and minds by Christ Jesus. Amen.

THE GLORIOUS GOSPEL OF THE BLESSED GOD

" According to the glorious gospel of the blessed God, which was committed to my trust."—1 Timothy i. 11.

THIS verse occurs just after a long list of sins, which the apostle declares to be contrary to sound doctrine; from which we gather that one test of sound doctrine is its opposition to every form of sin. That doctrine which in any way palliates sin may be popular, but is not sound doctrine : those who talk much of their soundness, but yet by their lives betray the rottenness of their hearts, need far rather to be ashamed of their hypocrisy than to be proud of their orthodoxy. The apostle offers us in the verse before us another standard by which to test the doctrines which we hear ; he tells us that sound doctrine is always evangelical—" sound doctrine according to the glorious gospel." Any doctrine which sets up the will or the merit of man, any doctrine which exalts priestcraft and ceremonial, any doctrine, in fact, which does not put salvation upon the sole footing of free grace, is unsound. These two points are absolutely needful in every teaching which professes to come from God ; it must commend, and foster holiness of life ; and, at the same time, it must, beyond all question, be a declaration of grace and mercy through the Mediator.

Our apostle was, by the drift of his letter, led incidentally to make mention of the gospel ; and then, in a moment, taking to himself wings of fire, he mounts into a transport of praise, and calls it " the glorious gospel of the blessed God." Such is his mode of writing generally, that if he comes across a favourite thought, he is away at a tangent from the subject that he was aiming at, and does not return until his ardent spirit cools again. In this case, or ever he was aware, his soul made him like the chariots of Ammi-nadib. His glowing heart poured forth the warmest eulogium upon that hidden treasure, that pearl of price immense, which he prized beyond all price, and guarded with a sacred jealousy of care. I think I see the radiant countenance of the apostle of the Lord, as with flashing eye he dictates the words, " The glorious gospel of the blessed God, which was committed to my trust."

Our subject affords us fine sea-room, but our time is short, our boat is small, and the atmosphere is so hot and heavy that scarcely a breath of air is to be had, and therefore I will keep to one straightforward track, and not distract you with many topics. To open up the text in all its length and breadth would be fit exercise for the loftiest intellect, but we must be content with a few experimental and practical remarks, and may the Lord enable us to weave them into a heart-searching discourse.

I. In the first place, then, Paul praises the gospel to the utmost by calling it " the glorious gospel of the blessed God "; HAVE WE EXPERIENCED ITS EXCELLENCE ?

It is needful to ask the question even in this congregation ; for even to great multitudes who attend our houses of prayer, the gospel is a dry, uninteresting subject. They hear the word because it is their duty ; they sit in the pew because custom requires an outward respect to religion ; but they never dream of the gospel having anything glorious in it, anything that can stir the heart or make the pulse beat at a faster rate. The sermon is slow, the service is dull, the whole affair is a weariness to which nothing but propriety makes men submit. Some people do their religion as a matter of necessity, as a horse drags a waggon ; but if that necessity of respectability did not exist, they would be as glad to escape from it as the horse is to leave the shafts and to miss the rumbling of the wheels. It is necessary, then, to ask the question ; and I shall put it before you in three or four ways. Paul calls the sacred message of mercy *the gospel.* Has it been the gospel to us ? The word is plain, and I hardly need remind you that it means " good news." Now, has the gospel been " good news " to us ? Has it ever been " *news* " to you ? " We have heard it so often," says one, " that we cannot expect it to be news to us. We were trained by godly parents ; we were taken to the Sunday-school ; we have learned the gospel from our youth up ; it cannot be news to us." Let me say to you, then, that you do not know the word of reconciliation unless it has been, and still is, news to you. To every man who is ever saved by the gospel, it comes as a piece of news as novel, fresh, and startling, as if he had never heard it before. The letter may be old, but the inward meaning is as new as though the ink were not dry yet in the pen of revelation. I confess to have been tutored in piety, put into my cradle by prayerful hands, and lulled to sleep by songs concerning Jesus ; but after having heard the gospel continually, with line upon line, precept upon precept, here much and there much, yet when the word of the Lord came to me with power, it was as new as if I had lived among the unvisited tribes of central Africa, and had never heard the tidings of the cleansing fountain filled with blood from the Saviour's veins. The gospel in its spirit and power always wears the dew of its youth ; it glitters with morning's freshness—its strength and its glory abide for ever. Ah ! my dear hearer, if thou hast ever felt thy guilt, if thou hast been burdened under a sense of it, if thou hast looked into thine own heart to find some good thing, and been bitterly disappointed, if thou hast gone up and down through the world to try this and that scheme of getting relief, and found them all fail thee like dry wells in the desert which mock the traveller, it will be a sweet piece of news to thy heart that there is present salvation in the Saviour. It is a most refreshing novelty to hear the voice of Jesus say, " Come unto Me and rest." Though thou hast heard the invitation outwardly thousands of times, yet Jesus' own voice, when He speaks to thy heart, will be as surprisingly fresh to thee as if these dumb walls should suddenly find a tongue, and reveal the mysteries which have been hidden from the foundation of the world. To every believer the gospel comes as news from the land beyond the river, God's mind revealed by God's Spirit to His chosen.

It is *good* news too. Now, has the gospel ever been experimentally *good* to you, my hearer? Good in the best sense, good emphatically, good without any admixture of evil, the gospel is to those who know it: is it so to you? Have you ever been deeply sensible of your overwhelming debt to the justice of God, and then gladly received the gracious information that your debts are all discharged? Have you trembled beneath the thunder-charged cloud of Jehovah's wrath, which was ready to pour forth its tempest upon you, and have you heard the gentle voice of mercy saying, " I have blotted out, as a thick cloud, thy transgressions, and, as a cloud, thy sins " ? Hast thou ever known what it is to be fully absolved, to stand before God without fear, accepted in the Beloved, received as a dear child, covered with the righteousness of Christ ? If so, the gospel has been " *good* " indeed to thee. Grasping it by the hand of faith, and feeling the power of it in thy soul, thou countest it to be the best tidings that ever came from God to man.

I shall now ask you earnestly to answer my question as in the sight of God ; let no man escape from this most vital enquiry, Has that which Paul calls the gospel, proved itself to be gospel to you ? Did it ever make your heart leap, just as some highly gratifying information excites and charms you ? Has it ever seemed to you an all-important thing ? If not, thou knowest not what the gospel means. O let my anxious questions tenderly quicken thee to be concerned about thy soul's affairs, and to seek unto the Lord Jesus for eternal life.

Paul having called the message of mercy " the gospel," then adds an adjective—" *the glorious gospel*," and a glorious gospel it is for a thousand reasons : glorious in its antiquity ; for before the beams of the first morning drove away primeval shades, this gospel of our salvation was ordained in the mind of the Eternal. It is glorious because it is everlasting—when all things shall have passed away as the hoar frost of the morning dissolves before the rising sun, this gospel shall still exist in all its power and grace. It is glorious because it reveals the glory of God more fully than all the universe beside. Not all the innumerable worlds that God has ever fashioned, though they speak to us in loftiest eloquence from their celestial spheres, can proclaim to us the character of our heavenly Father as the gospel does. " The heavens are telling the glory of God," but the gospel which tells of Jesus has a sweeter and a clearer speech. The poet talks of the great and wide sea wherein the Almighty form mirrors itself in tempest ; so, indeed, the finger of God may mirror itself, but a thousand oceans could not mirror the Infinite Himself—the gospel of Jesus Christ is the only molten looking-glass in which Jehovah can be seen. In Jesus we see not only God's train, such as Moses saw when he beheld the skirts of Jehovah's robe in the cleft of the rock, but the whole of God is revealed in the gospel of Jesus, so that our Lord could say, " He that hath seen Me, hath seen the Father." If the Lord be glorious in holiness, such the gospel reveals Him. Is His right hand glorious in power ? so the gospel speaks of Him. Is the Lord the God of love ? Is not this the genius of the gospel ? The gospel is glorious because every attribute of Deity is manifested in it with unrivalled splendour.

But I desire to come home to your consciences by asking, Is the gospel *to you* a glorious gospel ? Beloved friends, we may know our state very much by what answer we shall give to that question. The gospel, seen with these eyes and heard with these external ears, will be like the Lord Himself, " A root out of a dry ground, having no form nor comeliness " ; but the gospel understood by the renewed heart, will be quite a different thing. Oh, it will be a glorious gospel indeed, if you are raised up in newness of life, to enjoy the blessings which it brings to you. So, I beseech you, answer the question : and to help you, let me remind the people of God how glorious the gospel has been to them. Do you recollect the day when the gospel carried your heart by storm ? You never can forget when the great battering-ram of truth began to beat against the gates of Mansoul. You recollect how you strengthened the posts and bars, and stood out against the gospel, resolving not to yield. You were at times compelled to weep under impressions, but you wiped away your transient tears—your emotion was " as the morning cloud, and as the early dew." But eternal love would not relinquish its gracious assaults, for it was determined to save. Providence and grace together besieged the city of your soul, and brought divine artillery to bear upon it. You were straightly shut up till—as it was with Samaria, so it was with you—there was a great famine in your soul. You recollect how, Sabbath after Sabbath, every sermon was a fresh assault from the hosts of heaven—a new blow from the celestial battering-ram. How often, when the gates of your prejudice were dashed to shivers, did you set up fresh barricades ! Your heart trembled beneath the terrible strokes of justice, but, by the help of Satan, your depraved heart managed to secure the gates a little longer with iron clamps of pride, and brazen bars of insensibility ; till at last, one blessed day— do you remember it ?—one blessed day, the gospel battering-ram gave the effectual blow of grace, the gates flew wide open, and in rode the Prince of Peace, Immanuel, like a conqueror, riding in the chariots of salvation. Our will was subdued, our affections were overcome, our whole soul was brought into subjection to the sway of mercy. Jesus was glorious in our eyes that day, " the chief among ten thousand, and the altogether lovely." That day of days we have registered upon the tablets of our hearts : it was the true coronation-day of Jesus in us, and our birthday for eternity. When our glorious Lord entered into our souls, wearing His vesture dipped in blood, pardoning and blessing in the plenitude of His grace, then the bells of our heart rang merry peals ; the streamers of our joy floated in the fragrant air ; the streets of our soul were strewn with roses ; the fountains of our love ran with rich red wine, and our soul was as full of bliss as a heart could be this side of heaven ; for salvation has come to our house, and mercy's King had deigned to visit us. Oh, the sweet perfume of the spikenard, when, for the first time, the King sat at our table to sup with us ! how the savour of His presence filled every chamber of our inner man ! That day when grace redeemed us from our fears, the gospel was a glorious gospel indeed ! Ah ! dear hearer, you stood in the crowded aisle to hear the sermon, but you did not grow weary, the lips of the preacher refreshed you, for the truth dropped like sweet smelling myrrh. You could have gone over hedge and ditch to hear the gospel at that season of first love ; no matter how roughly it might have been served up by the preacher, you rolled the bread of heaven under your tongue as a sweet morsel, for it was the gospel of your salvation.

Christian, I will refresh your memory further. Do not forget the after conquests of that gospel. If you have made any advance in the divine life, it has been by the power of the gospel of Jesus Christ applied by the Holy Ghost. We make mistakes sometimes, for, having begun in the Spirit we hope to be made perfect in the flesh. I mean that frequently we try to battle with our inbred sins by smiting them with legal reasonings. No believer ever conquered sin by being afraid of the punishment of it—this is a weapon fit only for sons of the bond-woman. It is the blood of Jesus which is the conquering weapon in the holy war against natural corruption. " They overcame by the blood of the Lamb." Knowing that I am dead to sin and risen with Christ, it is in the power of resurrection life that I wrestle against the old man, and overcome him. Beloved, recollect that you are always weak when you get away from the cross, that it is only as a sinner saved by blood that you can hope to make any advance in sanctification. Do not attempt to flog yourself into grace, the new life must not be touched with the whip of bondage. Go to the cross for motive and energy as to holiness. Look to Jesus in the gospel as you did in the beginning of your *new* life. Know yourself to be saved in Him, and then go forth to battle with temptation, with the gospel as the standard of your lifelong warfare. If any of you have tried to make war with sin apart from the Captain of your salvation, you have either been wounded to your hurt already, or you will be ; but if Judah's Lion shall go up before you, and you follow with the gospel as your war-cry, your victory is sure, and you shall have another wreath to lay at the feet of Jesus and His glorious gospel.

Beloved, let me say that all true saints have found it to be a glorious gospel from its comforting us in our darkest hours. We are not without our troubles, for which we would be grateful ; they are flinty rocks which flow with oil. The roots of our soul might take too firm a hold upon this poor clay soil, if they were not roughly loosened by affliction ; this is not our rest, it is polluted, and our sorrows are useful because they remind us of this. But what has such power to calm the troubled spirit as the gospel ? Go ye to the Lord Jesus, ye daughters of grief ; know and understand once more your union with Him, and your acceptance in Him, and you will repine no more : you will bow your shoulder and cheerfully take up your cross when you have found out in your hour of need that the gospel has a glorious power to sustain those who are ready to sink.

Did you never perceive the glory of the gospel in its power to resist the attacks of the great enemy ? The soul has been beleagured by a thousand temptations ; Satan has howled, and all the fiends of hell have joined in horrible chorus, and your own poor distracted thoughts have said, " I shall perish notwithstanding all my high enjoyments and confidence." Have you never gathered, as John Bunyan would picture it, all your forces to the top of the wall to sling the great stones against the enemy ? Have you not felt that the castle would be taken, till, as a last resort, you ran up the blood-red flag of the cross, seized the sword of the Spirit, and went to the

rampart determined to hold the wall against the enemy ? Then when the scaling ladder touched the wall, and the foe leaped on the bulwarks, you dashed him down again in the name of Jesus by the power of the cross, and as often as he came up, so often did you hurl him down again, always overcoming in the power of the gospel ; keeping your ground against temptation from without, and corruption from within, by the energy which the gospel of Jesus Christ alone could give you.

One point may help us to see the glory of the gospel, namely, that it has saved us from tremendous ills. The ills which are to come upon the unbeliever, who shall describe them ? If a spirit could cross the bridgeless gulf which parts us from the land of darkness and the shadow of death, if he could tell us what are the pangs unutterable which are endured by guilty souls, then we might say, " Glorious indeed is that gospel which can lift us from the gates of hell, and preserve us from going down to the pit." Think, my brethren, of what the joys are for which the gospel is preparing us ! It is by the Holy Ghost, through the preaching of the word, that we are ripening for those joys which " eye hath not seen," and which " ear hath not heard." Meetness for heaven will not come to us by the law, but by the gospel. Not so much as one of the celestials came there by the deeds of the flesh, but altogether by the sovereign grace of God revealed to them in the gospel of Jesus Christ. A glorious gospel it is, for it brings its disciples to glory !

Let me ask you whether it is glorious to you at this hour ? I think I can say it is to me. I wish it were in my power to make it more glorious in my ministry ; but it is glorious to my own heart. After some years of experience, the Christian comes to know better than he did at first how much the gospel suits him. He finds that its simplicity suits his bewilderment ; its grace suits his sinfulness ; its power is suitable to his weakness ; its comfort is suitable to his despondency ; and the older he grows the more he loves the gospel of the grace of God. Give it up ? Ah ! never ; we will hold Christ the more firmly because men despise Him. To whom or whither should we go if we should turn aside from our Lord Jesus ?

Now, dear hearers, before I leave this point, I want to put to you again, with much loving solicitude. Is the gospel glorious to you ? Remember, if it be not, there can be no hope for you. There is no way of salvation except by the good news that " Jesus Christ came into the world to save sinners," and if that news should sound in your ears as a dry, dull thing, rest assured you are not on the way to heaven, for the gospel to every saved soul is sweeter than the sound of the best earthly music. Is it so to you ? God is pleased to-day to put up before your eyes the white flag of mercy, calling you to come to Jesus and live. But recollect if you do not yield to it, He will run up the red flag of threatening, and then the black flag of execution will not be far off. Perhaps some of you have been suffering under bodily disease, take that as a warning. When our vessels of war would stop a suspicious vessel, they fire a shot athwart her bows as a warning. If she does not haul to, perhaps they give another, and if no notice is taken of this, the gunners go to their business in real earnest, and woe to the offender. Your affliction is the gospel's warning gun. Pause awhile, I beseech you, ask the Lord in mercy to look upon you that you may be saved! As I think upon some of you here who are not saved, I feel something like the boy I read of yesterday in the newspapers. Last week there were two lads on the great rocks of Lundy Island, in the Bristol Channel, looking for sea-gulls' eggs ; one of them went far down the cliff, and lost his footing, and when his brother, hearing a faint voice, looked down, he saw him clinging to a jutting crag, and striving in vain to find a place for his feet. There stood the anxious brother, alarmed and paralysed with dread, quite unable to help the younger one in so much peril below, who soon relaxed his hold, and was dashed to pieces far beneath. I feel somewhat like that alarmed brother, only there is this happy difference : I *can* hope for you, and bid you hope for yourselves. You are clinging now, perhaps, to some false hope, and striving to find a rest where rest is not to be found ; but the strong-winged angel of the everlasting gospel is just underneath you this morning, crying, " Drop now ; simply drop into my arms ; I will take you and bear you aloft in safety." That angel is the Angel of the Covenant, the Lord Jesus Christ. You must be dashed to pieces for ever unless you rest in Him ; but cast yourself upon Him, I pray you, and then, as you are carried in safety far off from every fear, you will magnify the grace of God, and extol the glorious gospel.

I must leave that point, and observe that Paul recognized the gospel as being *the gospel of God.* Here arises another enquiry, by which we may know whether we are saved or not. Has the gospel been the gospel of God to you, my friends ? It is easy to receive the gospel as the gospel of " my minister." I am afraid there is a good deal of that sort of thing among us. We have great faith in our religious teachers, and very properly so, if we have received benefit from them ; but if the gospel only comes to us as the gospel of such-and-such a preacher, it will not save us ; it must come distinctly and directly as *God's* gospel, and we must receive it so. It is in solemn silence of the mind our privilege to hear the voice of God speaking to us, and to receive the truth in the love of it as coming with divine authority directly from God. Recollect that all religion which is not the work of the Holy Spirit in the heart will have to be unravelled, let it be woven ever so cunningly. We may build, as our little children do on the sea-shore, our sand houses, and we may pile them up very quickly too, and be very pleased with them, but they will all come down as the tide of time advances ; only that which God the Holy Ghost builds upon the foundation of Christ's finished work will stand the test of time and eternity. How is it with you ? If the Spirit of Christ be not in you ye are dead. If the gospel itself should come to you in a sort of power, but only because of the pathos of the preacher, or the eloquent manner of his speech, it has not brought eternal life to you.

If the gospel be indeed the gospel of God to us, it will exalt God in our estimation. The Father we shall love and adore, having chosen us to eternal life. The Son we shall love with warmest affection, having redeemed us with His precious blood. The Holy Spirit we shall constantly reverence, and we shall cherish Him as dwelling a welcome guest within these bodies of ours. By this we may tell whether we have received the truth of God, by its bringing us consciously into connection with God. Does

God dwell in you, my hearer ? for, if not, you will not dwell where God is. You must know the Holy Spirit, not as an influence to be poured out as some pray, but as dwelling within you, resting in your heart. I put that as a very important question, but I will not pause over it, for I have to close our first head by noticing that the gospel was to Paul the " *gospel of the blessed God.*" I believe William Knibb used to read this passage, " The gospel of the happy God," and it was not a mistake—it is the very gist of the matter. " The gospel of the happy God." Have you ever considered how happy God must be! how supremely happy ? No care, no sorrow, can ever pass across His infinite mind. He is serenely blessed evermore. Now, when a man is miserable, and of a miserable turn of mind, he as naturally makes people miserable, as a foul fountain pours out foul water ; but when a good man is superlatively happy, he imparts happiness. A happy face attracts many of us, and a happy temperament, a quiet mind, a serene disposition, why, a man who has these, inevitably tries to make others happy ; and it is, I suppose, because God is infinitely happy, that He delights in the happiness of His creatures. The fabled gods of the heathen were vexed with all sorts of ambitions, longings, and cravings, which they could not gratify, or which, when gratified, only made them crave the more, consequently they were pictured as revengeful and cruel, delighting in the miseries of men ; but our God is so perfectly blessed, that He has no motive for causing needless sorrow to His creatures. He has all perfection within Himself ; and, consequently, He delights to make us happy. How much satisfaction God finds in the happiness of creatures that are devoid of intellect ? You may have seen sometimes when the sea is going down, a little fringe at the edge of the wave which looks like mist ; but if you were carefully to examine it, you would find that there were countless multitudes of very tiny shrimps, all leaping up and casting themselves into all manner of forms of intense delight. Look again at the gnats, as you walk in your gardens in the summer's evenings—how they dance up and down— these little mirthful beings are all exhibiting to us the perfect blessedness that God would have to be manifested by all His creatures. He would have His people supremely blest, He would have every vessel of mercy full to the brim with the oil of joy, and the way to make us so is to give us the gospel. The gospel is sent, to use our Saviour's words, " that His joy may be in us, and that our joy may be full." We enjoy heaven upon earth as we sit at the feast of fat things on earth—what will be our glory when the gospel of the blessed God shall have turned out all our sin ; when we shall swim in the gospel as the fish swims in the sea ; when the gospel shall become our element in the next world. Oh! the happiness of the creatures that are full of the gospel spirit before the throne of God! Dear hearers, did the gospel ever come to you in that shape ? I am afraid that to most people the gospel is a bondage, because they do not know it in very deed. I am afraid that to many, gospel emotion is a sort of spasm ; they are satisfied with the truth sometimes, and at other times when they feel they must have a treat, they go into the world for it. Where you get your treats there your heart is ; whatever it is that gives you the most happiness, that is the master of your spirit. The Christian feels that he can sing with old Mason :—

" I need not go abroad for joys, I have a feast at home ;
　My sighs are turned into songs, my heart has ceased to
　　　roam.
　Down from above the bless'd Dove is come into my
　　　breast,
　To witness God's eternal love, and give my spirit rest.
　My God, I'll praise Thee while I live, and praise Thee
　　　when I die ;
　And praise Thee when I rise again, and to eternity."

The religion of the genuine Christian is calculated to impart perfect delight ; the truly regenerated man desires to have more and more of it, that his soul may be baptized in heavenly joy.

" The gospel of the happy God " also means the gospel of the God whom we must bless in return. As being happy, He makes us happy ; so we, being happy, desire to ascribe to Him all the glory of our happiness. Now, is the gospel to you, my dear young friend over there, the gospel of a God whom you bless from all your heart, because He has sent it to you, and made you willing to receive it ? If so, you are saved. But if not, if no emotions of sincere gratitude stirs the deeps of your soul, then the gospel has been to you no more than a sounding brass and a tinkling cymbal.

II. The apostle says, " The glorious gospel of the blessed God, which is committed to my trust " : DO YOU RECOGNISE YOUR RESPONSIBILITY ?

Paul speaks not here of himself alone ; he might have said, " which is committed to the trust of every believer in Christ." The gospel is a priceless treasure, and the saints are the bankers of it. It is committed to our trust as men commit business to their agents.

First, we are bound *to believe it all*. Take heed of receiving a divided and maimed gospel. It has been said that " only half the truth is a lie," and so it is. Most of the ill reports which distress the world have truth at the foundation of them, but they become false through the exaggeration of one part, and the omission of the next. It should be the duty of every enlightened Christian to labour to master the whole compass of truth so far as possible. I suppose none but the Infinite mind can know all the lengths and breadths of truth, but still we should not be warped by education, nor be kept from receiving truth by prejudice. We should strive against all partiality, and it should be, whenever we open this Book, one of our prayers, " Open Thou mine eyes, that I may behold wondrous things out of Thy law." To have a mind like molten metal, ready to be run into the mould of the truth ; to have a soul like a photographer's sensitive plate, ready to receive the light-writing of God at once, so that the truth may be there in its entirety ; to be willing to give up the most cherished dogma, the most flesh-pleasing form of teaching, when we find it to be contrary to Scripture, this is to be a true disciple. To sit at Jesus' feet and learn of Him, is the life-business of the Christian in this house of his pilgrimage. The gospel is in this sense committed to our trust, for we are to lay it up in our hearts. But some one demands, " How am I to know which is the gospel ? " You may know it by searching the Scriptures. " But one sect says this, and another sect says the reverse " ; what have you to do with the sects ? Read the Book of God for yourself. " But some men do read it and arrive at one opinion, and some maintain the opposite, and thus they contradict themselves, and yet are equally right." Who told you that ? That is

impossible. Men cannot be equally right when they contradict each other. There is a truth and there is a falsehood ; if *yes* be true, *no* is false. It may be true that good men have held different opinions, but are you responsible for what they may have held, or are you to gather that because they were good personally, therefore everything they believed was true ? No, but this Book is plain enough ; it is no nose of wax that everybody may shape to what form he likes. There is something taught here plainly and positively, and if a man will but give his mind to it, by God's grace he may find it out. I do not believe that this Book is so dark and mysterious as some suppose, or, if it were, the Holy Spirit who wrote it still lives, and the Author always knows His own meaning : you have only to go to Him in prayer, and He will tell you what it means. You will not become infallible, I trust you will not think yourself to be so, but you will learn doctrines which are infallibly true, and upon which you may put down your foot and say, " Now, I know this, and am not to be duped out of it." It is a grand thing to have the truth burnt into you, as with a hot iron, so that there is no getting it out of you. The priest, when he took away the Testament from the boy, thought he had done the work ; " But," said the boy, " sir, what will you do with the six-and-twenty chapters which I learned by heart ? You cannot take them away." Yet memory might fail, and, as the lad grew into an old man, he might forget the six-and-twenty chapters ; but suppose they changed his heart and made him a new creature in Christ, there would be no getting that away, even though Satan himself should attempt the task. Seek to carry out the sacred trust committed to you by believing it, and believing it all. Search the word to find out what the gospel is, and endeavour to receive it into your inmost heart, that it may be in your heart's core for ever.

Next, as good stewards we must *maintain the cause of truth* against all comers. " Never get into religious controversies," says one ; that is to say, being interpreted, be a Christian soldier, but let your sword rust in its scabbard, and sneak into heaven like a coward. Such advice I cannot endorse. If God has called you by the truth, maintain the truth which has been the means of your salvation. We are not to be pugnacious, always contending for every crotchet of our own ; but wherein we have learned the truth of the Holy Spirit, we are not tamely to see that standard torn down which our fathers upheld at peril of their blood. This is an age in which truth must be maintained zealously, vehemently, continually. Playing fast and loose as many do, believing this to-day and that to-morrow, is the sure mark of the children of wrath ; but having received the truth, to hold fast the very form of it, as Paul bids Timothy to do, is one of the duties of heirs of heaven. Stand fast for truth, and may God give victory to the faithful.

We must believe the gospel and maintain it, for it is committed to our trust. It seems to me, however, that the most of us may best fulfil our responsibility to the gospel by *adorning it* in our lives. Men give jewels to those whom they love ; and so, if we love the gospel, let our virtues be the jewels which shall display our love. A servant girl may adorn the gospel. She goes to a place of worship, and perhaps her irreligious mistress may object to her going. I remember Mr. Jay telling a story of such a case, where master and mistress had forbidden the girl to attend a Dissenting place of worship. She pleaded very hard, and at last determined to leave the house. The master said to his wife, "Well, you see our servant girl is a very excellent servant ; we never had such an industrious girl as she is. Everything in the house is kept so orderly, and she is so obedient, and so on. Now, she does not interfere with our consciences, it is a pity we should interfere with hers. Wherever she goes, it certainly does her no hurt—why not let her go ? " In the next conversation the wife said, " I really think, husband, that our servant gets so much good where she goes, that we had better go and hear for ourselves " ; and they were soon members of the very same church which they had thought so lightly of at first. Now, we can each of us in our station do that. We are not all called to preach in these boxes called pulpits, but we may preach more conveniently and much more powerfully behind the counter or in the drawing-room, or in the parlour, or in the field, or wherever else providence may have placed us. Let us endeavour to make men mark what kind of gospel we believe. Only a few weeks ago, a missionary in China took his gun to go up one of the rivers of the interior to shoot wild ducks ; and, as he went along in the boat he shot at some ducks, and down they fell ; unfortunately, they did not happen to be wild fowl, but tame ducks belonging to some of the neighbours. The owner was miles away, but the boat was drawn up to the side of the river, and the missionary went about carefully endeavouring to find out the owner of the ducks, for he could not rest until he had paid for the damage he had ignorantly done. The owner was much surprised, he had been so accustomed to have people shoot his ducks and never say a word about it, that he could not understand the honesty of the man of God, and he told others, until crowds of Chinese gathered round and stared at the missionary as if he had dropped from the moon ; a man so extremely honest as not to be willing to take away ducks when he had killed them ! They listened to the gospel with attention, and observed that the teaching must be good which made people so conscientious as the missionary had been. I should not wonder but what that little accident did more for the gospel than the preaching of twenty sermons might have done without it. So let it be with us ; let us so act in every position that we shall adorn the gospel which is committed to our trust.

Lastly, it is committed to our trust if we have received it that we may *spread it*—spread it personally by telling it abroad. If more could preach the gospel it would be well. We have in all our congregations young men who are hard at work—at this very moment I do not doubt but what we have a hundred preaching in the street—perhaps more ; but I have sometimes regretted that so few of the wealthier men enter into such labour. We could wish to see men of ten talents preaching—the men of large abilities consecrating themselves to Christ. Many of our young members are more useful at literary institutions than in the church. Other useful occupations are all very well in their way, but I wish we could get the strength of our men spent more in the preaching of the gospel. The first business of a Christian is his Christianity, all the rest, his patriotism even, must be kept subservient to that, for heaven is more his country than England is, and Jesus Christ is rather his King than any of the earth. " Seek ye first the kingdom of God and His righteousness." I would ask young men now present who love the Lord, whether they really are doing for the cause of God what they ought to to ? Whether they could not do something more by way of making manifest in every place the savour of Jesus Christ's name ? My sisters, your voices are exceedingly sweet, but we like to hear them better anywhere than from a pulpit ; but still you have your sphere— do you occupy it for Christ ? The Christian woman's first call is to serve Jesus in the family ; next to that to serve Christ in her neighbourhood. Are we doing so ? The " glorious gospel of the blessed God " is as much committed to your trust, Christian woman, as if there were not another Christian under heaven : how would it fare if it were so ? If all other Christians died, would you have done by the gospel what it might demand of you ? All the zeal and industry of ten thousand others cannot touch your personal responsibility as a Christian.

I have to ask you, this morning, to help me to spread the glorious gospel. Some years ago, having done my utmost to preach the word with my own mouth, finding that running up and down throughout the country, preaching ten or twelve times a week, I was still able to do but very little. I thought if I found other tongues and set them talking, found other brains and set them thinking, I might, perhaps, do more for the cause of my blessed Master. One young man was thrown in my way who was educated for me by an esteemed brother for the Christian ministry ; and when he was greatly owned of God as preacher, the desire to assist students grew within my heart, and that one young man gave place to ten, then twenty, then thirty, then fifty, then ninety, as at present. The pastors' college, for which I ask your contributions this morning, has grown to be a power for good. We have had for some successive years between eighty and ninety brethren in training for the ministry. The whole of the support for them is found by the gifts of God's people, which they voluntarily send, without being waited upon by any collector, or asked for annual subscriptions. I have nothing to depend upon but the providence of God, which directs the generosity of His people. Sometimes my funds run rather short, but never so short that I am really in need, for when the treasury is scantily furnished, we call the young men together and pray about it, and many a time we have had as distinct answers to prayer as though God had stretched His hand out of heaven to give the needful money. Some five thousand pounds a-year are spent in this way, which God always sends when it is wanted. We have built several places of worship ; we have formed and founded several fresh churches ; we have evangelized the darkest districts of London and the country ; and our men are now to be found in Australia, on the rock of St. Helena, in Southern Africa, in America, and all quarters of the earth. God has been pleased to bless them, and has given them souls for their hire, and we shall be glad if you feel moved to give towards their maintenance.

Before I dismiss you, I would like to press home to each one the question, " Dost thou believe in the Lord Jesus Christ ? Has the gospel become a glorious gospel to thee ? " I do not know you as I know my own people, but when I look along my galleries I mourn over those who have been hearing the word ten years, and are the same as if they never heard it. I suppose there are some of you in the like case, and my esteemed brother, Mr. Tucker, must cast his eye around the gallery, and the area, and see many who have grown gospel hardened. It is a horrible thing to think of! The same sun that melts wax hardens clay, and to some hearts the gospel becomes the savour of death unto death. If nothing comes of this morning's service but making every one enquire how it is with his own soul ; if it shall only constrain you to go to your solitary chamber and shut the door and pray, " O Lord, let me know this glorious gospel ; I have not understood it up till now, for it has not been glorious to me. Do make it so to me this day, that I may be saved ! "—my heart will be very glad if such shall be the case.

A SERMON ON A GRAND OLD TEXT

" This is a faithful saying, and worthy of all acceptation, that Christ Jesus came into the world to save sinners; of whom I am chief."—1 Timothy i. 15.

YOU will observe that Paul wrote this verse immediately after he had given a little outline of his own personal history. He had, he said, been " a blasphemer, and a persecutor, and injurious " ; and then he added this priceless gospel verse, as if he inferred it from God's grace to him, as well as received it by inspiration, " This is a faithful saying, and worthy of all acceptation, that Christ Jesus came into the world to save sinners ; of whom I am chief." It was an experimental text then, one which the apostle fetched out of the deeps of his own soul, as divers bring pearls from the ocean bed. He dipped his pen into his own heart when he wrote these words. No preaching or teaching can equal that which is experimental. If we would impress the gospel upon others, we must have first received it ourselves. Vainly do you attempt to guide a child in the pathway which you have never trodden, or to speak to adults of benefits of grace which you have never enjoyed. Happy is that preacher who can truly say he speaks what he doth know, and testifies what he hath seen.

The testimony of Paul is peculiarly forcible, because he was a very straightforward man. Before his conversion, he was second to none in opposing the gospel. He was a downright man who never did anything by halves. As the old Saxon proverb puts it, " It was neck or nothing with him." He threw his whole nature into anything which he espoused ; and it must have been indeed a mighty inward force which led him to speed forward so eagerly in the directly opposite way to that which he had pursued with enthusiasm throughout the early part of his life. He was an honest man, a man to whom it was impossible either to lie or to be neutral ; he was truthful, sincere, outspoken, wearing his heart upon his sleeve, and carrying his soul in his open hand. When we hear him say, as the outcome of his own personal experience, that Christ Jesus came into the world to save sinners, we may be sure that he believed it with his whole being, and we may receive his testimony as one which he lived to prove, and died to seal with his blood. Never had a fact a better witness ; he lost all for its sake, and counted that loss his greatest gain. Hear ye his words, for he speaks to you from the ground which received his blood : his blood speaketh better things than that of Abel, and it cries with a voice not less loud and clear.

The text, as we find it, is like a picture surrounded with a goodly border. We sometimes see paintings of the old masters in which the bordering is as full of art as the picture itself ; we might safely say as much of our text. We will look at its framework first ; here it is : " This is a faithful saying, and worthy of all acceptation." When we have carefully considered that, we will study the great masterpiece itself, meditating upon the matchless saying, " Christ Jesus came into the world to save sinners ; of whom I am chief." When we have noticed the preface and the saying, you will then allow me to preach a short sermon upon it.

I. First, then, THE FRAMEWORK. Paul says, " it is a saying."

When we declare a sentence to be a saying, we mean that it is commonly spoken, and usually said, so that everybody knows it ; it is town talk, " familiar in our mouths as household words." Those who like harder words explain that this is an axiom, a Christian axiom,—a self-evident truth, a thing which nobody doubts who is a Christian at all ; but I will keep to our own version, and add that I greatly wish that our text were more truly a saying among all Christian people at this day. That Jesus Christ came into the world to save sinners is a truth which we all believe, but do we all talk about it so frequently as to make it in very deed a saying ? Do you think that our servants, who have lived for months in our houses, would in their gossips say, " It was one of my master's sayings, that Jesus Christ came into the world to save sinners " ? I will even ask,—Do you think that, if a person attended our places of worship for years, he would be able conscientiously to say, " Why, it was our minister's ordinary saying, it was quite a proverb with him, he was always repeating that Jesus Christ came into the world to save sinners " ? Yet a sentence cannot be called " a saying " until it is often said. It does not get into the category of sayings, and is not called by that name unless it is a matter of ordinary common talk.

I gather, then, from this, that Christian people ought to talk more about the gospel than they do, and a great deal more about that primary and elementary truth of the gospel, the coming of Jesus Christ into the world to save the guilty. Believers ought so often to speak of it that it should be currently reported, amongst even ungodly people, as one of our common phrases and stock speeches. I should like them to be able to taunt us with it as a main part of our conversation ; it would even be a good sign if they complained that we wearied them with it. Let them say, " Why, they are always harping on that string ; even their children lisp it, their young men boast of it, and their matrons and their sires affirm it, and add their solemn seal thereunto, as if it were the sheet-anchor of their lives." O ye who know the wondrous story, talk ye of the gospel by the way, talk of it when ye sit in your houses, speak of it at your work, tell it to those who pass you in the street or in the fields ! Make the world hear it, make society ring with it. If there be a new saying, though it be but a jest, men report it, and every newspaper finds a corner for it ; are we to be silent about this oldest and yet newest saying ? Men rejoice in *bon mots*, and yet this is the best of words. We have the really good news ; let us publish it, let us popularize the gospel, and compel men to know what it is. If before some men we are less communicative upon the more mysterious truths, because we fear to cast pearls before swine, yet let this simple truth, since Scripture calls it " a saying," be spoken again and again and again till it shall be confessed to be a common word among us.

Now Paul did not merely write " it is a saying," but " *it is a faithful saying*," a saying worthy of faith, a saying full of truth, a saying about which no doubts may be entertained, a sure and certain saying, " that Christ Jesus came into the world to save sinners." Many sayings in the world had been much better left unsaid. There are proverbs which pass current amongst us as gold which are spurious metal, and no man can tell the mischief which an untruthful proverb may work ; but this is a saying fraught with unmingled benefit, it is pure truth, a leaf of the tree of life sent for the healing of the nations. Some matters which were important years ago are now worn out. Times have changed and circumstances have altered, and things are not now what they were to our forefathers ; but this is a faithful saying because it is as practically true to-day as when, eighteen hundred years ago, the apostle wrote it to the beloved Timothy. This is still a saying full of blessing to the nations, " that Christ Jesus came into the world to save sinners." Like the sun, it shines with the same golden light as in the ages past ; and, blessed be God, it will still shine when you and I have gone to our rest ; and if this crazy world holds out another thousand years, or even fifty thousand, the light of the gospel will not have grown dim. This coin of heaven will not have lost its image or its superscription when time shall be no more ; it is of God's minting, and will outlast the world : " Christ Jesus came into the world to save sinners." Ah, you heard it when you were a boy, and you did not think much of it. Your years are now many, and your life has almost run its course, and you are still unsaved ; but thank God that now, in your old age, we have the same truth to tell to you, though you rejected it in your boyhood, and it is quite as certain now as then that " Christ Jesus came into the world to save sinners." To the eleventh hour this precious sentence abideth sure. May none of you despise it or doubt it, but each one of you prove it to be God's own word of salvation !

Our apostle, however, adds yet another word : this saying " *is worthy of all acceptation*." I think he meant two things. It is worthy of all the acceptation anyone can give it ; and it is worthy of the acceptation of all men. Some sayings are not worth accepting : the sooner you have done with them, and forgotten them, the better for you ; but this saying you may receive as truth, and having received it as truth to other men, it will be a happy circumstance if you receive it as truth to yourself ; for it will be a blessed day to you when you appropriate it as your own. " Christ Jesus came into the world to save sinners." If I, feeling myself a sinner, infer that Jesus came to save me, I may without any fear rest assured that I am accepting a truth, for, believing in Jesus, I may safely rejoice that He came to save *me*. You may receive this truth not only into the ear,— it is worthy of that acceptation ; or into the memory, —it is worthy of that acceptation ; but you may receive it into your inmost heart,—it is worthiest of all of that acceptation ; and, receiving it, you may lay upon it all the stress of your soul's interests for the past, the present, and the future, for time and for eternity ; you may accept it as being the mainstay, the prop and pillar of your confidence ; for it is worthy of all the acceptation that you or any other man can possibly give to it.

It is worthy, we have said, of the acceptation of all mankind. The richest, the greatest, the most learned, the most innocent, the most pure,—speaking after the manner of men,—these may accept it ; it is worthy of their acceptation. In the sight of God they still are guilty, and need that Christ should save them. And, on the other hand, the lowest, the most ignorant, the most grovelling, depraved, debauched, abandoned, helpless, hopeless, lost, castaways may receive it, for it is true to them, emphatically to them ; for Jesus Christ came into the world to save just such offenders as they are. If I stood in Cheapside to-morrow, and any man out of the crowd should come to me, and say, " Is that sentence, ' Christ Jesus came into the world to save sinners,' worth my believing and accepting ? " I should not hesitate, but without knowing who spoke to me, I should reply, " Yes." If he stopped his carriage, and came to me, or if he took his hand off the costermonger's barrow, or left his shoe-blacking box, or came with his rags about him, or if he had escaped from the prison omnibus, it would not matter who he was, I might safely assure him that this saying is worthy of his acceptation. It is not a stoop for a king or a saint to receive it, and yet it meets the level of the poorest and the worst of characters. It is worthy of everybody's acceptance.

Beloved friends, no one can ever rightly accuse us of making too much of the gospel. However earnest we may be, we can never be too earnest, and however diligent to spread it, we can never be too diligent ; for it is a gospel worthy of every man's acceptance, and, therefore, worthy of every Christian's publication. Spread it ; let the winds bear it ; let every wave proclaim it ; write it everywhere, that every eye may see it ; sound it in all places, that every ear may hear it. Simple are the words, and to some men their meaning is despised as almost childish, but it is the great power of God. " A mere platitude," they say ; yet it is a platitude which has made heaven ring with sacred mirth, a platitude which will make earth's deserts blossom like a rose, a platitude which has turned many a man's hell into heaven, and his densest darkness into the brightness of glory. Ring out that note again, " Christ Jesus came into the world to save sinners " ; it is worthy of angelic trumpets, it is worthy of the orator's loftiest speech, and of the philosopher's profoundest thought. It is worthy of every Christian's publication, as surely as it is of the acceptance of every human being. God help us never to undervalue it, but to prize it beyond all price ! There is the frame of the picture ; the basket of silver which holds the apples of gold.

II. Our meditation now turns to THE SAYING ITSELF : " Christ Jesus came into the world to save sinners." Very briefly and simply I will open up this passage as if none of us had hitherto understood it. May the Holy Ghost instruct us!

Here is, first, *a Person coming*,—a Divine Person, —Christ Jesus the anointed Saviour. The Son of God, the second person of the ever-blessed Trinity, became the Saviour of sinners. " Very God of very God " was He. He created the earth, and upon His shoulders the pillars thereof still lean. Yes, He who was personally offended by human sin ; He, Himself, deigned to become the Saviour of men. Weigh this, and marvel and adore !

Next, you have *the deed He did*, He " came into the world." He was born a babe in Bethlehem ; it was thus He came into the world. " The Word was made flesh, and dwelt among us." Thirty years and more He lived in the world. sharing to the full its poverty and toil. He was a working-man. He wore the common garb of labour ; He wrought, He hungered, He thirsted, He was sick, He was weary ; He, in all these senses, came into the world, and became a man among men ; bone of our bone, and flesh of our flesh. As it was a sinful world, He was vexed with the transgressions of those about Him ; as it was a suffering world, He bore our sickness ; as it was a dying world, He died ; and as it was a guilty world, He died the death of the guilty, suffering in their stead the wrath of God.

Mark well *the object for which He came*, He came " to save." He came into this world because men were lost, that He might find them and save them. They were guilty, and He saved them by putting Himself into their place, and bearing the consequences of their guilt. They were foul, and He saved them by coming into the world, and giving His Holy Spirit, through whose agency they might be made new creatures, and so might have pure and holy desires, and escape the corruption which is in the world through lust. He came to sinners, to take them just where they are at hell's dark door, to cleanse them in His precious blood, and fit them to dwell with Himself in eternal glory, as saved souls for ever.

This is all wonderful. Angels marvel at it, so may we ; but the most wonderful fact of all is that He came into the world to save *sinners* ; not the righteous, but the ungodly. Remember His own words, " I came not to call the righteous, but sinners to repentance." The physician comes to heal the sick ; the Saviour comes to save the lost. To attempt to save those who are not lost would be a ridiculous superfluity ; to die to pardon those who are not guilty would be a gross absurdity. It is a work of supererogation to set free those who are not in bonds. Christ came not to perform an unnecessary deed. If you are not guilty, the Saviour will not save you. If you are not a sinner, you have no part in Christ. If you can say, " I have kept the law from my youth up, and am not a transgressor," then we have no gospel blessings to set before you. If you were blind, the Lord Jesus would open your eyes ; but as you say, " We see," your sin remaineth. If you are guilty, the text is full of comfort to you ; it drops with honey like a honey-comb : " Christ Jesus came into the world to save *sinners*."

Lest there should be any mistake, Paul added these words, " of whom I am chief," or, " of whom I am first " ; and Calvin warns us against supposing that the apostle laboured under a mistake or uttered an exaggeration. Paul was an inspired man writing inspired Scripture, and he spoke the truth. He was, in some respects, the chief of sinners. He went very, very far into sin. It is true that he did it ignorantly in unbelief ; but, then, unbelief is in itself the greatest of all sins. It is an atrocious thing for a man to be an unbeliever ; it is a damning sin, what if I say *the* damning sin ? We have heard of a man who had committed a violent assault, who, before the magistrate, pleaded that he was drunk. Now, it is sometimes the case that magistrates admit this as an extenuating circumstance ; but the magistrate, on that occasion, was a sensible man, and, therefore, he said, " Very well, then, I give you a month for the assault, and I fine you forty shillings for being drunk ; that is another offence, and it cannot diminish your guilt." So is it with unbelief. Though, from one point of view, it might be looked upon as a mitigating circumstance ; yet, from another, it is really an increase of sin, and Paul regarded it as such ; and, therefore, he believed himself to be the chief of sinners. Yet he declares that Christ Jesus came to save him. Now, if a great creature can pass through a certain door, a smaller creature can ; if a bridge is strong enough to bear an elephant, it will certainly bear a mouse ; if the greatest sinner who ever lived has entered into heaven by the bridge of the atoning sacrifice of Christ, no man who has ever lived may say, " My sin is beyond forgiveness." To-day, no mortal has a just pretence to perish in despair. Some of you continue to despair, but you have no ground for such a feeling, for this is the good news which is preached to you, that Jesus Christ has come to call the guilty, the lost, and the ruined to himself, and to save the vilest of them with a great salvation.

III. Thus we have looked at the setting of the text, and at the text itself. Now for A BRIEF SERMON upon it.

Our short homily shall begin with *the doctrine of the text ;* and we will handle it negatively. Notice that our text does not say that Jesus Christ has come to compliment, to encourage, and to foster the independent spirit of righteous men. It is not written that He has come to tell us that human nature is not so bad as some think it to be, or that He has to commend those who are self-reliant, and intend to fight their own way to heaven. Here is not a word of the kind ; and, what is more, there is not a word like it in the entire Book of God. There is no encouragement in Holy Scripture to the man who depends upon himself for salvation, or who imagines or conceives that eternal life can spring out of his own loins, or can be wrought out by anything that he can do ; and yet our human nature loves to do something to save itself.

I do not know that I ever felt my blood boil so with indignation, nor my heart melt so much with pity, as when I went to see the Santa Scala, at Rome, the holy staircase up which our Lord is said to have been brought by Pilate. On those very stairs, Martin Luther was crawling on his knees, trying to find pardon for his sins, when the text came to him, " The just shall live by faith." I stood at the foot of those marble stairs. They are very high, and they are covered with wood, lest the knees of the faithful should wear them out, and this wood has been worn away three different times by the kneelers. I saw men, and women, and children,—little children too, and aged women, going up from step to step upon their knees to find their way to heaven. On the first step there is a little hole in the wood so that the worshippers may kiss the marble, and they all kissed it, and touched it with their foreheads; the middle and top step are favoured in the same manner. It was an awful reflection to me to think that those poor creatures really believed that every step their knees knelt on there were so many days less of purgatory for them; that every time they went up the stairs there were so many hundreds of days of deliverance from the punishment of their sins. Oh, if they could but have understood this text, "This is a faithful saying, and worthy of all acceptation, that Christ Jesus came into the world to save sinners," —that men are not saved by crawling on their hands and knees, or by penances and self-inflicted misery, what a blessing it would have been to them, and how they would have turned with scorn from these infamous impostures with which priests seek to mislead and destroy the souls of men! No, the Scripture does not say that Jesus came to encourage the righteous, and to help those who are their own saviours.

Note, again, that it does not say in the text that Jesus Christ came to help sinners to save themselves. There is a gospel preached which is very like that; but it is not the gospel of Christ. The poor man who was wounded on the road to Jericho was found by the Samaritan half-dead. Now the Samaritan did not say to him, "I want you to come part of the way to me in this business"; but he came where he was lying wounded and half-dead, and poured the oil and wine into his wounds, bound up the gashes, took him and set him on his own beast, carried him to the inn, and did not even ask him to pay the reckoning, but said to the host, "If there be anything more, I will pay thee." If there were anything more to be done for sinners, Jesus would do it, for He would never let them have a share of the work of salvation. The sinner's business is to take the finished work of Christ, to give up all His own doings, and let Him, who came from heaven to save, do the saving which He came to do. It is not ours to interfere, but to let Jesus do His own work.

Another thought demands expression. The text does not say that Christ came to half-save sinners, intending, when He had completed half the work, to leave them to themselves. There is a notion abroad that men may be saved, and yet may fall from grace; that they may have eternal life, but it is eternal life of an odd kind, for it may die out; they may be pardoned, and yet punished; they may be children of God, and yet become children of the devil; members of Christ's body, and yet be cut off, and joined to Satan. Blessed be God, it is not so written in this precious Book! Jesus does not begin the saving work, and leave it unfinished. When He once puts His hand to it, He will go through with it; His wonderful salvation shall be completed, none shall say that He began, but was not able to finish. Glory be to His name, Jesus Christ came into the world to save sinners from top to bottom; He will be the Alpha and the Omega, He will be the beginning and the end to all who trust Him.

One other other reflection here. Christ, the real Saviour, came into the world to save real sinners. When Luther was under a bitter sense of sin, he said, "Oh, but my guilt is so great, I cannot believe that Christ can save me!" But one who was helping him much said to him, "If thou wert only the semblance of a sinner, then Christ would only

be the semblance of a Saviour; but if thou art a real sinner, then thou shouldst rejoice that a real Saviour has come to save thee." If we meet with a man who says, "Yes, I am a sinner, I know I am a sinner, but I do not know that I ever did much amiss; I have always been honest and correct"; such a person has a name to be a sinner, and no more. He is a sham sinner, and a sham saviour would suit him well. But for another who confesses that he has been a grievous transgressor, there is a real Saviour. Rejoice, O ye guilty ones, that the Christ of God Himself really came, with real blood, and presented a real atonement to take away real sins, such as theft, drunkenness, swearing, uncleanness, Sabbath-breaking, lying, murder, and things I need not mention, lest the cheek of modesty should blush; even these can be blotted out by the real Saviour who has come to save the chief of sinners from suffering what is due to their sins. Oh, that we could ring this great bell till the hills and valleys were filled with music! May the Lord open men's ears and hearts that those who hear the glad tidings may accept the Saviour who has come to save them!

My little sermon has dealt with the doctrine of the text, now it must treat of *the inferences from the text*, which are these.

First, it is a great and a difficult thing to save a sinner, for the Son of God must needs come into the world to do it. It could not have been accomplished by any other except Jesus Christ, and He Himself must leave the throne of heaven for the manger of earth, and lay aside His glories to suffer, and bleed, and die. If soul-saving be so great and difficult a work, let the Lord Jesus have all the glory of it now that it is accomplished; let us never put the crown on the wrong head, or neglect to honour the Lord who bought us so dearly. Unto the Lamd of God be honour and glory, for ever and ever! Amen.

And next, it must be a good thing to save a sinner, since Jesus would not have come from heaven to earth on an ill errand. It must be a great blessing to a sinner to be saved. Dear brethren, this ought to lead all of us to consecrate ourselves to be willing instruments in the hand of Christ in endeavouring to rescue the fallen. That work which filled the Saviour's heart and hand is noble work for us. It were worth living for and worth dying for to be the instruments in the Spirit's hands of bringing souls into a state of grace. Think much of the blessed service which Jesus allots you, though it be but to teach an infant class in the Sunday-school, or a few poor men and women whom you visit from house to house, or a group of sorry idlers at a lodging-house; mind not the degradation of the people, for to save them from sin is a work which God Himself did not disdain to undertake.

Another inference I draw is, that if Jesus came from heaven to earth to save sinners, depend upon it He can do it. If He has come into the world, and bled and died to be a Saviour, He can do it. The price He paid is enough to redeem us; the blood He shed suffices to cleanse us. If there be any man here who feels himself very foul and filthy, let him look up to Christ at the right hand of the Father, and dare to say in his soul, "He can save even me; He is exalted on high to give repentance and remission of sins, and He is able to save to the uttermost them that come unto God by Him. He must be able to save me." O soul, if thou canst say that, and venture thy soul on it, there is no risk in it ; thy faith shall save thee, and thou mayest go in peace, for he who can rely upon Christ shall not find the Saviour fail the faith which He Himself has wrought in the soul.

These are the inferences, then, which I gather from the text ; and I shall close by *an enquiry*, which my text very naturally raises in my mind, and suggests to you. If Jesus came to save sinners, has He saved *me*? Has He saved *you*?

Has He saved *me*? I dare not speak with any hesitation here ; I *know* He has. Many years ago, I understood by faith the plan of salvation. Hearing it simply preached, I looked to Jesus, and lived, and I am looking to Him now. I *know* His Word is true, and I *am* saved. My evidence that I am saved does not lie in the fact that I preach, or that I do this or that. All my hope lies in this, that Jesus Christ came to save sinners. I am a sinner, I trust Him, He came to save me, I am saved ; I live habitually in the enjoyment of this blessed fact, and it is long since I have doubted the truth of it, for I have His own Word to sustain my faith.

Now, beloved, can *you* say, if not positively, yet with some measure of confidence, " Yes,"—

" All my trust on Him is stayed,
All my help from Him I bring " ?

Ah, then, you are favoured, you are very favoured. Be happy, for God has highly blessed you. You ought to be as merry as the days are long in June. A man who can say, " Christ has saved me," has bells enough inside his heart to ring marriage peals for ever. Oh, be glad, be very glad, for you have the best inheritance in the world ; and if temporal matters are not quite as you would wish them to be, do not become discontented, but solace yourself with the fact that the Lord has saved you with a great salvation !

But are you compelled to answer, " No, I do not think that Christ has saved me " ? Then I will ask you another question,—May it not be, ere this day is finished, that you shall be able to say, " He has saved me " ? Look at the matter. It is written that He came to save *sinners*. Is that your name or not ? Spell it over. Are you a sinner ? I have distinguished between a sham sinner and a real sinner. Do you confess that you are guilty ? Then Jesus came to save such as you are. There is a passage of Scripture which says, " He that believeth on Him is not condemned." You know what to believe is ; it is to trust, to rely upon. Now soul, if thou reliest upon Christ Jesus, sinner as thou art, thou art a saved sinner. If thou dost lean on Him, thou art this moment saved, at this instant forgiven.

" Oh, but I, I——," ah ! you want to crawl up that Roman staircase, do you ? That is what you want, you are anxious to go up and down those steps. " No," you say, " I am not quite so foolish as that." But, indeed, if you are trying to be saved by your own works, you are quite as foolish. You make a Pilate's staircase for yourself, and toil up and down its steps. " Oh, but, sir," you say, " I must *be* something, I must *feel* something." Yes, yes, it is that staircase again, always that staircase. Now, the gospel is not that staircase, nor yet your feelings, nor yet your works ; its voice is, " He that believeth on Him is not condemned." " Believe on the Lord Jesus Christ, and thou shalt be saved." You smile at the folly of Romanists ; and yet Popery, in some form or other, is the natural religion of every unconverted man. We all want to do the crawling and penancing in some shape or another. We are so proud that we will not accept heaven for nothing. We want to pay, or do something or other, forgetting that, " if a man would give all the substance of his house for love, it would utterly be contemned." The one only plan of salvation is " Believe and live " ; trust, rest, depend upon, rely upon Jesus.

THE GLORIOUS GOSPEL

" This is a faithful saying, and worthy of all acceptation, that Christ Jesus came into the world to save sinners ; of whom I am chief."—1 Timothy i. 15.

I SUPPOSE that the message delivered by God's servants to the people must always be called " the burden of the Lord." When the old prophets came forth from their Master, they had such dooms, and threatenings, and lamentations, and woe to preach, that their countenances were wan with sorrow, and their hearts heavy within them. They usually commenced their discourses by announcing, " The burden of the Lord, the burden of the Lord." But now, our message is no heavy one. No threatenings and no thunders compose the theme of the gospel minister. All is mercy ; love is the sum and substance of our gospel—love undeserved ; love to the very chief of sinners. But it is still a burden to us. So far as the matter of our preaching is concerned, it is out joy and our delight to preach it ; but if others feel as I feel now, they will all acknowledge it to be a hard matter to preach the gospel. For now I am sore vexed, and my heart is troubled, not concerning what I have to preach, but how I shall preach it. What if so good a message should fail because of so ill an ambassador ? What if my hearers should reject this saying which is worthy of all acceptation, because I may announce it with lack of earnestness ? Surely —surely such a supposition is enough to draw the tears to the eyes of any man ! But may God in His mercy prevent a consummation so fearfully to be dreaded ; and, however I may now preach, may this word of God commend itself to every man's conscience ; and may many of you now gathered together, who have never as yet fled to Jesus for refuge, by the simple preaching of the word, now be persuaded to come in, that you may taste and see that the Lord is good.

Our text is one that pride would never prompt a man to select. It is quite impossible to flourish about it, it is so simple. Human nature is apt to cry, " Well, I cannot preach upon that text—it is too plain ; there is no mystery in it ; I cannot show my learning : it is just a plain, common-sense announcement—I scarcely would wish to take it, for it lowers the man, however much it may exalt the Master." So, expect nothing but the text from me this morning, and the simplest possible explanation of it.

We shall have two heads : first there is *the text* ; then there is *a double commendation* appended to the text—" This is a faithful saying, and worthy of all acceptation."

I. First, there is THE ANNOUNCEMENT OF THE TEXT—" Christ Jesus came into the world to save sinners." In that there are three things very prominent. There is *the Saviour*, there is *the sinner*, and there is *the salvation*.

1. There is, first of all, *the Saviour*. And in explaining the Christian religion, this is where we must begin. The person of the Saviour is the foundation-stone of our hope. Upon that person depends the usefulness of our gospel. Should some one arise and preach a Saviour, who was a mere man, he would be unworthy of our hopes, and the salvation preached would be inadequate to what we need. Should another preach salvation by an angel, our sins are so heavy that an angelic atonement would have been insufficient ; and therefore his gospel totters to the ground. I repeat it, upon the person of the Saviour rests the whole of the salvation. If he be not able, if he be not commissioned to perform the work, then, indeed, the work itself is worthless to us, and falls short of its design. But, men and brethren, when we preach the gospel, we need not stop and stammer. We have to show you this day such a Saviour that earth and heaven could not show his fellow. He is one so loving, so great, so mighty, and so well adapted to all our needs, that it is evident enough that He was prepared of old to meet our deepest wants. We know that Jesus Christ who came into the world to save sinners was God ; and that long before His descent to this lower world, He was adored by angels as the Son of the Highest. When we preach the Saviour to you, we tell you that although Jesus Christ was the Son of man, bone of our bone, and flesh of our flesh, yet was He eternally the Son of God, and hath in Himself all the attributes which constitute perfect Godhead. What more of a Saviour can any man want than God ? Is not He who made the heavens able to purge the soul ? If He of old stretched the curtains of the skies, and made the earth, that man should dwell upon it, is He not able to rescue a sinner from the destruction that is to come ? When we tell you He is God, we have at once declared His omnipotence and His infinity ; and when these two things work together, what can be impossible ? Let God undertake a work, it cannot meet with failure. Let Him enter into an enterprise, and it is sure of its accomplishment. Since, then, Christ Jesus the man was also Christ Jesus the God, in announcing the Saviour, we have the fullest confidence that we are offering you something that is worthy of all acceptation.

The name given to Christ suggests something concerning His person. He is called in our text, " Christ Jesus." The two words mean, the " Anointed Saviour." The Anointed Saviour " came into the world to save sinners.

Pause here, my soul, and read this o'er again :— He is the Anointed Saviour. God the Father from before all worlds anointed Christ to the office of a Saviour of men ; and, therefore, when I behold my Redeemer coming from heaven to redeem man from sin, I note that He does not come unsent, or uncommissioned. He has His Father's authority to back Him in His work. Hence, there are two immutable things whereon our soul may rest ;— there is the person of Christ, divine in itself ; there is the anointing from on high, giving in Him the stamp of a commission received from Jehovah His Father. O sinner, what greater Saviour dost thou want than He whom God anointed ? What more canst thou require than the eternal Son of God to be thy ransom, and the anointing of the Father to be the ratification of the treaty ?

Yet we have not fully described the person of the Redeemer, until we have noted that *He was man*. We read that He came into the world ; by which coming into the world we do not understand His usual coming ; for He often came into the world before. We read in Scripture, " I will go down now, and see whether they have done altogether according to the cry of it, which is come unto Me ; and if not, I will know." In fact, He is always here. The goings of God are to be seen in the sanctuary : both in providence and in nature they are to be seen most visibly. Does not God visit the earth when He makes the tempest His chariot, and rides upon the wings of the wind ? But this visitation was different from all these. Christ came into the world in the sense of the fullest and most complete union with human nature. Oh, sinner, when we preach a Divine Saviour, perhaps the name of God is so terrible to thee, that thou canst scarcely think the Saviour is adapted to thee. But hear thou again the old story. Although Christ was the Son of God, He left His highest throne in glory and stooped to the manger. There He is, an infant of a span long. See, He grows from boyhood up to manhood, and He comes forth into the world to preach and suffer ! See Him as He groans under the yoke of oppression ; He is mocked and despised ; His visage more marred than that of any other man, and His form more than the sons of men ! See Him in the garden, as He sweats drops of blood ! See Him in Pilate's chamber, in which He is scourged and His shoulders run with gore ! On the bloody tree behold Him ! See Him dying with agony too exquisite to be imagined, much less to be described ! Behold Him in the silent tomb ! See Him at last bursting the bonds of death, and rising the third day, and afterwards ascending up on high, " leading captivity captive ! " Sinner, thou hast now the Saviour before thee, plainly manifested. He who was called Jesus of Nazareth, who died upon the cross, who had His superscription written, " Jesus of Nazareth, King of the Jews," this Man was the Son of God, the brightness of His Father's glory, and the express image of His Father, " begotten by His Father before all worlds, begotten not made, being of one substance with the Father," He " thought it not robbery to be equal with God, but made Himself of no reputation, and took upon Him the form of a servant, and was made in the likeness of men ; and being found in fashion as a man, He humbled Himself and became obedient unto death, even the death of the cross." Oh, could I bring Him before you, could I now bring Him here to show you His hands and His side, if ye could now, like Thomas, put your fingers in the holes of the nails, and thrust your hand into His side, methinks you would not be faithless, but believing. This much I know, if there be anything that can make men believe under the hand of God's most Holy Spirit, it is a true picture of the person of Christ. Seeing is believing in His case. A true view of Christ, a right-looking at Him, will most assuredly beget faith in the soul. Oh, I doubt not if ye knew my Master, some of you who are now doubting, and fearing, and trembling, would say, " Oh, I can trust Him ; a person so divine, and yet so human, ordained and anointed of God, must be worthy of my faith, I can trust Him ; nay more, if I had a hundred souls I could trust Him with them all ; or, if I stood accountable for all the sins of all mankind, and were myself the very reservoir and sink of this world's infamy, I could trust Him even then—for such a Saviour must be ' able to save to the uttermost them that come unto God by Him.' " This, then, is the person of the Saviour.

2. Now, the second point is *the sinner*. If we had never heard this passage before, or any of similar import, I can suppose that the most breathless silence would reign over this place if for the first time I should commence to read them in your hearing, " This is a faithful saying, and worthy of all acceptation, that Christ Jesus came into the world to save —— " I know how you would thrust forward your heads ; I know how you would put your hand against your ear, and look as if you would hear with the eye as well as with the ear, to know for whom the Saviour died. Every heart would say, whom did He come to save ? And if we had never heard the message before, how would our hearts palpitate with fear lest the character described should be one unto which it would be impossible for us to attain ! Oh, how pleasant it is to hear again that one word which describes the character of those Christ came to save :— " He came into the world to save *sinners*." Monarch, there is here no distinction ; princes, He hath not singled you out to be the objects of His love ; but beggars and the poor shall taste His grace. Ye learned men, ye masters of Israel, Christ does not say He came specially to save you ; the unlearned and illiterate peasant is equally welcome to His grace. Jew, with all thy pedigree of honour, thou art not justified more than the Gentile. Men of Britain, with all your civilization and your freedom, Christ does not say He came to save you : He names not you as the distinguishing class who are the objects of His love—no, and ye that have good works, and reckon yourselves saints among men, He doth not distinguish you either. The one simple title, large and broad as humanity itself, is simply this ;—" Christ Jesus came into the world to save sinners." Now, mark, we are to understand this in a general sense when we read it, viz., that all whom Jesus came to save are sinners ; but if any man asks, may I infer from this that I am saved ; we must then put another question to him. To begin then, with the general sense :— " Christ Jesus came into the world to save sinners." The men whom Christ came to save were by nature sinners, nothing less and nothing more than sinners. I have often said that Christ came into the world to save *awakened* sinners. It is quite true ; so He did. But those sinners were not awakened sinners when He came to save them ; they were nothing but " sinners dead in trespasses and sins " when He came to them. It is a common notion that we are to preach that Christ died to save what are called sensible sinners. Now that is true ; but they were not sensible sinners when Christ died to save them. He makes them sensible or feeling sinners, as the effect of His death. Those He died for are described, without any adjective to diminish the breadth of it, as being sinners, and simply sinners, without any badge of merit or mark of goodness which could distinguish them above their fellows. Sinners ! Now, the term includes some of all kinds of sinners. There are some men whose sins appear but little. Trained up religiously, and educated in a moral way, they do not dash into the

deeps of sin ; they are content to coast along the shores of vice—they do not launch out into the depths. Now, Christ hath died for such as these, for many of these have been brought to know and love Him. Let no man think, because he is a less sinner than others, that therefore there is less hope for him. Strange it is that some have often thought that. " If I had been a blasphemer," says one, " or injurious, I could have had more hope ; though I know I have sinned greatly in my own eyes, yet so little have I erred in the eye of the world, that I can scarcely think myself included." Oh, say not so. It says, " Sinners." If thou canst put thyself in that catalogue, whether it be at the top or at the bottom, thou art still within it ; and the truth still holds good that those Jesus came to save were originally sinners, and thou being such, thou hast no reason to believe that thou art shut out. Again, Christ died to save sinners of an opposite sort. We have some men whom we dare not describe ; it would be a shame to speak of the things which are done by them in private. There have been men who have invented vices of which the devil himself was ignorant until they invented them. There have been men so bestial that the very dog was a more honourable creature than they. We have heard of beings whose crimes have been more diabolical, more detestable, than any action ascribed even to the devil himself. Yet my text does not shut out these. Have we not met with blasphemers so profane that they could not speak without an oath ? Blasphemy, which at first was something terrible to them, has now become so common that they would curse themselves before they said their prayers, and swear when they were singing God's praises. It has come to be part of their meat and drink, a thing so natural to them that the very sinfulness of it does not shock them, they so continually do it. As for God's laws, they delight to know them for the mere sake of breaking them. Tell them of a new vice and you will please them. They have become like that Roman emperor whose parasites could never please him better than by inventing some new crime—men who have gone head over ears in the Stygian gulf of hellish sin—men, who not content with fouling their feet while walking through the mire have lifted up the trap-door with which they seal down depravity, and have dived into the very kennel,—revelling in the very filth of human iniquity. But there is nothing in my text which can exclude even these. Many of these shall yet be washed in the Saviour's blood, and be made partakers of the Saviour's love.

Nor does this text make a distinction as to the age of sinners. I see many among you here whose hairs if they were the colour of your character would be the very reverse of what they are ; ye have become white without, but ye are blackened all within with sin. Ye have added layer to layer of crime ; and, now, if one were to dig down through the various deposits of numerous years, he would discover stony relics of youthful sins, hidden down in the depths of your rocky hearts. Where once all was tender, everything has become sere and hardened. You have gone far into sin. If you were to be converted now, would it not, indeed, be a wonder of grace ? For the old oak to be bent, oh, how hard ! Now, that it has grown so rugged and tough, can it be bent ? Can the Great Husbandman train it ? Can He graft on so old and so rough a stem something that shall bring forth heavenly fruit ? Ah, He can, for age is not mentioned in the text, and many of the most ancient of men have proved the love of Jesus in their latest years. " But," says one, " my sin has had peculiar aggravations connected with it. I have sinned against light and against knowledge. I have trampled on a mother's prayers ; I have despised a father's tears. Warnings given to me have been neglected. On my sick bed God Himself has rebuked me. My resolves have been frequent and as frequently forgotten. As for my guilt, it is not to be measured by any ordinary standard. My little crimes are greater than other men's deepest iniquities, for I have sinned against the light, against the prickings of conscience, and against everything that should have taught me better." Well, my friend, I do not see that thou art shut out here ; my text makes no distinction but just this : " Sinners ! " And as far as my text is concerned there is no limit whatever : I must deal with the text as it stands ; and even for you I cannot consent to limit it ; it says, " Christ Jesus came into the world to save sinners." There have been men of your sort saved ; why, then, should you not be saved ? There have been the grossest blackguards, and the vilest thieves, and the most debauched harlots saved ; then, why not you, even if you be such as they are ? Sinners a hundred years old have been saved ; we have instances on record of such cases ; then, why not you ? If from one of God's instances we may generally infer a rule, and if, moreover, we have His own word to back us, where lives the man who is so wickedly arrogant as to shut himself out, and close the door of mercy in his own face ? No, beloved, the text says " Sinners " ; and why should it not include you and me within its list ? " Christ Jesus came into the world to save sinners."

But I said, and I must return to it, if anyone wishes to make a particular application of the text to his own case, it is necessary he should read this text in another way. Every man in this place must not infer that Christ came to save him. Those whom Christ came to save were sinners ; but Christ will not save all sinners. There are some sinners who undoubtedly will be lost, because they reject Christ. They despise Him ; they will not repent ; they choose their own self-righteousness ; they do not turn to Christ ; they will have none of His ways and none of His love. For such sinners, there is no promise of mercy, for there remains no other way of salvation. Despise Christ, and you despise your own mercy. Turn away from Him, and you have proved that in His blood there is no efficacy for you. Despise Him, and doing so, die without giving your soul into His hands, and you have given a most awful proof that though the blood of Christ was mighty, yet never was it applied to you, never was it sprinkled on your hearts to the taking away of your sins. If, then, I want to know did Christ so die for me that I may now believe in Him, and feel myself to be a saved man, I must answer this question—Do I *feel* to-day that I am a sinner ? Not, do I *say* so, as a compliment, but do I feel it ? In my inmost soul is that a truth printed in great capitals of burning fire—I am a sinner ? Then, if it be so, Christ died for me ; I am included in His special purpose. The covenant of grace includes my name in the ancient roll of eternal election ; there my person is recorded, and I shall, without a doubt, be saved, if now, feeling myself to be a sinner, I cast myself upon that simple truth, believing it and trusting in it to be my sheet anchor in every time of trouble. Come, man and brother, are you not prepared to trust in Him. Are not many of you able to say that you feel yourself sinners ? Oh, I beseech you, whoever you are, believe this great truth which is worthy of all acceptation—Christ Jesus came to save you. I know your doubts ; I know your fears, for I have suffered them myself ; and the only way whereby I can keep my hopes alive is just this— I am brought every day to the cross ; I believe that to my dying hour I shall never have any hope but this :—

> " Nothing in my hand I bring ;
> Simply to Thy cross I cling."

And my only reason at this hour for believing Jesus Christ is my Redeemer is just this—I know that I am a *sinner* : this, I feel, and over this I mourn ; and though I mourn it much, when Satan tells me that I cannot be the Lord's, I draw from my very mourning the comfortable inference, that inasmuch as He has made me feel I am lost, He would not have done this if He had not intended to save me ; and inasmuch as He has given me to see that I belong to that great class of characters whom He came to save, I infer from that, beyond a doubt, that He will save me. Oh can you do the same, ye sin stricken, weary, sad, and disappointed souls, to whom the world has become an empty thing ? Ye weary spirits who have gone your round of pleasure, now exhausted with satiety, or even with disease, are longing to be rid of it—oh, ye spirits that are looking for something better than this mad world can ever give you here, I preach to you the blessed gospel of the blessed God—Jesus Christ the Son of God, born of the Virgin Mary, suffered under Pontius Pilate, was crucified, dead and buried, and raised again the third day to save you—even you, for He came into the world to save sinners.

3. And, now, very briefly, the third point : What is meant by *saving* sinners ? " Christ came to save sinners." Brethren, if you want a picture to show you what is meant by being saved, let me give it to you here. There is a poor wretch who has lived many a year in the grossest sin ; so inured to sin has he become, that the Ethiopian might sooner change his skin than he could learn to do well. Drunkenness, and vice, and folly have cast their iron net about him, and he has become loathsome and unable to escape from his loathsomeness. Do you see him ? He is tottering onwards to his ruin. From childhood to youth, from youth to manhood, he has sinned right on ; and now he is going towards his last days. The pit of hell is flaring across his path, flinging its frightful rays immediately before his face, and yet he sees it not : he still goes on in his wickedness, despising God and hating his own salvation. Leave him there. A few years have passed, and now hear another story. Do you see that spirit yonder— foremost among the ranks, most sweetly singing the praises of God ? Do you mark it robed in white, an emblem of its purity ? Do you see it as it casts its crown before the feet of Jesus, and acknowledges Him the Lord of all ? Hark ! do you hear it as it sings the sweetest song that ever charmed Paradise itself ? Listen to it, its song is this—

> " I, the chief of sinners am,
> But Jesus died for me."

" Unto Him that loved me, and washed me from my sins in His blood, unto Him be glory and honour, and majesty, and power, and dominion, world without end." And who is that whose song thus emulates the seraph's strain? The same person who a little while ago was so frightfully depraved, the selfsame man! But he has been washed, he has been sanctified, he has been justified. If you ask me, then, what is meant by salvation, I tell you that it reaches all the way from that poor, desperately fallen piece of humanity, to that high-soaring spirit up yonder, praising God. That is to be saved—to have our old thoughts made into new ones; to have our old habits broken off, and to have new habits given; to have our old sins pardoned, and to have righteousness imputed; to have peace in the conscience, peace to man, and peace with God; to have the spotless robe of imputed righteousness cast about our loins, and ourselves healed and cleansed. To be saved is to be rescued from the gulf of perdition; to be raised to the throne of heaven; to be delivered from the wrath, and curse, and the thunders of an angry God, and brought to feel and taste the love, the approval, and applause of Jehovah, our Father and our Friend. And all this Christ gives to sinners. When I preach this simple gospel, I have nothing to do with those who will not call themselves sinners. If you must be canonized, if you claim a saintly perfection of your own, I have nothing to do with you. My gospel is to sinners, and sinners alone; and the whole of this salvation, so broad and brilliant, and unspeakably precious, and everlastingly secure, is addressed this day to the outcast, to the offscouring—in one word, it is addressed to sinners.

Now, I think I have announced the truth of the text. Certainly, no man can misunderstand me unless he does so intentionally—" Christ Jesus came to save sinners."

II. And, now, I have but little to do, but yet I have the hardest work—THE DOUBLE COMMENDATION of the text. First, " it is a faithful saying "; that is a commendation to the *doubter*: secondly, " it is worthy of all acceptation "; that is a commendation to the *careless*—nay, to the *anxious* too.

1. First, " it is a faithful saying "; that is a commendation to the *doubter*. Oh, the devil, as soon as he finds men under the sound of the word of God, slips along through the crowd, and he whispers in one heart, " Don't believe it! " and in another, " Laugh at it! " and in another, " Away with it! " And when he finds a person for whom the message was intended—one who feels himself a sinner, he is generally doubly in earnest, that he may not believe it at all. I know what Satan said to you, poor friend, over there. He said, " Don't believe it—it's too good to be true." Let me answer the devil by God's own words: " This is a faithful saying." It is good, and it is as true as it is good. *It is* too good to be true if God had not Himself said it; but, inasmuch as He said it, it is not too good to be true. I will tell thee why thou thinkest it too good to be true; it is because thou measurest God's corn by thine own bushel. Please to remember, that His ways are not as thy ways, nor His thoughts as thy thoughts; for as the heavens are high above the earth, so are His ways high above thy ways, and His thoughts above thy thoughts. Why, thou thinkest that if any man had offended thee, thou couldst not have forgiven him. Aye, but God is not a man: He can forgive where thou canst not; and where thou wouldst take thy brother by the throat, God would forgive him seventy times seven. Thou dost not know Jesus, or else thou wouldst believe Him. We think that we are honouring God when we think great thoughts of our

sin. Let us recollect, that while we ought to think very greatly of our own sin, we dishonour God if we think our sin greater than His grace. God's grace is infinitely greater than the greatest of our crimes. There is but one exception that He has ever made, and a penitent cannot be included in that. I beseech you, therefore, get better thoughts of Him. Think how good He is, and how great He is; and when you know this to be a true saying, I hope you will thrust Satan away from you, and not think it too good to be true. I know what he will say to you next—" Well, if it is true, it is not true to you: it is true to all the world, but not to you. Christ died to save sinners; it is true you are a sinner, but you are not included in it." Tell the devil he is a liar to his face. There is no way of answering him except by straightforward language. We do not believe in the individuality of the existence of the devil, as Martin Luther did. When the devil came to him, he served him as he did other impostors; he turned him out of doors, with a good hard saying. Tell him on the authority of Christ Himself, that he is a liar. Christ says He came to save sinners; the devil says He did not. He says, virtually, He did not, for he declares that He did not come to save you, and you feel that you are a sinner. Tell him he is a liar, and send him about his business. At any rate, never put his testimony in comparison with that of Christ. He looks to-day on thee from Calvary's cross, with those same dear tearful eyes that once wept over Jerusalem. He looks on thee, my brother, my sister, and says through these lips of mine, " I came into the world to save sinners." Sinner! wilt thou not believe on Him, and trust thy soul in His hands? Wilt thou not say— " Sweet Lord Jesus, Thou shalt be our confidence henceforth! ' For Thee all other hopes I resign, Thou art, Thou ever shalt be mine.' " Come, poor timid one, I must endeavour to reassure you, by repeating again this text:—" Christ Jesus came into the world to save sinners." It is a true saying; I cannot have you reject it. You say you cannot believe it. Let me ask you, " Do you not believe the Bible? " " Yes," you say, " every word of it." Then, this is one word of it—" Jesus came into the world to save sinners." I charge thee by thy honesty —as thou sayest, " I believe the Bible," believe this. There it stands. Dost thou believe Jesus Christ? Come, answer me. Dost thou think He lieth? Would a God of Truth stoop to deceit? " No," thou sayest, " whatever God says, I believe." It is God that says it to thee, then, in His own book. He died to save sinners. Come, once again. Dost thou not believe facts? Did not Jesus Christ rise from the dead? Does not that prove His gospel to be authentic? If, then, the gospel be authentic, the whole of what Christ declares to be the gospel must be true. I charge thee, as thou believest His resurrection, believe that He died for sinners, and cast thyself upon this truth. Once again. Wilt thou deny the testimony of all the saints in heaven and of all the saints on earth? Ask every one of them, and they will tell you this is true—He died to save *sinners*. I, as one of the least of His servants, must bear my testimony. When Jesus came to save me, I protest He found nothing good in me. I know of a surety, that there was nothing in me to recommend me to Christ; and if He loved me, He loved me because He would do so; for there was nothing lovable, nothing that He could desire in me. What I am, I am by His grace; He made me what I am. But a sinner

He found me at first, and His own sovereign love was the only reason for His choice. Ask all the people of God, and they will all say the same.

But you say you are too great a sinner. Why, you are not greater than some in heaven already. You say that you are the greatest sinner that ever lived. I say you are mistaken. The greatest sinner died some years ago and went to heaven. My text says so—" Of whom I am chief." So, you see, the chief one has been saved before you ; and if the chief one has been saved, why should you not be ? There are the sinners standing in a line, and I see one starting out from the ranks, and He says, " Make way, make way ; I stand at the head of you, I am the chief of sinners ; give me the lowest place ; let me take the lowest room." " No," cries another, " not you ; I am a greater sinner than you." Then the apostle Paul comes, and says : " I challenge you all ; Manasseh and Magdalene, I challenge you. I will have the lowest place. I was a blasphemer, a persecutor, and injurious, but I have obtained mercy, that in me first God might show His long-suffering." Now, if Christ has saved the greatest sinner that ever lived, oh, sinner, great as you may be, you cannot be greater than the greatest, and He is able to save you. Oh, I beseech you by the myriads of witnesses around the throne, and by the thousands of witnesses on earth, by Jesus Christ, the witness on Calvary, by the blood of sprinkling that is a witness even now, by God Himself, and by His word which is faithful, I beseech you believe this faithful saying, that " Christ Jesus came into the world to save sinners."

2. And, now, to close. The second commendation of the text is to the *careless* and to the *anxious* too. To the careless one this text is worthy of all acceptation. Oh, man, thou scornest it. I saw thee curl thy lip in derision. The story was badly told, and therefore thou didst scorn it. Thou saidst in thine heart, " What is that to me ? If this be what the man preaches, I care not to hear it : if this be the gospel, it is nothing." Ah, sir, it is something, though thou knowest it not. It is worthy of thy acceptation : the thing I have preached, however poor the way in which it is preached, is well worthy of thy attention. I care not what orator may lecture to you, he can never have a subject greater than mine. Demosthenes himself might stand here, or Cicero, his later compeer, they could never have a weightier subject. Though a child should tell you of it, the subject might well excuse him, for it is so important. Man, it is not your house that is in danger, it is not your body only, it is your soul. I beseech you, by eternity, by its dreadful terrors, by the horrors of hell, by that fearful word, " Eternity—Eternity," I beseech thee as a man, thy brother, one who loves thee, and who would fain snatch thee from the burning, I beseech thee do not despise thine own mercies ; for this is worthy of thee, man, worthy of all thy attention, and worthy of thy heartiest acceptation. Art thou wise ? This is more worthy than thy wisdom. Art thou rich ? This is worthier than all thy wealth. Art

thou famous ? This is worthier than all thy honour. Art thou princely ? This is worthier than thine ancestry, or than all thy goodly heritage. The thing I preach is the worthiest thing under heaven, because it will last thee when all things else fade away. It will stand by thee when thou hast to stand alone. In the hour of death it will plead for thee when thou hast to answer the summons of justice at God's bar. And it shall be thine eternal consolation through never ending ages. It is worthy of thy acceptation.

And, now, dost thou feel anxious ? Is thy heart sad ? Dost thou say, " I desire to be saved. Can I trust to this gospel ? Is it strong enough to bear me ? I am an elephantine sinner ; will not its pillars crumble like leaves beneath my weight of sin ? " " I the chief of sinners am " ; will its portals be wide enough to receive me ? My spirit is diseased with sin ; can this medicine cure it ? Yes, it is worthy of you : it is equal to your disease, it is equal to your wants, it is all-sufficient for your demands. If I had a half-gospel to preach, or a defective one, I would not preach it earnestly ; but I have one that is worthy of all acceptation. " But, sir, I have been a thief, a whoremonger, a drunkard." It is worthy of thee, for He came to save sinners, and thou art one. " But, sir, I have been a blasphemer." It does not exclude even thee ; it is worthy of thy acceptation. But, mark ; it is worthy of all the acceptation you can give it. You may not only accept it in your head but in your heart ; you may press it to your soul and call it all in all ; you may feed on it, and live on it. And if you live for it, and suffer for it, and die for it, it is worthy of all.

I must let you go now ; but my spirit feels as if it would linger here. Strange it should be that many men should not care for their own souls, when your minister this day cares for you. What matters it to me whether men be lost or saved ? Shall I be any the better for your salvation ? Assuredly there is little gain there. And yet I feel more for you, many of you, than you feel for yourselves. Oh, strange hardenings of the heart, that a man should not care for his own salvation, that he should, without a thought, reject the most precious truth. Stay, sinner, stay, ere thou turnest from thine own mercy— stay, once more—perhaps this shall be thy last warning, or worse, it may be the last warning thou shalt ever feel. Thou feelest it now. Oh, I beseech thee, quench not the Spirit. Go not forth from this place to talk with idle gossip on thy way home. Go not forth to forget what manner of man thou art. but hasten to thy home ; seek thy chamber ; shut to the door ; fall on thy face by thy bedside ; confess thy sin ; cry unto Jesus ; tell Him thou art a wretch undone without His sovereign grace ; tell Him thou has heard this morning that He came to save sinners, and that the thought of such a love as that hath made thee lay down the weapons of thy rebellion, and that thou art desirous to be His. There on thy face plead with Him, and say unto Him, " Lord save me, or I perish."

The Lord bless you all for Jesus' sake. Amen.

PAUL AS PATTERN CONVERT

"Howbeit for this cause I obtained mercy, that in me first, Jesus Christ might show forth all long-suffering, for a pattern to them which should hereafter believe on Him to life everlasting."—1 Timothy i. 16.

IT is a vulgar error that the conversion of the apostle Paul was uncommon and exceptional even, and that we cannot expect men to be saved nowadays after the same fashion. It is said that the incident was an exception to all rules, a wonder altogether by itself. Now, my text is a flat contradiction to that notion, for it assures us that, instead of the apostle as a receiver of the long-suffering and mercy of God being at all an exception to the rule, he was a model convert, and is to be regarded as a type and pattern of God's grace in other believers. The apostle's language in the text, " for a pattern," may mean that he was what printers call a first proof, an early impression from the engraving, a specimen of those to follow. He was the typical instance of divine long-suffering, the model after which others are fashioned. To use a metaphor from the artist's studio, Paul was the ideal sketch of a convert, an outline of the work of Jesus on mankind, a cartoon of divine long-suffering. Just as artists make sketches in charcoal as the basis of their work, which outlines they paint out as the picture proceeds, so did the Lord in the apostle's case make, as it were, a cartoon or outline sketch of His usual work of grace. That outline in the case of each future believer He works out with infinite variety of skill, and produces the individual Christian, but the guiding lines are really there. All conversions are in a high degree similar to this pattern conversion. The transformation of persecuting Saul of Tarsus into the apostle Paul is a typical instance of the work of grace in the heart.

We will have no other preface, but proceed at once to two or three considerations. The first is that :—

I. IN THE CONVERSION OF PAUL THE LORD HAD AN EYE TO OTHERS, AND IN THIS PAUL IS A PATTERN.

In every case the individual is saved, not for himself alone, but with a view to the good of others. Those who think the doctrine of election to be harsh should not deny it, for it is Scriptural ; but they may to their own minds soften some of its hardness by remembering that elect men bear a marked connection with the race. The Jews, as an elect people, were chosen in order to preserve the oracles of God for all nations and for all times. Men personally elected unto eternal life by divine grace are also elected that they may become chosen vessels to bear the name of Jesus unto others. While our Lord is said to be the Saviour specially of them that believe, He is also called the Saviour of all men ; and while He has a special eye to the good of the person whom He has chosen, yet through that person He has designs of love to others, perhaps even to thousands yet unborn.

The apostle says, " I obtained mercy, that in me foremost Jesus Christ might show forth all long-suffering, for a pattern to them which should hereafter believe." Now, I think I see very clearly that *Paul's conversion had an immediate relation to the conversion of many others.* It had a tendency, had it not, to excite an interest in the minds of his brother Pharisees ? Men of his class, men of culture, who were equally at home with the Greek philosophers and with the Jewish rabbis, men of influence, men of rank, would be sure to enquire, " What is this new religion which has fascinated Saul of Tarsus ? That zealot for Judaism has now become a zealot for Christianity : what can there be in it ? " I say that the natural tendency of his conversion was to awaken enquiry and thought, and so to lead others of his rank to become believers. And, my dear friend, if you have been saved, you ought to regard it as a token of God's mercy to your class. If you are a working man, let your salvation be a blessing to the men with whom you labour. If you are a person of rank and station, consider that God intends to bless you to some with whom you are on familiar terms. If you are young, hope that God will bless the youth around you, and if you have come to older years, hope that your conversion, even at the eleventh hour, may be the means of encouraging other aged pilgrims to seek and find rest unto their souls. The Lord, by calling one out of any society of men, finds Himself a recruiting officer, who will enlist His fellows beneath the banner of the cross. May not this fact encourage some seeking soul to hope that the Lord may save him, though he be the only thoughtful person in all his family, and then make him to be the means of salvation to all his kindred.

We notice that *Paul often used the narrative of his conversion as an encouragement to others.* He was not ashamed to tell his own life-story. Eminent soul-winners, such as Whitefield and Bunyan, frequently pleaded God's mercy to themselves as an argument with their fellow-men. Though great preachers of another school, such as Robert Hall and Chalmers, do not mention themselves at all, and I can admire their abstinence, yet I am persuaded that if some of us were to follow their example, we should be throwing away one of the most powerful weapons of our warfare. What can be more affecting, more convincing, more overwhelming than the story of divine grace told by the very man who has experienced it ? It is better than a score tales of converted Africans, and infinitely more likely to win men's hearts than the most elaborate essays upon moral excellence. Again and again, Paul gave a long narrative of his conversion, for he felt it to be one of the most telling things that he could relate.

Whether he stood before Felix or Agrippa, this was his plea for the gospel. All through his epistles there are continual mentions of the grace of God towards himself, and we may be sure that the apostle did right thus to argue from his own case : it is fair and forcible reasoning, and ought by no means to be left unused because of a selfish dread of being called egotistical. God intends that we should use our conversion as an encouragement to others, and say to them, " Come and hear, all ye that fear God, and I will tell you what He has done for my soul." We point to our own forgiveness and say, " Do but trust in the living Redeemer, and you shall find, as we have done, that Jesus blotteth out the transgressions of believers."

Paul's conversion was an encouragement to him all his life long to have hope for others. Have you ever read the first chapter of the Epistle to the Romans ? Well, the man who penned those terrible verses might very naturally have written at the end of them, " Can these monsters be reclaimed ? It can be of no avail whatever to preach the gospel to people so sunken in vice." That one chapter gives as daring an outline as delicacy would permit of the nameless, shameless vices into which the heathen world had plunged, and yet, after all, Paul went forth to declare the gospel to that filthy and corrupt generation, believing that God meant to save a people out of it. Surely one element of his hope for humanity must have been found in the fact of his own salvation ; he considered himself to be in some respects as bad as the heathen, and in other respects even worse : he calls himself the *foremost* of sinners (that is the word) ; and he speaks of God having saved him foremost, that in him He might show forth all long-suffering. Paul never doubted the possibility of the conversion of a person however infamous, after he had himself been converted. This strengthened him in battling with the fiercest opponents—He who overcame such a wild beast as I was, can also tame others and bring them into willing captivity to His love.

There was yet another relation between Paul's conversion and the salvation of others, and it was this :—*It served as an impulse,* driving him forward in his life-work of bringing sinners to Christ. " I obtained mercy," said he, " and that same voice which spake peace to me said, I have made thee a chosen vessel unto Me to bear My name among the Gentiles." And he did bear it, my brethren. Going into regions beyond that, he might not build on another man's foundation, he became a master-builder for the church of God. How indefatigably did he labour ! With what vehemence did he pray ! With what energy did he preach ! Slander and contempt he bore with the utmost patience. Scourging or stoning had no terrors for him. Imprisonment, yea death itself, he defied ; nothing could daunt him. Because the Lord had saved him, he felt that he must by all means save some. He could not be quiet. Divine love was in him like a fire, and if he had been silent, he would ere long have had to cry with the prophet of old, " I am weary with restraining." He is the man who said, " Necessity is laid upon me, yea woe is unto me if I preach not the gospel." Paul, the extraordinary sinner, was saved that he might be full of extraordinary zeal and bring multitudes to eternal life. Well could he say :—

> " The love of Christ doth me constrain
> To seek the wandering souls of men ;
> With cries, entreaties, tears to save,
> To snatch them from the fiery wave.
>
> My life, my blood, I here present,
> If for Thy truth they may be spent ;
> Fulfil Thy sovereign counsel, Lord !
> Thy will be done, Thy name adored ! "

Now, I will pause here a minute to put a question. You profess to be converted, my dear friend. What relation has your conversion already had to other people ? It ought to have a very apparent one.

Has it had such ? Mr. Whitefield said that when his heart was renewed, his first desire was that his companions with whom he had previously wasted his time might be brought to Christ. It was natural and commendable that he should begin with them. Remember how one of the apostles, when he discovered the Saviour, went immediately to tell his brother. It is most fitting that young people should spend their religious enthusiasm upon their brothers and sisters. As to converted parents, their first responsibility is in reference to their sons and daughters. Upon each renewed man, his natural affinities, or the bonds of friendship, or the looser ties of neighbourhood should begin to operate at once, and each one should feel, " No man liveth unto himself."

If divine grace has kindled a fire in you, it is that your fellow-men may burn with the same flame. If the eternal fount has filled you with living water, it is that out of the midst of you should flow rivers of living water. You are blessed that you may bless ; whom have you blessed yet ? Let the question go round. Do not avoid it. This is the best return that you can make to God, that when He saveth you, you should seek to be the instruments in His hands of saving others. What have you done yet ? Did you ever speak with the friend who shares your pew ? He has been sitting there for a long time, and may, perhaps, be an unconverted person ; have you pointed him to the Lamb of God ? Have you ever spoken to your servants about their souls ? Have you yet broken the ice sufficiently to speak to your own sister, or your own brother ? Do begin, dear friend.

You cannot tell what mysterious threads connect you with your fellow-men and their destiny. There was a cobbler once, as you know, in Northamptonshire. Who could see any connection between him and the millions of India ? But the love of God was in his bosom, and Carey could not rest till, at Serampore, he had commenced to translate the word of God and preach it to his fellow-men. We must not confine our thoughts to the few whom Carey brought to Christ, though to save one soul is worthy of a life of sacrifice, but Carey became the forerunner and leader of a missionary band which will never cease to labour till India bows before Immanuel. That man mysteriously drew, is drawing, and will draw India to the Lord Jesus Christ. Brother, you do not know what your power is. Awake and try it.

Did you never read this passage : " Thou hast given Him power over all flesh, that He should give eternal life to as many as Thou hast given Him " ? Now, the Lord has given to His Son power over all flesh, and with a part of that power Jesus clothes His servants. Through you, He will give eternal life to certain of His chosen ; by you, and by no other means, will they be brought to Himself. Look about you, regenerate man. Your life may be made sublime. Rouse yourself ! Begin to think of what God may do by you ! Calculate the possibilities which lie before you with the eternal God as your helper. Shake yourself from the dust and put on the beautiful garments of disinterested love to others, and it shall yet be seen how grandly gracious God has been to hundreds of men by having converted you.

So far, then, Paul's salvation, because it had so clear a reference to others, was a pattern of all conversions. Now, secondly :—

II. PAUL'S FOREMOST POSITION AS A SINNER DID NOT PREVENT HIS BECOMING FOREMOST IN GRACE, AND HEREIN AGAIN HE IS A PATTERN TO US.

Foremost in sin, he became also foremost in service. Saul of Tarsus was a *blasphemer*, and he is to be commended because he has not recorded any of those blasphemies. We can never object to converted burglars and chimney-sweepers, of whom we hear so much, telling the story of their conversion; but when they go into dirty details, they had better hold their tongues. Paul tells us that he was a blasphemer, but he never repeats one of the blasphemies. We invent enough evil in our own hearts without being told of other men's stale profanities. If, however, any of you are so curious as to want to know what kind of blasphemies Paul could utter, you have only to converse with a converted Jew, and he will tell you what horrible words some of his nation will speak against our Lord. I have no doubt that Paul in his evil state thought as wickedly of Christ as he could—considered Him to be an impostor, called Him so, and added many an opprobrious epithet. He does not say of himself that he was an unbeliever and an objector, but he says that he was a blasphemer, which is a very strong word, but not too strong, for the apostle never went beyond the truth. He was a downright, thorough-going blasphemer, who also caused others to blaspheme. Will these lines meet the eye of a profane person who feels the greatness of his sin? May God grant that he may be encouraged to seek mercy as Saul of Tarsus did, for "all manner of sin and blasphemy" does He forgive unto men.

From blasphemy, which was the sin of the lips, Saul proceeded to *persecution*, which is a sin of the hands. Hating Christ, he hated his people, too. He was delighted to give his vote for the death of Stephen, and he took care of the clothes of those who stoned that martyr. He haled men and women to prison, and compelled them to blaspheme. When he had hunted all Judea as closely as he could, he obtained letters to go to Damascus, that he might do the same in that place. His prey had been compelled to quit Jerusalem and fly to more remote places, but "being exceeding mad against them, he persecuted them unto strange cities." He was foremost in blasphemy and persecution. Will a persecutor read or hear these words? If so, may he be led to see that even for him pardon is possible. Jesus, who said, "Father, forgive them; for they know not what they do," is still an intercessor for the most violent of His enemies.

He adds, next, that he was *injurious*, which, I think, Bengel considers to mean that he was a despiser: that eminent critic says—blasphemy was his sin towards God, persecution was his sin towards the church, and despising was his sin in his own heart. He was injurious—that is, he did all he could to damage the cause of Christ, and he thereby injured himself. He kicked against the pricks and injured his own conscience. He was so determined against Christ that he counted no cost too great by which he might hinder the spread of the faith, and he did hinder it terribly. He was a ringleader in resisting the Spirit of God which was then working with the church of Christ. He was foremost in opposition to the cross of Christ.

Now, notice that he was saved as a pattern, which is to show you that if you also have been foremost in sin, you also may obtain mercy, as Paul did: and to show you yet again that if you have not been foremost, the grace of God, which is able to save the chief of sinners, can assuredly save those who are of less degree. If the bridge of grace will carry the elephant, it will certainly carry the mouse. If the mercy of God could bear with the hugest sinners, it can have patience with you. If a gate is wide enough for a giant to pass through, any ordinary-sized mortal will find space enough. Despair's head is cut off and stuck on a pole by the salvation of "the chief of sinners." No man can now say that he is too great a sinner to be saved, because the chief of sinners was saved eighteen hundred years ago. If the ringleader, the chief of the gang, has been washed in the precious blood, and is now in heaven, why not I? why not *you*?

After Paul was saved, he became a foremost saint. The Lord did not allot him a second-class place in the church. He had been the leading sinner, but his Lord did not, therefore, say, "I save you, but I shall always remember your wickedness to your disadvantage." Not so: He counted him faithful, putting him into the ministry and into the apostleship, so that he was not a whit behind the very chief of the apostles. Brother, there is no reason why, if you have gone very far in sin, you should not go equally far in usefulness. On the contrary, there is a reason why you should do so, for it is a rule of grace that to whom much is forgiven, the same loveth much, and much love leads to much service.

What man was more clear in his knowledge of doctrine than Paul? What man more earnest in the defence of truth? What man more self-sacrificing? What man more heroic? The name of Paul in the Christian church stands in some respects the very next to the Lord Jesus. Turn to the New Testament and see how large a space is occupied by the Holy Spirit speaking through His servant Paul; and then look over Christendom and see how greatly the man's influence is still felt, and must be felt till his Master shall come. Oh! great sinner, if thou art even now ready to scoff at Christ, my prayer is that He may strike thee down at this very moment, and turn thee into one of His children and make thee to be just as ardent for the truth as thou art now earnest against it, as desperately set on good as now thou art on evil. None make such mighty Christians and such fervent preachers as those who are lifted up from the lowest depths of sin and washed and purified through the blood of Jesus Christ. May grace do this with thee, my dear friend, whoever thou mayest be.

Thus we gather from our text that the Lord showed mercy to Paul, that in him foremost it might be seen that prominence in sin is no barrier to eminence in grace, but the very reverse. Now I come to where the stress of the text lies.

III. PAUL'S CASE WAS A PATTERN OF OTHER CONVERSIONS AS AN INSTANCE OF LONG-SUFFERING.

"That in me foremost Jesus Christ might show forth all longsuffering for a cartoon or pattern to them which should hereafter believe." Thoughtfully observe the great long-suffering of God to Paul: he says, "He showed forth all long-suffering." Not only all the long-suffering of God that ever was shown to anybody else, but all that could be supposed to exist—*all* long-suffering.

"All Thy mercy's height I prove,
All its depth is found in me,"

as if he had gone to the utmost stretch of his tether in sin, and the Lord also had strained His long-suffering to its utmost.

That long-suffering was seen first *in sparing his life* when he was rushing headlong in sin, breathing out threatenings, foaming at the mouth with denunciations of the Nazarene and His people. If the Lord had but lifted His finger, Saul would have been crushed like a moth, but almighty wrath forbore, and the rebel lived on. Nor was this all; after all his sin, the Lord allowed mercy to be possible to him. He blasphemed and persecuted, at a red-hot rate; and is it not a marvel that the Lord did not say, " Now, at last, you have gone beyond all bearing, and you shall die like Herod, eaten of worms " ? It would not have been at all wonderful if God had so sentenced him; but He allowed him to live within the reach of mercy, and, better still, he in due time actually sent the gospel to him, and laid it home to his heart. In the very midst of his rebellion the Lord saved him. He had not prayed to be converted, far from it; no doubt he had that very day along the road to Damascus profaned the Saviour's name, and yet mighty mercy burst in and saved him purely by its own spontaneous native energy. Oh mighty grace, free grace, victorious grace! This was long-suffering indeed!

When divine mercy had called Paul, *it swept all his sin away*, every particle of it, his blood shedding and his blasphemy, all at once, so that never man was more assured of his own perfect cleansing than was the apostle. " There is therefore now," saith he, " no condemnation to them which are in Christ Jesus." " Therefore, being justified by faith, we have peace with God." " Who shall lay anything to the charge of God's elect ? " You know how clear he was about that; and he spoke out of his own experience. Long-suffering had washed all his sins away. Then that long-suffering reaching from the depths of sin lifted him right up to the apostleship, so that he began to prove God's long-suffering in its heights of favour. What a privilege if must have been to him to be permitted to preach the gospel. I should think sometimes when he was preaching most earnestly, he would half stop himself and say, " Paul, is this you ? " When he went down to Tarsus especially he must have been surprised at himself and at the mighty mercy of God. He preached the faith which once he had destroyed. He must have said many a time after a sermon, when he went home to his bed-chamber, " Marvel of marvels! Wonder of wonders, that I who once could curse have now been made to preach—that I, who was full of threatening and even breathed out slaughter, should now be so inspired by the Spirit of God that I weep at the very sound of Jesus' name, and count all things but loss for the excellency of the knowledge of Christ Jesus my Lord."

Oh! brothers and sisters, you do not measure long-suffering except you take it in all its length from one end to the other, and see God in mercy not remembering His servant's sin, but lifting him into eminent service in his church. Now, this was for a pattern, to show you that He will show forth the same long-suffering to those who believe. If you have been a swearer, He will cleanse your blackened mouth, and put His praises into it. Have you had a black, cruel heart, full of enmity to Jesus ? He will remove it, and give you a new heart and a right spirit. Have you dived into all sorts of sins ? Are they so shameful that you dare not think of them ? Think of the precious blood which removes every stain. Are your sins so many that you could not count them ? Do you feel as if you were almost damned already in the very memory of your life ? I do not wonder at it, but He is able to save to the uttermost them that come unto God by Him. You have not gone farther than Saul had gone, and therefore all long-suffering can come to you, and there are great possibilities of future holiness and usefulness before you. Even though you may have been a street-walker or a thief, yet if the grace of God cleanses you, it can make something wonderful out of you: full many a lustrous jewel of Immanuel's crown has been taken from the dunghill. You are a rough block of stone, but Jesus can fashion and polish you, and set you as a pillar in His temple.

Brother, do not despair. See what Saul was and what Paul became, and learn what you may be. Though you deserve the depths of hell, yet up to the heights of heaven grace can lift you. Though now you feel as if the fiends of the pit would be fit companions for such a lost spirit as yourself, yet believe in the Lord Jesus, and you shall one day walk among the angels as pure and white as they. Paul's experience of long-suffering grace was meant to be a pattern of what God will do for you.

" Scripture says, ' Where sin abounded,
There did grace much more abound ';
Thus has Satan been confounded,
And his own discomfit found.
Christ has triumph'd
Spread the glorious news around.

Again :—

Sin is strong, but grace is stronger;
Christ than Satan more supreme;
Yield, oh, yield to sin no longer,
Turn to Jesus, yield to Him—
He has triumph'd!
Sinners, henceforth Him esteem."

IV. THE MODE OF PAUL'S CONVERSION WAS ALSO MEANT TO BE A PATTERN, and with this I shall finish. I do not say that we may expect to receive the miraculous revelation which was given to Paul, but yet it is a sketch upon which any conversion can be painted. The filling up is not the same in any two cases, but the outline sketch. Paul's conversion would serve for an outline sketch of the conversion of any one of us. How was that conversion wrought ? Well, it is clear that *there was nothing at all in Paul to contribute to his salvation.* You might have sifted him in a sieve, without finding anything upon which you could rest a hope that he would be converted to the faith of Jesus. His natural bent, his early training, his whole surroundings, and his life's pursuits, all fettered him to Judaism, and made it most unlikely that he would ever become a Christian. The first elder of the church that ever talked to him about divine things could hardly believe in his conversion. " Lord," said he, " I have heard by many of this man, how much evil he hath done to Thy saints at Jerusalem." He could hardly think it possible that the ravening wolf should have changed into a lamb. Nothing favourable to faith in Jesus could have been found in Saul; the soil of his heart was very rocky, the ploughshare could not touch it, and the good seed found no roothold. Yet the Lord converted Saul, and He can do the like by other sinners, but it must be a work of pure grace and of divine power, for there is not in any man's fallen nature a holy spot of the size of a pin's point on which grace can light. Transforming grace can find no natural lodgment in our hearts, it must create its own soil ; and, blessed be God, it can do it, for with God all things are possible. Nature contributes nothing to grace, and yet grace wins the day. Humbled soul, let this cheer thee. Though there is nothing good in thee, yet grace can work wonders, and save thee by its own might.

Paul's conversion was an instance of divine power, and of that alone, and so is every true conversion. If your conversion is an instance of the preacher's power, you need to be converted again ; if your salvation is the result of your own power, it is a miserable deception, from which may you be delivered. Every man who is saved must be operated upon by the might of God the Holy Spirit : every jot and tittle of true regeneration is the Spirit's work. As for our strength, it warreth against salvation rather than for it. Blessed is that promise, " Thy people shall be willing in the day of Thy power." Conversion is as much a work of God's omnipotence as the resurrection ; and as the dead do not raise themselves, so neither do men convert themselves.

But Saul was changed immediately. His conversion was once done, and done at once. There was a little interval before he found peace, but even during those three days he was a changed man, though he was in sadness. He was under the power of Satan at one moment, and in the next he was under the reign of grace. This is also true in every conversion. However gradual the breaking of the day, there is a time when the sun is below the horizon, and a moment when he is no longer so. You may not know the exact time in which you passed from death to life, but there was such a time, if you are indeed a believer. A man may not know how old he is, but there was a moment in which he was born. In every conversion there is a distinct change from darkness to light, from death to life, just as certainly as there was in Paul's. And what a delightful hope does the rapidity of regeneration present to us ! It is by no long and laborious process that we escape from sin. We are not compelled to remain in sin for a single moment. Grace brings instantaneous liberty to those who sit in bondage. He who trusts Jesus is saved on the spot. Why, then, abide in death ? Why not lift up your eyes to immediate life and light ?

Paul proved his regeneration by his faith. He believed unto eternal life. He tells us over and over again in his epistles that he was saved by faith, and not by works. So is it with every man ; if saved at all, it is by simply believing in the Lord Jesus. Paul esteemed his own works to be less than nothing, and called them dross and dung, that he might win Christ, and so every converted man renounces his own works that he may be saved by grace alone. Whether he has been moral or immoral, whether he has lived an amiable and excellent life, or whether he has raked in the kennels of sin, every regenerate man has one only hope, and that is centred and fixed in Jesus alone. Faith in Jesus Christ is the mark of salvation, even as the heaving of the lungs or the coming of breath from the nostrils is the test of life. Faith is the grace which saves the soul, and its absence is a fatal sign. How does this fact affect you, dear friend ? Hast thou faith or no ?

Paul was very positively and evidently saved. You did not need to ask the question, Is that man a Christian or not ? for the transformation was most apparent. If Saul of Tarsus had appeared as he used to be, and Paul the apostle could also have come in, and you could have seen the one man as two men, you would have thought them no relation to one another. Paul the apostle would have said that he was dead to Saul of Tarsus, and Saul of Tarsus would have gnashed his teeth at Paul the apostle. The change was evident to all who knew him, whether they sympathize in it or not. They could not mistake the remarkable difference which grace had made, for it was as great as when midnight brightens into noon. So it is when a man is truly saved : there is a change which those around him must perceive. Do not tell me that you can be a child at home and become a Christian, and yet your father and mother will not perceive a difference in you. They will be sure to see it. Would a leopard in a menagerie lose his spots and no one notice it ? Would an Ethiopian be turned white and no one hear of it ? You, masters and mistresses, will not go in and out amongst your servants and children without their perceiving a change in you if you are born again. At least, dear brother or sister, strive with all your might to let the change be very apparent in your language, in your actions, and in your whole conduct. Let your conversation be such as becometh the gospel of Christ, that men may see that you, as well as the apostle, are decidedly changed by the renewal of your minds.

May all of us be the subjects of divine grace as Paul was : stopped in our mad career, blinded by the glory of the heavenly light, called by a mysterious voice, conscious of natural blindness, relieved of blinding scales, and made to see Jesus as one all in all. May we prove in our own persons how speedily conviction may melt into conversion, conversion into confession, and confession into consecration.

I have done when I have enquired, how far we are conformed to the pattern which God has set before us ? I know we are like Paul as to our sin, for if we have neither blasphemed nor persecuted, yet have we sinned as far as we have had opportunity. We are also conformed to Paul's pattern in the great long-suffering of God which we have experienced, and I am not sure that we cannot carry the parallel farther ; we have had much the same revelation that Paul received on the way to Damascus, for we, too, have learned that Jesus is the Christ. If any of us sin against Christ, it will not be because we do not know Him to be the Son of God, for we all believe in His deity, because our Bibles tell us so. The pattern goes so far : I would that the grace of God would operate upon you, unconverted friend, and complete the picture, by giving you like faith with Paul. Then will you be saved, as Paul was. Then also you will love Christ above all things, as Paul did, and you will say, " But what things were gain to me, those I counted loss for Christ. Yea, doubtless, and I count all things but loss for the excellency of the knowledge of Christ Jesus my Lord." He rested upon what Christ had done in His death and resurrection, and he found pardon and eternal life at once, and became, therefore, a devoted Christian.

What sayest thou, dear friend ? Art thou moved to follow Paul's example ? Does the Spirit of God prompt thee to trust Paul's Saviour, and give up every other ground of trust and rely upon Him ? Then do so and live. Does there seem to be a hand holding thee back, and dost thou hear an evil whisper saying, " Thou art too great a sinner " ? Turn round and bid the fiend depart, for the text gives him the lie.

" In me *foremost* hath Jesus Christ showed forth all long-suffering for a pattern to them which should hereafter believe on His name." God has saved Paul. Back, then, O devil ! The Lord can save any man, and He can save me. Jesus Christ of Nazareth is mighty to save, and I will rely on Him. If any poor heart shall reason thus, its logic will be sound and unanswerable. Mercy to one is an argument for mercy to another, for there is no difference, but the same Lord over all is rich unto all that call upon Him.

Now I have set the case before you, and I cannot do more ; it remains with each individual to accept or refuse. One man can bring a horse to the trough, but a hundred cannot make him drink. There is the gospel ; if you want it, take it, but if you will not have it, then I must discharge my soul by reminding you that even the gentle gospel—the gospel of love and mercy has nothing to say to you but this, " He that believeth not shall be damned."

> " How they deserve the deepest hell
> That slight the joys above ;
> What chains of vengeance must they feel
> Who break the bonds of love."

God grant that you may yield to mighty love, and find peace in Christ Jesus.

SALVATION BY KNOWING THE TRUTH

" God our Saviour ; who will have all men to be saved, and to come unto the knowledge of the truth."—1 Timothy ii. 3, 4.

MAY God the Holy Ghost guide our meditations to the best practical result this evening, that sinners may be saved and saints stirred up to diligence.

I do not intend to treat my text controversially. It is like the stone which makes the corner of a building, and it looks towards a different side of the gospel from that which is mostly before us. Two sides of the building of truth meet here. In many a village there is a corner where the idle and the quarrelsome gather together ; and theology has such corners. It would be very easy indeed to set ourselves in battle array, and during the next half-hour to carry on a very fierce attack against those who differ from us in opinion upon points which could be raised from this text. I do not see that any good would come of it, and, as we have very little time to spare, and life is short, we had better spend it upon something that may better tend to our edification. May the good Spirit preserve us from a contentious spirit, and help us really to profit by His word.

It is quite certain that when we read that God will have all men to be saved it does not mean that He wills it with the force of a decree or a divine purpose, for, if He did, then all men would be saved. He willed to make the world, and the world was made : He does not so will the salvation of all men, for we know that all men will not be saved. Terrible as the truth is, yet is it certain from holy writ that there are men who, in consequence of their sin and their rejection of the Saviour, will go away into everlasting punishment, where shall be weeping, and wailing, and gnashing of teeth. There will at the last be goats upon the left hand as well as sheep on the right, tares to be burned as well as wheat to be garnered, chaff to be blown away as well as corn to be preserved. There will be a dreadful hell as well as a glorious heaven, and there is no decree to the contrary.

What then ? Shall we try to put another meaning into the text than that which it fairly bears ? I trow not. You must, most of you, be acquainted with the general method in which our older Calvinistic friends deal with this text. " All men," say they,—" that is, *some men* " : as if the Holy Ghost could not have said " some men " if He had meant some men. " All men," say they ; " that is, some of all sorts of men " : as if the Lord could not have said " all sorts of men " if He had meant that. The Holy Ghost by the apostle has written " all men," and unquestionably He means all men. I know how to get rid of the force of the " alls " according to that critical method which some time ago was very current, but I do not see how it can be applied here with due regard to truth. I was reading just now the exposition of a very able doctor who explains the text so as to explain it away ; he applies grammatical gunpowder to it, and explodes it by way of expounding it. I thought when I read his exposition that it would have been a very capital comment upon the text if it had read, " Who *will not* have all men to be saved, nor come to a knowledge of the truth." Had such been the inspired language every remark of the learned doctor would have been exactly in keeping, but as it happens to say, " Who *will* have all men to be saved," his observations are more than a little out of place. My love of consistency with my own doctrinal views is not great enough to allow me knowingly to alter a single text of Scripture. I have great respect for orthodoxy, but my reverence for inspiration is far greater. I would soon a hundred times over appear to be inconsistent with myself than be inconsistent with the word of God. I never thought it to be any very great crime to seem to be inconsistent with myself, for who am I that I should everlastingly be consistent ? But I do think it a great crime to be so inconsistent with the word of God that I should want to lop away a bough or even a twig from so much as a single tree of the forest of Scripture. God forbid that I should cut or shape, even in the least degree, any divine expression. So runs the text, and so we must read it, " God our Saviour ; who will have all men to be saved, and to come unto the knowledge of the truth."

Does not the text mean that it is the wish of God that men should be saved ? The word " wish " gives as much force to the original as it really requires, and the passage should run thus—" whose wish it is that all men should be saved and come to a knowledge of the truth." As it is *my* wish that it should be so, as it is *your* wish that it might be so, so it is God's wish that all men should be saved ; for, assuredly, He is not less benevolent than we are. Then comes the question, " But if He wishes it to be so, why does He not make it so ? " Beloved friend, have you never heard that a fool may ask a question which a wise man cannot answer, and, if that be so, I am sure a wise person, like yourself, can ask me a great many questions which, fool as I am, I am yet not foolish enough to try to answer. Your question is only one form of the great debate of all the ages,—" If God be infinitely good and powerful, why does not His power carry out to the full all His beneficence?" It is God's wish that the oppressed should go free, yet there are many oppressed who are not free. It is God's wish that the sick should not suffer. Do you doubt it? Is it not your own wish? And yet the Lord does not work a miracle to heal every sick person. It is God's wish that His creatures should be happy. Do you deny that? He does not interpose by any miraculous agency to make us all happy, and yet it would be wicked to suppose that He does not wish the happiness of all the creatures that He has made. He has an infinite benevolence which, nevertheless, is not in all points worked out by His infinite omnipotence; and if anybody asked me why it is not, I cannot tell. I have never set up to be an explainer of all difficulties, and I have no desire to do so. It is the same old question as that of the negro who said, " Sare, you say the devil makes sin in the world." " Yes, the devil makes a deal of sin." " And you say that God hates sin." " Yes." " Then why does not He kill the devil and put an end to it?" Just so. Why does He not? Ah, my black friend, you will grow white before that question is answered. I cannot tell you why God permits moral evil, neither can the ablest philosopher on earth, nor the highest angel in heaven.

This is one of those things which we do not need to know. Have you never noticed that some people who are ill and are ordered to take pills are foolish enough to chew them? That is a very nauseous thing to do, though I have done it myself. The right way to take medicine of such a kind is to swallow it at once. In the same way there are some things in the word of God which are undoubtedly true which must be swallowed at once by an effort of faith, and must not be chewed by perpetual questioning. You will soon have I know not what of doubt and difficulty and bitterness upon your soul if you must needs know the unknowable, and have reasons and explanations for the sublime and the mysterious. Let the difficult doctrines go down whole into your very soul, by a grand exercise of confidence in God.

I thank God for a thousand things I cannot understand. When I cannot get to know the reason why, I say to myself, " Why should I know the reason why? Who am I, and what am I, that I should demand explanations of my God?" I am a most unreasonable being when I am most reasonable, and when my judgment is most accurate I dare not trust it. I had rather trust my God. I am a poor silly child at my very best: my Father must know better than I. An old parable-maker tells us that he shut himself up in his study because he had to work out a difficult problem. His little child came knocking at the door, and he said " Go away, John: you cannot understand what father is doing; let father alone." Master Johnny for that very reason felt that he must get in and see what father was doing—a true symbol of our proud intellects; we must pry into forbidden things, and uncover that which is concealed. In a little time upon the sill, outside the window, stood Master Johnny, looking in through the window at his father; and if his father had not with the very tenderest care just taken him away from that very dangerous position, there would have been no Master Johnny left on the face of the earth to exercise his curiosity in dangerous elevations. Now, God sometimes shuts the door, and says, " My child, it is so: be content to believe."

" But," we foolishly cry, " Lord, why is it so?" " It is so, My child," He says. " But why, Father, is it so?" " It is so, My child, believe Me." Then we go speculating, climbing the ladders of reasoning, guessing, speculating, to reach the lofty windows of eternal truth. Once up there we do not know where we are, our heads reel, and we are in all kinds of uncertainty and spiritual peril. If we mind things too high for us we shall run great risks. I do not intend meddling with such lofty matters. There stands the text, and I believe that it is my Father's wish that " all men should be saved, and come to the knowledge of the truth." But I know, also, that He does not will it, so that He will save any one of them, unless they believe in His dear Son; for He has told us over and over that He will not. He will not save any man except he forsakes his sins, and turns to Him with full purpose of heart: that I also know. And I know, also, that He has a people whom He will save, whom by His eternal love He has chosen, and whom by His eternal power He will deliver. I do not know how that squares with this; that is another of the things I do not know. If I go on telling you of all that I do not know, and of all that I do know, I will warrant you that the things that I do not know will be a hundred to one of the things that I do know. And so we will say no more about the matter, but just go on to the more practical part of the text. God's wish about man's salvation is this,—that men should be saved and come to the knowledge of the truth.

Men are saved, and the same men that are saved come to a knowledge of the truth. The two things happen together, and the two facts very much depend upon each other. God's way of saving men is not by leaving them in ignorance. It is by *a knowledge of the truth that men are saved;* this will make the main body of our discourse, and in closing we shall see how this truth *gives instruction to those who wish to be saved,* and also *to those who desire to save others.* May the Holy Spirit make these closing inferences to be practically useful.

Here is our proposition : IT IS BY A KNOWLEDGE OF THE TRUTH THAT MEN ARE SAVED.

Observe that stress is laid upon the article : it is *the* truth, and not every truth. Though it is a good thing to know the truth about anything, and we ought not to be satisfied to take up with a falsehood upon any point, yet it is not every truth that will save us. We are not saved by knowing any one theological truth we may choose to think of, for there are some theological truths which are comparatively of inferior value. They are not vital or essential, and a man may know them, and yet may not be saved. It is *the* truth which saves. Jesus Christ is *the* truth : the whole testimony of God about Christ is *the* truth. The work of the Holy Ghost in the heart is to work in us *the* truth. The knowledge of the truth is a large knowledge. It is not always so at the first : it may begin with but a little knowledge, but it is a large knowledge when it is further developed, and the soul is fully instructed in the whole range of the truth.

This knowledge of the grand facts which are here called the truth saves men, and we will notice its mode of operation. Very often it begins its work in a man by arousing him, and thus it *saves him from carelessness.* He did not know anything about the truth which God has revealed, and so he lived like a brute beast. If he had enough to eat and to drink he was satisfied. If he laid by a little money he was delighted. So long as the days passed pretty merrily, and he was free from aches and pains, he was satisfied. He heard about religion, but he thought it did not concern him. He supposed that there were some people who might be the better for thinking about it, but as far as he was concerned, he thought no more about God or godliness than the ox of the stall or the ostrich of the desert. Well, the truth came to him, and he received a knowledge of it. He knew only a part, and that a very dark and gloomy part of it, but it stirred him out of his carelessness, for he suddenly discovered that he was under the wrath of God. Perhaps he heard a sermon, or read a tract, or had a practical word addressed to him by some Christian friend, and he found out enough to know that " he that believeth not is condemned already, because he hath not believed on the Son of God." That startled him. " God is angry with the wicked every day : "—that amazed him. He had not thought of it, perhaps had not known it, but when he did know it, he could rest no longer. Then he came to a knowledge of this further truth, that after death there would be a judgment, that he would rise again, and that, being risen, he would have to stand before the judgment-seat of God to give an account of the things which he had done in the body. This came home very strikingly to him. Perhaps, also, such a text as this flamed forth before him,—" For every idle word that man shall speak he must give an account in the day of judgment." His mind began to foresee that last tremendous day, when on the clouds of heaven Christ will come and summon quick and dead, to answer at His judgment-seat for the whole of their lives. He did not know that before, but, knowing it, it startled and aroused him. I have known men, when first they have come to a knowledge of this truth, become unable to sleep. They have started up in the night. They have asked those who were with them to help them to pray. The next day they have been scarcely able to mind their business, for a dreadful sound has been in their ears. They feared lest they should stumble into the grave and into hell. Thus they were saved from carelessness. They could not go back to be the mere brute beasts they were before. Their eyes had been opened to futurity and eternity. Their spirits had been quickened—at least so much that they could not rest in that dolish, dull, dead carelessness in which they had formerly been found. They were shaken out of their deadly lethargy by a knowledge of the truth.

The truth is useful to a man in another way : *it saves him from prejudice.* Often when men are awakened to know something about the wrath of God they begin to plunge about to discover divers methods by which they may escape from that wrath. Consulting, first of all, with themselves, they think that, if they can reform—give up their grosser sins, and if they can join with religious people, they will make it all right. And there are some who go and listen to a kind of religious teacher, who says, " You must do good works. You must earn a good character. You must add to all this the ceremonies of our church. You must be particular and precise in receiving blessing only through the appointed channel of the apostolical succession." Of the aforesaid mystical succession this teacher has the effrontery to assure his dupe that he is a legitimate instrument ; and that sacraments received at his hands are means of grace. Under such untruthful notions we have known people

who were somewhat aroused sit down again in a false peace. They have done all that they judged right and attended to all that they were told. Suddenly, by God's grace, they come to a knowledge of another truth, and that is that by the deeds of the law there shall no flesh be justified in the sight of God. They discover that salvation is not by works of the law or by ceremonies, and that if any man be under the law he is also under the curse. Such a text as the following comes home, " Not of blood, nor of the will of the flesh, nor of the will of man, but of God " ; and such another text as this, " Ye must be born again," and then this is at the back of it—" that which is born of the flesh is flesh, and that which is born of the Spirit is spirit." When they also find out that there is necessary a righteousness better than their own —a perfect righteousness to justify them before God, and when they discover that they must be made new creatures in Christ Jesus, or else they must utterly perish, then they are saved from false confidences, saved from crying, " Peace, peace," when there is no peace. It is a grand thing when a knowledge of the truth stops us from trusting in a lie. I am addressing some who remember when they were saved in that way. What an opening of the eyes it was to you ! You had a great prejudice against the gospel of grace and the plan of salvation by faith ; but when the Lord took you in hand and made you see your beautiful righteousness to be a moth-eaten mass of rags, and when the gold that you had accumulated suddenly turned into so much brass, cankered, and good for nothing,—when you stood stripped naked before God and the poor cobwebs of ceremonies suddenly dropped from off you, oh, then the Lord was working His salvation in your soul, and you were being saved from false confidences by a knowledge of the truth.

Moreover, it often happens that a knowledge of the truth stands a man in good stead for another purpose ; *it saves him from despair.* Unable to be careless, and unable to find comfort in false confidences, some poor agitated minds are driven into a wide and stormy sea without rudder or compass, with nothing but wreck before them. " There is no hope for me," says the man. " I perceive I cannot save myself. I see that I am lost. I am dead in trespasses and sins, and cannot stir hand or foot. Surely now I may as well go on in sin, and even multiply my transgressions. The gate of mercy is shut against me ; what is the use of fear where there is no room for hope ? " At such a time, if the Lord leads the man to a knowledge of the truth, he perceives that though his sins be as scarlet they shall be as wool, and though they be red like crimson they shall be as white as snow. That precious doctrine of substitution comes in—that Christ stood in the stead of the sinner, that the transgression of His people was laid upon Him, and that God, by thus avenging sin in the person of His dear Son, and honouring His law by the suffering of the Saviour, is now able to declare pardon to the penitent and grace to the believing. Now, when the soul comes to know that sin is put away by the atoning blood ; when the heart discovers that it is not our life that saves us, but the life of God that comes to dwell in us ; that we are not to be regenerated by our own actions, but are regenerated by the Holy Ghost who comes to us through the precious death of Jesus, then despair flies away, and the soul cries exultingly, " There is hope. There is hope. Christ died for sinners : why should I not have a part in that precious death ? He came like a physician to heal the sick : why should He not heal me ? Now I perceive that He does not want my goodness, but my badness ; He does not need my righteousness, but my unrighteousness : for He came to save the ungodly and to redeem His people from their sins." I say, when the heart comes to a knowledge of this truth, then it is saved from despair ; and this is no small part of the salvation of Jesus Christ.

A saving knowledge of the truth, to take another line of things, works in this way. A knowledge of the truth *shows a man his personal need of being saved.* O you that are not saved, and who dream you do not need to be, you only require to know the truth, and you will perceive that you must be saved or lost for ever.

A knowledge of the truth *reveals the atonement by which we are saved :* a knowledge of the truth *shows us what that faith is by which the atonement becomes available for us :* a knowledge of the truth teaches us that faith is the simple act of trusting, that it is not an action of which man may boast ; it is not an action of the nature of a work, so as to be a fruit of the law ; but faith is a self-denying grace which finds all its strength in Him upon whom it lives, and lays all its honour upon Him. Faith is not self in action but self forsaken, self abhorred, self put away that the soul may trust in Christ, and trust in Christ alone. There are persons now present who are puzzled about what faith is. We have tried to explain it a great many times to you, but we have explained it so that you did not understand it any the better ; and yet the same explanation has savingly instructed others. May God the Holy Ghost open your understandings that you may practically know what faith is, and at once exercise it. I suppose that it is a very hard thing to understand because it is so plain. When a man wishes the way of salvation to be difficult he naturally kicks at it because it is easy : and, when his pride wants it to be hard to be understood, he is pretty sure to say that He does not understand it because it is so plain. Do not you know that the unlettered often receive Christ when philosophers refuse Him, and that He who has not called many of the great, and many of the mighty, has chosen poor, foolish, and despised things ? That is because poor foolish men, you know, are willing to believe a plain thing, but men wise in their own conceits desire to be, if they can, a little confounded and puzzled that they may please themselves with the idea that their own superior intellect has made a discovery ; and, because the way of salvation is just so easy that almost an idiot boy may lay hold of it, therefore they pretend that they do not understand it. Some people cannot see a thing because it is too high up ; but there are others who cannot see it because it is too low down. Now, it so happens that the way of salvation by faith is so simple that it seems beneath the dignity of exceedingly clever men. May God bring them to a knowledge of this truth : may they see that they cannot be saved except by giving up all idea of saving themselves ; that they cannot be saved except they step right into Christ, for, until they get to the end of the creature, they will never get to the beginning of the Creator. Till they empty out their pockets of every mouldy crust, and have not a crumb left ; they cannot come and take the rich mercy which is stored up in Christ Jesus for every empty, needy sinner. May the Lord be pleased to give you that knowledge of the truth !

When a man comes in very deed to a knowledge of the truth about faith in Christ, he trusts Christ, and he is there and then saved from the guilt of sin ; and he begins to be saved altogether from sin. God cuts the root of the power of sin that very day ; but yet it has such life within itself that at the scent of water it will bud again. Sin in our members struggles to live. It has as many lives as a cat : there is no killing it. Now, when we come to a knowledge of the truth, we begin to learn how sin is to be killed in us—how the same Christ that justifies, sanctifies, and works in us according to His working who worketh in us mightily, that we may be conformed to the image of Christ, and made meet to dwell with perfect saints above. Beloved, many of you that are saved from the guilt of sin, have a very hard struggle with the power of sin, and have much more conflict, perhaps, than you need to have, because you have not come to a knowledge of all the truth about indwelling sin. I therefore beg you to study much the word of God upon that point, and especially to see the adaptation of Christ to rule over your nature, and to conquer all your corrupt desires, and learn how by faith to bring each sin before Him that, like Agag, it may be hewed in pieces before His eyes. You will never overcome sin except by the blood of the Lamb. There is no sanctification except by faith. The same instrument which destroys sin as to its guilt must slay sin as to its power. "They overcame by the blood of the Lamb," and so must you. Learn this truth well, so shall you find salvation wrought in you from day to day.

Now, I think I hear somebody say, " I think I know all about this." Yes, you may think you know it, and may not know anything at all about it. " Oh, but," says one, " I do know it. I learned the ' Assembly's Catechism ' when I was a child. I have read the Bible ever since, and I am well acquainted with all the commonplaces of orthodoxy." That may be, dear friend, and yet you may not know the truth. I have heard of a man who knew how to swim, but, as he had never been in the water, I do not think much of his knowledge of swimming : in fact, he did not really know the art. I have heard of a botanist who understood all about flowers, but as he lived in London, and scarcely ever saw above one poor withered thing in a flower-pot, I do not think much of his botany. I have heard of a man who was a very great astronomer, but he had not a telescope, and I never thought much of his astronomy. So there are many persons who think they know and yet do not know because they have never had any personal acquaintance with the thing. A mere notional knowledge or a dry doctrinal knowledge is of no avail. We must know the truth in a very different way from that.

How are we to know it, then ? Well, we are to know it, first, by *a believing knowledge.* You do not know a thing unless you believe it to be really so. If you doubt it, you do not know it. If you say, " I really am not sure it is true," then you cannot say that you know it. That which the Lord has revealed in holy Scripture you must devoutly believe to be true. In addition to this, your knowledge, if it becomes believing knowledge, must be *personal knowledge*—a persuasion that it is true in reference to yourself. It is true about your neighbour, about your brother, but you must believe it about *yourself*, or your knowledge is vain—for instance, you must know that *you* are lost—that *you* are in danger of eternal destruction from the presence of God—that for *you* there is no hope but in Christ—that for *you* there is hope if you rest in Christ—that resting in Christ *you* are saved. Yes, *you*. You must know that because you have trusted in Christ *you* are saved, and that now *you* are free from condemnation, and that now in *you* the new life has begun, which will fight against the old life of sin, until it overcome, and you, even you, are safely landed on the golden shore. There must be a personal appropriation of what you believe to be true. That is the kind of knowledge which saves the soul.

But this must be *a powerful knowledge*, by which I mean that it must operate in and upon your mind. A man is told that his house is on fire. I will suppose that standing here I held up a *telegram*, and said, "My friend, is your name so-and-so ?" "Yes." "Well, your house is on fire." He knows the fact, does he not ? Yes, but he sits quite still. Now, my impression is about that good brother, that he does not know, for he does not believe it. He cannot believe it, surely : he may believe that somebody's house is on fire, but not his own. If it is his house which is burning, and he knows it, what does he do ? Why he gets up and goes off to see what he can do towards saving his goods. That is the kind of knowledge which saves the soul—when a man knows the truth about himself, and therefore his whole nature is moved and affected by the knowledge. Do I know that I am in danger of hell fire ? And am I in my senses ? Then I shall never rest till I have escaped from that danger. Do I know that there is salvation for me in Christ ? Then I never shall be content until I have obtained that salvation by the faith to which that salvation is promised : that is to say, if I really am in my senses, and if my sin has not made me beside myself as sin does, for sin works a moral madness upon the mind of man, so that he puts bitter for sweet and sweet for bitter, and dances on the jaws of hell, and sits down and scoffs at Almighty mercy, despises the precious blood of Christ and will have none of it, although there and there only is salvation to be found.

This knowledge when it comes really to save the soul is what we call *experimental knowledge*—knowledge acquired according to the exhortation of the Psalmist, "Oh, taste and see that the Lord is good "—acquired by tasting. Now, at this present moment, I, speaking for myself, know that I am originally lost by nature. Do I believe it ? Believe it ? I am as sure of it as I am of my own existence. I know that I am lost by nature. It would not be possible for anybody to make me doubt that : I have felt it. How many weary days I spent under the pressure of that knowledge ! Does a soldier know that there is such a thing as a cat when he has had a hundred lashes ? It would take a deal of argument to make him believe there is not such a thing, or that backs do not smart when they feel the lash. Oh, how my soul smarted under the lash of conscience when I suffered under a sense of sin ! Do I know that I could not save myself ? Know it ? Why, my poor, struggling heart laboured this way and that, even as in the very fire with bitter disappointment, for I laboured to climb to the stars on a treadwheel, and I was trying and trying and trying with all my might, but never rose an inch higher. I tried to fill a bottomless tub with leaking buckets, and worked on and toiled and slaved, but never

accomplished even the beginning of my unhappy task. I know, for I have tried it, that salvation is not in man, or in all the feelings, and weepings, and prayings, and Bible readings, and church goings, and chapel goings which zeal could crowd together. Nothing whatsoever that man does can avail him towards his own salvation. This I know by sad trial of it, and failure in it.

But I do know that there is real salvation by believing in Christ. Know it ? I have never preached to you concerning that subject what I do not know by experience. In a moment, when I believed in Christ, I leaped from despair to fulness of delight. Since I have believed in Jesus I have found myself totally new—changed altogether from what I was ; and I find now that, in proportion as I trust in Jesus, I love God and try to serve Him ; but if at any time I begin to trust in myself, I forget my God, and I become selfish and sinful. Just as I keep on being nothing and taking Christ to be everything, so am I led in the paths of righteousness. I am merely talking of myself, because a man cannot bear witness about other people so thoroughly as he can about himself. I am sure that all of you who have tried my Master can bear the same witness. You have been saved, and you have come to a knowledge of the truth experimentally ; and every soul here that would be saved must in the same way believe the truth, appropriate the truth, act upon the truth, and experimentally know the truth, which is summed up in few words :—" Man lost : Christ his Saviour. Man nothing : God all in all. The heart depraved : the Spirit working the new life by faith." The Lord grant that these truths may come home to your hearts with power.

I am now going to draw two inferences which are to be practical. The first one is this : in regard TO YOU THAT ARE SEEKING SALVATION. Does not the text show you that it is very possible that the reason why you have not found salvation is because you do not know the truth ? Hence, I do most earnestly entreat the many of you young people who cannot get rest to be very diligent searchers of your Bibles. The first thing and the main thing is to believe in the Lord Jesus Christ, but if you say, " I do not understand it," or " I cannot believe it," or if there be any such doubt rising in your mind, then it may be because you have not gained complete knowledge of the truth. It is very possible that somebody will say to you, " Believe, believe, believe." I would say the same to you, but I should like you to act upon the common-sense principle of knowing what is to be believed and in whom you are to believe. I explained this to one who came to me a few evenings ago. She said that she could not believe. " Well," I said, " now suppose as you sit in that chair I say to you, ' Young friend, I cannot believe in you ' : you would say to me, ' I think you should.' Suppose I then replied, ' I wish I could.' What would you bid me do ? Should I sit still and look at you till I said, ' I think I can believe in you ' ? That would be ridiculous. No, I should go and enquire, ' Who is this young person ? What kind of character does she bear ? What are her connections ? ' and when I knew all about you, then I have no doubt that I should say, ' I have made examination into this young woman's character, and I cannot help believing in her.' " Now, it is just so with Jesus Christ. If you say, " I cannot believe in Him," read those four blessed testimonies of Matthew,

Mark, Luke, and John, and especially linger much over those parts where they tell you of His death. Do you know that many, while they have been sitting, as it were, at the foot of the cross, viewing the Son of God dying for men, have cried out, " I cannot help believing. I cannot help believing. When I see my sin, it seems too great ; but when I see my Saviour my iniquity vanishes away." I think I have put it to you sometimes like this : If you take a ride through London, from end to end, it will take you many days to get an idea of its vastness ; for probably none of us know the size of London. After your long ride of inspection you will say, " I wonder how those people can all be fed. I cannot make it out. Where does all the bread come from, and all the butter, and all the cheese, and all the meat, and everything else ? Why, these people will be starved. It is not possible that Lebanon with all its beasts, and the vast plains of Europe and America should ever supply food sufficient for all this multitude." That is your feeling. And then, to-morrow morning you get up, and you go to Covent Garden, you go to the great meat-markets, and to other sources of supply, and when you come home you say, " I feel quite different now, for now I cannot make out where all the people come from to eat all this provision : I never saw such store of food in all my life. Why, if there were two Londons, surely there is enough here to feed them." Just so—when you think about your sins and your wants you get saying, " How can I be saved ? " Now, turn your thoughts the other way ; think that Christ is the Son of God : think of what the merit must be of the incarnate God's bearing human guilt ; and instead of saying, " My sin is too great," you will almost think the atoning sacrifice too great. Therefore I do urge you to try and know more of Christ ; and I am only giving you the advice of Isaiah, " Incline your ear, and come unto Me ; hear, and your soul shall live." Know, hear, read, and believe more about those precious things, always with this wish—" I am not hearing for hearing's sake, and I am not wishing to know for knowing's sake, but I am wanting to hear and to know that I may be saved." I want to be like the woman who lost her piece of silver. She did not light a candle and then say, " Bravo, I have lit a candle, this is enough." She did not take her broom and then sit down content, crying, " What a splendid broom." When she raised a dust she did not exclaim, " What a dust I am making ! I am surely making progress now." Some poor sinners, when they have been seeking, get into a dust of soul-trouble, and think it to be a comfortable sign. No, I'll warrant you, the woman wanted her groat : she did not mind the broom, or the dust, or the candle ; she looked for the silver. So it must be with you. Never content yourself with the reading, the hearing, or the feeling. It is Christ you want. It is the precious piece of money that you must find ; and you must sweep until you find it. Why, there it is ! There is Jesus ! Take Him ! Take Him ! Believe Him now, even now, and you are saved.

The last inference is for YOU WHO DESIRE TO SAVE SINNERS. You must, dear friends, bring *the truth* before them when you want to bring them to Jesus Christ. I believe that exciting meetings do good to some. Men are so dead and careless that almost anything is to be tolerated that wakes them up ; but for real solid soul-work before God, telling men that truth is the main thing. What truth ? It is gospel truth, truth about Christ that they want. Tell it in a loving, earnest, affectionate manner, for God wills that they should be saved, not in any other way, but in this way—by knowledge of the truth. He wills that all men should be saved in this way—not by keeping them in ignorance, but by bringing the truth before them. That is God's way of saving them. Have your Bible handy when you are reasoning with a soul. Just say, " Let me call your attention to this passage." It has a wonderful power over a poor staggering soul to point to the Book itself. Say, " Did you notice this promise, my dear friend ? And have you seen that passage ? " Have the Scriptures handy. There is a dear brother of mine here whom God blesses to many souls, and I have seen him talking to some, and turning to the texts very handily. I wondered how he did it so quickly, till I looked in his Bible, and found that he had the choice texts printed on two leaves and inserted into the book, so that he could always open upon them. That is a capital plan, to get the cheering words ready to hand, the very ones that you know have comforted you and have comforted others. It sometimes happens that one single verse of God's word will make the light to break into a soul, when fifty days of reasoning would not do it. I notice that when souls are saved it is by our texts rather than by our sermons. God the Holy Ghost loves to use His own sword. It is God's word, not man's comment on God's word, that God usually blesses. Therefore, stick to the quotation of the Scripture itself, and rely upon *the truth*. If a man could be saved by a lie it would be a lying salvation. Truth alone can work results that are true. Therefore, keep on teaching *the truth*. God help you to proclaim the precious truth about the bleeding, dying, risen, exalted, coming Saviour ; and God will bless it.

THE HEXAPLA OF MYSTERY

" And without controversy great is the mystery of godliness : God was manifest in the flesh, justified in the Spirit, seen of angels, preached unto the Gentiles, believed on in the world, received up into glory."—1 Timothy iii. 16.

THE apostle tells us in the preceding verse that the Lord has a double design in maintaining His church in the world. The first is that it may be the place of His abode, for the church of the living God is " the house of God," the home wherein He reveals Himself unto His own children, the resting-place of His love which He has of old appointed. Jehovah still inhabits the praises of Israel, and still He fulfills His promise to His chosen, " I will dwell in them and walk in them " (2 Cor. vi. 16). Blessed is the church which has realized this first design of God, and so has continued to enjoy the Lord's presence and power. May we in this place be a building fitly framed together, and grown unto a holy temple in the Lord, for a habitation of God through the Spirit. God's next purpose in sustaining a church in the world is that it may preserve and uphold His truth among men, for the church of the living God is " the pillar and ground of the truth." The gospel must be believed, practised, and proclaimed by men of God, or it will not have power. God does not trust the conservation of His truth to books, or to the most accurately written creeds, or to some one person supposed to be infallible, but He puts the incorruptible seed into the hearts of His chosen, and in such good soil its vitality and its growth secure its preservation. Even the inspired word, as a letter, has small power till it gains a lodging-place for the truth in a warm heart, and then it grows and yields fruit, till its boughs spread far and wide, and its seeds are wafted on the wings of every wind, to spring up on the hills and among the valleys where none had looked for them. As long as one copy of the Holy Scriptures remains in the world we shall have the pure truth among us, but it will be like an unplanted seed. For the propagation of the gospel, human voices are required ; for the establishment and confirmation of it among men, human lives are needed ; and God intends that His gospel shall be set forth and held up, published, defended, maintained, and supported in the world by His church ; not alone by His ministers, nor by hierarchical establishment, but by the entire company of faithful men. To the sacramental host of His elect has He committed the banner of the truth, which they are always to unfold, and carry on by the power of His Spirit, from victory to victory. In this sense, the church of the living God is, and ever must be, " the pillar and ground of the truth " ; let us take care, in our measure to make her so.

While dealing with this question, it was most fitting for the apostle to tell us what the truth is, and now is the most proper time for each one of us to learn what are the vital and essential truths which the church of God is for ever to maintain. Our text is for this reason deeply interesting ; it deals not with questionable and debatable topics, but with things verily, and, indeed, received among us. Its testimony is short, but weighty. We cannot spare a single word from it, and it would be a crime to add anything to it. The apostle calls it a " mystery," and so, indeed, it is, for exceeding greatness of meaning, but not for obscurity of language, for it is as plain as it is full. Neither is it a mystery because it speaks of recondite opinions, or philosophical theories, for it deals only with facts, and is an historical summary of actual occurrences.

Observe that the comprehensive summary of the gospel here given is contained in six little sentences, which run with such regularity of measure in the original Greek, that some have supposed them to be an ancient hymn ; and it is possible that they may have been used as such in the early church. There is a poetic form about the six sentences. You are aware, of course, that the Orientals do not consider it essential to sacred psalms and hymns that they should resound with jingling rhymes ; we are the slaves of mere sound in that respect, but they are free. Their fashion of verse-making has more respect to the sense than ours, and lies, as a rule, very much in introducing pleasant parallels and contracts. These you have here, whether the six paragraphs are verses of a hymn or no. Note that " manifest in *the flesh* " is contrasted with " justified in *the spirit*," " seen of angels," who are nearest to the throne of God, is fitly set by the side of " preached unto the Gentiles," who stand at the opposite pole, and are far off. And then the third duplicate is made up of the evident opposites, " believed on *in the world*," " received up *into glory*." Thus, all through, the lights and shades are set over against each other by evident design. Moreover, you will perceive an equally plain parallelism, if you will read attentively. The first two stanzas deal with the revealing of the Lord Jesus ;—He is manifest in the flesh, and He is yet more fully made manifest by being justified in the spirit. Then follows a making known of the Lord by sight to angels, and by hearing to the Gentiles ; and, in the third pair of lines, there is a two-fold reception,—the one by grace among men who believe, and the other into His actual glory in heaven. To all this add that pairs are also discernable in the first and last, the second and fourth, and the two middle lines. Just for an instant notice that the first clause of the series deals with Christ's descent, and the last with His ascent ; the second and the fifth are both intensely spiritual ; and the third and fourth have to do with the senses only. Thus you find another set of parallels, whose existence can hardly be a mere accident.

Note this, for it teaches us that our memories need to be helped and strengthened in every way, and so it is well to have condensed truth to carry about with us, and exceedingly advantageous to us to have it arranged for us in such a shape that we are likely to recollect it. The apostle has been led by the Spirit to give us goodly words, helping our infirmities ; of this help we should gratefully avail ourselves to the utmost. If we be somewhat instructed in the word we have here an example of practical usefulness ; we may for ourselves and for others, especially for the young, try to put truth into forms which will help it to retain its hold upon the memory.

I shall call my text a hexapla of essential truth, a sixfold mystery of godliness. You have six great points clearly set forth before you, and these constitute the main, the essential elements of our holy faith, which the church of God is for ever to set forth, and uphold to the end of time.

The apostle has said, " without controversy great is the mystery of godliness." When he says " without controversy," I suppose he means that there ought to be no controversy about these facts, though controversies have arisen concerning them, and always will, since the most self-evident truth will always find self-evident fools to contradict it. He means that, in the church of God, at any rate, there is no question about these fundamentals. Outside of the church these statements are denied, but inside the house of God no one ever questions them for a moment ; and he who does so is by that very act proven to have no part nor lot in the matter. Without controversy all Christians agree that these are truths, and also that they are no trifles, but involve a mystery, and a great mystery ; that is to say, that they were things hidden in themselves, and so concealed that reason could not have found them out ; and even now, though they be revealed, they concern matters so vast and so profound that none of us comprehend them to the full, and the best instructed scribe in the kingdom recognizes in them infinite deeps which he cannot hope fully to explore. The facts are unquestioned by the church of God, and are without dispute, among the faithful, regarded as containing in their inner depths a world of weighty meaning, even the great mystery of godliness.

Have you ever noticed that there are six New

Testament mysteries ? There may be more, but these six are the chief. The first is the mystery of the incarnation, which is now before us ; " Great is the mystery of godliness, God was manifest in the flesh." The next is the mystery of the union of Christ with His church, of which we read, in Ephesians v. 31, 32, " For this cause shall a man leave his father and mother, and shall be joined unto his wife, and they two shall be one flesh. This is a great mystery : but I speak concerning Christ and the church." Thrice blessed union with Jesus, may our souls find their heaven in thy holy mystery.

> " Oh teach us, Lord, to know and own
> This wondrous mystery,
> That Thou with us art truly ONE,
> And we are one with Thee ! "

The third mystery is the mystery of the calling of the Gentiles, to which Paul refers in Ephesians iii. 4–6, where he says, " Whereby, when ye read, ye may understand my knowledge in the mystery of Christ ; which in other ages was not made known unto the sons of men, as it is now revealed unto His holy apostles and prophets by the Spirit ; that the Gentiles should be fellow-heirs, and of the same body, and partakers of His promise in Christ by the gospel." Herein we have a joyful portion, for which we can never be too grateful. The fourth mystery concerns the Jews, and deals with the restoration of Israel, whom we ought to remember with abounding sympathy and brotherly love. Of this you will read in Romans xi. 25, 26 : " For I would not, brethren, that ye should be ignorant of this mystery, lest ye should be wise in your own conceits ; that blindness in part is happened to Israel, until the fulness of the Gentiles be come in. And so all Israel shall be saved ; as it is written, There shall come out of Sion the Deliverer, and shall turn away ungodliness from Jacob." For a fifth mystery I would bid you remember the doctrine of the removal of corruption from the body, and of its resurrection as spoken of in the famous passage, " Behold, I shew you a mystery ; we shall not all sleep, but we shall all be changed, in a moment, in the twinkling of an eye, at the last trump ; for the trumpet shall sound, and the dead shall be raised incorruptible, and we shall be changed." And then, alas ! to close the list, there is that mystery of iniquity which began to work so soon, and worketh yet more and more of evil.

Our text, then, is one of six mysteries, but it has this pre-eminence, that it is a *great* mystery, and is besides peculiarly *the* mystery. It is called " the mystery of godliness," because it most intimately concerns a godly life, because those who receive it in their hearts become thereby godly men ; and because, moreover, it builds up its believers in godliness, and is to them a grand motive for the reverent love and holy fear of the Lord their God.

Let so much as we have already spoken stand for our preface, and let us now, by the Holy Spirit's aid, consider one by one the six branches of the mystery which is now before us.

I. The first sentence is " GOD WAS MANIFEST IN THE FLESH." I believe that our version is the correct one, but the fiercest battlings have been held over this sentence. It is asserted that the word *Theos* is a corruption for " *Os* " ; so that, instead of reading " *God* was manifest in the flesh," we should read, " *who* was manifest in the flesh." There is very little occasion for fighting about this matter, for if the text

does not say " God was manifest in the flesh," who does it say was manifested in the flesh ? Either a man, or an angel, or a devil. Does it tell us that a man was manifest in the flesh ? Assuredly that cannot be its teaching, for every man is manifest in the flesh, and there is no sense whatever in making such a statement concerning any mere man, and then calling it a mystery. Was it an angel, then ? But what angel was ever manifest in the flesh ? And if he were, would it be at all a mystery that he should be " seen of angels " ? Is it a wonder for an angel to see an angel ? Can it be that the devil was manifest in the flesh ? If so, he has been " received up into glory," which, let us hope, is not the case. Well, if it was neither a man, nor an angel, nor a devil, who was manifest in the flesh, surely he must have been God ; and so, if the word be not there, the sense must be there, or else nonsense. We believe that, if criticism should grind the text in a mill, it would get out of it no more and no less than the sense expressed by our grand old version. God Himself was manifest in the flesh. What a mystery is this ! A mystery of mysteries ! God the invisible was manifest ; God the spiritual dwelt in flesh ; God the infinite, un-contained, boundless, was manifest in the flesh. What infinite leagues our thought must traverse between Godhead self-existent, and, therefore, full of power and self-sufficiency, before we have descended to the far-down level of poor flesh, which is as grass at its best, and dust in its essence ! Where find we a greater contrast than between God and flesh, and yet the two are blended in the incarnation of the Saviour. God was manifest in the flesh ; truly God, not God humanized, but God as God. He was manifest in real flesh ; not in manhood deified and made super-human, but in actual flesh.

> " Oh joy ! there sitteth in our flesh,
> Upon a throne of light,
> One of a human mother born,
> In perfect Godhead bright !
>
> For ever God, for ever man,
> My Jesus shall endure ;
> And fix'd on Him, my hope remains
> Eternally secure."

Matchless truth, let the church never fail to set it forth, for it is essential to the world's salvation that this doctrine of the incarnation be made fully known.

O my brethren, since it is " without controversy," let us not controvert but sit down and feed upon it. What a miracle of condescension is here, that God should manifest Himself in flesh. It needs not so much to be preached upon as to be pondered in the heart. It needs that ye sit down in quiet, and consider how He who made you became like you, He who is your God became your brother man. He who is adored of angels once lay in a manger ; He who feeds all living things hungered and was athirst ; He who oversees all worlds as God, was, as a man, made to sleep, to suffer, and to die like yourselves. This is a statement not easily to be believed. If He had not been beheld by many witnesses, so that men handled Him, looked upon Him, and heard Him speak, it were a thing not readily to be accepted that so divine a person should be manifest in flesh. It is a wonder of condescension !

And it is a marvel, too, of benediction, for God's manifestation in human flesh conveys a thousand blessings to us. Bethlehem's star is the morning star of hope to believers. Now man is nearest to

God. Never was God manifest in angel nature, but He is manifest in flesh. Now, between poor puny man that is born of a woman, and the infinite God, there is a bond of union of the most wonderful kind. God and man in one person is the Lord Jesus Christ ! This brings our manhood near to God, and by so doing it ennables our nature, it lifts us up from the dunghill and sets us among princes ; while at the same time it enriches us by endowing our manhood with all the glory of Christ Jesus in whom dwelleth all the fulness of the Godhead bodily. Lift up your eyes, ye down-trodden sons of man ! If ye be men ye have a brotherhood with Christ, and Christ is God. O ye who have begun to despise yourselves and think that ye are merely sent to be drudges upon earth, and slaves of sin, lift up your heads, and look for redemption in the Son of Man, who has broken the captives' bonds. If ye be believers in the Christ of God, then are ye also the children of God, and if children then heirs,—heirs of God, joint heirs with Jesus Christ.

What a fulness of consolation there is in this truth, as well as of benediction ; for if the Son of God be man, then He understands me and will have a fellow feeling for me. He knows my unfitness to worship sometimes—He knows my tendencies to grow weary and dull—He knows my pains, my trials, and my griefs :

> "He knows what fierce temptations mean
> For He has felt the same."

Man, truly man, yet sitting at the right hand of the Father, Thou, O Saviour, art the delight of my soul. Is there not the richest comfort in this for you, the people of God ?

And, withal, there is instruction, too, for God was manifest in the flesh ; and if you desire to see God, you must see Him in Christ Jesus. It does not say God was veiled in the flesh, though under certain aspects that might be true ; but God was " manifest in the flesh." The brightness of the sun might put out our eyes if we gazed upon it, and we must needs look through dim glass, and then the sun is manifested to us ; so the excessive glory of the infinite Godhead cannot be borne by our mind's eye till it comes into communication and union with the nature of man, and then God is manifest to us. My soul, never try to gaze upon an absolute God : the brightness will blind thine eye : even our God is a consuming fire ! Ask not to see God in fire in the bush, nor God in lightning upon Mount Sinai ; be satisfied to see God in the man Christ Jesus, for there God is manifested. Not all the glory of the sky, and of the sea, not the wonders of creation or provdence, can set forth the Deity as does the Son of Mary, who from the manger went to the cross, and from the cross to the tomb, and from the tomb to His eternal throne. Behold ye now the Lamb of God, for God is manifest in Him ! People of God, look ye nowhere else for God.

I shall leave the point when I have put a personal question. Have we each one of us seen God in Christ Jesus ? Remember, this is essential to salvation. We speak not now that which is harsh or severe, we only speak that which is honest and true ; if you rebel against it we still can say no less. Ye cannot be right anywhere unless ye are right about the person of the Lord Jesus. If you do not accept Him as the Son of God He cannot be a Saviour to you, and without Him for a Saviour you are as surely lost as you are born, whatever profession you may make. I trust we can say, many of us, " Yes, Jesus Christ is to us Lord, to the glory of God the Father, and we worship Him, and obey Him, putting all our trust in Him, and rendering our adoration to Him." If you be not now His worshippers, may the blessed Spirit bring you to Jesus, and not suffer you to attempt to go to the Father first, for the Lord Jesus hath told us " no man cometh unto the Father but by Me." May you go to the throne of God by the way of the cross, for this is the only open way, and may you go by that road at once.

II. The second clause concerns our Lord's vindication by the Spirit. He who was " manifest in the flesh " was also " JUSTIFIED IN THE SPIRIT." When our Lord came in human flesh and declared Himself to be the Son of God there were many reasons why His statement would be doubted, for He came in such poverty, weakness, and disrepute. In any case, the appearance of God in flesh would need great proof, but the circumstances which surrounded our Saviour were such as to cast, especially in carnal minds, great doubt upon His pretensions ; but our Lord, however the flesh might seem to cloud his claims, was " justified in the Spirit," which may mean, and perhaps does, that His spiritual nature as man was so elevated by His Godhead that it abundantly justified His claim to be the Son of God. What a spirit was His for purity and dignity ! What nobility ever came near to His ! What a mind was His, what wisdom dwelt in Him ! Even as a child He baffled Rabbis, and as a man He confounded all who would entrap Him in His speech. Was there ever such teaching as His ? Listen to Him, and you feel that the spirit which flashes from those eyes and distils from those lips justifies His claim to be the Son of the Highest.

Hearken also to His words of command, when His Godhead glows through His humanity and proves Him divine. He speaks, and it is done ; He commands and it stands fast. At His bidding waves sleep and winds rest ; pain flies, strength returns, health smiles and death lives ! Has not His spiritual nature, by deeds so astounding, fully justified Him ?

And see, dear friends, how He was justified—not only by His own spirit, which wrought beyond the reach and compass of all other spirits—but He was justified by the Holy Spirit which rested upon Him without measure, and made His human spirit strong. It was this anointing which made Him the chief of all prophets, teachers, and revealers of the mind of God. All who heard Him confessed His unrivalled power, even when they resisted it. The Spirit of God bore witness in Him—His words were full of unction ; the Spirit of God bore witness with Him—His words went to men's hearts. The Spirit of God bore witness to Christ, and justified all His claims at the time of His baptism, when out of the excellent glory there appeared the form of a dove, and a voice cried out of heaven, " This is My beloved Son." That same Spirit justifies Him audibly again in His transfiguration ; but silently, and yet more evidently, the seal of God was always on Him, everywhere the Spirit witnessed to Him. Only blind eyes, blinded by hate, refused to see the divine light which hung about His every word and act, as radiance enrobes a star. Above all, our Lord's claims were justified by the Spirit in His resurrection, when He was " declared to be the Son of God with power, according to the Spirit of holiness by His resurrection from the dead." Nor less so when, after forty days, He was received up into glory, and the Spirit of God justified all that Christ had said, by coming down like a rushing mighty wind and cloven tongues of fire, and resting upon His disciples. If Christ had not risen from the dead He would have been a convicted impostor, and after His rising from the dead, if the Spirit of God had not been given, His claim would still have remained under a cloud ; but now it is clear that " He hath ascended on high, and received gifts for men, yea, for the rebellious also, that the Lord God might dwell among them " ; for the scattering of the Spirit of God among men was that promised largess which our mighty Conqueror distributed among His people, when He entered upon the possession of His crown.

The Holy Spirit has justified Christ. This is a part of the testimony of the church—that Christ's claims are to be justified by the spirit of His teaching, and also by the Holy Spirit whose supernatural power will accompany the proclamation of the gospel. Now, let the church always stand to this. I am afraid we are on wrong ground when we begin to defend the gospel by mere reason. The true defence of the gospel is the spirit of Christ ; Jesus is justified in the Spirit, and needs no other justification. O, brethren, if we exhibit the Spirit of Christ we shall answer cavillers, and if the Spirit of God rests on the ministry of the church, cavillers will cease to cavil ; they will see her glory and they will be ashamed. The Holy Ghost is our strength, our glory, the abiding witness that our great Leader is Lord and God.

Brethren, has the Holy Spirit ever justified Christ in your soul ? He has come to save, has the Holy Spirit revealed Him as your Saviour ? He has come to blot out sin, has the Holy Ghost ever revealed Him in all His power to pardon you ? This is the sure vindication of Christ—your own personal experience of His preciousness and His power : if the Holy Ghost has given you that, none can confound you, but if you have it not you lack the one thing needful. God grant you may not lack it long !

III. The third clause of our hexapla is, " SEEN OF ANGELS." This is an important point, for angels had waited to see the Lord, patiently gazing on the mercy-seat. There had been rumours in heaven of this mystery of the manifold wisdom of God, but they had not understood it ; and it is now in Christ that the mystery of incarnate God has been revealed to them. If I may so say, the brightness of the Godhead had confounded even the angels ; they were not able to see God, but when God came and manifested Himself in the flesh, then God was seen of angels. The Godhead was seen in Christ by angels as they had never seen it before. They had beheld the attribute of justice, they had seen the attribute of power, they had marked the attribute of wisdom, and seen the prerogative of sovereignty ; but never had angels seen love, and condescension, and tenderness, and pity, in God as they saw these things resplendent in the person and the life of Christ. They were astounded to think that God was such a One. They knew Him to be thrice holy, for they had chanted " Holy, holy, holy," in their perpetual sanctus ; but they did not know Him to be love— essential love—as they knew it when they saw that " He spared not His own Son, but delivered Him up for us all." The angels, seeing God thus manifest in flesh, ministered to Him ; they watched around the manger ; they were messengers to His foster-parent to warn Him of intended evil to the child ; and they waited on the Redeemer in the desert of His temptation. One of their number strengthened Him in the garden, another rolled away the stone from His grave, while others sat at the head and foot of the sepulchre where Jesus had lain. I doubt not it is true as we sang just now :—

> " They brought His chariot from above,
> To bear Him to His throne ;
> Clapped their triumphant wings and cried,
> ' The glorious work is done.' "

Jesus was all along seen of angels, and this is one reason why they sing so sweetly of Him—why they tune their notes so heartily to the song, " Worthy is the Lamb that was slain " ; for they saw Him live, and die, saw Him labour and suffer ; and therefore is their song so vivid and so full of adoration. " Thou wast slain," say they, though they cannot add, " and hast redeemed us unto God by Thy blood." Now the joy of this truth lies here ; it brings the angel host so near to us, for they saw Jesus and waited on Him, and we see Him, and therefore our eyes and the angels' eyes meet upon the person of Christ. We have one common love, one common Lord ; and now the ministering spirits that waited upon Him are ready to wait upon us. They love the members for the sake of the Head. Beloved, we rejoice this day to know that Christ is head of angels and principalities and powers, as well as head of His church ; and so in Him broken unity is restored, and the household of God is one in Him. Angelic eyes beheld and loved ; they love on still, and wonder yet. Fair spirits, charmed with the beauty of our Bridegroom, ye rejoice with us, and make it your delight to swell His train !

One question, and we leave the point. Have you ever seen Jesus ? He was seen of angels. Has your eye seen Him—your inner, spiritual eye ? If not, the Lord help you this morning to look unto Him and be saved ! It is nothing that He was seen of angels, unless He be seen of me also, even as of one born out of due time. O ! to see Him as my Saviour, my all, and rest in Him ! This is the main business. May God grant us that gladness !

IV. Briefly, the fourth part of the great mystery does not look, at first sight, to be at all mysterious. There is much of mystery in the facts that God was " manifest in the flesh, justified in the Spirit, and seen of angels " ; but the next appears very commonplace—" PREACHED UNTO THE GENTILES." Yet it is not without a marvel : those who reflect will see a great mystery of grace in it. Until Christ came, nothing was " preached to the Gentiles." They were accounted dogs, and few were the crumbs that fell to them from the master's table ; but after our Lord had ascended on high He was proclaimed to the Gentiles. To a Jew especially this would seem a very strange thing. The Jew thought that if the Gentile perished, it was but a matter of course ; but for the Gentiles to be visited with the gospel was strange indeed. That God should work effectually in Peter to the apostleship of the circumcision was to them readily a matter of faith, but that the same should be equally mighty in Paul towards the Gentiles was incredible yet true. Well, blessed be God, you and I are partakers in this mystery, for we have heard and believed the love which God hath toward us. We are Gentiles also, but unto us has the gospel been preached as well as unto the ancient people ; yea, and we have been more highly favoured than they, for at this day, more are the children of the desolate than the children of the married wife. God hath multiplied the seed of Abraham after the Spirit among the Gentiles, whereas the seed of Abraham after the flesh have, in these times, rejected the Saviour. Rejoice then, in the mystery, that Christ is *preached* among the Gentiles. Mark you, *preached!* For He is to be set forth in that manner. The church is ever to maintain this great, uncontroverted mystery, that the setting forth of Christ to the Gentiles is to be by preaching, and not by any other means of man's devising. Suppose I could take my pencil now, and draw the Saviour, with such matchless skill, that a Raphael or a Titian could not rival me : God has never ordained that so Christ should be set forth to the Gentiles. Or, suppose I should perform the ceremony of the mass with all the exactness, and with all the gorgeousness which the church of Rome would require ; such a setting forth of Christ among the Gentiles would not be according to the divine mystery. Christ is to be *preached* among the Gentiles : the appointed way of manifesting the incarnate God to the sons of men is by preaching— the church must always maintain this. The strongest castle of the walls of Zion for offence and defence must ever be the pulpit. God is pleased by the foolishness of preaching to save them that believe. I hate to see, as I do sometimes, in certain modern buildings, the pulpit stuck in the corner, and the altar in the most conspicuous place. The altar of sacrifice, indeed, the place of defilement and remembrance of sin, how comes that to be in the holy place at all ? God has never ordained it to be there. Where in Holy Scripture have we mention of a material altar in the assemblies of believers ? Our only altar is spiritual altar of our Lord's person, whereof they have no right to eat that serve the tabernacle of outward forms of rites and ceremonies. Altars belong to Jews and heathens, and even they never bow before them ; none but your Popish idolaters have fallen so low as that. The most prominent agency in the church of God is the preaching of Christ—this is the trumpet of heaven and the battering-ram of hell ! By this door salvation comes, for faith cometh by hearing, and hearing by the word of God, and how shall they hear without a preacher ? God's way of creating faith in men's hearts is not by pictures, music, or symbols, but by the hearing of the word of God. This may seem a strange thing, and strange let it seem, for it is a mystery, and a great mystery, but a fact beyond all controversy ; for ever let the church maintain that Christ is to be preached unto the Gentiles. A part of the greatness of the mystery lies in the persons who preached the gospel. It was a strange thing that Jesus should be preached unto the Gentiles by unlearned and ignorant men. One of the apostles, it is true, was of another class, but he declares that he never preached with excellency of speech, but in all simplicity he laid bare the mystery of God in plain language. It was wonderful that Christ should be preached unto the Gentiles so rapidly. It was but the other day the hundred and twenty were in the upper room, and within a few years there was no part of the civilized globe which had not heard the name of Jesus ; they had penetrated Scythis, they had subdued the barbarians, their only weapon being the cross ; they had triumphed at Athens, in the stronghold of classic learning ; they had passed into Rome, and set up the cross amidst the luxurious vices of the capital. No place was

untrodden by the Christian missionary, and no place was unaffected by the power of the gospel which he preached. This is a great mystery : the Lord repeat the mystery again and again ! O that preaching might once again be recognized to be God's power unto salvation, and used everywhere—in the church, in the lecture hall, in the street—in foreign lands and at home ; for the voice of truth in the preaching of Jesus is the great power of God.

One question here, and we leave it—Have you reverently heard the. gospel ? for there goes with the declaration that God saves through preaching, the warning, " Take heed how ye hear," for if God waits to bless by hearing, woe unto the men who hear inattentively and disrespectfully, woe unto the hearers only who are not doers of the word ! A responsibility goes with hearing, and God grant that you may be obedient hearers, so that we who preach may give a good account of you at the last, that our ministry may not have been in vain, but may have been to you the voice of God to your salvation.

V. And now the fifth part of the mystery is a very remarkable one : like that which preceded, it does not appear to be mysterious on the surface, but it is so : " BELIEVED ON IN THE WORLD." This is the most glorious of all the six points, this wonderful fact that Jesus is " believed on in the world." Why, when the humble preachers went out first to tell of Jesus, their story was so strange you could not imagine that any would believe it. And then the doctrines that they taught were so contrary to all the prejudices of flesh and blood, so humbling to human pride, so insulting to all our self-esteem, that it was not probable that men would accept them. And the world, too, what a world it was ! It was steeped up to its throat in cruelty, in vice, in luxury, in sins infamous and unmentionable, and was it likely that a pure Saviour, with a perfect doctrine like His, would find followers ? But He did ; He was " believed on in the world." Why, I think the first preachers must have been ready to leap for joy when they found that men believed them. If I had been Peter, I should scarce have slept for joy for many a night if I had found three thousand willing to believe my testimony, and willing to be baptized into Christ ! And Paul—oh, methinks, with all his sorrows, he must have been a very happy man—must have been struck with wonder to see that though he went into idolatrous lands to tell this new, and strange, and incredible story, yet in every place there were found men or women who received it joyfully.

Mark well that the church is bound to maintain this mystery, that it is by believing in Christ that the efficacy of His sacrifice comes to men. The mystery is not that Christ is served in the world, that is not put here ; not that Christ is worshipped in the world, that is not the first point—those things will be sure to follow : but the vital mystery is that Christ is " believed on in the world," that is to say, trusted as the Saviour. Men leave all other trusts, and trust in Him ; they give up their self-righteousness, they leave their vaunted sacraments, they forsake all ways and modes of self-salvation, and come and trust in Christ—this is the great mystery. " Well," says one, " I do not see that there is a mystery in it." Have you ever believed in Jesus yourself, beloved friend ? If you have, you will say " this is the finger of God." Belief in Jesus is as great a work of divine power as the making of this globe. One of the visitors to this place lately said, " I am willing to be a believer, if the preacher can persuade me." Very likely, but no preacher can create true faith—it needs a mightier power than the preacher's, even the power of the Holy Ghost. God gives to His elect the blessing of faith, and others wilfully remain in unbelief. Faith, simple as it is, is supernatural, divine, and not to be attained by human aid, nor human eloquence ; they who have it know that it is a blessed mystery, this believing on Jesus Christ in the world.

Have you this faith ? Do you believe in Jesus ? Everything else in my text leads up to this. If He be manifest in the flesh what is that unless I believe in Him ? What if He be justified in the Spirit. What is that unless faith in Him justified me ? What if He be seen of angels, how does that help me unless I see Him too ? And even if He be preached among the Gentiles, that does but involve greater guilt upon my soul if, after hearing, I have not believed in Him ? O dear hearers, I may not long speak to you, and every time that I am kept away from addressing you I feel a deep anxiety that by some means my preaching may be made effectual to your salvation. Many of you have believed in my Lord—this is my comfort ; but, on the other hand, how many there are who still hear, and hear, and hear, and that is all. How long halt ye ? How long cause ye us to labour for nought ? No one is so worth trusting as the Saviour is, and nothing is so true as that He came to save sinners.

VI. The last point of the church's witness is that Jesus was " RECEIVED UP INTO GLORY." Only this word about it : He was so received because His work is finished. He would never have gone into His glory if He had not finished all His toil. He would have accepted no reward had He not fully earned it. My soul, believe thou that Christ is received up into glory ; that will let thee know that thou art resting in a finished work, an atonement which has put away all sin, a satisfaction which has made all believers accepted in the Beloved. He has gone into glory, thus He is personally rewarded ; and moreover, He has thus representatively taken possession of all that He has purchased. Is Christ in glory ? then the believer is in glory, not literally but in His covenant Head. What Christ takes possession of He claims in our name : " I go to prepare a place for you." O ye who sorrow over the present, rejoice also ; for even now at this moment heaven is yours,—your Jesus has taken possession in your name.

And oh, it is joyous to know that our great Lord is eternally exalted ! If He were not exalted what comfort could we have ? He is received up into glory ! Men say He is not God—they cannot hurt Him, for He is received up into glory ! They revile His gospel they cannot dim the lustre of His crown, He is received up into glory ! They would fain slay His people if they could, but *He* is received up into glory ! They struggle and they strive against His cause, and would fain overthrow it ; but O, what matters it, He is everlastingly exalted, and He will shortly come —that same Jesus who was received into glory shall so come, in like manner as He was seen to go up into heaven. Here are great wells of comfort. He has to His glory gone, and has taken to Himself His great power ; but every hour is bringing nearer the time when He shall lay bare His sword in the midst of His foes, and shall unveil His face in the midst of His friends. Let us rejoice in Him this day, and go our way to bear, with all the church of the living God, the six-fold testimony of our text concerning our precious Saviour. Amen.

THE PROFIT OF GODLINESS IN THE LIFE TO COME

" Godliness is profitable unto all things, having promise of the life that now is, and of that which is to come."— 1 Timothy iv. 8.

WE endeavoured, this morning, to prove the profitableness of godliness as to the life which now is, and to discriminate as to what the promise of this life really is. We tried to prove that " the promise " of the life that now is, its real and highest beauty and excellence, consists in peace of mind, peace with God, contentment, and happiness of spirit ; and while we pointed out that godliness did not ensure wealth, or health, or even a good name—for all these even to godly men might not be granted—yet we showed that the great end of our being, that for which we live and were created, that which will best make it worth while to have existed, shall certainly be ours if we are godly. We did not think it an unimportant matter to expound the bearing of true religion upon this present state, but I trust we did not exaggerate that view so as to keep those in countenance who dream that this world is the main consideration, and that the wisest man is he who makes it the be-all and the end-all of his existence.

Beloved friends, there is another life beyond this fleeting existence. This fact was dimly guessed by heathens. Strange as their mythology might be, and singular as were their speculations as to the regions of bliss and woe, even barbarous nations have had some glimmering light concerning a region beyond the river of death. Hardly yet have we been able to discover a people with no idea of an after-state. Man has scarcely ever been befooled into the belief that death is the finis of the volume of his existence. Few indeed have been so lost to natural light as to have forgotten that man is something more than the dog which follows at his heel. That which was dimly guessed by the heathen was more fully wrought out by the bolder and clearer minds among philosophers. They saw something about man that made him more than either ox or horse. They marked the moral government of God in the world, and as they saw the wicked prosper, and the righteous afflicted, they said, " There must be another state in which the GREAT AND JUST ONE will rectify all these wrongs—reward the righteous, and condemn the wicked." They thought it proved that there would be another life ; they could not, however, speak with confidence ; for reason, however right her inferences, does not content the heart, or give " the substance of things hoped for, the evidence of things unseen." That is reserved for faith. The best light of heathens was but twilight, yet was

THE TREASURY OF THE NEW TESTAMENT

there so much light in their obscurity that they looked beyond the stream of death, and thought they saw shades as of creatures that had once been here, and could not die. What was thus surmised and suspected by the great thinkers of antiquity, has been brought to light in the gospel of Jesus Christ. He has declared to us that we shall live again, that there will be a judgment and a resurrection both of the righteous and of the wicked, and that there will be awarded to the righteous a reward that shall know no end, while the wicked shall be driven into a banishment to which there shall be no close. We are not left now to speculate nor to rely upon unaided reason. We have been told upon the authority of God, sometimes by the lips of prophets, at other times by the lips of His own dear Son, or by His inspired apostles, that there is a world to come, a world of terrors to the ungodly, but a world of promised blessing to the righteous. My dear hearer, if it be so, what will the world to come be to you? Will you inherit its *promise?* You may easily answer that question by another— Have you godliness? If you have, you have the promise of the life that is to come. Are you ungodly? Do you live without God? Are you without faith in God, without love to God, without reverence to God? Are you without the pardon whch God presents to believers in Christ Jesus? Then are you without hope, and the world to come has nothing for you but a fearful looking for of judgment and of fiery indignation which will devour you.

I. GODLINESS CONCERNING THE LIFE TO COME POSSESSES A PROMISE UNIQUE AND UNRIVALLED.

I say a unique promise, for, observe, *infidelity makes no promise of a life to come.* It is the express business of infidelity to deny that there is such a life, and to blot out all the comfort which can be promised concerning it. Man is like a prisoner shut up in his cell, a cell all dark and cheerless save that there is a window through which he can gaze upon a glorious landscape. Infidelity comes like a demon into the cell, and with desperate hand blocks up the window, that man may sit for ever in the dark, or at best may have the boasted light of a farthing rushlight called free-thinking. All that infidelity can tell him is that he will die like a dog. Fine prospect for a man who feels eternity pulsing within his spirit! I know I shall not die like the beast that perisheth; and let who will propound the theory, my soul sickens and turns with disgust from it, nor would it be possible by the most specious arguments so to pervert the instincts of my nature as to convince me that I shall thus die, and that my soul, like the flame of an out-burnt candle, shall be quenched in utter annihilation. My inmost heart revolts at this degrading slander; she feels an innate nobility that will not allow her to be numbered with the beasts of the field, to die as they must do, without a hope. Oh, miserable prospect! How can men be so earnest in proclaiming their own wretchedness? Enthusiasts for annihilation! Why not fanatics for hell itself? Godliness hath promise of the life that is to come, but infidelity can do nothing better than deny the ennobling revelation of the great Father, and bid us be content with the dark prospect of being exterminated and put out of being. Aspiring, thoughtful, rational men, can ye be content with the howling wildernesses and dreary voids of infidelity? Leave them, I pray you, for the goodly land of the gospel which floweth with milk and honey; abandon extinction for immortality, renounce perishing for paradise.

Again; let me remark that this hope is unique because *Popery in any of its forms cannot promise us the life which is to come.* I know that it speaks as positively as Christianity does about the fact that there will be another life, but it gives us no promise of it, for what is the expectation of the Romanist, even of the best Romanist? Have I not aforetime remarked to you that we have heard—and therefore it is no slander for us to say it—of masses being said for the repose of the souls of the most eminent Romanists? Cardinals distinguished for their learning, confessors and priests distinguished for their zeal, and even Popes reputed to be remarkable for holiness and even infallibility, have when they died gone somewhere, I know not where, but somewhere where they have needed that the faithful should pray for the repose of their souls. That is a very poor look-out for ordinary people like ourselves; for if these superlatively good people are still uneasy in their souls after they die, and have in fact, according to their own statements, gone to purgatorial fires or to purgatorial chills, to be tossed, as certain of their prophets have informed us, from icebergs into furnaces, and then back again, until by some means, mechanical, spiritual, or otherwise, sin shall be burnt out, or evaporated from them; if that be their expectation, I think I should be inclined, as the Irishman said, to become a Protestant heretic, and go to heaven at once, if there be so sorry a prospect for the Catholic. Godliness hath the promise of the life which is to come, but it is altogether unique in possessing such a promise. No voice from the Vatican sounds one-half so sweetly as that from Patmos, which we unfeignedly accept: " I heard a voice from heaven saying unto me, Write, Blessed are the dead which die in the Lord from henceforth: Yea, saith the Spirit, that they may rest from their labours ; and their works do follow them." Our sorrow for the departed is not embittered by the absence of hope, for we believe that " them also which sleep in Jesus will God bring with Him." Neither superstition on the one hand, nor unbelief on the other, so much as dares to offer a promise as to the life to come.

No system based upon human merit ever gives its votaries a promise of the life to come, which they can really grasp and be assured of. No self-righteous man will venture to speak of the assurance of faith ; in fact, he denounces it as presumption. He feels that his own basis is insecure, and therefore he suspects the confidence of others to be as hollow as his own. He lives between hope and fear, a joyless, unsatisfied life : while the believer in Jesus, knowing that there is no condemnation to him, awaits the hour of his entrance into heaven with joyful expectancy. What is never promised to man's fancied righteousness is secured to all who possess the righteousness of Christ Jesus. " Come, ye blessed," is their assured welcome ; to be with Jesus, their entailed portion.

Godliness hath a monopoly of heavenly promise as to the blessed future. There is nothing else beneath high heaven to which any such promise has ever been given by God, or of which any such promise can be supposed. Look at *vice,* for instance, with its pretended pleasures—what does it offer you ? It offers pleasure in the life that now is ; but as it speaks, you detect the lie upon its face, for even in the life that now is vice gives but a hasty intoxication, to be followed by woe and redness of the eyes. 'Tis true it satiates with sweets, but in all its tables there is vomit; satiety follows its gluttony, dissatisfaction comes with discontent, loathing, remorse, and misery, like hounds at its heels. Vice dares not say, it never has had the effrontery yet to say, " Do evil and live in sin, and eternal life will come out of it." No, the theatre at its door does not proffer you eternal life, it invites you to the pit. The house of evil communications, the drunkard's settle, the gathering-place of scorners, the chamber of the strange woman—none of these has yet dared to advertise a promise of eternal life as among the boons that may tempt its votaries. At best sin gives you but bubbles, and feeds you upon air. The pleasure vanishes, and the misery is left. Even this side the tomb the hollowness of sinful mirth is clear to all but the most superficial, and he said truly who sang concerning merry worldlings—

" They grin ; but wherefore ? And how long the laugh ?
Half ignorance, their mirth ; and half a lie ;
To cheat the world, and cheat themselves, they smile.
Hard either task ? The most abandoned own
That others, if abandoned, are undone :
Then, for themselves, the moment reason wakes,
Oh, how laborious is their gaiety !
They scarce can swallow their ebullient spleen,
Scarce muster patience to support the farce,
And pump sad laughter till the curtain falls.
Scarce did I say ? Some cannot sit it out ;
Oft their own daring hand the curtain draws,
And show us what their joy by their despair."

If such the failure of the mirth of fools this side eternity, of what little benefit can it prove hereafter ?

So with other things not sinful in themselves— there is no promise of the life that is to come appended to them. For instance, *birth*. What would not some men give if they could but somehow trace their pedigree up to a distinguished Crusader, or up to a Norman knight reported of in the battle-roll of Hastings ? yet, nowhere in the world is there a promise of eternal life to blood and birth. " For when he dieth he shall carry nothing away : his glory shall not descend after him. Though while he lived he blessed his soul : and men will praise thee, when thou doest well to thyself. He shall go to the generation of his fathers ; they shall never see light." Genealogies and pedigrees are poor things ; trace us all up far enough, and we are all descended from that naked sinner who tried to cover his shame with fig-leaves, and owed his first true garment to the charity of offended heaven. Let the pedigree run through the loins of kings, yea, and of mighty kings, and let every one of our forefathers have been distinguished for his valour, yet no man shall pretend because of this that eternal life will be secured thereby. Ah ! no ; the king rots like a slave and the hero is devoured by the worm as though he had been but a swineherd all his days ; yea, and the flame unquenchable kindles on earl, and duke, and millionaire, as well as on serf and peasant.

And it is equally certain that no promise of the life that is to come is given to *wealth*. Men hoard it, and gather it, and keep it, and seal it down by bonds and settlements, as if they thought they could carry something with them ; but when they have gained their utmost, they do not find that wealth has the promise even of this life, for it yields small contentment to the man who possesses it. " Their inward thought is, that their houses shall continue for ever, and their dwelling places to all generations ; they call their lands after their own names. Nevertheless man being in honour abideth not." As for the life to come, is there any supposable connection between the millions of the miser's wealth and the glory that is to be revealed hereafter ? Nay, but by so much the more as the man lives for this world, by so much the more shall he be accursed. He said, " I will pull down my barns, and build greater " ; but God calls him a fool, and a fool he is, for when his soul is required of him, whose shall these things be which he had prepared ? Nay, ye may grasp the Indies if ye will ; ye may seek to compass within your estates all the lands that ye can see far and wide, but ye shall be none the nearer to heaven when ye have reached the climax of your avarice. There is no promise of the life that is to come in the pursuits of usury and covetousness.

Nor is there any such promise to *personal accomplishments and beauty*. How many live for that poor bodily form of theirs which so soon must moulder back to the dust ! To dress, to adorn themselves, to catch the glance of the admirer's eye, to satisfy public tastes, to follow fashion ! Surely an object in life more frivolous never engrossed an immortal soul. It seems as strange as if an angel should be gathering daisies or blowing soap-bubbles. An immortal spirit living to dress the body ! To paint, to dye, to display a ribbon, to dispose a pin, is this the pursuit of an immortal ? Yet tens of thousands live for little else. But ah ! there is no promise of the life to come appended to the noblest beauty that ever fascinated the eye. Far deeper than the skin is the beauty which is admired in heaven. As for earth's comeliness, how do time, and death, and the worm together, make havoc of it ! Take up yonder skull, just upturned by the sexton's careless spade, " and get you to my lady's chamber and tell her, though she paint an inch thick, to this complexion she must come at last," all her dressing shall end in a shroud, and all her washings and her dainty ornaments shall only make her but the sweeter morsel for the worm. There is no promise of the life to come to these frivolities ; wherefore then waste ye your time and degrade your souls with them ?

Nor even to *higher accomplishments than these* is there given any promise of the life to come. For instance, the attainment of learning, or the possession of that which often stands men in as good stead as learning, namely, cleverness, brings therewith no promise of future bliss. If a man be clever, if he can write interesting stories, if he can sketch the current fashions, if he can produce poetry that will survive among his fellow men—it matters not though his pen never wrote a line for Christ, and though he never uttered a sentence that might have led a sinner to the cross, though his work had no aim beyond this life, and paid no homage to the God of the gospel, yet even professed Christians will fall at the man's feet, and when he dies will canonize him as a saint, and almost worship him as a demi-god. I reckon that the meanest Christian that loved his God, though he could only speak stammeringly the profession of his faith, is nobler far than he who possessed the genius of a Byron or the greatness of a Shakespeare, and yet only used his ten talents for himself and for his fellow men, but never consecrated them to the great Master to whom the interest of them altogether belonged. No ; there is no promise of the life that is to come to the philosopher, or to the statesman, or to the poet, or to the literary man, as such. They have no preference before the Lord; not gifts but grace must save them. Humbly, penitently, and believingly they must find the promise of eternal life in godliness; and if they have not godliness, they shall find it nowhere. Godliness hath that promise, I say, and none besides. I saw in Italy standing at the corner of a road, as you may frequently see in Italy, a large cross, and on it were these words, which I had not often seen on a cross before: "Spes unica"—the only hope, the one unique hope, the one only hope of mankind. So would I tell you that on Christ's cross there is written this day, "Spes unica"—the one hope of men. "Godliness hath the promise of the life that now is, and of that which is to come," but to nothing else anywhere, search for it high or low, on earth or sea, to nothing else is the promise given save to godliness alone.

II. I pass on to notice, in the second place, that THE PROMISE GIVEN TO GODLINESS IS AS COMPREHENSIVE AS IT IS UNIQUE.

I have not time on this occasion to go into all the promises of the life that is to come which belong to godliness: who shall give an inventory where the treasure is boundless, or map out a land which has no limit? It will suffice if I give you the heads of this great theme. That promise is something of this kind. The godly man, unless Christ shall come, will die as others die, as to the matter of outward fact, but his death will be very different in its essence and meaning. He will pass gently out of this world into the world to come, and then he will begin to realise the promise which godliness gave him; for he will enter then, nay, he has entered now, upon an eternal life far other than that which belongs to other men. The Christian's life shall never be destroyed: "Because I live, ye shall live also," says Christ. There is no fear of the Christian's ever growing aged in heaven, or of his powers failing him. Eternal youth shall be to those who wear the unfading crown of life. Yon sun shall become black as a coal; yon moon shall fail until her pale beams shall never more be seen; the stars shall fall like withered figs; even this earth which we call stable, terming it terra firma, shall with yonder heavens be rolled up like a vestment that is worn out, and shall be laid aside among the things that were, but are not. Everything which can be seen is but a fruit with a worm at the core, a flower foredoomed to fade. But the believer shall live for ever, his life shall be coeval with the years of the Most High. God liveth ever, ever, ever, and so shall every godly soul. Christ having given him eternal life, he is one with Jesus, and as Jesus lives for ever, even so shall he.

In the moment of death the Christian will begin to enjoy this eternal life in the form of wonderful felicity in the company of Christ, in the presence of God, in the society of disembodied spirits and holy angels. I say in a moment, for from the case of the dying thief we learn that there is no halt upon the road from earth to heaven.

> "One gentle sigh the fetter breaks:
>   We scarce can say, 'He's gone!'
> Before the willing spirit takes
>   Its mansion near the throne."

How does Paul put it? "Absent from the body"; but you have hardly said that word, when he adds,

"present with the Lord." The eyes are closed on earth and opened again in heaven. They loose their anchor, and immediately they come to the desired haven. How long that state of disembodied happiness shall last it is not for us to know, but by-and-by, when the fulness of time shall come, the Lord Jesus shall consummate all things by the resurrection of these bodies. The trumpet shall sound, and as Jesus Christ's body rose from the dead as the first-fruits, so shall we arise, every man in his own order. Raised up by divine power, our very bodies shall be reunited with our souls to live with Christ, raised however, not as they shall be put into the grave to slumber, but in a nobler image. They were sown like the shrivelled seed, they shall come up like the fair flowers which decorate your summer gardens. Planted as a dull unattractive bulb, to develop into a glory like that of a lovely lily with snowy cup and petals of gold. Sown like the shrivelled barley or wheat, to come up as a fair green blade, or to become the golden ear. "It doth not yet appear what we shall be, but when He shall appear we shall be like Him, for we shall see Him as He is." Come, my soul, what a promise is given thee in God's word of the life that is to come! A promise for my soul, did I say? A promise for my body too. These aches and pains shall be repaid; this weariness and these sicknesses shall all be recompensed. The body shall be re-married to the soul, from which it parted with so much grief, and the marriage shall be the more joyous because there never shall be another divorce. Then, in body and in soul made perfect, the fulness of our bliss shall have arrived.

But will there not be a judgment? Yes, a judgment certainly; and if not in set ceremonial a judgment for the righteous, as some think, yet in spirit certainly. We shall gather at the great white throne, gather with the goats or gather with the sheep. But there is this promise to you who are godly, that you shall have nothing to fear in that day of judgment: you shall go to it with the blood-bought pardon in your bosom, to be shown before the judgment-seat. You shall go to that judgment to have it proclaimed to men, to angels, and to devils, that "there is now no condemnation to them that are in Christ Jesus," none being able to lay anything to the charge of those for whom Jesus Christ has died, and whom the Father justifieth. You need not fear the judgment, you need not fear the conflagration of the world, or whatever else of terror shall be attendant upon the coming of Christ as a thief in the night. You have the promise of the life that now is, and of that which is to come. Listen to me. You have the promise that you shall enjoy for ever the high dignity of being priests and kings unto God. You sons of toil, you daughters of poverty, you shall be peers in heaven, you shall be courtiers of the Prince Imperial, yourselves being princes of the blood-royal. Your heads shall wear crowns, your hands shall wave palms of triumph. And as you shall have glorious rank, so shall you have companions suitable to your condition. The worldling's haunt, the synagogue of Satan, shall be far away from you. No more shall you sojourn in Mesech and dwell in the tents of Kedar. No idle talk shall vex you, no blasphemies shall inflict themselves upon your ear. You shall hear the songs of angels; and as they charm you, you shall also charm them by making known unto them the manifold wisdom of God. The holiest and best of men, redeemed by Jesus' precious blood, shall commune with you, and, best of all—

> " He that on the throne doth reign
>   You for evermore shall feed ;
> With the tree of life sustain,
>   To the living fountain lead."

You shall have unbroken fellowship with God and with His Christ. What ravishing joy this will be we shall better be able to experience than to imagine. Communion with Jesus here below uplifts us far above the world, but what its delights are in the unclouded skies of face-to-face fellowship, hath not yet entered into the heart of man.

Hearken yet more, beloved. You shall have suitable occupation. I know not what you may have to do in heaven, but I do know it is written, " They shall see His face, and His name shall be in their foreheads, and His servants shall serve Him." They serve Him day and night in His temple. You would not be happy without occupation. Minds made like yours could not find rest except upon the wing ; delightful and honourable employment shall be allotted you, suitable to your perfected capabilities. But, mark you, you shall have rest as well as service. No wave of trouble shall roll over your peaceful bosoms. You shall for ever bathe your souls in seas of blissful rest—no care, no fear, no unsatisfied desire ; for all desires shall be consummated, all expectations be fulfilled. God shall be your portion, the infinite Spirit your friend, and the ever-blessed Christ your elder brother. Into the joy of heaven, which knoweth no bounds, shall you enter, according to his words, " Enter thou into the joy of thy Lord." And all this, and infinitely more than my tongue can tell you, shall be yours for ever and for ever, without fear of ever losing it, or dread of dying in the midst of it. " Eye hath not seen, nor ear heard, neither hath entered into the heart of man, the things that God hath prepared for them that love Him, but He hath revealed them unto us by His Spirit." All the kingdom which the Father has prepared, and the place which the Son has prepared, are yours, O believer, by the promise of the Lord ; for " whom He justified, them He also glorified." The promise goes with godliness, and if you have godliness there is nothing in heaven of joy, there is nothing there of honour, there is nothing there of rest and peace, which is not yours ; for godliness hath the promise of it, and God's promise never faileth.

> " Lo ! I see the fair immortals,
>   Enter to the blissful seats ;
> Glory opes her waiting portals,
>   And the Saviour's train admits.

> All the chosen of the Father,
>   All for whom the Lamb was slain,
> All the church appear together,
>   Wash'd from every sinful stain.

> His dear smile the place enlightens
>   More than thousand suns could do ;
> All around, His presence brightens,
>   Changeless, yet for ever new.

> Blessed state ! beyond conception !
>   Who its vast delights can tell ?
> May it be my blissful portion,
>   With my Saviour there to dwell."

Perhaps within the next ten minutes we may be there ! Who knows ? I had half said, " God grant it to me ! " No doubt, many anxious spirits would be glad to end so soon life's weary journey, and rest in the Father's home.

III. Now, very briefly, consider another point. I have shown you that the promise appended to godliness is unique and comprehensive, and now observe that IT IS SURE.

" Godliness hath promise " ; that is to say, it hath God's promise. Now, God's promise is firmer than the hills. He is God, and cannot lie. He will never retract the promise, nor will He leave it unfulfilled. He was too wise to give a rash promise : He is too powerful to be unable to fulfil it. " Hath He said, and shall He not do it ? " Already tens of thousands to whom the promise was made have obtained a measure of this bliss in the glorification of their perfect spirits. We are on the road to the same happy state. Some of us are on the river's brink. Perhaps the Lord may come suddenly, and we shall be changed, and so perfected without dying. Be that as the Lord wills, it is not a question which disturbs us. Our faith is strong and firm. We are sure that we, too, shall enter into the rest which remaineth, and with all the blood-washed multitude shall in wonder and surprise adore the God before whose throne we shall cast our crowns.

IV. But I shall not tarry upon that, for there comes a fourth thought. This promise is A PRESENT PROMISE.

You should notice the participle, " having promise." It does not say that godliness after awhile will get the promise, but godliness has promise now at this very moment. My dear hearer, if you are godly, that is, if you have submitted to God's way of salvation, if you trust God, love God, serve God, if you are, in fact, a converted man, you have now the promise of the life that is to come. When we get a man's promise in whom we trust, we feel quite easy about the matter under concern. A note of hand from many a firm in the city of London would pass current for gold any day in the week ; and surely when God gives the promise, it is safe and right for us to accept it as if it were the fulfilment itself, for it is quite as sure. We have the promise, let us begin to sing about it ; what is more, we have a part of the fulfilment of it, for " I give unto My sheep eternal life," says Christ : shall we not sing concerning that ? Believe in Jesus, you have eternal life now. There will be no new life given to you after death. You have even now, O Christian, the germ within thee which will develop into the glory-life above. Grace is glory in the bud. You have the earnest of the Spirit ; you have already a portion of the promise which is given to godliness. Now, what you should do is to live now in the enjoyment of the promise. You cannot enjoy heaven, for you are not there, but you can enjoy the promise of it. Many a dear child, if it has a promise of a treat in a week's time, will go skipping among its little companions as merry as a lark about it. It has not the treat yet, but it expects it ; and I have known in our Sunday-schools our little boys and girls months before the time came for them to go into the country, as happy as the days were long, in prospect of that little pleasure. Surely you and I ought to be childlike enough to begin to rejoice in the heaven that is so soon to be ours. I know to-morrow some of you will be working very hard, but you may sing :—

" This is not my place of resting,
  Mine's a city yet to come ;
  Onward to it I am hasting—
  On to my eternal home."

Perhaps you will have to fight the world's battles, and you will find them very stern. Oh! but you can sing even now of the palm-branch, and of the victory that awaits you ; and as your faith looks at the crown that Christ has prepared for it, you will be much rested even in the heat of the battle. When a traveller who has been long an exile returns home, it may be after walking many miles, he at last gets to the brow of the hill, where he can see the church of the little town, and get a bird's-eye view of the parish. He gazes awhile, and as he looks again and again, says to himself, " Yes, that is the High Street there, and yonder is the turning by the old inn, and there—yes, there I can see the gable of the dear old house at home." Though his feet may be blistered, the way may have been long, and the sweat may be pouring from his face, yet he plucks up courage at the sight of home. The last mile down hill is soon got over, for he has seen his long-loved home. Christians, ye may see it, ye may see the goodly land from Nebo even now :—

" How near
At times to faith's far-seeing eye,
The golden gates appear ! "

When the crusaders first came in sight of Jerusalem, though they had a hard battle before them ere they could win it, yet they fell down in ecstacy at the sight of the holy city. And do not you and I say—soldiers of the cross, my fellow crusaders in the holy war of righteousness, will you not in prospect of the coming glory sing :—

" O my sweet home, Jerusalem,
    Would God I were in Thee !
Would God my woes were at an end,
    Thy joys that I might see ! "

When the brave soldiers, of whom Xenophon tells us, came at last in sight of the sea, from which they had been so long separated, they cried out, " Thallassa! Thallassa ! "—" The sea ! the sea ! " and we, though death appears between us and the better land, can yet look beyond it and see the

" Sweet fields beyond the swelling flood
    Arrayed in living green,"

and bless God that a sight of what is to be revealed renders the burdens of the way light as we march towards glory. Oh! live, live in the foretaste of heaven. Let worldlings see that

" The thought of such amazing bliss
    Doth constant joys create."

V. Last of all. This promise which appended to godliness is A VERY NEEDFUL ONE.

It is a very needful one, for ah! *if I have no promise of the life that is to come, where am I? where am I? and where shall I be? where shall I be?* I live, I know ; I die, I know I must ; and if it all be true as this old Book, my mother's Book, tells me, that there is a hereafter, if I have no godliness, then woe worth the day to me! Oh! how much I want the promise of the life to come, for if I have not that *I have a curse for the life to come.* I cannot die, God has made my soul immortal. Even God Himself will never annihilate me, for He has been pleased to create me an immortal spirit, and on I must live for

ever. There be some who say, and I think the doctrine full of unnumbered perils to the souls of men, that God made man naturally mortal, and the soul can become extinct ; and they go on to teach that sinners are made to live after death on purpose to be tormented for a longer or shorter time, and then at last are annihilated. What a God must He be to give them a life they need not have, on purpose that He might torment them! I know no such God. But HE, whom I adore, in His unbounded goodness, gave to mankind what was in itself a wondrous blessing—immortality ; and if you, my hearer, choose to turn it into a curse for ever, it is you that are to be blamed for it, and not God who gave you the immortality which, if you believe in the appointed Saviour, will be to you an eternity of bliss. You are now past all recall an immortal being, and if you die without hope in Christ there will remain only this for you, to go on sinning in another state as you have gone on sinning here, but to get no pleasure from it as you think you do sometimes here—on the contrary, to be tortured with remorse concerning it, and vexed with angry passions to think that you cannot have your will, passions that will make you struggle yet worse against your God, and make your misery consequently the greater. The worm that never dies will be your own furious hatred of God. The fire that never shall be quenched is probably the flames of your own insatiate lust after evil. I say not that there will not be bodily pains, but the natural results of sin are the deepest hell to the soul. Sin has made you unhappy now. It will ripen ; it will increase ; when everything that checks it shall be taken off, your true character will be developed, and with that development will come enlarging wretchedness. Separated from the company of the righteous, and placed among the wicked, you will go on to be worse and worse, and every step in the increase of sin necessitates an increase of misery. It is not true that God will punish you in mere caprice. He has ordained, and right enough was He to ordain it, that sin should punish itself, that sin should be its own misery, and its own anguish. Sin will be to you a never-ending death. O wherefore will ye die? Wherefore will ye die? Wherefore will ye by the love of sin bring upon yourselves an eternity of sin, an eternity of suffering? Turn ye unto Christ. I pray His Spirit to turn you. Come ye now, come ye now, and lay hold on eternal life!

I have been thinking while I have been preaching to you, this evening, of my own self awhile, and I shall turn my thoughts to myself and any others who are preachers or teachers, and who try to do good to others. Years ago Hamburgh was nearly half of it burned down, and among the incidents that happened, there was this one. A large house had connected with it a yard in which there was a great black dog, and this black dog in the middle of the night barked and howled most furiously. It was only by his barking that the family were awakened just in time to escape from the flames, and their lives were spared ; but the poor dog was chained to his kennel, and though he barked and thus saved the lives of others, he was burned himself. Oh! do not you who work for God in this church perish in that fashion. Do not permit your sins to enchain you, so that while you warn others you become lost yourselves. Do see that you have the godliness which has the promise of the life that is to come.

And now, you who really desire to find godliness, remember, it is to be had in Christ, and only in Christ. I was in Windermere some three weeks ago, on a hot, dusty day, and I saw a little gushing stream of water, and a chain with a ladle to it for the passer-by to drink. I wanted to drink, and I went to it, but the ladle was cracked quite through, was very rusty, and would not hold a drop of water, neither was the water, if it had been held in it, fit to drink. There are ways of salvation chosen by some that are equally as deceptive. They mock the traveller. But oh! my Lord and Master, Jesus Christ, is a river of mercy, deep and broad. You have but to stoop and drink, and you may drink as much as you will, and none shall say you nay. Have you not His word for it, "Let him that is athirst come. And whosoever will, let him take the water of life freely"?

God grant you may with your heart believe the gospel of Jesus, for Christ's sake.

THE PROFIT OF GODLINESS IN THIS LIFE

"Bodily exercise profiteth little : but godliness is profitable unto all things, having promise of the life that now is, and of that which is to come. This is a faithful saying and worthy of all acceptation."—1 Timothy iv. 8, 9.

YOUR attention will be the more readily given to this passage, because Paul declares it to be a "faithful"—a most true and certain saying, and "worthy of all acceptation," that is to say, worthy to be received and practised by us all. Paul has four of these faithful sayings. The first occurs in 1 Timothy i. 15, "This is a faithful saying and worthy of all acceptation, that Christ Jesus came into the world to save sinners." The second is our text. The third is in 2 Timothy ii. 12, "It is a faithful saying, if we suffer, we shall also reign with Him"; and the fourth is in Titus iii. 8, "This is a faithful saying, that they which have believed in God might be careful to maintain good works." We may trace a connection between these faithful sayings. The first one lays the foundation of our eternal salvation in the free grace of God, as shown to us in the mission of the great Redeemer. The next affirms the double blessedness which we obtain through this salvation—the blessings of the upper and nether springs—of time and of eternity. The third shows one of the duties to which the chosen people are called; we are ordained to suffer for Christ with the promise that "if we suffer, we shall also reign with Him." The last sets forth the active form of Christian service, bidding us diligently to maintain good works. Thus we have the root of salvation in free grace ; next, the privileges of that salvation in the life which now is, and in that which is to come ; and we have also the two great branches of suffering with Christ, and serving with Christ, loaded with the fruits of the Spirit. Let us treasure up these faithful sayings. Let them be the guides of our life, our comfort, and our instruction. The apostle of the Gentiles proves them to be faithful, they are faithful still, not one word shall fall to the ground ; they are worthy of all acceptation, let us accept them now, and prove their faithfulness. Let these four faithful sayings be written on the four corners of your house.

To-day we consider the second of the four, and we will read the text again, "Bodily exercise profiteth little : but godliness is profitable unto all things, having promise of the life that now is, and of that which is to come." In the days when Paul wrote this epistle, the Greeks and others paid great attention to physical culture, the development of the muscles, the proportion of the limbs, the production of everything in the body which might conduce to the soundness of manhood. The philosophy of Greece all looked that way, and hence at the various gymnasia bodily exercises of an athletic and even violent kind were undergone by men with the view of developing the body, and so assisting the soul. It may be that Timothy being yet a young man, fancied that there was something in this philosophy ; and something indeed there is, and in the original the apostle Paul admits that it is so, for the passage might be read thus : "Bodily exercise verily profiteth a little," or thus, "Bodily exercise profiteth for a short time." Physical training is of some service ; attention to it is not sinful not to be condemned ; it is of some use and has its proper place, but still it has no very eminent position in the Christian system, it occupies a place far in the background in the teaching of Christ and His apostles ; it is but a minor part of a complete education. It profiteth a little, a little for a little time ; but godliness, the worship of God, the fear of God, hath a long and wealthy entail of blessing, having the promise both of the life that now is and of that which is to come ; its profiting is not little but great ; its benefit is not confined to the body, but is shared by the body and the soul, it is not limited by this mortal life, but overleaps the grave and brings its largest revenue of profit in the world where graves are all unknown.

This morning I am about to try and speak upon the profit of godliness to a man in this life. We will consider its having the promise of the life to come, in the evening, if God spare us.

With regard to this life, let it be remarked that *the religion of our Lord Jesus Christ neither undervalues nor overvalues this present life.* It does not sneer at this life as though it were nothing ; on the contrary, it ennobles it, and shows the relation which it has to the higher and eternal life. It does not overvalue it by making this life, and the secular pursuits of it, the main object of any man ; it puts it into an honourable but yet a secondary place, and saith to the sons of men, "Seek ye first the kingdom of God, and His righteousness ; and all these things shall be added unto you." It is not, however, very easy to keep to the middle point of exact truth as to a due estimate of this present life : he who does so is taught of God. There are many who undervalue this life ; let me mention some of them to you. Those undervalue it who sacrifice it to indulge their *passions,* or to gratify their *appetites.* Too many for the sake of monetary gratifications, have shortened their lives, and rendered their latter end bitterly painful to themselves. They conceived that the pleasures of the flesh were better than life ; they were mistaken in their estimate ; they made but a poor exchange when they chose lust and death, rather than purity and life. The drunkard has been known to take his cups, though he knew that in so doing he was virtually poisoning himself. The man of hot passions has been seen to plunge into uncleanness, though the consequences of his folly have been plainly set before him. Men who for a morsel of meat, or a flash of merriment, are selling this world as well as the world to come, are fools indeed. He that would have pleasure must not pursue it too furiously. Temperance is the rule here ; moderation and the use, not excess and the abuse, will secure to us the pleasure even of this mortal life. Value not, I pray you, the transient joys which the animal appetites can bring to you ; at least value them not so much as to shorten life for their sakes.

Some evidently undervalue their lives, because they make them wretched through *envy*. Others are richer than they are, and they think it a miserable thing to be alive at all while others possess more of this world's goods than they. They walk, they say, and toil, while yonder person, who has no more deserts than they, is riding in his chariot ; so, forsooth, they count the chariot the main thing and not the life, and they will not enjoy their life because they cannot have a certain coveted addition which another possesses. Haman is not grateful for all the mercies of life, while unbending Mordecai sits in the king's gate ; he counts his honey to be bitterness because he cannot lord it at his will. God gets not thankfulness at all from the man for the innumerable mercies which he has ; these are nothing, he pines for some particular supposed mercy which he has not ; he considers that the fact of his being alive and being favoured of God in many respects, is nothing at all to be considered, because he has not all thiat his avarice might wish for. O poison not life by the envy of others, for if you do so you miserably undervalue it !

The slaves of *avarice* undervalue their lives, for they do not care to make life happy, but pinch themselves in order to accumulate wealth. The miser who starves himself in order that he may fill his bags may well be reasoned with in this way : " Is not the life more than the meat, and the body than raiment ? Skin for skin, yea, all that other men have will they give for their lives ; but you give your life for this pelf, this glittering dust. You are willing to forego all the enjoyments that this life might afford you, that you may have a heap to leave to your uncertain heirs, who will probably squander it, and certainly forget the hands that scraped the hoard together." Why should I throw away myself for the sake of dying rich ? Is it true success in life to have enjoyed nothing, to have poisoned all my existence, merely that the world might be informed in a corner of the *Illustrated News* that I died worth so many thousands of pounds ? This is to undervalue life indeed.

So also do they undervalue it who in *foolhardiness* are ready to throw it away on the slightest pretext. He that for his country's sake, or for the love of his fellow creature, risks life and loses it, truly deserves to be called a hero ; but he who to provoke laughter and to win the applause of fools, will venture limb and life without need, is but a fool himself, and deserves no praise whatever. He undervalues life who will display an art which endangers it, or who will run the risk of it for anything whatever short of the laudable motive of preserving liberty to his country, or life to his fellow men. Holy Scripture never teaches us to undervalue our own lives. He that said, " Thou shalt not kill," meant that we were not to kill ourselves any more than others. We ought to seek by all we can do in the surroundings of our habitations, by our cleanliness, by carefully observing sanitary laws, by never encouraging dangerous exhibitions, and by every other means to show our care of the life that now is, for it is a precious thing.

Yet, my brethren, there can be such a thing as overvaluing this life, and multitudes have fallen into that error. Those overvalue it who prefer it to eternal life. Why, it is but as a drop compared with the ocean, if you measure time with eternity. Seventy or eighty years of dwelling here below, what are they when compared with infinite ages of existence in the presence of the Most High ? I reckon that this present life is not worthy to be compared with the glory that shall be revealed in us. When men in fearful moments have denied the faith for the sake of saving their lives, they have overvalued this life ; when to preserve themselves from the sword, or the fire, or the tortures of the rack, they have denied the name of Jesus, they have made a mistake, and exchanged gold for dross. Alas, how many of us, in like condition, might have fallen into the same error !

They overvalue this life who consider it to be a better thing than divine love, for the love of God is better than life—His lovingkindness is better than life itself. Some would give anything for their lives, but they would give nothing for God's love. If their lives were in danger, they would hasten to the physician, but though they enjoy not the love of God they yet sit at ease, and seek not the priceless boon. They who feel aright think it a cheap thing to die, but an awful thing to live apart from God ; they recognize that life would be but death, unless God were with us, and that death itself is but the vestibule of life while God is our joy and our strength ! Let us never set the present life before divine love, and never let it be compared even for a moment with the pursuit of God's glory. Every Christian man is to feel that he is to take care of his life in comparison with any earthly glory ; but if it comes to a choice between God's glory and his life, he is to have no timorous hesitation in the matter, but at once to sacrifice his life freely at his Lord's altar. This has been ever the spirit of true Christians. They have never been anxious to die, nor have they been fearful concerning the loss of life. They have not thrown away their lives, they have known their value too well, but they have not withheld their lives for Christ's sake, for they have esteemed Him to be better than life itself. So you see the Scripture teaches us that there is a proper middle course in estimating this present life, and if we follow its instructions, we shall neither undervalue nor overvalue it.

It appears from the text, that godliness influences this present life, puts it in its true position, and becomes profitable to it.

I. First, let me observe that GODLINESS CHANGES THE TENURE OF THE LIFE THAT NOW IS.

It hath " *the promise* of the life that now is." I want you to mark the word—" it hath *the promise* of the life that now is." An ungodly man lives, but how ? He lives in a very different respect from a godly man. Sit down in the cell of Newgate with a man condemned to die. That man lives, but he is reckoned dead in law. He has been condemned. If he is now enjoying a reprieve, yet he holds his life at another's pleasure, and soon he must surrender it to the demands of justice. I, sitting by the side of him, breathing the same air, and enjoying what in many respects is only the selfsame life, yet live in a totally different sense. I have not forfeited my life to the law, I enjoy it, as far as the law is concerned, as my own proper right : the law protects *my* life, though it destroys *his* life. The ungodly man is condemned already, condemned to die, for the wages of sin is death ; and his whole life here is nothing but a reprieve granted by the longsuffering of God. But a Christian man is pardoned and absolved ; he owes not his life now to penal justice ; when death comes to him it will not be at all in the sense of an infliction of a punishment ; it will not be death, it will be the transfer of his spirit to a better state, the slumbering of his body for a little while in its proper couch to be awakened in a nobler likeness by the trump of the archangel. Now, is not life itself changed when held on so different a tenure ? To live because I am now protected by the law, is not that better than to be living at the sufferance of the law ? To live the life of an absolved man, of a free man, the life of God's own child even in this present life, is not that a different thing from living the life of one to whom each hour measures out a nearer approach to the capital sentence, and to the execution of well-deserved punishment ? The first is a life of pleasure ; the second, disguise it as you may, is death in life, a life overshadowed with the darkness of eternal wrath.

" Godliness hath the promise of the life that now is." That word changes the tenure of our present life in this respect, that it removes in a sense the uncertainty of it. God hath given to none of you unconverted ones any promise of the life that now is. You are like squatters on a common, who pitch their tents, and by the sufferance of the lord of the manor may remain there for awhile, but at a moment's notice you must up tents and away. But the Christian hath the *promise* of the life that now is ; that is to say, he has the freehold of it ; it is life given to him of God, and he really enjoys it, and has an absolute certainty about it ; in fact, the life that now is has become to the Christian a foretaste of the life to come. Do you say that it is uncertain to the Christian whether he shall die or live ? I grant you in one sense his remaining here is uncertain ; yet is this certain to him, that he shall never die until it is best for him to die, and shall never depart this life till he is ripe for the life to come ; shall never, in fact, be removed from his present tabernacle till he himself, if he knew all, would be perfectly willing to be removed ; willing ! aye, far more, overjoyed that his tabernacle should be dissolved that he might enter into his " house not made with hands, eternal in the heavens." The tenure is very different between the uncertainty of the ungodly who has no rights, and no legal titles, and the blessed certainty of the child of God who lives by promise.

Let me add that this word seems to me to sweeten the whole of human life to the man that hath it. Godliness hath the *promise* of life that now is ; that is to say, everything that comes to a godly man comes to him by promise, whereas if the ungodly man hath any blessing apparent, it does not come by promise, it comes overshadowed by a terrible guilt which curses his very blessings, and makes the responsibilities of his wealth and of his health and position redound to his own destruction, working as a savour of death unto death through his wilful disobedience. Everything that comes to the Christian comes by promise. He sees his daily bread, and he saith, " It has my Father's mark on it ; he said my bread should be given me. Here comes the water from the crystal stream, it is flavoured with the love of God ; he said my water shall be sure." He puts on his raiment, and it may not be so comely as the dress of others, but he saith, " This is the livery my Father promised me." He sleeps, and it is beneath the canopy of divine protection. He wakes and he walks abroad, angels according to the promise bearing him up in their hands. Afflictions come to him by promise, the broad arrow of the great King is set on each one of them, for was it not said of old, " In the world ye shall have tribulation, but in Me ye shall have peace " ? He can see everywhere the trace of divine faithfulness in the keeping of the covenant promise. He lives not the life of Ishmael, who by-and-by may be banished to the wilderness with the bondwoman his mother, but he lives the life of Isaac, the child of the promise, who is ere long to inherit all things, and who even now is the darling child of his father, and rejoices in his father's love. There is a vast difference between having the life that now is, and having *the promise* of the life that now is—having God's promise about it to make it all gracious, to make it all certain, and to make it all blessed as a token of love from God.

II. It is time that we pass on to THE BENEFIT WHICH GODLINESS BESTOWS IN THIS LIFE.

Perhaps the fulness of the text is the fact that the flower of life, the crown of life, the highest blessedness and bliss of life, is secured to us by godliness. I have no doubt you have often heard interpretations of this text, very excellent, and it is not for me to judge or censure them, which lead to the belief that the way to make the best of both worlds is to be a Christian. I also subscribe to that, but I must demur to the way in which it is generally put. There is an excellent sermon by that notable divine, Saurin, in which he urges this text as a proof that the best hope of success in the world is enjoyed by the Christian. I demur to that being the teaching of this text. There may be some truth in it, but I do not think it is much to be insisted on. It has been said that he who fears God has the best guarantee of health. It is true, there is nothing in godliness to destroy the health of the body. The true Christian is preversed from many of those passions, and excitements, and indulgences, which tend to produce disease and to bring on early death. That much is true, but I do not believe that godliness inevitably ensures good health. I the rather believe that some godly man absolutely require for the highest perfection of their godliness, that they should be visited with sickness. It seems to me to be a very strange theory, to teach that godliness guarantees health, for it would lead to the supposition that all people who are unhealthy must necessarily be or have been deficient in godliness; and this is all the more untenable when we observe that some of the best people we have ever met with have been those who have for years been bedridden by affliction, which they certainly never brought upon themselves by any kind of sin. I would say to every young man, there is nothing in the pursuit of godliness that can injure your health, but I would not say to him, " If you are godly you have the promise of being a healthy man," for I do not believe it, since unhealthiness may come from a thousand other sources besides impropriety of conduct. I will go further, and affirm that godliness, when carried to its highest and most honourable degree of excellence, might sometimes render it necessary for a man to place himself where he would of necessity become unhealthy. I wot that it was the highest godliness which made our missionaries fix their abodes amongst the fever marshes of Fernando Po and Old Calabar to preach the gospel. When I heard from one of our missionaries, as I did personally, that he had at last become so acclimatised that he did not have the fever oftener than about two days out of three, I could not think that godliness in his case necessarily involved health; but I gathered that it might so happen that an eminently godly man might feel it needful to go where he might say, " Farewell, health, thou art not after all the promise of the life that now is. I can bear to suffer, I can bear to creep about this world sick and ready to die if I may but have what is better than health, the luxury of winning souls for Christ, the honour and joy of instructing the ignorant in the faith of the crucified Redeemer." It were wicked to think that a man has less of godliness who sacrifices his health for Christ's sake. He certainly would not be the man to miss the promise, and yet if health were such a promise he would evidently have missed it.

Again, we have heard it argued that the godly man has the best prospect of wealth in this world. Now, I will also grant that as godliness delivers us from a multitude of expenses into which riot and dissipation would lead us, and as godliness creates habits of sobriety and economy, as godliness begets honesty, and honesty is even in a worldly sense the best policy, there are some reasons why Christian traders should grow rich, and godly men have much in their favour. But I also cannot help recognizing, that while trade is as it is, there are many things which a Christian man cannot do, and dare not do, which some have done, and are to this day rich for having done them—dirty acts, mean, low, and grovelling, which have brought wealth to the creatures who have practised them: and yet more, I have known the best of Christians, and men, too, whose outward conduct has been fully conformable to their profession, who have lived and died poor. Now, if wealth be the promise of the life that now is, I venture to say that godliness does not infallibly or even generally secure it. The God-fearing man may have as fair an opportunity as any other in the race of life, but all things considered this is all we can say, for it may be that the godly man may be a poor man, and from a dozen circumstances not connected with his religion or his morals, may live and may die poor in this world, but rich in faith.

It has also been said that godliness has the promise of the life that now is, in the sense that a Christian man is the most likely to have a good name, fame, and reputation among his fellow men. That also is true in a measure. In well-regulated society, the believer in Christ through the holiness of his character, will be had in esteem, and even amongst the worst of men the excellence of his conduct will command a measure of respect. But for all that, I do not believe that repute among men is the promise of the life that now is: for what is it after all ? Good repute among men, if it be deserved, I shall not decry ; but if by any chance slander should come and take away the good man's name— and it has often done so—shall I say pity the calumniated saint as one who has lost the promise of the life that now is ? I dare not think it. Far rather would I bid him rejoice in that day, and leap for joy, for so persecuted they the prophets that were before him. And who is the most likely person to be slandered, is it not the man who is most consistent with his profession, and most zealous in the spread of the faith ? The apostle Paul certainly never accounted riches to be the promise of the life that now is, for he had nothing ; he had learned to be poor, and to labour with his hands. He certainly never reckoned health to be the promise of the life that now is, for he was in such circumstances of peril by land and sea, and among false brethren, that his life was in jeopardy for the gospel ; and as to a good name, he never regarded that as the promise of the life that now is, for he was willingly accounted as the offscouring of all things, some thought him mad, others thought him base, his repute with the multitude was gone.

I will repeat what I have said, lest I be misunderstood. Under ordinary circumstances it is true that godliness wears a propitious face both towards health, and wealth, and a name, and he who has respect to these things, shall not find himself, as a rule, injured in the pursuit of them by his godliness ; but still I disdain altogether the idea that all these three things together are, or even make up a part of the promise of the life that now is. I believe some persons have the life that now is in its fulness, and the promise of it in its richest fulfilment, who have neither wealth, health, nor fame ; for being blessed with the suffering Master's smile and presence, they are happier far than those who roll in wealth, who luxuriate in fame, and have all the rich blessings which health includes.

Let me now show you what I think is the promise of the life that now is. I believe it to be an inward happiness, which is altogether independent of outward circumstances, which is something richer than wealth, fairer than health, and more substantial than fame. This secret of the Lord, this deep delight, this calm repose, godliness always brings in proportion as it reigns in the heart.

Let us try and show that this is even so. A godly man, my brethren, is one who is at one with his Maker. *It must always be right with the creature when it is at one with the Creator.* The Creator is omnipotent, all just, all holy ; when the creature is out of gear, with the Creator it will always be dashing itself against the pricks, and wounding itself ; as the Creator will not change, if the creature runs not parallel to the divine will, the creature must suffer, must be unahppy, must be unrestful. But when godliness puts our will into conformity with the divine will, the more fully it does so the more certainly it secures to us happiness even in the life that now is. I am not happy necessarily because I am in health, but I am happy if I am content to be out of health when God wills it. I am not happy because I am wealthy, but I am happy if it pleases me to be poor because it pleases God I should be. I am not happy because I happen to be famous, but I am happy if, being all unknown, I count it my highest fame to be accepted in the Beloved. A heart reconciled to the divine will has full possession of the promise of the life that now is, for such peace with God is perfect happiness where it perfectly exists—conformity to

God's will is heaven below. I pray that godliness may work in all of you a conformity to the divine will, and then I am sure, whatever your outward lot may be, you will win the promise of the life that now is.

The Christian man starting in life as such, is best accoutred for this life. He is like a vessel fittingly stored for all the storms and contrary currents that may await it. The Christian is like a soldier, who must fain go to battle, but he is protected by the best armour that can be procured. He wears the helmet and the breastplate, he wears the entire divine panoply which heavenly wisdom has prepared to protect him from every dart of his adversaries. He has the promise of the life that now is already, just as the man with a good sword and good armour has the best promise of success in battle. O that God may grant us grace to know and feel that the best instruments and weapons of the warfare of this life are to be found in the arsenals of holiness, in the armouries of confidence in God! In this sense we have again the promise of the life that now is.

With a Christian *all things that happen to him work for good.* Is not this a rich part of the promise of the life that now is? What if the waves roar against him, they speed his bark towards the haven? What if the thunders and lightnings come forth? They clear the atmosphere and promote his soul's health. He gains by his losses, he grows healthy by his sicknesses, he lives by dying, he is enriched by being despoiled of his goods. Do you ask for any better promise than this? Is it not better that all things should work for my good, than that all things should be as I would wish to have them? They might all work my pleasure, and yet might all work my ruin; but now if they do not always please me, yet if they always benefit me, is not this the best promise of the life that now is?

The Christian enjoys his God under all circumstances. That, again, is the promise of the life that now is. I spoke of his being reconciled to God, he is much more than that—he delights himself in his God. He finds God in nature. The landscape glows for him with a diviner colour than any other eye can see. As for the heavens, with their starry glories, there is a light in them which hath not yet been beheld by the natural man. He sees God in his solitude, and peoples his loneliness with the spirits that are akin with the Most High. He is, wherever he may be, never debarred from the society he loves best; a wish will find his God, a tear will bring him his best Beloved. He has but to sigh and cry when on the bed of sickness, and God cometh and maketh his bed for him. Blessed man, he hath indeed the promise of the life that now is, for in it all, and over it all, he sees the divine love shining for him with a supernal splendour, and making earth but the porch of heaven. This is to have the life that now is in the fulness of the promise.

I am sure you will agree with me that the genuine possessor of godliness has the promise of the life that now is, in *his freedom from many of those cares and fears which rob life of all its lustre.* The man without godliness is weighted with the care of every day, and of all the days that are to come, the dread remembrance of the past, and the terror of the future as well. The godly man knows that all the past is forgiven, his transgressions are blotted out; as for the present, he casts that burden on the Lord; as for the future, he would not pry into it with anxious eye, but he leaves God to rule and govern as

He wills. He sits down, calmly content that his Father's will is right and good towards him.

And as he is thus free from care, so is he *free from the fear of men.* Ungodly men, many of them, truckle to their fellow men. It is to them a most important question whether they are smiled upon or frowned at by their fellow worms. The godly man has learned to lift his head above the common race of mankind, and when he lives as he should, he neither thinks a thing the better because men praise it, nor the worse because they censure it. His rule is not popular opinion, nor the dictates of the philosophy of the hour; he believes what God tells him to be true, and what God prescribes he knows to be right; and he does this careless of man's judgment, for none can judge him but his Master. That man has the promise of the life that now is who is in full enjoyment of the sweets of a clear conscience; who can afford to snap his fingers in the face of all mankind, and declare that if the heavens themselves should all, he would do the right, and dare all things for God. Oh, to have the yoke of human judgment from off your neck, and the bondage of man's domineering opinion from off your spirit! This is to receive the promise of the life that now is.

Moreover, the fear of death has gone from the Christian. This with many deprives the life that now is of everything that is happy and consoling. They are afraid in their merriest moments that the skeleton will disturb the feast; and when the dance is merriest they think they hear the sound of the trumpet that will silence all. But the Christian is not afraid; to him the prospect of departure is rather joyous than grievous, and the breaking up of this mortal state is an event he looks for as the clearing away of multitudes of sorrows and the bringing in of mighty joys. Brethren, to be free from the fear of death, is to make life truly life, and he has it who leans wholly upon Christ, and knows that Jesus is the resurrection and the life.

Put these things together, peacefulness with his fellow men, peace with God, a sense that all things are working for his good, fearlessness of man's judgment, communion with the Most High, and surely you have described in a few words the very flower of life, the thing that makes it worth while to live. This does not lie, as I have said before, in accumulated treasure; it does not blush in the rosy cheek; it does not dwell in the trump of fame; it resides within, when the man walks with God and subdues the earth beneath his feet; when the soul communes with the spiritual, and makes the visible to glow in the light of the unseen; when the man's peace and joy all stream from the deep springs of God's love, and the man lives in God, and God lives in him. Herein lies the highest kind of life; it is the flower of the life that now is, and godliness it is that has the promise of it.

I must not detain you longer, except to make an application of the subject to the present assembly. Brethren and sisters, you who have godliness, and live in the fear of God, let me entreat you to believe that there is provided for you in godliness, comfort, joy, and delight for the life that now is. You need not postpone your feasting upon Christ till you see Him face to face. Feed on Him this day. You need not wait for the joys of the Holy Spirit till you have shaken off this cumbrous clay; the joy of the Lord is your strength to-day. You need not think that your peace and rest remain as yet in the future, hidden from you ; eternal life with its blessings is a present possession. They that believe do enter into rest, and may enter into rest *now*. The clusters of Eshcol are before you, brought to you by a divine hand before you cross the Jordan.

> " The men of grace have found
>   Glory begun below,
> Celestial fruits on earthly ground
>   From faith and hope do grow."

We do not say that godliness has made all believers rich, for some here will be content always to be poor. The whole body of the faithful cannot claim that godliness has brought them earthly treasure, for some of the greatest of them have written that if in this life only they had hope, they would have been of all men the most miserable. But without exception, the whole of us can unanimously declare that we have found in godliness the highest happiness, the supremest delight, the richest consolation. I pray you, therefore, who profess godliness, be not content unless you have the promise of the life that now is. Believe that you can not only make this life sublime, but make it joyous ; believe that you can now be raised up together, and made to sit together in the heavenly places in Christ Jesus. Ye cannot find a heaven in things below, for the moth is there, and the rust that corrupted ; but you can, while here, if you set your affections upon things above, and not on things on the earth, find glory begun within you, and a young heaven already shining about your path. The life that now is, claim it. Up, ye sons of Israel, and slay the Amalekites that would take away from you your comfort. Arise, ye men that fear the Lord, and demand that doubts and fears, like the accursed Canaanites, shall be chased from the land ; for the promise of God ought to be believed, and in the believing of it, your peace shall be like a river, and your joy shall overflow.

Another application of the text is this. There is a bearing of it upon the sinner. It is quite certain, O ungodly man, that the promise of the life that now is belongs only to those who are godly. Are you content to miss the cream of this life ? I pray you, if you will not think of the life to come, at least think of this. You desire to be happy ; you have intelligence enough to know that happiness does not consist in externals, but in the state of your mind. I assure you, and there are thousands of my brethren who can affirm the same, that after having tried the ways of sin, we infinitely prefer the ways of righteousness for their own pleasure's sake even here, and we would not change with ungodly men even if we had to die like dogs. With all the sorrow and care which Christian life is supposed to bring, we would prefer it to any other form of life beneath the stars. There is no man like the Christian after all. Happy art thou, O Israel, a people saved of the Lord ! We do not come to you, and tell you that godliness will make you rich, although there is no need that it should make you poor. We do not tell you it will make you healthy ; it certainly will not make you the reverse. But these are not the things with which we would bribe you, these are inferior blessings, which we dare not set before you as worthy of your seeking after in the first instance. But we do tell you that if you will but seek the Lord while He may be found, and put your trust in His Christ, who came to put away sin, you shall have the happiest, best, noblest, most desirable life that can be enjoyed on earth. Now many of you believe this. I know you do. In your hearts you envy Christians—even poor Christians. You feel that you would gladly be as sick or as poor as yonder pious saint if you might have his hope, if you might have his God. Well, if you *know* which is best, have which is best. "May I have it ?" saith one. Who said you might not ? Doth not the Lord invite you to taste and see that He is good ? Hath not He even commanded you, and are not these His words, " Believe in the Lord Jesus Christ, and thou shalt be saved " ? Simply to trust, and to rely, this is to begin the divine life, and this will introduce you into a nobler sphere than mortals know of. They rejoice when corn and wine fill their barns and their vats, but you will say, " Lord, lift up the light of Thy countenance upon me," and in that you will find a richer joy than they. " Seek ye the Lord while He may be found, call ye upon Him while He is near : let the wicked forsake his way, and the unrighteous man his thoughts : and let him return unto the Lord, and He will have mercy upon him ; and to our God, for He will abundantly pardon." God bless you, for Christ's sake.

" TRUST IN THE LIVING GOD "

" We trust in the living God."—1 Timothy iv. 10.

IF we are inclined to grieve because everything around us changes, our consolation will be found in turning to our unchanging God. If we lament the ills of mortality, it will be wise for us to turn to Him " who only hath immortality." If our earthly joys fade and die, it is a blessed thing for us to be able to go to the fountain of undying joy, and there to drink deep draughts of bliss, which shall cause us to forget our misery.

Without any further preface, I ask you to follow me while, first, in a very simple manner, I speak upon *the great truth of the existence of the living God*, and then, secondly, while I draw *practical inferences from that existence*. Before I close my discourse, I shall have a question to put to you.

I. First, for a little while, let us think of THE GREAT TRUTH OF THE EXISTENCE OF THE LIVING GOD.

Paul wrote to Timothy, " Therefore we both labour and suffer reproach, because we trust in the living God."

He meant, by that expression, first, *that God is truly existing, and not like the dead gods of the heathen, which are no gods at all*,—which, in fact, have no existence as gods. Vast multitudes have bowed down before images of wood, or stone, or ivory, or gold ; but of them all it might truly be said, " Eyes have they, but they see not ; they have ears, but they hear not ; noses have they, but they smell not ; they have hands, but they handle not ; feet have they, but they walk not ; neither speak they through their throat." It is a sure sign that a man's understanding is dead when he can worship a dead god ; but you and I, beloved, " trust in the living God." He is the God who made heaven and earth, and all that in them is ; He is the God who supports the whole universe by the power of His almighty arm ; He is the God who rules and over-rules in nature, providence, and grace ; He is the true God, the only real God ;—no dream God, no phantom or myth conjured up by imagination, but a real God, the only living and true God. May we worship Him, then, with real worship, real adoration, and true sincerity of heart ! What a blessing it is for us that we are able to worship the true God ! We might have been left, as our remote ancestors were, to seek after God, if haply we might find Him, or to worship gods that are no gods, and be lost in the mazes of superstition, unable to find the Most High. But "God, who commanded the light to shine out of darkness, hath shined in our hearts, to give the light of the knowledge of the glory of God in the face of Jesus Christ," and, therefore, "we trust in the living God," the real God.

A second meaning of this expression, I have no doubt, lies in *the fact of God's self-existence and independence* : " We trust in the living God," who is " living " in a very emphatic sense. You and I are living, but our existence is entirely dependent upon the will of God. Although He has given us immortal spirits, yet that immortality only comes to us by reason of the divine decree ; and the glorious immortality of believers comes to them by virtue of their vital union with their ever-living Head, their Lord and Saviour Jesus Christ. We have no independent immortality ; it is not inherent in us, and it must be sustained by perpetual emanations of the divine power. It is a fire, which could not maintain its own glow ; it must be fed, or it would go out. But God is self-existent, the great I AM ; and if all His creatures could cease to be, He would be just as completely God without them as with them.

" He sits on no precarious throne,
    Nor borrows leave to be."

His is a fire which burns without fuel,—a sun which scatters light without itself diminishing. God is independent, self-existing, the only really " living " being in the entire universe in the fullest and most emphatic sense of the word "living."

What a joy it is to worship such a God as this, because nothing can diminish His life, His force, His power ! If His courts are sustained, not by the tribute of men, but by His own wealth ; if His sovereign state stands, not by the might of armies, but by His own omnipotence ; and if He Himself is all-sufficient, not because He gathers up all things into Himself, but because all things are from Him, and are all in Him in their germ and seed ; is He not a God whom we all ought to worship ;—and relying on whom we may be perfectly at rest, for He cannot fail us, neither can He fail Himself in any respect or degree ?

A third meaning of the expression "living" in Paul's declaration, "We trust in the living God," I have no doubt is to be found in *the fact of the existence of God through all eternity*. There was a time when you and I, who are now alive, were not alive ; and there will be a time when, as far as this world is concerned, we shall be numbered with the dead. But there never was a period in which God did not live. He always was, and always is, and always will be " the *living* God." Let your thoughts fly back to eternity if you can—for, mark you, all our ideas of eternity are very shallow and superficial. We cannot form any clear notion of what " eternity "

means ; and the very fact that we speak of a " past " eternity proves that we have to bring it down to our finite apprehension, and to use inaccurate words to express our imperfect and incorrect ideas. But far back, when the sun, and moon, and stars, and the whole universe slept in the mind of God, as a forest sleeps within an acorn cup, even then God was " the living God." Before the first ray of light had broken in upon the pristine darkness—aye, before there was any darkness,—ere anything was created,—God was " the living God," and was just as great and as glorious as He is now. Without an angel to sing His praise, or a human being to look up to Him with holy reverence or with tearful repentance,—yet still independent of them all, He was " the living God " then. What a blessing it is for us that it was so ! There was never a period, in which Satan could plot and plan against us, but what God had existed before him eternally. That evil spirit is but the infant of a day compared with God, the Eternal of all the ages, the everlasting Father, who was always able to anticipate everything that could possibly occur, knowing beforehand all that might be detrimental to us, counter-mining every mine of the arch-enemy, and baffling all the old serpent's cunning in such a way as, in the end, to add still more to His own glory.

And as He was " the living God " in the past, so He is " the living God " in the present, and just as truly living as He was ten thousand millions of years ago,—to speak of eternity after the fashion of men. Dr. Watts hit the mark when he sang,—

" He fills His own eternal NOW,
    And sees our ages pass."

Ages and years are past, or present, or future to us ; but they are all present to Him. When a man looks upon a map, he can cover a whole country with his hand ; but a traveller has to journey many weary miles before he can cross that country from one end of it to the other ; but on the map your hand covers it all ; and all eternity is under the hand of God like that country on the map covered by a human hand. God is " the living God " now as much as ever He was ; as powerful, as wise, as loving, as tender, as strong as ever He was, blessed be His holy name.

And so He will be throughout the whole of the future. We cannot tell all that will yet happen in this world, but one thing we know,—God will always be " the living God." It is probable that once-powerful nations will be utterly destroyed, and that there will be terrible disasters beyond anything that has yet been experienced ; we know that the present dispensation will utterly pass away, and that " the mountains shall depart, and the hills be removed ; " but this fact is sure, that He, who has been the dwelling-place of His people in all generations will be the dwelling-place of His people in all the generations that are yet to come. There will never be a funeral knell to tell us that our great Lord is dead. There will be no need of weeping amongst the blessed spirits above because He, who was their Creator, Protector, Preserver, and Friend, has ceased to be, for He ever will be " the living God." So, because of His eternal existence, He is right worthy to bear this title,—aye, and to monopolize it, for it belongs to Him alone.

" Great God ! how infinite art Thou !
    What worthless worms are we !
Let the whole race of creatures bow,
    And pay their praise to Thee.

" Thy throne eternal ages stood,
   Ere seas or stars were made ;
Thou art the ever-living God,
   Were all the nations dead.

" Eternity, with all its years,
   Stands present in Thy view ;
To Thee there's nothing old appears ;
   Great God ! there's nothing new."

The fourth meaning of the text seems to me to be this. *God is called " the living God " as being always Himself really and truly God in the full capacity of His being.* Sometimes we say of a man that he is " all alive." At another time, he does not appear to be fully quickened ; he has life to some extent, but not in its fulness. We say of the man, by-and-by, that he is dead ;—not that he has ceased to exist, for man will no more cease to exist than will God Himself ; but we speak of him as dead because his body, which is part of his being, lies mouldering in the tomb. But God is all life, and only life. No portion of Him, (I must use human language, though the words are incorrect which I am using, as our words always must be when we speak of God,) no faculty, no power, no attribute of God, can be smitten by any paralysis, or can, in any degree, or in the slightest measure, be subject to any failure which is at all akin to death. God is all alive, and altogether life, and nothing but life. God's wisdom is always infallible, His power is always almighty, His energy is at all time efficacious for everything that needs His attention. There never can come a time when He will be bowed down with age, or wearied with toil, or affected by suffering. " The living God " is the whole God, or, as the holy beings in heaven call Him —and it means the same thing,—" Holy, holy, holy, Lord God Almighty, which was, and is, and is to come." He is the whole God. Whatever the word " God " means,—and we do not know, nor shall we ever know, all that it means ; it is too vast to be conceived by anyone but God Himself ;—but, whatever that is, that is what God always is to the full measure, never in any degree diminished by what we call death. He is evermore " the living God."

I like to think of this truth, because God Himself speaks of it again and again. The Lord said to Moses in the wilderness, " Is the Lord's hand waxed short ? " In the prophecy of Isaiah we read, " Thus saith the Lord, . . Is My hand shortened at all, that it cannot redeem ? or have I no power to deliver ? " And, a little later, the prophet was inspired to write, " Behold, the Lord's hand is not shortened, that it cannot save ; " and, to-day, He is as mighty as He was in those glorious days when, in the van of Israel's host, He led His people in safety through the depths of the sea, and delivered them for ever from the iron bondage of Pharaoh. Aye, blessed be His holy name, He is still " the living God "—as full of life and power as ever He was.

Another meaning of this expression is, *that God is active and energetic, and not a mere name.* There are plenty of people who are willing to believe in a god of a certain sort, but I hardly know how to describe their god. They are not atheists ;—they would be horrified if we called them by that name ;— but their notion is that everything is regulated by what they call " the laws of nature." If you ask them what " nature " is, they give you some curious answers. One man says, " I do not go into your places of worship, and sit there, and hear you talk about God ; I like to walk about, and worship nature." If it is in London that a man talks like that, I should like to ask him what he calls " nature." Does he mean these miles of brick walls, and the dark lanes and alleys at the back of them ? If he means that, I should not like to worship his " nature." Or does he mean the grass in the meadows and the flowers of the field ? If so, I hardly think that I should like to worship what cattle eat ; it seems a degradation for a man to stoop as low as that. But they will say and do anything to get rid of the idea of the living and true God. " Nature "—" providence "—and so on, are the expressions they use, just as if " God " did not enter into their calculations, —or as if He had gone out of the business, and left the whole concern to go on by itself. I should not like to be the child of a father who, the moment I was born, had me washed and dressed by machinery, and had a cradle ready for me to be rocked by machinery, and fed me by machinery,—who, all the while that I was under his roof, dressed me by machinery, and fed me by machinery, and taught me by machinery, but I never saw him ;—in fact, I only knew that there was some mysterious force about somewhere, but I never saw him or it,—and never knew anything about his personality. That is the kind of dead force that many men call " God." But *our* God, in whom we trust, is a God with a great, warm, loving heart, a thinking God, an active God, a working, personal God, who comes into the midst of this world, and does not leave it to go on by itself. Although He is a stranger in the world, even as His people also are strangers and foreigners by reason of the revolt that men have made against their liege Lord and Sovereign, yet it is still His world, and He is still in it.

I like to think of " the living God " being in this world which He created ; for, now, when I look at the cowslip or the daffodil, I know that it is God who paints these flowers of the spring so delicately. When I gather the geranium or the fuchsia, I know that it is God's pencil which has been at work, and I love to look at the blossom, and feel that I am near to God,—just as I should feel if I were to go into a friend's studio, and see there some of his sketches and paintings. I know that he has been there, and that no other hand than his could paint that picture so well. And, in like manner, I know that no other hand but that of my God could paint these pictures of nature so beautifully, thus I am brought very near to " the living God." O dear brethren and sisters, it is such a joy to me to remember that God is not a mere dead force,—an abstract something or other which gives energy to the world, or which did give energy to it ages ago, but has now gone away, and left the old energies to work till they wear themselves out ! Oh, no ; I believe that the Lord God still walketh among the trees of this garden,—that the Lord God, like a shepherd, still watcheth over His sheep-fold,—that the Lord God still speaks to us in the thunder, smiles upon us in the sunlight, scatters His blessings down in the dew and the rain,—that he gives us the fruitful fields of harvest, and the golden days in which the sheaves can be gathered into the garner,—aye, and that He is just as truly at work for us in the winter months, sweetening the clods by the winds and the frost, and so preparing the earth to bring forth food for man and grass for the cattle. We delight to think that, in all these ways, God is still " the living God."

Yet once again, God is " the living God " in that *He is the Source of life, the Giver of life, and the Sustainer of life*. We are living creatures, but He is the living Creator. We are living dependents, but He is " the living God " upon whom we all depend. He spoke us out of nothing, and He could speak us back to nothing if He pleased to do so. We are just the creatures of His will, living on His estates as tenants who may, at any moment, be dismissed at His pleasure, receiving the very breath that is in our nostrils at His absolute discretion. But God is life itself, and after all the streams which have flowed from Him to His creatures, there is as much life in Him as at the first ; and when He saith, " Return, ye children of men," and we go back to Him, He will have no more life than He has now ; but He will be, as He always has been, " the living God."

> " Let them neglect Thy glory, Lord,
>   Who never knew Thy grace ;
> But our loud songs shall still record
>   The wonders of Thy praise.
>
> " 'Twas He, and we'll adore His name,
>   That form'd us by a word ;
> 'Tis He restores our ruin'd frame :
>   Salvation to the Lord ! "

Now, in these six ways, I have brought out only one thought, which I want to impress on your minds, because it has been such a sweet thought to me. I have, in imagination, looked upon all whom I know upon the earth, and I have said of them all, " They are dying creatures." This is always true, but it is often forgotten. Yet, when one is taken away who has been very precious to us, we begin to realize this truth. Thinking over this matter, I seem to see a procession going past me. I can remember many of those who have passed me. They have gone by while I have remained here, and I shall never see them here any more,—a long array of my Master's servants, some of them bearing His banner aloft, and others marching with their swords drawn, because of fear in the night. Some of them were weak and feeble folk, who had to be guarded on both sides by sturdy champions. And now, those of you who are before me as I speak, are also passing away ; and there are more coming on, but they are only coming that they may go. I said, just now, that I was looking on at this procession, but that was a mistake, for *I am in the procession, and I am passing on with the rest !* What shadows we all are ! What fleeting things ! What mists,— what paintings on a cloud ! We can scarcely say that we live, for, the moment we begin to live, that moment we begin to die, and—

> " Every beating pulse we tell
>   Leaves but the number less."

This earth is not " the land of the living." This world is a dying world ; the living world is beyond death's cold river. Here are graves innumerable. What part of the globe is there that has never yet been a cemetery ? Every particle of dust, which is blown in your face in the street, may once have formed a portion of some living being ? O death, thou rulest over all ! No, thou dost not, for there is One who rules over even thee, O death ! Thou canst have no power over " the living God " ; but thou art His servant, permitted to work out His purpose, for it is through death that we pass into life. By the

death of our redeeming Lord, we have been redeemed from destruction ; and, therefore, we can turn away from everything that wears the aspect of death and change, and turn to Him who is ever the same, and of whose years there is no end,—the Eternal, in whom we trust.

II. Thus have I set forth, as best I could, the great truth of the existence of " the living God." Now, in the second place, LET US DRAW SOME PRATICAL INFERENCES FROM THIS GREAT TRUTH.

And the first inference is this,—*an inference of reverential awe and holy trembling*. What a great God He is whom we have professed to worship ! When a poor pagan bows down before his wooden god, I should not wonder if what little sense he has should make him loathe and ridicule himself ; but we have gathered here to worship " the living God." Moses tells us, in the 5th of Deuteronomy, verse 26, that the Israelites said, when the law was given to them, " Who is there of all flesh, that hath heard the voice of the living God speaking out of the midst of the fire, as we have, and lived ? " Well might they stand there trembling because " the living God " had come down, and touched the mountains, so that they smoked like great altars of incense. This is the God whom we worship. Far hence be all trifling ! Vain thoughts, begone ! Before " the living God " we should prostrate ourselves in the very dust. O you, who profess to serve the Lord, mind that you serve Him faithfully, for it is " the living God "whom you serve, the God who is not to be mocked with the hypocritical service ! O you, who know that you are not reconciled to Him, remember that it is to " the living God " that you are not reconciled ; and recollect that solemn and true declaration, " It is a fearful thing to fall into the hands of the living God," and that other, " Our God is a consuming fire." So I say that our first inference should be that of reverential awe and holy trembling.

The next should be, to God's people, *an inference of holy courage*. Are we on the Lord's side ? Then, my brethren and sisters, let us never fear, for we are on the side of " the living God." Who can successfully defy Him ? Who dares to throw down the gage of battle against Him ? You remember what young David said to Saul concerning Goliath of Gath, " Thy servant slew both the lion and the bear ; and this uncircumcised Philistine shall be as one of them, seeing he hath defied the armies of the living God." It was grandly put, as though he had said, " This big fellow is only the servant of a dead god, and he and his god may both come out against me, and I, little as I am, yea, less than nothing in myself, will go to him in the name of the living God, and bring back his head as the trophy of victory. Let no man's heart fail because of him." So now, if the biggest Goliath that ever lived at Rome or anywhere else should come stalking out against us, let us say, " Who is he, that he should defy the armies of the living God ? " If the God of Israel is not now living, all is over with the cause of truth and righteousness ; but we may say, as David did on another occasion, " The Lord liveth ; and blessed be my rock." As long as He liveth, we may boldly say, " If God be for us, who can be against us ? "

This, too, should be *our great security in time of danger*. I like to recall that incident in the life of Hezekiah when he took that abominable Assyrian letter, " and spread it before the Lord." Do you ever take your letters to the Lord, brother ? That is the best thing in the world to do with them when they are very evil ones. Hezekiah spread his letter before the Lord, and said, " Lord, bow down Thine ear, and hear : open, Lord, Thine eyes, and see : and hear the words of Sennacherib, which hath sent him to reproach the living God." That was the point, and the king felt quite sure that Sennacherib would be overthrown because he had defied the living God. If God had been a dead god, Sennacherib might have done with Him as he did with other idol gods. He asked, " Have the gods of the nations delivered them which my fathers have destroyed ? " He did not realize that they were all broken to pieces because they were mere idols ; but, this time, he was defying " the living God." If, brother, " the living God " is on thy side, " no weapon that is formed against thee shall prosper ; and every tongue that shall rise against thee in judgment thou shalt condemn." If you, beloved, are walking before " the living God " in all sincerity, even if Sennacherib with a mighty host should come against you, the Lord your God would send His holy angel, and smite your foes, and you should surely be delivered. Have no doubt of fear, if your God is " the living God."

And this truth, brethren, *should always make us fearless of men* ; for, after all, what are men ? Remember what the Lord said to His servant, the prophet Isaiah, " Who art thou, that thou shouldest be afraid of a man that shall die ? " The most powerful and most cruel man, who ever dares to threaten you, is only a man that shall die, and the Lord Jesus says to you, " Be not afraid of them that kill the body, and after that have no more that they can do." Herod is soon eaten of worms. Persecuting monarchs soon disappear when God condemns them. Therefore, while " the living God " is your God, never be afraid of a dying man.

> " Fear Him, ye saints, and you will then
> Have nothing else to fear."

Another inference from this truth is this. *It should bring relief to us in times of bereavement.* Sorrow is natural to us, but to push sorrow to an extreme is wrong. I have heard of a good woman, who had lost her husband, and continued sorrowing over her loss for a very long time. Her little boy saw her weeping day after day, and, at last, plucking her by the gown, he said to her, " Mother, is God dead ? " " No, dear," she said ; " but your father is." But that question made her stay her grief, as it well might ; for, if God is not dead, our best Friend still lives, so let us be of good cheer. If people had to come here, and say, " That good woman, whom God so greatly blessed in the church's work, is dead ; and that dear brother, whom we all loved, is dead ; and the Pastor, too, is dead " ; who could help sorrowing ? But even then it would still be true that " the Lord liveth." Always get back to that great fact, " the Lord liveth." We shall have to put our beloved ones into the grave, but " the Lord liveth," blessed be His name ; and as long as God lives, we need never ask, " What shall we do ? " It is true that we shall not do much, but God will. We must never say, " Oh, there is such a great gap, it cannot be filled." God is alive, and He can fill it, so you must not give way to despondency or despair. We may grieve, for even Jesus wept, but let us never distrust the Lord ; for, as surely as He takes away one worker, He knows how to raise up another ; and if the Lord should take from thee thy husband, he will Himself be thy Husband ; if He should let thee be fatherless, He will be thy Father ; and if He should leave thee childless, good woman, He will say to thee, " Am I not better unto thee than ten sons ? " He can fill up every gap ; yea, and make your soul to overflow with supreme content.

> " ' Lo, I am with you,' saith the Lord,
> ' My church shall safe abide ;
> For I will ne'er forsake My own,
> Whose souls in Me confide.'

> " Through every scene of life and death,
> This promise is our trust ;
> And this shall be our children's song,
> When we are cold in dust."

This truth ought also to keep us from grieving too much over our losses and crosses in business. You have had a great loss to-day, friend, and your face looks very long over it ; or you have heard of someone who was the means of bringing you much business, who has removed or is dead. Well, but " the Lord liveth." " Trust in the living God." There have been times, in the little business I have had to do for the Lord in connection with the Orphanage and the College, when the funds have been very short, and sometimes have run quite out. I have scraped the bottom of the meal barrel a good many times, and I have had to squeeze the cruse to get a drop more oil out of it ; but we have trusted in the living God ; and, up till now, we have always found Him worthy of being trusted, and we believe we always shall. There have been failures and mistakes on our part, and on the part of our friends, but never any on God's part. We must all bear that testimony ; let us, therefore, all " trust in the living God." If an ill wind blows upon us, let us believe that, somehow or other, it will blow us some good ; and if a rough tide comes up, let us believe that it will, in some way or other, wash us nearer to our desired haven.

Once again, " we trust in the living God," and *this gives us the richest consolation concerning our departed Christian friends.* As " the Lord liveth," and He is their God, they are not dead. You remember Christ's argument with the Sadducees ; it was this,—God has said, " I am the God of Abraham and the God of Isaac, and the God of Jacob," " God is not the God of the dead, but of the living ; " so that the dead saints are not really dead. Whenever there comes out a new error, it generally breeds another, for errors are very prolific. Some people started the notion that the soul of man is not immortal, —that the soul of the wicked would die. I was quite sure that, when they got as far as that error, they would go still further ; and so the next notion was that every part of us will die when we die,—that there is no soul that is immortal, or no soul at all, and that the righteous dead are all in their graves, souls and bodies and everything. That is the beautiful materialistic notion that, after having received Christianity, we are expected to imbibe but we are not such idiots, whatever they may think of us. We shall never believe that all our beloved friends, who, according to the Scriptures, have been with Jesus these many years, have never been with Jesus at all ; in fact, do not exist at all, except whatever may be found of them in their coffins or in their graves. How could that be if God was their God, and if Christ's words are true, " God is not the God of the dead, but of the living " ? They are alive, brethren,—as much alive as they were alive here, with the exemption of that mortal part which they have left behind to be prepared for immortality, as Dr. Watts truly wrote,—

> "Corruption, earth and worms
> Shall but refine this flesh,
> Till My triumphant spirit comes
> To put it on afresh."

We go down to our graves, as Esther went to her bath of spices, to be prepared for the embrace of the great King ; and, in the morning of the resurrection, this poor body of ours, all fair and lustrous, shall be reunited with our glorified spirit, and we shall behold the face of the King in His beauty, and be with Him for ever and ever. " God is not the God of the dead ; " and, therefore, those of whom He is the God will never die. The inference is clear and forcible. Believe in it, hold to it, and rejoice in it, for it will comfort you to know that, as He is your God you will never die. " God is not the God of the dead ; " then, blessed be His holy name, I am not dead, though once I was dead, for He has quickened me into life ; and I never shall be dead any more, for Jesus said, " Because I live, ye shall live also." " The living God " is not the Father of dead souls, but He has an innumerable host of living children to be His heirs, and to dwell with Him for ever. Did you ever notice that passage where Joshua tells the people to be ready to go over the Jordan, and says that, when the priests' feet shall touch the river, it shall divide, and the ark shall be carried across ? " And then," saith he, " hereby ye shall know that the living God is among you, and that He will without fail drive out from before you the Canaanites, and the Hittites, and the Hivites, and the Perizzites, and the Girgashites, and the Amorites, and the Jebusites." The joyful triumphs of believers in death, when they metaphorically cross the Jordan, are proofs to us that God is with His people, that He will drive out all our enemies before us, and give us a triumphant entrance into the promised land above. Glory be to the name of " the living God " for ever !

III. Now I finish with the question which I said I might ask : it is this,—IS " THE LIVING GOD " YOUR GOD ?

If so, then *remember how near He is to you*, for Paul tells us, in 2 Cor. vi. 16, " Ye are the temple of the living God." I will not dwell on that sentence, though I am tempted to do so ; but what a wonderful thing it is that " the living God " should be willing to dwell inside our bodies ! Oh, let us keep these bodies pure, and let us see to it that we never fall under that terrible curse, " If any man defile the temple of God, him shall God destroy ; " but may our body, soul, and spirit be preserved blameless unto the coming of our Lord Jesus Christ !

And, dear brethren, if " the living God " be really ours, *let us thirst after Him*, let us say, as did the writer of the 42nd Psalm, " As the hart panteth after the water-brooks, so panteth my soul after Thee, O God. My soul thirsteth for God, for the living God." He is " the living God," so thirst after Him, and keep on thirsting after Him ; and do not be content to try to live without Him ; for, to live without " the living God ", is to have death in life, and not truly to live at all. Think, child of God, " the living God " dwells within you ; seek to realize His presence, long and pant to realize it more and more.

Are any of you obliged to answer my question truthfully by saying, " No, the living God is not mine " ? Then, I must repeat to you those two texts that I quoted earlier in my sermon : " It is a fearful thing to fall into the hands of the living God," " for our God is a consuming fire." That latter text has often been spoilt by being misquoted. I have many times heard it quoted, " God, *out of Christ*, is a consuming fire." That is not the text at all ; it is " *our* God "—the Christians' God—God *in* Christ, " is a consuming fire " ; and if He is a consuming fire to His own people, what will He be to the ungodly ? That is a wonderful question that is asked in Isaiah xxxiii. 14 : " Who among us shall dwell with the devouring fire ? who among us shall dwell with everlasting burnings ? " And the answer is, " Nobody can, except the man ' that walketh righteously, and speaketh uprightly,' " and so on. The prophet goes on to describe the man who has been renewed by grace, for he is the only man who can live in the everlasting burnings of the divine majesty and purity. He can live there because the devouring fire will only burn up everything in him that is unlike to God ; but the new life that is in the Christian, the grace that the Holy Spirit puts into us, will endure the fire. Everything that appertains to man and to man's work must be tried by fire ; and if God has built into us the gold, and silver, and precious stones of His grace, and if we have built upon them our life work, both we and our work will endure the trial by fire.

But, sinner, you will also have to go through that fire ; and seeing that there is nothing in you but the wood, and hay, and stubble of self and sin,—nothing in you but that which is foul and obnoxious to God, unholy and unrighteous,—or self-righteous, which is really unrighteous,—the fire will consume it. All your glory, your peace, your happiness, everything that makes life to be life, will be taken from you, and there shall remain for you nothing but existence, and this is the description of that existence, " These shall go away into everlasting punishment." Oh, may the Lord, who alone can give you life, give it to you now ; for, if not, there will remain nothing but an everlasting death to be your portion. From that may you now be delivered, of His infinite mercy, through trusting in the Lord Jesus Christ ! Amen.

ACCOMPLICES IN SIN

" Neither be partaker of other men's sins."—1 Timothy v. 22.

WE have all abundant reason to look at home, and see about our own sins. Nothing can be more absurd than for a man to take his hoe, and weed everybody else's garden, and leave all the thorns and thistles to flourish on his own plot. The old parable of the man who carried two bags, one behind and one in front, and who put other people's faults into the one in front, and his own into the one at his back, is a very correct representation of the folly of those who have their eyes widely open to see the faults of their neighbours, but are totally blind to their own imperfections. If, as our proverb puts it, " Charity begins at home," so should criticism ; and criticism concerning character had better stop there. There is so much dirty linen in our own house needing to be washed that none of us need to take in our neighbour's washing. " Mind your own business," is a command that might have been spoken by Solomon himself, and the apostle Paul was inspired to write to the Thessalonians, " Study to be quiet, and to do your own business " ; and he and Peter very sternly condemned those who were " busybodies in other men's matters."

So it is not my intention to bid any of you to cease to look to your own affairs ; but, at the same time, I want to remind you that we cannot, in this world, live altogether to ourselves. He who is most bent upon minding his own business cannot help knowing that his next-door neighbour has something to do with his garden. Even if he looks diligently after his own plot, thistle seeds from the left and the right may blow over into his garden, and trouble will come to him from the very fact that he has neighbours. Our dwelling-houses, in this life, are not all detached ; many of us have to live in streets ; and if our neighbour's house is on fire, it is not at all unlikely that the flames may spread to our dwelling. Let us never be so concerned about our own interests as to be selfish ; for, even if we try to be wholly wrapped up in ourselves, we shall be compelled to notice the actions of others, with whom we are more or less intimately linked, whether we wish to do so, or not. Hence, the message of the text is necessary, not to take us away from our own duty, but to help us to see that we are not " partakers of other men's sins."

The connection in which this text stands must be noticed. Timothy was exhorted by Paul to " lay hands suddenly on no man." There were certain upstarts who wrongly thought that they could preach, and there were others who thought that they could rule in the churches. These persons probably gained a few or many partisans to support their claims. There were some of their relatives, in the church, who thought a great deal of their sons, or brothers, or uncles, or cousins, or there were friends who heard some man speak, on a certain occasion, with considerable fluency, and being unwise, they judged him to be a man of master-mind, and would have put him into the front rank of the army at once if the power to do so had rested with them. Paul tells Timothy, whom he had sent to exercise a general oversight over the officers and members of the church, not to be in a hurry to lay his hands upon these men, so as to endorse their claims, but to let them wait a while until they were tried and tested ; because, if he allowed them to take office in the church, and they committed faults or follies, he would be responsible for them, and everybody would say, " We wonder that Timothy should have sent out such men as these." So he was bidden to be cautious, lest he should become, in any way, " a partaker of other men's sins." None of us are exactly in Timothy's position ; so we are not likely to fall into the fault against which Paul warned him, at least, not in precisely the same form ; yet the text has a message to us, and we may say to one another, " Be not partakers of other men's sins."

I. I shall first try to show you HOW WE CAN BE PARTAKERS OF OTHER MEN'S SINS ; and, in doing that, I am afraid that the various ways in which we can do this will seem to be very many ; and that, if I am not very careful, you will think that my sermon is like Ezekiel's valley of vision, in which the bones were " very many " and " very dry." I will not be more prolix than I can help ; but, at the same time, I must deal with the subject somewhat in detail.

As to how we can become accomplices in other people's sins,—*the preacher must first say to himself that he will be such a man if he is not true to his trust.* If he shall teach false doctrine, or if, teaching the true doctrines, he shall teach them erroneously ;— if he shall keep back unpalatable truths ;—if he shall allow sin to pass without reproof ;—if he shall see a great deficiency of spiritual life and service, and not point it out ;—if, in brief, he shall be an unfaithful servant of Christ, and his hearers shall thereby be kept in a low state of grace, inconsistent with their profession, and the unconverted shall be hindered from coming to Christ, he will become a partaker of other men's sins. Indeed, I know of no man who is more likely to fall into the fault indicated in the text than a minister of the gospel is. Oh, what grace we need, and what help from on high lest, if we fail in faithfulness to God and our hearers, the doom of souls should be laid at our door, and we should be partakers of other men's sins ! Brethren, pray for us that this may not be our unhappy lot.

> " 'Tis not a cause of small import
>   The pastor's care demands ;
> But what might fill an angel's heart,
>   And fill'd a Saviour's hands.
>
> " They watch for souls for which the Lord
>   Did heavenly bliss forgo ;
> For souls which must for ever live
>   In raptures or in woe.
>
> " May they *that* Jesus, whom they preach,
>   Their own Redeemer see ;
> And watch THOU daily o'er their souls,
>   That they may watch for THEE."

That piece is specially intended for myself and my brother-ministers ; the rest of my discourse will be for you as well as myself. So, next, I must remind you that we can all of us be partakers of other men's sins *by wilfully joining with them in any act of sin, and doing as they do,* like those sinners, mentioned by Solomon in the Book of Proverbs, who said, " Cast in thy lot among us ; let us all have one purse." We must have nothing to do with such men ; God forbid that we should ! If we sin alone, it is bad enough ; but if we sin in company, we have not only to answer for our own sins, but also for the sins of others, at least in part. If hand joins with hand in sin, there is a multiplication of its guilt ; for each man who has helped to lead a fellow-creature into iniquity will have his own transgression increased by the transgression of that other sinner. By their combination, the two will become capable of even greater guilt than they would have committed individually. God save us all from being accomplices in the sins of others by uniting with them in their sinful acts and deeds !

Further, we may be partakers of other men's sins *by tempting them to sin.* This is a most hateful thing, and makes the man who practises it to become the devil's most devoted drudge, servant, and slave.

I have known such tempters of others,—old men who, from their youth up, had sinned in such a shameful way that their very looks were full of lechery. There was a leer about their eyes that was almost enough to destroy all chastity that come beneath their glance ; and their speech was full of the *double entendre*, insinuations, and inuendos, which were almost worse than open profanity. I have known one such walking mass of putrefaction defile a whole parish ; and when I have seen a boy walking with such a demon incarnate, or sitting down with him in the public-house, I knew that the boy's character would be ruined if that vile doctor in devilry could only instruct him in the vices with which he is himself so shamefully familiar. There are such fiends in London, and we could almost wish to have them all buried straight away, for they are Satan's servants spreading wickedness all around them. I do not suppose I am addressing one such dreadful creature ; yet I know that some great sinners of that sort do come within these walls, and they will, of course, be very angry because of my allusion to them ; yet I never knew a thief who was fond of a policeman, and I do not expect or wish to secure the approval of scoundrels whose evil character I am exposing. If, sir, I have described thee, and thou wilt not repent of thy sin, I tell thee that the hottest place in hell is reserved for thee, for thou hast led young men to the alehouse, and taught them to drink the devil's drugs, and to repeat thy foul blasphemies, and to imitate thy scandalous lasciviousness. Yet, ere it is too late, I beseech thee to repent of thy sin, that it may be blotted out by the precious blood of Jesus Christ, God's Son, which cleanseth from all sin ; for, if not, "other men's sins" will cry out against thee for judgment at the bar of the Almighty. I solemnly charge all of you, who have not committed this iniquity, never to do so ; take care that you never say a word which might stain the innocence of a child's mind, and that you never let fall an expression which might, in any way, be the means of leading another person into sin, for it is an easy thing for us to become partakers of other men's sins by tempting them to commit iniquity.

If there is any evil worse than that, I think it is that of *employing others to sin*. It was one of the basest parts of David's great sin that, when he wanted to have Uriah killed, he did not slay him himself, but got Joab to expose him in a position where he was certain to be killed. It is horrible when a man is determined to be dishonest, yet gets someone else to commit the sin for him. It is a shameful thing that there are professedly "religious" employers, who try to get their young men to say across the counter what they know is not according to truth. Are there not some of these so-called "Christian" employers who want young men who are not "too particular" ? Do I not hear, every now and then, of young men who have been found to be too scrupulous, and who have been told that they had better get situations somewhere else ? They objected to describe the goods as their employer wanted them to do, because they knew it would be a lie. They were told, "It is the custom in the trade, and therefore must be so here" ; that is to say, because other persons are liars and cheats, these young men must be knaves, and their master must make money by their lying to his customers. Now, if I meant to thieve or deceive, I would do it myself, I would not employ young men and women, or old ones either, to lie and cheat for me. If any of you have done so, I pray God that He may lead you to repent of such abominable wickedness, for the sin is not one half theirs and the other half yours ; it is partly theirs, but it is far more yours, if they are doing wrong at your bidding. God save us all from being "partakers of other men's sins" in that way !

Some commit this great crime *by driving other men into sin*, by the fears which they have inspired, or by oppressing them in their wages, or by setting them to do what must involve them in sin. I remember the case of a man who was employed where it was well known that some of the parcels which he collected on his way, and carried to their destination, would never be booked by him, but the price paid for the carriage would be secretly dropped into his own pocket. The man's wages were so small that nobody, unless an idiot, ever believed that he lived on them ; so, tacitly, the understanding was that the man would sure to pilfer on his own account, so his wages were cut down below the point at which he could earn an honest living. I fear that there are many men who are dishonest for this reason ; I will not excuse them, but I hope that, if they are ever sent to prison for stealing, their masters will be sent with them, for they are equally guilty.

Yet again, we may become partakers of the sins of the others *by a misuse of our position over them*. This is especially the case with parents. When a father is a man of loose habits, if his son follows his evil example, who is to blame ? If a drunken father sees his child become a drunkard, whose fault is it ? If he is a swearer, and his son uses profane language, who taught the boy those oaths ? Is not the guilt of that swearing largely the father's ? "Oh !" say some of you, "we would not teach our children either drunkenness or profanity." Yet you are not yourselves Christians ; you may be moral and truthful, and so on, but you are not Christians ; and if your children are not converted, will they not say, "Our father never was converted, so why should we be ?" "But we always take them to a place of worship." I know you do, and your children say, "Father goes to a place of worship, but he does not believe in Christ, and he never prays" ; so, if they grow up in the same way, who is to blame ? You say that you trust they will not do so ; then ask the Lord to make you a Christian, for then it will be more likely that your children also will be Christians. When you blame your children for wrong-doing, you ought to blame yourselves even more ; for, after all, what are they doing but what you yourself are doing ? Plato, the philosopher, one day saw a boy in the street behaving in a very shameful manner, so he walked straight into the house where the boy's father lived, and began to beat him. When he said to Plato, "Why do you beat me ?" the philosopher replied, "I found your boy doing wrong ; I did not beat him, but I beat you, for he must have learnt it from you, or else it was your fault because you did not exercise proper discipline upon him at home." Have you never felt, when you have seen the faults of your own children, that you ought to lay the rod on your own back because, in some way or other, you were an accomplice in your children's sins ? How much of the ruin of many children's souls lies at their parents' door ! How sad it is that, in many cases, the influence of the mother and father is damning to their children ! Men and women, who have boys and girls at home who are very dear to you, can you bear the thought that you may, one day, have to say, " Our unchristian example has ruined our own children " ?

" Oh, but we are members of the church," say some. Yes, I know you are ; yet I speak to you as well as to others, for there are some of you who are bringing up your children in an improper manner. I do not see how they can be expected to love religion when they see your own household ordered so badly, or not ordered at all. The professor of religion, who does not live consistently with his profession, does more injury to the cause of Christ than a non-professor does. There are some who hang out the sign of " The Angel," but the devil keeps the inn. Someone has truly said that many a man's house is like Noah's ark in that it is pitched within and without with pitch. There is pitch in the dining-room,—gluttony and drunkenness ; and pitch in the bed-chamber,—lasciviousness and wantonness ; pitch in the drawing-room,—talk which is not even fit for the stables ; and pitch in the shop, for much that is " dirty " goes on there ; how can anyone expect good children to come out of such a house as that ? May none of us, like Eli, be accomplices in our children's sins through neglecting to rebuke them, or like David, through our evil example leading them into sin ! On the contrary, let us pray for them, as Abraham cried to the Lord, " O that Ishmael might live before thee ! " I like to present to God the petitions and pleas which are so well worded in that hymn in " Our Own Hymn Book " which is attributed to Rowland Hill—

" Thou, who a tender Parent art,
    Regard a parent's plea :
Our offspring, with an anxious heart,
    We now commend to Thee.

" Our *children* are our greatest care,
    A charge which Thou hast given :
In all Thy graces let them share,
    And all the joys of heaven.

" If a *centurion* could succeed,
    Who for his *servant* cried ;
Wilt Thou refuse to hear us plead
    For those so near allied ?

" On us Thou hast bestow'd Thy grace,
    Be to our *children* kind ;
Among Thy saints give *them* a place,
    And leave not *one* behind."

The injunction of the text of course applies, in a measure to the teacher of a class as well as the to parent of a family. If the teacher is inconsistent, and his scholars imitate him, the guilt of their wrong-doing will, at least in part, rest upon the teacher. The same principle applies to all persons who are in positions of the influence in the land. If I were preaching to the House of Commons and the House of Lords, I should probably have to say some things which they would not wish to hear again. Certain " honourable gentlemen " and " noble lords " talk very glibly about the necessity for the nation to be religious, yet their lives are not remarkably religious, so their talk is all hypocritical, and great sin lies at their door. God will certainly punish princes and so-called " nobles " if their example is not such as the common people can safely follow.

But even though we may not be of royal or exalted rank, all of us will become " partakers of other men's sins " *if we set them bad examples*. If they can quote us as having done certain wrong things which they have imitated, we must share in the guilt of their sin ; yet it is always a bad thing to follow a bad example. If I see anyone's example to be bad, it ought not to be a temptation to me ; and I am a partaker of that man's sins if, knowing that he has done amiss, I also do amiss simply because he has done so first. If I know that his course is wrong, I ought to shun the rock on which his bark has been wrecked.

We can also be " partakers of other men's sins " *by countenancing them*, and there are many ways in which that may be done ;—for instance, by associating with ungodly men, as though we did not think there was much harm in them ; and, worst of all, by laughing at and with them when their mirth is not pure fun. I fear that many a wicked man has been hardened in his sin because a professing Christian has laughed at his filthy jests.

We may also be " partakers of other men's sins " *by joining a church that holds unscriptural doctrines, or that does not act according to apostolic precedent*. Some people say, " We belong to such-and-such a church, but we don't approve of its teaching or its practice." What ! you belong to it, and yet you do not approve of its principles ? Out of your own mouth you are condemned. If I unite with a church, whose creed and catechism I do not believe, and whose ordinances I do not practise, I am guilty of my own share in all the error that is there. It is no use for me to say, " I am trying to undo the mischief "; I have no business to be there. If I join a pirate's crew, I shall be responsible for all that is done by the whole crew. I have no business to be on that vessel at all, and I must get out of it at the first opportunity, or even fling myself into the sea, rather than have a share in the pirates' wrong-doing.

But supposing you have joined a church whose doctrines are scriptural, you may be " partakers of other men's sins " if the discipline of the church is not carried out as it should be. If we know that members are living in gross sin, and do not deal with them either by way of censure or excommunication, in accordance with the teaching of Christ and His apostles, we become accomplices in their sin. I often tremble about this matter, for it is no easy task where we count our members by thousands ; but may we never wink at sin, either in ourselves or in others ! May you all, beloved, exercise a jealous oversight over one another, and so help to keep one another right ! And let each one pray Charles Wesley's prayer which we have often sung,—

" Quick as the apple of an eye,
    O God, my conscience make !
Awake, my soul, when sin is nigh,
    And keep it still awake."

Further, we may be " partakers of other men's sins " *by not rebuking them for sinning*, if it be our duty to do so, or *by not doing all we can towards their conversion ;*—for instance, by living in a certain neighbourhood, and never trying to bring the gospel to the people in that neighbourhood, or by not maintaining our consistent Christian walk as the separated people of God. In brief, let each one sing, from the heart, the rest of that hymn from which I began to quote just now,—

" I want a principle within
    Of jealous godly fear ;
A sensibility of sin,
    A pain to feel it near.

" I want the first approach to feel
    Of pride, or fond desire ;
To catch the wandering of my will,
    And quench the kindling fire.

" That I from Thee no more may part,
    No more Thy goodness grieve,
The filial awe, the fleshy heart,
    The tender conscience give.

" If to the right or left I stray,
    That moment, Lord, reprove ;
And let me weep my life away,
    For having grieved Thy love.

" Oh may the least omission pain
    My well-instructed soul ;
And drive me to the blood again,
    Which makes the wounded whole ! "

II. I must not say more upon this part of the subject, lest I should weary you ; so I pass on to ask in the second place, WHY SHOULD WE SEEK TO AVOID BEING PARTAKERS OF OTHER MEN'S SINS ? This will be a sufficient answer,—*Because we have more than enough sins of our own, and cannot also carry other people's ;* and also *because, if we are partakers in their sins, we shall also partake in their plagues ;* and also *because we do other men an injury by being accomplices with them ;* we steel and harden them in their sins.

The weightiest reason of all is this,—we should not be " partakers of other men's sins " *because, by so doing, we should grieve our holy and gracious God,* and no true lover of Christ ought ever to do that. remember what Paul wrote to the saints at Ephesus, " Grieve not the Holy Spirit of God, whereby ye are sealed unto the day of redemption."

III. My next question is,—How CAN WE AVOID BEING PARTAKERS IN OTHER MEN'S SINS ?

And I reply,—Only by the help of God's Spirit. First, *be very jealous about other men's sins.* I wish all parents acted as wisely as Job did concerning his children ; they went to one another's houses and feasted, so Job " rose up early in the morning, and offered burnt offerings according to the number of them all : for Job said, It may be that my sons have sinned, and cursed God in their hearts." O parents, do likewise, for that is the way to keep yourselves from participation in your children's sins.

Next to being thus jealous with a holy jealousy, *be always on the watch lest you should be " partakers in other men's sins."* The man who wants to avoid certain diseases will take care not to go to an infected house. So, go not where sinners go, lest you should catch the infection of their sin. Remember how careful Abraham was not to take anything from the king of Sodom, " from a thread even to a shoelatchet," even though it was his lawful share of the spoils of war. Be ye equally careful concerning even the least sin.

The next way to keep from being an accomplice in sin is *by prayer.* Augustine used to offer a short prayer which I commend to you all, " O Lord, save me from mine other men's sins ! " Put this down among your other confessions, " O Lord, I confess unto Thee mine other men's sins ! I mourn over mine other men's sins, I repent of mine other men's sins, I grieve on account of my participation in other men's sins." This will be a good way of keeping from committing them.

I think I had better close by saying that I do not think we have any of us escaped from the meshes of this sermon ; if we have done so, it is either my fault or the fault of our own consciences. I have tried to fire red-hot shot in all directions, not omitting myself ; and most of us have felt that there was a shot specially meant for us. What had we better do then ? I will call to your minds a verse which we often sing, and which we will again sing almost immediately,—

" There is a fountain filled with blood,
    Drawn from Immanuel's veins ;
And sinners, plunged beneath that flood,
    Lose all their guilty stains."

We are all stained with at least splashes from other men's sins as well as our own ; so let us all go to the fountain, and wash, let us renew our faith in the precious blood of Jesus ; for, if we never had any faith in it before, may God graciously grant it to us now ! If we had rebelled against the Queen, and had been at last subdued by force, and if there had been an Act of Oblivion passed for all who wished to claim an interest in it, perhaps some would say to themselves, " We do not know that we took any great part in the rebellion, yet it may be that we did ; and the safest thing for us all to do is, to put down our names, and so secure the benefit of the Act of Oblivion." So I, as one of the guilty ones, confessing that it is so, desire to say to the great King, " My Lord, I am guilty of sins of my own, and the sins of my children, and sins of my servants, and sins of my neighbours, and sins of my church, and sins of my congregation ;—but Thou hast said, ' I, even I, am He that blotteth out thy transgressions for Mine own sake, and will not remember thy sins.' Thou hast promised to plot out all sin from those who believe in Jesus Christ Thy Son. Lord, I believe in Him, so I claim the benefit of that Act of Oblivion." Dear hearer, will not you say the same ? Will not now obey that divine command, " Look unto Me, and be ye saved, all the ends of the earth " ? Though you have gone to the ends of the earth, yet God says to you, " Look unto Me, and be ye saved." Look ! *Look !* LOOK! It is little that you have to do ; indeed, it is nothing that *you* have to do, for God gives you grace to do all that He requires of you. So trust in Him, rest in Him ; the Lord help you so to do, and then, whatever your sins may have been, though they may have been " as scarlet, they shall be as white as snow " ; though they may have been " red like crimson, they shall be as wool." God bless you, and save you, for His name's sake ! Amen.

Now let us all sing the verse that I quoted just now,—

" There is a fountain filled with blood,
    Drawn from Immanuel's veins ;
And sinners, plunged beneath that flood,
    Lose all their guilty stains " ;—

and let all who can sing it from the heart join in the well-known chorus,—

" I do believe, I will believe,
    That Jesus died for me ;
That, on the cross, He shed His blood
    From sin to set me free."

"LAY HOLD ON ETERNAL LIFE!"

" Lay hold on eternal life."—1 Timothy vi. 12.

PAUL was very anxious about Timothy, his own son in the faith. He loved him greatly and he had much confidence in him ; but still he felt that the work of preaching the gospel was such a responsible undertaking, that he could not be too prayerful for him, nor too earnest in exhorting him to continued steadfastness in those things which he had received. So " the old man eloquent," whose very pen seems to have borrowed some of the burning fervour of his heart, pours out his very soul to young Timothy in the earnest desire that he may find in him a true successor ; one who, when he is compelled to lay down his trusteeship, will take it up, and be faithful to his Lord and to the gospel, when his father in Christ is taken away from him, We cannot be too anxious about our young brethren who are to preach the gospel of the grace of God. Pray for students always. Let them continually be mentioned in your private prayers, that, when those who have borne the burden and heat of the day shall rest with their fathers, God may raise up better men than they, who shall yet more faithfully proclaim His Word.

This passage of Scripture, " Lay hold on eternal life," is suggestive from its connection. In the same verse Timothy is told to " Fight the good fight of faith." From this it is evident that if he lays hold on eternal life, he will have to fight for it ; and that if he has to fight, he can only fight by laying hold upon eternal life with tenacious grip. Every Christian man is a soldier, and no man will war a good warfare unless he lays hold upon eternal life with all his heart and soul. A man may fight the battles of earth with the life of earth, but our warfare is of a different kind ; " For we wrestle not against flesh and blood, but against principalities, against powers, against the rulers of the darkness of this world, against spiritual wickedness in high places." With such foes we can only contend successfully when we are made invulnerable by the reception of the life of God within our souls. In classic story we read of one who was dipped in the river Styx ere he went forth to the battle, so that the arrows of the foe might fall harmless upon him. That fable becomes a fact for us when we " lay hold on eternal life." The fiery darts of the wicked are quenched by our shield of faith.

The whole chapter forms a sort of preface to the text. Three classes of people seem to have existed in the community where Timothy was called to labour, each with different views of the best method of teaching those around them. First of all, there were some who intermeddled with social politics. They told the slaves that they might conspire against their masters, and try to rectify the unquestionable wrongs which existed in that day. Paul desires, as much as anybody could do, that injustice should come to an end, and that slavery especially should be swept off the face of the earth, as it has largely been by the influence of the gospel. But, taught of God, and seeing that it was by the proclamation of the gospel that these evils would be most surely overcome, rather than by any hasty social change ;

he says to Timothy, " Leave that matter alone. Lay hold on eternal life. You are not sent to cleanse the Augean stable of politics, and to set things right socially ; let it be sufficient for you to lay hold on eternal life, and to call upon the people to do the same. Every man to his own calling, and that is yours. Lay hold on eternal life." Many a young preacher to-day, and perhaps some of the older ones, would do well to take heed to this advice of Paul given by the Spirit ; for while every real social improvement, based on the principles of right and justice, must have the sympathy of all Christian men, depend upon it that, in the long run, the surest way to raise men is to preach the gospel to them. This will change their character, and regenerated lives will soon result in altered social conditions.

Round about Timothy, too, there buzzed a set of men full of questions and difficulties, and discoveries of false science, which Paul calls " profane and vain babblings " ; these were in a most unhealthy state, " sick about questionings and disputes of words," as the apostle's language in verse four may be literally rendered. Concerning such he says to Timothy, " Do not answer such wranglings of men corrupted in mind and bereft of the truth. Do not worry yourself about them. Let the bees or the wasps buzz as much as they like ; as for you, lay hold on eternal life. Stick to your business. Go in for the one thing that God has called you, the glorious work of saving souls. Let those who like such questions fight them out to the bitter end ; but, as for you, lay hold on eternal life."

Then Paul had noticed that, at Ephesus, there were certain men who were striving to be rich, certain even of the members of the church who seemed to be sacrificing everything else to gain, counting that gain was godliness, and that if they could get rich they really were the better men for it. But Paul says to Timothy, " Leave money alone. Having food and raiment, let us be therewith content. Your hand is not big enough to lay hold of two things. Therefore, since you can only have one, see that it is the vital thing. Lay hold on eternal life." To use the rough old proverb, " Let the cobbler stick to his last." " Timothy, stick to your business ; lay hold on eternal life ; that is your main concern : ' Whereunto thou art also called and hast professed a good profession before many witnesses.' "

I like this plain dealing of the apostle. He seems to say, " Come to the all-important point, Timothy ; and keep to it. Let others go in for this, and that, and the other ; as for you, set before yourself the highest aim. Say to them, as I wrote to the Philippians last year from Rome, ' This one thing I do ' : ' Lay hold on eternal life.' "

The great complaint which we have to make against many is, that they seem to be looking after the odds and ends, the paraphernalia, the minor affairs of life ; but they do not seem to aim at this point—eternal life. Is it not so in praying ? Is there not much that passes by the name which is not real prayer ? We might often say, " Come to the point, man, and ask of God what you want. Come to real prayer, and downright grips with the angel; wrestle with him, and prevail." Paul seems also to hint that there was in the preaching, even in his day, a great deal that was extraneous, ornamental, superfluous; and so he says to young Timothy "Aim at the centre of the target. Go in for this, the main business, first of all. Lay hold on eternal life."

How much there is of our prayer which is only language; how much of our praise which is only music! How much there is in our churches which is something that may have to do with the betterment of the people, but is not salvation, not winning souls for Christ! How much there is of teaching which may be Christian teaching, but is not the teaching of Christ! But we clearly see here that the apostle focussed everything to this one point, and brought Timothy to this one thing—that he should "lay hold on eternal life"; and having laid hold on it himself, should then set it forth before others with such vehemence and strong emphasis, that they also might be persuaded to lay hold on it, and be saved.

Oh, my dear hearers! what does it matter what I have preached to you unless you get eternal life? What does it matter how I have said this or that to you, unless you have received, at the hand of my Master, that life-giving stream, which shall be in you "a well of water springing up into everlasting life"? With all your getting, I beseech you, get the understanding of the great mystery of godliness, and become wise as to the life which is life indeed.

I am going now to take this exhortation, and press it upon each one here present, asking God to bless it. "Lay hold on eternal life."

I. First, then, WHAT IS ETERNAL LIFE?

In attempting to answer this question, I remark what should be perfectly obvious: it is *a gift of God*, the fruit of a divine operation upon the heart. One of the first works of the grace of God is to put within us eternal life. No man can create it, either in himself, or in his fellow-men. Just as our physical life was bestowed upon us apart from any effort of our own, the divine life cannot be evolved by any device of man: it must be imparted by the Spirit of God. At first, God created man, "and breathed into his nostrils the breath of life; and man became a living soul"; and when, in Christ, man becomes a new creation, the work is as wholly and as really God's. Eternal life is what no man has by nature; for he is dead in sin. No man can earn it; for carnal works cannot purchase a spiritual gift; and if a man toiled for a whole eternity, he would be no nearer the possession of eternal life than when he began. That it does not come by effort is clear; for how shall the dead, by any kind of efforts or effort they could make, attain to life thereby? It does not come by outward ceremonies; these could never purchase that which God bestows freely. Yet how natural it is to the proud heart of man to seek to make payment for that which is to be obtained without money and without price! It is strange that men should expect God to take their gift, when they refuse to accept His. If they would but remember that all their giving cannot enrich God; that they cannot give Him anything that He does not already possess; it would be quite evident to them that eternal life can come in no other way than by the gift of God. It is foolish to try to fill an already full vessel; it is profane as well as foolish to seek to be saved by giving to God instead of receiving from Him, or by anything we can bring to attempt to buy this life eternal. This is to imitate Simon Magus, to whom Peter said, "Thy money perish with thee, because thou hast thought that the gift of God may be purchased with money." Neither with money nor with ceremonies can it be purchased. It is purely and solely the gift of God by Jesus Christ. "The wages of sin is death; but the gift"—the free gift—"of God is eternal life through Jesus Christ our Lord."

> "Life is found alone in Jesus,
>   Only there 'tis offered thee,—
> Offered without price or money,
>   'Tis the gift of God sent free;
>   Take salvation,
>   Take it now, and happy be."

This eternal life, given thus freely, is *a present possession*. "Eternal life" may sometimes be employed to set out the glories of heaven, but not often; it is a thing possessed here. In the day in which we are regenerated we receive the first germs of this life everlasting. When we are born again, it is "not of corruptible seed, but of incorruptible, by the Word of God, which liveth and abideth for ever." It is a gift of God, a gift not reserved for the future, but given now, the moment a sinner believes in Christ. One of the first tokens of eternal life being given is the cry of prayer, and then come repentance of sin, and faith in our Lord Jesus Christ. This is eternal life—the gift of God, and a present possession. Have you received it? I do not ask you whether you know exactly the day or the hour when you received it, but are you alive unto God with a life you had not by nature, but which has been planted in you by God the Holy Spirit?

This life is, in fact, *the life of God in the soul*. The Holy Spirit comes and breathes God's life into dead men. There is nothing everlasting in itself but God, and there is no life that is everlasting except that which comes from the everlasting One. The gift of God is not only the gift God gives, but God is the gift that is given. He it is who breathes into us this eternal life, which is really Christ living in us. He Himself is "that eternal life, which was with the Father, and was manifested unto us." The Holy Ghost comes and dwells in the man. "We will come to him," says Christ, "and take up our abode with him." The Father, the Son, and the Holy Ghost, each, in a certain way, come and dwell within the man; he becomes a temple of the Holy Ghost, and so he is alive unto God.

Again, eternal life is *a life which never dies*. We speak very positively here. Eternal life cannot have an end. If it can come to an end by any process whatever, then it is not eternal. This is as clear as words can make it. The life, then, which God gives to every soul in its regeneration, can never die out. Hear these words of Christ: "My sheep hear My voice, and I know them, and they follow Me: and I give unto them eternal life; and they shall never perish, neither shall any man pluck them out of My hand." We do not teach that if the life of God in a believer were to die out, he could nevertheless be saved. No scripture teaches that. But we teach that if there be the life of God in a man, it is eternal; not only that it is going to be eternal, but that now in its nature and essence it is eternal, and can be nothing but eternal life, and therefore can never come to an end. It may be lessened ; it may be sick ; it may be obscure ; but if it is there, since it is eternal life, it cannot come to an end. If it did, it could by no possibility be correctly said to be eternal life at all. See you, then, what a blessing is yours if you have received the gift of God ? If by grace you have received life through Jesus Christ, you have a life which will never die, a life which will outlast the sun and moon. You will see this world turned to a black coal ; you will see all things else expire ; but your life and the life of God shall run on for ever and ever. Well might Paul urge Timothy, and well may we urge you, to lay hold on such a life as this. So—

> " Take, with rejoicing, from Jesus at once
> The life everlasting He gives :
> And know, with assurance, thou never canst die,
> Since Jesus, thy righteousness, lives."

Once more, this eternal life is *the life that is perfected in glory.* It goes on developing, and matures, even in this world, to a very high degree. There is a very great difference between the new-born babe and the full-grown man, and there is a great difference between the believer who has just received eternal life and that riper saint who has come to the fulness of the stature of a man in Christ Jesus ; but it is the same life. It is the same life that says, " God be merciful to me a sinner," which afterwards says, " I know whom I have believed, and am persuaded that He is able to keep that which I have committed unto Him against that day." It is the same life, but a fuller measure therof. One is life, the other is life more abundant. As certainly as the life eternal begins, even in the tiniest bud, so will it blossom and become fruitful, until it comes to its full perfection in glory. The life of believers in heaven, the life that never sins, the life that is absolute obedience, the life that is undiluted bliss, is exactly the same life that is in the believer now. The same life that God gave him when he first believed is that wherewith he beholds the face of God, without a veil between, as he treads the golden streets of the New Jerusalem.

This, then, is eternal life—a new principle, a divine principle, an inexhaustible, unquenchable, immortal principle. He that hath it, is blessed indeed among the sons of men. He that hath it not, is dead while he liveth.

Having thus considered the nature of this possession, we come back to the question we have asked already : Have we this eternal life ? Have we received it as God's gift ? Is it within our hearts, a lamp burning there, never to be put out ? Do we know its present power and reality, and have we joy therein? Yea, do we delight ourselves in God, who has brought us out of death into life ; out of the region of the valley of the shadow of death into that great light which is the beginning of heaven, the dawn of the day that shall never end ? If we do, let us unitedly lift up our hearts in praise, and say, " Thanks be unto God for His unspeakable gift ! " Can we ever cease to adore His name, since He has bestowed such a treasure upon us ? But if you have not yet become a possessor of it, I beseech you at this moment to hold out your empty hand, and take the boon so freely offered. " And this is the record, that God hath given to us eternal life, and this life is in His Son. He that hath the Son hath life ; and he that hath not the Son of God hath not life."

II. In the second place, the apostle tells us to " lay hold on " eternal life. That is the main point of my present discourse. HOW DO WE LAY HOLD ON ETERNAL LIFE ? There are degrees in the reception of this life, but happy is the man who fully apprehends that for which also he is " apprehended of Christ Jesus." The Spirit of God lays hold of us, in order that we may lay hold on eternal life : how we are enabled to do this, is our present subject for consideration.

First, if you would grasp this gift, *believe in it as true.* The very beginnings of our hope is when the Lord leads us to believe that there is such a thing as eternal life ; and that it is a tangible thing, not a dream or a vision ; but a reality to be laid hold of. I certainly believe in the existence of a thing that I can lay hold upon. If " seeing is believing," laying hold is even a more thorough mode of believing. Believe, then, that there is a higher life than nature ever can create. If unconverted, you do not know anything about this in your own experience ; but there is such a thing. There is a life in Christ, which He can give you. There is life by the Holy Ghost, which He can work in you. He can strip you of those grave-clothes of sin, and raise you from your tomb. The words which Christ once addressed to Martha sound still in our ears : " I am the resurrection, and the life : he that believeth in Me, though he were dead, yet shall he live ; and whosoever liveth and believeth in Me shall never die. Believest thou this ? " Answer this question of my Master, " Believest thou this ? " If thou dost, there is hope that thou shalt yet be a partaker of His grace. Nothing can hinder when He begins to work. Though you feel as if you did not feel at all ; though you seem paralysed, and unable to repent or to believe ; this life shall be given unto you, and it shall be given unto you now, if you look unto Him who was lifted up upon the cross, that " whosoever believeth in Him should not perish, but have everlasting life."

Believe, my brethren, you that have this eternal life, in the power and reality of it ; and whenever Satan tempts you to think that it is a fiction, a dream, a piece of enthusiasm, an idea born of fanaticism, resist him by the plain testimony of the Word of God, and the abundant witness of those who have gone before you, rejoicing in the power of it. Every child of God has times when he questions himself ; but still he can truly say, " I am not what I used to be. I have feelings both of pain and joy that come not of the old life, but of the new, which has come to me by God's gracious gift."

> " Lord, I was dead : I could not stir
> My lifeless soul to come to Thee ;
> But now, since Thou hast quickened me,
> I rise from sin's dark sepulchre."

If any of you have not yet experienced such a change, begin as I have told you, by believing that there is such a thing as eternal life. I wish that you who have not yet obtained this blessing would make a point of regularly attending some place where the gospel is preached, saying, " It is to be had, and I will have it. It is to be had by faith. ' Faith cometh by hearing.' I will be an earnest hearer. ' Hearing comes by the Word of God.' I will take care to read and hear only the Word of God, that, so, faith may come to me, and life may come by faith ; for there is such a thing as receiving a new and spiritual life that shall make me far other than by nature I am. I believe it is true." That is the first way of laying hold.

But you do not lay hold of a thing by simply believing that there is such a thing. You must go farther. *Appropriate it.* There is a book, and I believe that it is there ; but if anybody told me that it was a present for me, and said, " All that you have to do in order to have it is to lay hold upon it," I should understand that he meant, not only that I was to believe in its existence, but that I was to take it up, and carry it home with me. That is how you are to " lay hold on eternal life." Strange as it is, this is a thing which, though it is so simple, we cannot make awakened sinners understand. That eternal life is God's free gift put within their reach, and that they are to take hold of it for their own salvation, seems harder for some to grasp, than if it was the most intricate puzzle. Yet this is, perhaps, the clearest aspect of the great matter of salvation. It was Dr. Chalmers, I think, who used to say, that he had no such comfort in the gospel as when he viewed it as a simple offer on the one side, and a simple acceptance on the other. God gives, and we take. The Lord who has been chastening you, and making you feel your sinnership, and showing you that you are condemned, and only fit to die, says now, " Lay hold on eternal life. Believe in the Lord Jesus Christ. Take Him to be yours. Accept Him as your Substitute, bearing the death justly your due ; and having given His life *for* you, now giving it *to* you. Make the exchange. Christ took your death : take His life. He bore your ill : take His good. Appropriate it. Lay hold on eternal life." When people are sinking in the water, and there is a life-buoy or a rope near, they do not need much exhorting to lay hold upon it, nor any elaborate explanation of the way. They simply grip anything that gives them half a hope of being saved from the devouring deep. Now, soul, thou art not to bring anything with thee. That would be to fill thy hand, and then thou couldst not lay hold of anything else. Thou art to come empty-handed, just as thou art, to Christ, who is set before thee. Be bold enough to take Him, and let Him be thine. Thou needest no worthiness. How couldst thou be worthy of Him ? He gives Himself freely to thine unworthiness and sinnership. Confess these, and lay hold on eternal life ; appropriate it to thyself.

The exhortation means more than that, however. Having appropriated it, keep it. *Hold to it,* and never let it go. Hide it in your heart as a choice treasure ; and, if any would rob you of it, or frown you out of it, or laugh at you because you prize so highly what they so lightly esteem, lay hold on it still more. This is the work of the grace of God, which enables you, first to take, and then to keep it. Oh, what efforts will be made, from within and from without, to get you to give up eternal life ! But here comes in the exhortation, " Cling to it. Hold fast by it constantly. As with a death-grip, grasp it with new energy. If you have held it with one hand, hold it with both hands. Yet more and more lay hold on eternal life."

And then, furthermore, *stay yourself upon it.* According to the text, you have to " Fight the good fight of faith." Every now and then you will get an ugly knock, a bruise, a bleeding wound from your enemy. What are you to do ? Always lay hold on eternal life again, and it will strengthen you, stanch your wounds, and make you once more strong in the day of battle. I would have you think much of this. If you believe in Christ, there is a life within you, like the life of God, which will never die ; a life within you which will bring you to stand before the glorious throne of Christ, " without spot, or wrinkle, or any such thing." Do not, therefore, ever give up hope. Do not be staggered by what you may have to suffer here. In the midst of all the agony of the way, stay your heart upon God, and upon the gift He hath given you. " Lay hold on eternal life." If between here and heaven you could be burned as a martyr every day, it would be worth your while to bear it, laying hold on eternal life.

" The King above in beauty,
  Without a veil is seen ;
It were a well-spent journey,
  Though ten deaths lay between ! "

If between here and heaven you had nothing to bear but the cruelty of men, and the unkindness of the enemies of Christ, you should bear it right manfully, and even joyfully, because you can say. " I know in myself that I have in heaven a better and an enduring substance. Even here I have a life which the world did not give me, and cannot take from me ; therefore I hold to it still, and I comfort myself with this sweet thought, that it is mine, the gift of God to me. It bears me up amid seas of grief. ' My flesh and my heart faileth, but God is the strength of my heart, and my portion for ever.' "

Further, I think that the apostle, by the exhortation, " Lay hold on eternal life," meant, *let other things go.* Here is a brother, lately converted, who has been accustomed to keep his shop open on Sundays. He lives in a street where the best business is to be done on that day, and if he shuts up his shop, he will very likely be a great loser. What should he do ? I thank God that the man has not asked anybody what he should do ; he has done the right thing, and trusted in his God. The apostle seems to say, " Let anything else go, let everything else go ; but lay hold on eternal life. Hold you to that." " Oh, but I should lose a living ! " Yes, but if you lost a living and saved your life, what would you lose ? Have you never heard of one who had a bag of gold on board a ship coming home from Australia ; the ship was sinking, and he went down to his cabin, put as much gold as he could into a belt, and then fastened the belt around his waist ? When he leaped for the boat, and missed it, it was not possible to pick him up, for he sank with the weight of his own gold round his loins. There was no hope for him ; his treasure was his ruin. And many a man, in like manner, is by all his toil but preparing sure destruction for himself ; toiling and working hard only that he may effectually ruin his own soul. Let these things go. " For what is a man advantaged, if he gain the whole world, and lose himself, or be cast away ? " Even for the fleeting life of the body, a man will sacrifice all, thankful if he can get out of the burning house alive, though all his worldly goods be destroyed ; glad to escape from the hands of the brigands, though they strip him of every possession : " All that a man hath will he give for his life." If this be wise for a transient life, how much more for the life which is eternal ! We shall be gainers by losing everything, if by the loss we gain everlasting bliss. Let all that opposes go—friends, kindred, comfort, this present life ; let them all go, if by the sacrifice we may more firmly lay hold on eternal life. To keep that, and hold fast to it amidst the stress of temptation, is the main business of the Christian man. " Lay hold on eternal life.' "

And it means, in my text, more than that. Fight, and as you fight lay hold upon the victory. While you are running for heaven, often *anticipate the joys of heaven.* I think you and I do not go to heaven often enough. "Well," says one, "I thought we should go there when we died." Yes, if you are a believer in Christ, that is secure ; but why not go there now ? The Christian's position is unique : he is in two worlds at once. Our Lord hath quickened us, " and hath raised us up together, and made us sit together in the heavenlies in Christ." Do you not know that the lower ends of all the streets of heaven are near here ? Victory—that is heaven ; well, we even now overcome through the blood of the Lamb. Peace with God—that is heaven ; and at this moment, "Being justified by faith we have peace with God." Holiness—that is heaven ; yes, but we are made holy now by the work of the Spirit of God in our hearts. Communion with God—that is heaven ; but even to-day, " Truly our fellowship is with the Father, and with His Son Jesus Christ." Is it not good sometimes to sit down, and anticipate the day when you will come into your inheritance ? You have heard of the young prince, who, when his father wakened one morning, was found putting on the king's crown. It was awkward in his case ; but your Father will not object to your often putting on your crown. Try it, and see how it fits you. You will have a new song to sing ; begin to sing it here. You will have holy work to do ; " They serve God day and night in His temple " ; serve Him here. Christ is to dwell among us in heaven ; let us know that He dwells among us here. I like that verse of our hymn—

> " I would begin the music here,
> And so my soul should rise :
> Oh, for some heavenly notes to bear
> My passions to the skies ! "

It was said of an old Puritan, that heaven was in him before he was in heaven ; that is necessary for all of us ; we must have heaven in us before we get into heaven. If we do not get to heaven before we die, we shall never get there afterwards. An old Scotchman was asked whether he ever expected to get to heaven ? " Why, man, I live there," was his quaint reply. Let us all live in those spiritual things which are the essential features of heaven. Often go there before you go to stay there. If you come down to-morrow morning, knowing and realizing that heaven is yours, and that you will soon be there, those children will not worry you half so much. When you go out to your business or to your work, you will not be half so discontented when you know that this is not your rest, but that you have a rest on the hills eternal, whither your heart has already gone, and that there your portion is in the everlasting dwellings. " Lay hold on eternal life." Get a hold of it now. It is a thing of the future, and it is a thing of the present ; and even your part of it that is future can be, by faith, so realized and grasped, as to be actually enjoyed while you are yet here. " Lay hold on eternal life."

I have not explained my text so fully or so clearly as I could wish. The life of which it speaks is beyond all language ; but if you will obey the exhortation of the text, that will be the best exposition of it. Let him that hath not this eternal life, believe that it is to be had. Let the man whose heart aches for it, grasp it and appropriate it now ; he need not be afraid that he will be repelled. Let him that hath it, hold it fast as a jewel, for which, sooner than part with it, he would sell house and home. Let him that hath it, enjoy it even now. God help you in this manner to " lay hold on eternal life " !

III. Now I have to finish with just a special word. WHO ARE THE PEOPLE THAT OUGHT CHIEFLY TO LAY HOLD ON ETERNAL LIFE ?

First, *those who are called.* This is the reason the apostle gives to Timothy : " whereunto thou art also called." Beloved, there are some of you that have been called. A boy, who had come upon an errand stood at my window this afternoon. Suddenly he ran away, and I thought, " What made him go ? " I found out that, though I had not heard the voice, some one had called him ; and therefore he was gone. Imitate that boy. Go about this world as men who have been called by a voice that nobody has heard but you. Has God called you to Himself. He means you to come away from your old self, and cease to live the old life : He would have you lay hold on life eternal. God never singles us out in this way unless He means to bless us. He never says, " Seek ye My face," in vain. Has God called you out from among men ? Do you feel what your parents and friends at home do not feel ? Is there a call to you like that call, " Samuel, Samuel," and have you responded, " Here am I ; for Thou didst call me. Speak ; for Thy servant heareth " ? Oh, if God has favoured you with a special and effectual call, then lay hold on eternal life with your whole heart and soul, and never let it go ! Come what may, resolve that you will hold to this gift of God in life, in death, and throughout eternity.

Next, *those who have confessed Christ* ought specially to lay hold on eternal life : " whereunto thou art also called, and hast professed a good profession before many witnesses." Timothy had been baptized, and probably there had been a great number of persons to encourage or watch him as he came forward to confess Christ. This, then, was a double reason why he should hold fast that on which he had laid hold. O you that have named the name of Christ, and have put Him on by that wonderful symbol of death and burial and resurrection, " Lay hold on eternal life." Do not play at baptism and the Lord's supper. Let these be stern, nay, sweet realities to you. Lay hold, not on the symbol alone, but on what the symbol means. Have you been " Buried with Him by baptism into death " ? Then, grasp the soul of the symbol. It is not a mere empty form, or only the badge of a sect, but a picture of the end of the old life of the flesh, dying to the world and sin, that we may rise in " newness of life " to walk before God in the land of the living. Of all men, he who has been baptized should " lay hold on eternal life " ; for, in proportion as his baptism is true, he has no other life to lay hold of, having died and been buried with Christ. Then, also, we come to his table, and there we eat His flesh and drink His blood after a spiritual sort, receiving not merely bread and wine as memorials, but Himself, by faith, into our hearts. " Lay hold on eternal life " ; for profession without eternal life is a fearful mockery. Without eternal life, to come to the Lord's supper will be to eat and drink condemnation to yourself, not discerning the Lord's body. You that have professed Him before many witnesses, " Lay hold on eternal life."

And, especially do I say this to *those who have been consecrated,* like Timothy, to the service of the

Christian ministry. You that have been permitted in any way, even in the Sunday-school, to speak of Christ to children ; you to whom the Lord has committed His gospel, that you may impart it to others, "Lay hold on eternal life." You will never do much in this work unless you have eternal life within your own soul. See to that first. A dead preacher—what is he but a mocker of dead souls ? A dead teacher—what can she teach ? A dead instructor of a Bible-class—how shall the word of life have free course and be glorified ? A blind man discoursing of colours, or a dumb man teaching music, is not more out of place than a man without eternal life trying to tell out the gospel. What can he do ? "Lay hold on eternal life," or else quit this false position ; lest when the Lord comes He should say to you, "What hast thou to do to declare My statutes, or that thou shouldest take My covenant in thy mouth ? " Ah ! I am speaking to myself now, and I will take it home. Will you also open your heart to whatever in the sermon belongs to you ? And when it is done, and my voice is silent to your ear, I pray that you may hear, for many a day, a gentle whisper saying to you, "Lay hold on eternal life."

You, poor sinner, as you go after your follies and amusements, may the call, "Lay hold on eternal life," come to you until you shall obey it, and quit such trifles ! And you, Christian man, when you get into the world, and are tempted to make gain by sin, while you will suffer loss by righteousness, may you hear a voice say, "Lay hold on eternal life " ! And any of you who get the "cold shoulder," and the rough side of men's tongues, when you begin to think that you cannot bear it, hear the voice saying again, "Lay hold on eternal life." Cling to that, for God, for Christ, for eternity, for heaven. The eternal life is the only life worth living for. God help you to live for it always ; and, if you do, it will be of His own grace, and to Him shall be all the glory, for ever and ever ! Amen.

ETERNAL LIFE WITHIN PRESENT GRASP

" Lay hold on eternal life."—1 Timothy vi. 12.
" Laying up in store for themselves a good foundation against the time to come, that they may lay hold on eternal life."—1 Timothy vi. 19.

"LAY hold on eternal life." Observe that this precept is preceded by another—"Fight the good fight of faith." Those who lay hold on eternal life will have to fight for it. The way of the spiritual life is no easy one : we shall have to contest every step of the way along which it leads us. "Contest the good contest of the faith" would be an accurate rendering of the passage ; and a contest it is against the world, the flesh, and the devil. If we live unto God we shall need to war a daily warfare, and tread down the powers of death and hell.

We fight the good fight by firm faith in the Lord our God ; "This is the victory that overcometh the world, even your faith." That fight is the fight of faith, fought for the faith, and by the faith. The article should be inserted, and then the words are—"Fight the good fight of the faith." "Contend earnestly for the faith once delivered to the saints." "Hold fast the form of sound words." It is worth fighting for, even if we come to resistance unto blood. He who dies for the faith has laid down his life in a worthy cause, and he shall find it unto life eternal. We can only hope that we shall be able to live unto God by faith in Him, and faith in the great truths which He has revealed to be the object of our faith. When I say unto you, "Lay hold on eternal life," do not imagine that this is to be done in a dream, or accomplished without arousing your utmost energies, nor even then without that divine assistance which only faith can receive.

As my text follows the command to "fight the good fight of the faith," it teaches us that the best way of contending for the faith is, for ourselves personally to lay hold on eternal life. You cannot defend the faith by mere reasoning : victory does not come through an array of arguments which have been aforetime used by men of learning ; you must yourself possess the inward life, and exhibit the force and power of it in your daily conduct, if you would be successful in the holy war. Men who forget the divine life soon cast away the divine truth. If the life be not in us, we may make what profession of orthodoxy we like, but we shall, in all probability, before long, turn aside, like others, unto crooked ways. Well are the two commands joined together : "Fight the good fight of the faith, lay hold on eternal life." It reminds me of our Lord's words, "I am the way, the truth, and the life."

My brethren, *there is a higher and a better life than that which is known to the most of men.* There is an animal life which we all possess ; there is a mental life which lifts us up above the beasts ; but there is another life as much above the mental life as the mental life is above the mere animal life. The bulk of men are not aware of this, and when they are told of it they do not believe the statement. Men whom they would believe upon any other subject, honest and true men are, nevertheless, regarded as a sort of madmen when they begin to talk about a spiritual life. How should the carnal mind discern that which is spiritual ? for it can only be spiritually discerned. But there is such a life, as many of us know assuredly, and this is the life eternal, which we are bidden to lay hold upon. The life of heaven is none other than the divine life which God's grace imparts to believers here below ; only it is developed and brought to perfection. There is no jerk to the believer in death : his line of life is unbroken. There is a change in his condition, for he drops this mortal body, and those tendencies to sin which cling to it ; but the same life is in him, in the body or out of it, unclothed or clothed upon with his house which is from heaven. His life is the same day, only here it is the dawn, and in glory it is full moon. His life is one, and flows on like a river, widening and deepening until at last it swells into a sea of joyous, perfected life in heaven.

Dream not that any of you will ever obtain eternal life hereafter unless you receive it in this life. Unless you are partakers of it now, tremble for the consequences. Where death finds you eternity will leave you. Thus I read the word of God, let others read as they may. The only laying hold on eternal life that can be practised by us must be commenced now ; it is now brought to light by Christ Jesus in the everlasting gospel ; beware how you put it from you. Grip it now : lay hold of it now ; and hold on to it at all hazards. Do my expressions sound strangely ? Let me remind you of that exhortation of Holy Scripture—" Awake, thou that sleepest, and arise from the dead, and Christ shall give thee light." Once obtained, we may rest assured that this life will not be wrenched from us in the pangs of departure from the body, nor in the day of judgment, nor throughout eternity. " Lay hold on eternal life." I would dwell upon this precept entreating the aid of the Holy Spirit that I may speak of this true life in a living and true manner.

I. " Lay hold on eternal life," that is, BELIEVE IN IT. You cannot lay hold on it unless you know it to be a reality. We do not lay hold on shadows, or fictions, or fancies ; there must be something substantial and tangible for us to lay hold upon. It is needful, therefore, to begin by a realizing faith.

That we may believe in this life, let me say that *Holy Scripture constantly describes men unrenewed by divine grace as being dead ;* they are " dead in trespasses and sins." They " shall not see life, but the wrath of God abideth on them." The natural life of fallen men, though it be cultivated to the highest degree, so that they become sages and philosophers, is nevertheless nothing better than death as compared with the inner life which is called eternal. The life which you possess to-day, if you are ungodly men, will be taken from you. How suddenly none of us can guess ! In this very house we have lately had a solemn reminder of our mortality. But if God gives to you the new life, if there be infused into you the life divine, it is eternal, a living and incorruptible seed which abideth for ever. It is the life of Christ in you : the sap of the undying vine flowing into the branches. Without this heavenly quickening you are dead while you live ; and as the tendency of death is to corruption, you will grow more and more sinful. Men who are dead in trespasses and sins by-and-by proceed to a further stage, and frequently become so corrupt that society itself cries out, " Bury my dead out of my sight." Without the quickening Spirit you will remain in spiritual death for ever.

The Scripture represents believers everywhere as possessing everlasting life. " He that believeth in Him hath everlasting life." Our death in sin has passed away when we have believed in Christ. That first look of the spiritual eye is sure proof that we possess within us the life of God ; and henceforth we are so linked with Jesus that because He lives we shall live also. " When Christ who is our life, shall appear, then shall we also appear with Him in glory."

This life is produced by the operation of the Holy Spirit within the heart. The Lord Jesus said to Nicodemus, " Except a man be born of water and of the Spirit, he cannot enter into the kingdom of God." It is by the new life wrought of the Spirit that we enter the kingdom. The infusion of the new life is the new birth, and the entrance into the kingdom. We are created anew in Christ Jesus ; or, to use another expression, we are quickened and raised from among the dead. Beloved hearers, do you know this change by personal experience ? I know that many here present have passed from death unto life, and I rejoice with them in Christ Jesus.

What a difference this quickening has made in those who have received it ! What a marvellous life it is ! It brings with it new perceptions, new emotions, new desires. It has new senses : there are new eyes, with which we see the invisible ; new ears, with which we hear the voice of God, before inaudible. Then we have a new touch, with which we lay hold hold on divine truth ; then have we a new taste, so that we " taste and see that the Lord is good." This new life ushers us into a new world, and gives us new relationships and new privileges. The Lord Jesus, who makes all things new, sits upon the throne of the soul, and is the centre of new power and rule. Do you know this life ? Some of us confidently bear witness of this life ; but what does this avail to dead men ? There is no change that can be comparable to that which is wrought in men when they are quickened by the infusion of the divine life : it is as though the dead quitted their graves ; and much more than that. The new life is a life of reconciliation ; the possessor of it is at peace with God. We are no longer enemies, but friends of God ; no longer heirs of wrath, but children of the Most High. The spirit of adoption within us cries, " Abba, Father." We delight ourselves in God, who becomes the spring of all our joys, the light of our delights. This delight in God draws us nearer and nearer to Him in communion and fellowship ; and this fellowship with God begets a new character in us like that of God. We are changed into the image of Him in whom we live, and with whom we have communion. The new life has about it a spirituality, an elevation, and a purity which are never found anywhere else. Under its power the man loves the things which are akin to the life of God and he enters into sympathy with God. The spiritual life has instinctive aspirations after holiness, even as the old natural life has desires after evil. It has new pains and new passions ; new joys and griefs. A heavenly fire burns upon the altar of the renewed soul which will utterly consume all that is contrary to holiness. As our God is a consuming fire, so is the life of God within the soul of man : ultimately it will destroy, by the spirit of burning, all the accumulated mass of original and acquired sinfulness. Much of smoke may blind our eyes, and make us weep during the process ; but the end is beyond measure to be desired. Do we know this life ? Does God live in us ? and are our bodies temples of the Holy Ghost ? If not, since the Lord liveth we can never see His face till we live. He is not the God of the dead, but of the living ; and only those that live unto Him in Christ Jesus can be in communion with Him.

I scarcely need to tell you that this life is one of high enjoyment. Truly it is a life of battle and of strife against the old death ; but the life itself is as peaceable as it is pure. The spiritual life has in it all the elements of heaven. There is a fulness of joy about it, inasmuch as it brings us into communion with the Ever-blessed One. On high days and holy days some of us have said, as a dear sister said to me last Thursday night, " I am happy as God Himself can make me." We can say, " God my exceeding joy." The Lord's visits fill us with such calm content and overflowing peace, that we rejoice with joy unspeakable. Those who know this happiness may truthfully be said *to live ;* but those who know it not have missed " the life which is life indeed."

I want you all to get this idea into your heads—I mean all of you who have not learned this fact as yet : there is a life superior to that of common men—a life eternal, to be enjoyed now and here. I want this idea to become a practical force with you. Stephenson got the notion of a steam-engine into his brain, and the steam engine soon became an actual fact with him. Palissy, the potter, had his mind full of his art, and for it he sacrificed everything till he gained his end ; so may you, by the teaching of the Holy Ghost, lay hold upon eternal life as being a blessed possibility ; and may you be moved to seek it ! There is an eternal life ; there is a life of God in the soul of man ; and I trust that you will each one resolve, " If it is to be had I will have it." Henceforth direct your thoughts and desires this way. When the heart begins to value this life, and to sigh after it, it is not far from the kingdom. The quickening Spirit is moving upon the soul when it begins to be restless in its fallen estate, and feels a hunger after higher things. Oh that the Lord Himself would convince you this morning that the life spiritual and eternal is no fancy of enthusiasts, but a literal fact, a matter worthy of your very best consideration ! In this way you will begin to " lay hold on eternal life."

II. But this is not enough : it is merely the door-step of the subject. " Lay hold on eternal life" ; that is to say, POSSESS IT. Get it into your own soul : be yourself alive. What am I saying ? My brethren, this eternal life must come to you ere you will come to it. The Holy Spirit must breathe upon you, or you will remain in your natural death. Behold, He sends me to cry, " Ye dry bones, live ! " and therefore I dare to speak as I have done. Apart from a divine commission I dare not speak thus to you.

How is eternal life grasped ? Well, *it is laid hold of by faith in Jesus Christ.* It is a very simple thing to trust the Lord Jesus Christ, and yet it is the only way of obtaining the eternal life. Jesus saith, " He that believeth in Me, though he were dead, yet shall he live ; and whosoever liveth and believeth in Me shall never die. Believest thou this ? " By faith we have done with self, and all the confidences that can ever grow out of self ; and we rely upon the full atonement made by the Lord Jesus, whom God has sent forth to be a propitiation : it is thus that we come to live. Faith and the new life go together and can never be divided. God grant that we may all lay hold on eternal life by laying hold of God in Christ Jesus !

This life once laid hold upon *is exercised in holy acts.* From day to day we lay hold on eternal life by exercising ourselves unto godliness in deeds of holiness and lovingkindness. Let you life be love, for love is life. Let you life be one of prayer and praise, for these are the breath of the new life. We still live the animal and mental life, but these must be the mere outer-courts of our being : our inner-most life must be spiritual, and be wholly consecrated to God. Henceforth be devotion your breathing, faith your heart-beat, meditation your feeding, self-examination your washing, and holiness your walking. Let your best life be most thought of, and most exercised. Be not content to use your eyes, but practice your faith in God ; neither be satisfied to exercise your limbs in moving your body, but in the power of the new life mount up with wings as eagles, run without weariness, walk without fainting. Lay hold on the eternal life by exercising it continually, and never allowing it to lie dormant.

In laying hold upon it, remember that it *is increased by growth.* Zealously grasp more and more of it. Do not be afraid of having too much spiritual life. Lay hold on it ; for Christ has come not only that we may have life, but that we may have it more abundantly. My brethren, we are none of us what we might be ; let us reach after something higher. " To him that hath shall be given, and he shall have abundance " ; let us not forget this encouraging word of our Lord. You that have much life have the promise of more. We may covet earnestly this heavenly treasure. We are quickened, but mayhap our life is sickly ; let us bask in the beams of the Sun of Righteousness, for He hath healing beneath His wings. Let us lay hold of the fullest measures of eternal life, and go from strength to strength.

Remember that spiritual life *is enjoyed in the fullest sense in close communion with God.* " This is life eternal, to know Thee the only true God, and Jesus Christ, whom Thou hast sent." " Acquaint now thyself with God, and be at peace." Do not think that those gates of heaven cut us off from God ; for they are never shut, and we may enjoy daily fellowship with Him who reigns within. In heaven or on earth we are in the same Father's house : yea, we will dwell in the house of the Lord for ever. We are not in heaven yet, but heaven may be in us. Men do not yet say of us, " He is with God " ; but we know that God is with us. Let us endeavour now to enjoy the life eternal by abiding in the love of Christ. Then do we live indeed when He sups with us, and we with Him. He being raised from the dead, dieth no more ; and we being raised with Him, live with Him, and for Him, and like Him. This Christ-life in us comes to the front and pushes back the lower order of things. We cry no longer, " What shall we eat ? or, What shall we drink ? or, Where-withal shall we be clothed " ; but we cry, " Lord, what wouldst Thou have me to do ? " Oh, to say with Paul, " I am crucified with Christ ; nevertheless I live ; yet not I, but Christ liveth in me : and the life which I now live in the flesh I live by the faith of the Son of God, who loved me, and gave Himself for me " !

III. Thirdly, " Lay hold on eternal life." That is, WATCH OVER IT, guard it, and protect it. Most men will preserve their lives at any cost. Unless they are drunk or mad, they will do anything for dear life : " Skin for skin, yea, all that a man hath will he give for his life." *Let every believer regard the life of God within him as being his most precious possession,* more valuable by far than the natural life. It would be wise to lay down a thousand natural lives, if we had them, in order to preserve the spiritual life. It is infinitely better to suffer than to sin, to lose property than purity. God has given us this priceless jewel, let us guard it as the apple of our eye. The other day we read in the newspapers of two persons in America being found dead from " starvation and cold," and we also read that each of these persons was possessed of a consider-able sum of money. We say, " What fools ! " Men with sums of money about their persons, or hidden away in their rooms, and yet suffering the ills of want till they actually die of hunger—what madness is this ! Are those more sane who injure and dwarf their spiritual life for the sake of intellectual pride, or carnal joy, or the esteem of men ? Is not the spirit infinitely more precious than the body ? Brethren, if we must starve at all, let us starve our bodies, and not our spirits. If anything must be stunted, let it be the baser nature. Let us not live eagerly for this world, and languidly for the world to come. Having the Divine life within us, let us not neglect to feed it and supply its wants. Here is a man that gives up attendance upon religious services in the week because he hungers to increase his business : he buys brass with gold. Another quits the place where he enjoys a gospel ministry to go at a larger salary to a place where his soul will be famished : he barters fine flour for husks. Another goes into all sorts of evil company, where he knows that his character is injured, and his soul imperilled, and his excuse is that it pays. O sirs, is it so after all, that this eternal life which you profess to possess is of trifling value in your eyes ? Then I protest before you that you do not possess it at all. How could you thus play the fool if the Lord had made you wise unto salvation ? " Lay hold on eternal life," for this is the chief good, for the sake of which you may quit inferior things. " Seek ye first the kingdom of God, and His righteousness ; and all these things shall be added unto you." First and foremost, guard beyond everything you life, your real life, wearing ever " the armour of light," " the whole armour of God." Here is a sinking ship, and none can escape but those who can swim. One man grasps a life-belt and puts it about him. Sensible man ! Another carefully makes up his gold into a girdle, and binds it about his waist. Madman ! He is treating himself as cruel wretches treat a dog whom they sink into the water with a stone about him. This last individual is the portrait of professing Christians who will be rich, and thereby drown themselves in perdition and destruction. See the ninth verse of the chapter before us. Hold you first and foremost on to eternal life, and guard it with all your power, as being yourself, your all.

To that end the apostle bade Timothy *flee from those things which are detrimental to that life.* " Thou, O man of God, flee these things." A man that is very careful of his life will not remain in a house where fever has been rife. He looks to the drains, and all other sanitary arrangements, and if these are hopelessly bad he quits the house. No measure of cheapness or convenience will make him risk his life. Have you heard of men in their senses who will hunt for dens of fever and cholera, and wantonly enter them ? On the contrary, visitors are scared from a city or district by the mere rumour of cholera or other infectious disease. You who profess to be men of God must flee these things which are injurious to purity, to truth, to godliness, to communion with God, for these are detrimental to your best life.

Then the apostle tells Timothy to *seek after everything that would promote his eternal life.* He says, "Follow after righteousness, godliness, faith, love, patience, meekness " : seek after that which will exercise and develop your highest life. Frequent those hills of holiness where the atmosphere is bracing for your new-born spirit. I notice how people who are sickly will quit their homes and journey far for health. Not only will they sojourn upon the sunny shore of the Mediterranean, but they will encounter the pitiless cold of the Alps in mid-winter at St. Maritz or Davoust in the hope of restoration. If physicians would only guarantee prolongation of life, men would emigrate to inhospitable Siberia or banish themselves to Greenland's icy mountains. Men will do anything for life. Shall we not be eager to do all that we can to foster our spiritual life ? Christian people, do nothing that will damage your heaven-born lives. Act in this according to the highest prudence.

God help us to lay hold on eternal life and to that end *above all things lay hold on Christ !* We only live in Him : He is our life. To be divided from Christ is as surely death to us as it would be death to the body to be separated from the head. Make Jesus the Alpha and the Omega of your existence, for without Him you can do nothing, nor even live. " This is the true God and eternal life." To believe in Jesus is to live ; to love Him much is to have life more abundantly. Cling to Jesus. Rest in the Lord, for He is our peace. Dwell on Calvary. Live between the first and second comings of the Lord. Lay hold on eternal life as a drowning man lays hold upon a spar, and will not relax his grasp. It is not a vain thing for you, for it is your life. " He that hath the Son hath life ; and he that hath not the Son of God hath not life " ; let us therefore steadfastly abide in the Son of God, and so know that we have eternal life.

IV. But now, fourthly (and with the same brevity) " Lay hold on eternal life," that is, FULFIL IT. Labour that the time of your sojourning here shall be occupied, not with this poor, dying existence, but with the eternal life. *Fulfil the higher and the eternal life in every position of society.* The chapter opens with advice to servants, who then were slaves. Their earthly life was wretched indeed, but the apostle bids them live, not for this present life, but for the eternal life. Inasmuch as they could glorify God by continuing to bear the yoke, and would not glorify Him by rising in insurrection against their masters, He bade them remain in their position until better times might come. He would have them by divine grace fulfil the relationship in which they found themselves. Christianity is the deadly foe of slavery, but it took time to destroy it, and in the meanwhile believing slaves were bidden to glorify God in their station. And this is what the gospel says to every one of us : Honour your station by glorifying God in it. When the famous Spartan warrior Brasidas complained that Sparta was so small a state, his mother replied to him, " My son, Sparta has fallen to your lot, and it is your duty to adorn it." Christian man, adorn the doctrine of God, your Saviour, in all things. Wherever you are found endeavour in that place to live out eternal life. Be not so anxious to change your position as to use it for eternal purposes. Art thou a preacher ? Seek not popularity by pleasing the times, but seek honour by pleasing God. Art thou a master ? Seek not to use thy position to please self, but to bless thy day and generation. Art thou a servant ? Be not perpetually lamenting because of thy hard work and scant wage, but let all men see what grace can do. The eternal life should gild the lower life as the sun lights up the landscape. It is a sad pity when we let the lower life rise above us ! Shall the horse ride the man ? Shall the bullock drive the husbandman ? Let the position be bettered, if it may be ; but if this cannot be improved, be thou thyself improved, and a greater thing is done. Live not for time, but for eternity. What if I am a servant, yet I am the Lord's freeman : let me live as such. What if I am poor, yet am I rich towards God, and let me enjoy my portion. Lay hold on eternal life all the more eagerly if in this temporal life thou hast little to lay hold on.

Fulfil this better life, also, by *leaving alone those questions which would swallow up the hour.* See how Paul destroys these devourers—" Questions and strifes of words whereof cometh envy, strife, railings, evil surmisings, perverse disputings of men of corrupt minds, and destitute of the truth, supposing that gain is godliness : from such withdraw thyself." He speaks in the end of the epistle of " profane and vain babblings, and oppositions of science falsely so called." We are overdone with these canker-worms at this hour. Brethren, you can go and interfere in all the controversies of the day if you like, but beware of the consequences. You can be a party politician if you like, or you can be a man of culture, loving speculation better than revelation, if you think fit ; but, if you take my advice, you will do nothing of the sort, but " lay hold on eternal life." I like that expression of Mr. Wesley's preachers when they were asked to interfere in this or that political struggle ; they replied, " Our work is to win souls and we give ourselves to it." Oh that churches would listen to this just now ! They are going in for amusements, and the church is vying with the theatre. Oh that we would lay hold on eternal life, and seek the salvation of men. Eternal life in our churches would soon cast out the rubbish which is now defiling them. Jesus in the churches would purify the temple of the puppets as once He cleansed it of the traders. We need to receive anew this conviction : that our one great business here below is to lay hold on eternal life, first making our own calling and election sure, and then seeking to bring others to Christ. Other questions compared with this are mere debates as to tweedledum and tweedledee. Let the potsherds strive with the potsherds of the earth until they break each other in their anger ; but we strive only for the kingdom of heaven, which lies not in trivial things. It is ours to lay hold upon eternal life ; as for the rest, the will of the Lord be done !

Further, the apostle bids us *do this so as to surmount the temptations of selfishness.* He warns us that " they that will be rich fall into temptation and a snare, and into many foolish and hurtful lusts, which drown men in destruction and perdition. For the love of money is the root of all evil ; which, while some coveted after, they have erred from the faith, and pierced themselves through with many sorrows." He whose life's object is to accumulate money is not a Christian. No man can serve two masters ; and if Mammon be his master Christ is not his Master. To prosper in business with the sincere desire of using everything for the honour and glory of God is laudable and proper ; but to make this the end rather than the means is a horrible prostitution and debasement of our energies. To live for this world is to be dead to the world to come. The apostle bids us " lay hold on eternal life " rather than on this life : to gain riches of grace rather than riches of gold. Furthermore, he has a word for us if we become rich—for he supposes that such a thing may be, and that it did happen in his own day. He says :— ' Charge them that are rich in this world, that they be not highminded, nor trust in uncertain riches, but in the living God, who giveth us richly all things to enjoy ; that they do good, that they be rich in good works, ready to distribute, willing to communicate ; laying up in store for themselves a good foundation against the time to come, that they may lay hold on eternal life." As the alchemist was said to transmute brass and copper into gold (though he did no such thing) so there is a real alchemy which can sublime gold and silver into everlasting treasure. These talents are not to be despised, but put out to interest for the Lord. They can be laid by where no rust doth corrupt, and where thieves do not break through and steal ; they can be traded with in a heavenly market, and turned to everlasting gains. We can use them for helping on the work of the Lord, and by distribution to the poor and needy. I would that all men at this hour abounded in almsgiving, but specially those who are followers of the loving Jesus. Regard your transactions from the standpoint of eternity. Weigh what you do, not as it may be thought of by men of the world, but as it will be judged by yourself when you behold in the heavenly country the face of Him you love. I do not want you to have to say when you come to die, " I have had large possessions, but I have been a bad steward. I have had a competence, and I have wasted my Master's goods. All I have done with my wealth was to furnish my house well, perhaps to buy expensive pictures, and to allow myself luxuries which did me more harm than good." I hope, on the contrary, you will have to say, " I am saved by grace alone ; but that grace enabled me to consecrate my substance, and put it to the best uses. I can render up my stewardship without fear. I did not live for the fleeting life which is now over, but for the life everlasting." Brethren, some men spend so much upon themselves, and so little for the Lord, that they seem to me to eat the apple and give Christ the parings : they hoard up the flour and give the Lord a little of the bran. Happy man who can carry out in life what he has dared to say in song—

" All that I am, and all I have,
    Shall be for ever Thine ;
Whate'er my duty bids me give,
    My cheerful hands resign.

" Yet if I might make some reserve,
    And duty did not call,
I love my God with zeal so great,
    That I should give Him all."

The apostle means when he says, " lay hold on eternal life," get beyond to-day and to-morrow ; leap out of this month, and this year ; live for the future ; range eternity. Live not as insects that die in a day, but as men that live for ever. This life is as a prick made on paper by a pin ; it is too small a thing to compare with the everlasting future. The for-ever, whether of misery or bliss, dwarfs this life to nothing.

Once more, let me say, the apostle urges us to fulfil the higher life by sundry arguments. He says, " whereunto thou art also called." Sovereign grace has called us to eternal life : we are elect according to the foreknowledge of God from among men, in order that we may live unto Him. We are bound to make eternal life our first and last consideration ; for God has called us thereto. Be not false to the call. If you are a minister or deacon you have an official call. Be not unmindful of it ; but live up to your high calling. The apostle adds : " and hast professed a good profession before many witnesses."

Many of you did this in your baptism, when as believers you were buried with Christ " by baptism into death : that like as Christ was raised up from the dead by the glory of the Father, even so we also should walk in newness of life." In that sacred act you professed that the old nature was there and then to be regarded as buried, and you would live for Christ and like Christ. Oh, be not false to your solemn vows ; but lay hold on eternal life, and not upon the miserable wretchednesses of the passing hour ! Then the apostle sets before us the great example, " I charge thee in the sight of God, who quickeneth all things, and before Christ Jesus, who before Pontius Pilate witnessed a good confession ; that thou keep this commandment." Christ sacrificed everything for us. He gave *Himself* for us. He laid hold on things eternal ; as for anything here below, He let it slip by for our sakes. Eternity was ever pressing upon the heart of Christ ; for the joy that was set before Him He endured the cross, despising the shame. Therefore, if thou be a Christian, professing to follow Christ, lay hold on eternal life, and let this fill thy grasp.

V.   Last of all, and I have done, EXPECT ETERNAL LIFE. By the two hands of faith and hope lay hold on eternal life as the great reward of the righteous. Look for the crown of life which fadeth not away. The time comes when this mortal life shall be utterly swallowed up in life eternal. Let me suggest to you, my beloved brothers and sisters, that we *think much about the life to come.* We shall soon be there in the endless home, let us send our thoughts thither like couriers in advance. Let the harps of angels ring out their music to our listening ears : let the songs of the redeemed awaken us to unite with them in the praises of our Lord. You will soon be there : anticipate the joy. Put on your white robes by faith, and even if a little imagination should come to the aid of faith it will do no harm. Your heads will soon wear the crown—the crown which you will delight to cast at Jesus' feet. To-day you know the straits of poverty, but you are going where the streets are paved with transparent gold. You now know the aches and pains of this frail flesh, but you are going where perpetual youth and vigour shall cause all pain to flee away. You are passing quickly along the journey, think much of that journey's end. Remember the rest which remaineth, the perfection which is promised, the victory which is secured, the communion which is provided, the glory which is dawning. " His servants shall serve Him, and they shall see His face." Think much of your home : every good child will do so.

When you think of it, and your heart grows warm with the thought, then *count it very near.* Suppose you are to live a comparatively long life, yet no human life is really long. Even to a young man, if he has to look forward to a grey old age, life is but a span. How brief it seems on looking back ! When I remember the brother who died in yonder pew last Sunday, I can but feel how near heaven is to some among us. We have touched the celestial country : one brother has just leaped on shore. The other day,

on a sudden, I saw the white cliffs of Dover. The swift ship had performed the passage so rapidly that the sea had been crossed before I had reckoned on reaching land. There were the cliffs. Just ahead. Brethren, heaven is just ahead ! Run to the bows ! Heaven ahoy ! Do not for ever continue gazing at the misty shores behind you. Look ahead ! You are far nearer than you think to the land of the immortal ! We are within speaking distance of heaven ! The Lord hears our cry, and we hear His promise.

" How near to faith's far-seeing eye
The golden gates appear ! "

In this way lay hold on eternal life by confident expectancy.

Rehearse eternal life ! Rehearse the service and joy of heaven ! They have rehearsals of fine pieces of music : let us have a rehearsal of heaven's harmonies. The thing is practicable. We have often enjoyed rehearsals of temple music in this Tabernacle. In this pulpit I have been within half an inch of heaven : and I hope you know the same nearness in the pews. Let us begin the music here and now. Glorified saints praise the Lamb, let us praise Him : they worship the great God with transports of joy, let us worship with them. They find their all in Jesus ; where else have we anything ? Let our Sabbaths be each of them an antepast of the Sabbath that shall have no end. Thus " lay hold on eternal life."

" Ah ! " says one, " I wish I were already in heaven." Do not be in a hurry. The best expectancy is that which doth with patience wait. Our esteemed brother, Mr. Lockhart, tells a story of one of his members, of the name of Carey—a royal name *that* ! She was very sick and near to die, but she expressed a desire to live, at which he was somewhat astonished, for he knew her to be so well prepared to depart. She wished to stay here a while for a good and laudable reason. There was one thing which she could see here on earth, which she could not see in heaven, and she wished to remain here to see it again and again. " What is that ? " Mr. Lockhart asked. " It is the tear of repentance on the sinner's cheek : I want to see a great many more of those before I go home." And so do I. O my unconverted hearers, I would willingly stop out of heaven to weep for you till you weep for sin. To see tears of repentance in all your eyes would be a heaven to me.

My brethren and sisters around me would be willing to wait also, even until Jesus comes, if we could, by our waiting, help to give you repentance. Tears of repentance bedewing the cheeks of sinners are the diamonds of angels and the jewels of saints. Oh, that my beloved helpers may see many drops of the dew of repentance this morning when they come round among you ; and may Jesus see them, and speak peace to repenting hearts. Poor sinners ! we would stop out of heaven for such as you, even as Jesus came out of heaven for such as you. Believe on the one appointed Saviour, and enter into eternal life, and we will dwell in heaven together. The Lord grant it.   Amen.

OUR GIFTS AND HOW TO USE THEM

" Wherefore I put thee in remembrance that thou stir up the gift of God, which is in thee by the putting on of my hands."—2 Timothy i. 6.

I SUPPOSE that Timothy was a somewhat retiring youth and that from the gentleness of his nature he needed to be exhorted to the exercise of the bolder virtues. He is bidden not to be ashamed of the testimony of our Lord, and to endure hardness as a good soldier of Jesus Christ. He is called to the front though his modesty would have kept him in the rear, and he is exhorted to command and teach, suffering no man to despise his youth. Perhaps, also, he was not a man of very vigorous action, and needed every now and then a little touch of the spur to induce him to put forth all his dormant energy and keep himself and his church thoroughly up to the mark in labour for Christ. His was a choice spirit, and therefore it was desirable to see it strong, brave, and energetic. No one would wish to arouse a bad man, for like a viper he is all the worse for being awake ; but in proportion to the excellence of the character is the desirability of its being full of force. The apostle Paul tells Timothy, in his first epistle, not to neglect the gift that is in him, and in the text before us he bids him stir up that gift : in each case he is sounding the trumpet in his ear, and summoning him to intense action.

He speaks of the gift that was conferred by the laying on of his hands, and in the former epistle he connects that with the hands of the presbytery. Now, it was no doubt the custom to lay on hands at the ordination of Christian ministers by the apostles, and there was an excellent reason for it, for gifts were thereby conveyed to the ordained, and when we can find anybody who can thereby confer some spiritual gift upon us, we shall be glad to have their hands laid on our heads ; but empty hands we care not for. Rites cease when their meaning ceases. If practised any longer they gender to superstition, and are fit instruments of priestcraft. The upholding of the hands of the eldership, when they give their vote to elect a man to the pastorate, is a sensible proceeding ; and is, I suspect, all the apostle means when he speaks of the presbytery ; but empty hands it seems to me are fitly laid on empty heads, and to submit to an empty ceremony is the idlest of all idle waste of time. If Paul were here, and could confer a gift, we should rejoice to receive it ; yea, and if the meanest man in Christendom, or woman either, could confer the smallest drachma of grace by the putting on of their hands, we would bow our heads in the lowliest manner ; till then we shall beg to decline submitting to the imposition, or assisting in it. For this reason, and others, we cannot use the text exactly as it stands in addressing this congregation, but leaving out the reference to laying on of hands, we may honestly, without violation of the current of inspiration, proceed to exhort each one of you to stir up the gift that is in you.

There are many kinds of gifts. All Christians have some gift. Some may have but one talent, but all have one at the least. The Great Householder has apportioned to every servant a talent. No single part of a vital body is without its office. True, there are some parts of the body whose office has not been discovered ; even the physician and the anatomist have not been able to tell why certain organs are in the human frame, or what office they serve, but as even these are found to be necessary, we are quite sure that they fulfil some useful purpose. Truly, there are some Christians who might be put in that category : it might puzzle anybody to know what they are capable of ; and yet it is certain they have some charge committed to them to keep, and that, if true believers, they are essential parts of the body of Christ. As every beast, bird, fish, and insect has its own place in nature, so has every Christian a fit position in the economy of grace. No tree, no plant, no weed, could be dispensed with without injury to nature's perfectness ; neither can any sort of gift or grace be lost to the church without injury to her completeness. Every living saint has his charge to keep—his talent, over which he is a steward. A measure of gift is in all of us, needing to be stirred up.

Some have gifts without them rather than within them—gifts, for instance, of worldly position, estate and substance. These ought to be well used, and considering that in these times we have a starving world to deal with, and that one of the great impediments to the spread of the gospel is with some of us the lack of means for the maintenance of those who should preach the word, it does seem a strange thing that professors should lay by God's money and use it as if it were their own. When for our orphans, our students, our colporteurs, and our missionaries, we need funds, how can men love the Lord with all their hearts, and yet keep their thousands cankering at their bankers, or their tens resting in their purses ? They have not learned to provide for themselves bags that wax not old. They do not understand that to keep their money they must give it away, that truly to preserve it they must dedicate it to God. For that which is kept by the miserly for themselves is not really preserved, but wasted. That which is expended in the Master's service is laid up in heaven, where neither moth nor rust can corrupt. But I am not going to speak about that : I have not much reason to speak upon that subject to those who are immediately connected with me, for I have rather to praise you than to upbraid. Most of our dear friends here do serve the Lord with the gifts that are outside of them— not all as we should, but many with more than ordinary liberality, and some up to the full measure of their means, if not beyond them. There are, however, exceptions to all rules : and there are a few who attend this place who need more than a gentle hint to excite anything like generosity in them. But we must go at once to the point in hand ;—" the gift that is *in* you," we have now to speak of.

First, *the gift that may be in each one of us* ; and then, secondly, *how we are to stir this gift up* ; and in conclusion, we will give *reasons for the stirring of it*.

I. First, then, WHAT GIFT IS THERE IN US ? In some here present there are gifts of mind, which are accompanied with gifts of utterance. It is no mean thing, to be able to read the Scriptures and to see their inner meaning, to be able to compare spiritual things with spiritual, and to be so taught in other matters, that we are able to see the hand of God in history, and can upon all such subjects speak to edification. It is not every one who has mind who has also the gift of utterance, but where God is pleased to give to any man mind and mouth, he possesses a gift which he ought abundantly to use. Many a man is mighty in the Scriptures, but not eloquent; when the two things meet, as in Apollos, and are combined with a fervent spirit, a man of God has power indeed. May I suggest that every Christian man here who is possessed of the faculty of eloquent discourse is bound to use it for Jesus Christ. Some young men spend their evenings in debating societies and the like, and I have not a word to say against that, but I have this to say—whatever you may do with this talent in other directions, the Lord who has bought you with His blood if you are a Christian man, has the first claim upon you, and you are bound to use your powers of utterance in His cause. " But I am not a minister!" What do you mean by that? Do you find anything in Scripture about clergy and laity? If so, you have read it with different eyes from mine. There were men called especially to the oversight of the Church and the preaching of the word, but everyone according to his gift had also a call, and there is no man in the Church of God who has ability to speak who has any license to be silent. Not only the golden-mouthed orators, but the silver-tongued speakers—men of the second as well as of the first order—should serve in the gospel of the Son of God. I shall not ask any young man whether he ought to preach, but whether he can prove that he ought not. Every man is bound to tell another who is in danger to escape from that danger. Everyone who has recovered from a dreadful disease is bound to tell others what remedy was made effectual in his case. Nothing can excuse us from, in some way or other, spreading abroad the gospel of Jesus Christ; and, if we have the ability to speak, it will go hard at last with us if we have been silent with our fellow men. The stones in the street might surely cry out against some religious professors who make the Houses of Parliament, the Council-chamber, the Courts of Justice, the Athenæum, or the Mechanics' Hall, ring with their voices, and yet preach not Jesus —who can argue points of politics and the like, but not speak a word for Christ,—eloquent for the world, but dumb for Jesus. From this may God deliver us! If thou hast any gift, young man, come out and use it—or old man either, if thou hast laid it by till late in the day. In these straightened times when the harvest is ripe and the labourers are few, let every man that has his sickle come forth into the field. Let no man say, " I pray thee have me excused," but by the blood that bought you, if ye have tasted of the water of life cry aloud and spare not, and be this your message—"Whosoever will, let him take the water of life freely."

There are numbers of believers who have not the gift of utterance with the tongue, who nevertheless can speak very fluently and admirably with the pen. If, then, you have the gift of the pen, are you using it for Christ as you ought? I want to stir up the gift that is in you. Letters have often been blessed to conversations; are you accustomed to write with that view? Perhaps you are a great contributor to the postal revenue; let me ask you what sort of matter it is with which you burden her Majesty's mails? Do you write letters to your children and friends full of loving testimony to what the grace of God has done for you? If you have not done so, dear friends, try at once. Jesus needs consecrated pens, and in His name I claim your service. The writing of tracts, and the dissemination of holy truth by means of the press, are most important,—any person who has any gifts in that direction should be sure to use them. Why are writers upon religion often so dull, while the world commands talent and vivacity? What thousands of pens are running every day upon the idlest nonsense, and making booksellers' shelves groan with the literature of fiction! Are there none who, with the splendour of diction or in humbler guise, could write interestingly of the gospel, and tell of its power among the sons of men? If there be in the tribe of Zebulun any that handle the pen of the ready writer, let them not keep back from the help of the Lord—the help of the Lord against the mighty.

Another form of gift that belongs to us is influence. We have all of us influence of some sort,—some more, some less. What an influence the parent has. To a great extent you mould your children's lives. Some of us owe what we never can repay to our mothers. What they have done for us shall make us grateful to them even when they shall slumber in the dust. The nurse girl who has the care of little children should be very careful, for a remark she may make without intention may shape the character, —ay, mar or bless the child's character throughout eternity. And you who associate daily with working men—is there enough among Christian masters of earnest zeal to use a holy and affectionate influence among the employed? If classes are alienated one from the other, as it is to be feared they are, is it not because we meet each other just as a matter of business, and that there is little of anything like Christian affection and communion between the one and the other? Indeed some scout the idea as ridiculous, and tell me I know very little of the world to dream of such a thing. I will leave that question to the day which shall reveal all things, and I think I know who will prove to be right. Let every one of us reckon up what influence he has, and having done so, let us ask God's grace that we may use it aright. I shall not go into details here. You are all affecting those round about you for good or evil. As Christian men you are either leading others to Christ even unconsciously, are else you are deadening their consciences, and leading them to think there is not much in religion after all; and surely you would not wish to do that. You have the gift of influence: I would stir you up to use it.

Many of the elder members of the church have another gift, namely, experience. Certainly, experience cannot be purchased, nor taught; it is given us of the Lord who teacheth us to profit. It is a peculiar treasure each man wins for himself as he is led through the wilderness. An experienced Christian is put in the church on purpose that he may guide the inexperienced; that he may help those who are distressed with a word of comfort derived from his own experience of God's helping hand in time of trouble, that he may warn the heedless by the mischiefs he himself has suffered through carelessness. Now, when an experienced Christian merely uses his experience for his own comfort, or as a standard by which to judge his fellow Christians, or makes use of it for self-exaltation as though he were infinitely superior to the most zealous young men, such a man mars his talent, does mischief with it, and makes himself heavily responsible. Dear brethren and sisters, I, who am so young in years compared with many of you, beseech you who have long walked in the ways of godliness to use your experience continually in your visitation of the sick, in your conversations with the poor, in your meetings with young beginners, in your dealings with backsliders, let your paths drop fatness ; let the anointing God has given you fall upon those who are round about you. May you be of such a sort as a certain clergyman I heard of the other day. I asked a poor woman " What sort of a man is he ? " She said, " He is such a sort of man, sir, that if he comes to see you you know he has been there." I understood what she meant : he left behind him some godly saying, weighty advice, holy consolation, or devout reflection, which she could remember after he had left her cottage door. May our venerable friends always have this said of them.

Another gift which many have is the gift of prayer—of prayer with power, in private for the church and with sinners. There be some who have learned by long practice how to knock at heaven's door, so as to get a readier opening of the door than others. Numbers of these have coupled with this the gift of utterance in public prayer. Such dear friends ought not to be absent from the prayer meeting, except when absolute necessity compels. They should not only be content with coming to prayer meetings which are established, but they should stir up the gift that is in them, and try to establish others in neglected places. There was never a period when the church had too much prayer. " The Sacraments," as they are called, may have been unduly exalted, but who has ever unduly exalted prayer. Bible-readings may degenerate into mere discussion, and even preaching into a show of oratory ; but prayer has vital elements about it which survive many an injury. Alas ! Alas ! for churches that have given up prayer meetings. You shall judge of the presence of God by the prayer meeting, as accurately as you shall judge the temperature of the air by the thermometer. It is one of the truest signs that God is with the people when they pray, and it is one of the darkest signs that He has departed when prayer is lacking. You who have sweet communion with God in private, look upon your prevalence on the knee not only as a blessing for yourselves, but as a gift that is bestowed upon you for the good of others.

There is another gift which is a very admirable one. It is the gift of conversation, not a readiness for chit chat and gossip—(he who has that wretched propensity may bury it in the earth and never dig it up again)—but the gift of leading conversation, of being what George Herbert called the " master-gunner " ; when we have that, we should most conscientiously use it for God. There lived some fifty years or so ago a set of great table-talkers, who were asked out to dine because of their lively conversational powers. Now if this be in any of you never waste it in mere pleasantries, but say something worth the saying and aim at the highest results. Remember Jesus was a mighty table-talker, as the Evangelists take care to note. I wish I could with discreet adroitness break in upon a conversation in a railway carriage and turn it round to the Saviour—

turn it round to something worth speaking of. I often envy those of my brethren who can go up to individuals and talk to them with freedom. I do not always find myself able to do so, though when I have been divinely aided I have had a large reward. When a Christian man can get hold of a man and talk to him, it is like one of the old men-of-war laying alongside a French ship and giving her a broadside, making every timber shiver, and at last sending her to the bottom. How many a soul has been brought to Christ by the loving personal exhortations of Christian people who know how to do it ? To be able, like Elijah, to stretch yourselves upon the dead child, to put you hands upon his hands, your feet upon his feet and breathe the life by God's help into the dead—oh, some of you can do this better, perhaps, than those who are called to speak to hundreds and thousands. Do use it if you have the ability ; and try to get the ability if you have it not. Peradventure you possess it, and have not found it out. No unconverted person should come to this place without your speaking to Him ; and as to a person attending the Tabernacle three Sabbath days without being spoken to by some Christian, it ought to be an impossibility, and would be if all were in a right warm-hearted state, earnestly desiring the salvation of others. May God teach us, if we can converse personally with individuals, to furbish up the gift, keep it in good condition, and continually use it.

My inventory of the gifts which are in us is not complete, nor is it intended to be. Each person may have a separate gift. Even the gift to be able to lie still and suffer is not a small one. The gift of being able to be poor and contented is not to be despised. The gift of nursing the sick, or of interesting children, should be lovingly employed, neither ought any talent to be wrapped in a napkin. But, whatever it is, the word is, " Stir up the gift which is in thee."

II. And this brings us, secondly, to the consideration of—HOW WE ARE TO STIR UP OUR GIFTS.

First, we should do it by examination to see what gifts we really have. There should be an overhauling of all our stores to see what we have of capital entrusted to our stewardship. May I ask you for a minute to sit quietly and take stock of all God has given you. Remember you shall assess yourself, for I am sure your manhood, not to say your self-esteem, will not let you put yourself down as utterly without gifts. If somebody were to speak of you depreciatingly, you would very soon defend yourself, and argue for your own capacity in many departments. I would put you on your mettle, and bring you to acknowledge your capabilities. Now think of all the abilities you have, dear brother, dear sister. What has God trusted you with ? Add up each item, and compute the total sum. What trading-money hast thou of thy Lord's ? To whom much is given, of him much will be required. What, then, has been given to thee ? Such an enquiry will help you to stir up the gift that is in you. The self-examination of every mental faculty, every spiritual attainment, every form of characteristic force or individual influence, will be an excellent commencement for a more vigorous course of action. Enquire what you can do, what more you could do, what more you might learn to do, what more you ought at least to attempt. Diminish nothing from the just amount of your possibilities ; and it will greatly tend to stir you up, if you then enquire, " How far have I done what I could do ? How far have I used all that has been committed to me ? How much of my life has been allowed to rust, and how much has been made bright by wear and tear in the service of the Master ? " It is not a pleasant duty to which I have invited you. You would be much more gratified if I asked you to consider some precious promise of the covenant, and certainly I should find it more consolatory to myself, but this is necessary. Sweet things are pleasant, but sharp things are often the more beneficial. Pillows for our heads are not our main desire ; we wish, as soldiers of the Cross, to be found faithful first of all and above all. We shall have to give an account before God. Oh, let us give an account before ourselves now, in the forum of our own conscience, and so stir up the gift that is in us.

The next mode of stirring up our gift is to consider to what use we could put the talents we possess. To what use could I put my talents in my family ? Am I doing all I could for the children ? Have I laboured all I ought for my wife's conversion—my husband's conversion ? Then about the neighbourhood—is there nothing more that I could do for the salvation of my poor godless neighbours ? Perhaps I see them drunken, profane, unchaste, irreligious, full of all manner of disobedience to God, can I not by God's grace uplift them ? They never come to a place of worship : have I done all I could to get them there ? I was not placed in that neighbourhood without an object. If it is a dark part of London, I am put there to be a lamp if I am a Christian. Am I shining, then ? Some people prefer to live where there is light, and for themselves the choice is wise ; but methinks, for usefulness, loving hearts might prefer to live in bad districts that they might do good. Are you doing all you can for Jesus ? Come, answer like an honest man ! Having done so, I have more work for your self-inspection. Will you examine yourself in every relation in which you stand. As a master, stir up your gift in reference to those you employ. As a servant, stir up the gift towards your fellow servants. As a trader, stir up your gift in reference to those with whom you come in contact. Are you a sailor ? Have you stepped in here to-night? What an opportunity you have, my friend, in landing on many shores, of doing something for Christ, here and there and everywhere. Are you a commercial traveller, and do you go to many places ? Surely you might travel for our Lord with gospel wares, to be distributed without money and without price, and yet attend to your own calling none the less. If our churches were in a right state of spiritual health, men would not first say, " What can I do to make money ? " but " What can I do to serve Christ, for I will take up a trade subserviently to that." But if we cannot bring men to that point, we must at least say (to all of you who profess to be Christians at any rate), in whatever condition you are placed, high or low, rich or poor, you should live unto Christ. You should each enquire, " What can I do for the Lord in my present condition ? What peculiar service does my position involve ? " In this way, dear friends, stir up the gift that is in you.

But, next, stir it up not merely by consideration and examination, but by actually using it. We talk of working, but working is better than talking about working : " to get really at it, and to do something for soul-winning and spreading abroad the glory of God, is infinitely better than planning and holding committees. Away with windbags, let us get to acts and deeds. None of us know what we can do till we try. The sportsman will tell you that there may be many birds in a field, but you know not how many till you walk through, and then you discover them and see them on the wing. When the wheel turns you will be able to see the force of the current. You will see the speed of the horse when you put him to his best. Work, work ! and the tool that is blunt will get an edge by being used. Shine, and the light you have shall grow in the very act of shining ! He who has done one thing will find himself capable of doing two ; and doing two will be able to accomplish four ; and having achieved the four will soon go on to twelve, and from twelve to fifty ; and so by growing multiples he will enlarge his power to serve God by using the ability he has.

Does this tire you ? Does my subject seem too much like salvation by works ? Nothing is further from my thoughts, I am not now speaking upon salvation at all, neither am I addressing those who are seeking after salvation ; I am speaking to you who have been saved already by the grace of God. You are saved, and on that point all is done. You are resting in the finished work of Christ. Should it ever seem hard to you to be stirred up to serve Him ? Let the vision of His tearful face come up to you. Behold His thorn-crowned brow ! Let Him turn His back on you, and mark the gashes the Roman scourges made. Look at Him—a spectacle of blood and love ! And is it possible that any service for Him can by you be considered hard ? To burn at a stake ! if we could do it a thousand times, He well deserves that we should make the sacrifice ! To give Him every pulse, and every drop of blood, and every breath we breathe—He well deserves it ; glory be to His name, He merits our all a thousand times over. I shall not fear to press upon you again and again, and again, that you use the gifts which are in you by actual service of so precious a master.

And then, dear friends, in addition to using our gift, every one of us should try to improve it. We have for years endeavoured to stir up the young Christians of this congregation to educate themselves. By our evening classes it is intended that young men who preach in the street may get education in order to preach better the gospel of Christ ; and out of this congregation have gone hundreds whom God has owned as ministers of Christ, and many such are being trained now ; I would have every man put himself in training. I think every man ought to feel, " I have been Christ's man with two talents ; I will be Christ's man with ten if I can. If now I do not thoroughly understand the doctrines of His gospel, I will try to understand them ; I will read, and search, and learn." We want an intelligent race of Christians, not an afflicted race of boasters of culture, mental fops, who pretend to know a great deal and know nothing ; but we need hard students of the word, adepts in theology, like the Puritans of old. Romanism will never do much with people who know the doctrines of the word of God ; it is a bat, and hates sunlight. Every one of us ought to be students and learners, trying to get more ability for usefulness as well as to be built up ourselves in our most holy faith. To the younger members of our churches especially we speak this. Give yourselves to reading, study, and prayer. Grow mentally and spiritually. You teach in the class ; you do well, but could you not do better if you knew more ? And if you address the children in the Sabbath schools we are glad of it, but would you not do that better if you studied more perfectly the truth of God ? Apollos was not ashamed to be taught, nor need the most successful labourer be ashamed to learn. Improve your gift, for that is one way of stirring it up.

And then pray over your gifts : that is a blessed way of stirring them up—to go before God, and spread out your responsibilities before Him. In my own case I have often to cry, " Lord, Thou hast given me this congregation, and O it is hard to be clear of the blood of them all, and to speak with affection, and prudence, and courage to all, so as not to leave one unwarned, unhelped, untaught. Help me, my Lord, that I may leave no one without his portion of meat in due season. Who is sufficient for these things ? Only Thy grace is sufficient for me." It stirs one up to preach with all his might, when he has laid before God in prayer his weakness, and the ability which God has given him, too, and asked that the weakness may be consecrated to God's glory and the ability accepted to the Lord's praise. Should we not do just the same, whatever our calling is—take it to the Lord and say, " Assist me, great God, to live to Thee. If Thy grace in me be only as a handful of meal and a little oil ; make it hold out— make it hold out. It is not much I can do, my Master ; help me to do it well, and to continue stead-fast and unwearied in it." Pray over yourself, as it were : put your whole self upon the altar, and then let the drink-offering be the pouring out of your tears before God in prayer that He would be pleased to accept you, to qualify you, to anoint you, to direct you, and bless you in all that you do. This would be the most excellent manner of stirring up the gift that is in you. O Spirit of the living God, lead all Thy people to downright earnest, and actual service of the Redeemer, and especially work in us to that end.

III. I will not linger longer there, but close with the third observation : WHY IS IT THAT WE SHOULD STIR UP THE GIFT THAT IS IN US. There are many replies to this. One or two will answer our purpose.

We should stir up the gift that is in us, because all we shall do when we have stirred ourselves to the utmost, and when the Spirit of God has strengthened us to the highest degree, will still fall far short of what our dear Lord and Master deserves at our hands. Ah ! what must Jesus think of us when He remembers His own love. Was there ever such a contrast between His furnace heated seven times hotter, and our iceberg spirits ? He spared not Himself, and we are always sparing ourselves. He gives us everything to the last rag, and hangs naked on the cross : we keep almost to ourselves, and count self-sacrifice to be hard. He labours, is weary, and yet ceases not : we are a little weary, and straightway we faint. He continued to preach on, notwith-standing all the ill return men made ; but we take offence and throw up our work, because we are not appreciated as we should be. Oh, the little things which put some workers out of temper and out of heart. Oh, the looks or the not-looks, the words, or the silence, that will make some spirits give up any place, and any service, and any work. " Forbearing one another " seems to have gone out of fashion with many people. " Forgiving one another even as God for Christ's sake hath forgiven you," is for-gotten. Brethren and sisters, if being door-mats for Christ for all the church to wipe their feet upon would honour Him, we ought to think it a great glory to be so used. Among genuine Christians the conten-tion is for the lowest place : among sham Christians the controversy is for the higher positions. Some will ask the question nowadays—" Which is the higher office—that of the elder or the deacon ? " and so on. Oh, what triviality ! When the Master was going up to Jerusalem to die, there was a contention among the disciples which of them should be the greatest ; and so it is with us ; at times when grace is low, our opinion of ourselves is very high, and then our love to Christ is little, so that we soon take affront, and are quick to resent any little insults, as we think them to be, where perhaps nothing of the kind was meant. Beloved, may we be saved from all this littleness of soul !

And remember what obligations we are under to our Master—how we should have been dead in tres-passes and sins but for Him—how we should have been in hell but for Him—how our expectations to-night would have been " a fearful looking for of judgment and of fiery indignation but for Him " ; but we are washed and cleansed, and on the way to heaven, and we owe it all to Him. Therefore let us stir up the gift that is in us, and serve Him with all our might.

Another reason is that these are stirring times. If *we* are not stirring everybody else is. The church of God, it seems to me, is travelling along the road to heaven in a broad-wheel waggon, and all the world is going its own way by express speed. If men become at all earnest in the cause of God, worldly critics shout out " Fanaticism ! Excitement ! " Did you ever stand on the Paris Bourse—ever hear the raving, raging excitement of those stock-jobbers as they are trying to buy various forms of script ! Nobody says, " Look at these men ! See how fanatical they are ! " No, they expect to see excitement on the Bourse ; but if we were half as excited for God and His gospel, there would be a hue and cry all over the country, " Here's a set of mad-men ! Here's a set of fanatics let loose." Of good Mr. Rowland Hill they said, " The dear old gentleman's too earnest." " Why," said he, " when I was at Wotton-under-Edge I saw a piece of gravel pit fall in upon two or three men, when I was walking by, so I went into Wotton as fast as my aged legs could carry me, and I shouted with all my might ' Help ! Help ! Help ! ' and nobody said ' the dear old man's too earnest.' " Oh, no ; you may be as earnest as you like about saving people's lives, but if their souls awaken your sympathy some lukewarm professor or other is sure to be ready with a wet blanket to cool your ardour. And yet were there ever times in which the wheels of life revolved so swiftly as now. The world marches with giant strides : everybody is up and awake, but the church is asleep to a great extent. For other things men labour, and tug, and toil, and make sacrifices ; for an idea they slaughter their fellow-creatures ; for the unity of a race they fatten fields with blood, and make rivers run with gore ; but to preach Christ, and snatch sinners from the jaws of hell, they require us to be chilled, and insist that we must not be too earnest, we must not go too fast ; we must be prudent, we must be cool ! From " prudence " and " coolness " good Lord deliver us ! From " decorum " and " propriety " (wherein they stand in the way of our winning souls) good Lord deliver us ! And from every conventionality, and every idol that has been set up among us, which prevents our being thoroughly useful and grandly serviceable to the cause of God, good Lord deliver us ! Because these are stirring times, we ought to stir up the gift that is in us.

And then, again, we must stir up our gift because it needs stirring. The gifts and graces of Christian men are like a coal fire which frequently requires stirring as well as feeding with fuel. You must not stir it up too much ; the poker does not give heat ; and, stirring up a man of itself does not make him better ; indeed, it is as injurious to a weak man to stir him up as it would be to an expiring fire in the grate ; but yet there must be stirring, and fires go out sometimes for the want of it. There are times with us when we become dull and heavy, doing little or nothing,—restless, indifferent,—and then it is that we require rebuking. If there be a solid bottom of real grace in us, we only need the poker that we be stirred up, and straightway the fire begins to burn. How I like to stir some of you up ! I remember a dear brother dropping in one Thursday night to hear the word preached—an excellent Christian, but sluggish, and the Lord touched his heart with the word spoken, and he began to preach in the streets of the city where he resides. He has now one of the largest houses of prayer, and God has given him hundreds of souls. He only wanted stirring up. Is there no other brother here, who, hearing this earnest word, shall find it like a live coal from off the altar, touching his lips and moving him to go forth and preach the word, and serve his Master according to his ability. We must then, dear friends, stir ourselves up, because if we do not, we may lose the faculty, and rob ourselves of the power of usefulness. The knife which is not used loses its edge, and the man who does not work for God loses much of his ability to do so in the future.

I shall give you another reason, and that is this. If we will but stir ourselves, beloved, or rather, if God's Holy Spirit will but stir us, we, as a church may expect very great things. I can hardly tell you how comforted I felt last Monday evening. I said on Sabbath day, " The Elders and Deacons will meet to pray, and those of you who love souls and are concerned about them will kindly come too, at six o'clock." I was glad to see many of you who I know love the Lord fervently, and through that warm prayer meeting which we had before our more public gathering, we felt that we had laid hold upon our God. I know there is a blessing coming. I am sure of it. I hear " a sound of a going in the tops of the mulberry trees." The Lord is with us. He never made His people agonize in secret, and join together publicly in deep soul earnestness, without intending to bless them. We might as well fear when the months are warm, that there will be no ripening of the wheat, as to say when Christian's hearts are warm towards God that there will be no conversions. It can't be. Enquiring saints always make enquiring sinners. If we enquire of God for sinners, sinners will soon enquire for themselves. Up, therefore ; up, therefore, beloved ! Bestir yourselves, for God is stirring us.

And remember, there will be a great stir by-and-bye. Business will all end ; politics will be done with, and all the matters in which you are concerned will be closed eternally. What a stir there will be in that day, when we shall stand before the Judgment seat of Christ to give an account of the deeds done in the body ! What a stir about ourselves ! What a stir about others ! Where will they be ? Will they be on the right hand, or on the left ? Shall I see my boys in heaven, or will they be cast out ? What a stir there will be about your husband or your wife ! What a stir there will be about your neighbours ! Think of it ! Think of it, I say, and be stirred now ! If they die as they are, they will be damned : they must be. They must sink into hell ! There is no hope of their escape if they die unsaved. What a stir there will be throughout all the nations in that day ! And, surely, if we look at it in the light of eternity, in the light of that tremendous day when Christ, with clouds, shall come ; we shall feel that there is nothing worth living for but serving God ; that the very core and centre of all life is to bring glory to God by bringing sinners to Jesus Christ. God grant you may live as if you expected to die. We ought always to preach as though we should go out of the pulpit into heaven ; always to pray in that way ; and always to spend every day as if we had not another day to spend. For this we need much of the Holy Spirit's power. But He rest upon His people. May He come and rest upon us now, for Jesus Christ's sake. Amen.

SALVATION ALTOGETHER BY GRACE

" Who hath saved us, and called us with an holy calling, not according to our works, but according to His own purpose and grace, which was given us in Christ Jesus before the world began."—2 Timothy i. 9.

IF we would influence thoughtful persons it must be by solid arguments. Shallow minds may be wrought upon by mere warmth of emotion and force of excitement, but the more valuable part of the community must be dealt with in quite another manner. When the apostle Paul was desirous to influence his son in the faith, Timothy, who was a diligent and earnest student and a man of gifts as well as of grace, he did not attempt to affect him by mere appeals to his feelings, but felt that the most effectual way to act upon him was to remind him of solid doctrinal truth which he knew him to have believed. This is a lesson for the ministry at large. Certain earnest preachers are incessantly exciting the people, and but seldom if ever instructing them ; they carry much fire and very little light. God forbid that we should say a word against appealing to the feelings ; this is most needful in its place, but then there is a due proportion to be observed in it. A religion which is based upon, sustained, and maintained simply by excitement, will necessary be very flimsy and unsubstantial, and will yield very speedily to the crush of opposition or to the crumbling hand of time. The preacher may touch the feelings by rousing appeals, as the harper touches the harp-strings ; he will be very foolish if he should neglect so ready and admirable an instrument ; but still, as he is dealing with reasonable creatures, he must not forget to enlighten the intellect and instruct the understanding. And how can he appeal to the understanding better than by presenting to it the truth which the Holy Ghost teacheth? Scriptural doctrine must furnish us with powerful motives to urge upon the minds of Christians. It seems to me that if we could by some unreasoning impulse move you to a certain course of action it might be well in its way, but it would be unsafe and untrustworthy, for you would be equally open to be moved in an opposite direction by other persons more skilful in such operations; but if God enables us by His Spirit to influence your minds by solid truth and substantial argument, you will then move with a constancy of power which nothing can turn aside. The feather flies in the wind, but it has no inherent power to move, and consequently when the gale is over it falls to the ground—such is the religion of excitement; but the eagle has life within itself, and its wings bear it aloft and onwards whether the breeze favours it or no—such is religion, when sustained by a conviction of the truth. The well-taught man in Christ Jesus stands firm where the uninstructed infant would fall or be carried away. "Be not carried about with every wind of doctrine," says the apostle, and those are least likely to be so carried who are well established in the truth as it is in Jesus.

It is somewhat remarkable—at least it may seem so to persons who are not accustomed to think upon the subject—that the apostle, in order to excite Timothy to boldness, to keep him constant in the faith, reminds him of the great doctrine that the grace of God reigns in the salvation of men. He gives in this verse—this parenthetical verse as some call it, but which seems to me to be fully in the current of the passage—he gives in this verse a brief summary of the gospel, showing the great prominence which it gives to the grace of God, with the design of maintaining Timothy in the boldness of his testimony for Christ. I do not doubt but that a far greater power for usefulness lies concealed within the doctrines of grace than some men have ever dreamed of. It has been usual to look upon doctrinal truth as being nothing more than unpractical theory, and many have spoken of the precepts of God's word as being more practical and more useful; the day may yet come when in clearer light we shall perceive that sound doctrine is the very root and vital energy of practical holiness, and that to teach the people the truth which God has revealed is the readiest and surest way of leading them to obedience and persevering holiness.

May the Holy Spirit assist us while we shall, first, *consider the doctrine taught by the apostle in this text;* and, secondly, *the uses of that doctrine.*

I. Very carefully let us CONSIDER THE DOCTRINE TAUGHT BY THE APOSTLE IN THIS TEXT.

Friends will remember that it is not our object to preach the doctrine which is most popular or most palatable, nor do we desire to set forth the view of any one person in the assembly; our one aim is to give what we judge to be the meaning of the text. We shall probably deliver doctrine which many of you will not like, and if you should not like it we shall not be at all surprised, or even if you should be vexed and angry we shall not be at all alarmed, because we never understood that we were commissioned to preach what would please our hearers, nor were expected by sensible, not to say gracious men, to shape our views to suit the notions of our audience. We count ourselves amenable to God and to the text; and if we give the meaning of the text, we believe we shall give the mind of God, and we shall be likely to have His favour, which will be sufficient for us, contradict us who may. However, let every candid mind be willing to receive the truth, if it be clearly in the inspired word.

1. The apostle in stating his doctrine in the following words, "Who hath saved us, and called us with an holy calling, not according to our works, but according to His own purpose and grace, which was given us in Christ Jesus before the world began," *declares God to be the author of salvation,*—"Who hath saved us and called us." The whole tenor of the verse is towards a strong affirmation of Jonah's doctrine, "that salvation is of the Lord." It would require very great twisting, involving more than ingenuity, it would need dishonesty, to make out salvation by man out of this text; but to find salvation altogether of God in it is to perceive the truth which lies upon the surface. No need for profound enquiry, the wayfaring man though a fool shall not err therein; for the text says as plainly as words can say, "God hath saved us, and called us with an holy calling." The apostle, then, in order to bring forth the truth that salvation is of grace declares that it is of God, that it springs directly and entirely from Him and from Him only. Is not this according to the teaching of the Holy Spirit in other places, where He affirms over and over again that the alpha and omega of our salvation must be found not in ourselves but in our God? Our apostle in saying that God hath saved us refers to all the persons of the Divine Unity. *The Father* hath saved us. "God hath given to us eternal life." 1 John v. 2. "The Father Himself loveth you." It was He whose gracious mind first conceived the thought of redeeming His chosen from the ruin of the Fall; it was His mind which first planned the way of salvation by substitution; it was from His generous heart that the thought first sprang that Christ should suffer as the covenant Head of His people, as saith the apostle, "Blessed be the God and Father of our Lord Jesus Christ, who hath blessed us with all spiritual blessings in heavenly places in Christ. According as He hath chosen us in Him before the foundation of the world, that we should be holy and without blame before Him in love: having predestinated us into the adoption of children by Jesus Christ to Himself, according to the good pleasure of His will, to the praise of the glory of His grace, wherein He hath made us accepted in the Beloved." Eph. i. 3-6. From the bowels of divine compassion came the gift of the only begotten Son: "For God so loved the world, that He gave His only begotten Son, that whosoever believeth in Him should not perish, but have everlasting life." The Father selected the persons who should receive an interest in the redemption of His Son, for these are described as "called according to His purpose." Rom. viii. 28. The plan of salvation in all its details sprang from the Father's wisdom and grace. The apostle did not, however, overlook the work of *the Son.* It is most certainly through the Son of God that we are saved, for is not His name Jesus, the Saviour? Incarnate in the flesh, His holy life is the righteousness in which the saints are arrayed; while His ignominious and painful death has filled the sacred bath of blood in which the sinner must be washed that he may be made clean. It is through the redemption which is in Christ Jesus that the

people of God become accepted in the Beloved. With one consent before the eternal throne they sing, "Unto Him that loved us, and washed us from our sins in His own blood, unto Him be glory"; and they chant that hymn because He deserves the glory which they ascribe to Him. It is the Son of God who is the Saviour of men, and men are not the saviours of themselves.

Nor did the apostle, I am persuaded, forget that Third Person in the blessed Unity—*the Holy Spirit.* Who but the Holy Spirit first gives us power to understand the gospel? for "the carnal mind understandeth not the things that be of God." Doth not the Holy Spirit influence our will, turning us from the obstinacy of our former rebellion to the obedience of the truth? Doth not the Holy Ghost renew us, creating us in Christ Jesus unto good works? Is it not by the Holy Spirit's breath that we live in the spiritual life? Is He not to us instructor, comforter, quickener, is He not everything, in fact, through His active operations upon our mind? The Father, then, in planning, the Son in redeeming, the Spirit in applying the redemption must be spoken of as the one God "who hath saved us."

Brethren, to say that we save ourselves is to utter a manifest absurdity. We are called in Scripture "a temple"—a holy temple in the Lord. But shall any one assert that the stones of the edifice were their own architect? Shall it be said that the stones of the building in which we are now assembled cut themselves into their present shape, and then spontaneously came together, and piled this spacious edifice? Should any one assert such a foolish thing, we should be disposed to doubt his sanity; much more may we suspect the spiritual sanity of any man who should venture to affirm that the great temple of the church of God designed and erected itself. No: we believe that God the Father was the architect, sketched the plan, supplies the materials, and will complete the work. Shall it also be said that those who are redeemed redeemed themselves? that slaves of Satan break their own fetters? Then why was a Redeemer needed at all? How should there be any need for Jesus to descend into the world to redeem those who could redeem themselves? Do you believe that the sheep of God, whom He has taken from between the jaws of the lion, could have rescued themselves? It were a strange thing if such were the case. Our Lord Jesus came not to do a work of supererogation, but if He came to save persons who might have saved themselves, He certainly came without a necessity for so doing. We cannot believe that Christ came to do what the sinners might have done themselves. No. "He hath trodden the winepress alone, and of the people there was none with Him," and the redemption of His people shall give glory unto Himself only. Shall it be asserted that those who were once dead have spiritually quickened themselves? Can the dead make themselves alive? Who shall assert that Lazarus, rotting in the grave, came forth to life of himself? If it be so said and so believed, then, nay, not even then, will we believe that the dead in sins have ever quickened themselves. Those who are saved by God the Holy Spirit are created anew according to Scripture; but who ever dreamed of creation creating itself? God spake the world out of nothing, but nothing did not aid in the creation of the universe. Divine energy can do everything, but what can nothing do? Now if we have a new creation, there must have been a creator, and it is

clear that not being then spiritually created, we could not have assisted in our own new creation, unless, indeed, death can assist life, and non-existence aid in creation. The carnal mind does not assist the Spirit of God in new creating a man, but altogether regeneration is the work of God the Holy Ghost, and the work of renewal is from His unassisted power. Father, Son, and Spirit we then adore, and putting these thoughts together, we would humbly prostrate ourselves at the foot of the throne of the august Majesty, and acknowledge that if saved He alone hath saved us, and unto Him be the glory.

2. We next remark that grace is in this verse rendered conspicuous when we see that *God pursues a singular method,* "Who hath saved us, and called us." The peculiarity of the manner lies in three things—first, in the *completeness* of it. The apostle uses the perfect tense and says, "who *hath* saved us." Believers in Christ Jesus *are* saved. They are not looked upon as persons who are in a hopeful state and may ultimately be saved, but they *are* already saved. This is not according to the common talk of professors nowadays, for many of them speak of being saved when they come to die; but it is according to the usage of Scripture to speak of us who *are* saved. Be it known this morning that every man and woman here is either saved at this present moment or lost, and that salvation is not a blessing to be enjoyed upon the dying bed and to be sung of in a future state above, but a matter to be obtained, received, promised and enjoyed now. God hath saved His saints, mark, not partly saved them, but perfectly saved them. The Christian is perfectly saved *in God's purpose;* God has ordained him unto salvation, and that purpose is complete. He is saved also as to the *price which has been paid for him;* for this is done not in part but in whole. The substitutionary work which Christ has offered is not a certain proportion of the work to be done, but "it is finished" was the cry of the Saviour ere He died. The believer is also perfectly saved *in His covenant Head,* for as we were utterly lost as soon as ever Adam fell, before we had committed any actual sin, so every man in Christ was saved in the second Adam when He finished His work. The Saviour completed His work, and in the sense in which Paul uses that expression, "He hath saved us." This completeness is one peculiarity —we must mark another. I want you to notice the *order* as well as the completeness; "who hath saved us and called us." What! saved us before He called us? Yes, so the text says. But is a man saved before he is called by grace? Not in his own experience, not as far as the work of the Holy Spirit goes, but he is saved in God's purpose, in Christ's redemption, and in his relationship to his covenant Head; and he is saved, moreover, in this respect, that the work of his salvation is done, and he has only to receive it as a finished work. In the olden times of imprisonment for debt, it would have been quite correct for you to step into the cell of a debtor and say to him, I have freed you, if you had paid his debts and obtained an order for his discharge. Well, but he is still in prison. Yes; but you really liberated him as soon as you paid his debts. It is true he was still in prison, but he was not legally there, and no sooner did he know that the debt was paid, and that receipt was pleaded before proper authorities, than the man obtained his liberty. So the Lord Jesus Christ paid the debts of His people before they knew anything about it. Did He not pay them on the cross more

than eighteen hundred years ago to the utmost penny ? and is not this the reason why, as soon as He meets with us in a way of grace, He cries, " I have saved thee ; lay hold on eternal life." We are, then, virtually, though not actually, saved before we are called. " He hath saved us and called us." There is yet a third peculiarity, and that is in connection with the calling. God has called us with an *holy calling*. Those whom the Saviour saved upon the tree are in due time effectually called by the power of God the Holy Spirit unto holiness ; they leave their sins, they endeavour to be like Christ, they choose holiness, not out of any compulsion, but from the stress of a new nature, which leads them to rejoice in holiness, just as naturally as aforetime they delighted in sin. Whereas their old nature loved everything that was evil, their new nature cannot sin, because it is born of God, and it loveth everything that is good. Does not the apostle mention this result of our calling in order to meet those who say that God calls His people because He foresees their holiness ? Not so ; He calls them to that holiness ; that holiness is not a cause but an effect ; it is not the motive of His purpose, but the result of His purpose. He neither chose them nor called them because they were holy, but He called them that they might be holy, and holiness is the beauty produced by His workmanship in them. The excellences which we see in a believer are as much the work of God as the atonement itself. This second point brings out very sweetly the fulness of the grace of God. First : salvation must be of grace, because the Lord is the author of it ; and what motive but grace could move Him to save the guilty ? In the next place, salvation must be of grace, because the Lord works in such a manner that our righteousness is for ever excluded. Salvation is completed by God, and therefore not of man, neither by man ; salvation is wrought by God in an order which puts our holiness as a consequence and not as a cause, and therefore merit is for ever disowned.

3. When a speaker desires to strengthen his point and to make himself clear, he generally puts in a negative as to the other side. So the apostle adds a negative :—" Not according to our works." The world's great preaching is, " Do as well as you can, live a moral life, and God will save you." The gospel preaching is this :—" Thou art a lost sinner, and thou canst deserve nothing of God but His displeasure ; if thou art to be saved, it must be by an act of sovereign grace. God must freely extend the silver sceptre of His love to thee, for thou art a guilty wretch who deserves to be sent to the lowest hell. Thy best works are so full of sin that they can in no degree save thee ; to the free mercy of God thou must owe all things." " Oh," saith one, " are good works of no use ? " God's works are of use when a man is saved, they are the evidences of his being saved ; but good works do not save a man, good works do not influence the mind of God to save a man, for if so, salvation would be a matter of debt and not of grace. The Lord has declared over and over in His word, " Not of works, lest any man should boast." " By the works of the law there shall no flesh living be justified." The apostle in the epistle to the Galatians is very strong indeed upon this point ; indeed he thunders it out again, and again, and again. He denies that salvation is even so much as in part due to our works, for if it be by works then he declares it is not of grace, otherwise grace is no

more grace ; and if it be of grace it is not of works, otherwise work is no more work. Paul assures us that the two principles of grace and merit can no more mix together than fire and water ; that if man is to be saved by the mercy of God, it must be by the mercy of God and not by works ; but if man is to be saved by works, it must be by works entirely and not by mercy mixed therewith, for mercy and work will not go together. Jesus saves, but He does all the work or none. He is Author and Finisher, and works must not rob Him of His due. Sinner, you must either receive salvation freely from the hand of Divine Bounty, or else you must earn it by your own unassisted merits, which last is utterly impossible. Oh that you would yield to the first ! My brethren, this is the truth which still needs to be preached. This is the truth which shook all Europe from end to end when Luther first proclaimed it. Is not this the old thunderbolt which the great reformer hurled at Rome—" Justified freely by His grace, through the redemption which is in Christ Jesus " ? But why did God make salvation to be by faith ? Scripture tells us—" Therefore it is of faith, that it might be by grace." If it had been by works it must have been by debt ; but since it is by faith, we can clearly see that there can be no merit in faith. It must be therefore by grace.

4. My text is even more explicit yet, for *the eternal purpose is mentioned*. The next thing the apostle says is this : " Who hath saved us, and called us with an holy calling, not according to our works but according to His own purpose." Mark that word—" according to His own purpose." Oh how some people wriggle over that word, as if they were worms on a fisherman's hook ! but there it stands, and cannot be got rid of. God saves His people " according to His *purpose*," nay, " according to His *own purpose*." My brethren and sisters, do you not see how all the merit and the power of the creature are shut out here, when you are saved, not according to *your* purpose or merit, but " according to *His* own purpose " ? I shall not dwell on this ; it is not exactly the object of this morning's discourse to bring out in full the great mystery of electing love, but I will not for a moment keep back the truth. If any man be saved, it is not because he purposed to be saved, but because God purposed to save him. Have ye never read the Holy Spirit's testimony : " It is not of him that willeth, nor of him that runneth, but of God that showeth mercy " ? The Saviour said to His apostles what He in effect says also to us, " Ye have not chosen Me, but I have chosen you, and ordained you, that ye might bring forth fruit." Some hold one and some another view concerning the freedom of the will, but our Saviour's doctrine is, " Ye will *not* come unto Me that ye might have life." Ye will not come ; your wills will never bring you ; if ye do come, it is because grace inclined you. " No man can come unto Me, except the Father which hath sent Me draw him." " Whosoever cometh to Me I will in no wise cast out," is a great and precious general text, but it is quite consistent with the rest of the same verse—" All that the Father giveth Me shall come to Me." Our text tells us that salvation is " according to His own purpose." It is a strange thing that men should be so angry against the purpose of God. We ourselves have a purpose ; we permit our fellow creatures to have some will of their own, and especially in giving away their own goods ; but my God is to be bound and fettered by men, and not

permitted to do as He wills with His own. But be this known unto ye, O men that reply against God, that He giveth no account of His matters, but asks of you, " Can I not do as I will with Mine own ? " He ruleth in heaven, and in the armies of this lower world, and none can stay His hand or say unto Him, " What doest Thou ? "

5. But then the text, lest we should make any mistake, adds, " according to His own purpose and grace." *The purpose is not founded on foreseen merit, but upon grace alone.* It is grace, all grace, nothing but grace from first to last. Man stands shivering outside, a condemned criminal, and God sitting upon the throne, sends the herald to tell him that he is willing to receive sinners and to pardon them. The sinner replies, " Well, I am willing to be pardoned if I am permitted to do something in order to earn pardon. If I can stand before the King and claim that I have done something to win His favour, I am quite willing to come." But the herald replies, " No: if you are pardoned, you must understand it is entirely and wholly as an act of grace on God's part. He sees nothing good in you, He knows that there is nothing good in you ; He is willing to take you just as you are, black, and bad, and wicked, and undeserving ; He is willing to give you graciously what He would not sell to you, and what He knows you cannot earn of Him. Will you have it ? " and naturally every man says, " No, I will not be saved in that style." Well, then, soul, remember that thou wilt never be saved at all, for God's way is salvation by grace. You will have to confess if ever you are saved, my dear hearer, that you never deserved one single blessing from the God of grace ; you will have to give all the glory to His holy name if ever you get to heaven. And mark you, even in the matter of the acceptance of this offered mercy, you will never accept it unless He makes you willing. He does freely present it to every one of you, and He honestly bids you come to Christ and live ; but come you never will, I know, except the effectual grace which first provided mercy shall make you willing to accept that mercy. So the text tells us it is His own purpose and grace.

6. Again, in order to shut out everything like boasting, *the whole is spoken of as a gift.* Do notice that ; lest (for we are such straying sheep in this matter)—lest we should still slip out of the field, it is added, " purpose and grace which He *gave us* " —not " which He sold us," " offered us," but " which He gave us." He must have a word here which shall be a death-blow to all merit,—" which He gave us "—it was given ; and what can be freer than a gift, and what more evidently of grace ?

7. *But the gift is bestowed through a medium which glorifies Christ.* It is written, " which was given us *in Christ Jesus.*" We ask to have mercy from the well-head of grace, but we ask not even to make the bucket in which it is to be brought to us ; Christ is to be the sacred vessel in which the grace of God is to be presented to our thirsty lips. Now where is boasting ? Why surely there it sits at the foot of the cross and sings, " God forbid that I should glory save in the cross of our Lord Jesus Christ." Is it not grace and grace alone ?

8. Yet further, a period is mentioned and added —" *before the world began.*" Those last words seem to me for ever to lay prostrate all idea of anything of our own merits in saving ourselves, because it is here witnessed that God gave us grace " before the world began." Where were you then ? What hand had you in it " before the world began ? " Why, fly back if you can in imagination to the ancient years when those venerable mountains, that elder birth of nature, were not yet formed ; when world, and sun, and moon, and stars, were all in embryo in God's great mind ; when the unnavigated sea of space had never been disturbed by wing of seraph, and the awful silence of eternity had never been startled by the song of cherubim—when God dwelt alone. If you can conceive that time before all time, that vast eternity—it was then He gave us grace in Christ Jesus. What, O soul, hadst thou to do with that ? Where were thy merits then ? Where wast thou thyself ? O thou small dust of the balance, thou insect of a day, where wert thou ? See how Jehovah reigned, dispensing mercy as He would, and ordaining unto eternal life without taking counsel of man or angel, for neither man nor angel then had an existence. That it might be all of grace He gave us grace before the world began.

I have honestly read out the doctrine of the text, and nothing more. If such is not the meaning of the text I do not know the meaning of it, and I cannot therefore tell you what it is, but I believe that I have given the natural and grammatical teaching of the text. If you do not like the doctrine why I cannot help it. I did not make the text, and if I have to expound it I must expound it honestly as it is in my Master's word, and I pray you to receive what He says whatever you may do with what I say.

II. I shall want your patience while I try to SHOW THE USES OF THIS DOCTRINE.

The doctrine of grace has been put by in the lumber chamber. It is acknowledged to be true, for it is confessed in most creeds ; it is in the Church of England articles, it is in the confessions of all sorts of Protestant Christians, except those who are avowedly Arminian, but how little is it ever preached ! It is put among the relics of the past. It is considered to be a respectable sort of retired officer, who is not expected to see any more active service. Now I believe that it is not a superannuated officer in the Master's army, but that it is as full of force and vigour as ever. But what is the use of it ? Why, first then, it is clear from the connection that it has a tendency to embolden the man who receives it. Paul tells Timothy not to be ashamed, and he gives this as a motive :—How can a man be ashamed when he believes that God has given him grace in Christ Jesus before the world was ? Suppose the man to be very poor. " Oh," says he, " what matters it ? Though I have but a little oil in the cruse, and a little meal in the barrel, yet I have a lot and a portion in everlasting things. My name is not in *Domesday Book* nor in *Burke's Peerage;* but it is in the book of God's election, and was there before the world began." Such a man dares look the proudest of his fellows in the face. This was the doctrine on which the brave old Ironsides fed ; the men who, when they rode to battle with the war-cry of " The Lord of hosts ! " made the Cavaliers fly before them like chaff before the wind. No doctrine like it for putting a backbone into a man, and making him feel that he is made for something better than to be trodden down like straw for the dunghill beneath a despot's heel. Sneer who will, the elect of God derive a nobility from the divine choice which no royal patent can outshine.

I would that free grace were more preached, because *it gives men something to believe with confidence.* The great mass of professing Christians know nothing of doctrine ; their religion consists in going a certain number of times to a place of worship, but they have no care for truth one way or another. I speak without any prejudice in this matter ; but I have talked with a large number of persons in the course of my very extensive pastorate, who have been for years members of other churches, and when I have asked them a few questions upon doctrinal matters it did not seem to me that they were in error ; they were perfectly willing to believe almost anything that any earnest man might teach them, but they did not know anything, they had no minds of their own, and no definite opinions. Our children, who have learned "The Westminster Assembly's Confession of Faith," know more about the doctrines of grace and the doctrine of the Bible than hundreds of grown-up people who attend a ministry which very eloquently teaches nothing. It was observed by a very excellent critic not long ago, that if you were to hear thirteen lectures on astronomy or geology, you might get a pretty good idea of what the science was, and the theory of the person who gave the lectures ; but that if you were to hear thirteen hundred sermons from some ministers, you would not know at all what they were preaching about or what their doctrinal sentiments were. It ought not to be so. Is not this the reason why Puseyism spreads so, and all sorts of errors have such a foothold, because our people as a whole do not know what they believe ? The doctrines of the gospel, if well received, give to a man something which he knows and which he holds and which will become dear to him, for which he would be prepared to die if the fires of persecution were again kindled.

Better still is it that this doctrine not only gives the man something to hold but *it holds the man.* Let a man once have burnt into him that salvation is of God and not of man, and that God's grace is to be glorified and not human merit, and you will never get that belief out of him ; it is the rarest thing in all the world to hear of such a man ever apostatizing from his faith. Other doctrine is slippery ground, like the slope of a mountain composed of loose earth and rolling stones, down which the traveller may slide long before he can even get a transient foothold ; but this is like a granite step upon the eternal pyramid of truth ; get your feet on this, and there is no fear of slipping so far as doctrinal standing is concerned. If we would have our churches in England well instructed and holding fast the truth, we must bring out the grand old verity of the eternal purpose of God in Christ Jesus before the world began. Oh may the Holy Spirit write it on our hearts !

Moreover, my brethren, this doctrine overwhelms as with an avalanche all the claims of priestcraft. Let it be told to men that they are saved by God, and they say at once, "Then what is the good of the priest ? " If they are told it is God's grace, then they say, "Then you do not want our money to buy masses and absolutions," and down goes the priest at once. Beloved, this is the battering ram that God uses with which to shake the gates of hell. How much more forcible than the pretty essays of many divines, which have no more power than bulrushes, no more light than smoking flax. What do you suppose people used to meet in woods for in persecuting times, meet by thousands outside the town of Antwerp, and such-like places on the Continent, in jeopardy of their lives ? Do you suppose they would ever have come together to hear that poor milk-and-water theology of this age, or to receive the lukewarm milk and water of our modern anti-Calvinists ? Not they, my brethren. They needed stronger meat, and more savoury diet to attract them thus. Do you imagine that when it was death to listen to the preacher, that men under the shadows of night, and amid the wings of tempest would then listen to philosophical essays, or to mere moral precepts, or to diluted, adulterated, soul-less, theological suppositions ? No, there is no energy in that kind of thing to draw men together under fear of their lives. But what did bring them together in the dead of night amidst the glare of lightning, and the roll of thunder—what brought them together? Why, the doctrine of the grace of God, the doctrine of Jesus, and of His servants Paul, and Augustine, and Luther, and Calvin ; for there is something in that doctrine which touches the heart of the Christian, and gives him food such as his soul loveth, savoury meat, suitable to his heaven-born appetite. To hear this men braved death, and defied the sword. And if we are to see once again the scarlet hat plucked from the wearer's head, and the shaven crowns with all the gaudy trumpery of Rome sent back to the place from whence they came—and Heaven grant that they may take our Puseyite Established Church with them—it must be by declaring the doctrines of the grace of God. When these are declared and vindicated in every place, we shall yet again make these enemies of God and man to know that they cannot stand their ground for a moment, where men of God wield the sword of the Lord and of Gideon by preaching the doctrines of the grace of God.

Brethren, let the man receive these truths ; let them be written in his heart by the Holy Spirit, and they will make him *look up.* He will say, " God has saved me ! " and he will walk with a constant eye to God. He will not for get to see the hand of God in nature and in providence ; he will, on the contrary, discern the Lord working in all places, and will humbly adore Him. He will not give to the laws of nature or schemes of state the glory due to the Most High, but will have respect unto the unseen Ruler. " What the Lord saith to me that will I do," is the believer's language. " What is His will that will I follow ; what is His word, that will I believe ; what is His promise, on that will I live." It is a blessed habit to teach a man to look up, look up to God in all things.

At the same time this doctrine makes a man look down upon himself. " Ah," saith he, " I am nothing, there is nothing in me to merit esteem. I have no goodness of my own. If saved, I cannot praise myself ; I cannot in any way ascribe to myself honour ; God has done it, God has done it." Nothing makes the man so humble ; but nothing makes him so glad ; nothing lays him so low at the mercy seat, but nothing makes him so brave to look his fellow man in the face. It is a grand truth : would God ye all knew its mighty power !

Lastly, this precious truth is full of comfort to the sinner, and that is why I love it. As it has been preached by some it has been exaggerated and made into a bugbear. Why, there are some who preach the doctrine of election as though it were a line of sharp pikes to keep a sinner from coming to Christ, as though it were a sharp, glittering halbert to be pushed into the breast of a coming sinner to keep him from mercy. Now it is not so. Sinner, whoever you may be, wherever you may be, your greatest comfort should be to know that salvation is by grace. Why man, if it were by merit, what would become of you ? Suppose that God saved men on account of their merits, where would you drunkards be ? where would you swearers be ? you who have been unclean and unchaste, and you whose hearts have cursed God, and who even now do not love Him, where would you be ? But when it is all of grace, why then all your past life, however black and filthy it may be, need not keep you from coming to Jesus. Christ receiveth sinners, God has elected sinners ; He has elected some of the blackest of sinners—why not you ? He receives everyone that comes to Him. He will not cast you out. There have been some who have hated Him, insulted Him to His face, that have burned His servants alive, and have persecuted Him in His members, but as soon as even they have cried, " God be merciful to me a sinner," He has given them mercy at once. and He will give it to you if you be led to seek lt. If I had to tell you that you were to work out your own salvation apart from His grace it were a sad look-out for you, but when it comes to you thus : black, there is washing for you ! dead ! there is life for you ! naked ! there is raiment for you ! All Undone and ruined ! here is a complete salvation for you ! O soul, mayest thou have grace to lay hold of it, and then thou and I together will sing to the praise of the glory of divine grace.

ASSURED SECURITY IN CHRIST

" I know whom I have believed, and am persuaded that He is able to keep that which I have committed unto Him against that day."—2 Timothy i. 12.

IN the style of these apostolic words there is a positiveness most refreshing in this age of doubt. In certain circles of society it is rare nowadays to meet with anybody who believes anything. It is the philosophical, the right, the fashionable thing nowadays to doubt everything which is generally received ; indeed those who have any creed whatever are by the liberal school set down as old-fashioned dogmatists, persons of shallow minds, deficient in intellect, and far behind their age. The great men, the men of thought, the men of high culture and refined taste, consider it wisdom to cast suspicion upon revelation, and sneer at all definiteness of belief. " Ifs " and " buts," " perhapses " and " peradventures," are the supreme delight of this period. What wonder if men find everything uncertain, when they refuse to bow their intellects to the declarations of the God of truth ? Note then, with admiration, the refreshing and even startling positiveness of the apostle—" I know," says he. And that is not enough—" I am persuaded." He speaks like one who cannot tolerate a doubt. There is no question about whether he has believed or not. " I know whom I have believed." There is no question as to whether he was right in so believing. " I am persuaded that He is able to keep that which I have committed unto Him." There is no suspicion as to the future ; he is as positive for years to come as He is for this present moment. " He is able to keep that which I have committed unto Him against that day." Now, there is a positiveness which is very disgusting, when it is nothing but the fruit of ignorance and is unattended with anything like thoughtfulness. But in the apostle's case, his confidence is founded not on ignorance, but on knowledge ; " I know," saith he. There are certain things which he has clearly ascertained, which he knows to be fact ; and his confidence is grounded on these ascertained truths. His confidence, moreover, was not the fruit of thoughtlessness, for he adds, " I am persuaded " ; as though he had reasoned the matter out, and had been persuaded into it—had meditated long upon it, and turned it over, and the force of truth had quite convinced him, so that he stood persuaded.

Where positiveness is the result of knowledge and of meditation, it becomes sublime, as it was in the apostle's case ; and being sublime it becomes influential ; in this case, it certainly must have been influential over the heart of Timothy, and over the minds of the tens of thousands who have during these nineteen centuries perused this epistle. It encourages the timid when they see others perserved ; it confirms the wavering when they see others steadfast. The great apostle's words, ringing out with trumpet tone this morning, " I know, and I am persuaded," cannot but help to cheer many of us in our difficulties and anxieties. May the Holy Spirit cause us not only to admire the faith of Paul, but to imitate it, and to attain to the same confidence.

Some speak confidently because they are not confident. How often have we observed that brag and bluster are only the outward manifestations of inward trembling—concealments adopted to cover cowardice ! As the schoolboy, passing through the churchyard, whistles to keep his courage up, so some people talk very positively because they are not positive, and make a pompous parade of faith because they desire to sustain the presumption which, as being their only comfort, is exceedingly dear to them. Now, in the apostle's case, every syllable he speaks has beneath it a most real weight of confidence which the strongest expressions could not exaggerate. Sitting there in the dungeon, a prisoner for Christ, abhorred by his countrymen, despised by the learned, and ridiculed by the rude, Paul confronted the whole world with a holy boldness which knew no quailing ; a boldness resulting from the deep conviction of his spirit. You may take these words and put what emphasis you can upon every one of them, for they are the truthful utterance of a thoroughly earnest and brave spirit. May we enjoy such a confidence ourselves, and then we need not hesitate to declare it, for our testimony will glorify God, and bring consolation to others.

This morning for our instruction, as the Holy Spirit may help us, we shall first consider *the matter in question*, that which Paul had committed to Christ ; secondly, *the fact beyond all question*, namely, that Christ was able to keep him ; thirdly, *the assurance of that fact*, or how the apostle was able to say, " I know and am persuaded " ; and fourthly, *the influence of that assurance* when it rules in the heart.

I.   First, then, dear friends, let us speak for a few minutes upon THE MATTER IN QUESTION.

1.   That matter was, *first* of all, *the apostle's deposit of all his interests and concerns into the hand of God in Christ.* Some have said that what Paul here speaks of was his ministry ; but there are many reasons for concluding that this is a mistake. A great array of expositors, at the head of whom we would mention Calvin, think that the sole treasure which Paul deposited in the hand of God was his eternal salvation. We do not doubt that this was the grandest portion of the priceless deposit, but we also think that as the connection does not limit the sense, it cannot be restricted or confined to any one thing. It seems to us that all the apostle's temporal and eternal interests were, by an act of faith committed into the hand of God in Christ Jesus.

To the Lord's gracious keeping the apostle committed *his body.* He had suffered much in that frail tabernacle : shipwrecks, perils, hunger, cold, nakedness, imprisonments, beatings with rods, and stoning, had all spent their fury upon him. He expected ere long that his mortal frame would become the prey of Nero's cruelty. None could tell what would then happen to him, whether he should be burned alive to light up Nero's gardens, or be torn to pieces by wild beasts to make a Roman holiday, or become the victim of the headsman's sword ; but in whatever way he might be called to offer up himself a sacrifice to God, he committed his body to the keeping of him who is the resurrection and the life, being well persuaded that in the day of the Lord's appearing he would rise again, his body having suffered no loss through torture or dismemberment. He looked for a joyful resurrection, and asked no better embalming for his corpse than the power of Christ would ensure it.

He gave over to Christ at that hour *his character* and reputation. A Christian minister must expect to lose his repute among men. He must be willing to suffer every reproach for Christ's sake. But, then, he may rest assured that he will never lose his real honour if it be risked for the truth's sake and placed in the Redeemer's hand. The day shall declare the excellence of the upright, for it will reveal all that was hidden, and bring to the light that which was concealed. There will be a resurrection of characters as well as persons. Every reputation that has been obscured by clouds of reproach, for Christ's sake, shall be rendered glorious when the righteous shall shine forth as the sun in the kingdom of their Father. Let the wicked say what they will of me, said the apostle, I commit my character to the Judge of quick and dead.

So also *his whole life-work* he delivered into the hands of God. Men said, no doubt, that Paul had made a great mistake. In the eyes of the worldly wise he must have seemed altogether mad. What eminence awaited him had he became a rabbi ! He might have lived respected and honoured among his countrymen as a Pharisee. Or if he had preferred to follow the Grecian philosophies, a man with such strength of mind might have rivalled Socrates or Plato, but instead thereof, he chose to unite himself with a band of men commonly reputed to be ignorant fanatics who turned the world upside down. Ah ! well, saith Paul, I leave the reward and fruit of my life entirely with my Lord, for He will at last justify my choice of service beneath the banner of His Son,

and the assembled universe shall know that I was no mistaken zealot for a senseless cause.

So did the apostle resign to the hands of God in Christ *his soul, whatever its jeopardy from surrounding temptations.* However great the corruptions that were within it, and the dangers that were without, he felt safe in the great Surety's hands. He made over to the divine trustee all his mental powers, faculties, passions, instincts, desires, and ambitions. He gave his whole nature up to the Christ of God to preserve it in holiness through the whole of life ; and right well did his life-course justify his faith.

He gave *that soul up to be kept in the hour of death*, then to be strengthened, sustained, consoled, upheld, and guided through the tracks unknown, up through the mysterious and unseen, to the throne of God even the Father. He resigned his spirit to Christ, that it might be presented without spot or wrinkle or any such thing in the last great day. He did, in fact, make a full deposit of all that he was, and all that he had, and all the concerned him, into the keeping of God in Christ, to find in his God a faithful guardian, a sure defender and a safe keeper.

This was the matter, then, about which the apostle was concerned.

2.   But next to this, the matter in question concerned *the Lord's ability to make good this guardianship.* The apostle did not doubt that Christ had accepted the office of keeper of that which he had committed to him. The question was never about Christ's faithfulness to that trust. The apostle does not even say that he was confident that Jesus would be faithful ; he felt that assertion to be superfluous. There was no question about Christ's willingness to keep the soul committed to him ; such a statement he felt it to be unnecessary to make. But the question with many was concerning the power of the once crucified Redeemer to keep that which was committed to Him. Oh, said the apostle, I know and am persuaded that He is able to do that. Mark, dear friends, that the question is not about the apostle's power to keep himself ; that question he does not raise. Many of you have been troubled as to whether you are able to endure temptation ; you need not debate the subject ; it is clear that apart from Christ you are quite unable to persevere to the end. Answer that question with a decided negative at once, and never raise it again. The enquiry was not whether the apostle would be found meritorious in his own righteousness in the day of judgment, for he had long ago cast that righteousness aside. He does not raise that point. The grand question is this, " Is Jesus able to keep me ? " Stand to that, my brethren, and your doubts and fears will soon come to an end. Concerning your own power or merit, write " despair " straightway upon its forehead. Let the creature be regarded as utterly dead and corrupt, and then lean on that arm, the sinews of which shall never shrink ; and cast your full weight upon that omnipotence which bears up the pillars of the universe. There is the point ; keep to it, and you will not lose your joy. You have committed yourself to Christ. The great question now is not about what *you* can do, but about what *Jesus* is able to do ; and rest assured that He is able to keep that which you have committed to Him.

3.   The apostle further carries our thoughts on to *a certain set period*, the keeping of the soul unto what he calls " *that day.*" I suppose he calls it " that day " because it was the day most ardently

expected and commonly spoken of by Christians. It was so usual a topic of conversation to speak of Christ's coming and of the results of it, that the apostle does not say, "the advent," he simply says, "that day." That day with which believers are more familiar than with any other day beside. That day, the day of death if you will, when the soul appears before its God. The day of judgment, if you please, that day when the books shall be opened and the record shall be read. That day, the winding up of all, the sealing of destiny, the manifestation of the eternal fate of each one of us. That day for which all other days were made. Christ Jesus is able to keep us against that day. That is to say, He is able to place us then at the right hand of God, to set our feet upon the rock when others sink into the pit that is bottomless ; to crown us when others shall be accursed ; to emparadise us when sinners shall be cast into hell.

Here was the matter of consideration—can the Great Shepherd of souls preserve His flock ? Ah ! brethren, if you have never searched into that question, I should not wonder but what you may. When you are very low and weak, and heart and flesh are failing, when sickness brings you to the borders of the grave, and you gaze into eternity, the enquiry will come to any thoughtful man, Is this confidence of mine in the Christ of God warranted ? Will He be able in this last article, when my spirit shivers in its unclothing, will He be able now to help me ? And in the more dreadful hour, when the trumpet peal shall awake the dead, shall I indeed find the Great Sinbearer able to stand for me ? Having no merit of my own, will His merit suffice ? From ten thousand sins will His blood alone cleanse me ? Nothing can ever equal this matter in importance ; it is one of most pressing urgency of consideration.

II. It is a happy circumstance that we can turn from it to our second point, to dwell for awhile upon THE FACT BEYOND ALL QUESTION, namely, that God in Christ is able to keep that which we have committed to Him.

The apostle's confidence was that Christ was an able guardian. So He meant, first, that Jesus is able *to keep the soul from falling into damning sin.* I suppose this is one of the greatest fears that has ever troubled the true believer. Have you never prayed that you might rather die than turn aside from Christ ? I know I have, and I have sung bitterly in my soul that verse,

> "Ah, Lord ! with such a heart as mine,
> Unless Thou hold me fast,
> I feel I must, I shall decline,
> And turn from Thee at last."

Now, troubled Christian, remember that your Lord is able to keep you under every possible form of temptation. Ah, say you, the apostle Paul had not the trials I have. I think he had ; but if he had not, Jesus had ; and Christ has ability to keep you under them. Do I hear one say, " I am the only one of my household that has been called by grace, and they all oppose me ; I am a lonely one in my father's house " ? Now, Paul was precisely in your condition. He was a Hebrew of the Hebrews, and he was regarded by his people with the extremest hate because he had come out from among them to follow the Crucified. Yet Paul felt that God was able to keep him, and you may depend upon it, though father and mother forsake, and brothers and sisters scoff, he

whom you trust will keep you also firm in the faith. " Ah," saith another, " but you do not know what it is to strive with the prejudices of an education hostile to the faith of Jesus ; when I seek to grow in grace, the things I learned in my childhood force themselves upon me and hinder me." And was not the apostle in this case ? As touching the law he had been a Pharisee, educated in the straitest sect, brought up in traditions that were opposed to the faith of Christ, and yet the Lord kept him faithful even to the end. None of his old prejudices were able so much as to make him obscure the simplicity of the gospel of Christ. God is able to keep you also, despite your previous prejudices. " Ah," saith one, " but I am the subject of many sceptical thoughts. I often suffer from doubts of the most subtle order." Thinkest thou that the apostle never knew this trial ? He was no stranger to the Greek philosophy, which consisted of a bundle of questions and scepticisms. He must have experienced those temptations which are common to thoughtful minds ; and yet he said, " I know that He is able to keep me " ; believe me, then, the Lord Jesus is equally able to keep you. " Yes," saith another, " but I have so many temptations in the world. If I were not a Christian, I should prosper much better. I have openings now before me, by which I might soon obtain a competence, and perhaps wealth, if I were not checked by conscience." Forget not that the apostle was in like case. What might he not have had ? A man of his condition in life—his birth and parentage being altogether advantageous—a man of his powers of mind and of his great energy, he might have seized upon any attractive position ; but those things which were gain for him, he counted loss for Christ's sake ; and he was willing to be less than nothing, because the power of divine grace kept him true to his profession. But you tell me you are very poor, and that poverty is a severe trial. Brother, you are not so poor as Paul. I suppose a few needles for his tentmaking, an old cloak, and a few parchments, made up all his wealth. A man without a home, a man without a single foot of land to call his own, was this apostle ; but poverty and want could not subdue him, Christ was able to keep him even then. " Ah," say you, " but he had not my strong passions and corruptions." Most surely he had them all, for we hear him cry, " I find then a law, that, when I would do good, evil is present with me. For I delight in the law of God after the inward man : but I see another law in my members, warring against the law of my mind, and bringing me into captivity to the law of sin which is in my members. O wretched man that I am ! who shall deliver me from the body of this death ? " He was tempted as you are, yet he knew that Christ was able to keep him. O trembling Christian, never doubt this soul-cheering fact, that your loving Saviour is able to keep you.

But the apostle did not merely trust Christ thus to keep him from sin, he relied upon the same arm to preserve him *from despair.* He was always battling with the world. There were times when he had no helper. The brethren often proved false, and those that were true were frequently timid. He was left in the world like a solitary sheep surrounded with wolves. But Paul was not faint-hearted. He had his fears, for he was mortal : he rose superior to them, for he was divinely sustained. What a front he always maintains ! Nero may rise before him, a horrible monster for a man even to dream of, but Paul's courage does not give way. A Jewish mob may surround him, they may drag him out of the city, but Paul's mind is calm and composed. He may be laid in the stocks after having been scourged, but his heart finds congenial utterance in a song rather than a groan ; he is always brave, always unconquerable, confident of victory. He believed that God would keep him, and he was kept. And you, my brother, and sister, though your life may be a very severe conflict, and you sometimes think you will give it up in despair, you never shall relinquish the sacred conflict. He that has borne you onward to this day will bear you through, and will make you more than conqueror, for He is able to keep you from fainting and despair.

Doubtless, the apostle meant, too, that Christ was able to keep him from *the power of death*. Beloved, this is great comfort to us who so soon shall die. To the apostle death was a very present thing. " I die daily," said he. Yet was he well assured that death would be gain rather than loss to him, for he was certain that Christ would so order all things that death should be but like an angel to admit him into everlasting life. Be certain of this too, for He who is the resurrection and the life will not desert you. Do not, my brethren and sisters, fall under bondage through fear of death, for the living Saviour is able to keep you, and He will. Do not, I pray you, look too much at the pains and groans and dying strife ; look rather to that kind Friend, who, having endured the agonies of death before you, can sympathise with your sufferings, and who, as He ever liveth, can render you available assistance. Cast this care on Him, and fear no more to die than you fear to go to your bed when night comes on.

The apostle is also certain that Christ is able to preserve *his soul in another world*. Little is revealed in Scripture by way of detailed description of that other world. Imagination may be indulged, but little can be proved. The spirit returns to God who gave it, this we know ; and in the instant after death the righteous soul is in Paradise with Christ ; this too is clear. Yet whether we know the details or no, we are assured that the soul is safe with Christ. Whatever of danger from evil spirits may await us on our journey from this planet up to the dwelling-place of God, whatever there may be of conflict in the last moment, Jesus is able to keep that which we have committed to Him. If I had to keep myself, I might, indeed, tremble with alarm at the prospect of the unknown region, but he that is the Lord of death and of hell, and hath the keys of heaven, can surely keep my soul on that dread voyage across a trackless sea. It is all well ; it must be well with the righteous, even in the land of death-shadow, for our Lord's dominion reaches even there, and being in His dominion we are safe.

Paul believed, lastly, that Christ was able to preserve *his body*. Recall to mind my statement that Paul committed all that he had and was to God in Christ. We must not despise this body ; it is the germ of the body in which we are to dwell for ever ; it shall be raised from corruption into incorruption, but it is the same body. Developed from weakness into power, from dishonour into glory, it never loses its identity. The marvel of the resurrection will not fail of accomplishment. It may seem an impossibility that the body which has rotted in the tomb, and, perhaps been scattered in dust over the face of the soil, which has been absorbed by vegetables, which has been digested by animals, which has passed through countless circles of change, should be raised again, yet impossible as it seems, the Lord Jesus Christ will perform it. It must be as easy to construct a second time as to create out of nothing at the first. Look at creation, and see that nothing is impossible with God. Think of the Word, without whom was not anything made that was made, and straightway you will talk no longer of difficulties. With man it may be impossible, but with God all things are possible. In your entirety, my brethren, in the integrity of your manhood, spirit, soul, and body, all that is essential to your nature, to its happiness, to its perfection, every part of you and every power of you, you having placed all in the hand of Christ, shall be kept until that day, when in His image you shall stand, and prove it your own persons the power which in your faith you do, this day, devoutly trust.

III. We shall, in the third place, pass on to notice THE ASSURANCE OF THAT FACT, or how the apostle Paul attained to it.

" I cannot talk like that," saith one ; " I cannot say, ' I know, and I am persuaded,' I am very thankful that I can say, I hope, I trust, I think." Dear friends, in order to help you to advance, we will notice how the apostle Paul attained to such assurance. One main help to Him was His habit, as seen in this text, of *always making faith the most prominent point of consideration*. Faith is twice mentioned in the few lines before us. " I know whom I have *believed*, and am persuaded that He is able to keep that which I have *committed unto Him*." Paul knew what faith was, namely, a committal of his precious things into the custody of Christ. He does not say, " I have served Christ." No ; he does not say, " I am growing like Christ, therefore I am persuaded I shall be kept." No ; he makes most prominent in his thought the fact that he believed, and so had committed himself to Christ. I would to God, dear friends, that you who are subject to doubts and fears, instead of raking about in your hearts to find out evidences and marks of growth in grace and likeness to Christ, and so on, would first make an investigation concerning a point which is far more vital ; namely, this, have you believed ? Dear anxious heart, begin thy search on this point. Dost thou commit thyself to Christ ? If thou dost, what though marks should be few, and evidences for awhile should be obscure, he that believeth on Him hath everlasting life ; he that believeth and is baptized shall be saved. The evidences will come, the marks will be cleared in due time, but all the marks and evidences between here and heaven are not worth a single farthing to a soul when it comes to actual conflict with death and hell. Then, it must be simple faith that wins the day. Those other things are good enough in brighter times ; but if it be a question whether thou art safe or not, thou must come to this, " I have rested with all my heart on Him that came into the world to save sinners, and though I be the very chief of sinners, I believe He is able to save me." You will get to assurance if you keep clear about your faith.

The next help to assurance, as I gather from the text, is this ; the apostle maintained most clearly *His view of a personal Christ*. Observe how three times he mentioned his Lord. " I know *whom* I have believed, and am persuaded that *He* is able to keep that which I have committed unto *Him*." He does not say, " I know the doctrines I believe." Surely he did, but this was not the main point. He does not say, " I am certain about the form of sound words which I hold." He was certain enough about that, but this was not His foundation. No mere doctrines can ever be the stay of the soul. What can a dogma do ? What can a creed do ? Brethren, these are like medicines, but you need a hand to give you them ; you want the physician to administer them to you ; otherwise you may die with all these precious medicines close at hand. We want a person to trust to. There is no Christianity to my mind so vital, so influential, so true, so real, as the Christianity which deals with the person of the living Redeemer. I know Him, I know He is God, I know that He is mine ; I trust not merely in His teaching but in Himself ; not on His laws, rules, or teachings am I depending so much as on Himself as a person. Dear brother, is that what thou art doing now ? Hast thou put thy soul into the keeping of that blessed Man who is also God, and sitteth at the right hand of the Father ? Canst thou come in faith to His feet, and kiss the prints of the nails, and then look up into His dear face and say, " Ah, thou Son of God, I rely upon the power of Thy arm, on the preciousness of Thy blood, on the love of Thy heart, on the prevalence of Thy plea, on the certainty of Thy promise, on the immutability of Thy character, I rest on Thee, and on Thee alone." You will get assurance readily enough now. But if you begin to fritter away your realisation of the person of Christ, and live merely on dogmas and doctrines, you will be far removed from real assurance.

Brethren, furthermore, the apostle attained this full assurance through *growing knowledge*. He did not say, " I am persuaded that Christ will save me, apart from anything I know about Him " ; but he begins by saying, " I know." Let no Christian among us neglect the means provided for obtaining a fuller knowledge of the gospel of Christ. I would that this age produced more thoughtful and studious Christians. I am afraid that, apart from what many of you gather from the sermon, or from the reading of the Scriptures in public, you do not learn much from the word of God, and from those innumerable instructive books which godly men have bequeathed to us. Men are studious in various schools and colleges in order to obtain knowledge of the classics and mathematics, but should we not be even more diligent that we may know Christ, that we may study Him, and all about Him, and no longer be children, but in knowledge may be men ? Many of the fears of Christians would be driven away if they knew more. Ignorance is not bliss in Christianity, but misery ; and knowledge sanctified, and attended by the presence of the Holy Spirit, is as wings by which we may rise out of the mists and darkness into the light of full assurance. The knowledge of Christ is the most excellent of sciences, seek to be masters of it, and you are on the road to full assurance.

Once, again, the apostle, it appears from the text, gained his assurance from *close consideration* as well as from knowledge. " I know and am persuaded." As I have already said, persuasion is the result of argument. The apostle had turned this matter over in his mind ; he had meditated on the *pros* and *cons* ; he had carefully weighed each difficulty, and he felt the preponderating force of truth which swept every difficulty out of the way. O Christian, if you made your mind more familiar with divine truth, you would, under the guidance of the Holy Spirit, have much more assurance. I believe it is the doctrine which we have least studied in the word which gives us the most trouble in our minds. Search it out and look. The divisions among Christians nowadays are not so much the result of real difference of opinion as of want of accurate thought. I believe we are getting closer and closer in our theology, and that on the whole, at least amongst the Nonconforming churches of England, very much the same theology is preached by all evangelical ministers ; but some are not careful of their terms and words, and use them incorrectly, and so seem to preach wrong doctrines, when in their hearts they mean rightly enough. May we come to be more thoughtful, each of us, for a thousand benefits would flow therefrom. Thinking of the deity of Christ, considering of the veracity of the divine promise, meditating upon the foundations of the eternal covenant, revolving in our minds what Christ hath done for us, we should come at last, by the Spirit's teaching, to be fully persuaded by the power of Christ to keep the sacred charge which we have given to Him. Doubts and fears would vanish like clouds before the wind. How many Christians are like the miser who never feels sure about the safety of his money, even though he has locked up the iron safe, and secured the room in which he keeps it, and locked up the house, and bolted and barred every door ! In the dead of night, he thinks he hears a footstep, and tremblingly he goes down to inspect his strong-room. Having searched the room, and tested all the iron bars in the window, and discovered no thief, he fears that the robber may have come and gone, and stolen his precious charge. So he opens the door of his iron safe, he looks and pries, he finds his bag of gold all safe, and those deeds, those bonds, they are safe too. He puts them away, shuts the door, locks it, bolts and bars the room in which is the safe and all its contents ; but even as he goes to bed, he fancies that a thief has just now broken in. So he scarcely ever enjoys sound, refreshing sleep. The safety of the Christian's treasure is of quite another sort. His soul, not under bolt and bar, or under lock and key of his own securing, but he has transferred his all to the King eternal, immortal, invisible, the only wise God, our Saviour—and such is his security that he enjoys the sleep of the beloved, calmly resting, for all is well. If Jesus could fail us, we might wear sackcloth for ever, but while He is immutable in His love and omnipotent in His power, we may put on the garments of praise. Believing as we do that eternal love neither can nor will desert a soul that reposes in its might, we triumph in heart and find glory begun below.

IV. Now, to close, what is THE INFLUENCE OF THIS ASSURANCE when it penetrates the mind ?

As time fails me, I shall but say that, as in the apostle's case, it enables us to bear all the obloquy which we may incur in serving the Lord. They said Paul was a fool. " Well," replied the apostle, " I am not ashamed, for I know whom I have believed ; I am willing to be thought a fool." The ungodly may laugh at us now, but their laugh will soon be over, and he will laugh that wins for ever. Feel perfectly confident that all is safe, and you can let the world grin at you till its face aches. What does it matter what mortals think ? What signifies it what the whole universe thinks if our souls are beloved of God ? You will, my dear friends, as you live in full assurance of God's love, grow quite indifferent to the opinions of the carnal. You will go about your heavenly service with an eye only to your Master's will: and the judgment of such as cavil and carp will seem to you to be too inconsiderable to be worth a thought. If you doubt and fear, you will be hard put to it; but if you are serenely confident that He is able to keep you, you will dare the thickest of the fray, fearless because your armour is of proof. Assurance will give you a serenity within, which will qualify you for doing much service. A man who is always worrying about his own soul's salvation, can have little energy with which to serve his Lord. But when the soul knows the meaning of Christ's word, " It is finished," it turns all its strength into the channels of service, out of love to such a blessed Saviour. O you that doubt, and therefore fret and care, and ask the question, " Do I love the Lord or no? Am I His, or am I not ? " how I wish this suspense were over with you. O you who fear lest after all you be castaways, you lose your strength for serving your God. When you are sure that He is able to keep what you have committed to Him, then your whole manhood, excited by gratitude, spends itself and is spent in your Master's cause. God make you men to the fulness of vigour, by giving you a fulness of assurance.

Those who are unsaved in this place may well envy those who are. That which attracted me to Christ—I have not heard of others brought in this way, but this brought me to Christ mainly—was the doctrine of the safety of the saints. I fell in love with the gospel through that truth. What! I thought, are those who trust in Jesus safe ? shall they never perish, and shall none pluck them out of Christ's hand ? Everybody esteems safety. One would not insure his life where he thought there was a doubt as to the safety of the insurance. Feeling that there was perfect safety if I gave myself up to the Redeemer, I did so; and I entertain no regrets this day that I committed my soul to Him. Young people, you cannot do better than early in life entrust your future with the Lord Jesus. Many children at home appear to be very excellent, many lads

before they leave their father's house are amiable and commendable in character; but this is a rough world, and it soon spoils the graces that have been nurtured in the conservatory of home-life. Good boys very often turn out very bad men; and girls who were so lovely and pure at home have been known to become very wicked women. O children, your characters will be safe if you trust them with Jesus. I do not say you will be rich if you trust Christ, nor that you will prosper after the manner of men, but I do say that you shall be happy in the best sense of that word, and that your holiness shall be preserved through trusting yourself with Jesus. I pray that you may be led to desire this, especially any of you who are leaving your father's house, or are setting up in business on your own account, commit yourselves to God. This first Sabbath of a new year, what time more suitable for beginning aright! O may the Holy Spirit softly whisper in your ear reasons that shall persuade you to give yourselves to Christ. I say, again, my testimony is that you cannot do a wiser or a better thing. Oh! the happiness my soul has known in resting on my Lord. I wish you knew it. I would not cease to be a Christian, if I might be made a king or an angel. No character can be to me so suitable or so happy as that of a humble dependant upon the faithful love of my redeeming Lord. O come and trust Him, dear young friends! You older ones, do you need that I should speak to you, when you are getting so near your grave ? You are now out of Christ—how soon may you be in hell ? You younger ones, I say, embrace this flying hour, and let this be the day of which you shall have to sing in after years —

> " 'Tis done; the great transaction's done;
>   I am my Lord's and He is mine:
> He drew me, and I followed on,
>   Charmed to confess the voice divine.
>
> High heaven, that heard the solemn vow,
>   That vow renewed shall daily hear:
> Till in life's latest hour I bow,
>   And bless in death a bond so dear."

A GOOD SOLDIER OF JESUS CHRIST

" A good soldier of Jesus Christ."—2 Timothy ii. 3.

MANY men, many minds. In reference to what a Christian is there have been very many and diverse opinions. According to the notions of some, a Christian is an exquisite of remarkably delicate tastes; he cannot worship except it be in a place whose architecture is correctly Gothic, otherwise his dainty soul will be shocked; he is unable to offer prayer aright unless his devotions are uplifted upon the wings of the choicest music; and, even then, scarcely will he be successful unless he be aided by sundry gentlemen, whose pedigree, like that of racehorses, can be clearly traced, and whose garments the tailor has fashioned according to the directions of the ecclesiastical fashion book for the various seasons of the year. If this be to be a Christian in these days, it must be confessed that Paul has said little concerning this delicate and artistic sort of creature, unless, indeed, he had reference to it in Galations iv, 9, 10, 11, which

read at your leisure; neither would Paul's Master acknowledge it.

With some a Christian is a spiritual gourmand. He attends upon the ministry of the word for no purpose but to be fed; he strongly denounces every sermon that is aimed at the conversion of sinners, for he looks upon the Bible itself as a book solely intended to yield him personal consolation. The more any doctrinal teaching promises him a monoply of good things, and the more it excludes others, the better he enjoys it, it being to him a particular part of the sweetness of the feast to believe that but a very slender company may dare to partake of it. For him to live is to enjoy and not to serve. To gratify his selfishness he would blot out the free invitations of the gospel. He is not a hearer only, but certainly he is not also a doer, he is a hearer and a feeder, in a certain coarse sense, upon the word of God, and nothing more. That is not Paul's ideal of a Christian.

He does not picture him with his napkin in his hand, sitting at a banquet, but rather with a sword girt upon his thigh, ready for the conflict.

To some the highest form of Christian is a great reader, a profound student of the best of books, for the purpose of composing spiritual riddles. He reads for no practical end. He is a picker out of words, a speller over of syllables, a magnifier of microscopic points, a proficient in Biblical hair-splitting. The more a passage perplexes others the more sure he is of its meaning. He cares most for things which have the least practical bearing. He is a peeper through the spiritual spyglasses, fancying that he can interpret what wiser men leave to God to expound. He is a hunter after spiritual conies, which, if caught, would never pay the huntsman for his toil, while the weightier matters he holds in small esteem. This does not seem to have been Paul's conception of a Christian ; for the apostle was no lover of foolish and unlearned questions which gender strife.

And I am afraid I must add that with some the *beau ideal* of a Christian is that of a man who can sleep out his existence in blissful serenity ; a man who, having believed, or professed to believe, in Christ, has settled his life-work for ever, and henceforth can say, " Soul, take thine ease, thou hast henceforth much goods laid up for many years in thine own security, eat, drink, be merry in the gospel ; but as for feeding the hungry or clothing the naked, art thou thy brother's keeper ? What is that to thee ? See thou to thyself, and if thou thyself be right, let fate, or providence, or sovereignty, take care of the rest." Paul does not appear to have pictured true believers as sluggards sound asleep upon the downiest beds ; his description of a Christian in the text is that of a soldier, and that means something very far different either from a religious fop, whose best delight is music and millinery, or a theological critic who makes a man an offender for a word, or a spiritual glutton who cares for nothing but a lifelong enjoyment of the fat things full of marrow, or an ecclesiastical slumberer who longs only for peace himself. He represents him as a soldier, and that, I say, is quite another thing. For what is a soldier ? A soldier is a practical man, a man who has work to do, and hard, stern work. He may sometimes when he is at his ease wear the fineries of war, but when he comes to real warfare he cares little enough for them ; the dust and the smoke, and the garments rolled in blood, these are for those who go a soldiering ; and swords all hacked, and dented armour, and bruised shields, these are the things that mark the good, the practical soldier. Truly to serve God, really to exhibit Christian graces, fully to achieve a life-work for Christ, actually to win souls, this is to bear fruit worthy of a Christian. A soldier is a man of deeds, and not of words. He has to contend and fight. In war times his life knows little of luxurious ease. In the dead of night perhaps the trumpet sounds to boot and saddle, just at the time when he is most weary, and he must away to the attack just when he would best prefer to take his rest in sleep. The Christian is a soldier in an enemy's country always needing to stand on his watchtower, constantly to be contending, though not with flesh and blood, with far worse foes, namely, with spiritual wickednesses in high places.

The Christian is a self-sacrificing man as the soldier must be. To protect his country the soldier must expose his own bosom ; to serve his king he must be ready to lay down his life. Surely he is no Christian who never felt the spirit of self-sacrifice. If I live unto myself I am living unto the flesh, and of the flesh I shall reap corruption. Only he who lives to his God, to Christ, to the truth, to the church, and to the good old cause, only he is the man who can reckon himself at all to be a soldier of Jesus Christ.

A soldier is a serving man. He does not follow his own pleasure ; he is under law and rule ; each hour of the day has its prescribed duty ; and he must be obedient to the word of another and not to his own will and whim. Such is the Christian. We serve the Lord Jesus Christ. Though no longer the slaves of man so as to dread his frown, we are servants of Christ who has loosed our bonds.

The soldier is full often a suffering man. There are wounds, there are toils, there are frequent lyings in the hospitals, there may be ghastly cuts which let the soul out with the blood. Such the Christian soldier must be, ready to suffer, enduring hardness, not looking for pleasure of a worldly kind in this life, but counting it his pleasure to renounce his pleasure for Christ's sake.

Once again, the true soldier is an ambitious being. He pants for honour, seeks for glory. On the field of strife he gathers his laurels, and amidst a thousand dangers he reaps renown. The Christian is fired by higher ambitions than earthly warrior ever knew. He sees a crown that can never fade ; he loves a King who best of all is worthy to be served ; he has a motive within him which moves him to the noblest deeds, a divine spirit impelling him to the most self-sacrificing actions. Thus you see the Christian is a soldier, and it is one of the main things in Christian life, to contend earnestly for the faith, and to fight valorously against sin.

Paul does not exhort Timothy to be a common, or ordinary soldier, but to be a " *good* soldier of Jesus Christ " ; for all soldiers, and all true soldiers, may not be *good* soldiers. There are men who are but just soldiers and nothing more ; they only need sufficient temptation and they readily become cowardly, idle, useless and worthless ; but he is the good soldier who is bravest of the brave, courageous at all times, who is zealous, does his duty with heart and earnestness. He is the good soldier of Jesus Christ who, through grace, aims to make himself as able to serve his Lord as shall be possible, who tries to grow in grace and to be perfected in every good word and work, that he may be in his Master's battles fit for the roughest and sternest service, and ready to bear the very brunt of the fray. David had many soldiers, and good soldiers too, but you remember it was said of many, " These attained not unto the first three." Now Paul, if I read him rightly, would have Timothy try to be of the first three, to be a good soldier. And surely I would this morning say to my dear comrades in the little army of Christ meeting here, let each one of us try to attain unto the first three ; let us ask to be numbered among the King's mighties, to do noble work for Him and honourable service, that we may bring to our Master's cause fresh glory. Be it ours to covet earnestly the best gifts, and as we have had much forgiven, let us love much, and prove that love by signs following.

Before I proceed fully to open up this metaphor, let me say that though we shall use military terms this morning, and stirring speech, it should ever be recollected that we have no war against persons, and that the weapons which we use are not such as are forged for the deadly conflicts of mankind. The wars of a Christian are against principles, against sins against the miseries of mankind, against that evil one who has led man astray from his Maker, against the iniquity which keeps man an enemy to himself; and the weapons that we use are holy arguments and consecrated lives, devotion and prayer to God, and teaching and example among the sons of men. Ours is battling for the peace, and fighting for rest. We disturb the world to make it quiet, and turn it upside down to set it right; we pull down strongholds that they may not pull down the Zion of God; we dash down the mighty that the humble and the meek may be established. We have no sympathy with any other war, but count it an evil of the direst sort, let it be disguised as it may. Now with that caution, whatever I shall seem to say will not sound as though I loved or excused ordinary warfare, for nothing can be more abhorrent to the Christian man than wholesale slaughter; nothing can be more desired by us than the promised era, when men shall beat their swords into ploughshares, and their spears into pruning hooks.

Now let us come to the work of this morning. First, we shall *describe a good soldier of Jesus Christ,* and when we have done so, we shall *exhort you to be such.*

I. First, then, this morning, we shall endeavour to DESCRIBE A GOOD SOLDIER OF JESUS CHRIST. We must begin with this fundamental—*he must be loyal to his King.* A soldier of Jesus Christ owns the divine Redeemer as his King, and confesses his sole and undivided sovereignty in the spiritual kingdom. He abhors Antichrist in all its forms, and every principle that opposes itself to the reign of the beloved Prince of Peace. Jesus is to him both Lord and God. The day when he enlisted, he did, as it were, put his finger into *the print of the nails,* and say with Thomas, " My Lord and my God." This was his enlistment declaration, and he remains true to it. " Christ is all," is his motto, and to win all men to obedience to Immanuel is his lifework. Till he sheathes his sword in the last victory, the Crucified is sole monarch of his soul; for Him he lives, for Him he would even dare to die. He has entered into solemn league and covenant, to maintain against all comers that Jesus Christ is Lord to the glory of God the Father.

Moreover, the Christian soldier not only acknowledges Jesus to be his King, but his heart is full of loving devotion to Him as such. Nothing can make his heart leap like the mention of that august, that more than royal name. He remembers who Jesus is, the Son of God, " the Wonderful, the Counsellor, the Mighty God." He remembers what Jesus did, how He loved him, and gave Himself for him; he looks to the cross, and remembers the streams of blood whereby the elect were redeemed, even when they are enemies to God. He remembers Christ in heaven, enthroned at the right hand of the Father, he loves Him there, and it ravishes his heart to think that God hath highly exalted the once-despised and rejected One, and given Him a name that is above every name, that at the name of Jesus every knee shall bow, of things in heaven, and things in earth, and things under the earth. He pants for the time when the Crucified shall come in His glory, and rule the nations as their liege Lord. He loves Jesus so that he feels he belongs to Him altogether,

bought with His blood, redeemed by His power, and comforted by His presence; he delights to know that he is not his own, for he is bought with a price. And since he loves his King, and loves Him with an ardour unquenchable, for many waters cannot drown his love, neither can the floods quench it, he loves all the King's brethren and servants for the King's sake; he hails his brethren in arms with hearty affection; he loves the grand old banner of the gospel; he prays for the wind of the Holy Spirit to expand its furls, that all eyes may behold its beauties; he is steadfast in the faith once delivered to the saints, and rejoices so much at every doctrine of the gospel that he would gladly lay down his life to preserve it to the world. Above all, he loves the crown of his King, and the cause of his Master. Oh, could he set the Captain of his salvation higher among men, he would be content to die in the ditch of neglect and scorn; could he but see the King come to His own, and the heir of all things loyally acknowledged by His revolted provinces, he would be satisfied whatever might become of himself. His heart is more than loyal, it is full of personal affection for the chief among ten thousand. I ask you, brethren, whether it is so with you? Believing, yea, knowing that it is so with many, I would to God it were thus with all. Brethren, I know you love Jesus well, no music sounds to your ears so sweetly as His charming name; no song of choicest minstrel is half so sweet. The very thought of Him with rapture fills your breasts. Assuredly you have one of the first marks of good soldiers; go on, I pray you, to that which lies beyond.

The next characteristic of a good soldier is that *he is obedient to his captain's commands.* He would be no soldier at all who would not take his marching orders from his leader, but must needs act after his own mind; he would soon be dismissed the service, if not shot, by order of a court martial, for crimes which military rule cannot tolerate. Now, without enlarging on that illustration, let me ask every Christian here, and myself first of all, are we doing all the Master's will? Do we wish to know the Master's will? I should not like that any part of the Scripture should be distasteful to me. I would tremble if there were portions of my Lord's testimony which I feared to read, or found it convenient to forget. It is terrible when men are obliged to pass over certain texts, or else to cut and square them to make them agree with their beliefs. We should not practise an ordinance merely because our church teaches it, or our parents believed in it; we must read the Scriptures, and search the question for ourselves, or we are not respectful to our Lord. The soldier who did not take the trouble to read the orders of his superior, might justly be suspected of mutinous intentions. Disobedience rankles in any heart where there is carelessness about knowing the Lord's will. Be courageous enough always to look Scripture in the face, it is after all nothing more than your bare duty. Better for us that we changed our sentiments every day in order to be right, than that we held to them obstinately while we had some fear that perhaps we were wrong. To live a life of obedience is a greater matter than some suppose. Obedience is no second-rate virtue: " to obey is better than sacrifice, and to hearken than the fat of rams." " If ye love me "—what saith Jesus, " Go to the stake for me," or, " Preach before kings for me "? No, neither of these things is expressly selected, but " If ye love me, keep my commandments," as though this were the surest and most accepted test of love. May you thus, then, being loyal to the King, be in the second place obedient to His commands.

The third matter for a good soldier to mind is this, if he be indeed a first-class soldier, worthy of the service, *to conquer will be his ruling passion.* The fight is on, and the soldier's blood is up, and now he feels " I must drive the enemy from his entrenchment, I must take yonder redoubt. I must plant our conquering standard on the castle of the foe, or I must die. Accursed be the sun if he go down this day and see me turn my back upon the enemy." He is resolved that he will win or lie cold and stark upon the battlefield. The Christian man, in order that he may win for Christ the souls of others, may make known Christ's truth, may establish Christ's church on fresh ground, is quite as ready to suffer or die as is the boldest member of the most renowned regiment. To do this he disentangles himself as much as he can from all other ambitions and aims, " for he that warreth entangleth not himself with the affairs of this life." With a good soldier of Christ the master passion is to spread the gospel, to save souls from perishing, and he would sooner do this and be poor than be rich and neglect it ; he would sooner be useful and live unknown than rank among the great ones of the earth and be useless to his Lord. A truly good soldier of Jesus Christ knows nothing about difficulties except as things to be surmounted. If his Master bids him perform exploits too hard for him, he draws upon the resources of omnipotence, and achieves impossibilities. Wellington sent word to his troops one night, " Ciudad Rodrigo must be taken to-night." And what do you think was the commentary of the British soldiers appointed for the attack ? " Then," said they all, " we will do it." So when our great Captain sends round, as He doth to us, the word of command, " Go ye into all the world and preach the gospel to every creature," if we are all good soldiers of the cross, we should say at once, " We will do it." However hard the task, since God Himself is with us to be our Captain, and Jesus the Priest of the Most High is with us to sound the trumpet, we will do it in Jehovah's name. May such dauntless resolution fire your breasts, my brethren and sisters, and may you thus prove yourselves " good soldiers of Jesus Christ."

The passion for victory with the soldier often makes him forget everything else. Before the battle of Waterloo, Picton had had two of his ribs smashed in at Quartre Bras, but he concealed this serious injury, and, though suffering intensest agony, he rode at the head of his troop, and led one of the great charges which decided the fortunes of the day. He never left his post, but rode on till a ball crushed in his skull and penetrated to the brains. Then in the hot fight the hero fell. How few among us could thus endure hardness for Jesus. O that we felt we could suffer anything sooner than be turned aside from accomplishing our life-work for Him we love. In that same battle one of our lieutenants, in the early part of the day, had his left fore-arm broken by a shot ; he could not, therefore, hold the reins in his hand, but he seized them with his mouth, and fought on till another shot broke the upper part of the arm to splinters, and it had to be amputated ; but within two days there he was, with his arm still bleeding, and the wound all raw, riding at the head of his division. Brave things have been done amongst the soldiers of our country— O that such brave things were common among the armed men of the church militant ! Would to God, that in the teeth of suffering we could all persevere in living the holy life He bids us live, and in zealously spreading abroad that glorious gospel which has saved our souls and which will save the souls of others. Great Master, by Thine own example inspire us with this valour. I desire to see in this our beloved church more of you who are resolved that Christ's gospel shall conquer this South of London, that it shall conquer the world, that Christ *shall* see of the travail of His soul and be satisfied. I long to witness more of that dogged perseverance amongst Christians which would make them work on and on, even without success, and persevere under every discouragement, until at last their Master shall give them their reward on earth, or else take them away to their reward in heaven. To be a good soldier of Jesus Christ, there must be a passion for victory, an insatiable greed for setting up the throne of Jesus in the souls of men.

Fourthly, *a good soldier is very brave at a charge.* When the time comes and the orders are given for the good soldier to advance to the attack, he does not wish himself away ; though a perfect hail of hurtling shot whistles all around, and the ranks of the army are thinned, he is glad to be there, for he feels the stern joy that flushes the face in the light of battle, and he only wants to be within arm's length of the foe and to come to close quarters with him. So is it with the genuine Christian when his heart is right with God. If he be bidden to advance, let the danger be what it may, he feels he is honoured by having such a service allotted to him. But are we all such ? I fear not. How many of us are silent about Jesus Christ in private conversation, how little do we show forth our light before men. If we were good soldiers, such as we ought to be, we should select every favourable opportunity in private as well as in public intercourse with our fellow men, and prudently but yet zealously press the claims of Jesus Christ and His gospel upon them. Oh, do you this, beloved, and good will come of it. We should each one be seeking to have his own special work for Jesus, and if no one else were attempting the task we should, like the brave men who rush into the storming of a battery, carry the flag first and plant it, knowing that there are hundreds of others who will follow the first brave man, who might not be able perhaps to lead the way themselves. My beloved, may you and I be ready for anything, and bold to bear witness for Christ before a scoffing world. In the pulpits where we preach, in the workshops where we labour, in the markets where we trade, in every company amidst which we are called to move ; wherever we may be, may we be brave enough to own our Lord and to uphold His cause.

But this is not all that goes to make a good soldier. *A good soldier is like a rock under attack.* So British soldiers have been ; they have stood in solid squares against the enemies' cavalry until their foes have dashed upon them madly, gnashed their teeth, fired in their faces, thrown their guns at them, and yet might just as well have ridden against granite rocks ; for our soldiers did not know how to yield, and would not retreat ; as fast as one fell another filled up the gap, and there stood the square of iron defying the rush of the foe. We want this kind of fixed, resolved, persevering godliness in our churches, and we shall have it if we are good soldiers of Jesus Christ. Alas ! too many are exhausted by the zeal at first exhibited ; for a time they can reach the highest point, but to continue on, and on, and on, this is too difficult a task for them. How many young people will join the church, and for awhile seem very zealous and then grow cold ! Alas ! it is not always the young, there be some among yourselves who were once most diligent in your various forms of service ; what doth hinder you that you are not diligent in your Master's business now ? Has Christ given you leave to retire into inglorious ease ? Does He exempt you from service ? Take heed, lest you are also exempt from reward. No, we must through life still maintain our integrity, still resist temptation, still tread the separated path, and, withal, still seek the souls of men with undying ardour, with indefatigable earnestness, still wrestling with God for men and with men for God. Oh, for more of this stern determination to stand, and having done all to stand !

The last mark of a really good soldier of Jesus Christ is that *he derives his strength from on high.* This has been true even of some common soldiers, for religious men when they have sought strength from God have been all the braver in the day of conflict. I like the story of Frederick the Great ; when he overheard his favourite general engaged in prayer, and was about to utter a sneering remark, the fine old man, who never feared a foe, and did not even fear his majesty's jest, said, " Your Majesty, I have just been asking aid from your Majesty's Great Ally." He had been waiting upon God. This is how Christians get the victory ; they seek it from the church's Great Ally, and then go to the conflictsure that they will win the day. He is the best Christian who is the best intercessor, he shall do the most who shall pray the best. In the battle of Salamanca, when Wellington bade one of his officers advance with his troops and occupy a gap which the Duke perceived in the lines of the French, the general rode up to him, and said, " My lord, I will do the work, but first give me a grasp of that conquering right hand of yours." He received a hearty grip, and away he rode to the deadly encounter. Often has my soul said to her Captain, " My Lord, I will do that work if Thou wilt give me a grip of Thy conquering right hand." Oh, what power it puts into a man when he gets a grip of Christ, and Christ gets a grip of him ! Fellowship with Christ is the fountain of the church's strength. Her power did never lie in her wealth, nor in the eloquence of her preachers, nor in aught that comes of man ; the strength of the church is divine, and if she fails to draw strength from the everlasting hills, she becomes weak as water. Good soldiers of Jesus Christ, watch unto prayer, " praying in the Holy Ghost," for so shall you be strong in the Lord, and in the power of His might.

II. Thus I have in a very poor way described a good soldier of Jesus Christ. Give me a few minutes while I EXHORT YOU TO BE SUCH ; and, mark you I shall speak especially to the members of this Christian church.

I exhort you, dear brethren, who are soldiers of Christ, to be good soldiers, because *many of you have been so.* Paul was wont to commend the churches when he could, and I feel I may honestly and from my heart commend many of you, for you have served your Lord and Master well. I know you have nothing whereof to glory, for when you have done all, you are unprofitable servants ; but still I do rejoice, and will rejoice when I see the work of the Holy Spirit in you : and I will venture to say that I have seen here instances of apostolic ardour and self-sacrifice such as I have read of in ancient records, but hardly ever expected to see. There are those in this house this day who will shine as stars for ever and ever, for they have turned many to righteousness. Dishonour not your past, I beseech you, fall not from your high standing. " Forward " be your motto ; never think of declining, but rather advance in love to God, and in the ardour of your zeal. Be good soldiers still, and depart not from your first love. I am sure *there is greater need of good soldiering now than ever.* Ten years ago or sixteen years ago, when first I addressed you, the power of popery in this land was nothing to what it is now. In those days the Church of England was more generally Protestant, now it is so frequently popish that I may broadly say that now we are afflicted with two popish churches, that of Rome and that of Oxford, the second not one whit better than the first, only more crafty and insidious, inasmuch as it attracts to itself a number of godly and gracious men, who protect the villains who bear a Protestant name and who are doing the Pope's work. I grieve to know that the evangelical clergy of England, by their continued union with the Church of England are acting as a shield to the ritualistic or popish party, and giving them every opportunity to work out their schemes for leading the nation back to popery *en masse.* Around this very spot a battle will have to be fought between the sacramentarians and the lovers of the gospel. At your very doors the battle is come at last ; it was not so till but lately, but here it is, and ye that are men must show your colours, and serve your Master against innumerable and constantly active foes. Ye have never failed me, ye have always been bold and steadfast, and laborious, and so let it be, for the time requires it. I can see on all hands that many of your young men are being attracted by the worldly amusements which surround us, for our dangers are not only those of popery, but those of the world, the flesh, and the devil. There must be greater earnestness and a deeper-toned piety among you, or the next generation will become unworthy of yourselves, your grief and not your joy. I pray you see to this.

Be good soldiers, for *much depends upon it.* Your country will be blest in proportion as you are earnest. Nonconformity in England will lose all its power if it loses its godliness. I do not care much for our political strength—I was about to say I am almost indifferent to our political rights—I care for them, but only so much as to occupy a very minor place in my consideration ; but our spirituality is the main matter, it is this alone that can make us a blessing to our country. Sons of the Puritans, ye must walk with God, or your day is past, ye will be swept away as Esther would have been, who came to the kingdom for the salvation of her nation, if she had not fulfilled the office for which God had exalted her. You have grown in numbers, grown in strength. O that you may grow in grace, love the gospel better, and love Christ better, for your country needs it, your children need it, yourselves need it. The times are perilous, and yet they are hopeful ; by their peril, and by their hopefulness, I beseech you be good soldiers of Jesus Christ.

Good soldiers we ought to be, for *it is a grand old cause that is at stake.* It is the kingdom of God, it is the church of Christ, it is the word, the truth, the doctrine of the gospel, the crown of Jesus, that are all at stake. I grant you that none shall ever shake the throne of Jesus, for though "the heathen rage, and the people imagine a vain thing," yet shall His throne be established. But we now speak according to the manner of men. God has been pleased to leave this matter to His church, which is the pillar and ground of the truth. Oh then, stand up manfully, and fight earnestly when so much rests upon it ! God grant that you may not be as the children of Ephraim, who being armed and carrying bows turned their backs in the day of battle.

I implore you, my brethren, and mostly myself, to be good soldiers of Jesus, when you consider *the fame that has preceded you.* A soldier when he receives his colours finds certain words embroidered on them, to remind him of the former victories of the regiment in which he serves. Look at the eleventh chapter of Hebrews, and see the long list of the triumphs of the faithful. Remember how prophets and apostles served God ; recollect how martyrs joyfully laid down their lives ; look at the long line of the reformers and the confessors ; remember your martyred sires and covenanting fathers, and by the grace of God I beseech you walk not unworthy of your noble lineage.

Be good soldiers because of *the victory which awaits you.* Oh, it will be a grand thing to share in the ultimate triumph of Christ, for triumph He will ; when all His soldiers shall come back from the war, and the King Himself at their head with the spoils of the victory, when they shall come back to the metropolitan city, to the ivory palaces of the great Captain, when the song is heard, " Lift up your heads, O ye gates, and be ye lifted up, ye everlasting doors," when the question shall be answered, " Who is the King of glory ? " by the reply, " The Lord of Hosts, the Lord mighty in battle, He is the King of glory " ; it will be a glorious thing to have shared the fight, for so surely you shall share the honours of that coronation day. A crown is prepared for that head though it be now made to ache with care for the cause, a palm branch for that hand which now toils in the fight, silver sandals for those feet which have now to march over weary miles for Christ's sake, honour and immortality not to be imagined till they are enjoyed, await every faithful soldier of the cross.

Besides, and lastly, if I want another argument to make you good soldiers, *remember your Captain,* the Captain whose wounded hands and pierced feet are tokens of His love to you. Redeemed from going down to the pit, what can you do sufficiently to show your gratitude ? Assured of eternal glory by-and-by, how can you sufficiently prove that you feel your indebtedness ? Up, I pray you now. By Him whose eyes are like a flame of fire, and yet were wet with tears, by Him on whose head are many crowns, and who yet wore the crown of thorns, by Him who is Kings of kings and Lord of lords, and yet bowed His head in death for you, resolve that to life's latest breath you will spend and be spent for His praise. The Lord grant that there may be many such in this church—good soldiers of Jesus Christ.

Two or three words and I will close. At this present time I contemplate exhorting you to engage in fresh efforts for Christ. I do not know that you are relaxing, neither have I complaints to make of any, but I would wish that we would commence with renewed vigour this day, if God so wills it. As I myself commence a new year of Sabbaths as to my own age, I desire to see a new era of greater exertion in the cause of Jesus Christ ; and, in order that it may be successful, let not a single man or woman on the church-roll be missing from his or her post in the spiritual conflict. It is a remarkable fact that on the eve of a great battle in the Peninsular war the officers read the muster-roll, and noted that " not a man was missing." They had all good stomach for the fight, and were all there. You that are in the Sabbath school, you that distribute your tracts, you that preach in the street, every man to his post ; and if you have no post as yet, find one—let there not be one idler, not one single loiterer, for a single sluggard may mar the work.

Then if we are to be successful let nothing divide us. The motto of one of our most famous regiments embroidered on their banner is, " *Quis separavit.*" Who shall separate us ? We are but mortals, and, therefore, little jealousies may spring up, and among us there may be little causes of personal pique, but brave warriors in the olden times who had fallen out have been known to come together on the eve of battle, and say, " Come, let us be reconciled, we may die to-morrow ; besides, we join in common hatred of the foe and love to the king." Let your peace be unbroken, your union indissoluble, and God will bless you.

To help us to succeed now, let us lay down this one rule, let no low standard of work, or virtue, or spiritual attainment, content any one of us ; let us resolve to be as good Christians as can be beneath the stars, as fond of Christ as human hearts can be, doing and giving as much for Christ as we can do or give, consistently with other duties. Let us spare nothing, and keep back no part of the price ; let there be no Ananias and Sapphira among us, but all be as John, who loved his Lord ; and Paul, who counted all things but loss for the excellency of Christ Jesus his Lord.

Next, let me say, *let the present moment be seized.* I should like to saturate this district with a mass of tracts simply teaching the gospel and protesting against the bastard popery around us. Heaven and earth are being raised around us just now ; our poor are being bribed, the houses of our members are being systematically visited with the view of decoying them from our worship. We are told that a certain small building used by the Episcopal body is the parish church, and we ought to attend it. I might far more truthfully assert this to be the church of the parish by the choice of a far more numerous body, but I care not to make pretensions which prove nothing. The true question is—do we follow Christ, and uphold the teachings of Scripture, and if so, our standing is unassailable. Doubtless the word has gone forth that Dissent must be crushed, but if we live near to God, and maintain our zeal, Dissent will rise invincible from every attack. Foreseeing the gathering storm, it is our consolation that we know where He dwells who is Master of the tempest, and can walk the waters for our help, and calm the sea around the weather-beaten bark. It becomes us now at this present moment to be indefatigable, to put forth all our strength for the truth, even the Lord's pure word in doctrine and in ordinance. *Let no man's heart fail him.* There is no fear of defeat. Lo, these many years the Lord of Hosts has been with us as a church, and He will be still our helper. We have seen the rise and fall of many who blazed for a while, but are now quenched in darkness, while we have increased from a handful to this mass ; and God who has been our trust, and is still our stay, will not forsake us now. He has not drawn you together, and held you in one body by cords of love, that after all you may prove to be a powerless unwieldy mass of associated Christians ; He intends to direct and strengthen you for nobler ends and purposes. God, even our own God, will bless us. Immanuel, God with us, leads the van. The truth, like the virgin daughter of Zion, shakes her head at boastful error, and laughs it to scorn. Let falsehood put on her tawdry garments, and think herself a queen, and say that she shall sit alone, and see no sorrow ; let error come forth in her panoply and wave her flaunting banner before the sun. She draws near her end. Her armour—what is it ? It is but pasteboard, and the lance of truth shall pierce it through and through. Her banner, what is it but a foul rag of the Roman harlot ? It shall be laid in the dust. Nay, let error bring forth all her hosts, and let them stand in their serried ranks, and through them the faithful soldiers of Jesus will ride and bow the columns like reeds in the wind. In these days, the doctrines and traditions of men compass us about, yea, like bees they compass us about, but in the name of the Lord will we destroy them. Only let us have confidence in God, and the victory is sure. As for the thought of turning back, that can never be endured. A message came to Sir Colin Campbell at the Alma, that Her Majesty's Guards were falling thick and fast beneath the shot, had they not better retire for a little while into safe quarters ? The answer was, " It was better, sir, that every one of Her Majesty's Guards should lie dead on this battlefield than turn their backs on the enemy." And it is so. Let us die, yea, it were to be devoutly wished rather than that we lived a coward's life ! Let the preacher first of all be carried to his grave, let him never live to see the shame of this Israel. Let these eyes be sealed in death rather than behold " Ichabod " written on these walls. No, brethren, it shall not be ; you will serve Jesus, you will love Him, and " Onward to victory " shall be your watchword from to-day. Be more in prayer, for this is the great matter. Seek out each one your own sphere of action ; give yourselves wholly to it ; and if any grow cold or careless, let him remember Jesus saith, " I stand at the door, and knock : if any man hear My voice, and open the door, I will come in to him, and will sup with him, and he with Me." This blessed supping with Jesus will restore you ; though you be like Laodicea, " neither cold nor hot." Fellowship with Jesus will renew the love of your espousals. Oh, then, my brethren, in Jesus' name I bid you be strong in the Lord, and in the power of His might.

I have not preached to sinners, but you will do that if you catch the spirit of this sermon ; there will be many thousands of words to sinners spoken as the result of this exhortation, if God, the Holy Spirit, make it answer my design. Only this word to those who are not soldiers of Jesus Christ ; trust Him now, come now and kiss His silver sceptre of grace ; He will forgive the rebel, and take him to be His servant. God bless you. Amen.

THE RESURRECTION OF OUR LORD JESUS

" Remember that Jesus Christ of the seed of David was raised from the dead according to my gospel."—2 Timothy ii. 8.

FROM long sickness my mind is scarcely equal to the work before me. Certainly, if I had ever sought after brilliance of thought or language, I should have failed to-day, for I am almost at the lowest stage of incapacity. I have only been comforted in the thought of preaching to you this morning by the reflection that it is the doctrine itself which God blesses, and not the way in which it may be spoken ; for if God had made the power to depend upon the speaker and his style, He would have chosen that the resurrection, grandest of all truths, should have been proclaimed by angels rather than by men. Yet He set aside the seraph for the humbler creature. After angels had spoken a word or two to the women their testimony ceased. The most prominent testimony to the resurrection of the Lord was at the first that of holy women, and afterwards that of each one of the guileless men and women who made up the five hundred or more whose privilege it was to have actually seen the risen Saviour, and who therefore could bear witness to what they had seen, though they may have been quite unable to describe with eloquence what they had beheld. Upon our Lord's rising, I have nothing to say, and God's ministers have nothing to say, beyond bearing witness to the fact that Jesus Christ of the seed of David was raised from the dead. Put it in poetry, tell it out in sublime Miltonic verse, it will come to no more ; tell it out in monosyllables, and write it so that little children may read it in their first spelling-books, and it will come to nothing less. " The Lord is risen indeed " is the sum and substance of our witness when we speak of our risen Redeemer. If we do but know the truth of this resurrection, and feel the power of it, our mode of utterance is of secondary consequence ; for the Holy Spirit will bear witness to the truth, and cause it to produce fruit in the minds of our hearers.

Our present text is found in Paul's second letter to Timothy. The venerable minister is anxious about the young man who has preached with remarkable success, and whom he regards in some respects as his successor. The old man is about to put off his tabernacle, and he is concerned that his son in the gospel, should preach the same truth as his father has preached, and should by no means adulterate the gospel. A tendency showed itself in Timothy's day, and the same tendency exists at this very hour, to try to get away from the simple matters of fact upon which our religion is built, to something more philosophical and hard to be understood. The word which the common people heard gladly is not fine enough for cultured sages, and so they must needs surround it with a mist of human thought and speculation. Three or four plain facts constitute the gospel, even as Paul puts it in the fifteenth chapter of his first Epistle to the Corinthians : " For I delivered unto you first of all that which I also received, how that Christ died for our sins according to the Scriptures ; and that He was buried, and that He rose again the third day according to the Scriptures." Upon the incarnation, life, death, and resurrection of Jesus our salvation hinges. He who believes these truths aright hath believed the gospel, and believing the gospel he shall without doubt find eternal salvation therein. But men want novelties ; they cannot endure that the trumpet should give forth the same certain sound, they crave some fresh fantasia every day. " *The gospel with variations* " is the music for them. Intellect is progressive, they say ; they must, therefore, march ahead of their forefathers. Incarnate Deity, a holy life, an atoning death, and a literal resurrection,—having heard these things now for nearly nineteen centuries they are just a little stale, and the cultivated mind hungers for a change from the old-fashioned manna. Even in Paul's day this tendency was manifest, and so they sought to regard facts as mysteries or parables, and they laboured to find a spiritual meaning in them till they went so far as to deny them as actual facts. Seeking a recondite meaning, they overlooked the fact itself, losing the substance in a foolish preference for the shadow. While God set before them glorious events which fill heaven with amazement they showed their foolish wisdom by accepting the plain historical facts as myths to be interpreted or riddles to be solved. He who believed as a little child was pushed aside as a fool that the disputer and the scribe might come in to mystify simplicity, and hide the light of truth. Hence there had arisen a certain Hymenæus and Philetus, " Who concerning the truth have erred, saying that the resurrection is past already ; and overthrow the faith of some." Turn to verse seventeen and read for yourselves. They spirited away the resurrection ; they made it to mean something very deep and mystical, and in the process they took away the actual resurrection altogether. Among men there is still a craving after new meanings, refinements upon old doctrines, and spiritualizations of literal facts. They tear out the bowels of the truth, and give us the carcase stuffed with hypotheses, speculations, and larger hopes. The golden shields of Solomon are taken away, and shields of brass are hung up in their stead : will they not answer every purpose, and is not the metal more in favour with the age ? It may be so, but we never admired Rehoboam, and we are old-fashioned enough to prefer the original shields of gold. The Apostle Paul was very anxious that Timothy at least should stand firm to the old witness, and should understand in their plain meaning his testimonies to the fact that Jesus Christ of the seed of David rose again from the dead.

Within the compass of this verse several facts are recorded : and, first, there is here the great truth that Jesus, the Son of the Highest, was anointed of God ; the apostle calls Him " Jesus *Christ*," that is, the anointed one, the Messiah, the sent of God. He calls Him also " *Jesus*," which signifies a Saviour, and it is a grand truth that He who was born of Mary, He who was laid in the manger at Bethlehem, He who loved and lived and died for us, is the ordained and anointed Saviour of men. We have not a moment's doubt about the mission, office, and design of our Lord Jesus ; in fact, we hang our soul's salvation upon His being anointed of the Lord to be the Saviour of men.

This Jesus Christ was really and truly man ; for Paul says He was " *of the seed of David*." True He was divine, and His birth was not after the ordinary manner of men, but still He was in all respects partaker of our human nature, and came of the stock of David. This also we do believe. We are not among those who spiritualize the incarnation, and suppose that God was here as a phantom, or that the whole story is but an instructive legend. Nay, in the very flesh and blood did the Son of God abide among men : bone of our bone and flesh of our flesh was He in the days of His sojourn here below. We know and believe that Jesus Christ has come in the flesh. We love the incarnate God, and in Him we fix our trust.

It is implied, too, in the text that *Jesus died* ; for He could not be raised from the dead if He had not first gone down among the dead, and been one of them. Yes, Jesus died : the crucifixion was no delusion, the piercing of His side with a spear was most clear and evident proof that He was dead : His heart was pierced, and the blood and water flowed therefrom. As a dead man He was taken down from the cross and carried by gentle hands, and laid in Joseph's virgin tomb. I think I see that pale corpse, white as a lily. Mark how it is distained with the blood of His five wounds, which make Him red as the rose. See how the holy women tenderly wrap Him in fine linen with sweet spices, and leave Him to spend His Sabbath all alone in the rock-hewn sepulchre. No man in this world was ever more surely dead than He. " He made His grave with the wicked, and with the rich in His death." As dead they laid Him in the place of the dead, with napkin and grave-clothes, and habiliments fit for a grave : then they rolled the great stone at the grave's mouth and left Him, knowing that He was dead.

Then comes the grand truth, that as soon as ever the third sun commenced his shining circuit, *Jesus rose again*. His body had not decayed, for it was not possible for that holy thing to see corruption ; but still it had been dead ; and by the power of God— by His own power, by the Father's power, by the power of the Spirit—for it is attributed to each of these in turn, before the sun had risen His dead body was quickened. The silent heart began again to beat, and through the stagnant canals of the veins the life-flood began to circulate. The soul of the Redeemer again took possession of the body, and it lived once more. There He was within the sepulchre, as truly living as to all parts of Him as He had ever been. He literally and truly, in a material body, came forth from the tomb to live among men till the hour of His ascension into heaven. This is the truth which is still to be taught, refine it who may, spiritualize it who dare. This is the historical fact which the apostles witnessed ; this is the truth for which the confessors bled and died. This is the doctrine which is the key-stone of the arch of Christianity, and they that hold it not have cast aside the essential truth of God. How can they hope for salvation for their souls if they do not believe that " the Lord is risen indeed " ?

This morning I wish to do three things. First, let us *consider the bearings of the resurrection of Christ upon other great truths* ; secondly, let us consider *the bearings of this fact upon the gospel*, for it has such bearing, according to the text—" Jesus Christ of the seed of David was raised from the dead according to my gospel " ; thirdly, let us *consider it bearings on ourselves,* which are all indicated in the word " Remember."

I. First, then, beloved, as God shall help us, let us CONSIDER THE BEARINGS OF THE FACT THAT JESUS ROSE FROM THE DEAD.

It is clear at the outset that *the resurrection of our Lord was a tangible proof that there is another life.* Have you not quoted a great many times certain lines about " That undiscovered country from whose bourne no traveller returns " ? It is not so. There was once a traveller who said that " I go to prepare a place for you, and if I go away I will come again, and receive you unto Myself ; that where I am there ye may be also." He said, " A little time and ye shall see Me, and again a little time, and ye shall not see Me, and because I go to the Father." Do you not remember these words of His ? Our divine Lord went to the undiscovered country, and He returned. He said that at the third day He would be back again, and He was true to His word. There is no doubt that there is another state for human life, for Jesus has been in it, and has come back from it. We have no doubt as to a future existence, for Jesus existed after death. We have no doubt as to a paradise of future bliss, for Jesus went to it and returned. Though He has left us again, yet that coming back to tarry with us forty days has given us a sure pledge that He will return a second time when the hour is due, and then will be with us for a thousand years, and reign on earth amongst His ancients gloriously. His return from among the dead is a pledge to us of existence after death, and we rejoice in it.

His resurrection is also a pledge that the body will surely live again and rise to a superior condition ; for the body of our blessed Master was no phantom after death any more than before. " Handle Me, and see." Oh wondrous proof I He said, " Handle Me, and see " ; and then to Thomas, " Reach hither thy finger, and behold My hands ; and reach hither thy hand and thrust it into My side." What deception is possible here ? The risen Jesus was no mere spirit. He promptly cried, " A spirit hath not flesh and bones, as ye see Me have." " Bring Me," said He, " something to eat " ; and as if to show how real His body was, though He did not need to eat, yet He did eat, and a piece of a broiled fish and of an honeycomb were proofs of the reality of the act. Now, the body of our Lord in its risen state did not exhibit the whole of His glorification ; for otherwise we should have see John falling at His feet as dead, and we should have seen all His disciples overcome with the glory of the vision ; but, still, in a great measure, we may call the forty days' sojourn— " The life of Jesus in His glory upon earth." He was no longer despised and rejected of men ; but a glory surrounded Him. It is evident that the raised body passed from place to place in a single moment, that it appeared and vanished at will, and was superior to the laws of matter. The risen body was incapable of pain, of hunger, thirst, and weariness during the time in which it remained here below,— fit representative of the bulk of which it was the firstfruits. Of our body also it shall be said ere long, " It was sown in weakness, it is raised in power ; it was sown in dishonour, it is raised in glory." Let us, then, as we think of the risen Christ, rest quite sure of a future life, and quite sure that our body will exist in it in a glorified condition.

I do not know whether you are ever troubled with doubts in connection with the world to come as to whether it can be true that we shall live eternally. Here is the respect which makes death so terrible to doubters ; for while they have realized the grave, they have not realized the life beyond it. Now, the best help to that realization is a firm grip of the fact that Jesus died and Jesus rose again. This fact is proved better than any other event in history ; the witness to it is far stronger than to anything else that is written either in profane or sacred records. The rising of our Lord Jesus Christ being certain, you may rest assured of the existence of another world. That is the first bearing of this great truth.

Secondly, *Christ's rising from the dead was the seal to all His claims.* It was true, then, that He was sent of God, for God raised Him from the dead in confirmation of His mission. He had said Himself, " Destroy this body, and in three days I will raise it up." Lo, there He is : the temple of His body is rebuilt I He had even given this as a sign, that as Jonas was three days and three nights in the whale's belly, so should the Son of man be three days and three nights in the heart of the earth, and should then come forth to life again. Behold His own appointed sign fulfilled I Before men's eye the seal is manifest I Suppose He had never risen. You and I might have believed in the truth of a certain mission which God had given Him ; but we could never have believed in the truth of such a commission as He claimed to have received—a commission to be our Redeemer from death and hell. How could He be our ransom from the grave if He had Himself remained under the dominion of death ?

Dear friends, the rising of Christ from the dead proved that this man was innocent of every sin. He could not be holden by the bands of death, for there was no sin to make those bands fast. Corruption could not touch His pure body, for no original sin had defiled the Holy One. Death could not keep Him a continual prisoner, because He had not actually come under sin ; and though He took sin of ours, and bore it by imputation, and therefore died, yet He had no fault of His own, and must, therefore, be set free when His imputed load had been removed.

Moreover, Christ's rising from the dead proved His claim to Deity. We are told in another place that He was proved to be the Son of God with power by the resurrection from the dead. He raised Himself by His own power, and though the Father and the Holy Spirit were co-operative with Him, and hence His resurrection is ascribed to them, yet it was because the Father had given Him to have life in Himself, that therefore He arose from the dead. Oh, risen Saviour, Thy rising is the seal of Thy work I We can have no doubt about Thee now that Thou hast left the tomb. Prophet of Nazareth, Thou art indeed the Christ of God, for God has loosed the bands of death for Thee I Son of David, Thou art indeed the elect and precious One, for Thou ever livest I Thy resurrection life has set the sign-manual of heaven to all that Thou hast said and done, and for this we bless and magnify Thy name.

A third bearing of His resurrection is this, and it is a very grand one,—*The resurrection of our Lord, according to Scripture, was the acceptance of His sacrifice.* By the Lord Jesus Christ rising from the dead evidence was given that He had fully endured the penalty which was due to human guilt. " The soul that sinneth it shall die "—that is the determination of the God of heaven. Jesus stands in the sinner's stead and dies : and when He has done *that* nothing more can be demanded of Him, for he that is dead is free from the law. You take a man who has been guilty of a capital offence ; he is condemned to be hanged, he is hanged by the neck till he is dead—what more has the law to do with him ? It has done with him, for it has executed its sentence upon him ; if he can be brought back to life again he is clear from the law ; no writ that runs in Her Majesty's dominions can touch him—he has suffered the penalty. So when our Lord Jesus rose from the dead, after having died, He had fully paid the penalty that was due to justice for the sin of His people, and His new life was a life clear of penalty, free from liability. You and I are clear from the claims of the law because Jesus stood in our stead, and God will not exact payment both from us and from our Substitute : it were contrary to justice to sue both the Surety and those for whom He stood. And now, joy upon joy ! the burden of liability which once did lie upon the Substitute is removed from Him also ; seeing He has by the suffering of death vindicated justice and made satisfaction to the injured law. Now both the sinner and the Surety are free. This is a great joy, a joy for which to make the golden harps ring out a loftier style of music. He who took our debt has now delivered Himself from it by dying on the cross. His new life, now that He has risen from the dead, is a life free from legal claim, and it is the token to us that we whom He represented are free also. Listen ! " Who shall lay anything to the charge of God's elect ? It is God that justifieth, who is He that condemneth ? It is Christ that died, yea rather, that is risen again." It is a knockdown blow to fear when the apostle says that we cannot be condemned because Christ has died in our stead, but he puts a double force into it when he cries, " Yea rather, that is risen again." If Satan, therefore, shall come to any believer and say, " What about your sin ? " tell him Jesus died for it, and your sin is put away. If he come a second time, and say to you, " What about your sin ? " answer him, " Jesus lives, and His life is the assurance of our justification ; for if our Surety had not paid the debt He would still be under the power of death." Inasmuch as Jesus has discharged all our liabilities, and left not one farthing due to God's justice from one of His people, He lives and is clear, and we live in Him, and are clear also by virtue of our union with Him. Is not this a glorious doctrine, this doctrine of the resurrection, in its bearing upon the justification of the saints ? The Lord Jesus gave Himself for our sins, but He rose again for our justification.

Bear with me, while I notice, next, another bearing of this resurrection of Christ. *It was a guarantee of His people's resurrection.* There is a great truth that never is to be forgotten, namely, that Christ and His people are one just as Adam and all his seed are one. That which Adam did he did as a head for a body, and as our Lord Jesus and all believers are one, so that which Jesus did He did as a Head for a body. We were crucified together with Christ, we were buried with Christ, and we are risen together with Him ; yea, He hath raised us up together and made us sit together in the heavenly places in Christ Jesus. He says, " Because I live ye shall live also." If Christ be not raised from the dead your faith is vain, and our preaching is vain,

and ye are yet in your sins, and those that have fallen asleep in Christ have perished, and you will perish too ; but if Christ has been raised from the dead then all His people must be raised also ; it is a matter of gospel necessity. There is no logic more imperative than the argument drawn from union with Christ. God has made the saints one with Christ, and if Christ has risen all the saints must rise too. My soul takes firm hold on this and as she strengthens her grasp she loses all fear of death. Now we bear our dear ones to the cemetery and leave them each one in his narrow cell, calmly bidding him farewell and saying—

" So Jesus slept : God's dying Son
Pass'd through the grave, and blest the bed ;
Rest here, dear saint, till from His throne
The morning break, and pierce the shade."

It is not merely ours to know that our brethren are living in heaven, but also that their mortal parts are in divine custody, securely kept till the appointed hour when the body shall be reanimated, and the perfect man shall enjoy the adoption of God. We are sure that our dead men shall live ; together with Christ's dead body they shall rise. No power can hold in durance the redeemed of the Lord. " Let My people go " shall be a command as much obeyed by death as once by the humbled Pharaoh who could not hold a single Israelite in bonds. The day of deliverance cometh on apace.

" Break from His throne, illustrous morn !
Attend, O earth, His sovereign word ;
Restore thy trust, a glorious form :
He must ascend to meet His Lord."

Once more, *our Lord's rising from the dead is a fair picture of the new life which all believers already* enjoy. Beloved, though this body is still subject to bondage like the rest of the visible creation, according to the law stated in Scripture, " the body is dead because of sin," yet " the spirit is life because of righteousness." The regeneration which has taken place in those who believe has changed our spirit, and given to it eternal life, but it has not affected our body further than this, that it has made it to be the temple of the Holy Ghost, and thus it is a holy thing, and cannot be obnoxious to the Lord, or swept away among unholy things ; but still the body is subject to pain and weariness, and to the supreme sentence of death. Not so the spirit. There is within us already a part of the resurrection accomplished, since it is written, " And you hath He quickened who were dead in trespasses and sins." You once were like the ungodly, under the law of sin and death, but you have been brought out of the bondage of corruption into the liberty of life and grace ; the Lord having wrought in you gloriously. " according to the working of His mighty power, which He wrought in Christ, when He raised Him from the dead, and set Him at His own right hand in the heavenly places."

Now, just as Jesus Christ led, after His resurrection, a life very different from that before His death, so you and I are called upon to live a high and noble spiritual and heavenly life, seeing that we have been raised from the dead to die no more. Let us joy and rejoice in this. Let us behave as those who are alive from the dead, the happy children of the resurrection. Do not let us be money-grubbers, or hunters after worldly fame. Let us not set our affections on the foul things of this dead and rotten world, but let our hearts fly upward, like young birds that have broken loose of their shells—upward towards our Lord and the heavenly things upon which He would have us set our minds. Living truth, living work, living faith, these are the things for living men : let us cast off the graveclothes of our former lusts, and wear the garments of light and life. May the Spirit of God help us in further meditating upon these things at home.

II. Now, secondly, LET US CONSIDER THE BEARINGS OF THIS FACT OF THE RESURRECTION UPON THE GOSPEL ; for Paul says, "Jesus Christ was raised from the dead *according to my gospel.*" I always like to see what way any kind of statement bears on the gospel. I may not have many more opportunities of preaching, and I make up my mind to this one thing, that I will waste no time upon secondary themes, but when I do preach it shall be the gospel, or something very closely bearing upon it. I will endeavour each time to strike under the fifth rib, and never beat the air. Those who have a taste for the superfluities may take their fill of them, it is for me to keep to the great necessary truths by which men's souls are saved. My work is to preach Christ crucified and the gospel, which gives men salvation through faith. I hear every now and then of very taking sermons about some bright new nothing or another. Some preachers remind me of the emperor who had a wonderful skill in carving men's heads upon cherry stones. What a multitude of preachers we have who can make wonderfully fine discourses out of a mere passing thought, of no consequence to anyone. But we want the gospel. We have to live and die, and we must have the gospel. Certain of us may be cold in our graves before many weeks are over, and we cannot afford to toy and trifle : we want to see the bearings of all teachings upon our eternal destinies, and upon the gospel which sheds its light over our future.

The resurrection of Christ is vital, because first it tells us that *the gospel is the gospel of a living Saviour.* We have not to send poor penitents to the crucifix, the dead image of a dead man. We say not, "These be thy gods, O Israel ! " We have not to send you to a little baby Christ nursed by a woman. Nothing of the sort. Behold the Lord that liveth, and was dead, and is alive for evermore, and hath the keys of hell and of death ! Behold in Him a living and accessible Saviour who out of the glory still cries with loving accents, " Come unto Me, all ye that labour and are heavy laden, and I will give you rest." " He is able also to save them to the uttermost that come unto God by Him, seeing He ever liveth to make intercession for them." I say we have a living Saviour, and is not his a glorious feature of the gospel ?

Notice next that *we have a powerful Saviour* in connection with the gospel that we preach ; for He who had power to raise Himself from the dead, has all power now that He is raised. He who in death vanquishes death, can much more conquer by His life. He who being in the grave did, nevertheless, burst all its bonds, can assuredly deliver all His people. He who, coming under the power of the law, did, nevertheless, fulfil the law, and thus set His people free from bondage, must be mighty to save. You need a Saviour strong and mighty, yet you do not want one stronger than He of whom it is written that He rose again from the dead. What a

blessed gospel we have to preach,—the gospel of a living Christ who hath Himself returned from the dead leading captivity captive.

And now notice, that we have *the gospel of complete justification* to preach to you. We do not come and say, " Brethren, Jesus Christ by His death did something by which men may be saved if they have a mind to be, and diligently carry out their good resolves." No, no ; we say Jesus Christ took the sin of His people upon Himself and bore the consequences of it in His own body on the tree, so that He died ; and having died, and so paid the penalty, He lives again ; and now all for whom He died, all His people whose sins He bore, are free from the guilt of sin. You ask me, "Who are they ? " and I reply, as many as believe on Him. Whosoever believeth in Jesus Christ is as free from the guilt of sin as Christ is. Our Lord Jesus took the sin of His people, and died in the sinner's stead, and now being Himself set free, all His people are set free in their Representative. This doctrine is worth preaching. One may well rise from his bed to talk about perfect justification through faith in Christ Jesus. One might as well keep asleep as rise to say that Jesus accomplished little or nothing by His passion and His rising. Some seem to dream that Jesus made some little opening by which we have a slight chance of reaching pardon and eternal life, if we are diligent for many years. This is not our gospel. Jesus has saved His people. He has performed the work entrusted to Him. He has finished transgression, made an end of sin, and brought in everlasting righteousness, and whosoever believeth in Him is not condemned, and never can be.

Once again, the connection of the resurrection and the gospel is this, *it proves the safety of the saints,* for if when Christ rose His people rose also, they rose to a life like that of their Lord, and therefore they can never die. It is written, " Christ being raised from the dead dieth no more ; death hath no more dominion over Him," and it is so with the believer : if you have been dead with Christ and are risen with Christ, death has no more dominion over you ; you shall never go back to the beggarly elements of sin, you shall never become what you were before your regeneration. You shall never perish, neither shall any pluck you out of Jesus' hand. He has put within you a living and incorruptible seed which liveth and abideth for ever. He says Himself, " The water that I shall give him shall be in him a well of water springing up into everlasting life." Wherefore hold ye fast to this, and let the resurrection of your Lord be the pledge of your own final perseverance.

Brethren, I cannot stop to show you how this resurrection touches the gospel at every point, but Paul is always full of it. More than thirty times Paul talks about the resurrection, and occasionally at great length, giving whole chapters to the glorious theme. The more I think of it the more I delight to preach Jesus and the resurrection. The glad tidings that Christ has risen is as truly the gospel as the doctrine that He came among men and for men presented His blood as a ransom. If angels sang glory to God in the highest when the Lord was born, I feel impelled to repeat the note now that He is risen from the dead.

III. And so I come to my last head, and to the practical conclusion : THE BEARING OF THIS RESURRECTION UPON OURSELVES. Paul expressly bids us

" Remember " it. " Why," says one, " we don't forget it." Are you sure you do not ? I find myself far too forgetful of divine truths. We ought not to forget, for this first day of the week is consecrated for Sabbatic purposes to constrain us to think of the resurrection. On the seventh day men celebrated a finished creation, on the first day we celebrate a finished redemption. Bear it, then, in mind. Now, if you will remember that Jesus Christ of the seed of David rose from the dead, what will follow ?

First, you will find that *most of your trials will vanish*. Are you tried by your sin ? Jesus Christ rose again from the dead for your justification. Does Satan accuse ? Jesus rose to be your advocate and intercessor. Do infirmities hinder ? The living Christ will show Himself strong on your behalf. You have a living Christ, and in Him you have all things. Do you dread death ? Jesus, in rising again, has vanquished the last enemy. He will come and meet you when it is your turn to pass through the chill stream, and you shall ford it in sweet sompany. What is your trouble ? I care not what it is, for if you will only think of Jesus as living, full of power, full of love, and full of sympathy, having experienced all your trials, even unto death, you will have such a confidence in His tender care and in His boundless ability that you will follow in His footsteps without a question. Remember Jesus, and that He rose again from the dead, and your confidence will rise as on eagles' wings.

Next remember Jesus, for then you will see how your present sufferings are as nothing compared with His sufferings, and you will learn to *expect victory over your sufferings even as He obtained victory*. Kindly look at the chapter, and you will find the apostle there saying in the third verse, " Thou therefore endure hardness, as a good soldier of Jesus Christ," and further on in the eleventh verse, " It is a faithful saying : For if we be dead in Him, we shall also live in Him : if we suffer, we shall also reign with Him." Now, then, when you are called to suffer, think,—" Jesus suffered, yet Jesus rose again from the dead ; He came up out of His baptism of griefs the better and more glorious for it, and so shall I ! " Wherefore go you into the furnace at the Lord's bidding, and do not fear that the smell of fire shall pass upon you. Go you even down into the grave, and do not think that the worm shall make an end of you any more than it did of Him. Behold in the risen One the type and model of what you are and are to be ! Wherefore fear not, for He conquered ! Stand not trembling, but march boldly on, for Jesus Christ of the seed of David rose from the dead, and you who are of the seed of the promise shall rise again from all your trials and afflictions, and live a glorious life.

We see here, dear brethren, in being told to remember Jesus that *there is hope even in our hopelessness*. When are things most hopeless in a man ? Why, when he is dead. Do you know what it is to come down to that, so far as your inward weakness is concerned ? I do. At times it seems to me that all my joy is buried like a dead thing, and all my present usefulness and all my hope of being useful in the future are coffined and laid underground like a corpse. In the anguish of my spirit, and the desolation of my heart, I could count it better to die than to live. You say it should not be so. I grant you it should not be so, but so it is. Many things happen within the minds of poor mortals which should not happen ; if we had more courage and more faith they would not happen. Aye, but when we go down, down, down, is it not a blessed thing that Jesus Christ of the seed of David died, and was raised from the dead ? If I sink right down among the dead men, yet will I hold to this blessed hope, that as Jesus rose again from the dead, so also shall my joy, my usefulness, my hope, my spirit rise. " Thou, which hast showed us great and sore troubles shalt quicken us again, and bring us up from the lowest depths of the earth." This downcasting and slaying is good for us. We take a deal of killing, and it is by being killed that we live. Many a man will never live till his proud self is slain. O proud Pharisee, if you are to live among those whom God accepts, you will have to come to the slaughter-house and be cut in pieces as well as killed. " This is dreadful work," saith one, " this dividing of joints and marrow, this spiritual dismemberment and destruction." Assuredly it is painful, and yet it were a grievous loss to be denied it. Alas, how many are so good and excellent, and strong and wise, and clever, and all that, that they cannot agree to be saved by grace through faith. If they could be reduced to less than nothing it would be the finest thing that ever happened to them. Remember what Solomon said might be done with the fool, and yet it would not answer—he was to be brayed in a mortar among wheat with a pestle,— pretty hard dealing that, and yet his folly would not depart from him. Not by that process alone, but through some such method, the Holy Spirit brings men away from their folly. Under His killing operation this may be their comfort that, if Jesus Christ rose literally from the dead (not from sickness, but from death), and lives again, even so will His people. Did you ever get, where Bunyan pictures Christian as getting, right under the old dragon's foot ? He is very heavy, and presses the very breath out of a fellow when he makes him his footstool. Poor Christian lay there with the dragon's foot on his breast ; but he was just able to stretch out his hand and lay hold on his sword, which, by a good providence, lay within his reach. Then he gave Apollyon a deadly thrust, which made him spread his dragon wings and fly away. The poor crushed and broken pilgrim, as he gave the stab to his foe, cried, " Rejoice not over me, O mine enemy ; though I fall, yet shall I rise again." Brother, do you the same. You that are near despair, let this be the strength that nerves your arm and steels your heart. " Jesus Christ of the seed of David was raised from the dead according to Paul's gospel."

Lastly, this proves *the futility of all opposition to Christ*. The learned are going to destroy the Christian religion. Already, according to their boastings, it has pretty nearly come to an end. The pulpit is effete, it cannot command public attention. We stand up and preach to empty benches ! As you see— *or do not see*. Nothing remains for us but to die decently, so they insinuate. And what then ? When our Lord was dead, when the clay-cold corpse lay, watched by the Roman soldiery, and with a seal upon the enclosing stone, was not the cause in mortal jeopardy ? But how fared it ? Did it die out ? Every disciple that Jesus had made forsook Him, and fled ; was not Christianity then destroyed ? Nay, that very day our Lord won a victory which shook the gates of hell, and caused the universe to stand astonished. Matters are not worse with

Him at this hour! His affairs are not in a sadder condition to-day than then. Nay, see Him to-day and judge. On His head are many crowns, and at His feet the hosts of angels bow! Jesus is the Master of legions to-day, while the Cæsars have passed away! Here are His people—needy, obscure, despised, I grant you, still, but assuredly somewhat more numerous than they were when they laid Him in the tomb. His cause is not to be crushed, it is for ever rising. Year after year, century after century, bands of true and honest hearts are marching up to the assault of the citadel of Satan. The prince of this world has a stronghold here on earth, and we are to capture it ; but as yet we see small progress, for rank after rank the warriors of the Lord have marched to the breach and disappeared beneath the terrible fire of death. All who have gone before seem to have been utterly cut off and destroyed, and still the enemy holds his ramparts against us. Has nothing been done, think you ? Has death taken away those martyrs, and confessors, and preachers, and laborious saints, and has nothing been achieved ? Truly if Christ were dead I would admit our defeat, for they that are fallen asleep in Him would have perished : but as the Christ liveth so the cause liveth, and they that have fallen are not dead : they have vanished from our sight for a little, but if the curtain could be withdrawn, every one of them would be seen to stand in His lot unharmed, crowned, victorious ! " Who are these arrayed in white robes, and whence came they ? " These are they that were defeated ! Whence, then, their crowns ? These are they that were dishonoured ! Whence, then, their white robes ? These are they who clung to a cause which is overthrown. Whence, then, their long line of victors, for there is not a vanquished man among them all ? Let the truth be spoken. Defeat is not the word for the cause of Jesus, the Prince of the house of David. We have always been victorious, brethren ; we are victorious now. Follow your Master on your white horses, and be not afraid! I see Him in the front with His blood-stained vesture around Him, fresh from the winepress where He has trodden down His foes. You have not to present atoning blood, but only to conquer after your Lord. Put on your white raiment and follow Him on your white horses, conquering and to conquer. He is nearer than we think, and the end of all things may be before the next jibe shall have come forth from the mouth of the last new sceptic. Have confidence in the risen One, and live in the power of His resurrection.

SUFFERING AND REIGNING WITH JESUS

" If we suffer, we shall also reign with Him : if we deny Him, He also will deny us."—2 Timothy ii. 12.

MY venerable friend who has hitherto sent me a text for the new year, still ministers to his parish the word of life, and has not forgotten to furnish the passage for our meditation to-day. Having preached from one of a very similar character a short time ago, I have felt somewhat embarrassed in preparation ; but I will take courage, and say with the apostle, " To write the same things to you, to me indeed is not grievous, but for you it is safe." If I should bring forth old things on this occasion, be ye not unmindful that even the wise householder doth this at times. For oft-recurring sickness the same wine may be prescribed by the most skilful physician without blame ; no one scolds the contractor for mending rough roads again and again with stones from the same quarry ; the wind which has borne us once into the haven, is not despised for blowing often from the same quarter, for it may do us good service yet again; and therefore, I am assured that you will endure my repetitions of the same truths, since they may assist you to suffer with patience the same trials.

You will observe that our text is a part of one of Paul's *faithful sayings*. If I remember rightly, Paul has four of these. The first occurs in 1 Timothy i. 8, that famous, that chief of all faithful sayings, " This is a faithful saying, and worthy of all acceptation, that Christ Jesus came into the world to save sinners ; of whom I am chief." A golden saying, whose value Paul himself had most marvellously proved. What shall I say of this verse, but that, like the lamp of a lighthouse, it has darted its ray of comfort through leagues of darkness, and guided millions of tempest-tossed spirits to the port of peace ? The next faithful saying is in the same epistle, at the fourth chapter, and the ninth verse: " Godliness is profitable unto all things, having promise of the life that now is, and of that which is to come. This is a faithful saying, and worthy of all acceptation." This, too, the apostle knew to be true, since he had learned in whatsoever state he was therewith to be content. Our text is a portion of the third faithful saying ; and the last of the four you will find in Titus iii : 8, " This is a faithful saying, and these things I will that thou affirm constantly, that they which have believed in God might be careful to maintain good works. These things are good and profitable unto men." We may trace a connection between these faithful sayings. The first one which speaks of Jesus Christ coming into the world to save sinners, lays the foundation of our eternal salvation in the free grace of God, as shown to us in the mission of the great Redeemer. The next affirms the double blessedness which we obtain through this salvation —the blessings of the upper and nether springs—of time and of eternity. The third faithful saying shows one of the duties to which the chosen people are called ; we are ordained to suffer for Christ with the promise that " if we suffer, we shall also reign with Him." The last faithful saying sets forth the active form of Christian service, bidding us diligently to maintain good works. Thus you have the root of salvation in free grace ; you have next the privileges of that salvation in the life which now is, and in that which is to come ; and you have also the two great branches of suffering with Christ and service of Christ loaded with the fruit of the Spirit of all grace. Treasure up, dear friends, those faithful sayings, " Lay up these words in your heart ; bind them for a sign upon your hand, that they may be as frontlets between your eyes." Let these choice sayings be printed in letters of gold, and set up as tablets upon the door posts of our house and upon our gates. Let them be the guides of our life, our comfort, and our instruction. The apostle of the Gentiles proved them to be faithful; they are faithful still, not one word shall fall to the ground; they are worthy of all acceptation, let us accept them now, and prove their faithfulness, each man for himself.

This morning's meditation is to be derived from a part of that faithful saying which deals with suffering. We will read the verse preceding our text. "It is a faithful saying: For if we be dead with Him, we shall also live with Him." All the elect were virtually dead with Christ when He died upon the tree—they were on the cross, crucified with Him. In Him, as their representative, they rose from the tomb, and live in newness of life: because He lives, they shall live also. In due time the chosen are slain by the Spirit of God, and so made dead with Christ to sin, to self-righteousness, to the world, the flesh, and the powers of darkness; then it is that they live with Jesus, His life becomes their life, and as He was, so are they also in this world. The Spirit of God breathes the quickening grace into those who were once dead in sin, and thus they live in union with Christ Jesus. When believers die, though they may be sawn in sunder, or burnt at the stake, yet, since they sleep in Jesus, they are preserved from the destruction of death by Him, and are made partakers of His immortality. May the Lord make us rooted and grounded in the mysterious but most consolatory doctrine of union with Christ Jesus.

We must at once advance to our text—" If we suffer, we shall also reign with Him: if we deny Him, He also will deny us." The words naturally divide themselves into two parts; *suffering with Jesus, and its reward—denying Jesus, and its penalty.*

I. SUFFERING WITH JESUS, AND ITS REWARD. To suffer is the common lot of all men. It is not possible for us to escape from it. We come into this world through the gate of suffering, and over death's door hangs the same escutcheon. We must suffer if we live, no matter in what style we spend our existence. The wicked man may cast off all respect for virtue, and riot in excess of vice to the utmost degree, yet, let him not expect to avoid the well-directed shafts of sorrow; nay, rather let him look for a tenfold share of pain of body and remorse of soul. "Many sorrows shall be to the wicked." Even if a man could so completely degrade himself as to lose his intellectual powers, and become a brute, yet even then he could not escape from suffering; for we know that the brute creation is the victim of pain, as much as more lordly man; only, as Dr. Chalmers well remarks, the brutes have the additional misery that they have no mind endowed with reason and cheered by hope to fortify them under their bodily affliction. Seest thou not, O man, that however thou mayest degrade thyself, thou art still under the yoke of suffering: the loftiest bow beneath it, and the meanest cannot avoid it. Every acre of humanity must be furrowed with this plough. There may be a sea without a wave, but never a man without sorrow. He who was God as well as man, had His full measure pressed down and running over; let us be assured that if the Sinless One was not spared the rod, the sinful will not go free. " Man that is born of woman is of few days and full of trouble." " Man is born unto trouble as the sparks fly upward."

If then, a man hath sorrow, it doth not necessarily follow that he shall be rewarded for it, since it is the common lot brought upon all by sin. You may smart under the lashes of sorrow in this life, but this shall not deliver you from the wrath to come. Remember you may live in poverty and drag along a wearisome existence of illrequited toil; you may be stretched upon a bed of sickness, and be made to experience an agony in every single member of your body; and your mind, too, may be depressed with fears, or plunged in the depths of despair; and yet, by all this you may gain nothing of any value to your immortal spirit; for, " Except a man be born again, he cannot see the kingdom of God ; " and no amount of affliction upon earth can alter that unchanging rule, so as to admit an unregenerate man into heaven. To suffer is not peculiar to the Christian, neither doth suffering necessarily bring with it any recompense of reward. The text implies most clearly that we must suffer *with Christ* in order to reign with Him. The structure of the preceding verse plainly requires such a reading. The words, " with Him," may be as accurately supplied at the close of the one clause as the other. The suffering which brings the reigning with Jesus, must be a suffering with Jesus. There is a very current error among those poor people who are ignorant of true religion, that all poor and afflicted people will be rewarded for it in the next state. I have heard working men refer to the parable of the rich man and Lazarus, with a cruel sort of satisfaction at the pains of Dives, because they have imagined that, in the same manner, all rich people would be cast into the flames of hell without a drop of water to cool their tongue, while all poor persons like Lazarus, would be triumphantly carried into Abraham's bosom. A more fearful mistake could not be made. It was not the suffering of Lazarus which entitled him to a place in Abraham's bosom; he might have been licked by all the dogs on earth and then have been dragged off by the dogs of hell. Many a man goes to hell from a dunghill. A drunkard's hovel is very wretched: is he to be rewarded for bringing himself to rags? Very much of the beggary we see abroad is the result of vice, extravagance, or folly—are these things so meritorious as to be passports to glory? Let no man deceive himself so grossly. On the other hand, the rich man was not cast into hell because he was rich and fared sumptuously; had he been rich in faith, holy in life, and renewed in heart, his purple and fine linen would have done him no hurt. Lazarus was carried above by the angels, because his heart was in heaven; and the rich man lifted up his eyes in hell, because he had never lifted them up towards God and heavenly things. It is a work of grace in the heart and character, which shall decide the future, not poverty or wealth. Let intelligent persons combat this notion whenever they meet with it. Suffering here does not imply happiness hereafter. It is only a certain order of suffering to which a reward is promised, the suffering which comes to us from fellowship with the Lord Jesus, and conformity to His image.

A few words here, by way of aiding you in making the distinction. *We must not imagine that we are suffering for Christ, and with Christ, if we are not in Christ.* If a man be not a branch of the living vine, you may prune and cut until the sap flows, and the branch bleeds, but he will never bring forth heavenly fruit. Prune the bramble as long as ever you like, use the knife until the edge is worn away, the brier will be as sharp and fruitless as ever; you cannot by any process of pruning translate it into one of the vines of Eschol. If a man remain in a state of nature, he is a member of the earthly Adam, he will not therefore escape suffering, but ensure it ; he must not, however, dream that *because* he suffers he is suffering with Christ ; he is plagued with the old Adam ; he is receiving with all the other heirs of wrath the sure heritage of sin. Let him consider these sufferings of his to be only the first drops of the awful shower which will fall upon him for ever, the first tingling cuts of that terrible whip which will lacerate his soul for ever. If a man be in Christ, he may then claim fellowship with the second Man, who is the Lord from heaven, and he may expect to bear the image of the heavenly in the glory to be revealed. O my hearers, are you in Christ by a living faith ? Are you trusting to Jesus only ? If not, whatever you may have to mourn over on earth, you have no hope of reigning with Jesus in heaven.

Supposing a man to be in Christ, yet it does not even then follow that all his sufferings are sufferings with Christ, for *it is essential that he be called by God to suffer*. If a good man were, out of mistaken views of mortification and self-denial, to mutilate his body, or to flog his flesh as many a sincere enthusiast has done, I might admire the man's fortitude, but I should not allow for an instant that he was suffering with Christ. Who called men to such austerities ? Certainly not the God of love. If, therefore, they torture themselves at the command of their own fancies, fancy must reward them, for God will not. If I am rash and imprudent, and run into positions for which neither providence nor grace has fitted me, I ought to question whether I am not rather sinning than communing with Christ. Peter drew his sword, and cut off the ear of Malchus. If somebody had cut *his* ear off, what would you say ? He took the sword, and he feels the sword. He was never commanded to cut off the ear of Malchus, and it was his Master's gentleness which saved him from the soldiers' rage. If we let passion take the place of judgment, and self-will reign instead of Scriptural authority, we shall fight the Lord's battles with the devil's weapons, and if we cut our own fingers we must not be surprised. On several occasions, excited Protestants have rushed into Romish cathedrals, have knocked down the priest, and dashed the wafer upon the ground, trod upon it, and in other ways exhibited their hatred of idolatry ; now when the law has interposed to punish such outrages, the offenders are hardly to be considered as suffering with Christ. This I give as one instance of a class of actions to which overheated brains sometimes lead men, under the supposition that they will join the noble army of martyrs. The martyrs were all chosen to their honourable estate ; and I may say of maryrdom as of priesthood, " No man taketh that honour upon himself but he that is called thereunto as was Aaron." Let us mind we all make a distinction between things which differ, and do not pull a house down on our heads, and then pray the Lord to console us under the trying providence.

Again, *in troubles which come upon us as the result of sin, we must not think we are suffering with Christ*. When Miriam spoke evil of Moses, and the leprosy polluted her, she was not suffering for God. When Uzziah thrust himself into the temple, and became a leper all his days, he could not say he was afflcted for righteousness' sake. If you speculate and lose all your property, do not say that you are losing all for Christ's sake ; when you unite with bubble companies and are duped, do not whine about suffering for Christ—call it the fruit of your own folly. If you will put your hand into the fire and it gets burned, why it is the nature of fire to burn you or anybody else ; but be not so silly as to boast as though you were a martyr. If you do wrong and suffer for it, what thanks have ye ? Go behind the door and weep for your sin, but come not forth in public to claim a reward. Many a hypocrite, when he has had his deserts, and has been called by his proper name, has cried out, "Ah ! I am persecuted." It is not an infallible sign of excellence to be in bad repute among men. Who feels any esteem for a cold-blooded murderer ? Does not every man reprobate the offender ? Is he, therefore, a Christian because he is spoken against, and his name cast out as evil ? Assuredly not ; he is a heartless villain and nothing more. Brethren, truthfulness and honesty should stop us from using expressions which involve a false claim ; we must not talk as if we suffered nobly for Jesus when we are only troubled as the result of sin. Oh, to be kept from transgression ! then it mattereth not how rough the road of obedience may be, our journey shall be pleasant because Jesus walks with us.

Be it observed, moreover, that suffering such as God accepts and rewards for Christ's sake, *must have God's glory as its end*. If I suffer that, I may earn a name, or win applause among men ; if I venture into trial merely that I may be respected for it, I shall get my reward ; but it will be the reward of the Pharisee, and not the crown of the sincere servant of the Lord Jesus.

I must mind too, that love to Christ, and love to His elect, is ever the main-spring of all my patience ; remembering the apostle's words. "Though I give my body to be burned, and have not charity, it profiteth me nothing." If I suffer in bravado, filled with proud defiance of my fellow-men ; if I love the dignity of singularity, and out of dogged obstinacy hold to an opinion, not because it is right —and I love God too well to deny His truth—but because I choose to think as I like, then I suffer not with Jesus. If there be no love to God in my soul ; if I do not endure all things for the elect's sake, I may bear many a cuff and buffeting, but I miss the fellowship of the Spirit, and have no recompense.

I must not forget also that *I must manifest the Spirit of Christ, or else I do not suffer with Him.* I have heard of a certain minister, who, having had a great disagreement with many members in his Church, preached from this text, " And Aaron held his peace." The sermon was intended to portray himself as an astonishing instance of meekness ; but as his previous words and actions had been quite sufficiently violent, a witty hearer observed, that the only likeness he could see between Aaron and the preacher, was this, " Aaron held his peace, and the preacher did not." It is easy enough to discover some parallel between our cases and those of departed saints, but not so easy to establish the parallel by holy patience and Christlike forgiveness. If I have, in the way of virtue, brought down upon myself shame and rebuke ; if I am hot to defend myself and punish the slanderer ; if I am irritated, unforgiving, and proud, I have lost a noble opportunity of fellowship with Jesus. I must have Christ's spirit in me, or I do not suffer acceptably. If like a sheep before her shearers, I can be dumb ; if I can bear insult, and love the man who inflicts it ; if I can pray with Christ, " Father, forgive them, for they know not what they do "; if I submit all my case to Him who judgeth righteously, and count it even my joy to suffer reproach for the cause of Christ, then, and only then, have I truly suffered with Christ.

These remarks may seem very cutting, and may take away much false but highly-prized comfort from some of you. It is not my intention to take away any true comfort from the humblest believer who really suffers with my Lord ; but God grant we may have honesty enough not to pluck flowers out of other men's gardens, or wear other men's honours. Truth only will be desired by true men.

I shall now very briefly show what are the forms of real suffering for Jesus in these days. We have not now to rot in prisons, to wander about in sheep-skins and goat-skins, or to be stoned, or to be sawn in sunder, though we ought to be ready to bear all this, if God wills it. The days of Nebuchadnezzar's furnace are past, but the fire is still upon earth. *Some suffer in their estates.* I believe that to many Christians it is rather a gain than a loss, so far as pecuniary matters go, to be believers in Christ ; but I meet with many cases—cases which I know to be genuine, where persons have had to suffer severely for conscience sake. There are those present who were once in very comfortable circumstances, but they lived in a neighbourhood where the chief of the business was done on a Sunday ; when grace shut up their shop, trade left them ; and I know some of them are working very hard for their bread, though once they earned abundance without any great toil ; they do it cheerfully for Christ's sake, but the struggle is a hard one. I know other persons who were employed as servants in lucrative positions involving sin, but upon their becoming Christians, they were obliged to resign their former post, and are not at the present moment in anything like such apparent prosperity as they were. I could point to several cases of persons who have really suffered to a very high degree in pecuniary matters for the cross of Christ. Brethren, ye may possess your souls in patience, and expect as a reward of grace that you shall reign with Jesus your beloved. Those feather-bed soldiers who are broken-hearted if fools laugh at them, should blush when they think of those who endure real hardness as good soldiers of Jesus Christ. Who can waste his pity over the small griefs of faint hearts, when cold, and hunger, and poverty are cheerfully endured by the true and brave. Cases of persecution are by no means rare. In many a country village squires and priests rule with a high hand, and smite the godly villagers with a rod of iron. " No blankets, no coals, no almshouse for you, if you venture into the meeting-house. You cannot live in my cottage if you have a prayer-meeting in it. I will have no religious people on my farm. We who live in more enlightened society, little know the terrorism exercised in some of the rural districts over poor men and women who endeavour conscientiously to carry out their convictions and walk with Christ. True Christians of all denominations love each other and hate persecution, but nominal Christians and ungodly men would make our land as hot as in the days of Mary, if they dared. To all saints who are oppressed, this sweet sentence is directed—" If we suffer, we shall also reign with Him.

More usually, however, the suffering takes the form of *personal contempt.* It is not pleasant to be pointed at in the streets, and have opprobrious names shouted after you by vulgar tongues ; nor is it a small trial to be saluted in the workshop by opprobrious epithets, or to be looked upon as an idiot or a madman ; and yet this is the lot of many of the people of God every day in the week. Many of those who are of the humbler classes have to endure constant and open reproach, and those who are richer have to put up with the cold shoulder, and neglect, and sneers, as soon as they become true disciples of Jesus Christ. There is more sting in this than some dream ; and we have known strong men who could have born the lash, brought down by jeers and sarcasms, even just as the wasp may more thoroughly irritate and vex the lion than if the noblest beast of prey should attack him. *Believers have also to suffer slander and falsehood.* It is not expedient for me, doubtless, to glory, but I know a man who scarcely ever speaks a word which is not misrepresented, and hardly performs an action which is not misconstrued. The press at certain seasons, like a pack of hounds, will get upon his track, and worry him with the basest and most undeserved abuse. Publicly and privately he is accustomed to be sneered at. The world whispers, " Ah ! he pretends to be zealous for God, but he makes a fine thing of it ! " Mark you, when the world shall learn what he does make of it, maybe it will have to eat its words. But I forbear ; such is the portion of every servant of God who has to bear public testimony for the truth. Every motive but the right one will be imputed to him ; his good will be evil spoken of ; his zeal will be called imprudence—his courage, impertinence—his modesty, cowardice—his earnestness, rashness. It is impossible for the true believer in Christ, who is called to any eminent service, to do anything right, He had better at once learn to say with Luther, " The world hates me, and there is no love lost between us, for as much as it hates me, so heartily do I hate it," He meant not the men in the world, for never was there a more loving heart than Luther's ; but he meant the fame, the opinion, the honour of the world he trod beneath his feet. If in your measure, you bear un-deserved rebuke for Christ's sake, comfort your-selves with these words, " If we suffer, we shall also reign with Him : if we deny Him, He also will deny us."

Then again, if in your service for Christ, you are enabled so to sacrifice yourself, that you bring upon yourself *inconvenience and pain, labour and loss,* then I think you are suffering with Christ. The missionary who tempts the stormy deep—the herald of the cross who penetrates into unknown regions among savage men—the colporteur toiling up the mountain-side—the teacher going wearily to the class—the village preacher walking many toilsome miles—the minister starving on a miserable pittance —the evangelist content to break down in health— all these and their like, suffer with Christ. We are all too much occupied with taking care of ourselves ; we shun the difficulties of excessive labour. And frequently behind the entrenchments of *taking care of our constitution,* we do not half as much as we ought. A minister of God is bound to spurn the suggestions of ignoble ease, it is his calling to labour ; and if he destroys his constitution, I for one, only thank God that He permits us the high privilege of so making ourselves living sacrifices. If earnest ministers should bring themselves to the grave, not by imprudence, for that we would not advocate, but by honest labour, such as their ministry and their consciences require of them, they will be better *in* their graves than *out of* their graves, if they come there for the cause of Christ. What, are we never to suffer ? Are we to be carpet-knights ? Are God's people to be put away in wadding, perfumed with lavender, and boxed up in quiet softnesses ? Nay, verily, unless they would lose the reward of true saints !

Let us not forget that *contention with inbred lusts,* denials of proud self, resistance of sin, and agony against Satan, are all forms of suffering with Christ. We may, in the holy war within us, earn as bright a crown as in the wider battle-field beyond us. O for grace to be ever dressed in full armour, fighting with principalities and powers, and spiritual wickedness of every sort.

There is one more class of suffering which I shall mention, and that is, *when friends forsake, or become foes.* Father and mother forsake sometimes. The husband persecutes the wife. We have known even the children turn against the parents. "A man's foes are they of his own household." This is one of the devil's best instruments for making believers suffer ; and those who have to drain this cup for the Lord's sake, shall reign with Him.

Brethren, if you are thus called to suffer for Christ, will you quarrel with me if I say, in adding all up, what a very little it is compared with reigning with Jesus ! "For our light affliction, which is but for a moment, worketh for us a far more exceeding and eternal weight of glory." When I contrast our sufferings of to-day with those of the reign of Mary, or the persecutions of the Albigenses on the mountains, or the sufferings of Christians in Pagan Rome, why ours are scarcely a pin's prick : and yet what is the reward ? We shall reign with Christ. There is no comparison between the service and the reward. Therefore it is all of grace. We do but little, and suffer but little—and even that little grace gives us —and yet the Lord grants us "A far more exceeding and eternal weight of glory." We are not merely to sit with Christ, but we are *to reign* with Christ. All that the pomp imperial of His kingship means ; all that the treasure of His wide dominions can yield ; all that the majesty of His everlasting power can bestow—all this is to belong to you, given to you of His rich, free grace, as the sweet reward of having suffered for a little time with Him. Who would draw back then ? Who among you will flinch ? Young man, have you thought of flying from the cross ? Young woman, has Satan whispered to you to shun the thorny pathway ? Will you give up the crown ? Will you miss the throne ? O beloved, it is so blessed to be in the furnace with Christ, and such an honour to stand in the pillory with Him, that if there were no reward, we might count ourselves happy ; but when the reward is so rich, so superabundant, so eternal, so infinitely more than we had any right to expect, will we not take up the cross with songs, and go on our way rejoicing in the Lord our God ?

II. DENYING CHRIST, AND ITS PENALTY. "If we deny Him, He also will deny us," Dreadful "if," and yet an "if" which is applicable to every one of us. If the apostles, when they sat at the Lord's Supper, said, "Lord, is it I ?" surely we may say as we sit here, "Lord, shall I ever deny Thee ?" You who say most loudly, "Though all men shall deny Thee, yet will not I "—you are the most likely to do it. In what way can we deny Christ ? Some deny Him openly as scoffers do, whose tongue walketh through the earth, and defieth heaven. Others do this wilfully and wickedly in a doctrinal way, as the Arians and Socinians do, who deny His deity : those who deny His atonement, who rail against the inspiration of His Word, these come under the condemnation of those who deny Christ. There is a way of denying Christ, without even speaking a word, and this is the more common. In the day of blasphemy and rebuke, many they hide their heads. They are in company where they ought to speak up for Christ, but they put their hands upon their mouths ; they come not forward to profess their faith in Jesus ; they have a sort of faith, but it is one which yields no obedience. Jesus bids each believer to be baptized. They neglect His ordinance. Neglecting that, they also despise the weightier matters of the law. They will go up to the house of God because it is fashionable to go there ; but if it were a matter of persecution, they would forsake the assembling of themselves together. In the day of battle, they are never on the Lord's side. If there be a parade, and the banners are flying, and the trumpets are sounding, if there are decorations and medals to be given away, here they are ; but if the shots are flying, if trenches have to be carried, and forts to be stormed, where are they ? They have gone back to their dens, and there will they hide themselves till fair weather shall return. Mind, mind, mind, for I am giving a description, I am afraid, of some here ; mind, I say, ye silent ones, lest ye stand speechless at the bar of judgment. Some, after having been long silent, and so practically denying Christ, go farther, and apostatize altogether from the faith they once had. No man who hath a genuine faith in Christ will lose it, for the faith which God gives will live for ever. Hypocrites and formalists have a name to live while yet they are dead, and after a while they return like the dog to its vomit, and the sow which was washed to her wallowing in the mire. Certain professors who do not run this length, yet practically deny Christ by their lives, though they make a profession of faith in Him. Are there not here some who have been baptized and who come to the Lord's table. but what is their character ? Follow them home. I would to God they never had made a profession, because in their own houses they deny what in the house of God they have avowed. If I see a man drunk ; if I know that a professor indulges in lasciviousness ; if I know a man to be harsh, and overbearing, and tyrannical to his servants ; if I know another who cheats in'his traffic, and another who adulterates his goods, and if I know that such men profess allegiance to Jesus, which am I to believe, their words or their deeds ? I would believe that which speaks loudest ; and as actions always speak louder than words, I will believe their actions—I believe that they are deceivers whom Jesus will deny at the last. Should we not find many present this morning, belonging to one or other of these grades ? Does not this description suit at least some of you ? If it should do so, do not be angry with me, but stand still and hear the word of the Lord. Know, O man, that you will not perish even if you have denied Christ, if now you fly to Him for refuge. Peter denied, but Peter is in heaven. A transient forsaking of Jesus under temptation will not bring on everlasting ruin, if faith shall step in, and the grace of God shall intervene ; but persevere in it, continue still in a denial of the Saviour, and my terrible text will come upon you, " He also will deny you."

In musing over the very dreadful sentence which closes my text, " He also will deny us," I was led to think of various ways in which Jesus will deny us. He does this sometimes on earth. You have read, I suppose, the death of Francis Spira. If you have ever read it, you never can forget it to your dying day. Francis Spira knew the truth ; he was a reformer of no mean standing ; but when brought to death, out of fear, he recanted. In a short time he fell into despair, and suffered hell upon earth. His shrieks and exclamations were so horrible, that their record is almost too terrible for print. His doc m was a warning to the age in which he lived. Another instance is narrated by my predecessor, Benjamin Keach, of one who, during Puritanic times, was very earnest for Puritanism : but afterwards, when times of persecution arose, forsook his profession. The scenes at his death-bed were thrilling and terrible. He declared that though he sought God, heaven was shut against him ; gates of brass seemed to be in his way, he was given up to overwhelming despair. At intervals he cursed, at other intervals he prayed, and so perished without hope. If we deny Christ, we may be delivered to such a fate. If we have stood highest and foremost in God's Church, and yet have not been brought to Christ, if we should become apostates, a high soar will bring a deep fall. High pretensions bring down sure destruction when they come to nought. Even upon earth Christ will deny such. There are remarkable instances of persons who have sought to save their lives and lost them. One Richard Denton, who had been a very zealous Lollard, and was the means of the conversion of an eminent saint, when he came to the stake, was so afraid of the fire that he renounced everything he held, and went into the Church of Rome. A short time after his own house took fire, and going into it to save some of his money, he perished miserably, being utterly consumed by that fire which he had denied Christ in order to escape. If I must be lost, let it be anyhow rather than as an apostate. If there be any distinction among the damned, those have it who are wandering stars, trees plucked up by the roots, twice dead, for whom Jude tells us, is " reserved the blackness of darkness for ever." *Reserved !* as if nobody else were qualified to occupy that place but themselves. They are to inhabit the darkest, hottest places, because they forsook the Lord. Let us, my dear friends, then rather lose everything than lose Christ. Let us sooner suffer anything than lose our ease of conscience and our peace of mind. When Marcus Arethusus was commanded by Julian the apostate to subscribe towards the rebuilding of a heathen temple which his people had pulled down upon their conversion to Christianity, he refused to obey ; and though he was an aged man, he was stripped naked, and then pierced all over with lancets and knives. The old man still was firm. If he would give but one halfpenny towards the building of the temple, he could be free—if he would cast in but one grain of incense into the censer devoted to the false gods, he might escape. He would not countenance idolatry in any degree. He was smeared with honey, and while his innumerable wounds were yet bleeding, the bees and wasps came upon him and stung him to death.

He could die, but he could not deny his Lord. Arethusus entered into the joy of his Lord, for he nobly suffered with Him. In the olden times when the gospel was preached in Persia, one Hamedatha, a courtier of the king, having embraced the faith, was stripped of all his offices, driven from the palace, and compelled to feed camels. This he did with great content. The king passing by one day, saw his former favourite at his ignoble work, cleaning out the camels' stables. Taking pity upon him he took him into his palace, clothed him with sumptuous apparel, restored him to all his former honours, and made him sit at the royal table. In the midst of the dainty feast, he asked Hamedatha to renounce his faith. The courtier, rising from the table, tore off his garments with haste, left all the dainties behind him, and said, " Didst thou think that for such silly things as these I would deny my Lord and Master ? " and away he went to the stable to his ignoble work. How honourable is all this ! But how shall I execrate the meanness of the apostate, his detestable cowardice, to forsake the bleeding Saviour of Calvary to return to the beggarly elements of the world which he once despised, and to bow his neck again to the yoke of bondage ? Will you do this, O followers of the Crucified ? You will not ; you cannot ; I know you cannot, if the spirit of the martyrs dwells in you, and it must dwell in you if you be the children of God. What must be the doom of those who deny Christ, when they reach *another world.* Mayhap, they will appear with a sort of hope in their minds, and they will come before the judge, with " Lord, Lord, open to us ? " " Who are you ? " saith He. " Lord, we once took the Lord's Supper—Lord, we were members of the Church, but there came very hard times. My mother bade me give up religion ; father was angry ; trade went bad ; I was so mocked at, I could not stand it. Lord, I fell among evil acquaintants and they tempted me—I could not resist. I was Thy servant—I did love Thee—I always had love towards Thee in my heart, but I could not help it— I denied Thee and went to the world again," What will Jesus say ? " I know ye not, whence ye are." " But, Lord, I want Thee to be my advocate." " I know you not ! " " But, Lord, I cannot get into heaven unless Thou shouldst open the gate—open it for me." " I do not know you ; I do not know you." " But, Lord, my name was in the Church Book." " I know you not—I deny you." " But wilt Thou not hear my cries ? " " Thou didst not hear Mine— thou didst deny Me, and I deny thee." " Lord, give me the lowest place in heaven, if I may but enter and escape from wrath to come." " No, thou wouldst not brook the lowest place on earth, and thou shalt not enjoy the lowest place here. Thou hadst thy choice, and thou didst choose evil. Keep to thy choice. Thou wast filthy, be thou filthy still. Thou wast unholy, be thou unholy still." O sirs, if ye would not see the angry face of Jesus ! O sirs, if ye would not behold the lightning flashing from His eye, and hear the thunder of His mouth in the day when He judges Thee, and the unbelieving, and the hypocrite ; if you would not have your portion in the lake which burneth with fire and brimstone, cry this day mightily unto God, " Lord, hold me fast, keep me, keep me. Help me to suffer with Thee, that I may reign with Thee ; but do not, do not let me deny Thee, lest Thou also shouldst deny me."

ETERNAL FAITHFULNESS UNAFFECTED BY HUMAN UNBELIEF

" If we believe not, yet He abideth faithful : He cannot deny Himself."—2 Timothy ii. 13.

THIS is one of the five faithful sayings which the apostle mentions. All those faithful sayings are weighty and important. I suppose that they may have come into the possession of the church by having been uttered by some of those prophets who were raised up to cherish the infancy of the church, such as Agabus, and the daughters of Philip, and others. These may have been some of their more remarkable sayings which laid hold upon the minds of good men, were quoted by the preachers and teachers, and so became current throughout the church. Such golden sayings were minted into proverbs, and passed from hand to hand, enriching all who received them : to the saints they became " familiar. in their mouths as household words," and were specially named faithful or true sayings. No doubt the apostle Paul gave his endorsement to many of these holy proverbs, but five of them he has encased in the amber of inspiration, and handed down for our special note. Perhaps it may interest you to notice them as they occur. The first one, the best one probably, is in the First Epistle of Timothy, first chapter, and the fifteenth verse, " This is a faithful saying, and worthy of all acceptation, that Christ Jesus came into the world to save sinners ; of whom I am chief." I can suppose that the good news was frequently conveyed by humble-minded Christians to the outside world in that short and compact form—"Jesus Christ came into the world to save sinners," so that it was commonly known to be a saying among Christians. It was the way in which those who could not preach a sermon, and, perhaps, could scarcely compose a sentence for themselves, learned the pith and marrow of the gospel, and had it by them in a concise and simple form for instructing others. Converts were in the habit of telling this to their heathen friends and acquaintances wherever they went, that so they might know what Jesus Christ had come to do, and might be led to believe on His name. The next faithful or true saying is in the First Epistle of Timothy, the third chapter, and the first verse. " This is a true saying, If a man desire the office of a bishop, he desireth a good work." Any man who desireth to oversee the church of God, and to be in the midst of the people as a shepherd, desireth a good work. He will bring upon himself great anxiety, labour, and travail, but the work is honourable, and has so large a spiritual reward that a man is wise to choose it, and to give his whole life to it. Another of these faithful sayings will be found in the First Epistle of Timothy, the fourth chapter, and the eighth verse, for so the words run, " For bodily exercise profiteth little : but godliness is profitable unto all things, having promise of the life that now is, and of that which is to come. This is a faithful saying and worthy of all acceptation. For therefore we both labour and suffer reproach, because we trust in the living God, who is the Saviour of all men, specially of those that believe." Godliness hath the profit of this life and the next, and therefore godly men are content to suffer, because they expect and do receive an abundant blessing as the result thereof at the hands of God. Such a proverb as this was greatly needed in persecuting times, and it is valuable still in these greedy days, when men find godliness a hindrance to their hasty snatching at wealth, and therefore turn aside unto ways of dishonesty and falsehood. The next is the one which constitutes our text. We will not, therefore, read it until we come to handle it. But the fifth is in Titus, the third chapter, and the eighth verse, " This is a faithful saying, and these things I will that thou affirm constantly, that they which have believed in God might be careful to maintain good works. These things are good and profitable unto men." That those who believe in Jesus should manifest the holy character of their faith by their lives is another one of these faithful sayings, which comes with all the greater force from Paul because he above all men was free from any suspicion of legality, or the putting of human merit into the place of the grace of God which is received by faith.

And now, coming to the faithful saying before us, it may not strike you at first, but scholarly men have observed that the eleventh, twelfth, and thirteenth verses assume the form of a hymn. The Hebrew hymns were written in parallelisms, not, of course, in rhymes ; and these three verses are thought to have been one of the oldest of Christian hymns.

> " It is a faithful saying :
> For if we be dead with Him, we shall also live with Him :
> If we suffer, we shall also reign with Him :
> If we deny Him, He also will deny us :
> If we believe not, yet He abideth faithful :
> He cannot deny Himself."

This is a miniature psalm—one of those psalms and hymns and spiritual songs with which the saints of God were wont to edify one another.

I am sure this last part of this brief hymn is well worthy to be regarded as a faithful saying among ourselves. Brethren, we may often mention it ; we may frequently quote it ; we may roll it under our tongue as a sweet morsel ; we may pass it from one to another as a classic saying of Christian wisdom—" If we believe not, yet He abideth faithful : He cannot deny Himself."

In handling it at this time I would divide it into two folded parts. The first double portion is, *the sad possibility, with the consoling assurance.* " If we believe not,"—sad possibility : " yet He abideth faithful,"—consoling assurance. The second part of our subject is *the glorious impossibility, and the sweet inference that we may draw from it.* The glorious impossibility is,—" He cannot deny Himself," and the inference we draw from it is the obverse or converse of our text—If we believe, He abideth faithful : He cannot deny Himself.

I. To begin, then, with THE SAD POSSIBILITY,

AND THE CONSOLING ASSURANCE—" If we believe not, yet He abideth faithful."

I must take the *sad possibility* first,—" if we believe not," and I shall read this expression as though, first of all, it concerned *the world in general*, for I think it may so be fairly read. If we believe not—if mankind believe not, if the race believe not, if the various classes of men believe not—yet He abideth faithful. *The rulers* believe not, and there are some that make this a very great point. They said concerning Jesus, " Have any of the rulers believed on Him ? " If Lord So-and-so hears the preacher there must be something in what he says. Englishmen are wonderfully impressed with the judgment of a duke or an earl, and even with that of titled folk of lower degree. If any of the rulers believe in Him, who among worshippers of rank would raise a question ? Is it published under authority ? Do the great ones subscribe to it ? " Oh, then," says one, " it must be good, and it must be true." Now, I venture to say that all history proves that the truth has very seldom been accepted by the rulers of this world, and that for the most part the poorest of the poor have been more able to perceive the truth than the greatest of the great have ever been. There would have been no Christianity in the world at the present moment if it had not found a shelter in workshops and in cottages. It has flourished amongst the despised poor when it has been scouted by the great ones of the earth. Well, sirs, if we believe not—that is, if our greatest men, if our senators and magistrates, princes and potentates, believe not—it does not affect the truth of God in the smallest conceivable degree— " yet He abideth faithful."

Many, however, think it more important to know on which side *the leaders of thought* are enlisted and there are certain persons who are not elected to that particular office by popular vote, who nevertheless take it upon themselves to consider that they are dictators in the republic of opinion. They are advanced men and far ahead of the old school of divines. Some of us think that they are advancing in the direction of going backwards, and that they are putting ignorant guess-work into the room of proved doctrine and solid, experimental, Scriptural teaching. Still, as in their own opinion they are our superiors, and pioneer the way of progress, we will for a moment think of them as such. Now, in our Lord's day, the advanced thinkers were not on His side at all ; they were all against Him, and after He had departed, the gravest peril of the church of God arose from the advanced thought of the period. The Gnostics, and other Grecian thinkers, came forward, and they threw their philosophical mud into the pure stream of the gospel till there was no plain statement which was not rendered mythical, mystical, confused, and clouded, so that only the initiated could possibly understand it. The gospel of Jesus Christ was meant to be the plainest truth that ever shone upon the sons of men. It was meant to be legible in its own light by the young, the unlearned, and the simple ; but the advanced thinkers took the gospel, and twisted it, coloured it, adorned it, and bedaubed it till by the time it came through their various processes you would not have known it to be the same thing at all ; and, in fact, Paul said that it was not the same thing, for he called it " another gospel," and then he corrected himself, and said it was not another :

" But there be some," said he, " that trouble you." However, we need not care because of these wise men, for if they believe not, but becloud the gospel, yet God abideth faithful. If over there in the groves where Socrates and Plato gathered disciples by their philosophy, if over there, I say, there should not be found a single philosopher who believes in God, so much the worse for the philosophers, but it does not affect the gospel or our faith in it : if they believe not, He abideth faithful. If Paul at the Areopagus gets no sympathy except from two or three, and in fact they have only asked him there to " hear what this babbler saith," and though they all as they go home say that Paul is beside himself, and mad, and a setter forth of strange gods, yet Paul is right, and the Lord abideth faithful.

Yes, and I venture to enlarge this thought a little more. If the rulers do not believe, and if the philosophical minds do not believe, and if in addition to this *public opinion*, so called, rejects it, yet the gospel is still the same eternal truth. Public opinion is not the test and gauge of truth, for it has continually altered, and it will continue to alter. The aggregate thinking of fallible men is less than nothing when set against the one solitary mind of God, who is infallible, as He reveals it to us by the Holy Ghost in the words of truth in the Scriptures. But some think that the old gospel cannot be right, because, you see, everybody says that it is out of date and wrong. That is one reason for being the more sure that it is right, for the world lieth in the wicked one, and its judgment is under his sway. What are multitudes when they are all under the influence of the father of lies ? The grandest majority in the world is a minority of one when that man is on God's side. Count heads, do you ? Well count by the millions, if you like, but I shall rather weigh than count ; and if I speak the truth of God, I have more weight on my side than can be found in a million who believe not. I wish we all partook of the spirit of Athanasius when he said, defending the deity of his great Master, " I, Athanasius, against the world." You must learn to stand alone. When you know that you have a grip of revealed truth you may not set all the judgments of men in comparison with the eternal and infallible judgment of the mighty God. No, though we believe not, that is, the mass of us and nations of us, " yet He abideth faithful : He cannot deny Himself."

I want to ask your thoughtful attention to one consideration here. Have you not often heard it said that ministers ought to be abreast of the times, that theology should be always toned and varied so as to suit the advanced thought of the wonderful period in which we live ? And as this is a time when infidelity appears to be in the very air, we are told that we ought to sympathize with it very earnestly and heartily, for it is a form of struggling for the light which we ought to encourage. Now, this is another sort of talk from what I hear from the apostle Paul. He has no sympathy with it. He puts his foot on it. " Let God be true and every man a liar "—that is the style in which he speaks. As to going in to study the philosophies in order to tune the gospel to their note, he says, " I determined not to know anything among you save Jesus Christ and Him crucified." When he finds that this style of doctrine does not please the Jew, and that it is to him a stumbling-block, and that it does not please the Greek, but makes him sneer and call it foolishness, does the apostle, therefore, say, " Come hither, dear Jewish friend. I have a way of putting this which will show you that I do not quite mean what you thought I did. I used the word ' cross ' in a certain sense not at all objectionable to Judaism " ? Does he gently whisper, " Come to me, my learned Greek friend, and I will show you that your philosophers and I mean the same thing " ? Not a bit of it ; but he stands fast and firm to Christ crucified and salvation by His blood, as, by God's grace, I trust we are resolved to do. Though we believe not—that is, though the whole world believe not—yet God's gospel is not to be altered to suit human whims and fancies, but in all its angularity and singularity, in all its divine authority, unpared, uncut, wrought out as a whole, it is still to be proclaimed, for " He abideth faithful : He cannot deny Himself."

Now, having spoken of our text as referring to the world in general, it is, perhaps, a more sorrowful business to look at it as referring to the visible church in particular. The apostle says, " Though *we* believe not," and surely he must mean the *visible church of God.*

And does the church of God ever fall into such a state that we may say of it, " It believes not " ? Yes, the visible church has many and many a time fearfully turned aside. Go back for a type of it to the wilderness. The children of Israel were brought up out of Egypt with a high hand and an out-stretched arm, and they were fed in the wilderness with angels' food, and made to drink of water from the rock ; but they were continually doubting their God.

> " Now they believe His word
> While rocks with rivers flow ;
> Anon with sin they grieve the Lord,
> And judgments lay them low."

But what happened ? Did God depart from His purpose to give the land that flowed with milk and honey to the seed of Abraham ? Did He break up the covenant and grow weary of it ? No ; but Abraham's seed inherited the land, and they dwelt therein every man under his own vine and fig-tree. Though the visible people of God rejected Him full often, so that for their unbelief they died in the wilderness, yet He remained faithful : He did not, He could not, deny Himself. Well, now, it comes to pass sometimes, according to this type, that the visible church of God apostatizes from the truth of God. The doctrines of grace, the truths of the gospel are obscured, beclouded, scarcely preached, preached with gaudy words, or hid behind ceremonies and rites, and all sorts of things. And what happens ? Are the foundation truths removed ? Is the eternal verity reversed ? Has God recalled His promise ? Oh no. " He abideth faithful : He cannot deny Himself."

Alas ! the church of God seems to lose sometimes her faith in prayer. Her pleading assemblies become scant. Her prayer for men's conversion is scarcely raised. Few come together to supplicate the Lord and besiege the mercy-seat. But what then ? Does God change ? Does He forsake His cause ? Oh, no : " He abideth faithful : He cannot deny Himself." At such times the church almost loses her faith in the Holy Spirit and looks upon preaching as, perhaps, a necessary evil to be borne with, but not as the vehicle by which the Holy Ghost saves men.

They have small confidence in God's word that " by the foolishness of preaching " He will " save them that believe." They do not expect the kingdom of Christ to be predominant, but they say, " Since the fathers fell asleep what long ages have dragged along, and what slow progress Christianity has made. It is a hopeless cause. Let us be content to let the heathen world alone." At such time they lose all heart and all faith in God. Have we not seen large portions of the visible church of God decline into such a state as this till we have been ready to say with our Master, " When the Son of man cometh shall He find faith on the earth ? " But what then, my brethren ? Suppose we should live to see every-where a degenerate church ? Suppose it should become like Laodicea, till the Lord should seem to spew the visible church out of His mouth, because she has become neither hot nor cold ? Suppose He should say of the professing church of to-day as He did of Shiloh of old—" Go now to Shiloh where My place was at the first, and see if there be one stone left upon another that is not cast down " ? He took the candlestick away from Rome, and He may take that candlestick away from other churches too. But would that prove that God was unfaithful, or that He had denied Himself ? No, beloved ; no. His faithfulness would be seen then in the judgment with which He would visit an unfaithful church. Aye, and it is seen to-day. You shall see a church which does not believe in the simple gospel grow few and feeble. According as the churches cease to be evangelical they are minished and brought low. A church that neglects prayer becomes disunited, scattered, lethargic, all but dead. A church that has no faith in the Holy Ghost may carry on her ordinances, but it will be with barren formality and without power from on high : all of which proves the faithfulness of Him who said, " If ye walk contrary to Me, I will walk contrary to you." If they cast away from them that which is their strength, it is but faithfulness on God's part that they should become weak. All the history of the church, if you read it, from the days of Christ till now, will go to show that He deals with His church in such a way as to make her see that He is faithful, whatever she may be. He will help her when she turns to Him, He will bless her when she trusts Him, He will crown her when she exalts Him, but He will bring her low and chasten her when she turns in any measure aside from the simplicity of her faith. Thus does He prove that He still is faithful.

Once more, my brethren, I will read the text in a somewhat narrower circle. " If we believe not "— that is to say, if the *choicest teachers*, and preachers, and writers believe not, yet He abideth faithful.

One of the most shocking trials to young Christians is the fall of an eminent teacher. I have known some that have been almost ready to give up their faith when some one who appeared to be very earnest and faithful has suddenly apostatized. Such things have happened in our memory, to our intense grief : and I want, therefore, to put it very, very plainly. If it should come to pass that any one whom you revere as having been blest to your soul—whom you love because you have received from Him the word of life—if such a one upon whom you may, perhaps, have leaned too much, should in the future turn out not to be true and faithful, and should not believe, do not follow his unbelief, for " if we believe not, yet *He* abideth faithful : He cannot deny Himself."

Peter denies his Master : do not follow Peter when he is doing that, for he will have to come back weeping, and you will hear him preaching his Master again. Worse still, Judas sells his Master : do not follow Judas, for Judas will die a wretched death, and his destruction shall be a warning to others to cling more closely to the faith. You may see the man who stood like a cedar in Lebanon fall by one stroke of the devil's axe, but do not, therefore, think that the trees of the Lord, which are full of sap, will fall too. He will keep His own, for He knows them that are His. Pin not your faith to any man's sleeve. Let not your confidence rest on any arm of flesh, neither say " I believe because of the testimony of such a one, and I hold to the form of sound words because my minister has held it " ; for .all such props may be smitten away, and on a sudden may fail you. Do let me put this very, very plainly,—if *we* believe not—if those that seem to be the choice teachers of the age, if those that have been the most successful evangelists of the period, if those who stand high in the esteem of God's people, should, in an evil hour, forsake the eternal verities and begin to preach to you some other gospel which is not the gospel of Jesus Christ, I beseech you follow us not whoever we may be, or whatever we may be. Suffer no teachers, however great they may be, to lead you to doubt, for God abideth faithful. Keep you to the revealed will and mind of God—for " He cannot deny Himself."

Here, then, is the fearful possibility ; and side by side with it runs *this most blessedly consoling assurance*—" He abideth faithful." Jesus Christ *abideth :* there are no shifts and changes in Him. He is a rock, and not a quicksand. He is the Saviour whether the rulers and the philosophers believe in Him or refuse Him, whether the church and her ministers are true to Him or desert Him. He is the same Saviour, God-man, sitting supreme upon the throne. " Why do the heathen rage, and the people imagine a vain thing ? The kings of the earth set themselves, and the rulers take counsel together, against the Lord, and against His anointed. He that sitteth in the heavens shall laugh : the Lord shall have them in derision. Yet," saith He, " have I set My king upon My holy hill of Zion." They cannot affect the imperial throne of our immortal Lord. He still is " the blessed and only Potentate," and so He must be, let them say what they will.

And as Christ remains the same Saviour, so we have the same gospel. They have improved upon it, they tell us ! Well, well, I feel so satisfied with the gospel as I get it from Paul and the inspired apostles that I would rather not have this improved gospel if they will allow me to keep to the old original. But so it is, like babies pleased with new toys they cry up their " modern thought," and culture and advanced ideas. He that has once tasted the old wine does not desire the new, because he saith, " The old is better." Our Saviour and His gospel abide the same. The gospel of Paul, the gospel of Augustine, the gospel of Calvin, the gospel of Whitefield, the gospel of any succession of faithful men you like to strike out abundantly suffices us. " He abideth faithful."

And as the gospel is the same, so does Christ remain faithful to His engagements to His Father. He has promised to keep those whom the Father gave Him, and He will keep them even to the end ; and when the sheep shall pass again under the hand of Him that telleth them He will say, " Of all whom Thou gavest Me I have lost none." " He abideth faithful " ; to sinners all over the world He says that if they come to Him He will not cast them out, and He is faithful to that. He graciously promises that " whosoever calleth upon the name of the Lord shall be saved " ; and He will be faithful to that. He is also faithful to His saints. He has promised to preserve them to His eternal kingdom and glory, and He will preserve them. He says, " I give unto My sheep eternal life, and they shall never perish, neither shall any pluck them out of My hands " : and He has held them in His loving grasp, and He will hold them even to the end ; and all this, though all the unbelief in the world should rise against Him. He will stand to every word He has spoken, and carry out every promise He has declared, though all should distrust and deny. " Yea and amen in Christ Jesus " are all the promises, henceforth and for ever, and we shall find it so.

II. And now we have but a little time to spend upon the second very important part of our text, which is A GLORIOUS IMPOSSIBILITY WITH A SWEET INFERENCE THAT MAY BE DRAWN FROM IT. " He cannot deny Himself."

Three things God cannot do. He cannot die, He cannot lie, and He cannot be deceived. These three impossibilities do not limit His power, but they magnify His majesty ; for these would be infirmities, and infirmity can have no place in the infinite and ever blessed God.

Here is one of the things impossible with God— " He cannot deny Himself." What is meant by that ? It is meant, first, that *the Lord Jesus Christ cannot change* as to His nature and character towards us, the sons of men, for if He were to change He could only change from one state to another—from a better to a worse or from a worse to a better. If from a better to a worse, that were to deny Himself indeed by ceasing to be as good as He is by nature ; and if from a worse to a better, that were to deny Himself by proving that He was not before so good as He might have been. In no one point can Jesus Christ be changed, for He is " Jesus Christ, the same yesterday, to-day, and for ever." If in any point He changed, He would, in that point, deny Himself : but He cannot do this, for being God He changeth not.

His word cannot alter. I want you to notice this, because His word is so conspicuously Himself. His name shall be called the Word of God ; yea, He is Himself the Logos, the eternal Word ; and that Word cannot change. " The grass withereth, and the flower thereof falleth away, but the word of the Lord endureth for ever, and this is the word which by the gospel is preached unto you." O servant of the Lord, the assurance which Paul and Peter gave you may give. That same word of mercy which those first messengers of heaven went forth to declare you may declare, for it still stands the same. He cannot deny His word, since that word is Himself, and He cannot deny Himself.

He cannot, beloved friends, *withdraw the salvation which He has presented to the sons of men,* for that salvation is indeed Himself. Jesus is the salvation of Israel. If a sinner wants to know where salvation lies, we point him to the Christ of God. He is not only a Saviour, but He is salvation itself ; and His salvation cannot be changed, for if *it* were changed He would be Himself changed or denied, and He cannot deny Himself. There is still the same pardon for the chief of sinners, still the same renewing for the hardest hearts, still the same generous response to those who have strayed most, still the same adoption into the family for aliens and foreigners. His salvation, as Peter preached it at Pentecost, is the salvation which we preach to sinners now. " He cannot deny Himself."

And then *the atonement is still the same*, for that, too, is Himself : He has by Himself purged our sins. He Himself is the sacrifice. Well did the poet say,—

> " Dear dying Lamb, Thy precious blood
> Shall never lose its power."

Because it is *His* blood it must be unchanged in efficacy. He cleanses away our sins by Himself. His blood is His life, and He ever liveth, and since He ever liveth He is " able to save to the uttermost them that come unto God by Him." Blessed be His name, the atoning sacrifice has not, even in the smallest degree, lost its efficacy. It is just as mighty as when it washed the dying thief from the foulness of hell into the purity of heaven, and carried him from a gibbet to a throne. Oh, how blessed must its power be to have cleansed so foul a wretch, and to have placed him with the Master Himself in paradise the self-same day. The atonement cannot change, for that would involve that Jesus had denied Himself.

And *the mercy-seat*, the place of prayer, still remains ; for if that were altered He would have denied Himself, for what was the mercy-seat, or propitiatory, that golden lid upon the covenant ark ? What was it but Christ Himself, who is our propitiatory, the true mercy-seat ? You may always pray, brethren, for if prayer were denied its efficacy, God would have denied Himself. This is His memorial, " The God that heareth prayer " ; and if He does not hear prayer He has denied Himself and ceased to be what He was. Jehovah will never so deny Himself as to become like Baal, a deaf god ; to imagine it would be blasphemy.

And here is another sweet thought : *Christ's love to His church, and His purpose towards her cannot change*, because He cannot deny Himself, and His church is Himself. I mean not that visible church of which I spoke just now, which is a mixed multitude, but I mean that invisible church, that spiritual people, that bride of Christ, which no man seeth, for she is prepared in darkness, and curiously wrought in the lowest parts of the earth ; and her Lord Himself will never see her actually till she is perfected, even as Adam never saw Eve, but slept until the great God had finished his bride, and presented her in all her matchless beauty to be His sister and spouse. The day comes when the Lord Jesus Christ shall thus receive His perfected bride, and meanwhile He cannot change towards her, but His espousals shall be confirmed. She was taken out of His side when in deep sleep of death He lay, and she is fashioned to be like to Him, so that when in joy He shall behold her His joy and her joy shall be full. No, He will never, never deny her, for He cannot deny Himself. His plan of love shall be carried out and all His thoughts of grace fulfilled.

Nor will any one of *His offices towards His church and people ever fail*. The Prophet shall be Prophet for ever,—" He cannot deny Himself." The Priest shall be a Priest for ever after the order of Melchizedec,

and will never refuse to offer our prayers and praises, and to cleanse our souls, for He cannot deny Himself. The King will never cease to reign, or doff His crown, or lay down His sceptre, for He cannot deny Himself. The Shepherd will for ever keep the flock. The Friend will eternally stick closer than a brother. The Husband will still love his spouse. All that He is in relation to His people shall continue and abide, for He abideth faithful. " He cannot deny Himself."

Now, my last word is about *an inference*. The text says, " If we believe not, yet He abideth faithful " : it runs on that supposition. Now, brethren, take the other supposition :—Suppose we do believe. Will He not be faithful in that case ? And will it not be true that He cannot deny Himself ?

I will suppose that a sinner is at this moment saying, " I believe that Christ can save me : I will go and ask Him, I will go and trust Him." Ah, He will not deny Himself by rejecting your cry. I tell you, if He were to shut you out, dear soul, whoever you may be, if you go to Him, He would deny Himself. He never did deny Himself yet. Whenever a sinner comes to Him He becomes His Saviour. Whenever He meets a sick soul He acts as his Physician. Now, I have heard of persons who have been physicians, who were ill, or weary and wanted rest : an accident has happened, and they have felt inclined to get out of the way if they could, because they were very hard-worked and worn out. They have told their servant to say, " My master is not at home ! " but my Master never denied Himself. He will never get out of the way of a sinner. If you go to Him you will find Him at home and on the look-out for you : He will be more glad to receive you than you will be to be received, for He " waiteth to be gracious." As Matthew sat at the receipt of custom, waiting for the people to pay their dues, so does Christ sit at the receipt of sinners waiting for them to mention their wants. He is watching for you. I tell you again that He cannot reject you : that would be to alter His whole character and un-Christ Himself. To spurn a coming sinner would un-Jesus Him, and make Him to be somebody else, and not Himself any longer. " He cannot deny Himself." Go and try Him : go and try Him. I wish some trembling soul would at this moment go and cast himself upon Christ, and then report to us the result. Come, poor quivering seekers, sing in your heart, unbelieving as you are, that hymn of ours—

> " I can but perish if I go,
> I am resolved to try ;
> For if I stay away, I know
> I must for ever die."

Oh, but if you were to perish at His feet, you would be the first that ever did so out of all those who have ever come to Him ; and that first man has never been seen yet. Go and try my Lord and see for yourselves.

Well now, you Christian people, I want you to come also. If you believe your Lord He will be faithful to you. Suppose it is a time of trouble with you : He will be faithful to you ; go and cast your burden upon Him. Suppose at this time you are much exercised with spiritual distress : go to the Lord as you did at first, as poor, guilty, rebellious sinners, and cast yourself upon Him, and you will find Him faithful. " He cannot deny Himself." If my Lord were not kind to me to-night when I go to Him with my burden I should think that I had knocked at the wrong door ; because the Lord has been so good and so faithful to me hitherto that it would take my breath away if I found Him changed. Oh, how good, how exceeding good is my Lord! Did not we sing just now—

"He by my side has always stood :
His lovingkindness, oh, how good ! "

I could sing that with all my heart, and I hope many of you could earnestly join with me. You have a dear mother, or a fond wife, or a choice friend, and none of them has ever spoken anything but kindness to you ; and therefore if in some dark hour you were to go to them, and instead of showing sympathy they gave you sharp words, and you could evidently see that they did not love you, how surprised you would be! So should I be if I were to meet anything but love from my dear Lord after all these years of tenderness. There is no fear of it, for "He cannot deny Himself."

So I finish by saying that we shall find it so in connection with the things of His kingdom and the concerns of His truth. There is a great uproar just now about the God of providence, and they call me I know not by what names for speaking the truth for my Master. Well, what comes of it? Shall we, therefore, be afraid? No ; but if we believe we shall find Him faithful. He will not deny Himself. Is the good old cause really in danger from scepticism and superstition? Speaking after the manner of men, it may seem so ; but it never really is so. Even if it were tottering we must not put our hand upon the ark of the Lord to steady it. God's cause is always safe. I do not know whether we may live to see it, but as surely as the Lord lives the truth will be triumphant in England yet. They may tell us that Puritanism is thrust to the wall, but it will take the crown of the causeway yet. The old cause goes back a little to take breath, but she will make such a leap in this land as shall utterly surprise the soothsayers ; for the Lord will make the diviners mad, and they that count the towers and say that Zion is utterly fallen shall not know where to hide their heads. The devil once flew all over Europe, and said, " It is all mine. Here they are selling indulgences and the Pope and I are master of it all." But there was a poor monk who had not himself seen the light any long time, who nailed his theses on the door of a church, and from that hour the light began to spread all over Europe. And do you think the Lord is short of Luthers? Do you imagine that He has no sword or spear left in His armoury? I tell you He has as many instruments within reach as there are stars in the sky. When the influence of the gospel appears to recede it is like the tide when it is ebbing out. Steadily it goes back, and if we did not know better we should begin to think that the silver waves would all give place to mire and shingle : yet when the hour comes, at the very minute, the waters pause and remain at one point awhile. Then up comes the first wave of the wash, and another, and another, and another, and another, rising, advancing, conquering the shore, till the sea has come to her fulness again. So must it be, and so shall it be with the ocean of truth ; only let us have faith, and we shall see the gospel at the flood again, and old England covered with it. Doubt what you like, brethren, but do not doubt divine truth, or doubt God. Hold you on to the side that is most disgraced and dishonoured, and that has the worst word from men ; for Christ and His church usually have the bleak side of the hill. Be content to breast the stream with courage learned from your Redeemer and Lord, for the day comes when to have stood with the truth and with the Son of the Highest will be the grandest honour that a creature can have worn. May that honour be ours, for Jesus' sake. Amen.

RIGHTLY DIVIDING THE WORD OF TRUTH

" Rightly dividing the word of truth."—2 Timothy ii. 15.

TIMOTHY was to divide rightly the word of God. This every Christian minister must do if he would make full proof of his ministry, and if he would be clear of the blood of his hearers at the last great day. Of the whole twenty years of my sermons, I can honestly say that this has been my aim—rightly to divide the word of truth. Wherein I have succeeded I magnify the name of the Lord, wherein I have failed I lament my faultiness. And now once more we will try again, and may God the Holy Spirit, without whose power nothing can be done aright, help us rightly to divide the word of truth.

The expression is a very remarkable one, because it bears so many phases of meaning. I do not think that any one of the figures by which I shall illustrate it will be at all strained, for they have been drawn from the text by eminent expositors, and may fairly be taken as honest comments, even when they might be challenged as correct interpretations of the text. " Rightly dividing the word of truth " is our authorised version, but we leave it for a little to consider other renderings. Timothy was neither to mutilate, nor twist, nor torture, nor break in pieces the word, nor keep on the outside of it, as those do who never touch the soul of a text, but rightly to divide it, as one taught of God to teach others.

I. The vulgar version translates it—and with a considerable degree of accuracy—" Rightly HANDLING the word of truth." What is the right way, then, to handle the word of truth? It is like a sword, and it was not meant to be played with. That is not rightly to handle the gospel. It must be used in earnest and pushed home. Are you converted, my friends? Do you believe in Jesus Christ? Are you saved, or not? Swords are meant to cut and hack, and wound, and kill with, and the word of truth is for pricking men in the heart and killing their sins. The word of God is not committed to God's ministers to amuse men with its glitter, nor to charm them with the jewels in its hilt, but to conquer their souls for Jesus. Remember, dear hearers, if the preacher does not push you to this— that you shall be converted, or he will know the reason why ; if he does not drive you in this—that you shall either wilfully reject, or cheerfully accept Christ, he has not yet known how rightly to handle the great " sword of the Spirit, which is the word of God." Now, then, where are you personally at this moment? Are you unbelievers, upon whom the wrath of God abideth, or are you believers, who may lay claim to that gracious word, " Verily, verily, I say unto you, he that believeth in Me hath everlasting life." Oh that the Lord would make His all-discerning word go round this place and strike at every conscience and lay bare every heart with its mighty power.

He that rightly handles the word of God will *never use it to defend men in their sins*, but to slay their sins. If there be a professing Christian here who is living in known sin, shame upon him ; and if there be a non-Christian man who is living in sin, let his conscience upbraid him. What will he do in that day when Christ comes to judge the hearts of men, and the books shall be opened, and every thought shall be read out before an assembled universe ? I desire to handle the word of God so that no man may ever find an excuse in my ministry for his living without Christ, and living in sin, but may know clearly that sin is a deadly evil, and unbelief the sure destroyer of the soul. He has indeed been made to handle the word aright who plunges it like a two-edged sword into the very bowels of sin.

The gospel ought *never to be used for frightening sinners from Christ*. I believe it is so handled sometimes. Sublime doctrines are rolled like rocks in the sinner's way, and dark experiences set up as a standard of horror which must be reached before a man may believe in Jesus : but rightly to handle the word of life is to frighten men *to* Christ rather than *from* Him, yea, to woo them to Him by the sweet assurance that He will cast out none that come, that He asks no preparations of them, but if they come at once as they are He will assuredly receive them. Have I not handled the word of truth in this way hundreds of times in this house ? Has it not been a great magnet attracting sinners ? As a magnet has two poles, and with one pole it repels, so, no doubt, the truth of God repels the prejudiced, rebellious heart, and thus it is a savour of death unto death ; but our object is so to handle it that the attractive pole may come into operation through the power of the Spirit of God, and men may be drawn to Christ.

Moreover, if we rightly handle the word of God *we shall not preach it so as to send Christians into a sleepy state*. That is easily done. We may preach the consolations of the gospel till each professor feels " I am safe enough ; there is no need to watch, no need to fight, no need for any exertion whatever. My battle is fought, my victory is won, I have only to fold my arms and go to sleep." No, no, men, this is not how we handle the word of God, but our cry is, " Work out your own salvation with fear and trembling ; for it is God which worketh in you both to will and to do of His good pleasure. Watch and pray that ye enter not into temptation. Reckon not yourselves to have attained unto perfection, but forget the things that are behind, and reach forward to that which is before, ever looking unto Jesus." This is rightly to handle the word of God.

And, oh, beloved, there is one thing that I dread above all others—lest I should ever handle the word of God *so as to persuade some of you that you are saved when you are not*. To collect a large number of professors together is one thing ; but to have a large number of true saints built together in Christ is quite another thing. To get up a whirl of excitement, and to have people influenced by that excitement, so that they think full surely that they are converted, has been done a great many times ; but the bubble has, by-and-by vanished. The balloon has been filled

until it has burst. God save us from that. We want sure work, lasting work, a work of divine grace in the heart. If you are not converted, pray do not pretend that you are. If you have not known what it is to be brought down to see your own nothingness, and then to be built up by the power of the Spirit upon Christ as the only foundation, oh, remember that whatever is built upon the quicksand will fall with a crash in the hour of trial. Do not be satisfied with anything short of a deep foundation, cut in the solid rock of the work of Jesus Christ. Ask for real vital godliness, for nothing else will serve your turn at the last day. Now, this is rightly to handle the word of God ; to use it to push truth home upon men for their present conversion, to use it for the striking down of their sins, to use it to draw men to Christ, to use it to arouse sinners, and to use it to produce, not mere profession, but a real work of grace in the hearts of men. May the Holy Ghost teach all the ministers of Christ after this fashion to handle the two-edged sword of the Spirit, which is the word of God.

II. But now, secondly, my text has another meaning. It has an idea in it which I can only express by a figure. " Rightly dividing, or STRAIGHT CUTTING." A ploughman stands here with his plough, and he ploughs right along from this end of the field to the other, making a straight furrow. And so Paul would have Timothy make a straight furrow right through the word of truth. I believe there is no preaching that God will ever accept but that which goes decidedly through the whole line of truth from end to end, and is always thorough, honest, and downright. As truth is a straight line, so must our handling of the truth be straightforward and honest, without shifts or tricks. There are two or three furrows which I have laboured hard to plough. One is the furrow of *free grace*. " Salvation is of the Lord,"— He begins it, He carries it on, He completes it. Salvation is not of man, neither by man, but of grace alone. Grace in election, grace in redemption, grace in effectual calling, grace in final perseverance, grace in conferring the perfection of glory ; it is all grace from beginning to end. If we say at any time anything which is really contrary to this distinct testimony that salvation is of grace, believe us not. This furrow must be ploughed fairly, plainly, and beyond all mistake. Sinner, you cannot be saved by any merit, penance, preparation, or feeling of your own. The Lord alone must save you as a work of gratis mercy, not because you deserve it, but because He wills to do it to magnify His abundant love. That is the straight furrow of the word.

We endeavour always to make a straight furrow upon the matter of *human depravity*—to preach that man is fallen, that every part and passion of his nature is perverted, that he has gone astray altogether, is sick from the crown of his head to the sole of his foot, yea, is dead in trespasses and sins, and corrupt before God. " There is none that doeth good, no, not one." I have noticed some preachers ploughing this furrow very crookedly, for they say, " There are some very fine points about man still, and many good things in him which only need developing and educating." You may have read in the history of Mr. Whitefield's time what a howl was made at him because he once said that man was half beast and half devil. I do not think he ever got nearer the truth than when he said that ; only I would beg the beast's pardon, for a beast would scarcely become so evil and vile as human nature becomes when it is left alone fully to develop itself. O pride of human nature, we plough right over thee! The hemlock stands in thy field, and must be cut up by the roots. Thy weeds smile like fair flowers, but the ploughshare must go right through them all till all human beauty is shown to be a painted Jezebel, and all human glorying a bursting bubble. God is everything, man is nothing. God in His grace saves men, but man by his sin utterly ruins himself until God's grace interposes. I like to plough a straight furrow here.

Another straight furrow is that of *faith*. We are sent to tell men that he that believeth and is baptized shall be saved, and our duty is to put it so. "Salvation is not of works"; that is not the furrow; not of prayers, that is not the furrow: not of feelings—that is not the gospel furrow: not of preparations and amendments and reforms: but by faith in Jesus Christ. He that believeth on Him is not condemned. As we begin the new life by faith, we must abide in it by faith. We are not to be saved by faith up to a certain point, and then to rely upon ourselves. Having began in the gospel we are not to be perfected by the law. "The just shall live by faith." We live by faith at the wicket-gate, and we live by faith until we enter into our eternal rest. *Believe!*—that is the grand gospel precept, and we trust we have never gone out of this furrow, but have tried to plough right across the gospel field from end to end, crying, "Look unto Me and be ye saved, all ye ends of the earth, for Jehovah is God, and beside Him there is none else."

Another furrow which some do not much like to plough, but which must be distinctly marked if a man is an honest ploughman for God, is that of *repentance*. Sinner, you and your sins must part. You have been married long, and you have had a merry time of it perhaps; but you must part. You and your sins must separate, or you and your God will never come together. Not one sin may you keep. They must all be given up: they must be brought out like the Canaanitish kings from the cave, and hanged up before the sun. Not one darling must be spared. You must forsake them, loathe them, abhor them, and ask the Lord to overcome them. Do you not know that the furrow of repentance runs right through the Christian's life? He sins, and as long as he sins he repents of his sin. The child of God cannot love sin: he must loathe it as long as he sees any of it in existence.

There is the furrow of *holiness*, that is the next turn the ploughman takes. "Without holiness no man shall see the Lord." We have preached salvation by grace, but we do not preach salvation to those who still continue in sin. The children of God are a holy people, washed, purged, sanctified, and made zealous for good works; and he who talks about faith, and has no works to prove that his faith is a living faith, lies to himself and lies before God. It is faith that saves us, not works, but the faith that saves us always produces works: it renews the heart, changes the character, influences the motives, and is the means in the hand of God of making the man a new creature in Christ Jesus. No nonsense about it, sirs: you may be baptized and re-baptized, you may attend to sacraments, or you may believe in an orthodox creed; but you will be damned if you live in sin. You may become a deacon, or an elder, or a minister, if you dare; but there is no salvation for any man who still harbours his sins. "The

wages of sin is death"—death to professors as well as to non-professors. If they hug their sins in secret God will reveal those sins in public, and condemn them according to the strict justice of His law. These are the furrows we have tried to plough—deep, sharp cut, and straight. Oh, that God might plough them Himself in all your hearts that you may know experimentally how the truth is rightly divided.

III. There is a third meaning to the text. "Rightly dividing the word of truth" is, as some think, an expression taken from the priests dividing the sacrifices. When they had a lamb or a sheep, a ram or a bullock to offer, after they had killed it, it was cut to pieces, carefully and properly; and it requires no little skill to find out where the joints are, so as to cut up an animal discreetly. Now, the word of truth has to be taken to pieces wisely; it is not to be hacked or torn as by a wild beast, but rightly divided. There has to be DISCRIMINATION AND DISSECTION. It is a great part of a minister's duty to be able to dissect the gospel—to lay one piece there, and another there, and preach with clearness, distinction, and discrimination.

Every gospel minister must divide between the covenant of works and the covenant of grace. It is a very nice point that, and many fail to discern it well; but it must always be kept clear, or great mischief will be done. Confusion worse confounded follows upon confusing grace and law. There is the covenant of works—"This do, and thou shalt live," but its voice is not that of the covenant of grace which says, "Hear and your soul shall live." "You shall, for I will": that is the covenant of grace. It is a covenant of pure promise unalloyed by terms and conditions. I have heard people put it thus—"Believers will be saved if from this time forth they are faithful to grace given." That savours of the covenant of works. "God will love you"—says another,—"if you—." Ah, the moment you get an "if" in it, it is the covenant of works, and the gospel has evaporated. Oil and water will sooner mix than merit and grace. When you find the covenant of works anywhere, what are you to do with it? Why, do what Abraham did, and what Sarah demanded, "cast out the bondwoman and her son, for the son of the bondwoman shall not be heir with my son, even with Isaac." If you are a child of the free-grace promise, do not suffer the Hagar and Ishmael of legal bondage and carnal hope to live in your house. Out with them; you have nought to do with them. Let law and gospel keep their proper places. The law is the schoolmaster to bring us to Christ, but when we have come to Christ we are no longer under a schoolmaster. Let the law principle go its way to work conviction in sinners, and destroy their ill-grounded hopes, but do you abide in Christ Jesus even as you have received Him. If you are to be saved by works then it is not of grace, otherwise work is no more work; and if saved by grace then it is not of human merit, otherwise grace is no more grace. To keep clear here is of the first importance, for on the rocks of legality many a soul has been cast away.

We need also to keep up a clear distinction between the efforts of nature and the work of grace. It is commendable for men to do all they can to improve themselves, and everything by which people are made more sober, more honest, more frugal, better citizens, better husbands, better wives, is a good thing; but that is nature and not grace. Reformation is not regeneration. "Ye must be born again" still stands for the good as well as for the bad. To be made a new creature in Christ Jesus is as necessary for the moral as for the debauched; for, when flesh has done its best, "that which is born of the flesh is flesh"; and men must be born of the Spirit, or they cannot understand spiritual things, or enter into heaven. I have always tried to keep up this distinction, and I trust none of you will ever mistake the efforts of nature for the works of divine grace. Do what you can for human reformation, for whatsoever things are honest and of good repute you are to foster; but, still, never put the most philanthropic plan, or the most elevating system in the place of the work of sovereign grace, for, if you do, you will do ten times as much mischief as you can possibly do good. We must rightly divide the word of truth.

It is always well, too, for Christian men to be able to distinguish one truth from another. Let the knife penetrate between the joints of the work of Christ for us, and the work of the Holy Spirit in us. Justification, by which the righteousness of Christ is imputed to us, is one blessing; sanctification, by which we ourselves are made personally righteous, is another blessing. I have known some describe sanctification as a sort of foundation, or at least a buttress for the work of justification. Now, no man is justified because he is sanctified: he is justified because he believeth in Him that justifieth the ungodly. Sanctification follows justification. It is the work of the Spirit of God in the soul of a believer, who first of all was justified by believing in Jesus while as yet he was unsanctified. Give Jesus Christ all the glory for His great and perfect work, and remember that you are perfect in Christ Jesus and accepted in the Beloved, but, at the same time, give glory to the Holy Spirit, and remember that you are not yet perfect in holiness, but that the Spirit's work is to be carried on and will be carried on all the days of your life.

One other point of rightly dividing should never be forgotten, we must always distinguish between the root and the fruit. He is a very poor botanist who does not know a bulb from a bud, but I believe that there are some Londoners who do not know which are roots and which are fruits, so little have they seen of anything growing; and I am sure there are come theologians who hardly know which is the cause and which is the effect in spiritual things. Putting the cart before the horse is a very absurd thing, but many do it. Hear how people will say—"If I could feel joy in the Lord I would believe." Yes, that is the cart before the horse, for joy is the result of faith, not the reason for it. "But I want to feel a great change of heart, and then I will believe." Just so; you wish to make the fruit the root. "Believe in the Lord Jesus Christ," that is the root of the matter; change of life and joy in the Lord will spring up as gracious fruits of faith, and not otherwise. When will you discriminate?

Thus I have given you three versions of my text —rightly handling, straightly furrowing, and wisely discriminating.

IV. The next interpretation of the apostle's expression is, practically CUTTING OUT the word for holy uses. This is the sense given by Chrysostom. I will show you what I mean here. Suppose I have a skin of leather before me, and I want to make a saddle. I take a knife and begin cutting out the shape. I do not want those parts which are dropping off on the right, and round this corner; they are very good leather, but I cannot just now make use of them. I have to cut out my saddle, and I make that my one concern. Or, suppose I have to make a pair of reins out of the leather. I must take my knife round, and work away with one object, keeping clearly before me what I am aiming at. The preacher, to be successful, must also have his wits about him, and when he has the Bible before him he must use those portions which will have a bearing upon his grand aim. He must make use of the material laid ready to his hand in the Bible. Every portion of the word of God is very blessed, and exceedingly profitable, but it may not happen to be connected with the preacher's immediate subject, and therefore he leaves it to be considered another time; and, though some will upbraid him for it, he is much too sensible to feel bound to preach all the doctrines of the Bible in each sermon. He wants to have souls saved and Christians quickened, and therefore he does not for ever pour out the vials, and blow the trumpets of prophecy. Some hearers are crazy after the mysteries of the future. Well, there are two or three brethren in London who are always trumpeting and vialing. Go and hear them if you want it, I have something else to do. I confess I am not sent to decipher the Apocalyptic symbols, my errand is humbler but equally useful, I am sent to bring souls to Jesus Christ. There are preachers who are always dealing with the deep things, the very deep things. For them the coral caves of mystery, and the far descending shafts of metaphysics have a mighty charm. I have no quarrel with their tastes, but I do not think the word of God was given us to be a riddle-book. To me the plain gospel is the part which I cut out, and rightly cut out of the word of God. There is a soul that wants to know how to find peace with God. Some other brother can tell him where predestination falls in with free agency, I do not pretend to know; but I do know that faith in Jesus Christ brings peace to the heart. My business is to bring forth that which will save souls, build up saints, and set Christians to work for Christ. I leave the mysteries, not because I despise them; but because the times demand that we first, and above all other things, seek the souls of men. Some truths press to be heard; they must be heard now, or men will be lost. The other truths they can hear to-morrow, or by-and-by, but now escape from hell and fitness for heaven are their immediate business. Fancy the angels sitting down with Lot and his daughters inside Sodom, and discussing predestination with them, or explaining the limits of free agency. No, no, they cry, "Come along," and they take them by the arm and lead them out, saying, "Flee, flee, flee, for fire is coming down from heaven, and this city is to be destroyed." This is what the preacher has to do; leaving certain parts of truth for other times, he is now rightly dividing the word of truth when he brings out that which is of pressing importance. In the Bible there are some things that are essential, without which a man cannot be saved at all: there are other things which are important, but still men are saved, notwithstanding their ignorance of those things; is it not clear that the essentials must have prominence? Every truth ought to be preached in its turn and place, but we must never give the first place to a second truth, or push that to the front which was meant to be in the background of the picture. "We preach Christ," said the apostle, "Christ and Him crucified," and

I believe that if the preacher is rightly to divide the word, he will say to the sinner, " Sinner, Christ died, Christ rose again, Christ intercedes ; look to Him. As for the difficult questions and nice points, leave them for awhile. You shall discuss them by-and-by, so far as they are profitable to you, but just now believing in the Lord Jesus Christ is the main matter." The preacher must thus separate the vital from the secondary, the practical from the speculative, and the pressing and immediate from that which may be lawfully delayed ; and in that sense he will rightly divide the word of truth.

V. I have given you four meanings. Now I will give you another, leaving out some I might have mentioned. One thing the preacher has to do is to ALLOT TO EACH ONE HIS PORTION ; and here the figure changes. According to Calvin, the intention of the Spirit is to represent one who is the steward of the house, and has to apportion food to the different members of the family. He has rightly to divide the loaves so as not to give the little children and the babes all the crust ; rightly to supply each one's necessities, not giving the strong men milk, nor the babes hard diet ; not casting the children's bread to the dogs, nor giving the swine's husks to the children, but placing before each his own portion. Let me try and do it.

Child of God, your portion is the whole word of God. Every promise in it is yours. Take it : feed on it. Christ is yours ; God is yours ; the Holy Spirit is yours ; this world is yours, and worlds to come. Time is yours ; eternity is yours ; life is yours ; death is yours ; everlasting glory is yours. There is your portion. It is very sweet to give you your royal meat. The Lord give you a good appetite. Feed on it ; feed on it. Sinner, you who believe not in Jesus, none of this is yours. While you remain as you are the threatenings are yours. If you refuse to believe in Jesus, neither this life nor the next is yours, nor time, nor eternity. You have nothing good. Oh, how dreadful is your portion now, for the wrath of God abideth on you. Oh, that you were wise, that your character might be changed, for until it is, we dare not flatter you, there is not a promise for you, not a single approving sentence. You get your food to eat and your raiment to put on ; but even that is given to you by the abounding long-suffering of God, and it may become a curse to you unless you repent. I am sorry to bring you such a portion but I must be honest with you. That is all that I can give you. God has said it—it is an awful sentence—" I will curse their blessings." Oh, sinner, the curse of the Lord is in the house of the wicked.

We have also to divide a portion to the mourners, and oh, how sweet a task that is, to say to those that mourn in Zion that the Lord will give them beauty for ashes. " Blessed are they that mourn, for they shall be comforted." The Lord will restore peace unto His mourners. Fear not, neither be dismayed, for the Lord will help you. But when we have given the mourners their sweet meats we have to turn round upon the hypocrites and say to them, " You may hang your heads like bulrushes, you may rend your garments and pretend to fast, but the Lord, who knows your heart, will suddenly come and unmask you, and if you are not sincere before Him, if you are weighed in the balances and found wanting, He will deal out the gall of bitterness to you for ever. For His mourners there is mercy, but for the deceiver and the hypocrite there is judgment without mercy."

It is a very pleasant thing, moreover, to deal out a portion to the seeker—when we say, " He that seeketh, findeth, and to Him that knocketh it shall be opened." " Come unto Me all ye that labour and are heavy laden," saith Christ, " and I will give you rest." Take your portion and be glad.

We have to turn round, and say to others who think they are seekers, aut who are delaying, " How long halt ye between two opinions ? " How is it that you continually hesitate and refuse to believe in Jesus, and stay in the condition of unbelief, when the gospel mandate is, " Believe—believe now and live !" So we have to give to one comfort, to another counsel ; to one reproof, to another encouragement : to one the invitation, to another the warning ; and this is rightly to divide the word of truth.

Yes, and sometimes God enables His servants to give the word very remarkably to some men. I believe that if I were to tell a few of the things which have happened to me during the last one-and-twenty years they would not be believed, or if I were to tell you of passages of history which are known to me that have occurred in this Tabernacle to people who have come here, and to whom I have spoken the exact word, not knowing them for a moment, the facts would sound like fictions. I will give you one instance. Some of you will remember my preaching from the text, " What if thy father answer thee roughly ? " There came into the vestry after that sermon a venerable Christian gentleman, bringing with him a young foreigner whom he was anxious to satisfy upon one point. He said, " Sir, I want you kindly to answer this question—have you seen me concerning this young gentleman ? " " No, sir, certainly not," I said ; and assuredly, though I knew the gentleman who addressed me, he had never spoken to me about the foreign stranger whose very existence was up to that moment unknown to me. Said he, " This young gentleman is almost persuaded to be a Christian. His father is of quite another faith and worships other gods, and our young friend knows that if he becomes a Christian he will lose his father's love. I said to him, when he conversed to me, come down and hear Mr. Spurgeon this morning. Here we came, and your text was, ' What if thy father answer thee roughly ? ' Now, have you ever heard a word from me about this young gentleman ? ' " No, never," I said, " Well," said the young man, " it is the most extraordinary thing I ever heard in my life." I could only say, " I trust it is the voice of God to your soul. God knows how to guide His servants to utter the word most fitted to bless men."

Some time ago a town missionary had in his district a man who never would suffer any Christian person to come into his house. The missionary was warned by many that he would get a broken head if he ventured on a visit. He therefore kept from the house, though it troubled his conscience to pass it by. He made a matter of prayer of it, and one morning he boldly ventured into the lion's den, and the man said, " What have you come here for ? " " Well, sir," he said, " I have been conversing with people in all the houses along here, and I have passed you by because I heard you objected to it ; but somehow I thought it looked cowardly to avoid you, and therefore I have called." " Come in," the man said ; " sit down, sit down. Now, you are going to talk to me about the Bible. Perhaps you do not know much about it yourself. I am going to ask you a question, and if you can answer me you shall come again. If you do not answer it, I will bundle you downstairs. Now," said he, " do you take me ? " " Yes," said the other, " I do take you." " Well, then," said he, " this is the question—where do you find the word ' girl ' in the Bible, and how many times do you find it ? " The city missionary said, " The word ' girl ' occurs only once in the Bible, and that is in the Book of Joel, the third chapter and the third verse. ' They sold a girl for wine.' " " You are right," said he, " but I would not have believed you knew it, or else I would have asked you some other question. You may come again." " But," said the missionary, " I should like you to know how I came to know it. This very morning I was praying for direction from God, and when I was reading my morning chapter I came upon this passage, ' And they sold a girl for wine '; and I took down my concordance to see whether the word ' girl ' was to be found anywhere else. I found that the word ' girls ' occurs in the passage, ' There shall be boys and girls playing in the streets of Jerusalem,' but the word did not occur as ' girl ' anywhere but in Joel." The result, however, of that story, however odd it seems, was that the missionary was permitted to call, and the man took an interest in his visits, and the whole family were the better; the man, and his wife, and one of his children becoming members of a Christian church some time afterwards. What an extraordinary thing it seems ; yet, I can assure you that such extraordinary things are as commonplaces in my experience. God does help His servants rightly to divide the word, that is to say, to allot a special portion to each special case, so that it comes as pat upon the man as if everything about him was known. Before I came to London, a man met me one Sunday, in a dreadful state of rage. He vowed he would horsewhip me for bullying him from the pulpit. What had I said, I asked. " What have you said ? You looked me in the face and said, ' What more can God do for you ? Shall he give you a good wife ? You have had one : you have killed her by bad treatment : you have just got another, and you are likely to do the same by her.' " " Well," I said, " did you kill your wife by your bad treatment ? " " They say so ; but I was married on Saturday," said he. " Did you not know it ? " " No, I did not, I assure you," I replied ; " I have no knowledge whatever of your family matters, and I am sure I wish you joy of your new wife." He cooled down a great deal ; but I believe that I had struck the nail on the head that time—that he had killed his wife with his unkindness, and he scarcely liked to bring his new wife to the place of worship to be told of it. The cap fitted him ; and if any cap fit you, I pray you wear it, for so far from shrinking from being personal, I do assure you I try to be as personal as ever I can, for I long to see the word go home to every man's conscience, and convict him and make him tremble before God and confess his sin and forsake it.

VI. You must give me a few more minutes while I take the last point, which is this. Rightly to divide the word of truth means to TELL EACH MAN WHAT HIS LOT AND HERITAGE WILL BE IN ETERNITY. Just as when Canaan was conquered, it was divided by lot among the tribes, so the preacher has to tell of Canaan, that happy land, and he has to tell of the land of darkness and of death-shade, and to let each man know where his last abode will be. You do know it ; you who come here do know it. Need I repeat a story that we have gone over and over a thousand times ? As many as believe in Jesus, and are renewed in heart, and are kept by the grace of God through faith unto salvation, shall inherit eternal life ; but as for those who believe not on God, who reject His Son, who abide in their sins, there remaineth nothing for them but " a fearful looking for judgment and of fiery indignation." " The wicked shall be turned into hell with all the nations that forget God." " These shall go away into everlasting punishment ; but the righteous into life eternal." " Beware," saith God,—" Beware, ye that forget God, lest I tear you in pieces and there be none to deliver." Oh, the wrath to come ! the wrath to come !

Believer, there is your portion—in the blessed land. Sinner, except you repent, there is your portion—in the land of darkness and of weeping, and of wailing, and of gnashing of teeth. I take a religious newspaper from America, and the last copy I had of it bore on it these words at the end, in good large type, printed in a practical, business-like, American way : " If you do not want to have this paper, discontinue it NOW. If you wish to have it for the year 1875, send your subscription NOW. If you have any complaint against it, send your complaint NOW. If you have removed, send a notice of your change of residence NOW." There was a big " NOW " at the end of every sentence. As I read it I thought, well, that is right : that is common sense. And it struck me that I would say to you on this last night of the year, if you wish to forsake your sins, forsake them NOW. If you would have mercy from God through Jesus Christ, believe on Him NOW. What fitter time than ere the dying year is gone—NOW, NOW, NOW ? In that very paper I read a story concerning Messrs. Moody and Sankey to the same point. The story is that, while they were preaching in Edinburgh, there was a man sitting opposite to them who was very deeply interested, and was drinking it all in. There was a pause in the service, and the man went out with his friend ; but when he reached the door he stopped, and his friend said, " Come away, Jamie." " No," he said, " I will go back. I came here to get good to may soul, and I have not taken it all in yet, I must go back again." He went back, and sat in his old place, and listened again. The Lord blessed him. He found Christ, and so found salvation. Being a miner, he went down the pit the next day to his work, and a mass of rock fell on him. He was taken out ; but he could not recover. He said to the man who was helping him out, " Oh, Andrew, I am so glad it was all settled last night. Oh, mon," said he, " it was all settled last night." Now, I hope those people who were killed in the railway accident on Christmas Eve could say—" It was all settled the night before." What a blessed thing it will be for you, if you should meet with an accident to-morrow, to say, " Blessed be God, it was all settled last night. I gave my heart to Jesus, I yielded myself to His divine love and mercy, and I am saved." O Holy Spirit, grant it may be so, and Thou shalt have the praise. Amen and Amen.

THE GREAT HOUSE AND THE VESSELS IN IT

" But in a great house there are not only vessels of gold and of silver, but also of wood and of earth ; and some to honour and some to dishonour. If a man therefore purge himself from these, he shall be a vessel unto honour, sanctified, and meet for the Master's use, and prepared unto every good work."—2 Timothy ii. 20, 21.

ONE of the most serious calamities which can befall a church is to have her own ministers teaching heresy : yet this is no new thing, it has happened from the beginning. Paul and Peter and James and John in their epistles had to speak of seducers in the church, even in those primitive days, and ever since then there have arisen in the very midst of the house of God those who have subverted the faith of many, and led them away from the fundamental truths into errors of their own inventing. The apostle compares this to a gangrene, which is one of the most dangerous and deadly mischiefs which can occur to the body. It is within the body, it eats into the flesh deeper and deeper, festering and putrefying, and if it be not stopped it will continue its ravages till life is extinguished by " black mortification." False doctrine and an unchristian spirit in the midst of the church itself must be regarded as such a gangrene, a silent wolf ravenously gnawing at the heart, the vulture of Prometheus devouring the vitals : no external opposition is one-half so much to be dreaded. Yet here is our comfort when distressed at the evils of the present age, among which this one is one of the chief, that the truth abides for ever the same, " The foundation of God standeth sure." There is no moving that. Whether ten thousand oppose it or promulgate it, the truth is still the same in every jot and tittle ; even as the sun shineth evermore, as well when clouds conceal its brightness as when from a clear sky it pours abroad a flood of glory. The lovers of profane and vain babblings have not taken away from us, nor can they take from us, the eternal verities : the Lord liveth, though they have said, " There is no God." The precious blood of Jesus has not lost its efficacy, though divines have beclouded the atonement ; the Spirit of God is not less mighty to quicken and to console though men have denied His personality ; the resurrection is as *sure* as if Hymeneus and Philetus had never said that it is passed already ; and the eternal covenant of grace abides for ever unbroken though Pharisees and Sadducees unite to revile it. The foundation of God standeth sure, and moreover the foundation of the church remains sure also, for, blessed be God, " the Lord knoweth them that are His." All that God has built upon the foundation which He Himself has laid keeps its place, not one living stone that He ever laid upon the foundation has been lifted from its resting place. Earthquakes of error may test the stability of the building and cause great searching of heart, but sooner shall the mountains which are round about Jerusalem start from their seats than the work or word of the Lord be frustrated. The things which cannot be shaken remain unaltered in the very worst times.

" After all," says the apostle in effect, though in fewer words, " it is not such a very great wonder that there should be persons in the church who are not of the sterling metal of sincerity, nor of the gold and silver of truth, which endures the fire. You must not look at Hymeneus and Philetus as if they were prodigies, there have been many like them and there will be many more ; these ill weeds grow apace, in all ages they multiply and increase." Where, dear brethren, beneath the skies shall we find absolute purity in any community ? The very first family had a Cain in it, and there was a wicked Ham even in the select few within the ark. In the household of the father of the faithful there was an Ishmael ; Isaac, with all his quiet walk with God, must be troubled with an Esau, and ye know how in the house of Jacob there were many sons that walked not as they should. When the church of God was in the wilderness and had a barrier of desert between it and the outer world, yet ye know how Korah, Dathan, and Abiram were there, beside many other troublers in Israel ; yea, even amidst the most select part of the visible church of God, in the priesthood, there were found those that had dishonoured it. Nadab and Abihu were slain with fire before the Lord ; and Hophni and Phineas died in battle, because they had made themselves vile, though God's anointed priests. Even when our divine Master had formed for Himself

" A little garden, walled around,
Chosen, and made peculiar ground,"

in which there were but twelve choice trees, yet one of them bore evil fruit. " I have chosen you twelve, and one of you is a devil." In the great field which Christ had sown, tares will spring up among the wheat, for the enemy takes pains to sow them ; neither is it possible for us to root them up. In the king's garden briars will grow, thorns also and thistles will the most sacred soil yield to us. Even the lilies of Christ grow among thorns. You cannot keep the best of churches altogether pure, for though the Lord Himself has prepared a vineyard, and made a winepress, and built a wall about it, yet the foxes come and spoil the vines ; and though our great Lord has an orchard which yieldeth rare fruit, yet when He cometh to visit it He finds a barren fig tree, digged about and dunged it is true, but barren still. Look to Christ's fold on earth, and behold there are wolves in sheep's clothing there ; look to the net which His servants draw to shore, and there are both good and bad fish therein. Yea, lift your eyes even to the skies, and though there be myriads of stars, yet ye shall mark wandering stars among them, and meteors which are and are not, and are quenched in the blackness of darkness for ever. Until we shall come to the heaven of the Most High we must expect to find chaff mixed with the wheat, dross with the gold, goats with the sheep, and dead flies with the ointment ; only let us see to it that we be not of that ill character, but be precious in the sight of the Lord.

Coming to the text, the apostle suggests the encouragement I have already given, under a certain metaphor. He says that in a great house there will naturally be varieties of furniture, and there will be vessels and utensils of many kinds ; some of them will be of wood, and of earthenware, for meaner purposes; and others of gold and silver, for state occasions, when the honour and glory of the great proprietor are to be displayed. There are vessels of precious metal in a great house, and these are its honour, decking the tables on high festivals when the Master is at home; but there are others of baser stuff, kept in the background, never displayed at times of rejoicing, but meant for common drudgery. There are cups and flagons of solid silver prized as perpetual heirlooms of the family, which are carefully preserved, and trenchers and pots which are soon worn out and are only of temporary use, many sets of them being broken up in the lifetime of a family. The like is true in the church of God, which being in the world has its common side and its common vessels, but being also a heavenly house has also its nobler furniture, far more precious than gold which perisheth though it be tried with fire.

For our instruction, may the Holy Spirit help us while we look first at *the great house;* secondly, at *the meaner vessels,* peeping into the scullery; thirdly, at the *nobler vessels,* going into the plate chamber to look at the silver and gold; and then, fourthly, before we leave the house, let us ask for an interview with *the Master Himself.*

I. First, let us consider THE GREAT HOUSE

The apostle compares the church to a great house. We feel sure he is not speaking of the world; it did not occur to him to speak about the world, and it would have been altogether superfluous to tell us that in the world there are all sorts of people,— everybody knows that. The church is a great house *belonging to a great personage,* for the church is the house of God, according to the promise—" I will dwell in them, and walk in them." The church is the temple in which the Lord is worshipped, the palace in which He rules; it is His castle, and place of defence for His truth, the armoury out of which He supplies His people with weapons. The church is God's mansion house in which He abides—" This is my rest for ever, here will I dwell, for I have desired it." There it is that He rests in His love, and in infinite condescension manifests Himself as He doth not unto the world. King Solomon built for himself a house in the forest of Lebanon, and behold, the Lord hath of living stones builded for Himself a far more glorious house wherein He may abide. It is a great house because it is the house of the great God. Who can be so great as He?

It is a great house because *planned and designed upon a great scale.* I fear that some who live in the house have no idea how great it is. They have a very faint notion of its length and breadth. The great thoughts of God are far beyond their most elevated conception, so that He might say to them as He has said to others, " My thoughts are not your thoughts, neither are My ways your ways, saith the Lord." The palace of the King of kings is " exceeding magnifical," and for spaciousness far excelleth all the abodes of earthly princes. We read of the golden palace of Nero, that it reached from hill to hill, and enclosed lakes and stream and gardens beneath its wondrous roof; but behold, the Lord has stretched the line of His electing grace over nations and kindreds even to the ends of the earth: His house taketh in a mighty sweep of humanity. Many are the rooms in the house, and there are dwellers in one room who have never yet seen any part of the great house but the little chamber in which they were born, never walked through the marvellous corridors, or moved in the vast halls which God hath builded with cedar pillars and cedar beams, and carved work of heavenly workmanship. Some good men hardly care to see the long rows of polished columns, quarried by grace from the rough mass of nature, which now shine resplendent as monuments of divine love and wisdom. Colossal is the plan of the Eternal, the church of God is worthy of the infinite mind. Angels and princi- palities delight to study the stupendous plan, and well they may: as the great Architect unrolls His drawings piece by piece to let them see the various sections of the complete design, they are struck with admiration, and exclaim, " Oh the riches of the wisdom and the knowledge of God." The church is no narrow cottage wherein a few may luxuriate in bigotry, but is a great house, worthy of the infinite heart of Jehovah, worthy of the blood of Jesus, the incarnate God, and worthy of the power of the ever-blessed Spirit.

It is a great house because *it has been erected at great cost, and with great labour.* The cost of this mansion who can tell? It is a price beyond price, for God has given His only-begotten Son—He had but one, and heaven could not match Him—that He might redeem unto Himself a people who should be His dwelling-place for ever. Solomon's temple, now that they have laid bare a part of the foundations, even though it be in utter ruin, astonishes all beholders as they mark the enormous size and accurate adjust- ment of the stones; what must it have been in its glory? What cost was lavished on that glorious house. But think of the labour and the skill, the divine art and engineering with which Jehovah has hewn out of the rock of sinful nature the stones with which He builds up His spiritual house. What energy has the Holy Spirit displayed! What resurrection power! Harder than any granite we were by nature, yet has He cut us away from the rock of which we formed a part, and fashioned and squared us, and made us to be builded together for an habitation of God, through the Spirit. Tell it to the praise of the glory of His grace, that the Lord's omnipotent power and boundless wealth of love are revealed in His church. When our eyes shall see the church of God at last in all her beauty descending out of heaven from God, having the glory of God, and her light like unto a stone most precious, even like unto a jasper stone; when we shall see that the length and the breadth and the height of it are equal; when we shall see its deep foundations laid in the eternal purpose, and its walls upbuilt with lofty pinnacles of glory, high as the divine person of her Lord; and when we shall mark its wondrous compass, broad enough to hold the glory and honour of the nations,— then shall we shout for joy as we behold the riches and the power and the splendour of the great King of kings, who has builded for Himself this great house.

It is a great house, again, because *its household arrangements are conducted on a great scale.* You know the country people, when there is some rich lord living in the village, speak always of his mansion as " the great house." It is the great house for which those bullocks are being fattened, and those sheep and lambs will be consumed at the great house, for there are many in the family, and none are allowed to want. Solomon kept a great house. When you read the account of the daily provision for his table you see that it was a great house indeed, a vast and truly royal establishment. Aye, but neither for quality nor quantity could Solomon's palace match with the great house of God in its plenty. Speak of fine flour—behold, He has given us angels' food: speak of royal dainties—behold, the Lord hath given us fat things full of marrow, wines on the lees well refined. What a perpetual feast doth the Lord Jesus keep up for all His followers. If any of them hunger it is not because their rations are stinted ; if there be any complaining it is not because the Master's oxen and fatlings are not freely provided. Ah, no ; to every man there is a good piece of flesh and a flagon of wine dealt out, even as David dealt it out in the day when he removed the ark unto the hill of Zion. Glory be to God, He hath said, " Eat, O friends ; drink, yea, drink abundantly, O beloved." In this mountain shall the hand of the Lord rest, and He will make unto all nations a feast of fat things. Behold, His oxen and fatlings are killed, all things are ready. It is a great house, where great sinners are fed on great dainties, and filled with the great goodness of the Lord.

It is a great house *for the number of its inhabitants.* How many have lived beneath that roof-tree for ages. " Lord," say they like a great host, " Thou hast been our dwelling place throughout all generations." God is the home of His people, and His church is the home of God ; and what multitudes are dwelling there now. Not only the companies that we know of, with whom it is our delight to meet for solemn worship, but all over the world the Lord hath a people who dwell in the midst of His church ; and, though men have disfigured their Master's house by chalking up odd signs over some of the rooms, and calling them by other names than those of the owner, yet the Lord's people are all one church, and to whatever part or party they may seem to belong, if Christ is in them they belong to Him of whom the whole family in heaven and earth is named, and they make up but one spiritual house. What a swarm there is of the Lord's children, and yet not one of the family remains unfed. The church is a great house wherein thousands dwell, yea, a number that no man can number.

Once more, it is a great house, *because of its importance.* People speak of " the great house " in our remoter counties because to the whole neighbourhood it bears a special relationship, being connected with some of its most vital interests : county politics and police, dignity and wealth find their centre at "the great house." The church is a great house because it is God's hospice, where He distributes bread and wine to refresh the weary, and entertains wayfarers that else had been lost in the storm. It is God's hospital, into which He takes the sick, and there He nourishes them till they renew their youth like the eagle's. It is God's great pharos with its lantern flashing forth a directing ray so that wanderers far away may be directed to the haven of peace. " Out of Zion, the perfection of beauty, God hath shined." It is the seat of God's magistracy, for there are set thrones of the house of David. Behold, the Lord hath set His King upon His holy hill of Zion, and thence shall the power of His sceptre go forth to the ends of the earth. The great house of the church is the university for teaching all nations, the library wherein the sacred oracles are preserved, the treasury wherein the truth is deposited, and the registry of new-born heirs of heaven. It is important to heaven as well as to earth, for its topmost towers reach into glory, and there is in it a ladder the foot whereof doth rest on earth, but the top thereof doth reach

to heaven, up and down which the angels come and go continually. Said I not well that the apostle had wisely chosen the figure when he called the church a great house ?

II. We will now go inside the great house, and we at once observe that it is well furnished. Our text, however, invites us to note that it contains a number of MEANER VESSELS, articles of the coarser kind for ordinary and common uses. Here are trenchers and buckets of wood, and pitchers and pots and divers vessels of coarse pottery. Some have thought that this figure of vessels to dishonour relates to Christians of a lower grade, persons of small grace and of less sanctified conversation. Now, although believers may from some points of view be comparable to earthen vessels, yet I dare not look upon any child of God, however low in grace, as a vessel to dishonour. Moreover, the word " *these* " refers to the earthen and wooden vessels, and surely they cannot represent saints, or we should never be told to purge ourselves from them. If a man be God's child, into whatever state and condition he may fall, it is our business to look after him and endeavour to restore him, remembering ourselves also, lest we also be tempted ; but it cannot be right to purge ourselves from even the least of our believing brethren. Besides, that is not the run of the chapter at all. The real meaning is that in a church of God there are unworthy persons serving inferior and temporary purposes, who are *vessels to dishonour.* They are in the church, but they are like vessels of wood and vessels of earth, they are not the treasure of the mansion, they are not brought out on state occasions, and are not set much store by, for they are not " precious in the sight of the Lord." The apostle does not tell us how they came there, for it was not his intent to do so, and no parable or metaphor could teach everything ; neither will I stay to describe how some professors have come into the church of God, some by distinct falsehood and by making professions which they knew were untrue, others through ignorance, and others again by being self-deceived, and carried away with excitement. The parable does not say how they got there, but there they are, and yet they are only vessels of wood and vessels of earth. It is no credit to them that they are where they are, for they are not vessels to honour though in an honourable place. It is no honour to any man to be a member of a Christian church if he be in himself intrinsically worthless : though they make a minister of him, or elect him deacon, it is no honour to him to be in office if the metal he is made of does not fit him for so honourable a purpose. He is an intruder in an honourable position, and it is a dishonour to him to be where he is. It is no honour to a weed to grow in the best part of the garden, no honour for a barren figtree to cumber the finest ground in the vineyard. Ah, dear friend, if you are in the church of God, but not truly one of the Lord's people, it is a dishonourable thing of you to have come there, and it is equally dishonourable for you to remain there without fulfilling that great requisite which is demanded of every one who names the name of Jesus, that he depart from all iniquity.

The vessels in the great house are, however, *of some use,* even though they are made of wood and earth ; and so there are persons in the church of God whom the Lord Jesus will not own as His treasure, but He nevertheless turns them to some temporary purpose. Some are useful as the scaffold to a house, or the dogshores to a ship, or the hedges to a field. I believe that some unworthy members of the church are useful in the way of watch dogs to keep others awake, or lancets to let blood, or burdens to try strength. Some quarrelsome members of the church help to scour the other vessels, lest they should rust through being peaceful. The church is made up of men who are yet in the body, and it has to deal with the outside world, and sometimes the worldly men who are in her serve some purpose in connection with this her lowest need. Judas made a good treasurer, for his economy saved more than he stole. Joab was a good warrior for David, though he was by no means a saint. False professors do not make the gospel untrue, and sometimes when they have spoken it God has blessed it. You may see, if you go down the Kennington-park-road to-day, a row of young trees planted by the road : how are they kept up while yet they are slender ? Why, small posts of dead timber hold them up ; and even so a dead Sunday-school teacher may yet be useful to a really Christian child, and a dead deacon may be the financial support of a living church. Aye, and there are dead preachers, too, who nevertheless serve to fill up a space, but what vessels to dishonour they are. It is a dreadful thing, however, for those who are like the posts I just now mentioned, because the quicker the young tree grows the sooner will the post be taken away, being no participant in the life which it helped to support. You see, then, that the base professors who get into the church are turned to some account by our great Master ; the servants of the great house can use the wooden ware and the earthenware for awhile for rough every-day purposes, even as mere formalists can be employed in some scullery work or another.

There is one thing noticeable, viz., that the wooden and earthen vessels are *not for the Master's use*. When He holds high festival His cups are all of precious metal. " All King Solomon's drinking vessels were of gold." Would you have the King of kings set an earthen pot upon His royal table ? Shall the guests at His table eat from wooden bowls ? So false professors are only useful to the servants, not to the Master ; they serve base purposes, and are not to be seen on those great days when He manifests His glory. The great Master overrules all things, being the Master of the servants, and so far that which answers the purpose of His servants is serviceable to Him, but personally between the King at His table and the wooden vessel there is no congruity : it would be an insult to hand Him wine in any but a sumptuous cup of precious metal, or to bring Him butter in any but a lordly dish. How sad it is that many Christians are useful to the Church in various ways, but as for personal service rendered to the Lord Jesus Christ Himself, in that they have no share whatever and never can have till grace changes them from wood to silver, or from earth to gold.

Note that in these vessels of which the apostle speaks *the substance is base*. They are wood, or they are earth, nothing more. So are we all by nature of base material, and grace must make us into silver or into golden vessels, or the Master cannot Himself use us, nor can our use in the church ever be to honour. The wooden vessels in the church are very easily hacked and carved and spoiled ; if a man be inclined to mischief he can put his knife to them and can cut great notches in them, ruin their character, and render them worthless. Cunning teachers can soon take away from merely nominal Christians what they professed to believe, for they are very readily cut and hacked by those who play at such games. As for the earthen vessels, how soon they are broken. Outside of any great house there are the remains of many broken pots, which fell to the ground and went to pieces ; and, I am sorry to say, we also can find enough of such relics to sadden us all. There were some in this house once who were comely to look upon, but there came a temptation and brushed them from the table, and they were shivered in a moment. Others of precious metal have endured far more shocks and tests of a severer kind, but these being only of earth were broken at once. Heaps of crockery accumulate outside every great house, and certainly outside the great house of Christ.

These vessels unto dishonour, though turned to some account, *require a great deal of care on the part of the servants*. When our forefathers used to eat from wooden trenchers, the time the good wives used to spend in scalding and cleaning to keep them at all sweet to eat upon was something terrible, and there are members of the church who take a world of time from pastors and elders to keep them at all decent : we are continually trying to set them right, or keep them right, in the common relationships of life. There are quarrels in their families which must be settled lest they become scandals, and these occupy the careful thought of their fellow Christians who have to watch for their good ; or they get lax in their doctrines, or foolish in their habits, or loose in their business transactions, and we have to be scouring and cleaning them times without number. Certain sorts of earthen vessels you have to be very particular in handling. Like egg-shell china, you may hardly look at them. Thank God I have not many in this church, perhaps none of that sort, as far as *my* handling is concerned, but other people's touches, though quite as wise, are not so welcome. Certain earthen vessels get dreadfully chipped unless they have dainty handling. If a brother does not take his hat off to them in very lowly style, and behave very reverently, they are ready to take offence. They feel themselves hurt and slighted when no such thing was intended ; they stand upon their dignity and expect the fullest recognition of it. These are real earthen pots, very apt to be chipped, perhaps a little cracked already, and needing a deal of care and trouble on the part of the Lord's servants, lest they should go to pieces and spill everything that is put into them.

There are such in all great houses, and in the Master's great house there are, I fear, not a few. They are useful up to a certain point, but they bring no honour to the house, because there are plenty as good as they in other houses, every cottage can have common earthen pitchers in it. They are vessels in which is no pleasure, they are not peculiar, or precious ; nobody ever sounds abroad the Master's fame because He has so many thousands of wooden bowls or earthen pots. No, the king's honour comes from the plate, the gold and silver vessels, the peculiar treasure of kings. People speak about these rich goods and say, " You should see the sideboards loaded down with the massive services of gold and silver ; you should see how the tables groan beneath the splendour of the royal feast when the king brings forth his treasures." True Christians are the glory of Christ, but false professors at their very best are unto dishonour. Better the smallest silver vessel than the largest earthen one ; better the least of all the saints than the greatest of vain professors. So much upon the vessels to dishonour.

III. We are now going into the treasury, or plate room, and will think of THE NOBLER VESSELS.

These are, first of all, *of solid metal*, vessels of silver and vessels of gold. They are not all equally valuable, but they are all precious. Here is weight for you; here is something that is worth treasuring, something which will last for ages, and at any time will endure the fire. Now, in real Christians, those who really love the Lord, there is something substantial and weighty, and when you get hold of them you know the difference between them and the wooden professor. Even those who do not like them —strange taste that which does not appreciate silver and gold—are nevertheless compelled to say, "That is a genuine article, worth a great deal, weighty and substantial." Now, we shall none of us ever be vessels of silver and gold unless the Lord make us so by divine grace. Vessels of earth are things of nature, any potter can make them; vessels of wood are common enough, the cooper soon produces a pail; but a vessel of silver or of gold is a rarer thing; it costs mining and searching, furnace work and fashioning, toil and skill. On each vessel unto honour Jesus Himself has put His hand to mould and fashion it, and to cause it to be "prepared unto glory." Did you ever hear how vessels come to be golden? Listen to this, and you shall know. One very dear to me has put the story into rhythm.

> "'Oh, that I were a cup, a golden cup
> Meet for the Master's use!
> Brimming and trembling with that draught of joy
> (The love of His belov'd and purchas'd ones)
> Which fills His heart with gladness.'
>
> * * * * *
>
> So spake a poor, vile, broken, earthly thing,
> A worthless castaway.
> The Master heard, and when He passed that way
> He stoop'd and touch'd it with his *wounded* hand—
> When lo! its baseness vanish'd, and instead
> There stood a *golden* chalice wondrous fair,
> And overflowing with deep love for Him.
> He raised it to His gracious lips, and quaffed
> 'The wine that maketh glad the heart of God,'
> Then took the cup to heaven."

On the vessel to honour you can see *the hall mark*. What is the hall mark which denotes the purity of the Lord's golden vessels? Well, He has only one stamp for everything. When He laid the foundation what was the seal He put upon it? "The Lord knoweth them that are His, and let every one that nameth the name of Christ depart from all iniquity." That was God's seal, the impress of the great King upon the foundation-stone. Do we find it here? Yes, we do. "If a man, therefore, purge himself from these he shall be a vessel unto honour." You see that the man who is the golden or silver vessel departs from all iniquity, and that is the token of his genuine character. The man who is truly the Lord's seeks to be cleansed not only from the open sin of the world, but from the common sin of professing Christians; he labours to be purged from that which the wooden vessel and the earthen vessel would delight in; he wants to be pure within and without, he desires perfection, he labours daily to conquer every sin, and strives with all his might to serve his Lord. He is not content to have a fair appearance, as wood and earth may have—he wishes to be solid, substantial metal, purged and purified to the utmost

possible degree, and fit for the highest purposes. Now, this seeking after purity is the hall mark of the King's vessels of gold and silver.

Notice, however, that *they are purged*, for the Lord will not use filthy vessels be they what they may. He will only use those that are clean, and He would have His true people purged, as I have said before, not only from gross sin, but from doctrinal error, and from association with the perverse minded. We are to be purged from Hymeneus and Philetus, and from the vain babblings of which the apostle has been speaking in the previous part of the chapter. I fear that Christian men do a great deal of mischief by their complicity with those who are teaching what is downright falsehood. If we are to serve the Lord in the matter of advancing His truth we must be true to truth ourselves; but if we join hand in hand with others, and so form a confederacy when the very pillars of the temple are being pulled down by rude hands, it may be we shall be partakers of other men's sin. We must be clean-handed in this matter.

And then notice that *these gold and silver vessels are reserved* as well as purged. They are made meet for the Master's use. Nobody is to drink out of them but the King Himself. This is the blessedness of the child of God when he comes to be what he should be, that he can sing as we did just now,

> "I am Thine and Thine alone,
> This I gladly, fully own;
> And, in all my works and ways,
> Only now would seek Thy praise."

As Joseph had a cup out of which he alone drank, so the Lord taketh His people to be His peculiar treasure, for His personal use. Brethren, I count it an honour to be useful to the meanest child of God, but I confess that the honour lies mainly in the fact that I am thereby serving the Master Himself. Oh, to be used by God! This is to answer the end of our being. If you can feel that *God* has used you, then may you rejoice indeed. There are some Christians whom the Lord cannot much use because, first of all, they are not cleansed from selfishness, they have an eye to their own honour or aggrandisement. The Lord will not be in complicity with selfish aims. Some men are self-confident: there is too much of the "I" about them, and the Master will not use them. He will have our weakness, but not our strength, and if we are great somebodies He will pass us by and take some little nobody and make use of him. The Lord cannot use some men because they are too apt to be proud; if He were to give them a little success it would be dangerous to their Christian existence; their poor brain would begin to swim, and they would think the Lord could hardly do without them; indeed, when they meet with a little encouragement they swell into such wonderful people that they expect everybody to fall down and worship them. God will not use them, neither will He set upon His tables vessels which are in any way defiled. There must be purity, and a man may work his heart out in the ministry or the Sunday-school, but if he is practising some secret sin he cannot prosper; it is not possible that God should honour him. There may be a measure of apparent success for a time, and divine sovereignty may use the truth itself despite the man, but the man himself will not be useful to the Master. Littleness of grace and contentedness with that spiritual poverty also puts many a man aside. We must be full if God is to pour out of us to the thirsty, we must be full of His light if we are to illuminate the darkness of others : we cannot reveal to the world what the Lord has not revealed to us.

Oh, for a holy character and holy communion with God ; then we shall be golden vessels fit for the Master's use, and so, according to the text, we shall be *ready for good work*, ready *for* the work when it comes, and ready *at* the work when it has come, because completely consecrated to God and subject to His hand. In this readiness for whatever comes we shall be honoured. Men may despise us, as they will, but what matters it if God honours us ? This height of grace may cost us a sharp experience, but must not gold be tried with fire ? As thieves are most anxious to steal, not the pots and wooden vessels, but the gold and the silver, so we may expect to be exposed to greater temptations and greater persecutions than others. More grace involves more trials, but then we shall have the delight of glorifying God more. Oh, to be vessels unto honour ! Beloved members of this church, do aspire to this. You have given in your names as Christians, you have been baptized into the sacred name of the divine Trinity, you have borne hitherto a consistent moral character, but oh, see to it that the inner substance is the real metal, the gold and silver. Do see to it that you are reserved for the Lord's own special use. Be as consecrated to Him as were the bowls before the altar. Never let the world drink out of you, as Belshazzar did out of the vessels taken at Jerusalem. May the Lord grant that you may never be defiled, but may be kept by His grace pure and consecrated to Him.

IV. Fourthly, for a moment we must speak about THE MASTER.

He is introduced here, you see, as having certain vessels meet for His use, and this shows that He is in the house. There would be no need to reserve vessels for His use if He were not there, but He is in the midst of His church by His indwelling Spirit. How this ought to make us wish to be purged, sanctified, and ready for Him. Your Master is not far away. His presence in the church is promised :

"Lo, I am with you alway, even to the end of the world." What manner of persons, therefore, ought you to be ?

Secondly, the Master knows all about the house, and knows the quality of all the vessels. There is no deceiving Him with the wooden trencher, He knows it is not gold : and as for that earthen cup, though it may be gilt all over, He knows it is not gold. He reads the heart of everyone here present ; wood or earth, silver or gold, the Master understands us.

And then reflect that the Master will use us all as far as we are fit to be used. We are in God's house, and if we are wood, He will put us to wooden use. There are many wooden preachers. If we are earth and earthly minded He may put us to earthly uses, as He did Judas, who carried the bag, but had no grace. If you are silver He will give you silver use, and if you are gold He will give you golden service, in which you shall be happy, and honoured, and blessed.

What comes of this, then, lastly ? Why, brethren, let us bestir ourselves that we are purged, for the text says, " If a man therefore purge himself." It throws this business upon each one of us personally—a man must purge himself from ill company ; but when we have confessed the responsibility let us turn to God in prayer, and feel that thorough purging is a work which we cannot achieve, and therefore we cry, " Cleanse me, O God, sanctify me ; make me meet for Thy service, and prepared to every good work."

Beloved, finish with earnest prayer. Pray God that ye may not be hypocrites : beseech the Lord to search you and try you, that you be not found deceivers, and when you are sure that you are His, then ask Him to make you not merely silver, for it is very apt to tarnish, but even the precious gold, which when exposed to the worst influences scarcely shows a trace of dulness. Pure unalloyed gold may we be, and then may the Master both in secret and public use us to His own joy. May He refresh Himself with our love and faith, yea, may His joy be fulfilled in us, that our joy may be full. God grant it may be so, for Christ's sake.

THE FORM OF GODLINESS WITHOUT THE POWER

" Having a form of godliness, but denying the power thereof : from such turn away."—2 Timothy iii. 5.

PAUL warns us of certain characters which will appear in the last times. It is a very terrible list. The like have appeared in other days, but we are led by his warning to apprehend that they will appear in greater numbers in the last days than in any previous age. " Lovers of their own selves, covetous, boasters, proud, blasphemers, disobedient to parents, unthankful, unholy, without natural affection, truce-breakers, false accusers, incontinent, fierce, despisers of those that are good, traitors, heady, highminded, lovers of pleasures more than lovers of God." These will swarm like flies in the decay of the year, and will make the times exceeding perilous. We are nearing that period at this very time. That these people would, some of them, be within the church is the most painful part of it ; but they will be so, for they are comprehended in this last clause of the black catalogue, which we have taken for our text—" Having a form of godliness, but denying the power thereof."

Paul does not paint the future with rose-colour : he is no smooth-tongued prophet of a golden age, into which this dull earth may be imagined to be glowing. There are sanguine brethren who are looking forward to everything growing better and better and better, until, at last, this present age ripens into a millennium. They will not be able to sustain their hopes, for Scripture gives them no solid basis to rest upon. We who believe that there will be no millennial reign without the King, and who expect no rule of righteousness except from the appearing of the righteous Lord, are nearer the mark. Apart from the second Advent of our Lord, the world is more likely to sink into a pandemonium than to rise into a millennium. A divine interposition seems to me the hope set before us in Scripture, and, indeed, to be the only hope adequate to the occasion. We look to the darkening down of things ; the state of mankind, however improved politically, may yet grow worse and worse spiritually. Certainly, we are assured in verse thirteen that " evil men and seducers shall wax worse and worse, deceiving, and being deceived." There will spring up in the Christian church, and round about it, a body of faithless men who profess to have faith ; unsaintly men who will unite with the saints ; men having the form of godliness, but denying the power. We may call these hard times, if we will, but we have hardly yet come to the border of those truly harder times when it will go hard with the church, and she shall need, even more than to-day, to cry mightily unto the Lord to keep her alive.

With this cloud upon our spirit, we come to the text itself. Let us consider it carefully, and may the Holy Spirit help us ! True religion is a spiritual thing, but it necessarily embodies itself in a form. Man is a spiritual creature, but the human spirit needs a body in which to enshrine itself ; and thus, by this need, we become allied to materialism ; and if not " half dust, half Deity," as one has said, we are certainly both matter and soul. In each of us there is the form or body, and the soul or power. It is so with religion : it is essentially a spiritual thing, but it requires a form in which to embody and manifest itself. Christian people fall into a certain outward method of procedure, a peculiar outward mode of uttering their faith, which becomes to true godliness what the body is to the soul. The form is useful, the form is necessary, the form ought to be vitalized ; just as the body is useful, and is necessary, and is vitalized by the soul. If you get both the form, as modelled in the Word of God, and the power, as bestowed by the Spirit of God, you do well, and are living Christians. If you get the power alone, without the ordained form, you somewhat maim yourself ; but if you get the form without the power, then you dwell in spiritual death. The body without the spirit is dead ; and what follows upon death with flesh ? Why, corruption, corruption so horrible, that even love itself has to cry, " Bury my dead out of my sight." So that if there be in any the body of religion without the life of religion, it leads to decay, and this to corruption ; and that has a tendency to putridity of character. The raw material of a devil is an angel bereft of holiness. You cannot make a Judas except out of an apostle. The eminently good in outward form, when without inward life, decays into the foulest thing under heaven. You cannot wonder that these are called " perilous times," in which such characters abound. One Judas is an awful weight for this poor globe to bear, but a tribe of them must be a peril indeed. Yet, if not of the very worst order, those are enough to be dreaded who have the shadow of religion without its substance. Of such I have to speak at this time : from such may God give you grace to turn away ! May none of us ever be spots in our feasts of love, or clouds without water carried about of winds ; but this we shall be if we have the form of godliness without the power thereof. With great solemnity of soul I approach this subject, seeking from the Lord the aid of His Spirit, who makes the Word to be a discerner of the thoughts and intents of the heart.

First, I shall speak of *the men*, and secondly, of *their folly,* and when I have done that, I shall have some words of instruction to give by way of conclusion.

I. First, let us talk awhile of THE MEN. They had the form of godliness, but denied the power thereof. Note *what they had*, and then observe *what they had not.*

They had a form of godliness. What is the form of godliness ? It is, first of all, *attention to the ordinances of religion.* These, so far as they are Scriptural, are few and simple. There is baptism, wherein, in figure, the believer is buried with Christ, that he may rise into newness of life ; and there is the Lord's Supper, wherein, in type and emblem, he feeds upon Christ, and sustains the life which came to him by fellowship with Christ's death. Those who have obeyed the Lord in these two ordinances have exhibited in their own persons the form of godliness. That form is every way instructive to others, and impressive to the man himself. Every baptized person, and every communicant at the Lord's table, should be godly and gracious ; but neither baptism nor the communion will secure this. Where there is not the life of God in the soul, neither holiness nor godliness follows upon the ordinances ; and thus we may have around us baptized worldlings, and men who go from the table of the Lord to drink the cup of devils. It is sad that it should be so. Such persons are guilty of presumption, falsehood, sacrilege, and blasphemy. Ah me ! We sit beside such every Sabbath-day !

The form of godliness *involves attendance with the assemblies of God's people.* Those who have professed Christ are accustomed to come together at certain times for worship, and, in their assemblies, they join in common prayer and common praise. They listen to the testimony of God by His servants whom He calls to preach His Word with power. They also associate together in church fellowship for purposes of mutual help and discipline. This is a very proper form, full of blessing both to the church and to the world, when it does not die down into mere form. A man may go to heaven alone, but he will do better if he travels thither with Mr. Greatheart, and Father Honest, and Christiana, and the children. Christ's people are called sheep for one reason, that they love to go in flocks. Dogs do very well separately, but sheep do best in company. The sheep of Christ love to be together in the same pasture, and to follow in a flock the footsteps of the good Shepherd. Those who constantly associate in worship, unite in church-fellowship, and work together for sacred purposes, have the form of godliness, and a very useful and proper form it is. Alas ! it is of no value without the power.

Some go further than public worship, for they *use a great deal of religious talk.* They freely speak of the things of God in Christian company. They can defend the doctrines of Scripture, they can plead for its precepts, and they can narrate the experience of a believer. They are fondest of talking of what is doing in the church : the tattle of the streets of Jerusalem is very pleasant to them. They flavour their speech with godly phrases when they are in company that will relish it. I do not censure them ; on the contrary, I wish there were more of holy talk among professors. I wish we could revive the old habit, " They that feared the Lord spake often one to another." Holy conversation causes the heart to glow, and gives to us a foretaste of the fellowship of the glorified. But there may be a savour of religion about a man's conversation, and yet it may be a borrowed flavour, like hot sauces used to disguise the staleness of ancient meat. That religion which comes from the lips outward, but does not well up from the deep fountains of the heart, is not that living water which will spring up unto eternal life. Tongue-godliness is an abomination if the heart be destitute of grace.

More than this, some have a form of godliness *upheld and published by religious activity.* It is possible to be intensely active in the outside work of the church, and yet to know nothing of spiritual power. One may be an excellent Sunday-school teacher after a fashion, and yet have need to be taught what it is to be born again. One may be an eloquent preacher, or a diligent officer in the church of God, and yet know nothing of the mysterious power of the Spirit of truth upon the heart. It is well to be like Martha in service; but one thing is needful, and that is, to sit at the Master's feet and learn, as Mary did. When we have done all the work our position requires of us, we may only have displayed the form of godliness; unless we hearken to our Lord, and from His presence derive power, we shall be as a sounding brass and a tinkling cymbal. Brethren, I speak to myself and to each one of you in solemn earnestness; if much speaking, generous giving, and constant occupation could win heaven, we might easily make sure of it; but more than these are needful. I speak to each one of you; and if I singled out any one more than another to be the pointed object of my address, it would be the best among us—the one who is doing most for his Master and who, in his inmost soul, is thinking, "That warning does not apply to me." O my active and energetic brother, remember the word, "Let him that thinketh he standeth take heed lest he fall." If any of you dislike this searching sermon, your dislike proves how much you need it. He that is not willing to search himself should stand self-suspected by that unwillingness to look at his affairs. If you are right, you will not object to be weighed in the balances. If you are indeed pure gold, you may still feel anxiety at the sight of the furnace, but you will not be driven to anger at the prospect of the fire, for your prayer will be, "Search me, O God, and know my heart: try me, and know my thoughts: and see if there be any wicked way in me, and lead me in the way everlasting."

I need not enlarge further. You all know what a form of godliness is, and most of us who are here present hold fast that form: may we never dishonour it! I trust we are anxious to make that form accurate according to Scripture, so that our form of godliness may be that into which the earliest saints were delivered. Let us be Christians of a high type, cast in our Lord's own mould. But do not become sticklers for the form and neglect the inner life: that will never do. Shall we fight about a man's clothes, and allow the man himself to die?

But now, as these people had not the power of godliness, *how did they come to hold the form of it?* This needs several answers.

Some come by the form of godliness in *an hereditary way.* Their ancestors were always godly people, and they almost naturally take up with the profession of their fathers. This is common, and where it is honest, it is most commendable. It is a great mercy when, instead of the fathers, shall be the children;

and we may hopefully anticipate that our children will follow us in the things of God, if by example, instruction, and prayer, we have sought it before the Lord. We are unhappy if we do not see our children walking in the truth. Yet the idea of birthright membership is an evil one, and is as perilous as it is unscriptural. If children are taken into the church simply because of their earthly parentage, surely this is not consistent with that description of the sons of God which is found in the inspired Scripture—"Which were born, not of blood, nor of the will of the flesh, nor of the will of man, but of God." Not generation, but regeneration, makes the Christian. You are not Christians because you can trace a line of fleshly descent throughout twenty generations of children of God; but you must, yourselves, be born again; for except a man be born from above, he cannot see the kingdom of God. Many, no doubt, lay hold naturally on the form of godliness because of family ties: this is poor work. Ishmael is a sorry son of Abraham, and Esau of Isaac, and Absalom of David. Grace does not run in the blood. If you have no better foundation for your religion than your earthly parentage, you are in a wretched case.

Others have accepted the form of godliness *by the force of authority and influence.* They were, as lads, put apprentice to godly men; as girls, they were under the guidance of pious teachers; and, as they grew up, they came under the influence of persons of superior intelligence and character, who were on the Lord's side. This accounts for their form of godliness. Many persons are the creatures of their surroundings; religion or irreligion is with them the result of circumstances. Such persons were led to make a profession of faith in Christ because others did so, and friends encouraged them to do the same. The deep searching of heart, which they ought to have exhibited, was slurred over, and they were found among the people of God without having to knock for entrance at the wicket-gate. I do not wish any one to condemn himself because he was guided to the Saviour by godly friends—far from it; but, nevertheless, there is danger lest we fail to have personal repentance and personal faith, and are content to lean upon the opinions of others.

So have I seen the form of godliness taken up *on account of friendships.* Many a time courtship and marriage have led to a formal religiousness, lacking heart. The future husband is induced to make a profession of religion for the sake of gaining one who was a sincere Christian, and would not have broken her Lord's command to be unequally yoked together with an unbeliever. Godliness should never be put on in order that we may put a wedding ring upon the finger: this is a sad abuse of religious profession. Other kinds of friendship, also, have led men and women to profess a faith they never had, and to unite themselves visibly with the church, while in spirit and in truth they were never truly a part of it. I put these things to you that there may be great searchings of heart among us all, and that we may candidly consider how we have come by our form of godliness.

Certain persons assume the form of godliness from *a natural religious disposition.* Do not suppose that all unconverted people are without religion. Much religiousness is found in the heathen, and there are races which have naturally more of reverence than others. The German, with his profound philosophy, is often free, not only from superstition, but from reverence ; while the Russian is by race naturally religious, not to say superstitious. I am speaking after the manner of men : the usual Russian takes off his hat to holy places, pictures, and persons, and he is little inclined to disbelieve or scoff. We perceive like differences among our own acquaintances : one man is readily fooled by sceptics, while another is ready, with open mouth, to believe every word. One is naturally an infidel, another is as naturally credulous. I mean, then, that to some the form of godliness commends itself, because they have a natural leaning that way. They could not be happy unless they were attending where God is worshipped, nor unless they were reckoned among the believers in Christ. They must play at religion, even if they do not make it their life business. Let me remind you of the questionable value of that which springs out of fallen human nature. Assuredly, it brings no one into the spiritual kingdom, for " that which is born of the flesh is flesh," and only " that which is born of the Spirit is spirit." " Ye must be born again." Beware of everything which springs up in the field without the sowing of the husband-man, for it will turn out to be a weed. O sirs, the day will come when God will try us as with fire, and that which comes of unregenerate nature will not stand the test, but will be utterly consumed.

I do not doubt that, in these silken days, many have a form of godliness *because of the respect it brings them.* Time was when to be a Christian was to be reviled, if not to be imprisoned, and, perhaps, burned at the stake. Hypocrites were fewer in those days, for a profession cost too much ; yet, strange to say, there were some who played the Judas even in these times. To-day religion walks forth in her velvet slippers ; and in certain classes and ranks, if men did not make some profession of religion, they would be looked upon with suspicion, and therefore men will take the name of Christian upon them, and wear religion as a part of full dress. The cross is at this day worn as a decoration. The cross as the instrument of our Saviour's shame and death is forgotten, and instead thereof, it is made the badge of honour, a jewel wherewith ungodly men may adorn themselves. Is this indicative of the deceit-fulness of the age ? Beware of seeking respect by a hypocritical godliness. Honour gained by a heartless profession is, in God's sight, the greatest disgrace. The actor may strut in his mimic royalty, but he must take off his crown and robes when the play is over ; and what will he then be ?

From the days of Iscariot until now, some have taken up the form of godliness *to gain thereby.* To make gain of godliness is to imitate the son of perdition. This is a perilous road, and yet many risk their souls for the lucre which they find therein. Apparent zeal for God may really be zeal for gold. The Emperor Maximilian showed great zeal against idolatry, and published a decree that images of gold and silver should be melted down. He was extremely zealous about this. The images were all to be melted down, and the metal forfeited to the emperor. It was shrewdly suspected that this great iconoclast was not altogether swayed by unselfish motives. When a business brings grist to the mill, it is not hard to keep to it. Some love Christ because they carry His bag for Him. Beware of that kind of godliness which makes a man hesitate until he sees whether a duty will pay or not, and then

makes him eager because he sees it will answer his purpose.

Once more : I do not doubt that a form of godliness has come to many because *it brings them ease of conscience,* and they are able, like the Pharisee, to thank God that they are not as other men are. Have they not been to church ? Have they not paid for their pew ? They can now go about their daily business without those stings of conscience which would come of neglecting the requirements of religion. These people profess to have been con-verted, and they are numbered with believers ; but, alas ! they are not of them. Of all people these are the hardest to reach, and the least likely to be saved. They hide behind the earthworks of a nominal religion ; they are out of reach of the shot and shell of gospel rebukes ; for these fly among the sinners, and they have taken up their quarters among the saints. Sad is that man's plight who wears the name of life but has never been quickened by the Holy Spirit.

Thus, I have very feebly tried to show what these men had, and why they had it.

Let us now remember *what they did not have.* They had " the form " of godliness ; but they denied "the power." *What is that power ?* God Himself is the power of godliness. The Holy Spirit is the life and force of it. Godliness is the power which brings a man to God, and binds him to Him. Godliness is that which creates repentance towards God, and faith in Him. Godliness is the result of a great change of heart in reference to God and His character. Godliness looks towards God, and mourns its distance from Him ; godliness hastens to draw nigh, and rests not till it is at home with God. Godliness makes a man like God. Godliness leads a man to love God, and to serve God ; it brings the fear of God before his eyes, and the love of God into his heart. Godliness leads to consecration, to sanctification, to concentra-tion. The godly man seeks first the kingdom of God and His righteousness, and expects other things to be added to him. Godliness makes a man commune with God, and gives him a partnership with God in His glorious designs ; and so it prepares him to dwell with God for ever. Many who have the form of godliness are strangers to this power, and so are in religion worldly, in prayer mechanical, in public one thing, and in private another. True godliness lies in spiritual power, and as they are without this, they are dead while they live.

What is the general history of those who have not this power ? Well, dear friends, their course usually runs thus : they do not begin with denying the power, but they begin by trying to do without it. They would like to become members of the church, and as they fear that they are not fit for it, they look about for something which looks like conversion and the new birth. They try to persuade themselves that they have been changed : they accept emotion as regeneration, and a belief of doctrine for belief in Christ. It is rather hard at first to reckon brass as gold, but it grows easier as it is persisted in. Patch-ing up a conversion, and manufacturing a regeneration, they venture forward. At the first they are a good deal suspicious of themselves, but they industriously kill every question by treating it as a needless doubt. Thus, by degrees, they believe a lie.

The next step is easy : *they deceive themselves,* and come to believe that they are surely saved. All is now right for eternity, so they fancy ; and they fold their arms in calm security. Meeting with godly people, they put on a bold front, and speak up as bravely as if they were the true soldiers of King Jesus. Good people are charmed to meet with fresh brethren, and at once take them into their confidence. Thus they deceive others, and help to strengthen themselves in their false hope. They use the choice phrases of earnest Christians. Mixing with them, they pick up their particular expressions, and pronounce Shibboleth in the most approved fashion.

At last they take the daring step of *denying the power*. Being without it themselves, they conceive that others are without it also. Judging from their own case, they conclude that it is all an affair of words. *They* get on very well without any supernatural power, and others, no doubt, do the same ; only they add a little cant to it to please the very godly folk.

They practically deny the power in their lives, so that those who see them and take them for Christians say, " There really is nothing in it ; for these people are as we are. They have a touch of paint here, and a little varnish there, but it is all the same wood." Practically, their actions assure the world that there is no power in Christianity ; it is only a name. Very soon, *privately, in their hearts* they think it is so, and they invent doctrines to match. Looking about them, they see inconsistent Christians and faulty believers, and they say to themselves, " There is not much in faith, after all. I am as good as any of these believers, and perhaps better, though I am sure there is no work of the Spirit in me." Thus, within their own hearts they believe, what, at first, they dare not speak : they count godliness an empty thing. By-and-by, in some cases, these people *profanely deny the divine power* of our holy faith, and then they become the greatest enemies of the cross of Christ. These traitors, nourished in the very house of God, are the worst foes of truth and righteousness. They ridicule that which once they professed to reverence. They have measured Christ's corn with their own bushel ; and because they never felt the powers of the world to come, they imagine that no one else has done so. Look at the church of the present day ; the advanced school, I mean. In its midst we see preachers who have a form of godliness, but deny the power thereof. They talk of the Lord Jesus, but they deny His Godhead, which is His power ; they speak of the Holy Spirit, but deny His personality, wherein lies His very existence. They take away the substance and power from all the doctrines of revelation, though they pretend still to believe them. They talk of redemption, but they deny substitution, which is the essence of it ; they extol the Scriptures, but deny their infallibility, wherein lies their value ; they use the phrases of orthodoxy, and believe nothing in common with the orthodox. I know not which to loathe the most, their teachings or their spirit : surely they are worthy of each other. They burn the kernel and preserve the husk. They kill the truth, and then pretend to reverence its sepulchre ; " they say they are Jews, and are not, but do lie." This is horrible, but the evil is widely spread, and in the presence of it the children of God are framing compromises, selling their Lord, and becoming partakers with the despisers of His truth. " Having a form of godliness, but denying the power thereof."

It is the sin of the age—the sin which is ruining the churches of our land.

II. In the second place, we are to observe THE WICKED FOLLY of this hypocritical conduct. Those who rest in the mere show of godliness are acting in a shameless manner, and I will try to expose it.

First, *they degrade the very name of Christ.* Brethren, if there is no spiritual power in godliness, it is worth nothing. We want no clouds without rain. Of shams and mere pretences we have more than enough. Those who have not the power of godliness, show us a very damaging picture of religion. They make out our Lord's religion to be comparable to a show at a country fair, with fine pictures and loud drumming on the outside, and nothing within worth a moment's consideration. The best of the show is on the outside ; or if there be anything within, it is a masquerade where all act borrowed parts, but no one is what he seems to be. Gracious Lord, never suffer us so to act as to make the world think that our Redeemer is nothing more than the clever manager of a theatre, where nothing is real, but all is pantomime. Men and brethren, if you pray at all, pray God to make you real, through and through. May you be made of true metal ! It were better for you that you had never been born than that you should make Christ dishonourable among the sons of men, by leading them to conclude that religion is all a piece of acting.

The folly of this is illustrated by the fact that *there is no value in such a dead form.* The form of godliness without the power is not worthy the trouble it takes to put it together, and keep it together. Imitation jewels are pretty and brilliant ; but if you take them to the jeweller he will give you nothing for them. There is a religion which is all paste gems—a godliness which glitters, but is not gold ; and in that day when you will want to realize something from it, you will be wretchedly disappointed. A form of godliness joined to an unholy heart is of no value to God. I have read that the swan was not allowed to be offered upon the altar of God, because, although its feathers are as white as snow, yet its skin is black. God will not accept that external morality which conceals internal impurity. There must be a pure heart as well as a clean life ; the power of godliness must work within, or else God will not accept our offering. There is no value to man or to God in a religion which is a dead form.

Next, *there is no use in mere formality.* If your religion is without spiritual life, what is the use of it ? Could you ride home on a dead horse ? Would you hunt with dead dogs ? Would any one like to go into battle with a pasteboard helmet ? When the sword fell on it, what use would such a helmet be ? What an outcry has been raised about bad swords ! Is false religion any better ? In the depth of winter, can you warm yourself before a painted fire ? Could you dine off the picture of a feast when you are hungry ? There must be vitality and substantiality, or else the form is utterly worthless ; and worse than worthless, for it may flatter you into deadly self-conceit.

Moreover, *there is no comfort in it.* The form without the power has nothing in it to warm the heart, to raise the spirits, or to strengthen the mind against the day of sickness, or in the hour of death. O God, if my religion has been a mere form, what shall I do in the swelling of Jordan ? My fine profession will all disappear, and nothing will come of it wherewith I may face the last enemy. Peter called hypocrites " wells without water." You are thirsty, and you gladly spy a well. It is well surrounded with a curb, and provided with a windlass and bucket. You hasten to draw water. What ! Does the bucket come up empty ? You try again. How bitter is your disappointment ! A well without water is a mockery. It is a mere pit of destruction, a deadly delusion. Are some of you possessors of a religion which never yields you a drop of comfort ? Is it a bondage to you ? Do you follow Christ as a slave follows his master ? Away with such a religion ! The godliness which is worth having is a joy to a man : it is his choice, his treasure, his all. When it does not yield him conscious joy, yet he prizes it as the only source from which joy is expected by him. He follows after Christ *con amore*, out of his heart's desire after Him, and not from the force of fashion, or the power of fear.

To have the form of godliness without the power of it is to *lack constancy* in your religion. You never saw the mirage, but those who have travelled in the East, when they come home are sure to tell you about it. It is a very hot and thirsty day, and you are riding on a camel. Suddenly there rises before you a beautiful scene. Just a little from you are brooks of water, flowing between beds of osiers and banks of reeds and rushes. Yonder are palm trees and orange groves. Yes, and a city rises on a hill, crowned with minarets and towers. You are rejoiced, and ask your guide to lead you nearer to the water which glistens in the sun. He grimly answers, " Take no notice, it is the mirage. There is nothing yonder but the burning sand." You can scarce believe him, it seems so real ; but lo, it is all gone, like a dream of night. So unsubstantial is the hope which is built upon the form of godliness without the power. The white ants will eat up all the substance of a box, and yet leave it standing, till a touch causes the whole fabric to fall in dust : beware of a profession of which the substance has been eaten away. Believe in nothing which has not the stamp of eternity upon it. Go to, poor child ; thou mayest blow thy bubble, and the sunlight may paint it with rainbows ; but in an instant it is gone, and not a trace of it remains. Thy transient globe of beauty is for thee and thy fellow children, and not for men.

In reality, this kind of religion is *in opposition to Christ*. It is Jannes and Jambres over again : the magician of hypocrisy is trying to work miracles which belong to God only. In appearance he would produce the same marvels as the finger of God ; but he fails. God grant we may never be guilty of resisting the truth by a lying profession. False men do serious injury to true godliness ; for, like Ehud, they come with a pretended message from God, and with their dagger sharpened at both edges, they strike vital godliness in its very bowels. Nobody can do so much damages to the church of God as the man who is within its walls, but not within its life.

This nominal godliness, which is devoid of power, *is a shameful thing*. I close with that. It is a shameful thing for this life, for the Lord Jesus loathes it. When He passed by the fig-tree, which was so early with its leaves, but so empty of fruit, He saw therein the likeness of the vainglorious professor who has no real holiness, and he said, " Henceforth let no fruit grow on thee for ever." His word withered it at once : it stood a terrible emblem of the end of a false profession. How shameful will such a fruitless,

lifeless professor be in eternity, when the secrets of all hearts shall be revealed ! What shame and everlasting contempt will await him when his falsehood shall be detected, and his baseness shall fill all holy minds with horror ! What will be the hell of the false professor !

I have done when I have added a few words of *instruction*. The form of godliness is most precious ; let those who feel the power of godliness honour it and use it. Do not despise it because others have damaged it. Come forth, and make an open profession of religion ; but see that you have the power of it. Do cry to God that you may never wear a sleeve which is longer than your arm : I mean, may never go beyond what is really and truly your own. It will be better for you to go to God as a lost soul, and cry for mercy, than to profess yourself saved when you are not. Yet do confess Christ without fail or fear. Do not be ashamed of Jesus because of the ill manners of His disciples. Regard the ill savour of false professors as a part of the cross which you will have to bear for your Lord. To be associated with some who are not true seems inevitable in this life, however carefully we choose our company.

My next is a word of *discrimination*. Those to whom my text has nothing to say will be the first to take it home to themselves. When I discharge my heart with a faithful sermon, certain trembling souls whom I would fain comfort are sure to think that I mean *them*. A poor woman, in deep distress, comes to me, crying, " Sir, I have no feeling." Dear heart, she has ten times too much feeling. Another moans out, " I am sure I am a hypocrite." I never met with a hypocrite who thought himself one ; and I never shall. " Oh ! " said another, " I feel condemned." He that feels himself condemned may hope for pardon. If you are afraid of yourselves I am not afraid of you. If you tremble at God's word, you have one of the surest marks of God's elect. Those who fear that they are mistaken are seldom mistaken. If you search yourselves, and allow the word of God to search you, it is well with you. The bankrupt trader fears to have his books examined. The sound man even pays an accountant to overhaul his affairs. Use discrimination, and neither acquit nor condemn yourself without reason. If the Spirit of God leads you to weep in secret for sin, and to pray in secret for grace ; if it leads you to seek after holiness ; if it leads you to trust alone in Jesus, then you know the power of godliness, and you have never denied it. You who cry, " Oh, that I felt more of the power of the Holy Spirit, for I know that He could comfort and sanctify me, and make me live the life of heaven on earth ! " You are not aimed at either by the text or the sermon ; for you have not denied the power. No, no, this text does not belong to you, but to quite another class of people.

Let me give you a word of *admonition*. Learn from the text that there is something in godliness worth the having. The " form " of godliness is not all : there is a blessed " power." The Holy Ghost is that power, and He can work in you to will and to do of God's good pleasure. Come you to Jesus Christ, dear souls. Do not come to the minister, nor to the church, in the first place ; but come to Jesus. Come and lay yourselves at His feet, and say, " Lord, I will not be comforted unless Thou comfort me." Come, and take everything at first hand from your crucified Lord. Then shall you know the power of godliness. Beware of second-hand religion, it is never worth the carrying home. Get your godliness direct from heaven by the personal dealing of your own soul with your Saviour. Profess only what you possess, and rest only in that which has been given you from above. Your heavenly life, as yet, may be very feeble, but the grain of mustard seed will grow. You may be the least in Israel, but that is better than being the greatest in Babylon. The Lord bless these words, and apply them to each one in His own way by His Holy Spirit. You can make either a blister of them, or a plaster of them, as conscience shall direct. God guide you, for Jesus Christ's sake. Amen.

THE SUNDAY SCHOOL AND THE SCRIPTURES

" And that from a child thou hast known the Holy Scriptures, which are able to make thee wise unto salvation through faith which is in Christ Jesus."—2 Timothy iii. 15.

NOW very remarkably the times repeat themselves ! As I said just now, in the reading of the chapter, the warning which Paul gave concerning his own times is quite as needful for this present age. Again darkness thickens, and the mists hang heavily around our footsteps. Evil men and seducers wax worse and worse, and very many have turned away their ears from the truth to hearken to fables. Nor do we wonder that it is so. History must repeat itself so long as we have the same human nature to deal with, the same sins to ensnare mankind, the same truth to be trifled with, and the same devil to stir men up to the same mischief.

But, brethren, when the same evils come, we must apply to them the same remedies. When a disease appears which has done deadly mischief in past times, physicians enquire for medicines which on a former occasion curbed the enemy. We are bound to do the same in spiritual matters. We must see what Paul did in his day when the malaria of false doctrine was in the air. It is remarkable how very simple, as a rule, everything is that is really effective. If a discovery is made in science or machinery, it is complicated at first, and that for the very reason that it is imperfect ; but all improvements are in the direction of simplicity. It is just the same with spiritual teachings. When we get at reality we cut off superfluity. Let us not talk of inventing wise measures for the present distress in the spiritual world, but let us use the great remedy which was so effectual in Paul's day. Paul taught young Timothy the gospel himself : he made him not only hear his doctrine, but see his practice. We cannot force truth upon men, but we can make our own teaching clear and decided, and make our lives consistent therewith. Truth and holiness are the surest antidotes to error and unrighteousness. The apostle said to Timothy, " Continue thou in the things which thou hast learned and hast been assured of, knowing of whom thou hast learned them."

He then dwelt upon another potent remedy which had been of great service to the young preacher, namely, the knowing of the holy scriptures from his earliest childhood. This was to young Timothy one of his best safeguards. His early training held him like an anchor, and saved him from the dreadful drift of the age. Happy young man, of whom the apostle could say, " From a child thou hast known the holy scriptures, which are able to make thee wise unto salvation through faith which is in Christ Jesus " !

Brethren, to be prepared for the coming conflict, we have only to preach the gospel, and to live the gospel ; and also take care that we teach the children the word of the Lord. This last is specially to be attended to, for it is by the mouth of babes and sucklings that God will still the enemy. It is idle to dream that human learning must be met by human learning, or that Satan must cast out Satan. No. Lift up the brazen serpent wherever the fiery serpents are biting the people, and men shall look to it and live. Bring the children out, and hold them up, and turn their little eyes towards the divinely ordained remedy ; for still there is life in a look—life as against the varied venoms of the serpent which are now poisoning the blood of men. There is no cure after all for midnight but the rising sun ; no hope remains for a dark world but in that light which lighteneth every man. Shine forth, O Sun of Righteousness, and mist, and cloud, and darkness must disappear. Brethren, keep to the apostolic plans, and rest assured of apostolic success, Preach Christ ; preach the word in season and out of season ; and teach the children. One of God's chief methods for preserving His fields from tares, is to sow them early with wheat. Upon that I am going to speak this morning as the Holy Spirit shall help me.

In tracing the gracious work of God upon the heart of Timothy, and upon others who are favoured as he was, I shall notice that this work *commenced with early instruction*—" From a child thou hast known the holy scriptures " ; and secondly, it was *quickened and made effectual by saving faith*—" The holy scriptures which are able to make thee wise unto salvation through faith which is in Christ Jesus." Then we shall notice that the effect of this early teaching upon Timothy was that it *created a solid character*, and, furthermore, that it *produced great usefulness*.

I. The work of God's grace in Timothy COMMENCED WITH EARLY INSTRUCTION—" From a child thou hast known the holy scriptures."

Note the time of instruction. The expression, " from a child," might be better understood if we read it, " from a very child ; " or, as the Revised Version has it, " from a babe." It does not mean a well-grown child, or youth, but a child just rising out of infancy. From a very child Timothy had known the sacred writings. This expression is, no doubt, used to show that we cannot begin too early to imbue the minds of our children with scriptural knowledge. Babes receive impressions long before we are aware of the fact. During the first months of a child's life it learns more than we imagine. It soon learns the love of its mother, and its own dependence ; and if the mother be wise, it learns the meaning of obedience and the necessity of yielding its will to a higher will. This may be the key-note of its whole future life. If it learns obedience and submission early, it may save a thousand tears from the child's eyes, and as many from the mother's heart. A special vantage-ground is lost when even babyhood is left uncultured.

The holy scriptures may be learned by children as soon as they are capable of understanding anything. It is a very remarkable fact, which I have heard asserted by many teachers, that children will learn to read out of the Bible better than from any other book. I scarcely know why : it may, perhaps, be on account of the simplicity of the language ; but I believe it is so. A Biblical fact will often be grasped when an incident of common history is forgotten. There is an adaptation in the Bible for human beings of all ages, and therefore it has a fitness for children. We make a mistake when we think that we must begin with something else and lead up to the Scriptures. The Bible is the book for the peep of day. Parts of it are above a child's mind, for they are above the comprehension of the most advanced among us. There are depths in it wherein leviathan may swim ; but there are also brooks in which a lamb may wade. Wise teachers know how to lead their little ones into the green pastures beside the still waters.

I was noticing, in the life of that man of God whose loss presses very heavily upon many of our hearts, namely, the Earl of Shaftesbury, that his first religious impressions were produced by a humble woman. The impressions which made him Shaftesbury —the man of God, and the friend of man—were received in the nursery. Little Lord Ashley had a godly nurse who spoke to him of the things of God. He tells us that she died before he was seven years of age ; clear proof that early in life his heart had been able to receive the seal of the Spirit of God, and to receive it by humble instrumentality. Blessed among women was she whose name we know not, but who wrought incalculable service for God and man by her holy teaching of the chosen child. Young nurses, note this.

Give us the first seven years of a child, with God's grace, and we may defy the world, the flesh, and the devil to ruin that immortal soul. Those first years, while yet the clay is soft and plastic, go far to decide the form of the vessel. Do not say that your office, you who teach the young, is in the least degree inferior to ours, whose main business is with older folks. No, you have the first of them, and your impressions, as they come first, will endure last : oh that they may be good, and only good ! Among the thoughts that come to an old man before he enters heaven, the most plentiful are those that aforetime visited him when he sat upon his mother's knee. That which made Dr. Guthrie ask for a " bairn's hymn " when he was dying is but an instinct of our nature, which leads us to complete the circle by folding together the ends of life. Childlike things are dearest to old age. We shuffle off a portion of the coil that doth surround and hamper us, and go back again to our more natural selves ; and therefore the old songs are on our lips, and the old thoughts are in our minds. The teaching of our childhood leave clean cut and sharp impressions upon the mind, which remain after seventy years have passed. Let us see that such impressions are made for the highest ends.

It is well to *note the admirable selection of instructors.* We are not at a loss to tell who instructed youthful Timothy. In the first chapter of this epistle Paul says, " When I call to remembrance the unfeigned faith that is in thee, which dwelt first in thy grandmother Lois, and thy mother Eunice ; and I am persuaded that in thee also." No doubt grandmother Lois and mother Eunice united in teaching the little one. Who should teach the children but the parents ? Timothy's father was a Greek, and probably a heathen, but his child was happy in having a venerable grandmother, so often the dearest of all relatives to a little child. He had also a gracious mother, once a devout Jewess, and afterwards also a firmly believing Christian, who made it her daily pleasure to teach her own dear child the word of the Lord. O dear mothers, you have a very sacred trust reposed in you by God ! He hath in effect said to you, " Take this child and nurse it for me, and I will give thee thy wages." You are called to equip the future man of God, that he may be throughly furnished unto every good work. If God spares you, you may live to hear that pretty boy speak to thousands, and you will have the sweet reflection in your heart that the quiet teachings of the nursery led the man to love his God and serve Him. Those who think that a woman detained at home by her little family is doing nothing, think the reverse of what is true. Scarcely can the godly mother quit her home for a place of worship ; but dream not that she is lost to the work of the church ; far from it, she is doing the best possible service for her Lord. Mothers, the godly training of your offsprings is your first and most pressing duty. Christian women, by teaching children the holy scriptures, are as much fulfilling their part for the Lord, as Moses in judging Israel, or Solomon in building the temple.

Nowadays, since the world has in it, alas ! so few of Christian mothers and grandmothers, the church has thought it wise to supplement the instruction of home by teaching held under her fostering wing. Those children who have no such parents the church takes under her maternal care. I regard this as a very blessed institution. I am thankful for the many of our brothers and sisters who give their Sabbath days, and many of them a considerable part of their week evenings also, to the teaching of other people's children, who somehow grow to be very much their own. They endeavour to perform the duties of fathers and mothers, for God's sake, to those children who are neglected by their own parents ; and therein they do well. Let no Christian parents fall into the delusion that the Sunday-school is intended to ease them of their personal duties. The first and most natural condition of things is for Christian parents to train up their own children in the nurture and admonition of the Lord. Let holy grandmothers and gracious mothers, with their husbands, see to it that their own boys and girls are well taught in the book of the Lord. Where there are no such Christian parents, it is well and wisely done for godly people to intervene. It is a Christly work when others undertake the duty which the natural doers of it have left undone. The Lord Jesus looks with pleasure upon those who feed His lambs, and nurse His babes ; for it is not His will that any of these little ones should perish. Timothy had the great privilege of being taught by those whose natural duty it is ; but where that great privilege cannot be enjoyed, let us all, as God shall help us, try to make up to the children the terrible loss which they endure. Come forward, earnest men and women, and sanctify yourselves for this joyful service.

Note the subject of the instruction. " From a child thou hast known the holy scriptures " : he was led *to treat the book of God with great reverence.* I lay stress upon that word " *holy* scriptures." One of the first objects of the Sabbath-school should be to teach the children great reverence for these holy writings, these inspired Scriptures. The Jews esteemed the Old Testament beyond all price ; and though unfortunately many of them fell into a superstitious reverence for the letter and lost the spirit of it, yet were they much to be commended for their profound regard to the holy oracles. Especially is this feeling of reverence needed nowadays. I meet with men who hold strange views, but I do not care one-half so much about their views, nor about the strangeness of them, as I do about a certain something which I spy out at the back of this novel thinking. When I find that, if I prove their views to be unscriptural, I have nevertheless proved nothing to them, for they do not care about Scriptures, then I have found out a principle far more dangerous than mere doctrinal blundering. This indifference to Scripture is the great curse of the church at this hour. We can be tolerant of divergent opinions, so long as we perceive an honest intent to follow the Statute-book. But if it comes to this, that the Book itself is of small authority to you, then we have no need of further parley : we are in different camps, and the sooner we recognize this, the better for all parties concerned. If we are to have a church of God at all in the land, Scripture must be regarded as holy, and to be had in reverence. This Scripture was given by holy inspiration, and is not the result of dim myths and dubious traditions ; neither has it drifted down to us by the survival of the fittest as one of the human books. It must be given to our children, and accepted by ourselves, as the infallible revelation of the Most Holy God. Lay much stress upon this ; tell your children that the word of the Lord is a pure word, as silver tried in a furnace of earth, purified seven times. Let their esteem for the Book of God be carried to the highest point.

Observe that Timithy was taught, not only to reverence holy things in general, but especially to *know the Scriptures.* The teaching of his mother and his grandmother was the teaching of holy scripture. Suppose we get the children together on Sabbath days, and then amuse them and make the hours to pass away pleasantly ; or instruct them, as we do in the week-days, in the elements of a moral education, what have we done ? We have done nothing worthy of the day, or of the church of God. Suppose that we are particularly careful to teach the children the rules and regulations of our own church, and do not take them to the Scriptures ; suppose that we bring before them a book which is set up as the standard of our church, but do not dwell upon the Bible—what have we done ? The aforesaid standard may or may not be correct, and we may, therefore, have taught our children truth or have taught them error ; but if we keep to holy scripture we cannot go aside. With such a standard we know that we are right. This Book is the word of God, and if we teach it, we teach that which the Lord will accept and bless. O dear teachers—and I speak here to myself also—let our teaching be more and more scriptural ! Fret not if our classes forget what *we* say, but pray them to remember what the Lord says. May divine truths about sin, and righteousness, and judgemnt to come, be written on their hearts ! May revealed truths concerning the love of God, the grace of our Lord Jesus Christ, and the work of the Holy Ghost never be forgotten by them ! May they know the virtue and necessity of the atoning blood of our Lord, the power of His resurrection, and the glory of His second

coming ! May the doctrines of grace be graven as with a pen of iron upon their minds, and written as with the point of a diamond upon their hearts, never to be erased ! Brethren, if we can secure this, we have not lived in vain. The generation now ruling seems bent on departing from the eternal truth of God : but we shall not despair if the gospel be impressed upon the memory of the rising race.

Once more upon this point : it appears that young Timothy was so taught as a child that *the teaching was effectual.* "Thou hast *known* the holy scriptures," says Paul. It is a good deal to say of a child that he has "known the holy scriptures." You may say, "I have taught the children the Scriptures," but that they have known them is quite another thing. Do all of you who are grown up know the Scriptures ? I fear that although knowledge in general increases, knowledge of the Scriptures is far too rare. If we were now to hold an examination, I am afraid that some of you would hardly shine in the lists at the end. But here was a little child who knew the holy scriptures : that is to say, he had a remarkable acquaintance with them. Children can get that : it is by no means an impossible attainment. God blessing your efforts, dear friends, your children may know all of Scripture that is necessary to their salvation. They may have as true an idea of sin as their mother has : they may have as clear a view of the atonement as their grandmother can have ; they may have a distinct a faith in Jesus as any of us can have. The things that make for our peace require no length of experience to prepare us for receiving them ; they are among the simplicities of thought. He may run that readeth them ; and a child may read them as soon as he can run. The opinion that children cannot receive the whole truth of the gospel is a great mistake ; for their child-condition is a help rather than a hindrance : older folk must become as little children before they can enter the kingdom. Do lay a good groundwork with the children. Let not Sunday-school work be slurred, nor done in a slovenly manner. Let the children know the holy scripture. Let the Scriptures be consulted rather than any human book.

II. Our second head was to be that this work WAS QUICKENED BY A SAVING FAITH. The Scriptures do not save, but they are able to make a man wise unto salvation. Children may know the Scriptures, and yet not be children of God. *Faith in Jesus Christ is that grace which brings immediate salvation.* Many dear children are called of God so early, that they cannot precisely tell when they were converted ; but they were converted : they must at some time or other have passed from death to life. You could not have told this morning, by observation, the moment when the sun rose, but it did rise ; and there was a time when it was below the horizon, and another time when it had risen above it. The moment, whether we see it or not, in which a child is really saved, is when he believes in the Lord Jesus Christ. Pehaps for years Lois and Eunice had been teaching the Old Testament to Timothy, while they themselves did not know the Lord Jesus ; and, if so, they were teaching him the type without the antitype—the riddles without the answers : but it was good teaching for all that, since it was all the truth which they then knew. How much happier, however, is our task, since we are able to teach concerning the Lord Jesus so plainly, having the New Testament to explain the Old ! May we not hope that even earlier in life than Timothy, our dear children may catch the thought that Christ Jesus is the sum and substance of holy scripture, and so by faith in Him may receive power to become the sons of God ? I mention this, simple as it is, because I want all teachers to feel that if their children do not as yet know all the doctrines of the Bible, and if there be certain higher or deeper truths which their minds have not yet grasped, still children are saved as soon as they are wise unto salvation through faith which is in Christ Jesus. Faith in the Lord Jesus, as He is set forth in Scripture, will surely save. " If thou believest with all thine heart, thou mayest," said Philip to the eunuch ; and we say the same to every child : thou mayest confess thy faith if thou hast any true faith in Jesus to confess. If thou believest that Jesus is the Christ, and so dost put thy trust in Him, thou art as truly saved as though grey hairs adorned thy brow.

Notice, that *by this faith in Christ Jesus we continue and advance in salvation.* The moment we believe in Christ we are saved ; but we are not at once as wise as we may be, and hope to be. We may be, as it were, saved unintelligently ; I mean, of course, comparatively so ; but it is desirable that we should be able to give a reason for the hope that is in us, and so be wise unto salvation. By faith children become little disciples, and by faith they go on to become more proficient. How are we to go on to wisdom ? Not by quitting the way of faith, but by keeping to that same faith in Christ Jesus by which we began to learn. In the school of grace faith is the great faculty by which we make advances in wisdom. If by faith thou hast been able to say A and B and C, it must be by faith that thou shalt go on to say D and E and F, until thou shalt come to the end of the alphabet, and be an expert in the Book of wisdom. If by faith thou canst read in the spelling book of simple faith, by the same faith in Christ Jesus thou must go on to read in the classics of full assurance, and become a scribe well instructed in the things of the kingdom. Keep therefore close to the practice of faith, from which so many are turning aside. In these times men look to make progress by what they call *thought*, by which they mean vain imagination and speculation. We cannot advance a step by doubt ; our only progress is by faith. There are no such things as " stepping-stones of our dead selves " ; unless, indeed, they be stepping-stones down to death and destruction ; the only stepping-stones to life and heaven are to be found in the truth of God revealed to our faith. Believe God, and thou hast made progress. So let us pray for our children, that constantly they may know and believe more and more ; for the Scripture is able to make them wise unto salvation, but only through faith which is in Christ Jesus. Faith is the result to aim at ; faith in the appointed, anointed, and exalted Saviour. This is the anchorage to which we would bring these little ships, for here they will abide in perfect safety.

Observe that the text gives us a plain intimation that *by faith knowledge is turned into wisdom.* Exceedingly practical is the difference between knowledge and wisdom. See it in the text, " From a child thou hast known " ; but it is faith, faith alone, that turns that knowledge into wisdom ; and thus the holy scriptures are " able to make wise unto salvation." " Knowledge is power," but wisdom is the application of that power to practical ends. Knowledge may be bullion, but wisdom is the minted gold, fit for circulation among men. You can give your children knowledge without their having faith ; but they must have faith given them of the Holy Ghost before that knowledge can become wisdom. Scriptural knowledge is wisdom when it influences the heart, when it rules the mind, when it affects the daily life, when it sanctifies the spirit, when it renews the will. O teachers, pray for your dear children, that God would give them faith in Christ Jesus, that so the knowledge which you have given them may turn to wisdom ! Go as far as you can go with the teaching ; but ever cry mightily unto the Lord, that His Holy Spirit may work regeneration, create faith, impart wisdom, and give salvation.

Learn yet again, that *faith finds her wisdom in the use of knowledge conferred by the Scriptures.* " From a child thou hast known the holy scriptures, which are able to make thee wise unto salvation through faith." Faith never finds her wisdom in the thoughts of men, nor in pretended revelations ; but she resorts to the inspired writings for her guidance. This is the well from which she drinks, the manna on which she feeds. Faith takes the Lord Jesus to her be wisdom. The knowledge of Christ is to her the most excellent of the sciences. She asks only—What is written ? and when that question is answered, her difficulties are ended. I know it is not so with this unbelieving age ; and this it is which causes me to go mourning and lamenting. Alas for a church which rejects the testimony of the Lord ! As for us, we abide by the word of the Lord, and from it we will not stir an inch.

See then, my hearers, what is wanted for all of you who are unconverted. The holy scriptures must be made the means of your salvation through faith. Know the Bible, read the Bible, search the Bible ; and yet that alone will not save you. What did out Lord Himself say ? " Ye search the Scriptures, for in them ye think ye have eternal life ; and they are they which testify of Me ; and ye will not come unto Me that ye might have life." If you come not to Jesus, you will miss eternal life. Searching the Scriptures is able to make you wise unto salvation " through faith which is in Christ Jesus " ; but not without that faith. Pray, ye Sunday-school teachers, that ye may see this faith wrought in the children whom you teach. What a blessed ground-work for faith your teaching of the holy scriptures will be ; but never mistake it for the building itself, which is of faith alone.

III. Time fails me ; I cannot dwell as I would upon other points ; but I beg you to notice, in the third place, that sound instruction in holy scripture, when quickened by a living faith, CREATES A SOLID CHARACTER. The man who from a child has known the holy scriptures, when he obtains faith in Christ will be grounded and settled upon the abiding principles of the unchanging word of God. I wish it were so with the bulk of those who profess and call themselves Christians. In these days we are surrounded by unsettled minds, " ever learning, but never coming to a knowledge of the truth." These are carried about by every wind of doctrine. What numbers of professors I have known who go into one place of worship and hear one form of doctrine and apparently approve it because the preacher is " a clever man ! " They hear an opposite teaching, and they are equally at home, because again it is " a clever man ! " They join with a church, and you ask them, " Do you agree with the views of that community ? " They neither know nor care what those views may be ; one doctrine is as good as another to them. Their spiritual appetite can enjoy soap as well as butter ; they can digest bricks as well as bread. These religious ostriches have a marvellous power of swallowing everything ; they have no spiritual discernment, no appreciation of truth. They follow any " clever " person, and in this prove that they are not the sheep of our Lord's pasture, of whom it is written, " A stranger will they not follow ; for they know not the voice of strangers." We desire to build up a church with those who know what they do know, and can give a reason for what they believe. The true believer's great reason for his faith is, " It is written." Christ our Master met the tempter in the wilderness with, " It is written." Though He was Himself inspired, yet His teaching was full of the Old Testament ; He was always quoting the words of the inspired Book, and therein setting us an example. If you and I would contend with Satan, and with an evil world, so as to overcome in the conflict, we must take care to take our stand squarely and firmly upon the Scriptures. Let us treat our opponents to volleys of Scripture. Let us fire point-blank with sacred texts. These are arguments which wound and kill. Our own reasonings are mere paper pellets ; but scriptural proofs are bullets of steel. Our opponents will find it useless to try to lead us away from the old faith when they perceive that we will not budge an inch from holy scripture. We are bomb-proof when we shelter beneath the word of the Lord. The cunning craftiness of deceivers is foiled by the clear simplicity of " Thus saith the Lord."

Those who know the Scriptures, and so believe in Jesus, are pillared upon a personal acquaintance with the foundations of their faith. " From a child thou hast known the holy scriptures " : they were not treated with an ignorant reverence, but with an intelligent homage. How much I desire that each one of you may be a personal student of the holy scriptures ! We need to know them for ourselves. Personally grasping them as a revelation to himself, the godly man loves them, studies them, feels them, lives upon them, and so knows them. By this means he becomes independent of other men. Paul is to die. Poor Timothy ! Yes, it will be " poor Timothy ! " if he carries his faith in Paul's bosom, and has none in his own heart. But Timothy's Bible is not going to die. Timothy's knowledge of Scripture is not going to be taken from him ; nor is the Holy Spirit about to depart from him. Look at some of our churches : while a well-instructed gospel minister leads the way, the brethren abide in their steadfastness. The good man dies, and where is the church ? No doubt, those who are instructed in the Scriptures remain in their places, but the more ignorant are scattered like chaff. There are numbers now in this part of London wandering about, who were once zealous for the faith, but are now almost indifferent to it. I will not mention names, but I could do so readily enough—I mean the names of esteemed brethren who gathered an earnest following about them ; but they are gone, and with their going, numbers of their followers have gone, too. I fear there could not have been a sound knowledge of the word, or these people would have survived the great loss of their teacher. Oh, to have a good personal building up upon the solid word of God ! then you will know what you do know, and you will hold fast to it, and there will be no driving you away from the standards of the faith. I labour for this among you, and I pray that I may not labour in vain.

The man who has been taught the Scripture from his youth is anchored by the divine influences of that Scripture. It has so operated upon him that he knows for himself its divine power. He knows the difference between truth and error by the effect produced on his heart and life. Without any boasting, he is able to discern between things that differ ; because about scriptural truth there is a strange, mysterious unction, which does not attend the teachings of the most learned of men. I cannot explain to you what this unction is, but every child of God knows it. When I read a text of Scripture, even if I do not know it to be a text of Scripture by memory, I perceive its divine origin at once by a mystic influence which it exerts over my heart. The most striking passages of any sermon are texts well placed. A sentence from the mouth of God will have more permanent power over a Christian man than the best composed of human statements. God's word is living, and powerful, and has a power to enter the heart beyond that of any other word. The words of the Bible strike and stick : they enter and abide. He that has been taught in Scripture, steeped in Scripture, saturated with Scripture, is conscious of its permeating influence, and it gives him permanence of conviction. Like the crimson dye in cloth, the tint of Scripture is not to be got out of the soul when once fixed there ; it is dyed ingrain, it enters into the very nature of the man. Bible truth influences his thoughts, words, and deeds : it is all-pervading ; he begins to eat, and drink, and sleep holy scripture. The man's heart is fixed on God, fixed in the truth, fixed in holy living. He will stand fast, however evil the days. Though all the rest should apostatize, this man cannot ; for the divine word through faith has bound Him to the altar of the Lord, and in the truth He must and will both live and die, come what weathers there may.

Besides, a man that has once been taught in the Scripture, and to whose soul the Spirit has blessed that teaching, has come to yield himself to the supremacy of the Scripture, and this must operate to the shaping of his character. I confess that sometimes I come across a text which does not at the first blush agree with other teachings of Scripture which I have already received, and this startles me for the moment. But one thing is settled in my heart, namely, that I will follow the Scripture wherever it leads me, and that I will renounce the most cherished opinion rather than shape a text or alter a syllable of the inspired Book. It is not mine to make God's word consistent, but to believe that it is so. When a text stands in the middle of the road I drive no further. The Romans had a god they called " Terminus," who was the god of landmarks. Holy scripture is my sacred landmark, and I hear a voice which threatens me with a curse if I remove it. Sometimes I say to myself, " I did not think to find this truth to be just so ; but as it is so, I must bow. It is rather awkward for my theory, but I must alter my system, for the Scripture cannot be broken." " Let God be true, but every man a liar." We want our children to have this deep reverence for Scripture, even as we have it ourselves. There it stands : the eternal pen has written it : we accept it. If God has said it, we have no desire to question it, lest the Scripture should say to us, "Nay but, O man, who art thou that repliest against God ?" We must bow before the infallibility of the Holy Ghost, and say, "Lord, teach me what this means. What I know not, teach Thou me." He who goes through the world with an intense reverence for Scripture will be a man indeed. The Lord will make good in him that word—"Them that honour me I will honour." Angels and men ere long reverence the man who reverences the word of God. Feed your mind on the pulse of Scripture, and, like Daniel and his comrades, your countenance shall appear fairer and fatter in the flesh than all the children who eat the portion of the king's meat from the philosophic tables of the world.

While on this point I would also say, that this kind of instruction will hold a man fast against the differing seductions of the age. Here I go into one place of worship, and I see a pretty little doll's-house at the further end, and people are bowing down before some paper flowers and candlesticks. Around the building I see pictures of virgins and saints ; but he who has read his Bible enters not into this modern idolatry. A priest once said to a poor Irishman, "There will be no good come of your reading the Bible." "Why," replied the man, "It is written, 'Search the Scriptures.' Please, your Reverence, I was just reading ' Ye shall read it to your children,' and the priests have no children : how can you account for that ?" "Ah !" replied the priest, "the like of you cannot understand the book." "Well," said the man, "if I cannot understand it, it will do me no harm ; and if I can understand it, it will do me great good." Just so : the Bible is a very dangerous book to superstition, but to nothing else. Spread it, then, to the winds of heaven ; and read it, every one of you. To the law and to the testimony ; if we speak not according to this word, it is because there is no light in us. He that holds to the Bible will be equally free from the dangers of rationalism which are now so abundant ; and he will keep himself clean from the ravings of anarchy which now sound like the cries of dragons from the dark places of the earth. People are beginning to forget the commandment, "Thou shalt not steal," and they are planning various methods of political thievery, by which the foundations of society will be shaken. Love of holy scripture will be the sheet-anchor of the State as well as of the Church. If men are thoroughly grounded in holy scripture, we shall undergo political changes with great advantage ; but if not, there is mischief brewing. That book is the corner-stone of our future hope.

IV. Now, lastly. As this early teaching creates a fine solid character, so will it PRODUCE GREAT USEFULNESS. I will say nothing more than just this. Thus Timothy became above all others a choice companion for Paul, one upon whom Paul looked with love, and remembered with joy.

Companions for apostles are only to be produced in the school of holy scripture. Those who have communed with Moses, and David, and the prophets, are fit to associate with an apostle. It is something to produce out of a child a comrade for a veteran servant of the living God. Let a man of God get side by side with a youth who knows the Scriptures and he feels, "This is fit company for me." Paul, worn with years of persecution, strokes his grey beard, and his eyes light up with joy as he looks on that young Timothy. What is there about him more than any other ? Why, only that he knows the Scriptures, and they have made him wise unto salvation. There were, no doubt, fine young fellows to be found who gloried in preferring the advanced thought of philosophers to the stereotyped teachings of holy scripture ; but had they begun to talk to the apostle upon their new theories, Paul would have dismissed them with words of warning. He knew nothing of them or of their " other gospel," except that they troubled him and the churches. Without a scriptural training a convert has no grit, no backbone, and no soul in him. But when Paul looked on a gracious youth who knew the Scriptures, and held fast to them, he thanked God, and took courage.

This young man became a minister and an evangelist. He was a preacher of such a sort that we should have been glad to have heard him. God send us many such ! Perhaps we might have said, "The young man's opinions were rather crude, and his expressions were somewhat rough ; but we can put up with that from so young a man. On the other hand, what a richness of Scripture there was in him ! What depth of thought ! Did you not notice he had not got through a dozen sentences before he had quoted a Scripture ? and when he came to prove his point he did not give half-a-dozen rationalistic arguments, but he brought out a single word from the Lord, and the point was settled." You must agree with a man who is at home with his Bible. This is the kind of preacher that we need more of. Instruct your children well, beloved teachers, that they also may become scriptural teachers in due time.

Timothy became, also, a great champion for the faith. He came forward, and in the midst of all those who were preaching false doctrine he stood firm to the end ; steadfast, unmovable, courageous, because as a child he had known the Scriptures. O teachers, see what you may do ! In your school sits our future Evangelists. In that infant class sits an apostle to some distant land. There may come under your training hand, my sister, a future father in Israel. There shall come under your teaching, my brother, those that are to bear the banners of the Lord in the thick of the fray. The ages look to you each time your class assembles. Oh, that God may help you to do your part well ! We pray with one heart and one soul that the Lord Jesus Christ may be with our Sunday-schools from this day and till He cometh. Amen and Amen.

A LAST LOOK-OUT

The time of my departure is at hand."—2 Timothy iv. 6.

SO near, so very near the change—his removal from this to another world; and so very conscious of it; yet Paul looked back with calm satisfaction; he looked forward with sweet assurance; and he looked round with deepest interest on the mission that had engaged his life. As you must have noticed while we were reading the chapter, in his case " the ruling passion was strong in death." Writing what he well knows is the last letter he shall ever write, its main topic is care for the church of God—anxiety for the promotion of the truth—zeal for the furtherance of the gospel. When he is dead, and gone from the post of service, the scene of suffering, the field of enterprise, on whom shall his mantle fall ? He desires that in Timothy he may find a worthy successor, strong in the faith, sincere of heart, and having dauntless courage withal, one who will wield the sword and hold the banner when his hand is palsied in death. Men have usually shown us what lies at the bottom of their heart when they have come to die. Often their last expiring expressions have been indicative of their entire character. Certainly you have before you in the last sentences of Paul's pen a fair epitome of his entire life. He is trusting in the Saviour; he is anxious to show his love for that Saviour. The welfare of the Christian church and the advancement of the holy cause of the gospel are uppermost in his mind. May it be yours and mine to live wholly for Christ, and to die also for Him. May this ever be foremost in our thoughts, " How can I advance the kingdom of our Lord and Saviour ? By what means can I bless His church and people ? " It is very beautiful to observe the way in which Paul describes his death in this verse. According to our translation he speaks of it as an offering. " I am now ready," saith he, " to be offered." If we accept this version he may be supposed to mean that he felt as one standing like a bullock or a lamb, ready to be laid on an altar. He foresaw he would die a martyr's death. He knew he could not be crucified as his brother Peter had been, for a Roman citizen was, as a rule, exempt from that ignominious death. He expected to die in some other manner. Probably he guessed it would be by the sword, and so he describes himself as waiting for the sacrificial knife to be used, that he might be presented as a sacrifice. So I say the words of our translation would lead us to think. But the original is far more instructive. He here likens himself, in the Greek, not to an offering, but to the drink-offering. Every Jew would know what that meant. When there was a burnt-sacrifice offered, the bullock or the victim then slain was the main part of the sacrifice. But sometimes there was a little, what if I say an unimportant, supplement added to that sacrifice—a little oil and a little wine were poured on to the altar or the bullock, and thus a drink-offering was said to be added to the burnt-offering. Now, Paul does not venture to call himself an offering—Christ is his offering. Christ is, so to speak, the sacrifice on the altar. He likens himself only to that little wine and oil poured out as a supplement thereto, not necessary to its

perfection, but tolerated in performing a vow, or allowed in connection with a free-will offering, as you will find if you refer at leisure to the fifteenth chapter of Numbers, from the fourth to the eighth verses. The drink-offering was thus a kind of addendum, by which the person who gave it showed his thankfulness. So Paul is resolved to show his thankfulness to Christ, the great sacrifice, and he is willing that his blood should be poured as a drink-offering on the altar where his Lord and Master was the great burnt-offering. He rejoices when he can say, " I am ready to be presented as a drink-offering unto God."

We have mainly to do with the second description which he gives of his death. What does he say when the hour that this grim monster must be grappled with is at hand ? I do not find him sad. Those who delight in gloomy poetry have often represented death in terrible language. " It is hard," says one—

" To feel the hand of death arrest one's steps,
Throw a chill blight on all one's budding hopes,
And hurl one's soul untimely to the shades."

And another claims—

" O God, it is a fearful thing
To see the human soul take wing,
In any shape, in any mood !
I've seen it rushing forth in blood,
I've seen it on the breaking ocean.

Not so the apostle Paul. I do not even hear him speak of flying through the gate as our grand old poet has described death. He does not say, " The hour of my dissolution is at hand "—a very proper word if he had used it ; but he is not looking so much at the process as at the result of his dying. He does not even say, " The hour of my death is at hand," but he adopts a beautiful expression, " The time of my departure "—words which are used sometimes to signify the departure of a vessel from the port ; the pulling up of the anchor so that it looses its moorings, when about to put out to sea—so he feels himself like a ship lying at the harbour for awhile—but he says, " The time for pulling up the anchor, the time for letting loose the cable, and cutting from the mooring is at hand ; I shall soon be launched upon my voyage." And he knew right well where that voyage would end, in the fair havens of the port of Peace in the better country, whither his Lord had gone before him.

Now we will proceed very briefly to say a word about *departure* ; and then a shorter word still about *the time* of our departure ; and then a little more about the time of our departure *being at hand*—trying here, especially, to bring forward some lessons which may be of practical usefulness to each one of us.

I. First, then, dear brethren, let us think a little about OUR DEPARTURE.

It is quite certain we shall not dwell here for ever : we shall not live here below as long as the first man did, or as those antediluvian fathers, who tarried some eight or nine hundred years. The length of human life then led to greatness of sin. Monstrosities of evil were ripened through the long continuance of physical strength, and the accumulating force of eager passions. All things considered, it is a mercy that life is abridged and not prolonged to a thousand years. Amidst the sharp competition of man with man, and class with class, there is a bound to every scheme of personal aggrandisement, a limit to all the spoils of individual despotism, a restraint upon the hoardings of any one's avarice. It is well, I say, that it should be so. The narrow span of life clips the wings of ambition, and baulks it of its prey. Death comes in to deprive the mighty of his power, to stay the rapacity of the invader, to scatter abroad the possessions of the rich. The most reprobate men must end their career after they have had their three score years and ten, or their four score years of wickedness. And as for the good and godly, though we mourn their exit, especially when we think that they have been prematurely taken from us, we remember how the triumphs of genius have been for the most part achieved in youth, and how much the world has been enriched by the heads and hearts of those who have but sown the seeds of faith and left others to reap the friuts. If into less than the allotted term they have crowded the service of their generation, we may save our tears, for our neglects are needless. The summons will reach each one of us ere long. We cannot stop here as long as the grey fathers of our race : we expect, and it is meet that we should prepare, to go. The world itself is to be consumed one day. "The elements shall melt with fervent heat." The land on which we stand we are wont to call *terra firma*, but beneath it is probably an ocean of fire, and it shall itself feel the force of the ocean. We must not marvel, the house being so frail, that the tenants are unsettled and migratory. Certainly, whether we doubt it or not, we shall have to go. There will be a departure for us. Beloved believer in Christ Jesus, to you the soft term, "Departure," is not more soft than the truth it represents. To die is to depart out of this world unto the Father. What say you about your departure ? What say you of that from which you go, and what think you of that land to which you go ? Well, of the land from which we go, my brethren, we might say many hard things if we would, but I think we had better not. We shall speak more correctly if we say the hard things of ourselves. This land, my brethren, has been a land of mercy to us : there have been sorrows in it ; but in bidding it farewell we will do it justice and seek the truth concerning it. Our sorrows have usually sprung up in our bosoms, and those that have come from the soil itself would have been very light if it had not been for the plague of our hearts, which made us vex, and fret over them. Oh, the mercy you and I have enjoyed even in this life ! It has been worth while to live for us who are believers. Even had we to die like a dog dieth, it has been worth while to live for the joy and blessedness which God has made to pass before us. I dare not call that an evil country in which I have met my Saviour, and received the pardon of my sin. I dare not call that an ill life in which I have seen my Saviour, though it be through a glass darkly. How shall I speak ill of that land where Zion is built, beautiful for situation, the joy of the whole earth, the place of our solemn assemblies, where we have worshpiped God ? No ; cursed of old as the earth was to bring forth the thorn and the thistle, the existence of the church of God in that land seems to a great degree to have made reparation for the blight to such as know and love the Saviour. Oh, have we not gone up to the house of God in company with songs of ecstatic joy, and have we not when we have gathered round the table of the Lord—though nothing was upon it but the type and emblem—have we not felt it a joyous thing to be found in the assembly of the saints, and in the courts of the Lord's house even here ? When we loose our cable, and bid farewell to earth, it shall not be with bitterness in the retrospect. There is sin in it, and we are called to leave it ; there has been trial in it, and we are called to be delivered from it ; there has been sorrow in it, and we are glad that we shall go where we shall sorrow no more. There have been weakness, and pain, and suffering in it, and we are glad that we shall be raised in power ; there has been death in it, and we are glad to bid farewell to shrouds and to knells ; but for that there has been such mercy in it, such lovingkindness of God in it, that the wilderness and the solitary place have been made glad, and the desert has rejoiced and blossomed as a rose. We will not bid farewell to the world, execrating it, or leaving behind us a cold shudder and a sad remembrance, but we will depart, bidding adieu to the scenes that remain, and to the people of God that tarry therein yet a little longer, blessing Him whose goodness and mercy have followed us all the days of our life, and who is now bringing us to dwell in the house of the Lord for ever.

But, dear brethren, if I have had to speak in a somewhat apologetic manner of the land from which we depart, I shall need to use many apologies for my own poor talk about the land to which we are bound. Ah, whither goest thou, spirit loosened from thy clay—dost know ? Whither goest thou ? The answer must be, partly, that we know not. None of us have seen the streets of gold of which we sang just now ; those harpings of the harpers, harping with their harps, have never fallen on these ears ; eye hath not seen it, ear hath not heard it : it is all unrevealed to the senses ; flesh and blood cannot inherit it, and, therefore, flesh and blood cannot imagine it. Yet it is not unknown, for God hath revealed it unto us by His Spirit. Spiritual men know what it is to feel the spirit, their own new-born spirit, living, glowing, burning, triumphing within them. They know, therefore, that if the body should drop off they would not die. They feel there is a life within them superior to blood and bone, and nerve and sinew. They feel the life of God within them, and none can gainsay it. Their own experience has proven to them that there is an inner life. Well, then, when that inner life is strong and vigorous, the spirit often reveals to it what the world of spirits will be. We know what holiness is, do we not, brethren ? Are we not seeking it ? That is heaven—perfect holiness is heaven. We know what peace means ; Christ is our peace. Rest—He gives us rest : we find *that* when we take His yoke. Rest is heaven. And rest in Jesus tells us what heaven is. We know, even to-day, what communion with God is. If any one should say, " I do not know it," I should reply to him thus : Suppose I said to you, " You know not what it is to eat and drink " : the man would tell me that I belied him, for he knew, as he knew his own existence, what it was to eat and drink ; and, as surely as I live, I have communion with God. I know it as certainly as you know that I have declared it to you. Well, friends, that is heaven. It has but to be developed from the germ to the produce, and there is heaven in its full development.

Communion with saints in like manner—know we not what that is ? Have we not rejoiced in each other's joys, been made glad with the experience of our brethren ? That, too, carried to perfection, will be heaven. Oh, to throw yourself into the bosom of the Saviour and lie there taken up with His mind and His love, yielding all things to His supremacy, beholding your king in Him ! When you have been in that state you have had an antepast of heaven. Your view may have been but as one seeing a man's face in shadow, yet you would know that man again even by the shadow ; so know we what heaven is. We shall not be strangers in a strange land when we get there. Though, like the Queen of Sheba, we shall say, " The half has not been told me," yet we shall reflect on it thus : " I did surmise there would be something of this sort. I did know from what I felt of its buddings in my soul below that the full-blown flower would be somewhat of this kind." Whither away, then, spirit that art departing to soar through tracks to thyself unknown ? Thine answer is, " I am away : away to the throne of Him whose cross first gave me life, and light, and hope. I am away to the very bosom of my Saviour, where I hope to rest and to have fellowship with the church of the Firstborn, whose names are written in heaven." This is your departure that you have in near prospect.

Suppose, dear friend, the thought of departing from this world to the glory-world should ever startle you, let me remind you that you are not the first that ever went that way. Your vessel is in the pool, as it were, or in the dock ; she is going out on her voyage ; oh, but you will not go alone, nor have to track your course through paths unnavigated or unknown before ! When the Portuguese captain first went by the Cape of Storms it was a venturous voyage, and he called it the Cape of Good Hope when he had rounded it. When Columbus first went in search of the New World, his was a brave spirit that dared cross the unnavigated Atlantic. But oh, there are tens of thousands that have gone whither you go. The Atlantic that severs us from Canaan is white with the sails of the vessels that are on voyage thither. Fear not, they have not been wrecked ; we hear good news of their arrival ; there is good hope for you. There are no icebergs on the road, no mists, no counter currents, and no sunken vessels or quicksands ; you have but to cut your moorings, and with Christ on board you shall be at your desired haven at once.

Remember, too, your Saviour went that way. Have you to depart ? So Christ departed too. Some of my brethren are always so pleased—pleased as some children are with a new toy—at the idea that they shall never die ; that Christ will come, it may be before the time of their decease ; for, " we shall not all sleep, but we shall all be changed." Well, let Him come, aye, let Him come ; come quickly. But if I had my choice, were it permitted me to choose, I would prefer to pass through the portals of the grave. Those that are alive and remain unto the coming of the Lord will not prevent, go before, or steal a march on them which are asleep. But surely they will lack one point of conformity to their Lord, for He disdained not to sojourn awhile in the tomb, though it was impossible that He should be holden of death. Let the seal of death, then, be set upon this face of mine, that my fate in the matter may be like His. Enoch and Elias were exempt from this privilege—privilege, I call it—of conformity to His death. But it is safe to go by the beaten track, and desirable to travel by the ordinary route to the heavenly city. Jesus died. Through the valley of shadows, the vale of death-shades, there are the footprints of Immanuel all the way along : go down into it and fear not. Bethink you, too, dear brethren and sisters, that we may well look forward to our departure, and look forward to it comfortably too ? Is it not expedient by reason of nature ? Is it not desirable by reason of grace ? Is it not necessary by reason of glory ? I say, is not our departure needful by reason of nature ? Men are not, when they come to hoary age, what they were in the prime of their days. The staff is needed for the foot, and the glass is wanted for the eye ; and after a certain number of years, even those on whom Time hath gently laid his hand, find the taste is gone. They might proclaim, like old Barzillai, that they know not what they eat or drink. The hearing fails, the daughters of music are silent, the whole tenement gets very crazy. Oh, it were a melancholy thing if we had to continue to live ! Perhaps there is no more hideous picture than that which the satirist drew of men who lived on to six or seven hundred years of age—that strange satirical man, Swift. Be thankful that we do not linger on in imbecility. Kind Nature says we may depart ; she gives us notice, and makes it welcome by the decays that come upon us. Besides, grace desires it ; for it were a poor experience of His kindness as our best and truest Friend that did not make us long to see our Saviour's face. It is no mere drivelling sentiment, I hope, when we join to sing—

" Father, I long, I faint to see
    The place of Thine abode ;
I'd leave Thy earthly courts, and flee
    Up to Thy seat, my God ! "

I must confess that there was one verse in the hymn we sung just now which I could not quite chime in with. I am not eagerly wishing to go to heaven this night. I have a great deal more to do here ; therefore I do not want to take a hasty leave of all below. To full many of us, I suppose, there are times of quiet contemplation and times of rapt devotion, when our thoughts surmount these lower skies, and look within the veil ; and then, oh, how we wish to be there ! Yet there are other times ; times of strenuous activity when we buckle on the armour and press to the front ; and then we see such a battle to be waged, such a victory to be won, such a work to be wrought, that we say : " Well ; to abide in the flesh, to continue with you all for the joy and furtherance of your faith, seems more loyal to Christ, more needful for you, and more in accord with our present feelings." I think it is idle for us to be crying to go home ; it is too much like the lazy workman, that wants Saturday night to come when it is only Tuesday morning. Oh, no ; if God spare us to do a long life's work, so much the better. At the same time, as a spark flies upward to the sun, the central source of flame, so does the new-born spirit aspire towards heaven, towards Jesus, by whom it was kindled. And, I add, that glory demands it, and makes our departure needful. Is not Christ in heaven praying that we may be with Him where He is ? Are not the saints in heaven, of whom it is said, they without us cannot be perfect ? The circle of the skies cannot be completed until all the redeemed be there. The grand orchestra of glory misses some notes as yet. What if the bass be full, there are wanting still some trebles and tenors ! There are some sopranos that will be requisite to swell the enshanting melodies, and consummate the worship of the Eternal ! What, therefore, nature prepares for, grace desires, and glory itself demands, we have no just cause to shudder at. Our departure need not make us afraid.

II. Having thus occupied so much time on this point, I have little or no room to enlarge on the second.

THE TIME OF OUR DEPARTURE, though unknown to us, is fixed by God, unalterably fixed ; so rightly, wisely, lovingly settled, and prepared for, that no chance or haphazard can break the spell of destiny. The wisdom of divine love shall be proven by the carefulness of its provision. Perhaps you will say : " It is not easy to discern this ; the natural order of things is so often disturbed by casualties of one kind or another." Let me remind you, then, that it is through faith, only through faith, we can understand these things ; for it is as true now of the providence of God as it was of old of the creation of God that " *things* which are seen were not made of things which do appear." Because the *mode* of your departure is beyond your own ken, it does not follow that the *time* of your departure is not foreseen by God. " Ah ! but," say you, " it seems so shocking for any one to die suddenly, unexpectedly, without warning, and so come to an untimely end ! " I answer you thus. If you take counsel with death your flesh will find no comfort ; but if you trust in God your faith will cease to parley with these feverish anxieties, and your spirit will enjoy a sweet calm. Dire calamities befel Job when he was bereaved of his children and his servants, his herds and his flocks. Yet he took little heed of the different ways in which his troubles were brought about ; whether by an onslaught of the Sabeans or by a raid of the Chaldeans ; whether the fire fell from heaven, or the wind came from the wilderness ; it mattered little. Whatever strange facts broke on his ear, one thought penetrated his heart, and one expression broke from his lips. " The Lord gave, and the Lord hath taken away ; blessed be the name of the Lord." So, too, beloved, when the time of your departure arrives—be it by disease or decay, be it by accident or assault, that your soul quits its present tenement—rest assured that " thy times are in His hand " ; and know of a surety that " all His saints are in His hand " likewise. Besides this, dear friends, since the time of our departure must come, were the manner of it at our own disposal, I think we should most of us say, " What I shall choose, I wot not." Fevers and agues, the pangs and tortures of one malady and another, or the delirium incident to sickness, are not so much to be preferred to the shock of a disaster, or the terror of a wreck at sea, because one is the prolonging of pain, and the other the despatch of fate, that we need to covet, and desire weeks or months spent in the vestibule of the grave. Rather should we say, Let the Lord do with me as seemeth Him good. To live in constant communion with God is a sure relief from all these bitter frettings. Those who have walked with Him have often been favoured with such presentiments of their departure as no physician could give them. Survivors will tell you that though

death seemed to come suddenly to the godly merchant, he had in the last acts of his life appeared to expect and prepare for it, and even to have taken an affecting farewell of his family while in the vigour of health, as though he were aware that he was setting out on his last journey, which a few hours afterwards it proved to be. So, too, the minister of Christ has sometimes fallen, expiring in his pulpit with a *nunc dimittis*, " Now lettest Thou Thy servant depart in peace " on his lips ; secretly, but surely, made ready to depart and to be with his Lord. There is a time to depart ; and God's time to call me is my time to go.

III. Now, to our third point—THE TIME IS AT HAND. " The time of my departure is at hand."

In a certain sense, every Christian here may say this ; for whatever interval may interpose between us and death, how very short it is ! Have you not all a sense that time flows faster than it did ? In our childish days, we thought a year was quite a period of time, a very epoch in our career ; now as for weeks —one can hardly reckon them ? We seem to be travelling by an express train, flying along at such a rate that we can hardly count the months. Why, the past year only seemed to come in at one door and go out at the other ; it was over so soon. We shall soon be at the terminus of life, even if we live for several years ; but in the case of some of us, God knows of whom, this year, perhaps this month, will be our last. I think to-morrow night we shall have to report at the church meeting the deaths of nine members of this church within the last eight or nine days. Since these have gone, some of us may expect to follow them. There are those who will evidently go ; disease has set in upon them. Some of those disorders that in this land seem to be always fatal, tell these dear friends that the time of their departure is undoubtedly at hand. And then old age, which comes so gracefully and graciously to many of our matrons and our veterans, shows, past all dispute, " the time of your departure is at hand." The lease of your life is almost up. Not indeed that I would address myself to such special cases only. I speak to every brother and sister in Christ here. " The time of our departure is at hand." What then, dear friends ?

Is not this a reason for surveying our condition again ? If our vessel is just launching, let us see that she is seaworthy. It would be a sad thing for us to be near departing, and yet to be just as near discovering that we are lost. Remember, dear friends, it is possible for anyone to maintain a decent Christian profession for fifty years, and be a hypocrite after all ; possible to occupy an office in the church of God, and that of the very highest, and yet to be a Judas ; and one may not only serve Christ, but suffer for him too, and yet, like Demas, may not persevere to the end ; for all that looks like grace is not grace. Where true grace is, there it will always be ; but where the semblance of it is, it will ofttimes suddenly disappear. Search thyself, good brother ; set thine house in order, for thou must die and not live. Hast thou the faith of God's elect ? Art thou built on Christ ? Is thy heart renewed ? Art thou verily an heir of heaven ? I charge every man and woman within this place, since the time of his departure may be far nearer than he thinks, to take stock, and reckon up, and see whether he be Christ's or no.

But if the time of my departure be at hand, and I am satisfied that it is all right with me, is there

not a call for me to do all I can for my household ?
Father, the time of your departure is at hand ; is
your wife unsaved ? Will you pass another night
without lovingly speaking to her of her soul ? Are
those dear boys unregenerate ? Is that girl still
thoughtless ? The time of your departure is at
hand. You can do little more for the lads and lasses ;
you can do little more for the wife and the brother.
Oh ! do what you can now. Sister, you are consumptive ; you will soon be gone. You are the only
Christian in the family. God sent you there to be a
missionary. Do not have to say, when you are
dying, " The last hope of my family is going out,
for I have not cared for their souls." Masters, you
that have servants about you, you must soon be
taken away. Will you not do something for their
souls ? I know if there were a mother about to go
to Australia, and she had to leave some of her children
behind, she would fret if she thought, " I have not
done all that needs to be done for those poor children.
Who will care for them now their mother is gone ? "
Well, but to have neglected something necessary for
their temporal comfort would be little in comparison
with not having cared for their souls ! Oh, let it
not be so ! Let it not be a thorn in your dying pillow
that you did not fulfil the relations of life while you
had the opportunity. " The time of my departure
is at hand."

Then there is a third lesson. Let me try to
finish all my work, not only as regards my duty to
my family, but in respect to all the world so far as
my influence or ability can reach. Rich men, be
your own executors. Do what you can with your
substance while it is your own. Men of talent,
speak for Jesus before your tongue has ceased to
articulate, and becomes a piece of clay. George
Whitefield may supply us with a fine model of this
uniform consistency. He was so orderly and precise
in his habits, and so scrupulous and holy in his life,
that he used to say he would not like to go to bed if
there were a pair of gloves out of place in the house,
much less were his will not made, or any part of his
duty unfulfilled to the best of his knowledge. He
wished to have all right, and to be fully prepared for
whatever might happen, so that, if he never woke
again from the slumbers of the night, nobody would
have cause to reflect upon anything he had left
undone, entailing needless trouble on his wife or his
children. Such care bestowed on what some account
to be trifles is a habit worthy of our imitation. The
main work of life may be sadly spoiled by negligence in
little things. This is a striking test of character.
" He that is faithful in that which is least is faithful
also in much : and he that is unjust in the least is
unjust also in much." Oh, then ! time is fleeting,
despatch is urgent ; gather up your thoughts, quicken
your hands, speed your pace, for God commandeth
thee to make haste. If you have ought to do, you
must do it soon. The wheels of eternity are sounding
behind you. Press on ! If you are to run a race
you must run it fast, for Death will soon overtake
you. You may almost feel the hot breath of the
white horse of Death upon your cheeks already.
O God, help us to do something ere we go hence and
be no more seen. It was grand of the apostle that
in the same breath, when he said, " The time of my
departure is at hand," he could also say, " I have
fought a good fight, I have finished my course, I have
kept the faith." So may we be able to say when the
time of our departure has arrived.

If the time of our departure is at hand, let it
cheer us amid our troubles. Sometimes, when our
friends go to Liverpool to sail for Canada, or any
other distant region, on the night before they sail
they get into a very poor lodging. I think I hear
one of them grumbling, " What a hard bed ! What
a small room ! What a bad look-out ! " " Oh,"
says the other, " never mind, brother ; we are not
going to live here ; we are off to-morrow." Bethink
you in like manner, ye children of poverty, this is not
your rest. Put up with it, you are away to-morrow.
Ye sons of sorrow, ye daughters of weakness, ye
children of sickness, let this cheer you :—

> " The road may be rough,
> But it cannot be long,
> And I'll smooth it with hope,
> And cheer it with song."

Oftentimes when I have been travelling on the
Continent I have been obliged to put up at an hotel
that was full, where the room was so inconvenient,
that it scarcely furnished any accommodation at all.
But we have said, " Oh, never mind : we are off in
the morning ! What matters it for one night ? "
So, as we are soon to be gone, and the time of our
departure is at hand, let us not be ruffling our tempers
about trifles, nor raise evil spirits around us by
cavilling and finding fault. Take things as you find
them, for we shall soon be up and away.

And if the time of my departure is at hand, I
should like to be on good terms with all my friends
on earth. Were you going to stop here always,
when a man treated you badly, apart from a Christian
spirit, you might as well have it out with him ; but
as we are going to stop such a little while, we may
well put up with it. It is not desirable to be too
ready at taking an offence. What if my neighbour
has an ugly temper, the Lord has to put up with
him, and so I may. There are some people with
whom I would rather dwell in heaven for ever than
abide with them half an hour on earth. Nevertheless,
for the love of the brethren, and for the peace of the
church, we may tolerate much during the short
time we have to brook with peevish moods and
perverse humours. Does Christ love them, and
shall not we ? He covers their offences ; why, then,
should we disclose them or publish them abroad ?
If any of you have any grievances with one another,
if there is any bickering or jealousy between you,
I should like you to make it up to-night, because the
time of your departure is at hand. Suppose there
is some one you spoke harshly to, you would not
like to hear to-morrow that he was dead. You
would not have minded what you said to him if he
had lived, but now that the seal is set upon all your
communications one with another, you could wish
that the last impress had been more friendly. There
has been a little difference between two brothers—a
little coldness between two sisters. Oh, since
one or other of you will soon be gone, make it up !
Live in love, as Christ loved you and gave himself
for you. If one of you were going to Australia
to-morrow, never to come back again, and you had
had a little tiff with your brother, why I know before
you started you would say," Come, brother, let us
part good friends." So now, since you are so soon
to depart, end all strife, and dwell together in blessed
harmony till the departure actually occurs.

If the time of my departure is at hand, then let
me guard against being elated by any temporal

prosperity. Possessions, estates, creature comforts dwindle into insignificance before this out-look. Yes, you may have procured a comfortable house and a delightful garden, but it is not your rest : your tenure is about to expire. Yes, you may say, " God did prosper me last year, the bank account did swell, the premises were enlarged, and the business thrived beyond all expectation." Ah ! hold them loose. Do not think they are to be your heaven. Be very jealous lest you should get your good things here, for if you do you will not have them hereafter. Be not lifted up too much when you grasp the gain, of which you must so soon quit your hold. As I said of the discomfort of the hotel, we did not think much of it, because we were going away. So, if it happens to be very luxurious, do not be enamoured of it, for you must go to-morrow. " These are the things," said one, when he looked at a rich man's treasures, " that make it hard to die." But it need not be so if you hold them as gifts of God's kindness, and not as gods to be worshipped with self-indulgence, you may take leave of them with composure ; " knowing in yourselves that ye have in heaven a better and an enduring substance."

Lastly, if the time of our departure is at hand, let us be prepared to bear our testimony. We are witnesses for Christ. Let us bear our testimony before we are taken up and mingle with the cloud of witnesses who have finished their course and rested from their labours. Dost thou say, " I hope to do that on my dying bed ? " Brother, do it now : do it now, for you may never have opportunity to do it then. Mr. Whitefield was always desirous that he might bear a testimony for Christ in the hour of death ; but he could not do so at that momentous crisis, for as you well know, he was suddenly taken ill after preaching, and very soon expired. Was this to be grievously deplored ? Ah, no. Why, dear friends, he had borne so many testimonies for his Lord and Master while he was alive, there was no need to add anything in the last few moments before his death, or to supply the deficiences of a life devoted to the proclamation of the gospel. Oh, let you and I bear our testimony now ! Let us tell to others wherever we can what Christ hath done for us. Let us help Christ's cause with all our might while it is called to-day. Let us work for Jesus while we can work for Him. As to thinking we can undo the effect of our idleness by the spasmodic effort of our dying breath, that were a vain hope indeed compared with living for Jesus Christ. Your dying testimony, if you are able to bear it, will have the greater force if it is not a sickly regret, but a healthy confirmation of your whole career.

I only wish these words about departure were applicable to all here. " Precious in the sight of the Lord is the death of His saints." But, " As I live, saith the Lord God, I have no pleasure in the death of the wicked, but that the wicked turn from his ways, and live." O unconverted man, the time for letting loose your cable draws nigh ; it is even at the door. You must shortly set sail for a far country. Alas ! then yours is not the voyage of a passenger, with a sweeter clime, a happier home, a brighter prospect in view. Your departure is the banishment of a convict, with a penal settlement looming in the distance ; fear all rife, and hope all blank, for the term of your banishment is interminable. I fear there are some of you who may depart ere long full of gloom with a fearful looking for of judgment and of fiery indignation. I seem to see the angel of death hovering over my audience. He may, perhaps, select for his victim an unconverted soul. If so, behind that death-angel attends there something far more grim. Hell follows death to souls that love not Christ. Oh, make haste, make haste ! Seek Christ. Lay hold on eternal life ; and may infinite mercy save you, for Jesus Christ's sake. Amen and Amen.

WHAT GOD CANNOT DO!

" God, that cannot lie."—Titus i. 2.

TRUTH once reigned supreme upon our globe, and then earth was Paradise. Man knew no sorrow while he was ignorant of falsehood. The Father of Lies invaded the garden of bliss, and with one foul lie he blighted Eden into a wilderness, and made man a traitor to his God. Cunningly he handled the glittering falsehood and made it dazzle in the woman's eyes—" God doth know that in the day ye eat thereof, then your eyes shall be opened, and ye shall be as gods, knowing good and evil." Proud ambition rode upon that lie as a conqueror in his chariot, and the city of Mansoul opened its gates to welcome the fascinating enemy. As it was a lie which first subjugated the world to Satan's influences, so it is by lies that he secures his throne. Among the heathen his kingdom is quiet and secure, because the minds of the people are deluded with a false mythology. The domains of Mahomet and the Pope are equally the kingdom of Satan, and his reign is undisturbed, for human merit, priestly efficacy, and a thousand other deceptions buttress his throne. The darkness of ignorance, the dungeons of falsehood, and the chains of superstition, are the main reliance of that monster who oppresses all the nations with his infernal tyranny.

Since by the lie Satan now holds the world and maintains his power, he everywhere encourages lies and aids their propagation. Look about you and see what a prolific family falsehood has ! The children of the untrue are as many as the frogs of Egypt, and like those plagues they intrude into every chamber. The slime of falsehood may be seen upon most things, both in secular and religious life. You have lying news and garbled reports in print ; and as for the flying gossip of the tongue, if it touches the characters of good men, beware of believing a word it utters. If you would not have complicity with those who make the lie, be not hasty to entertain it. From the high places of the earth falsehood is not excluded. The untruth glides right royally from the kingly tongue, but is as much a lie as if the ragged mendicant had blurted it forth with low-lived oaths and curses. What is diplomacy for the most part ? Is it not " the art of lying ? " Was not he thought to be the best politician who used language to conceal his thoughts ? In how many a conference have the plenipotentiaries laboured which could overreach, dissimulate, and intrigue to the greatest degree? In the commerce of courts, who knows not that flatteries and lies are the most abundant commodities? The art of king-craft, as practised by the Most High and Mighty Prince James, whose name dishonours our English Bible, was only and simply the science of lying in the neatest possible manner. In these modern times, the difference between the promises at the hustings and the performances in the House of Commons, proves that the lie is still commonly patronized. Falsehood is everywhere; it is entertained both by the lowest and the highest; it permeates all society; it has ruined the whole of our race, and so defiled the entire world, that upright men exclaim, " Woe is me, that I sojourn in Mesech, that I dwell in the tents of Kedar ! " In the so-called religious world, which should be as the holy of holies, here too, the lie has insinuated itself. Of old there were prophets who prophesied lies, and dreamers of false dreams; and there were others who spoke the word of God with such bated breath; and after such a fashion, that it was no longer the truth as it came from God, but truth alloyed with human falsehood. It is so to-day. There are those wearing the vestments of God's priests who do not hesitate to profess what they do not believe. Such men are the priests of hell. To wear a bishop's mitre and teach infidelity—how shall I stigmatize it ?—it is nothing less than detestable hypocrisy and robbery. And what shall I say of men of all creeds, all subscribing to the same articles and catechism, when all the world knows they cannot all honestly believe the same thing, and yet differ as much from one another as light from darkness? What shall I say but that shame covers my face that there should be so many ministers of God who are untrue to their convictions, and continue to do and say what they feel to be unscriptural? In other quarters philosophy is believed and Christianity professed : the traditions of men are put in the place of God's truth. The prophets prophesy lies, and the people love to have it so. Brethren, we have everywhere to battle with falsehood, and if we are to bless the world, we must confront it with sturdy face and zealous spirit. *God's* purpose is to drive the lie out of the world, and be this *your* purpose and mine. His Holy Spirit has undertaken to drive falsehood out of our hearts; be this our determination, in His strength, that it shall be cut up root and branch, and utterly consumed; then let us walk in the truth; " Buy the truth, and sell it not "; hold fast the truth, speak the truth in love, and act the truth in all our deeds, for so shall we be known to be the children of that God of whom our text asserts that He is " God, that cannot lie." After wandering over the sandy desert of deceit, how pleasant is it to reach our text, and feel that one spot at least is verdant with eternal truth. Blessed be Thou, O God, for Thou canst not lie.

We will use our text in the following manner this morning; first, while we do not attempt to prove it, *we will remind you of a few things which may confirm your confidence that God cannot lie,* so that our opening remarks shall be *upon the truth of the text;* then secondly, we will speak upon *the breadth of the text;* endeavouring to show that we must give no narrow interpretation to the words before us, but must receive them with an extent of meaning not usual to the expression; and then, thirdly, *we will try to use the text for our own improvement,* arguing from it that if God cannot lie He ought to receive our loving confidence.

I. First, then, let us commune together awhile concerning THE TRUTH OF THE TEXT, not, as we have said, to prove it, because we all believe it, but to confirm our confidence thereon.

Methinks we shall feel assured that God cannot lie, when we remember that *He is not subject to those infirmities which lead us into falsehood.* Lord Bacon has said, " There are three parts in truth : first, the enquiry, which is the wooing of it; secondly, the knowledge of it, which is the presence of it; and thirdly, the belief, which is the enjoyment of it." In each of these three points, by reason of infirmity, men fail to be perfectly true. In *the search* after truth, our moral eye is not altogether clear, and therefore we fail to see what we love not; we do not follow truth in a straight line, but are very liable to turn aside to the right hand or to the left, either to obey our prejudices or advance our profit. " Truth lies in a well," said the old philosopher; many go down into that well to find truth, but looking into the water they see their own faces, and become so desperately enamoured of their own beauty that they forget poor truth, or dream that she is the counterpart of themselves. Now the great God cannot be liable to this error, because there is no discovery of truth with Him. He needeth not to search anything out, for " all things are naked and opened unto the eyes of Him with whom we have to do." When in Scripture that term is sometimes used—" Shall not God search this out ? " when we hear Him spoken of as " searching the heart and trying the reins of the children of men," it is not because He is not perfectly acquainted with all things, but only to set forth the certainty and accuracy of divine knowledge. God having no need to search, or if He had, having nothing in Him which should lead Him to make a dishonest search, therefore He doth not lie. When we have searched out the truth there is *the knowing of* it; and here the falsehood gets a footing in the form of a sin of omission, for we often refuse to know all that we might know. It would be inconvenient, perhaps, for us to be too well acquainted with certain arguments, for then our prejudices must be given up, and therefore we close our eyes to them for fear of knowing the truth. Do not many men leave passages of Scripture altogether unread because they have no wish to receive the doctrines which are taught therein ? Every time you refuse to give a hearing to God's truth, you do in effect lie; because you prefer not to know the truth, which is really to prefer to hold error. Now nothing of this kind can ever happen with our only wise God. He knows all truth, seeing it all at a glance, and retaining it ever in His mind. In nothing is He ignorant, either wilfully or otherwise. He receives truth as His own beloved, and when the world casts her out, she finds a happy shelter beneath His shield. We are quite clear that we frequently fall into the lie through a defect *in our believing,* for we sometimes know more than we care to believe. Truth is grasped by the understanding, but thrust out by the affections. We know her as Peter knew his Lord, and yet deny it after the same fashion as that disciple did his Master. Moreover, through weakness, we are led to doubt what we know to be God's truth, and even to speak unadvisedly with our lips. Now this can never occur with God, since God is one, and is not to be divided into parts and passions, and His tongue can never be diverse from His heart. God's tongue is His heart, and God's heart is His hand. God is one. You and I are such that we can know in the heart, and yet with the tongue deny; but God is one and indivisible; God is light, and in Him is no darkness at all; with Him is no variableness, neither shadow of turning.

Then, again, *the Scriptural idea of God forbids that He should lie.* Just review your thoughts about God, if you can. What idea have you formed of Him? If you have read Holy Scripture, and have gotten the slightest shadow of an idea of God, I think you will see that it is utterly inconsistent with the thrice Holy One, whose kingdom is over all, that He should lie. Admit the very possibility of His speaking an untruth, and to the Christian there would be no God at all. The depraved mind of the heathen may imagine a monster to be a god who can live in adultery, and in theft, and in lying, for such the gods of the Hindoos are described as being; but the enlightened mind of the Christian can conceive no such thing. The very word "God" comprehendeth everything which is good and great. Admit the lie, and to us at once there would be nothing but the black darkness of atheism for ever. I could neither love, worship, nor obey a lying God.

Again, *we all know that God is too wise to lie.* Falsehood is the expedient of a fool. It is only a short-sighted man who lies. For some present advantage the poor creature who cannot see the end as well as the beginning states that which is not, but no wise man who can look far into the future ever thinks a lie to be profitable; he knows that truth may suffer loss at first, but that in the long run she is always successful. He endorses that worldly-wise proverb, that "Honesty is the best policy" after all; and the man, I say, who has anything like foresight, or judgment, or wisdom, prefers always the straight line to the curve, and goes directly to the mark, believing that this is in the end the best. Do you suppose that God, who must know this, with an intensity of knowledge infinitely greater than ours, will choose the policy of the witless knave. Shall God, only wise, who seeth the end from the beginning, act as only brainless fools will choose to behave themselves? Oh! it cannot be, my brethren. God, the all-wise, must also be all-true.

And the lie, again, *is the method of the little and the mean.* You know that a great man does not lie; a good man can never be false. Put goodness and greatness together, and a lie is altogether incongruous to the character. Now God is too great to need the lie, and too good to wish to do such a thing; both His greatness and His goodness repel the thought.

My dear friends, *what motive could God have for lying?* When a man lies it is that he may gain something, but "the cattle on a thousand hills" are God's, and all the beasts of the forest, and all the flocks of the meadows. He says, "if I were hungry I would not tell thee." Mines of inexhaustible riches are His, and treasures of infinite power and wisdom. He cannot gain aught by untruth, for "the earth is the Lord's, and the fulness thereof"; wherefore, then, should He lie? Men are false ofttimes to win applause. See how the sycophant cringes to the tyrant's foot, and spawns his villanies. But God needs no honour and no fame, especially from the wicked. To Him it were the greatest

disgust of His righteous soul to be loved by unholy creatures. His glory is great enough even if there were no creatures; His own self-contained glory is such that if there were no eye to see it, and no ear to hear it, He would be infinitely glorious; He asketh nothing, no respect and no honour of man, and therefore hath He no need to stoop to the lie to gain it. And of whom, again, could He be afraid? Men will sometimes, under the impulse of fear, keep back or even contradict the truth, but can fear ever enter into the heart of the eternal God? He looketh down upon all nations who are in rebellion against Him, and He doth not even care to rise to put them down. "He that *sitteth* in the heavens shall *laugh:* the Lord shall have them in derision!" Are not the chariots of the Lord twenty thousand, even thousands of angels? Even these are but as a drop of a bucket, when compared with the deep and infinite sea of His own power. Who, then, shall think that Jehovah needs to be afraid? "Fear" and "Jehovah" are two words which cannot meet together. Therefore, since there can be no motive whatever which should possibly lead God to lie, we feel well assured that the declaration of Paul is most certainly true—"God, that cannot lie."

Moreover, dear friends, we may add to all this *the experience of men with regard to God.* It has been evident enough in all ages that God cannot lie. He did not lie when Adam fell. It seemed a strange thing, that after all the skill and labour which had been spent in making such a world as this, so fair and beautiful, God should resign it to the dominion of Satan, and drive the man whom He had made in His own image, out of his home, his Eden, to labour in sweat, and toil and suffering, until he came to his grave. But God did it, and the fiery sword at the gate of Eden was proof that God could not and would not lie. He might come to Adam, and bemoan Himself, crying, "Adam, where art thou?" as if He pitied him, and would, if it had been possible, have spared the stroke; but still it must be done, and Eden is blasted, and Adam becomes a wanderer upon the fruitless earth. Then afterwards, to quote a notable instance of God's faithfulness, when the Flood swept away the race of men, and Noah came forth the heritor of a new covenant, we have clear proof that God cannot lie. No flood has ever destroyed the earth since then. Partial floods there have been, and parts of provinces have been inundated, but no flood has ever come upon the earth of such a character as that which Noah saw; hence the rainbow, every time it is painted upon the cloud, is an assurance to us that God cannot lie. Then He made an oath with Abraham that he should have a son, and that his seed should become possessors of all the land in which the patriarch had sojourned. Did not that come true? They waited in Egypt two hundred years; they smarted under the tyrant's lash; they lay among the pots, and yet, after all, with a high hand and with an outstretched arm He brought forth His people, led them through the wilderness, and divided Canaan by lot to them, having driven out the inhabitants of the land before them. Since that time He made His covenant with David, and how fast has that stood! All the threatenings which He has uttered against the enemies of Israel, how surely have they been fulfilled! Last of all, and best of all, when the fulness of time was come, did not God send forth His own Son, born of a woman, made under the law? Did He not, according to His ancient promise, lay upon Him the iniquity of us all ? Were not the incarnation and death of our Lord Jesus the grandest proof of the truthfulness of God which could be afforded. His own Son must leave heaven emptied of its glory, must be given up to be despised and rejected of men, must be nailed to the accursed wood, and be forsaken in the hour of His bitterest grief : herein is truth indeed. I say, if this *must be* according to the promise, and if this *was* according to the fact, then we have the clearest and the surest evidence that God cannot by any possibility be false to His own word. Rightly hath He earned the title which His nature claims—" God, that cannot lie." May I not add as another argument, that *you have found Him true* ! You have been to Him, dear friends, in many times of trial ; you have taken His promise and laid it before His mercy-seat ; what say you, has He ever broken His promise ? You have been through the floods—did He leave you ? You have passed through the fires—were you burned ? You have cried to Him in trouble—did He fail to deliver you ? O ye poor and needy ones, ye have been brought very low, but has He not been your helper ? You have passed hard by the gates of the grave, and hell has opened its horrid jaws to swallow you up, but are you not to-day the living monuments of the fidelity of God to His promise, and the veracity of every word of the Most High God ? Let these things, then, refresh your memories, that you may the more confidently know that He is " God, that cannot lie."

II. Let us pass on to look at THE BREADTH OF MEANING IN THE TEXT.

When we are told in Scripture that God cannot lie, there is usually associated with the idea the thought of immutability. As for instance—" He is not a man that He should lie, nor the son of man that He should repent." The word " lie," here includes beyond its ordinary meaning the thought of change, so that when we read that God cannot lie, we understand by it, not only that He cannot say what is untrue, but that having said something which is true *He never changes* from it, and does not by any possibility alter His purpose or retract His word. This is very consolatory to the Christian, that whatever God has said in the divine purpose is never changed. The decrees of God were not written upon sand, but upon the eternal brass of His unchangeable nature. We may truly say of the sealed book of the decrees, " Hath He said, and shall He not do it ? hath He purposed and shall it not come to pass ? " We read in Scripture of several instances where God apparently changed, but I think the observation of the old Puritan explains all these ; he says, " God may will a change, but He cannot change His will." Those changes of operation which we sometimes read of in Scripture did not involve any change in the divine purpose. God, for instance, sent to warn Hezekiah that according to the common course of nature he must die, and yet afterwards fifteen years were added to his life, God's purpose having been all along that Hezekiah should live till the end of the fifteen years ; but still his purpose equally included that he should be brought so near to the gates of death, that in the ordinary course of nature he must die ; and then that the miracle should come in as still in part of the purpose, that Hezekiah might be cured in a supernatural manner, and be made to live nearer to his God in consequence. God wills a change, but He never changes His will ; and when the last great day shall

come, you and I shall see how everything happened according to that hidden roll wherein God had written with His own wise finger every thought which man should think, every word which he should utter, and every deed which he should do. Just as it was in the book of decree, so shall it transpire in the roll of human history.

God never changes, then, as to His purpose, and here is our comfort. If He has determined to save us, and we know He has, for all who believe in Him are His elect ; then we shall be saved. Heaven shall never by any possibility be defeated by hell. Hell and earth may combine together to destroy a soul which rests upon Christ, but while God's decree standeth fast and firm, that chosen soul is safe, and since that decree never can be removed, let us take confidence and rejoice. No promise has ever been altered, and no threatening either. Still is His promise sure. " I have not said unto the seed of Jacob, seek ye My face in vain." No new decrees have been passed, repealing the past. We can never say of God's Book, as we can of old law books, that such and such an Act is obsolete. There is no obsolete statute in God's Book. There stand promises, as fresh, as new, as vigorous, and as forceful to-day, as when they first dropped from the mouth of God. The words, then, " God, that can not lie," include the very gracious and precious doctrine that He cannot by any possibility change.

But we must not, while talking in this manner, forget the primary meaning, that He cannot *be false* in His thoughts, words, or actions. There is no shadow of a lie upon anything which God thinks, or speaks, or does. He cannot lie in His *prophecies.* How solemnly true have they been ! Ask the wastes of Nineveh ; turn to the mounds of Babylon ; let the traveller speak concerning Idumea and Petra ; turn even to the rock of Sidon, and to Thy land, O Immanuel. We may boldly ask the traveller, " Hath He said, and hath He not done it ? Have His words fallen to the ground ? Has God's curse been an idle word ? " No, not in one single case. All the words of the Lord are sure. The prophecies will be as true as they have been, and the Book of Revelation, though we may not comprehend it to-day, will doubtless be fulfilled in every stroke and in every line, and we shall marvel how it was that we did not know its meaning, but at present it is enough for us to know its truth—its meaning shall only be learned as the events explain the prophecy.

As God is true in His prophecies, so is He faithful to His *promises.* Have you and I, dear friends, a confidence in these ? If so, let us try them this morning. Sinner, weeping and bemoaning thyself, God will forgive thee thy sin if thou believest in Jesus. If thou wilt confess that He is faithful and just to forgive thee, He hath promised so to do, and He cannot lie. Christian, if you have a promise to-day laid upon your heart, if you have been pleading it, perhaps for months, and it has not been fulfilled, I pray you gather fresh courage this morning, and again renew thy wrestling. Go and say, " Lord, I know Thou canst not lie, therefore fulfil Thy word unto Thy servant." If the promises of God were not kept God would lie, they must therefore be fulfilled ; and let us believe that they will be, and go to God, not with a wavering spirit, which half hopes that the word may be true, but with the full assurance that they cannot fail. As certainly as we know that day and night shall not cease, and that summer will not fail, so surely let us be convinced that every word of the Lord shall stand.

His *threatenings* are true also. Ah! sinner, thou mayest go on in thy ways for many a day, but thy sin shall find thee out at the last. Seventy years God's longsuffering may wait over thee, but when thou shalt come into another world thou shalt find every terrible word of Scripture fulfilled; thou shalt then know that there is a place "where their worm dieth not, and the fire is not quenched"; thou shalt then experience the "wailing and gnashing of teeth" except thou repentest. If thou wilt believe in Jesus thou shalt find the promise true, but if thou wilt not, equally sure shall be the threatening. This is a dreadful part of the subject to those who are out of Christ, who have never been partakers of the Holy Ghost. It will be in vain for you to cry to Him then, and ask Him then to change His mind. No, though you should weep oceans of tears, hell's flames cannot be quenched, nor can your soul escape from the place to which it is finally doomed. To-day, while mercy is preached to you, lay hold upon it, but remember, if not, as God cannot lie He cannot suffer you to escape, but you must feel the weight and terror of His arm.

We might thus go through everything which concerns God, from prophecy to promises, and threatenings, and onwards, and multiply observations, but we choose to close this point by observing that *every word of instruction from God is most certainly true.* It is astounding how much sensation is caused in the Christian Church by the outbreak every now and then of fresh phases of infidelity. I do not think that these alarms are at all warranted. It is what we must expect to the very end of this dispensation. If all carnal minds believed the Bible, I think the spiritual might almost begin to doubt it; but as there are always some who will attack it, I shall feel none the less confidence in it. Really, the Book of God has stood so many attacks from such different quarters, that to be at all alarmed about it shows a very childish fear. When a rock has been standing all our lifetime, and has been known to stand firmly throughout all the ages of history, none but foolish people will think that the next wave will sweep it away. Within out own short life—say some five-and-twenty years' recollection—have we not remembered, I was about to say almost as many as five-and-twenty shapes of infidelity? You know it must change about every twenty years at least, for no system of infidelity can live longer than that. There was the witty system of objection which Voltaire introduced; and how short-lived was that! Then came the bullying, low-lived, blackguard system of Tom Paine; and how short-lived was its race! Then, in more modern times, unbelief took the shape of Secularism: what particular shapes it takes now we scarcely know—perhaps Colensoism is the most fashionable; but that is dying out, and something else will follow it. These creations of an hour just live their little day, and they are gone. But look at belief in Scripture, and at Scripture itself. The Bible is better understood, more prized, and I believe, on the whole, more practised than ever it was since the day when its Author sent it abroad into the world. Its course is still onward; and after all which has been done against it, no visible effect has been produced upon the granite-wall of Scriptural truth by all the pickaxes and boring rods which have been broken upon it. Walking through our museums now-a-days, we smile at those who think that Scripture is not true. Every block of stone from Nineveh, every relic which has been brought from the Holy Land, speaks with a tongue which must be heard even by the deaf adder of Secularism, and which says, "Yes, the Bible is true, and the word of God is no fiction." Beloved, we may rest assured that we have not a word in the Book of God which is untrue. There may be an interpolation or two of man's which ought to be revised and taken away, but the Book as it comes from God is truth, and nothing but truth; not only containing God's word, but being God's word; being not like a lump of gold inside a mass of quartz, but all gold, and nothing but gold; and being inspired to the highest degree, I will not say verbally inspired, but more than that, having a fulness more than that which the letter can convey, having in it a profundity of meaning such as words never had when used by any other being, God having the power to speak a multitude of truths at once. And when He means to teach us one thing according to our capability of receiving it, He often teaches us twenty other things, which for the time we do not comprehend, but which by-and-by, as our senses are exercised, reveal themselves by the Holy Spirit. Every time I open my Bible I will read it as the word of "God, that cannot lie"; and when I get a promise or a threatening, I will either rejoice or tremble because I know that these stand fast.

Dear friends, this leads us, in closing this point, to say that when we read that passage—"God, that cannot lie"—we understand that *His very nature cannot lie*, for He hates lies; wherever there is a lie God is its enemy. It was to overcome the lie of sin that God sent His Son to bleed; and every day the thoughts of God are centred upon the extermination of evil and the extension of His own truth. Nothing can set forth in words to us the hatred and detestation which God has in His heart of anything which is untrue. O that we knew and felt this, and would glow with the same anger, seeking to exterminate the false, slaying it in our own hearts, and giving it nothing to feed upon in our temper, our conversation, or our deeds.

III. But I shall now come to make a practical use of the text, in the third place, by observing HOW WE OUGHT TO ACT TOWARDS GOD IF IT BE TRUE THAT HE IS A "GOD, THAT CANNOT LIE."

Brethren, if it be so that God cannot lie, then *it must be the natural duty of all His creatures to believe Him.* I cannot resist that conclusion. It seems to me to be as clear as noonday, that it is every man's duty to believe truth, and that if God must speak and act truth, and truth only, it is the duty of all intelligent creatures to believe Him. Here is "Duty-faith" again, which some are railing at, but how they can get away from it, and yet believe that God cannot lie, I cannot understand. If it be not my duty to believe in God, then it is no sin for me to call God a liar. Will anyone subscribe to that—that God is a liar? I think not; and if to think God to be a liar would be a most atrocious piece of blasphemy, then it can only be so on the ground that it is the natural and incumbent duty of every creature understanding the truthfulness of God to believe in God. If God has set forth the Lord Jesus Christ as the propitiation for sin, and has told me to trust Christ, it is my duty to trust Christ, because God cannot lie; and though my sinful heart will never believe in Christ as a matter of duty but only through the work of the Holy Spirit, yet faith does not cease to be a duty ; and whenever I am unbelieving and have doubts concerning God, however moral my outward life may be, I am living in daily sin ; I am perpetrating a sin against the first principles of morality. If I doubt God, as far as I am able I rob Him of His honour, and stab Him in the vital point of His glory ; I am, in fact, living an open traitor and a sworn rebel against God, upon whom I heap the daily insult of daring to doubt Him. O my hearers, there are some of you who do not believe in Christ ; I wish you would look at your character and position in this light. You are not trusting in Christ for your salvation. Remember, " He that believeth not God hath made Him a liar " ; those are John's own inspired words, and you are, every day that you are not a believer in Christ, virtually writing upon your doorpost, and saying with your mouth, " God is a liar ; Christ is not able to save me ; I will not trust Him ; I do not believe God's promise ; I do not think He is sincere in His invitation to me to come to Christ ; I do not believe what God says." Remember that you are living in such a state as this, and may God the Holy Ghost impress you with a sense of the sin of that state, and feeling this your sin and misery, I pray God to lead you to cry, " Lord, I believe, help Thou my unbelief." This then, is our first practical conclusion from the fact that God cannot lie.

Other thoughts suggest themselves. *If we were absolutely sure that there lived on earth a person who could not lie, how would you treat him ?* You know there cannot be such a man ; there may be a man who *will not* lie, but there cannot be a man of whom it may be said that he *cannot* lie ; for alas ! we have all the power of evil in us, and we can lie, and to a certain degree it is quite true that " all men are liars." But if you could be certain that there was a man, out of whose heart the black drop had been wrung, and that he could not lie, how would you act towards him ? Well, I think *you would cultivate his acquaintance.* If you be true yourselves, you would desire his friendship ; you would say, " He is the friend for me ; I have trusted in such-and-such a man, and he has played the Judas ; I asked counsel of another, and he was an Ahithophel ; but if this man cannot lie, he shall be my bosom companion, if he will accept me ; and he shall be my counsellor, if he will but have the goodness to direct me." I should expect to see a *levee* of all the good in the world waiting at the man's door. You know how the world, with all its sinfulness, does reverence the man who is true. We had an instance in our streets the other day, of the good man, and the true, who received homage of all, and yet that man *could* lie ; but inasmuch as we never have seen *that he did*, but his life has been straightforward, therefore have we paid him honour, and deservedly so. Well now, if such be the case, should not all Christians seek more and more the friendship of God ? " O Lord, be Thou my familiar Friend, my Counsellor, my Guide ; if Thou canst not lie I will lay bare my heart to Thee ; I will tell Thee all my secrets ; I will trust Thee with all the desires of my heart ; I know Thou canst never betray me, or be unfaithful ; let there be a union established betwixt my soul and Thine, and let it be broken never." Let communion with God be the desire of your hearts on the ground that He cannot lie.

If we knew a man who could not lie, *we should believe him, methinks, without an oath.* I cannot suppose that when *he* came into the court of justice they would pass *him* the Bible ; no, his word would be better than the oath of ordinary men if he could not lie. You would not want any sign or evidence to prove what he said ; you would take his word at once. So should it be with God. Ah ! dear friends, God has given us more than His word, He has given us His oath : and yet, strange is it, that we who profess to be His children are vile enough to distrust our own Father ; and sometimes, if He does not give us signs and evidences, we begin to distrust Him, so that after all I am afraid we rather trust the signs than trust God, and put more confidence in frames and evidences than we do in the naked promise, which is an atrocious sin indeed. Many believers cannot be comfortable without signs and evidences. When they feel in a good frame of mind—ah ! then God's promise is true ; when they can pray heartily, when they can feel the love of God shed abroad in their hearts, then they say, " How God has kept His promise." Ah ! but, my brother, that is a seeing-faith : " Blessed are they that have not seen, and yet have believed." Faith is to believe in God when my heart is as hard as the nether millstone, when my frames are bad, when I cannot pray, when I cannot sing, when I can do nothing good. To say, " He has promised and will perform ; He has said that whosoever believeth in Christ is not condemned ; I do believe in Christ, and therefore I am not condemned "—this is genuine faith.

Again, if we knew a man who could not lie, *we should believe him in the teeth of fifty witnesses the other way.* Why, we should say, " they may say what they will, but they *can* lie." You might have good evidence that they were honest men usually, but you would say, " They *can* lie, they have the power of lying ; but here is a man who stands alone, and cannot lie ; then his word must be true." This shows us, beloved, that we ought to believe God in the teeth of every contradiction. Even if outward providence should come to you, and say that God has forsaken you, that is only one ; and even if another, and another, and another should come, and fifty trials should all say that God has forsaken you, yet, as God says, " I will never leave thee, nor forsake thee," which will you take—the one promise of God who cannot lie, or the fifty outward providences which you cannot interpret ? I know what the devil has been whispering in your ear—

" The Lord hath forsaken thee quite,
Thy God will be gracious no more."

But then, recollect who hath said, " Fear thou not ; for I am with thee : be not dismayed ; for I am thy God." Which will you believe—the devil's insinuation, or God's own testimony ? My dear sister, you have been praying for a certain thing for years ; you pray, you pray, and you pray again, and now discouragement arises ; unbelief says, " God will not hear that prayer ; that prayer of yours does not come up before the throne of God, and there will be no answer." But the Lord has said, " Ask, and it shall be given you ; seek, and ye shall find ; knock, and it shall be opened unto you." Which will you believe—your unbelief, the long months of weariness, and the anxieties which prompted you to discouragement, or will you believe in the naked promise ? Why, if God cannot lie, let us give Him what we would give to a man if he were of the same character—our full confidence even in the teeth of contradiction—for He is " God, that cannot lie."

If a man were introduced to us, and we were certain that he could not lie, *we should believe everything he said, however incredible it might appear to us at first sight to be.* I shall have an appeal to every soul here present. It does seem very incredible at first sight that God should take a sinner, full of sin, and forgive all his iniquities in one moment, simply and only upon the ground of the sinner believing in Christ. I recollect the time when it seemed to me utterly impossible that I could ever have my sins forgiven. I had a clear sense of the value of pardon, and this thought would be always ringing in my ears—" It is too good to be true that *you* should be pardoned ; that *you*, an enemy, should be made into a child ; that *you* who have gone on sinning against light and against knowledge, should yet rejoice in union to Christ ; the thing is too good to be true." But, beloved friends, supposing it should seem too good to be true, yet since you have it upon the testimony of one who " cannot lie," I pray you believe it. " *But, sir,*"—No, none of your " buts," He cannot lie. " *Ah ! but* "—Away with your " ahs " or your " buts," for Jehovah cannot lie. He has said it, " He that believeth and is baptized shall be saved." To believe is to trust Christ. If therefore you are trusting Christ, you must be saved ; and whatever you may be, or whatever you may have done, if you will now trust Jesus Christ you have God's word for it, and He cannot lie, that you shall be saved. Come, now, will you kick against the promise because of its greatness ? Do not so, but let your doubts and fears be hushed to sleep, and now, with the promise of God as your pillow, and God's faithfulness as your support, lie down in peace, and behold in faith's open vision the ladder, the top whereof leads to heaven. Trust the promise of God in Christ, and depend upon it that He will be as good to you, even to you, as His own word, and in heaven you shall have to sing of the " God, that cannot lie."

I would that these weak words of mine, for I am very conscious of their feebleness this morning, may nevertheless have comfort in them for any who have been doubting and fearing, that they may trust my Lord ; and sure I am that if they begin a life of faith they will being a life of happiness and of security. " The just shall live by faith," and well may they do so, when they have to trust in a " God, that cannot lie."

FIVE LINKS IN A GOLDEN CHAIN

" To Titus, mine own [or, " true "] son after the common faith : Grace, mercy, and peace, from God the Father and the Lord Jesus Christ our Saviour."—Titus i. 4.

AMONG the friends of Paul, Titus was one of the most useful and one of the best beloved. Paul was the apostle to the Gentiles, and Titus was a Gentile. I should suppose that both his parents were Gentiles, and in this respect he differed from Timothy, whose mother was a Jewess. Timothy would well serve as a preacher to the circumcision, but Titus would be a man after Paul's heart as a preacher to the Gentiles. He seems to have been a man of great common sense ; so that, when Paul had anything difficult to be done, he sent Titus. When the collection was to be made at Corinth on behalf of the poor saints at Jerusalem, Paul sent Titus to stir the members up, and with him another brother to take charge of the contributions. Titus appears to have been a man of business capacity and strict probity, as well as a man who could order the church aright, and preach the gospel with power. Paul was, on one occasion, comforted by the coming of Titus. At another time, he was sad because Titus was not where he had hoped to meet with him. Though we know little about him from the Acts of the Apostles, or anywhere else, he appears to have been in every way one of the ablest of the companions of Paul, and the apostle takes care to mention him over and over again in his Epistles to the Galatians and to the Corinthians, rendering honour to whom honour is due. It is a great pity when eminent men forget those who help them, and it is a sad sign when any of us do not gratefully feel how much we owe to our coadjutors. What can any servant of God do unless he has kind friends to bear him up by their prayers and their help ? Paul did not forget to mention his friend and helper, Titus.

Dear Brethren, in this particular verse, which I have chosen for my text, it seems to me that Paul has brought together five points in which he was one with Titus. It is a great blessing when Christian men are in union with each other, and when they are willing to talk about the bonds that unite them. The more we can promote true unity among Christian men, the better. " First pure, then peaceable," must be our motto ; first, the truth ; afterwards, unity in the truth. We must not be content with merely contending for the faith ; we must next fight the battles of life, and do all we can to note the points in which true Christians are agreed. I desire, at this time, to " stir up your pure minds by way of remembrance," to refresh your memories in regard to all the love that we have borne to one another in days and years that are now past, and to exhort you to a still closer union in heart unto the glory of God.

There are five things in which Paul seems to me to bring out clearly his union with Titus ; I might call them, " five links in a golden chain." I shall only briefly speak of each of the five, and try to apply them to ourselves.

I. First, Paul says of himself and Titus, that THERE WAS A CLOSE RELATIONSHIP BETWEEN THEM : " Titus, mine own son."

This was a very close relationship ;—not that Titus was Paul's son after the flesh, for there was no natural relationship between them at all. Probably, in the early part of their lives, they had been total strangers to one another ; but now, *Paul views Titus as his son.* We know, beloved, many of us, that the grace of God creates relationships of a very near and tender kind, relationships which will endure through life, relationships which will outlast death, and be, perhaps, even more strong and vivid in eternity than they are here. Up yonder, where they neither marry nor are given in marriage, I should think that the relationships which come of the flesh will, to a large degree, be merged in their celestial condition ; but there, the sonship of Titus towards Paul is even stronger than it was when they twain were here below.

How comes that sonship ? It comes often through God blessing a ministry to the conversion of a soul. Henceforth, he who has spoken the word with power to the heart bears to him who has heard it the relationship of a father to a son. There are many in this place to whom I stand in this most hallowed relationship. You recognize it, I know, and I desire to express my intense and fervent love to the many of you who have been born unto God by the preaching of the word here. I do not know of anything that has more greatly comforted me during the last week or two, in the time of sharp contention for the faith, than the reception of so many letters, from persons of whom I have never before heard, saying, " You do not know me, but you are my spiritual father ; and now, at such a time of trial as this is to you, I must write and send you a word of good cheer." It is always a marvel to me that my feeble testimony should ever be blessed to the conversion of a seeking soul ; but when I think of the hundreds, and the thousands,—ay, I am not exaggerating when I say thousands,—whom I have met with here on earth, and the many more, at present unknown to me, whom I hope to meet with either here or in heaven, I do rejoice, yea, and I will rejoice ; and I cannot help expressing my great love to all those who have been brought to the Saviour by the word which I have preached and published.

The apostle Paul not only said of Titus that he was his son, but *he called him his " true " son.* The Revised version correctly translates it, " My true child." We have, alas! some who have called us "father" in a spiritual sense, of whom we have cause to be ashamed. There are converts *and* converts. There are those who say they have received the word, and perhaps they have after the poor fashion in which the brain can receive it, but they have never received it in the heart ; so, after running well for a while, they grow weary, and turn aside, and then the gainsayer says, " That is one of your converts! " They throw this in our teeth, and we do not wonder that they should do so. These base-born ones, these who have no part nor lot in the matter, though they pretend to have it, these are a perpetual grief to us, a wound in our spirit, which is hard to bear. But, oh, what a mercy it is when we know that many of our converts are our " true " spiritual children, in whom the work of repentance was deep, and whose profession of faith was sincere, who are not the products of free will, but the products of the Holy Spirit, and who bring forth fruit, not of themselves, but their fruit is found in Christ Jesus to whom they are eternally joined! Oh! those of you, between whom and myself there is this intimate relationship, let us feel some touch of this sacred kinship, and rejoice before God that we do feel it.

But, beloved, many of you are joined together by spiritual ties in other relationships ; you also have been the means of bringing souls to Christ, and there are those sitting by your side who, for that reason, look upon you with great love. Others of you are brethren in Christ ; there is a brotherhood, produced by the Christian life, that will remain when other brotherhoods have all disappeared. An ungodly man may be the literal brother of a saint ; but they will be separated in that day when there shall be weeping at the judgment seat of Christ, and they shall be eternally separated, for, though they seemed to be of one family, they were really of two families, the one an heir of wrath, the other receiving grace to become a child of God. But beloved, as many of you as believe in Jesus Christ, are members of one family ; you are related to one another in the highest possible way through the kinship of the spiritual life. Wherefore, let us now salute each other in the Lord ; standing or sitting in our places, and without using any outward sign or symbol, let our hearts go out to one another in loving greeting. One family we dwell in Christ, knit to one another by ties of sympathy, and love, and mutual delight, because knit to Christ Jesus the Lord. I want you to feel that blessed union. Let us make this service a sort of family gathering, as when the father stands up at the head of the table, at Christmas time, or on New Year's day, and says that he is glad to see all the family at home once more. I seem to stand among you thus, not as the oldest in years, but still the chief official member of this church, and I salute you all, and bid you rejoice together because of ties of love which time cannot loose, and death itself cannot dissolve.

II. Then the apostle, wishing to show how real was the union between himself and Titus, next mentioned that THEY WERE BRETHREN BY A COMMON FAITH : " Titus, my true son after the common faith."

Yes, beloved, and our faith is also common. It is the same faith in two respects ; first, because *we believe the same truths ;* and, secondly, because we believe them with " like precious faith." We who are rightly members of this Tabernacle Church have believed the same truths ; there is no dispute or discussion among us about the fundamentals of our faith. To us, there is one God,—Father, Son, and Holy Ghost. To us, there is one Mediator,—Jesus Christ the Saviour. We believe in the election of grace by the Divine Father ; we believe in the vicarious sacrifice of the Eternal Son ; we believe in the regenerating work of the Holy Spirit, and in the need of it in the case of every living man, and woman, and child. We believe in " one Lord, one faith, one baptism." I feel intensely grateful for this unity of faith. A church divided in its doctrine,—what can it do ? If it has to spend its strength in continual debate, what force has it with which to conquer the world ? But knowing, as we do know, that the Scriptures are our unerring guide, that the Holy Spirit is the infallible Explainer of the Scriptures, we come to one common fount to learn what we are to receive and we receive it with one common anointing, even the anointing of the Spirit of God.

This unity of faith is one of the things in which we ought continually to rejoice. I hope that I love all Christians ; yet I cannot help saying that, when I sit down and talk with a brother who believes the doctrines of grace, I feel myself a great deal more at home than I do when I am with one who does not believe them. Where there is the unity of the faith, there seems to be a music which creates harmony, and that harmony is delightful to the renewed spirit. God grant, dear friends, that none of us may err from the faith ; but that we may be steadfast, immovable, firmly fixed in our belief of the great doctrines of the gospel, for this is the way in which we are made truly one.

Then, Paul says that he and Titus were one

" after the common faith "; that is, *the one faith was believed by them in the same way.* There is only one faith worth having ; Paul calls it, in the first verse, " the faith of God's elect." It is real faith cordial faith, childlike faith, God-given faith. It is not a faith that springs out of human nature unaided by the Holy Ghost ; but it is precious faith, faith which is the gift of God, and the work of the Holy Spirit. Now, if we believe only intellectually, we do not enter into sympathy with one another as we do when we both believe spiritually, with heart and soul, from the very depths of our being. Beloved, I trust that I can say of myself, and of you also, that we have received faith as a gift from God ; here, then, is another sacred tie binding us together. You have that jewel of faith gleaming on your bosom, and here are others who have the same precious gem, so by that very fact you are drawn to each other. Your faith and my faith, if they are both true faith, are " the common faith." I may have very little faith, and you may have the full assurance of understanding ; but your faith and mine are of the same sort. Your faith may be but as a grain of mustard seed, and your friend's faith may have grown into a tree ; but it is the same faith : it clings to the same Christ, and will produce the same eternal results in the salvation of the soul. Come, then, let us spiritually shake hands again over this second point. First, we are closely related to one another ; secondly, we possess a common faith which is a wonderful bond of union between us.

III. Carefully note the third link. It is this : WE HAVE A MUTUAL BENEDICTION, for Paul wishes for Titus, " Grace, mercy, and peace."

This is just what Titus would have wished for Paul if he had been sending him a benediction ; and I wish to you, beloved, " Grace, mercy, and peace " ; and I think you are in your hearts wishing for me also, " Grace, mercy, and peace." We all alike need these three choice favours.

First, we need *" grace " to help.* I know how it is with the weak believer ; he sees some brave Christian doing mighty works for God, and he says, " Oh, I wish that I were like him ! Oh, that I were as strong as he is ! " and he gets the notion that this more prominent worker has no fainting fits or weaknesses such as he has. Oh, no ! he supposes that his brother's head is bathed in everlasting sunshine, and that his heart is continually flooded with rivers of delight. That shows, my friend, that you are greatly mistaken, for the most eminent saint has no more grace to give away than the least in the family of God has. I sometimes wish that I could disabuse the minds of our dear trembling friends, Miss Muchafraid and Mr. Despondency, of the ideas they have concerning some of us to whom they look up with esteem. I am not going to let you into all our secrets ; but, believe me, our heads ache as much as yours and our eyes are sometimes as wet with tears as ever yours are, aye, and our hearts get quite as heavy as yours do. " Yes," you say, " very likely, but then, somehow or other, you are stronger than we are." Just so, but suppose you have to carry fifty pounds weight, and you can carry that, and no more ; well, you have strength enough for your task. If another man has to carry a hundred pounds weight, and he can just carry that, and no more, he is in exactly the same condition as you are. Here is a brother who has a large measure full of manna, which he is carrying for the supply of his family. Here is another, who

has quite a small measure and as he carries it into his tent, he says to himself, " Oh ! I wish that I had that great bushel of manna that my brother took into his tent just now." Yes, but listen : " he that gathered much had nothing over, and he that gathered little had no lack." Mark you, I do not discourage the attempt to gather much grace, I would urge you to get all you can of it ; for, however much you gather, you will have none too much ; but I would discourage your despair if there should seem to be but little falling to your share, for you shall have no lack. The fact is, all of us need grace. You who preach the gospel, you who are deacons, you who are elders, you who teach the infant class, you who can only give away a tract, you must do all these works with grace, or else you will not really do them at all ; and our need of grace is a common meeting place for us all. Only grace can save you, and only grace can save me ; and the grace of God shall be given to us and all believers as we have need of it.

Our next want is, *" mercy " to forgive.* Titus perhaps thought to himself, " Well, Paul wishes mercy for me, but can hardly wish it for himself, for he is such an eminent servant of God, so holy, so consecrated, so zealous, so self-denying, that he does not need mercy. I reminded you, in our reading, that Paul, in writing to a church says, " Grace be to you, and peace " ; but when he writes to a minister, he says, " Grace, *mercy,* and peace." It looks as though ministers needed more mercy than their people do ; and it is my firm conviction that the more eminent is their office, and the more remarkable is their usefulness in the service of God, the more mercy do they require. Brethren, how can we meet our responsibilities unless we constantly cry, " Lord, have mercy upon us " ? How can we deal faithfully with the souls committed to our charge, and be clear of the blood of all men, unless the Lord shall have mercy upon us, and upon us beyond all others ?

All of us, then, need mercy. I do ; do not you ? You are only a plain man, with a family growing up around you ; but you need mercy for your sins as the head of the household. Perhaps you are only a domestic servant, my sister ; but you need mercy even in that humble calling of yours. You, perhaps, dear friend, are very rich, oh, you need much mercy ! And you, on the other hand, are very poor ; I am sure that you need mercy. Some of you are in full health ; you need mercy lest you should pervert that strength to an evil purpose. Others of you are very sickly ; you may well cry for mercy, that you may bear up under your many pains and depressions of spirit. We all need mercy ; so that is another point in which we are one.

The third word of the benediction is *" peace " to comfort.* I hope that many of us know what peace of conscience means, what peace with God means, and what peace with man means. If God has given us His peace, it is a treasure of untold value, " the pearl of great price." To be at peace with God is better than to be a millionaire, or Czar of all the Russias. Peace of mind, restfulness of heart, quiet of spirit, deliverance from care, from quarrelling, from complaining.—I know that I want that kind of peace, and you want it too, do you not ? You need it in your family, in your business, in your own hearts. Well, then, here we meet again, having this same want of peace ; and, when we get it, we meet once more in finding the same delicious enjoyment of it. I wish to you, beloved, now and henceforth, grace, mercy, and peace ; and I believe that you wish the same to me ; and herein again we join our hands, and bless God that we feel true union of heart.

IV. Upon the next part of my subject, which is more weighty still, I must say but little. It is this : "Grace, mercy, and peace, from God the Father and the Lord Jesus Christ." That is, WE ARE ONE IN THE SOURCE OF EVERY BLESSING.

All good comes to us from God the Father, through the one Mediator, the Lord Jesus Christ our Saviour. I love to think of this,—that all the grace, mercy, and peace that come to you, and all the grace, mercy, and peace that come to me, come from the heart of God. How many waggons there are upon the road of grace, and all of them heavily laden ! One stops at that brother's door, and another waits at this sister's gate ; but they all started from one spot. Look on the side of the waggons, and you will see the name of the same Proprietor on every one. "The chariots of God are twenty thousand," but they are all the Lord's ; so that whatever grace, mercy, and peace come to us at all, come from the same place. Get to the very foundation of this truth, and you will see that we who believe all eat bread baked in the same oven, our clothes come out of the same wardrobe, the water that we drink comes from the same rock, aye, and the shoes that we wear were made by the same mighty Worker who bade Moses say to Israel of old, " Thy shoes shall be iron and brass ; and as thy days, so shall thy strength be." You have not anything that is worth having but what your Father gave to you ; and your Father is my Father, and the hand that passeth the blessing to you passeth the blessing to me and to the whole family of believers.

These blessings not only all come from the same source, but *they all come by the same channel :* " the Lord Jesus Christ." There is the sacred blood-mark on every covenant blessing, whether you have it, or your brother has it, or some Christian far away in India gets it. It all comes by the same divinely-appointed channel,—the man, the God, Christ Jesus our Lord. I do not know how you feel about this matter, but it seems to me as if this ought to bind us very closely together. I recollect when first I left my grandfather, with whom I had been brought up as a little child, how grieved I was to part from him ; it was the great sorrow of my little life. Grandfather seemed very sorry, too, and we had a cry together ; he did not quite know what to say to me, but he said, " Now, child, to-night, when the moon shines, and you look at it, don't forget that it is the same moon your grandfather will be looking at " ; and for years, as a child, I used to love the moon because I thought that my grandfather's eyes and my own somehow met there on the moon. How much better it is to think that you, dear friend, going right away to Australia, are looking to the Saviour, while we are doing the same thing here, and so our eyes meet ! You go to God at the mercy-seat in prayer, and that is just where we go ; so, after all, we pray at the same sacred spot, and our petitions meet at the great throne of mercy. Thus we are made to feel our blessed union in Christ.

Some people say that they try to recollect other people ; but if you really love them, you will not " try " to recollect them, you will not be able to keep from remembering them. Their image will come up before your mind's eye ; you cannot avoid it, and you will not wish to avoid it. So, dear friends, we will nor say that we will try to remember each other while we are parted a while ; but every blessing that comes to us shall remind us that it comes from our Father, through Jesus Christ our Mediator, and so we shall feel that we are truly one.

V. Then, to close, there is one more point of union, and that lies in OUR COMMON RELATIONSHIP TO OUR LORD JESUS CHRIST. See how Paul put it, " The Lord Jesus Christ our Saviour."

I must dwell briefly upon every word of this title. First, Jesus is *Lord* to all His people. and equally *to be obeyed by them all, and adored by them all.* It is important that, with bowed knee, and reverent love, we call Him Lord and God. We put our finger into the print of the nails, and the wound in His side, confessing that He is and must be real man ; but, at the same moment, we cry with Thomas, " My Lord and my God." I cannot pretend to have any union with the man who cannot from his heart say that. If thou dost not count Christ to be God, well, go thy way, my fellow-man, and I will go mine ; but thy way and my way cannot be the same. We know that this is the Christ of God. and he who does not know it needs to be taught of God the very first principles of the gospel. So, you see, we have a true unity in the lordship of Christ ; we desire, as one man, to be obedient to all His commands, and to worship Him as " very God of very God."

Then comes the next word, " the Lord *Jesus* Christ." That will come over again when I speak of the word " Saviour," so I pass on to the following word, " the Lord Jesus *Christ.*" He is, to all of us who believe, the Anointed One, so anointed that every Word that Jesus Christ has spoken is to us infallibly inspired. We believe in Jesus, not only as men say they do to-day ; but we believe really in Jesus, for we believe in His doctrine, in that which He Himself spoke, and in that which He spoke by His inspired apostles. We cannot separate between Christ and the truth He came to preach, and the work he came to do ; nor will we attempt to do so. He is to us the Anointed of God, as Prophet, Priest, and King, and we accept Him in all the offices for which He bears that anointing ; do we not, my brethren ? I know that we do ; as brethren in one common faith, we rejoice in the common Christ whose anointing has fallen upon us, too. Though we are but as the skirts of the garment of our Great High Priest, yet the holy oil upon His head has come down even to us, as it is written, " ye have an unction from the Holy One."

The apostle further writes, " The Lord Jesus Christ *our Saviour.*" Sometimes, in the Bible, we find the Lord Jesus Christ called " *a* Saviour." " Unto you is born in the city of David a Saviour, which is Christ the Lord." That is good, but it is not good enough for what poor sinners need. Our Lord Jesus Christ is not *a* Saviour among other saviours, though He does instrumentally make His people saviours, as it is written, " saviours shall come up on Mount Zion ; " and happy are they who, as instruments in His hands, save souls from death, and hide multitudes of sins. But Jesus is also called " *the* Saviour." He is " the Saviour of all men, specially of those that believe,"—the Saviour, *par excellence.* Then next, He is *my* Saviour, as Mary sang, " My spirit hath rejoiced in God my Saviour." Oh, that is sweet indeed,—to get a personal grip of Him, and to know that He has saved *me* from despair, from sin, from the power of evil, from death, from hell. But there is, in some respects, a superior sweetness in this plural pronoun, "*our* Saviour." Selfishness is gone when we come to feel an intense delight in this truth, that the Lord Jesus Christ is the Saviour of many more beside ourselves. "Our Saviour "—does not this bind us to one another ? A common delight in one person is one of the strongest bands of sympathetic union that can bind men together ; and a common obligation to some one superior being becomes a great reason for our being knit together in love. My Saviour, your Saviour, our Saviour : "The Lord Jesus Christ *our* Saviour." Whenever we feel any disposition to break off from this brother and from that, whom we know to be, after all, saved in the Lord, let us come together with a fresh clasp of the hands as we say to one another, "We rejoice in *our* Saviour, and we are one in Him."

What I want to say,—as a parting word, before I leave you once more for my season of rest,—is just this. Let us keep close together now, shoulder to shoulder, if ever we did so in all our lives. "Close your ranks ! " must be the message to the faithful in those evil days. Let us feel heart touching heart in the deepest and truest Christian affection ; for, in proportion as we are welded together in love. we shall be strong for all the practical purposes for which the Holy Spirit intends a church to be used.

These thirty-four years,—is not that the number ? —they are so many, I begin to forget the figures,—a third of a century have I served among you as a preacher of the gospel. I am always fearing that I shall get "flat, stale, and unprofitable," and that my voice will cease to have music for you, but there is one thing I know, from the first day I came among you until now, I have preached nothing but "the glorious gospel of the blessed God,"—"Jesus Christ and Him crucified," and I am not afraid that that gospel will ever get "flat, stale, or unprofitable," and this is the golden chain which has bound us together in holy fellowship. This is the foundation on which we have built,—"One Lord, one faith, one baptism." Yes, one baptism ; there are others who hold another baptism, but we know of no outward baptism but the immersion of the believer into the name of the Father, the Son, and the Holy Ghost ; and upon this point we are all agreed, as we are upon the rest of the articles of our faith.

So, being one, let us show to all the world what the power of Christian unity really is. Keep together in the prayer-meetings. Never let those precious gatherings decay or drop. If you have come together in large numbers,—and you have in my presence,—

do so much more in my absence ; let each one feel bound to meet with his brothers and sisters in prayer. I am longing for a genuine revival of religion,—a revival of religion everywhere ; and I think I can see signs that it is coming ; I find that many of the Baptist ministers who love the gospel are going over the groundwork, preaching the fundamental doctrines more than ever they did ; that is a good thing. I find that the churches are meeting together for prayer at this juncture, more than they have done, seeking that God will help and guide them to be faithful ; that also is a good thing. And people are talking about the plan of salvation,—on the tops of omnibuses, and in the railway carriages,—everywhere it comes up as a subject of debate. In the daily papers, the same theme is brought forward, for which I thank God ; and though I have had to bear my share of reproach for the truth's sake, yet I joyfully accept it. Anything which can call public attention to the gospel of Christ is a help to us ; and I believe that the attention called to this question is hopeful, that the discussion of it by so many is still more hopeful, and that the firm adherence to the faith, which I see in so many, will be attended by an intense zeal for the conversion of souls, and then we shall see a revival. God has been hindered and hampered by the false doctrine and heresy that have been cherished in so many of the churches ; and the Spirit of God has been grieved and driven away by the utter rottenness of worldliness that has been indulged in by so many professing Christians. We have let a little light into this darkness ; we have opened a door here and there, and a clear cold draught is blowing out some of the miasma, and the ill gases of the stagnant atmosphere that has been poisoning our people far too long.

Now is our time, brethren. Let us, as one man, pray God to send this benediction from on high,— "grace, mercy, and peace." I charge you, while I am away, to be instant in and out of season about this matter ; and to let this be a special object of supplication with the members of this church, that we should have a revival of religion here, at any rate, while the pastor is away. It is better for it to come while he is away, for nobody will then put the credit of it upon any instrument. Break out, heavenly fire ! Descend ! Descend ! Descend ! Let the sacrifice be consumed !

As for you who do not know and love the Lord, we love you, we desire to bring you into the blessed circle of love by the door of faith in Christ. Look alone to Jesus Christ, who is the only way of salvation for you as for us. Oh, that you would look to Him, and live ! God grant it, for Christ's sake ! Amen.

THE MAINTENANCE OF GOOD WORKS

" For we ourselves also were sometimes foolish, disobedient, deceived, serving divers lusts and pleasures, living in malice and envy, hateful, and hating one another. But after that the kindness and love of God our Saviour toward man appeared, not by works of righteousness which we have done, but according to His mercy He saved us, by the washing of regeneration, and renewing of the Holy Ghost; which He shed on us abundantly through Jesus Christ our Saviour; that being justified by His grace, we should be made heirs according to the hope of eternal life. This is a faithful saying, and these things I will that thou affirm constantly, that they which have believed in God might be careful to maintain good works. These things are good and profitable unto men."—Titus iii. 3-8.

LAST Thursday evening my sermon was based upon the contrast, in the second chapter of Ephesians, between the expressions "not of works" and "created in Jesus Christ unto good works." I tried to show the true place of good works in connection with salvation. Many of you were not present then, and I felt that the subject was of such extreme importance that I must return to the same line of thought in this greater congregation. I shall endeavour by another text, which contains the same contrast, to set before you the usefulness, the benefit, yea, and the absolute necessity for our abounding in good works, if indeed we are saved by faith in Christ Jesus.

Let us come at once to our text. Our apostle tells us that we are to speak evil of no man, but to show meekness unto all men; and he adds this as an all-sufficient reason—we ourselves also were sometimes like the very worst of them. When we look upon the world at this day, it pains us by its folly, disobedience, and delusion. He that knows most of this modern Babylon, whether he observes the richer or the poorer classes of society, will find the deepest cause for grief. But we cannot condemn with bitterness, for such were some of us. Not only can we not condemn with bitterness, but we look upon our sinful fellow-creatures with great compassion, for such were some of us. Yea more, we feel encouraged to hope for ungodly men, even for the foolish and disobedient, for we ourselves also were, not long ago, like them. We feel that we must give the thought of our heart and the energy of our lives to the great work of saving men, out of gratitude to the Lord our God, who, in His kindness and love, has saved us. " I am a man," said one, " and everything that has to do with men concerns me ": but the child of God adds to this, " I am also a sinful man, and owe my cleansing to the loving favour of the Lord. I was in the same mire of sin as these are in; and if I am now washed in the laver of regeneration, and renewed by the Holy Ghost, I owe it all to sovereign grace, and am bound by love to man and love to God to seek the cleansing and renewal of my fellow-men." Eyes that have wept over our own sin will always be most ready to weep over the sins of others. If you have judged yourselves with candour, you will not judge others with severity. You will be more ready to pity than to condemn, more anxious to hide a multitude of sins than to punish a single sinner. I will give little for your supposed regeneration if there is not created in you a tender heart, which can truly say—

> " My God, I feel the mournful scene;
> My bowels yearn o'er dying men;
> And fain my pity would reclaim,
> And snatch the firebrands from the flame."

With this feeling towards mankind at large, we are led to consider the divine remedy for sinfulness, and to look with pleasure upon what God has devised for the creation of holiness in a fallen race. He at first created man a pure and spotless being. When He placed Adam in the garden, He made a friend of him; and though Adam has fallen, and all his race are depraved, God is still aiming at the same thing, namely, to create holy beings, purified unto Himself, to be a peculiar people, zealous for good works. What has the Lord done? What is He still doing to this end? How far have we participated in those processes of grace which work towards this glorious design?

I ask your attention this morning while I speak, first, *of what we were ;* and here let the tears stand in your eyes: secondly, *of what has been done for us ;* and here let grace move in your hearts: and, thirdly, *of what we wish to do ;* and here let care be seen in your lives.

I. First, beloved, let us think for a few minutes only OF WHAT WE ONCE WERE. Think, I say, with tears of repentance in our eyes. " For we ourselves also were sometimes foolish, disobedient, deceived, serving divers lusts and pleasures, living in malice and envy, hateful, and hating one another." The apostle does not say, " Ye yourselves," as if he spoke to Titus and the believing Cretians, but *we* ourselves, thus including himself. Beloved apostle, thou dost humbly present to us this bitter cup of confession, drinking of it thyself with us, and putting thyself on a level with us—" We ourselves also." Come, then, pastor, elders, deacons, and members of the church, you that have served your Lord for many years, hesitate not to join in this humiliating confession.

A threefold set of evils is here described. The first set consists of *the evils of the mind :* " We were sometimes foolish, disobedient, deceived." We were *foolish.* We thought we knew, and therefore we did not learn. We said, " We see," and therefore we were blind, and would not come to Jesus for sight. We thought we knew better than God; for our foolish heart was darkened, and we imagined ourselves to be better judges of what was good for us than the Lord our God. We refused heavenly warnings because we dreamed that sin was pleasant and profit-Table. We rejected divine truth because we did not care to be taught, and disdained the lowly position of a disciple sitting at Jesus' feet. Our pride proved our folly. What lying things we tried to believe ! We put bitter for sweet, and sweet for bitter; darkness for light, and light for darkness. In thought, desire, language, and action " we were sometimes foolish." Some of us were manifestly foolish, for we rushed headlong into sins which injured us, and have left that in our bones which years have not been sufficient to remove. Every lover of vice is a fool writ large. O my brother, I suppose you have no photograph of yourself as you used to be; but if you have, take it down, and study it, and bless

God that He has made you to differ so greatly from your former self.

In addition to being foolish, we are said to have been *disobedient*; and so we were, for we forsook the commands of God. We wanted our own will and way. We said, "Who is the Lord, that we should obey His voice?" There is a touch of Pharaoh about every one of us. Obedience is distasteful to the obstinate; and we were such. "I knew," said God, "that thou wast very obstinate, and hadst an iron sinew." Our necks by nature refuse to bow to the yoke of our Creator. We would, if we could, be the Lords of Providence, for we are not content with the divine allotment. We wish that we were the legislators of the universe, that we might give license to our own lusts, and no longer be hampered with restrictions. To the holy law of God we were disobedient. Ah, how long some of us were disobedient to the gospel? We heard it as though we heard it not; or when it did touch the heart, we did not allow its influence to remain. Like water, which retains no mark of a blow, so did we obliterate the effect of truth. We were determined not to be obedient to the faith of the Lord Jesus. We were unwilling to yield God His due place either in providence, law, or gospel.

Paul adds that we were *deceived*, or led astray. As sheep follow one another, and go away from the pasture, so did we follow some chosen companion, and would not follow the good Shepherd. We were deceived. Perhaps we were deceived in our thoughts, and made to believe a lie; certainly we were deceived in our idea of happiness; we hoped to find it where it did not exist, we searched for the living among the dead. We were the dupes of custom and of company. We were here, there, and everywhere in our actions: no more to be relied upon than lost sheep.

Children of God, remember these errors of your minds, lay them upon your consciences, and let your souls plead guilty to them; for I feel assured that we have all, in some measure, been in this triple condition—foolish, disobedient, deceived.

The next bundle of mischief is found in *the evils of our pursuits*. The apostle says we were "serving divers lusts and pleasures." The word for "serving" means being under servitude. We were once the slaves of divers lusts and pleasures. By *lusts* we understand desires, longings, ambitions, passions. Many are these masters, and they are all tyrants. Some are ruled by greed for money; others crave for fame; some are enslaved by lust for power; others by the lust of the eye; and many by the lusts of the flesh. We were born slaves, and we live slaves until the great Liberator emancipates us. No man can be in worse bondage than to be enslaved by his own evil desires.

We were also the bondslaves of *pleasure*. Alas! alas! that we were so far infatuated as to call it pleasure! Looking back at our former lives, we may well be amazed that we could once take pleasure in things whereof we are now ashamed. The Lord has taken the very name of our former idols out of our mouths. Some who are now saints were once the slaves of drunkenness, or of "chambering and wantonness." Some were given up to evil company and rioting, or to pride and self-seeking. Many are the evils which array themselves in the silken robes of pleasure, that they may tempt the hungry heart of man. Once we took pleasure in those sins which are now our misery as we look back on them. O my brethren, we dare not deny our base original! To-day we drink from the well of holiness undefiled pleasures which delight our souls; but we blush as we remember that aforetime yonder foul and putrid pools seemed sweet to our vitiated taste. Like Nebuchadnezzar in the failure of his mind, we fed among beasts in the madness of our sin. Unlike the Egyptians, who loathed to drink of the river when God had smitten it with His curse, we took all the more delight in draughts of unhallowed pleasure because it yielded a fearful intoxication to know that we were daring to defy a law.

Do not let me talk about these things this morning while you listen to me without feeling. I want you to be turning over the pages of your old life, and joining with Paul and the rest of us in our sad confession of former pleasure in evil. A holy man was wont to carry with him a book which had three leaves in it, but never a word. The first leaf was black, and this showed him his sin; the second was red, and this reminded him of the way of cleansing by blood; while the third was white, to show how clean the Lord can make us. I beg you just now to study that first black page. It is all black; and as you look at it, it shows blacker and blacker. What seemed at one time to be a little white darkens down as it is gazed upon, till it wears the deepest shade of all. Ye were sometimes erring in your minds and in your pursuits. Is not this enough to bring the water into your eyes, O ye that now follow the Lamb whithersoever He goeth?

The apostle then mentions *the evils of our hearts*. Here you must discriminate, and judge, each one for himself, how far the accusation lies. He speaks of "living in malice and envy, hateful and hating one another." That is to say, first, we harboured *anger* against those who had done us evil; and, secondly, we lived in envy of those who appeared to have more good than we had ourselves. The first sin is very common: many abide year after year in the poisonous atmosphere of an angry spirit. All are not alike in this, for some are naturally easy and placable; but in all of us there is that proud spirit which resents injuries, and would revenge them. Men may sin against God, and we are not indignant; but if they sin against us, we are very angry. To the spirit of Christ it is natural and even delightful to forgive: but such is not the spirit of the world. I have heard of men who would not forgive their own children, and of brothers who were implacable towards each other. This is the spirit of the devil. Revenge is the delight of the wicked, but to do kindness in return for injury is the luxury of a Christian. One main distinction between the heirs of God and the heirs of wrath is this: the unregenerate are in the power of self, and so of hate, but the regenerate are under the dominion of Christ, and so of love. Thou mayest judge thyself by this, whether thy prevailing spirit is that of wrath or of love: if thou art given to anger, thou art a child of wrath; and if thou art full of love, thou art a child of God, whose name is *love*. God help us to stamp out the last spark of personal animosity! Let us remove the memories of injury, as the incoming tide washes out the marks on the sand. If any of you have disputes in your family, end them at once, cost what it may. How can you love God whom you have not seen, if you do not love your brother whom you have seen? Grace makes a great change in this respect in those who by nature are malicious.

The other form of evil is *envy* of those who seem to have more of good than we have. Frequently envy attacks men because of their wealth. How dare they have luxuries when we are poor ? At other times envy spits its venom against a man's good repute, when he happens to be more praised than we are. How can any man venture to be better thought of than we are ? Truly this is the spirit of the devil, the spirit which now worketh in the children of disobedience. The child of God is delivered from envy by the grace of God ; and if it ever does arise, he hates himself for admitting it. He would wish to see others happy, even if he were unhappy himself. If he be in the depths of poverty, he is glad that everybody is not so pinched as he is. If he has received unjust censure, he is willing to hope that there was some mistake ; and he is glad that everybody is not quite so unfairly dealt with. He rejoices in the praise of others, and triumphs in their success. What ! do you wince at this, and feel that you have not reached so far ? May grace enable you to get into this spirit, for it is the spirit of Jesus.

Beloved, sin takes different shapes in different people, but it is in us all. This darkness once beclouded those who to-day shine like stars among the godly. Sin is often restrained by circumstances, and yet it is in the heart. We ought not to take credit for ourselves because of our freedom from evils into which we had no chance of falling. We have not been so bad as others because we could not be. A certain boy has run away from home. Another boy remained at home. Is he, therefore, a better child ? Listen ? he had broken his leg, and could not get out of bed. That takes way all the credit of his staying at home. Some men cannot sin in a certain direction, and then they say to themselves, " What excellent fellows we are to abstain from this wickedness ! " Sirs, you would have done it if you could, and therefore your self-praise is mere flattery. Had you been placed in the same position as others, you would have acted as others have done, for your heart goes after the same idols. Sin in the heart of every man defiles everything that he does. Even if an ungodly man should do what in itself might be a good action, there is a defilement in his motive which taints it all. You cannot draw pure water from a foul well. As is the heart, such is the life. Listen to this, ye that have never passed under the processes of divine grace. See what you are, and where you are, if left to yourselves, and cry to the Lord to save you.

II. Now for a more cheerful topic. We are now to think OF WHAT HAS BEEN DONE FOR US ; and here let us feel the movements of grace in our hearts. What has been done for us ?

First, *there was a divine interposition.* " The kindness and love of God our Saviour toward man appeared." Man was in the dark, plunging onward to blacker midnight every step he took. I do not find, as I read history, any excuse for the modern notion that men are longing for God, and labouring to find Him. No, the sheep were never seeking the Shepherd, but all were going astray. Men everywhere turn their backs to the light, and try to forget what has been handed down by their forefathers : they are everywhere feeling after a great lie which they may raise to the throne of God. We do not by nature long after God, nor sigh for His holiness.

The gracious Lord came in uncalled for and unsought, and in the bounty of His heart, and in the great love of His nature, He determined to save man. Methinks I hear Him say, " How shall I give thee up ? " He sees mankind resolved to perish unless an almighty arm shall intervene ; and He interposes in fulness of pity and power. You know how, in many ways, the Lord has intervened on our behalf ; but, especially, you remember how He came down from heaven, took our nature, lived among us, mourned our sin, and bore it in His own body on the tree. You know how the Son of God interposed in that grand *Avatar*, that marvellous incarnation in which the Word became flesh, and dwelt among us. Then broke He what would else have been an everlasting darkness ; then snapped He the chain which must have fettered our humanity throughout all the ages. The love and kindness of God our Saviour, which had always existed, at length " appeared " when God, in the person of His Son, came hither, met our iniquities hand to hand, and overcame their terrible power, that we also might overcome.

Note well that *there was a divine salvation.* In consequence of the interposition of Jesus, believers are described as being saved : " not by works of righteousness which we have done, but according to His mercy He saved us." Hearken to this. There are men in the world who are saved : they are spoken of, not as " to be saved," not as to be saved when they come to die, but saved even now—saved from the dominion of the evils which we described under our first head : saved from folly, disobedience, delusion, and the like. Whosoever believeth in the Lord Jesus Christ, whom God has set forth to be the propitiation for sin, is saved from the guilt and power of sin. He shall no longer be the slave of his lusts and pleasures ; he is saved from that dread bondage. He is saved from hate, for he has tasted love, and learned to love. He shall not be condemned for all that he has hitherto done, for his great Substitute and Saviour has borne away the guilt, the curse, the punishment of sin ; yea, and sin itself. O my hearer, if thou believest in the Lord Jesus Christ this morning, thou art saved ! As surely as once thou wast lost, being led astray, so surely art thou now saved, if thou art a believer, being found by the great Shepherd, and brought back again upon His shoulders. I beg you to get hold of this truth, that according to His mercy the Lord has saved us who believe in Jesus. Will you tell me, or rather tell yourselves, whether you are saved or not ? If you are not saved, you are lost ; if you are not already forgiven, you are already condemned. You are in the ruin of fallen nature, unless you are renewed by the Holy Ghost. You are a slave to sin, unless your liberty has been procured by the great ransom. Examine yourselves on these points, and follow me in the next thought.

There was a motive for this salvation. Positively, " According to His mercy He saved us " ; and negatively, " Not by works of righteousness which we have done." Brethren, we could not have been saved at the first by our works of righteousness ; for we had not done any. " No," says the apostle, " we were foolish, disobedient, deceived," and therefore we had no works of righteousness, and yet the Lord interposed and saved us. Behold and admire the splendour of His love, that " He loved us even when we were dead in sins." He loved us, and therefore quickened us. God does not come to men to help them when they are saving themselves ; but He comes to the rescue when they are damning themselves. When the heart is full of folly and disobedience, the good God visits it with His favour. He comes, not according to the hopefulness of our character, but according to His mercy ; and mercy has no eye except for guilt and misery. The grace of God is not even given according to any good thing that we have done since our conversion : the expression before us shuts out all real works of righteousness which we have done since regeneration, as all supposed ones before it. The Lord assuredly foreknew these works, but He also foreknew our sins. He did not save us according to the foreknowledge of our good works, because these works are a part of the salvation which He gave us. As well say that a physician healed a sick man, because he foreknew that he would be better ; or that you give a beggar an alms, because you foresee that he would have the alms. Works of righteousness are the fruit of salvation, and the root must come before the fruit. The Lord saves His people out of clear, unmixed, undiluted mercy and grace, and for no other reason. " I will have mercy on whom I will have mercy, and I will have compassion on whom I will have compassion. So then it is not of him that willeth, nor of him that runneth, but of God that showeth mercy." Oh, how splendidly is the grace of God seen in the whole plan of salvation ! How clearly is it seen in our cases, for " we ourselves also were sometimes foolish, disobedient, deceived," yet He saved us, " not by works of righteousness which we have done, but according to His mercy " ! Will not some self-convicted sinner find comfort here? O despairing one, does not a little hope come in by this window ? Do you not see that God can save you on the ground of mercy ? He can wash you and renew you according to the sovereignty of His grace. On the footing of merit you are hopelessly lost, but on the ground of mercy there is hope.

Observe, next, that *there was a power by which we were saved.* " He saved us by the washing of re-generation, and renewing of the Holy Ghost ; which He shed on us abundantly through Jesus Christ our Saviour." The way in which we are delivered from the dominion of sin is by the work of the Holy Ghost. This adorable Person is very God of very God. This divine Being comes to us, and causes us to be born again. By His eternal power and Godhead, He gives us a totally new nature, a life which could not grow out of our former life, nor be developed from our nature— a life which is a new creation of God. We are saved, not by evolution, but by creation. The Spirit of God creates us anew in Christ Jesus unto good works. We experience regeneration, which means—being gener-ated over again, or born again. Remember the result of this as set forth in covenant terms—" A new heart also will I give you, and a new spirit will I put within you : and I will take away the stony heart out of your flesh, and I will give you an heart of flesh." This great process is carried out by the Holy Ghost.

After we are regenerated, He continues to renew us ; our thoughts, feelings, desires, and acts are constantly renewed. Regeneration as the com-mencement of the new creation can never come twice to any man, but renewal of the Holy Ghost is constantly and perpetually repeated. The life once given is revived : the light once kindled is fed with holy oil, which is poured upon it continually. The new-born life is deepened and increased in force by that same Holy Spirit who first of all created it. See then, dear hearers, that the only way to holiness is to be made anew, and to be kept anew. The washing of regeneration and the renewing of the Holy Ghost are both essential. The name of Jesus has been engraved in us, even on our hearts, but it needs to be cut deeper and deeper, lest the letters be covered up by the moss of routine, or filled up by the bespat-terings of sin. We are saved " by the washing of regeneration and renewing of the Holy Ghost "—one process in different stages. This is what our God has done for us : blessed be His name ! Being washed and renewed we are saved.

There is also mentioned a blessed privilege which comes to us by Jesus Christ. The Spirit is shed on us abundantly by Jesus Christ, and we are " justified by His grace." Both justification and sanctification come to us through the medium of our Lord Jesus Christ. The Holy Spirit is shed on us abundantly " through Jesus Christ our Saviour." Beloved, never forget that regeneration is wrought in us by the Holy Spirit, but comes to us by Jesus Christ. We do not receive any blessing apart from our Lord Jesus. In all works of the Spirit, whether regeneration or renewal, it is the Lord Jesus who is putting forth His power, for He saith, " Behold, I make all things new." The Mediator is the conduit-pipe through which grace supplies us day by day with the water of life. Everything is by Jesus Christ. Without Him was not anything made that was made, either in grace or in nature. We must not think it possible for us to receive anything from God apart from the appointed Mediator. But, oh, think of it ! in Jesus Christ we are to-day abundantly anointed by the Holy Spirit ; the sacred oil is shed upon us abund-antly from Him who is our Head. We are sweet to God through the divine perfume of the Holy Spirit, who comes to us by Jesus Christ. This day we are just in the sight of God in Christ's righteousness, through which we are " justified by grace." Jehovah sees no sin for which He must punish us ; He has said, " Take away his filthy garments from him, and set a fair mitre upon his head " ; and this is done. We are accepted in the Beloved. Since Jesus has washed our feet, we are " clean every whit "—clean in the double sense of being washed with water and with blood, and so cleansed from the power and guilt of sin. What a high privilege is this ! Can we ever sufficiently praise God for it ?

Once more, *there comes out of this a divine result.* We become to-day joint-heirs with Christ Jesus, and so heirs of a heavenly estate ; and then out of this heirship there grows a hope which reaches forward to the eternal future with exceeding joy. We are " made heirs according to the hope of eternal life." Think of that ! What a space there is between " foolish, disobedient, deceived "—right up to " heirs according to the hope of eternal life " ! Who thought of bridging this great gulf ? Who but God ? With what power did He bridge it ? How, but by the divine power and Godhead of the Holy Ghost ? Where was the bridge found by which the chasm could be crossed ? The cross of our Lord Jesus Christ, who loved us and gave Himself for us, has made a way over the once impassable deep.

I have thus very briefly set before you an outline of the work of grace within the human heart. Do you understand it ? Have you ever felt it ? Do you feel the life of regeneration pulsing within you this morning ? Will you not bless God for it ?

" We raise our Father's name on high,
  Who His own Spirit sends
To bring rebellious strangers nigh,
  And turn His foes to friends."

III. We will now speak of WHAT WE WISH TO DO ; and here let us show care in our lives. Mark well these words, " This is a faithful saying, and these things I will that thou affim constantly, that they which have believed in God might be careful to maintain good works. These things are good and profitable unto men."

" Be careful to maintain good works." This precept is *full in its meaning*. In another Scripture you are told to be careful for nothing, but here you are bidden to be careful to maintain good works. We read, " casting all your care upon Him ; for He careth for you " ; but do not cast off your care to maintain good works. You have a number of cares about you ; slip a bridle over their heads, and train them to plough in the field of good works. Do not let care be wasted over food and raiment and such temporary matters—these may be left with God ; but take sacred cares upon you—the cares of holy and gracious living. Yoke your best thoughts to the car of holiness—" be careful to maintain good works."

What are good works ? The term is greatly inclusive. Of course we number in the list works of charity, works of kindness and benevolence, works of piety, reverence, and holiness. Such works as comply with the two tables of command are good works. Works of obedience are good works. What you do because God bids you do it, is a good work. Works of love to Jesus, done out of a desire for His glory, these are good works. The common actions of every-day life, when they are well done, with a view not to merit, but out of gratitude—these are good works. " Be careful to maintain good works " of every sort and kind. You are sure to be working in some way, mind that your works are good works. If you have commenced well, be careful to *maintain* good works ; and if you have maintained them, go on to increase them. I preached last Thursday night as now—salvation by grace, and by grace alone ; and if I know how to speak plainly, I certainly did speak plainly then, and I hope I do so now. Remember, you are saved by grace, and not by works of righteousness ; but after you are saved there comes in this precept, " Be careful to maintain good works."

This precept is *special in its direction*. To the sinner, that he may be saved, we say not a word concerning good works, except to remind him that he has none of them. To the believer who is saved, we say ten thousand words concerning good works, beseeching him to bring forth much fruit, that so he may be Christ's disciple. There is all the difference between the living and the dead : the living we arouse to work ; the dead must first receive life. Exhortations which may most fittingly be addressed to the regenerate may be quite out of place when spoken to those who are under the power of unbelief, and are strangers to the family of grace. The voice of our text is to them that have believed in God ; faith is pre-supposed as the absolutely indispensable foundation of good works. You cannot work that which will please God if you are without faith in Him. As there is no coming to God in prayer without believing that He is and that He is the rewarder of them that diligently seek Him, so there is no bringing

any other sacrifice to Him without a faith suitable to the business in hand. For living works you must have a living faith, and for loving works you must have a loving faith. When we know and trust God, then with holy intelligence and sacred confidence we work His pleasure. Good works must be done freely : God wants not slaves to grace His throne ; He seeks not from us the forced works of men in bondage. He desires the spontaneous zeal of consecrated souls who rejoice to do His will, because they are not their own, but bought with the precious blood of Jesus. It is the heartiness of our work which is the heart of it. To those who have renewed hearts, this exhortation is addressed—" Be careful to maintain good works."

This precept is *weighty in importance*, for it is prefaced thus : " This is a faithful saying." This is one among four great matters thus described. It is not trivial, it is not a temporary precept which belongs to an extinct race and a past age. " This is a faithful saying "—a true Christian proverb, " that they which have believed in God might be careful to maintain good works." Let the ungodly never say that we who believe in free grace think lightly of a holy life. O you who are the people of my care, I charge you before God and the holy angels that, in proportion as you hold the truth of doctrine, you follow out the purity of precept ! You hold the truth, and you know that salvation is not of man, nor of man's work : it is not of merit, but of mercy; not of ourselves, but of God alone ; I beseech you to be as right in practice as in doctrine, and therefore be careful to maintain good works. Dogs will open their mouths, but do not find bones for them : the enemies of the faith will cavil at it, but do not give them ground of accusation. May God the Holy Spirit help you so to live that they may be ashamed, having no evil thing to say of you !

I am afraid that this precept of being careful to maintain good works is *neglected in practice*, or else the apostle would not have said to Titus, " These things I will that thou affirm constantly." Titus must repeat perpetually the precept which commands the careful maintenance of good works. Beloved, I fear that preachers often think too well of their congregations, and talk to them as if they were all perfect, or nearly so. I cannot thus flatter you. I have been astounded when I have seen what professing Christians can do. How some dare call themselves followers of Jesus I cannot tell ! It is horrible. We condemn Judas, but his fellow is to be found in many. Our Lord is still sold for gain. He still has at His heels sons of perdition who kiss Him and betray Him. There are still persons in our churches who need to have the ten commandments read to them every Sabbath-day. It is not a bad plan of the Church of England, to put up the ten commandments near the communion table where they can be clearly seen. Some people need to see them ; though I am afraid, when they come in their way, they wink hard at some of the commands, and go away and forget that they have seen them. Common morality is neglected by some who call themselves Christians.

My brethren, such things ought not to be, but as long as they are so we must hear Paul saying : " I will that thou affirm constantly that they which have believed in God might be careful to maintain good works." Certain people turn on their heel, and say, " That is legal talk. The preacher is preaching up works instead of grace." What! will you dare to say that? I will meet you face to face at God's right hand at the last day if you dare to insinuate so gross a libel. Dare you say that I do not preach continually salvation by the grace of God, and by the grace of God only? Having preached salvation by grace without a moment's hesitation, I shall also continually affirm that they which have believed in God must be "careful to maintain good works."

This, mark you, is *supported by argument*. The apostle presses home his precept by saying: "These things are good and profitable unto men." He instances other things which are neither good nor profitable, namely, "Foolish questions, and genealogies, and contentions, and strivings about the law." In these days some are occupied with questions about the future state, instead of accepting the plain testimony of Scripture, and some give more prominence to speculations drawn from prophecy than to the maintaining of good works. I reverence the prophecies; but I have small patience with those whose one business is guessing at their meaning. One whose family was utterly unruly and immoral met with a Christian friend, and said to him: "Do you quite see the meaning of the Seven Trumpets?" "No," answered his friend, "I do not; and if you looked more to your seven children the seven trumpets would suffer no harm." To train up your children and instruct your servants, and order your household aright, are "things which are good and profitable unto men." A life of godliness is better than the understanding of mysteries. The eternal truth of God is to be defended at all hazards, but questions which do not signify the turn of a hair to either God or man may be left to settle themselves. "Be careful to maintain good works," whether you are a babe in grace or a strong man in Christ Jesus. A holy household is as a pillar to the church of God. Children brought up in the fear of God are as cornerstones polished after the similitude of a palace. You, husbands and wives, that live together in holy love,

and see your children serving God, you adorn the doctrine of God our Saviour! Tradesmen who are esteemed for integrity, merchants who bargain to their own hurt but change not, dealers who can be trusted in the market with uncounted gold, your acts are good and profitable both to the Church and to the world! Men are won to Christ when they see Christianity embodied in the good and the true. But when religion is a thin veneer or a mere touch of tinsel, they call it "humbug"; and rough as the word is, it is worthy of the contemptible thing which it describes. If our religion comes from the very soul, if our life is the life of Christ in us, and we prove that we have new hearts and right spirits by acting the honourable, the kindly, the truly Christian part, these things are good and profitable unto those who watch us, for they may induce them to seek for better things.

I pray you, my beloved, be careful to maintain good works. I thus stir up your pure minds by way of remembrance: if your minds were not pure I would not stir them up, for it would be of no use to raise the mud which now lies quiet. I stir you up because I am not afraid to do so, but am sure that it will do you good. You will take home this exhortation, and you will say, each one to himself, "What can I do more for Jesus? How can I walk more worthy of my profession? How can I be careful to maintain good works?" So may God bless you!

You who do not believe in God, who have not come to trust in His dear Son, I am not talking to you. To you, I must say, first, that you must be made new creatures. I do not talk to a crab-tree, and say, "Bear apples," It cannot. The tree must first become good before the fruit can be good. "Ye must be born again." You will never be better till you are made new creatures. You must be spiritually slain, and then made alive again. There must be an end of you, and there must be a beginning of Christ in you. God grant that this may happen at once, and may you immediately believe in the Lord Jesus! Amen.